ADVANCED ECONOMIC THEORY

MICROECONOMIC ANALYSIS

H L AHUJA

MA, PhD (DSE)

Formerly, Associate Professor
Department of Economics
Zakir Husain Delhi College
University of Delhi,
Delhi

S. CHAND
PUBLISHING
empowering minds

S Chand And Company Limited

(ISO 9001 Certified Company)

RAM NAGAR, NEW DELHI - 110 055

S Chand And Company Limited
(ISO 9001 Certified Company)
Head Office: 7361, RAM NAGAR, QUTAB ROAD, NEW DELHI - 110 055
Phone: 23672080-81-82, 66672000 Fax: 91-11-23677446
www.**schandpublishing.com**; e-mail: **info@schandpublishing.com**

S. CHAND PUBLISHING
empowering minds

Branches:

Ahmedabad : Ph: 27541965, 27542369, ahmedabad@schandpublishing.com
Bengaluru : Ph: 22268048, 22354008, bangalore@schandpublishing.com
Bhopal : Ph: 4209587, bhopal@schandpublishing.com
Chandigarh : Ph: 2625356, 2625546, 4025418, chandigarh@schandpublishing.com
Chennai : Ph: 28410027, 28410058, chennai@schandpublishing.com
Coimbatore : Ph: 2323620, 4217136, coimbatore@schandpublishing.com (Marketing Office)
Cuttack : Ph: 2332580, 2332581, cuttack@schandpublishing.com
Dehradun : Ph: 2711101, 2710861, dehradun@schandpublishing.com
Guwahati : Ph: 2738811, 2735640, guwahati@schandpublishing.com
Hyderabad : Ph: 27550194, 27550195, hyderabad@schandpublishing.com
Jaipur : Ph: 2219175, 2219176, jaipur@schandpublishing.com
Jalandhar : Ph: 2401630, jalandhar@schandpublishing.com
Kochi : Ph: 2809208, 2808207, cochin@schandpublishing.com
Kolkata : Ph: 23353914, 23357458, kolkata@schandpublishing.com
Lucknow : Ph: 4065646, lucknow@schandpublishing.com
Mumbai : Ph: 22690881, 22610885, 22610886, mumbai@schandpublishing.com
Nagpur : Ph: 2720523, 2777666, nagpur@schandpublishing.com
Patna : Ph: 2300489, 2260011, patna@schandpublishing.com
Pune : Ph: 64017298, pune@schandpublishing.com
Raipur : Ph: 2443142, raipur@schandpublishing.com (Marketing Office)
Ranchi : Ph: 2361178, ranchi@schandpublishing.com
Sahibabad : Ph: 2771235, 2771238, delhibr-sahibabad@schandpublishing.com

First Edition 1970
Subsequent Editions 1971, 73, 75, 80, 85, 90, 92, 95, 96, 97, 98, 2000, 2001, 2003, 2004, 2005
2006 (Twice), 2007, 2008, 2009, 2010, 2011, 2012, 2013, 2014, 2016
Twenty-First Edition 2017
Reprint 2017 (Twice)
Reprint 2018 (Twice)

ISBN : 978-93-525-3332-9

PRINTED IN INDIA

By Vikas Publishing House Pvt. Ltd., Plot 20/4, Site-IV, Industrial Area Sahibabad, Ghaziabad-201010 and Published by S Chand And Company Limited, 7361, Ram Nagar, New Delhi-110 055.

Dedicated to

the memory of my mother

Nihal Bai

with reverence and affection

PREFACE TO THE TWENTY-FIRST EDITION

It gives me immense pleasure to bring out the 21st edition of this popular book. As mentioned in the previous editions, my efforts have been to incorporate in this book the latest trends and tendencies in microeconomic theory. In keeping with this approach, I have explained the various important economic concepts and theories such as theory of demand, cost, production, price and output determination under perfect competition, monopoly and oligopoly in mathematical terms. Further, to enable the students to understand better the mathematical exposition of the theories, I have added Chapter 5 which explains the **Basic Mathematical Concepts and Optimisation Techniques**.

In the present revised 21st edition of the book, some significant changes have been made in some chapters. Among them, mention may be made of the following:

- ***Chapter 1***: The meaning of *economic efficiency* has been clearly explained distinguishing between production efficiency, allocative efficiency and distributive efficiency.
- ***Chapter 7***: The *concept of utility* and its *critique by Prof. Amartya Sen* has been explained.
- ***Chapter 8***: The Hicksian substitution effect and Slutsky substitution effect have been clearly distinguished.
- ***Chapter 17***: The attitudes towards risk of different individuals have been explained and the choice by risk-averter and risk lover under risky and uncertain situations has been shown. It has been clearly shown why a risk-averter generally buys insurance and a risk lover indulges in gambling.
- ***Chapter 28***: The chapter explains how economic efficiency is claimed to be achieved under perfect competition and have shown that even in a perfectly competitive economy, there are *market failures* to achieve economic efficiency when there exist *externalities*, both positive and negative, *public goods* and *imperfect information*. Besides, it has been made clear how a perfectly competitive economy fails to achieve *equity* in distribution of goods and services.
- ***Chapter 65***: The *Bergson-Samuelson social welfare function* has been critically examined and how it differs from *Classical utilitarian social welfare* function and *Rawl's social welfare function* which gives the highest weight to the welfare of the poorest people in a society has been brought out.
- ***Chapter 67***: The impact of imperfect and asymmetric information on individual's choice has been explained and the problems of adverse selection and moral hazard under conditions of imperfect and asymmetric information has been clarified.

With the above changes, I hope the students will find the book more useful for them. The book is intended to meet the requirements of the students of MA (Economics), MCom, MBA and related courses, BA (Hons) and candidates preparing for competitive examinations such as IAS, IES and Public Service Examinations of different States. I shall greatly appreciate the suggestions for further improvement of the book from fellow teachers. The author can be approached at ***drhlahuja@gmail.com***

H L AHUJA

PREFACE TO THE FIRST EDITION

There have been significant developments in economic theory in recent years, but the tendency has been to make it more mathematical. Postgraduate and Honours students of Indian universities, having poor background of mathematics, find it difficult to understand the various theories and concepts involving use of advanced mathematics. Moreover, the matter pertaining to advanced topics in economic theory is scattered in many economic journals to which most of the students of Indian universities have no access. I have endeavoured to help them. So, in this book an effort has been made to discuss the various theories of microeconomics without making use of advanced mathematics. The merit of this book is that it explains the advanced theories and concepts with the help of geometry and simple mathematics.

The book is intended to meet the requirements of MA and Honours students of Indian universities and of candidates who are preparing for IAS, IES and Allied Civil Services competitive examinations, for their paper on advanced economic theory. In this book, I have confined myself only to microeconomic theory and have covered the theories of demand, production, value and distribution.

I am deeply indebted to Dr K K Dewett, formerly Head of Economics Department, Punjab University, and Dr J D Varma, former Professor and Head, Department of Economics, Punjab University, Chandigarh, who have been my teachers as well as colleagues, for inspiring me to write this book. I am also grateful to my wife Prem Ahuja, teacher in Cambridge School, without whose generous cooperation and help, this book would not have been possible.

Suggestions for making improvements in the book from fellow teachers are most welcome.

January 26, 1970

H L AHUJA

CONTENTS

PART – I

SCOPE AND METHODOLOGY OF ECONOMICS

1. Nature and Scope of Economic Theory 3–30

The Economic Problem: Scarcity and Choice. The Scope of Economic Theory and Basic Economic Problems. The Problem of Allocation of Resources. Choice of a Production Method. The Problem of Distribution of National Product. The Problem of Economic Efficiency. The Problem of Full Employment of Resources. The Problem of Economic Growth. Problem of Scarcity vs. Problem of Affluence. Critical Evaluation of Robbin's Definition of Economics, Positive Economics, Normative Economics and Welfare Economics. Production Possibility Curve: A Basic Tool of Economics. Economic Growth and Shift in Production Possibility Curve. Production Possibility Frontier and the Law of Increasing Opportunity Cost. Production Possibility Curve and Basic Economic Questions.

2. Micro and Macro-Economics 31–43

Microeconomics. Importance and Uses of Microeconomics. Macroeconomics distinguished from Microeconomics. Why a Separate Study of Macroeconomics. Interdependence between Micro and Macroeconomics.

3. Methodology of Economics 44–55

Nature of Scientific Theory. Derivation of Economic Theories and Nature of Economic Reasoning. Deductive Method. Merits and Demerits of Deductive Method. The Inductive Method. Conclusion: Integration of Two Methods. Role of Assumptions in Economic Theory: Friedman's View. The Concept of Equilibrium: Partial Equilibrium Analysis; General Equilibrium Analysis. Model Building in Economics. Endogenous and Exogenous Variables in Economic Models.

4. Methodology of Economics: Economic Statics and Dynamics 56–67

Nature of Economic Statics. Static Analysis and Functional Relationships. Micro-Statics and Macro-Statics. Assumptions of Static Analysis. Relevance of Static Analysis. Comparative Statics. Economic Dynamics. Endogenous Changes and Dynamic Analysis. Hicks' Definition of Economic Dynamics. Expectations and Dynamics. Need and Significance of Economic Dynamics.

5. Basic Mathematical Concepts and Optimisation Techniques 68–94

Introduction. Functions: Linear and Power Functions-Slopes of Functions. Optimisation Techniques: Differential Calculus. The Concept of a Derivative. Rules of Differentiation. Differentiation of Functions with Two or More than Two Independent Variables. Applications of Differential Calculus (Derivatives) to Optimisation Problems: Use in Profit Maximisation; Minimisation Problem. Multivariate Optimisation. Constrained Optimisation. Lagrange Multiplier Technique.

PART – II

DEMAND ANALYSIS AND THEORY OF CONSUMER'S CHOICE

6. Demand and Demand Function 97–114

Significance of Demand Function. Individual Demand. Demand Function. Law of Demand. Reasons for the Law of Demand: Why does Demand Curve Slope Downward? Market Demand Function. Inverse demand function. Relationship between Demand Function and Demand Curve. Factors Determining Demand. Demand for Durable Goods. Derived Demand. Network Externalities: Bandwagon Effect and Snob Effect.

7. Consumer's Behaviour: Cardinal Utility Analysis 115–133

Introduction. The Concept of Utility. Amartya Sen's Critique of the Concept of Utility. Law of Diminishing Marginal Utility; Consumer's Equilibrium: Principle of Equi-marginal Utility. Derivation of Demand Curve and Law of Demand. Critical Evaluation of Marshall's Cardinal Utility Analysis.

8. **Indifference Curve Analysis of Demand** 134–185

Consumer Preferences. Indifference Curve Approach. What are Indifference Curves? Marginal Rate of Substitution. Properties of Indifference Curves. Some Non-normal Cases of Indifference Curves: Goods, Bads and Neuters. Budget Line or Budget Constraint. Consumer's Equilibrium: Maximising Satisfaction. Consumer's Equilibrium: Corner Solutions. Income Effect: Income Consumption Curve. Income Consumption Curve and Engel Curve. Substitution Effect. Price Effect: Price Consumption Curve. Breaking Up Price Effect into Income and Substitution Effects. Price-Demand Relationship: Deriving Law of Demand. Derivation of Individual's Demand Curve from Indifference Curve Analysis. Questions and Problems for Review.

Appendix A to Chapter 8: Slutsky Substitution Effect 186–190

Slutsky Substitution Effect and Cost Difference: Slutsky Substitution Effect for a Decline in Price; Slutsky Substitution Effect for a Rise in Price. A Numerical Example.

Appendix B to Chapter 8: Mathematical Treatment of the Theory of Consumer's Choice 191–198

Mathematical Derivation of Conditions for Consumer's Equilibrium: Lagrangian Method. Optimum Values of the Goods. Derivation of Demand Function. Slutsky Equation: Decomposing Price Effect.

9. **Demand for Complementary and Substitute Goods** 199–207

Edgeworth-Pareto Definition of Complementary and Substitute Goods. Hicksian Explanation of Complementary and Substitute Goods. Compensated Demand Curve. Relationship between Compensated and Ordinary Demand Curves. Measurement of Consumer Surplus with Ordinary and Compensated Demand Curves.

10. **Marshallian Cardinal Utility Analysis vs. Indifference Curve Analysis** 208–221

Similarity between the Two Analyses. Superiority of Indifference Curve Analysis. Is Indifference Curve Analysis "Old Wine in a New Bottle" ? A Critique of Indifference Curve Analysis Limitations of Maximising Behaviour.

11. **Applications and Uses of Indifference Curve** 222–244

Exchange between Two Individuals: Gain from Trade. Subsidies to Consumers: Price Subsidy vs. Lump Sum Income Grant. Rationing and Indifference Curve Analysis. Rationing of both the Commodities. Income-Leisure Choice. Need for Higher Overtime Wage Rate. Wage Offer Curve and the Supply of Labour. Income Effect and Substitution Effect of the Change in Wage Rate. Backward-Bending Supply Curve of Labour. Food Stamp Programmer: In-Kind Food Subsidy. Welfare Effects of Direct and Indirect Taxes. Economic Theory of Index Numbers: Assessing Changes in Standards of Living. Conclusion.

12. **Revealed Preference Theory of Demand** 245–262

Behaviouristic Approach to Demand Analysis. Preference Hypothesis and Strong Ordering. Deriving Demand Theorem from Revealed Preference Hypothesis. Critical Appraisal of Revealed Preference Theory. Derivation of Indifference Curves through Revealed Preference Approach. Convexity of Indifference Curve and Revealed Preference Approach.

13. **Hicks' Logical Ordering Theory of Demand** 263–278

Need for Revision of Demand Theory. Preference Hypothesis and Logic of Ordering Strong and Weak Orderings Distinguished. Hicks' Criticism of the Logic of Strong Ordering. The Logic of Weak Ordering. The Direct Consistency Test. Derivation of Law of Demand through Logical Weak Ordering Approach: Deriving Law of Demand by the Method of Compensating Variation. Deriving Law of Demand by Cost Difference Method. Inferior Goods, Giffen Goods and Law of Demand. Appraisal of Hicksian Weak Logical Ordering Theory of Demand.

14. **Elasticity of Demand** 279–321

Various Concepts of Demand Elasticity. Price Elasticity of Demand. Perfectly Inelastic and Perfectly Elastic Demand. Measurement of Price Elasticity. Finding Price Elasticity from a Demand Function. Price Elasticity of Demand and Changes in Total Expenditure. Measurement of Price Elasticity of Demand at a Point on a Demand

Curve. Comparing Price Elasticity at a given Price on the Two Demand Curves with Different Slopes. Determinants of Price Elasticity of Demand. Cross Elasticity of Demand. Income Elasticity of Demand. Measuring Income Elasticity at a Point on an Engel Curve. Engel Curve and Income Elasticity: Necessities, Luxuries and Inferior Goods. Sum of Income Elasticities, Budget Constraint and Expenditure. The Elasticity of Substitution. Relationship between Price Elasticity, Income Elasticity and Substitution Elasticity.

15. Consumer Surplus 322–342

Meaning of Consumer Surplus. Marshall's Measure of Consumer Surplus. Consumer Surplus and Changes in Price. Measurement of Consumer's Surplus through Indifference Curves. Hicksian Four Concepts of Consumer Surplus: Price-Compensating Variation; Price-Equivalent Variation; Quantity Compensating Variation; Quantity Equivalent Variation. Critical Evaluation of the Concept of Consumer's Surplus. Applications of Consumer Surplus: Water-Diamond Paradox, Evaluating Loss of Benefit from Tax; Evaluating Gain from a Subsidy; Use of Consumer Surplus in Cost-Benefit Analysis. Numerical Problems on Consumer's Surplus.

16. Attribute Approach to Consumer's Behaviour 343–351

Attribute or Characteristics Approach: Introduction. Indifference Curves of Attributes. The Budget Constraint and the Efficiency Frontier. Maximising Satisfaction from Attributes. Equilibrium with a Mixed Bundle of Products. Attribute Approach and the Price Effect. Attribute Approach and Law of Demand. Pricing a Product Out of the Market. Introduction of a New Product. An Evaluation of the Attribute Approach to Consumer Theory.

17. Individual Choice Under Risk and Uncertainty 352–378

Introduction. The Concept of Risk. St. Petersburg Paradox and Bernoulli's Hypothesis. Utility Theory and Attitude Toward Risk: Risk Averter. Choice of a Risk Averter Under Conditions of Risk and Uncertainty. Risk Lover. Risk Neutral. Risk Aversion and Fair Bets. Risk Aversion and Insurance. Risk Preference and Gambling: Why Do Some Individuals Gamble? An Application: Farmer's Gambling Against Nature. Friedman-Savage Hypothesis. Measuring Risk: Probability of an Outcome: Expected Value. Risk-Return Trade off and Choice of a Portfolio. Decision Making Under Risk when Investment Projects differ in their Expected Values: Some Numerical Problems.

Appendix to Chapter 17: Neumann-Morgenstern Method of Constructing Utility Index under Risky Conditions 379–381

PART – III

THEORY OF PRODUCTION AND COST ANALYSIS

18. Theory of Production: Returns to a Variable Factor 385–407

Introduction. Production Function. Production Function with One Variable Factor: Total, Average and Marginal Physical Products. Output Elasticity of an Input. Law of Variable Proportions: Three Stages of Production. The Stage of Operation. Causes of Initial Increasing Marginal Returns to a Variable Factor. Causes of Diminishing Marginal Returns. Causes of Negative Marginal Returns. General Applicability of the Law of Diminishing Returns.

19. Production Function with Two Variable Inputs 408–456

Isoquants. Marginal Rate of Technical Substitution. General Properties of Isoquants. Isoquants of Perfect Substitutes and Complements. Fixed Proportion and Variable Proportion Production Functions. Linear Homogeneous Production Function. Cobb-Douglas Production Function. Cobb-Douglas Production Function and Returns to Scale. Elasticity of Technical Substitution (Between Factors). The Economic Region of Production. Production Function and Technological Change. Returns to Scale—Changes in Scale and Factor Proportions. Constant Returns to Scale. Divisibility of Factors/Constant Returns to Proportionality and Scale. Increasing Returns to Scale. Decreasing Returns to Scale. Varying Returns to Scale in a Single Production Function. Returns to Scale and Marginal Returns to a Variable Factor. Important Production Functions Exhibiting Constant Returns to Scale. Constant Elasticity of Substitution

(CES) Production Function. Numerical Problems on Returns to Scale. The Estimation of Production Function. Problems in Estimation of Production Functions.

20. Optimum Factor Combination 457–478

Iso-Cost Line. Least-Cost Combination of Factors. Output Maximisation Subject to Cost Constraint. Numerical Problems. Expansion Path. Derivation of Equation for Expansion Path (in Cobb-Douglas Production Function). Numerical Problems. Profit Maximisation and Optimum Input Combination. Effect of Changes in Factor Prices: Factor Substitution. Substitute and Complementary Factors. The Expansion Path of a Linear Homogeneous Production Function.

Appendix to Chapter 20: Mathematical Treatment of Production Theory 479–481

Choice of Inputs: Cost-Minimisation for a Given Output. Duality of Cost-Minimisation Problem: Output-Maximisation with a Given Cost.

21. Cost Analysis 482–536

Introduction. Technological Efficiency Versus Economic Efficiency. The Concepts of Cost: Opportunity Cost; Historical Costs as Sunk Costs; Accounting Costs and Economic Costs. Theory of Cost. Cost Functions: Short Run and Long Run. Total, Fixed and Variable Costs in the Short Run. The Short-Run Average and Marginal Cost Curves. Relationship Between Marginal Cost and Marginal Physical Product. Derivation of Short-Run Average and Marginal Cost Curves from their Total Cost Curves. Theory of Long-Run Costs: Long-Run Average Cost Curve. Long-Run Average Cost Curve in Case of Constant Returns to Scale. Minimum Efficient Scale. Explanation of the U-shape of the Long-Run Average Cost Curve: Economies of Scale; Internal Diseconomies of Scale. Long-Run Marginal Cost Curve. Relationship between STC and LTC and between LAC and SAC Curves. Long-Run Total Costs and Expansion Path. External Economies and Diseconomies and Cost Curves. Modern Developments in Cost Theory: L-shaped Long-Run Average Cost Curve.The Learning Curve. Algebraic Forms of Cost Functions: Cubic Cost Function. Quadratic Cost Function. Linear Cost Function. Numerical Problems on Cost Function.

Appendix to Chapter 21: Derivation of Long-Run Cost Function 537–538

22. Linear Programming 539–559

Introduction. Meaning of Linear Programming. Basic Concepts and Terms of Linear Programming. Choice of Products: Constrained Profit Maximisation. Choice of a Process: Output Maximisation Subject to Some Constraints. Choice of a Process: Output Maximisation with Cost-Outlay Constant. Cost Minimisation for a Given Output. Multiple Optimal Solutions. Choice of a Process: Output Maximisation with Two Inputs as Constraints. Some Additional Problems and their Linear Programming Solutions. A Special Problem of Cost Minimisation: Diet Problem.

23. Supply and its Elasticity 560–570

The Meaning of Supply. Supply Function. The Relation between Price and Quantity Supplied: Law of Supply. Why Does Supply Curve Generally Slope Upward? Shift in Supply Curve: Increase and Decrease in Supply. Elasticity of Supply. Supply Function and Elasticity of Supply. Elasticity along the Supply Curve. Factors Determining Elasticity of Supply.

PART – IV

PRICE AND OUTPUT DETERMINATION IN VARIOUS MARKET STRUCTURES

24. Market Structures and Concepts of Revenue for a Firm 573–595

Meaning of Market. Classification of Market Structures. Market Classification and Cross Elasticity of Demand. Total, Average and Marginal Revenue and their Relationship. Deriving Average and Marginal Revenue Curves from Total Revenue Curve. Relationship between AR and MR Curves. Price Elasticity, Total Revenue and Marginal Revenue. Average Revenue. Marginal Revenue and Price Elasticity of Demand: Geometric Proof. Mathematical Derivation of Relationship between Marginal Revenue, Average Revenue and Price Elasticity of Demand. Demand Function, MR and Price Elasticity. Some Numerical Problems on MR, TR and Price Elasticity of Demand.

25. **Firm: A General Analysis of its Nature, Objectives and Equilibrium** 596–621

Introduction: The Nature of Firm: The Firm as an Agent of Production; Organising Economic Activity by a Firm: Market Coordination Vs. Managerial Coordination. Why Does a Firm Exist: Coase's View. Objectives of a Firm: Profit Maximization Objective; A Critique of Profit Maximisation Objective: The Objective of Securing a Steady Flow of Profits. Sales-maximization Objective; Maximization of Utility Function with Leisure as a Desirable Object; Hall and Hitch's Mark-up Pricing Approach and Profit Maximisation. Utility Maximisation by Managers of Corporate Business Firms: Satisficing Behaviour; Staff Maximisation. Case for Maximisation of Profits. Equilibrium of the Firm: Total Revenue-Total Cost Approach, Marginal Revenue-Marginal Cost Approach. Second Order Condition for Equilibrium of the Firm. A Numerical Example of Profit Maximisation.

26. **Pricing in Competitive Markets: Demand-Supply Analysis** 622–634

Marshallian Versus Walrasian Approaches to Price Theory: Marshall's Partial Equilibrium Analysis, Walras' General Equilibrium Analysis. Price Determination: Static Equilibrium Between Demand and Supply. Walrasian Price Adjustment and Marshallian Quantity Adjustment. Are Demand and Supply Final Answers to the Pricing Problem? Demand-Supply Model of Price-Output Determination: Mathematical Analysis. Marshall's Theory of Value: Time-Period Analysis.

27. **Applications of Demand and Supply Analysis** 635–651

Introduction. Price Control and Rationing. Rent Control. Minimum Support Price. Paradox of Poverty Amidst Plenty. Crop Restriction Programme and Farmers' Income. Why did OPEC Fail to Keep the Price of Oil High for Long? Fight Against Use of Drugs. Incidence of Taxation.

28. **Equilibrium of the Firm and Industry Under Perfect Competition** 652–686

Conditions of Perfect Competition. Demand Curve of a Product Facing a Perfectly Competitive Firm. Short-run Equilibrium of the Competitive Firm. Shutting Down in the Short-run. Long-run Equilibrium of the Firm Under Perfect Competition. Long-run Equilibrium Adjustment of a Competitive Firm. Why Do Competitive Firms Stay in Business if they Make Zero Economic Profits in the Long Run? Short-run Supply Curve of the Perfectly Competitive Firm. Short-run Supply Curve of the Competitive Industry. The Equilibrium of the Competitive Industry. Economic Efficiency of Perfectly Competitive Market. Consumer Surplus and Producer Surplus. Economic Efficiency and Perfect Competition: Pareto Efficiency Analysis. Market Failures of a Perfectly Competitive Economy: Externalities and Market Failure. Public Goods and Market Failure. Imperfect Information. Distribution of Goods and Economic Inefficiency. Numerical Problems on Perfect Competition Model.

Appendix to Chapter 28: Competitive Equilibrium Under Differential Cost Conditions 687–691

Short-run Equilibrium of the Firm: Differential Cost Conditions. Long-run Equilibrium of Firm: Differential Cost Conditions. Differential Cost Conditions and Economic Rent.

29. **Comparative Static Analysis of Equilibrium and Long-Run Supply Curve of the Competitive Industry** 692–705

Introduction. Comparative Static Analysis. The Concept of Supply Curve. Long-run Supply Curve under Perfect Competition: Long-run Supply Curve in Increasing-Cost Industry; Long-run Supply Curve in the Constant-Cost Industry; Long-run Supply Curve in the Decreasing-Cost Industry. Change in Competitive Equilibrium in Response to Changes in Input Prices and Technology Response of Price and Output of the Competitive Industry to Changes in Technology.

30. **Existence and Stability of Equilibrium under Perfect Competition** 706–716

Existence of Equilibrium. Multiple Equilibria. Stability of Equilibrium. Walrasian Price Adjustment and Marshallian Quantity Adjustment. Static Stability Vs. Dynamic Stability. Dynamic Stability with Lagged Adjustment: Cobweb Model. Stability of Equilibrium: Policy Implications.

31. **Kaldor and Sraffa on Incompatibility of Equilibrium with Perfect Competition** 717–731

Controversy: Incompatibility of Firm's Equilibrium Under Perfect Competition and Decreasing Costs (Increasing Returns to scale). Incompatibility of Competitive Firm's Equilibrium with Constant Costs (Constant Returns). Kaldor on Incompatibility of Firm's Long-Run Static Equilibrium with Perfect Competition. Sraffa on Incompatibility of Competitive Equilibrium with Increasing Returns. Sraffa's Challenge to Perfect Competition Model and his Advocacy of the Adoption of Monopoly Model. Comments over Sraffa's Analysis.

32. **Price and Output Determination under Monopoly** 732–758

Monopoly: Its Meaning and Conditions. Sources or Causes of Monopoly. The Nature of Demand and Marginal Revenue Curves under Monopoly. Relation between Marginal Revenue and Price. MR, Price and Elasticity of Demand under Monopoly. Price-Output Equilibrium under Monopoly. Price and Marginal Cost under Monopoly. Monopoly Equilibrium and Price Elasticity of Demand. Monopoly Equilibrium in Case of Zero Marginal Cost. Long-Run Equilibrium under Monopoly. Monopoly Equilibrium and Perfectly Competitive Equilibrium Compared. Absense of Supply Curve under Monopoly. Monopoly, Resource Allocation and Social Welfare. Numerical Problem on Dead-Weight Loss.

33. **Price Discrimination** 759–776

Meaning of Price Discrimination. Degrees of Price Discrimination : Price Discrimination of the First Degree, Price Discrimination of the Second Degree, Price Discrimination of the Third Degree. When is Price Discrimination Possible ? When is Price Discrimination Profitable? Price and Output Equilibrium under Price Discrimination. International Price Discrimination and Dumping. Perfect Price Determination: Output Determination. Case when Output of a Commodity is Possible Only under Price Discrimination. Price Discrimination and Social Welfare. Numerical Problem on Price Discrimination.

34. **Measurement of the Degree of Monopoly Power** 777–783

Elasticity of Demand as a Measure of Monopoly Power. Lerner's Measure of Monopoly Power, Lerner's Index of Monopoly Power and Price Elasticity of Demand. Critique of Lerner's Measure of Monopoly Power. Cross Elasticity of Demand as a Measure of Monopoly Power. Criticism.

35. **Price and Output under Bilateral Monopoly** 784–789

Price and Output under Bilateral Monopoly. Price and Output under Bilateral Monopoly Explained with the Help of Contract Curve.

36. **Price and Output Determination under Monopolistic Competition** 790–808

Imperfect Competition: Monopolistic Competition and Oligopoly. Product Differentiation and Monopolistic Competition, Important Features of Monopolistic Competition. Price-Output Equilibrium under Monopolistic Competition. Individual Firm's Equilibrium under Monopolistic Competition. Long-Run Firm's Equilbrium and Group Equilibrium under Monopolistic Competition. Excess Capacity under Monopolistic Competition. Price-Output Equilibrium under Monopolistic Competition Compared with that under Perfect Competition. Monopolistic Competition and Economic Efficiency.

37. **A Critique of Chamberlin's Theory of Monopolistic Competition** 809–822

Superiority of Chamberlin's Approach. Uniformity Assumption Challenged. Symmetry Assumption Criticised. Challenge to Chamberlin's Concept of Group by Stigler and Triffin. Monopolistic Competition and the Concept of Marginal Revenue. Number of Firms, Demand Elasticity and Market Imperfection. Monopolistic Competition and Increasing Returns (Economies of Scale). Freedom of Entry and Monopolistic Competition. Excess Capacity Criticism. Conclusion.

38. **A Critical Evaluation of Excess Capacity of Doctrine Monopolistic Competition Theory** 823–834

Cassel's Two Concepts of Excess Capacity. Chamberlin's Concepts of Proportional and Perceived Demand Curves. Short-run Firm's Equilibrium under Monopolistic Competition : Chamberlin's Alternative Approach. Chamberlin's Concepts of Ideal

Output and Emergence of Excess Capacity. Harrod's Critique of the Excess Capacity Doctrine. Kaldor's Critique of the Theory of Excess Capacity. Conclusion.

39. Chamberlin's Monopolistic Competition vs. Joan Robinson's Imperfect Competition Theories 835–842

Introduction. Chamberlin Views: Real-World Market Situations as Blend of Competition and Monopoly. Chamberlin Lays Stress on Product Differentiation. Chamberlin's Penetrating Analysis of Non-Price Competition, that is, Product Variation and Selling Costs. Analysis of Oligopoly Problem Neglected in Robinson's Imperfect Competition Theory. According to Chamberlin, Perfect Competition cannot be Regarded as Welfare Ideal. Differences Regarding the Concept of Exploitation of Labour.

40. Price and Output Determination under Oligopoly 843–866

Introduction. Characteristics of Oligopoly: Interdependence, Importance of Advertising and Selling Costs, Group Behaviour, Indeterminateness of Demand Curve Facing an Oligopolist. Causes for the Existence of Oligopolies. Are Price and Output under Oligopoly Indeterminate? Various Approaches to Determination of Price and Output under Oligopoly. Cooperative Vs Non-Cooperative Behaviour: Basic Dilemma of Oligopoly. Collusive Oligopoly: Cartels as a Cooperative Model. Price Leadership: Types of Price Leadership; Price-Output Determination under Low-Cost Price Leadership; Price Leadership by the Dominant Firm. Difficulties of Price Leadership. Kinked Demand Curve Theory of Oligopoly. Prof. Stigler's Critique of Kinked Demand Curve and his Empirical Study.

41. Classical Models of Oligopoly 867–888

Introduction; Cournot's Duopoly Model: Cournot's Approach to Equilibrium; Comparison of Cournot's Equilibrium with Perfectly Competitive Equilibrium and Monopoly Equilibrium. Cournot's Duopoly Equilibrium as an Example of Nash Equilibrium. Cournot's Duopoly Model: Mathematical Illustration. Cournot's Duopoly Equilibrium Explained with the Aid of Reaction Curves. Bertrand's Duopoly Model. Edgeworth Duopoly Model. Comments over the Classical Models of Duopoly (Oligopoly.) Chamberlin's Oligopoly Model. Stackelberg Model: Folloer's Problem; Leader's Profit Maximising Problem.

42. Non-Price Competition: Selling Cost and Advertising 889–901

Introduction. Selling Costs Distinguished from Production Costs. Importance of Advertising and other Selling Costs under Monopolistic Competition and Oligopoly. Effect of Selling Costs (Advertising Expenditure) on Demand. The Curve of Average Selling Cost. Optimum Level of Advertising Outlay (Selling Costs): With Price and Product Variety as Constant. Optimum Level of Advertising Expenditure or Selling Costs when Both Price and Output are Variables. Effect of Advertising (Selling Costs) on Elasticity of Demand. Effect of Advertising (Selling Costs) on Price and Output.

43. Cost-Plus (or Mark-up) Pricing Theory 902–910

Adding Mark up to Average Cost. Cost-Plus Pricing: A Critique of Cost-Plus Pricing.

44. Theory of Games and Strategic Behaviour 911–929

Introduction. Cooperative and Non-Cooperative Games. Dominant Strategy. Choice of an Optimal Strategy in the Absence of a Dominant Strategy. Nash Equilibrium. Neumann-Morgenstern's Game Theory: Maximin and Minimax Strategies. Equilibrium (Saddle) Point. Critical Appraisal of Maximin Strategy. The Prisoners' Dilemma and Oligopoly Theory. Prisoners' Dilemma and Instability of a Cartel. Repeated Games and Tit-for-Tat Strategy. Strategic Moves. Entry Deterrence.

45. Sales Maximisation Model of Oligopoly Firm 930–937

Rationale for Sales Maximization Hypothesis. Sales Maximisation Model: Price-Output Determination of a Product without Advertising. Optimal Advertising Outlay. Sales Maximization Model: Pricing and Changes in Fixed Costs. Emphasis on Non-Price Competition in Sales Maximization Model. Critical Appraisal of Sales Maximization Model.

46. Managerial Theories of the Firm: Marris and Williamson's Models 938–950

Managerial Models: Separation of Control from Ownership. Marris's Managerial Theory of the Firm; Equilibrium of the Firm. Instrument Variables in Marris' s

Model. Evaluation of Marris's Model. Williamson's Managerial Theory of the Firm: Williamson's Managerial Discretional Model; Managerial Utility Maximization. Graphic Representation of Williamson's Managerial Discretionary Model.

47. **Behavioural Theory of the Firm: Satisficing Model** 951–958

Introduction. The Firm as a Coalition of Group with Conflicting Multiple Goals. The Aspiration Level and Satisficing Behaviour. Organisational Slack. The Process of Decision Making by the Firm. Price and Output Determination in the Behavioural Theory. Critical Evaluation of Behavioural Theory.

48. **Theory of Limit Pricing** 959–971

Introduction. Basics of the Theory of Limit Pricing: Bain's Model. Barriers to Entry and Limit Price. Sylos-Labini Model of Limit Pricing: Fixation of Limit Price. Modigliani's Model of Limit Pricing: Generalisation of Sylos's Model. Bhagwati's Extension of Modigliani's Model. Critical Evaluation of the Theory of Limit Pricing.

49. **Government Policies Towards Monopoly and Competition** 972–983

Introduction, The Drawbacks of Monopolies and Limited Competition. Public Policy towards Monopoly and Competition. Problems of Nationalised Industries. Regulation of Natural Monopolies: Public Interest Theory and Marginal-Cost Pricing; Average Cost Pricing ; Capturing Regulators, Encouraging Competition.

PART – V

THEORY OF DISTRIBUTION (PRICING OF FACTORS)

50. **Theory of Distribution: A General View** 987–1009

Functional vs. Personal Distribution. Micro and Macro Theories of Distribution. Theory of Distribution as a Special Case of Price Theory. Marginal Productivity Theory of Distribution: Marginal Productivity Theory: Clark's Version. Marginal Productivity Theory: Marshall-Hick's Version. Critical Evaluation of Marginal Productivity Theory. Euler's Theorem and Product Exhaution Problem or Adding-up Problem. Wicksteed's Solution of Product Exhaustion Problem. Wicksell, Walras, Barone, Samuelson and Hicks' Solution of Product Exhaustion Problem. Interrelationships between Value, Production and Distribution.

51. **Neo-Classical Macro-Theory of Relative Distributive Shares** 1010–1024

Relative Shares of Labour and Capital - Changes in Absolute Shares of Labour and Capital - Elasticity of Substitution and Changes in Relative Factor Shares in Neo-Classical Distribution Theory. Technological Progress and Factor Shares in Income. Cobb - Douglas Production Function and Distributive Shares of Labour and Capital. Solow's and SMAC Production Functions and Relative Shares of Labour and Capital - Critical Evaluation of Neo-Classical Theory of Relative Shares.

52. **Pricing of Factors in Competitive Markets** 1025–1073

Concepts of Factor Productivity. Marginal Revenue Product (MRP) and Value of Marginal Product (VMP). Factor-Employment Equilibrium of a Firm: General Conditions. Derived Demand for a Factor. Factor-Employment Equilibrium of a Firm in Competitive Markets. The Average Revenue Product and the Decision to Employ a Factor. Derivation of Demand Curve for a Single Variable Factor. Demand for a Factor (Labour) with more than One Variable Factor. Competitive Industry's Demand Curve for Labour. Determinants of Demand for Factors. Factors Determining Elasticity of Factor Demand. The Nature of Supply of Factors: Supply of Land, Supply of Labour, Indifference Curves between Income and Leisure: Attitude towards Work and Leisure. Effect of Wage Increase on Work Effort: Income Effect and Substitution Effect. Wage Offer Curve and Supply Curve of Labour. Wage Determination in a Perfectly Competitive Labour Market.

53. **Pricing of Factors in Imperfectly Competitive Markets** 1074–1090

Wage Determination in Case of Perfect Competition in Labour Market and imperfect Competition in Product Market. Factor Pricing (Wage Determination) Under Monopsony. Wage Determination when there is Monopsony in the Labour Market and Perfect Competition in the Product Market. Wage Determination when there is Monopsony in the Labour Market and Monopoly in the Product Market. Exploitation of Labour: How Can Labour Exploitation be Removed?

54. **Trade Unions, Collective Bargaining and Wages** 1091–1111

Superfluous Role of Trade Unions in Traditional Wage Theories: Perfect Competition in the Labour Market. Trade Union and Wages. The Effect of a Trade Union in Case of Monopsony in the Labour Market. Alternative Union Goals. Positive Role of Trade Unions in Raising Wages. Wage Determination under Collective Bargaining. Bilateral Monopoly Model. Wage Determination under Collective Bargaining: Bilateral Monopoly Model. Hicksian Analysis of Wage Determination under Collective Bargaining.

55. **Theory of Rent** 1112–1134

Introduction. Ricardian Theory of Rent: Scarcity Rent: Rent as Surplus over Cost of Production - Differential Rent. Critical Evaluation of Ricardian Theory of Rent. Quasi-rent.

56. **Theories of Interest** 1135–1163

Introduction. Classical Theory of Interest. Critical Appraisal of the Classical Theory of Interest. Loanable Funds Theory of Interest. Critical Evaluation of Loanable Funds Theory. Keynes's Liquidity Preference Theory of Interest. Critical Appraisal of Keynes's Liquidity Preference Theory of Interest. Synthesis between Classical and Keynes's Theories of Interest: LS-LM Curve Model. Why Money Interest Rate is Positive; Keynes's View; Fisher's Analysis.

57. **Theory of Profits** 1164–1174

Introduction. Profit as a Dynamic Surplus. Innovations and Profits: Schumpeter's Theory of Profits. Risk, Uncertainty and Profits: Knight's Theory of Profits. Monopoly Theory of Profits.

58. **Alternative Macro-Theories of Distribution** 1175–1199

Problem of Distributive Shares. Ricardian or Classical Theory of Income Distribution. Criticism of Ricardian Macro-Theory of Distribution. The Marxian Theory of Income Distribution. Critique of the Marxian Theory of Distribution. Kalecki's 'Degree of Monopoly' Theory of Distributive Shares. Kaldor's or Keynesian Theory of Income Distribution. Critical Appraisal of Kaldor's Theory of Distribution.

PART – VI

GENERAL EQUILIBRIUM ANALYSIS AND WELFARE ECONOMICS

59. **General Equilibrium Analysis** 1203–1221

Partial Equilibrium and General Equilibrium Analysis. General Equilibrium of Exchange and Consumption: A Pure Exchange Economy Model. General Equilibrium of Production. Transformation Curve and General Equilibrium of Production. General Equilibrium of Production and Exchange. General Equilibrium and Initial Endowments. General Equilibrium Determines only Relative Prices. General Equilibrium and Perfect Competition.

60. **Welfare Economics: An Introduction** 1222–1228

What Welfare Economics is about. Individual Welfare and Social Welfare. Three Concepts of Social Welfare. Role of Value Judgements in Welfare Economics.

61. **Concept and Conditions of Pareto Optimality** 1229–1255

Pareto Criterion of Social Welfare: Equilibrium Approach. Marginal Conditions of Pareto Optimum: The Optimum Distribution of Products among the Consumers: Efficiency in Exchange. The Optimum Allocation of Factors: The Optimum Direction of Production. The Optimum Degree of Specialisation; The Optimum Factor-Product Relationship. The Optimum Allocation of a Factor's Time; Inter-temporal Optimum Allocation of Money Assets. The Second Order and Total Conditions. A Critical Evaluation of Pareto Criterion and Pareto Optimality. Perfect Competition and Pareto Optimality. Perfect Competition and Optimum Distribution of Goods or Efficiency in Exchange. Perfect Competition and the Optimum Allocation of Factors between Firms.

Perfect Competition and Optimum Degree of Specialisation. Perfect Competition and Allocative Efficiency (Optimum Direction of Production). Perfect Competiton and Optimum Factor-Product Relationship. Fundamental Theorem of Welfare Economics – Does Perfect Competition always ensure Pareto Optimality and Maximum Social Welfare? Failures of Market and Role of Government.

62. **New Welfare Economics: Compensation Principle** 1256–1263

Introduction. Kaldor-Hicks Welfare Criterion: Compensation Principle. Scitovsky Paradox. Scitovsky's Double Criterion of Welfare. A Critique of the Compensation Principle.

63. **Grand Utility Possibility Frontier and Welfare Maximization** 1264–1269

Introduction. From Factor Endowments and Production Functions to the Production Possibility Curve. From the Production Possibility Curve to the Grand Utility Possibility Frontier. From the Grand Utility Possibility Frontier to the Point of Constrained Bliss.

64. **Market Failures, Externalities and Public Goods** 1270–1284

Monopoly as an Obstacle to the Attainment of Pareto Optimality. Externalities and Market Failure. Positive or Beneficial Externalities in Production. Externalities in Consumption. How Externalities Cause Market Failure ? Government Intervention and Externalities. Public Goods and Market Failure: Free-Rider's Problem, Public Goods and Pareto Efficiency. Theory of the Second Best.

65. **Social Welfare Function and Theory of Social Choice** 1285–1302

Introduction. The Classical Social Welfare Function. Pareto Social Welfare Function. Maximin or Rawlsian Social Welfare Function. Bergson-Samuelson's Social Welfare Function. Representation of Bergson-Samuelson Social Welfare Function through Social Indifference Curves. Maximum Social Welfare: Point of Constrained Bliss. A Critical Evaluation of Bergson-Samuelson Social Welfare Functions. Prof. Amartya Sen's Critique. Arrow's Theory of Social Choice. Arrow's Impossibility Theorem. Arrow's Consequences. Amartya Sen on Arrow's Impossibility Theorem. Alternative Social Choice Theories: Classical Utilitarian Welfare Criterion. Rawl's Concept of Social Justice and Welfare Criterion.

PART – VII

INTERTEMPORAL CHOICE AND MARKETS WITH ASYMMETRIC INFORMATION

66. **Interest, Saving and Investment: Intertemporal Choice** 1305–1323

Introduction. Intertemporal Choice: Lending. Supply Curve of Lending. Intertemporal Choice: Borrowing. Borrowing-Lending Equilibrium. Saving-Investment Equilibrium. Determination of Market Interest Rate with Saving and Investment, Borrowing and Lending. Investment Decisions and Present Value Rule. Application of Present Value Rule to Education or Human Capital.

Appendix to Chapter 66: Cost-Benefit Analysis 1324–1329

Meaning. The Use of Cost-Benefit Analysis. Cost-Benefit Criterion. General Steps (or Stages) of Cost-Benefit Analysis. Importance of Cost-Benefit Analysis.

67. **Information Problem and Markets with Asymmetric Information** 1330–1347

The Information Problem. The Market for Lemons and Adverse Selection. Asymmetric Information. Adverse Selection. Measures Adopted to Solve the Problem of Adverse Selection. The Insurance Market and Adverse Selection. The Problem of Moral Hazard. Moral Hazard and Allocative Inefficiency. Market Signalling. The Principal-Agent Problem. The Principal-Agent Problem in Private Sector. Efficiency Wage Theory.

PART–I

SCOPE AND METHODOLOGY OF ECONOMICS

- Nature and Scope of Economic Theory
- Micro and Macro-Economics
- Methodology of Economics
- Methodology of Economics: Economic Statics and Dynamics
- Basic Mathematical Concepts and Optimisation Techniques

CHAPTER

1

Nature and Scope of Economic Theory

The Economic Problem : Scarcity and Choice

Economic theory enunciates the laws and principles which govern the functioning of an economy and its various parts. An economy exists because of two basic facts. First, human wants for goods and services are unlimited, and secondly, productive resources with which to produce goods and services are scarce. With our wants being virtually unlimited and resources scarce, we cannot satisfy all our wants and desires by producing everything we want. That being the case, a society has to decide how to use its scarce resources to obtain the maximum possible satisfaction of its members. It is this basic problem of scarcity which gives rise to many of the economic problems which have long been the concern of economists.

Since it is not possible to satisfy all wants with the limited means of production, every society must decide some way of selecting those wants which are to be satisfied. The necessity for economising arises therefore from the fact that we have limited productive resources such as land, raw materials, skilled manpower, capital equipment etc. at our disposal. These resources being found in limited quantity (the quantity may however increase over time), the goods they can produce are also limited. Goods are thus scarce because the productive resources are scarce. Since the resources are limited in relation to our wants, we should get most out of what we have. Thus ***a society is faced with the problem of choice—choice among the vast array of wants that are to be satisfied.*** If it is decided to use more resources in one line of production, then resources must be withdrawn from the production of some other goods. The scarcity of resources therefore compels us to choose among the different channels of production to which resources are to be devoted. In other words, ***we have the problem of allocating scarce resources so as to achieve the greatest possible satisfaction of wants of the people. This is the economic problem.*** It is also called the economising problem.

The scarcity of resources relative to human wants gives rise to the struggle of man for sustenance and efforts by him to promote his well-being. That the scarcity of resources in relation to human wants is the fundamental economic problem can be easily understood in the context of poor and developing countries like India where quite a large number of population live at a bare subsistence level. The struggle for existence due to the scarcity of resources is too obvious in them to need any elaborate explanation. However, to say that the developed countries, such as the U.S.A., where affluence and prosperity have been brought about also confront the scarcity problem raises some doubts. But the fact is, despite their affluence and riches, developed societies too face the problem of scarcity. Of course, their possession of goods and services has enormously increased, but so have their wants. Indeed, their wants for goods and services have been multiplying during the course of economic growth so that their present wants still remain ahead of their resources and capability to produce. As has been said above, the problem of scarcity of resources is not only the result of availability of limited resources and capability to produce but also of human wants. So long as human wants for goods and services remain ahead of the resources, both natural and acquired, the economic problem of scarcity would exist. If Americans today, for example, were content to live at the level of the Indian middle class people, all their wants would probably be fully satisfied with their available resources and capacity to produce. In that situation they would face little or no scarcity and economic problem for them would disappear. However, it needs to be emphasized again that the affluent and developed countries of the U.S.A. and Western Europe face the problem of scarcity even today as their present wants run ahead of their increased resources and capability to produce.

Since all wants cannot be satisfied due to scarcity of resources we face the problem of choice–choice among multiple wants which are to be satisfied. If it is decided to use more resources in one line of production, some resources must be withdrawn from another commodity. Thus, the problem of choice from the viewpoint of the society as a whole refers to which goods and in what quantities are to be produced and productive resources allocated for their production accordingly so as to achieve greatest possible satisfaction of the people. An eminent English economist Lord Robbins defines economics in terms of this basic economic problem. According to him, ***"Economics is a science which studies human behaviour as a relationship between ends and scarce resources which have alternative uses."***[1] Here ends refer to wants which are considered to be unlimited. The use and allocation of scarce resources to produce goods and services have to be such as would maximise satisfaction. This applies both to the behaviour of the individual and of the society as a whole.

The scarcity of resources also compels us to decide how the different goods should be produced, that is, what production methods should be chosen for the production of goods so as to make best possible use of the available resources. If the resources were unlimited, the problem of how goods should be produced would not have arisen. This is because with unlimited resources it would not matter whichever method, efficient or inefficient, was employed for production of goods.

Further, due to scarcity of resources goods cannot be produced in abundant quantities to satisfy all wants of all the people of a society. This raises another problem of choice, namely, who should get how much from the national output. This means how the national product is distributed among various members of a society.

Thus, problem of scarcity gives rise to some problems generally known as **basic economic problems** which a society has to solve so as to promote material well-being of its people. These basic economic problems relate to what commodities are to be produced, how they are to be produced, how the national product is to be distributed among the people, and how much to provide for future growth. It is with regard to these problems of resource allocation, the choice of production methods, distribution and economic growth, which have their roots in scarcity of resources, that economists have been asking questions from time to time and providing answers for them. Besides, economists have also been raising questions about the ***efficiency of the resource allocation*** for the production of goods and their distribution among them people. This question of economic efficiency is aimed at knowing whether or not a particular allocation of resources to the production of various goods and distribution of income among them ensures maximum social welfare.

The knowledge of the scope and purpose of economic theory can be obtained from the type of relevant questions that have been asked by the economists from time to time and their mode of answering them.

---

1. L. Robbins, *Essay on the Nature and Significance of Economic Science*, London, 1932, p. 15.

The Scope of Economic Theory and Basic Economic Problems

There has been a lot of controversy among economists about the true scope of economic theory or its subject-matter. The subject-matter of economics or economic theory has been variously defined. According to Adam Smith, ***economics enquires into the nature and causes of the wealth of nations.*** According to Ricardo, economics studies "*how the produce of the earth is distributed*", that is, economics deals with the distribution of income and wealth. According to Marshall, economics is a study of mankind in the ordinary business of life and examines that part of individual and social action which is connected with material requisites of well-being. A. C. Pigou says, "***economics studies that part of social welfare which can be brought directly or indirectly into relationship with the measuring rod of money***". Gustav Cassel has defined economics as dealing with markets, prices and market exchange. Professor Lionel Robbins defines economics as a study of the allocation of scarce resources among competing ends or uses. Ludwig Von Mises has defined economics as "the logic of rational action".

Each definition of economics given above is incomplete and inadequate since they do not indicate the true scope and subject-matter of economics. Moreover, some of them are "too wide'' and some "too narrow". Professor Boulding aptly remarks about some of the above definitions : "To define it (economics) as a study of mankind in the ordinary business of life" is surely too broad. To define it as the study of material wealth is too narrow. To define it as the study of human valuation and choice is again probably too wide, and to define it as the "study of that part of human activity subject to the measuring rod of money is again too narrow"

A great confusion has been created about the true nature and scope of economics because of these numerous and conflicting definitions of economics. J. N. Keynes was right when he said, "***Political economy is said to have strangled itself with definitions.***"[2] In view of the present author, the subject-matter of the science of economics has grown so wide and vast that it is extremely difficult to put it in a "nutshell" of a definition. It is because of this fact that modern economists have now stopped discussing the proper way of defining economics. In fact, they think any attempt to define economics is a useless and futile exercise. They are of the view that what economics is about can be better explained by pointing out the various issues and questions with which economists are concerned. It is because of the difficulties in putting the whole subject-matter of economics in a definition of a few words that Jacob Viner has given a pragmatic definition of economics. According to him, "*Economics is what economists do.*" In other words, what economics is, can be better understood from what economists do and what they have been doing. That is to say, what type of questions economists ask and have been asking and what answers they have provided for them. Thus, what economics is about or, in other words, what is the scope and subject-matter of economics can be better known by spelling out the questions economists have been asking and the basic economic problems they have been concerned with.

The following are the main questions which have been asked by the economists from time to time. It is worth remembering that all these fundamental questions arise because of the basic problem of scarcity confronting an economy.

1. What goods are produced and in what quantities by the productive resources which the economy possesses ?
2. How are the different goods produced ? That is, what production methods are employed for the production of various goods and services ?
3. How is the total output of goods and services of a society distributed among its people ?

2. J. N. Keynes, *Scope and Method of Political Economy*, p. 3.

4. Are the use of productive resources economically efficient?
5. Whether all available productive resources of a society are being fully utilized, or are some of them lying unemployed and unutilized ?
6. Is the economy's productive capacity increasing, declining or remaining static over time ?

The six questions listed above have been the concern of economic theory from time to time. As said above, all of them arise from the fundamental problem of scarcity. All economies whether they are capitalist, socialist or mixed, must take decision about them. Economic theory studies how these decisions are arrived at in various societies. It is worth mentioning that ***economic theory has been mainly evolved and developed in the framework of capitalist institutions where free market mechanism plays a dominant role in solving the above basic problems***. Therefore, mainstream economic theory assumes free market system and explains how the above six problems are solved by it and with what degree of efficiency. We shall explain below above six problems and questions in detail and see how they are related to the problem of scarcity.

1. The Problem of Allocation of Resources

The first and foremost basic problem confronting an economy is "What to produce" so as to satisfy the wants of the people. The problem of what goods are to be produced and in what quantities arises directly from the scarcity of resources. If the resources were unlimited, the problem of what goods are to be produced would not have arisen because in that case we should have been able to produce all goods we wanted and also in the desired quantities. But because resources are in fact scarce relative to human wants, an economy must choose among various goods and services. Wants for those goods which society decides not to produce will remain unsatisfied. Thus the question of selecting goods for production implies which wants should be satisfied and which ones to be left unsatisfied.

If the society decides to produce a particular good in a larger quantity, it will then have to withdraw some resources from the production of other goods and devote them to the production of the good which is to be produced more. The greater the quantity of a good which is desired to be produced, the greater the amount of resources allocated to that good. The question of what goods are produced and in what quantities is thus a question about the ***allocation of scarce resources among the alternative uses.***

Thus, with the given scarce resources, if the society decides to produce one good more, the production of some other goods would have to be cut down. For instance, at times of war, when the society decides to produce more war goods like guns, jet planes and other armaments, some resources have to be withdrawn from the production of civilian goods and devoted to the production of war goods. Because of the scarcity of resources we cannot have more 'guns' and more 'butter'; some 'butter' has to be scarified for the sake of more 'guns'.

What determines the allocation of resources and what are the results of attempts made to change the allocation has occupied the minds of economists from the very beginning of our economic science. Whatever the type of economy, be it capitalist, socialist or mixed, a decision has to be made regarding allocation of resources. In a capitalist economy, decisions about the allocation of resources or, in other words, about what goods are to be produced and in what quantities are made through the free-market price mechanism. A capitalist or free-market economy uses impersonal forces of demand and supply to decide what goods are to be produced and in what quantities and thereby determines the allocation of resources. The producers in a free-market economy, motivated as they are by profit considerations, take decisions regarding what goods are to be produced and in what quantities by taking into account the relative prices of various goods. Therefore, the relative prices of goods, which are determined by free play of forces of demand and supply in a free market economy, ultimately determine the production of goods and the allocation of resources.

The branch of economic theory which explains how the relative prices of goods are determined is called ***Microeconomic Theory or Price Theory*** and has been the concern of economists from the earliest days of economics.

2. Choice of a Production Method

There are various alternative methods of producing goods and a society has to choose among them. For example, cloth can be produced either with automatic looms or with powerlooms or with handlooms. Similarly, fields can be irrigated (and hence wheat can be produced) by building small irrigation works like tubewells and tanks or by building large canals and dams. Therefore, it has to decide whether cloth is to be produced by handlooms or powerlooms or automatic looms. Similarly, it has to decide whether the irrigation has to be done by small irrigation works or by large canals. Obviously, it is a problem of the choice of production techniques. Different methods or techniques of production would use *different quantities of various resources.* For instance, the production of cloth with handloom would make use of relatively more labour and less capital. On the other hand, production with automatic looms uses relatively more capital and less labour. Therefore, production with handlooms is a *labour-intensive* technique while production with automatic looms is a *capital-intensive technique* of producing cloth. Thus, a society has to choose whether it wants to produce with labour-intensive methods or capital-intensive methods of production.

More generally, the ***problem of 'how to produce' means which combination of resources is to be used for the production of goods and which technology is to be made use of for their production.*** Scarcity of resources demands that goods should be produced with the most efficient method. If the economy uses its resources inefficiently, the output will be less and there will be unnecessary loss of goods which otherwise would have been available. The choice between different methods of production by a society depends on the available supplies and the prices of the factors of production. The criterion for the choice of a method of production should therefore be the cost of production per unit of output involved in various methods. We have noted above that economic resources are scarce relative to demand. But economic resources are unequally scarce; some are more scarce than others. Therefore, it is in society's interest that those methods of production be employed that make the greatest use of the relatively plentiful resources and economises as much as possible on the relatively scarce resources.

Why one method of production is used rather than another and consequences of the method used are dealt with in the **Theory of Production**. In the theory of production we study the physical relationship between inputs and outputs. This physical relationship between inputs and outputs along with prices of factors goes to determine the cost of production. Cost of production governs the supply of goods which together with demand for them determines their prices. The theory of production thus becomes a part of microeconomic theory (*i.e.* theory of price) and will be explained in detail in the present work.

It is worth noting here that the *choice of technique* of production is dealt with not only in microeconomic theory but is also an important issue in the *theory of economic growth.* This is because the choice of a production technique determines not only the cost of production of a commodity but also the *surplus* which can become a source for further investment.[3] The greater the surplus, the higher the rate of investment and therefore the higher the rate of growth of output and employment. An eminent economist, Prof. Amartya Sen, currently of

3. See Amartya Sen, *Choice of Techniques*, Basil Blackwell, Oxford, 1960.

Harvard University, has analysed the choice of technique as an important issue in economics of growth of the developing countries.

3. The Problem of Distribution of National Product

This is the problem of *sharing of the national product among the various individuals and classes* in the society. The question of distribution *of* national product has occupied the attention of economists since the days of Adam Smith and David Ricardo who explained the distribution of national product between different social groups such as workers and capitalists in a free market society. ***Who should get how much from the total output of goods and services is a question concerning social justice or equity.*** Economists' interest in this subject has increased very much' in recent years. It is important to note that the distribution of national product depends upon the distribution of money income. Those people who have larger incomes would have larger capacity to buy goods or to use Prof. Amartya Sen's phrase, would have larger ***entitlement for goods*** and hence will get greater share of output. Those who have low incomes, would have less purchasing power to buy things and will therefore be able to obtain a small share of output. More equal is the distribution of income, more equal will be the distribution of national product.

Now, the incomes can be earned either by doing some work or by lending the services of one's property such as land, capital. Labour, land and capital are factors of production and all of them contribute to the production of national product and get prices or rewards for their contribution. The question as to how the prices or rewards of factors of production are determined is the subject-matter of the ***Theory of Distribution.*** After the marginalist revolution in economic theory, theory of distribution has been boiled down to the theory of factor pricing which is an important part of the price theory or what is now popularly called microeconomic theory. The old division of factors into land, labour and capital is retained in modern economic theory but their old association with *'social classes'*, such as capitalist and working classes as was made by classical economists has been given up.

The theory of distribution viewed as the theory of pricing of factors of production is merely an extension of the theory of price or value. Prof. A. K. Dassgupta rightly remarks,"*Distribution appears an extension of the theory of value, being just a problem of pricing of factors of production.* The two aspects of the economic problem are then integrated into a unified and logically self-consistent system. *Value of commodities is derived in the ultimate analysis from utility, and value of factors derived from productivity imputed by the commodities which they help in producing.* The old tripartite division of factors into land, labour and capital is retained but their old association with social 'classes' is lost. Factors are conceived as just productive agents independently of the institutional framework within which they operate."[4]

The theory of distribution viewed as the theory of factor pricing deals with the functional distribution of income rather than the personal distribution of income, since it explains only how the prices of factors, that is, wages of labour, rent of land, interest on capital and profits of entrepreneur are determined. But the question which we raised, namely, "how the national product is distributed among the various individuals that comprise a society" is not fully answered by the theory of functional distribution. It is the personal distribution of income that determines who would get how much from the national product. Now, the income of a person depends not only on the price of a factor he owns and the amount of work he does but also on how much property or assets in the form of factors of production such as land and capital he owns. Private ownership of the means of production is a *sine qua non* of the capitalist system. Therefore, the *personal distribution of income is greatly affected by the distribution of the*

4. *Tendencies in Economic Theory,* Presidential Address to the 43rd Annual Conference of the Indian Economic Association held at Chandigarh, December, 1960.

ownership of property. A person who owns a large amount of property will be enjoying a higher income. In the free market capitalist economies because of the large inequalities in the ownership of the property there are glaring inequalities of income. As a result, the distribution of national product is very much unequal in capitalist economies. In recent years, the governments of the capitalist countries, like U.S.A., Great Britain have taken various steps to reduce inequalities of income and property and have accordingly tried to influence the distribution of national product. Since the distribution of the ownership of property is an institutional factor, it will not be discussed in this book which deals with pure economic theory. We shall, therefore, confine ourselves to the analysis of the theory of functional distribution which is an integral part of the microeconomic theory.

4. The Problem of Economic Efficiency

Resources being scarce, it is desirable that they should be most efficiently used. It is therefore important to know whether a particular economy works efficiently. It is important to note that concept of economic efficiency is related to the well-being of the members of a society. *When allocation of resources is such that no one can be made better off without making anyone else worse off, economic efficiency is said to have been achieved*. This concept of economic efficiency was put forward by Italian economist and sociologist, Vilfredo Pareto (1848–1923) and is therefore often called *Pareto efficiency* or *Pareto optimality*. The achievement of economic efficiency requires that the allocation of resources and the production and distribution of goods by an economy is Pareto optimal. Having asked what and how goods are being produced and how the total national product is distributed, it is but proper to ask further whether the production and distribution decisions of an economy are efficient ones. The production is said to be efficient if the productive resources are used for production of various goods in such a way that through any rearrangement it is impossible to produce more of one good without reducing the output of any other good. The production would be economically inefficient if it is possible by reorganising the use of resources to increase the production of one good without reducing the output of any other. Likewise, the distribution of the goods among individuals of a society is efficient if it is not possible to make, through any redistribution of goods, some individuals or any one person better off without making any other person worse off.

It is not enough to use resources efficiently for production of goods and distribute them efficiently among individuals for consumption. The achievement of these production and distribution efficiencies will not ensure maximum well-being if the economy is allocating resources in the production of goods which do not correspond to the preferences of the people. *For attaining economic efficiency, optimum product-mix must be produced, that is, allocation of resources among production of various goods should be in accordance with the preferences of people, given their incomes*. If the economy is producing wrong-mix of goods, then through reallocation of resources among them it will be possible to make some people better off without any one worse off.

In the later chapters of the book we will explain how under perfect competition where individual firms have no control over the price of the product, the three efficiencies, productive, allocative and distributive, are achieved. Therefore, perfect competition is considered as an ideal market form. On the other hand, under conditions of monopoly, monopolistic competition and oligopoly where individual firms have market power to set price, economic efficiency in production, distribution and allocation of resources is not achieved causing loss of social welfare. Further, it may be noted that these may prevail productive efficiency but the product-mix produced may not conform to the consumers' preferences so that there are long queues outside the markets or stores selling commodities whose level of production has been quite insufficient or inadequate as compared to the wants of the consumers for them. Such was the case in erstwhile USSR before the collapse of communism in late nineteen eighties. In our opinion, it is the failure to achieve economic or allocative efficiency which was the chief economic cause of the downfall of communism in erstwhile USSR and East European countries.

It may however be noted that *attainment of economic efficiency also involves the achievement of productive efficiency.* This is because if productive efficiency in the use of resources is not achieved, it would then be possible to make some people better off by increasing production through fuller and better utilisation of resources without making others worse off. Thus with the achievement of economic efficiency a society not only produces the largest possible output with the available resources but also allocates its resources for the production of goods in such a way that conforms to consumers' preferences.

5. The Problem of Full Employment of Resources

Whether all available resources of a society are fully utilized is a highly significant question because answer to it would determine whether or not there will exist involuntary unemployment of labour as well as of capital stock. In view of the scarcity of resources to satisfy all wants of the people, it may look strange to ask a question whether or not all available resources of a community are being fully utilized. This is because resources being scarce, a community will try to use all the available resources to achieve maximum possible satisfaction of the people. Thus a community will not consciously allow the resources to lie idle. But in a capitalist free market society it so happens that at times of depression available resources are not fully utilised. At times of depression, many workers are rendered unemployed; they want to be employed but no jobs are there for them. At such times, factories which can employ people are there, but they are not working. Thus, at times of depression in capitalist economies, even the scarce available resources are not fully employed.

This question assumed great importance in economic theory during the depression of nineteen thirties when, on the one hand, about 25 per cent of labour force in the USA, Britain and other industrialised countries was rendered unemployed and, on the other, a number of factories representing a lot of capital stock remained idle and unused. How did it come about became a controversial question at that time. An eminent British economist, J.M. Keynes put forward a different explanation from the then popularly held view advocated by neo-classical economists led by A. C. Pigou. Thanks to J.M. Keynes who in his book ***"General Theory of Employment, Interest and Money"*** published in 1936, explained what caused such involuntary unemployment of resources. Keynes' explanation was that unemployment of labour at that time was found not because money wages were fixed at higher levels by the activities of strong labour unions and intervention of the Government but because ***of the fall in aggregate effective demand for goods and services***. His theory of deficiency of effective demand causing recession and resulting in involuntary unemployment of labour and underutilisation of capital stock has played an important role in the formulation of economic policies to control fluctuations in economic activity. Keynesian analysis has greatly widened the scope of economic theory and improved our understanding of the working of the capitalist economic system which suffers from large fluctuations in economic activity. This branch of economic theory which deals with the problem of employment of resources (and thus with the determination of national income) is called ***Macroeconomic Theory.*** This macroeconomic theory has been greatly developed beyond the Keynesian perception in recent years and several alternative models of macroeconomics have been put forward.

6. The Problem of Economic Growth

It is very important to know whether the productive capacity of an economy is increasing. If the productive capacity of the economy is growing, it will be able to produce progressively more and more goods and services with the result that the living standards of its people will rise. The increase in the capacity to produce goods over time is called economic growth. Now, the analysis of the factors on which the rate of economic growth depends has interested economists since the days of Adam Smith who in his book ***"An Enquiry into the Nature and Causes of the Wealth of Nations"*** threw light on the subject. But after the classical economists and with the advent of marginalism the economists' interest in the problem of economic growth almost disappeared and the marginalist theory of relative prices and resource allocation with its emphasis on scarcity and choice occupied the central position in economic theory for a long time. In the thirties and forties, with the publication of Keynes' ***General Theory of Employment, Interest and Money,*** the problem of depression and business cycles occupied the minds of the economists.

But the need for balanced equilibrium growth rate in the developed capitalist countries on the one hand and the urge to remove mass poverty, hunger and chronic unemployment in the developing countries after their achievement of political independence have once again aroused the interests of economists in the problems of economic growth and numerous growth and development models have been put forward. Some of these growth models such as Harrod-Domar model, Neo-classical growth models of Solow and Swan, Cambridge growth models of Kaldor and Joan Robinson etc. have been propounded to explain and analyse the growth problem of the industrialised developed countries.[5] Likewise, to initiate and accelerate the process of growth in developing countries, the various theories and models of growth and development have been offered.[6] However, it is worth noting that till 1980s the concept of economic development generally implied the active intervention of the government and the public sector in the field of production. And, with the fall of communism in the USSR and East European countries and dismal experience of the working of public sector in the developing countries, the trend all over the world today is to adopt *market friendly approach* to development. To what extent free-market economy approach would generate greater economic growth and ensure economic efficiency in the developing countries, only the future will tell.

Two Views about Development Economics

However, it is worth mentioning that in the scope of development economics today we are not only concerned with the promotion of growth of GNP (gross national product) and raising standards of material living of the people at the present but also with bringing out the adverse and disastrous consequences of depletion of natural resources. Besides, economists are also interested in preventing environmental pollution which occurs through reckless industrialisation and economic growth. If the interests of the future generation are to be promoted, the resources, especially energy resources, have to be conserved and also if *quality of life* has to be improved, the environment has to be protected and saved from pollution. It is

5. Those who are interested in knowing the various growth models concerning the industrialised developed countries may read "*Growth Economics*" (Penguin Modern Economics Readings) edited by Amartya Sen.
6. The various leading theories and models of development relating to the developing countries have been brought together in an edited work "*Leading Issues in Economic Development*" by Gerald M. Meier (Oxford University Press, 8th edition, 2005.) Another two-volume World Bank Publication "*Pioneers in Economic Development*", edited by Gerald Meier and Dudley Seers (Oxford University Press, 1989) is a highly useful work describing the contributions of various pioneers in development theories and models of development. Mention may be made of Ragnar Nurkse's *Capital Formation in Underdeveloped Countries,* Lewis" *Economic Development with. Unlimited Supplies of Labour,* Rostow's *Take off into Self-Sustained, Growth,* Hirschman's *Strategy of Economic Development,* Sen's *Choice of Techniques.*

with this regard that the concept of *sustainable growth* or *smtainable development* has been put forward which implies that if severe damage is done to the *environment* and *resources* and if because of reckless industrialisation resources are not conserved for future, economic growth in the future will be limited.

PROBLEM OF SCARCITY VS. PROBLEM OF AFFLUENCE

It may be pointed out here that recently some economists in the industrially developed countries, especially USA, have pointed out that the important problem now confronting them is the problem of *affluence* rather than scarcity. During the past century or two there has been a rapid economic growth in these countries which has brought about unprecedented riches and prosperity to their citizens. As a result, the standards of living of their people have gone up very high. It is said, they have won over the problem of scarcity and poverty and are now facing the problems created by affluence and growth, such as problems of mental tension, optimum use of leisure, environment pollution etc. Thus having achieved growth and affluence they are now thinking with reference to what might be called *"beyond economic growth"*. The economist who has put forward this point of view is a noted American economist Professor J. K. Galbraith, the former United States Ambassador to India. He presented this viewpoint in his revolutionary book ***"The Affluent Society"***.

The use of the term "The Affluent Society" looks strange, since economists have always been laying a great stress on the point that the basic economic problem a society has to encounter is the problem of scarcity, which is the mother of all economic problems that arise in the society. Economists have remained so much preoccupied with scarcity and poverty that it is now difficult for them to believe that economics is concerned with problems of affluence. It is precisely because of economists' preoccupation with the problems of scarcity even today in Western Europe and the USA that Professor Galbraith has pointed out that their concern with problems of scarcity and poverty has become outdated. According to him, the conventional economic ideas and wisdom are inadequate because the problem has changed from scarcity to affluence, from poverty to prosperity. Emphasizing the affluence of Western European countries and the United States of America he remarks, "the experience of nations with well-being is exceedingly brief. Nearly all throughout all history have been poor... in the last few generations in the comparatively small corner of the world populated by Europeans.... and especially in the United States, there has been great and quite unprecedented affluence.[7] And urging the economists to change their traditional ideas about the economic world since it has fundamentally changed, he says, "The ideas by which the people of this favoured part of the world interpret their existence, and in a measure guide their behaviour, were not forged in a world of wealth. These ideas were the product of a world in which poverty had always been man's normal lot."[8]

Speaking about that old ideas about economic behaviour and conventional prescriptions about rational behaviour formed in the world of poverty have become irrelevant and obsolete in today's world of affluence, he asserts, "No one would wish to argue that the ideas which interpreted the world of grim scarcity would serve equally well for the contemporary United States. Poverty was an all pervasive fact of that world. Obviously, it is not of ours. One would not expect that preoccupations of a poverty-ridden world be relevant in one where the ordinary individual has access to amenities– food, entertainment, personal transportation and plumbing– in which not even the rich rejoiced a century ago. So great has been the change that many of the desires of the individual are no longer even evident to him. They become so only as they synthesized, elaborated and nurtured by advertising and salesmanship."[9]

7. J. K. Galbraith, *The Affluent Society* (1958). p. 1.
8. *Ibid, p. 2.*
9. Ibid, p. 2.

It is true that United States and Western European countries have eliminated general mass poverty from their people and, with the phenomenal progress of science and technology, have achieved unprecedented affluence and enormous production of goods with which they have been able to satisfy their wants to a greater extent. But from this it should not be construed that the economic problem of scarcity has ceased to exist in the so-called affluent world of Western Europe and the USA. **The term scarcity in economics is used in a *relative* sense,** that is, in the sense of scarcity of resources relative to the wants of the people. With technological advancement, it is no doubt that developed and rich countries have greatly increased their resources and production but with growth and development new wants and desires have also been created. In view of this, it cannot be said that resources have become abundant in relation to wants in these affluent countries.

Of course, it is true that mass poverty as a general phenomenon has disappeared in the affluent societies. ***But scarcity in the economic sense and poverty are two different things.*** Therefore, the affluent countries still confront the economic problem of scarcity—the problem of using resources in such a fashion as to attain the maximum possible satisfaction of wants. The problem of economic scarcity would have been won only if the resources would have become abundant in relation to wants which have been multiplying during the process of growth. Besides, the basic economic problems which arise due to the scarcity of resources in relation to wants still confront the affluent societies and they have to solve them in one way or the other. These basic economic problems are: what goods to be produced and in what quantities (that is, how the resources are to be allocated to the production of various goods), what methods or techniques of production to be employed for the production of various goods, how the total national product to be distributed and how much investment or capital accumulation should take place so as to achieve further growth. All these problems arise because of the fundamental scarcity of resources in relation to wants and therefore still require rational and optimum solutions by the affluent societies so that the maximum possible satisfaction of wants of the people is achieved.

How the prices are determined in a market is still a subject of economic enquiry in these affluent societies. This phenomenon of pricing is enquired into because goods and services that are priced are scarce in relation to wants for them. Further, ***it is scarcity again that causes conflict*** between parties to exchange, popularly known as classes such as, industrialists, workers, landlords, traders. Given the national cake, that is, total national output of goods and services, when one class gets more share, the other has less of it. This causes conflict and clashes. The fact that, wages to labour are paid and capital earns interest further goes to show that the problem of scarcity has been quite there. Thus, the problem of scarcity still dominates the economic scene in the so-called affluent societies. Of course, the unprecedented affluence and prosperity enjoyed by the people has given rise to several problems such as depletion of valuable resources, pollution of environment and consequently worsening the quality of life.

We, of course, admit that because of the achievement of prosperity the affluent and developed countries can now afford *some waste in the use of resources,* which the poor world cannot. Some loss in economic efficiency (that is to say, inefficiency in the use of resources) will not make much difference in their production or standards of living which have risen very high. We further admit that the affluent societies have *reduced their problem of scarcity* in the sense that they have been able to reduce *the gap between resources and basic wants* by expanding their production potential enormously. But the fundamental problem of scarcity has not been completely overcome by these affluent societies and probably it will never be since wants will always remain ahead of resources and production. When the problem of scarcity ceases to exist, there will be no need for the science of economics which will then disappear. Thus, economics will disappear only in a world so rich that wants were unfulfilled for lack of resources. Such a world is not imminent and may be impossible.

It is important to note that the two-thirds of the world is still living in poverty. This two-thirds part of the world includes the developing countries of Asia, Africa and Latin America. The per capita income of these countries is so low that a large chunk of their population is living at the subsistence or near subsistence level. The abysmal poverty, hunger, disease, squalor and unemployment rule the land there. The problem of scarcity is present there in its full strength and affluence for them is still a far cry. In view of the scarcity of resources and unlimited wants for more and more production, these countries must utilise their resources so as to get more out of them. Thus they encounter the ***economic problem of allocation of the scarce resources*** so as to achieve the maximum satisfaction of their people.

CRITICAL EVALUATION OF ROBBIN'S DEFINITION OF ECONOMICS

We have explained above the various questions and problems which are discussed by economists. Therefore, we are now in a position to examine Robbins' definition of economics, which for a long time, was regarded as a correct, adequate and scientific definition. We shall see to what extent it covers the various questions with which modern economists are concerned.

Robbins not only criticised Marshall's definition and other welfare definitions of economics but also provided a new definition which he considered to be more scientific and correct. He has given this definition in his famous book "*Nature and Significance of Economic Science*" which he brought out in the year 1932. According to Robbins, economics studies the problems which arise because of the scarcity of resources. Nature has not provided mankind sufficient resources to satisfy all its wants. Therefore, the people have to choose for satisfaction of which wants the resources are to be utilised. Thus, according to Robbins, economics is the science of scarcity and it studies how the scarce resources are allocated among their different uses. Thus, he has defined economics in the following words: ***"Economics is the science which studies human behaviour as a relationship between ends and scarce means which have alternative uses."*** This definition is based upon the following three facts.

1. Unlimited Wants. The first fact on which Robbins' definition is based is that man's wants are unlimited. In this definition ends imply wants for which the man uses resources. That man's wants are unlimited is a very important and fundamental fact of economic life of the people. If man's wants were limited, then no economic problem would have arisen. But in the real life of the people there is no end and limit to their wants; when one want is satisfied another crops up. An important thing to know about wants is that all are not of equal intensity; some are more intense than others. It is because of the different intensities of the wants for goods and services that people are able to allocate the scarce resources to satisfy some of their wants.

2. Scarce Means. The second element which gives rise to economic problem is that resources are scarce in relation to wants. If the resources like wants were unlimited no economic problem would have arisen because in that case all wants could have been satisfied and there would have been no problem of choosing between the wants and allocating the resources between them. Because the resources are in a fact scarce all wants cannot be satisfied. Therefore, human beings have to decide for the satisfaction of which wants the resources should be used and which wants should be left unfulfilled. It should be noted that means or resources here refer to natural productive resources, financial resources, man-made capital goods, consumer goods, time available with man, etc. If the means or resources were unlimited then we would have obtained goods in the desired quantity because, in that state of affairs, goods would have been free goods. But in actual life we cannot obtain goods free of cost or without price; we have to pay price for them and do labour to obtain them.

3. Alternative Uses of Means. The third fact on which Robbins' definition is based is that resources or means have various alternative uses. In other words, the resources can be put into various uses. For instance, coal can be used as a fuel for the production of industrial goods, it can be used for running trains, it can be used for domestic cooking purposes and for so many other purposes. Likewise, financial resources can be utilised for the production of consumer goods, for the production of capital goods and for so many other goods. It has to be decided for which uses the resources have to be allocated. The man or society has therefore to choose the uses for which resources have to be employed. If the resources would have one use only, then the question of choice would not have arisen at all. In the case of single uses of different resources. They will be employed for the uses for which they are meant. It is because of the various alternative uses of the resources that we have to decide which would be the best allocation of resources.

We thus see that Robbins' definition stands on the above mentioned three facts, namely, ***unlimited wants, scarce resources and alternative uses of them***. According to him, economics studies human behaviour in regard to how he satisfies his wants with the scarce resources. According to him, economics is a *human science* and not a *social science* ; it studies man in a society as well as without a society when he is confronted with the problem of allocating scarce resources to satisfy his wants.

An important thing to note about Robbins' definition is that he ***does not draw distinction between material and non-material commodities, between welfare and non-welfare activities.*** According to Robbins, economics studies man's activities in regard to all goods and services, whether they are material or immaterial, provided they satisfy the wants of the people. Besides, whether the goods and services are conducive to human welfare or not, economics would study them if they satisfy the wants of some men. It is also worth noting that in view of Robbins economics does not deal with the question as to what ends should be achieved *i.e,* what wants should be satisfied and what not because in this regard man himself has to decide. Economics itself does not make a choice. Economist only tells in what ways the given ends or wants can be achieved with the minimum possible resources. What ends or wants have been selected for satisfaction is no concern of economics. Whether the ends chosen by man are good or bad, noble or ignoble, economics would study them because the task of economist is not to praise or condeon but only to analyse and explain. To decide about the desirability or otherwise of a thing is beyond the scope of economics. Therefore, according to Robbins, ***economics is neutral between ends.***

It follows from the definition of Robbins that ***economics is a science of choice.*** It deals with how the resources of society should be allocated to the satisfaction of different wants. Whenever the resources are scarce and the wants are many the question of choice arises. The man has to choose between the wants to which resources are to be allocated. Thus, Robbins remarks, "When time and means for achieving ends are limited and capable of alternative application and the ends are capable of being distinguished in order of importance, then behaviour necessarily assumes the form of choice."[10] It is thus clear that economics is the science of choice.

Like Robbins many other economists have also defined economics in terms of scarcity of resources and choice. Thus Wicksteed says that economics is a "study of those principles on which the resources of a community should be so regulated and administered as to secure communal ends without waste."[11] Likewise, G.J. Stigler defines economics in the following words : "Economics is the study of the principles governing the allocation of scarce means

10. L. Robbins, *Nature and Significance of Economic Science*, p. 114.
11. Philip Wicksteed, *Commonsense of Political Economy*, p. 12.

among competing ends when the objective of allocation is to maximise the attainment of the ends.[12] Similarly, Scitovosky says, "Economics is a social science concerned with the administration of scarce resources"[13] Professor Erich Roll has also defined economics in terms of scarcity of resources and choice. Thus according to him, "The economic problem is essentially a problem arising from the necessity of choice ; choice of the manner in which limited resources with the alternative uses are disposed of. It is the problem of the husbandry of resources .... economics studies the activity of husbandry."[14]

It is thus clear that after Robbins economics has assumed character of the science which is concerned with the scarcity of resources and the problem of choice which arises because of the scarcity. Robbins' definition has been claimed to be more scientific. It has broadened the scope of economics whereas the material-welfare definition had narrowed down the scope of economic study. Moreover, with this definition which lays stress on scarcity of resources and the problem of choice, economics ***can no longer be called dismal science.*** Economics has no responsibility about the choice of ends. Ends may be good or bad, economics has no concern with it. When the ends are many and resources scarce the science of economics is required to study this problem.

A Critical Appraisal

No doubt Robbins has made economics a scientific study and his definition has become very popular among the economists. This definition brings to light the basic economic problem which confronts the society. But Robbins' definition has also been criticised on several grounds. The main charge against Robbins is that he has made economics quite impersonal, colourless and devoid of any normative element. He says, equilibrium is just an equilibrium. He does not seek to make economics a study of welfare. Therefore, many economists like Durbin, Fraser, Beveridge and Wootton have tried to defend Marshall's idea about the true scope of economics and its objective of promoting social welfare. Thus, Wootton has said that "It is very difficult for economists to divest their discussions completely of all normative significance."

Economics is an Instrument of Promoting Social Welfare. It is not justified on the part of Robbins to oppose making economics an engine of social welfare. In fact, it has been contended that even in Robbins' definition itself the idea of welfare is present. If we closely analyse the Robbins' definition we would come to the conclusion that it says that economics is concerned with how a man and society use its scarce resources so as to achieve maximum possible satisfaction of human wants. But this maximum satisfaction of wants is nothing else but maximum welfare. Robbins' definition implies that allocation of resources to the satisfaction of wants has to be made in such a way that maximum satisfaction is achieved. Thus, without the satisfaction or welfare being brought into consideration the question of allocation of scarce resources does not arise. Thus, it is not correct on the part of Robbins to assert that economics is neutral between ends.

Many economists are of the view that if economics has to be made a means of promoting social welfare and economic growth it has to give its decision what is good and what is bad to achieve these ends. In other words, if economics is to serve as an engine of social betterment, then it would have to abandon the neutrality between ends or objectives. Economist would have to tell what is good or bad for welfare and progress and what steps should be taken to attain these ends. Thus, in the opinion of Robbins, that economists should eschew the term welfare from the scope of economics is quite uncalled for. Thomas rightly remarks, "the function of the economist is not only to explain and explore but also to evaluate and condemn".

12. G. J. Stigler, *The Theory of Price,* 1949, p. 12.
13. T. Scitovosky, *Welfare and Competition, 1952,* p. 3.
14. Erich Roll, *The Elements of Economic Theory,* 1950, p. 16.

Economics is a Social Science. As noted above, Robbins viewed economics as a human science and not a social science. In one sense the scope of economics has been unnecessarily widened by Robbins. In accordance with Robbins' view economist would also study a sadhu who lives in a cave of Himalaya because that sadhu would also be faced with the problem of how to distribute his time between various ends. That is, a sadhu has also to face the problem of choice and therefore comes within the purview of Robbins' definition. But many economists are of the view that economics is a social science and it should study the problem of choice when it has a social aspect *i.e.,* when a man's choice affects other members of the society. Therefore, many economists though laying stress on the scarcity of resources and the problem of choice have described it as a social science and not a human science as Robbins treats it. Thus, Sictovosky defines economics as "a social science concerned with the administration of scarce resources." Likewise, according to Cairncross, "***Economics is a social science studying how people attempt to accommodate scarcity to their wants and how these attempts interact through exchange***." It is thus clear, contrary to the views of Robbins, economics has been regarded by many economists as a social science. Economics studies the problem of choice if it has social implications.

Economics is more than a Study of Resource Allocation. A serious objection against Robbins' definition is that it has reduced economics to a mere value theory. In other words, economics has to study only how the prices of goods and factors are determined and consequently how the allocation of resources to the production of various goods is decided. But the scope of economics is wider than the allocation of resources and the price theory. These days the importance of macroeconomics has increased in which we study how the national income of country and its total employment are determined. But the determination of national income and employment does not fall within the purview of Robbins' definition which only lays stress on the allocation of resources. The history of western economies has revealed that there has been great instability in them. There has been periodic occurrence of mass unemployment and depression. On the other hand, at other times, these economies have encountered the problems of boom and inflation. It is the task of economics to explain this instability and short-run fluctuations in the levels of income, prices, output and employment. But Robbins' definition leaves this untouched. It is thus clear that macroeconomics which has become more important these days does not come within the purview of Robbins' definition.

Robbins' definition also does not cover the theory of economic growth and development. The theory of economic growth and development studies how the national income and per capita income of a country increase over a long period of time and what factors cause such increases. With economic growth productive capacity of the country expands which brings about an increase in national income, per capita income and level of employment. While Robbins takes the resources as given and talks about their allocation, the theory of economic growth implies how to minimise the problem of scarcity by expansion of capacity to produce more goods and services. In developing countries the question of economic growth is more important because these countries are making efforts to remove poverty from their people and to raise their living standards through economic growth. In the recent years, many theories regarding how to initiate economic growth and also how to accelerate it in the developing countries have been propounded. The theory of economic growth has become the core of the science of economics both in the developed and. developing countries. Robbins' definition is defective because it does not cover an important subject like economic growth.

Joan Robinson's Critique of Robbins' Definition

A prominent British economist, Joan Robinson has asserted that the existence of involuntary unemployment at times of slump, as occurred in the early thirties and explained by J. M. Keynes, contradicts the principle of scarcity and choice which Robbins considered as the subject of economics. According to her, the ***existence of involuntary unemployment of labour on the one hand and the idle capital stock on the other in the situation of depression represent indeed the situation of abundance of resources in the sense that we do not have to forego one thing in order to have another*** since with the use of unemployed and idle resources we can produce some goods more without sacrificing others provided there is sufficient demand for them. Referring to Robbins book "***Essay on the Nature and Significance of Economic Science***" wherein he described economics as the subject that deals with the allocation of scarce means between alternative uses. Joan Robinson writes, "By the time the book came out there were 3 million workers unemployed in Great Britain and statistical measure of GNP in USA had recently fallen to half its former level. It was just a coincidence that the book appeared when means for any end at all had rarely been less scarce."[15]

Defending Robbins definition against the onslaught of Joan Robinson Late Prof. A. K. Dassgupta writes, "Keynesian involuntary unemployment does by no means suggest a failure of the scarcity postulate; it is due, on the other hand, to one of those vagaries of the capitalist system which segregates the act of investment from the act of saving."[16] He further writes, "the abundance that Keynesian economics denotes is an apparent abundance, not real. The fact is that even at the depth of depression labour is paid a wage and capital earns interest. Keynesian involuntary unemployment, far from being a sign of the failure of the scarcity principle, ***is rather to be explained by a feature of the capitalist system***". In view of the present author Prof. A. K. Dassgupta misses the real point in Joan Robinson's criticism of Robbins definition of economics. The real import of Robinson's critique of Robbins' definition is that the nature of the basic economic problem faced in the period of slump was not one of scarcity of resources and their allocation among alternative uses, but of the use of massive amount of idle and involuntarily unemployed human and capital resources in the economy. These resources were lying idle because investment in a private enterprise economy was lacking not because of scarce resources or small savings but due to the deficiency of effective demand for goods which lowered the expected rate of return from investment.

Thus, if the purpose of economic theory is to raise relevant questions and provide answer to them, economics of Robbins' definition which concerns itself with only allocation of scarce resources among alternative ends did not cover the paramount economic problem, namely, the existence of involuntary unemployment on a massive scale faced by the private enterprise economy at times of depression. In our view the significance of the economic problem highlighted by Keynes lies in describing that massive unemployment of labour and gross underutilisation of capital stock at times of depression is not due to the supply-side factor, namely, the scarcity of resources but due to the fact that economic system failed to generate sufficient effective demand to ensure full employment of resources. The investment was lacking not because of scarce savings but due to the deficiency of effective demand for goods, the expected rate of profits on the new investment was not enough to ensure the amount of investment equal to the saving gap corresponding to full employment level of national product. We therefore agree with Joan Robinson that the economic problem facing a private enterprise economy at times of depression

15. Joan Robinson, The Second Crisis of Economic Theory, printed in her *Selected Economic Writings*, Oxford University Press, 1974, p. 237.

16. See his article "The Purpose of Economic Theory" in *Reflections on Economic Development and Social Change*, Essays in Honour of Dr. V.K.R.V. Rao edited by Hanumantha Rao and P, C. Joshi (Oxford, 1960).

underwent a sea change; it was of a different nature from ***the problem of allocation of scarce resources among alternative*** *uses* and required an answer different from the economic theory described by Robbins' definition.

In defense of Robbins' definition Late Prof. A. K. Dassgupta further argues that the theory of growth involves a choice of resource allocation and therefore can be described within the framework of Robbins' definition. According to him, growth is essentially a choice between the present and future output and consumption. Thus, according to Neo-Classical economics as defined by Robbins, economic growth depends upon rate of investment which is governed by saving. Therefore, how much to grow depends upon how much to consume out of current national income and how much to save for investment purposes so as to expand production and consumption in the future. To put in terms of physical resources, the decision regarding saving and investment implies how much of the available resources should be allocated for the production of consumer goods and how much for making capital goods. And, the greater the amount of resources devoted to the production of capital goods, the greater the rate of growth of output. Thus, Prof. A. K. Dassgupta writes, "it is not true that the theory of growth eschews choice. It very much involves choice. Is not the problem of growth one of allocation of scarce resources among outputs at different points of time ? And, is not such allocation a function of the relation between current output and future output ? ***Growth rightly understood is essentially an extension of allocation problem to cover time.***"[17]

However, in our view, the scarcity of resources and the choice about their optimum allocation, between the present and future does not tell the full story of economic growth. There is no dispute about the fact that economic growth in an economy to an extent depends on investment but whether investment is determined by the savings as Prof. Dassgupta and other economists who view the process of growth as an allocation of scarce resources between the present and future is a doubtful proposition. In fact, Keynes and his followers such as Joan Robinson have argued that ***in the dynamics of growth it is investment that determines saving rather than the other way round.*** Investment depends upon expectations of profits from the sale of goods produced with the capital goods in which investment has been made and these expectations of profits from investment depend on the level of aggregate demand. Investment leads to increase in national income and, given the propensity to save, at a higher income more is saved.

As has been brought out by Harrod and Domar who extended the Keynesian short-run analysis to the long-term problem of growth that ***steady growth in the presently developed countries can be achieved if demand for goods is increasing sufficiently to match the expanding productive capacity due to investment that is currently taking place.*** Thus, the sustained and steady growth in the present-day industrialised countries is not merely a problem of allocation of scarce resources between the present and future but also hinges on whether adequate demand for goods is forthcoming or not. This is not to deny the crucial importance of scarcity of resources and the need for its proper allocation among products and between the present and future. What is being suggested is that this does not tell the whole story about economics; the demand side of the problem is also important.

Likewise, in developing countries in the initial years of planned development the growth of GNP was described as the prime objective and for promotion of growth stress was laid on raising the rate of saving so as to mobilise scarce resources for investment. However, the experience of six decades of development in these countries reveals that, as in developed countries, the growth in the developing countries can also be constrained by effective demand apart from scarcity of resources for investment.

17. *Op Cit*, p. 7.

Further, it has now been realised that economic growth in developing countries is not function of investment in capital alone but also depends on technological progress, expansion in education and health care, and institutional changes such as land reforms in agriculture. Moreover, the real problem of developing countries is not merely to generate and promote high growth rate in GNP but also to eradicate mass poverty and chronic unemployment. Thus *raising the rate of saving and allocating scarce resources efficiently to generate higher rate of economic growth is necessary but not a sufficient condition of eliminating mass poverty and large–scale chronic unemployment.*

Of course, in the fifties and sixties it was widely believed that benefits of growth would trickle down to the poor and unemployed and therfore once growth takes place; the problem of poverty and unemployment faced by the developing countries would automatically be solved. This has been belied by the actual experience. For removal of poverty and unemployment what is required is not only the growth of output but also of what is being produced and how the output is being distributed. Thus, Joan Robinson writes, "***But a growth in wealth is not at all the same thing as reducing poverty. A universal paean was raised in praise of growth. Growth was going to solve all problems. No need to bother about poverty. Growth will lift up the bottom and poverty will disappear without any need to pay attention to it. The economists who should have known better, fell in with the same cry.***"[18]

To sum up, Robbins' definition which lays stress on allocation of scarce resources to meet various ends does not fully bring in its ambit the problems of growth, poverty and unemployment faced by the developing countries like India. For a long time Robbins' definition was accepted as a proper one.but nowadays it is felt that Rabbins' definition does not indicate adequately the content, scope and the subject-matter of economics. As we have pointed out above, Robbins' definition does not cover the theory of income and employment determination as well as the theory of economic growth. According to Charles Schultze of the University of Maryland, ***"Robbins' definition of economics is misleading, in particular it does not fully reflect two of the major concerns of modern economics, namely, growth and instability."***[19]

Economic is What Economists Do

However in recent years economists have stopped discussing the problem of giving proper definition of economics and the controversy regarding its proper and adequate definition has almost stopped. Many modern economist think that for explaining what economics is about, there is no necessity for defining it. What economics is about can he better understood by knowing subjects with which economists have been concerned and with which they are concerned to day. Therefore, Professor Jacob Viner has remarked," Economics ***is what economists do."*** This means what economists is about can be better understood from knowing the questions which economists have raised and discussed. What economics is about can therefore be better understood from the study of its subject–matter. We have discussed above the various questions and issues with which economists are concerned.

POSITIVE ECONOMICS, NORMATIVE ECONOMICS AND WELFARE ECONOMICS

It is important to know the difference between positive economics and normative economics. Positive economics is concerned with explaining what is, that is, it describes theories and laws to explain observed economic phenomena, whereas normative economics is concerned

18. Joan Robinson, The Second Crisis of Economic Theory, printed in her *Selected Economic Writings*, Oxford University Press, 1974, p. 245.
19. Charles L. Schulze, *National Income Analysis* (Foundatioons of Modern Economics), 1965, p.2.

with what *should be* or what *ought to be* the things. J. N. Keynes draws the distinction between the two types of economics in the following manner : "A positive science may be defined as a body of systematized knowledge concerning what is, normative science or a regulative science is a today of systematized **knowledge** relating to criteria of what ought to be, and is concerned with the ideal as distinguished from the actual......The objective of a positive science is the establishment of uniformities, of a normative science, the determination of the ideals."[20] Thus, in positive economics we derive propositions, theories and laws following certain rules of logic. These theories, laws and propositions explain the cause and effect relationship between economic variables.

In positive microeconomics, we are broadly concerned with explaining the determination of relative prices and the allocation of resources between different commodities. In positive macroeconomics we are broadly concerned with how the level of national income and employment, aggregate consumption and investment and the general level of prices are determined. In these parts of positive economics, what should be the prices, what should be the saving rate, what should be the allocation of resources, and what should be the distribution of income are not discussed. These questions of what should be and what ought to be fall within the purview of normative economics. Thus, given the profit maximization assumption, positive economics states that monopolist will fix a price which will equate marginal cost with marginal revenue. The question what price should be or ought to be fixed so that maximum social welfare is achieved lies outside the purview of positive economics. Similarly, given the monopoly in the labour market, positive economics explains what actual wage rate is determined. It does not go into the question how much wage rate should be paid to the workers so that they should not be exploited. Likewise, how national income between different individuals is distributed falls within the domain of positive economics. But positive economics is not concerned with the question of how income should be distributed. On the other hand, normative economics is concerned with describing what should be the things. It is, therefore, also called ***prescriptive economics***. What price for a product should be fixed, what wage rate should be paid, how income should be distributed, etc., fall within the purview of normative economics.

It should be noted that normative economics involves ***value judgements*** or what are simply known as ***values***. By value judgements or values is meant the conceptions of the people about what is good or bad. These conceptions regarding values of the people are based on the ethical, political, philosophical and religious beliefs of the people and are not based upon any scientific logic or law. Because normative economics involves value judgements, eminent economist L. Robbins contended that economics should not become normative in character.[21] He opined that it was unscientific to include the value judgements in the economic analysis. To quote him, "the role of the economist is more and more conceived of as that of the expert, who can say what consequences are likely to follow certain actions, but who cannot judge as an economist the desirability of ends".[22] While drawing difference between economics and ethics he further writes, "economics deals with ascertainable facts, ethics with valuations and obligations. The two fields of inquiry are not on the same plane of discourse. Between the generalisations of positive and normative economics, there is a logical gulf fixed which no ingenuity can disguise and no juxtaposition in space or time bridge over. Propositions involving the verb 'ought' are different in kind from propositions involving the verb 'is'[23]

Value judgements of various individuals differ and their rightness or wrongness cannot be decided on the basis of scientific logic or laws. Therefore, in our view, positive economics

20. J.N. Keynes, *Scope and Method of Political Economy*, Macmillan, London, 1930, p. 46.
21. L. Robbins, *"Nature and Significance of Economic Science"*, Macmillan, London, 2nd Edition, 1938.
22. *Ibid.*
23. *Ibid.*

should be kept separate and distinct from normative economics. However, from the fact that normative economics involves value judgements, it does not mean that it should be considered as useless or not meaningful and should not be the concern of economics. As a matter of fact, many vital issues concerning economic welfare of the society necessarily involve some value judgements. If economics is to become an 'engine for social betterment, it has to adopt certain norms, ideals or criteria with which to evaluate economic policies and pass judgements on what is good and what is bad from the viewpoint of social welfare. We agree with A. C. Pigou, "our impulse is not the philosopher's impulse, knowledge for the sake of knowledge but rather the physiologist's knowledge for the healing that knowledge may help to bring."[24]

As is clear from above, normative economics is concerned with welfare propositions, since what is good or what is bad ultimately depends upon its effect on the welfare of the individual and the society. In recent years, a branch of economics known as welfare economics, has been developed. This welfare economics seeks to evaluate the social desirability of alternative social states or economic organisations. Thus, Sotitovsky writes, "welfare economics is that branch of economic analysis which is concerned primarily with establishment of criteria that can provide a positive basis for adopting policies which are likely to maximise social welfare".[25] In short, welfare economics is to prescribe criteria or norms with which to judge the desirability of certain economic re-organisatiom and prescribe policies on that basis.

However, an important difference between positive economics and welfare economics may be noted. The propositions or laws of positive economics are derived from a set of axioms. Whereas the propositions or laws so derived are capable of being tested and verified by observations of the facts in the real world, the propositions of welfare economics cannot be so tested and verified because we cannot know whether welfare has actually increased or not. This is because welfare is not an observable quantity like price or quantities of goods, "it is a bird of an other sort".[26] We cannot measure welfare in cardinal terms. Being subjective, welfare or satisfaction resides in the mind of an individual and, therefore, it is not capable of being measured in quantitative terms. Further, there are still more difficulties in testing a proposition regarding social welfare because propositions regarding social welfare generally involve value judgements of some sort. Thus Graff is very right when he states, "the normal way of testing a theory in positive economics is to test its conclusions, 'the normal way of testing a welfare proposition is to test its assumptions."[27] Therefore, to judge the validity of the welfare propositions we must test its assumptions or premises which invariably involve value judgements. To quote Graff again, "in positive economics, the proof of the pudding is indeed in the eating. The welfare cake, on the other hand, is so hard to taste, that we must test its ingredients before baking".[28]

From the above it seems that difference between positive and welfare economics is quite clear; in one case *what man does* without considering the favourable or unfavourable effects on others while in the other it is *what he should do* and must consider the favourable or unfavourable effects on others. But the distinction between positive and welfare economics is not as clear as it is supposed to be. Every man does what he thinks is the best for him. It may be that he does often what others do not consider to be best for him. But in such cases the probability of a faulty judgement by others is equal to is own faulty judgement. Thus, fault being a common factor in both the cases it is reasonable to conclude that "what a man does' and 'what he should do' are one and the same thing in every case and that there is no difference

24. A.C. Pigou, *Economics of Welfare*, 4th Edition, Macmillan, London, 1932, p.5.
25. Tibor Scitovsky, *Papers on Welfare and Growth*, 1962, p. 1974.
26. J. De V. Graff, *Theoretical Welfare Economics*, Cambridge University Press, 1957, p.2,
27. *Ibid*, p. 2.
28. *Ibid*, p.2.

between positive and normative or welfare economics when judged from the individual's point of view.

Although there is no difference between positive and welfare economics when judged fim the individual point of view, yet it is possible to make out a difference between the two by adopting a social point of view. Any course of action which may be best for an individual may not be best for the society. Thus, there is a difference between what a man thinks best for him and what is best for the society. When a man does what he thinks best for him, he does not necessarily do what is best for the society. If the word 'should' is given a social connotation, the difference between 'what is done' and 'what should be done' becomes clear. Thus only by adopting the social point of view, the positive and welfare economics can be differentiated from each other.

PRODUCTION POSSIBILITY CURVE : A BASIC TOOL OF ECONOMICS

The nature of basic economic problems explained above can be better understood and distinguished from each other with the aid of an important tool of modern economics known as production possibility curve. Production possibility curve is also called the ***production possibility frontier.*** We shall explain below the concept of the production possibility curve and bring out its relation with the basic economic problems stated above.

Production possibility curve (frontier) is a graphic representation of alternative production possibilities facing an economy. As the total productive resources of the economy are limited, the economy has to choose between different goods. The productive resources can be used for the production of various alternative goods. It has, therefore, to be decided which goods are to be produced more and which ones less. In deciding what amounts of different goods are to be produced, the society would in fact be deciding about the allocation of resources among different possible goods. How much labour should go into raising wheat on the farms and how much should be employed in manufacturing cloth. How many factories would produce armaments for the army and how many should produce consumer goods for the civilians. In order to simplify our analysis we shall assume that two types of goods—wheat and cloth—are to be produced. We shall explain the production possibilities with these two goods but the analysis made will equally apply to the choice between any other two goods.

Let us assume that there is a given amount of productive resources and they remain fixed. Although resources are fixed in quantity, yet they can be shifted from the production of one good to another. Further, we assume that the given resources are being used fully and with utmost technical efficiency. In other words, we assume that resources are neither unemployed and under-employed, nor inefficiently utilized. That means that economy is working at the level of full-employment and achieving maximum possible production. We also presume that technology does not undergo any change. In other words, we rule out any progress in technology. In short, we assume fixed resources, full-employment, complete technical efficiency and a given technology. All these assumptions imply that we are looking at our economy at some particular point in time or over a very short period of time. This is because it will be very unrealistic to rule out progress in technology and growth in the supply of resources over a long period of time.

With the given amount of resources and a given technology, we have constructed the following table showing various production possibilities between wheat and cloth. If all the given resources are employed for the production of wheat, it is supposed that 15 thousand quintals of wheat are produced. On the other hand, if all the resources are devoted to the production of cloth, 5 thousand metres of cloth are made. But these are the two extreme production possibilities. In between these two, there will be many other production possibilities such as *B*, *C*, *D* and *E*.

With production possibility *B*, the economy can produce, with given resources, 14 thousand quintals of wheat, and one thousand metres of cloth and with production possibility *C*, the economy can have 12 thousand quintals of wheat and 2 thousand metres of cloth and so on. As we move from possibility *A* towards *F*, we draw away some resources from the production of wheat and devote them to the production of cloth. In other words, we give up some units of wheat in order to have some more units of cloth. As we move from alternative A to *B*, we sacrifice one thousand quintals of wheat for one thousand metres of cloth. Again, our movement from alternative *B* to *C*, involves the sacrifice of two thousand quintals of wheat for the sake of one thousand more metres of cloth. A look at the Table 1.1 shows that our sacrifice of wheat

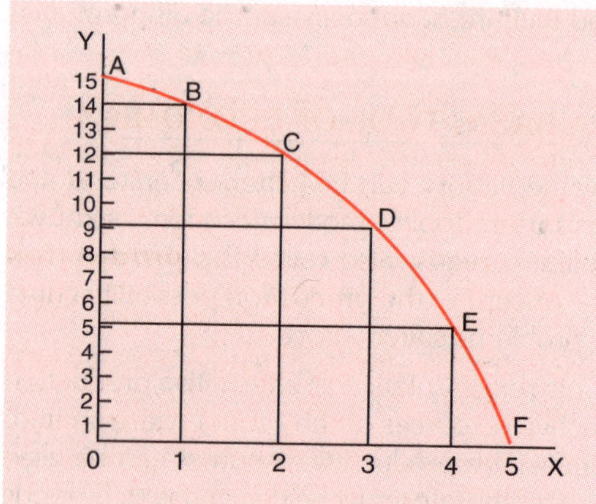

Fig. 1.1. *Production Possibility Curve*

Table 1.1. Alternative Production Possibilities

Production possibilities	Cloth (in thousand (metres	Wheat (in thousand quintals)
A	0	15
B	1	14
C	2	12
D	3	9
E	4	5
F	5	0

goes on increasing as we move further from *C* towards *F*. It is, therefore, clear that in a fully employed economy more of one good can be obtained only by cutting down the production of another good. Thus, we conclude that a fully employed and technically efficient ***economy must always give up something of one good to obtain some more of another.*** The basic fact that resources are limited prevents an economy from having more of both the goods.

The alternative production possibilities can be illustrated graphically by plotting the data of the Table 1.1. The curve *AF* in Figure 1.1 is obtained when the data of the table are plotted. This curve *AF* is called the production possibility curve which shows the various combinations of two goods or two classes of goods which the economy can produce with a given amount of resources. This production possibility curve *AF* like the Table 1.1 illustrates that, in a fully employed economy, an increase in the amount of cloth necessitates a decrease in the amount of wheat. As we move from *A* towards *F* on the curve we sacrifice some units of wheat for having more of cloth. On the other hand, if we move up from *F* towards *A*, we will be giving up some amount of cloth for the sake of more wheat.

The production possibility curve is also called ***transformation curve*** because in moving from one point to another on it, one good is "transformed" into another, not physically but by transferring resources from one use to the other. With the given resources being fully employed and utilized, the combination of two goods produced can lie anywhere on the production possibility curve *AF* but not inside or outside it. For example, the combined output of two goods produced can neither lie at *U*, nor at *H* (see Figure 1.2). This is so because at point *U* the economy would not be utilizing its resources fully, and the output of two goods represented by point *H*, given the productive resources, would lie beyond the capacity of the economy to produce.

The Problem of Unemployment and Under-utilisation of Resources. However, during those periods when the economy is not fully utilizing its resources, or not using them most efficiently, that is, when there is either unemployment or inefficiency in the use of resources, output combination of two products will lie below the economy's production possibility frontier, such as at a point like U in Figure 1.2., where the economy can produce more of both the goods or more of either of the two goods (as indicated by arrows) by putting the unemployed resources to work. As shown by arrows in Figure 1.2, if the economy is working at U, *then by using its idle resources fully and most efficiently, it can move from* U to Q, or to R, or to S on the production possibility curve.

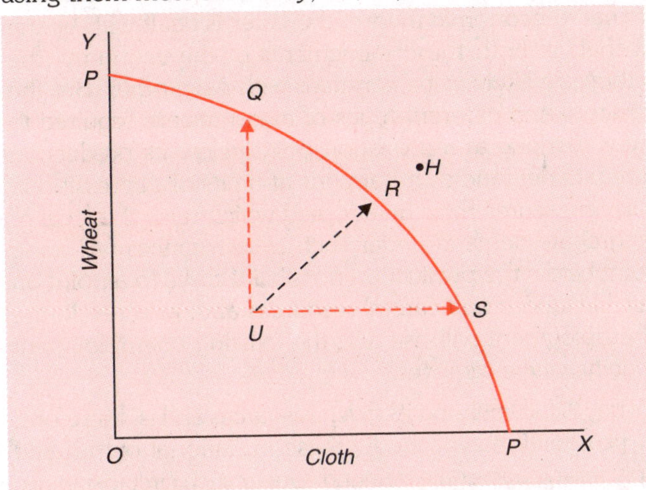

Fig. 1.2. *The Problem of Under-utilisation of Resources*

Economic Growth and Shift in Production Possibility Curve

Let us turn to the question of economic growth and see what happens to the production possibility curve when the economy's productive capacity increases over time. As already pointed out, the production possibility curve is drawn with a given amount of productive resources like land, labour and capital equipment. Now, if the productive resources increase, the production possibility curve will shift outward and to the right showing that more of both goods can be produced than before. Further, when the economy makes progress in technology, that is, when the scientists and engineers discover new and better ways of doing things, the production possibility curve will shift to the right and will indicate the possibility of producing more of both the goods. Technological progress by improving productive efficiency allows the society to produce more of both the goods with a given and fixed amount of resources.

From above it follows that when the supply of resources increases or an improvement in technology occurs, the production possibility curve shifts outwards such as from PP to $P'P'$, in Figure 1.3. On production possibility curve $P'P'$, the economy can produce more goods than on curve PP. The increase in the amount of capital, natural and human resources and progress in technology are determinants of economic growth. Thus, with the growth of the economy, the production possibility curve shifts outward.

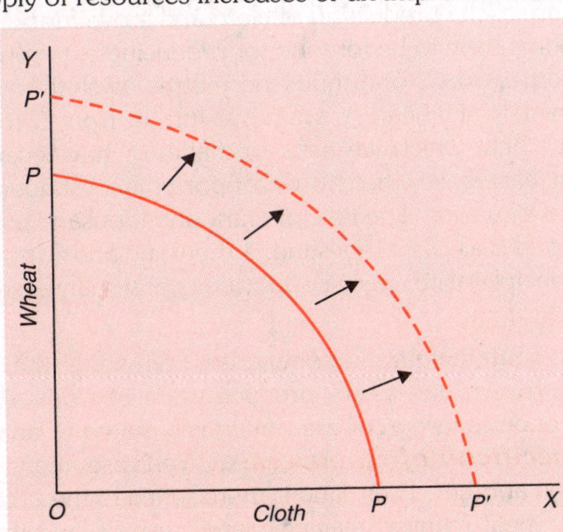

Fig. 1.3. *Shift in Production Possibility Curve due to Economic Growth*

It is very important to understand the distinction between (i) the movement of the economy from a point inside the production possibility curve to a point on it, such as from point U to point Q in Figure 1.2 and (ii) the movement of the economy from one production possibility curve to another. In both these cases national product or output of goods and services increases. But the former involves fuller employment of given resources while the latter involves the increase in resources or productive capacity. While the first type of movement is dealt with by the short-run Keynes' theory of income and employment or rnacro-economic theory, the latter is dealt with by the theory of economic growth. The fact that, in both these movements of the economy, the national product or income increases they are likely to be confused with each other. But the two movements are of quite different nature and different types of measures are required to bring them about. When the economy is working at a utilization point below its production possibility curve due to the lack of aggregate demand as it happens at times of depression in the capitalist countries, then those policy measures have be adopted which raise the level of aggregate demand. The increase in aggregate demand under such circumstances will bring about a shift of the economy from a point below the production possibility curve to a point on it. This will mean full utilisation of available labour and capital resources and, as a result, the levels of national income, output and employment will rise and the existing unemployment and under-utilisation of productive capacity will be removed.

On the other hand, when the economy is fully utilising its given resources and is, therefore, working at a point on the production possibility curve, the increase in national output and employment cannot be achieved by simply raising aggregate demand. Under such circumstances, national income and employment can be increased by adopting measures which generate economic growth. The measures aimed at generating economic growth will involve stepping up of the rate of capital accumulation and making progress in technology.

Production Possibility Frontier and the Law of Increasing Opportunity Cost

The production possibility frontier *AF* in Figure 1.1 shows an important principle of economics. That principle is the law of increasing opportunity cost. ***The opportunity cost of a commodity means the amount of a next best commodity foregone for producing an extra unit of the commodity.*** The reduction in output of a commodity foregone releases productive resources which can be used for the production of additional units of the other commodity. From looking at the Table 1.1 it will be clear that, as we move from possibility *A* to possibility *B*, we have to give up one thousand quintals of wheat in order to have one thousand metres of cloth. It means, in other words, that a first thousand metres of cloth have the opportunity cost of one thousand quintals of wheat to the society. But as we step up the production of cloth and move further from *B* to *C*, extra two thousand quintals of wheat have to be forgone for producing extra one thousand metres of cloth. Thus, in moving from *B* to *C*, one thousand metres of cloth involve the opportunity cost of two thousand quintals of wheat. As we move further from *C* to *D*, *D* to *E* and *E* to *F*, the sacrifice in terms of wheat which we have to make for having extra one thousand metres of cloth goes on increasing. In other words, opportunity cost goes on increasing as we have more of cloth and less of wheat. The cost of extra one thousand metres of cloth as we move from *C* to *D*, *D* to *E* and *E* to *F* is 3 thousand, 4 thousand and 5 thousand quintals of wheat respectively. It is this principle of increasing opportunity cost that makes the production possibility curve concave to the origin.

But the question now arises: Why does the sacrifice of wheat or the opportunity cost of cloth increases as we produce more of cloth. A simple answer to this question is that the economic resources are not equally suited or adaptable to alternative uses. This is known as ***specificity of resources:*** a given resource is more suited to the production of one good than another. Thus, land is more suited to the production of wheat than cloth. The production of wheat requires relatively larger use of land than cloth. As we increase the production of cloth, resources which are less and less adaptable or productive in the production of cloth would have to be pushed in that line of production. As we move from *A* towards *F*, we will first transfer those resources which are more productive in making cloth. As we move further from *B to C, C to D* and so forth, we will have to transfer those resources to the production of cloth which are sucessively more productive for producing wheat and less productive for making cloth. It is, therefore, obvious that as the resources that are more suited to the production of wheat are withdrawn, extra loss of wheat for the sake of producing extra one thousand metres of cloth will go on increasing. This law equally holds good if we move from *F* towards *A*, successively more amount of cloth would have to be given up for the sake of a given extra increase in the amount of wheat.

Production Possibility Curve and Basic Economic Questions

Scarcity, Choice, and Resource Allocation. Production possibility frontier or curve is an important concept of modern economics. This concept is used to explain the various economic problems and theories. The basic economic problem of scarcity, on which Robbins' definition of economics is based, can be explained with the aid of production possibility curve. According to the problem of scarcity, because of the limited availabilities of the resources, all wants of the society for goods cannot be satisfied; if a society decides to allocate more resources to the production of one good, it has to withdraw resources from the production of another good, as has been seen above. Given the amount of resources, the economy has to operate on the given production possibility curve. As has been brought out above, when we increase the production of one commodity by moving along the production possibility curve, we have to reduce the production of some other commodity. If the given resources are being fully used and technology remains constant, an economy cannot increase the production of both the goods represented on the two axes. This illustrates the basic economic problem. Thus, the basic economic problem is that, in view of the scarcity of resources, at what point on the production possibility curve the economy should produce so as to maximise social welfare.

The problem of resource allocation involves what and how the goods will be produced. Which goods to be produced and in what quantities implies that on what point of the production possibility curve the economy should operate. A glance at Figure 1.1 will reveal that if the economy is operating at point *B* on the production possibility curve *AF*, then one thousand metres of cloth and fourteen thousand quintals of wheat are being produced. If the economy operates at point *E* on this curve, four thousand metres of cloth and five thousand quintals of wheat are being produced. Thus, operation at different points of the production possibility curve implies different allocation of resources between the production of two goods. At which point of the production possibility curve, a free-market economy will operate depends upon the consumers' demand for different gbods. In other words, in a free-market economy, how the resources are allocated between the two goods on a given production curve is determined by the demand of the consumers.

How the goods are to be produced implies which methods or techniques should be employed for the production of various goods. In other words, what resource combination be used for the production of goods so as to maximise the output or to minimise the cost. A factor would be used for the production of a product for which it is more efficient. It is obvious that this is the problem of technical efficiency. If for producing goods such resource combinations as will minimise cost of production are not employed, the economy will be operating at a point below the given production possibility curve. Thus, if in the production of various goods, efficient methods are not used or if the resources are not employed in their efficient uses, the economy will not be operating at a point on the production possibility curve, instead it will be operating at a point below the production possibility curve such as *U* in Figure 1.2. The working of the economy below the production possibility curve indicates that less than maximum possible production is being done which will lower the welfare and standards of living of the people. This loss of production is the result of inefficient use of the resources.

Distribution and Production Possibility Curve. For whom to produce or how the national product is being distributed is not directly revealed by the production possibility curve. However, we can obtain some knowledge of the distribution of goods from the production possibility curve. If such a production possibility curve is constructed in which necessaries are represented on one axis and luxuries on the other, we can know from the actual position of the economy on this curve that how the national output is being distributed. Consider Figure 1.4 where on the X-axis necessary goods and on the *Y*-axis luxury goods have been shown. If the economy is working at point *R* on the production possibility curve *PP* in this figure, the economy would be producing relatively more of luxury goods such as refrigerators, televisions, motor cars, airconditioners and would be producing relatively less quantities of ncessary consumer goods such as foodgrains, cloth, edible oil, which indicates that distribution of national income would be very much uneven and the richer sections of the society will be getting relatively more of luxury goods,whereas the poorer sections would be deprived of even the necessaries of life.

On the contrary, if the economy is operating at point *S* on the production possibility curve *PP*, then it implies that essential consumer goods are being produced relatively more and luxury goods relatively less by the economy. This indicates that the distribution of income and output in the society in this case will be relatively more equal.

What quantities of various goods will be produced in a free enterprise economy *i.e.*, how much of luxury goods and how much of necessaries would be produced, depends upon the pattern of demand of the consumers. In other words, pattern of production will correspond to the pattern of demand.

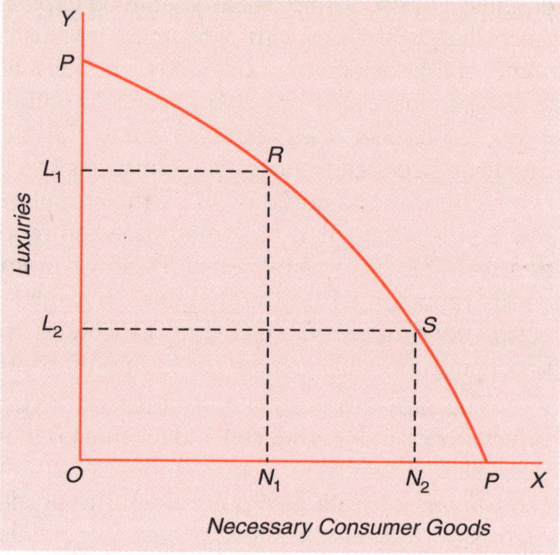

Fig 1.4. *Resource Allocation between Necessary Consumer Goods and Luxuries*

But it should be remembered that the pattern of demand depends not only on the ***preferences of the consumers*** comprising a society but also upon the ***distribution of income*** in a society. The more unequal is the distribution of income in the society, the greater the amount of luxury goods produced in it.

The Problem of Unemployment and Under-utilisation of Resources. As we have studied above, the problem of unemployment and under-employment of resources can be illustrated and understood with the aid of the production possibility curve. When all resources are being fully used, the economy will operate at a point on the production possibility curve. But the economy will operate at a point on the production possibility curve if the aggregate demand is large enough to buy the total output produced by the full employment of resources. If the aggregate demand is somehow smaller, the economy will not be able to use its productive capacity fully, that is, it will not be able to utilize its resources fully, which will result in unemployment and under-employment of resources.

In the case of unemployment and under-employment of resources, the economy will be working at a point below the production possibility curve (such as point *U* in Figure 1.2). In such a situation if the aggregate demand for goods increases, the demand for resources and, therefore, their employment will increase and as a result unemployment and under-employment will disappear and national income will increase. Thus, it follows that as a result of increase in aggregate demand the economy moves from a point below the production possibility curve to a point on the production possibility curve. Renowned economist J. M. Keynes, who attributed unemployment and under-employment to the lack of aggregate demand recommended construction of public works on a large scale by the government, financed by deficit financing, so as to raise the aggregate demand which will help in utilising resources fully and therefore in solving the problem of unemployment and under-employment.

The Problem of Economic Growth. Another important use of the production possibility curve is that we can explain with it the problem of capital formation and economic growth. In order to explain the problem of capital formation we have to construct such a production possibility curve in which on one axis capital goods and on the other axis consumer goods are measured. This has been done in Figure 1.5 in which along the X-axis consumer goods and on Y-axis capital goods are measured. If the economy is allocating the available resources between capital and consumer goods in such a way that it operates at point A on the production possibility curve *PP*, it will be producing OC_1 of consumer goods and OK_1 of capital goods.

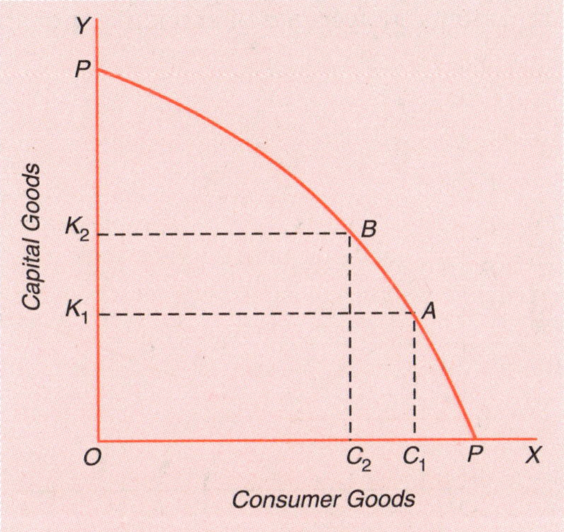

Fig. 1.5. *Resource Allocation between Consumer and Capital Goods*

Now, suppose that the society decides to produce more of capital goods. To implement this decision, society will have to withdraw some resources from the production of consumer goods and use them for the production of capital goods. As a result of this, the production of consumer goods will decline. It is clear from Figure 1.5, that if the economy reallocates its resources between consumer and capital goods and shifts from point *A* to point *B* on the production possibility curve *PP*, it will now produce OK_2 of capital goods and OC_2 of consumer goods. That is, K_1K_2 amount of capital goods will be produced more and C_1C_2 amount of consumer goods will be produced less than before. We, therefore, conclude that in order to step up the rate of capital formation the production of consumer goods and therefore consumption has to be reduced.

But the above conclusion is based on the assumption that the economy is using its resources fully and most efficiently and is operating at a point on the production possibility curve. However, if some available resources are lying unemployed and idle or the economy is not using them more efficiently, the economy will be working below the production possibility curve. When the economy is working at a point below the production possibility curve, then more capital goods can be produced without the reduction in the production of consumer goods because by employing idle and unemployed resources, economy can produce more of capital goods. But, as has been explained above, if the economy is utilising its resources fully, the rate of capital formation cannot be increased without the reduction in consumption. But it is worth noting that when the rate of capital formation is raised, this does not mean that amount of consumption is reduced for ever. The accumulation of more capital enables the economy to increase its production of consumer goods in the future. That is, the accumulation of capital raises the productive capacity of the economy which will enable it to produce more consumer goods in future. Thus, capital accumulation implies that ***"less jam today for more jam tomorrow".***

Since the accumulation of capital raises the productive capacity, national production will increase, that is, economic growth will take place. As a result, the economy will not remain on the same production possibility curve and its production possibility curve will shift outward which indicates that the economy will be able to produce more than before. The greater the rate of capital formation, the greater the extent of shift in the production possibility curve, and the greater the rate of economic growth. Consider Figure 1.6 in which in the beginning the economy is producing OC_1 of consumer goods and OK_1 of capital goods on the production possibility curve P_1P_1. If the economy maintains this rate of capital formation, the production possibility curve will go on shifting and the economy will be growing annually at a certain fixed rate. It should be noted that in Figure 1.6 as a result of low rate of capital formation, production possibility curve shifts outward at a relatively low speed. Thus, growth path OR in Figure 1.6 represents a lower rate of economic growth.

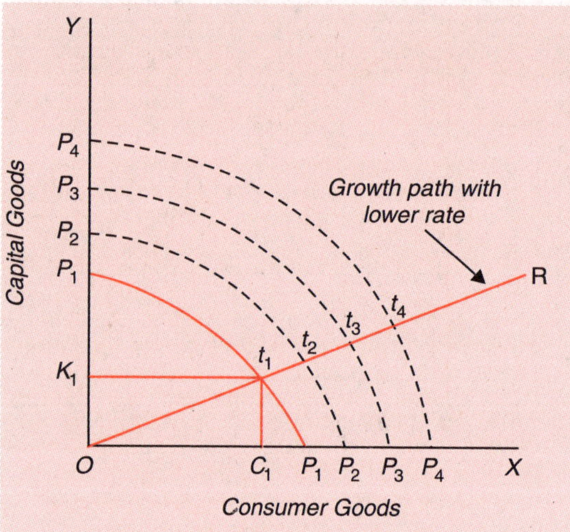

Fig. 1.6. *Growth Path with a Lower Rate due to Lower Rate of Capital accumulation*

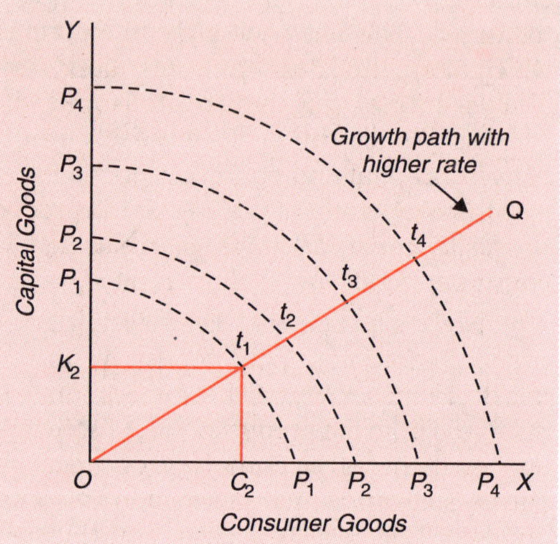

Fig. 1.7. *Growth Path with a Higher Rate due to Higher Rate of Capital Formation*

If the society wants to obtain a higher rate of economic growth, it will have to raise its rate of capital formation. This is shown in Figure 1.7 in which economy is producing at point t_1 on the production possibility curve P_1P_1, OK_2 of capital goods and OC_2 of consumer goods. If economy maintains this rate of capital formation, production possibility curve will go on shifting outward to a greater extent than in Figure 1.6. This means that the rate of economic growth will now be relatively greater than in Figure 1.6. In the two Figures 1.6 and 1.7, it will be noticed that, in the beginning, in Figure 1.7, the production of consumer goods is less than in Figure 1.6, but when as aresult of higher rate of economic growth, production possibility curve reaches at position P_4P_4 at time t_4, it will be producing more consumer goods in Figure 1.7 exhibiting higher rate of capital formation than in Figure 1.6, where the rate of capital formation and therefore the rate of economic growth is relatively less.

We have explained above economic growth which has been brought about by capital formation. Besides capital formation, there are other factors which determine the rate of economic growth. Progress in technology and expansion in education also favourably affect the rate of economic growth and cause the production possibility curve to shift outward.

We have explained above only some important uses of production possibility curve. There are several other uses of production possibility curve. We can understand better the concept of opportunity cost with the aid of production possibility curve. The concept of production possibility curve has also been extensively used in welfare economics and in the theory of international trade. In the modern economic theory, gains from international trade have also been explained with the aid of production possibility curve.

CHAPTER

2

Micro and Macro-economics

The subject-matter of economics has been divided into two parts : Microeconomics and Macroeconomics. These terms were first coined and used by Ragnar Frisch and have now been adopted by the economists all the world over. Nowadays one can hardly come across a text-book on modern economic analysis which does not divide its analysis into two parts, one dealing with microeconomics and the other with macroeconomics. The term microeconomics is derived from the 'Greek word ***mikros***, meaning "small" and the term macroeconomics is derived from the Greek word ***makros***, meaning "large." Thus microeconomics deals with the analysis of small individual units of the economy such as individual consumers, individual firms and small aggregates or groups of individual units such as various industries and markets. On the other hand, macroeconomics concerns itself with the analysis of the economy as a whole and its large aggregates such as total national output and income, total employment, total consumption, aggregate investment. Thus, according to K. E. Boulding, "Microeconomics is the study of particular firms, particular households, individual prices, wages, incomes, individual industries, particular commodities."[1] About macroeconomics he remarks, "Macroeconomics deals not with individual quantities as such but with aggregates of these quantities; not with individual incomes but with the national income; not with individual prices but with the price level; not with individual outputs but with the national output."[2]

MICROECONOMICS

As stated above, microeconomics studies the economic actions and behaviour of *individual units* and *small groups* of individual units. In microeconomic theory we discuss how the various cells of economic organism, that is, the various units of the economy such as thousands of consumers, thousands of producers or firms, thousands of workers and resource suppliers in the economy do their economic activities and reach their equilibrium states. In other words, in microeconomics we make a ***microscopic study*** of the economy. But it should be remembered that microeconomics does not study the economy *in its totality*. Instead, in microeconomics we discuss equilibrium of innumerable units of the economy *piecemeal* and their inter-relationship to each other. Professor Lerner rightly says, "Microeconomics consists of looking at the economy through a microscope, as it were, to see how the millions of cells in the body economic–the individuals or households as consumers, and the individuals or firms as producers—play their part in the working of the whole economic organism."[3] For instance, in microeconomic analysis we study the demand of an individual consumer for a good and from there go on to derive the *market demand* for the good (that is, demand of a group of individuals consuming a

1. K.E.Boulding, *A Reconstruction of Economics, (1950), p.3.*
2. K.E. Boulding, *Economic Analysis, p. 25*
3. Abba P. Lerner, Microeconomic Theory, printed in *Perspectives in Economics, edited by Brown, Neuberger and Palmatier (Preliminary edition, 1968)*, p.29.

particular good). Likewise, microeconomic theory studies the behaviour of the individual firms in regard to the fixation of price and output and their reactions to the changes in the demand and supply conditions. From there we go on to establish price-output fixation by an industry (Industry means a group of firms producing the same product).

Thus, microeconomic theory seeks to determine the mechanism by which the different economic units attain the position of equilibrium, proceeding from the individual units to a *narrowly defined group such as a single industry or a single market.* Since microeconomic analysis concerns itself with narrowly defined groups such as an industry or market. However it does not study the *totality of behaviour of all units in the economy* for any particular economic activity. In other words, the study of economic system or economy as a whole lies outside the domain of microeconomic analysis.

Microeconomic Theory Studies Resource Allocation, Product and Factor Pricing. Microeconomic theory takes the total quantity of resources as given and seeks to explain how they are allocated to the production of particular goods. It is the allocation of resources that determines what goods shall be produced and how they shall be produced. The allocation of resources to the production of various goods in a free-market economy depends upon the prices of the various goods and the prices of the various factors of production. Therefore, to explain how the allocation of resources is determined, microeconomics proceeds to analyse how the relative prices of goods and factors are determined. Thus the theory of product pricing and the theory of factor pricing (or the theory of distribution) fall within the domain of microeconomics. The theory of product pricing explains how the relative prices of cotton cloth, foodgrains, jute, kerosene oil and thousands of other goods are determined. The theory of distribution explains how *wages* (price for the use of labour), *rent* (payment for the use of land), *interest* (price for the use of capital) and *profits* (the reward for the entrepreneur) are determined. Thus, the theory of product pricing and the theory of factor pricing are the two important branches of microeconomic theory.

Prices of the products depend upon the forces of demand and supply. The demand for goods depends upon the consumers' behaviour pattern, and the supply of goods depends upon the conditions of production and cost and the behaviour pattern of the firms or entrepreneurs. Thus the demand and supply sides have to be analysed in order to explain the determination of prices of goods and factors. Thus the theory of demand and the theory of production are two subdivisions of the theory of pricing.

Microeconomics as a Study of Economic Efficiency. Besides analysing the pricing of products and factors and the allocation of resources based upon the price mechanism, microeconomics also seeks to explain whether the allocation of resources determined is *efficient.* Efficiency in the allocation of resources is attained when the resources are so allocated that maximises the satisfaction of the people. Economic efficiency involves three efficiencies; ***efficiency in production, efficiency in distribution*** of goods among the people (This is also called ***efficiency in consumption) and allocative economic efficiency,*** that is, efficiency in the ***direction of production***. Microeconomic theory shows under what conditions these efficiencies are achieved. Microeconomics also shows what factors cause departure from these efficiencies and result in the decline of social welfare from the maximum possible level.

Economic efficiency in production involves minimisation of cost for producing a given level of output or producing a maximum possible output of various goods from the given amount of outlay or cost incurred on productive resources. When such productive efficiency is attained, then it is no longer possible by any reallocation of the productive resources or factors among the production of various goods and services to increase the output of any good without a reduction in the output of some other good. Efficiency in consumption consists of distributing the given amount of produced goods and services among millions of the people for consumption in such a way as to maximize the total satisfaction of the society. When such efficiency is achieved it is no longer possible by any redistribution of goods among the people to make some people better off[4] without making some other ones worse off.[5] Allocative economic efficiency or optimum direction of production consists of producing those goods which are most desired by the people, that is, when the direction of production is such that maximizes social welfare.

In other words, ***allocative economic efficiency implies that pattern of production (i.e, amounts of various goods and services produced) should correspond to the desired pattern of consumption of the people.*** Even if efficiencies in consumption and production of goods are present, it may be that the goods which are produced and distributed for consumption may not be those preferred by the people. There may be some goods which are more preferred by the people but which have not been produced and *vice versa.* To sum up, allocative efficiency (optimum direction of production) is achieved when the resources are so allocated to the production of various goods that the maximum possible satisfaction of the people is obtained. Once this is achieved, then by producing some goods more and others less by any rearrangement of the resources will mean loss of satisfaction or efficiency. The question of economic efficiency is the subject-matter of ***theoretical welfare economics*** which is an important branch of microeconomic theory.

That microeconomic theory is intimately concerned with the question of efficiency and welfare is better understood from the following remarks of A. P. Lerner, a noted American economist. "In microeconomics we are more concerned with the avoidance or elimination of waste, or with inefficiency arising from the fact that production is not organised in the most efficient possible manner. Such inefficiency means that it is possible, by rearranging the different ways in which products are being produced and consumed, to get more of something that is scarce without giving up any part of any other scarce item, or to replace something by something else that is preferred. Microeconomic theory spells out the conditions of efficiency *(i. e.* , for the elimination of all kinds of inefficiency) and suggests how they might be achieved. These conditions (called Pareto-optimal conditions) can be of the greatest help in raising the standard of living of the population."[6]

The four out of six basic economic questions listed in the first chapter and with which economists are concerned, namely, (1) what goods shall be produced and in what quantities, (2) how they shall be produced, (3) how the goods and services produced shall be distributed, and (4) whether the production of goods and their distribution for consumption is efficient fall within the domain of microeconomics. The whole content of microeconomic theory is presented in the following chart :

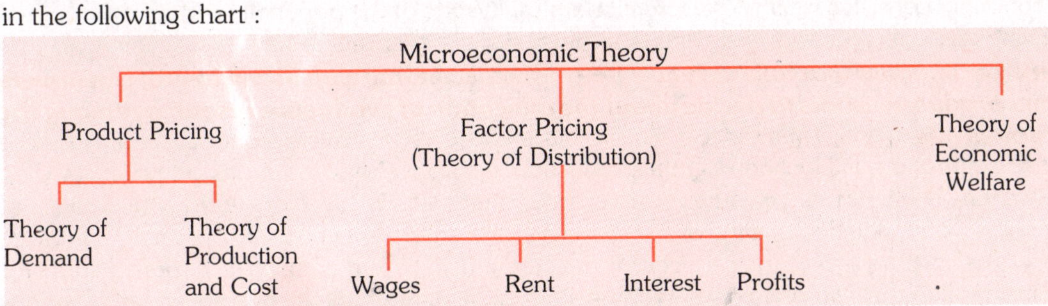

4. Making some people *better off* means increasing their satisfaction.
5. Making some people *worse off means* reducing their satisfaction.
6. Abba P. Lerner: Microeconomic Theory, printed in *Perspectives in Economics,* edited by Brown, Neuberger and Palmatier (Preliminary edition, 1968), p. 30.

Microeconomics and the Economy as a Whole. It is generally understood that microeconomics does not concern itself with the economy as a whole and an impression is created that microeconomics differs from macroeconomics in that whereas the latter examines the economy as a whole, the former is not concerned with it. But this is not fully correct. That microeconomics is concerned with the economy as a whole is quite evident from its discussion of the problem of allocation of resources in the society and judging the efficiency of the same. Both microeconomics and macroeconomics analyse the economy but with two different ways or approaches. Microeconomics examines the economy, so to say, *microscopically,* that is, it analyses the behaviour of individual economic units of the economy, their inter-relationships and equilibrium adjustment to each other which determine the allocation of resources in the society. This is known as ***general equilibrium analysis.***

No doubt, microeconomic theory mainly makes particular or partial equilibrium analysis, that is, the analysis of the equilibrium of the individual economic units, taking other things remaining the same. But microeconomic theory, as stated above, also concerns itself with general equilibrium analysis of the economy wherein it is explained how all the economic units, various product markets, various factor markets, money and capital markets are interrelated and interdependent to each other and how through various adjustments and readjustments to the changes in them, they reach a general equilibrium, that is, equilibrium of each of them individually as well as collectively to each other. Professor A. P. Lerner rightly points out, "Actually microeconomics is much more intimately concerned with the economy as a whole than is macroeconomics, and can even be said *to examine the* whole *economy microscopically*. We have seen how economic efficiency is obtained when the "cells" of the economic organism, the households and firms, have adjusted their behaviour to the prices of what they buy and sell. Each cell is then said to be 'in equilibrium.' But these adjustments in turn affect the quantities supplied and demanded and therefore also their prices. This means that the adjusted cells then have to readjust themselves. This in turn upsets the adjustment of others again and so on. An important part of microeconomics is examining whether and how *all* the different cells get adjusted at the same time. This is called ***general equilibrium analysis* in contrast with *particular equilibrium* or *partial equilibrium analysis.*** General equilibrium analysis is the microscopic examination of the inter-relationships of parts within the economy as a whole. Overall economic efficiency is only a special aspect of this analysis."[7]

Importance and Uses of Microeconomics

Microeconomics occupies a vital place in economics and it has both theoretical and practical importance. It is highly helpful in the formulation of economic policies that will promote the welfare of the masses. Until recently, especially before Keynesian Revolution, the body of economics consisted mainly of microeconomics. In spite of the popularity of macroeconomics these days, microeconomics retains its importance, theoretical as well as practical. It is ***microeconomics that tells us how a free-market economy with its millions of consumers and producers works to decide about the allocation of productive resources among the thousands*** of goods and services. As Professor Watson says, "microeconomic theory explains the composition or allocation of total production, why more of some things are produced than of others."[8] He further remarks that microeconomic theory "has many uses. The greatest of these is depth in understanding of how a free private enterprise economy operates."[9] Further, it tells us *how the goods and services produced are distributed among the various people* for consumption through price or market mechanism. It shows how the relative prices of various products and factors are determined, that is, why the price of cloth is what it is and why the wages of an engineer are what they are and so on.

7. Abba P. Lerner, *op. cit.*, pp 36-37.
8. D. S. Watson, *Price Theory and its Uses* (1963), p. 5.
9. *Ibid.*, p. 11.

Moreover, as described above, microeconomic theory *explains the conditions of efficiency in consumption and production* and highlights the factors which are responsible for the departure from the efficiency or economic optimum. On this basis, microeconomic theory *suggests suitable policies* to promote economic efficiency and welfare of the people. Thus, not only does microeconomic theory describe the actual operation of the economy, it has also a normative role in that it suggests policies to eradicate "inefficiency" from the economic system so as to maximize the satisfaction or welfare of the society. The usefulness and importance of microeconomics has been nicely stated by Professor Lerner. He writes, "Microeconomic theory facilitates the understanding of what would be a hopelessly complicated confusion of billions of facts by constructing simplified models of behaviour which are sufficiently similar to the actual phenomena to be of help in understanding them. These models at the same time enable the economists to explain the degree to which the actual phenomena depart from certain ideal constructions that would most completely achieve individual and social objectives. They thus help not only ***to describe*** the actual economic situation but ***to suggest policies*** that would most successfully and most efficiently bring about desired results and to predict the outcomes of such policies and other events. Economics thus has descriptive, normative and predictive aspects."[10]

We have noted above that microeconomics reveals how a decentralised system of a free private enterprise economy functions without any central control. It also brings to light the fact that the functioning of a complete centrally directed economy with efficiency is impossible. Modern economy is so complex that a central planning authority will find it too difficult to get all the information required for the optimum allocation of resources and to give directions to thousands of production units with various peculiar problems of their own so as to ensure efficiency in the use of resources. To quote Professor Lerner again, "Microeconomics teaches us that completely 'direct' running of the economy is impossible—that a modern economy is so complex that no central planning body can obtain all the information and give out all the directives necessary for its efficient operation. These would have to include directives for adjusting to continual changes in the availabilities of millions of productive resources and intermediate products, in the known methods of producing every thing everywhere, and in the quantities and qualities of the many items to be consumed or to be added to society's productive equipment. The vast task can be achieved, and in the past has been achieved, *only by the development of a decentralised system whereby the* millions of producers and consumers are induced to act in the general interest without the intervention of anybody at the centre with instructions as to what one should make and how and what one should consume."[11]

Microeconomic theory shows that welfare optimum of economic efficiency is achieved when there prevails perfect competition in the product and factor markets. Perfect competition is said to exist when there are so many sellers and buyers in the market so that no individual seller or buyer is in a position to influence the price of a product or factor. Departure from perfect competition leads to a lower level of welfare, that is, involves loss of economic efficiency. It is in this context that a large part of microeconomic theory is concerned with showing the nature of departures from perfect competition and therefore from welfare optimum (economic efficiency). The power of giant firms or a combination of firms over the output and price of a product constitutes the problem of monopoly. ***Microeconomics shows how monopoly leads to misallocation of resources and therefore involves loss of economic efficiency or welfare.*** It also makes important and useful policy recommendations to regulate monopoly so as to

10. A. P. Lerner, *op cit.*, p. 29.
11. A. P. Lerner, *op. cit.*, p. 33.

attain economic efficiency or maximum welfare. Like monopoly, *monopsony* (that is, when a single large buyer or a combination of buyers exercises control over the price) also leads to the loss of welfare and therefore needs to be controlled. Similarly, microeconomics brings out the welfare implications of oligopoly (or oligopsony) whose main characteristic is that individual sellers (or buyers) have to take into account, while deciding upon their course of action, how their rivals react to their moves regarding changes in price, product and advertising policy.

Another class of departure from welfare optimum is the problem of *externalities.* Externalities are said to exist when the production or consumption of a commodity *affects other people* than those who produce, sell or buy it. These externalities may be in the form of either *external economies or external diseconomies.* External economies prevail when the production or consumption of a commodity by an individual benefits other individuals and external diseconomies prevail when the production or consumption of a commodity by him *harms other individuals.* ***Microeconomic theory reveals that when the externalities exist, free working of the price mechanism fails to achieve economic efficiency***, since it does not take into account the benefits or harms made to those external to the individual producers and the consumers. The existence of these externalities requires government intervention for correcting imperfections in the price mechanism in order to achieve maximum social welfare.

Several Practical Applications of Microeconomics for Formulating Economic Policies. Microeconomic analysis is also usefully applied to the various applied branches of economics such as Public Finance, International Economics. It is the microeconomic analysis which is used to explain the factors which determine the distribution of the *incidence* or *burden* of a commodity tax between producers or sellers on the one hand and the consumers on the other. Further, microeconomic analysis is applied to show the *damage* done to the social welfare or economic efficiency by the imposition of a tax. If it is assumed that resources are optimally allocated or maximum social welfare prevails before the imposition of a tax, it can be demonstrated by microeconomic analysis that what amount of the damage will be caused to the social welfare. The imposition of a tax on a commodity *(i.e.,* indirect tax) will lead to the loss of social welfare by causing deviation from the optimum allocation of resources, the imposition of a direct tax (for example, income tax) will not disturb the optimum resource allocation and therefore will not result in loss of social welfare. Further, microeconomic analysis is applied to show the *gain from international trade* and to explain the factors which determine the distribution of this gain among the participant countries. Besides, microeconomics finds application in the various problems of international economics. Whether devaluation will succeed in correcting the disequilibrium in the balance of payments depends upon the elasticities of demand and supply of exports and imports. Furthermore, the determination of the foreign exchange rate of a currency, if it is free to vary, depends upon the demand for and supply of that currency.

We thus see that microeconomic analysis is a very useful and important branch of modern economic theory.

MACROECONOMICS

Macroeconomics is a Study of Aggregates. We now turn to explain the approach and content of macroeconomics. 'As said above, word macro is derived from the Greek word *'makros' meaning 'large'and therefore macreoconomic is concerned* with the economic activity in the large. Macroeconomic analyses the behaviour of the whole economic system in totality or entirety. In other words, macroeconomic studies the behaviour of the large aggregates such as total employment, the national product or income,the general price level of the economy. Therefore, macroeconomics is also known as aggregative economics. Macroeconomics analyses and establishes the functional relationship between these large aggregates. Thus Professor

Boulding says, "Macroeconomics deals not with individual quantities as such but with the aggregates of these quantities; not with individual incomes but with the national income; not with individual prices but with the price level; not with individual output but with the national output.[12] In his other famous book, ***Economic Analysis,*** he similarly remarks, ."Macroeconomics, then, is that part of the subject which deals with large aggregates and averages of the system rather than with particular items in it and attempts to define these aggregates in a useful manner and to examine their relationships."[13] Professor Gardner Ackley makes the distinction between the two types more clear and specific when he writes, "macroeconomics concerns itself with such variables as the aggregate volume of output in an economy, with the extent to which its resources are employed, with the size of the national income, with the "general price level". Microeconomics, on the other hand, deals with the *division* of total output among industries, products and firms and the allocation of resources among competing uses. It considers problems of income distribution. Its interest is in relative prices of particular goods and services.[14]

Macroeconomics Distinguished from Microeconomics. Macroeconomics should be carefully distinguished from microeconomics. It should be noted that microeconomics also deals with some "aggregates" but not of the type with which macroeconomics is concerned. Microeconomics examines the behaviour of the industry in regard to the determination of its product price, output and employment, and the industry is an *aggregate of the various firms* producing the same or similar product. Likewise, microeconomic theory seeks to explain the determination of price of a ptoduct through the interaction of the market demand for and market supply of a product. Market demand for a product is the aggregate of the individual demands of all consumers wishing to buy the product and the market supply of a product is the aggregate of the productions of many firms producing that product. Similarly, demand for and supply of labour in an industry of a city through which microeconomics explains wage determination are aggregative concepts.

But the aggregates with which macroeconomics deals with are of somewhat different variety. Macroeconomics concerns itself with those *aggregates which relate to the whole economy.* Macroeconomics also discusses the sub-aggregates, unlike the aggregates of microeconomics which examines aggregates relating to a particular product, a particular industry or a particular market, But macroeconomics is concerned with those aggregates that cut across various products and industries. For example, the total production of consumer goods (*i.e.,* total consumption) and the total production of capital goods (*i.e.,* total investment) are two important sub-aggregates dealt with in macroeconomics but these aggregates are not confined to a single product or a single industry but instead they refer to all industries producing consumer goods and all industries producing capital goods. Moreover, the sub-aggregates, discussed in macroeconomics, add up to an aggregate for the whole economy. For instance, total consumption and total investment, two important sub-aggregates in macroeconomics, together constitute the total national product. Likewise, the total wage income (*i.e.,* total share of labour) and total profits (defined as total property income) add up to the national income. Professor Ackley thus says, "Macroeconomics also uses aggregates smaller than for the whole economy but only in a context which makes them sub-divisions of an economy wide total. Microeconomics also uses aggregates, but not in a context which relates them to ***an economy-wide total.***[15]

As we said above, the subject-matter of microeconomics consists in explaining the determination of relative prices of products and factors and the allocation of resources based upon them. On the other hand, the subject-matter of macroeconomic analysis is to explain

12. K. E. Boulding, *A Reconstruction of Economics* (1950), p. 3.
13. K. E. Boulding, *Economic Analysis,* p. 259.
14. Gardner Ackley, *Macroeconomic Theory,* 1961, p. 4.
15. Op. cit. P-5

what determines the ***level of national income and employment,*** and what *causes* ***fluctuations*** in the level of national income, output and employment. Further, it also explains the ***growth*** of national income over a long period of time. In other words, macroeconomics examines the determination of the level, fluctuations (cycles) and trends (growth) in the overall economic activity *(i.e.,* national income, output and employment).

Neo-Classical Economists Neglected Macroeconomic Analysis. It is worth mentioning that classical economic theory of Adam Smith, Ricardo, Malthus and J. S. Mill was *mainly* macro-analysis, for they discussed the determination of growth of national income and wealth, the division of national income among broad social classes (total wages, total rent and total profits), the general price level and the effects of technology and population increase on the growth of the economy. On the other hand, neo-classical economics, in which writings of Pigou and Marshall predominate, is mainly micro-analysis. Neo-classical writers assumed that full-employment of resources prevailed in the economy and concentrated mainly upon showing how the resources were allocated to the production of various goods and how the relative prices of products and factors were determined. It is mainly because of their full-employment assumption and their preoccupation with the problem of determination of prices, outputs and resource employments in individual industries that they could not explain the existence of involuntary unemployment and under-utilisation of the productive capacity at times of depression in the private-enterprise capitalist countries. They thus could not provide adequate explanation of the occurrence of the trade cycles in a private enterprise economy. What is worse, the neo : classical writers tried to apply the economic generalisations valid in the case of an individual industry to the case of the behaviour of the whole economic system and macroeconomic variables. For instance, Pigou asserted that involuntary unemployment existing at the time of depression could be eliminated and employment expanded by cutting down wages. This is quite incorrect. While the cut in wages may expand employment in an individual industry, the reduction in wages throughout the economy will mean the fall in incomes of the working classes which will result in the decrease in the level of aggregate demand. The fall in aggregate demand will tend to lower the level of employment rather than expand it.

Macroeconomic Analysis : Keynesian Revolution. There were no doubt pre-Keynesian theories of business cycles and the general price level which were "macro" in nature but it was late Lord J. M. Keynes who laid great stress on macroeconomic analysis and put forward a general theory of income and employment in his revolutionary book, *A General Theory of Employment, Interest and Money* published in 1936. Keynes's theory made a genuine break from the neo-classical economics and produced such a fundamental and drastic change in economic thinking that his macroeconomic analysis has earned the names "***Keynesian Revolution***" and "***New Economics***". Keynes in his analysis made a frontal attack on the neo-classical "***Say's Law of Markets***" which was the basis of full-employment assumption of neo-classical economics and challenged the neo-classical dictum that involuntary unemployment could not prevail in a free private enterprise economy. He showed how the equilibrium level of national income and employment was determined by aggregate demand and aggregate supply and further that this is achieved at far less than full-employment level in a free private enterprise economy and thereby causing involuntary unemployment of labour on the one hand and excess productive capacity *(i.e.,* under-utilization of the existing capital stock) on the other. His macroeconomic model revealed how consumption function, investment function, liquidity preference function, conceived in aggregative terms, interact to determine income, employment, interest and the general price level.

Therefore, before showing how the level of income and employment is determined, we have to study the determinants of consumption function and investment function. The analysis of consumption function and investment function are the important subjects of macroeconomic theory. It is the total consumption demand and total investment demand taken together that constitute the level of aggregate demand which is the crucial determinant of the level of income and employment in the advanced industrialised countries.

Macroeconomics and the General Level of Prices. Besides studying how the level of income and employment is determined in the economy, macroeconomics also concerns itself with showing how the general level of prices is determined. Keynes made a significant improvement over the quantity theory of money by showing that the increase in the supply of money does not always bring about the rise in prices. Important topic in this field is to explain the causes of inflation. Keynes, who before the Second World War showed that involuntary unemployment and depression were due to the deficiency of aggregate demand, during the Second World War period when prices rose very high he explained in a booklet entitled *"How to Pay for War"* that just as unemployment and depression were caused by the deficiency of aggregate demand, inflation was due to the excessive aggregate demand. Since Keynes the theory of inflation has been further developed and many types of inflation depending upon various causes have been pointed out. The problem of inflation is a serious problem faced these days, both by the developed and developing countries of the world. Theory of inflation is an important subject of macroeconomics.

Macroeconomics and Theory of Economic Growth. Another distinct and more important branch of macroeconomics that has been developed recently is the ***theory of economic growth,*** or what is briefly called ***growth economics.*** The problem of growth is a long-run problem and Keynes did not deal with it. In fact, Keynes is said to have once remarked that "in the long run we are all dead". From this remark of Keynes it should not be understood that he thought long run to be quite unimportant. By this remark he simply emphasised the importance of the short-run problem of fluctuations in the level of economic activity (involuntary cyclical unemployment, depression, inflation). It was Harrod[16] and Domar[17] who extended the Keynesian analysis to the long-run problem of growth with stability. They pointed out the dual role of investment; one of **income generating**, which Keynes considered, and the second of ***increasing capacity*** which Keynes ignored because of his pre-occupation with the short run. In view of the fact that investment adds to the productive capacity *(i.e.,* capital stock), if growth with stability (i.e. without secular stagnation or secular inflation) is to be achieved, income or demand must be increasing at a rate sufficient enough to ensure full utilization of the increasing capacity. Thus, macroeconomic models of Harrod and Domar have revealed the required rate of growth of income that must take place if the steady growth of the economy is to be achieved. These days growth economics has been further developed and extended a good deal. Though a general growth theory applies to both the developed and developing economies, special theories which explain the causes of under-development and poverty in developing countries and which also suggest strategies for initiating and accelerating growth in them have been propounded. These special growth theories relating to developing countries are generally known as ***Economics of Development.***

Macro-theory of Relative Shares in National Income. Still another important subject of macroeconomic theory is to explain what determines the *relative shares* from the total national income of the various classes, especially workers and capitalists, in the society. The interest in this subject goes back to Ricardo who not only emphasised that how the produce of

16. R. F. Harrod, *Towards a Dynamic Economics* (1948).
17. E. D. Domar, Expansion and *Employment, American Economic Review* (March 1947).

earth is distributed among the three social classes—landlords, workers and capitalists is the principal problem in economics but also propounded a theory explaining the determination of relative shares of rent, wages and profits in the total national income. Like Ricardo, Marx also showed a deep interest in this problem of determination of relative shares in a capitalist economy. But after Marx interest in this subject very much declined and the theory of distribution came to be discussed mostly in micro-terms, that is, the theory of distribution merely assumed the role of explaining the determination *of* ***factor prices*** rather than the relative aggregative shares of the social classes. Thanks to the efforts of M. Kalecki and Nicholas Kaldor, the interest in this macro-theory of distribution has again been revived. Kalecki advanced the view that the relative shares of wages and profits in the national income are governed by the degree of monopoly in the economy. On the other hand, Kaldor has applied the Keynesian analysis and has shown that the relative shares of wages and profits in the national income depend upon the propensity to consume and the rate of investment in the economy.

We have now stated, in brief, all aspects of macroeconomic theory. These various aspects of macroeconomic theory are shown in the following chart :

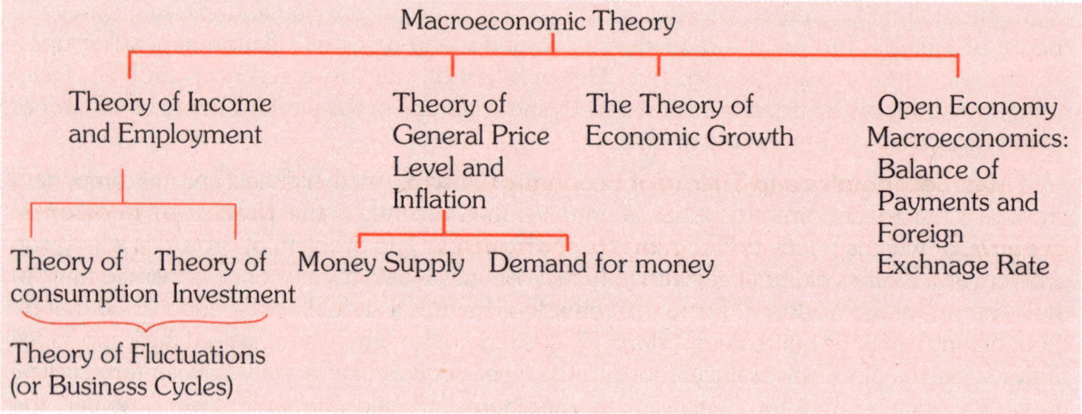

Why a Separate Study of Macroeconomics

Now, an important question which arises is why a separate study of the economic system as a whole or its large aggregates is necessary. Can't'we generalise about the behaviour of the economic system as a whole or about the behaviour of large aggregates such as aggregate consumption, aggregate saving, aggregate investment from the economic laws governing the behaviour patterns of the individual units found by microeconomics. In other words, can't we obtain the laws governing the macroeconomic variables such as total national product, total employment and total income, general price level etc. by simply adding up, multiplying or averaging the results obtained from the behaviour of the individual firms and industries. The answer to this question is that the behaviour of the economic system as a whole or the macroeconomic aggregates is not merely a matter of addition or multiplication or averaging of what happens in the various individual parts of the whole. As a matter of fact, in the economic system what is true of parts is not necessarily true of the whole. Therefore, the application of micro-approach to generalise about the behaviour of the economic system as a whole or macroeconomic aggregates is incorrect and may lead to misleading conclusions. Therefore, a separate macro-analysis is needed to study the behaviour of the economic system as a whole as well as in respect of various macroeconomic aggregates. When laws or generalisations are true of constituent individual parts but untrue and invalid in case of the whole economy, paradoxes seem to exist. K.E. Boulding has called these paradoxes as ***macroeconomic paradoxes.*** It is because of the existence of these macroeconomic paradoxes that there is a justification for making macro-analysis of the behaviour of the whole economic system or its large economic aggregates. Thus, Professor Boulding rightly remarks, "It is these paradoxes more than any other factor, which justify the separate study of the system as whole, not merely as an inventory or list of particular items, but as a complex of aggregates."[18]

Professor Boulding further elaborates his point by comparing the economic system with a forest and the individual firms or industries with the trees in the forest. Forest, he says, is the aggregation of trees but it does not reveal the same properties and behaviour patterns as the individual trees. It will be misleading to apply the rules governing the individual trees to generalise about the behaviour of the forest.

Various examples of ***macroeconomic paradoxes*** (that is, what is true of parts is not true of the whole) can be given from the economic field. We shall give two such examples which are concerned with savings and wages, on the basis of which Keynes laid stress on using and applying macroeconomic analysis as a separate and distinct approach from microeconomic analysis. Take savings first. Savings are always good for an individual since they save with some purpose in view, for old age, for education of their children, for purchasing durable things like houses and cars etc. in the future, accumulation of money to start or expand business, for lending money to others including banks to earn interest. But savings are not *always* good for the society as a whole. If an economy is in the grip of depression and unemployment caused by the deficiency of aggregate effective demand, the increase in savings by individuals will lead to a fall in aggregate consumption demand of the society which will cause aggregate demand to fall. As a result, national income will decline. Given the propensity to save, at the lower level of national income, the agtgregate saving will fall to the original level of aggregate saving. The paradox of thrift arises because the acts of all the people to save more does not actually lead to the increase in national saving. Besides, as their decision to save more causes fall in national income, consumption of the people is less than before which implies they will become worse off than before. Therefore, this has been called a ***paradox of thrift***.

Another common example to prove that what is true for the individual may not be true for the society as a whole is the wage-employment relationship. As pointed out above, classical and neo-classical economists, especially A. C. Pigou, contended that the cut in money wages at times of depression and unemployment would lead to the increase in employment and thereby eliminate unemployment and depression. Now, whereas it is true that a cut in money wages in an individual industry will lead to more employment in that industry but it is not a valid proposition for the economy as a whole. It is quite common-place conclusion of microeconomic theory that, given the demand curve for labour, at a lower wage rate more men will be employed. But for the society or economy as a whole this is highly misleading. If the wages are cut all round in the economy, as was suggested by Pigou and others on the basis of wage-employment relationship in an individual industry, the aggregate demand for goods and services in the society will decline, since wages are incomes of the workers which constitute majority in the society. The decline in aggregate demand will mean the decrease in demand for goods of many industries. Because the demand for labour is a derived demand, *i.e.* derived from the demand for goods, the fall in aggregate demand of goods will result in the decline in demand for labour which will create more unemployment rather than reduce it.

We thus see that the laws or generalisations which hold good for the behaviour of an individual consumer, firm or industry may be quite invalid and misleading when applied to the behaviour of the economic system as a whole. There is thus ***a fallacy of composition***. This is so because what is true of individual components is not true of their collective whole. As

18. K. E. Boulding, *A Reconstruction of Economics* (1952), p.173.

mentioned above, these are called macroeconomic paradoxes and it is because of these paradoxes that a separate study of the economic system as a whole is essential.

Macroeconomic analysis takes account of many relationships which are not applicable to individual parts at all. For instance, an individual may save more than that he invests or he may invest more than he saves, but for the economy as a whole it is one of the important principles of Keynesian macroeconomics that **actual savings are always equal to actual investment.** Likewise, for an individual, expenditure may be more or less than his income but the national expenditure of the economy must be equal to the national income. In fact, the national expenditure and national income are two identical things. Similarly, in the case of full employment, an individual industry may increase its output and employment by bidding away the workers from other industries, but the economy cannot increase its output and employment in this way. Thus, what applies to an individual industry does not do so in case of the economic system as a whole.

We therefore conclude that a separate and distinct macroeconomic analysis is essential if we want to understand the true working of the economic system as a whole. From this it should not be understood that microeconomic theory is worthless and should be abandoned. As a matter of fact, ***microeconomics and macroeconomics are complementary to each other rather than being competitive.*** The two types of theories deal with different subjects, one deals mainly with the explanation of relative prices of goods and factors and the other with the short-run determination of income and employment of the society as well as its long-run growth. The study of both micro and macroeconomics is therefore necessary. Professor Samuelson rightly says, "There is really no opposition between micro and macroeconomics. Both are absolutely vital. And you are only half-educated if you understand the one while being ignorant of the other."[19]

Interdependence between Micro and Macroeconomics

Actually micro and macroeconomics are interdependent. The theories regarding the behaviour of some macroeconomic aggregates (but not all) are derived from theories of individual behaviour. For instance, the theory of investment, which is a part and parcel of the microeconomic theory, is derived from the behaviour of individual entrepreneur. According to this theory, an individual entrepreneur in his investment activity is governed by the expected rate of profit on the one hand and rate of interest on the other. And so is the aggregate investment function. Similarly, the theory of aggregate consumption function is based upon the behaviour patterns of individual consumers. It may be noted that we are able to draw aggregate investment function and aggregate consumption function because in this respect the behaviour of the aggregate is in no way different from the behaviour patterns of individual components. Moreover, we can derive the behaviour of these aggregates only if either the composition of aggregates is constant or the composition changes in some regular way as the size of aggregates changes. From this it should not be understood that behaviour of all macroeconomic relationship is in conformity with behaviour patterns of individuals composing them. As we saw above, saving-investment relationship and wage-employment relationship for the economic system as a whole are quite different from the corresponding relationships in case of individual parts.

Microeconomic theory contributes to macroeconomic theory in another way also. The theory of relative prices of products and factors is essential in the explanation of the determination of general price level. Even Keynes used microeconomic theory to explain the rise in the general price level as a result of the increase in the cost of production in the economy. According

19. Paul A. Samuelson, *Economics.*, 11th edition, 1980.

to Keynes, when as a result of the increase in money supply and consequently the aggregate demand, more output is produced, the cost of production rises. With the rise in the cost of production, the prices rise.

According to Keynes, cost of production rises because of (1) the law of diminishing returns operates and (2) wages and prices of raw materials may rise as the economy approaches full-employment level. Now, the influence of cost of production, diminishing returns, etc., on the determination of prices are the parts of microeconomics.

Not only does macroeconomics depend upon to some extent on microeconomics, the latter also depends upon to some extent on macroeconomics. The determination of the rate of profit and the rate of interest are well-known microeconomic topics, but they greatly depend upon the macroeconomic aggregates. In microeconomic theory, the profits are regarded as reward for uncertainty bearing but microeconomic theory fails to show the economic forces which determine the magnitude of profits earned by the entrepreneur and why there are fluctuations in them. The magnitude of profits depends upon the level of aggregate demand, national income, and the general price level in the country. We know that at times of depression when the levels of aggregate demand, national income and price level are low, the entrepreneurs in the various fields of the economy suffer losses. On the other hand, when aggregate demand, incomes of the people, the general price level go up and conditions of boom prevail, the entrepreneurs earn huge profits.

Now, take the case of the rate of interest. Strictly speaking theory of the rate of interest has now become a subject of macroeconomic theory. Partial equilibrium theory of interest which belongs to microeconomic theory would not reveal all the forces which take part in the determination of the rate of interest. Keynes showed that the rate of interest is determined by the liquidity preference function and the stock (or supply) of money in the economy. The liquidity preference function and the stock of money in the economy are macroeconomic concepts. No doubt, the Keynesian theory has also been shown to be indeterminate, but in the modern theory of interest Keynesian aggregative concepts of liquidity preference and stock of money play an important role in the determination of the rate of interest. Moreover, in the modern interest theory (*i.e* determination of interest rate through intersection of *LM* and *IS* curves) along with liquidity preference and the supply of money, the other two forces which are used to explain the determination of interest are saving and investment functions which are also conceived in aggregative or macro terms.

It is thus clear from above that the determination of profits and rate of interest cannot be explained without the tools and concepts of macroeconomics. It follows that though microeconomics and macroeconomics deal with different subjects, but there is a good deal of interdependence between them. In the explanation of many economic phenomena, both micro and macro-economic tools and concepts have to be applied. About interdependence between microeconomics and macroeconomics, Professor Ackley's remarks are worth quoting. He says, "The relationship between macroeconomics and theory of individual behaviour is a two-way street. On the one hand, microeconomic theory should provide the building blocks for our aggregate theories. But macroeconomics may also contribute to microeconomic understanding. If we discover, for example, empirically stable macroeconomic generalisations which appear inconsistent with microeconomic theories, or which relate to aspects of behaviour which microeconomics has neglected, macroeconomics may permit us to improve our understanding of individual behaviour."[20]

---

20. Gardner Ackley, op.cit.

CHAPTER

3

Methodology of Economics

Every science derives hypotheses, generalisations, principles, laws and theories which explain the behaviour of phenomena it studies. For deriving generalisations and theories it has to adopt a certain methodology. One of the controversies in economics relates to the kind of methods to be adopted to discover generalisations and theories about the relationship between economic variables. Economists have in fact adopted both deductive and inductive methods of reasoning. Recently econometrics, that is, application of statistical methods have gained much popularity among economists. These different methods will be explained below. Besides, the concept of equilibrium and role of equilibrium analysis in deriving economic theories will also be explained. Further, the role of model building in economics to explain the behaviour of individuals and the economy will be brought out. The other aspect of the method or technique of economic analysis is whether it should be of the nature of statics, comparative statics or dynamics. These methods will be explained in the next chapter.

Nature of Scientific Theory

A scientific theory sets up relationship between facts or, in other words, it explains cause and effect relationship between various variables. The variables with which economists are concerned are prices, quantities demanded and supplied, the money supply, national income, employment, wages, profits, etc. Every theory is based upon a set of assumptions, often called premises or postulates. It is worth mentioning that some assumptions are taken merely to simplify the analysis, though they may not be entirely realistic. In economics, the assumptions may be behavioural, that is, relating to the behaviour of economic variables or they may be technological pertaining to the production technology and the availability of productive factors. From the assumptions or postulates some implications or conclusions are deduced through logical process of reasoning. The process of logical deduction to discover relevant conclusions from a set of definitions and assumptions is carried out either in words or in the language of symbolic logic or it may be done with the aid of geometry or more formal mathematics. It is these conclusions drawn from the assumptions through deductive logic which are called *hypotheses*.

It is worth noting that a ***scientific hypothesis states the proposition about relationship between facts or variables in a form that is testable or falsifiable, that is, propositions which are capable of being refuted.*** If the predictions based on a hypothesis are refuted by the direct observation of actual facts or through the statistical methods of interpreting actual facts, a hypothesis stands rejected. If on testing the predictions based on a given hypothesis are proved correct, it stands established as a scientific theory. For instance, the quantity demanded varies inversely with price is one of the important economic hypotheses established in economics. If a sales tax is imposed on a commodity and as a result the price of the commodity rises, the prediction will be that the quantity demanded will decline, other things remaining constant. This has not been falsified and in fact has been corroborated by the facts of the real world. So the law of demand stating that there is inverse relationship between price and quantity demanded is a scientific economic hypothesis.

Likewise, the generalisation regarding the direct relationship between price and quantity supplied, that is, the higher the price, the greater will be the quantity supplied, has also been found to be consistent with facts in several cases. Further, the Keynesian hypothesis that under conditions of less than full-employment of resources, levels of national income and employment are determined by the magnitude of aggregate effective demand is also a well established economic hypothesis regarding the developed capitalist economies. The predictions based on the above Keynesian theory that the increase in aggregate demand through deficit budgeting by the Government under conditions of less than full-employment will lead to the rise in national income and employment has been generally found to be consistent with facts. Therefore, Keynesian theory of effective demand has been proved to be valid for the advanced capitalist economies by empirical evidence.

If the predictions based on a hypothesis are falsified by the facts of the real world, either some error would have been committed during the process of logical deduction or the assumptions made would have been too unrealistic, wrong or irrelevant to the subject of economic enquiry. Thus, in order to establish scientific economic hypotheses, error in logic and mistake of making unrealistic assumptions be avoided. It is worth emphasising that every hypothesis or theory is based upon some simplifying assumptions which are not quite realistic, that is, it is an abstraction from reality. But good hypotheses and theories abstract from reality in a useful and significant way. Indeed, if we do not abstract from reality we would merely duplicate the real world in a camera like manner and will not gain any understanding of it. The crucial test of a hypothesis or theory is that whether predictions which follow from it are falsified or not by the empirical evidence, that is, by the facts in the real world. If the predictions of the hypothesis or theory are found to be consistent with the facts, its assumptions would be justified even if they are unrealistic. Thus, a hypothesis or theory should not be criticised simply because assumptions it makes are unrealistic. The hypothesis is valid if its predictions are found to be consistent with the facts.

DERIVATION OF ECONOMIC THEORIES AND NATURE OF ECONOMIC REASONING

After having explained the scientific nature of economic hypothesis we are now in position to explain in detail how the generalisations in economics are derived and to clearly bring out the nature of economic reasoning. Economic generalisations describe the laws or ***statements of tendencies*** in various branches of economics such as production, consumption, exchange and distribution of income. In the view of Robbins, economic generalisations and laws are statements of uniformities which describe human behaviour in the allocation of scarce resources between alternative ends. The generalisations of economics, like the laws of other sciences, state relationship between variables and describe those economic hypotheses which have been found consistent with facts or, in other words, have been found to be true by empirical evidence. But a distinction may be drawn between a generalisation (law) and a theory. A generalisation or law ***just describes*** the relationship between variables; it does not provide any explanation of the described relation. On the other hand, ***a theory provides an explanation of the stated relation between the variables,*** that is, it brings out the logical basis of the generalisation. An economic theory or a model derives a generalisation through process of logical reasoning and explains the conditions under which the stated generalisation will hold true.

Deductive Method

Generalisations in economics have been derived in two ways: (1) *Deductive Method,* (2) *Inductive Method.* We shall first explain the deductive method of deriving economic generalisations. The deductive method is also called *abstract, analytical* and *a priori* method and represents an abstract approach to the derivation of economic generalisations and theories. The principal steps in the process of deriving economic generalisations through deductive logic are: (a) perception of the problem to be enquired into; *(b)* defining precisely the technical terms and making appropriate assumptions, often called postulates or premises; (c) deducing hypotheses, that is, deriving conclusions from the premises through the process of logical reasoning; and *(d)* testing of hypothesis deduced.

(a) **Perception of the Problem.** In any scientific enquiry, the analyst or theorist must have a clear idea of the probtem to be enquired into. He must know the significant variables regarding whose behaviour and interrelationship he wants to derive generalisations. The perception of the problem is by no means an easy task.

(b) **Defintion of Technical Terms and Making of Assumptions.** The next step in the process of deriving generalisations is to define precisely and unambiguously the various technical terms to be used in the analysis as well as to state clearly the assumptions or postulates one makes to derive generalisations. As mentioned above, assumptions may be behavioural pertaining to the behaviour of the economic variables or they may be technological relating to the state of technology and the factor endowments. The crucial assumptions are made on the basis of observations or introspection. A crucial assumption that has been made in economics is that consumers try to maximise their satisfaction and producers try to maximise their profits. Likewise, it is assumed that investors try to minimise their risk and maximize the expected rate of return. Some of the assumptions are made merely to simplify the analysis and may not be quite realistic. The actual economic world is quite complex and full of details in which numerous factors play a part and act and interact on each other. The introduction of simplifying assumptions is quite necessary in order to bring out the importance of really significant factors having a bearing on the problem under investigation. According to Prof. Boulding, economic theory represents just a 'map' of real world phenomenon and not a perfect picture of it. To quote him, "Just as we do not expecf a map to show every tree, every blade of grass in a landscape, so we should not expect economic analysis to take into account every detail and quirk of real economic behaviour."[1]

It, therefore, follows that each and every assumption made by a theory may not be realistic. The crucial factor in building up a valid theory is whether its predictions are corroborated by the facts in the world. A correct scientific theory or generalisation must be expressed in the form of a hypothesis that is conceivably refutable. As mentioned above, Professor Friedman in his now well-known article, *"The Methodology of Positive Economics"* has expressed the view that undue importance should not be given to the 'realism' of assumptions. What matters most from the viewpoint of scientific theory, according to him, is whether it enables us to predict accurately.

(c) **Deducing Hypotheses through Logical Deduction.** The next step in deriving a generalisation through deductive logic is deducing hypothesis from the assumptions or premises taken. An hypothesis describes the relationship between factors affecting a phenomenon; it establishes cause and effect relationship between the variables having a bearing on the phenomenon. Then through logical process, hypothesis is deduced from the assumptions made. This logical reasoning may be carried out verbally or it may be conducted in symbolic

1. K. E. Boulding, *Economic Analysis,* Hamish Hamilton, New York, 1956, p. 11.

terms using the language of what is known as symbolic logic. The geometric or graphic technique is also usually employed to deduce the hypothesis about the relationship between factors. Besides, the process of logical deduction may be done with the help of more formal mathematics. Nowadays in almost all branches of modern economics, the mathematics as a tool of analysis for deriving economic theories and generalisations is being increasingly used. The use of mathematics in economic analysis proves extremely useful where geometrical methods make the analysis more complicated to comprehend. Besides, the use of mathematical method makes the derivation of economic hypotheses more rigorous and exact.

It is worthwhile to note that in deriving analytically sound hypotheses, one should guard against committing ***logical fallacy*** in the process of logical deduction. For instance, it is inappropriate to conclude that A must be the cause of B, if A happens to precede B. Further, it is logically fallacious to argue that since there exists a high degree of correlation between the two factors, say between the supply of money and the general price level, the former must be the cause of the latter, unless the causation must be logically developed.

(d) **Testing or Verification of Hypotheses.** Hypotheses obtained above have to be verified before they are established as generalisations or principles of economics. For the verification of hypotheses, economists cannot make controlled experiments, because they have to discern uniformities in behaviour patterns of man. As we cannot make experiments with man under controlled conditions, such as in laboratories as physical scientists make experiments with inanimate objects of nature and biologists make these with animals and plants. Therefore, economists have to rely on uncontrolled experiences and observations. This information regarding uncontrolled experiments about the behaviour patterns concerning variables about man and the economy are quite amply available.

The reliance by economists on uncontrolled experiences, however, does increase the number of observations required to verify the hypotheses or to establish the generalisations. Besides, the need to rely on uncontrolled experiences complicates the analysis and requires that facts must be carefully interpreted to discern successfully the significant relationship between relevant economic variables. Prof. Baur rightly remarks, "The need to rely on uncontrolled experiences does, however, increase the number of observations required, and also complicates their successful analysis and interpretation, before we can discern successfully the significant uniformities and ascertain their limits."[2] He points out that in spite of the complexities and difficulties involved in verifying economic hypotheses through successful analysis and proper interpretation of uncontrolled experiences and observations, several useful and significant generalisations have been established in economics.

In the field of microeconomics, the well-established generalisations relate to the inverse relationship between price and quantity demanded, the direct relation between price and quantity supplied, the tendency of the price of the product to be equal to the marginal cost under conditions of perfect competition, and the tendency for the wages to be equal to the value of marginal product under conditions of perfect competition and several others. In the field of macroeconomics, established generalisations relate to the determination of the level of national income by aggregate demand and aggregate supply in a capitalist economy, the multiple increase in income and employment as a result of a given initial increase in investment depending upon the size of marginal propensity to consume, the dependence of the amount of investment on the marginal efficiency of capital and the rate of interest and several others.

"It is worth noting that the absence of controlled or contrived experiments in economics affects the forms of various generalisations in different degrees."[3] This means that the generalisations in economics are not as exact as those of physical sciences and they are

2. P. T. Baur, *Economic Analysis and Policy in Under-developed Countries*, Routledge and Kegan Paul Ltd. 1957, p. 8.
3. P.T. Bour, *op., cit.* P.9.

therefore not universally applicable under all circumstances. Because of the absence of contrived experiments economic generalisations lack in firmness. Economic generalisations are therefore not easily accepted by all. Even generalisations that are refuted by empirical evidence are not abandoned for good by all. Prof. Baur rightly points out, "the absence of the vivid and dramatic evidence provided by the contrived experiments adds greatly to the difficulty of securing acceptance for generalisations which are amply justified by the analysis of the available evidence."[4] Likewise, absence of controlled experiments, according to Friedman, "renders the weeding out of unsuccessful hypotheses slow and difficult. They are seldom downed for good and are always cropping up again."[5]

In regard to framing and testing of economic generalisations, two related distinctions must be borne in mind. First, functional relationship between economic variables and a historically sequence of events must be distinguished. For instance, the law of demand stating inverse relationship between price and quantity demanded does not become invalid in view of the fact that both prices and quantities sold of many commodities increase during a boom period. This is because certain other forces such as a rise in aggregate investment demand operates which causes increase in both the price and quantity sold during a boom period. Second, predictions of a generalisation to show its validity must be carefully differentiated from the forecasting of future events; actual events may not exactly come about as predicted by a generalisation and yet that generalisation may be correct. This is because, as mentioned above, the actual course of events is governed by several other factors assumed by a generalisation which remains constant under the qualification "other things remaining the same". Thus, "even if the prediction that producers of a particular crop respond to a higher price by producing more is correct, this prediction does not enable us to forecast accurately next year's output (still less the harvest in the more distant future), which in the event will be affected by many factors besides changes in price."[6]

It follows from above that in the absence of controlled experiments, for the verification of their generalisations economists have to rely on the direct observations of the events in the real world. By direct observations we mean "gathering of information personally or reliance on comparatively unprocessed material such as files of business firms and government departments, locally published reports, proceedings of representative assemblies, newspapers, advertisements, market reports, auction notices and the like." In order to prove the validity of hypotheses and therefore to establish generalisations, importance of direct observations cannot be underrated. Thus Prof. Baur assets, "The depth and significance of economic generalisations depend on the quality of the underlying observations and analysis."[7]

Testing of Economic Hypotheses through Econometrics. In recent years a very useful method to test economic hypothesis has been developed. This is the *statistical method* or what is now popularly called econometric method. The statistical or econometric method to verify and establish the theoretical generalisations occupies an important place because there is limited applicability of controlled experimentation in economics. The various statistical methods such as regression analysis have been developed to empirically test the economic hypotheses on the basis of collected economic data. The merit of econometrics is that the degree of functional relationship between relevant economic variables in precise quantitative terms is obtained by it and also the level of significance of the results can also be estimated. Recently, econometric method has been used to establish the precise relationships between money supply and the price level, quantity of money and the national income, consumption and income, capital accumulation and rate of economic growth and so forth.

4. *Ibid*, p. 9.
5. Milton Friedman, *Essays in Positive Economics*, Chicago, 1953, p. 11.
6. P. T. Baur, *op. cit.*, pp. 10-11.
7. P. T. Baur, *op. cit.*, p. 9.

It may, however, be pointed out that statistical analysis or econometrics alone cannot be used to derive and establish economic principles and theories. Economic hypotheses or theories must be developed logically before we can meaningfully use statistical analysis to test and verify them. Indeed, theory or hypothesis is needed before the selection of the relevant facts and data regarding relevant variables which can be subjected to empirical testing through the methods of econometrics. Prof. Myrdal is quite right, when he says, "Theory, therefore, must always be *a priori* to the empirical observation of facts. Facts come to mean something only as ascertained and organised in the frame of a theory. Indeed, facts as part of scientific knowledge have no existence outside such a frame. Questions must be asked before answers can be obtained and, in order to make sense, the questions must be part of a logical co-ordinated attempt to understand social reality as a whole. A non-theoretical approach is, in strict logic, unthinkable."[8]

Merits and Demerits of Deductive Method

The deductive approach to establish economic generalisations was extensively used by Classical and Neo-Classical economists such as Ricardo, Malthus, Senior, J.S. Mill, Marx, Marshall and Pigou. It still remains popular with modern economists as it has several merits. First, useful mathematical techniques can be employed to derive generalisations of economics. With the aid of rigorous mathematical logic, economic theories can be developed through the process of deduction which can successfully explain economic phenomena. Secondly, through deductive logic useful economic theorems can be derived without the tenuous and detailed collection and analysis of data which are required under the alternative inductive method. Thus, as compared to inductive method, method of deduction is less time-consuming and less expensive. Thirdly, in view of the limited scope for controlled experimentation in economics, the method of deduction is an extremely useful method of deriving generalisations. This is because multiplicity of forces acts simultaneously on an economic phenomenon and it is not possible to eliminate some of these by means of a controlled experiment. This indicates the crucial importance of deductive logic for building up economic principles or generalisations. Fourthly, the use of sophisticated mathematical methods in the deductive approach enables the economists to introduce accuracy and exactness in economic principles and theories.

In spite of the above merits, shortcomings of the deductive approach should not be overlooked. The use of deductive method in deriving economic generalisations requires the use of a high-level competence in logic and theoretical abstraction. A good deal of care and objectivity is needed to avoid bad logic or faulty economic reasoning. Prof. Blaug rightly opines, "It is perfectly true that economists have often deceived themselves and their readers by engaging in what Leontief once called "implicit theorising" presenting tautologies in the guise of substantive contributions to economic knowledge." Besides, most economists have preconceived notions or biases on several economic issues. If sound and valid economic generalisations are to be established, economists must dissociate themselves from normative preconceptions and biases in their logical process of deducing valid economic generalisations. Further, a great demerit of deductive approach is that with it highly sophisticated theoretical models based on highly unrealistic assumptions may be developed which do not have any operational significance. Indeed, such highly irrelevant analytical models with little empirical content and incapable of being used for policy formulation have in fact been developed by economists. Such models are no more than mere "intellectual toys". If economics is to serve as an instrument of social betterment, building of such theoretical models having no operational use should be avoided.

8. Gunnar Myrdal, *Value in Social Theory,* Routledge and Kegan Paul Ltd., London, 1958, p. 233.

Lastly, in the derivation of economic hypotheses and conclusions through deductive logic, assumptions play a crucial role. If the assumptions made are such that when on removing them, economic hypothesis based on them is refuted, then making of these assumptions is not valid. Thus, one who uses deductive approach should always keep in mind to what extent the validity of generalisations derived depends on the assumptions made. For instance, the Keynesian macro-analysis is based upon the assumption of a depression-ridden capitalist economy with a lot of excess productive capacity. Therefore, a positive harm has been done in applying the Marxian theories in the context of developing countries such as ours where the assumptions made by Marx do not hold good. Hence, mere "deductive arm-chair analysis" should be avoided, if the scientific character of economics is to be maintained.

The Inductive Method

The indicative method which is also called empirical method derives economic generalisations on the basis of experience and observations. In this method detailed data are collected with regard to a certain economic phenomenon and effort is then made to arrive at certain generalisations which follow from the observations collected. But, it is worth mentioning that the number of observations has to be large if it can yield a valid economic generalisation. One should not generalise on the basis of a very few observations. There are three ways which can be used for deriving economic principles and theories. They are: (a) experimentation, (b) observations, (c) statistical or econometric method. As has been mentioned above, the experimentation, that is, the use of controlled experiments is of limited applicability in economics. First, unlike natural sciences which are concerned with analysing the behaviour of either inanimate objects or obedient animals such as rats and rabbits under the influence of chloroform, economics deals with the behaviour of man who is quite fickle, sensitive, wayward and unmanageable. Besides, man cannot tolerate the idea of being experimented upon, either individually or collectively. Further, an economic phenomenon is the result of multiplicity of factors and causes acting and inter-acting upon each other. Therefore, economic phenomenon does not repeat itself in the same uniform pattern. Numerous factors acting on an economic phenomenon 'disturb' it and make its exact repetition unlikely.

Thus, as compared with the natural phenomena, economic phenomena are of less uniform pattern, less repetitive and more variable. Furthermore, economists study the economic phenomena in which pressure groups such as employers' associations, trade unions, farming lobbies, political parties with their different ideologies play a crucial part and their activities render it difficult to make controlled experiments in the economic world. However, in spite of these difficulties, experimental method can be used in some fields. For instance, experiments have been conducted to find out which law of production is valid, that is, whether law of diminishing returns, law of constant returns or law of increasing returns operates in the real world. Besides, public undertakings or big industrial firms often try to assess the effect of the changes in the prices of their products on the demand for it and thus find out the demand elasticity of their products.

As has been explained above, observations of facts through collection of detailed data and the use of statistical methods to arrive at economic generalisations describing relationship between facts are being increasingly made. Some of the recent researches in the field of macro-economics, such as the nature of consumption function describing the relation between income and consumption, the principle of acceleration describing the factors which determine investment in the economy have been obtained through the use of mainly inductive method. However, it needs to be emphasized again that the use of induction or empirical method is not of much value if it is not supported by the economic hypothesis or theory developed by deductive logic. The inductive or statistical method can at best be used to empirically test the theory or hypothesis as to whether it is consistent with or refuted by facts. The inductive method has another limitation in that there is a great risk of conclusions being drawn from insufficient data. To obtain generalisations through empirical method, one should take care that sufficient number of observations or data has been taken into account. Besides, the collection of data itself is also not an easy task. And a researcher who wants to employ the inductive method to arrive at generalisations must have good knowledge of statistical methods, that is, he must know the art of collecting, processing and interpreting data. It is obvious that as compared with the deductive method, the inductive method is time-consuming and expensive.

Conclusion : Integration of Two Methods

Now, the controversy which existed among the earlier economists as to whether deductive or inductive approach is more appropriate in developing economic theories and principles has been resolved. The modern viewpoint in this regard is that both are needed for the proper development of scientific economic theories. Indeed, the two are complementary rather than competitive. The modern economists first derive economic hypotheses through the process of logical deduction and then empirically test them through statistical or econometric methods. Marshall rightly pointed out, "induction and deduction are both needed for scientific thought as the right and left foot are both needed for walking."[9]

Empirical studies made through statistical or inductive method without a theoretical hypothesis to serve as a guide for the selection of data are quite useless. The derivation of economic generalisations through the approach of deductive logic without empirically testing them through inductive method is also not quite proper. Empirical studies made in inductive approach also bring to light significant economic facts or phenomena which require analytical explanation through deductive logic. For instance, *Farm Management Studies* in India in the mid fifties led to the discovery of a fact that output per acre on the small-sized farms is higher than that on large farms. This led to the various theoretical explanations of the phenomenon observed in the empirical studies. On the other hand, a theory or hypothesis is first developed through deductive logic from some assumptions and then predictions based on the hypothesis are tested through inductive or statistical method. If the predictions are found to be consistent with facts, the hypothesis or theory stands proved and if the predictions of the theory are found to be inconsistent with facts, it stands rejected.

Role of Assumptions in Economic Theory : Friedman's View

As has been pointed out above, every law and generalisation of economics is based upon some assumptions. Now, the question is whether for the formulation of proper economic laws these assumptions should be realistic or not. One view is that laws of economics if they are to be realistic must be based upon assumptions which are realistic too. Thus, according to this view, making unrealistic assumptions and establishing laws on their basis will make these laws invalid. However, a contrary view has been put forward by Prof. Milton Friedman of Chicago University in his now well-known article, ***"The Methodology of Positive Economics."*** In this context Prof. Friedman draws a distinction between positive economics and normative economics. According to Prof. Friedman, positive economics explains "a system of generalisations that can be used to make correct predictions about the consequences of any change in circumstances."[10] Because the predictions of this positive economics have to be tested with the empirical evidence it is as much a science as any other physical science even though the assumptions made may be unrealistic.

---

9. Alfred Marshall, *Principles of Economics*, 8th edition, p. 29.

10. Milton Friedman, *op. cit.*

The crucial point is whether the predictions based on economic generalisations of positive economics are confirmed by the facts and empirical evidence. According to Friedman, assumptions cannot be realistic; since they are made merely to simplify the analysis. However, it may be pointed out that while drawing conclusions from economic theories and laws regarding economic policies it must be known whether the assumptions made do not make the policy conclusions invalid if these assumptions are removed. Dr. K. N. Raj has rightly said, "some of the differences between economists of policy questions can be traced to the assumptions they choose to make when faced with the problems of this kind."[11] He further adds, "it is, however, essential in the interest of clarity and intellectual honesty that economists state clearly the assumptions on which one set of policies and programmes is advanced in preference to another and the reasons for making these assumptions"[12]

THE CONCEPT OF EQUILIBRIUM

In the methodology of economics, concept of equilibrium occupies an important place. The concept of equilibrium is employed in almost every theory of economics in the fields of price, income and growth. Word equilibrium means a state of balance. When two opposing forces working on an object are in balance so that the object is held still, the object is said to be in equilibrium. In other words, when the object under the pressure of forces working in opposite directions has no tendency to move in either direction, the object is in equilibrium. Thus, a system can be said to be in equilibrium when the various important variables in it show no change, and when there are no pressures or forces working which will cause any change in the values of important variables. Thus, by consumer's equilibrium we mean that in regard to the allocation of money expenditures among various goods the consumer has reached the state where he has no tendency to re-allocate his money expenditure. Similarly, a firm is said to be in equilibrium when it has no tendency to change its level of output, that is, when it has no tendency either to increase or to contract its level of output.

Whether it is the price, level of income or employment, solution always lies in the equilibrium value. Thus, the important topic in microeconomics is that how the prices of goods are determined and the prices are in equilibrium when the quantity demanded and the quantity supplied of the goods are equal. At the market price at which the quantity demanded and the quantity supplied are equal, both buyers and sellers would be satisfied. Therefore, that price would be ultimately settled in the market and there would be no tendency for it to change unless some changes in the determining conditions of demand and supply occur. Likewise, the levels of income and employment in advanced capitalist countries are determined by their equilibrium levels at which aggregate demand is equal to aggregate supply.

It may, however, be pointed out that equilibrium in economic activities may never be realised in actual practice. But the importance of the equilibrium analysis lies in the fact that if other things remain the same the economy would tend towards the equilibrium values. What happens is that before the final equilibrium is reached changes occur in the determining factors so that the system tends to move towards new equilibrium value corresponding to the new changed conditions.

Partial Equilibrium Analysis

Two types of equilibrium have been distinguished: (1) *Partial Equilibrium*, (2) *General Equilibrium*. In partial equilibrium approach to the pricing, we seek to explain the price determination of a commodity, keeping the prices of other commodities constant and assuming

11. See his Presidential Address at the 55th Annual Conference of the Indian Economic Association, held at Bodh Gaya, Magadh University, Dec. 1972, reprinted in the *Indian Economic Journal*. Vol. XX, No. 3.
12. *Ibid.*

that demands of various commodities are not interdependent. In explaining partial equilibrium approach, Marshall writes: "The forces to be dealt with are, however, so numerous that it is best to analyse a few at a time and to work out a number of partial solutions as auxiliaries to our main study. Thus we begin by isolating the primary relations of supply, demand and price in regard to a particular commodity. We reduce to inaction all other forces by the phrase, *'other things being equal.'* We do not suppose that they are inert, but for the time being we ignore their activity. This scientific device is a great deal older than science. It is the method by which consciously or unconsciously sensible men dealt from the time immemorial with every difficult problem of everyday life."

Thus, in Marshallian explanation of pricing under perfect competition, demand function (or a demand curve) for a commodity is drawn with the assumption that prices of other commodities remain constant. Similarly, supply curve of a commodity is constructed by assuming that prices of other commodities, prices of resources or factors and production function remain the same. Then the Marshall's partial equilibrium analysis seeks to explain the price determination of a single commodity through the intersection of demand and supply curves, prices of other goods and resources etc. remaining constant. That is, the data of the system are taken as given and kept the same and the determination of price-output equilibrium of a single commodity is explained. Given the assumption of ***ceteris paribus*** it explains the determination of the price of a good independently of the prices of all other goods. With the change in the data, new demand and supply curves will be formed and, corresponding to these, new price of the commodity will be determined. This partial equilibrium analysis of price determination also studies how the equilibrium price changes as a result of change in the data. But, given the independent data, the partial equilibrium analysis discusses only the price determination of a commodity in isolation and does not analyse how the prices of various goods are inter-dependent and inter-related and how they are simultaneously determined.

It should be noted that partial equilibrium analysis is based on the assumption that the changes in a single sector do not significantly affect the rest of the sectors. Thus, in partial equilibrium analysis, if the price of a good changes, it will not affect the demand for other goods. Prof. Lipsey rightly writes: "All partial equilibrium analyses are based on the assumption of *ceteris paribus*. Strictly interpreted, the assumption is that all other things in the economy are unaffected by any changes in the sector under consideration (say sector *A*). This assumption is always violated to some extent, for anything that happens in one sector must cause changes in some other sectors. What matters is that the changes induced throughout the rest of the economy are sufficiently small and diffuse so that the effect they in turn have on the Sector A can be safely ignored."[13]

General Equilibrium Analysis

In general equilibrium analysis, the price of a good is not explained to be determined independently of the prices of other goods. Since the changes in price of a good X affect the prices and quantities demanded of other goods and in turn the changes in prices and quantities of other goods will affect the quantity demanded of the good X, the general equilibrium approach explains the mutual and simultaneous determination of prices of all goods and factors. Thus, general equilibrium analysis looks at ***multi-market equilibrium.*** It considers the way in which the prices of all goods in an economic system are determined simultaneously, each in its own free market.

As stated above, partial equilibrium approach assumes that the effect of the change in price of a good X will be so diffused in the rest of the economy *(i. e.,* over all other goods) as

13. R. G. Lipsey, *Introduction to Positive Economics*, 3rd edition, p. 404.

to have negligible effect on the prices and quantities of other individual goods. Therefore, where the effect of a change in the price of a good on the prices and quantities of some other goods is significant, as is there in the case of inter-related goods, the partial equilibrium approach cannot be validly applied in such cases and therefore the need for applying general equilibrium analysis which explains the mutual and simultaneous determination of their prices and quantities.

General equilibrium analysis deals with inter-relationship and inter-dependence between equilibrium adjustment of prices and quantities of various goods and factors with each other. General equilibrium exists when, at the going prices, the quantities demanded of each product and each factor are equal to their respective quantities supplied. A change in the demand or supply of any good or factor would cause changes in prices and quantities of all goods and factors and there will begin adjustment and readjustment in demand, supply and prices of other goods and factors till the new general equilibrium is established. Indeed, the general equilibrium analysis is solving a system of simultaneous equations.

MODEL BUILDING IN ECONOMICS

In order to explain the behaviour of individual consumer, producer or industry or the economy *as* a whole the economists have constructed analytical models. An economic model usually consists of a set of equations that express relationships between variables that are relevant for the problem to be investigated. Each equation attempts to explain the behaviour of one variable, that is, it seeks to establish cause and effect relationship in respect of an individual variable. It is worth mentioning that causation does not always run in one direction. There is a mutual relationship among various variables, that is, a variable influences the other variables and in turn is influenced by them. For instance, consumption depends upon income and also consumption being an important constituent of aggregate demand influences income. Therefore, in such a system values of various variables are to be determined simultaneously. Therefore, models which involve more than one equation attempt to solve these equations simultaneously.

Another noteworthy point about a model is that it does not represent the real economic world in its entirety; it only represents its main significant features. Thus, a model is an abstraction from reality. In order to build a model, one has to make some unrealistic assumptions to simplify it. Indeed, the real economic world is too complex to be represented by a model which would reflect all its features. Therefore, one has to abstract from reality to some extent so that some useful and meaningful features of reality are brought out. However, a model is not a complete abstraction from reality; it abstracts from reality is some ways in order to pinpoint those features of reality which are significant and useful for explaining the behaviour of a consumer, producer or the economic system as a whole.

Now, an important question is why economists are interested in building models. Economic models are built for purposes of (a) ***analysis*** and (b) ***prediction***. By analysis we mean how adequately we can explain the behaviour of an economic agent, that is, consumer, producer or the economic system. From a set of assumptions we derive through deductive logic certain laws which describe the behaviour of an economic agents (consumer, producer or the whole economy) and which have a quite general application. On the other hand, prediction implies the ability of a model to forecast the effects of changes in some magnitudes in the economy. For instance, a model of price determination through demand and supply is generally used to forecast the effect of imposition of an excise duty or sales tax on the price of a commodity.

The validity of a model may be judged on the basis of either its explanatory or predictive power, or the realism of its assumptions, or the extent of its applicability *(i.e.* its generality). Economists differ as to what is more important attribute of a valid model. According to Milton Friedman, the most important attribute of a model is its predictive power, that is, to what extent it can correctly predict the behaviour of an economic unit. If the model has a good predictive power, then, according to his view, it is immaterial whether its assumptions are realistic or not. On the contrary, Paul Samuelson is of the view that realism of assumptions and the analytical power of the model to explain the behaviour of consumers, producers or the economic system, are the essential attributes of a valid and satisfactory model. It may be noted that the general view among economists is that the most important attribute of a model depends on its purpose, that is, whether the model builder wants to use it for predicting the effect of a change in some variable or for analysing and explaining the particular behaviour of an economic agent (consumer, producer or economic system). Realism of assumptions and explanatory power are important features of a good model if the purpose of the model is the explanation of why a system behaves as it does. However, as mentioned above, some unrealistic assumptions have to be made to simplify the analysis of model building.

As said earlier, economic models express inter-relationship among variables. In the field of microeconomics the variables with which economists are generally concerned are demand, supply, prices of goods and factors such as labour, capital, land and so on. On the other hand, in macroeconomics, the important variables are national income, aggregate consumption, aggregate investment, general price level, aggregate supply and so on.

Endogenous and Exogenous Variables in Economic Models

Let us make clear the meaning of endogenous and exogenous variables in economic models. For example, in the demand-supply model of pricing described above, price *(p)* and quantity *(q)* are inter-related; the value of one depends on the value of the other. Therefore, in solving the equations of demand and supply we obtain the value of p and then find out the value of q by substituting the value of p in either the demand or supply equation. The price and quantity are therefore endogenous variables; the value of one depends on the value of the other and are therefore determined *within the system*.

On the other hand, the exogenous variables are those whose values are not determined by other variables within the model. Let us take an example. As is well known, apart from the price of output, the supply of agricultural output depends to a great extent on the amount of rainfall in a place. Thus, writing the supply function of agricultural output including rainfall as a variable we have

$$Q_s = a + b\,P + cR$$

Where a is the intercept term, R stands for the average rainfall in a place. Rainfall is an exogenous variable as it is not determined by other variables, Q and P in the system. Changes in price of the agricultural output or the quantity of output *do not affect* the rainfall. It is worth mentioning that the changes in the exogenous variables such as rainfall would cause a shift in the whole supply curve.

In the Keynesian macro-model of income determination, investment (I) has been treated as an exogenous variable as it is taken to be independent of income or consumption, that is, other variables in the system. However, if instead of a given investment-independent of income, it is taken as a function of income, it would then be an endogenous variable. It should be further noted that investment is an exogenous variable in the simple Keynesian model of determination of income. In the complete Keynesian model the money market is considered along with the goods market to determine jointly the level of national income and the rate of interest. In this complete Keynesian model, the other variables such as rate of interest, demand for money are also included as endogenous variables. Investment is determined by the rate of interest which in turn depends on the demand for and supply of money. Thus, in this complete Keynesian model, investment becomes an endogenous variable.

CHAPTER

4

Methodology of Economics: Economic Statics and Dynamics

In the methodology of economics, techniques of economic statics and dynamics occupy an important place, A greater part of economic theory has been formulated with the aid of the technique of economic statics. However, during the last eighty years (since 1925) dynamic technique has been increasingly applied to the various fields of economic theory. J. M. Clark's principle of acceleration and Aftalion theory of business fluctuations resulting from the lagged over-response of output to previous capital formation are some examples of dynamic models which appeared before 1925. But prior to 1925, dynamic analysis was mainly confined, with some exceptions, to the explanation of business cycles. After 1925, dynamic analysis has been used extensively not only for the explanation of business fluctuations but also for income determination, growth and price theories. Economists like R. Frisch, C. F. Roos, J. Tinbergen, M. Kalecki, Paul Samuelson and many others have formulated dynamic models which give rise to cycles of varying periodicity and amplitude.

English writers such as Robertson, Keynes, Haberler, Kahn, and Swedish economists such as, Myrdal, Ohlin, Lindahl and Lunberg have laid a great stress on economic dynamics in the sphere of income analysis. More recently, economists like Samuelson, Goodwin, Smithies, Domar, Metzler, Haavelmo, Klein, Hicks, Lange, Koopmans and Tinter have further extended and developed dynamic models concerning the stability and fluctuations around any equilibrium point or path and which cover the four important fields of economic theory, namely, cycles, income determination, economic growth and price theory.

We shall explain below the meaning and nature of economic statics, dynamics and comparative statics and shall bring out the distinction between them. There has been a lot of controversy about their true meaning and nature, especially about economic dynamics.

NATURE OF ECONOMIC STATICS

The method of economic statics is very important since, as noted above, a large part of economic theory has been formulated with its aid. Besides, the conception of economic dynamics cannot be understood without being clear about the meaning of statics, because one thing which is certain about economic dynamics is that it is 'not statics'. J. R. Hicks aptly remarks, "The definition of Economic Dynamics must follow from the definition of Economic Statics; when we have defined one, we have defined the other."[1]

In order to make the difference between the natures of economic statics and dynamics quite clear, it is essential to bring out the distinction between two sorts of phenomena, *stationary* and *changing*. An economic variable is said to be stationary, if the value of the variable does not change over time,

1. J. R. Hicks, *Capital and Growth*, Oxford ClarendonPress, 1965, p. 7.

that is, its value is constant over time. For instance, if the price of a good does not change as time passes, price will be called stationary. Likewise, national income is stationary if its magnitude does not change through time. On the other hand, the variable is said to be changing (non-stationary) if its value does not remain constant through time. Thus, the whole economy can be said to be *stationary (changing),* if values of all important variables are constant through time (are subject to change). It may be noted that the various economic variables whose behaviour over time is studied are prices of goods, quantity supplied, quantity demanded, national income, level of employment, the size of the population, the level of investment, etc.

It is worth mentioning that it is quite possible that whereas a variable may be changing from the micro point of view, but stationary from the macro point of view. Thus, the prices of individual goods may be changing, of which some may be rising and some falling, but the general price level may remain constant over time. Likewise, the national income of a country may be stationary while the incomes generated by various industries may be changing. On the other hand, the particular variables may be stationary, while the economy as a whole may be changing. For example, even if the level of net investment in the economy is stationary, the economy as a whole may not be stationary. When there is a *constant amount* of net positive investment per annum, the economy will be growing (changing) since addition to its stock of capital will be occurring.

It should be carefully noted that there is no necessary relationship between stationary phenomenon and economic statics, and the changing phenomenon and dynamics. Although economic dynamics is inherently connected with only a changing phenomenon but the static analysis has been extensively applied to explain the changing phenomena. ***The distinction between statics and dynamics is the difference between the two different techniques of analysis and not the two different sorts of phenomena.*** Prof. Tinbergen rightly remarks, "The distinction between Statics and Dynamics is not a distinction between two sorts of phenomena but a distinction between two sorts of theories, *i.e.,* between two ways of thinking. The phenomena may be stationary or changing, the theory (the analysis) may be Static or Dynamic".[2]

Static Analysis and Functional Relationships

The test of economic theory is to explain the functional relationships between a system of economic variables. These relationships can be studied in two different ways. ***If the functional relationship is established between two variables whose values relate to the same point of time or to the same period of time, the analysis is said to be static.*** In other words, the static analysis or static theory is the study of static relationship between relevant variables. A functional relationship between variables is said to be static if the values of the economic variables relate to the same point of time or to the same period of time. Numerous examples of static relationships between economic variables and the theories or laws based upon them can be given. Thus, in economics the quantity demanded of a good at a time is generally thought to be related to the price of the good at the same time. Accordingly, the law of demand has been formulated to establish the functional relationship between the quantity demanded of a good and its price *at a given moment of time.* This law states that, *other things remaining the same,* the quantity demanded varies inversely with price at a given point of time. Similarly, the static relationship has been established between the quantity supplied and the price of goods, both variables relating to the same point of time. Therefore, the analysis of this price-supply relationship is also static.

Micro-Statics and Macro-Statics

Generally, economists are interested in the equilibrium values of the variables which are

2. J. Tinbergen, Significant Developments in General Economic Theory, *Econometrica,* 1934.

attained as a result of the adjustment of the given variables to each other. That is why economic theory has sometimes been called ***equilibrium analysis.*** Until recently, the whole price theory in which we explain the determination of equilibrium prices of products and factors in different market categories was mainly static analysis, because the values of the various variables, such as demand, supply, price were taken to be relating to the same point or period of time. Thus, according to this micro-static theory, equilibrium at a given moment of time under perfect competition is determined by the intersection of given demand and the supply functions (which relate the values of variables at the same point of time). Thus in Figure 4.1 given the demand function as demand curve *DD* and the supply function *SS*, the equilibrium price *OP* is determined. The equilibrium amount supplied and demanded so determined is *OM*. This is a static analysis of price determination, for all the variables such as, quantity supplied, quantity demanded and the price refer to the same point or period of time. Moreover, the equilibrium price and quantity determined by their interaction also relate to the same time as the determining variables.

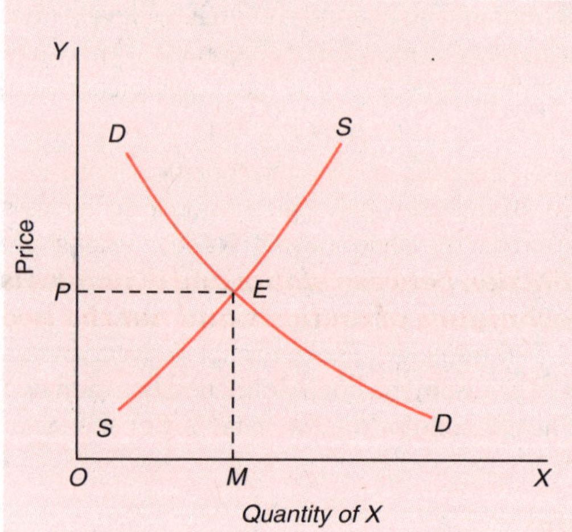

Fig. 4.1. Micro-Static Equilibrium

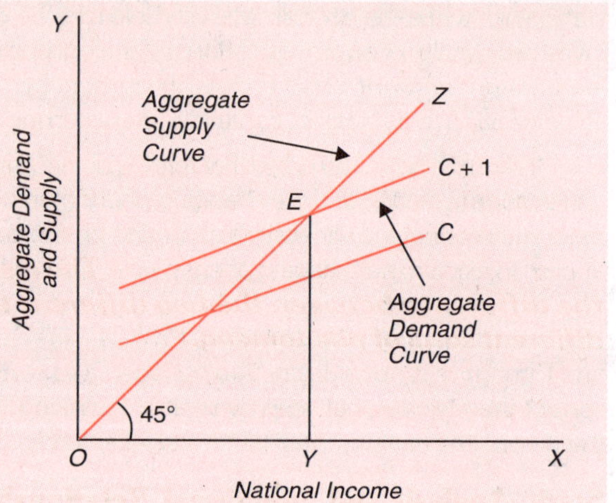

Fig. 4.2. Keynesian Model of Macro-Static Equilibrium

Examples of static analysis can also be given from macroeconomic theory. Keynesian macro model of the determination of level of national income is also mainly static. According to this model, national income is determined by the intersection of aggregate demand curve and aggregate supply curve (45° line) as is depicted in Figure 4.2 where the. vertical axis measures consumption demand plus investment demand *(C + I)* and aggregate supply, and the X-axis measures the level of national income. Aggregate demand equals aggregate supply at point *E* and income *OY* is determined. This is static analysis since aggregate demand (consumption and investment) and aggregate supply of output refer to the same point of time and element of time is not taken into account in considering the adjustment of the various variables in the system to each other. In other words, this analysis refers to instantaneous or timeless adjustment of the relevant variables and the determination of equilibrium level of national income. Professor Schumpeter describes the meaning of static analysis as follows: "By static analysis we mean method of dealing with economic phenomena that tries to establish relations between elements of the economic system—prices and quantities of commodities all of which have the same time subscript, that is to say, refer to the same point of time. The ordinary theory of demand and supply in the market of an individual commodity as taught in every textbook will illustrate this case: it relates demand, supply and price as they are supposed to be at any moment of observation."[3]

3. J. A. Schumpeter, *History of Economic Analysis*, Oxforcl, 1954.

Assumptions of Static Analysis

A point worth mentioning about static analysis is that in it certain determining conditions and factors are assumed to remain *constant* at the point of time for which the relationship between the relevant economic variables and the outcome of their mutual adjustment is being explained. Thus, in the analysis of price determination under perfect competition described above, the factors such as incomes of the people, their tastes and preferences, the prices of the related goods which affect the demand for a given commodity are assumed to remain constant. Similarly, the prices of the productive resources and production techniques which affect the cost of production and thereby the supply function are assumed to remain constant. These factors or variables do change with time and their changes bring about shift in the demand and supply functions and therefore affect prices. But because in static analysis we are concerned with establishing the relationship between certain given variables and their adjustment to each other at a given point of time, changes in the other determining factors and conditions are ruled out. We, in economics, generally use the term *data* for the determining conditions or the values of the other determining factors. Thus, in static analysis, **data** are assumed to be constant and we find out the eventual ***consequence*** of the mutual adjustment of the given variables.

It should be noted that assuming the data to be constant is very much the same thing as considering them at a moment of time or in other words allowing them a very short period of time[4] within which they cannot change. Moreover, the crucial point about static analysis is that the given conditions or data are supposed to be independent of the behaviour of variables or units in the given system between which functional relationship is being studied. Thus, in the above static price analysis it is assumed that variables in the system, that is, price of the good, quantity supplied and quantity demanded do not influence the determining conditions or data of incomes of the people, their tastes and preferences, the prices of the related goods, etc. Thus, the relationship between the data and the behaviour of the economic variables in a given system is assumed to be one-way relationship ; the data influence the variables of the given system and not the other way around. On the contrary, we shall see below that in dynamic analysis the determinant data or determining conditions are not assumed to be constant. In dynamic analysis, certain elements in the data are not independent of the behaviour of the variables in a given system. In fact, in a fully dynamic system, it is hard to distinguish between *data* and *variables* since in a dynamic system over time "today's determinant data are yesterday's variables and today's variables become tomorrow's data. The successive situations are interconnected like the links of a chain."[5]

Since in static analysis, we study the behaviour of a system at a particular time, or in other words, in economic statics, we do not study the behaviour of a system over time. Therefore how the system has proceeded from a previous position of equilibrium to the one under consideration is not studied in economic statics. Prof. Stanley Bober rightly remarks, "A static analysis concerns itself with the understanding of what determines an equilibrium position at any moment in time. It focuses attention on the outcome of economic adjustments and is ***not concerned with the path by which the system,*** be it the economy in the aggregate or a particular commodity market, has proceeded from a previous condition of equilibrium to the one under consideration."[6]

---

4. Time does not wait or remain constant; it is always passing. Therefore, by a 'moment' or point of time, we actually mean a very short period of time. A point or moment of time may be a day, a week or a month.
5. Haberler, *Prosperity and Depression*, p. 249.
6. Stanley Bober, *The Economics of Cycles and Growth*, First Wiley Eastern Reprint Edition, 1971, p.2.

Relevance of Static Analysis

Now, the question arises as to why the technique of static analysis is used which appears to be unrealistic in view of the fact that determining conditions or factors are never constant. Static techniques are used because it makes the otherwise complex phenomena simple and easier to handle. To establish an important causal relationship between certain variables, it becomes easier if we assume other forces and factors constant, not that they are inert but for the time it is helpful to ignore their activity. According to Robert Dorfman, "Statics is much more important than dynamics, partly because it is the ultimate destination that counts in most human affairs, and partly because the ultimate equilibrium strongly influences the time paths that are taken to reach it, whereas the reverse influence is much weaker".[7]

To sum up, in static analysis we ignore the passage of time and seek to establish the causal relationship between certain variables relating to the same point of time, assuming some determining factors as remaining constant. To quote Samuelson who has made significant contributions to making clear the distinction between the methods of economic statics and dynamics, "Statics concerns itself with the simultaneous and instantaneous or timeless determination of economic variables by mutually interdependent relations. Even a historically changing world may be treated statically, each of its changing positions being treated as successive states of static equilibrium." [8] In another article he says, "Statical then refers to the form and structure of the postulated laws determining the behaviour of the system. An equilibrium defined as the intersection of a pair of curves would be statical. Ordinarily, it is ***'timeless' in that, nothing is specified concerning the duration of the process,*** but it may very well be defined as holding over time."[9]

COMPARATIVE STATICS

We have studied above static and dynamic analysis of the equilibrium position. To repeat, static analysis is concerned with explaining the determination of equilibrium values with a given set of data and the dynamic analysis explains how with a change in the data the system gradually grows out from one equilibrium position to another. Midway between the static and dynamic analyses is the comparative static analysis. Comparative static analysis compares one equilibrium position with another when the data have changed and the system has finally reached another equilibrium position. It does not analyse the whole path as to how the system grows out from one equilibrium position to another when the data have changed; it merely explains and compares the initial equilibrium position with the final one reached after the system has adjusted to a change in data. Thus, in ***comparative static analysis, equilibrium positions corresponding to different sets of data are compared.*** Professor Samuelson writes:

"It is the task of comparative statics to show the determination of the equilibrium values of given variables (unknowns) under postulated conditions (functional relationships) with various data (parameters) specified. Thus, in the simplest case of a partial equilibrium market for a single commodity the two independent relations of supply and demand, each drawn up with other prices and institutional data being taken as given, determine by their interaction the equilibrium quantities of the unknown price and quantity sold. If no more than this could be said, the economist would be truly vulnerable to that he is only a parrot, taught to say 'supply and demand.' Simply to know that there are efficacious 'laws'

7. M. Robert Dorfman, *Prices and Markets,* Prentice-Hall of India Private Limitd, 2nd edition, New Delhi, 1972.
8. Paul A. Samuelson, "Dynamic Process Analysis'" printed in *The Collected Scientific Papers of Paul A. Samuelson* (M.I.T. Press, 1966). p. 354.
9. Paul A. Samuelson, Dynamics, Statics and the Stationary State, printed in *The Collected Scientific Papers of Paul A. Samuelson.*

determining equilibrium tells us nothing of the character of these laws. In order for the analysis to be useful it must provide information concerning the way in which our equilibrium quantities will change as a result of changes in the parameters— taken as independent data".[10]

It should be noted that for better understanding of the changing system, comparative statics studies the effect on the equilibrium position of a change in *only a single datum at a time* rather than the effects of changes in the many or all variables constituting the data. By confining ourselves to the adjustment in the equilibrium position as a result of alteration in a single datum at a time, we keep our analysis simple, manageable and at the same time useful, instructive as well as adequate enough to understand the crucial aspects of the changing phenomena. To quote Erich Schneider :

'The set of data undergoes changes in the course of time, and each new set of data has a new equilibrium position corresponding to it. It is therefore of great interest to compare ***the different equilibrium positions corresponding to different sets of data.*** In order to understand the effect of a change in the set of data on the corresponding position of equilibrium, we must only alter *a* ***single datum at a time.*** Only in this way it is possible to understand fully the effects of alterations in the individual data. We ask, to start with, about set I of the data, and the equilibrium position corresponding to it, then study next equilibrium position corresponding to set II of the data, where set II differs from set I only in the alteration of a single datum. In this way we compare the equilibrium values for the system corresponding to the two equilibrium positions with one another. This sort of comparative analysis of two equilibrium positions may be described as comparative-static analysis, since it studies the alteration in the equilibrium position corresponding to an alteration in a single datum".[11]

Let us give some examples of comparative static analysis from the microeconomic theory. We know that given the data regarding consumer's tastes, incomes, prices of other goods on the one hand and the technological conditions, costs of machines and materials, and wages of labour we have given demand and supply functions which by their interaction determine the price of a good. Now suppose that other things remaining constant, incomes of consumers increase. With the increase in incomes, the demand function would shift upward. With the change in the demand as a result of the change in the income, the supply would adjust itself and final new equilibrium position would be determined. To explain the determination of new equilibrium price and how it differs from the initial one is the task of comparative statics. In Figure 4.3, initially the demand and supply functions are *DD* and *SS* and with their interaction price OP_1 is determined. When the demand function changes to *D'D'* as a result of changes in consumers' income, it intersects the given supply function at E_2 and the new equilibrium price OP_2 is determined. In comparative-static analysis, we are concerned only with explaining the new equilibrium position E_2 and comparing it with E_1, and not with the whole path the system has traversed as it gradually grows out from E_1 to E_2.

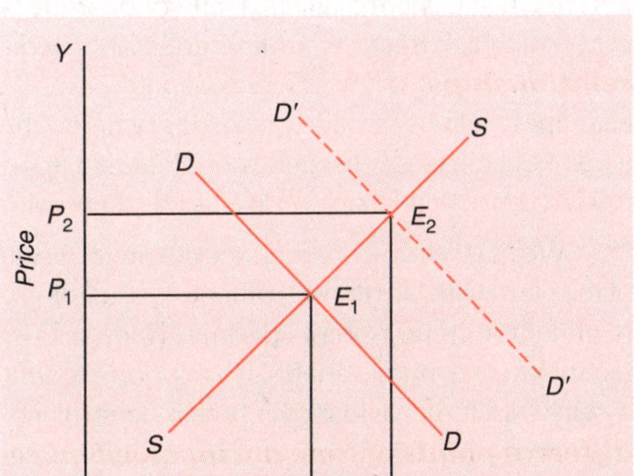

Fig. 4.3. Comparative Static Analysis

10. Paul A. Samuelson, *Foundations of Economic Analysis,* Cambridge, Mass., 1947, p. 257.
11. Erich Schneider, *Pricing and Equilibrium,* George Allen and Unwin, Ltd.,1962,pp.235-36.

As we shall study in the part of price theory, comparative static analysis was extensively used by Alfred Marshall in his time-period analysis of pricing under perfect competition.

Importance of Comparative Statics

No doubt, more realistic, complete and true analysis of the changing phenomena of the real world would be the dynamic analysis, nevertheless comparative statics is a very useful technique of explaining the changing phenomena and its crucial aspects without complicating the analysis. To quote Schneider again. "This sort of dynamic analysis of the influence of a change in data is much more comprehensive and informative than the mere static analysis of two different sets of data and of the equilibrium positions corresponding to them. Nevertheless, the comparative static treatment provides some important insights into the mechanism of the exchange economy".[12] Likewise, Professors Stonier and Hague write, "The construction of a truly dynamic theory of economics, where more continuous changes in demand and supply conditions, like those which occur in the real world, are analysed, is the ultimate goal of most theories of economics.... However, so far as the determination of price and output is concerned, simple comparative static analysis.... is as powerful an analytical method as we need".[13]

ECONOMIC DYNAMICS

Now, we turn to the method of Economic Dynamics which has become very popular in modern economics. Economic dynamics is a more realistic method of analysing the behaviour of the economy or certain economic variables through time. The definition of economic dynamics has been a controversial issue and it has been interpreted in various different ways. We shall try to explain the standard definitions of economic dynamics.

The course thorough time of a system of economic variables can be explained in two ways. One is the method of economic statics described above, in which the relations between the relevant variables in a given system refer to the same point or period of time. On the other hand, if the analysis considers the relationship between relevant variables whose values belong to *different* points *of time* it is known as Dynamic Analysis or Economic Dynamics. The relations between certain variables, the values of which refer to the different points or different periods of time, are known as ***dynamic relationships.*** Thus, J.A. Schumpeter says, "We call a relation dynamic if it connects economic quantities that refer to different points of time. Thus, if the quantity of a commodity that is offered at a point of time (t) is considered as dependent upon the price that prevailed at the point of time($t-1$), this is a dynamic relation."[14] In a word, economic dynamics is the analysis of dynamic relationships.

We thus see that in economic dynamics we duly recognize the element of time in the adjustment of the given variables to each other and accordingly analyse the relationships between given variables relating to different points of time. Ragnar Frisch who is one of the pioneers in the use of the technique of dynamic analysis in economics defines economic dynamics as follows: "A system is dynamical if its behaviour over time is determined by functional equations in ***which variables at different points of time are involved in a essential way."***[15] In dynamic analysis, he further elaborates, "We consider not only a set of magnitudes in a given point of time and study the interrelations between them, but we ***consider the magnitudes of certain variables in different points of time, and we introduce*** certain equations which embrace at the same time several of those

12. *Op. cit.*,p.236.
13. Stonier and Hague, A *Textbook of Economic Theory,* Fourth edition 1972, p. 188.
14. J.A. Schumpeter, *History of Economic Analysis,* Oxford, 1954.
15. Ragnar Frisch, Propagation Problems and Impulse Problems in Dynamic Economics, *Economic Essays in Honour of Gustav Cassel,* George Alien and Unwin, Ltd., London, 1933, pp. 171-172.

magnitudes belonging to different instants. This is the essential characteristic of a dynamic theory. Only by a theory of this type we can explain ***how one situation grows out of the foregoing.***"[16]

Many examples of dynamic relationships from both micro and macro economic fields can be given. If one assumes that the supply *(S)* for a good in the market in the given time *(t)* depends upon the price that prevails in the preceding period (that is, $t-1$), the relationship between supply and price is said to be dynamic. This dynamic functional relation can be written as :

$$S_t = f(P_{t-1})$$

where S_t stands for the supply of a good offered in a given period t and P_{t-1} for the price in the preceding period. Likewise, if we grant that the quantity demanded (*D*) of a good in a period t is a function of the expected price in the succeeding period ($t+1$), the relation between demand and price will be said to be dynamic and the analysis of such relation would be called dynamic theory or economic dynamics.

Similarly, examples of dynamic relationship can be given from the macro field. If it is assumed that the consumption of the economy in a given period depends upon the income in the preceding period ($t-1$), we shall be conceiving a dynamic relation. This can be written as:

$$C_t = f(Y_{t-1})$$

When macroeconomic theory (theory of income, employment and growth) is treated dynamically, that is, when macroeconomic dynamic relationships are analysed, the theory is known as ***"Macro dynamics"***. Samuelson, Kalecki, Post-Keynesians like Harrod, Hicks have greatly dynamized the macroeconomic theory of Keynes.

Endogenous Changes and Dynamic Analysis

It should be noted that the change or movement in a dynamic system is *endogenous,* that is, it goes on independently of the external changes in it; one change grows out of the other. There may be some *initial* external shock or change but in response to that initial external change, the dynamical system goes on moving independently of any fresh external changes, successive changes growing out of the previous situations. In other words, the development of a dynamic process is self-generating. Thus, according to Paul Samuelson, "It is important to note that each dynamic system generates its own behaviour over time either as an autonomous response to a set of 'initial conditions'. or as a response to some changing external conditions. ***This feature of self-generating development over time is the crux of every dynamic process.***[17] Likewise,Professor J. K. Mehta remarks,"In simple words, we can say that an economy can be said to be in a dynamical system when the various variables in it such as output, demand, prices have values at any time dependent on their values at some other time. If you know their values at one moment of time, you should be able to know their values at subsequent points of time. Prices of goods in a causal dynamic system do not depend on any outside exogenous forces. A dynamic system is self-contained and self-sustained."[18]

It is thus clear that a distinctive feature of dynamic analysis is to show how a dynamic process or system is self-generating, how one situation in it grows out of a previous one or how one situation moves on independently of the changes in external conditions. As Schneider, a German economist, has aptly and precisely put it, "A dynamic theory shows how in the course of time a condition of the

16. *Ibid.*
17. Paul A. Samuelson, Dynamic Process Analysis, printed in *The Collected Scientific Papers of Paul A. Samuelson,* Vol. 1 , edited by Joseph E. Stiglitz (MIT Press 1966), p. 590.
18. J- K. Mehta, *Lectures on Modern Economic Theory,* 3rd edition 1967, p. 212.

economic system has grown out of its condition in the previous period of time. It is this form of analysis which has the central importance for the study of the process of economic developments, be they short-run or long-run processes."[19]

An illustration of dynamic analysis may be given. As described earlier, level of national income is determined by the equilibrium between given aggregate demand curve and the aggregate supply curve. Now, if the aggregate demand increases, due to the increase in investment, the aggregate demand curve will shift upward and as a consequence the new equilibrium point will be reached and level of national income will rise. In static analysis, the new equilibrium is supposed to occur instantaneously (timeless) and no attention is paid how the new equilibrium position of income has grown out of the original through time when the increase in aggregate demand has taken place. That is to say, the ***dynamic analysis traces out the whole path through which the system passes over time to reach the new equilibrium position.*** We present in Figure 4.5 the common macro model of income determination. Given the aggregate demand $C + I$, the level of national income OY_0 is determined in time t. Suppose now the aggregate demand curve shifts upward due to the increase in investment in time period t. As the investment increases in time-period t, the income will rise in time period $t + 1$ by the amount of the investment. Now, this increase in income will push up the consumption demand. To meet this increase in consumption, output will be increased with the result that income will further rise in period $t + 2$. This additional increase in income will induce further increase in consumption with the result that more output will be produced to meet the rise in demand and the income in period $t + 3$ will still further rise. In this way, the income will go on rising; one increase in income giving rise to another till the final equilibrium point H is reached in the time period $t + n$ in which the level of income OY_n is determined. The path by which the income increases through time is shown in the figure by dotted arrow lines. This illustration of macro-dynamics makes it clear that the dynamic analysis is concerned with how magnitude of variables in a period (income and consumption in the present illustration) depends upon the magnitudes of the variables in the previous periods.

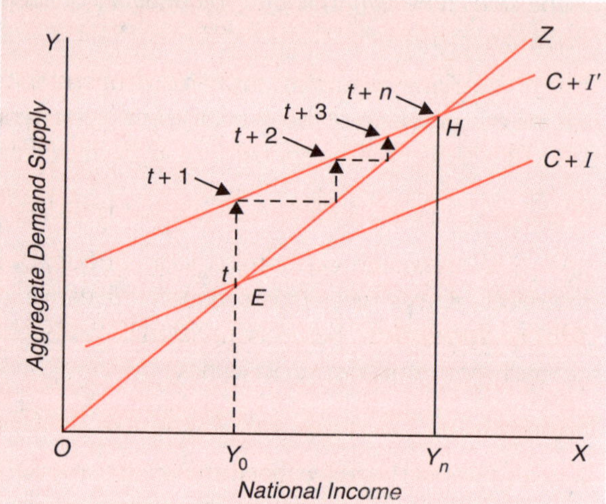

Fig. 4.5. Macro-Dynamic Equilibrium

Hicks' Definition of Economic Dynamics

In the light of our above explanation of the meaning of the method of economic dynamics, we are in a position to examine the definition of dynamics given by J. R. Hicks in his book *'Value and Capital'*. Hicks says, "I call Economic Statics those parts of economic theory where we do not trouble about dating, ***Economic Dynamics those parts where every quantity must be dated.***[20] This is a very simple way of defining dynamics. When the magnitude of variables does not change with time, the dating of the quantities of variables is not necessary. In the absence of change in the economic variables determining the system, an equilibrium position that applies to the present will apply equally well to the future.

---

19. Erich Schneider, *Pricing and Equilibrium, An Introduction to Static and Dynamic Analysis*, 2nd English edition (1962), p. 230.

20. J. R. Hicks, *Value and Capital*, Oxford University Press, London, 1953, p. 115.

But in our view, this is not a satisfactory definition of economic dynamics. A system may be statical, but still may be dynamic according to Hicksian definition if some dates are attached to variables. Thus, a statical system may be converted into Hicksian dynamics by merely assigning some dates to the variables. But this is not true meaning of economic dynamics, as is now generally conceived. Mere dating of variables is not enough. As has been made clear by Ragnar Frisch, variables in the system must relate to different dates or different points of time, if it is to be a truly dynamic system. Secondly, as has been contended by Paul Samuelson, this "Hicksian definition is too general and insufficiently precise. According to Paul Samuelson, Hicksian definition of dynamics would cover *a* ***historical static system*** of variables. An historically moving static system certainly requires dating of the variables but it would not thereby become dynamic.[21] A system of variables to be called dynamic must involve functional relationships between the variables, that is, the variables at one point of time must be shown to be dependent upon the variables at other points of time. Thus, according to Samuelson," a system is dynamical if its behaviour over time is determined ***by functional equations*** in which ***variables at different points of time*** are involved in an essential way ."[22]

Thus, Samuelson's emphasis is on functional relationships as well as on different points of time. We therefore conclude that a dynamical system involves ***functional relationships between variables at different points of time.*** A historically moving system does not necessarily involve the functional relationships between the variables at different historical times. The historical movement of a system may not be dynamical. For instance, as has been pointed out by Samuelson, if one year crop is high because of good monsoons, the next year low because the monsoons fail, and so forth, the system will be statical even though not stationary.

The concept or technique of economic dynamics which we have explained above was first of all clarified by Ragnar Frisch in 1929. According to his view, like static analysis, ***economic dynamics is a particular method of explanation of economic phenomenon,*** economic phenomena themselves may be stationary or changing. Although technique of dynamic analysis has great scope in a changing and a growing system but it may also be applied even to stationary phenomena. A system or phenomenon may be stationary in the sense that the values of relevant economic variables in it may remain constant through time, but if the values of the variables at a time are dependent upon the values at another time, then dynamic analysis can be applied. But, as stated above, the greater scope of economic dynamics lies in the field of changing and growing phenomena. Schneider aptly brings out the distinction between statics and dynamics on the one hand and stationary and changing phenomena on the other when he writes," It is essential to understand that in modern theory 'statics' and 'dynamics' refer to a ***particular mode of treatment or type of analysis of the phenomena*** observed, while the adjectives 'stationary' and 'changing' describe the actual economic phenomena. A ***static or dynamic theory is a particular kind of explanation of economic phenomena, and, indeed, stationary and changing phenomena can be submitted either to a static or to a dynamic analysis."***[23]

Expectations and Dynamics

We have described above that economic dynamics is concerned with explaining dynamic relationships, that is, the relationships among variables relating to different points of time. The variables at the present moment may depend upon the variables at other times, past and future. Thus, when the relationship between the economic variables belonging to different points of time is considered, or when rates of change of certain variables in a growing economy are

21. Paul A. Samuelson, "Dynamics, Statics and Stationary State", printed in the *Collected Essays of Paul A. Samuelson* (Vol. 1) edited by Joseph E. Stiglitz, p. 204.

22. *Op. cit*, p. 59.

23. *Op.cit.*,p.228.

under discussion, the question of future creeps into the theoretical picture. The economic units (such as consumers, producers and entrepreneurs) have to take decisions about their behaviour in the present period. The consumers have to decide what goods they should buy and what quantities of them. Similarly, producers have to decide what goods they should produce, what factors they should use and what techniques they should adopt. These economic units decide about their present course of action on the basis of their *expected values* of the economic variables in the future. When their expectations are realised, they continue behaving in the same way and the dynamic system is in equilibrium. In other words, when the expectations of the economic units are fulfilled, they repeat the present pattern of behaviour and there exists what has been called **dynamic equilibrium,** unless some external shock or force disturbs the dynamic system.

The expectations or anticipations of the future held by the economic units play a vital role in economic dynamics. In a purely static theory expectations about the future have practically no part to play since static theory is mainly concerned with explaining the conditions of equilibrium positions ***at a point of time*** as well as under the assumptions of ***constant tastes, techniques and resources.*** Thus, in static analysis expectations about the future play little part since under it no **processes over time** are considered. On the other hand, since dynamic analysis is concerned with dynamic processes over time, that is, changing variables over time and their action and interaction upon each other through time, expectations or anticipations held by the economic units about the future have an important place.

But from the intimate relation between dynamics and expectations it should not be understood that mere introduction of expectations in static analysis would make it dynamic. Whether the analysis is dynamic or not depends upon whether the relationship between variables belonging to different points or periods of time is considered or not, or whether rates of change of certain variables over time are considered or not. German economist Schneider rightly says, "A theory is not to be considered as dynamic simply because it introduces expectations, whether that is the case or not depends simply on whether or not the expected values of the single variables relate to different periods or points of time."[24]

Moreover, it is important to note that a theory becomes truly dynamic only if in it the expectations are taken as a variable and not as a given data. In other words, in a really dynamic theory, expectations should be considered as changing over time rather than remaining constant. A dynamic theory should tell us what would happen if, the expectations of the economic units are realised and what would happen if they have not come true. In Harrod's macro-dynamic model of a growing economy that if the entrepreneurs expect the rate of growth of output equal to $\frac{S}{C}$, (whereas S stands for rate of saving and C for capital-output ratio) their expectations would be realised and as a result the relevant variables in the system will move in equilibrium over time and there will be a steady growth in the economy. If their expectations about the rate of growth are smaller or larger than $\frac{S}{C}$, they will not be realised and as a consequence there will be instability in the economy.

When the expectations of the individuals turn out to be incorrect, they will revise or change their expectations. Because of the changing nature of these expectations they should not be taken as given data or given conditions in a dynamic theory. To take expectations as given data means that they remain constant even if they turn out to be incorrect. That is to say, even when the individuals are surprised by the actual events because their expectations have not been fulfilled, they will continue to have the same expectations. But that will amount to be assuming

24. *Op.cit.*,p.223.

irrationality on the part of the individuals. We, therefore, conclude that expectations must be taken as changing in the dynamic system and not as a given condition.

Need and Significance of Economic Dynamics

The use of dynamic analysis is essential if we want to make our theory realistic. In the real world, various key variables such as prices of goods, the output of goods, the income of the people, the investment and consumption are changing over time. Both Frischian and Harrodian dynamic analyses are required to explain these changing variables and to show how they act and react upon each other and what results flow from their action and interaction. Many economic variables take time to make adjustment to the changes in other variables. In other words, there is a lag in the response of some variables to the changes in the other variables, which make it necessary that dynamic treatment be given to them. We have seen that changes in income in one period produce influence on consumption in a later period. Many similar examples can be given from micro and macro-economics.

Besides, it is known from the real world that the values of certain variables depend upon the *rate of growth* of other variables. For example, we have seen in Harrod's dynamic model of a growing economy that investment depends upon expected rate of growth in output. Similarly, the demand for a good may depend upon the rate of change of prices. Similar other examples can be given. In such cases where certain variables depend upon the rate of change in other variables, the application of both the period analysis and the rate of change analysis of dynamic economics become essential if we want to understand their true behaviour.

Until recently, dynamic analysis was mainly concerned with explaining business cycles, fluctuations or oscillations. But, after Harrod's[25] and Domar's[26] path-breaking contributions, the interest in the problems of growth has been revived among economists. It is in the study of growth that dynamic analysis becomes more necessary. Now-a-days economists are engaged in building dynamic models of optimum growth both for developed and developing countries of the world. Thus, in recent years, the stress on dynamic analysis is more on explaining growth rather than cycles or oscillations. Prof. Hansen is right when he says, "In my own view mere oscillation represents a relatively unimportant part of economic dynamics. Growth, not oscillation, is the primary subject-matter for study in economic dynamics. Growth involves changes in technique and increases in population. Indeed that part of cycle literature (and cycle theories are a highly significant branch of dynamic economics) which is concerned merely with oscillation is rather sterile."[27]

---

25. R. F. Harrod, *Towards a Dynamic Economics*, Macmillan & Co. Ltd. (London), 1948.
26. E. Domar, Capital Expansion, Rate of Growth and Employment, *"Econometrica"*, Vol. 14, 1946, pp. 137-47.
27. Alvin H. Hansen, '*A Guide to Keynes*, McGRAW-HILL (New York), 1953, pp. 49-50.

CHAPTER

5

Basic Mathematical Concepts and Optimisation Techniques

Introduction

Managers of a firm have to take decisions regarding the level of output of a product to be produced, the price for a product to be charged, the size of the sales force to be engaged, the technique to be used for the production, the level of advertising expenditure to be incurred and many other such things. In business decision making a large number of options are open to a manager from which he has to make a choice. Obviously, a manager will try to make a best choice from among different options available to him. A best or optimum choice is one that best achieves the desired goal or objective of the firm. For example, a manager might consider what level of output of a product he should produce. Manager will produce the level of output which maximises firm's profit if he has set before himself the objective of profit-maximisation. This is a maximisation problem which he has to solve. Similarly, he may be considering to choose among the various combinations of factors or inputs that can be used for producing a level of output. To maximise profits he will choose the combination of inputs that minimises cost for producing a given level of output. Evidently, this is a minimisation problem which he has to solve.

Decision making that involves solving of maximisation and minimisation problems is called **optimisation**. Therefore, for making efficient decision it is neccessary for a successful manager to learn the techniques of optimisation. It may however he noted that popular techniques of optimisation are mathematical in nature. In recent year the use of analytical models of business decision making has increased the importance of the knowledge of techniques of optimisation for the students of economics. Mathematical formulations of these analytical models of decision-making are expressed in terms of **functions** which describe economic relationship between various variables. Therefore, to begin with we will explain the concept of a function and its various important types. Besides, optimisation techniques involve the use of differential calculus and its concepts of deserivatives. Therefore, after studying the concept of function and its various types we will proceed to explain the concept of a derivative and rules of differentiation. At the end of this chapter we will give some examples of how differential calculus is used for optimisation problems in economics.

FUNCTIONS

A function describes the relation between two or more than two variables. That is, a function expresses dependence of one variable on one or more other variables. Thus, if the value of a variable Y depends on another variable X, we may write

$$Y = f(X) \qquad .....(1)$$

Where f stands for function.

This expression (1) is read as 'Y is function of X'. This implies that every value of the variable Y is determined by a unique value of the variable X. In the function (1), Y is known as the dependent variable and X is the independent variable. Thus in function (1) Y is called the dependent variable and its value depends on the value of X. Further, the independent variable is interpreted as the cause and the dependent variable as the effect. An important function which is extensively used in economics is a demand function which expresses quantity demanded of a commodity is a function of its price, other factors being held constant. Thus, demand for a commodity X is described as under

$$D_x = f(P_x)$$

Where D_x is the quantity demanded of commodity X and P_x is its price.

Similarly, supply function of a commodity X is expressed as

$$S_x = f(P_x)$$

When the value of the variable Y depends on more than two variables $X_1, X_2 ....X_n$ this function is written in general form as :

$$Y = f(X_1, X_2, X_3, X_4 ....X_n)$$

This shows the variable Y depends on several independent variables $X_1, X_2, ...X_n$ where n is the number of independent variables. Again note that in economics we write '*causes*' as the independent variables and '*effect*' as the dependent variable.

For example, demand for a product is generally considered to be a function of its own price, prices of other commodities (which may be substitutes or complements), income of the consumers, tastes and preferences of the consumers and advertising expenditure made by a firm to promote its product. Thus,

$$D_x = f(P_x, P_y, M, T, A)$$

Where

D_x = demand for the commodity X
P_x = price of the commodity X.
P_y = price of a substitute product Y.
M = income of the consumers
T = tastes and preferences of the consumer for the product.
A = advertising expenditure incurred by the firm.

The exact nature of relation of dependent variable with the independent variables can be known from the *specific form* of the function. The specific form of a function can take a variety of mathematical forms. We explain below some specific types of functions.

Linear and Power Functions

A widely used mathematical form of a function is a *linear function*. A linear function can be stated in the following general form :

$$Y = a + bX$$

Where a and b are positive constants and are called *parameters* of the function. Note that parameters of a function are variables that are fixed and given in a specific function. The values of constants a and b determine the specific nature of a linear function. The linear demand function with price as the only independent variable is written as

$$Q_d = a - bP$$

The minus sign before coefficient b indicates that quantity demanded of a commodity is negatively related with price of the commodity. That is, if price of a commodity falls, its quantity demand increases and vice versa. If a equals 7 and b equals 0.5, the linear demand function can be expressed in the following specific form :

$$Q_d = 7 - 0.5\,P$$

The above specific demand function shows that a unit fall in price of the commodity will cause 0.5 units increase in the quantity demanded of the commodity. If price (P) is zero, the second term ($0.5P$) in the demand function drops out and the quantity demanded is equal to 7.

We can take various values of P and find out different quantities (Q_d) of a commodity demanded at them. In Figure 5.1 we have noted these price-quantity combinations on a graph and have obtained demand curve DD of the commodity representing the given demand function ($Q_d = 7 - 0.5P$).

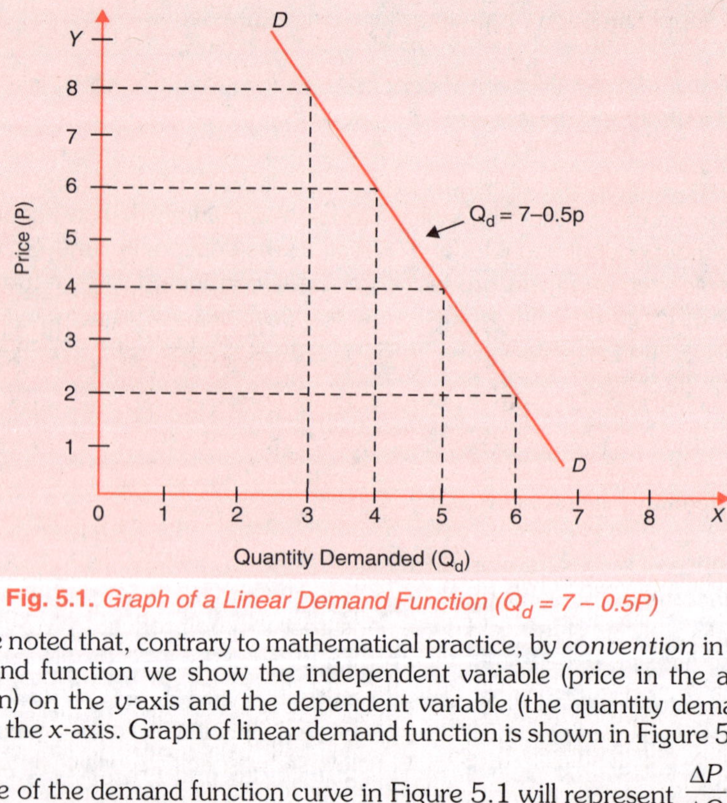

Fig. 5.1. *Graph of a Linear Demand Function ($Q_d = 7 - 0.5P$)*

It should be noted that, contrary to mathematical practice, by *convention* in economics to represent demand function we show the independent variable (price in the above case of demand function) on the y-axis and the dependent variable (the quantity demanded in the present case) on the x-axis. Graph of linear demand function is shown in Figure 5.1. It is worth noting that slope of the demand function curve in Figure 5.1 will represent $\frac{\Delta P}{\Delta Q}$. However, if we represent quantity demanded (Q_d) on the y-axis, and price (P_x) on the x-axis; the slope of the demand curve so drawn would be equal to $\frac{\Delta Q}{\Delta P}$.

Multivariate Linear Demand Function

Linear demand function with more than one independent variables, can be written in the following way

$$Q_x = a + b_1\,Px + b_2\,P_y + b_3\,M + b_4\,T + b_5\,A$$

Where b_1, b_2, b_3, b_4 are the coeffieients of the respective variables. In economics the effect of variables other than the own price of a commodity in the demand function are depicted by *shifts in the demand curve*. For instance when income (M) of the consumers increases consumers will demand more of the product X at a given price. This implies shifting of the demand curve to the right.

The linear multivariate function is written in the following form

$Y = 4 - 0.4X_1 + 0.2X_2 + 0.3X_3 + 0.5\,X_4$

In this function the coefficients 0.4, 0.2, 0.3 and 0.5 show the precise impact of the independent variables X_1, X_2, X_3, X_4 on the dependent variable Y.

Power Functions

The linear functions stated above are known as first degree functions where the independent variables X_1, X_2, X_3, etc are raised to the first power only. We now turn to explain power functions. In economics power functions of the quadratic and cubic forms are extensively used.

Quadratic Functions : In quadratic function one or more of the independent variables are squared, that is, raised to the second power. Note that power is also referred to as *exponent*. A quadratic function may be written as

$$Y = a + b\,X + c\,X^2$$

This implies that value of the dependent variable Y depends on the constant *a* plus the coefficient *b* times the value of the independent variable X plus the coefficient c times the square of the variable X. Suppose *a* = 4, *b* = 3 and c = 2 then quadratic function takes the following specific form.

$$Y = 4 + 3X + 2\,X^2$$

We can obtain the different values of Y for taking different values of the independent variable X. Quadratic functions are of two types : convex quadratic functions and concave quadratic functions. The form of quadratic function depends on the sign of the coefficient c of X^2. The quadratic function, $Y = a + bX + cX^2$, where the coefficient c of X^2 is positive (i.e. c > 0) is called ***convex*** quadratic function, because its graph is U-shaped as shown in Figure 5.2. On the other hand, if coefficient of X^2 is negative (c < 0), that is, when $Y = a + bX - cX^2$, then we have ***concave*** quadratic function because its graphs is of inverted U- shape (*i.e.* ∩-shaped) as shown in Figure 5.3.

It is worth noting that slope of the curve of convex quadratic functions as is evident from U-shaped graph in this case where coefficient of X^2 is positive, slope is increasing every

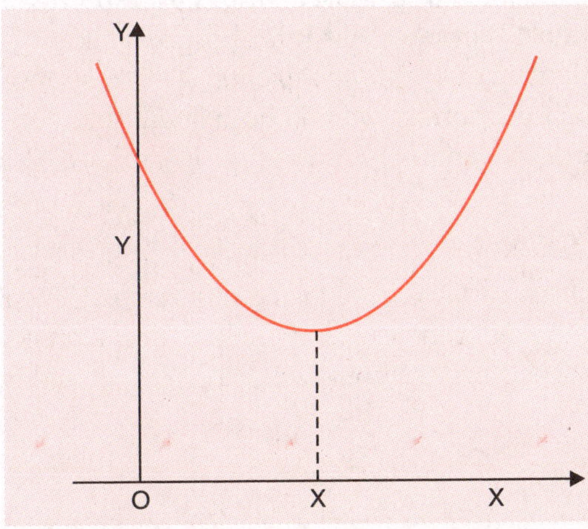

Fig.5.2. *Convex Quadratic function*

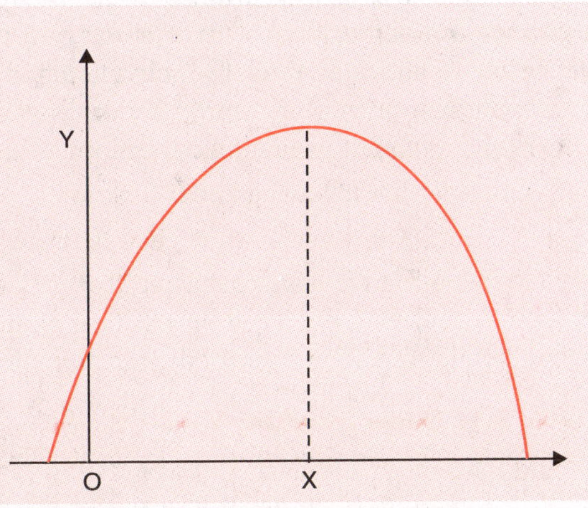

Fig.5.3. *Concave Quadratic Function*

where. On the other hand, in case of concave quadratic function where coefficient of X^2 is negative ($c < O$), slope of its graph is decreasing every where. It should be further noted that in analytical geometry it is proved that graph of any quadratic function is a **parabola** which may be be either convex or concave. A parabola is a curve which has a turning point and unlike the curve of a linear function, its slope is changing at different values of X.

Multivariable Quadratic Function. When there are more than one independent variable such as X_1, X_2, and they have a quadratic relationship with the dependent variable Y, such a function is called multivariable quadratic function. In case of two independent variables X_1 and X_2 such a function may be expressed as under:

$$Y = a + bX_1 - cX^2{}_1 + dX_2 - eX_2{}^2$$

If such a function is graphically shown, it will be represented by a three dimensional surface and not a two dimensional curve.

Cubic Function. A cubic function is the power function in which there is a *third degree term* relating to an independent variable. Thus, a cubic functions may have first degree, second degree and third degree terms. A cubic function may have the following form :

$$Y = a + bX + cX^2 + dX^3$$

a is the intercept term, the dependent variable X has the first degree, second degree and third degree terms. When the signs of all the coefficients a, b, c and d are positive, then the values of Y will increase by progressively larger increments as the value of X increases. However, when the *signs* of various coefficients differ in the cubic function, that is, some have positive signs and some have negative signs, then the graph of the function may have both convex and concave segments depending on the values of the coefficients. Such a cubic function where signs of the coefficients of variables differ may be expressed as follows :

$$Y = a + bX - cX^2 + dX^3$$

in which the sign of the coefficient c of variable X^2 is negative whereas the coefficients of others are positive.

SLOPES OF FUNCTIONS

In economics it is important to know *the rate at which a variable changes* in response to a change in another variable, the slope of a variable measures this rate. For example, it is important to know the rate at which quantity demanded of a commodity changes in response to a change in price of a commodity. In the field of economics we find both linear and non-linear functions. Let us first take the slope of a linear function.

Consider the following linear function.

$$Y = f(X) = 2 + 0.5\,X$$

In Table 5.1 we have calculated the values of the variable Y by taking different values of X such as 1, 2, 3, 4 etc. Further, we have plotted the different values of Table 5.1 on a graph shown in Fig. 5.4. The slope of the function. ($Y = 2 + 0.5X$) between two points, say, A and B

Table 5.1. Linear Function, $Y = 2 + 0.5X$

Value of X	0	1	2	3	4	5	6	7
Value of Y	2	2.5	3	3.5	4	4.5	5	5.5

in Figure 5.4 is given by the ratio of change in Y to the change in X. That is, slope = $\frac{\Delta Y}{\Delta X}$. For example, at point A of the given function value of variable X is 3 and corresponding to it the value of variable Y is 3.5. When value of X rises from 3 to 4, value of Y increases from 3.5 to 4. Thus, the slope of the function ($Y = 2 + 0.5X$) is :

$$\frac{\Delta Y}{\Delta X} = \frac{4-3.5}{4-3} = \frac{0.5}{1} = 0.5$$

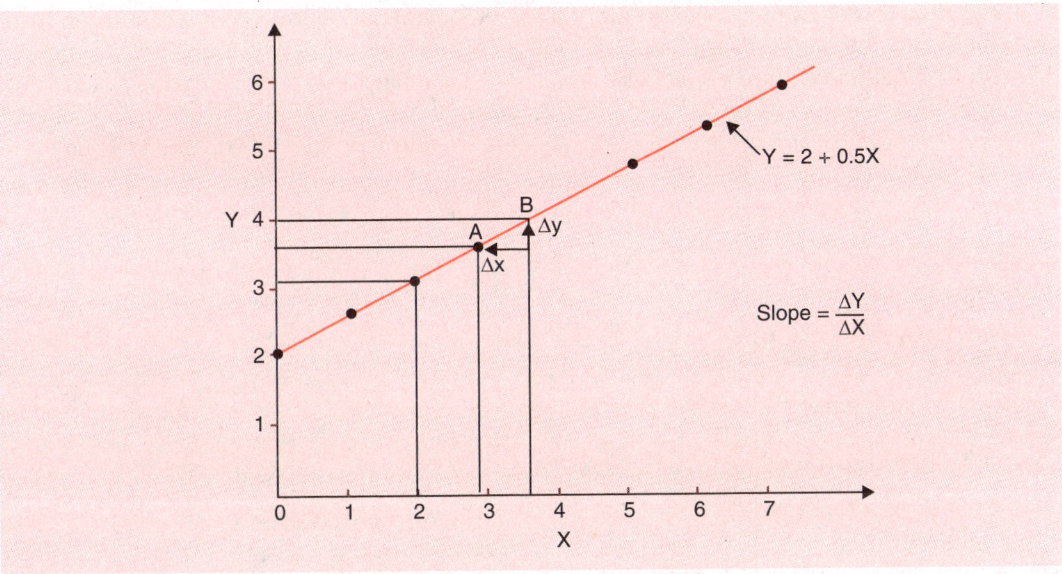

Fig. 5.4. *Graph of Y = 2 + 0.5X*

This implies that value of Y increases by 0.5 when value of X increases by 1. It should be noted that slope of a linear function is constant throughout.

However, the slope of a linear function can be directly known from the linear function itself and for that purpose there is no need to plot the data. Consider the following linear function

$$Y = a + bX$$

It will be seen from this linear function that when the value of X is zero, the value of Y will be equal to a. Thus a is Y intercept. Further, in this function b is the coefficient of X and measures change in Y due to change in X, that is, $\frac{\Delta Y}{\Delta X}$. Thus, b represents the slope of the linear function. In linear function $Y = 2 + 0.5X$, 2 is the Y-intercept, that is, value of Y when X is zero, 0.5 is the b coefficient which measures the slope $\frac{\Delta Y}{\Delta X}$ of the linear function.

Slope of a Non-linear Function

We now turn to explain how slope of a non-linear function, say, a quadratic function ($Y = a + bX + cX^2$) can be measured. On plotting the non-linear function in a graph, we get a non-linear curve. Let us take the following specific quadratic function :

$$Y = 5 + 3X + X^2$$

In Table 5.2 we have calculated the various values of Y by taking different values of X (0, 1, 2, 3, etc)

Table 5.2. Quadratic Function : $Y = 5 + 3X + X^2$

Value of X	0	1	2	3	4	5	6
Value of Y	5	9	15	23	33	45	59

The data so obtained have been plotted to get a curve in Figure 5.5. It will be seen from this Figure 5.5 that slope of the line AB which connects two points A and B on a curve representing quadratic function can be measured by taking the change in the value of Y divided by the change in value of X. At point A, value of X is 1 and the corresponding value of Y is 9 and at point B, the value of X is 4 to which the corresponding value is 33. Thus, here $\Delta X = 4 - 1 = 3$ and $\Delta Y = 33 - 9 = 24$.

Thus, the slope of the line AB is

$$\frac{\Delta Y}{\Delta X} = \frac{24}{3} = 8$$

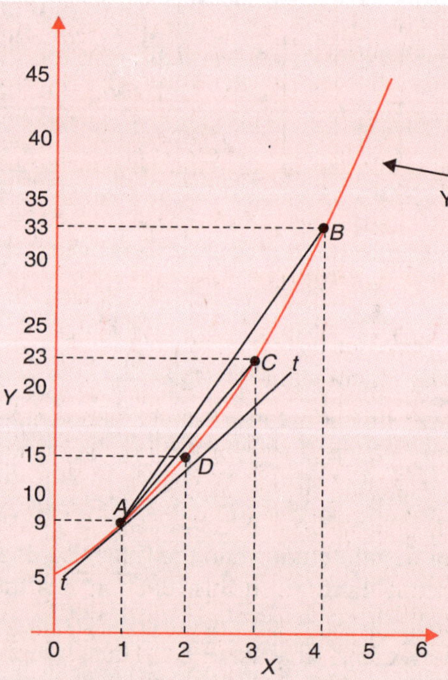

Fig. 5.5. *Slope of a Quadratic Function*

Similarly, slope of straight line AC in Fig.5.5. can be measured. Between two points A and C, $\Delta X = 3 - 1 = 2$ and $\Delta Y = 23 - 9 = 14$, Thus, the slope of straight line AC is

$$\frac{\Delta Y}{\Delta X} = \frac{14}{2} = 7$$

In a similar fashion, the slope of the straight line AD connecting points A and D on the non-linear quadratic function curve in Figure 5.5 is given by

$$\frac{\Delta Y}{\Delta X} = \frac{15-9}{2-1} = \frac{6}{1} = 6$$

It will thus be seen that as ΔX decreases; it was 3 between *A* and *B*, 2 between *A* and *C* and 1 between *A* and *D*, slope of the non-linear curve goes on declining. It was 8 of the line *AB*, 7 of the line *AC* and 6 of the line *AD*. As ΔX further decreases, slope of the line connecting two points of the non-linear curve will further decline,. It should also be noticed that the slope of the straight line *AD* connecting points *A* and *D* is very close to the slope of the tangent drawn to the curve at point *A*. As ΔX becomes smaller and smaller slope of the line connecting the two points on a curve will be come extremely close to the slope of the tangent *tt* drawn to the curve at point *A*. Therefore, ***the slope at a point on the non-linear function curve can be measured by the slope of a tangent drawn to the curve at that point.***

OPTIMISATION TECHNIQUES : DIFFERENTIAL CALCULUS

Optimisation techniques are an important set of tools required for efficiently managing firm's resources. In what follows we will focus on the use of differential calculus to solve certain types of optimisation problems. In a later chapter we will explain linear programming technique used for solving constrained optimisation problem.

Diffential Calculus : The Concept of a Derivative

In explaining the slope of a continuous and smooth non-linear curve we explained above that when a change in the indpendent variable, that is, ΔX gets smaller and approaches zero, $\frac{\Delta Y}{\Delta X}$ becomes better approximation of the slope the function, $Y = f(X)$, at a particular point. Thus, if ΔX is infinitesimally small, $\frac{\Delta Y}{\Delta X}$ measures the slope of the function at a particular point and is called the derivative $\frac{dY}{dX}$ of the function with respect to X. *The derivative* $\frac{dY}{dX}$ *or more precisely the first derivative of a function is defined as limit of the ratio* $\frac{\Delta Y}{\Delta X}$ *as* ΔX *approaches zero*. Thus

$$\frac{dY}{dX} = \lim_{\Delta x \to 0} \frac{\Delta Y}{\Delta X}$$

It is thus evident that derivative of a function shows the change in value of the dependent variable when change in the independent variable (ΔX) becomes infinitesimally small. Note that derivative of a function $[Y = f(X)]$ is also written as $\frac{d(fX)}{dX}$ or $f'(X)$.

As explained above, the derivativey of a function at a point measures the slope of the tangent at that point. Consider Figure 5.6 when $\Delta X = X_3 - X_1$, the slope of the corresponding straight line *AB* is equal to $\frac{Y_3 - Y_1}{X_3 - X_1}$. When ΔX becomes smaller and is equal to $X_2 - X_1$, slope of that corresponding line AC is equal $\frac{Y_2 - Y_1}{X_2 - X_1}$. It will be seen from Figure 5.6 that slope of line AC is more near to the slope of the tangent *tt* drawn at point A to the function curve. Similarly, if ΔX is reduced further, slope of the straight line between the two corresponding points will go on becoming closer and closer to the slope of the tangent *tt* drawn at point A to the curve. At the limit of $\frac{\Delta Y}{\Delta X}$ *when ΔX approaches zero, slope of the tangent such as tt at a point on a function becomes the derivative* $\frac{dY}{dX}$ *of the function with respect to X.*

Thus, derivative $\frac{dY}{dX}$ is slope of a function whether it is linear or non-linear and represents a change in the dependent variable due to a small change in the independent variable. The concept of a derivative is extensively used in economics and managerial decision making,

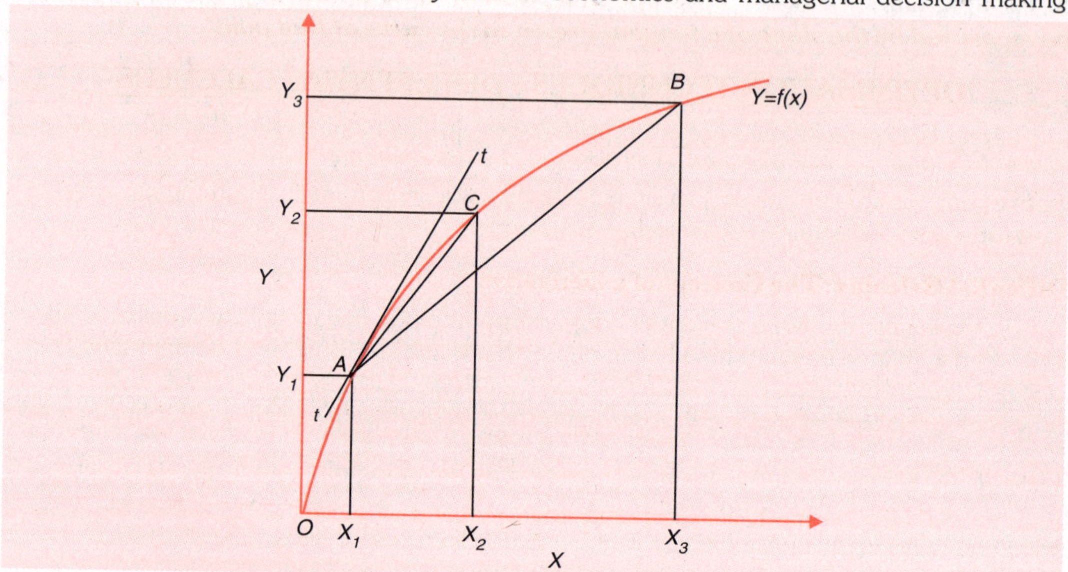

Fig 5.6. *Finding Derivative of a Function (Y = f(X) at a point*

especially in solving the problems of optimisation such as those of profit maximisation, cost minimisation, output and revenue maximisation.

There are various types of functions and for them there are different rules for finding the derivatives. We will explain below the basic rules of finding derivatives of the various types of functions.

RULES OF DIFFERENTIATION

Process of finding the derivative of a function is called **differentiation.** As stated above, derivative of a function represents the change in the dependent variable due to a infinitesimally small change in the independent variable and is written as $\frac{dY}{dX}$ for a function $Y = f(X)$. A series of rules have been derived for differentiating various types of functions. We describe below these rules of differentiation.

Derivative of a Constant Function. A constant function is expressed as

$$Y = f(X) = a$$

Where 'a' is constant. The constant 'a' implies that Y does not vary as X varies, that is, Y is independent of X. Therefore, the derivative of a constant function is equal to zero. Thus, in this constant function

$$\frac{dy}{dx} = 0$$

For example, let the constant function be

$$Y = 2.5$$

This is graphed in Figure 5.7(a). It will be seen that a constant function is a horizontal straight line (having a zero slope) which shows that irrespective of the value of the variable X, the value of Y does not change at all. Therefore, derivative $\frac{dY}{dX} = 0$.

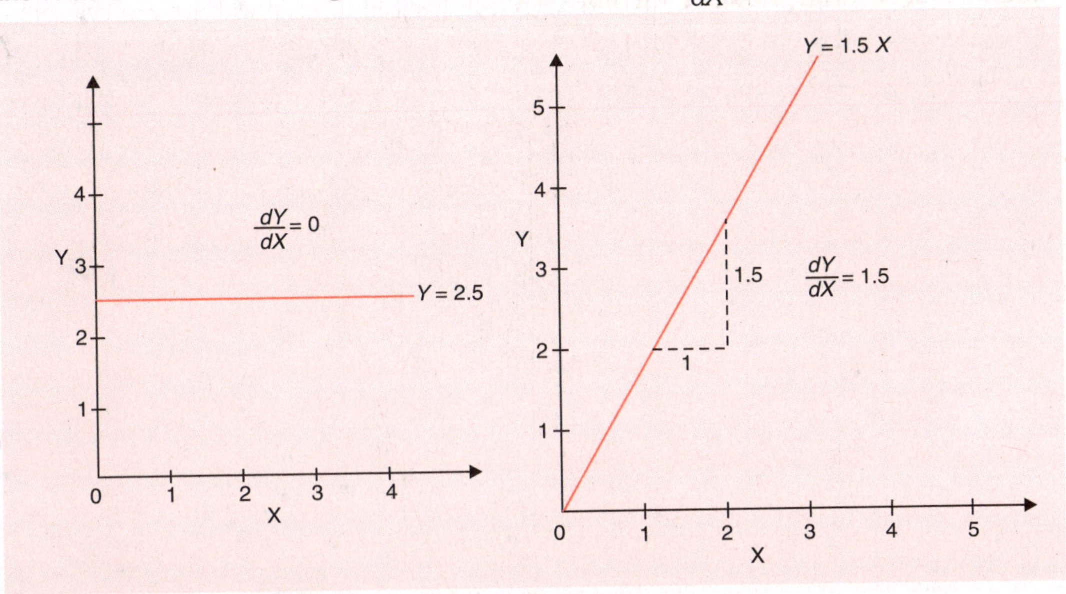

Fig. 5.7. (*a*) *Graph of a Constant Function* **Fig. 5.7.** (*b*) *Graph of a Linear Function*

Derivative of a Power Function

A power function takes the following form :

$$Y = aX^b$$

Where *a* and *b* are constants. Here *a* is the coefficient of the X term and the variable X is raised to the power *b*. The derivative of this power function is equal to the power *b* multiplied by the coefficient *a* times the variable X raised to the power *b* – 1. Thus rule for the derivative of power function ($Y = a X^b$) is

$$\frac{dY}{dX} = b.a.X^{b-1}$$

Let us take some examples of determining the derivative of a power function.

First, take the following power function :

$$Y = 1.5 X$$

In this function 1.5 is the coefficient of variable X, that is, *a* and the power *b* of X is 1 (implicit). Using the above rule for the derivative of a power function we have

$$\frac{dY}{dX} = 1 \times 1.5 X^{1-1} = 1 \times 1.5 X^0 = 1.5$$

This is graphically shown in Figure 5.7(*b*). It will be seen from this figure that slope of the linear function (Y = 1.5 X) is constant and is equal to 1.5 over any range of the values of the variables X.

Quadratic Power Function. Let us take the following example of a power function which is of quadratic type.

$$Y = X^2$$

$$\text{Its derivative,} \quad \frac{dy}{dx} = 2X^{2-1} = 2X^1 = 2X$$

To illustrate it we have calculated the values of Y, associated with different values of X such as 1, 2, 2.5 and –1, –2, –2.5 and have been shown in Table 5.3.

Table 5.3. Quardratic Power Function $Y = X^2$

Value of X	–2.5	–2	–1	+1	+2	+2.5
Value of Y	–6.25	–4	–1	+1	+4	+6.25

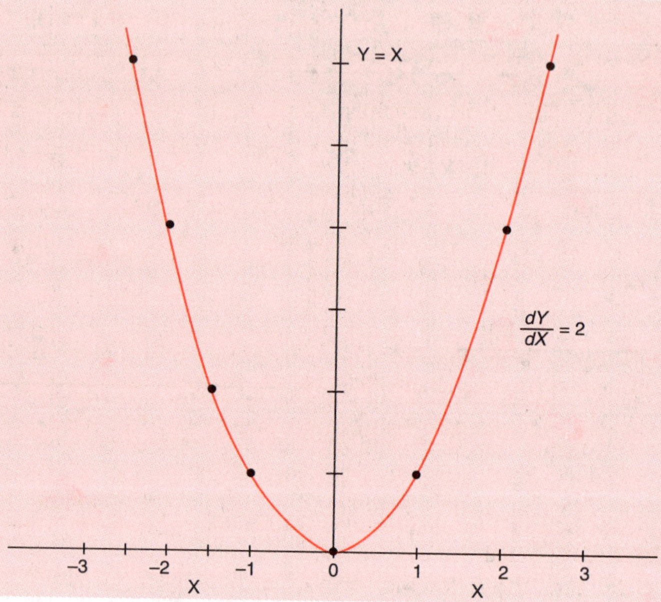

Fig. 5.8. *Graph of a Quadratic function*

We have plotted the values of X and corresponding values of Y to get a U-shaped parabolic curve in Figure 5.8. It will be seen that derivative $\frac{dY}{dX}$ or, in other words, slope of this quadratic function is changing at different values of X. Some other examples of power function and their derivatives are :

For power function,

$$Y = 3X^2$$

$$\frac{dy}{dx} = 2 \times 3.X^{2-1} = 6X$$

For power function; $Y = X^5$

$$\frac{dY}{dX} = 5 \times 1.X^{5-1} = 5X^4$$

For power function; $Y = X$

$$\frac{dY}{dX} = 1 \times 1\,X^{1-1} = 1 \times 1.X^0 = 1$$

It should be noted that any variable raised to the zero power (as in our example X^0) is equal to 1

For power function, $Y = 3X^{-2}$

$$\frac{dY}{dX} = -2 \times 3.X^{-2-1} = -6X^{-3}$$

Derivative of a Sum or Difference of Two Functions

The derivative of a sum of the two functions is equal to the *sum* of the derivatives obtained separately of the two functions.

Suppose, $Y = f(X) + g(X)$

Where $f(X)$ and $g(X)$ are the two unspecified functions and Y is the sum of the two functions. Then the derivative of their sum is

$$\frac{dY}{dX} = \frac{df(X)}{dX} + \frac{dg(X)}{dX}$$

Likewise, the derivative of the difference of the two or more different functions is the difference of their separate derivatives. Thus, if

$$Y = f(X) - g(X)$$

then
$$\frac{dY}{dX} = \frac{df(X)}{dX} - \frac{dg(X)}{dX}$$

To illustrate, we take some examples.

If, $Y = 4X^2 + 5X$

then $\frac{dY}{dX} = 2 \times 4X^{2-1} + 1 \times 5X^{1-1} = 8X + 5$

If $Y = 5X^2 - 2X^5$

$$\frac{dY}{dX} = 10X - 10X^4$$

Now, consider the following profit function where each of the three terms represents a function

$$\pi = -40 + 140Q - 10Q^2$$

Where π stands for profit and Q for level of output. Then, derivative of profit (π) with respect to output (Q) is

$$\frac{d\pi}{dQ} = 0 + 140 - 20\,Q$$

$$= 140 - 20\,Q$$

Note that derivative of a constant (–40) is zero, derivative of 140 Q is 140 and derivative 10 Q^2 = 20 Q.

Derivative of a Product of the Two Functions

Suppose Y is the product of the two separate functions $f(X)$ and $g(X)$.

$$Y = f(X).\, g(X)$$

The derivative of the product of these two functions is equal to the first function multiplied by the derivative of the second function plus the second function multiplied by the derivative of the first function. Thus,

$$\frac{dY}{dX} = f(X).\frac{dg(X)}{dX} + g(X).\frac{df(X)}{dX}$$

For example, take the following function

$$Y = 5X^2 (2X + 3)$$

$f(X) = 5X^2$ and $g(X) = (2X + 3)$ are the two functions. Then, derivative of the product of these two functions,

$$\frac{dY}{dX} = 5X^2.\frac{d(2X+3)}{dX} + (2X+3).\frac{d(5X^2)}{dX}$$

$$\frac{dY}{dX} = 5X^2.2 + (2X + 3).10X$$

$$= 10X^2 + 20X^2 + 30X$$

$$= 30X^2 + 30X$$

$$= 30(X^2 + X)$$

Take another example of the product rule. Let

$$Y = (X^3 + X^2 + 5)(2X^2 + 3)$$

then, $$\frac{dY}{dX} = (X^3 + X^2 + 5).\frac{d(2X^2+3)}{dX} + (2X^2 + 3).\frac{d(X^3+X^2+5)}{dX}$$

$$= (X^3 + X^2 + 5).4X + (2X^2 + 3).(3X^2 + 2X)$$

$$= (4X^4 + 4X^3 + 20X) + 6X^4 + 9X^2 + 4X^3 + 6X$$

$$= 10X^4 + 8X^3 + 9X^2 + 26X$$

Derivative of the Quotient of the Two Functions

Suppose the variable Y is equal to the quotient of the two functions $f(X)$ and $g(X)$. That is,

$$Y = \frac{f(X)}{g(X)}$$

The derivative of the quotient of the two functions is equal to the denominator times the derivative of the numerator minus the numerator times the derivative of the denominator and the whole divided by the denominator squared. Thus,

$$\frac{dY}{dX} = \frac{g(X).\frac{df(X)}{d(X)} - f(X).\frac{dg(X)}{dX}}{[g(X)]^2}$$

To illustrate, consider the following example

$$Y = \frac{5X+2}{X-1}$$

Here Y is a quotient of two functions

$$f(X) = 5X + 2 \text{ and } g(X) = X - 1$$

$$\frac{dY}{dX} = \frac{(X-1).\frac{d(5X+2)}{dX} - (5X+2).\frac{d(X-1)}{dX}}{(X-1)^2}$$

$$= \frac{(X-1)\times 5-(5X+2)\times 1}{(X-1)^2}$$

$$\frac{dY}{dX} = \frac{(5X-5)-(5X+2)}{(X-1)^2}$$

$$= \frac{dY}{dX} = \frac{5X-5-5X-2}{(X-1)^2}$$

$$= \frac{dY}{dX} = \frac{-7}{(X-1)^2}$$

Take another example. Let

$$Y = \frac{5-2X}{2X^2}$$

then,
$$\frac{dy}{dx} = \frac{2x^2.\frac{d(5-2X)}{dX} - (5-2X).\frac{d(2X^2)}{dX}}{(2X^2)^2}$$

$$= \frac{2X^2.(-2)-(5-2X).4X}{4X^4}$$

$$= \frac{-4X^2-20X+8X^2}{4X^4}$$

$$= \frac{4X^2-20X}{4X^4} = \frac{4X\,(X-5)}{4X\,(X^3)}$$

$$= \frac{X-5}{X^3}$$

Derivative of Function of a Function (Chain Rule)

When a variable Y is function of a variable U which in turn is related to another variable X, and if we wish to obtain a derivative of Y with respect to X, then we use chain rule for this purpose. Suppose variable Y is a function of the variable U, that is, $Y = f(U)$ and variable U is a function of variable X, that is, $U = g(X)$. Then, to obtain the derivative of Y with respect to X, that is $\frac{dY}{dX}$, we first find the derivative of the two functions, $Y = f(U)$ and $U = g(X)$ separately and then multiply them together. Thus,

For function,
$$Y = f(U)$$

$$\frac{dY}{dU} = \frac{df(U)}{dU}$$

For function,
$$U = g(X)$$

$$\frac{dU}{dX} = \frac{dg(X)}{dX}$$

Then
$$\frac{dY}{dX} = \frac{dY}{dU} \cdot \frac{dU}{dX}$$
$$= \frac{df(U)}{dU} \cdot \frac{dg(X)}{dX}$$

Thus, ***according to the chain rule if Y = f(U) and U = g(X), then derivative of Y with respect X, can be obtained by multiplying together the derivative of Y with respect to U and the derivative of U with respect to X***

Let us take some examples to illustrate this chain rule

Suppose $Y = U^3 + 15$ and $U = 3X^2$

$$\frac{dY}{dX} = \frac{dY}{dU} \cdot \frac{dU}{dX}$$

then
$$\frac{dY}{dX} = \frac{d(U^3 + 15)}{dU} \cdot \frac{d(3X^2)}{dX} = 3U^2 \,.\, 6X$$

Substituting $U = 3X^2$ in the above we have

$$\frac{dY}{dX} = 3.(3X^2)^2 \,.\, 6X$$
$$= 3 \,.\, 9X^4 \,.\, 6X$$
$$= 27X^4 \,.6X$$
$$= 162X^5$$

SUMMARY OF RULES OF DIFFERENTIATION

Function	Derivative
1. **Constant Function :** $y = f(x) = a$	$\frac{dy}{dx} = 0$
2. **Power Function :** $y = ax^b$	$\frac{dy}{dx} = b.a.\, x^{b-1}$
3. **Sum of functions :** $y = f(x) + g(x)$	$\frac{dy}{dx} = \frac{df(x)}{dx} + \frac{dg(x)}{dx}$
4. **Product of two Function :** $y = f(x).\, g(x)$	$\frac{dy}{dx} = f(x) \,.\, \frac{dg(x)}{dx} + g(x) \,.\, \frac{df(x)}{dx}$
5. **Quotient of two Finctions** $y = \frac{f(x)}{g(x)}$	$\frac{dy}{dx} = \frac{g(x) \,.\, \frac{df(x)}{dx} - f(x) \,.\, \frac{dg(x)}{dx}}{[g(x)]^2}$
6. **Function of a Function** $y = f(u)$, and $u = g(x)$	$\frac{dy}{dx} = \frac{dy}{du} \cdot \frac{du}{dx}$

DIFFERENTIATION OF FUNCTIONS WITH TWO OR MORE THAN TWO INDEPENDENT VARIABLES

Partial Derivatives

So far we have been concerned with the differentiation of functions with one independent variable. However, in economics relations contain two or more than two independent variables about whose use economists and managers of business firms have to take decisions. For example, demands for the product of a firm depends on its price, income of the consumers, price of its substitute, advertising outlay made by the firm to promote the sales of its product and some others. Further, output of a product depends on the amounts of labour, capital, raw materials etc used for the production of a commodity. Other examples of functions from economics and business with two or more independent variables can be given.

When a function has two or more independent variables and each of them has an effect on the value of the dependent variable, we use the concept of a partial derivative. It is called partial derivative because in this the effect of only a part of influences on the dependent variable is examined. ***A partial derivative of a function measures the marginal effect of a change in one variable on the value of the dependent variable, holding constant all other variables.*** Thus,in a function, $y = f(x_1, x_2, x_3)$, partial derivative of y with respect to x_1, will show the marginal effect of a very small change in x_1, keeping constant x_2, x_3. By convention and to distinguish it from derivative of a function with one independent variable, for partial derivative we use lower case delta (∂) instead of lower case d. However, rules of differentiation in finding partial derivatives are the same as explained above in case of derivative of a function with a single independent variable.

It is worth nothing that in multivariable function, the partial derivative of one independent variable depends on the values at which other independent variables are held constant. That is why the expression for partial derivative of profit function of a firm with two independent variables, products x and y, indicates that $\frac{\partial \pi}{\partial x}$ depends on the level at which the variable y is held constant. Similarly, the partial derivative of profit function with respect to y, indicates that it depends on the value of the variable x which is held constant. The economic reasoning for this will become clear if we take a two factor production function $q = f(L, K)$. In this partial derivative of production function with respect to labour (L), that is, $\frac{\partial q}{\partial L}$ implies marginal product of labour. Now, as is well known, marginal product of labour depends not only on its own skill and efficiency, but also on with how much capital (K) he has to work with. Generally, the greater the amount of capital, the higher will be marginal productivity of labour, the other things remaining the same.

To illustrate the concept of partial derivative we take the example of profit function with sales of two products as independent variables

$$\pi = f(x, y) = 50x - 3x^2 - xy - 4y^2 + 60y$$

where π represents profits, x and y are the sales of the two products being produced by a firm. The function represents that profits of a firm depend on the sales of two products produced by it.

Determining the partial derivative of profit (π) function with respect to sales of the product x treating sales of y as constant from the above profit function we obtain

$$\frac{\partial \pi}{\partial x} = 50 - 6x - y$$

Thus, with partial derivative we are able to isolate the marginal effect on profit (π) of the change in the sales of the product x, keeping the sales of products y as constant.

Note that in finding partial derivative of the profit function with respect to x, fourth and fifth terms in the profit function are not considered because they do not contain the variable x.

Likewise through partial derivative we can separate the marginal effect of the variation in sales of the product y on profit (π) while holding x constant.

Thus, partial derivative of profit (π) function with respect to y is

$$\frac{\partial \pi}{\partial y} = -x - 8y + 60.$$

APPLICATIONS OF DIFFERENTIAL CALCULUS (DERIVATIVES) TO OPTIMISATION PROBLEMS

We have explained above the concept of a derivative and rules for its differentiation in different types of functions because they are widely used in solving the problems of optimisation in economics. *The process of optimisation often requires us to determine the maximum or minimum value of a function*. For a function to be a maximum (or minimum) its first derivative is zero. As explained above, derivative of a function measures its slope. Therefore, maximization of a function occurs where its derivative is equal to zero, Thus, an important optimisation problem facing a business manager is to produce a level of output which maximises firm's profits. Similarly, optimum use of resources requires that cost be minimised for producing a given level of output. These problems of maximisation and minimisation can be solved with the use of the concept of derivative.

Use in Profit Maximisation

For example, consider the following profit function :

$$\pi = -100 + 160Q - 10Q^2$$

where π = profits and Q is units of output

For the profit (π) function to be maximum, its first derivative must be equal to zero.

Therefore, to find the profit-maximising level of output we find the derivative of the given profit function and set it equal to zero. Thus

$$\frac{d\pi}{dQ} = 160 - 20Q.$$

Setting it equal to zero.

$$\frac{d\pi}{dQ} = 160 - 20\,Q = 0$$

$$20Q = 160$$

$$Q = \frac{160}{20} = 8$$

At 8 units of output profits will be maximum. Maximisation of profits through the use of derivative is graphically shown in Figure 5.9. It will be seen that profit maximisation curve reaches its maximum point at point H. Therefore, at point H, the slope of the tangent (which measures the value of derivative $\frac{d\pi}{dQ}$) drawn to the profit curve at this point is equal to zero. It will be seen that corresponding to maximum profit point H on the profit function level of output is 8 units.

Total profits made at 8 units of output can be obtained by substituting 8 for Q in the given profit function. Thus

$$\pi = -100 + 160 \times 8 - 10\,(8)^2$$
$$= 1280 - 740 = 540$$

Thus at output level of 8 units profits are equal to 540.

Graphical analysis *cannot tell us easily* exactly at what level of output, profits will be maximum, for it takes time to draw a graph and conclude from it. However, it is easier to use differential calculus to find the profit-maximising output. For this we simply find the first derivative of the profit function and set it equal to zero.

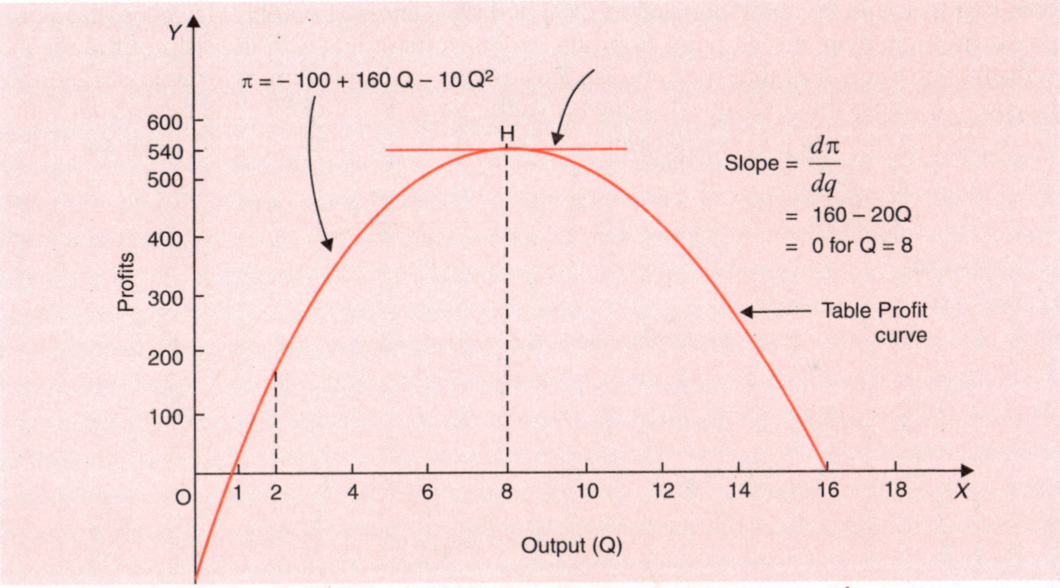

Fig. 5.9. *Profit Maximisastion is reached at output level where* $\frac{d\pi}{dQ} = 0$

Second Derivative and Second Order Condition for Optimisation

A problem arises when we use the first derivative of a function to determine its maximum or minimum value. For setting the first derivative of a function equal to zero and solving the resulting equation for the optimum value of the independent variable does not guarantee that optimum value (maximum or minimum as the case may be) will in fact he obtained. For the optimum value, the first derivative being equal to zero is a necessary condition for maximum or minimum, but it is not a sufficient condition : For example, in a profit function, first derivative is equal to zero, both it at maximum and minimum profit levels. To ensure that the derivative is zero at the profit maximising level of the decision variable (*i.e.* output in the present case), we require to apply the second order condition. According to the second order condition, for profit *maximisation*, the second derivative of the profit function must be negative, that is, $\frac{d^2\pi}{dQ^2} < 0$. Thus, if optimisation requires maximisation of function say, $y = f(x)$, then the second derivative, which is written as $\frac{d^2y}{dx^2}$, must be negative.

It should be noted that the second derivative of a function is obtained by differenting the first derivative with respect to the independent variable. In case optimisation requires minimisation of a function as in case of minimisation of cost for producing a given level of output, the second derivative must be positive, that is, $\frac{d^2y}{dx^2} > 0$.

Consider again the case of profit maximisation explained above. A profit function curve such as the one drawn in Figure 5.10 may have both minimum point and maximum points. It will be seen from Figure 5.10 that point L represents the minimum point and H represents the maximum point of the profit curve. Important thing to note is that at both minimum point L and maximum point H, first order condition, that is, first derivative $\frac{d\pi}{dQ}$ be zero is satisfied at both points, L and H, corresponding to OQ_1 and OQ_2 levels of output. However, at point L profits are minimum and at point H profits are maximum. It is with the help of the second derivative of a function that we can distinguish between maximum and minimum along a function. Whereas the first derivative measures the slope of a function, the second derivative measures the slope of the first derivative. Thus, in case of profit function, whereas first

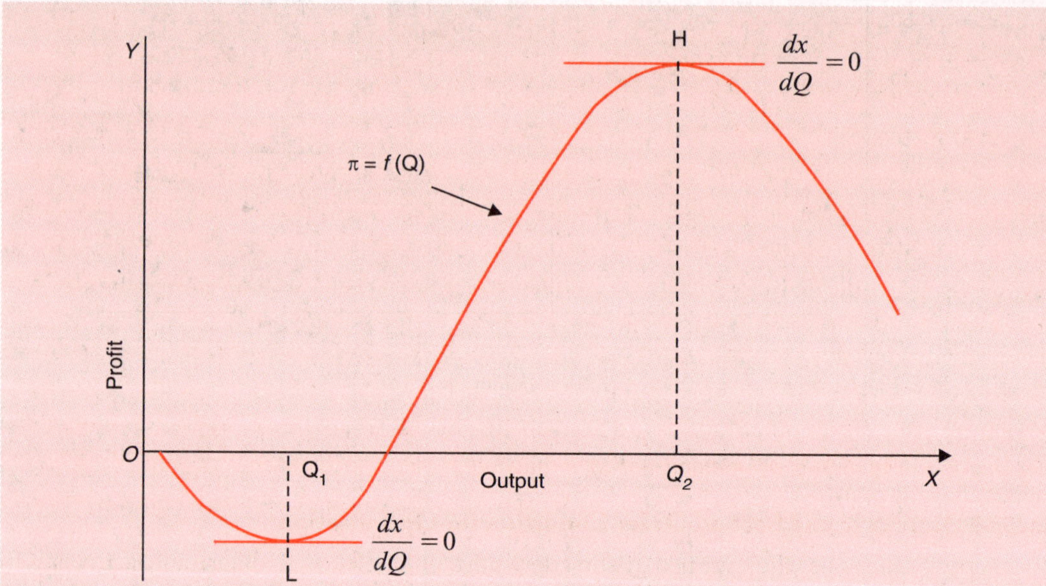

Fig. 5.10. *Second Order Condition for Optimisation*

derivative, $\frac{d\pi}{dQ}$, measures the slope of the profit function curve, That is, marginal profit, its second derivative, $\frac{d^2\pi}{dQ^2}$, measures slope of the marginal profit function curve.

Since the second derivative of a function when measured at the maximisation level is always negative and when measured at the minimisation level is always positive, it can be used to distinguish between points of maximum and minimum. For example, if the second derivative in our profit function curve is negative, it implies that profits are maximum at the level where first derivative is equal to zero. On the other hand, if the second derivative at a point on a profit function where first derivative is zero is positive, it shows profits are in fact minimum rather than maximum. It can be easily known from having a look at Figure 5.10. It will be seen from this figure that up to point L, marginal profit $\left(\frac{d\pi}{dQ}\right)$, that is, slope of the total profit curve, is negative and has been causing the total profits to fall (in fact, up to L, due to negative marginal profits loses have been increasing. At point L, marginal profit $\left(\frac{d\pi}{dQ}\right)$ becomes zero and thereafter it becomes positive and therefore it will causes the total profit to increase.

Hence, point L beyond which the second derivative (*i.e.* the slope of the first derivative) is positive, and since profits will be increasing beyond this point, it cannot be point of maximum profits.

Now consider point H on the total profit corresponding to output level OQ_2. At point H, first derivative $\left(\frac{d\pi}{dQ}\right)$ is again equal to zero but after that marginal profit $\frac{d\pi}{dQ}$ becomes negative as the slope of total profit curve is negative as output is expanded beyond Q_2. This causes the total profits to fall. This shows that point H at which first derivative, $\frac{d\pi}{dQ}$ is zero and also beyond which second derivative $\left(\frac{d^2\pi}{dQ^2}\right)$, that is, slope of the first derivative becomes negative is indeed the point of maximum profit.

To conclude, we get a following general test for maximum and minimum.

(1) If the second derivative $\frac{d^2y}{dx^2}$ of a function is negative (< 0) at the point where the first derivative $\left(\frac{dy}{dx}\right)$ is zero, it will represent a point of maximum.

(2) If the second derivative $\left(\frac{d^2y}{dx^2}\right)$ of a function is positive (> 0) at the point where first derivative is zero, it will represent a point of minimum.

Coming back to our profit function ($\pi = -100 + 160Q - 10Q^2$) in which case the first derivative is zero at 8 units of output, we test for the sign of second derivative. Thus,

$$\frac{d\pi}{dQ} = 160 - 20Q$$

$$\frac{d^2\pi}{dQ^2} = -20.$$

Thus, we find that at 8 units of output profits will in fact be maximum.

Minimisation Problem

In some decision making problems the objective of a manager is to minimise the objective function. For example, efficiency in the use of resources requires that a firm should produce at the minimum possible cost per unit of output. For example, the following average cost function of a firm is given :

$$AC = 25{,}000 - 180Q + 0.50Q^2$$

A manager is interested to find what level of output the firm will minimise its average cost. This can be obtained by differentiating the AC function with respect to output (Q) and setting it equal to zero, Thus

$$\frac{d(AC)}{dQ} = -180 + 1.0Q$$

Setting it equal to zero and solving for Q we have

$$-180 + 1.0\,Q = 0$$

$$Q = 180$$

Applying the second order condition to ensure whether it is really minimum we take the second derivative of AC function

$$\frac{d^2(AC)}{dQ^2} = +1.0$$

Since second derivative of AC function is positive, $\frac{d^2(AC)}{dQ^2} > 0$, output of 180 units of output is one that minimises average cost of production.

Multivariate Optimisation

As has been explained earlier, when a dependent variable is a function of many independent variables we use the concept of a partial derivative. Partial derivatives are therefore used to find optimal solution to maximisation or minimisation problem in case of two or more independent variables. Rules for finding maximisation and minimisation problems are the same as described above in case of one independent variable. To maximise or minimise a multivariate function we set partial derivative with respect to each independent variable equal to zero and solve the resulting set of simultaneous equations.

Consider that a firm is producing two products X and Y. Its profit function may be written as

$$\pi = f(X, Y).$$

Consider a firm producing the two products whose function is given below

$$\pi = 50X - 2X^2 - XY - 4Y^2 + 75Y$$

Where X and Y are two independent variables representing levels of outputs of two products. It is to decide what levels of output of the two products will maximise profits.

Differentiating the profit function with respect to X while holding Y constant we have

$$\frac{d\pi}{dX} = 50 - 4X - Y$$

Differentiating the profit function with respect to y while holding X constant we have

$$\frac{d\pi}{dY} = -X - 8Y + 75$$

For maximisation of profits ***we must set each partial derivative equal to zero*** and then solve the resulting set of simultaneous equations for optimal values of independent variables x and Y. Thus,

$$\frac{\partial\pi}{\partial X} = 50 - 4X - Y = 0 \qquad \text{.... }(i)$$

$$\frac{\partial\pi}{\partial Y} = 75 - X - 8Y = 0 \qquad \text{.... }(ii)$$

To solve the above two equations simultaneously we multiply equation (*i*) by – 8 and adding (*i*) and (*ii*) we have

$$-400 + 32X + 8Y = 0$$
$$75 - X - 8Y$$
$$\overline{-325 + 31X = 0}$$
$$31x = 325$$
$$X = \frac{325}{31} = 10.45$$

Substituting $X = 10.45$ in equation (i) we have

$$50 - 4 \times 10.45 - Y = 0$$
$$50 - 41.80 - Y = 0$$

or $$Y = 50 - 41.80 = 8.20$$

Thus the firm will maximise profits of it produces and sells 10.45 units of product X and 8.2 units of product Y.[1]

CONSTRAINED OPTIMISATION

So far we have been concerned with explaining unconstrained optimisation, that is, maximisation or minimisation of an objective function when there are *no constraints*. However, consumers and managers of business firms quite often face decision problems when there are constraints which limit the choice available to them for optimisation. For example, a business firm may face a constraint with regard to the limited availability of some crucial raw material, skilled manpower. Constraint may be of the limited productive capacity as determined by the size of the plant and capital equipment installed. Besides, quite often marketing managers are required to maximise sales subject to the constraint of a given advertising expenditure at their disposal. Further, financial managers also work under the constraint of a given *investment requirements* of a firm and they are required to minimise the cost of raising capital for that purpose. Managers of business firms also face legal and environmental constraints.

In all these cases when individuals face constraints in their decision making to maximise or minimise their objective functions we have a problem of *constrained optimisation*. It is worth nothing that the existence of constraints prevents the achievement of the unconstrained optimal. There are two techniques of solving the constrained optimisation problem[2]. They are : (1) substitution method, (2) Lagrangian multiplier technique. We explain them below.

1. **Constrained Optimasation : Substitution Method.** Substitution method to solve constrained optimisation problem is used when constraint equation is simple and not too complex. For example substitution method to maximise or minimise the objective function is

1. It should be noted that the second order condition for maximisation is also satisfied. Recall that the second order condition which is based on the value of the second order derivative is used to distinguish between a maximum and minimum. However, the second-order condition in case of maximisation or minimisation of a multivariable function is very complex and therefore we do not attempt to explain that in this text in all maximisation and minimisation problems involving multivariable functions explained in this chapter. We therefore assume that the point at which all partial derivatives are zero, the second order condition for maximisation or minimisation is satisfied. Those readers who are interested in knowing the second order condition in case of multivariable functions may consult a textbook on differential calculus.

2. In this chapter we explain the techniques of solving the problems of unconstrained optimisation in those cases when constraints are expressed in the form of equations. Quite often constraints faced refer only to the upper or lower limits on the decision makers. These constraints are expressed as *inequalities*. A technique of linear programming has been development to deal with the problems of constrained optimisation in case constraints of inequality type are present. We will explain linear programming technique in a separate chapter of this book.

used when it is subject to only one constraint equation of a very simple nature. In this method, we solve the constraint equation for one of the decision variables and substitute that variable in the objective function that is to be maximised or minimised. In this way this method converts the constrained optimisation problem into one of unconstrained optimisation problems of maximisation or minimisation. Then, the same procedure of optimisation is applied as the explained earlier in this chapter.

An example will clarify the use of substitution method to solve constrained optimisation problem. Suppose a manager of a firm which is producing two products x and y, seeks to maximise total profits function which is given by the following equation

$$\pi = 50x - 2x^2 - xy - 3y^2 + 95y$$

where x and y represent the quantities of the two products. The manager of the firm faces the constraints that the total output of the two products must be equal to 25. That is, according to the constraint,

$$x + y = 25$$

To solve this constrained optimisation problem through substitution we first solve the constraint equation for x. Thus

$$x = 25 - y$$

The next step in the substitution method is to substitute this value of $x = 25 - y$ in the objective function (*i.e.* the given profit function) which has to be maximised. Thus, substituting the constrained value of x in the profit function we have

$$\begin{aligned}\pi &= 50\,(25 - y) - 2\,(25 - y)^2 - (25 - y)\,y - 3y^2 + 95y\\ &= 1250 - 50y - 2\,(625 - 50y + y^2) - 25y + y^2 - 3y^2 + 95y\\ &= 1250 - 50y - 1250 + 100y - 2y^2 - 25y + y^2 - 3y^2 + 95y\\ &= 120y - 4y^2\end{aligned}$$

To maximise the above profit function converted into the above unconstrained form we differentiate it with respect to y and set it equal to zero and solve for y. Thus,

$$\frac{d\pi}{dy} = 120 - 8y = 0$$

or,

$$8y = 120$$

$$y = 15$$

Substituting $y = 15$ in the given constraint equation $(x + y = 25)$ we have

$$X + 15 = 25$$

$$X = 25 - 15 = 10$$

Thus, given the constraint, profit will be maximised if the manager of the firm decides to produce 10 units of the product x and 15 units of the product y. We can find the total profits in this constrained optimum situation by substituting the values of x and y obtained in the given profit function. Thus,

$$\begin{aligned}\pi &= 50x - 2x^2 - xy - 3y^2 + 95y\\ \pi &= 50 \times 10 - 2(10)^2 - 10 \times 15 - 3(15)^2 + 95 \times 15\\ &= 500 - 200 - 150 - 675 + 1425\\ &= 1925 - 1025\\ &= 900\end{aligned}$$

Lagrange Multiplier Technique

The substitution method for solving constrained optimisation problem cannot be used easily when the constraint equation is very complex and therefore cannot be solved for one of the decision variable. In such cases of constrained optimisation we employ the Lagrangian Multiplier technique. In this Lagrangian technique of solving constrained optimisation problem, a combined equation called Lagrangian function is formed which incorporates both the original objective function and constraint equation. This Lagrangian function is formed in a way which ensures that when it is maximised or minimised, the original given objective function is also maximised or minimised and at the same time it fulfils all the constraint requirements. In creating this Lagrangian function, an artificial variable λ (Greek letter Lamda) is used and it is multiplied by the given constraint function having been set equal to zero. λ is known as ***Lagrangian multiplier.***

Lagrangian Multiplier

Since Lagrangian function incorporates the constraint equation into the objective function, it can be considered as unconstrained optimisation problem and solved accordingly. Let us illustrate Lagrangian multiplier technique by taking the constrained optimisation problem solved above by substitution method. In that problem manager of a firm was to maximise the following profit function :

$$\pi = 50x - 2x^2 - xy - 3y^2 + 95y$$

subject to the constraint,

$$x + y = 25$$

where x and y are the outputs of two products produced by the firm.

In order to constitute Lagrangian function we first set the constraint function equal to zero by bringing all the terms to the left side of the equation. In doing so we have

$$x + y - 25 = 0$$

The next step in creating the Lagrangian function is to multiply this form of the constraint function by the unknown artificial factor λ and then adding the result to the given original objective function. Thus combining the constraint and the objective function through Lagrangian multplier (λ) we have

$$L_\pi = 50x - 2x^2 - xy - 3y^2 + 95y + \lambda\,(x + y - 25)$$

where L_π stands for the expression of Lagrangian function.

As stated above, the Lagrangaion function can be considered as unconstrained optimisation function. It will be seen that in this function there are three unknowns x, y and λ. Note that the solution that maximises Lagrangian function (L_π) will also maximise profit (π) function :

For maximising L_π, we first find partial derivatives of L_π with respect to three unknown x; y and λ and then set them equal to zero. Thus

$$\frac{\partial L_\pi}{\delta x} = 50 - 4x - y + \lambda = 0 \quad \text{..... (i)}$$

$$\frac{\partial L_\pi}{\delta y} = -x - 6y + 95 + \lambda = 0 \quad \text{..... (ii)}$$

$$\frac{\partial L_\pi}{\delta \lambda} = x + y - 25 = 0 \quad \text{..... (iii)}$$

Note that the last equation (iii) is the constraint subject to which the original profit function has to be maximised. In fact, Lagrangian function is so constructed that the partial derivative of L_π with respect to λ (Lagrangian multiplier) always yields the original constraint function. Further, since the partial derivative of L_π with respect to λ is set equal to zero, it not only ensures that the constraint of the optimisation problem is fulfilled but also converts the Lagrangian function into original constrained profit maximisation problem so that the solution to both of them will yield the same result.

Let us now solve the above system of three equations with three unknowns to find the optimal values of x and y. To do so we first substract the equation (ii) from equation (i) and get

$$-45 - 3x + 5y = 0 \qquad \text{..... (iv)}$$

Now, multiplying equation (iii) by 3 and adding it to equation (iv) we have

$$\begin{aligned} -45 - 3x + 5y &= 0 \\ -75 + 3x + 3y &= 0 \\ \hline -120 + 8y \quad - &= 0 \end{aligned}$$

Thus,

$$8y = 120$$

$$y = 15$$

Substituting the value of $y = 15$ in the constraint function $x + y = 25$ we get x equal to 10. Thus, we find the same optimal values of x and y as we obtained in the substitution method.

Lagrange technique of solving constrained optimisation is highly significant for two reasons. First, as noted above, when constraint conditions are too many or too complex, it is not feasible to use substitution method and therefore in such cases it is easy to use Lagrange technique for solution of constrained optimisation problems. Second, the use of Lagrangian multiplier technique also provides the decision maker as additional important information. This information is the value of λ that is, Lagrangian multiplier itself. The value of λ has a significant economic interpretation. The value of λ shows the marginal effect on the solution of the objective function when there is a unit change in the constraint. Thus, in our example of profit maximization, value of λ indicates the *marginal profit* caused by a one unit change in the output of products, that is, change in the total profit when output constraint either increases from 25 to 26 or decreases from 25 to 24.

The value of λ can be obtained by substituting the solved values of x and y in a partial derivative equation containing λ in the Lagrangian function. Thus, in our above example, the value of λ can be obtained by substituting $x = 10$ and $y = 15$ in equation (ii) above

Thus, in the above equation (*ii*)

$$-x - 6y + 95 + \lambda = 0$$

$$\lambda = x + 6y - 95$$

$$\lambda = 10 + 90 - 95$$

$$\lambda = +5$$

Here λ can be interpreted as marginal profit at the production level of 25 units. It shows if the firm is required to produce 24 units instead of 25 units, its profits will fall by 5. On the other hand, if firm were to produce 26 instead of 25 units, its profits will increase by about 5.

Note that Lagrange technique maximises profits under a constraint. It does not solve **unconstrained** profit maximization.

QUESTIONS FOR REVIEW

1. What is meant by optimisation ? Explain its significance in managerial decision making.

2. Define the following terms

(*i*) Function

(*ii*) Dependent Variable

(*iii*) Independent Variable

(*iv*) Constant

(*v*) Intercept

3. (*a*) What is a linear function ? What factors determine a specific form of a linear function ? How does its graph look like ?

(2) (a) Write a linear demand function with a single independent variable.

(*b*) Give an example of a specific linear demand function with a single independent variable.

(*c*) How will you interpret the coefficient of the independent variable in a linear demand function ?

4. (*a*) Write a multivariable linear demand function ? How will you interpret the coefficients of various independent variables ?

(*b*) How is the effect of non-price variables on demand for a commodity depicted in economics?

5. What is a quadratic function ? Distinguish between a convex and concave quadratic functions. How will their graphs look like ? Show them with diagrams.

6. Write a quadratic function with two independent variables. How will its graph look like ?

7. What is a cubic function ? Write a general form of a cubic function. Can a cubic function contain first degree, second degree and third degree terms in it ?

8. What does slope of a function indicate ? Plot the following linear function and measure its slope.

$$y = 5 + 0.8x$$

9. Draw a curve representing a quadratic function : How will you measure slope at a point on it? Does slope of a quadratic function remain constant along it ?

OPTIMISATION TECHNEQUES

10. (a) Explain the concept of a derivative of a function. Explain the logic of using the derivative of a function to find the maximum or minimum of that function.

(b) What is the significance of the concept of derivative in business applications ?

11. Why is derivative of a constant function equal to zero? Draw a graph of a constant function.

12. You are given the following linear supply function :

$$Q = 2 + 1.5P$$

Draw its graph and show the value of its derivative.

13. Describe the following rules of differentiation

(1) Power rule of differentiation

(2) Function of a function rule of differentiation

(3) Chain rule of differentiation

(4) Product rule of differentiation

14. What is a partial derivative of a function ? In which type of function the concept of a partial derivative is applied ? What is the assumption that underlies the interpretation of any one variable?

15. What is a second derivative ? How is the second derivative used in distinguishing between a maximium and minimum point ?

16. Find the first and second derivative of the following total revenue (*TR*) and total cost (*TC*) functions. Find the values of these derivatives at the level of output of 10 units. Also interpret the values of the first and second derivatives so obtained

1. $TR = 40\,Q - 2Q^2$
2. $TR = 150 + 25Q + 10Q^2$
3. $TC = 300 + 15Q$
4. $TC = 150 + 7Q - 3Q^2 + Q^3$

17. You are given the following production functions where Q stands for output, L and K for units of labour and capital respectively used in the production process. Find the first and second derivatives of these functions with respect to labour and explain what these derivatives imply :

1. $Q = 3L^2 + 2\,LK - 5K^2$
2. $Q = 5L^2 + 10\,LK + 2K$
3. $Q = 100L^{0.5}\,K^{0.5}$

18. Consider the following demand function of a product facing a firm

$$P = 25 - Q$$

Where P = price and Q = quantity demand of the product measured in units

(*a*) Express the total revenue function

(*b*) Express the marginal revenue function

(*c*) At what quantity demanded total. revenue will be maximised.

19. How does the manager of a business firm determine the profit maximising level of output ? Use concept of derivatives.

20. Suppose objective function of a firm is to maximise its sales. How will it determine sales-maximisation level of output ?

(**Hints.** Sales is considered in value terms. Thus sales mean total revenue received from the output produced and sold) Take inverse demand function (that is, price expressed as a function of quantity demanded (Q) and multiply it with Q to get total revenue. Then use the concept of derivatives to determine sales maximisation level of output).

21. What is meant *by* partial derivative ? How is it obtained ? Can the partial derivative of a function with respect to one independent variable depend also on the value of the other independent variable ? If so, why ?

PROBLEMS ON CONSTRAINED OPTIMISATION

22. (a) What is meant *by* 'constrained optimisation'? What is its significance in managerial decision making ? How can a constrained optimisation problem be solved through Lagrangian multiplier technique?

23. Explain Lagrangian mutiplier method of solving constrained optimisation problem. How is Lagrangian function formed ? What is the economic significance of Lagrangian multiplier λ ?

24. Suppose that a firm is producing two models of a car, model J and model T. The total revenue function from the sales of two cars is

$$TR = J.T$$

where both J and T are measured in thousands of units Due to limited productive capacity the maximum number of cars (J models + T models) that can be produced is 10 thousands.

Using lagrangion multiplier method determine the quantities of the two models is J and T that should be produced to maximise revenue. Also interpret the value of Lagrangian multiplier (λ) in this case.

PART–II

DEMAND ANALYSIS AND THEORY OF CONSUMER'S CHOICE

- Demand and Demand Function
- Consumer's Behaviour: Cardinal Utility Analysis
- Indifference Curve Analysis of Demand
- Demand for Complementary and Substitute Goods
- Hicks's Logical Ordering Theory of Demand
- Elasticity of Demand
- Consumer Surplus
- Attribute Approach to Consumer's Behaviour
- Individual Choice Under Risk and Uncertainty
- Marshallian Cardinal Utility Analysis vs. Indifference Curve Analysis
- Applications and Uses of Indifference Curve
- Revealed Preference Theory of Demand

CHAPTER

6

Demand and Demand Function

Significance of Demand Function

This chapter provides an introduction to the theory of demand and explains the various factors that determine demand for a product of a firm and an industry. In this context we will explain demand function and law of demand and the factors that account for it. We will also explain the effects of changes in factors that influence demand for products. Demand for products plays crucial role in the determination of a firm's profitability. Therefore, estimates of future demand for a product are important for planning production activity and its expansion and also of marketing the product. For example, if demand for a firm's product is stable, then the same production schedule per period may be planned. On the other hand, if demand fluctuates very much, then flexible production processes must be used or arrangements for carrying large inventories of the product and raw materials must be made.

Demand conditions for a firm's product have also profound influence on its financial decisions. If product demand is strong and growing, the firm's financial manager must plan to arrange for sufficient funds to meet the growing capital requirements of the firm. The expansion of a firm needs not only increased finance but also increased human resources, especially skilled manpower. Therefore, human resource (HR) manager must plan not only to make arrangements for the recruitment of the new personnel but also for training programmes to ensure the availability of trained work force required for production and marketing the product. Further, demand conditions for a product together with the production technologies allow efficient production by a small-sized firm. If demand for a product is quite large, then it may cause a large number of firms producing a product which ensures a high level of competition in the industry. And if demand and production technology are such that lead to the existence of monopoly or oligopoly, then degree of competition will be low and firms will exercise large control over the price of the product. We will discuss in later chapters of this book the various forms of market structure and pricing and output decisions of the firms working in them.

INDIVIDUAL DEMAND

It is useful to know what economists mean by the demand for the goods by consumers. The demand for a commodity is consumer's desire to have it for which he is willing and able to pay. Demand for a good is in fact a photographic picture of consumers' attitude towards a commodity. This consumers' attitude gives rise to his actions in purchasing a certain number of units of a commodity at various given prices. ***Precisely stated, the demand for a commodity is the amount of it that a consumer will purchase it at various given prices during a period of time.*** This time period may be a week, a month, a year or any other given time period. The demand in economics implies both the desire to purchase and the ability to pay for a good. It is noteworthy that mere desire for a commodity does not constitute demand for it, if it is not backed by the ability to pay. For example, if a poor man who hardly makes both ends meet, wishes to have a car, his wish or desire for a car will not constitute the demand for the car because he cannot afford to pay for it, that is, he has no purchasing power to make his wish or desire effective in the market.

Thus, in economics unless demand is backed by purchasing power or ability to pay it does not constitute demand. Demand for a good is determined by several factors such as price of a commodity, the tastes and desires of the consumer for a commodity, income of the consumer, the prices of related goods, substitutes or complements. When there is a change in any of these factors, demand of the consumer for a good changes. Individual consumer's demand and market demand for a good may be distinguished. Market demand for a good is the total sum of the demands of individual consumers, who purchase the commodity in the market. We shall discuss in detail later in this chapter the various factors which determine the demand for a commodity and also how a market demand curve for a commodity is obtained.

Demand and Utility. People demand goods because they satisfy the wants of the people. The utility means the amount of satisfaction which an individual derives from consuming a commodity. It is also defined as want-satisfying power of a commodity. Utility of a good is the important determinant of demand of a consumer for the good. It is assumed that Individuals will try to maximise their utility or satisfaction from the goods they buy for consumption. Consumers' demand for consumer goods for their own satisfaction is called ***direct demand.*** Utility is a subjective entity and resides in the minds of men. Being subjective, it varies with different persons, that is, different persons derive different amounts of utility from a given good. People know utility of goods by means of introspection.

The desire for a commodity by a person depends upon the utility he expects to obtain from it. The greater the utility he expects from a commodity, the greater his desire for that commodity. It should be noted that no question of ethics or morality is involved in the use of the word, 'utility' in economics. Thus desire to consume alcohol may be considered immoral by some relegious prople but no such meaning is attached to it in economics. ***Thus, in economics the concept of utility*** is ethically neutral. Further a commodity may not be useful in the ordinary sense of the term, even then it may provide utility to some people. For instance, alcohol and cigarettes may actually harm persons but it possesses utility for those whose want they satisfy.

Consumer's choice of goods he buys is a difficult task in the modern economic system as thousands of goods and services are available in the market. But the quantities of goods consumers buy are constrained by their income or budget. Who would not like to 'buy City Honda Car, dine at Taj Hotel and live in a good bungalow in South Delhi. It is income which constrains consumers to buy goods they might want. Thus **consumers face constrained optimisation problem.**

Demand and Quantity Demanded. Demand for a good is determined by several factors such as tastes and desires of the consumer for a commodity, income of the consumer, the prices of related goods, substitutes or complements. When there is a change in any of these factors, demand of the consumer for a good changes. Individual consumer's demand and market demand for a good may be distinguished. ***Market demand for a good is the total sum of the demands of all individual consumers who purchase the commodity at various prices in the market in a period.*** We shall discuss in detail later in this chapter the various factors which determine demand for a commodity.

It is worth noting that the demand for a commodity and quantity demanded are two different concepts. Whereas, demand refers to the quantities of a commodity which consumers plan to buy at *various prices of a good* during a period of time, the quantity demanded is the amount of a good or service which consumers plan to buy at a *particular price*. It is worth mentioning that quantity demanded is not necessary the amount *actually bought by* the consumers. Sometimes, the quantity demanded is greater than the quantity of the good available so that quantity of the good actually bought is less than the quantity demanded of it. The second thing worth mentioning about quantity demanded is that it is a *flow concept*. This means that quantity demanded is measured as an amount that consumers wish to buy per unit of time, which may be a day, a week a month or a year. Thus if you consume 5 cups of tea in a day, then your quantity demanded of tea is expressed as 5 cups per day or 35 cups per week or 150 cups per month and so on. Without specifying the time period, it is not possible to say whether the quantity demanded is large or small.

Demand Function

The demand function for a commodity describes the relationship between the quantity demanded of it and the factors that influence it. Individual's demand for a commodity depends on its own price, his income, prices of related commodities (which may be either substitutes or complements), his tastes and preferences, and advertising expenditure made by the producers for the commodity in question. Individual demand function for a commodity can be expressed in the folllowing *gereral form* :

$$Q_d = f(P_x, I, P_r, T, A) \quad \ldots(1)$$

where P_x = Own price of the commodity X

I = Income of the individual

P_r = Prices of related commodities

T = Tastes and preferences of the individual consumer

A = Advertising expenditure made by the producers of the commodity.

We will explain in detail the above factors that determine demand later in this chapter.

For many purposes in economics, it is useful to focus on the relationship between quantity demanded of a good and its own price while ***keeping other determining factors such as consumer's income, prices of other goods, his tastes and preferences constant.*** With this we write the demand function of an individual in the following way.

$$Q_d = f(P_x) \quad \ldots(2)$$

This implies that quantity demanded of a good X is function of its own price, other determinants remaining constant. As has been explained above, there is inverse relationship between price of a commodity and its quantity demanded. Thus, when price of a commodity falls, its quantity demanded will increase and when its price rises, its quantity demanded will decrease. Therefore, when we express this relationship through a curve we get a downard-sloping demand curve of a commodity as shown in Figure 6.1.

The individual's demand functon in (2) above is in *general* functional form and does not show how much quantity demanded of a consumer will change following a unit change in price (P_x). For the purpose of actually estimating demand for a commodity we need a specific form of the demand function. Generally, demand function is considered to be of a *linear* form. The specific demand function of a linear form is written as

$$Q_d = a - b\,P_x \quad \ldots(3)$$

where a is a constant intercept term on the X- axis and b is the coefficient showing the slope of the demand curve. The coefficient of price (P), that is, b being negative implies that there is a negative relationship between price and quantity demanded of a commodity.

If on estimating the demand functon (3) from the information about yearly quanties demanded of sugar at its various prices by an individual consumer, we find the constant a to be equal to 70 and the constant b to be equal to 2 we can write individual's demand function as

$$Q_d = 70 - 5P \qquad \text{... (4)}$$

The above demand equation (4) is interpreted as one rupee fall in price of sugar will cause its quantity demanded to increase by 5 units of sugar and vice versa. It is this demand function that we have plotted on a graph and shown in Figure 6.1.

It should be noted that when there is a change in the other determining factors which are held constant such as income, tastes, prices of related commodities, the whole demand curve will shift. For example, if income increases, the whole demand curve will shift to the right and, on the contrary, if income decreases, the whole demand curve will shift to the left. Similarly, changes in other determining factors such as tastes, prices of related commodities, advertising expenditure cause shift in the demand curve and are therefore called ***shift factors.***

The demand function expressed in equation (1) above is of a general form and merely states the factors or variables that affect demand for a commodity. But to be useful for a manager of a firm in his decision making a demand function must be stated in explicit form which should show the precise effect on demand of changes in various individual variables. To illustrate an important form of a demand function that is generally used is the following linear form.

$$Q_d = a + b_1 P_x + b_2P_1 + b_3P_2 + b_4I + b_5I + b_6A \qquad \text{...(5)}$$

In the demand function (5), coefficient b_1, b_2, b_3, b_4 etc. shows the changes in quantity demanded of the commodity caused by one-unit change in the associated variables such as P, I T, price P_1 of a substitute, price P_2 of a complement and so on. Thus, if price of a product X is measured in rupees, the value of b will indicate the amount or quantity demanded of the commodity X resulting from a unit change in its price (P_x). For example, if $b_1 = -5$, then a fall in price of the commodity by one rupee will cause 5 units increase in the quantity demanded of the commodity. If we know the values of coefficients of various variables of the demand function for a commodity we can accurately predict the demand for that commodity in the next year or in some other future years.

LAW OF DEMAND

An important information about demand is described by the law of demand. This law of demand expresses the functional relationship between price and quantity demanded. The law of demand or functional relationship between price and quantity demanded of a commodity is one of the best known and most important laws of economic theory. ***According to the law of demand, other things being equal, if the price of a commodity falls, the quantity demanded of it will rise, and if the price of the commodity rises, its quantity demanded will decline.*** Thus, according to the law of demand, there is inverse relationship between price and quantity demanded, other things remaining the same. These other things which are assumed to be constant are the tastes and preferences of the consumer, the income of the consumer, and the prices of related goods. If these other factors which determine demand also undergo a change at the same time, then the inverse price-demand relationship may not hold good. Thus, the constancy of these other things which is generally stated as ceteris paribus is an important qualification of the law of demand.

Demand Curve and the Law of Demand. The law of demand can be illustrated through a demand schedule and a demand curve. A demand schedule of an individual consumer is presented in Table 6.1. It will be seen from this demand schedule that when the price of a commodity is Rs. 12 per unit, the consumer purchases 10 units of the commodity. When the price of the commodity falls to Rs. 10, he purchases 20 units of the commodity. Similarly, when the price further falls, quantity demanded by him goes on rising until at price Rs. 2, the quantity demanded by him rises to 60 units. We can convert this demand schedule into a demand curve by graphically plotting the various price-quantity combinations, and this has been done in Fig. 6.1 where along the X-axis, quantity demanded is measured and along the Y-axis price of the commodity is measured.

Table 6.1. Demand Schedule of an Individual Consumer

Price (Rs.)	*Quantity Demanded*
12	10
10	20
8	30
6	40
4	50
2	60

By plotting 10 units of the commodity against price 12, we get a point in Fig. 6.1. Likewise, by plotting 20 units of the commodity demanded against price 10, we get another point in Fig. 6.1. Similarly, other points are plotted representing other combinations of price and quantity demanded of the commodity and are shown in Fig. 6.1. By joining these various points, we get a curve *DD*, which is known as the demand curve. Thus, this demand curve is a graphic representation of quantities of a good which are demanded by the consumer at various possible prices in a given period of time.

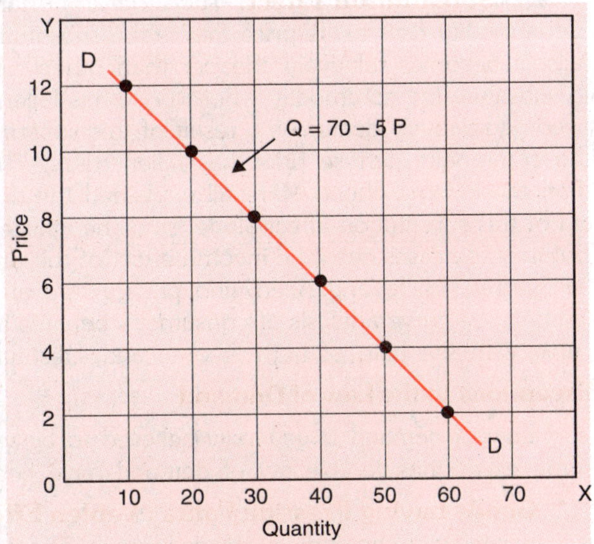

Fig. 6.1. *The Demand Curve of an Individual ($Q^d = 70 - 5P$)*

It should be noted that a demand schedule or a demand curve does not tell us what the price is; it only tells us how much quantity of the good would be purchased by the consumer at a various possible prices. Further, it will be seen from both the demand schedule and the demand curve that as the price of a commodity falls, more quantity of it is purchased or demanded. Since more is demanded at a lower price and less is demanded at a higher price, the demand curve slopes downward to the right. Thus, ***the downward-sloping demand curve is in accordance with the law of demand which, as stated above, describes inverse price-demand relationship.***

It is important to note here that behind this demand curve or price-demand relationship always lie the tastes and preferences of the consumer, his income, the prices of substitutes and complementary goods, all of which are assumed to be constant in drawing a demand curve. If any change occurs in any of these other factors, the whole demand schedule or demand curve will change and new demand schedule or a demand curve will have to be drawn. Further, in drawing a demand curve, we assume that the buyer or consumer does not exercise any influence over the price of a commodity, that is, he takes the price of the commodity as given and constant for him.

Reasons for the Law of Demand : Why does Demand Curve Slope Downward?

We have explained above that when price falls the quantity demanded of a commodity rises and *vice versa,* other things remaining the same. It is due to this law of demand that demand curve slopes downward to the right. Now, the important question is why the demand curve slopes downward, or in other words, why the law of demand which describes inverse price-demand relationship is valid. We can prove this with marginal utility analysis which we shall explain in the next chapter. It may however be mentioned here that there are two factors due to which quantity demanded increases when price falls: (1) Income effect, (2) Substitution effect.

(1) **Income Effect.** When the price of a commodity falls the consumer can buy more quantity of the commodity with his *given income.* Or, if he chooses to buy the same amount of quantity as before, some money will be left with him because he has to spend less on the commodity due to its lower price. In other words, as a result of fall in the price of a commodity, consumer's real income or purchasing power increases. This increase in real income induces the consumer to buy more of that commodity. This is called *income effect* of the change in price of the commodity. This is one reason why a consumer buys more of a commodity when its price falls.

(2) **Substitution Effect.** The other important reason why the quantity demanded of a commodity rises as its price falls is the substitution effect. When price of a conmmodity falls, it becomes relatively cheaper than other commodities . This induces the consumer to substitute the commodity whose price has fallen for other commodities which have now become relatively dearer.As a result of this *substitution effect,* the quantity demanded of the commodity, whose price has fallen, rises. This substitution effect is more important than the income effect. Marshall explained the downward-sloping demand curve with the aid of this substitution effect alone, since he ignored the income effect of the price change. But in some cases even the income effect of the price change is very significant and cannot be ignored. Hicks and Allen who put forward an alternative theory of demand called as indifference curve analysis of consumer's behaviour explain this downward-sloping demand curve with the help of both income and substitution effects.

Exceptions to the Law of Demand

Law of demand is generally believed to be valid in most of the situations. However, some exceptions to the law of demand have been pointed out.

Goods having Prestige Value : Veblen Effect. One exception to the law of demand is associated with the name of the economist, Thorstein Veblen who propounded the doctrine *of conspicuous consumption.* According to Veblen, some consumers measure the utility of a commodity entirely by its price *i.e.,* for them, the greater the price of a commodity, the greater its utility. For example, diamonds are considered as prestige good in the society and for the upper strata of the society the higher the price of diamonds, the higher the prestige value of them and therefore the greater utility or desirability of them. In this case, some consumers will buy less of the diamonds at a lower price because with the fall in price its prestige value goes down. On the other hand, when price of diamonds goes up, their prestige value goes up and therefore their utility or desirability increases. As a result, at a higher price the quantity demanded of diamonds by a consumer will rise. This is called *Veblen effect.* Besides diamonds, other goods such as mink coats, luxury cars have prestige value and Veblen effect works in their case too.

Giffen Goods. Another exception to the law of demand was pointed out by Sir Robert Giffen who observed that when price of bread increased, the low-paid British workers in the early 19th century purchased more bread and not less of it and this is contrary to the law of demand described above. The reason given for this is that these British workers consumed a diet of mainly bread and when the price of bread went up they were compelled to spend more on given quantity of bread. Therefore, they could not afford to purchase as much meat as before. Thus, they substituted even bread for meat in order to maintain their intake of food. After the name of Robert Giffen, such goods in whose case there is a direct price-demand relationship are called *Giffen goods.* It is ***important to note that with the rise in the price of a Giffen good, its quantity demand increases and with the fall in its price its quantity demanded decreases, the demand curve will slope upward to the right and not downward.***

MARKET DEMAND FUNCTION

So far we have been primarily concerned with an individual's demand for a commodity. However, for determination of price of a commodity we are more interested in the size of total market demand for the commodity. Apart from the factors affecting individual's demand such as price of a product, his income, prices of related commodities, individual's preferences, market demand for a product depends on an additional factor, namely the *number of consumers* which in turn depends on the population of a region or city or country (for which demand is being considered) who consume the product. Mathematically, market demand function of a product can be expressed in the general functional form as under.

$$Q_D = f(P_x, I, P_r, T, A, N)$$

where the additional factor is N which stands for the number of consumers or population.

As explained above, for the purpose of estimation of demand for a product we need a specific form of the above market demand function. Generally, it is the linear form which is chosen for estimating market demand function. So in the linear form, the market demand function is given below :

$$Q_D = C + b_1 P_x + b_2 I + b_3 P_y + b_4 T + b_5 A + b_6 N$$

C is a constant term which shows the intercept of the market demand curve on the X-axis. b_1, b_2, b_3 etc. are coefficients (these are generally called parameters) which show the quantitative relationship of various independent variables with the market demand. In other words, these coefficients, b_1, b_2, b_3 show how much market demand changes as a result of a unit change in various variables such as price, income, advertising expenditure, population (*i.e.*, the number of consumers).

Suppose we are interested in market demand for a specific brand of tea, say Brooke Bond Tea. We assume that tastes (T) and the number of consumers for tea (N) remain the same and further if we have estimated the coefficients of various variables determining the market demand for Brooke Bond Tea we can write market demand function for Brooke Bond Tea as follows

1. T Veblen, ***The Economics of Leisure Class.***

$$Q_D = 2.0 - 1.5\ P_x + 0.6\ I + 0.8\ P_y - 0.7\ P_s + 1.5\ A$$

where Q_D represents market demand for Brooke Bond Tea, P_x is the price of brooke bond Tea per kilogram, I is disposable per capita income of the country, P_y is the price of Tata Tea which is the competitor of Brooke Bond Tea, P_s is the price of sugar which is complementary with tea. A is advertisement expenditure made by manufacturers of Brooke Bond Tea.

From the above market demand function, it follows that change of Re. 1 of Brooke Bond Tea will cause 1.5 unit change in quantity demanded of Brooke Bond Tea. Similarly, a fall in price by one rupee of Tata Tea, a competing product, will cause 0.8 unit reduction in quantity demanded of Brooke Bond Tea. On the other hand, one rupee fall in price of sugur will cause 0.7 unit change in the quantity demanded of Brooke Bond Tea and similarly for other variables. Given these values of the coefficients, if we write the values of defferent determining variables such as price of Brooke Bond Tea, per capita personal disposable income, price of sugur (P_s) we can calculate the change in market demand for Brooke Bond Tea.

As pointed out in case of individual demand, in economics it is considered important and useful to focus on the relationship between quantity demanded of a product and its price, holding other factors constant. Therefore, if income (*I*), prices of other related commodities (P_r), tastes or preferences of the people (*T*), advertising expenditure are held constant at certain given values, the market demand function can be written as

$$Q_D = a - b_1 P_x$$

where a is the constant term in the function or intercept of the market demand curve on the *X*-axis, b_1 is the coefficient which indicates how much quantity demanded of product *X* in the market will change as a result of a unit change in its own price, other factors held constant.

The above demand function ($Q_D = a - bP_x$ or specifically $Q_D = 70 - 5P$ shows how the change in price of a commodity affects the quantity demanded of it and is called **direct demand function.** In economics we are also interested in knowning how a change in quantity affects the price of a commodity, that is, ***price as a function of quantity demanded*** of a commodity and is called **inverse demand function.** Thus manipulating the direct demand function, $Q^d = 70 - 5\ P_x$ we get the following inverse demand function.

$$P_x = 14 - 0.20\ Q_d$$

Market Demand Curve

We have drawn above an individual's demand curve of a commodity. We can graphically obtain the market demand curve by making horizontal addition of the demand curves of all individuals buying the commodity. In order to do so we add the various quantities demanded by the number of consumers in the market. In this way we can obtain the *market demand curve* for a commodity which like the individual consumer's demand curve will slope downward to the right. How this summation is done is illustrated in Fig. 6.2. Suppose there are two individual buyers of a good in the market. Fig. 6.2 (*a*) and (*b*) show the demand curves of the two independent individual buyers. Now, the market demand curve can be obtained by adding together the amounts of the goods which individuals wish to buy at each price. Thus, at price P_1, the individual A wishes to buy 2 units of the goods; individual *B* wishes to buy 3 units of the goods. The total quantity of the goods that the two individuals plan to buy at price P_1 is therefore 2 + 3 = 5, which is equal to OQ_1 in Fig. 6.2(*c*).

Now, as shall be seen from the figure, at price OP_2, individual *A* demands 4 units and individual *B* demands 6 units of the commodity. So the market demand at price OP_2 of the commodity is 4 + 6 = 10 units or OQ_2. Similarly, we can plot the quantity of the goods that

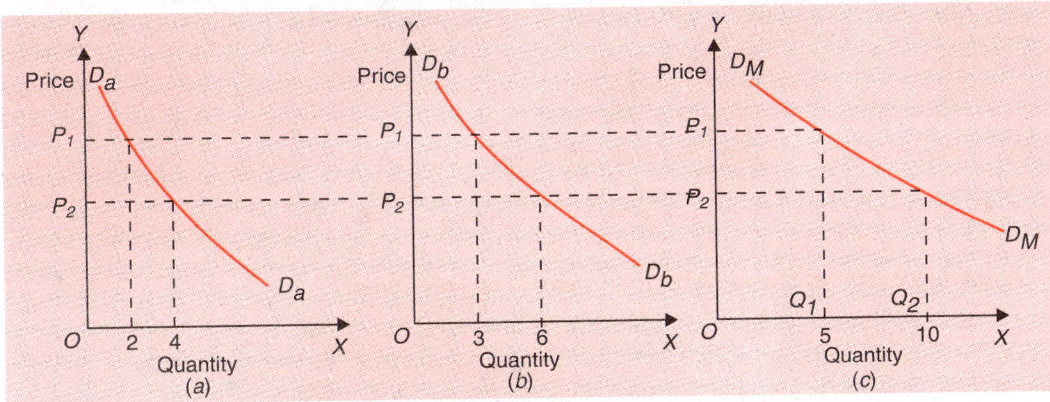

Fig. 6.2. *Horizontal Addition of Individual Demand Curves to get Market Demand Curve*

will be demanded by the two individuals at every other price of the good. When all the points showing the amounts demanded of the good by the two individuals at various prices are joined we get a market demand curve for the goods. For the sake of convenience we have supposed that there are two individuals or buyers in the market for a good. Whatever be the number of individuals in the market, their demand curves can be added together, as illustrated above, to get a market demand curve for the good.

The market demand curve slopes downward to the right, since the individual demand curves whose lateral summation gives us the market demand curve, normally slope downward to the right. Besides, as the price of the goods falls, it is very likely that the new buyers will enter the market and will further raise the quantity demanded of the goods. This is another reason why the market demand curve slopes downward to the right.

As in case of individuals' demand curves, factors other than price which affect market demand such as prices of related goods, per capital income of the individuals, their preferences for goods, number of consumers, etc are held constant while drawing the demand curve.

INDIVIDUAL DEMAND FUNCTIONS AND MARKET DEMAND FUNCTION

Market Demand Function

Adding up Individual Demand Functions. Demand for commodity by an individual depends on price of the commodity, his income, prices of related commodities. A simple demand function is expressed in terms of own price of the commodity, keeping other factors constant. Thus, such a linear demand function is

$$Q_A = 40 - 2P \qquad \ldots(i)$$

where Q_A is the quantity demanded of the commodity by individual A and *P* is the price of the commodity in rupees and 40 is constant (the intercept term). The above demand function shows that a rise in price of the commodity by one rupee causes 2 units decrease in quantity demanded by the individual A and vice-versa.

Likewise, demand functions of individuals *B* and *C* are as under :

$$Q_B = 25.5 - 0.75P \qquad \ldots(ii)$$
$$Q_C = 36.5 - 1.25P \qquad \ldots(iii)$$

If we are now required to determine the market demand for the commodity when there are above three individuals demanding the commodity, how will we do it ?

Note that market demand (Q_m) is the *sum* of the demands of indviduals who want to purchase the commodity.

Thus,

$$Q_m = Q_A + Q_B = Q_C = (40.0 - 2P) + (25.5 - 0.75P) + (36.5 - 1.25P)$$
$$= 40.0 + 25.5 + 36.5 - (2 + 0.75 + 1.25) P$$
$$= 102 - 4P$$

If P is in rupees, the market demand function shows that rise in price of the commodity by one rupee will result in fall in its quantity demanded by 4 units.

Relationship between Demand Function and Demand Curve

It is important to know the relationship between demand function and demand curve. While a complete demand function specifies the relationship between quantity demanded of a product and many variables such as the own price of the product, income of consumers, prices of related commodities, tastes and preferences, expected future prices etc. ($Q_x{}^d = f(P_x, I, P_x, T, A, N)$), the demand curve is a graphic representation of only a part of this demand function, namely, $Q_x{}^d = f(P)$, holding other independent variables in the demand function as constant. That is, while drawing a demand curve values of other variables in the demand function are kept constant at *particular levels*. The complete demand function with many variables cannot be shown by the two dimensional curve, the effect of changes in other variables or factors on the quantity demanded of a product is shown by shifts

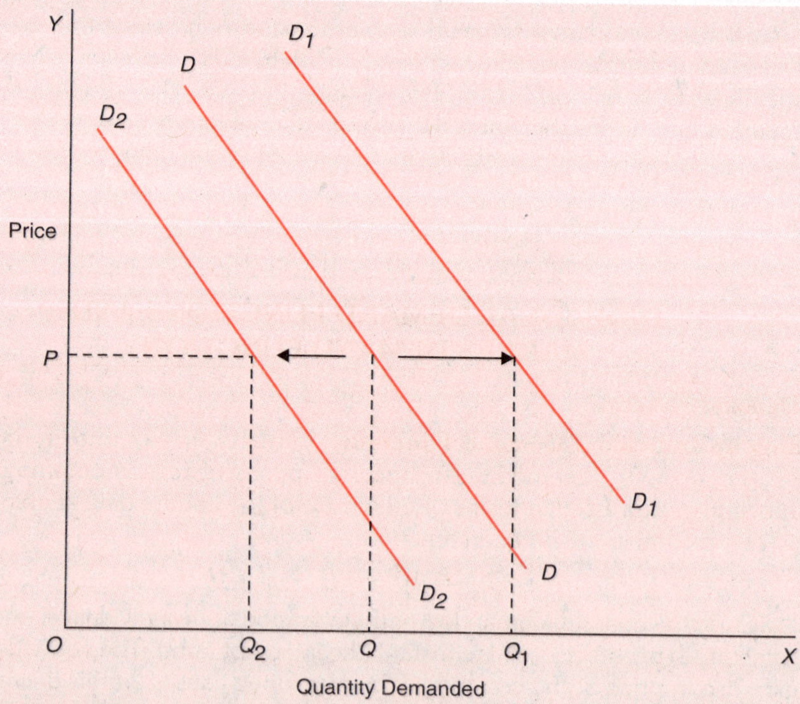

Fig. 6.3. *Shifts in Demand curve due to Changes in Variables other than Price*

in the whole demand curve. This is illustrated in Figure 6.3. To begin with *DD* is the market demand curve. Now, suppose income of consumers increases, say due to the hike in their wages and salaries. As a result, they will demand more of a product at each price causing a shift in the demand curve to the right as from *DD* to D_1D_1 in Figure 6.3. It will be seen that at a given price *OP*, with demand curve *DD* the consumers were buying *OQ* quantity of the product and with rightward shift in the demand curve to D_1D_1 they demand greater quantity OQ_1 of the product. Similarly, at other prices more is demanded at D_1D_1 as compared to the demand curve *DD*.

Similarly, increase in price of a substitute of a product, favourable change in preferences of consumers for a product, expectations of rise in price of a product in future will cause increase in the quantity demanded of a product and will therefore lead to the shift in demand curve for the product to the right.

On the other hand, decrease in consumers' income, fall in price of a substitute product, unfavourable change in consumers' preference for the product, aggressive advertisement expenditure by competitive firms will cause a decrease in demand for the product resulting in leftward shift in the demand curve from *DD* to D_2D_2. With lower demand curve D_2D_2 at each price consumers will demand less quantity of the product than before. Thus at price *OP* on demand curve D_2D_2 the consumers would now demand OQ_2 quantity of the product which is smaller than OQ.

To conclude, whereas demand function specifies relationship between quantity demanded of a product with many independent variables, demand curve of a product is a graphic representation of only a part of the demand function with price of the product as the only independent variable. The effects of change in variables other than price, as explained above, are shown through a shift in the demand curve.

FACTORS DETERMINING DEMAND

We have explained above how the demand changes as a result of changes in price, other factors determining it being held constant. We shall explain below in detail how these other factors determine market demand for a commodity. These other factors determine the position or level of demand curve of a commodity. It may be noted that when there is a change in these non-price factors, the whole curve shifts rightward or leftward as the case may be. The following factors determine market demand for a commmodity.

1. Tastes and Preferences of the Consumers. An important factor which determines the demand for a good is the tastes and preferences of the consumers for it. A good for which consumers' tastes and preferences are greater, its demand would be large and its demand curve will therefore lie at a higher level. People's tastes and preferences for various goods often change and as a result there is change in demand for them. The changes in demand for various goods occur due to the changes in fashion and also due to the pressure of advertisements by the manufacturers and sellers of different products. On the contrary, when certain goods go out of fashion or people's tastes and preferences no longer remain favourable to them, the demand for them decreases.

2. Income of the People. The demand for goods also depends upon the incomes of the people. The greater the incomes of the people, the greater will be their demand for goods. In drawing the demand schedule or the demand curve for a good we take income of the people as given and constant. When as a result of the rise in the income of the people, the demand increases, the whole of the demand curve shifts upward and *vice versa*. The greater income means the greater purchasing power. Therefore, when incomes of the people increase, they can afford to buy more. It is because of this reason that increase in income has a positive effect on the demand for a good. When the incomes of the people fall, they would demand less of a good and as a result the demand curve will shift downward. For instance, as a result of economic growth in India the incomes of the people have greatly increased owing to the large investment expenditure on the development schemes by the Government and the private sector. As a result of this increase in incomes, the demand for goodgrains and other consumer goods has greatly increased. Likewise, when because of drought in a year the agriculture production greatly falls, the incomes of the farmers decline. As a result of the decline in incomes of the farmers, they will demand less of the cotton cloth and other manufactured products.

3. Changes in Prices of the Related Goods. The demand for a good is also affected by the prices of other goods, especially those which are related to it as substitutes or complements. When we draw the demand schedule or the demand curve for a good we take the prices of the related goods as remaining constant. Therefore, when the prices of the related goods, substitutes or complements, change, the whole demand curve would change its position; it will shift upward or downward as the case may be. ***When the price of a substitute for a good falls, the demand for that good will decline and when the price of the substitute rises, the demand for that good will increase.*** For example, when price of tea and incomes of the people remain the same but the price of coffee falls, the consumers would demand less of tea than before. Tea and coffee are very close substitutes. Therefore, when coffee becomes cheaper, the consumers substitute coffee for tea and as a result the demand for tea declines. The goods which are complementary with each other, the fall in the price of any of them would favourably affect the demand for the other. For instance, if price of milk falls, the demand for sugar would also be favourably affected. When people would take more milk, the demand for sugar will also increase. Likewise, when the price of cars falls, the quantity demanded of them would increase which in turn will increase the demand for petrol.

4. Advertisement Expenditure. Advertisement expenditure made by a firm to promote the sales of its product is an important factor determining demand for a product, especially of the product of the firm which gives advertisements. The purpose of advertisement is to influence the consumers in favour of a product. Advertisements are given in various media such as newspapers, radio, television. Advertisements for goods are repeated several times so that consumers are convinced about their superior quality. When advertisements prove successful they cause an increase in the demand for the product.

5. The Number of Consumers in the Market. We have already explained that the market demand for a good is obtained by adding up the individual demands of the present as well as prospective consumers of a good at various possible prices. The greater the number of consumers of a good, the greater the market demand for it. Now, the question arises on what factors the number of consumers for a good depends. If the consumers substitute one good for another, then the number of consumers for the good which has been substituted by the other will decline and for the good which has been used in place of the others, the number of consumers will increase. Besides, when the seller of a good succeeds in finding out new markets for his good and as a result the market for his good expands, the number of consumers for that good will increase. Another important cause for the increase in the number of consumers is the growth in population. For instance, in India the demand for many essential goods, especially foodgrains, has increased because of the increase in the population of the country and the resultant increase in the number of consumers for them.

6. Consumers' Expectations with Regard to Future Prices. Another factor which influences the demand for goods is consumers' expectations with regard to future prices of the goods. If due to some reason, consumers expect that in the near future prices of the goods would rise, then in the present they would demand greater quantities of the goods so that in the future they should not have to pay higher prices. Similarly, when the consumers expect that in the future the prices of goods will fall, then in the present they will postpone a part of the consumption of goods with the result that their present demand for goods will decrease.

Increase in Demand and Shifts in Demand Curve

When demand changes due to the factors other than price, there is a shift in the whole demand curve. As mentioned above, apart from price, demand for a commodity is determined by incomes of the consumers, his tastes and preferences, prices of related goods. Thus, when there is any change in these factors, it will cause a shift in demand curve. For example, if incomes of the consumers increase, say due to the hike in their wages and salaries or due to the grant of dearness allowance, they will demand more of a good, say cloth, at each price. This will cause a shift in the demand curve to the right. Similarly, if preferences of the people for a commodity, say colour TV, become greater, their demand for colour TV will increase, that is, the demand curve will shift to the right and, therefore, at each price they will demand more colour TV.

The other important factor which can cause an increase in demand for a commodity is the expectations about future prices. If people expect that price of a commodity is likely to go up in future, they will try to purchase the commodity, especially a durable one, in the current period which will boost the current demand for the goods and cause a shift in the demand curve to the right. As seen above, the prices of related commodities such as substitutes and complements can also change the demand for a commodity. For example, if the price of coffee rises, other factors remaining the constant, this will cause the demand for tea, a substitute for coffee, to increase and its demand curve to shift to the right.

Decrease in Demand and Shift in the Demand Curve

If there are adverse changes in the factors influencing demand, it will lead to the decrease in demand causing a shift in the demand curve to the left as shown in Fig. 6.3. For eample, if due to inadequate rainfall agricultural production in a year declines, this will cause a fall in the incomes of the farmers. This fall incomes of the farmers will cause a decrease in the demand for industrial products, say cloth, and will result in a shift in the demand curve to the left. Similarly, change in preferences for commodities can also affect the demand. For example, when colour TVs came to India people's greater preference for them led to the increase in their demand. But this brought about decrease in demand for black and white TVs causing leftward shift in demand curve for these black and white TVs. The decrease in demand does not occur due to the rise in price but due to the changes in other determinants of demand. Decrease in demand for a commodity may occur due to the fall in the prices of its substitutes, rise in the prices of complements of that commodity and if the people expect that price of a good will fall in future.

DEMAND FOR DURABLE GOODS

Nature of demand for durable goods is of special interest in demand theory. Demand for durable goods is more volatile than the demand for non-durable goods. ***In economics durable goods are defined as those goods that go on yielding services to the consumers over a number of periods in future.*** Further, because of their durability they can be stored for longer periods of time. It is due to the use of services of durable goods for a relatively long term that consumers' demand for them is more volatile, that is, fluctuates very much.

Now what accounts for the large volatility in demand for durable goods. First, since durable goods can be stored, producers, distributors and consumers usually keep a large inventories of such goods. Therefore, increase in demand for them may not show up in more production of such goods for quite some time because the greater demand for them can be met by drawing upon their inventories. On the other hand, when inventories of durable goods are low even a small increase in demand for them by their consumers may actually lead to greater market demand because producers and distributors would also tend to increase their demand for holding more inventories to accommodate their large demand in future.

The other factor responsible for volatility in demand for durable goods is that *replacement of these durable goods can be deferred* by undertaking additional maintenance expenditure on existing durable goods possessed by them. For example, an old car may be got replaced or its old model may be used for a longer period. Similarly, the purchase of new furniture may be postponed by tolerating the use of old furniture for one more year. Thus, analysis of demand for durable goods must consider not only new consumers' demand for them but also consider the need for building up their inventories by distributors and producers and replacement demand for them which may be deferred. It is not mere physical deterioration which calls for replacement of durable goods but more important is the fact that models of the durable goods being currently used may go out of fashion and therefore lose their prestige value.

However, the important difference between non-durable and durable goods is that non-durables are purchased for current consumption only, whereas durables are demanded for getting their services in future periods. Consequently, their demand for them crucially depends on consumers' expectations regarding their future incomes, especially when they buy them on credit, availability of these durables in future, expectations regarding future prices, rate of change in technology that make them obsolete. Thus, fluctuations in demand for durables is relatively greater as it depends on expectations of consumers about future developments. If the expectations of consumers are such that prices of durables will rise in future due to their short supply, their demand for them will increase not only to meet their current consumption needs but also for storing them for future use. Similarly, if consumers expect their prices will fall in future, they will postpone their purchases resulting in large decline in their demand.

Derived Demand

There are some goods which are not demanded by individuals to satisfy their wants directly but for using them to produce other consumer goods which directly satisfy their wants. Demand for them is called derived demand as its is derived from the demand for other goods. Thus, demand for car and housing loans is not determined directly but is derived from the demand for cars or houses which are purchased with the loan money. However, the important case of derived demand is demand for producers' goods such as raw materials, machines and other types of capital equipment, spare parts etc. These producers goods are not consumed directly by individuals to satisfy their wants. For example, demand for copper does not solely depend on individuals' desire for copper itself but rather for using it to produce products which are wholly or partly made of copper. In fact individuals, wants for them may be quite independent of the fact that copper is used in their production.

Therefore, for the analysis of demand for the products for which there is derived demand we must consider the factors that affect demand for altimate goods in the production of which producer goods are used.

NETWORK EXTERNALITIES : BANDWAGON EFFECT AND SNOB EFFECT

In our analysis of demand we have assumed that demand for goods of different individuals are independent of one and another. That is, demand for Pepsi by Amit depends on his own tastes, his income, price of Pepsi etc and does not depend on Swati or Amitab Bachchan's demand for Pepsi. The ***assumption of independence of demands of different individuals*** enabled us to derive a market demand curve for a good by simply summing up horizontally the demands of different individuals consuming a good. However, in the real world, demand for some goods of an individual depends on other individuals' demand for them. In such cases of interdependence of demands of different individuals economists say *network externalities* are present. Network externalities may be positive or negative. ***Network externalities are a special kind of externalities in which one individual's utility for a good depends on the number of other people who consume the commodity.*** For example, a consumer's demand for 'telephone' depends on the number of other people owning the telephone connections. People wants telephone connection so that they can communicate with each other. If no one else has a telephone connection, it is certainly not useful for you to demand a telephone connection. The same applies to demand for fax machines, mobile phones, modems, internet connection etc. Internet connection is very useful to you if there are some other individuals or institutions have internet facilities with whom you can communicate.

Network externalities can arise through a fashion or stylishness. The desire or demand for wearing jeans by girls is influenced by the number of other girls who have chosen to wear them. Wearing jeans have become a fashion among the college going girls at metropolitan cities in India. To be in keeping with the fashion, more and more girls have opted for wearing jeans. This has led to the increase in demand for jeans. However, it may be noted that network effects here go two ways. It is better if there are some others who have adopted the fashion, but if too many people go in for this, the fashion falls out of style and this adversely affects the demand for the good by others.

Another type of network externalities arises in case of complementary goods. The intrinsic value of a good is greater if its complementary good is available. Thus, it is not worthwhile to open a CD discs store in a locality if only one person in the area has a CD player. If the number of people owning CD players increases significantly, desire for opening CD (discs) store or for manufacturing CD (discs) will increase. Thus, the more the number of individuals who own CD players, the more CD (discs) will be produced. In this case the demand for CD players depends on the number of CD (discs) available and the demand for CD discs depends on the number of people having CD players., Thus this is a more general form of positive network externalities.

Bandwagon Effect[2]

The existence of positive network externalities gives rise to Bandwagon effect. ***Bandwagon effect refers to the desire or demand for a good by a person who wants to be in style because possession of a good is in fashion and therefore many others have it.*** It may be noted that this bandwagon effect is the important objective of marketing and advertising strategies of several manufacturing companies who appeal to go in for a good as people of style are buying it.

2. Bandwagon effect and Snob effect were introduced in economic theory by Harvey Lebstein. See his Bandwagon Effect, Snob Effect and Veblen Effect and Consumer Behavour, in *Quarterly Journal of Economics* Vol. 62, (Feb. 1948) pp. 165-201.

Let us explain how to derive a demand curve for a good incorporating the bandwagon effect. This is illustrated in Figure 6.4 on whose X-axis, we measure the number of units of a good in question. Suppose consumers think that only 10 thousand people in Delhi have purchased the good. This is a relatively small number of people compared to the total population of Delhi. So the other people have little incentive to buy the good to satisfy their instinct of living in style. However, some people may still purchase because it has a intrinsic value for them. In this case the demand for the good is given by the demand curve D_{10}. Now suppose that they think that 20 thousand people have purchased the good. This increases the attractiveness of the good for them. As a result, they are induced to buy more of the good to keep themselves to live in fashion or style.

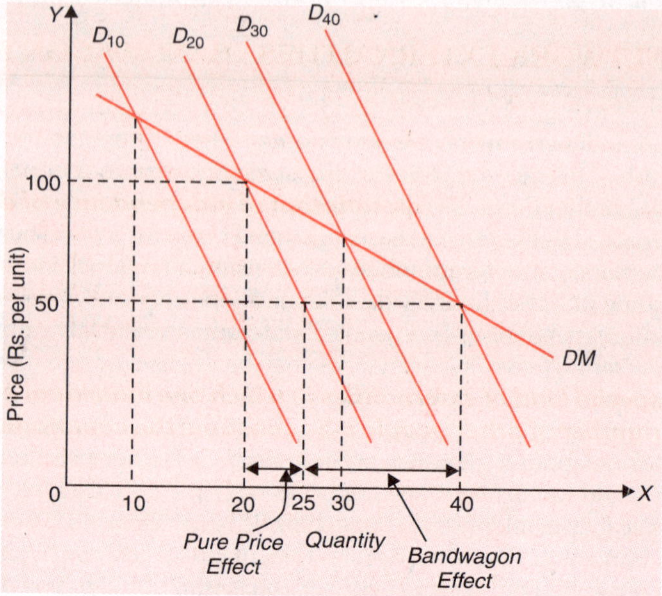

Fig. 6.4. *Bandwagon Effect*

This leads to the increase in the demand for the good which causes the demand curve for the good to shift to the right, say to D_{20}. If the people believe that 30 thousand people have purchased the good in question, this further raises the attractiveness of the good and as a result people's demand curve for the good further shifts to the right, say to D_{30}. Thus, more the number of people the consumers find have bought the good, the greater the demand for the good in question and further to the right demand curve for the good lies. This is a bandwagon effect. Thus, ***a bandwagon effect is an example of a positive network externality in which the quantity demanded of a good that an individual buys increases in response to the increase in the quantity purchased by other individuals.***

In due course of time people come to know how many people actually buy the good. However, in addition to the bandwagon effect, the quantity demanded of the good depends on the price of the good. If price of the good in question is Rs. 100, and at it 20 thousand people buy 20 thousand units of the good, the relevant demand curve is D_{20}. Now, if the price of the good falls to Rs. 50, 40 thousand people buy 40 thousand units of the good and the relevant demand curve is D_{40}. Thus, actual market *demand curve* D_M incorporating the Bandwagon effect *is obtained by joining the points on the demand curves* D_{10}, D_{20}, D_{30}, D_{40} *that correspond to the quantities 10 thousand, 20 thousand, 30 thousand and 40 thousand units of the good.*

It should be noted that the movement along the demand curves D_{10}, D_{20}, D_{30}, and D_{40} individually represent how much quantity of a commodity is demanded at various prices if no bandwagon effect is operating. Thus, if price of a good falls from Rs. 100 to Rs. 50 per unit, the quantity demanded of the good will increase to 25 units of the good along a given demand curve D_{20} as a result of pure price effect when no bandwagon effect is working. However, actually as a result of fall in price and resultant increase in the quantity purchased of the good by others has created a bandwagon effect and as a result at price of Rs. 50 per unit, quantity bought of the good increases to 40 thousand units. Thus, the 15 thousand units increase in the the quantity demanded is the result of bandwagon effect. It is also evident from this analysis that bandwagon effect makes the demand curve more elastic. It will be seen that demand curve D_M which incorporates the bandwagon effect is more elastic than the demand curves D_{10}, D_{20}, D_{30} and D_{40}.

Snob Effect

In case network externalities are negative, snob effect arises. ***Snob effect refers to the desire to possess a unique commodity having a prestige value.*** Snob effect works quite contrary to the bandwagon effect. The quantity demanded of a commodity having a snob value is greater, the *smaller* the number of people owning its. Rare works of art, specially designed sport cars, specially designed clothing made to order, very expensive luxury cars. For example, the utility one gets from a very expensive luxury car is mainly due to the presitge and status value of it ***which results from the fact that only few others own it.***

Snob effect is illustrated in Figure 6.5 where on the X-axis we measure the quantity demanded of a snob good and on the y-axis price of the good in lakhs (Rs.).

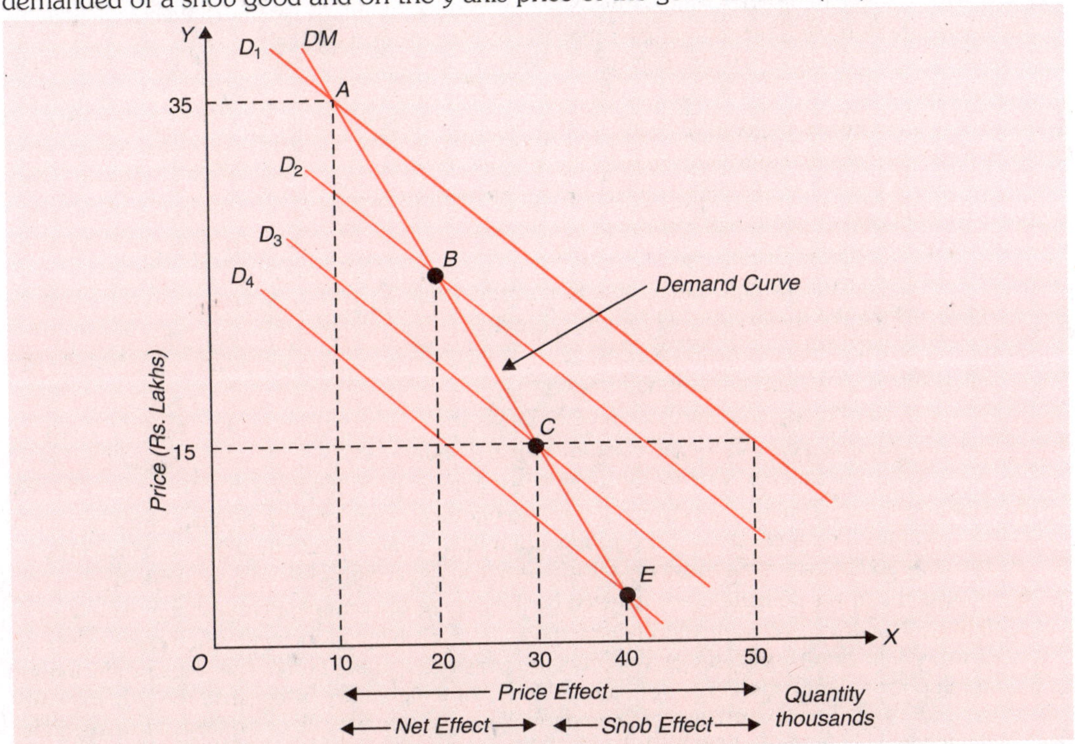

Fig. 6.5. *Negative Externality and Snob Effect*

Suppose D_1 is the relevant demand curve when people think that one thousand people own the commodity having a snob value. Now suppose that people think that 20 thousand people are having this good, its snob-value is lowered and as a result demand for the good decreases and demand curve shifts to the left to D_2 position. Again, if people believe that 30 thousand people happen to own the commodity, its snob value or prestige value is further reduced. As a result, desire or demand for it is further reduced and demand curve further shifts to the left. Further, if it is thought that 40 thousand people possess the good, the relevant demand curve is D_4. Thus, as a result of snob effect, the quantity demanded of the good falls as more people are believed to own it. Ultimately people come to know how many people actually own the good. If we join the points *A, B, C* and *E* which represent the quantities demanded at different number of people owning the commodity and thus incorporating snob effect we have the market demand curve D_M.

It is important to note that snob effect makes the demand curve less elastic. Thus at price Rs. 35 lakhs per luxury car, its quantity demand is 10 thousands. Now, if price is reduced to Rs. 15 lakhs per luxury car, its quantity demanded would increase to 50 thousands per year, and if snob effect was not present we had moved down more along the demand curve D_1 But in the presence of snob effect quantity demand increases from 10 thousand to only 30 thousand cars. Thus, in Figure 6.5 the snob effect has reduced the full effect of the fall in price so that net effect is the increase in quantity demanded from 10 thousand to 30 thousand units.

QUESTIONS AND PROBLEMS FOR REVIEW

1. Distinguish between a demand function and demand curve. What are the factors that cause a shift in the demand curve?
2. Distinguish between the movement along a demand curve and shift in the demand curve.
3. State the law of demand. How would you explain it with substitution effect and income effect? Are there any exceptions to this law?
4. Given the following market demand function for the commodity X

   $$Q_x = f(P_x, P_y, P_z, I, T, A)$$

   where

   P_x = Price of the commodity *X*
   P_y = Price of a substitute commodity *Y*
   P_z = Price of commodity *Z* which is complement of *X*
   I = Level of per capita income of consumers
   T = Tastes and preferences of consumers
   A = Advertising expenditure by a firm producing *X*

   How will the consumer demand for a commodity *X* change ?

   (*i*) if price of the commodity *X* rises,
   (*ii*) if price of the substitute good *Y* rises,
   (*iii*) if price of complementary commodity Z falls,
   (*iv*) per capita income (*I*) of the consumers rises, and
   (*v*) the firm producing *X* increases its advertisement expenditure.
5. Distinguish between industry demand curve and demand curve for the product of a single firm. Do you think demand curve for the product of a firm is more elastic than the demand curve for the commodity facing the industry? Give reasons.
6. How is the firm's demand curve affected by the degree of competition existing in its industry? (**Hint :** The degree of competition depends on the availability of substitutes and number of rival firms. When close substitutes of a product are available and the number of firms producing the commodity is very large, degree of competition is very high and consequently the demand curve for a firm's product is very elastic. When perfect competition prevails and different firms produce homogeneous product which are perfect substitutes of each other, though the demand curve for the industry as a whole slopes downward, demand curve for a firm is perfectly elastic at the price determined by the intersection of demand curve for industry and supply curve of the industry.)
7. What are the factors which determine market demand for a commodity? Explain what additional factors affect demand for individual firm's product.
8. Exaplain the nature of demand for durable goods. What factors are responsible for higher volatility in demand for them?
9. What is meant by derived demand? How is demand for producer goods a derived demand?
10. What is bandwagon effect and snob effect? How do they affect the demand for goods?
11. Explain 'Giffen Paradox' and Veblen Effect. Does usual law of demand apply in their case?

CHAPTER

7

Consumer's Behaviour : Cardinal Utility Analysis

Introduction

The price of a product depends upon the demand for and the supply of it. In this part of the book we are concerned with the theory of consumer's behaviour, which explains his demand for a good and the factors determining it. Individual's demand for a product depends upon price of the product, income of the individual, the prices of related goods. It can be put in the following functional form:

$$D_x = f(P_x, I, P_y, P_z, T \text{ etc.})$$

where D_x stands for the demand of good X, P_x for price of good X, I for individual's income, P_y, P_z, for the prices of related goods and T for tastes and preferences of the individual. But among these determinants of demand, economists single out price of the good in question as the most important factor governing the demand for it. Indeed, the function of a theory of consumer's behaviour is to establish a relationship between quantity demanded of a good and its own price and to provide an explanation for it. From time to time, different theories have been advanced to explain consumer's demand for a good and to derive a valid demand theorem. Cardinal utility analysis is the oldest theory of demand which provides an explanation of consumer's demand for a product and derives the law of demand which establishes an inverse relationship between price and quantity demanded of a product. Recently, cardinal utility approach to the theory of demand has been subjected to severe criticisms and as a result some alternative theories, namely, ***Indifference Curve Analysis, Samuelson's Revealed Preference Theory, and Hicks' Logical Weak Ordering Theory*** have been propounded. We shall discuss indifference curve analysis of demand revealed preference approach and Hicks's logical weak ordering theory of demand in the next few chapters, while in the present chapter we shall be concerned with the cardinal utility analysis of consumer's demand. Though cardinal utility approach to the theory of demand is very old, its final shape emerged at the hands of Alfred Marshall. Therefore, it is Marshallian cardinal utility analysis of demand which has been discussed in this chapter.

THE CONCEPT OF UTILITY

Which combination of goods from the given opportunity set, the consumer will choose depends on utilities he gets from different combinations of goods. While making a decision, the consumer weights the utility of different goods. ***Utility is defined as satisfaction that a consumer derives from consuming a good or combination of goods.*** When an individual has a desire for a good or service and when he gets it and consumes it, his desire is fulfilled. Thus utility was also defined as "fulfillment of desire". Besides, an English philosopher Jeremy Benthan (1748–1832), defined utility as the property of a good that provides pleasure or happiness to the people and in this way promotes their welfare. The goal of the society, according to him, is the achievement of *the greatest happiness* of the greatest number.

Though, the economists called as utilitarians believed that utility was a psychic feeling, they thought it can be measured directly in cardinal terms with some kind of psychological or imaginary units called "*utils*". However, Alfred Marshall provided a measure of utility in cardinal terms in a different and relatively better way. According to him, the utility of a quantity of a good is the amount of money that a consumer is *willing to pay for it* instead of defining in terms of subjective units of 'utils'.

However, prior to Marshall, William Stanley Jevons (1835–82) extended Bentham's utility concept to explain consumer's behaviour. He conceived utility as value that a consumer places on a good. The major contribution of Jevons has been his contribution to development of marginal utility analysis. He demonstrated that rational consumers in their decision making regarding choice of goods for consumption would take into account the marginal utility of each good. It is Jevon's pioneering work together with Carl Menger, Leon Walras and Alfred Marshall that led to the neoclassical revolution that established the marginal analysis as the core of economics.

Ordinal Utility: It may however be noted that the cardinal concept of utility was subjected to severe criticism by renowned English economist J.R. Hicks who pointed out that one could not preisely read consumer's mind and measure utility in cardinal terms. He put forward the concept of ordinal utility according to which a person could give only *ranking* or *order* (that is, I, II, III etc.) to the utilities he derived from various goods or combination of goods. Hicks explained his concept of ordinal utility through indifference curves. With his indifference curves Hicks explained how a consumer's choice could be explained without measuring marginal utility cardinally. In fact, according to him, to explain consumers' choice cardinal measurement of utility was not required; only measuring utility in ordinal terms was sufficient. We will explain Hick's indifference curve analysis of consumer's behaviour in detail in a later chapter.

AMARTYA SEN'S CRITIQUE OF THE CONCEPT OF UTILITY

It is worth mentioning that utility defined as satisfaction, happiness or fulfillment of a desire which has been considered as a measure of welfare or well-being in neoclassical economics has been criticised by Amartya Sen. According to him, utility defined as psychic satisfaction or desire fulfillment, happiness or pleasure does not correctly measure welfare or well-being of the deprived sections of the society who have psychologically adjusted to persistent exploitation and therefore may derive a higher psychological satisfaction from small gains accruing to them. He is of the view that it is not correct to identify welfare or well-being with utility. To quote him, ***"To judge the well-being of a person exclusively in metric of hapiness or desire fulfillment has some obvious limitations.*** These limitations are particularly damaging in the context of interpersonal comparison of well-being".[1] He is of the view that people living a life of great misfortune with little hope and opportunities may get more utility or happiness even from small gains. But that should not be interpreted that there is significant improvement in their well-being. To quote him again, "The hopeless beggar, precarious landless labourers, the dominant housewife, the hardened unemployed or the over-exhausted coolie may all take pleasures in small mercies and manage to suppress intense suffering for the necessity of contunued survival but it could be ethically deeply mistaken to attach correspondingly small value to the loss of their welfare because of their survival strategy".[2]

---

1. Amartya Sen, *On the Ethics and Economics*, Oxford University Press, 1990, p. 31-32.
2. *Ibid*, p. 45-46.

The same problem, according to Sen, arises in the case of desire fulfillment because the hopelessly deprived lack the courage to desire much and their deprivation are muted and deadened in scale of desire fulfillment.

Despite the shortcomings of the concept of utility, we will confine ourselves to using utility as satisfaction derived by the consumers from consumption of goods. The goal of the consumer is to maximise his satisfaction subjected to his budget constraint.

Assumptions of Cardinal Utility Analysis

Cardinal utility analysis of demand is based upon certain important assumptions. Before explaining how cardinal utility analysis explains consumer's equilibrium in regard to the demand for a good, it is essential to describe the basic assumptions on which the whole utility analysis rests. As we shall see later, cardinal utility analysis has been criticised because of its unrealistic assumptions. The basic assumptions or premises of cardinal utility analysis are as follows:

The Cardinal Measurability of Utility. The exponents of cardinal utility analysis regard utility to be a cardinal concept. In other words, they hold that utility is a measurable and quantifiable entity. According to them, a person can express utility or satisfaction he derives from the goods in the quantitative cardinal terms. Thus, a person can say that he derives utility equal to 10 units from the consumption of a unit of good *A*, and 20 units from the consumption of a unit of good *B*. Moreover, the cardinal measurement of utility implies that a person can compare utilities derived from goods in respect of size, that is, how much one level of utility is greater than another. A person can say that the utility he gets from the consumption of one unit of good *B* is double the utility he obtains from the consumption of one unit of good *A*.

According to Marshall, marginal utility ***is actually measurable in terms of money.***[3] Money represents the general purchasing power and it can therefore be regarded as a command over alternative utility-yielding goods. Marshall argues that the amount of money which a person is prepared to pay for a unit of a good rather than go without it is a measure of the utility he derives from that good. Thus, according to him, money is the measuring rod of utility. Some economists belonging to the cardinalist school measure utility in imaginary units called "utils". They assume that a consumer is capable of saying that one apple provides him utility equal to 4 utils. Further, on this ground, he can say that he gets twice as much utility from an apple as compared to an orange.

The Hypothesis of Independent Utilities. The second important tenet of the cardinal utility analysis is the hypothesis of *independent utilities*. On this hypothesis, the utility which a consumer derives from a good is the function of the quantity of that good and of that good only. In other words, the utility which a consumer obtains from a good does not depend upon the quantity consumed of other goods; it depends upon the quantity purchased of that good alone. On this assumption, then the total utility which a person gets from the whole collection of goods purchased by him is simply the total sum of the separate utilities of the goods. Thus, the cardinalist school regards utility as ***'additive'***, that is, separate utilities of different goods can be added to obtain the total sum of the utilities of all goods purchased.

Constancy of the Marginal Utility of Money. Another important assumption of the cardinal utility analysis is the constancy of the marginal utility of money. Thus, while the cardinal utility analysis assumes that marginal utilities of commodities diminish as more of them are purchased or consumed, but the marginal utility of money remains constant throughout when the individual is spending money on a good and due to which the amount of money with him

---

3. Emil Kauder, *A History of Marginal Utility Theory*, (Princeton, New Jersy, 1965). p. 120.

varies. Daniel Bernoulli first of all introduced this assumption but later Marshall adopted this in his famous book "***Principles of Economics***'. As stated above, Marshall measured marginal utilities in terms of money. But measurement of marginal utility of goods in terms of money is only possible if the marginal utility of money itself remains constant. It should be noted that the assumption of constant marginal utility of money is very crucial to the Marshallian analysis, because otherwise Marshall could not measure the marginal utilities of goods in terms of money. If money which is the unit of measurement itself varies as one is measuring with it, it cannot then yield correct measurement of the marginal utility of goods.

When price of a good falls and as a result the real income of the consumer rises, marginal utility of money to him will fall but Marshall ignored this and assumed that marginal utility of money did not change as a result of the change in price. Likewise, when price of a good rises, the real income of the consumer will fall and his marginal utility of money will rise. But Marshall ignored this and assumed that marginal utility of money remains the same. Marshall defended this assumption on the ground that "his (the individual consumer's) expenditure on any one thing.....is only a small part of his whole expenditure."

Introspective Method. Another important assumption of the cardinal utility analysis is the use of introspective method in judging the behaviour of marginal utility. "Introspection is the ability of the observer to reconstruct events which go on in the mind of another person with the help of self-observation. This form of comprehension may be just guesswork or intution or the result of long lasting experience."[1] Thus, the economists construct with the help of their own experience the trend of feeling which goes on in other men's mind. From his own response to certain forces and by experience and observation one gains understanding of the way other people's minds would work in similar situations. To sum up, in introspective method we attribute to another person what we know of our own mind. That is, by looking into ourselves we see inside the heads of other individuals. So the law of diminishing marginal utility is based upon introspection. We know from our own mind that as we have more of a thing, the less utility we derive from an additional unit of it. We conclude from it that other individuals' mind will work in a similar fashion, that is, marginal utility to them of a good will diminish as they have more units of it.

With the above basic premises, the founders of cardinal utility analysis have developed two laws which occupy an important place in economic theory and have several applications and uses. These two laws are : (1) Law of Diminishing Marginal Utility and (2) Law of Equi-Marginal Utility. It is with the help of these two laws about consumer's behaviour that the exponents of cardinal utility analysis have derived the law of demand. We explain below these two laws in detail and how law of demand is derived from them.

LAW OF DIMINISHING MARGINAL UTILITY

An important tenet of cardinal utility analysis relates to the behaviour of marginal utility. This familiar behaviour of marginal utility has been stated in the Law of Diminishing Marginal Utility according to which marginal utility of a good diminishes as an individual consumes more units of a good. In other words, as a consumer takes more units of a good, the extra utility or satisfaction that he derives from an extra unit of the good goes on falling. It should be carefully noted that it is the marginal utility and not the total utility that declines with the increase in the consumption of a good. The law of diminishing marginal utility means that the total utility increases at a decreasing rate.

Marshall who has been a famous exponent of the cardinal utility analysis has stated the law of diminishing marginal utility as follows:

"The additional benefit which a person derives from a given increase of his stock of a thing diminishes with every increase in the stock that he already has."

This law is based upon two important facts. First, while the total wants of a man are virtually unlimited, *each single want is satiable*. Therefore, as an individual consumes more and more units of a good, intensity of his want for the good goes on falling and a point is reached where the individual no longer wants any more units of the good. That is, when saturation point is reached, marginal utility of a good becomes zero. Zero marginal utility of a good implies that the individual has all that he wants of the good in question. The second fact on which the law of diminishing marginal utility is based is that the different goods are not perfect substitutes for each other in the satisfaction of various wants. When an individual consumes more and more units of a good, the intensity of his particular want for the good diminishes but if the units of that good could be devoted to the satisfaction of other wants and yielded as much satisfaction as they did initially in the satisfaction of the first want, marginal utility of the good would not have diminished.

It is obvious from above that the law of diminishing marginal utility describes a familiar and fundamental tendency of human nature. This law has been arrived at by introspection and by observing how consumers behave.

Illustration of the Law of Diminishing Marginal Utility

Consider Table 7.1. where we have presented the total and marginal utilities derived by a person from cups of tea consumed per day. When one cup of tea is taken per day, the total utility derived by the person is 12 utils. And because this is the first cup its marginal utility is also 12 utils. With the consumption of 2nd cup per day, the total utility rises to 22 utils but marginal utility falls to 10. It will be seen from the table that as the consumption of tea increases to six cups per day, marginal utility from the additional cup goes on diminishing (*i.e.* the total utility goes on increasing at a diminishing rate). However, when the cups of tea consumed per day increases to seven, then instead of giving *positive* marginal utility, the seventh cup gives *negative* marginal utility equal to - 2 utils. This is because too many cups of tea consumed per day (say more than six for a particular individual) may cause acidity and gas trouble. Thus, the extra cups of tea beyond six to the individual in question gives him disutility rather than positive satisfaction.

Table 7.1. Diminishing Marginal Utility

Cups of tea consumed per day (Q)	*Total Utility (utils)* TU	*Marginals Utility (utils)* $\frac{\Delta TU}{\Delta Q}$
1	12	12
2	22	10
3	30	8
4	36	6
5	40	4
6	41	1
7	39	–2
8	34	–5

Figure 7.1 illustrates the total utility and the marginal utility curves. The total utility curve drawn in Figure 7.1 is based upon three assumptions. First, as the quantity consumed per period by a consumer increases **his total utility increases but at a decreasing rate.** This implies that as the consumption per period of a commodity by the consumer increases, marginal utility diminishes as shown in the lower panel of Figure 7.1. Secondly, as will be observed from the figure, when the rate of consumption of a commodity per period increases to Q_4, the total utility of the consumer reaches its maximum level. Therefore, the quantity Q_4, of the commodity is called **satiation quantity or satiety point.** Thirdly, the increase in the quantity consumed of the good per period by the consumer beyond the satiation point has an adverse effect on his total utility, that is, his total utility declines if more than Q_4 quantity of the good is consumed. This means beyond Q_4 marginal utility of the commodity for the consumer becomes negative as will be seen from the lower panel of Figure 7.1 beyond the satiation point Q_4 marginal utility curve *MU* goes below the *X*-axis indicating it becomes negative beyond quantity Q_4 per period of the commodity consumed.

It is important to understand how we have drawn the marginal utility curve. As stated above, marginal utility is the increase in total utility of the consumer caused by the consumption of an additional unit of the commodity per period. We can directly find out the marginal utility of the successive units of the commodity consumed by measuring the additional utility which a consumer obtains from successive units of the commodity and plotting them against their respective quantities. However, in terms of calculus, marginal utility of a commodity *X* is the slope of the total utility function $U = f(Q_x)$. Thus, we can derive the marginal utility curve by measuring the slope at various points of the total utility curve *TU* in the upper panel of Figure7.1 by drawing tangents at them. For instance, at the quantity Q_1 marginal utility (*i.e.* $\frac{dU}{dQ} = MU_1$) is found out by drawing tangent at point *A* and measuring its slope which is then plotted against quantity Q_1 in the lower panel of Figure 7.1. In the lower panel we measure marginal utility of the commodity on the *Y*-axis. Likewise, at quantity Q_2 marginal utility of the commodity has been obtained by measuring slope

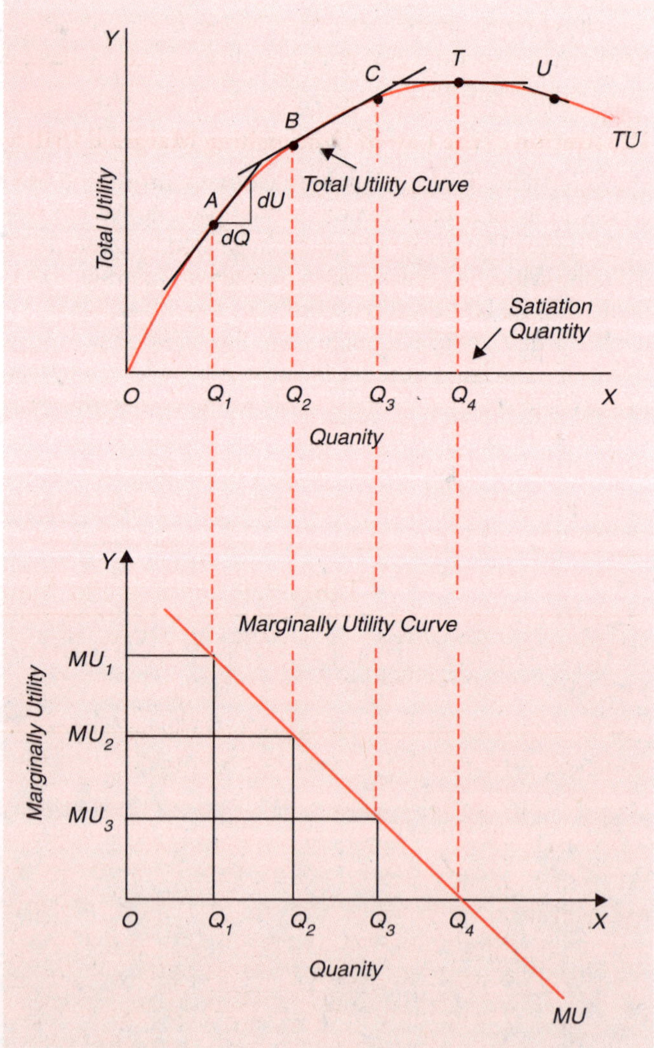

Fig. 7.1. *Total Utility and Marginal Utility*

of the total utility curve TU at point B and plotting it in the lower panel against the quantity Q_2. It will be seen from the figure that at Q_4 of the commodity consumed, the total utility reaches at the maximum level T. Therefore, at quantity Q_4 the slope of the total utility curve is zero at this point. Beyond the quantity Q_4 the total utility declines and marginal utility becomes negative. Thus, quantity Q_4 of the commodity represents the satiation quantity.

Another important relationship between total utility and marginal utility is worth noting. At any quantity of a commodity consumed the *total utility is the sum of the marginal utilities*. For example, if marginal utility of the first, second, and third units of the commodity consumed are 15, 12, and 8 units, the total utility obtained from these three units of consumption of the commodity must equals 35 units (15 + 12 + 8 = 35). Similarly, in terms of graphs of total utility and marginal utility depicted in Figure 7.1 the total utility of the quantity Q_4 of the commodity consumed is the *sum of the marginal utilities* of the units of commodity up to point Q_4. That is, the entire area under the marginal utility curve MU in lower panel up to the point Q_4 is the sum of marginal utilities which must be equal to the total utility Q_4T in the upper panel.

Marginal Utility and Consumer's Tastes and Preferences

The utility people derive from consuming a particular commodity depends on their tastes and preferences. Some consumers like oranges, others prefer apples and still others prefer bananas for consumption. Therefore, the utility which different individuals get from these various fruits depends on their tastes and preferences. An individual would have *different marginal utility curves* for different commodities depending on his tastes and preferences. Thus, *utility which people derive from various goods reflect their tastes and preferences for them.* However, it is worth noting that we cannot compare utility across consumers. Each consumer has a unique subjective utility scale. In the context of cardinal utility analysis, *a* change in consumer's tastes and preferences means a shift in his one or more marginal utility curves. However, it may be noted that a consumer's tastes and preferences do not frequently change, as these are determined by his habits. Of course, tastes and preferences can change occasionally. Therefore, in economic theory we generally assume that tastes or preferences are given and relatively stable.

Significance of Diminishing Marginal Utility

The significance of the diminishing marginal utility of a good for the theory of demand is that it helps us to show that the quantity demanded of a good increases as its price falls and *vice versa*. Thus, it is because of the diminishing marginal utility that the demand curve slopes downward. This will be explained in detail later in this chapter. If properly understood the law of diminishing marginal utility applies to all objects of desire including money. But it is worth mentioning that *marginal utility of money* is generally never zero or negative. Money represents purchasing power over all other goods, that is, a man can satisfy all his material wants if he possesses enough money. Since man's total wants are practically unlimited, therefore, the marginal utility of money to him never falls to zero.

The marginal utility analysis has a good number of uses and applications in both economic theory and policy. The concept of marginal utility is of crucial significance in explaining determination of the prices of commodities. The discovery of the concept of marginal utility has helped us to explain the *paradox of value* which troubled Adam Smith in "*The Wealth of Nations.*" Adam Smith was greatly surprised to know why water which is so very essential and useful to life has such a low price (indeed no price), while diamonds which are quite unnecessary, have such a high price. He could not resolve this water-diamond paradox. But modern economists can solve it with the aid of the concept of marginal utility. According to the modern economists, the total utility of a commodity does not determine the price of a commodity and it is the marginal utility which is crucially important determinant of price. Now, the water is available in abundant quantities so that its relative marginal utility is very low or even zero. Therefore, its price is low or zero. On the other hand, the diamonds are scarce and therefore their relative marginal utility is quite high and this is the reason why their prices are high. Prof. Samuelson explains this paradox of value in the following words:—***"The more there is of a commodity, the less the relative desirability of its last little unit becomes, even though its total usefulness grows as we get more of the commodity. So, it is obvious why a large amount of water has a low price Or why air is actually a free good despite its vast usefulness. The many later units pull down the market value of all units."***[4]

Besides, the Marshallian concept of consumer's surplus is based on the principle of diminishing marginal utility.

CONSUMER'S EQUILIBRIUM : PRINCIPLE OF EQUI-MARGINAL UTILITY

Principle of equi-marginal utility occupies an important place in cardinal utility analysis. It is through this principle that consumer's equilibrium is explained. A consumer has a given income which he has to spend on various goods he wants. Now, the question is how he would allocate his given money income among various goods, that is to say, what would be his equilibrium position in respect of the purchases of the various goods. It may be mentioned here that consumer is assumed to be 'rational', that is, he carefully calculates utilities and substitutes one good for another so as to maximise his utility or satisfaction.

Suppose there are only two goods X and Y on which a consumer has to spend a given income. The consumer's behaviour will be governed by two factors: first, the marginal utilities of the goods and secondly, the prices of two goods. Suppose the prices of the goods are given for the consumer. ***The law of equi-marginal utility states that the consumer will distribute his money income between the goods in such a way that the utility derived from the last rupee spent on each good is equal.*** In other words, consumer is in equilibrium position when marginal utility of money expenditure on each good is the same. Now, the marginal utility of money expenditure on a good is equal to the marginal utility of a good divided by the price of the good. In symbols,

$$MU_m = \frac{MU_x}{P_x}$$

where MU_m is marginal utility of money expenditure and MU_x is the marginal utility of X and P_x is the price of X. The law of equi-marginal utility can therefore be stated thus: the consumer will spend his money income on different goods in such a way that marginal utility of money expenditure on each good is equal. That is, consumer is in equilibrium in respect of the purchases of two goods X and Y when

$$\frac{MU_x}{P_x} = \frac{MU_y}{P_y}$$

Now, if $\frac{MU_x}{P_x}$ and $\frac{MU_y}{P_y}$ are not equal and $\frac{MU_x}{P_x}$ is greater than $\frac{MU_y}{P_y}$, then the consumer will substitute good X for good Y. As a result of this substitution, the marginal utility of good X will fall and marginal utility of good Y will rise. The consumer will continue substituting good X for good Y until $\frac{MU_x}{P_x}$ becomes equal to $\frac{MU_y}{P_y}$. When $\frac{MU_x}{P_x}$ becomes equal to $\frac{MU_y}{P_y}$ the consumer will be in equilibrium.

4. Paul Samuelson, *Economics*, McGraw-Hill, 8th edition, p. 417.

But the equality of $\frac{MU_x}{P_x}$ with $\frac{MU_y}{P_y}$ can be achieved not only at one level but at different levels of expenditure. The question is how far does a consumer go in purchasing the goods he wants. This is determined by the size of his money income. With a given income and money expenditure a rupee has a certain utility for him: this utility is the marginal utility of money to him. Since the law of diminishing marginal utility applies to money income also, the greater the size of his money income the smaller the marginal utility of money to him. Now, the consumer will go on purchasing goods until the marginal utility of money expenditure on each good becomes equal to the marginal utility of money to him. Thus, the consumer will be in equilibrium when the following equation holds good:

$$\frac{MU_x}{P_x} = \frac{MU_y}{P_y} = MU_m$$

where MU_m is marginal utility of money expenditure (that is, the utility of the last rupee spent on each good).

If there are more than two goods on which the consumer is spending his income, the above equation must hold good for all of them. Thus

$$\frac{MU_x}{P_x} = \frac{MU_y}{P_y} = \ldots\ldots\ldots\ldots = \frac{MU_n}{P_n} = MU_m$$

Let us illustrate the law of equi-marginal utility with the aid of an arithmetical table given below:

Table 7.2. Marginal Utility of Goods X and Y

Units	MU_x *(Utils)*	MU_y *(Utils)*
1	20	24
2	18	21
3	16	18
4	14	15
5	12	9
6	10	3

Let the prices of goods X and Y be Rs. 2 and Rs. 3 respectively. Reconstructing the above table by dividing marginal utilities (MU_x) of X by Rs. 2 and marginal utilities (MU_y) of Y by Rs. 3 we get the Table 7.3.

Table 7.3. Marginal Utility of Money Expenditure

Units	$\frac{MU_x}{P_x}$	$\frac{MU_y}{P_y}$
1	10	8
2	9	7
3	8	6
4	7	5
5	6	3
6	5	1

Suppose a consumer has money income of Rs. 24 to spend on the two goods. It is worth noting that in order to maximise his utility the consumer will not equate *marginal utilities of the goods* because prices of the two goods are different. He will equate the marginal utility of the last rupee (*i.e.* marginal utility of money expenditure) spent on these two goods. In other words, he will equate $\frac{MU_x}{P_x}$ with $\frac{MU_y}{P_y}$ while spending his given money income on the two goods. By looking at the Table 7.3 it will become clear that $\frac{MU_x}{P_x}$ is equal to 5 utils when the consumer purchases 6 units of good X and $\frac{MU_y}{P_y}$ is equal to 5 utils when he buys 4 units of good Y. Therefore, consumer will be in equilibrium when he is buying 6 units of good X and 4 units of good Y and will be spending (Rs. 2 × 6 + Rs. 3 × 4) = Rs. 24 on them that are equal to consumer's given income. Thus, in the equilibrium position where the consumer maximises his utility,

$$\frac{MU_x}{P_x} = \frac{MU_y}{P_y} = MU_m$$

$$\frac{10}{2} = \frac{15}{3} = 5$$

Thus, marginal utility of the last rupee spent on each of the two goods he purchases is the same, that is, 5 utils.

Consumers' equilibrium is graphically protrayed in Fig. 7.2. Since marginal utility curves of goods slope downward, curves depicting $\frac{MU_x}{P_x}$ and $\frac{MU_y}{P_y}$ also slope downward. Thus, when the consumer is buying *OH* of *X* and *OK* of *Y*, then

$$\frac{MU_x}{P_x} = \frac{MU_y}{P_y} = MU_m$$

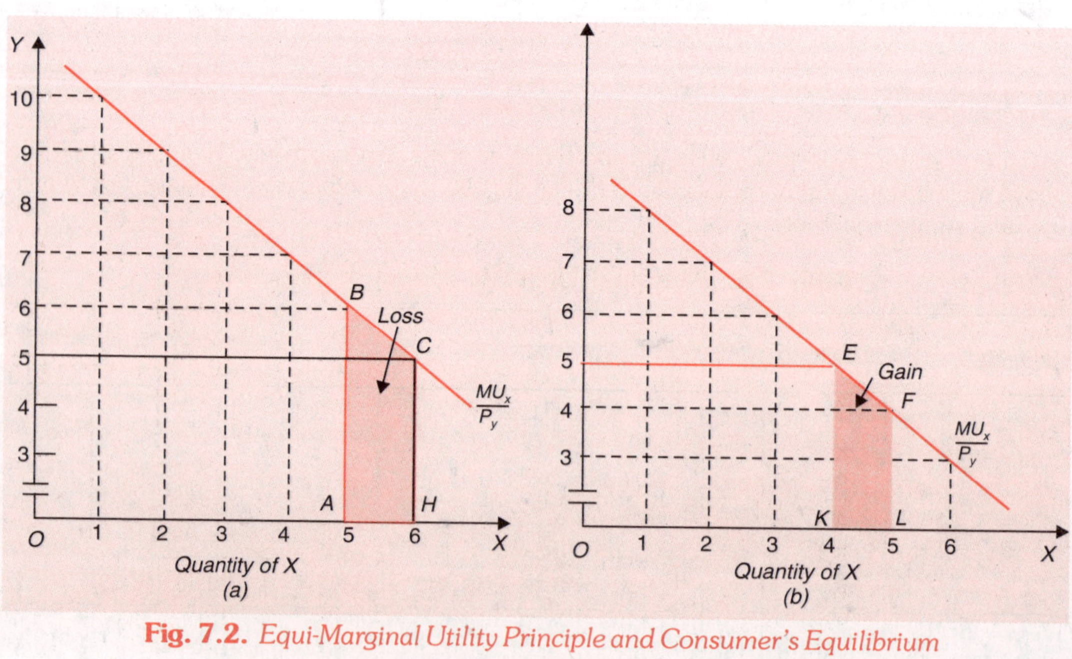

Fig. 7.2. *Equi-Marginal Utility Principle and Consumer's Equilibrium*

Therefore, the consumer is in equilibrium when he is buying 6 units of X and 4 units of Y. No other allocation of money expenditure will yield him greater utility than when he is buying 6 units of commodity X and 4 units of commodity Y. Suppose the consumer buys one unit less of good X and one unit more of good Y. This will lead to the decrease in his total utility. It will be observed from Figure 7.2 (a) that the consumption of 5 units instead of 6 units of commodity X means a loss in satisfaction equal to the shaded area *ABCH* and from Fig. 7.2(b) it will be seen that consumption of 5 units of commodity Y instead of 4 units will mean gain in utility equal to the shaded area *KEFL*. It will be noticed that with this rearrangement of purchases of the two goods, the loss in utility *ABCH* exceeds gain in utility *KEFL*. Thus, his total satisfaction will fall as a result of this rearrangement of purchases. Therefore, when the consumer is making purchases by spending his given income in such a way that $\frac{MU_x}{P_x} = \frac{MU_y}{P_y}$, he will not like to make any further changes in the basket of goods and will therefore be in equilibrium situation by maximizing his utility.

Limitations of the Law of Equi-Marginal Utility

Like other laws of economics, law of equimarginal utility is also subject to various limitations. This law, like other laws of economics, brings out an important tendency among the people. This is not necessary that all people exactly follow this law in the allocation of their money income and therefore all may not obtain maximum satisfaction. This is due to the following reasons:-

(1) For applying this law of equi-marginal utility in the real life, consumer must weigh in his mind the marginal utilities of different commodities. For this he has to calculate and compare the marginal utilities obtained from different commodities. But it has been pointed out that the ordinary consumers are not so rational and calculating. Consumers are generally governed by habits and customs. Because of their habits and customs they spend particular amounts of money on different commodities, regardless of whether the particular allocation maximises their satisfaction or not.

(2) For applying this law in actual life and equate the marginal utility of the last rupee spent on different commodities, the consumers must be able to measure the marginal utilities of different commodities in cardinal terms. However, this is easier said than done. It has been said that it is not possible for the consumer to measure utility cardinally. Being a state of psychological feeling and also there being no objective units with which to measure utility, it is cardinally immeasurable. It is because of the immeasurability of utility in cardinal terms that the consumer's behaviour has been explained with the help of ordinal utility by J.R. Hicks and R.G.D. Allen. Ordinal utility analysis involves the use of indifference curves which we shall explain in the next chapter.

(3) Another limitation of the law of equi-marginal utility is found in case of *indivisibility* of certain goods. Goods are often available in large indivisible units. Because the goods are indivisible, it is not possible to equate the marginal utility of money spent on them. For instance, in allocating money between the purchase of car and foodgrains, marginal utilities of the last rupee spent on them cannot be equated. An ordinary car costs about Rs. 300,000 and is indivisible, whereas foodgrains are divisible and money spent on them can be easily varied. Therefore, the marginal utility of rupee obtained from cars cannot be equalised with that obtained from foodgrains. Thus, indivisibility of certain goods is a great obstacle in the way of equalisation of marginal utility of a rupee from different commodities.

DERIVATION OF DEMAND CURVE AND LAW OF DEMAND

We now turn to explain how the demand curve and law of demand is derived in the marginal utility analysis. As stated above, the demand curve or law of demand shows the relationship between price of a good and its quantity demanded. Marshall derived the demand curves for goods from their utility functions. It should be further noted that in his utility analysis of demand Marshall assumed the utility functions of different goods to be independent of each other. In other words, Marshallian technique of deriving demand curves for goods from their utility functions rests on the hypothesis of *additive utility functions*, that is, utility function of each good consumed by a consumer does not depend on the quantity consumed of any other good. As has already been noted, in case of independent utilities or additive utility functions, the relations of substitution and complementarity between goods are ruled out. Further, in deriving demand curve or law of demand Marshall assumes the marginal utility of money expenditure (MU_m) *in general* to remain constant.

We now proceed to derive demand curve from the law of equi-marginal utility. Consider the case of a consumer who has a certain given income to spend on a number of goods. According to the law of equi-marginal utility, the consumer is in equilibrium in regard to his purchases of various goods when marginal utilities of the goods are proportional to their prices. Thus, the consumer is in equilibrium when he is buying the quantities of the two goods in such a way that satisfies the following proportionality rule:

$$\frac{MU_x}{P_x} = \frac{MU_y}{P_y} = \text{MU}_m$$

where MU_m stands for marginal utility of money income in general.

With a certain given income for money expenditure the consumer would have a certain *marginal utility of money* (MU_m) *in general*. In order to attain the equilibrium position, according to the above proportionality rule, the consumer will equalise his marginal utility of money (expenditure) with the ratio of the marginal utility and the price of each commodity he buys. It follows therefore that a rational consumer will equalise the marginal utility of money (MU_m) with $\frac{MU_x}{P_x}$ of good X, with $\frac{MU_y}{P_y}$ of good Y and so on. Given *Ceteris Paribus* assumption, suppose price of good X falls. With the fall in the price of good X, the price of good Y, consumer's income and tastes remaining unchanged, the equality of the $\frac{MU_x}{P_x}$ with $\frac{MU_y}{P_y}$ and MU_m in general would be disturbed. With the lower price than before $\frac{MU_x}{P_x}$ will be *greater than* $\frac{MU_y}{P_y}$ or MU_m (It is assumed of course that the marginal utility of money does not change as a result of the change in the price of one good). Then, in order to restore the equality, marginal utility of X or MU_x must be reduced. And the marginal utility of X or MU_x can be reduced only by the consumer buying more of the good X. It is thus clear from the proportionality rule that as the price of a good falls, its quantity demanded will rise, other things remaining the same. This will make the demand curve for a good downward sloping. How the quantity purchased of a good increases with the fall in its price and also how the demand curve is derived in the cardinal utility analysis is illustrated in Fig. 7.3.

In the upper portion of Fig. 7.3, on the *Y*-axis $\frac{MU_x}{P_x}$ is shown and on the *X*-axis the quantity demanded of good *X* is shown. Given a certain income of the consumer, marginal utility of money *in general* for him is equal to *OH*. The consumer is buying Oq_1 of good *X* when price is P_{x1}, since at the quantity Oq_1 of X, marginal utility of money *OH* is equal to $\frac{MU_x}{P_{x1}}$. Now, when price of good *X* falls to P_{x2}, the curve will shift upward to the new position $\frac{MU_x}{P_{x2}}$. In order to equate marginal utility of money (*OH*) with the new $\frac{MU_x}{P_{x2}}$ the consumer increases the quantity demanded to Oq_2. Thus, with the fall in price of good *X* to P_{x2}, the consumer buys more of it. It should be noted that no account is taken of the increase in real income of the consumer as a result of fall in price of good X. This is because if change in real income is taken into account, then marginal utility of money will also change and this would have an effect on the purchases of goods. Marginal utility of money can remain constant in two cases. First, when the elasticity of marginal utility curve (price elasticity of demand) is unity so that even with increase in the purchase of a commodity following the fall in price, the money expenditure made on it remains the same. Second, marginal utility of money will remain approximately constant for small changes in price of unimportant goods, that is, goods which account for negligible part of consumer's budget. In case of these unimportant goods increase in real income following the fall in price is negligible and therefore can be ignored.

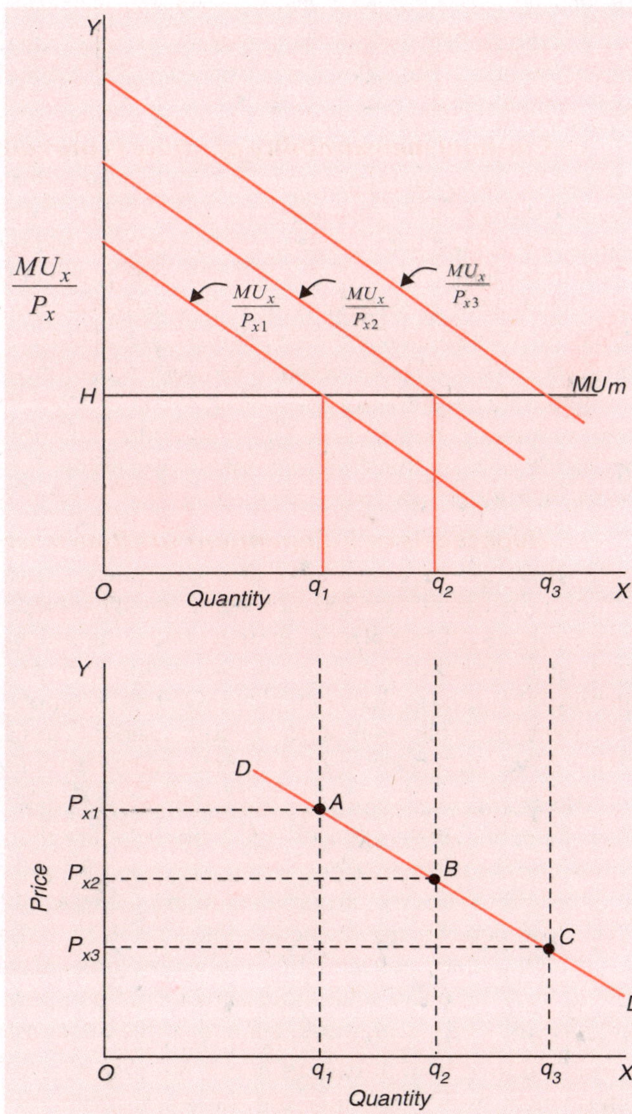

Fig. 7.3. *Derivation of Demand Curve*

At the bottom of Figure 7.3 the demand curve for *X* is derived. In this lower panel, price is measured on the *Y*-axis. As in the upper panel, the *X*-axis represents quantity. When the price of good *X* is Px_1, the relevant curve of $\frac{MU}{P}$ is $\frac{MU_x}{P_{x1}}$ which is shown in the upper panel. With $\frac{MU_x}{P_{x1}}$, as explained earlier, he buys Oq_1 of good X. Now, in the lower panel this quantity Oq_1 is directly shown to be demanded at the price P_{x1}. When price of X falls to Px_2, the curve of $\frac{MU}{P}$ shifts upward to the new position $\frac{MU_x}{P_{x2}}$. With $\frac{MU_x}{P_{x2}}$ the consumer buys Oq_2 of X. This quantity Oq_2 is directly shown to be demanded at price Px_2 in the lower panel. Similarly, by varying price further we can know the quantity demanded at other prices. Thus, by joining points A, B and C we obtain the demand curve DD. The demand curve DD slopes downward which shows that as price of a good falls, its quantity purchased rises.

CRITICAL EVALUATION OF MARSHALL'S CARDINAL UTILITY ANALYSIS

Cardinal utility analysis of demand which we have studied above has been criticised on various grounds. The following shortcomings and drawbacks of cardinal utility analysis have been pointed out:

(1) ***Cardinal measurability of utility is unrealistic.*** Cardinal utility analysis of demand is based on the assumption that utility can be measured in absolute, objective and quantitative terms. In other words, it is assumed in this analysis that utility is cardinally measurable. According to this, how much utility a consumer obtains from goods can be expressed or stated in cardinal numbers such as 1, 2, 3, 4 and so forth. But in actual practice utility cannot be measured in such quantitative or cardinal terms. Since utility is a psychic feeling and a subjective thing, it cannot be measured in quantitative terms. In real life, consumers are only able to *compare* the satisfactions derived from various goods or various combinations of the goods. In other words, in the real life consumer can state only whether a good or a combination of goods gives him more or less, or equal satisfaction as compared to another. Thus, economists like J.R. Hicks are of the opinion that the assumption of cardinal measurability of utility is unrealistic and therefore it should be given up.

(2) ***Hypothesis of independent utilities is wrong.*** Utility analysis also assumes that utilities derived from various goods are independent. This means that the utility which a consumer derives from a good is the function of the quantity of that good and of that good alone. In other words, the assumption of independent utilities implies that the utility which a consumer obtains from a good does not depend upon the quantity consumed of other goods; it depends upon the quantity purchased of that good alone. On this assumption, the total utility which a person gets from the whole collection of goods purchased by him is simply the total sum of the separate utilities of various goods. In other words, utility functions are *additive*.

Neo-classical economists such as Jevons, Menger, Walras and Marshall considered that utility functions were additive. But in the real life this is not so. In actual life the utility or satisfaction derived from a good depends upon the availability of some other goods which may be either substitutes for or complementary with each other. For example, the utility derived from a pen depends upon whether ink is available or not. On the contrary, if you have *only* tea, then the utility derived from it would be greater but if along with tea you also have the coffee, then the utility of tea to you would be comparatively less. Whereas pen and ink are *complements* with each other, tea and coffee are *substitutes for each other*.

It is thus clear that various goods are related to each other in the sense that some are complements with each other and some are substitutes for each other. As a result of this, the utilities derived from various goods are interdependent, that is, they depend upon each other. Therefore, the utility obtained from a good is not the function of its quantity alone but also depends upon the existence or consumption of other related goods (complements or substitutes). It is thus evident that the assumption of the independence of utilities by Marshall and other supporters of marginal utility analysis is a great defect and shortcoming of their analysis. As we shall see below, the hypothesis of independent utilities along with the assumption of constant marginal utility of money reduces the validity of Marshallian demand theorem to the one-commodity model only.

(3) ***Assumption of constant marginal utility of money is not valid.*** An important assumption of cardinal utility analysis is that when a consumer spends varying amount on a good or various goods or when the price of a good changes, marginal utility of money remains unchanged. But in actual practice this is not correct. As a consumer spends his money income on the goods, money income left with him declines. With the decline in money income of the consumer as a result of increase in his expenditure on goods, the marginal utility of money to him rises. Further, when price of a commodity changes, the real income of the consumer also changes. With this change in real income, marginal utility of money will change and this would have an effect on the demand for the good in question, even though the total money income available with the consumer remains the same.

But utility analysis ignores all this and does not take cognizance of the changes in real income and its effect on demand for goods following the change in price of a good. As we shall see below, it is because of the assumption of constant marginal utility of money that Marshall ignored the income effect of the price change which prevented Marshall from understanding the ***composite character of the price effect*** (that is, price effect is the sum of substitution effect and income effect). Moreover, as we shall see later, the assumption of constant marginal utility of money together with the hypothesis of independent utilities, renders the Marshall's demand theorem to be valid in case of one comodity. Further, it is because of the constant marginal utility of money and therefore the neglect of the income effect by Mashall that ***he could not explain Giffen Paradox.***

As has been explained earlier, according to Marshall, utility from a good can be measured in terms of money (that is, how much money a consumer is prepared to sacrifice for a good). But, to be able to measure utility in terms of money marginal utility of money itself should remain constant. Therefore, assumption of constant marginal utility of money is very crucial to Marshallian demand analysis. On the basis of constant marginal utility of money Marshall could assert that "utility is not only measurable in principle" but also "measurable in fact". But, as we shall see below, in case a consumer has to spread his money income on a number of goods, there is a necessity for revision of marginal utility of money with every change in price of a good. In other words, in a multi-commodity model marginal utility of money does not remain invariant or constant.Now, when it is realised that marginal utility of money does not remain constant, then Marshall's belief that utility is 'measurable in fact' in terms of money does not hold good. However, if in marginal utility analysis, utility is conceived only to be 'measurable in principle' and not in fact, then it practically gives up cardinal measurement of utily and comes near to the ordinal measuremnet of utility.

(4) ***Marshallian demand therem cannot genuinely be derived except in a one commodity case :*** J.R. Hicks and Tapas Majumdar have criticised Marshallian utility analysis on the ground that "Marshallian demand theorem cannot genuinely be derived from the marginal utility hypothesis except in a one-commodity model without contradicting the assumption of constant marginal utility of money".[5] In other words, Marshall's demand theorem and constant marginal utility of money are incompatible except in a one commodity case. As a result, Marshall's demand theorem cannot be validily derived in the case when a consumer

---

5. Tapas Majumdar, *Measurement of Utility*, p. 55.

spends his money on more than one good. In order to know the truth of this assertion consider a consumer who has a given amount of money income to spend on some goods with given prices. According to utility analysis, the consumer will be in equilibrium when he is spending money on goods in such a way that the marginal utility of each good is proportional to its price. Let us assume that, in his equilibrium position, consumer is buying q_1 quantity of a good X at a price p_1. Marginal utility of good X, in his equilibrium position, will be equal to its price p_1 multiplied by the marginal utility of money (which, in Marshallian utility analisis, serves as the unit of measurement). Thus, in the equilibrium position, the following equation will be fulfilled :

$$MU_x = MU_m \times p_1$$

Since the consumer is byuing q_1 quantity of good X at price P_1, he will be spending P_1q_1 amount of money on it. Now, suppose that the price of good X rises from p_1 to p_2. With this rise in price of X, all other things remianing the same, the consumer will at once find himself in disequilibrium state, for the marginal of good X will now be less than the higher price p_2 multiplied by the marginal utility of money (MU_m) wihich is assumed to remain unchanged and constant. Thus, now there will be

$$MU_x < MU_m.P_2$$

In order to restore his equilibrium, the consumer will buy *less* of good X so that the marginal utility of good X (MUx) would rise and become equal to the product of p_2 and MU_m. Suppose in this new equilibrium position, he is buying q_2 of good X which will be less than q_1. With this he will now be spending p_2q_2 amount of money on good X. Now the important thing to see is that whether his new expenditure p_2q_2 on good X is equal to, smaller or greter than p_1q_1. This depends upon the elasticity of marginal utility curve i.e., price elasticity of demand. If the elastictiy of marginal utility curve of good X is unity, then the new expenditure on good X (i.e. p_2q_2) after the rise in its price from p_1 to p_2 will be equal to the initial expenditure p_1q_1. When the monetary expenditure made on the good remains constant as a result of change in price, then the Marshallian theory is valid. But constant monetary expenditure following a price change is only a rare phenomenon. However, the Marshallian demand theory breaks down when the new expenditure p_2q_2 after the rise in price, instead of being equal, is smaller or greater than the initial expenditure p_1q_1. If elasticity of marginal utility curve is greater than one (that is, price demand for the good is elastic), then the new expenditure p_2q_2, after the rise in price from p_1 to p_2, will be less than the initial expenditure p_1q_1. On the other hand, if the elasticity of marginal utility curve is less than unity, then the new expenditure p_2q_2 after the rise in price will be greater than the initial expenditure p_1q_1.

Now, if the new expenditure p_2q_2 on good X is less than the initial expenditure p_1q_1 on it, it means more money will be left with the consumer to spend on goods other than X. And if the new expenditure p_2q_2 on good X is greater than the initial expenditure p_1q_1 on it, then less money would be left with him to spend on goods other than X. In order that the consumer spends the entire amount of money available with him, then in case of new expenditure p_2q_2 on good X being smaller or greater than initial expenditure p_1q_1 on it, the expenditure on goods other than X and therfore consumer's demand for them will change.But in Marshallian theoretical framework, this further adjustment in consumer's expenditure on goods other than X can occur only if the unit of utility measurement, that is, the marginal utility of money is revised or changed. But Marshall assumes marginal utility of money to remain constant.

Thus, we see that marginal utility of money cannot be assumed to remain constant when the consumer has to spread his money income on a number of goods. In case of more than one good, Marshallian demand theorem cannot be genuinely derived while keeping the marginal utility of money constant. If, in Marshallian demand analysis, this difficulty is avoided "by giving up the assumption of constant marginal utility of money, then money can no longer provide the measuring rod, and we can no longer express the marginal utility of a commodity in units of money. If we cannot express marginal utility in terms of common *numeraire* (which money is defined to be) the cardinality of utility would be devoid of any operational significance."[6]

Only in case there is one good on which the consumer has to spend his money, Marshallian demand theorem can be validity derived. To conclude, in the words of Majumdar, ***"Except in a strictly one-commodity world, therefore, the assumption of a constant marginal utility of money would be incompatible with the Marshallian demand theorem.*** Without the assumption of an invariant unit of measurement, the assertion of measurability would be entirely meaningless. The necessity and the possibility of revision of the unit of utility measurement, following every change in price, had been assumed away in Marshallian theory under the cover of 'other things remaining the same' clause."[7]

(6) Cardinal utility analysis does not split up the price affect into substitution and income effects: The third shortcoming of the cardinal utility analysis is that it ***does not distinguish between the income effect and the substitutional effect of the price change.*** We know that when the price of a good falls, the consumer becomes better off than before, that is, a fall in price of a good brings about an increase in the real income of the consumer. In other words, if with the fall in price the consumer purchases the same quantity of the good as before, then he would be left with some income. With this income he would be in a position to purchase more of this good as well as other goods. This is the income effect of the fall in price on the quantity demaded of a good. Besides, when the price of a good falls, it becomes relatively cheaper than other goods and as a result the consumer is induced to substitute that good for others. This results is increase in quantity demanded of that good. This is the substitution effect of the price change on the quantity demanded of the good.

With the fall in price of a good, the quantity demanded of it rises because of income effect and substitution effect. But cardinal utility analysis does not make clear the distinction between the income and the substitution effects of the price change. In fact, Marshall and other exponents of marginal utility analysis ignored income effect of the price change by assuming the constancy of marginal utility of money. Thus, according to Tapas Majumdar, "the assumption of constant marginal utility of money obscured Marshall's insight into the truly *composite character* of the unduly simplified price-demand relationship".[8] They explained the changes in demand as a result of change in the price of a good on the basis of substitution effect on it. Thus, marginal unility analysis does not tell us about how much quantity demanded increases due to income effect and how much due to substitution effect as a result of the fall in price of a good. J.R. Hicks rightly remarks, ***"that distinction between income effect and substitution effect of a price change is accordingly left by the cardinal theory as an empty box which is crying out to be filled."***[9] In the same way, Tapas Majumdar says,"The efficiency and precision with which the Hicks-Allen approach can distinguish between the income and subsitutuion effects of a price change really leaves the cardinal argument in a very poor state indeed."[10]

(7) **Marshall could not explain Giffen Paradox:** By not visualizing the price effect as a combination of substitution and income effects and ignoring the income effect of the price change,Marshall could not explain the Giffen Paradox. He treated it merely as an exception to his law of demand. In contrast to it, indifference curve analysis has been able to explain

6. **Tapas Majumdar, *op. cit.*, p. 56.**
7. ***Ibid.*,p. 60.**
8. ***Ibid.*,p. 57.**
9. **J.R. Hicks *A Revision of Demand Theory***
10. ***Op. cit.*, p.57**

satisfactorily the Giffen good case. According to indifference curve analysis, in case of a Giffen Paradox or the Giffen good negative income effect of the price change is more powerful than substitution effect so that when the price of a Giffen good falls the negative income effect outweighs the substitution effect with the result that quantity demanded of it falls. Thus, in case of a Giffen good, quantity demanded varies directly with the price and the Marshall's law of demand does not hold good. It is because of the constant marginal utility of money and therefore the neglect of the income effect of price change that Marshall could not explain why the quantity demanded of the Giffen good falls when its price falls and rises when its price rises. This is a serious lacuna in Marshalllian's utility analysis of demand.

(8) **Marginal utility analysis assumes too much and explains too little :** Marginal untility analysis is also criticised on the ground that it takes more assumptions and also more severe ones than those of ordinal utility analysis of indifference curve technique. Marginal utility analysis assumes, among others, that utility is cardinally measurable and also that marginal utility of money remains constant. Hicks-Allen's indifference curve analysis does not take these assumptions and even then it is not only able to deduce all the theorems which cardinal utiltiy analysis can but also deduces a *more general theorem of demand*. In other words, indifference curve analysis explains not only that much as cardinal utility analysis does but even goes further and that too with fewer and less severe assumptions. Taking less severe assumption of ordinal utility and without assuming constant marginal utility of money, indifference curve analysis is able to arrive at the condition of consumer's equilibrium, namely, equality of marginal rate of substitution (MRS) with the price ratio between the goods, which is similar to the proportionality rule of Marshall. Further, since indifference curve analysis does not assume constant marginal utility of money, it is able to derive a valid demand theorem in a more than one commodity case.

It shall be explained in the next few chapters that indifference curve analysis is able to explain *Giffen Paradox* which Marshall with his marginal utility analysis could not. In other words, indifference curve analysis clearly explains why in case of Giffen goods, quantity demanded increases with the rise in price and decreases with the fall in price. Indifference curve analysis explains even the case of ordinary inferior goods (other than Giffen goods) in a more analytical manner. It may be noted that even if the valid demand theorem could be derived for the Marshallian hypothesis, it would still be rejected because "*better hypothesis*" of indifference preference analysis was available which can enunciate *more general demand theorem* (covering the case of Giffen goods) with fewer, less severe and more realistic assumptions.

Because of the above drawbacks, cardinal utility analysis has been given up in modern economic theory and demand is analysed with new approaches to demand theory. We shall discuss these modern approaches to the demand theory in the following chapters.

QUESTIONS FOR REVIEW

1. State and explain the law of diminishing marginal utility? How is law of demand derived from it ?
2. What is meant by consumer's equilibrium? How does a consumer reach his equilibrium position in cardinal utility analysis ?
3. Explain the Law of Equi-marginal utility? How does it explain consumer's equilibrium?
4. You are given the following marginal utilities of goods X and Y obtained by a consumer. Given that price of X = Rs. 5, price of Y = Rs. 2 and income = Rs. 22, find out the optimal combination of goods.

Number of units consumed of a commodity	MU_x (utils)	MU_y (utils)
1	30	20
2	25	18
3	20	16
4	15	14
5	10	12
6	5	10
7	1	8

(**Hint**: Divide marginal utilities of goods X and Y by their prices and then compare.)

5. Distinguish between cardinal utility and ordinal utility. On what grounds Marshall's cardinal utility analysis has been criticised?
6. How is a demand curve for a commodity derived in Marshall's Cardinal Utility Analysis? How does cardinal utility analysis explain the downward sloping nature of a demand curve?
7. Explain hypothesis of independent utilities adopted by Alfred Marshall. How does this hypothesis rendered Marshall unable to explain the substitute and complementary goods.
8. In Marshallan cardinal utility analysis law of demand cannot be genuinely derived except in a one commodity model. Critically examine.
9. "The distinction between income effect and substitution effect of a price change is left by the cardinal theory as an empty box which is crying out to be filled" (J.R. Hicks). Discuss.
10. "The assumption of constant marginal utility of money obscured Marshall's insight into the truly composite character of simplified price-demand relationship". (Tapas Majumdar). Explain and examine critically.
11. What is *Giffen Paradox*? Explain why Marshall could not resolve it with his cardinal utility analysis.
12. Cardinal utility analysis assumes too much and explains too little of consumer's demand. Discuss.
13. Deduce the inverse relationship between the quantity demanded of a commodity and its price in tems of Marshallian analysis, indicating the underlying assumption. How would you explain, in terms of this analysis, the phenomenon that a fall in price of salt does not make a consumer buy more of it ?
14. Why is the marginal utility of money assumed to be constant in the Marshallian analysis of the therory of cusumer's behaviour ? Does the dropping of this assumption negate the inverse relationship between the quantity demanded of a commodity and its price ? Give arguments in support of your answer.

CHAPTER

8

Indifference Curve Analysis of Demand

Introduction

In the earlier two chapters we explained the demand for products and the factors that determine it. In the last chapter we explained and critically examined cardinal utility approach to consumer's demand. In the present chapter we shall explain the indifference theory of *consumer choice* underlying consumer's demand for products. Theory of *consumer choice* helps us to predict consumer's responses to changes in prices, income, tastes and preferences, prices of related goods, and advertising expenditure. With this understanding manager of a firm is better able to know the changes in firm's revenue consequent to the change in variables that the firm can control such as price of its product, advertising expenditure to promote its sales as well as consumer's responses to changes in variables such as consumer's income, prices of products of other rival firms and their promotional strategies. The indifference curve analysis is a popular theory of consumer's demand which forms the subject-matter of the present chapter. The technique of indifference curves was first of all invented by a classical economist Edgeworth but he used it only to show the possibilities of exchange between two persons and not to explain consumer's demand. Two English economists, J.R. Hicks and R.G.D. Allen in their now well-known paper '*A Reconsideration of the Theory of Value*' severely criticized Marshall's cardinal utility analysis based upon cardinal measurement of utility and put forward the indifference curve approach based on the notion of ordinal utility to explain consumer's behaviour. In 1939 Hicks reproduced the indifference curve theory of consumer's demand in his book ***'Value and Capital'*** modifying somewhat the version of the original paper.

CONSUMER PREFERENCES

The analysis of consumer behaviour is concerned with the choice he makes among different goods or bundles of goods, given his budget constraint. It is from the choices of quantities of goods, given their prices, that consumers make that we derive demand curve for a good. In economics it is assumed that consumers behave rationally in the choice of goods or bundle of goods for satisfaction of their wants. To explain consumer behaviour economists assume that consumers have a set of preferences which guide them in choosing among goods for their consumption. The preferences of different individuals differ substantially. For example, some individuals prefer white shirts while others may prefer coloured shirts. Likewise, some prefer apples, others may like bananas and so on. In real life, the consumers have to make a choice among several goods but the use of two dimensional diagrams compel us to limit us to two goods. However, economists use the concept of a *composite commodity* which represents all other goods and the choice is between two goods while one of them is composite good. Since money represents general purchasing power which can buy other goods, it is taken as a *composite commodity*. Thus with the help of the composite commodity, we can consider consumer choice involving may goods and still use two dimensional diagrams.

Let us explain how we explain consumer preferences. Let x_1 denote the quantity of good 1 and x_2 quantity of good 2. Thus a bundle of two goods containing x_1 of good 1 and x_2 of good 2 is generally denoted by (x_1, x_2) and is called X bundle. Similarly, the other bundle may consists of y_1 amount of good 1 and y_2 amount of the good 2 and therefore is denoted by (y_1, y_2) and is called Y bundle. In the theory of consumer preferences it is assumed that, given the two bundles of goods, (x_1, x_2) and (y_1, y_2), the ***consumer is able to rank*** them in order of his preference. In other words, the consumer can determine whether he ***strictly prefers*** one bundle of goods to the other one or he is indifferent between the two bundles. "***strictly prefers***' implies that he definitely likes the one over the other. This preference relation has an operational significance. If a person strictly prefers one bundle over the other, he will choose that one over the other if there is opportunity for him to have any of them. Thus, the consumer's choice and demand for goods will depend on whether he strictly prefers one bundle over another. Thus, if a consumer always chooses a bundle (x_1, x_2) when bundle (y_1, y_2) is available, it shows he prefers (x_1, x_2) to (y_1, y_2).

Further, if the consumer shows his ***indifference*** between any two bundles of goods, it means he derives the some satisfaction from consuming bundle (x_1, x_2) as the other bundle (y_1, y_2) of the goods.

There is a third case which occurs if the consumer either prefers or is indifferent between the two bundles of goods, it is then said that the consumer ***weakly prefers*** one basket (x_1, x_2) to the other available basket (y_1, y_2) of the two goods.

This weak preference has been used by J.R. Hicks in his revision of demand theory based on logical ordering. In his analysis of weak-ordering preference hypothesis Hicks assumes that when a person chooses one bundle of two goods from among the several bundles of two goods available to him, it means he either prefers the chosen combination over all others available or he will be indifferent between the chosen one and some others available. Thus, Hicks in his revised demand theory does not rule out the indifference of the chosen bundle with any other bundle of the two goods available to the consumer but not chosen. Thus weakly preference implies that choice of a bundle of goods among several available to the consumer means that he does not strictly prefer the bundle he chooses among the various alternative bundles available to him; it is likely, according to weakly preference hypothesis, that he may be indifferent between the chosen bundle and some other alternative bundles available to him.

Assumptions about Consumer Preferences.

In analysing consumer behaviour economists usually make some crucial assumptions about the nature of consumer preferences. Some of these assumptions about consumer preferences are so fundamental that they are referred to as '*axioms*' of consumer theory. There are following three such assumptions made about consumer preferences.

Completeness. According to this assumption, the consumer is *capable of ranking alternative bundles* of goods for his consumption. This implies that between two bundles of goods a consumer can rank them so that he either prefers one bundle to another or is indifferent between them. This assumption about consumer preferences rules out the possibility that the consumer cannot decide which bundle is preferable. For example, if a person is offered a choice between an apple and orange and he chooses the apple, it means he prefers the apple. If he has no preference, he would not care which fruit, apple or orange, is given to him since either of them will leave him equally satisfied (that is, he will be indifferent between the two).

(2) Transitivity. The second assumption about preferences of consumers is that consumers' preference over bundles of goods is consistent. According to this, if a consumer prefers bundle *A* to an alternative bundle *B* and prefers the bundle *B* to another bundle *C*, then he will also prefer bundle A to bundle *C*. Similarly, if a consumer is indifferent between bundles *A* and *B* and between bundles *B* and *C*, then he will also be indifferent between bundles *A* and *C*. Thus, this assumption of transitivity of preferences implies that the consumer is *able to rank all available bundles of goods in a consistent manner.* In fact, transitivity principle implies that the consumer behaviour is rational.

3. More is Better. The third assumption about consumer preferences is that, all else remaining the same, more of a commodity is better than less of it, that is, more of the commodity is preferred to less of it. This implies that the person is *not already satiated* because if a person has already consumed so much of the good that he is fully satiated, then the extra amount of it would not give him more satisfaction.

It may however he noted that there are some things for which *less of them is preferred to more.* They are called *bads* in economics. For example, pollution, smog, germs are bads and less of them is preferred to more. However, the standard economic theory does not deal with bads and explains consumer choice with regard to desirable combinations of goods.

INDIFFERENCE CURVE APPROACH

Indifference curve method has been evolved to supersede the cardinal utility analysis of demand which was discussed in the last chapter. The indifference curve method seeks to derive all rules and laws about consumer's demand that are derivable from the cardinal utility analysis. At the same time the inventors and supporters of new method contend that their analysis is based on fewer and more reasonable assumptions. The indifference curve analysis has, however, retained some of the assumptions of Marshall's cardinal utility analysis. Thus, the indifference curve approach, like the old cardinal utility approach, assumes that the *consumer possesses 'complete information'* about all the relevant aspects of economic environment in which he finds himself. For example, the prices of goods, the markets in which they are available, the satisfaction to be obtained from them etc. are all known to the consumer. Further, it is assumed that the *consumer acts rationally* in the sense that, given the prices of goods and the money income, he will choose the combination from among the various possible combinations that gives him maximum satisfaction. Moreover, the *assumption* of *'continuity'* has also been retained by Hicks-Allen indifference curve method. Continuity assumption means that the consumers are capable of ordering or ranking all *conceivable combinations of goods* according to the satisfaction they yield.

Ordinal Utility

The fundamental approach of indifference curve analysis is that it has abandoned the concept of cardinal utility and instead has *adopted the concept of ordinal utility*. According to the supporters of the indifference curves theory, utility is a psychic entity and it cannot therefore be measured in quantitative cardinal terms. In other words, utility being a psychological feeling is not quantifiable. The concept of cardinal utility, according to the exponents of the indifference curve theory, is therefore untenable. On the other hand, the assumption of ordinal utility, according to them, is quite reasonable and realistic. ***The ordinal utility implies that the consumer is capable of simply 'comparing the different levels of satisfaction'.*** In other words, according to the ordinal utility hypothesis, while the consumer may not be able to indicate the exact amounts of utilities that he derives from commodities or any combination of them, but he is capable of judging whether the satisfaction obtained from a good or a combination of goods is equal to, lower than, or higher than another.

Notions of Preference and Indifference

For deriving the theory of consumer's behaviour, it is sufficient to assume that the consumer is able to rank his preferences consistently. Thus, the basis of indifference curve analysis of demand is the preference-indifference hypothesis. This means that if the consumer is presented with a number of various combinations of goods, he can order or rank them according to his '*scale of preferences*'. If the various combinations are marked *A, B, C, D, E*, etc. the consumer can tell whether he prefers *A* to *B*, or *B* to *A*, or is indifferent between them. Similarly, he can indicate his preference or indifference between any other pair of combinations. ***The concept of ordinal utility implies that the consumer cannot go beyond stating his preference or indifference.*** In other words, if a consumer happens to prefer *A* to *B*, he cannot tell by how much he prefers *A* to *B*. Thus, under ordinal utility hypothesis, the consumer cannot tell the '*quantitative differences*' between various levels of satisfaction; he can simply compare them 'qualitatively', that is, he can merely judge whether one level of satisfaction is higher than, lower than or equal to another. Further, according to the supporters of indifference-curve method, by 'how much' one combination of goods is preferred to another is not even needed for deriving laws concerning consumer's behaviour. It is sufficient to assume that the consumer is able to tell whether one combination of goods gives him greater, equal, or less satisfaction than another.

It may be noted that the consumer formulates his scale of preferences independently of the market prices of goods keeping in view only the satisfaction which he hopes to get from various combinations of goods. In consumer's scale of preferences some combinations will occupy the *same place*, *i.e.*, the consumer will be indifferent among them. Combinations occupying a higher place in his scale will be preferred to the combinations occupying lower places in the scale. Moreover, the indifference curve analysis assumes that the preference and indifference relations are '*transitive*'. The transitivity of preferences or indifference relations means that if a consumer prefers *A* to *B*, and *B* to *C*, then he will also prefer *A* to *C* and, likewise, if he is indifferent between *A* and *B*, and between *B* and *C*, then he will also be indifferent between *A* and *C*.

Assumptions of Indifferent Curve Analysis

Before explaining the properties or attributes which the indifference curves normally possess. It will be userful if we first mention the assumptions about the behaviour of the consumer which are generally made in indifference curve analysis.

1. More of a commodity is better than less. It is assumed that the consumer will always prefer a larger amount of a good to a smaller amount of that good, provided that the other goods at his disposal remains unchanged. This is a very reasonable and realistic assumption. This assumption implies that the consumer is not over-supplied with any good. When a consumer is over-supplied or over-satiated with one good, he will prefer a smaller quantity of that good to its larger quantity. It is thus assumed that the consumer has not yet reached the point of satiety in the consumption of any good. This assumption is therefore known as *non-satiety assumption*.

2. Preferences or indifferences of a consumer are transitive. Suppose there are three combinations of two goods *A*, *B* and *C*. If the consumer is indifferent between *A* and *B* and also between *B* and *C*, it is then assumed that he will be indifferent between *A* and *C* too. This condition implies that consumer's tastes are quite consistent. This assumption is known as *assumption of transitivity*.

3. Diminishing marginal rate of substitution. In indifference curve analysis the principle of diminishing marginal rate of substitution is assumed. In other words, it is assumed that as more and more units of *X* are substituted for *Y*, the consumer will be willing to give up fewer and fewer units of *Y* for each additional unit of *X*, or when more and more of *Y* is substituted for *X*, he will be willing to give up successively fewer and fewer units of *X* for each additional unti of *Y*. This rule about consumer's behaviour is described as the principle of diminishing, marginal rate of substitution. This principle follows as a matter of logical necessity from the assumption that particular wants are satiable and that various goods are not perfect substitutes for one another.

WHAT ARE INDIFFERENCE CURVES ?

The basic tool of Hicks-Allen ordinal utility analysis of demand is the indifference curve which represents all those combinations of goods which give same satisfaction to the consumer. Since all the combinations on an indifference curve give equal satisfaction to the consumer, he will be indifferent between them, that is, it will not matter to him which one he gets. In other words, all combinations of two goods lying on a consumer's indifference curve are equally desirable to or equally preferred by him. To understand indifference curves, it is better to start with indifference schedules. In Table 8.1, two indifference schedules are given. In each schedule the amounts of goods *X* and *Y* in each combination are so much that the consumer is indifferent among the combinations in each schedule. In schedule 1, the consumer has to start with 1 unit of *X* and 12 units of *Y*. Now, the consumer is asked to tell how much of good *Y* he will be willing to give up for the gain of an additional unit of *X* so that his level of satisfaction remains the same. If the gain of one unit of *X* compensates him fully for the loss of 4 units of *Y*, then the next combination of 2 units of *X* and 8 units of *Y* (2*X* + 8*Y*) will give him as much satisfaction as the initial combination (1*X* + 12*Y*). Similarly, by asking the consumer further how much of *Y* he will be prepared to forgo for successive increments in his stock of *X* so that his level of satisfaction remains unaltered, we get combinations 3*X* + 5*Y*, 4*X* + 3*Y*, and 5*X* + 2*Y*, each of which provides him same satisfaction as combination 1*X* + 12*Y* or 2*X* + 8*Y*. Since his satisfaction is the same whichever combination of goods in the schedule is offered to him, he will be indifferent among the combinations of two goods included in the schedule.

Table 8.1. Two Indifference Schedules

I		II	
Good X	*Good Y*	*Good X*	*Good Y*
1	12	2	14
2	8	3	10
3	5	4	7
4	3	5	5
5	2	6	4

In schedule II, the consumer has initially 2 units of *X* and 14 units of *Y*. By asking the consumer how much of *Y* he will be prepared to abandon for the successive additions of X in his stock so that his satisfaction remains equal to what he derives from the initial combination (2*X* + 14*Y*), we get combinations 3*X* + 10*Y*, 4*X* + 7*Y*, 5*X* + 5*Y* and 6*X*+ 4*Y*. Thus, each of the combinations in schedule II will be equally desirable to the consumer and he will be indifferent among them. But it should be borne in mind that the consumer will prefer any combination in schedule II to any combination in schedule I. That is, any combination in schedule II will give him more satisfaction than any combination in shcedule I. This is because it is assumed that more of a commodity is preferable to less of it (in other words, the greater quantity of a good

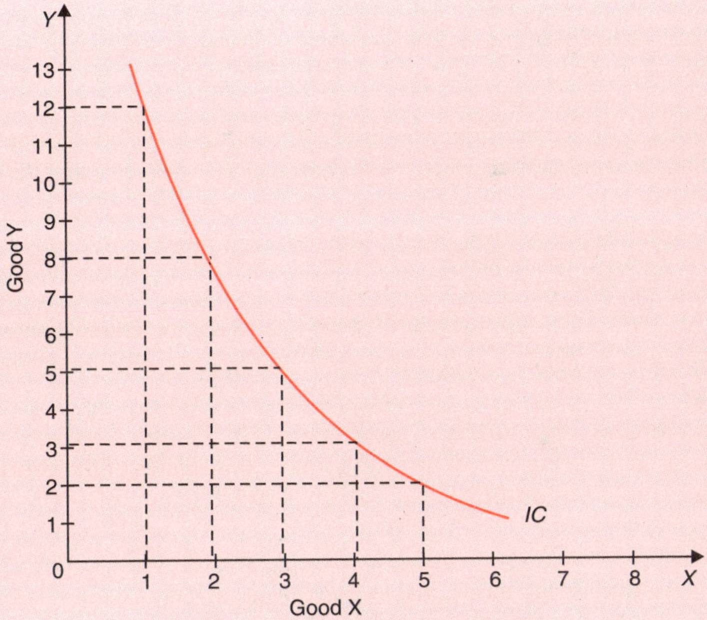

Fig. 8.1. An Indifference Curve

gives an individual more satisfaction than the smaller quantity of it), the quantities of other goods with him remaining the same. Initial combination in schedule II contains more of both the goods than the initial combination in schedule I, therefore the former will give greater satisfaction to the consumer than the latter. Now, since each of the other combinations in indifference schedule II provides the consumer same satisfaction as the initial combination (2*X* + 14*Y*) of this schedule and also each of other combinations in indifference schedule I gives the same satisfaction as the initial combination (1*X* + 12*Y*), any combination of the schedule II will be preferred to (will yield greater satisfaction) than any combination of schedule I.

Now, we can convert the indifference schedules into indifference curves by plotting the various combinations on a graph paper. In Fig. 8.1 an indifference curve *IC* is drawn by plotting the various combinations of the indifference schedule I. The quantity of good *X* is measured on the horizontal axis, and the quantity of the good *Y* is measured on the vertical axis. As in an indifference schedule, combinations lying on an indifference curve will also be equally desirable to the consumer, that is, will give him the same satisfaction. The smoothness and continuity of an indifference curve mean that goods in question are assumed to be perfectly divisible. If the indifference schedule *II* is also converted into indifference curve, this will lie above the indifference curve *IC*.

Any combination on a higher indifference curve will be preferred to any combination on a lower indifference curve. It is thus clear that the indifference curve lying above and to the right of an indifference curve will indicate a higher level of satisfaction. It may be noted that while an indifference curve shows all those combinations of two goods which provide equal satisfaction to the consumer, it does not indicate *exactly how much* satisfaction is derived by the consumer from those combinations. This is because the concept of ordinal utility does not involve the quantitative measurability of utility. Therefore, no attempt is made to label an indifference curve by the amount of satisfaction it represents.

Mathematically, utility function represented by indifference curve of an individual in case of two goods *X* and *Y* can be written as

$$U(x, y) = a$$

where a is some constant in the ordinal sense,
utility function, $U(x, y)$ of indifference curves can also take the following form :

$$U(x, y) = xy = a$$

According to the above utility function indifference curves will be convex and sloping downward. For different and higher values of a there will be successively higher indifference curves.

Note further that even utility function, $U(x, y) = x^2y^2$ will represent typical indifference curves. We can easily slow this as follows

$$U(x, y) = x^2y^2 = (xy)^2 = U(x, y)^2$$

It is thus clear that $U(x, y)^2$ is just the square of the utility function $U(x, y)$ being its *monotonic transformation*. Similarly, $U(x, y) = \sqrt{xy}$ will also be the utility function of typical indifference curves.

It may be noted that *Marshallian Cardinal utility model* suffered from a serious shortcoming as it rested on the restrictive assumption that the utilities of the various goods were *independent of each* other and *additive*. The additive utility function of cardinal utility analysis takes the following form

$$U = U_x(x) + U_y(y)$$

where $U_x(x)$ is the total utility derived from the consumption of x units of good X, $U_y(y)$ is the total utility derived from the consumption of y units of good Y and U is the aggregate utility.

As mentioned above, the advocates of indifference curve analysis has *rejected* the view of cardinal utility analysis that utilities of various goods are independent and additive.

It is important to note that the economists use the concept of utility function to study about consumer behaviour, but utility functions of individuals are not easily known. To obtain utility function of individuals a researcher askes a sufficiently large number of questions about their choices of bundles of goods in order to construct a utility function that correctly represents their preferences. Usually, *consumers can easily answer questions about whether they prefer one bundle of goods to another*. But they find it difficult to answer question about *how much more* they prefer one bundle to another because they do not have a measure in which they can express their level of satisfaction or utility. Therefore, we are able to know only his *rank-ordering* of bundles of goods and do not know how much more the consumer prefers one bundle to another. In other words, we know only *ordinal preferences* of individuals and not cardinal measures of their utility. However, in the indifference curves analysis, it is thought sufficient to know only ordinal preferences of consumers for deriving the condition of consumer choice and derive the demand theorem stating the relation between changes in price of a good and its quantity demanded.

Indifference Map

A complete description of consumer's tastes and preferences can be represented by an *indifference map* which consists of a set of indifference curves. Because the field in a two-dimensional diagram contains an infinite number of points, each representing a combination of goods X and Y, there will be an infinite

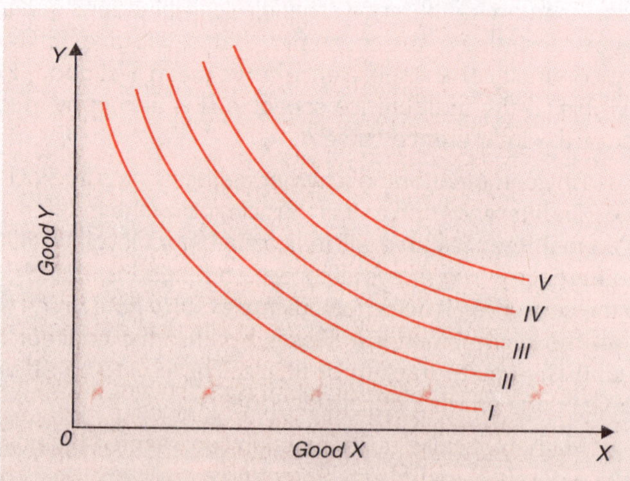

Fig. 8. 2. *Indifference Map*

number of the indifference curves each passing through combinations of goods that are equally desirable to the consumer. In Fig.8.2 an indifference map of a consumer is shown which consists of five indifference curves. The consumer regards all combinations on the indifference curve *I* as giving him equal satisfaction. Similarly, all the combinations lying on indifference curve *II* provide the same satisfaction but the level of satisfaction on indifference curve *II* will be greater than the level of satisfaction on indifference curve *I*. Likewise, all higher indifference curvs, *III*, *IV* and *V* represent progressively higher and higher levels satisfaction. It is importnat to remember that while the consumer will prefer any combination on a higher indifference curve to any combination on a lower indifference curve, but by *how much he prefers* one combination to another cannot be said. In other words, a higher indifference curve represents a higher level of satisfaction than a lower indifference curve but by *"how much higher"* cannot be indicated. This is because the indifference curve system is based upon the concept of ordinal utility according to which the consumer is able to state only the '*qualitative*' differences in his various levels of satisfaction. It is not possible for the consumer to specify '*quantitative*' differences in his various levels of satisfaction (*i.e.*, by how much more or by how much less cannot be stated by him). Therefore, in an indifference map successively higher indifference curves can be denoted by any ascending series, 1,3,7, 9...; or 1, 4, 6, 8, 13...; or 1, 2, 5, 8, 10...; etc., the magnitude of these various numbers and the quantitative differences among them having no relevance. It is more usual to label the indifference curves by ordinal numbers as *I*, *II*, *III*, *IV*, *V* as is done in Fig. 8.2.

An indifference map of a consumer represents, as said earlier, his tastes and preferences for the two goods and his preferences between different combinations of them. In other words, ***an indifference map portrays consumer's scale of preferences.*** Scale of preferences of indifference curve analysis replaces Marshall's utility schedule. So long as consumer's tastes and preferences remain unchanged, the whole indifference map will remain the same. If the consumer's tastes and preferences undergo a change, then a new indifference map corresponding to new tastes and preferences will have to be drawn. If, for instance, good Y is eggs and good X is bread, and if the doctor advises our consumer to take more of eggs to overcome some diseases, the shapes of all his indifference curves will change and his indifference map will have to be redrawn. Since the doctor's advice will intensify our consumer's desire for eggs, now a smaller quantity of eggs than before will be given up by him for a given increment in bread.

MARGINAL RATE OF SUBSTITUTION

The concept of marginal rate of substitution is an important tool of indifference curve analysis of demand. The rate at which the consumer is prepared to exchange goods X and Y is known as marginal rate of substitution. In our indifference schedule I above, which is reproduced in Table 8.2, in the beginning the consumer gives up 4 units of Y for the gain of one additional unit of X and in this process his level of satisfaction remains the same. It follows that one unit gain in X fully compensates him for the loss of 4 units of Y. It means that at this stage he is prepared to exchange 4 units of Y for one unit of X. Therefore, at this stage consumer's marginal rate of substitution of X for Y is 4. Thus, ***we may define the marginal rate of substitution of X for Y as the amount of Y whose loss can just compensate the consumer for one unit gain in X.*** In other words, marginal rate of substitution of X for Y represents the amount of Y which the consumer has to give up for the gain of one additional unit of X *so that his level of satisfaction remains the same*.

In Table 8.2, when the consumer moves from combination *B* to combination *C* on his indifference schedule he forgoes 3 units of Y for additional one unit gain in X. Hence, the marginal rate of substitution of X for Y is 3. Likewise, when the consumer moves from *C* to *D*, and then from *D* to *E* in his indifference schedule, the marginal rate of substitution of X for Y is 2 and 1 respectively.

Table 8.2. Indifference Schedule

Combination	Good X	Good Y	MRS_{xy}
A	1	12	
B	2	8	4
C	3	5	3
D	4	3	2
E	5	2	1

How to measure marginal rate of substitution on an indifference curve ? Consider Fig. 8.3 where an indifference curve is shown. When the consumer moves from point *A* to *B* on this indifference curve he gives up *AS* of *Y* and takes up *SB* of *X* and remains on the same indifference curve (or, in other words, at the same level of satisfaction). It means that the loss of satisfaction caused by giving up *AS* of *Y* equals the gain in satisfaction due to the increase in good *X* by *SB*. It follows that the consumer is prepared to exchange *AS* of *Y* for *SB* increase in *X*. In other words, marginal rate of substitution of X for Y (MRS_{xy}) is equal to $\frac{AS}{SB}$. Now, a small change in the amount of *Y* such as *AS*, along an indifference curve can be written as ΔY and the change in the amount of *X* as ΔX. Thus, ΔY shows the amount of *Y* which the consumer has to give up for the ΔX increase in *X* if he is to remain on the same indifference curve. Therefore, it follows that :

$$\text{Marginal rate of substitution of } X \text{ for } Y\ (MRS_{xy}) = \frac{AS}{SB} = \frac{\Delta Y}{\Delta X}$$

Now, suppose that points *A* and *B* are very close to each other so that it can be assumed that both of them lie on the same tangent *tT* (Fig. 8.3). Now, in a right-angled traingle *ASB*, $\frac{AS}{SB}$ is equal to the tangent of the angle *ABS*. It therefore follows that :

$$MRS_{xy} = \frac{AS}{SB} = \frac{\Delta Y}{\Delta X} = \text{tangent of } \angle ABS$$

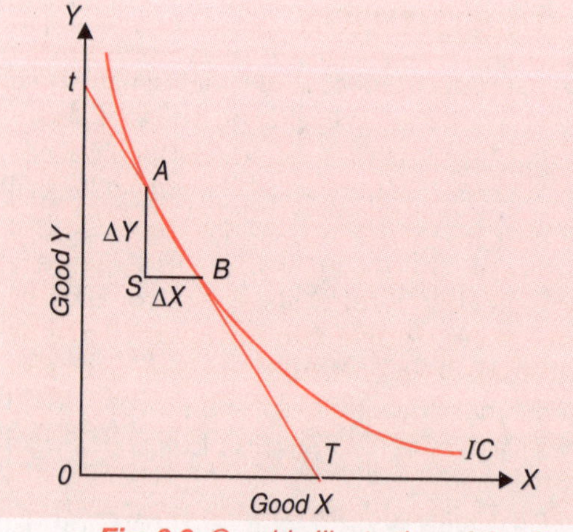

Fig. 8.3. Graphic Illustration of the Concept of Marginal Rate of Substitution

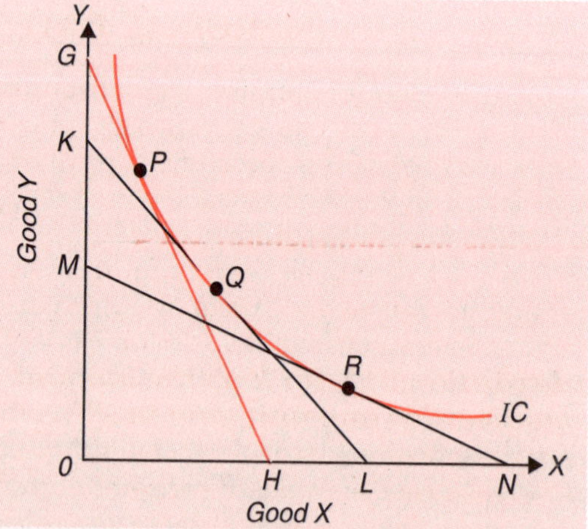

Fig. 8.4. Diminishing Marginal Rate of Substitution

But in Fig. 8.3 $\angle ABS = \angle tTO$

Hence MRS_{xy} = tangent of $\angle tTO$

But the tangent of $\angle tTO$ is equal to $\frac{Ot}{OT}$

Thus tangent of $\angle tTO$ indicates the slope of the tangent line tT drawn at point A or B on the indifference curve. In other words, the slope of the indifference curve at point of A or B is equal to the tangent of $\angle tTO$. It therefore follows:

$$MRS_{xy} = \text{tangent of } \angle tTO = \text{slope of the indifference curve on } A \text{ or } B = \frac{Ot}{OT}$$

It is thus clear from above that if we have to find out the MRS_{xy} at a point on the indifference curve we can do so by drawing a tangent at the point on the indifference curve and then measuring the slope by estimating the value of the tangent of the angle which the tangent line makes with the X-axis.

Principle of Diminishing Marginal Rate of Substitution

An important principle of economic theory is that marginal rate of substitution of X for Y diminishes as more and more of good X is substituted for good Y. In other words, as the consumer has more and more of good X, he is prepared to forego less and less of good Y. The principle of diminishing marginal rate of substitution is illustrated in Fig. 8.4.

That marginal rate of substitution falls is also evident from the Table 8.2. In the beginning the marginal rate of substitution of X for Y is 4 and as more and more of X is obtained and less and less of Y is left, the MRS_{xy} keeps on falling. Between B and C it is 3; between C and D, it is 2; any finally between D and E, it is 1. It means from Table 8.2 that as the consumer's stock of X increases and his stock of Y decreases, he is willing to forego less and less of Y for a given increment in X. In other words, marginal rate of substitution of X for Y falls as the consumer has more of X and less of Y. That the marginal rate of substitution of X for Y diminishes can also be known from drawing tangents at different points on an indifference curve. As explained above, marginal rate of substitution at a point on the indifference curve is equal to the slope of the indifference curve at that point and can therefore be found out by measuring the slope of tangent drawn at a point. In Fig. 8.4 three tangents GH, KL and MN are drawn at the points P, Q and R respectively to the given indifference curve. Slope of the tangent GH is equal to $\frac{OG}{OH}$. Hence, marginal rate of substitution of X for Y at point P is equal to $\frac{OG}{OH}$. Likewise, marginal rate of substitution at point Q is equal to $\frac{OK}{OL}$ and at point R it is equal to $\frac{OM}{ON}$. It will be noticed that $\frac{OK}{OL}$ is smaller than $\frac{OG}{OH}$ and $\frac{OM}{ON}$ is smaller than $\frac{OK}{OL}$. It follows that MRS_{xy} diminishes as the consumer slides down on his indifference curve.

Reasons for Diminishing MRS_{xy}

Now, the question is what accounts for the diminishing marginal rate of substitution. In other words, why is it that the consumer is willing to give up less and less of Y for a given increment in X as he slides down on the curve? The following three factors are responsible for diminishing marginal rate of substitution.

First, *the want for a particular good is satiable* so that as the consumer has more and more of a good the intensity of his want for that good goes on declining. It is because of this fall in the intensity of want for a good, say X, that when its stock increases with the consumer, he is prepared to forego less and less of good Y for every increment in X. In the beginning, when the consumer's stock of good Y is relatively large and his stock of good X is relatively small, consumer's marginal significance for good Y is low, while his marginal significance for good X is high. Owing to higher marginal significance of good X and lower marginal significance of good Y in the beginning the consumer will be willing to give up a larger amount of Y for one unit increase in good X. But as the stock of good X increases and intensity of desire for it falls, his marginal significance of good X will diminish and, on the other hand, as the stock of good Y decreases and the intensity of his desire for it increases, his marginal significance for good Y will go up. As a result, therefore, as the individual substitutes more and more of X for Y, he is prepared to give up less and less of Y for one unit increase in X.

The second reason for the decline in marginal rate of substitution is that the *goods are imperfect substitutes of each other.* If two goods are perfect substitutes of each other, then they are to be regarded as one and the same good, and therefore increase in the quantity of one and decrease in the quantity of the other would not make any difference in the marginal significance of the goods. Thus, in case of perfect substitutability of goods, the increase and decrease will be virtually in the same good which cancel out each other and therefore the marginal rate of substitution remains the same and does not decline.

Relationship Between MRS and Marginal Utilities

It can be shown mathematically that MRS_{xy} between goods is equal to the ratio of marginal utilities of goods X and Y.

An indifference curve can be represented by

$$U(x, y) = a \qquad \text{......}(i)$$

where *a* represents a constant utility along an indifference curve. Taking total differential of (i) above, we have :

$$\frac{\partial U}{\partial X} dX + \frac{\partial U}{\partial Y} dY = 0$$

$$\frac{dY}{dX} = \frac{\frac{\partial U}{\partial X}}{\frac{\partial U}{\partial Y}}$$

$\frac{\partial U}{\partial X}$ and $\frac{\partial U}{\partial Y}$ are marginal utilities of goods X and Y respectively. Thus,

$$\frac{dY}{dX} = \frac{MU_x}{MU_y}$$

$\frac{dY}{dX}$ is the slope of indifference curve and represents MRS_{xy}. Thus,

$$MRS_{xy} = \frac{MU_x}{MU_y}$$

PROPERTIES OF INDIFFERENCE CURVES

We now proceed to deduce from the above-mentioned assumptions the important properties of typical indifference curves.

Property I. Indifference curves slope downward to the right.

This property implies that an indifference curve has a negative slope. This property follows from assumption I. Indifference curve being downward sloping means that when the amount of one good in the combination is increased, the amount of the other good is reduced. This must be so if the level of satisfaction is to remain the same on an indifference curve. If, for instance, the amount of good X is increased in the combination, while the amount of good Y remains unchanged, the new combination will be preferable to the original one and the two combinations will not therefore lie on the same indifference curve provided more of a commodity gives more satisfaction.

Property II : Indifference curves are convex to the origin.

Another important property of indifference curves is that they are usually convex to the origin. In other words, the indifference curve is relatively flatter in its right-hand portion and relatively steeper in its left-hand portion. This property of indifference curves follows from assumption 3, which is that the marginal rate of substitution of X for Y (MRS_{xy}) diminishes as more and more of X is substituted for Y. Only a convex indifference curve can mean a diminishing marginal rate of substitution of X for Y. If indifference curve was concave to the origin it would imply that the marginal rate of substitution of X for Y increased as more and more of X was substituted. for Y.

As shown in Fig. 8.4, when the indifference curve is convex to the origin, MRS_{xy} diminishes as more of X is substituted for Y. We therefore conclude that indifference curves are generally convex to the origin.

Our assumption regarding diminishing MRS_{xy} and the convexity of indifference curves is based upon the observation of actual behaviour of the normal consumer. *If indifference curves were concave or straight lines, the consumer would succumb to monomania, that is, he would buy and consume only* one good. We know that consumers in actual world do not generally buy and consume *one good*. It is for this reason that we reject indifference curves of concave or straight-line shapes and assume that indifference curves are normally convex to the origin. The degree of convexity of an indifference curve depends on the rate of fall in the marginal rate of substitution of X for Y. As stated above, when two goods are perfect substitutes of each other, the indifference curve is a straight line on which marginal rate of substitution remains constant. The better substitutes the two goods are for each other, the closer the indifference curve approaches to the straight line so that when the two goods are perfect substitutes, the indifference curve is a straight line.

Property III: Indifference curves cannot intersect each other.

Third important property of indifference curves is that they cannot intersect each other. In other words, only one indifference curve will pass through a point in the indifference map. This property can be easily proved by first making the two indifference curves cut each other and then showing the absurdity or self-contradictory result it leads to. In Fig. 8.5 two indifference curves are shown cutting each other at point C. Now take point A on indifference curve IC_2 and point B on indifference curve IC_1 vertically below A. Since an indifference curve represents those combinations of two commodities which give equal satisfaction to the consumer, the combinations represented by points A and C will give equal satisfaction to the consumer because both lie on the same indifference curve IC_2.

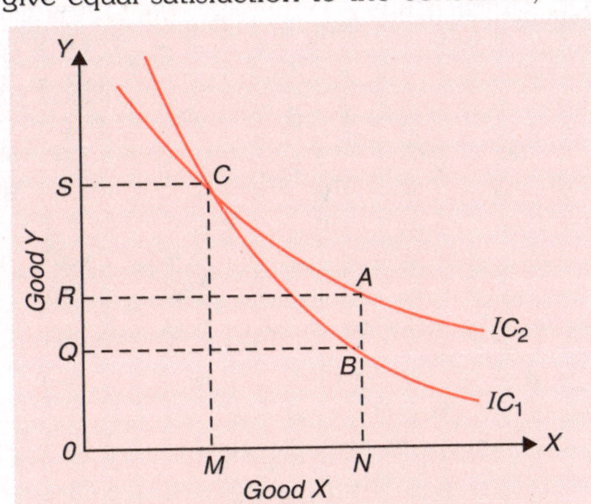

Fig. 8.5. Indifference curves cannot cut each other.

Likewise, the combinations B and C will give equal satisfaction to the consumer; both being on the same indifference curve IC_1. If combination A is equal to combination C in terms of satisfaction, and combination B is equal to combination C, it follows that the combination A will be equivalent to B in terms of satisfaction. But a glance at Fig.8.5 will show that this is absurd conclusion since combination A contains more of good Y than combination B, while the amount of good X is the same in both the combinations. Thus, the consumer will definitely prefer A to B, that is, A will give more satisfaction to the consumer than B. But the two indiffference curves cutting each other lead us to an absurd conclusion of A being equal to B in terms of satisfaction. We therefore conclude that indifference curves cannot cut each other.

Another point which is worth mentioning in this regard is that indifference curves cannot even meet or touch each other or be tangent to each other at a point.The meeting of two indifference curves at a point will also lead us to an absurd conclusion. The same argument holds good in this case as developed above in the case of intersection of indifference curves.

Property IV: A higher indifference curve represents a higher level of satisfaction than a lower indifference curve.

The last property of indifference curve is that a higher indifference curve will represent a higher level of satisfaction than a lower indifference curve. In other words, the combinations which lie on a higher indifference curve will be preferred to the combinations which lie on a lower indifference curve. Consider indifference curves IC_1 and IC_2 in Fig. 8.6. IC_2 is a higher indifference curve than IC_1. Combination Q has been taken on a higher indifference curve IC_2 and combination S on a lower indifference curve IC_1. Combination Q on the higher indifference curve IC_2 will give a consumer more satisfaction than combination S on the lower indifference curve IC_1 because the combination Q contains more of both goods X and Y than the combination S. Hence the consumer must prefer Q to S. And by transitivity assumption, he will prefer any other combination such as combination R on IC_2 (all of which are indifferent with Q) to any combination on IC_1 (all of which are indifferent with S). We, therefore, conclude that a higher indifference curve represents a higher level of satisfaction and combinations on it will be preferred to the combinations on a lower indifference curve.

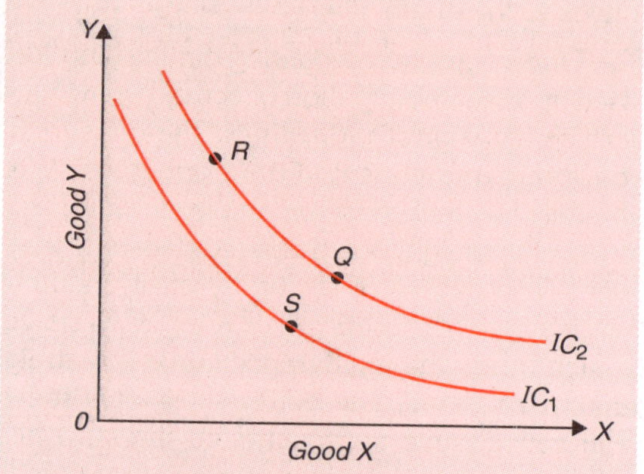

Fig. 8.6. *A higher indifference curve shows a higher level of satisfaction.*

Indifference Curves of Perfect Substitutes and Perfect Complements

The degree of convexity of an indifference curve depends upon the rate of fall in the marginal rate of substitution of X for Y. As stated above, when two goods are perfect substitutes of each other, the indifference curve is a straight line on which marginal rate of substitution remains constant. Straight-line indifference curves of perfect substitutes are shown in Fig. 8.7. The better substitutes the two goods are for each other, the closer the indifference curve approaches to the straight-line so that when the two goods are perfect substitutes, the indifference curve is a straight line. In case of perfect substitutes, the indifference curves are parallel straight lines because the consumer equally prefers the two goods and is willing to exchange one good for the other at a constant rate. As one moves along a straight-line indifference curve of perfect substitutes, marginal rate of substitution of one good for another remains constant. Examples of goods that are perfect substitutes are not difficult to find in the real world. For example, Dalda and Rath Vanaspati, two different brands of cold drink such as Pepsi Cola and Coca Cola are generally considered to be perfect substitutes of each other.

The greater the fall in marginal rate of substitution, the greater the convexity of the indifference curve. The less the ease with which two goods can be substituted for each other, the greater will be the fall in the marginal rate of substitution. At the extreme, when two goods cannot at all be substituted for each other, that is, when the two goods are perfect complementary goods, as for example gasoline and coolant in a car, the indifference curve will consist of two straight lines with a right angle bent which is convex to the origin as shown in Fig. 8.8. Perfect complementary goods are used in a certain fixed ratio.

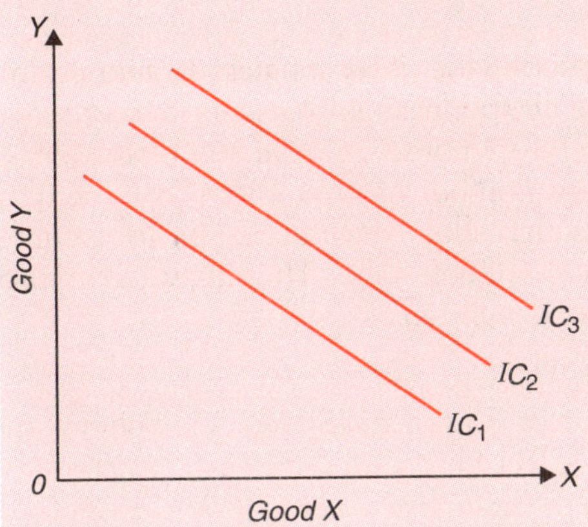

Fig. 8.7. *Indifference Curves of Perfect Substitutes*

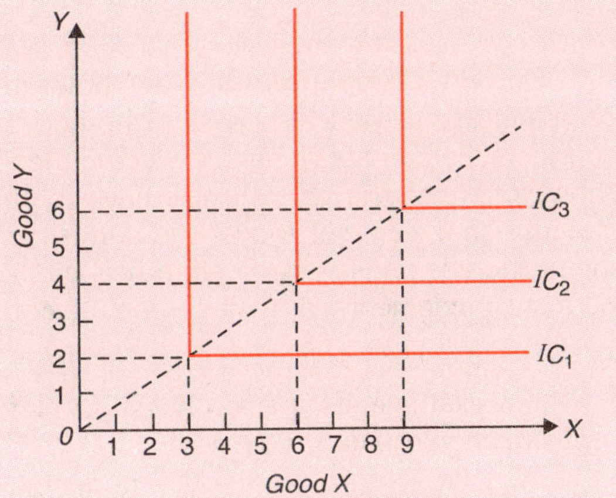

Fig. 8.8. *Indifference Curves of Perfect Complements*

As will be seen in Fig. 8.8, the left-hand portion of an indifference curve of the perfect complementary goods is a vertical straight line which indicates that an infinite amount of Y is necessary to substitute one unit of X, and the right-hand portion of the indifference curve is a horizontal straight line which means that an infinite amount of X is necessary to substitute one unit of Y. All this means that the two perfect complements are used in a certain fixed ratio and cannot be substituted for each other. In Fig. 8.8 two perfect complements are consumed in the ratio, $3X : 2Y$. ***Complements are thus those goods which are used jointly in a fixed ratio in consumption so that their consumption increases or decreases simultaneously.*** Pen and ink, right shoe and left shoe, automobile and petrol, sauce and hamburger, type writer and typists are some examples of perfect complements.

Utility Functions of Perfect Substitutes and Perfect Complements

Perfect Substitutes. In general utility function of perfect substitutes can be written as

$$U(x, y) = ax + by$$

where x and y are the quantities of two goods X and Y and a and b are some positive numbers that measure the values of goods to the consumer. The slope of indifference curve representing the above utility function of perfect substitutes is equal to $-\frac{a}{b}$.

If the consumer is willing to substitute good X and Y at the rate of *one-to-one*, the utility function of the perfect substitute goods can be written as

$$U(x, y) = x + y$$

The indifference curves of such substitute goods with one-to-one relationship in consumption has a slope of -1.

Further, if a consumer is willing to accept two units of good Y to compensate him for the loss of one unit of good X, then utility function of these two perfect substitutes can be written as

$$U(x, y) = 2x + y$$

This means that good X is *twice as valuable* to the consumer than good Y. Now, the indifference curve representing such utility function will have a slope of –2.

Besides, the squares of the quantities of two goods in the utility function [$U(x, y) = x + y$] of perfect substitutes will also give us the following utility function of the perfect substitutes

$$U(x, y) = (x + y)^2$$

Perfect Complements. Now, how can we describe the utility function of two perfect complements such as left shoe and right shoe. In case of two perfect complements, the consumer considers the *pairs* of shoes for wearing them. Therefore, in order to have complete pairs of shoes for wearing a person must have the *minimum* number of right shoes (call them x). Because, in the case of shoes, one right shoe and one left shoe constitute a pair for wearing them, there is one-to-one relation between right shoe and left shoe. The utility function of perfect complements with one-to-one relationship can be written as

$$u(x, y) = min\ (x, y)$$

For example, if a person has a bundle of goods of 5 right shoes and 5 left shoes, the utility function can be written as

$$u(x, y) = min\ (5, 5)$$

If the person is provided with one more unit of right shoe, then his utility will not increase because the left shoe is not available to him to make up the pair for wearing. Therefore, the extra one right shoe, keeping the number of left shoes remaining the same, will not cause any increase in the utility of the person. Thus in this case utility function can be written as

$$u(x, y) = min\ (5, 5) = min\ (6, 5)$$

The above cases of complements relate to when there is one-to-one relation of the two perfect complements. However, there are cases of perfect complements when the consumer consumes goods in proportion other than one-to-one. For example, consider a consumer who always uses two teaspoons of sugar with each cup of tea. Thus in this case appropriately sweetened cups of tea will be minimum $(x, \frac{1}{2}y)$ and in this case of perfect complements utility function can be written as

$$u(x, y) = min\ (x, \frac{1}{2}y)$$

In general, the utility functions of two perfect complements can be written as

$$u(x, y) = min\ (ax + by)$$

where a and b are the proporitions in which the two goods are consumed.

SOME NON-NORMAL CASES OF INDIFFERENCE CURVES : GOODS, BADS AND NEUTERS

We have drawn and explained the indifference curves of commodities which are "**goods**", that is, desirable objects. If a commodity is 'good', then more of it is preferred to less of it. As seen above, indifference curves between two commodities which are "goods" slope downward and are convex to the origin. However, when for a consumer a commodity is a '***bad***', that is, undesirable object, the more of it will lower his satisfaction. Thus, if a commodity which is bad, less is preferable to more. Pollution, risk, tenacious work, and illness are some examples of bads. In the case of bads, indifference curves are of different shape. Suppose a bad (for example, pollution) is represented on the X-axis and a commodity which is "good" is represented on the Y-axis, then the indifference curve will be sloping upward (that is, will have a positive slope) as displayed in Figure 8.9. This is because in this case a movement towards the right along an indifference curve implies more of pollution which will reduce consumer's satisfaction and, therefore, in order to keep his level of satisfaction constant, the quantity of a commodity which'is "good" such as clothing will have to be increased. The direction of preference in this case is upward and to the left.

An important application of indifference curve analysis in recent years relates to the problem of **portfolio selection**. Portfolio selection by an individual means his choice of a particular distribution of his wealth among several assets such as equity shares, debentures, real estate, etc. These different assets yield different rates of return and involve varying degree of riskiness. In the analysis of portfolio selection, the *average or mean return* from a portfolio enters as a "good" or a desired object, whereas degree of risk involved enters as a bad or an undesired object. In Figure 8.10 we depict indifference curves of an investor who wants or prefers high average return and low risk. The higher the average return, the higher the

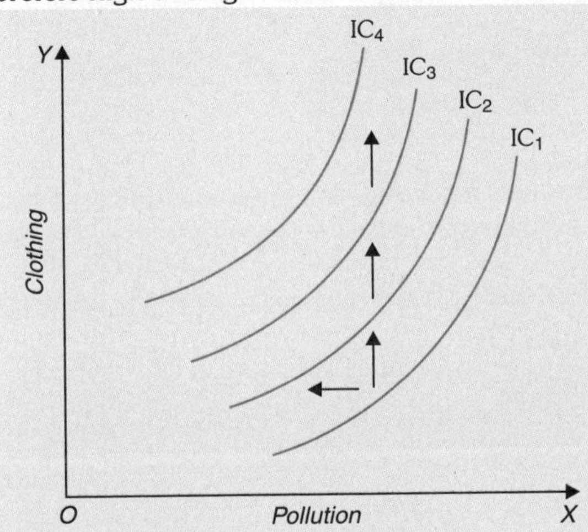

Fig. 8.9. *Indifference, Curves between 'Bad' and 'Good'*

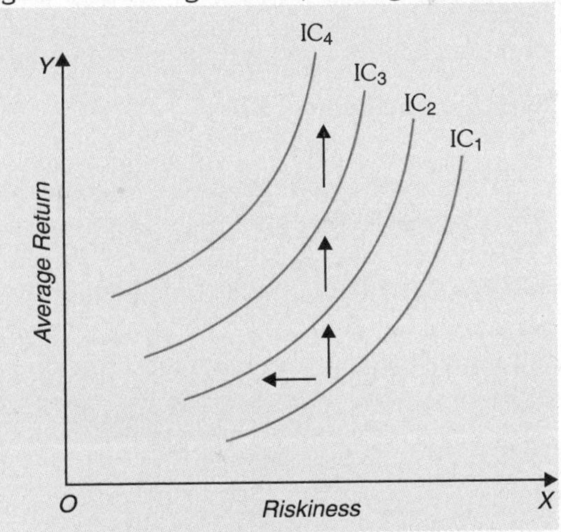

Fig. 8.10. *Indifference Curves between Riskiness and Average Return*

Neuter. A commodity can be neuter (or a neutral good) in which case the consumer does not care whether he has more or less of that commodity. That is, more or less of a neuter does not affect his satisfaction in any way. If a commodity X is a neuter good and Y a normal good,

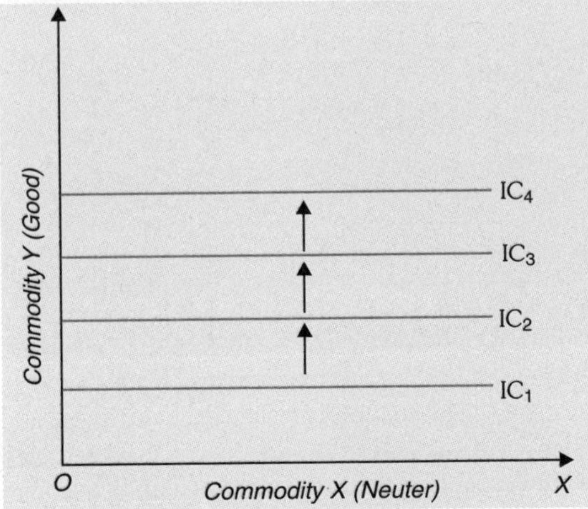

Fig. 8.11. *Indifference Curves between a Neuter and Good*

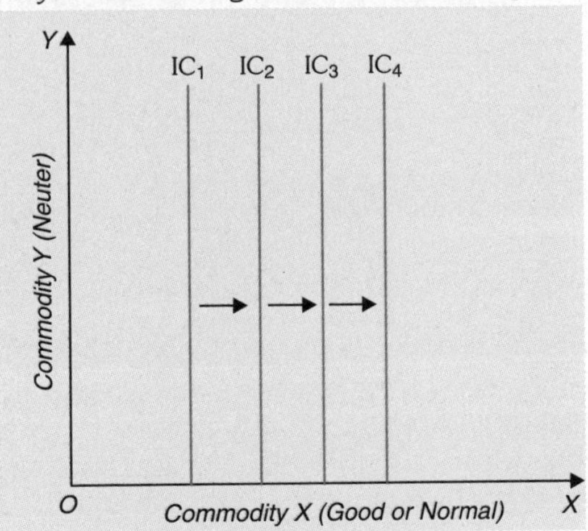

Fig. 8.12. *Indifference curves between Good and Neuter*

satisfaction of the investor; and higher the degree of risk involved in a portfolio, the lower the satisfaction of the investor. Therefore, in this case also, the indifference curve between riskiness (*i.e.*, bad) and rate of return (*i.e.*, a good) slopes upward. This is because as we move rightward satisfaction declines due to greater risk and to compensate for the decline in satisfaction due to greater risk and to keep the level of satisfaction constant, rate of return (*i.e.*, 'good') has to be increased. It may be noted that direction of preference in this case also will be northward and westward as indicated in the diagram. then *indifference curves will be horizontal lines* as depicted in Figure 8.11 and the direction of preference will be upward to the north indicating thereby that the higher level of indifference curve will mean higher level of satisfaction because upward movement will mean a 'good' commodity is increasing, the quantity of a neuter good remaining the same.

On the other hand, if commodity Y is neuter, while commodity X is good or normal, then indifference curves will be vertical straight lines as depicted in Figure 8.12. The direction of preference in this case will be towards the east (i.e. rightward).

Satiation and Point of Bliss

Our observations in the real world tell us that a commodity can be good only upto a point, called the point of satiation and becomes bad for a consumer if he is forced to increase his consumption beyond that point. There is a combination or bundle of the commodities which contains the optimal or most preferred quantities of the commodities for a consumer and any increase in the quantity of each of them beyond that best or optimal quantity will make the consumer worse off (that is, reduce his satisfaction), quantities of other commodities remaining the same. Too much of everything is bad. Therefore, commodity X becomes bad beyond the quantity X_1 and commodity Y becomes bad beyond the quantity Y_1. Two goods case is represented in Figure 8.13 where the circular indifference curves between the two commodities X and Y are drawn. Suppose X_1 and Y_1, are the quantities of two commodities which the consumer considers as the best or optimal quantities beyond which the two commodities become bad. Point S represents these most preferred quantities of the two commodities and is therefore the *point of satiation or bliss*. In zone 1, the portions of indifference curves between the two commodities have negative slope and, therefore, the two commodities are good in this zone.

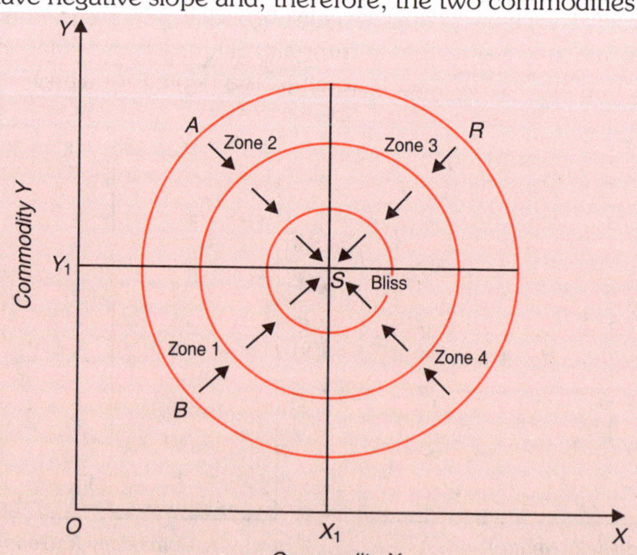

Fig. 8.13. *Different zones of Goodness and Badness and Point of Bliss*

Let us now consider point A in zone 2 which contains more of Y than regarded optimal or best by our consumer. Therefore, in order to keep his satisfaction constant, he has to be compensated by increase in the quantity of X (Note that in zone 2 the quantity of X remains less than X_1 and increase in its quantity is desirable and adds to his satisfaction. In zone 2, indifference curves have positive slope and here while commodity X is too little, the commodity Y is too much. Therefore, in zone 2, the commodity Y becomes bad while the commodity X remains good. It may be further noted that as the consumer moves toward the point S or his indifference curves approach closer to this point, his satisfaction is increasing and at point S of satiation his satisfaction is maximum. Satiation point S is also called the *point of bliss*.

Now, consider point R on indifference curve IC_1 in zone 3 in which indifference curves have also negative slope. As the consumer moves from point R to S, the quantities of both the commodities decrease but he reaches nearer to the point S of his satiation or bliss. ***In this case both the commodities are bad.*** The sum and substance of the whole matter is that as a consumer moves nearer to his most preferred combination S, his satisfaction increases.

In zone 4, whereas the commodity X is more than the desirable quantity X_1, the quantity of commodity Y is less than its optimal quantity. Indifference curves in this region are positively sloping indicating that, commodity X being bad in this region increase in its quantity has to be compensated by the increase in the quantity of Y which is desirable in this region to keep the level of consumer's satisfaction constant.

It follows from above that a consumer has some optimal or most preferred combination of commodities and closer he is to that combination, the better off he is. The combinations of two commodities, say chocolate and ice cream, which are nearer to the point of satiation or bliss point, lie on higher indifference curves and the combinations lying further away from the satiation point, would lie on lower indifference curves. There will be some optimal combination of chocolate and ice cream which a consumer would like to eat per week. Consumers would not voluntarily like to consume too much of them, that is, more than what they want. Thus, the interesting and relevant region for consumer's choice of commodities is where he has less than optimal quantities of both these commodities. In Figure 8.13 this region is represented by zone 1 in which the consumer has less of the two goods than he wants and therefore increase in the quantities of the two goods in this region will cause increase in his satisfaction and will move him nearer to the point of satiation.

BUDGET LINE OR BUDGET CONSTRAINT

The knowledge of the concept of *budget line*[1] or what is also called *budget constraint* is essential for understanding the theory of consumer's equilibrium. As explained above, a higher indifference curve shows a higher level of satisfaction than a lower one. Therefore, a consumer in his attempt to maximise his satisfaction will try to reach the highest possible indifference curve. But in his pursuit of buying more and more goods and thus obtaining more and more satisfaction he has to work under two constraints: first, he has to pay the prices for the goods and, secondly, he has a limited money income with which to purchase the goods. Thus, how far he would go in for his purchases depends upon the prices of the goods and the money income which he has to spend on the goods. As explained above, indifference map represents consumer's scale of preferences between the two goods. Now, in order to explain consumer's equilibrium there is also the need for introducing into the indifference curve analysis the budget line which represents the prices of the goods and consumer's money income.

Suppose our consumer has got income of ₹ 50 to spend on two goods X and Y. Let price

1. The budget line has been variously named by different authors. Other names in the literature for the budget line are price line, price opportunity line, price-income line, outlay line, budget constraint, expenditure line and consumption possibility line.

of good X in the market be ₹ 10 per unit and that of Y ₹ 5 per unit. If the consumer spends his whole income of ₹ 50 on good X, he would buy 5 units of X; if he spends his whole income of ₹ 50 on good Y he would buy 10 units of Y. If a straight line joining 5X and 10Y is drawn, we will get what is called the price line or the budget line. ***Thus budget line shows all those combinations of two goods which the consumer can buy by spending his given money income on the two goods at their given prices.*** A look at Fig. 8.14 shows that with ₹ 50 and the prices of X and Y being Rs 10 and ₹ 5 respectively the consumer can buy 10Y and 0X, or 8Y and 1X; or 6Y and 2X, or 4Y and 3X etc. In other words, he can buy any combination that lies on the budget line with his given money income and given prices of the goods. It should be carefully noted that any combination of the two goods such as H (5Y and 4X) which lies above and outside the given budget line will be beyond the reach of the consumer. But any combination lying within the budget line such as K (2X and 2Y) will be well within the reach of the consumer, but if he buys any such combination he will not be spending all his income of ₹ 50. Thus, with the assumption that whole of the given income is spent on the given goods and at given prices of them, the consumer has to choose from all those combinations which lie on the budget line.

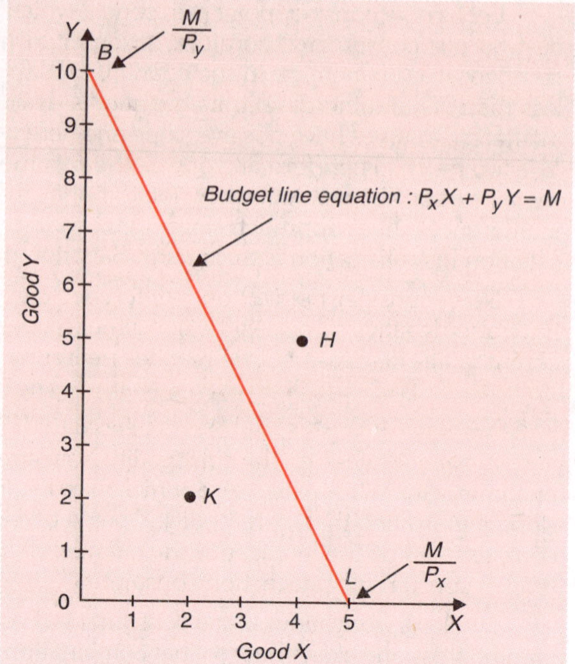

Fig. 8.14. *Budget Line or Budget Constraint*

It is clear from above that budget line graphically shows the *budget constraint*. The combinations of commodities lying to the right of the budget line are *unattainable* because income of the consumer is not sufficient to buy those combinations. Given consumer's income and prices of the two goods, the combinations of goods lying to the left of the budget line are *attainable*, that is, the consumer can buy any one of them. It is also important to remember that the intercept OB on the Y-axis in Fig. 8.14 equals the amount of his entire income (M) divided by the price (P_Y) of commodity Y. That is, $OB = M/Py$. Likewise, the intercept OL on the X-axis measures the total income divided by the price of commodity X. Thus $OL = M/P_x$.

The budget line can be written algebraically as follows :

$$P_x X + P_y Y = M \qquad \text{... (1)}$$

or

$$Y = \frac{M}{P_Y} - \frac{P_x}{P_Y}.X$$

where P_x and P_y denote prices of goods X and Y respectively and M stands for money income:

The above budget-line equation (1) implies that, given the money income of the consumer and prices of the two goods, every combination lying on the budget line will cost the same amount of money and can therefore be purchased with the given income. The budget line can be defined as *a* ***set of combinations of two commodities that can be purchased if***

whole of the given income is spent on them and its slope is equal to the negative of the price ratio.

Budget Space

It should be carefully understood that the budget equation $P_xX + P_yY = M$ or $Y = M/P_y - Px/P_y.X$ depicted by the budget line in Fig. 8.14 only describes the budget line and not the budget space. ***A budget space shows a set of all combinations of the two commodities that can be purchased by spending the whole or a part of the given income.*** In other words, budget space represents the ***opportunity set*** for the consumer, that is, all those combinations of two commodities which he can buy, given his budget constraint. Thus, the budget space implies the set of all combinations of two goods for which income

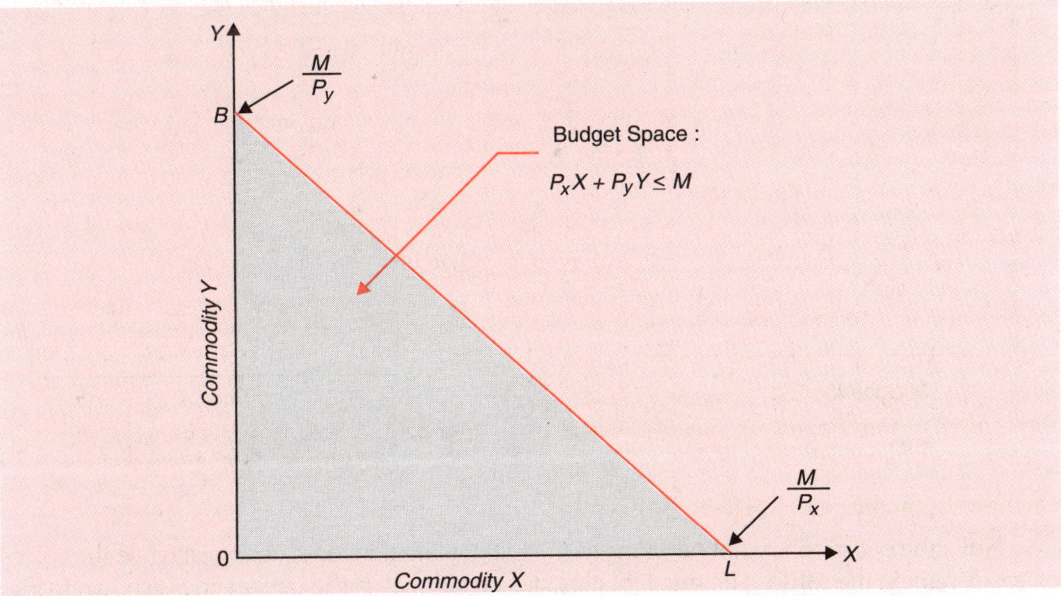

Fig. 8.15. *Budget Space or Opportunity Set*

X (*i.e.*, P_xX) and income spent on good Y (*i.e.* P_yY) *must not exceed* the given money income. Therefore, we can algebraically express the budget space in the following form of inequality :

$$P_xX + PyY \leq M, \text{ or } M \geq P_xX + P_yY$$

The budget space has been graphically shown in Fig. 8.15 as the shaded area. The budget space is the entire area enclosed by the budget line *BL* and the two axes.

Changes in Price and Shift in Budget Line

Now, what happens to the budget line if either the prices of goods change or the income changes. Let us first take the case of the changes in prices of the goods. This is illustrated in Fig. 8.16. Suppose the budget line in the beginning is *BL*, given certain prices of goods *X* and *Y* and a certain income. Suppose price of *X* falls, the price of *Y* and income remaining unchanged. Now, with a lower price of *X* the consumer will be able to purchase more quantity of *X* than before with his given income. Let at the lower price of *X*, the given income purchases *OL'* of *X* which is greater than *OL*. Since price of *Y* remains the same, there can be no change in the quantity purchased of good *Y* with the same given income and as a result there will be no shift in the point *B*. Thus, with the fall in price of good *X*, the consumer's money income and the price of Y remaining constant, the budget line will shift to the right to the new position *BL′*.

Now, what will happen to the budget line (initial budget line *BL*) if price of good *X* rises, the price of good *Y* and income remaining unaltered. With higher price of good *X*, the consumer can purchase smaller quantity of *X*, say *OL″* than before. Thus, with the rise in price of *X* the budget line will shift to the left to the new position *BL″*.

Figure 8.17 shows the changes in the budget line when price of good *Y* falls or rises, with the price of *X* and income remaining the same. In this the initial budget line is *BL*. With fall in price of good *Y*, other things remaining unchanged, the consumer could buy more of *Y* with the given money income and therefore budget line will shift above to *LB′*. Similarly, with the rise in price of *Y*, other things being constant, the budget line will shift below to *LB″*.

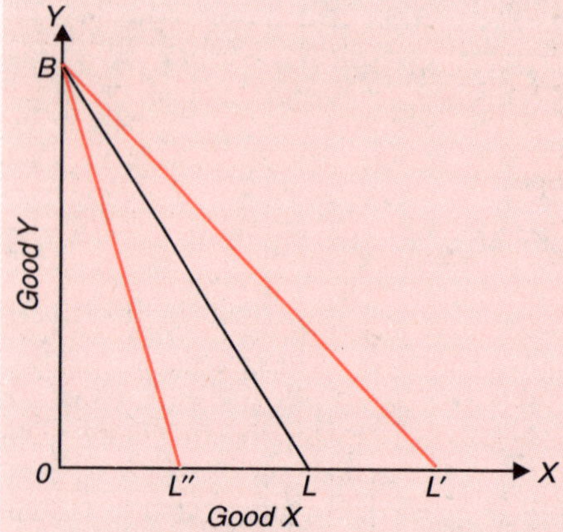

Fig. 8.16. *Changes in Budget Line as a Result of Changes in Price of Good X*

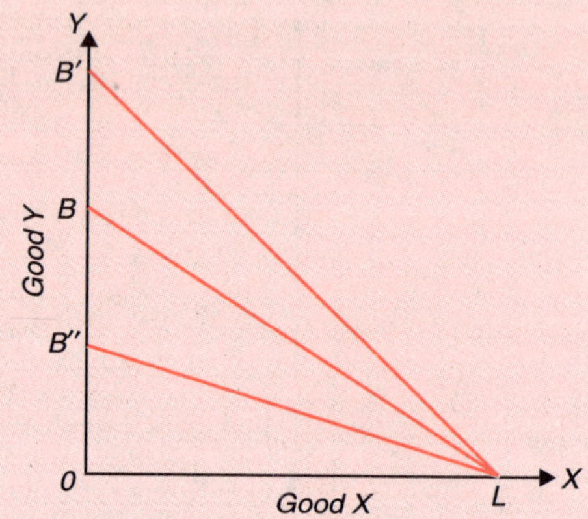

Fig. 8.17. *Changes in Budget Line as Result Changes in Price of Good Y*

Changes in Income and Shifts in Budget line

Now, the question is what happens to the budget line if income changes, while the prices of goods remain the same. The effect of changes in income on the budget line is shown in Fig. 8.18. Let *BL* be the initial budget line, given certain prices of goods and income. If consumer's income increases while prices of both goods *X* and *Y* remain unaltered, the price line shifts upward (say, to *B′L′*) and is parallel to the original budget line *BL*. This is because with the increased income the consumer is able to purchase proportionately larger quantity of good X than before if whole of the income is spent on *X*, and proportionately greater quantity of good Y than before if whole of the income is spent on Y. On the other hand, if income of the consumer decreases, prices of both goods *X* and *Y* remaining unchanged, the budget line shifts downward (say, to B″L″) but remains parallel to the original price line *BL*. This is because a lower income will purchase a proportionately smaller quantity of good *X* if the whole of the income is spent on *X* and proportionately smaller quantity of good *Y* if the whole of the income is spent on *Y*.

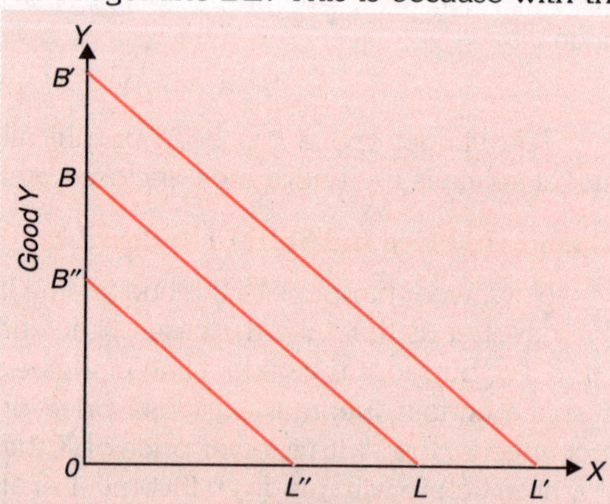

Fig. 8.18. *Shifts in Budget Line as a Result of Changes in Income*

It is clear from above that the budget line

will change if either the prices of goods change or the income of the consumer changes. Thus, the two determinants of the budget line are : (a) the prices of goods, and (b) the consumer 's income to be spent on the goods.

Slope of the Budget Line and Prices of Two Goods

It is also important to remember that the *slope* of the budget line is equal to the ratio of the prices of two goods. This can be proved with the aid of Fig. 8.14. Suppose the given income of the consumer is *M* and the given prices of goods X and Y are P_x and P_y respectively. The slope of the budget line *BL* is $\frac{OB}{OL}$. We intend to prove that this slope is equal to the ratio of the prices of goods X and Y.

The quantity of good *X* purchased if whole of the given income *M* is spent on it is *OL*.

Therefore, $OL \times P_x = M$

$$OL = \frac{M}{P_x} \quad \text{...}(i)$$

Now, the quantity of good *Y* purchased if whole of the given income *M* is spent on it is *OB*. Therefore,

$$OB \times P_y = M$$

$$OB = \frac{M}{P_y} \quad \text{...}(ii)$$

Dividing (*ii*) by (*i*) we have

$$\frac{OB}{OL} = \frac{M}{P_y} \div \frac{M}{P_x} = \frac{M}{P_y} \times \frac{P_x}{M} = \frac{P_x}{P_y}$$

$$\text{Thus, slope of budget line } = \frac{OB}{OL} = \frac{P_x}{P_y}$$

It is thus proved that *the slope of the budget line BL is equal to the ratio of prices of two goods.*

CONSUMER'S EQUILIBRIUM : MAXIMISING SATISFACTION

We are now in a position to explain with the help of indifference curves how a consumer reaches equilibrium position. *A consumer is said to be in equilibrium when he is buying such a combination of goods as leaves him with no tendency to rearrange his purchases of goods*. He is then in a position of balance in regard to the allocation of his money expenditure among various goods. In the indifference curve technique the consumer's equilibrium is discussed in respect of the purchases of two goods by the consumer. As in the cardinal utility analysis, in the indifference curve analysis also it is assumed that the consumer tries to maximise his satisfaction. In other words, the consumer is assumed to be rational in the sense that he aims at maximising his satisfaction. Besides, we shall make the following assumptions to explain the equilibrium of the consumer:

(1) The consumer has a given indifference map exhibiting his scale of preferences for various combinations of two goods, *X* and *Y*.
(2) He has a fixed amount of money to spend on the two goods. He has to spend whole of his given money on the two goods.
(3) Prices of the goods are given and constant for him. He cannot influence the prices of the goods by buying more or less of them.
(4) Goods are homogeneous and divisible.

To show which combination of two goods, X and Y, the consumer will decide to buy and will be in equilibrium position, his indifference map and budget line are brought together. As seen above, while indifference map portrays consumer's scale of preferences between various possible combinations of two goods, the budget line shows the various combinations which he can afford to buy with his given money income and given prices of the two goods. Consider Fig. 8.19 in which we depict consumer's indifference map together with the budget line BL. Good X is measured on the X-axis and good Y is measured on the X-axis. With a given money to be spent and given prices of the two goods, the consumer can buy any combination of the goods which lies on the budget line BL. Every combination on the budget line BL costs him the same amount of money. In order to maximise his satisfaction the consumer will try to reach the highest possible indifference curve which he could with a given expenditure of money and given prices of the two goods. Budget constraint forces the consumer to remain on the given budget line, that is, to choose a combination from among only those which lie on the given budget line.

It will be seen from Fig. 8.19 that the various combinations of the two goods lying on the budget line BL and which therefore the consumer can afford to buy do not lie on the same indifference curve; they lie on different indifference curves. The consumer will choose that combination on the budget line BL which lies on the highest possible indifference curve. The highest indifference curve to which the consumer can reach is the indifference curve to which the budget line BL is tangent. Any other possible combination of the two goods either would lie on a lower indifference curve and thus yield less satisfaction or would be unattainable.

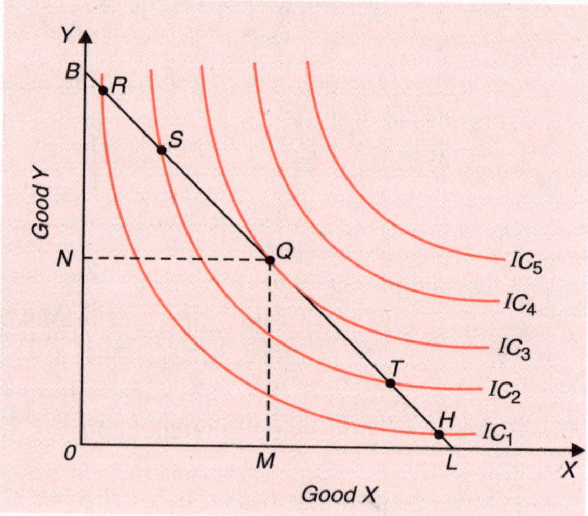

Fig. 8.19. *Consumer's Equilibrium*

In Fig. 8.19 budget line BL is tangent to indifference curve IC_3 at point Q. Since indifference curves are convex to the origin, all other points on the budget line BL, above or below the point Q, would lie on lower indifference curves. Take point R which also lies on the budget line BL and which the consumer can afford to buy. Combination of goods represented by R costs him the same as the combination Q. But, as is evident, R lies on the lower indifference curve IC_1 and will therefore yield less satisfaction than Q. Likewise, point S also lies on the budget line BL but will be rejected in favour of Q since S lies on the indifference curve IC_2 which is also lower than IC_3 on which Q lies. Similarly, Q will be preferred to all other points on the budget line BL which lies to the right of Q on the budget line, such as T and H. It is thus clear that of all possible combinations lying on budget line BL, combination Q lies on the highest possible indifference curve IC_3 which yields the consumer maximum possible satisfaction. Of course, combinations lying on indifference curves IC_4 and IC_5 will give greater satisfaction to the consumer than Q, but they are unattainable with the given money income and the given prices of the goods as represented by the budget line BL. It is therefore concluded that with the given money expenditure and the given prices of the goods as shown by BL the consumer will obtain maximum possible satisfaction and will therefore be in equilibrium position at point Q at which the budget line BL is tangent to the indifference curve IC_3. In this equilibrium position at Q the consumer will buy OM amount of good X and ON amount of good Y.

At the tangency point Q, the slopes of the budget line BL and indifference curve IC_3 are equal. Slope of the indifference curve shows the marginal rate of substitution of X for Y (MRS_{xy}), while the slope of the budget line indicates the ratio between the prices of two goods P_x/P_y. Thus, at the equilibrium point Q.

$$MRS_{xy} = \frac{\text{Price of good } X}{\text{Price of good } Y} = \frac{P_x}{P_y}$$

When the marginal rate of substitution of X for Y (MRS_{xy}) is greater or less than the price ratio between the two goods, it is advantageous for the consumer to substitute one good for the other. Thus, at points R and S in Fig. 8.19, marginal rates of substitution (MRS_{xy}) are greater than the given price ratio[2], the consumer will substitute good X for good Y and will move down along the budget line BL. He will continue to do so until the marginal rate of substitution becomes equal to the price ratio, that is, the given budget line BL becomes tangent to an indifference curve.

On the contrary, marginal rates of substitution at points H and T in Fig. 8.19 are less than the given price ratio. Therefore, it will be to the advantage of the consumer to substitute good Y for good X and accordingly move up the budget line BL until the MRS_{xy} rises so as to become equal to the given price ratio.

We can therefore express the condition for the equilibrium of the consumer by either saying that the given budget line must be tangent to the indifference curve, or the marginal rate of substitution of good X for good Y must be equal to the ratio between the prices of the two goods.

Second Order Condition for Consumer Equilibrium

The tangency between the given budget line and an indifference curve or, in other words, *the equality between MRS_{xy} and the price ratio is a necessary but not a sufficient condition of consumer's equilibrium.* The second order condition must also be fulfilled. ***The second order condition is that at the point of equilibrium indifference curve must be convex to the origin, or to put it in another way, the marginal rate of substitution of X for Y must be falling at the point of equilibrium.*** It will be noticed from Fig. 8.19 above that the indifference curve IC_3 is convex to the origin at Q, Thus at point Q both conditions of equilibrium are satisfied. Point Q in Fig. 8.19 is the optimum or best choice for the consumer and he will therefore be in stable equilibrium at Q.

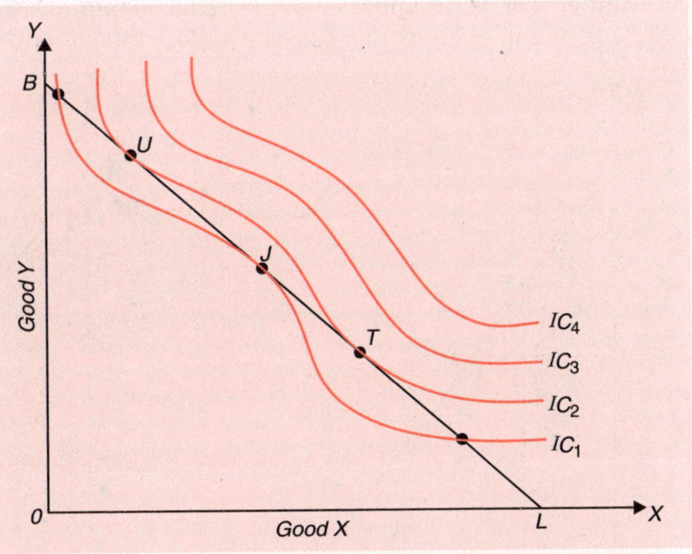

Fig. 8.20. *Second Order Condition for Consumer's Equilibrium*

But it may happen that while budget line is tangent to an indifference curve at a point

2. Tangents drawn at point R and S on indifference curves IC_1 and IC_2 respectively in Fig. 8.19 have greater slopes than the given slope of the budget line BL.

but the indifference curve may be concave at that point. Take for instance, Fig. 8.20 where indifference curve IC_1 is concave to the origin around the point J. Budget line BL is tangent to the indifference curve IC_1 at point J and MRS_{xy} is equal to the price ratio, P_x/P_y. But J cannot be a position of equilibrium because consumer's satisfaction would not be maximum there. Indifference curve IC_1 being concave at the tangency point J, there may be some points on the given budget line BL such as U and T, which will lie on an indifference curve higher than IC_1. Thus the consumer by moving along the given budget line BL can go to points such as U and T and obtain greater satisfaction than at J. We therefore conclude that for the consumer to be in equilibrium, the following two conditions are required:

1. A given budget line must be tangent to an indifference curve, or marginal rate of substitution of X for Y (MRS_{xy}) must be equal to the price ratio of the two goods $\frac{P_x}{P_y}$.

2. Indifference curve must be convex to the origin at the point of tangency.

The above explanation of consumer's equilibrium in regard to the allocation of his money expenditure on the purchases of two goods has been made *entirely in terms of the consumer's relative preferences of the various combinations of two goods.* In this indifference curve analysis of consumer's equilibrium no use of cardinal utility concept has been made which implies that satisfaction or utility obtained from the goods is measurable in the quantitative sense.

Differences in Preferences and Consumer's Equilibrium and Choice of Goods

The differences in shapes of indifference curves of the individuals causing difference in their marginal rates of substitution of one good for another at any given market basket of goods furnish us with the information about their preferences and tastes for goods. In panel (a) of Figure 8.21 the indifference curves depicting preferences and tastes of Amit and in panel (b) the indifference curves depicting preferences of Rajiv between wine and soft drinks have been drawn. As will be seen, whereas indifference curves of Amit between wine and soft drinks are relatively flat which implies that his marginal rate of substitution between the two goods (MRS_{WS}), at any given market basket, say M, of the goods is low, the indifference curves of

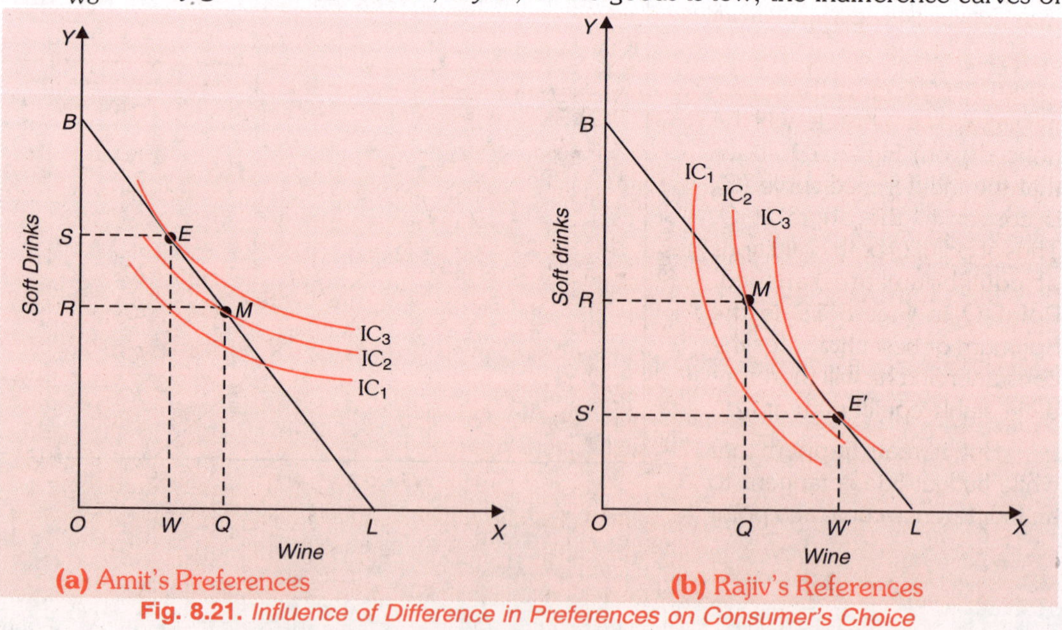

Fig. 8.21. *Influence of Difference in Preferences on Consumer's Choice*

Rajiv are steeper and his marginal rate of substitution *(MRS_{WS})* at the same market basket *M* is high showing that he strongly prefers wine to soft drink. Suppose both the individuals face the same prices of these goods and the same income to spend on them which mean that they have the same budget line *BL*.

It will seen from Figure 8.21 that at a given market basket *M* both the individuals are not in equilibrium. This is so because whereas at *M* in the panel (a) Amit's marginal rate of substitution of wine for soft drink *(MRS_{WS})* is lower than the given price ratio (P_w/P_S) of the two goods, in panel (b) marginal rate of substitution of wine for soft drinks *(MRS_{WS})* of Rajiv is greater than the given price ratio P_w/P_s).

Now, it is important to understand how the differences in preferences and tastes of the individuals between the goods would affect their equilibrium or choice of the two goods. In the analysis of consumer's equilibrium, as we have seen above, a consumer is in equilibrium and chooses a basket of goods where his indifference curve is tangent to the given budget line. A glance at Figure 8.21 will reveal that, with the budget line *BL*, since Amit strongly prefers soft drinks to wine, he is in equilibrium at point *E* where he chooses relatively a large quantity *OS* of soft drinks and relatively a small quantity of wine *OW* whereas Rajiv who prefers wine to soft drinks is in equilibrium at *E′* in panel (b) where he chooses a relatively large quantity *OW′* of wine and a smaller quantity *OS′* of soft drink. Thus the choice of basket of goods by the two individuals are determined by their respective preferences between the two goods. It is worth noting that the MRS_{ws} of both the individuals in their *equilibrium position* is the same, though their preferences between the two goods differ. This is so because to maximise satisfaction each of them equates his MRS_{WS} with the given price rates (P_w/P_s) of the two goods which has been assumed to be the same for the two individuals.

Thus, it follows from above that whereas differences in preferences of the individuals cause differences in MRS_{ws} of the individuals at any given market basket of goods and result in *choice of different market baskets of goods* in their equilibrium position, MRS_{ws} of the two individuals at these different baskets of goods in their equilibrium solution is the same.

CONSUMER'S EQUILIBRIUM : CORNER SOLUTIONS

When a consumer's preferences are such that he likes to consume some amount of both the goods, he reaches an equilibrium position at the point of tangency between the budget line and his indifference curve. This equilibrium position at the poinf of tangency which lies within commodity space between the two axes is often called *interior solution*. The economic implication of the interior solution is that consumer's pattern of consumption is *diversified*, that is, he purchases some amount of both the commodities. Our knowledge of the real world tells us that consumers' pattern of consumption is quite diversified and they often buy a basket or bundle of several different goods instead of spending their entire income on a single commodity.

In the context of two commodity model which is generally assumed in indifference curve analysis, assumption of diversification in consumption and an interior solution, which imply that consumer purchases some amount of both goods, is correct. However, in the real world of many commodities we often find that a typical consumer does not buy positive amounts of all the goods and services available in the market. In fact, a typical consumer buys only a small number of goods available in the market. How to explain this real world phenomena ?

Convex Indifference Curves and Corner Equilibrium

The reason for not purchasing a commodity by a consumer may be that the price or opportunity cost of that particular commodity may be too high for him. One may like to have

Maruti car, air conditioner or a colour TV, but may not actually have it on account of their prices being too high. The indifference curve analysis enables us to explain even this phenomenon. Consider Figure 8.22 where indifference map between two goods X and Y and budget line BL are such that the interior solution is not possible and consumer in its equilibrium position at point B will not consume any quantity of commodity X.

This is because as seen in the Figure 8.22 the price of commodity X is so high that budget line is steeper than the indifference curves between the two commodities. In economic terms it means that the price or opportunity cost of commodity X in the market is greater than

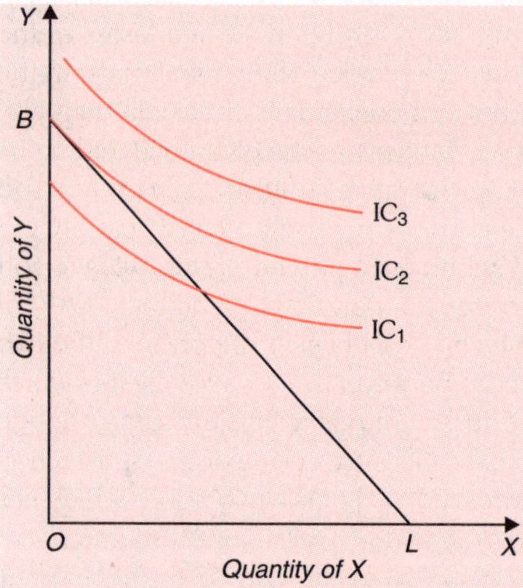

Fig. 8.22 *Corner Equilibrium in case of Convex Indifference Curves: Only commodity Y is bought*

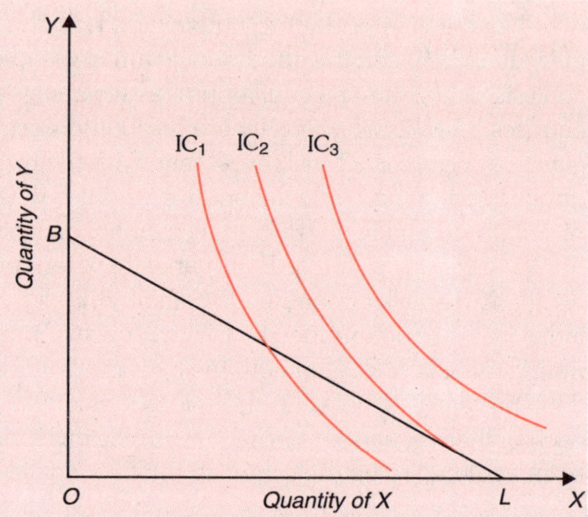

Fig. 8.23 *Corner Equilibrium in case of Convex Indifference Curves: Only commodity X is purchased*

the marginal rate of substitution of X for Y which indicates willingness to pay for the commodity X. The price of good X is so high as compared to marginal rate of substitution (willingness to pay for X or the marginal valuation of the first unit of the commodity X that the consumer does not purchase even one unit of the commodity X ($P_x/P_y > MRS_y$). Thus the consumer maximises his satisfaction or is in equilibrium at the corner point B where he buys only commodity Y and none of commodity X. Thus we have a corner solution for consumer's equilibrium,

On the other hand, in Figure 8.23. the indifference map between the two goods is such that the budget line BL is less steep than the indifference curves between the two goods so that the $MRS_y > P_x/P_y$ for all levels of consumption along the budget line BL. Therefore, he maximizes his satisfaction at the corner point L where he buys only commodity X and none of Y. In this case price of commodity Y and willingness to pay (*i.e. MRS*) for it are such that he does not consider it worthwhile to purchase even one unit of it.

Corner Equilibrium and Concave Indifference Curves

As said above, indifference curves are usually convex to the origin. Convexity of indifference curves implies that the marginal rate of substitution of X for Y falls as more of X is substituted for Y. Thus, indifference curves are convex to the origin when principle of diminishing marginal rate of substitution holds good and which is generally the case. But the possibility of indifference curves being concave to the origin cannot be ruled out in some exceptional cases. Concavity of the indifference curves implies that the marginal rate of substitution of X for Y increases when more of X is substituted for Y. It will be clear from the analysis made below that in case of indifference curves being concave to the origin, the consumer will choose or buy only one good. In other words, concavity of indifference curves implies that the consumer has a distaste for variety, that is, does not like diversification in consumption. However, distaste for variety cannot be considered a normal or model behaviour, so we regard convexity to be the general case. But when consumers have a distaste for variety and diversification the case of concave indifference curves will occur.

In case of concave indifference curves, the consumer will not be in equilibrium at the point of tangency between budget line and indifference curve, that is, in this case interior solution will not exist. Instead, we would have *corner solution* for consumer's equilibrium. Let us take Fig. 8.24 here indifference curves are sfiown to be concave. The given budget line *BL* is tangent to the indifference curve IC_2 at point *Q*. But the consumer cannot be in equilibrium at *Q* since by moving along the given budget line *BL* he can get on to higher indifference curves and obtain greater satisfaction than at *Q*. Thus by moving to *K* on the given budget line *BL*, he will get more satisfaction than at *Q* since *K* lies on a higher indifference curve than Q. He can increase his satisfaction still more by moving to point *Z* on the budget line *BL*.Thus, as he moves upward from tangency point *Q* on the budget line his satisfaction will go on increasing until he reaches the extremity point *B*. Likewise, if from *Q* he moves downward on the budget line, he will get on to higher indifference curves and his satisfaction will go on increasing till he reaches the other extremity point *L*. In these circumstances the consumer will choose only one of two goods: he will buy either *X* or *Y* depending upon whether *L* or *B* lies on the higher indifference curve. In the situation depicted in Fig. 8.24 point *B* lies on a higher indifference curve than point *L*.Therefore, the consumer will choose only *Y* and will buy *OB* of *Y*. It should be carefully noted that at *B* the budget line is not tangent to the indifference curve IC_5, even though the consumer is here in equilibrium. It is clear that when a consumer has concave indifference curves, he will succumb to monomania, that is, he will consume only one good.

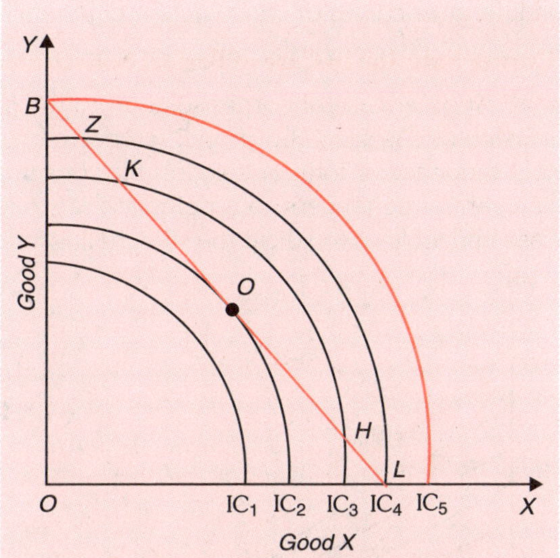

Fig. 8.24. Consumer Equilibruim in Case of Concave Indifference Curves

Conclusion

In our analysis above, we have shown that corner solution of consumer's equilibrium is possible even when his indifference curves between goods are convex. It is worth noting that in case of convex indifference curves, corner equilibrium is however not inevitable, it occurs only when price of a commodity is too high as compared to the marginal rate of substitution of even the first unit of the commodity. However, ***when the indifference curves are concave, consumer's equilibrium will inevitably be a corner solution.*** This implies that more of commodity *X* a consumer has the more useful or significant in terms of satisfaction an extra unit of it becomes. Therefore, the concave indifference curves do not seem to be plausible or realistic. Now, as seen above, the concavity of indifference curves for a consumer implies that the consumer spends his entire income on a commodity and therefore buys only one commodity. However, consumption of one good only by a consumer which the concavity of indifference curves leads us to believe is quite unrealistic. Observations in the real world reveal that consumers do not spend their entire income on a single commodity and in fact purchase a multitude of different goods and services. This rejects the existence of concave indifference curves.

Our analysis of inevitability of corner equilibrium in case of concave indifference curves provides us an important *economic rationale for indifference curves being convex rather than concave.* If indifference curves were predominantly concave the consumers would spend their entire income on a single commodity alone and thus consume only one commodity. This is quite inconsistent with the observed behaviour of consumers. This reinforces our belief that indifference curves of consumers are generally convex.

Corner Solution in Case of Perfect Substitutes and Perfect Complements

Another case of corner solution to the consumer's equilibrium occurs in case of perfect substitutes. As seen above, indifference curves for perfect substitutes are linear. In their case too, tangency or interior solution for consumer's equilibrium is not possible since the budget line cannot be tangent to a point of the straight-line indifference curve of substitutes. In this case budget line would cut the straight-line indifference curves. Two possibilities can be visualised :

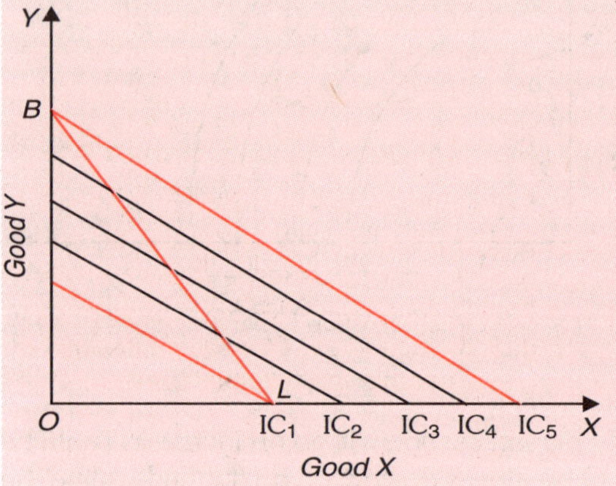

Fig. 8.25. *Corner Equilibrium in Case of Perfect Substitutes*

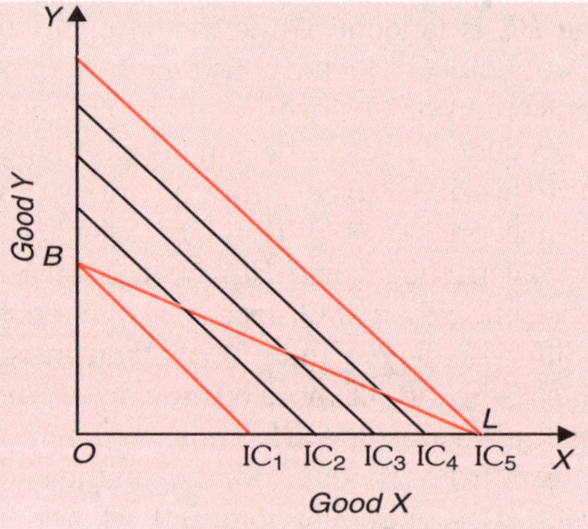

Fig. 8.26 *Corner Equilibrium in Case of Perfect Substitutes*

either the slope of the budget line *BL* can be greater than the slope of indifference curves, as in Fig. 8.25 or the slope of the budget line can be less than the slope of indifference curve, as in Fig. 8.26. If the slope of the budget line is greater than the slope of indifference curves, *B* would lie on a higher indifference curve than *L* and the consumer will buy only *Y*. If the slope of the budget line is less than the slope of indifference curves, *L* would lie on a higher indifference curve than *B* and the consumer will buy only *X*. It should be noted that in these cases too, the consumer will not be in equilibrium at any point between *B* and *L* on the price line since in case of Figure 8.25 of all the points on the given budget line extremity point *B* would lie on the highest possible indifference curve and in case of Figure 8.26 of all the points of the budget line extremity point *L* would lie on the highest

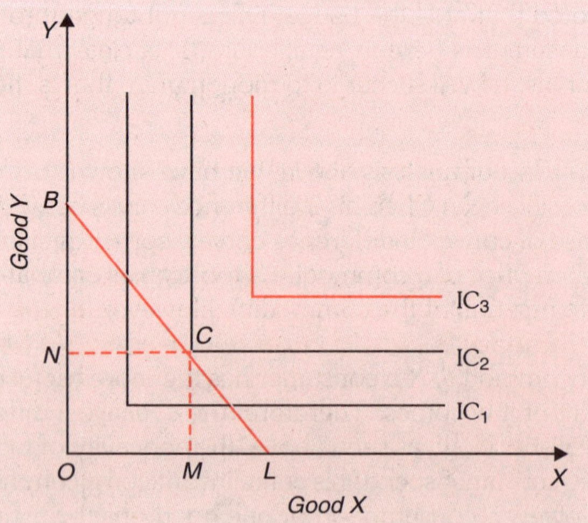

Fig. 8.27. *In case of perfect complements equilibrium exists at the corner of an indifference curve*

possible indifference curve. It is thus manifest that even in case of perfect substitutes, the consumer will succumb to monomania.

Another non-normal case is of *perfect complementary goods,* is depicted to Figure 8.27. Indifference curves of perfect complementary goods have a right-angled shape. In such a case the equilibrium of the consumer will be determined at the corner point of the indifference curve IC_2 which is just touching the budjet line *BL* at point *C* Indefference curve IC_2 is the highest possible indiffernce curve to which the consumer can go. In Figure 8.27, given the budget line *BL* the consumer will be in equilibrium at point *C* on indifference curve IC_2 and will be consuming *OM* of *X* and *ON* of *Y*.

INCOME EFFECT : INCOME CONSUMPTION CURVE

With a given money income to spend on goods, given prices of the two goods and given an indifference map (which portrays given tastes and preferences of the consumers), the consumer will be in equilibrium at a point in an indifference map. We are now interested in knowing how the consumer will react in regard to his purchases of the goods when his money income changes, prices of the goods and his tastes and preferences remaining unchanged. Income effect shows this reaction of the consumer. Thus, *the income effect means the change in consumer's purchases of the goods as a result of a change in his money income*. Income effect is illustrated in Fig. 8.28.

With given prices and a given money income as indicated by the budget line P_1L_1, the consumer is initially in equilibrium at point Q_1 on the indifference curve IC_1 and is having OM_1 of *X* and ON_1 of *Y*. Now suppose that income of the consumer increases. With his increased income, he would be able to purchase larger quantities of both the goods. As a result, budget line will shift upward and will be parallel to the original budget line P_1L_1. Let us assume that the consumer's money income increases by such an amount that the new budget line is P_2L_2 (consumer's income has increased by L_1L_2 in terms of *X* or P_1P_2 in terms of Y). With budget line P_2L_2, the consumer is in equilibrium at point Q_2 on indifference curves IC_2 and is buying OM_2 of *X* and ON_2 of *Y*. Thus, as a result of the increase in his income the consumer buys more quantity of both the goods. Since he is on the higher indifference curve IC_2 he will be better off than before *i.e.*, his satisfaction will increase. If his income increases further so that the budget line shifts to P_3L_3, the consumer is in equilibrium at point Q_3 on indifference curve IC_3 and is having greater quantity of both the goods than at Q_2. Consequently, his satisfaction further increases. In Fig. 8.28 the consumer's equilibrium is shown at a still further higher level of income and it will be seen that the consumer is in equilibrium at Q_4 on indifference curves IC_4 when the budget line shifts to P_4L_4. As the consumer's income increases, he switches to higher indifference curves and as a consequence enjoys higher levels of satisfaction.

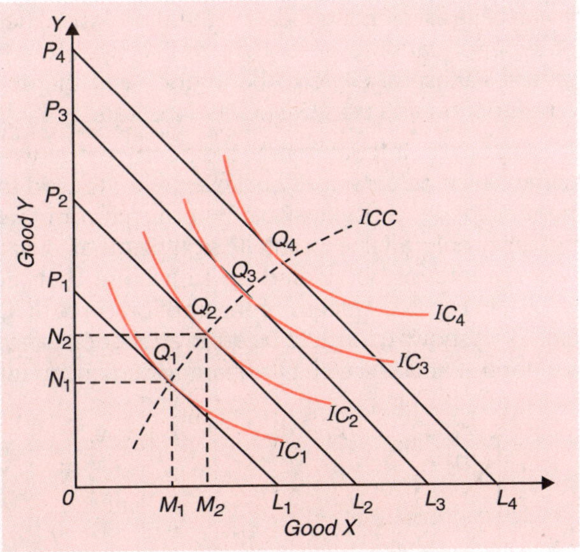

Fig. 8.28. *Income Consumption Curve: Income Effect*

If now various points Q_1, Q_2, Q_3 and Q_4 showing consumer's equilibrium at various levels of income are joined together, we will get what is called *Income Consumption Curve (ICC)*.

Income consumption curve is thus the locus of equilibrium points at various levels of consumer's income. ***Income consumption curve traces out the income effect on the quantity consumed of the goods. Income effect can either be positive or negative. Income effect for a good is said to be positive when with the increase in income of the consumer, his consumption of the good also increases.*** This is the normal good case. When the income effect of both the goods represented on the two axes of the figure is positive, the income consumption curve (*ICC*) will slope upward to the right as in Fig. 8.28. Only the upward-sloping income consumption curve can show rising consumption of the two goods as income increases.

However, for some goods, income effect is negative. ***Income effect for a good is said to be negative when with the increases in his income, the consumer reduces his consumption of the good.*** Such goods for which income effect is negative are called *Inferior Goods*. This is because the goods whose consumption falls as income of the consumer rises are considered to be some way 'inferior' by the consumer and therefore he substitutes superior goods for them when his income rises. When with the increase in his income, the consumer begins to consume superior goods, the consumption or quantity purchased by him of the inferior goods falls. When the people are poor, they cannot afford to buy the superior goods which are often more expensive. Hence as they become richer and can afford to buy more expensive goods they switch to the consumption of superior and better quality goods. For instance, most of the people in India consider cheaper common foodgrains such as maize, jawar, bajra as inferior goods and therefore when their income rises, they shift to the consumption of superior varieties of foodgrains like wheat and rice. Similarly, most of the Indian people regard Vanaspati Ghee to be inferior and therefore as they become richer, they reduce its consumption and use '*Desi Ghee*' instead.

In case of inferior goods, indifference map would be such as to yield income consumption curve which either slopes backward (*i.e.*, toward the left) as in Fig. 8.29, or downward to the right as in Fig. 8.30. It would be noticed from these two figures that income effect becomes negative only after a point. It signifies that only at higher ranges of income, some goods become inferior goods and up to a point their consumption behaves like those of normal goods. In Fig. 8.29 income consumption curve (*ICC*) slopes backward *i.e.*, bends toward the *Y*-axis. This shows good *X* to be an inferior good, since beyond point Q_2, income effect is negative for good *X* and as a result its quantity demanded falls as income increases. In Fig.8.30 income

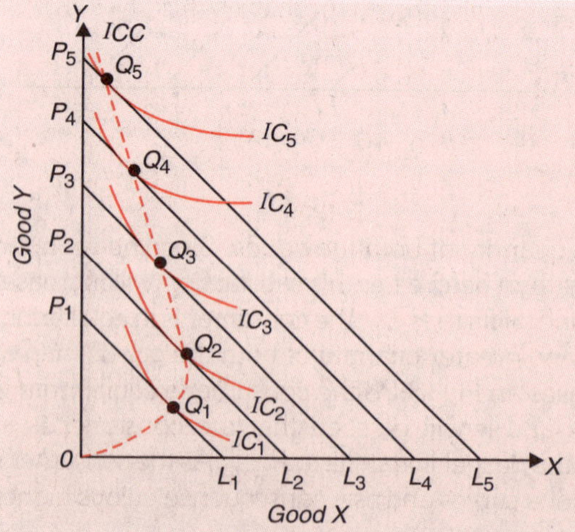

Fig. 8.29. *Income Consumption Curve in Case of Good X being Inferior Good*

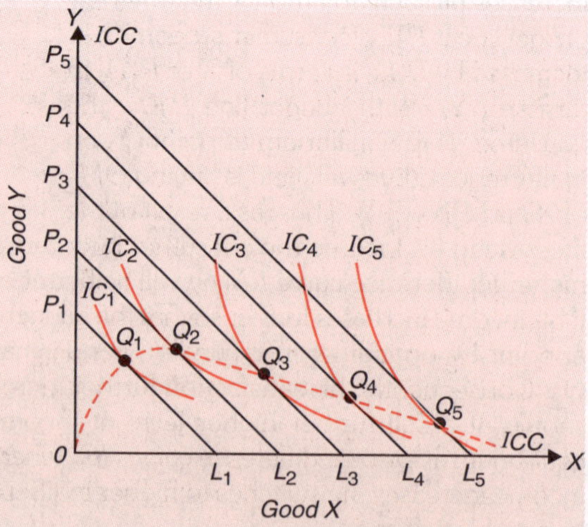

Fig. 8.30. *Income Consumption Curve in Case of Good Y being Inferior Good*

consumption curve (*ICC*) slopes downward to the right beyond point Q_2 *i.e.*, bends towards the *X*-axis. This signifies that good *Y* is an inferior good because beyond point Q_2, income effect is negative for good *Y* and as a result its quantity demanded falls as income increases. It follows from above that the income consumption curve can have various possible shapes.

But normal goods can be either necessities or luxuries depending upon whether the quantities purchased of the goods by the consumers increase less than or more than proportionately to the increases in income. If the quantity purchased of a commodity rises less than proportionately to the increases in consumer's income, the commodity is known as a *necessity*. On the other hand, if the quantity purchased of a commodity increases more than proportionately to the increases in income, it is called a *luxury*. In Fig. 8.31, the slope of income consumption curve ICC_1 is increasing which implies that the quantity purchased of the commodity *X* increases less than proportionately to the increases in consumer's income. Therefore, in this case of ICC_1, good *X* is a necessity and good *Y* is luxury. On the other hand, the slope of income consumption curve ICC_3 is decreasing which implies that the quantity purchased of good *X* increases more than proportionately to increases in income and therefore in this case good *X* is luxury and good *Y* is necessity. It will be seen from Fig. 8.31 that the income consumption curve ICC_2 is a *linear* curve passing through the origin which implies that the increases in the quantities purchased of both the goods are rising in proportion to the increase in income and therefore neither good is a luxury or a necessity.

If income effect is positive for both the goods *X* and *Y*, the income consumption curve will slope upward to the right as in Fig. 8.28 given earlier. But upward-sloping income consumption curves to the right for various goods may be of different slopes as shown in Fig. 8.31 in which income consumption curves, with varying slopes, are all sloping upward and therefore indicate both goods to be normal goods having positive income effect. ***If income effect for good X is negative, income consumption curve will slope backward to the left as ICC' in Fig. 8.32. If good Y happens to be an inferior good and income consumption curve will bend towards X-axis as shown by ICC" in Fig. 8.32.*** In Figs. 8.31 and 8.32, various possible shapes which income consumption curve can take are shown *bereft of indifference curves and budget lines* which yield them. It may however be pointed out that given an indifference map and a set of budget lines there will be one income consumption curve.

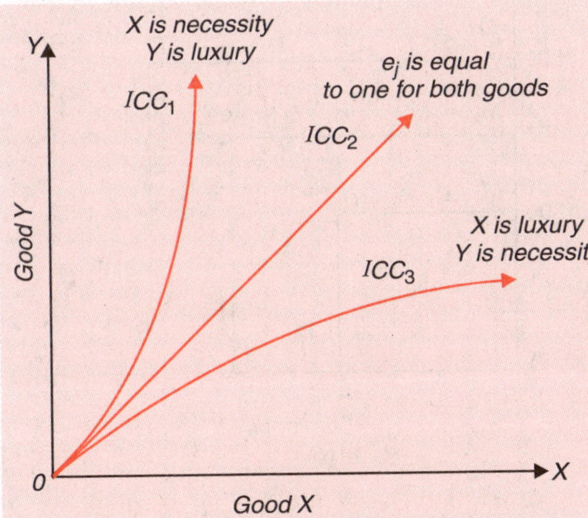

Fig. 8.31. *Income Consumption Curves of Normal Goods*

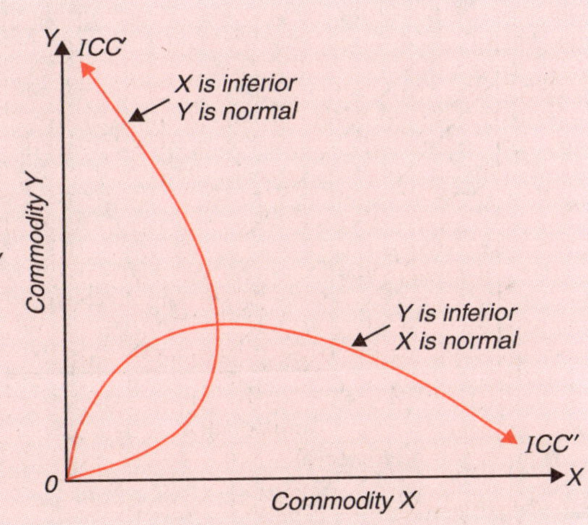

Fig. 8.32. *Income Consumption Curves of Inferior Goods*

A noteworthy point is that it is not the indifference curves which explain why a good happens to be an inferior good. In other words, indifference curves do not explain why income effect for a good is negative. Indifference curves can only illustrate the inferior-good phenomenon.

INCOME CONSUMPTION CURVE AND ENGEL CURVE

As seen above, in indifference curve map income consumption curve is the locus of the equilibrium quantities consumed by an individual at different levels of his income. Thus, the income consumption curve (*ICC*) can be used to derive the relationship between the level of consumer's income and the quantity purchased of a commodity by him. A nineteenth century German statistician Ernet Engel (1821-1896) made an empirical study of family budgets to draw conclusions about the pattern of consumption expenditure, that is, expenditure on different goods and services by the households at different levels of income. The conslusions he arrived at are still believed to be generally valid. According to Engel's studies, as the income of a family increases, the proportion of its income spent on necessities such as food falls and that spent on luxuries (consisting of industrial goods and services) increases. In other words, the poor families spend relatively large proportion of their income on necessities, whereas rich families spend a relatively a large part of their income on luxuries. ***This change in the pattern of consumption expenditure (that is, decline in the proportion of income spent on food and other necessities and increase in the proportion of income spent on luxuries) with the rise in income of the families has been called Engel's law.***

Though Engel dealt with the relationship between *income and expenditure* on different goods, in order to keep our analysis simple we will describe and explain the *relationship between income and quantities purchased of goods*. However, both types of relations will convey the same information about individual's consumption behaviour as in our analysis of Engel's curve, the prices of goods are held constant. The curve showing the relationship between the levels of income and quantity purchased of particular commodities has therefore been called Engel curve. In what follows we explain how an Engel curve is derived from income consumption curve. In our analysis of Engel curve we relate *quantity purchased* of a commodity, rather than *expenditure* on it, to the level of consumer's income.[3]

It is worth noting that like the demand curve depicting relationship between price and quantity purchased, other factors remaining the same, Engel curve shows relationship between

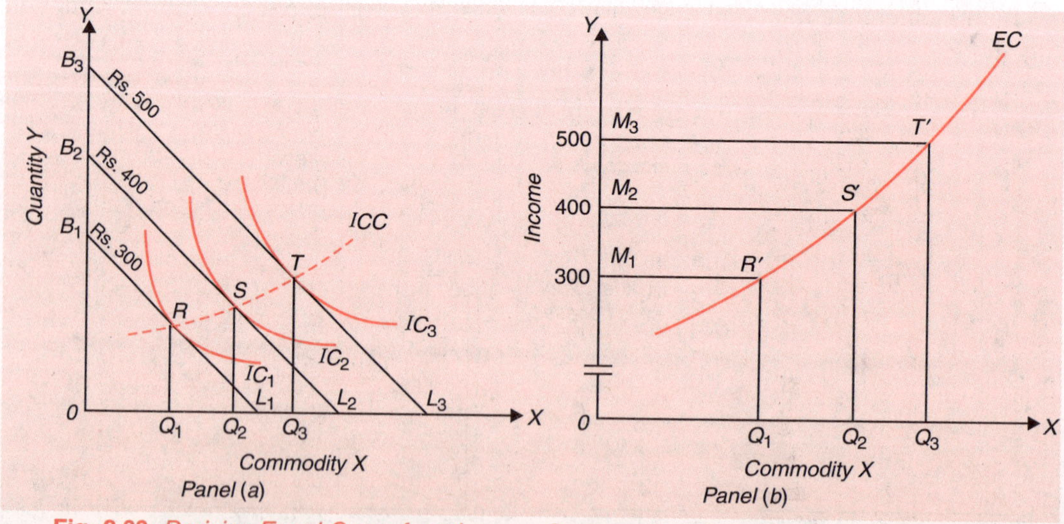

Fig. 8.33. *Deriving Engel Curve from Income Consumption Curve in Case of Necessities*

3. It may be noted that modern economists also study the relationship between expenditure and level of income and represent this by a curve which they call Engel Expenditure Curve. When they study the relationship between income and quantity purchased and derive a curve of this relationship, they call it simply Engel Curve as we are doing in the present chapter.

income and quantity demanded, other influences on quantity purchased such as prices of goods, consumer preferences are assumed to be held constant.

For deriving Engel curve from income consumption curve we plot level of income on the Y-axis and quantity purchased of a commodity on the X-axis. Consider panel (*a*) in Fig. 8.33. Given the indifference map representing the preferences of a consumer and the prices of two goods X and Y, *ICC* is the income consumption curve showing the equilibrium quantities purchased of commodities by the consumer as his income increases from Rs. 300 to Rs. 400 and to Rs. 500 per day. It will be seen from panel (*a*) of Fig. 8.33 that when income is Rs. 300, given prices of goods X and Y, the consumer is buying OQ_1 quantity of the commodity X. In panel (*b*) of Fig. 8.33 in which level of income is represented on the vertical axis and quantity purchased of commodity X on the horizontal axis we directly plot quantity OQ_1 against income level of Rs. 300. As income increases to Rs. 400, prices of goods remaining constant, the budget line in panel (*a*) shifts outward to the left to the new position B_2L_2 with which consumer is in equilibrium at point S and the consumer buys OQ_2 quantity of good X. Thus, in panel (*b*) of Fig. 8.33 we plot quantity purchased OQ_2 of commodity X against income level of Rs. 400. Likewise, as income further rises to Rs. 500, budget line in panel (*a*) shifts to B_3L_3 and the consumer buys OQ_3 quantity of X in his new equilibrium position at T. Therefore, in panel (*b*) of Fig. 8.33. OQ_3 we plot OQ_3 against income of Rs. 500. Thus equilibrium points constituting the income consumption curve in consumer's indifference map have been transformed into Engel curve depicting quantity-income relationship. Each point of an Engel curve corresponds to a relevant point of income consumption curve. Thus R' of the Engel curve *EC* corresponds to point R on the *ICC* curve. As seen from panel (*b*), **Engel curve for normal goods is upward-sloping which shows that as income increases, consumer buys more of a commodity.**

The slope of Engel curve *EC* drawn in panel (*b*) of Figure 8.33 equals $\Delta M/\Delta Q$ where ΔM stands for chnage in income and ΔQ for change in quantity demanded of good X and has a positive sign. It is important to note that **the slope of the Engel curve in Fig. 8.33 (panel (b)) increases as income increases.** This indicates that with every equal increase in income, expansion in quantity purchased of the good successively declines. This upward-sloping Engel curve with increasing slope as income rises depicts the case of necessities, consumption of which increases relatively less as income rises. For instance, in Fig. 8.33 when

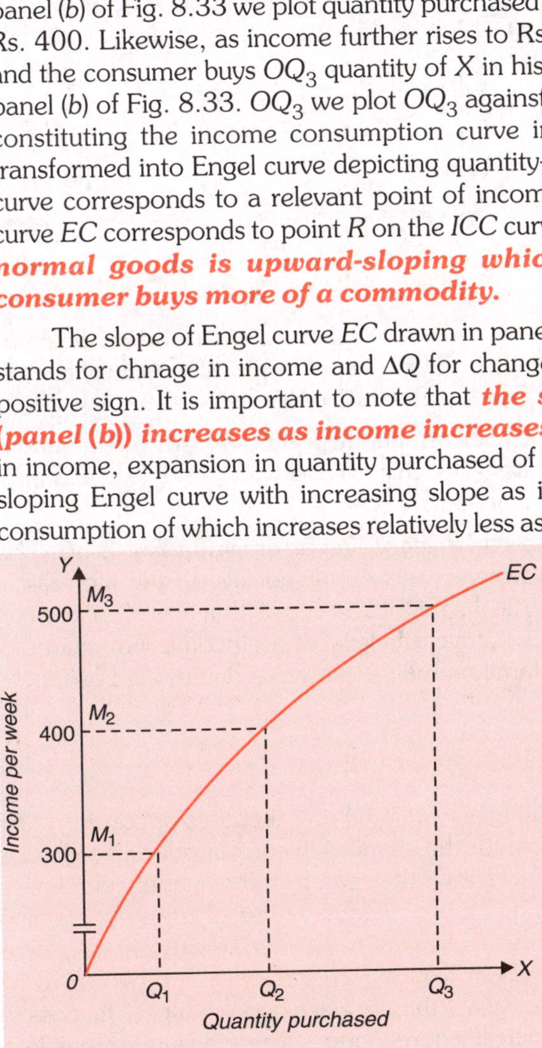

Fig. 8.34. *Engel Curve of a Luxury*

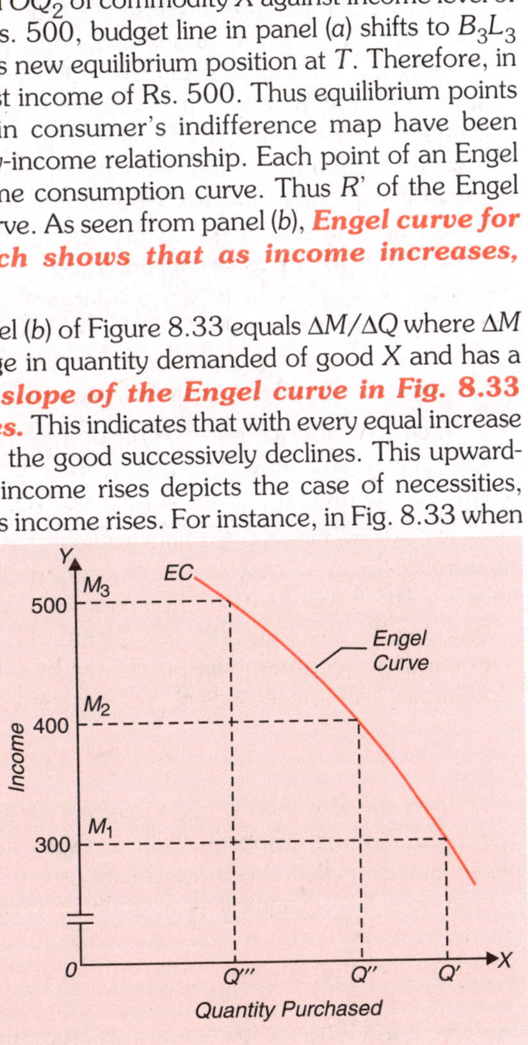

Fig. 8.35. *Backward Bending Engel Curve of an Inferior Good*

income is initially ₹ 300 (= M_1) per week, the quantity purchased of the good X equals OQ_1 and when income rises by ₹ 100 to ₹ 400 (= M_2) per week he increases his consumption to OQ_2, that is, by quantity $Q_1 Q_2$. Now, when his income per week further increases by ₹ 100 to ₹ 500 per week, the quantity consumed increases to OQ_3, that is, by Q_2Q_3 which is less than Q_1Q_2. Thus, in Engel curve drawn in panel (*b*) of Fig. 8.33 quantity purchased of the commodity increases with the increase in income but at a *decreasing rate*. This shape of the Engel curve is obtained for *necessities*.

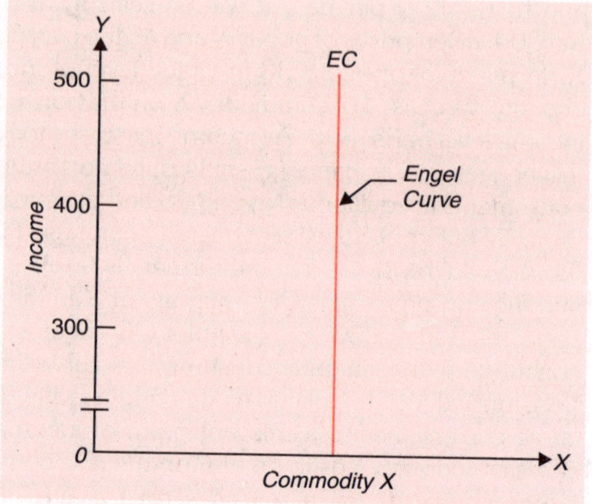

Fig. 8.36. Engel Curve of a Neutral Good

The Engel curve drawn in Fig.8.34 is upward-sloping but is concave. This implies that slope of the Engel curve ($\Delta M/\Delta Q$) is declining with the increase in income. That is, in the Engel curve of a commodity depicted in Fig. 8.34 the equal increments in income result in successively larger increases in the quantity purchased of the commodity. Thus, in Fig. 8.34 at income of ₹ 300 the consumer purchases OQ_1 quantity of a commodity. The increase in income by ₹ 100 to ₹ 400 results in increase in quantity purchased of the commodity equal to Q_1Q_2. With the further increase in income by the same amount of ₹ 100 to ₹ 500, the quantity purchased increases by Q_2Q_3 which is much larger than Q_1Q_2. This implies that ***as a consumer becomes richer he purchases relatively more of the commodity. Such commodities are called luxuries.*** Example of luxuries are air travel, luxury cars, costly woollen suits, air conditioners, costly fruits, etc.

In case of *inferior goods*, consumption of the commodity declines as income increases. Engel curve of an inferior good is drawn in Figure 8.35 which is backward bending indicating a fall in the quantity purchased of the good as income increases.

An extreme case of Engel curve is *a vertical straight* line as drawn in Fig. 8.36. This represents the case of a *neutral* commodity which is quite unresponsive to the increase in income. The Engel curve of the shape of a vertical straight line shows that a person goes on consuming the same amount of a commodity whatever the level of his income. For example, the quantity of common salt purchased by a family remains the same, determined as it is by food habits, with the increase in their income.

SUBSTITUTION EFFECT

We have explained above the effect of changes in income on purchases or consumption of a good. Another important factor responsible for the changes in consumption of a good is the substitution effect. Whereas the income effect shows the change in the quantity purchased of a good by a consumer as a result of change in his income, prices of goods remaining constant, ***substitution effect means the change in the quantity purchased of a good as a consequence of a change in its relative price alone, real income or level of satisfaction remaining constant.*** When the price of a good changes, he goes to a different indifference curve and his level of satisfaction changes.The Consumer goes to a different indifference curve as a result of a change in price because with this the real income or purchasing power of a consumer also changes. To keep the real income of the consumer constant so that the effect due to a change in the relative price alone may be known, price change is compensated by a simultaneous change in income. For example, when price of a good, say X, falls, real income of the consumer would increase and he would be in equilibrium at a higher indifference curve showing a higher level of satisfaction. In order to find out the substitution effect *i.e.*, change in the quantity of X purchased which has come about due to the change only in its relative price, the consumer's money income must be reduced by an amount that cancels out the gain in real income that results from the decrease in price. Now, two slightly different concepts of substitution effect have been developed; one by J.R. Hicks and the other by E. Slutsky. These two concepts of substitution effect have been named after their authors. Thus, the substitution effect which is propounded by Hicks and Allen is called the ***Hicksian Substitution Effect*** and that developed by E. Slutsky is known as ***Slutsky Substitution Effect.*** The two concepts differ in regard to the magnitude of the change in money income which should be effected so as to neutralise the change in real income of the consumer which results from a change in the price. We shall explain here the Hicksian substitution effect.

In the Hicksian substitution effect price change is accompanied by a so much change in money income that the consumer is neither better off nor worse off than before, that is, he is brought to the original level of satisfaction. In other words, money income of the consumer is changed by an amount which keeps the consumer on the same indifference curve on which he was before the change in the price. Thus the Hicksian substitution effect takes place on the same indifference curve. ***The amount by which the money income of the consumer is changed so that the consumer is neither better off nor worse off than before is called compensating variation in income.*** In other words, compensating variation in income is a change in the income of the consumer which is just sufficient to compensate the consumer for a change in the price of a good.

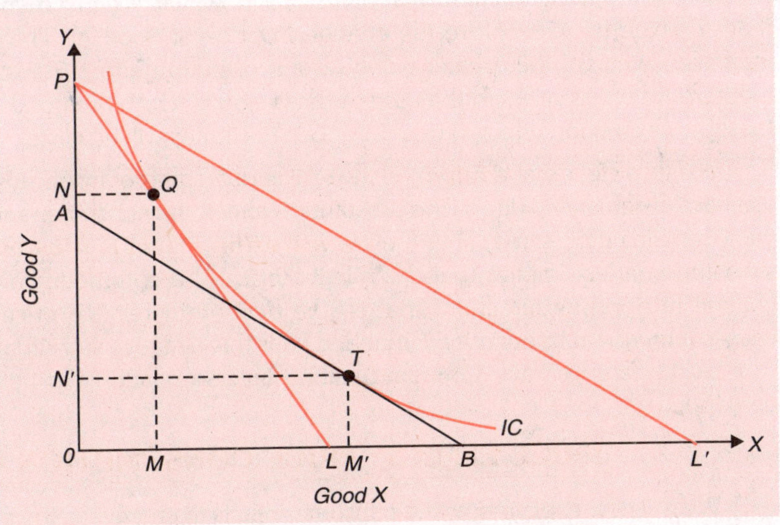

Fig. 8.37. *Hicksian Substitution Effect*

Thus, in the Hicksian type of substitution effect, income is changed by the magnitude of the *compensating variation in income.* Hicksian substitution effect is illustrated in Fig. 8.37. With a given money income and given prices of the two goods as represented by the budget line *PL*, the consumer is in equilibrium at point *Q* on the indifference curve *IC* and is purchasing *OM* of good X and *ON* of good Y. Suppose that the price of good X falls (price of Y remaining unchan-ged) so that the budget line now shifts to *PL'*. With the fall in price of X the consumer's real income or purchasing power would increase. In order to find out the substitution effect, this gain in real income should be wiped out by reducing the money income of the consumer by such an amount that forces him to remain on the same indifference curve *IC* on which he was before the change in price of the good X. When some money is taken away from the consumer to cancel out the gain in real income, then the budget line which shifted to position *PL′* will now shift downward but will be parallel to *PL′*. In Fig.8.37 a budget line *AB* parallel to *PL′* has been drawn at such a distance from *PL′* that it touches the indifference curve *IC*. It means that reduction of consumer's income by the amount *PA* (in terms of *Y*) or *L′B* (in terms of *X*) has been made so as to keep him on the same indifference curve. *PA* or *L′B* is thus just sufficient to cancel out the gain in the real income which occurred due to the fall in the price of *X*. *PA* or *L′B* is therefore compensating variation in income.

Now, budget line *AB* represents the new relative prices of goods *X* and *Y* since it is parallel to the budget line *PL′* which was obtained when price of good *X* had fallen. In comparison to the budget line *PL*, *X* is now relatively cheaper. The consumer would therefore rearrange his purchases of *X* and *Y* and will substitute *X* for *Y*. That is, since *X* is now relatively cheaper and *Y* is now relatively dearer than before, he will buy more of *X* and less of *Y*. It will be seen from Fig. 8.37 that budget line *AB* represents the changed relative prices but a lower money income than that of *PL*, since consumer's income has been reduced by compensating variation in income.

It will seen from Fig. 8.37 that with budget line *AB* the consumer is in equilibrium at point *T* and is now buying *OM′* of *X* and *ON′* of *Y*. Thus in order to buy *X* more he moves on the same indifference curve *IC* from point *Q* to point *T*. This increase in the quantity purchased of good *X* by *MM′* and the decrease in the quantity purchased of good *Y* by *NN′* is due to the change only in the relative prices of goods *X* and *Y*, since effect due to the gain in real income has been wiped out by making a simultaneous reduction in consumer's income. Therefore, movement from *Q* to *T* represents the substitution effect. Substitution effect on good *X* is the increase in its quantity purchased by *MM′* and substitution effect on *Y* is the fall in its quantity purchased by *NN′*. It is thus clear that as a result of the Hicksian substitution effect the consumer remains on the same indifference curve; he is however in equilibrium at a different point from that at which he was before the change in price of good *X*. The less the convexity of the indifference curve, the greater will be the substitution effect. As is known, the convexity of indifference curve is less in the case of those goods which are good substitutes. It is thus clear that the substitution effect in case of good substitutes will be large.

It is thus clear that a **fall** in relative price of a commodity always leads to the **increase** in its quantity demanded due to the substitution effect, the consumer's satisfaction or indifference curve remaining the same. Thus the ***substitution effect is always negative.*** The negative substitution effect implies that the relative price of a commodity and its quantity demanded change in opposite direction, that is, the *decline* in relative price of a commodity always causes *increase* in its quantity demanded. It is this negative substitution effect which lies at the root of the famous law of demand stating inverse relationship between price and quantity demanded.

PRICE EFFECT: PRICE CONSUMPTION CURVE

We will now explain how the consumer reacts to charges in the price of a good, his money income, tastes and prices of other goods remaining the same. Price effect shows this reaction of the consumer and measures the full effect of the change in the price of a good on the quantity purchased since no compensating variation in income is made in this case. When the price of a good charges, the consumer would be either better off or worse off than before, depending upon whether the price falls or rises. In other words, as a result of change in price of a good, his equilibrium position would lie at a higher indifference curve in case of the fall in price and at a lower indifference curve in case of the rise in price.

Price effect is shown in Fig. 8.38. With given prices of goods X and Y, and a given money income as represented by the budget line PL_1, the consumer is in equilibrium at Q on indifference curve IC_1. In this equilibrium position at Q, he is buying OM_1 of X and ON_1 of Y. Let price of good X fall, price of Y and his money income remaining unchanged. As a result of this price change, budget line shifts to the position PL_2. The consumer is now in equilibrium at R on a higher indifference curve IC_2 and is buying OM_2 of X and ON_2 of Y. He has thus become

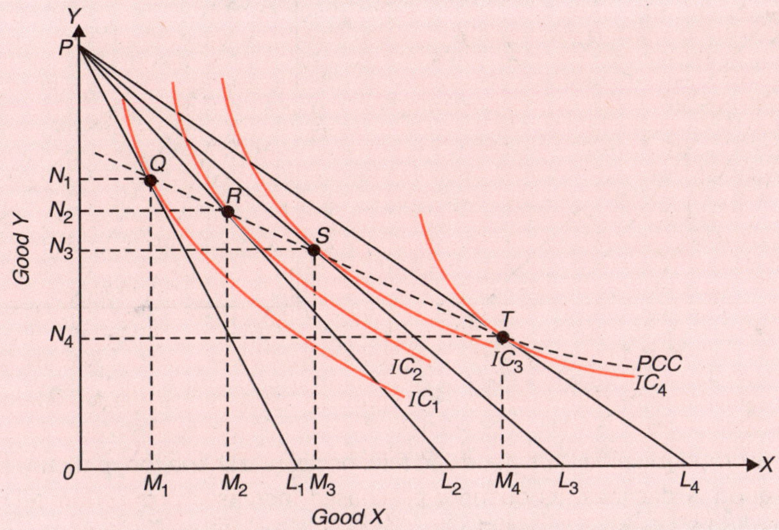

Fig. 8.38. *Downward-Sloping Price Consumption Curve*

better off, that is, his level of satisfaction has increased as a consequence of the fall in the price of good X. Suppose that price of X further falls so that PL_3 is now the relevant budget line. With budget line PL_3 the consumer is in equilibrium at S on indifference curve IC_3 where he has OM_3 of X and ON_3 of Y. If price of good X falls still further so that budget line now takes the position of PL_4, the consumer now attains equilibrium at T on indifference curve IC_4 and has OM_4 of X and ON_4 of Y. When all the equilibrium points such as Q, R, S, and T are joined together, we get what is called Price Consumption Curve (PCC). ***Price consumption curve traces out the price effect. It shows how the changes in price of good X will affect the consumer's purchases of X, price of Y, his tastes and money income remaining unaltered,***

In Fig.8.38 price consumption curve (*PCC*) is sloping downward. Downward-sloping price consumption curve for good X means that as price of good X falls, the consumer purchases a larger quantity of good X and a smaller quantity of good Y. This is quite evident from Fig. 8.38. As we shall discuss in detail in the chapter concerning elasticity of demand, we obtain downward-sloping price consumption curve for good X when demand for it is elastic (*i.e.*, price elasticity is greater than one). But downward sloping is one possible shape of price consumption curve. Price consumption curve can have other shapes also. In Fig. 8.39 upward-sloping price consumption curve is shown. Upward-sloping price consumption curve for X means that when the price of good X falls, the quantity demanded of both goods X and Y rises. We obtain the upward-sloping price consumption curve for good X when the demand for good is inelastic, (*i.e.*, price elasticity is less than one).

Price consumption curve can also have a backward-sloping shape, which is depicted in Fig. 8.40. Backward-sloping price consumption curve for good X indicates that when price of

X falls, after a point smaller quantity of it is demanded or purchased. We shall see later in this chapter that this is true in case of exceptional type of goods called Giffen Goods.

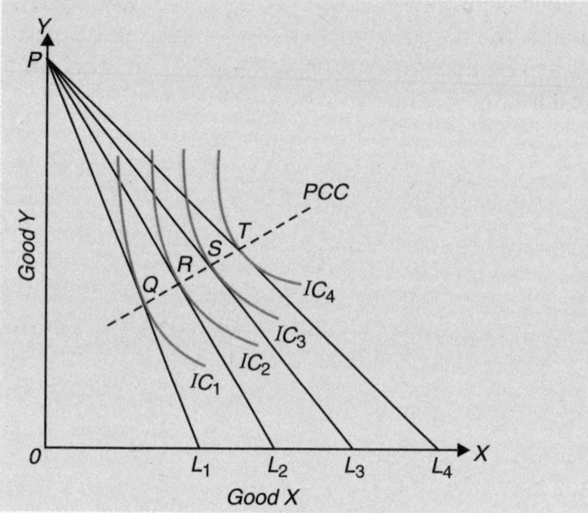

Fig. 8.39. *Upward-Sloping Price Consumption Curve*

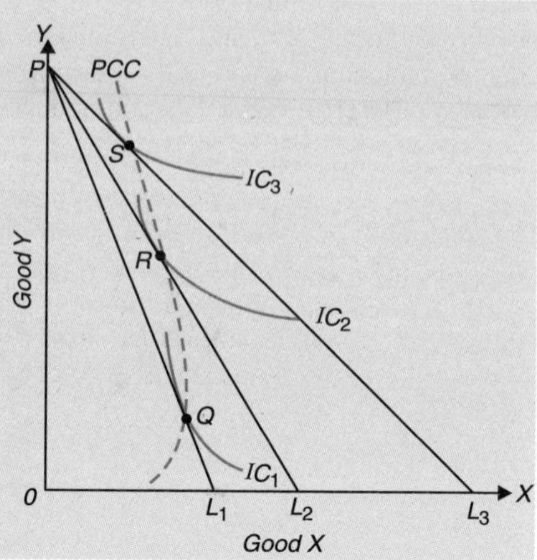

Fig. 8.40. *Backward-Sloping Price Consumption Curve in Case of Giffen Goods*

Price consumption curve for a good can take horizontal shape too. It means that when the price of the good X declines, its quantity purchased increases proportionately but quantity purchased of good Y remains the same. Horizontal price consumption curve is shown in Fig. 8.41. We obtain horizontal price consumption curve of good X when the price elasticity of demand for good X is equal to unity.

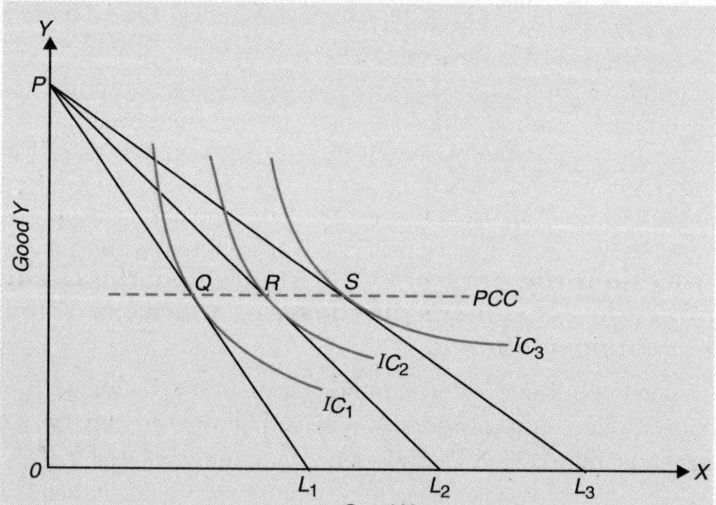

Fig.8.41. *Horizontal Price Consumption Curve*

But it is rarely found that price consumption curve slopes downward throughout or slopes upward throughout or slopes backward throughout. More generally, price consumption curve has different slopes at different price ranges. At higher price levels it generally slopes downward, and it may then have a horizontal shape for some price ranges but ultimately it will be sloping upward. For some price ranges it can be backward sloping as in case of Giffen goods. A price consumption curve which has different shapes or slopes at different price ranges is drawn in Fig. 8.42. Such a type of price consumption curve means that price elasticity of demand varies at different price ranges.

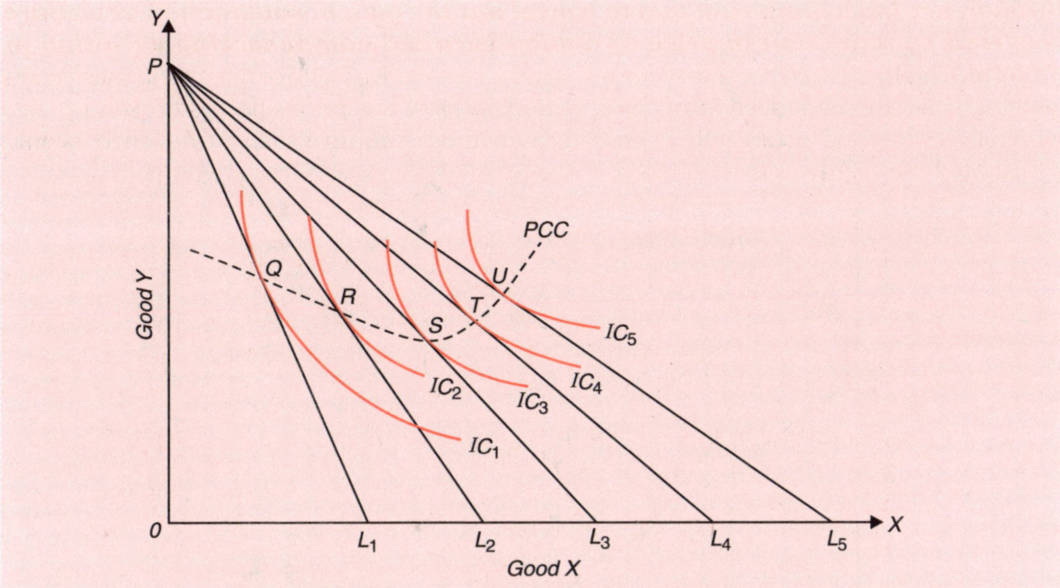

Fig. 8.42. *Price Consumption Curve with Varying Slopes*

BREAKING UP PRICE EFFECT INTO INCOME AND SUBSTITUTION EFFECTS

It has been explained above that as price of a good *X* falls, other things remaining the same, consumer would move to a new equilibrium position at a higher indifference curve and would buy more of good *X* at the lower price unless it is a Giffen good. Thus, in the Fig. 8.43 the consumer who is initially in equilibrium at *Q* on indifference curve IC_1 moves to the point *R* on indifference curve IC_2 when the price of good *X* falls and the budget line twists from PL_1 to PL_2. The movement from *Q* to *R* represents the price effect. It is now highly important to understand that this price effect is the net result of two distinct forces, namely, substitution effect and income effect. In other words, price effect can be split up into two different parts, one being the substitution effect and the other income effect.

There are two approaches for decomposing price effect into its two parts, substitution effect and income effect. They are the Hicksian approach and Slutsky approach. Further, Hicksian approach uses two methods of splitting the price effect, namely (*i*) ***Compensating variation in income (ii) Equivalent variation in income.*** Slutsky uses *cost-difference method* to decompose price effect into its two component parts. How the price effect can be decom-posed into income effect and substitution effect by the Hicksian methods is explained below, whereas Slutsky's cost-difference method will be explained in an appendix to this chapter.

1. Breaking Up Price Effect: Compensating Variation in Income

In the method of breaking up price effect by compensating variation we adjust the income of the consumer so as to offset the change in satisfaction resulting from the change in price of a good and bring the consumer back to his original indifference curve, that is, his initial level of satisfaction which he was obtaining before the change in price occurred. For instance, when the price of a commodity falls and consumer moves to a new equilibrium position at a higher indifference curve his satisfaction increases. To offset this gain in satisfaction resulting from a fall in price of the good we must take away from the consumer enough income to force him to come back to his original indifference curve. ***This required reduction in income (say,***

through levying a lump sum tax) to cancel out the gain in satisfaction or welfare occurred by reduction in price of a good is called compensating variation in income. This is so called because it compensates (in a negative way) for the gain in satisfaction resulting from a price reduction of the commodity. How the price effect is broken up into substitution effect and income effect through the method of compensating variation in income is illustrated in Fig 8.43.

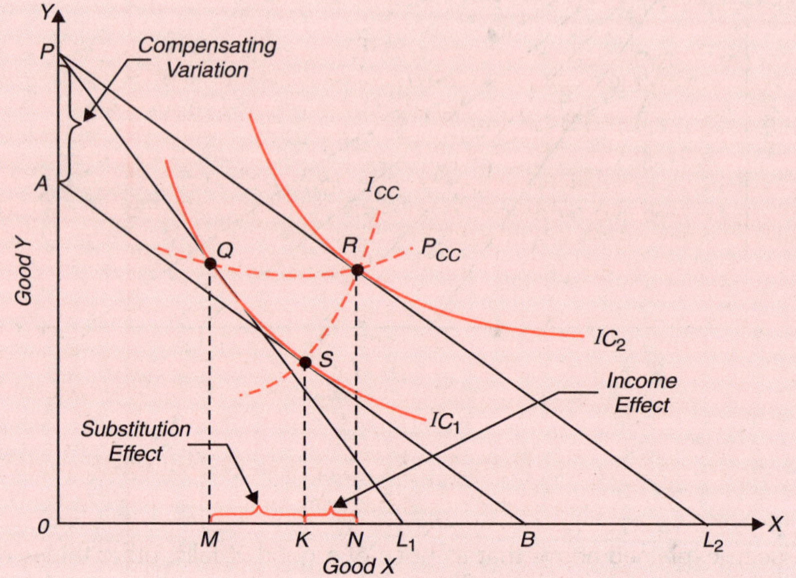

Fig. 8.43. *Price Effect Split up into Substitution and Income Effects through Compensating Variation Method*

When price of good *X* falls and as a result budget line shifts to PL_2, the real income of the consumer rises, *i.e.*, he can buy more of both the goods with his given money income. That is, price reduction enlarges consumer's opportunity set of the two goods. With the new budget line PL_2 he is in equilibrium at point *R* on a higher indifference curve IC_2 and thus gains in satisfaction as a result of fall in price of good *X*. Now, if his money income is reduced by the compensating variation in income so that he is forced to come back to the original indifference curve IC_1 he would buy more of *X* since *X* has now become relatively cheaper than before. In Fig. 8.43 as result of the fall in price of *X*, price line switches to PL_2. Now, with the reduction in income by compensating variation, budget line shifts to *AB* which has been drawn parallel to PL_2 so that it just touches the indifference curve IC_1 where he was before the fall in price of *X*. Since the price line *AB* has got the same slope as PL_2, it represents the changed relative prices with *X* being relatively cheaper than before. Now, *X* being relatively cheaper than before, the consumer in order to maximise his satisfaction in the new price-income situation substitutes *X* for *Y*. Thus, when the consumer's money income is reduced by the compensating variation in income (which is equal to *PA* in terms of *Y* or L_2B in terms of *X*), the consumer moves along the same indifference curve IC_1 and substitutes *X* for *Y*. With price line *AB*, he is in equilibrium at *S* on indifference curve IC_1 and is buying *MK* more of *X* in place of *Y*. This movement from *Q* to *S* on the same indifference curve IC_1 represents the substitution effect since it occurs due to the change in relative prices alone, real income remaining constant.

If the amount of money income which was taken away from him is now given back to him, he would move from *S* on indifference curve IC_1 to *R* on a higher indifference curve IC_2. The movement from S on a lower in difference curve to R on a higher in difference curve is the result of income effect. Thus the movement form Q to R due to price effect can be regarded as having been taken place into two steps : first from Q to S as a result of substitution effect and second from S to R as a result of income effect. In is thus mainfest that price effect is the combined result of a substitution effect and an income effect.

In Fig. 8.43 me various effects on the purchases of good X are:

	Price effect	=	MN
	Substitution effect	=	MK
	Income effect	=	KN
	MN	=	$MK + KN$
or	Price effect	=	Substitution effect + Income effect

From the above analysis, it is thus clear that price effect is the sum of income and substitution effects.

2. Breaking up Price Effect: Equivalent Variation in Income

As mentioned above, price effect can be split up into substitution and income effects through an alternative method of equivalent variation in income. The reduction in price of a commodity increases consumer's satisfaction as it enables him to reach a higher indifference curve. Now, the same increase in satisfaction can be achieved through bringing about an increase in his income, prices remaining constant. ***The increase in income of the consumer, prices of goods remaining the same, so as to enable him to move to a higher subsequent indifference curve at which he in fact reaches with reduction in price of a good is called equivalent variation in income*** **because it represents the variation in income that is equivalent in terms of gain in satisfaction to a reduction in price of the good.** Thus, in this equivalent income-variation method substitution effect is shown along the subsequent indifference curve rather than the original one. How this price effect is decomposed into income and substitution effects through equivalent variation in income is shown in Fig. 8.44.

When price of good X falls, the consumer can purchase more of both the goods, that is, the purchasing power of his given money income rises. It means that after the fall in price of X, if the consumer buys the same quantities of goods as before, then some amount of money will be left over. In other words, the fall in price of good X will release some amount of money. Money thus released can be spent on purchasing more of both the goods. It therefore follows that a change in price of the good produces an income effect. When the power to purchase goods rises due to the income effect of the price change, the consumer has to decide how this increase in his purchasing power is to be spread over the two goods he is buying. How he will spread the released purchasing power over the two goods depends upon the nature of his income consumption curve which in turn is determined by his preferences about the two goods.

From above it follows, that, as a result of the increase in his purchasing power (or real income) due to the fall in price, the consumer will move to a higher indifference curve and will become better off than before. It is as if price had remained the same but his money income was increased. In other words, a fall in price of good X does to the consumer what an equivalent rise in money income would have done to him. As a result of fall in price of X, the consumer can therefore be imagined as moving up to a higher indifference curve along the income consumption curve as if his money income had been increased, prices of X and Y remaining unchanged. Thus, a given change in price can be thought of as an equivalent to an appropriate change in income.

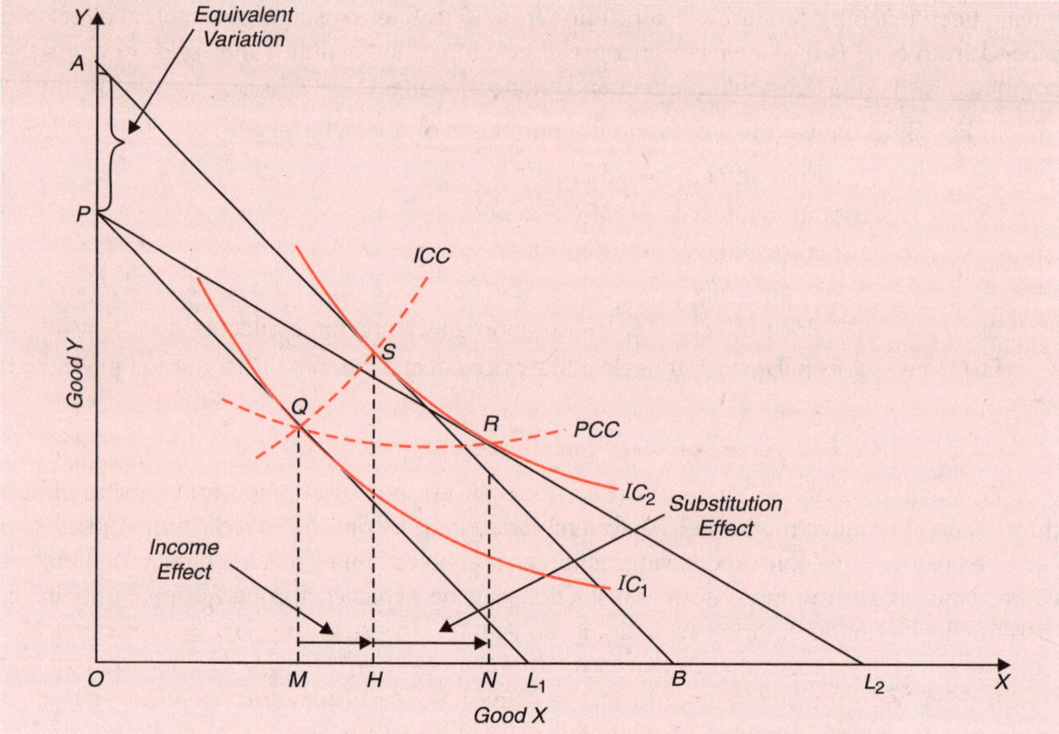

Fig. 8.44. *Price Effect Split Up into Income and Substitution Effects through Equivalent Variation Method*

It will be seen from Fig. 8.44 that with price line PL_1, the consumer is in equilibrium at Q on indifference curve IC_1. Suppose price of good X falls, price of Y and his money income remaining unaltered, so that budget line is now PL_2. With budget line PL_2, he is in equilibrium at R on indifference curve IC_2. Now, a line AB is drawn parallel to PL_1 so that it touches the indifference curve IC_2 at S. It means that the increase in real income or purchasing power of the consumer as a result of the fall in price of X is equal to PA in terms of Y or L_1B in terms of X. Movement of the consumer from Q on indifference curve IC_1 to S on the higher indifference curve IC_2 along the income consumption curve is the result of income effect of the price change. But the consumer will not be finally in equilibrium at S. This is because now that X is relatively cheaper than Y, he will substitute X, which has become relatively cheaper, for good Y, which has become relatively dearer. It will be gainful for the consumer to do so. Thus the consumer will move along the indifference curve IC_2 from S to R. This movement from S to R has taken place because of the change in relative prices alone and therefore represents substitution effect. Thus the price effect can be broken up into income and substitution effects, showing in this case substitution along the subsequent indifference curve. In Fig 8.44 the magnitudes of the various effects are :

$$\text{Price effect} = MN$$

$$\text{Income effect} = MH$$

$$\text{Substitution effect} = HN$$

$$\text{In Fig. 8.44, } MN = MH + HN$$

or

$$\text{Price effect} = \text{Income Effect} + \text{Substitution Effect}$$

PRICE-DEMAND RELATIONSHIP: DERIVING LAW OF DEMAND

Indifference curve analysis with its technique of looking upon the price effect as a combination of income effect and substitution effect explains relationship between price and quantity demanded in a better and more analytical way. A distinct advantage of viewing the price effect as a sum of income effect and substitution effect is that through it the nature of response of quantity purchased to a change in the price of a good can be better and easily explained. In case of most of the goods, the income effect and substitution effect work in the same direction. But, in some cases, they may pull in different directions. The direction of substitution effect is quite certain. A fall in the relative price of a good always leads to the increase in quantity demanded of the good. In other words, substitution effect always induces the consumer to buy more of the cheaper good.

But the direction of income effect is not so certain. With a rise in income, the individual will generally buy more of a good. But with the rise in income the individual will buy less of a good if it happens to be an inferior good for him since he will use better or superior substitutes in place of the inferior good when his income rises. Thus the income effect may be either positive or negative. For normal goods, the income effect is positive. Therefore, when price of a normal good falls and results in increase in the purchasing power, income effect will act in the same direction as the substitution effect, that is, both will work towards increasing the quantity demanded of the good whose price has fallen. For the inferior good in which case income effect is negative, income effect of the price change will work in opposite direction to the substitution effect. The net effect of the price change will then depend upon the relative strengths of the two effects. To sum up, price effect is composed of income effect and substitution effect and further that the direction in which quantity demanded will change as a result of the change in price will depend upon the direction and strength of the income effect on the one hand and strength of the substitution effect on the other.

Price Demand Relationship : Normal Goods

In order to understand the way in which price-demand relationship is established in indifference curve analysis, consider Fig 8.43. Given the price of two goods and his income represented by the budget line PL_1, the consumer will be in equilibrium at Q on indifference curve IC_1. Let us suppose that price of X falls, price of Y and his money income remaining unchanged so that budget line now shifts to PL_2. The consumer will now be in equilibrium at a point on the new budget line PL_2. If the equilibrium position on PL_2 lies to the right of Q such as at R in Fig. 8.43, it will mean that the consumer buys more quantity of good X than at Q. Now, it can be proved that in case of normal goods the ***new equilibrium point on budget line PL_2 will lie to the right of Q, meaning thereby that the quantity demanded of the good X will increase as its price falls.***

As seen above, the direction and magnitude of the change in quantity demanded as a result of fall in price of a good depend upon the direction and strength of income effect on the one hand and substitution effect on the other. As for normal goods, the income effect is positive, it will work towards increasing the quantity demanded of good X when its price falls. The substitution effect which is always negative and operates so as to raise the quantity demanded of the good if its price falls and reduces the quantity demanded of the good if its price rises. Thus, in case of normal goods both the income effect (when positive) and negative substitution effect work in the same direction and cause increase in the quantity purchased of good X whose price has fallen with the result that the new equilibrium point will lie to the right of the original equilibrium point Q such as point R in Fig. 8.43 above. Substitution effect causes MK

increase in quantity demanded. Income effect which is positive here also leads to the increase in quantity demand by *KN*. Each effect therefore reinforces the other. As a result, the total effect of a fall in price of *X* from the level indicated by PL_1 to the level indicated by PL_2 is the rise in quantity demanded of good *X* from *OM* to *ON*, that is, quantity demanded increases by *MN* which is equal to *MK* + *KN*. To sum up, ***the income effect and substitution effect in case of normal goods work in the same direction and will lead to the increase in quantity demanded of the good whose price has fallen.*** In other words, quantiy purchased of a normal good will vary inversely with its price as in its case income effect is positive.

Price-Demand Relationship : Inferior Goods. In case of inferior goods the income effect will work in opposite direction to the substitution effect. When price of an inferior good falls, its negative income effect will tend to reduce the quantity purchased, while the substitution effect will tend to increase the quantity purchased. But normally it happens that negative income effect of change in price is not large enough to outweigh the substitution effect. This is so because a consumer spends a very small proportion of his income on a single commodity and when price of a commodity falls, a very little income is released. In other words, income effect even when negative is generally too weak to outweigh the substitution effect. It follows therefore that as a result of fall in price of a good the substitution effect which always induces

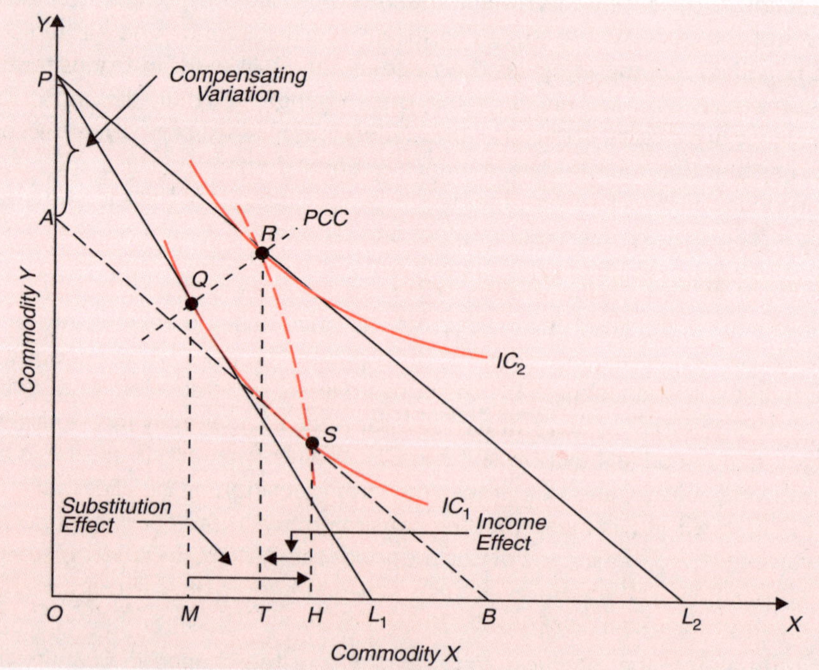

Fig. 8.45. *Price-Demand Relationship in Inferior Good*

the consumer to buy more of the good whose price has fallen will usually outweigh the negative income effect. Thus even in most cases of inferior goods the net result of the fall in price will be increase in its quantity demanded. It is thus clear that in a majority of inferior goods quantity demanded of the good will vary inversely with price and the Marshallian law of demand will hold good.

The price-demand relationship in case of inferior goods having weaker income effect is illustrated in Figure 8.45. It will be seen from Fig. 8.45 that the fall in price of good *X* makes the consumer to shift from equilibrium at *Q* to a new equilibrium at *R*. As a result, quantity purchased of good X increases from OM to OT. But the income effect is negative and is equal to HT. If income effect alone was working, it would have caused the consumer to buy HT less of good X. But substitution effect is universally present and always induces the consumer to buy more of the relatively cheaper good. In Fig. 8.45 substitution effect is equal to MH and is greater than negative income effect HT. Therefore, the net effect of the fall in price of good X is the increase in quantity demanded by MT. Hence we conclude that **in case of inferior goods, quantity demanded varies inversely with price when negative income effect is weaker than the substitution effect.** In other words, even in case of inferior goods having weaker income effect, the demand curve will be downward sloping.

Price-Demand Relationship: Giffen Goods or Giffen Paradox. There is a third possibility. This is that there may be some inferior goods for which the negative income effect is strong or large enough to outweigh the substitution effect. In this case, quantity purchased of the good will fall as its price falls and quantity purchased of the good will rise as its price rises. In other words, in this case quantity purchased or demanded will vary directly with price. Now, the income effect can be substantial only when the consumer is spending a very large proportion of his income on the good in question so that when price of the good falls, a good amount of income is released. If that good happens to be inferior good, the income effect will be negative as well as strong and may outweigh the substitution effect so that with the fall in price, the consumer will buy less of the good. **Such an inferior good in which case the consumer reduces its consumption when its price falls and increases its consumption when its price rises is called a Giffen good** named after the British statistician, Sir Robert Giffen, who in the mid-nineteenth century is said to have claimed that when price of cheap common foodstuff like bread went up the people bought and consumed more bread. A rise in the price of bread caused such a large decline in the purchasing power of the poor people that they were forced to cut down the consumption of meat and other more expensive food. Since bread even when its price was higher than before was still the cheapest food article, people consumed more of it and not less when its price went up. Similarly, when price of an inferior good, on which people spend a large proportion of their income, falls people will purchase less than before. This is because the fall in price of an inferior good on which they spend a very large portion of their income causes such a large increase in their purchasing

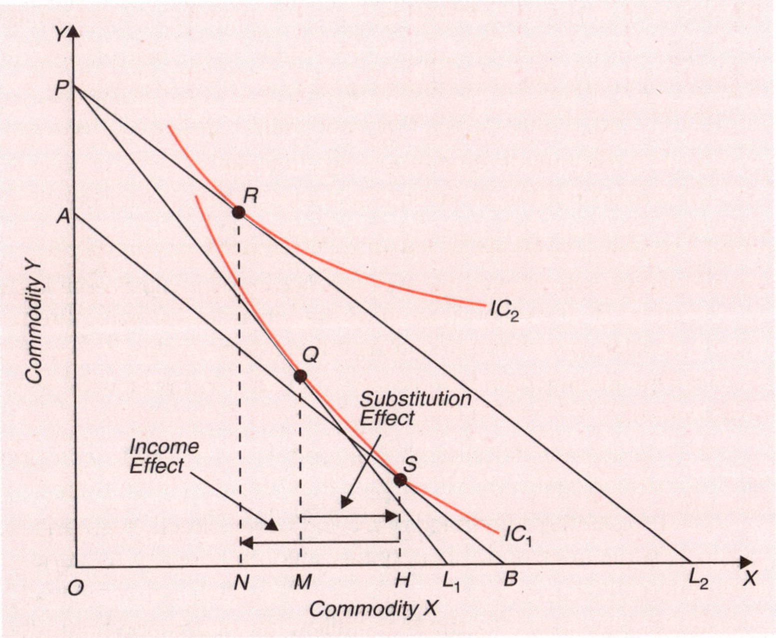

Fig. 8.46. *Price-Demand Relationship in Case of a Giffen Good*

power that creates a large negative income effect. They will therefore reduce the consumption of that good when its price falls since large negative income effect outweighs the substitution effect.

The price-demand relationship in case of a Giffen good is illustrated in Fig. 8.46. With a certain given price-income situation depicted by the budget line PL_1, the consumer is initially in equilibrium at Q on indifference curve IC_1. With a fall in price of the good, the consumer shifts to point R on indifference curve IC_2. It will be seen From Fig. 8.46 that with the fall in price and, as a result, the shift of the budget line from PL_1 to PL_2 the consumer reduces his consumption of the good X from OM to ON. This is the net effect of the negative income effect which is here equal to HN which induces the consumer to buy less of good X and the substitution effect which is equal MH which induces the consumer to buy more of the good. Since the negative income effect HN is greater than the substitution effect MH, the net effect is the fall in quantity purchased of good X by MN with the fall in its price. Thus, ***the quantity demanded of a Giffen good varies directly with price.*** Therefore, if a demand curve showing price-demand relationship of a Giffen good is drawn, it will slope upward.

Thus, the quantity demanded of a Giffen good varies directly with price. For a good to be a Giffen good, the following three conditions are necessary:[4]

(1) The good must be inferior good with a large negative income effect;

(2) The substitution effect must be small; and

(3) The proportion of income spent upon the inferior good must be very large.

Three Demand Theorems Based on Indifference Curve Analysis

It follows from above that, indifference curve analysis enables us to derive a more general law of demand in the following composite form, consisting of three demand theorems to which the Marshallian law of demand constitutes a special case.[5]

(*a*) The quantity demanded of a good varies inversely with price when the income effect is positive or nil.

(*b*) The quantity demanded of a good varies inversely with price when the income effect for the good is negative but is weaker than the substitution effect.

(*c*) The quantity demanded of a good varies directly with price when the income effect for the good is negative and this negative income effect of a change in price is larger than the substitution effect.

In the case, (*a*) and (*b*) the Marshallian law of demand holds good and we get a downward sloping demand curve. The case (*a*) applies to normal goods in which income effect and substitution effect work *in the same direction*. The case (*b*) applies to inferior goods which are not Giffen goods. When the third case occurs, we get a Giffen good of positively sloping demand curve. Marshallian law of demand does not hold true in the third case. Marshall mentioned a Giffen good case as an exception to his law of demand. Thus the indifference curve analysis is superior to Marshallian analysis in that it yields a more general law of demand which covers the Giffen-good case. The explanation for the occurrence of a Giffen good is that in its case the negative income effect outweighs the substitution effect. Since Marshall ignored the income effect of the change in price, he could not provide a satisfactory explanation for the reaction of the consumer to a change in price of a Giffen good.

However, it may be pointed out that it is very hard to satisfy the above mentioned third conditions for the occurrence of the Giffen good, namely, the consumer must be spending a

4. J.R. Hicks, *A Revision of Demand Theory*, p. 66.
5. Tapas Majumdar, *Measurement of Utility*, pp. 74-75.

very large proportion of his income on an inferior good. Therefore, although Giffen good case is theoretically possible the chance of its occurrence in the actual world is almost negligible.[6] This is because consumption of the people is generally diversified so that people spend a small proportion of their income on a single commodity with the result that price-induced income effect even when negative is generally small and cannot therefore outweigh the substitution effect. As mentioned earlier, Marshall believed that quantity demanded could vary directly with price, and, as mentioned above, Sir Robert Giffen is said to have actually observed this phenomenon. But there is a controversy about the intrepretation of this so-called Giffen good. But from our analysis it is clear that Giffen good case can occur in theory. As explained above, when negative income effect of the fall in the price of an inferior good is larger than substitution effect we get a positively-sloping demand curve of Giffen good. Thus Giffen good is theoretically quite possible. But, since income effect of the change in price of a single commodity in the real world is small, the negative income effect of the change in price of an inferior good is too weak to outweigh the substitution effect and therefore a Giffen good, although theoretically conceivable, rarely occurs in practice.

DERIVATION OF INDIVIDUAL'S DEMAND CURVE FROM INDIFFERENCE CURVE ANALYSIS

Price consumption curve traces the effect of a change in price on the quantity demanded of a good. But price consumption curve does not directly relate price with quantity demanded. In indifference curve diagram price is not explicitly shown on the *Y*-axis. On the other hand, demand curve directly relates price with quantity demanded, price being shown on the *Y*-axis and quantity demanded on the *X*-axis. A demand curve shows how much quantity of a good will be purchased or demanded at various prices, assuming that tastes and preferences of a consumer, his income, prices of all related goods remain constant. This demand curve showing explicit relationship between price and quantity demanded can be derived from price consumption curve of indifference curve analysis.

In Marshallian utility analysis, demand curve was derived on the assumptions that utility was cardinally measurable and marginal utility of money remained constant with the change in price of the good. In the indifference curve analysis, demand curve is derived without making these dubious assumptions.

Let us suppose that a consumer has got income of ₹ 300 to spend on goods. In Fig. 8.47 money is measured on the *Y*-axis, while the quantity of the good *X* whose demand curve is to be derived is measured on the *X*-axis. An indifference map of a consumer is drawn along with the various budget lines showing different prices of the good *X*. Budget line PL_1 shows that price of the good *X* is ₹ 15 per unit. As price of good *X* falls from ₹ 15 to ₹ 10, the budget line shifts to PL_2. Budget line PL_2 shows that price of good *X* is ₹10. With a further fall in price to ₹ 7.5 the budget line takes the position PL_3. Thus PL_3 shows that price of good *X* is ₹ 7.5. When price of good *X* falls to ₹ 6, PL_4 is the relevant budget line. The various budget lines obtained are shown in the column 2 of the Table 8.3. Tangency points between the various budget lines and indifference curves, which when joined together by a line constitute the price consumption curve shows the amounts of good *X* purchased or demanded at various prices.

With the budget line PL_1 the consumer is in equilibrium at point Q_1 on the price consumption curve *PCC* at which the budget line PL_1 is tangent to indifference curve IC_1. In his equilibrium position at Q_1 the consumer is buying *OA* units of the good *X*. In other words, it means that the

6. J.R. Hicks, *op.cit*, p. 67.

consumer demands *OA* units of good *X* at price ₹ 15. When price falls to ₹ 10 and thereby the budget line shifts to PL_2, the consumer comes to be in equilibrium at point Q_2 of the price-consumption curve *PCC* where the budget line PL_2 is tangent to indifference curve IC_2. At Q_2, the consumer is buying *OB* units of good *X*. In other words, the consumer demands *OB* units of the good *X* at price ₹ 10. Likewise, with budget lines PL_3 and PL_4, the consumer is in equilibrium at points Q_3 and Q_4 of price consumption curve and is demanding *OC* units and *OD* units of good *X* at price ₹ 7.5 and ₹ 6 respectively. It is thus clear that from the price consumption curve we can get information which is required to

Table 8.3. Demand Schedule

Price of good X ₹	Budget Line	Quantity Demanded
15	PL_1	*OA*
10	PL_2	*OB*
7.5	PL_3	*OC*
6	PL_4	*OD*

draw the demand curve showing directly the amounts demanded of the good *X* against various prices. With the above information we draw up the demand schedule in Table 8.3 given above :

The above demand schedule which has been derived from the indifference curve diagram can be easily converted into a demand curve with price shown on the *Y*-axis and quantity demanded on the *X*-axis. It is easier to understand the derivation of demand curve if it is drawn rightly below the indifference curve diagram. This has been done so in Fig 8.47. In the diagram at the bottom, where on the *X*-axis the quantity demanded is shown as in indifference curves diagram in the top pannel, but on the *Y*-axis in the diagram in the bottom panel *price per unit* of the good *X* is shown instead of

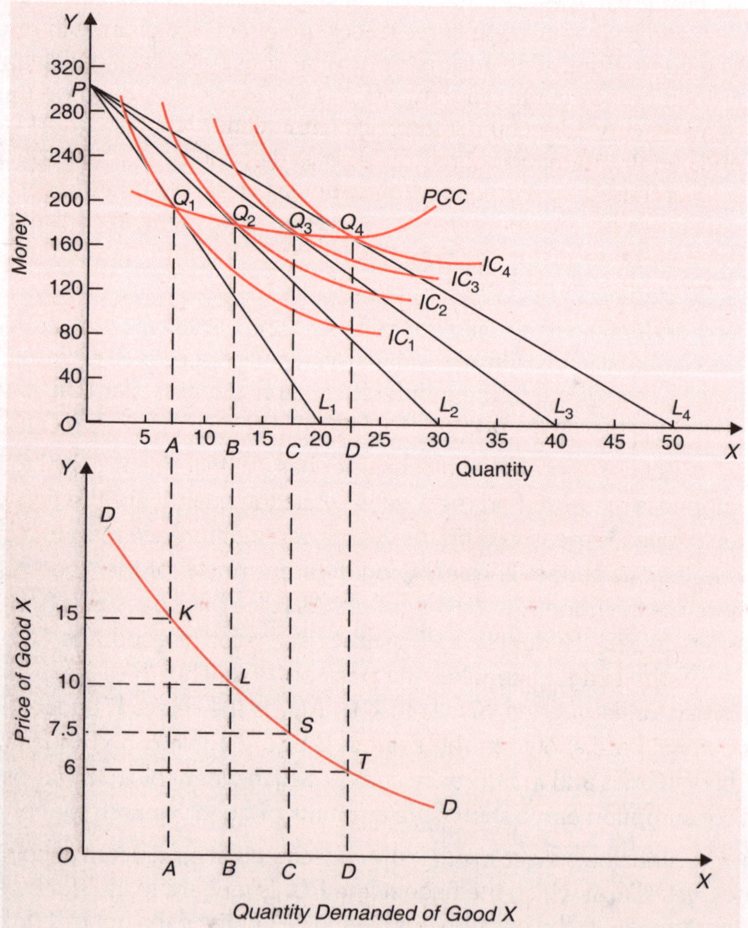

Fig. 8.47. *Derivation of individual's Demand Curve*

total money. In order to obtain the demand curve, various points *K*, *L*, *S* and *T* representing the demand schedule of the above table are plotted. By joining the points *K*, *L*, *S* and *T* we get the required demand curve *DD*. In most cases the demand curve of individuals will slope downward to the right, because as the price of a good falls both the substitution effect and income effect pull together in increasing the quantity demanded of the good. Even when the income effect is negative, the demanded curve will slope downward to the right if the substitution effect is strong enough to overwhelm the negative income effect. Only when the negative income effect is powerful enough to outweigh the substitution effect can the demand curve slope upward to the right instead of sloping downward to the left.

Deriving Demand Curve For a Giffen Good

The demand curve *DD* in Fig. 8.47 is sloping downward. As explained in a previous section, the demand curve slopes downward because of two forces, namely, income effect and substitution effect. Both the income effect and substitution effect usually work towards increasing the quantity demanded of the good when its price falls and this makes the demand curve slope downward. But in case of Giffen good, as explained in a previous section, the demand curve slopes upward from left to right. This is because in case of a Giffen good income effect, which is negative and works in opposite direction to the substitution effect, outweighs the substitution effect. This results in the fall in quantity demanded of the Giffen good when its price falls and therefore the demand curve of a Giffen good slopes upward from left to right. In Fig. 8.48 the derivation of demand curve of a Giffen good from indifference curves diagram is explained.

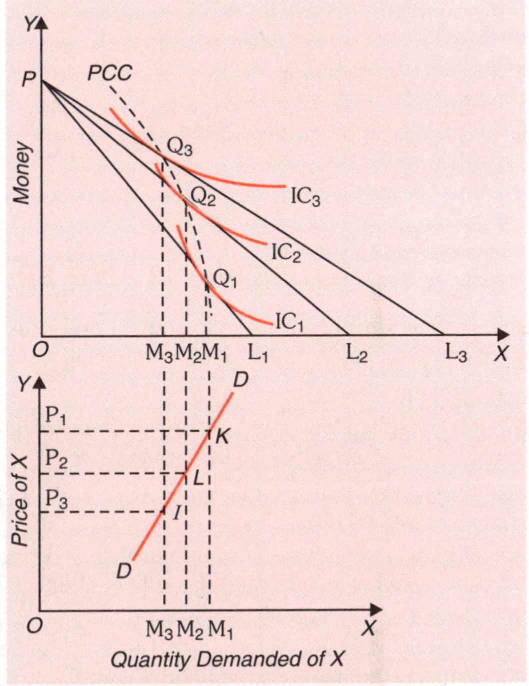

Fig. 8.48 *Upward Sloping Demand Curve for a Giffen Good*

In Fig. 8.48 the Indifference curves of a Giffen good are drawn along with the various budget lines showing various prices of the good. Price consumption curve of a Giffen good slopes backward. In order to simplify the discussion in this figure we have avoided the numerical values of prices and have instead used symbols such as, P_1, P_2, P_3 and P_4 for various levels of the price of good *X*.

It is evident from Fig. 8.48 (the upper portion) that with budget line PL_1 (or price P_1) the consumer is in equilibrium at Q_1 on the price consumption curve *PCC* and is purchasing *OM*) amount of the good. With the fall in price from P_1 to P_2 and shifting of budget line from PL_1 to PL_2, the consumer goes to the equilibrium position Q_3 at which he buys OM_2 amount of the good. OM_2 is less than OM_1. Thus with the fall in price from P_1 to P_2 the quantity demanded of the good falls. Likewise, the consumer is in equilibrium at Q_3 with price line PL_3 and is purchasing OM_3 at price P_3. With this information we can draw the demand curve, as is done in the lower portion of Fig. 8.48 It will be seen from Fig. 8.48 (lower part) that the demand curve of a Giffen good slopes upward to the right indicating that the quantity demanded varies directly with the changes in price. With the rise in price, quantity demanded increases and with the fall in price quantity demanded decreases.

Demand Schedule

Budget Line	*Price of good X* ₹	*Quantity Demanded*
PL_1	$\frac{OP}{OL_1}$ or p_1	OM_1
PL_2	$\frac{OP}{OL_2}$ or p_2	OM_2
PL_3	$\frac{OP}{OL_3}$ or p_3	OM_3

To sum up, *in most cases (that is, in case of normal goods) the demand curve of individuals will slope downward to the right, because as the price of a good falls both the substitution effect and income effect pull together in increasing the quantity demanded of the good. Even in case of inferior goods for which the income effect is negative, the demand curve will slope downward to the right if the substitution effect is strong enough to overwhelm the negative income effect. Only in case of Giffen goods for which the negative income effect is powerful enough to outweigh the substitution effect, the demand curve slopes upward to the right instend of sloping downward to the left.*

QUESTIONS AND PROBLEMS FOR REVIEW

1. Distinguish between cardinal utility and ordinal utility? Which is more realistic?
2. What are indifference curves? What are the assumptions on which indifference curve analysis of demand is based?
3. (*a*) Explain why consumer's indifference curves (*i*) have negative slope, (*ii*) do not intersect and (*iii*) are convex to the origin.

   (*b*) Show that if indifference curves are concave, a consumer will consume only one of the two goods.
4. What is budget line? What does its intercept on X-axis show ? What does its intercept on Y-axis show? What does slope of the budget line measure ?
5. Amit's budget line relating good *X* and good Y has intercepts of 50 units of good *X* and 20 units of good Y. If the price of good *X* is 12, what is Amit's income? What is the price of good. *Y* ? What is the slope of the budget line ?
6. What is marginal rate of substitution? An indifference curve of Sonia contains the following market baskets of apples and bananas. Each of these baskets gives her equal satisfaction.

Market basket	*Apples*	*Bananas*
1	2	16
2	3	11
3	4	7
4	5	4
5	6	2
6	7	1

   Find out marginal rate of substitution of Sonia. How does marginal rate of substitution vary as she consumes more of apples and less of bananas? Give reasons.
7. Explain consumer's equilibrium condition with the help of indifference curve approach. How will a change in consumer's income affect his equilibrium ?
8. Explain why a consumer will choose a market basket so that marginal rate of substitution (*MRS*) equals price ratio of the goods.
9. A consumer spends all her income on food and clothing. At the current prices of P_f = ₹ 10 and P_c = ₹ 5, she maximises her utility by purchasing 20 units of food and 50 units of clothing.

(a) What is the consumer's income?

(b) What is the consumer's marginal rate of substitution of food for clothing at the equilibrium position ?

10. *Priya spends all her monthly income of ₹ 5000 on food and clothing. Price of food is ₹ 250 and price of clothing is ₹ 100 and her monthly consumption of food is 10 units and that of clothing is 25. With this consumption of the two commodities her marginal rate of substitution of food for clothing is* $MRS_{fc} = \frac{1C}{1F}$. *Is she in equilibrium with this consumption? Which commodity she will substitute for the other to reach equilibrium position ? Illustrate diagrammatically with indifference curves.*

11. What is the inferior good? How is it different from normal goods? Show them with the help of indifference curves.

12. Use indifference curves to explain what happens to the demand for an inferior good as consumer's real income increases at constant relative prices.

13. (a) What is price consumption curve? What is the relationship between price consumption curve and price elasticity of demand ?

(b) Derive demand curve from Price Consumption Curve.

14. What is income consumption curve. Draw indifference curve diagrams showing the income consumption curve in case of (a) normal good, (b) inferior good.

15. (a) What is an Engel curve? How is Engel curve derived from income consumption curve ?

(b) Draw an Engel curve for (*i*) a necessary good, (*ii*) luxury good (*iii*) neutral good.

16. Using indifference curve analysis, show how price effect of a commodity is decomposed into income effect and substitution effect.

17. With the help of indifference curve analysis, derive demand curve for a normal commodity? Explain why it slopes downward to the right.

18. What is Giffen good? How does indifference curve analysis explain Giffen Paradoix? What is the shape of price consumption curve for a Giffen good? Illustrate it with an indifference curve diagram.

19. Why demand curve for a Giffen good has a positive slope ?

20. What is an inferior good ? What is the shape of a demand curve for an inferior good which is not a Giffen good ?

21. What is compensating variation in income ? Using the concept of compensating variation in income distinguish between income and substitution effects of a fall in price of a commodity with the help of indifference curve technique in case of (*a*) normal good, and (*b*) an inferior good.

22. An individual's marginal utilities for commodities are given by the following relations:

$$MU_x = 40 - 5x \text{ and } MU_y = 20 - 3\,Y.$$

What is his marginal rate of substitution in consumption at the consumption basket X = 3, Y = 5? If P_x = ₹ 5 and P_y = Re. 1. Does the basket represent consumption equilibrium?

APPENDIX A TO CHAPTER 8

SLUTSKY SUBSTITUTION EFFECT

Slutsky Substitution Effect and Cost Difference

Slutsky has given a slightly different version of substitution effect. In this version when the price of a good changes and consumer's real income or purchasing power increases, the income of the consumer is changed by the amount equal to the change in its purchasing power which occurs as a result of the price change. His purchasing power changes by the amount equal to the change in the price multiplied by the number of units of the good which the individual used to buy at the old price. In other words, in Slutsky's approach, income is reduced or increased (as the case may be) by the amount which leaves the consumer to be just able *to purchase the same combination of goods,* if he so desires, which he was having at the old price. That is, the income is changed by the difference between the cost of the amount of good X purchased at the old price and the cost of the same quantity of X at the new price. Income is then said to be changed by the *cost difference*. Thus, in Slutsky substitution effect, income is reduced or increased not by the compensating variation but by the cost difference.

Now, an important question is how to determine the exact magnitude of cost difference by which money income of the consumer has to be adjusted to arrive at Slutsky substitution effect. The reduction in price of a commodity, say *X*, can be represented as ΔP_x. If the consumer is buying quantity Q_x of the commodity X before the reduction in price of the commodity, then $\Delta P_x \cdot Q_x$ will represent the cost difference by which money income of the consumer is to be adjusted so as to enable him to buy the quantity Q_x of commodity *X* (and the same original quantity of *Y*) which he was buying before the change in price. Suppose, with a given money income, a consumer is buying Q_x of X and Q_y of *Y* at given prices of P_{X1}, and Py_1 respectively. Now, if the price of X falls from Px_1 to Px_2, the money income and price of Y remaining the same, the cost difference will thus be equal to

$$Px_1\,Q_x - Px_2\,Q_x = \Delta\,P_x\,Q_x$$

Let us give a numerical example. If at a price of ₹ 10, a consumer is buying 15 units of the commodity X along with a certain quantity of *Y* at the given price of *Y.* If now the price of X falls to ₹ 8, the cost difference will be

$$10 \times 15 - 8 \times 15 = 2 \times 15 = 30$$

In this hypothetical case, with the fall in price from ₹ 10 to ₹ 8 per unit, the money income that is required to be reduced is ₹ 30 so as to enable the consumer to buy the original combination of goods *(i.e., Ox* of X and *Oy* of *Y).* With this reduction in money income the budget line will pass through the original equilibrium combination of the two goods.

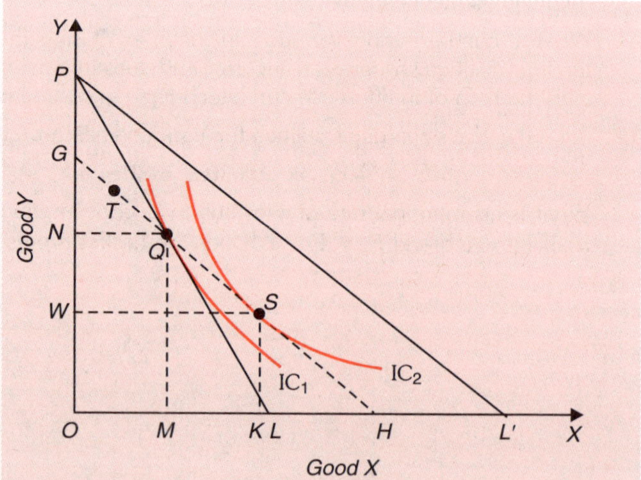

Fig. 8A.1. *Slutsky Substitution Effect (for a Fall in Price)*

Slutsky Substitution Effect for a Decline in Price

Slutsky substitution effect is illustrated in Fig. 8A.1. With a given in other words, by the amount which will leave him to be just able to purchase the old combination *Q* of the goods if he so desires. For this, a price line *GH* parallel to *PL′* has been drawn which passes through the point *Q*. It means that income equal to *PG* in terms of *Y* or *L′H* in terms of X has been taken away from the consumer and as a result he can buy the combination *Q*, if he so desires, since *Q* also lies on the price line *GH*.

Actually, he will not how buy the old combination Q since X has now become relatively cheaper and *Y* has become relatively dearer than before. The change in relative prices will induce the consumer to rearrange the purchases of X and Y. He will substitute X for Y. But in this *Slutsky substitution* case, he will not move along the same indifference curve IC_1, since the budget line *GH,* on which the consumer has to remain due to price-income circumstances, is nowhere tangent to the indifference curve IC_1. The price line *GH* is tangent to the indifference curve IC_2 at point *S*. Therefore, the consumer will now be in equilibrium at point *S* on higher indifference curve IC_2. This movement from *Q* to *S* represents Slutsky substitution effect according to which the consumer moves not on the same indifference curve, but from one indifference curve to another. A noteworthy point is that movement from *Q* to *S* as a result of Slutsky substitution effect is due to the change in relative prices alone, since the effect due to the gain in his the purchasing power has been eliminated by making a reduction in his money income equal to the *cost-difference*. At *S*, the consumer is buying *OK of X* and *OW* of *Y; MK* of *X* has been substituted for *NW* of Y. Therefore, Slutsky substitution effect on X is the increase in its quantity purchased by *MK* and Slutsky substitution effect on *Y* is the decrease in its quantity purchased by *NW.*

It is important to note that with Slutsky substitution effect, consumer chooses new combination *S* on the budget line *GH* rather than the original combination *Q* which he could buy if he so desired. This choice implies that he prefers combination *S* to combination *Q*. That is why combination *S* lies on his higher indifference curve IC_2. It is also worth noting that *S* must lie on the line segment *QH* on the budget line *GH* which shows that under the influence of fall in relative price of *X,* the consumer buys more of *X* and less of Y. That is, ***Slutsky substitution effect must always be negative.*** On the budget line *GH,* the consumer cannot be in equilibrium or choose a combination on the line segment *QG*. This is because if he did, the consumer would be inconsistent. Suppose with budget line *GH* the consumer chooses point *T*. This means that he prefers *T* to any point on the budget line *GH* particularly even point *Q* which also lies on *GH*. But he had earlier chosen point *Q* (that is, he was in equilibrium at point *Q*) which also lies on the budget line *GH*. Since the consumer cannot both prefer *Q* to *T* and *T to Q,* we conclude that his equilibrium point on the budget line *GH* must lie somewhere along segment *QH*. His equilibrium somewhere along segment *QH* means that as a result of fall in relative price of *X,* he buys more of X and less of Y. We thus eoncude that ***Slutsky substitution effect must always be negative.***

Slutsky Substitution Effect for a Rise in Price

We have graphically explained above Slutsxy substitution effect for a fall in price of good X. It will be instructive to explain it also for a rise in price of *X*. This is demonstrated in Fig. 8A.2 Initially, the consumer is in equilibrium at point *Q* on the indiference curve IC_1, prices of the two goods and his money income being given. Now suppose that the price of *Y* good *X* rises, price of *Y* remaining unchanged. As a result of the rise in price of *X*, budget line will shift downward to *PL′* and consumer's real income or purchasing power of his given money income will fall. Further, with this price change, good *X* has become relatively dearer and good *Y* relatively cheaper than before. In order to find out Slutsky substitution effect in this present case, consumer's money income must be increased by the *'cost- difference'* created by the price change to compensate him for the rise in price of X. In other words, *his money income must be increased to the extent which is just large enough to permit him to purchase the old combination Q, if he so desires,* which he was buying before. For this, a budget line *GH* has been drawn which passes through point *Q*. It will be evident from the figure that *PG* (in terms of *Y)* or *L′H* (in terms of *X)* represents 'cost-difference' in this case. With budget line *GH* he can buy if he so desires the old combination *Q*, which he was buying at the old price of *X*. But actually he will not buy the old combination *Q*, since on budget line *GH, X* is relatively dearer than before. He will therefore replace some *X* by *Y (i.e.,* he will substitute *Y* for *X)*. As is shown in Fig. 8A.2 with budget line *GH* he is in equilibrium position at *S* on higher indifference curve IC_3 and is buying *OK* of *X* and *OW* of *Y; MK* of *X* has been replaced out by *NW* of *Y*. Movement from point *Q* to *S* is the result of Slutsky substitution effect; the effect due to the fall in the purchasing power has been cancelled out by giving him money equal to *PG* of *Y* or *L′H* of *X*. In this present case of stipulated rise in price of *X*, Slutsky substitution effect on *X* is the fall in its quantity bought by *MK* and Slutsky substitution effect on *Y is* the increase in its quantity bought by *NW*.

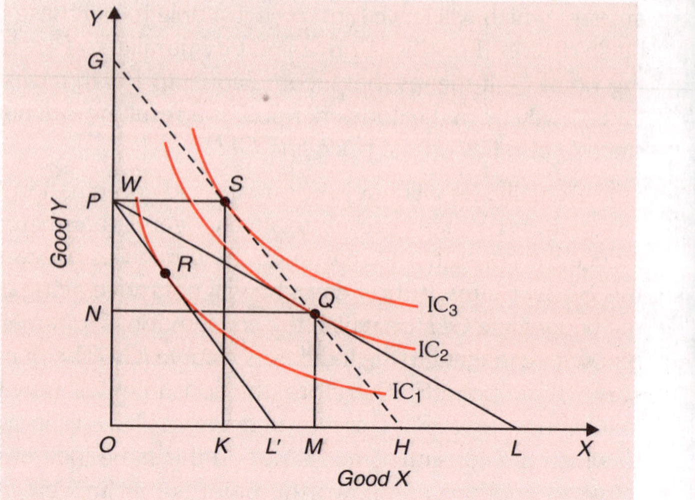

Fig.8A.2. *Slutsky Substitution Effect for a Rise in Price*

From the above analysis it is clear that, whereas Hicksian substitution effect takes place on the same indifference curve, Slutsky substitution effect involves the movement from one indifference curve to another curve, a higher one. For the proper understanding of the difference between the two versions of the substitution effect we have shown them below together in one figure 8A.3 and 8A.4.

A glance at these Figs. 8A.3 *(a)* and *8A.***4** *(b)* which respectively show the two substitution effects in the case of both a fall and a rise in the price of good X will reveal that the movement from *Q* to *T on* the same indifference curve represents Hicksian substitution effect and the movement from *Q* on the original indifference curve to a point *S* on a higher indifference curve represents Slutsky substitution effect. The difference between the two versions of the substitution effect solely arises due to the magnitude of money income by which income is reduced or increased to compensate for the change in his real income. Hicksian approach just restores to the consumer his initial level of satisfaction, whereas the Slutsky approach "over-compensates" the consumer by putting him on a higher indifference curve. Prof, J. R. Hicks points out that the method of adjusting the level of money income by the compensating variation "has the merit that on this interpretation, the substitution effect measures the effect of change in relative price, ***with real income constant***, the income effect measures the effect of the *change in real income*. Thus the analysis which is based upon the compensating variation is a resolution of the price change into two fundamental economic 'directions', we shall not encounter a more fundamental distinction upon any other route".[1]

1. J. R. Hicks, *A Revision of Demand Theory,* 1956 p. 62.

But Slutsky method has a distinct advantage in that it is easier to find out the amount of income equal to the 'cost difference by which income of the consumer is to be adjusted. On the other hand, it is not so easy to know the compensating variation in income. The cost-difference method has the advantage of being dependent on observable market data, while for knowing the amount of compensating variation in income, knowledge of indifference curves (about tastes and preferences) of the consumer between various combinations of goods is required. Prof. J. R. Hicks himself recognizes this merit of Slutsky approach *(i.e.*, adjustment of income by the cost-difference) and remarks :

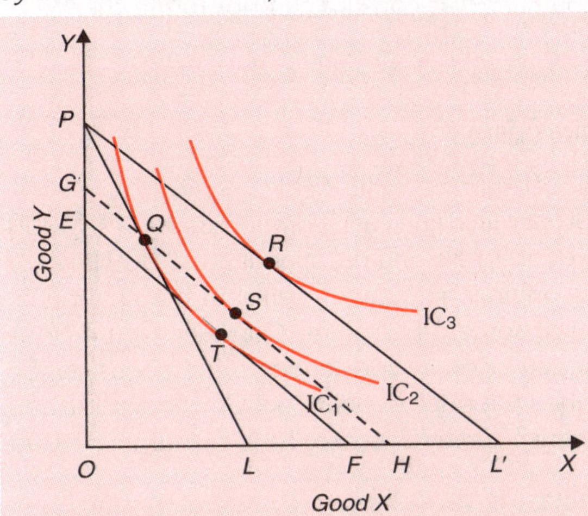

Fig. 8A.3. (*a*) *Two Types of Substitution Effects Compared (for a Fall in Price of X)*

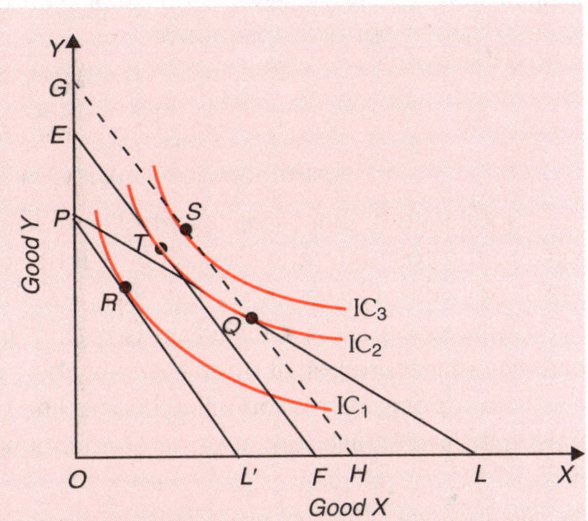

Fig. 8A.4. (*b*) *Two Types of Substitution Effects Compared (for a Rise in Price of X)*

"The difference between two methods is solely a matter of the magnitude of the rise in income, which leads to the income effect; and on this point the method of cost difference has a distinct advantage. For, while the magnitude of the compensating variation is quite a problem... the magnitude of the cost difference raises no problem at all. It can be read off at once from the data of the situation under discussion."[2]

It follows from what has been said above that both the cost-difference and compensating variation methods have their own merits. While the law of demand can be easily and adequately established by the method of cost-difference, method of compensating variation is very useful for analysis of consumer's surplus and welfare economics. With the help of the cost-difference, the income effect can be easily separated from the substitution effect but the substitution effect so found out involves some gain in real income (since it causes movement from a lower indifference curve to higher indifference curve). It is because of this that in cost-difference method substitution effect is not theoretically distinct concept. To quote J. R. Hicks again on this point, "The merit of the cost difference method is confined to the property.....that its income effect is peculiarly easy to handle. The compensating variation method does not share in this particular advantage; but it makes up for its clumsiness in relation to income effect by its convenience with relation to the substitution effect."[3]

A Numerical Example. Let us explain the concept of cost-difference and Slutsky substitution effect with a numerical example stated below:

2. *Ibid*, p. 64.
3. *Ibid* p. 69.

When the price of petrol is ₹ 20.00 per litre, Amit consumes 1,000 litres per year. The price of petrol rises to ₹ 25.00 per litre. Calculate the cost difference equal to which the Government should give him extra money income per year to compensate him for the rise in price of petrol. Will Amit be better or worse off after the price rise plus the cash compensation equal to the cost difference than he was before ? What will happen to petrol consumption ?

As explained above, the cost difference is equal to $\Delta P.\ Q$ where ΔP stands for the change in price and Q stands for the quantity of commodity he was consuming prior to the change in price. Thus, in our example above,

$$\Delta P = ₹\ 25 - 20 = ₹\ 5$$

$$Q = 1{,}000 \text{ litres per year}$$

$$\text{Cost-difference} = \Delta P.Q = ₹\ 5 \times 1{,}000 = ₹\ 5{,}000.$$

Now, with higher price of petrol of ₹ 25.00 per litre and cash compensation of ₹ 5,000 equal to the cost difference he can buy, if he so desires, the original quantity of 1,000 litres of petrol per year. However, he may not buy this original quantity of petrol in the new price-income situation if his satisfaction is maximum at some other point. Consider Figure 8A.5 where we measure petrol on the X-axis and money income representing other goods on the Y-axis. Suppose, BL_1 is the initial budget line when the price of petrol is ₹ 20.00 per litre and consumer is in equilibrium at point Q on indifference curve IC_1 where he is consuming 1,000 litres of petrol per year. Now, with the rise in price of petrol to ₹ 25.00 per litre, suppose the budget line shifts to BL_2. Now, if to compensate the rise in price, his money income is raised by ₹ 5,000, that is, equal to the cost difference, the budget line shifts parallel to BL_2 so that it reaches the position GH which passes through the original point of consumption Q. A glance at Fig. 8A.5 will reveal that the consumer with higher price of petrol and having received monetary compensation equal to the cost difference of ₹ 5,000 will not be in equilibrium at the original point Q and instead he will be maximizing his satisfaction in the new situation at point S on higher indifference curve IC_2 where his consumption of petrol has decreased to ON litres (that is, the decrease in consumption of petrol by MN is the Slutsky substitution effect.) Since, with the rise in price and simultaneous increase in his income equal to the cost-difference has enabled him to attain higher indifference curve, he has become better off than before the rise in price.

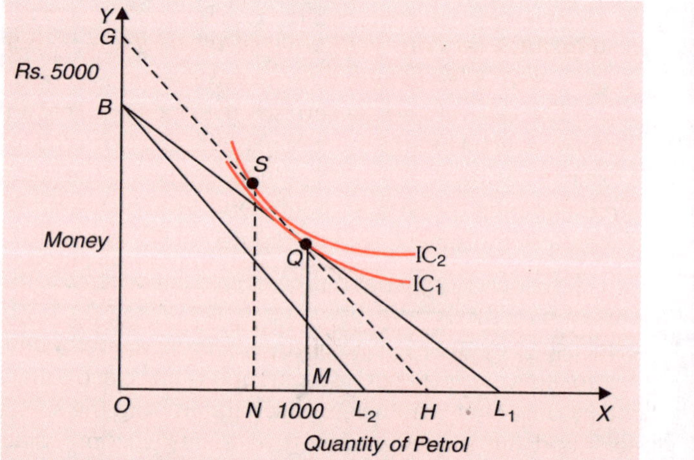

Fig. 8A.5. *Cash Compensation for a Rise in Price of Petrol*

APPENDIX B TO CHAPTER 8

MATHEMATICAL TREATMENT OF THE THEORY OF CONSUMER'S CHOICE

In this appendix we will study the mathematical derivation of consumer's equilibrium, the demand function and Slutsky equation which describes decomposition of price effect into substitution effect and income effect. We will also solve some numerical problems based on these concepts.

Mathematical Derivation of Conditions for Consumer's Equilibrium : Lagrangian Method

Those who know mathematics can understand the condition for consumer's equilibrium easily with the Lagrangian multiplier method which seeks to solve the maximisation and minimisation problems subject to some constraints.

Consider a consumer who intends to spends his entire given income (I) on the two goods, X and Y. P_x and P_y are the prices of two goods respectively which the consumer takes as given and constant for him. Consumer's budget constraint can be written by means of the following budget equation.

$$I = P_x . X + P_y . Y \quad ...(1)$$

where X and $Y$are the quantities of the two goods X and Y. The budget equation (1) describes that the expenditure on the two goods $P_x.X + P_y . Y$ equals his given income I.

The general ordinal utility function visualised by indifference curve analysis is given by

$$U = f(X, Y) \quad ...(2)$$

Equation (2) postulates that total utility (U) derived from consumption depends on the quantities X and Y of the two goods X and Y respectively. Note that in the indifference curve ordinal utility approach, total utility is not the *sum* of independent utilities derived separately from the two goods X and Y.

The aim of the consumer is to purchase such quantities of the two goods which maximise his total utility as given by the equation $U = f(X, Y)$ subject to the budget constraint as given by equation (1). So this is a *constrained maximisation problem* which can be solved through a mathematical technique called Lagrangian method which is explained below.

First Step in this method is to form Lagrangian function from the above two equations which is as under :

$$L = f(X, Y) + \lambda(I - P_xX - P_yY)$$

where λ is Lagrangian multiplier. For maximisation of utility it is necessary that partial dirivative of L with respect to X, Y and λ of the above Lagraugian function be zero. Thus, for maximisation of utility.

$$\frac{\partial L}{\partial X} = \frac{\partial f}{\partial X} - \lambda P_x = 0 \quad ...(4)$$

$$\frac{\partial L}{\partial Y} = \frac{\partial f}{\partial Y} - \lambda P_y = 0 \quad ...(5)$$

$$\frac{\partial L}{\partial \lambda} = I - P_xX - P_yY = 0 \quad ...(6)$$

(Note that '*f*' in the above equation represents the utility function).

It will be noticed that equation (6) coincides with the budget equation (1). Knowing that $\frac{\partial f}{\partial x} = MU_x$ and $\frac{\partial f}{\partial y} = MU_y$ the above equations can be rewritten as

$$MU_x - \lambda P_x = 0 \quad ...(7)$$
$$MU_y - \lambda P_y = 0 \quad ...(8)$$
$$I - P_x X - P_x Y = 0 \quad ...(9)$$

Rewritting the above equations we have

$$MU_x = \lambda P_x \quad ...(7)$$
$$MU_y = \lambda P_y \quad ...(8)$$
$$I = P_x . X + P_y . Y \quad ...(9)$$

The above three equations can be solved simultaneously to obtain the values of X and Y. In order to do so we divide (7) by (8) we have

$$\frac{MU_x}{MU_y} = MRS_{xy} = \frac{\lambda P_x}{\lambda P_y}$$

or
$$MRS_{xy} = \frac{P_x}{P_y} \quad ....(10)$$

In order to maximise satisfaction subject to the budget constraint, the equation (10) must be met along with the budget constraint equation (9).

It will be recalled that equality of MRS_{xy} with the price ratio is the necessary condition of consumer's equilibrium.

In order to obtain the values of *X* and *Y* we find out the value of *X* or *Y* from equation (10) and then substitute its value in the budget equation (9) to obtain the value of the other. This will become clear from the numerical problems solved below. Note that Lagrangean multiplier (λ) is equal to the marginal utility or satisfaction obtained from the last rupee spent on each commodity.

Numerical Problem 1

Utility function of an individual is given by $U = f(x, y) = x^{3/4}y^{1/4}$. Find out the optimal quantities of the two goods using Lagrangian method, if it is given that price of good x is ₹ 6 per unit, price of good y is ₹ 3 per unit and income of the individual (I) is equal to ₹ 120.

Solution:

Given : $U = x^{3/4}y^{1/4}$

$P_x = 6$, $P_y = 3$ and $I =$ Rs. 120

Lagrangian expression for the above problem is

$$L = x^{3/4}y^{1/4} + \lambda(120 - 6x - 3y)$$

Differentiating the Legrangian function (*L*) with respect to *x*, *y*, λ and setting them equal to zero we have

$$\frac{\partial L}{\partial x} = \frac{3}{4}x^{-1/4}y^{1/4} - 6\lambda = 0 \quad ...(1)$$

$$\frac{\partial L}{\partial y} = \frac{1}{4}x^{3/4}y^{-3/4} - 3\lambda = 0 \qquad ...(2)$$

$$\frac{\partial L}{\partial \lambda} = 120 - 6x - 3y = 0 \qquad ...(3)$$

Through rearrangement we have

$$\frac{3}{4}x^{-1/4}y^{1/4} = 6\lambda \qquad ...(4)$$

$$\frac{1}{4}x^{3/4}y^{-3/4} = 3\lambda \qquad ...(5)$$

$$6x + 3Y = 120 \qquad ...(6)$$

To solve for x we divide the equation (4) by equation (5). Thus

$$\frac{\frac{3}{4}x^{-1/4}\,y^{1/4}}{\frac{1}{4}x^{3/4}y^{-\frac{3}{4}}} = \frac{6\lambda}{3\lambda}$$

$$3x^{-1}\cdot y = \frac{6}{3}$$

or $$\frac{3y}{x} = 2 \text{ or } x = \frac{3y}{2}$$

Substituting the value of $x = \frac{3y}{2}$ in the budget equation (6) we have

$$6\frac{3y}{2} + 3y = 120$$

$$12y = 120$$

$$y = 10$$

Now, substituting the value of y = 10 in the budget equation (6) we have

$$6x + 30 = 120$$

$$x = 15$$

Thus the optimal quantities of x and y which maxise utility are x = 15 and y = 10.

Note. We can also find out the values of λ by substituting the values of x and y either in equation (4) or equation (5).

Numerical Problem 2

There are two commodities X_1 and X_2 on which a consumer spends his entire income in a day. He has utility function $U = \sqrt{X_1X_2}$. Find out the optimal quantities of X_1 and X_2 if prices of X_1 and X_2 are ₹ 5 and ₹ 2 respectively and his daily income equals ₹ 500.

Solution

Given utility function : $$U = \sqrt{X_1X_2}$$

or $$U = X_1^{1/2}X_2^{1/2}$$

and with $P_{x1} = 5$, $P_{x2} = 2$ and I = ₹ 500, budget equation is

$$500 = 5X_1 + 2X_2$$

Defferentiating the given utility function with respect to X_1 and X_2 we have

$$MU_{x1} = \frac{\partial U}{\partial X_1} = \frac{1}{2} X_1^{-1/2} X_2^{1/2} \quad ...(1)$$

$$MU_{x2} = \frac{\partial U}{\partial X_2} = \frac{1}{2} X_1^{1/2} X_2^{-1/2} \quad ....(2)$$

Dividing equations (1) by equation (2)

$$MRS_{xy} = \frac{MU_{x1}}{MU_{x2}} = \frac{\frac{1}{2} X_1^{-1/2} . X_2^{1/2}}{\frac{1}{2} X_1^{1/2} . X_2^{-1/2}} = X_1^{-1} X_2 = \frac{X_2}{X_1}$$

For maximisation of utility it is required that

$$MRS_{xy} = \frac{P_{x1}}{P_{x2}}$$

or $$\frac{X_2}{X_1} = \frac{5}{2}$$

$$X_2 = \frac{5X_1}{2}$$

Substituting the value of X_2 in the budget equation, we have

$$I = X_1 P_{x1} + X_2 P_{x2} \text{ (Budget Equation)}$$

$$500 = X_1\, 5 + \frac{5X_1 .2}{2}$$

$$10\, X_1 = 500$$

$$X_1 = 50$$

Now substituting the value of X_1 in the budget equation

$$500 = 50 \times 5 + 2X_2$$

$$500 = 250 + 2X_2$$

$$2X_2 = 250$$

$$X_2 = 125$$

Thus the optimal quantities of X_1 and X_2 are 50 and 125 respectively.

DERIVATION OF DEMAND FUNCTION

In the above example we have found the optimal values (i.e. utility-maximising values) of the goods for *specific* values of prices and income. A two variable demand function represents how quantity demanded of a good changes when prices and income change. In other words, for deriving a demand function prices and income are treated as variables. This demand function can be derived with Lagrangian method.

To Illustrate the derivation of demand function, we take the utility function $U = f(x, y) = x^{3/4} y^{1/4}$ considered above. Thus, for derivation of demand function constrained maximisation problem is

Maximise $U = x^{3/4} y^{1/4}$

Subject to $P_x.x + P_y.y = I$ (Budget equation)

Differentiating the utility function with respect to x and y we have

$$\frac{\partial U}{\partial x} = \frac{3}{4} x^{-1/4} . y^{1/4}$$

$$\frac{\partial U}{\partial y} = \frac{1}{4} x^{3/4} . y^{-3/4}$$

$\frac{\partial U}{\partial x}$ and $\frac{\partial U}{\partial y}$ represent marginal utility of X and Y respectively

For maximisation of utility :

$$MRS_{xy} = \frac{MU_x}{MU_y} = \frac{P_x}{P_y} \quad \text{... (i)}$$

$$MRS_{xy} = \frac{MU_x}{MU_y} = \frac{\frac{3}{4} x^{-1/4} . y^{1/4}}{\frac{1}{4} x^{\frac{3}{4}} . y^{-\frac{3}{4}}} = 3x^{-1} y = \frac{3y}{x}$$

Substituting the value of MRS_{xy} in equation (1) we have

$$\frac{3y}{x} = \frac{P_x}{P_y} \text{ or } y = \frac{x}{3} \frac{P_x}{P_y}$$

Substituting the value of $y = \frac{x}{3} \frac{P_x}{p_x}$ in the budget equation, we have

$$I = P_x \cdot x + P_y \cdot \frac{x}{3} \frac{P_x}{P_y}$$

or

$$I = P_x \left(x + \frac{1}{3} x \right) = P_x \left(\frac{4}{3} x \right)$$

$$x = \frac{3}{4} \frac{I}{P_x} \quad \text{...(2)}$$

x represents the quantity demanded of good x. The above equation (2) represents the demand function which states that quantity demanded of a good depends on its own price (P_x) and income (I)of the consumer, keeping the prices of other goods constant.

Likewise we can derive the demand function for y as

$$y = \frac{1}{4} \frac{I}{P_y} \quad \text{...(3)}$$

It is important to note that in the demand functions for goods X and Y, price of the good appear in the denominator which shows that the quantity demanded of the good is inversely related to the price of the good. That is, demand curve of a good shopes downward to the right. Besides, I appear in the numerator of equations (2) and (3) which shows demand for a good varies directly with income.

Example 2. *Let us take another type of utility function and explain the mathematical derivation of demand function for a good following detailed procedure of Lagrangian method.*

Suppose a general utility function $U = xy$ is given. I stands for income, and P_x and P_y denote prices of the two goods. Writing the constrained utility maximisation problem in this case we have

$$\text{Maximise } U = xy \qquad ...(1)$$

$$\text{Subject to } P_x . x + P_y . y = I \qquad ...(2)$$

Lagrangian expression for the above problem is

$$L = xy + \lambda(I - P_x . x - P_y y)$$

For maximisation of utility we differentiate the Lagrangian function with respect to x, y and λ and set them equal to zero.

$$\frac{\partial L}{\partial x} = \frac{\partial U}{\partial x} - \lambda P_x = 0 \qquad ...(3)$$

$$\frac{\partial L}{\partial y} = \frac{\partial U}{\partial y} - \lambda P_y = 0 \qquad ...(4)$$

$$\frac{\partial L}{\partial \lambda} = I - P_x \cdot x + P_y y = 0 \qquad ...(5)$$

Note that derivative $\frac{\partial U}{\partial x}$ of the utility function $U = xy$ is equal to y and derivative $\frac{\partial U}{\partial y}$ of the utility function $U = xy$ is equal to x. Further note that these derivatives represent marginal utilities of the goods. Rewriting the equation (3) and (4), we have

$$\frac{MU_x}{P_x} = \lambda$$

$$\frac{MU_y}{P_y} = \lambda$$

or $$\frac{MU_x}{P_x} = \frac{MU_y}{P_y} \qquad ...(6)$$

Since in the given utility function $MU_x = y$ and $MU_y = x$ we have

$$\frac{y}{P_x} = \frac{x}{P_y} \qquad ...(7)$$

or $$y = x\frac{P_x}{P_y} \qquad ...(8)$$

Putting the value of y into the budget equation (2) we have

$$P_x \cdot x + P_y \cdot \frac{P_x}{P_y} \cdot x = I$$

$$P_x(x + x) = I$$

or $$P_x . 2x = I$$

$$x = \frac{I}{2P_x} \qquad ...(9)$$

The equation (9) represents the demand function for good x with shows that quantity demanded (x) of good X is directly related to income (I) and inversely related to its own price (P_x), price of the other goods remaining constant.

Likewise, it can be shwn that demand function for y is given by :

$$y = \frac{I}{2P_y} \qquad ...(10)$$

SLUTSKY EQUATION : DECOMPOSING PRICE EFFECT

In Appendix A to this chapter on indifference curve analysis we have graphically shown according to Slutsky how the effect of change in price of a good can be broken up into its two component parts, namely, substitution effect and income effect. The decomposition of price effect into its two components can be derived and expressed mathematically. Suppose price of good X falls, its substitution effect on quantity demanded of the good arises due to substitution of the relatively cheaper good X for the now relatively dearer good Y so that his level of *real income* remains constant. The overall effect of change in its own price of a commodity on its quantity demanded can be expressed as $\frac{dq_x}{dp_x}$ and the substitution effect can be expressed as $\left.\frac{\partial q_x}{\partial p_x}\right|_{U=\bar{U}}$. The term $\left.\frac{\partial q_x}{\partial p_x}\right|_{U=\bar{U}}$ shows change in quantity demanded resulting from a relative change in price of X while real income of the consumer remains constant.

However, expressing income effect of the price change mathematically is rather a ticklish affair. Suppose a unit change in income (∂I) causes a (∂q_x) change in quantity demanded of the good X. This can be written as $\frac{\partial q_x}{\partial I}$. But how much income changes due to a change in price of the good is determined by how much quantity of the good (q_x) the consumer was purchasing on the one hand and change in price of the good (∂p_x) that has taken place on the other. The change in income due to a change in price can be measured by $q_x.(\partial p_x)$. How much this change in income will affect the quantity demanded of the good X is determined by $\frac{\partial q_x}{\partial I}$ which shows the effect of a unit change in income on the quantity demanded of the good X. Thus the overall effect of change in price of the good X on its quantity demanded can be expressed by the following equation which is generally called *Slutsky equation* because it was Russian economist Slutsky who first of all divided the price effect into substitution and income effect.

$$-\frac{\partial q_x}{\partial p_x} = -\left.\frac{\partial q_x}{\partial p_x}\right|_{U=\bar{U}} - q_x \cdot \partial P_x \frac{\partial q_x}{\partial I} \qquad .... (i)$$

The first term on the right hand side of the equation represents the substitution affect obtained after income of the consumer has been adjusted to keep his level of real income or purchasing power constant. Since under the substitution effect, the *fall* in price of good leads to the *increase* in its quantity demanded, its sign is negative. The second term on the right hand side of the equation shows the income effect of the fall in price of the good X. The term $q_x.\partial p_x$ measures the increase in income or purchasing power caused by the fall in price of good X and

$\frac{\partial q_x}{\partial I}$ measures the change in quantity demanded resulting from a unit increase in income (I).

Therefore, income affect of the price change is given by $q_x . \partial p_x \frac{\partial q_x}{\partial I}$. Since the *fall* in price of a good *increases* real income or purchasing power of the consumer which in case of normal goods leads to the ***increase in quantity demanded*** of the good, sign of the income affect has also been taken to be negative (–). Though income effect for a normal good as such is positive, but in the present case it is real income effect produced by fall in price that leads to ***increase in quantity demanded*** of good X which in mathematical terms is negative. Thus viewed from the viewpoint of ***relationship between price and quantity*** demanded both the effects are negative in mathematical terms and work in the *same direction* in case of normal goods. It should be noted that price effect *i.e.* $\frac{\Delta Q_x}{\Delta P_x}$ is itself negative showing the inverse relationship between price and quantity demanded. Remember that negative relationship in mathematics does not necessarily mean decrease in the variable, it means that the variables change in opposite directions.

Further, a point needs to be clarified. In the analysis of decomposing price effect into substitution and income effects Hicks considered substitution effect when with a change in price, consumer is so compensated as to keep his utility constant. However, in obtaining Slutsky substitution affect income of the consumer is adjusted to *keep his purchasing power constant* so that he could buy the original combination of goods if he so desires. This difference was later emphasised by J.R. Hicks. Since it was Slutsky who first of all split up the price effect into substitution effect and income effect the above equation (*i*) is popularly known as Slutsky equation. It is proper to call it ***Slutsky-Hicks equation.***

The second important conclusion which follows from Slutsky equation is that as the quantity of commodity (q_x) becomes smaller and smaller, the income effect of the price change will become smaller and smaller. Thus, if the quantity consumed of a commodity is very small, then the income effect is not very significant.

QUESTIONS FOR REVIEW

1. What is Slutsky Substitution effect ? Explain Slutsky substitution effect for a fall in price of good X.
2. Distingusih between Hicks and Slutsky approach to the measurements of income and substitution effects.
3. Show graphically the substitution and the real income effects by Hicks and Slutsky. What is the advantage of Slutsky measure ?
4. A consumer spends all his income on two goods X and Y. When the price of goods X is ₹ 2 he consumes 100 units of good X. If price of goods X increases to ₹ 3 and income is increased by ₹ 100 to enable him to purchase the original bundle, price of Y remaining constant, explain (*i*) would the level of satisfaction of the consumer change; and (*ii*) what would happen to the quantity consumed of X ?
5. State the Slutsky equation algebraically and explain each term in it. Using the equation explain (*i*) what must be the sign and magnitude of the income effect for a downward-sloping demand curve.

CHAPTER

9

Demand for Complementary and Substitute Goods

Edgeworth-Pareto Definition of Complementary and Substitute Goods

Marshall did not give any definitions of substitute and complementary goods. However, before Marshall, Edgeworth and Pareto had provided the definitions of substitute and complementary goods in terms of marginal utility. According to Edgeworth-Pareto definition, **"*Y* is a complementary with *X* in the consumer's budget if an increase in the supply of *X* (*Y* constant) raises the marginal utility of *Y*; *Y* is competitive with *X* (or is a substitute for *X*) if an increase in the supply of *X* (*Y* constant) lowers the marginal utility of *Y*."**[1]

According to the above Edgeworth-Pareto definition, complementary and substitution relations are reversible, that is, if good *Y* is complementary with *X*, *X* is complementary with *Y*; and if *Y* is substitute for *X*, *X* is substitute for *Y*. Secondly, assuming that marginal utility of money remains constant, from the above definition it follows that if the price of good *X* falls and consequently the quantity demanded of good *X* increases, this will bring about an increase in the marginal utility of good *Y* if goods' *X* and *Y* are complementary, and will therefore raise the demand for *Y*. On the contrary, if goods *X* and *Y* are substitutes, according to Edgeworth-Pareto definition, the fall in the price of good *X* and consequently the increase in the quantity demanded of *X* will lower the marginal utility of *Y* and thereby bring about a decline in the demand for *Y*. Thus, it is in this way that Edgeworth and Pareto explained the demand for inter-related goods—complementary and substitute goods.

However, Pareto encountered difficulties when he tried to express his definitions of complementary and substitute goods in terms of indifference curves. He opined that the indifference curves between the two complementary goods (according to the above definition) are ***very bent,*** as shown in Fig. 9.1 and the indifference curves between two substitutes (according to the above definition) are ***very flat*** as shown in Figure 9.2. Thus Pareto traced parallelism between the complementary goods and the "very bent" shape indifference curves; and between substitutes and very flat indifference curves. But while the definitions make clear-cut distinction between complementary and substitute goods, their translation into indifference curves makes the distinction vague, inexact, and imprecise. This is because the difference between the indifference curves diagrams in Figures 9.1 and 9.2 is not one of kind but of degree. These two diagrams differ only in the ***curvature of indifference curves***; indifference curves in Figure 9.1 have greater curvature than those of Figure 9.2. Now, the pertinent question is what degree of curvature marks the dividing line between substitutes and complementary goods. Therefore, criticizing Pareto's aforesaid parallelism Hicks remarks, "the parallelism is not at all exact, as is made evident at once by the impossibility of discovering what degree of curvature of the indifference curves corresponds to the *distinction* between

1. J. R. Hicks, *Value and Capital*, second edition, 1946, p. 42.

complementary and substitute goods—which ought, on the above definition, to be a perfectly clear-cut distinction."[2]

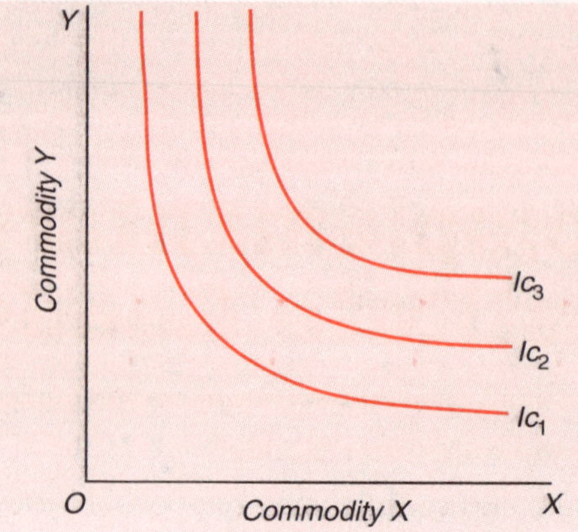

Fig. 9.1. *Complementary Goods*

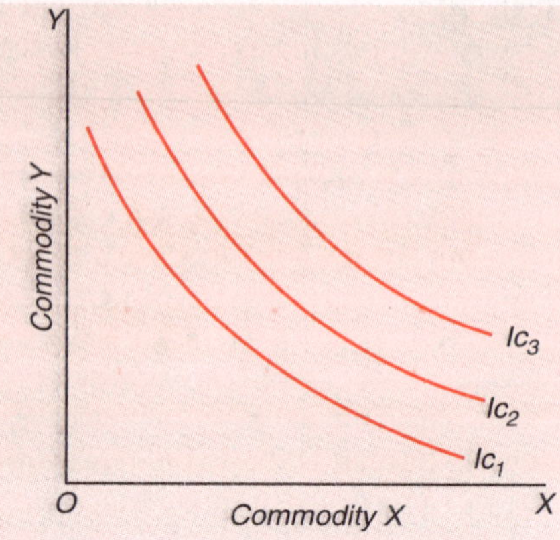

Fig. 9.2. *Subsitute Goods*

Further, the above Edgewdrth-Pareto definition of complementary and substitute goods is based on the assumption that utility is measurable. But Pareto regarded the utility to be immeasurable in cardinal or quantitative sense. Therefore, Pareto contradicted himself by defining complementary and substitute goods in terms of measurable utility. Thus, according to Hicks, "Edgeworth-Pareto definition errs against Pareto's own principle of the immeasuarability of utility. If utility is not a quantity, but only an index of the consumer's scale of preferences, his definition of complementary goods has a precise meaning. The distinction between complementary and competitive goods will differ according to the arbitrary measure of utility which is adopted."[3]

Hicksian Explanation of Complementary and Substitute Goods

With indifference curve analysis of demand in which price effect was bifurcated into substitution effect and income effect, Hicks was able to explain in a satisfactory way the cases of substitute and complementary goods. Before Hicks, substitutes and complementary goods were generally explained in terms of ***total price effect*** (or in other words, with the concept of *cross elasticity of demand).* According to this total price-effect approach, if the price of a good *X* falls and as a result the quantity demanded of good *X* increases, the quantity demanded of good *Y* decreases, then *Y* is a substitute for *X*. On the other hand, *Y* is a complement of *X*, if with the fall in price of *X* and resultant increase in quantity demanded of *X*, the quantity demanded of *Y* also increases.

Now, according to Hicks, if income effect is taken into account, then even if with the fall in price of *X*, the quantity demanded of good *Y* may also increase even though the good *Y* may be substitute or competitive good. This is when with the fall in price of good, there is a large income effect which more than offsets the substitution effect. Income effect of the fall in price of good *X* tends to increase the quantity demanded of good *Y* (as also of the good *X)* and the substitution effect of the fall in price of *X* works in favour of *X* (that is, tends to increase its quantity demanded) and against good *Y* (that is, tends to reduce its quantity demanded). When this income effect for *Y* is stronger than substitution effect, then the quantity demanded of *Y* increases as a result of the fall in price of *X*, even though the two may be substitute goods.

2. J. R. Hicks, *op. cit.*, p. 42.
3. *Op. cit.*, p. 43.

Therefore, when the income effect is strong enough to swamp the substitution effect for the commodity *Y* which has become relatively dearer due to the fall in price of good *X*, the purchases of both goods *X* and *Y* increase as a result of the fall in price of good *X*. Then, on the basis of total price effect, the goods would be described as complements, even though they are in fact substitute goods. Therefore, according to Hicks, goods can be classified as substitutes or complements more accurately by reference to the substitution effect or preference function alone. Hence, in the opinion of Hicks, we can define substitute and complementary goods correctly and precisely only in a situation when we have eliminated the income effect of the price change by making a compensating variation in income. When with a change in price compensating variation in income is also made, the effect which remains is the substitution effect.

Since indifference curve analysis splits up the price effect into income and substitution effects, it is greatly helpful in analyzing the relations of substitution and complementarity. Take two goods *X* and *Y*. If the price of good *X* falls, price of *Y* remaining constant, the quantity demanded of good *X* will increase due to the substitution effect and income effect (we suppose that good *X* is not an inferior good). Now, if after the income of the consumer is reduced by compensating variation in income so that with reduced price of good *X* he is no better off than before, the quantity demanded of *X* increases and the quantity demanded of Y declines, then good *Y* is a substitute for X. In this case, due to the relative fall in its price, good *X* has been substituted for good *Y* and because of compensating variation in income, consumer is no better off than before.

Now, if the price of good *X* falls and after making compensating variation in income, the quantity demanded of *X* increases due to the substitution effect and if with it the quantity demanded of *Y* also increases, then *Y* is a complement of *X*. Thus, in this case of complements, the quantity purchased of both the goods increases and *both of them substitute some other good*. Consumer is no better off than before, since compensating variation in income having been made the quantities purchased of two complementary goods has increased due to the substitution effect alone. In view of the above analysis, Prof. Hicks defines the substitutes and complements in the following way :

"I shall say, *Y* is a substitute of *X* if a fall in the price of *X* leads to a fall in the consumption of *Y*; *Y* is a complement of *X if* a fall in the price of *X* leads to a rise in the consumption of *Y*; ***a compensating variation in income being made, of course in each case.*** Thus a fall in the price or X, combined with a compensated variation in income, which must tend to increase the consumption of *X* itself (by the first substitution theorem), will increase the consumption of complements, but diminish the consumption of substitutes."[4]

We have seen above that the relation of substitutability or complementarity depends on the substitution effect. To determine the substitution effect is quite simple if there are only two commodities on which the consumer has to spend his money income. We know that a fall in the price of good *X* always leads to the substitution of *X* for the other goods; and if *Y* was the only other good available to the consumer, then the substitution effect of the fall in price of good *X*'must necessarily reduce the quantity demanded of *Y*. However, when there are more than two goods, a fall in the price of good *X* may not reduce the quantity demanded of *Y*; it may in fact increase the quantity purchased of good *Y*, if the two goods *X* and *Y* happen to be complements. Here, the two goods *X* and *Y* are substituted for some ***other goods***.

From the above description, it is clear that the definition and proper analysis of substitutes and complementary goods require three goods. That is why J. R. Hicks in his *Value and*

4. J. R. Hicks, *A Revision of Demand Theory*, Oxford University Press, 1956, p. 128.

Capital defined them by taking three commodities, X, Y and money and in terms of the concept of marginal rate of substitution. It should be remembered that money stands for all other goods lumped together and is known as *composite commodity*. Hicks defined substitute and complementary goods in his book "Value and Capital" in the following way :

"Y is a substitute for X if the marginal rate of substitution of Y for money is diminished when X is substituted for money in such a way as to leave the consumer no better off than before."

"Y is complementary with X if the marginal rate of substitution of Y for money is increased when X is substituted for money in such a way as to leave the consumer no better off than before."[5]

In order to understand the above definitions, let us assume that a consumer is in equilibrium between *X*, *Y* and money so that marginal rates of substitution between them is equal to their respective prices. Now suppose that the price of *X* falls, prices of *Y* and money remain the same (price of money is unity). With the fall in price of *X*, consumer will substitute *X* for money so that the quantity of *X* increases and that of money decreases; *X* is substituted for money. This will disturb the equality of marginal rate of substitution between *Y* and money, price of *Y* being constant. With this, if the marginal rate of substitution of *Y* for money declines, the consumer must reduce his consumption of *Y* (that is, he either substitutes *X* or money for *Y)* so that the consumer's marginal rate of substitution of *Y* for money rises to the level of the unchanged price ratio between *Y* and money. Therefore, in this case, good *Y* would be substitute for *X* since fall in the price of *X* and consequent increase in its quantity demanded leads to the fall in quantity of *Y*.

On the other hand, if price of X falls, and consumer substitutes X for money, and as a result of this, the marginal rate of substitution of *Y* for money increases, consumer will increase the consumption of *Y* (he will substitute *Y* for money) so that consumer's marginal rate of substitution of *Y* for money falls to the unchanged price ratio between money and *Y*. Therefore, in this case, *Y* would be complementary with *X* since the fall in the price of *X* and consequent increase in its quantity demanded has led to the increase in quantity demanded of *Y*.

We thus see that ***whereas the case of substitutes can be depicted and analysed on a two-dimensional indifference curves diagram, the case of complementarity cannot be done so***. This is because in case of analyzing the relation between two complementary goods, at least one other good must be brought into the picture against whom substitution of two complements takes place. So the case of complementarity cannot arise on a two-dimensional indifference curve diagram. In indifference curve analysis, the case of two complementary goods is generally shown by right-angled indifference curves which show that two goods are used in a given fixed proportion. However, the right-angled indifference curves do not indicate the true nature of complements. When the price of one complement falls and compensating variation in income is made, the quantities of two complementary goods remain the same, that is, the substitution effect between them is zero, as is shown in Figure 9.3 where as result of the fall in price of good *X*, the price line

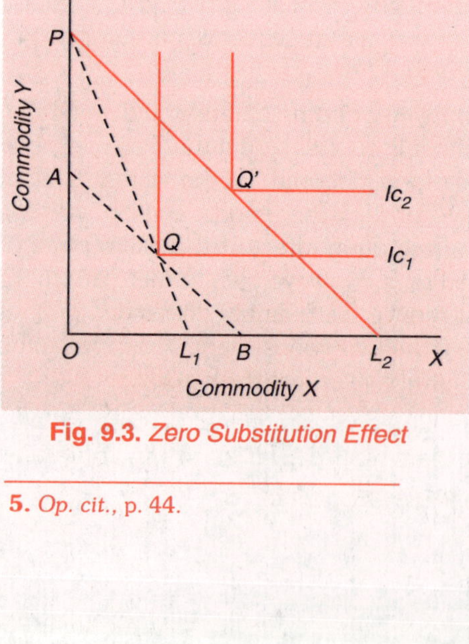

Fig. 9.3. *Zero Substitution Effect*

5. *Op. cit.*, p. 44.

shifts from PL_1 to PL_2 and the consumer shifts from equilibrium position Q to Q'. Line AB is drawn to bring about compensating variation in income (PA in terms of Y is the compensating variation in income). It will be seen from the figure that the price line AB is tangent to the indifference curve IC_1 at the same point Q at which he was in equilibrium before the fall in price of X. Hence, the substitution effect is zero.

However, as we have seen above, in case of two complementary goods, substitution effect between them is not only zero but when the quantity purchased of one good rises due to the compensated price falls, the quantity purchased of the other good also increases. And both these goods substitute some other good. Further, for the consumer to be indifferent (or no better off) between the two situations, when the quantities "purchased of two complements increase as a result of the compensated price fall of one of them, the quantity purchased of some other good must decline against which the two complements are substituted. Therefore, the case of complementarity can arise when there are more than two goods..... at least three goods among which two are complements and one their substitute.

It follows from the above analysis that while substitutes can occur in case of only two goods, complementary goods cannot be so. When there are only two goods on which the consumer has to spend his income, substitution effect always works in favour of the good whose price has fallen and against the other (that is, it tends to increase the quantity purchased of one and tends to reduce the quantity purchased of the other.) Thus, ***if there were only two goods on which the consumer had to spend his income, they would necessarily be substitute goods.*** Thus, case of complementarity can arise only if there are at least three goods. To quote J. R. Hicks, "If consumer is dividing his income between purchases of two goods only and cannot possible buy any goods other than these two, then there cannot be anything else but a substitution relation between the two goods. For if he is to get more of one of them and still be no better off than before, he must have less of the other. But when he is dividing his income between more than two goods, other kinds of relation become possible."[6] Likewise, Prof. Hicks writes in his later book *"A Revision of Demand Theory"*: "If income is being spent upon two goods only, it is impossible that these two goods should be complements. A fall in the price of X must tend to increase the consumption of X (by the first substitution theorem); if it, increases the consumption of Y and there are no other goods in the budget, the consumer will have moved to a position in which case he has more Y and no less X; by the consistency theory, this cannot be indifferent with his initial position. Thus in the two goods case, the relation between the two goods must be that of substitution; a compensated price change, if it has any effect at all, must lead to more consumption of one good and less of the other."[7]

Another significant point to be noted regarding the relations of substitutability that ***whereas all goods in a consumer's budget can be substitutes for each other, all cannot be complements.*** Suppose the price of good X falls and consumer's money income is reduced by the compensating variation in income so as to wipe out the income effect. As a result of this compensated price fall, the quantity purchased of some other goods will decline, that is, good X will be substituted for some other goods. These 'some other goods' whose consumption declines as a result of the compensated price fall of X, are substitutes for X. It is possible that the quantity purchased of some of the other goods may increase as a result of this compensated price fall of X and these would be the complements of X. But while it is possible that all other goods may be substitutes of X, *all other goods* cannot be complements of X; *at least one of the other good* must be substitute of X so that substitution of X for it may be done. To quote J. R.

6. J. R. Hicks, *Values and Capital.*
7. J. R. Hicks, *A Revision of Demand Theory*, p. 129.

Hicks again, "It is still possible that all other goods may be simply substitutes for one of the goods (say *X*). This will happen if, when the supply of X is increased, there has to be reduction in the quantities of *all* other goods.....Here the substitution in favour of X is a substitution against each of the other commodities taken separately. But it is possible that......there must be an increase in *some* of the other commodities—commodities complementary with X since the consumer cannot get more of all commodities and still be left no better off than before."[8]

COMPENSATED DEMAND CURVE

The ordinary demand curve for a consumer which we derived from the price consumption curve includes the effect of both the substitution and income effects of the changes in price of a good on its quantity purchased. As a consumer moves downward along the ordinary demand curve, he goes to a higher indifference curve on the price consumption curve and his satisfaction or real income increases. It may be noted that in deriving ordinary demand curve, money income of the consumer is held constant. However, for certain problems such as measurement of consumer surplus, the use of ordinary demand curve is not appropriate. This is because for the proper analysis of consumer surplus we need a **demand curve that is based on the real income (i.e., satisfaction) being held constant** as price of a good changes rather than *money income* being kept constant.

Such demand curve which incorporates the effects of changes in price of a commodity, *real income remaining constant* is called **income compensated demand curve or simply compensated demand curve.** In the derivation of compensated demand curve, following the changes in price of the commodity, real income is held constant by making appropriate compensating variation in income.

Thus, whereas ordinary demand curve describes the effects of both the substitution and income effects of the changes in price of a commodity, compensated demand curve includes the effect of only substitution effect.

How a compensated demand curve is derived is illustrated in Fig. 9.4. In the upper panel (a) the consumer has money income equal to *OB*. With initial price of the commodity equal to $P_0, \left(\text{slope of } \frac{OB}{OL} = P_0\right)$, budget line is *BL* which is tangent to the indifference curve *IC* at point *E* where consumer is buying Ox_1 quantity of the commodity. Now, suppose price of a commodity X falls to price $P_1, \left(P_1 = \text{slope of budget line } B'L' = \frac{OB'}{OL'}\right)$ and together with this fall in price, consumer's income is reduced so that the budget line representing the lower price of *X* is again tangent to indifference curve *IC*, although at a different point indicating that real income (or utility) remains constant as at point *E*. Note that with the fall in price we have reduced the consumer's money income by compensating variation in income so that he remains on the same indifference curve as before. At the new equilibrium point *S* is achieved after the fall in price, real income remaining constant, the consumer buys Ox_2 quantity of the commodity.

---

8. *Op. cit.*, p. 47. It should be noted that the condition of "no better off than before" or in other words constant level of satisfaction or real income is essential to judge the relation of substitution or complementarity, since, these relations, as explained above, are to be judged with reference to the substitution effect alone after eliminating the income effect by making compensating variation in income. And under Hicksian-substitution effect, as has been seen earlier, consumer's satisfaction remains the same, that is, he remains neither better off, nor worse off.

In the lower panel *(b)* corresponding to points E and S against prices P_0 and P_1 quantities demanded Ox_1 and Ox_2 are shown. Similarly, we can derive other points corresponding to different prices of commodity X, real income being held constant. By joining points such as E' and S' we get the compensated demand curve which includes the influence of substitution

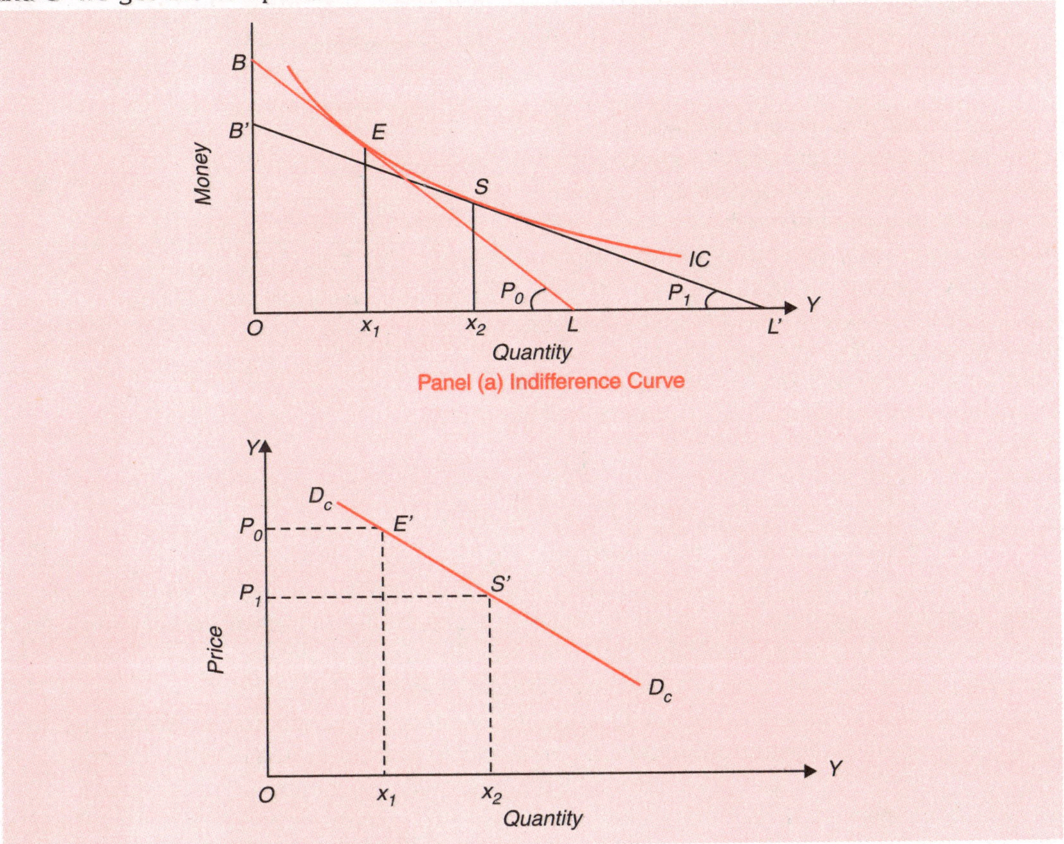

Panel *(b)* **Compensated Demand Curve**

Fig. 9.4. *Derivation of Compensated Demand Curve*

effect only, real income remaining the same or, in other words, compensated demand curve corresponds to the different equilibrium points achieved at different prices of the good X on the same indifference curve representing a given level of real income (i.e. level of satisfaction or utility) after compensating variation in income has been made.

It should be noted that a different compensated demand curve can be derived corresponding to each of a set of indifference curves (that is, for each level of real income or utility). This is because, as seen before, each point on the ordinary demand curve corresponds to a different indifference curve of price consumption curve representing different levels of real income.

Relationship Between Compensated and Ordinary Demand Curves

It is important to note the relationship between the compensated demand curve and the ordinary demand curve in case of a *normal* commodity which is illustrated in Fig. 9.5. On the ordinary demand curve D_0D_0, we take a point E corresponding to the tangency point of a given budget line and an indifference curve which represents a given level of real income *(i.e.,* satisfaction). At price P_0, quantity demanded of the commodity is Ox_0. Now suppose price of the commodity falls from P_0 to P_1. *In the absence of compensating variation in income*, at the lower price P_1, the consumer moves downward along the ordinary demand curve D_0D_0 and buys Ox_2 quantity of the commodity.

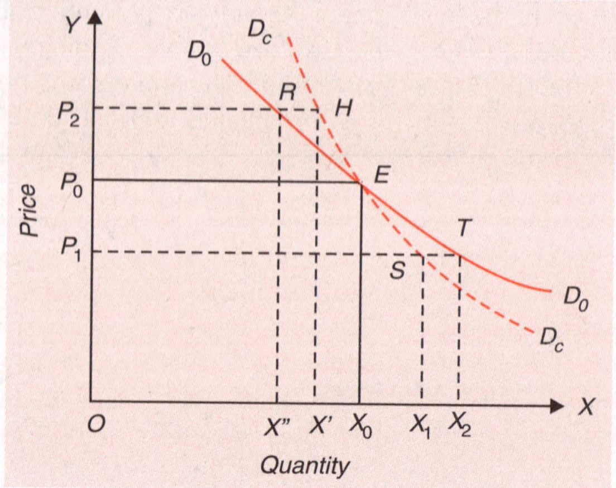

Fig. 9.5. *Comparison Between Compensated and Ordinary Demand Curves in Case of a Normal Commodity*

Note that, in the absence of compensating variation in income, at a lower price P_1 and quantity Ox_2 on the ordinary demand curve, real income will increase as he would move to a higher indifference curve on the price consumption curve. However, in order to prevent him from gaining in real income his money income is reduced large enough to keep him on the same indifference curve, he will buy less than Ox_2 quantity of the commodity. It will be seen from Fig. 9.5. that at a lower price P_1 together with compensation variation in income the consumer buys Ox_1 quantity of the commodity which corresponds to point *S*. Thus, point *S* is the relevant point on the compensated demand curve corresponding to price P_1 and quantity Ox_1.

Now, suppose price of the commodity X rises from P_0 to P_2. In the absence of compensating variation in income, the consumer moves upward along the ordinary demand curve to point *R* and buys Ox'' quantity and with this his real income will decrease as his new position will lie on a lower indifference curve than before. In order to keep his real income constant, if he is compensated by increase in money income, the quantity purchased of *X* by him will not decline as much as in the absence of compensating variation in income. Therefore, with compensating variation in income his new equilibrium position will lie to the right of *R*, say at *H*, at which he buys Ox'quantity of the commodity. By joining points such as *H, E, S,* we get a compensated demand curve along which real income remains constant. Thus, ***whereas along ordinary demand curve, a consumer's money income remains constant, along compensated demand curve, his real income remains constant.***

As is seen from Fig. 9.5 for a normal commodity, ordinary demand curve is *flatter* than compensated demand curve. This is because, as explained above, with the fall in price *without* compensating reduction in money income, the quantity purchased of a normal commodity will increase to a greater extent than what he buys when compensating reduction in income is made. On the other hand, when price rises from P_0 to P_2, in the absence of compensating increase in his income, his quantity demanded of the commodity will decrease to a greater extent as compared to the quantity he buys when his money income is increased together with rise in price of the commodity so as to keep his real income constant.

However, ***it may be noted that the above condition that ordinary demand curve is flatter than the compensated demand curve is valid in case of normal goods.*** It may be recalled that normal goods are those whose demand increases when consumer's income increases and vice-versa, that is, in their case income effect is positive. *In case of inferior goods,* the opposite is the case and for them ordinary demand curve is *steeper* than the compensated demand curve. This is because income effect in case of inferior goods is negative.

Measurement of Consumer Surplus with Ordinary and Compensated Demand Curves

As noted above, the concept of compensated demand curve is needed to obtain the exact value of consumer surplus. Marshall measures consumer surplus as an area under the ordinary demand curve which includes the influence of both the substitution and income effects of price changes. The concept of consumer surplus is based on the marginal valuation of the units of a commodity and represents the excess of the sum of marginal valuations of the units of commodity purchased over the total price he pays for them. Now, for the purpose of accurate measurement of marginal valuation of the commodity and therefore the consumer surplus which a consumer derives from his purchases, the concept of compensated demand curve is better than the ordinary demand curve as the former does not include the income effects of changes in price of a commodity. As explained above, the concept of compensated demand curve is based on the exclusion of income effect of price changes.

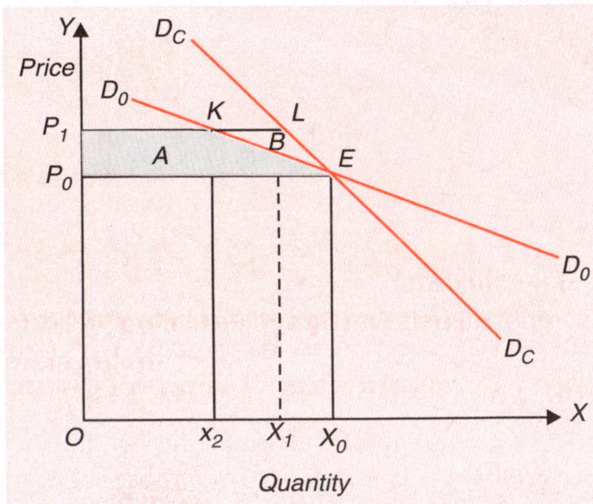

Fig. 9.6. *Compensated Vs. Marshallian Consumer Surplus*

Let us illustrate with the help of a diagram how much error is introduced in the estimate of consumer surplus by using ordinary demand curve rather than compensated demand curve. In Fig. 9.6, we have reproduced the compensated demand curve $D_C D_C$ and ordinary demand curve D_0 D_0 of a normal commodity. Suppose initially the price of commodity is P_0 at which the consumer is buying x_0 quantity of the commodity on the ordinary the demand curve D_0 D_0. With the rise in price from P_0 to P_1 and the ordinary demand curve as the measure of marginal valuation, the consumer suffers a loss of welfare (as measured by decline in consumer surplus) by the area P_0 P_1 *KE* which is marked as *A*. However, if we use compensated demand curve, which more accurately represents marginal valuation of a commodity, loss of consumer surplus as a result of rise in price from P_0 to P_1 is equal to the area $P_0 P_1$ *LE* (*i.e.*, areas *A* + *B*) which is greater by the area marked as *B* than $P_0 P_1$ *KE* obtained by using the concept of Marshallian ordinary demand curve concept.

It follows from above that ***in case of a normal commodity,*** the use of ordinary demand curve rather than compensated demand curve leads to the *underestimation* of the loss of consumer surplus. Likewise, ***in case of an inferior commodity*** use of ordinary demand curve rather than compensated demand curve leads to the *overestimation* of the loss of consumer surplus associated with a rise in price of a commodity. It is worth mentioning that the difference in loss of welfare (*i.e.*, consumer surplus) associated with the use of the concepts of compensated and the ordinary demand curves depends on the magnitude of income effect of the changes in price of the commodity. To the extent income effect is small, the difference in welfare loss in using ordinary demand curve and compensated demand curve will tend to be small. It should be noted that size of income effect of the changes in price depends on the importance of a commodity in consumer's budget. Since in the actual world, for many commodities budget share spent on a single commodity is very small, income effect of price changes does not make much difference in the two cases. Therefore, in most cases, economists regard Marshallian measure of consumer surplus as a good approximation to the exact measure derived from the use of compensated demand curve.

CHAPTER

10

Marshallian Cardinal Utility Analysis Vs. Indifference Curve Analysis

SIMILARITY BETWEEN THE TWO ANALYSES

We are now in a position to compare the indifference curve analysis with Marshallian Cardinal utility analysis. Barring some economists like Dennis Robertson, W. E. Armstrong, F. H. Knight, it is now widely believed that indifference curve analysis makes a definite improvement upon the Marshallian cardinal utility analysis. It has been asserted that whereas Marshallian utility analysis assumes 'too much', it explains 'too little', on the other hand, the indifference curve analysis explains more by taking fewer as well as less restrictive assumptions. Though the two types of analyses are fundamentally different approaches to the study of consumer's demand, they nonetheless, have some common points which are as follows :

(*a*) Both the analyses assume that the consumer is rational in the sense that he tries to maximize utility or satisfaction. The assumption of indifference curve analysis that the consumer tries to reach the highest possible indifference curve and thus seeks to maximize his level of satisfaction is similar to the assumption made in Marshallian utility analysis that the consumer attempts to maximize utility.

(*b*) In Marshallian utility analysis, condition of consumer's equilibrium is that the marginal utilities of various goods are proportional to their prices. In other words, a consumer is in equilibrium when he is distributing his money income among various lines of expenditure in such a way that,

$$\frac{MU \text{ of } X}{\text{Price of } X} = \frac{MU \text{ of } Y}{\text{Price of } Y} \text{ and so on.}$$

According to indifference curve analysis, consumer is in equilibrium when his marginal rate of substitution between the two goods is equal to the price ratio between them. That is,

$$MRS_{xy} = \frac{\text{Price of } X}{\text{Price of } Y}$$

That the equality of the marginal rate of substitution with the price ratio is equivalent to the Marshallian condition that marginal utilities are proportional to their prices is shown below:

In equilibrium, according to indifference curve analysis :

$$MRS \text{ of } X \text{ for } Y = \frac{\text{Price of } X}{\text{Price of } Y} \quad .....(i)$$

But *MRS* of *X* for *Y* is defined as the ratio between the marginal utilities of the two goods. Therefore,

$$MRS \text{ of } X \text{ for } Y = \frac{MU \text{ of } X}{MU \text{ of } Y} \qquad \text{....}(ii)$$

From (*i*) and (*ii*), it follows that

$$\frac{MU \text{ of } X}{MU \text{ of } Y} = \frac{\text{Price of } X}{\text{Price of } Y}$$

which can be written as

$$\frac{MU \text{ of } X}{\text{Price of } X} = \frac{MU \text{ of } Y}{\text{Price of } Y} \qquad \text{....}(iii)$$

It is evident that (*iii*) is the same proportionality condition of consumer's equilibrium as enunciated by Marshall.

(*c*) The third similarity between the two types of analysis is that some form of diminishing utility is assumed in each of them. In Hicksian indifference curve analysis, indifference curves are assumed to be convex to the origin. The convexity of the indifference curves implies that the marginal rate of substitution of *X* for *Y* diminishes as more and more of X is substituted for Y. This principle of diminishing marginal rate of substitution is equivalent to the Marshallian law of diminishing marginal utility.

(*d*) Another similarity between the two approaches is that both employ psychological or introspective method. In the introspective method, as has been seen already, we attribute a certain psychological feeling to the consumer by looking into and knowing from our own mind. In Marshallian analysis, observed law of demand is explained by *the psychological law* of diminishing marginal utility which is based upon *introspection*. In Hicks-Alien indifference curve technique, indifference curves are usually obtained through psychological-introspective method. Though some attempts have been made recently by some economists to obtain indifference curves from the observed data of the consumer's behaviour, but with limited success. As things are, in the Hicks-Alien indifference curve analysis, indifference curves are derived through *hypothetical* experimentation. Thus, the method of indifference curve analysis is fundamentally psychological and introspective. "The basic methodological approach of Hicks-Alien is same as in the Marshallian marginal utility hypothesis : It is, that is to say, mainly, introspective".[1]

SUPERIORITY OF INDIFFERENCE CURVE ANALYSIS

So far we have pointed out the similarities between the two types of analyses, we now turn to study the difference between the two and to show how far indifference curve analysis is superior to the Marshallian cardinal utility analysis.

1. Ordinal vs. Cardinal Measurability of Utility. In the first place, Marshall assumes utility to be *cardinally measurable*. In other words, he believes that utility is *quantifiable*, both in principle and in actual practice. According to this, the consumer is able to assign specific amounts to the utility obtained by him from the consumption of a certain amount of a good or a combination of goods. Further, these amounts of utility can be manipulated in the same manner as weights, lengths, heights, etc. In other words, the utilities can be compared and

1. Tapas Majumdar, *Measurement of Utility, op. cit., p.* 70.

added. Suppose, for instance, utility which a consumer gets from a unit of good *A* is equal to 15, and from a unit of good *B* equal to 45. We can then say that the consumer prefers *B three times as strongly as A and* the utility obtained by the consumer from the combination containing one unit of each good is equal to 60. Likewise, even the differences between the utilities obtained from various goods can be so compared as to enable the consumer to say *A* is preferred to *B* twice as much as *C* is preferred to *D*.

According to the critics, the Marshallian assumption of cardinal measurement of utility is very strong ; he demands too much from the human mind. They assert that utility is a psychological feeling and the precision in measurement of utility assumed by Marshall is therefore unrealistic. Critics hold that the utility possesses only ordinal magnitude and cannot be expressed in quantitative terms.

According to the sponsors of the indifference curve analysis, utility is mere *orderable* and not quantitative. In other words, indifference curve technique assumes what is called ***'ordinal measurement of utility'***. According to this, the consumer need not be able to assign specific amounts to the utility he derives from the consumption of a good or a combination of goods but he is capable *of comparing* the different utilities or satisfactions in the sense whether one level of satisfaction is equal to, lower than, or higher than another. He cannot say by how much one level of satisfaction is higher or lower than another. That is why the indifference curves are generally labelled by the ordinal numbers such as I, II, III, IV, etc., showing successively higher levels of satisfaction. The advocates of indifference curve technique assert that for the purpose of explaining consumer's behaviour and deriving the theorem of demand, it is quite sufficient to assume that the consumer is able to *rank his preferences consistently.*

It is obvious that the ordinal measurement of utility is a less severe assumption and sounds more realistic than Marshall's cardinal measurement of utility. This shows that the indifference curve analysis of demand which is based upon the ordinal utility hypothesis is superior to Marshall's cardinal utility analysis. The superiority of indifference curve analysis is rather overwhelming since even by taking less severe assumption it is able to explain not only as much as Marshall's cardinal theory but even more than that as far as demand theory is concerned.

2. Analysis of Demand Without Assuming Constant Marginal Utility of Money. Another distinct improvement made by indifference curve technique is that unlike Marshall's cardinal utility approach it explains consumer's behaviour and derives demand theorem without the assumption of constant marginal utility of money. In indifference curve analysis, it is not necessary to assume constant marginal utility of money. As has already been seen, Marshall assumed that the marginal utility of money remains constant when there occurs a change in the price of a good. It has been shown in the last chapter that the Marshallian demand analysis based upon constancy of marginal utility of money is not self-consistent. In other words, "the Marshallian demand theorem cannot genuinely be derived from the marginal utility hypothesis except in one commodity model, without contradicting the assumption of constant marginal utility of money."[2] It means that "the constancy of marginal utility of money is incompatible with the proof of the demand theorem in a situation where the consumer has more than a single good to spread his expenditure on."[3] To overcome this difficulty in Marshallian utility analysis, if the assumption of constant marginal utility of money is abandoned, then money can no longer serve as a measuring rod of utility and we can no longer measure marginal utility of a commodity in units of money.

2. Tapas Majumdar, *op. cit.*, p. 55.
3. *Ibid.*, *pp.* 55-56

Thus, Marshall's cardinal utility theory finds itself in a dilemma; if it adopts the assumption of constancy of marginal utility of money, as it actually does, it leads to contradiction and if it gives up the assumption of constancy of marginal utility of money, then utility is not measurable in terms of money and the whole analysis breaks down. On the other hand, indifference curve technique using ordinal utility hypothesis can validly derive the demand theorem without the assumption of constant marginal utility of money. In fact, as we shall see below, the abandonment of the assumption of constant marginal utility of money enables the indifference curve analysis to enunciate a *more general* demand theorem.

3.Greater Insight into Price Effect. The superiority of indifference curve analysis further lies in the fact that it makes greater insight into the effect of the price change on the demand for a good by distinguishing between income and substitution effects. The indifference technique splits up the price effect analytically into its two component parts—substitution effect and income effect. The distinction between the income effect and the substitution effect of a price change enables us to gain better understanding of the effect of a price change on the demand for a good. The amount demanded of a good generally rises as a result of the fall in its price due to two reasons. Firstly, real income rises as a result of the fall in price (income effect) and, secondly, the good whose price falls becomes relatively cheaper than others and therefore the consumer substitutes it for others (substitution effect). In indifference curve technique, income effect is separated from the substitution effect of the price change by the methods of 'compensating variation in income' and 'equivalent variation in income'.

But Marshall by assuming constant marginal utility of money ignored the income effect of a price change. He failed to understand the composite character of the effect of a price change. Prof. Tapas Majumdar rightly remarks, "the assumption.of constant marginal utility of money obscured Marshall's insight into the truly composite character of the unduly simplified price-demand relationship".[4] In this context, remarks made by J. R. Hicks are worth noting, "The distinction between direct and indirect effects of a price change is accordingly left by the cardinal theory as an empty box, which is crying out to be filled. But it can be filled. The really important thing which Slutsky discovered in 1915 and which Alien and I rediscovered in the nineteen thirties, is that content can be put into the distinction by tying it up with actual variations in income, so that the direct effect becomes the effect of the price change combined with a suitable variation in income, while the indirect effect is the effect of an income change."[5]

Commenting on the improvement made by Hicks-Alien indifference curve approach over the Marshallian utility analysis, Prof. Tapas Majumdar says : "The efficiency and precision with which' the Hicks-Alien approach can distinguish between the 'income' and 'substitution' effects of a price change really leaves the cardinalist argument in a very poor state indeed."[6]

4. Enunciation of a more general and adequate 'Demand Theorem". A distinct advantage the technique of dividing the effect of a price change inlo income and the substitution effects employed by the indifference curve analysis is that it enables us to enunciate a *more general* and a *more inclusive* theorem of demand than the Marshallian law of demand. In the case of most of the normal goods in this world, both the income effect and the substitution effect work in the same direction, that is to say, they tend to increase the amount demanded of a good when its price falls. The income effect ensures that when the price of a good falls, the consumer buys more of it because he can now afford to buy more; the substitution effect ensures that he buys more of it because it has now become relatively cheaper and is, therefore, profitable to substitute it for others. This thus accounts for the inverse price-demand relationship (Marshallian law of demand) in the case of normal goods.

4. Tapas Majumdar, *op cit.*, p. 76.
5. J. R. Hicks, *A Revision of Demand Theory*, p. 14.
6. Tapas Majumdar, *op. cit.*, p. 57.

When a certain good is regarded by the consumer to be an inferior good, he will tend to reduce its consumption as a result of the increase in his income. Therefore, when the price of an inferior good falls, the income effect so produced would work in the opposite direction to that of the substitution effect. But so long as the inferior good in question does not claim a very large proportion of consumer's total income, the income effect will not be strong enough to outstrip the substitution effect. In such a case, therefore, the net effect of the fall in price of an inferior good will be to raise the amount demanded of the good. It follows that even for most of the inferior goods, the Marshallian law of demand holds good as much as for normal goods.

But it is possible that there may be inferior goods for which the income effect of a change in price is larger in magnitude than the substitution effect. This is the case of Giffen goods for which the Marshallian law of demand does not hold good. In such cases, the negative income effect outweighs the substitution effect so that the net effect of the fall in price of the good is the reduction in quantity demanded of it. Thus, amount demanded of a Giffen good varies directly with price.

It is clear from above that by breaking the price effect into income effect and substitution effect, the indifference curve analysis enables us to arrive at a general and a more inclusive theorem of demand in the following composite form[7]:

(*a*) The demand for a commodity varies *inversely* with price when the income elasticity of demand for that commodity is nil or positive.

(*b*) The demand for a commodity varies *inversely* with price when the income elasticity is negative but the income effect of the price change is smaller than the substitutton effect.

(*c*) The demand for a commodity varies *directly* with price when the income elasticity is negative and the income effect of the price change is larger than the substitution effect.

In the case of (a) and *(b),* the Marshallian law of demand holds while in (c) we have a Giffen-good case which is exception to the Marshallian law of demand. Marshall could not account for 'Giffen Paradox', Marshall was not able to provide explanation for 'Giffen Paradox' because by assuming constant marginal utility of money, he ignored the income effect of the price change. The indifference curve technique by distinguishing between the income and substitution effects of the price change can explain the Giffen-good case. According to this, the Giffen paradox occurs in the case of an inferior good for which the negative income effect of the price change is so powerful that it outweighs the substitution effect, and hence when the price of a Giffen good falls, its quantity demanded also falls instead of rising. Thus, a great merit of Hicks-Alien indifference curve anajysis is that it offers an explanation for the Giffen-good case, while Marshall failed to do so.

It is quite manifest from above that Hicks-Alien indifference curve analysis, though based upon fewer as well as less severe assumptions, yet it enables us to enunciate a more general demand theorem covering the Giffen-good case. To quote Prof. Tapas Majumdar on this point: "The ordinal theory succeeds in stating the relationship between a given change in the price of a commodity and its demand in a composite form distinguishing between the income and the substitution effects which fills in a genuine gap in the Marshallian statement of 'law of demand'."

5. Implications of a Price Change in terms of Income and Welfare Increments. Another distinct improvement of Hicks-Allen ordinal theory is that, through it, the welfare consequences of a change in price can be translated into those of a change in income. As seen above, a fall in the price of a good enables the consumer to shift from a lower to a higher level

7. Tapas Majumdar, *op. cit*, pp., 74-75.

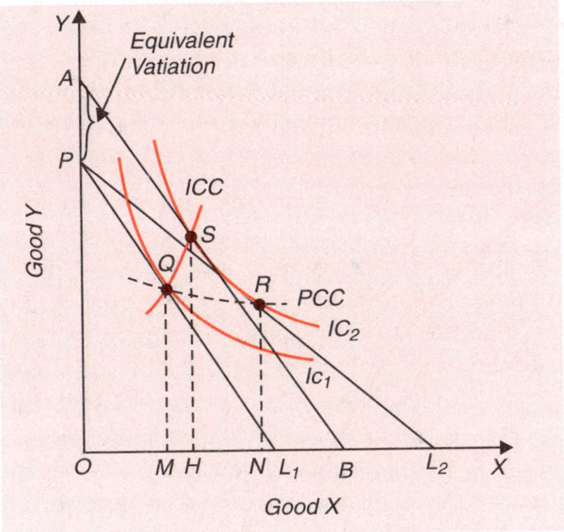

Fig. 10.1. *Income Variation Equivalent to a Price Change*

of welfare (or satisfaction). Likewise, a rise in the price of the good would cause the consumer to shift down to a lower indifference curve and therefore to a lower level of welfare. This means that a fall in price of a good causes a change in consumer's welfare exactly as the rise in income would do. In other words, the consumer can be thought of reaching higher level of welfare through an equivalent rise in income rather than the fall in price of a good. In Fig. 10.1, with the fall in price of good X from PL_1 to PL_2 the consumer shifts from indifference curve IC_1 to the indifference curve IC_2 showing an increase in his level of welfare. Now, if instead of the fall in price from PL_1 to PL_2 the consumer's income is increased by the amount equal to PA or L_1B, he will reach the indifference curve IC_2. Thus the increase in consumer's welfare due to the rise in income by PA or L_1B is equal to that of the change in price of X from PL_1 to PL_2. Therefore, PA (in terms of commodity *Y)* and L_1B (in terms of commodity *X)* is called *Equivalent Variation in Income* or simply Equivalent variation. ***"The equivalence of a given change in price to a suitable change in income is a major discovery of ordinal utility analysis."***[8] This fundamental relation necessarily remains obscure in cardinal utility analysis with its single good model and the assumption of constant marginal utility of money.

The discovery of a suitable change in income equivalent in terms of welfare to a given change in price has enabled Hicks to extend Marshall's concept of consumer's surplus. Marshall's concept of consumer's surplus was based upon the assumption that utility was cardinally measurable and also that the marginal utility of money remained constant when the price of a good is changed. Thus, in Figure 10.1, equivalent variation *PA* is surplus income or gain in welfare accrued to the consumer as a result of fall in price of a commodity. Hicks has freed the concept of consumer's surplus from these dubious assumptions and by using ordinal utility hypothesis along with the discovery that the welfare effect of a price change can be translated into a suitable change in income, he has been able to rehabilitate and extend the concept of consumer's surplus.

6. Hypothesis of Independent Utilities Given Up. Marshall's cardinal utility analysis is based upon the *hypothesis of independent utilities.* This means that the utility which the consumer derives from any commodity is a function of the quantity of that commodity and of that commodity alone. In other words, the utility obtained by the consumer from a commodity is independent of that derived from any other. ***By assuming independent utilities, Marshall completely bypassed the relation of substitution and complementarity between commodities.***

Demand analysis based upon the hypothesis of independent utilities, as shown in the last chapter, leads us to the conclusion "that in all cases a reduction in the price of one commodity only will either result in an expansion in the demand for *all* other commodities or in a contraction in the demands for *all* other commodities." But this is quite contrary to the common cases

8. Tapas Majumdar, *op. cit.*, p. 72.

found in the real world. In the real world, it is found that as a result of the fall in price of a commodity, the ***demand for some commodities expands while the demand for others contracts.*** We thus see that Marshall's analysis based upon 'independent utilities' does not take into account the complementary and substitution relations between goods. This is a great flaw in Marshall's cardinal utility analysis.

On the other hand, this flaw is not present in Hicks-Allen indifferenpe curve analysis which does not assume independent utilities and duly recognizes the relation of substitution and complementarity between goods. Hicks-Allen indifference curve technique by taking more than one commodity model and recognizing interdependence of utilities is in a better position to explain related goods. By breaking up price effect into substitution and income effects by employing the technique of compensating variation in income, Hicks succeeded in explaining complementary and substitute goods in terms of substitution effect alone. Accordingly, it can define and explain substitutes and complements in a better way. According to Hicks, *Y* is a substitute for *X* if a fall in the price of *X* leads to a fall in the consumption of *Y*; *Y* is a complement of *X* if a fall in the price of *X* leads to a rise in the consumption of *Y*, *a compensating variation in income being made in each case so as to maintain indifference*.

7. Analysing Consumer's Demand with Less Severe and Fewer Assumptions. It has been shown above that both the Hicks-Allen indifference curve theory and Marshall's cardinal theory arrive the same condition for consumer's equilibrium. Hicks-Allen condition for consumer's equilibrium, that is, *MRS* must be equal to the price ratio amounts to the same thing as Marshall's proportionality rule of consumer's equilibrium. But even here, ordinal approach of indifference curve analysis is an improvement upon the Marshall's cardinal theory in so far as the former arrives at the same equilibrium condition with less severe and fewer assumptions. Dubious assumptions such as (*i*) utility is quantitatively measurable, (*ii*) marginal utility of money remains constant, and (*iii*) utilities of different goods are independent of each other, on which Marshall's cardinal utility theory is based, are not made in indifference-curves' ordinal utility theory.

Is Indifference Curve Analysis "Old Wine in a New Bottle" ?

But superiority of indifference curve theory has been denied by some economists, foremost among them are D. H. Robertson, F. H. Knight, W. E. Armstrong. Knight remarks, "indifference curve analysis of demand is not a step forward; it is in fact a step backward." D. H. Robertson is of the view that the indifference curve technique is merely *"the old wine in a new bottle."* The indifference curve analysis, according to him, has simply substituted new concepts and equations in place of the old ones, while the essential approach of the two types of analyses is the same. Instead of the concept of 'utility', the indifference curve technique has introduced the term 'preference' and scale of preferences. In place of cardinal number system of one, two, three, etc., which is supposed to measure the amount of utility derived by the consumer, the indifference curve have the ordinal number system of first, second, thrid etc. to indicate the order of consumer' s preferences. The concept of marginal utility has been substituted by the concept of marginal rate of substitution. And against the Marshallian 'proportionality rule' as a condition for consumer's equilibrium, indifference curve approach has advanced the condition of equality between the marginal rate of substitution and the price ratio.

Robertson's view that the concept of marginal rate of substitution of indifference curve analysis represents the reintroduction of the concept of marginal utility in demand analysis requires further consideration. Robertson says : "In his earlier book ***Value and Capital*** Hicks's treatment involved making an assumption of the convexity of the 'indifference curves' which appeared to some of us to involve reintroduction of marginal utility in disguise.[9]" It has thus been held that the ***use of marginal rate of substitution implies the presence of cardinal element in indifference curve technique.*** In going from one combination to another on an indifference curve, the consumer is assumed to be able to tell what constitutes his compensation in terms of a good for the loss of a marginal unit of another good. In other words, the consumer is able to tell his marginal rate of substitution of one good for another. Now, the marginal rate of substitution has been described by Hicks and others as the *ratio* of the marginal utilities of two goods $\left(MRS_{xy} = \frac{MU_x}{MU_y} \right)$. But ratio cannot be measured unless the two marginal utilities in question are at least measurable in principle. One cannot talk of a ratio if one assumes the two marginal utilities (as the numerator and denominator) to be non-quantifiable entities. It has, therefore, been held that the concept of marginal rate of substitution and the idea of indifference based upon it essentially involves an admission that utility is quantifiable in principle.

Against this, Hicks contends that we need not assume measurability of marginal utilities in principle in order to know the marginal rate of substitution. He says, "All that we shall be able to measure is what the ordinal theory grants to be measurable— namely the *ratio* of the marginal utility of one commodity to the marginal utility of another." This means that *MRS* can be obtained without actually measuring marginal utilities. If a consumer, when asked, is prepared to accept 4 units of good *Y* for the loss of one marginal unit of *X*, *MRS* of *X* for *Y* is 4 : 1. We can thus directly derive the ratio indicating *MRS* by offering him how much compensation in terms of good *Y* the consumer would accept for the loss of a marginal unit of *X*. Commenting on this point Tapas Majumdar writes : "The marginal rate of substitution in any case can be so defined as to make its meaning independent of the meaning of marginal utility. If marginal utilities are taken to be quantifiable, then their ratios certainly give the marginal rate of substitution; if the marginal utilities are not taken to be quantifiable the marginal rate of substitution can still be derived as a meaningful concept from the logic of the compensation principle."[10] The contention that the concept of marginal rate of substitution is a mere reintroduction of the marginal utility (a cardinal concept) in disguise is therefore not valid. It follows from above that "if we do not assume that marginal utilities are measurable even in principle, we can still have the marginal rates of substitution which is another distinct advantage of the ordinal formulation."[11]

It has been further contended by Robertson and Armstrong that it is not possible to arrive at the Hicksian *principle of diminishing marginal rate of substitution* without making use of the 'Marshallian scaffolding' of the concept of marginal utility and the principle of diminishing marginal utility. It is asked why *MRS of X* for *Y* diminishes as more and more of *X* is substituted for *Y* ? The critics say that the marginal rate of substitution (MRS_{xy}) diminishes and the indifference curve becomes convex to the origin, because as the consumer's stock of X increases, the marginal utility of X falls and that of *Y* increases. They thus hold that Hicks and Allen have not been able to derive the basic principle of diminishing marginal rate of substitution independently of the law of diminishing marginal utility. They contend that by a stroke of terminological manipulation, the concept of marginal utility has been relegated to the background, but it is there all the same. They, therefore, assert that "the principle of diminishing marginal rate of substitution is as much determinate or indeterminate as the poor law of diminishing marginal utility".

9. Sir Dennis Robertson, *Lectures on Economic Principles,* The Fontana Library Edition, 1963, p. 85.
10 & **11**. Tapas Majumdar, *Measurement of Utility.*

However, even this criticism of indifference curve approach advanced by the defenders of the Marshallian cardinal utility analysis is not valid. As shown above, the derivation of marginal rate of substitution does not depend upon the actual measurement of marginal utilities. While the law of diminishing marginal utility is based upon the cardinal utility hypothesis *(i.e.,* utility is quantitiable and actually measurable), the principle of marginal rate of substitution is based upon the ordinal utility hypothesis *(i.e.,* utility is mere orderable). As a consumer gets more and more units of good *X*", his strength of desire for it (though we cannot measure it in itself) will decline and therefore he will be prepared to forego less and less of *Y* for the gain of a marginal unit of *X*. It is thus clear that the principle of diminishing marginal rate of substitution is based upon purely ordinal hypothesis and is derived independently of the cardinal concept of marginal utility, though both laws reveal essentially the same phenomenon. The derivation of the principle of diminishing marginal rate of substitution by using ordinal utility hypothesis and quite independent of the concept of marginal utility is a great achievement of the indifference curve analysis. We therefore agree with Hicks who claims that ***"the replacement of the principle of diminishing marginal utility by the principle of diminishing marginal rate of substitution is not a mere translation. It is a positive change in the theory of consumer's demand".***

Further, in favour of ordinal indifference curve analysis, it is sometimes claimed that it is better since it can explain with fewer assumptions what cardinal utility theory explains with a larger number of assumptions. An eminent mathematical economist, N. Georgescu-Rogen, has argued that this point of view is very weak scientifically. He remarks, "Could we refuse to take account of animals with more than two feet, on the ground that only two feet are needed for walking."[11] However, it may be pointed out that indifference curve analysis is held to be superior not merely because it applies fewer assumptions but because it is based upon more realistic and less severe assumptions. Apart from this, indifference curve theory is considered to be superior because, as explained above, it explains more than the cardinal theory.

It follows from what has been said above that indifference curve analysis of demand is an improvement upon the Marshallian utility analysis and the objections that the former too involves cardinal elements are groundless. It is of course true that the indifference curve analysis suffers from some drawbacks and has been criticized on various grounds, as explained below, but as far as the question of indifference curve technique versus Marshallian utility analysis is concerned, the former is decidedly better.

A CRITIQUE OF INDIFFERENCE CURVE ANALYSIS

Unrealistic Assumptions. Indifference curve analysis has come in for criticism on several grounds, especially it has been alleged that it is based on unrealistic assumptions. In the first place, it is argued that the indifference curve approach for avoiding the difficulty of measuring utility quantitatively is forced to make ***unrealistic assumption that the consumer possesses complete knowledge of all his scale of preferences or indifference map.*** The indifference curve approach, so to say, falls from the frying pan into the fire. The indifference curve analysis envisages a consumer who carries in his head innumerable possible combinations of goods and relative preferences in respect of them. It is argued that carrying into his head all his scales of preferences is too formidable a task for a frail human being ? Hicks himself admits this drawback. When revising his demand theory based on indifference curves, he says that "one of the most awkward assumptions into which the older theory appeared to be impelled by its geometrical analogy was the notion that the consumer is capable of ordering all conceivable alternatives that might possibly be presented to him—all the positions which might be

11. N. Georgescu-Rogen, A Diagrammatic Analysis of Complementarity, *Southern Economic Journal.*

represented by points on his indifference map. This assumption is so unrealistic that it was bound to be a stumbling block."[12] This is one of the reasons that Hicks has given up indifference curves in his *Revision of Demand Theory*.

Further, another unrealistic element present in indifference curve analysis is that ***such curves include even the most ridiculous combinations*** which may be far removed from his habitual combinations. For example, while it may be perfectly sensible to compare whether three pairs of shoes and six shirts would give a consumer as much satisfaction as two pairs of shoes and seven shirts, the consumer will be at a loss to know and compare the desirability of an absurd combination such as eight pairs of shoes and one shirt. The way the indifference curves are constructed, they include absurd combinations like the one just indicated.

A further shortcoming of the indifference curve technique is that it can *analyse consumer's behaviour effectively only in simple cases, especially those in which the choice is between the quantities of two goods only*. In order to demonstrate the case of three goods, three-dimensional diagrams are needed which are difficult to understand and handle. When more than three goods are involved geometry altogether fails and recourse has to be taken to the complicated mathematics which often tends to conceal the economic point of what is being done. Hicks also admits this shortcoming of indifference curve technique.

Another demerit of indifference curve analysis because of its geometrical nature is that it involves the ***assumption of continuity*** "a property which the geometrical field does have, but which the economic world, in general, does not". The real economic world exhibits discontinuity and it is quite unrealistic and analytically bad if we do not recognize it. That is why Hicks too has abandoned the assumption of continuity in his *A Revision of Demand Theory*.

Armstrong's Critique of the Notion of Indifference and the Transitivity Relations. Armstrong has criticized the relation of transitivity involved in inditterence curve technique. He is of the view that in most cases, the consumer's indifference is due to his imperfect ability to perceive difference between alternative combinations of goods. In other words, the consumer indicates his indifference between the combinations which differ very slightly from each other not because they give him equal satisfaction but because the difference between the combinations is so small that he is unable to perceive the difference between them. If this concept of indifference is admitted, then the relation of indifference becomes non-transitive. Now, with non-transitivity of indifference relation; the whole system of indifference curves and the demand analysis based upon it breaks down.

The viewpoint of Armstrong is illustrated in Fig. 10.2 Consider combinations *A, B* and *C* which lie continuously on indifference curve *IC*. According to Hicks-Allen indifference curve analysis, consumer will be indifferent between *A* and *B*, and between *B* and *C*. Further, on the assumption of transitivity, he will be indifferent between *A* and *C*. According to Armstrong, the consumer is indifferent, say, between. *A* and *B* not because the total utility of combination *A* is equal to the total utility of combination *B* but because the difference between the total utilities is so small as to be imperceptible to the consumer. However, if we compare *A* with *C*, the difference between the total utilities becomes large enough to become perceptible. Thus, the consumer will not remain indifferent between *A* and *C*; he will either prefer *A* to *C*, or *C* to *A*. So on Armstrong's interpretation, the relation of indifference between *A* and *B, B* and *C* which was due to the fact that the difference in utilities was *imperceptible will not hold between A and C since the difference in utilities between A and C* becomes perceptible. If Prof. Armstrong's interpretation is admitted; the indifference relation becomes non-transitive and the theory of consumer's demand based on the indifference system falls to the ground.

12. J. R. Hicks, *A Revision of Demand Theory*, p. 20.

It may, however, be pointed out that Armstrong's interpretation of indifference is not correct. Actually, the relation of indifference in the ordinal theory is the exact equivalent of the relation of 'equality' in the cardinal sense. In other words, the consumer is said to be indifferent between *A* and *B*, for instance, because he derives *equal utility* from the two combinations and not because the difference between the utilities from *A* and *B* is imperceptible. If such is the case then "the axiom of transitivity of ordinal indifference emerges automatically and is no more subject to dispute than is the axiom of transitivity of numerical equality".

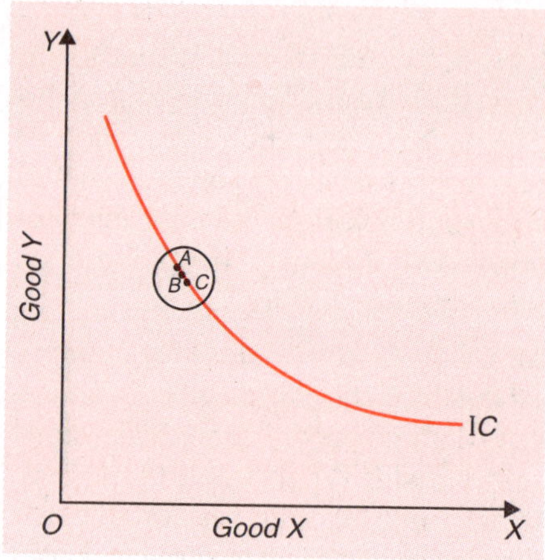

Fig. 10.2 *Imperceptible Differences between A, B and C Combinations of Goods*

Another way in which Armstrong's argument has been refuted is the adoption of *'statistical definition'* of indifference, as suggested by Charles Kennedy.[13] According to the statistical definition, the consumer is said to be indifferent between the two combinations when he is offered to choose between those two combinations several times and he chooses each combination 50 per cent of the time. However, there are some serious difficulties in adopting the statistical definition. But if the statistical definition of indifference is adopted, then also the indifference relation between *A* and *B*, *B* and *C*, *C* and *D* etc., becomes transitive and in that case, therefore, Armstrong's criticism does not hold good.

Cardinal Utility is Implicit in Indifference Curve Analysis : Robertson's View. Further, another criticism of indifference curve analysis is made by D.H. Robertson who asserts that indifference curve analysis implicitly involves the cardinal measurement of utility. He points out that Pareto and his immediate followers who propounded ordinal indifference curve analysis continued to use the law of diminishing marginal utility of individual goods and certain other allied propositions with regard to complements and substitutes. In order to do so, Robertson asserts that "you have got to assume, not only that the consumer is capable of regarding one situation as preferable to another situation, but that he is capable of regarding ***one change in situation as preferable to another change in situation.***[14] Now, while the first assumption does not, it appears that the second assumption really *does* compel you to regard utility as being not merely orderable but a measurable entity. He explains this point with the help of Fig. 10.3. According to him, if the consumer can compare one change in situation with another change in situation, he can then say that he rates the change *AB* more highly than the change *BC*. If such is the case, it is then always possible to find the point *D* so that he rates the change *AD just* as highly as the change *DC* and "that seems", says Robertson, "to be equivalent to saying that the interval *AC is twice* the interval *AD*, we are back in the world of cardinal measurement."[15] How far Robertson's contention is valid is however a matter of opinion.

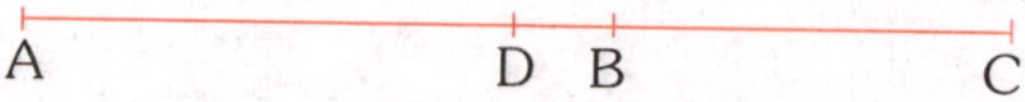

Fig. 10.3

13. Charles Kennedy, The Common Sense of Indifference Curves, *Oxford Economic Papers*, Jan. 1950, pp. 123-31.
14. D. H. Robertson. *Lectures on Economic Principles*. The Fontana Library Edition, 1963, p. 83.
15. *Ibid.*

Indifference Curve Analysis is a midway house. Further, indifference curve analysis has been criticised for its limited empirical nature. Indifference curve analysis is neither based upon purely imaginary and subjective utility functions, nor is based upon purely empirically derived indifference functions. It is because of this fact that Schumpeter has dubbed indifference curve analysis as *'a midway house'*. It would have been quite valid if indifference curve analysis was based upon experimentally obtained quantitative data in regard to the observed market behaviour of the consumer. But, in Hicks-Allen theory, indifference curves are based upon *hypothetical experimentation*. The indifference curve theory of demand is, therefore, based upon imaginarily drawn indifference curves. Commenting on Hicks-Allen theory of demand, Schumpeter remarks, "If they use nothing that is not observable *in principle* they do use "potential" observations which so far nobody has been able to make *infact:* from a practical standpoint we are not much better off when drawing purely imaginary indifference curves than we are when we speak of purely imaginary utility functions."[16]

It may, however, be pointed out that attempts have recently been made by some economists and psychologists to derive or measure indifference curves experimentally. But a limited success has been achieved in this regard. This is because such experiments have been made under controlled conditions which render these experiments quite unfit for drawing conclusions regarding real consumer's behaviour in 'free circumstances'. So, for all intents and purposes, indifference curves still remain imaginary.

Failure to analyse Consumer's Bahaviour Under Uncertainty. An important criticism against Hicks- Allen ordinal theory ot demand is that it cannot formalise consumer's behaviour when uncertainty or risk is present. In other words, consumer's behaviour cannot be explained by ordinal theory when he has to choose among alternatives involving risk or 'uncertainty of expectation'. Von Neumann and Morgenstern[17] and also Armstrong[18] have asserted that while cardinal utility theory can, the ordinal utility theory cannot formalise consumer's behaviour when we introduce "uncertainty of expectations with regard to the consequences of choice." Let us consider an individual who is faced with three alternatives *A, B* and *C*. Suppose that he prefers *A* to *B,* and *C* to *A*. Suppose also that while the chance of his getting *A* is certain, the chance of his getting *B* or *C* is fifty-fifty. Now, the question is which alternative will the consumer choose. It is obvious that the choice he will make depends on *how much* he prefers *A* to *B* and *C* to *A*. If, for example, *A* is very much preferred to *B,* while C is only just preferred to *A*, then he will surely choose *A* (certain) rather than fifty-fifty chance of *C* or *B*. But unless the consumer *can say how large* his preferences for *A* over *B,* and for *C* over *A* are, we cannot know which alternative he is likely to choose. It is obvious that a consumer who is confronted with the choice among such alternatives, will often compare the relative degree of his preference of *A* over *B* and the relative degree of his preference for *C* over *A* with the respective chances of getting *B* or *C*. Now, a little reflection will show that ordinal utility system cannot be applied to such a situation, for in such a situation, the choice is determined if the consumer knows the differences in the amounts of utility or satisfaction he gets from various alternatives. According to ordinal utility theory, individual cannot tell *how much more* utility he derives from *A* than *B,* or, in other words, he cannot tell whether the extent to which he prefers *A* to *B* is greater than the extent to which he prefers *C* to *A*.

We thus find that Hicks-Allen ordinal utility system cannot formalise consumer's behavior when there exists uncertainty of expectation with regard to the consequences of choice. On the other hand, cardinal utility theory can formalise consumer's behavior in the presence of

16. J. Schumpeter, *History of Economic Analysis, p.* 1067.
17. *The Theory of Games and Economic Behaviour.*
18. Uncertainty and the Utility Function, *Economic Journal,* March, 1948

uncertainty of expectations since it involves quantitative estimates of utilities or preference intensities. Commenting on indifference preference hypothesis, Neumann and Morgenstern remark : "If the preferences are not all comparable, then the indifference curves do not exist. If the individual preferences are all comparable, then we can even obtain a (uniquely defined) numerical utility which renders the indifference curves superfluous."[19]

Drawback of Weak-ordering Hypothesis and Introspective Approach. An important point be noted regarding indifference curves is that it is based upon the weak ordering hypothesis. According to this hypothesis, the consumer *can be* indifferent between certain combinations. Though the possibility of relation of indifference is not denied, it is pointed out that indifference curve analysis has exaggerated the role of indifference in demand theory. The innumerable positions of indifference, assumed by Hicks-Allen theory, is quite unrealistic. Hicks himself later realised this shortcoming of indifference curve analysis, as is clear from the following remarks in his "Revision of Demand Theory, "The older theory may have exaggerated the omnipresence of indifference; but to deny its possibility is purely to run to the other extreme."

Further, Paul A. Samuelson has criticized the indifference curves approach as being predominantly introspective. Samuelson himself has developed a behaviourist method of deriving the theory of demand. He seeks to enunciate demand theorem from observed consumer's behaviour. His theory is based upon the strong-ordering hypothesis, namely, 'choice reveals preference'. Samuelson thinks that his theory sloughs off the last vestiges of the psychological analysis in the explanation of consumer's demand.

Limitations of Maximizing Behaviour

In the last place, indifference curve analysis has been criticized for its assumption that the consumer ***'maximizes his satisfaction'.*** Since Marshall also assumed this maximizing behavior on the part of the consumer, this criticism is equally valid in the case of Marshallian utility analysis also. It is asserted that it is quite unrealistic to assume that the consumer will maximize his satisfaction or utility in his purchases of goods. This means that the consumer will try to reach the highest possible indifference curve. He will get maximum satisfaction when he is equating the marginal rate of substitution between the two goods with their price ratio. It is pointed out that the consumer of the real world is guided by custom and habit in his daily purchases whether or not they provide him maximum satisfaction. The real consumers are slaves of custom and habit. The housewife, it is said, purchases the same amount of milk, even if its price has gone up a bit, though on the basis of maximizing postulate this change in price should have made her readjust her purchases of milk. If a housewife is asked about her marginal rate of substitution of milk for bread, she will show complete ignorance about this. Further, if you ask her whether she equates the marginal rate of substitution with the price ratio while making purchases; she is sure to tell you that she never indulges in achieving such mathematical equality.

But this criticism is not very much valid. *A* theory will be true even if the individuals unconsciously behave in the way assumed by the theory. Robert Dorfman rightly remarks: "It is only the result that counts for a descriptive theory, not the conscious intent. The strands of a bridge cable do not know what they are supposed to do in the form of a caternary, they just do it".[20] Thus the question of the indifference curve theory to be valid or not hinges upon whether the consumers behave in the way assumed by the theory. The answer is yes; the consumers do behave in the way asserted by the theory. Taking the above example, when the

19. *Op. cit.*, pp. 19-20.
20. R. Dorfman, *The Price System*, p. 69.

price of milk goes up and high price persists, the housewives will notice that their milk bills are getting out of line and will take steps to save on milk here and there in their daily consumption. This will ultimately reduce the quantity demanded of milk.

The reactions to changes in the prices of other goods are similar. If the price of a durable consumer good rises, the consumers may continue to use the present stock of it for a longer time than they had planned to replace it. If the close substitutes of the good in question exist, then they may give it up and replace it by any relatively cheaper substitutes. In these and various other ways the consumers will prevent prices of goods from getting far out of line from their marginal rates of substitution. It is, therefore, clear that consumers do actually behave in accordance with the maximizing postulate though unconsciously, and roughly equate marginal rate of substitution of money for a good with the price of the good, though they may not be knowing what the marginal rate of substitution is. However, it may be noted that while examining the question as to whether or not consumer's behavior is in accordance with the maximization assumption, the theory should not be taken too literally. The ordinary consumer cannot be expected to equate *precisely* the marginal rate of substitution of money for a good with the price of the good. In the first place, many goods in the real world are *indivisible* (*i.e.*, available only in large units). This indivisibility of goods renders precise adjustment of the quantities of goods impossible and thus prevents the equality of the marginal rate of substitution of money for a good with its price. The two main examples of indivisible goods are cars and television sets. In such cases, if we want to be precise we must make a *more elaborate* statement about consumer's equilibrium, namely, a consumer will purchase such a number of units of good that an addition of one more unit to it would cause the marginal rate of substitution of money for the good lower than its price. "But this elaboration" as rightly asserted by Dorfman, "is only a detail and not a change in principle."[21]

Secondly, another fact that prevents the equality of marginal rate of substitution with the price is that no consumer buys all goods. For instance, bachelors do not buy diapers; non-drivers do not buy gasoline. The marginal rate of substitution of money for diapers for bachelors is equal to zero and thus is not equal to price. In such cases also, if we want to be precise we have to make another modification in our theory of consumer's equilibrium: "If the marginal rate of substitution of money for a commodity is less than its price when no units are purchased, then none will be purchased."[22] But this modification also is simply a refinement and not a change in basic principle.

21. *Ibid*, p. 69
22. Dorfman, *op. cit.*, pp. 69-70.

CHAPTER

11

Applications and Uses of Indifference Curve

We have studied the indifference curve analysis of demand. But the technique of indifference curves has been used not only to explain consumer's behaviour and demand but also to analyse and explain several other economic phenomena. In other words, besides analysing consumer's demand, indifference curves have several other applications. Thus, indifference curves have been used to explain the concept of consumer's surplus, supply curve of labour of an individual, several principles of welfare economics, burden of different forms of taxation, gain from foreign trade, welfare implications of subsidy granted by the Government, index number problem, mutual advantage of exchange of goods between two individuals and several other things. We shall discuss applications of indifference curves in some of the above stated fields in the relevant chapters. We shall explain here only few of the applications.

EXCHANGE BETWEEN TWO INDIVIDUALS : GAIN FROM TRADE

An important application of indifference curves is to explain the mutual exchange between two individuals of two goods possessed by each. When the two individuals have to exchange two things, the case is one of bilateral monopoly. It should be noted that inventor of indifference curves, Y. F. Edgeworth applied them to explain exchange of goods between two individuals. Suppose there are two individuals, *A* and *B*. Both individuals *A* and *B* have some amount of goods *X* and *Y*. They are to exchange these goods between themselves.

Fig. 11.1. *Indifference Map of Individual A*

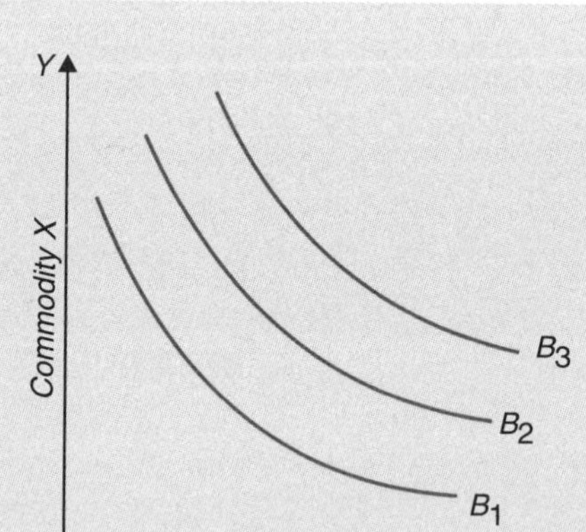

Fig. 11.2. *Indifference Map of Individual B*

Now, with the help of indifference curves it can be proved that the exchange of two goods between the two individuals will be of mutual advantage to both of them, that is, the exchange of goods between the two individuals will add to their combined welfare. This can be illustrated with the help of Figures 11.1 and 11.2. In Figure 11.1, indifference map depicting the scale of preferences of individual *A* between the two goods X and Y is drawn. Likewise in Figure 11.2 indifference-map of individual *B* depicting his scale of preferences between the two goods X and *Y* is drawn. Now, the exchange problem between the two individuals and its resultant welfare implications can be analysed with the help of ***Edgeworth Box*** diagram which has been named after its inventor Y. F. Edgeworth who first of all discussed this exchange problem.[1]

In order to make the Edgeworth Box diagram, we have to turn upside down (that is, turning around 180°) the indifference map of one individual. So in Figure 11.3, we have turned around 180° the indifference map of individual *B* with *O ′* as the origin. Suppose individual *A* has *OM* quantity of X and *ON* quantity of *Y*. The individual *B* has *O ′M ′* of good X and *O ′N ′* of good *Y*. Thus *OQ* and *OT* are the dimensions of the rectangular Edgeworth Box. A_1, A_2, A_3, A_4, etc. are the successive indifference curves between two goods of individual *A*, and B_1, B_2, B_3, and B_4 are the successive indifference curves between the two goods of individual *B*. Thus,

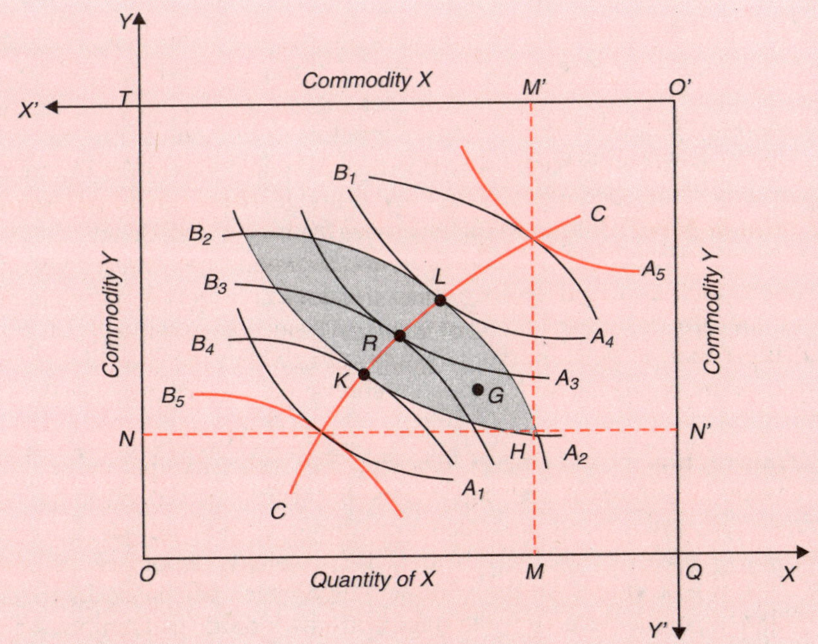

Fig. 11.3. *Region of Mutual Advantage and Gain From Trade*

in the Edgeworth Box diagram, the indifference maps of two individuals are combined by turning the indifference map of one individual upside down. There are several points at which the indifference curves of two individuals are tangent to each other. If all these tangency points between the two sets of indifference curves are joined together we get a curve CC which is called the *Contract Curve.*[2] It is at any point on this contract curve that the exchange or trade of goods between the two individuals will take place. Further, it will be to the mutual advantage of the individuals to move from a point away from the contract curve to a point *on* the contract

1. Y. F. Edgeworth, *Mathematical Psychics,* Kegan Paul, London, 1881, p. 176.
2. The concept of contract curve was also put forward by Y. F. Edgeworth in his *Mathematical Psychics* (London, Kegan Paul, 1881) already referred to.

curve. This will be understood from the following analysis.

Since the initial distribution of two goods is that individual *A* has *OM* of good *X* and *ON* of good *Y* and individual *B* has *O′M′* of X and *O′N′* of *Y*, the two will be at point *H* in the Edgeworth Box. Now, every point within or on the boundaries of the shaded area represents a possible act of exchange to the mutual advantage of both individuals because it leaves them either at their initial indifference curves A_3 or B_3 respectively as the case may be and possibly on the higher indifference curves of both of them. Therefore, the shaded region has been called the *region of mutual advantage*. With initially at point *H* on which the individuals *A* and *B* are respectively at their indifference curves A_2 and B_2, if the two individuals move to the point *L* after exchanging some quantities of the two goods, then the individual A has been put on higher indifference curve A_4 and individual *B* remains at same indifference curve B_2. Thus, with the contemplated exchange, individual *A* has been made better off than before (his welfare or satisfaction has increased), while individual *B* is no worse off than before *(i.e., his* welfare or satisfaction remains the same). Likewise, if the two individuals move to the point *K* after exchanging some quantities of the goods, individual *B* has been put on a higher indifference curve B_4 and therefore he has become better off than before, whereas individual *A* remains at A_2 and therefore no worse off than before.

It is thus clear that exchange of goods between the two individuals involved in moving from point *H* to either *L* or *K* is to their advantage; it makes one better off without making other worse off than before (that is, it increases the welfare of one without reducing the welfare of the other). However, *K* and *L* are the points on the boundary lines of the shaded region. If the two individuals exchange such quantities of two goods that they move from point *H* to any point within the boundaries such as point *G* and *R*, ***then both individuals will be better off than before.*** For instance, if they move from *H* to *R*, both individuals *A* and *B* are put at higher indifference curves A_3 and B_3 respectively and both are better off than at *H* where they are on their lower indifference curves A_2 and B_2 respectively. Similarly, in moving from *H* to *G*, welfare of both of them will increase since they will be put on the higher indifference curves than at *H*. Even point *G*, which lies within the shaded region but off the contract curve, will be on the higher indifference curves of the two individuals than *H*, because the indifference curves are convex to the origin.

Though moving from point *H* to a point such as G which lies within the boundaries would mean the increase in welfare of both individuals, but it will not be equilibrium point, since corresponding to any point off the contract curve, there will be points on the contract curve which will be better than it *(i.e.,* will mean higher level of welfare for both). Thus, corresponding to point G, there will be points on the contract curve which will lie on higher indifference curves and will mean higher level of welfare for both the individuals than point G. In welfare economics, the points on the contract curve are known as ***Pareto optimum***, since they indicate the situation of maximum social welfare where no individual can be made better off without making other worse off, and the points off the contract curve are known as *Pareto sub-optimum* where there is possibility of making all individuals better off or some better off without making others worse off. Therefore, it follows that the two individuals will voluntarily exchange goods *X* and *Y* until they reach a point such as *K, R* or *L* on the contract curve where their indifference curves are tangent to each other. Having reached the contract curve, no further changes of mutual benefit can be made. Thus, in ***equilibruim, exchange of goods (that is, trading) between the two individuals will occur at a point on the contract curve within the shaded region relative to the initial point H.***

Though when the individual moves from point *H* to a point on the contract curve between *K* and *L*, he will be better off than at *H*, all points on the contract curve are not equally advantageous to both the individuals. As we move from point *K* towards *L* on the contract curve, individual *A* will be going to his higher indifference curves but individual *B* will be going to his lower indifference curves. Thus while trading individual *A* will want to go to the point *L*, while individual *B* will try to go to the point *K*. On the contract curve, where the two individuals will end up in their exchange depends on their ***respective bargaining strengths which will determine the rate of exchange*** between the two goods possessed by them.

It follows therefore that the trade or exchange between the two individuals will ultimately take place at any point on the contract curve between *K* and *L*. The greater the bargaining strength of individual *A*, the trading point will be nearer to *L*. On the other hand, the greater the bargaining strength of individual *B*, the trading point will be nearer to *K*. Thus moving along the contract curve means the increase in the satisfaction or welfare of one and reduction in the welfare of the other. That is why contract curve is also known as *Conflict Curve*.

For assessing whether the aggregate welfare (that is combined welfare of the two individuals) increases or decreases as we move along the contract curve, we have to make interpersonal comparison of utility which following Pareto most of the economists refuse to do so. Thus, according to economists, so far as movement from a point ***off the contract curve*** to the point *on the contract curve* is concerned, it definitely and unambiguously increases the aggregate welfare of the two individuals. But the changes in aggregate social welfare cannot be assessed when the contemplated move is from one point of the contract curve to another on it, unless we are willing to make interpersonal comparison of utility. To conclude, "An unwillingness to make interpersonal comparison of utility means that the only changes that can be evaluated are those that make everyone better off or that makes at least one person better off without anyone else worse off. An improvement in some people's welfare at someone else's expense cannot be judged in quantitative utility terms. A movement toward the contract curve always represents an unambiguous improvement of aggregate welfare but a movement along the contract curve alters the distribution of aggregate welfare among the participants in the market."[3]

It is now clear from above that with the help of indifference curves why the exchange or trade between the two individuals will take place and what gain from this exchange or trading of goods they will obtain in terms of increment in their welfare can be ascertained. Further, indifference curve analysis clearly brings out that it is to the advantage of both individuals to exchange goods between themselves.

SUBSIDIES TO CONSUMERS : PRICE SUBSIDY VS. LUMP SUM INCOME GRANT

Another important application of indifference curves is to analyse with its aid the effect of subsidies to the consumers. Several kinds of subsidies are paid to the individuals these days by the Government for promoting social welfare. Let us take the case of food subsidy which is given by the Government to help the needy families. Suppose that under food-subsidy programme, the needed families are entitled to purchase food at half the market price, the other half of the market price is paid by the Government as subsidy. The effect of this subsidy on consumer's welfare and money value of this subsidy to the consumer is illustrated in Figure 11.4 where the quantity of food is measured on the X-axis and money on the *Y*-axis.

Let us suppose that the individual has *OP* money income. Given this money income and given the market price of food, the budget line is PL_1. Since we are assuming that subsidy paid by the Government is half the market price of food, the consumer would pay half the market price. Therefore, with subsidy the individual will face the budget line PL_2 where $OL_1 = L_1L_2$.

3. M. Blaug, *Economic Theory in Retrospect*, p. 72.

With budget line PL_2, the individual is in equilibrium at point *R* on the indifference curve *IC* at which he is purchasing *OA* quantity of food. By purchasing *OA* quantity of food, the individual is spending *PT* amount of money.

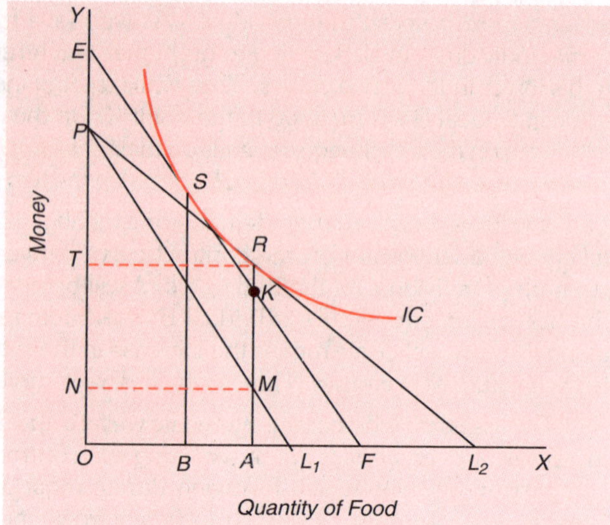

Fig. 11.4. *Subsidies to Consumers : Price Subsidy versus Cash Grant*

Now, if no food subsidy was given and therefore the budget line was PL_1 then for buying *OA* quantity of food, the individual would have spent *PN* amount of money. In other words, *PN* is the market price of *OA* quantity of food. Since *PT* amount of money is paid by the individual himself, the remaining amount *TN* or *RM* (the vertical distance between the budget lines PL_1 and PL_2 at *OA* amount of food) is paid by the Government as food subsidy for the individual.

Now, the important question is what is the ***money value of this food subsidy*** *(RM)* to the individual. When no food subsidy is paid, the individual faces the budget line PL_1. In order to find the money value of the subsidy to the individual, draw a line *EF* parallel to PL_1 so that it touches the same indifference curve *IC* where the individual comes to be in equilibrium when subsidy is paid. It will be seen from Figure 11.4 that budget line *EF* touches the indifference curve *IC* at a point *S* and is buying *OB* quantity of food. This means that if individual is paid *PE* amount of money (say as a cash grant), he reaches the same indifference curve *IC* (same level of welfare) at which he is when subsidy is paid by the Government. Thus *PE,* is money value of the subsidy to the individual. It will be seen from Flgure 11.4 than *PE* is less than *RM* which is the amount of money paid by the Government as subsidy. In our Figure, *PE* = *MK* (the vertical distance between two parallel lines) and *RM* is greater than *MK*. Therefore, *RM* is also greater than *PE*. It follows that *PE* is less than *RM*. If instead of giving *RM* as price subsidy on food, Government ***pays the individual cash money equal to PE,*** the individual will reach the same level of welfare as he does with *RM* subsidy. Thus, the ***money equivalent of the subsidy to the individual is less than the cost of the subsidy to the Government.*** "In fact, it would always be so whatever the subsidy and whatever the preferences of consumers so long as only the indifference curves remain convex and smooth. Thus the cost of giving subsidies to consumers is always greater than the money equivalent of the subjective gain to the consumers".[4] Likewise Scitovsky remarks, ***"The value of the subsidy to the subsidised person is smaller than the cost of subsidy to the Government. This is so whatever the shape of a particular indifference curve as long as it has a smooth curvature.***[5]

Now, if instead of providing price subsidy on food, the Government gives lump-sum cash grant to the consumer equivalent to the cost of price subsidy on food, what will be its impact

4. D, S. Watson, *Price Theory and Its Uses,* 1963, p. 94.
5. Tibor Scitovsky, *Welfare and Competition,* Revised Edition, 1971, p. 70.

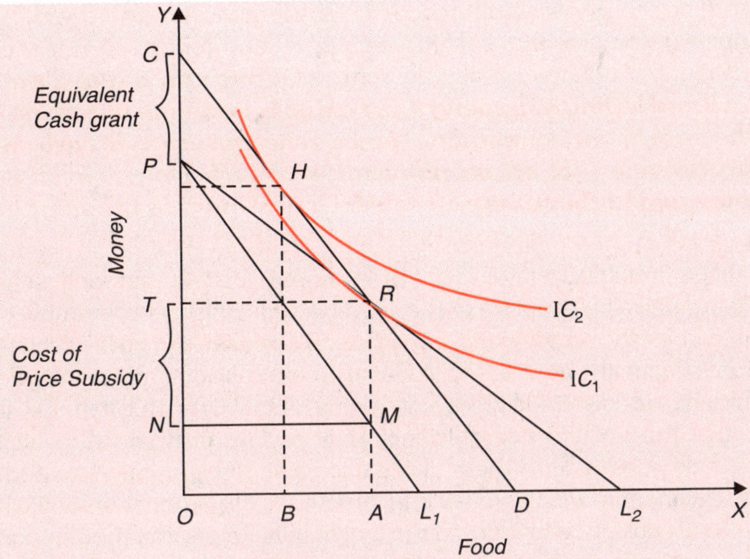

Fig. 11.5. *Lump-Sum Cash Grant is Better than Price Subsidy*

on the individual's welfare and consumption of food by him. As explained above, cost of price subsidy on food to the Government equals *RM* amount of money. If the Government provides the consumer lump-sum cash grant of *RM* instead of price subsidy on food, this will amount to increasing the money income of the consumer by *RM* amount. With this extra cash transfer equal to *RM* (= *PC*), the budget line will shift to the right to the position *CD and pass through point R*. It will be seen from Figure 11.5 that with the budget line *CD* though the individual *can buy the same market basket R, if he so desires,* which he was purchasing with price subsidy on food, he is actually in equilibrium at point *H* on higher indifference curve IC_2. Thus, the cash transfer equivalent to the cost of price subsidy has led to the greater increase in welfare or satisfaction of the individual as compared to the price subsidy. Further, as will be seen from Figure 11.5, ***with a cash grant the individual buys less food and more of other goods relative to the situation under price subsidy with equivalent monetary cost.***

That the individual with cash transfer must be better off and his food consumption must be less as compared to price subsidy on food is due to the fact that indifference curves being convex, the budget line *CD* obtained with cash transfer *must intersect* the indifference curve IC_1 at point *R* reached with equivalent price subsidy. Therefore, given that the consumer is free to spend money as he likes, with cash grant his new equilibrium position must be to the left of point *R on the budget line CD* where it will be tangent to the higher indifference curve than IC_1. This implies that ***in case of lump-sum cash transfer, the consumer will be better off and consume less food relative to*** the equilibrium position under price subsidy on food.

The superiority of cash grant in terms of its impact on the welfare of the individuals can be explained in a slightly different way. Though both the lump-sum cash transfer and price subsidy on a commodity produces income effect making the individual better off, under ***cash grant, the individual is free to buy different goods according to his own tastes and preferences which ensures higher level of welfare as compared to the policy of price subsidy on food which imposes a certain pattern of consumption favouring food.*** Besides, a lower price of food due to price subsidy on it induces the consumer to substitute food for other goods causing greater consumption of food as compared to the scheme of lump-sum cash grant which have no such substitution effect and permits free choice of goods to the individual according to his own preference. Thus, to quote Watson again, *"you can make someone happier if you give him cash instead of a commodity, even if the commodity is something he wants."*[6] Likewise, Scitovsky remarks, ***"one can make a man happier by giving him cash and letting him spend it as he thinks best than by forcing him to take all his relief in the form of one commodity. Hence, relief payments in cash are preferable to a food subsidy because they are economically more efficient, giving the relief receipts either a greater gain at the same cost to the Government or the same gain at a lower cost."***[7]

But the above principle regarding the programme of subsidised food, subsidised housing etc. cannot always be validly applied to the Government subsidy programme since the above principle is based upon the **subjective benefits to the individuals** which is not always the correct criterion to judge the desirability of Government subsidy programme. For instance, the aim of Government's food subsidy programme may be that the needy families should consume more food so that their health and efficiency may be improved. It will be seen from Figure 11.5 that with food subsidy *RM,* the individual is having *OA* amount of food, whereas with equivalent cash payment of *PC* the indi-vidual purchases *OB* amount of food which is less than *OA*. Thus the food subsidy has inducecd the individual to consume more food than in case of cash payment. Similarly, if a country has food surpluses and wants to dispose them off, then the food subsidy to the needy families will be the ideal measure to increase the consumption of foodgrains and thereby to dispose or the food surpluses.[8]

RATIONING AND INDIFFERENCE CURVE ANALYSIS

Indifference curve analysis can be used to explain under what conditions rationing of goods by the Government can act as binding or a constraint on consumer's choices and further how it affects his welfare. It may be noted that income of a consumer along with the prices of goods serves as a constraint on his choices and is often called a **budget constraint.** This budget constraint can be written as follows :

$$Px.X + Py.Y \leq M$$

The above inequality implies that consumer can choose a combination of goods from within or on the *market opportunity set.* With given income of the consumer and prices of the two goods, we draw a budget line *BL* in Figure 11.6. The shaded region bounded by the budget line *BL* and the coordinate axes represents market opportunity set from which the consumer can make a choice of the two commodities. If now the Government introduces a rationing for commodity *X* and fixes a ration of *X* equal to OR_x (At point R_x we have shown a vertical line showing the constraint or ration limit imposed by the rationing fixed at OR_x). It will be seen that with ration limit fixed at OR_x, rationing does not act as a binding at all and prove to be quite

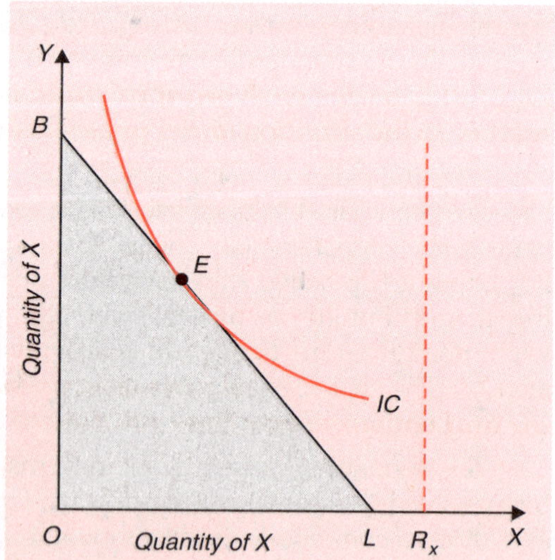

Fig. 11.6. *Ration is not binding.*

6. D. S. Watson, *Price Theory and Its Uses,* 1963, p. 94.
7. Tibor Scitovsky, *Welfare and Competition,* Revised Edition, 1971, p. 70.
8. In 1939, U.S. Government introduced food subsidy programme called 'food stamp programme' which besides helping the needy families had an important objective of disposing off the agricultural surpluses.

ineffective in restricting the consumption of good X which is the objective of the policy. Such a situation is relevant in case of a poor family whose income is so small that it cannot buy even the rationed quantity. It is the income that serves as a binding on his consumption choice and not the ration limit.

Now consider Figure 11.7 where ration limit is fixed at R_x which lies to the left of L. This ration limit reduces or truncates his market opportunity set *(i.e.* set of attainable combinations of two goods X and Y) as shown by the reduced shaded area in Figure 11.7 and therefore in

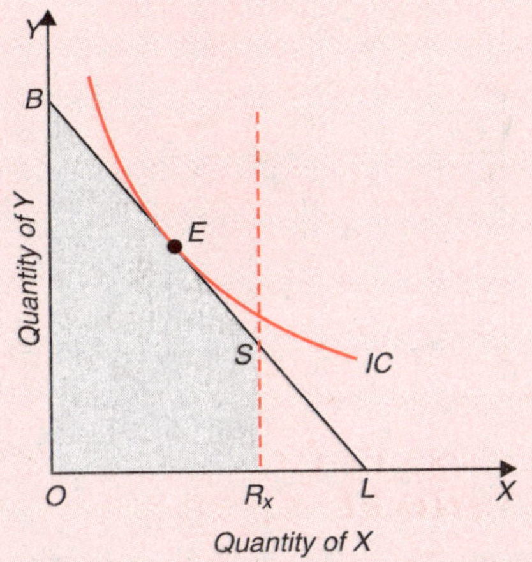

Fig. 11.7 *Ration is potentially binding.*

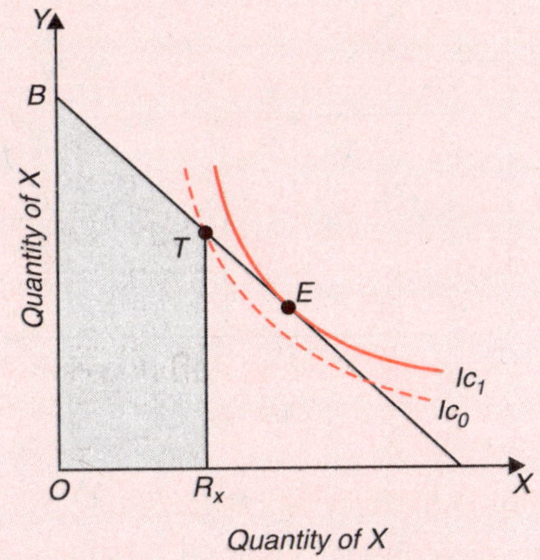

Fig. 11. 8. *Ration is binding.*

this case the ration limit is only *potentially binding* on him. Though the consumer can buy the ration amount, that is, ration limit is attainable but he is not willing to consume good X as much as the ration limit permits him. He is in equilibrium at point E where he consumes quantity of good X which is smaller than the ration amount $R_{x'}$. Thus, his preferences are such that rationing is not actually binding for him.

However, the more important and relevant case of rationing is depicted in Figure 11.8. In this case, ration limit fixed R_x lies to the left of his equilibrium position E. Without the restriction of rationing he will consume a larger amount of commodity X and is at indifference curve IC_1. With the budget line BL and the rationed quantity R_x, he will be at point T which lies at lower indifference curve IC_0. Thus ration limit serves as a binding for him and forces him to consume less of good X and more of good Y than he prefers. That is why at point T in Fig.11.8 he is at lower indifference curve IC_0 indicating his lower level of welfare. Thus, in this case, rationing is actually binding for the consumer and reduces his welfare.

Rationing of both the Commodities

We will now explain the consequences if both the commodities X and Y are rationed. In particular we are interested in knowing whether it is the ration limits or income of the consumer that is binding, that is, which forces the consumer to consume less amounts of the goods. In Figure 11.9 with a given income and prices of the two goods X and Y the consumer is in equilibrium at E buying OM of commodity X and ON of commodity Y. Now, suppose with the introduction of rationing, ration limit R_x is fixed for good X and R_y for good Y. It will be seen from Figure 11.9 that ration amounts of R_x and R_y of goods X and Y respectively are greater than OM and ON which the consumer is buying with his price-income situation. Therefore, the ration limits in this case are *not actually binding* since these do not anyway constraint his consumption. Of course, these ration limits narrow down or truncate his market opportunity set at both ends on the X and Y axes, and in this way they are ***potentially binding*** but they are ***not effective*** in restraining his consumption. Therefore, this can be interpreted to be the case of a poor family whose optimum consumption basket of the two goods is small because of low income and therefore remains unaffected if ration limits are set at higher levels.

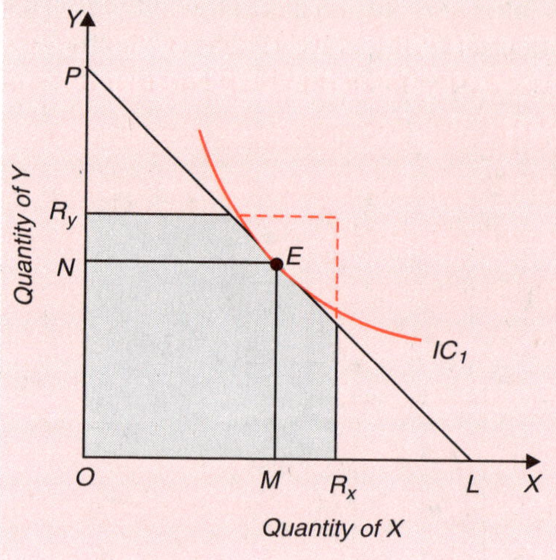

Fig. 11.9. *Ration Not Binding*

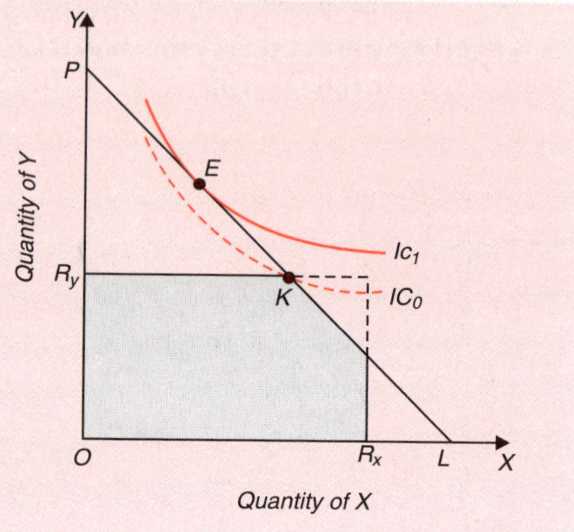

Fig. 11.10. *Y Ration is Binding, X Ration not Binding*

Now, consider Figure 11.10 where it will be seen that ration limit R_y is smaller than consumer's optimum consumption of Y as indicated by combination E of the two goods on the budget line PL which has been drawn with his given income and prices of two goods. But ration limit R_x for good X is larger than his optimum or equilibrium consumption quantity of good X. It follows therefore that for good Y ration limit is ***actually binding*** as it forces the consumer to point K on a lower' indifference curve IC_0 than optimum point E on indifference curve IC_1, at which he would have been without the restriction of rationing. On the other hand, in case of good X in Figure 11.10 the ration limit does not seem to be effective, though it is potentially binding as it truncates his market quantity set. It will be observed that binding by rationing lowers his level of welfare as he is forced to come to the point K on a lower indifference IC_0 where he consumes less of good Y than he prefers.

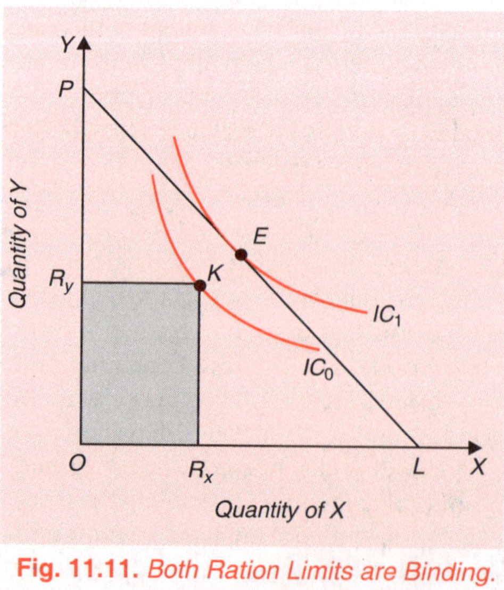

Fig. 11.11. *Both Ration Limits are Binding.*

In Figure 11.11. both ration limits R_x and R_y are actually binding and force the individual to consume less of both the commodities than he consumes at his equilibrium position E in the absence of rationing of the two commodities. Figure 11.11 depicts the case of a rich person who without the binding of rationing is at point E on indifference curve IC_1 and is consuming greater quantity of the two goods than the ration amounts. Introduction of rationing limits forces him to come to point K on lower indifference curve IC_0 and consume less amounts of both the goods than he would do without the restriction of rationing. Thus in this case rationing is actually binding on him and reduces his welfare.

INCOME-LEISURE CHOICE

Indifference curve analysis can be used to explain an individual's choice between income and leisure and to show why higher overtime wage rate must be paid if more hours of work is to be obtained from the workers. It is important to note that income is earned by devoting some of the leisure time to do some work. That is income is earned by sacrificing some leisure. The greater the amount of this sacrifice of leisure, that is, the greater the amount of work done, the greater income an individual earns. Further, income is used to purchase goods, other than leisure for consumption. Leisure time can be used for resting, sleeping, playing, listening to music on radios and television etc. all of which provide satisfaction to the individual. Therefore, in economics leisure is regarded as a normal commodity the enjoyment of which yields satisfaction to the individual. While leisure yields satisfaction to the individual directly, income represents general purchasing power capable of being used to buy goods and services for satisfaction of various wants. Thus income provides satisfaction indirectly. Therefore, we can draw indifference curves between income and leisure, both of which give satisfaction to the individual. An indifference map between income and leisure is'depicted in Figure 11.12 and have all the usual properties *of* indifference curves. They slope downward to the right, are convex to the origin and do not intersect. Each indifference curve represents various alternative combinations'of income and leisure which provide equal level of satisfaction to the individual and the farther away an indifference curve is from the origin, the higher the level of satisfaction it represents for the individual. The slope of the indifference curve measuring marginal rate of substitution between leisure and income (MRS_{LM}) shows the *trade off between income and leisure.* This trade-off means how much income the individual is willing to accept for one hour sacrifice of leisure time. In geometric terms, it will be seen from Figure 11.12 that on indifference curve IC_1 at point A the individual is willing to accept ΔM (= AC) income for sacrificing an hour (ΔL) or BC of leisure. Thus the trade-off between income and leisure at this point is $\frac{\Delta M}{\Delta L}$. At different income-leisure levels, the trade-off between leisure and income varies. Indifference curves between income and leisure are therefore also called *trade-off curves*.

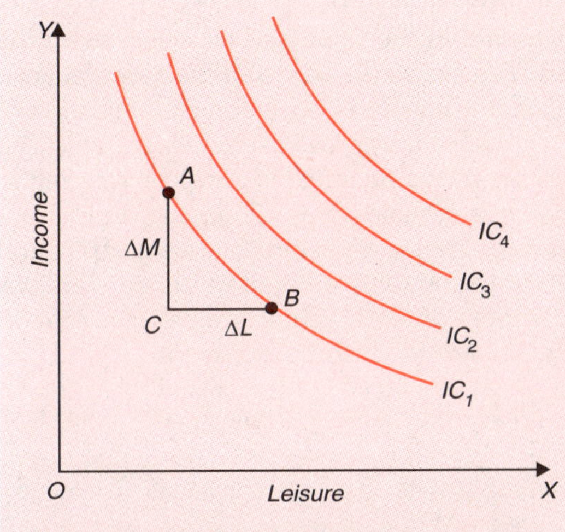

Fig. 11.12. *Trade-off Curves: Indifference Curves between Income and Leisure*

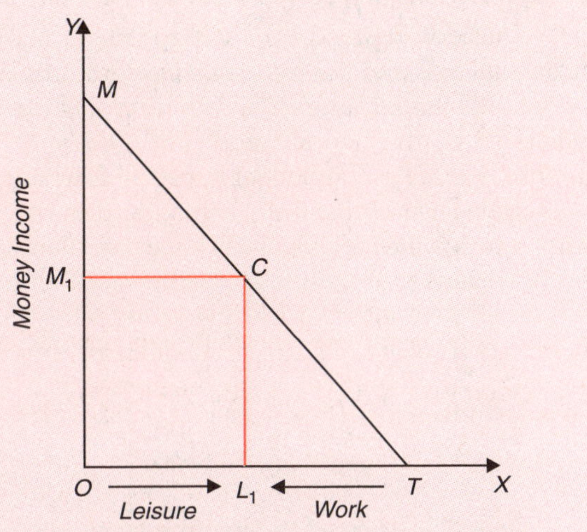

Fig. 11.13. *Income-Leisure Constraint*

Income-Leisure Constraint. However, the actual choice of income and leisure by an individual would also depend upon what is the market rate of exchange between the two, that is, the wage rate per hour of work. It is worth noting that *wage rate is the opportunity cost of leisure.* In other words, to increase leisure by one hour, an individual has to forego the opportunity of earning income (equal to wage per hour) which he can earn by doing work for an hour. This leads us to income-leisure constraint which together with the indifference map between income and leisure would determine the actual choice by the individual. The maximum amount of time available per day for the individual is 24 hours. Thus, the maximum amount of leisure time that an individual can enjoy per day equals 24 hours. In order to earn income for satisfying his wants for goods and services, he will devote some of his time to do work.

Consider Figure 11.13 where leisure is measured in the rightward direction along the horizontal axis and the maximurn leisure time is OT (equal to 24 hours). If'the individual can work for all the 24 hours in a day, he would earn income equal to OM. Income OM equals OT multiplied by the hourly wage rate ($OM = OT.w$) where w represents the wage rate. The straight line MT is the budget constraint, which in the present context is generally referred to as income-leisure constraint which shows the various combinations of income and leisure among which the individual will have to make a choice. Thus, if a person chooses combination C, this means that he has OL_1 amount of leisure time and OM_1 amount of income. He has earned OM_1 amount of income by working TL_1 hours of work. Choice of other points on income-leisure line MT will show different amounts of leisure, income and work.

Income $\quad OM = OT.w$

$$\frac{OM}{OT} = w$$

Thus, the slope of the income-leisure curve OM/OT equals the wage rate.

Income-Leisure Equilibrium. Now, we can bring together the indifference map showing ranking of preferences of the individual between income and leisure and the income-leisure line to show the actual choice of leisure and income by the individual in his equilibrium position. We will further show how much work effort (*i.e.* supply of labour in terms of hours worked) he would put in this optimal situation. Our analysis is based on two assumptions. First, he *is free to work as many hours per day as he likes.* Second, wage rate is the same irrespective of the number of hours he chooses to work.

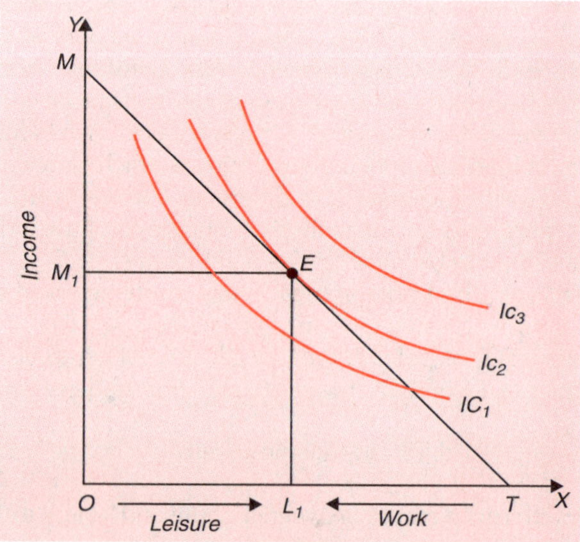

Fig. 11.14 Income-Leisure Equilibrium

Figure 11.14 displays income-leisure equilibrium of the individual. With the given wage rate, the individual will choose a combination of income and leisure lying on the income-leisure line MT that maximises his satisfaction. It will be seen from Figure 11.14 that the given income-leisure line MT is tangent to the indifference curve IC_2 at point E showing choice of OL_1 of leisure and OM_1 of income. In this optimal condition, income-leisure trade off (*i.e. MRS* between income and leisure) equals the wage rate (w), that is, the market exchange rate between the two. In this equilibrium position the individual works for TL_1 hours per day (TL_1, = $OT - OL_1$). Thus, he has worked for TL_1 hours to earn OM_l amount of income.

Need for Higher Overtime Wage Rate

It will be interesting to know why there is need for paying higher wage rate than the normal wage rate for getting more or overtime work from the individuals. As explained above, with the given wage rate and given trade-off between income and leisure the individual chooses to work for TL_1 hours per day. To do overtime work, he will have to sacrifice more leisure-time and therefore to provide him incentive to forego more leisure and thus to work for more hours it is required to pay him higher wage rate. This is depicted in Figure11.15 where at the equilibrium point E a steeper leisure-income line EK than MT *has* been drawn. TL_1 is the hours worked at the wage rate w represented by the slope of the income-leisure line MT. If the higher overtime wage rate w' represented by the line EK is fixed, the individual is in equilibrium at point H on indifference curve IC_2 where he chooses to have OL_2 leisure time and OM_2 amount of income. Thus, he has sacrificed L_1L_2 more leisure to do overtime work and earns M_1M_2 more income than before. He now works for TL_2 hours per day, TL_1, at hourly wage rate w and L_1L_2 at higher wage rate w'. Further, he is better off than before as he is now at higher indifference curve IC_2.

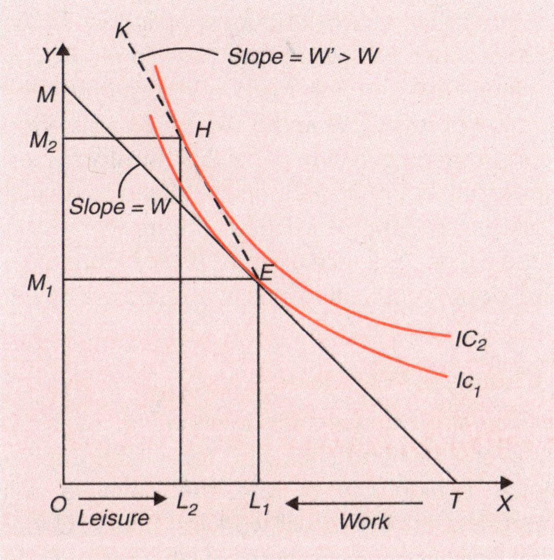

Fig. 11.15. *Need for higher overtime wage rate*

Wage offer Curve and the Supply of Labour

Now with the analysis of leisure-income choice, it is easy to derive supply curve of labour.

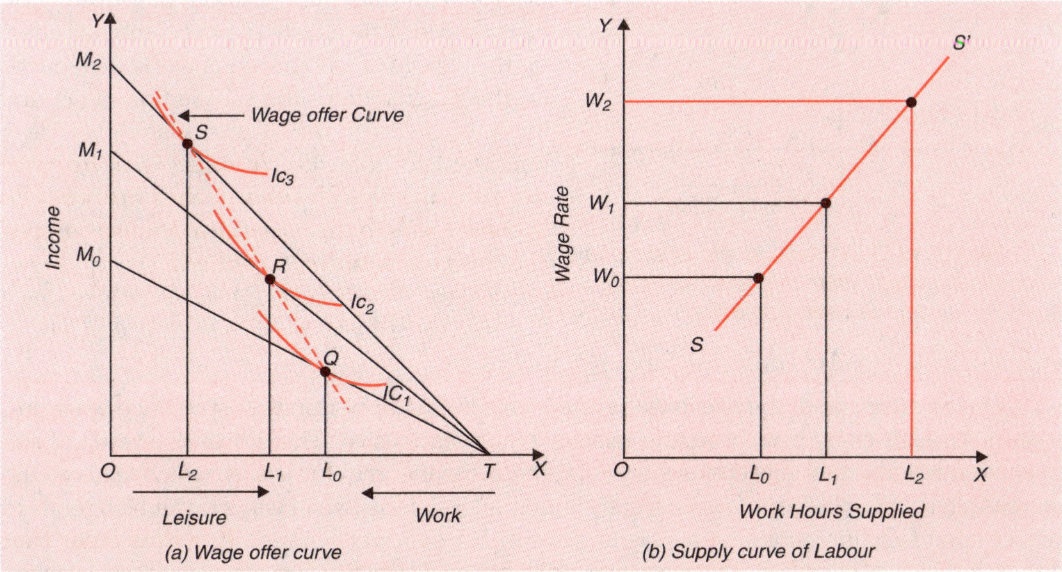

Fig. 11.16. *Supply Curve of Labour*

Supply curve of labour shows how an individual's work effort responds to changes in the wage rate. The derivation of supply curve of labour is depicted in Figure 11.16. In panel *(a)* of this figure it will be seen that at the wage rate w_0 ($w_0 = OM_0/OT$), the wage line or income-leisure line is TM_0 and the individual is in equilibrium at point *Q* where he chooses OL_0 leisure time and works for TL_0 hours. That is, at wage rate w_0 he supplies TL_0 amount of labour. This supply of labour is directly shown against wage rate w_0 in panel *(b)* of Figure 11.16. Now, when the wage rate rises to w_1, wage line or income-leisure line shifts to TM_1 ($w_1 = OM_1/OT$), the individual reduces his leisure to OL_1 and supplies TL_1 hours of work; L_1L_0 more than before (see Panel *(a)* in Figure 11.16). Thus, L_1 number of work-hours supplied is shown against w_1, in panel *(b)* of Figure 11.16. Likewise, when the wage rate rises to w_2 (w_2, $= OM_2/OT$), income-leisure line shifts to TM_2 the individual chooses to have leisure time OL_2 and supplies TL_2 work-hours. In panel (a) on joining points *Q*, *R* and *S* we get what is often called *wage-offer curve* which is similar to price-consumption curve. In panel *(b)*, the information supplied by the wage-offer curve, that is, the supply of labour (work-hours) by the individual at different wage rates is shown directly as, in this panel, supply of labour (hours worked) is measured along the *X*-axis and wage rate along the y-axis. A glance at panel *(b)* of Figure 8.16 will reveal that supply curve of labour is upward sloping indicating positive response of the individual to the rise in wage rate.

Income Effect and Substitution Effect of the Change in Wage Rate

Now the supply curve of labour does not always slope upward as shown in Fig. 11.16. It can slope or bend backward too which implies that at a higher wage rate, the individual will supply less labour (*i.e.* will work less hours). Under what conditions supply curve of labour (*i.e.* work-hours) slopes upward and under what circumstances it bends backward can be explained in terms of income effect and substitution effect of a change in wage rate. As in case of change in price, rise in wage rate has both the substitution effect and income effect. The net combined effect on the supply of labour (hours worked) depends on the magnitude of the substitution effect and income effect of the rise in wage rate. It is important to note that ***leisure is a normal commodity which means that increase in income leads to the increase in leisure enjoyed (i.e. less work-hours supplied).*** That is, income effect of the rise in wage rate on leisure is positive, that is, leads to the *increase in the hours of leisure enjoyed* (that is, tends to *decrease labour supply*).

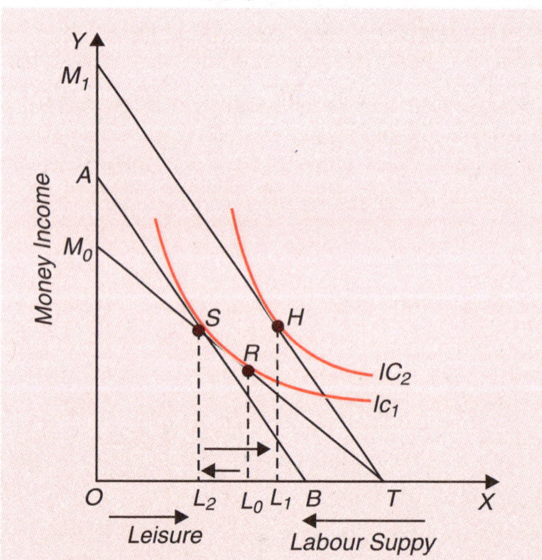

Fig. 11.17 *Decomposing the Effect of Rise in Wage Rate into Income Effect and Substitution Effect*

On the other hand, the rise in wage rate increases the opportunity cost or price of leisure, that is, it makes enjoyment of leisure relatively more expensive. Therefore, as a result of rise in wage rate individual substitutes work (and therefore income) for leisure which leads to the increase in supply of labour. This is a substitution effect of the rise in wage rate which tends to reduce leisure and *increase labour supply (i.e. number of hours worked)*. **It is thus clear that *for an individual supplier of labour, income effect and substitution effect work in opposite***

directions[9]. Whereas income effect of the rise in wage rate tends to reduce supply of labour substitution effect tends to increase it. ***If the income effect is stronger than the substitution effect, the net combined effect of rise in wage rate will be to reduce labour supply.*** On the other hand, if substitution effect is relatively larger than the income effect, the rise on wage rate will increase labour supply.

How the effect of rise in wage rate is split up into income effect and substitution effect is shown in Fig 11.17. In this figure we measure money income on the *Y*- axis and leisure (reading from left to right) and labour supply (reading from right to left) on the X-axis. Suppose to begin with the wage rate is w_0 and if all the available hours *OT* are used to do work, OM_0 money income is earned. This gives us TM_0 as the budget constraint or which in the present context is also called leisure-income constraint. It will be seen from Figure 11.17 that TM_0 is tangent to indifference curve IC_1 between leisure and income at point *R*. Thus, with wage rate w_0 the individual is in equilibrium when he enjoys OL_0 leisure and therefore he is supplying TL_0 work hours of labour. Now suppose that wage rate rises to w_1 with the result that income-leisure constraint line rotates to TM_1. Now, with TM_1 as new income-leisure constraint line, the individual is in equilibrium at point *H* at which he supplies TL_1 work-hours of labour which are less than TL_0.

Thus, with the rise in wage rate, supply of labour has decreased by L_0L_1. To break up this wage effect on labour supply, we reduce his money income by compensating variation in income. To do so we take away so much income from the individual that he comes back to the original indifference curve IC_1. *AB* is such line obtained after reducing his money income by compensating variation. *AB* is tangent to indifference curve IC_1 at point *S* at which he supplies TL_2 hours for work. This shows with change in wage rate from w_0 to w_1, resulting in leisure becoming relatively more expensive, he substitutes work (*i.e.* labour supply) L_0L_2 for leisure. This is substitution effect which tends to increase labour supply by L_0L_2, Now, if the money taken from him is given back to him so that the income-leisure line again shifts back to TM_1. With TM_1, he reaches his old equilibrium position at point *H* where he supplies TL_1 work-hours. Thus, movement from point *S* to *H* represents the income effect of the rise in wage rate and as a result labour supply decrease by L_2L_1.

Thus, while income effect of the increase in wage rate causes decrease in labour supply by L_2L_1 the substitution effect causes increase in labour supply by L_2L_1. It will be seen from Fig. 11.17 that in this case income effect is stronger than substitution effect so that the net result is reduction in labour supply by L_0L_1 work-hours and therefore in this case labour supply curve bends backward. Now, if substitution effect had been larger than income effect, work-hours supplied would have increased as a result of rise in wage rate and labour supply curve would slope upward.

Backward Bending Supply Curve of Labour

It may, however, be noted that on theoretical grounds it cannot be predicted which effect will be stronger. It has, however, been empirically observed that when the wage rate is small so that the demand for more income or goods and services is very strong, substitution effect is larger than the income effect so that the net effect of rise in wage rate will be to reduce leisure and increase the supply of labour. But when he is already supplying a large amount of labour and is earning sufficient income, further increases in wage rate may induce the individual to demand more leisure so that income effect may outweigh the substitution effect at higher wage rates. This implies that at higher wage rates, labour supply may be reduced in response

9. Note that thjis is unlike the case of *price effect of normal goods* in which case substitution effect of a change in price and income effect work in the *same* direction.

to further rise in wage rates. This means up to a point substitution effect is stronger than income effect so that labour supply curve slopes upward, but beyond that at higher wage rates, supply curve of labour bends backward. This is illustrated in Fig 11.18 where in panel (a) wage

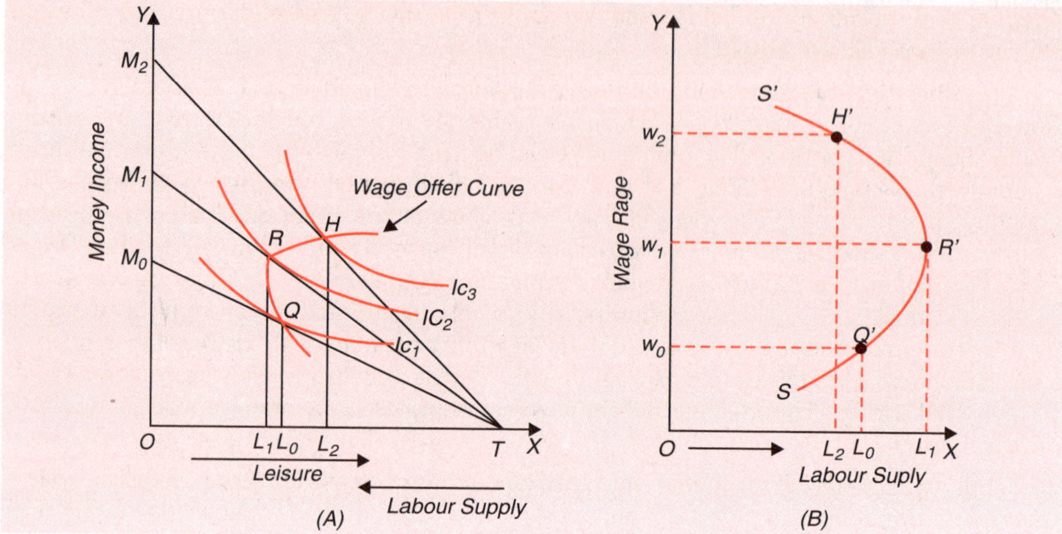

Fig. 11.18. *Backward-Bending Supply Curve of Labour*

offer curve is shown, and in panel (b) supply curve of is drawn corresponding to leisure-work equilibrium in panel (a). Thus, to start with at wage rate w_0 (*i.e.* TM_0 as budget constraint) L_0 amount of work-hours (labour) are supplied. This is directly plotted against the wage rate w_0 in panel (b) of Fig. 11.18. When the wage rate rise to w_1(budget constraint becomes TM_1 in panel (a) of Fig.11.18 the greater amount of labour L_1 is supplied. Amount of labour L_1 is directly plotted against higher wage rate w_1 in panel (b) of Fig. 11.18. With the further increase in wage rate to w_2, the income-leisure constraint rotates to TM_2 and the individual is in equilibrium when he supplies L_2 work-hours which are smaller than L_1. Thus, with the rise in wage rate above w_1 labour supply decreases. In other words, upto wage rate w_1, labour supply curve slopes upward and beyond that it starts bending backward. This is quite evident from panel (b) of Fig. 11.18.

FOOD STAMP PROGRAMMER : IN-KIND FOOD SUBSIDY

Food stamp programme is a type of food subsidy to provide poor people with adequate quantity of food. It is a form of *in-kind food subsidy* in contrast to the subsidy provided in the form of cash income, often called *cash subsidy*. In the United States it was introduced in 1964 and was amended in 1979 and since then it continues there in the amended form. In India also food stamp programme has been suggested in recent years as an anti-poverty measure. Under food stamp programme, some stamps or coupons are given to the eligible persons or households. With these stamps, the recipient can buy food and only food. That is, these food stamps cannot be used to buy non-food goods. Further, these stamps cannot be traded or transferred to the other people.

Let us explain how a receipt of food stamps affects the budget line, consumption of food and welfare of the individual. We will also demonstrate how the effect of food stamp subsidy differs from cash subsidy. Consider Fig. 11.19 where along the *X*-axis we measure quantity of food and along the *Y*-axis we measure money which represents all other goods, (*i.e.* goods other than food). With a given income of an individual and given market price of food, B_1L_1 is the budget line whose slope represents the price of food (Note that price of money represented on the Y-axis is Re. 1, that is, price of rupee one is Re. 1.). OB_1, is the given money income of the individual. Before the receipt of food stamps the individual is in equilibrium at point E_1 on indifference curve IC_1, and is consuming OF_1, quantity of food and ON_1 quantity of other goods per week.

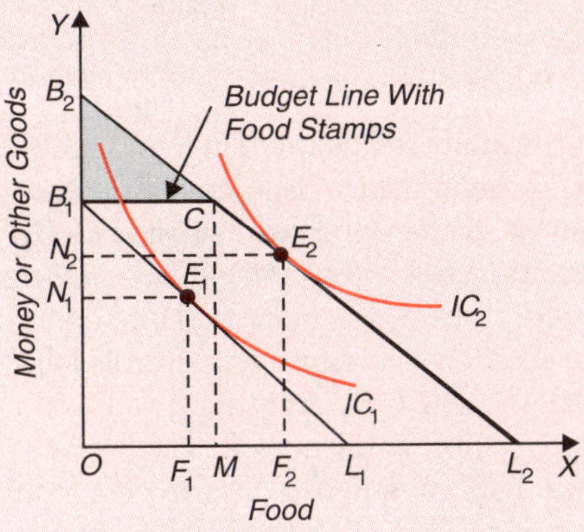

Fig. 11.19. *Effect of Food Stamp Programme on Consumption and Welfare*

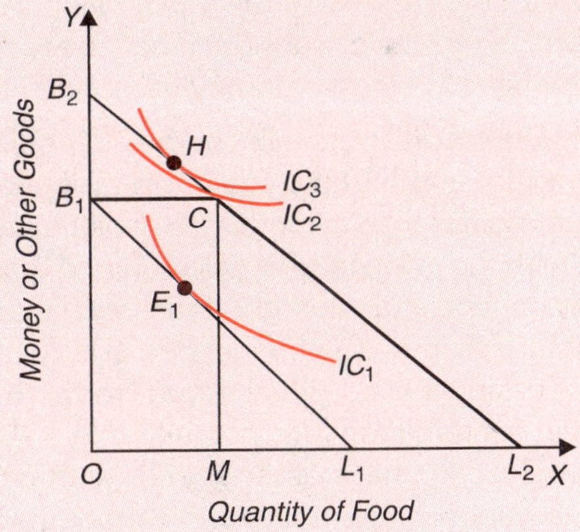

Fig. 11.20. *Effects of Food Stamp Subsidy and Cash Subsidy on Consumption and Welfare*

Now, suppose the individual is given food stamps of Rs. 200 per week, which he can spend on food alone. Suppose further that price of food is Rs. 10 per kg. With stamps of Rs. 200 he can therefore buy 20 kg of food. Since the consumer cannot use food stamps to buy non-food items (other goods), he cannot spend more than his initial income OB_1, on other goods. Thus above the horizontal line B_1C, the combinations of other goods and food are not attainable when he is given food stamps of Rs. 200. Suppose at the given market price of food, he can buy B_1C amount of food with the food stamps of Rs. 200 provided to him, while spending his entire income OB_1 on other goods. For instance, if price of food is Rs. 10 per kg., then with Rs. 200 he can buy 20 kg of food. In this case, therefore, B_1C will be equal to 20 kg. If the individual wants to buy more foodgrains than B_1C, then he will spend some part of his initial income to purchase additional food. Since the food stamps are in addition to his initial income OB_1 his budget line with food stamps becomes a kinked line B_1CL_2.

The food stamp programme can affect the recipient in two ways. One possibility is that with the food-stamp subsidy and resultant kinked budget line B_1CL_2, in Fig. 11.19 the individual maximises his satisfaction at point E_2 where his budget line is tangent to indifference curve IC_2. At this new equilibrium point E_2 he is purchasing OF_2 quantity of food and ON_2 of other goods. Thus, as compared to the situation prior to food-stamp subsidy, he is on higher indifference curve showing a greater level of satisfaction or welfare and consuming greater quantities of food and other goods. Thus, ***food stamp subsidy has led him to buy not only more food but also more of other goods. This means that food stamp subsidy has been indirectly used for financing the purchases of non-food commodities.***

It is important to note that in this possible case, the effect of food stamp subsidy is exactly the same as would be the case if cash subsidy is granted to the individual. Thus, if instead of food stamps the individual is given cash income of B_1B_2 (Note that with given market price of food, cash income of B_1B_2 can buy B_1C quantity of food and thus the two are equivalent), the budget line will shift from B_1L_1 to B_2L_2. But given the preferences of the individual between food and other goods, he is in equilibrium at the same point E_2 at which his budget line B_2L_2 is tangent to the indifference curve IC_2. Thus, in this possibility, the effect of equivalent cash subsidy is exactly the same as the effect of food stamp subsidy. This happens because the preferences of the individual between food and other commodities are such that he wants to have more than B_1C quantity of food which is the quantity of food provided under the food stamp subsidy.

Another important conclusion from this possible case is that with either food stamp subsidy or cash subsidy the individual buys more of both food and other goods than he buys before the grant of subsidy. This is because food and other goods are here considered as normal goods whose quantity demanded increase with the increase in income.

The second possibility of the effect of food stamp subsidy is illustrated in Fig. 11.20. Prior to grant of any subsidy, and given his budget line B_1L_1 the individual is in equilibrium at point E_1 on indifference curve IC_1. Now let us assume that he is given the cash subsidy of B_1B_2 so that with the given market price of food, budget line shifts to B_2L_2. The individual's preferences between food and other goods are such that with this cash subsidy the individual is in equilibrium at point H where the budget line B_2L_2 is tangent to indifference curve IC_3. In this case with cash subsidy the individual spends more than his initial income OB_1 on other goods. As noted above, combination H is not available under food stamp subsidy because food stamps cannot be used to purchase other goods. With equivalent food stamp subsidy of B_1C, the individual has to choose a point which must be on the kinked budget line B_1CL_2. With the budget line B_1CL_2 ***with food stamp subsidy, the best that the individual can do is to choose the corner point C*** of budget line B_1CL_2 which lies on the highest possible indifference curve IC_2 passing through the point C.

Therefore, from the point of individual welfare we reach our earlier conclusion that ***cash subsidy is superior to in-kind subsidy represented by food stamps programme.*** This is because cash subsidy does not limit a person that he must purchase a certain amount of food and he is therefore free to spend as he likes. But it should be noted that the consumption of food in case of cash subsidy is less than under the food stamp subsidy programme. If the purpose is to increase the consumption of food and therefore provide adequate diet to the people, then food stamp subsidy is better than cash subsidy as under the former, the individual is constrained to buy at least a given quantity of food.

Another important result obtained from our above analysis is that even with food stamps programme the individual increases the consumption of all other goods *(i.e.,* non-food items) too. This shows that a part of food stamp subsidy is *indirectly* used to finance the increased consumption of other goods. This is because some part of the income which the individual was spending on food prior to food stamp subsidy get released because of the food stamps being used for its purchase and this released income is spent on non-food items. This increases the consumption of non-food items also. This result is of special importance because supporters of food stamp subsidy have been emphasising that food subsidy should not be used to finance any part of non-food unnecessary items such as liquor. However, as seen above, in practice it is difficult to make a plan that will increase the consumption of subsidised food and will not affect the consumption of other goods.

Lastly, out of the two possibilities of the effects of food stamp subsidy and cash subsidy which is the most common result, that is, the most common outcome of the two possible cases presented in Fig. 11.19 and Fig. 11.20. However, the final result of the two types of subsidies depends on the value of food stamps relative to preferences and incomes of the individuals whom subsidies are granted. We cannot predict the specific result purely on theoretical grounds. Empirical research conducted in the USA however reveals that most recipients of food stamps porogramme represent situation depicted in Fig. 11.20. This means for most of the recipients, food stamp programme has the same effect as a cash subsidy.

WELFARE EFFECT OF DIRECT AND INDIRECT TAXES

An important application of indifference curves is to judge the welfare effects of direct and indirect taxes on the individuals. In other words, if the Government wants to raise a given amount of revenue whether it will be better to do so by levying a direct tax or an indirect tax from the viewpoint of welfare of the individuals[10]. As shall be proved below an indirect tax such as excise duty, sales tax causes *'excess burden'* on the individuals, that is, indirect tax reduces welfare more than the direct tax, say lump-sum tax, when an equal amount of revenue is raised through them. Consider Figure 11.21 where on the X-axis, good *X* and on the *Y*-axis money is measured. With a given income of the individual and the given price of good *X*, the price line is PL_1 which is tangent to indifference curve IC_3 at point Q_3 where the individual is in equilibrium position.

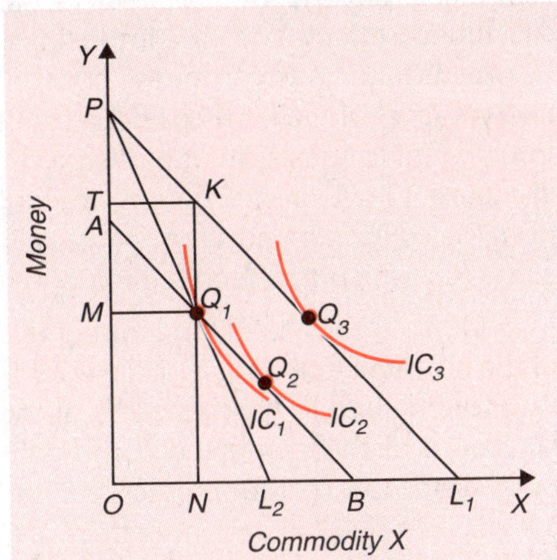

Fig. 11.21. *Indirect tax is more burdensome than lump-sum tax*

Suppose now that Government levies an excise duty (an indirect tax) on good X. With the imposition of excise duty, the price of good *X* will rise. As a result of the rise in price of good X, the price line rotates to a new position PL_2 which is tangent to indifference curve IC_1 at point Q_1. It is thus clear that as a result of the imposition of excise duty, the individual has shifted from a higher indifference curve IC_3 to a lower one IC_1, that is, his level of satisfaction or welfare has declined. It is worth noting that the movement from Q_3 on indifference curve IC_3 to Q_1 on indifference curve IC_1 is the combined result of the income effect and substitution effect caused by the excise duty.

It should be further noted that at point Q_1 (that is, after the imposition of excise duty), the individual is purchasing *ON* amount of good *X* and has paid *PM* amount of money for it. At the old price (before the excise duty was imposed), that is, with budget line PL_1, he could purchase *ON* quantity of good *X* for *PT* amount of money. Thus, the difference *TM* (or KQ_1) between the two is the amount of money which the individual is paying as the excise duty.

Now, suppose that instead of excise duty, Government levies lump-sum tax on the individual when the individual is initially at point Q_3 on indifference curve IC_3. With the imposition of lump-sum tax, the price line will shift below but will be parallel to the original price line PL_1. Further, if the same amount of revenue is to be raised through lump-sum tax as with excise duty, then the new price line *AB* should be drawn at such a distance from the original price line PL_1 that it passes through the point Q_1. So, it will be seen from Figure 11.21 that with the imposition of lump-sum tax equivalent in terms of revenue raising to the excise duty, we have drawn the budget line *AB* which is passing through the point Q_1. However, with *AB* as the price line, individual is in equilibrium at point Q_2 on indifference curve IC_2 which lies at a higher level than IC_1 In other words, at point Q_2 individual's level of welfare is higher than at Q_1,. Lump-sum tax has reduced the individual's welfare less than that by the excise duty. Thus, indirect tax (excise duty) causes an excess burden on the individual.[11]

Now, the important question is why an indirect tax (an excise duty or a sales tax on a commodity) causes excess burden on the consumer in terms of loss of welfare or satisfaction. The basic reason for this is that whereas both the lump-sum tax (or any other general income

11. Direct taxes are those taxes whose incidence cannot be shifted to others. Lump-sum tax, proportionate and progressive income taxes, wealth tax, death duty are the examples of direct tax. On the other hand, an indirect tax is one which can be passed on or shifted to others by raising the prices of the goods. The excise duty, sales tax are the examples of indirect tax.

tax) and an indirect tax reduce consumer's income and produce income effect, the indirect tax in addition to the income effect, also raises the relative price of the good on which it is levied and therefore causes substitution effect. The imposition of a lump-sum tax (or any income tax) does not affect the prices of goods because it is not levied on any saleable goods. Since lump-sum tax or any income tax does not alter the relative prices of goods it will not result in any substitution effect. With the imposition of a lump-sum tax (or any other income tax), a certain income is taken away from the consumer and he is pushed to the lower indifference curve (or a lower level of welfare) but he is free to spend the income he is left with as he likes without forcing him to substitute one commodity for another due to any change in relative prices. Thus in Figure 11.21, imposition of an equivalent lump-sum or income tax, the consumer moves from the equilibrium position Q_3 on indifference curve IC_3 to the new position Q_2 on indifference curve IC_2 which represents the income effect.

On the other hand, an indirect tax not only reduces the purchasing power or real income of the consumer causing income effect, but also produces price-induced substitution effect and thus forcing him to purchase less of the commodity on which indirect tax has been levied and buy more of the non-taxed commodity. And this later substitution effect caused due to the price-distortion by the indirect tax further reduces his welfare. As will be seen from Figure 11.21, as a result of income effect of the indirect tax the consumer moves from point Q_3 on indifference curve IC_3 to point Q_2 on lower indifference curve IC_2 and as a result of substitution effect he is further pushed to point Q_1on still lower indifference curves IC_1.

ECONOMIC THEORY OF INDEX NUMBERS : ASSESSING CHANGES IN STANDARDS OF LIVING

A significant use of indifference curve analysis is made in the economic theory of index numbers. First, let us make it clear what is the index number problem in economic theory. To make the analysis simple let us assume an individual consumer purchases two commodities, X and Y, in two different time periods, zero and one. In period zero, the consumer purchases 25 units of good X at price Rs. 10 per unit and 15 units of good Y *at* price Rs. 12 per unit. Suppose the prices of goods X and Y change in period one and at price of X equal to Rs. 15 the consumer purchases 20 units of good X, and at price of Y equal to Rs. 9 he purchases 22 units of good Y. Thus in period one the quantity purchased of good X has fallen while the quantity purchased of good Y has increased. Now, the problem of index number is *whether the economic welfare or standard of living of the individuals has increased or decreased in period one as compared with period zero.* If indifference map of individual is known, then with its aid we can know whether welfare of the individual has increased or decreased. Let us restate the index number problem in notational form. Suppose in period zero individual buys x° quantity of commodity X at price $p^0{}_x$ and y^0quantity of commodity Y at price $P_y{}^{\circ}$. Similarly, in period one, individual purchases X^1 quantity of commodity X at price $P^1{}_x$ and Y^1 quantity of commodity Y at price $p^1{}_y$. We have to assess whether the standard of living or welfare of the individual has increased or decreased during the period one as compared with period zero with the change in relative prices and income of the individual. To make this assessment we assume that individual's tastes and preferences, that is, his indifference map remains constant

11. This conclusion regarding excess burden of indirect tax compared with the direct tax is however based on several assumptions about initial conditions. Whether or not indirect tax reduces welfare more than direct tax depends upon so many initial conditions before the taxes are introduced. For knowing the analysis regarding welfare implications of direct and indirect taxes, see (1) I.M.D. Little, Direct Versus Indirect Taxes, *Economic Journal*, Sept. 1951. (2) Milton Friedman, The Welfare Effects of Taxes, *Essays in Positive Economics*. University of Chicago Press, 1953 and (3) Musgrave, *Theory of Public Finance.*

and unchanged over the time period under consideration. Indifference curves IC_1, IC_2 and IC_3 depict the indifference map of the individual between commodity X and Y.

In the period zero (called the base period), individual's given money income and the prices p_x^0 and p_y^0 give rise to the budget line P_0L_0. It will be seen from Figure 11.22 that with budget line P_0L_0 individual is in equilibrium at point Q_0 on indifference curve IC_2. As a result of the changes in income and prices of goods in period one, the budget line changes to P_1L_1 (the relative price of X has risen). The new budget line P_1L_1 is tangent to indifference curves IC_3 at point Q_1 where the individual is now in equilibrium. It will be seen from the figure that in this new equilibrium position reached after the change in income and prices of goods and the consequent changes in the bundle of goods X and Y from Q_0 *to* Q_1, the individual becomes better off (that is, his standard of living in terms of utility or satisfaction has increased), since he has shifted to a higher indifference curve IC_3 from IC_2. In other words, he has enjoyed a gain in real income by the above changes in prices and quantities, for they have pushed him to a higher indifference curve.

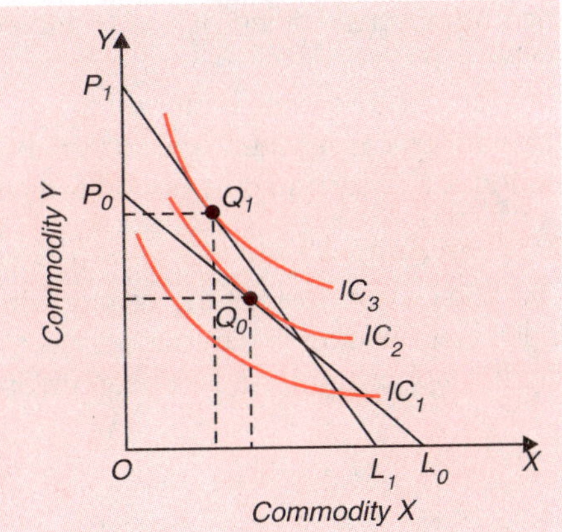

Fig. 11.22. *Theory of Index Numbers*

But it should be noted that we are able to judge the increment in real income or economic welfare ***only when the indifference-curves map of the individual is actually known.*** However, if the indifference curves are not known, as is usually the case, and we know only the budget lines and the consumption points Q_0 and Q_1, we ***cannot assess with the aid of indifference curve analysis*** whether the real income, or standard of living or welfare of the individual has increased or decreased by the above stated changes in prices and quantities purchased of the commodities, for in the absence of indifference curves depending upon his subjective preferences we cannot know whether or not individual has shifted to a higher indifference curve.

Fortunately, in several cases even in the absence of knowledge about individual's indifference curves we can judge whether with the changes in income and relative prices, he has become better off in period 1 as compared to the base period by simply observing the behaviour of the individual regarding his choice of bundle of goods in different periods. In this analysis only assumption which we make is that the ***individual makes rational choice.*** Consider the situation depicted in Figure 11.22 now reproduced in Figure 11.23 without the indifference curves. With the given income and prices of goods in period 0 *(i.e.* the base period) the budget line is *A A′*. Suppose with a certain change in income and price of goods, the individual's budget line becomes *BB′* in period 1. It is observed that the consumer chooses bundle of goods Q_0 in period 0 on the budget line *AA′* and the bundle Q_1 in period 1 on budget line *BB′*. Now, we have to assess whether the consumer has become better off in period 1 as compared to period

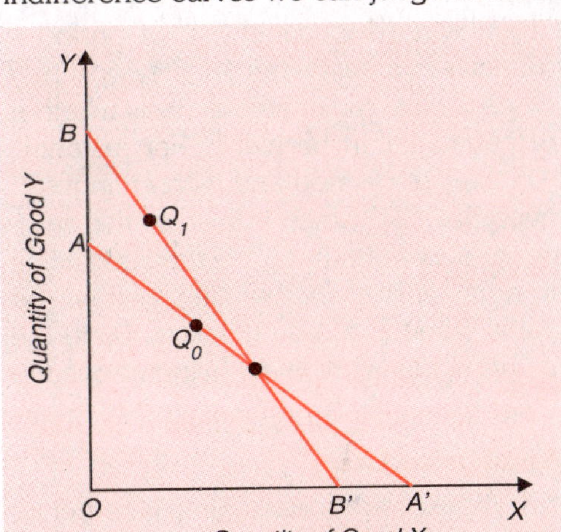

Fig. 11.23. *The Economic Theory of Index Numbers*

0. It will be seen that in period 1 the bundle Q_0 is available (that is, Q_0 lies within market opportunity set or budget space of the budget line *BB′* of period 1 but the consumer actually chooses the bundle Q_1 implying that he prefers bundle Q_1. In other words, he has become better off (that is, his real income has increased) in period 1 as a result of changes in prices and income occurred since period 0. However, as we shall discuss later in all cases of changes in income and prices we cannot assess without the knowledge of indifference curves whether the individual has become better off in period 1 as compared to the base period. We explain below the various cases when we can infer about whether the consumer has become better off in period 1 as compared to period 0 as a result of changes in income and prices.

1. When Budget Line of Period 1 Lies Entirely Outward to the Base Period's Budget Line

First, we consider the case when prices and money income have so changed that the individual's budget line in period 1 lies outward to the budget line in period 0 implying that his market opportunity set has been enlarged. For instance, consider Figure11.24 where *AA′* is the budget line in the base period and with the change in income and relative prices of goods, the budget line in period 1 shifts entirely outward to the position *BB′* with greater intercepts on both the axes.

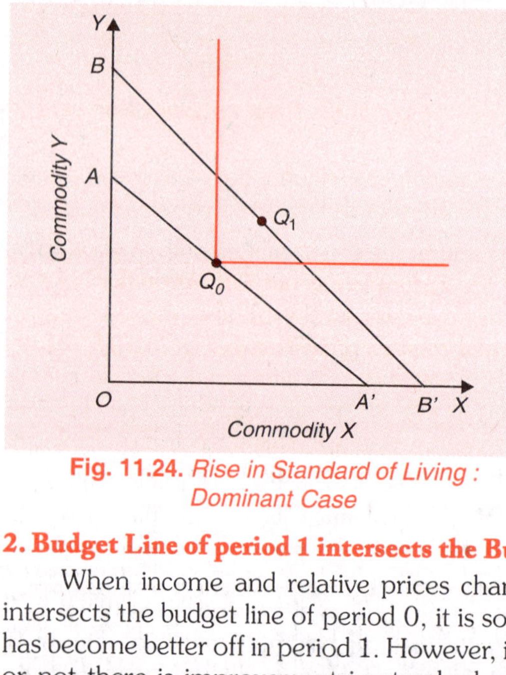

Fig. 11.24. *Rise in Standard of Living : Dominant Case*

Note that we are assuming that both the commodities are *'goods'* and further that the consumer behaves rationally, that is, he prefers more to less of a good. Suppose the consumer chooses bundle Q_0 on budget line *AA′* in period 0 and bundle Q_1 on budget line *BB′* in period 1. Since bundle Q_1 in period 1 *is lying in the north east of* Q_0 contains more of both the goods. We can unambiguously say that he has become better off or his standard of living has risen in period 1 as compared to the period 0.

2. Budget Line of period 1 intersects the Budget line of period

When income and relative prices change in such a way that budget line of period 1 intersects the budget line of period 0, it is somewhat difficult to assess whether the consumer has become better off in period 1. However, in some cases we can say unambiguously whether or not there is improvement in standard of living of consumer in period 1. For instance, consider Figure 11.25 where *AA′* is the budget line in the base period and with changes in income and relative prices, budget line in period 1 becomes *BB*' which intersects the base-period budget line *AA′*. In the base period the consumer chooses bundle Q_0 on the budget line *AA′* and in period 1 his choice is the bundle Q_1 lying north east of the bundle Q_0. It will be noticed that the bundle Q_1 contains more of both goods *X* and *Y* as compared to Q_0 in the base period. We can therefore say unambiguously that his standard of living has improved in period 1.

3. Budget Lines of the Two Periods Intersect: The Ambiguous Cases

The situation depicted in Figure 11.26 poses a difficult problem for assessing whether or not there is improvement in the standard of living in period 1. In this case, as will be seen from Figure 11.26, the budget lines intersect and the consumer chooses the bundle Q_0 in period 0 and the bundle Q_1 in period 1 which lies to the north-west of Q_0. This is an ambiguous case

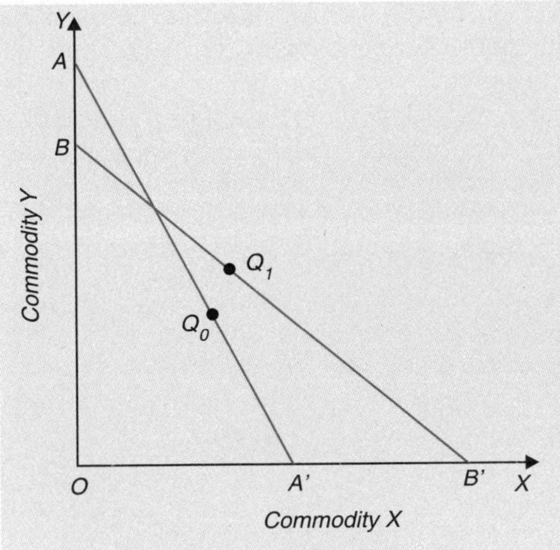

Fig. 11.25. *Rise in Standard of Living : Q_1 demonates Q_0*

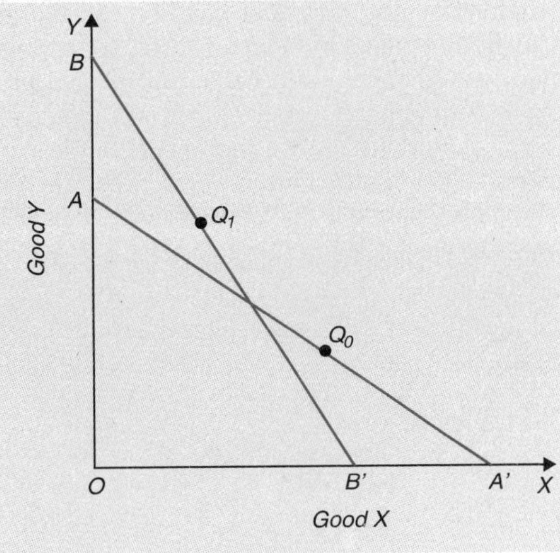

Fig. 11.26. *Assessing a Standard of Living Change : Ambiguous Case*

because without the knowledge of consumer's indifference curves we cannot infer form his observed behaviour whether or not he has become better off. This is because both situations are possible depending on the shapes and location of his indifference curves. As will be seen from Figure 11.27 (panels *a* and *b*) with Q_1 living northwest of Q_0, it would be possible to construct indifference curves so that Q_0 lies on a higher indifference curve than Q_1 as in (panel *a)* but is equally possible to construct indifference curves so that Q_1 of period 1 lies on a higher indifference curve than Q_0 (as in panel *b)*. If the indifference curves of our consumer are those that are depicted in panel (*a*), then change in situation from AA' to BB' will make him worse off and if his indifference curves are such that are shown in panel *b*, then he would become better off in period 1.

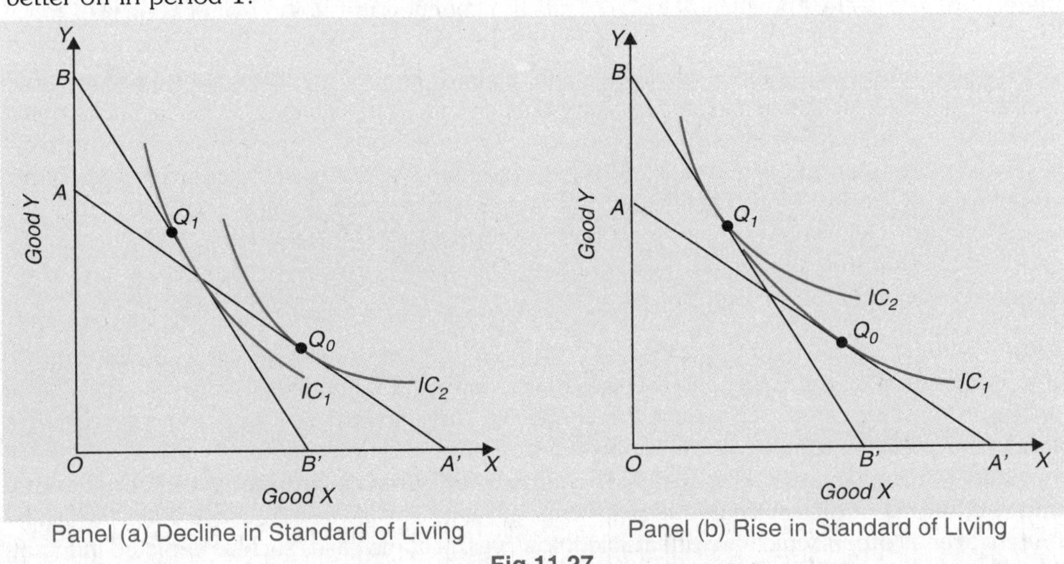

Panel (a) Decline in Standard of Living

Panel (b) Rise in Standard of Living

Fig.11.27

4. Budget Lines of the Two Periods Intersect : Non-Dominant Cases

There are certain situations when we cannot at first glance conclude unambiguously whether or not individual has become better off in period 1 . For example, consider the situation depicted in Figure 11.28. To start with, consumer chooses Q_0 on AA' in period 0 and with changes in income and relative prices he chooses Q_1 on BB' in period 1 . The dominance criteria to assess improvement in standard of living cannot be applied. Here bundle Q_1 of period 1 contains more of X but less of Y as compared to the bundle Q_0 in the base period (Note that neither Q_1 dominates Q_0 nor Q_0 dominates Q_1), Nevertheless, we can infer about the change in standard of living in period 1 from his observed behaviour and attainable

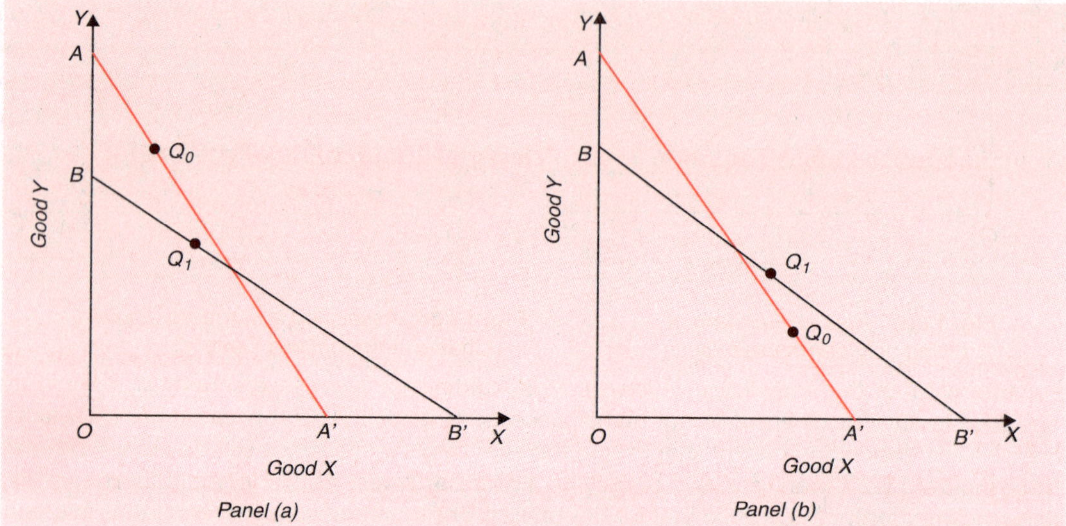

Fig. 11.28. *Assessing Change in Standard of living in Non-Dominant Cases*

bundles in each period. In period 0, the budget line is AA' and the consumer chooses Q_0 when Q_1 is attainable, that is, Q_1 lies within the budget space or market opportunity set of the budget line AA', thus the consumer could have chosen Q_1but, instead he chose Q_0 implying thereby that he prefers bundle Q_0 to Q_1. Thus the change in situation from Q_0 on AA' to Q_1 on BB' in Panel (a) of Fig. 11.28 means that he has become worse off in period 1.

Now, a similar situation is depicted in panel (*b*) of Figure 11.28 where also the relative prices of goods and income of the consumer change in such a way that the budget lines of the two periods intersect and the consumer chooses Q_0 in period *0* and Q_1 in period 1. And Q_1 lies to the north-west of Q_0. Here Q_1 does not dominate Q_0 as it contains more of good *Y* but less of good *X*. Since Q_0 also lies within the budget space of the budget line *BB'* in period 1 and is therefore available in this period but the consumer does not choose it but instead he chooses Q_1 This means that he prefers Q_1 to Q_0 and we can unambiguously say that his standard of living has improved in period 1.

Conclusion

It follows from our foregoing analysis that following the changes in income and relative prices, in most cases we can assess the change in the standard of living from the observed behaviour of the consumer without the knowledge of his indifference curves or his preference map. Only assumptions we make are that **the consumer behaves rationally and consistently and further his choice reveals his preference.** That is, he always chooses a bundle which he prefers over all others which are attainable. However, in some cases such as depicted in Figure 11.27 we cannot assess whether his standard of living has improved or not without the knowledge of indifference curves.

CHAPTER

12

Revealed Preference Theory of Demand

BEHAVIOURISTIC APPROACH TO DEMAND ANALYSIS

In the previous two chapters the Marshallian utility theory and Hicks-Allen indifference curve theory of demand have been discussed. In both these theories, introspective method has been applied to explain the consumer's behaviour. In other words, both these theories provide psychological explanation of consumer's demand; they derive laws about consumer's demand from how he would react psychologically to certain hypothetical changes in price and incomes. But the Revealed Preference Theory which has been put forward by Paul Samuelson seeks to explain consumer's demand from his actual behaviour in the market in various price-income situations. Thus, in sharp contrast to psychological or introspective explanation Prof. Samuelson's revealed preference theory is behaviouristic explanation of consumer's demand. Besides, revealed preference theory is based upon the concept of ordinal utility. In other words, revealed preference theory regards utilities to be merely comparable and not quantifiable. Tapas Majumdar has described Samuelson's revealed preference theory as "Behaviourist Ordinalist."[1] The description "Behaviourist Ordinalist" highlights the two basic features of the revealed preference theory : first, it applies behaviouristic method, and secondly it uses the concept of ordinal utility.

The revealed preference theory is regarded as "scientific" (meaning behavioristic) explanation of consumer's behaviour as against the psychological explanation provided by Marshallian and Hicks-Allen theories of demand. This shift from psychological to behavioristic explanation of consumer's behaviour is a landmark in the development of the theory of demand. The urge among economists to have scientific explanation led to the emergence of the behaviouristic method which seeks to derive the demand theorem from actually observed consumer's behaviour.

PREFERENCE HYPOTHESIS AND STRONG ORDERING

Samuelson's revealed preference theory has ***preference hypothesis*** as a basis of his theory of demand. According to this hypothesis, when a consumer is observed to choose a combination *A* out of various alternative combinations open to him, then he 'reveals', his preference for *A* over all other alternative combinations which he could have purchased. In other words, when a consumer chooses a combination *A*, it means he considers all other alternative combinations which he could have purchased to be inferior to *A*. That is, he rejects all other alternative combinations open to him in favour of the chosen combination *A*. Thus, according to Samuelson, ***choice reveals preference.*** Choice of the combination A reveals his

1. Tapas Majumdar, *Measurement of Utility*, Chapter VII.

definite preference for A over all other rejected combinations. From the hypothesis of 'choice reveals preference' we can obtain definite information about the preferences of a consumer from the observations of his behaviour in the market. By comparing preferences of a consumer revealed in different price-income situations we can obtain certain information about his preference scale.

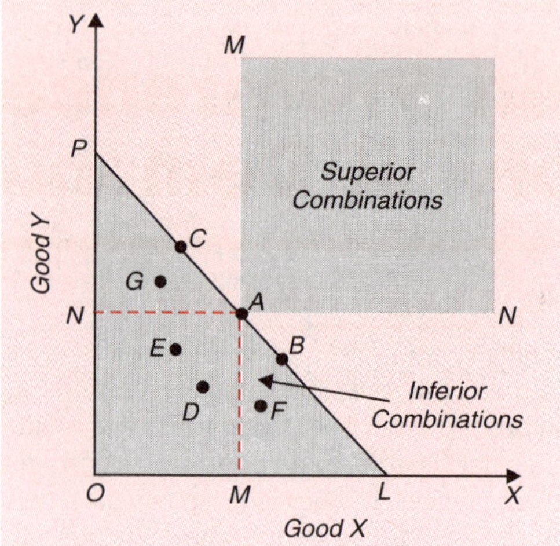

Fig. 12.1. Choice reveals preference

Let us graphically explain the preference hypothesis. Given the prices of two commodities *X* and *Y* and the income of the consumer, price line *PL* is drawn in Fig. 12.1. The price line *PL* represents a given price-income situation. Given the price-income situation as represented by *PL*, the consumer can buy or choose any combination lying within or on the triangle *OPL*. In other words, all combinations lying on the line *PL* such as *A*, *B*, *C* and lying below the line *PL* such as *D*, *E*, *F* and *G* are alternative combinations open to him, from among which he has to choose any combination. If our consumer chooses combination *A* out of all those open to him in the given price-income situation, it means he reveals his preference for *A* over all other combinations such as *B*, *C*, *D*, *E* and *F* which are rejected by him. As is evident from Fig. 12.1, in his observed chosen combination *A*, the consumer is buying *OM* quantity of commodity *X* and *ON* quantity of commodity *Y*.

It can be inferred from this choice of the consumer that he prefers *A* to other baskets of goods lying on the budget line *AB* or within the budget space. Thus, with the given *price-income situation PL*, when the consumer chooses *A* it is inferred that all other combitions of goods lying within the triangle *OPL* or on the line *PL* which he can afford to buy are revealed to be *inferior* to his chosen combitions *A*. Besides, we can infer more from consumer's observed choice. As it is assumed that a rational consumer prefers more of both the goods to less of them or prefers more of at least one good, the amount of the other good remaining the same, we can infer that all combitions lying in the **rectangular shaded area** drawn above and to the right of chosen combination *A* are superior to *A*. Since in the rectangular shaded area there lie those combinations (baskets) of two goods which contain either more of both the goods or at least more of one good, the amount of the other remaining the same, this means that the consumer would prefer all combitions in the rectangular shaded area to the chosen combination *A*. In other words, all combitions in the shaded area *MAN* are superior to the chosen combination *A* .

As seen above, all other combinations lying in the budget-space *OPL* are attainable or affordable but are rejected in favour of *A* and are therefore revealed to be *inferior* to it. It should be carefully noted that Samuelson's revealed preference theory is based upon the strong form of preference hypothesis. In other words, in revealed preference theory, strong-ordering preference hypothesis has been applied. Strong ordering implies that there is *definite ordering* of various combinations in consumer's scale of preferences and therefore the choice of a combination by a consumer reveals his definite preference for that over all other alternatives open to him. ***Thus, under strong ordering, relation of indifference between various alternative combinations is ruled out.*** When in Fig. 12.1 a consumer chooses a combination *A* out of various alternative combinations open to him, it means he has a definite preference for *A* over all others; the possibility of the chosen combination *A* being indifferent to any other possible combination is ruled out by strong ordering hypothesis.

J. R. Hicks in his "*A Revision of Demand Theory*" does not consider the assumption of strong ordering as satisfactory and instead employs weak ordering hypothesis. Under weak ordering hypothesis (with an additional assumption that the consumer will always prefer a larger amount of a good to a smaller amount of it), the chosen combination A is preferred over all positions that lie within the triangle *OPL* and further that the chosen position *A* will be either preferred to or indfferent to the other positions on the price-income line *PL*. "The difference between the consequnces of strong and weak ordering, so interpreted amounts to no more than this that under strong ordering the chosen position is shown to be preferred to all other positions *in* and *on* the triangle, while under weak ordering it is preferred to all positions *within* the triangle, but may be indifferent to other positions *on* the same boundary as itself."[2]

The revealed preference theory rests upon a basic assumption which has been called the **'*consistency postulate*'**. In fact, the consistency postulate is implied in the strong ordering hypothesis. The consistency postulate can be stated thus : **'*no two observations of choice behaviour are made which provide conflicting evidence to the individual's preference.*"** In other words, consistency postulate asserts that if an individual chooses *A* rather than *B* in one particular instance, then he cannot choose *B* rather than *A* in any other instance when both are available to the consumer. If he chooses *A* rather than *B* in one instance and chooses *B* rather than *A* in another when *A* and *B* are present in both the instances, then he is not behaving consistently. Thus, consistency postulate requires that if once *A* is revealed to be preferred to *B* by an individual, then *B* cannot be revealed to be preferred to *A* by him at any other time when *A* and *B* are present in both the cases. Since comparison here is between the two situations consistency involved in this has been called ' *two term consistency*' by J.R. Hicks[2].

Weak Axiom of Revealed Preference (WARP)

If a person chooses combination *A* rather than combination *B* which he could purchase with the given budget constraint, then it cannot happen that he would choose (i.e. prefer) *B* over *A* in some other situation in which he could have bought A if he so wished. This means his choices or preferences must be consistent. This is called ***revealed preference axiom.*** We illustrate, revealed preference axiom in Figure 12.2. Suppose with the given prices of two goods *X* and *Y* and given his money income to spend on the two goods, *PL* is the budget line facing a consumer. In this budgetary situation *PL*, the consumer chooses *A* when he could have purchased *B* (note that combination *B* would have even cost him less than *A*). Thus, his choice of *A* over *B* means he prefers the combination *A* to the combination *B* of the two goods.

Now suppose that price of good *X* falls, and with some income and price adjustments, budget line changes to *P'L'*. Budget line *P'L'* is flatter than *PL* reflecting relatively lower price of *X* as compared to the budget line *PL*. With this new budget line *P'L'*, if the consumer chooses combination *B* when he can purchase the combination *A* (as *A* lies below the budget line *P'L'* in Fig. 12.2), then the consumer will be inconsistent in his preferences, that is, he will be violating the axiom of revealed preference. Such inconsistent consumer's behaviour is ruled out in revealed preference theory based on strong ordering. This axiom of revealed preference according to which consumer's choices are consistent is also called ' *Weak Axiom of Revealed Preference* or simply WARP. To sum up, according to the weak axiom of revealed preference,

2. J.R. Hicks, *A Revision of Demand Theory* (1956), p. 43.

"if combination A is directly revealed preferred to another combination B, then in any other situation, the combination B cannot be revealed preferred to combination A by the consumer when combination A is also affordable". [3]

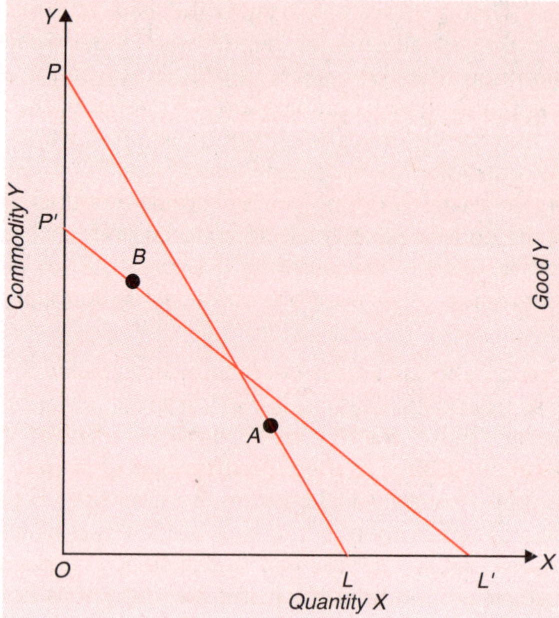

Fig.12.2. *Consumer's Preferences are Inconsistent*

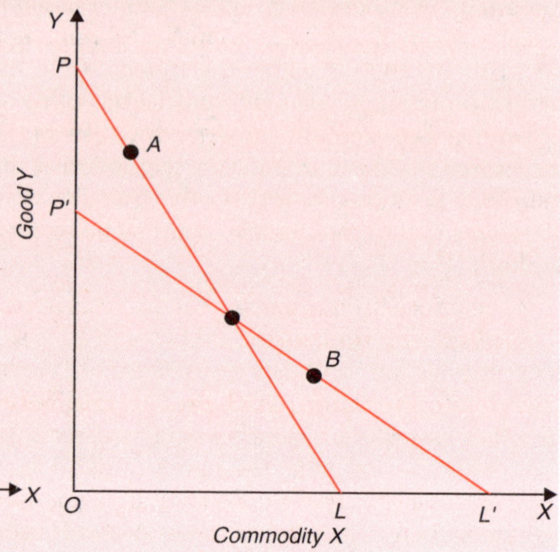

Fig. 12.3. *Consumer's choices satisfy weak axiom of revealed preference*

Now consider Figure 12.3 where to start with a consumer is facing budget line *PL* where he chooses combination *A* of two goods *X* and *Y*. Thus, consumer prefers combination *A* to all other combinations within and on the triangle *OPL*. Now suppose that budget constraint changes to *P'L'* and consumer purchases combination *B* on it. As combination *B* lies outside the budget line *PL* it was not affordable when combination *A* was chosen. Therefore, choice of combination *B* with the budget line *P'L'* is consistent with his earlier choice *A* with the budget constraint *PL* and is in accordance with the weak axiom of revealed preference.

Transitivity Assumption of Revealed Preference

The axiom of revealed preference described above provides us a consistency condition that must be satisfied by a rational consumer who makes an optimum choice. Apart from the axiom of revealed preference, revealed preference theory also assumes ***that revealed preferences are transitive.*** According to this, if an optimising consumer prefers combination *A* to combination *B* of the goods and combination *B* to combination *C* of the goods, then he will also prefer combination *A* to combination *C* of the goods. To put it briefly, assumption of transitivity of preferences requires that if $A > B$ and $B > C$, then $A > C$.

In this way we say that combination *A* is *indirectly* revealed to be preferred to combination *C*. Thus, if a combination *A* is either directly or indirectly revealed preferred to another combination we say that combination *A* is revealed to be preferred to the other combination. Consider Figure 12.4 where with budget constraint *PL*, the consumer chooses *A* and therefore reveals his preference for *A* over combination *B* which he could have purchased as combination

3. Hal Varian, *Intermediate Microeconomics*, 1963, p. 94.

B is affordable in budget constraint *PL*. Now suppose budget constraint facing the consumer changes to *P′L′*, he chooses *B* when he could have purchased *C*. Thus, the consumer prefers *B* to *C*. From the transitivity assumption it follows that the consumer will prefer combination *A* to combination *C*. Thus, combination *A* is indirectly revealed to be preferred to combination *C*. We therefore conclude that the consumer prefers *A* either directly or indirectly to all those combinations of the two goods lying in the shaded regions in Figure 12.4.

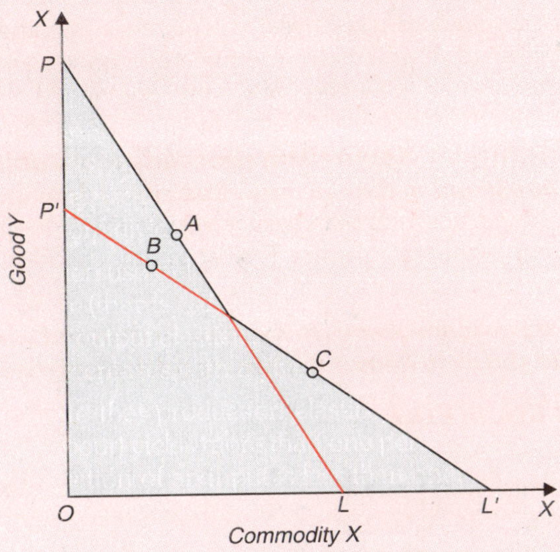

Fig. 12.4. *Revealed preferences are transitive*

It is thus evident from above that concept of revealed preference is a very significant and powerful tool which provides a lot of information about consumer's preferences who behave in an optimising and consistent manner. By merely looking at the consumer's choices in different price-income situations we can get a lot of information about consumer's preferences.

It may be noted that the consistency postulate of revealed preference theory is the counterpart of the utility maximisation assumption in both Marshallian utility theory and Hicks-Allen indifference curve theory. The assumption that the consumer maximises utility or satisfaction is known as rationality assumption. It has been said that a rational consumer will try to maximise utility or satisfaction. Recently, some economists have challenged this assumption. They assert that consumers in actual practice do not maximise utility. The revealed theory has the advantage that its rationality assumption can be easily realised in actual practice. The rationality on the part of the consumer in revealed preference theory only requires that he should behave in a 'consistent' manner. Consistency of choice is a less restrictive assumption than the utility maximisation assumption. This is one of the improvements of Samuelson's theory over the Marshallian cardinal utility and Hicks-Allen indifference curve theories of demand.

It is important to note that Samuelson's revealed preference is not a statistical concept. If it were a statistical concept, then the preference of an individual for a combination A would have been inferred from giving him opportunity to exercise his choice several times in the same circumstances. If the individual from among the various alternative combinations open to him chooses a particular combination more frequently than any other, only then the individual's preference for A would have been statistically revealed. But in Samuelson's revealed preference theory preference is said to be revealed from a *single act of choice*. It is obvious that no single act of choice on the part of the consumer can prove his indifference between the two situations. Unless the individual is given the chance to exercise his choice several times in the given circumstances, he has no way of revealing his indifference between various combinations. Thus, because Samuelson infers preference from a single act of choice the relation of indifference is inadmissible to his theory. Therefore, the rejection of indifference relation by Samuelson follows from his methodology. "The rejection of indifference in Samuelson theory is, therefore, not a matter of convenience but dicated by the requirements of his methodology."[4]

4. Tapas Majumdar, *Measurement of Utility*, p. 82

DERIVING DEMAND THEOREM FROM REVEALED PREFERENCE HYPOTHESIS

Revealed preference hypothesis can be utilised to establish the demand theorem. Samuelson has derived the Marshallian law of demand from his revealed preference hypothesis. Marshallian law of demand, as is well known, states that a rise in the price of a good must, if income and other prices are held constant, results in the reduction of amount demanded of the good, and *vice versa*. In other words, according to Marshall's law of demand, there is inverse relation between price and amount demanded of a good. ***Samuelson proceeds to establish relationship between price and demand by assuming that income elasticity of demand is positive.*** From positive income elasticity, he deduces the Marshallian inverse price-demand relationship. He states the demand theorem what he calls the Fundamental Theorem of Consumption Theory as under :

"Any good (simple or composite) that is known always to increase in demand when money income alone rises must definitely shrink in demand when its price alone rises".

Fundamental Consumption Theorem and Rise in Price

It is clear from the above statement of Fundamental Theorem that positive income elasticity of demand has been made a necessary qualification to the inverse price-demand principle. The geometrical proof of the Fundamental Theorem is illustrated in Fig. 12.5. Let us suppose that the consumer spends his entire income on the two goods *X* and *Y*. Further suppose that his income in terms of good *X* is *OB*, and in terms of good *Y* is *OA*. Now, the price line *AB* represents the price-income situation confronting the consumer. All the combinations of goods *X* and *Y* lying within or on the triangle *OAB* are available to the consumer, from which he can buy any combination. Suppose that the consumer is observed to choose the combination *Q*. This means that *Q* is revealed to be preferred to all other combinations that lie within or on the triangle *OAB*.

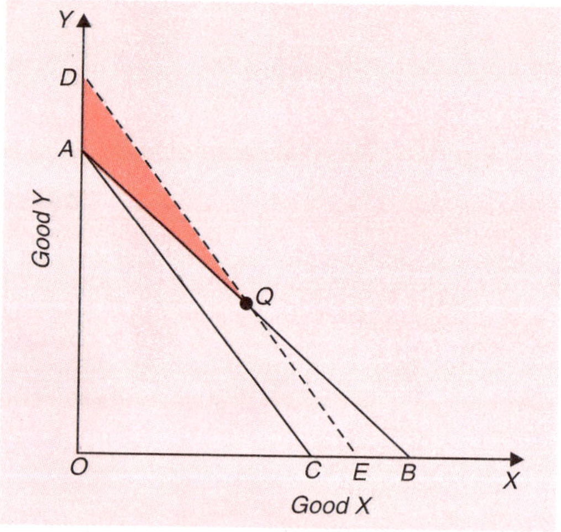

Fig. 12.5. *Deriving Law of Demand through Revealed Preference Hypothesis*

Now, suppose that the price of good *X* rises, his income and price of *Y* remaining unchanged. With the rise in price of *X* the price line shifts to the new position *AC*. The price line *AC* represents new price-income situation. We now want to know what is the effect of this rise in price of good *X* on its quantity demanded, assuming that demand varies directly with income (*i.e.*, income elasticity of demand is positive). It is evident from Fig. 12.5 that combination *Q* is not available to the consumer in price-income situation *AC*. Let us compensate the consumer for the higher price of *X* by granting him extra money so that he can buy the same combination *Q* even at the higher price of *X*. The amount of money which is required to be granted to the consumer so that he could buy the original combination *Q* at the higher price of *X* has been called **Cost-difference** by J. R. Hicks. In Fig.12.5. a line *DE* parallel to *AC* has been drawn so that it passes through *Q*. *DE* represents higher price of *X* and the money income after it has been increased by the cost difference.

Now, the question is which combination will be chosen by the consumer in price-income situation *DE*. The original combination *Q* is available in price-income situation *DE*. It is evident from Figure 12.5, that he will not choose any combination lying below *Q* on the line *DE*. This is because if he chooses any combination below *Q* on the line *DE*, his choice would be inconsistent. All combinations below *Q* on *DE*, that is, all combinations on *QE* could have been bought by the consumer but had been rejected by him in price-income situation *AB* in favour of *Q*. (All points on *QE* were contained in the original choice triangle *OAB*.). Since we are assuming consistency of choice behaviour on the part of the consumer he will not choose, in price-income situation *DE*, any combination below *Q* on *QE* in preference to *Q* when *Q* is available in the new situation. It follows, therefore, that in the price-income situation *DE* the consumer will either choose the original combination *Q* or any other combination on *QD* portion of *DE* or any combination within the shaded area *QDA*. (It should be noted that choice of any other combination on *QD* or within the shaded area *QDA* in preference to *Q* by the consumer will not be inconsistent since combinations lying above *Q* on *QD* or within the shaded region *QDA* were not available in price-income situation *AB*.)

In price-income situation *DE* if the consumer chooses the original combination *Q*, it means he will be buying the same amount of goods *X* and *Y* as before, and if he chooses any combination above *Q* on *QD* or within the shaded area *QDA*, it means that he will be buying less amount of commodity *X* and greater amount of *Y* than before. Thus, even after sufficient extra income has been granted to the consumer to compensate him for the rise in price of good *X*, he purchases either the *same* or the *smaller* quantity of *X* at the higher price. Now, if the extra money granted to him is *withdrawn*, he will definitely buy the smaller amount of *X* at the higher price, if the demand for good *X* is known always to fall with the decrease in income (that is, if income elasticity of demand for *X* is positive). In other words, when the price of good *X* rises and no extra money is granted to the consumer so that he faces price-income situation *AC*, he will purchase less amount of good *X* than at *Q*. Thus assuming a positive income-elasticity of demand, the inverse price-demand relationship is established through revealed preference hypothesis so far as rise in price is concerned.

Proving Consumption Theorem in Case of Fall in Price

That the inverse price-demand relationship holds good in case of a fall in price also is demonstrated in Fig.12.6. Let us suppose that *AB* represents original price income situation and further that the consumer reveals his preference for *Q* over all other combinations within or on the triangle *OAB*. Now, suppose that price of good *X* falls so that the price line shifts to the right to the position *AC′*. Let us take away some amount of money from the consumer so that he is left with just sufficient amount of money which enables him to purchase the original combination *Q* at the lower price of good *X*. Thus, in Figure.12.6, a line *DE* is drawn parallel to *AC* so that it passes through *Q*. Price line *DE* represents lower price of *X* as given by *AC′* and the money income after it has been reduced by the cost difference. It is obvious that in price-income situation *DE*, the consumer cannot choose any combination above *Q* on *QD*, since all such combinations were available to him in the original price-income situation *AB* and were rejected by him in favour of *Q*. The consumer will, therefore, choose either *Q* or any other combination on *QE* or from within the shaded region *QEB*. In price-income situation *DE*, his choice of *Q* means that he buys the same quantity of goods *X* and *Y* as in original price-income situation *AB*, and his choice of any other combination on *QE* or from ***within the shaded region QEB*** means that he buys larger amount of good *X* and smaller amount of good *Y* than in the original price-income situation *AB*. Thus, even after consumer's income has been reduced, he buys either the same quantity of *X* or more at the lower price. And if we give him back the amount of money taken away from him so that he confronts price-income situation AC' he will definitely buy more of X at the lower price, provided that his demand for X rises with the rise in income (*i.e.* his income elasticity of demand for good X is positive).

The two demonstrations given above together prove the fundamental theorem of consumption theory, according to which any good whose demand varies directly with income must definitely shrink in demand when its price rises and expands in demand when its price falls. It may be noted that Samuelson's theory involves two implicit assumptions which have not been explicitly stated. In the first place the consumer is always shown to choose a combination on the budget line. In other words, he is never shown to choose a combination from within the triangle. This is based upon the assumption that a **consumer always prefers a larger collection of goods to a smaller one.** Secondly, another implicit assumption involved in Samuelson's theory is that the consumer is shown to choose only one combination of goods in every price-income situation. With these two implicit assumptions the inverse price-demand relationship is deduced by Samuelson by making explicit assumptions of consistency of choice and a positive income- elasticity of demand.

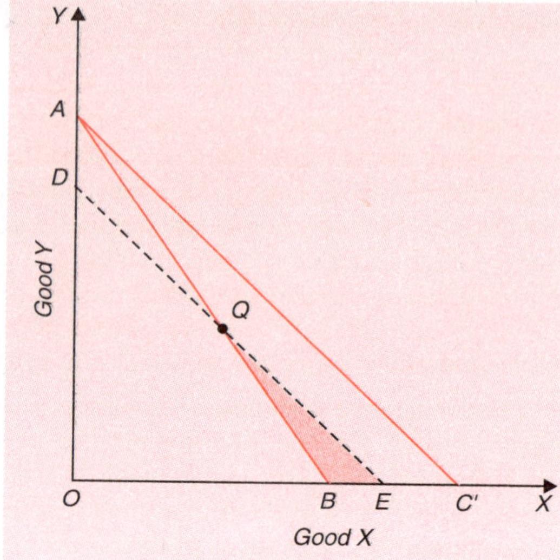

Fig. 12.6. *Proof of Consumption Theorem through Revealed Preference Approach*

Breaking up Price Effect into Substitution Effect and Income Effect

Having now explained the derivation of law of demand from revealed preference approach we are now in a position to show how in the revealed preference approach price effect can be broken up into substitution and income effects. We will explain this by considering the case of fall in price of a commodity. Now consider Figure 12.7 where, to begin with, price income situtation faced by a consumer is given by the budget line AB. With price income situation represented by the budget line AB, suppose the consumer chooses combination Q and buys OM quantity of commodity X.

Now, suppose price of commodity X falls and as a result budget line shifts to the new position AC. Now, income of the consumer is reduced so much that the new budget line DE passes through the original chosen combination Q. That is, income is reduced equal to the cost difference so that gain in real income caused by the fall in price of commodity X is cancelled out. As seen above, with the new budget line DE, to be consistent in his behaviour the consumer can either choose the original combination Q or any combination lying on the segment QE of the budget line DE or from within the shaded area QEB. If he chooses again the original combination Q, the Slutsky substitution effect will be zero. However, suppose that the consumer actually chooses combination S on the segment QE of the new budget line DE.

Now, choice of the combination S shows that there will be substitution effect due to which the consumer will buy MN more of good X. Note that subsitution effect is negative in the sense that the relative *fall* in price of good X has led to the *increase in quantity demanded* of X, that is, change in quantity demanded *is in opposite direction* to the change in price. It should be noted that choice of combination S on segment QE in preference to combination Q of the budget line DE is not inconsistent because combinations on QE segment and within the shaded area QEB were not available before when combination Q was earlier chosen in price-income situation *AB*. Thus, with the new budget line *DE* after consumer's income has been adjusted to cancel out the gain in real income resulting from a relative fall in price of *X*, the consumer chooses either *Q* (when substitution effect is zero or a combination such as *S* on segment *QE* when substitution effect leads to the increase in quantity demanded of good *X* by *MN*. This is generally known as **Slutsky theorem which states that if income effect is ignored substitution effect will lead to the increase in quantity demanded of the good whose price has fallen.** *Therefore, according to Slutsky theorem, due to the negative substitution effect, the Marshallian law of demand describing inverse relationship between quantity demanded and price of a good will hold good, that is, due to substitution effect alone demand curve slopes downward.*

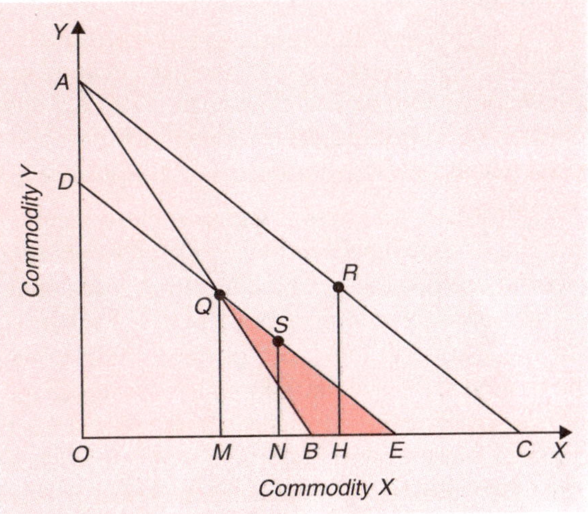

Fig. 12.7. *Breaking up Price Effect into Substitution and Income Effects*

Now, if the consumer chooses the combination *S* on the line segment *QE* of budget line *DE*, it means that he buys *MN* more due to the substitution effect. Thus he prefers combination *S* to combination *Q*. In other words, his choice of *S* instead of *Q* reveals that he will be *better off* at *S* as compared to *Q*. Now, if money income withdrawn from him is restored to him so that he is faced with the budget line *AC*. If income effect is positive, he will choose a combination, say *R*, on the budget line *AC* to the right of point *S* indicating that as a result of income effect he buys *NH* more of the commodity *X*. Thus quantity demanded of commodity *X* increases by *MN* as a result of substitution effect and by *NH* as a result of income effect. This proves the law of demand stating inverse relationship between price and quantity demanded.

On budget line *DE*, if the consumer chooses combination *Q* and consequently substitution effect is zero, the whole increase in quantity demanded *MH* as a result of decline in price of good *X* will be due to positive income effect. However, it is more likely that the substitution effect will lead to the choice by a consumer a combination such as *S* that lies to the right of *Q* on the line segment *QE* and will therefore cause increase in quantity demanded. This substitution effect is reinforced by the positive income effect and as result we get a downward-sloping demand curve.

It needs to be emphasised that **in revealed preference theory it is not possible to locate exact positions of points S and R obtained as a result of substitution effect and income effect respectively.** It will be recalled that with indifference curve analysis we could obtain precise points to which a consumer moves as a result of substitution and income effects and as we saw in the previous chapter that these were the points of tangency of indifference curves with the relevant budget lines. As explained above, revealed preference theory is based on the assumption that all points on or below the budget line are *strongly ordered* and relation of indifference of a consumer between some combinations of goods is therefore ruled out. In revealed preference theory, choice of a consumer reveals his preference for a chosen position; it cannot reveal indifference of the consumer between combinations. Therefore, in revealed preference theory we can only say about the *direction* of substitution effect through logical ordering and cannot measure the exact size of it, nor we can measure the exact amount of income effect of the change in price.

Besides, the substitution effect obtained through variation in income through cost difference method, does not represent *pure* substitution effect in the Hicksian sense in which the consumer's satisfaction remains constant. In substitution effect obtained by the revealed preference theory through Slutskian method of cost difference, the consumer moves from point *Q* to point *S* on budget line *DE*. His choice of *S* on budget line *DE* instead of *Q* under the influence of substitution effect shows that he prefers *S* to *Q*. That is, he is ***better off*** in position *S* as compared to the position *Q*. Therefore, it is maintained by some economists that the substitution effect obtained in revealed preference theory is not a pure one and contains also some income effect.[5]

However, the present author is of the view that the two types of substitution effect (Hicksian and the one obtained in revealed preference theory) differ with regard to the *concept of real income* used by them. In indifference curve analysis the term real income is used in the sense of level of satisfaction obtained by the consumer, whereas in revealed preference theory real income is used in the sense of purchasing power. Thus, Hicksian substitution effect involves the change in the quantity demanded of a good when ***its relative price alone changes, level of his satisfaction remaining the same.*** On the other hand, ***revealed preference theory*** considers substitution effect as the result of change in relative price of a good on its quantity demanded, ***consumer's purchasing power remaining the same.*** In Fig.12.7. when we obtain budget line *DE* after reduction in income by the cost difference so that it passes through the original combination *Q* chosen by the consumer before the fall in price. This implies that with budget line *DE*, he can buy, if he so desires, the original combination *Q*, that is, the gain in purchasing power or real income caused by fall in price of *X* has been cancelled out by the reduction in his money income.

CRITICAL APPRAISAL OF REVEALED PREFERENCE THEORY

Samuelson's revealed preference theory has gained some advantages over the Marshallian cardinal utility theory and Hicks-Allen indifference curve theory of demand. It is the first to apply behaviouristic method to derive demand theorem from observed consumer's behaviour. In contrast, both the earlier theories, namely, Marshallian utility analysis and Hicks-Allen indifference curve theory were psychological and introspective explanations of consumer's behaviour. Both these earlier theories have been considered to be unsatisfactory by Samuelson who remarks, "For just as we do not claim to know by introspection the behavior of utility, many will argue we cannot know the behaviour of ratio of marginal utilities or of indifference directions."[6] He further says, "The introduction and meaning of the marginal rate of substitution as an entity independent of any psychological, introspective implications would be, to say the least, ambiguous and would seem an artificial convention in the explanation of price behaviour."[7] Samuelson thinks that his revealed preference theory casts away the last vestiges of the psychological analysis in the explanation of consumer's behaviour.

It has been claimed that behaviouristic method is more scientific than the introspective method. In fact, the behaviouristic method has been called 'the scientific method'. Now, the question is whether it is the behaviouristic approach or the psychological approach which is more correct to explain consumer's demand. Two opinions are held in this regard. Prof. Samuelson and others of his way of thinking contend that the behaviouristic method is the only valid method of explaining consumer's demand. On other hand, Knight who beongs to the philosophical-psychological school of thought has called the scientific (behaviouristic)

---

5. See Stonier and Hague, *A Textbook of Economic Theory*, Orient Longman, 5th edition.
6. Samuelson. A Note on the Pure Theory of Consumer's Behaviour, *Economica*, Feb. 1938, p. 61.
7. *Ibid*, p. 62

approach as the 'recourse' of those who worship the occam's razor.[8]

We are of the opinion that no prior grounds for choosing between behaviourist and introspective methods can be offered which would be acceptable irrespective of personal inclinations. Commenting on the behaviourist-ordinalist controversy, Tapas Majumdar says, ***"Behaviourism certainly has great advantages of treading only on observed ground; it cannot go wrong."*** But whether it goes far enough is the question. It may also be claimed for the method of introspection that operationally it can get all the results which are obtained by the alternative method, and it presumes to go further, ***it not only states, but also explains its theorems."***[9] We therefore conclude that which of the two methods is better and more staisfactory depends upon one's personal philosophical inclinations. However, behaviourist method has recently gained wide support from the economists and has become very popular.

Samuelson's revealed preference theory also marks an advance over the earlier theories of demand by giving up the dubious assumptions underlying them. Both the Marshallian utility analysis and Hicks-Allen indifference curve theory were based upon the utility-maximisation postulate. In these theories, rational behaviour on the part of consumer is interpreted as the attempt on his part to maximise utility or satisfaction. But this utility-maximising postulate has been objected to on the ground that it is very severe and is therefore difficult of realisation in actual practice. Samuelson has given up utility maxmisation assumption and has instead employed consistency postulate to derive the demand theorem. Now, his assumption of consistency of choice in the consumer's behavior is much less severe and conforms more to the real world behavior of the consumers.

Samuelson has likewise abandoned the assumption of continuity. The indifference curve theory involved the assumption of continuity. Indifference curves are continuous curves in which lie all conceivable combinations, whether they are actually available in the market or not. It may happen under indifference curve analysis that the budget line comes to be tangent to an indifference curve on the point which represents a combination which is not actually available. Thus, continuity assumption is quite unrealistic. The real economic world exhibits discontinuity. Now, the continuity assumption is not involved in the revealed preference theory. Of course, in the graphic explanation of the revealed preference theory a continuous price-income line, that is, a budget line is drawn within or on which the consumer has to choose any combination. But since the theory is based upon the actual observed choice of the consumer, and the consumer will choose a combination among all those actually available in the given price-income situation the continuity is not involved in the revealed preference theory.

The concept of reveal preference is a powerful tool which can provide a significant information about consumer's preferences from which we can derive law of demand or downward-sloping demand curve. Revealed preference theory does this without assuming that a consumer possesses complete information about his preferences and indifferences. In indifference curve analysis it is supposed that consumers have complete and consistent scale of preferences reflected in a set of indifference curves. His purchases of goods are in accordance with his scale of preferences. It is as if consumers were carrying complete indifference maps in their mind and purchasing goods accordingly. Therefore, it was considered better to derive demand theorem by observing consumer's behaviour in making actual choices. Most economists now-a-days believe that it is unrealistic to assume that a consumers have complete knowledge of their scale of preferences depicted in a set of indifference curves. The merit of revealed preference theory is that it has made possible to derive law of demand (*i.e.* downward-sloping

8. *Introduction to Carl Menger's Principles of Economics*, p. 20.
9. Tapas Majumdar, *Measurement of Utility* (Italics Supplied).

demand curve) on the basis of revealed preference without using indifference curves and associated restrictive assumptions. Further, it has enabled us to divide the price effect into its two component parts, namely, substitution and income effects through cost difference method and axiom of revealed preference. Cost difference method requires only market data regarding changes in price and quantities purchased of goods in different market situations. Cost difference (ΔC) can be simply measured by change in price (ΔP) multiplied by the quantity initially purchased by him. Thus,

$$\Delta C = \Delta P_x Q_x$$

where ΔC stands for the cost difference, ΔP_x stands for the change in price of good X, Q_x is the quantity purchased by the consumer before the change in price of the good X.

Further, with revealed preference theory we can even establish the *existence* of indifference curves and their important property of *convexity*. However, it is noteworthy that indifference curves are not required for deriving law of demand or downward-sloping demand curve. Indifference curve analysis requires less information than Marshall's cardinal utility theory. But it still requires a lot of information on the part of a consumer since indifference curve analysis requires him to be able to rank consistently all possible combinations of goods. On the other hand, in Samuelson's revealed preference theory of demand the consumer does not require to rank his preferences on the basis of his introspection. It is based on the preferences revealed by his purchases or choices in the different market situations and on the axiom of revealed preference. If consumer's preferences and tastes do not change, revealed preference theory enables us to derive demand theorem just from observation of his market behaviour, that is, what purchases or choices he makes in different market situations. It is however assumed that his preference pattern or tastes do not change. As said above, we can even construct indifference curves from consumer's revealed preferences even though they are not required for establishing law of demand.

A Critique of Revealed Preference Theory

Although Samuelson's revealed preference approach has made some important improvements upon the earlier theories of demand but it is not free from all flaws. Various criticisms have been levelled against it.

First, Samuelson does not admit the possibility of indifference in consumer's behaviour. As has been explained above, the rejection of indifference by Samuelson follows from his strong ordering preference hypothesis. J.R. Hicks in his later work "*A Revision of Demand Theory*" does not consider the assumtion of strong ordering as satisfactory and instead employs weak ordering from of preference hypothesis. Whereas under strong ordering, the chosen combination is shown to be preferred to all other combinations within and *on* the triangle, under weak ordering the chosen combination is preferred to all positions *within* the triangle but ***may be either preferred to or indifferent to other combinations on*** the same triangle (*i.e.* on the budget line).

Further, in Samuelson's theory, preference is considered to be revealed from a single act of choice. It has been pointed out that if preference is to be judged from a large number of observations, then the possibility of indifference also emerges. Thus, an individual reveals preference for *A* over *B* if he chooses *A* rather than ***B more frequently*** than he chooses B rather than *A* over a given number of observations. Now, we can say that an individual is indifferent between the two situations *A* and *B* if a definite preference for either does not emerge from a sufficiently large number of observations. Thus only because Samuelson regards preference to be revealed from a single act of choice that indifference relation is methodologically inadmissible to his theory. The possibility of indifference relation clearly emerges if the existence of preference or otherwise is to be judged from a sufficiently large number of observations.

Furthermore, if we assume that an ***individual is able to compare his ends***, which is a very valid assumption to be made about the individual's behaviour, then the possibility of indifference or in other words, remaining at the same level of satisfaction by sacrificing some amount of one good for a certain amount of another good will emerge clearly. Thus, commenting on the Samuelson's revealed preference theory from 'welfare' point of view Tapas Majumdar remarks : "It may be remembered that in all forms of welfare theory, indeed in any integral view of human activity, we have to assume that the individual can always compare his ends. If this axiom is not granted, the whole of welfare economics falls to the ground. And if this axiom is granted, then the idea of remaining on the same level of welfare while sacrificing something of one commodity for something else of another will emerge automatically."[10]

Again, Armstrong has propounded the view that there are points of indifference on every side of a given chosen point. Thus, according to his view, the collection of goods actually selected by the consumer is one of the few between which the consumer is inidfferent. If this contention of Armstrong is granted, then the proof which Samuelson's theory offers to establish the Fundamental Theorem of Consumption Theory breaks down. This is illustrated in Fig. 12.8. In price-income situation *AB*, the consumer chooses the combination *Q*. According to Armstrong's notion, points around *Q* (within the circle) such as *S*, *T* etc. would be indifferent to *Q*. Suppose that the price of good *X* rises so that the price-income situation is now *AC*. If an extra grant of money is given to the consumer so that he can buy the same combination *Q*, the price-income situation is *DE*. Now, in price-income situation *DE*, the consumer can pick up a point like *S* below *Q* on *QE*.

Thus, choice of *S* instead of *Q*, or *T* (or any other point in the circle) is not inconsistent to his previous choice because he was indifferent between points such as *Q*, *T*, *S* etc. But the choice of *S* in price income situation *DE* means that the consumer buys more of *X* now when its price is higher (since *DE* is parallel to *AC*, it represents the higher price of *X* as represented by *AC*). It follows, therefore, that if Armstrong's notion about points of indifference around the chosen point is granted, Samuelson's proof that the demand for a good shrinks when its price rises breaks down.

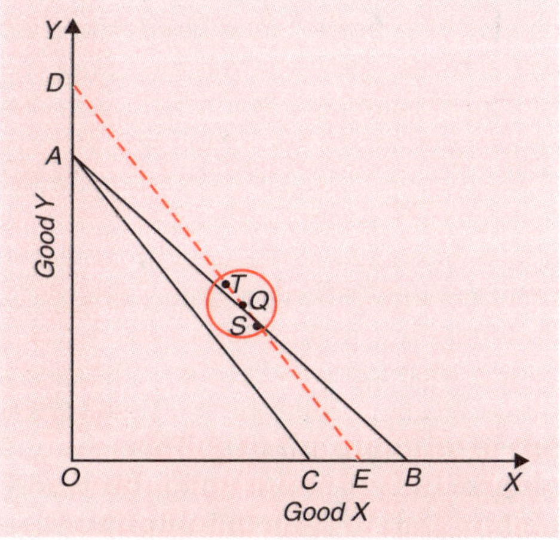

Fig. 12.8. *Armstrong's Notion of Indifference and Samuelson's consumption TheoremConsumption Theorem*

Further, it has been argued that Samuelson, because of his ruling out the relation of indifference, does not recognise or admit the substitution effect which is the operational consequence of the non-observable indifference hypothesis. It has been pointed out that Samuelson's revealed preference theory is based upon observed consumer's behaviour and on the plane of observation substitution effect cannot be distinguished from income effect. Since response of demand to a change in price is a composite of income and substitution effects, it is concluded, that Samuelson's theory offers a partial explanation of change in demand as a result of change in price. But to the present author, it seems that this criticism of Samuelson's theory is misplaced. In his article ***"Consumption Theorems in Terms of Over Compensation,'***[11] Samuelson draws clear distinction between income effect and

10. Tapas Majumdar, *Measurement of Utility*, p. 90
11. See *Economica*, February 1953, p. 2.

what he calls over-compensation effect as a result of change in price. His over-compensation effect is similar to Slutsky's substitution effect which involves the movement of the consumer from one level of satisfaction to another (that is, from one indifference curve to another). Therefore, what Samuelson rejects is Hicksian type substitution effect which permits only movement along the same indifference curve (that is, level of satisfaction remains the same). And Samuelson's rejection of Hicksian type substitution effect follows from his rejection of the relation of indifference in consumer's behaviour.

Since Samuelson proves his demand theorem on the basis of positive income elasticity of demand, it cannot enunciate the demand theorem when income effect or income elasticity is negative. Thus, Samuelson is able to enunciate the demand theorem in the case in which, in terms of Hicksian indifference curve theory, substitution effect has been reinforced by positive income effect of the price change. When the income elasticity is negative, Samuelson's revealed preference theory is unable to establish the demand theorem. In other words, given negative income elasticity of demand, we cannot know on the basis of revealed preference theory as to what will be the direction of change in demand as a result of change in price. Thus, Samuelson's revealed preference theory cannot enunciate the demand theorem when (*i*) the income elasticity is negative and the negative income effect is smaller than the substitution effect; and (*ii*) the income elasticity is negative and the negative income effect is greater than the substitution effect.

From above it follows that Samuelson's theory cannot account for Giffen's Paradox. The case of Giffen goods occurs when the income effect is negative and this negative income effect is so powerful that it outweighs the substitution effect. In case of Giffen goods, demand varies directly with price. Since he assumes income elasticity to be positive in his establishment of demand theorem, his theory cannot include the Giffen-good case. Samuelson denies the validity of Giffen goods in which case demand seems to vary directly with price. He thus says, "but the phenomenon of Giffen's Paradox reminds us that the Marshallian proposition is not a true theorem and it is rather to a theory's credit than discredit if it refuses to enunciate a false theorem."[12] According to Samuelson, only valid theorem in demand theory is the one that establishes inverse relationship between price and demand. Against this we may, however, point out that Giffen good may not really exist in the world, but it is theoretically conceivable. Its theoretical possibility is clear when negative income effect of a change in price of an inferior good outweighs the substitution effect with the result that demand changes in the same direction as the price. Thus Hicks-Allen theorem of demand is more general than the Samuelson's Fundamental Theorem of Consumption since the former includes Giffen good case, while the latter does not. We thus conclude that though Samuelson makes improvement over the Hicks-Allen indifference curves theory of demand in respect of methodology adopted (that is, its behaviouristic method is superior to Hicks-Allen introspective method) but in respect of the content of the demand theorem enunciated by it, it is a few steps backward than the Hicks-Allen demand theorem.

In the end, we may emphasize the point that superiority of Samuelson's theory lies in his applying scientific or behaviouristic method to the consumer's demand and his enunciation of preference hypothesis.

DERIVATION OF INDIFFERENCE CURVES THROUGH REVEALED PREFERENCE APPROACH

In revealed preference theory, we establish law of demand without deriving and using indifference curves of consumers. However, revealed preference approach provides us an

12. 'Consumption Theorems in Terms of Over-compensation', *Economica*, February 1953, p. 2.

alternative method to the Hicksian introspective method of deriving indifference curves of a consumer. In the Hicksian method, indifference curves are obtained by asking the consumer to express his preference among all possible combinations or baskets of two commodities. However it has been found that consumers are unable to provide reliable answers to direct questions about their preferences between various baskets or combinations of goods. Further, in the Hicksian analysis some stringent assumptions are made about consumer for deriving indifference curves. For instance, in the Hicksian method of deriving indifference curves it is assumed that consumer is able to give ranking to or order consistently all possible combinations of two commodities. This implies that consumer has a complete knowledge of his precise preferences between various baskets of goods. This is indeed a very strong assumption about a consumer.

On the other hand, in revealed preference approach it is not needed to assume that consumer can rank or order his preferences or to provide other information about his tastes and likings. It is worth noting that in Samuelson's revealed preference approach, no assumptions about consumer's preferences or tastes are made. In fact, in revealed preference approach information about consumer's preferences is inferred from observing his actual behaviour or choice of goods in the market. Thus, in revealed preference approach we can derive indifference curves of consumers from observing his behaviour in the market or his actual choice of commodities in the market. For deriving indifference curves by means of revealed preference hypothesis we make the following assumptions :

1. Choices of a consumer are *consistent*. This implies that if a consumer is once observed to prefer combination *A* to combination *B*, then he will never prefer *B* to *A*.
2. Consumer's tastes and preferences remain constant over a time period his behaviour is being observed.
3. Consumer's preferences are *transitive*. This means that if a consumer prefers basket *A* to basket *B*, basket *B* to basket *C*, then he will prefer *A* to *C*.
4. A consumer behaves *rationally* in Pareto sense, that is, *he prefers more of a good to a less of* it.

In the procedure to derive indifference curves with revealed preference approach we make repeated experiments by varying prices of goods and observe consumer's choices. It is assumed that consumer's chosen combination of goods is preferred by him over all other alternative combinations which he could afford to buy. Thus, the combinations of goods not chosen, would be either those which are inferior (in terms of ranking or preferences) or those which lie outside the budget space. Now, consider Figure 12.9 where *AB* is the initial budget line with a given income and prices of the two goods. Suppose it is observed that the consumer chooses combination *R*. It can be inferred from this behaviour or choice of the consumer that he prefers *R* to other baskets of goods lying on the budget line *AB* or within the budget space. Thus, with the given price-income situation *AB*, when the consumer chooses *R* it is inferred that all other combinations of goods which he can afford to buy are revealed to be inferior to his chosen combination *R*.

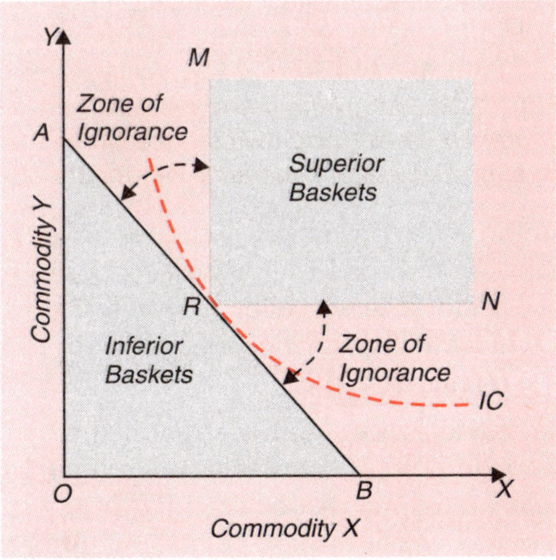

Fig. 12.9. *Derivation of Indifference curve through Revealed Preference Approach*

Besides, we can infer more from consumer's observed choice. As it is assumed that a rational consumer prefers more of both the goods to less of them or prefers more of at least one good, the amount of the other good remaining the same, we can infer that all combinations lying in the ***rectangular shaded area*** drawn above and to the right of chosen combination *R* are superior to *R* since in the rectangular shaded area there lie those combinations (baskets) which contain either more of both the goods or at least more of one good, the amount of the other remaining the same. This means that the consumer would prefer all combinations in the rectangular shaded area to the chosen combination *R*. In other words, all combinations in the shaded area *MRN* are superior to the chosen combination *R* and therefore cannot lie on an indifference curve (which represent baskets of goods yielding the same level of satisfaction) passing through the chosen combination *R*.

As seen above, all other combinations lying in the budget-space *OAB* in Fig. 12.9 are attainable or affordable but are rejected in favour of *R* and are therefore revealed to be *inferior* to *R*. We now have some information about the location of indifference curve passing through the chosen combination *R* and other combinations of goods yielding equal satisfaction as combination *R*. This indifference curve passing through *R* will lie somewhere in between the budget line AB and the shaded area *MRN* drawn directly above and to the right of point *R*. The region in between the budget line *AB* and the shaded area *MRN* is known as *zone of ignorance* within which an indifference curve can possibly lie. To find the exact location of the indifference curve in the zone of ignorance, we can narrow down this zone of ignorance by making changes in prices of the goods and then observing consumer's choice. This is illustrated in Figure 12.10 where initially budget line is *AB* and consumer chooses point *R*. As explained above, all combinations lying above and to the right of point *R* will be preferred to the chosen combination. And all other combinations lying on the budget line *AB* and to the left of it are shown to be inferior to *R* since the consumer chooses *R* when they are affordable. In order to reduce the zone of ignorance let us assume that price of *X* falls so that the new budget line is *CD*. The consumer will not choose any combination to the left of *T* on the budget line *CD* because such a choice would be inconsistent as combinations on *CD* to the left of *T* being below the initial budget line *AB* are inferior to *T*. Therefore, the consumer will choose either *T* or any point to the right of *T* on the segment *TD*. Suppose the consumer actually chooses *T* on the budget line *CD*. Using the postulate of transitive preference we have : *R* is preferred to *T* in the initial budget situation, *T* is preferred to the combinations in shaded area *(TBD)* in the new budget situation. Hence, *R* is preferred to the combinations in the shaded area *(TBD)*.

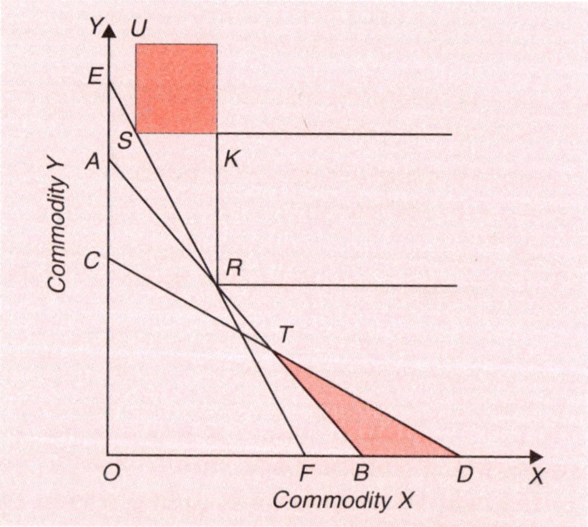

Fig. 12.10. *Narrowing down the Zone of Ignorance for Deriving Indifference Curve through Revealed Preference Approach*

It follows from above that combinations in the shaded area *TBD are* revealed to be inferior to point *R* and therefore indifference curve through point *R* cannot go to this area. In this way from the lower zone of ignorance we have eliminated the shaded area *(TBD)* where the indifference curve through *R* cannot be located. In the similar fashion by making further experiments of reducing price of good *X and* observing consumer's choice in the new situation we can eliminate more area where the indifference curve through *R* cannot possibly go till we find in the lower ignorance zone the exact location of the indifference curve through point *R*.

Likewise, we make experiments for the points (or baskets of goods) lying above and to the left of point *R (i.e.* in the upper zone of ignorance). For this, to begin with, we draw a new budget line *EF* which passes through the original chosen point *R* on the initial budget line *AB*. On the new budget line *EF*, the consumer will either choose *R* or a point such as *S* to the left of *R*. Suppose the consumer actually chooses combination *S* and thus reveals his preference for *S* to the combination *R*. Using Pareto's rational assumption that a person prefers more to less of a good, all the baskets (combinations) of goods in the shaded area *USK* would be preferred to the basket *S* since the baskets of goods lying in this shaded area as compared to *S* contain either more of both the goods or more of one good, the amount of the other remaining the same. We now have

Baskets in *(USK)* are preferred to *S*

Basket *S* is preferred to the basket *R*

Hence, by transitivity, baskets in *(USK)* are preferred to *R*.

Thus, we have been able to rank combinations in *(USK)* as preferred to *R* and therefore indifference curve through *R* cannot pass through the shaded area *(USK)*. In this way we eliminate the area *(USK)* from the upper zone of ignorance. We can continue making more such experiments for eliminating more areas and narrowing down the zone of ignorance till we find the exact position of the indifference curve through *R*. Hence revealed preference hypothesis enables us to derive indifference curve from the actual choice and behaviour of the consumer in different market situations.

Convexity of Indifference Curve and Revealed Preference Approach

In the Hicksian ordinal utility analysis we prove the convexity of a typical indifference curve on the basis of diminishing marginal rate of substitution. The importance of revealed preference approach also lies in that it enables us to establish the convexity of indifference curve without involving the diminishing marginal rate of substitution. This is shown in Figure 12.11 where we have drawn a budget line *AB* on which the consumer chooses basket *R*. As seen above, all baskets of goods on the budget line *AB* or below it are revealed to be inferior to *R* and all those baskets in the area *(MRN)* are revealed to be superior to the basket *R*. Further, as explained above, the indifference curve through *R* must lie somewhere in the zone of ignorance. Now, the indifference curve cannot be straight line *AB* since all other baskets of goods, lying on the line *AB* are revealed to be inferior to the basket *R* when this *R* is chosen and therefore the consumer cannot be indifferent between *R* and any of them. The indifference curve cannot be a curve such as *LK* cutting the budget line *AB* at *R* since this would imply the point on *LK* below *R* as being indifferent with *R* while the consumer has already revealed is preference for *R* over them when he chose *R*. Further, points on *RK*, as explained above, are superior to *R* and cannot therefore lie on an indifference curve passing through *R*. The

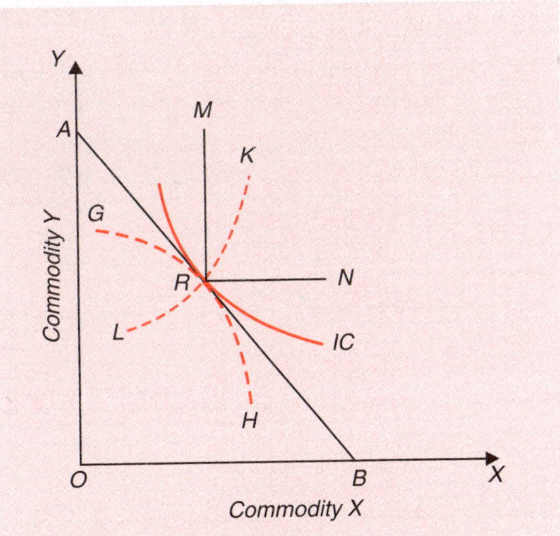

Fig. 12.11. *Proving Convexity of Indifference Curve through Revealed Preference Approach*

indifference curve also cannot be concave such as *GH* through *R* because all points on it have been ranked inferior to *R* when choice of *R* is made by the consumer (Note that all other points on *GH* contain less of the goods as compared to *R*). Thus with the revealed preference hypothesis we reach the conclusion that only possible shape of the indifference curve is its being convex to the origin such is the curve *IC* drawn in Figure 10.11.

QUESTIONS FOR REVIEW

1. What is meant by 'revealed preference hypothesis' ? Explain Samuelson's revealed preference theory of demand based on it.
2. Carefully state the assumptions of the revealed preference theory of demand. Explain how law of demand is derived from these assumptions.
3. Define substitution effect. ***Substitution effect is always negative.*** How can you prove it with revealed preference approach to demand theory ?
4. Distinguish between strong-ordering and weak ordering forms of preference hypothesis.
5. What is Slutsky theorem? How will you establish it with the help of revealed preference approach to demand analysis ?
6. Explain how price effect is broken up into income effect and substitution effect with the aid of revealed preference theory of demand.
7. The price of a good increases. We know that the substitution effect is always negative. Does it follow that the income and substitution effects of the price rise always work in the same direction if the income elasticity of demand for the good is negative? Will the demand curve be downward sloping? Explain.
8. Show with the help of a diagram that the substitution effect of a fall in price of a commodity will make a consumer either consume the same quantity or more but not less of it.
9. (*a*) State Samuelson's "Weak Axiom of Revealed Preference" (WARP)

   (*b*) Consider two commodities, apples and oranges. Initially when both apples and oranges cost Re. 1 per unit each, a consumer buys 4 apples and 6 oranges. When the price of apples rises to Rs. 2 per unit and that of oranges falls to Rs. 0.50 per unit, she buys 8 apples and 3 oranges. Does she violate WARP ?
10. Revealed preference theory makes a major advancement in the study of consumer's behaviour. Discuss.
11. What are indifference curves ? Explain how indifference curves can be derived using revealed preference approach. State clearly the assumptions made in this regard.
12. What is the significance of the convexity of indifference curves? Prove the convexity of indifference curves using the revealed preference approach.

CHAPTER

13

Hicks' Logical Ordering Theory of Demand

Need For Revision of Demand Theory

Prof. Hicks brought out a book[1] in 1956 in which he revised his demand theory which he presented in his earlier work *Value and Capital.* Now, the question that arises at the very outset is what prompted Professor Hicks to undertake the revision of his earlier demand theory? Among the chief reasons for undertaking the revision are the emergence of Samuelson's "Revealed Preference Approach", the rise of econometrics, the appearance of mathematical theories of strong and weak orderings, and the discovery of a more closely reasoned derivation of demand from a few simple propositions of logic.

Hicks was deeply influenced by the revealed preference hypothesis and the logic of strong ordering used by Samuelson and his followers (Arrow, Little and Houthaker) to derive theory of demand. It may, however, by pointed out that though Hicks' revision of demand theory was greatly influenced by the works of Samuelson and his followers, he was nevertheless sceptical about the 'revealed preference' approach. He thus remarks, "All this I owe to Samuelson and the Samuelsonians, though I can hardly count myself of their member since I retain a considerable scepticism about the Revealed Preference Approach."[2]

Prof. Hicks in his revision of demand theory emphasises econometric approach to the theory of demand. He holds that the demand theory which is useful for econometric purposes is definitely superior to the one which does not serve such purposes. "There can be no doubt that econometrics is now a major form of economic research; a theory which can be used by econometrists is to that extent a better theory than one which cannot."[3] Prof. Hicks says that the demand theory which he represented in his book *Value and Capital* contained only potential econometric reference. The defect of demand theory in *Value and Capital* was that econometric reference was not made explicit. It was in Samuelson's revealed preference theory, he says, that econometric reference was made explicit. But Hicks wants to make econometric reference of his new theory of demand more explicit than Samuelson's theory. "In Samuelson, the whole form of the theory is allowed to be dictated by the reference to econometrics. Great and beautiful simplifications follow. But I am not convinced that even in Samuelson the econometric reference is quite explicit as it should be, so that the present work, deeply influenced by Samuelson as it is, will not follow him at all exactly. In technique we shall keep quite close to him, but our methodology will be more explicitly econometric even than his."[4]

It is important to note that Hicks in his ***'A Revision of Demand Theory'*** once again rejects the concept of cardinal utility and the hypothesis of independent utilities. He continues

1. *A Revision of Demand Theory,* Oxford University Press, 1956.
2. J. R. Hicks, *op. cit.,* p. VI.
3. *Ibid,* p. 3.
4. *Ibid,* p. 4.

to believe that utility is purely ordinal. Prof. Hicks holds that more elementary parts of the theory can be established almost as well by the cardinal method as by the ordinal method but in the more difficult branches of the theory 'cardinal utility becomes a nuisance.'[5] Further, he holds that if one rejects the hypothesis of independent utilities and if one admits the possibility and usefulness of breaking up the effect of a price change into those of substitution effect and income effect one has in effect eliminated the cardinalism from the argument. He, therefore, continues to make use of the concept of ordinal utility in his *Revision of Demand Theory* as well.

But it is important to remember that Hicks who popularised the use of indifference curves in demand theory has given them up in his ***Revision of Demand Theory.*** There are no indifference curves in any of the 22 diagrams in this new book, though there are positions which are equally preferred by the consumer. He discusses even his concept of consumer's surplus without the help of indifference curves. He now points out the various disadvantages of the indifference curves technique. First, he points out that this geometrical method of indifference curves is fully effective and useful for representing only quite simple cases, especially, those in which the choice concerns two commodities. When the analysis is extended to three commodities, complicated three-dimensional diagrams are to be drawn and if analysis is extended to more than three commodities, then recourse has to be made to elaborate mathematics which often conceals the economic point of what is being done.

The second disadvantage of the geometrical method of indifference curves, according to Hicks, is that "it forces us at the start to make assumptions of continuity, a property which the geometrical field does have but which economics in general does not." He therefore gives up the assumption of continuity in his revision of demand theory. However, Hicks thinks that neither of these disadvantages provides sufficient reason to abandon the indifference curves method which has its own advantages and which has been widely used by economists. Now, what prompted Hicks to adopt a new method is that it is more effective in clarifying the nature of preference hypothesis. "The consideration which decides me in favour of the new method, **at least as an essential complement to the old, if not as a substitute**, is its greater effectiveness in clarifying the nature of the preference hypothesis itself'[6]. We shall now explain below how Hicks develops his new method of preference hypothesis and bases his new demand theory on it.

Any factual or empirical data regarding the demand for a good is determined by non-economic factors (such as population changes, age distribution of population, social habits etc.) as well as by economic factors (such as current prices and incomes). The task of the econometrists is to estimate the effects on the empirical data of demand which are due to the changes in current prices and incomes. But to make such estimates, the econometrist needs a technique for separating out the effects due to current prices and incomes from those due to the non-economic factors. But "such a technique cannot be provided without a theory. The econometric purpose of the theory of demand is to give assistance in making this separation."[7]

The theory of demand which is useful for econometric purposes is, therefore, one which will tell us something about the ways in which consumers will likely to react if variations in current prices and incomes were the only causes of changes in consumption. Such a demand theory starts by assuming an ideal consumer who by definition is influenced by the current prices and incomes alone and then proceed to show how such a consumer is expected to behave.

5. *Ibid*, p. 9.
6. *Op. cit.* p. 19.
7. *Op. cit.* p. 17.

PREFERENCE HYPOTHESIS AND LOGIC OF ORDERING

In order to explain the behaviour of an ideal consumer Prof. Hicks assumes preference hypothesis as a principle which governs the behaviour of such a consumer. ***The assumption of behavior according to a scale of preferences is known as preference hypothesis.*** Hicks explains the meaning of preference hypothesis or behaviour according to the scale of preference as follows:

"The ideal consumer (who is not affected by anything else than current market conditions) chooses that alternative out of the various alternatives open to him, which he most prefers, or ranks most highly. In one set of market conditions he makes one choice, in others other choices; but the choices he makes always express the same ordering, and must, therefore, be consistent with one another. This is the hypothesis made about the behaviour of the ideal consumer."[8]

The above statement of Hicks implies that the consumer in a given market situation chooses the most preferred combination and he will choose different combinations in different market situations but his choices in different market situations will be consistent with each other. It is important to remember that Hicks' demand theory presented in '*Value and Capital*' was also based upon the preference hypothesis but there he expressed the given scale of preferences at once in the form of a set of indifference curves. This direct introduction of geometrical device has, as already noted above, various disadvantages and has, therefore, been given up. In '*Revision of Demand Theory*' Hicks begins from the logic of ordering itself rather than starting from the geometrical application of it. According to him, "the demand theory which is based upon the preference hypothesis turns out to be nothing else but an economic application of the logical theory of ordering."[9] Therefore, before deriving demand theory from preference hypothesis he explains the "logic of order". In this context he draws out difference between strong ordering and weak ordering. He then proceeds to base his demand theory on **weak-ordering form of preference hypothesis.**

Strong and Weak Orderings Distinguished

A set of items is *strongly* ordered, if *each item has a place of its own in the order* and each item could then be given a number and to each number there would be one item and only one item which would correspond. A set of items is weakly ordered if the items are clustered into groups but none of the items within a group can be put ahead of the others. ***"A weak ordering consists of a division into groups, in which sequence of groups is strongly ordered, but in which there is no ordering within the groups."***[10]

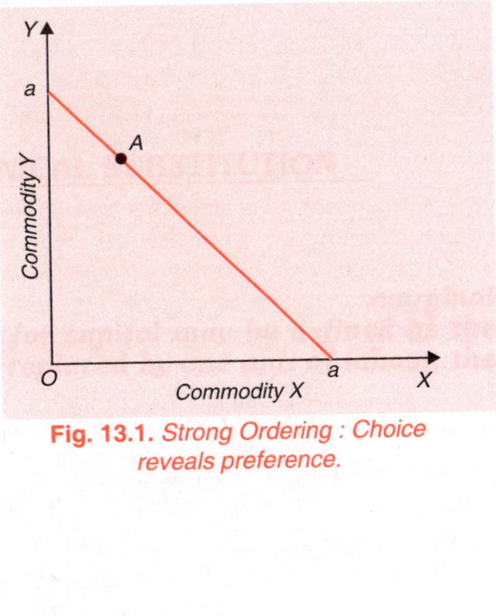

Fig. 13.1. *Strong Ordering : Choice reveals preference.*

It should be noted that indifference curves imply weak ordering in as much as all the points on a given indifference curve are equally desirable and hence occupy same place in the order. On the other hand, revealed preference approach implies strong ordering since it assumes that the choice of a combination reveals

8. *Ibid*, p. 18.
9. *Ibid*, p. 18.
10. *Ibid*, p. 19.

consumer's preference for it over all other alternative combinations open to him. Choice can reveal preference for a combination only if all the alternative combinations are strongly ordered. Weak ordering implies that the consumer chooses a position and rejects others open to him, then the rejected positions need not be inferior to the position actually chosen but may have been indifferent to it. Hence, under weak ordering, actual choice fails to reveal definite preference. The strong ordering and weak-ordering as applied to the theory of demand are illustrated in Fig. 13.1. If the consumer is confronted with the price-income situation *aa,* then he can choose any combination that lies in or on triangle *aOa*. Suppose that our consumer chooses the combination *A*. Let us assume that our consumer is an ideal consumer who is acting according to his scale of preferences. Now, the question is how his act of choice of *A* from among the available alternatives within and on the triangle *aOa* is to be interpreted. If the available alternatives are strongly ordered, then the choice of *A* by the consumer will show that he prefers *A* over all other available alternatives. In Samuelson's language he 'reveals his preference' for *A* over all other possible alternatives which are rejected. Since, under strong ordering, the consumer shows definite preference for the selected alternative, there is no question of any indifferent positions to the selected one.

Hicks' Criticism of the Logic of Strong Ordering

Hicks criticises the logic of strong ordering. "If we interpret the preference hypothesis to mean strong ordering, we cannot assume that all the geometrical points, which lie within or on the triangle *aOa* represent effective alternatives. A two-dimensional continuum point cannot be strongly ordered." Prof. Hicks further says that if commodities are assumed to be available only in discrete units, so that the diagram is to be conceived as being drawn on squared paper and the only effective alternatives are the points at the corners of squares and therefore the selected point must also lie at the corner of a square, then the strong ordering hypothesis is acceptable. Since in the real world, commodities are available in discrete units, therefore the strong ordering hypothesis should not present any difficulty. But Hicks contends that the actual commodities may be available in integral number of units but this cannot be said of the composite commodity money, which is usually measured on the *Y*-axis, when demand for a single commodity is under discussion. Hicks regards money to be finally divisible. To quote him:

"If everyone of the actual commodities into which *M* can be exchanged is itself only available in discrete units; but if the number of such commodities is large, there will be a large number of ways in which a small increment of *M* can be consumed by rearrangement of consumption among the individual commodities, whence it will follow that the units in which *M* is to be taken to be available must be considered as exceedingly small. And as soon as any individual commodity becomes available in units that are finally divisible, *M* must be regarded as finally divisible. In practice, we should usually think of M as being money, held back for the purchase of other commodities than *X;* though money is not finally divisible in a mathematical sense, the smallest monetary unit (farthing or cent) is so small in relation to the other units with which we are concerned that the imperfect divisibility of money is in practice a thing of no importance. For these reasons, while it is a theoretical improvement to be able to regard the actual commodity *X* as available in discrete units it is no improvement at all to be oblidged to impute same indivisibility to the composite commodity *M.* It is much better to regard money as finally divisible".[11]

So, according to Hicks, where the choice is between any good which is available in discrete units and money whtich is finally divisible, the possibility of equally desired combinations

11. Hicks, *op. cit*, pp. 40-41.

must be accepted and strong ordering has, therefore, to be given up. Why the strong ordering hypothesis is not valid when the choice is between money which is finally divisible and is represented on the Y-axis and the commodity X which is imperfectly divisible and is represented on the X-axis is illustrated in Fig. 13.2. This is because when money measured on Y-axis is taken to be finally divisible, the effective alternatives will no longer be represented by square corners, they will appear in the diagram as a series of parallel lines (or stripes) as shown in Fig. 13.2. All points on the stripes will be effective alternatives but such alternatives cannot be strongly ordered "unless the *whole* of one stripe was preferred to the *whole* of the next stripe, and so on; which means that the consumer would always prefer an additional unit of X whatever he had to pay for it."[12] But this is quite absurd. Thus, the effective alternatives appearing on the stripes cannot be strongly ordered. Again, suppose there are two alternatives P and Q on a given stripe which are such that P is preferred to R on another stripe, while R is preferred to Q. Given that, we can always find a point between P and Q on a given stripe which is indifferent to R.

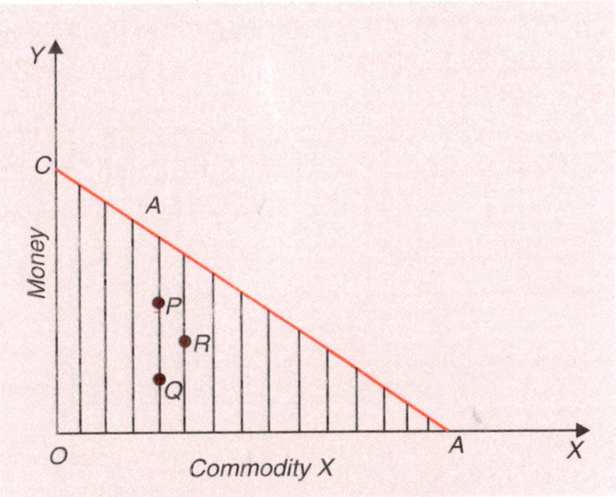

Fig. 13.2. *Strong ordering cannot be maintained when one commodity is money*

It is thus evident that when various alternatives appear as a series of stripes, there can be a relation of indifference between some of them. Thus strong ordering cannot be maintained when various alternative combinations consist of the composite commodity money which is finally divisible and actual commodity which is available only in discrete units. "As soon as we introduce the smallest degree of continuity (such as is introduced by the 'striped' hypothesis) strong ordering has to be given up."[13]

The Logic of Weak Ordering

After rejecting the strong ordering hypothesis, Hicks proceeds to establish the case for the adoption of the weak ordering hypothesis. As noted above, the weak ordering hypothesis recognizes the relation of indifference, while the strong ordering hypothesis does not. In the words of Hicks, "If the consumer's scale of preferences is weakly ordered, then his choice of a particular position A does not show (or reveal) that A is preferred to any rejected position within or on the triangle: ***all that is shown is that there is no rejected position which is preferred to A.*** It is perfectly possible that some rejected position may be indifferent to A; the choice of A instead of that rejected position is then a matter of 'chance'."[14]

From the above statement of Hicks it is clear that, under the weak ordering hypothesis, the choice of a particular combination does not indicate preference for that particular combination over another possible alternative combination but it only shows that all other possible alternative combinations within or on the choice triangle cannot be preferred to the chosen combination. There is possibility of some rejected combinations being indifferent to the selected one. If preference hypothesis in its weak ordering form is adopted, then it yields so little information about the consumer's behavior that the basic propositions of demand theory cannot be derived from it. Therefore, Hicks has felt it necescary to introduce an

12. *Ibid*, p. 41.
13. J. R. Hicks, *op. cit*, p. 41.
14. *Ibid*, p. 42 *(italics supplied).*

additional hypothesis along with the adoption of the weak ordering hypothesis so as to derive basic propositions of demand theory. This additional hypothesis which is introduced is simply that **'the consumer will *always prefer a* larger amount of money to a smaller amount of money,** provided that the amount of good *X* at his disposal is unchanged."[15] It should be carefully noted that it is not necessary to make this additional hypothesis if strong ordering form of preference hypothesis is adopted. But this additional hypothesis which has been introduced by Hicks is very reasonable and is always implicit in economic analysis, even though it is not explicitly stated everytime.

Now the question is what positive information is provided by weak ordering approach when supported by the above additional hypothesis. Let us consider Fig. 13.3. From all the available combinations within and on the triangle *aOa* the consumer chooses A. Under weak ordering hypothesis alone the choice of A rather than *B* which lies within the triangle *aOa* does not show that A is preferred to *B*; it only shows that *B is not preferred to A.* In other words, under weak ordering alone, the choice of A rather than *B* means that either A is preferred to *B*, or the consumer is indifferent between A and *B*.

Now, consider the position *L* which lies where the stripe through *B* meets the line *aa*. On the additional hypothesis made, *L* is preferred to *B*, since *L* contains more amount of money than *B*, amount of *X* being the same in both the positions. If A and *B* are indifferent, then from the transitivity it follows that *L* is preferred to A. But *L* was available when A was selected. Therefore, though *L* can be indifferent to A, it cannot be preferred to A. Thus, it follows that the possibility that A and *B* are indifferent must be ruled out. Hence, when we adopt the weak ordering along with the additional hypothesis we come to the conclusion that the chosen combination A is preferred to any combination such as *B* which lies *within* the triangle. What cannot be said with certainty under weak ordering even with the additional hypothesis is whether the chosen combination A is preferred to a combination such as *L* which lies *on* the triangle, that is, on the line *aa*. *A* can be either preferred to *L* or indifferent to it. Drawing the difference between the implications of strong and weak orderings, Hicks says. "The difference between the consequences of strong and weak ordering so interpreted amounts to no more than this: that under strong ordering the chosen position is shown to be preferred to all other positions within and *on* the triangle, while under weak ordering it is.preferred to all positions *within* the triangle, but may be indifferent to other positions *on* the same boundary as itself."[16]

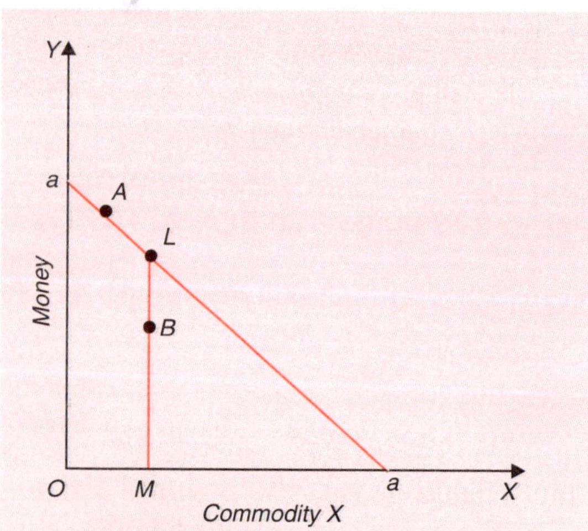

Fig. 13.3. *Weak-ordering Approach along with an additional hypothesis about money*

It will be evident from above that the difference between the effects of the strong and weak orderings is very small and that it only affects a class of limiting cases (*i.e.*, positions lying *on* the triangle). The weak ordering theory, Hicks says, "has a larger tolerance and, therefore, it deals with these limiting cases rather better". Apart from this, weak ordering hypothesis, contends Hicks, is more useful and desirable. "If we take the strong ordering approach, we are

15. *Op. cit.*, p. 42.
16. *Op. cit.*, p. 43.

committing ourselves to discontinuity not merely to the indivisibility of the particular commodity, demand for which is being studied, but also to the indivisibility of the composite commodity used as a background. If, on the other hand, we take the weak ordering approach, we are committing ourselves to some degree of continuity but divisibility of the background commodity is itself quite sufficient to ensure that the weak ordering approach is practicable."

As stated above, the weak ordering approach to be useful for demand theory requires an additional assumption to be made, namely, that the consumer prefers a larger amount of money to a smaller amount. Further, another assumption which is to be necessarily made when the weak ordering approach is adopted is that *the* ***preference order is transitive.*** These two additional assumptions are not required in the case of strong ordering approach.

THE DIRECT CONSISTENCY TEST

Following Samuelson, Hicks also assumes consistency of choice behaviour on the part of the ideal consumer whose scale of preferences remains unchanged when prices of goods and his income vary. So, in order to derive laws about consumer's demand, Hicks applies the consistency test which has been applied by Samuelson in his revealed preference approach. Hicks calls this consistency test as the Direct Consistency Test. It should be remembered that the direct consistency is nothing else but the economic expression of the two-term consistency condition of the theory of the logic of order.

Consistency test, as applied by Samuelson, in his revealed preference theory is quite simple. But Hicks has elaborated the consistency idea by considering the consistency or inconsistency involved in numerous alternative cases. Consider Fig. 13.4 where commodity X is measured on the X-axis and the composite commodity, money (which represents all other commodities) on the Y-axis. The price of good X and income of the consumer being given, the alternative combinations which are open to the consumer are represented by the points within or

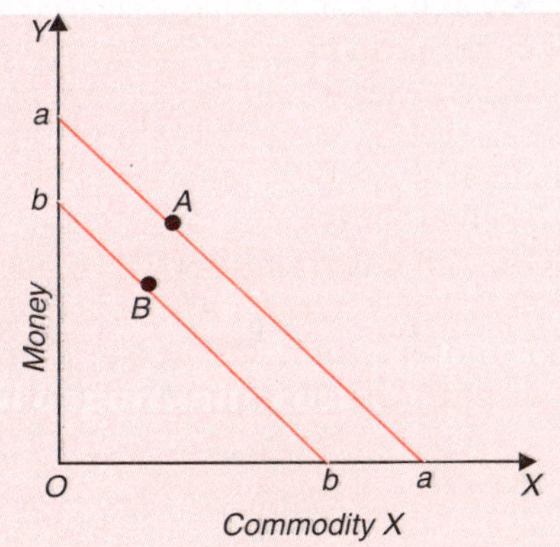

Fig.13.4. *A is preferred to B both under Strong and Weak Orderings.*

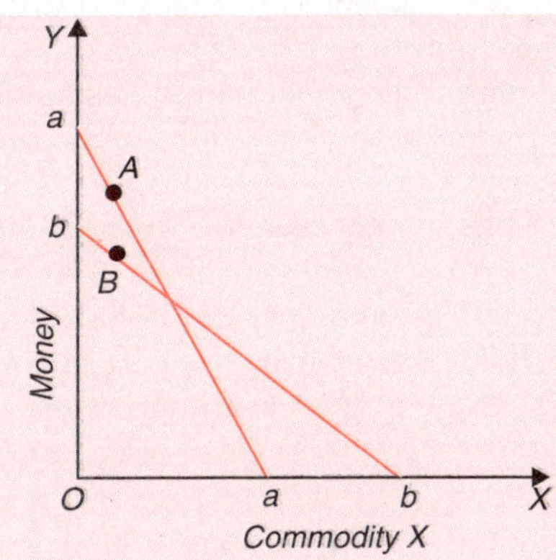

Fig. 13.5. *Consumer prefers A to B both under Strong and Weak Orderings.*

on the triangle *aOa*. The point *A* on the line *aa* represents the actually chosen combination. As seen earlier, under strong ordering A is shown to be preferred to all other available combinations within or on the triangle. But, under weak ordering, *A* is shown to be preferred to all the combinations *within* the triangle *aOa* and is either preferred or indifferent to other combinations on the line *aa*. Now, take another price-income situation *bb* in which price of good X is different, while the income of the consumer may or may not be different. The various alternative combinations open to the consumer in the new situation are those lying within or on the triangle *bOb*. Point *B* on the line *bb* represents the actually selected combination in this new situation. Similar kind of preferences, as in situation *A*, will follow in situation *B* under strong and weak forms of preference hypothesis.

Since the consumer is assumed to be acting according to the **unchanged scale of preferences** in both situations, the preferences by him in the two situations must be consistent with each other. The consumer's behaviour will be inconsistent if he reveals his preference for combination *A* over combination *B* in *A* situation, while in *B* situation he prefers combination *B* over combination *A*, *when both the combinations A and B are available in both the situations*. But, under weak ordering, the possibility of indifference has also to be taken into account.

The various possible cases in which consistency or otherwise has to be judged are the following:

(a) First, it is conceivable that one of the two price income lines lies wholly outside the other, as in Fig. 13.4, where *aa* lies wholly outside *bb*. In this case point *B* lies within the triangle *aOa*. Therefore, in the *A* situation, *A* is preferred to *B* both under strong and weak orderings. In the *B* situation, *A* is not available. Therefore, the consumer's choice of *A* in the *A* situation is quite consistent with his choice of *B* in the *B* situation.

(b) Secondly, if one of the two price-income lines does not lie wholly outside the other, then the two will intersect each other at some point. Let us suppose that the price income line *aa* lies outside the price-income line *bb* on the left of the cross. When the two price-income lines intersects each other, then the following are the four possible cases:

(i) Both the selected positions *A* and *B* respectively in "the two situations lie to the left of cross, such as points *A* and *B* in Fig. 13.5. In this case, the choice of *B* in the *B* situation is quite consistent with the preference for A over *B* in the *A* situation. Position *B* lies within the triangle *aOa* and therefore the choice of *A* in *A* situation shows consumer's preference for *A* over *B*, both under strong and weak orderings. But in the *B* situation *A* is not available, and therefore the choice of *B* in the *B* situation is quite consistent with the choice of *A* in the *A* situation.

(ii) Both the selected postitions *A* and *B* respectively in the two situations lie to the right of the cross as in Fig. 13.6. Here also the choice of *B* rather than *A* in *B* situation is quite consistent with the choice of *A* in *A* situation. The position *A* lies within the triangle *bob* and therefore under strong as well as weak ordering *B* is revealed to be preferred to *A* in the *B* situations. But the consumer chooses *A* in the *A* situation since *B* is not available in the *A* situation. Thus, in this case too the consumer's choice behaviour is quite consistent.

(iii) The two chosen positions *A* and *B* respectively in the two situations lie outside the cross, *A* to the left and *B* to the right of it, as in Fig. 13.7 In this case, in *A* situation when *A* is chosen, *B* is not available, and in *B* situation when *B* is chosen, *A* is not available. Therefore, the choices made in the two situation are consistent, whether the strong or weak ordering is adopted.

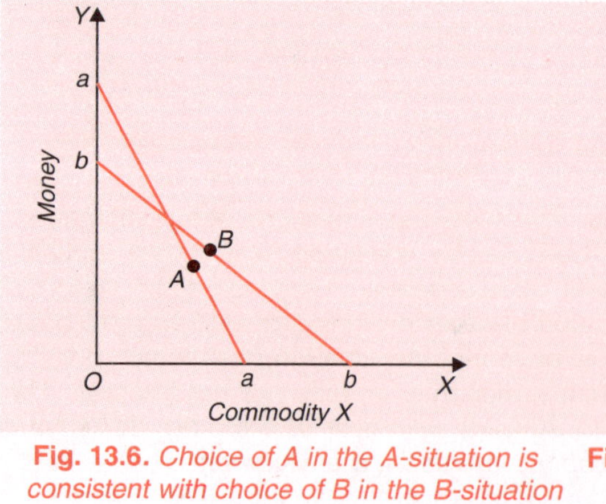

Fig. 13.6. *Choice of A in the A-situation is consistent with choice of B in the B-situation*

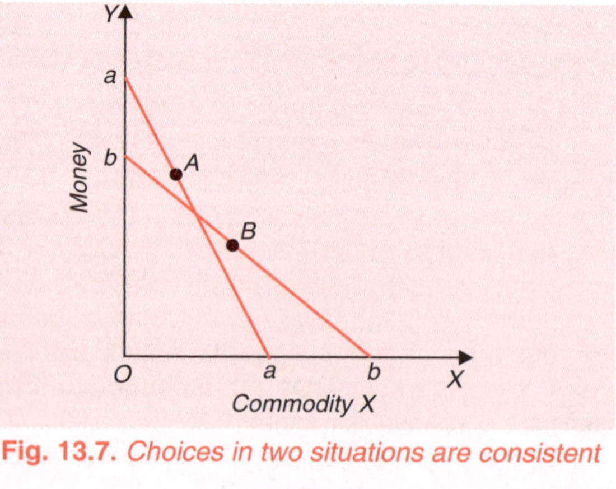

Fig. 13.7. *Choices in two situations are consistent*

(*iv*) The two selected positions *A* and *B* respectively in the two situations lie inside the cross, *A* to the right and *B* to the left of it, as shown in Fig. 13.8. In this case, there is inconsistency. In the *A* situation when *A* is chosen, *B* lies within the triangle *aoa,* therefore *A* is revealed to be preferred to *B*. But in the *B* situation where *A* is also availble and lies within the triangle *bob*, position *B* is chosen rather than *A*, showing consumer's preference for *B* over *A*. Thus in this case, at one time the consumer prefers *A* to *B* and at another he prefers *B* to *A*. Hence his choice is quite inconsistent, both under weak ordering and strong ordering.

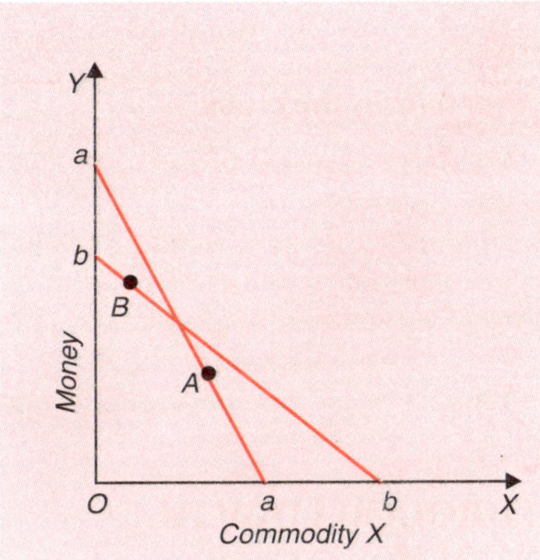

Fig. 13.8. *Inconsistency of Choices in the Two Situations*

(*c*) Finally, we have a group of special cases when the two price-income lines intersect each other, but one of the two choice positions lies at the cross while the other chosen position may lie either outside or inside the cross. Thus, there are two possibilities in this respect.

(*i*) One chosen position *A* lies at the cross while the other one outside the cross. Suppose for instance chosen position *A* lies at the cross and chosen position *B* lies outside the cross as shown in Fig. 13.9. In this case, *B* is not available in the *A*-situation. Therefore, the choice of *A* in *A*-situation is not inconsistent. It should be noted that in the *B*-situation both *A* and *B* are present, *B* is actually chosen rather than *A*. Under weak ordering hypothesis it means that *B* is either preferred to *A* or indifferent to *A* (*A* also lies on the line *bb*). But in the *A* situation, the choice of *A* does not mean inconsistency since *B* is not available in the *A*-situation.

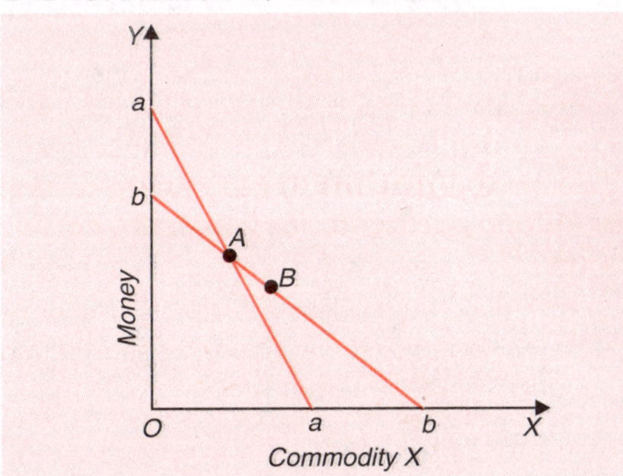

Fig. 13.9. *Choices are consistent.*

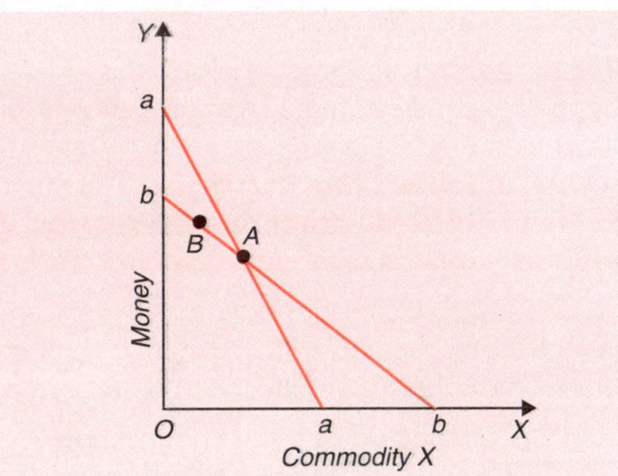

Fig. 13.10. *Choices are incosistent.*

(*ii*) One chosen position lies at the cross, while the other one inside the cross. Suppose the selected position *A* lies at the cross and the selected position *B* inside the cross as shown in Fig. 13.10. In this case, position *B* lies *within* the triangle *aOa*. Therefore, the choice of *A* in the *A* situation shows, even under weak ordering, that *A* is preferred to *B*. But in the *B* situation the choice of *B*, under weak ordering, shows that either *B* is either preferred to *A* or *B* is indifferent to *A* (*A* also lies on the line *bb*) either of these is inconsistent with the definite preference for *A* over *B*. Hence if one chosen point lies at the cross, while the other inside the cross, there is inconsistency of choice in consumer's behavior.

17. See Hicks, *op. cit.*, p. 51.

It is evident from the above analysis that we reach the same conclusion in all cases from the direct consistency test whether we are adopting strong or weak ordering hypothesis. On either hypothesis, there is inconsistency in the following two cases[17]:

(i) When both positions A and B lie within the cross.

(ii) When one position lies at the cross and the other within the cross.

Though the weak and strong forms of preference hypothesis yield the same result in regard to the consistency tests but it should be remembered that the arguments by which they achieve the result are different. It may, however, be pointed out that the same identity or result under weak and strong orderings will not occur "when we proceed to generalise" (that is, when we take more commodities besides good *X* and composite commodity *M* and allow the price of more than one good to vary). But as long as we are limiting our analysis to the demand for a single commodity, we reach, the same conclusion in respect of the presence or absence of consistency whether we assume strong or weak ordering.

DERIVATION OF LAW OF DEMAND THROUGH LOGICAL WEAK ORDERING APPROACH

From the logic of weak ordering (along with the additional hypothesis) and the theory of direct consistency test based upon it, Hicks proceeds to deduce all major propositions of the theory of consumeur's demand. Hicks first derives theory of demand for a single commodity, that is, for the behavior of a consumer confronted with a market in which the price of no more than one good is liable to change. The primary task in a theory of demand is to derive the law of demand, that is, "the principle that the demand curve for a commodity is downward sloping". As in indifference curve approach the technique adopted by Hicks in *Revision of Demand Theory* to derive the law of demand is that of dividing the effect of a price change into two parts: income effect and substitution effect.

In the present work, the substitution effect is deduced by Hicks from the consistency theory while the income effect, according to him, is based upon empirical evidence. He points out that there is a good deal of empirical evidence about the effects of 'pure' changes in income. ***"It follows that in strictness the law of demand is a hybrid; it has one leg resting on theory and the other on observation. But, in this particular instance, the double support happens to be quite exceptionally strong."***[18]

Let us now consider how the law of demand is derived by dividing the effects of a price change into substitution effect and income effect. The real task is to separate out the substitution effect. The substitution effect can be separated by means of two methods.

(1) The method of the compensating variation, and
(2) The method of the cost difference.

How the substitution effect is separated from the income effect by these two methods and how the law of demand is derived is explained below.

Deriving Law of Demand by the Method of Compensating Variation

Let us consider the demand for a commodity *X* which is measured on the X-axis in Fig. 13.11. As before the composite commodity *M (i.e.,* money) is measured on the *Y*-axis. Given a certain *price* of the good and income of the consumer, the opportunity line *(i.e.,* price income line) *aa* is drawn. Now suppose that in this initial price-income situation the consumer chooses the combination *A* on *aa*. Suppose that the price of good *X* falls, money income remaining unchanged. As a result, the opportunity line will be *bb* starting from the same point

18. *Op. cit.*, p. 47.

on the vertical axis as the line *aa* but will be lying outside *aa*. The consumer will now choose a position on *bb* in this new situation. It follows from the consistency theory that so long as some amount of X is consumed any position on line *bb* must be preferred to *A*. In other works, whether the choosen position *B* on *bb* lies to the left of or to the right of or exactly above *A*, it will be preferred to *A*. This is because *A* lies within the triangle *bob*. But, as Hicks says, "this is all we learn from consistency theory when it is applied to these two positions. It is perfectly *consistent* for there to be a rise, or fall, or no change in the consumption of X between *A* and *B*"[19].

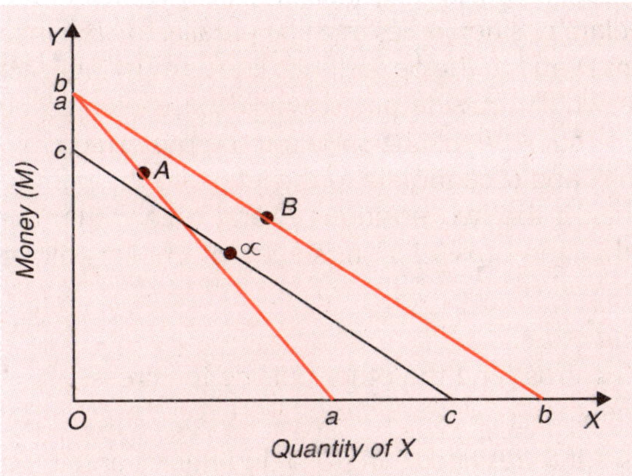

Fig. 13.11. *Deriving Law of Demand through Hicksian Logical Ordering Approach*

Now the question is where the position *B* on *bb* will lie, that is, whether it will lie to the right of *A*, or to the left of *A* or exactly above it. The position *B* lying to the right of *A* means that the amount demanded of good X rises as a result of fall in its price, and the position *B* lying to the left of *A* means that the amount demanded of good X falls with the fall in its price, and further the position *B* lying exactly vertically above *A* means the amount demanded of the good X remains the same with the fall in price. Thus, the question is whether the amount demanded of good X rises or falls or remains unchanged with a fall in its price. The answer to this question, as a whole, cannot be deduced from the consistency theory. As explained above, it is perfectly consistent for there to be a rise or a fall or no change in the amount demanded of a good as a result of the fall in its price. However, if the fall in price of good X is accompanied by an appropriate reduction in consumer's income, then it can be shown from the consistency theory that the amount demanded of good X must rise or remain the same; it cannot fall. When the income of the consumer is reduced by an appropriate amount along with a fall in price of X, the remaining effect of the change in price on the demand of the good will be due to the relative fall in price of good X. The effect on the demand for a commodity due to only the relative change in its price is called substitution effect. It follows, therefore, that it can be shown from the consistency theory that due to substitution effect of the fall in price of good X the consumption of X must rise or remain the same; it cannot diminish. The rest of the effect of the change in price is the income effect. In which direction the income effect of the fall in price works cannot be proved with the aid of consistency theory. Our knowledge about income effect is based upon observation.

It follows from above that in order to show the influence of substitution effect on the demand for a commodity we have to construct an ***intermediate position*** and making suitable reduction in income along with a fall in price of X.

The movement from *A* on aa to *B* on *bb* as a result of the change in price represents the price effect. In order to separate out the substitution effect, income is reduced by ***compensating variation***, that is, income is reduced by such an amount that gain in the real income accruing to the consumer due to the fall in price of good *X* is wiped out. In other words, income of the consumer is reduced by so much amount that in the intermediate position α he chooses at the new lower price but with lower income is ***indifferent to the position A.*** "On this interpretation, the substitution effect measures the effect of the change in relative prices, *with real income constant'*, the income effect *measures the effect of the changes in real income."*

19. *Op., cit.*, p.60.

If the intermediate position can be obtained by the method of compensation variation, it is easy to show from the consistency theory that in what direction the substitution effect works. As the price of good X is the same in the intermediate position as indicated by the line *bb*, the price opportunity line *cc* on which the intermediate position α lies must be parallel to *bb*. Since the consumer is indifferent between the positions *A* and α, the opportunity line *cc* must intersect the line *aa*. This is because if *cc* were to lie wholly outside *aa*, α would be shown to be preferred to A; and if it were to lie wholly inside *aa*, *A* would be shown to be preferred to α. Similarly, if A and α are to be indifferent, both A and α cannot lie to the left or to the right of the cross of the lines on which they lie. Further, if the two positions A and α lie within the cross, or one at the cross and the other within the cross, inconsistency of choice will be involved. Thus, the only alternatives left are:

(i) Both positions A and α lie outside the cross.
(ii) From position A and α, one lies at the cross and the other outside the cross.
(iii) Both positions A and α lie at the cross.

The above three are the only possible cases if the A and α are to be indifferent and if the consumer's choice is to be consistent. In any of these cases it should be noted that either the consumption of *X* increases or remains the same. It, therefore, follows that if the fall in the price of good *X* is accompanied by the reduction in income by the compensating variation, the quantity demanded of good *X* will increase or at least will remain the same. In other words, as a result of substitution effect the quantity demanded of good *X* whose price falls will increase or at least will remain the same.

In Fig.13.11 when the income is reduced by the compensating variation, the new opportunity line *cc* intersects the opportunity line *aa* below the point *A*. On the opportunity line *cc*, the consumer actually chooses the position α which lies outside the cross (It should be noted as explained already that the intermediate position α cannot lie to the left of the cross on the line cc, since in that case the consumer cannot be indifferent between α and *A*). The movement from A to α represents the substitution effect and results in the increase in quantity demanded of X. This is one part of the price effect.

Let the money income which was taken away from the consumer by the amount of compensating variation be now restored to him. With this rise in income whether the consumer will buy more of good *X* or less than at α cannot be proved with the aid of consistency theory or any other theoretical rule. But from the empirical evidence we know that in case of most of the goods, the consumption of a good increases with the rise in income. "There is no theoretical rule which tells us that rise in income must 'tend to increase' the consumption of *X* but it is safe to conclude from the empirical evidence that it will do so in most cases, that the cases in which it does not do so may fairly be regarded as exceptional."[20]

Thus, when consumer is at position α and his income is raised by the amount which was previously withdrawn from him (so that he is once again on the opportunity line *bb*), he will further increase his consumption of good *X*. In other words, he will buy more of good *X* than at position α when his income is increased so that he faces the opportunity line *bb*. That is why the chosen position *B* on *bb* lies to the right of α, showing that the consumption of good *X* increases between α and *B*. The movement from α to *B* represents the income effect.

It follows from above that quantity demanded of a good increases with the fall in its price due to substitution effect and income effect. Thus the basic law of demand, namely, that the demand curve is downward sloping has been proved.

20. J.R. Hicks, *op. cit.*, p.61.

Deriving Law of Demand by Cost-Difference Method

While the method of compensating variation is perfectly valid and is very useful in dividing the price change into two parts which have 'special economic significance', the alternative method of cost difference is more convenient for the purpose of deriving the law of demand. The cost-difference method which was evolved by Samuelson has also been adopted by Hicks.

The cost-difference method and how the law of demand is established with its aid is illustrated in the Fig. 13.12. As before, the composite commodity, money *(M)* is measured on the *Y*-axis and the commodity *X* whose demand is under consideration is measured on the X-axis. *aa* is the initial opportunity line and point *A* on it represents the actually selected position. Now, suppose the price of good *X* falls, money income of the consumer remaining the same. As a result of this, the opportunity line now takes up the position *bb*. Under the cost-difference method, the fall in price of good *X* is accompanied by the ***reduction in income of the consumer by such an amount which will leave the consumer just able to purchase the original combination A.*** In other words, income is reduced by the difference between the cost of his original consumption of *X* (that is, in position A) at the old price and at the new price. In terms of Fig. 13.12 this means that income is reduced by such an mount that the ***intermediate opportunity line cc passes through point A. (In Fig. 13.12 the cost difference = ca or cb).***

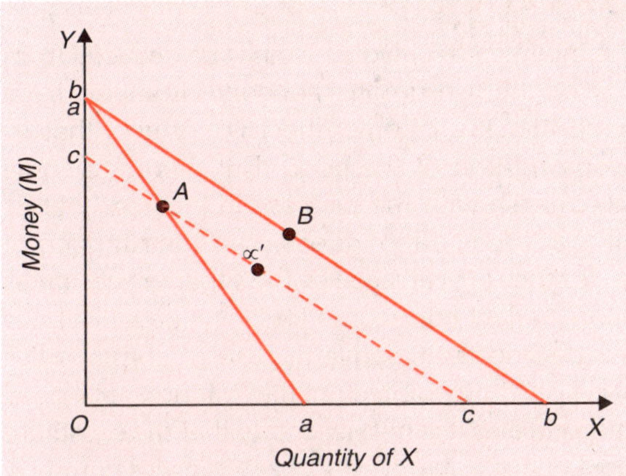

Fig. 13.12. *Derving Law of Demand through Hicksian Logical Ordering Approach and Cost-difference Method*

Now the question is where the intermediate position on the opportunity line *cc* will lie. The two opportunity lines are *aa* and *cc* and one of the two positions now lies at the cross of the two lines, so that the possible cases in which consistency tests have to be applied are few. The intermediate position α′ lies to the right of *A* and (*ii*) that α' and *A* coincide. In case (*i*) the consumption of *X* will increase between *A* and α' and in case *(ii)* the consumption of *X* will remain the same. The movement from *A* to α' represents the substitution effect. It follows from above that as a result of substitution effect, the consumption of *X* must rise or remain the same; it cannot diminish. Now, if the income taken away from the consumer is given back to him, he will further increase the consumption of *X*, ***if the increase in income is known to raise the consumption of X.*** Thus the point *B* will lie to right of α′ showing the increase in consumption of *X* between α′ and *B* as a result of the income effect.

It is clear from above that the choice of an intermediate position through the cost-difference method provides an alternative method of dividing the effect of a price change into income effect and substitution effect. Although the intermediate positions in the two methods are not exactly the same, the parts into which they break up the price effect have substantially similar properties. By whichever method we divide the price effect it remains true that as a result of the substitution effect the consumption of good whose price falls must rise or remain the same; it cannot diminish. This conclusion about the direction in which the substitution effect operates follows from the consistency theory.

Hicks admits the superiority of cost-difference method over the compensating variation method for the purpose of deriving the law of demand. Commenting on them, he remarks, "The difference between the two methods is solely a matter of the magnitude of the rise in income, which leads to the income effect; and on this point the method of cost difference has a distinct advantage. For while the magnitude of the compensating variation is quite a problem... the magnitude of the cost-difference raises no problem at all. It can be read off at once from the data of the situation under discussion."[21]

INFERIOR GOODS, GIFFEN GOODS AND LAW OF DEMAND

As stated above, the direction in which the income effect works cannot be deduced from any theory. The effect of the increase of income on the consumption of goods is known from empirical evidence. In most cases it is observed that the income effect is positive, that is, increase in income leads to the increase in consumption of the good. But there are some goods of which the consumption is known to diminish with the increase in income, that is, income effect for them is negative. Such goods are called inferior goods. The consumption of inferior goods decreases with the rise in income, for they are replaced by the superior substitutes at higher levels of income. The goods with income effect (or income elasticity) negative have been called *inferior goods,* since income effect is mostly negative in case of commodities which are of physically *inferior quality.* It may however be pointed out that inferior good need not be one which is of physically inferior quantity and also it is not necessary that the substitute which replaces the so called inferior goods should have any physical characteristics common with them. Furthermore, it is not even essential that the 'wants' which are satisfied by the inferior good and the substitute which replaces it should be the same. Suppose an individual is induced to buy a car by a small rise in income, he will then be forced to economize on several goods which he was previously consuming. As a result, the consumption of the goods on which the individual ordinarily spends his income will fall as a result of the particular small rise in income which induced the individual to buy the car. Thus, for the particular rise in income which has occurred, all the ordinary types of goods on which the individual spends his income will become 'inferior goods'.

Let us now consider the effect of a change in price of an inferior good on its consumption or demand. Substitution effect of the *fall* in price of a good, as proved above, *always* tends to increase the consumption of the good. But the income effect of the fall in price of an inferior good will diminish the consumption of the good. Therefore, in case of inferior goods the income effect will work in the opposite direction to the substitution effect. But the income effect of the change in price of a good is generally quite small. This is so because a person spends no more than a small proportion of his income on a single good with the result that not even a large proportional fall in the price of a good will produce a cost difference which is more than a small fraction of his income. Thus, unless the demand for a good is exceedingly responsive to the changes in income, that is, unless the income elasticity of demand is extremely large, the income effect of the change in price must be quite small in relation to previous consumption. Therefore, in case of an inferior good although the income effect works in the opposite direction to the substitution effect, it is unlikely that it will outweigh the substitution effect. The netresult of the fall in price of an inferior good will then be the rise in its consumption because the substitution effect is larger than the negative income effect. Thus, the law of demand *(i.e.,* inverse price-demand relationship) usually holds good in case of inferior goods

21. J. R. Hicks, *op. cit.,* p. 61.

too. Hicks rightly remarks, "Though the law of demand does not necessarily hold in the case of inferior goods, it *is in practice likely* to."[22]

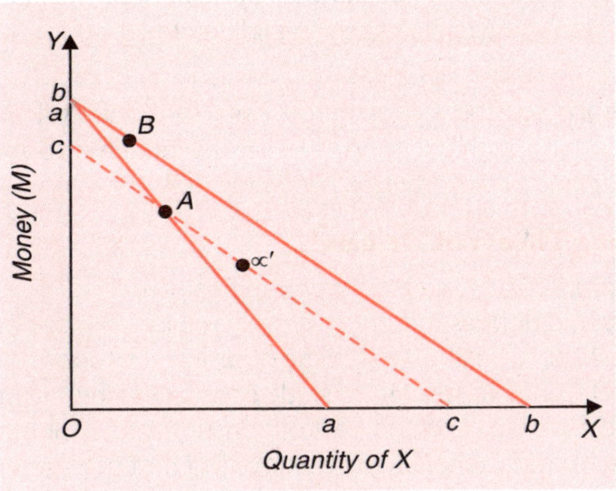

Fig. 13.13. *Demand for an Inferior Good*

The case of inferior goods in which inverse price-demand relationship holds good is depicted in Fig 13.13 in which good X represented on X-axis is assumed to be an inferior good. Suppose the price of good X falls so that the opportunity line shifts from position *aa* to *bb*. As before, the amount demanded of the good increases between A and α'. In other words, substitution effect leads to the increase in the consumption of good X. But, since the good X is now supposed to be an inferior good, the income effect of the price change will tend to diminish the demand. Therefore, the amount demanded will fall between α' and B. In other words, *B* will lie to the left of α'. But since the income effect is usually small and substitution effect much larger than it, position *B*, though lying to the left of α', will remain to the right of *A* indicating that amount demanded increases as a net result of the working of substitution effect and negative income effect. It is evident from Fig. 13.13 that when the price of an inferior good falls, its quantity demanded can rise even though the income effect is negative. Thus inverse price-demand principle will also hold in most cases of the inferior goods.

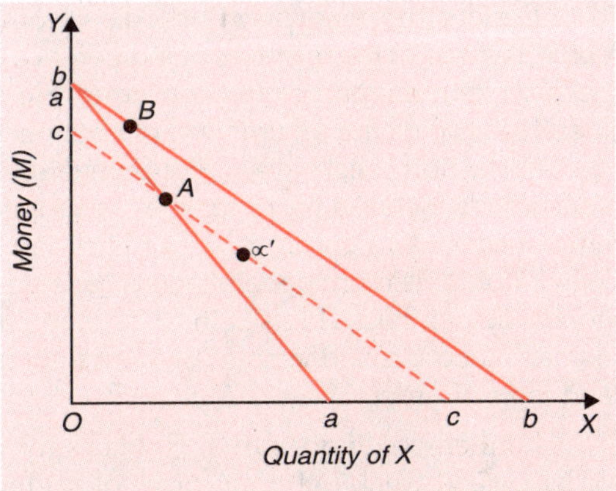

Fig. 13.14. *Demand for a Giffen Good*

If follows from the above analysis that exception to the law of demand can occur if in the case of an inferior good the negative income effect is so large that it outweighs the substitution effect. Now, the income effect can be very large if the income elasticity of demand is very high and also the proportion of income spent on the good is quite large. When the negative income effect overwhelms the substitution effect, the net result of the fall in price will be to diminish the amount demanded. The ***inferior goods for which there is direct price-demand relationship are known as Giffen goods.*** Thus Giffen goods, which are exceptions to the Marshallian law of demand can occur when the following three conditions are fulfilled[23]:

(i) The commodity must be inferior with a negative income elasticity of significant size.

(ii) The substitution effect must be small.

(iii) The proportion of income spent upon the inferior good must be large.

The Giffen good case is demonstrated in Fig.13.14. Here the position *B* lies to the left of original position *A* indicating that there is decrease in amount demanded of the good *X* as a

22. Hicks, *op. cit.*, p. 66.
23. *Op. cit.*, p. 66 *(italics supplied)*

result of the fall in price. Since substitution effect always tends to increase the amount demanded of the good whose price falls, in this case too the amount demanded increases between *A* and α'. Owing to the negative income effect, *B* lies to the left of α'. Since negative income effect is larger than the substitution effect, *B* lies even to the left of *A* showing fall in consumption of *X* as a result of the fall in its price.

It is very unlikely that the three conditions for the Giffen good case to occur will be satisfied in the case of any ordinary good. Thus "although exceptions to the law of demand are theoretically possible the chance of their occurrence is in practice negligible."[24]

Appraisal of Hicksian Weak Logical Ordering Theory of Demand

J. R. Hicks in his *Revision of Demand Theory* based on weak logical ordering goes deeper into the foundations of demand theory and derives in a more closely reasoned manner law of demand from a few simple and self-evident propositions of 'logic of order'. He does not follow Samuelson's behaviouristic revealed preference approach to study consumer's behavior but instead adopts the technique of weak logical ordering on the part of consumer to establish the theorems of demand. To establish law of demand, he takes the assumption that consumer behaves according to a scale of preferences. Thus, it is the weak logical ordering and preference hypothesis which are the hallmarks of the methodology of Hicks in his new theory of demand as distinct from indifference curve approach. Commenting on Hicks' *Revision of Demand Theory*, Fritz Machlup remarks, "The methodological position underlying Hicks approach is eminently sound. He is free from positivist behaviouristic restrictions on the study of consumer's behavior, and he also avoids contentions about the supposedly empirical assumptions regarding rational action. Instead he starts from a fundamental postulate, the preference hypothesis."[25]

Besides the innovation of logic of order and preference hypothesis, J. R. Hicks also corrects some of the mistakes of indifference curve analysis, namely, continuity and maximizing behaviour on the part of the consumer. He now abandons the use of indifference curves and therefore avoids the assumption of continuity. Instead of assuming that consumer maximizes the satisfaction, Hicks now, like Samuelson, relies on *consistency in the behaviour* of the consumer which is a more realistic assumption. Further, indifference curves could be usefully employed for two goods case, but Hicksian new theory based on preference hypothesis and logic of order is more general and is capable of being easily applied in cases of more than two goods. In fact, Hicks himself in his second part of this book presented a generalised version of demand theory covering cases of more than two goods by deducing from preference hypothesis and logic of order.

Further, credit goes to J. R. Hicks for distinguishing, for the first time, between strong ordering and weak ordering forms of preference hypothesis. By basing his theory on weak ordering which recognises the possibility of indifference in consumer's scale of preferences, Hicks succeeds in retaining the merits of indifference curve analysis in his new theory also.

Thus even by giving up the unrealistic assumption of indifference curve analysis, Hicks in his new logical weak ordering theory decomposes the price effect into income and substitution effects and is therefore able to account for Giffen goods which Samuelson's revealed preference theory cannot. Further, by separating substitution effect from income effect with the weak ordering approach, Hicks has been able to explain complementary and substitute goods in his generalised version of demand theory. Hence, in our view, Hicks has been able to improve upon his own indifference curve analysis of demand and Samuelson's revealed preference approach.

24. J. R. Hicks, *op. cit.*, p. 67.
25. Fritz Machlup, " Professor Hicks' Revision of Demand Theroy" *American Economic Review*, 1957.

CHAPTER

14

Elasticity of Demand

Various Concepts of Demand Elasticity

We have discussed in the preceding chapter that when price of a good falls, its quantity demanded rises and when price of it rises, its quantity demanded falls. This is generally known as *law of demand.* This law of demand indicates only the *direction of change in quantity demanded* of a commodity in response to a change in its price. This does not tell us by *how much* or *to what extent* the quantity demanded of a good will change in response to a change in its price. This information as to how much or to what extent the quantity demanded of a good will change as a result of a change in its price is provided by the concept of price elasticity of demand.

But, besides price elasticity of demand, there are various other concepts of demand elasticity. As we have seen in the previous chapter, demand for a good is determined by its price, income of the people, prices of related goods, etc. Quantity demanded of a good will change as a result of change in any of these determinants of demand. The concept of elasticity of demand therefore refers to the **degree of responsiveness of quantity demanded of a good to** a change in its price, consumers' income and prices of related goods. Accordingly, there are three concepts of demand elasticity : price elasticity, income elasticity, and cross elasticity. Price elasticity of demand relates to the degree of responsiveness of quantity demanded of a good to the change in its price. Income elasticity of demand refers to the sensitivenes of quantity demanded to a change in consumers' income. Cross elasticity of demand means the degree of responsiveness of demand of a good to a change in the price of a related good, which may be either a substitute for it or a complementary with it.

The concept of elasticity of demand has a very great importance in economic theory as well as formulation of suitable economic policies.

PRICE ELASTICITY OF DEMAND

As mentioned above, price elasticity of demand indicates the degree of responsiveness of quantity demanded of a good to the change in its price, other factors such as consumers' income, prices of related commodities that determine demand are held constant. Precisely, *price elasticity of demand is defined as the ratio of the percentage change in quantity demanded of a commodity to a given percentage change in price. Thus*

$$e_p = \frac{\text{Percentage change in quantity demanded}}{\text{Percentage change in price}}$$

For example, suppose 5 per cent rise in price of eggs causes its quantity demanded to fall by 10 per cent, we calculate price elasticity of demand for eggs as

$$\text{Price elasticity of demand} = \frac{10}{5} = 2$$

Strictly speaking, since as price of a commodity rises, its quantity demanded falls we should put negative sign before 10 and since price rises, we should put positive sign before 5., then we obtain the value of price elasticity as

$$\text{Price elasticity of demand} = \frac{-10}{+5} = -2$$

Thus, we get –2 as the price elasticity of demand. For the same changes in price and quantity demanded, we will get the same value of price elasticity of demand if price *falls* by 5 percent and quantity demanded *rises* by 10 percent. In this case we have

$$e_p = \frac{+10}{-5} = -2$$

However, it may be noted that a convention has been adopted in economics that price elasticity be expressed with a positive sign despite the fact that change in price and change in quantity demanded are inversely related to each other. This is because we are interested in measuring the *magnitude of responsiveness* of quantity demanded of a good to changes in its price.

It follows from the above definition of price elasticity of demand that when the percentage change in quantity demanded a commodity is greater than the percentage change in price that brought it about, price elasticity of demand (e_p) will be greater than one and in this case demand is said to be *elastic*. On the other hand, when a given prercentage change in price of a commodity leads to a smaller percentage change in quantity demanded, elasticity will be less than one and demand in this case is said to be *inelastic*. Further, when the percentage change in quantity demanded of a commodity is equal to the percentage change in price that caused it, price elasticity is equal to one. Thus. in case of elastic demand, a given percentage change

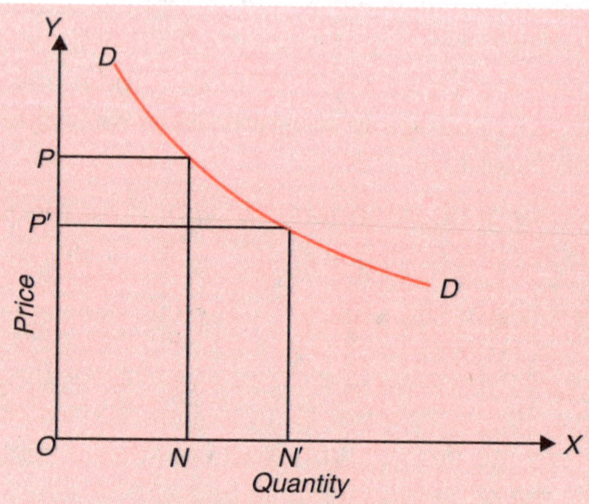

Fig. 14.1. *Elastic Demand*

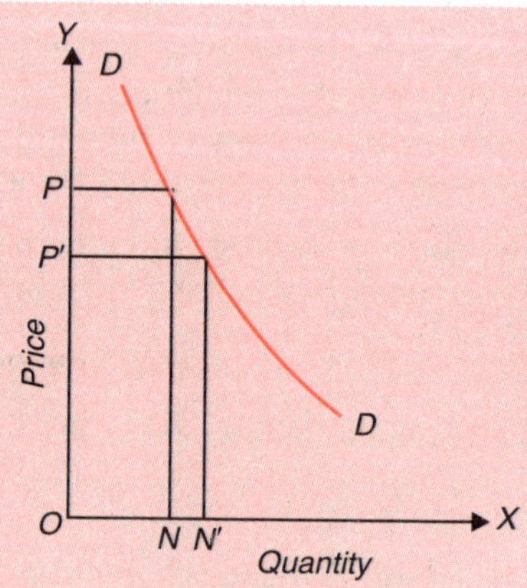

Fig. 14.2. *Inelastic Demand*

in price causes quite a large change in quantity demanded. And in case of inelastic demand, a given percentage change in price brings about a very small change in quantity demanded of a commodity.

It is a matter of common knowledge and observation that there is a considerable difference between different goods in regard to the magnitude of response of demand to the changes in price. The demand for some goods is more responsive to the changes in price than those for others. In terminology of economics, we would say that demand for some goods is *more elastic* than those for the others or *the price elasticity of demand of some* goods is greater than those of the others. Marshall[1] who introduced the concept of elasticity into economic theory remarks that the elasticity or responsiveness *of demand in a market is great or small according as the amount demanded increases much or little for a given fall in price, and diminishes much or little for a given rise in price.* This will be clear from Figures 14.1 and 14.2 which respresent two demand curves. For a *given fall* in price, from *OP* to *OP′*, increase in quantity demanded is much greater in Figure 14.1 than in Figure 14.2. Therefore, demand in Figure 14.1 is more elastic than the demand in Figure in 14.2 for a given fall in price for the portion of demand curves considered. Demand for the good represented in Fig. 14.1 is generally said to be elastic and the demand for the goods in Fig. 14.2 to be inelastic.

It should, however, be noted that *terms elastic and inelastic demand are used in the relative sense.* In other words, elasticity is a matter of degree only. Demand for some goods is only more or less elastic than others. Thus, when we say that demand for a good is elastic, we mean only that the demand for it is relatively more elastic. Likewise, when we say that demand for a goods is inelastic, we do not mean that its demand is absolutely inelastic but only that it is relatively less elastic. In economic theory, elastic and inelastic demands have come to acquire precise meanings. Demand for a goods is said to be *elastic* if price elasticity of demand for it is *greater than one.* Similarly, the demand for a goods is called *inelastic* if price elasticity of demand for it is *less than one.* Price elasticity of demand equal to one, or in other words, *unit elasticity* of demand therefore represents the dividing line between elastic and inelastic demands. It will now be clear that by inelastic demand we do not mean perfectly inelastic but only that price elasticity of demand is less than unity, and by elastic demand we do not mean absolutely elastic but that price elasticity of demand is greater than one.

Thus,

Elastic demand : $e_p > 1$

Inelastic demand : $e_p < 1$

Unitary elastic demand : $e_p = 1$

Price Elasticity of Demand for Different Goods Varies a Good Deal

As said above, goods show great variation in respect of elasticity of demand *i.e.*, their responsiveness to changes in price. Some goods like common salt, wheat and rice are very unresponsive to changes in their prices. The demand for common salt remains practically the same for a small rise or fall in its price. Therefore, demand for common salt is said to be 'inelastic'. Demand for goods like televisions, refrigerators etc., is elastic, since changes in their prices bring about large changes in their quantity demanded. We shall explain later at length those factors which are responsible for the differences in elasticity of demand of various goods. It will suffice here to say that the main reason for differences in elasticity of demand is the *possibility of substitution i.e.*, the presence or absence of competing substitues. The greater the ease with which substitutes can be found for a commodity or with which it can be substituted for other commodities, the greater will be the price elasticity of demand of that commodity.

Goods are demanded because they satisfy some particular wants and in general wants can be satisfied in a variety of alternative ways. For instance, the want for entertainment can be gratified by having television set, or by possessing a gramophone, or by going to cinemas or by visiting theatres. If the price of a television set falls, the quantity demanded of television

1. Alfred Marshall, *Principles of Economics*, 8th Edition, Vol. 2.

sets will rise greatly since fall in the price of television will induce some people to buy television in place of having gramophones or visiting cinemas and theatres. Thus the demand for televisions is elastic. Likewise, if price of 'Lux' falls, its demand will greatly rise because it will be substituted for other varieties of soap such as Jai, Hamam, Godrej, Nirma etc. On the contary, the demand for a necessary goods like common salt is inelastic. The demand for common salt is inelastic since it satisfies a basic human want and no substitutes for it are available. People would consume almost the same quantity of salt whether it becomes slightly cheaper or dearer than before.

Perfectly Inelastic and Perfectly Elastic Demand

We will now explain the two extreme cases of price elasticity of demand. First extreme situation is of perfectly inelastic demand which is depicted in Fig.14.3. In this case changes in price of a commodity does not affect the quantity demand of the commodity at all. In this perfectly inelastic demand, demand curve is a vertical straight line as shown in Fig.14.3. As will be seen from this figure, whatever the price the quantity demanded of the commodity remains unchanged at *OQ*. An approximate example of perfectly inelastic demand is the demand of acute diabetic patient for insulin. He has to get the prescribed doze of insulin per week whatever its price.

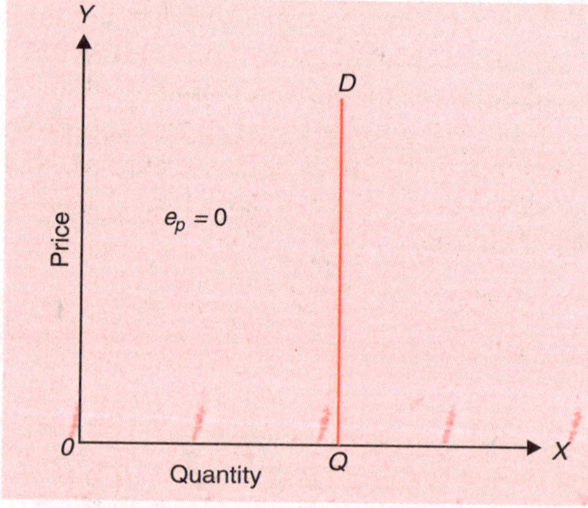

Fig. 14.3. *Perfectly Inelastic Demand ($e_p = 0$)*

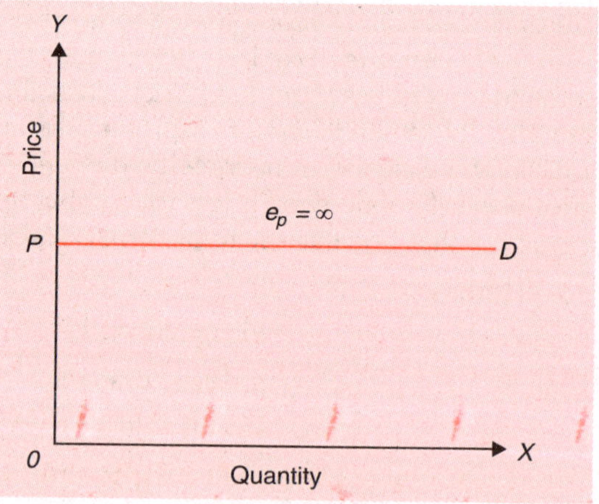

Fig. 14.4. *Perfectly Elastic Demand, $e_p = \infty$*

The second extreme situaiton is of perfectly elastic demand in which case demand curve is a horizontal straight line as shown in Fig.14.4. This horizontal demand curve for a product implies that a small reduction in price would cause the buyers to increase the quantity demanded from zero to all they wanted. On the other hand, a small rise in price of the product will cause the buyers to switch completely away from the product so that its quantity demanded falls to zero. We will see in later chapters that perfectly elastic demand curve is found for the product of an individual firm working under perfect competition. Products of different firms working under perfect competition are completely identical. If any perfectly competitive firm raises the price of its product, it would lose all its customers who would switch over to other firms, and if it reduces its price somewhat it would get all the customers to buy the product from it.

MEASUREMENT OF PRICE ELASTICITY

As said above, price elasticity of demand expresses the response of relative change in quantity demanded of a good to relative changes in its price, given the consumer's income, his tastes and prices of all other goods. Thus price elasticity means the degree of responsiveness or sensitiveness of quantity demanded of a good to a change in its price. An important method to measure price elasticity of demand is the percentage method which we explain below.

Price elasticity can be precisely measured by dividing the percentage change in quantity demanded by the given percentage change in price that caused it. Thus we can measure price elasticity by using the following formula:

$$\text{Price Elasticity} = \frac{\text{Percentage change in quantity demanded}}{\text{Percentage change in price}}$$

$$= \frac{\text{Change in quantity demanded / Quantity demanded}}{\text{Change in price /Price}}$$

or, in symbolic terms

$$e_p = \frac{\Delta q / q}{\Delta p / p} = \frac{\Delta q}{q} \div \frac{\Delta p}{p}$$

$$= \frac{\Delta q}{q} \times \frac{p}{\Delta p}$$

$$= \frac{\Delta q}{\Delta p} \times \frac{p}{q}$$

where e_p stands for price elastictity
q stands for quantity demanded
p stands for price
Δ stands for infinitesimal small change

Mathematically speaking, price elasticity of demand (e_p) is negative, since the change in quantity demanded is in opposite direction to the change in price; when price falls, quantity demanded rises and *vice versa.* But for the sake of convenience in understanding the *magnitude of response* of quantity demanded to the change in price we ignore the negative sign and take into account only the *numerical value* of the elasticity. Thus, if 2% change in price leads to 4% change in quantity demanded of good *A* and 8% change in that of good *B*, then the above formula of elasticity will give the value of price elasticity of good *A* equal to 2 and of good *B* equal to 4. It indicates that the quantity demanded of good *B* changes much more that of good A in response to a given change in price.

Midpoint Method of Calculating Percentage Changes

When we calculate the price elasticity of demand through percentage or proportionate method we face a problem whether to use the *initial price* as the base for calculating percent change in price and *initial quantity* as the base for calculating the percent change in quantity demanded in response to a given percent change in price. For example, suppose price of a commodity rises from Rs. 4 to Rs. 6 per unit and as a result, the quantity demanded falls from 120 units to 80 units. If we take initial price Rs. 4 as the base for change in price, then change in price by Rs. 2 amounts to 50 percent change in price $\left(\frac{6-4}{4} \times 100 = \frac{1}{2} \times 100 = 50\right)$ And taking initial quantity 120 units as the base for calculating percent change in quantity demanded, then there is 33.3 percent change in quantity demanded $\left(\frac{120-80}{120} \times 100 = \frac{1}{3} \times 100 = 33.3\right)$.

Thus we get price elasticity of demand as

$$e_p = \frac{33}{50} = 0.66$$

Let us now reverse the direction. Suppose the price of the commodity falls from ₹ 6 to ₹ 4 per unit, and as a result quantity demanded increases from 80 units to 120 units, then now taking initial ₹ 6 as the base for calculating percentage change in price, then there is 33.3 per cent change in price $\left(\frac{6-4}{6} \times 100 = \frac{2}{6} \times 100 = 33.3\right)$ and taking 80 units as the base for calculating percentage change in quantity, then the quantity demanded rises by 50 percent $\left(\frac{120-80}{80} \times 100 = \frac{40}{80} \times 100 = 50\right)$. Thus, we will now get $\frac{50}{33.3} = 1.5$ as the price elasticity of demand. It therefore follows that for the same absolute change in price and absolute change in quantity demanded we get different values of price elasticity of demand if we use ₹ 4 or ₹ 6 as the base for calculating percentage change in price and 120 units or 80 units as the base for calculating percentage change in quantity demanded. To avoid this problem we use ***midpoint method*** for calculating the percentage changes in price and quantity demanded. In midpoint method we calculate the percentage change in price or quantity demanded by *taking midpoint of the initial and final values of price and quantity demanded* respectively as the base. Thus, in our above example, midpoint (or, in other words, average) of prices of ₹ 4 and ₹ 6 is $\frac{4+6}{2} = 5$ and midpoint (or average) of quantities demanded is $\frac{80+120}{2} = 100$. Using this midpoint method, the percentage change in price is $\frac{6-4}{5} \times 100 = 40$ and percentage change in quantity demanded is $\frac{120-80}{100} \times 100 = 40$. With these percentage changes in price and quantity demanded price of elasticity of demand will be

$$e_p = \frac{40}{40} = 1$$

It should be carefully noted that for ***large changes in price, we must use midpoint method of calculating price elasticity of demand***. If change in price is *very small*, then we can use initial price and initial quantity demanded.

It p_1 stands for initial price and p_2 for the new price and q_1 for the initial quantity and q_2 for the new quantity, then midpoint formula for calculating price elasticity of demand (e_p) can be written as

$$e_p = \frac{(q_2 - q_1)}{\frac{q_1 + q_2}{2}} \div \frac{p_2 - p_1}{\frac{p_1 + p_2}{2}}$$

$$= \frac{\Delta q}{\frac{q_1 + q_2}{2}} \times \frac{\frac{p_1 + p_2}{2}}{\Delta p}$$

$$= \frac{\Delta q}{\Delta p} \times \frac{p_1 + p_2}{q_1 + q_2}$$

In a later section we will explain the concept of *arc elasticity of demand* which should be distinguished from the *point elasticity of demand.* Point elasticity of demand refers to the price elasticity at a point on a demand curve or, in other words, it refers to the price elasticity when the changes in the price and the resultant changes in quantity demanded are infinitestimally small. In this case if we take the initial or the original price and original quantity or the subsequent price and quantity after the change in price as the basis of measurement, there will not be any significant difference in the coefficient of elasticity.

Some Numerical Problems of Price Elasticity of Demand

Let us solve some numerical problems of price elasticity of demand (both point and arc) by percentage method.

Problem 1. *Suppose the price of a commodity falls from ₹ 6 to ₹ 4 per unit and due to this the quantity demanded of the commodity increases from 80 units to 120 units. Find out the price elasticity of demand.*

Solution : Change in quantity demand $(Q_2 - Q_1) = 120 - 80$

$$\text{Percentage change in quantity demanded} = \frac{Q_2 - Q_1}{\frac{Q_2 + Q_1}{2}} \times 100$$

$$= \frac{40}{\frac{200}{2}} \times 100$$

$$= 40$$

Change in price $= P_2 - P_1 = 4 - 6 = -2$

$$\% \text{ Change in price} = \frac{P_2 - P_1}{\frac{P_2 + P_1}{2}} \times 100 = \frac{-2}{\frac{10}{2}} \times 100$$

$$= -40$$

$$\text{Price elasticity of demand} = \frac{\% \text{ change in quantity demanded}}{\% \text{ Change in price}}$$

$$= \frac{40}{-40} = -1$$

We ignore the minus sign. Therefore, price elasticity of demand is equal to one.

Problem 2. *A consumer purchases 80 units of a commodity when its price is Re. 1 per unit and purchases 48 units when its price rises to ₹ 2 per unit. What is the price elasticity of demand for the commodity?*

Solution : It should be noted that the change in price from Re. 1 to ₹ 2 in this case is very large (*i.e.*, 100%). Therefore, to calculate the elasticity coefficient in this case midpoint elasticity formula should be used.

Change is price (Δp) = ₹ 2 – 1 = 1

Average of the original and subsequent prices = $\dfrac{p_1 + p_2}{2}$

$$= \frac{1+2}{2} = \frac{3}{2} = 1.5$$

Change in quantity demanded (Δq) = 80 – 48 = 32

Average of the original and subsequent quantities $= \dfrac{q_1 + q_2}{2} = \dfrac{80 + 48}{2} = \dfrac{128}{2} = 64$

$$e_p = \frac{\Delta q}{\frac{q_1 + q_2}{2}} \div \frac{\Delta p}{\frac{p_1 + p_2}{2}}$$

$$= \frac{32}{64} \div \frac{1}{1.5}$$

$$= \frac{32}{64} \times \frac{1.5}{1} = \frac{1}{2} \times \frac{15}{10} = \frac{3}{4} = 0.75$$

Thus, the price elasticity of demand obtained is equal to 0.75.

Problem 3. *Suppose a seller of a textile cloth wants to lower the price of its cloth from ₹ 150 per metre to ₹ 142.5 per metre. If its present sales are 2000 metres per month and further it is estimated that its price elasticity of demand for the product is equal to 0.7. Show*

(a) Whether or not his total revenue will increase as a result of his decision to lower the price; and

(b) Calculate the exact magnitude of its new total revenue.

Solution (*a*) Price elasticity $= \dfrac{\Delta q}{\Delta p} \cdot \dfrac{p}{q}$

p = ₹ 150

q = 2000 metres

Δp = 150 – 142.5 = 7.5

e_p = 0.7

Δq = ?

Substituting the values of p, q, Δp and e_p in the price elasticity formula we have

$$0.7 = \frac{\Delta q}{7.5} \cdot \frac{150}{2000}$$

$$\Delta q = \frac{0.7 \times 7.5 \times 2000}{150} = 70$$

Since the price has fallen, the quantity demanded will increase by 70 metres. So the new quantity demanded will be 2000 + 70 = 2070.

(*b*) Total Revenue before reduction in price = 2000 × 150 = ₹ 3,00,000

Total revenue after price reduction = 2070 × 142.5 = 2,94,975

Thus with reduction in price his total revenue has decreased.

Finding Price Elasticity from a Demand Function

Linear demand function for a commodity is of the following form

$$Q = a - bP \qquad \text{... }(i)$$

where Q stands for the quantity demanded and P for price of the commodity, a and b are constants.

Note that b represents the slope of the demand function which is negative and shows the ratio of change in quantity to a change in price, that is, $\frac{\Delta Q}{\Delta P}$.

Now, $$e_p = \frac{\Delta Q}{\Delta P} \cdot \frac{P}{Q}$$

Writing b for $\frac{\Delta Q}{\Delta P}$ we have

$$e_p = b\frac{P}{Q} \qquad \text{...... }(ii)$$

With the expression of above equation (*ii*) we can measure price elasticity from a given demand function. Let us take a numerical example.

Suppose we are given the following demand function for milk in the city of Delhi.

$$Q = 720 - 25\,P$$

Q is in thousands of litres. It is required to find out the price elasticity at price of ₹ 15 per litre.

b or $\frac{\Delta Q}{\Delta P}$ in the given demand function is 25. To obtain price elasticity we have first to calculate the quantity demanded at the given price of ₹ 15 per litre. Substituting 15 for P in the given demand function, we have

$$Q = 720 - 25 \times 15$$

$$Q = 720 - 375 = 345$$

Now, substituting $P = 15$, $Q = 345$ and $b = 25$ in the elasticity expression of equation (*ii*) along we have

$$e_p = b.\frac{P}{Q} = 25 \times \frac{15}{345} = 1.08$$

Thus price elasticity at price ₹ 15 per litre is 1.08 and quantity demanded of milk is equal to 345 thousand litres

Price Elasticity of Demand and Changes in Total Expenditure

It is often useful to know what happens to total expenditure made by the consumers on a good when its price changes. In Figure 14.5 a demand curve *DD* of a good is shown. When the price of good is OP, its quantity demanded is OQ. Since the total expenditure is price multiplied by the quantity of the good purchased, therefore

Consumer's total expenditure

$$= OP \times OQ = \text{area } OQRP$$

Now, whether the total expenditure rises or falls or remains the same with the change in the price of the good depends upon the price elasticity of demand. The total expenditure bears an important relationship with the price elasticity of demand and this relationship is of great significance in the theory of price. The following is the relationship between changes in total expenditure and price elasticity of demand.

The relationship between price elasticity of demand for goods and total expenditure or outlay made on it is of great significance because with this knowledge of relationship a producer or seller of the goods can estimate how his total revenue will change with the fall or rise in the price of the goods. As seen above, the price elasticity of demand measures the ratio of proportionate change in quantity demanded to the proportionate change in price. That is, ignoring signs,

$$e_p = \Delta Q/Q/\Delta P/P \text{ or } \%\ \Delta Q/\%\ \Delta P.$$

If price elasticity of demand is greater than one, then ignoring the signs, $\%\Delta Q > \%\ \Delta P$. On the other hand, if price elasticity of demand is less than one, $\%\ \Delta Q < \%\ \Delta P$. And if price elasticity equals one or, in other words, demand is unitary elastic, $\%\ \Delta Q = \%\ \Delta P$. For the sake of convenience, we write the results of this relationship in Table 14.1.

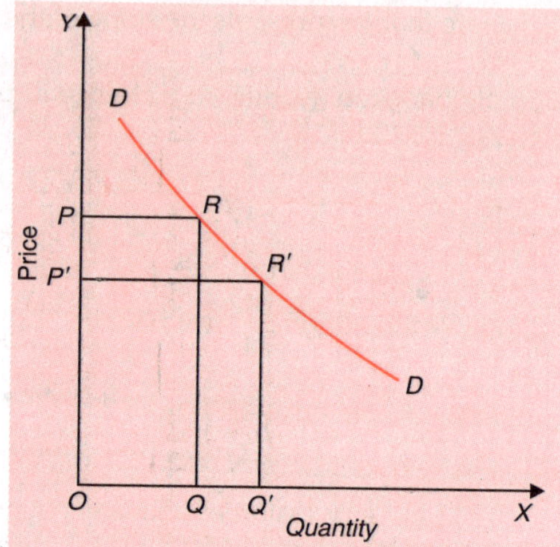

Fig. 14.5. *Changes in Price and Total Expenditure*

Table 14.1 Relationship Between Price Elasticity (e_p) and Total Expenditure (*TE*)

Price change	Elasticity greater than one ($e_p > 1$)	elasticity less than one ($e_p < 1$)	Elasticity equal to one ($e_p = 1$)
Price falls	*TE* increases	*TE* decreases	No change in *TE*
Price rises	*TE* decreases	*TE* increases	No change in *TE*

Proof of the Relation Between Price Elasticity and Total Expenditure

We can graphically prove the above-mentioned relationship between price elasticity of demand and the total expenditure. Consider Figure. 14.6. Suppose the price of a commodity falls from P to P_1 and in the response to it the quantity demanded increases from Q to Q_1. Since the total expenditure on a good equals the quantity demanded (Q) multiplied by the price of the good (P), that is, $TE = P.Q$, it will be seen from the diagram that at price OP the total expenditure equals the area of the rectangle $OPRQ$ and with the fall in price of the good the total expenditure equals OP_1TQ_1. Whereas the fall in price ($-\Delta P$) exerts a downward pressure on the total expenditure causing a decline in expenditure equal to $\Delta P.Q$. The increase in the quantity demanded caused by it ($+\Delta Q$) exerts an upward pressure on the total expenditure causing a gain in expenditure equal to ΔQP. If net total expenditure *increases* as price falls, then, as will be seen from Figure 14.6, the gain in expenditure ($+\Delta QP$) measured by the area

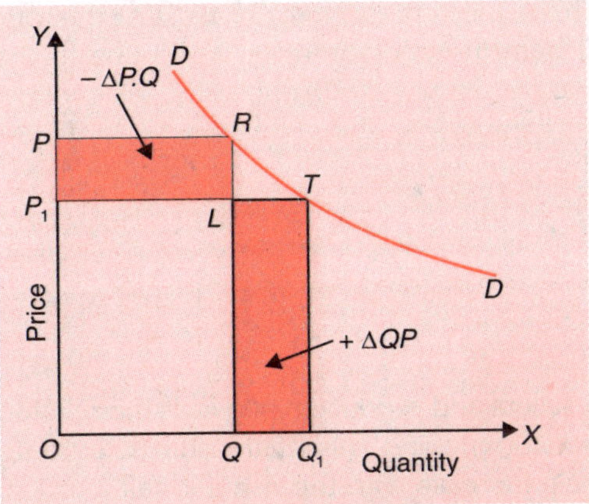

Fig. 14.6. *When total expenditure increases with the fall in price, e_p is greater than one*

of the rectangle $QLTQ_1$ must be greater than the decline in expenditure (– ΔP. Q) as measured by the area of the rectangle $PRLP_1$. Thus, if with the fall in price from P to P_1, the total expenditure increases, we have

$$\Delta QP > \Delta PQ.$$

Rearranging we have

$$\frac{\Delta QP}{\Delta PQ} > 1$$

Now, as seen above, $\frac{\Delta Q \cdot P}{\Delta P \cdot Q}$ measures the price elasticity of demand. It follows therefore that if the total expenditure increases

$$\frac{\Delta QP}{\Delta PQ} = e_p > 1$$

It is thus proved that if the total expenditure on a commodity increases resulting from a fall in its price, the price elasticity of demand is greater than one.

Likewise, we can show that if with the fall in price of a good the total expenditure on it declines, price elasticity will be less than one. Consider Figure14.7 where it will be seen that with the fall in price from P to P_1 the total *net* expenditure decreases because as the decline in expenditure (– ΔPQ) due to fall in price (– ΔP) exceeds the gain in expenditure (+ ΔQP) due to the increase in quantity demanded (+ ΔQ) caused by it.

Thus, when total expenditure (*TE*) decreases with the fall in price we have

$$\Delta QP < \Delta PQ$$

Rearranging we have

$$\frac{\Delta QP}{\Delta PQ} < 1$$

$$\frac{\Delta QP}{\Delta PQ} = e_p < 1$$

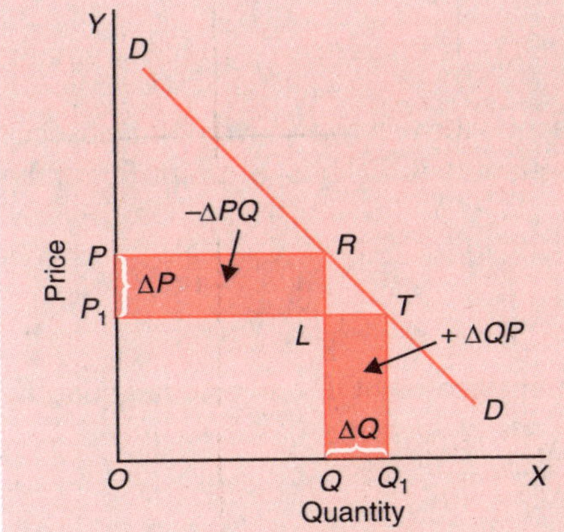

Fig.14.7. *When with the fall in price of a commodity total expenditure decreases, price elasticity of demand is less than one*

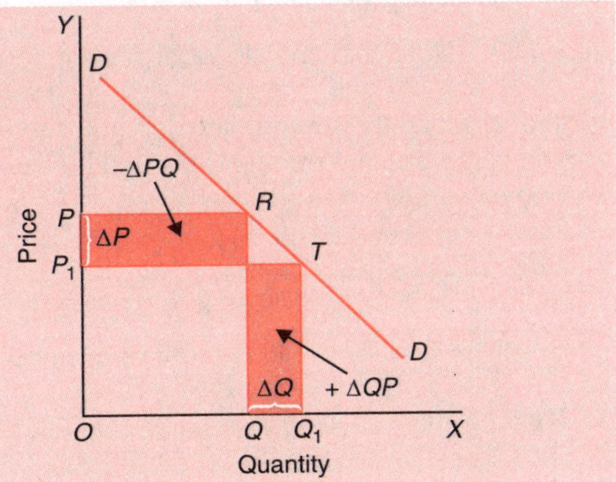

Fig.14.8. *When with the fall in price of a commodity, total expenditure remains the same, price elasticity of demand is equal to unity*

Similarly, as will be seen from Figure 14.8, with the fall in price from OP to OP_1, the total expenditure on the good remains constant as the gain in expenditure ($+ \Delta QP$) due to the increase in quantity demanded equals the decline in expenditure ($-\Delta PQ$) due to the fall in price. Thus, with the fall in price, constant total expenditure implies

$$\Delta QP = \Delta PQ$$

$$\frac{\Delta QP}{\Delta PQ} = 1$$

$$e_p = 1$$

As mentioned above, from the point of view of sellers and producers of goods the relation between price elasticity and total expenditure is of great importance. This relationship determines whether or not the seller's revenue or earnings would increase with the rise and fall in price. Total expenditure on a goods made by the consumers is revenue for the sellers. It is evident from the above relationship, that if a seller of a product *plans to cut the price* of his product, the total expenditure on it and therefore the total revenue of the seller will increase only if the demand for its product is elastic ($e_p > 1$) and his total revenue would decrease if the demand for its product is inelastic ($e_p < 1$). On the other hand, if the firm plans to raise the price of its product in a bid to increase its total revenue with the increase in its price, his total revenue will increase if the demand for its product is inelastic ($e_p < 1$).

MEASUREMENT OF PRICE ELASTICITY OF DEMAND AT A POINT ON A DEMAND CURVE

Let a straight line demand curve DD' is given and it is required to measure price elasticity at a point R on this demand curve. It will be seen from Fig. 14.9 that corresponding to point R on the demand curve DD', price is OP and quantity demanded at it is OQ.

The measure of price elasticity of demand is given by :

$$e_p = \frac{\Delta Q}{\Delta P} \cdot \frac{P}{Q}$$

The first term in this formula, namely, $\frac{\Delta Q}{\Delta P}$ is the reciprocal of the slope of the demand curve DD' (Note that the slope of the demand curve DD' is equal to $\frac{\Delta P}{\Delta Q}$ which remains constant all along the straight-line demand curve). The second term in the above point elasticity formula is the original price (P) divided by the original quantity (Q). Thus, at point R, on the demand curve DD'

$$e_p = \frac{1}{\text{slope}} \cdot \frac{P}{Q}$$

It will be seen from Fig. 14.9 that at point R, original price $P = OP$ and original quantity $Q = OQ$. Further, slope of the demand curve DD', is $\frac{\Delta P}{\Delta Q} = \frac{PD}{PR}$

Substituting these values in the above formula we have

$$e_p = \frac{1}{\frac{PD}{PR}} \times \frac{OP}{OQ}$$

$$= \frac{PR}{PD} \times \frac{OP}{OQ}$$

A glance at Figure 14.9 reveals that $PR = OQ$ and they will therefore cancel out in the above expression.

Therefore, $$e_p = \frac{OP}{PD} \quad ...(1)$$

Measuring price elasticity by taking the *ratio of these distances on the vertical axis,* that is, $\frac{OP}{PD}$ is called *vertical axis formula.*

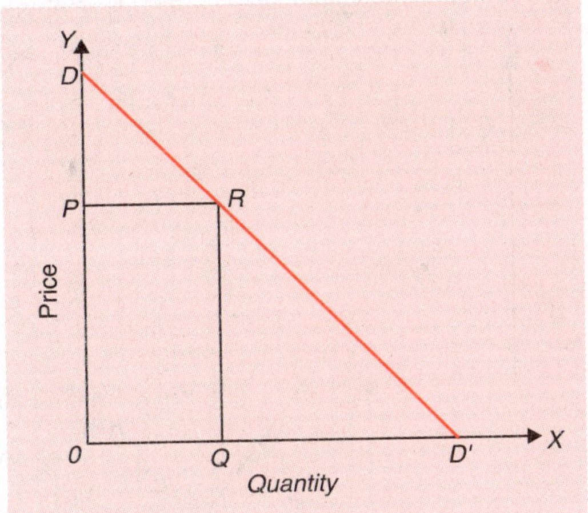

Fig. 14.9. *Measuring Price Elasticity at a point on a Straight-Line Demand Curve*

In a right-angled triangle ODD', PR is parallel to OD'. Therefore,

$$e_p = \frac{OP}{PD} = \frac{RD'}{RD}$$

RD' is the lower segment of the demand curve DD' at point R and RD is its upper segment. Therefore,

$$e_p = \frac{RD'}{RD} = \frac{\text{lower segment}}{\text{upper segment}}$$

Measuring price elasticity at a point on the demand curve by measuring the ratio of the distances of lower segment and upper segment is a popular method of measuring point price elasticity on a demand curve.

Measuring price elasticy on a non-linear demand curve. If the demand curve is not a straight line like DD' in Fig. 14.9 but is, as usual, a non-linear curve, then how to measure price elasticity at a given point on it? For instance, how price elasticity at point R on the demand curve DD in Fig. 14.10 is to be found. In order to measure price elasticity in this case, we have to draw a tangent TT' at the given point R on the demand curve DD' and then measure price elasticity by finding out the value of $\frac{RT'}{RT}$.

On a linear demand curve price elasticity varies from zero to infinity. Now again, take the straight-line demand curve DD' (Fig. 14.11). If point R lies exactly at the middle of this straight-line demand curve DD', then the distance RD will be equal to the distance RD'. Therefore, elasticity which is equal to $\frac{RD'}{RD}$ will be equal to one at the middle point of the straight-line demand curve. Suppose a point S lies above the middle point on the straight-line demand curve DD'. It is obvious that the distance SD' is greater than the distance SD and price

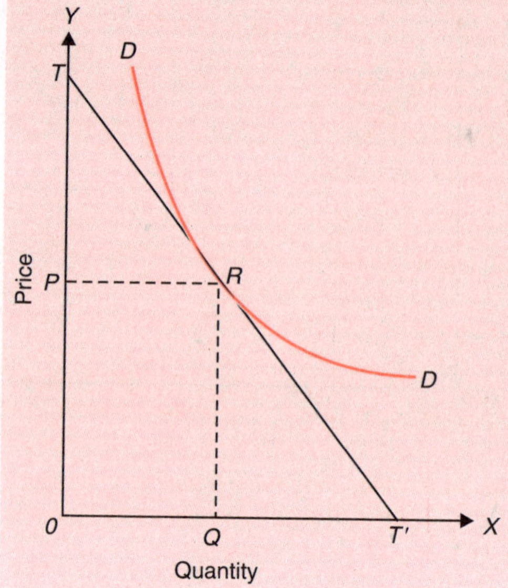

Fig. 14.10. *Measuring Price Elasticity at a Point on a Non-Linear Demand Curve*

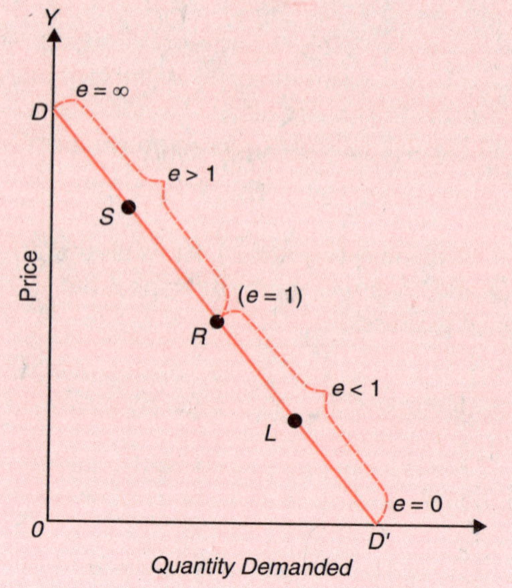

Fig.14.11. *On a linear demand curve price elasticity varies from infinity to zero.*

elasticity, which is equal to $\frac{SD'}{SD}$ at point S, will be more than one. Similarly, at any other point which lies above the middle point on the straight-line demand curve, price elasticity will be greater than unity. Moreover, price elasticity will go on increasing as we move further towards point D and at point D price elasticity will be equal infinity. This is because price elasticity is equal to $\frac{\text{lower segment}}{\text{upper segment}}$ and as we move towards D the lower segment will go on increasing while the upper segment will become smaller and smaller. Therefore, as we move towards D on the demand curve, the price elasticity will be increasing. At point D, the lower segment will be equal to the whole DD', and the upper segment will be zero. Therefore,

$$\text{Price elasticity at point } D \text{ on the demand curve } DD' = \frac{DD'}{0} = \text{infinity.}$$

Now, suppose a point L lies below the middle point on the linear demand curve DD' in Fig. 14.11. In this case, the lower segment LD' will be smaller than the upper segment LD and therefore price elasticity at point L which is equal to $\frac{LD'}{LD}$ will be less than one.

Moreover, price elasticity will go on decreasing as we move towards point D'. This is because whereas lower segment will become smaller and smaller, the upper one will be increasing as we move towards point D'. At point D' the price elasticity will be zero, since at D' the lower segment will be equal to zero and the upper one equal to the whole DD'. At point D',

$$e_p = \frac{0}{DD'} = 0$$

Price Elasticity Varies at Different Points on a Non-linear Demand Curve

From above it is clear that price elasticity at different points on a given demand curve (or, in other words, price elasticity at different prices) is different. This is not only true for a straight-line demand curve but also for a non-linear demand curve. Take, for instance, demand curve *DD* in Fig. 14.12. As explained above, price elasticity at point *R* on the demand curve *DD* will be found out by drawing a tangent to this point.

Thus elasticity at *R* will be $\frac{RT'}{RT}$. Since distance RT' is greater than RT, price elasticity at point *R* will be more than one. How exactly it is equal to will be given by actual value which is obtained from dividing RT' by RT. Likewise, price elasticity at point *S* will be given by $\frac{SJ'}{SJ}$. Because SJ' is smaller than SJ, elasticity point at *S* will be less than one. Again,how exactly it is, equal to will be found from actually dividing SJ' by SJ. It is thus evident that elasticity at point *S* is less than that at point *R* on the demand curve *DD*. Similarly, price elasticity at other points of the demand curves *DD* will be found to be different.

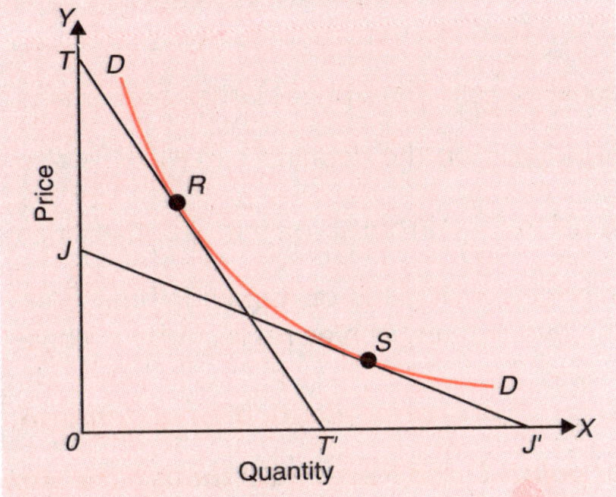

Fig. 14.12. *Price elasticity declines as we move down on a demand curve.*

Comparing Price Elasticity at a Given Price on the Two Demand Curves with Different Slopes

Having explained the measurement of price elasticity on a demand curve we will now explain how to compare price elasticity on two demand curves.

Let us take the case of two *demand curves with different slopes* starting from a given point on the *Y*-axis. This case is illustrated in Fig. 14.13 where two demand curves *DA* and *DB* which have different slopes but are starting from the same point *D* on the *Y*-axis. Slope of demand curve *DB* is less than that of *DA*. Now, it can be proved that at any given price the price elasticity on these two demand curves would be the same. If price is *OP*, then according to demand curve *DA*, quantity *OL* of the good is demanded and according to demand curve *DB*, quantity *OH* of the good is demanded . Thus, at price *OP* the corresponding points on the two demand curves are *E* and *F* respectively. We know that price elasticity at a point on the demand curve is equal to $\frac{\text{lower segment}}{\text{upper segment}}$. Therefore, the price elasticity of demand at point *E* on the demand curve *DA* is equal to $\frac{EA}{ED}$ and the price elasticity of demand at point *F* on the demand curve *DB* is equal to $\frac{FB}{FD}$.

Now, take triangle *ODA* which is a right-angled triangle in which *PE* is parallel ot *OA*.

It follows that in it, $\frac{EA}{ED}$ is equal to $\frac{OP}{PD}$. Thus, the price elasticity at point *E* on the demand curve DA is equal to $\frac{OP}{PD}$.

Now, in the right-angled triangle ODB, PF is parallel to OB. Therefore, in it $\frac{FB}{FD}$ is equal to $\frac{OP}{PD}$. Thus, price elasticity of demand at point F on the demand curve DB is also equal to $\frac{OP}{PD}$. From above it is clear that price elasticity of demand on points E and F on the two demand curves respectively is equal to $\frac{OP}{PD}$, that is, ***price elasticities of demand at points E and F are equal though the slopes of these two demand curves are different. It therefore follows that price elasticity is not the same thing as slope.*** Therefore, price elasticity on two demand curves should not be compared by considering their slopes alone.

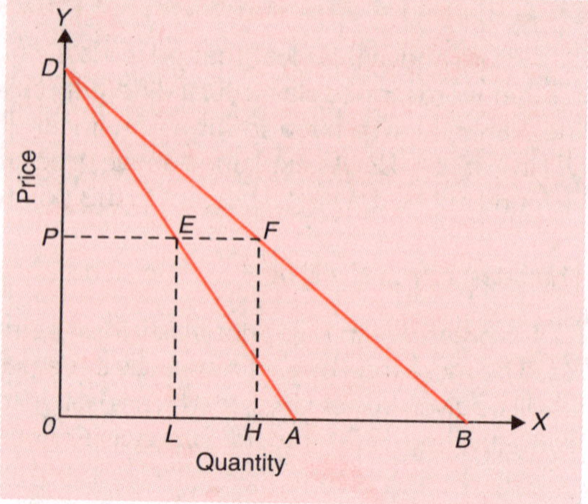

Fig. 14.13. *Comparing Price Elasticity on the Two Demand Curves with Different Slopes*

DETERMINANTS OF PRICE ELASTICITY OF DEMAND

We have explained above the concept of price elasticity of demand and also how it is measured. Now an important question is what are the factors which determine whether the demand for a goods is elastic or inelastic. The following are the main factors which determine price elasticity of demand for a commodity.

The Availabilty of Substitutes. Of all the factors determining price elasticity of demand the availability of the number and kinds of substiutes for a commodity is the most important factor. If for a commodity close substitutes are available, its demand tends to be elastic. If price of such a commodity goes up, the people will shift to its close substitutes and as a result the demand for that commodity will greatly decline. The greater the possibility of substitution, the greater the price elasticity of demand for it. If for a commodity good, substitutes are not available, people will have to buy it even when its price rises, and therefore its demand would tend to be inelastic.

For instance, if price of Coca Cola were to increase sharply, many consumers would turn to other kind of cold drinks, and as a result, the quantity demanded of Coca Cola will decline very much. On the other hand, if price of Coca Cola falls, many consumers will change from other cold drinks to Coca Cola. Thus, the demand for Coca Cola is elastic. It is the availability of close substitutes that makes the consumers senstive to the changes in price of Coca Cola and this makes the demand for Coca Cola elastic. Likewise, demand for common salt is inelastic because good substitutes for common salt are not available. If the price of common salt rises slightly, people would consume almost the same quantity of common salt as before since good substitutes are not available. The demand for common salt is inelastic also because people spend a very little part of their income on it and even if its price rises, it makes only negligible difference in their budget allocation for common salt.

The Proportion of Consumer's Income Spent. Another important determinant of the elasticity of demand is how much it accounts for in consumer's budget. In other words, the proportion of consumer's income spent on a particular commodity also influences price elasticity of demand for it. The greater the proportion of income spent on a commodity, the greater will generally be its price elasticity of demand, and vice versa. The demand for common salt, soap, matches and such other goods tends to be highly inelastic because the households spend only a fraction of their income on each of them. When price of such a commodity rises, it will not make much difference in consumers' budget and therefore they will continue to buy almost the same quantity of that commodity and, therefore, demand for them will be inelastic. On the other hand, demand for cloth in a country like India tends to be elastic since households spends a good part of their income on clothing. If price of cloth falls, it will mean great saving in the budget of many households and therefore this will tend to increase the quantity demanded of the cloth. On the other hand, if price of cloth rises, many households will not afford to buy as much quantity of cloth as before, and therefore, the quantity demanded of cloth will fall.

The Number of Uses of a Commodity. The greater the number of uses to which a commodity can be put, the greater will be its price elasticity of demand. If price of a commodity having several uses is very high, its demand will be small and it will be put to the most important uses and if price of such a commodity falls it wil be put to less important uses also and consequently its quantity demanded will rise significantly. To illustrate, milk has several uses. If its price rises to a very high level, it will be used only for essential purposes such as feeding the children and sick persons. If price of milk falls, it would be devoted to other uses such as preparation of curd, cream, ghee and sweets. Therefore, the demand for milk tends to be elastic.

Complementarity Between Goods. Complementarity between goods or joint demand for goods also affects the price elasticity of demand. Households are generally less sensitive to the changes in prices of goods that are complementary with each other or which are jointly used as compared to those goods which have independent demand or used alone. For example, for the running of automobiles, besides petrol, lubricating oil is also used. Now, if price of lubricating oil goes up, it will mean a very small increase in the total cost of running the automobile, since the use of oil is much less as compared to other things such as petrol. Thus, the demand for lubricating oil tends to be inelastic. Similarly, the demand for common salt is inelastic, partly because consumers do not use it alone but along with other things.

It is worth mentioning here that for assessing elasticty of demand for a commodity all the above three factors must be taken into account. The three factors mentioned above may reinforce each other in determining the elasticity of demand for a commodity or they may operate against each other. The elasticity of demand for a commodity will be the net result of all the forces working on it.

Time and Elasticity. The element of time also influences the elasticity of demand for a commodity. Demand tends to be more elastic if the time involved is long. This is because consumers can substitute goods in the long run. In the short run, substitution of one commodity by another is not so easy. The longer the period of time, the greater is the ease with which both consumers and businessmen can substitute one commodity for another. For instance, if price of fuel oil rises, it may be difficult to substitute fuel oil by other types of fuels such as coal or cooking gas. But, given sufficient time, people will make adjustments and use coal or cooking gas instead of the fuel oil whose price has risen. Likewise, when the business firms find that the price of a certain material has risen, then it may not be possible for them to substitute that material by some other relatively cheaper one. But with the passage of time they can undertake research to find substitute material and can redesign the product or modify the machinery employed in the production of a commodity so as to economize in the use of the dearer material. Therefore, given the time, they can substitute the material whose price has risen. We thus see that demand is generally more elastic in the long run than in the short run.

CROSS ELASTICITY OF DEMAND

Very often demand for two goods are so related to each other that when price of any of them changes, the demand for the other goods also changes, when its own price remains the same. Therefore, the degree of responsiveness of change in the demand for one good in response to change in price of another good represents the corss elasticity of demand of one goods for the other.

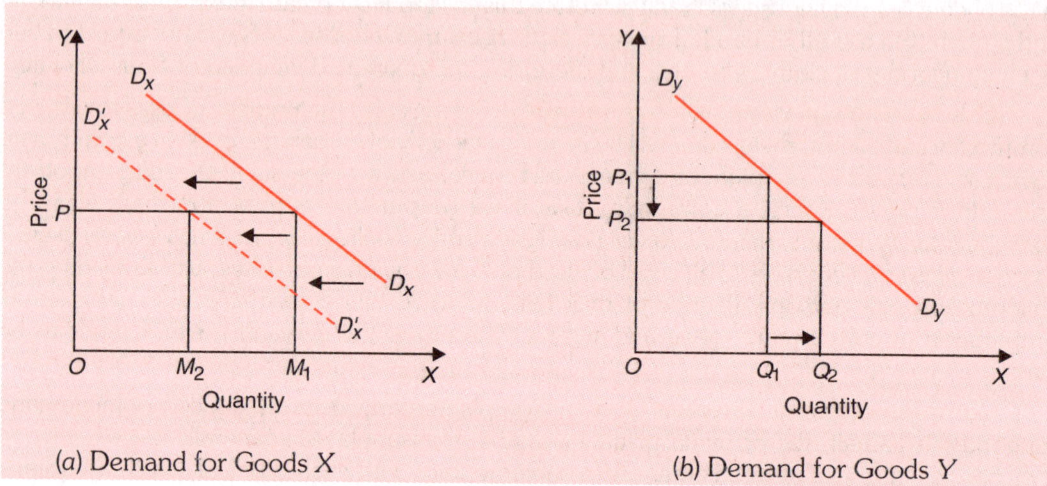

Fig. 14.14. *Demand Relations Between Two Substitutes Goods*

The concept of cross elasticity of demand is illustrated by Figure 14.14 where demand curves of two goods *X* and *Y* are given. Initially, the price of goods *Y* is OP_1 at which OM_1 quantity of it is demanded.

Now suppose that the price of goods *Y* falls from OP_1 to OP_2, while price of goods *X* remains constant at *OP*. As a consequence of fall in price of good *Y* from OP_1 to OP_2, its quantity demanded rises from OQ_1 to OQ_2. In drawing the demand curve $D_x D_x$ for good *X*, it is assumed that the prices of other goods (including good *Y*) remains the same. Now that the price of good *Y* has fallen and as *Y* is a substitute for good *X*, then as a result of the fall in price of good *Y* from OP_1 to OP_2, demand curve of good *X* will shift to the left, that is, demand for good *X* will decrease. This is because, as we have seen in the chapter on cardinal utility analysis, as the quantity of a good increases, the marginal utility of its substitute good declines and therefore the entire marginal utility curve of the substitute good shifts to the left. As shall be seen from the Figure 14.14 that as a result of the fall in price of good Y, the demand curve of good *X* shifts from D_xD_x to the dotted position $D_x'D_x'$ so that now at price *OP* less quantity OM_2 of good *X* is demanded; M_1M_2 of good *X* has been substituted by Q_1Q_2, quantity of good *Y*.

It should be noted that if good *X* instead of being substitute is ***complement*** of good Y, then the fall in price of good *Y* and resultant increase in its quantity demanded would have caused the increase in the demand for good *X* and as a result the entire demand curve of good *X*, instead of shifting to the left, would have shifted to the right. This is because, as has been explained in the chapter on cardinal utility analysis, when the price of a good falls and consequently its quantity demanded increases, the marginal utility of its complements increases and therefore the entire demand curve of the good *X* would shift to the right. With the rightward shift of the demand curve of goods X, greater quantity of it would be demanded at price *OP*. It should be noted again that in the concept of cross elasticity of demand, in response to the change in price of *one*, the quantity demanded of *another good* changes.

When the quantity demanded of good X rises as a result of the fall in the price of good Y, the coefficient of cross elasticity of demand of X for Y will be equal to the relative change in the quantity demanded of goods X in response to a given relative change in the price of good Y. Therefore,

$$\text{Coefficient of cross elasticity of demand of X for Y} = \frac{\text{Proportionate change in the quantity demanded of X}}{\text{Proportionate change in the price of good Y}}$$

$$\text{or, } e_c = \frac{\frac{\Delta q_x}{q_x}}{\frac{\Delta p_y}{P_y}} = \frac{\Delta q_x}{q_x} \div \frac{\Delta p_y}{p_y}$$

$$= \frac{\Delta q_x}{q_x} \times \frac{p_y}{\Delta p_y}$$

$$= \frac{\Delta q_x}{\Delta p_y} \times \frac{p_y}{q_x}$$

where e_c stands for cross elasticity of demand of X for Y.

q_x stands for the original quantity demanded of good X

Δq_x stands for change in quantity demanded of good X

p_y stands for the original price of good Y

Δp_y stands for a small change in the price of good Y

When change in price is large, we should use midpoint method for estimating cross elasticity of demand. We can write midpoint formula for measuring cross elasticity of demand as

$$e_c = \frac{q_{x2} - q_{x1}}{\frac{q_{x2} + q_{x1}}{2}} \div \frac{p_{y2} - p_{y1}}{\frac{p_{y2} + p_{y1}}{2}}$$

Numerical Problems

Problem 1. If *price of coffee rises from Rs. 45 per pack to Rs. 55 per pack of 250 grams and as a result the consumers demand for tea increases from 600 packs to 800 packs of 250 grams, then find the cross elasticty of demand of tea for coffee.*

Solution. We use midpoint method to estimate cross elasticity of demand.

Change in quantity demanded of tea = $q_{t2} - q_{t1}$ = 800 – 600

Change in price of Coffee = $P_{C2} - P_{C1}$ = 55 – 45

Substituting the values of the various variables in the cross elasticity formula we have

$$\text{Gross elasticity of demand} = \frac{800-600}{\frac{800+600}{2}} \div \frac{55-45}{\frac{55+45}{2}} = \frac{200}{700} \times \frac{50}{10} = \frac{10}{7} = 1.43$$

Problem 2. *Suppose the following demand function for coffee in terms of price of tea is given. Find out the cross elasticity of demand when price of tea rises from ₹ 50 per 250 grams pack to ₹ 55 per 250 grams pack.*

$$Q_c = 100 + 2.5P_t$$

where Q_c is the quantity demand of coffee in terms of packs of 250 grams and P_t is the price of tea per 250 grams pack.

Solution. The positive sign of the coefficient of P_t shows that rise in price of tea will cause an increase in quantity demanded of coffee. This implies that tea and coffee are substitutes.

The demand function equation implies that coefficient $\frac{dQ_c}{dP_t} = 2.5.$

In order to determine cross elasticity of demand between tea and coffee, we first find out quantity demanded of coffee when price of tea is ₹ 50 per 250 grams pack. Thus,

$$Q_c = 100 + 2.5 \times 50 = 225$$

$$\text{Cross elasticity,} \qquad e_c = \frac{dQ_c}{dP_t} \times \frac{P_t}{Q_c}$$

$$= 2.5 \times \frac{50}{225} = \frac{125}{225} = 0.51.$$

Cross Elasticity of Demand : Substitutes and Complements

As we have seen in the example of tea and coffee above, when two goods are substitutes of each other, then as a result of the rise in price of one good, the quantity demanded of the other good increases. Therefore, the cross elasticity of demand between the two substitute goods is *positive,* that is, in response to the *rise in price* of one good, the *demand for the other good rises.* Substitute goods are also known as *competing goods.* On the other hand, when the two goods are complementary with each other such as bread and butter, tea and milk, etc., the *rise in price* of one good brings about the *decrease* in demand for the other. Therefore, the cross elasticity of demand between the two complementary goods is *negative.* Thus, ***according to the classification based on the concept of cross elasticity of demand, goods X and Y are substitutes or complements according as the cross** elasticity of demand is positive or negative.* However, these definitions of substitute and complementary goods in terms of cross elasticity of demand are not very satisfactory. While goods between which cross elasticity of demand is positive can be called substitutes, but the goods between which cross elasticity is negative are not always complements. This is because positive cross elasticity is also found when income effect of the price change is very strong.

Take two goods X and Y where the demand for good X is inelastic. Suppose the price of good X falls and as a result real income of the consumer increases. Since the demand for good X is inelastic, the less moeny would now be spent on good X when its price has fallen. In this way, a good amount of money income would now be released from good X which will be spent on good Y. Thus, the income effect of the fall in price of X on the demand for good Y will be very large and, as a result, the quantity demanded of good Y will increase (the demand curve for good Y will shift to the right). We thus see that the ***fall in price of good X has resulted in the increase in demand for good Y*** and therefore the cross elasticity and demand of *good Y* for good *X* is negative. But this negative cross elasticity of demand of *Y* for *X* is not due to the complementary relationship between the two but due to the strong income effect as compared to the substitution effect on the demand for good *Y* produced by the fall in price of good *X* [2].

This can be easily understood from the aid of indifference curve diagram (Figure 14.15). With given prices of goods *X* and *Y* and a given money income as represented by the budget line *PL*, the consumer is in equilibrium at point *Q* on indifference curve IC_1, where he is purchasing OM_1 of good *X* and ON_1 of good *Y*. Now, suppose that the price of good *X* falls so that the budget line switches to the right to the position *PL'*. With *PL'* as the budget line, the consumer is in equilibrium at point *R* at which he is buying more of good *X* as well as more of good *Y*. This increase in the demand for good *Y* has come about as a result of stronger income effect on *Y* as compared to substitution effect on *Y*. Thus, in this case of strong income effect for good *Y*, the *quantity demanded of good Y increases* as a result of the fall *in price of good X,* and therefore the cross elasticity between the two is negative even though they are not complements.[3]

We have explained above important case where the cross elasticity between the two goods is negative even when they are not complements of each other. Thus, though the cross elasticity between the complements is negative, *but* ***negative cross elasticity, as we have seen above, cannot always be associated with complements,*** since negative cross elasticity is also associated with relatively powerful income effect. Thus, Ryan writes, "While we shall generally find that where the cross elasticity is negative, the goods would be regarded as complemntary in everyday usage.... We may associate negative cross elasticities of demand not only with complementarity but also with relatively strong income effect.[4]

It would be clear from the above analysis that cross elasticity approach to classify the goods as substitutes and complements is based upon the *total price effect on the quantity* demanded of a good resulting from a change in another good's price *without compensating for the change in the level of real* income, that is, without eliminating income effect. Thus, to quote Ferguson,"the cross elasticity approach to commodity classification, directs attention to the change in quantity demanded resulting from a change in price without compensating for the change in the level of real income. The *total effect* of a price change is thus the criterion used in this classification scheme".[5]

It is because of this inherent shortcoming that cross elasticity approach to classify goods as substitutes and complements leads to misleading conclusions regarding complementary goods. Therefore, in his important work '*Value and Capital*', Hicks pointed out that more

---

2. *It should be noted that the income effect and substitution effect on good Y produced by the fall in price of good X, work in the opposite direction. While the income effect on Y of the fall in price of X tends to increase the quantity demanded of Y, the substitution effect tends to reduce the quantity demanded of Y. This is because consumers would tend to substitue relatively cheaper good X for good Y. But if the income effect on Y is stronger, it would outweigh the substitution effect.*
3. *That the two goods X and Y are not complements is evident from the shape of their indifference curves in Figure 14.15. As has been explained in the chapters on Indifference Curve Analysis of Demand, the shape of the indifference curves of two complements is angular.*
4. W.J.L. Ryan *Price Theory,* Macmillan and Co. Ltd, London, 1959, p. 41.
5. C.F. Ferguson, *Microeconomic Theory.* Richard D. Irwin Inc., Illinois, 1967.

accurate classification of substitutes and complements can be obtained on the basis of *substitution effect alone* of the price change, after the income effect has been eliminated. However, on an empirical level, it is very difficult to employ substitution effect alone, since it is based on individual's preference function about which data are not readily available. Thus, according to Ferguson, a more accurate classification can be obtained by analysing the *substituion effect* alone. But while the latter method is more accurate, it is also more difficult to utilize on an empirical level. Thus in actual problems the older and less precise method must usualy be used.[6] He further says, "On an empirical level the cross elasticity approach is the only feasible method of commodity classification because market demand function can be computed while individual preference function cannot be from readily available data."

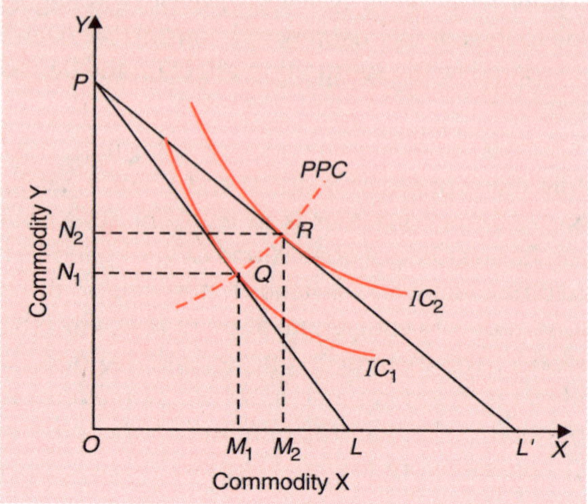

Fig. 14.15. *Demand for goods Y increases due to stronger income effect of change in Price*

Moreover, cross elasticity approach to commodity classification is very useful in applied economic problems because in such problems we are generally interested in knowing the *market relations* among various commodities rather than the relation among commodities as considered from the viewpoint of consumer preference functions."Thus the cross-elasticity classification of commodity relations is *the one* most frequently encountered in applied studies."[7]

The concept of cross elasticity of demand can be better understood with the aid of indifference curve analysis. Three indifference curves diagrams (Figure 14.16, 14.17 and 14.18) are drawn below in which the difference is found in the *shapes* of indifference curves. As explained in the chapter on indifference curves, the shapes of the indifference curves between two commodities reflect the consumer's scale of preferences between two commodities. With given prices of two goods and given income of the consumer, the budget line, to begin with, is PL_1. Suppose, with the fall in price of good *X*, consumer's income and price of *Y* remaining the same, price line shifts to the position PL_2. As a result of this fall in price of *X* in Figure 14.16 the consumer buys more of good *X* and *less of good Y*. In other words, cross elasticity between goods *X* and *Y* in Figure 14.16 is *positive*. It should be noted that **in case of positive cross elasticity, price consumption curve slopes downward** as in Figure 14.16.

Similarly, in Figure 14.17 with price line PL_1, the consumer is in equilibrium at point *Q* on indifference curve IC_1. As a result of fall in price of *X*, price of *Y* and consumer's income remaining the same, the budget line switches to the position PL_2 and consumer comes to be in equilibrium position at *R* where he is buying greater quantity OM_2 of *X but the same quantity of good Y*. In other words, with the fall in price of *X*, the quantity demanded of good *Y* has not changed at all. Therefore, in this Figure 14.17 cross elasticity of demand between *X* and *Y* is *zero*. It should be noted that **in case of zero cross elasticity of demand, price consumption curve is a horizontal straight line, that is, it is parallel to the X-axis.**

6. *Ibid*, p. 60.
7. *Ibid*, p. 63

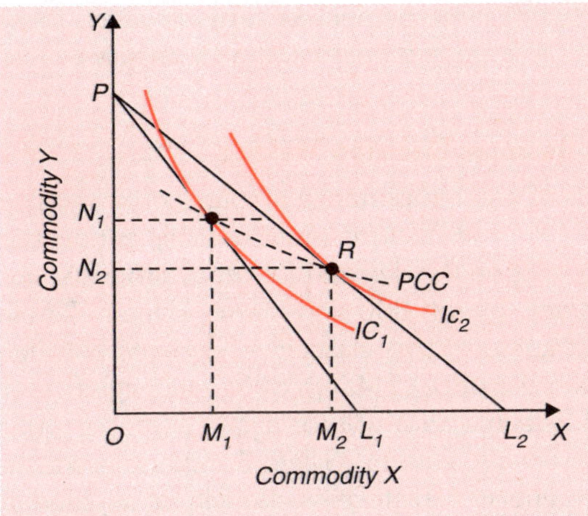

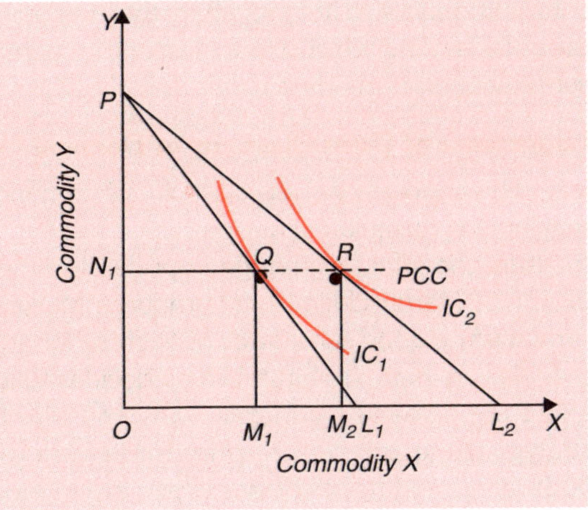

Fig. 14.16. *Substitute Goods : e_c is positive* **Fig. 14.17.** $e_c = 0$

Now consider Figure 14.18 where with the fall in price of good *X* and consequently shifting of the price line from PL_1 to PL_2, the consumer's equilibrium position shifts from *Q* to *R*. It will be seen from Figure14.18 that as a result of fall in price of *X*, consumer is buying more not only of *X* but also of *Y*. In other words, *fall in price of X* has resulted in the increase in *quantity demanded of* good *Y*. Therefore, the cross elasticity of demand between *X* and *Y* in Figure 14.18 is negative. It should be noted that ***in case of negative cross elasticity of demand, price consumption curve slopes upward.***

It is worth mentioning here that through indifference curves analysis, we can only know whether cross elasticity is negative, zero or positive, we cannot precisely measure the magnitude of cross elasticity of demand.

The concept of cross elasticity of demand is very important in economic theory. The substitutes and complementary goods, as we have seen above, are defined in terms of cross elasticity of demand. The goods between which cross elasticity of demand is positive are known as substitute goods and the goods between which cross elasticity of demand is negative are complementary goods. Besides, classification of various types of market structures is made on the basis of cross elasticity of demand. Triffen has employed the concept of cross elasticity of demand in distinguishing the various forms of markets. Perfect competition is defined as that in which the cross elasticity of demand between the products produced by many firms in it is infinite. Monopoly is said to exist when a producer produces a product, the cross elasticity of whose product with any other product is very low. In fact, the pure or absolute monopoly is often defined as the production by a single producer of a product whose cross elasticity of demand product with any other product is zero. Monopolistic

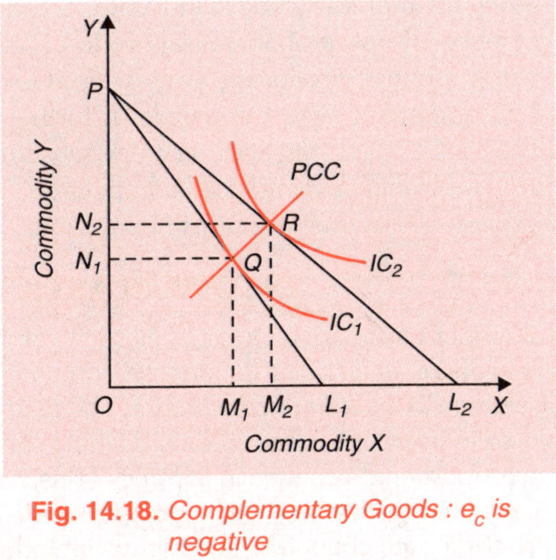

Fig. 14.18. *Complementary Goods : e_c is negative*

competition is said to prevail in the market when a large number of firms produce those products among which cross elasticity of demand is large and positive, that is, they are close substitutes of each other.

Importance of Cross Elasticity of Demand for Business Decision Making

The concept of cross elasticity of demand is of great importance in managerial decision making for formulating proper price strategy. Multiproduct firms often use this concept to measure the effect of change in price of one product on the demand for other products. For example, Maruti Udyog Ltd. produces Maruti Vans, Maruti 800 and Maruti Esteem. These products are good substitutes of each other and therefore cross elasticity of demand between them is very high. If Maruti Udyog decides to lower the price of Maruti 800, it will significanty affect the demand for Maruti Vans and Maruti Esteem. So it will formulate a proper price strategy fixing appropriate price for its various products. Further, Gillete Company produces both razors and razors blades which are complements with high cross elasticity of demand. If it decides to lower the price of razors, it will greatly increase the demand for razor bladdes. Thus there is need for adopting a proper price strategy when it produces products with high positive or negative cross price-elasticity of demand.

Second, the concept of cross elasticity of demand is frequently used in defining the boundaries of an industry and in measuring interrelationship between industries. An industry is defined as a group of firms producing similar products (that is, products with a high positive cross elasticity of demand. For example, cross elasticity of demand between Maruti Esteem, Hyundai Assent, Opel Astra is postiive and quite high. They therefore belong to the same industry (*i.e.*, automobiles). It should be noted that because of interrelationship of firms and industries between which cross price-elasticity of demand is positive and high, any one cannot raise price of its product without losing sales to other firms in the related industries.

Further, the concept of cross elasticity of demand is extremly used in the United States in deciding cases relating to Anti-trust laws and monopolistic practices used by firms. It so happens that in order to reduce competition that one dominant firm producing a product with a high cross elasticity of demand with the products of other firms tries to take over them and thereby establish a monopoly or different firms try to merge with each other to form a cartel to enjoy monopolistic profits. These actions are held illegal by Anti-trust or anti-monopoly laws. An interesting attempt was made in India by Coca-Cola in 1995 when it returned to India following the adoption of policy of liberalisation. In order to reduce competition, Coca-Cola company purchased the firm producing Thums Up, Gold Spot Limca which have high positive cross elasticity of demand with Coca-Cola. It further made efforts to take over 'Pure Drinks', the producer of Campa-Cola, another close substitutes but failed. If it had succeeded in its venture it could have significantly reduced competition. With this its competition would have been only with other multinational rival firm *Pepsi-Cola*.

INCOME ELASTICITY OF DEMAND

Another important concept of elasticity of demand is income elasticity of demand. Income elasticity of demand shows the degree of responsiveness of quantity demanded of a good to a small change in income of consumers. The degree of responsiveness of quantity demanded to a change in income is measured by dividing the proportionate change in quantity demanded by the proportionate change in income. Thus, more precisely, the income elasticity of demand may be defined as the ratio of the proportionate change in the quantity purchased of a good to the proportionate change in income which induces the former.

$$\text{Income Elasticity} = \frac{\text{Proportionate change in purchases of a good}}{\text{Proportionate change in income}}$$

Thus, if the proportionate change in purchases or quantity demanded of a good exceeds that of proportionate change in income, income elasticity will be greater than one. For example, if a 2 per cent change in income leads to 5 per cent change in quantity demanded of a good, income elasticity of the demand for the good will be 5%/2%=2.5.

Let M stand for an initial income, ΔM for a small change in income, Q for the initial quantity purchased demand, ΔQ for a change in quantity purchased as a result of a change in income and e_i for income elasticity of demand. Then

$$e_i = \frac{\frac{\Delta Q}{Q}}{\frac{\Delta M}{M}} = \frac{\Delta Q}{Q} \times \frac{M}{\Delta M}$$

$$= \frac{\Delta Q}{\Delta M} \cdot \frac{M}{Q}$$

Midpoint formula for measuring income elasticity of demand when changes in income are quite large can be written as

$$e_i = \frac{Q_2 - Q_1}{\frac{Q_2 + Q_1}{2}} \div \frac{M_2 - M_1}{\frac{M_2 + M_1}{2}}$$

$$= \frac{\Delta Q}{Q_2 + Q_1} \times \frac{M_2 + M_1}{\Delta M}$$

$$= \frac{\Delta Q}{\Delta M} \times \frac{M_2 + M_1}{Q_2 + Q_1}$$

Income Elasticity, Normal Goods and Inferior Goods

It is important to note that the value of *zero income elasticity of demand is of great significance.* Zero income elasticity of demand for a good implies that a given increase in income does not at all lead to any increase in quantity demanded of the good or increase in expenditure on it. In other words, zero income elasticity signifies that quantity demanded of the good is quite unresponsive to changes in income. Besides, zero income elasticity is significant because it represents a dividing line between positive income elasticity on the one side and negative income elasticity on the other. When income elasticity is more than zero (*that is, positive*), then an increase in income leads to the increase in quantity demanded of the goods. This happens in case of normal goods. On the other side there are all those goods which have income elasticity less than zero (that is, negative) and in such cases increase in income leads to the fall in quantity demanded of the goods. ***Goods having negative income elasticity are known as inferior goods.*** We thus see that zero income elasticity is a significant value, for it represents a dividing line between positive income elasticity and negative income elasticity and therefore helps us in distinguishing normal goods from inferior goods.

Income Elasticity, Luxuries and Necessities

Another significant value of income elasticity is unity. This is because when income elasticity of demand for a good is equal to one, then proportion of income spent on the good remains the same as consumer's income increases. Income elasticity of unity also represents a useful dividing line. If the income elasticity for a good is greater than one, the proportion of consumer's income spent on the good rises as consumer's income increases, that is, that good bulks larger in consumer's expenditure as he becomes richer. On the other hand, If income elasticity for a good is less than one, the proportion of consumer's income spent on it falls as his income rises, that is, the good becomes relatively less important in consumer's expenditure as his income rises. ***A good having income elasticity more than one and which therefore bulks larger in consumer's budget as he becomes richer is called a luxury. A good with an income elasticity less than one and which claims declining proportion of consumer's income as he becomes richer is called a necessity.*** It should, however, be noted that the definitions of luxuries and necessities on the basis of income elasticity may not conform to their definitions in English dictionary because the dictionary's luxuries may be necessities and its necessities may be luxuries according to the above definition. But in economic theory it is useful to call the goods with income elasticity greater than one as luxuries and goods with income elasticity less than one as necessities.

Income Elasticity Defined in Terms of Expenditure

We can also express the income elasticity in terms of changes in expenditure made on the good rather than the change in quantity purchased of the good as a result of a change in income. It should be noted that expenditure is equal to the quantity purchased of the good multiplied by the price of the good. If Q is the quantity purchased of the good and P the price of the good, the expenditure made on the good will be equal to QP.

As defined above,

$$e_i = \frac{\Delta Q}{Q} \div \frac{\Delta M}{M} = \frac{\Delta Q}{Q} \times \frac{M}{\Delta M}$$

Multiplying the numerator and denominator by P, we get

$$e_i = \frac{\Delta Q \,.\, P}{Q \,.\, P} \times \frac{M}{\Delta M}$$

Now, as explained above, $Q.P$ is the expenditure made on the good and $\Delta Q \,.\, P$ is the change in expenditure made as a result of change in income. Let E stand for the expenditure made on the good. Then the above equation will become:

$$e_i = \frac{\Delta E}{E} \times \frac{M}{\Delta M}$$

or $$e_i = \frac{\Delta E}{\Delta M} \cdot \frac{M}{E}$$

$$\text{Thus, income elasticity} = \frac{\text{Change in expenditure on a good}}{\text{Change in income}} \times \frac{\text{Income}}{\text{Expenditure on a good}}$$

It is important to note that the value of *zero income elasticity* of demand is of great significance. Zero income elasticity of demand for a good implies that a given increase in income does not at all lead to any increase in quantity demanded of the good or increase in expenditure on it. In other words, zero income elasticity signifies that quantity demanded of the good is quite unresponsive to changes in income. Besides, zero income elasticity is significant because it represents a dividing line between positive income elasticity on the one side and negative income elasticity on the other. On the one side, when income elasticity is more than zero (that *is, positive)*, then an increase in income leads to the increase in quantity demanded of the good. This happens in case of normal goods. On the other side of zero income elasticity are all those goods which have income elasticity less than zero (that is, negative) and in such cases increase in income will lead to the fall in quantity demanded of the goods. ***Goods having negative income elasticity are known as inferior goods.*** We thus see that zero income elasticity is a significant value, for it represents a dividing line between positive income elasticity and negative income elasticity and therefore help us in distinguishing normal goods from inferior goods.

Another important value of income elasticity is ***the reciprocal of proportion of consumer's income spent on a good,*** that is $1/K_x$ where K_x stands for the proportion of consumer's income spent on a good X. The value of $1/K_x$ for the income elasticity of demand seems to be significant because when income elasticity for a good equals $1/K_X$, then the whole of the increase in consumer's income will be spent on the increase in quantity purchased of the good X.

Proof: It is easy to show that when whole of the increase in income is spent on any good X, then income elasticity is equal to the reciprocal of the proportion of income spent on the good, that is, $1/K_x$.

We know that $e_i = \frac{M}{E} \cdot \frac{\Delta E}{\Delta M}$

Suppose the whole of the increase in income (ΔM) is spent on the good X, then change in expenditure (ΔE) on the good X would be equal to ΔM, price of good X remaining the same. Substituting ΔM for ΔE in the above measure of income elasticity, we get

$$e_i = \frac{M}{E} . \frac{\Delta M}{\Delta M} = \frac{M}{E} = \frac{1}{E/M}$$

$$= \frac{1}{K_x} \text{ (where } K_x = E/M = \text{proportion of income spent on good } X\text{).}$$

It may be further noted that if income elasticity of demand for a good is greater than $1/K_x$, then more than the increase in consumer's income would be spent on the good and *vice versa*.

Measuring Income Elasticity at a Point on an Engel Curve

An Engel curve shows the relationship between quantity demanded of a good and level of consumer's income. Since with the increase in income normally more quantity of the good is demanded, Engel curve slopes upward *(i.e.* it has a positive slope). As seen in a previous chapter, though Engel curve for normal goods slopes upward but it is of different shape for different goods. It is convex or concave, depending on whether the good is a necessity or a luxury. In case of an inferior good for which income effect is negative, that is, less is demanded when income rises. Engel curve is backward bending. We will first explain how income elasticity

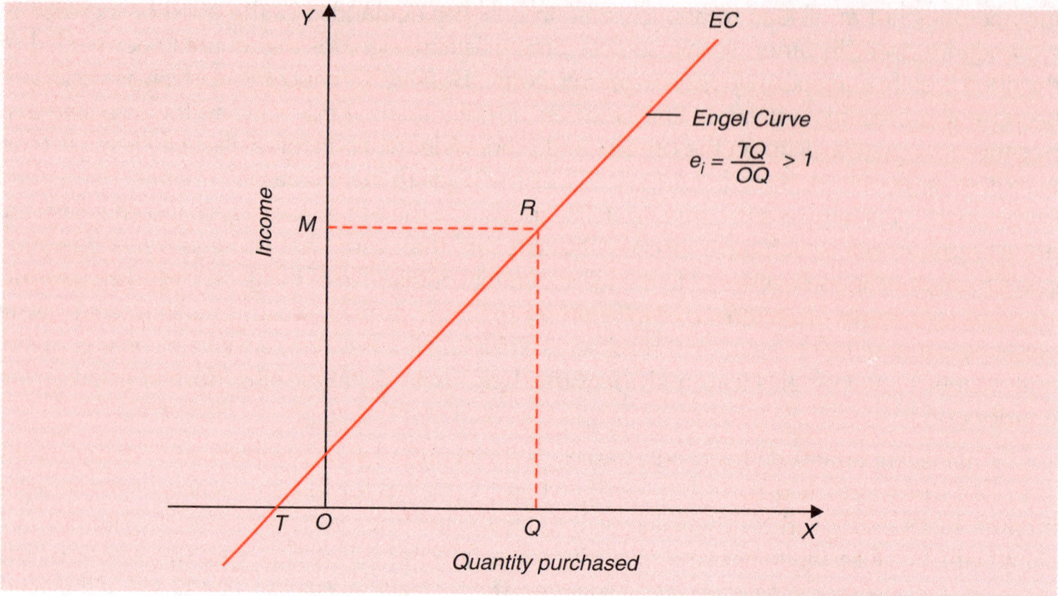

Fig. 14.19. *Measuring Income Elasticity at Point R on the Engel Curve*

is measured at a point on a linear Engel curve *EC* in Fig. 14.19 which is sloping upward. It is required to measure income elasticity at point *R* on this Engel curve. It will be seen that at point *R*, the quantity of a good *OQ* is purchased at the income level *OM*. Let us extend the Engel curve *EC* downward so that it meets the *X*-axis at point *T*.

$$e_i = \frac{\Delta Q}{\Delta M} \cdot \frac{M}{Q} \quad \text{....(i)}$$

$\Delta Q/\Delta M$ is the reciprocal of the slope ($\Delta M/\Delta Q$) of the Engel curve *EC*.
Rewriting the income elasticity measure we have

$$e_i = \frac{1}{\Delta M / \Delta Q} \cdot \frac{M}{Q} \quad \text{....(ii)}$$

It will be seen from the Engel curve *EC* in Figure 14.19 that at point *R* on it, its slope (*i.e.* $\Delta M/\Delta Q$) equals *RQ/TQ* and level of income (*M*) equals *RQ* and quantity purchased at this income level equals *OQ*. Substituting these in (*ii*) above we have

$$e_i = \frac{1}{\Delta M / \Delta Q} \cdot \frac{M}{Q} = \frac{1}{RQ / TQ} \cdot \frac{RQ}{OQ}$$

$$= \frac{TQ}{RQ} \cdot \frac{RQ}{OQ} = \frac{TQ}{OQ}$$

Thus, income elasticity at point *R* on the Engel Curve *EC* in Figure 14.19 can be obtained by measuring the lengths *TQ* and *OQ* and dividing the former by the latter. Since in Figure 14.19 *TQ* is larger than *OQ*, income elasticity at point *R* is greater than one (However, the exact magnitude of income elasticity can be found by actually dividing *TQ* by *OQ*). We therefore conclude that ***if Engel curve on being extended downward meets X-axis to the left of the point of origin income elasticity will be greater than one.***

In Figure 14.20 at point R on Engel curve EC, income elasticity is equal to TQ'/OQ'. Since TQ' is less than OQ', income elasticity will be here less than one. ***We therefore conclude that if Engel curve when extended downward meets the X-axis to the right of the point of origin, income elasticity will be less than one.***

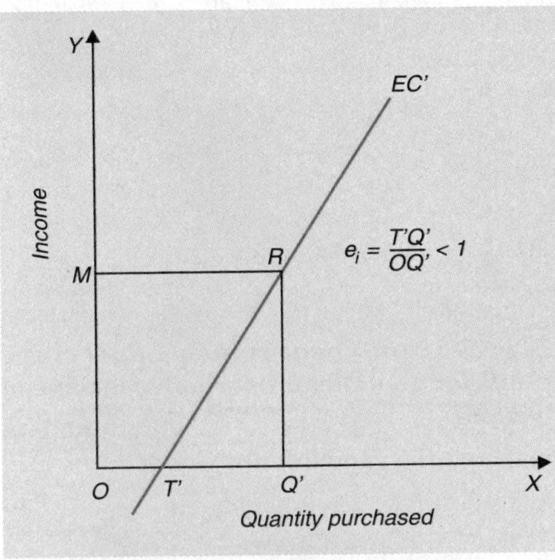

Fig. 14.20. *Income elasticity is less than one*

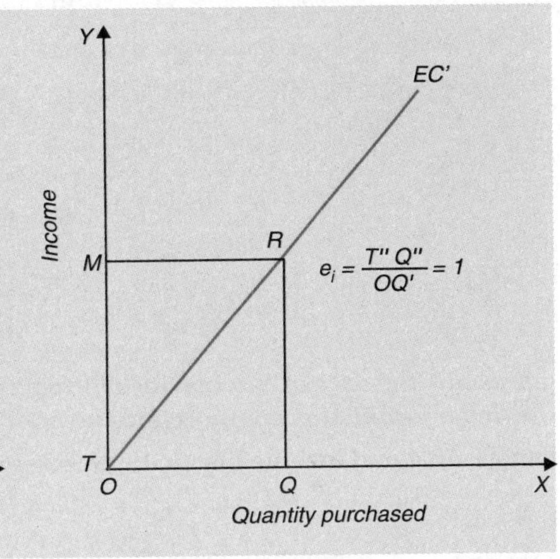

Fig. 14.21. *Income elasticity is equal to one*

In Figure 14.21 Engel curve when extended meets the point of origin, income elasticity at point R is equal to one (TQ/OQ in Figure 14.21 equals one).

Measuring Income Elasticity at a Non-Linear Engel Curve

If Engel curve is non-linear as is usually the case in the real world, the income elasticity can be measured at a point on the Engel curve by drawing a tangent at the point and extending it to meet the X-axis. Suppose we are required to measure income elasticity at K on the non-linear Engel curve EC drawn in Figure 14.22 where at income level OM, quantity OQ is being demanded. We draw a tangent $T\ T$ at point K and extend it to meet the X-axis at point T.

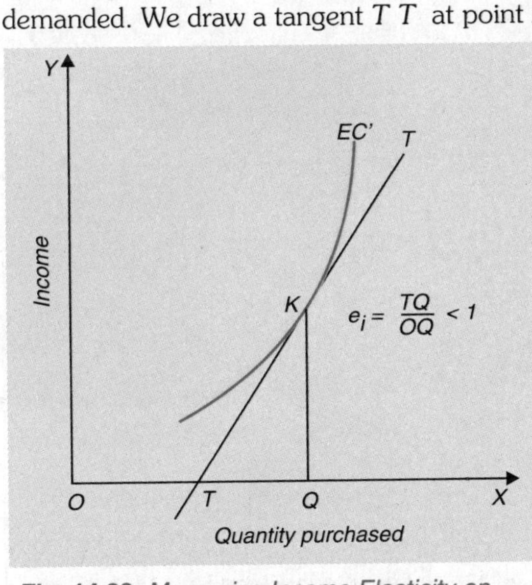

Fig. 14.22. *Measuring Income Elasticity on a Non-Linear Engel Curve of a Necessity*

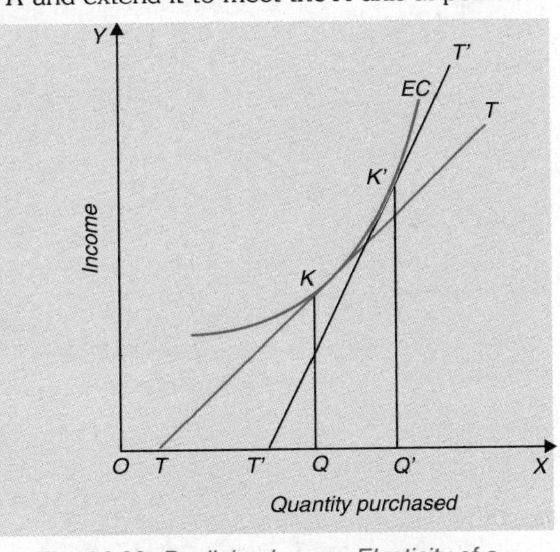

Fig. 14.23. *Declining Income Elasticity of a necessity as income increases*

Applying the income elasticity formula we have

$$e_i = \frac{\Delta Q}{\Delta M} \cdot \frac{M}{Q} = \frac{1}{\Delta M / \Delta Q} \cdot \frac{M}{Q}$$

$$= \frac{1}{KQ / TQ} \cdot \frac{KQ}{OQ} = \frac{TQ}{KQ} \cdot \frac{KQ}{OQ}$$

$$= \frac{TQ}{OQ}$$

A glance at Figure 14.22 shows that the length TQ is less than OQ. Therefore, income elasticity at point K on the non-linear and outwardly convex Engel curve of a necessity is less than one. Income elasticity will vary at different levels of income. And further in the case of Engel curve having outwardly convex slope, the income elasticity of the good is declining as income increases as will be seen from Fig. 14.23. This indicates the responsiveness of demand to increase in income falls as a consumer becomes richer. ***Non-linear convex Engel curve represents the case of a necessity which accounts for a smaller proportion of income of the richer families as compared to the poor people.***

Engel Curve and Income Elasticity: Necessities, Luxuries, and Inferior Goods

As stated above, the Engel curve shows the relationship, between quantity demanded of a good and changes in levels of consumer's income. An Engel curve can take various shapes depending upon whether the good is a necessity, luxury or an inferior good. As explained above, in case of a necessity, income elasticity is positive but less than unity and the quantity demanded increases less than proportionately to increase in income. Therefore, the Engel curve of a necessity will be convex as shown in Figure 14.23.

On the other hand, in case of luxuries, income elasticity is greater than one, As income increases the consumer spends more than proportionate increase in income on them. Income elasticity of a luxury good increases at higher levels of income. Therefore, for luxuries, Engel curve is concave as shown in Figure 14.24. Finally, in case of inferior goods, income elasticity is negative and consumer's quantity demanded of these goods declines as their income increases.

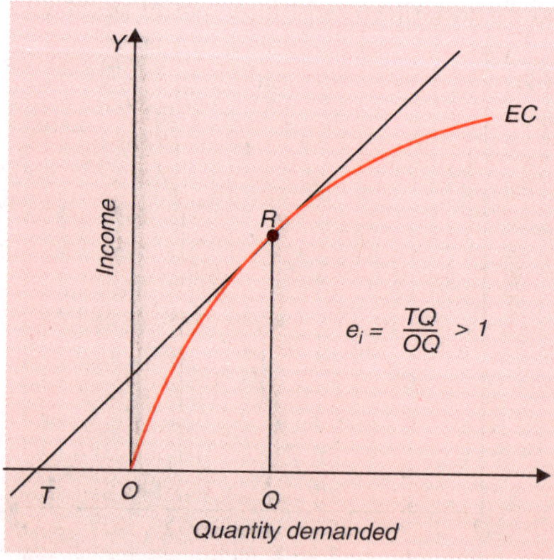

Fig. 14.24. *Income Elasticity and Engel Curve of a Luxury*

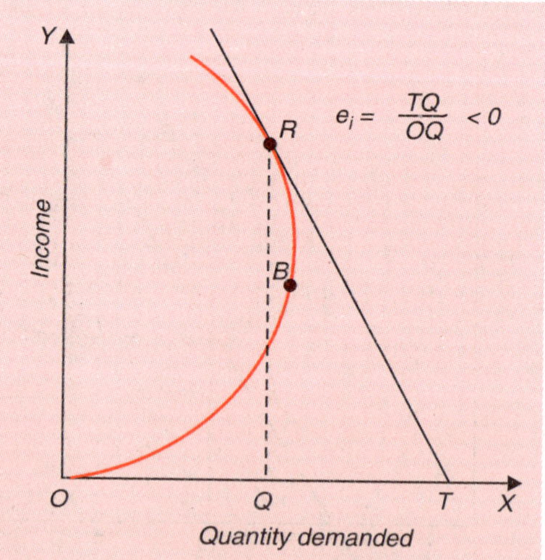

Fig. 14.25. *Backward-Bending Engel Curve of an Inferior Good*

Engel curve bends backward and has a negative slope beyond a certain level of income as illustrated in Figure 14.25. It will be observed from figure 14.25 that an inferior good behaves like a necessity in the initial ranges of income and therefore the slope of its Engel curve is initially positive, and only after a particular level of income, it bends backward. Thus, in Figure 14.25, it is only after point *B* that Engel curve bends backward indicating that beyond this point if income increases, quantity demanded of the good declines. Therefore, if we calculate income elasticity at point *R* on the backward-bending portion using the income elasticity measure *TQ/OQ*, we get a negative *TQ* distance over the positive distance *OQ*. Hence $e_i = TQ/OQ < 0$.

Income Elasticity and Proportion of Income Spent

There is a useful relationship between income elasticity for a good on the one hand and proportion of income spent on it. The relationship between the two is described in the following three propositions:

1. If proportion of income spent on the good remains the same as income increases, then income elasticity for the good is equal to one.

2. If proportion of income spent on the good increases as income increases, then the income elasticity for the good is greater than one.

3. If proportion of income spent on the good decreases as income rises, then income elasticity for the good is less than one.

We give below proofs of the above three propositions.

Theorem 1: *If proportion of income spent on a good remains the same as income increases, income elasticity for the good is equal to one.*

Let *E* stand for the income spent on a good and *M* for a level of income. The proportion of income spent will then be $\frac{E}{M}$. If the income increases by ΔM and as a result expenditure on the good rises by ΔE, new proportion of income spent on the good will be $E + \Delta E/M + \Delta M$. Now, if proportion of income spent on the good remains the same as income increases, then

$$\frac{E + \Delta E}{M + \Delta M} = \frac{E}{M}$$

or, $$M(E + \Delta E) = E(M + \Delta M)$$

$$EM + M.\Delta E = EM + E\Delta M$$

Since *EM* occurs on both sides of the equation, it will cancel out. Therefore, $M\,\Delta E = E\,\Delta M$

or $$\frac{\Delta E}{\Delta M} \cdot \frac{M}{E} = 1$$

But $\frac{\Delta E}{\Delta M} \cdot \frac{M}{E}$ is an expression for income elasticity of demand. We therefore conclude that when with the change in income, proportion of income spent on a good remains constant income elasticity for it is equal to unity ($e_I = 1$). Likewise, we can prove the other two theorems.

Theorem 2 : If the proportion of income spent on the good rises as income increases, the income elasticity is greater than unity.

As stated above, *E/M* is the proportion of income spent on a good, *E* stands for expenditure made on the good and *M* for consumer's income. Suppose income increases by ΔM and as a result the income spent on the good rises by ΔE, the new proportion of income spent on the good will equal to

$$\frac{E + \Delta E}{M + \Delta M}.$$

Now, if proportion of income spent on the good is to rise with the increase in income, then

$$\frac{E + \Delta E}{M + \Delta M} > \frac{E}{M}$$

or $$M(E + \Delta E) > E(M + \Delta M)$$

$$EM + M.\Delta E > EM + E.\Delta M$$

$$M.\Delta E > E.\Delta M$$

$$\frac{\Delta E}{\Delta M}.\frac{M}{E} > 1$$

Hence, $e_t > 1$.

We, therefore, conclude that if proportion of income spent on the good increases as income increases, income elasticity is greater than one.

Theorem 3 : ***If the proportion of income spent on the good decreases as income increases, income elasticity is less than one.***

If the proportion of income spent on a good has to decrease with the increase in income, then $\frac{E + \Delta E}{M + \Delta M}$ should be less than the initial proportion E/M

or, $$\frac{E + \Delta E}{M + \Delta M} < \frac{E}{M}$$

$$M(E + \Delta E) < E(M + \Delta M)$$

$$EM + M.\Delta E < EM + E.\Delta M$$

$$M.\Delta E < E.\Delta M$$

$$\frac{M}{E}.\frac{\Delta E}{\Delta M} < 1$$

Hence $e_i < 1$

We, therefore, conclude that when proportion of income spent on the good falls as income increases, income elasticity is less than unity.

Sum of Income Elasticities, Budget Constraint and Expenditure

Increase in income can be spent on a number of goods and services demanded by a consumer. Given the budget constraint, when some part of an increase in income is not spent on a good, it must be spent on other goods and services, assuming that there is no saving and borrowing by the consumer. From this, a relationship can be derived which shows that ***the sum of income elasticities for all goods and services must be unity and further that income elasticity of demand for a good depends on income elasticity of other goods and services.***

Suppose that consumer has an income equal to M and further that all his income is spent on two goods X and Y. Let P_x and P_y represent the prices of two goods X and Y respectively. Let income increases by ΔM and as a result quantities purchased of two goods increase by ΔQ_x and ΔQ_y. Then, budget constraint can be written as

$$\Delta M = P_x . \Delta Q_x + P_y . \Delta Q_y$$

Dividing both sides of the budget equation by ΔM we have

$$\frac{\Delta M}{\Delta M} = \frac{P_x . \Delta Q_x}{\Delta M} + \frac{P_y . \Delta Q_y}{\Delta M}$$

or, $$\frac{P_x . \Delta Q_x}{\Delta M} + \frac{P_y . \Delta Q_y}{\Delta M} = 1 \quad \ldots (i)$$

The above equation implies that the sum of the proportion of increase in income spent on good X (*i.e.* $P_x \Delta Q_x / \Delta M$) and the proportion of increase in income spent on good Y (i.e. $P_y \Delta Q_y / \Delta M$) must be equal to one. Multiplying the first term on the left side of equation (i) by Q_x/Q_x and M/M and multiplying the second term by Q_y/Q_y and M/M, we have

$$\frac{P_x . Q_x}{M} . \frac{\Delta Q_x}{\Delta M} . \frac{M}{Q_x} + \frac{P_y . Q_y}{M} . \frac{\Delta Q_y}{\Delta M} . \frac{M}{Q_y} \quad \ldots (ii)$$

It will be seen that the term $P_x Q_x / M$ represents the proportion of income spent on good X and $\frac{\Delta Q_x}{\Delta M} . \frac{M}{Q_x}$ is the income elasticity of demand for good X. Similarly, term $P_y Q_y / M$ is the proportion of income spent on goods Y, and the term $\frac{\Delta P_Y}{\Delta M} . \frac{M}{Q_Y}$ is the income elasticity of demand for good Y. Using K_x to denote proportion of income spent on good X, K_y for the proportion of income spent on good Y, e_{xi} for income elasticity of demand for good X, and e_{yi} for income elasticity of demand for good Y, then from equations (*i*) and (*ii*) we have :

$$K_x e_{xi} + K_y e_{yi} = 1$$

The above equation reveals that the weighted sum of the income elasticities of demand for all goods (weights being the proportion of income spent on goods) must equal unity. This for example, means that when income increases by 10 per cent, the budget constraint requires that purchases or consumption of goods as a whole must also increase by 10 per cent. If there is a 10 per cent increase in income, if the consumption of some goods increases by less than 10 per cent, the consumption of others must increase by more than 10 per cent so that the increase in income must somehow be spent on the goods. That is, the increase in consumption of goods whose income elasticity of demand is less than one must be offset by increase in consumption of others for which income elasticity of demand is greater than one. Thus, on the average, consumption of goods must increase by the same proportion as income. If there are two goods X and Y, then the above equation $K_x e_{xi} + K_y e_{yi} = 1$ must hold. This equation implies that given the two goods on which a consumer spends his income, if we know the proportion of income spent of one good and the income elasticity for that good, we can calculate the income elasticity of demand for the other good.

Numerical Example

Assume that there are two commodities, rice and milk. If rice accounts for 75% of the budget and has income elasticity equal to 0.8, what would be the income elasticity of milk?

Let us call rice as commodity X and milk as commodity Y :

$$K_x.e_{xi} + k_y.e_{yi} = 1$$

$$0.75\ (0.8) + 0.25\ (e_{yi}) = 1$$

$$.600 + 0.25\ (e_{yi}) = 1$$

$$0.25(e_{yi}) = 1 - 0.6 = 0.4$$

$$e_{yi} = 0.4/0.25 = 1.6$$

Thus, income elasticity of demand for milk equals 1.6.

Importance of Income Elasticity for Business Firms

The concept of income elasticity is important for decision making both by business firms and industries. First, the firms producing products which have a high income elasticity have great potential for growth in an expending economy. For example, if for a firm's product income elasticity of demand is greater than one, it means that it will gain more than proportionately to the increase in national income. Thus firms which are producing products having high income elasticity are more interested in forecasting the level of aggregate economic activity (*i.e.*, level of national income) because the demand for their products greatly depends on the level of overall economic activity. Further, as seen above, the demand for luxuries is highly income elastic. Therefore, the demand for luxuries fluctuates very much during different phases of business cycles. During boom periods, demand for luxuries increases very much and declines sharply during recessionary periods.

On the other hand, the demand for products with low income elasticity will not be greatly affected by the fluctuations in aggregate economic activity. During booms the demand for these products will not increase much and during recessions it will not decrease sharply. Therefore, the firms with low income elasticity for their products would not be much interested in forecasting future business activity. Remember it is generally necessities for which demand is not much income elastic. However, there is one good thing for the firms which produce goods having low income elasticity. They are to a good extent recession-proof. In the periods of recession, their incomes do not fall to the extent of decline in aggregate income. Of course, to share the benefits of increasing national income firms currently producing products with low income elasticity would try to enter the industries demand for whose products is highly income elastic as this would ensure better growth opportunities.

The knowledge of income elasticity of demand also plays a significant role in designing marketing strategies of the firms. If income of people is an important determineant of demand for a product, the firms producing products with high income elasticity of demand will be located in those areas or set up their sales outlets in those cities or regions where incomes are increasing rapidly. Besides, the firms will direct their advertising campaigns and other sales promotion activities to those segments of people whose income is high and also increasing rapidly. This is to ensure higher growth of sales of their products.

The concept of income elasticity of demand shows clearly why farmers' income do not rise equal to that of urban people engaged in manufacturing industries. Income elasticity of demand for agricultural products such as foodgrains is less than one. This implies that it is difficult for the farmers' income from agriculture to increase in proportion to the expanding national income. Thus farmers' income cannot keep face with the urban people who derive their income from industries producing goods with high income elasticity of demand.

Some Numerical Problems on Income Elasticity

Problem 1. If a consumer's daily income rises from Rs. 300 to Rs. 350, his purchase of a good X increases from 25 units per day to 35 units, find income elasticity of demand for X.

Solution. Change in quantity demand (ΔQ) = ($Q_2 - Q_1$) = 35 – 25 = 10

Change in income (ΔM) = $M_2 - M_1$ = 350 – 300 = 50

$$e_i = \frac{\%\text{ Change in quantity demanded}}{\%\text{ Change in price}}$$

$$e_i = \frac{\Delta Q}{\Delta M} \times \frac{M_2 + M_1}{Q_2 + Q_1}$$

$$= \frac{10}{50} \times \frac{350 + 300}{25 + 35}$$

$$= \frac{10}{50} \times \frac{650}{60} = 2.17$$

Income elasticity of demand in this case is 2.17.

Problem 2. *Suppose demand for cars in Bombay as a function of income is given by the following equation :*

$$Q = 20{,}000 + 5M$$

where Q is quantity demanded, M is per capita level of income in rupees.

Find out income elasticity of demand when per capita annual income in Bombay is ₹ 15,000.

Solution.

$$\text{Income elasticity } (e_i) = \frac{\Delta Q}{\Delta M} \cdot \frac{M}{Q}$$

In order to obtain income elasticity, we have to first find out quantity demanded (Q) at income level of ₹ 15,000. Thus.

$$Q = 20{,}000 + 5 \times 15{,}000 = 95{,}000$$

It will be seen from the given income demand function that coefficient of income (M) is equal to 5. This implies that $\frac{\Delta Q}{\Delta M} = 5$. With this information we can calculate income elasticity.

$$e_i = \frac{\Delta Q}{\Delta M} \times \frac{M}{Q} = 5 \times \frac{15{,}000}{95{,}000} = 0.8$$

Problem 3. *The following demand function for readymade trousers has been estimated*

$$Q = 2{,}000 + 15Y - 5.5P$$

where Y is income in thousands of rupees, Q is the quantity demanded in units and P is the price per unit.

(a) *When P = ₹ 150 and Y = 15 thousand rupees, determine the following :*

1. *Price elasticity of demand*
2. *Income elasticity of demand*

(b) *Determine what effect a rise in price would have on total revenue.*

(c) *Assess how sale of trousers would change during a period of rising incomes.*

Solution.

(*a*) Coefficient of *P*, *i.e.*, $\frac{\Delta Q}{\Delta P} = 5.5$

Price elasticity of demand $\frac{\Delta Q}{\Delta P} \cdot \frac{P}{Q} = 5.5 \times \frac{150}{Q}$

Let us first find out the quantity demanded (*i.e.*, *Q*) at the given income (*Y* = 15 thousands) and given price (*P* = ₹ 150 per unit). Substituting the values of income and price in the given demand function, we have :

$$Q = 2{,}000 + 15 \times 15 - 5.5 \times 150$$
$$= 2{,}000 + 225 - 825 = 1{,}400$$

Thus, $$e_p = \frac{\Delta Q}{\Delta P} \times \frac{P}{Q} = 5.5 \times \frac{150}{1400} = \frac{82.5}{140} = 0.59$$

Income elasticity $= \frac{\Delta Q}{\Delta Y} \times \frac{Y}{Q}$

$$\frac{\Delta Q}{\Delta Y} = 15,\ Q = 1400,\ Y = 15 \text{ thousand rupees}$$

$$e_i = 15 \times \frac{15}{1400} = \frac{9}{56} = 0.16$$

(*b*) Since price elasticity of demand for trousers is less than one, rise in price would cause increase in total revenue.

(*c*) Since income elasticity of demand for trousers is less than one, trousers are a necessity and therefore the increase in income of the people will lead to less than a proportionate increase in their sales.

SOME FURTHER EXERCISES ON ELASTICITY OF DEMAND

Exercise 1. *Two goods have a cross price elasticity of demand of + 1.2. (a) Would you describe the goods as substitutes or complements? (b) If price of one of the goods rises by 5 percent, what will happen to the demand for the other good, holding other factors constant?*

Ans. (*a*) The goods with positive cross-price elasticity of demand are substitute goods. Therefore, the above two goods with cross-price elasticity of demand equal to + 1.2 will be substitute goods. (b) If price of one of the two goods increases by 5 per cent, it will be substituted by the other good so that the quantity demanded of it will rise. With positive cross-price elasticity being equal to 1.2, the quantity demanded of the good will increase by 1.2 × 5 = 6 per cent.

Exercise 2. *In an attempt to increase revenues and profits, a firm is considering 5 per cent increase in price of its good and 15 per cent increase in advertising expenditure. If the price elasticity of demand is –1.5 and advertising elasticity of demand is + 0.6, would you predict an increase or decrease in total revenue? Explain.*

Ans. To answer this question, students should know the interpretation of the concept of elasticity. The price elasticity of demand equal to –1.5 means that 5 percent *increase* in price will result in 5 × 1.5 = 7.5 per cent *decrease* in quantity demanded of the good. On the other hand, advertising elasticity of demand being equal to + 0.6 means that 15 per cent increase in advertising expenditure will cause 1.5 × 0.6 = 9 per cent increase in quantity demanded. Therefore, there will be net 1.5 percent increase in quantity demanded of the good. Besides, there is 5 per cent rise in price. We therefore predict increase in revenue.

Exercise 3. *For the following demand functions, determine whether demand is elastic, inelastic or unitary elastic at the given price:*

(*i*) $Q = 100 - 4P$ and the given $P = ₹\ 20$

(*ii*) $Q = 1500 - 20P$ and the given $P = ₹\ 5$

(iii) $P = 50 - 0.1Q$ *and the given* $P = ₹\ 20$

Solution. (*i*) $Q = 100 - 4P$ where $P = ₹\ 20$

In this demand function the derivative $\frac{dQ}{dP} = 4.$

Substituting the value of P in this demand function (*i*)

$$Q = 100 - (4 \times 20) = 20$$

$$e_p = \frac{dQ}{dP} \times \frac{P}{Q} = 4 \times \frac{20}{20} = 4.$$

Since $e_p > 1$, demand is elastic.

(*ii*) $Q = 1500 - 20P$ where $P =$ Rs 5

In this demand function equation, the derivative $\frac{dQ}{dP} = 20$

Substituting the value of P in this demand function

$$Q = 1500 - (20 \times 5) = 1400$$

$$e_p = \frac{dQ}{dP} \times \frac{P}{Q} = 20 \times \frac{5}{1400} = \frac{5}{70} = 0.07$$

Since $e_p < 1$, demand is inelastic.

(*iii*) $P = 50 - 0.1Q$ where $P = ₹\ 20$

Let us first express this demand function in terms of quantity demanded as a function of price.

$$P = 50 - 0.1Q$$

$$0.1Q = 50 - P$$

$$Q = 50 \times 10 - 10P$$

$$Q = 500 - 10P$$

With given price equal to ₹ 20,

$$Q = 500 - (10 \times 20) = 300$$

The derivative $\frac{dQ}{dP} = 10$

$$e_p = \frac{dQ}{dP} \times \frac{P}{Q} = 10 \times \frac{20}{300} = \frac{2}{3} = 0.66$$

Since $e_p < 1$, demand is inelastic.

Exercise 4. *Demand for "Advanced Economic Theory" by Dr H.L. Ahuja is given by $Q = 20{,}000 - 60P$.*

(a) Compute the point price elasticity of demand at price = ₹ 200.

(b) If the objective is to increase total revenue from the sales of the book, should the price be increased or reduced?

Solution. The given demand function is

$$Q = 20{,}000 - 60P$$

Substituting the value of $P = 200$ in the demand function equation

$$Q = 20{,}000 - (60 \times 200) = 8{,}000$$

The derivative $\frac{dQ}{dP} = 60$

$$e_p \text{ at ₹ } 200 = \frac{dQ}{dP} \times \frac{P}{Q} = 60 \times \frac{200}{8{,}000} = \frac{3}{2} = 1.5$$

Since price elasticity of demand is greater than one, reduction in price will increase revenue. Therefore, price of the book should be reduced to increase revenue from the sales of the book.

THE ELASTICITY OF SUBSTITUTION

The elasticity of substitution is another important concept of demand elasticity. The elasticity of substitution between two goods is a measure of the ease with which one can be substituted for the other. Just as price elasticity of demand is a relative measure of the price effect; income elasticity is a relative measure of the income effect; similarly, the elasticity of substitution is a relative measure of the substitution effect.

When it is difficult to substitute one good for another, a small change in the proportion of the two goods will bring about a large change in the marginal rate of substitution between the two goods. When the substitution between the two goods is easy, a small change in the proportion of two goods possessed by the consumer, the change in the marginal rate of substitution between the two goods will not be much. It is thus clear that from the change in the proportion of two goods and the resultant change in the marginal rate of substitution we can know the elasticity of substitution. Therefore, elasticity of substitution can be expressed as follows:

$$\text{Elasticity of substitution} = \frac{\text{Proportionate Change in the amount of } X \text{ with respect to } Y}{\text{Proportionate decrease in the marginal rate of substitution } X \text{ for } Y}$$

$$e_s = \frac{\Delta (Q_x / Q_y)}{Q_x / Q_y} \div \frac{\Delta(\Delta Y / \Delta X)}{\Delta Y / \Delta X}$$

$\frac{Q_x}{Q_y}$ stands for the original proportion between the quantities of goods X and Y.

$\Delta\left(\dfrac{Q_x}{Q_y}\right)$ stands for the change in the proportion of goods X and Y.

$\dfrac{\Delta Y}{\Delta X}$ stands for the original marginal rate of substitution of good X for good Y.

$\Delta\left(\dfrac{\Delta Y}{\Delta X}\right)$ stands for the small change in the marginal rate of substitution of good X for good Y.

The concept of substitution elasticity of demand can be easily understood with the aid of indifference curves. We have given below two diagrams of indifference curves. In Figure 14.26 an indifference curve between two close substitutes has been drawn. Being close substitutes their indifference curve is nearer to a straight line. On the other hand, in Figure 14.27 the indifference curve between two complementary goods has been drawn. Since the substitution between the two complementary goods is difficult, the convexity of the indifference curve between two goods is very large.

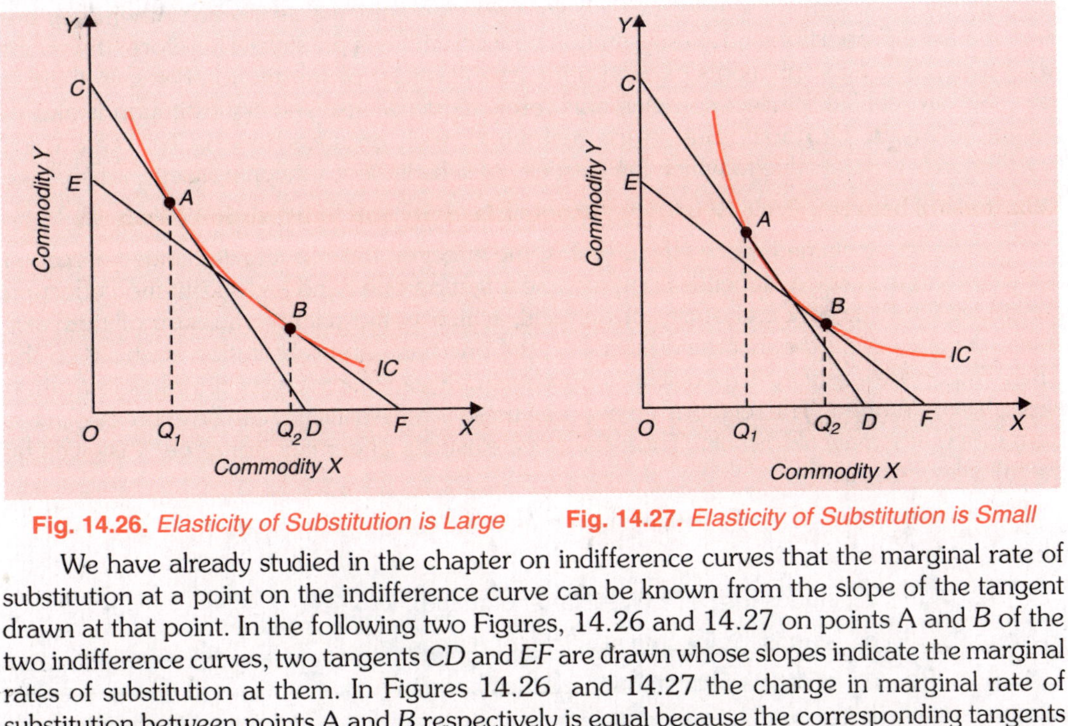

Fig. 14.26. *Elasticity of Substitution is Large* **Fig. 14.27.** *Elasticity of Substitution is Small*

We have already studied in the chapter on indifference curves that the marginal rate of substitution at a point on the indifference curve can be known from the slope of the tangent drawn at that point. In the following two Figures, 14.26 and 14.27 on points A and *B* of the two indifference curves, two tangents *CD* and *EF* are drawn whose slopes indicate the marginal rates of substitution at them. In Figures 14.26 and 14.27 the change in marginal rate of substitution between points A and *B* respectively is equal because the corresponding tangents in the two figures are parallel to each other, that is, *CD* in Figure 14.27 is parallel to *CD* of Figure 14.26 and *EF* of Figure 14.26 is parallel to *EF* of Figure 14.27. In other words, in both the indifferences curves, on switching from *A* to *B* there is same charge in the marginal rate of substitution. Whereas in both the indifference curves, the fall in the marginal rate of substitution of *X* for *Y* between *A* to *B* is the same, the increase in the quantity of *X* in indifference curve in Figure 14.26 is much greater than the increase in quantity of *X* in indiffernce curve of Figure 14.27. A glance at the two figures will show that the distance Q_1Q_2 in Figure 14.26 is much greater than the distance Q_1Q_2 in Figure 14.27. It is thus clear than in Figure

14.26 the same relative change in marginal rate of substitution as that in Figure 14.27 brings about a relatively large increase in quantity demanded of X, that is, elasticity of substitution between the two goods depicted in Figure 14.26 is very large. On the other hand, in Figure 14.27 with the same relative change in marginal rate of substitution as in Figure 14.26 the increase in quantity of X is very small, that is, between the two goods shown in Figure 14.27 the elasticity of substitution is very low.

When the two goods *X and Y* are perfect substitutes of each other, then the proportion between them (that is, Q_x/Q_y) can be increased infinitely without any change in the marginal rate of substitution between them, that is, elasticity of substitution between the perfect substitutes is infinite. That is why the indifference curve of the two perfectly substitute goods is a straight line. But in real life it is very difficult to find the examples of perfectly substitute goods, and if such goods do exist, then from the economic point of view they should be considered as the same goods. But in the real life goods are often found which, though not perfect substitutes, are very close substitutes of each other, such as tea and coffee, travel by railway and travel by bus, between which the elasticity of substitution is very large, and therefore, the indifference curve between them is very near to the straight line, that is, the indifference curve between the two is very much less convex to the origin.

On the other hand, the goods which are perfect complements to each other, they are used in a fixed proportion and no substitution between them is possible. Therefore, the goods which are perfect complements of each other, the elasticity of substitution between them is zero. But, in real life, perfect complements rarely exist because some substitution is always possible between the goods. But, in the real world, such products do exist between which substitution is very less due to which the elasticity of substitution, though not zero, is very less.

Relationship between Price Elasticity, Income Elasticity and Substitution Elasticity

As already explained, price effect, that is, the effect on the quantity demanded of a good due to a change in price, depends upon income effect on one hand and substitution effect on the other. Similarly, price elasticity of demand, which is the relative measure of the price effect, depends upon the income elasticity on the one hand and substitution elasticity on the other. *Thus, price elasticity in a way is a compromise between income elasticity and substitution elasticity of demand.* The relationship between these three elasticities can be expressed in the form of a mathematical formula. Thus, the price elasticity of demand for good X is given by the following formula:

$$e_p = K_x . e_i + (1 - K_x)\, e_s$$

where

e_p stands for price elasticity of demand.

e_i stands for income elasticity of demand.

e_s stands for substitution elasticity of demand.

k_x stands for the proportion of consumer's income spent on good X.

The first part of the equation, that is, $K_x . e_i$ shows the influence of income effect on the price elasticity of demand. In other words, it shows that the change in quantity demanded of good X due to the fall in its price depends in part upon the magnitude of income effect of the change in price. This income effect of the change in price depends, on the one hand, on the proportion of income spent on good X (that is, K_x) and income elasticity of demand for good X (that is, e_i) on the other. The proportion of income spent on good X determines what amount of the income spent on good X will be released as a result of fall in price of good X. The income thus released will be spent on increasing the purchases of good X as well as of other goods. Given the income elasticity of demand, the greater the proportion of income spent on good X, the greater the amount of income released for purchase of X and consequently greater the increase in amount demanded of good X. Besides the proportion of income spent on good X, the increase in amount demanded of good X due to income effect of the price fall depends on the income elasticity of demand for good X. This is because income elasticity of demand for good X determines how much of the income released by the fall in price of good X will be spent on good X whose price has fallen and how much will be spent on other goods. Proportion of income spent on good X being given, greater the income elasticity of demand for good X, greater the part of income released will be spent on good X and consequently there will be a greater increase in quantity demanded of good X. We thus see that first part of the equation, that is, $K_x e_i$, shows the impact of income effect on the price elasticity of demand.

The quantity demanded of the good does not increase only because of the income effect of the fall in price, it also increases because of the substitution effect. As the price of good X falls, more of it is purchased at the expense of others because good X has now become relatively cheaper than others. The second part of the equation, that is $(1 - K_x)\, e_s$, shows the influence of the substitution effect on the price elasticity of demand for good X. The magnitude of substitution effect in turn depends in part on the elasticity of substitution (e_s), that is, the extent to which good X can be substituted for other goods now that it is relatively cheaper. The substitution effect also depends on the amount of other goods which were being purchased before the fall in price of good X. This is because only to the extent one was already purchasing other goods, the substitution of X for other goods is possible. Elasticity of substitution being given, the greater the amount of other goods being purchased by the consumer, the greater is the possibility of substitution of good X for other goods when X becomes cheaper. Since K_x stands for the proportion of income spent on good X, $(1 - K_x)$ will give the proportion of income not being spent on good X. In other words, $(1 - K_x)$ stands for the proportion of income spent on goods other than X. Therefore, $(1 - K_x)$ indicates the proportion of consumer's income within which substitution of A for other goods is possible.

From the above analysis it follows that the price elasticity of demand for a good is determined by the following four factors:

1. *Proportion of income spent on the good*
2. *Income elasticity of demand*
3. *Elasticity of substitution*
4. *Proportion of income spent on other goods*

Price elasticity can be known if the first three factors are known. Let us consider the following examples.

Suppose that a consumer is spending l/5th of this income on any good X and the income elasticity of demand for the good X is 2 and elasticity of substitution between good X and all other goods is 3. What will be the price elasticity of demand in this case?

$$
\begin{aligned}
e_p &= K_x \cdot e_i + (1 - K_x)\, e_s \\
&= 1/5 \times 2 + (1 - 1/5) \times 3 \\
&= 2/5 + 4/5 \times 3 \\
&= 2/5 + 12/5 \\
&= 14/5 = 2.8
\end{aligned}
$$

Thus, price elasticity of demand for good X is equal to 2.8.

From the above formula of price elasticity of demand, it follows that whatever the proportion of income spent on a good, if income elasticity and substitution elasticity are equal to one, then price elasticity will also be equal to one. For instant, if a proportion of income spent on a good is I/ 5 and income and substitution elasticities are equal to one, then price elasticity will be:

$$\begin{aligned} e_p &= K_x \cdot e_i + (1 - K_x)\, e_s \\ &= 1/5 \times 1 + 4/5 \times 1 \\ &= 1/5 + 4/5 = 1 \end{aligned}$$

Likewise, if proportion of income spent on a good is 1/3, and given that both the income and substitution elasticities are equal to one, price elasticity will be found to be equal to one.

QUESTIONS FOR REVIEW

1. (*a*) How would you measure point price elasticity of demand at a point on the demand curve?

   (*b*) What happens to point price elasticity at a given price when the demand curve shifts to the right in a parallel manner?

2. What are the factors which determine price elasticity of demand? What role does price elasticity of demand play in decision-making by business firms?

3. What would you say about the price elasticity of demand for a good when

   (*a*) price consumption curve slopes downward,

   (*b*) price consumption slopes upward,

   (*c*) price consumption curve slopes backward.

4. Suppose that in a year the excise duty on cigarettes is doubled and as a result of this total revenue from the excise duty decreases. What conclusions about the price elasticity of demand for cigarettes would you draw?

5. Do you think that price elasticity of demand would be greater for car industry as a whole or for Maruti 800 of Maruti firm?

6. Demand for a firm's product has been estimated to be $Q_d = 1000 - 200/P$

   If the price of the product is Rs 3 per unit, find out the price elasticity of demand at this price.

7. *Given*: $P \,.\, Q = 500$, What happens to price elasticity of demand as price falls (P = *price*, and Q = quantity purchased)?

   [**Hints:** $P.\,Q$ represents expenditure on a commodity which remains constant at 500 even when price falls. When expenditure on a commodity remains constant as price changes, its price elasticity of demand is equal to one.]

8. An individual spends all his income on two goods, X and Y. If with the rise in price of good X, the quantity purchased of good Y remains unchanged, what is the price elasticity of demand for X?

   [**Hints:** Quantity purchased of good Y remaining the same even when price of good X rises, means that expenditure on good Y, that is $P_y . Q_y$, remains constant with a given income to spend on the two goods. This also means expenditure on good X remains constant when its price rises. This implies that price elasticity of demand for good X equals one.]

9. The price elasticity of demand for colour TVs is estimated to be – 2.5. If the price of colour TVs is reduced by 20 per cent, how much percentage increase in the quantity of colour TVs sold do you expect?

   [**Hints:** Price elasticity of demand being equal to –2.5 means that one per cent change in price causes 2.5 per cent change in quantity demanded or sold. Besides, minus sign only indicates there is *inverse* relationship between price and quantity sold. Thus, 20 percent *reduction in price* of colour TVs will cause *increase in quantity sold* by 2.5 × 20 = 50 per cent.]

10. In an attempt to increase sales and profits, a firm is considering 5 per cent increase in price and 15

per cent increase in advertising expenditure. If the price elasticity of demand is -1.5 and advertising elasticity of demand is + 0.6, would there be increase or decrease in total revenue?

[**Hints:** 5 per cent increase in price will cause 5 × 1.5 = 7.5 per cent *decrease* in quantity sold. However, 15 per cent increase in advertising will cause 0.6 × 15 = 9 per cent *increase* in quantity sold. Thus, there is 1.5 per cent net increase in quantity sold. Since there is also 5 per cent rise in price, the total revenue (which is equal to *P.Q.*) will increase.

11. Explain the relationship between the total revenue of a firm and the price elasticity of demand for price reduction.

12. *(a)* Explain why a firm facing a downward sloping demand curve would never produce in the inelastic ($e_p < 1$) portion of the demand curve.

(b) When would the firm operate at the point where demand curve is unitary elastic?

13. Show that on a linear demand curve, price elasticity of demand decreases continuously from infinity at the price axis to zero at the quantity axis.

14. From the demand schedule given below calculate price elasticity of demand and total revenue.

Price (Rs)	*Quantity demanded*	*Price elasticity*	*Total revenue*
10	20	—	—
8	30	—	—
6	35	—	—
4	40	—	—

15. Explain the concept of cross elasticity of demand. Using concept of cross elasticity of demand, define substitutes and complements.

16. Colgate sells its standard size toothpaste for ₹ 25. Its sales have been on an average 8000 units per month over the last year. Recently, its close competitor Binaca reduced the price of its same standard size toothpaste from ₹ 35 to ₹ 30. As a result Colgate sales declined by 1500 units per month.

(i) Calcualte the cross elasticity between the two products, (ii) What does your estimate indicate about the relationship between the two?

17. Explain the importance of the concept of cross elasticity of demand in (a) formulating proper price strategy, *(b)* in analysing the degree of competition prevailing in an industry.

18. Suppose the following demand function for coffee in terms of price of tea is given. Find out the cross elasticity of demand when price of tea rises from ₹ 50 per 250 grams pack to ₹ 55 per 250 grams pack.

$$Q_c = 100 + 2.5P_t$$

where Q_c is the quantity demanded of coffee in terms of packs of 250 grams and P_t is the price of tea per 250 grams pack. .

19. Two goods have a cross-price elasticity of demand of+1.2 (a) Would you describe the goods as substitute or complements? *(b)* If the price of one of the goods rises by 5 per cent, what will happen to the demand for the other good, holding other factors constant?

20. Explain the concept of income elasticity of demand. How would you define necessities and luxuries on the basis of income elasticity of demand?

21. Explain the importance of income elasticity of demand for business firms especially in designing marketing strategies.

22. If a consumer's daily income rises from ₹ 300 to ₹ 350, his purchase of a good X increases from 25 units to 40 units per day. Find income elasticity of demand for X.

CHAPTER

15

Consumer Surplus

Meaning of Consumer Surplus

The concept of consumer surplus was first formulated by Dupuit in 1844 to measure social benefits of public goods such as canals, bridges, national highways. Marshall further refined and popularised this in his *'Principles of Economies"* published in 1890. The concept of consumer surplus became the basis of old welfare economics. Marshall's concept of consumer's surplus was based on the cardinal measurability and interpersonal comparisons of utility. According to him, every increase in consumer's surplus is an indicator of the increase in social welfare. As we shall see below, ***consumer's surplus is simply the difference between the price that 'one is willing to pay' and 'the price one actually pays' for a particular product.***

Concept of consumer's surplus is a very important concept in economic theory, especially in theory of demand and welfare economics. This concept is important not only in economic theory but also in formulation of economic policies such as taxation by the Government and price policy pursued by the monopolistic seller of a product. The essence of the concept of consumer's surplus is that a consumer derives extra satisfaction from the purchases he daily makes over the price he actually pays for them. In other words, people generally get more utility from the consumption of goods than the price they actually pay for them. It has been found that people are prepared to pay more price for the goods than they actually pay for them. This extra satisfaction which the consumers obtain from buying a good has been called consumer surplus. Thus, Marshall defines the consumer's sruplus in the following words: ***"excess of the price which a consumer would be willing to pay rather than go without a thing over that which he actually does pay is the economic measure of this surplus satisfaction.... it may be called consumer's surplus."***[1]

The amount of money which a person is willing to pay for a good indicates the amount of utility he derives from that good; the greater the amount of money he is willing to pay, the greater the utility he obtains from it. Therefore, the marginal utility of a unit of a good determines the price a consumer will be prepared to pay for that unit. The total utility which a person gets from a good is given by the sum of marginal utilities *(ΣMU)* of the units of a good purchased and the total price which he actually pays is equal to the price per unit of the good multiplied by the number of units of it purchased. Thus:

Consumer's surplus = What a consumer is willing to pay minus what he actually pays.

= Σ Marginal utility – (Price × Number of units of a commodity purchased)

1. Alfred Marshall, *Principles of Economics*, 8th edition, p. 103.

The concept of consumer surplus is derived from the law of diminishing marginal utility. As we purchase more units of a good, its marginal utility goes on diminishing. It is because of the diminishing marginal utility that consumer's willingness to pay for additional units of a commodity declines as he has more units of the commodity. The consumer is in equilibrium when marginal utility becomes equal to the given price. In other words, consumer purchases the number of units of a commodity at which marginal utility is equal to price. This means that at the margin what a consumer will be willing to pay (*i.e.*, marginal utility) is equal to the price he actually pays. But for the previous units which he purchases, his willingness to pay (or the marginal utility he derives from the commodity) is greater than the price he actually pays for them. This is because the price of the commodity is given and constant for him.

Marshall's Measure of Consumer Surplus

Consumer surplus measures extra utility or satisfaction which a consumer obtains from the consumption of a certain amount of commodity over and above the utility of its market value. Thus the total utility obtained from consuming water is immense while its market value is negligible. It is due to the occurrence of diminishing marginal utility that a consumer gets total utility from the consumption of a commodity greater than the utility of its market value. Marshall tried to obtain the monetary measure of this surplus, that is, how many rupees this surplus of utility is worth to the consumer. It is the monetary value of this surplus that Marshall called consumer surplus. To determine this monetary measure of consumer surplus we are required to measure two things. First, the total utility in terms of money that a consumer expects to get from the consumption of a certain amount of a commodity. Second, the total market value of the amount of commodity consumed. It is quite easy to measure the total market value as it is equal to market price of a commodity multiplied by its quantity purchased (*i.e. P.Q.*). An important contribution of Marshall has been the way he devised to determine the monetary measure of the total utility a consumer obtains from the commodity. Consider Table 15.1 which has been graphically shown in Figure 15.1.

Suppose the price of a commodity is ₹ 20 per unit. At price of ₹ 20, the consumer is willing to buy only one unit of the commodity. This implies that utility which the consumer gets from this first unit is at least worth ₹ 20 to him otherwise he would not have purchased it at this price. When the price falls to ₹ 18, he is prepared to buy the second unit also. This again implies that the second unit of the commodity is at least worth ₹ 18 to him. Further, he is prepared to buy third unit at price ₹ 16. which means that it is at least worth ₹ 16 to him.

Table 15.1. Marginal Valuation and Consumer Surplus

No of Units	Marginal Valuation	Price		Net Marginal Benefit
1	₹ 20	₹ 12		₹ 8
2	₹ 18	₹ 12		₹ 6
3	₹ 16	₹ 12		₹ 4
4	₹ 14	₹ 12		₹ 2
5	₹ 12	₹ 12		₹ 0
6	₹ 10	₹ 12		– 2
			Total Consumer Surplus	20

Likewise, the fourth and fifth units of the commodity are at least worth ₹ 14 and ₹ 12 as he is prepared to pay these prices for the fourth and fifth units respectively, otherwise he would not have demanded them at these prices.

Now, we can interpret the demand prices of these units in a slightly different way. The prices that the consumer is prepared to pay for various units of the commodity means the *marginal valuation* which he places on these units of the commodity demanded by him. This marginal valuation of a unit of a commodity shows the *willingness of the individual to pay for* it. However, actually he has not to pay the sum of money equal to the marginal valuation he places on them. For all the units of the commodity he has to pay the current market price. Suppose the current market price of the commodity is ₹ 12. It will be seen from the Table 15.1 and Figure 15.1 that the consumer will buy 5 units of the commodity at this price because his marginal valuation of the fifth unit just equals the market price of ₹ 12. This shows that his marginal valuation of the first four units is greater than the market price which he factually pays for them. He will therefore obtain surplus or, net marginal benefit of ₹ 8 (₹ 20 – 12) from the first unit, ₹ 6 (= ₹ 18 – 12) from the second unit, ₹ 4 on the third unit and ₹ 2 from the fourth unit and zero on the fifth unit. He thus obtains total consumer surplus or total net benefit) from 5 units equal to ₹ 20.

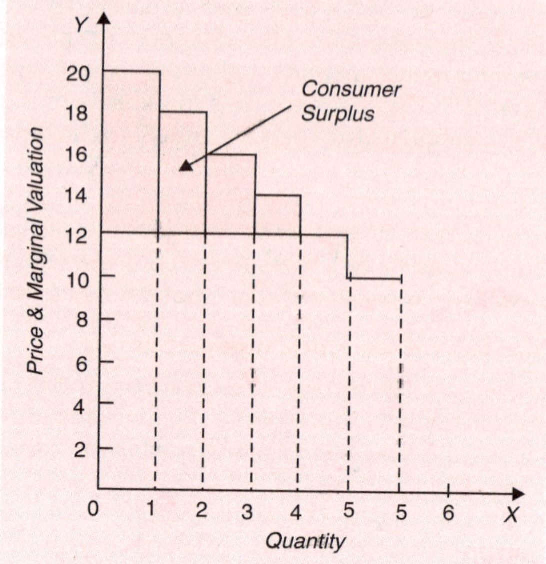

Fig. 15.1. *Consumer Surplus*

Measurement of Consumer Surplus as Area Under the Demand Curve

The analysis of consumer surplus made above is based on discrete units of the commodity. If we assume that the commodity is perfectly divisible, which is usually made in economic theory, the consumer surplus can be represented by the area under the demand curve.

The measurement of consumer surplus from a commodity from the demand curve is illustrated in Fig.15.2 which along the *X*-axis the amount of the commodity has been measured and on the *Y*-axis the marginal utility (or willingness to pay for the commodity) and the price of the commodity are measured. *DD* is the demand or marginal utility curve which is sloping downward, indicating that as the consumer buys more units of the commodity, his willingness to pay for the additional units of the commodity or, in other words, marginal utility which he gets from the commodity falls. As said above, marginal utility shows the price which a person will be willing to pay for the different units rather than go without them. If *OP* is the price that prevails in the market, then the consumer will be in equilibrium when he buys *OM* units of the commodity, since at *OM* units, marginal utility is equal to the given price *OP.* The *M*th unit of the commodity does not yield any consumer' s surplus to the consumer since this is the last unit purchased and for this price paid is equal to the marginal utility which indicates the price he will be prepared to pay rather than go without it. But for the intra-marginal units *e.i.* units before *M*th, marginal utility is greater than the price and therefore, these units yield consumer's surplus to the consumer. The total utility of a certain quantity of a commodity to a consumer can be known by summing up the marginal utilities of the various units purchased.

In Figure 15.2, the total utility derived by the consumer from *OM* units of the commodity will be equal to the area under the demand or marginal utility curve up to point *M*. That is, the total utility of *OM* units in Fig. 15.2 is equal *to ODSM.* In other words, for *OM* units of the

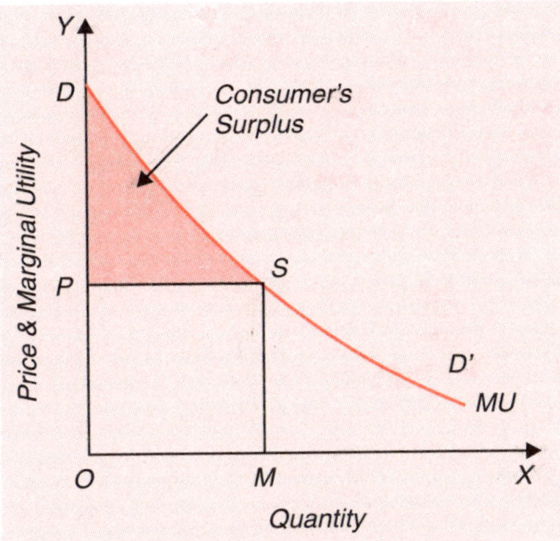

Fig. 15.2. Marshall's Measure of Consumer's Surplus

good the consumer will be prepared to pay the sum equal to Rs. *ODSM*. But, given the price *OP*, the consumer will actually pay for *OM* units of the good the sum equal to Rs. *OPSM*. It is thus clear that the consumer derives extra utility equal to *ODSM* minus *OPSM* = *DPS*, which has been shaded in Figure 15.2. To conclude when we draw a demand curve, the monetary measure of consumer surplus can be obtained by the area under the demand curve over and above the rectangular area representing the total market value *(i.e. P. Q)* of the amount of the commodity purchased.

If the market price of the commodity rises above *OP*, the consumer will buy fewer units of the commodity than *OM*. As a result, consumer's surplus obtained by him from his purchase will decline. On the other hand, if the price falls below *OP*, the consumer will be in equilibrium when he is purchasing more units of the commodity than *OM*. As a result of this, the consumer's surplus will increase. Thus, given the marginal utility curve of the consumer, the higher the price, the smaller the consumer's surplus and the lower the price, the greater the consumer's surplus.

It is worth noting here that in our analysis of consumer's surplus, we have assumed that perfect competition prevails in the market so that the consumer faces a given price, whatever the amount of the commodity he purchases. But if the seller of a commodity discriminates the prices and charges different prices for the different units of the good, some units at a higher price and some at a lower price, then in this case consumer's surplus will be smaller. Thus, when the seller makes price discrimination and sells different units of a good at different prices, the consumer will obtain smaller amount of consumer's surplus than under perfect competition. If the seller indulges in perfect price discrimination, that is, if he charges price for each unit of the commodity equal to what any consumer will be prepared to pay for it, then in that case no consumer's surplus will accrue to the consumer.

Consumer Surplus and Changes in Price

In our above analysis consumer's surplus has been explained by considering the surplus of utility or its money value which a consumer obtains from a given quantity of the commodity rather than nothing at all. However, viewing consumer surplus derived by the consumer from the consumption of a comniodity by considering it in an all or none situation has rather limited uses. In a more useful way, consumer' s surplus can be considered as net benefit or extra utility which a consumer obtains from the changes in price of a good or in the levels of its consumption.

Consider Figure 15.3 where *DD* shows the demand curve for food. At a market price *OP* of the food, the consumer buys *OQ* quantity of the food. The total market value which he pays for *OQ* food equals to the area *OPEQ*, that is, price *OP* multiplied by quantity *OQ*. *The total benefit, utility or use-value of OQ quantity of food is the area ODEQ*. Thus, consumer's surplus obtained by the consumer would be equal to the area *PED*. Now, if the price of food falls to *OP′*, the consumer will buy *OQ′* quantity of food and consumer surplus will increase to *P′TD*. The net increase in the consumer's surplus as a result of fall in price is the shaded area *PETP′*. *(P′TD – PED = PETP′)*. This measures the net benefit or extra utility obtained by the consumer from the fall in price of food. This net benefit can be decomposed into two parts.

First, the increase in consumer surplus arising on consuming previous OQ quantity of food due to fall in price. Second, the increase in consumer surplus equal to the small triangle EST arising due to the increase in consumption of good following the lowering of its price ($PETP' = SEPP' + EST$).

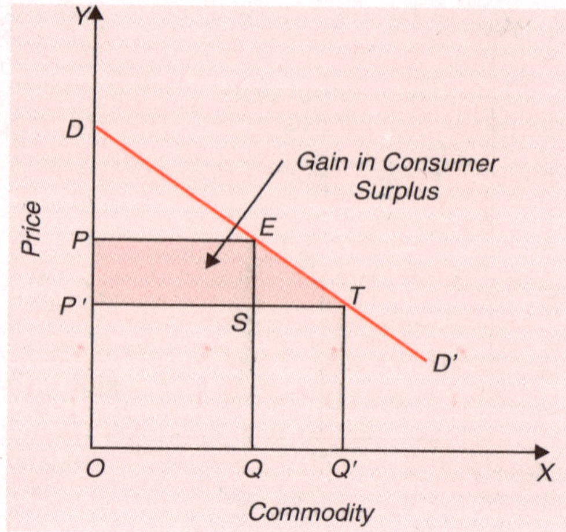

Fig. 15.3. *Gain in Consumer Surplus with a Fall in Price.*

Measurement of Consumer's Surplus through Indifference Curves

We have explained above the Marshallian method of measuring consumer's surplus. Marshallian method has been criticised by the advocates of ordinal utility analysis. Two basic assumptions made by Marshall in his measurement of consumer's surplus are: (1) utility can be quantitatively or cardinally measured, and (2) when a person spends more money on a commodity, the marginal utility of money does not change or when the price of a commodity falls and as a result consumer becomes better off and his real income increases, the marginal utility of money remains constant. Economists like Hicks and Allen have expressed the view that utility is a subjective and psychic entity and, therefore, it cannot be cardinally measured. They further point out that marginal utility of money does not remain constant with the rise and fall in real income of the consumer following the changes in price of a commodity. The implication of Marshallian assumption of constant marginal utility of money is that he neglects the income effect of the price change. But in some cases, income effect of the price change is very significant and cannot be ignored. Marshall defended his assumption of constancy of marginal utility of money on the ground that an individual spends a negligible part of his income on an individual commodity and, therefore, this does not make any significant change in the marginal utility of money. But this need not be so in case of all commodities.

Prof. J. R. Hicks rehabilitated the concept of consumer's surplus by measuring it with indifference curve technique of his ordinal utility analysis. Indifference curve technique does not make the assumption of cardinal measurability of utility, nor does it assume that marginal utility of money remains constant. However, without these invalid assumptions, Hicks was able to measure the consumer's surplus with his indifference curve technique. The concept of consumer's surplus was criticised mainly on the ground that it was difficult to measure it in cardinal utility terms. Therefore, Hicksian measurement of consumer's surplus in terms of ordinal utility went a long way in establishing the validity of the concept of consumer's surplus.

Measurement of Consumer Surplus With Indifference Curves

How consumer's surplus is measured with the aid of indifference curve technique is illustrated in Figure 15.4. In Figure 15.4, we have measured the quantity of commodity X along the X-axis, and money along the Y-axis. It is worth noting that money represents *other goods* except the commodity X. We have also shown some indifference curves between the given commodity X and money for the consumer, the scale of his preferences being given. Note that the assumption of constant marginal utility of money requires that indifference curves are vertically parallel to each other. We know that consumer's scale of preferences depends on his tastes and is quite independent of his income and market prices of the good. This will help us in understanding the concept of consumer's surplus with the aid of indifference curves.

Suppose, a consumer has *OM* amount of money which he can spend on the commodity X and the remaining amount on other goods. The indifference curve IC_1 touches this point *M* indicating thereby that all combinations of money and commodity X represented on IC_1 give the same satisfaction to the consumer as *OM* amount of money. For example, take combination *R* on an indifference curve IC_1. It follows that *OA* amount of commodity X and *OS* amount of money will give the same satisfaction to the consumer as *OM* amount of money because both *M* and *R* combinations lie on the same indifference curve IC_1. In other words, it means that the consumer is willing to pay *MS* amount of money for *OA* amount of the commodity X. It is thus clear that, given the scale of preferences of the consumer, he derives the same satisfaction from *OA* amount of the commodity X as from *MS* amount of money. In other words, he is prepared to give up *FR* (or *MS*) for *OA* amount of commodity X.

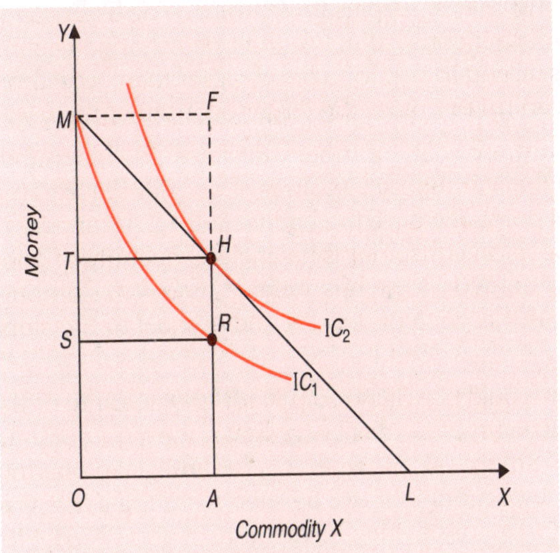

Fig. 15.4. *Measurement of Consumer Surplus with Indifference Curves*

Now, suppose that the price of commodity X in the market is such that we get the budget line *ML* (price of X is equal to $\frac{OM}{OL}$). We know from our analysis of consumer's equilibrium that consumer would be in equilibrium where the given budget line is tangent to an indifference curve. It will be seen from Fig. 15.4 that the budget line *ML* is tangent to the indifference curve IC_2 at point *H*, the consumer is having *OA* amount of commodity X and *OT* amount of money. Thus, given the market price of the commodity X, the consumer has spent *MT* amount of money for acquiring *OA* amount of commodity X. But, as mentioned above, he was pre-pared to forgo *MS* (or *FR*) amount of money for having *OA* amount of X. Therefore, the consumer pays *TS* or *HR* less amount of money than he is prepared to pay for *OA* amount of the commodity X rather than go without it. Thus, *TS* or *HR* is the amount of consumer's surplus which the consumer derives from purchasing *OA* amount of the commodity. In this way, Hicks explained the consumer's surplus with his indifference curves technique without assuming cardinal measurability of utility and without assuming constancy of the marginal utility of money. Since Marshall made these dubious assumptions for measuring consumer surplus, his method of measurement is regarded as invalid and Hicksian method of measurement with the technique of indifference curves is regarded as superior to Marshallian method.

Consumer's Surplus with Declining Marginal Utility of Money

The magnitude of Marshallian consumer's surplus as measured by the area under the demand curve is equal to the measure of consumer's surplus as measured by the vertical distance between the two indifference curves as obtained in Figure 15.4 subject to an assumption which was actually made by Marshall. It is that the marginal utility of money income remains constant when price of a commodity falls and consumer spends more money income on that particular good. In terms of indifference curve analysis this implies that income effect of the price change on the quantity consumed of the commodity is zero. In our above analysis of consumer's surplus through indifference curves, this means that indifference curves are vertically parallel, that is, have the same slope vertically above a given quantity of commodity measured on the X-axis. For example, slope of the indifference curves IC_1 and IC_2 at the quantity OA must be the same for Marshall's measure of consumer's surplus to be true[1]. The assumption of vertically parallel indifference curves or the zero income effect of the price change ensures that the amount of money that the consumer is willing to pay for a good rather than go without it does not change as the money income is given up to obtain the larger quantity of the good.

Now, if instead of remaining constant, marginal utility of money declines, the magnitude of consumer of surplus is smaller than the Marshallian theory visualises. Consider Figure 15.5 where the consumer is initially in equilibrium at point H where the budget line ML is tangent to the indifference curve IC_2. In this equilibrium position consumer is having OQ quantity of good X and has given up MT amount of money. In other words, he has spent $P_x.OQ = MT$ amount of money on OQ quantity of good X where P_x is the price of good X and is equal to the slope of the budget line ML.

To know how much money the consumer would be willing to pay for OQ quantity of the good X rather than go without it, an indifference curve IC_1 has been drawn through point M. This indifference curve IC_1, is flatter (that is, of smaller slope) than IC_2 for any given quantity of good X indicating decrease in marginal utility of money. It will be seen from the curve that the consumer is willing to pay MK amount of money for having OQ quantity of good X. But for quantity OQ he actually pays MT amount of money. Thus TK or HJ is the consumer surplus enjoyed by the consumer in this case when the assumption of constant marginal utility of money has been dropped.

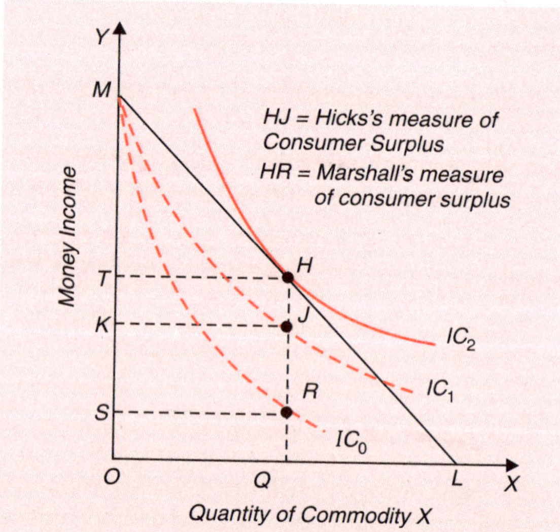

Fig. 15.5. *Consumer Surplus with Declining Marginal Utility of Money*

To compare this with the Marshallian measure of consumer's surplus which takes marginal utility of money to remain constant, we draw through point M another indifference curve IC_0 which is vertically parallel to the indifference curve IC_2, that is, has the same slope as IC_2 for a given quantity of X indicating *same* marginal utility of money as on IC_2. It will be seen from Figure 15.5 that on indifference curve IC_0, to obtain OQ quantity of good X the consumer is willing to surrender MS amount of money. Thus Marshall's measure of consumer's surplus is TS or HR which is larger than consumer's surplus TK or HJ obtained under the assumption of declining marginal utility of money income.

Hicksian Four Concepts of Consumer Surplus

We have explained above Hicksian analysis of consumer's surplus which is equivalent to the Marshallian concept of consumer's surplus. In defining consumer's surplus in terms of money in his well-known book '*Value and Capital*', Hicks pointed out that the Marshallian concept of consumer' s surplus was similar to the *compensating variation in income* of his indifference curve analysis of demand. But soon after Henderson showed that Hicksian compensating variation in income is not the same thing as the Marshallian consumer's surplus.

2. In case of zero income effect, we get income consumption curves as a vertical straight line.

According to Henderson[3], Marshallian concept of consumer's surplus related to the amount of money that the consumer was prepared to pay for the privilege of being able to buy at the existing price *the quantity of a commodity that he was already buying at this price.* On the other hand, according to Henderson, Hicksian concept of compensating variation in income refers to the amount of money that a consumer was prepared to pay for the privilege of buying the commodity at the existing price *in whatsoever quantities he desired.* Thus, the difference between compensating variation in income and the Marshallian consumer's surplus rests on the quantity of the commodity purchased; whereas Marshallian consumer surplus involves a quantity constraint, in Hicksian compensating variation in income, there is no such quantity constraint. Henderson showed that Hicksian compensating variation in income is greater than Marshallian consumer's surplus. Consider Figure 15.6. As explained above, the Marshallian consumer's surplus is *QR* whereas compensating variation in income is equal to *MG*. It will be seen from the figure that *MG* (which is equal to *QL)* is greater than *QR*. Henderson in his paper further pointed out that Hicksian compensating variation would differ according to whether the consumer had *to pay* for the privilege of buying the commodity at a lower price, or whether he was to *be paid* for making him to forgo the opportunity of buying at a lower price.

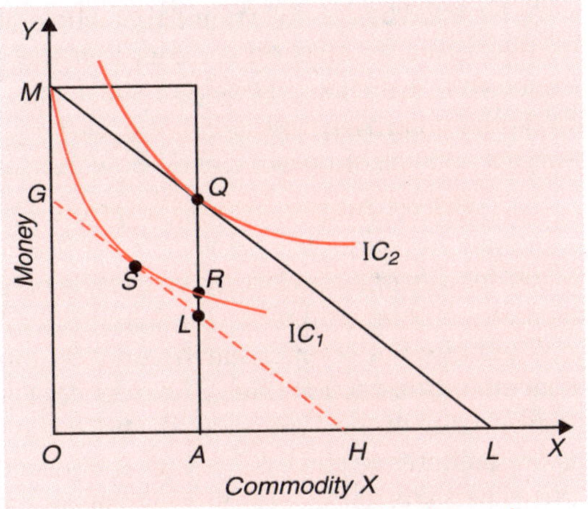

Fig. 15.6. *Consumer's Surplus and Compensating Variation in Income*

Hicks accepted these suggestions of Prof. Henderson and made a deeper study of the concept of consumer's surplus and further extended and developed it. Following the suggestions of Henderson, Hicks drew a distinction between the four concepts of consumer's surplus. Firstly, he distinguished between *compensating variation* for a *fall* in price and *equivalent variation* for a fall in price. Whereas compensating variation refers to the amount of money which is to be paid to the consumer so as to leave him in his *initial* level of satisfaction or welfare, equivalent variation refers to the amount of money which the consumer has to pay for buying the commodity at the lower price such as to leave him in the *subsequent* level of satisfaction or welfare following the change in price. Secondly, he drew distinction between *price* compensating variation or *price* equivalent variation on the one hand and *quantity* compensating variation or *quantity* equivalent variation on the other. In these the difference rests on whether there is a quantity constraint or not; whereas price compensating variation and price equivalent variation involve no quantity constraint, the quantity compensating variation and quantity equivalent variation like the original Marshallian concept of consumer's surplus involve a quantity constraint. Thus, the following four concepts of consumer's surplus were propounded *by* Hicks:

(1) Price Compensating Variation

(2) Price Equivalent Variation

(3) Quantity Compensating Variation

(4) Quantity Equivalent Variation

3. A. Henderson, "Consumer's Surplus and. the Compensating Variation" *Review of Economic Studies*, Vol. VIII, No. 2, p. 117.

It should be carefully noted that whole of the analysis of these four concepts of consumer's surplus of Hicks rests on the fact that the best way to look at the consumer's surplus is to conceive it as the extra benefit or satisfaction (welfare) a consumer will obtain as a result of the fall in the price of a commodity. We shall now explain below these four concepts of consumer's surplus and will bring out clearly how they are different from each other.

(1) **Price Compensating Variation.** *Price Compensating Variation is defined by Hicks as the maximum amount of money the consumer will be willing to pay for the privilege of buying a commodity at a lower price so that he obtains the initial level of welfare*, that is, the level of welfare he obtained before the fall in price. The concept of price compensating variation is nothing else but compensating variation in income explained earlier in connection with the concept of substitution effect. This concept is explained in Figure 15.7. In this figure, given the market price of the commodity X, price line is PL_1 and the consumer is in equilibrium at point Q on indifference curve IC_1. Now, suppose that the price of commodity X falls and as a result price line shifts to PL_2. Thus, as a result of the given fall in price, the consumer moves to a new

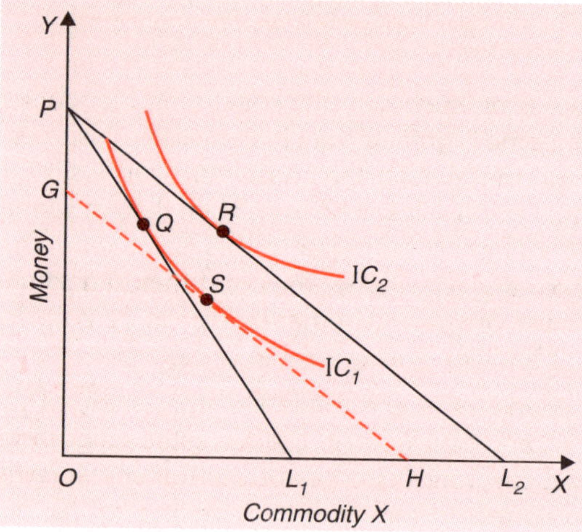

Fig. 15.7. *Price Compensating Variation*

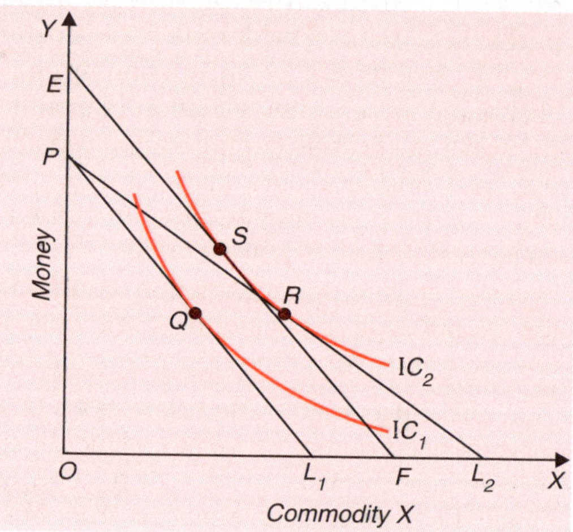

Fig. 15.8. *Price Equivalent Variation*

equilibrium position R on indifference curve IC_2. And in this move he has gained in satisfaction or welfare. Now, the question is how much amount of money the consumer will be prepared to pay for the opportunity of buying the good at this lower price and yet get the initial level of satisfaction as at point Q on IC_1. In order to know this, we need to draw a budget line parallel to PL_2 which touches the indifference curve IC_1. Such a line GH has been drawn in Figure 15.7. It will be seen from the figure that the price line GH represents the lower price of X as PL_2 but smaller amount of money income, since a part of money income has been taken away from the consumer. This means that the consumer will be prepared to pay PG amount of money for the privilege of buying the commodity at the lower price since he is indifferent between combination Q and S; the combination S he purchases with the lower price of X but with the smaller amount of money and combination Q he buys at higher price but with greater money income. Thus, PG is the price compensating variation.

(2) Price Equivalent Variation. Four concepts of consumer's surplus, price equivalent variation is the most important and has recently gained much popularity and prominence. ***Price equivalent variation is defined by Hicks as the minimum sum of money the consumer will accept to receive (that is, will have to be paid) for forgoing the opportunity of buying at a lower price so that he obtains the subsequent level of welfare (or satisfaction) which he reaches with the lower price.*** Let us illustrate this with Figure 15.8. Given the price of the commodity X in the market, the price line is PL_1. Some indifference curves of the consumer depicting his scale of preferences have also been drawn in Figure 15.8. It will be seen from this figure that the price line PL_1 is tangent to the indifference curve IC_1, at point Q. Now suppose that the price of commodity X falls so that we get a new price line PL_2. As a result of this fall in the price of X, the consumer will move to a new equilibrium position at a point *R* on a higher indifference curve IC_2. Since he has moved from a lower indifference curve to a higher indifference curve as a result of the fall in price of the commodity X, his satisfaction or welfare has increased. Now, the same increment in satisfaction or welfare could be obtained by the consumer if instead of the given fall in price of X, his money income would be increased by *PE*. With *PE* as the compensation and with the old price represented by the price line PL_1, he will move along *EF* (*EF* is parallel to PL_1) and will be in equilibrium at point *S* on indifference curve IC_2 at which he will get the level of welfare which he gets with the lower price at point *R*.

Thus, another measure of increment in satisfaction or welfare obtained by the consumer from the given fall in price of X, is equal to the amount of money income *PE*. *PE* is price equivalent variation. The consumer will be indifferent between the given fall in price and the increment in money income by *PE,* since with the lower price of X, he reaches point *R* on indifference curve IC_2 and at original price with extra amount of money he reaches point *S* on the subsequent indifference curve IC_2 at which *R* lies. Hence *PE* amount of money is required to compensate the consumer for depriving him of the privilege of buying the commodity X at the reduced price represented by the price line PL_2.

(3) Quantity Compensating Variation. *Quantity compensating variation is defined by Hicks as the maximum amount of money a consumer will be willing to pay for the privilege of buying a good at a lower price, if along with this privilege he is constrained to buy the quantity of the good which he would buy at the lower price, in the absence of any compensating payment*. Consider Figure 15.9 . Consumer is initially in equilibrium at point Q on indifference curve IC_1, given *OP* amount of money income and the price of X as represented by PL_1. Suppose the price of X falls and the consumer moves to the new equilibrium position *R* on indifference curve IC_2, at which he is buying *OB* amount of commodity X. Now, the question

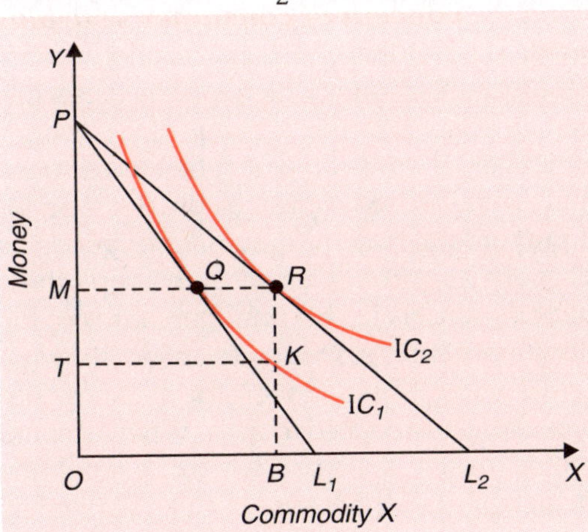

Fig. 15.9. *Consumer's Surplus : Quantity Compensating Variation*

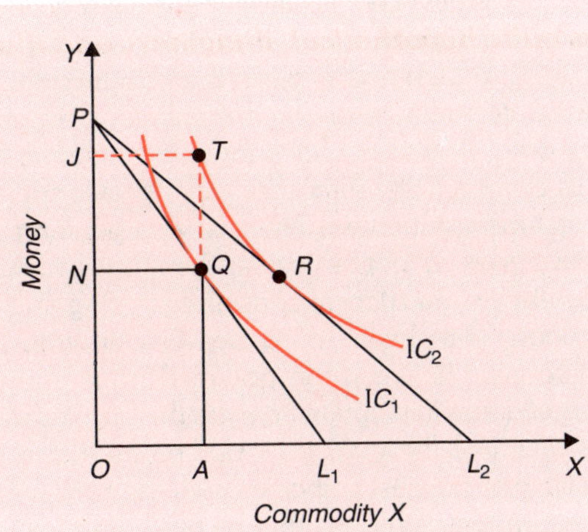

Fig. 15.10. *Consumer's Surplus : Quantity Equivalent Variation*

is how much amount of money the consumer will be willing to pay for buying good at the lower price so that he again reaches the original level of welfare represented by IC_1, if along with this he is constrained to buy *OB* amount of the commodity *X*. It will be seen from the Fig. 15.9 that if *RK* amount of the money is taken away from the consumer, he will be at point

K on indifference curve IC_1, his initial level of welfare and will buy *OB* amount of money. *Thus RK* is another measure of gain in welfare as a result of the fall in price of the good *X*. *RK* is the quantity compensating variation.

(4) Quantity Equivalent Variation. *The Quantity Equivalent Variation is defined as the minimum sum of money that the consumer will accept (or will have to be paid) for forgoing the opportunity of buying the commodity at the lower price, provided he is constrained to buy the quantity of X which he actually buys at the old higher price*. Consider Figure 15.10, where the consumer is initially in equilibrium at point *Q* on indifference curve IC_1, with the given money income *OP* and the price of X as represented by the budget line PL_1. In this equilibrium position, he is buying *OA* amount of commodity X. Now, suppose the price of X falls and the budget line shifts to PL_2. With this he will reach the higher indifference curve IC_2 at the new equilibrium position *R*. Thus, his satisfaction or welfare will be increased. But at *R*, he will be buying greater amount of commodity *X* than *OA*. However, if the consumer is constrained to buy *OA* amount of *X*, he will accept *QT* amount of money for giving up the opportunity of buying the commodity at the lower price *(i.e.* budget line PL_2). *This* is because combination *T* gives same satisfaction as combination *R* at which point the consumer reaches with the lower price of *X*. *Thus QT is quantity equivalent variation*. Increase in money income by *QT* is equivalent to the given fall in price in terms of increment in welfare.

Critical Evaluation of the Concept of Consumer's Surplus

The concept of consumer's surplus has been severely criticised ever since Marshall propounded and developed it in his *Principles of Economics*. Critics have described it as quite imaginary, unreal and useless. Most of the criticism of the concept has been levelled against the Marshallian method of measuring it as the area under the demand curve. However, some critics have challenged the validity of the concept itself. Marshallian concept of consumer's surplus has also been criticised on the ground of its being based upon unrealistic and questionable assumptions. We shall explain below the various criticisms levelled against this concept and will critically appraise them.

(1) It has been pointed out by several economists that the ***concept of consumer's surplus is quite hypothetical, imaginary and illusionary.*** They say that a consumer cannot afford to pay for a commodity more than his income. The maximum amount which a person can pay for a commodity or for a number of commodities, is limited by the amount of his money income. And, as is well known, a consumer has a number of wants on which he has to spend his money. Total sum of money actually spent by him on the goods cannot be greater than his total money income. Thus, what a person can be prepared to pay for a number of goods he purchases cannot be greater than the amount of his money income. Viewed in this light, there can be no question of consumer getting any consumer's surplus for his total purchases of the goods. Thus Prof. A. K. Das Gupta writes, "Taking consumer's surplus to mean simply a difference between the potential price and the actual price, Ulisse Gobbi, for instance, has argued that in ultimate analysis this surplus must necessarily be reduced to zero. When account is taken of the totality of purchases that a consumer makes, the price which he would be willing to pay just coincides with the price which he actually pays; because both are limited by the amount of money that he has command over, that is to say, by his income. If an individual starts with a given income he may be supposed to be willing to spend the whole of it on one good. As, however, he secures the good for a smaller sum, he turns to a second good, this time offering only what it is left with after the purchase of the first good. If again there arises a margin he turns to a third good and so on—the margin between the offer price and the actual price becoming narrower as the series of actions is extended, until it vanishes as he completes his final purchases."[4]

4. A. K. Das Gupta, *The Concept of Surplus in Theoretical Economics*, p. 120.

But, in our view, the above criticism misses the real point involved in the concept of consumer's surplus. The essence of the concept of consumer's surplus is that consumer gets excess psychic satisfaction from his purchases of the goods. It is not contended by the advocates of consumer's surplus that he gets monetary benefits from his purchases. It is true that with his limited money income, consumer cannot pay more for his total purchases than that he actually pays. But nothing prevents him from feeling and thinking that he derives more satisfaction from the goods than the price he pays for them and if he had the means he would have been prepared to pay much more for the goods than he actually pays for them.

(2) Another criticism against consumer's surplus is that it ***is based upon the invalid assumption that different units of the goods give different amounts of satisfaction to the consumer.*** We have explained above how Marshall calculated consumer's surplus derived by the consumer from a good. Consumer purchases the amount of a good at which marginal utility is equal to its price. It is assumed that marginal utility of a good diminishes as the consumer has more units of it. This means that while at the margin of the purchase, marginal utility of the good is equal to its price, for the previous intra-marginal units, marginal utility is higher than the price and on these intra-marginal units, consumer obtains consumer's surplus. Now, the critics point out that when a consumer takes more units of a commodity it is not only the utility of the marginal unit that declines but also all previous units of the commodity he has taken. Thus, as all units of a commodity are assumed alike, all would have the same utility. And when at the margin price is equal to the marginal utility of the last unit purchased, the price will also be equal to the utility of the previous units and consumer would, therefore, not get any consumer's surplus. Let us take an example. Suppose a consumer has six units of the commodity, marginal utility is equal to 10 and is equal to the given price. The critics argue that when the consumer has 6 units, it is not only the utility of the 6th unit that will be equal to 10, but all the previous five units will also yield utility equal to 10 each, since all units are alike. The total utility derived from 6 units will be equal to ₹ 60. The total price he actually pays for 6 units of the good, is also 60 and therefore he does not derive any excess utility from his purchases.

But this criticism is also not acceptable, because even though all units of a commodity may be alike, they do not give same satisfaction to the consumer; as consumer takes the first unit, he derives more satisfaction from it and when he takes up the second unit, it does not give him as much satisfaction as the first one, because while taking the second unit, a part of his want has already been satisfied. Similarly, when he takes the third unit, it will not give him as much satisfaction as the previous two units, because now a part of his want has been satisfied by two units. If we accept the above criticism that when a consumer takes more units of a commodity, it is not only the utility of the marginal unit but also of the previous units declines, we then deny the law of diminishing marginal utility. As has been seen in he previous chapter, diminishing marginal utility from a good describes the fundamental human tendency and has also been confirmed by observation of actual consumer's behaviour. The concept of consumer's surplus, as has been mentioned before, is derived from the law of diminishing marginal utility. If law of diminishing marginal utility is valid, the validity of the Marshallian concept of consumer's surplus can also not be challenged.

(3) The concept of consumer's surplus has also been criticised on the ground that *it ignores the interdependence between the goods,* that is, the relations of substitute and complementary goods. Thus, it is pointed out that if only tea were available and no other substitute drinks such as milk, coffee, etc., then the consumer would have been prepared to

pay much more price for tea than that in the presence of substitute drinks. Thus, the magnitude of consumer's surplus derived from a commodity depends upon the availability of substitutes. This is because if only tea were available, consumer will have no choice and would be afraid that if he does not get tea, he cannot satisfy his given want from any other commodity. Therefore, he will be willing to pay more for a cup of tea rather than go without it. But if substitutes of tea are available he would not be prepared to pay as much high price since he will think that if he is deprived of tea, he will take other substitute drinks like milk and coffee.

Thus, it is said that ***consumer's surplus is not a definite, precise and unambiguous concept,*** it depends upon the availability of substitutes. The degree of substitutability between different goods is different for different consumers, and this makes the concept of consumer's surplus little vague and ambiguous. Marshall was aware of this difficulty and, to overcome this, he suggested that for the purpose of measuring consumer's surplus, substitute products like tea and coffee be clubbed together and considered as one single commodity.

(4) Prof. Nicholson described the concept of consumer's surplus as hypothetical and imaginary. He writes "of what avail is it to say that the utility of an income of (say) £ 100 a year is worth (say) £ 1000 a year." According to Prof. Nicholson and other critics, it is difficult to say how much price a consumer would be willing to pay for a good rather than go without it. This is because consumer does not face this question in the market when he buys goods; he has to pay and accept the price that prevails in the market. It is very difficult for him to say how much he would be prepared to pay rather than go without it. However, in our view, this criticism only indicates that it is difficult to measure consumer's surplus precisely. That a consumer gets extra satisfaction from a good than the price he pays for it is undeniable.

Moreover, as J. R. Hicks has pointed out "the best way of looking at consumer's surplus is to regard it as a means of expressing it in terms of money income gain which accrues to the consumer as a result of a fall in price."[5] When price of a commodity falls, the money income of the consumer being given, the budget line will switch to the right and the consumer will be in equilibrium at a higher indifference curve and as a result his satisfaction will increase. Thus, consumer derives more satisfaction at the lower price than that at the higher original price of the good. This implies that fall in the price of a commodity, and, therefore, the availability of the commodity at a cheaper price adds to the satisfaction of the consumer and this is in fact the change in consumer's surplus brought about by change in the price of the good. As has been seen above, J. R. Hicks has further extended the concept of consumer's surplus, considering it from the viewpoint of gains which consumer gets from the fall in price of a good. Moreover, the concept of consumer's surplus is useful and meaningful and not unreal because it indicates that he gets certain extra satisfaction and advantages from the use of amenities available in civilized towns and cities.

(5) The concept of consumer's surplus has also been criticised on the ground that ***it is based upon questionable assumptions of cardinal measurability of utility and constancy of the marginal utility of money.*** Critics point out that utility is a psychic entity and cannot be measured in quantitative cardinal terms. In view of this, they point out that consumer's surplus cannot be measured by the area under the demand curve, as Marshall did it. This is because Marshallian demand curve is based on the marginal utility curve in drawing which it is assumed that utility is cardinally measurable. Further, as has been explained in earlier chapters, by assuming constant marginal utility of money, Marshall ignored income effect of the price change. Of course, income effect of the price change in case of most of the commodities is negligible and can be validly ignored. But in case of some important commodities such as

5. J. R. Hicks, *Value and Capital*, Oxford University Press, 2nd edition 1946, p. 40.

foodgrains, income effect of the price change is quite significant and cannot be validly ignored. Therefore, the Marshallian method of measurement as area under the demand curve, ignoring the income effect, is not perfectly correct. However, this does not invalidate the concept of consumer's surplus. As has been explained above, J. R. Hicks has been able to provide *a money measure of consumer's surplus* with his indifference curves technique of ordinal utility analysis which does not assume cardinal measurement of utility and constant marginal utility of money. Hicks has not only rehabilitated the concept of consumer's surplus but also extended and developed it further.

Conclusion

Despite some of the shortcomings of the concept of consumer surplus, some of which are based on wrong interpretation of the concept of consumer surplus, it is of great significance not only in economic theory but also in the formulation of economic policies by the Government. The concept of consumer's surplus has a great practical importance in the formulation of economic policies by the Government and the producers of commodities especially monopolists. First, consumer's surplus brings out quite clearly that the price which a consumer pays for a good does not exactly measure the utility or satisfaction he derives from it; utility is often more than the price paid for them. Adam Smith emphasized the distinction between ***value-in-use*** and ***value-in-exchange***, and pointed out that value-in-use of a commodity is much more than the value-in-exchange. Value-in-use of a commodity signifies the utility or satisfaction which it provides to the consumer, while value-in-exchange means the price paid by the consumer. The difference between the two is the amount of consumer's surplus derived by the consumer from the consumption of the good. There are several things in daily life such as common salt, match boxes, newspapers whose utility or value-in-use is much greater than the price people actually pay for them. That shows these goods provide a good deal of consumer's surplus to the people.

People living in the modern civilised areas get so may amenities and recreation facilities for which they will be prepared to pay much higher prices, if they are to be deprived of them. Thus, the increment in welfare by these amenities and recreation facilities is much greater than the prices they pay for them. Prof. Samuelson rightly remarks that "The important thing is to see how lucky the citizens of modern efficient communities really are. The privilege of being able to buy a vast array of goods at low prices cannot be overestimated."[6] Thus, the concept of consumer surplus clearly indicates the difference in value-in-use and value-in-exchange of the commodities and clearly brings out that the welfare derived from the consumption of good is greater than the price paid for them.

Marshall used the concept of consumer surplus for prescribing a suitable fiscal policy by the Government which will maximize the welfare of the people. Marshall regarded the long-run equilibrium position under perfect competition as one of ensuring maximum satisfaction. With this he proved that the total welfare of the community will increase by imposing taxes on the product of the increasing-cost industry and giving subsidies to the product of the decreasing-cost industry.

Besides, the concept of consumer surplus has been extensively used in explaining the excess burden of an indirect tax, cost-benefit analysis of the various projects and market structure. The consumer surplus has also been used to bring out loss in social welfare or misallocation of resources under monopoly and other forms of imperfect competition. Further, it has been applied to show the gain from exchange of goods between two individuals or between countries. We discuss below some important applications of the concept of consumer

6. P. A. Samuelson, *Economics*, McGraw-Hill, 8th edition, 1970, p. 418.

surplus both in economic theory and for formulation of economic policy which clearly bring out the importance of consumer surplus.

APPLICATIONS OF CONSUMER SURPLUS

The concept of consumer surplus has several applications both in economic theory and economic policy. This concept has been used to resolve water-diamond paradox of value theory, to explain the effects of taxes and subsidies on people's welfare, to make cost-benefit analysis of public projects, to show gains from trade etc. We will explain below some of the applications of the concept of consumer surplus.

Water-Diamond Paradox

One of the most famous puzzles in economic theory is why diamonds are more expensive than water. Water is essential for life; it is so useful that without its consumption one cannot live or survive. On the other hand, diamonds, though attractive and beautiful, satisfy less important human needs than water. Then, how it can be that in the market less useful commodity like diamonds are so expensive and a highly useful commodity as water is very cheap. Some thinkers in the past therefore complained that something was wrong with the market system which determines high price of commodities such as diamond, gold etc. which are least useful and low price of a commodity which is necessary and highly useful such as water. Therefore, this came to be known as water-diamond paradox. However, for modern economists there is no paradox about it as they are able to explain the large price differential of water and diamond. The notion of marginal valuation of a commodity and the concept of consumer surplus based on it, can be used to resolve the water-diamond paradox. The marginal benefit or marginal valuation per litre of water for the consumer is very low as the actual supply of water per period is relatively very large. On the other hand, the marginal valuation or marginal benefit of diamonds is very high because the amount of diamond actually available is very small. If, in fact, only few litres of water were available marginal valuation of water would have been much greater than that of diamonds. Note that ***marginal valuation of a commodity reflects how much amount of money consumer is prepared to pay for a commodity.*** This indicates marginal benefit or use value of the commodity for the consumer.

In is worth noting that downward-sloping demand curve for a commodity can be interpreted as showing the marginal valuation or marginal benefit in terms of money to the consumer of various units of a commodity. If the quantity actually available of a commodity in the market is very large, its marginal valuation or marginal benefit will be very small, though its total use-value or total benefit may be very large. On the other hand, as the actually available quantity of a commodity such as diamonds, gold etc. is very small, its marginal valuation or marginal benefit would be high, though its total value-in-use or total benefit is small. *Market price of a commodity is determined not by its total use-value but by its marginal valuation or marginal benefit which in turn depends on the actually available quantity*. The total use-value or total benefit which a consumer gets from a quantity of a commodity equals the amount actually paid and the consumer surplus he obtains from it. In case of water market price as determined by its marginal benefit is low but consumer surplus from it is very large. On the other hand, in case of diamond due to their greater scarcity, marginal benefit and hence its price is large but consumer surplus from it is very small. Thus, the concept of consumer's surplus shows that price should not be confused with use-value of a commodity and this helps us to resolve the water-diamond paradox.

This is illustrated in Figure 15.11 where consumers' demand curve D_d depicts the marginal valuation curve for diamonds. On the X-axis quantity of diamonds in grams per time period and along the Y-axis marginal benefit and price of diamonds are measured. Since the total use-value *(i.e.* total benefit) of diamond is small, the demand curve is at a low level. Suppose the quantity of diamond actually available is Q_d and, as will be seen from the figure, price of diamond determined by demand and supply is P_d which is quite high, whereas the consumer surplus equal to LAP_d (shaded area) obtained by the consumers over and above what they actually pay is small.

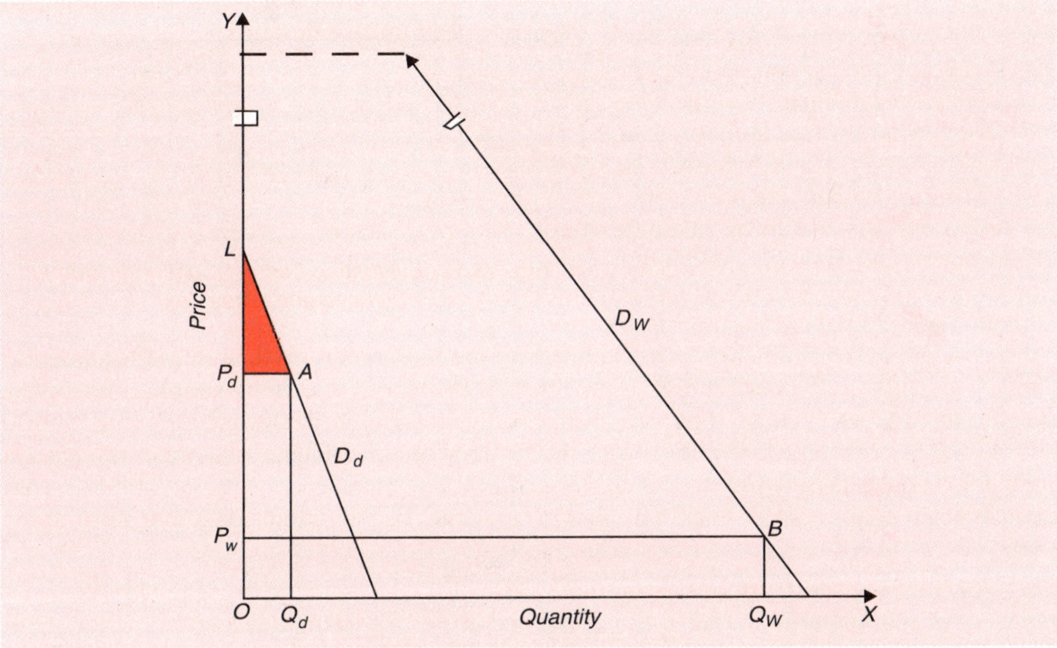

Fig. 15.11. Water-Diamond Paradox

Figure 15.11 also illustrates the price determination ot water. Demand curve D_w representing marginal valuation or marginal benefit of different quantities of water is at a higher level. If the quantity of water available is a very large quantity OQ_w, its marginal benefit equals Q_wB and therefore price determined is OP_w. Though the market price of water is very low, consumer surplus obtained by the consumers will be the whole shaded area (not fully shown) above the price line PwB wliich is very large compared with those of diamonds.

To sum up, the total valuation or satisfaction derived from water consumed is much greater compared with diamonds but its marginal valuation is low due to its abundant supply. The difference is large consumer surplus. On the other hand, total valuation (value in use) of diamonds consumed is very small but due to its scarcity its marginal benefit and therefore its price is very high compared with water. The difference is very small consumer surplus.

Evaluating Loss of Benefit from Tax

The notion of consumer surplus is applied for evaluating benefits and losses from certain economic policies. Chapter 13 showed the impact of taxes and subsidies on consumer's welfare using indifference curve analysis. The losses and gains from taxes and subsidies to the consumers can also be analysed using market demand curve and the concept of consumer's surplus. First, we explain the loss in consumer's surplus or welfare caused by the imposition of an indirect tax (say, sales tax) on cars. We assume that supply curve of cars is perfectly elastic, indicating constant cost conditions under which the car industry is working. Under these conditions, imposition of a sales tax, say ₹ 10,000 per car sold would raise the price of car by exactly this amount, say from ₹ 1,60,000 to ₹ 1,70,000. The rise in price of car will result in fall in its quantity demanded and sold. The loss in benefits incurred by the consumers as a result of the sales tax is illustrated in Figure 15.12. The *DD* represents the demand curve for cars. This demand curve for cars can also be interpreted as marginal benefit or marginal valuation curve of the cars for the consumers. Before the imposition of a sales tax *PS* is the supply curve of cars. The demand and supply for cars are in equilibrium at quantity Q_1 and price *OP*. Thus Q_1 quantity of cars is sold at price *OP*. In this situation consumers obtain *APD* amount of consumer surplus which measures net benefit to the consumers from the use of Q_1 number of cars. Now, with the imposition of sales tax of ₹ 10,000 (or *PP′* = *T*) the supply curve of cars shifts to *P′S′*. Consequently, the price of car rises from *OP* (₹ 1,60,000) to *OP′* (₹ 1,70,000) and number of cars sold falls to Q_2. With the rise in price and fall in the number of cars sold consumer surplus is now reduced to *BP′D* and consumers incur a loss in consumer surplus (benefit) equal to the ares *APP′B*. This loss in consumer surplus can be decomposed into two parts.

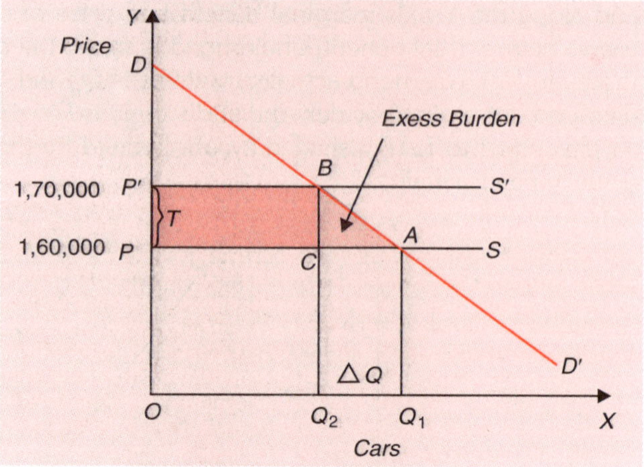

Fig. 15.12. *Evaluating Loss of Consumer Surplus by Imposing Sales Tax*

The first part is the rectangular area, *PP′BC* which is equal to the tax (*T*) multiplied by the reduced number of cars Q_2, ($PP'BC = T.Q_2$) and arises due to the increased expenditure on Q_2 number of cars consequent to the imposition of the sales tax. The area *PP′BC* or Q_2T also represents the revenue collected by the Government from levying sales tax. The second component of loss in consumer's surplus is the triangular area *ABC* which measures the loss in consumer surplus on account of the decrease in number of cars sold, that is, ΔQ or Q_1Q_2 as a result of levying of sales tax. In this way, the total loss in net benefit or consumer sur-plus is $PP'BA = PP'BC + ABC$. Where *PP′BC* is also equal to tax per car (*i.e.* *T*) multiplied by the reduced numbers of card sold (*i.e.* Q_2), that is, TQ_2 and the triangular area *ABC* which equals $1/2\ T\Delta Q$. Thus, loss in consumer surplus ($PP'BA$) $= T.Q_2 + 1/2\ T\Delta Q$.

It is worth noting that the loss in consumer surplus *PP′ BA* is greater than the revenue collected by the Government which is equal to the area *PP′BC* and this extra loss in consumer surplus is equal to the triangular area *ABC*. This area *ABC* represents the **excess burden of sales taxation**. It measures the net loss in welfare or consumer surplus in excess of tax revenue received by the Government and *is also called* **dead weight loss**. If instead of sales tax, a *lump sum tax of* the equal amount were levied, there would have been no excess burden. Thus, sales tax distorts the price of cars, reduces the number of cars sold and thereby results in loss in consumer welfare in excess of the amount of tax collected. Therefore, economists dub indirect taxes such as sales tax or excise duty as economically inefficient.

Thus, it follows that the burden of indirect tax (such as sales tax or excise duty) is greater than the direct tax such as lump-sum tax or income tax. Therefore, many economists hold that from the viewpoint of social welfare or optimum allocation of resources, the *direct taxes* such as a lump-sum tax or income tax is superior to an indirect tax such as sales tax or excise duty. Let us show and illustrate it with the help of Figure 15.12 *which represents the case of constant-cost industry, with* the given demand and supply curves DD' and PS' respectively price OP and equilibrium quantity OQ_1 are determined. This is the position before the imposition of the tax and represents the maximum satisfaction or welfare of the people. Now, if the sales tax equal to PP' per unit of the commodity is imposed, the supply curve will shift upward to the position $P'S'$. As a result, the price will rise to OP' and the quantity demanded and sold will fall to Q_2. As explained above, tax collected by the Government in this case will be equal to $PP'BC$, but the loss in consumer's surplus suffered by the consumer will be equal to $PP'BA$. Now, if the Government takes away the sum equal to $PP'BC$ through a direct tax, say lump-sum tax or income tax, then the people would not have to suffer the loss equal to the area ABC. This is so because where an ***indirect tax distorts the price of a commodity (i.e. it raises the price), a lump-sum or income tax does not affect the price.*** Thus, it is clear that a direct tax causes less loss of welfare than a price-distorting indirect tax. However, it should be remembered that this conclusion is based on the assumption that the total welfare is maximum before the imposition of any tax.

Evaluating Gain from a Subsidy

The concept of consumer surplus can also be used to evaluate the gain from subsidies. The Government these days provide subsidies on many commodities such as foodgrains, fertilizers, power. Let us take the example of subsidy on foodgrains production being given by the Government. Suppose the subsidy reduces the price of foodgrains from ₹ 400 to ₹ 300 per quintal. As a result of the fall in price of foodgrains due to subsidy being provided for its production, the quantity demanded of foodgrains increases from 10 thousand quintals Q_1 to 12 thousand quintals Q_2. Now, the question to be answered is what will be net social benefit or gain from this subsidy. Consider Figure 15.13 where DD is the demand curve for foodgrains which, as explained above, can also be interpreted as *marginal benefit (or marginal valuation) curve*. To begin with, PS is the supply curve, assuming constant cost conditions. Price determined is OP or ₹ 400 per quintal. With the grant of subsidy equal to ₹ 100 per quintal, supply curve shifts below to P_1S_1 and as a result price falls to OP_1 or ₹ 300 per quintal. With the reduction in price to OP_1 (*i.e.* ₹ 300 per quintal) quantity demanded increases to from OQ_1 to OQ_2. It will be seen from Figure 15.13 that the total gain in consumer surplus is equal to the area $PACP_1$ which can be divided into two parts, namely, the area $PABP_1$ (= $R.Q_1$) where R is the subsidy per quintal of foodgrains plus triangle ABC, which equals $1/2\ R\Delta Q$.

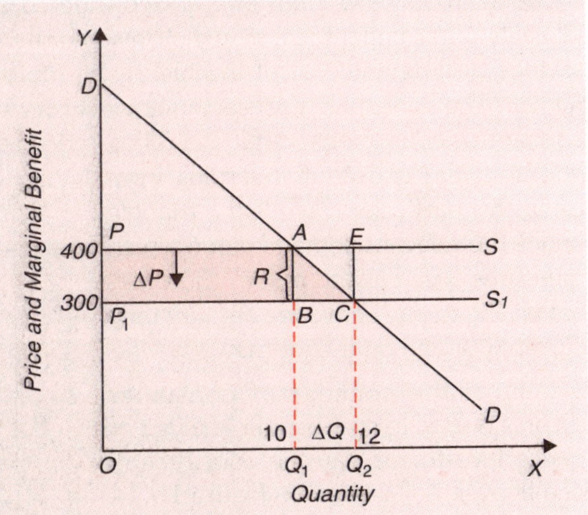

Fig. 15.13. *Gain from a Price Subsidy*

$$\text{Thus, the gain in consumer surplus} = R.Q_1 + \frac{1}{2} R.\Delta Q.$$

Where $R.Q_1$ represents the reduction in expenditure on the quantity Q_1 that would have cost Rs. R (= ₹ 100) per quintal more without subsidy. Thus $R.Q_1$ represents the benefit or gain in consumer surplus to those who were purchasing foodgrains before the grant of subsidy but would now do so at a lower price. The amount $1/2\ R\Delta Q$ represents the gain in consumer surplus due to the increase in quantity demanded at a lower price made possible by the grant of subsidy. Thus, the total gain in consumer surplus is the-area $PACP_1$, which equals $R.Q_1 + 1/2\ R\Delta Q$.

But the cost of subsidy to the Government is $R.Q_2$ or the area P_1PEC which is greater than the gain in consumer surplus by the area of the triangle *ACE*. Thus, if the buyers would have been given the lump-sum grant of $PACP_1$ they would have been as well off as in case of subsidy which costs more to the Government. Thus, *subsidy causes excess burden equal to the area of triangle ACE.*

Use of Consumer Surplus in Cost-Benefit Analysis

An important application of consumer surplus is its use in cost-benefit analysis, especially of public investment projects. In fact, Dupuit, the originator of the idea of consumer surplus in his paper. *"On the Measurement of Public Works"* in 1944 used the concept of consumer surplus for describing the impact of public investment projects on social welfare. In recent years, E. J. Mishan has based his cost-benefit analysis on consumer surplus approach. Consumer's surplus has been treated as benefits in various cost-benefits analysis of investment projects. The cost-benefit analysis has become very popular these days to judge the desirability of public investment in particular projects. It should be noted that ***costs and benefits in cost-benefit analysis do not merely mean money costs and money benefits but real costs and real benefits in terms of satisfaction and resources.*** Further, cost-benefit analysis looks at costs and benefits from social point of view; it is concerned with social benefits and social costs. The amount of consumer's surplus expected to be derived from certain projects such as a bridge, road park, dam etc. are considered as an important benefit flowing from these projects[7]. The benefit of a new motor way or flyover is estimated by reference to the expected savings of time and'cost of the fuel by all motorists who will make use of the new road or flyover. The concept of cost-saving however, as we shall see below, is derived directly from the concept of consumer's surplus ... Thus, prior to the introduction of, say the new flyover in question, the consumer's surplus from using this particular route is the triangle under the relevant demand curve which measures the maximum sum motorists are willing to pay above the amount they currently spend on the journey."[8]

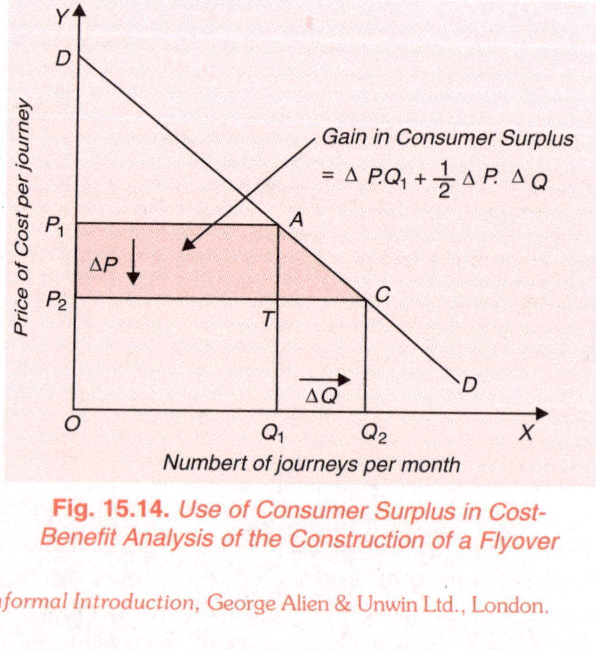

Fig. 15.14. *Use of Consumer Surplus in Cost-Benefit Analysis of the Construction of a Flyover*

How the concept of consumer surplus is used in cost-benefit analysis of public investment, say the construction of a flyover, is illustrated in Figure 15.14 where on the X-axis we measure the number of journeys made per month on a particular route where flyover is proposed to be undertaken and on the X-axis we measure the price or cost per journey. *DD* is the demand curve for the journey in that route which, as explained above, shows the maximum price the

7. See Mishan, E. J., *Cost-Benefit Analysis: An Informal Introduction*, George Alien & Unwin Ltd., London.
8. Mishan, E. J. *op., cit.*, p. 33.

motorists are willing to pay for making journeys on that route. If the current price or cost per journey, that is, prior to the construction of flyover is OP_1, the motorists make OQ_1 number of journeys on that route and pay $OP_1.OQ_1$ as the total cost for the OQ_1 journeys made. It will be seen from the demand curve that the total amount of money that the motorists will be willing to pay for OQ_1 journeys equals the area $ODAQ_1$ and thus the triangle P_1DA represents the consumer surplus they derive from making OQ_1 journeys. Now suppose the flyover is constructed which by reducing their fuel consumption reduces the cost per journey to OP_2. At the lower price or cost per journey, they will make OQ_2 number of journeys and their consumer surplus will increase by the shaded area P_1ACP_2. This is the benefit the motorists receive from the construction of flyover.

This increase in consumer surplus can be divided into two parts. First, we have the cost-saving component equal to the rectangular area P_1P_2TA which is calculated as the saving per journey multiplied by the original number of journeys OQ_1. The other part of the increase in consumer surplus is represented by the area of the triangle ATC which is the gain in consumer's surplus obtained from the additional journeys made by the same motorists or the new ones. It is worth noting that it is the cost-saving segment of the increment in consumer surplus that often enters into the cost-benefit calculations of the investment projects. But, as we have just seen, this cost-saving is the main component of the addition to the consumer surplus due to fall in the cost per journey brought about by the construction of the flyover.

We have seen above that the concept of consumer's surplus in the context of an individual and in the context of a particular good is a meaningful and useful idea. However, it is worth noting here that the use of the concept of consumer's surplus as a tool for formulation of policies, such as choice of investment projects based on cost-benefit calculation, requires the summation of consumer's surpluses derived from a good or project by various consumers belonging to different income groups. Such summation and comparison of consumer's surplus of different individuals can be validly made if one rupee worth of consumer's surplus means the same thing to different individuals. However, this is based on the assumption that marginal utility of money is the same for all individuals regardless of the size of their income. This lands us into interpersonal comparison of the utility which is not regarded as scientific and justified by many economists.

NUMERICAL PROBLEMS ON CONSUMER'S SURPLUS

It will be worthwhile to explain how to solve numerical problems on consumer surplus. Let us take some problems:

Problem 1: *Swati's demand for chocolate is given by the following demand function:*

$$Q = 30 - 2P$$

Where Q represents quantity demanded and P represents price.

If market price for a chocolate is ₹ 5 per piece, calculate her consumer's surplus.

Solution: We have to first construct a demand from the given demand function which is linear. For this purpose we have to find out the intercepts of the demand curve on the X-axis and on the Y-axis.

It will be observed from the demand function that intercept on the X-axis is given to be equal to 30 which indicates the quantity demanded at price zero of the commodity. Intercept of the demand curve on the Y-axis is the price at which *no quantity* of the commodity will be demanded. Thus putting the demand function equal to zero we have

$$30 - 2P = 0$$
$$2P = 30$$
$$P = 15$$

With 15 as the intercept on the Y-axis and 30 as the intercept on *X-axis*, demand curve

DD has been drawn in Figure 15.15. Now, from the given demand function or the demand curve *DD* we can obtain the quantity demanded at the given price ₹ 5 per chocolate. Thus,

$$Q = 30 - 2P$$
$$P = 5$$
$$Q = 30 - 2 \times 5 = 20$$

Consumer's surplus = Area *ADB*

$$= (\text{base} \times \text{height})\ \frac{1}{2}$$

$$= (\ 20 \times (15 - 5)\ \frac{1}{2}$$

$$= \frac{1}{2}\ (\ 20 \times 10\ ) = 100$$

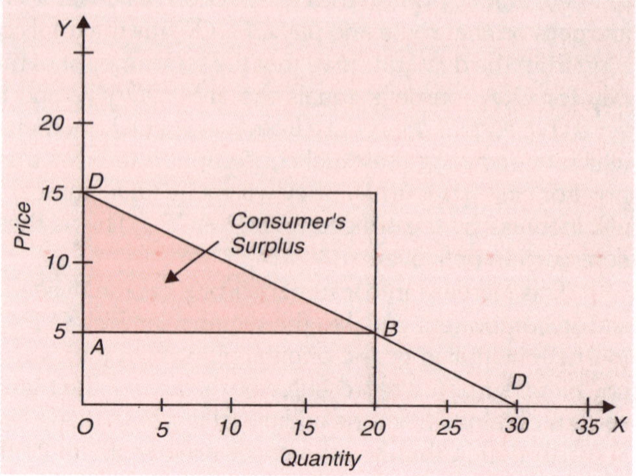

Fig. 15.15. *calculating consumer's surplus*

Problem 2: *A producer raises the price of his product from ₹ 10 per unit to ₹ 15 per unit. As a result, the quantity demanded and sold by him decreases from 250 units to 200 units. Calculate the loss in consumers surplus to the buyers of his product. Also calculate the dead-weight loss to the society.*

Solution: We have drawn the demand curve for the producer so that at ₹ 10 per unit, 250 units are demanded and at ₹ 15 per unit 200 units of commodity are demanded. It will be seen from Figure15.16. that with the rise in price from ₹10 to 15 loss of consumer's surplus by the buyers is equal to the area *ABCE*. This loss in consumer's surplus can be broken into two parts. First as a result of rise in price, the producer gains some income at the expense of consumers. This gain in income by the producer is equal to the area of rectangle *ABCF*.

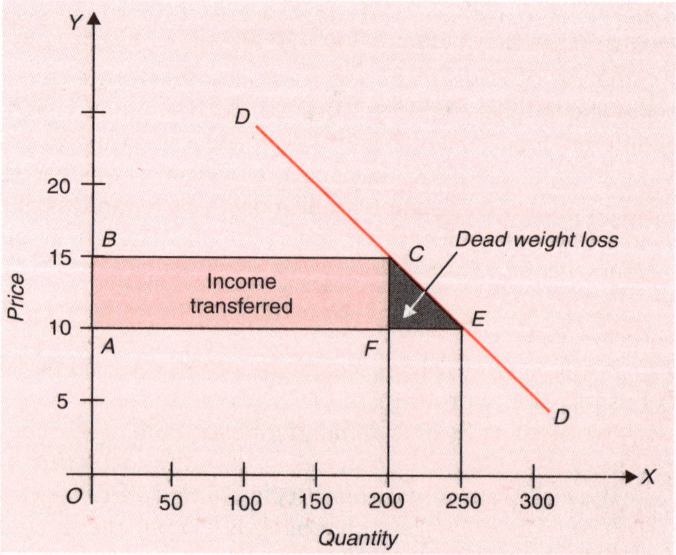

Fig. 15.16. *Loss of Consumer's Surplus and Dead Weight Loss of the Rise in Price*

The second part of loss of consumer's surplus is small triangle *CEF* which measures the dead weight loss to the society. This is called dead-weight loss because no member of the society gains income due to this loss by the consumers. It is a pure waste.

Gain in income by the producer = Area *ABCF* = Base × height

= [200 × (15 – 10)] = 1000.

Dead weight loss = Area of triangle *CEF*

= (base × height)/2

$$= 50 \times (15 - 10)/2 = 250 \times \frac{1}{2} = 125.$$

CHAPTER

16

Attribute Approach to Consumer's Behaviour

Attribute or Characteristics Approach : Introduction

In recent years a new approach to consumer's demand for products has been put forward. This new approach[1] lays stress on the attributes or characteristics which various products possess rather than products themselves. The traditional theories of demand, namely, Marshallian utility analysis, indifference curve theory of demand and revealed preference approach suffer from several short-comings which prevent them to offer explanatory or predictive models to explain why, for instance, some consumers prefer brand A of a product, while others prefer brand *B*. Further, the traditional models fail to predict whether or not the improvement in its product by a firm will increase its market share. Again, the traditional theories do not help us to explain and predict whether a firm will lose its sales to another when the latter introduces a new product. The new approach lays its emphasis on the attributes possessed by the alternative products or the alternative brands of a product. For example, the attributes of a house refer to its size, number of its rooms, its floor and location, quality of bathrooms, quality of its construction and so on. The attributes of a car include its outlook, fuel economy, its pick-up, interior space and others. It is worth noting that attributes cannot be purchased by themselves; they are contained in goods. For instance, an apple contains iron, vitamins and other nutrients. Most consumers would like to have iron by consuming apples rather taking iron-pills.

Thus the new approach to consumer's demand emphasizes that consumers do not want goods directly but rather they desire attributes which the goods provide. For example, a person who buys a woollen suit, does not do so because he desires to own a woollen suit for its own sake but because of the utility which its attributes provide him such as warmth, protection, beauty and so on. Likewise, an individual does not want just to own a house but for the sake of various attributes such as bedroom space, cooking facilities of its kitchen, its bathroom facilities, drawing room etc it provides. The reason some individuals would buy one type of house, whereas others would purchase other types of houses having almost the same price is their varying preferences of attributes provided by the various types of houses. Thus, "the novelty of this approach is the notion that attributes of goods provide utility to individuals and that goods themselves provide utility only to the extent that they contain desirable attributes."[2]

Indifference Curves of Attributes

Just as an individual can express his preference or indifference between various combinations of two commodities, similarly he can express his preference or indifference between attributes. Suppose an individual is interested in two attributes of food he buys, namely

1. For the original statement of this new approach to consumer theory, See Lancaster K. J. "A New Approach to Consumer Theory" *Journal of Political Economy,* 74, April 1966, pp. 132.157.
2. Nicholson, Walter, *Microeconomic Theory,* 3rd edition, The Dryden Press, 1989, p. 160.

(i) the amount of calories and (ii) the amount of vitamins it contains. The different types of food would provide different amounts and proportions of calories and vitamins. As mentioned above, an individual cannot buy these attributes directly. Instead, he must buy the various food articles that contain these attributes. We can graphically represent the ranking of preferences or indifferences of various combinations of these two attributes, calories and vitamin, from the various food articles through an indifference curve map. Such an indifference map between the amounts of calories and vitamins is shown in Figure 16.1. We measure the amounts of calories on the X-axis and the amount of vitamins along the vertical axis.

In explaining how an individual will choose a combination of two attributes and consequently of two food products in order to maximize his satisfaction an important concept called ***product ray*** needs to be introduced. Let us take the example of consumption of a food product "rice". One kilogram of rice contains a particular combination of calories and vitamins and two kilograms of rice would contain double the amounts of calories and vitamins. Given the price of rice, the various amounts of rice (and therefore varying amounts of attributes of rice, calories and vitamins) are represented along a product ray. In Figure 16.1. a product ray *OA* is drawn which shows increasing expenditure on rice and therefore the increasing amounts of rice consumption providing greater amounts of calories and vitamins. Thus point *Q* on ray *OA* shows the expenditure or consumption of rice which provides OC_1 amount of calories and OV_1 amount of vitamins which would yield a level of satisfaction represented by I_2. Thus a movement upward along the ray *OA*, would mean how the satisfaction or utility of the individual will increase from the attributes provided by greater expenditure *X* on rice.

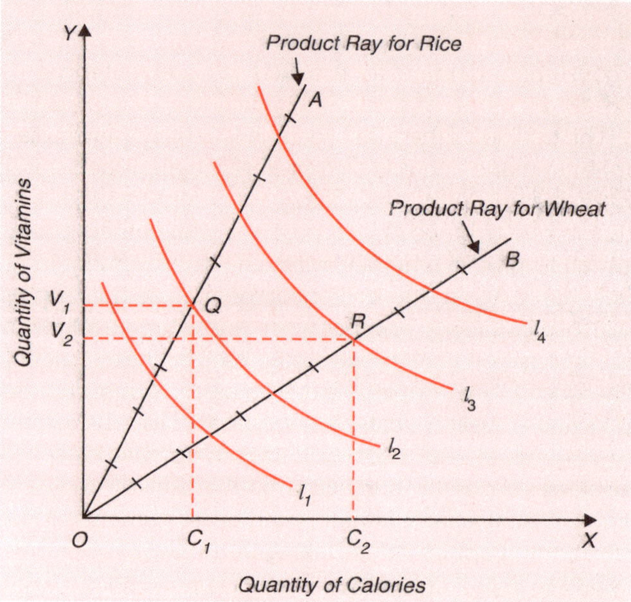

Fig.16.1. *An Indifference Map and Product Rays in Attribute Approach*

Similarly, a product ray *OB* has been drawn which shows the enjoyment of various combinations of attributes (calories and vitamins) provided by another food product wheat. A kilogram of wheat would provide different amounts of calories and vitamins from those of rice. Hence, a different product ray for wheat. As we move upward along the ray *OB* for wheat the individual would get increasing amounts of both calories and vitamins derived from the successively greater expenditure on wheat and therefore its large consumption. Likewise, other product rays representing various combinations of these attributes provided by other products such as fish, milk, mutton can be drawn.

The Budget Constraint and the Efficiency Frontier

Now, an important issue is how far along each ray a consumer can go, that is, how much amounts of the two attributes from a food product he can afford to buy. That depends upon his income and the prices of food products that determines his budget constraint. The budget constraint in the present context is often called the *efficiency frontier.* A budget constraint or an efficiency frontier represents the various alternative combinations of the maximum amounts of two attributes provided by various products which our consumer, given his income and prices of products, can buy. Consider Figure 16.2 where four product rays are drawn to show the various levels of consumption of four food products. If the individual spends his entire income on product A, he can purchase such amount of product *A* that can provide him the combination of calories and vitamins as shown by point *Q*. Similarly, if he spends his entire income on the food product *B*, with the given price of product *B*, he can have combination of the two attributes represented by point *R*. Likewise, he can go up to point *S* if he spends his entire income on product *C* and upto point *T* if he spends his entire income on the food product *D*. On joining the points *Q*, *R*, *S* and *T* we obtain a budget constraint or the efficiency frontier curve in the attribute space. He has to make a choice from the various alternative combinations of attributes on this efficiency frontier in order to maximize utility.

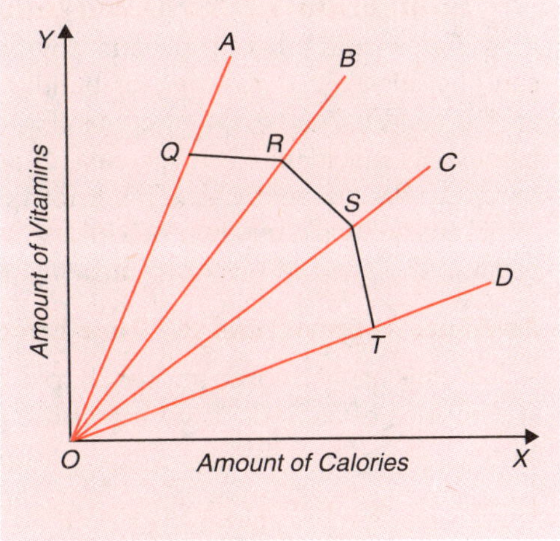

Fig. 16.2. *The Efficiency Frontier in the Attribute Space*

Maximising Satisfaction from Attributes

In order to find which combination of attributes on the efficiency frontier (*i.e.* budget constraint) the individual will choose to maximize his utility, we have to bring together the

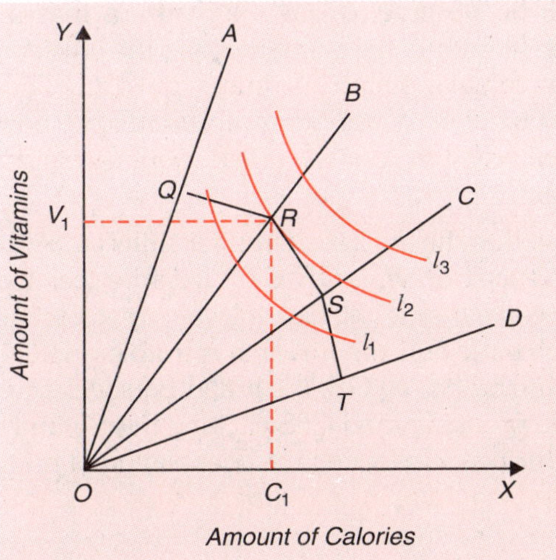

Fig. 16.3. *Maximizing Utility from Attributes*

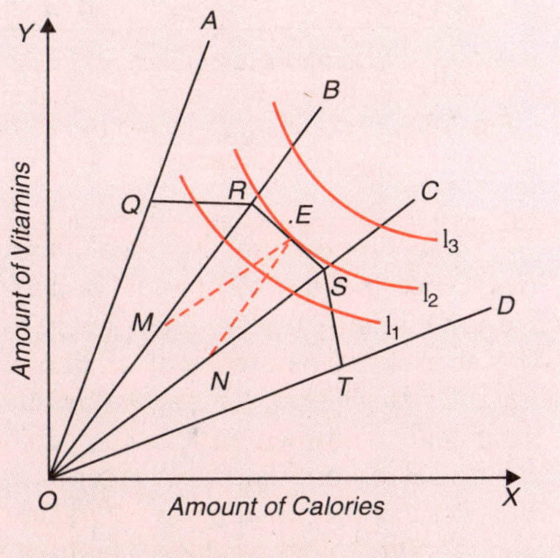

Fig. 16.4. *Equilibrium with a mixed Bundle of Products*

indifference map of the attributes and the efficiency frontier. We can superimpose the indifference map of the individual on the efficiency frontier since both are drawn in the attribute space. This has been done in Figure 16.3 where it will be seen the highest attainable indifference curve I_2 is tangent to the efficiency frontier at point *R* lying on the product ray *OB* at which he will be maximising the level of his satisfaction. Thus, in this optimal equilibrium position he will purchase the product *B* and will enjoy combination of attributes, OC_1, of calories and OV_1 of vitamins.

Equilibrium with a Mixed Bundle of Products. It is however not necessary that the individual should buy one product to get his utility-maximising combination of attributes. He can buy even a combination or bundle of two products to get the required amount of two attributes. This has been depicted in Figure 16.4 where the efficiency frontier is tangent to the highest attainable indifference curve at point *E* which lies on the segment *RS* between the two product rays *OB* and *OC*. This implies that in his maximum-satisfaction combination *E* of attributes he would buy two products *B* and *C* and would spend *OM* on product B and *ON* on product *C*. Line *EM* has been drawn parallel to *OC* and line *EN* parallel to *OB*.

Attribute Approach and the Price Effect

In this new attribute approach to consumer's demand, we can also explain how a change in the price of a product will effect the purchases of a product. Let us take the example of colour television of which five brands say, *A*, *B*, *C*, *D* and *E* are available in the market. Two desired attributes of a TV brand, namely, clarity of its sound and the quality of its picture are to be considered by a consumer. Rays, *OA*, *OB*, *OC*, *OD* and *OE* drawn in Figure 16.5 depict the varying proportions of these two attributes present in the various brands of television. The efficiency frontier and two indifference curves depicting his preference pattern between attributes are also shown in Figure 16.5. To begin with, prices of the various brands are such that we get the efficiency frontier *QRSTJ*. It will be observed from the diagram that the indifference curve I_2 is tangent to the efficiency frontier at point *S* on brand ray *OC*. Thus, combination of attributes represented by point *S* on brand ray *C* is the satisfaction-maximizing point.

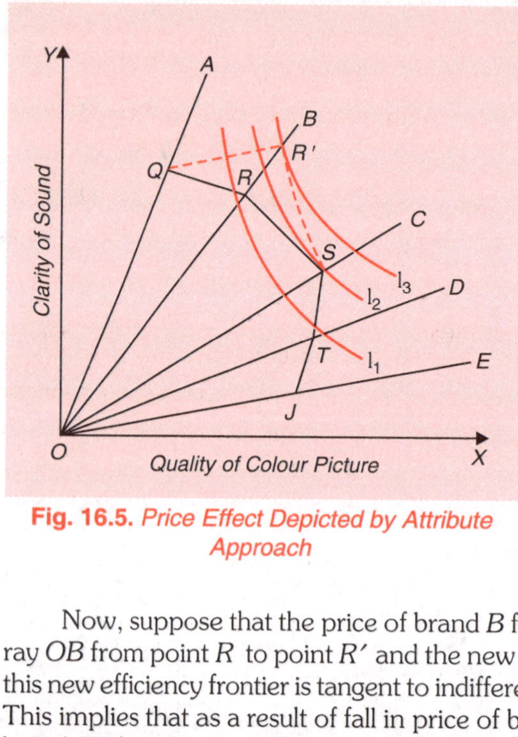

Fig. 16.5. *Price Effect Depicted by Attribute Approach*

Now, suppose that the price of brand *B* falls so that the efficiency frontier shifts along the ray *OB* from point *R* to point *R′* and the new efficiency frontier is *QR′STJ*. It will be seen that this new efficiency frontier is tangent to indifference curve I_3 showing higher levels of satisfaction. This implies that as a result of fall in price of brand *B*, the consumer switches from brand *C* to brand *B* of television. As is shown by the slope of the brand ray *OB*, the brand *B* provides two attributes in a different ratio to the earlier preferred product brand C. Switching from brand *C* to brand *B* representing various ratios of the two attributes following the cheapening of brand *B* implies that the *consumer is willing to trade off some quality of colour picture* for some extra amount of the other attribute 'clarity of sound'.

Attribute Approach and Law of Demand

In the above example we have shown that as a result of change in price of a product or a brand, the consumer entirely switches from one brand (product) to another embodying the desired attributes to increase his satisfaction. The law of demand, that is, a consumer would reduce the consumption of a product whose price has risen and *vice versa* can be more clearly proved in the attribute approach by considering a case in which consumer is initially purchasing a mix of the two products to obtain the desired attributes and maximizing his satisfaction. Suppose the two desired attributes are *X* and *Y* and four brands *A*, *B*, *C* and *D* of a product are available which are shown by rays, *A, B, C* and *D* representing different ratios of the two desired attributes in Figure 16.6. A consumer's tastes and preference patterns are represented by indifference curves I_1 and I_2. It will be seen that the indifference curve I_1 just touches the efficiency frontier at point *E* on the line segment *R$*. Thus consumer is initially in equilibrium and maximizing his satisfaction by obtaining a combination *E* of attributes from a mix of two products, *OK* of product *B* and *OL* of product *C*.

Now, if the price of product *B* falls and the efficiency fontier moves out from point *R* to the point *R′* along the ray *OB* so that the efficiency frontier switches to *QR′ ST*. It will be observed from the diagram that now the indifferent curve I_2 of the consumer is tangent to point *E′* of the efficiency frontier *QR′ ST* and therefore the consumer will increase his satisfaction by moving to combination *E′* of the two attributes purchasing a greater quantity *OK′* of product *B* and less quantity *OL′* of product *C* than before. Thus, the quantity purchased of product *B* has risen and that of product *C* decreased following the fall in price of product *B*. This gives the proof of law of demand in the attribute analysis of demand. This further shows that with the fall in price of product *B* the consumer obtains a greater amount of desired attributes from product *B* as compared to the product *C* than he was previously getting from them.

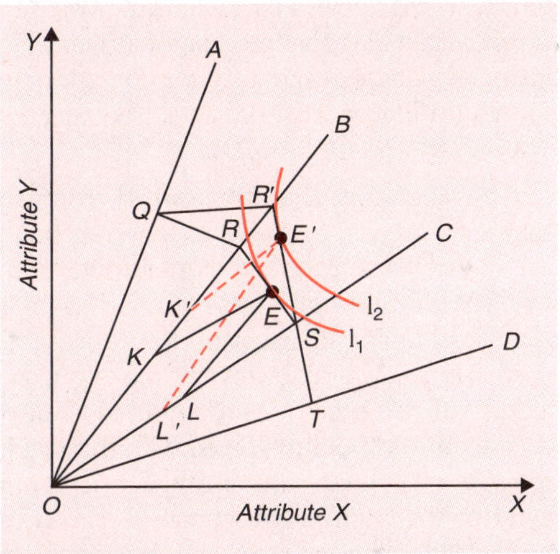

Fig. 16.6. *Law of Demand Proved with Attribute Approach*

Pricing a Product out of the Market

Now, we shall demonstrate how a product is priced out of the market for a consumer, even if that product acutely represents his tastes and preference pattern. Given his perception of attributes contained in a product, there is a certain maximum price that a consumer is prepared to pay for a commodity. If the price of the product rises higher than this maximum, the consumer would stop purchasing it and instead would go in for other products. Figure 16.7 displays a case where three products, soyabean, fish, and poultry provide two desired attributes, proteins and fats, in different proportions. Three rays from the origin depicting the ratios of the two attributes which the consumer hopes to obtain from these three products have been drawn. Prices of the three products are such that we get the efficiency frontier *ABC*. Given his tastes and preference pattern between the two attributes, fats and protein, his indifference curves are IC_1,IC_2. The consumer maximises his satisfaction by buying only product fish; the efficiency frontier is tangent to his indifference curve IC_2 at point *B* on the product ray of fish.

Suppose that price of fish is raised so that the efficiency frontier is now represented by a straight line *AB′C*. The consumer is now in equilibrium at point *B′* still purchasing only fish. But at position *B′* on the ray of fish, he will be purchasing smaller amount of fish due to its higher price, his budget remaining the same.

If price of fish is further increased so that with the given income he can buy such an amount of fish that provides him the combination of the two attributes represented by point *B″*. But it is worth noting that point *B″* does not lie on the efficiency frontier; in fact point *B″*

has fallen inside the efficiency frontier. The efficiency frontier still remains $AB'C$. This is because B' has fallen inside the efficiency frontier. The efficiency frontier still remains $AB'C$. This is because the combination of attributes at point B' can be obtained by purchasing a mix of the two products, soyabeans and poultry. The total amount of two attributes at B' will be the same as the amount of attributes derived from combination OM from soyabeans and ON from poultry. It will be seen that with his given budget he can obtain OM combination of attributes from buying soyabeans and ON combination from poultry (In Figure 16.7 it should be noted that $OM = NB'$ and $ON = MB'$).

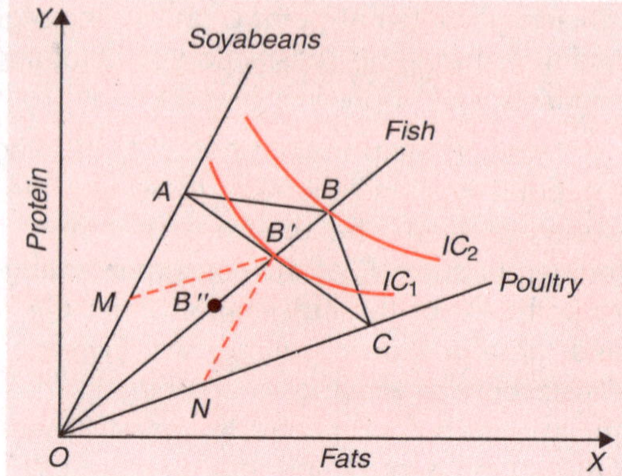

Fig. 16.7. *Pricing a Product out of the Market*

It is thus clear that the point B' represents the maximum price at which he would buy fish and if the price goes up higher than this, he would no longer purchase any units of fish because combination of attributes represented by point B' cannot be obtained from the fish at a higher price with his given income or budget. However, as explained above, with his unchanged budget he can obtain the combination of desired attributes of point, B' by buying a mix of soyabeans and poultry. Thus, with the rise in the price of fish beyond a point, fish disappears from the efficiency frontier and is priced out of the reach for this consumer. However, it may be noted that some other consumers may continue to buy fish even at a higher price at which the former consumer stops purchasing the commodity. This is because these other consumers expect or perceive to get greater amount of the two attributes in each unit of fish as compared to the perception of our consumer whose behaviour has been explained above. Further, some consumers may continue to buy fish even at higher price due to the presence of another attribute present in fish which they prefer but is quite unimportant for our consumer discussed above.

Introduction of a New Product

The attribute approach to consumer's behaviour explains with regard to the impact of the introduction of a new product in a better way than the traditional approach. The introduction of a new product to the existing products in the market can be represented in the diagram by a new product ray. If the ratio of the attributes provided by the new product is the same in any of the existing product, then the ray of the new product would coincide with that of the existing product. But, even though embodying the same ratio of attributes the new product may provide the greater quantities of the attributes per rupee as compared to the existing product, the entry of the new product would push the efficiency frontier outward by eclipsing the existing product in the perception of consumers. Since the new product provides more of the two attributes per rupee rational consumers would stop purchasing the existing product and switch over to the new product.

On the other hand, if the new product that is launched which furnish the two attributes in a different ratio, there will be a new product ray in the diagram. Further, if with the given total money income, the highest attainable point in the attribute space occurs outside the existing efficiency frontier, then the frontier will be pushed outward from its existing flat portion. In both of the above cases some consumers who perceive the new product favourably will switch over to it adversely affecting the sales of the existing products. This is because their favourable perception of the new product and consequently outward shifting of the efficiency frontier enable them to reach their higher indifference curves.

The entry of the new product to the existing range of products and its influence on the choice of consumers and impact on the sales of the existing products is illustrated in Figure 16.8. Suppose there are three existing product brands of colour T.V. namely, Videocon, Sony and Akai. As will be seen there are three product rays depicting the two attributes (clarity of sound and quality of picture) furnished by them. The existing efficiency frontier is *A B C*. The consumer maximizes his satisfaction by attaining indifference curve I_1 which is tangent to the efficiency frontier at point *B* and purchasing the TV brand 'Sony'. Now suppose a new product BPL is introduced which competes with the three existing products. Suppose new brand BPL offers the two attributes in a different ratio but between those of Sony and Akai. Consequently, the product ray of BPL lies between the ray of Sony and Akai. Suppose further that colour TV brand, BPL, is so priced and the magnitudes of the two attributes provided by it are such that, given the money expenditure of the consumer, the efficiency frontier shifts outward to the new position *ABNC*. It will be noticed that consumer is now able to reach higher indifference curve I_2 by switching over to the new product BPL. Thus, the new product would take away the customers from Sony and Akai and would adversely affect their sales. However, the new product would have no effect on the third product Vidoecon unless there are more than two attributes desired by the consumers (For instance consumers have also a desire for a good cabinet of TVs.).

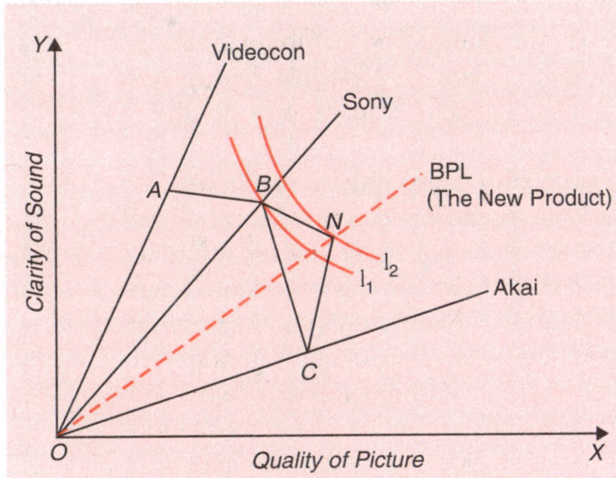

Fig. 16.8. *Addition of a New Product to the Existing Products*

However, in the real world, consumers do want more than two attributes. Therefore, the addition of a new product to the existing range of products would affect the sales of all the existing products.

AN EVALUATION OF THE ATTRIBUTE APPROACH TO CONSUMER THEORY

This new attribute approach to consumer theory has some distinct merits for studying consumer behaviour. By focussing on attributes or characteristics possessed by goods it gives a clear and precise explanation of why people obtain utility from various goods. According to this approach, it is the possession of desirable attributes or characteristics which provide utility to the goods. The consumers demand goods because they have desirable attributes and more desirable attributes a good contains more utility it will provide to the consumer.

This attribute approach also explains in a better way than both the cardinal and ordinal utility approaches to demand as to why people choose a commodity which is newly introduced. As explained above, people switch over to the new product if it contains greater quantity of attributes yielding higher level of utility per rupee spent on it. Thus, the attribute approach easily explains why people buy new product whereas the earlier cardinal and ordinal approaches to consumer's behaviour found it difficult to explain this phenomenon.

Lancaster's new approach can also explain why people generally prefer to buy *mixed bundles of goods* rather than a single good. For example, several people buy both rice and wheat, that is, a mixed bundle rather than a single grain. The attribute analysis makes it clear that people buy mixed bundle of goods because it provides them higher level of utility. This is illustrated in Figure 16.9. Suppose a consumer has Rs. 100 to spend on rice and wheat. If he has to buy a single grain, he can afford to buy *OA* of rice or *OB* of wheat. Then budget line *AB* represents various possible combinations of maximum amounts of calories and vitamins to be obtained by purchasing a mixed bundle of wheat and rice with a given amount of expenditure. It is worth noting that any combination of two grains on line *AB* would cost him the same ₹ 100. Now, the question is what will be consumer's choice to maximise satisfaction. Given the budget constraint the consumer will choose the mixed bundle of rice and wheat containing C_1 of calories and V_1 of vitamins. It will be seen that the consumer is achieving a higher level of satisfaction (he is on higher indifference curve IC_4) by buying the mixed bundle *E*. Given the budget constraint, if he buys rice he reaches point *A* on the rice ray at indifference curve IC_2, if he buys wheat he reaches the point *B* on the wheat ray which lies on indifference curve IC_3. This shows people prefer mixed bundle of goods because the mixed bundle provides greater quantity of attributes as compared to the single grain and therefore yields higher level of satisfaction.

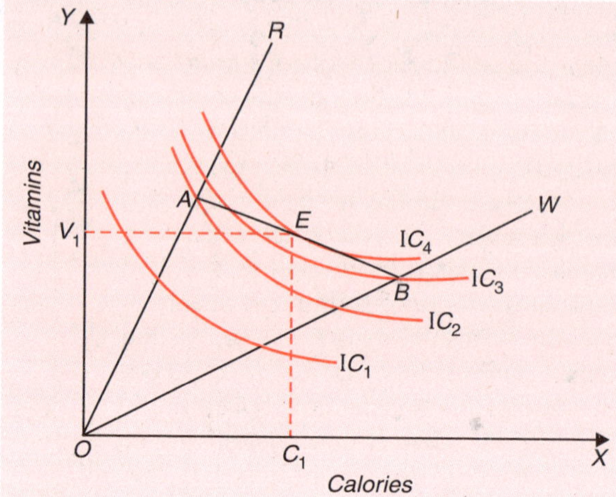

Fig. 16.9. *Choice of a Mixed Bundle of Goods*

The new attribute approach also brings out clearly the concept of implicit prices of the various attributes which show particular attributes can be traded for each other by substituting one good for another in consumption. Let us assume that point *A* on rice ray represents 200 vitamins and 100 calories and point *B* on wheat ray represents 150 vitamins and 200 calories. In switching from *A* on rice ray to *B* on wheat ray, the consumer foregoes 50 vitamins for 100 calories. Hence the implicit price of an additional calories is half a vitamin. Since ***AB* is a straight line this *trade off rate* or *implicit price* is the same all along *AB*.** It follows therefore that the relative price of an additional calorie is implicit in the relative magnitudes of attributes contained in rice and wheat. We can go further and assign monetary values to the implicit prices of calories and vitamins by taking the given market prices of goods.

Another significant advance made by the new attribute approach to demand theory is that it explains substitutes and complements with greater clarity and precision. ***The goods containing common attributes are substitutes.*** For example, beer and wine are substitutes because both contain a common attribute an 'intoxicant'. On the other hand, complementarity between goods exists when certain attributes can be obtained by combining two or more goods. Examples of complementary goods are milk and tea leaves, ink and pen etc.

The new attribute approach also has some drawbacks. An important shortcoming of the new approach is that between buyers and sellers it is goods that are visibly traded and not the attributes. Therefore, it is the prices of goods that are determined in the market. Prices of attributes are not readily known; they have to be inferred from the prices of goods. Besides, the attributes of goods may not be clearly defined and are often of subjective nature. For instance, some attributes of a complex good such as a house or car are of highly subjective nature. The various individuals would differ with regards to what constitutes a desirable attribute of a house or a car and how it might be measured. For example, how a style of a car or design of a house is to be measured. Therefore, the approach to consumer's behaviour based on attributes always tends to be somewhat more subjective than theories based on goods. However, these shortcomings of the new attribute approach are only minor ones. As explained above, Prof. Lancaster's attribute approach is a landmark in the theory of demand. It gives a better explanation of how a new product is successfully introduced in the market, the concept of product differentiation, the notion of implicit prices, the concept of substitutes and complements in addition to establishing the law of demand. It is important to note that this attribute theory of demand is not the rival of the theories of cardinal utility, ordinal utility and revealed preference; instead by focussing on attributes it only supplements them.

CHAPTER

17

Individual Choice Under Risk and Uncertainty

Introduction

So far in our analysis of consumer's behaviour we have assumed that while making a choice the consumers do not face any uncertainty. For example, when consumers buy goods they know with certainty what they are getting and how much utility they will get from their consumption. However, in the real world situations this assumption of certainty is not valid. This is due to three factors. First, some goods that individuals buy are in the nature of ***games or lotteries*** for which outcome is quite uncertain. For example, in case of some games such as horse racing, buying insurance, playing gambles outcome is quite uncertain. You may veiw a gamble and get a certain amount of money which will increase your utility. On the other hand, you may lose the game which will reduce money with you and cause a loss of utility. Buying of such goods such as gambles does not guarantee an individual any particular outcome with certainty.

Secondly, individuals who make investment in assets face uncertainty as the outcome (*i.e.* return) from the assets or from any combination (*i.e.* portfolio) of assets cannot be known with certainty. This is because cost conditions and future prices can vary and cannot be known with certainty. Therefore, the individuals have to make a choice of assets or investment portfolio of assets in uncertain and therefore risky situation.

The third case in which the individuals face uncertainty is when there is lack of information about the quality of goods they buy for example, while buying cars, colour TVs, referigerators, the individuals are not quite sure the car referigerator or colour TV they buy will offer best quality for money. The problem of uncertainty arising out of lack of information is more true when individuals buy used or second-hand cars or second-hand bikes.

Of the above three cases of uncertainty we will be concerned with individual choice in the first two cases of uncertainty of outcomes. Choice or decision making in case of uncertainty due to lack of information on the part of buyers will be analysed in the last part of the book.

The Concept of Risk

The risk refers to a situation when the outcome of a decision is uncertain but when the probability of each possible outcome is known or can be estimated. The analysis of decision making and choice involving risk or uncertainty requires that the individual knows all the possible outcomes and also have some idea of the probability of occurrence of each possible outcome. For example, in tossing a coin there is equal 50-50 chance of getting either a head or tail. Likewise, when an individual invests in the shares of a company, the probability of outcome (that is, how much dividend it will be yield and how much its price will rise in a year) can be estimated from the past experience. The outcome can vary a good deal. ***The greater the variability of possible outcome, the greater the risk involved in making the investment***

decision. Therefore, in the theory of choice or decision making under uncertainty it is necessary to know the meaning of probability of outcome and its variability.

It is important to mention the distinction between risk and uncertainty. ***The uncertainty refers to the situation when there is more than one possible outcome of a decision but where the probability of occurrence of each particular outcome is not known or even cannot be estimated.*** This may be due to lack of sufficient past information or the great instability of the variables involved that determine the outcome. In some extreme cases even outcomes themselves are not known. For example, in case of drilling for exploration of oil in an *unproven field,* investor does not know either the probability of oil being struck or the possible output of oil from it. Though the distinction between risk and uncertainty is theoretically significant the two terms will be here used with the same meaning.

ST. PETERSBURG PARADOX AND BERNOULLI'S HYPOTHESIS

As said above, Daniel Bernoulli evinced great interest in the problem known as St. Petersburg paradox and tried to resolve this. **St. Petersburg paradox refers to the problem why most people are unwilling to participate in a fair game or bet.** For example, offer of participating in a gamble in which a person has *even chance* (that is, 50-50 odds) of winning or loosing ₹ 1000 is a fair *game.* To put in mathematical terms, a gamble whose expected value is zero, or more generally, the game in which the fee for the right to play is equal to its expected value is a fair one. Thus, according to St. Petersburg in an uncertain game a most individuals will not make a fair bet or, in other words, will not play the fair game.

Daniel Bernoulli[1] provided a convincing explanation of the said behaviour of rational individual. According to him, a rational individual will take decisions under risky and uncertain situations on the basis of ***expected utility*** rather than ***expected monetary value.*** He further contended that *marginal utility of money to the individual declines* as he has more of it. Since the individual behaves on the basis of expected utility from the extra money if he wins a game and the marginal utility of money to him declines as he has extra money, most individuals will not 'play the game',that is, will not make a bet. It is in this way that Bernoulli resolved 'St. Petersburg paradox'.

A graphic illustration will make clear Bernoulli's solution to the paradox. Consider Figure 17.1 in which on the *X*-axis, the quantity of money (thousands of rupees) and on the *Y*-axis, marginal utility of money (rupees) to an individual are measured. Suppose an individual has 20 thousands of rupees with him and can make a bet at even odd *(i.e.,* 50-50 chance) of winning or losing rupees one thousand. If he wins the bet, money with him will rise to 21 thousand (20 + 1) rupees. If as a result of an increase in money with him, his expected marginal utility of money declines, then the expected marginal utility of extra one thousand rupees to him which is depicted by the rectangle *CDFE* is less than the extra marginal utility of the previous one thousand *(i.e.,* 20th thousand) rupees which is measured by the rectangle *ABDC.* In other words, the gain in utility in case of his winning the bet is less than the loss of utility in case of his losing the bet, though the gain and loss is the same in terms of monetary amount *(i.e.,* ₹ one thousand). Thus, ***given the diminishing marginal utility of money the expected gain in utility is less than the expected loss of utility from one thousand rupees involved in the bet, a rational individual will therefore not make a bet with 50-50 odds.***

It may be further noted that *a rational individual would even be unwilling to bet or gamble even at favourable odds if his marginal utility of money declines very rapidly.* For

1. D. Bernoulli, Exposition of a New Theory on the Measurement of Risk, *Econometrica*, Jan. 1954, pp. 23-36.

example, if a person is offered a bet; if he wins the bet, he will be given ₹ 1500 and if he loses it, he has to pay ₹ 1000, then, as in case of rapid decline in marginal utility of money, he may be unwilling to agree to make the bet. Consider Figure17.2 where the individual has ₹ 20,000 at present. In case he wins the bet, his monetary gain will be ₹ 1500 which will raise his money income to ₹ 21,500 and gain in his total utility will be given by the black-shaded area and if he loses the bet, his income falls by ₹ 1000 to ₹ 19,000 and as a result he suffers a loss in total utility equal to the red-shaded area. It will be observed from Figure 17.2 that despite a smaller loss in money terms, the loss in terms of total utility is greater than the gain in total utility despite a greater increase in money in case he wins the bet. This happened due to the rapid decline in marginal utility of money as individual's money increases.

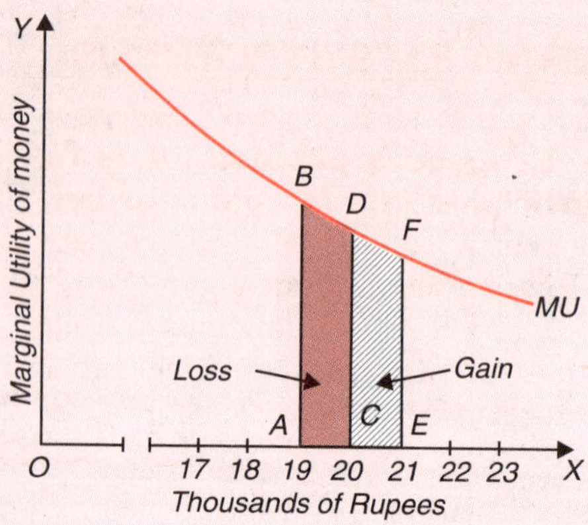

Fig 17.1. *Bernoulli's hypothesis:unwillingness to participate in a 'fair game'*

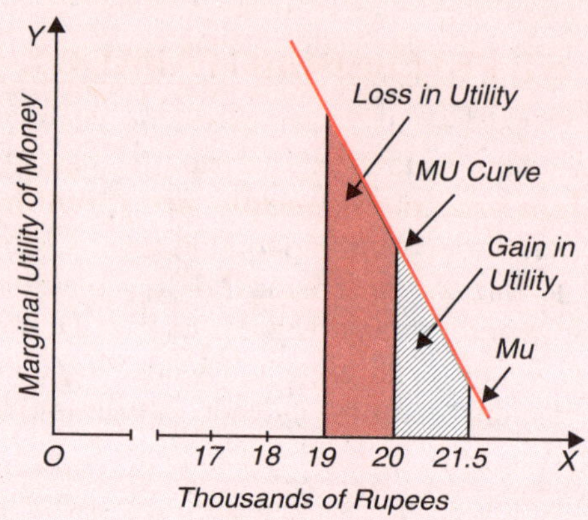

Fig. 17.2. *Unwillingness to participate at favourable when MU of money declines rapidly.*

It may be pointed out that in our discussion above about the individual's betting it is assumed that individual derives no pleasure from gambling, that is, he does not enjoy gambling for its own sake. This is another way of saying that the individual behaves rationally in the sense that *he will behave on the basis of expected gains and losses of utility* from winning and losing money through gambling.

Although Bernoulli's hypothesis that individual decision to participate in a gamble or not, depends on his expected utility rather than expected money value of the game is of crucial significance in any discussion of individual's behaviour under risky and uncertain situations. So long as there is no upper bound on the utility function, the prize in a gamble can be appropriately adjusted so that the paradox is regenerated. Further Bernoulli's main point that an individual considers expected utility from the extra money rather than monetary value of the gain itself has found wide acceptance among economists.

However, a major drawback of *Bernoulli's expected utility hypothesis is that it assumes cardinally measurable utility* which economists today find it difficult to believe. As will be explained later, J. Von Neumann and O. Morgenstern adopted an entirely new approach to assigning numerical values to the utilities obtained from extra money by the individuals behaving in risky or uncertain situations, such as in case of gambling and insurance and they based their method of constructing utility index (which is arrived at in a different way from the cardinal measurement of utility by neoclassical economists) on the expected utility hypothesis of Bernoulli. They showed that we can analyse the choice by an individual under risky and uncertain situation on the basis of $N - M$ utility index.

Neumann-Morgenstern Utility Concept Index Under Risky Situations

Making use of Bernoulli's idea that under risky and uncertain prospects as in betting, gambling and purchasing lottery tickets etc., a rational individual will go by the expected utilities rather than expected money values, Neumann and Morgenstern in their now famous work "***Theory of Games and Economic Behaviour***"[2] gave a method of numerically measuring expected utility from winning prizes. On the basis of such utility index, called N-M index rational decisions are made by the individuals in case of risky situations. Thus, Neumann-Morgenstern method seeks to assign a utility number or in other words, construct N-M utility index of the total utility of money which a person gets as his stock of money wealth increases. The choices by an individual under risky and uncertain situations depend on N-M utility index (*i.e.* expected numerical utilities) and with changes in money income.

How N–M utility index is calculated will be explained in the Appendix to this chapter. In what follows we shall first explain different attitude towards risk using the concept of N-M utility functions. Having explained attitude toward risk , we shall explain with N-M utility functions why most people avoid fair bets (*i.e* fair gambles) and buy insurance. Besides, we shall explain why some people prefer gambling.

UTILITY THEORY AND ATTITUDE TOWARD RISK

We analysed the problem of investment choice to describe how people makes a choice among alternative investments involving different degree of risk involved. But the underlying principles of making a choice in risky and uncertain situation, namely, expected return and the degree of risk involved apply equally well to other choices. In this section we focus on examining individual's choices in the face of risk. In the various earlier theories of consumer's behaviour we saw that in making choices among commodity bundles when there is no risk and uncertainty, the consumer maximises his utility. We will analyse below how an individual maximises his expected utility when risk or uncertainty is present.

People's preferences toward risk greatly differ. Most individuals generally prefer the less risky situation (that is, the situation with less variability in outcomes or rewards). In other words, most individuals seek to minimise risk and are called *risk averter* or *risk averse.* However, some individuals prefer risk and are therefore called *risk-seekers* or *risk lovers.* Some other individuals are indifferent toward risk and are called *risk-neutral.* But it is important to note that these different preferences toward risk depend on whether for an individual ***marginal utility of money diminishes or increases or remains constant.*** As shall be explained below, ***for a risk averse individual marginal utility of money diminishes as he has more money, while for a risk-seeker marginal utility of money increases as money with him increases. In case of risk-neutral individual marginal utility of money remains constant as he has more money.***

Risk Averter. To explain the attitude toward risk we will consider a single *composite commodity, namely, money income*. An individual's money income represents the market basket of goods that he can buy. It is assumed that the individual knows the probabilities of making or gaining money income in different situations. But the outcomes or payoffs are measured in terms of utility[3] rather than rupees.

In Fig. 17.3 we have drawn a curve *OU* showing utility function of money income of an

2. John Von Neumann and Oskar Morgenstern, *Theory of Games and Economic Behaviour,* 2nd ed., Princeton University Press, Princeton, 1947.
3. As mentioned above, Neumann and Mrgenstern in their important contribution. "*The Theory of Games and Economic Behaviour*" suggested a way of measuring utility in quantitative terms in situations involving risk and uncertainty. They construct index numbers, termed as *N-M Index Numbers,* to measure utility. However, to simplify our analysis we just assume that utility can be measured in some units.

individual who is risk-averse. In this Fig. 17.3 money income of the individual has been measured on the X-axis and utility from money income on the Y-axis. It will be seen from this figure that the utility function of the individual who is risk averter is *concave* towards the income axis (i.e. X-axis) indicating that the though the total utility of the risk-averse individual increases as his income increases but at a adiminishing rate (that is, slope of total utility function *OU* decreases as the money income of the individual increases). It will be seen from Fig. 17.3 that as money income of the individual increases from 10 to 20 thousand rupees, his total utility increases from 45 units to 65 (that is, by 20 units) and when his money increases from 20 thousand to 30 thousand rupees, his total utility increases from 65 to 75 units (that is, by 10 units).

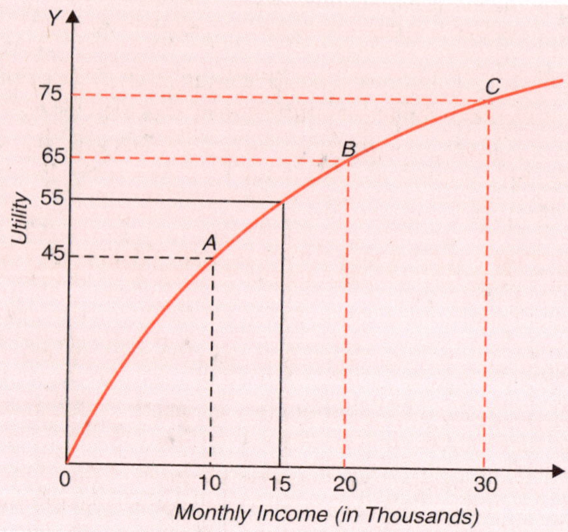

Fig. 17.3. *Utility Function of a Risk Averter*

Choice of a Risk Averter Under Conditions of Risk and Uncertainty

Now, an important question is what choice a risk-averse individual whose utility function is concave will make when faced with a situation of risk and uncertainty. Suppose the individual is currently employed on a fixed monthly salary basis of ₹ 20,000. There is no uncertainty about the income from this present job on a the fixed salary basis and hence no risk. Now, suppose that the individual is considering to join a new job of a salesman on a *commission basis*. This new job involves risk because his income in this case is not certain. This is because if he proves to be a successful salesman his income may increase to ₹ 30 thousand per month but if he does not happen to be a good salesman his income may go down to ₹ 10 thousand per month. Suppose in this new job there is 50-50 chance of either earning ₹ 30 thousands or ₹ 10 thousands (that is, each has a probability of 0.5). When there is uncertainty, the individual does not know the actual utility from making a particular choice.

But given the *probabilities* of alternative outcomes, we can calculate the expected utility. Whether the individual will choose the new risky job or retain the present salaried job with *a certain income* can be known by comparing the *expected utility* from the new risky job with

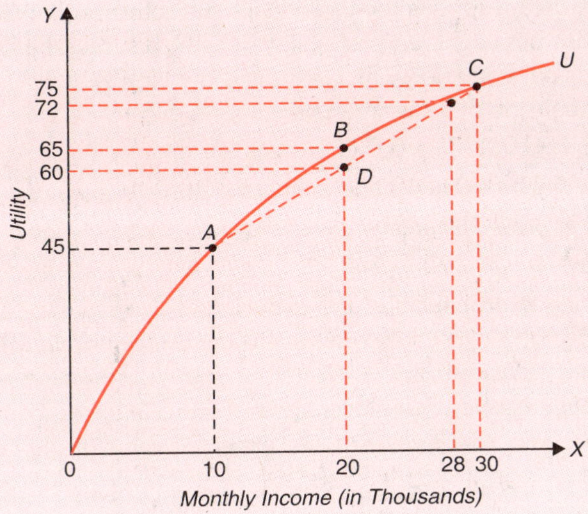

Fig. 17.3(a). *Choice of a Risk-Averse Individual*

the utility of the current job. To explain the choice of a risk-averse individual consider Fig. 17.3(a). It will be seen from the utility function curve *OU* in Fig. 17.3(a) that the utility of money income of ₹ 20,000 with *certainty* is 65. Further, in case of new risky job if he is proved to be a successful salesman and his income increases to ₹ 30 thousands, his utility from ₹ 30 thousands is 75, and if he fails as a good salesman, his income falls to ₹ 10 thousands which yields him utility of 45. (Note that in the new risky job, the expected value of income is 20,000 which is given by $E(X) = 0.5 \times 10{,}000 + 0.5 \times 30{,}000 =$ ₹ 20,000). Now, a chord *AC* is drawn joining points *A* corresponding to ₹ 10 thousands and point *C* corresponding to ₹ 30 thounsands. Given that the probability of success or failure as a salesman is 0.5, the expected utility of the new job is given by

$$E(U) = 0.5\, U\,(10{,}000) + 0.5\, U\,(30{,}000)$$

Since utility of ₹ 10,000 is 45 and utility of ₹ 30,000 is 75, we have

$$E(U) = 0.5 \times \times 45 + 0.5 \times 75$$
$$= 22.5 + 37.5$$
$$= 60.0$$

This can be seen from Fig. 17.3(a) that corresponding to expected value of income of ₹ 20 thousands, the expected utility is 60 (point *D* on the chord *AC*).

Thus with the present job with a fixed salary of ₹ 20,000 with no uncertainty utility is 65, whereas the expected utility of the new job or salesman on commission basis is 60. (Note that it is by coincidence that expected value of income, i.e. ₹ 20 thousands equals income of ₹ 20 thousands with certainty though they are conceptually different.)

Thus with the present job with a fixed salary of ₹ 20,000 with no uncertainty his utility is 65, whereas the expected utility of the new job as salesman on commission basis expected utility is 60 at point *D* corresponding to expected income of ₹ 20,000 in Fig. 17.3 (a). Since the expected utility of the new risky job is less than the utility of the present job with a certain income, he will reject the offer of new job involving risk.

Let us change the data, suppose the individual's subjective probability of proving to be a successful salesman is 90 per cent (*i.e.*, probability of being a successful salesman is 0.9), then given the above income data and utility function (as shown in Fig. 17.3 (a)), then the expectd utility from joining the new job of a salesman on a commission basis is:

$$E(U) = 0.1\,U(10{,}000) + 0.9\,U(30{,}000)$$

Since the utility of ₹ 10,000 is 45 and utility of ₹ 30,000 is 75, we have:

$$E(U) = 0.1 \times 45 + 0.9 \times 75$$
$$= 4.5 + 67.5 = 72$$

Now, in these changed probabilities, the expected utility (equal to 72) of a riskier choice is greater than the utility of a certain income of 20,000, *the individual even though he is risk-averse will choose the risker option*. Note that in this case the *expected value* is much greater than the previous case with 50 per cent probability of each outcome. Now with 90 per cent chances of being a successful salesman, the expected value of the outcome is:

$$E(V) = 0.1 \times 10{,}000 + 0.9 \times 30{,}000$$
$$= 1{,}000 + 27{,}000 = 28{,}000 \text{ or } 28 \text{ thousand}$$

In Fig. 17.3 (a), it will be seen that corresponding to expected income from a new job equal to ₹ 28 thousands at which expected utility is 72 exceeds utility of 65 of certain income of ₹ 20 thousands. It will be seen from chord *AC* that corresponding to new expected income of ₹ 28 thousands utility of the individual is 72. To conclude a *risk averter will choose a riskier option only if it has a sufficiently large expected value and therefore higher expected utility from the new option.* This happens only if the individual's subjective probability of being a successful salesman is very high, that is, he is more confident of being a successful salesman.

Risk Lover. On the other hand, ***a person is risk-preferer or risk-loving who prefers a risky outcome with the same expected income as a certain income.*** In case of a risk-loving individual, *marginal utility of income to the individual increases* as his money income increases as shown by the convex total utility function curve *OU* in Fig. 17.4. Suppose

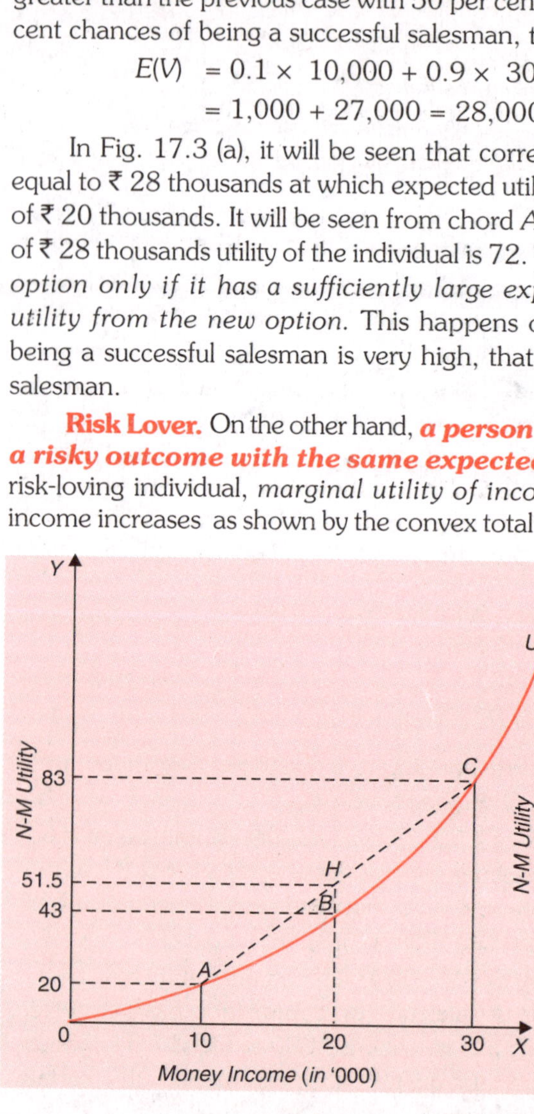

Fig. 17.4. *Utility Function of a Risk-Seeker*

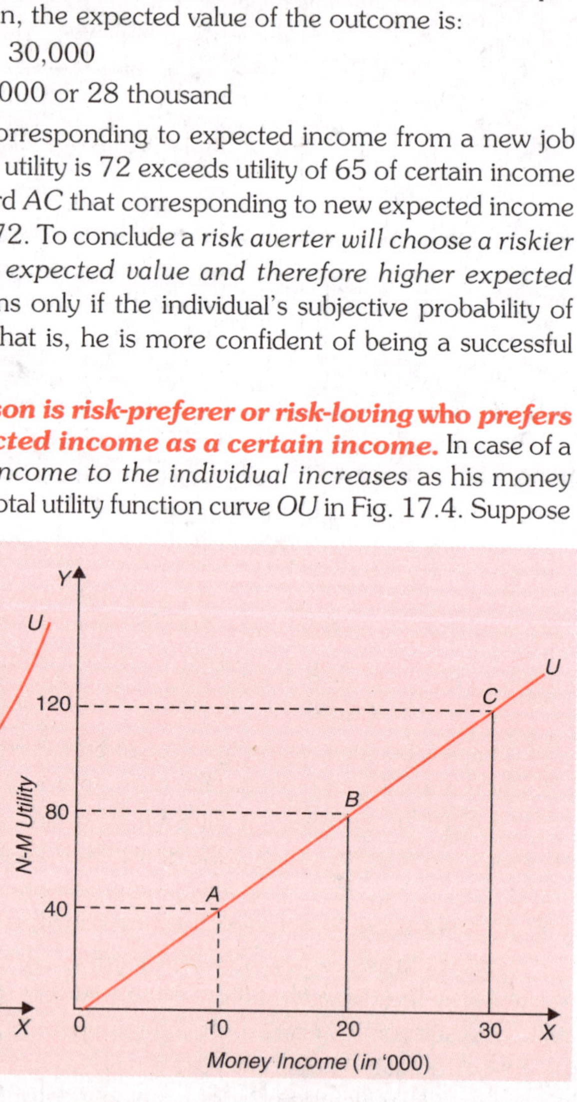

Fig. 17.5. *Utility Function of a Risk Neutral*

this risk-loving individual has a present job with a certain income of ₹ 20 thousands. It will be seen from Fig. 17.4 that the utility of ₹ 20 thousands is 43 units to this individual. Now, if he is offered a risky job with his income of ₹ 30 thousands if he happens to be highly efficient and ₹ 10 thousands if he happens to be not so efficient in the new job with the equal probability of 0.5 in these two jobs, then the expected utility from the new job is given by

$$E(U) = 0.5\, U\,(10{,}000) + 0.5\, U\,(30{,}000)$$

It will be seen from Fig. 17.4 that the utility of ₹ 10 thousands to this individual is ₹ 20 while utility of ₹ 30 thousands to him is 83. Therefore,

$$\begin{aligned} E(U) &= 0.5\,(20) + 0.5\,(83) \\ &= 10 + 41.5 \\ &= 51.5 \end{aligned}$$

Since the expected utility from the new risky job is 51.5 which is greater than the utility of 43 from the present job with a certain income of ₹ 20 thousands, the ***risk-loving individual will prefer the new risky job even though the expected income in the new risky job is also ₹ 20,000*** as (0.5 × 10,000) + 0.5 (30,000) = ₹ 20,000).

As mentioned above, most of the individuals are risk averse but there is a good deal of evidence of people who are risk seekers. It is risk-loving individuals who indulge in gambling, buy lotteries, engage in criminal activities such as robberies, big frauds even at risk of getting heavy punishment if caught. We will explain gambling by a risk-loving individual in a later section.

Risk-Neutral. ***A person is called risk neutral, if he is indifferent between a certain given income and an uncertain income with the same expected value.*** An individual will be risk neutral if his marginal utility of money income remains constant with the increase in his money. The total utility function of a risk neutral person is shown in Fig. 17.5. It will be seen from this figure that utility of a *certain income* of ₹ 20 thousands is 80. Now, in a risky job when income increases to ₹ 30 thousands if he proves to be a successful salesman, the utility of ₹ 30 thousands is 120 units.

On the other hand, if in a new risky job, he proves to be a bad salesman, his income goes down to ₹10,000 whose utility to the individual is 40 units. We assume that there is equal probability of high and low income in the new risky job. Note that expected value of income in the new job with an uncertain income is 20,000 as (0.5 × 10,000 + 0.5 (30,000) = 20,000. The expected utility of the new risky job is given by

$$\begin{aligned} E(U) &= 0.5\, U\,(10{,}000) + 0.5\, U\,(30{,}000). \\ &= 0.5\,(40) + 0.5\,(120) \\ &= 20 + 60 \\ &= 80 \end{aligned}$$

It is seen from above that in case of risk-neutral person expected utility of an uncertain income with the same expected value (₹ 20,000 in the present case), is equal to utility of an assured or a certain income. That is, risk-neutral person is indifferent between them.

Risk Aversion and Fair Bets

People differ greatly in their attitudes towards risk. In Bernoulli's hypothesis we have seen that a person whose marginal utility of money declines will refuse to accept a fair gamble. *A fair game or gamble is one in which the expected value of income from a gamble is equal to the same amount of income with certainty.* ***The person who refuses a fair bet is said to be risk averse.*** Thus, the risk averter is one who prefers a given income with certainty to a risky gamble with the same expected value of income. Risk aversion is the most common attitude towards risk. It is because of the attitude of risk aversion that many people insure against various kinds of risk such as burning down of a house, sudden illness of a severe nature, car accidence and also prefer jobs or occupations with stable income to jobs and occupations with uncertain income.

This attitude of risk aversion can be explained with Neumann-Morgenstern method of measuring expected utility. It may be noted that marginal utility of income of a risk-averter diminishes as his income increases. In Figure 17.6 Neumann-Morgenstern utility function curve *U (I)* has been drawn. It will be seen from this figure that *N-M* utility curve starts from the origin and has a positive slope throughout indicating that the individual prefers more income to less. Further, the *N-M* utility curve shown in Figure 17.6 is **concave which shows the marginal utility of income of a person diminishes as his income increases.** Therefore, the utility curve in Figure 17.6 represents the case of a risk averter or the attitude of risk aversion. With ₹ 2,000 income, the person's utility is 50 which rises to 70 when his income increases to ₹ 3,000. As his income further increases to ₹ 4,000, his utility rises to 75.

Now suppose the person's current income is ₹ 3,000 and he is offered a fair gamble in which he has a 50-50 chance of winning or losing ₹ 1,000. Thus, the probability of his winning is 1/2 or 0.5. If he wins the game, his income will rise to ₹ 4,000 and if he loses the gamble, his income will fall to ₹ 2,000. The expected money value of his income in this situation of uncertain outcome is given by:

$$E(V) = \frac{1}{2} \times 4000 + \frac{1}{2} \times 2000 = ₹\ 3000$$

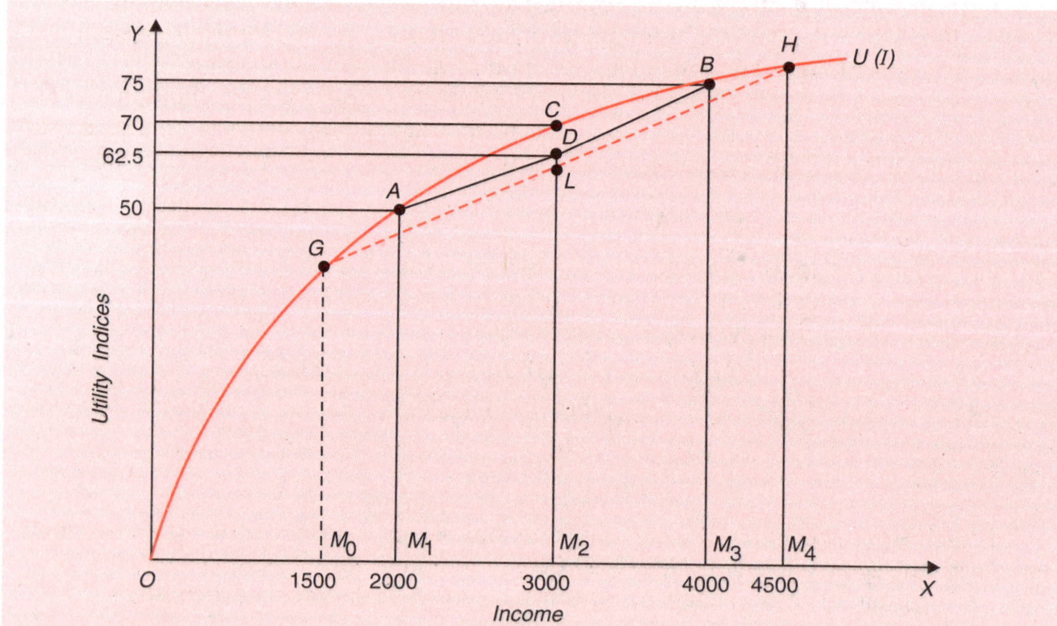

Fig. 17.6 *The Neumann-Morgenstern Concave Utility Curve of a Risk-Averter*

If he rejects the gamble he will have the present income *(i.e.,* ₹ 3,000) with certainty. Though the expected value of his *uncertain income prospect* is equal to his income with certainty, a risk averter will not accept the gamble. This is because as he acts on the basis of *expected utility* of his income in the uncertain situation (that is, ₹ 4,000 if he wins and ₹ 2,000 if he loses) can be obtained as under:

Expected Utility (EU) = πU (₹ 4000) + 1 – π U (₹ 2000)

where π denotes probability.

As will be seen from Figure 17.6 the utility of the person from ₹ 4,000 is 75 (point B on the utility curve and utility from 2000 is 50 (point A in Figure 17.6), the expected utility from this uncertain prospect will be:

$$E(U) = \frac{1}{2}(75) + \frac{1}{2}(50)$$

$$= 37.5 + 25 = 62.5$$

In the N–M utility curve $U(I)$ in Figure 17.6 the expected utility can be found by joining point A (corresponding to ₹ 2,000) and point B (corresponding to ₹ 4,000) by a straight line segment AB and then reading a point on it corresponding to the expected value of the gamble ₹ 3,000, the expected value of the utility is M_2D (= 62.5) which is less than M_2C or 70 which is the utility of income of ₹ 3,000 with certainty. Therefore, the person will refuse to accept the gamble (that is, he will not gamble). It should be carefully noted that his rejection of gamble is due to diminishing marginal utility of money income for him. The gain in utility from ₹ 1,000 in case he wins is less than the loss in utility from ₹ 1000 if he loses the gamble. That is why his expected utility from the uncertain income prospect has been found to be lower than the utility he obtains from the same income with certainty.

It follows from above that in case marginal utility of money income diminishes a person will avoid fair gambles. Such a person is called risk averter as he prefers an income with certainty (*i.e.*, whose variability or risk is zero) to the gamble with the same expected value (where variability or risk is greater than zero). Let us illustrate it with another example. Suppose to our person with a certain income of ₹ 3,000, two fair gambles are offered to him. First, a 50:50 chance of winning or losing ₹ 1000 as before and the second a 50:50 chance of winning or losing ₹ 1,500. With the even chance of winning and losing the expected value of income in the second gamble will be 1/2(1500) + 1/2 (4500) = ₹ 3000. On the N- M utility curve $U(I)$ in Figure 17.6 we draw a straight line segment GH joining point G (corresponding to income of ₹ 1500) and H corresponding to income of ₹ 4500). It will be seen from this straight-line segment GH that the expected utility from the expected money value of ₹ 3,000 from the second gamble is M_2L which is less than M_2D of the first gamble.

Thus the person will prefer the first gamble which has lower variability to the second gamble which has a higher degree of variability of outcome. It should be remembered that risk in this connection is measured by the degree of variability of outcome. In the first gamble, the degree of variability of outcome is less and therefore the risk is less and in the second gamble, the degree of variability is greater which makes it more risky. And in case of income with certainty there is no variability of outcome and therefore involves no risk at all. A risk-averse person therefore prefers the income with certainty to any gamble with the same expected money value as the income with certainty.

RISK AVERSION AND INSURANCE

Our foregoing analysis shows why most people buy insurance when they are faced with a risky and uncertain situation. As mentioned above, most people are risk averters and therefore they buy insurance to avoid risk. Now an important question is how much money or premium a risk-averse individual will pay to the insurance company to avoid risk and uncertainty facing him. Suppose the individual buys a house which yields him income of ₹ 30 thousands per month. But if the house catches fire and due to the damage caused, his income from it falls to ₹ 10 thousands per month and thus he suffers a loss of income. For the sake of simplifying analysis suppose there is 50 per cent chance of the house catching fire. Then the expect value of income in this risky and uncertain situation is

$$E(X) = 0.5 \times 30{,}000 + 0.5 \times 10{,}000$$
$$= 15{,}000 + 5{,}000$$
$$= 20{,}000$$

It is important to note that expected income of ₹ 20,000 is the weighted average of the two uncertain alternatives (30 thousands and 10 thousands) using their probabilities as weights. Different probabilities of the occurring of these incomes (30 and 10 thousands) would yield different expected income. Further note that the expected income is not the actual income that a person would get; it is weighted average of the two uncertain outcomes.

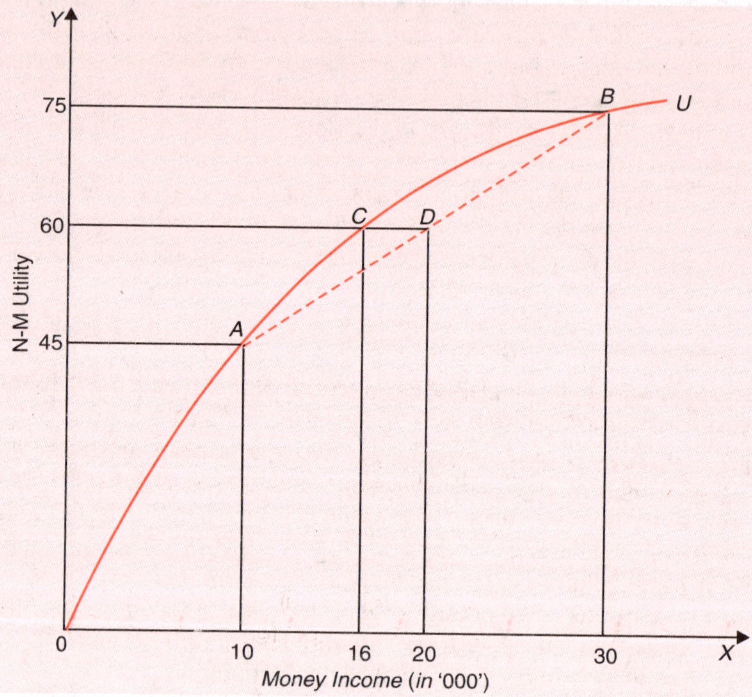

Fig. 17.7. *Insurance and Risk Premium*

The utility function *OU* with a diminishing marginal utility of money income of a risk-averse individual is shown in Fig. 17.7. With money income of ₹ 30 thousands, his utility is 75 and with his lower income of 10 thousands his utility is 45. Given that there is probability of 0.5 for each outcome, expected utility of the two outcomes is given by

$$E(U) = 0.5\,U(30{,}000) + 0.5\,U(10{,}000)$$
$$= 0.5 \times 75 + 0.5 \times 45$$
$$= 37.5 + 22.5$$
$$= 60$$

It will be seen from Fig. 17.7 that we have drawn a straight line *AB* joining the utilities of 75 and 45. It is on this straight line or chord *AB* that the amount of expected utility will be corresponding to the expected value of income in the present risky and uncertain situation. It will be seen from Fig.17.7 that on this straight line *AB* and corresponding to the expected value of income of ₹ 20 thousands, the expected utility is 60 which corresponds to point *D* on the straight line *AB*. But it will be seen from the individual's utility function *OU*, that utility of 60 is equal to that of *an assured and certain income* of ₹ 16 thousands. Thus the individual with an expected uncertain income of ₹ 20 thousands will be willing to forego ₹ 4 thousands (or *DC*) to get a certain or guaranteed income of ₹ 16 thousands as the expected utility of uncertain expected income of ₹ 20 thousands is equal to the utility of a certain income of ₹ 16 thousands. This means that if the individual gives up ₹ 4 thousands (20 – 16 = 4) from his uncertain expected income he will get the same utility of 60 as with a certain income of ₹ 16 thousands. ₹ 4 thousands equal to distance *DC* is called the *risk premium*. Therefore, ***the risk premium is the amount of money that a risk-averse individual will be willing to pay to avoid the risk.*** By paying the risk premium the individual can insure himself against a large loss from a fire and to get an assured or certain income.

It is clear from above why people buy insurance for fire, accident, ill health and even life.

RISK PREFERENCE AND GAMBLING : WHY DO SOME INDIVIDUALS GAMBLE ?

In sharp contrast to risk-averse individual, the risk lover or risk preferrer will play a gamble. As stated above, a risk lover prefers uncertain outcome having the same *expected value of income* to the equivalent income with certainty. In case of risk preferring or loving individual, marginal utility of money increases as his income increases. In fig. 17.8 the N–M utility curve of a risk lover has been drawn that is convex. The convexity of the utility curve implies that marginal utility of money income increases as his money income increases. Now suppose that present income of the individual is 25 thousand rupees and is offered a gamble with 50-50 chance of winning or losing ₹ 15 thousand rupees. Therefore, if he wins, his money

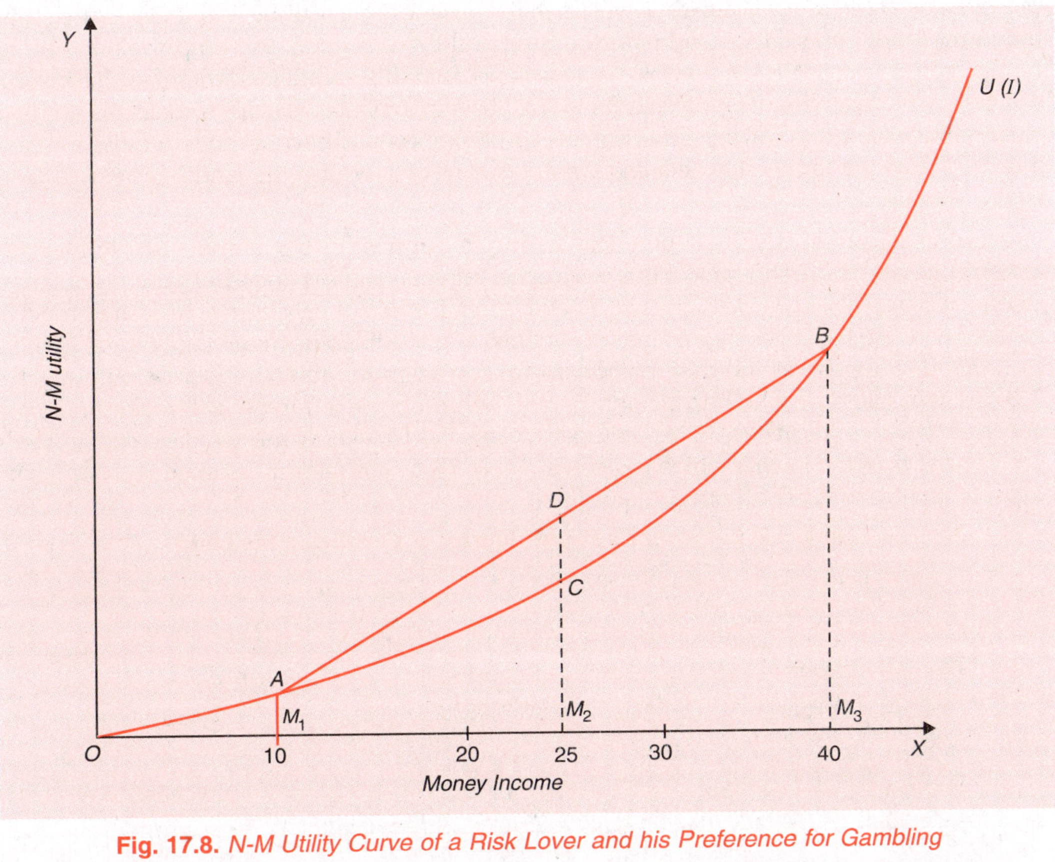

Fig. 17.8. *N-M Utility Curve of a Risk Lover and his Preference for Gambling*

income will rise to ₹ 40,000 and if be loses, his money income will fall to ₹ 10 thousand rupees. The expected money value of the gamble is given by.

$$E(X) = 0.5 \times 40{,}000 + 0.5 \times 10{,}000$$
$$= 20{,}000 + 5000$$
$$= 25{,}000$$

In order to find out the expected utility of 25 thousand rupees we draw a chord AB which connects the utility M_1A at income of ₹ 10 thousand and utility M_3B at income level of ₹ 40 thousand. Corresponding to the expected value of income of ₹ 25 thousand the expected utility is M_2D whereas point D lies on the chord AB corresponding to income of ₹ 25 thousand. It will be seen from Fig. 17.8 that expected utility M_2D of expected income of ₹ 25 thousand is greater than the utility M_2C of certain income of ₹ 25 thousand.

Since his expected utility from gamble is greater than that from his income with certainty, he will accept the gamble. Further, it can be shown that risk lover, a person whose marginal utility of money increases with increase in his income will prefer a gamble having greater risk, that is, the gamble which has a larger variability of outcome to a gamble with less risk (that is, with smaller variability of outcome).

An Application: Farmer's Gambling Against Nature

We will now provide an interesting and useful application of choice under risk and uncertainty to the case of a farmer who in the absence of irrigation has to face an uncertain situation regarding outcome of his use of fertilizers which yields higher output only in the presence of water, the availability of which, in the absence of irrigation, depends on the rain. If the farmer fertilizes his land and nature is kind and there is good and timely rainfall, he will reap a bumper crop. On the contrary, if it does not rain, his output (and therefore his income) will be low because the use of fertilizers in the absence of water is likely to burn his seed and damage his soil. If the farmer does not use fertilizers, he will have a moderate but a certain income. Thus the farmer for deciding whether or not to fertilize the land is playing a game against nature.

Let us illustrate it with a numerical example. Suppose if our farmer uses fertilizer his income rises to ₹ 5000 but only if there is a good rainfall. And if it does not rain, his output or income will be small because in the absence of water, the use of fertilizers may destroy much of his seed and also cause damage to his soil. Let his output or income in this case comes about to be ₹ 2500. Suppose in the case of non-use of fertilizers, he has a moderate output worth ₹ 3750 regardless of whether it rains or not. What choice a farmer will make under this uncertain situation depends on his attitude towards risk. To know this we have constructed a pay off matrix of the farmer which is given in Table 17.1. It is further assumed that the farmer expects that there is 50:50 chance of rainfall.

Table 17.1. Farmer's Payoff Matrix of Fertilizing his Land

Choice	Outcome	
	Rain	No Rain
Using Fertilizers	₹ 5000	₹ 2500
Not using Fertilizers	₹ 3750	₹ 3750
Probability of a rainfall	$\frac{1}{2}$ or 0.5	$\frac{1}{2}$ or 0.5

The choice of not using fertilizers yields a certain income of ₹ 3750. The choice by the farmer in favour of using fertilizers yields expected value equal to 1/2 (5000) + 1/2 (2500) = ₹ 3750. Thus the choice facing the farmer is between a certain income of ₹ 3750 and a gamble of using fertilizers with an expected value of ₹ 3750. This is quite a fair game. But whether or not the farmer will choose to fertilize his land depends upon his attitude towards risk. His choice is between a certain income of ₹ 3750 from not using fertilizers and a gamble of using the fertilizers the expected money value of which also equals ₹ 3750. If the farmer is risk averter, he will choose not to fertilize the land, that is, he will not gamble. On the other hand, if a farmer is risk lover, as depicted in Figure 17.4 he will fertilize the land that is, he will gamble. Of course, if he is a risk neutral, he will be indifferent between the two choices.

FRIEDMAN-SAVAGE HYPOTHESIS

We studied above that, according to Bernoulli, marginal utility of money diminishes for most of the people and therefore they are unwilling to make fair bets. But if the marginal utility of money always diminishes for all the people, then the widespread practice of gambling found among the people all over the world cannot be explained . Moreover, why some people actually prefer to make choices under very risky situations such as in a gamble or a race. Are these people irrational and thoughtless ? Do they gamble for the sake of fun and pleasure ? Watson provides an answer to this. According to him, "To point to the entertainment and pleasure that many people find in gambling is not enough, nor does it suffice to dismiss gambling and other decisions under risk as "irrational". Though the world abounds with people who are thoughtless and scatter-brained in their decisions, much gambling is done with cold and careful calculations. Remember, too, that gambling has flourished for centuries and in many cultures, whatever its morals and legality might be, gambling is not an aberration in the behaviour of a part of the population."[4]

As explained above, Neumann-Morgenstern provided the method of measuring numerically the marginal utility of money. Based on Neumann-Morgenstern cardinal utility analysis, Milton Friedman and L. J. Savage in their well-known article[5] put forward a hypothesis that explains why the same persons buy insurance and also engage in gambling. In buying insurance they seek to avoid risk and in engaging in gambling they take risk. In other words, people behave both as risk averters (*i.e.*, when they buy insurance), and also as risk lovers when they gamble by buying lottery tickets or bet at horse races. This seemingly contradictory behaviour on the part of the people could not be explained with Bernoullian hypothesis of diminishing marginal utility of money.

Friedman and Savage abandoned Bernoullian hypothesis of diminishing marginal utility of money *for all ranges of income* and instead adopted another hypothesis. ***According to Friedman-Savage hypothesis, for most people marginal utility of money income diminishes up to a certain level of money income, it increases from that middle level to a certain higher level of money income and thereafter at very high levels of income it again diminishes.*** With this hypothesis and using Neumann-Morgenstern Utility Curve Friedman and Savage[6] explain both types of behaviour of buying insurance to avoid risk and of indulging in gambling and thereby to take risks. Friedman-Savage hypothesis is depicted in Figure 17.9 where the Neumann-Morgenstern Utility Curve having both the concave and convex portions has been drawn. It will be observed from this figure that the section of this *N-M* utility curve *U(I)*

---

4. D.S. Watson, *Price Theory and its Uses. op. cit.*, p. 128.
5. "The Utility Analysis of Choices Involving Risk" in *Journal of Political Economy*, Vol. LVI, 1948, reprinted in Stigler and Boulding (ed.,) *Reading's in Price Theory*, AEA, Ch. 3.
6. M. Friedman and L.J. Savage, "The Utility Analysis of Choices Involving-Risk", *Journal of Political Economy*, Aug. 1948, pp. 279-304.

up to point K is concave and in the middle portion from E to F is convex, and beyond point F, that is, at higher levels of income, it again becomes concave. This implies that at the lower levels of income marginal utility of income of the person diminishes and between middle incomes corresponding to point E and F, marginal utility of income is increasing and beyond B onwards marginal utility of income again diminishes with further increases in income.

Let us now explain how Friedman and Savage explain the behaviour of the *same person* as risk averter (as when he buys insurance) and risk lover (when he buys a lottery ticket). Suppose the person's present income is 35 thousand rupees which lies at the concave part of the *N–M* utility curve corresponding to point C where marginal utility of income is diminishing. Suppose the individual feels that he has a 50:50 chance of losing the sum of money income equal to 30. This means that there is probability of 0.5 or $\frac{1}{2}$ that he may have income of 35 and probability of 0.5 that his income may fall to 5 thousand rupees. As explained in the preceding section, the person with diminishing marginal utility of money will try to avoid this uncertain prospect (which is a kind of gamble) and will therefore buy insurance to eliminate risk and thereby have an income with certainty giving the insurance premium.

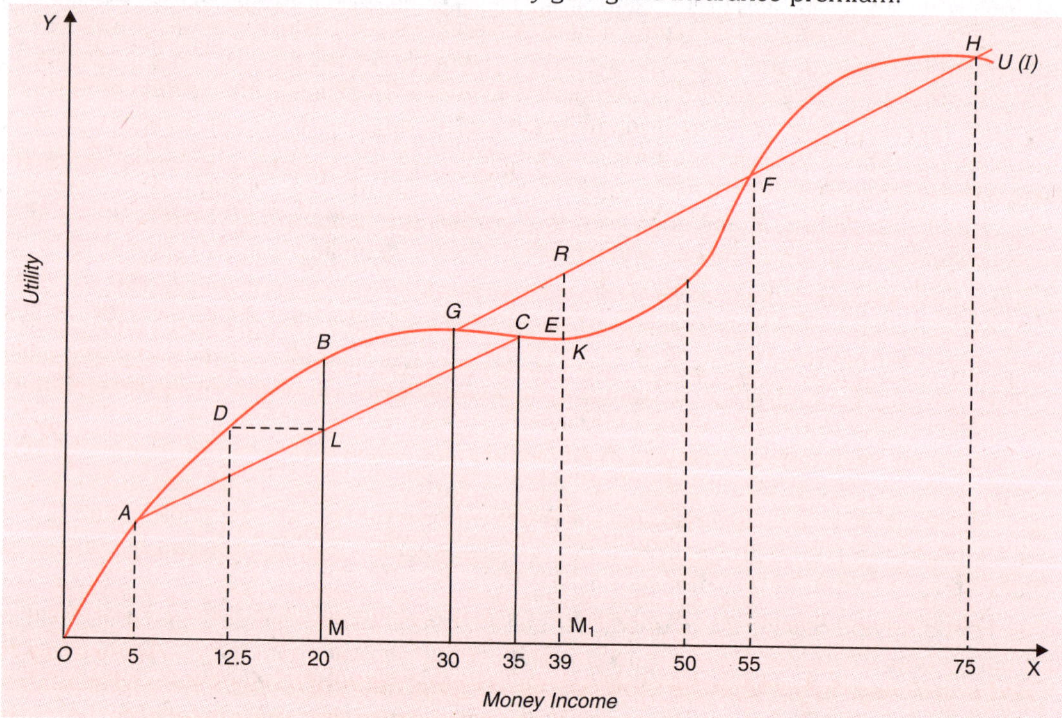

Fig. 17.9. *Friedman–Savage Hypothesis*

Note that his expected value of income in this case is

$$E(X) = 0.5 \times 35 + 0.5\ (5)$$
$$= 17.5 + 2.5 = 20 \text{ thousands}$$

It will be seen from Figure 17.9 that expected utility from ₹ 20 thousand is *ML* lying at chord *AC* which is less than utility *MB* of income of ₹ 20 thousand with certainty. To avoid risk, he can pay insurance premium *LD* or 7.5 thousand to have *certain* income of ₹ 12.5 thousands.

Now, assume that the same person with the present income of ₹ 35 thousands is considering to buy a lottery ticket that offers him chance of winning a large sum of money, say 40 thousand rupees, the first prize of the lottery and thereby raising his income to ₹ 75 thousands. If he does not win, his income will fall to ₹ 30 thousands; 5 thousands being the price of the lottery ticket. Now, if there is 20 per cent chance of winning the lottery, its expected value will also be equal to $0.2 \times 75 + 0.8\ (30) = 15 + 24 = 39$ and as it will be seen from Figure 17.9 the *expected utility* from the sum of ₹ 39 thousands is M_1R (note that point R lies on the straight line segment GH) which is greater than utility M_1K which he gets from income of ₹ 39 thousands with certainty. Thus, the person would purchase the lottery ticket, that is, he will gamble.

Now, suppose the individual's income is ₹ 50 thousands which lies in the middle income segment where the marginal utility of money income is increasing. With ₹ 50 thousands income the individual will be willing to buy lottery tickets, indulge in gambling or undertake risky investment since the gain in utility from extra money will be much greater (marginal utility of money income is rising) than the loss of utility from the small payment for a lottery ticket or from equal monetary loss in a gamble.

A person with an income beyond 55 or in the segment *FH* enjoys quite high income and therefore marginal utility of money to him is declining. As a result of this he would be unwilling to take risk either in a gamble or in undertaking risky investment except at very favourable odds.

Friedman-Savage think that the *N*–M utility curve of money indicates the behaviour or attitude of people towards risk in different socio-economic groups. They of course admit that there are many differences between the persons within a same socio-economic group; some have great preference for gambling and others are unwilling to take any risk at all. Even then Friedman and Savage think the curve describes the propensities of broad classes. The middle income group with increasing marginal utility of money are those, they argue, who are eager to take risks to improve their economic conditions. The expectation of more money means much to this group of persons: if their efforts succeed, they will lift themselves up into the next upper socio-economic class. These persons want not just more consumer goods; they have ambition to look up in the social scale. They want to rise, to change their life styles. No wonder that marginal utility of money increases for them.

MEASURING RISK: PROBABILITY OF AN OUTCOME

We have seen above that risk refers to the situation when there is more than one possible outcome of a decision and the probability of each outcome is either known or can be estimated. Therefore, to measure the degree of risk we need to know the probability of each possible outcome of a decision. ***The probability means the likelihood of occurring of an event.*** Thus, if possibility of an outcome occurring is 1/4 or 0.25, this means that there is 1 chance in 4 or 25 per cent chance for the outcome to occur. For example, suppose a person is considering to invest in a company which is engaged in the new exploration of offshore oil. If the exploration is successful, the price of company's stock will rise to ₹ 50 per share and if its exploration meets with a failure, the company's stock will fall to ₹ 10 per share. Given these two possible outcomes, namely, ₹ 50 per share price and ₹ 10 per share price, if the past information reveals that the chance of oil exploration being successful is $\frac{1}{4}$ or 25 per cent and chance of its failure is $\frac{3}{4}$, then we say the probability of success of oil exploration is 25 per cent and the probability of its failure is 75 per cent (The success and failure are the two possible outcomes). Thus ***probability is a number that indicates the likelihood of an event or outcome occurring.***

These are two concepts of probability depending on how it is measured. The first is the *frequency concept of probability*. If past information or data is available regarding occurrence of outcomes or events, the probability is defined as the proportion of times an outcome occurs if the situation is repeated in the long run over and over again. In general, if a situation is repeated over a large number of times, say M, and if an outcome, say X, occurs m times, then

$$P(X) = \frac{m}{M}$$

Thus, in our example if we know from the past data of oil exploration that rate of success is 25 per cent, then the probability of getting success is 1/4 or 0.25. The measurement of probability based on the past experience is generally known as the **objective measure of probability.**

But in many cases there are no similar past situations which help us in measuring probability. In that case the ***concept of subjective probability*** is used. The subjective probability is an individual's personal view about the chance of an outcome to occur and is based on his personal judgement, experience or knowledge about the subject and not on the frequency with which outcome actually took place in the past. Obviously, when probability is subjectively determined and not based on the past data, the different individuals will attach different probabilities to the occurrence of various outcomes and therefore they will make different choices. In whatever way the probability is arrived at, it helps us to measure two important concepts, namely, ***expected value and variability of outcome.*** With the use of these two concepts we compare the profitability of various strategies involving risk and uncertainty which helps us to make a choice among them. We explain below the meaning of these two concepts.

Measuring Risk with Probability Distribution

As explained above, the probability of an outcome is the likelihood that an event will occur. ***Probability distribution describes the occurrence of all possible outcomes of an event and the probability of occurrence of each outcome.*** It is worth noting that the sum of probabilities of all possible outcomes must equal *unity* because probabilities of all outcomes together must equal certainty. Thus, in Table 17.2 we give *all possible cash flows* that will occur from an investment project A in the *next year* and the probabilities of their occurrence. It will be seen from Table 17.2 that there are five possible cash flows in the next year depending on the state of the economy which is determined by general economic conditions, nature of competition in the industry to which the firm belongs. If all conditions are favourable for the firm, its cash flow will be 70 lakhs whose probability is 0.1 or 10 per cent. On the other hand, if all conditions are unfavourable for the firm, its cash flow from the investment project will be ₹ 30 lakhs whose probability of occurrence is also 0.1 or 10 per cent. One of the other three cash flows will occur if some factors work in favour of the firm's project A and others

Table 17.2. *Probability Distribution*

Cash flows (in ₹ Lakh) (X_i)	*Probability (P_i)*	*Expected Value (P_iX_i)*
30	0.1	3
40	0.2	8
50	0.4	20
60	0.2	12
70	0.1	7
		$\Sigma P_iX_i = 50$
	$E(X)$ or $\bar{X} = 50$	

unfavourable to it. The probability distribution shows that there is 10 per cent probability that all determining conditions work in favour of the investment project which yields cash flow of ₹ 70 lakhs in the next year. Similarly, there is 10 per cent probability that all conditions will be unfavourable and yields cash flow of ₹ 30 lakhs in the next year. It is more probable that some conditions will be favourable and others unfavourable for firm's project so that intermediate cash flows such as ₹ 40 lakhs, 50 lakhs and ₹ 60 lakhs would occur.

In Table 17.3 we give the cash flows that will occur in the next year and their associated probabilities from an investment project B. It will be seen that *cash flows from investment project B are more dispersed as compared to the cash flows from investment project A.*

Table 17.3. *Cash Flows from Investment Project B*

Cash Flows (in ₹ Lakhs) (X_i)	*Probability* (P_i)	(P_iX_i)
20	0.10	2
35	0.25	8.75
50	0.30	15
65	0.25	16.25
80	0.10	8
		$\Sigma P_iX_i = 50$
	$E(X)$ or $\bar{X} = 50$	

The concept of probability distribution is required for evaluating and comparing investment projects when managers have to take decisions under conditions of risk. From the probability distribution of outcomes we can calculate two values which are essential for decision making under conditions of risk. They are : (1) *expected value* of all possible outcomes (cash-flows in our above example), and (2) a value that measures the *degree of risk* involved. We explain below both of these.

Expected Value

As stated above, individuals and firms face situations where a number of outcomes can occur each of which results in a certain payoff or cash flow, that is, monetary gain or loss. ***If the probability of each outcome is known we*** can find out the expected monetary value in this uncertain situation (that is, when a variety of outcomes can occur). ***The expected monetary value is the weighted average of payoffs of all possible outcomes with the probability of each outcome used as weights.*** Thus the expected value of an uncertain income is the average payoff of the various outcomes. For example, it investment in offshore oil exploration, there are two possible outcomes, namely, the success of the project yielding a payoff of ₹ 50 per share with a probability of 0.25 and the failure yielding a payoff ₹ 10 per share with a probability of 0.75. Thus in this case, expected value of investment per share

$$= 0.25 \times 50 + 0.75 \times 10$$
$$= 12.5 + 7.5$$
$$= ₹\ 20$$

In general terms if there are two possible outcomes with payoffs of X_1 and X_2 and the probability of each possible outcome is denoted by P_1 and P_2, then the expected value of investment is given by

$$E(X) \text{ or } \bar{X} = P_1X_1 + P_2X_2$$

Similarly, if there are n possible outcomes, then the expected value is

$$E(X) \text{ or } \bar{X} = P_1X_1 + P_2X_2 + P_2X_3 \ldots\ldots P_nX_n$$

or in condense form, expected value in case of n possible outcomes with their associated probabilities can be written as

$$E(X) = \sum_{i=1}^{n} P_iX_i$$

In the data given in Table 17.2 regarding 5 possible cash flows from an investment project, the expected value is obtained by multiplying the possible cash flows with their associated probabilities and then adding them. This we have done in the last column of Table 17.2 whose sum yields 50. Thus

$$E(X) \text{ or } \bar{X} = (0.1 \times 30) + (0.2 \times 40) + (0.4 \times 50) + (0.2 \times 60) + (0.1 \times 70)$$

$$= 3 + 8 + 20 + 12 + 7 = 50$$

Risk and Probability Distribution

In addition to the expected value, the probability distribution of outcomes also helps us in measuring risk involved in a project. In fact, ***the variability of outcomes measures the degree of risk involved in any choice of a project or strategy from the various alternative projects or strategies.*** In economics and finance, risk is the measured by the extent of dispersion (*i.e.* deviation) of possible outcomes from the expected value. The greater the variability or dispersion of payoff of various outcomes from the expected value of payoff means the greater risk involved. ***The variability of outcomes may be measured by the average deviation of actual values of payoffs of various outcomes from the expected value of payoff with probability of each being used as weights.*** Let X_1 and X_2 are the payoffs of two outcomes and the probability of each is P_1 and P_2, then the average deviation (V) as a measure of risk is given by

$$V = P_1[X_1 - E(X_1)] + P_2[X_2 - E(X_2)]$$

However, the most widely used measure of dispersion or variability is the standard deviation. The standard deviation (d or σ) is defined as the square root of the weighted average of the squared deviation of all possible outcomes from the expected value with probabilities of various possible outcomes used as weights. Thus, in case of three possible outcomes

$$\sigma = \sqrt{P_1(X_1 - E(X))^2 + P_2[X_2 - E(X)]^2 + P_3[X_3 - E(X)]^2}$$

Where σ is standard deviation and X_1, X_2, X_3 are outcomes and $E(X)$ is the expected value of outcomes.

In general terms, when there are n outcomes, standard deviation (σ) of outcomes is given by

$$\sigma = \sum_{i=1}^{n} \sqrt{(X_i - E(X))^2 P_i}$$

RISK-RETURN TRADE-OFF AND CHOICE OF A PORTFOLIO

The theory of choice under risk and uncertainty is also applicable in case of an investor who has to invest his savings in various types of assets having varying degrees of risk to get optimum return from them. For instance, if an investor does not want to bear risk at all he may go in for investing in Fixed Deposits of the State Bank of India which carry a fixed rate of interest. If he is prepared to take risk he may be interested in buying shares from the stock market whose value and dividend can vary a good deal. From these shares he can get much higher return if the stock market goes well or his return may be very low if the stock market is gripped by depression. Obviously, he faces a choice problem of combining the assets with assured fixed returns such as Fixed Deposits in Banks, debentures of reputed companies with some equity shares to arrive at an ***optimum portfolio of investment.***

For analysis of choice of a portfolio of assets by individuals or firms we require to explain the concept of risk-return trade-off function which are represented by indifference curves between degree of risk and rate of return from investment. The indifference curve between expected income or return (measured along the vertical axis) and the degree of risk (measured by standard deviation and shown on the horizontal axis). Each indifference curve or what is also called ***risk-return trade off*** *curve* shows all those combinations of degree of risk (i.e. standard deviation) and expected return that give the individual same level of utility. As riskiness is 'bad' or undesirable and therefore more of it yields less satisfaction and therefore as we move rightward indicating greater risk or standard deviation of the variability of return, the investor should receive higher expected return to give him equal utility or satisfactions. Therefore, indifference curves (*i.e.* risk - return trade off curves) between degree of risk and expected return slope upward (*i.e.* are positively sloped).

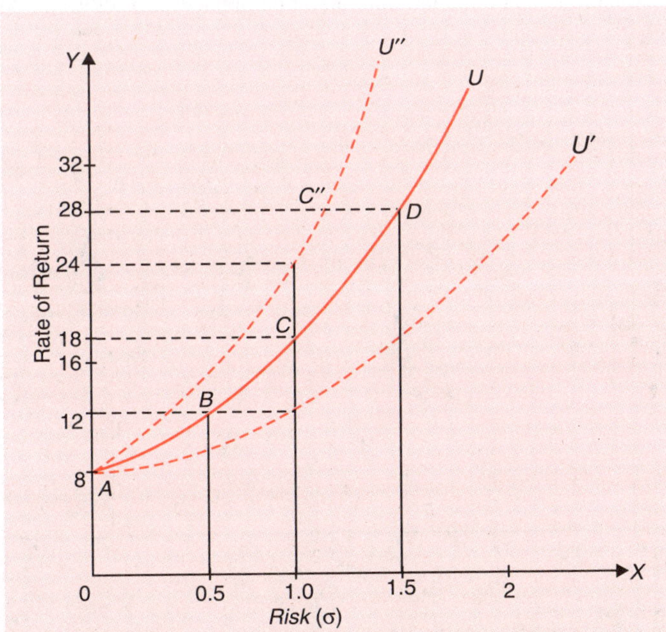

Fig. 17.10. *Indifference Curves or Risk-Return Trade off Curves*

The concept of indifference curve or risk-return trade-off function can be better explained with Fig. 17.10 where on the X-axis, we measure risk in terms of standard deviation (σ) of probability distribution, and rate of return as per cent of investment is measured along the Y-axis. An upward-sloping solid curve *AU* has been drawn from point *A*. Point *A* represents risk-free return of 8 per cent. This *AU* curve represents the risk-return trade off function of an individual or a firm and shows that 4 per cent extra return over and above risk-free return of 8 per cent is required to compensate him for the degree of risk given by $\sigma = 0.5$ (Note that 12 – 8 = 4).

Here 8 per cent is a risk-free return as corresponding to it standard deviation (σ), which measures the level of risk, is zero. ***The difference between the required rate of return on a risky investment and the return on risk-free investment is called risk premium.*** Thus in the trade-off curve *AU* rate of return of 4 per cent is required on an investment with a risk of $\sigma = 0.5$. Similarly, as will be seen from *AU* trade off curve in Figure 17.10 that to compensate the individual for undertaking an investment with a risk of $\sigma = 1.0$, return of 18 per cent is required (that is, risk premium on this investment is 10 per cent, 18 –

8 = 10). 28 per cent rate of return is required or expected on risky investment with σ = 1.5.

For a *more risk-averse individual* the higher rate of return is required for a risky investment with a given standard deviation. Therefore, for a more risk-averse manager risk-return trade-off curve will be steeper than *AU* curve. Thus, with a more risk-averse individual, a steeper indifference curve or risk-return trade-off curve *AU″* (dotted) has been drawn. With *AU″* risk-return trade off curve to compensate for risky investment with σ = 1.0, 24 per cent return is required, that is, his risk premium is 16 per cent as compared to 10 per cent of the previous individual.

Similarly, for a less risk-averse individual trade-off curve will be less steep such as *AU′* (dotted). A individual with trade off curve *AU* ′, to compensate him for risky investment with σ = 1.0, return of 12 per cent is required, (that is, 4 per cent risk premium is needed for a risk of σ = 1.0).

It is evident from above that different individuals will have different indifference curves between expected returen and degree of risk depending upon their risk aversion. The individuals who are highly risk averse have more steeply indifference curves as shown in Fig. 17.11 and those who are less risk-averse they have flatter indifference curves as shown in Fig. 17.12.

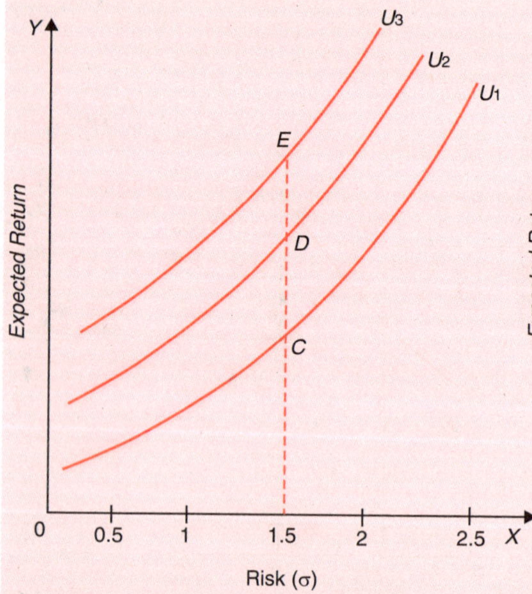

Fig. 17.11 *Indifference Curves between Expected Return and Risk of a Highly Risk-averse Individual*

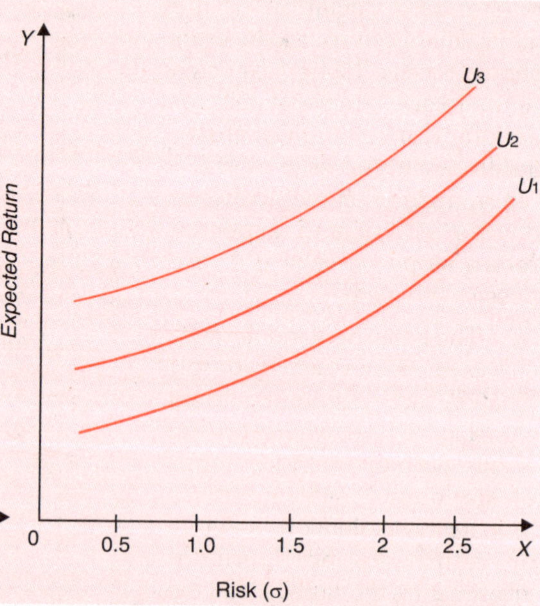

Fig. 17.12. *Indifference Curves between Expected Return and Risk of a Less Risk-averse Individual*

It should be understood why we get higher indifference Curves such as U_2, U_3 of the individuals. When *with a given degree of risk such* as 1.5 σ in Fig. 17.11 expected return from investment increases the individuals shifts from a point *C* on indifference curve U_1 to point *D* on the higher indifference curve U_2. The similar reasoning holds good in case of individuals with flatter indifference curves. It needs to be re-emphasised that it is differences in attitudes towards risk of various individuals that make their indifference curves between risk and return of different slopes and concavity.

The Choice of an Investment Portfolio

As explained above, the individuals try to reduce risk by diversification. Towards that end the firms produce different types of products, that is, invest in different lines of business.

Similarly, individuals investors choose a portfolio of assets to reduce overall risk of their investment. We have explained above how risk is measured by standard deviation and risk-return trade off curve is obtained. Now, the investors choose a risky portfolio of assets if it provides them adequate return.

To explain the choice of an optimum portfolio we need another concept generally called a *budget frontier*. ***A budget frontier which represents the combinations of risk and return that are obtainable with the given available funds from mixed portfolios of two assets, say, shares of Reliance Industries and Tata Steel.***

Suppose the expected returns from these assets are 20 per cent and 10 per cent respectively. If a portion W_i of the given available funds are invested in Reliance Industries and the remaining funds W_t are invested in Tata Steel, the expected return of the portfolio of these two assets is given by

$$r_p = W_i r_i + W_t . r_t \qquad ...(1)$$

where r_p = expected return of the portfolio of two assets.

r_i = the expected return of investment in Reliance Industries

r_t = the expected return from Tata Steel.

W_i = the proportion of the given funds invested in Reliance Industries

W_t = the remaining portion of the given funds invested in Tata Steel.

Note that $W_i + W_t = 1$ and different portfolios or combinations of two assets will involve different degrees of risk (σ) and also yield different returns. Note that ***rate of return from a portfolio is the weightage average of the returns from the two assets*** as *given by equation (1)*. It is worth noting that any linear weighted combinations of returns from two assets with the given returns, r_i and r_t shows the rate of return from a portfolio of these two assets. We draw in Figure 17.13 such a budget frontier *BF* which shows the combinations or portfolios of two assets which are obtainable with the given funds. It will be seen from Figure 17.13 that budget frontier *BF* is tangent to the trade-off function curve U_2 at point *E* which represents the optimum portfolio of two assets which yield return of r_p and involve a risk (σ) of 1.0. The combination of two assets represented by *E* is an optimally diversified portfolio containing a mix of the two assets.

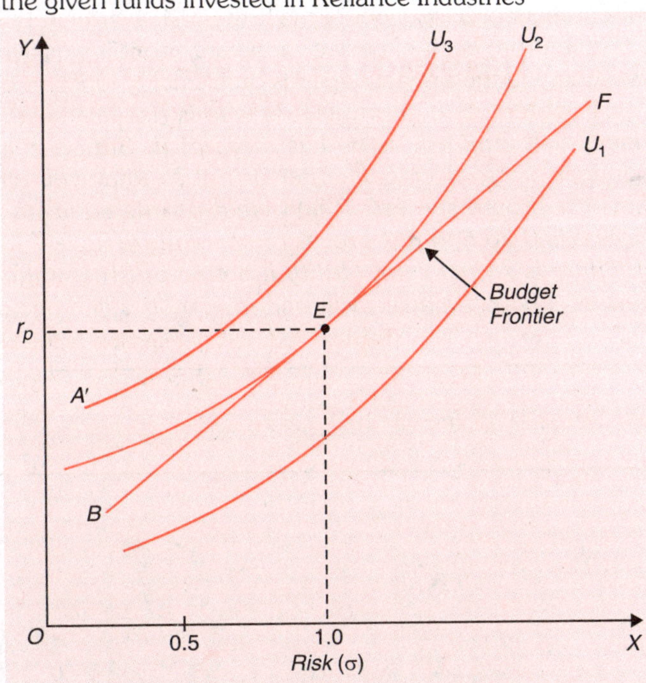

Fig. 17.13. *Choice of an Investment Portfolio*

If the rate of return on shares of Reliance Industries is 20 per cent and return on Tata Steel shares is 10 per cent. Suppose in the optimum portfolio, the individual spends 40 per cent of its investible funds on shares of Reliance Industries and the remaining 60 per cent on shares of Tata Steel, the rate of return on the portfolio can be calculated as follows

$$r_p = W_r\ r_i + W_t\ r_t$$
$$= 0.40 \times 20 + 0.60 \times 10$$
$$= 8 + 6 = 14$$

Thus rate of return of the portfolio of the two assets is 14 per cent.

DECISION MAKING UNDER RISK WHEN INVESTMENT PROJECTS DIFFER IN THEIR EXPECTED VALUES : SOME NUMERICAL PROBLEMS

Having discussed the utility approach to risk measurement we are in a position to explain how a manager faced with investment projects with different expected values and different degrees of risk will choose an investment project. From the viewpoint of utility approach, an individual is *risk-averse* whose total utility curve of money is concave (*i.e.* face downward) as shown in Fig. 17.3 in which marginal utility of money for an individual diminishes. When not only degrees of risk differ but also expected values of profits from investment projects are different, on what basis the individual or manager will make a choice among the investment projects ? If the manager of a firm is risk neutral or risk seeker he will choose to undertake the investment project whose expected monetary value is positive. However, if the individual entrepreneur or a manager of the firm is risk-averter, it is not necessary that he will choose the investment project if expected monetary profit is positive. Whether or not he will undertake investment in the project depends on his utility function of money. Let us take an example.

Problem 1. *If an individual who is risk averse and therefore his marginal utility of money will diminish as he has more of it. Suppose such a risk averse entrepreneur or manager has to decide whether or not to undertake investment in a project. It is given that if it proves success, it will yield profits equal to 175 lakhs and the probability of success is 0.25 and if it proves to be a failure he will lose ₹ 50. lakhs and the probability of failure is 75 per cent. Utility function of firm's manager is given in Table 17.3. in the form of a payoff matrix. Whether a manager will decide to invest in the project ?*

Table 17.3. Utility Function of the Firm's Manager

Money Income (in ₹ lakhs)	*Total Utility*
–50	–10
0	0
+50	15
+100	25
+150	32
+175	35
+200	37.5

In order to assess whether a manager will decide to invest in the project, we calculate below the expected monetary value of the profits of the investment.

Table 17.4. Payoff from Investment (in lakhs)

Decision	*Investment is a success*	*Investment is is a failure*
Invest in the project	175	–50
Do not invest in the project	0	0
Probability	0.25	0.75

Expected monetary value of profits $= 175 \times 0.25 + (-50 \times 0.75)$

$= 43.75 - 37.5 = 6.25$

Thus expected monetary value of profits is positive, a risk neutral and risk-seeker will decide in favour of undertaking investment in the project. Now whether a risk averse manager will undertake investment in this project. For this we require utility function of the firm's manager which is given above in Table 17.3. It will be seen from the total utility function of Table 17.3 that marginal utility of money income of the firm's manager is declining and that means he is risk averter. Now we can calculate the expected utility of the manager from investing in the project.

Thus, $E(U) = U(175) \times 0.25 + U(-50) \times 0.75$.

It will be seen from Table 17.3 that utility of ₹ 175 laks of the manager is 35 and the utility of loss of ₹ 50 lakh (i.e. – 50 lakh) for the manager is –10.

Putting them in the expression for expected utility we have

$$E(U) = 0.35 \times 0.25 + (-10) \times 0.75$$
$$= 0.08 - 7.5$$
$$= -7.42$$

Since the expected utility from the project is negative, a risk-averse manager will not invest in the project. Thus even though expected monetary gain for the manager from the investment project is positive, his expected utility from it is negative. It may however be noted that utility functions of different risk-averse managers are quite different and marginal utility of money income for different managers diminish at different rates. It is therefore possible that for some risk-averse managers the utility function of money may be such that expected utility from the above investment project may turn out to he positive and therefore he will decide to undertake investment in the project.

Problem 2. A manager of a firm is faced with the problem in which of the two products A and B he should invest. The market studies estimate the following net present values of all future profits under three possible states of the economy.

State of the	*Investment in Product A*		*Investment in Product B*	
Economy	*Probability*	*Profit*	*Probability*	*Profit*
Boom	0.2	50	0.2	30
Normal	0.5	20	0.4	20
Recession	0.3	0	0.4	10

The manager's utility function for money is : $U = 100\,M - M^2$ where M stands for money profits.

(a) Determine whether manager is risk-averse, risk neutral or risk, seeker.

(b) If manager's objective is to maximise money profits irrespective of risk, in which product he should invest?

(c) What is the relative level of risk involved in each investment?

(d) If the manager's objective were to maximise utility, in which product he should invest ?

Solution

(*a*) To determine whether manager is risk-seeker, risk neutral or risk averter, we find the marginal utility of money from the given utility function of money of the manager. Thus

$$U = 100\,M - M^2 \qquad \text{...(1)}$$

Taking the first derivative of (1), which will indicate the marginal utility of money, we have

$$\frac{dU}{dM} = 100 - 2M \qquad \text{...(2)}$$

Taking the second derivative

$$\frac{d^2U}{dM^2} = -2$$

The negative value of the second derivative implies that marginal utility of money for the manager diminishes. Therefore he is a risk averter

(*b*) To find in which product investment will yield him more profits we find the expected values of money profits for investment in the two products.

Investment in Product A

State of the Economy	P_i	π_i	$P_i\pi_i$	$\pi - \bar{\pi}$	$(\pi - \bar{\pi})^2$	$(\pi - \bar{\pi})^2 . P_i$
Boom	0.2	50	10	30	900	180
Normal	0.5	20	10	0	0	0
Recession	0.3	0	0	–20	400	120
			$E(\pi)$ or $\bar{\pi} = 20$			300

Expected profits from $A = 20$

$$\text{Standard deviation } (\sigma) \text{ of } A = \sqrt{\sum_{i=1}^{n} =(\pi_i - \bar{\pi})^2 . P_i}$$

$$= \sqrt{300} = 17.32$$

Relative risk is obtained by coefficiation of variation $= \frac{\sigma}{\bar{\pi}} = \frac{17.32}{20} = 0.866$

Investment in Product B

State of the Economy	P_i	π_i	$P_i\pi_i$	$\pi_i - \bar{\pi}$ $(\bar{\pi} = 18)$	$(\pi_i - \bar{\pi})^2$	$(\pi_i - \bar{\pi})^2 . P_i$
Boom	0.2	30	6	+12	144	28.8
Normal	0.4	20	8	+2	4	1.6
Recession	0.4	10	4	–8	64	25.6
			$\bar{\pi} = 18$			$\Sigma(\pi_i - \bar{\pi})^2 . P_i = 56.0$

$$E(\pi) = 18$$

$$\sigma = \sqrt{\sum_{i=1}^{n} (\pi_i - \pi)^2 . P_i} = \sqrt{56} = 7.48$$

$$\text{Coefficient of Variation} = \frac{7.48}{18} = 0.41$$

It follows from above that if manager's objective is to maximise profits, he will choose to invest in product A as expected value of profits for it (20) is greater as compared to expected value of profits (18) for product B.

(c) Relative risk is measured by coefficient of variation (V) which in the present case will indicate standard deviation per rupee of profits. Coefficient of variation of investment in product

$$A = \frac{\sigma}{\pi} = \frac{17.32}{20} = 0.866$$

Coefficient of variation of investment in product $B = \frac{7.48}{18} = 0.41$

Thus investment in product A involves more risk, though it yields higher expected money profits.

(d) To find expected utility we first calculate utilities of money profits and then multiply them by their associated probabilities. For calculating utilities obtained from money profits, we use the given utility function $U = 100\,M - M^2$.

Calculating Expected Utility from Investment in A

π_i	U_i	P_i	P_iU_i
50	$100 \times 50 - (50)^2 = 2500$	0.2	500
20	$100 \times 20 - (20)^2 = 1600$	0.5	800
0	0	0.3	0
			$\Sigma P_iU_i = 1300$

Calculating Expected Utility from Investment in B

π_i	U_i	P_i	P_iU_i
30	$100 \times 30 - (30)^2 = 2100$	0.2	420
20	$100 \times 20 - (20)^2 = 1600$	0.4	640
10	$100 \times 10 - (10)^2 = 900$	0.4	360
			$\Sigma P_iU_i = 1420$

Thus, if manager's objective is to maximise utility, he will invest in product A

Problem 3. An oil drilling company offers the opportunity of investing ₹ 5,000 with 20 per cent probability of return of ₹ 20,000 if oil-drilling operation is successful (that is, if oil is struck) and if it is a failure (that is, oil is not found), the individual loses ₹ 5,000.

(a) Calculate expected monetary value of return on investment.

(b) The utility schedules of three individuals A, B and C are given. What is the expected utility for each of these individuals ? Who will invest in this oil-drilling operations ?

Money →	– ₹ 5000	0	₹ 5000	₹ 10,000	₹ 15,000	₹ 20,000
Utility of A	–5	0	4	7	9	10
Utility of B	–5	0	5	10	15	20
Utility of C	–5	0	6	13	21	30

Solution :

Expected monetary return $E(X) = \sum_{i=1}^{n} P_iX_i$

$$= 0.20 \times 20{,}000 + 0.80 \times -5000$$
$$= 4000 - 4000$$
$$= 0$$

(Note that if there is 20 per cent probability of being successful, there will be 80 per cent probability of its failure)

Now consulting the given utility schedule we find that for individual *A* utility of return of ₹ 20,000 is 10 and utility of loss of ₹ 5,000 for him is –5. Thus

$$E(U) \text{ of } A = 0.20\,(10) + 0.80\,(-5)$$
$$= 2.0 - 4.0 = -2$$

Similarly,

$$E(U) \text{ of } B = 0.2\,(20) + 0.8\,(-5)$$
$$= 4.0 - 4.0 = 0$$
$$E(U) \text{ of } C = 0.2\,(30) + 0.8\,(-5)$$
$$= 6.0 - 4.0 = +2.0$$

It will be seen from expected utility of the three individuals that for individual *C*, the expected utility from investment in drilling operations is positive. Therefore, only individual *C* will invest in the project. It is worth noting that as revealed by the given utility schedule for individual *C*, his marginal utility of money increases and therefore he is risk seeker. The utility functions of *A* reveals that he is risk averter, and that of *B* reveals that he is risk neutral.

QUESTIONS FOR REVIEW

1. What is meant by risk ? How does it differ from uncertainty ?
2. What is a fair gamble ? Why most individuals refuse to play a fair gamble ?
3. What is meant by risk and uncertainty ? Why are these concepts important in the theory of consumer choice ?
4. What is St. Petersburg paradox? How did Daniel Bernoulli solve it ?
5. What is Bernoulli's hypothesis ? How did he explain that most people do not accept fair bets (*i.e.* play fair games) ?
6. What is Neumann -Morgenstern concept of utility index under risky conditions? How is it constructed ?
7. Explain the attitde of risk-averter, risk lover and risk neutral with the help N-M utility functions of money.
8. How does the process of utility maximisation by an individual differ in the case of risk or uncertainity from the case of certainty.
9. How is risk measured ? In this connection explain the concepts of expected value, standard deviation and coefficient of variation.
10. Explain the process of decision making in a situation involving risk and uncertainty. Is maximisation of the expected value valid criterion for decision making in a risky economic situation.
11. What is meant by risk aversion, risk loving and risk neutrality ? How are these concepts related to the individual's utility function of money income ?
12. What is risk premium ? How is it measured ?
13. Why do people buy insurance ? Explain.
14. How can risk be reduced by businessmen ?
15. What is meant by when it is said that a person is risk averse ? Why are most people risk averse while some are risk lovers ?
16. How is risk measured through probability distribution of outcomes. Explain standard deviation as a measure of risk.
17. Distinguish between discrete and continuous probability distribution. How is probability distribution useful in risk analysis ?
18. Why do some people indulge in gambling as it may bring heavy losses to them ? Illustrate graphically.

APPENDIX TO CHAPTER 17

NEUMANN-MORGENSTERN METHOD OF CONSTRUCTING UTILITY INDEX UNDER RISKY CONDITIONS

Introduction

Making use of Bernoulli's idea that under risky and uncertain prospects as in betting, gambling, purchasing lottery tickets etc a rational individual will go by the expected utility rather than expected money values, Neumann and Morgenstern in their now famous work, ***"Theory of Games and Economic Behaviour"*** gave a method of cardinally measuring expected utility from win and prizes. On the basis of such a cardinal utility index called *N–M* index, rational decisions are made by the individuals in case of risky situations. Thus, Neumann-Morgenstern method seeks to assign a utility number, or in other words, construct a *N–M* utility index of the marginal utility of money which a person gets from extra amounts of money income. The choices by an individual under risky and uncertain situations depend on the *N–M* utility index *(i. e.,* expected numerical utilities) and changes in it with the changes in money income.

Assumptions of Constructing N-M Utility Index

Before explaining the Neumann-Morgenstern method of measuring utility from money or the construction *of N-M* utility index, it will be better to describe the assumptions on which the method is based. Firstly, it is assumed that the individual possesses a scale of preferences that is quite comprehensive and complete. This is similar to the assumption of indifference curve analysis of demand that the individual knows fully his indifference map depicting his scale of preferences. But unlike the indifference curve analysis of demand, the question here is the choices of "events". The events refer to the amounts of money some of which are "certain" and others uncertain, monetary amounts with probabilities or odds attached to them. Secondly, it is assumed that the individual can always say whether he prefers one event to another or he is indifferent between the two. This means that he can make probability calculations and on their basis can make comparison between the alternative events. For instance, he can compare the event of receiving ₹ 5,000 for sure, or ₹ 10,000 with 60 - 40 odds or any other probability, and can say whether he prefers one to the other or is indifferent between the two. Lastly, it is assumed that individual's choices are consistent.

Constructing Neumann-Morgenstern Utility Index

First step in the Neumann-Morgenstern method of measurement of utility of money is to state the numerical probabilities of uncertain events of acquiring additional money. Suppose the purchase of a lottery ticket is under consideration of an individual. Let the prize be ₹ 5,000 which he will get if he wins and suppose if he loses, he will get the consolation prize of ₹ 10. Further, suppose that odds are 60:40, that is, the probability of his winning is 0.6 and the probability of his losing (and therefore getting the consolation prize) is 0.4. With this the *expected monetary value (generally called standard acturial evaluation) of lottery ticket*;

$$= \pi (W) + (1 - \pi) F$$

where π stands for probability of winning and W the monetary amount of the first prize and $(1 - \pi)$ the probability of his losing and therefore of getting the consolation prize of the monetary value of F.

In our above numerical example, expected monetary value of lottery ticket

$$= 0.6 (5000) + (0.4) 10$$
$$= 3,000 + 4$$

= 3,004.

But, as said above, Neumann and Morgenstern seek to measure the *expected utility* from the monetary gain rather than the expected value of monetary gain itself. Thus the problem is to convert the monetary value of gains into expected utility terms. In *N-M* utility analysis, the lottery ticket would be evaluated from the following formula.

Expected utility of the above lottery ticket with the aforesaid two prizes

$$= \pi.U(W) + (1 - \pi) \,.\, U(F)$$

where *U(W)* is the expected utility of the first prize in case of winning and *U(F)* the utility of the consolation prize, if he loses. Thus in our above numerical example, the expected utility of lottery ticket is:

$$= 0.6 \times U(₹\ 5{,}000) + 0.4 \times U(₹\ 10)$$

Now in Neumann and Morgenstern method we have to assign utility numbers to ₹ 5,000 and ₹ 10 ***arbitrarily*** and then with reference to these, utility of a certain sum of money has to be evaluated. Let the utility of ₹ 5,000 to the individual be 500 utils and ₹10 be 1 util. With this the expected utility of the above lottery ticket is

= 0.6 × 500 utils + 0.4 × 1 util

= 300 utils + .4 util

= 300.4 utils

But the objective of Neumann-Morgenstern method is to evaluate the utility of a certain sum of money. For this, tool of ***certainty equivalent*** is used. A certainty equivalent is the sure sum of money. **An individual is *indifferent* between certainty equivalent and the probable amount of money with a certain probability in an uncertain and risky situation such as in a lottery ticket or gamble.** For finding out the certainty equivalent, we have to interrogate the individual and to know his mind.

Take the above example of lottery ticket of the first prize of ₹ 5,000 with a probability of 0.6 of winning and 0.4 of losing (getting consolation prize of ₹ 10). We ask the individual *X* as to how much *sure sum* of money and the above lottery ticket with the given prize and probabilities he would be indifferent. Suppose the individual reveals that he is indifferent between ₹ 3,000 and the above lottery ticket with the aforesaid prize and probabilities. Then, in this individual's case, certainty equivalent is ₹ 3,000. With this we can calculate the marginal utility of ₹ 3,000.

Since the individual is indifferent between the aforesaid lottery ticket and the *sure sum* of ₹ 3,000, the expected utility of the lottery ticket will be equal to the utility of ₹ 3,000. Therefore,

Utility of ₹ 3,000 = Expected utility of the lottery ticket

$$₹\ 3{,}000 = \pi.U(W) + (1 - \pi)\ U(F)$$

= 0.6 × 500 utils + 0.4 × 1 util

= 300 utils + 0.4 utils

= 300.4 utils

Thus, for the individual utility index of ₹ 3,000 is 300.4 utils. Hence:

Amount	₹ 10	₹ 5,000	₹ 3000
Expected utility	1 util	500 utils	300.4 utils

Likewise, by using the above procedure utility index of other sums of money by taking the examples of other lottery tickets and gambles with *other probabilities* and *different amounts* of prizes can be calculated. In this way a series of *N - M* utility indices can be converted into a schedule prepared at different levels of income, which then can be converted into a curve.

Neumann-Morgenstern Utility Measure is not the same as Neoclassical Cardinal Measurement of Utility

It should be noted that Neumann-Morgenstern method of measuring utility cardinally is not the same thing as neoclassical cardinal measurement of utility. The neoclassicals sought to measure the strength of psychic feelings of individuals towards goods and services. In fact the word 'cardinal' in these two types of analysis means two entirely different things. The Neumann-Morgenstern method does not measure the individual's quantities of satisfaction or pleasure from goods and services; it is intended to measure the utility of money with respect to predicting how an individual will make choices in risky and uncertain situations. The Neumann-Morgenstern index is constructed by asking the consumer to choose among risky alternatives *to know about individual's attitude towards gambling* and not the evaluation of amount of pleasure or satisfaction he obtains from the outcome of his choice. Thus, according to Professor Baumol, "The *N-M* utility index is cardinal in this very specific sense—it is intended to be used for making predictions. It is employed to predict which of two lottery tickets (or which of two other risky alternatives) a person will prefer. We are given this individual's ranking of the alternative prizes offered by the lottery tickets and the odds on each prize. From this we wish to be able to infer by numerical calculation, and without actually asking the person, which lottery ticket he will choose.

Further, he writes, "It is *not* the purpose of the Neumann-Morgenstern utility index to set up any sort of measure of introspective pleasure intensity. Such a measure of "strength of feelings" is totally unnecessary in the theory of games for which the *N - M* utility theory was constructed. Rather, the utility measure was set up for purposes of calculation, or rather of prediction (in the subtler sense of the word) to permit the theorist to determine in *the absence of the player* which of several risky propositions the player will *prefer*". Thus we see that in Neumann-Morgenstern method an individual's preferences among risky alternatives and lotteries come prior to constructing utility index. In this analysis it is not said that the individual prefers alternative *A* to alternative *B* because *A* gives him greater utility than *B*. Instead, because individual prefers A to *B*, the higher utility number is assigned to it.

PART–III

THEORY OF PRODUCTION AND COST ANALYSIS

- Theory of Production: Returns to a Variable Factor
- Production Function with Two Variable Inputs
- Optimum Factor Combination
- Cost Analysis
- Linear Programming
- Supply and its Elasticity

CHAPTER

18

Theory of Production: Returns to a Variable Factor

Introduction

So far we have been discussing the demand side of the pricing problems. In this chapter and the next few ones we shall be discussing the supply side of the pricing of products. The supply of a product, as we shall see in a later chapter, depends upon its cost of production, which in turn depends upon (a) the physical relationship between inputs[1] and output, and (b) the prices of inputs. The physical relationship between inputs and output plays an important part in determining the cost of production. It is the general description of this physical relation between inputs and output which forms the subject-matter of the theory of production. In other words, the theory of production relates to the physical laws governing production of goods.

The act of production involves the transformation of inputs into outputs. ***The word production in economics is not merely confined to effecting physical transformation in the matter, it is creation or addition of value.*** Therefore, production in economics also covers the rendering of services such as transporting, financing, marketing. Laws of production, or in other words, the generalisations regarding relations between inputs and outputs developed in this chapter will apply to all these types of production. *The theory of production provides a formal framework to help the managers of firms in deciding how to combine various factors or inputs most efficiently to produce the desired output of a product or service.*

The relation between inputs and output of a firm has been called the ***'Production Function'.*** Thus, the theory of production is the study of production functions. The production function of a firm can be studied by holding the quantities of some factors fixed, while varying the amount of other factors. This is called *short-run production function.* The time period in which at least one factor or input is fixed and production is increased by varying other factors is called the *short run*. The study of short-run production function when at least one factor is kept fixed forms the subject of ***law of diminishing returns*** which is also known as *law of Variable Proportions.* On the other hand, the time period when *all factors* are variable is called the *long run.* The lenght of the long run, that is, the time period required for changes in all inputs depends on the industry. For some industries such as making of wooden chairs or tables the long run may be few weeks or months but for production of steel, it may be many years as it takes several yours to expend the capacity of steel production. The behaviour of production when all factors are varied proportionately is the subject-matter of ***returns to scale***. Thus, in the theory of production, the study of (a) the returns to a variable factor and

1. The words "inputs" and "factors" of production are most often used interchangably. But, to some economists, meaning of inputs is broader. Inputs are all the things that firms buy, while the factors of production are taken to mean such things as labour, capital, land, entrepreneur.

(b) the returns to scale is included. Besides this, the theory of production is also concerned with explaining ***which combination of inputs (or factors of production) a firm will choose*** so as to minimize its costs of production for producing a given level of output or to maximize output for a given level of cost.

PRODUCTION FUNCTION

Production, as said above, is transformation of physical inputs into physical outputs. The output is thus a function of inputs. The functional relationship between physical inputs and physical output of a firm is known as production function. Algebraically, production function can be written as :

$$q = f(a, b, c, d \ldots\ldots\ldots\ldots\ldots) \quad \ldots (i)$$

where q stands for the quantity of output, a, b, c, d etc., stand for the quantities of factors A, B, C, D respectively. This function shows that the quantity (q) of output produced depends upon the quantities, a, b, c, d of the factors A, B, C and D respectively. The above function shows that there exists *some relationship* between output q and the quantites of inputs a, b, c, d etc., but it does not tell us the specific form of this relationship. This unspecified relationship is denoted here by the letter f. If the form of the function f is given, that is, if right-hand side of the equation (*i*) is given in a *specific* mathematical form[2], we can then fully find out precisely the quantity of output that the firm would produce with each set of inputs such as labour and capital.

"The production function is the name given to the relationship between the rates of input of productive services and the rate of output of product. It is the economist's summary of technological knowledge."[3] Thus, the production function expresses the relationship between the quantity of output and the quantity of various inputs used for the production. More precisely, the production function states the *maximium* quantity of output that can be produced from any given quantities of various inputs per period of time or, in other words, it states the *minimum* quantities of various inputs that are required to yield a given quantity of output per period of time, the technology being assumed to remain constant. It is important to note that when a change in technology occurs such as introduction of a new automated machine or the substitution of skilled labour for unskilled labour we will get a new production function. If a small firm produces wooden tables in a day, its production function will consist of the *maximum* number of tables that can be produced from *given quantities* of various inputs such as wood, varnish, labour time, machine time, floor space. Or, the production function of that firm may also be defined as the *minimum* quantites of wood, varnish, labour time, machine time, floor space, etc., that are required to produce a *given number* of tables per day.

Knowledge of the production function is a technological or engineering knowledge and is provided to the firm by its engineers or production managers. Two things must be noted in respect of production function. First, production function, like the demand function, must be considered with reference to a ***particular period of time, Production function expresses a flow of inputs resulting in a flow of output in a specific period of time.*** Secondly, production function of a firm is determined by the state of technology. When there is advancement in technology, the production function changes with the result that the new production can yield greater flow of output from the given inputs, or smaller quantities of inputs can be used for producting a given quantity of output.

---

2. A function is said to be in a specific form if we are able to find out the value of output q when the values of the independent variables (a, b, c, d etc.) are given.
3. G.J. Stigler, *The Theory of Price*, 1953, p.106.

In economic theory we, are intersted in two types of input-output relations or production functions. First , we study the production function when the quantities of some inputs are kept constant and the quantity of one input (or quantities of few inputs) are varied. This kind of input-output relation forms the subject-matter of the law of variable proportion. Since only in the short run, some factors are required to be held constant, the law of variable proportions relates to the short-run production function. Secondly, we study the input-output relation by varying all inputs proportionally. This forms the subject-matter of returns to scale. Since in the long run all factors can be varied, the question of returns to scale relates to *long-run production function.*

Production function can be represented in various forms; it can be represented by tables, graphs, mathematical equations, showing the maximum quantity of output that a firm can produce per period of time with various combinations of factors (*i.e.*, inputs). When two factors have to be explicity shown, production function can be represented by isoquants (*i.e.*, equal product curves). Production function can also be represented by ***input-output tables.*** However, it is worth mentioning that although production function provides quite a useful information about the production possibilities open to a firm, it does not give all the information required for efficient combination of inputs to produce a given level of output or to determine the profit-maximising rate of output. As mentioned above, production function describes a physical relationship which must be combined with prices of inputs to determine the efficient resource combination of producing a specific level of output.

PRODUCTION FUNCTION WITH ONE VARIABLE FACTOR

As mentioned above, in economic theory we are interested in two types of input-output relations or production functions. First, we study the production function when the quantities of some inputs are kept constant and the quantity of one input (or quantities of few inputs) are varied. This kind of input-output relations forms the subject-matter of the law of diminishing marginal returns which is also called *law of variable proportions* and describes *returns to a factor.* Secondly, we study the input-output relation by varying all inputs, that is, production function with two or more than two variable factors. The latter forms the subject-matter of the *returns to scale.* In the present chapter, we shall explain the production function with one variable factor and in the next chapter we shall analyse returns to scale. It may be noted that concept of returns to a variable factor is relevent for the short run because in the short run some factors such as capital equipment, machines, land remain fixed and factors such as labour, raw materials are increased to expand output. Thus the short-run two factor prooduction function can be written as

$$Q = f(L, \overline{K})$$

where Q stands for output, L for labour and K for capital which is held constant in the short run. (Note that bar on K indicates that it is held constant). An important specific form of production function known as Cobb-Douglas production function which is most widely used in economics is written as

$$Q = A\,L^{\alpha}\,K^{\beta}$$

Where L is the amount of labour, K is the amount of capital used in the production process and A, α, β are constants. Either K or L can be held constant and the amount of the other factor can be a increased to study the returns to a factor. The concept of returns to a factor is concerned with the study of how output (Q) changes when the amount of a variable factor, such as labour, is increased. In what follows we will first explain some concepts of physical product that are generally used for the study of returns to a variable factor.

Total, Average and Marginal Physical Products

Regarding physical production of factors there are three concepts : (1) Total Product, (2) Average Product, and (3) Marginal Product. To study these concepts of a productivity relating to the use of a variable factor, say labour, we assume that a firm leases a machine with 1000 horse power and employs it in the production process as a fixed factor. Depending on the amount of a labour (*i.e.*, the number of workers) employed to operate the given machine, various quantities of output of the product will be produced. In Table 18.1 we give the quantities of output that is, produced by employing more workers with the given machine (*i.e.*, the fixed capital). Thus the data of Table 18.1 represents the production function with one variable input (labour), holding capital constant. We shall now explain the concepts of total product, marginal product and average product of labour with the help of Table 18.1 and the curves.

Table 18.1 Total Product, Marginal Product, Average Product of Labour

Labour (*i.e.* No. of workers) L	Total Product (TP) Q	Marginal Product (MP) $\left(\frac{\Delta Q}{\Delta L}\right)$	Average Product (AP) $\left(\frac{Q}{L}\right)$	Output Elasticity of Labour (E_L)
1	80	80	80	1
2	170	90	85	1.06
3	270	100	90	1.11
4	368	98	92	1.06
5	430	62	86	0.72
6	480	50	80	0.62
7	504	24	72	0.33
8	504	0	0	0
9	495	–9	55	–0.16
10	480	–15	48	–0.31

Total Product (TP). The total product of a variable factor is the amount of total output produced by a given quantity of the variable factor, keeping the quantity of other factors such as capital, fixed. As the amount of the variable increases, the total output increases. But the rate of increase in total output varies at different levels of employment of the variable factor. It will be seen from Table 18.1 that as more workers are employed with a given quantity of capital (*i.e.*, the given machine), the total output of the product (*TP*) increases. When one worker is employed with a machine, total output is 80 units of output, with employment of 2 workers with the machine, the total output increase to 170 units, with employment of three workers, the total output incresases to 270. It will be seen from Table 18.1 that when more than 3 workers are employed, total output (*TP*) starts increasing at a diminishing rate and when more than 8 workers are employed, total output (*TP*) starts decreasing.

The behaviour of total product is graphically shown by the total product curve *TP* in Figure 18.1 where it will be seen that in the beginning total product curve rises at an increasring rate, that is, the slope of *TP* curve is rising in the beginning. After a point, total product curve starts increasing at a diminishing rate as the employment of the variable factor labour is increased. The fact that ultimately total product increases at a diminishing rate has been proved to be valid on the basis of empirical evidence, as will be seen later in our discussion of the law of diminishing returns.

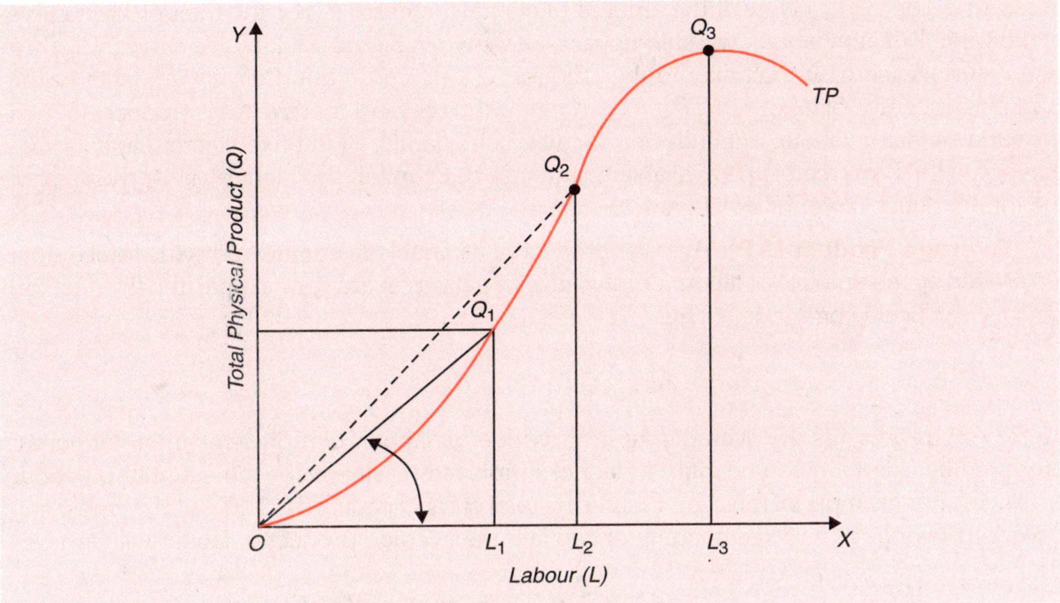

Fig. 18.1. *Total Product Curve of Labour*

It may be emphasized again that the total product curve shows how the total output of the firm changes by increasing the quantities of a variable factor, say, labour assuming that the fixed factor (capital) is held constant. The total product curve of labour starts from the origin O because it is reasonable to assume that the fixed factor capital alone cannot produce any output. When the firm uses OL_1 amount of labour along with a fixed amount of capital, the total product equals $L_1 Q_1$ units of total output. As employment of labour is increased to OL_2 the total product rises to $L_2 Q_2$. Likewise, total product of the variable factor along with a fixed amount of capital continues to increase until OL_3 units of labour are employed at which the total production of labour with a given amount of capital reaches the maximum level L_3Q_3. Further increases in employment of labour cause total product to decline. We shall discuss in detail later why total product of the variable labour decreases beyond a point.

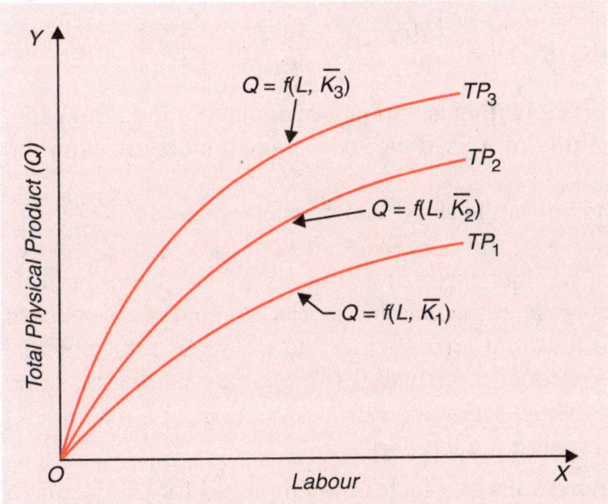

Fig. 18.2. *Shift in Total Product Curve Due to Increase in the Fixed Capital* $(\bar{K}_1 < \bar{K}_2 < \bar{K}_3)$

Shift in the Total Product Curve. The total product curve of a variable factor (labour) is drawn on the assumption that the amount of a fixed factor capital is held constant. Now, any change in the magnitude of the fixed factor capital will cause a shift in the total physical product curve of labour, the variable factor.

In Figure 18.2 the total product curve TP_1 of labour is drawn assuming that capital is held constant at a given amount K_1 of capital. (Note that for the sake of simplicity we have drawn in Fig. 18.2 the total product curves with decreasing slope only.) Now, if the amount of capital increases to K_2, the total product curve of the variable factor, labour, will shift upward as shown in Figure 18.2 by the curve TP_2, ($K = K_2$). A further increase in capital to the amount K_3 will cause a further upward shift in the total product curve of labour to TP_3, ($K = K_3$). It is thus evident that the total product curve of the variable factor, labour, depends upon how much quantity of the fixed factor capital it has to work with. The greater the available quantity of the capital, the higher will be the level of the total product curve *TP* of labour.

Average Product (AP). Average product of a variable factor (labour) is the total output (*Q*) divided by the amount of labour employed with a given quantity of capital (the fixed factor) used to produce a commodity. Thus

$$AP_L = \frac{Q}{L}$$

where AP_L represents the average physical product of labour, *Q* represents the total output produced by using a given quantity of labour employed, *L* stands for the quantity of labour employed. For example in Table 18.1 when the total output produced is 170 units by employing 2 workers (along with a fixed quantity of capital), the average product of labour will be

$$AP_L = \frac{Q}{L} = \frac{170}{2} = 85$$

Similarly, in Table 18.1 when three workers are employed with the given capital, 270 units of output are produced, average product of labour,

$$AP_L = \frac{270}{3} = 90$$

It will be seen from Table 18.1 that average product of labour (*AP*) is increasing until 4 workers are employed and beyond that average product (*AP*) of labour starts declining.

Derivation of Average Product (AP) Curve From the Total Product (TP) Curve. The average physical product curve can be easily derived from the total product curve of labour. This is illustrated in Fig. 18.3 where when OL_1 amount of labour is used, the total output is L_1Q_1. Thus, the average product of labour is equal to $\frac{L_1Q_1}{OL_1}$. But $\frac{L_1Q_1}{OL_1}$ is equal to the *slope of the line* connecting Q_1 with the point of origin (that is, tangent of angle $Q_1 OL_1$). Similarly, average product of labour when OL_2 quantity of it used can be obtained by connecting the point Q_2 with a line to the origin and finding out its slope which will be equal to $\frac{L_2Q_2}{OL_2}$. In Fig. 18.3, it will be seen that the average product curve of labour, as derived from the total product curve *TP*, is changing with the increase in the variable factor, labour. As we increase the amount of labour from L_1 to L_5, we find that lines connecting points of total physical products, Q_1, Q_2, Q_3, Q_4 etc. on the total product curve with the origin have increasing slope up to Q_5 and then have a decreasing slope. Thus, average physical product of labour increases up to OL_5 quantity of labour used and thereafter it decreases.

It has been generally found that as more units of a factor are employed for producting a commodity with a fixed quantity of another, average product first rises and then it falls. As will be seen from Figure 18.3, the average product of labour first rises and then it diminishes That is, the average product curve of a factor would have an inverted U-shape.

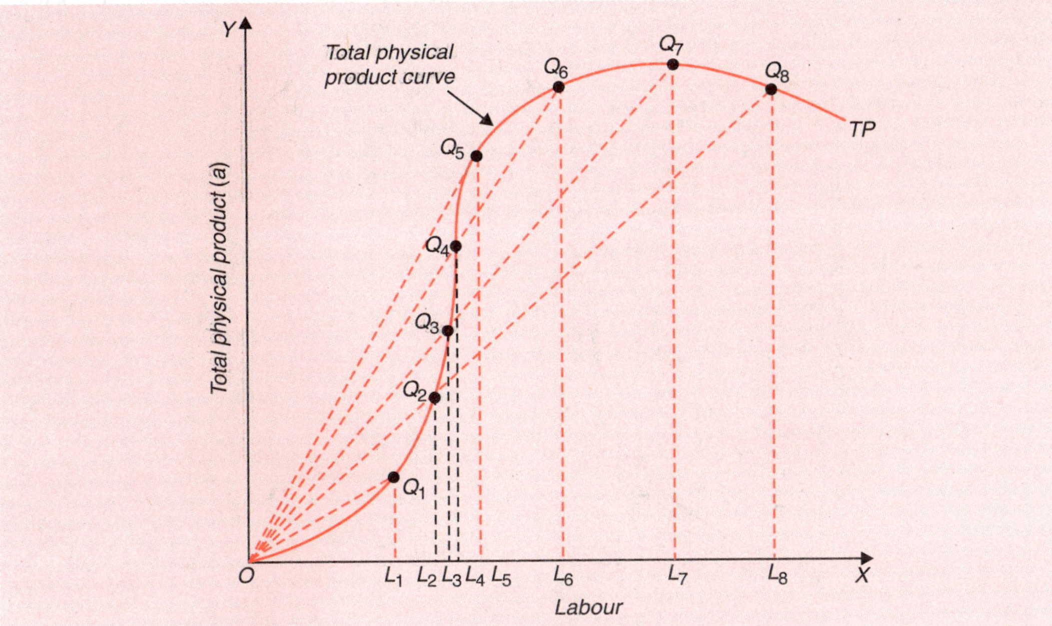

Fig. 18.3. Changing Average Physical Product of Labour

Marginal Product (MP). Marginal product of a variable factor is the addition made to the total production by the employment of an extra unit of a factor. Suppose in Table 18.1 when two workers are employed to produce the product and they produce 170 units of output. Now, if instead of two workers, three workers are employed and as a result total product increases to 270 units metres of cloth, then the third worker has added 100 metres to the total production. Thus 100 metres is the marginal physical product of the third worker. Similarly, when four workers are employed with the given machine (capital), the total product increases to 368, that is, fourth factor has added 98 metres to total output. Thus, marginal product of workers has declined to 98. It will be seen from Table 18.1 that marginal product (*MP*) of labour rises initially but after 3 workers are employed marginal product of workers diminishes. When more than 8 workers are employed, *MP* of labour has declimed to zero and on employing more than 8 workers, *MP* of labour has become negative.

In general, if employment of labour increases by ΔL units yielding increases in total output by ΔQ units, the marginal product of labour* is given is by $\frac{\Delta Q}{\Delta L}$. That is,

$$MP_L = \frac{\Delta Q}{\Delta L}$$

The marginal product curve of a variable factor can also be derived from the total physical product curve of labour. At any given level of employment of labour, marginal product of labour can be obtained by measuring the slope of the total product curve at the given level of labour employment. For example, in Figure 18.4 when OL_1 units of labour are employed, the marginal physical of labour is given by the slope of the tangent drawn at point *A* to the total product curve *TP*. Again, when OL_2 units of labour are employed, marginal product of labour is obtaned by measuring the slope of the tangent drawn to the total product curve *TP* at point *B* which corresponds to OL_2 level of labour employment.

* For *Infinitesimal changes* in labour, the marginal product of labour is the first derivative of the production function with respect to labour and is written as $\frac{dQ}{dL}$.

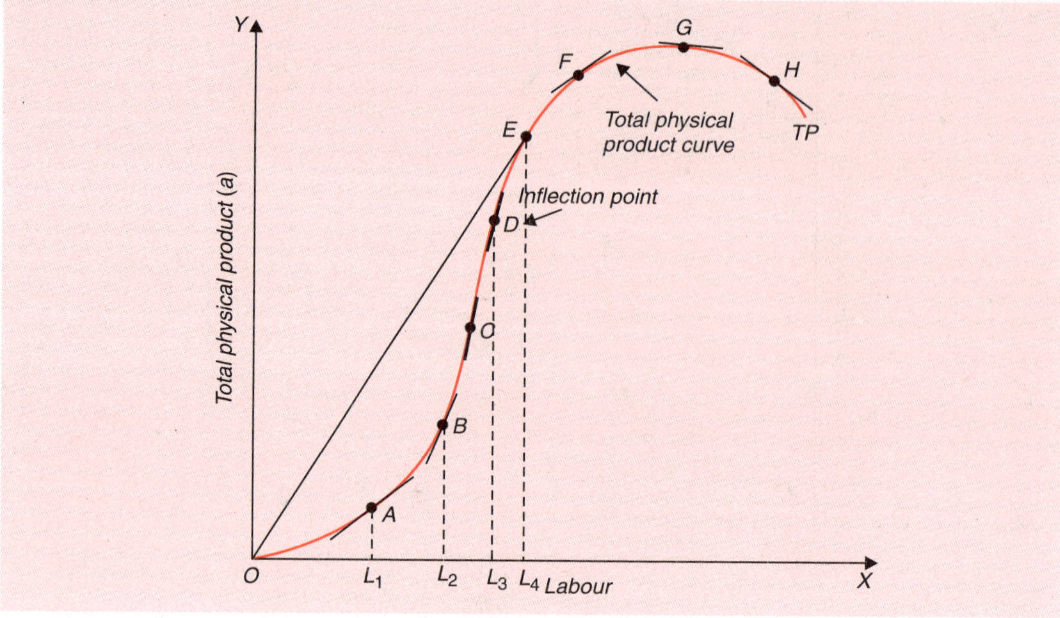

Fig. 18.4. *Deriving Mariginal Physical Product Curve*

The marginal product of a factor will change at different levels of employment of the factor. It has been found that marginal product of a factor rises in the beginning and then utimately falls as more of it is used for production, other things remaining the same. That is why in Fig. 18.4 marginal product (*MP*) has been shown to be rising in the beginning upto point *D*, that is, when OL_3 workers are employed and beyond that it starts diminishing. Point *D* is known as *point of inflection*. Marginal product of labour goes on diminishing beyond the inflection point *D* until it becomes negative beyond point G.

The relationship with average product and marginal product curves and how both of them are related to the total product curve has been graphically shown in Figure 18.5.

Output Elasticity of an Input

An important concept relating to production function with one variable input is output elasticity of an input. Just as price elasticity of demand for a good is defined as percentage change in quantity demanded of it that results from a given percentage change in price, the output elasticity of a variable input, say labour, is the percentage change in output that is brought about by a given percentage change in the quantity of variable input used, other factors such as capital remaining the same. That is,

$$E_L = \frac{\% \Delta Q}{\% \Delta L} \quad \text{....(1)}$$

where E_L stands for output elasticity of labour

Rewriting equation (1) we have

$$E_L = \frac{\Delta Q}{Q} \div \frac{\Delta L}{L} = \frac{\Delta Q}{Q} \times \frac{L}{\Delta L}$$

$$E_L = \frac{\Delta Q}{\Delta L} \cdot \frac{L}{Q} \quad \text{....(2)}$$

Since $\frac{\Delta Q}{\Delta L}$ represents marginal product of labour and $\frac{Q}{L}$ represents average product of labour, the equation (2) can be written as

$$E_L = \frac{MP_L}{AP_L}$$

Thus, output elasticity of labour is the ratio of marginal product of labour to its average product. In the last column of Table 18.1 we have calculated the output elasticity of labour from dividing MP_L by AP_L.

When use of labour, with a given quantity of capital is increased from one unit to 2 units of labour (that is, $\Delta L = 1$), output increases more than proportionately (i.e. by 1.06). The negative output elasticity of labour when more than 8 units of labour are employed means that output decreases with a given percentage increase in labour input.

Note that production elasticity greater that one means that one percentage change in input (labour) yields more than one percentage increase in output of the commodity. If elasticity of production of an input is less than one, it implies that one per cent increase in the variable input, keeping other factors constant, causes less than one per cent increase in output. Thus, the ***elasticity of production of a variable input being less than one indicates diminishing returns to that factor.*** Production elasticity of zero means that output does not change at all when a given percentage change in a variable input, keeping other factors constant, is used in the production process. If elasticity of production is less than zero (that is, it is negative), this implies that output of the commodity *decreases* as a result of a given percentage increase in the variable input.

Problem. *You are given the following production function*

$$Q = L^{0.75} K^{0.25}$$

(*i*) *Find the marginal product of labour.*

(*ii*) *If the fixed quantity of capital in the short run equals 10,000 units, what is the short-run production function ?*

(*iii*) *Show that marginal product of labour (MP_L) is less than average product of labour (AP_L)in the short-run production function in* (ii) *above*

Solution. (*i*) To get marginal product of labour, we differentiate the given production fuction with respect to labour. Thus

$$MP_L = \frac{\partial Q}{\partial L} = 0.75L^{-0.25}K^{0.25}$$

$$= 0.75\left(\frac{K}{L}\right)^{0.25}$$

(*ii*) Note that in the short-run producton function, one factor is variable with the quantity of other fixed factor. Thus

$$Q = L^{0.75} K^{0.25}$$

$$Q = L^{0.75} (10{,}000)^{0.25}$$

Since the fourth root of 10,000 is 10

$$Q = L^{0.75} . 10 = 10L^{0.75}$$

Thus, short-run production function is $Q = 10 L^{0.75}$.

(iii) $$MP_L = \frac{\partial Q}{\partial L} = 10 \times 0.75 L^{-0.25}$$

$$= \frac{7.5}{L^{0.25}}$$

$$AP_L = \frac{Q}{L} = \frac{10L^{0.75}}{L} = 10L^{0.75-1}$$

$$= \frac{10}{L^{0.25}}$$

Comparing the values of MP_L and AP_L we find that $MP_L < AP_L$

Algebraic Determinination of Marginal Product and Average Product of a Factor from Short-run Production Function

It is useful to determine marginal and average products from the short-run production function. Let the following short-run algebraic production function of a business firm has been estimated. We have to determine the marginal and average products of labour

$$Q = 6L^2 - 0.4L^3$$

where Q is output and L is the quantity of labour used.

Note that the above function is short-run production function as there is no fixed term in it ; all terms in it contain the variable factor, labour (L).

To determine *marginal product of labour* (MP_L) we take the first derivative of output with respect to labour

$$MP_L = \frac{dQ}{dL} = 2 \times 6L - 3 \times 0.4L^2$$

$$= 12L - 1.2L^2$$

To determine *average product of labour,* we divide the total output by L. Thus,

$$AP_L = \frac{Q}{L} = \frac{6L^2 - 0.4L^3}{L} = 6L - 0.4L^2$$

We can find out the value of the variable factor L that maximises output (Q) and also the value of labour (L) at which its average product is maximum.

Value of *L* that maximises output (Q) : The value of variable input L that maximises output (Q) can be obtained by setting marginal product function of the variable input equal to zero. We have found above that . $MP_L = 12L - 1.2L^2$. Setting it equal to zero we have

$$12L - 1.2L^2 = 0$$

$$1.2L^2 = 12L$$

$$\frac{1.2L^2}{L} = 12$$

$$1.2L = 12$$

$$L = 12 \times \frac{10}{12} = 10$$

At 10 units of labour, value of Q will be maximum.

Value of L at which its AP is maximum : Value of average product function will be maximised where its first derivative equals zero.

AP of labour obtained above = $6L - 0.4L^2$

$$\frac{dAP}{dL} = 6 - 0.8L = 0$$

$$0.8L = 6$$

$$L = 6 \times \frac{10}{8} = \frac{60}{8} = 7.5$$

Thus, when 7.5 units of labour are used, its average product will be maximum.

Determination of Marginal and Average Products of a Variable Factor in Cobb-Douglas Production Function

An important production function called Cobb-Douglas production function widely used in empirical studies is of the following form

$$Q = AL^{\alpha} K^{\beta}$$

Let us first find out marginal products of labour, holding capital constant. This can be found by the first derivative of the function with respect to labour. Thus,

$$MP_L = \frac{\partial Q}{\partial L} = A\alpha\, L^{\alpha-1}\, K^{\beta}$$

$$= \alpha\, \frac{AL^{\alpha}K^{\beta}}{L} = \alpha \frac{Q}{L}$$

Marginal product of capital, holding labour constant, can be obtained by obtaining the first derivative of the function with respect to capital. Thus,

$$MP_k = \frac{\partial Q}{\partial K} = A\beta\, L^{\alpha}K^{\beta-1}$$

$$= B\frac{AL^{\alpha}K^{\beta}}{K} = \beta\frac{Q}{K}$$

Average product of labour, $AP_L = \dfrac{Q}{L} = \dfrac{AL^{\alpha}K^{\beta}}{L}$

$$= AL^{\alpha-1}K^{\beta}$$

Average product of capital, $AP_L = \dfrac{Q}{L} = \dfrac{AL^{\alpha}K^{\beta}}{K}$

$$= AL^{\alpha}K^{\beta-1}$$

Exercise. Suppose a firm producing cotton cloth has the following production function.

$$Q = 2K^{1/2}\, L^{1/2}$$

Determine the marginal products of labour and capital.

Solution. This is Cobb-Douglas production function with the given specific values of exponents.

$$MP_L = \frac{\partial Q}{\partial L} = 2\left(\frac{1}{2}\right) K^{1/2} L^{1/2-1}$$

$$= K^{1/2} L^{-1/2}$$

$$= \left(\frac{K}{L}\right)^{1/2} = \sqrt{\frac{K}{L}}$$

$$MP_K = \frac{\partial Q}{\partial K} = 2.\left(\frac{1}{2}\right) K^{1/2-1} L^{1/2}$$

$$= K^{-1/2} L^{1/2} = \left(\frac{L}{K}\right)^{1/2}$$

$$= \sqrt{\frac{L}{K}}.$$

NUMERICAL PROBLEM ON ELASTICITY OF OUTPUT

Problem : *Given the following production function*

$$Q = 1.50\, L^{0.75} K^{0.25}$$

Determine the elasticity of output with respect to (1) labour and (2) capital. Give an economic interpretation of these output elasticities.

Solution. Given production function is

$$Q = 1.50\, L^{0.75} K^{0.25}$$

Output elasticity of labour (E_L) = $\dfrac{MP_L}{AP_L}$

$$MP_L = \frac{\partial Q}{\partial L} = 0.75 \times 1.50\, L^{-0.25} K^{0.25}$$

$$= 1.125\, L^{-0.25} K^{0.25}$$

$$AP_L = \frac{Q}{L} = \frac{1.50 L^{0.75} K^{0.25}}{L}$$

$$\frac{Q}{L} = 1.50\, L^{-0.25} K^{0.25}$$

$$E_L = \frac{MP_L}{AP_L} = \frac{1.125 L^{-0.25} K^{0.25}}{1.50\, L^{-0.25} K^{0.25}}$$

$$= 0.75$$

Output elasticity of capital (E_K) = $\dfrac{MP_K}{AP_K}$

$$MP_K = \frac{\partial Q}{\partial K} = 0.25 \times 1.50\, L^{0.75}\, K^{-0.75}$$

$$= 0.375\, L^{0.75}\, K^{-0.75}$$

$$AP_K = \frac{Q}{K} = \frac{1.50 L^{0.75}\, K^{0.25}}{K}$$

$$= 1.50\, L^{0.75}\, K^{-0.75}$$

$$E_K = \frac{MP_K}{AP_K} = \frac{0.375\, L^{0.75}\, K^{-0.75}}{1.50\, L^{0.75}\, K^{-0.75}} = 0.25$$

From the value of output elasticity of labour equal to 0.75 it follows that 1 per cent increase in employment of labour causes 0.75 increase in output, that is, less than proportionately. Similarly, output elasticity of capital being equal to 0.25 implies that one per cent increase in capital causes 0.25 per cent increase in output of the commodity.

LAW OF VARIABLE PROPORTIONS

Law of variable proportions occupies an important place in economic theory. This law examines the production function with one factor variable, keeping the quantites of other factors fixed. In other words, it refers to the input-output relation when output is increased by varying the quantity of one input. When the quantity of one factor is increased keeping the quantity of the other factors constant, the proportion between the variable factor and the fixed factor is altered; the ratio of employment of the variable factor to that of the fixed goes on increasing as the quantity of the variable factor is increased also. Since under this law we study the *effects on output of variations in factor proportions*, this is known as the *law of variable proportions*. Since according to this law when one factor increases, other factors held constant, after a point, marginal returns to the variable factor diminishes, this is also called law of diminishing returns. This law has played a vital role in the history of economic thought and occupies an equally important place in modern economic theory and has been supported by the empirical evidence about the real world. The law of diminishing returns has been stated by various economists in the following manner : G. J. Stigler, a Nobel prize winner in economics writes, **"*As equal increments of one input are added ; the inputs of other productive services being held constant, beyond a certain point the resulting increments of product will decrease, i.e., the marginal products will diminish.*[4]**

***Similarly, Samuelson, another Nobel Laureate, writes"An increase in some inputs relative to other fixed inputs will, in a given state of technology, causes output to increase; but after a point the extra output resulting from the same additions of extra inputs will become less and less".*[5]**

Assumptions of the Law. The law of variable proportions or diminishing returns as stated above holds good under the following conditions:

1. First, the state of technology is assumed to be given and unchanged. If there is improvement in technology, then marginal and average product may rise instead of diminishing.

2. Secondly, there must be some other inputs such as capital must be kept fixed. It is only in this way then that we are able to measure the changes in output caused by increase in a

4. G.J. Stigler, *Theory of Price*, The Macmillan Co., 1953, p.111.
5. P.A . Samuelson, *Economics*, 8th edition, p.25.

variable factor that we can alter the factor proportions and know its effects on output. This law does not apply in case all factors are proportionately varied. Behaviour of output as a result of the variations in all inputs is discussed under "returns to scale".

3. Thirdly, the law is based upon the possibility of varying the proportions in which the various factors can be combined to produce a product. The law does not apply to those cases where the factors must be used in fixed proportions to yield a product. When the various factors are required to be used in rigidly fixed proportions, then the increase in one factor would not lead to any increase in output, that is, the marginal product of the factor will then be zero and not diminishing. It may however be pointed out that products requiring fixed proportions of factors are quite uncommon. Thus the law of diminishing marginal returns also known as law of variable proportions applies to most of the cases of production.

Returns to a variable factor, say labour, keeping the quantity of a fixed factor land as constant is illustrated in Table 18.1 and Figure18.5. We shall first explain it by considering Table 18.1. Assume that there is a given fixed amount of land with which more variable factor, labour, is used to produce wheat. With a given fixed quantity of land, as a farmer raises employment of labour from one unit to 7 units, total product increases from 80 quintals to 504 quintals of wheat. Beyond the employment of 8 units of labour, total product diminishes. It is worth noting that up to the use of 3 units of labour, total product increases at an increasing rate and afterwards it increases at a diminishing rate. This fact is clearly revealed from column 3 which shows successive marginal products of labour as extra units of labour are used. Marginal product of labour, it may be recalled, is the increment in total output due to the use of an extra unit of labour.

It will be seen from col. 3 of Table 18.1 that the marginal product of labour initially rises and beyond the use of three units of labour, it starts diminishing. Thus when three units of labour are employed, marginal product of labour is 100 and with the use of 4th and 5th units of labour marginal product falls to 98 and 62 respectively. Beyond the use of eight units of labour, total product diminishes and therefore marginal product of labour becomes negative. As regards average product of labour, it rises up to the use of fourth unit of labour and beyond that it is falling throughout.

Three Stages of Production

The behaviour of output when the varying quantity of one factor is combined with a fixed quantity of the other can be divided into three distinct stages. In order to understand these three stages it is better to graphically illustrate the production function with one factor variable. This has been done in Fig. 18.5. In this figure, on the *X*-axis we measure the quantity of the variable factor and on the *Y*-axis we measure the total product, average product and the marginal product. How the total product, average product and marginal product of the variable factor change as a result of the increase in the quantity of one factor to a fixed quantity of the others will be seen from Fig. 18.5. The total product curve *TP* goes on increasing to a point and after that it starts declining. Average and marginal product curves also rise in the beginning and then decline; marginal product curve starts declining earlier than the average product curve. The behaviour of these total, average and marginal products of the variable factor consequent to the increase in its amount is generally divided into three stages which are explained below :

Stage 1: In this stage, total product increases at an increasing rate to a point. In Fig. 18.5 from the origin to the point *F*, slope of the total product curve *TP* is increasing, that is, up to the point *F*, *the total product increases at an increasing rate* (the total product curve *TP* is concave upwards to the point *F*), which means that the marginal product *MP* rises. From the point *F* onwards during the stage 1, the total product goes on rising but its slope is declining which means that ***from point F to the point H the total product increases at a diminishing rate*** (total product curve is concave downwards), i.e., marginal product falls but is positive. The point *F* where the total product stops increasing at an increasing rate and starts increasing at the diminishing rate is called the *point of inflection*. Corresponding vertically to this point of inflection marginal product is maximum, after which it starts diminishing.

The stage 1 ends where the average product curve reaches its highest point. During the stage 1, when marginal product of the variable factor is falling, it still exceeds its average product and so continues to cause the average product curve to rise. Thus, during the stage 1, whereas marginal product curve rises in a part and then falls, the average product curve rises throughout. In the first stage, the quantity of the fixed factor is too much relative to the quantity of the variable factor so that if some quantity of the *fixed factor* is withdrawn, the total product would increase. Thus, in the first stage *marginal product of the fixed factor is negative.* Stage 1 is called by some economists as the *stage of increasing returns* because average product of the variable factor increases throughout this stage. It is notable that the marginal product in this stage initialy increases and in a later part it starts declining but remains greater than the average product throughout in stage 1 so that the average product continues to rise.

Stage 2: In stage 2, the total product continues to increase at a diminishing rate until it reaches its maximum point *H* where the second stage ends. In this stage, both the marginal product and average product of the variable factor are diminishing but are positive. At the end of the second stage, that is, at point *M* marginal product of the variable factor is zero (corresponding to the highest point *H* of the total product curve *TP*). Stage 2 is very crucial and important because the firm will seek to produce in its range. This stage is known as *the stage of diminishing returns* as both the average and marginal products of the variable factor continuously fall during this stage.

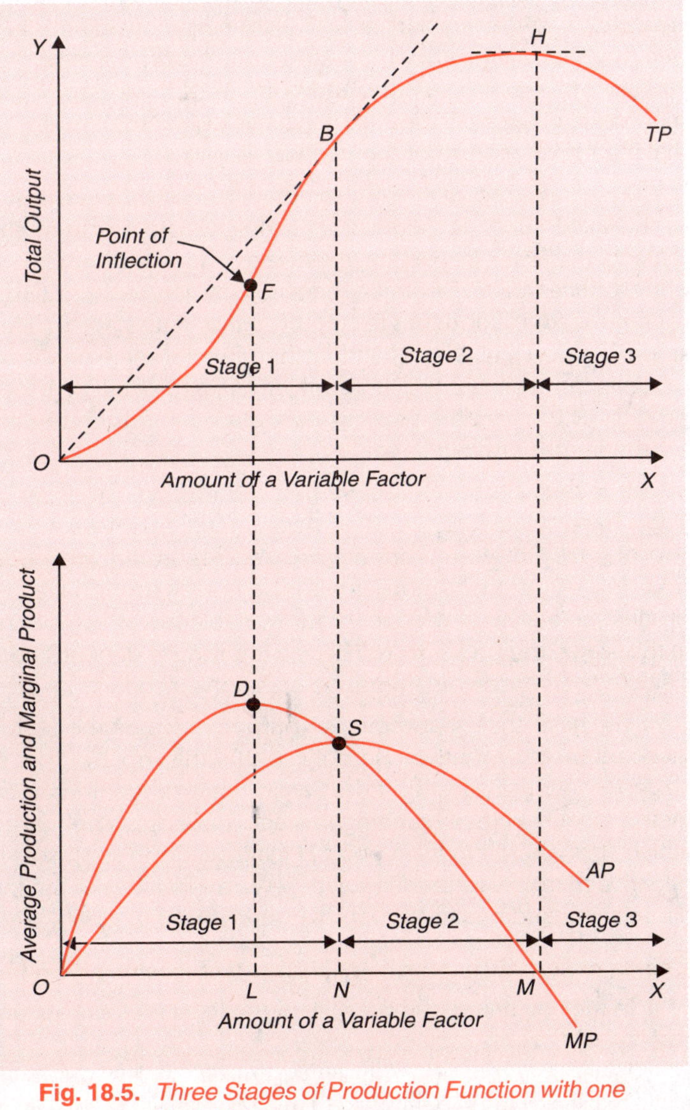

Fig. 18.5. *Three Stages of Production Function with one Variable Factor*

Stage 3: In stage 3, total product declines and therefore the total product curve *TP* slopes downward. As a result, marginal product of the variable factor is negative and the marginal product curve *MP* goes below the X-axis. In this stage, variable factor is too much relative to the fixed factor. This stage is called the *stage of negative returns,* since the marginal product of the variable factor is negative during this stage.

It may be noted that stage 1 and stage 3 are *completely symmetrical*. In stage 1 the fixed factor is too much relative to the variable factor. Therefore, in stage 1, marginal product of the fixed factor is negative. On the other hand, in stage 3, variable factor is too much relative to the fixed factors. Therefore, in stage 3, the marginal product of the variable factor is negative.

The Stage of Operation

Now an important question is in which stage a rational producer will seek to produce. A rational producer will never choose to produce in stage 3 where marginal product of the variable factor is negative. Marginal product of the variable factor being negative in stage 3, a producer can always increase his output by reducing the amount of variable factor. It is thus clear that a rational producer will never be producing in stage 3. Even if the variable factor is free, the rational producer will stop at the end of stage 2 where the marginal product of the variable factor is zero. At the end point *M* of the second stage where the marginal product of the variable factor is zero, the producer will be maximizing the total product and will thus be making maximum use of the variable factor.

A rational producer will also not choose to produce in stage 1 where the marginal product of the fixed factor is negative. A producer producing in stage 1 means that he will not be making the best use of the fixed factor and further that he will not be utilizing fully the opportunities of increasing production by increasing quantity of the variable factor whose average product continues to rise throughout the stage 1. Thus a rational entrepreneur will not stop in stage 1 but will expand further. Even if the fixed factor is free (i.e., costs nothing), the rational entrepreneur will stop only at the end of stage 1 (i.e., at point *N*) where the average product of the variable factor is maximum. At this end point *N* of stage 1 he will be making maximum use of fixed factor.[6]

It is thus clear from above that the rational producer will never be found producing in stage 1 and stage 3. Stage 1 and stage 3 may, therefore, be called stages of economic absurdity or economic nonsense. Thus stages 1 and 3 represent ***non-economic region in production*** *function*. A rational producer will always seek to produce in stage 2 where both the marginal product and average product of the variable factor are diminishing. At which particular point in this stage, the producer will decide to produce depends upon the price the of variable factor. The stage 2 represents the range of rational production decisions.

We have thus seen how the output varies as the factor proportions are altered at any given moment. We have also noticed that this input-output relation can be divided into three stages. Now the question arises as to what causes increasing marginal returns to a variable factor, labour, in the beginning in stage 1, diminishing marginal returns to the variable factor which start operating from point *D* in stage 1 and continues in stage 2 and ultimately we have negative marginal returns in stage 3. We explain below the factors which cause the increasing, diminishing and nagetive marginal returns to the variable factor.

Causes of Initial Increasing Marginal Returns to a Variable Factor

In the beginning, the quantity of the fixed factor is abundant relative to the quantity of the

6. The statement in respect of the non-operation by a rational producer in stage 1 applies to the producer who is working under perfect competition in both the product and factor markets where the price of product sold by him and the prices of factors bought by him remain fixed. In monopoly and imperfect competition in product and factor markets where the prices of product and factors do not remain fixed with the changes in the level of output and employment, the producer might find his most profitable level of output in stage 1.

variable factor. Therefore, when more and more units of the variable factor are added to the constant quantity of the fixed factor, then the fixed factor is more intensively and effectively utilized, that is, the efficiency of the fixed factor increases as additional units of the variable factors are added to it. This causes the production to increase at a rapid rate. When, in the beginning, the variable factor is relatively smaller in quantity, some amount of the fixed factor may remain unutilized and, therefore, when the variable factor is increased fuller utilisation of the fixed factor becomes possible with the result that increasing returns to a variable factor are obtained. The question arises as to why the fixed factor is not initially taken in a quantity which suits the available quantity of the variable factor. Answer to this question is provided by the fact that generally those factors are taken as fixed which are ***indivisible.***[7]

Indivisibility of a factor means that due to technological requirements, a minimum amount of it must be employed whatever the level of output. Thus, as more units of the variable factor are employed to work with an indivisible fixed factor, output greatly increases due to fuller and more effective utilization of the latter. Thus we see that it is the indivisibility of some factors which causes increasing returns to a variable factor in stage 1.

The second reason why we get increasing returns to a factor at the initial stage is that as more units of the variable factor are employed, the efficiency of the variable factor itself increases. This is because when there is a sufficient quantity of the variable factor, it becomes possible to introduce specialization or division of labour which results in higher productivity. The greater the quantity of the variable input, the greater the scope for specialization and hence greater will be the level of productivity and efficiency.

Causes of Diminishing Marginal Returns

The stage of diminishing returns in the production function with one factor variable is the most important. The question arises as to why we get diminishing marginal returns after a certain amount of the variable factor has been added to the fixed quantity of the other factor. It is important to note that the famous law of diminishing returns is in fact concerned with *diminishing marginal returns* and not diminishing total returns *i.e.* total product of a factor.

Scarcity of the fixed factor. As explained above, increasing returns to a factor occur in the first stage primarily because of the more effective and efficient use of the fixed factor as more units of the variable factor are combined to work with it. Once the point is reached at which the amount of the variable factor is sufficient to ensure the efficient utilization of the fixed factor, further increases in the variable factor will cause *marginal and average products to decline because the fixed factor then* ***becomes inadequate relative to the quantity of the variable factor.*** In other words, the ***contributions to the production made by the variable factor after a point becomes less and less because the additional units of the variable factor have less and less of the fixed factors to work with.*** *The production is the result of the co-operation of various factors aiding each other*. In the beginning in stage 1, the fixed factor is abundant relative to the number of the variable factor and the former provides much aid to the latter. On the other hand, when with the increase in the variable factor the fixed factor becomes more and more scarce in relation to the variable factor so that as the units of the variable factor are increased they receive less and less aid from the fixed factor. As a result, the marginal and average products of the variable factor decline.

Indivisibility of the Fixed Factor. The phenomenon of diminishing marginal returns, like that of increasing marginal returns, rests upon the indivisibility of the fixed factor. As explained above, the important reason for increasing returns in stage 1 is the fact that the fixed factor is indivisible which has to be employed whether the output to be produced is small

7. Moreover, a factor has to be taken in a fixed quantity because this is one way in which we can alter the factor proportion and judge its effect on output.

or large. In stage 1 when the indivisible fixed factor is not being fully used, successive increases in the variable factor add more and more to output since fuller and more efficient use is made of the indivisible fixed factor. But there is generally a limit to the range of the employment of the variable factor over which its average product will increase. There will usually be a level of employment of the variable factor at which indivisible fixed factor is being as fully and efficiently used as possible and therefore the marginal product of the variable factor is maximum. It will happen when the variable factor has increased to such an amount that the fixed indivisible factor is being used in the '***best or optimum proportion***' with the variable factor. Once the optimum proportion is disturbed by further increases in the variable factor, marginal returns to the variable factor (*i.e.*, marginal product) will diminish primarily because the indivisible factor is being used in wrong proportion with the variable factor. Just as the marginal product of the variable factor increases in the beginning when better and fuller use of the fixed indivisible factor is being made, so the marginal product of the variable factor diminishes when the fixed indivisible factor is being worked too hard.

If the fixed factor was finely divisible, neither the increasing nor the diminishing marginal returns would have occurred. If the factors were perfectly divisible, then there would not have been the necessity of taking a large quantity of the fixed factor in the beginning to combine with the varying quantities of the other factor. ***In the presence of perfect divisibility of the factors, the optimum proportion between the factors could be achieved in every case.*** Perfect divisibility of the factors implies that a small farm with a miniature combine and one worker would be as efficient as a large farm with a large combine and many workers. The productivity would be the same in the two cases.

Thus we see that if the factors were perfectly divisible the question of varying factor proportions would not have arisen and hence the phenomena of increasing and diminishing marginal returns to a factor would not have occurred. It has been rightly said, "Let divisibility enter through the door, law of variable proportions rushes out through the window."

Imperfect Substitutability of the Factors. Joan Robinson goes deeper into the causes of diminishing returns. She holds that ***the diminishing returns occur because the factors of production are imperfect substitutes for one another.*** As seen above, diminishing marginal returns occur after a point since the fixed factor becomes inadequate relatively to the variable factor. Now, a factor which is scarce in supply is taken as fixed. When there is a scarce factor, quantity of that factor cannot be increased in accordance with the varying quantities of the other factors which beyond the optimum proportion of factors will result in diminishing marginal returns. If now some variable factor was perfect substitute of the scarce fixed factor, then the paucity of the scarce fixed factor after a stage would have been made up by increasing the supply of this perfect substitute with the result that output could be expanded without diminishing marginal returns. Thus, even if the variable factor which we add to the fixed factor were perfect substitute of the fixed factor, then when the fixed factor becomes relatively deficient, its deficiency would be made up on account of the increase in the variable factor which is its perfect substitute.

Thus Joan Robinson says, "What the Law of Diminishing Returns really states is that there is limit to the extent to which one factor of production can be substituted for another, or, in other words, that the elasticity of substitution between factors is not infinite. If this were not true, it would be possible when one factor of production is fixed in amount and the rest are in perfectly elastic supply, to produce part of the output with the aid of the fixed factor, and then, when the optimum proportion between this and other factors was attained, to substitute some other factor for it and to increase output at constant cost."[8] **We therefore see that *diminishing***

8. Joan Robinson, *The Economics of Imperfect Competition*, p. 330.

marginal returns operate because the elasticity of substitution between factors is not infinite.

Causes of Negative Marginal Returns

As the amount of the variable factor continues to be increased to the constant quantity of the other, a stage is reached when the total product declines and the marginal product becomes negative. This phenomenon of negative marginal returns to the variable factor is due to the fact that the amount of the variable factor becomes excessive relative to the fixed factor so that they get in each other's way with the result that the total output falls instead of rising. Besides, too large a number of the variable factor also impairs the efficiency of the fixed factor. The proverb "too many cooks spoil the broth" aptly applies to this situation. In such a situation, a reduction in the units of the variable factor will increase the total output. Just as in the first stage, marginal product of the fixed factor was negative due to its abundance, in the third stage the marginal product of the variable factor is negative due to its excessiveness.

GENERAL APPLICABILITY OF THE LAW OF DIMINISHING RETURNS

We have discussed above, the law of diminishing returns which states marginal physical product eventually diminishes, even if it is increasing in the beginning. Uptil Marshall, it was thought that three laws of production–diminishing, constant and increasing returns were quite distinct and separate. Now, modern economists have veered round to the view that diminishing, constant and increasing returns are not three separate laws but they are three phases of one general law of variable proportions. Moreover, uptil Marshall it was thought that law of diminishing returns applied to agriculture and the manufacturing industries were characterised by increasing or constant returns. But this is no longer believed; law of diminishing returns has vast general applicability. This law applies as much to industries as to agriculture. Whenever some factors are fixed and the amount of other increases, then the technology remaining the same, diminishing returns to a factor are bound to occur eventually both in agriculture and industries. We have given above the various definitions of law of diminishing returns which lay stress on its general applicability.

It is important to note that law of diminishing returns is ***empirical generalization*** and not the law of economics derived through deductive logic. As for its validity is concerned, we have given the various reasons for the occurrence of diminishing returns. The occurrence of diminishing marginal physical returns to a factor after a point has been confirmed by the overwhelming empirical evidence. Indeed, if the diminishing returns did not occur we could grow sufficient amount of foodgrains even in a flower pot by using more dozes of labour and capital. If the constant returns could be obtained by applying more labour on a given piece of land, then as the population is increased we could use more labour on that land to get proportionate increase in agricultural output. In that case, world, especially developing countries like India, would not have to face problems of food shortage and overpopulation. R. G. Lipsey is right when he says, "Indeed, were the hypothesis of diminishing returns incorrect, there would need to be no fear that the present population explosion will bring with it a food crisis. If the marginal product of additional workers applied to a fixed quantity of land were constant, then world food production could be expanded in proportion to the increase in population merely by keeping the same proportion of the population on farms. As it is, diminishing returns mean an inexorable decline in the marginal product of each additional laborer as an expanding population is applied, with static techniques, to a fixed world supply of agricultural land.[9]"

9. Richard, G. Lipsey, *Introduction to Positive Economics,* 3rd edition p. 216.

Thus, it should not be understood that because of diminishing returns there can be no hopes for raising the living standards of mankind, especially of the people in developing countries. Owing to the gloomy prognosis about the future of mankind made by the classical economists, especially Thomas Malthus, on the basis of diminishing returns, the subject of economics came to be called as a **dismal science.** However, to predict such a gloomy prospects for the future of mankind on the basis of law of diminishing returns is wholly unwarranted. Some people have misunderstood the law and have asserted that as the population will increase, the quantity of land remaining unchanged, the productivity per person will decline. But this is quite wrong. Law of diminishing returns, as stated above, has a great provision that technology, equipment, etc. remain the same. In the present-day developed countries, though population has increased, agricultural productivity has greatly gone up instead of diminishing. This is so because present-day developed countries have made an impressive progress in technical knowledge, resulting in new and superior machinery and other equipment, and the use of fertilizers. Capital equipment per worker engaged in agriculture has greatly increased. As a result, agricultural productivity has registered a phenomenal increase in the present-day advanced countries.

On the other hand, developing countries have not made much progress in technical knowledge and capital accumulation. Therefore, they do use sufficient capital and equipment like machinery, tools, fertilizers, etc. It is no wonder, therefore, that agricultural productivity in them has not risen significantly. In fact, marginal productivity of labour has gone down. The phenomenon of disguised unemployment found in agriculture of developing countries reveals that marginal productivity of a worker is zero or nearly zero. It is thus clear that actual experience regarding the behaviour of agricultural productivity in both developed and developing countries is in no way a contradiction to the law of diminishing returns, the operation of which is subject to the condition that technical knowledge, capital equipment and other aids of production remain the same.Even in developing countries such as India where new agricultural technology represented by the use of HYV seeds, fertilizers, irrigation has been adopted, the productivity of labour and land has greatly increased which is described as Green Revolution. For India attaining food self-sufficiency, credit goes to the adoption of this new agricultral technology.

Of course, if we fail to improve our technology sufficiently and to bring about rapid capital accumulation, diminishing returns would assert themselves and create the problems of food crisis and starvation. We therefore conclude ***"unless there is continual and rapidly accelerating improvement in the techniques of production, the population explosion must bring with it declining living standards over much of the world and the eventual widespread famine."***[10]

Numerical Problem 1 : *The production function for the firm is* $Q = 20\,K^{0.5}L^{0.5}$ *Suppose the quantity of capital is fixed at* 100. *If the wage rate is Rs. 20 and price of output is Rs 2 per unit, determine the optimal use of labour input.*

Solution. In order to determine the optimal use of labour we first find out marginal product of labour from the given production function. Taking the first derivative of the given production function with respect to labour we have

The given production function is

$$Q = 20\,K^{0.5}L^{0.5}$$

$$MP_L = \frac{dQ}{dL} = 20 \times \frac{1}{2} K^{\frac{1}{2}} L^{-\frac{1}{2}}$$

10. R.G. Lipsey, *op.cit.*

$$MP_L = 10\,K^{\frac{1}{2}}L^{-\frac{1}{2}}$$

$$= 10\,\frac{\sqrt{K}}{\sqrt{L}}$$

Since $K = 100$ we have

$$MP_L = 10\,\frac{\sqrt{100}}{\sqrt{L}}$$

$$MRP_L = \text{Price of output} \times MP_L$$

$$= 2 \times 10\,\frac{\sqrt{100}}{\sqrt{L}} = 20\frac{\sqrt{100}}{\sqrt{L}}$$

To determine optimal use of labour we equate MRP_L = wage rate. Thus

$$20\frac{\sqrt{100}}{\sqrt{L}} = 20$$

$$\frac{200}{\sqrt{L}} = 20$$

$$= \sqrt{L} = \frac{200}{20} = 10$$

$$= L = 100$$

Numerical Problem 2. *The following short-run production function of a firm is given*

$$Q = 10L - 0.5L^2$$

Where Q = output and L is the variable input. Price at which output can be sold is Rs 10 per unit and given wage rate of labour for the firm is Rs 20 per labour unit.

(1) find the marginal revenue product function of labour.

(2) What is marginal factor cost function of labour.

(3) Determine the optimum amount of labour used if the objective of the firm is to maximize profits.

Solution :

The given short-run production function is

$$Q = 10\,L - 0.5L^2$$

(1) To find the marginal revenue product of labour (MRP_L) we have to first find out the total revenue generated by labour. Thus

$$TR = PQ = 10.P.\,L - 0.5P.\,L^2$$

The given price of output (P) = Rs 10. Therefore

$$TR = 10.10.L - 0.5.10\,L^2$$

$$= 100L - 5L^2$$

$$MRP_L = \frac{\Delta\,TR}{\Delta\,L} = 100 - 10L$$

(2) To obtain marginal factor cost function of labour we first find total factor cost function of labour. The given wage rate of labour is Rs 20 per unit of labour. Thus

$$\text{Total Factor cost } (TFC_L) = 10.W.L - 0.5\,WL^2$$
$$= 10 \times 20\,L - 0.5 \times 20L^2$$
$$= 200L - 10L^2$$

$$MFC_L = \frac{\Delta\,TFC}{\Delta\,L} = 200 - 20L$$

(3) In order to maximize profits, the firm will equate MRP_L with MFC_L. Thus,

$$MRP_L = MFC_L$$
$$100 - 10L = 200 - 20L$$
$$20L - 10L = 200 - 100 = 100$$
$$10L = 100$$
$$L = 10$$

Thus optimum use of labour is to employ 10 units of labour.

QUESTIONS FOR REVIEW

1. What is production function? Distinguish between fixed inputs and variable inputs. Is the distinction between the two relevant in the long run ?
2. Explain the concept of production function? Why is it useful in the analysis of firm's behaviour?
3. What is the relationship between marginal product and average product of labour (or a variable input) ?
4. State the law of diminishing returns. Why does diminishing marginal returns to a variable input occur eventually? Can they become negative? If so, why ?
5. What are the three stages of short-run production function? Why does it not make any economic sense to produce in stage 1 or stage 3 ?
6. How is the law of diminishing returns reflected in the shape of the total product curve? If the total product increases at a decreasing rate from the very beginning what would be the shapes of corresponding marginal and average product curves ?
7. Explain the law of diminishing returns. Mention on what assumptions it is based. How Malthus used the law to predict gloomy forecast for future mankind? What mistake did he commit in making this gloomy forecast ?
8. If the law of diminishing marginal product did not hold, the world's food supply could be grown in a flower pot. Discuss.
9. The marginal revenue product function of factor is the demand curve for that factor. Explain
10. Fill in the blanks in the following table:

Number of variable input	*Total output (number of units)*	*Marginal product of the variable input*	*Average product of the variable input*
3	–	18	30
4	–	20	–
5	130	–	–
6	–	5	–
7	–	–	19½

Does the production function stated in the table given above exhibit diminishing returns? If so, at what number of units of the variable input do diminishing marginal returns begin to set in?

11. *As the quantity of a variable input increases, explain why the point where marginal product begins to decline is reached before the point where average product begins to decline. Also explain why*

the point where average product begins to decline is reached before the point where ***total output*** *begins to decline.*

[**Hints:** This is due to the usual average-marginal relationship in the production process. Due to the operation of diminishing marginal returns, marginal returns begin to decline at some point but for some range though diminishing it remains greater than average product. Therefore, average product continues to increase. Only when in its diminishing phase marginal product becomes less than average product, average product starts declining. That is why marginal product curve cuts the average product curve at the latter's highest point.

Marginal product continues diminishing after it is equal to the maximum average product but remains positive which causes the total output to continue increasing. Only when marginal product becomes zero, the total product reaches its maximum level. As a result, total output continues increasing after the maximum average product point and begins to decline only when marginal product becomes negative.]

12. Consider the following short-run production function (where X is the variable input and Q is the output).

$$Q = 6X^2 - 0.2X^3$$

(a) *Determine the marginal product function (MP_x).*

(b) *Determine the average product function (AP_x).*

(c) *Find the value of X that maximises Q.*

(d) *Find the value of X at which its average product takes on its maximum value.*

13. What is meant by output elasticity of an input ? Given the following production function, find the output elasticities of labour and capital.

$$Q = 50\,L^{0.70}\,K^{0.40}$$

where Q = output, L = labour and K = capital

14. Explain the condition for optimum use of a variable factor if the objective of the firm is to maximise profits.

15. Explain what considerations manager of a firm will keep in view while hiring labour. Explain and illustrate graphically how much labour a firm will employ to maximise profits ?

CHAPTER

19

Production Function with Two Variable Inputs

In the last chapter we explained the production function with a single variable factor, holding other factors constant.In the present chapter we are concerned with the analysis of production function when two variable factors as used in the production process. For the analysis of a production function with two variable factors we make use of a concept called *isoquants* or *iso-product curves* which are similar to indifference curves of the theory of consumption.

ISOQUANTS

Isoquants, which are also called equal-product curves, are similar to the indifference curves of the theory of consumer's behaviour. An isoquant represents all those input combinations which are capable of producing the same level of output. The isoquants are thus contour lines which trace the loci of equal outputs. Since an isoquant represents those combinations of inputs which are capable of producing an equal quantity of output, the producer would be indifferent between them. Therefore, another name which is often given to the equal product curves is *production-indifference curves.*

The concept of isoquant can be easily understood from Table 19.1. It is presumed that two factors labour and capital are being employed to produce a product. Each of the factor combinations *A*, *B*, *C*, *D* and *E* produces the same level of output, say 100 units. To start with, factor combination *A* consisting of 1 unit of labour and 12 units of capital produces the given 100 units of output. Similarly, combination *B* consisting of 2 units of labour and 8 units of capital, combination *C* consisting of 3 units of labour and 5 units of capital, combination *D* consisting of 4 units of labour and 3 units of capital, combination *E* consisting of 5 units of labour and 2 units of capital are capable of producing the same amount of output, *i.e.,* 100 units. In Fig. Fig.19.1 we have plotted all these combinations and by joining them we obtain an isoquant showing that every combination represented on it can produce 100 units of output.

Table 19.1. Factor combinations to produce a given level of output

Factor Combinations	*Labour*	*Capital*
A	1	12
B	2	8
C	3	5
D	4	3
E	5	2

Though isoquants are similar to the indifference curves of the theory of consumer's behaviour, there is one important difference between the two. An indifference curve represents all those combinations of two goods which provide the same satisfaction or utility to a consumer but no attempt is made to specify the level of utility it stands for in exact quantitative terms. This is so because the cardinal measurement of satisfaction or utility in unambiguous terms is not possible. That is why we usually label indifference curves by ordinal numbers as I, II, III, etc. indicating that a higher indifference curve represents a higher level of satisfaction than a lower

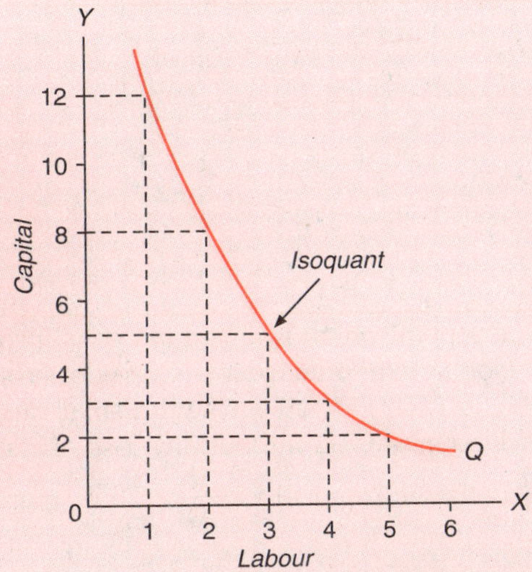

Fig. 19.1. *Isoquant*

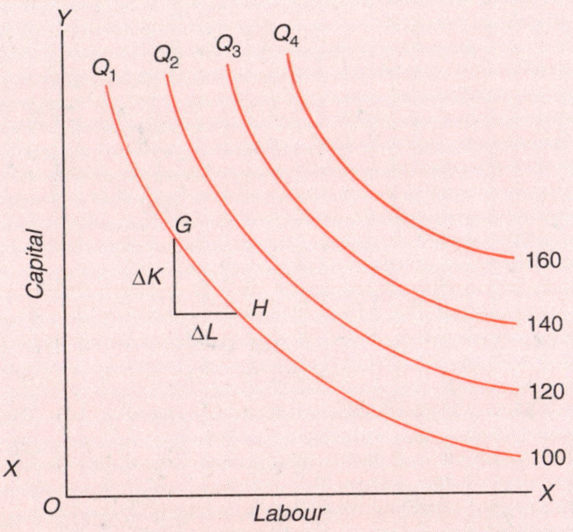

Fig. 19.2. *Isoquant Map*

one, but the information as to by how much one level of satisfaction is greater than another is not provided. On the other hand, we can label isoquants in the physical units of output without any difficulty. Production of a good being a physical phenomenon lends itself easily to absolute measurement in physical units. Since each isoquant represents specified level of production, it is possible to say by how much one isoquant indicates greater or less production than another. In Fig. 19.2 we have drawn *an isoquant-map or equal-product map* with a set of four isoquants which represent 100 units, 120 units, 140 units and 160 units of output respectively. Then, from this set of isoquants it is very easy to judge by how much production level on one isoquant curve is greater or less than another.

MARGINAL RATE OF TECHNICAL SUBSTITUTION

Marginal rate of technical substitution in the theory of production is similar to the concept of marginal rate of substitution in the indifference curve analysis of consumer's demand. Marginal rate of technical substitution indicates the rate at which factors can be substituted at the margin without altering the level of output. More precisely, ***marginal rate of technical substitution of labour for capital may be defined as the number of units of capital which can be replaced by one unit of labour, the level of output remaining unchanged.*** The concept of marginal rate of technical substitution can be easily understood from Table 19.2.

Each of the input combinations *A*, *B*, *C*, *D* and *E* yields the same level of output. Moving down the table from combination *A* to combination *B*, 4 units of capital are replaced by 1 unit of labour in the production process without any change in the level of output. Therefore, marginal rate of technical substitution of labour for capital is 4 at this stage. Switching from input combination *B* to input combination C involves the replacement of 3 units of capital by an additional unit of labour, output remaining the same. Thus, the marginal rate of technical substitution is now 3. Likewise, marginal rate of technical substitution of labour for capital between factor combinations C and D is 2, and between factor combinations D and E is 1.

Table 19.2. Marginal Rate of Technical Substitution

Factor Combinations	Units of Labour (L)	Units of Capital (K)	MRTS of L for K
A	1	12	
B	2	8	4
C	3	5	3
D	4	3	2
E	5	2	1

The marginal rate of technical substitution at a point on an isoquant (an equal product curve) can be known from the slope of the isoquant at that point. Consider a small movement down the equal product curve from G to H in Fig. 19.2 where a small amount of capital, say ΔK is replaced by an amount of labour say ΔL without any loss of output. The slope of the isoquant curve Q_1 at point G is therefore equal to $\frac{\Delta K}{\Delta L}$. Thus, marginal rate of technical substitution of labour for capital is equal to slope which is measured by $\frac{\Delta K}{\Delta L}$.

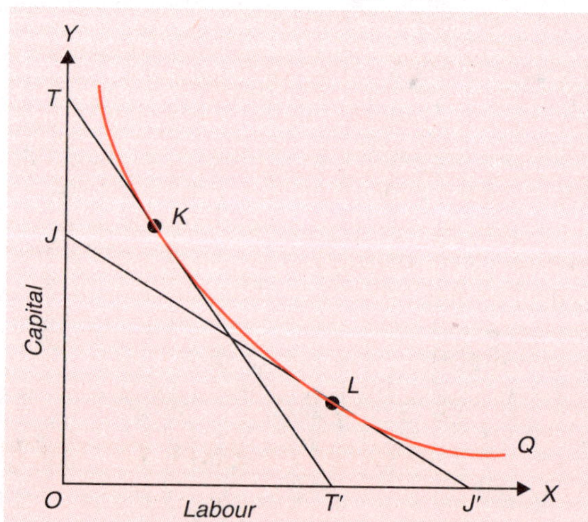

Fig. 19.3. *MRTS is given by the slope of the equal product curve.*

Slope of the isoquant at a point and hence the marginal rate of technical substitution (*MRTS*) between factors can also be known by the slope of the tangent drawn on the isoquant at that point. In Fig. 19.3 the tangent TT' is drawn at point K on the given equal product curve Q. The slope of the tangent TT' is equal to $\frac{OT}{OT'}$. Therefore, the marginal rate of substitution at point K on the equal product curve Q in Fig. 19.3 is equal to $\frac{OT}{OT'}$. JJ' is the tangent at point L on the isoquant Q. Therefore, the marginal rate of technical substitution of labour for capital at point L is equal to OJ/OJ'.

An important point to be noted about the marginal rate of technical substitution is that it is equal to the ratio of the marginal physical products of the two factors. Since, by definition, output remains constant on an isoquant, the loss in physical output from a small reduction in capital will be equal to the gain in physical output from a small increment in labour. The loss in output is equal to the marginal physical product of capital (*MP*) multiplied by the amount of reduction in capital. The gain in output is equal to the marginal physical product of labour (*MP*) multiplied by the increment in labour.

Accordingly, along an isoquant

$$\Delta K.MP_k + \Delta L \,.\, MP_L = 0$$

$$\Delta K \times MP_k = \Delta L \times MP_L$$

$$\frac{\Delta K}{\Delta L} = \frac{MP_L}{MP_K}$$

But $\frac{\Delta K}{\Delta L}$, by definition, is the marginal rate of technical substitution of labour for capital

$$\therefore \qquad MRTS_{LK} = \frac{MP_L}{MP_K}$$

We thus see that marginal rate of technical substitution of labour for capital is the ratio of marginal physical products of the two factors.

Diminishing Marginal Rate of Technical Substitution. An important characteristic of marginal rate of technical substitution is that it diminishes as more and more of labour is substituted for capital. In other words, as the quantity of labour used is increased and the quantity of capital employed is reduced, the amount of capital that is required to be replaced by an additional unit of labour so as to keep the output constant will diminish. This is known as the *Principle of Diminishing Marginal Rate of Technical Substitution*. This principle of diminishing marginal rate of technical substitution is merely an extension of the Law of Diminishing Returns to the relation between the marginal physical productivities of the two factors. Along an isoquant as the quantity of labour is increased and the quantity of capital is reduced, the marginal physical productivity of labour diminishes and the marginal physical productivity of capital increases. Therefore, less and less of capital is required to be substituted by an additional unit of labour so as to maintain the same level of output.

It may also be noted that the rate at which the marginal rate of technical substitution diminishes is a measure of the extent to which the two factors can be substituted for each other. The smaller the rate at which the marginal rate of technical substitution diminishes, the greater the degree of substitutability between the two factors. If the marginal rate of substitution between any two factors does not diminish and remains constant, the two factors are *perfect substitutes* of each other.

GENERAL PROPERTIES OF ISOQUANTS

The isoquants normally possess properties which are similar to those generally assumed for indifference curves of the theory of consumer's behaviour. Moreover, the properties of isoquants can be proved in the same manner as in the case of indifference curves. The following are the important properties of isoquants.

1. Isoquants, like indifference curves, slope downward from left to right (*i.e.*, they have a negative slope.) This is so because when the quantity of factor, say labour, is increased, the quantity of other capital *i.e.*, capital must be reduced so as to keep output constant on a given isoquant. This downward-sloping property of isoquants follow from a valid assumption that the marginal physical products of factors are *positive*, that is, the use of additional units of factors yield *positive increments* in output. In view of this, when one factor is increased yielding positive marginal products, the other factor must be *reduced* to hold the level of output constant; otherwise the output will increase and we will switch over to a higher isoquant.

The assumption that the marginal physical product of a factor is positive is quite reasonable. In the discussion of the law of variable proportions we saw that in the stage III, when the units of the variable factor, say labour, become excessive, it causes such an overcrowding on a fixed capital equipment (or on a given piece of land if land is the fixed factor) that they obstruct each other resulting in negative marginal products of labour, that is, the use of additional units of labour reduces total output. This could happen but no rational producer who aims to minimise costs or maximise profits will employ units of a factor to the point where its marginal product has become negative because *positive prices* have to be paid for them. Thus, in view of the positive prices that have to be paid for the units of a factor, we rule out the use of the units of the factor that have negative or zero marginal products.

Thus, with labour measured on the *X*-axis and capital on the *Y*-axis, if the isoquant is a horizontal straight line, this would indicate that the marginal products of labour (MP_L) are zero. Likewise, vertical isoquant would indicate marginal products of capital (MP_K) are zero. Further, an upward-sloping isoquant implies that either the marginal products of the two factors are zero or one of the two factors has negative marginal products and the other has positive marginal products. It is also worth noting that the *upward-sloping isoquant implies that the same output can be produced with the use of less of both the factors,* that is, marginal products of at least one factor is negative. In this situation, when every reduction in both the factors used does not affect output, the producer will not reach an equilibrium position. It follows from above that over the economically relevant stage of production when the marginal products of the factors are positive we have *downward-sloping isoquants*.

2. No two isoquants can intersect each other. If the two isoquants, one corresponding to 20 units of output and the other to 30 units of output intersect each other, there will then be a common factor combination corresponding to the point of intersection. It means that the same factor combination which can produce 20 units of output according to one equal product curve can also produce 30 units of output according to the other equal product curve. But this is quite absurd. How can the same factor combination produces two different levels of output, techniques of production remaining unchanged.

3. Isoquants, like indifference curves, are convex to the origin. The convexity of isoquant curves means that as we move down the curve, successively smaller units of capital are required to be substituted by a given increment of labour so as to keep the level of output unchanged. Thus, the convexity of equal product curves is due to the diminishing marginal rate of technical substitution of one factor for the other.

If the isoquants were concave to the origin, it would mean that the marginal rate of technical substitution increased as more and more units of labour substitute capital. This could be valid if the law of increasing returns is applied. Since it is the law of diminishing returns to a factor which is more true of the real world, the principle of diminishing marginal rate of technical substitution generally holds good and it makes the isoquants convex to the origin. We have seen above that marginal rate of technical substitution diminishes because of diminishing marginal returns to a factor as we increase its quantity used. Therefore, ***the convexity of isoproduct curves implies the diminishing returns to a variable factor.*** We have seen that there are diminishing returns to a factor because of the fact that different factors are *imperfect substitutes* of each other in the production of a good.

In general, convexity of isoquants implies that it ***becomes progressively more difficult or harder to substitute one factor for another*** as we move along an isoquant and increase the use of one factor substituting the other factor. Thus, when it is difficult to substitute a factor, say labour, for capital, it will then require a relatively larger amount of labour to replace one unit of capital, level of output being held constant.

The Rationale for Convexity of Isoquants

The main economic justification for the convexity of isoquants is that the producer's equilibrium in case of both concave isoquants or linear isoquants cannot occur with both factors used and instead it would occur when only one factor is being employed for production. Therefore, in case of concave or linear isoquants, we would have *corner solution* where only one factor is being used for the production of a commodity. Since in practice more than one factor is used for production, both in the agricultural and industrial sectors, the isoquants are actually convex to the origin.

The convexity of isoquants follows from a valid assumption that marginal physical products of factors are positive, that is, the use of additional units of inputs (factors) yields positive increments in output. In view of this, when only factor with positive marginal products is increased, the other factor in the production function must be reduced so as to keep the level of output constant, otherwise total output will increase and we will switch over to a higher isoquant. The assumption that marginal physical product of a factor is positive is quite reasonable. In the discussion of the law of variable proportions, we saw that in stage III when the amount of a variable factor, labour, becomes excessive, it causes such an overcrowding in a given industrial plant or a given piece of agricultural land that workers obstruct each other in production resulting in negative marginal product. Of course, this could happen but no rational producer will employ a factor to the point where its marginal product has become negative (or even zero). This is because factors have to be paid *positive prices* and if they yield negative marginal returns, the producer will have to incur losses if he employs them. Thus, in view of the positive prices that have to be paid to the factors, we rule out the use of factors which have negative or zero marginal products.

Isoquants of Perfect Substitutes and Complements

There are two exceptions to this general property of the convexity of isoquants. One is the case of factors which are perfect substitutes of each other. When the two factors are perfect substitutes of each other, then each of them can be used equally well in place of the other. For all intents and purposes, they can be regarded as the same factor. Therefore, the marginal rate of technical substitution between two perfect substitute factors remains constant. Since marginal rate of technical substitution remains the same throughout, the isoquants of perfect substitutes are straight lines, as shown in Fig. 19.4 instead of being convex to the origin.

Another exceptional case is of factors which are *perfect complements* and for which the isoquants are right-angled as shown in Fig. 19.5. The perfect complementary factors are those which are jointly used for production in a *fixed proportion*. Thus, in Fig. 19.5, *OA* of factor *X* and *OB* of factor *Y* are used to yield a level of output represented by isoquant Q_1. An increase in one factor without the required proportional increase in the other factor will yield no additional output whatsoever. That is why, the isoquant is right-angled (with two arms, one is a vertical straight line and the other is a horizontal straight line) at the combination consisting of a given proportion of the two factors.

Consider isoquant or equal product curve Q_1 in Fig. 19.5 where output can be produced by the combination *H* consisting of *OA* of factor *X* and *OB* of factor *Y*. If now the amount of factor *X* is increased beyond OA without the increase in the factor *Y*, output will not rise and hence the lower portion of isoquant is a horizontal straight line. Likewise, if the amount of factor *Y* is increased beyond *OB* without the increase in factor *X*, the output will remain the same and hence the upper portion of the equal product curve is a vertical straight line. In case of perfect complementary factors, output can be increased only by increasing the amount of both the factors by the required given proportion. Thus in Fig. 19.5 if the amount of factor X is increased to OR (which is twice OA), then the amount of factor Y will have to increase by OS (which is twice OB) so that we have the same factor proportion. Output also increases by the same proportion as the increase in factors and we have a new isoquant Q_2 . It should be noted that no substitution is possible in case of perfect complements.

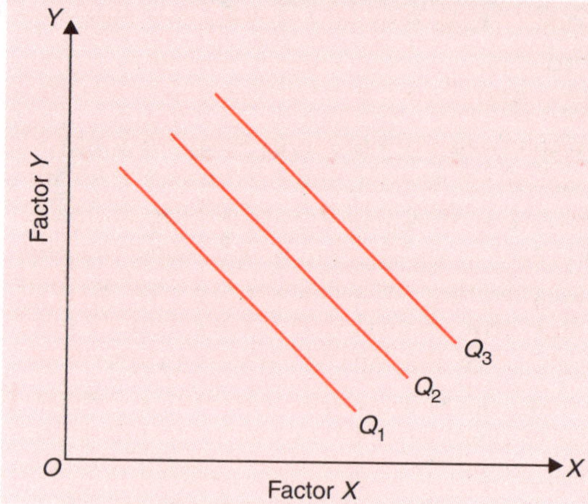

Fig. 19.4. *Perfect Substitutes*

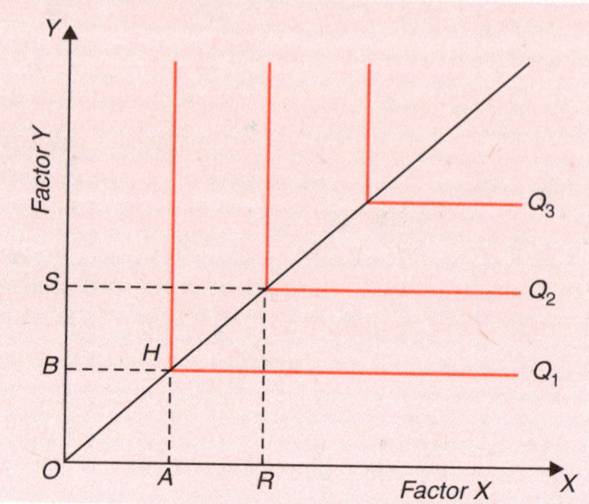

Fig.19.5. *Perfect Complementary Factors*

Fixed-Proportion and Variable-Proportion Production Functions

Production function is of two qualitatively different forms. It may be either ***fixed-proportion production function or variable-proportion production function.*** Whether production function is of a fixed-proportions form or a variable-proportions form depends upon whether technical coefficients of production are fixed or variable. The amount of a productive factor that is essential to produce a unit of product is called the technical coefficient of production. For instance, if 25 workers are required to produce 100 units of a product, then 0.25 is the technical coefficient of labour for production. Now, if the technical coefficient of production of labour is fixed, then 0.25 of labour must be used for producing a unit of product and its amount cannot be reduced by using in its place some other factor. Therefore, in case of fixed-proportion production function, the factors or inputs, say labour and capital, must be used in a definite fixed proportion in order to produce a given level of output.

On the other hand, when technical coefficient of production is variable, that is, when the amount of a factor required to produce a unit of product can be varied by substituting in its place some other factor, the production function is of variable proportion form. Therefore, in case of variable-proportion production function, a given amount of a product can be produced by several alternative combinations of factors (inputs). The isoquant map shown in Fig. 19.2 represents variable proportion production function, since each isoquant drawn in it shows that various different combinations of factors, labour and capital, can be used to produce a given level of output. Several commodities in the real world are produced under conditions of variable- proportion production function.

The fixed-proportion production function can also be illustrated by isoquants. As in fixed-proportions production function, the two factors, say capital and labour, must be used in fixed ratio, the isoquants of such a production function are right-angled. Suppose in the production of a commodity, capital-labour ratio that must be used to produce 100 units of output is 2:3. In this case, if with 2 units of capital, 4 units of labour are used, then extra one unit of labour would be wasted; it will not add to total output. The capital-labour ratio must be maintained whatever the level of output. If two hundred units of output are required to be produced, then, given the capital-labour ratio of 2 : 3, 4 units of capital and 6 units of labour will have to be used, if three hundred units of output are to be produced, then 6 units of capital and 9 units of labour will have to be used. Given the capital-labour ratio of 2 : 3, an isoquant map of fixed-proportions production function has been drawn in Fig. 19.6. The slope of the ray *OR* represents the given capital-labour ratio.

It should be noticed that along each isoquant of complements with fixed proportion marginal product of a factor is zero. For instance, if we are at *B* on isoquant of 200, then capital being held constant at 4 units, use of more labour does not make any addition to total output, that is, marginal product of labour is zero. Likewise, if labour is held constant at 6 units, increase in the quantity of capital does not add to output. On the other hand, in a fixed-proportion production function, doubling the quantities of capital and labour at the required ratio doubles the output, trebling their quantities at the required ratio trebles the output.

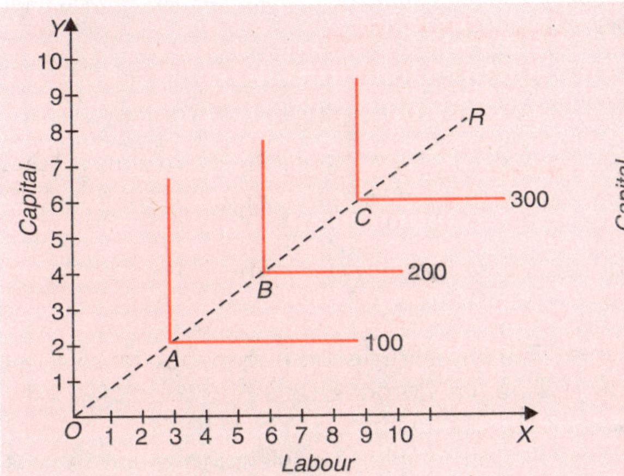

Fig. 19.6. *Isoquant Map of Fixed-Proportion Production Function*

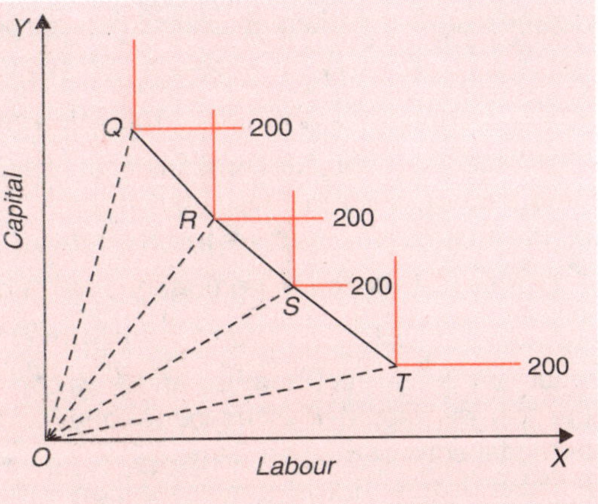

Fig.19.7. *Four Fixed-Proportion Production Functions*

However, in the real world, instead of a single fixed-proportion production process, many (but not infinite) fixed-proportion production processes to produce a commodity are available, each process involves a given fixed factor ratio. Within one production process, no factor substitution is possible. However, different processes use various factors in different proportions, since they involve different fixed-factor ratios. Such a production function of a commodity for which four fixed-proportion processes are available is depicted in Fig. 19.7 where four isoquants representing four processes *i.e.*, four different capital-labour ratios have been drawn and all yield 200 units or output of the commodity. *OQ*, *OR*, *OS* and *OT* are the process-rays whose slopes represent different capital-labour ratios. By joining points *Q*, *R*, *S* and *T* by right-line segments we get a kinked (segmented) line *QRST*, each of the four points on which represents a factor-combination which can produce 200 units of the commodity. The kinked line *QRST* is similar to the ordinary isoquant, but there is an important difference between the two. Whereas every point on the ordinary isoquant is a feasible factor combination which itself is directly capable of producing a specified level of output, but every point on the kinked line *QRST* is not a feasible factor-combination capable of producing 200 units of output. Thus, factor combinations lying between *Q* and *R*, *R* and *S*, and *S* and *T* on the kinked line are not feasible factor combinations and cannot directly produce 200 units of output, for we have assumed that only four factor-combinations *Q*, *R*, *S* and *T* corresponding to four available processes are feasible factor-combinations capable of directly producing 200 units of output.

However, factor ratio corresponding to any point between Q and R, R and S, and S and T can be achieved by properly combining the two production processes. Thus, if factor ratio represented by a point between R and S is to be achieved, it can be done so by using a proper combination of two processes represented by R and S, that is, producing a part of the output with process R and a part with process S.

Linear Homogeneous Production Function

Production function can take several forms but a particular form of production function enjoys wide popularity among the economists. This is a linear homogeneous production function, that is, production function which is homogeneous of the first degree. Homogeneous production function of the first degree implies that if all factors of production are increased in a given proportion, output also increases in the same proportion. Hence linear homogeneous production function represents the case of constant returns to scale. If there are two factors X and Y, then homogeneous production function of the first degree can be mathematically expressed as :

$$mQ = f(mX, mY)$$

where Q stands for the total production and m is any real number.

The above function means that if factors X and Y are increased by m-times, total production Q also increases by m-times. It is because of this that homogeneous function of the first degree yields constant returns to scale.

More generally, a homogeneous production function can be expressed as

$$Qm^k = (mX, mY)$$

where m is any real number and k is constant. This function is homogeneous function of the kth degree. If k is equal to one, then the above homogeneous function becomes homogeneous of the first degree. If k is equal to two, the function becomes homogeneous of the 2nd degree. If k is greater than one, the production function will yield increasing returns to scale. If on the other hand, k is less than 1, it will yield decreasing returns to scale.

Linear homogeneous production function is extensively used in empirical studies by economists. This is because in view of the limited analytical tools at the disposal of the economists, it can be easily handled and used in empirical studies. Further, because of its possessing highly useful economic features and properties, (for instance, constant returns to scale is a very important property of homogeneous production function of the first degree), it is easily used in calculations by computers and on account of this it is extensively employed in linear programming and input-output analysis. Moreover, because of its simplicity and close approximation to reality, it is widely used in model analysis regarding production, distribution and economic growth

As we shall prove in the next chapter, the expansion path of the homogeneous production function of the first degree is always a straight line through the origin. This implies that in case of homogeneous production function of the first degree, with constant relative factor prices, optimal proportions between the factors that will be used for production will always be the same whatever the amount of output to be produced. Because of the simple nature of the homogeneous production function of the first degree, the task of the entrepreneur is quite simple and convenient; he requires only to find out just one optimum factor proportions and so long as relative factor prices remain constant, he has not to make any fresh decision regarding factor proportions to be used as he expands his level of production. Moreover, the use of the same optimum factor proportions (with constant relative factor prices) at different levels of output in homogeneous production function of the first degree is also very useful in input-output analysis. Homogeneous production function of the first degree, which, as said above, implies constant returns to scale, has been actually found in agriculture as well as in many manufacturing industries. In India, farm management studies have been made for various States and data have been collected for agricultural inputs and outputs. Analysing the data collected in these farm management studies, Dr. A.M. Khusro reached the conclusion that constant returns to scale prevailed in Indian agriculture[1]. Likewise, empirical studies conducted in the United States and Britain have found that many manufacturing industries are characterized by a long phase of constant long-run average cost (*LAC*) curve which again implies constant returns to scale and homogeneous production function of the first degree.

COBB-DOUGLAS PRODUCTION FUNCTION

Many economists have studied actual production functions and have used statistical methods to find out relations between changes in physical inputs and physical outputs. A most familiar empirical production function found out by statistical methods is the *Cobb-Douglas production function.* Originally, Cobb-Douglas production function was applied not to the production process of an individual firm but to the whole of the manufacturing industry. Output in this function was thus originally whole manufacturing production. In Cobb-Douglas production function, there are two inputs, labour and capital, Cobb-Douglas production function takes the following mathematical form:

$$Q = AL^{\alpha}K^{\beta}$$

where Q is the manufacturing output, L is the quantity of labour employed, K is the quantity of capital employed, and A and α are positive constants. Roughly speaking, Cobb-Douglas production function found that about 75% of the increase in manufacturing production was due to the labour input and the remaining 25% was due to the capital input. It is evident from the form of Cobb-Douglas production function that it is a multiplicative production function which implies that both the factors are required to produce an output. That is, if amount of one factor is zero, no output can be produced.

It is important to note that originally it was found that the sum of exponents of Cobb-Douglas production was equal to one, that is, $\alpha + \beta = 1$. However, from further research and analysis it was generalized and found that the sum of exponents $(\alpha + \beta)$ could be equal to one, more than one and less than one. As we shall prove later, when sum of exponents $(\alpha + \beta)$ is equal to one, constant returns to scale (i.e., linear homogeneous production function) occur, when $\alpha + \beta > 1$, we get increasing returns to scale and when $\alpha + \beta < 1$, decreasing returns to scale occur.

Essential Features of Cobb-Douglas Production Function

Let us explain some of the essential features of linear homogeneous production function with special reference to Cobb-Douglas production, which is an important example of linear homogeneous production function.

Average Product of Factors in Cobb-Douglas Production Function. The first important feature of Cobb-Douglas production function when the sum of its exponents is equal to one (*i.e.*, $\alpha + \beta = 1$) and therefore it is linear homogeneous production function is that the *average and marginal products of factors depend upon the ratio in which factors are combined for the production of a commodity.*

Linear Cobb-Douglas function can be written as

$$Q = A\,L^{\alpha}K^{1-\alpha}, \qquad (\alpha + 1 - \alpha = 1)$$

Average product of labour can be obtained from dividing the production function by the amount of labour L. Thus,

1. See his article "Returns to Scale in Indian Agriculture", *The Indian Journal of Agricultural Economics*, Vol. XIX, July-Dec. 1964, reprinted in "*Readings in Agricultural Development*, edited by A.M. Khusro, Allied Publishers, 1968.

$$\text{Average product of labour} = \frac{AL^{\alpha}K^{1-\alpha}}{L} = \frac{AK^{1-\alpha}}{L^{1-a}}$$

$$= A\left(\frac{K}{L}\right)^{1-\alpha}$$

Since A and α are constants, average product of labour will depend on the *ratio of the factors* $\left(\frac{K}{L}\right)$ and will not depend upon the *absolute quantities* of the factors used. Let us take a numerical example: Suppose the constant term A in the Cobb-Douglas production is equal to 50 and constant exponent α is equal to $\frac{1}{2}$ and the quantity of capital used is 8 units and quantity of labour used is 2 so that, we get the capital-labour ratio equal to 4:1. The average product of labour will be equal to:

$$AP_L = A\left(\frac{K}{L}\right)^{1-\alpha}$$

$$= 50\left(\frac{8}{2}\right)^{1-\frac{1}{2}} = 50\times(4)^{\frac{1}{2}} = 50.\sqrt{4} = 100$$

Now, if the quantities of factors used are increased to K = 400 and L = 100, *keeping the factor-ratio constant* at 4:1, the average product of labour will still remain equal to 100.

$$AP_L = A\left(\frac{K}{L}\right)^{1-\alpha} = 50\left(\frac{400}{100}\right)^{\frac{1}{2}} = 50.\sqrt{4} = 100$$

Marginal Product of Factors and Cobb-Douglas Production Function. Like the average product of a factor, the marginal product of a factor of *a linear* Cobb-Douglas production function also depends upon the *ratio of the factors* and is independent of the absolute quantities of the factors used. Note that marginal product of a factor, say labour, is the first derivative of the production function with respect to labour. The marginal product of labour from linear Cobb-Douglas production can be obtained as under:

$$Q = AL^{\alpha}K^{1-\alpha}$$

$$\text{Marginal Product of labour} \frac{dQ}{dL} = A\alpha L^{\alpha-1}K^{1-\alpha}$$

$$= \frac{A\alpha L^{\alpha}k^{1-\alpha}}{L}$$

$$= \frac{A\alpha L^{\alpha-\alpha}K^{1-\alpha}}{L^{1-\alpha}} = \frac{A\alpha K^{1-\alpha}}{L^{1-\alpha}}$$

$$= A\alpha\left(\frac{K}{L}\right)^{1-\alpha}$$

Since A and α are constants, marginal product of labour will depend on captial-labour ratio, that is, capital per worker and is independent of the magnitudes of the factors employed.

Cobb-Douglas Production Function and Law of Diminishing Returns to a Factor. An important feature of Cobb-Douglas production is that in it law of diminishing returns to a variable factor holds. This is shown as under :

Let us consider a Cobb-Douglas production, $Q = AL^{0.75}K^{0.25}$. The first derivative of this function with reference to a factor, say labour (L) which will give us marginal product of labour (MP_L) is given by

$$\frac{\partial Q}{\partial L} = MP_L = 0.75\ AL^{0.75-1}K^{0.25}$$
$$= 075AL^{-0.25}K^{0.25}$$

Now MP_L or $\frac{\partial Q}{\partial L}$ will diminish if its second derivative is negative. Thus taking the second derivative of the given Cobb-Douglas production function with respect to labour we have

$$\frac{\partial^2 Q}{\partial L^2} = -0.25 \times 0.75AL^{-1.25}K^{0.25}$$

Since the second derivative of Cobb-Douglas production with respective to a variable factor (labour) is *negative* marginal returns to labour will be diminishing as more labour is used with a constant amount of capital.

Cobb-Douglas Production Function and Marginal Rate of Substitution. Marginal rate of substitution is an important concept which is extensively used in the analysis of cost-minimizing choice of inputs for producing a given level of output of a commodity. As has been shown above, marginal rate of substitution between factors is equal to the ratio of the marginal physical products of the factors. Therefore, in order to derive marginal rate of substitution from Cobb-Douglas production function we need to obtain the marginal physical products of the two factors from the Cobb-Douglas production function. We now proceed to derive them below:

$$Q = AL^{\alpha}K^{\beta}$$

Differentiating this with respect to L we have

$$\frac{dQ}{dL} = aAL^{\alpha-1}K^{\beta}$$
$$= \frac{a\left(AL^{\alpha}K^{\beta}\right)}{L}$$

Now, $AL^{\alpha}K^{\beta} = Q$. Therefore,

$$\frac{dQ}{dL} = a\left(\frac{Q}{L}\right)$$

$\frac{dQ}{dL}$ represents marginal product of labour and $\frac{Q}{L}$ stands for the average product of labour.

Thus,

$$MP_L = a(AP_L) \quad \text{... } (i)$$

Similarly, by differentiating Cobb-Douglas production function with respect to captial we can show that marginal product of captial,

$$\frac{dQ}{dK} = \beta\frac{Q}{K}$$

or,
$$MP_K = \beta(AP_K) \quad \text{... } (ii)$$

It follows from (*i*) and (*ii*) above, that

$$MRS_{LK} = \frac{MP_L}{MP_K} = \frac{\alpha.Q/L}{\beta.Q/K} = \frac{\alpha}{\beta}\cdot\frac{K}{L} \quad \text{... } (iii)$$

Cobb-Douglas Production Function and Elasticity of Substitution: Now, we can show that in *Cobb-Douglas production function, elasticity of factor substitution* (e_s or σ) *is equal to unity.*

$$e_s \text{ or } \sigma = \frac{\text{Proportionate Change in Capital – Labour Ratio}\left(\frac{K}{L}\right)}{\text{Proportionate Change in } MRS_{LK}}$$

$$e_s \text{ or } \sigma = \frac{d\frac{K}{L}/\frac{K}{L}}{d(MRS_{LK})/MRS_{LK}}$$

Substituting the value of marginal rate of substitution obtained in (*iii*) above we have

$$e_s \text{ or } \sigma = \frac{d\left(\frac{K}{L}\right)/\left(\frac{K}{L}\right)}{d\left(\frac{\alpha}{\beta}.\frac{K}{L}\right)/\left(\frac{\alpha}{\beta}.\frac{K}{L}\right)}$$

Since $\frac{\alpha}{\beta}$ is constant and would not affect the derivative, it can therefore be factored out. Therefore,

$$\sigma = \frac{d\left(\frac{K}{L}\right).\frac{\alpha}{\beta}}{\frac{\alpha}{\beta}.d\left(\frac{K}{L}\right)} = 1$$

Cobb-Douglas Production Function and Returns to Scale

An important property of Cobb-Douglas production function is that the sum of its exponents measures returns to scale. Cobb-Douglas production function in general from, that is, when the sum of exponents is not necessarily equal to zero is given below :

$$Q = AL^{\alpha}K^{\beta}$$

In this production function the sum of exponents ($\alpha + \beta$) measures returns to scale. Multiplying each input, labour (L) and capital (K), by a constant factor g, we have

$$Q' = A(gL)^{\alpha}(gK)^{\beta}$$

$$= g^{\alpha}g^{\beta}\left(AL^{\alpha}K^{\beta}\right)$$

$$= g^{\alpha+\beta}\left(AL^{\alpha}K^{\beta}\right)$$

Expression in bracket, $AL^{\alpha}K^{\beta} = Q$. Therefore

$$Q' = g^{\alpha+\beta}Q$$

This means that when each input is increased by a constant factor g, output Q increases by $g^{\alpha+\beta}$ Now, if $\alpha + \beta = 1$, then in this production function

$$Q' = g^1 Q$$

$$Q' = gQ$$

This is, when $\alpha + \beta = 1$, output (Q) also increases by the some factor g by which both inputs are increased. This implies that production function its *homogenous of first degree or,* in other words, returns to scale are constant.

When $\alpha + \beta > 1$, say it is equal to 2, then, in this production function new output

$$Q' = g^{\alpha+\beta}AL^{\alpha}K^{\beta} = g^2Q$$

In this case, multiplying each input by constant g, then output (Q) increases by g^2, that is by more than g. Therefore, when $\alpha + \beta > 1$, *Cobb-Douglas production function exhibits increasing returns to scale.*

When $\alpha + \beta < 1$, say it is equal to 0.8, then in this production function new output

$$Q' = g^{\alpha+\beta} AL^{\alpha}K^{\beta} = g^{0.8}Q$$

That is, increasing each input by constant factor g will cause output to increase by $g^{0.8}$, that is, less than g. Returns to scale in this case are decreasing.

It therefore follows from above that the sum of the exponents of Cobb-Douglas production function, that is, $\alpha + \beta$ measures returns to scale.

If $\alpha + \beta = 1$, returns to scale are constant.

If $\alpha + \beta > 1$, returns to scale are increasing.

If $\alpha + \beta < 1$, returns to scale are decreasing.

Cobb-Douglas Production Function and Output Elasticities of Factors

Thirdly, the exponents of labour and capital in Cobb-Douglas production function measure output elasticities of labour and capital. Output elasticity of a factor refers to a percentage change in output caused by a given percharge change in a variable factor, other factors and inputs remaining constant. Thus,

$$\text{Output elasticity of labour} = \frac{\partial Q}{Q} \div \frac{\partial L}{L} = \frac{\partial Q}{\partial L} \cdot \frac{L}{Q}$$

$\frac{\partial Q}{\partial L}$ = marginal product of labour and $\frac{Q}{L}$ = average product of labour

$$\text{Thus, output elasticity of labour} = \frac{MP_L}{AP_L}$$

We write Cobb-Douglas production function as under:

$$Q = AL^{\alpha}K^{\beta} \qquad \text{......(1)}$$

Since output elasticity of labour is the ratio of its marginal product to the average product. Therefore, in order to find out the output elasticity of labour in Cobb-Douglas production function we have to first obtain marginal and average products of labour.

Taking the first derivative of the Cobb-Douglas production function with respect to labour:

$$MP_L = \frac{\partial Q}{\partial L} = A\alpha L^{\alpha-1}K^{\beta}$$

Average product of labour in the Cobb-Douglas production function:

$$AP_L = \frac{AL^{\alpha}K^{\beta}}{L}$$

$$= AL^{\alpha-1}K^{\beta}$$

Now, by taking the ratio of marginal and average products of labour we get elasticity of output of labour. Thus

$$E_L = \frac{MP_L}{AP_L} = \frac{A\alpha L^{\alpha-1}K^{\beta}}{AL^{\alpha-1}K^{\beta}}$$

$$= \alpha$$

Thus, output elasticity of labour in Cobb-Douglas production is *constant* and is equal to its exponent α. This means that one percentage increase in labour input results in α increase in output.

Similarly, output elasticity of capital $= \frac{\partial Q}{\partial K} \cdot \frac{K}{Q} = \frac{MP_K}{AP_K}$

We take the first derivative of Cobb-Douglas production function ($Q = AL^{\alpha}K^{\beta}$) with respect to capital. Thus

$$MP_K = \beta A L^{\alpha} K^{\beta-1}$$

Average product of capital, $\quad AP_K = \frac{AL^{\alpha}K^{\beta}}{K} = AL^{\alpha}K^{\beta-1}$

Output elasticity of capital, $E_K = \frac{\beta A L^{\alpha} K^{\beta-1}}{AL^{\alpha}K^{\beta-1}} = \beta$

Thus in Cobb-Douglas production function the exponents of inputs, labour and capital, measure their elasticities of output respectively.

Note that if output elasticity of a factor, that is, the value of α or β above is less than one, this will show diminishing marginal returns to a factor. Thus, if the value of α, that is, output elasticity of labour is less then one (say, it is equal to 0.7), this will mean, for example, one per cent increase in labour will cause 0.7 per cent increase in output. Therefore, when in Cobb-Douglas production function the sum of exponents ($\alpha + \beta$) equals one, then the individual values of exponents α and β labour and capital respectively are less than one and Cobb-Douglas production function shows diminishing returns to a variable factor.

Cobb-Douglas Production Function and Euler Theorem

Cobb-Douglas production function, $Q=AL^{\alpha}K^{\beta}$ where $\alpha + \beta = 1$ helps to prove Euler theorem. According to Euler theorem, total output Q is exhausted by the distributive shares of all factors when each factor is paid equal to its marginal physical product. We give below a formal proof of it

As we saw above,

$$MP_L = A\alpha\left(\frac{K}{L}\right)^{\beta} \qquad \dots (1)$$

fiberise,

$$MP_K = A\beta\left(\frac{L}{K}\right)^{\alpha} \qquad \dots (2)$$

According to Euler theorem, if production function is homogeneous of first degree, then

$$\text{Total output, } Q = L.MP_L + K.MP_K.$$

Substituting the values of MP_L and MP_K we have

$$Q = L.A\alpha\left(\frac{K}{L}\right)^{\beta} + K.A\beta\left(\frac{L}{K}\right)^{\alpha}$$

$$Q = A\alpha L^{1-\beta}K^{\beta} + A\beta L^{\alpha}K^{1-\alpha} \qquad \dots (3)$$

Now, in Cobb-Douglas production function with constant returns to scale, $a + b = 1$ and therefore $a = 1 - b$, and $b = 1 - a$. Substituting these in equation (3) we have

$$Q = AaL^{\alpha}K^{\beta} + AbL^{\alpha}K^{\beta}$$

$$= AL^{\alpha}K^{\beta}(\alpha + \beta)$$

Since $\alpha + \beta = 1$, we have

$$Q = AL^{\alpha}K^{\beta}$$

$$= Q.$$

Thus, in Cobb-Douglas production with $\alpha + \beta = 1$ if wage rate $= MP_L$ and rate of return on capital $(K) = MP_K$, then total output will be exhausted.

Cobb-Douglas Production Function in the Extended Form

Cobb-Douglas production function can be extended to include more than two factors. For example, agricultural production depends not only on labour and capital used but also on the use of other inputs such as land, irrigation, fertilisers. Incorporating these inputs in the Cobb-Douglas production function we have:

$$Q = AL^a K^{b_1} D^{b_2} G^{b_3} F^{b_4}$$

where Q stands for output, L and K for labour and capital respectively, a and b are exponents of labour and capital respectively. D stands for land, G stands for irrigation, F for fertiliser and b_2, b_3, b_4 are exponents of land, irrigation and, fertilisers respectively.

The above Cobb-Douglas Production can be estimated by regression analysis by first converting it into the following log form.

$$\log Q = \log A + a \log L + b_1 \log K + b_2 \log D + b_3 \log G + b_4 \log F$$

Cobb-Douglas production function in log form is a linear function and therefore it can be estimated by least squares regression technique.

Cobb-Douglas production function is used in empirical production studies to estimate returns to scale in various industries as to whether they are increasing, constant or decreasing. Further, Cobb-Douglas production function is also frequently used to estimate output elasticities of labour and capital.

ELASTICITY OF TECHNICAL SUBSTITUTION (BETWEEN FACTORS)

In the theory of production, we are concerned with the elasticity of substitution between factors (or inputs) in the production of goods. Thus, in the theory of production we are concerned with what may be called *elasticity of technical substitution*.

As seen above, marginal rate of technical substitution (*MRTS*) of factor X for factor Y declines as factor X is substituted for factor Y along an isoquant. In other words, marginal rate of technical substitution is different at different factor-proportions (*i.e.*, input ratios) used in the production of a good. This responsiveness of the proportions or ratios in which factors (or inputs) are used as there is a movement along an isoquant may be compared with the change in production possibilities as measured by the change in the marginal rate of technical substitution. ***The relative change in the factor-proportions (or input ratios) as a consequence of the relative change in the marginal rate of technical substitution is known as elasticity of substitution between factors.***

The concept of elasticity of substitution has been widely discussed in economic literature in connection with the substitution between labour and capital. Therefore, we shall also explain the concept of elasticity of substitution with reference to capital and labour as factors of production. If K stands for the quantity of capital, L for the quantity of labour and σ for the elasticity of substitution, then in accordance with the above definition, elasticity of substitution of capital for labour can be expressed as follows:

$$\sigma = \frac{\text{proportionate change in the ratio of inputs } (K \text{ and } L) \text{ used}}{\text{proportionate change in the marginal rate of technical substitution of } L \text{ for } K}$$

$$= \frac{\text{proportionate change in } K/L}{\text{proportionate change in } MRTS_{LK}}$$

$$= \frac{\dfrac{\Delta(K/L)}{K/L}}{\Delta(MRTS_{LK})/(MRTS_{LK})}$$

$$= \frac{\Delta(K/L)}{K/L} \cdot \frac{MRTS_{LK}}{\Delta(MRTS_{LK})}$$

$$= \frac{\Delta(K/L)}{\Delta(MRTS_{LK})} \cdot \frac{MRTS_{LK}}{K/L}$$

In order to understand the concept of elasticity of substitution, consider Fig. 19.8 where an isoquant or equal product curve q has been drawn. It will be seen that a point A on the given isoquant q, the capital-labour ratio used *is* K_1/L_1 which is equal to the slope of the ray OA. As labour is substituted for capital and therefore we move down along the isoquant q from point A to B, capital-labour ratio used is changed to K_2/L_2 which is equal to the slope of the ray OB. If further substitution of labour for capital takes place and we come down to point C on the isoquant q, capital-labour ratio further falls to K_3/L_3 which is equal to the slope of the ray OC. It is therefore clear that as we substitute more labour for capital along the isoquant, capital-labour ratio is decreasing.

Now, as we have already seen, marginal rate of technical substitution at point A is given by the slope of the isoquant at that point (which is equal to the slope of the tangent t_1/t_1 drawn at that point). At point B, the $MRTS_{LK}$ is equal to the slope of tangent t_2/t_2 and at point C, the $MRTS_{LK}$ is equal to the slope of tangent t_3/t_3. It will be seen that the slope of tangent t_2/t_2 is less than that of t_1/t_1; slope of t_3/t_3 is less than that of t_2/t_2.

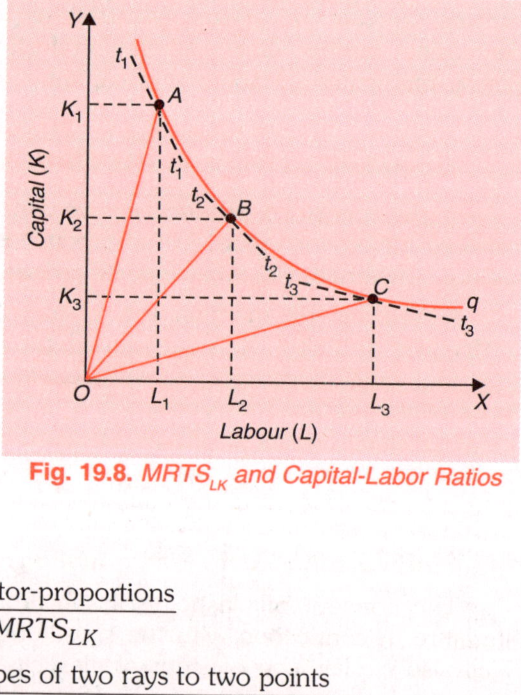

Fig. 19.8. *$MRTS_{LK}$ and Capital-Labor Ratios*

It follows from above that geometrically the elasticity of substitution between factors is the ratio of proportionate change in the slopes of two rays from the origin to the two points on an isoquant to the proportionate change in the slopes of isoquants at those points. Thus

$$\sigma_{LK} = \frac{\text{proportionate change in the factor-proportions}}{\text{proportionate change in } MRTS_{LK}}$$

$$= \frac{\text{proportionate change in the slopes of two rays to two points}}{\text{porportionate change in the slopes of the tangents drawn to the isoquants at these points}}$$

Convexity of Isoquants and Elasticity of Substitution. The magnitude of the elasticity of substitution varies inversely with the curvature of the isoquants. The greater the convexity of isoquants, the less will be the substitution elasticity and *vice versa*. In the extreme case when the two factors are perfect complements and their isoquants are right-angled, the substitution elasticity between them is zero. On the other extreme, when the two factors are perfect substitutes and the isoquants between them are straight lines, substitution elasticity between them is equal to infinity. Moreover, since there is inverse relationship between marginal rate of technical substitutor and factor-ratio (as marginal rate of technical substitution of labour for capital *falls*, the labour-capital ratio *increases*), the elasticity of substitution is always negative.

Elasticity of Substitution and Factor-Price Ratio. Since, in equilibrium position the marginal rate of technical substitution is equal to the ratio of factor prices, the marginal rate of substitution in the formula for elasticity of substitution may therefore be replaced by the ratio of factor-prices.

Let r represent price of capital and w represent wage rate or price of labour. Thus,

$$\sigma_{LK} = \frac{\text{proportionate change in capital-labor ratio}}{\text{proportionate change in the ratio of } r/w}$$

$$\sigma = \frac{\Delta(K/L)}{K/L} \div \frac{\Delta(r/w)}{(r/w)} = \frac{\Delta(K/L)}{(K/L)} \cdot \frac{(r/w)}{\Delta(r/w)}$$

$$\sigma = \frac{\Delta(K/L)}{\Delta(r/w)} \cdot \frac{(r/w)}{(K/L)}$$

The replacement of factor-price ratio for marginal rate of technical substitution in the formula of elasticity of substitution is greatly helpful in practical application of the concept of elasticity of substitution. This is because information regarding prices is more easily available than the information regarding marginal rate of technical substitution. Further, changes in factor-proportions in which factors are used are generally induced by the changes in relative factor prices. The sign of the elasticity of substitution is always negative (unless $\sigma = 0$). This is because *when r/w rises,* capital becomes relatively more costly and as a result it is substituted by labour so that *capital-labour (K/L) decreases.* On the other hand, a fall in *r/w* will lead to the increase in capital-labour (*K/L*) ratio.

Elasticity of factor substitution occupies an important place in the theory of distribution. According to the neo-classical theory of distribution, distributive shares of labour and capital in national income depend on the elasticity of factor substitution.

THE ECONOMIC REGION OF PRODUCTION

Before explaining which factor combination a firm will use for production, it will be useful to demonstrate the region in which the optimal factor combination will lie. The economic theory focuses on only those combinations of factors which are technically efficient and the marginal products of factors are diminishing but positive. According to this, isoquants are sloping downward (*i.e.* their slope is negative) and convex to the origin. However, there are regions in a production function, where isoquants may have positively-sloping segments, that is, bend backwards. In Fig. 19.9 we represent a production function through isoquants and measure labour along the *X*-axis and capital along the *Y*-axis. It will be seen from this figure that above the line *OA* and below the line *OB* slope of the isoquants is *positive* which means that *increases in both capital and labour are required to produce a given fixed quantity of output.* Obviously the production techniques (that is, factor combinations) lying on these positively-sloping segments of the isoquants are technically inefficient. It may be recalled that a technique or factor combination is technically inefficient if it requires more quantity of both the factors for producing a given level of output. The positively-sloping segments of isoquants implies that marginal product of one of the factors has become negative. Thus, above the line *OA*, marginal product of capital has become negative, which means output decreases by using more capital, if the amount of labour is held constant. Therefore, to keep output constant along an isoquant when capital with negative marginal product increases, labour with positive marginal product has to be increased.

On the other hand, to the right of the line *OB*, marginal product of labour becomes negative, which means to keep output constant capital with positive marginal product has to be increased with the increase in labour input having negative marginal product. The lines *OA* and *OB* are called the *ridge lines* which bound a region in which marginal products of the two factors are positive. The ridge line *OA* connects those points of the isoquants where marginal product of capital is zero ($MP_k = 0$). On the other hand, the ridge line *OB* connects those points of the isoquants where marginal product of labour is zero ($MP_L = 0$). Thus, ***the ridge lines are the locus of points of isoquants where marginal product of one of the factors is zero.***

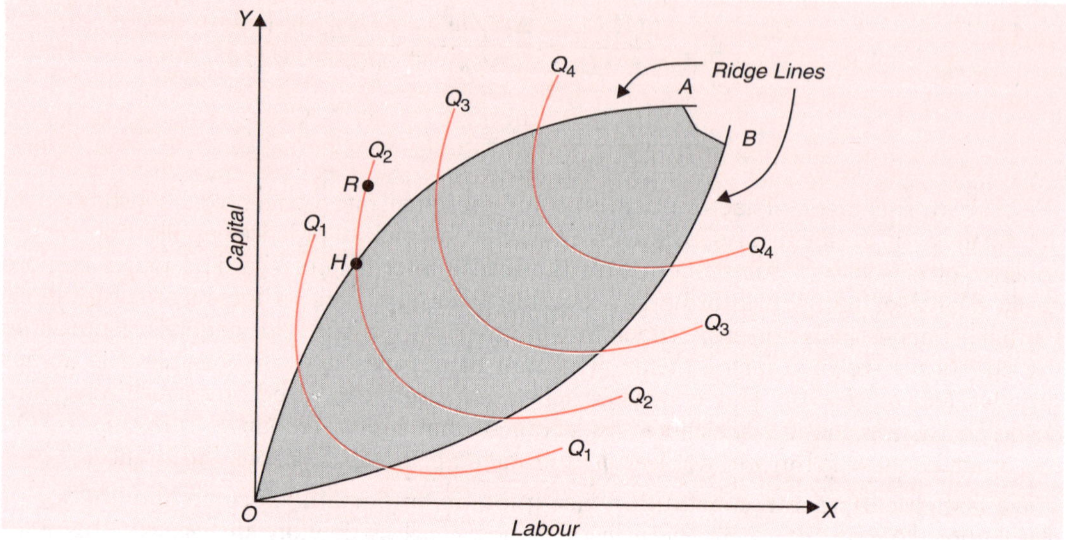

Fig. 19.9. *The Economic Region of Production*

The above analysis also shows that there is a limit to which one factor can be substituted for another. As the substitution of one factor for another is carried out more and more, it becomes progressively more difficult until a point is reached beyond which substitution between factors becomes impossible. As a result, the marginal product of the increasing factor first becomes zero and then it becomes negative so that isoquant becomes positively sloping.

No rational entrepreneur will operate at a point outside the ridge lines since marginal product of one of the factors is negative and production is technically inefficient. In other words, production outside the ridge lines is inefficient because ***same output can be produced with less of the factors which therefore must be cheaper.*** This can be better understood from Fig. 19.9. Consider point *R* on isoquant Q_2. It will be seen that *R* is the point where the isoquant is positively sloping and therefore lies outside the ridge line. It will be seen from Fig. 19.9 that at point *R* to produce output Q_2 requires more of both capital and labour than some other points, such as point *H* on the same isoquant. Since, both capital and labour have to be paid positive prices, it will be cheaper to produce a given quantity of output at point *H* than at point *R*.

Thus, since production outside the ridge lines is technically inefficient and marginal product of one of the factors is negative, no rational entrepreneur will like to operate outside the ridge lines if he aims at minimizing cost to produce a given output. Thus, *regions outside the ridge lines are called regions of economic nonsense.* A rational producer will produce in the region bound by the two ridge lines *OA* and *OB* where the isoquants are negatively sloping and marginal products of factors are diminishing but positive. Therefore, the region bound by the two ridge lines, *OA* and *OB* is called *economic region of production* which has been shaded. Exactly at what point in the economic region, a firm will operate depends on the outlay it has to make on purchasing the factors (or the level of output it wants to produce) and also on prices of the factors.

PRODUCTION FUNCTION AND TECHNOLOGICAL CHANGE

For producing goods a firm tries to use the best available production process, given the state of technological knowledge. ***Advance in technological knowledge that enables the firms to produce more output with the same quantities of inputs is called technical change or technological innovation.*** It is important to note that technical progress changes or shifts the production function. Suppose this year a firm produces output of a product which is given by

$$Q_1 = f(L,K)$$

It uses L units of labour and K units of capital to produce Q_1 units of output. Now suppose in the next year due to *technical change* the firm is able to produce 10 per cent more output from the *given inputs,* the output next year will be

$$Q_2 = 1.1\, f(L,K)$$

The firm's rate of growth of output in our example is 10 per cent as $\dfrac{1.1f(L,K) - f(L,K)}{f(L,K)}$ = 0.1 or 10 per cent.

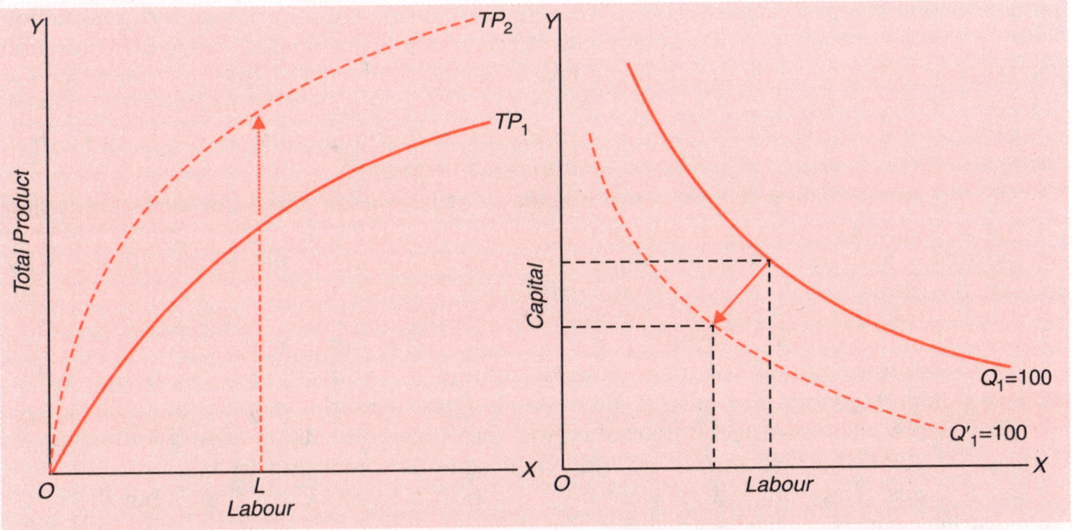

Fig. 19.10. *Upward Shift in the Total Product Curve of Labour due to Technological Change*

Fig. 19.11. *Downward Shift in the Isoquant due to Technological Change*

This increase in productivity in a year is due to technical change. As noted above, the technical change brings about a shift in the production function and will therefore cause a shift in the productivity curve of factors and isoquant as shown in Fig. 19.10 and 19.11. It will be seen from Fig. 19.10 that total product curve of labour shifts upward to a higher level indicating that from a given quantity of labour such OL, the firm can produce more, that is, productivity of labour has risen. In Fig. 19.11 the isoquant Q_1 representing output of 100 units has shifted downward Q'_1 due to technological advancement that shows use of lower amounts of labour and capital can now yield 100 units of output. That is, productivity of both labour and capital or what is often called *total factor productivity* has gone up. In recent years, various empricial studies have been made to measure technical change or growth in productivity. In Table 19.3 we have given the estimates of growth in productivity during 1949-1983 in the USA. The growth in productivity varies in different industries.

It will be seen from Table 19.3 that in the manufacturing sector as a whole in the United States, productivity increased at the rate of 1.1 per cent annum during 1949-1983.

Table 19.3 Industry Annual Rate of Productivity Growth in United States, 1949-83

Industry	*Growth rate (%)*
Food and Kindred products	0.7
Tobacco manufactures	0.2
Lumber and Wood Products	1.3
Paper and Allied Products	1.5
Total Manufacturing	1.1

Source: Gullickson and Harper, "*Multi-Factor Productivity in US Manufacturing,*1949-83"

Growth in productivity or technical change over years is an important factor in determining rate of economic growth of a country. The lower growth of productivity causes slowdown in economic growth. If developing countries such as India have to catch up with the presently developed countries the key factor to achieve this is to bring about adequate technical change.

Since technological change raises productivity of inputs, it reduces average cost of producing output. Empirical evidence shows that possibilities of reducing cost of production through choice among available techniques of production are limited, while cost per unit can be reduced significantly through new inventions and innovations, that is, cost reduction through technological change is substantial. Lipsey and Chrystal rightly write, "*improvements by inventions and innovations are potentially limitless. Hence growth in living standards is critically linked to technological change.*[2]

It may be noted that technological change is of two kinds. First type of technological change is the introduction of ***product innovations,*** that is, new and superior products. The second type of technological change is ***process innovation*** which occurs when new improved techniques of production are developed.

Endogenous Technological Change

An important feature of technological change in the last 50 years is that it has occurred as endogenous response of firms to changes in market signals, that is, changes in factor prices. The past technological change took place mainly in a random fashion as a result of scientific discoveries by individual scientists working in labouratories and technical shops. These inventions were not in response to economic signals but the result of individual efforts to find something new.

On the other hand, *endogenous technological changes are brought about within firms through a systematic research and development (R & D) activity undertaken in response to market signals.*[3] For example, when in the 1973-74, price of petrol shot up, car manufacturing firms directed their R & D activity to develop more fuel efficient cars.Similarly,when prices of natural rubber rose, firms through their research and development activity developed synthetic rubber and plastic to substitute natural rubber. Thus, Lipsey and Chrystal write, "Changes in technology are often *endogeneous responses to changing economic signals,* that is, they result from *responses by firms* to the same things that induce substitution of one input for another."[4] That is, as firms substitute one input for another within the confines of a given technology in response to change in

2. Richard G. Lipsey, K. Alex Chrystal, *Economics,* 10th edition, 2004, p. 152.
3. Lipsey and Chrystal, *op. cit.* p. 152.
4. *Ibid,* p. 153
5. In clarifying the concept of nature of technological change, N. Rosenberg has made an important contribution. See his work, *Inside the Black Box: Technology and Economics* (Cambridge University Press, 1982).

relative prices of these inputs, similarly in the very long-run, firms develop new technologies in response to changes in market prices of inputs[5].

Regarding endogeneous technological change a significant example is furnished by Japanese experience. Japanese car manufacturing firms developed a new flexible manufacturing technology in response to scale disadvantage they suffered as compared to the car producers of the United States and Europe. Japanese firms could not attain the *minimum efficient scale* because they were then producing for home market with a small-size plants. But even *within the confines of small-scale plants,* they introduced new innovations which enabled them to produce superior cars at lower prices and almost drived out the American firms from competition within the United States. Production on a small-scale but using a superior and efficient technology has been called '***Flexible Manufacturing***'. They repeated this same experience with regard to production of electronic products. This shows that for the introduction and use of new and improved technology, the production on a large scale is not necessary.

Conclusion. So far most of microeconomic theory explains the short-run and long-run responses of the firms to changes in prices of output and inputs within the confines of fixed plant and equipment. It has generally ignored the development of new technologies by the firms in response to economic signals. Thus, the response of firms to changes in prices of products and inputs should be analyzed at three levels.

1. In the short run, the firms can change their output by changing the amounts of variable factors, fixed factors such as plant and equipment remaining the same.
2. In the long run, the firmss can change all inputs or factors, that is, both variable and fixed inputs but within the *confines of given* technology.
3. In the very long run firms respond to economic signals to introduce new inventions and innovations (*i.e.*, new technologies) through their research and development activity.

Types of Technical Change

Technical change has been classified into three categories: (1) Neutral technical change, (2) Labour-saving technical change and (3) Capital-saving technical change. *The technical*

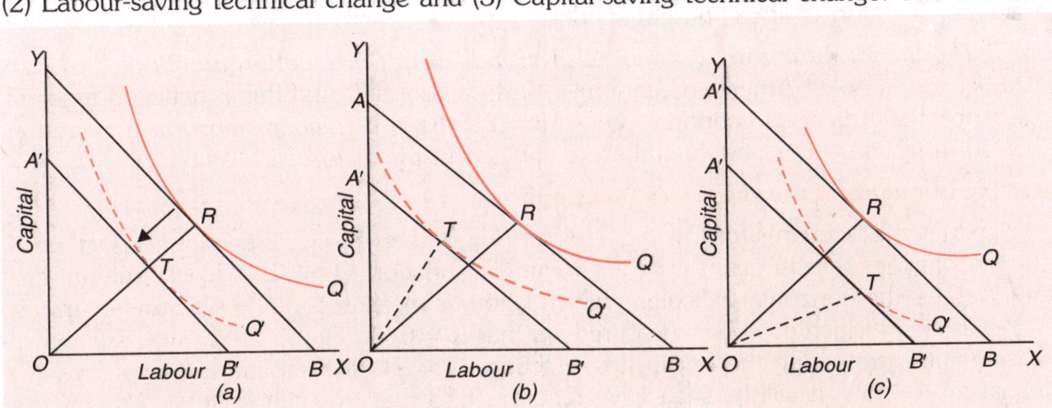

Fig. 19.12(a) Neutral Technological Change

Fig. 19.12(b) Labour-Saving (or Capital-Bias) Technological Change

Fig. 19.12(c) Capital-Saving (or Labour-Bias) Technological Change

change is neutral if more output can be produced by using the same ratio of inputs, say labour and capital. This is depicted in Fig. 19.12 (a) where with the shift in production function, capital-labour ratio remains the same at a given MRS_{LK}.

5. In clarifying the concept of nature of technological change, N. Rosenberg has made an important contribution. See his work, *Inside the Black Box: Technology and Economics* (Cambridge University Press, 1982).

On the other hand, if due to a technical change, the firm produces more output by using relatively less labour per unit of capital; the technological change will be labour-saving. For example, if a printing press that required two workers per machine is substituted by the production process that requires one worker per machine to produce the given quantity of printing material so that capital-labour ratio rises or labour-capital ratio falls, it will be labour saving. Thus, as a result of labour-saving technical change labour productivity increases with the increase in capital intensity. This is shown in Fig. 19.12 (b) where with the technological change, capital-labour ratio rises at a given MRS_{LK}.

On the other hand, ***if as a result of technological change relatively less capital than labour is used to produce a given output so that capital-labour ratio falls, it will be capital-saving technological change.*** As a result of capital-saving technical change, productivity of capital rises more than that of labour. This is depicted in Fig. 19.12 (c) where with the shift in production function capital-labour ratio falls at a given MRS_{LK}.

NUMERICAL PROBLEMS

Problem 1. *You are given the following production functions. What types of production function they are ? Draw the isoquants for these production functions.*

(i) $Q = 2L + K$

(ii) $Q = Min\ (2L, K)$

Ans. (i) *Production function,* $Q = 2L + K$ is a *linear production* function. This is proved as under. Let L and K are increased by a given number λ

$$Q' = 2\lambda L + \lambda K$$

λ can be factored out. Thus,

$$Q' = \lambda(2L + K) = \lambda Q$$

Thus, increasing each inputs by λ, output also increases by λ. This shows this production function is linear homogeneous.

(ii) *Production function,* $Q = \text{Min}\ (2L, K)$ is a *Leontief production function.* This is so called because a noted American economist Wassily Leontief used this production function to describe the American economy. $Q = \text{Min}\ (2L, K)$ is a *fixed proportion production function* in which labour and capital are combined in the ratio of $2L$ and $1K$.

Drawing isoquants of the above two functions

To draw the isoquants for $Q = 2L + K$, let $K = 0$, then $L = Q/2$ and let $L = 0$, then $K = Q$. This implies that isoquant for the production function $Q = 2L + K$ is a straight line that intersects the horizontal axis along which labour is measured at $L = Q/2$ and intersects the Y-axis along which capital is measured, so that $K = Q$. In Figure 19.13 we have drawn the isoquant representing the production function, $Q = 2L + K$ assuming output level (Q) is equal to 10 units. It will be seen from Figure 19.13 that isoquant for $Q = 2L + K$ is a downward-sloping straight line.

Drawing Isoquant of production function, $Q = \text{Min}\ (2L, K)$

This production function indicates that capital and labour are used in fixed proportion so that $\frac{K}{L} = \frac{1}{2}$, that is, for each unit of capital (K), minimum 2 units of labour (L) are employed to produce an output, Isoquant of such a fixed factor proportion production function is right-angled at the point $\frac{K}{L} = \frac{1}{2}$ as shown in Figure 19.14.

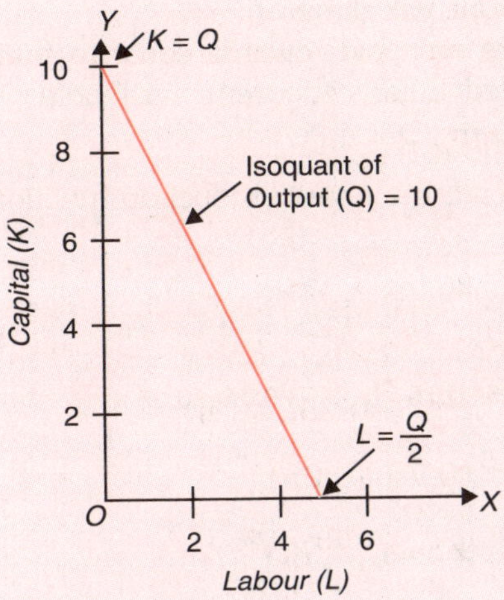

Fig. 19.13. *Straight line Isoquant of Q = 2L + K*

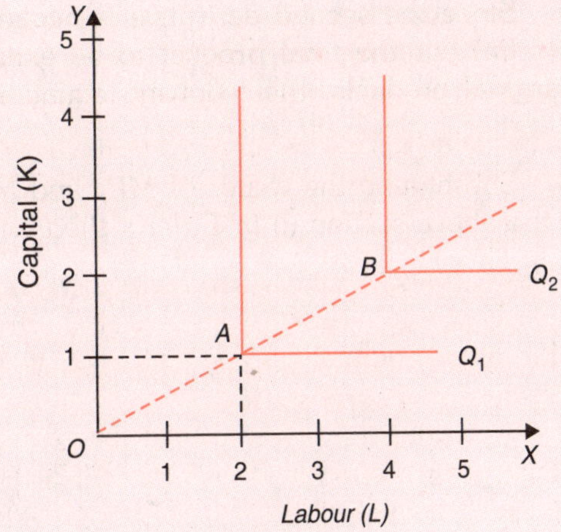

Fig. 19.14. *Isoquant of Q = Min. 2L, K)*

Problem 2. *The following production function is given:*

$$Q = L^{0.75}K^{0.25}$$

(*i*) *Find the marginal product of labour, and marginal product of* capital

(*ii*) *Show that law of diminishing returns holds*

(*iii*) *Show that if labour and capital are paid rewards equal to their marginal products, total product would be exhausted*

(*iv*) *Calculate the marginal rate of technical substitution of capital for labour*

(*v*) *Find out the elasticity of substituion.*

Ans. (*i*)

$$MP_L = \frac{\partial Q}{\partial L} = 0.75L^{0.75-1}K^{0.25}$$

$$= 0.75L^{-0.25}K^{0.25}$$

$$= 0.75\left(\frac{K}{L}\right)^{0.25}$$

$$MP_K = \frac{\partial Q}{\partial K} = 0.25.L^{0.75}K^{0.25-1}$$

$$= 0.25.L^{0.75}.K^{-0.75} = 0.25\left(\frac{L}{K}\right)^{0.75}$$

(*ii*) *Law of diminishing returns holds, that is, marginal product of labour declinces with increases in the amount of labour, given the amount of capital.* Marginal product of labour will diminish if the second derivative of the Cobb-Douglas production $Q = L^{0.75}K^{0.25}$ with respect to a factor is negative. As found above, the first derivative of the given production function with respect to labour (i.e., MP_L) is given by :

$$\frac{\partial Q}{\partial L} = MP_L = 0.75L^{-0.25}K^{0.25}$$

Its second derivative is

$$\frac{\partial^2 Q}{\partial L^2} = -\,0.25 \times 0.75\, L^{-0.25-1}K^{0.25} = -\,1875L^{-1.25}K^{0.25}$$

Since the second derivative is negative MP of labour will diminish.

(*iii*) For the total product to be exhausted if factors are paid rewards equal to their marginal products, the following equation which is called Euler's theorem must hold:

$$Q = MP_L.L + MP_K.K$$

Substituting the values of MP_L and MP_K obtained from the given production function in the above section (*i*) *in Euler's theorem* we have

$$Q = 0.75\left(\frac{K}{L}\right)^{0.25}.L + 0.25\left(\frac{L}{K}\right)^{0.75}.K$$

$$Q = 0.75K^{0.25}L^{0.75} + 0.25L^{0.75}K^{0.25}$$

$$Q = L^{0.75}K^{0.25}(0.75 + 0.25),$$

$$Q = L^{0.75}K^{0.25} \times 1 = L^{0.75}K^{0.25}$$

Since $L^{0.75}K^{0.25} = Q$ (given)

Therefore, $Q = Q$

Thus, product exhaustion of Euler's theorem applies to the given production function.

(*iv*) $MRTS_{LK}$ is equal to the ratio of marginal products of labour and capital. Using the marginal products of labour and capital we have

$$MRTS_{LK} = \frac{MP_L}{MP_K} = \frac{0.75\left(\frac{K}{L}\right)^{0.25}}{0.25\left(\frac{L}{K}\right)^{0.75}} = 3\left(\frac{K}{L}\right)$$

(*v*) Elasticity of substitution $= \dfrac{\Delta\left(\frac{K}{L}\right)/\frac{K}{L}}{\Delta MRS/MRS}$

Substituting the value of $MRS = 3\left(\frac{K}{L}\right)$ we have

$$\text{Elasticity of substitution} = \frac{\Delta\left(\frac{K}{L}\right)/\frac{K}{L}}{3\Delta\left(\frac{K}{L}\right)/3\frac{K}{L}} = 1$$

RETURNS TO SCALE

Changes in Scale and Factor Proportions

In the previous section we explained the behaviour of output when alteration in factor proportions is made. Factor proportions are altered by keeping the quantity of one or some factors fixed and varying the quantity of the other. The changes in output as a result of the variation in factor proportion, as seen before, forms the subject-matter of the "law of variable proportions." We shall now undertake the study of changes in output when *all factors or inputs* in a particular production function are increased together *proportionately*. In other words, we shall now study the behaviour of output in response to the changes in the scale. The scale of production in the context of two factor production function means a *given amount of labour and capital* used in the production process. The proportionate changes in both the factors bring about a change in the scale. Thus **an increase in the scale means that all inputs or factors used in a production process are increased in the same proportion.** Increase in the scale thus occurs when all factors or inputs are increased keeping factor proportion unaltered. The term returns to scale refers to the degree by which output changes as a result of a given proportionate change in the amounts of all factors (inputs) used in production.

Before explaining returns to scale it will be instructive to make clear the distinction between changes in the scale and changes in factor proportion. The difference between the changes in scale and changes in factor proportion will become clear from the study of Fig. 19.15 where the two factors, labour and capital, have been measured on *X*-axis and *Y*-axis respectively. We suppose that only labour and capital are required to produce a particular product. An isoquant map has been drawn. *A* point *S* has been taken on the *Y*-axis and the horizontal line *ST* parallel to *X*-axis has been drawn. *OS* represents the amount of capital which remains fixed along the line *ST*. As we move towards right on the line *ST*, the amount of labour varies while the amount of capital remains fixed at *OS*. In other words, proportion between the two factors undergoes a change along the line *ST*; the ratio of the variable factor 'labour' to the fixed factor 'capital' rises as we move to the right on the line *ST*. Thus, the movement along the line *ST* represents variation in factor proportion. Likewise, a vertical line *GH* parallel to the *Y*-axis is drawn which will also indicate changes in factor proportion. But in this case the quantity of labour will remain fixed while the quantity of capital will vary.

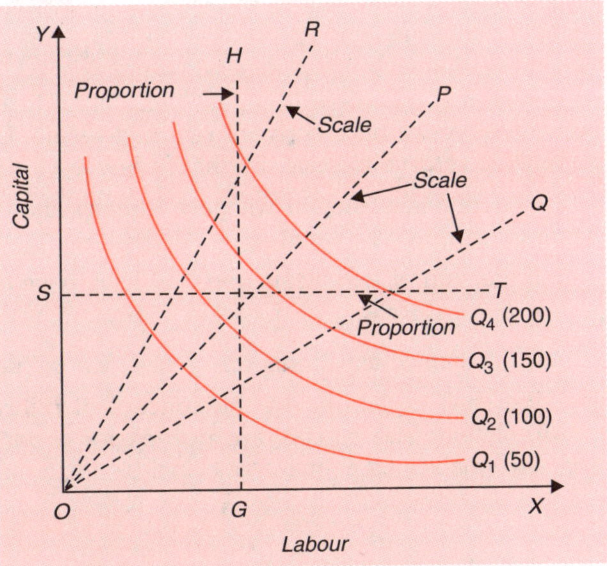

Fig. 19.15. *Changes in Scale and Factor Proportions*

Now, draw a straight line *OP* passing through the origin. It will be seen that along the line *OP* the inputs of both the factors, labour and capital, vary proportionately. Morover, because the line *OP* is a straight line through the origin, the ratio between the two factors along *OP* will remain the same throughout. Thus, the upward movement along the line *OP* indicates the increase in the absolute amounts of two factors employed with the proportion between two factors remaining unchanged. Assuming that only labour and capital are needed to produce a product, then the increase in the two factors along the line *OP* represents the *increase in the scale* since along the line *OP* both the factors increase in the same proportion and therefore proportion between the two factors remains unaltered. If any other straight line through the origin such as *OQ* or *OR* is drawn, it will show, like the line *OP*, the changes in the scale but it will represent a *different given proportion* of factors which remains the same along the line. That is, the various straight lines through the origin will indicate different proportions between the two factors but on each line the proportion between the two factors will remain the same throughout.

Returns to Scale. Let us explain further the meaning of returns to scale taking two factors (inputs) Cobb-Douglas production function, $Q = 100\, L^{0.5} K^{0.5}$. As explained above, returns to scale refer to the response of output to proportionate changes in all inputs used in production. For example, if the amounts of both labour and capital used in production are 10 in the above given production function, we have

$$Q = 100(10)^{0.5}(10)^{0.5}$$

$$= 100\sqrt{100} = 1000$$

Now if we double the amounts of both factors (*i.e.*, if 20 units of labour and 20 units of capital) are used in production, then output will be

$$Q = 100(20)^{0.5}.(20)^{0.5}$$

$$= 100\sqrt{400} = 100 \times 20 = 2000$$

Thus in this case, doubling of both inputs results in doubling of output. Thus this is a case of constant returns to scale. But we do not have always constant returns to scale. The output may increase more than in proportion to the increase in inputs when we will have *increasing returns to scale*. On the other hand, output may increase less than in proportion to the increase in inputs and this case we will have decreasing returns to scale.

Returns to scale are formally defined as follows. Let us take the general production function,

$$Q = f(L,K)$$

If both capital and labour are increased by some factor λ and output increases by factor h, we write it as follows :

$$hQ = f(\lambda L, \lambda K)$$

Now if $h = \lambda$, then it implies that output increases in the same proportion as inputs and therefore we have constant returns to scale. On the other hand, if $h > \lambda$, we will have *increasing returns* to scale. Further, if $h < \lambda$ we will have *decreasing returns* to scale.

In a previous section we have already shown that in Cobb-Douglas production of general form, that is, when $Q = AL^{\alpha}K^{\beta}$,

If the sum of exponents $a + \beta = 1$ we have constant returns to scale.

If the sum of exponents $a + \beta > 1$ we have increasing returns to scale.

If the sum of exponents $\alpha + \beta < 1$, we get decreasing returns to scale.

We shall explain below the concept of returns to scale by assuming that only two factors, labour and capital, are needed for production. This makes our analysis simple and also enables us to make our analysis in terms of isoquants.

CONSTANT RETURNS TO SCALE

Returns to scale may be constant, increasing or decreasing. If we increase all factors (*i.e.*, scale) in a given proportion and the output increases in the same proportion, returns to scale are said to be constant. Thus, if a doubling or trebling of all factors causes a doubling or trebling of output respectively, returns to scale are constant. But, if the increase in all factors leads to a more than proportionate increase in output, returns to scale are said to be increasing. Thus, if all factors are doubled and output increases by more than a double, then returns to scale are increasing. On the other hand, if increase in all factors leads to a less than proportionate increase in output, returns to scale are decreasing. We shall explain below these various types of returns to scale.

As said above, the constant returns to scale mean that with the increase in the scale or the amounts of all factors leads to a proportionate increase in output, that is, doubling of all inputs doubles the output. In mathematics, the case of constant returns to scale is called ***linear homogeneous production function or homogeneous production function of the first degree.*** Production function exhibiting constant returns to scale possesses very convenient mathematical properties which make it very useful for theoretical analysis. There are a number of special theorems which apply when production function exhibits constant returns to scale. Empirical evidence suggests that production function for the economy as a whole is not too far from being homogeneous of the first degree Empirical evidence also suggests that in the production function for an individual firm there is a long phase of constant returns to scale.

Let us illustrate diagrammatically the constant returns to scale with the help of equal product curves *i.e.* isoquants. Fig. 19.16 depicts an isoquant map. It is assumed that, in the production of a good, only two factors, labour and capital, are used. In order to judge whether or not returns to scale are constant, we draw some straight lines through the origin. As shown above, these straight lines passing through the origin indicate the increase in scale as we move upward. It will be seen from the figure that successive isoquants showing equal increments in output are equidistant from each other along each straight line drawn from the origin. Thus, along the line *OP*, *AB* = *BC* = *CD*, and along the line *OQ*, *A′ B′* = *B′C′* = *C′D′* and along the ray *OR*, *A″ B″* = *B″ C″* = *C″ D″*. The distance between the successive isoquants being the same along any straight line through the origin, means that if both labour and capital are increased in a given proportion, output expands by the same proportion. Therefore, Fig. 19.16 displays constant returns to scale.

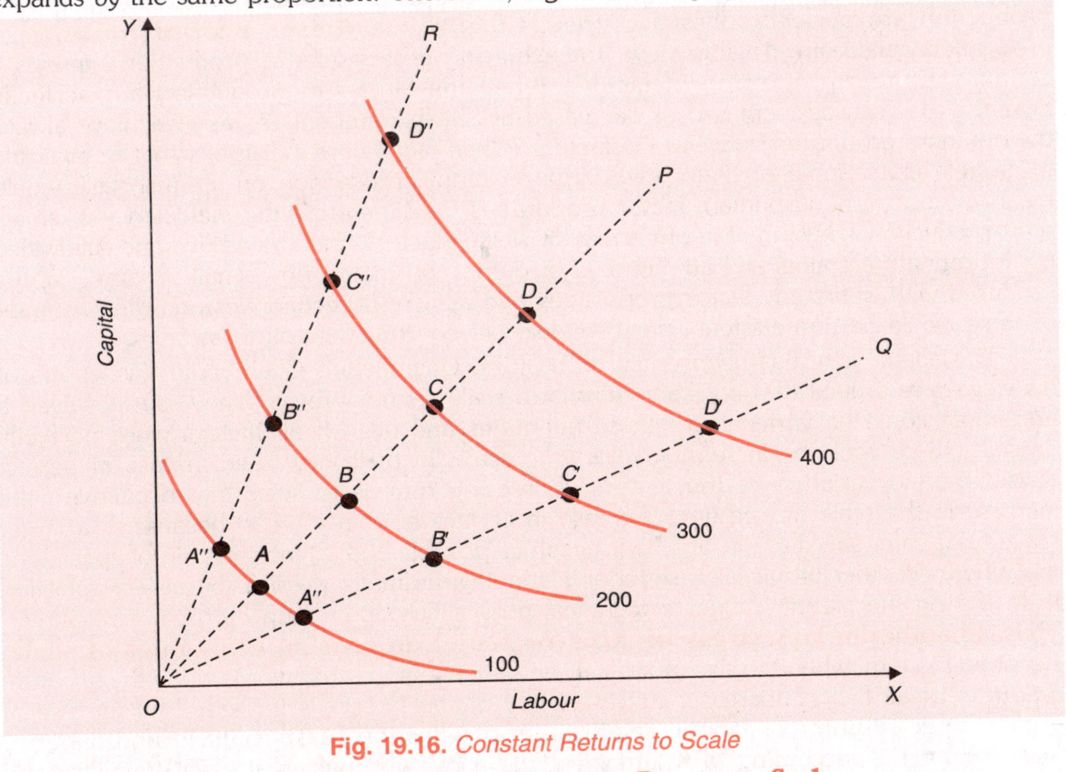

Fig. 19.16. *Constant Returns to Scale*

Divisibility of Factors, Proportionality and Constant Returns to Scale

Some economists are of the view that if the factors of production are perfectly divisible, production function must necessarily exhibit constant returns to scale. It is thus argued by them that if, for instance, all factors or inputs are doubled, then what is there to prevent the output from being doubled. Suppose we build three exactly same types of factories by using exactly same type of workers, capital equipment and raw materials, will we not produce three times the output of a single factory? Economists such as Joan Robinson, Nicholas Kaldor, A.P. Lerner, F.H. Knight who hold this view argue that if it is possible to increase or diminish all factor inputs in the same proportion, then the constant returns to scale must occur. They say that if constant returns to scale does not prevail in some industries it is because it is not possible to increase or diminish factors used in them in exactly the same proportion.

They advanced two reasons for our inability to vary the factors in the same proportion. First, there are some factors whose amount cannot be increased in a given proportion because their supplies are scarce and limited. The scarcities of these factors cause diminishing returns to scale. Secondly, it is pointed out that some factors are *indivisible* and full use of them can be made only when production is done on quite a large scale. Because of the indivisibility, they have to be exploited even at a small level of output. Therefore, when output is sought is to be expanded, these indivisible factors will not be increased since they are already not being fully utilized. Thus, with the increase in output, cost per unit will fall because of the better utilization of indivisible factors. Indivisibilities are a source of a good many economies of large-scale production. It is thus clear that in the presence of indivisible factors their amount cannot be varied in the required proportion. According to this view, if the limited supply of some factors and the existence of indivisibilities would not have stood in the way of increasing the amounts of all factors in the same proportion, then there must have been constant returns to scale.

The above explanation of the absence of economies of scale when the factors of production are perfectly divisible, stresses the role of ***factor proportionality*** in production. According to this view, for achieving best results in production there is a certain *optimum proportion* of factors. When the factors of production are perfectly divisible, they can be increased or decreased by suitable amounts so as to achieve always the optimum proportion between the factors. When factors are indivisible, that is, available in discrete units, some of them quite large or lumpy, production on a small scale would mean the use of non-optimum factor proportions and therefore the inefficiency of small-scale production. Thus, in case of perfect divisibility, factors could be divided and subdivided by appropriate amounts and any amount of output, no matter how small or large, can be produced with optimum factor proportions and as a result economies and diseconomies of scale would be non-existent and we would get constant returns to scale.

The above view has been criticized by E.H. Chamberlin. Chamberlin and others of his view have argued that constant returns to scale cannot prevail. They say that even if all factors could be varied in required quantities and even if all factors were perfectly divisible, there could be increasing returns to scale. In their view even in case of perfect divisibility and variation of the factors, increasing returns to scale can occur with the increase in the scale or size (*i.e.*, increase in all factors or resources) because at a larger scale, (1) greater specilization of labour becomes possible and (2) introduction of specialized machinery or other inputs of a superior technology is made possible by a wise selection from among the greater range of technical possibilities opened up by greater resources. Thus, **Chamberlin lays stress on *size* (or *scale*), in causing economies of scale.** According to him, when the size or scale of operations, or in other words when the *absolute amounts* of all factors increase, the efficiency of the factors is increased by the use of greater specialization of labour and by the introduction of specialized and superior machinery. Thus, according to Chamberlin, the above view which stresses divisibility and proportionality neglects the effect of *scale* on the efficiency of factors.[6]

It has been further pointed out that one cannot meaningfully speak of doubling all

6. For the views of Professor Chamberlin regarding the controversial question of divisibility, proportionality and economies of scale, see his article in *Quarterly Journal of Economics*. Vol. LXII, Feb. 1948.

the factors in a given situation. For instance, two factories existing nearby is simply not the same thing as doubling of one factory in isolation. The existence of another factory in close distance affects labour discipline, air pollution, cost of labour training etc. It is thus argued that in practice it is not possible to vary all the factors in a given proportion and obtain increases in output in the same proportion.

More significantly, it is pointed out that if a large single factory is more efficient than two small factories (the two having total capacity equal to the large one), then there would be no incentive on the part of an entrepreneur to double or duplicate his factors in the sense of setting up another small factory near to his previous one. In other words, when the entrepreneur sees the opportunity of getting increasing returns to scale by setting up a large factory, then he would not set up a duplicate factory of his previous size and obtain constant returns to scale. In this connection, it is pointed out that there are many types of economies of scale due to which there is a great possibility of getting, at least in the beginning, increasing returns to scale.

INCREASING RETURNS TO SCALE

As stated above, increasing returns to scale means that output increases in a greater proportion than the increase in inputs. If, for instance, all inputs are increased by 25%, and output increases by 40%, then the increasing returns to scale will be prevailing. When a firm expands, the increasing returns to scale occur at least in the initial stages.

Indivisibility of the Factors. Many economists, such as Joan Robinson, Kaldor, Lerner and Knight ascribe increasing returns to scale to the indivisibility of factors. Some factors are available in large and lumpy units and can therefore be utilized with utmost efficiency at a large level of output. Therefore, in the case of some indivisible and lumpy factors, when output is increased from a small level to a large one, indivisible factors are better utilized and therefore increasing returns are obtained. According to this view, as stated above, if all factors are perfectly divisible, increasing returns to scale would not occur.

Greater Possibilities of Specialization of Labour and Machinery. As stated above, Chamberlin is of the view that returns to scale increase because of greater possibilities of specialization of labour and machinery. According to him, even if the factors were perfectly divisible, with the increase in the scale, returns to scale can increase because the firm can introduce greater degree of specialization of labour and machinery (because now greater resources or amounts of factors become available) and also because it can install technologically more efficient machinery.

At a larger scale of production, instead of being generalists, workers can specialise in performing a particular task in the production process. Generally, a worker who does one task repeatedly will do it more efficiently and accurately than the one who has to perform various tasks in the production process. By concentrating on one task, the time of the worker is also saved as he does not have to move from one machine to another.

Similarly, the use of techologically superior machine and specialized equipment is cost effective at larger scale of production as at smaller scale its capacity will not be fully utilized. For example, installing an expensive automated binding machine for books will make little sense for use by small book-binding firm as it will not be using its full capacity.

Dimensional Economies. Another important cause of increasing returns to scale lies in dimensional relations, which have been emphasized by Professor Baumol.[7] A wooden box of 3 foot-cube contains 9 times greater wood than the wooden box of 1 foot-cube, that is, 3 foot-cube wooden box contains 9 times greater input. But the capacity of the

7. W.J. Baumol, *Economic Theory and Operations Analysis*, 3rd edition, p. 382.

3 foot-cube wooden box is 27 times greater than that of 1 foot-cube. Another example is the construction of warehouse. Suppose a rectangular warchouse is proposed to be constructed. Most important input used in this construction work is the number of bricks and other inputs which almost vary in proportion to the number of bricks used. The number of bricks used depends upon the wall area of the building. The elementary mathematics tells us that the wall area will increase equal to the square of the perimeter of the warehouse, while its volume, that is, its storage area will increase equal to the cube of the perimeter. In other words, double the number of bricks and other inputs that go with them, the storage capacity of the warehouse will be more than doubled. This is thus a case of increasing returns to scale. Similarly, if the diameter of a pipe is doubled, the flow through it is more than doubled.

Increasing returns to scale can be shown through isoquants. When increasing returns to scale occur, the successive isoquants representing equal increments in output will lie at successively smaller distances along a straight line ray *OR* through the origin. In Fig. 19.17 the various isoquants Q_1, Q_2, Q_3, are drawn which represent 100, 200 and 300 units of output respectively. It will be seen that distances between the successive isoquants decrease as we expand output by increasing the scale. Thus, increasing returns to scale occur since $AB < OA$ and $BC < AB$ which means that equal increases in output are obtained by successively smaller increments in inputs.

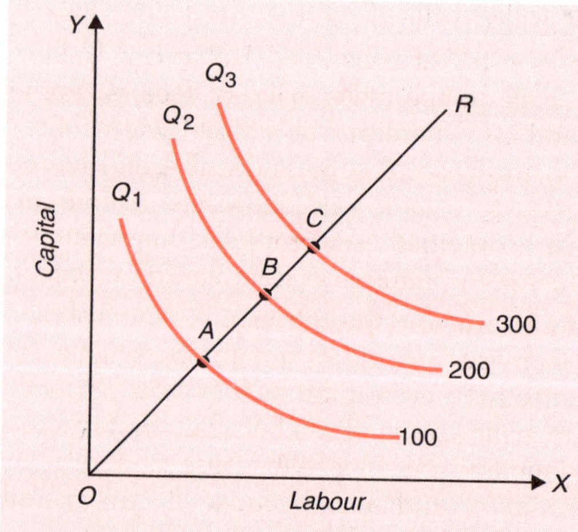

Fig. 19.17. *Increasing Returns to Scale*

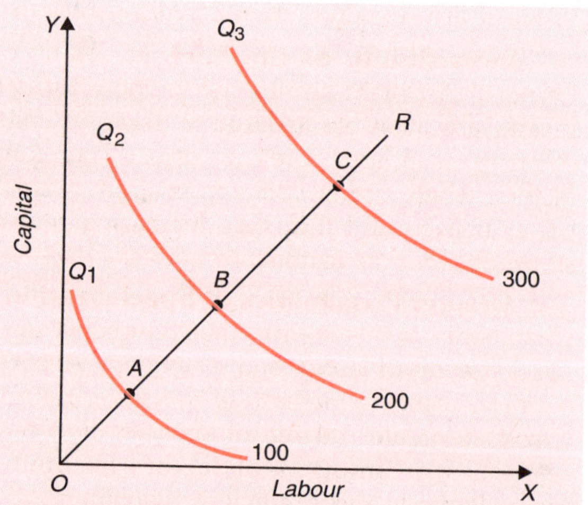

Fig. 19.18. *Decreasing Returns to Scale*

DECREASING RETURNS TO SCALE

As stated above, when output increases in a smaller proportion than the increase in all inputs, decreasing returns to scale are said to prevail. When a firm goes on expanding by increasing all his inputs, *eventually* diminishing returns to scale will occur. But among economists there is no agreement on a cause or causes of diminishing returns to scale. Some economists are of the view that the entrepreneur is a fixed factor of production; while all other inputs may be increased, he cannot be. According to this view, decreasing returns to scale is therefore actually a special case of the law of variable proportions. Thus, they point out that we get diminishing returns to scale beyond a point because varying quantities of all other inputs are combined with a fixed entrepreneur. Thus, according to this view, decreasing returns to scale is a special case of the law of variable proportions with entrepreneur as the fixed factor. Other economists do not treat decreasing returns to scale as the special case of the law of variable proportions and argue that decreasing returns to scale eventually occur because of the ***increasing difficulties of management, co-ordination and control.*** When the firm has expanded to a too gigantic size, it is difficult to manage it with the same efficiency as previously. For example, managing a large number of workers and coordinating the activities of several divisions of the firm is quite difficult and results in decline in productivity of inputs used.

The case of decreasing returns to scale can be shown on an isoquant map. When successive isoquants representing equal increments in output lie at progressively larger and larger distance on a ray through the origin, returns to scale will be decreasing. In Fig. 19.18 successively decreasing returns to scale occur since $AB > OA$, and $BC > AB$. It means that ***more and more of inputs (labour and capital) are required to obtain equal increments in output.***

Varying Returns to Scale in a Single Production Process

It should be noted that it is not always the case that different production functions should exhibit different types of returns to scale. It generally happens that there are three phases of increasing, constant and diminishing returns to scale in a single production function. In the beginning when the scale increases, increasing returns to scale are obtained because of greater possibilities of specialization of labour and machinery. After a point, there is a phase of constant returns to scale where output increases in the same proportion as inputs. Empirical evidence suggests that the phase of constant returns to scale is quite

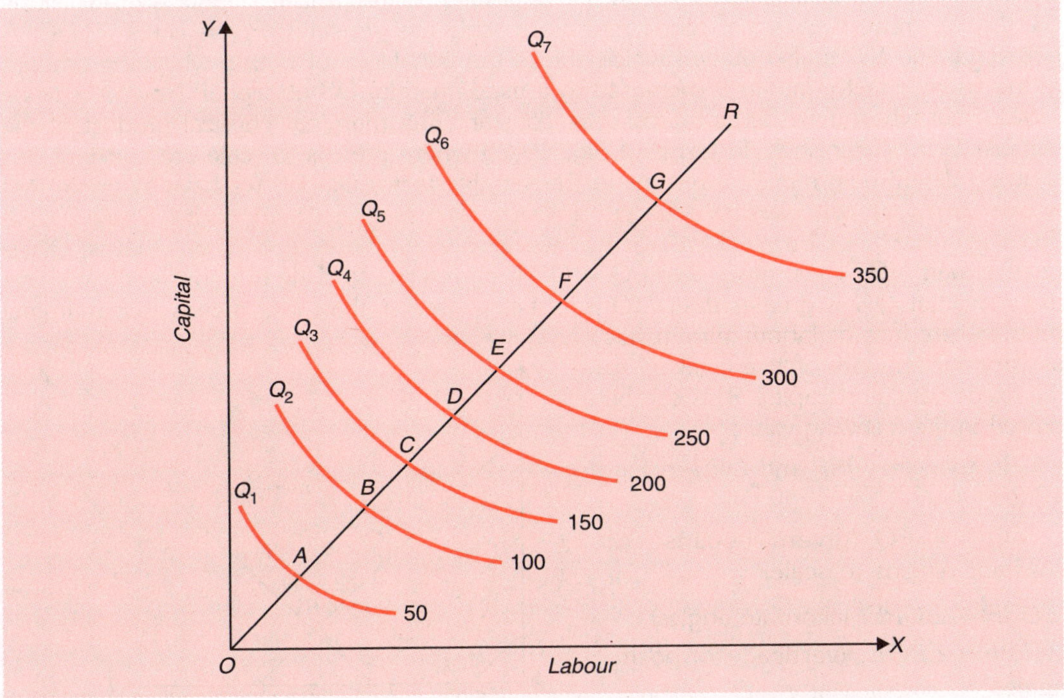

Fig.19.19. *Varying Returns to Scale in a Single Production Process*

long. If the firm continues to expand, then eventually a point will be reached beyond which decreasing returns to scale will occur due to the mounting difficulties of co-ordination and control. These varying returns to scale have been shown in Fig. 19.19. It will be seen from Fig. 19.19 that upto point C on a ray OR from the origin, the distance between the successive isoquants showing equal increments in output goes on decreasing. This implies that upto point C equal increments in output are obtained from the use of successively smaller increases in inputs (labour and capital). Thus, upto point C on ray OR increasing returns to scale occur. Further, it will be seen form Fig.19.19 that from point *C* to point *E* constant returns to scale are obtained as the same proportionate increments in output are obtained from the proportional increase in inputs of labour and capital. Beyond point *E*, the distance between the successive isoquants representing equal increments in output is decreasing along the ray *OR* from the origin which implies that less than proportionate increase in output is obtained from the same proportionate increments in the use of the two factors, labour and capital on the ray *OR* from the origin; *EF* > *DE* and *FG* > *EF*. Thus decreasing returns to scale occur beyond point *E* on the process ray *OR*.

RETURNS TO SCALE AND MARGINAL RETURNS TO A VARIABLE FACTOR

Constant Returns to Scale and Returns to a Variable Factor

We now turn to study the relationship between returns to scale and marginal returns to a variable factor. In other words, we want to study whether marginal productivity of a factor diminishes or rises when the returns to scale are constant, diminishing and increasing. We first take the case of constant returns to scale. As seen above, in case of constant returns to scale, or what is called in mathematics, homogeneous production function of the first degree, the distance between the successive isoquants showing equal increments in output along a straight line through the origin is always the same. Consider Fig. 19.20 in which three equal product curves showing 100, 200 and 300 units of output respectively are drawn. A straight line *OL* through the origin and cutting the isoquants is drawn. Line *OL* displays returns to scale. Since returns to scale are constant, *PQ* is equal to *QR*. A horizontal line *ST* is also drawn, which shows the behaviour of output when the amount of the variable factor labour is increased to a fixed quantity *OS* of capital. Now, it is to be proved that when the returns to scale are constant, the marginal physical product of the variable factor diminishes. In terms of Fig. 19.20 where returns to scale are constant, for showing diminishing marginal returns to the variable factor (labour) we have to prove that ***more units of the variable factor labour will be required to be added to a fixed quantity of capital to obtain equal increments in output,*** that is, *QN* is greater than *MQ*. Thus, given that *PQ* = *QR* (*i.e.*, returns to scale are constant), we have to prove that *QN* is greater than *MQ*. *QN* being greater than *MQ* means that marginal physical product of labour diminishes as varying amounts of it are added to the fixed quantity of capital. This can be proved in the following way :

In triangles *QRF* and *QPE* in Fig. 19.20

QR = *PQ* (given, because of constant returns to scale)

∠*QRF* = ∠*QPE*, (alternate angles)

∠*RQF* = ∠*PQE*, (vertically opposite angles)

Therefore, triangles *QRF* and *QPE* are congruent, *i.e.*, equal in every respect.

Hence, *QF* = *EQ*

It will be seen from Fig. 19.20 that *MQ* is less than *EQ* and *QN* is greater than *QF*.

Therefore, *QN* is greater than *MQ*.

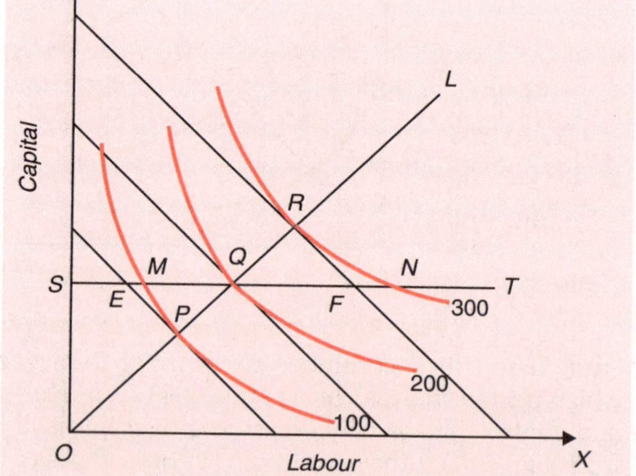

Fig. 19.20. *When Returns to Scale are Constant, Returns to a Variable Factor Diminish.*

It is thus proved that ***when returns to scale are constant, (or when production function is homogenors of the first degree), marginal physical product (i.e., marginal returns) to a variable factor diminishes.*** In other words, constant returns to scale implies diminishing returns to a variable factor.

Relation between Constant Returns to Scale and Marginal Product of a Variable Factor : Mathematical Proof

When returns to scale are constant, marginal product of a variable factor, say labour, diminishes. We can prove it mathematically. Let us take *Cobb-Douglas production function* with sum of exponents equal to 1 which implies constant returns to scale. Such a Cobb-Douglas production function can be written as

$$Q = AL^{a}K^{1-a}$$

Since their sum $a + 1 - a$ equals 1, this represents constant returns to scale.

In order to obtain marginal product of labour, we differentiate the given production function with respect to labour. Thus,

$$MP_L = \frac{\partial Q}{\partial L} = aAL^{a-1}K^{1-a}$$

$$= \frac{aAL^{a}K^{1-a}}{L}$$

Dividing L term in both the numerator and denominator by a

$$MP_L = \frac{aAL^{a-a}K^{1-a}}{L^{1-a}} = \frac{aAK^{1-a}}{L^{1-a}}$$

$$= aA\left(\frac{K}{L}\right)^{1-a}$$

In the above equation for marginal product of labour, a and A are constants. Now, if with the given and constant K, the quantity of labour (L) increases, the ratio $\frac{K}{L}$ falls and therefore MP of labour diminishes with increasing quantity of the variable factor, labour. Likewise, it can be shown that with a given quantity of labour, if capital increases, marginal product of capital will diminish.

Decreasing Returns to Scale and the Marginal Physical Product of the Variable Factor

It also follows from above that when returns to scale are decreasing, the marginal physical product of the variable factor will diminish more than in the case of constant returns to scale. In Fig. 19.21 returns to scale are diminishing, since *QR* is greater than *PQ*. It is quite obvious from Fig. 19.21 that along the horizontal line *ST* which represents the varying quantities of factor *X* with a fixed quantity of factor *Y*, the intercept *QN* is much greater than the intercept *MQ*. It follows therefore ***that when returns to scale are diminishing, marginal physical product of the variable factor falls rapidly.***

Increasing Returns to Scale and Marginal Physical Product of the Variable Factor

Finally, how the marginal physical product of the variable factor behaves when returns to scale are increasing. This case is illustrated in Fig. 19.22 where returns to scale are increasing strongly. *QR* is much smaller than *PQ*. It will be seen from Fig. 19.22 that along the horizontal line *ST, QN* is less than *MQ*. It means that as the varying quantities of factor *X* are successively added to the given quantity of the fixed factor *Y*, smaller quantity of factor X than before is required to be increased to get an equal increment in output. Thus, *QN* being less than *MQ* means that marginal physical product of the variable factor *X* increases.

It is therefore concluded that when returns to scale are *strongly* increasing, the marginal returns to a variable factor (used with a fixed quantity of the other factor) increases.

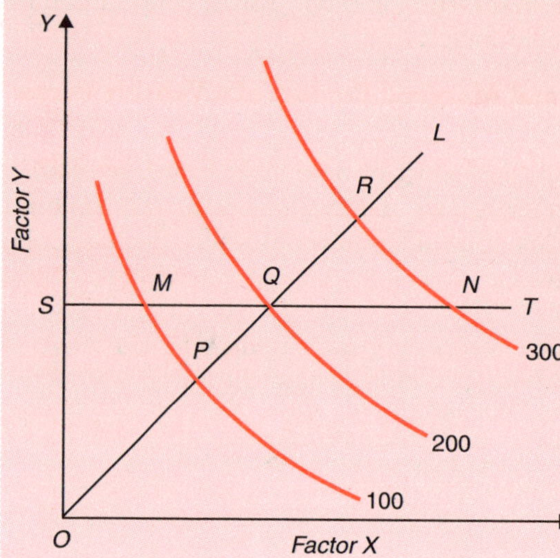

Fig. 19.21. *When Returns to Scale are Decreasing, Returns to a Variable Factor Diminish Rapidly.*

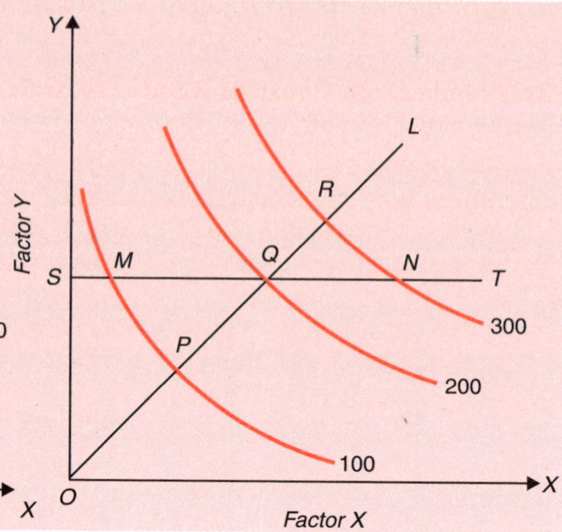

Fig. 19.22. *Marginal Physical Product of a factor increases when Returns to Scale are Increasing.*

However, when the returns to scale are slightly increasing, then the marginal returns of the variable factor will be diminishing. *Thus, the law of diminishing marginal returns to a factor is even consistent with increasing returns to scale. As just seen above, increasing returns to scale can yield increasing marginal returns as well as diminishing marginal returns to a variable factor depending upon whether returns to scale are strongly increasing or slightly increasing.*

From the foregoing analysis we conclude that ***if returns to scale are constant the marginal physical product of a variable factor used in combination with a fixed factor will always diminish as more of the variable factor is used. Similarly, when returns to scale are decreasing, marginal physical product of a variable factor will always diminish, and when returns to scale are increasing marginal physical product of a factor will still diminish unless the returns to scale are increasing sufficiently strongly.***

IMPORTANT PRODUCTION FUNCTIONS EXHIBITING CONSTANT RETURNS TO SCALE

There are four types of important production functions which yield constant returns to scale. These productions are also distinguished by a different elasticity of technical substitution between factors. They are the production functions with elasticity of technical substitution (1) equals to infinity ($\sigma = \infty$), (2) equals to zero ($\sigma = 0$), (3) equals to one ($\sigma = 1$) and (4) equals to any positive constant. We explain these four production functions below.

Production Function with Elasticity of Substitution (σ) = ∞

This production function is of the following form

$$Q = aK + bL$$

where Q is output, K and L are capital and labour inputs respectively, and a and b are constants.

The graph of this production function yields downward sloping parallel straight lines with a slope equal to $\frac{b}{a}$. The isoquant map of such a production function is shown in

Figure 19.23 This is a case of perfect substitutes with elasticity of substitution being equal to infinity ($\sigma = \infty$) This can be easily shown that elasticity of substitution in the production function $(Q = aK + bL)$ is equal to infinity

$$\sigma = \frac{\%\text{ Change in } K/L}{\%\text{ Change in } MRS_{LK}}$$

Now since the production function ($Q = aK + bL$) yields straight line isoquants, $MRTS_{LK}$ being equal to the slope of an isoquant will be constant along a straight line. Therefore, change in marginal rate of technical substitution in this type of production function in zero. Hence in this case

$$\sigma = \frac{\%\text{ Change in } K/L}{\%\text{ Change in } MR\,S_{LK}} = \frac{\%\,\Delta\,K/L}{0} = \infty$$

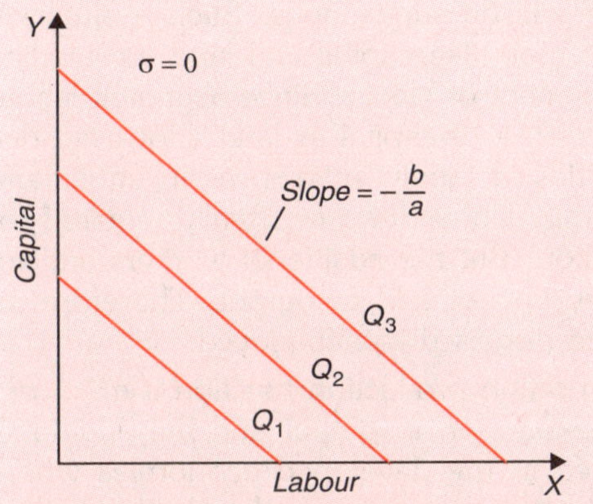

Fig. 19.23. *Production Function with elasticity of Substitution equal to infinity ($\sigma = \infty$)*

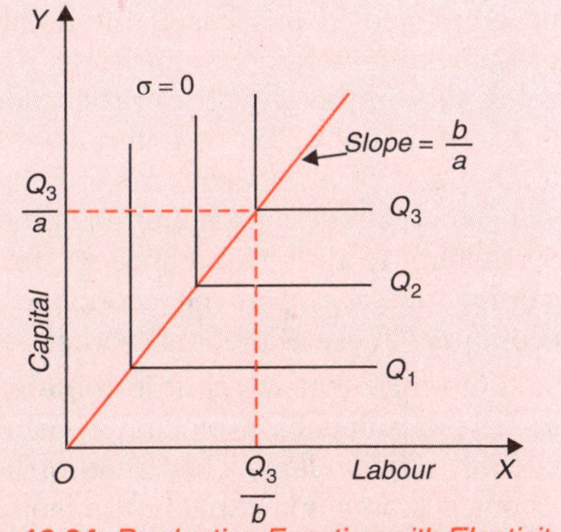

Fig. 19.24. *Production Function with Elasticity of Factor Substitution Equal to Zero ($\sigma = 0$)*

It may however be noted that such a linear production function with infinite elasticity of substitution is an extreme case and rarely exists in the real world because there are few production processes in which factors can be substituted with perfect ease. For example, two important factors, labour and capital, cannot be perfect substitutes of each other, because in no industry production work can be done either with *capital alone* or *labour alone*. Indeed, every machine requires some labour to start it and on the other hand every labourer requires some capital equipment or tool, however simple, to work with.

Production Function with Elasticity of Substitution being equal to zero ($\sigma = 0$)

Another important case of production function exhibiting constant returns to scale is provided *by fixed proportion production function* in which factors are used for production in a fixed ratio. As seen earlier, the isoquants for this type of production function are right-angled or L-shaped. They are shown again in Fig. 19.24. If in an industry such a fixed proportion production function prevails, the firms will always operate along the ray from the origin where capital-labour rate (K/L) is fixed at $\frac{b}{a}$, that is, at a vertex of an isoquant. This is because production in such a production function at a point other than a vertex of an isoquant would be inefficient because the same output can be produced with the smaller quantity of the factors by moving along an isoquant to the point of the vertex. It can be easily shown that elasticity of substitution between the factors in this fixed proportion production function is zero ($\sigma = 0$). As in this the factor ratio (K/L)

remains constant and therefore no change in it is possible for optimum production, the numerator in the substitution-elasticity formula is zero which will make the value of substitution elasticity equal to zero. Thus

$$\sigma = \frac{\%\text{Change in } K/L}{\%\text{ Change in } MRS_{LK}} = \frac{0}{\%\,\Delta\, MRS_{LK}} = 0$$

The fixed proportion production function can be mathematically expressed in the following form:

$$Q = \min\,(aK,\ bL) \qquad a,\ b > 0$$

In the above formulation of this production function, the operator *"min"* implies that output Q is determined by the smaller of the two values, aK or bL, in the bracket. If $aK < bL$, then output $Q = aK$ which would mean that capital acts as binding constraint in the production process; the increase in the use of labour would not raise output (that is, marginal product of labour will be zero). If due to some reasons additional labour has to be employed in this case, this additional labour will be superfluous. Such a situation prevails in developing countries like India where factors like capital and land are binding constraint on the growth of production and employment of labour. Since abundant labour is available, the output is determined by the given stock of capital or land. However, due to the lack of alternative employment opportunities in family enterprises in agriculture with limited land and capita) equipment, more family labour than is actually required for agricultural work is to be engaged for the production. But the additional workers are not gainfully employed in the economic icnse as they do not add to output. Therefore, in economics these additional workers are said to be disguisedly unemployed.

On the other wand, it in the above fixed proportion production function if $aK > bL$, then labour acts as a binding constraint on the expansion in output and the additional capital is redundant. This situation is encountered in the developed economies where labour is scarce and capital abundant and for production processes of several commodities $aK > bL$. That is, why recently some American companies have set up some production units in India by bringing their additional capital equipment and machines in India to increase their output by using cheap and surplus Indian labour.

That in the fixed proportion production function constant returns to scale are obtained can be proved as under. Let us increase the inputs of capital and labour by a certain positive number m (*i.e.* $m > 0$),

$$f(mK,\ mL) = \min\,(amK,\ bmL)$$

Now, m can be factored out.

$$\min\,(amb,\ bmL) = m.\ \min\,(ak,\ bL), \text{ for any } m > 0.$$
$$= m.Q$$

Thus, in the fixed proportion production function, when inputs K and L are increased by m, output (Q) also increases by m. The fixed proportion production function has been widely used in empirical studies, especially in input-output analysis. Prior to the choice of technology or technique of production or type of machine to be used for production, there are several possibilities of choosing different labour-capital combinations. However, once the technique is chosen or machine is purchased the capital-labour ratio becomes almost fixed. This is because many machines are of such a type that require a fixed number of workers per machine.

Cobb-Douglas Production Function: Production Function with Unit Elasticity of Substitution

The third important production function exhibiting constant returns to scale is Cobb-Douglas production function which has been explained above. As shown above, for Cobb-

Douglas production the elasticity of factor substitution (σ) is equal to unity and is thus an intermediate case between the two extreme cases of zero and infinite substitution elasticity between factors. The mathematical form of Cobb-Douglas production is given by

$$Q = AK^aL^b$$

where *A*, *a* and *b* are positive constants.

Now, as explained above, when the sum of exponents, $a + b = 1$ in Cobb-Douglas production function, it exhibits returns to scale are constant. If the sum of exponents, $a + b > 1$, we get increasing returns to scale and if $a + b < 1$, decreasing returns to scale are obtained. The isoquants of Cobb-Douglas production function are convex to the origin and are of rectangular hyperbola shape as shown in Figure 19.25. Cobb-Douglas production function has been used in empirical studies for estimating the type of returns to scale in various industries and for estimating *elasticities of output with respect to various inputs* such as labour and capital.

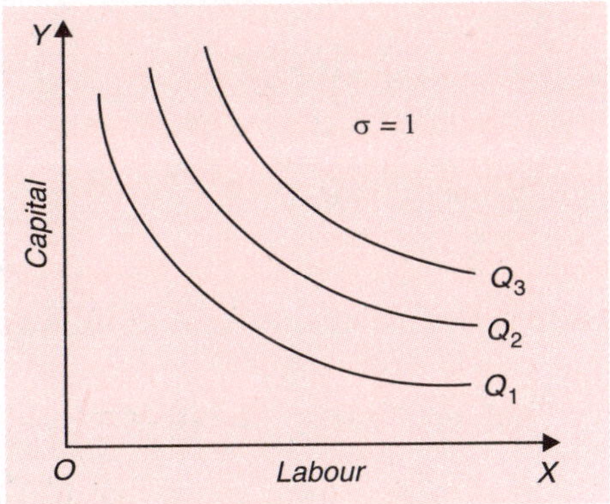

Fig. 19.25. *Isoquants of Cobb-Douglass Production Function*

CONSTANT ELASTICITY OF SUBSTITUTION (CES) PRODUCTION FUNCTION

A general production function which can have any constant value of elasticity of factor substitution has been developed jointly by Arrow, Chenery, Minhas and Solow is the Constant Elasticity of Substitution (CES) Production Function.[8] The two types of production function with either elasticity of factor-substitution equal to zero, and infinity are rarely found in the production processes of the industrial world. Cobb-Douglas production function with elasticity of factor substitution being equal to one has been found to be approximately valid for several industries and agricultural crops. But it is still restrictive and is lacking in general application. CES production function is quite a general production function wherein elasticity of factor-substitution can take any positive constant value. However, CES production function is of complex mathematical form given below :-

$$Q = \gamma[\delta K^{-p} + (1 - \delta)L^{-p}]^{-1/p}$$

where

γ is an efficiency parameter

δ is a distribution parameter

p is a substitution parameter.

and where $\delta > 0$

$0 \leq \delta \leq 1$

$p \geq 1$

It may be noted that a change in efficiency parameter γ causes a shift in the production function that can occur as a result of technological or organizational changes. The distribution parameter δ indicates the relative importance of capital (*K*) and labour (*L*) in various production processes.

8. A. J. Arrow, H. B Chenery, B. S. Minhas and R. M Solow, "Capital-Labour Substitution and Economic Efficiency". *The Review of Economics and Statistics.* August, 1961, pp. 225-250.

Lastly, the substitution parameter p indicates the substitution possibilities in the production processes. The elasticity of substitution between factors (σ) for this production function depends upon this parameter. Thus, for this production function,

$$\sigma = \frac{1}{1+p}$$

When $p = 0, \sigma = 1$, as $\sigma = \frac{1}{1+p} = \frac{1}{1+0} = 1$

When $p = \infty, \sigma = 0$, as $\sigma = \frac{1}{1+p} = \frac{1}{1+\infty} = 0$

When $p = -1, \sigma = \infty$, as $\sigma = \frac{1}{1+p} = \frac{1}{1+(-1)} = \frac{1}{0} = \infty$

It is evident from above that CES production is quite general and it includes $\sigma = 1$, $\sigma = 0$, and $\sigma = \infty$ as special cases.

Isoquants of CES production are also of normal convex shape. Further, CES production also exhibits constant returns to scale which can be proved as under

$$Q = \gamma\,[\delta K^{-p} + (1-\delta)L^{-p}]^{-\frac{1}{p}}$$

Let capital (K) and labour (L) inputs be increased by a positive number m. Thus

$$Q = f(mk, mL) = \gamma\,[\delta\,(mk)^{-p} + (1-\delta)\,(mL)^{-p}]^{-\frac{1}{p}}$$

In this $[m^{-p}]^{-\frac{1}{p}}$ can be factored out and we have

$$Q = f(mk, mL) = \gamma\,[m^{-p}]^{-\frac{1}{p}}\;[\delta K^{-p} \times (1-\delta)L^{-p}]^{-\frac{1}{p}}$$
$$= mf(K, L)$$

In recent years, economists are making extensive use of CES production function in their empircal studies of production processes because this production function permits the determination of the value of elasticity of factor-substitution from the data itself rather than prior fixing of the value of substitution elasticity (σ).

NUMERICAL PROBLEMS ON RETURNS TO SCALE

Problem 1. *Given the production function $Q = f(x_1, x_2) = x_1^2 x_2^3$ where x_1, x_2 are two inputs and Q is production. Does this show constant, decreasing or increasing returns to scale ?*

Solution. $Q = x_1^2 x_2^3$

Increasing both inputs x_1 and x_2 by m, we get

$$Q' = (mx_1)^2 \,.\, (mx_2)^3 = m^2 m.^3\, x_1^2 x_2^3$$
$$Q' = m^5 x_1^2 x_2^3 = m^5 Q$$

Thus, increase in both inputs by m causes output to increase by m^5. Hence, increasing returns to scale prevail in this case. (Students should see that the sum of the exponents of two inputs x_1 and x_2 is 2 + 3 = 5. As explained above, in the case of Cobb-Douglas production function, if the sum of exponents is greater than one, increasing returns to scale occur. Note further that $Q = x_1^2 x_2^3$ is a production function of Cobb-Douglas variety).

Problem 2. *Consider production function $Q = 5L^{0.5}K^{0.3}$. Does it represent increasing, decreasing or constant returns to scale ?*

Solution. Increasing both labour and capital inputs by m, we have :

$$Q' = 5\,(mL)^{0.5}.\,(mK)^{0.3}$$

$$Q' = m^{0.5}m^{0.3}\,5L^{0.5}K^{0.3}$$

$$Q' = m^{0.8}\,Q$$

That is, by increasing labour and capital by m, output increases by $m^{0.8}$, that is, less than m. Thus, in this case decreasing returns to scale occur.

Problem 3. *Do each of the following production functions exhibit decreasing, constant or increasing returns to scale ?*

(a) $Q = 0.5KL$ *(b)* $Q = 2K + 3L$

Solution. (*a*) $Q = Q.5KL$

Increasing K and L by m, we have :

$$Q' = 0.5mK\,.\,mL$$

$$Q' = m^1m^1\,0.5KL$$

$$= m^2.0.5KL = m^2Q$$

Increasing K and L by m, output increases by m^2, that is, increasing returns to scale operate in this case.

(*b*) $Q = 2K + 3L$

Increasing K and L by m, we have :

$$Q' = 2mK + 3mL$$

$$Q' = m(2K + 3L) = mQ$$

That is, increasing K and L by m in this production function results in increase in output also by m. That is, constant returns to scale occur in this case.

Problem 4. *Suppose a commodity is produced with two inputs, labour and capital, and the production function is given by*

$$Q = 10\sqrt{LK}$$

where Q is output and L and K are amounts of labour and capital. What type of returns to scale does it exhibit ?

Solution. The above production function can be rewritten as

$$Q = 10L^{1/2}K^{1/2}$$

Hence, this is a Cobb-Douglas production function. To show the nature of returns to scale, let us multiply L and K by λ

$$Q' = 10(\lambda L)^{1/2}(\lambda K)^{1/2}$$

$$= \lambda^{1/2}\lambda^{1/2}10L^{1/2}K^{1/2}$$

$$Q' = \lambda Q$$

Increasing L and K by λ results in increase in output (Q) by λ. Hence, this shows constant returns to scale.

Problem 5. *Econometric studies of jute industry in India show that Cobb-Douglas production function can be applied and the exponent of labour is 0.84 and exponent of capital is 0.14. If both labour and capital are increased by one per cent, by what amount output of jute will increase ?*

Solution. As shown above, an exponent of an input in Cobb-Douglas production function can be interpreted as the percentage increase in output resulting from one per cent in increase in input. Thus, the exponent of 0.84 of labour means that one per cent increase in labour leads to 0.84 per cent expansion in output of jute. Similarly, the exponent of 0.14 of capital means *one per cent increase in capital* leads to 0.14 per cent increase in output. Thus, one per cent increase in both labour and capital will result in 0.84 + 0.14 = 0.98 per cent expansion in output.

Problem 6. *Suppose you find that a paper mill which uses capital and labour is subject to the production function $Q = L^{0.75} K^{0.25}$. Will it be right to say that in the paper mill, output per worker will be a function of capital per worker ?*

Solution. Note that capital per worker means capital-labour ratio $\left(\frac{K}{L}\right)$. The given production function $Q = L^{0.75}K^{0.25}$ is a Cobb-Douglas production function where sum of exponents is equal to one (0.75 + 0.25 = 1). Let a represent 0.75, then 0.25 will be $1 - a$. Now, rewriting the production function

$$Q = L^a K^{1-a}$$

Now, Average Product of Labour (*AP*) $= \frac{Q}{L} = \frac{L^a K^{1-a}}{L}$

Now, dividing the term L in both numerator and denominator by a, we have:

$$AP_L \left(\text{or } \frac{Q}{L}\right) = \frac{L^{a-a}K^{1-a}}{L^{1-a}}$$

Since $L^{a-a} = L^0 = 1$, we have

$$AP_L = \frac{K^{1-a}}{L^{1-a}} = \left(\frac{K}{L}\right)^{1-a}$$

Since a is constant, it follows that average product of labour or output per worker depends on capital-labour ratio, that is, capital per worker.

Problem 7. *Suppose we are interested in determining the returns to scale of Britannia Company whose production function is as follows:*

$$Q = 10XY - 2X^2 - Y^2$$

where Q = output, X and Y are inputs.

Solution. Multiplying each input in the above production function by a constant g, we have

$$\begin{aligned} Q' &= 10(gX)(gY) - 2(gX)^2 - (gY)^2 \\ &= 10g^2 XY - 2g^2X^2 - g^2y^2 \\ &= g^2 (10XY - 2X^2 - Y^2) \end{aligned}$$

Note that expression in bracket = Q

Thus, $Q' = g^2Q$

This means that output increases by a factor *more than* g, that is, by a factor g^2.

Thus production function of Britannia Company shows increasing returns to scale.

Problem 8. The production function of a firm is given by :

$$Q = 0.6X + 0.2Y$$

where Q = output, X and Y are inputs.

Determine returns to scale.

Solution. To determine returns to scale we multiply each input by a constant factor g. Thus,

$$Q' = 0.6gX + 0.2gY$$

g can be factored out

Therefore, $$Q' = g(0.6X + 0.2Y)$$

or $$Q' = gQ.$$

Thus, increasing each input by a constant g leads to increase in output by the same constant g. Thus, it shows that production function is *homogeneous of first degree* and returns to scale are constant.

Problem 9. *Determine returns to scale of the following production function*

$$Q = aL + bK.$$

Solution. To determine returns to scale we multiply each input by a constant factor g. Thus,

$$Q' = a \cdot gL + b \cdot gK$$
$$= g(aL + bK)$$
$$= gQ.$$

This shows returns to scale are constant.

THE ESTIMATION OF PRODUCTION FUNCTION

Having explained the theory of production, we now turn to explain how the economists estimate production function. The estimation of production function which applies to the productive activity of the firm is one of the important tasks of its manager. In what follows we will discuss the possible forms of production function and its implications for the productive activity of a firm. Second, we shall explain the estimation of Cobb-Douglas production which is most commonly used by the economists. Third, we will examine the data required for estimation of production function. Finally, we will present the estimates of the production function studies made by some economists.

Various Forms of Production Functions

There are many forms of production functions and therefore the first task of a manager is to select *a form of production function* that applies well to the productive activity of the firm. It may be noted that a functional form of production describes the *specific relationship among the factors* used in the production process.

In our analysis of production theory the distinction has been drawn between the short-run production function and long-run production function. The short-run production function describes the existence of a fixed factor to which the different amounts of a variable factor are added to produce output. In the short-run production function of a manufacturing industry, the economists generally take capital as a fixed factor and labour as a variable factor. Thus, the form of this two factor production function can be written as

$$Q = f(L)_k \qquad \text{....(1)}$$

According to this, output of a product in the short-run is determined by the amount of the variable factor labour (L), given the quantity of the fixed factor capital (k).

In the discussion of general production function with one factor variable we have seen that in the beginning we get increasing marginal returns and beyond a point we have diminishing marginal returns to a variable factor. This implies a cubic form of production function which can be written as where a is constant (intercept term), b, c and d are the coefficients. This cubic production function with labour as the variable factor is shown in Fig. 19.26 where panel (a) depicts the total product curve of labour and panel (b) shows the average and marginal product.

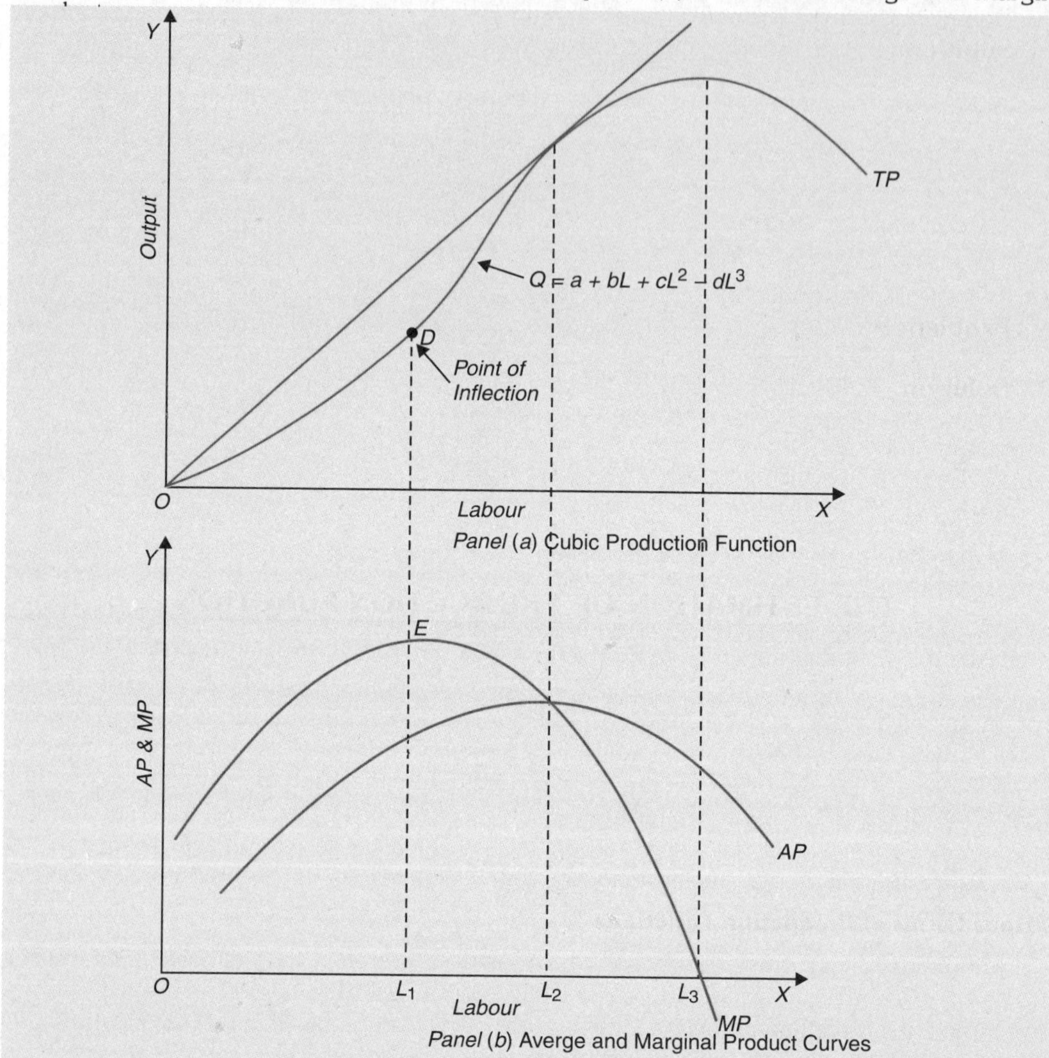

Fig. 13.21. *Cubic Production Function and its Associated Average and Marginal Product Curves*

$$Q = a + bL + CL^2 - dL^3 \quad \text{....(2)}$$

It may be noted that total product curve (*TP*) of labour has been drawn beginning from the origin. This is because it is assumed that no production is possible without the use of a variable factor. However, in the cubic production function equation (2), an intercept term a appears. This is because when such a production function is estimated we are likely to get the fitted curve with a positive or negative constant term.

It is possible that production data used to estimate the production function may exhibit only diminishing marginal returns to a variable factor (*i.e.* the absence of stage 1.). In such a situation the short-run production function is represented by a quadratic production function as given below

$$Q = a + bL - CL^2 \quad \text{....(3)}$$

This quadratic production function is shown in Figure 19.27 where in panel (*a*) we have drawn the total product curve (*TP*) of labour which is concave inside indicating that both average and marginal product curves will be sloping downward as shown in panel (*b*) of Fig. 19.27. This shows that stage of increasing marginal returns to the variable factor is not present in the quadratic production function.

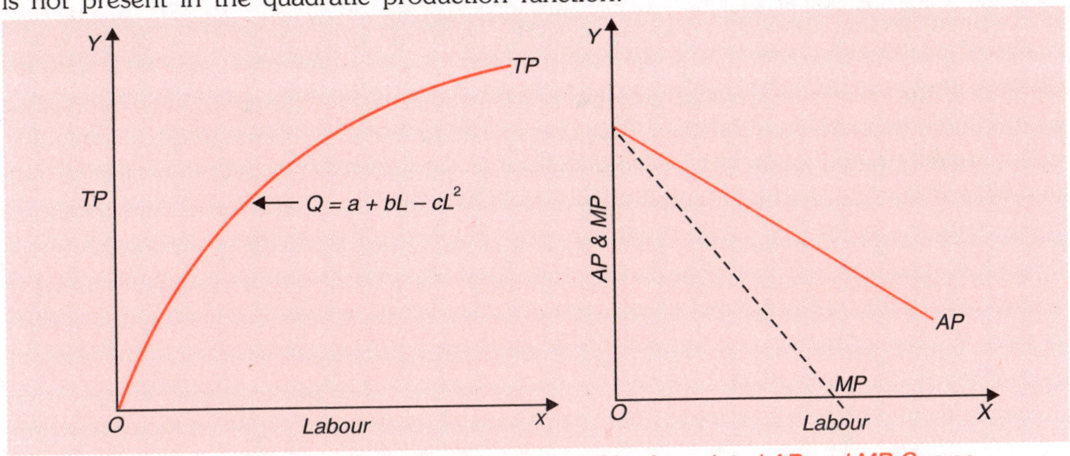

Fig. 19.27. *Quadratic Production Function and its Associated AP and MP Curves*

Finally, in an empirical study it is likely that data used exhibits no increasing or diminishing marginal returns to a variable factor. Thus production function obtained by an empirical study may indicate linear production function of the following type :

$$Q = a + bL \quad .....(3)$$

In this case of linear production function with one variable factor we get a straight-line total product curve with slope (*b*) equal to average product (*AP*) and marginal product as shown in Figure 19.28. Therefore, in this linear production function *AP* and *MP* curves will coincide and are horizontal straight line as shown in panel (*b*) of Fig. 19.28. A linear production function may be obtained in some real situations. However, given the fact that there is a fixed factor in the short-run production function, linear production function may not hold over a wide range of output.

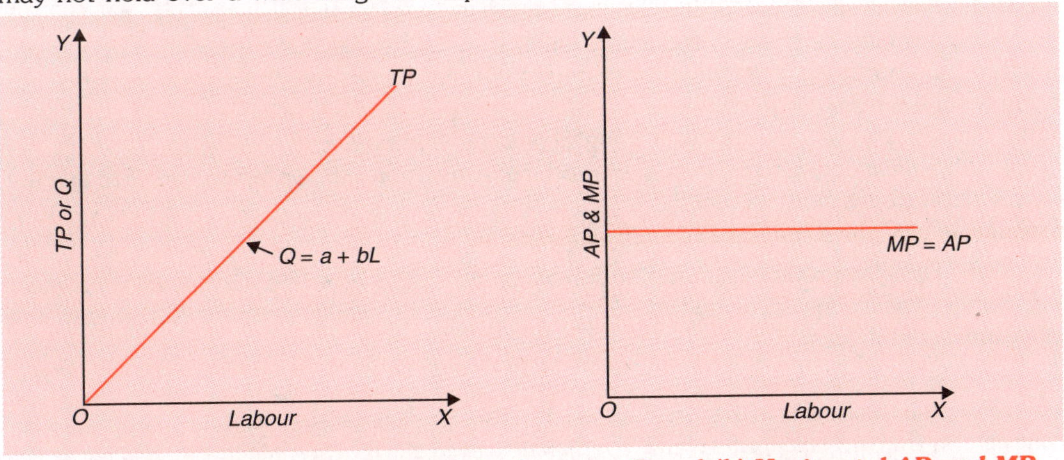

Panel (a) Total Product Curve of a Linear Production Function ***Panel (b) Horizontal AP and MP Curves***

Fig. 19.28. *Linear Production Function and its Associated AP and MP Curves*

Power Production Function

Another important form of production function usually obtained in empirical studies is power function which can be written as

$$Q = a L^b \qquad ..... (4)$$

The shape of power production function depends on the value of exponent b. If $b = 1$ in the above power production function, the marginal product of the variable factor (*e.g.* labour) will be straight line from the origin as shown in Fig. 19.29. by line *OA* . If $b > 1$ the marginal product of labour will be increasing and the shape of power function will be convex towards the *X*-axis as shown by line *OB* in Fig. 19.29. Finally if b < 1, marginal product of labour will be diminishing and the shape of the power production function will be concave towards the *X*-axis as shown by the curve *OC* in Fig. 19.29.

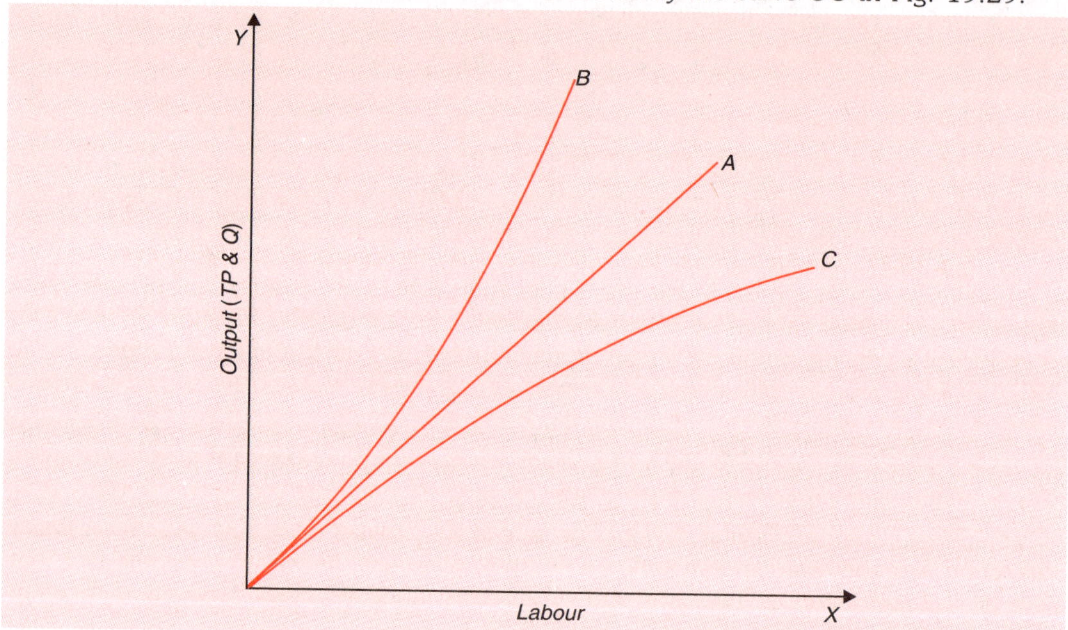

Fig. 19.29. *Power Production Function with Increasing, Constant and Diminishing Marginal Returns*

An advantage of power production function is that it can be converted into a linear function by expressing it in logarithmic terms. Thus writing power function equation (4) in log form we have

$$\log Q = \log a + b \log L$$

In this linear log form the power production function can be estimated through the least squares regression method.

Estimation of Cobb-Douglas Production Function

Cobb-Douglas production function introduced in 1928 by Cobb and Douglas[9] is most commonly used in empirical studies for the estimation of production function. It is of the following general form[10] :

$$Q = AL^a K^b \qquad ... (i)$$

Note that estimation of production function requires to estimate the values of parameters, that is, constant *A* and coefficient *a* and *b*. To estimate these measures we

9. See C.W. Cobb and P.H. Douglas, 'A Theory of Production, *American Economic Review* 8, (March 1928)
10. Originally Cobb-Douglas production used was of the form where the sum of exponents was equal to one, that is, it was of the form, $Q = AL^aK^{1-a}$ where (a + 1 – a = 1).Later on it was generalized so that the sum of exponents may be equal to one, greater than one or less than one.

use the time series data of inputs and output of a firm or industry or cross section analysis of firm in an industry. The time series data of inputs and output of the whole manufacturing can be used. The value of the parameters A, a and b will measure the production relationship between inputs (L and K) and output (Q). An important feature of Cobb-Douglas production is that it is of multiplicative form. This implies that both inputs must be used to get a positive output[11] (Q).

It is worth mentioning that as proved in the analysis of the theory of production function, the marginal products of labour and capital are functions of the parameters A, a, and b and the quantities of labour (L) and capital (K) inputs used for production. Thus

$$MP_L = \frac{\partial Q}{\partial L} = a\,AL^{a-1}K^b = \frac{a\,AL^aK^b}{L}$$

$$MP_K = \frac{\partial Q}{\partial K} = b\,AL^aK^{b-1} = \frac{b\,AL^aK^b}{K}$$

Further, as shown earlier, the sum of exponents of Cobb-Douglas ($a + b$) shows the returns to scale. Thus

If $a + b = 1$, returns to scale are constant. If $a + b > 1$, returns to scale are increasing.

If $a + b < 1$, returns to scale are decreasing.

Since Cobb-Douglas production function describes non-linear relationship between inputs and output, it cannot be directly estimated by the least squares regression technique. Therefore, for estimation of Cobb-Douglas production we have to first transform it in logarithmic form. That is,

$$\log Q = \log A + a \log L + b \log K \qquad \text{... (ii)}$$

In this logarithmic form, Cobb-Douglas production is linear and therefore can be estimated through least squares method of regression analysis[12].

A merit of Cobb-Douglas production function is that it can be used not only for just two variable inputs but for any number of independent input variables. Thus

$$Q = AX_1^{b_1}.X_2^{b_2}.X_3^{b_3}.X_4^{b_4}..............X_n^{b_n}$$

It may be noted that in theoretical discussion of Cobb-Douglas production function, it is assumed that technology remains constant. However, when using a time series data of a firm or industry, it may be found that technology has progressed over time. To capture the effect of technological change on output a trend variable can be included in the production function where $t = 1$, $t = 2$, $t = 3$, etc. over a time span can be taken.

On estimating Cobb-Douglas production function we can easily know the elasticities of output and marginal products. Note that the elasticity of output with respect to any input shows the percentage change in output in response to one per cent change in an input. As mentioned above, the exponents such as a and b of independent variables (L and K) measure the output elasticities of labour and capital.

Having estimated the parameters of functional equation (*ii*) we can obtain from these equations marginal products of labour and capital by using the specified values of inputs, labour and capital.

11. On the other hand, if additive function such as $Q = a + bL + CK$ is used, output could be positive even if one of the two inputs is zero

12. There are many software packages such as Excel of Microsoft, SPSS which are available to estimate the values of parameters through least squares regression. The use of these software packages has made the calculation involved in estimating Cobb-Douglas production quite easier.

For example, using time series data in natural log form of the Indian jute manufacturing industry the following estimate of Cobb-Douglas production function in log form has been obtained

$$\log Q = 2.501 + 0.84 \log L + 0.14 \log K \qquad R^2 = 0.98$$

The estimated value of coefficient $a = 0.84$ and $b = 0.14$. To determine the value of A we take antilog of 2.501 (which is equal to 12.19). Thus estimated Cobb-Douglas production function can be written as

$$Q = 12.19\, L^{0.84}\, K^{0.14}$$

The returns to scale are 0.84 + 0.14 = 0.98 which is very close to one. This means that the Indian jute industry exhibits constant returns to scale. Output elasticity of labour is 0.84 and output elasticity of capital 0.14. The marginal products of labour and capital are given by

$$MP_L = \frac{\partial Q}{\partial L} = 0.84\,(12.19).L^{-0.16}K^{0.14}$$

$$MP_K = \frac{\partial Q}{\partial L} = 0.14\,(12.19).L^{0.84}K^{-0.86}$$

Now MP_L and MP_K can be obtained by substituting the specified values of labour and capital (say 50 units of labour and 10 units of capital) in the above marginal product functions of labour and capital.

Estimates of production function made for some industries of India and the USA are given in the following table. It is useful to know the estimates of parameters especially β_1, β_2. For example, the estimate of β_1 shows elasticity of production with respect to labour, that is, it shows how much per cent output increases when there is one percentage increase in labour input. Likewise, estimate of β_2 shows the production elasticity with respect to capital input. Thus, the β_1 coefficient of labour equal to 0.59 obtained for sugar industry shows that one percentage increase in labour causes 0.59 per cent expansion in sugar output in India. Similarly, the value of β_2 coefficient of 0.33 of capital for Indian sugar Industry show that one percentage increase in capital input leads to 0.33 per cent increase in sugar output.

Table 19.4. Estimates β_1 and β_2 for Some Industries

Industry	*Country*	β_1	β_2	β_3	$\beta_1 + \beta_2$
Cotton	India	0.92	0.12		1.04
Jute	India	0.84	0.14		0.98
Sugar	India	0.59	0.33		0.92
Coal	India	0.71	0.44		1.15
Paper	India	0.64	0.45		1.09
Chemicals	India	0.80	0.37		1.17
Electricity	India	0.20	0.67		0.87
Food	United States	0.63	0.44		1.07
Paper	United States	0.62	0.37		0.99
Rail Roads	United States	0.70	0.41		1.11
Aircraft	United States	0.54	0.38	0.11	1.03
Gas	France	0.83	0.10		0.93
Coal	U.K.	0.79	0.29		1.08

Source. A.A. Walters, "Production and Cost Function", *Econometrica*, January 1963, and J. Moroney, "Cobb-Douglas Production Function and Returns to Scale in U.S. Manufacturing". *Western Economic Journal*, 1967.

In the last column of Table 19.4, we have shown the sum of the exponents of labour and capital of the two-factor Cobb-Douglas production function. A look at this table will reveal that in 7 out of 13 cases, the sum of the parameters ($\beta_1 + \beta_2$) is greater than one and therefore increasing returns to scale occur in these cases. In the two cases (jute industry in case of India and paper industry in case of the USA), the sum of $\beta_1 + \beta_2$ is *near unity* (0.98 and 0.99 respectively) and hence constant returns to scale occur in these cases. In the remaining cases, decreasing returns to scale are obtained as the sum of $\beta_1 + \beta_2$ is less than one.

Problems in Estimation of Production Functions

Some important problems encountered in the production function studies are noteworthy. First, whereas production function theoretically includes only technically efficient combinations of inputs and output, the actual data used for measurement of production function may not actually represent the efficient input combinations. This may cause some error in the estimation of production function.

The second important problem in estimating production function relates to the measurement of capital input. The main difficulty in this regard is that stock of capital is heterogeneous, that is, it is composed of different types of machines, buildings and inventories. to obtain *a single measure* of the quantity of capital input used poses a very difficult problem.

A third problem which arises in case of time series and cross-section studies of production function is that errors can arise because the various data-points which are assumed to be on the same production function may belong in fact to different production functions.

Cobb-Douglas production function cannot show the changes in marginal product of a variable factor *over all the three stages of short-run production function in one specification*. As explained above, a cubic type of production function is needed to represent all the three stages of production function with one variable factor. Thus Cobb-Douglas production when estimated for a firm or an industry cannot represent changes in marginal returns over stages of increasing, constant and decreasing returns. As seen above, the estimation of Cobb-Douglas function can show either increasing or constant or decreasing returns to scale.

Ideally, inputs should be measured as *'flow'* rather than *'stock'* variables. However, this is not always possible, especially in case of measurement of capital used in production. This is because capital which is of heterogenous type is available in stock and it is difficult to measure *how much capital is actually* utilized during a period for producing a commodity. Thus, like other production functions the estimation of Cobb-Douglas production is also not without problems.

QUESTIONS FOR REVIEW

1. Distinguish between returns to scale and returns to a variable factor with the help of isoquants.
2. What are isoquants ? Why does an isoquant slope downward? Why do they cannot cut each other ? Why are they convex to the origin ?
3. What is meant by marginal rate of technical substitution between factors ($MRTS_{LK}$)? How is it related to marginal products of factors ? Why does marginal rate of technical substitution of labour for capital diminishes as more labour is used by substituting capital?
4. "The slope of an isoquant is a measure of the relative marginal productivities of the factors." Explain.
5. Distinguish between fixed proportion and variable-proportion production function. Draw the isoquants of fixed-proportion production function.

6. Define substitute and complementary factors. Draw isoquants of perfect substitutes and perfect complements in production. Give examples.

7. What are increasing returns to scale? Show them on an isoquant map. Explain the causes of increasing returns to scale.

8. Show the increasing, constant and decreasing returns to scale through isoquants. What causes decreasing returns to scale beyond a certain point?

9. Is increasing marginal returns to a variable factor compatible with increasing returns to scale?

10. Show that when returns to scale are constant, marginal returns to a variable factor diminishes, (*a*) Prove geometrically, (*b*) Give an algebraic proof of it using a linear homogeneous production function.

11. What are ridge lines? Draw an isoquant map showing ridge lines. Why does a rational producer not operate outside the ridge lines? Indicate in the isoquant map the area where a rational producer will possibly operate.

12. What is linear homogeneous production function? What are its properties ?

[**Hint:** Cobb-Douglas production function is linear homogeneous when sum of its exponents, $a + b = 1$. Therefore, the properties of Cobb-Douglas production function explained in the chapter are the properties of linear homogeneous production function.]

13. What is Cobb-Douglas production function ? What are its useful properties ? Why is it extensively used in empirical studies for estimation of production ?

14. When the sum of exponents $(a + b)$ of two factor Cobb-Douglas production function is equal to one, it shows constant returns to scale. Prove it ?

15. What is meant by constant returns to scale? Show them with an isoproduct map. Is it correct to say that returns to scale would have been constant if the factors of production had been perfectly divisible?

16. You are given the following production functions. Which ones represent constant returns to scale, which ones increasing returns to scale and decreasing returns to scale and why?

(*a*) $Q = AK^{0.5} L^{0.7}$ (*b*) $Q = AK^{0.25} L^{0.75}$

(*c*) $Q = AK^{0.3} L^{0.6}$ (*d*) $Q = 10\sqrt{L}\sqrt{K}$

17. A firm has the following production function:

$$Q = 2K^{\frac{1}{2}}L^{\frac{1}{2}}$$

Calculate marginal product functions for labour and capital.

18. (*a*) What would the isoquants look like if both inputs are perfect substitutes in the production process? What if there was zero substitutability between inputs?

(*b*) What does the isoquants of perfect substitutes imply for the least-cost combination of inputs ?

19. Consider the production function represented by $Y = AL^{\alpha} K^{\beta}$ where Y is output and α. and β are positive constants.

(*a*) Show that this production function exhibits constant returns to scale when $\alpha + \beta = 1$.

(*b*) Show that marginal product of labour depends on the input ratio $\frac{K}{L}$ only.

(*c*) When is the expansion path linear ?

20. State the form of Cobb-Douglas production function which exhibits constant returns to scale. Prove that returns to a variable factor diminishes in this production function.

CHAPTER

20

Optimum Factor Combination

Introduction

In the last three chapters we explained the law of variable proportions and returns to scale which underlie the process of production. An important problem facing an enterpreneur is to decide about the particular combination of factors which should be employed for producing a product. There are various technical possibilities open to a firm from which it has to choose, that is, there are various combinations of factors which can yield a given level of output and from among which producer has to select one for production. As explained in an earlier chapter, various combinations of factors which produce equal level of output are represented by an equal product curve or what is also called insoquant. An isoquant map or isoproduct map represents various technical possibilities of producing different levels of output.

It is assumed that the entrepreneur aims at maximizing his profits. A profit-maximizing entrepreneur will seek to minimize his cost for producing a given output, or to put it in another way, he will try to maximize his output for a given level of cost outlay. The choice of a particular combination of factors by an entrepreneur depends upon (*a*) technical possibilities of production, and (*b*) the prices of factors used for the production of a particular product. Technical possibilities of production are represented by the isoquant map. Before explaining how producer will arrive at the least-cost combination of factors, we shall first explain how the prices of factors can be introduced, in our analysis.

ISO-COST LINE

The prices of factors are represented by the iso-cost line. The iso-cost line plays an important role in determining what combination of factors the firm will choose for production. An iso-cost line shows various combinations of two factors that the firm can buy with a given outlay. How the iso-cost line is drawn is shown in Fig.20.1 where on the *X*-axis we measure units of labour and on the *Y*-axis we measure units of capital. We assume that prices of factors are given and constant for the firm. In other words, we are considering a firm which is working under perfect competition in the factor markets. Further suppose that the firm has ₹ 300 to spend on the factors, labour and capital and price of labour is ₹ 4 per labour hour and the price of capital is ₹ 5 per machine hour. With outlay of ₹ 300 he can buy 75 units of labour or 60 units of machine hours (*i.e.*, capital). Let *OB* in Fig.20.1 represent 75 units of labour and *OA* represent 60 units of capital. In other words, if the firm spends its entire outlay of ₹ 300 on labour it buys 75 units or *OB* of labour hours and if it spends its entire outlay of ₹ 300 on capital it buys 60 units or *OA* of machine hours. The straight line *AB* which joins points *A* and *B* will pass through all combinations of labour and capital which the firm can buy with cost outlay of ₹ 300 , if it spends the entire sum on them at the given prices. This line *AB* is called *iso-cost* line, for whichever combination lying on it the firm buys it has to incur the same cost-outlay at the given prices. ***An iso-cost line is defined as the locus of various combinations of factors which a firm can buy with a constant outlay. The iso-cost line is also called the price line or outlay line.***

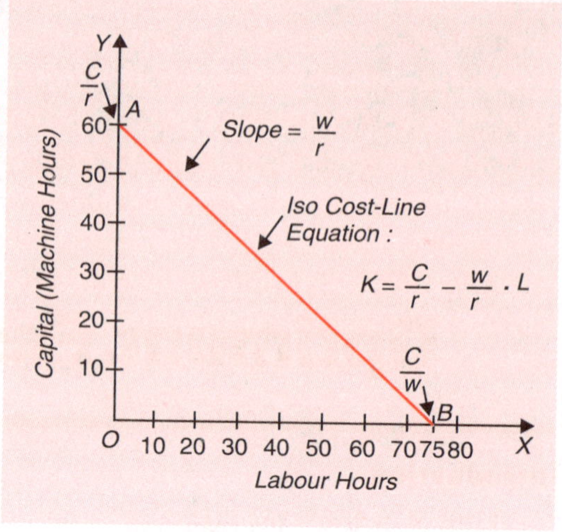

Fig. 20.1. *Iso-Cost Line*

The Equation of the Iso-Cost Line. The total cost incurred on the factors of production for production of a commodity is equal to the sum of the payments made for labour and capital. Now, payment for the labour used is equal to the wage rate (w) multiplied by the amount of labour used (L). Thus $W.L$ represents the total payment made for labour. Similarly, rK is the total payment made for capital where r is the price per unit of capital and K is the quantity of capital used. The total cost equation can therefore be described as follows.

$$C = w.L + rK$$

Where C is the total cost incurred by the firm on purchasing the quantities of factors used for production. Given the prices of factors, the iso-cost equation can be rearranged as under to express it in the intercept-slope form :

$$C = wL + rK$$
$$rK = C - w.L$$
$$K = \frac{C}{r} - \frac{w}{r}.L \qquad ...(ii)$$

Where $\frac{C}{r}$ represents the intercept of the isocost line on the Y-axis and $\frac{w}{r}$ represents the factor price ratio and is equal to the slope of the is-cost line.

Slope of the Iso-Cost Line. The slope of the isocost line can be proved to be equal to the ratio of price of labour (w) and price of capital (r). Let, according to the iso-cost line AB, which, given the factor prices, represents the total cost-outlay incurred on the two factors, labour and capital, the total cost equals C.

As explained above, the vertical intercept OA that represents the quantity of factor capital if entire costoutlay is spent on it is equal to $\frac{C}{r}$. Similarly, the horizontal intercept OB representing the quantity of labour purchased if entire cost-outlay is incurred on purchasing it is equal to $\frac{C}{w}$.

Now, the slope of the iso-cost line is

$$\frac{OA}{OB} = \frac{C}{r} \div \frac{C}{w} = \frac{C}{r}.\frac{w}{C} = \frac{w}{r}$$

Thus the slope of the iso-cost line $\frac{OA}{OB}$ is equal to the ratio of factor-prices $(\frac{w}{r})$

Shift in the Iso-Cost Line

Now, the iso-cost line will shift if the total outlay which the firm wants to spend on the factors changes. Suppose if the total outlay to be made by the firm increases to ₹ 400, prices of factors remaining the same, then it can buy 100 units of labour hours (*i.e.*, *OB′* of labour) or 80 units of machine hours (*i.e.*, *OA′* of capital) if it spends the entire sum on either of them. Thus, the new iso-cost line will be *A′B′* which will be parallel to the original iso-cost line *AB* as shown in Fig. 20.2. If the outlay which the firm intends to make further increases to ₹ 500, then iso-cost line will shift to the position *A″B″*. Thus any number of iso-cost lines can be drawn, all parallel to one another, and each representing the various combinations of two factors that can be purchased for a particular outlay. The higher the outlay, the higher the corresponding iso-cost line.

The iso-cost line will also change if the prices of factors change, outlay remaining the same. Suppose the firm's outlay is ₹ 300 and the prices of labour and capital are ₹ 4 and ₹ 5 respectively the iso-cost line will then be *AB* as shown in Fig. 20.3. If now the price of labour falls to ₹ 3, then with the outlay of ₹ 300 and ₹ 3 as the price of labour, the firm can buy 100

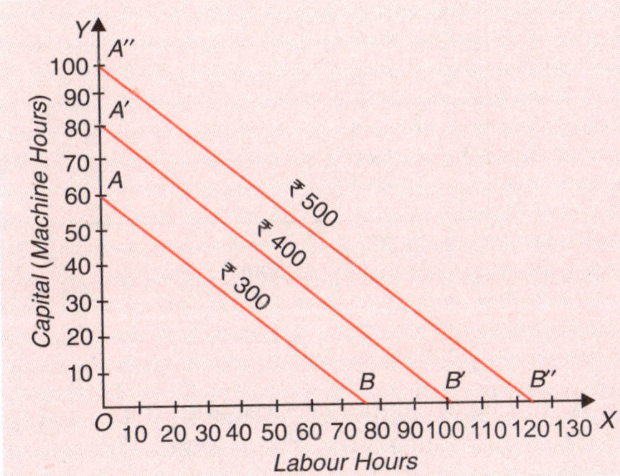

Fig. 20.2. *Shift in Iso-cost Line Resulting from Increase in Outlay or Total Cost*

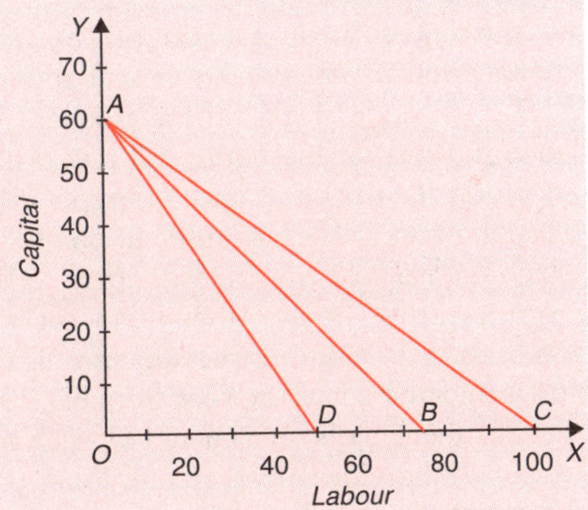

Fig. 20.3. *Changes is Iso-cost Line as a Result of Changes in the Price of Labour*

units of labour if it spends the entire outlay on it. *OC* represents 100 units of labour. Therefore, as a result of the fall in price of labour from ₹ 4 to 3, the price line changes from *AB* to *AC*. If price of labour rises from ₹ 4 to ₹ 6 per hour the iso-cost line will shift to *AD*. Likewise, if price of capital changes, the outlay and price of labour remaining the same, the iso-cost line will shift.

It is clear from above that the iso-cost line depends upon two things : (i) prices of the factors of production, and (ii) the total cost outlay which the firm has to make on the factors. Given these two things, an iso-cost line can be drawn. It should also be noted that the slope of the iso-cost line, like that of the price line in indifference curve analysis and demand, is equal to the ratio of prices of two factors. Thus, slope of the iso-cost line *AB*

$$= \frac{\text{Price of Labour}}{\text{Price of Capital}} = \frac{w}{r}$$

LEAST-COST COMBINATION OF FACTORS

An equal product map of isoquant map represents the various factor combinations which can yield various levels of output, every isoquant showing those factor combinations each of which can produce a specified level of output. Thus, an isoquant map represents the production function of a product with two variable factors. Therefore, an isoquant map represents the technical conditions of production for a product. On the other hand, a family of iso-cost line represents the various levels of total cost outlay, given the prices of two factors. The entrepreneur may desire to minimize his cost for producing a given level of output, or he may desire to maximize his output level for a given cost outlay. Let us suppose that the entrepreneur has already decided about the level of output to be produced. Then the question is with which factor combination the entrepreneur will try to produce the given level of output. To produce a given level of output, the entrepreneur will choose the combination of factors which minimizes his cost of production, for only in this way he will be maximizing his profits. Thus a producer will try to produce a given level of output with **least-cost combination of factors.** This least-cost combination of factors will be optimum for him.

Which will be the least-cost combination of factors can be understood from considering Fig. 20.4. Suppose the entrepreneur has decided to produce 500 units of output which is represented by isoquant *Q*. The 500 units of output can be produced by any combination of labour and capital such as *R.,S.,E.,T.* and *J* lying on the isoquant *Q*. Now, a glance at the figure will reveal that for producing the given level of output (500 units) the cost will be minimum at point *E* at which the iso-cost line *CD* is tangent to the given isoquant. At no other point such as *R,S,T.* and *J*, lying on the isoquant *Q*, the cost is minimum. It will be seen from Fig.20.4 that all other points on isoquant *Q*, such as *R, S, T, J* lie on higher iso-cost lines than *CD* and which will therefore mean greater total cost-outlay for producing the given output. Therefore, the entrepreneur will not chose any of the combinations *R, S, T* and *J*.

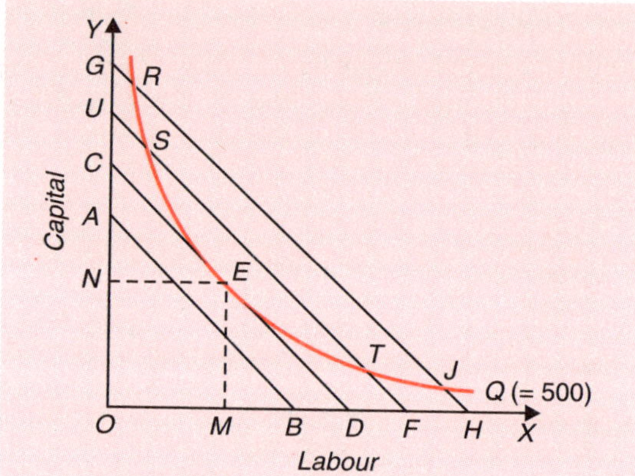

Fig. 20.4. *Minimizing Cost for a Given Level of Output*

We thus see that factor combination *E* is the least-cost combination of labour and capital for producing a given output. Factor combination *E* is therefore an optimum combination for him under the given circumstances. Hence we conclude that the entrepreneur will choose factor combination *E* (that is, *OM* units of labour and *ON* units of capital) to produce 500 units of output. It is thus clear that the tangency point of the given isoquant with an iso-cost line represents the least-cost combination of factors for producing a given output.

How the entrepreneur will arrive at the least-cost factor combination can also be explained with the help of the concept of marginal rate of technical substitution (*MRTS*) and the price ratio of the two factors. As has been shown earlier, the marginal rate of technical substitution (*MRTS*) is given by the slope of the isoquant at its various points. On the other hand, the price ratio of the factors is given by the slope of the iso-cost line. The entrepreneur will not choose to produce the given output at point *R* because at point *R* marginal rate of technical substitution of labour for capital is greater than the price ratio of the factors (at point *R* the slope of the isoquant *Q* is greater than the slope of the iso-cost line *GH*). Therefore, if he is at point *R*, he will be reducing his cost by using more of labour in place of capital and go down on the isoquant *Q*. Likewise, he will not stop at point *S*, since the marginal rate of technical substitution of labour for capital is still greater than the price ratio of the factors; slope of the isoquant at point *S* being greater than the slope of the iso-cost line *EF*. Therefore, the entrepreneur will further substitute labour for capital and will go down further on the isoquant Q.

When the entrepreneur reaches point E, the marginal rate of technical substitution of labour for capital is there equal to the price ratio of the factors, since the slopes of the isoquant and the iso-cost line CD are equal to each other. The entrepreneur will have no incentive to go down further, for he will not be lowering his cost in this way, but in fact he will be reaching higher iso-cost lines. At points J and T on the isoquant Q the marginal rate of technical substitution of labour for capital is smaller than the price ratio of the factors and the entrepreneur will try to substitute capital for labour and move upward on the isoquant Q until he reaches the point of tangency E, where marginal rate of technical substitution is equal to the price ratio of the factors. It is thus clear that the entrepreneur will be minimizing his cost when he is using the factor combination for which his marginal rate of technical substitution is equal to the price ratio of the factors. Thus at his equilibrium point E'.

$$MRTS_{LK} = \frac{w}{r}$$

where w stands for the wage rate of labour and r for the price of capital

But, as we saw in the last chapter, marginal rate of technical substitution of labour for capital is equal to the ratio of the marginal physical products of the two factors.

Therefore

$$MRTS_{LK} = \frac{MP_L}{MP_k} = \frac{w}{r}$$

$$\frac{MP_L}{MP_k} = \frac{w}{r}$$

We can rearrange the above equation to have

$$\frac{MP_L}{w} = \frac{MP_K}{r}$$

We therefore reach an important conclusion about the entrepreneur's choice of the quantities of the two factors. The entrepreneur will be in equilibrium in regard to his use and purchases of the two factors when he is using such quantities of the two factors that the marginal physical products of the two factors are proportional to the factor prices. If, for instance, the price of factor X is twice as much as that of factor Y, then the entrepreneur will purchase and use such quantities of the two factors that the marginal physical product of factor X is twice the marginal physical product of factor Y.

We can extend the above condition for least-cost combination of factors when more than two factors are involved. Suppose there are three factors, labour, capital and land. From the above condition for least cost or optimal combination of factors to produce a given level of output, it follows that in case of these three factors also the ratio of marginal physical product of factor to its price will be the same in case of all the three factors. Thus, the equilibrium to produce a given level of output will be achieved when the following condition holds :

$$\frac{MP_L}{w} = \frac{MP_K}{r} = \frac{MP_D}{t}$$

where

w = price of labour, *i.e.*, its wage rate

r = price of capital

t = price of the use of land, that is, rent of land

MP_D = the marginal physical product of land

It is quite clear from above that the entrepreneur's behaviour in choosing the quantities of factors is exactly symmetrical with the behaviour of the consumer. Both the entrepreneur and the consumer purchase things in such quantities as to equate marginal rate of substitution with the price ratio. The consumer, to be in equilibrium, equates his marginal rate of substitution (or the ratio of the marginal utilities of two goods) with the price ratio of the goods. The entrepreneur equates the marginal rate of technical substitution (or, the ratio of the marginal physical products of the two factors) with the price ratio of the factors.

Output Maximisation Subject to Cost Constraint

The dual of cost-minimisation problem for a given level of output is of output maximisation for a given level of cost or outlay. Suppose the firm has decided upon the cost which it has to incur for the production of a commodity. With a given level of cost-outlay, there will be a single iso-cost line that represents the outlay that the firm has decided to spend. The firm will have to choose a factor combination lying on the given iso-cost line. Obviously, with a given cost- outlay, a rational producer will be interested in maximizing output of the commodity. Consider Fig. 20.5. Suppose the firm has decided to incur an outlay of ₹ 5000 on labour and capital which is represented by the iso-cost line *AB*. The firm has a choice to use any factor combination of labour and capital such as *R, S, E, T, J* etc. lying on the given iso-cost line *AB* to produce the product, An isoquant map showing a set of isoquants that represents various levels of output (200, 300, 400, 500 units) has been superimposed on the given iso-cost line *AB*. A glance at the Fig. 20.5 reveals that the firm will choose the factor combination *E* consisting of *ON* of labour and *OH* of capital. This is because of all the factor combinations that lie on the given iso-cost line *AB*, only the factor combination *E* enables the firm to reach the highest possible isoquant Q_3 and thus produce 400 units of output. All other combinations of labour and capital on the given iso-cost line *AB* such as *R, S, T, J* etc., lie on lower isoquants showing lower level of output than 400 units.

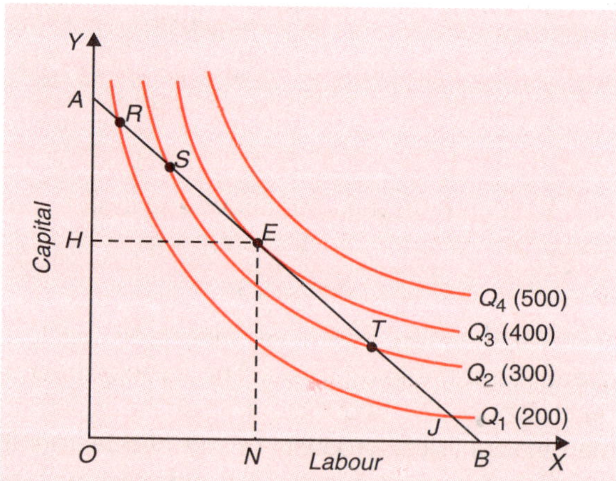

Fig. 20.5. *Maximization of Output for a Given Cost*

NUMERICAL PROBLEMS

Problem 1. *A firm is producing output using labour and capital in such quantities that marginal product of labour is 15, and marginal product of capital is 8. The wage rate of labour is ₹ 3 and price of capital is ₹ 2. Is the firm using efficient factor combination for production? If not, what it should do to achieve economic efficiency ?*

Solution :

Efficiency condition for factor use (that is, optimal factor combination) requires that the following condition should be fulfilled:

$$\frac{MP_L}{w} = \frac{MP_K}{r}$$

Now, $$\frac{MP_L}{w} = \frac{15}{3} \text{ and } \frac{MP_K}{r} = \frac{8}{2}$$

Now, $$\frac{15}{3} > \frac{8}{2}$$

The given factor combination cannot therefore be efficient or optimal factor combination because the firm is getting more output from a rupee spent on labour than on capital. To achieve economic efficiency in use of resources and maximising profits the firm should substitute labour for capital so that $\frac{MP_L}{w}$ becomes equal to $\frac{MP_K}{r}$.

Problem 2. *The wage rate of labour is ₹ 6 and price of raw materials is ₹ 2. The marginal product of labour is 16 while the marginal product of raw materials is 4. Can a firm operating under these conditions be maximizsing profits ?*

Solution : Profit maximisation is achieved when resources are efficiently used. Efficiency in resource use requires the following condition :

$$\frac{MP_L}{w} = \frac{MP_{RM}}{P_{RM}}$$

$$\frac{MP_L}{w} = \frac{16}{6}, \frac{MP_{RM}}{P_{RM}} = \frac{4}{2}$$

$$\frac{16}{6} > \frac{4}{2} \text{ or } \frac{MP_L}{w} > \frac{MP_{RM}}{P_{RM}}$$

Thus, the firm will not be maximising profits. To maximise profits it should substitute labour for raw materials.

Problem 3. *A firm reports that marginal product of labour is 5 and marginal rate of technical substitution of labour for capital is 2. What is the marginal product of capital ?*

Solution : $$MRTS_{LK} = \frac{MP_L}{MP_K}$$

$$2 = \frac{5}{MP_K}$$

$$MP_K = \frac{5}{2} = 2.5$$

Problem 4. *A firm employs labour as the only variable factor along with a fixed quantity of capital. Wage rate of labour is ₹ 100 per day and its marginal product is 20 units of output. What is marginal cost of the product ?*

Solution : Marginal cost is the additional cost incurred on producing an extra unit of output. Marginal cost can be obtained from dividing the wage that has to be paid to the additional unit of labour by the number of units of output produced by it (that is, marginal product). Thus,

$$MC = \frac{w}{MP_L}$$

$$= \frac{100}{20} = 5.$$

Problem 5. *A biscuit producing company reports the following data about its production and factors used:*

Q	K	L	Q	K	L
490	15	99	470	14	100
500	15	100	500	15	100

where Q = output, K = capital, L = labour.'

If wage rate of labour is ₹ 5 and price of capital is ₹ 10, does the input combination of 15K and 100L represents the least-cost factor combination? If not, should it use more labour and less capital or less labour and more capital ?

Solution :

Least-cost factor combination requires that the following condition must be met

$$\frac{MP_L}{w} = \frac{MP_K}{r},$$

where w is wage rate and r is price of capital.

Now, in the problem when factor combination is changed from $15K + 100L$ to $15K + 99L$, the output declines by 10 units (500 – 490 = 10). Thus, MP_L = 10. Similarly, when factor combination is changed from $15K + 100L$, to $14K + 100L$, output declines by 30 (500 – 470 = 30). Thus, MP_k= 30. Substituting these values of marginal products of labour and capital and the factor prices in the condition for least-cost factor combination, we have

$$\frac{MP_L}{w} = \frac{MP_K}{r}$$

$$\frac{10}{5} \neq \frac{30}{10} \text{ or } \frac{10}{5} < \frac{30}{10}$$

The company will use more capital and less labour as output per unit of a rupee (3) spent on it is greater than the output per unit of a rupee $\left(\frac{10}{5} \text{ or } 2\right)$ spent on labour.

EXPANSION PATH

We explained above which factor combination a firm will choose to produce a specified level of output, given the prices of the two factors. We are now interested in studying how the entrepreneur will change his factor combination as he expands his output, given the factor prices. To begin with, suppose the prices of the two factors labour and capital are such that are represented by the slope of the iso-cost line AB. In Fig. 20.6 four iso-cost lines, AB, CD, UF and GH are drawn which show different levels of total cost outlay. All iso-cost lines are parallel to one another indicating that prices of two factors remain the same. If the firm wants to produce the output level denoted by Q_1 (= 100 units of output), it will chose the factor combination E_1 which minimizes cost of production; E_1 being the point of tangency between the isoquant Q_1 and the iso-cost line AB. Now, if a firm wants to produce a higher level of output denoted by the isoquant Q_2 (=200), it will choose the factor combination E_2 which is the least-cost combination for new output. Likewise, for still higher output levels denoted by Q_3 and Q_4 , then firm will choose tangency combination E_3 and E_4 respectively which minimize cost for the given outputs.

The line joining the minimum cost combinations such as E_1, E_2, E_3, E_4 is called the *expansion path* because it shows how the factor combination with which the firm produces will alter as the firm expands its level of output. Thus ***the expansion path may be defined as the locus of the points of tangency between the iso product curves (i.e., isoquants) and the iso-cost lines***. The expansion path is also known as *scale-line* because it shows how the entrepreneur will change the quantities of the two factors when it increases the level of output. The expansion path can have different shapes and slopes depending upon the relative prices of the productive factors used and the shape of the isoquants. As we shall prove below, when the production function exhibits constant returns to scale, the expansion path will be a straight line through the origin. Further, for a given isoquant map there will be a different expansion path for each different relative prices of the factors.

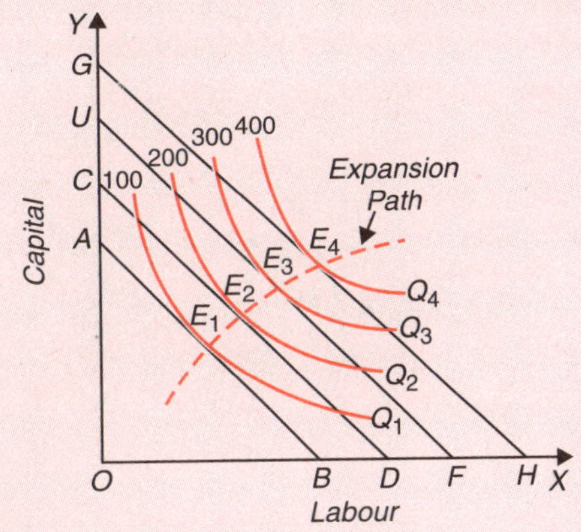

Fig. 20.6. *Expansion Path.*

Since expansion path represents minimum cost combinations for various levels of output, it shows the cheapest way of producing each output, given the relative prices of the factors. When two factors are variable, the entrepreneur will choose to produce at some point on the expansion path. One cannot say exactly at which particular point on the expansion path the entrepreneur will in fact be producing unless one knows either the output which he wants to produce or the size of the cost-outlay it wants to incur. But this is certain that when both factors are variable and the prices of factors are given, a rational entrepreneur will seek to produce at one point or the other on the expansion path.

Derivation of Equation for Expansion Path (in Cobb-Douglas Production Function)

As explained above, expansion path shows how *optimal factor combination changes* when a firm expands its level of output *at the given factor prices*. We can mathematically derive equation for expansion path which plays an important role in the production analysis. To derive the equation for expansion we take the following Cobb-Douglas production function.

$$Q = 100\, K^{0.5}\, L^{0.5}$$

We have seen above at optimal factor combinations the following condition holds :

$$MRTS_{LK} = \frac{w}{r} \qquad \text{......(1)}$$

and

$$MRTS_{LK} = \frac{MP_L}{MP_K} \qquad \text{......(2)}$$

To obtain MP_L or $\frac{\partial Q}{\partial L}$ we differentiate the given production function ($Q = 100\, K^{0.5}\, L^{0.5}$) with respect to labour. Thus

$$MP_L = 100 \times \frac{1}{2} K^{1/2} L^{-1/2} = 50 \frac{K^{1/2}}{L^{1/2}}$$

and $$MP_K \text{ or } \frac{\partial Q}{\partial K} = 100 \times \frac{1}{2} K^{-1/2} L^{1/2} = 50 \frac{L^{1/2}}{K^{1/2}}$$

Therefore, $$MRTS_{LK} = \frac{MP_L}{MP_K} = \frac{50 \frac{K^{1/2}}{L^{1/2}}}{50 \frac{L^{1/2}}{K^{1/2}}} = \frac{K}{L} \qquad .....(3)$$

Substituting $\frac{K}{L}$ for $MRTS_{LK}$ in equation (1), we have

$$\frac{K}{L} = \frac{w}{r}$$

or $$K = \frac{w}{r} . L \qquad ....(4)$$

The expression in equation (4) is the equation for expansion path for the production function, $Q = 100K^{1/2}L^{1/2}$. If the prices of labour and capital, *i.e.*, w and r respectively are known, equation (4) defines the *optimal combinations of factors* (that is, least-cost combinations of factors for various levels of output or output-maximizing factor combinations for various cost-outlays)

The equation (4) for expansion path reveals that the quantities of labour and capital used to produce a level of output, given the production function, depends on prices of factors, w and r. For example, if prices of labour and capital are equal, say ₹ 50 per hour as wage rate (w) of labour and ₹ 50 per hour as rental (r) of machine (*i.e.*, capital) used, then from the expansion path equation (4) we obtain

$$K = \frac{w}{r} . L = \frac{50}{50} L$$

$$K = L$$

That is, when prices of two factors are the same, given the Cobb-Douglas production function, equal quantities of the two factos will be used.

Suppose the wage rate of labour rises to ₹ 100 per hour, while rental of the machine remains fixed at ₹ 50 per hour, we obtain the following equation for expansion path

$$K = \frac{w}{r} . L = \frac{100}{50} L$$

$$K = 2L$$

This means that with rise in wage rate of labour from ₹ 50 per hour to ₹ 100 per hour, the quantity of capital used will be two times labour input. That is, rise in wage rate has resulted in substitution of capital for labour in the production process.

Finding Output Level with given Factor Prices

It should be noted that expansion path $\left(K = \frac{w}{r} L\right)$ shows various optimal factor combinations for the given factor prices, *it does not indicate the specific level of output for a given optimal factor combination.* However, the level of output produced with an optimal factor combinations can be determined by substituting the equation for expansion path into the original production function. Thus, in our example, to determine the specific level or rate of output, we substitute the equation for expansion path $\left(K = \frac{w}{r}.L\right)$ into the production function $Q = 100\ K^{1/2}.\ L^{1/2}$ we have

$$Q = 100\left(\frac{w}{r}.L\right)^{1/2} L^{1/2}$$

$$Q = 100\ L\left(\frac{w}{r}\right)^{1/2}$$

If the value of L and $\frac{w}{r}$ are known, we can find out the value of Q.

Numerical Problem : *Given the production function $Q = 100\ K^{0.5}\ L^{0.5}$. Determine the optimal input combination for producing 1444 units of output if wage rate of labour (w) is ₹ 30 and price per unit of capital (r) is ₹ 40. What is the minimum cost of production?*

Solution : The given production function is

$$Q = 100K^{0.5}\ L^{0.5}$$

$$MP_L = \frac{\partial Q}{\partial L} = 100 \times 0.5\ K^{0.5}\ L^{-0.5}$$

$$= 50K^{0.5}L^{-0.5}$$

$$MP_K = \frac{\partial Q}{\partial K} = 100 \times 0.5K^{-0.5}L^{0.5}$$

$$= 50\ K^{-0.5}\ L^{0.5}$$

$$\frac{MP_L}{MP_K} = \frac{50K^{0.5}L^{-0.5}}{50K^{-0.5}\ L^{0.5}} = \frac{K}{L}$$

In equilibrium, $MRS_{LK} = \frac{MP_L}{MP_K} = \frac{w}{r}$ Thus, in optimal input combination, $\frac{K}{L} = \frac{w}{r}$

or
$$K = \frac{w}{r}L.$$

To obtain the value of L we substitue $K = \frac{w}{r}L.$ in the production function with $Q = 1444$ units. Thus

$$1444 = 100\ K^{0.5}\ L^{0.5}$$

$$= 100\left(\frac{w}{r}L\right)^{0.5} L^{0.5}$$

$$1444 = 100\,L \left(\frac{w}{r}\right)^{0.5}$$

Substituting $w = 30$ and $r = 40$

$$1444 = 100L \times \left(\frac{30}{40}\right)^{0.5}$$

$$1444 = 100\,L \times (0.75)^{0.5}$$
$$= 100\,L \times 0.866 = 86.6L$$

$$L = \frac{1444}{86.6} = 16.67$$

Now, using the equation for expansion path ($K = \frac{w}{r}L$) we can obtain the value of K by substituting the values of L, w and r. Thus

$$K = \frac{30}{40} \times 16.67$$
$$= 0.75 \times 16.67$$
$$= 12.5$$

Thus optimum combination of inputs consists of 16.67 units of labour and 12.5 units of capital. This will ensure minimum possible cost for producing 1444 units of output.

In order to determine this minimum cost we substitute the optimum values of L and K obtained above and the given prices of labour and capital (*i.e.*, w and r) in the cost function. Thus

$$C = wL + rK$$
$$= 30 \times 16.67 + 40 \times 12.50$$
$$= 500 + 500$$
$$= ₹\ 1000$$

Thus minimum cost of producing 1444 units of output is ₹ 1000.

Numerical Problem 2. *Given : $Q = 100K^{0.5}L^{0.5}$, C = ₹ 1200, $w = 30$ and $r = 40$. Determine the quantity of labour and capital that the firm should use in order to maximize output. What is this level of output ?*

Solution. The problem of constrained maximisation is :

$$\text{Maximize } Q = 100\,K^{\frac{1}{2}}\,L^{\frac{1}{2}}$$

Subject to cost constraint : $1200 = 30\,L + 40\,K$

$$MP_K = \frac{\partial Q}{\partial K} = \frac{1}{2}\,100\,K^{-1/2}\,L^{1/2}$$

$$MP_L = \frac{\partial Q}{\partial L} = \frac{1}{2}\,100\,K^{1/2}\,L^{-1/2}$$

$$\frac{MP_K}{MP_L} = \frac{50K^{-1/2}\,L^{1/2}}{50K^{1/2}\,L^{-1/2}} = \frac{L}{K} \quad ...(1)$$

For output maximisation :

$$\frac{MP_K}{MP_L} = \frac{r}{w} \qquad ...(2)$$

Substituting $\frac{MP_K}{MP_L} = \frac{L}{K}$ and $w = 30$ and $r = 40$ in equation (2) we have

$$\frac{L}{K} = \frac{4}{3} \text{ or } L = \frac{4K}{3} \qquad ...(3)$$

Putting the value of $L = \frac{4}{3}K$ in cost-constraint equation we get

$$1200 = wL + rK$$

$$= 30 \times \frac{4K}{3} + 40K = 80\,K$$

$$K = \frac{1200}{80} = 15$$

Substituting $K = 15$ in the cost-constraint equation we have

$$1200 = 30 \times L + 40 \times 15$$

$$30L + 600 = 1200$$

$$L = \frac{1200 - 600}{30} = 20$$

Thus output-maximizing amounts of capital and labour are 15 and 20 respectively. To get the level of output produced we substitute these amounts of capital and labour in the given production function

$$Q = 100K^{1/2}\,L^{1/2}$$

$$Q = 100\sqrt{15}\,\sqrt{20}$$

$$= 100\sqrt{300}$$

$$= 100 \times 17.32$$

$$= 1732$$

PROFIT MAXIMISATION AND OPTIMUM INPUT COMBINATION

The optimum combination of factors (inputs) is a necessary but not sufficient for profit maximisation which is the objective of the firm. If a firm is not working with an optimum input combination it can substitute one for another to reduce cost for a given output and thereby to increase its profits. But there are several optimum input combinations depending on the level of output to be produced . For example, on expansion path in Figure 20.6 there are several points of tangency between isoquants and iso-costs such as E_1, E_2 and E_3 which are all optimum or efficient input combinations. The problem is to determine which one of these optimum input combinations will ensure maximum profits for the firm. Thus, for determining profit maximisation only optimum combination lying on the expansion need to be considered.

To arrive at profit maximisation we should consider *the optimum use of each variable factor* explained earlier . As shown above, for optimum use of a variable factor it must be used until marginal revenue product (*MRP*) of the factor is equal to marginal factor cost (*MFC*) of the factor. When the price of an input such as wage rate of labour or rental cost (*r*) of capital is given and constant for the firm marginal factor cost for the firm equals the price of the factor or input (that is, wage rate of labour or rental cost of capital). Thus, for a perfectly competiive firm to achieve profit maximisation labour and capital should be used in such amounts that marginal revenue product of each should be equal to wage rate and rental cost of capital respectively. Thus, the conditions for profit maximisation with regard to the use of the factors when the factor prices for the firm are given and constant are :

$$MRP_L = w \qquad \text{...(1)}$$

and

$$MRP_K = r \qquad \text{...(2)}$$

Marginal revenue product of a factor is the additional revenue generated by using an extra unit of a factor (input). Thus, if the use of an additional unit of a factor generates more revenue than the price of the factor, the firm's profits will rise by hiring and using it . And the profits will increase until marginal revenue product of each variable factor equals the price of the factor. That is, for maximisation of profits, in case of two factor production function the above condition (1) and (2) must be satisfied.

The above conditions for profit maximisation imply that the condition for optimum factor combination, namely, $MP_{Ls}/w = MP_k/r$ will also be fulfilled. This can be proved as follows.

As explained earlier, marginal revenue product of a factor, given the price of output, is equal to the marginal physical product of the factor times the *price of output* in the market. Keeping this in view, we rewrite the above conditions (1) and 2) for profit maximisation. Thus

$$MP_L.P = w \qquad \text{... (3)}$$

and

$$MP_K.P = r \qquad \text{...(4)}$$

where P is price of output,
Dividing equation (3) by (4) we get

$$\frac{MP_L}{MP_K} = \frac{w}{r} \qquad \text{...(5)}$$

The equation 5 is the condition for optimum factor combination which can also be written as

$$\frac{MP_L}{w} = \frac{MP_K}{r} \qquad \text{...(6)}$$

Thus, from equation (1) and (2) and (6) we conclude that *if a firm is maximizing profits, it will also be working with optimum input combination and thus working efficiently.*

Numerical Problem. *The following production function of a firm is given*

$$100\ L^{0.5}K^{0.5}$$

It is also given that K = 100 and price (P) of output is ₹ 2 per unit, wage rate of labour is ₹ 50 and rental cost (r) of capital is ₹ 40 per machine hour. Determine the quantity of labour the firm should hire to maximise profits. Find the maximum profits of the firm.

Solution :

To maximize profits, the firm will hire labour until MRP_L equals its wage rate. Thus

$$MRP_L = w$$

or

$$P.MP_L = w \qquad \text{...(1)}$$

Similarly, the firm will equate marginal revenue product of capital with rental cost of capital

$$MRP_K = r$$

or $$P.MP_K = r \quad ....(2)$$

Dividing equation (1) by (2) we have

$$\frac{P.MP_L}{P.MP_K} = \frac{w}{r}$$

or $$\frac{MP_L}{MP_K} = \frac{w}{r} \quad ...(3)$$

From the given production function $Q = 100\ L^{0.5}\ K^{0.5}$ we obtain marginal products of labour and capital by differentiating it with respect to labour and capital. Thus

$$MP_L = 50L^{-0.5}\ K^{0.5}$$

and $$MP_K = 50L^{0.5}\ K^{-0.5}$$

Dividing MP_L by MP_K we have

$$\frac{MP_L}{MP_K} = \frac{50L^{-0.5}K^{0.5}}{50\ L^{0.5}K^{-0.5}}$$

$$= \frac{K}{L}$$

Substituting $\frac{K}{L}$ for $\frac{MP_L}{MP_K}$ in equation (3)

$$\frac{K}{L} = \frac{w}{r}$$

$$L = K.\frac{r}{w} \quad ...(4)$$

Substituting the given values of K and $\frac{r}{w}$ in the expansion path equation (4) we have

$$L = 100\ \frac{40}{50}$$

$$= 80$$

Now, substituting values of L and K in the given production function we have

$$Q = 100\ (80)^{0.5}\ (100)^{0.5}$$

$$= 100 \times 8.944 \times 10$$

$$= 8944$$

The profit (π) function can be stated as under

$$\pi = TR - TC$$

$$TR = PQ \text{ and } TC = wL + rK$$

Therefore $$\pi = P.Q. - wL - rK$$

$$= 2 \times 8944 - 50 \times 80 - 40 \times 100$$

$$= 17888 - 4000 - 4000$$
$$= 9888$$

Thus 80 units of labour will be employed and total profits made are ₹ 9888.

EFFECT OF CHANGES IN FACTOR PRICES : FACTOR SUBSTITUTION

We have seen above that the cost-minimizing factor combination depends on the relative prices of factors used. As shown above, given the prices of factors, the cost of producing a level of output is minimized by using a factor combination at which

$$MRTS_{LK} = \frac{w_0}{r_0}$$

or, where
$$\frac{MP_L}{w_0} = \frac{MP_K}{r_0}$$

Now, if either the price of labour (w) or the price of capital (r) changes, the producer will respond to this change in factor prices as his cost-minimisation state will be disturbed. For example, if wage rate rises from w_0 to w_1, then at the initial equilibrium position,

$$\frac{MP_L}{w_1} < \frac{MP_K}{r_0} \quad \text{or,} \quad \frac{MP_K}{r_0} > \frac{MP_L}{w_1}$$

This will induce a rational producer to substitute capital for relatively more expensive labour. That is, he will try to use more capital and less labour and continue substituting capital for labour until $MRTS_{LK} = \frac{w_1}{r_0}$ *or* $\frac{MP_L}{w_1} = \frac{MP_k}{r_0}$. Substitution of one factor for another is graphically illustrated by using isoquants in Fig. 20.7 where with factor prices w_0 and r_0 respectively of labour and capital, *AB*, which is the iso-cost line for a given amount of outlay, is tangent to the isoquant Q_0 at point *E*. In this equilibrium situation, he is using OL_0 of labour and OK_0 of capital. Now, suppose price of labour (*i.e.*, wage rate) rises so that the iso-cost line, price of capital (r) and outlay remaining constant, rotates to the new position *AC*. It will be seen from Fig. 20.7 that none of the factor combinations lying on the iso-cost line *AC* will be sufficient to produce the level of output Q_0 as the iso-cost line *AC* lies at a lower level than the isoquant Q_0. In other words, with higher wage rate w_1, the given amount of outlay is not enough to buy the required amounts of the two factors to produce the level of output Q_0. Thus, if producer wants to produce the same level of output Q_0 it will have to increase its outlay. The increase in outlay on factors implies moving to a higher iso-cost line that will be parallel to the new iso-cost line *AC*. Now, with the new relative prices of labour and capital, the iso-cost line *GH* is drawn parallel to *AC* so that it is tangent to the isoquant Q_0. It will be seen from the Fig. 20.7 that the iso-cost line *GH* will not be tangent at the initial equilibrium point *E* since its slope reflecting the new relative factor prices differs from the slope of the initial iso-cost line *AB*. Thus, *the initial point E no longer minimises cost in the context of new relative factor prices*. Now that the wage rate is higher, that is, the labour is relatively more expensive, to produce the initial level of output, the producer will substitute capital for labour by moving upward along the isoquant Q_0.

It will be observed from Fig.20.7 that the new iso-cost line *GH* which is parallel to *AC* and therefore reflects the relatively higher wage rate as compared to the iso-cost line *AB*, is tangent to the isoquant Q_0 at point R showing that in order to minimize cost with the new relative factor prices, the producer has substituted $K_0 K_1$ amount of capital for $L_0 L_1$ amount of labour to reach the new cost-minimizing factor combination R where he uses smaller amount OL_1 of labour and larger quantity OK_1 of capital. It may be noted again that substitution of capital for labour and thereby changing the factor-proportion used to reach the equilibrium point R for producing a given level of output Q_0 involves the increase in cost of production resulting from the rise in the price of labour (iso-cost line GH lies further away from the iso-cost line AC when viewed from the origin).

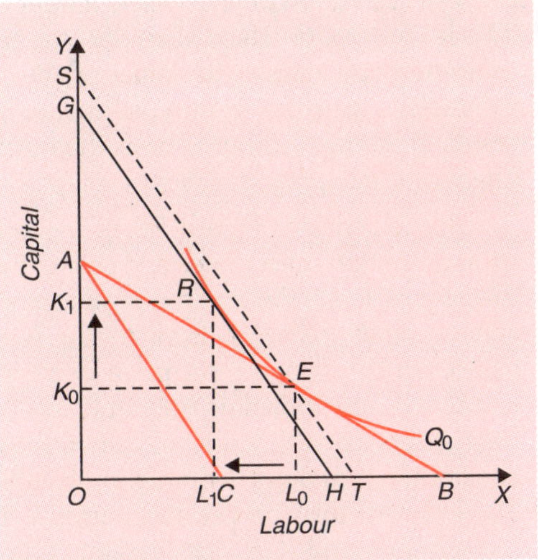

Fig. 20.7. *Rise in wage rate (price) of labor causes substitution of capital for labor*

However, if with the new higher price of labour, the producer had used the original factor combination E, he would have incurred still higher cost or expenditure for producing the output level Q_0. An iso-cost line ST that is drawn parallel to AC reflecting new relative factor prices passes through the original factor combination point E but lies still further away from GH indicating that if with new relative prices of labour and capital the firm uses the same labour-capital combination E to produce the initial level of output Q_0, it will involve still higher cost. Thus, by changing the factor combination from E to R, following the rise in price of labour by substituting capital for now relatively more expensive labour, the firm has succeeded in lowering its cost than it would have incurred if it had continued to use the original factor combination E to produce output Q_0 even after the change in the factor price situation.

From the foregoing analysis we arrive at the conclusion that change in relative factor prices causes a substitution of a factor that has become relatively more expensive by a factor that has become relatively cheaper. In the real world, there are several examples of factor substitution in response to changes in relative factor prices. When price of petroleum increased many countries tried to substitute other types of energy resources using inputs such as coal, electricity to reduce costs of production. Again, in the United States the firms use more machines (*i.e.*, capital) and relatively less labour as labour is very costly there than is the case in some developing countries where wages are comparatively low. Further, recently when prices of computers have fallen, there has been substitution of manual labour for doing such work as book-keeping, making architectural maps, composing books and journals by computers (*i.e.*, capital).

SUBSTITUTE AND COMPLEMENTARY FACTORS

When a fall in the price of one of the two variable factors leads to the decline in the quantity purchased of the other factor, the two factors are said to be substitutes of each other in production. The substitute factors are also called *rival factors*. It should be carefully understood why when the price of a factor falls and as a result its quantity used increases, the quantity employed of its substitute factor decreases. The answer is that ***in case of substitute factors, the increase in the use of one factor actually reduces the marginal physical product of its substitute factor.*** This reduction in marginal physical product of the factor, given its price, causes the decrease in its quantity used to attain cost-mimimising or optimal factor combination. The examples of substitute or rival factors are male and female labour, capital and labour in several production processes, jumbo jets and small jets, electronic typewriter and word processors etc.

The Fig. 20.8. illustrates the case of two factors which are substitute of each other. The effect of change in price of a factor on the use of the factors can be divided into two parts, namely, the substitution effect and output effect. The fall in price (wage rate) of labour, price of capital and cost-outlay remaining the same, makes it relatively cheaper than capital. This causes substitution of relatively cheaper labour for capital which becomes relatively expensive. This is substitution effect. Besides, the fall in price of labour enables the producer to produce more output because with lower price of labour the producer can buy more quantities of both the factors with the same cost-outlay. This leads to the increase in use of both the factors resulting in more output. This is the output effect of the change in price of a factor.

Now consider Figure 20.8. to begin with, given the factor prices and cost outlay, the iso-cost line is *AB* and the producer is in equilibrium at point *R* on isoquant Q_1. Now, with the fall in wage rate, price of capital and cost outlay remaining the same, iso-cost line shifts to *AC* and the producer's equilibrium is at point *T* on higher isoquant Q_2 and with this the producer uses L_1L_2 more labour and K_1K_2 less capital. This is the factor price effect of the fall in wage rate of labour. To separate the two effects we reduce the cost-outlay of the producer so that iso-cost -line shifts to *GH* which is tangent to the original isoquaut Q_1 at new point *S*. It should be noted that the fall in the price of labour has led to the decline in quantity used of capital, because the substitution effect of the fall in wage rate which causes substitution of capital by labour is greater than the output effect. We may therefore say *two factors X and Y are substitutes if the substitution effect on Y of the change in price of X is greater than the output effect on it.* Fig. 20.8 the substitution effect of the fall in the price of labour on the use of capital is K_1 *M* which is greater than the output effect MK_2 on it which tends to increase the use of capital. The two effects work in opposite direction on the quantity used of capital; the substitution effect tends to reduce it and output effect tends to increase it. Since the substitution effect on capital is greater than the output effect, the net result is the fall in the quantity used of capital by K_1K_2. Thus Fig. 20.8 represents the case of the two factors which are substitutes of each other.

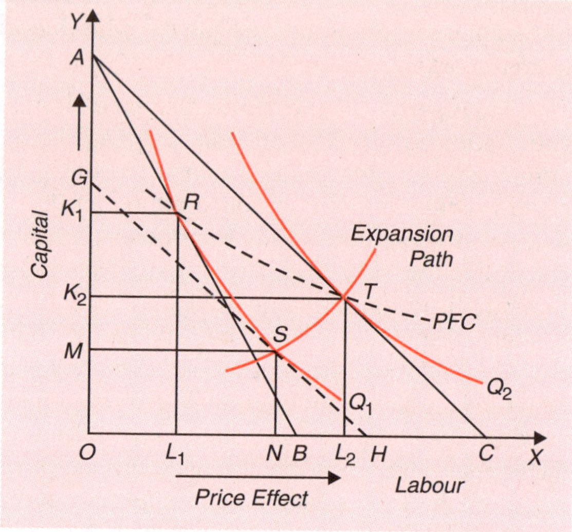

Fig. 20.8. *Substitution and Output Effects of the Change in Factor Price*

In Fig. 20.9 the marginal rate of technical substitution diminishes rapidly along the isoquants, that is, the isoquants are highly convex when looked from origin. In this case, therefore, the substitution effect will be very small. Thus, in Fig. 20.9 the output effect of the fall in price of factor *X* on the quantity used or purchased of factor *Y* is greater than the substitution effect and therefore the net effect of the fall in price of *X* on *Y* is the increase in the quantity purchased of *Y*. In Fig 20.9 the substitution effect on *Y* as a result of the fall in the price of factor *X* is decrease in *Y* by K_1M, whereas the output effect is increase in *Y* by MK_2 which is greater than K_1M. In this case, therefore, the fall in price of *X* leads to the increase in the quantity purchased and used of both the factors. ***When a fall in the price of one of the two factors causes the increase in quantity purchased of both the factors, they are said to be complementary. Thus Fig. 20.9 illustrates the complementary factors. In terms of output and technical substitution effects, the complementary***

factors may be defined as those factors in which case the output effect of the relative fall in the price of one factor on the purchases of the other is greater than the substitution effect.

Why is the output effect large and substitution effect very small in case of some factors which brings about the increase in the quantity used of both the factors when the price of one falls? ***Complementarily signifies a mutually advantageous cooperation of factors. Therefore, in case of complementary factors, when the price of one factor falls resulting in increase in its quantity used, it also leads to the increase in the quantity of its complementary factors because its marginal physical productivity rises due to the greater use of the other factor.*** The examples of complementary factors in the real world are irrigation and fertilizers, land and labour, air planes and air pilots, brick layers and bricks, computers and computer programmers.

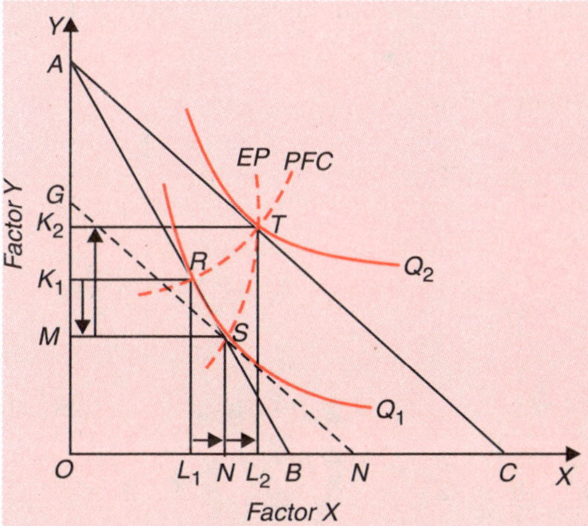

Fig. 20.9. *Complementary Factors*

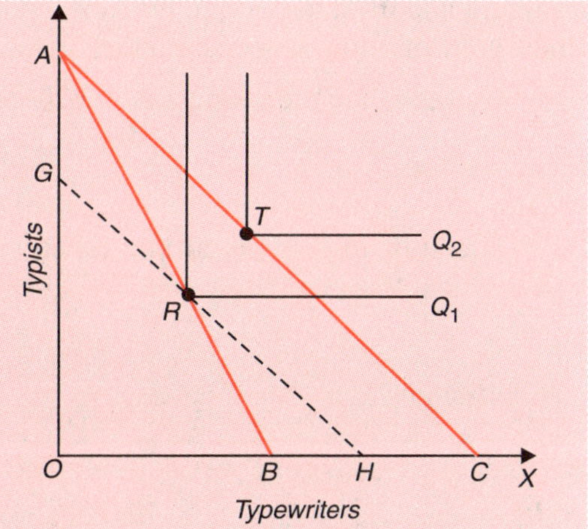

Fig. 20.10. *Perfect Complimentsary Factors*

It should be noted that the factors represented in Fig.20.9 are complements but not perfect complements. The two perfect complementary factors are used in a given fixed proportion and, as explained in the previous chapter, the isoquants of the two perfect complementary factors are right-angled and the *technical substitutions effect in case of the two perfect complements* is therefore zero. The case of perfect complements is illustrated in Fig. 20.10 where substitution effect being nil, price effect consists of only the output effect and the quantities of both factors change in a given proportion as a result of the fall in price of a factor and the resultant change in the iso-cost line from *AB* to *AC*. It will be seen from Fig. 20.10 that when iso-cost line *GH* is drawn parallel to *AC* so as to be tangent to the initial isoquant Q_1, it touches the same point *R* where the original iso-cost *AB* is tangent to the isoquant Q_1. This shows that substitution effect is zero and price effect contains only the output effect.

THE EXPANSION PATH OF THE LINEAR HOMOGENEOUS PRODUCTION FUNCTION

We shall now establish an important relationship between the linear production function exhibiting constant returns to scale and the nature of the expansion path. The following proposition holds good in this connection:

The expansion path in case of the linear homogeneous production function (i.e., production function with constant returns to scale) is always a straight line through the origin.

Whether expansion path is linear or non-linear, depends on the nature of technology involved in the production function. ***Expansion path of a linear homogeneous production path is a straight line from the origin.*** This is an important property of linear homogeneous production function. Recall that expansion path shows optimal factor combinations as firm expands its output, given the prices of factors. Since at optimal factor combination $MRS_{LK} = \frac{w}{r}$, given the constant factor prices along an expansion path, this implies that given the factor price ratio, *MRS* will remain the same. Expansion path being a straight line from the origin implies that $\frac{K}{L}$ ratio remains constant as we move from one optimal point to another on it. To prove that expansion path of a linear homogeneous production function is a straight line from the origin, we take Cobb-Douglas production function ($Q = AK^{1/2} L^{1/2}$) which is linear homogeneous production function.

Differentiating the production function with respect to labour

$$\frac{\partial Q}{\partial L} = \frac{1}{2} AK^{1/2} L^{-1/2} \qquad ...(1)$$

Differentiating the production function with respect to capital

$$\frac{\partial Q}{\partial K} = \frac{1}{2} AK^{-1/2} L^{1/2} \qquad ...(2)$$

Dividing (1) by (2), we have

$$MRTS_{LK} = \frac{MP_L}{MP_K} = \frac{\frac{\partial Q}{\partial L}}{\frac{\partial Q}{\partial K}} = \frac{\frac{1}{2} AK^{1/2} L^{-1/2}}{\frac{1}{2} AK^{-1/2} L^{1/2}} = \frac{K}{L} \qquad ...(3)$$

Thus, $MRTS_{LK}$ in linear homogeneous Cobb-Douglas production is equal to $\frac{K}{L}$. Since, as explained above, at optimal factor combinations on the expansion path,

$$MRTS_{LK} = \frac{w}{r}$$

As $MRTS_{LM}$ in linear homogeneous Cobb-Douglas production is equal to $\frac{K}{L}$, it follows that on expansion path

$$\frac{K}{L} = \frac{w}{r}$$

With given prices of labour and capital, *w* and *r*, capital-labour $\left(\frac{K}{L}\right)$ ratio will remain constant. This means that expansion path of this production function is a straight line from the origin.

We therefore conclude that, in a linear homogeneous production function, $MRTS_{LK}$ *depends on the capital-labour ratio which remains constant*. This is graphically illustrated in Figure 20.11 where linear homogeneous production has been represented by isoquants Q_1 (=100), Q_2 (= 200) and Q_3 (=300) units of output. Two rays *OR* and *OS* from the origin have been drawn which represent two different capital-labour ratios but along each ray capital-labour ratio remains the same. Now, on the ray *OR* from the origin which passes though *A*, *B* and *C* on the isoquants Q_1,Q_2 and Q_3, tangents have been drawn at points *A*, *B*, and *C*.

These tangents depicting the slopes of the isoquants (i.e. $MRTS_{LK}$) at points A, B, and C on the isoquants Q_1, Q_2 and Q_3 respectively are parallel to each other. Thus the marginal rate of technical substitution ($MRTS_{LK}$) along the straight-line ray OR, which depicts a given and constant capital-labour ratio $\left(\frac{K}{L}\right)$ as we move along it, remains the same. Likewise, on a straight-line ray OS with a new a constant capital-labour ratio (K/L), from the origin the tangents representing slope of the isoquants drawn at the points E, F and G on the successive isoquants Q_1, Q_2 and Q_3 are parallel to each other which show that the marginal rate of substitution remains the same, given the new capital-labour ratio.

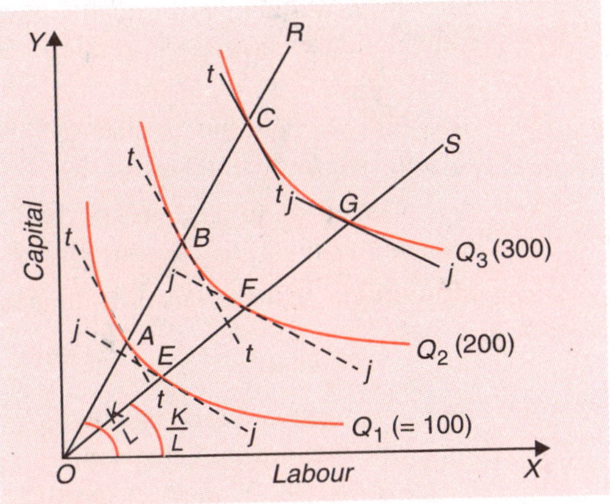

Fig. 20.11. Expansion path in case of a Linear Homogeneous Production Function is a straight line from the origin

Now, since the marginal rate of technical substitution on a straight-line ray from the origin in a linear homogeneous production function remains the same and, given the factor prices, the successive iso-cost lines have the same slope at the cost-minimisation points the expansion path of the firm will be located on the given straight line from the origin at which $MRTS_{LX}$ will be equal to the factor price ratio (w/r) at the tangency points of the successive isoquants and iso-cost lines. Thus, it is evident that expansion path of a linearly homogeneous production function is a straight line through the origin. However, it is important to notice that with a different factor price ratio, the expansion path of a linear homogeneous production function will be a different straight line from the origin. Thus in Fig. 20.11. If the factor-price ratio is given by the slope of the tangent tt, the expansion path will be the straight line OR from the origin and if the factor price ratio is given by the slope of the tangent jj, the expansion path will be the straight line OS from the origin.

It follows from above that the expansion path of a production function exhibiting constant returns to scale will always be a straight line through the origin. But, as is known, all points on a straight line through the origin involve the same proportion between the two factors. It follows therefore that with constant returns to scale and given factor prices there will be only one *optimum factor proportion (say, 5 units of a particular raw material per unit of labour which remains the same whatever the firm's level of output. Thus, in case of constant returns to scale, the task of an entrepreneur is quite simple and convenient. He requires only to find out just one optimum factor proportion and so long as factor prices do not change he does not face any decision-making problem regarding factor proportion to be used for production*. Moreover, this result is also very useful for input-output analysis in economics.

QUESTIONS FOR REVIEW

1. Explain the concept of production function. The information about production function facing a firm is inadequate for making decision regarding economically efficient use of factors or resources. Explain

   [**Hints :** Production function describes the technological aspect of production, that is, maximum possible output that can be produced by various combination of factors. On the other hand, economic efficiency in resource use implies least-cost combination of factors to produce a given output or alternatively it implies maximisation of output for a given cost. Thus, for deciding about optimal or economically efficient resource use we require not only the data about the production function but also about prices of factors.]

2. What is meant by efficient or optimum factor combination in production? Explain with the help of isoquants and iso-cost lines how a producer achieves this combination of factors.
3. Show with the help of isoquants that a firm will be in equilibrium regarding use of a factor combination when marginal rate of technical subsititution (*MRTS*) between factors is equal to the ratio of factor prices.
4. Given the prices of the two factors for the individual firm, explain the conditions for producing a given output at the least cost.
5. Capital-labour ratio has been increasing in the Indian manufacturing industry over time. What possible explanations can be offered for this increase in capital intensity?

   [**Hints:** One possible reason is that the rise in wage rate of labour due to which factor price ratio $\frac{w}{r}$ has been increasing inducing the producers to substitute capital for labour. As a result, capital-labour ratio has risen. An alternative explanation can be the nature of technology used which determines the nature of production function which, with given factor prices, influences the shape of the expansion path. Besides, change in technology over time can be such that makes the production function capital-biased. In both these, the nature of production function and therefore the expansion path is such that, with given prices of labour and capital, capital-labour ratio will be increasing).
6. Show with the help of isoquant diagram how a rise in wage rate of labour, price of capital remaining the same, will affect the use of labour and capital.
7. Show with the isoquant-iso-cost apparatus, a firm is in equilibrium with regard to the use of factors when the ratios of marginal products of factors to their respective prices are equal.
8. Show that maximisation of output subject to a given cost constraint and minimisation of cost subject to a given output yield identical results.
9. What is an expansion path? Show that expansion path of a linear homogeneous production function is a straight line from the origin.
10. Explain using isoquants (*a*) the effect of rise in wage rate of labour, price of capital remaining constant, on the use of labour and capital, (*b*) the effect of fall in price of capital, wage rate of labour remaining the same.
11. Explain using isoquants-iso-cost apparatus how a change in price of a factor is split up into output effect and substitution effect.
12. A firm is operating with a optimum factor combination of labour and capital. How will it be affected if wage rate of labour rises ?
13. Given the two factor product in, $Q = 150\ L^{0.5}\ K^{0.5}$, wage rate of labour equal to ₹ 50 and rental cost of capital equal to ₹ 40. Determine the amounts of labour and capital that will minimize the cost of producing 1118 units of output.

APPENDIX TO CHAPTER 20

MATHEMATICAL TREATMENT OF PRODUCTION THEORY

This appendix deals with the mathematical derivation of cost minimisation and its dual output maximisation problems of production theory.

Choice of Inputs : Cost Minimisation for a Given Output

Consider a firm that uses labour (L) and capital (K) to produce output (Q). Let w is the price of labour, that is, wage rate and r is the price of capital and C the cost incurred to produce a level of output is given by

$$C = wL + rK \quad \text{...(i)}$$

The objective of the firm is to minimize cost for producing a given level of output. Let the production function is given by the following

$$Q = f(L,K)$$

In general, there are several labour-capital combinations to produce a given level of output. A firm will choose combination of factors which will minimize its total cost of production to produce a given level of output. Thus, the problem of constrained minimisation is :

$$\text{minimize } C = wL + rK$$

subject to produce a given level of output, say Q_1, that satisfies the following production function

$$Q = f(L, K)$$

The choice of an optimal factor combination can be obtained through using Lagrangian method. Let us first form the Lagrangian function which is given below

$$Z = wL + rK + \lambda\,[Q_1 - f(L, K)] \quad \text{...(ii)}$$

where λ is Lagrangian multiplier

For minimisation of cost it is necessary that partial derivatives of Z with respect to L, K and λ be zero

$$\frac{\partial Z}{\partial L} = w - \frac{\lambda \partial f(L,K)}{\partial L} = 0 \quad \text{...(iii)}$$

$$\frac{\lambda \partial Z}{\partial K} = r - \frac{\lambda \partial f(L,K)}{\partial K} = 0 \quad \text{...(iv)}$$

$$\frac{\partial Z}{\partial \lambda} = Q_1 - f(L, K) = 0 \quad \text{...(v)}$$

Note that $\frac{\partial f(L,K)}{\partial L}$ and $\frac{\partial f(L,K)}{\partial K}$ are the marginal physical products of labour and capital respectively. It will also be noticed that the equations (*v*) is the given production function. Rewriting the above equations we have

$$w - \lambda\, MP_L = 0 \quad \text{...(vi)}$$

$$r - \lambda\, MP_K = 0 \quad \text{...(vii)}$$

$$Q_1 = f(L, K) \quad \text{...(viii)}$$

By combining the two equations (*vi*) and (*vii*) we have

$$\frac{w}{r} = \frac{MP_L}{MP_K} \quad \text{.....(ix)}$$

Equation (*ix*) shows that total cost is minimized when the factor price ratio $\frac{w}{r}$ equals the ratio of marginal physical products of labour and capital. Since the ratio of marginal products of the two factors equals the marginal rate of technical substitution (*MRTSxy*), optimal or cost-minimising quantities of the two factors are obtained when we have

$$\frac{w}{r} = \frac{MP_L}{MP_K} = MRTS_{LK}$$

By rearranging the equation (*ix*) we get the following necessary condition for choice of optimal factor combination :

$$\frac{MR_L}{w} = \frac{MR_K}{r} \qquad ...(x)$$

From the above equation (x) it follows that when price of capital (r) falls, wage rate remaining constant, $\frac{MR_K}{r} > \frac{MR_L}{w}$. This will induce the firm to substitute capital for labour so that MP_K falls and in this way $\frac{MP_K}{r}$ becomes equal to $\frac{MP_K}{w}$ again to obtain a new cost-minimizing factor combination.

Finally, we combine the two equations (vi) and (vii) in an alternative way to obtain the value of Lagrangian multiplier λ. Thus

$$\lambda = \frac{w}{MP_L} \text{ and } \lambda = \frac{r}{MP_K}$$

$$\lambda = \frac{w}{MP_L} = \frac{r}{MP_K}$$

Suppose output is increased by one unit. Since the marginal product of labour measures the extra output obtained by using an additional unit of labour, $\frac{1}{MP_L}$ represents the extra labour required to produce one unit of output, $\frac{w}{MP_L}$ measures the extra or marginal cost on labour of producing an additional unit of output. Similarly, $\frac{r}{MP_K}$ measures the marginal cost of producing an extra unit of output by using an additional unit of capital. It is thus clear that Lagrange multiplier (λ) equals marginal cost of output because it tells us how much addition to cost occurs when an extra unit of output is produced by using an additional unit of labour or capital.

Duality of Cost-Minimisation Problem : Output-Maximisation With a Given Cost

In the field of both consumer theory and production theory, for every minimisation problem there is corresponding maximisation problem and vice versa. In other words, for every minimisation problem there is corresponding dual problem of maximisation and vice versa. The solution of both the primal problem and its dual is the same. We explain below the dual nature of optimal choice of factor combination used for production of a commodity.

The dual of the primal problem of cost-minimisation for producing a given level of output *is maximisation of output for a given cost*. In other words, for a given iso-cost line the dual problem for a firm is to choose a factor combination that enables it to reach the highest production isoquant which is tangent to the given iso-cost line. Thus the dual problem of cost minimisation is of the following type

$$\text{Maximise } Q = f(L, K) \qquad \ldots(i)$$

Subject to cost constant: $C_0 = r.L + rK$ ...(*ii*)

Lagrangian expression for the above constrained maximisation problem is

$$Z = f(L, K) + \lambda (C_0 - w.L - rK)$$

where C_0 is the given amount of cost, λ is the Lagrangian multiplier. For maximisation of output with a given cost, the necessary conditions are that partial derivatives of Lagrangian function with respect to L, K and λ be zero, Thus

$$\frac{\partial Z}{\partial L} = \frac{\partial f(L,K)}{\partial L} - \lambda w = 0 \qquad \ldots(iii)$$

$$\frac{\partial Z}{\partial K} = \frac{\partial f(L,K)}{\partial K} - \lambda r = 0 \qquad \ldots(iv)$$

$$\frac{\partial Z}{\partial \lambda} = C_0 - w.L - rK = 0 \qquad \ldots(v)$$

Note that $\frac{\partial f(L,K)}{\partial L} = MP_L$ and $\frac{\partial f(L,K)}{\partial K} = MP_K$. Further, note that the equation (*v*) represents the budget constraint (that is, the equation of the iso-cost line). Rewriting the above equations we have

$$MP_L - \lambda w = 0 \qquad \ldots(vi)$$

$$MP_K - \lambda r = 0 \qquad \ldots(vii)$$

$$wL + rK = C_0 \qquad \ldots(viii)$$

Combining the equations (*vi*) and (*vii*) we have

$$\frac{MP_L}{MP_K} = \frac{w}{r}$$

or

$$\frac{MP_L}{w} = \frac{MP_K}{r} \qquad \ldots(ix)$$

It will be seen from equation (*ix*) that necessary condition for output maximisation with a given cost is the same for as the one we obtained for cost-minimisation problem for a given level of output.

CHAPTER

21

Cost Analysis

Introduction

In the last two chapters we studied the nature of production function underlying the production process of goods. The production function, along with the prices of factors, and the state of technology determine to an appreciable degree, the supply of goods. In this chapter we carry further the analysis of the forces determining supply of goods. We shall examine here how the costs of production of the firm depend on the nature of physical production function. We will be mainly concerned with how the cost of production varies with the increase in the level of output of the firm. In other words, we shall study how the cost and level of output are related to each other. The relation between cost and output is called "*cost function*". The *cost function of the firm depends upon the nature of physical production function, the prices of the factors used for production and the technology used for production*. How much cost a firm will incur on production depends on the level of output, given the factor prices and the state of technology. The quantity of a product that will be offered by the firm for supply in the market will depend to a great degree upon the cost of production incurred on the various possible levels of output. Cost of production is the most important factor governing the supply of a product. It should be pointed out here that it is assumed that for each level of output, the firm chooses least-cost combination of factors. We shall explain below the various concepts of costs that are used in modern economic theory and then turn to study the derivation of the short-run and the long-run cost curves. However, to begin with, we shall draw distinction between technological efficiency and economic efficiency as they are intimately connected with the study of costs of production.

TECHNOLOGICAL EFFICIENCY VERSUS ECONOMIC EFFICIENCY

Before explaining the theory of cost, it is worthwhile to make clear the notion of economic efficiency in the use of resources as it is intimately related to the cost of production. In the last few chapters we have studied the concepts of physical production function and isoquants. In the study of both the production function and the isoquants representing it, economists take it granted that resources are used by the producers with technological efficiency. By ***technological efficiency we mean that the maximum possible output is obtained from a given set of inputs***. It may be noted that in the description of production function and in drawing the isoquants it is assumed that producer has in fact attained the technical efficiency in the use of resources or factors. If the use of resources is not technological efficient, it will involve the *waste of resources*. However, it is primarily the concern of management and engineers to attain this technological efficiency in the use of resources so that scarce resources are not wasted.

Though this question of technological efficiency is highly important, economists are not generally concerned with it. Economists examine the question that with the given prices of various resources or factors, which production process or factor combination, a producer will employ for producing a *given level of output* of a commodity that minimises the cost of production. **The economic efficiency therefore implies the use of production process or resource combination which ensures the minimization of cost incurred on using resources to produce a given level of output.** Thus whereas engineers are primarily concerned with getting *maximum output* from a given amount of physical inputs, economists are essentially concerned with *maximizing the output from a given level of cost* (i.e. value of inputs used) or *minimizing cost for a given level of output*. Economic efficiency is achieved when a rupee's worth of inputs yields largest possible output. In the theory of production and cost, the prices of inputs and outputs are assumed to be given and constant for the producer. As explained in a previous chapter, for deciding which factor combination or production process a firm will choose to produce a level of output, given the prices of inputs, the problem which a firm faces is not of technological efficiency but of economic efficiency. Indeed, in that analysis, it was taken for granted that technological efficiency of resources had already been attained and the isoquants depicting the production function drawn represented only the technically efficient combinations of factors; each isoquant represents various technologically efficient factor combinations to produce a given level of output. The achievement of economic efficiency requires that the firm should choose a factor combination that minimises cost of production for producing a given level of output or that maximises output for a given level of cost-outlay. We saw in a previous chapter that the producer achieves economic efficiency in resource use when for the production of a commodity he chooses a factor combination at which marginal rate of substitution between two factors equals the ratio of factor prices $(MRS_{LK} = \frac{w}{r})$. It is thus clear that to make economically efficient use of resources, the producer has to take into account not only the physical productivity of factors (*i.e.* MRS_{LK} which is equal to the ratio of $\frac{MPP_L}{MPP_K}$) but also the prices of factors employed for production.

It is important to note that in the theory of cost we assume that for each level of output a producer uses economically efficeint production process or the least-cost factor combination. In other words, a producer chooses a factor combination which lies on the expansion path corresponding to a given level of output. In fact, as we will explain later, how the long-run total cost curve is derived from the firm's expansion path which represents economically efficient factor combinations for the production of different levels of output.

THE CONCEPTS OF COST

The term 'cost' has different meaning. Accountants view of cost is different from that of economists. The accountants tend to focus on the explicit and historical costs. On the other hand, economists emphasize that for efficient decision making by the firm it is the *opportunity cost* rather than explicit and historical cost that must be considered. And, as will be explained below, the opportunity cost concept includes both the explicit and implicit costs. It is therefore necessary that we should explain the meaning of cost as used by economists and which is relevant for decision-making by a producer.

Opportunity Cost

The concept of opportunity cost is a basic concept of cost in economics. As the resources of the society are scarce, we cannot produce all goods that the people may desire. Therefore, when more resources are allocated to one product, some other product has to be foregone or sacrificed. The opportunity cost of a product is therefore the value of the next best alternative product that is forgone so as to release resources for greater production of the former.

The knowledge of opportunity cost is essential for decision making by a firm as it is also faced with the problem of constrained optimization. It works with a budget constraint. Whenever more resources are allocated by it to one division or department they have to be withdrawn from another and therefore the opportunity cost is involved. For example, if some resources are allocated to Research and Development (R & D) Division, it may result in withdrawal of resources from Production Department which means reduction in the current output of the product, though allocation of more resources to R & D may result in more and better products in future yielding more profits to the firm in future. Of course, such a decision should be made if the manager of the firm is quite sure that greater profits in future will outweigh the loss of output and profits in the current period.

However, in the theory of costs we are more concerned with opportunity cost of a factor of production used in the production of a commodity. In this sense, the opportunity cost of an input or factor of production is *its value* (*i.e. earnings*) *in the next best alternative use or employment.* The firm must consider the opportunity cost of all inputs and factors of production. If a firm pays lower price for a factor than it can get in any other firm or use, it will not be able to retain it. That is, actual payment to an input or a factor of production which is called explicit cost must not be less than its opportunity cost, otherwise it will not be able to retain it.

Similarly, it will not be worthwhile for the firm to use a self-owned factor in its business if it can get a higher price by *selling* it to others, or hiring it out to others. For example, if an entrepreneur has set up his firm and manages his own business, he foregoes the salary that he could have earned for working as a manager in another's firm. Similarly, if an entreprenur invests his own financial capital in his firm, he foregoes interest or return that he could earn by investing that in fixed deposits in banks or purchasing shares of companies. The interest which he could earn on fixed deposits or return which he could get by making investment of his financial capital in shares of other companies is the opportunity cost of financial capital which he invests in his own business. The salary which an entrepreneur gets elsewhere by working as a manager and return on his own financial capital which he can get by investing elsewhere are the implicit costs which are not generally considered by accountants in their financial statement of the firm must be taken into account in rational decision making by management of the firm.

It follows from above that economic opportunity costs include both explicit and implicit costs and therefore both should be taken into account in rational decision making by management. Thus, both the explicit and implicit costs are relevant and therefore must be considered while making decision regarding whether to produce a product or use inputs for its production. The failure to consider the opportunity cost and rely on historical cost will lead to inefficient decision. An example will bring out the importance of the opportunity cost in making optimal managerial decisions. Let us consider the problem of *inventory evaluation*. Suppose a firm purchased a raw material at price of ₹ 1000 per quintal. The accountant would continue to consider the value of the inventory of raw material at its historical cost, namely, ₹1000 per quintal. However, the economists would consider the value of inventory of raw material at its current price at which it can be presently replaced. If a firm considers the historical cost of inventories of raw materials rather than their current replacement value, it may take a wrong decision. For example, on the basis of higher historical cost of the raw material it may decide not to produce the commodity in whose production it is used because it would involve losses. But if the raw material is valued at its current replacement price of Rs. 600 per quintal it may be profitable to produce the commodity.

The resources which are used for the manufacture of armaments may also be used for the production of cars or other automobiles. Therefore, the opportunity cost of production of an armament is the output of cars and other automobiles foregone or sacrificed, which could have been produced with the same amount of factors that have gone into the making of an armament. To take another example, a farmer who is producing wheat, can also produce potatoes with the same factors. Therefore, the opportunity cost of a quintal of wheat is the amount of output of potatoes given up. Thus, the opportunity-cost of anything is the next best alternative that could be produced instead by the same resources having the same monetary value.

The alternative or opportunity cost of a good can be given a money value. In order to produce a good the producer has to employ various factors of production and has to pay them sufficient prices to get their services. These factors have alternative uses. The factors must be paid at least the price they are able to obtain in the alternative uses. The opportunity cost of a factor to a firm is its earnings in the next best alternative use. For instance, consider the case of a farmer who works on his own farm. While calculating cost he must take into account the wages of his own labour rendered on his farm. These wages must be equal to the maximum wages that he would earn if he worked as hired labour on other farms. The maximum wages earned elsewhere by a farmer is the opportunity cost of his labour rendered on his own farm. The total alternative earnings in the next best use of the various factors, both supplied by others to the entrepreneur and those supplied by the entrepreneur himself employed in the production of a good will constitute the opportunity cost of the good.

A significant fact worth mentioning is that ***relative prices of goods tend to reflect their opportunity costs.*** The resources will remain employed in the production of a particular good when they are being paid at least the money rewards that are sufficient to induce them to stay in the industry, *i.e.*, equal to the value they are able to obtain and create elsewhere. In other words, a collection of factors employed in the production of a good must be paid equal to their opportunity costs. The greater the opportunity cost of the collection of factors used in the production of a goods, the greater must be the price of the goods. Thus, if the same collection of factors can produce either one tractor or 2 scooters, then the price of one tractor will be twice that of one scooter.

However, it may be noted that ***market prices of goods do not always reflect their true social opportunity costs.*** This is because the market prices of factors or resources used for the production of commodities may fail to reflect their opportunity costs from the social point of view (*i.e.* their true scarcity value or the true cost of diverting resources from alternative uses in the economy as a whole). This may occur for a number of reasons such as government regulation and control of prices of some inputs and resources, imposition of indirect taxes on various inputs, presence of monopoly or imperfect competition in the production and supply of resources or inputs under which higher prices are charged than justified on the basis of their scarcity values. For example, labour in India is abundant and a large magnitude of unemployment of labour prevails in the Indian economy and therefore its scarcity value is zero, that is, from the social point of view, opportunity cost of labour is zero. But due to several social and institutional factors, labour commands a price in the market which the entrepreneurs will have to include in their private costs of production. Similarly, in India due to the cheap credit policy, liberal depreciation allowance on investment granted to the business entrepreneurs in the corporate taxation policy and until recently before the policy of liberalization the higher exchange rate of rupee kept by the government had made the effective price of capital lower than warranted by its scarcity in the Indian economy. Thus, the higher market price of labour and the lower price of capital than their social opportunity costs or their scarcity values have encouraged the choice of capital-intensive techniques and production processes in the Indian industries. This has stood in the way of minimizing social opportunity costs which is generaly assumed in the economic theory.

Historical Costs as Sunk Costs. There is an important difference between the approach of economists from accountants regarding the treatment of fixed costs incurred on durable capital goods such as machines, buildings. The accountants take *historical costs* of these capital goods, that is, the price at which they were originally purchased and a given percentage of the original price is taken as *depreciation* which is charged to current costs of production per year. However, economists consider the historical costs as *sunk cost* which is irrelevant to the current costs of production and therefore cannot be the basis of decision-making with regard to production and pricing of commodities. Sunk costs are those expenditures that cannot be recovered. The economists adopt the principle that "bygones are bygones" and consider the current opportunity costs of these capital goods after they have been acquired that is relevant for decision making in the current period. If the capital goods can be put to an alternative use or can be let out to others, the earnings in the next best alternative or the rental value of the machines if they are hired by others would constitute the opportunity costs of these capital goods and could be counted by the economists as part of the current cost of production. However, if the durable capital goods, especially specialized equipment such as machines, have no alternative use, their opportunity cost will be zero and economists would not include them in current costs of production, despite their depreciation during a year. It may, however, be noted that conventional accounting method of including depreciation charge in current cost of production may be useful for other purposes, for instance, for determining income tax liability. But economists look at things from the point of view of opportunity costs which affect the decision-making process. Thus, when determining the rental value of specialized capital equipment, economists consider its opportunity cost and ignore its historical price.

Accounting Costs and Economic Costs

The difference between accounting costs and economic costs requires further consideration. This difference also makes clear the meaning of economic profits. The accounting costs are called *explicit costs* which include wages to hire labour, prices of raw materials, fuel and semi-finished products purchased for use in production and rental price of capital equipment and buildings. When an entrepreneur undertakes an act of production, he has to pay prices for the factors which he employs for production. He thus pays wages to the labourers employed, prices for the raw materials, fuel and power used, rent for the building he hires for the production work, and the rate of interest on the money borrowed for doing business. All these are included in his cost of production. *An accountant will take into account only the* expenditure incurred on buying or hiring various inputs or factors for use in production.

But an economist's view of cost is somewhat different from this. It generally happens that the entrepreneur invests a certain amount of his own money capital in his business. If the money capital invested by the entrepreneur in his own business had been invested elsewhere, it would have earned a certain amount of interest or dividends. Further, an entrepreneur devotes times to his own work of production and contributes his entrepreneurial and managerial ability to it. If the entrepreneur had not set up his own business, he would have worked as manager in some other's firm on salary basis. The economists, therefore, also include in his costs of production the opportunity costs of the self-owned factors. Thus, in calculation of costs the economists will include *(i) the normal return on money capital* invested by the entrepreneur himself in his own business, which he could have earned if invested elsewhere. Normal return on his own capital invested by the entrepreneur in his own business is in fact the opportunity cost of his money capital, and *(ii) the wages or salary* he could have earned if he sold his services to others as a manager or consultant. The accountants do not include these two items in cost of production but the economists consider them as bonafide costs and will accordingly include them. Likewise, the money rewards for other factors such as building owned by the entrepreneur himself and employed by him in his own business are also considered by the economists as costs of production.

Thus, the accountants consider those costs which involve actual *cash payments by the entrepreneur of the firm to others*, the economists take into account all of these *accounting costs*, but in addition, they also take into account the amount of money the entrepreneur could have earned if he had invested his money capital and sold his own services and other factors in the next best alternative uses. ***The accounting costs or actual contractual cash payments which the firm makes to other factor owners for purchasing or hiring the various factors are also known as explicit costs.*** The normal return on money capital invested by the entrepreneur and the wages or salary for his services and the opportunity costs of the other factors the entrepreneur himself owns and employs them in his firm are known as ***implicit costs or imputed costs.*** The economists take into consideration both the explicit and implicit costs. Therefore,

Economic Costs = Accounting costs (i.e. explicit costs) + Implicit costs

It is worthwhile to note that the concept of opportunity cost explained above is not confined to the firm's implicit cost alone. The concept of opportunity cost applies to the explicit costs also. Thus, when a firm buys or hire labour, capital, land for its production, it must pay prices for them equal to their earnings in the next best use or industry. The earnings in the next best use represent their opportunity costs.

It may be pointed out that the firm will ***earn economic profits only if it is making revenue in excess of the total of explicit and implicit costs.*** Thus, when the firm is in no profit and no loss position, it means that the firm is making revenue equal to the sum of explicit and implicit costs and no more. Therefore,

Economic Profits = Total Revenue – Economic Costs

Since the economic costs are sum of the explicit and implicit costs, economic profits can be defined and measured as under:

Economic Profits = Total Revenue – (Explicit costs + Implicit costs)

Among the implicit costs which economists take into account but accountants ignore them, mention may be made of *normal profits*. These normal profits are not the true profits as understood in economics. The normal profits are defined as the necessary payments that must be made to the entrepreneur in order to retain him in the present business or industry. Obviously, if the entrepreneur leaves his own business, he can be employed by another firm as a manager or executive which is generally taken to be his next best occupation or job. If the entrepreneur in his next best job of a manager earns ₹ 50,000 per month as salary or wages, he must earn this much amount in his own business and therefore this would constitute his normal profits. As a matter of fact, in his own business he does perform certain managerial functions such as bringing together various factors, bringing about coordination among them to do a particular work of production and supervising them. Thus normal profits are actually wages or salary for managerial services rendered by the entrepreneur in his own business which he must earn if he is to stay in his own business. If he is unable to get this normal reward for this managerial services performed, he will go to his next best alternative as a manager in another's firm. It is thus clear that normal profits are his opportunity costs or transfer earnings and like other opportunity costs of other productive services, they should also be included in the implicit costs of production.

THEORY OF COST

Cost Functions : Short-Run and Long-Run

From the viewpoint of the changes in cost of production, the economists draw distinction between the short-run costs and long-run costs. The short-run costs are those costs which are incurred by the firm during a period in which some factors, especially, capital equipment, land and management are held constant. The short-run costs are incurred on the purchases of labour, raw materials, chemicals, fuel etc. which vary with the changes in the level of output. On the other hand, the long-run costs are the costs incurred during a period which is sufficiently long to allow the variation in all factors of production including capital equipment, land and managerial staff to produce output.

As explained earlier, the long-run cost function refers to the change in cost when output is varied by changing the quantities of all factors used for the production of a commodity. Besides, as emphasized earlier, the long-run cost function represents the minimum cost incurred on factors used for producing various levels of output, given the prices of factors or inputs. Further, the level of technology is also assumed to remain constant in deriving the long-run cost function. We shall explain later how a *long-run average cost curve representing the long-run cost function is derived from the expansion path* of the firm. Recall that expansion path is the locus of optimum or least-cost factor combinations used for producing various levels of output.

It is important to note that ***effect of changes in technology and factor prices on cost of production are shown to cause a shift in the function,*** either downward or upward as the case may be. For instance, the improvement in technology raises the productivity of factors and will therefore cause the long-run cost function to shift downward. On the other hand, increase in factor prices will raise the cost of production and shift the cost function upward. Therefore, the determinants of cost of production other than the level of output are called *shift factors.*

Short-Run Cost Function

The short-run is defined as a period of time in which output of a firm can be increased or decreased by changing the amounts of variable factors such as labour, raw materials, chemicals, fuel etc. while the quantity of such factors as capital equipment, building remaining fixed. Thus, in the short-run a firm's manager cannot decide to build a new plant or abondon an old one. If a firm wants to increase output in the short-run, it can do so only by using more labour and raw materials. It cannot increase output in the short run by expanding the capacity of the existing plant or building a new plant with a larger capacity. Therefore, the short-run cost function relates the cost of production with level of output where capital (and other fixed factors) are held constant along with the given technology and given factor prices. The difference between the short-run and long-run cost function is that whereas in the former, the cost-output relation is studied with a certain amount of capital or land fixed, the long-run cost function examines the relation between cost and output when capital and land also vary along with the variable factors such as labour, raw materials. In both the short-run and long-run cost functions we study the relation between the cost and level of output *i.e.*, $C = f(Q)$, the difference lies in factors that are varied to expand or contract output . Whereas in the long-run, the advancement in technology and changes in factor prices cause a shift in the long-run cost function, in the short run, besides technology and factor prices some fixed factors such as capital or land also bring about a shift in the cost function.

As has been pointed out above, in deriving the cost function or cost curve, especially in the long run, it is assumed that every level of output of a commodity is produced at the minimum possible cost. This implies that it is assumed that the firm employs optimum or economically efficient resource combinations. Thus every point on the long-run cost function or long-run cost curve represents the use of optimum resource combination so as to ensure minimum cost of production for each level of output. Even in the short run, it is assumed that given the size of the plant (*i.e.*, capital equipment), the firms operate to minimise cost for producing various levels of output.

Total Fixed and Variable Costs in the Short Run

There are some inputs or factors which can be readily adjusted with the changes in the output level. Thus, a firm can readily employ more workers, if it has to increase output. Likewise, it can secure and use more raw materials, more chemicals without much delay if it has to expand production. Thus, labour, raw materials, chemicals etc., are the factors which can be readily varied with the change in output. Such factors are called variable factors. On the other hand, there are factors such as capital equipment, factory building, top management personnel which cannot be so readily varied. It requires a comparatively long time to make variations in them. It takes time to expand a factory building or to build a new factory building with larger area or capacity. Similarly, it also takes time to order and install new machinery. The factors such as raw materials, labour, etc., which can be readily varied with the change in the output level are known as variable factors and the factors such as capital equipment, building which cannot be readily varied and require comparatively a long time to make adjustment in them are called fixed factors.

Corresponding to this distinction between variable factors and fixed factors, economists distinguish between the short run and the long run. ***The short-run is a period of time in which output can be increased or decreased by changing only the amount of variable factors such as labour, raw materials, chemicals,*** etc,. In the short run, quantities of the fixed factors such as capital equipment, factory building etc., cannot be varied for making changes in output. Thus, in the short run, the firm cannot build a new plant or abandon an old one. If the firm wants to increase output in the short run, it can only do so by using more labour and more raw materials, it cannot increase output in the short run by expanding the capacity of its existing plant or building a new plant with a larger capacity. Thus, the short run is a period of time in which only the quantities of variable factors can be varied, while the quantities of the fixed factors remain unaltered.

On the other hand, ***the long run is defined as the period of time in which the quantities of all factors may be varied.*** All factors being variable in the long run, the fixed and variable factors dichotomy holds good only in the short run. In the long run, the output can be increased not only by using more quantities of labour and raw materials but also by expanding the size of the existing plant or by building a new plant with a larger productive capacity. It may be noted that the word 'plant' in economics stands for a collection of fixed factors, such as factory building, machinery installed, the organization represented by the manager and other essential skilled personnel. As mentioned above, even in the long run, it is assumed that while calculating costs and drawing cost curves, *prices* of inputs, (*i.e.*, the prices of resources and factors) and the *technology* (*i.e.*, the state of arts) remain constant. Whenever there is change in prices of inputs or the progress in technology, even the long run cost curves will shift.

Total Fixed Costs. Having explained the difference between the fixed factors and the variable factors and also between the short run and the long run, we are in a position to distinguish between the fixed costs and the variable costs which when added together make up total costs of a business. Fixed costs are those which are independent of output, that is, they do not change with changes in output. These costs are a 'fixed' amount which must be incurred by a firm in the short run, whether the output is small or large. Even if the firm closes down for some time in the short run but remains in business, these costs have to be borne by it. Fixed costs are also known as *overhead costs* and include charges such as contractual rent, insurance fee, maintenance costs, property taxes, interest on the borrowed funds, minimum administrative expenses such as manager's salary, watchman's wages etc. Thus fixed costs are those which are incurred in hiring the fixed factors of production whose amount cannot by altered in the short run.

Total Variable Cost. Variable costs, on the other hand, are those costs which are incurred on the employment of variable factors of production whose amount can be altered in the short run. Thus, the total variable costs change with changes in output in the short run, *i.e.*, they increase or decrease when output rises or falls. These costs include payments to labour employed, the prices of the raw materials, fuel and power used, the expenses incurred on transportation and the like. If a firm shuts down for sometime in the short run, it will not use the variable factors of production and will not therefore incur any variable costs. Variable costs are made only when some amount of output is produced and the total variable costs increase with the increase in the level of production. Variable costs are also called *prime costs or direct costs*. Total costs of a business are the sum of its total variable costs and total fixed costs. Thus:

$$TC = TFC + TVC$$

Because one component, *i.e.*, the total variable cost (*TVC*) varies with the change in output, the total cost of production will also respond to changes in the level of output. The total cost increases as the level of output increases. The way in which fixed, variable and total costs are estimated are shown in Table 21.1 where for the sake of convenience it is assumed that labour is the only variable factor and daily wage per worker is ₹ 60. The second column gives how the output changes with the increase in the number of workers to produce cloth. It is further assumed that "fixed cost is ₹ 120 per day whether or not cloth is produced on any day. By multiplying the wage rate *W* (₹ 60) with the number of workers (*L*) employed for the production of cloth we get the total variable costs (*W.L*) in the short-run which is given in the column IV. By adding the fixed cost of ₹ 120 to the variable costs at different levels of labour employment we get the short-run total cost (*STC* = *TVC* + *TFC*) which is given in column VI. It will be seen from column V that total fixed costs remain fixed at ₹ 120 whatever the level of output. Column VI reveals that short-run total cost increases as output is expanded by increasing the employment of workers. The short-run total fixed and variable costs curves are portrayed in Fig. 21.1 where output is measured on the *X*-axis and cost on *Y*-axis. Since the total fixed cost remains constant whatever the level of output, the total fixed cost curve (*TFC*) is parallel to the X-axis. It will be seen from Fig. 21.1 that total fixed cost curve (*TFC*) starts from a point on the *Y*-axis meaning thereby that the total fixed cost will be incurred even if the output is zero. On the other hand, the total variable cost curve (*TVC*) rises upward showing thereby that as the output is increased, the total variable cost also increases. The total variable cost curve *TVC* starts from the origin which shows that when output is zero the variable costs are also nil.

Table .21.1 Fixed, Variable and Total Costs in the Short-Run

Number of Workers (L)	*Output (Metres of Cloth Produced Per Day) (Q)*	*Daily Wages Per Worker (W)*	*Total Variable Costs (W.L.)*	*Total Fixed Costs (TFC)*	*Short-Run Total Cost (TVC+TFC)*
I	II	III	IV	V	VI
0	0	Rs. 60	0	Rs. 120	Rs. 120
1	10	60	Rs. 60	120	180
2	22	60	120	120	240
3	36	60	180	120	300
4	52	60	240	120	360
5	70	60	300	120	420
6	86	60	360	120	480
7	100	60	420	120	540
8	112	60	480	120	600
9	122	60	540	120	660
10	130	60	600	120	720
11	137	60	660	120	780
12	143	60	720	120	840
13	148	60	780	120	900
14	152	60	840	120	960
15	155	60	900	120	1020

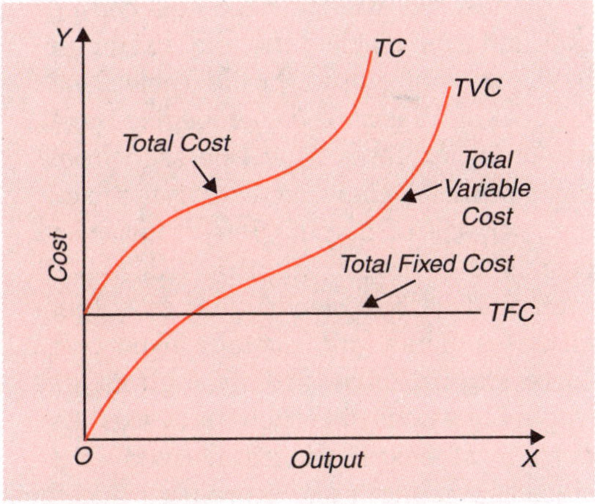

Fig. 21.1. *Short-Run Total Cost Curves*

It should be noted that cost (*TC*) is function of output (*Q*); the greater the output, the graeter will be the total cost. In symbols, we write

$$TC = f(Q)$$

We can prove this as follows :

$$TC = TFC + TVC$$

Suppose *TFC* is equal to *K* which is a constant amount whatever the level of output. TVC is equal to the amount used of the variable factor, say labour, multiplied by the given price of the variable factor, say, *w*,

$$TVC = L.w$$

$$TC = \overline{K} + L.w. \quad \ldots(i)$$

Now, *L.w.*, that is, *TVC* must rise with the increase in output in the short run because only by increase in the amount of variable factor, that is, by increase in *L*, that the output can be increased. From equation (*i*) it follows that with the increase in *L.w* as output rises, *TC* must also rise. In other words, total cost (*TC*) is a function of total output (*q*) and varies directly with it.

Total cost curve (*TC*) has been obtained by adding up vertically total fixed cost curve and total variable cost curve because the total cost is sum of total fixed cost and total variable cost at various levels of output. It will be seen that the vertical distance between the *TVC* and *TC* curves in Fig. 21.1 is constant throughout. This is because the vertical distance between the *TVC* and *TC* curve represents the amount of total fixed cost which remains unchanged as output is increased in the short run. It should also be noted that the vertical distance between the total cost curve (*TC*) and total fixed cost curve (*TFC*) represents the amount of total variable costs which increase with the increase in output. The shape of the total cost curve (*TC*) is exactly the same as that of total variable cost curve (*TVC*) because the same vertical distance always separates the two curves.

THE SHORT-RUN AVERAGE AND MARGINAL COST CURVES

We have explained above the short-run total cost curves. However, the cost concept is more frequently used both by businessmen and economists in the form of cost per unit, or average costs rather than total costs. We, therefore, pass on to the study of short-run *average cost curves*.

Average Fixed Cost (*AFC*)

Average fixed cost is the total fixed costs divided by the number of units of output produced. Therefore,

$$AFC = \frac{TFC}{Q}$$

where *Q* represents the number of units of output produced.

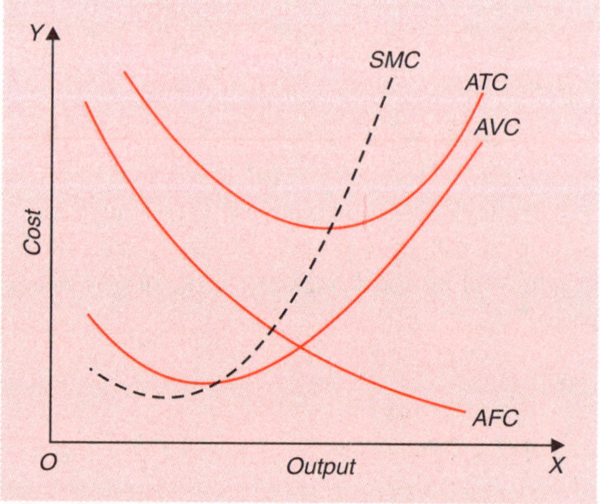

Fig. 21.2. *Short-run Average and Marginal Cost Curves*

Thus, the average fixed cost can be obtained from dividing the total fixed cost by the level of output. In the Table 21.2 the column *VI* gives the average fixed cost as output increases. It will be seen from the table that average fixed cost is the fixed cost per unit of output. Since total fixed cost is a constant quantity (Rs. 120) average fixed cost steadily falls as output increases. Therefore, average fixed cost curve slopes downward throughout its length but it does not touch the *X*-axis. As output increases, the total fixed cost spreads over more and more units and therefore average fixed cost becomes less and less. When output becomes very large average fixed cost approaches zero. Average fixed cost curve (*AFC*) is shown in Fig. 21.2. It will be seen that average fixed cost curve continuously falls throughout. Mathematically speaking, average fixed cost curve approaches both axes asymptotically. In other words, the *AFC* curve gets very nearer to but never touches either axis.

The average fixed cost curve, *AFC*, possesses another important property. If we pick up any point on the average fixed cost curve and multiply the average fixed cost at that point with the corresponding quantity of output produced, then the product is always the same. This is because the product of the average fixed cost and the corresponding quantity of output will yield the total fixed cost which remains constant throughout. A curve with such a property is called ***rectangular hyperbola.***

Table 21.2. Average Variable Cost, Average Fixed Cost, Average Total Cost and Marginal Cost

Number of Workers (L) I	Output of Cloth (Q) II	TVC (w= ₹ 60) w.L III	AVC $\frac{TVC}{Q}$ IV	TFC V	AFC $\left(\frac{TFC}{Q}\right)$ VI	ATC $\left(\frac{TVC+TFC}{Q}\right)$ VII	MC $\left(\frac{\Delta TVC}{\Delta Q}\right)$ VIII
0	0	0	0	₹ 120	0	0	—
1	10	60	6	120	12	18	6.0
2	22	120	5.45	120	5.45	10.9	5
3	36	180	5.0	120	3.35	8.33	4.28
4	52	240	4.61	120	2.30	6.92	3.75
5	70	300	4.28	120	1.71	6.00	3.33
6	86	360	4.19	120	1.39	5.58	3.75
7	100	420	4.20	120	1.20	5.40	4.28
8	112	480	4.29	120	1.07	5.36	5.00
9	122	540	4.42	120	0.98	5.41	6.00
10	130	600	4.62	120	0.92	5.54	7.50
11	137	660	4.82	120	0.87	5.69	8.57
12	143	720	5.03	120	0.84	5.87	10.00
13	148	780	5.27	120	0.81	6.08	12.00
14	152	840	5.52	120	0.79	6.32	15.00
15	155	900	6.00	120	0.77	6.58	20.00

Average Variable Cost (AVC)

Average variable cost is the total variable cost divided by the number of units of output produced. Therefore,

$$AVC = \frac{TVC}{Q}$$

where *Q* represents the total output produced.

Thus average variable cost is variable cost per unit of output. In Table 21.2 we have obtained the average variable cost per unit of output from dividing column III which gives total variable cost (*TVC*) by column *II* which gives total output (*Q*). It will be seen that average variable cost falls until 86 units of output and thereafter it increases. The average variable cost will generally fall as output increases from zero to the normal capacity output due to the occurrence of increasing returns. But beyond the normal capacity output the average variable cost will rise steeply because of the operation of diminishing returns. The average variable cost curve is shown in Fig. 21.2 by the curve *AVC* which first falls, reaches a minimum and then rises.

Average total cost (*ATC*) is the sum of the average variable cost and average fixed cost. Therefore, as output increases and average fixed cost becomes smaller and smaller, the vertical distance, representing average fixed cost between the average total cost curve (*ATC*) and average variable cost curve (*AVC*) goes on diminishing and the average variable cost curve approaches the average total cost curve (*ATC*).

Average variable cost bears an important relationship with the average product per unit of the variable factor. Let Q stand for quantity of total product produced, L for the amount of the variable factor, say labour, used and w for the price per unit of the variable factor and AP for the average product of the variable factor. We assume that the price of the variable factor remains unaltered as more or fewer units of it are employed.

Total product (or output Q) $= AP.L$

Average variable cost, $AVC = \dfrac{TVC}{Q}$

Since the total variable cost (*TVC*) is equal to the amount of the variable factor (L) employed multiplied by the price per unit (w) of the variable factor, ($TVC = L.w$). Therefore,

$$AVC = \frac{L.w}{Q}$$

Since $$Q = AP.L,$$

$\therefore$ $$AVC = \frac{L.w}{AP.L}$$

$$= \frac{w}{AP}$$

$$= w\left(\frac{1}{AP}\right)$$

Thus, given the price of the variable factor w, the average variable cost is equal to the reciprocal of the average product ($\frac{1}{AP}$ is the reciprocal of AP) multiplied by the constant w. It follows that average variable cost and average product vary inversely with each other. Therefore, when average product rises in the beginning as more units of the variable factor are employed, the average variable cost must be falling. And when the average product of the variable factor falls, the average variable cost must be rising. At the level of output at which the average product is maximum, the average variable cost is minimum. Thus, the average variable cost (*AVC*) curve looks like the average product (*AP*) curve turned upside down with minimum point of the *AVC* curve corresponding to the maximum point of the *AP* curve.

Average Total Cost (ATC)

The average total cost or what is called simply average cost is the total cost divided by the number of units of output produced. Thus

$$\text{Average total cost} = \frac{\text{total cost}}{\text{output}}$$

or $$ATC = \frac{TC}{Q}$$

Since the total cost is the sum of total variable cost and total fixed cost, the average total cost is also the sum of average variable cost and average fixed cost. This can be proved as follows :

$$ATC = \frac{TC}{Q}$$

Since $$TC = TVC + TFC$$

Therefore, $$ATC = \frac{TVC + TFC}{Q}$$

In Table 21.2 we have obtained the average total cost by first adding up the total variable cost and total fixed cost (*TVC* + *TFC*) and then dividing it by total output. Thus, in Table 21.2 we have calculated the average total cost by adding up column *III* and *V* and then dividing by output figures of column *II*. Since average total cost is sum of average variable cost and average fixed cost, we can also compute the average total cost by adding up the average variable cost, *AVC* (given in Column *IV*) and average fixed cost, *AFC* (given in Column VI). Thus :

$$ATC = \frac{STC}{Q}$$

$$= \frac{TVC + TFC}{Q} = AVC + AFC$$

It will be seen from Table 21.2 that as output increases in the initial stages, that is, upto 112 meters of cloth production average total cost falls and thereafter it is rising. This implies that short-run average total Cost (*ATC*) curve will have a U-shape, which is shown in Figure 21.2

ATC Curve. It needs to be emphasized that the behaviour of the average total cost curve will depend upon the behaviour of the average variable cost curve and average fixed cost curve. In the beginning, both *AVC* and *AFC* curves fall, the *ATC* curve therefore falls sharply in the beginning. When *AVC* curve begins rising, but *AFC* curve is falling steeply, the *ATC* curve continues to fall. This is because during this stage the fall in *AFC* curve weighs more than the rise in the *AVC* curve. But as output increases further, there is a sharp rise in *AVC* which more than offsets the fall in *AFC*. Therefore, the *ATC* curve rises after a point. Therefore, the average total cost curve (*ATC*) like the *AVC* curve first falls, reaches its minimum value and then rises. The average total cost curve (*ATC*) is therefore almost of a 'U'-shape.

Short-Run Marginal Cost (SMC)

The concept of marginal cost occupies an important place in economic theory. ***Marginal cost is addition to the total cost caused by producing one more unit of output.*** In other words, marginal cost is the addition to the total cost of producing *n* units instead of *n* – 1 units (*i.e.*, one less) where *n* is any given number. In symbols:

$$MC_n = TC_n - TC_{n-1}$$

Suppose the production of 5 units of a product involves the total cost of ₹ 206. If the increase in production to 6 units raises the total cost to ₹ 236, then marginal cost of the sixth unit of output is ₹ 30, (236 – 206 = 30). Let us illustrate the computation of marginal cost from a table of total cost and output.

Since marginal cost is a change in total cost as a result of a unit change in output, it can also be written as:

$$MC = \frac{\Delta\, TC}{\Delta\, Q}$$

where ΔTC represents a change in total cost and ΔQ represents a small change in output.

In the Table 21.3 we have explained the method of computing short-run marginal cost. When output is zero in the short run, the producer is incurring total cost of ₹ 120 which represents the total fixed cost of production. When 10 units of output are produced, the total cost rises to ₹ 180. The marginal cost of a unit of output is therefore ₹ 6 which has been obtained from dividing change in total cost (₹ 180 – 120 = 60) by change in total output ΔQ *i.e.*, 10 – 0 = 10). Thus $MC = \frac{\Delta\, TC}{\Delta\, Q} = \frac{60}{10} = 6$. When output increases to 22 metres of cloth, the total cost increases to ₹ 240. This gives us short-run marginal cost to be equal to $\frac{240-180}{22-10} = \frac{60}{12} = 5$. Similarly, for further increases in output, the short-run marginal cost can be computed.

Table 21.3 Computation of Short-Run Marginal Cost

Output of Cloth in metres (Q)	Change in Output (ΔQ)	Total Cost (TC)	Change in Total Cost (ΔTC)	Marginal Cost (MC) $\left(\frac{\Delta\, TC}{\Delta\, Q}\right)$
0	—	₹ 120	—	—
10	10	180	₹ 60	₹ 6
22	12	240	60	5
36	14	300	60	4.28
52	16	360	60	3.75
70	18	420	60	3.33
86	16	480	60	3.75
100	14	540	60	4.28
112	12	600	60	5.00
122	10	660	60	6.00
130	8	720	60	7.50
137	7	780	60	8.57
143	6	840	60	10.00
148	5	900	60	12.00
152	4	960	60	15.00
155	3	1020	60	20.00

It will be seen from Table 21.3 that the short-run marginal cost declines until output of 70 metres of cloth is produced. With the further increases in output beyond 70 metres, short-run marginal cost rises. This means that short-run marginal cost will have a U-shape. This short-run marginal cost has been shown in Fig. 21.2 by the curve labelled as *SMC*.

If we consider the total cost curve, $\frac{\Delta\, TC}{\Delta\, Q}$ represents the slope of it. Therefore, if we want to measure the marginal cost at a certain output level, we can do so by measuring the slope of the total cost curve corresponding to that output by drawing a tangent to it.

It is worth pointing out that *marginal cost is independent of the fixed costs.* Since fixed costs do not change with the change in output, there are no *marginal fixed costs* when output is increased in the short run. It is only the variable costs that vary with output in the short run. Therefore, the marginal costs are in fact due to the change in variable costs, and whatever the amount of fixed cost, the marginal cost is unaffected by it.

The independence of the marginal cost from the fixed cost can be proved algebraically as follows :

$$\begin{aligned} MC_n &= TC_n - TC_{n-1} \\ &= (TVC_n + TFC) - (TVC_{n-1} + TFC) \\ &= TCN_n + TFC - TVC_{n-1} - TFC \\ &= TVC_n - TVC_{n-1} \end{aligned}$$

Hence marginal cost is the *addition to the total variable costs* when output is increased from $n - 1$ units to n units of output. It follows, therefore, that the marginal cost is independent of the amount of the fixed costs.

Relationship Between Marginal Cost and Marginal Physical Product

It should be noted that marginal cost of production is intimately related to the marginal product of the variable factor. As explained above,

$$MC = \frac{\Delta TC}{\Delta Q}$$

Since MC is independent of fixed cost and is directly attributed to the change in total variable cost,

$$MC = \frac{\Delta TVC}{\Delta Q}$$

Since price of the variable factor *i.e.*, w is assumed to be constant, the change in total variable cost can occur due to the change in the amount of the variable factor. Therefore,

$$MC = \frac{w \cdot \Delta L}{\Delta Q} = w \cdot \frac{\Delta L}{\Delta Q} \qquad ...(i)$$

From our prior study of the theory of production we know that marginal product of the variable factor is the change in total product as a result of a unit change in the variable factor

$$MP = \frac{\Delta Q}{\Delta L},$$

where ΔQ stands for change in total product, ΔL stands for the change in the amount of the variable factor.

The reciprocal of the marginal product of the variable factor is

$$\frac{1}{MP} = \frac{\Delta L}{\Delta Q}$$

Substituting $\frac{1}{MP}$ for $\frac{\Delta L}{\Delta Q}$ in equation (*i*), we get

$$MC = w. \frac{1}{MP} = \frac{w}{MP} \qquad ...(ii)$$

Thus, marginal cost of production is equal to the reciprocal of marginal product of the variable factor multiplied by the price of the variable factor. Therefore, marginal cost varies inversely with marginal product of the variable factor. Now, if price of the variable factor i.e. w is assumed constant, then from the relation between *MC* and *MP* represented in equation (*ii*), we can ascertain the shape of the marginal cost curve. We know from the study of the law of variable proportions that as output increases in the beginning, marginal product of the variable factor rises. This means that the constant w in equation (ii) is being divided by increasingly larger *MP*. This will cause the marginal cost (*MC*) to decline as output increases in the beginning. Further, according to the law of variable proportions, marginal product declines after a certain level of output, which means that now the constant w in equation (ii) is being divided by increasingly smaller *MP*. This causes the marginal cost (*MC*) to rise after a certain level of output. Thus, the fact that marginal product rises first, reaches a maximum and then declines, ensures that the marginal cost curve of a firm declines first, reaches a minimum level and then rises. In other words, marginal cost curve of a firm has a U-shape.

It is clear from above that the law of variable proportions, or in other words, the behaviour of marginal product (*MP*) curve determines the shape of marginal cost (*MC*) curve. Indeed, marginal cost (*MC*) curve is an inversion of the marginal product (*MP*) curve, with the maximum of marginal product corresponding to the minimum of marginal cost. Marginal cost is simply the transformation of marginal product from physical terms into money terms. The relation between marginal product and marginal cost is quite similar to the relationship between average product and average cost.

Three points are worth noting in regard to our above analysis of marginal cost. First, marginal cost is due to the changes in variable cost and is, therefore, independent of the fixed cost. Secondly, the shape of the marginal cost curve is determined by the law of variable proportions, that is, by the behaviour of the marginal product of the variable factor. Thirdly, the assumption that the price of variable factor remains constant as the firm expands its output is greatly significant since a change in factor price may disturb our conclusion.

DERIVATION OF SHORT-RUN AVERAGE AND MARGINAL COST CURVES FROM THEIR TOTAL COST CURVES

In a previous chapter we explained how average and marginal physical product curves were derived from a total physical product curve. Likewise, average and marginal cost curves can be derived from the total cost curves. In the short run there are three types of total costs: (*i*) Total Fixed Cost (*TFC*), (*ii*) Total Variable Cost (*TVC*) and Short-Run Total Cost (*STC*) which is equal to the sum of total fixed cost and total variable cost ($STC = TFC + TVC$). Accordingly, there are three types of total cost curves in the short run, *TFC*, *TVC* and *STC* curves.

We will derive the average fixed curve, average variable cost and short-run average total cost curves from their respective total cost curves. This analysis of derivation of average and marginal cost curves from their total cost curves will reveal how the average and marginal cost curves are related to the total cost curves.

Derivation of Average Fixed Cost Curve from Total Fixed Cost Curve

We have seen above that the total fixed cost is a fixed amount of expenditure per time period incurred on some fixed factors such as managerial staff, capital and land. The total fixed cost curve is invariant to the changes in the level of output in the short run and is therefore a horizontal straight line. How the average fixed cost curve is derived from the *TFC* curve is illustrated in Figure 21.3. It will be seen from this figure that at all levels of output the total fixed cost remains constant at ₹ 100 per period. At the level of output OQ_1 (or 10 units), the average fixed cost is given by $\frac{AQ_1}{OQ_1}$ or $\frac{100}{10} = 10$. Geometrically, the average fixed cost at OQ_1 level of output is given by the *slope of the ray OA* drawn from the origin to the point *A* on the total fixed cost curve *TFC* which is equal to $\frac{AQ_1}{OQ_1}$ or 100/10 =10 in the Figure 21.3.

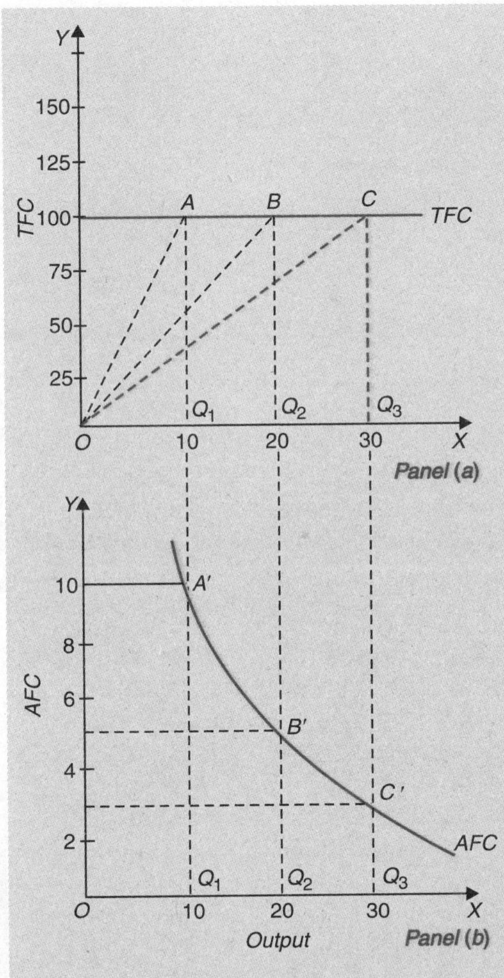

Fig.21.3. *Derivation of Average Fixed Cost Curve from Total Fixed Cost Curve*

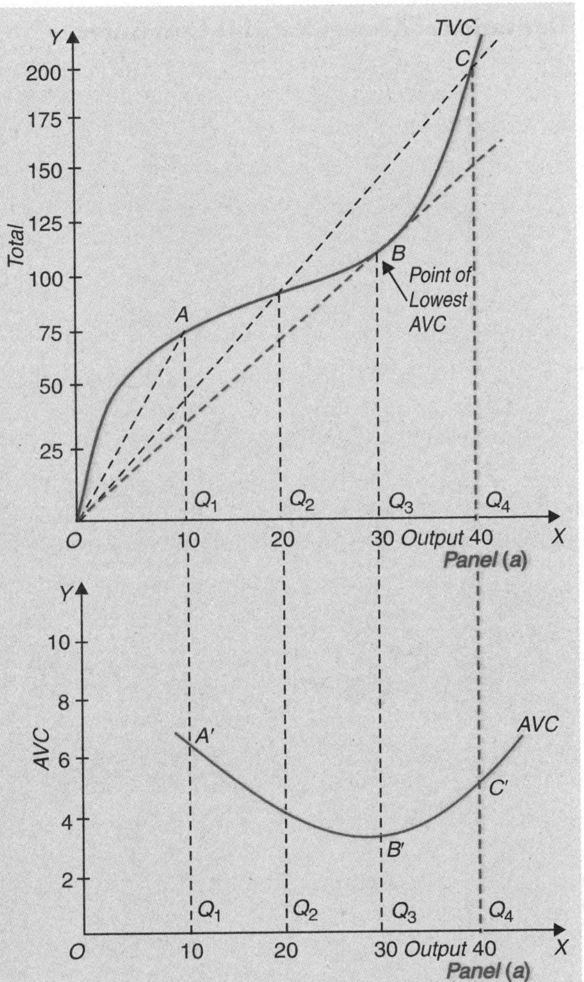

Fig.21.4. *Derivation of Average Variable Cost Curve from Total Variable Cost Curve*

In the lower panel (*b*) of Fig. 21.3 we have directly plotted this average fixed cost of ₹10 or AQ_1/OQ_1 as point *A′* against the output level of OQ_1 or 10 units. Note that in the lower panel (*b*) the scale on the vertical axis is different from that in the upper panel (*a*). Similarly, at output level of OQ_2 or 20 units, the average fixed cost is given by the slope of the ray *OB* which equals BQ_2/OQ_2 or 100/20 = ₹ 5. Again, this average fixed cost is plotted in the lower panel (*b*) as point *B′* against the output level OQ_2 or 20 units. Further, at output level OQ_3 or 30 units of output, the average fixed cost is given by slope of the ray *OC* which equals $\frac{CQ_3}{OQ_3} = \frac{100}{30}$ = ₹ 3.33 which is plotted as point *C′* in the lower panel (*b*) against output level

OQ_3 or 30 units. On joining points A', B' and C' in the lower panel (*b*) of Figure 21.3 we get the average fixed cost curve *AFC* as derived from the total fixed cost curve *TFC*. Since total fixed cost equals *AFC* multiplied by output, the area at every point under the average fixed cost curve *AFC* will be equal to the total fixed cost. As the total fixed cost does not vary with the change in output in the short run, the area under every point of the average fixed cost curve will be equal to the constant total fixed cost. It follows therefore that the shape of the average fixed cost curve is of *rectangular hyperbola*.

Derivation of Average Variable Cost Curve

The average variable cost (*AVC*) curve can be derived from the total variable cost (*TVC*) curve. Unlike the total fixed cost curve, the total variable cost is function of output, that is, it varies with the changes in the level of output. The total variable cost curve is drawn as *TVC* curve in panel (*a*) of Figure 21.4. Since average variable cost at any given level of output is given by the total variable cost divided by the quantity of output produced, it can be measured by the slope of the ray (i.e., straight line) from the origin to a point on the *TVC* curve corresponding to a given level of output. Thus, in Figure 21.4 at output level OQ_1 the average variable cost curve is given by $\frac{AQ_1}{OQ_1} = \frac{75}{10} = 7.5$ which is equal to the slope of the ray *OA* drawn from the origin. The average variable cost so obtained is plotted in the panel (*b*) below as Q_1A' (= ₹ 7.5). Note that the scale on the vertical axis in panel (*b*) is not the same as in panel (*a*) above. Similarly, at a higher level of output OQ_3, the average variable cost is given by the slope of the ray *OB* drawn from the origin which equals BQ_3/OQ_3 or 110/30 = ₹ 3.7 which in panel (*b*) is plotted as Q_3B' (= ₹ 3.7). Again, at a still' higher level of output OQ_4, the average variable cost is measured by the slope of the ray *OC* drawn from the origin which is equal to CQ_4/OO_4 or $\frac{200}{40}$ = ₹ 5 and this is plotted in the lower panel (*b*) as Q_4C'.

It will be seen from panel (*a*) of Figure 21.4 that the slope of the ray drawn from the origin to a point on the *TVC* curve goes on declining until the output level OQ_3 is reached. It should be carefully noted that the slope of the ray *OB* from the origin at point *B* or output level OQ_3 is also the tangent to the *TVC* curve. This implies that beyond output level OQ_3, or point *B* on the *TVC* curve, the slope of the ray from the origin starts increasing. Thus, at point *C* on the *TVC* curve corresponding to the output level OQ_4, the slope of ray *OC* from the origin is greater than the slope of the ray *OB*. Thus, until output level OQ_3 the average variable cost curve, as will be seen from panel (*b*) below, is declining and beyond output level Q_3 it rises. This implies that the *AVC* curve is roughly of U-Shape.

Derivation of the Short-Run Average Total Cost (ATC) Curve

Derivation of the short-run average total cost curve from the short-run total cost curve (*STC*) is similar to the derivation of *AVC* curve from the *TVC* curve as explained above.It can be derived by drawing *rays from the origin to the points on total short-run cost curve (STC)* corresponding to various levels of output and then *measuring the slope* of these rays from the origin. Since the short-run total cost (*STC*) curve is generally of *S* shape as the total variable cost curve *TVC* in Fig. 21.4, the average total cost curve (*ATC*) which we will get will also be of U shape, that is, first sloping downward and then rising. Besides, since average total cost is the sum of average fixed cost and average variable cost (*ATC* = *AFC* + *AVC*), average total cost (*ATC*) curve falls in the beginning because both *AFC* and *AVC* decline upto a point and then *ATC* rises beyond a point because due to diminishing returns to the variable factors, average variable cost (*AVC*) curve rises more rapidly than the fall in the average fixed cost (*AFC*) curve.

Derivation of Short-Run Marginal Cost Curve

Since marginal cost is defined as $\frac{\Delta TC}{\Delta Q}$, that is, addition made to the total cost resulting from a small change in output, it can be derived form the total cost curve. The derivation of the marginal cost curve from the total cost curve is illustrated in Figure 21.5 in which *STC* is the short-run total cost curve with its usual shape. As output increases from OQ_1 to OQ_2, the producer moves from point *A* to *B* on the total cost curve *STC* and his total cost increases from C_1 to C_2. From this, marginal cost is obtained as under :

$$MC = \frac{\Delta TC}{\Delta Q} = \frac{C_2 - C_1}{Q_2 - Q_1} = \frac{BH}{AH}$$

Now, if point *A* is brought closer to point *B* on the total cost curve, the distance between *A* and *B* becomes smaller so that the slope of the tangent drawn at point *B* becomes a better measure of the $\frac{BH}{AH}$, that is, marginal cost. Thus movement in the small neighbourhood around point *B*, the slope of the tangent geometrically measures the marginal cost of production at the output level Q_2.

Now, consider the *STC* curve in Figure 21.5. It will be seen that the slope of the tangents drawn to the *STC* curve at various points corresponding to successively higher levels of output, diminishes until output Q_3 is reached. Thereafter, the slope of the tangent, that is, marginal cost increases. Thus, as output increases up to Q_3, marginal cost decreases and beyond that it increases. This implies that the marginal cost is minimum at output level OQ_3. It should be further noted that at point *D* on the short-run total cost curve (*STC*) corresponding to output level Q_4, the ray from the origin is also the tangent at this point. This means that at output level Q_4, the marginal cost which is given by the slope of the tangent drawn to the *STC* curve becomes equal to the average cost which is given by the slope of the ray from the origin to a point on *STC*. Beyond point *D*, the slope of the tangent at a point on the total cost curve, for instance, at point *E* becomes greater than the slope of the ray from

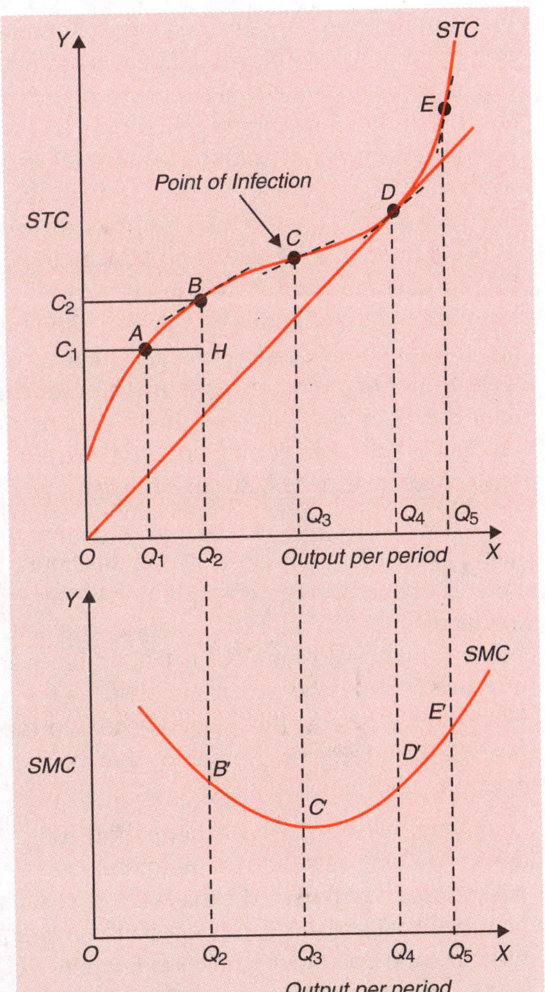

Fig. 21.5. *Derivation of Short-Run Marginal Cost Curve from Short-Run Total Cost Curve*

the origin drawn to that point. This implies that beyond point *D* on the short-run total cost curve, marginal cost curve would lie above the average cost curve, cutting the latter from its minimum point. Figure 21.5 therefore also brings out the relationship between the marginal cost and average cost curves. The slope of short-run total cost curve (*STC*) at any point to the left of point *D* is less than the slope of the ray from the origin which means that marginal cost curve (*SMC*) would lie below the average cost curve. In fact, it is the lower marginal cost than the average cost before point *D* that pushes down the average cost. On the other hand, to the right of point *D*, the slope of the total cost curve at any point is greater than the slope of the ray drawn from the origin, which means that the marginal cost is greater than the average cost to the right of point *D*. As a matter of fact, the higher marginal cost than average cost pushes up the latter.

The Relation Between the Average and Marginal Cost Curves

We have explained above the concepts of average and marginal cost curves. There is an important relation between the two. The relationship between the marginal cost and average cost is the same as that between any other marginal-average quantities. When marginal cost is less than average cost, average cost falls and when marginal cost is greater than average cost, average cost rises. This marginal-average relationship is a matter of mathematical truism and can be easily understood by a simple example. Suppose that a cricket player's batting average is 50. If in his next innings he scores less than 50, say 45, then his average score will fall because his marginal (additional) score is less than his average score. If instead of 45, he scores more than 50, say 55, in his next innings, then his average score will increase because now the marginal score is greater than his previous average score. Again, with his present average runs as 50, if he scores 50 also in his next innings, then his average score will remain the same i.e. 50, since his marginal score is just equal to the average score. Likewise, a producer is producing a certain number of units of a product and his average cost is ₹ 20. Now, if he produces one unit more and his average cost falls, it means that the additional unit must have cost him less than ₹ 20. On the other hand, if the production of the additional unit raises his average cost, then the marginal unit must have cost him more than ₹ 20. And finally, if as a result of production of an additional unit, the average cost remains the same, then marginal unit must have cost him exactly ₹ 20, that is, marginal cost and average cost would be equal in this case.

The relationship between average and marginal cost can be easily remembered with the help of Fig. 21.6. It is illustrated in this figure that when marginal cost (*MC*) is above average cost (*AC*), the average cost rises, that is, the marginal cost (*MC*) pulls the average cost (*AC*) upward. On the other hand, if marginal cost (*MC*) is below the average cost (*AC*), average cost falls, that is, the marginal cost pulls the average cost downward. When marginal cost (*MC*) stands equal to the average cost (*AC*), the average cost remains the same, that is, the marginal cost pulls the average cost horizontally.

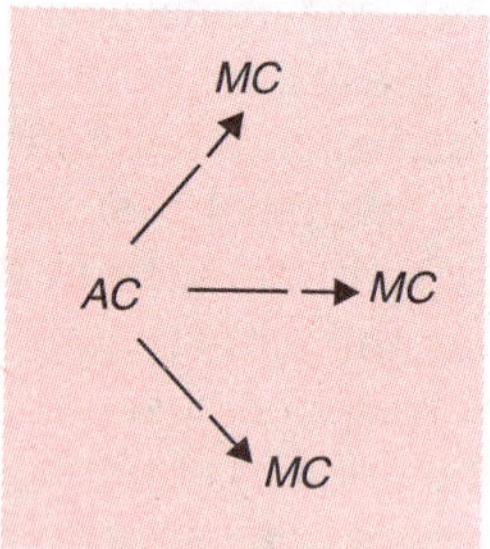

Fig. 21.6

Now, take Fig. 21.7 where short-run average cost curve *AC* is drawn. As long as short-run marginal cost curve *MC* lies *below* short-run average cost curve *AC*, the average cost curve *AC* is falling. When marginal cost curve *MC lies above* the average cost curve *AC*, the average cost curve *AC* is rising. At the point of intersection *L* where *MC* is equal to *AC*, *AC* is neither falling nor rising, that is, at point *L*, *AC* has just ceased to fall but has not yet begun to rise. It follows that point *L*, where the *MC* curve crosses the *AC* curve to lie above the *AC* curve, is the minimum point of the *AC* curve. Thus marginal cost curve cuts the average cost curve at the latter's minimum point.

It is important to note that we cannot generalize about the *direction* in which marginal cost is moving from the way average cost is changing, that is, when average cost is falling we cannot say that marginal cost will be falling too. When average cost is falling, what we can say definitely is only that the marginal cost will be *below* it but marginal cost itself may be either rising or falling. Likewise, when average cost is rising, we cannot deduce that marginal cost will be rising too. When average cost is rising, the marginal cost must be *above* it but the marginal cost itself may be either rising or falling. Consider Fig. 21.7 where up to the point *K*, marginal cost is falling as well as below the average cost. As a result, the average cost is falling. But beyond point *K* and up to point *L*, marginal cost curve lies below the average cost curve with the result that the average cost curve is falling. But it will be seen that between *K* and *L* when the marginal cost is rising, the average cost is falling. This is because though *MC* is rising between *K* and *L*, it is below *AC*. It is therefore clear that when the average cost is falling, marginal cost may be either falling or rising. This can also be easily illustrated by the example of batting average. Suppose a cricket player's present batting average is 50. If in his next innings he scores less than 50, say, 45, his batting average will fall. But his marginal score of 45, though less than the average may have risen. For instance, he might have scored 35 in his previous innings so that his present marginal score of 45 is much greater than his previous marginal score. Thus one cannot deduce about the *direction* of marginal cost as to whether it will be falling or rising when the average cost is falling or rising.

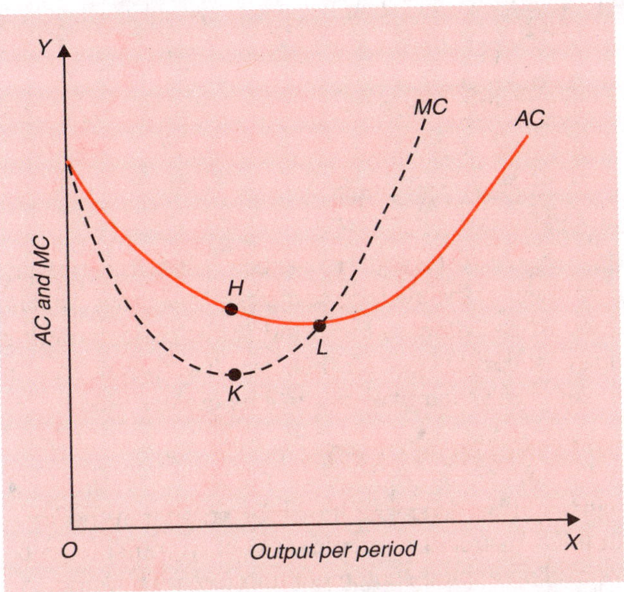

Fig. 21.7. The Relation between *AC* and *MC* curves

The relationship between average cost and marginal cost can be easily proved with the aid of differential calculus. Let *AC* stand for average cost per unit and *Q* for total output,

$$\text{Then, total cost } (TC) = AC.Q$$

$$MC = \frac{d(TC)}{dQ}$$

$$\text{Since } TC = \text{output x average cost}$$
$$= AC.Q$$

$$MC = \frac{d(AC.Q)}{dQ}$$

$$MC = Q\,\frac{d(AC)}{dQ} + AC \qquad \text{...(i)}$$

$\frac{d(AC)}{dQ}$ measures the slope of the average cost curve. Because total output Q is positive, from equation (*i*) above, it follows that when

$$\frac{d(AC)}{dQ} < 0, MC < AC \quad ...(ii)$$

$$\frac{d(AC)}{dQ} > 0, MC > AC \quad ...(iii)$$

$$\frac{d(AC)}{dQ} = 0, MC = AC \quad ...(iv)$$

From the condition (iv), it follows that marginal cost is equal to average cost at its minimum. From condition (*ii*), it follows that when the slope of the average cost curve is negative, that is, when *AC* is falling, marginal cost (*MC*) would be below it. From the above condition (*iii*) it follows that when the slope of the average cost curve is greater than zero (*i.e.*, positive) or, in other words, when the average cost curve is rising, marginal cost will be greater than it.

THEORY OF LONG-RUN COSTS

We now begin to explain the cost curves in the long run. It may be noted that the long-run refers to a time period during which full adjustment to a change in environment can be made by the firm by varying all inputs, including capital equipment and factory building. An important aspect of the long run is that it represents a *planning horizon* because in it the firm plans its size of the plant which is appropriate to the specific level of output. However, all production is done in the short run during which the size of plant (*i.e.*, the capital equipment, factory building) is given. Thus, the long run consists of all possible short run situations among which a firm has to choose to produce a target level of output. It needs to be carefully understood that *before* an investment is made, a firm is in a long-run situation; it can choose among a number of possible sizes of plant in which to invest. But once investment is made in a particular capital equipment and plant has been set up, the firm operates in the short run.

In what follows we shall first explain how a long run average and marginal cost curves are derived from a number of short-run average cost and marginal cost curves. Having done so we shall explain why the long-run average cost curve is of approximately U-shape. Further we shall show how the long-run total cost curve is derived from the production function or the expansion path of the theory of production.

Long-Run Average Cost Curve

We now turn to explain the cost curves in the long run. The long run, as noted above, is a period of time during which the firm can vary all its inputs. In the short run, some inputs are fixed and others are varied to increase the level of output. In the long run, none of the factors is fixed and all can be varied to expand output. The long run production function has therefore no fixed factors and the firm has no fixed costs in the long run. It is conventional to regard the size or scale of plant as a typical fixed input. The term 'plant' is here understood to be as consisting of capital equipment, machinery, land, etc. In the short run, the size of the plant is fixed and it cannot be increased or reduced. That is to say, one cannot change the amount of capital equipment in the short run, if one has to increase or decrease output. On the other hand, long run is a period of time sufficiently long to permit changes in plant, that is, in capital equipment, machinery, land, etc. in order to expand or contract output. Thus, whereas in the short run the firm is tied with a given plant, in the long run the firm moves from one plant to another; the firm can make a larger plant if it has to increase its output and a smaller plant if it has to reduce its output. The long-run cost of production is the least possible cost of producing any given level of output when all inputs are variable, including of course the size of the plant. A long-run cost curve depicts the functional relationship between output and the long-run cost of production, as just defined.

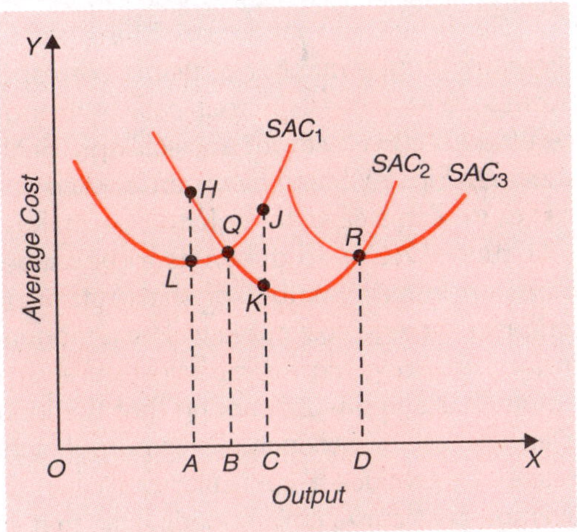

Fig. 21.8. *Plant Curves*

Long-run average cost is the long-run total cost divided by the level of output. Long-run average cost curve depicts the least possible average cost for producing various levels of output. In order to understand how the long-run average cost curve is derived, consider the three short run average cost curves as shown in Fig. 21.8. These short run average cost curves are also called *plant curves,* since in the short run plant is fixed and each of the short-run average cost curves corresponds to a particular plant. In the short run, the firm can be operating on any short-run average cost curve, given the size of the plant. Suppose that only these three are technically possible sizes of plant and that no other size of the plant can be built. Given the size of the plant or short run average cost curve the firm will increase or decrease its output by varying the amount of the variable inputs. But, in the long run, the firm can choose among the three possible sizes of plant as depicted by short run average cost curves SAC_1, SAC_2 and SAC_3. In the long run the firm will examine with which size of plant or on which short run SAC_2 curve it should operate to produce a given level of output at the minimum possible cost.

It will be seen from Fig. 21.8 that upto *OB* amount of output, the firm will operate on the short-run average cost curve SAC_1, though it could also produce with short-run average cost curve SAC_2, because upto *OB* amount of output, production on SAC_1 curve entails lower cost than on SAC_2. For instance, if the level of output *OA* is produced with SAC_1 it will cost *AL* per unit and if it is produced with SAC_2 it will cost *AH* per unit. It will be seen from the figure that *AL* is smaller than *AH*. Similarly, all other output levels up to *OB* can be produced more economically with the smaller plant SAC_1 than with the larger plant SAC_2. It is thus clear that in the long run the firm will produce any output upto *OB* on SAC_1. If the firm plans to produce an output which is larger than *OB* (but less than *OD*), then it will not be economical to produce on SAC_1. It will be seen from Fig. 21.8 that the outputs larger than *OB* but less than *OD*, can be produced at a lower cost per unit on SAC_2 than on SAC_1. Thus, the output *OC* if produced on SAC_2 costs *CK* per unit which is lower than *CJ* which is the cost incurred when produced on SAC_1. Therefore, if the firm plans to produce between outputs *OB* and *OD*, it will employ the plant corresponding to the short-run average cost curve SAC_2. If the firm has to produce an output which exceeds *OD*, then the cost per unit will be lower on SAC_3 than on SAC_2. Therefore, for outputs larger than *OD*, the firm will employ plant corresponding to the short-run average cost curve SAC_3.

It is thus clear that in the long-run the firm has a choice in the employment of a plant, and it will employ that plant which yields minimum possible unit cost for producing a given output. The long-run average cost curve depicts the least possible average cost for producing various levels of output when all factors including the size of the plant have been adjusted. Given that only three sizes of plants as shown in Fig. 21.8 are technically possible, then the long-run average cost curve is the curve which has scallops in it. This heavily scalloped long-run average cost curve consists of some segments of all the short-run average cost curves as explained above.

Suppose now that the size of the plant can be varied by infinitely small gradations so that there are infinite number of plants corresponding to which there will be numerous short-run average cost curves. In that case, the long-run average cost curve will be a smooth and continuous curve without any scallops. Such a smooth long-run average cost curve has been shown in Fig. 21.9 and has been labelled as *LAC*. There will be infinite short-run average cost curves in such a case, though only seven have been shown in Fig. 21.9. This long-run average cost curve *LAC* is so drawn as to be tangent to each of the short-run average cost curves. Since an infinite number of short-run average cost curves is assumed, every point on the long-run average cost curve will be a tangency point with some short-run average cost curve. In fact, the long-run average cost curve is nothing else but the locus of all these tangency points. It is again worth noting that the long-run average cost curve shows the least possible average cost of producing any output, when all productive factors are variable. If a firm desires to produce a particular output in the long run, it will pick a point on the long-run average cost curve corresponding to that output and it will then build a relevant plant and operate on the corresponding short-run average cost curve.

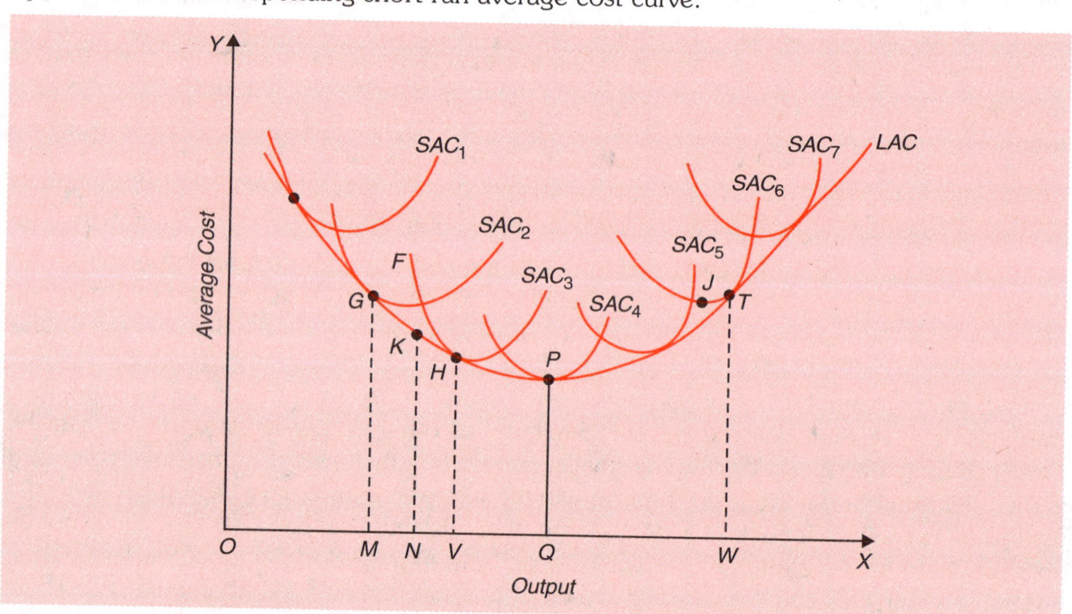

Fig. 21.9. ***Deriving Long-Run Average Cost Curve from a Family of Short-Run Average Cost Curves***

In the situation as depicted in Fig. 21.9 for producing output *OM* the corresponding point on the long-run average cost curve *LAC* is *G* at which the short-run average cost curve SAC_2 is tangent to the long-run average cost curve *LAC*. Thus, if a firm desires to produce output *OM*, the firm will construct a plant corresponding to SAC_2 and will operate on this curve at point *G*. Similar would be the case for all other outputs in the long run. Further, consider that the firm plans to produce output *ON*, which corresponds to point *K* on the long-run average cost curve LAC. As already noted, ***every point on the long-run average cost curve is a tangency point with some short-run average cost curve and that there are infinite number of short-run average cost curves,*** so there will be some short-run average cost curve (not shown in Fig. 21.9) which will be tangent to the long-run average cost curve LAC at the point K corresponding to ON output. Thus, for producing output ON, the firm will build a plant which will correspond to that short-run average cost curve which is tangent to the long-run average cost curve LAC at point K corresponding to output ON. The long-run average cost curve LAC is also called '***envelope***' since it envelops or supports a family of short-run average cost curves from below.

It is evident from Fig. 21.9 that larger outputs can be produced at the lower cost with the larger plants, whereas smaller outputs can be produced at the lower cost with smaller plants. Thus, output OM can be produced with the lowest possible cost with the plant represented by SAC_2. To produce OM output with a larger plant corresponding to SAC_3 will entail higher unit cost than that of SAC_2. But a larger output OV can be produced most economically with a larger plant represented by SAC_3, while to produce OV with the smaller plant of SAC_2 will mean higher unit cost. This is as it will be expected. A larger plant with a greater productive capacity is more expensive when employed to produce a small output as it will not be fully utilized and its under-utilization will cause higher unit cost. In other words, using a larger plant and to operate it much below its capacity in order to produce a small output will naturally mean higher average cost. On the other hand, a large output with a small-sized plant will also involve higher cost per unit because of its limited capacity.

It will be seen from Fig. 21.9 that the long-run average cost curve first falls and then beyond a certain point it rises, that is, the long-run average cost curve is U-shaped, though the U-shape of the long-run average cost curve is less pronounced than that of the short-run average cost curve. In Fig. 21.9 long-run average cost is minimum at output OQ. The long-run average cost falls upto the output OQ and it rises beyond it. Why the long-run average cost first declines and then rises will be explained a little later.

An important fact about the long-run average cost curve is worth mentioning. It is that the ***long-run average curve LAC is not tangent to the minimum points of the short-run average cost curves.*** When the long-run average cost curve is declining, that is, for output less than OQ, it is tangent to the *falling portions* of the short-run average cost curves. This means that for any output smaller than OQ, it will not pay to operate a plant at its minimum unit cost. Consider, for instance, the plant corresponding to the short-run average cost curve SAC_2, which is operated at point G in the long run to produce output OM. The point G lies on the falling portion of the short-run average cost curve SAC_2 which has a minimum point F, By working on point G of SAC_2, the firm is using the given plant below its full capacity. The plant of SAC_2 will be utilized to its full capacity if it is operated at minimum unit cost point F to produce a larger output than OM. But, in the long run, it does not pay the firm to produce with the plant of SAC_2 an output larger than OM. This is because output larger than OM can be produced at a lower unit cost with a plant larger than the plant of SAC_2. It is thus clear that for producing an output less than OQ at the lowest possible unit cost the firm will construct an appropriate plant and will operate it at less than its capacity, that is, at less than its minimum average cost of production.

On the other hand, when the long-run average cost curve is rising, it will be tangent to the *rising portions* of the short-run average cost curves. This implies that output larger than OQ will be produced most cheaply by constructing a plant with a given optimal capacity and operating it to produce larger than its capacity, that is, using it to produce at more than its minimum unit cost of production. Consider, for instance, the short-run average cost curve SAC_6 which is tangent to the long-run average cost curve *LAC* at point *T*. Point *T* lies on the rising portion of SAC_6 which has a minimum unit cost point *J* to the left of the point *T*. This means that the firm is producing output *OW* by operating at point *T* on the plant of SAC_6 which has a optimum capacity less than *OW*. That is, for producing output *OW* at lowest possible cost the firm has built a plant corresponding to SAC_6 and works it at more than its capacity.

Long-run average cost curve is often called the ***'planning curve'*** of the firm by some economists because a firm plans to produce any output in the long run by choosing a plant on the long-run average cost curve corresponding to the given output. The long-run average cost curve reveals to the firm that how large should be the plant for producing a certain output at the least possible cost. Thus, while making decisions regarding the choice of a plant, the firm has to look at its long-run average cost curve enveloping a family of plant curves. What different sizes of plants are available at a time and what short-run average cost curves they will have on being used for production are known to the firm either from experience or from engineering studies.

Long-Run Average Cost Curve in Case of Constant Returns to Scale

If the production function is linear and homogeneous (that is, homogeneous of the first degree) and also the prices of inputs remain constant, then the long-run average cost will remain constant at all levels of output. As explained in the previous chapter, linear homogeneous production function implies constant returns to scale which means that when all inputs are increased in a certain proportion, output increases in the same proportion. Therefore, with the given prices of inputs, when returns to scale are constant, cost per unit of output remains the same. In this case, the long-run average cost curve will be a horizontal straight line as depicted in Fig. 21.10. Though there will be infinite number of short-run average cost curves as we continue to assume that the size of the plant can be varied by infinitely small gradations, only the *SAC* curves of three plants have been shown in Fig. 21.10

It will be noticed from Fig. 21.10 that all short-run average cost curves such as SAC_1, SAC_2, SAC_3 have the same minimum average cost of production. This means whatever the size of the plant, the minimum average cost of production is the same. This implies that all factors can be adjusted in the long-run in such a way that the proportions between them always remain optimum. In such a case, the optimum size of the firm is indeterminate, since all levels of output can be produced at the same long-run average cost which represents the same minimum short-run average cost throughout. It is useful to note that though all levels of output will be produced at the same minimum cost of production the different sizes of plants will be used for producing different levels of output. Thus, for producing output *OA*, the plant of SAC_1 will be employed; for output *OB*, the plant of SAC_2 will be employed; and for output *OC* the plant of SAC_3 will be employed. This is because the production at the lowest possible cost for output *OA* is possible with plant SAC_1, and for output *OB* with plant SAC_2 and for output *OC* with plant SAC_3.

Some economists like Kaldor, Joan Robinson, Stigler are of the view that when all factors of production are "*perfectly divisible*" then there would be no internal economies of scale (and no internal diseconomies). Therefore, according to them, in case of 'perfect divisibility' of all factors, the long-run average cost curve will be a horizontal straight line showing that the long-run average cost is constant whatever the level of output. In their view, all internal economies of scale are due to the indivisibility of some factors. Therefore, they argue that if perfect divisibility of factors is assumed, then it implies the absence of internal economies of scale and therefore in such a case the long-run average cost curve will be a horizontal straight line. But E.H. Chamberlin has challenged this viewpoint. According to him, perfect divisibility has nothing to do with efficiency, that is to say, perfect divisibility does not mean the absence of internal economies of scale. Thus, according to him, even if all

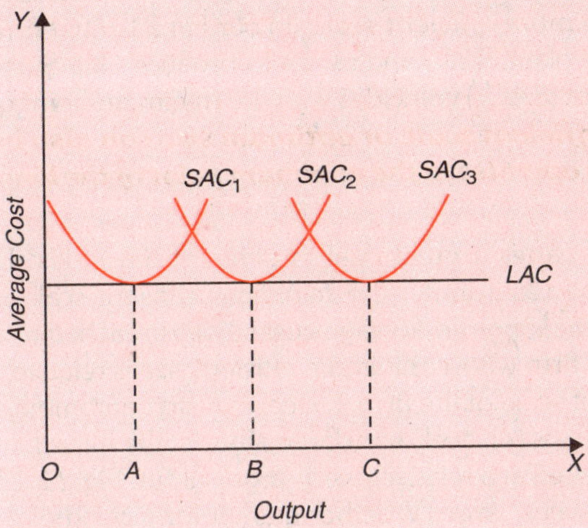

Fig. 21.10. *When Returns to Scale are Constant, Long-run Average Cost Curve is a Horizontal Straight Line*

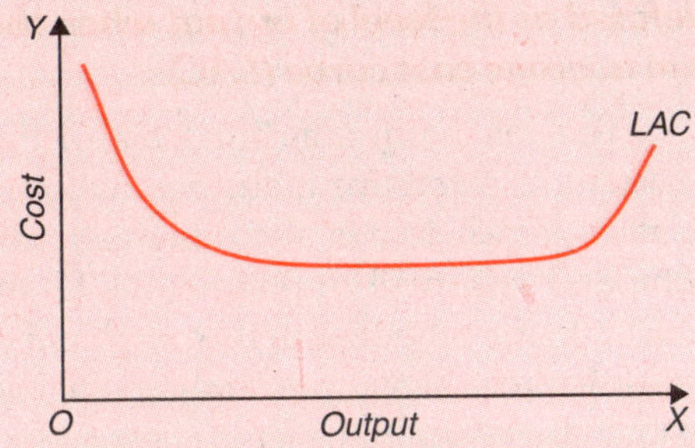

Fig . 21.11. *Saucer-Shaped Long-Run Average Cost Curve*

factors were perfectly divisible, the economies of scale will be reaped due to the use of more specialized machinery and a greater degree of division of labour at higher levels of output. Therefore, according to Chamberlin, constant returns to scale cannot exist and long-run average cost cannot remain constant even when factors are perfectly divisible.

However, many empirical studies have shown that U-shape of the long-run average cost curve is not smooth and regular but a wavy and irregular one. Further, a very important feature of long-run average cost curve revealed by empirical studies is that there is a relatively very large flat portion or, in other words, a large horizontal region in the centre of long-run average cost curve, as is depicted in Figure 21.11. In such a real case, long-run average cost curve has a saucer-shaped appearance. Such a long-run cost curve with a very large flat portion in the centre can arise if the economies of scale are exhausted at a very modest scale of operation and then for a relatively large further expansion in output, diseconomies of scale do not occur. Only after a very large increase in output, diseconomies of scale exert themselves and bring about a rise in the long-run average cost. A long horizontal or flat section in the long-run average cost curve can also occur because economies of scale which are mostly of technological type may offset the diseconomies over a wide range of output.

Minimum Efficient Scale

It is clear from Fig. 21.9 that in the continuous long-run average cost curve both for outputs less than *OQ* and more than *OQ* no plant is used at its point of minimum cost. It is only the plant, the minimum point of whose short-run average cost curve coincides with the minimum point of the long-run average cost curve, which is operated at the point of its minimum average cost of production. In Fig. 21.9 for producing output *OQ*, the plant of SAC_4 is being efficiently utilized to produce output with minimum long-run average cost, that is, it is being used at its full capacity. The *minimum efficient scale* of plant is the level of output at which long-run average cost is minimum. This is also called the *optimum size* of a firm.

It should be noted that in Fig 21.9 the plant of SAC_4 is optimum plant, since its minimum cost of production is the lowest of the minimum costs of all other plants. If the size of the plant is increased beyond SAC_4, it results in higher average cost of production. Similarly, if the size of the plant is smaller than SAC_4, average cost of production is higher. Further, the least-cost output of plant SAC_4 is OQ. Now, if the firm produces output OQ with the optimum plant SAC_4, it is said to have achieved the *minimum efficient scale*. In our Fig 21.9 the firm will be working with efficient scale if it employs plant SAC_4 and uses it to produce OQ. Since the point of minimum cost of the optimum plant (SAC_4) coincides with the minimum point of the long-run average cost curve, the ***minimum efficient scale or optimum size can also be defined as the level of output when the firm operates at the minimum point of the long-run average cost curve (LAC).***

The minimum efficient scale of the firm varies a great deal in different industries. In agriculture, extractive industries, wholesale and retail trade, the minimum efficient scale is relatively small, that is, the minimum point of the long-run average cost curve is reached at a comparatively small output. Fig.21.12 shows a firm whose minimum efficient size is relatively small. On the other hand, the minimum efficient scale of the firm in steel industry, automobile industry, other heavy industries and public utilities is relatively very large, that is, the minimum point of their long-run average cost curve is reached at a relatively very large output. Fig.21.13 depicts a firm whose minimum efficient size is very large. Whether market for a good of a

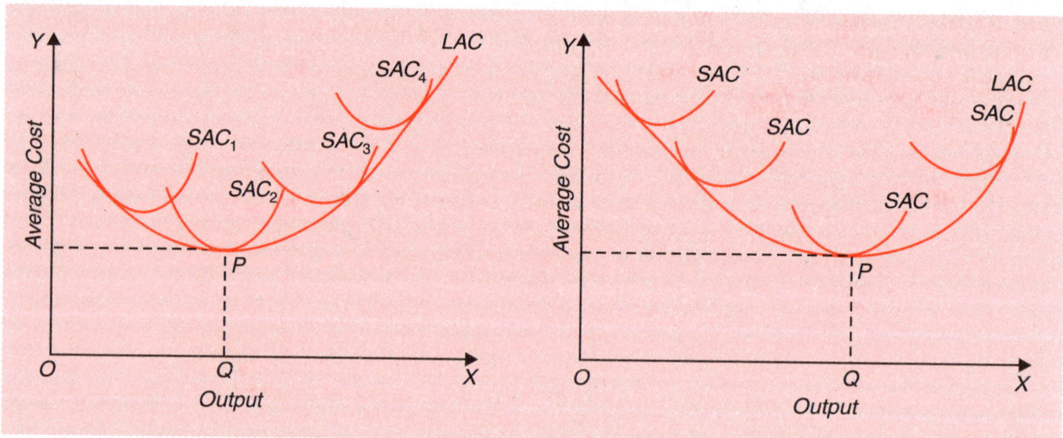

Fig. 21.12. *Small Minimum Efficient Scale* **Fig. 21.13.** *Large Minimum Efficient Scale*

given size is supplied by a large number of relatively small-scale firms or by a small number of relatively large size firms depends on the minimum efficient scale of firms in the industry. And this minimum efficient scale is largly determined by the technology of production of an industry. In the industry in which the efficient size of the firm is very large, there are generally a few number of firms, each with a large size.

EXPLANATION OF THE U-SHAPE OF THE LONG-RUN AVERAGE COST CURVE

In Fig. 21.9 we have drawn the long-run average cost curve as having an approximately U-shape. It is generally believed by economists that the long-run average cost curve is normally U-shaped, that is, the long-run average cost first declines as output is increased and then beyond a certain point it rises. Now, what is the proper explanation for such a behaviour of the long-run average cost?

We saw above that the U-shape of the short-run average cost curve is explained with the law of proportions. But *the long run average cost curve depends upon the returns to scale*. In the long run all inputs including the capital equipment can be altered. Therefore, the relevant principle governing the shape of the long-run average cost curve is that of returns to scale. In a previous chapter we explained that returns to scale increase at the initial increases in output and after remaining constant for a while, the returns to scale decrease. It is because of the increasing returns to scale in the beginning that the long-run average cost of production falls as output is increased and, likewise, it is because of the decreasing returns to scale that the long-run average cost of production rises beyond a certain level of output.

Economies of Scale

But the question is why we first get increasing returns to scale due to which cost falls and why after a certain point we get decreasing returns to scale that result in rise in cost per unit of output. In other words, what are the reasons for the firm to enjoy *economies of scale* up to a certain point and then beyond it why it encounters *diseconomies of scale*. The following factors are said to be responsible for the economies of scale which accrue to the firm and due to which cost per unit falls.

Use of Technically Efficient Machines : First, as the firm increases its scale of operations, it becomes possible to *use more specialized and technically more efficient form of all factors, especially capital equipment and machinery*. For producing higher levels of output, a technically more efficient machinery is generally available which when employed to produce a larger output yields a lower cost per unit of output. Thus, the use of technological specialized equipment, for example, automated buiding machine for a book publishing company, is cost effective at a large scale of production.

Division of Labour : Secondly, when the scale of operations is increased and the amount of labour and other factors becomes larger, *introduction of a greater degree of division of labour or specialization becomes possible* and as a result the long-run cost per unit declines. Thus, whereas in the short run, decreases in cost (the downward sloping segment of the short-run average cost curve) occur due to the fact that the ratio of the variable input comes nearer to the optimum proportion, decreases in the long-run average cost (downward segment of the long-run average cost curve) take place due to the use of a greater degree of division of labour in the production process. At a large scale of production, instead of being generalists workers can specialize in performing a particular task in the production process. Generally, a worker who has to perform one task in the production process of a commodity can do it more efficiently than the one who has to perform several tasks in it. Besides, under division of labour, time of the workers is also saved as they do not have to move from one machine to another.

Indivisibility and Economies of Scale. Some economists as Nicholas Kaldor and Joan Robinson explain economies of scale as arising from the *imperfect divisibility of factors*. In other words, they think that the economies of scale occur and therefore the long-run average cost falls because of the 'indivisibility' of factors. They argue that most of the factors are 'lumpy'. That is, they are available in *large indivisible units*, which can therefore yield lower cost of production when they are used to produce a large output. If a small output is produced with these costly indivisible units of the factors, the average cost of production will naturally be high. If the factors of production were perfectly divisible, they say, then suitable adjustment in the factors could be made so that the optimum proportions between the factors were maintained even for producing small outputs and hence the average cost of production would not have been higher. Thus, according to them, if the factors were perfectly divisible the small-scale production would be as good and efficient as the large-scale production and the economies of scale would be non-existent. Thus, Kaldor writes: "It appears methodologically convenient to treat all cases of large-scale economies under the heading 'indivisibility.'"[1] Likewise, Joan Robinson remarks,[2] "if all the factors were finely divisible, like sand, it would be possible to produce the smallest output of any commodity with all the advantages of large-scale industry."

We have outlined above the two different opinions regarding the emergence of economies of scale and hence the downward sloping segment of the long-run average cost curve. Both the above views are currently held by economists, some economists aligning themselves with the first line of reasoning which is associated with the name of Chamberlin and some other economists believe in the second view which is advanced by Joan Robinson, Nicholas Kaldor, J. Stigler and some others.

Financial Economies. In addition to the above technological factors accounting for economies of scale there are financial reasons for reduction in unit cost of production as the size of the firm increases. Due to bulk purchases large firms generally get large quantity discounts in buying raw materials and intermediate products than the small-sized firms. Similarly, large firms can borrow funds from the commercial banks at relatively lower interest rate than smaller firms. Further, large firms can sell bonds and stocks in the capital market at more favourable terms. This reduces the cost of raising funds required for business purposes. Finally, large firms are able to take advantage of economies that result from spreading out of advertisiment and other promotional costs.

Economies of Scope. Economies of scope should be distinguished from economies of scale. Economies of scope refer to the reduction in costs that occur when a firm produces two or more commodities together rather than a single one. Many examples of economies of scope can be given. For example, a passanger airline can profitably extend its operations by using the same air plane for providing cargo services which lowers its cost of operation. In such an aeroplane seats have to be removed and packets and bags containing goods can be placed to carry to their places of destination.

Another example of benefit from economies of scope which is often cited is when a firm extends its product line by utilizing its waste product to produce a useful commodity for which there is demand in the market. Before this, the firm may be disposing of its waste product at a cost. Besides, a firm may have excess capacity that can be utilised to produce other products with little or no increase in capital cost. This results in lowering cost per unit of output of a firm.

In the real world, the firms greatly benefit from their comparative advantage in the production of related products. For example, Hindustan Lever does not produce only bathing soap 'Lux' but a whole range of detergents and cleansing products. This is quite cost effective and lowers the overall unit cost of products.

Diseconomies of Scale

So much for the downward-sloping segment of the long-run average cost curve. As noted above, beyond a certain point the long-run average cost curve rises which means that the long-run average cost increases as output exceeds beyond a certain point. In other words, beyond a certain point a firm experiences *net diseconomies of scale*. There is also divergence of views about the proper explanation for this upward-sloping segment of the long-run average

1. Nicholas Kaldor, The Equilibrium of the Firm, *Economic Journal*, Vol. 44, reprinted in *Readings in Price Theory* (A.E.A.).
2. Joan Robinson, *The Economics of Imperfect Competition*, p.334.

cost curve. The first view as held by Chamberlin and his followers is that when the firm has reached a size large enough to allow the utilization of almost all the possibilities of division of labour and the employment of more efficient machinery, further increase in the size of the plant will entail higher long-run unit cost because of the difficulties of management. When the scale of operations exceeds a certain limit, the management may not be as efficient as when the scale of operations is relatively small.

With too large a scale of operations, it becomes difficult for the top management to exercise control and to bring about proper coordination. When the scale of operations is enlarged, it ordinarily becomes necessary to employ more assistants and supervisors and to carry out more delegation of powers. Thus, increase in the firm's plant beyond a certain size involves more bureaucracy, more red tape, and lengthens the chain of communication and command between the top management and the men on the production line. Thus, increase in the plant beyond a certain sufficiently large size makes the managerial structure more cumbersome and reduces the overall efficiency of management. After a certain sufficiently large size these inefficiencies of management more than offset the economies of scale and thereby bring about the rise in long-run average cost and make the *LAC* curve upward-sloping. It should be noted that this view regards the entrepreneurial or managerial functions to be divisible and variable and explains the diseconomies of scale or the rising part of the long-run average cost curve as arising from the mounting difficulties of management (i.e., of supervision and coordination) beyond a certain sufficiently large scale of operations.

The Entrepreneur as a Fixed and Indivisible Factor. The second view regards the entrepreneur to be a fixed and indivisible factor. In this view, though all other factors can be increased, the entrepreneur cannot be. The entrepreneur and his functions of decision-making and ultimate control are indivisible and cannot be increased. Therefore, when a point is reached where the abilities of the fixed and indivisible entrepreneur are best utilized, further increases in the scale of operations *by increasing other inputs* cause increases in the cost per unit of output. In other words, there is a certain optimum proportion between an entrepreneur and other inputs and when that optimum proportion is reached, further increases in the other inputs to the fixed entrepreneur means the proportion between the inputs is moved away from the optimum and, therefore, results in the rise in the long-run average cost. Thus, in this view, increases in the long-run average cost is explained by the law of variable proportions. Economists who hold this view think that the decreasing returns to scale or rising long-run average cost is actually a special case of variable proportions, with entrepreneur as the fixed factor.

LONG-RUN MARGINAL COST CURVE

In a previous section we explained what is the marginal cost and how the short-run marginal cost curve is obtained and what relation it bears to the short-run average cost curve. Since marginal cost curve is important both from the viewpoint of the short-run and the long-run, it will be useful to know how the long-run marginal cost curve can be directly derived from the long-run total cost curve, since the long-run marginal cost at a level of output is given by the slope of the total cost curve at the point corresponding to that level of output. Besides, the long-run marginal cost curve can also be derived from the long-run average cost curve, because the long-run marginal cost curve is related to the long-run average cost curve in the same way as the short-run marginal cost curve is related to short-run average cost curve. In Fig.21.14, it is depicted how the long-run marginal cost curve *LMC* is derived from a long-run average cost curve *LAC* enveloping a family of short-run average and marginal cost curves.

If the output OA is to be produced in the long-run, then it must be produced on the long-run average cost curve LAC at point H which is a tangency point with the short-run average cost curve SAC_1. Thus, when output OA is to be produced in the long run, it will be produced with the plant corresponding to the short-run average cost curve SAC_1 and the short-run marginal cost curve SMC_1.

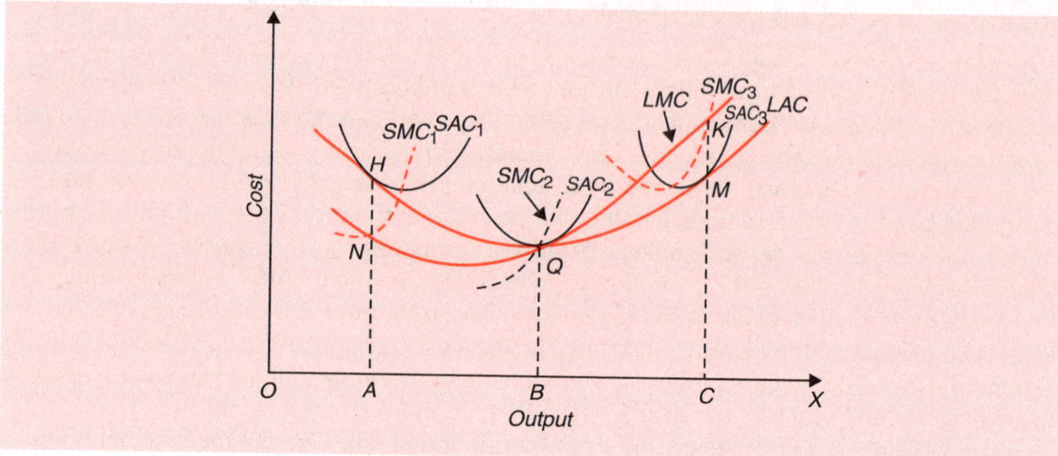

Fig.21.14. *Derivation of Long-Run Marginal Cost Curve*

Corresponding to the tangency point H between the short-run average cost curve SAC_1 and the long-run average cost curve LAC, there is point N on the short run marginal cost curve SMC_1. This means that the production of output OA in the long run involves the marginal cost AN. Therefore, point N must lie on the long-run marginal cost curve corresponding to output OA. If output OB is to be produced in the long run, it will be produced at point Q which is the tangency point between LAC and SAC_2. Q is also the point on the shortrun marginal cost curve SMC_2 corresponding to output OB. (Q is the common point between SAC_2 at which the SMC_2 cuts it from below). Thus Q must also lie on the long-run marginal cost curve corresponding to output OB. Similarly, if output OC is to be produced in the long run, it will be produced at point M which is the tangency point between LAC and SAC_3. Corresponding to point M, the relevant point on the SMC_3 is K which means that the long-run marginal cost of producing OC is CK. Thus point K must lie on the long-run marginal cost curve corresponding to output OC. By connecting points N, Q and K we obtain the long-run marginal cost curve LMC.

It will be seen from Fig. 21.14. that long-run marginal cost curve LMC, like the long-run average cost curve LAC, is U-shaped. It will be further seen that the long-run marginal cost curve LMC is flatter than the short-run marginal cost curves. This is what one would expect because the long-run average cost curve LAC is flatter than the short-run average cost curves. It should also be remembered that the relationship between the long-run marginal cost curve LMC and the long-run average cost curve LAC is the same as that between the short-run marginal cost curve and the short-run average cost curve. Thus, when the long-run marginal cost (LMC) curve lies below the long-run average cost (LAC) curve, the latter is falling and when longrun marginal cost (LMC) lies above the long-run average cost curve, the latter will be rising. When the long run marginal cost is equal to the long-run average cost, the latter will be neither rising nor falling. In other words, the long-run marginal cost curve will cut long-run average cost curve at the latter' s minimum point.

RELATIONSHIP BETWEEN STC AND LTC AND BETWEEN LAC AND SAC CURVES

It is useful to note that *LAC* and *SAC* curves are related in an important way with the *SMC* and *LMC* curves. This relationship shows, as will be seen from Fig. 21.14, that *at the level of output at which a particular SAC curve is tangent to the LAC curve, the corresponding SMC curve intersects the LMC curve*. In other words, the level of output where the short-run average cost is equal to the long-run average cost, the corresponding short-run marginal cost is equal to the long-run marginal cost at that level of output. This proposition can be proved with the graphical technique using a short-run total cost curve and the long-run total cost curve and this has been done in Fig. 21.15 where a short-run total cost curve *STC* and the long-run total cost curve *LTC* are drawn. It will be seen from top panel of Fig.21.15 that long-run total cost curve *LTC* lies below the short-run total cost curve *STC* (dotted) at all levels of output except at output *OQ* at which the two curves are tangent. This means that at output level *OQ*, the slope of the ray *OP* measures both the short-run average cost (*SAC*) and long-run average cost, (*LAC*). Therefore, in the panel at the bottom of Fig. 21.15 at output *OQ* and corresponding to tangency point *P* in the top panel, *SAC* and *LAC* curves are tangent to each other at point *E* indicating that *SAC* equals *LAC* at the output level *OQ* at which *STC* is tangent to *LTC*.

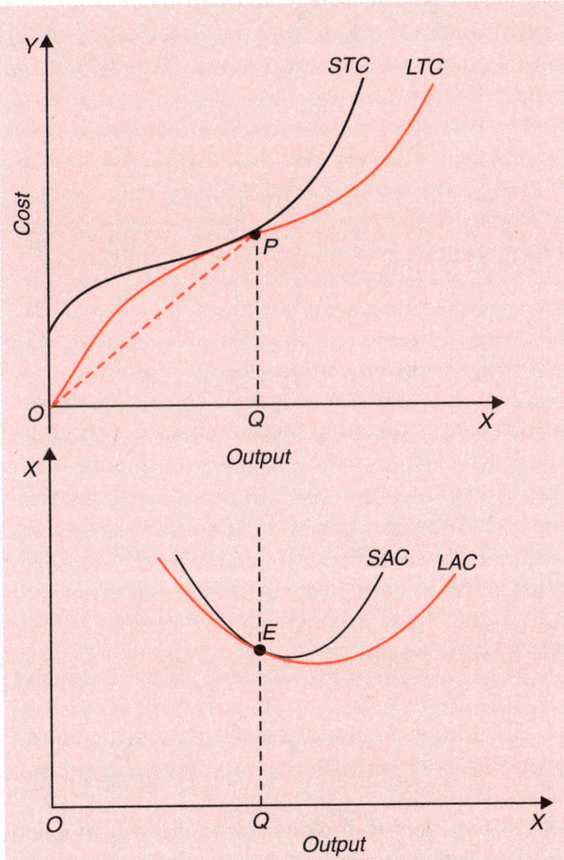

Fig. 21.15. *Relationship between STC and LTC and between SAC and LAC*

Further, the above relation implies that *LAC* is less than *SAC* at all levels of output until *OQ* is reached, as can be ascertained by drawing rays from the origin to *LTC* and *STC* at various levels of output before point *Q*. Beyond *OQ* output, *SAC* becomes greater than *LAC* as will be known by drawing rays from the origin to the corresponding points on the *STC* and *LTC* curves at a given level of output beyond *OQ*. As will be seen from the panel at the bottom of Fig. 21.15, the long-run average cost *LAC* is therefore equal to the short-run average cost *SAC* at output *OQ* at which *LTC* is tangent to the *STC*. How do we explain this relationship between short-run and long-run cost curves? In the long-run adjustment is made in all factors including fixed factors such as capital equipment to minimise cost of production. In the short-run some factors remain fixed and therefore cannot be suitably adjusted to minimise cost of production. As a result, short-run cost, both total and average, exceed long-run cost except at one point where the given quantity of the fixed factor is in optimum proportion with the variable factor. A glance at the Figure 21.15 will make this point quite clear.

But the long-run marginal cost *LMC* must also be equal to short-run marginal cost *SMC* at output *OQ i.e.* the tangency point *P* of *STC* and *LTC* in Fig.21.15. This is because marginal cost is given by the slope of the total cost curve at any point, and the *LTC* curve and *STC* curve have the same slope at the tangency point *P*. It is thus clear that at output level *OQ*, where the *SAC* is equal to the *LAC*, *SMC* is also equal to the *LMC*. **Though *SMC* and *LMC* will be equal to each other at output level *OQ*, they will be less than *SAC* and *LAC* because the slope of the tangent at point *P* is less than the slope of the ray *OP* from the origin.** Thus the long-run marginal cost (*LMC*) curve will cut the short-run marginal cost (*SMC*) at output level *OQ*, that is, exactly vertically below the point of equality of *SAC* and *LAC*.

LONG-RUN TOTAL COSTS AND EXPANSION PATH

Costs are related to the expansion path of the isoquant analysis of the production theory. We can derive the total cost curve from the expansion path. It may be recalled that given the nature of production function and factor prices, expansion path depicts the combinations of factors which an entrepreneur uses to produce various levels of output at the minimum possible cost. Once the long-run total cost curve is derived from the expansion path we can then derive the long-run average cost and marginal cost curve from the long-run total cost curve in a similar way that was adopted in case of derivation of short-run average and marginal cost curves. Let us take two factor production function which is assumed in the isoquant analysis. These two factors which we take are labour and capital. To minimise cost for a given level of output an entrepreneur will use such capital-labour ratio which equates marginal rate of technical substitution with factor price ratio. This is realised at the tangency point between an isoquant (representing a given level of output) with an iso-cost curve. Now, we are interested in knowing how the total cost changes when output is expanded by the entrepreneur along the expansion path as this would enable us to derive the long-run total cost curve. This is illustrated in Figure 21.16. We select three isoquants Q_1, Q_2, Q_3, representing three levels of output.

To find out the minimum-cost combination of capital and labour to produce a level of output Q_1, we draw an iso-cost line (which has a slope equal of price of labour and capital, $\frac{w}{r}$) which is tangent to the given isoquant Q_1. It will be seen from Figure 21.16 that resulting iso-cost line is C_1L_1. This will give us the total cost incurred on producing rate of output Q, equal to K.r or L.w which we call as TC_1. Now, we take the higher isoquant representing a higher rate of output Q_2. With factor prices remaining the same we draw an iso-cost line which is tangent to the isoquant Q_2. We find that the iso-cost line C_2L_2 giving us total cost equal to TC_2 is tangent to the isoquant Q_2. Next we draw an iso-cost line which is tangent to the isoquant representing higher level of output Q_3 and find that this iso-cost line C_3L_3 is tangent to it which gives us total cost equal to TC_3. Connecting the tangency points A, B, and C we get the expansion path.

It is thus evident from the expansion path that when output level is Q_1, the minimum total cost to produce it is TC_1. When rate of output is Q_2, the minimum total cost to produce it is TC_2 and when output expands to Q_3, the minimum total cost for its production rises to TC_3. Now, plotting TC_1, TC_2 and TC_3 against output levels Q_1 Q_2 and Q_3 respectively in panel (*b*) of Figure 21.16 we get the long-run total cost curve (*LTC*). Note that on an expansion path in the input space of panel (*a*) of Figure 21.16, there are numerous points of tangency

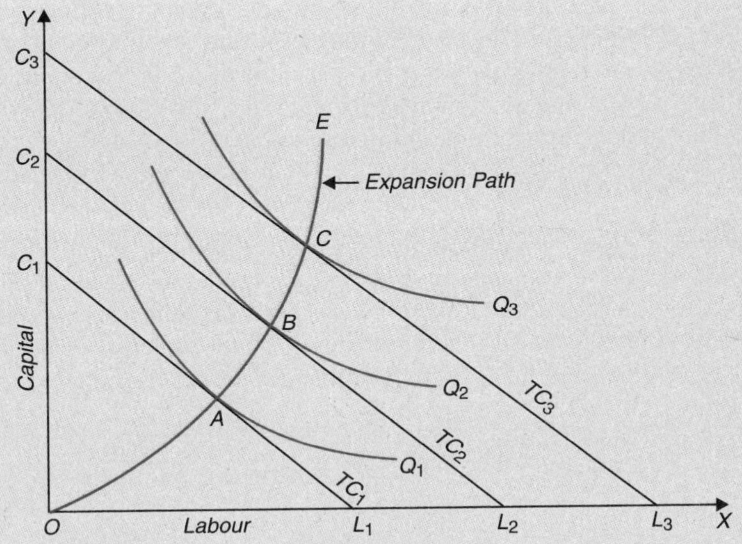

(a) Expansion Path

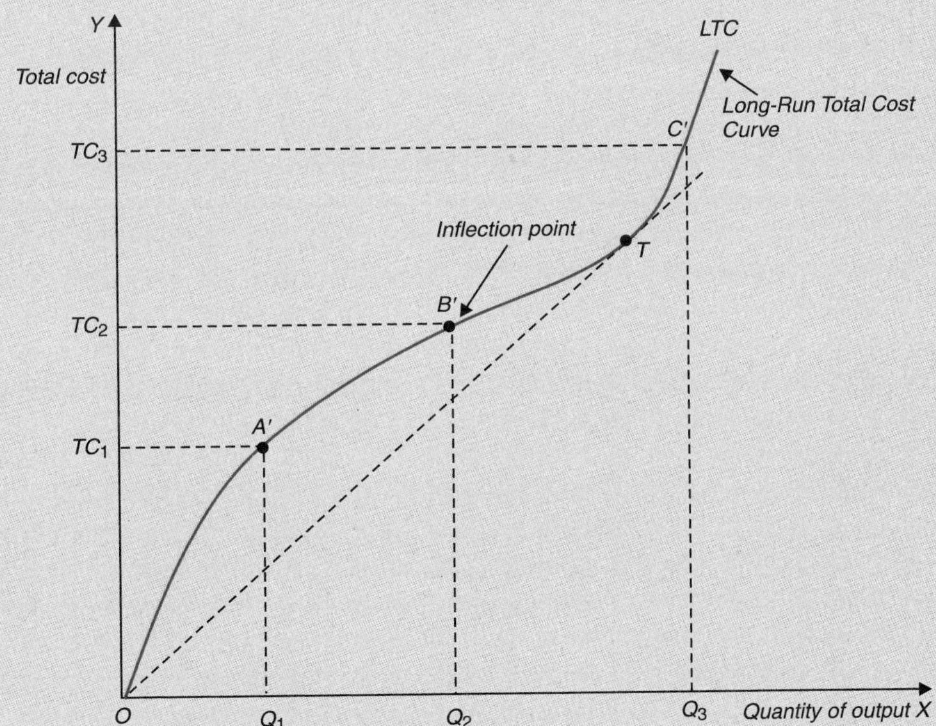

(b) Long-run Total Cost Curve

Fig. 21.16. *Derivation of Long-Run Total Cost Curve from the Expansion Path*

of isoquants and iso-cost lines (only three are actually shown) which give us the combinations of long-run total cost and different rates of output. This gives us a smooth long-run total cost curve *LTC* in panel (*b*) of Figure 21.16.

It is now easy to derive the long-run average cost curve and marginal cost curve from the total cost curve. The long-run average cost curve can be derived from the long-run total cost curve by *measuring the slopes of the rays* drawn from the origins to various points on the *LTC* curves corresponding to different levels of output, as we have explained above in case of the derivation of short-run average cost curve from the short-run total cost curve (*STC*). The long-run marginal cost (*LMC*) curve is derived by *measuring slopes of LTC curve* by drawing tangents at various points corresponding to different levels of output. We have derived the *LAC* and *LMC* curves from the *LTC* in Figure 21.17. This also shows not only the relationship between the *LAC* and *LMC* curves with the *LTC* curve but also between the *LAC* and *LMC* curves. The relationship between *LAC* and *LMC* is the same as between *SAC* and *SMC* curves explained above.

It is important to note that at different points of the expansion path, that is, at different levels of output, the firm may use a different capital-labour ratio as we are here concerned with the long run in which quantities of both capital and labour can be changed. Thus entirely

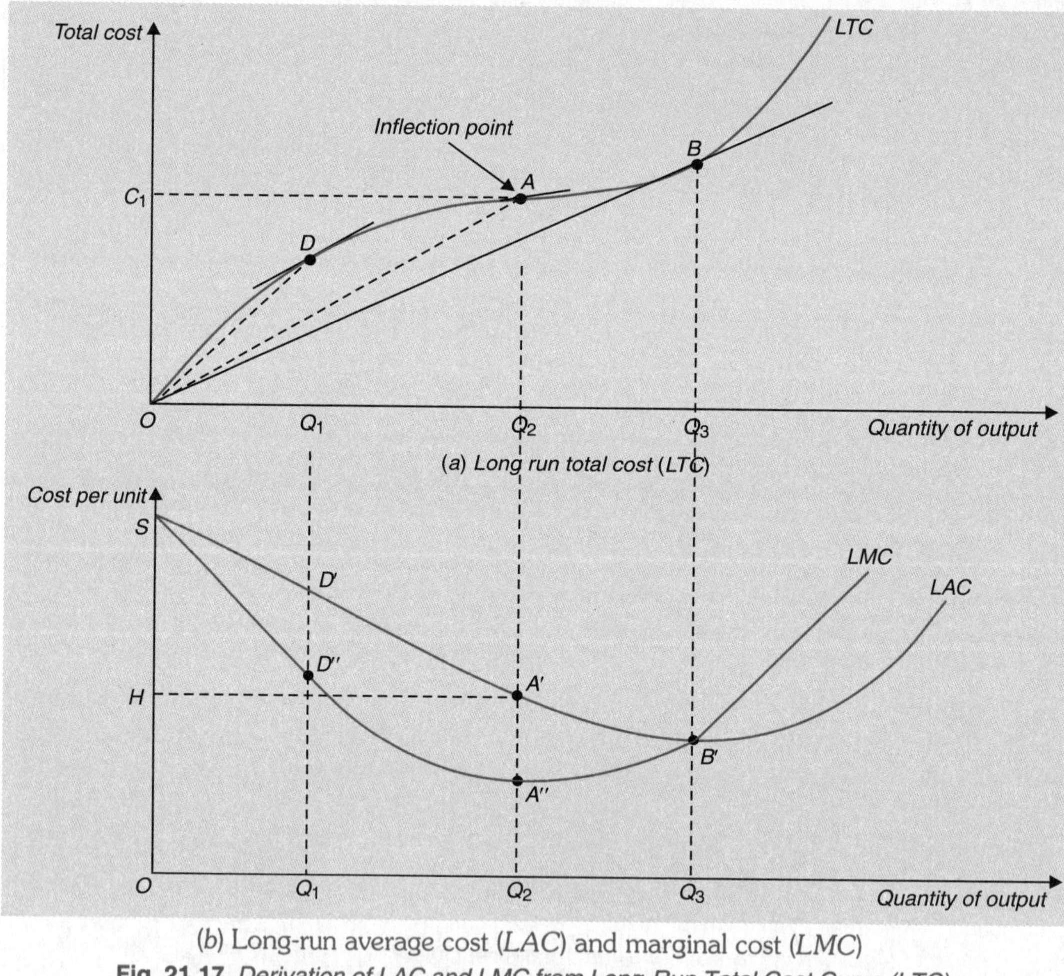

(*b*) Long-run average cost (*LAC*) and marginal cost (*LMC*)

Fig. 21.17. *Derivation of LAC and LMC from Long-Run Total Cost Curve (LTC)*

different factor-ratio, that is, the production process may be used to minimise cost for producing output levels Q_1, Q_2, and Q_3 respectively. It is only when production function is linearly homogeneous and expansion path is a straight line from the origin, that the same factor ratio or the production process will be used to produce different levels of output. It needs to be emphasised that the long run represents a planning horizon where all productive factors (in our case both labour and capital) are variable, except factor prices and technology (*i.e.* the state of arts) and the firm has to decide which combination of factors (capital and labour) it has to choose. Whereas the change in factor prices will shift the iso-cost line, a change in technology will cause a change in the production function which will require a different isoquant map. This will change the expansion path and the long-run total cost curve derived from it.

EXTERNAL ECONOMIES AND DISECONOMIES AND COST CURVES

We have explained above that the long-run average cost curve falls downward in the beginning because of economies of scale, namely, the use of greater degree of division of labour and the specialised machinery at higher levels of output. The uses of greater degree of division of labour and the specialized machinery at higher levels of output are the *internal economies*. They are internal in the sense that they accrue to the firm when *its own output* or *scale* increases. Besides internal economies, Marshall introduced the concept of *external economies* which play an important role in Marshall's partial equilibrium theory of value, especially in his analysis of equilibrium problem under conditions of increasing returns or decreasing cost. Costs of a firm depend not only on its own output level but also on the output level of the industry as a whole. External economies and diseconomies are those economies and diseconomies which accrue to the firms as a result of the expansion in the output of the whole industry and they are not dependent on the output level of individual firms. They are external in the sense that they accrue to the firms not out of its internal situation but from outside it *i.e.*, output of the industry. Marshall defined external economies as "those dependent on the general development of the industry.[3]". In a more precise manner Jacob Viner has defined **external economies as "*those which accrue to particular concerns as the result of expansion of output by the industry as a whole and which are independent of their own individual output.*"[4]**

External economies accrue to the individual firms, if the increase in the output of industry *lowers* the cost curves of each firm in the industry. On the other hand, external diseconomies accrue to the firms, when the expansion of the output of the industry *raises* the cost curves of each firm. Thus, when the industry expands and as a result certain external economies accrue to the firms, the cost curves of a firm will shift down as is shown in Figure 21.18. It should be noted that external economies will cause all types of firm's cost curves—long-run average and marginal cost curves, short-run average and marginal cost curves—to shift down. In Figure 21.18, initially the long-run average cost curve is *LAC* (thick curve) and as a result of the expansion of whole industry and the creation of external economies it shifts down to new position *LAC′* (dotted).

On the other hand, when the external diseconomies accrue to the firms as a result of expansion of the industry, cost curves of the individual firms will shift upward as is depicted in the Fig.21.19. In the beginning, the long-run average cost curve is *LAC* and with the expansion of the industry output and consequent emergence of external diseconomies cause the long-run average cost curve (along with its short-run average and marginal cost curves) to shift upward to new position *LAC′* (dotted).

We noted above in a previous section that internal economies and diseconomies of scale affect the shape that the long-run average cost curve takes; internal economies of scale cause the long-run average cost to fall as output is increased in the initial stage and internal

3. A Marshall, *Principles of Economics*, 8th ed., p. 266.
4. Jacob Viner, Cost Curves and Supply Curves, *Readings in Prices Theory*, AEA, p. 217.

diseconomies of scale cause the long-run average cost curve to rise. On the other hand, external economies and external diseconomies cause the long-run average cost curve to shift *down or up* as the case may be. Moreover, when we are considering the effect of external economies and external diseconomies on the cost curves, it is not only the long-run cost curves, but all short-run and long-run cost curves, whether total, average or marginal, shift together up or down as the case may be. In this connection, it is also worth noting that shifts in cost curves of a firm are not always, nor necessarily brought about by the expansion or contraction of an industry's output. For instance, a *general increase* in the prices of machinery and equipment, an all-round increase in wages and interest rates in the economy will also shift up the cost curves of a firm. Therefore, in microeconomics when we speak of increasing-

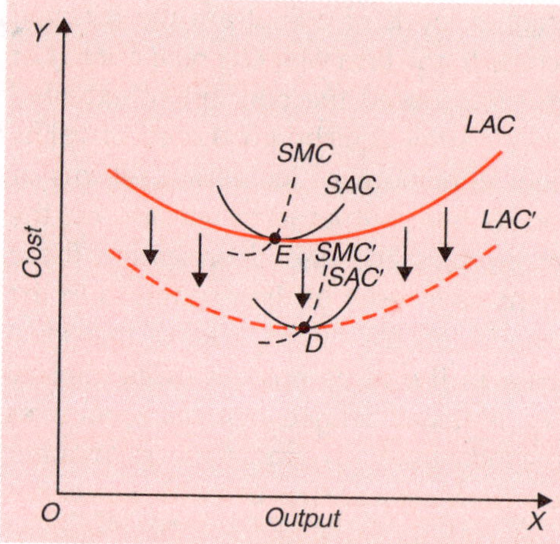

Fig. 21.18. *Downward Shift of the Cost Curves due to External Economies*

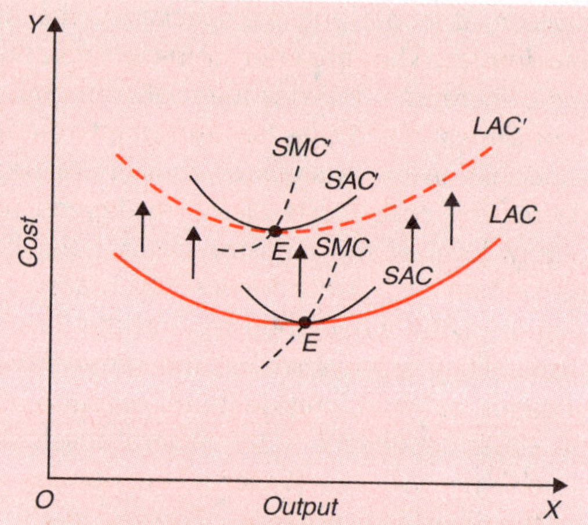

Fig. 21.19. *Upward Shift of the Cost Curves due to External Diseconomies*

cost industries, and decreasing-cost industries, we consider *only the effect of expansion of industry's own output* on costs of materials, labour, capital equipment etc. incurred by the firms in that industry's and rule out any general increase in these costs in the whole economy.

Now, the question arises when an industry grows or expands its output, what types of external economies it generates which reduce the costs of all firms in it. The chief examples of external economies provided by Marshall are :

(*i*) "improved methods or machinery which are accessible to the whole industry"[5] when it expands;

(*ii*) economies which result from "development of mechanical appliances, of division of labour and of the means of transport and improved organization of all kinds"[6] with the growth of an industry;

(*iii*) economies which result from the growth of correlated branches of industry which mutually assist one another and "being concentrated in the same localities"[7] encourage the development of 'hereditary skill"[8], 'the growth of subsidiary trades supplying it with implements and machinery and the "economic use of expensive machinery."[9]

5. A Marshall, *Principles of Economics*, 8th edition, p.615.
6. *Ibid*, p. 808.
7. *Ibid*, p. 317.
8. *Ibid*, p. 217.
9. *Ibid*, p. 267.

(*iv*) economies which are "connected with the growth of knowledge and the progress of arts, especially in matters of trade knowledge: newspapers, trade and technical publications[10].

Like Marshall, Joan Robinson who analyzed the *phenomenon of increasing returns* (i.e., decreasing costs) in the context of partial equilibrium analysis, provided the following main examples of external economies:

(*i*) the cases "where the machinery can be bought more cheaply when the industry presents a large market to the machine-making industry"[11] and

(*ii*) the cases "where a large labour force is accustomed to work at a certain trade" and develops "traditional skill"[12]

From the above examples mentioned by Marshall and Joan Robinson we explain below some of important external economies which accrue to the firms and reduce their costs of production.

1. Cheaper Materials and Capital Equipment. First, the expansion of an industry may lead to new and cheaper raw materials, machinery and other types of capital equipment. The expansion of an industry means that demand for the various kinds of materials and capital equipment required by it increases. This makes it possible to produce them on a large-scale by other industries. This large-scale production of materials and capital equipment lowers their costs of production and hence their prices. Thus the firms in the industry which use these materials and capital equipment will be able to get them at lower prices. This will favourably affect their costs of production. This, of course, will happen in cases where there are increasing returns (i.e. decreasing costs) in the industries supplying the materials and capital equipment.

2. Technological External Economies. Secondly, with the growth of an industry some external economies of technological type may accrue to the firms of an industry. In our discussion of returns to scale we mentioned that as an individual firm expands its scale, it may become possible for it to use more specialized and productive machinery and to introduce greater degree of division of labour. These are internal technological economies which change the technical coefficients of production and improve the firm's productivity. Similarly, when the whole industry expands, it may lead to the discovery of new technical knowledge and in accordance with that the use of improved and better machinery than before becomes possible. This will also change the technical coefficients of production and will enhance the productivity of the firms in the industry and will reduce their costs of production.

3. Development of Skilled Labour. Another example of external economies that has been suggested is the development of hereditary or traditional skills among labour. When an industry expands in an area, the labour in that area is well accustomed to do the various productive processes and learns a good deal from the experience. As a result, with the growth of an industry a region a pool of trained labour equipped with the traditional skills is developed which has a favorable effect on the level of productivity and costs of the firms in the industry.

4. The Growth of Subsidiary and Correlated Industries. Another external economy accruing to the firms from the growth of an industry is the growth of subsidiary and correlated industries. These subsidiary and correlated industries may specialize in the production of raw materials, tools and machinery and therefore can provide them at lower prices to the main industry. Likewise, some specialized firms may come into existence, which process the 'waste product' of the industry into some useful product as a result of expansion of the industry

10. *Ibid*, p. 284.
11. Joan Robinson, *The Economics of Imperfect Competition*, p.340.
12. *Ibid*, p. 341.

when the waste product is large enough to make it worthwhile to set up separate plants for transforming the waste products into useful ones. When this happens, then the firms of the industry can sell their waste products at a good price. This will tend to reduce their cost of production.

5. Improved Transportation and Marketing Facilities. These external economies are greatly relevant when an infant industry grows up in a new territory. In the beginning, transportation and marketing facilities both for the purchase of materials and for the sale of its product may not be well-developed. However, the expansion of the industry by the entry of new firms in it may make possible the development of transportation and marketing facilities which will greatly reduce the costs of the firms.

6. Development of Industry Information Services. As an industry expands, the firms may form a trade association that distributes information regarding technical knowledge and market possibilities about the industry through publication of trade and technical journals. With the expansion of the industry the firms may jointly set up a central research institute which will be engaged in discovering new improved techniques for the firms in the industry. Thus, besides providing market information, the growth of the industry may help in discovering and spreading improved technical knowledge.

External Diseconomies

We have explained above the external economies which accrue to the firms as a result of the growth of the industry. But, as said above, the expansion of an industry is also likely to generate external diseconomies which raise the cost curves of the firms. The main example of external diseconomies is the *rise in some factor prices* when the industry expands and its demand for various factors needed by it increases. The expansion of an industry will definitely raise the prices of those raw materials and capital goods which are in short supply. Likewise, the expansion of the industry is likely to raise the wages of skilled labour, at least in the short run, since it always takes time for the labour to get training and acquire specialized skills needed in a particular industry.

Since the productive factors such as various types of raw materials, cement, steel, various kinds of machinery and tools and skilled labour are scarce, the increase in demand for them resulting from the expansion in the industry is likely to push up their prices. In the context of scarcity of resources, an industry in an attempt to snatch away the resources from other industries, will bid up their prices. Thus, in the real world of scarcity, an expanding industry will create more external diseconomies than external economies. Therefore, most industries in the real world encounter rising costs when they expand.

MODERN DEVELOPMENTS IN COST THEORY

Until recently it was widely believed that both the short-run and long-run average costs are of roughly U-shape. But in recent years, U-shape of the cost curve has been questioned by some economists, mainly on the empirical grounds. This challenge to U-shape average cost curve relates to both the short-run and long-run average cost curve. We first explain the shape of the short-run average variable cost according to the modern developments in economic theory.

Saucer-Shaped Short-Run Average Variable Cost Curve (SAVC)

The recent empirical studies have found that the short-run average variable cost curve has a saucer-type shape rather than U-shape of the traditional economic theory. The saucer-type shape of the average variable cost curve implies that there is a *flat stretch over a certain range of output* in it. It has been pointed out that this flat stretch in the short-run average cost curve is due to the reserve capacity that is consciously built in the plant size while designing it. This reserve capacity is built in the plant size with a view to impart flexibility in production so that the firm can expand output over a certain range without a rise in unit cost to meet any greater demand for its output in the future. On the contrary, the traditional theory assumes that there is single optimum level of output of a plant or firm after which unit cost starts rising. This short-run average variable cost curve with a saucer shape has been shown in Fig.21.20 where it will be seen that in the beginning the short-run average variable cost declines and the remains constant over the range of output $Q_1 Q_2$ and thereafter it rises. Corresponding to the output range $Q_1 Q_2$, the short-run average variable cost curve has a flat stretch.

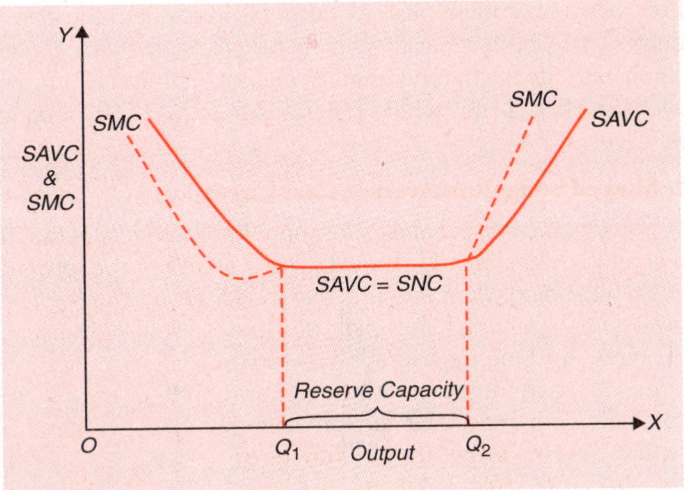

Fig. 21.20. *Saucer-Shaped Average Variable Cost Curve*

The decline in average variable cost as output is expanded in the beginning has been explained to be the result of (1) better utilization of the fixed factor with increase in the variable factor, (2) the improvement in skills and productivity of labour, and (3) reduction in waste of raw materials due to better skills and productivity of both management and labour ensuring better efficiency in the operation of the firm. On the other hand, the rising part of the *SAVC* curve after a flat stretch has been attributed to the fall in labour productivity as a result of long hours of work, overtime payment to labour, wastage in raw materials and more frequent breakdown of machinery as plant is operated for a longer time or with more shifts per day.

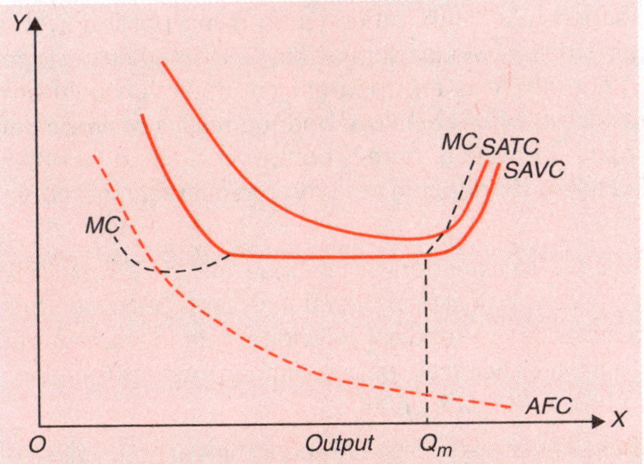

Fig. 21.21. *Short-Run Average Total Cost Curve when Average Variable Cost Curve has a Saucer-Shape*

In the initial stages, when *SAVC* curve falls, marginal cost curve (*MC*) lies below it, in its flat stretch portion the marginal cost curve coincides with it and ultimately when *SAVC* curve rises after the full utilization of the reserve capacity of the plant, the marginal cost curve lies above it.

Average Total Cost Curve

Now, it is interesting to note that what will be the shape of the short-run average total cost curve when average variable cost curve has a saucer-type shape. Average total cost is obtained by adding the average fixed cost to the average variable cost. Since average fixed cost falls continuously as output is expanded, the *SATC* curve declines up to the level of output at which reserve capacity is fully exhausted. Beyond that level of output, *SATC* will be rising with the further increases in output. This *SATC* curve when *SAVC* is of saucer-shape is shown in Fig. 21.21 which illustrates how *SATC* is obtained by adding vertically *SAVC* and *AFC*.

L-Shaped Long-Run Average Cost Curve

A significant recent development in cost theory is that the long-run average cost theory is L-shaped rather than U-shaped. The L-shape of the long-run average cost curve implies that in the beginning when output is expanded through increase in plant size and associated variable factors, cost per unit falls rapidly due to economies of scale. Even after a sufficiently large-scale of output, the long-run average cost curve does not rise; it may either remain constant or it may even go on falling slightly. ***At a very large scale of production, the managerial cost per unit of output may rise, but the technical or production economies more than offset the managerial diseconomies so that the total long-run average cost does not rise or even falls continuously though at a very small rate.*** Thus the empirical evidence gathered by economists in recent years does not indicate any U-shape in the long-run average cost curve. Empirical evidence indicates that the long-run average cost rapidly falls but after a point it remains flat throughout or at its right-hand end it may even slope gently downward.

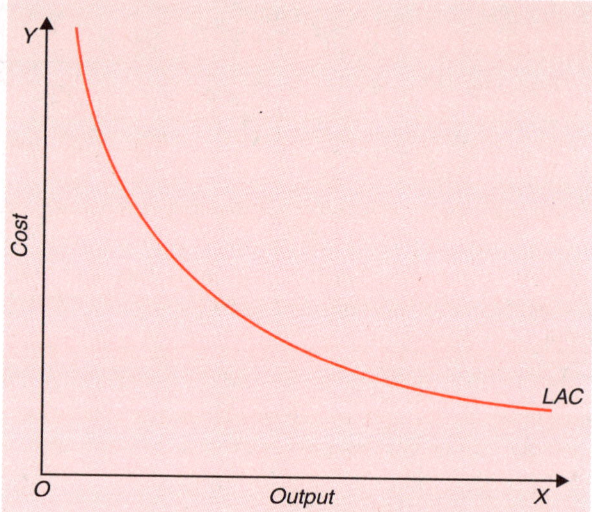

Fig. 21.22. *L-Shaped Long-Run Average Cost Curve*

L-shaped long-run average cost curve is illustrated in Fig.21.22. The difference between L-shaped *LAC* of Fig.21.22 and the U-shaped *LAC* is that there is no rising portion in the former. Indeed, as stated just above, the empirical evidence shows that *LAC* may even slope gently downward at its right-hand end. Thus, there is an apparent contradiction between traditional economic theory according to which *LAC* is U-shaped and the results of empirical investigations which find *LAC* to be L-shaped. However, there is controversy about whether the long-run average cost is really L-shaped when for deriving the long-run average cost curve usual assumptions made in traditional theory hold.

Two explanations have been given for the explanation of L-Shape of *LAC*. First, it is pointed out that a firm continues to enjoy some technical or production economies even after a *minimum optimal scale* is reached. Secondly, the modern developments in managerial science ensuring optimal managerial set-up for a larger scale of production prevents the long-run average cost to rise. We explain them below in some detail.

Production or Technical Economies. These are substantial economies of scale enjoyed by a firm when it expands its scale of output in the beginning. This causes the long-run average cost to fall steeply with the initial increases in scale of production. However, it has been asserted that even after most of the economies of scale have been achieved and the firm reaches a minimum optimal scale, given the technology of the industry, the unit cost of production may fall due to some technical eonomies which it can continue to enjoy even after the minimum optimal scale. First, the *new techniques* of production are adopted at a large scale of production due to which cost per unit falls. But even with the existing known techniques some economies can always be obtained due to (1) decentralization and improved skills and productivity of labour, (2) lower repair costs after a certain scale is achieved, and (3) manufacturing by a firm itself some of the materials and equipment at lower cost which it needs for its production process instead of buying them from other firms.

Managerial Costs. In the traditional cost theory, the rising part of the *LAC* is explained by the difficulties in management, supervision, coordination and control which pushes up the unit cost of production after a certain scale of production is attained. In this regard, it has been pointed out that modern management science has developed for each plant size appropriate organizational and managerial set-up for efficient working of the firm. For different scales of plant and sizes of firms different appropriate management techniques have been evolved and each management technique is applicable to a range of output. Only at a very large scale, managerial costs may rise. However, it has been claimed that any rise in managerial costs after a very large-scale of output may be offset by production economies.

L-Shape Long-Run Cost Curve and Empirical Evidence : A Critical Evaluation

Now, the question is how L-Shaped long-run average cost curve can be explained and apparent contradiction between traditional theory and empirical evidence be removed. The following two explanations have been provided for the existence of L-shaped long-run average cost curve.

1. Technical Progress. One reason why empirical studies don't find U-shaped long-run average cost curve is that whereas economic theory assumes that technology remains unchanged or there is no technological progress, but, in the real world, technological progress does take place over time. As a result of technological progress in the real world, long-run average cost curve will shift downward over time. The empirical investigations which are based on time series data would not find the rising average cost in view of the existence of technological progress. Thus while in the case of unchanged technology, as is assumed in traditional economic theory, long-run average cost curve (*LAC*) is U-shaped, empirical studies conducted on the basis of data belonging to different points of time between which technological progress had taken place would find the average cost falling. In view of the technological progress, they could not find the average cost rising. This is illustrated in Fig. 21.23. Suppose initially the firm is producing output OQ_1 at aveage cost OK_1 by operating on LAC_1. If the demand for the firm's product increases to OQ_2, then in the context of unchanged technology the firm will expand production along LAC_1 and will produce OQ_2 output at average cost *OH*. Now, if the technological progress has taken place and in

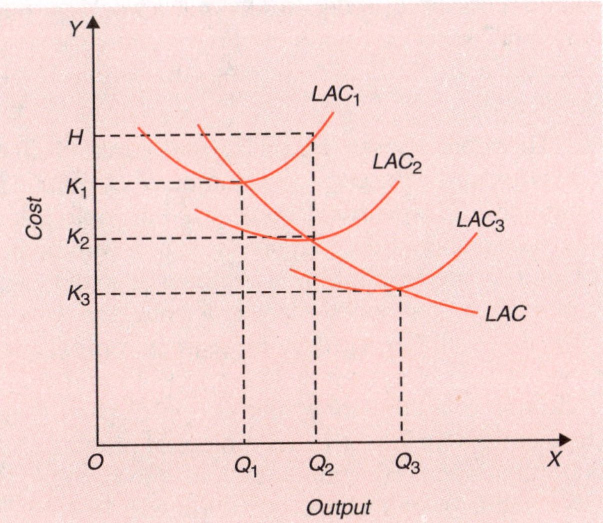

Fig. 21.23. *L-Shaped Long-Run Average Cost Curve*

accordance with new technology the firm has a new plant whose long-run average cost is LAC_2, the firm will produce on the new curve LAC_2 output OQ_2 at OK_2 cost per unit which is less than both OK_1 and OH.

Likewise, when the firm at some later date has expanded output to OQ_2 in response to the increase in demand for its product, the technology might have advanced in the mean time so that the firm produces OQ_3 at OK_3 cost per unit which is less than OK_2. By joining the minimum points of long-run average cost curves we get a curve LAC which gently slopes downward due to technological progress that has taken place over time, whereas with unchanged technology long-run average cost curves LAC_1, LAC_2 and LAC_3 each with a different but unchanged technology is U-shaped.

Empirical studies made by economists at different points of time would estimate OK_1, OK_2 and OK_3 costs at output OQ_1, OQ_2 and OQ_3 respectively and would therefore suggest that long-run average cost curve was like the L-shaped curve LAC. We therefore conclude that while with a given and unchanged technology long-run average cost curves are U-shaped, empirical studies would find L-shaped long-run average cost curve due to technological progress that takes place over time. "The fact that technology changes does not in itself contradict our contention that, if only because it is harder to manage a larger firm than a smaller one, long-run average cost curves will be U-shaped in a given state of technology. What the empirical evidence does suggest is that technological progress may often be rapid enough to reduce unit costs even in a situation where, with given technology, the problem of managing a bigger firm would increase unit costs."[13]

Learning by Doing. Learning by doing is another factor which causes the long-run average cost to slope downward throughout. It is now common knowledge that a person learns while doing some productive work, the greater the amount of work he has done since the time he started doing a particular work, the greater the experience he attains and with the experience he learns to do things in a better way than before. This tends to reduce the cost per unit. A firm learns to produce a commodity more efficiently as the aggregate amount of output produced by it increases over time. A good deal of empirical evidence is available which goes to prove that firm's cost of production depends not only on the amount of output of a commodity it produces each month or year but also on the aggregate amount of that commodity produced since the time it started its production. This is because the aggregate output by a firm to date determines the degree of learning it has acquired and the efficiency gained by it.

Therefore, we can draw a learning curve which relates the average cost of production of a commodity to the *aggregate amount* of output produced over time by a firm of that commodity. This learning curve will be sloping downward indicating thereby that as the aggregate amount of output produced of a commodity by a firm increases over time, cost per unit goes on declining. This is because, as said above, with greater production, a firm learns to produce a commodity more efficiently and therefore cost per unit declines. It should be noted that with the increase in aggregate production of a commodity over time, learning gained by a firm is not only in respect of improving efficiency in physical operations in the production of a commodity but also in respect of improving the organization of the plant. Thus, besides the factor of technological progress, learning provides us another reason why long-run average cost curve is L-shaped rather than U-shaped. To quote Stonier and Hague, "Even with a given technology, a firm can 'learn' to produce at a lower unit cost the longer the period of time that has elapsed since a previous observation and the greater the aggregate

13. Stonier and Hangue, *A Textbook of Economic Theory*, 4th edition, 1972, p.140.

amount of that product that has consequently been made. It may be, therefore, that technological change is not the only reason why long-run average cost curves are L-shaped rather than U-shaped."[14]

Validity of Empirical Evidence Regarding the Behaviour of Long-Run Average Cost

We have stated above that according to empirical evidence gathered by economists long-run average cost is L-shaped rather than U-shaped. In other words, according to the empirical evidence, long-run average cost after the initial rapid fall, either remains constant or declines throughout; it does not rise. That is, long-run average cost does not turn up as is required if it is U-shaped. C.A. Smith who has examined empirical evidence in this connection has concluded that with a very large size of firm, labour costs, assembly costs and distribution costs increase very much and therefore large-sized plants with *increasing average cost are not set up in actual practice* and therefore empirical evidence cannot assess the cost situation in them. Therefore, according to Smith, empirical evidence does not refute the U-shaped nature of long-run average cost curve. To quote him, "(1) With increasing size of plant, at least from small to medium size, average cost of production declines as size increases if factor costs are held constant. (2) There is no substantial evidence that the decline in unit costs stops before the maximum size of plant available for study if factor costs are held constant and the product is the same. On the other hand, the *little evidence available does not refute the idea that the long-run average cost curves even with factor prices constant turns up at some attainable size*. We can hardly hope to find an answer to this question as to whether there is in practice a plant so large that the cost of producing specific products does not increase even if factor prices are held constant because : (*a*) Factor costs, especially labour cost, seem to vary with size of plant : (*b*) Assembly costs and distribution costs per unit decline for a time with increasing size of plant but usually start to increase within the range of size of plant available for study"[15].

From his analysis of empirical evidence, he concludes that "increases in factor prices and in assembly and distribution costs result in cost increases which make it impractical to build plants which might be large enough to have higher average cost. Therefore, *we have no opportunity to study the costs of such plants*. The hypothesis that the long-run cost function for the production of a product typically turns up at some very large size cannot be subjected to empirical verification."[16]

In view of the limited empirical evidence about the correct shape of the long-run average cost curve we shall continue to assume in our analysis throughout that the typical shape of the long-run average cost curve is U-shaped, though its U-shape is less pronounced than that of short-run average cost curve. However, there is in fact a long flat region *i.e.*, horizontal portion in this long-run average cost curve, which we shall not be showing in the diagrams.

THE LEARNING CURVE

The learning curve is an important modern concept according to which cumulative experience by a firm in the production of a product over time increases efficiency in the use of inputs such as labour and raw materials and thereby lowers cost per unit of output. Arrow, one of the pioneers in putting forward this concept calls it "*Learning by Doing*"[17]. According

14. Op. cit, p. 141.
15. C.A. Smith, *Empirical Evidence of Economies of Scale,* printed in Business Concentration and Price Policy, Universities National Bureau Committee for Economic Research, Princeton University press, 1955.
16. Op. cit, p. 42.
17. K.J. Arrow, "The Economic Implications of Learning by Doing", *Review of Economic Studies*, Vol. 29 (June 1962) pp. 154-179.

to Arrow, as a firm or its manager produces successive lots of output over various periods of time, it learns to produce more with a given quantity of resources or it is capable of producing a given output by using lesser quantities of inputs or resources than before. Thus, either with the increase in efficiency of resources or with saving in resources such as labour and raw materials, cost per unit of output declines as a firm gathers more experience over time. This learning curve effect mostly occurs in the reduction of labour requirements per unit of output.

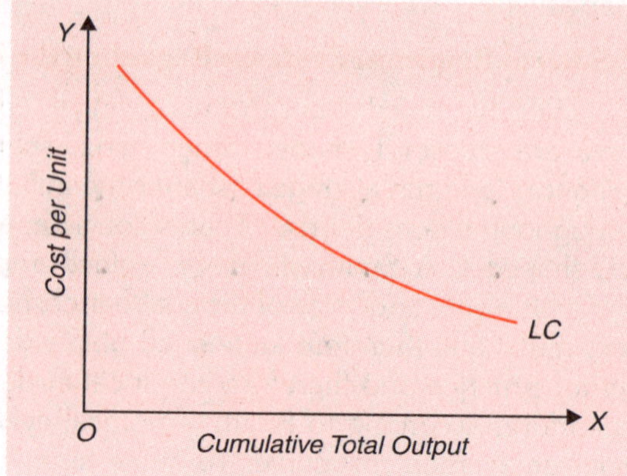

Fig. 21.24. *The Learning Curve*

A number of factors bring this learning curve effect. As cumulative volume of output over successive periods of time increases, labour and supervisors become more familiar with the work methods or the production process, which leads to the reduction in the amount of scrap and other types of wastes. Besides, raw materials cost per unit of output may also decline as cumulative volume of output in successive periods over time increases and as a result a firm gains more experience in doing a production process repeatedly over successive time periods. The learning curve is graphically shown in Fig, 21.24. where on the X-axis cumulative total output over successive periods of time and on the Y-axis cost per unit of output are measured. It will be seen from Fig. 21.24 that the learning curve slopes downward which shows declining cost per unit of output as cumulative output increases over time and the firm learns from its work experience.

The learning curve effect is usually expressed as a *constant percentage*. This percentage represents the proportion by which cost per unit of output declines with the increase in cumulative output in each successive time period. For example, if in a production process labour-input cost experiences 80 per cent learning-curve effect, this means that if in the first period production of a unit of output requires labour cost of ₹ 1000, in the next period labour cost per unit will decline to ₹ 800 and so forth. This learning curve relationship between cost and output is expressed algebraically as follows

$$C = aQ^b$$

where C is the input cost of Qth unit of output, Q is successive unit of output produced, a is the input cost per unit of output in the first period and b is the rate of decline in cost per unit of output in the successive periods. Since the learning curve is downward-sloping, the value of b is negative.

It is important to note that reduction in cost per unit due to the learning-curve effect is different from economies of scale. Whereas economies of scale refer to decline in cost per unit of output as a *firm's output per time period* increases, the learning curve describes the reduction in cost per unit of output as a *firm's cumulative output over successive time periods increases, while output per period* may remain the same.

ALGEBRAIC FORMS OF COST FUNCTIONS

Cubic Cost Function. Economists generally use polynomial functions to represent the relationships between costs and output. The algebraic form of the total cost function used in standard economic theory represents a *cubic relationship* between costs and output which can be written as

$$TC = a + bQ + cQ^2 + dQ^3 \qquad \text{...}(i)$$

where TC is total cost, Q is level of output, a, b, c, d are constants of the function. Note that cost function (i) is a short-run cost function because the term 'a' does not contain Q element which means that 'a' represents fixed cost which has to be borne even if output produced is zero. Therefore, cubic total variable cost (TVC) function can be written as

$$TVC = bQ + CQ^2 + dQ^3$$

From the above total cost function, marginal cost function can be derived by taking the first derivative of the total cost function in equation (i) with respect to output Q. Thus, marginal cost function is

$$MC = \frac{d\,(TC)}{dQ} = b + 2cQ + 3dQ^2$$

When graphically represented, the marginal cost function yields a U-shaped marginal cost curve.

Average cost function from the cubic total cost function can be obtained from dividing the latter by the output level.

$$AC = \frac{TC}{Q}$$

$$= \frac{a + bQ + cQ^2 + dQ^3}{Q}$$

$$= \frac{a}{Q} + b + cQ + dQ^2$$

When graphically represented, the average cost function yields a U-shaped average total cost curve.

Quadratic Cost Function. Some econometric studies of cost functions in some industries have found that cubic term (Q^3) is not statistically significant. With the deletion of this cubic term the following quadratic relationship between cost and output is obtained.

$$TC = a + bQ + cQ^2$$

In this quadratic cost function *total cost increases at an increasing rate* throughout as output is expanded. The marginal and average cost functions corresponding to the above quadratic total cost functions are

$$MC = \frac{d(TC)}{dQ} = b + 2cQ \qquad \text{....}(iv)$$

$$AC = \frac{TC}{Q} = \frac{a + bQ + cQ^2}{Q} = \frac{a}{Q} + b + cQ$$

It will be observed from equation (iv) that the marginal cost increases linearly (that is, at a constant rate) as output is expanded.

Linear Cost Function. When econometric studies find that both the cubic (Q^3) and quadratic (Q^2) terms in a cost function are statistically insignificant, we get linear cost function which is written as

$$TC = a + bQ$$

From the above linear total cost function associated marginal cost and average cost functions can be obtained as under :

By taking the first derivative of the linear cost function, we have the following marginal cost function.

$$MC = \frac{d(TC)}{dQ} = b \qquad ....(v)$$

By dividing the linear total cost function by output, we get average cost function. Thus

$$AC = \frac{TC}{Q} = \frac{a + bQ}{Q}$$

$$= \frac{a}{Q} + b \qquad ....(vi)$$

Two important implications of linear total cost functions are noteworthy. First, as can be seen from equation (v) above, *its associated marginal cost is constant.* If a curve representing this marginal cost curve is drawn, it will be a horizontal straight line. Secondly, associated average cost of the linear total cost function, as will be seen from equation (vi), continuously decreases as output is expanded and has no upward rising part. It may however be noted that both of the above implications are contrary to the law of diminishing returns according to which, with one or more fixed inputs short-run marginal and average cost curves will eventually begin decreasing.

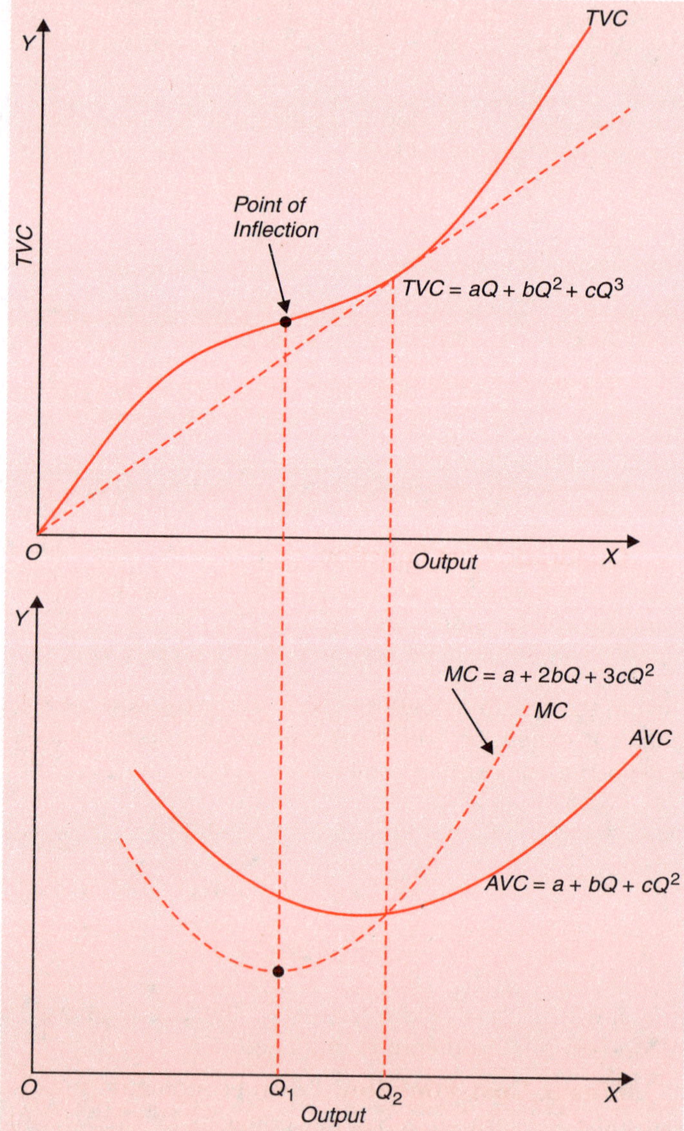

Fig. 21.25. *Cubic Total Variable Cost Function and Corresponding AVC and MC Function*

The Cubic TVC Function

In economic theory, it is generally hypothesized that *TVC* function is *S*, shaped (*i.e.* cubic) which corresponds to U-shaped *AVC* and *MC* curves as indicated in Fig. 21.26. The empirical data about output and cost may also indicate cubic form of *TVC* function and hence U-shaped *AVC* and marginal cost functions are given by

$$TVC = aQ + bQ^2 + cQ^3 \qquad AVC = \frac{TVC}{Q} = a + bQ + cQ^2$$

$$MC = \frac{dTVC}{dQ} = a + 2bQ + 3cQ^2$$

Though the variable cost functions are non-linear in variables Q, Q^2 and Q^3 but are linear in parameters a, b and c. Therefore, these parameters can be estimated by least squares regression technique without transformation of the functional equations. The cubic total variable cost function and its associated *AVC* and *MC* functions are shown in Fig.21.25. In the upper panel of this figure, S-shaped *TVC* curve has been drawn and in the lower panel corresponding to it, U-shaped *AVC* and *MC* curves have been shown. It should be noted that *AVC* and *MC* curves are equal at the level of output corresponding to which the tangent drawn to the *TVC* curve meets the point of origin. Further note that up to the inflection point of the *TVC* curve *MC* is falling and beyond that *MC* will be rising. It is worth noting that actual shapes of these cost functions depend on the values of estimated parameters (*i.e.* a, b and c)

Explanation of Flat AVC and MC Curves

It will be noticed from Fig. 21.26 that *MC* curve is a horizontal straight line and *AVC* curve is flat over a wide range of output and the two coincide over a wide range of output. Empirical studies of short-run cost functions have found that marginal cost and average variable cost are constant over a wide range of output rates. This seems to be inconsistent to the convenional economic theory according to which average variable cost and marginal cost curves are U-shaped, that is, in the beginning they slope downward and beyond a certain level of output, they rise due to diminishing returns to the variable factors. How can we then explain this inconcistency between economic theory and empirical studies? One explanation that is offerred is that average variable cost and short-run marginal cost curves are saucer-shaped as shown in Fig.21.26. The saucer-shape of these curves show that they have a negative slopes at low levels of output and positive slopes (rising) at high levels of output with a flat portion over a wide range of output in between. Since efficient working generally requires that firms in the real world should operate in the flat portion of these curves, most of the data regarding actual production rates and costs would reveal approximately constant costs.

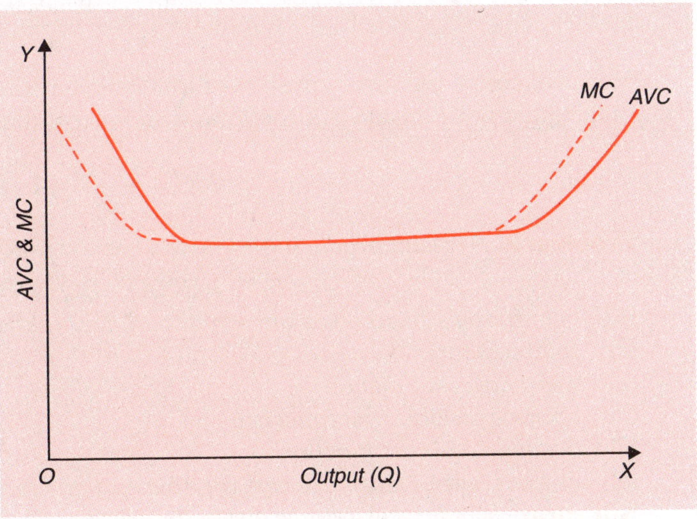

Fig. 21.26. *Saucer Shaped AVC and MC Curves*

According to another explanation given for flat *AVC* and *MC* cost functions found in empirical studies is that in the short run the fixed factors such as physical capital may not be really fixed in the short run as is assumed in economic theory. Economic theory explains that short-run marginal and average variable costs rise because in the short run, as a greater quantity of a variable factor is used along with a fixed amount of capital, diminishing marginal returns to the variable factor occur. It is due to this diminishing marginal returns to the variable factors that short-run marginal and average variable costs rise beyond a certain level of output. However, in the actual world, the firms have usually a fixed stock of capital (*i.e.* the number of machines) which is not fully used at small rates of output and in fact some of them may lie idle at lower output rates. Thus, in response to greater demand for output, output is increased by employing more variable factors and using the *idle* capital stock. In this way even in the short run, labour-capital ratio is not likely to increase which suggests that both short-run marginal cost and average variable cost will remain approximately constant.

NUMERICAL PROBLEMS ON COST FUNCTIONS

Problem 1. *Suppose a firm faces a cost function of* $C = 8 + 4q + q^2$

(*i*) *What is the firm's fixed cost ?*

(*ii*) *Derive an expression for the firm's average variable cost and marginal cost.*

Solution. (*i*) As fixed cost of the firm does not vary with output, the term in the given cost function which has no output (*q*) term will be the fixed cost. From the given cost function it is evident that fixed cost is 8.

(*ii*) Total variable cost (*TVC*) $= TC - TFC$

$$= (8 + 4q + q^2) - 8 = 4q + q^2$$

and

$$AVC = \frac{TVC}{Q} = \frac{4q+q^2}{q} = 4 + q$$

Marginal cost is the first derivative of total cost function or total variable cost function. Thus, taking the first derivative of the total variable cost function we have

$$MC = \frac{\Delta TVC}{\Delta q} = 4 + 2q$$

Problem 2. *A biscuit producing company has the following variable cost function :*

$$TVC = 200Q - 9Q^2 + 0.25Q^3$$

If the company's fixed costs are equal to ₹ 150 lakhs, find out :

(*a*) *total cost function*

(*b*) *marginal cost function*

(*c*) *average variable cost function*

(*d*) *average total cost function*

(*e*) *at what output levels average variable cost and marginal cost will be minimum.*

Solution. Since total cost is the sum of total fixed cost and total variable cost ($TC = TFC + TVC$), we get the total cost function as under:

$$TC = 150 + 200Q - 9Q^2 + 0.25Q^3$$

To determine the marginal cost we take the first derivative of the total variable cost function with respect to output Q. Thus,

$$MC = \frac{d\,(TC)}{dQ} = 200 - 18Q + 0.75Q^2$$

To derive the average total cost and average variable cost we divide the respective total costs by the output level.

$$AC = \frac{TC}{Q} = \frac{150}{Q} + \frac{200Q}{Q} - \frac{9Q^2}{Q} + \frac{0.25Q^3}{Q}$$

$$= \frac{TC}{Q} = \frac{150}{Q} + 200 - 9Q + 0.25Q^2$$

and
$$AVC = \frac{TVC}{Q} = 200 - 9Q + 0.25Q^2$$

It is also useful to know at what level of output, average variable cost takes on its minimum value. To determine the level of output at which average variable cost is minimum, we have to take first derivative of the average variable cost (*AVC*) function and set this derivative equal to zero.

Thus, taking the first derivative of *AVC* function ($AVC = 200 - 9Q + 0.25Q^2$), we have :

$$\frac{d\,(AVC)}{dQ} = -9 + 0.50Q$$

Setting it equal to zero we have

$$-9 + 0.50Q = 0$$

$$0.50Q = 9$$

$$\frac{1}{2}Q = 9$$

$$Q = 18$$

Thus, at output level equal to 18, average variable cost will be minimum.

Output at which MC Function is Minimum

$$MC = 200 - 18Q + 0.75Q^2$$

To find the output level at which *MC* is minimum, we have to set the first derivative of *MC* function equal to zero. The first derivative of *MC* function is

$$\frac{d\,(MC)}{dQ} = -18 + 1.50\,Q$$

Setting $\frac{d\,(MC)}{dQ}$ equal to zero, we have :

$$-18 + 1.50\,Q = 0$$

$$1.50Q = 18$$

$$Q = 18 \times \frac{10}{15} = 12$$

Thus, at output level 12, *MC* is minimum.

It is thus clear from above that marginal cost takes on the minimum value at an output level smaller than that at which *AVC* is minimum.

Problem 3. *A firm producing hockey sticks has a production function given by* $Q = 2\sqrt{KL}$. *In the short-run, the firm's amount of capital equipment is fixed at* $K = 100$. *The rental rate* *for K is Re. 1 and the wage rate is ₹4.*

(*i*) *Calculate the firm's short-run total and average costs.*

(*ii*) *What are STC, SAC and SMC for producing 25 sticks.*

Solution. The given production function of the firm is

$$Q = 2\sqrt{KL}$$

With $K = 100$ in the short run the short-run production function is

$$Q = 2\sqrt{100L} = 2 \times 10\sqrt{L} = 20\sqrt{L}$$

Cost, $C = wL + rK$

Given that $w = 4$ and $r = 1$

$$C = 4L + 1K$$

With the given $K = 100$

$$C = 4L + 100 \quad ...(1)$$

The short-run production function when $K = 100$ as obtained above is:

$$Q = 20\sqrt{L}$$

Taking square of both sides we have

$$Q^2 = 400\, L$$

or $$\frac{Q^2}{400} = L. \quad ...(2)$$

Substituting (2) in (1) we have

$$C = 100 + 4.\frac{Q^2}{400}$$

$$C = 100 + \frac{Q^2}{100} \quad ...(3)$$

The above equation (3) represents the short-run total cost function.

To get the short-run average cost function, we divide the short-run total cost function in (3) by output (Q). Thus,

$$SAC = \frac{100 + \frac{Q^2}{100}}{Q} = \frac{100}{Q} + \frac{Q}{100}$$

Short-run Marginal Cost Function :

Short-run marginal cost function can be obtained by taking the first derivative of the short-run total cost function.

Short-run total cost function as found above is

$$C = 100 + \frac{Q^2}{100}$$

$$SMC = \frac{dC}{dQ} = \frac{2Q}{100} = \frac{Q}{50}$$

(*ii*) If output of hockey sticks = 25, then

$$STC = 100 + \frac{(25)^2}{100} = 100 + \frac{625}{100}$$

$$STC = 106.25$$

$$SAC = \frac{STC}{Q} = \frac{106.25}{25} = 4.25$$

$$SMC = \frac{Q}{50} = \frac{25}{50} = 0.5$$

Problem 4. *If $Q = A(KL)^{0.5}$, what is short-run cost function when $K = 100$? What is MC function ?*

Solution. With $K = 100$, the short-run production function can be written as

$$Q = A\,(100\,L)^{0.5} = 10A\,(L)^{0.5}$$

Squaring both sides, we have

$$Q^2 = 100A^2L \qquad \ldots(i)$$

Now, the short-run cost function is

$$C = TFC + TVC$$

$$\text{Since } TVC = w.L \text{ and } TFC = K.r = 100\,r$$

where r is the rental price of capital and w is wage rate of labour and given $K = 100$

Therefore, $C = 100r + wL$ ...(*ii*)

From equation (*i*) we have

$$L = \frac{Q^2}{100A^2}$$

Substituting the value of L in (*ii*) we get the following short-run cost function :

$$C = 100r + w.\frac{Q^2}{100A^2} \qquad \ldots(iii)$$

Note that total variable cost function is $w\dfrac{Q^2}{100A^2}$

Differentiating the total variable cost (*TVC*) function with respect to output (*Q*) we have the following marginal cost function :

$$MC = \frac{dTVC}{dQ} = \frac{2wQ}{100A^2}$$

QUESTIONS FOR REVIEW

1. Distinguish between economic costs and accounting costs. Which should be taken into account for calculating the economic profits of the firm?
2. What is the difference between explicit costs and implicit costs? Should both be considered for optimal business decision-making by the firm?
3. Explain the concepts of total fixed cost, total variable costs and total costs. How are they related

to each other? Illustrate them through curves. Is the distinction between the fixed costs and variable costs relevant in the long run ?

4. Explain the following concepts of cost:

   (*a*) Average fixed cost (*AFC*)

   (*b*) Average variable cost (*AVC*)

   (*c*) Average total cost (*ATC*)

   (*d*) Marginal cost (*MC*)

   Why does *ATC* curve reach its lowest point after the *AVC* curve? Why does the *MC* curve intersect below the *AVC* and *ATC* curves at their minimum points ?

5. Derive long-run total cost curve from expansion path. How are average cost curve and marginal cost curve derived from total cost curve.

6. Short-run total and average cost will exceed *long-run* total and average cost respectively. Explain and illustrate graphically.

7. We give below short-run total cost function :

$$TC = 100 + 50Q - 12Q^2 + Q^3$$

   where *TC* is total cost and *Q* is level of output.

   (*i*) Determine : (*a*) total fixed cost function, (*b*) total variable cost function, (*c*) average variable cost function, (*d*) marginal cost function.

   (*ii*) Calculate total cost, *ATC*, *AVC* and *MC* when the firm produces 10 units of output.

   (*iii*) Calculate the level of output at which *AVC* is minimum.

8. What is the relationship between average cost and marginal cost? If the marginal cost is rising, does it mean that average cost must also be rising?

9. Derive long-run average cost curve from short-run average cost curves. How are they related to each other? Does the curve joining the minimum points of the short-run average cost curves constitutes long-run average cost curve? Give reasons.

10. Give reasons for the U-shape of long-run average cost curve. Why is long-run average cost curve usually called 'planning curve'?

11. Explain the various economies of scale and diseconomies of scale that accrue to the firm when it expands its scale of production.

12. Modern empirical studies have found that long-run average cost curve (*LAC*) is L-shaped. How would you explain it? Does it not contradict the U-shaped long-run average cost curve of the traditional cost theory?

13. What would be the shape of long-run average cost (*LAC*) curve when constant returns to scale occur? How would you explain the occurrence of constant returns to scale?

14. What is the Learning Curve? What are the factors that bring about learning curve effect? How does reduction in cost per unit due to the learning curve effect differ from economies of scale?

15. (a) Describe relationship between *AVC* and average product and between marginal cost and marginal product.

    (b) How is U-shape of average variable cost curve explained by law of variable proportions?

16. Define marginal cost. How is it related to marginal product of a factor? As output is increased, marginal cost first falls and then beyond a certain point it rises. How would you explain it ?

APPENDIX TO CHAPTER 21

DERIVATION OF LONG-RUN COST FUNCTION

Total cost incurred by a firm is the sum of costs of all the inputs or factors used. In symbolic terms for the two factor production function, total cost is given by

$$C = L \,.\, w + K \,.\, r$$

where L and K are the quantities of labour and capital employed and w and r are the prices of these factors respectively. As has been discussed in the chapters on production theory that a profit-maximizing firm must seek to use the specific combination of factors (or inputs) that minimizes its cost and to adjust its use of factors as it increases its level of output along a particular expansion path which is determined by the underlying production function and relative factor prices. Points along that expansion path then determine the specific relation between costs and output constituting the firm's cost function which can be expressed as

$$C = f(Q)$$

As the cost function is essentially the relationship between costs and outputs along an expansion path, it is strictly defined for the *given factor prices*. This means that any change in factor prices causes a change in the expansion path and, therefore, causes a shift in the associated cost function.

In the light of the above, we proceed to derive the long-run cost function. We are given the following production function.

$$Q = L^{1/2} K^{1/2} \qquad \text{...}(i)$$

and cost equation is given by

$$C = w \,.\, L + rK \qquad \text{...}(ii)$$

It may be reiterated that long-run cost function depicts the expenditure incurred on cost-minimizing combinations of factors (labour and capital in our example) to produce various levels of output. We explain below step-wise procedure of deriving long-run cost function.

First step in deriving the long-run cost function from a given production function and cost equation is to obtain the value of $MRTS_{LK}$ or ratio of marginal products of the factors. Thus, for the given production function,

$$MP_L = \frac{1}{2} L^{-1/2} K^{1/2}$$

$$MP_K = \frac{1}{2} L^{1/2} K^{-1/2}$$

$$MRTS_{LK} = \frac{MP_L}{MP_K} = \frac{\frac{1}{2}L^{-1/2} K^{1/2}}{\frac{1}{2} L^{1/2} K^{-1/2}} = \frac{K}{L} \qquad \text{...}(iii)$$

The *second step* is to substitute the value of $MRTS_{LK}$ in the condition for minimizing cost, namely, $MRTS_{LK} = \frac{w}{r}$ and to find out the equation for expansion path. Thus, in our example

$$\frac{K}{L} = \frac{w}{r}$$

$$K = \frac{w \,.\, L}{r} \qquad \text{.....}(iv)$$

The equation (*iv*) describes the expansion path of the firm

The *third step* is to substitute the equation for expansion path, $K = \frac{w.L}{r}$ in the given production function to obtain the cost-minimizing quantity of labour to produce an output. In our example

$$Q = L^{1/2}\left(\frac{w.L}{r}\right)^{1/2}$$

or $$L = w^{-1/2}.\, r^{1/2}\,.\, Q \qquad ...(v)$$

The *fourth step* is to estimate the cost-minimizing quantity of capital to produce an output. The equation for expansion path derived above can be rewritten as $L = \frac{Kr}{w}$. In order to obtain the cost-minimizing quantity of capital to produce an output substitute $L = \frac{Kr}{w}$ in the given production function. Thus, in our example

$$Q = \left(\frac{Kr}{w}\right)^{1/2} K^{1/2}$$

or $$K = r^{-1/2}.\, w^{1/2}\,.\, Q \qquad ...(vi)$$

The final step in the derivation of cost function is to substitute the cost-minimising quantities of inputs (labour and capital) as given by equation (v) and (vi) in the iso-cost equation.

$$C = w.L + rK$$

$$C = w \times (w^{-1/2}\,.\, r^{1/2}\, Q) + r\,(r^{-1/2}\,.\, w^{1/2}\, Q)$$

$$= 2w^{1/2}\, r^{1/2}\, Q \qquad ...(vii)$$

The equation (*vii*) **represents the long-run cost function according to which long-run cost depends on factor prices and output.** It is evident from equation (*vii*) that, *given the factor prices*, we can find out the cost by taking different amounts of output (*i.e.*, Q). It will also be noticed from the cost function that rise in price of either factor will cause the total cost to increase. This can be easily shown by differentiating the cost function ($C = 2w^{1/2}\, r^{1/2}\, Q$) with respective to wage, the price of labour. Thus

$$\frac{\partial C}{\partial w} = w^{-1/2}\, r^{1/2}\, Q$$

It will be seen that this partial derivative of cost function with respect to wage rate is positive ($w^{-1/2}\, r^{1/2}\, Q > 0$). The positive partial derivative with respect to wage rate shows that cost increases with the rise in wages. It will also be noticed this partial derivative of the cost function with respect to wage equals the cost-minimizing quantity of labour (described by equation (*v*) above). This is an important finding. ***In general, the derivative of cost function with respect to a factor price is the cost-minimizing quantity of that factor.***

CHAPTER

22

Linear Programming

Introduction

The central problem of economics is how the maximum possible satisfaction of the people can be achieved through proper allocation of scarce or limited resources among different uses. Several economists attempted to analyse this central problem of economics with the use of marginal analysis. But the marginal analysis involves several practical difficulties due to which it has not succeeded in solving some practical economic problems. In order to solve some practical problems, especially decision-making by the business firms, the technique of linear programming has been developed. First of all, an American mathematician, D.B. Dantzig developed the technique of linear programming after the Second World War in 1946. A Russian mathematician L.V. Kantorvich also had evolved independently the technique of linear programming. Linear Programming has also been called ***mathematical programming and activity analysis.***

Linear programming technique is concerned with constrained optimisation problem. In such problem, there is one objective function and one or more constraints. In the theory of production we dealt with such problem when we explained how to minimize cost subject to the production of *a given level of output*. Here minimisation of cost was the objective function and a given level of output was the constraint. Another common example of constrained optimisation problem is maximization of profits subject to the constraints such as the capacity of machine used in production, availabilty of raw materials etc.

An important feature of linear programming technique is that in it both the objective function and constraints are linear, that is, they describe linear relationship between the variables. Hence the name of the technique is linear programming, Since all managers of business firms face constrained optimisation problems, linear programming technique is used in solving a number of business problems. Linear programming problem is also widely used in agriculture, especially agribusiness. Such problems as determination of least cost minimisation of feeds given to animals that meet their minimum nutritional requirements, the problem of allocation of land to different crops subject to constraints such as fixed land area, limited availability of irrigation facilities. We will explain the use of linear programming technique to some important problems of constrained optimisation facing producers and managers of business firms. Both graphical and algebraic methods will be used to solve linear programming problems.

Meaning of Linear Programming

The term 'Linear Programming' consists of two words: (a) linear and (2) programming. The linear programming considers only *linear relationship* between two or more variables. By linear relationship we mean that relations between the variables can be represented by straight lines. Programming means planning or decision-making in a systematic way. "Linear programming refers to a technique for the formulation and solution of problems in which some linear function of two or more variables is to be optimized subject to a set of linear constraints, at least one of which must be expressed as inequality." The American mathematician George B. Dantzig who invented the linear programming technique used it for the purpose of scheduling the procurement activities of the United States Air Force. Since 1946 linear programming has been greatly developed both in theory and its application to several practical problems of the firm, industry and the economy. Since linear programming requires a lot of numerical calculations, the development of electronic computer after the Second World War has contributed to the development of this method and its application to practical problems.

Since leading concepts, principles and ideas of linear programming involve the use of advanced mathematics, a complete analysis of linear programming theory and its application cannot be given here. We shall confine ourselves to the explanation of linear programming technique with special reference to the theory of the firm and will briefly describe its applications to other fields at the end. Further, we shall only make graphical and simple mathematical analysis of linear programming and will avoid the use of higher mathematics as far as possible. A firm has to face two important production problems. In the first place, a firm has to decide about which particular production process from several alternative processes available it should choose for the production of a commodity. This problem has been successfully analysed with linear programming technique. Second important production problem which a firm faces is what amounts of output of various products it should produce so as to maximise its profits. Linear programming technique also helps to solve this problem of the firm. But before explaining the applications of linear programming to these aspects of the theory of the firm, we shall explain the basic concepts and terms used in linear programming.

BASIC CONCEPTS AND TERMS OF LINEAR PROGRAMMING

The linear programming as applied to the theory of the firm explains decision-making by a firm about output and processes it will choose, given the prices of both inputs and products. Thus in the analysis of the firm conducted through the linear programming, it is assumed that prices for the products as well as the inputs used by them will remain constant. With the given constant prices of inputs and outputs, the linear programming provides numerical solution to the problem of making optimum choice by the firm when it has to work within certain given constraints. The optimisation can refer to either maximization or minimisation. For instance, objective may be maximization of profits for a given level of outlay or minimisation of cost for a given level of output. Optimizaton and choice are thus central features of linear programming problem.

The Linearity Assumption. The principal characteristic of a problem that can be solved through linear programming technique is linearity. By linearity we mean that the problem which is to be analysed through linear programming must be formulated in terms of *linear functions* of two or more variables which are also subject to a set of *linear constraints*, at least one of which must be expressed as inequality. That is, the problem to be analysed through linear programming is expressed entirely in terms of linear equations and inequalities. It may be noted that the correctness of the solution reached through linear programming depends crucially upon the validity of this assumption of linearity. The assumption of linearity makes the complicated mathematical programming simpler than it otherwise would have been. Linearity is not only a merely simplifying assumption but also a realistic description of the real world situation.

The economic implications of linearity in the field of production are that constant returns to scale prevail and average cost is constant and consequently marginal products and average products are equal. Empirical evidence has revealed that over a wide range of output, constant returns to scale prevail and average cost curve is horizontal over this range. Besides, the implications of linearity assumption are that prices of inputs and outputs are given for the firm. It is because of the constant prices of inputs and outputs that they can also be shown by straight lines on price-quantity diagrams. Even though returns and costs may not be exactly linear they may be so close to it that it may be justified to make the linearity assumption.

Objective Function. Objective function, also called criterion function, describes the "determinants of the quantity to be maximised or to be minimized."[1] If the objective of a firm is to maximise output or profits, then this is the objective function of the firm. If the linear programming requires the minimisation of cost, then this is the objective function of the firm. An objective function has two parts—*the primal and dual*. If the primal of the objective function is to maximise output subject to a cost-outlay, then its dual will be the minimisation of cost subject to a given output.

Constraints. The maximization of the objective function is subject to certain limitations which are called constraints. The budget or income of a consumer is constraint on him for maximizing his satisfaction. A firm which aims to maximise its output is constrained by the fact that it has, say, only 13 machines to work with and a certain limited floor space on which work has to be performed. Besides, constraints on a firm may be of the type that for a particular machine, say A, at least two labourers are needed to operate it, and for another machine B, at least 5 labourers are required to operate it. *Constraints are also called inequalities* because they are generally expressed in the form of inequalities. The constraint regarding the availability of 10 machines for production is generally expressed as 10 or fewer machines (that is, $\leq$ 10 machines) are available for production. If the constraint is that at least two workers are required to operate a machine, then it is written as $\leq$ 2 workers are needed to operate a machine.

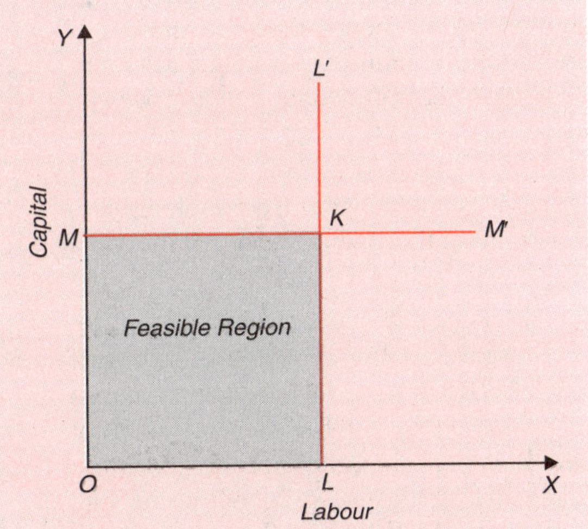

Fig. 22.1. *Region of Feasible Solutions.*

Feasible Region. After knowing the constraints, feasible solutions of the problem for a consumer, a producer, a firm or an economy can be ascertained. Feasable region contains those solutions which *meet or satisfy the constraints of the problem* and therefore it is possible to attain them. For a consumer which aims to maximise his satisfaction from his purchases of goods, feasible solutions are those which lie at or to the left of the given budget line, which in turn is determined by the constraints of the given income and the given prices of goods. Likewise, feasible solutions for a firm using two inputs, labour and capital, and seeking to maximise his output are those possible combinations of inputs which lie on or to the left of the given iso-cost line which in turn is determined by the given total outlay and given prices of the two inputs. The shape of the area or region of feasible solutions depends upon the nature of constraints.

Some Illustrations. The constraints of a firm for the production of a commodity are given by a certain amount of physical capital, say, *OM* and a certain amount of labour, say, *OL*, then the region of feasible solutions is represented in Figure 17.1 by the area *OMKL*.

1. D. S. Watson, *Price Theory and Its Uses*, 4th edition, p. 206.

Since no more than *OL* amount of labour and no more than *OM* amount of capital is available, in Figure 22.1 a vertical line *LL′* at *OL* amount of labour has been drawn to represent the constraint of labour and a horizontal straight line *MM′* at the amount of capital *OM* has been drawn to represent the constraint of capital. Any combination of factors which lies on or within the rectangle *OMKL* is feasible to be used for production. And any combination of inputs which is outside the region *OMKL* is not feasible to be used for production.

Another example of the region of feasible solutions is depicted in Figure 22.2. It has been assumed that two goods *X* and *Y* are to be produced. The machine *A* which is used for the production of a commodity has the capacity to work for 12 hours a day and the machine *B* has the capacity to work for eight hours a day. The production of a unit of commodity *X* requires 2 hours work each on machine *A* and *B*. To produce a unit of commodity *Y* requires three hours work on machine A and one hour work on machine *B*. These constraints can be expressed in the form of following inequalities :-

$$2X + 3Y \leq 12$$

$$2X + 1Y \leq 8$$

These constraints are represented in Figure 22.2. If the entire capacity of 12 machine hours of machine *A* is devoted to production of X, then 6 units of commodity *X* are produced. If entire capacity of 12 hours of machine *A* is used for the production of commodity *Y*, then 4 units of product *Y* are produced. Thus, the line *AB* in Figure 22.2 represents the constraint imposed by machine *A*, that is, it represents $2X + 3Y \leq 12$. The area to the left of the line *AB* represents the feasible region from the viewpoint of the given capacity of machine *A*.

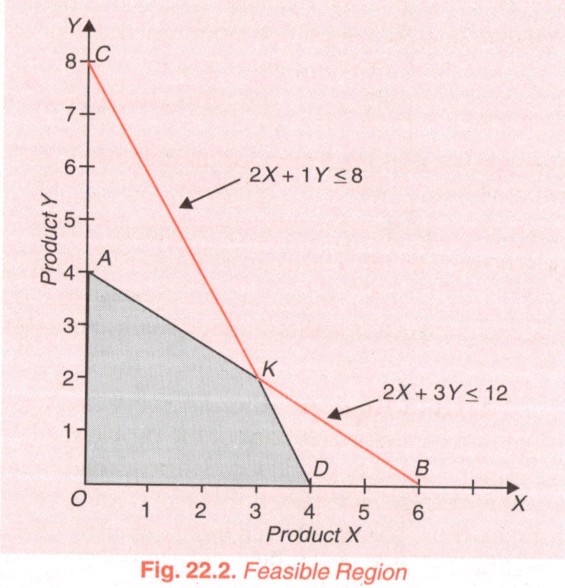

Fig. 22.2. *Feasible Region*

In the same way, constraint $2X + 1Y \leq 8$ regarding the available capacity of machine *B* has been represented in Figure 22.2 by the line *CD*, the area to the left of which represents the area of feasible solutions from the viewpoint of the capacity of machine *B*. But from the viewpoint of the constraints imposed by the two machines together, the region of feasible solutions is given by the shaded area *OAKD*.

We have given above some examples of region of feasible solutions. The shape of the feasible region would differ as the number and nature of constraints vary.

Optimum Solution

The best of all feasible solutions is the optimum solution. In other words, of all the feasible solutions, the solution which maximises or minimizes the objective function is the optimum solution. For instance, if the objective function is to maximise profits from the production of two goods, then the optimum solution will be that combination of two products that will maximise the profits for the firm. Similarly, if the objective function is to minimize cost by the choice of a process or combination of processes, then the process or a combination of processes which actually minimizes the cost for a given level of output will represent the optimum solution. It is worthwhile to repeat that optimum solution must lie within the region of feasible solutions.

In linear programming, there are two alternative methods of finding the optimum solution. One is the non-mathematical or graphical method of obtaining the optimal solution. This graphical method can handle only simple linear programming problems. The other method of finding the optimum solution of the linear programming problem is the ***simplex method***. The simplex method involves a set of successive mathematical calculations with which feasible solutions are successively tested during which the poorer solutions (*i.e.* which are not optimal) are successively eliminated until ultimately the optimum solution is obtained. Thus, the simplex method uses a mathematical and computational procedure to find out the optimal solution for the problem in question. Though the graphical and simplex methods follow different procedures to obtain the optimal solution for the problem, they reach identical numerical results.

CHOICE OF PRODUCTS : CONSTRAINED PROFIT MAXIMISATION

An important linear programming relates to the maximization of profits in the production of two products when it is subject to some contraints. That is, what quantities of the two products are produced so that the profits of the firm are maximised when their production is subject to some constraints. Such analysis is highly relevant for a multiple product firm *i.e.* for a firm which produces more than one product. In this regard, it is worthwhile to know that production is subject to what constraints.

The Problem : *Let us suppose that the production of two products X and Y requires the use of two machines I and II. The available capacity of machine I is to work for 12 hours in a day and the capacity of machine II is to work for eight hours a day. The other constraint relates to the machine hours required for the production of each unit of commodities X and Y. Let us assume that to produce a unit of product X, 2 hours work each on machine I and II is required and to produce a unit of product Y, 3 hours work is required to be done on machine 1 and 1 hour work is needed to be done on machine II.*

Solution. We can write these two constraints in the following manner :

$$2X + 3Y \leq 12 \quad \ldots(i)$$

$$2X + 1Y \leq 8 \quad \ldots(ii)$$

Graphical Method. As stated above, the linear programming problem can be solved both by graphical and algebraic methods. We will first explain the graphical method of solving the above constrained profit-maximization problem. In this graphical method we first graph the feasible region as defined by the system of linear constraints and then draw linear profit-function curves to determine the optimum solution.

The first constraint is shown by the straight line *AB* and the second constraint is shown by another straight line *CD* in Fig. 22.3 (How these straight lines representing the constraints are drawn has been explained above). The area to the left of the thick line *AQD* in Fig. 22.3 represents the region of feasible solutions.

To show which combination of two products *X* and *Y*, the firm will produce so as to maximise its profits, it is necessary to explain first the concept of *iso-profit curves* which represent the given profit function. To draw iso-profit curves one needs to know the profit per unit produced of the two products. ***The profits or net revenue earned per unit of a product that can be obtained by deducting the average variable cost from the price pet unit of the product.*** Let us assume that profits obtained in this way from product *X* are Rs. 10 per unit of output and from product *Y* are Rs. 6 per unit of output. We can therefore write the objective function as follows:

$$\pi = 10X + 6Y$$

where π (i.e. profits) are to be maximised subject to the constraints stated above in (i) and (*ii*), and X and Y represent the quantities of two products.

In order to represent the profits through iso-profit curves we shall have to fix the various amounts of profits. With different amounts of profits, the level of iso-profit curve will vary; the larger the amount of profits to be earned, the higher the level of iso-profit curve. If the amount of profits to be made is ₹ 30, then the equation of the objective function will be as follows :

$$30 = 10X + 6Y$$

If product X is not to be produced at all and therefore its amount is zero, we will get the following equation of the objective function :

$$30 = 10(0) + 6Y$$
$$Y = 5$$

This means that with the production of 5 units of product Y and none of product X, amount of profits made will be ₹ 30. The point 5 is plotted on the Y-axis in Fig. 22.4 Likewise, if no amount of product Y is produced, then

$$30 = 10X + 6(0)$$
$$X = 3$$

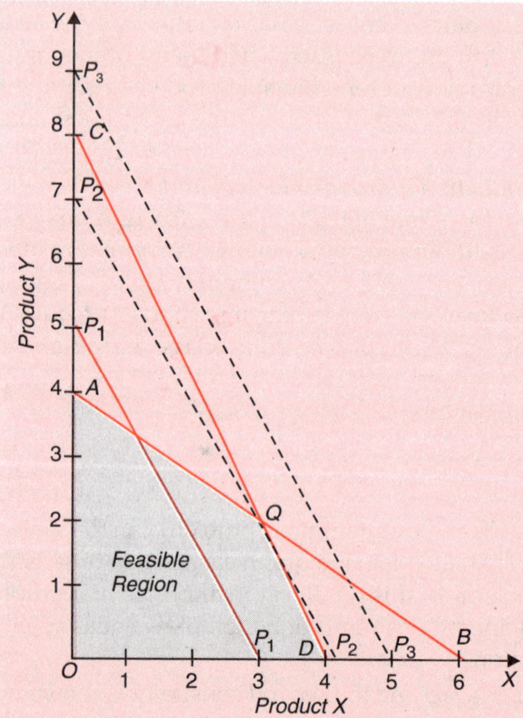

Fig. 22.3. *Optimal Solution : Constrained Profit Maximisation*

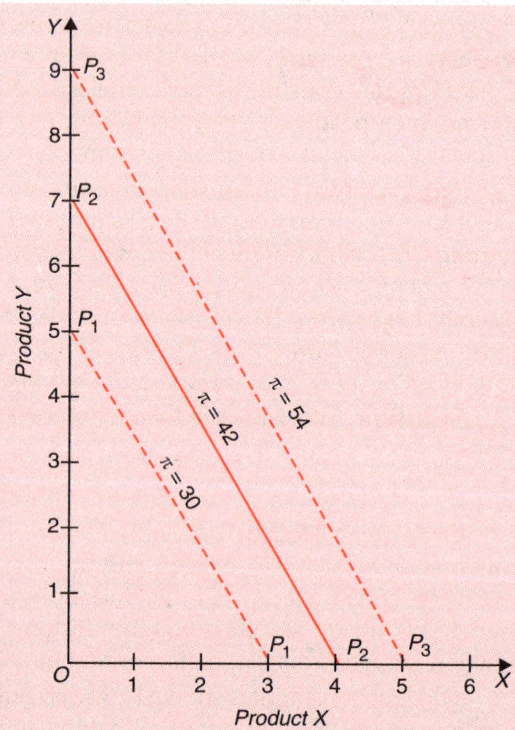

Fig. 22.4. *Iso-Profit Curves*

This means that the production of 3 units of X alone and none of Y will fetch the profit of ₹ 30. Therefore, point 3 is plotted of the X-axis. Thus, in Fig. 22.4 by joining the points 5 on the Y-axis and point 3 on the X-axis through a straight line, we get an iso-profit curve P_1P_1 representing the amount of profits equal to ₹ 30. All combinations of two products lying on the iso-profit curve P_1P_1 will yield profit equal to ₹ 30. Similarly, in Fig. 22.4 iso-profit curves P_2P_2,P_3P_3 showing successively higher levels of profits can be drawn. Given that profits per unit of products X and Y remain unchanged, various iso-profit curves will be parallel to each other.

Now, consider again Figure 22.3 where iso-profit curves have been superimposed on the region of feasible solutions. As noted above, the higher the level of iso-profit curve, the greater the amount of profits. Therefore, a firm whose objective is to maximise profits, will seek to go to the highest possible iso-profit curve. However, it cannot go beyond the region of feasible solutions because constraints prevent it to do so. A glance at Figure 22.3 will reveal that the firm will make maximum possible profits by producing at point *Q* where an iso-profit curve P_2P_2 is touching the boundary of the region of feasible solutions. The firm will not produce at any other point since any point other than *Q* on or within the region of feasible solutions will lie at a lower iso-profit curve.

It is worthwhile to note that the optimum solution of the linear programming problem will always lie at the boundary of the region of feasible solutions. This follows from a simple logic even without reference to the iso-profit curves. It may be recalled that in linear programming constant returns to scale are assumed to be prevailing and also prices of products and inputs are assumed to remain constant. Therefore, if the production of a commodity is profitable, a firm will continue to expand output because neither diminishing returns to scale will occur nor there will be any adverse effects on the prices of output and inputs. Therefore, it will always be worthwhile to increase output until some capacity limit is reached, that is, until the boundary of the feasible region is reached. Point *Q* is a corner point of the region of feasible solutions. The firm cannot go beyond the point *Q* because of the constraints. Hence, we conclude that by producing outputs of *X* and *Y* as represented by the point *Q*, the firm will make maximum profits. In other words, the production of combination of products of *X* and *Y* represented by point *Q* is an optimum solution for it. ***Point Q is a corner point of the feasible region. It is worth remembering that when there is a single solution for the linear programming problem, it will always lie at the corner point.***

Algebraic Solution

The graphic method to solve the linear programming problem can be used to solve the problem when there are two decision variables for example, the quantities of the two products in our above example. The graphic approach cannot be used when more than two decision variables are involved. There is algebraic method of solving the constrained optimisation problem when two or more than two decision variables are involved. However, for explaining the algebraic method we will explain the above profit maximization problem when the quantities of two products are to be chosen, subject to constraints. The problem considered above involves an objective function, two constraints and non-negativity requirements. We formulate the above problem in linear programming form.

Maximise : $\pi = 10X + 6Y$ (Objective function)

Subject to : $2X + 3Y \leq 12$

Non negativity requirements

$$X \geq 0$$
$$Y \geq 0$$

The general algebraic approach to solve the problem is to ***identify the corners*** (*i.e.* extreme points including the zero value of each decision variable) of the feasible region by graphing the constraints. The corner points are either extreme points of zero value of the variables or the intersection points of the two constraints. We then solve the two constraint equations for the values of the decision variables (the quantities of the two products to be produced at the point of the intersection. With the values of the decision variables so obtained we solve the objective function. In our example, we calcuate the profits for each set of the values of decision variables corresponding to different corner or extreme points. This is explained below.

Consider Fig. 22.3 where the feasible region has been shown with corner points *A*, *Q* and *D*. Thus the present linear programming problem can be solved by calculating the profits for the quantities of the two products at these corner points,

(1) The given profit function is $\pi = 10X + 6Y$. At point *A* of the feasible region the quantity of *X* is zero and the quantity of *Y* is 4. Thus, at point *A*

$$\pi = 10(0) + 6(4)$$
$$= 24 \quad \quad ...(i)$$

(2) At corner point *D* of the feasible region, the quantity of product *X* is 4 and the quantity of product *Y* is zero. Thus at corner point *D*

$$\pi = 10(4) + 6(0)$$
$$= 40 \quad \quad ...(ii)$$

(3) Now at the corner point *Q*, the two constraint equation curves intersect. That is, point *Q* satisfies the two constraint equations. The values of variables (*i.e.* outputs of the two products corresponding to this can be obtained by solving them simultaneously. The two constraint equations are :

$$2X + 3Y = 12 \quad \quad ...(a)$$
$$2X + 1Y = 8 \quad \quad ...(b)$$

Subtracting equation (*b*) from equation (*a*), we have

$$2Y = 4$$
$$Y = 2$$

Substituting the value of *Y* into equation (*a*), we have

$$2X + 3(2) = 12$$
$$2X = 12 - 6 = 6$$
$$X = 3$$

Thus at the corner point *Q*, the outputs of *X* and *Y* are 3 and 2 units respectively. Now substituting these values of *X* and *Y* in the profit-function equation we can find the profits at the corner points *Q*.

Thus

$$\pi = 10X + 6Y$$

with $X = 3$ and $Y = 2$ we have

$$\pi = 10 \times 3 + 6 \times 2 = ₹\ 42 \quad \quad ....(iii)$$

Given the profit function, profits at the corner points *A*, *D* and *Q* are ₹ 24, 40 and 42 respectively. Thus, given the constraints, profits at corner point *Q* are the maximum and corresponding to this the firm produces 3 units of *X* and 2 units of *Y*. It is thus clear in linear programming solution optimal solution occurs at a corner of the feasible region. This is because both the objective function and constraints are linear.

Let us take another linear programming problem and solve it by algebraic method. An important thing the students should understand is how to formulate the given problem as a linear programming problem, that is, to write the objective function and the constraints in the ***form of equations or inequalities.*** Let us first state the problem.

Problem 2

Suppose a firm produces two products X_1 and X_2. Each unit of product X_1 contributes ₹ 30 to profit and each unit of product X_2 contributes 40 to profits. The production of these products require inputs A, B and C and their available quantities are 14, 10 and 4 respectively. It is given that production of one unit of product X_1 requires 2 units of *input A, 1 unit of input B and does not require input C. And the production of one unit of product X_2 requires 2 units of input A, 2 units of input B and 4 units of input C.*

Formulate the above problem as a linear programming problem and solve it by algebraic method.

Solution:

We write below the above problem as a linear programming problem.

Maximise : $\pi = 30X_1 + 40X_2$ (objective function)

Subject to :

$2X_1 + 2X_2 \leq 14$ (Input A constraint)

$1X_1 + 2X_2 \leq 10$ (Input B constraint)

$X_2 \leq 4$ (Input C constraint)

$X_1, X_2 \geq 0$ (non-negativity constraint)

In order to solve the above linear programming problem by algebraic method we first determine feasible region and its extreme or corner points. This has been done in Fig. 22.5. Three constraint lines *AB*, *CD* and *EG* representing input constraints have been drawn to get the area *EFKB* as the feasible region. There are three *E, F, K,* and *B* corner points of this feasible region.

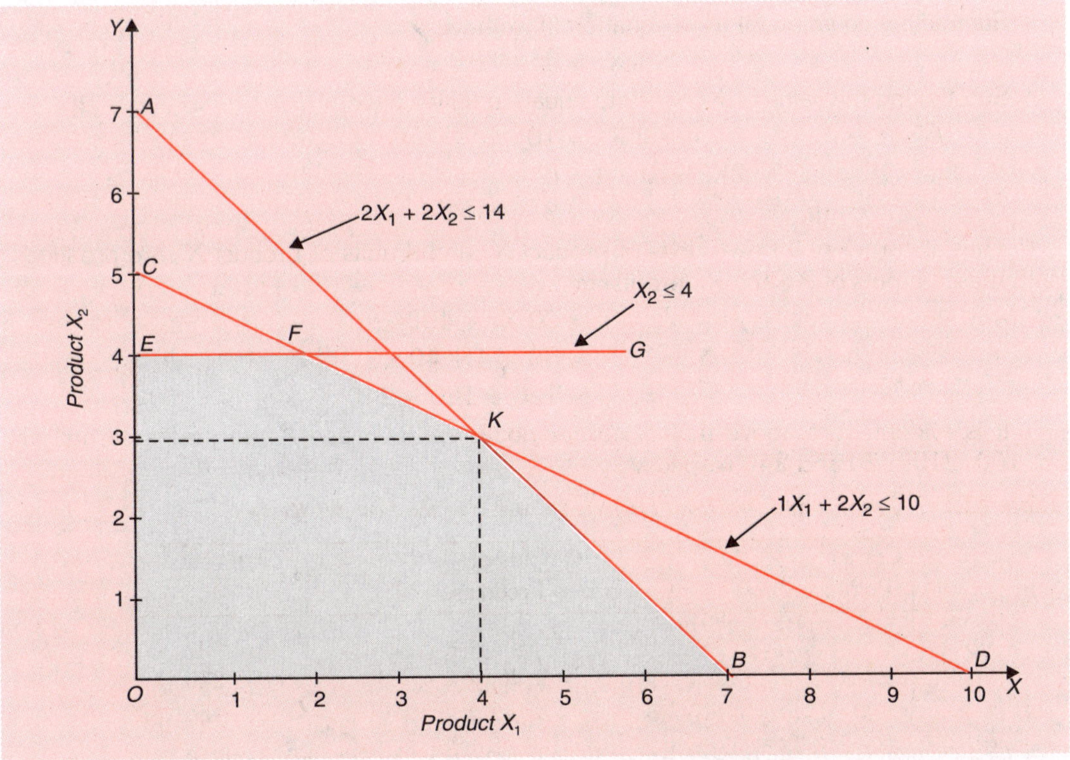

Fig. 22.5. *Feasible Region and Corner Points*

The corner point *E* is determined by only one constraint of input *C* and according to it 4 units of product X_2 and 0 amount of X_1 are produced. Substituting this in profit function we get profits at corner point *E*.

Thus profits at corner point $E = 30\times 0 + 40 \times 4 = 160$.

At corner point *B*, 7 units of product X_1 and zero output of product X_2 are produced. Thus

π at corner point $B = 30 \times 7 + 40 \times 0 =$ ₹ 210

The corner point *F* is determined by the intersection of constraints of inputs *B* and *C*.

As will be seen from the feasible region, according to the corner point *F*, 4 units of product X_2 are produced. To get the quantity produced of product X_1 we substitute $X_2 = 4$ in the constraint equation of input *B*

Thus,

$$X_1 + 2 \times 4 = 10$$
$$X_1 = 10 - 8 = 2$$

Now with $X_1 = 2$ and $X_2 = 4$ at the corner point *F*, profits are

$$\pi = 30\,X_1 + 40\,X_2$$
$$= 30 \times 2 + 40 \times 4 = 60 + 160 = 220$$

Now, take corner point *K* which is determined by intersection of the constraints of inputs *A* and *B*. The output of two products at the corner point can therefore be obtained by solving the constraints equation of the input *A* and *B*. Thus

$$2\,X_1 + 2\,X_2 = 14 \quad \text{...(i)}$$
$$1\,X_1 + 2\,X_2 = 10 \quad \text{...(ii)}$$

Subtracting equation (ii) from equation (i) we have

$$1\,X_1 = 4$$

Substituting the value of $X_1 = 4$ into equation (*ii*) we have

$$4 + 2\,X_2 = 10$$
$$2X_2 = 10 - 4 = 6$$
$$X_2 = 3$$

Thus at corner point *K*, 4 units of product X_1 and 3 units of product X_2 are produced. With these outputs of X_1 and X_2 profits are :

$$\pi = 30\,X_1 + 40\,X_2$$
$$= 30 \times 4 + 40 \times 3$$
$$= 120 + 120 = 240$$

It is evident from above that at corner points *E*, *B*, *F* and *K* the profits earned are Rs. 160, 210, 220 and 240 respectively.

Table 22.1 : ***Outputs and Profits at Different Corners of the Feasible Region***

Corner Point	Outputs of Two Products	Profits ₹
E	$X_1 = 0; X_2 = 4$	160
F	$X_1 = 2; X_2 = 4$	220
K	$X_1 = 4; X_2 = 3$	240
B	$X_1 = 7; X_2 = 0$	210

K represents the optimum or profit-maximizing outputs of two products, namely, 4 units of product X_1 and 3 units of product X_2. We summarize these results in the Table 22.1.

CHOICE OF A PROCESS : OUTPUT MAXIMISATION SUBJECT TO SOME CONSTRAINTS

Another important problem of firm which can be solved through the method of linear programming is that of choosing a best process for production of a commodity. In this analysis of choice of a process it is generally assumed that a firm seeks to maximise its output subject to the constraint of (*i*) a given cost outlay or (*ii*) some available inputs. On the other hand, if the level of output is given, the choice of a process by a firm is analysed by assuming that a firm will aim to minimize cost for the given level of output. We shall discuss all these cases of choice of a best process. But before we explain the optimal solution in these cases we will explain the various concepts in this regard.

Processes and Process Rays. A process is another fundamental concept of linear programming as applied to the theory of production and firm. A process is a particular method of producing goods and requires various inputs (or factors) in fixed proportions. A process is also called *activity* or *complex*. The constant or fixed proportion between inputs to produce a particular product is an essential property of a production process. Thus, a process is a complex of workers and capital equipment. Since each process requires the use of fixed proportion between factors, say between capital and labour, no substitution within a process is possible. This is in sharp contrast to the neo-classical theory of production which assumes easy substitution among factors of production and accordingly a smooth isoquant is drawn. If a production process *A* involves 8 machine hours and one worker (that is, per unit of labour time) and another production method *B* involves 5 machine hours per unit of labour, they are by definition two different production processes. The level of a process means how many machine hours and units of labour within that process are used for production. The assumption of linearity implies that 16 machine hours and 2 workers will produce twice as much as 8 machine hours and 1 worker and so on in case of process *A*. Similarly, for process *B*. Some processes used for the production of a commodity are capital-intensive and some are labour-intensive.

The concept of a process is technological in nature. Depending upon available technologies, several processes are available to a firm for producing a particular product. Each production process can be used at several levels to produce a particular product. The higher the level at which the process is used, the greater the output produced. It is worth mentioning that one process can be substituted for another. Besides, when a commodity is produced with two or more processes at the same time in a community, it is generally assumed that the two processes do not interfere with each other or do not increase the productivity of one another. A typical linear programming is to choose a process or a combination of processes, given the constraints, that minimizes cost of production for producing a given level of output.

Representation of Process : Process Rays. Given the linearity assumption, in each production process proportion between factors remains fixed or constant. As a result, each production process can be expressed through a straight line passing through the origin. In a diagram whose two axes represent the two factors, say labour and capital, the straight line passing through the origin which is the locus of points involving fixed proportion between the two factors is called a process ray. In Figure 22.6 a process ray *OA* has been drawn which represents a fixed ratio between capital and labour which is given by the slope of the ray. It may be noted that on the process ray *OA* points Q_1, Q_2, Q_3 etc are the various levels at which the given process can be used. It will be further noticed that the process *A* is a relatively capital-intensive method of production. Similarly, in Fig.22.6 process rays *OB*, *OC* and *OD* representing different factor proportions and therefore representing different processes *B*, *C* and *D* have been drawn which are respectively less and less capital-intensive. R_1, R_2, R_3 etc are the different levels of the process *B*. S_1, S_2, S_3 etc are the different levels of process *C*, and T_1, T_2, T_3 etc are the different levels of process *D*. Because linear relationship between inputs and outputs has been assumed, as the amounts of inputs or factors are increased along a given process ray, output will increase in the same proportion as inputs, that is, constant returns to scale will occur. Since point Q_1, Q_2, Q_3 and Q_4 have been taken at the same distance from each other, the increment in output between them will also be the same.

On process ray OB, points R_1 R_2, R_3 and R_4 lying on it represent a different factor proportion (*i.e.* capital-labour ratio) from that on various points at process ray OA. It is worth mentioning that it is not necessary to produce a given output along process ray B, one has to work at the same level of process B as of A, that is, distance OR_1 on OB may not be equal to the distance OQ_1 on OA ; both O_1, and R_1 yielding the same level of output. Likewise, factor combination R_2 and Q_2 which yield the same level of output may not be equidistant from the origin O. Similarly, points S_1, S_2, S_3 and S_4 have been taken on process ray OC and points T_1, T_2, T_3 and T_4 have been taken on process ray OD. With factor combination S_1 of process C, T_1 of process D, output equal to that of Q_1 or R_1 is obtained. With factor combination S_2 of process C and factor combination T_2 of process D, output equal to that of Q_2 or R_2 is obtained.

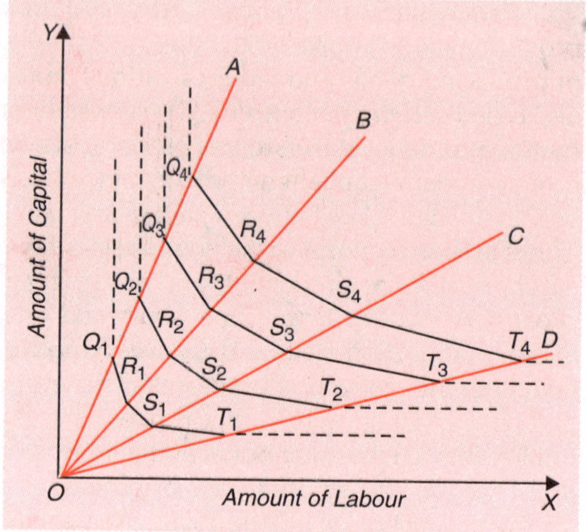

Fig. 22.6. *Process Rays*

Likewise, on process ray OD, points T_1, T_2, T_3, T_4 represent output equal to Q_1, Q_2, Q_3 and Q_4 respectively. On joining points Q_1, R_1, S_1 and T_1, we get a kinked curve (with right linear segments) $Q_1R_1S_1T_1$ which is called isoquant which is similar to equal product curves of the traditional production theory. Further, points Q_2, R_2, S_2 and T_2 are joined together to obtain another isoquant representing a higher level of output. Likewise, higher isoquants are obtained by joining points on different process rays. In order to make it more similar to the iso-product curves of traditional production theory, the extremes of isoquants of linear programming theory are usually extended by vertical and horizontal lines as shown in Figure 22.6 by the dotted lines. Another point worth mentioning is that iso-product curves or isoquants of traditional production theory are smooth or continuous, whereas isoquants in linear programming theory are kinked having right-line segments.

Combination of Processes. As mentioned above, more than one processes are generally available to produce a commodity and various levels of output of the commodity can be produced by working at different levels of the process. It is worthwhile to note that instead of producing a commodity with a single production process, a combination of two processes can also be used to produce a commodity. A part of the output of a commodity can be produced with one process and a part with another process. This happens when a firm is working at a point like K on segment QR in Figure 22.7. In this figure, three process rays, OA, OB, and OC have been depicted and an isoquant QRS has been drawn. If a firm decides to work at point K to produce

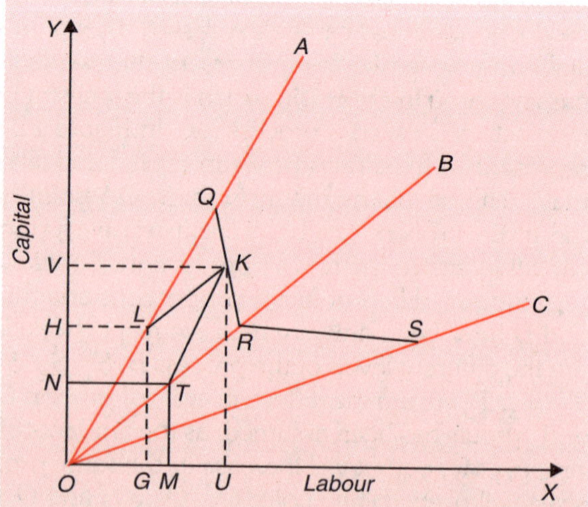

Fig. 22.7. *Combination of Processes*

a given level of output represented by the isoquant *QRS*, it will employ two processes *A* and *B* to produce the commodity. Now, the question is at what levels of the processes *A* and *B*, the firm will work when it is producing at *K*. In order to know that a line from point *K* parallel to *OB* is drawn which meets *OA* at *L* and, similarly, a line from *K* parallel to *OA* is drawn which meets *OB* at *T*. Thus, to produce the output corresponding to point *K* on isoquant *QRS*, the firm will work at the level of *OL* of process *A* and at *OT* of process *B*.

It can be proved that the total amounts of factors, labour and capital, used at point *L* and *T* will be equal to the factor combination represented by *K* (*i.e.* *OV* of capital and *OU* of labour). That is, *OG* + *OM* = *OU* of labour and *OH* + *ON* = *OV* of capital.[2]

In the same way, working at any point on the straight line segment between *R* and *S* will mean that a combination of two processes *A* and *B* will be used for the production of the commodity. However, it may be noted that working at the corner points such as *Q*, *R* or *S* means that only one process will be used for the production of the commodity ; working at point *Q* involves the use of process *A* only, point *R* involves the use of process *B* only, and point *S* involves the use of process *C* only.

Choice of a Process: Output Maximisation with Cost-Outlay Constant

Let us suppose that a firm uses two inputs, labour and capital, to produce a commodity X. Further, three production processes *A*, *B* and *C* are available to the firm for the production of the commodity X. Each process uses a particular ratio of two inputs capital and labour. Thus process *A* uses 2 units of capital for each unit of labour, process *B* uses one unit of capital for each unit of labour and process *C* uses 0.5 units of capital for each unit of labour. The slope of the each process ray measures the ratio of the two inputs, capital and labour. These processes are represented by the process rays *OA*, *OB*, and *OC* in Figure 22.8 wherein along X-axis amount of labour is measured and along the *Y*-axis amount of capital is measured. The process rays, *OA*, *OB* and *OC* are successively more and more labour-intensive. Points *L*, *M* and *N* on the process rays *OA*, *OB* and *OC* represent the levels of these processes respectively, the working at which yields the same level of output, say 40. By joining these points we get an isoquant *LMN* representing 40 units of commodity X. Likewise, we join points *J*, *H*, *G* on various process rays to represent an isoquant representing output level of 60 units of commodity X.

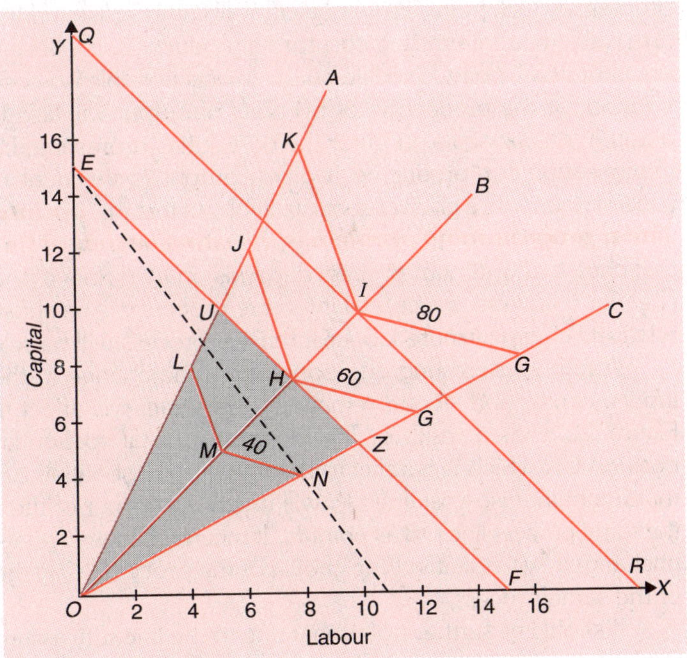

Fig. 22.8. *Optimum Choice of Processes*

Let us assume that with a given cost-outlay, say *T* (= Rs 300) the firm can buy *OF* amount of labour at its given price or wage rate *w* or *OE* amount of capital at its given price *r*.

2. For proof Sec J. Baumol, *Economic Theory and Operations Analysis*, 4th edition, p. 305.

Then, in Fig. 22.8 on a straight line EF, called an iso-cost line, any combination of two factors can be purchased with the given cost-outlay (= ₹ 300). Writing this in the from of equation :

$$T\ (= ₹\ 300) = L.w + Kr$$

$$\text{or } 300 = L.\ w + Kr$$

where T stands for the given cost-outlay, L for the amount of labour, w for the given price of labour, K for the amount of capital and r for the given price of capital. With the constraint of given total cost-outlay, the area to the left or on the line EF represents the feasible region. But, as noted above, since only three processes of production represented by process rays OA, OB and OC are available, choice of process will be confined to the area within process rays OA and OC. With these constraints imposed by the availability of only 3 production processes, the feasible region is reduced to the shaded area OUZ. Since with a given cost-outlay, a firm will seek to maximise production the actual choice of process will be made from among the process lying on segment UZ of the iso-cost line EF.

It will be seen from the Figure 22.8 that the iso-cost line is touching the corner point H of isoquant JHG representing 60 units of output. No point other than H lying on the given iso-cost line EF will yield greater output. Thus, the factor combination H is the optimum solution of the problem, that is, output-maximizing combination for the given cost-outlay. It will be observed that point H lies on the process ray OB. It follows therefore that firm will employ process B for the production of the commodity.

Cost–Minimisation for a Given Output

It is worthwhile to mention here that if the problem is to choose a process subject to the given output of 60 units of product X, even then the firm will choose the point H on the process ray OB. In this case, output of 60 units or isoquant JHG will be the constraint and the firm will aim at minimizing cost for its production. It will be seen from Figure 22.8 that on the isoquant JHG, point H will lie on the lowest possible iso-cost line EF. It means cost-minimizing solution for the production of 60 units of output will also be H which, as seen above, is the output-maximizing solution for the cost outlay represented by the iso-cost line EF. Since cost-minimisation for producing a given output is the dual of the primal problem of output maximization with a given cost-oulay, it follows that the ***optimum solution for the dual of the linear programming problem is the same as that of its primal problem.*** It should be noted that choice of optimum process depends on the relative prices of inputs. If capital is relatively cheaper than labour, a capital intensive process will be chosen. On the other hand, if labour is relatively cheaper, more labour intensive process will be selected for production.

Another interesting question is how the change in the total cost-outlay, prices of both inputs, capital and labour, remaining the same, will affect the choice of process. Suppose in Figure 22.8, as a result of the increase in total cost-outlay, iso-cost line shifts to a higher position QR which is parallel to the initial iso-cost outlay EF. It will be seen from Figure 22.8 that the higher iso-cost line QR will touch the corner of the higher isoquant and but will lie on the same process line OB as point H. It means change in total-cost outlay, input prices remaining unchanged, will not affect the choice of the process ; only the firm will now be at different level of the same process.

It should be further noted that due to the linearity assumption in linear programming that the higher isoquants are so drawn as to reflect the operation of constant returns to scale. For example in our Fig. 22.8 when we increase inputs by 50 percent (from $8K + 4L$ to $12K + 6L$) on process ray OC we obtain higher isoquant JHG of 60 units of output which is 50 per cent greater than 40 units of output of lower isoquant LMN.

It is also clear from the above analysis that when there exists only one constraint, namely, total cost-outlay in the above case, there will be only one process which will be optimal and will be used by the firm for the production of the goods.

Multiple Optimal Solutions

It may be noted that in linear programming, there is usually a *single* optimum solution for the choice of process. But there can be an unusual case where there are *multiple optimum* solutions of the problem. This can happen when the factor prices are such that the given iso-cost line coincides with a segment of an iso-cost line. This is depicted in Figure 22.9 where it is assumed that four processes *A, B, C* and *D*, represented by process rays *OA, OB, OC*, and *OD* respectively, are available for the production of a commodity. Factor prices are such that *EF* is the iso-cost line. It will be observed that the iso-cost line *EF* coincides with the segment *RS* of the isoquant *QRST*. It is thus obvious that either processes *B* or *C* or any other combination of these processes lying on segment *RS* are optimum solution for the firm; any of which can be used to maximise production. Thus, in this case, there are more than one optimum solution. However, normally there is one optimum solution which may be at the corner or an extreme point of the isoquant.

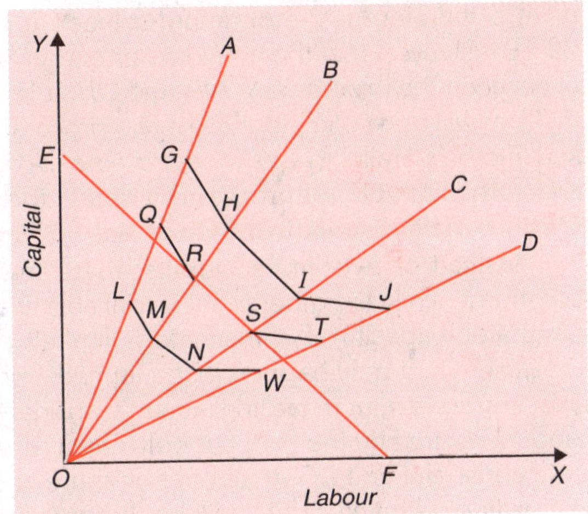

Fig. 22.9. *Choice of a Process : Mulitiple Optimum Solutions*

Choice of a Process: Output Maximisation with Two Inputs as Constraints

Now, if instead of cost-outlay as constraint, the firm is faced with constraints of two inputs which are available to it in limited quantities. Evidently, with the given amounts of inputs, the firm will try to maximise output so as to maximise its profits. Let us assume that three processes *A, B* and *C* are available for the production of the commodity produced by the firm. In Figure 22.10 process rays *OA* , *OB* and *OC* represent the three processes *A* , *B* and *C*. *OL* and *OK* are the available quantities of labour and capital, Thus, the horizontal straight line *KT* represents the constraint of available capital and the vertical line *LG* represents the constraint of available labour. These two lines interact at point *S*. The area *OKSL* represents the region of feasible solutions.

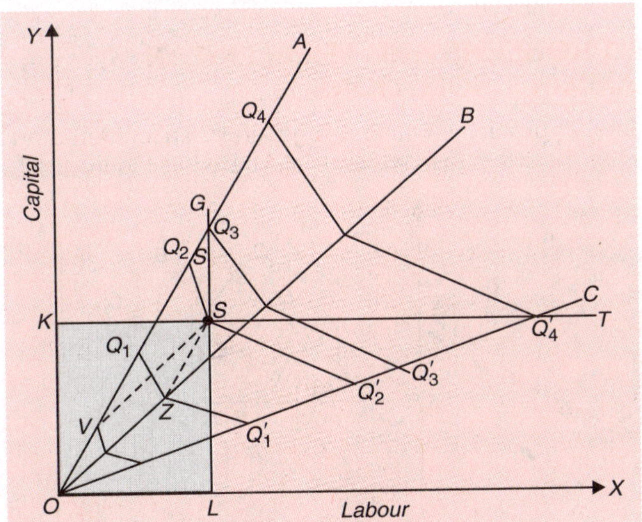

Fig. 22.10. *Output Maximisation with Two Inputs as Constraints*

As the firm will be interested in maximising output; with the given constraints it will try to reach the highest attainable isoquant. So it will go to the boundary of the feasible region because production at this will ensure its maximum output which is possible within the constraints. It will be observed from the Figure 22.10 that the feasible region is touching the isoquant $Q_2Q'_2$ at the corner point *S*. So the firm will produce maximum possible output represented by isoquant $Q_2Q'_2$ by working at point *S*. The point S therefore is the optimum solution for the choice of the process. A glance at Figure 22.10 will reveal that the boundary or corner point *S* lies at the segment of the isoquant Q_2Q_2 in between the process rays *OA* and *OB*. It is thus clear that at the optimum solution point *S*, the firm will use a combination of two processes *A* and *B*. By drawing a line *SV* parallel to *OB* and line *SZ* parallel to *OA* we determine that the firm will work at the level *OV* of process *A* and at the level *OZ* of process *B* to attain the optimum input combination *S*.

Output-Maximisation with One Limited Input

Instead of two limited inputs, there may be one limited input which constitutes the constraint, while the other input is available in any desired amount. It may happen that in case of capital, capacity of a machine is limited or a warehouse of a limited given capacity is available. Or, it may happen that a limited amount of capital is available while there does not exist any constraint regarding labour. Consider Figure 22.10 again. If labour is available in any amount desired by the firm but only *OK* amount of capital is available for production. In this case constraint line *LG* would not be there and only the horizontal line *KT* representing the constraint of limited capital will be there. A firm with its objective of maximization of output will move along the capital-constraint line *KT* so as to reach highest achievable isoquant $Q_4Q'_4$. Since only three processes are available, the firm cannot go to the right of process ray *OC*. It will be observed that with *OK* as limited capital at the most the firm will go upto point Q'_4 on process *C*. Thus Q'_4 will be the optimum solution with only *OK* amount of capital as the constraint.

If there were no limitations in regard to the availability of capital, while labour was available only in limited quantity, such as the amount *OL* in Figure. 22.10. Now, the vertical line *LG* representing the given labour constraint meets the ray *OA* at point Q_3. Since only three process rays are available, the firm cannot go above (*i.e.* to the right) of process ray *OA*, Thus, with *OL* as the maximum amount of labour available, the firm will use the process *A* and work at its level OQ_3.

SOME ADDITIONAL PROBLEMS AND THEIR LINEAR PROGRAMMING SOLUTIONS

We shall now explain some additional problems which are generally encountered and their linear programming solutions. First, take the case which is illustrated in Figure 22.11

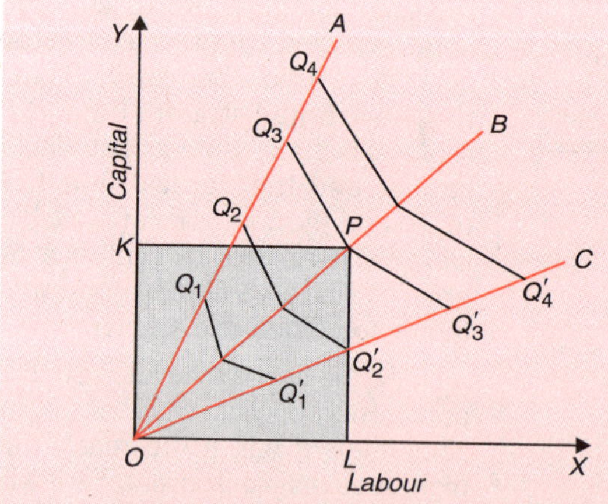

Fig. 22.11. *Full Utilization of Given Input*

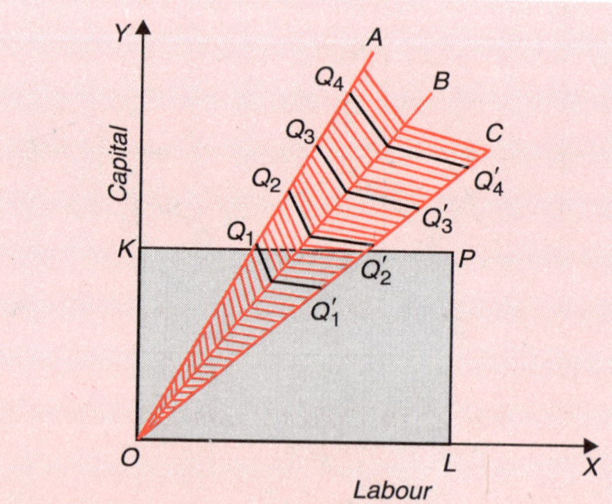

Fig. 22.12. *Labour as Slack Variable*

where three processes *A*, *B* and *C* represented by process rays *OA*, *OB* and *OC* respectively are available. Furthermore, labour and capital are available in limited quantities, *OL* and *OK* respectively. *OKPL* is thus feasible region $Q_1Q'_1$, $Q_2O'_2$, $Q_3Q'_3$, $Q_4Q'_4$, are the isoquants indicating various levels of output. It will be seen from Fig. 22.11 that in this case the upper right-hand comer of the feasible region *OKPL* happens to touch the process ray *OB* at corner point *P*. This means that optimal linear programming solution will be to use only one production process *B*; *the other two processes, A and C will not be used at all*. In equilibrium, the firm will work with the process *B* at the level *OP* and produce the amount of the product indicated by the isoquant $Q_3Q'_3$. It will also be seen that with the corner point *P* as the production point, the available quantities of both the factors, labour and capital, are being fully used.

Now, consider the problem represented in Fig.22.12. In this there are two constraints regarding the availabilities of factors, labour and capital. *OL* is the amount of labour available and *OK* is the amount of capital available. Consequently, *OKPL* is the feasible region. It will be further seen that three processes, *A, B* and *C* are available and striped region *AOC* between them represents the cone of production possibilities as permitted by the availability of three production processes. In this case which represents a rather common situation in real economic life, the upper right hand corner (*i.e.* point *P*) of the feasible region lies outside the cone of production possibilities *AOC*. *In this case, the corner point P does not represent the optimal solution of the problem.* Instead, point Q'_2, from where the feasible region passes through provides the optimal solution. It will be noticed from Figure 22.12 that in this case with O'_2 as the optimal production point labour will not be fully used. The magnitude of labour unused is equal to PO'_2. Further, in this case also only one process *C* will be employed for production.

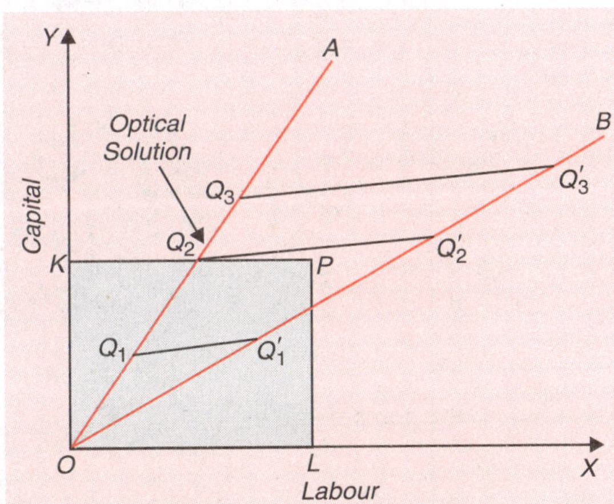

Fig. 22.13. *Inefficiency of Labor-intensive Process and Labor Surplus*

Another similar case which is commonly found is represented in Figure 22.13. Here there are two factors, labour and capital. Their available quantities yield *OKPL* as the feasible region. *A* and *B* are the two production processes represented by the process rays *OA* and *OB*. The process *A* is relatively capital-intensive and process *B* is relatively labour-intensive. The special thing about this case is that labour-intensive method is highly inefficient with the result that *isoquants*, Q_1Q_1, $Q_2Q'_2$,*etc, are positively sloping*. Because of this, for instance, on the same isoquant higher level point O_2 on the labour-intensive process ray *OB* yields the same output as the lower level point Q_2, on the relatively capital-intensive process ray *OA*. Point Q'_2 yields the same output as does point Q_2 but since point Q'_2 is above and to the right of point Q_2, it requires more of the two factors than does Q_2 to produce the same output. In this case, though the *upper right-hand corner point P of the feasible region lies within the cone of production possibilities* permitted by the available processes, yet it will be uneconomic and unprofitable to use the relatively labour-intensive process *B*.

Hence, it will pay the firm to use only more efficient process *A* and to use it to the full extent permitted by the firm's capital resources. Thus the optimal solution in this case will be point Q_2 on process ray *OA* where the shaded feasible region touches the highest possible isoquant Q_2Q_2'. It will be observed from Figure 22.13 that with optimal production at point Q_2,the available labour will not be fully used; PQ_2 amount of labour will remain unemployed.

A SPECIAL PROBLEM OF COST MINIMISATION : DIET PROBLEM

In the modern days linear programming technique has been used to solve several types of business and social problems. A social problem in which linear programming has been used to find an optimum solution relates to the problem of feeding diet to the animals. The problem of feeding optimum diet is the problem in minimizing cost of feeding various grains so that the animals are provided with minimum nutritional requirements which constitute the constraints. Various grains or foodstuffs have different prices and a pound of each grain contains different amounts of various nutrients—vitamins, minerals, calories, proteins, etc. Thus the problem is to find a least-cost combination of various grains which meet the minimum nutritional requirements.

Suppose a farmer feeds two types of grains *A* and *B* to the animals reared by him. Constraint facing him is that the animals must be fed with certain minimum amounts of three nutrients-proteins, carbohydrates and calcium. Thus in this simplified example there are two variables, each with a price, represented by grains, three constraints regarding the minimum quantities of three nutrients which must be provided. The objective function is minimisation of cost of providing the required diet to the animals.

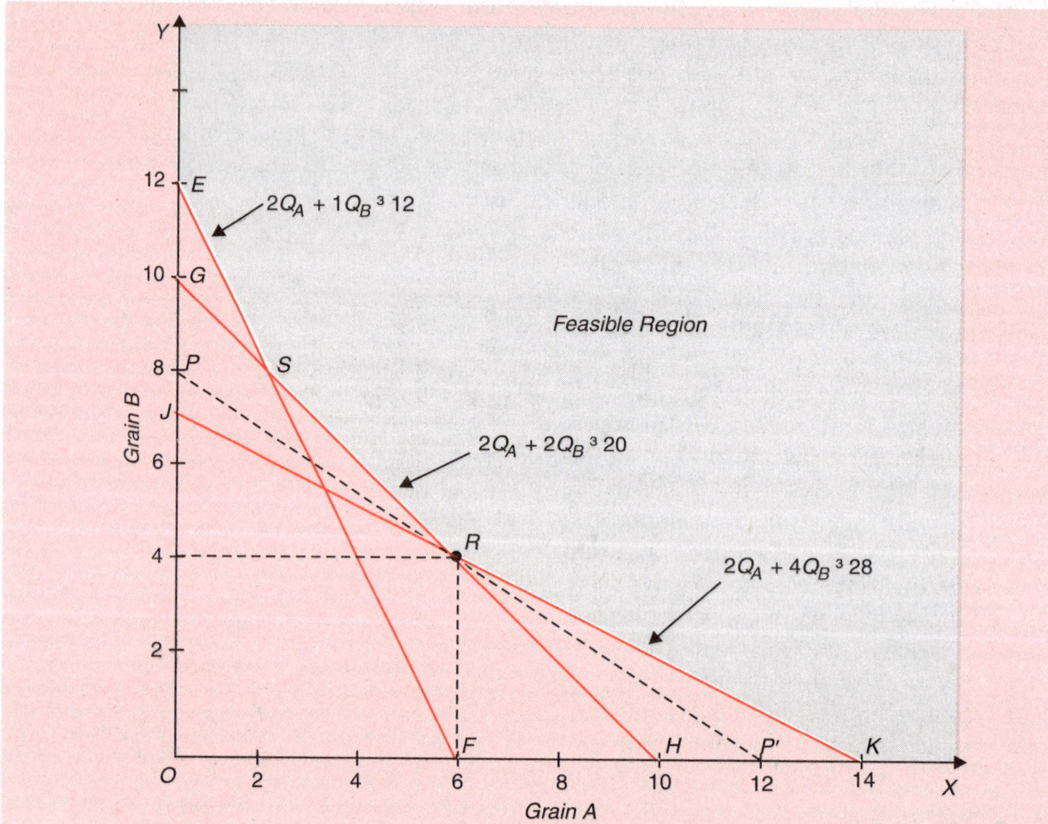

Fig. 22.14. *Solution of Diet Problem through Linear Programming*

What is the feasible region in this case and what will be the optimum solution is illustrated in Figure 22.14 where the *X*-axis measures the quantity of grain *A* and the *Y*-axis measures the quantity of grain *B*. The line *EF* represents the protein constraint ($2Q_A + 1Q_B \geq 12$) and shows the various combinations of quantities of grains *A* and *B* which meet the minimum requirements of protein. Similarly, the line *GH* represents calcium constraint ($2Q_A + 2\ Q_B \geq 20$) and shows the combinations of two grains which provide the minimum requirements of calcium and the line *JK* represents the combinations which fulfil the minimum requirements of carbohydrates. It should be noted that the steeper slope of the line *EF* shows that one pound of grain A contains relatively more amount of proteins than grain B. We write below the cost-minimizing problem of providing proper diet to the animals.

Minimise : $C = 2\,Q_A + 3Q_B$

Subject to :

$$2Q_A + 1Q_B \geq 12$$
$$2Q_A + 2Q_B \geq 20$$
$$2Q_A + 4Q_B \geq 28$$
$$Q_A, Q_B \geq 0$$

Now, we are interested in obtaining the region of feasible solutions. Since any combination of grains lying *below the lines* showing the three constraints will not meet the minimum nutritional requirement, the outer segments of the three lines which have been thickened constitute the boundary, the combinations lying on it and to the right of it will be feasible solutions. The thick line *ESRK* consisting of linear segments and shaded area to the right of it will form the region of feasible solutions and therefore any combination of it will ensure that when it is given to the animal it will provide the minimum amounts of nutrients required. But the farmer who is rearing the animals for the sake of making profits would like to minimise cost of providing the minimum required diet.

In order to find out the optimum or cost-minimizing combination of grains we need to bring in prices of two grains. An iso-cost line *PP′* with slope 2/3 has been drawn. In order to minimize cost, the farmer would try to reach the lowest possible iso-cost line. Price of grain A is ₹ 2 per unit and price of grain B is ₹ 3 per unit. Thus the cost function is given by $C = 2Q_A + 3Q_B$. The several iso-cost lines can be drawn with slope 2/3. The given cost function reveals that the slope of the iso-cost line will be 2/3 which is the ratio of price of grain A to the price of grain B. It will be noticed from the figure that the boundary of the feasible region consisting of linear segments is hitting the iso-cost line *PP′* at point R. Thus given the grain prices as indicated by the iso-cost line *PP′*, combination R occupies the lowest position in the zone of feasible solution. Therefore, combination of grains represented by point R is the optimum when the prices of grains are given by the slope of the iso-cost line *PP′*. It will be seen from the slope of the iso-cost line *PP′* that the price of grain A is relatively lower. Therefore, in the optimal solution R, the greater quantity of grain A is being fed.

An important point to note is that with iso-cost line *PP'* and optimum solution-R, if the prices of grains change somewhat so that the iso-cost line changes a little but still hits the corner R, the optimum solution will remain unchanged. In other words, the prices can change somewhat without changing the optimum solution. However, if there is a drastic change in prices, the optimum solution will change. It should be further noted that if the prices of two grains are such that the slope of the iso-cost line is identical with the line segment *SR* of the thick boundary line, then there will be *no single* optimum solution of the diet problem; either R or S or any other point between them on the line segment *SR* will be the optimum.

Algebraic Solution

The cost minimisation problem to provide minimum required neutrients to the animals which we have graphically explained above can be solved by algebraic method. For doing so we do not have to draw iso-cost lines but consider only the corner points of the feasible region and then compare the costs at the corner points. The corner point at which the total cost will be minimum will give us the optimum solution.

It will be seen from the boundary of the feasible region that we have to compare the costs at corner points E, S, R and K. At corner point E only 12 units of grain B are fed to the animal ($Q_A = 0$; $Q_B = 12$) which will cost $C = 3 \times 12 =$ ₹ 36

Now consider the corner point S which is formed by the intersection of the constraints of protein and calcium. We solve the equations of these two nutrients simultaneously

Thus

$$2Q_A + 2Q_B = 20 \quad \text{...(i)}$$
$$2Q_A + 1Q_B = 12 \quad \text{...(ii)}$$

Subtracting equation (*ii*) from equation (i), we have

$$1Q_B = 8$$

Now, substituting $Q_B = 8$ into equation (*ii*) we have

$$2Q_A + 8 = 12$$
$$Q_A = 2$$

Now we can calculate the cost of combination S of two grains, $Q_A = 2$, $Q_B = 8$

Thus, the cost at corner point $S = 2 \times (2) + 3\ (8) = 4 + 24 = 28$

Now we consider corner point R which is formed by the intersection of constraints of calcium ($2Q_A + 2Q_B \geq 20$) and of carbohydrates ($2Q_A + 4Q_B \geq 28$). In order to find the quantities of two grains A and B at the corner point R, we solve these two constraint equations. Thus

$$2Q_A + 4Q_B = 28 \quad \text{...(a)}$$
$$2Q_A + 2Q_B = 20 \quad \text{...(b)}$$

Subtracting equation (*b*) from equation (*a*) we have

$$2Q_B = 8$$
$$Q_B = \frac{8}{2} = 4$$

Substituting the value $Q_B = 4$ in equation (*b*) above we have

$$2Q_A + 2 \times 4 = 20$$
$$2Q_A = 20 - 8 = 12$$
$$Q_A = 6$$

The cost of combination of two grains at corner point R is $C = 2 \times (6) + 3\ (4) =$ **24**

Now consider corner point of the boundary. K containing only 14 units of grain A and zero grain B. Thus cost of grains at corner point K is $C = 2 \times 14 =$ **28**

It is evident from above that given the cost-function and the constraints, the corner point R where the quantity of grain A is 6 units and the quantity of grain B is 4 units which provides the optimal solution where the cost is minimum.

QUESTIONS FOR REVIEW

1. Explain the linear programming technique to solve the problems of constrained optimisation. Why is the assumption of linearity important in linear programming?
2. Explain the following concepts as used in linear programming technique.
   1. Objective function
   2. Feasible region
   3. Constraints

Write some objective functions and give some examples of different forms of feasible region

3. State the three broad types of problems for which linear programming is used and solve them. A firm is producing two products *A* and *B* and face constraints in the form of limited quantities of two inputs *X* and *Y* which are available for use in the production of two commodities. Explain the linear programming techniques in general to solve the profit maximization problem given the constraints in the form of limited availabilities of two inputs.

4. Explain the primal and dual problems in the theory of linear programming technique. Is optimum solution of the dual problem the same as of the primal problem? Explain.

5. Why does optimum solution in linear programming always lie at the corner of the feasible region? When do we get multiple optimal solutions in the linear programming. Show graphically

6. A firm uses two machines *A* and *B* to produce two products *X* and *Y*. Each unit of product *X* requires two hours of time on both machines. Each unit of product *Y* requires three hours of time on machine A and one hour on machine *B*. The profit contribution of product X is ₹ 6 per unit and of product *Y* is ₹ 7 per unit.

Assuming that the objective is to maximise profits, how many units of product X and Y should be produced. Formulate this problem as linear programming problem and solve graphically and by algebraic method.

7. You are given the following linear programming problem.

Maximise : $\pi = 2Q_A + 5Q_B$

Subject to

$$1Q_A + 3Q_B \leq 16$$

$$4Q_A + 1Q_B \leq 20$$

$$1Q_B \leq 4$$

$$Q_A, Q_B \geq 0$$

π stands for profits, Q_A and Q_B are the quantities of two products. 16, 20, 4 are the quantities of three inputs available for use in production.

Solve the above problem graphically.

8. A manager of a milk producing firm has to decide how much of two feeds *A* and *B* be given to milch cattle to minimize cost. The minimum requirement of adequate feed intake of a milch cattle consists of 40 units of protein, 60 units of calcium and 60 units of carbohydrates. It is given that price of feed *A* is ₹ 100 per ton and price of feed *B* is ₹ 200 per ton.

Find the quantities of two feeds to be purchased for feeding milk cows that minimizes cost subject to the minimum nutritional requirements of feed intake. Formulate the above problem as linear programming problem and solve both by graphic and algebraic methods.

CHAPTER

23

Supply and its Elasticity

The Meaning of Supply

As demand is defined as a schedule of the quantities of good that will be purchased at various prices, similarly the supply refers to the schedule of the quantities of a good that the firms are able and willing to offer for sale at various prices. How much of a commodity the firms are able to produce depends on the resources available to them and the technology they employ for producing a commodity. How much of a commodity the firms will be willing to offer for sale depends on the profits they expect to make on producing and selling the commodity. Profits in turn depends on the price of the commodity on the one hand and unit cost of production on the other.

Supply should be distinguished from the *quantity supplied*. Whereas supply of a commodity is the entire schedule of the quantities of a commodity that would be offered for sale at all possible prices during a period of time, for example, a day, a week, a month and so on, the quantity supplied refers to the quantity of a commodity which the firms are able and willing to sell at a *particular price* of the commodity. Thus the term 'supply' refers to the entire relationship between the price of a commodity and the quantity supplied at various possible prices and is illustrated by the entire supply curve or supply schedule as given in Figure 23.1 and Table 23.1, where the term 'quantity supplied' refers to a *point* on a given supply curve, that is, quantity supplied at a particular price.

Two things are worth mentioning about the concept of supply. First, supply is a *flow concept*, that is, it refers to the amount of a commodity that the firms produce and offer for sale in the market *per period of time*, say a week, a month or a year. Without specifying the time period, supply of a commodity has a little meaning. Second, the quantity supplied at a commodity which the producers plan to produce and sell at a price is not necessarily the same as the *quantity actually sold*. Sometimes, the quantity which the firms are willing to produce and sell at a price is greater than the quantity demanded, so the quantity actually bought and sold is less than the quantity supplied.

Supply Function

The quantity of a commodity that firms will be able and willing to offer for sale in the market depends on several factors. The important factors determining supply of a commodity are :

1. The price of the commodity
2. The prices of inputs (*i.e.*, resources) used for the production of the commodity
3. The state of technology
4. The number of firms producing and selling the commodity

5. The prices of related goods produced.
6. Future expectations regarding prices.

We will explain these factors determining supply of a commodity in detail in a later section. However, it may be noted that out of the above determinants of supply the own price of the commodity, the prices of inputs (*i.e.*, resources) used to produce the commodity, and the technology used in production are three important factors and therefore the supply function of a commodity is often written taking these factors as independent variables. *Thus, supply function of a commodity is written as*

$$Q_x^s = S\,(P_x, F_1, F_2 \,\ldots\ldots\ldots\ldots\, F_m)$$

where $Q^s{}_x$ is the quantity supplied of the commodity X, P_x is it own price, $F_1, F_2,\ldots F_m$ are the prices of inputs used to produce the commodity X. The state of technology determines the form of supply function S. It must be noted that the form of the function refers to the precise quantitative relation between the independent variables such as the own price of the commodity P_x and prices of factors such as, F_1, F_2 etc.

The Relation between Price and Quantity Supplied : Law of Supply

Supply of a commodity is functionally related to its price. The law of supply relates to this functional relationship between price of a commodity and its quantity supplied. In contrast to the inverse relationship between the quantity demanded and the changes in price, ***the quantity supplied of a commodity generally varies directly with price.*** That is, the higher the price, the larger is the quantity supplied of a commodity.

The supply schedule and the upward-sloping supply cruve reflect the law of supply. According to the law of supply, *when the price of a commodity rises, the quantity supplied of it in the market increases, and when the price of the commodity falls, its quantity supplied decreases, other factors determining supply remaining the same*. Thus, according to the law of supply, the quantity supplied of a commodity is directly or positively related to price. It is due to this positive relationship between price of a commodity and its quantity supplied that the supply curve of a commodity slopes upward to right as seen from supply curve *SS* in Figure. 23.1. When price of wheat rises from ₹ 520 to ₹ 530 per quintal, the quantity supplied of wheat in the market increases from 200 quintals to 225 quintals per period.

Table 23.1. Supply Schedule of Wheat

Price Per Quantity (₹)	*Quantity Supplied (in quintals)*
500	100
510	150
520	200
530	225
540	250
550	275

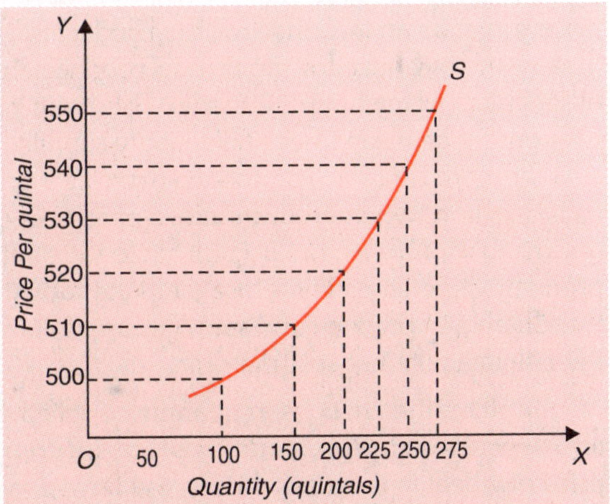

Fig. 23.1. *Supply Curve Showing Direct Relationship Between Price and Quantity Supplied*

Similar to the demand schedule we can construct an individual's supply schedule. Also by totalling up the quantity supplied at various prices by all the sellers in a market, we can obtain the supply schedule of the market. Supply schedule represents the relation between prices and the quantities that the firms are able and willing to produce and sell at various prices. We have given in Table 23.1 a supply schedule of wheat per day in a market.

It will be seen from the above table that when price of wheat is ₹ 500 per quintal, the 100 quintals of wheat are supplied in the market. When price of wheat rises to ₹ 510 per quintal, 150 quintals of wheat are supplied. When price of wheat goes up to ₹ 550 per quintals, its quantity supplied in the market rises to 275 quintal. By plotting the above supply schedule of wheat on a graph paper we have obtained supply curve *SS* in Fig. 23.1. In Fig. 23.1, the quantity supplied has been measured along the *X*-axis and price of wheat has been measured along the *Y*-axis. It will be seen from this figure that supply curve slopes upward from left to right, which indicates that as price of wheat rises, quantity supplied increases and vice versa. This is in a sharp contrast to the demand curve of a commodity which slopes downward from left to right.

Explanation of the Law of Supply: Why does Supply Curve Generally Slope Upward ?

It has been observed that price of a product and quantity supplied of it by firms producing it are positively related to each other, that is, at a higher price more is supplied and vice versa, other things remaining the same. In analyzing the relation between price of a commodity and the quantity supplied, given *ceteris parilbus* assumption, we are in fact dealing with the supply function, $Q^s_x = f(P_x)$. This positive relationship between price and quantity supplied is an important law of economics. How do we explain it? It should be remembered that firms are driven by profit motive. The higher price of a product, given the cost per unit of output, makes it profitable to expand output and offer more quantity of the product for sale. Thus, higher price serves as an incentive for the producer to produce more of it. The higher the price, the greater the incentive for the firm to produce and supply more of a commodity in the market, other things remaining the same. The basic reason behind the law of supply (*i.e.,* positive relationship between price and quantity supplied) is the way cost changes as output is expanded to offer more for sale. To produce more of a product, firms have to devote more resources to its production. When production of a product is expanded by using more resources, diminishing returns to variable factors occur. Due to the diminishing returns, average and marginal costs of production increase. Therefore, at higher additional cost of producing more units of output; it is profitable to produce and supply more units of output *only at a higher price* so as to cover the rise in additional cost per unit.

Further, the changes in quantity supplied of a product following the changes in its price also depends on the *possibilities of substitution of one product for an other.* For example, if price of wheat in the market rises, the farmers will alter the cropping pattern so as to produce more of wheat by withdrawing land and other resources from the cultivation of gram and devoting them to the production of wheat. This is because high market price for wheat relative to gram induces farmers, who aim at maximizing profits, to use more resources for production of wheat and fewer resources for the production of gram.

Shifts in Supply : Increase and Decrease in Supply

As stated above, the supply of a commodity in economics means the entire schedule or curve depicting the relationship between price and quantity supplied of the commodity, given the other factors influencing supply. These other factors are the state of technology, prices of inputs (resources), prices of other related commodities, etc., which are assumed constant when the relationship between price and quantity supplied of a commodity is examined. It is the change in these factors other than price that cause a shift in the supply curve. For example, when prices of inputs such as labour and raw materials used for the production of a commodity decline, this will result in lowering the cost of production which will induce the producers to produce and make available a greater quantity of the commodity in the market at each price. This increases in supply of a commodity due to the reduction in prices of inputs will cause the

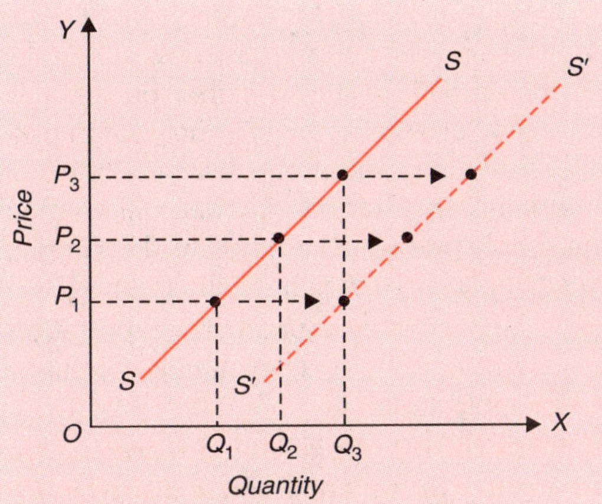

Fig. 23.2. *Increase in Supply Causing a Rightward Shift in the Supply Curve*

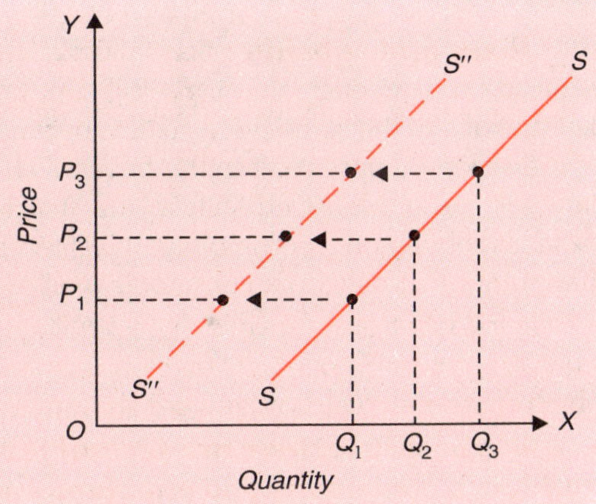

Fig. 23.3. *Decrease in Supply Causing a Leftward Shift in the Supply Curve*

entire supply curve to shift to the right as shown in Figure 23.2 where the supply curve shifts from SS to $S'S'$. As shown by arrow marks, at price P_1, P_2 and P_3 quantity supplied increases when supply increases causing a rightward shift in the supply curve. Similarly, progress in technology used for production of a commodity which increases productivity and reduces cost per unit will also cause the supply curve to shift to the right.

On the other hand, ***decrease in supply means the reduction in quantity supplied at each price of the commodity*** as shown in Figure 23.3 where as a result of decrease in supply the supply curve shifts to the left from SS to $S''S''$. As shown by the arrow marks, at each price such as P_1, P_2, P_3, the quantity supplied on the supply curve $S''S''$ has declined as compared to the supply curve SS. The decrease in supply occurs when the rise in prices of factors (inputs) used for the production of a commodity produced leads to higher cost per unit of output which causes a reduction in quantity supplied at each price. Similarly, the imposition of an excise duty or sales tax on a commodity means that each quantity will now be supplied at a higher price than before so as to cover the excise duty or sales tax per unit. This implies that quantity supplied of the commodity at each price will decrease as shown by the shift of the supply curve to the left.

Another important factor causing a decrease in supply of a commodity is the *rise in prices of other commodities* using the same factors. For example, if the price of wheat rises sharply, it will become more profitable for the farmers to grow it. This will induce the farmers to reduce the cultivated area under other crops, say pulses, and devote it to the production of wheat. This will lead to the decrease in supply of pulses whose supply curve will shift to the left.

Further, agricultural production in India greatly depends on the rainfall due to monsoons. If monsoon come in time and rainfall is adequate, there are bumper crops, the supply of agricultural products increases. However, in a year when monsoons are untimely or highly inadequate, there is a sharp drop in agricultural output which causes a shift in the supply curve of agricultural output to the left.

The supply of a commodity in the market at any time is also determined by ***sellers' expectations of future prices.*** If, as happens during inflationary periods, sellers expect the prices to rise in future, they would reduce current supply of a product in the market and would instead hoard the commodity. The hoarding of huge quantities of goods by traders is an important factor in reducing their supplies in the market and thus causing further rise in their prices.

Taxes and subsidies also influence the supply of a product. If an excise duty or sales tax is levied on a product, the firms will supply the same amount of it at a higher price or less quantity of it at the same price. This is because excise duty on a commodity is included in price by the sellers to pass it on to the buyers. This implies that imposition of a sales tax or excise duty will cause a leftward shift in the supply curve. On the other hand, when government provides subsidy on a commodity, it will reduce the supply price of a commodity. This implies that grant of subsidy on a commodity will cause the supply curve to shift to the right.

It follows from above that technology, prices of factors and products, expectations regarding future prices and taxes and subsidies are the important determinants of supply which cause rightward or leftward shift in the whole supply curve.

We thus see that ***there are several factors other than price which determine the supply of a commodity and any change in these other factors will cause a shift in the entire supply curve.***

ELASTICITY OF SUPPLY

The concept of elasticity of supply, like the elasticity of demand, occupies an important place in price theory. The elasticity of supply is the degree of responsiveness of supply to changes in price of a good. More precisely, the *elasticity of supply can be defined as a percentage change in quantity supplied of a good in response to a given percentage change in price of the good*. Therefore :

In terms of symbols, we can write :

$$e_s = \frac{\Delta q}{q} \div \frac{\Delta p}{p} = \frac{\Delta q}{q} \times \frac{p}{\Delta p} = \frac{\Delta q}{\Delta p} \times \frac{p}{q}$$

For an accurate measure of elasticity of supply *midpoint method*, as explained in case of elasticity of demand, should be used. Using midpoint formula, elasticity of supply can be measured as

$$e_s = \frac{q_2 - q_1}{\frac{q_1 + q_2}{2}} \div \frac{p_2 - p_1}{\frac{p_1 + p_2}{2}},$$

where $q_2 - q_1 = \Delta q$ and $P_2 - P_1 = \Delta P$

Therefore, $$e_s = \frac{\Delta q}{q_1 + q_2} \times \frac{p_1 + p_2}{\Delta P} = \frac{\Delta q}{\Delta P} \times \frac{p_1 + p_2}{q_1 + q_2}$$

The elasticity of supply depends upon the ease with which the output of an industry can be expanded and the change in marginal cost of production. Since there is greater scope for increase in output in the long run than in the short run, the supply of a good is more elastic in the long run than in the short run.

Measurement of Elasticity of Supply at a Point on the Supply Curve

The elasticity of supply at a point on the supply curve can be easily measured by a formula. We shall derive this formula below.

In Fig. 23.4 supply curve *SS* is given and elasticity of supply at point *A* is required to be measured. At price *OP*, the quantity supplied is *OQ*. With the rise in price from *OP* to *OP'*, the quantity supplied increases from *OQ* to *OQ'*. Extending supply curve *SS* downward so that it meets *X*-axis at point *T*.

Then, elasticity of supply at point $A = \frac{\Delta q}{q} \div \frac{\Delta p}{p} = \frac{\Delta q}{\Delta p} \times \frac{p}{q}$

A glance at Figure 23.4 reveals that $\Delta q = QQ'$, $\Delta p = PP'$. Therefore, writing QQ' for Δq, PP' for Δp, we have elasticity of supply equal to

$$e_s = \frac{\Delta q}{\Delta p} \cdot \frac{p}{q} = \frac{QQ'}{PP'} \times \frac{OP}{OQ}$$

It will be further seen from Figure 23.4 that $QQ' = AC$, $PP' = BC$ and $OP = QA$. Therefore, substituting *AC* for *QQ'*, *BC* for *PP'* and *QA* for *OP* we have

$$e_s \text{ at point } A = \frac{\Delta q}{\Delta p} \cdot \frac{p}{q} = \frac{QQ'}{PP'} \times \frac{OP}{OQ} = \frac{AC}{BC} \cdot \frac{QA}{OQ} \quad ..(i)$$

Now, in triangles *ACB* and *TQA*

$\angle ACB = \angle TQA$ (rt. angles)

$\angle BAC = \angle ATQ$ (corresponding angles)

$\angle ABC = \angle TAQ$ (corresponding angles)

Therefore, triangles *ABC* and *TAQ* are similar.

Hence, $\frac{AC}{BC} = \frac{TQ}{QA}$

Substituting $\frac{TQ}{QA}$ for $\frac{AC}{BC}$ in (*i*) above, we have

$$e_s \text{ at } A = \frac{TQ}{QA} \cdot \frac{QA}{OQ}$$

$$= \frac{TQ}{OQ}$$

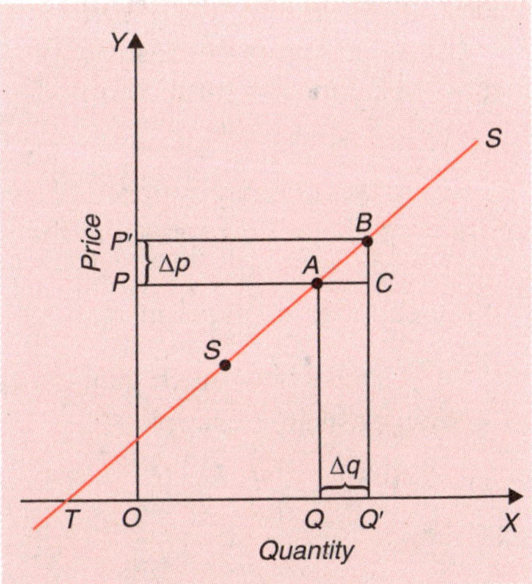

Fig. 23.4. *Measurement of elasticity of supply at a point on a linear supply curve*

Thus, we can measure the value of elasticity of supply from dividing *TQ* by *OQ*. Since in Fig. 23.4, *TQ* is greater than *OQ*, supply elasticity $\frac{TQ}{OQ}$ will be greater than one.

In Fig. 23.5 supply curve when extended meets the *X*-axis to the right of the point of origin so that *TQ* is smaller than *OQ*. Therefore, in Fig. 23.5 the elasticity of supply at point A, which is equal to $\frac{TQ}{OQ}$ is less than unity. In Fig. 23.6 supply curve *SS* when extended meets

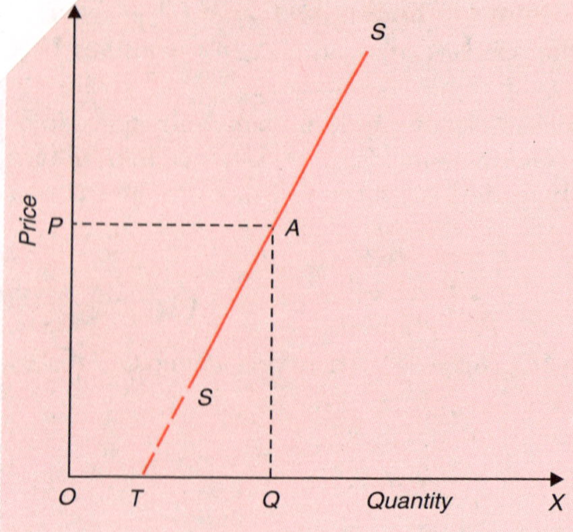

Fig. 23.5. $e_s < 1$

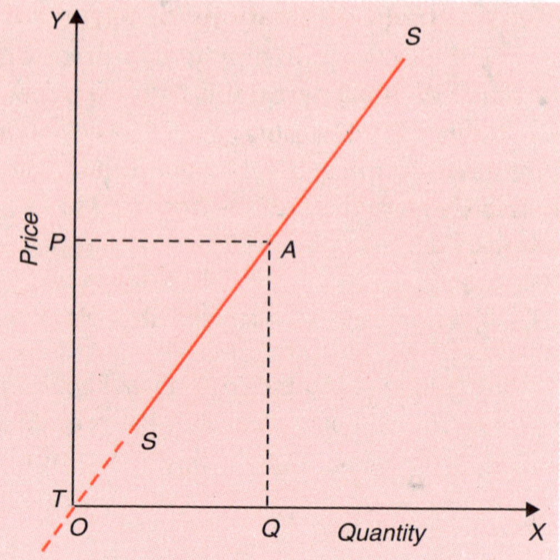

Fig. 23.6. $e_s = 1$

the X-axis exactly at the point of origin so that TQ is equal to OQ. Therefore, in Fig. 23.6 elasticity of supply at point A will be equal to one.

Supply Function and Elasticity of Supply

Let us explain price elasticity of supply using the supply function for a commodity. The linear supply function for a commodity is of the following form :

$$Q = c + dP$$

where Q is quantity supplied of a commodity, P is its price and c and d are constants. The constant coefficient d represents the slope of the supply function and indicates how much quantity supplied changes in response to a change in price. That is, $d = \frac{\Delta Q}{\Delta P}$. Since d is positive, it shows how much quantity supplied of a commodity increases as its price rises.

Now, elasticity of supply is

$$e_s = \frac{\Delta Q}{\Delta P} \cdot \frac{P}{Q}$$

Substituting d for $\frac{\Delta Q}{\Delta P}$ we have $e_s = d\frac{P}{Q}$

We take the following specific supply function to estimate elasticity of supply.

$$Q = 90 + 15P$$

It is required to estimate elasticity of supply at price ₹ 20 per unit of the commodity from the above supply function. In the above supply function, 90 is the constant intercept term c and 15 measures slope of the function (d) and is equal to $\frac{\Delta Q}{\Delta P}$.

In order to obtain elasticity of supply at price of ₹ 20, we first find out the quantity supplied at this price. Therefore, substituting 20 for P in the supply function we get

$$Q = 90 + 15 \times 20 = 390$$

Now, as shown above, elasticity of supply is

$$e_s = b\frac{P}{Q} = 15 \times \frac{20}{390} = \frac{20}{26} = 0.77$$

This means 1 per cent rise in price will lead to 0.77 per cent increase in quantity supplied.

Elasticity along the Supply Curve

We have explained above the measurement of point elasticity of supply on a supply curve. The elasticity of supply may vary along a supply curve. The supply function of a linear supply curve is

$$Q = c + dP$$

As explained above, the constant d measures $\frac{\Delta Q}{\Delta P}$ and elasticity of supply is $\frac{\Delta Q}{\Delta P} \times \frac{P}{Q}$.

Since d or $\frac{\Delta Q}{\Delta P}$, which measures *inverse* of the slope of the supply curve, remains constant along a linear supply curve, elasticity of supply will vary with the change in $\frac{P}{Q}$. As the ratio $\frac{P}{Q}$ along a linear supply curve rises, the supply elasticity rises. Let us take the linear supply curve *SS* in Fig. 23.7. which starts from the Y-axis above the point of origin. As we move from point

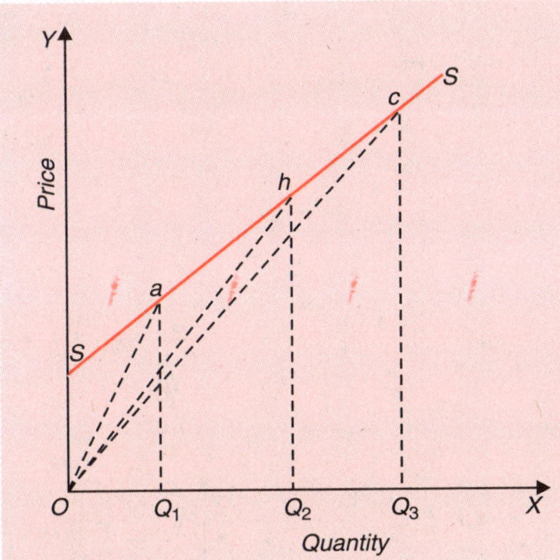

Fig. 23.7. Elasticity of supply along a linear supply curve is falling

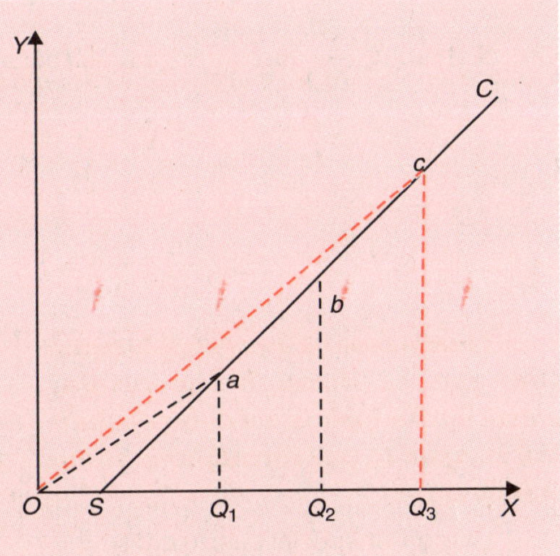

Fig. 23.8. Elasticity of supply rises along a linear supply curve

a to *b* and to *c*, slope of the supply curve falls. Slope of the supply curve *SS* at points *a*, *b* and *c* is given by the slopes of the rays drawn from the origin to these points. It will be seen that in this case (Fig. 23.7) slope of rays $\left(\frac{P}{Q}\right)$ falls as we move upward on it. With constant $\frac{\Delta P}{\Delta P}$ on a linear supply curve, the fall in the ratio $\frac{P}{Q}$ implies that the elasticity of supply will be falling along it though it will remain greater than one.

Now take the case of linear supply curve drawn in Fig. 23.8 which starts from the X-axis to the right of point of origin. In this case, slope of rays which measures the ratio of $\frac{P}{Q}$ is *rising* as we move upward along it. With constant $\frac{\Delta Q}{\Delta P}$, the rise in the ratio $\frac{P}{Q}$ implies that *supply elasticity will be rising* in this case though it will remain less than one.

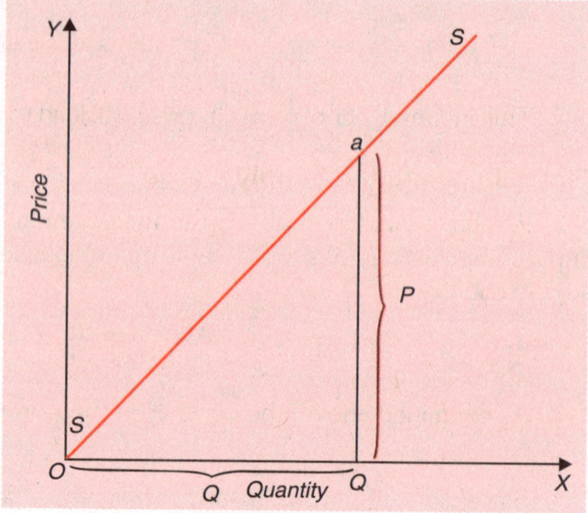

Fig. 23.9. Constant Elasticity of Supply Equal to Unity

Now, a special case of linear supply curve is when it passes through the origin as shown in Fig. 23.9. In this case, not only *inverse* of the slope, $\frac{\Delta Q}{\Delta P}$ is constant but ratio $\frac{P}{Q}$ is also constant and is *equal to the slope of the supply curve itself*, that is, $\frac{\Delta P}{\Delta Q}$.

On substituting $\frac{\Delta P}{\Delta Q}$ for $\frac{P}{Q}$ in the elasticity formula we have

$$e_s = \frac{\Delta Q}{\Delta P} \cdot \frac{P}{Q}$$

$$= \frac{\Delta Q}{\Delta P} \cdot \frac{\Delta P}{\Delta Q} = 1$$

Thus in case of linear supply curve that passes through the origin, elasticity of supply is not only constant but is equal to one throughout along supply curve.

Two other special cases where the supply elasticity remains constant are (*i*) *a vertical straight-line supply curve along which supply* ***elasticity*** is equal to zero throughtout.

(2) *a horizontal straight-line* supply curve along which supply elasticity remains equal to infinity throughtout.

Now we explain how supply elasticity varies along a non-linear supply curve. Consider Fig. 23.10 where a non-linear supply curve has been drawn and

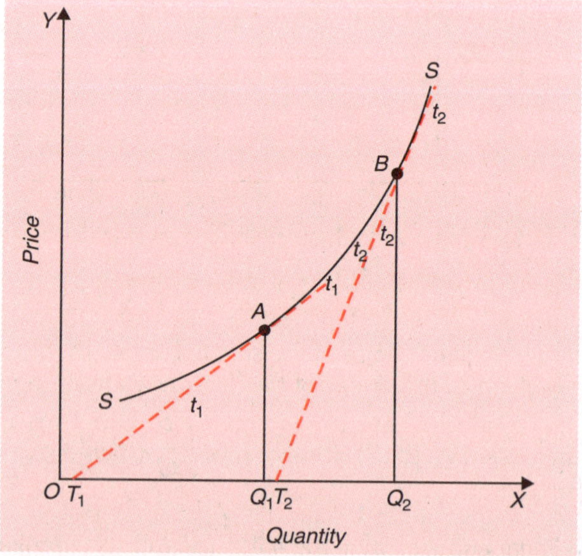

Fig. 23.10. Varying Price Elasticity at Different Points on a Non-Linear Supply Curve

it is required to measure eleasticity at point A on it. The general principle involved is the same as derived above. In order to apply the above principle for estimating the point elasticity at point A on the supply curve SS, we have to draw a tangent to it. Now, a tangent t_1t_1 has been drawn at point A. On being extended, tangent t_1t_1 meets the X-axis at point T_1. Therefore, elasticity of supply at point A on the supply curve is $\frac{T_1Q_1}{OQ_1}$.

Likewise, we can find out the elasticity of supply at point B on the supply curve. For estimating the supply elasticity the tangent t_2t_2 has been drawn at point B and has been extended to meet the X-axis at point T_2. Thus, the elasticity at point B on the supply *curve SS* is equal to $\frac{T_2Q_2}{OQ_2}$. It is also evident from Figure 23.7 that elasticity of supply at point A and B is different. Since $\frac{T_2Q_2}{OQ_2}$ is less than $\frac{T_1Q_1}{OQ_1}$, the price elasticity of supply at point B is less than that at A.

FACTORS DETERMINING ELASTICITY OF SUPPLY

Elasticity of supply plays an important role in determining prices of products. To what extent price of a product will rise following the increase in demand for it depends on the elasticity of supply. The greater the elasticity of supply of a product, the less the rise in its price when demand for it increases. We explain below the factors which determine elasticity of supply of a product.

Changes in Marginal Cost of Production. Elasticity of supply of a commodity depends upon the ease with which increases in output can be obtained without bringing about rise in cost of production. If with the increase in production, the marginal cost of production goes up the elasticity of supply to that extent would be less. In the short run, with some factors of production being fixed, the increase in the amount of a variable factor eventually causes diminishing marginal returns and as a result with the expansion of output marginal cost of production rises. This causes supply of a commodity in the short run less elastic. However, in the long run, the firms can increase output by varying all factors and also the new firms can enter the industry and thereby add to the supply of a commodity. Therefore, the long run supply curve of a commodity is more elastic than that of the short run.

In the increasing-cost industry, that is, the industry which experiences increases in cost when industry expands through the entry of new firms, the long-run supply curve, like the short-run one, is upward sloping, but will be more elastic than that of the short-run. In the constant-cost industry, *i.e.*, the industry wherein costs do not change with the expansion of the industry as a whole, the longrun supply curve is perfectly elastic, because in this case increases in the industrial output can be obtained at the same cost of production. In the decreasing-cost industry, that is, industry which is subject to increasing returns, long-run supply curve is downward sloping and has therefore a negative elasticity of supply. This is because in the case of decreasing-cost industry, expansion in the industry brings down the cost of production and therefore additional output is forthcoming at a lower supply price.

Response of the Producers. Besides the change in cost of production, the elasticity of supply for a product depends on the responsiveness of producers to changes in its price. If the producers do not respond positively to the increase in prices, the quantity supplied of a product would not increase as a result of rise in its price. A profit-maximizing producer will increase the quantity supplied of a product following the rise in its price. However, producers who not always exhibit profit-maximizing behaviour may not raise supply in response to the rise in price. For example, it has been argued by some with some empirical evidences that farmers in developing countries respond negatively to the rise in prices of their agricultural products. They point out that with the higher agricultural prices, their need for fixed money income is met by selling smaller quantities of foodgrains and therefore at higher prices they may produce and sell smaller quantities rather than more. However, recent evidence does not indicate this negative response of farmers in the developing countries.

Availability of Inputs for Expanding Output. The extent to which the producers would raise supply of their products also depends on the availability of inputs required for the production of goods. If inputs used in the production of a commodity are easily available at going market prices, then output of the commodity can be easily expanded with little rise in price. This would show price elasticity of supply is relatively large. On the other hand, if production capacity for producing a product is limited or infrastructure facilities for expanding output of a commodity are not adequately available, then even sharp increase in price of the product will cause only a small expansion in output. This indicates relatively inelastic supply. For example, when there is lack of fertilizers and irrigation facilities, the farmers would not be able to raise the supplies of agricultural products in response to the rise in their prices even if they want to do so. Likewise, in the industrial field if there is shortage of power, fuel, essential raw materials, the expansion in supply would not be forthcoming in response to the rise in prices of industrial products.

Possibilities of Substitution of one Product for the Others. The change in quantity supplied of a product following the change in its price also depends on the possibilities of substitution of one product for others. For example, if market price of wheat rises, the farmers will try to shift resources such as land, labour, fertilizers away from other products such as pulses to devote them to the production of wheat. The greater the extent of possibilities of shifting of resources from the other products to the production of a given product, the greater the elasticity of supply of wheat.

The Length of Time. The elasticity of supply of a product also depends on the length of time during which producers have to respond to a given change in price of a product. Generally, the longer the time producers get to make adjustments for changing the level of output in response to the change in price, the greater the response of output, that is, the greater the elasticity of supply. In the immediate and short period following a rise in price of a commodity, it may not be possible for the firms to increase the inputs of labour (especially skilled labour), materials and capital and therefore the supply may be price inelastic. However, over a long period the firm can hire more labour, build new capacity to expand output. This means long-run supply is price elastic. From the viewpoint of the influence of the length of time on the elasticity of supply we distinguish between three time periods : (1) market-period or very short-run, (2) short run and (3) long run. The market period is a very short period and during this no more production is possible. Therefore, market-period supply curve is a vertical straight line (*i.e.*, perfectly inelastic). In the short run, firms can change output by changing the amounts of only variable factors, short run supply curve is somewhat elastic. In the long-run since firms can adjust all factors of production and also new firms can enter or leave the industry, long-run supply curve is more elastic.

PART–IV

PRICE AND OUTPUT DETERMINATION IN VARIOUS MARKET STRUCTURES

- Market Structures and Concepts of Revenue for a Firm
- Firm: A General Analysis of its Nature, Objectives and Equilibrium
- Pricing in Competitive Markets: Demand-Supply Analysis
- Applications of Demand and Supply Analysis
- Equilibrium of the Firm and Industry Under Perfect Competition
- Comparative Static Analysis of Equilibrium and Long-Run Supply Curve of the Competitive Industry
- Existence and Stability of Equilibrium under Perfect Competition
- Kaldor and Sraffa on Incompatibility of Equilibrium with Perfect Competition
- Price and Output Determination under Monopoly
- Price Discrimination
- Measurement of the Degree of Monopoly Power
- Price and Output under Bilateral Monopoly
- Price and Output Determination under Monopolistic Competition
- A Critique of Chamberlin's Theory of Monopolistic Competition
- A Critical Evaluation of Excess Capacity of Doctrine Monopolistic Competition Theory
- Chamberlin's Monopolistic Competition vs. Joan Robinson's Imperfect Competition Theories
- Price and Output Determination under Oligopoly
- Classical Models of Oligopoly
- Non-Price Competition: Selling Cost and Advertising
- Cost-Plus (or Mark-up) Pricing Theory
- Theory of Games and Strategic Behaviour
- Sales Maximisation Model of Oligopoly Firm
- Managerial Theories of the Firm: Marris and Williamson's Models
- Behavioural Theory of the Firm: Satisficing Model
- Theory of Limit Pricing
- Government Policies Towards Monopoly and Competition

CHAPTER

24

Market Structures and Concepts of Revenue for a Firm

The determination of prices and outputs of various products depends upon the type of market structure in which they are produced, sold and purchased. In this connection, economists have classified the various markets prevailing in a capitalist economy into (*a*) perfect competition or pure competition, (*b*) monopolistic competition, (*c*) oligopoly and (*d*) monopoly. Three market forms, monopolistic competition, oligopoly and monopoly, are generally grouped under the general heading of imperfect competition, since these three forms of market differ with respect to the degree of imperfection in the market. Monopolistic competition is slighly imperfect and monopoly is the most imperfect form of market structure.

But before explaining the salient features of various market forms, it will be useful to explain what is meant by market in economics.

Meaning of Market

Market is generally understood to mean a particular place or locality where goods are sold and purchased. However, in economics, by the term 'market' we do not mean any particular place or locality in which goods are bought and sold. The idea of a particular locality or geographical place is not necessary to the concept of the market. What is required for the market to exist is the contact between the sellers and buyers so that transaction (*i.e.*, sale and purchase of a commodity) at an agreed price can take place between them. The buyers and sellers may be spread over a whole town, region or a country but if they are in close communication with each other either through personal contact, exchange of letters, telegrams, telephones, etc. so that they can sell and buy a good at an agreed price, the market would be said to exist. Further, it is noteworthy that because in a market, there is close and free communication between various buyers and sellers, price of a homogeneous commodity settled between different sellers and buyers tends to be the same. Thus, in the words of Cournot, a French economist, ***"Economists understand by the term market not any particular market place in which things are bought and sold but the whole of any region in which buyers and sellers are in such free intercourse with one another that the price of the same good tends to equality easily and quickly".***

Thus, the essentials of a market are: (*a*) commodity which is dealt with, (*b*) the existence of buyers and sellers, (*c*) a place, be it a certain region, a country or the entire world, and (*d*) such communication between buyers and sellers that only one price should prevail for the same commodity at the same time.

CLASSIFICATION OF MARKET STRUCTURES

The popular basis of classifying market structures rests on three crucial elements, (1) the number of firms producing a product, (2) the nature of product produced by the firms, that is, whether it is homogeneous or differentiated, and (3) the ease with which new firms can enter the industry. The price elasticity of demand for a firm's product depends upon the number of competitive firms producing the same or similar product as well as on the degree of substitution which is possible between the product of a firm and other products produced by rival firms. Therefore, a distinguishing feature of different market categories is the degree of price elasticity of demand faced by an individual firm.

We present in the table given below the classification of market forms based on the number of firms, the nature of product produced by them and price elasticity of demand.

1. Perfect Competition. As is evident from Table 18.1 perfect competition is said to prevail when there is a large number of producers (firms) producing a homogeneous product. The maximum output which an individual firm can produce is very small relatively to the total demand of the industry's product so that a firm cannot affect the price by varying its supply of output.

There are following four important features of perfect competition :

1. There is a large number of firms (producers and sellers) and buyers of a product,
2. Products of all firms are homogeneous,
3. There is freedom of new firms to enter the industry and old ones to leave it,
4. All firms and buyers have perfect information about the prevailing market price of the product.

With many firms and homogenous product under perfect competition, no individual firm in it is in a position to influence the price of the product and therefore the demand curve facing it will be a horizontal straight line at the level of prevailing price of the product in the market, that is, price elasticity of demand for a single firm will be infinite. Mrs. Joan Robinson writes: "Perfect competition prevails when the demand for the output of each producer is perfectly elastic. This entails, first, that the number of sellers is large so that the output of any one seller is negligibly small proportion of the total output of the commodity, the second, that the products of various sellers are homogeneous from the viewpoint of consumers[1].

2. Imperfect Competition. Imperfect competition is an important market category wherein individual firms exercise control over the price to a smaller or larger degree depending upon the degree of imperfection present in a case. Control over price of a product by a firm and therefore the existence of imperfect competition can be caused either by the 'fewness' of the firms or by the product differentiation. Therefore, imperfect competition has several sub-categories.

(a) Monopolistic Competition. The first important sub-category of imperfect competition is monopolistic competition on which E.H. Chamberlin laid a great stress in his original thought-provoking work "*The Theory of Monopolistic Competition*". Monopolistic Competition, as is now understood, is characterised **by a large number of firms and product differentiation.**[2] That is, in *monopolistic competition* a large number of firms produce somewhat different

1. Joan Robinson, *The Economics of Imperfect Competition.* Macmillan and Co., London, 1954, p. 18.
2. It should be carefully noted that E.H. Chamberlin called any market structure, which was a blend of monopoly and competition as monopolistic competition. A blend of monopoly and competition could be there if there was either a few firms producing an identical or differentiated product or there was a large number of firms producing differentiated products. The former is the case of oligopoly with and without product differentiation and the latter is the monopolistic competition with many firms. Thus, in Chamberlin's terminology, the concept of monopolistic competition covers both oligopoly (with as well as without product differentiation) and monopolistic competition with a large number of firms producing differentiated products. However, in standard modern economic theory, the term monopolistic competition is used only for the latter.

products which are close substitutes of each other. As a result, demand curve facing a firm under monopolistic competition is highly elastic and this indicates that a firm working in it enjoys some control over the price. Besides, there is freedom of entry and exit under monopolistic competition.

Table 24.1. The Classification of Market Structures

Form of Market Structure	*Number of Firms*	*Nature of Product*	*Price Elasticity of Demand for an Individual Firm*	*Degree of Control over Price*	*Ease of Entry*
(*a*) **Perfect Competition**	A large number of firms	Homogeneous product	Infinite	None	Free Entry
(*b*) **Imperfect Competition**					
(*i*) Monopolistic Competition	A large number of firms	Differentiated Products (but they are close substitutes of each other)	Large	Some	Free entry but for producing close substitutes
(*ii*) Pure Oligopoly, (*i.e.*, Oligopoly without Product Differentiation)	Few firms	Homogeneous Product	Small	Some	Limited entry
(*iii*) Differentiated Oligopoly (*i.e.*, Oligopoly with Product Differentiation)	Few firms	Differentiated Products (which are close substitutes of each other)	Small	Large	Limited entry
(*c*) **Monopoly**	One	Unique Product without Close Substitutes	Very Small	Very Large	Strong Barriers to Entry

(*b*) Pure Oligopoly. The second sub-category of imperfect competition is **oligopoly without product differentiation** which is also known as *pure oligopoly*. Under it there is competition among the few firms producing homogeneous or identical product. The fewness of the firms ensures that each of them will have some control over the price of the product and the demand curve facing each firm will be downward sloping which indicates that the price elasticity of demand for each firm will not be infinite.

(*c*) Differentiated Oligopoly. The third sub-category of imperfect competition is **oligopoly with product differentiation** which is also called *differentiated oligopoly*. As its name shows, it is characterised by competition among the few firms producing differentiated products which are close substitutes of each other. The demand curve facing individual firms under oligopoly with product differentiation is downward sloping[3] and the firms have fairly large control over the price of their individual products.

3. The nature of demand curve under oligopoly is, however, a controversial matter. In some models of oligopoly without product differentiation, it is assumed that the demand curve for an oligopolist is perfectly elastic (*i.e.*, horizontal straight line). Further, another important model of oligopoly assumes a kinked demand curve (with a kink at the prevailing price) for an oligopoly firm.

Monopoly.[4] Monopoly, as is now generally understood, means the existence of a *single producer or seller which is producing or selling a product which has no close substitutes*. Since a monopoly firm has a sole control over the supply of a product, which can have only remote substitutes, it has a very large control over the price of its product. The expansion and contraction in output of the product by a monopolist will considerably affect the price of the product, contraction in output will raise its price and expansion in output will lower it. Therefore, the demand curve facing a monopolist is downward sloping and has a steep slope. Thus, according to F. Machlup, "Monopolistic competition would then comprise the cases of closer substitutes and more elastic demand curves, while monopoly would comprise those of remote substitutes and steeper demand curves."[5] Besides, in monopoly there are strong barriers to the entry of new firms in the industry.

The classification of market forms made on the basis of *(i) number af firms in the industry, (ii) the nature of product (i.e., the closeness or remoteness of substitution among products and (iii) the ease with which new firms can enter the industry or the old ones can leave it, which we have explained above, is quite adequate and satisfactory.*

Market Classifications and Cross Elasticity of Demand

The concept of cross elasticity of demand has been used by Robert Triffin[6] to measure the amount and kind of competition among firms and therefore for classifying market structures. "In perfect competition the cross elasticity of demand for the product of a *single firm with respect* to a change in the price of the rest of the industry will be infinite. That is to say, the proportionate fall in the *demand for the product of a single* firm will be infinitely large compared with any given proportionate fall in the price of the product of the whole industry. Similarly, in monopolistic competition the cross elasticity of demand for the product of a single firm with respect to a change in the price of other products made in the monopolistic 'group' will be very high. The cross elasticity of demand for the product of a monopolist with respect to a fall in the price of other products in the economy will be very low."[7] We present below the different market categories and the cross elasticity of demand (e_c) found in them in a tabular form.

Table 24.2: Market Classification on the Basis of Cross-Elasticity of Demand

Market Form	Cross-Elasticity of Demand
1. Perfect Competition	Cross-elasticity is infinite ($e_c = \infty$)
2. Monopolistic Competition	Cross-elasticity (e_c) is very high
3. Monopoly	Cross elasticity (e_c) is very low or zero

The concept of cross elasticity of demand as a measure of classifying market forms is very much inadequate and sometimes leads to erroneous conclusions. "The basic objection to the concept of cross-elasticity is that it causes neglect of the two basic determinates of market structure : the degree of closeness or remoteness of substitution among products and the

4. For monopoly, sometimes the terms *absolute* monopoly, *pure* monopoly, *complete* monopoly are used. All these terms have the same meaning since all visualise a single producer or seller producing a product which has no close substitutes. However, Sraffa used the term 'Pure Monopoly' in a different 'sense. *By pure monopoly Sraffa means that a single seller of a product is so powerful that he is in a position to take the whole income of all the consumers whatever the level of his output. Obviously, such a pure or absolute monopoly cannot exist in the real world.*
5. Fritz Machlup, Monopoly and Competition: A Classification of Market Positions, *American Economic Review,* September 1937, p.448.
6. R. Triffin *Monopolistic Competition and General Equilibrium Theory.*
7. Stonier and Hague, *A Textbook of Economic Theory,* 4th edition, 1972, p. 244.

number of firms in the relevant group or industry. The concept of cross-elasticity leads to the neglect of the two elements which ... are fundamental to an understanding of market structure."[8]

It has been pointed out by several economists[9] such as E. H. Chamberlin, W. Fellner, E. F. Beach and A. G. Papandreou that crosselasticity of demand of any perfectly competitive firm, instead of being infinity, is zero. Now, as said above, under pure monopoly, cross-elasticity of demand is also zero. Thus in two market situations of pure competition and pure monopoly which are two opposite extreme cases, cross-elasticity is found to be the same. Therefore, cross-elasticity of demand is a very unsatisfactory measure of a market structure. The cross elasticity of demand of a perfectly competitive firm is zero because it produces a product that has a very large number of homogeneous substitutes produced by other firms in the competitive industry. The number of firms producing homogeneous products, that is, perfect substitutes, is so large that *no one of them* will be noticeably affected when a single firm changes its price or output. If a perfectly competitive firm tries to raise its price unilaterally, its output will be substantially substituted by the homogeneous products of other firms. But the crucial point worth noting is that no other single firm will perceive any noticeable change because the number of firms involved is so large. M. Olson and D. Mcfarland rightly write :

"The coefficient of cross-elasticity neglects the closeness or remoteness of substitution among products most glaringly when it is used to classify pure competition and pure monopoly. The cross-elasticity of demand between a pure monopolist and any other firm is obviously zero, for the output or price of the pure monopolist will not be noticeably affected by the output or price of any other firm. Similarly, in pure competition, the cross-elasticity of any pure competitor, *i,* with any other firm; will be zero, at least so long as the rising marginal costs essential to pure competition are recognized. The output, q_i of any firm *i* in pure competition will not be significantly affected by the price, p_t of any firm *j* : in short cross-elasticity is zero. Even if firm *j* should reduce its price to deprive other firms of sales, it would because of its rising marginal costs be unable to satisfy the demand at the lower price, so the sales of firm *i* would not be perceptibly affected. In pure competition by definition no firm is large enough to influence perceptibly the sales of any other firm"[10]

We therefore conclude that cross-elasticity of demand as a means of market classification is unsatisfactory. The classification of market forms made on the basis of *(i)* number of firms in the industry and (H) the nature of product *(i. e.* the closeness or remoteness of substitution among products), which we have explained above, is quite adequate and satisfactory.

TOTAL, AVERAGE AND MARGINAL REVENUE AND THEIR RELATIONSHIP

Relationship between total, average and marginal concepts is highly useful in marginal analysis of optimum decision making. This relationship between total, average and marginal numbers holds in case of all concepts such as revenue, cost of production, profit, utility. We explain here the relationship by taking total, average and marginal revenue concepts. ***Total revenue from the production and sale of a product of a firm is the total quantity of the***

8. M. Olson and D. Mcfarland "The Restoration of Pure Monopoly and the Concept of Industry", *Quarterly Journal of Economics* Vol. 76 (November 1962), pp. 613-31.

9. E. H. Chamberlin, *Toward a More General Theory of Value,* pp. 79-81 : W. Fellner. *Competition among the Few,* pp. 50-54 E. F. Beach, Triffin's Classification of Market Positions, *Canadian Journal of Economics and Politics,* Feb. 1943. pp. 69-74. A. G. Papandreou, Market Structure and Monopoly Power, *American Economic Review,* September 1949, p. 883-97.

10. M.Olson and D. Mcfarland, *op. cit.*

product produced and sold multiplied by price of the product. Thus

$$TR = P.Q \quad ...... (1)$$

where TR stands for total revenue, P for price and Q for quantity of the product produced and sold.

Average revenue is the revenue earned per unit of output produced and sold. Thus

$$AR = \frac{TR}{Q} \quad ...... (2)$$

Average revenue (AR) is equal to price when a firm sells all units of output produced at the same price (that is, when it is not discriminating prices.

However, it is marginal revenue concept that is of crucial importance in marginal analysis. ***Marginal revenue is defined as the extra revenue earned by producing and selling an extra unit of output.*** Stating algebraically, marginal revenue is the difference between total revenue earned by producing and selling 'n' units of a product instead of 'n-1' units. Thus

$$MR = TR_n - TR_{n-1} \quad ...... (3)$$

Marginal revenue can also be defined in terms of differential calculus as

$$MR = \frac{\Delta TR}{\Delta Q}$$

Or $$MR = \frac{dTR}{dQ}, \text{ that is, limit of } \frac{\Delta TR}{\Delta Q} \text{ when } \Delta Q \Rightarrow O,$$

$\frac{\Delta TR}{\Delta Q}$ or $\frac{dTR}{dQ}$ indicates that marginal revenue is given by the slope of the total revenue curve. The relationship between total, average and marginal revenue can be illustrated through equations, tables or graphs. We have explained the relation between these three concepts in Table 24.3 where we have given the data representing the following specific total revenue equation:

$$TR = 50Q - 5Q^2$$

By substituting the value of Q (0 to 7), we have obtained the total revenue, marginal revenue, average revenue figures at various levels of output or sales. It will be seen from the table that when output is zero and nothing is sold, total revenue is zero and therefore marginal and average revenue (AR) are zero. As output is expanded and we substitute higher values of output (Q) in the total revenue equation, total revenue goes on increasing as will be seen from Col. III of Table 24.3. An important fact to be noted is that ***when one unit of output is produced and sold, total revenue, marginal revenue and average revenue are equal.*** All these are equal to Rs.45. This is quite obvious from the definition of total revenue, marginal revenue and average revenue and needs no explanation. It will be seen from Table 24.3 that if output is increased beyond five units of output, total revenue (TR) starts declining and marginal revenue (MR) becomes negative.

Relation between Total Revenue and Marginal Revenue

As stated above, marginal revenue is the addition to total revenue associated with a unit increase in output or sales. Therefore, total revenue (TR) increases when marginal revenue (MR) is positive and total revenue (TR) decreases when marginal revenue (MR) is negative. It will be seen from Table-24.3 that up to 5 units of output and sales, marginal revenue is positive and as a result total revenue increases with output over this range. Marginal revenue

Table 24.3. Relation between Total Revenue, Marginal Revenue and Average Revenue

Output (Q)	Equation $TR = 50Q - 5Q^2$		Total Revenue TR	Marginal Revenue (MR) $TR_n - TR_{n-1}$	Average Revenue (AR) TR/Q
0	$50(0) - 5(0)^2$	=	0	0	0
1	$50(1) - 5(1)^2$	=	45	45	45
2	$50(2) - 5(2)^2$	=	80	35	40
3	$50(3) - 5(3)^3$	=	105	25	35
4	$50(4) - 5(4)^2$	=	120	15	30
5	$50(5) - 5(5)^2$	=	125	5	25
6	$50(6) - 5(6)^2$	=	120	–5	20
7	$50(7) - 5(7)^2$	=	105	–15	15

of the 6th and 7th units of output are negative, it therefore causes total revenues (*TR*) to decrease. From this it follows that total revenue function will be maximized (or any function for that matter) at the point where marginal revenue (*MR*) changes from being positive to be negative. That is, total *revenue is maximised when marginal revenue (MR) is zero.* This is an important rule of marginal analysis.

Another important rule of marginal analysis can be derived from the relation between total revenue (*TR*) and marginal revenue (*MR*). Since marginal revenue is addition to total revenue by each successive units of output, ***total revenue (TR) can be obtained by suming up marginal revenues of all the preceding units of output (including the last one). Thus TR = ΣMR*** of all the units of output produced and sold.

Thus with regard to relation between total revenue and marginal revenue we arrive at the following important rules:

1. Total revenue increases when marginal revenue is positive.
2. Total revenue is maximized at the output level where marginal revenue (*MR*) is equal to zero.
3. Total revenue at a certain level of output (or sales) is equal to the sum of all the preceding marginal revenues (including the last one) of the total units of output produced and sold.

The above relationships between total and marginal number apply equally to all the total and marginal concepts whether they relate to revenue, cost, profit or utility.

Relationship between Average and Marginal Revenue

There is an important arithmetical relationship between average and marginal revenue which is extensively used in optimization analysis. Since a marginal revenue represents the change in total revenue as a result of a unit change in output, it follows that when marginal revenue is greater than average revenue, average revenue increases (that is, higher *MR* pulls up *AR*). When marginal revenue is less than average revenue, average revenue declines. And when marginal revenue is equal to average revenue, average revenue remains unchanged.

It will be seen from Table 24.3 that when output increases from 2 units to 7 units, average revenue (*AR*) decreases from Rs. 40 to Rs. 15. This is because marginal revenue is less than average revenue over this range and therefore pulls down the average revenue. This relation between average and marginal numbers is more clearly evident is case of average and marginal costs. In the beginning when output increases, average cost of production falls because marginal cost remains less than average cost. Beyond a point average cost rises because marginal cost exceeds average cost of production. Marginal cost is equal to average cost when it stops falling and has not yet started rising. That is, marginal cost is equal to average cost at the latter's minimum point.

However, this relationship between average and marginal numbers is often misunderstood. It is often stated that when an average quantity *falls,* marginal quantity must also be *falling* and when average quantity *rises,* marginal quantity *must also be rising.* This is quite false. In fact what the relation between the two states is that *when average quantity falls* marginal quantity must be *less* than the average quantity; marginal quantity though remaining less than the average quantity may itself may be falling, rising on remain constant. If an average quantity is rising, marginal quantity need not be rising. What is true in this case is that when average is rising marginal *must be greater than average,* marginal number itself may be rising, falling or remaining constant. The relation between an average quantity (*A*) and marginal quantity (*M*) is illustrated in Figure 24.1.

It is worth noting that above relationship between average and marginal quantities is a purely arithmetical relation and does not represent any proposition or law of economics.

DERIVING AVERAGE AND MARGINAL REVENUE CURVES FROM TOTAL REVENUE CURVE

The relationship between total, average and marginal quantities can be illustrated geometrically. We explain this relationship by taking total revenue curve and deriving average and marginal revenue curves from it. Total revenue curve *TR* has been drawn in the upper panel of Fig. 24.1. This total revenue curve *TR* shows that total revenue (*P.Q*) earned increases with the increase in output up to output level OQ_3 and decreases beyond it. Average revenue is the total revenue (*TR*) divided by the corresponding level of output (that is, $AR = \frac{TR}{Q}$). Therefore, geometrically average revenue at a given level of output is given by the slope of a line from the origin to the corresponding point on the total revenue curve. For example, in Figure 24.1 at output level OQ_1, the corresponding point on the total revenue curve *TR* is *R*. Thus, average revenue at this point is given by the slope of the line *OR*, which is $\frac{RQ_1}{OQ_1}$, in the bottom panel of Figure 24.1, taken to be equal to Q_1r, (that is, $\frac{RQ_1}{OQ_1} = Q_1r$). Now, at output level OQ_2 corresponding to point *S* on the total revenue curve *TR*, average revenue is given by the slope of line *OS*, that is, $\frac{SQ_2}{OQ_2}$ which in the bottom panel is taken to be equal to Q_2S. Similarly, at point *T* on the total revenue curve *TR* or output level OQ_3 in the top panel of Figure 24.1, average revenue is given by the *slope of the line OT*, that is, $\frac{TQ_3}{OQ_3}$ which in the bottom panel has been taken to be equal to Q_3t. Thus, **at any point on the total revenue curve, the corresponding average revenue is given by the slope of a straight line from the origin to that point.**

Now, in the bottom panel of Figure 24.1 by joining points *r*, *s* and *t* we get average revenue curve *AR* which we have extended to the *Y*-axis.

Deriving Marginal Revenue Curve from the Total Revenue Curve

As stated above, marginal revenue is the addition to total revenue associated with a unit increase in output or sales by a firm. Therefore, marginal revenue (*MR*) at a point on the total revenue curve is given by the slope of the total revenue curve at that point. The slope of the total revenue curve at a point is measured by the slope of the tangent drawn at that point to the total revenue curve. For example, at point *R* corresponding to output level OQ_1 in the top panel of Figure 24.1, marginal revenue at output level OQ_1 or point *R* on the *TR* curve can be obtained by measuring the slope of the tangent *tt′* drawn at point *R* which in the bottom panel of Figure 24.1 is taken to be equal to Q_1m_1. Similarly, at point *S* on the total revenue curve corresponding to output level OQ_2, marginal revenue can be measured by the slope the tangent *JJ′* drawn to the total revenue curve at point *S*, which is taken to be equal to Q_2m_2 in the bottom panel of Figure 24.1.

Further, at the highest point *H* on the total revenue curve *TR* corresponding to output level OQ_3, the slope of the tangent *kk′* drawn at point *H* is a horizontal straight line which implies that slope of the total revenue curve *TR* at this point is zero. Therefore, marginal revenue at OQ_3 in bottom panel is taken to be equal to zero. Now, joining points m_1, m_2, and Q_3 in the bottom panel gives us marginal revenue curve *MR* which we extend to the *Y*-axis. Thus, ***at the point at which total revenue (TR) is maximum, marginal revenue (MR) is zero.***

It is important to note from Figure 24.1 that beyond output level OQ_3, total revenue curve is sloping downward. This implies that beyond output level OQ_3, marginal revenue will be negative. Therefore, it *will* be seen from the bottom panel of Figure 24.1 that beyond output OQ_3 marginal revenue curve goes below the *X*-axis.

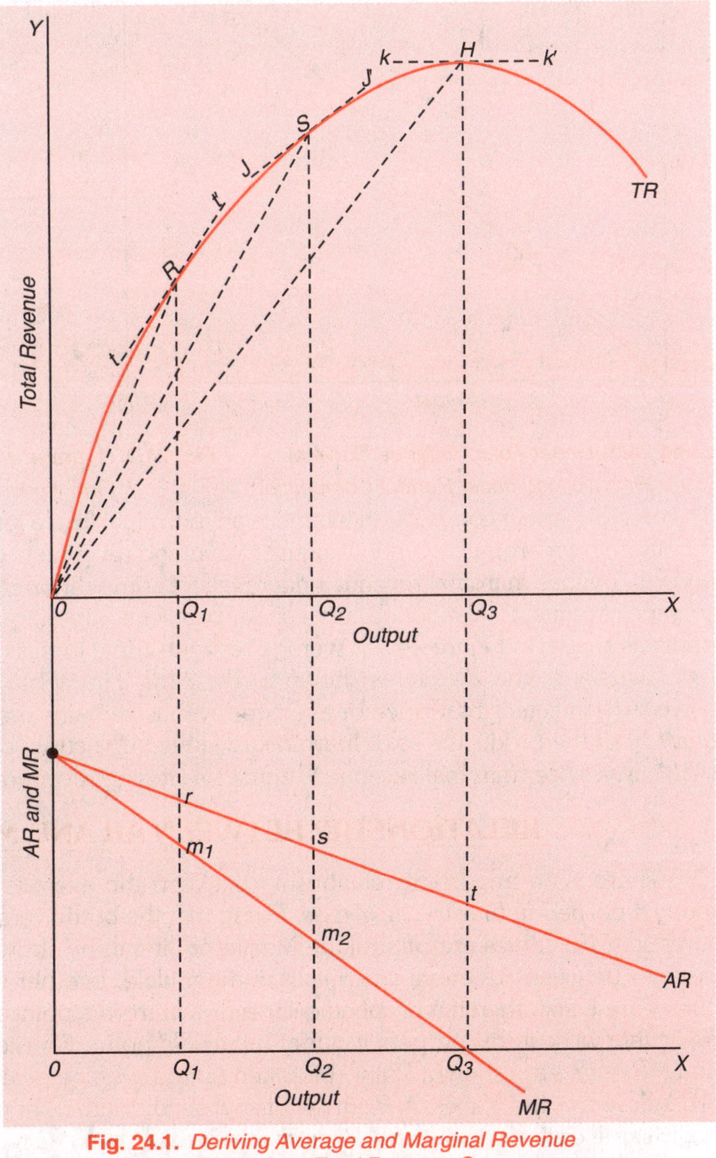

Fig. 24.1. *Deriving Average and Marginal Revenue Curves from Total Revenue Curve*

Average Revenue and Marginal Revenue Under Perfect Competition

We have explained above the concepts of total revenue, average revenue and marginal revenue when with the increase in output or sales by a firm, price of its product falls. However, when there prevails a perfect competition in the market for a product, price of the product is beyond the control of the firm, and it takes price as given and constant. As a result, demand curve facing a firm working in a perfectly competitive market is a horizontal straight-line at the given level of price of the product. Thus, a perfectly competitive firm can sell as much as it likes at the prevailing price in the market. If the price or average revenue remains the same when more units of the good are sold, the marginal revenue will be equal to average revenue. This is so because if one more unit is sold and the price does not fall, the addition made to the total revenue by that unit will be equal to the price at which it is sold, since no loss in revenue is incurred on the previous units in this case.

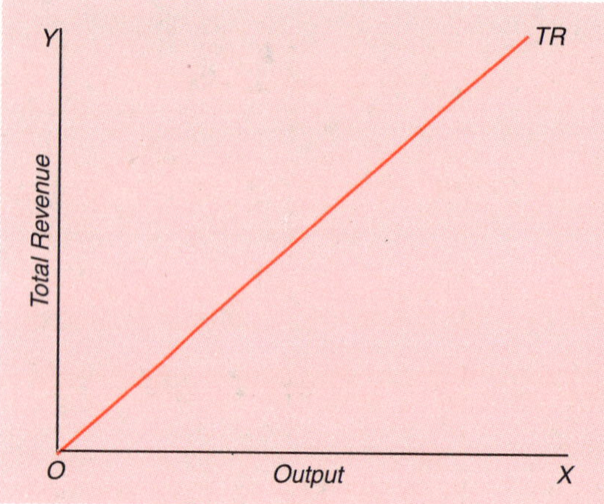

Fig 24.2. *Linear Total Revenue Curve of a Firm working under Perfect Competition*

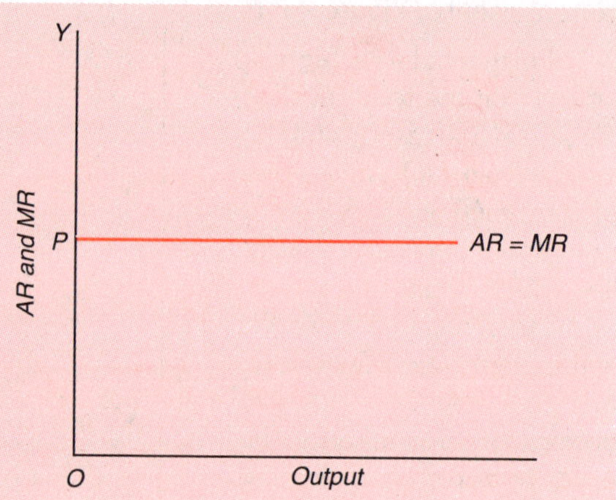

Fig. 24.3. *Average and Marginal Revenue Curves of a Firm working under Perfect Competition*

The case of perfect competition when for an individual firm average revenue (or price) remains constant and marginal revenue is equal to average revenue is graphically shown in Fig. 24.2 and 24.3. Since marginal revenue under perfect competition remains constant and is equal to average revenue, total revenue curve under perfect competition will be a straight-line from the origin as shown in Figure 24.2. Average revenue curve in this case is a horizontal straight line (*i.e.*, parallel to the *X*-axis) as shown in Fig.24.3. Horizontal straight-line average revenue curve (*AR*) indicates that price or average revenue remains the same at *OP* level when more quantity of the product is sold. Marginal revenue (*MR*) curve coincides with average revenue (*AR*) curve since marginal revenue is equal to average revenue.

RELATIONSHIP BETWEEN AR AND MR CURVES

There is an important relationship between the average and marginal revenue curves *along a perpendicular to the Y-axis.* Given that the both average revenue (*AR*) and marginal revenue (*MR*) curves are of straight-line shape, it can be shown that (*MR*) curve will cut the distance between *AR* curve and *Y*-axis in the middle. In other words, when both *AR* and *MR* curves are linear, then if a perpendicular is drawn from a point on the *AR* curve to the *Y*-axis, *MR* curve will cut this perpendicular at its middle point. Consider Fig.24.4, where linear *AR* and *MR* curves are shown. Point *A* is taken on the average revenue curve and a perpendicular *AB* is drawn to the *Y*-axis. *MR* curve cuts perpendicular *AB* at point *C*. Now, if *MR* curve cuts halfway the distance between *AR* curve and *Y*-axis, then *AC* must be equal to *BC*. So in order to show that MR cuts halfway the distance between AR and Y-axis, we have to prove in Fig.24.4 that $AC = BC$.

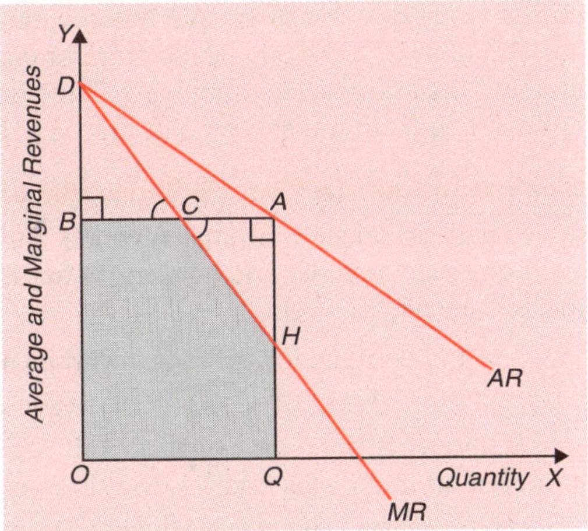

Fig.24.4. *MR curve cuts half-way the distance between AR curve and the Y-axis.*

Draw a vertical straight line from A so as to meet the X-axis at Q. It means that when OQ quantity of the good is sold, average revenue is equal to AQ. Now, there are two ways in which we can find out the total revenue earned by the sale of OQ units of the good. First, **total revenue (TR) can be obtained from the quantity of the product sold multiplied by the average revenue earned at that quantity sold.** Thus

$$TR = AR \times \text{quantity sold}$$
$$= AQ \times OQ$$
$$= \text{area } OQAB \quad \text{..... (1)}$$

Secondly, **total revenue can also be obtained by taking a sum of marginal revenues of all units of the good sold.**

Thus, total revenue (TR) $= \Sigma MR$

$$= \text{area } OQHD$$

Since total revenue for a given quantity of the good sold will be the same whichever way it may be found, it follows that

$$OQAB = OQHD$$

But it will be noticed from the Figure 24.4 that

$$OQAB = OQHCB + ACH$$

And also $\quad OQHD = OQHCB + BDC$

From above, it follows that

$$OQHCB + ACH = OQHCB + BDC$$

Or $\quad ACH = BDC$

Thus triangles ACH and BDC are equal in area

Now, in Δs ACH and BDC

$\angle HAC = \angle DBC$ (right angles)

$\angle ACH = \angle BCD$ (vertically opposite angles)

$\angle BDC = \angle AHC$ (alternate angles)

Therefore, ΔACH and ΔBDC are similar.

We have proved above that triangles ACH and BDC are equal in area as well as similar. Now, when the two triangles are both equal in area and similar, they are congruent (i.e. equal in all respects)

Therefore, Δs ACH and BDC are congruent

Hence, $AC = BC$

It is thus proved that given the linear average and marginal revenue curves, the marginal revenue curve will lie halfway on the perpendicular drawn from the average revenue curve to the Y-axis. ***In other words, the slope of a marginal revenue curve is twice that of the average revenue curve.***

From above relationship between average revenue and marginal revenue, in case of a downword-sloping linear average revenue curve we can construct a marginal revenue curve corresponding to the given average revenue curve. For this purpose we draw any horizontal line AB (that is, a perpendicular from any point on the average revenue curve to the Y-axis) and find the midpoint C of line AB. Then draw a line MR *passing through this mid-point* C and starting from the same point on the Y-axis at which average revenue curve meets it.

Slope of Linear *MR* Curve is Twice that of *AR* Curve: Mathematical Proof

That the linear marginal revenue curve has the same intercept on the Y-axis as the average revenue curve and its slope is twice that of average revenue curve of the firm can be mathematically proved.

Let the demand (or average revenue) curve be

$$P = a - bQ \qquad \text{.....}(i)$$

where P is price and Q is quantity demanded, 'a' is a constant term representing the intercept on the Y-axis and b is the slope of the demand or average revenue curve.

The total revenue curve (function) is

$$TR = P \,.\, Q = aQ - bQ^2$$

Differentiating the above total revenue function with respect to Q, we have

$$\frac{d(TR)}{dQ} = \frac{d(PQ)}{dQ} = a - 2bQ$$

Since
$$\frac{d(TR)}{dQ} = MR$$

Therefore,
$$MR = a - 2bQ \qquad \text{.....}(ii)$$

Comparing equations (i) and (ii), we see that intercept of the marginal revenue function (curve) on Y-axis is the same as of average revenue curve and the slope coefficient of the marginal revenue function is two times the slope coefficient b of the average revenue function. This implies that marginal revenue curve will cut halfway the distance between the Y-axis and the average revenue curve.

Non-Linear *AR* and *MR* Curves

Marginal revenue curve corresponding to a *convex or concave* average revenue curve is not of straight-line shape but is either convex or concave to the origin. What relationship MR curve will bear to AR curve when average and marginal revenue curves are either convex or concave ? In either of these cases the marginal revenue curve will not lie halfway on the perpendicular from the average revenue curve to the Y-axis. If the average revenue curve is convex to the origin as in Fig.24.5 the marginal revenue curve MR will also be convex to the origin and will cut any perpendicular drawn from AR curve to the Y-axis *more than halfway* as measured from the average revenue curve. On the other hand, if the average revenue curve is *concave* to the origin as in Fig.24.6, the marginal revenue curve will also be concave and will cut any perpendicular line from the average revenue curve to the Y-axis *less than halfway* as measured from the average revenue curve. In Fig. 24.5 and 24.6, C is the middle point on the perpendicular line AB drawn to the Y-axis.

PRICE ELASTICITY, TOTAL REVENUE AND MARGINAL REVENUE

The importance of price elasticity of demand for a business firm lies in the fact that it provides a useful measure of the effect of a change in price of its product by a firm on the total revenue obtained from it. Note that the total revenue (TR) is equal to the price (P) multiplied by

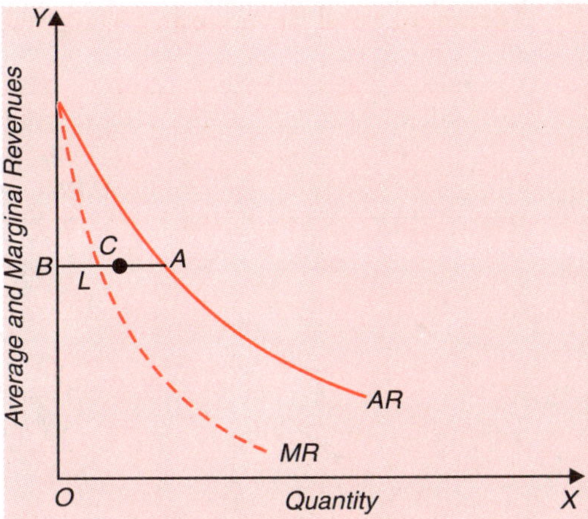

Fig. 24.5. *MR curve cuts the perpendicular from the AR curve to the Y-axis more than half-way from AR curve when AR curve is convex*

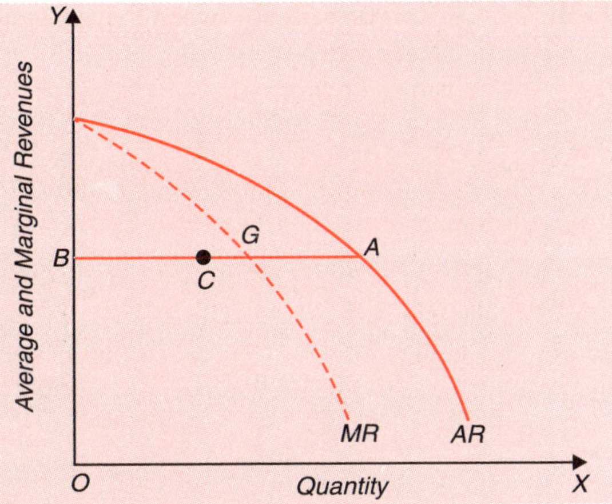

Fig. 24.6. *Marginal Revenue curve cuts the perpendicular drawn from AR curve to the Y-axis less than half way from the AR curve when AR curve is concave*

the quantity sold ($TR = P.Q$). Further, since the quantity demanded and sold (Q) is inversely related to price, that is, when price falls, the quantity demanded sold increases and vice versa, the change in total revenue (PQ) depends on the price elasticity of demand, This is because $e_p = \frac{\%\Delta Q}{\%\Delta P}$. When demand is unitary elastic (e_p= 1), a given percentage fall in price (P) is offset by an equal percentage increase in the quantity demanded, therefore the total revenue remains unchanged.

When demand is elastic (*i.e.* $e_p > 1$), a given percentage in price leads to a larger percentage increase in the quantity demanded (Q) and as a result total revenue (TR) increases.

On the other hand, when demand is inelastic (*i,e.*$e_p < 1$), a given percentage fall in price causes a smaller percentage increase in quantity demanded, the total revenue decreases. The effect of price elasticity of demand on changes in total revenue is illustrated in Table 24.4 where in the third column we have calculated price elasticity of demand corresponding to various quantities demanded in response to changes in price of the commodity. It should be further noted that we use the formula, namely, $e_p = \frac{Q_2 - Q_1}{p_2 - p_1} \times \frac{P_2 + P_1}{Q_2 + Q_1}$ for measuring price elasticity.

It will be seen from the Table 24.4 that in the range of the demand function where price of the commodity falls from ₹ 50 to ₹ 30 per unit, price elasticity of demand exceeds unity ($e_p > 1$), total revenue (TR) increases over the range. When price falls from ₹ 30 to ₹ 25, price elasticity is equal to unity ($e_p = 1$) total revenue remains constant. When price falls from ₹ 25 per unit downwards price elasticity is less than one ($e_p < 1$), and total revenue decreases.

In the last column of Table 24.4, we give marginal revenue earned from sale of additional units of output at different prices. It will be seen from Table 24.4, that over the range where $e_p > 1$ and total revenue (TR) is increasing, marginal revenue is positive and over the range of the demand function where price elasticity is less than one ($e_p < 1$) and total revenue deceases

Table 24.4. Relationship between Price Elasticity of demand, Total Revenue and Marginal Revenue

Price (*P*)	Quantity Demanded (*Q*)	Price Elasticity (e_p) $\frac{\Delta Q}{\Delta P} \cdot \frac{P_1+P_2}{Q_1+Q_2}$	Total Revenue (*TR*)	Marginal Revenue (*MR*)
50	1	–	50	50
45	2	$\frac{1}{5} \times \frac{95}{3} = 6.33$	90	40
40	3	$\frac{1}{5} \times \frac{85}{5} = 3.40$	120	30
35	4	$\frac{1}{5} \times \frac{75}{7} = 2.14$	140	20
30	5	$\frac{1}{5} \times \frac{65}{9} = 1.44$	150	10
25	6	$\frac{1}{5} \times \frac{55}{11} = 1.00$	150	0
20	7	$\frac{1}{5} \times \frac{45}{13} = 0.69$	140	– 10
15	8	$\frac{1}{5} \times \frac{35}{15} = 0.47$	120	– 20
10	9	$\frac{1}{5} \times \frac{25}{17} = 0.29$	90	– 30

marginal revenue (*MR*) is negative. When in the middle marginal of this demand function price falls from ₹ 30 to ₹ 25 per unit, price elasticity is equal to one, total revenue remains unchanged and therefore marginal revenue is zero.

TR, AR and MR : Graphic Illustration. The relationship between price elasticity, total revenue and marginal revenue is further clarified through Figure 24.7 where in the upper panel, a linear demand curve *DD′* has been drawn along with the marginal revenue (*MR*) curve lying below it. In the bottom panel of this figure total revenue curve has been drawn which first rises, reaches at the maximum point *H* at output level *OQ* and then falls downward. As we have been seen above, point price elasticity at the mid-point of the linear demand curve is equal to one and at points above it is greater than one and goes on increasing to the point at which the demand curve intercepts the vertical axis where it is equal to infinity.

On the other hand, below the *midpoint* of a demand curve price elasticity is less than one and goes on decreasing as we *move* downwards on *the demand curve DD′* in Figure 24.7 till it reaches zero at the point at which demand curve intercepts the *X*-axis.

Now, starting from point *D* as we move *downwards* to the midpoint *C*, absolute value of the elasticity of demand, though declining *remains* greater than one which causes total revenue (*P.Q*) to increase with the fall in price of the product. While reduction in price per unit (*P*) of the commodity *tends* to reduce revenue, increase in quantity sold caused by it tends to increase the revenue. Price elasticity *remaining* greater than one above the mid-point *C* implies that the percentage increase in quantity demanded exceeds the percentage fall in price which causes the total revenue (*PQ*) *to increase. Therefore, upto the level of output Q which corresponds to the mid-point C* of the demand curve, total revenue (*TR*) curve goes on increasing (see the bottom panel of Figure 24.7).

Now, as we move *downword* from the mid-point C of the demand curve DD', price elasticity being less than one implies that relative increase in the quantity demanded is less than relative fall in price which causes total revenue curve to decline. Therefore beyond output OQ corresponding to the mid-point C of the demand curve, total revenue (TR) curve is sloping downward as can be seen from the bottom panel of Figure 24.7. Since on a demand curve up to the mid-point C at which price elasticity is equal to one, total revenue goes on increasing as price elasticity is greater than one and below the mid-point C, total revenue decreases as price elasticity of demand is less than one, it follows therefore that the total revenue will be maximum at output OQ corresponding to the mid-point C of the demand curve at which price elasticity is equal to one.

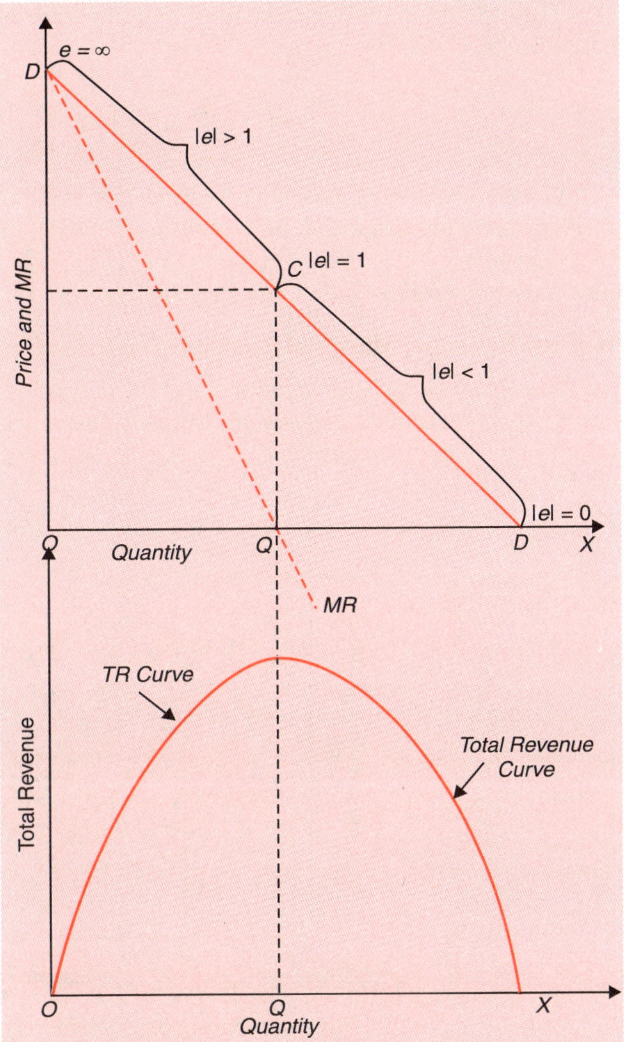

Figure 24.7. *Relationship between Price Elasticity of Demand, Total Revenue and Marginal Revenue*

Marginal Revenue and Total Revenue

Marginal revenue (MR) has an important relationship with total revenue (TR) as both depend on price elasticity of demand. Marginal revenue is defined as the additional revenue obtained when one more unit of output is sold. It will be seen from MR curve in Figure 24.7 that marginal revenue is positive in the range of the demand curve above the mid-point C where price elasticity is greater than one and marginal revenue is negative below the mid-point C of the demand curve where price elasticity is less than one, and marginal revenue is zero corresponding to the mid-point C where price elasticity (e_p) is equal to one. How can we explain this?

Since marginal revenue is the extra revenue earned from the sale of an additional unit of output where total revenue from the sale increases over the elastic *range* of a demand curve, it implies that marginal revenue (MR) is positive, and when *total revenue declines* over the inelastic raange that is, below the mid-point of the demand curve, it means marginal revenue is negative. When at the unitary elastic mid-point of the demand curve total revenue remains the same for a small change in price, it impiles that marginal revenue (MR) is zero. That is, at a unitary elastic mid-point of the linear demand curve, where total revenue is maximum, marginal revenue is zero.

The relationship between marginal revenue and price elasticity can be expressed algebraically as under.

$$MR = P\left(1 - \frac{1}{e_p}\right)$$

We can use this relationship to show that when demand is price elastic ($e_p > 1$), MR is positive and when demand is unitary elastic ($e_p < 1$), MR is equal to zero and when demand is price-inelastic ($e_p < 1$), MR is negative. We first derive below the above relationship between price elasticity and marginal revenue algebraically.

Average Revenue, Marginal Revenue and Price Elasticity of Demand : Geometric Proof

There is a very useful relationship between price elasticity of demand, average revenue and marginal revenue *at any level of output.* We will make use of this relation extensively when we come to the study of price determination under different market conditions. Let us study what this relation is.

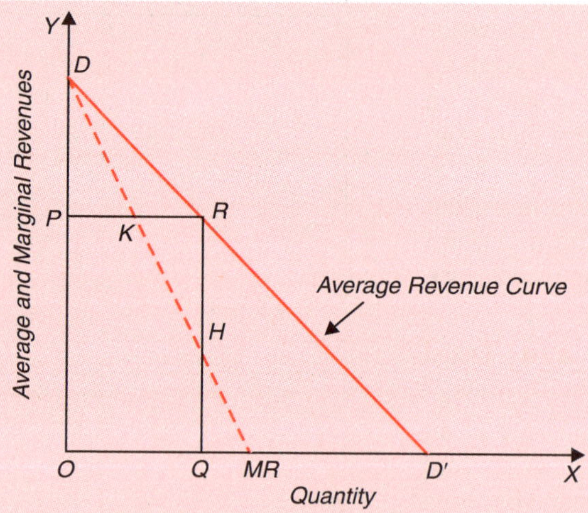

Fig. 24.8 *Derivation of relationship between AR, MR and Price elasticity of demand*

We have stressed above that the average revenue curve of a firm is really the same thing as the demand curve of consumers for the firm's product. Therefore, elasticity of demand at any point on consumers' demand curve is the same thing as the elasticity of demand on the given point on the firm's average revenue curve. We know that price elasticity of demand *(e_p)* at point *R* on the average revenue curve *DD′* in Fig. *24.8* national is equal to $\frac{RD'}{RD}$. With this measure of point elasticity of demand we can derive the relationship between average revenue, marginal revenue and price elasticity at any level of output.

In Fig. 24.8, *AR* and *MR* are respectively average and marginal revenue curves. Price Elasticity of demand *(e_p)* at point *R* on the average revenue curve :

$$e_p = \frac{RD'}{RD}$$

Now, in triangles *PDR* and *QRD′*

$\angle DPR = \angle RQD'$ (*right* angles)

$\angle DRP = \angle RD'Q$ (corresponding angles)

Third $\angle PDR = \angle QRD'$

Therefore, triangles *PDR* and *QRD'* are equiangular.

Hence, $$\frac{RD'}{RD} = \frac{RQ}{PD} \qquad ...(i)$$

In the triangles *PDK* and *KRH*

$PK = RK$

$\angle PKD = \angle RKH$ (vertically opposite angles)

$\angle DPK = \angle KRH$ (right angles)

Therefore, triangles *PDK* and *KRH* are congruent (*i.e.*, equal in all respects).

Hence $PD = RH$ ...(*ii*)

From (*i*) and (*ii*), we get

Price elasticity at $\frac{RD'}{RD} = \frac{RQ}{PD} = \frac{RQ}{RH}$

Now, it is seen from Fig. 24.8 that

$$\frac{RQ}{RH} = \frac{RQ}{RQ - HQ}$$

Hence, price elasticity at $R = \frac{RQ}{RQ - HQ}$

It will also be clear from the figure that *RQ* is average revenue and *HQ* is the marginal revenue at the level of output *OQ* which corresponds to the point *R* on the average revenue curve. Therefore,

$$\text{Price Elasticity at } R = \frac{\text{Average Revenue}}{\text{Average Revenue} - \text{Marginal Revenue}}$$

If, *A* stands for average revenue

M stands for marginal rgvenue

e stands for point price elasticity on the average revenue curve,

then $$e = \frac{A}{A - M} \qquad ...(iii)$$

$$eA - eM = A$$

$$eA - A = eM$$

$$A(e - 1) = eM$$

$$A = \frac{eM}{e - 1}$$

Hence, $$A = M\left(\frac{e}{e - 1}\right) \qquad ...(iv)$$

And also, $$M = A\left(\frac{e-1}{e}\right) \qquad \ldots(v)$$

Thus we obtain the three alternative formulations (*iii*), (*iv*) and (v) which describe the relationship between average revenue, marginal revenue and price elasticity of demand at a level of output of a firm. With the help of these formulae we can find out marginal revenue at any level of output from average revenue at the same output provided we know the point elasticity of demand on the average revenue curve. If the demand elasticity of a firm's average revenue curve at a point is equal to one, marginal revenue equals zero. This can be shown as under:

$$M = A\left(\frac{e-1}{e}\right)$$
$$= A\left(\frac{1-1}{1}\right)$$
$$= A \times 0$$
$$= 0$$

Similarly, when price elasticity of demand on a firm's average revenue curve is 2, the marginal revenue equals half the average revenue. Thus putting the value of price elasticity equal to 2 in formula (*iii*) we have

$$M = A\left(\frac{e-1}{e}\right)$$
$$= A\left(\frac{2-1}{2}\right)$$
$$= A\left(\frac{1}{2}\right)$$
$$= \frac{1}{2}A.$$

If follows from above that marginal revenue from the scale of a product depends on the average revenue and price elasticity of demand at any given level of output.

By applying the formula for various elasticities of demand at different points (or at different levels of output) on the average revenue curve it will be found that marginal revenue is always positive at any point or output where the elasticity of the average revenue curve is greater than one, and marginal revenue is always negative where the elasticity of the average revenue curve is less than one. Thus

$$|e_p| > 1, MR > 0$$
$$|e_p| = 1, MR = 0$$
$$|e_p| < 1, MR < 0$$

Mathematical Derivation of Relationship between Marginal Revenue, Average Revenue and Price Elasticity of Demand

There exists an important relationship between marginal revenue, price (*i.e.*, *AR*) and price elasticity of demand which is extensively used in making price decisions by the firms. This relationship can be written algebraically as

$$MR = P\left(1 + \frac{1}{-e}\right)$$

where P = price and e = point price elasticity of demand.

This relationship is mathematically derived as follows :

Marginal revenue (MR) is defined as the first derivative of total revenue (TR). Thus,

$$MR = \frac{d(TR)}{dQ} \quad ...(1)$$

Now, TR is the product of price and the quantity of the product sold ($TR = P.Q$). Thus,

$$MR = \frac{d(P.Q)}{dQ}$$

Using the rule of differentiation of a product, we have

$$MR = P\frac{dQ}{dQ} + Q\frac{dP}{dQ}$$

$$MR = P + Q\frac{dP}{dQ} \quad ......(2)$$

This equation (2) can be rewritten as

$$MR = P\left(1 + \frac{Q}{P} \cdot \frac{dP}{dQ}\right) \quad ......(3)$$

Now, recall that point price elasticity of demand $= \frac{P}{Q} \cdot \frac{dQ}{dP}$.

It will thus be noticed that the expression $\frac{Q}{P} \cdot \frac{dP}{dQ}$ in the equation (3) above is the reciprocal of point price elasticity of demand $\left(\frac{P}{Q} \cdot \frac{dQ}{dP}\right)$. Thus,

$$\frac{Q}{P} \cdot \frac{dP}{dQ} = \frac{1}{e} \quad ......(4)$$

Substituting equation (4) into equation (3), we obtain

$$MR = P\left(1 + \frac{1}{e}\right)$$

Remember that price elasticity of demand has a negative sign which is generally ignored. However, recognizing it, we have

$$MR = P\left(1 + \frac{1}{-e}\right)$$

or

$$MR = P\left(1 - \frac{1}{e}\right)$$

Demand Function, MR and Price Elasticity

Let us use the above relationship between marginal revenue and price elasticity of demand to show that when price elasticity of demand is greater than one, marginal revenue will be positive and when it is less than one, MR is negative and when price elasticity equals one, MR is zero. To illustrate these relationships – we take the following demand function

$Q_d = 1000 - 200\,P$

At price ₹ 3 per unit,

$Q_d = 1000 - 200 \times 3 = 400$

Price elasticity (e_p) at price ₹ 3 and associated quantity of ₹ 400 = $\dfrac{\Delta Q}{\Delta P} \cdot \dfrac{P}{Q}$

$$= 200 \times \frac{3}{400} = 1.5$$

MR at price (₹ 3) and quantity (400) = $P\left(1+\dfrac{1}{e}\right) = 3\left(1+\dfrac{1}{-1.5}\right)$

$$= 3\left(1-\frac{1}{1.5}\right) = 1$$

Thus when price elasticity exceeds one, MR is positive

In the same demand function ($Q = 1000 - 200\,P$) at price ₹ 2.50, price elasticity is equal to one. MR at this price is

$$= P\left(1+\frac{1}{-1}\right) = 2.5\left(1-\frac{1}{1}\right) = 0$$

Again at price ₹ 2, quantity demanded is 600 units and price elasticity is equal to 2/3, then MR at price ₹ 2 is

$$= P\left(1+\frac{1}{-\frac{2}{3}}\right) = 2\left(1-\frac{3}{2}\right) = -1$$

Thus at price elasticity of less than one, (e.g. $\frac{2}{3}$ in this case) marginal revenue is found to be negative.

Having clarified the relationship between marginal revenue and price elasticity of demand we solve some important problems concerning this relationship.

SOME NUMERICAL PROBLEMS ON MR, TR AND PRICE ELASTICITY OF DEMAND

Problem 1. *The demand function equation faced by HCL for its personal computers is given by*

$$P = 50{,}000 - 4Q$$

1. *Write the marginal revenue equation.*
2. *At what price and quantity marginal revenue will be zero ?*
3. *At what price and quantity will total revenue be maximized ?*

1. Students should note that in each case given a price, we have found the quantity demanded (Q) by substituting the value of the given price in the demand function. Then with price and quantity demanded (Q) we have calculated e_p by using elasticity formula $\dfrac{dQ}{dP} \cdot \dfrac{P}{Q}$. The value of $\dfrac{dQ}{dP}$ is the same (*i.e* 200) in all cases as the given demand function is linear.

Solution. To obtain total revenue function, we multiply the given demand equation by Q.

$$TR = PQ = 50{,}000Q - 4Q^2 \qquad \text{... (1)}$$

Taking the first derivative of the total revenue function would give us marginal revenue equation. Thus,

$$MR = \frac{d(TR)}{dQ} = \frac{d(PQ)}{dQ} = 50{,}000 - 8Q \qquad \text{... (2)}$$

(2) Setting MR function equal to zero would give us the quantity at which MR is zero. Thus,

$$50{,}000 - 8Q = 0$$
$$8Q = 50{,}000$$
$$Q = 6250$$

Now, to obtain price associated with the quantity (6250), we substitute the value of Q into the demand equation ($P = 10{,}000 - 4Q$). Thus.

$$P = 50{,}000 - (4 \times 6250)$$
$$= 50{,}000 - 25{,}000 = 25{,}000$$

(3) To obtain quantity at which TR is maximum, we set the first derivative of TR function (1) equal to zero.

$$TR = 50.000Q - 4Q^2$$

$$\frac{d(TR)}{dQ} = 50{,}000 - 8Q = 0$$

$$8Q = 50{,}000$$
$$Q = 6250$$

Thus, at the quantity of 6250 units the total revenue is maximum.

It follows from above that at the quantity of 6250 units and price of ₹ 25,000 per computer, marginal revenue is zero.

Important Conclusion. It is clear from the answers to the questions (2) and (3) of this problem that the ***quantity at which MR is equal to zero, total revenue is maximum.*** This is because, as stated above, it follows from the very definition of marginal revenue. Marginal revenue is the increase in total revenue resulting from the sale of an additional unit of output. As long as marginal revenue is positive, total revenue is increasing and beyond the output level where total revenue is maximum, marginal revenue becomes negative and, therefore, total revenue declines. Thus, at the output level where marginal revenue is zero, total revenue is maximum.

Problem 2. *From the demand function equation given in problem 1 show that price elasticity of demand is equal to one when total revenue is maximum.*

Solution. Total revenue is maximum at quantity 6250 units of computers and it at price is ₹ 25,000 per computer.

$$e_p = \frac{dQ}{dP} \cdot \frac{P}{Q} \qquad \text{... (i)}$$

The given demand function is

$$P = 50{,}000 - 4Q \qquad \text{... (ii)}$$

In order to obtain $\frac{dQ}{dP}$, we express demand function expressed in terms of quantity demanded as a function of price. Thus, rearranging the given demand function

$$4Q = 50{,}000 - P$$

$$Q = 12{,}500 - \frac{1}{4}P \qquad \text{..... (iii)}$$

From the demand function equation (*iii*), we find that the coefficient of P is $-\frac{1}{4}$ which means that $\frac{dQ}{dP} = -\frac{1}{4}$.

Further we found in problem I above that at the quantity (Q) equal to 6250 and price equal to 25,000, total revenue is maximum.

$$e_p = \frac{dQ}{dP} \times \frac{P}{Q}$$

$$= -\frac{1}{4} \times \frac{25{,}000}{6250} = -1$$

Thus, we find that output and price level at which TR is maximum, Price elasticity of demand is equal to one ($e_p = 1$)

Problem 3. *Outside an airport, a shopkeeper is running a coffee shop. The demand function for coffee cups is*

$$Q = 150 - 10P$$

where Q is the quantity demanded of coffee cups and P is price per coffee cup.

1. Write total revenue function and determine at what quantity of coffee cups sold and price fixed, total revenue is maximised.

2. Find out value of marginal revenue at the quantity at which total revenue is maximised.

3. Show that at the quantity sold where total revenue is maximised, price elasticity of demand is equal to unity.

Solution. 1. Total Revenue and Price. The given demand function is

$$Q = 150 - 10P \qquad \text{...... (i)}$$

In order to determine the total revenue, demand function can be rewritten in terms of price as a function of quantity demanded.

$$10P = 150 - Q$$

$$P = 15 - \frac{Q}{10} \qquad \text{...... (ii)}$$

Now,

$$TR = PQ$$

$$= Q\left(15 - \frac{Q}{10}\right)$$

$$TR = 15Q - \frac{Q^2}{10} \qquad \text{..... (iii)}$$

Taking the first derivative of the TR function

$$\frac{d(TR)}{dQ} = 15 - \frac{2}{10}Q = 15 - \frac{1}{5}Q$$

In order to find out quantity sold at which TR is maximized, we set first derivative of TR equal to zero.

$$15 - \frac{1}{5}Q = 0$$

$$\frac{1}{5}Q = 15$$

$$Q = 75$$

Substituting the value of Q into the demand equation (ii)

$$P = 15 - \frac{1}{10}.75 = 15 - 7.5$$

$$= ₹\,7.5$$

Thus, the quantity at which total revenue is maximized is 75 and associated price is ₹ 7.5 per coffee cup.

2. *MR* Function

MR is obtained by taking the first derivative of TR function Thus,

$$TR = 15Q - \frac{Q^2}{10}$$

$$MR = \frac{d(TR)}{dQ} = 15 - \frac{1}{5}Q$$

Substituting the revenue-maximising quantity (= 75) into marginal revenue function

$$MR = 15 - \frac{1}{5}Q = 15 - \frac{1}{5} \times 75 = 0$$

Thus at the quantity sold at which TR is maximum, marginal revenue is zero.

3. Price elasticity of demand (e_p) = $\frac{dQ}{dP}.\frac{P}{Q}$

From the demand function equation (i), we find that $\frac{dQ}{dP} = 10$.

We have found above that TR–maximizing quantity is 75 and associated price is 7.5. Substituting these values into the price elasticity formula

$$e_p = \frac{dQ}{dP}.\frac{P}{Q} = 10 \times \frac{7.5}{75} = 1$$

Thus, price elasticity of demand at the TR–maximizing quantity is equal to one.

CHAPTER

25

Firm: A General Analysis of its Nature, Objectives and Equilibrium

Introduction

In a previous chapter we discussed the environment in which firm works, that is, the various forms of market in which a producer or firm may sell his product. Analysis of equilibrium of the firm and the industry under various market forms occupies an important place in economic theory. The theory of product pricing with which we are concerned in this part of the book is primarily an analysis of equilibrium of the firm and the industry under various market forms. When different firms are producing differentiated products, it is difficult to define an industry and the analysis of equilibrium of the industry under such conditions is full of conceptual difficulties. When different firms are producing differentiated products, each would have its separate demand and supply of its particular product. Therefore, in this case we cannot sum up the demand and supply of the various firms producing differentiated products to obtain the supply of and the demand for the product of the industry. It was in connection with the industry composed of various firms producing homogenous, undifferentiated products that the concepts of supply and demand were forged by Marshall. It is because of this difficulty of viewing supply and demand as a whole for a group of firms producing differentiated products and also because of greater importance of the behaviour of individual firms who exercise a great deal of control over the supply of their own product as against the behaviour of the whole industry or group that in recent years emphasis has been shifted from the equilibrium to the industry to the equilibrium of the firm. However, equilibrium of the industry under conditions of perfect competition where various firms produce homogenous products retains its importance and usefulness.

In the present chapter we will study in general terms the conditions of equilibrium of the firm with regard to the magnitude of output it will produce and the price of the product it will fix. For analysis of the equilibrium of the firm we require the information about the type of the total, average and marginal revenue curves of the firms working in different market structures and also the objective or goal it pursues. Until recently, it was generally assumed that rational behaviour on the part of a firm or entrepreneur was to maximise its money profits. However, the profit maximisation hypothesis has recently been challenged and various alternative objectives which the firms seek to achieve have been proposed. Therefore, before explaining the equilibrium of the firm, we will first discuss the objective of profit maximisation and then critically evaluate the various alternative objectives of the firm which have been suggested in recent years. However, to begin with we explain the nature of the firm and how it organises its activity.

THE NATURE OF FIRM : THE FIRM AS AN AGENT OF PRODUCTION

The firm is an agent in the economy that produces goods and services to satisfy wants of the people. In its productive activity, it transforms inputs such as labour, raw materials, natural resources into useful products which are demanded by the consumers. Firms exist to use scarce resources of the society efficiently and thus help the economy to cope with the basic problem of scarcity. Business firms exist for three main reasons. (1) They exploit the economies of mass production, (2) They raise funds to finance its productive activities and (3) They organise the production process. The most important reason for organization of production in firms is that *it enables us to take advantage of the economies of mass production*. Efficient production of goods requires the use of specialised machines and factories, assembly lines and division of labour into small operations which are performed by special groups of labour adequately trained for the operations done by them. Firms coordinate the process of production. They hire labour, get land or building and capital on rent, purchase raw materials, arrange for electric power to undertake the process of production. Emphasizing the need for organising production in firms, Prof. Samuelson writes ***"If there were no need for specialisation and division of labour, we could each produce our own electricity, digital watch and fine-spun shirt in our backyard. We obviously cannot perform such feats, so efficiency generally requires large-scale production in business firms."***[1]

The second important function of firm is *raising of resources* for large-scale production of goods and services. A modern steel plant requires more than 100 crores of rupees to be set up, the expenditure on research and development to devise and develop a new type of aircraft might require even more funds. The supply of such a huge amount of funds cannot possibly come from wealthy individuals who in the past used to provide resources for production. Today, in a private-enterprise economy, the business firms are able to raise a large amount of funds through selling shares or bonds to the millions of people, borrowing funds from financial institutions and ploughing back their own profits for financing production.

The third important reason for the existence of firms is *management by someone* who organises production, arrange the required financial resources, introduce new products and processes, makes other business decisions and is responsible for the success or failure of the business venture. To quote Prof. Samuelson again, "*Production is organised in firms because efficiency generally requires large-scale production, the raising of significant financial resources and careful management and monitoring of ongoing activities.*"[2]

Decisions by Firms

To maximise profits and to use its resources for production of goods and services to satisfy wants of the buyers, the firm must make the following decisions :

1. Which goods and services to produce and in what quantities?
2. Which production technique to use for production of a product?
3. Which production resources or inputs to use and in what quantities?
4. How to organize its management structure so as to coordinate the various activities of the process of production?
5. How to finance its productive activity, that is, how to raise resources or money capital to finance its investment in machines and factory building and pay wages to the workers and prices to the suppliers of other inputs?

1. Paul, A. Samuelsun & William D. Nordhaus, *Economics*, Fourteenth edition, 1992 McGraw Hill, p. 104.
2. Samuelson & Nordhaus, *op. cit*, p. 105.

ORGANISING ECONOMIC ACTIVITY BY A FIRM

Market Coordination Vs. Managerial Coordination. The primary objective of firms is to make maximum possible profits. Therefore, a firm makes the above decisions in a way that minimizes its cost to produce a given level of output. The basic problem facing a firm is to organize the production of goods and services by combining and coordinating the productive resources it employs. Production in a modern economy is based on vast division of labour and specialisation among individuals. For efficient production of goods a firm must coordinate the activities of the individuals employed by it. According to Coase[3], firms organise or coordinate its activities in the following two ways.

1. Market Coordination
2. Managerial Coordination or Command System.

We explain below these two ways of coordinating economic activity of a firm.

Market Coordination. Which goods and services a firm should produce is a significant decision a firm has to make and this decision relies on the market price system that serves as a source of incentives and information network. As relative market prices of goods or services change due to the changes in their demand and supply, the buyers or users will substitute the relatively cheaper goods or services for the expensive ones. In response to the changes in demand for goods and guided by price signals, a firm will adjust the production of various goods produced by it. Besides, changes in relative prices of goods create new profit opportunities for firms who can plan for expanding production of goods which are in greater demand and have higher prices. All these adjustments in productive activity of the firms is accomplished through changes in *market demand, supply and prices of goods* without any central coordinating authority issuing commands to the firms to change their production structure.

Managerial Coordination or Command System. There are many areas of firm's activity which do not rely on market system and instead are coordinated by management hierarchy. That is, these activities are coordinated within a firm by various layers of management. A senior manager issues commands or directions to their subordinates to do things in a way desired by him. Therefore, coordination by management within a firm is also called *command system*. At the top of managerial hierarchy within a firm is the Chief Executive Officer (CEO) who issues directions to the senior managers. The senior managers in turn give instructions to the middle-level managers and then middle-level managers directs the operation managers. The operation managers represent the lowest level of management that controls the workers who produce goods and services as directed by the managers. While commands or directions pass downward through top management to the lowest level of workers, information passes upward. Managers at different levels of management hierarchy not only directs their subordinates but also collect and process information about the performance of the individuals under their control and supervision. They also ensure that the commands issued to their subordinates must be implemented properly and effectively. In the modern corporate form of business organization, there are many layers of management and coordination of activities and collecting information and monitoring the activities of workers by them have become quite complex. However, since the 1980s, with the invention of micro computers and information revolution that has accompanied it has made the task of collecting information and coordinating efforts within a firm relatively much easier than before.

It is important to note that despite the enormous efforts made by owners and top-level management and the recent information revolution, top managers lack the necessary and

3. Ronald E. Coase, The Nature of the Firm, *Economica*, New Series, 4 (Nov. 1937) 386-405.

complete information about what is happening at the lowest level of actual implementation of commands issued. This affects the efficient working of the firm. Therefore, *large firms use incentive systems at various levels along with the command system to operate efficiently*. There is a need for the use of incentives for efficient operation because firm's owners and top level managers cannot have full information for efficient working of the firms. The use of incentives is necessary because contribution made by managers at various lower levels and workers at the floor level is very difficult to measure directly. At the floor level, some workers are more efficient and hard-working but for owners and managers it is often difficult to know who is efficiently working and who is shirking work. It is due to the lack of adequate information on the part of owners and CEO that it is difficult to fix responsibility on the sales-force when sales of the firm decline.

The above factors induce the firms to devise incentive systems within the organisation so as to ensure that all including managers, workers and sales-force work efficiently for better performance of the firm. It is due to the lack of complete information that firms do not simply employ productive resources and pay for them certain prices as if they were buying tangible goods with well-known qualities. Instead, they enter into contracts with managers of various levels, technical staff such as engineers, skilled labour and ordinary workers and pay them suitable compensation packages that give them adequate incentives so as to raise productivity. These contracts and incentive packages are known as **agency relationship**. These steps are adopted to solve what is called **principal-agent problem**. The principal-agent problem arises because managers and workers do not always work in the best interests of the owners or shareholders in case of corporate form of business organisation. Instead, managers and workers often attempt to pursue their own goals which may conflict with the efficient and profitable working of the firm. To solve this principal-agent problem, suitable compensation packages that provide adequate incentives to the agents (*i.e.* managers and workers) to work in the interests of the principal (*i.e.* owners of the firm). In a later chapter, we will discuss *agency theory of the firm* which is concerned with this principal-agent problem.

Why does a Firm Exist : Coase's View

In a famous article in 1937, Ronald Coase[4], a Nobel Prize winner in economics in 1991 explained why a firm exists. In theory, the existence of a firm is not really necessary. One can think of separate contracts made by various individuals between them to produce a product without the existence of any institution of the firm. For example, consider production of a car. One individual can make a part of the car and sell it to another individual who could produce another part and add another part to the part bought from the first individual. Then, the second individual can sell these two parts of the car together to a third individual who in turn can add another part of car and then sell the three parts of the car together to a fourth individual and so on the chain of individuals adding their parts continue until the complete car is manufactured and sold to the ultimate buyer. In this way, assembly line of manufacturing car will be replaced by a series of individual contracts made between various individuals selling and buying different parts of the car. This entire process of producing and selling different parts by individuals of the car is coordinated by prices at which different parts are bought and sold. In this way, the firm is eliminated from the process.

Coase explained the existence of a firm producing the complete car in a single organisation rather than a series of contracts between individuals working independently to produce different parts and selling them to each other. Coase gives two reasons for the existence of firms. These are : (1) *Reduction of transaction costs*, (2) *higher productivity under team work with division of labour*.

4. Ronald E. Coase, *op.cit.*

Transaction costs are costs of obtaining information about prices of components and inputs and also include the costs of negotiating contracts with the suppliers of inputs and purchasers of goods, writing bills and records and expenses made on getting contracts, if necessary, settled through courts and tribunals. The firm's transaction costs are reduced through bilateral contracts made by the firm. Each individual deals with the firm on bilateral basis rather than with other several individuals on a multilateral basis from whom the firm buys inputs and sells the products.

The second reason for the existence of a firm is that *production in it is done on a mass scale by a group or team of workers* among whom work is divided on the basis of their specialisation which greatly enhances productivity. Of course, there are some disadvantages of production by a group or team but its benefits outweigh its cost or disadvantages. Therefore, in modern times, it is team or group production with proper division of labour and specialization in a firm that has made it possible to enjoy economies of scale and consequently lower cost per unit.

OBJECTIVES OF A FIRM

Profit Maximisation Objective

In the analysis of equilibrium of the firm, an important assumption is made about the objective of the enterpreneur. It is that the entrepreneur aims at maximisation of his profits. Profit maximisation assumption about the behaviour of the firm is one of the most fundamental assumptions of economic theory. The attempt of the entrepreneur to maximise his profits is regarded as a rational behaviour. It has been said that as the rationality on the part of the consumer means that he tries to maximise his satisfaction, the rationality on the part of the entrepreneur implies that he tries to maximise his profits. In our analysis of equilibrium of the firm below, we will assume that the entrepreneur maximises his profits.

It should be carefully noted as to what the entrepreneur is supposed to maximise under profit maximisation principle. An entrepreneur's income consists of two elements. First, he gets wages for his work of routine management and supervision which he is supposed to pay to himself and include in his regular cost calculations. Thus the total costs of output comprise not only the costs incurred on other factors by the entrepreneur, that is, explicit costs but also the entrepreneur's own wages of routine management and supervision, *i.e.* the implicit costs. When we say that the entrepreneur tries to maximise the difference between total revenue and total costs, these total costs also include entrepreneur's wages of management and supervision. Thus the entrepreneur's wages of management do not form part of that income which the entrepreneur has to maximise. Besides, market rate of return on self-owned capital invested by the entrepreneur in his business is also a part of normal profits and therefore do not from part of income that come under the profit maximising category. Secondly, the entrepreneur gets what is left after meeting all explicit and implicit costs (including his own wages of routine management). This is surplus of total revenue over total explicit and implicit costs which is called his *pure* or *economic profits*. These pure profits are profits of entrepreneurship proper. It is always only his pure or economic profits that the entrepreneur is assumed to maximise. Thus we see that the entrepreneur's income comprises his own wages of routine management *(i.e.,* his own opportunity cost) and the pure profits which accrue to him.

Marshall called entrepreneur's wages of management and supervision as *normal profits,* and the residual income as *super-normal profits.* This dichotomy of entrepreneur's income is very fundamental in the theory of firm. ***The normal profits are the minimum income***

which the entrepreneur must get in order to stay in a business or industry. As has been just said above, the normal profits are included in costs and do not come under the maximizing problem. It is the supernormal profits, *i.e.*, economic profits which is the residual income which the entrepreneur aims at maximizing. *These true or pure profits are of the nature of economic rent* since they are over and above the normal profits which must be paid to the entrepreneur to make him to remain in the industry or business. Another important thing to note is that in the traditional theory of the firm maximisation of pure profits is considered to be maximisation of short-run profits. This short run in generally considered to be a year.

A CRITIQUE OF PROFIT MAXIMISATION OBJECTIVE

The profit maximisation hypothesis has been subjected to severe criticisms in recent years. It has been pointed out that in the real world firms do not maximise profits. Some economists have proposed alternative objectives to profit maximisation. First, K.W. Rothschild has asserted that entrepreneurs try to achieve a steady flow of profits for a long time. Prof. Baumol has put forward the view that firms try *to maximise sales i.e.,* the money value of the sales. Scitovsky, Reder and B. Higgins have asserted that firms or owner-entrepreneurs try to *maximise utility or satisfaction.*

Baumol[5] is of the view that firms attempt to maximise sales (i.e. total revenue) subject to minimum profit constraint. Williamson[6] argues that in case of corporate business firms, managers maximise their own utility function rather than maximising profits for shareholders who are the owners of the firm. On the other hand, H.A. Simon and Cyert and March express the view that rather than maximise any thing the firms just *satisfice*, that is, want satisfactory performance regarding profits, market share and sales revenue.

With the growth of managerial capitalism, the two developments have taken place which have been the basis of criticism of profit maximisation objective. The traditional assumption of profit maximisation implies that a firm was owned by an entrepreneur himself and therefore it was perfectly rational for him to maximise profits. Now, in large corporate firms it is managers who make business decisions while the corporate firm is owned by shareholders. In other words, there is separation between **control** and **ownership**. It has been asserted that managers who make business decisions may not be interested in maximising profits; instead they may try to achieve their own goals or objectives which may not be in the interests of owners *i.e.* shareholders. This situation has been described as **managerial capitalism**. Prof. Nellis and Parker rightly write "With managers in control it is easy to question the validity of the profit maximisation assumption of traditional theory. Some managers may seek to keep shareholders happy by reporting a certain level of profit while leaving themselves the flexibility to achieve, perhaps personal objectives (such as business growth, diversification, salary, etc)".[7]

The second development on the basis of which the validity of profit maximisation has been questioned is the emergence of oligopoly as the most common form of market structure. In the traditional theory the firms which were assumed to work under condition of perfect competition and monopoly, they were assumed to work *independently* and possess full and accurate information about demand and cost conditions. They could therefore easily determine profit maximisation by equating marginal cost with marginal revenue. However, the assumption of perfect maximisation fails to provide a satisfactory explanation decision making under oligopoly because in this type of market structure (1) the firms are quite **interdependent** and (2) there exists a **lot of uncertainly** about demand and cost conditions. Mutual interdependence

5. W.J. Baumol, *Business Behavaiour, Value and Growth*, p.49
6. O.E. Williamson, *The Economics of Discretionary Behaviour: Managerial Objectives in a Theory of the Firm*, Marsham Publishing Co. Chicago, 1967.
7. Joseph G. Nellis and David Parker, *"The Essence of Business Economics"* Prentice-Hall of India, New Delhi, 2002

arises in oligopoly because there are a few firms in this market structure and each of them produces a sufficiently large proportion of the industry's output so that its price-output decisions affect the market share of its rival firms which are expected to retaliate. Uncertainty exists because under oligopoly form of market structure a firm's decision is influenced not just by what its competitors are doing but also by what it thinks its rivals might do in reponse to its initiative regarding change in price, quantity of output, product variation and advertising.

In the context of development of managerial capitalism and the emergence of oligopoly as the chief form of market structure, Baumol put forward the view that managers, of firms, maximise sales value (*i.e.* total revenue) rather than profits, O.E. Williamson laid stress on the view that managers or business executives of large corporate firms are motivated by self-interest and therefore they **maximise their own utility function** rather than profits for the shareholders. Still another view has been presented by Marris[8] according to whom the managers try to **maximise growth of their companies** which raise their status, power and prestige rather than maximising profits which are mostly bagged by shareholders.

In addition to the above altrenative maximising objectives in place of profit maximisation, there are two other theories of the firm which emphasize that managers or firms **do not maximise any thing but pursue non-maximising goals.** There are mainly two non-maximising approaches to firm's behaviour. First, on the basis of empirical study two Oxford economists professors Hall and Hitch expressed the view that businessmen do not maximise profits but charge price according to what is called **mark-up principle** to achieve normal profit. According to this principle, firms calculate average cost on the basis of expected output or sales of the product and add to it, (*i.e.* mark up) a normal profit margin. In this way they can prevent the entry of new firms in the industry which enable them to earn a steady flow of profits over time.

The second approach to non-maximising behaviour is the behaviourist theory initially put forward by Professor H.A. Simon[9] but was further developed by R.M. Cyert and J.C. March.[10] According to this behaviourist approach, managers of the firms **do not try to maximise any thing,** whether it is profits, sales value, utility or growth. They just pursue the goal of **satisficing.** According to this, they try to achieve only a **satisfactory performance** with regard to profits, sales, market share. We shall explain these approaches in detail later. We explain below alternative objectives of the firm which have been proposed by some economists.

The Objective of Securing a Steady Flow of Profits

First, it has been pointed out that in deciding about his price and output policy the entrepreneur does not aim at maximizing his profits at a particular time or for a particular period of time, instead he tries to have *a steady flow of profits for a long time.* In this connection, it is worth quoting K. W. Rothschild who subscribes to this view : "*Profit maximisation has up till now served as the wonderful master key that opened all the doors leading to an understanding of the entrepreneur's behaviour. True, it was always realised that family pride, moral and ethical considerations, poor intelligence and similar factors may modify the results built on the maximum profits assumption; but it was rightly assumed that these 'disturbing' phenomena are sufficiently exceptional to justify their exclusion from the main body of price theory .... But there is another motive which cannot be so lightly dismissed and which is probably of a similar order of magnitude as the desire for maximum profits : the desire for secure profits.*"[11]

8. R. Marris, A Model of Managerial Enterprise, *Quarterly Tournal of Economics*, 1963.
9. H.A. Simon, A Behavioural Model of Rational Choice, *Quarterly Journal of Economics*, Feb-1955.
10. R.M. Cyert and J.C. March, *A Behavioural Theory of the Firm*, Prentice Hall, 1963.
11. K.W. Rothschild, Op. Cit 299-320.

Rothschild is of the view that profit maximisation assumption is valid for explaining the behaviour of a firm which is working under conditions of perfect competition or monopolistic competition with a large number of firms or when a firm enjoys absolute monopoly because, in these cases, the problem of having secure profits does not arise. He says that to the absolute monopolist security against competition is ensured by virtue of its monopoly position. And for a small firm working under perfect competition or monopolistic competition for whom the question of having secure question is a very urgent one, the market conditions are such an overwhelming force that he alone cannot do anything to safeguard his position. Maximisation of short-term profits is therefore a legitimate assumption about the behaviour of an entrepreneur in such cases. But Rothschild asserts that in the field of oligopoly the profit maximisation assumption is no longer sufficient. "Here is both the desire for achieving a secure position as well as the power to act on his desire."[12] He laments that in spite of the growth of numerous oligopolies in the real world, economists have ignored this additional motive and have relied exclusively on the profit-maximisation principle.

Sales Maximisation Objective

Prof. Baumol has also challenged the assumption of profit maximisation. He has argued that maximisation of sales rather than profits is the ultimate objective of the firm. He says that the firm tries to promote sales not merely as a means to further its other objectives, namely, operational efficiency and profits, but for businessman *"sales have become an end of themselves."* He therefore thinks that sales maximisation is the most valid assumption about the behaviour of the firm. ***By sales he means the revenue earned by selling the product.*** He therefore calls his hypothesis as Sales Maximisation Hypothesis or Revenue Maximisation Hypothesis.

Baumol thinks that empirical evidence for his hypothesis that sales rank ahead of profits as the main object of the oligopolist's concern is quite strong. He says, *Surely it is common experience that when one asks an executive, 'How's business ?' he will answer that his sales have been increasing (or decreasing), and talk about profits only as an after-thought, if at all. And I am told the requirements for acceptance to membership in Young Presidents' Organization (an honorific society) are that the applicant be under 40 years of age and president of a company whose annual sales volume is over a million dollars. Presumably it makes no difference if this firm is in imminent danger of bankruptcy ..... Almost everytime I come across a case of conflict between profits and sales the businessmen with whom I worked left little doubt as to where their hearts lay. It is not unusual to find a profitable firm, in which some segment of its sales can be shown to be highly unprofitable..... when such a case is pointed out to management, it is usually quite reluctant to abandon its unprofitable markets. Businessmen may consider seriously proposals which promise to put these sales on a profitable basis...... But a programme which explicitly proposes any cut in sales volume, whatever the profit considerations, is likely to meet a cold reception."*[13] This long quotation has been given to show to the reader that Prof. Baumol very strongly believes that sales maximisation has become the ultimate objective of the entrepreneur or the manager of a firm and therefore they direct their energies in promoting and maximising sales instead of profits.

Constrained Revenue Maximisation. But Prof. Baumol softens his sales or revenue maximisation hypothesis by pointing out that in their attempt to promote sales businessmen do not completely disregard costs incurred on output and profits to be made. He also concedes that there is some conflict between the firm's sales goal and its profit objective. He points out

12. Ibid.
13. W. J. Baumol, *Business Behaviour, Value and Growth*, pp. 47-48.

that in the actual world, businessmen usually promote sales subject to the limitation that costs incurred are covered plus a usual rate of return on investment made. According to him, "management is not concerned to obtain profits higher than this. Once this minimum profit level is achieved, sales rather than profits become the overriding goal".[14] To quote him again "the typical oligopolist's objective can usefully be characterized approximately ***as sales maximisation subject to minimum profit constraint.*** Doubtless this premise overspecifies a rather vague set of attitudes but I believe it is not too far from truth. So long as profits are high enough to keep stockholders satisfied and contribute adequately to the financing of company growth, management will bend its efforts to the augmentation of sales revenues rather than to further increase profits".[15]

Is Sales Maximisation Irrational Behaviour ? It may be objected that maximisation of sales instead of profits means irrational behaviour of the entrepreneur or a manager. But Prof. Baumol rightly points out that his hypothesis in no way conflicts with the assumption of rationality. He presents a different conception of rationality which is more scientific. According to him, ***rationality does not consist in choosing the ends, it only means pursuing the ends efficiently and consistently,*** He says, "People's objectives are whatever they are. Irrationality surely must be defined to consist in decision patterns which make it more difficult to attain one's own ends that are for some reason considered to be right. Unless we are prepared to determine other people's values, or unless they pursue incompatible objectives, *we must class behaviour as rational if it efficiently pursues whatever goals happen to have been chosen*[16]. Thus he thinks that given the sales maximisation as objective, the entrepreneur will be rational if he works most efficiently and consistently towards maximizing his sales.

Thus the whole concept of rationality has undergone a change these days. Rationality refers to the efficiency and consistency with which one pursues the ends. If profit maximisation is considered to be the objective of the firm, then the attempt on the part of the firm to maximise profits will be quite rational. But if some other end or objective is considered to be most valid, then the maximisation of that end will mean rationality. Prof. Papandreou rightly remarks that "Profit maximisation does imply rationality of course; but rationality is consistent with maximisation of other things as well as profits."Rationality "implies maximisation of ends with a given set of means or minimisation of means in the attainment of a given set of related ends"[17]. We therefore conclude that rationality is implicit in profit maximisation but if the maximisation of sales is the goal of the entrepreneur or a manager, then maximising sales will be a rational behaviour rather than maximising profit.

Baumol's revenue maximisation hypothesis is an alternative to the principle of profit maximasation. Among the various alternatives to profit maximisation put forward, Baumol's hypothesis of sales maximisation has one great merit — it revises and modifies the older principle of profit maximisation in the direct of realism and plausibility while still permitting a rather general theoretical analysis. We shall see in a later chapter that under the sales maximisation objective, the output is greater and price lower than obtained under the objective of profit maximisation. Therefore, to the extent the business firms are actually guided by the sales or revenue maximisation objective, their price and output policies will come nearer to the welfare maximisation of the consumers. Empirical research is needed to find out how far the business firms in the actual world are guided by the considerations of sales maximisation. So far not much empirical research has been done in this connection.

14. *Ibid*, P.49.
15. *Ibid.*, pp. 49-50 (italics added)
16. *Ibid.*, p. 47 (italics added)
17. Papandreou, Basic Problems in the Theory of the Firm, *Survey of Contemporary Economics.*

Maximisation of Utility Function with Leisure as a Desirable Object

Since satisfaction or utility is the ultimate end which an individual aspires to get, therefore some economists like Prof. Benjamin Higgins, Melvin Reder, Tibor Scitovsky have argued that in case of small unincorporated business firms, the entrepreneur who happens to be owner-manager of the firm pursues the objective of *utility maximisation* or what is called *preference function maximisation* in which *leisure* appears to be the desirable thing to have apart from making money profits. It has been pointed out by these economists that profit maximisation does not necessarily mean utility or satisfaction maximisation. If the entrepreneur is supposed to maximise his satisfaction, then not only the satisfaction which he gets from material goods, that is, material necessaries and comforts of life which are obtained with the money profits earned from putting in entrepreneurial activity or work but also the satisfaction which he obtains from the leisure at his disposal. According to them, the ***leisure or what Hicks calls 'quiet life' is an essential ingredient of an individual's welfare.*** The more activity or work put in by the entrepreneur will mean the less leisure he will be able to enjoy. The preference for leisure must be incorporated into the analysis of an entrepreneur who is supposed to maximise his satisfaction or utility.

We now proceed to show that as long as we do not make a special assumption about the entrepreneur's psychology or behaviour pattern regarding income, work and leisure, maximisation of profits will not ensure maximisation of utility function when leisure enters into the function as a desirable entity. Let us draw the entrepreneur's indifference curves IC_1, IC_2, and IC_3 between pure economic profits and the entrepreneurial activity which will indirectly show perference for leisure. In Fig.25.1 money profits are measured on the Y-axis and entrepreneurial activity or output (from left to right) is measured on the X-axis. An indifference curve in such a diagram will represent the various combinations of economic profits and entrepreneurial activity (and indirectly leisure) which will give the entrepreneur an equal amount of satisfaction. The higher the level of such an indifference curve towards the left, the greater the level of entrepreneur's satisfaction.

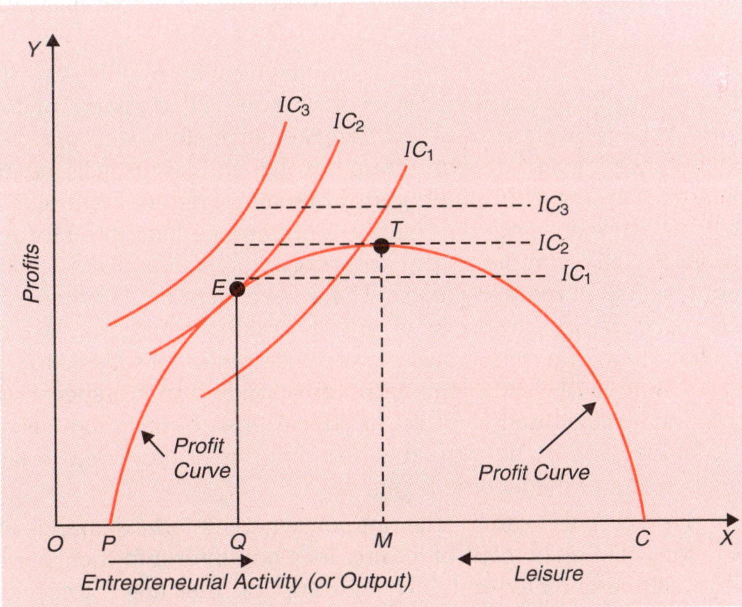

Fig. 25.1 Utility Maximisation Vs. Profit Maximisation

We further assume that entrepreneurial activity (*i.e.*, work) is a variable factor, that is, we assume entrepreneurship to be divisible but whose quantity per unit of output is fixed. In this way, we can measure entrepreneurial activity in terms of output also. The greater the amount of output made, the greater the amount of entrepreneurial activity to earn pure economic profits. The greater entrepreneurial activity will mean less leisure. In Fig. 25.1 the curve *PC* is the profit curve. For any activity or output less than *OP* and more than *OC* there are no profits. When a person puts in some entrepreneurial activity, he sacrifices some leisure, will produce some output and will earn some pure economic profits. These pure economic profits are the difference between his total revenue and total costs and in these total costs are also included his own wages of routine management *(i.e.,* normal profits). In Fig. 25.1 economic profit curve *PC* starting from *P* is drawn which shows the profits made by the entrepreneur by producing various levels of output, or in other words, by putting in various amounts of entrepreneurial activity by sacrificing leisure.

Now, the entrepreneur who wants to maximise his satisfaction or utility would try to reach the highest possible indifference curve. He would get maximum possible satisfaction where his profit curve is tangent to an indifference curve. It will be seen from the figure that the profit curve is tangent to indifference curve IC_2 at point *E*. Therefore, at point *E* he is getting maximum possible satisfaction. In this maximum satisfaction position, he is getting totai money profits equal to *QE*. *OQ* represeni entrepreneurial activity in terms of output he will be putting in for earning money profits, it should be noted that at point *E* where his satisfaction is maximum, his money profits are not maximum. Profits are maximum when he is producing *OM* output or putting in entrepreneurial activity equal to *OM*. *MT* is the greatest difference between profit curve and X-axis, *T* being the highest point of the economic profit curve. It is therefore clear that satisfaction-maximizing output (activity) which is equal to *OQ* is less than profit maximizing output (activity) which is equal to *OM*. We thus see that when leisure enters into preference function of the entrepreneur he will fix the level of output below the profit-maximizing output level.

A little reflection will show that maximisation of utility or satisfaction can be achieved at the profit-maximizing point *T*, only if we assume that instead of convex indifference curves the entrepreneur has horizontal indifference curves (between profits and leisure). But horizontal indifference curves between money profits and leisure will mean that it does not make any difference to the entrepreneur's satisfaction whether he has more or less leisure. In other words, leisure does not enter into his preference function. Horizontal indifference curve also means that the entrepreneur's choice between more and less activity or in other words between more income or more leisure must be independent of his income. In other words, it means that income elasticity of supply of entrepreneurship is zero. We thus see that in order that maximisation of profits should mean maximisation of satisfaction, the entrepreneur must have a special type of psychology and corresponding to it a special type of indifference map. In order that maximisation of profit should ensure maximum satisfaction, the entrepreneur's psychology should be such that the amount of work and energy put in by him remains independent of the income he earns.

However, this can be true not only when material demands of businessmen are insatiable but also when enjoyment of leisure does not enter into their preference function. Further, as Scitovsky has pointed out, "The assumption that the entrepreneur's willingness to work is independent of his income need not imply that he is not interested in the material rewards of his work. It may also mean that he is so keen on making money that his ambition cannot be damped by a rising income. The latter interpretation seems to be the more realistic one of those businessmen who regard the income they earn as an index of their success and efficiency; and their ambition of excelling in their profession manifests itself in the desire to make more money, not in order to have more to spend, but for its own sake, because it is an index and token of their success in life. He, who wants success for its own sake and measures it in terms of money is likely to keep working unabated even after his income has risen. This is likely to be the case, partly because the desire for success is more insatiable than the demand for material goods and partly because it is not a high but a rising income that is a sign of business success."[1]

Given the assumption that entrepreneur's willingness to work is independent of the level of his income, maximizing profits is identical with maximizing satisfaction. By attributing to the entrepreneur the psychology of valuing money for its own sake, and not for the enjoyments and comforts it might yield, Prof. Scitovsky justifies the assumption of profit maximisation as most valid since in such a case it amounts to maximizing satisfaction. When the entrepreneur does not have this psychology and preference for leisure enters into their utility function, then the level of output at which profits are maximum will be greater than that at which satisfaction is maximum. To quote Prof. Scitovsky again, "Only when he is more susceptible to the attractions of leisure than to those of his work and is consequently induced by a higher income to take life easier, will the entrepreneur's optimum behaviour be, not to maximise profits but to keep his exertions and output below the point at which profits would be at a maximum.[18]

Hall and Hitch's Mark-up Pricing Approach and Profit Maximisation

Further, reference may also be made to the empirical study made by Oxford economists, Hall and Hitch who interviewed some thirty-eight entrepreneurs on price policy. From their empirical study, Hall and Hitch have concluded that businessmen do not try to maximise profits by equating marginal cost with marginal revenue, which they seldom know. They also concluded from their study that businessmen charged prices according to what is known as *"mark-up pricing principle"*. According to this principle, businessmen charge prices that cover their average cost of production and to this average cost they *add profit mark-up* (i.e., profit margin) to fix the price of their products. According to this principle, businessmen do not seek abnormal profits, that is, more than conventional profits which are considered as reasonable. Thus the mark-up or full-cost principle, observance of which Hall and Hitch found in their enquiry, is claimed to be opposed to the principle of profit maximisation. It may however be pointed out that the market situation in which businessmen of Hall and Hitch enquiry were placed was one of monopolistic competition with an admixture of oligopoly elements. In such a market situation, the desire to obtain secure profits in the long run greatly governs the businessmen in charging prices of their products. In order to earn large economic profits if they charge high prices, new firms will invade their field. Thus in a market situation where the obstacles for new comers to enter the field are very small and as a result the businessmen already in the field fear that new comers will invade, they will not seek to maximise economic profits.

It is thus asserted that the practice of mark-up pricing contradicts the hypothesis of profit maximisation. However, it may be noted that a relevant question in this regard is what will determine the profit mark-up on the basis of which price will be fixed. On the face of it, it appears that since in this mark-up pricing principle demand is not taken into account in determining the profit mark-up it cannot possibly lead to the maximisation of profits. However, in our view this profit mark-up is not a fixed magnitude but varies depending on the price elasticity of demand or the intensity of competition in the market. In actual practice, businessmen determine this profit mark-up keeping in view the price elasticity of demand for their product or the intensity of competition from rival products, Empirical studies made in USA confirm this varying profit mark-up in case of different products. For example, an empirical study made for pricing by the U.S Steel Corporation, it has been found that profit mark-up or margins fixed in case of steel rails was relatively high because this was the product in which US steel faced little competition. On the other hand, profit mark-up fixed in case of stainless steel and tin plates was low because for them competition from aluminium and lumber products were quite strong. We thus see that mark-up principle of price fixation can be consistent with the hypothesis of profit maximisation.

18. Tibor Scitovsky : A Note on Profit Maximization and Implications, *The Review of Economic Studies.* Vol. XI (1943), Reprinted in *Readings in Price Theory* (AEA)

Managers of Corporate Firms and Alternatives to Profit Maximisation

Whether the firms try to maximise profits also depends upon who control their business conducted by them. That is, whether the owner himself or their hired manager controls and directs the business is a very relevant question in this regard. In case of individual proprietorship and partnership, it is the owners themselves who take price and output decisions and perform other entrepreneurial functions. But these days the organizational set up of the firms, especially in case of big firms, is of the nature of a business corporation which is also called joint stock company. In the case of corporations we find a ***separation between ownership and management.*** It is the shareholders who are the owners of the joint stock company and bear the risks of business. But price and output decisions are taken by hired managers. Under such a set up, profits of the business go to the shareholders and the managers are paid usually fixed salaries. Now, it has been pointed out that it may be expected of the owners-entrepreneurs of individual proprietorship and partnership that they will try to maximise profits since it is in their interest to do so. But hired managers of joint stock companies cannot be expected to try to maximise profits since these profits are not to go to them; they are to go to the shareholders. It may be true that when managers are able to earn more profits for shareholders, they may be rewarded by them in some farm or the other, but there is great force and truth in the argument regarding managers not maximizing profits. Not only the incentive to maximise profits is weak on the part of managers of these corporate firms but also, it has been claimed, that they pursue other alternative goals or objectives. We explain below some of these alternative goals of corporate managers.

Utility Maximisation by Managers of Corporate Business Firms

According to O.E. Williamson, managers or business executives of large firms are motivated by self-interest and they maximise their own utility function. Williamson argued that managers of large firms have enough discretion to pursue those polices which increase their personal utility. Utility function of managers include their salaries, the number of staff under their control, lavishly furnished office, *discretional* non-essential investment expenditure. However, the objective of utility maximisation by managers is subject to the constraint that after-tax profits are large enough to pay acceptable dividends to shareholders and also to pay for necessary investment expenditure. According to Williamson, utility maximisation by self-seeking managers depend on the following factors.

1. **Salaries.** The higher the salaries and other forms of monetary compensation which the managers receive from the business firms, the greater the utility they have. The high salaries ensure them high standard of living and high status.

2. **Staff under their control.** The utility desired by managers also depend upon the number of staff under their control. The greater the number of staff under the control of a manager, the higher his status, power and prestige.

3. **Managerial Slack.** Mananger utility also depends on what Williamson calls 'managerial slack' which consists of non-essentical eapenditure and includes such benefits such as lavishly furnished office, a luxurious company car, free air travel.

4. **The Discretionary Investment Expenditure-** This includes expenditure which a manager can spend according to his discrection. This discretionary expenditure is over and above the essential investment expenditure which is necessary for the growth of the firm.

The utility function of the managers and the factors on which it depends can be written as under:

$$U = f(S, N, M, I_d)$$

where, U = utility of a manager,

S = the salary and other forms of monetary compensation which a manager obtains from a business firm,

N = the number of staff under the control of a manager,

M = **management slack** which means the amount of non-essential expenditure by management such as lavishaly furnished offices, luxurious company car, large expense accounts, etc.

I_d = the amount of discretionary non-essential investment expendiutre by the manager.

Thus the managers maximise the above utility function, that is, the composite utility derived from the above mentioned four factors. However, as mentioned above, the objective of utility maximization by a manager is subject to the constraint that after-tax profits are large enough to pay acceptable dividends to the shareholders and also to pay for economically necessary investments (as discretionary investment expenditure by the managers).

Growth Maximisation

According to another important theory the managers of corporate firms try to **maximise the growth rate of their firms** rather than maximisation of profits. This theory was put forward by the Cambridge economist Robert Marris[19] in 1960s, Prof. Marris also considers the case of market structure in which competition is limited. Besides, he is concerned with the behaviour of the corporate firm where management is separated from ownership so that there is ample scope for managerial discretionary behaviour. Prof. Marris regards the corporator firm as a typically bureaucratic organisation where corporate growth and the security associated with it is a desirable goal. According to him, the goal of the corporate manager is to achieve balanced rate of growth of the firm which requires maximising rate of growth of demand for the products on the one hand and rate of growth of capital supply for increase in investment on the other.

Rationale for Maximising Growth of the Firm. Now, an important question is why managers seek to maximise the balanced growth rate of the firm, that is, why do they jointly maximise the rate of growth of demand for firm's products and the growth rate of capital supply. This is because by doing so they maximise their own utility function and the utility function of their owners. Before Marris, it was generally argued by the management theorists that the goals of the manager and the owner often cash because the utility functions which they try to maximise greatly differ. The utility function which managers seek to maximise include variables such as salaries, status, job security. On the other hand, utility function which owners seek to maximise include variables such as profits, capital supply, size of output, market share and image or reputation in the public.

According to Marris, despite the difference in the variables in the utility functions of managers and owners, the most of the variables included in both of them are positively correlated with a single variable, namely, the growth rate of the firm. Further, according to him, the growth of the firm may be measured by the increase in the level of output, capital supply, sales revenue or market share. However, Marris regards steady balanced growth rate over time as the objective of the managers because most of the variables such as sales, output, capital supply, included in their utility function increase simultaneously so that maximising long-run growth of any variable amounts to maximising long-run growth of others.

19. R. Marris, A Model of Managerial Enterprise, *Quarterly Journal of Economics* (1963). Also R. Marris, *Theory of Managerial Capitalism*, Macmillan, 1964.

It is evident from above that Marris thinks that corporate managers would recognise the relationship between the growth of the company with profits being ploughed back into investment for expansion of production capacity on the hand and their own personal goals (such as increased status, power and salary) on the other. Besides, according to Marris, managers try to balance growth against the impact of their decision on profits and dividends. They are expected to be aware of the risk of low dividends lowering share prices which put the firms vulnerable to being taken over by the rival companies. Thus, according to Marris, minimisation of risk requires Prudent approach in deciding about investment and ralsing of capital. Prof. Nellis and Parker[20] rightly state that there may be trade off between securing profits to pay dividends and taking risk when investing to increase the growth of the firm at the same time while profits provide the retained earnings to help finance. New investment which leads to growth of excessive company liquidity may attract predators. Cash rich companies attract takeover bids In Marris's model this conflict is summarised as management seeking "**optimal dividend-to-profit retention ratio**".

It may be noted that a noted American economist, J. K. Galbraith who has made an indepth study of big modern corporations has found that managers, which he calls technostructure, pursue *multiple goals* in which along with sales maximisation and utility maximisation, the objective of achieving the highest possible growth of output is paramount[21]. Further, Galbraith points out that managers of the big business corporations make every effort to increase their prestige, market power and technical superiority. In his view, the corporate technocrats who are highly skilled persons are able to pursue these multiple goals as they can greatly influence the consumers through effective advertizing on a large scale. Galbraith further points out that the highly salaried managers or technocrats of the modern business corporations desire to have an easy life for themselves and try to avoid risk and for that purpose extensive business planning is done by them for taking appropriate decisions.

Satisficing Behaviour

According to the satisficing hypothesis, corporate managers aim at achieving *satisfactory performance regarding rate of profit, sales, market share etc.* rather than maximizing profits. The advocates of this hypothesis say that a corporate manager sets for itself a minimum standard for performance or what is called the aspiration level. Once this satisfactory rate of profit according to this *aspiration level* is achieved, the firm will slack off.

H. A. Simon[22], one of the pioneers of the behavioural approach to the theory of the firm points out that most psychological theories assume that instead of *maximising,* rational men normally *satisfice.* Applying this to the business decisions of the firm, he suggests that instead of *maximizing profits,* firms aim at *satisficing,* that is, want to achieve *satisfactory level or rate of profit, satisfactory sales, satisfactory market share of the product.* Simon has further postulated that a firm has normally an *"aspiration level'*. An aspiration level of a firm is based on its goal as well as its past experience, and in fixing it uncertainties are duly taken into account. If the actual performance of the firm reveals that a given aspiration level can be easily achieved, it will be revised upward. On the other hand, if it is found that a given aspiration level is difficult to be achieved, it will be lowered. Simon points out that when the actual performance of a firm falls short of an aspiration level, *'search*[23] *activity* is started to find out the ways of

20. R. Marris, A Model of Managerial Enterprise, *Quarterly Journal of Economics* (1963). Also R. Marris, *Theory of Managerial Capitalism*, Macmillan, 1964.
21. See his well known works *The New Industrial State and Economics and the Public Purpose.*
22. Ibid.
23. Important works by H. A. Simon, in which he has developed his behavioural theory of the firm are : (1) A Behavioural Model of Rational Choice, *Quarterly Journal of Economics,* Feb. 1955. (2) Theories of Decision Making in Economic and Behavioural Sciences, *American Economic Review,* June 1959. (3) *Models of Men,* Wiley, New York, 1957.

better performance in the future and therefore achieving the aspiration level. But, according to Simon, there is a limit to 'searching activities' which a firm will undertake because for searching activities such as obtaining of information firms have to incur cost. And therefore the gain from search activity must be balanced against its cost. That is why if searching activities relatively cost more, aspiration level is adjusted downward to a level which is more likely to be achieved. Since the firm limits its searching activity on account of its cost, it does not maximise profits. Therefore, the firms behaving rationally aim at *'satisficing'* rather than *'maximising'*.

According to an other prominent satisficing theory put forward by Cyert and March[24], in these days of large-scale corporate type of business firms, we can no longer consider them as a *single major decision maker (i.e.,* the entrepreneur), but instead we should look at them as complex group or complex organisation composed of various individuals whose interests may conflict with each other. Cyert and March call this complex organisation or group an *organisational coalition* which may include managers, stock holders, workers, customers and so on. They assert that all of these different individuals participate in setting the *goals* of the organisation. Another argument for satisficing behaviour on the part of the corporate managers advanced is that top management serves as trustees of the organisation which has a responsibility not only to shareholders but also to employers, customers creditors, suppliers etc. Thus, corporate managers pursuing a satisficing goal strike a statesman like balance among the claims of shareholders for dividends and higher share price, the demands of employees for higher wages, the pressures from consumers for lower prices and better quality products.

Thus, the hypothesis of satisficing behaviour implies that instead of maximising profits for owners, corporate managers strive for attaining satisfactory rate of profit. The satisficing model of behaviour of the corporate managers rightly stresses that the problem of decision making in large firms, especially in oligopoly environment, is quite complex as they have to reconcile the interests of various pressure groups in the organisation. But the major problem with the satisficing hypothesis is that it does not provide a clear definition of *satisfactory rate of profits.* A number of standards of profits which may be considered as satisfactory may be mentioned. Thus, on the one hand, the satisfactory rate of profit may be that which is *high enough* to attract outside capital on sustained basis. On the other hand, the firms may fix their satisfactory rate of profit at a *low level* so as to prevent the entry of new firms which may offer a strong competition and erode their profits. The satisfactory rate of profits may be fixed at a low level in order to prevent the government control and regulation. Thus the standard of satisfactory profit may vary a good deal depending on the nature of competition and environment in which a particular firm may find itself. The satisficing model, therefore, does not provide us any general guideline for determination of satisfactory rate of profits for the fixation of output and price.

Staff Maximisation

In the present days of corporate form of business organisation, where there is separation of management from ownership managers, do not always work in the best interest of owners *i.e.* the shareholders, and try to maximise their utility. This is also so because monitoring and controlling the managers by the owners also involve a good amount of cost and therefore in actual practice this is not done. Therefore, complex organisational and managerial setup of modern corporate firms which Prof. J. K. Galbraith calls as 'technostructure' wields a great deal of power and influence with regard to policies pursued by these firms. In their bid to maximise utility managers often sacrifice *some* profits of the owners. The two important factors, namely, sales maximisation and a desire for adequate leisure and quiet life on the part of the

24. R. M. Cyert and J. C March, *A Behavioural Theory of the Firm,* Prentice-Hall, 1963.

managers have been discussed above, another important factor which enhances the utility of the managers of large corporate firms is the number of subordinate staff under their supervision and control. The greater the number of subordinate staff, the greater their utility.

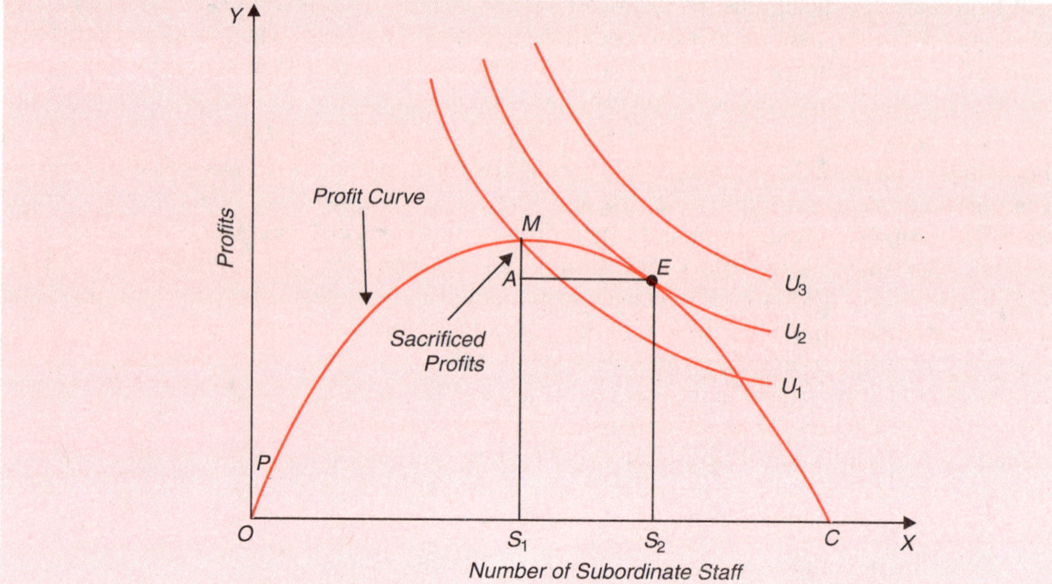

Fig. 25.2. *Staff Maximisation versus Profit Maximisation*

Thus, given the separation of ownership from control, the managers often strive to maximise their utility by employing more subordinate staff and in this process they even sacrifice some profits of the owners.

We can depict the *trade-off* between owners' profits and the number of subordinate staff for the managers in terms of indifference curves, U_1, U_2, U_3 in Figure 25.2 where on the horizontal axis the number of subordinate staff of a manager and on the vertical axis profits are measured. It will be seen from this figure that manager's indifference curves between owners' profits and number of subordinate staff are convex to the origin. It will be further seen that up to OS_1 number of staff, profits to the owners increase. This implies that addition of staff up to OS_1 improves efficiency and therefore causes profits to increase until OS_1 staff is employed at which maximum profits equal to S_1M are earned. With staff OS_1 and profits equal to S_1M, manager's utility is indicated by indifference curve U_1. When the number of staff increases beyond OS_1, profits to the owners decrease but manager's utility increases until he reaches the higher indifference U_2 which is tangent to the profit curve at point E. In the absence of effective monitoring and control by the owners, the manager would like to operate at point E where he is employing OS_2 number of staff and, given the owners profits curve, at the highest possible indifference curve U_2. It will be seen as compared to the profits S_1M with the staff equal to OS_1, profits with OS_2 staff are lower. This means that profits equal to MA have been sacrificed for the additional employment of AE staff by the manager so as to the increase his utility.

Case for Maximisation of Profits

We have explained above the various alternatives to profit maximisation hypotheses. However, the various alternatives to profit maximisation are not free from drawbacks and no comprehensive theory of the firm has been developed on the basis of non-profit maximising assumption so that till now the theory of the firm based on profit maximising behaviour dominates the economic theory. Several reasons can be given in favor of the assumption of profit maximising behaviour of the firms.

In the first place, there is a question of *survivorship.* The firm which is working in a very competitive environment and does not maximise profits will run the risks of not being able to survive in the long run. Thus, profit maximising is quite a rational behaviour in the fields where intense competition prevails. It may appear under certain circumstances that the firms are not maximising profits, but they may be doing so only for the short run. For instance, the firms working in oligopolistic or monopolistic market structures do not maximise profits in the short run in order to prevent the potential competitors to enter industry. Under these circumstances, the firms are only *maximising profits in the long run.* Similarly, some other goals such as maximising the growth of output, sales maximisation, increasing the market share are only means to achieve maximum profits in the long run and therefore from the long-run point of view, they are not inconsistent with the goal of profit maximisation.

In defence of profit maximisation hypothesis, it may also be noted that the managers are not permanent in a firm and are likely to be changed by the owners (shareholders in the corporate firms) if they feel that managers are not providing them adequate return or profits on their investment. Thus, given the fact that managers are liable to be changed, if they deviate much from profit maximisation, they will not be allowed to continue for long in the firm. Of course, if control over management is absent, the managers may continue to behave in a non-profit maximising manner. However, if the managers of corporate firms are not maximising profits in the long run, the prices of its shares will fall greatly and it may be taken over by others who will change the current management and install a new team of managers who are efficient and try to maximise profits in the long run.

Finally, it may be said that no model, nor its assumptions can be completely *realistic.* Models are built and assumptions are made so as to bring out the crucial aspects and relations of the economic phenomena. For this purpose we need not fully take into account the massive and confusing details of the real world. We must abstract from reality to draw purposeful conclusions which can adequately explain the economic phenomenon. This is true of the profit maximisation assumption. The profit maximisation may not fully reflect the behaviour of the managers in the real world but on the basis of the profit maximisation assumption, correct predictions regarding determination of prices and outputs of commodities have been made. In this regard we may refer again to the viewpoint of Friedman[25] who has argued that the ultimate test of the validity of an assumption is its *capability to predict correctly;* the assumption itself may be unrealistic. Defending the assumption of profit maximisation on these grounds he writes, "unless the behaviour of businessmen in some way or other is approximated behaviour consistent with the maximisation of returns, it seems unlikely that they would remain in business for long"[18]. He points out that profit maximisation assumption is valid because predictions regarding changes in prices and output based on it have been shown to be correct.

EQUILIBRIUM OF THE FIRM

Word 'equilibrium' means a state of balance. When two opposing forces working on an object are in balance so that the object is held still, the object is said to be in equilibrium. In other words, when the object under the pressure of forces working in opposite directions has no tendency to move in either direction, the object is in equilibrium. Thus, by consumer's equilibrium we mean that in regard to the allocation of money expenditures among various goods the consumer has reached the state where he has no tendency to reallocate his money expenditure. Similarly, ***a firm is said to be in equilibrium when it has no tendency to change its level of output, that is, when it has no tendency either to increase or***

25. Milton Friedman "The Methodology of Positive Economics", *Essays in Positive Economics,* University of Chicago Press, Chicago, 1953.

26. Ibid,

to contract its level of output. The firm will produce the equilibrium level of output and will charge the price at which the equilibrium output can be sold in the market. In fact in a previous chapter, we explained the equilibrium of the firm in respect of the combination of factors it has to employ for producing a given level of output. But the problem for a producer is not simply what combination of factors it has to choose for producing a given level of output but it goes further to decide what level of output it should produce. Therefore, equilibrium of the firm has also to be achieved in respect of output it has to produce. In this regard, to repeat what has been just said above, the firm is in equilibrium, when given certain demand and cost conditions, it has struck upon the level of output at which it will stick on and will have on tendency to change it.

The Goal of Profit Maximisation

Equilibrium of the firm depends upon what objective it wants to achieve. We have explained earlier various alternative objectives suggested by several economists. However, the goal of profit maximisation by the firm is still believed to be the most important and the theory of the firm has been extensively developed with maximisation of profits as the objective of the firm. Therefore, is our analysis of equilibrium of the firm, we will assume that it aims at maximizing its profits. The firm will therefore be in equilibrium when it is producing a level of output at which it is making maximum money profits. Now, profits are the difference between total revenue and total cost. So, in order to be in equilibrium, the firm will attempt to maximise the difference between total revenue and total cost.

In order to simplify our analysis, we also assume that our firm produces a single product. It is true that a firm in the real world may produce more than one product and our assumption of the sinlgle product firm may therefore be unrealistic. But the assumption of multi-product firm which seems to be more realistic will not, given the assumption of profit maximisation, involve any significant modification in the method or results of analysis. It is to make our analysis simple that we are making the assumption of a single-product firm. It should be noted that in the present chapter we are concerned with the analysis of equilibrium of firm in general terms. We shall explain the equilibrium of firm with reference to specific market forms, namely, perfect competition, monopoly, monopolistic competition when we take up their separate detailed study. Here, we shall derive general conditions of equilibrium which are valid under all types of market. An old method of explaining the equilibrium of the firm is to draw the total revenue and total cost curves of the firm and locate the maximum profit point. But with the development of the approach of marginal analysis, equilibrium of the firm in modern micro-economic theory is explained with the aid of marginal revenue and marginal cost curves. We shall explain below the equilibrium of the firm in both these ways.

Equilibrium of the Firm : Total Revenue – Total Cost Approach

A firm is in equilibrium when it is earning maximum profits. A firm will go on increasing its output if its profits are thereby increasing. It will fix output at the level where it is making maximum money profits. Profits are the difference between total revenue (*TR*) and total cost (*TC*). Thus the firm will be in equilibrium at the level of output where the difference between total revenue and total cost is the greatest. Fig. 25.3 portrays what is called break-even chart by businessmen. In this are shown total revenue curve *TR* and total cost curve *TC*. Total revenue curve *TR* starts from the origin which means that when no output is produced revenue is zero. Total revenue goes on increasing as more output is produced. However, it will be noticed that total cost curve *TC* starts from a point *F which lies above the origin*. In other words, it is assumed that even when there is no production, the firm has to incur some costs equal to *OF.* For instance, when the firm has to stop production in the short run, it has to bear the fixed costs. Thus, Fig. 25.3 depicts short-run total revenue and total cost curves of the firm. As a firm starts from zero output and increases its production of the good, in the initial stages total cost is greater than total revenue and the firm is not making any profits at all. When it is producing *OL* level of output, total revenue just equals total cost and the firm is therefore making neither profits nor losses, that is, the firm is only *breaking even*. Thus the point *S* corresponding to output *OL* is called *Break-Even Point*.

When the firm increases its output beyond *OL*, total revenue becomes larger than total cost and profits begin to accrue to the firm. It will be seen from the figure that profits are rising as the firm increases production to *OM*, since the distance between the total revenue curve *(TR)* and total cost curve *(TC)* is widening. At *OM* level of output, the distance between the *TR* curve and *TC* curve is the greatest and therefore the profits are maximum. Thus the firm will be in equilibrium at the *OM* level of output. The firm will not produce any output larger than *OM* since after it the gap between *TR* and *TC* curves goes on narrowing down and therefore the total profits will be declining. At *OH* level of output, *TR* and *TC* curves again intersect each other, which means that total revenue is equal to total cost at output *OH*. Thus point *K* (corresponding to output *OH*) is again a break-even point. Beyond output *OH*, total revenue is less than total cost and the firm will make losses if it produces any output larger than *OH*.

From above it is clear that the firm will be in equilibrium at level of output *OM* where the total revenue exceeds total cost by the largest amount and hence profits are maximum. Now the question is how to locate this profit-maximizing output level. By vision it is not easy to locate where exactly is the largest distance between *TR* and *TC* curves. In order to do so we have to draw tangents to the various points on the *TR* and *TC* curves. Where the tangents to the corresponding points on the *TR* and *TC* curves are parallel to each other, as is shown in Fig. 25.3 by tangents to points *E* and *N* on *TR* and *TC* curves respectively, the distance between *TR* and recurves will be the largest and hence profits the maximum.

Another way to find out the profit maximizing output is to draw directly total profit curve showing the difference between total revenue and total cost at various levels of output. In Fig. 25.3 *TP* is such total profit curve which indicates the difference between total revenue and total cost at various levels of output. The level of output at which this profit curve stands highest from the X-axis will be the profit-maximizing level of output. It will be noticed from Fig. 25.3 *TP* that total profit curve *TP* lies below the X-axis upto point *L* which shows that the firm is making negative profits *(i.e.* losses) upto *OL* level of output. At *L*, the profit curve cuts the *X*-axis indicating that at output *OL*, the profits are equal to zero. As the firm increases its output beyond *OL*, profits curve is rising which indicates that total profits are increasing. At output *OM*, profit curve stands highest from the X-axis and beyond *OM* the profit curve slopes downward indicating that total profits are declining when output is raised beyond *OM*. It may also be pointed out that tangent drawn to point *D* on the profit curve (corresponding to output *OM*) will be parallel to the X-axis which indicates the greatest distance between the profit curve and the *X*-axis at output level *OM*. It follows that at output *OM* the firm will be making maximum profits and hence will be in equilibrium position.

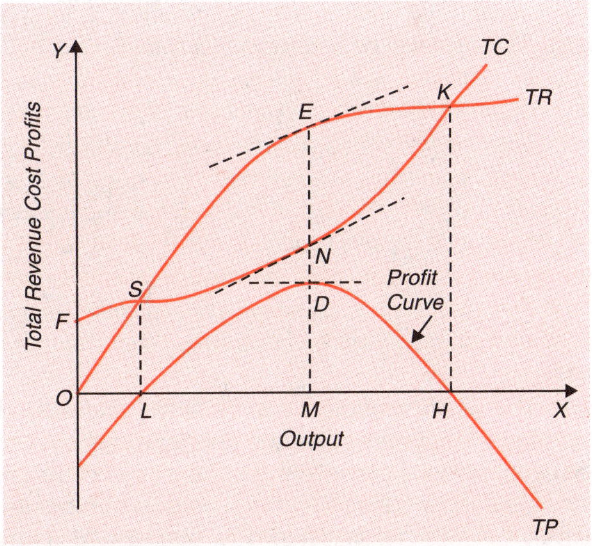

Fig. 25.3. *Profit Maximising by a Firm : TC–TC Approach*

The profits earned at *OM* level of output are equal to *NE* or *MD*.

This method of finding out the profit-maximizing level of output by curves of total revenue and total cost seems to be quite reasonable and is also often employed by businessmen too, but it has some limitations. In the first place, the greatest vertical distance between total revenue and total cost curves is difficult to find out at a glance. Many tangents have to be drawn before one finds the corresponding tangents to two curves to be parallel to each other indicating the level of output which yields maximum money profits. Of course, when profit curve is also drawn, it is relatively less difficult to locate the maximum profit point, because output corresponding to the highest point of profit curve is profit-maximizing output. Secondly, in this method, price per unit of output cannot be known at first sight from the diagram since price is not directly shown in the diagram. In order to know the price we have to divide the total revenue at the profit-maximizing point by the total output. Thus in Fig. 25.3 at maximum profit output *OM* the total revenue is *ME*. The price charged by the firm will be equal to $\frac{\text{total revenue}}{\text{total output}} = \frac{ME}{OM}$. With these limitations, complicated problems of the equilibrium analysis of the firm cannot be easily discussed with this method of showing equilibrium of the firm. In modern economic theory, marginal analysis involving marginal cost and marginal revenue curves are therefore employed for explaining the equilibrium of the firm. We now turn to explain this alternative method.

Equilibrium of the Firm : Marginal Revenue-Marginal Cost Approach

In an earlier chapter we explained in detail the concepts of marginal revenue and marginal cost. Marginal revenue means the addition made to the total revenue by producing and selling an additional unit of output and marginal cost means the addition made to the total cost by producing an additional unit of output. Now, a firm will go on expanding its level of output so long as an extra unit of output adds more to revenue than to cost, since it will be profitable to do so. The firm will not produce an additional unit of the product which adds more to cost than to revenue because to produce that unit will mean losses. In other words, it will pay the firm to go on producing additional units of output so long as the marginal revenue exceeds marginal cost. The firm will be increasing its total profits by increasing its output to the level at which marginal revenue just equals marginal cost. It will not be profitable for the firm to produce a unit of output of which marginal cost is greater than marginal revenue.

The firm will be making maximum profits by expanding output to the level where marginal revenue is equal to marginal cost. If it goes beyond the point of equality between marginal revenue and marginal cost, it will be incurring losses on the extra units of output and therefore will be reducing its total profits. Thus, the firm will be in equilibrium position when it is producing the amount of output at which marginal revenue equals marginal cost. It will be earning maximum profits at the point of equality between marginal revenue and marginal cost. Therefore, the condition for equilibrium of the firm is that the marginal revenue should be equal to marginal cost.

The whole argument can be better understood with the aid of Fig. 25.4 which depicts hypothetical marginal revenue and marginal cost curves of the firm. In this Fig. 25.4 firm's marginal revenue curve *MR* is sloping downward and firm's marginal cost curve *MC* which in the beginning is falling but after a point is sloping upward. The two curves intersect each other at point *E* which corresponds to output *OM*. Upto *OM* level of output, marginal revenue exceeds marginal cost and at *OM* the two are just equal to each other. The firm will be maximizing its profits by producing output *OM*. The total profits will be less if it produces less than or more than *OM*. For instance, if the firm produces *OL* level of output (which is less than

OM), its total profits will be less than at *OM*, because by producing *OL*, it will be foregoing the opportunity to earn more profits which it can if it raises output to *OM*. This is so because additional units between *L* and *M* add more to revenue than to cost (*i.e.*, their *MR* is greater than *MC*) and it will therefore be profitable for the firm to produce them. The extra units between *L* and *M* can give to the firm extra profits equal to the area *ABE* which it would be foregoing if it produces *OL* output.

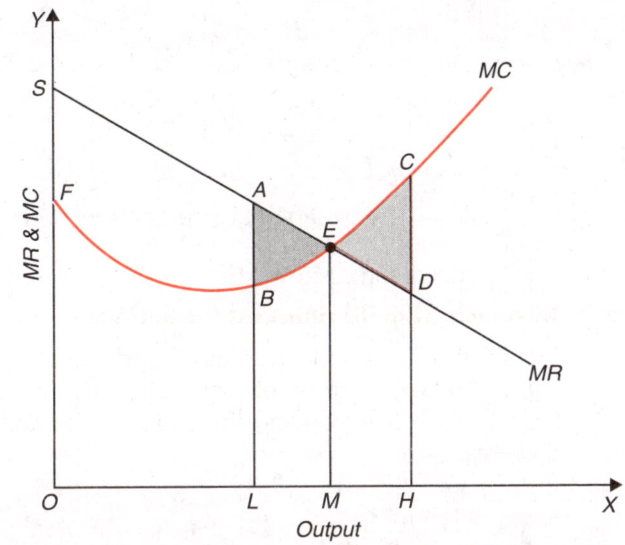

Fig. 25.4. *Equilibrium of the Firm: MR – MC Approach*

To conclude, the firm will be making maximum profits and will therefore be in equilibrium at the level of output at which marginal revenue is equal to marginal cost, or where the marginal revenue and marginal cost curves intersect each other. The amount of total profits earned by the firm in its equilibrium position at *OM* output will be equal to the area *SFE*. A point about profits is worth noting. It will be seen from figure that as the output is approaching near to point *M*, the gap between *MR* and *MC* curves is narrowing down till it disappears at output *OM* . Since gap or distance between *MR* and *MC* indicates the amount of profit earned on the additional unit of output, it means therefore the amount of profit earned on successive units of output goes on declining and is equal to zero at *OM*. Thus at *OM* output, amount of profit on marginal unit is zero but total profits will be maximum. It means that by expanding output to *OM* level, the firm has availed the whole opportunity of making profits and therefore its profits are maximum at *OM*.

The students who have some knowledge of mathematics may better understand the argument in the following way :

Let *R* stand for total revenue, *C* for total cost and *q* for the quantity produced of the good. Since marginal revenue is the rate of change of total revenue (*i.e.* , slope of the total revenue curve), it can be written as $\frac{dR}{dq}$. Similarly, marginal cost is the rate of change of total cost (*i.e*, slope of the total cost curve), it can be written as $\frac{dC}{dq}$.

Let π represent total profits

Total profits = Total Revenue – Total cost

or, $$\pi = R - C$$

To make π maximum it is necessary to fix that level or quantity of output at which small variation in output will cause no change in profit (*i.e.*, where rate of change of total profits will be zero).

Thus, in order that π be maximum

$$\frac{d\pi}{dq} = 0$$

But $$\frac{d\pi}{dq} = \frac{dR}{dq} - \frac{dC}{dq}$$

Therefore, for π to be maximum,

$$\frac{dR}{dq} - \frac{dC}{dq} = 0$$

$$\frac{dR}{dq} = \frac{dC}{dq}$$

But $\frac{dR}{dq}$ and $\frac{dC}{dq}$ represent marginal revenue and marginal cost respectively. Hence, for profits (π) to be maximum, $MC = MR$.

Profit-Maximising Equilibrium Output and Price

In Fig. 25.4 only marginal revenue and marginal cost curves are shown and price cannot be directly read or known from this figure. In order to read price directly from the figure, it is customary to draw corresponding average revenue and average cost curves along with the marginal curves.

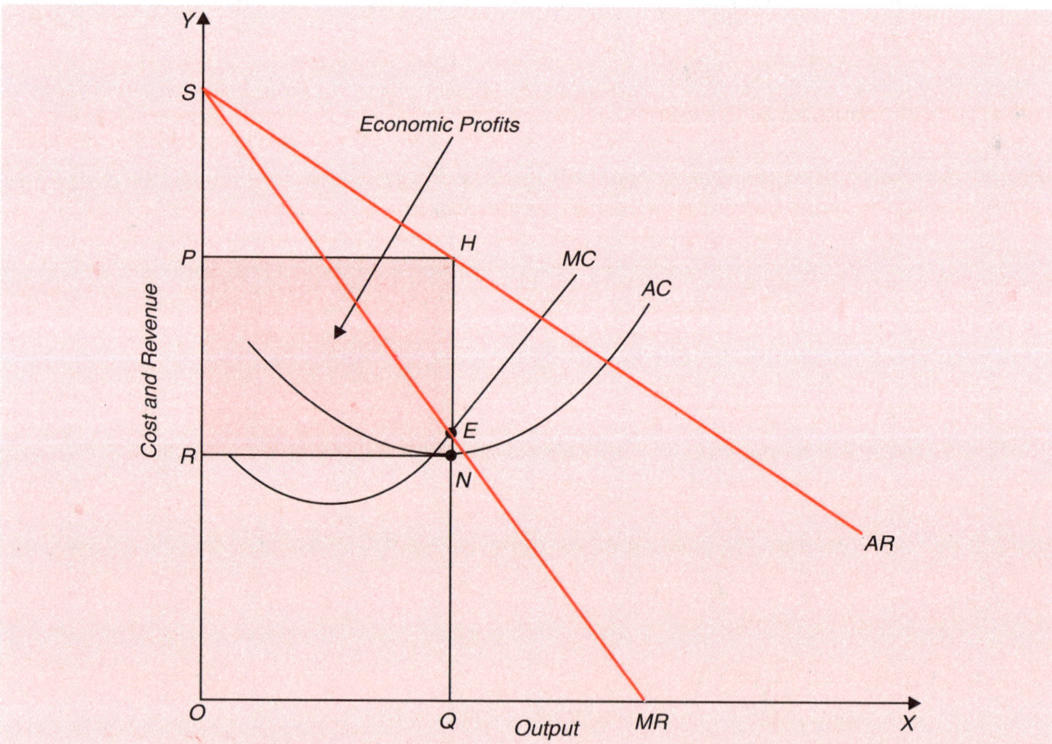

Fig. 25.5 *Equilibrium of the Firm: Equilibrium Output, Price and Profits*

This is exhibited in Fig. 25.5. The firm is in equilibrium at output *OQ* at which marginal revenue and marginal cost curves intersect each other. It will be seen from *AR* curve that *OQ* output yields *QH* (= *OP*) as average revenue or, in other words, *OQ* output can be sold at price *QH* (= *OP*).

Thus, we can directly read the price at which the firm sells its output from this figure. In Fig. 25.5 the total profits made by the firm can also be represented and known in a different way from that of Fig. 25.3.

Total profits = Total Revenue – Total Cost
= AR (or Price) x Output – AC × Output

In Fig. 25.5, AR or Price = QH, output = OQ
average cost or $AC = QN$

Total profits = $QH \times OQ - QN \times OQ$
= area $OQHP$ – area $OQNR$
= *area RNHP*

Second Order Condition for Equilibrium of the Firm

The first order condition for the equilibrium output of the firm is that its marginal revenue should be equal to marginal cost. There is a second order condition which must also be fulfilled if the firm is to be in a stable equilibrium position. Thus, equality between marginal revenue and marginal cost is a necessary but not a sufficient condition of firm's equilibrium. The ***second order condition requires that for a firm to be in equilibrium marginal cost curve must cut marginal revenue curve from below at the point of equilibrium.*** If at the point of equality between *MR* and *MC*, the *MC* curve is cutting *MR* curve from above, then beyond this equality point, *MC* would be lower than *MR* and it will be profitable for the firm to expand output beyond this equality point. It is thus clear that the output at which marginal revenue is equal to marginal cost but marginal cost curve is cutting marginal revenue curve from above cannot be the position of equilibrium because the firm will have a tendency to increase its output further in spite of the equality between marginal revenue and marginal cost. For instance, consider Fig. 25.6. Here *MR* curve is a horizontal straight line and *MC* curve is U-shaped and is cutting *MR* curve at two points, *F* and *E*. The firm cannot be in equilibrium at point *F* (or output *ON*) at which *MC* is equal to *MR*. This is because *MC* curve is cutting *MR* curve from above at point *F* corresponding to *ON* output with the result that beyond *ON* output *MC* is lower than *MR* and it is therefore profitable for the firm to expand output beyond *ON*. Actually, at *ON* output the firm is making losses equal to the area between *MC* curve and *MR* curve. (*MC* curve lies above *MR* curve up to *F*). It is thus clear that in spite of the fact that marginal revenue and marginal cost are equal at output *ON*, the firm is not in equilibrium since it is profitable for it to expand further.

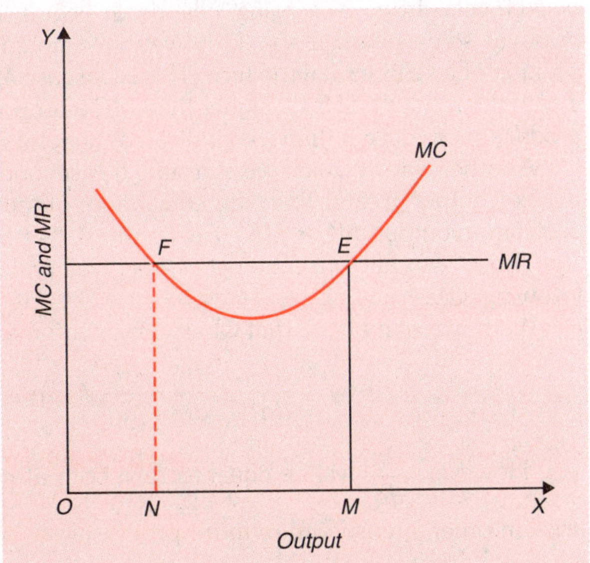

Fig. 25.6 *MC curve must cut MR Curve from below at the point of equilibrium.*

At output *OM* (or point *E*) where marginal cost and marginal revenue are equal and also marginal cost curve is cutting marginal revenue curve *from below*, the firm will be in equilibrium position. This is so because beyond *OM*, marginal cost curve lies above marginal revenue curve and therefore it will not be worthwhile to produce more than *OM*. The firm will not stop short of *OM* output for it can increase its profits by expanding output up to *OM*. To conclude, in Fig. 25.6 the firm is in equilibrium at *OM* output (point *E*) and not at output *ON* (point *F*).

Similarly, point *C* in Fig. 25.7 (*a*) cannot be the position of equilibrium though *MC* equals *MR*. This is because at *C*, *MC* curve is cutting *MR* curve from above with the result that *MC* is lower than *MR* after *C*. The firm will go on expanding output beyond *C* since the additional

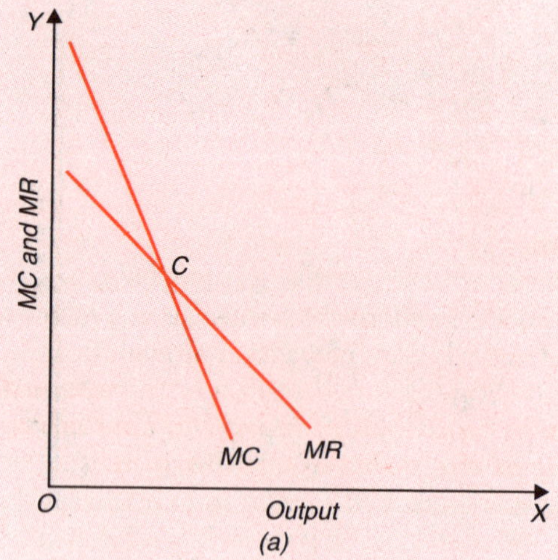

Fig. 25.7 (a). Equilibrium cannot exist

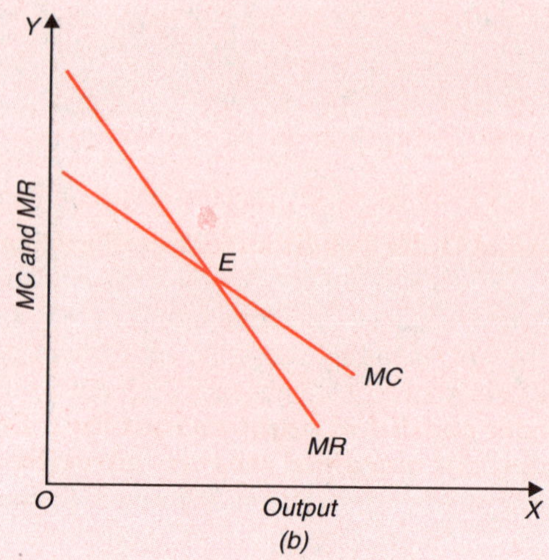

Fig. 25.7 (b). Equilibrium exists

units will add more to revenue than to cost. In the situation depicted in Fig. 25.7 (*a*), there is no determinate position of firm's equilibrium. In this figure determinate position of equilibrium can only be established if marginal cost curve begins to rise so that it then cuts *MR* curve from below at some point. It should however be noted that point *E* in Fig. 25.7(*b*) denotes the position of equilibrium of the firm. This is because *MC* curve is cutting *MR* curve from below at *E* with the result that *MC* is higher than *MR* after point *E*. It will not therefore be worthwhile to produce more output than that indicated by point *E*.

Another way in which we can state this second order condition of firm's equilibrium is:

For output greater than the equilibrium output, $MC > MR$ and for output less than the equilibrium output, $MC < MR$

Those who know mathematics may well understand the second order condition in the following way:

We have seen above that when profits are maximised,

$$\frac{d\pi}{dq} = \frac{dR}{dq} - \frac{dC}{dq} = 0$$

However, $\frac{d\pi}{dq}$ will be equal to zero both at minimum profit level and maximum profit level. In order to ensure *maximum* profits, its second derivative must be negative, that is,

$$\frac{d^2\pi}{dq^2} = \frac{d^2R}{dq^2} - \frac{d^2C}{dq^2} < 0$$

or, $$\frac{dMR}{dq} - \frac{dMC}{dq} < 0; \qquad \frac{dMR}{dq} < \frac{dMC}{dq}.$$

This means that at profit-maximising level, the slope of *MR* curve must be less than the slope of *MC* curve. In Fig. 25.6 at point *F* the second order condition is not fulfilled since at *F* slope of marginal revenue curve is zero which is greater than the slope of marginal cost curve which is negative (*i.e.*, less than zero). Point *E* in Fig. 25.6 satisfies this second-order condition as the slope of marginal revenue curve which is still equal to zero is less than the slope of marginal cost curve which is positive (*i.e.*, more than zero). At point *C* in Fig. 25.7(*a*) both *MR* and *MC* curves have *negative slopes* but *MR* curve is falling less rapidly than *MC* curve which means that algebraic value of the slope of *MR* curve is greater than that of *MC* curve. Thus point *C* in Fig. 25.7(*a*) does not satisfy the second-order condition and therefore cannot represent equilibrium position. On the other hand, point *E* in Fig. 25.7(*b*) satisfies the second-order condition.

To sum up, for a firm to be in equilibrium, the following two conditions must be satisfied.

(1) *MR* = *MC*,

(2) Slope of *MR* curve must be less that of *MC* curve or *MC* Curve must cut *MR* curve from below.

A Numerical Example of Profit Maximisation

Problem. *A firm has the following total revenue and total cost function.*

$$TR = 320\,Q - 2Q^2$$
$$TC = 1800 + 50\,Q + 3Q^2$$

Find out to determine

1. *The level of output at which the firm will be maximising profits.*
2. *The level of output at which total revenue will be maximum.*

Solution. The profit-maximising output can be found by obtaining *MR* and *MC* from the given total revenue and total cost functions respectively. As has been noted above, marginal revenue (*MR*) and marginal cost (*MC*) are measured by the slopes at a point on these curves. Further, as has been explained in the previous chapter, slope at a point of a function is measured by the first derivative of the function. Taking the first derivative of the given total revenue function :

$$MR = \frac{\Delta TR}{\Delta Q} = 320 - 4Q$$

Taking the first derivative of the total cost function,

$$MC = \frac{\Delta TC}{\Delta Q} = 50 + 6Q$$

$$\text{Setting } MR = \text{MC we have}$$
$$320 - 4Q = 50 + 6Q$$
$$10Q = 320 - 50 = 270$$
$$Q = 27$$

Thus, profit-maximising level of output is 27.

It should be noted that if we use total revenue total cost approach to obtain optimum level of output, we will get the same results. Thus

$$\text{Profits } (\pi) = TR - TC$$
$$\pi = (320Q - 2Q^2) - (1800 + 50Q + 3Q^2)$$
$$= 320Q - 2Q^2 - 1800 - 50Q - 3Q^2$$
$$\pi = 270Q - 5Q^2 - 1800 \quad \ldots (i)$$
$$\frac{d\pi}{dQ} = 270 - 10Q \quad \ldots (ii)$$

Now, profits will be maximised when the first derivative of total profit function is zero.

Thus, setting $\frac{d\pi}{dQ} = 0$, we have

$$270 - 10Q = 0$$
$$10Q = 270; \quad Q = 27$$

The second order condition requires that the second derivative of profit function in equation (i) above with respect to output must be negative. The second derivative of profit function is

$$\frac{d^2\pi}{dQ^2} = -10$$

Thus at output level of 27, the second order condition is satisfied.

CHAPTER

26

Pricing in Competitive Markets: Demand-Supply Analysis

We are now in a position to explain how price is determind under perfect competitive markets. In the preceding chapters we have explained in detail the forces of demand and supply which by their interaction determine the price of the product. In the discussion of the theory of demand it was assumed that an individual buyer is unable to influence the price of the product and therefore took the prevailing price of the product as a given datum for him. Further, the consumer spends his given money income on various goods so as to obtain maximum satisfaction from his total outlay. On this assumption we derived the demand curve for a product with the aid of Marshallian cardinal utility analysis as well as with indifference curve technique. Likewise, we explained the theory of production by assuming that an individual entrepreneur or a firm could not individually affect the prices of the factors and took the ruling prices in the market as given and constant for him and used the various factors in such a ratio that minimised cost of production for a given level of output. It is the cost of production, especially marginal cost of production that determines the supply of a product in the market at a given price.

Now, the intersection of demand and supply curves determines the price of the product. It is not the demand of a single buyer and the supply of a single seller that go to determine the price of the product, but the demand of all buyers of a product taken together (*i.e.*, market demand curve) and the supply of all firms selling the product taken together (*i.e.*, the supply curve of the industry) that determine the price of the product in competitive markets. The market demand curve shows the various quantities of the good which will be demanded at different prices. On the other hand, the industry's supply curve of a product shows the various quantities of the good that the industry will be ready to supply at different prices. The particular price at which quantity demanded is equal to quantity supplied will finally settle down in the market.

MARSHALLIAN VERSUS WALRASIAN APPROACHES TO PRICE THEORY

Marshall's Partial Equilibrium Analysis

In regard to pricing under perfect competition, two main approaches have been adopted. One approach has been followed by famous English economist Alfred Marshall who propounded the *partial equilibrium analysis* and the second approach has been advanced by Walras and is called *general equilibrium analysis*. In partial equilibrium approach to the pricing, we seek to explain the price determine of a commodity, *keeping the prices of other commodities constant and also assuming that the various commodities are not interdependent*. In explaining partial equilibrium approach. Marshall writes :

"The forces to be dealt with are, however, so numerous that it is best to analyse a few at a time and to work out a number of partial solutions as auxiliaries to our main study. Thus we begin by isolating the primary relations of supply, demand and price in regard to a particular commodity. We reduce to inaction all other forces by the phrase 'other things being equal'. We do not suppose that they are inert, but for the time we ignore their activity. This scienctific device is a great deal older than science; it is the method by which consciously or unconsciously sensible men dealt from time immemorial with every difficult problem of everyday life."[1]

Thus in Marshallian explanation of pricing under perfect competition, demand function (or a demand curve) for a commodity is drawn with the assumption that prices of other commodities, tastes and incomes of the consumers remain constant. Similarly, supply curve of commodity is constructed by assuming that prices of other commodities, prices of resources or factors and production function remain the same. Then Marshall's partial equilibrium analysis seeks to explain the price determination of a single commodity through the intersection of demand and supply curves, with prices of other goods, resource prices etc., remaining the same. Prices of other goods, resource prices, income, *etc*., are the *data* of the system which are taken as given and the determination of price-output equilibrium of a single commodity is explained. Given the assumption of *ceteris paribus* it explains the determination of a price of a good, say X, independently of the prices of all other goods. With the change in the data, new demand and supply curves will be formed and, corresponding to these, new price of the commodity will be determined. Thus partial equilibrium analysis of price determination also studies how the equilibrium price changes as a result of change in the data. But given the independent data the partial equilibrium analysis explains only the price determination of a commodity in isolation and does not analyse how the prices of various goods are interdependent and inter-related and how they are *simultaneously* determined.

It should be noted that partial equilibrium analysis is based on the assumption that the changes in a single industry do not significantly affect the rest of the industries. Thus, in partial equilibrium analysis, if the price of a good changes, it will not affect the demand for other goods. Prof. Lipsey rightly writes: "All partial equilibrium analyses are based on the assumption of *ceteris paribus*. Strictly interpreted, the assumption is that all other things in the economy are unaffected by any changes in the sector under consideration (say sector *A*). This assumption is always violated to some extent, for anything that happens in one sector must cause changes in some other sectors. What matters is that the changes induced throughout the rest of the economy are sufficiently small and diffiuse so that the effect they in turn have on the sector A can be safely ignored".[2]

Walras' General Equilibrium Analysis

In general equilibrium analysis, the price of a good is not explained to be determined independently of the prices of other goods. Since the changes in price of good X affect the prices and quantities demanded of other goods and in turn changes in prices and quantities of other goods will affect the quantity demanded of the good X, the *general equilibrium approach explains the simultaneous determination of prices of all goods and factors*. Thus, general equilibrium analysis "looks at ***multi-market equilibrium.*** It considers the way in which the prices of all goods in an economic system are set simultaneously, each in its own flex-price market."[3]

As stated above, partial equilibrium approach assumes that the effect of the change in price of a good X will be so diffused in the rest of the economy (*i.e.*, over all other goods) so as

1. Alfred Marshall, *Principles of Economics*, Eighth Edition, Macmillan, 1949.
2. R.G. Lipsey, *An Introduction to Positive Economics, Sixth edition 1990, p.404.*
3. Stonier and Hague, *A Textbook of Economic Theory*, 4th edition, 1972, p.383.

to have negligible effect on the prices and quantities of other individual goods. Therefore, where the effect of a change in the price of a good on the prices and quantities of some other goods is significant, as is there in the case of inter-related goods, the partial equilibrium approach cannot be validly applied in such cases and therefore the need for applying general equilibrium analysis which should explain the mutual and simultaneous determination of their prices and quantities. Hence, if goods X and Y are either strongly complementry or close substitutes, a fall in the price of good X can significantly influence the demand for Y. General equilibrium analysis attempts to take account of such relationships.

General equilibrium analysis deals with inter-relationship and inter-dependence between equilibrium adjustment with each other. General equilibrium exists when, at the going prices, the quantities demanded of each product and each factor are equal to their respective quantities supplied. A change in the demand or supply of any good, or factor would cause changes in prices and quantities of all goods and factors and there will begin adjustment and readjustment in demand, supply and prices of other goods and factors till the new general equilibrium is established. Indeed, the general equilibrium analysis is solving a system of simultaneous equations. In a general equilibrium system, the quantity demanded of *each good* is described by an equation in which its quantity demanded is a function of *prices of all goods*. That is,

$$q_i^d = D_i \ (p_1, p_2, p_3, \ldots\ldots p_n), \qquad \ldots.(i)$$

where $i = 1, 2, 3, \ldots. n$

In the above equation q_i^d stands for the quantity demanded for a good, p_1, p_2, p_3 etc. stand for the prices of various goods, and D_i denotes function for a good. The above equation (*i*) means that quantity demanded of each of *n* goods is a function of (*i.e.*, depends upon) prices of all goods.

Likewise, in general equilibrium analysis, quantity supplied of each good is considered to be the function of price of all factors of production. Thus,

$$q_i^s = S_i \ (f_1, f_2, f_3, \ldots\ldots f_m), \qquad \ldots.(ii)$$

where $i = 1, 2, 3, \ldots. m$

That is, quantity supplied of each of the *n* goods (q_i^s) is a function of the prices of various factors f_1, f_2, f_3 etc.

The above function (*i*) means that the prices of *n goods* affect the quantity demanded of *each* of the *n* goods. The above function (*ii*) means that the prices of the *m* factors affect the quantity supplied of each of the *n* goods. Besides these crucial equations, there will be equations determining ***the price of each of the factors of production.*** As noted above, a change in any of the demand or supply equations would cause changes in prices and quantities of all goods and as a result the system will tend to move to the new general equilibrium.

To explain the inter-relationship and interdependence among the prices and quantities of goods and factors and ultimately to explain the determination of the relative prices of all goods and factors, the proportion in which different goods are being produced and different factors are being used for the production of different goods is the essence of general equilibrium analysis.Professor Ryan explains the gist of general equilibrium in the following words :

"Let us suppose that the whole economy is initially in 'general' equilibrium: that is, that at the going prices the planned sales of each commodity and productive service are equal to the planned purchases...... When a 'general' equilibrium is disturbed by some economic event there will ensue a process of adjustment and readjustment during which each price affects, and is in turn affected by each other price. The changing pattern of prices is in part the cause, and in part the consequence, of revision in the purchases and sales plans of individuals, households and firms.. . . ultimately, a new equilibrium will emerge, in which the planned sales of each commodity and productive service will again be equal to the planned purchases. In the new 'general' equilibrium, full adjustment will have been made to the new conditions. In our example, there will be a new pattern of relative product and factor prices ; the proportion in which the different productive services are being used by firms will have altered ; the distribution of skills amongst the different members of the labour-force and the composition of the economy's stock of durable goods and equipment may both have changed and there will have been changes in the composition of the flow of goods and services that is being produced in each period and in the manner in which this flow is being distributed between households."[4]

PRICE DETERMINATION : STATIC EQUILIBRIUM BETWEEN DEMAND AND SUPPLY

Before Marshall there was a dispute among earlier economists as to whether it is supply of a good or the demand for it that determines its price. Broadly speaking, there were two schools of thought in this regard. One school of thought believed that it is cost of production, that is, the force working on the supply side, which determines the price of the product. The other school of thought held the view that it is the utility or more precisely the marginal utility that determines the demand and therefore the price of the product. But each school of thought took one-sided view of the pricing problem. The credit of finding the true answer to the pricing problem goes to Marshall who held that both demand and supply were equally important in determining the price of a good. In other words, Marshall said that both the marginal utility of a good and the cost of producing it took part in determining price. He compared the price determination to the cutting of a piece of a paper by a pair of scissors. This famous analogy is worth quoting here. "We might as reasonably dispute whether it is the upper or the under blade of a pair of scissors that cuts a piece of paper as whether value is governed by utility or cost of production. It is true that when one blade is held still and the cutting is effected by moving the other, we may say with careless brevity that the cutting is done by the second, but the statement is not strictly accurate and is to be excused only so long as it claims to be merely a popular and not a strictly scientific account of what happens."[5]

Neither the upper blade nor the lower one taken individually can cut the paper; both are required to do the work of cutting. The lower blade may be held stationary and only the upper one may be moved, yet both are indispensable for cutting the paper. Similarly, both demand and supply are essential forces for determining price. The only right answer to the question whether it is supply or demand which determines price is that it is both. At sometimes it appears that one is more important than the other, because one is active and the other passive. Thus, if demand remains constant but supply conditions change, it is demand which is passive and supply active. But both are equally important in determining price.

In the chapters on theory of demand we have explained that the demand curve of a commodity normally slopes downward. In other words, with the fall in price, quantity demanded of a good rises and *vice versa*. In the theory of production and cost we have studied that the supply curve of a commodity usually slopes upward. In other words, an industry will offer to

4. W.J.L. Ryan, *Price Theory*, Macmillan & Co., 1958, pp. 244, 246-47.

5. A. Marshall, *Principles of Economics*, 8th edition, p. 344.

sell more quantity of a good at a higher price than at a lower one. The level of price at which demand and supply curves intersect each other will finally come to stay in the market. In other words, the price which will come to prevail in the market is one at which quantity demanded is equal to quantity supplied.

Marshallian Quantity Adjustment. Marshall explained the adjustments of market to the equilibrium situation through the *changes in quantity*. In his analysis of equilibrium, Marshall put forward the view that buyers and sellers should be viewed as *adjusting quantity when there is disequilibrium* between demand and supply and according to him, changes in price occur to bring quantity demanded of a good equal to its quantity supplied. ***The price at which quantity demanded of a good equals quantity supplied is called equilibrium price,*** for at this price the two forces of demand and supply exactly balance each other. ***The quantity of the good which is purchased and sold at this equilibrium price is called equilibrium amount.*** Thus, the intersection of demand and supply curves determines price-quantity equilibrium. This price-quantity equilibrium is ***static equilibrium*** because, other factors influencing demand and supply have been held constant.

Equilibrium Price. Only at the equilibrium price wishes of both the buyers and sellers are satisfied. If price was greater or less than the equilibrium price the buyers' and sellers' wishes would be inconsistent: either the buyers would demand more than the amount offered by sellers, or the sellers would be ready to supply more than the amount demanded by the buyers. If price was greater than the equilibrium price, quantity supplied would exceed quantity demanded and thus giving rise to *excess supply* of the good at the current price. It means some of the sellers will not be able to sell the amount of the good they wanted to supply. These unsatisfied sellers would try to dispose of the unsold goods by bidding price down. The price will go on declining until the quantity demanded equals quantity supplied.

On the other hand, if price were lower than the equilibrium price, the quantity demanded would exceed quantity supplied giving rise to *excess demand* for the commodity. Some buyers would not be able to obtain the amount of the good they wanted to purchase at the prevailing price. They will therefore bid price up in their effort to get all that they desired to buy. The price will go on rising until the quantity demanded and quantity supplied are again equal. We thus see that the price which will settle down can be neither greater nor less than the equilibrium price. It is the equilibrium price which will finally come to stay in the market.

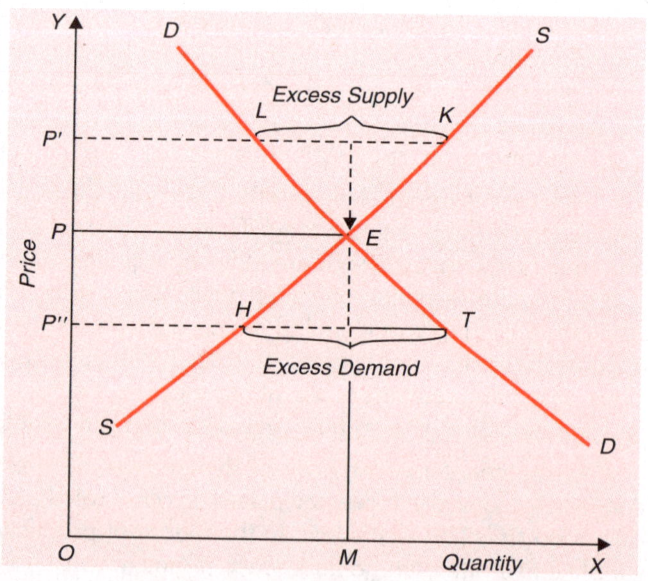

Fig. 26.1 *Determination of Price Through Intersection of Demand and Supply Curves*

Graphic Illustration

We illustrate below the process of price determination with the aid of demand and supply curves which will make the whole pricing process in perfectly competitive markets very clear. The equilibrium between demand and supply is depicted in Fig. 26.1 where demand curve *DD* of a good is sloping downward and the supply curve *SS* of the good is sloping upward. Demand and supply are in equilibrium at point *E* where two curves intersect each other. It means that only at price *OP* (corresponding to the intersection point), the quantity demanded is equal to quantity supplied. *OM* is the equilibrium quantity which is exchanged at price *OP*. If price is greater than the equilibrium price, say *OP′*, the quantity demanded by the buyers is *P′L*, while the quantity offered to supply by the sellers is *P′K*. Thus *LK* is the excess supply which the buyers will not take off the market at price *OP′*. In order to dispose of this excess supply, the sellers will compete with each other and in doing so they will bring down the price. Thus there will be tendency for the price to fall to the level of equilibrium price *OP*.

At price *OP″*, which is less than the equilibrium price, the buyers demand *P″T*, the sellers are prepared to supply only *P″H*. The quantity *HT* represents excess demand. The unsatisfied buyers will compete with each other to obtain the limited supply of cloth and in this effort they will bid up the price. Thus there will be tendency for the price to rise to the level of equilibrium price *OP* where all wanting to buy and all wanting to sell will be satisfied.

From above it follows that if the price was above or below the equilibrium price, certain forces in the system would operate to bring the price to the level of the equilibrium price *OP*. We thus see that price is determined by the equilibrium between demand and supply. The price at which demand and supply curves intersect each other will eventually come to prevail in the market.

Walrasian Price Adjustment. Method of adjustment of market to the equilibrium position explained above considers change in price as the driving force in the process. It is changes in price that bring about adjustment to bring about equilibrium between demand and supply. In this process of adjustment to equilibrium between demand and supply, when buyers and sellers (firms) find themselves in disequilibrium, they move along their respective demand and supply curves until the equilibrium price-quantity combination is reached. As seen above, when price is above equilibrium price, quantity demanded falls short of quantity supplied (that is, the excess demand is negative, $ED < 0$.) As a result of this excess supply, price falls. On the other hand, when price is below the equilibrium price, the quantity demanded exceeds the quantity supplied (that is, excess demand is positive, $ED > 0$). This pulls up the price of the product.

Marshallian Quantity Adjustment. On the other hand Marshall explained the adjustment of the market to the equilibrium position through the *changes in quantity of a good*. In his analysis of equilibrium Marshall but forward the view that buyers and sellers should be viewed as ***adjusting quantity when there is disequilibrium*** between demand and supply and according to him changes in price occur due to the changes in the quantity demanded and supplied. Marshallian process of quantity

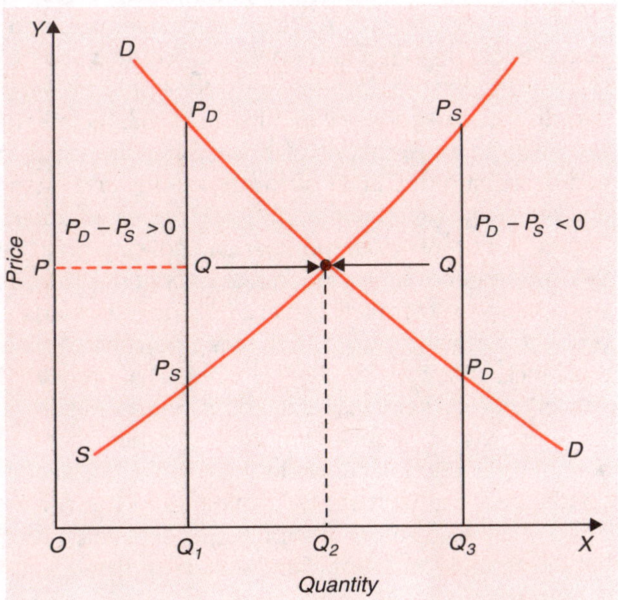

Fig. 26.2 *Marshallian Quantity Adjustment*

adjustment to bring the market to the equilibrium state is illustrated in Figure 26.2. It will be seen from this figure that when quantity of the commodity is smaller than the equilibrium quantity Q_2, say equal to Q_1, the price at which the buyers want to buy this quantity Q_1, equals P_D (that is, demand price is P_D) and the sellers wish to supply the quantity Q_1 at price P_s (P_s is therefore the supply price). It will be seen at quantity Q_1, the demand price (P_D) exceeds the supply price (P_s). This will serve as incentive for the sellers to increase the quantity supplied until the equilibrium is reached at the quantity Q_2. On the other hand, if the quantity is somehow Q_3 which is more than the equilibrium quantity Q_2. It will be seen from the figure that at the disequilibrium quantity Q_3, supply price (P_s) exceeds the demand price (P_D) of the good, which will induce the sellers to reduce the quantity until it reaches the equilibrium level Q_2 and consequently equilibrium price is established at the level *OP*.

It is evident from the analysis of Walrasian and Marshallian approaches to adjustment of market to the price-quantity configuration usually involve changes in both price and quantity. The difference in the two approaches is which of the two variables, price or quantity, is adjusted by the buyers and suppliers and the other follows. Walras is of the view that when there is disequilibrium between demand and supply it is the price that is adjusted so as to bring demand and supply in equilibrium, whereas Marshall thinks that it is the quantity that is adjusted. This, however, still remains an unsettled question. Recent economic researches however show that it is the *transaction costs* that greatly influence the adjustment process. These transaction costs arise because both buyers and suppliers need to acquire information about demand and supply conditions, prevailing prices and the difficulties involved in adapting behaviour to the information gathered. We will discuss these transaction costs involved in the adjustment process to the equilibrium state at length in a later chapter.

Are Demand and Supply Final Answers to the Pricing Problem ?

From above it follows that price is determined by equilibrium between demand and supply. But it is worth mentioning that demand and supply do not provide final answers to the pricing problem. Demand and supply which by their intersection determine price are themselves governed by several factors. There are many forces or factors which work behind demand and supply to determine price of a product. 'Demand and supply' is only a superficial formula. The ultimate factors that determine the prices of goods are those upon which demand and supply themselves depend. But demand and supply are very useful concepts serving outer covers for two distinct categories of factors. Prof. Samuelson rightly remarks: "Supply and demand are not ultimate explanations of price. They are simply useful catch-all categories for analyzing and describing multitude of forces, causes and factors impinging on price. Rather than final answers, supply and demand simply represent initial questions. Our work is not over but just begun."[6] For instance, market demand for a good depends upon the incomes of the people, their preferences for the good, the total population, availability and prices of substitute goods. Any change in them will cause a change in demand and hence in the equilibrium price of the product. Similarly, supply depends upon the availability and price of labour, raw materials, machines, chemicals etc., and techniques of production, all of which govern cost of production. Any change in them will bring about change in cost of production that governs supply and will therefore alter the equilibrium price. It is thus clear that factors like availability of raw materials, cost of production, incomes of the people, the size of population, consumers' preferences for goods, etc., are ultimate determinants of the prices of various goods but all of them work through either demand or supply. For explaining the price behaviour of a good we have to go behind demand and supply and search for those factors which are responsible for the changes in its price.

6. P.A. Samuelson, *Economics*, 8th edition, 1970, pp. 369-70.

Demand-Supply Model of Price-Output Determination: Mathematical Analysis

As we have seen both demand for and supply of a commodity determine price and the quantity sold and purchased in a competitive market. In this model quantity demanded is inversely related to price, that is, demand curve for a commodity slopes downward to the right. On the other hand, quantity supplied of a commodity is directly related to price, that is, supply curve slopes upward to the right.

Thus, assuming that both demand and supply curves are linear, demand-supply model can be stated in the form of the following three equations:

$$q^d = a - bp \quad \text{...(1)}$$

$$q^s = c + dp \quad \text{...(2)}$$

$$q^d = q^s \quad \text{...(3)}$$

where q^d and q^s are the quantities demanded and supplied respectively, a and c are intercept coefficients of demand and supply curves respectively, b and d are the coefficients that measure the slopes of these curves and (3) is the equilibrium condition. Thus, in equilibrium

$$a - bp = c + dp$$

$$a - c = dp + bp = p\,(d + b)$$

Dividing both sides by $d + b$ we have

$$\frac{a-c}{d+b} = \frac{p(d+b)}{d+b}$$

or equilibrium price $$p = \frac{a-c}{b+d} \quad \text{...(4)}$$

Substituting (4) into (1) we have

equilibrium quantity $$q^d = a - b\frac{a-c}{b+d} = a - \frac{ab+ac}{b+d} = \frac{a(b+d)-ab+ac}{b+d}$$

$$= \frac{ab+ad-bc}{b+d} = \frac{ad+bc}{b+d} \quad \text{...(5)}$$

Equations (4) and (5) describe the qualitative results of the model. If the values of parameters a, b, c and d are given we can obtain the equilibrium price and quantity by substituting the values of these parameters in the qualitative results of equations (4) and (5).

A Numerical Example

Suppose the following demand and supply functions of a commodity are given which is being produced under conditions of perfect competition. Find out the equilibrium price and quantity

$$q^d = 750 - 25p$$

$$q^s = 300 + 20p$$

Solution. There are two alternative ways of solving for equilibrium price and quantity. First, we can find out the equilibrium price and quantity by using the equilibrium condition, namely, $q^d = q^s$. Secondly, we can obtain equilibrium price and quantity by using the qualitative results of the demand-supply model, $p = \frac{a-c}{b+d}$ and $q = \frac{ad+bc}{b+d}$

1. Since in equilibrium, $q^d = q^s$

$$750 - 25p = 300 + 20p$$

$$45p = 750 - 300$$

$$p = \frac{450}{45} = 10$$

Now, substituting the value of p in the demand equation

$$q^d = 750 - 25 \times 10$$
$$= 500$$

Alternative Method

$$p = \frac{a-c}{b+d}$$
$$a = 750,\ b = 25,\ c = 300,\ d = 20$$
$$p = \frac{750-300}{25+20} = \frac{450}{45} = 10$$
$$q^d = \frac{ad + bc}{b + d}$$
$$= \frac{750 \times 20 + 25 \times 300}{25 + 20} = \frac{15000 + 7500}{45}$$
$$= \frac{22500}{45} = 500$$

Thus both methods yield the same results.

MARSHALL'S THEORY OF VALUE : TIME PERIOD ANALYSIS

Marshall, who propounded the theory that price is determined by both demand and supply, also gave a great importance to the time element in the determination of price. Time element is of great relevance in the theory of value since one of the two determinants of price, namely supply, depends on the time allowed for its adjustment. It is worth mentioning that Marshall divided time into different periods from the viewpoint of supply and not from the viewpoint of demand. Time is short or long according to the extent to which supply can adjust to the changes in demand. Marshall felt it necessary to divide time into different periods on the *basis of response of supply* because it always takes time for the supply to adjust fully to the changed conditions of demand. The reason why supply takes time to adjust itself to a change in the demand condition is that the nature of technical conditions of production is such as to prohibit instantaneous adjustment of supply to changed demand conditions. A period of time is required for changes to be made in the size of plant, new machinery to be installed, and for the new firms to enter the industry or the old ones to leave the industry.

Another point is worth noting. When Marshall distinguished short and long periods he was not using clock or calendar time as his criterion, but *'operational'* time in terms of economic forces at work. In this regard, as said above, supply forces were given the major attention and a time was short or long according to the extent of adjustment in the forces of supply. The greater the adjustability of the supply forces, the greater the length of the time, irrespective of the length in clock-time.

Marshall divided time into following three periods on the basis of response of supply to a given and permanent change in demand.

(1) Market Period. The market period is very short period in which the supply is fixed, that is, no adjustment can take place in supply conditions. In other words, supply in the market period is limited by the existing stock of the good. The maximum that can be supplied in the market period is the stock of the good which has already been produced. In this period more good cannot be produced in response to an increase in demand. This market period may be a day or a few days or even a few weeks depending upon the nature of the good. For instance, in case of perishable goods, like fish, the market period may be a day and for a cotton cloth, it may be a few weeks.

(2) Short Run. Short run is a period in which supply can be adjusted to a limited extent. During the short period the firms can expand output with given equipment by changing the amounts of variable factors employed. Short period is not long enough to allow the firm to change the plants or given capital equipment. The plant or a capital equipment remains fixed or unaltered in the short run. Output can be expanded by making intensive use of given plant or capital equipment by varying the amounts of variable factors.

(3) Long Run. The long run is a period long enough to permit the firms to build new plants or abandon old ones. Further, in the long run, new firms can enter the industry and old ones can leave it. Since in the long run all factors are subject to variation, none is a fixed factor. During the long period forces of supply fully adjust themselves to a given change in demand; the size of individual firms as well as the size of the whole industry expands or contracts according to the requirements of demand.

From above, it is clear that because of the varying response of supply over a period of time to, a sudden and once-for-all increase in demand that Marshall found it necessary and useful to study the pricing process in *(a)* the market period, *(b)* the short run, and (c) the long run depending respectively upon whether the supply conditions have time to ***make (i) no adjustment, (ii) some adjustment of labour and other variable factors, and (iii) full adjustment of all factors and all costs.*** Therefore, Marshall explained how the equilibrium between demand and supply was established in three time periods which consequently determine market price, short-run price and long-run price.

Determination of Market Price. Market-period price or what is simply called market price is determined by the momentary equilibrium between demand and supply at a time. In the market period, as has been already mentioned, the supply of the good is limited by the available stock of the good. But the quantity that may be supplied in the market period may not be equal to the given stock of the good. Whether or not the whole stock of the good is offered for sale depends upon whether the good in question is perishable or durable. The perishable goods like fish, milk, cannot be stored or kept back ; they will go waste if stored. Therefore, the whole of the given stock of a perishable good has to be supplied in the market, whatever the price of the good. As a result, the market-period supply curve of a perishable commodity is perfactly inelastic or a vertical straight line.

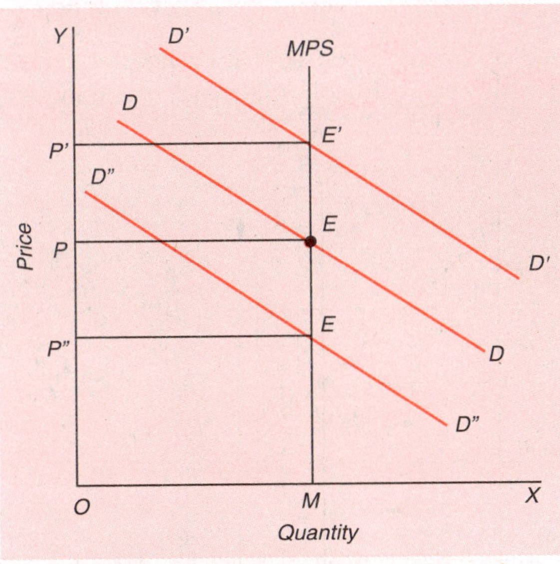

Fig. 26.3 *Determination of Market Price of a Perishable Commodity.*

On the other hand, the sellers can hold back a durable good and wait for the time when price of the good rises. Out of a given stock of the good, they will be prepared to sell a lesser amount at lower price, and a greater amount at a higher price. At some price, they will be willing to supply the whole stock of the good and beyond that price the supply of the good will be completely inelastic.

Consequently, the supply curve of a durable commodity slopes upward to a point but becomes a vertical straight line after that.

Fig, 26.3 illustrates the determination of market price of a perishable commodity. *OM* is the given stock of the good and *MPS* is the market-period supply curve. Suppose, to begin with, *DD* is the demand curve of the commodity. Demand and supply are in equilibrium at price *OP*. Therefore, *OP* is the equilibrium market price. Now, if the demand increases from *DD* to *D′D′*, the market price will sharply rise from *OP* to *OP′*, the supply of the good remaining fixed at *OM*. On the contrary, if the demand decreases from *DD* to *D″D″*, the market price will fall from *OP* to *OP″*, the supply again remaining constant at *OM*. We thus see that changes in demand produce sharp changes in price in the market period, supply being constant during this period.

Short-Run and Long-Run Price. The price of a commodity that will prevail in the market depends upon the time period under consideration. If a sudden and a once-and-for-all increase in demand takes place, the market price will register a sharp increase, since supply cannot increase in the market period. In this market period, firms can sell only the output that has already been produced. However, in the short run some limited adjustment in supply will take place as a result of the firms moving along their short-run marginal cost curves by expanding output with the increase in the amount of variable factors. Consequently, the short-run price will come down from the new high level of the market price. But this short-run price will stand above the level of original market price which prevailed before the increase in demand occurred. In the long run the firms would expand by building new plants, that is, by increasing the size of their capital equipment. In other words, firms would expand along the long-run marginal cost curves. Besides this, new firms will enter the industry in the long run and will add to the supply of output. As a result of these long-run adjustments in supply, the price will decline. Thus the long-run price will be lower than the short-run price. But this long-run price will be higher than the original price which ruled before the increase in demand took place, *if the industry happens to be increasing-cost industry.*

The adjustment of supply over a period of time and consequent changes in price is illustrated in Figure 26.4 where long-run supply curve *LRS* of an increasing-cost industry along with the market-period supply curve *MPS* and the short-run supply curve *SRS* has been drawn. Originally, demand curve *DD* and market period supply curve *MPS* intersect at point *E* and price *OP* is determined. Now suppose that there is a once-for-all increase in demand from *DD* to *D″D″*. Now, supply cannot increase in the market period, it remains the same at *OM*. Market-period supply curve *MPS* intersects the new demand curve *D″D″* at point *Q*. Thus the market price sharply rises to *OP″*. Short-run supply curve *SRS* intersects the new demand curve *D″D″* at point *R*. The short-run price will therefore be *OP″* which is lower than the new market price *OP′*. As a result of the long run adjustment

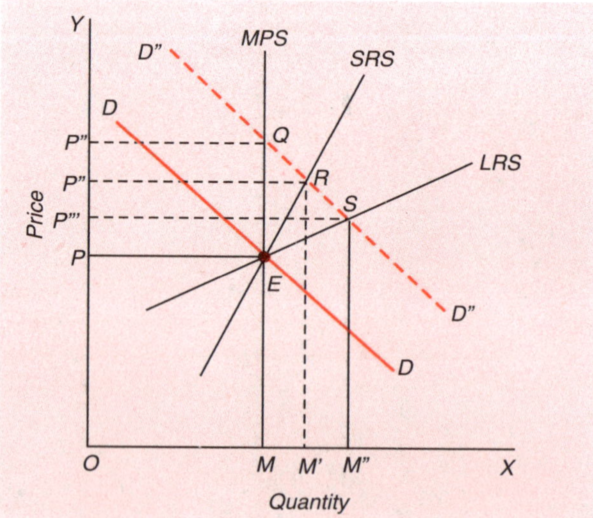

Fig. 26.4. *The role of time element in the determination of price*

the price will fall to OP''' at which the long-run supply curve *LRS* intersects the demand curve $D'D''$. The long-run price OP''' is lower than the new market price OP' and the short-run price OP'', but is higher than the original *price OP* which prevailed before the increase in demand took place. This is so because we are assuming an increasing-cost industry whose long-run supply curve *LRS* slopes upward. If the industry is subjected to constant costs, the long-run supply curve *LRS* will be a straight line and the long-run price will be equal to the original price. Further, if the industry is subject to decreasing costs, the long-run supply curve will be sloping downward and therefore the long-run price will be lower than the original price.

It follows from above that the price which prevails in the market depends upon the period under consideration. It is thus clear that time plays an important role in the determination of price.

Another significance of the time-period analysis of pricing is that it enabled Marshall to resolve the controversy among economists whether it is demand or supply which determines price. Marshall propounded the view that both demand and supply took part in the determination of price. But, "as a general rule", said Marshall, "the shorter the period which one considers the greater must be the share of our attention which is given to the influence of demand on value, and the longer the period the more important will be the influence of cost of production on value. Actual value at any time–the market value as it is often called–is often influenced by passing events and causes whose action is fitful and short-lived than by those which work persistently. But in the long run these fitful and irregular causes in a large measure efface one another's influence so that in the long-run persistent causes dominate value completely."[7]

From the above quotation from Marshall it follows that in the market period, demand exercises a predominant influence over price but in the long run it is the supply which is of overwhelming importance as a determinant of price. Roughly speaking, we can say that in the market period it is the force of demand which determines price and in the long period it is the force of supply which governs price. Thus those economists who held that value was governed by demand were in a way right and so were those who contended that cost of production *(i.e.* force working on the supply side) determined price. The difference in the two views was due to the fact that one group of economists was emphasizing the determination of the *market price* over which demand has an important influence and over which cost of production does not exercise much influence, while the other group was stressing on the determination of *long-run price* over which cost of production has got paramount influence. It is thus clear that Marshall by putting forth the view that both demand and supply determine price by their interaction brought about synthesis between the views of earlier economists.

Both the two opposite views of earlier economists were in a way right but each was one-sided. Each view provided us with a force which governed price. The two forces of supply and demand furnished by the two opposing views were sufficient determining factors. Therefore, Marshall gave equal importance to both demand and supply as determinants of price, though the influence of the two varied in different time periods. Marshall introduced time period analysis into pricing process to bring out the varying influence of each of two forces over price of the product in different time periods.

It follows from what has been said above that Marshall and modern economists following him study the effect of the varying response in supply in different time periods on price to a sudden and permanent change in demand conditions. On the contrary, *economists do not study the effect on price of adjustment in demand over a period of time in response to a*

7. Marshall, *Principles of Economics*, 8th edition, pp. 349-50.

change in supply conditions. The reason why we do not study adjustment in demand- in response to a change in supply and its consequent effect on price is better brought out in the words of Professors Stonier and Hague, "There is no reason why, if supply conditions change, demand conditions should change as well, or if they do, why they should change differently in the short run and the long run. Change in consumer's tastes are not dependent on technology in the way that supply conditions are. Admittedly, consumers' tastes may and probably will change as time goes on. But this will be a change of data and not a change induced by changed supply conditions. There is no necessary reason why the long-run demand curve should differ from the short-run demand curve, however odd the behaviour of supply has been —we must expect that the longer is the period during which demand and supply are coming into equilibrium, the more changes will have time to take place. If we were to study the changes in demand and supply which would take place in respect to any change of data during many successive very short periods of time, we should find that we had introduced unnecessary and intolerable complexity into the analysis."[8]

QUESTIONS FOR REVIEW

1. Distinguish between partial equilibrium analysis and general equilibrium analysis of pricing. Why Marshall's partial equilibrium analysis has been more widely adopted than Walras' general equilibrium analysis?
2. Explain determination of equilibrium price of a good using Walras' price adjustment mechanism and Marshall's quantity adjustment mechanism. Which do you think is more realistic?
3. "Supply and demand are not the ultimate explanation of price. They are simply useful catch-all categories for analysing and describing multitude of forces, causes and factors impinging on price. Rather than final answers supply and demand represent initial questions" (Samuelson). Discuss.
4. Explain Marshall's theory of value with special reference to the role of time element in his analysis of determination of price of products in competitive markets.
5. On what basis Marshall divided time into three periods, namely, market period, short run and long run. What is their importance in the determination of price of goods in a competitive market?
6. Before Marshall some classical economists argued that it was cost of producing goods that determined price, others were of the view that it was utility of goods that determined price. Explain how Marshallian time-period analysis of value helped to resolve this controversy.
7. Suppose there is a permanent increase in demand for a good. Explain how it will affect the price of the good in the (1) market period, (2) short run, and (3) long run. Assume the case of increasing cost industry.

8. Stonier and Hague, *A Textbook of Economic Theory*, Fifth edition, pp. 178-179.

CHAPTER

27

Applications of Demand and Supply Analysis

Introduction

In the last chapter we have explained how prices of goods are determined by demand and supply. The analysis of price determination in terms of demand and supply is not merely of great theoretical significance but it has important several practical applications in economic life of a country. This analysis of demand and supply has been used to explain the implications of price control and rationing, minimum price fixation, incidence of taxes, several other economic problems and policies. In the present chapter we shall explain some of these applications of demand and supply analysis.

In the analysis of the previous chapter we have assumed that market mechanism is allowed to function without interference by the government. But government in the modern mixed economies interferes with the functioning of the market system to influence prices so as to promote social welfare when it is felt that free working of market will not produce desirable results. The government can interfere with the working of the economy in two main ways. The first government fixes the *maximum price* (often called *price ceiling)* or fix the *minimum price* often called *floor price*). *Price control* of foodgrains, rent controls are the examples of fixation of maximum price or price ceiling above which the sellers cannot charge the price. *Agricultural price support programme* is the example of fixation of minimum price to assure minimum remunerative prices to farmers so as to protect their interests.

The second way in which government interferers with the price or market system is *working through the market.* In the second way government can impose taxes on the commodities or provide subsidies. These taxes and subsidies affect the market supply or demand curves which determine prices of goods and services. Imposition of heavy excise duties on cigarettes or other drugs and providing subsidies on agricultural products are examples of interference by government through market. In what follows we will explain both types of intervention with the functioning of markets by government. We begin our analysis with the imposition of price control and rationing by government. In addition to above, elasticities of demand and supply have important applications for formulation of proper economic polices to be adopted by the government and also to explain several economic events.

PRICE CONTROL AND RATIONING

In times of war imposition of price control is quite common and was introduced by several countries during the Second World War. Even in peace time, price controls on essential commodities have been introduced in several countries to help the poor against inflation. *Under price control the maximum price of a good is fixed* above which the sellers cannot charge from the consumers. Price control is imposed or price ceiling is set below the equilibrium price. This is because if the price ceiling is set above the equilibrium price that balances supply and demand, it will have no effect or in other words, *it will not be binding*. Consider Figure 27.1. where demand and supply balance each other at price P_1. At this equilibrium price both buyers and sellers are satisfied, buyers are getting the quantity of the good they want to buy at this equilibrium price and the sellers are selling what they want to sell at this price. Therefore, the higher price P_2 fixed by governmenc will have no effect. When it is realised that the equilibrium price of a commodity is too high and consequently some buyers go unsatisfied, for they lack the means to pay for it, the Government may pass a law through which ***it fixes the maximum price of the commodity* at a level** below the equilibrium price. Now, at a price lower than the equilibrium price, quantity demanded will be larger than the quantity supplied and thus *shortage* of the commodity will emerge; some consumers who are willing and able to buy at that price will go unsatisfied. Buyers would, if permitted, bid up the price to the equilibrium level. But under price control by the Government, price is not free to move to equate quantity

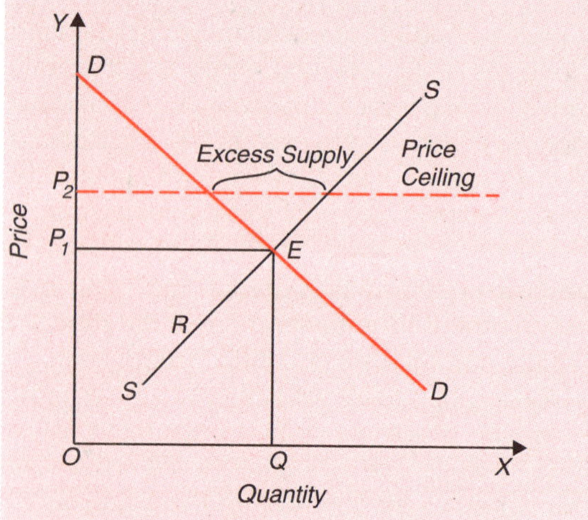

Fig. 27.1. *Price Ceiling above the Equilibrium Price is not Binding and is Ineffective.*

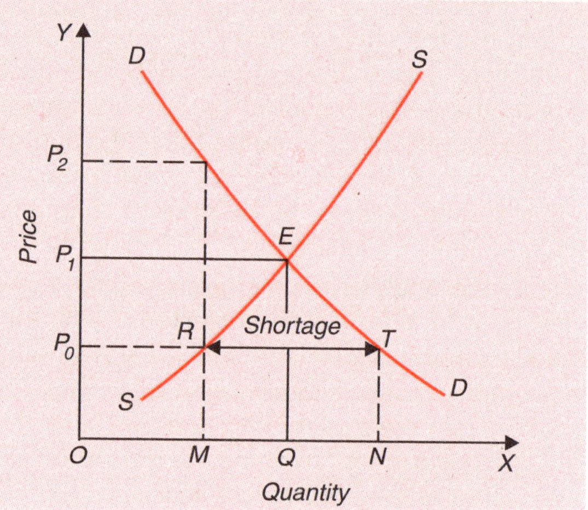

Fig. 27.2. *Effect of Price Control (i.e. Fixing Price Ceiling below the Equilibrium Level)*

demanded with the quantity supplied. Thus, when the Government intervenes to fix the maximum price for a commodity, price loses its important function of a rationing device.

Price control and problems raised by it are graphically illustrated in Figure 27.2 where demand and supply curves, *DD* and *SS* of sugar are given. As will be seen from this figure that demand and supply curves intersect at point *E* and accordingly OP_1 is the equilibrium price of sugar. Suppose that this equilibrium price OP_1 of sugar is very high so that many poor people are not able to obtain any quantity of it. Therefore, the Government intervenes and fixes the maximum price of sugar at the level OP_0 which is below the equilibrium price OP_1. As will be seen from Figure 27.2 at the controlled price OP_0 the quantity demanded exceeds the quantity supplied. At price OP_0, whereas the producers offer to supply $P_0 R$ quantity of sugar, the consumers are prepared to buy P_0T quantity of it. As a result, shortage of sugar equal to the amount *RT* has emerged and some consumers will go unsatisfied.

In the absence of Government intervention fixing the maximum price at OP_0 level, the excess demand equal to *RT* would have led to the rise in price to the equilibrium level OP_1 where quantity demanded is equal to quantity supplied. ***But, under price control by the government, to charge a price higher than the legally fixed maximum price*** OP_0 is punishable under the law. Therefore, the available supply *OM* at the fixed price OP_0 has to be somehow allocated or rationed between the consumers. The rationing can take many forms. This task of rationing the available supply *OM may* be done by the producers or sellers themselves. The sellers may adopt the principle *of* ***"first come first served"*** and distribute the available supply of sugar among those who are *first in the queue* before their shops. This system of rationing is therefore called ***queue rationing.*** *The* second method of rationing or allocating the scarce supply of the good is to distribute it on the basis of what has been called, ***"allocation by sellers' preferences".*** Under this, the available supply of good is sold by the sellers to certain preferred consumers at the controlled price. The sellers may sell the good at the controlled price to their regular customers. They may also adopt the policy of selling the available supply to the buyers belonging to certain caste, religion, colour etc. and not to others.

If the Government does not like the rationing of a commodity among the population on the basis of either "first come first served" or arbitrary allocation by sellers' preferences, it may introduce ***coupon rationing*** of the commodity. Under the coupon rationing system consumers are given ration coupons just sufficient to buy the available quantity of the commodity. The number of ration coupons issued to a family may depend on the age of its members, sex, and the number of family members or on any other criterion considered desirable.

Black Market. A point worth noting is that price control with or without rationing is likely to give rise to the black-market in the commodity. ***By black market we mean the sale of a commodity by the producers or sellers at a price higher than the controlled price.*** As mentioned above, at the controlled maximum price fixed below the equilibrium price, the quantity demanded would exceed the quantity supplied and consequently shortage of the commodity would develop. It is thus clear that some buyers of the commodity will not be fully satisfied as they will not be able to get the quantity of the good they wish to buy at the controlled price. Therefore, they will be prepared to pay a higher price for getting more quantity of the good, but they can do so only in the black market. Sellers will also be interested in selling the commodity, at least some quantity of it, in the black market at a higher price as it will fetch them larger profits.

Even when coupon rationing is introduced there will be pressure for the black market to develop. This is because the consumers are willing to buy more quantity of the commodity than is available at the controlled price, whereas rationing only distributes the available quantity of the commodity. Therefore, the consumers who want to procure larger quantity than the rationing amount will be prepared to pay a higher price to get some quantity in the black market.

There is sufficient evidence in India and abroad to confirm the predictions based on demand and supply analysis. ***When price control and rationing system for some commodities which were in shortage were introduced during the Second World War and after, black markets developed in spite of punitive measures taken by the authorities.***

RENT CONTROL

Rent controls is an other example of maximum price that Government fixes on the rental price of housing units. Under rent control, the Government fixes the rent per month per housing unit of a standard size which is ***below the equilibrium rent*** that would otherwise prevail in the market. The maximum rent fixed by the Government helps the tenants, who generally belong to lower and middle income groups and intend to prevent their exploitation by rich landlords who would charge a very high market determined rates of rent. Market determined equilibrium rent rate happens to be high because demand for rental housing tend to be relatively greater than supply of it. In several important cities such a New York, London,

Mumbai, Delhi. Government has imposed rent control to help the lower and middle income people by ensuring rental houses at fair rents. In Delhi, Delhi Rent Control Act, 1958 which has now been amended by the recently passed New Rent Control Act 1995 specifies some monthly rental rates of housing units of some standard sizes above which the landlord cannot charge rent. Besides, the landlord cannot evict the tenants easily except under some conditions laid down in the law. It is however important to understand both the short-run and long-run effects of rent control.

Economists often point out the adverse effects of rent control and hold the view that it is highly inefficient way of helping the poor and lower middle class people. The adverse effects of rent control are evident only in the long run because it always takes time to construct new housing units/apartments and also for the tenants to adjust to the rent and housing accommodation available on rent. So the long-run effect of rent control is different from the short-run effect. In the short run the land-lords have almost a fixed number of housing units/appartments to give on rent. Therefore, the supply curve of rental units is inelastic in the short run. On the other hand, people searching for rental-housing units are also not very responsive in the short-run as it always take time for them to adjust their housing arrangements. Thus, even demand for rental housing is relatively inelastic in the short run.

Therefore, in Fig. 27.3, short-run supply curve of housing units is perfectly inelastic at Q_0 number of housing units available for renting. D_s is the short-run demand curve which is also relatively inelastic. If left free to the market force, rent equal to R_0 will be determined at which there is equilibrium between demand and supply. Suppose R_0 is too high for the poor and middle class people to pay. To help them, government fixes ceiling on rent at R_1. It will be seen from Figure 27.3 that at R_1, people demand R_1L housing units whereas supply of them remains at R_1K or OQ_0. Thus, KL shortage of housing units has emerged. Since the demand and supply of housing units in the short run is inelastic, shortage caused by rent control is small. The main effect of rent control in the short run is to reduce rents.

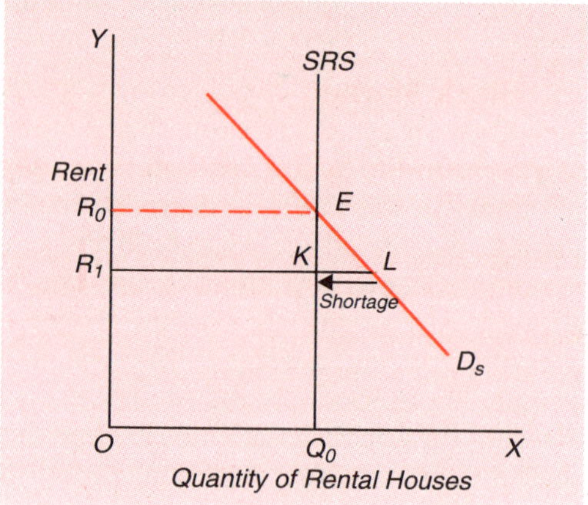

Fig. 27.3. *Effect of Rent Control in the Short Run*

Although in the short run, landlords cannot do much to the lowering of rent through control, ***further investment in constructing houses and apartments*** by them will be reduced causing reduction in the supply of rental houses in the long run. In addition to this, the landlords will not spend any money *on repairs and maintenance* of rental houses when rents are lowered. These steps will ultimately lead to the poor quality of rental houses and apartments. Thus, ***in the long run, rent control has an important effect on the availability or supply of rental houses and their quality.*** It will be seen from Fig. 27.4 that at the lower controlled rent OR_1 the quantity demanded of rental housing increases to OQ_2 and the quantity supplied of rental housing units falls to OQ_1. Thus, fixation of lower controlled rent OR_1 results in increase in the quantity demanded and decrease in the quality supplied of rental houses and thereby leads to the emergence of the large shortage of rental houses equal to Q_1Q_2 or KL as will be seen from Fig 27.4. ***The greater the elasticity of supply and demand for rental housing in the long run, the greater will be the shortage of rental housing units as a result of imposition of rent control act.***

It may be noted that this shortage of rental housing represents the conditions of excess demand for rental housing. An important question is whether fixation of maximum rent which is lower than the equilibrium rent can be effectively enforced when conditions of excess demand or shortage of rental housing units emerges. Of course, no one can openly or explicitly charge a rent higher than the controlled rate. However, the emergence of the conditions of excess demand or shortage of rental housing will tend to put upward pressure on the actual rents received. Due to the excess demand conditions landlords have devised various ways to circumvent the rent control act and charge higher actual rents, Consider Fig. 27.4 where it will be seen that at the controlled rent OR_1 of rental housing the quantity supplied of rental housing is OQ_1. Further, for OQ_1 rental housing units tenants are willing to pay rent equal to OR_2. **Under these conditions of excess demand and shortage of rental housing units, landlords tend to extract side payments from tenants, though explicitly they charge controlled rent.** For example, in Delhi and New York, two of the important world cities where rent control law operates, landlords require tenants to make a large non-refundable pay deposits or a large advance payments adjustable against monthly rents. Further, landlords may also require from tenants to make costly fittings or get expensive wood work done in the rental houses as a condition for rent and further also requiring them to pay for the repairs and maintenance of the rental housing units. All these ways of evading the rent control act have been observed. Unless the law explicitly prohibits such practices, they will be operating and will have the effect of nullifying the rent control policy. That is, tenants will pay controlled rent OR_1 explicitly but extra expenditure and payments they are required to incur may add up to R_1R_0 per month so that the actual effective monthly rent may amount to the equilibrium rent OR_0.

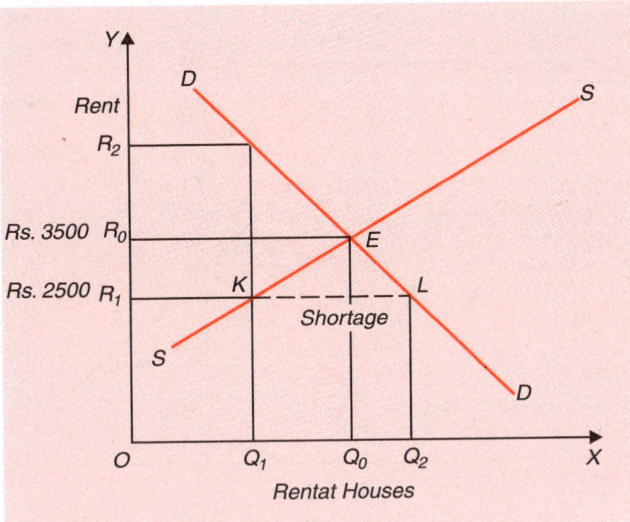

Fig. 27.4. Effects of Rent Control in the Long Run

When landlords fail to extract such extra concealed payments to raise the effective rent, another alternative way has been adopted by them to protect their interests. It has been observed that landlords of rent controlled housing units or apartments have a tendency to convert their rental housing units into owner occupied units or condominium, some of which may sold to the existing tenants at a discount. It may be noted that conversion of rental housing units into condominium results in reducing the supply of *rental* housing.

It is evident from above that the consequence of rent control, like that of any other price control, is the emergence of shortage. However, in case of shortage of rental housing units those who are unable to get them, will make efforts to make another living arrangements. They may decide to live in other cities or satellite towns which are not covered by rent controls. Further, the disappointed seekers of rental housing may turn to the construction of their own self-occupied houses. But this requires a lot of finance which have to be arranged by them.

MINIMUM SUPPORT PRICE

In the price control we examined the case when the government fixed a *price ceiling* (that is, *maximum price)* to prevent it from rising to the equilibrium level. For many agricultural products the Government policy has been to fix *a price floor,* that is, the *minimum support price* above the equilibrium level which is considered to be low and unremunerative to the farmers. While in case of price control or fixation of price ceiling the Government simply announces the maximum price above which price cannot be charged by the producers or sellers of a product, in case of minimum support price, the Government becomes an active buyer of the product in the market. It is not only in India but also in the developed countries such as the USA that price support policy for agricultural products has been adopted to provide reasonable prices to the farmers and increase their income. From 1930 to 1973, the federal government in the USA operated a price suppport policy under which it fixed the minimum price. The effects of imposition of minimum support price for wheat, an important agricultural product, in India is llustrated in Figure 27.5 where demand curve *DD* and supply curve *SS* of wheat intersect at point *E*. Thus if price of wheat is allowed to be determined by the free working of demand for and supply of wheat, equilibrium price is *OP* and equilibrium quantity determined is *OQ*.

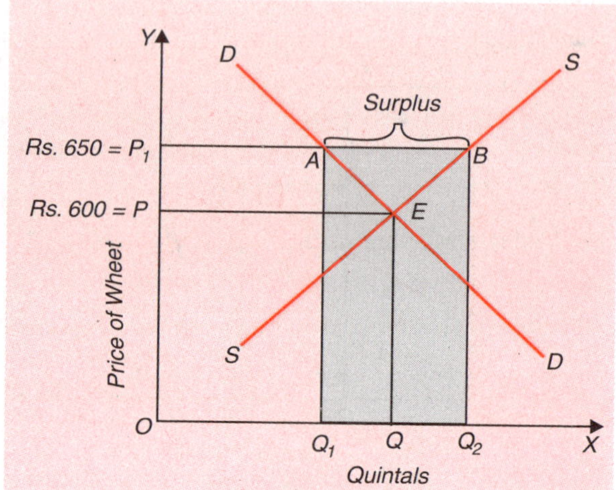

Fig. 27.5 *Minimum Support Price for Agriculture*

Now suppose this free market determined equilibrium price *OP* (= ₹ 600 per quintal) is considered to be unremunerative which does not provide incentives to the farmers to produce wheat or expand its production. Therefore, to promote the interests of the farmers, the Government intervenes and fixes a higher minimum support price OP_1 (₹ 650 per quintal) for wheat. It will be seen from Figure 27.5 that at price OP_1 of wheat, the quantity demanded of wheat decreases to OQ_1 (= P_1A). On the other hand, at higher price OP_1 farmers expand their output and supply a greater quantity OQ_2 (= P_1B) of wheat. Thus at minimum support price OP_1 the quantity of wheat supplied by the farmers exceeds the quantity demanded of it by the consumers in the market. This means that the imposition of minimum support price of wheat higher than the equilibrium price *OP* leads to the emergence of ***surplus of wheat*** equal to *AB* or Q_1Q_2. If the Government does not purchase this surplus, this will tend to depress the price of wheat. Therefore, in order to ensure this minimum price of wheat OP_1 (= ₹ 650 per quintal) to the farmers the Government will have to purchase the entire surplus *AB* or Q_1Q_2 from the farmers. It should be noted that to purchase the surplus Q_1Q_2 from the farmers, the Government will have to make expenditure equal to $OP_1 \times Q_1Q_2$, that is, equal to the area Q_1ABQ_2. This expenditure on purchase of wheat surplus by government may be financed by taxation of the people.

It follows from above that under minimum support price OP_1 the farmers sell OQ_1 quantity of wheat in the free market and quantity Q_1Q_2 to the-Government. At the free market determined equilibrium price *OP* and quantity *OQ*, the total income of the farmers will be equal to the area *OPEQ*. Now, with minimum support price equal to OP_1 and the total quantity sold equal to OQ_2, the income of the farmers has increased to OP_1BQ_2. Thus minimum support price policy has greatly benefited the farmers both in terms of price they receive for their product and the income they are able to earn.

A major problem facing the Government is how to dispose of the surplus it purchases from the farmers at the higher minimum support price. If the Government sells it in the market, the price of wheat in the market will fall which will defeat the purpose of price support policy. Alternatively, the Government may store the surplus and in this case the Government will incur storage costs. Besides, the wheat and any other foodgrains get rottened if kept for longer time in storage bins. Thus while to produce surplus requires valuable resources such as labour, fertilizers, irrigation and other inputs, yet it is quite often left to decay in government warehouses. In America, one important way of disposing of surplus was to give them to the developing countries as food aid. But this food aid is not without problems. The American food aid to developing countries has tended to depress prices of foodgrains in these countries and therefore has harmed the interests of farmers of these developing countries.

In India Food Corporation of India on behalf of the Government procures surplus of wheat and rice production created as a result of fixation of minimum procurement or support prices of wheat and rice. Food Corporation of India then keeps it in its warehouses. The food surpluses are then used for distribution through Public Distribution System (PDS) at a lower price. Since Government procures these food grains at a higher rate and sells to the consumers at lower issue prices, the Government subsidises the foodgrain consumption and has to incur several thousand crores on food subsidy annually.

Besides, food surplus procured by the Government is also used for giving to the workers under '***food for work***' programme, and other such special employment schemes launched in India. A part payment of wages is made in food and a part in form of money. Some years ago food surplus of wheat posed a problem for government in India. The food surplus with the Government had been mounting. It was estimated to about 50 million tons in June 2004. On the other hand, off-take from public distribution system was quite small. There was a real danger of these food surpluses getting rottened in warehouses of the Food Corporation of India. Therefore, Government of India decided to export some wheat.

It should be noted that in India Government has been raising year after year the procurement or support prices for wheat and rice. This raises the food cost in every sector of the economy which must lead to higher prices all round. Thus, increase in procurement prices of wheat and rice have been an important factor that has created inflationary pressures in the Indian economy.

We summarise below the important results of price support policy :-

1. Price paid by the consumers who buy from the open market *increases* when the minimum support price of the agricultural product is fixed at a higher level than the equilibrium price. This is because supply of the agricultural product in the open market decreases as a result of Government purchases of it from the farmers.
2. Fixation of minimum support price *(i.e.,* price floor) leads to the emergence of wheat surplus which the Government has to purchase from the farmers. This is quite obvious from the Indian experience where fixation of higher minimum support price (MSP) has resulted in mountain of foodgrains with Food Corporation of India.
3. Taxpayers pay more tax money to finance the Government's wheat purchases as well as storage costs.
4. How to dispose of the surplus purchased from the farmers poses a big problem.

There are several ways to dispose of the surplus procured. One way is to sell it at subsidised rate to the persons below the poverty line through public distribution system. Second, the surplus can be used to make a part payment of wages in terms of foodgrains under *'food for work''* programme. Third, food surplus can be given to other countries as foreign aid or it can be exported.

5. Incomes of the farmers *increase* as a result of minimum support price fixed at a higher level than the free market equilibrium price. As a result of price support, they receive higher price than that which would prevail in the free market and also they produce and sell more than before. They sell a part of their larger production in the market and a part to the Government.

PARADOX OF POVERTY AMIDST PLENTY

A good news of a good weather or good monsoon which will substantially increase agricultural production may possibly be bad news for the farmers. The bumper crop as a result of good weather may cause such a large fall in prices of agricultural products that the sales revenue or income of the farmers falls. Similarly, if due to research there is improvement in agricultural technology which leads to the substantial increase in agricultural output instead of raising farmers' income may actually bring about reduction in it. This strange phenomenon is due to the ***inelastic nature of demand for agricultural products*** and is illustrated in Fig 27.6. Suppose initially the demand curve *DD* and supply curve S_1 determine price of an agricultural crop, say wheat, equal to P_1 (or ₹ 500 per quintal) at which the quantity Q_1 (or 100 quintals) are bought and sold. Suppose due to good weather (or in case of India due to good monsoon), there is bumper crop of wheat and as result supply curve of wheat shifts from S_1 to S_2. The new supply curve S_2 intersects the inelastic demand curve *DD* at point *B* and determines price P_2 (or ₹ 400 per quintal) and quantity bought and sold increases to Q_2 or 110 quintals. Thus, there is a large fall (₹ 100 per quintal) in price of wheat but due to inelastic demand of the agricultural product there is only a small increase in quantity bought and sold. Now, as explained above, in an earlier chapter, total sales revenue made by the farmers is equal to the price of product multiplied by the quantity sold *(TR = P × Q)*. In view of the fact that demand for agricultural product is inelastic, small expansion in output (*Q*) causes a relatively large fall in price resulting in *decrease* in total revenue of the farmers. It will be seen from Fig. 27.6 that increase in supply from S_1 to S_2 causes price to fall from P_1 (= ₹ 500 per quintal) to P_2 (= ₹ 400 per quintal). As a result, total revenue which was equal to the area OP_1AQ_1 (or 500 × 100 = 50,000) falls and is now equal to the area OP_2BQ_2 (or 400 × 110 = 44,000). Thus, good news of a bumper crop has led to the fall in total revenue or income of the farmers. This is usually described as farmers facing a *'paradox of poverty amongst plenty'* or a good news

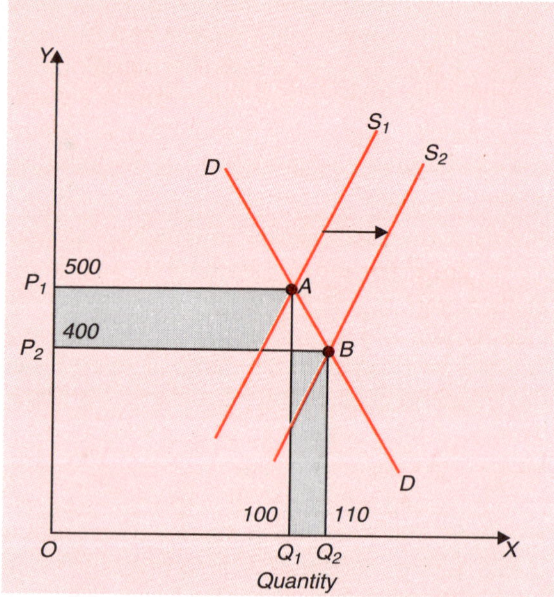

Fig. 27.6. Bumper Crop leads to lower income of the farmers.

(in the form of good weather or good monsoon) turns out to be actually a bad news for the farmers as it leads to the decline in their incomes and they have become worse off[1].

CROP RESTRICTION PROGRAMME AND FARMERS' INCOME

In the previous section we explained through demand and supply analysis that govrnment often helps the farmers by giving them subsidy for every bushel of wheat or any other crop such as rice produced by the farmers. However, during the last over three decades, government in the United States helps farmers by requiring them to restrict production. To induce them to restrict output government provides subsidy to them for not planting crops on all their land (that is, for keeping some land uncultivated). The purpose of restricting production in this way is to reduce their supply in the market so that price of the agricultural product in the market rises. In view of the fact that demand for agricultural product is inelastic a fall in production will cause their revenue or income to rise and will thus make them better off. Consider Fig. 27.7. where without intervention by government demand curve *DD* and supply curve S_1 determine equilibrium price P_1 and the farmer's sales revenue is equal to the area $OP_1E_1Q_1$. As a result of crop restriction programme of government supply curve shifts to the left to S_2 (For sake of simplicity we have assumed perfectly inelastic supply curve). With the intersection of new supply curve S_2 with the given inelastic demand curve *DD*, price of agricultural product rises to P_2 and the quantity sold has fallen to Q_2 so that the new total revenue is $OP_2E_2Q_2$ which is greater than the initial revenue $OP_1E_1Q_1$ *before crop restriction*. Thus crop restriction programme of government has led to the increase in total revenue and hence it will raise the incomes of the farmers.

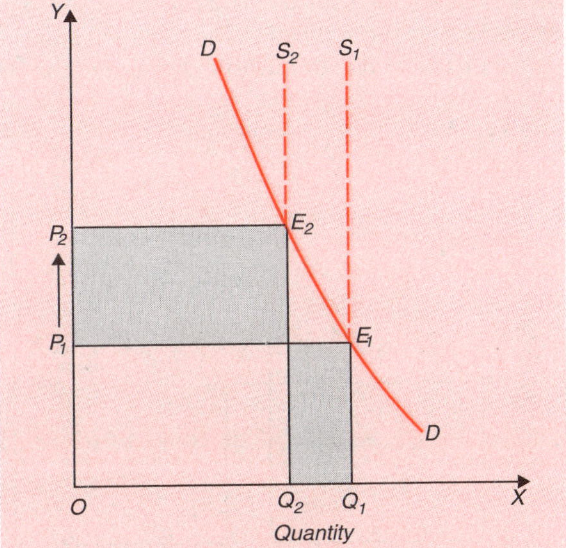

Fig. 27.7 *Crop restriction programme raises both price and income of the farmers.*

It should be noted that whereas crop restriction has raised the incomes of the farmers, it has hurt the consumers as they have to pay higher prices for foodgrains as they would if flood or drought conditions had created shortage of foodgrains. Thus, interests of farmers and consumers clash with each other.

WHY DID OPEC FAIL TO KEEP THE PRICE OF OIL HIGH FOR LONG ?

Petroleum exporting countries have formed a cartel to promote their interests and raise their incomes. This certel is known as OPEC (Organisation of Petroleum Exporting Countries). In the early 1970s OPEC gave a shock to the world when it decided to raise the price of oil by jointly deciding to reduce the supply of oil they supply. In 1973 and 1974, OPEC raised the

1. Strictly speaking, our analysis indicates decline in sales revenue. From decline in sales revenue we are concluding the fall in farmers' income. However, income is equal to total revenue minus cost. In our analysis however we have assumed that costs do not change much.

price of oil by more than 50 per cent that created energy crisis in the world. Again price of crude oil was raised by 14 per cent in 1979, 34 per cent in 1980 and further 34 per cent in 1981. However, after 1981, OPEC failed to maintain high price of oil and from 1982 to 1985, oil prices fell by about 50 per cent. In 1986 cooperation among OPEC countries completely failed that caused a further decline in price of oil by 45 per cent. In 1990, price of crude oil (adjusted for overall inflation) came down to the level of 1970. Price of crude oil remained at the low level throughout the decade of 1990s.

Now, the important question is why OPEC failed to maintain high price ? Why was it not able to raise oil prices in 1990s by reducing the supply of oil. The model of elasticities of demand and supply answers this question. As explained earlier, both demand and supply of oil are inelastic in the short run. The rise in oil price by reducing supply brought about a substantial rise in price and due to inelastic demand in the short run, the quantity demanded and sold fell

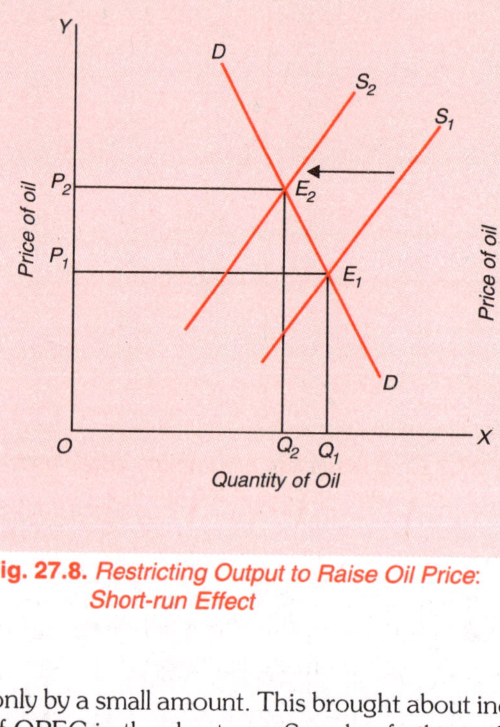

Fig. 27.8. *Restricting Output to Raise Oil Price: Short-run Effect*

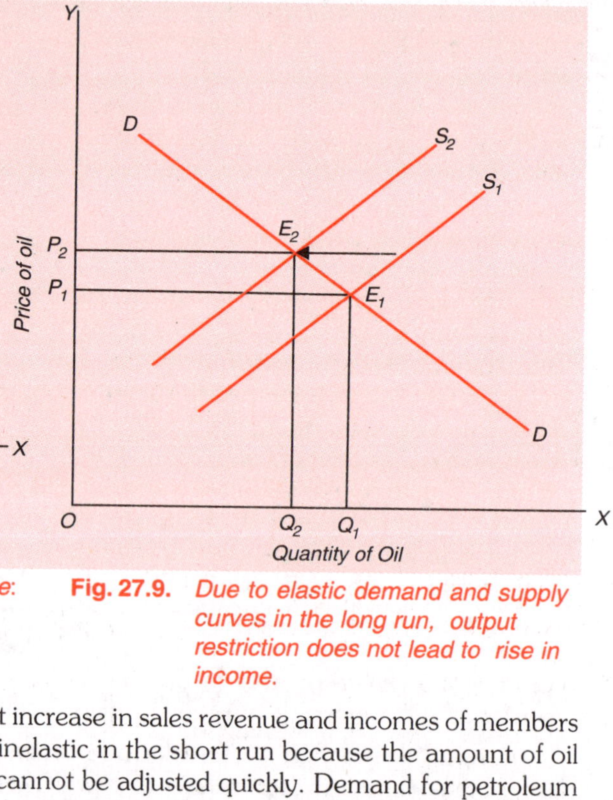

Fig. 27.9. *Due to elastic demand and supply curves in the long run, output restriction does not lead to rise in income.*

only by a small amount. This brought about increase in sales revenue and incomes of members of OPEC in the short run. Supply of oil is inelastic in the short run because the amount of oil in reserves and capacity for extracting oil cannot be adjusted quickly. Demand for petroleum oil in the short run is also inelastic because buying habits of consumers of oil also could not be adjusted quickly to changes in price of this oil. This helps to explain the rise in revenue or income of OPEC when they succeeded in raising price of crude oil by cutting down production and supply of it in the market. This is illustrated in Figure 27.8 where *DD* is the demand curve of oil which is quite steep (i.e. inelastic) and S_1 is the initial supply curve and the two determine price P_1 of oil and quantity Q_1 sold. The total revenue of members of OPEC is given by the area $OP_1E_1Q_1$. Now, with reduction in production by members of OPEC, supply curve shifts to the left to S_2 and given the inelastic demand curve *DD* causes a substantial rise in oil price to P_2 and the quantity sold falls by only a small amount from Q_1 to Q_2 As result, the new total revenue earned $OP_2E_2Q_2$ is greater than the revenue $OP_1E_1Q_1$ earned before the reduction in production. Thus joint action by OPEC resulted in rise in incomes of members of OPEC in the short run.

However, the situation in the long run is different. In the long run, the producers who were not members of OPEC tried to raise their production by increasing oil exploration and also by expanding their extraction capacity. This response of producers makes supply curve quite elastic in the long run as is shown in Fig. 27.9. Similarly, in the long run consumers responded to high oil prices by making attempts to conserve oil. For example, they replaced old fuel-inefficient cars with more fuel-efficient ones. As a result, demand for oil is also elastic in the long run as shown in Figure 27.9. Now, with elastic supply and demand curves in the long run the same reduction in production by OPEC bringing about leftward shift in the supply curve by the same amount as in Fig. 27.8 causes only a small rise in price. As will be seen from Fig 27.9 the reduction in output by OPEC and shift in supply curve from S_1 to S_2 by the same horizontal distance as in Fig. 27.8 price rises only a little from P_1 to P_2 and quantity sold declines from Q_1 to Q_2. It will be seen that in the long run reduction in production has resulted in fall in revenue (the area $OP_2E_2Q_2$ is less than the area $OP_1E_1Q_1$ in Fig. 27.9) and therefore it is not profitable to make a cut in oil production in the long run. That is why OPEC could not succeed to maintain high oil prices in the long run.

FIGHT AGAINST USE OF DRUGS

An important problem faced by a modern society is the extensive use of illegal drugs such as cocaine, heroine, etc. The use of these harmful drugs not only impairs the health of individuals who consume them but they also ruin the families as the drug addicts often spend a lot of incomes of their families. Besides, drug-addicts often commit burglaries and robberies to make

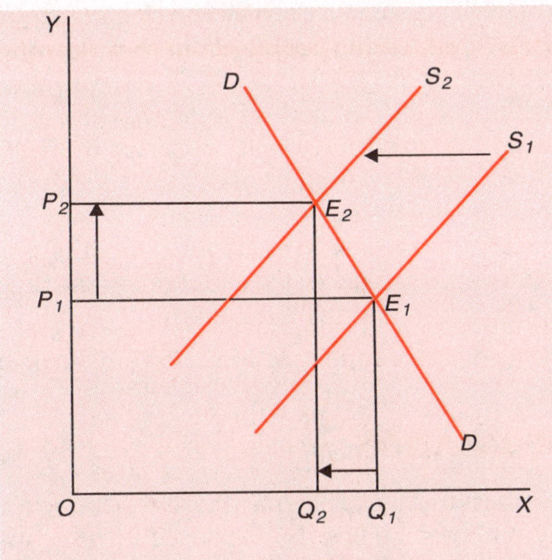

Fig. 27.10. *Reducing Supply to Check the Use of Drugs*

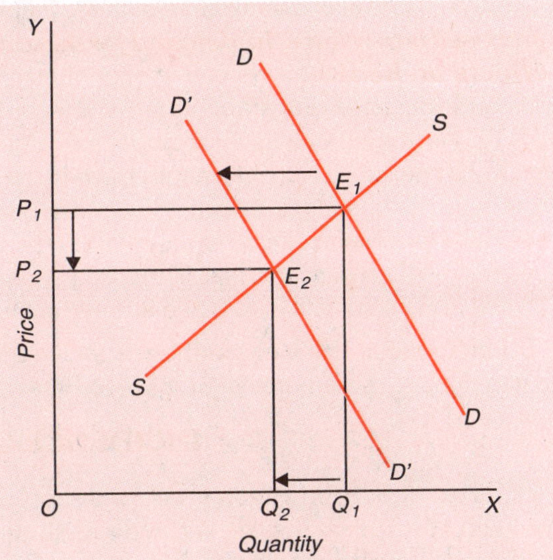

Fig. 27.11. *Reducing Demand for Drugs through Education*

quick money to spend on drugs. There are other drug-related crimes. Therefore, governments of different countreis including India often adopt measures to discourage the use of drugs. There are two main strategies to discourage and prevent the use of these harmful and illegal drugs. ***The first strategy is to reduce the supply of drugs and thereby raising prices of drugs. The second strategy is to reduce the demand for drugs by giving education to the people, especially the young ones about the harmful effects of these drugs.*** To reduce the use of these illegal drugs governments of various countries (including India) prohibit the flow of drugs into their countries and arrest and put heavy penalties on smugglers of these drugs. As a result, cost of selling these drugs rises which reduces the supply of these drugs in a country. This policy of discouraging the use of these harmful drugs by reduction in their supply is depicted in Fig. 27.10. It will be seen from this figure that initially with the given demand curve *DD* and supply curve S_1, the equilibrium price is P_1 at which quantity Q_1 is bought and sold. Now, as a result of various measures adopted by government to reduce the supply of these drugs, supply curve shifts to the left to S_2. It will be seen that with the leftward shift in supply curve to S_2, price of drug rises to P_2 and quantity demanded and sold falls to Q_2.Thus, reduction in drug supply has led to reduction in the drug use.

However, some economists have criticized this strategy of reducing drug use by reducing supply. According to them; this will not prevent the drug-related crimes. This is because demand for drugs is likely to be inelastic as has been drawn in Fig. 27.10. It has been pointed out that drug users are unlikely to forego their habits of using drugs in response to higher price of these drugs. In fact, given the inelastic demand, at a higher price P_2 of these drugs the users of these drugs will be spending more money than before. In Fig. 27.10 the total expenditure as measured by the area $OP_2E_2Q_2$ is greater than the area $OP_1E_1Q_1$ before the reduction in supply. Thus, to meet the need for money to fulfil their desire for these drugs they will commit more crimes to make sufficient money. Besides, high price of drugs make them very profitable to produce or sell these drugs. The persons engaged in this business will make efforts to procure these drugs from whatever sources they can do so.

Due to the above drawbacks of the strategy of reducing supply, the ***alternative strategy proposed is to reduce the demand for these drugs by educating people about their harmful effects on health.*** If education about harmful effects of drugs is successful, it will reduce the demand for these drugs and cause a leftward shift in their demand curve as shown in Fig. 27.11. As a result of education about harmful effects, demand curve shifts to the left from *DD* to *D′D′*. The equilibrium price falls from P_1 to P_2 and as will be seen from Fig. 27.11 the total revenue which is equal to price times the quantity ($P \times Q$) also declines. Thus, by bringing down the price, alternative strategy of drug education makes it less profitable to produce, sell or smuggle these illegal drugs. Thus drug education not only reduces the use of drugs and drug related crimes but will also make it unattractive to produce and sell these drugs.

However, in our view, both the supply-reducing measures and drug education are required if war against these harmful drugs is to be won.

INCIDENCE OF TAXATION

A significant application of demand-supply model is that it explains the problem of incidence of indirect taxes such sales tax and excise duty on commodities. By incidence of taxes we mean who bear the money burden of taxes. For example, if sale tax is imposed on a commodity the question is whether the producers will bear the burden of the tax or the consumers who buy the commodity or the money burden of the sales tax would be distributed in some way between the producers and the consumers. We will confine ourselves to the explanation of incidence of indirect taxes, that is, taxes which are levied on either production or sale or purchase of commodities.

It is worthwhile to note that the price of a commodity is determined by demand and supply only when perfect competition prevails in the market. Supply curve of a commodity slopes upward as it is assumed that law of diminishing returns operates. The upward sloping supply curve implies that as the price of a commodity rises the producer would offer more quantity for sale in the market. If no tax is levied on the commodity, the seller or producer will receive the whole amount of the price. Now, if the sales tax is imposed equal to ₹ 5 per unit, then the supply price of each unit of the quantity offered for sale in the market will rise by ₹ 5. In this case, the producer would receive the market price.minus the amount of the tax per unit. Thus, if the producer is to receive the same amount of price as prior to the imposition of the sales tax, then the supply price of each unit of the commodity sold will rise by the full amount of the tax. This implies that the supply curve of the commodity will now shift upward by the amount of the tax as a result of the imposition of the sales tax.

Figure 27.12 illustrates the incidence of a sales tax under conditions of perfect competition. *DD* is the demand curve for a commodity and *SS* is its supply curve before the imposition of tax on it. Interaction of these demand and supply curves determines price *OP* of the commodity and *OM* is the quantity sold and purchased. Suppose a unit sales tax, that is, sales tax per unit of the commodity equal to *SS′*(= *LQ*) is levied by the Government on the commodity in question. This will raise the supply price of the commodity by the sellers as the unit tax *SS′* will now be included by the sellers in their supply price. As a result, the supply curve of the commodity will shift to the left by the magnitude of tax *SS′*. The new supply curve *SS′* intersects the demand curve *DD* at the point *Q* and determines the new price *OP′* and quantity exchanged *OT*. It will be seen from the Figure 27.12 that price has risen by *PP′* or *RQ* which the buyers will bear whereas the tax per unit is *SS′* or *LQ*. It may be noted that the buyers will bear the burden of a tax to the extent that they have to pay the higher price than before. Thus the incidence of the tax borne by the buyers will be equal to *RQ*. The remaining part of the tax equal to *RL*, will be borne by the sellers. Thus of the tax *SS′* or *LQ*, *RQ* is incidence of the tax on the buyers and *RL* is the incidence on the sellers. Now, we can show that the incidence of the tax *RL* and *RQ* on the sellers and buyers respectively is equal to the ratio of the elasticity of demand and the elasticity of supply.

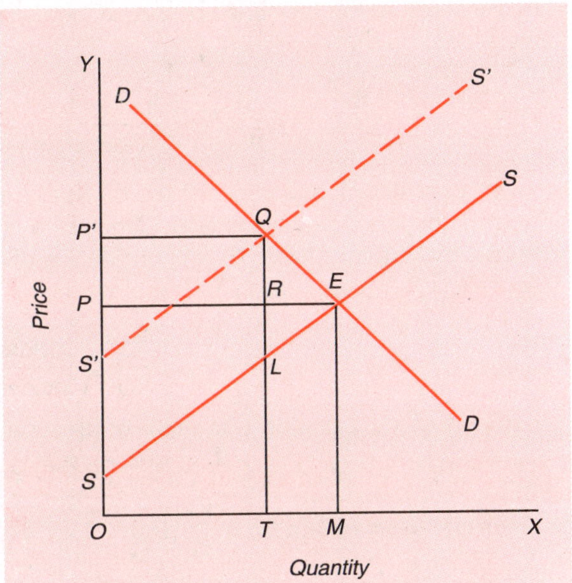

Fig. 27.12. *Incidence of an Indirect Tax.*

$$\frac{RL}{RQ} = \frac{\text{Incidence of tax on the sellers}}{\text{Incidence of tax on the buyers}}$$

$$\text{Price elasticity of demand} = \frac{\Delta q}{\Delta p} \cdot \frac{p}{q}$$

By referring to Figure 27.3, elasticity of demand when the price rises from *OP* to *OP′* for the buyers will be

$$e_d = \frac{\Delta q_d}{\Delta p} \cdot \frac{p}{q} = \frac{MT}{RQ} \cdot \frac{OP}{OM} \quad ...(1)$$

Likewise, elasticity of supply when the price received by the sellers falls from *OP* (= *ME*) to *TL* and the quantity sold declines from *OM* to *OT* can be found out. Thus :

$$e_s = \frac{\Delta q_s}{\Delta p}.\frac{P}{q} = \frac{MT}{RL}.\frac{OP}{OM} \quad .....(ii)$$

$$\frac{e_d}{e_s} = \frac{\frac{MT}{RQ}.\frac{OP}{OM}}{\frac{MT}{RL}.\frac{OP}{OM}} = \frac{RL}{RQ}$$

Since RL is the incidence of the tax on the sellers and RQ is the incidence of tax on the buyers, we find that

$$\frac{RL}{RQ} = \frac{\text{Incidence of tax on seller}}{\text{Incidence of tax on buyers}} = \frac{\text{Price elasticity of demand}}{\text{Price elasticity of sypply}}$$

To conclude, to what extent the burden of the tax will be shifted and the proportion in which the buyers will share the incidence of a commodity tax depends on the elasticities of demand and supply. What exactly incidence of tax on buyers RQ and incidence of tax on sellers RL will be equal to is shown below :-

$$\frac{e_d}{e_s} = \frac{RL}{RQ} = \frac{\text{Incidence of tax on seller}}{\text{Incidence of tax on buyer}} \quad .....(iii)$$

Suppose tax per unit 't' is levied on the commodity. Then.

$$t = RL + RQ \quad ....(iv)$$

From (*iii*) we obtain $RL= \frac{e_d}{e_s}.RQ$

Putting this value of RL in (*iv*) above we get $t=\frac{e_d}{e_s}RQ + RQ$

$$t = RQ\left(\frac{e_d}{e_s}+1\right) = RQ\left(\frac{e_d+e_s}{e_s}\right)$$

$$RQ = t\left(\frac{e_s}{e_d+e_s}\right) \quad ......(v)$$

(Note that in the above formula we have taken the absolute value of elasticity of demand and ignored the minus sign).

Thus the incidence of tax on the buyers RQ, that is, increase in price (ΔP) paid by the buyers is equal to the tax per unit multiplied by $\left(\frac{e_s}{e_d+e_s}\right)$

From equation (*v*) it follows that given the elasticity of supply, the greater the elasticity of demand, the lower the incidence of tax on buyers'.

Likewise, we can obtain $RL = t\left(\frac{e_d}{e_d+e_s}\right)$ .....(*vi*)

That is, incidence of tax on the sellers, RL will be equal to the tax per unit (t) multiplied by the $\frac{e_d}{e_d + e_s}$. Given the elasticity of demand, the greater the elasticity of supply, the lower the incidence of tax on the sellers.

If elasticity of demand for a commodity is zero, then from (*vi*) it follows that the incidence of tax on the sellers *RL* will be zero and from (*v*) above it follows that incidence of tax *RQ* on buyers will be equal to the whole tax *t* per unit. On the other hand, if the elasticity of supply is zero, then it follows from (vi) above that the incidence of tax on sellers *RL* will be equal to the whole amount of the tax *t* and as a result the incidence of tax on the buyers will be zero in this case. (This also follows from (*v*) above).

If elasticity of demand is infinity ($e_d = \infty$), then it also follows from (*vi*) above that *RL* = *t*, that is, the whole burden of the tax will fall on the sellers. On the other hand, if elasticity of supply is infinity, then it follows from (*v*) above that *RQ* = *t*, that is, the whole burden of the tax will fall on the buyers. Let us graphically explain these cases of incidents of tax.

A commodity tax, excise duty or sales tax drives a wedge between the price paid by the buyers and the price received by the sellers. Consider Figure 27.13 where the demand curve *DD* is inelastic and supply curve S_1S_1 is relatively elastic. Suppose now sales tax equal to *CB* per unit is imposed. The producers or sellers will be willing to sell a *given quantity of a commodity*, if they receive the same *net price* as before. That is, the producers or sellers will treat the sales tax *CB* per unit as an extra cost of production and therefore, they would add it to the cost per unit. As a result of the imposition of a sales tax per unit of the commodity, supply curve will shift upward to S_2 and will be parallel to the supply curve S_1S_1 without a tax. Demand curve *DD* will remain unaffected as a result of the imposition of sales tax. It will be seen from Fig 27.13 that the new supply curve S_2S_2 intersects the demand curve *DD* at point *B* and determines higher equilibrium price OP_2 and the quantity sold falls to OQ_2 It will be seen from Fig. 27.13

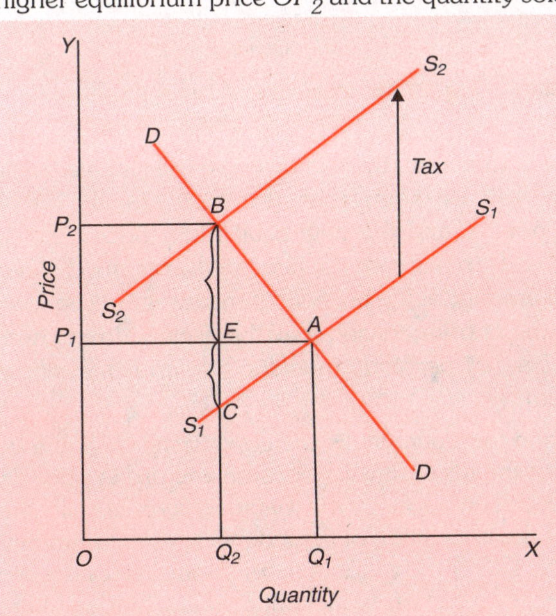

Fig. 27.13. *In case of inelastic demand the burden commodity tax falls more on buyers.*

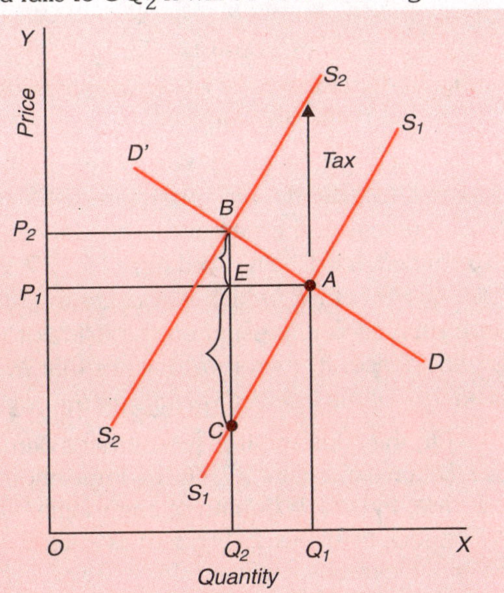

Fig.27.14. *In case of elastic demand the burden of a commodity tax falls more on the sellers.*

that in this present case when demand is inelastic and supply is relatively elastic, the burden of the tax falls more on the buyers and less on the sellers. The buyers have to pay *EB* more price than before and sellers receive *EC* less price than before. And *EB* > *EC*.

Now consider Fig. 27.14 where demand curve *DD* is elastic and supply curve $S_1 S_1$, is relatively inelatic. Before the imposition of tax P_1 is the price at which quantity Q_1 is being bought and sold. Consequent to imposition of scales tax equal to *CB*, supply curve shifts to S_2S_2. Price rises from P_1 to P_2 and equilibrium quantity sold and bought falls to Q_2. In this case when demand is elastic and supply relatively inelastic, burden of tax *EB* per unit borne by the buyers is much less than *CE* borne by the sellers. It follows from above that the burden or ***the incidence of taxes borne by the producer and the consumer will depend upon the elasticity of demand as well as elasticity of supply. The lower, elasticity of demand, the greater will be the incidence of tax borne by the consumer.***

If the demand for a commodity is perfectly inelastic the whole of the burden of the commodity tax will fall on consumer. This is shown in figure 27.15. In this figure demand curve *DD* is a vertical straight line showing that demand for the commodity is completely inelastic. As a result of the intersection of the demand and supply curves, price *OP* is determined.

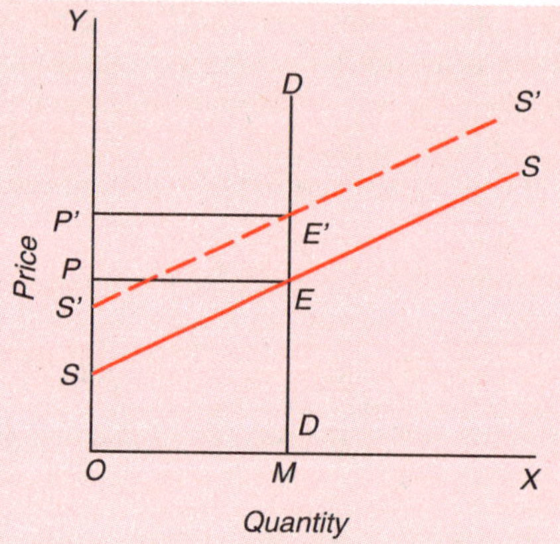

Fig. 27.15. *Incidence of Tax in Case of Perfectly Inelastic Demand*

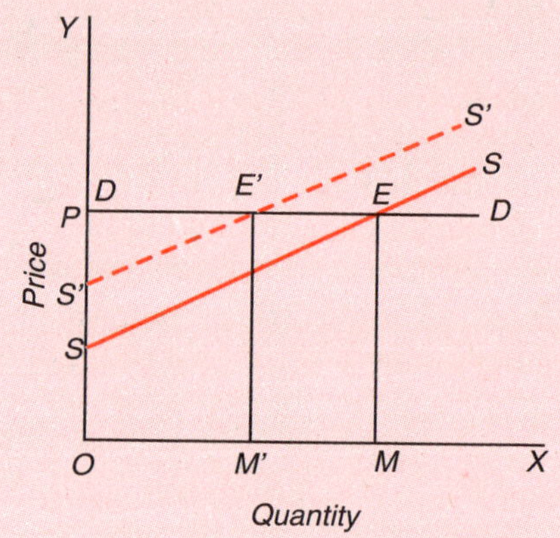

Fig. 27.16. *Incidence of Tax in Case of Perfelectly Elastic Demand*

If now the tax equal to *SS′* is imposed on the commodity, the supply curve will shift vertically upward to the dotted position *S′S′*. It will be seen that the new supply curve *S ′S ′* intersects the demand curve *DD* at point *E′*and the new equilibrium price *OP ′* is determined. It will be noticed from Fig. 27.15 that in this case the price of the commodity has risen by *PP ′* or *EE ′*which is equal to the full amount ol the tax *SS″*. It means that producers have succeeded in passing on the full tax to the consumers and they themselves do not bear any incidence. It, therefore, follows that *in case of perfectly inealstic demand, the whole incidence of the indirect tax falls on the consumer.*

On the contrary, if theconsumer's demand for a quantity is perfectly elastic, as is shown by *DD* curve in Figure 27.16 the imposition of the tax on it will not cause any rise in price. In this case, the whole burden of commodity tax will be borne by the manufacturers or sellers. It will be seen from Fig. 27.16 that as a result of the imposition of the indirect tax by the amount *SS′* and the resultant upward shift in supply curve to *S′S′* the equilibrium price remains unchanged at the leve *OP*. Since the price has not risen, the consumers would not bear any burden of the tax in this case. Therefore, the whole incidence of the tax will fall on the producers or sellers in case of perfectly elastic demand. *It should be noted that the more inelastic the demand for a commodity, the greater the rise in the price paid by the consumers and the vice versa.*

We have explained above how the burden of a tax on a commodity is shared between the sellers (or producers) and buyers of the commodity. We are now interested in showing a the burden of a commodity tax on buyers and sellers depends on the elasticities of demand and supply. Two important taxes are levied on a commodity and a part of these taxes is passed on to the consumers. First, the excise duty is imposed on the production of a commodity. The producers of the commodity try to shift the burden of excise duty to the buyers by raising the price of the commodity. Secondly, sales tax is levied on the sales of a commodity on the sellers of the commodity.. Sellers also try to shift the burden of sales tax to the buyers by including it in the price of the commodity. However, whatever the intentions of the producers or sellers to shift the burden of a commodity tax, *actual burden borne by buyers and sellers depends on the elasticities of demand and supply.* The money burden of a tax on buyers and sellers is called *incidence of a tax.*

The predictions about the incidence of taxes borne by zthe consumers and the producers have been generally found to be true in the real world situation when the commodities on which taxes are imposed are sold under competitive conditions.

QUESTIONS FOR REVIEW

1. Explain the effect of price control on a commodity ? Why is it necessary to introduce rationing when price control is imposed on a commodity ?
2. What is black market ? Why do black markets often arise when price control and rationing of a commodity is introduced ?
3. What would happen if government imposes a ceiling on the retail price of a commodity, say patrol. Why do advocates of price control also recommend rationing ?
4. Explain the effect of setting a minimum support price for an agricultural product. Does it lead to the increase in income of the farmers ?
5. Examine the effects of setting by government *procurement price of wheat higher than the free market price. Explain with special reference to rising stocks of foodgrains in India.*
6. Explain how rent control leads to the shortage of housing units available on rent.
7. Do rent controls help those who wish to find cheap housing ?
8. Explain the effect of imposition of excise duty on the quantity bought and sold of the commodity and its price. Do buyers of the commodity bear the whole burden of the excise duty ?
9. Explain with reference to agriculture 'Paraxdox of poverty amongst plenty', Illustrate diagrammatically.
10. How a good news of forecast of good wealther for agriculture can be a bad news for farmers ?
11. How does a crop-restriction programe by government of the Untied States help farmers ?
12. Show that what is good for farmers is not necessarily good for the society as a whole
13. In the 1970s, OPEC caused a dramatic increase in the price of oil. What prevented it from maintaining the high price through 1980s ?
14. What strategies can be adopted to reduce the use of drugs ? Comment on the efficiency of each strategy.
15. Analyse the incidence of a per unit tax imposed on a commodity with perfectly inelastic demand. Assume that the conditions in the market are perfectly competitive.
16. A unit excise duty is imposed on a firm in a competitive market. Examine its short-run and long-run effects on industry and firm.
17. Analyse the incidence of a per unit tax imposed on a commodity with *(i)* perfectly elastic demand and *(ii)* perfectly inelastic demand.
18. Explain the circumstances under which rise in price of a commodity as a result of the imposition of a per unit tax on it is more than the tax.
    [**Hints.** This happens in case of a decreasing-cost industry where supply curve slopes downward].
19. How is a specific duty imposed on a commodity is shared between the consumers and producers? Show that the lower the price elasticity of demand, the higher is the incidence of a specific commodity tax on the consumers.

CHAPTER

28

Equilibrium of the Firm and Industry Under Perfect Competition

Conditions of Perfect Competition

In an earlier chapter we made a general analysis of the equilibrium of the firm and its conditions. In this chapter we will study the equilibrium of the firm and industry under conditions of perfect competition and explain how price and output are determined under it. It would be in the fitness of things if we first describe what we mean by perfect competition. As mentioned in a previous chapter, perfect competition, as is generally understood, is said to prevail when the following conditions are found in the market:

1. There are a large number of firms producing and selling a product. .
2. The product of all firms is homogeneous.
3. Both the sellers and buyers have perfect information about the prevailing price in the market.
4. Entry into and exit from the industry is free for the firms.

We shall discuss below in detail the above four conditions of perfect competition.

A Large Number of Firms. The first condition of perfect competition is that there are a large number of firms in the industry. The position of a single firm in the industry containing numerous firms is just like a drop in the ocean. The existence of a large number of firms producing and selling the product ensures that an individual firm exercises no influence over the price of the product. The output of an individual firm constitutes a very small fraction of the total output of the whole industry so that any increase or decrease in output by an individual firm has a negligible effect on the total supply of the product of industry. As a result, a single firm is not in a position to influence the price of the product by increasing or reducing its output. The individual firm under perfect competition therefore takes the price of the product as a given datum and adjusts its output to earn maximum profits. In other words, a firm under perfect competition is price-taker and output-adjuster.

Homogeneous Products. The second condition of perfect competition is that the products produced by all firms in the industry are fully homogeneous and identical. It means that the products of various firms are indistinguishable from each other; they are perfect substitutes for one another. In other words, cross elasticity between the products of the firms is infinite. In case of homogeneous products, trade marks, patents, special brand labels etc. do not exist since these things make the products differentiated. It should be noted that if there are many firms, but they are producing differentiated products, each one of them will have influence over the price of his own variety of the product. The control over price is completely eliminated only when all firms are producing homogeneous products.

But whether or not products are homogeneous should be judged from the viewpoint of the buyers. Products would be homogeneous only when the buyers consider them to be so. Even if the buyers find some imagined differences between the products, the products would not be homogeneous, howsoever physically alike they may be. Anything which makes buyers prefer one seller to another, be it personality, reputation, convenient location, or the tone of his shop, differentiates the product to that degree, since what is bought is really a bundle of utilities of which these things are a part. Therefore, for the products to be homogeneous utilities offered by all sellers to buyers must be identical. If the bundle of utilities offered by all sellers is not the same, then the buyers would have a preference for some sellers who will have a degree of control over their individual prices. Thus the existence of homogeneous products signifies that the products of all sellers are completely identical in the eyes of consumers who therefore do not have any preference for one seller over another. Under such conditions it is evident that "buyers and sellers will be paired in random fashion in a large number of transactions. It will be entirely a matter of chance from which seller a particular buyer makes his purchases, and purchases over a period of time will be distributed among all sellers according to the law of probability. After all this is only another way of saying that the product is homogeneous."[1]

Perfect Information about the Prevailing Price. Another condition for perfect competition to prevail is that both the buyers and sellers are fully aware of the ruling price in the market. Because only when all buyers know fully the current price of the product in the market, sellers cannot charge more than the prevailing price. If any seller tries to charge a higher price than that ruling in the market, the buyers will shift to some other sellers and buy the good at the ruling price since they know what the ruling price in the market is. Similarly, all sellers are also aware of the prevailing price in the market and no one will charge less price than this.

Free Entry and Exit. Lastly, perfect competition requires that there must be complete freedom for the entry of new firms or the exit of the existing firms from the industry in the long run. There must be no barriers to the entry of firms. Since, in the short run, firms can neither change the size of their plants, nor new firms can enter or old ones can leave the industry, the condition of free entry and free exit therefore applies only to the long-run equilibrium under perfect competition. If the existing firms are making super-normal profits in the short run, this condition requires that in the long run new firms will enter the industry to compete away the profits. If, on the other hand, firms are making losses in the short run, some of the existing firms will leave the industry in the long run with the result that the price of the product will go up and the firms left in the industry will be earning at least normal profits.

Demand Curve of a Product Facing a Perfectly Competitive Firm

The first three conditions ensure that a single price must prevail under perfect competition and demand curve or average revenue curve faced by an individual firm under perfect competition is perfectly elastic at the ruling price in the market. Perfectly elastic demand curve signifies that the firm does not exercise any control over the price of the product but can sell any amount of the product as it likes at the ruling price. If the firm raises its price slightly above the ruling price, it will lose all its customers to its rivals. Because it can sell as much as it likes at the prevailing price it has no incentive to lower it. Without being able to raise the price and having no incentive to lower it, the firm is content to accept the ruling price in the market. Once the price in the market is established, a firm accepts the price as a given datum and adjusts its output at the level which gives it maximum profits. Consider Fig.28.1. To begin with, demand curve *DD* and supply curve *SS* intersect at point *E* and determine price *OP*. Now, the firm, having no influence over the price, will take the price *OP* as given and therefore average-marginal revenue curve facing it will be a horizontal straight line at the level of *OP*.

1. E.H. Chamberlin, *Theory of Monopolistic Competition*, 7th ed, p.8.

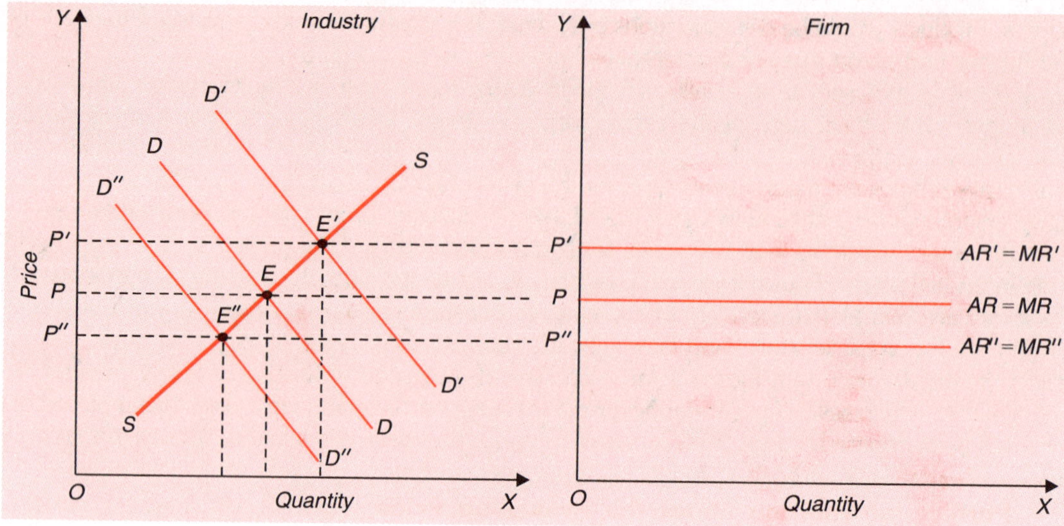

Fig. 28.1. *Demand Curve Facing a Perfectly Competitive Firm is Perfectly Elastic*

When demand increases and as a result price rises to OP', the firm will now confront average-marginal revenue curve at the level of OP'. And if the demand decreases and price falls to OP'', the firm's average-marginal revenue curve will shift below to the level of OP''.

SHORT-RUN EQUILIBRIUM OF THE COMPETITIVE FIRM

As explained in a previous chapter, the short run means a period of time within which the firms can alter their level of output only by increasing or decreasing amounts of variable factors such as labour and raw materials, while fixed factors like capital equipment, machinery etc. remain unchanged. Moreover, in the short run, new firms can neither enter the industry, nor the existing firms can leave it. Before explaining competitive equilibrium we assume that a firm tries to maximize money profits. We shall explain the equilibrium of a perfectly competitive firm in two stages : first, by assuming that all firms are working under identical cost conditions and, secondly, by assuming that they are working under differential cost conditions.

The working of firms under identical cost conditions implies that all firms are facing same cost conditions, that is, their average and marginal cost curves are of the same level and shapes. This would be so if the entrepreneurs of all firms are of equal efficiency and also the other factors of production used by them are perfectly homogeneous and are available to all of them at the same prices.

As explained earlier, under perfect competition, an individual firm is a *price taker*, that is, it has to accept the prevailing price as a given datum. It cannot influence the price by its individual action. As a result, demand curve or average revenue curve of the firm is a horizontal straight line (*i.e.*, perfectly elastic) at the level of the prevailing price. Since a perfectly competitive firm sells additional units of output at the same price, marginal revenue curve coincides with average revenue curve. That the marginal revenue of a perfectly competitive firm equals price or average revenue can be mathematically shown as under

$$MR = \frac{\Delta TR}{\Delta Q}$$

Now, $$\Delta TR = \Delta (P.Q)$$

Since price of the product (*P*) for a perfectly competitive firm is a given datum and is independent of its level of output (*Q*), therefore,

$$\Delta TR = P \,.\, \Delta Q$$

Thus, $$MR = \frac{\Delta TR}{\Delta Q} = \frac{P.\Delta Q}{\Delta Q} = P$$

Marginal cost curve of the firm, as usual, is U-shaped. Now, in order to decide about its equilibrium output, the firm will compare marginal cost with marginal revenue. It will be in equilibrium at the level of output at which marginal cost equals marginal revenue and marginal cost curve is cutting marginal revenue curve *from below*. At this level it will be maximizing its profits. Since marginal revenue is the same as price (or average revenue) under perfect competition, the firm will equate marginal cost with price to attain equilibrium output. Consider Fig. 28.2 in which price *OP* is prevailing in the market. *PL* would then be the demand curve or the average and marginal revenue curve of the firm. It will be seen from Fig. 28.2 that marginal cost curve cuts average and marginal revenue curve at two different points, *F* and *E*. *F* cannot be the position of equilibrium, since at *F* second order condition of firm's equilibrium, namely, that the marginal cost curve must cut marginal revenue curve from below at the point of equilibrium is not satisfied. The firm will be increasing its profits by producing beyond *F* because marginal revenue is greater than marginal cost. The firm will be in equilibrium at point *E* or output *OM* since at *E* marginal cost equals marginal revenue (or price) as well as marginal cost curve is cutting marginal revenue curve from below. As under perfect competition marginal revenue curve is a horizontal straight line, the marginal cost curve must be rising so as to cut the marginal revenue curve from below. Therefore, in case of perfect competition the second order condition of firm's equilibrium requires that marginal cost curve must be rising at the point of equilibrium. Hence the twin conditions of firm's equilibrium under perfect competition are:

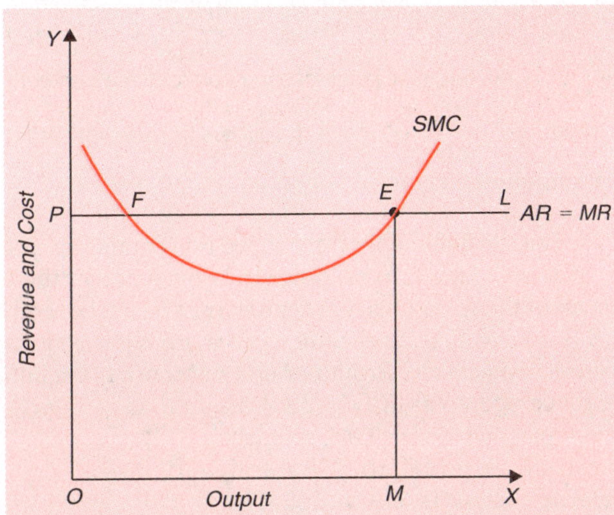

Fig. 28.2. *Firm's Equilibrium Under Perfect Competition*

(1) *MC* = *MR* = *Price*

(2) *MC* curve must be rising at the point of equilibrium.

Conditions for Profit Maximization; Algebraic Analysis. That a competitive firm will maximise its total profits when marginal cost (*MC*) equals price (*P*) can be easily proved with differential calculus. Note that both the total cost (*TC*) and total revenue (*TR*) are functions of output (*Q*). This implies that total profits are also function of output (*Q*). Let π represent total profits. Thus

$$\pi = f(Q)$$

$$\pi = TR - TC = P.Q - TC \qquad \ldots(i)$$

For maximisation of profits, the first derivative of the profit function has to be set equal to zero.

Thus, for maximum profits $\frac{d\pi}{dQ} = 0$

Since $d\pi = d(P.Q) - dTC$, for maximisation of profits

$$\frac{d\pi}{dQ} = \frac{d(P.Q)}{dQ} - \frac{dTC}{dQ} = 0 \qquad \text{....}(ii)$$

$\frac{d(P.Q)}{dQ}$ represents marginal revenue, and $\frac{d(TC)}{dQ}$ represents marginal cost.

Assuming that second order condition for profit maximisation holds, it follows from (*ii*) above that for maximisation of profits

$$\frac{d(P.Q)}{dQ} = \frac{dTC}{dQ} \text{ or } MR = MC$$

Now, because price of the product for a perfectly competitive firm is constant, marginal revenue, $\frac{d(P.Q)}{dQ}$ = Price. It follows therefore that for maximisation of profits by a perfectly competitive firm,

$$\text{Price} = MC$$

But the fulfilment of the above two conditions does not guarantee that positive profits will be earned by the firm. In order to know whether the firm is making profits or losses and how much of them, average cost curve must be introduced in the figure. This has been done in Fig. 28.3, where *SAC* and *SMC* curves are short-run average cost and short-run marginal cost curves respectively. Profit per unit of output is the difference between average revenue (price) and average cost. In Fig. 28.3 at the equilibrium output *OM*, average revenue is equal to *ME*, and average cost is equal to *MF*. Therefore, the profit per unit of output is *EF*, the difference between *ME* and *MF*. The total economic profits earned by the firm will be equal to *EF* (profit per unit) multiplied by *OM* or *HF* (total output). Thus the total profits will be equal to the area *HFEP*. Because normal profits are included in average cost, the area *HFEP* indicates super-normal or economic profits.

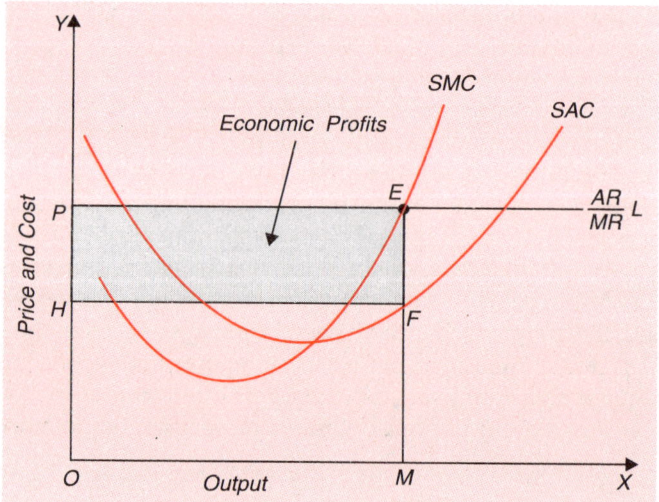

Fig. 28.3. *Short-Run Equilibrium with Profit*

Since we are assuming that all firms in the industry are working under same cost conditions and also for all of them price is *OP*, all will be earning super-normal or economic profits equal to the area *HFEP*. Thus while all firms in the industry will be in short-run equilibrium, but the industry will not be in equilibrium since there will be a tendency for the new firms to enter the industry to compete away the super-normal profits. But the short run is not a period long enough for the new firms to enter the industry. The existing firms will therefore continue earning super-normal profits equal to *HFEP* in the short period. It is evident that in the situation depicted in Fig. 28.3 all firms will be in equilibrium at *E* and each will be producing *OM* output, but the industry will not be in equilibrium since the tendency for the new firms to enter the industry will be present, though they cannot enter during the short period.

Short-Run Equilibrium of a Firm in Case of Losses

Now suppose that the prevailing market price of the product is such that the price line or average and marginal revenue curve lies below average cost throughout. This case is illustrated

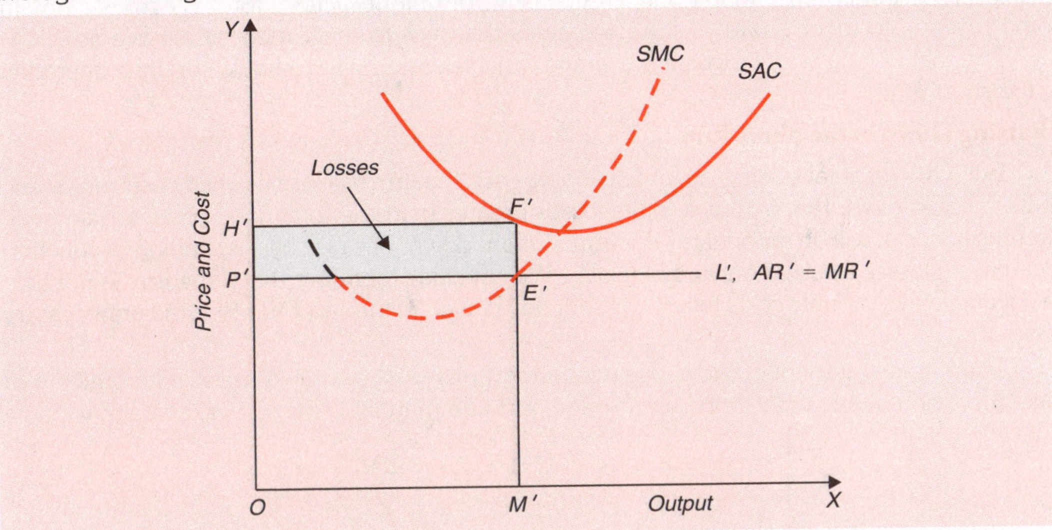

Fig. 28.4 *Short-Run Equilibrium: Minimising Losses*

in Fig. 28.4 where the ruling price is *OP'* which is taken as given by the firm. *P'L'* is the price line which lies below *AC'* curve at all levels of output. The firm will be in equilibrium at point *E'* at which marginal cost is equal to price (or marginal revenue) and marginal cost curve is rising. Firm would be producing *OM'* output but would be making losses, since average revenue, (or price) which is equal to *M'E'* is less than average cost which is equal to *M'F'*. The loss per unit of output is then equal to *E'F'* and total loss will be equal to *P'E'F'H'* which is the minimum loss that a firm can make under the given price-cost situation. Since all the firms are working under same cost conditions, all would be in equilibrium at point *E'* or output *OM'* and every one will be making losses equal to *P'E'F'H'*. As a result, the firms will have a tendency to quit the industry in order to make a search for earning at least normal profits elsewhere. We thus see that at price *OP'* firms will be in equilibrium at *E'*.

But the question arises as to why at all the firms should continue producing the product if they are to make losses. In the short run if they cannot go out of the industry by disposing of the plant, why do they not at least close down, that is, stop producing, when they are making losses. In other words, why do they not suspend production during the short period while remaining in the industry. This is because they cannot alter the fixed capital equipment in the short run and will therefore have to incur losses equal to the fixed costs even if they choose to shut down and stop producing the product. We thus see that if *the firm shuts down in the short run, it can avoid only variable costs, fixed costs have to be borne by it in the short run whether it is producing or not*. Therefore, if the firm can earn revenue which covers variable costs as well as a part of the fixed costs, it will be quite rational for it to keep operating and go on producing the product since stopping production under such circumstances will mean greater losses. ***If the firm stops production in the short run, losses will be equal to the fixed cost.*** Losses will be less than the fixed costs if a firm while operating earns revenue which covers variable costs fully as well as a part of the fixed costs.

It is thus quite rational for the firm to continue producing in the short run when it is earning more than variable costs even though it may be producing at a loss. For by doing so it will be *minimizing its losses in* the short run. It is prudent to continue working in the short run if the firm is covering variable costs and also making something to meet a part of the fixed costs. The saying 'half a loaf is better than none' is suggestive of rational action, for it is better to obtain some revenue to meet a part of the fixed costs than not to meet them at all. We conclude therefore that as long as price exceeds average variable cost, the firm should continue operating in the short run.

Shutting Down in the Short Run

But if the price falls below average variable cost, the firm will lose its fixed costs plus some of its variable costs, that is, it will make losses greater than the total fixed costs. Under such circumstances, it will be rational for the firm to close down, because by suspending production it can avoid losses incurred on variable costs. We conclude therefore that if the firm is not able to cover even its variable costs fully it will shut down even in the short run to avoid unnecessary losses.

The whole argument of the above two paragraphs can be easily grasped with the help of Fig.28.5 where along with short-run average cost and marginal cost curves, average variable

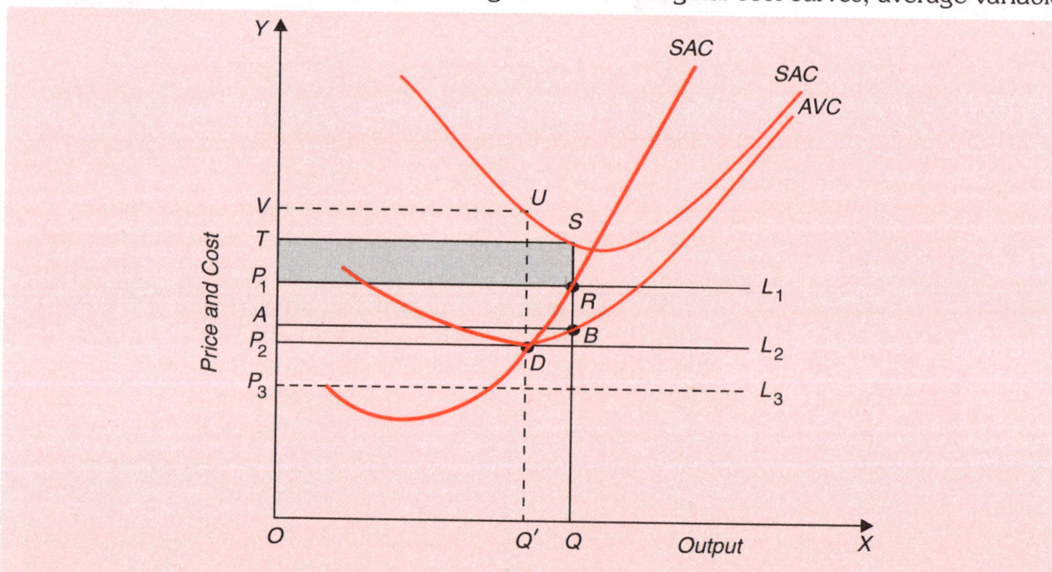

Fig. 28.5. *Shut-Down Point for the Perfectly Competitive Firm*

cost curve is also drawn. When the price in the market is OP_1, the firm will be in equilibrium at point R and will therefore produce output OQ . Since average cost which is equal to QS is greater than the average revenue or price which is equal to QR or OP_1, the firm will be making losses equal to P_1RST. But it will be in the interest of the firm to continue producing at point R because the price OP_1 or QR is greater than the average variable cost which is here equal to QB. By operating at price OP_1, the firm is covering total variable costs (area $OQBA$) and a part of the fixed costs (area $ABRP_1$). The part of the fixed costs equal to area P_1RST is not being covered. The firm should operate and bear the losses equal to P_1RST because by closing down in the short run the firm will have to bear the losses equal to the whole fixed costs, the area $ABST$. Thus the losses will be smaller in case the firm is working than if it stops producing. If price in the market happens to be OP_2, the firm will be in equilibrium at point D. Price is here equal to average variable cost. At point D the firm is covering the variable costs fully, but it is not meeting any part of the fixed costs. Therefore, its losses are equal to the whole fixed costs equal to the area P_2DUV. Even if the firm stops operating, its losses will be equal to the whole fixed cost, therefore it will be a matter of indifference for the firm to operate at price OP_2 or not. But if the price falls below average variable cost or OP_2, for instance, if price falls to OP_3, the firm will simply shut down since the firm will not cover even its variable costs fully. Therefore, the firm will suspend production at price OP_3 or any other price below OP_2 and will wait for some good time to come.

From the above analysis of equilibrium of the competitive firm in the short run, it follows that the firm in the short run may earn supernormal profits or losses or normal profits depending upon the price prevailing in the market. Firm's short-run equilibrium is possible in all these three situations. If the prevailing price is such that the price line is tangent to the minimum point of the average cost curve, then the firm would make only normal profits even in the short run.

LONG-RUN EQUILIBRIUM OF THE FIRM UNDER PERFECT COMPETITION

The long run is a period of time which is sufficiently long to allow the firms to make changes in all factors of production. In the long run, all factors are variable and none fixed. The firms, in the long run, can increase their output by changing their capital equipment; they may expand their old plants or replace the old lower-capacity plants by the new higher-capacity plants or add new plants. Besides, in the long run, new firms can enter the industry to compete the existing firms. On the other hand, in the long run, the firms can contract their output level by reducing their capital equipment; they may allow a part of the existing capital equipment to wear out without replacement or sell out a part of the capital equipment. Moreover, the firms can leave the industry in the long run. The long-run equilibrium then refers to the situation when free and full adjustment in the capital equipment as well as in the number of firms has been allowed to take place. It is therefore long-run average and marginal cost curve which are relevant for deciding about equilibrium output in the long run. Moreover, in the long run, it is the average total cost which is of determining importance since all costs are variable and none fixed.

As explained above, a firm is in equilibrium under perfect competition when marginal cost is equal to price. But for the firm to be in long-run equilibrium, besides marginal cost being equal to price, the price must also be equal to average cost. For, if the price is greater or less than the average cost, there will be tendency for the firms to enter or leave the industry. If the price is greater than the average cost, the firms will earn more than normal profits. These supernormal profits will attract other firms into the industry. With the entry of new firms in the industry the price of the product will go down as a result of the increase in supply of output and also the cost will go up as a result of more intensive competition for factors of production. The firms will continue entering the industry until the price is equal to average cost so that all firms are earning only normal profits.

On the contrary, if the price is lower than the average cost, the firms would make losses. These losses will induce some of the firms to quit the industry. As a result, the output of the industry will fall which will raise the price. On the other hand, with some firms going out of the industry cost may go down as a result of fall in the demand for certain specialised factors of production. The firms will continue leaving the industry until the price is equal to average cost so that the firms remaining in the field are making only normal profits. It, therefore, follows that for a perfectly competitive firm to be in long-run equilibrium, the following two conditions must be fulfilled.

1. Price = Marginal Cost

2. Price = Average Cost

If price is equal to both marginal cost and average cost, then we have a double condition of long-run perfectly competitive equilibrium :

Price = Marginal Cost = Average Cost

But from the relationship between marginal cost and average cost we know that marginal cost is equal to average cost only at the minimum point of the average cost curve. Therefore, the condition for long-run equilibrium of the firm can be written as :

Price = Marginal Cost = Minimum Average Cost

Fig. 28.6 represents long-run equilibrium of the firm under perfect competition. The firm cannot be in the long-run equilibrium at a price greater than *OP* in Fig.28.6. This is because if price is greater than *OP*, then the price line (demand curve) would lie somewhere above the minimum point of the average cost curve so that marginal cost and price will be equal where the firm is earning super-normal profits. Since there will be tendency for new firms to enter and compete away these super-normal profits, the firm cannot be in long-run equilibrium at any price higher than *OP*. Likewise, the firm cannot be in long-run equilibrium at a price lower than *OP* in Fig. 28.6 under perfect competition. If price is lower than *OP*, the average and marginal revenue curve will lie below the average cost curve so that the marginal cost and price will be equal at the point where the firm is making losses. Therefore, there will be tendency for some of the firms in the industry to go out with the result that price will rise and the firms left in the industry make normal profits. We therefore conclude that the firm can be in long-run equilibrium under perfect competition only when price is at such a level that the horizontal demand curve (that is, *AR* curve) is tangent to the average cost curve so that price equals average cost and firm makes only normal profits.

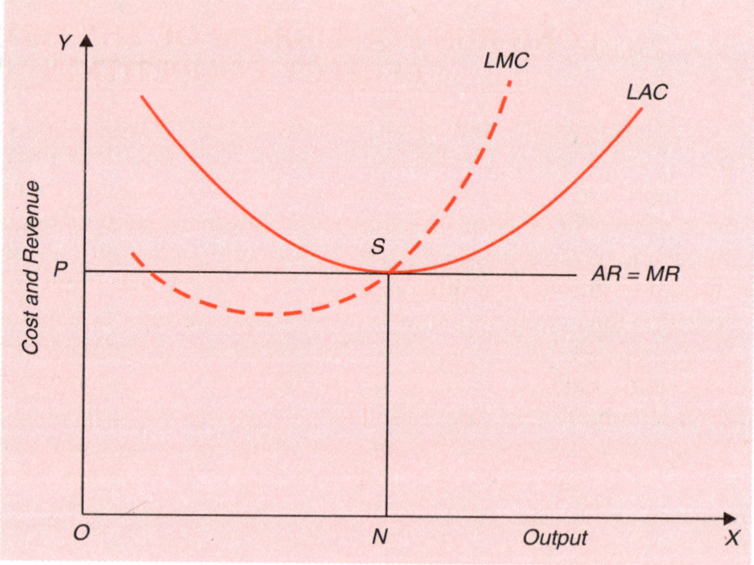

Fig. 28.6. *Long-run Equilibrium of the Firm*

It should be noted that a horizontal demand curve can be tangent to a U-shaped average cost curve only at the latter's minimum point. Since at the minimum point of the average cost curve the marginal cost and average cost are equal, price in long-run equilibrium is equal to both marginal cost and average cost. In other words, double condition of long-run equilibrium is fulfilled at the minimum point of the average cost curve.

It is clear from above that ***long-run equilibrium of the firm under perfect competition is established at the minimum point of the long-run average cost curve.*** Working at the minimum point of the long-run average cost curve signifies that the firm is producing with the plant of optimum scale, that is, with lowest possible level of short-run average cost curve. Besides, the perfectly competitive firm by producing at the minimum point of the long-run average curve *LAC is enjoying all possible economies of scale,* or in other words, it has exhausted the economies of scale and has no incentive to move to any other point on the long-run average cost curve *LAC*. Working at the minimum point of long-run average cost curve implies that it is working ***at the optimum or efficient scale.*** The fact that the firm working under conditions of perfect competition tends to be working with optimum scale plant and at the minimum point of *LAC* in the long run is beneficial from the social point of view in two ways.

First, by working at the minimum point of long-run average cost curve by a perfectly competitive firm means that it works with utmost technical efficiency and thus resources are being used most efficiently. Secondly, since at the minimum point of long-run average cost curve marginal cost equals average cost this ensures price is also equal to marginal cost (Price = *MC*). We will explain later that *producing output at which price equals marginal cost ensures allocative efficiency*. Allocative efficiency means that resources are allocated to the production of goods which maximise satisfaction of the people. Having achieved allocative efficiency, we cannot make some people better off without making some others worse off.

LONG-RUN EQUILIBRIUM ADJUSTMENT OF A COMPETITIVE FIRM

We have explained above the conditions of long-run equilibrium of a perfectly competitive firm. In what follows the process of adjustment of a perfectly competitive firm to attain its long-run equilibrium position is analysed. In the long run a firm can change all factors including the size of plant by installing more or new machines. More specifically, in the long run a firm can choose an appropriate size of the plant for the production of a product depending upon the price of the product and the long-run average and marginal cost of production. In the long run, a firm can even decide to leave the industry to avoid losses or if it thinks it can earn more profits elsewhere. The long-run equilibrium adjustment of competitive firm is illustrated in Fig. 28.7.

As in the short run, in the long run also a competitive firm faces a perfectly elastic (horizontal) demand curve as being incapable of influencing the price, it takes the market price as given. In Fig.28.7, the price of the product in the market, to begin with, is equal to OP_1 and therefore the demand curve facing the firm is P_1L_1. Suppose the firm is working with a plant of the size having short-run average cost curve, SAC_1, with its short run marginal cost curve SMC_1. With P_1L as the demand curve, the firm will maximise its profits in the short run by producing level of output equal to OQ_1 where its SMC = Price OP_1. With this short-run equilibrium

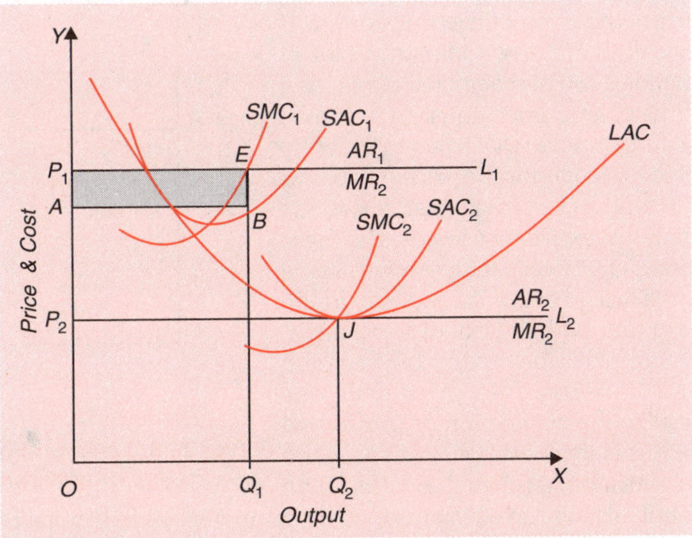

Fig. 28.7. *Long-run Adjustment of a Competitive Firm*

output OQ_1, the firm is making positive economic profits equal to the area of the rectangle $ABEP_1$ (Note that EB is the difference between AR and AC and therefore represents profit per unit).

Though the firm is making positive economic profits in the short run by producing output OQ_1, this does not represent its long-run equilibrium position. This is because the firm can increase its profits by expanding the size of plant and other associated factors. The decision regarding which plant size to employ and what level of output to produce with it is governed by the long-run average and marginal cost curves. The long-run average cost curve is also U-shaped which shows that as the firm expands the size of its plant and output there are economies of scale up to an output level OQ_2 and beyond this the diseconomies of scale occur. As long as the firm is earning economic profits and economies of scale exist, the firm will expand its scale.

It will be seen from Figure 28.7 that if firm can reduce its average cost of production by expanding output to the level OQ_2 and installing a plant of scale whose short-run average cost curve is SAC_2. Thus, the firm will tend to shift to SAC_2 and produce output OQ_2. However, at the same time lured by the economic profits made by the existing firms, new firms having same costs as the existing firm will enter the industry which will cause the supply of output to increase. Thus supply of output of the product increases in two ways: First, the existing firms expand their size to take advantage of the economies of scale and secondly new firms enter the industry to take advantage of the profit opportunities in the industry.

As a consequence of the expansion of output by all the existing firms and the entry of new firms in the industry, the supply of the product of the industry will increase which will cause a reduction in its price. The entry of new firms will continue and price go on falling under the pressure of more supply until the price falls to OP_2 equal to the level of minimum long-run average cost curve. It will be seen from Fig.28.7 that with price OP_2, the competitive firm will be in equilibrium by producing output equal to OQ_2 where the following conditions hold good:

Price (OP_2) = LMC = SMC = Minimum LAC

Since price is equal to average cost, the competitive firms will earn no economic profits. Thus, eventually, as a result of the entry of new firms and expansion of scale by the existing firms, the competitive equilibrium is established at the minimum point of the long-run average cost curve, and firms charge price equal to it. It may be further noted that if due to the entry of too many firms the price falls below the long-run average cost curve, the firms will experience losses. But these losses will be only temporary as some firms will go out of the industry in the long run. With the exit of some firms, the supply of the product will decrease and consequently price will rise resulting in elimination of profits and with this the existing firms can hope to earn only normal profits. The eventual long-run equilibrium of the competitive firm when it makes zero economic profits or in other words, earns only normal profits has been shown in Fig. 28.8.

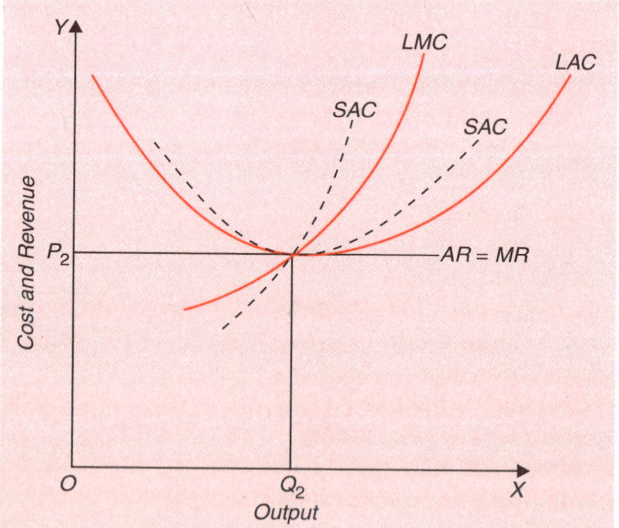

Fig. 28.8. *Long-run Equilibrium of the Competitive Firm with Zero Economic Profits*

Why do Competitive Firms Stay in Business if They Make Zero Economic Profits in the Long Run ?

The earning of zero economic profits by the competitive firms in the long run poses a great puzzle for the students of economics. The competitive firms which aim to maximize profits and adjust their plant size to increase profits in the long run finally end up in zero economic profits. As has been explained above, this is mainly due to the free entry and exit of the firms which is an important feature of perfect competition model. In the perfect competition model it is assumed that there are no legal restrictions on the entry of new firms and further that there are no entry costs apart from the direct cost of production and capital investment. Besides, the zero economic profit situation arises because we have assumed that all firms have the same cost functions which implies that not only all the factors used by the firms are homogeneous and equally productive but also the owner-entrepreneurs themselves are equally efficient.

But the most important issue raised by zero economic profits in the long-run competitive equilibrium is one of survival of the firms. In view of zero-economic profits, how do they survive ? Further, why don't these firms quit the industry to search for profits elsewhere ? To understand this issue one should remember the distinction between *economic profits* and *accounting profits*. As has been explained in the chapter on costs, the *accounting profits* are measured by the difference between the revenue and the explicit costs (*i.e.*, actual expenditure incurred by the firms for buying and hiring factors plus depreciation), whereas economic profits also take into account the *opportunity costs* of self-owned factors employed by the entrepreneur in his firm. The two important factors supplied by the owner-entrepreneurs to their firms are capital investment and the managerial services rendered by them. Economists include the opportunity costs of capital invested (*i.e.*, the reasonable rate of return on capital which can be earned elsewhere) and the opportunity costs of managerial services rendered by the owner-entrepreneurs (*i.e.*, wages of management), which are generally called normal profits, in the costs of production. Thus, when the competitive firms earn zero economic profits, it means that they are in fact earning a fair rate of return on capital invested and wages for the managerial services performed which are included in the average cost of production. Thus, in long-run competitive equilibrium, all factors including the capital investment and the managerial services by the entrepreneurs are rewarded equal to their opportunity costs. That is why the firms survive and also stay in the competitive industry.

Of course, the firms would like to earn positive economic profits. The goal of earning positive economic profits motivates the entrepreneurs to innovate and develop new ideas for commercial use so that they can either lower the cost of production or raise the demand for their product. But, as seen above, in competitive markets as a result of adjustment expansion of output by all firms and the entry of new firms, economic profits tend to be zero in the long run. But it takes time for the full adjustment to take place and economic profits to be reduced to zero. Therefore, by introducing innovations and also as a result of frequent changes in tastes, incomes and demand of the people entrepreneurs can earn positive economic profits in the short run as depicted in Figure 28.3 by the area *PEFH*. Indeed, the long run, like tomorrow, never comes as the demand and supply conditions change frequently as a result of changes in both the external and the internal factors. For example, innovations introduced by the entrepreneurs themselves cause the emergence of economic profits in the short run.

SHORT-RUN SUPPLY CURVE OF THE PERFECTLY COMPETITIVE FIRM

As is known, the short run is a period in which more quantity of the good is produced by working the given capital equipment or plant more intensively by employing more amounts of the variable factors. We have seen above that the firm under perfect competition produces that amount of the good at which marginal cost equals price. Since the price for a perfectly competitive firm is given and constant for it, price line will be a horizontal straight line. The horizontal coordinate of a point on the rising marginal cost curve measures the quantity of the good that the firm will produce at that price. The short-run marginal cost curve of the firm therefore indicates the quantities which the firm will produce in the short run at different prices.

Consider Figure 28.9. At price OP_3 the firm will produce and offer for sale *OM* quantity of the good, because at *OM* quantity of the good, price OP_3 equals marginal cost. Similarly, at price OP_4 the quantity produced or supplied will be *ON*, since price OP_4 equals marginal cost at output *ON*. Likewise, at price OP_2 the firm will produce and supply *OL* quantity of the product. It is thus clear that *short-run marginal cost curve of the firm is in fact the short-run supply curve of the firm*. The firm will not produce any output at a price below OP_1, since it will not be fully recovering its variable costs at a price below OP_1. Thus, ***only the part of the short-run marginal cost curve which lies above the average variable cost forms the short-run supply curve of the firm.*** In Fig. 28.9 thick portion of the short-run marginal cost curve *SMC* represents the short-run supply curve of the firm. Since under perfect competition marginal cost must be rising above the minimum point of the average variable cost curve ***the short-run supply curve of the firm must always slope upward to the right.***

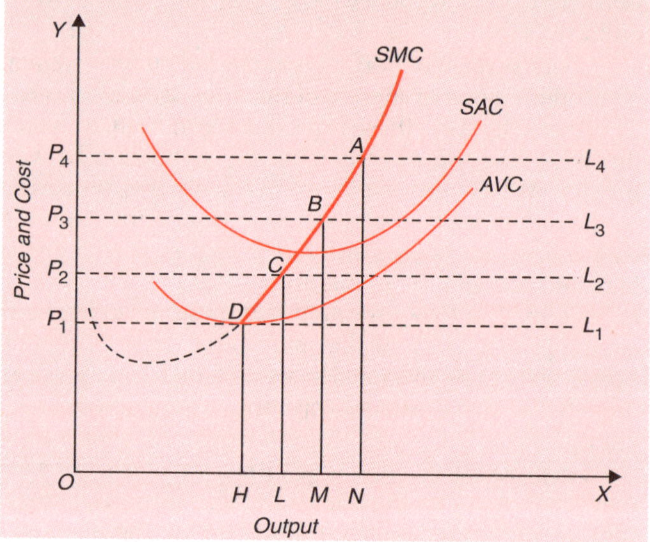

Fig. 28.9. *Short-run Supply Curve of the Firm*

It should be noted that in our analysis of deriving short-run supply curve of the firm, we have assumed that following the rise in price when the firm expands its output or supply, prices of resources or inputs it uses for production do not go up. It is a valid assumption because an individual firm under perfect competition is only one among many and its demand for inputs or resources is insignificant part of the total market demand for them and therefore the increase in demand for these resources by the firm as it expands will have no effect on their prices.

SHORT-RUN SUPPLY CURVE OF THE COMPETITIVE INDUSTRY

We now proceed to derive the short-run supply curve of the competitive industry. As the market demand curve is found by the horizontal summation of demand curves of all individual consumers of a product, similarly ***the short-run supply curve of the industry is obtained by lateral summation (horizontal addition) of short-run supply curves of all individual firms in the industry.*** How the short-run supply curves (short-run marginal cost curves) of the firms are added to obtain the short-run supply curve of the competitive industry is illustrated in 28.10 Suppose there are 200 firms in the competitive-industry. We further assume that all firms are alike in respect of cost of production. In Fig. 28.10 (a), *SMC* represents short-run supply curve of an individual firm. At price OP_1 an individual firm will produce and supply OM_1 quantity of the product. Since there are 200 such firms in the industry, the whole industry will produce and supply $200 \times OM_1$ quantity of the product. Therefore, in Fig. 28.10(*b*), $200 \times OM_1$, quantity is plotted against the price OP_1; ON_1 is equal to $200 \times OM_1$. It should be

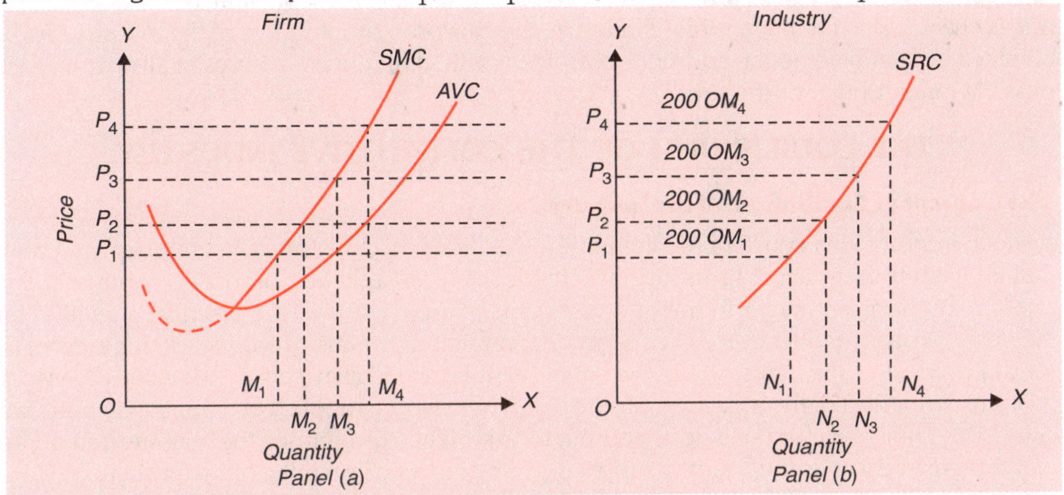

Fig. 28.10. *Derivation of the Short-Run Supply Curve of the Perfectly Competitive Industry*

in Fig.28.10 (*a*) and (*b*) while the scale on *X*-axis is the same, the scale on *Y*-axis differs carefully noted that very much. The scale on *X*-axis in Fig. 28.10, has been compressed very much to accommodate large quantities. At price OP_2 an individual firm will produce and supply OM_2 amount of the good, while the whole industry will supply ON_2 which is equal to $200 \times OM_2$ amount of the product. In the same way, industry will produce and supply $(200 \times OM_3) = ON_3$ output at price OP_3 , and $(200 \times OM_4)$ or ON_4 at price OP_4. Likewise, the industry's supply can be determined for all other prices. ***The short-run supply curve of the industry will always slope upward.*** This is because the short-run marginal cost curves of the firms (*i.e.*, their short-run supply curves) always slope upward above the minimum point of the average variable cost curves. The slope and the elasticity of short-run supply curve of the industry will obviously depend upon the slope and elasticity of the short-run marginal cost curves of individual firms in the industry.

That the short-run supply curve of the industry under perfect competition is a lateral or horizontal summation of the short-run marginal cost curves (*i.e.*, *SMC*) of the firms in it is subject to an important qualification. This is that the simultaneous expansion of output by all the firms in it (*i.e.*, the expansion of output by the industry) in the short run and therefore the increase in demand for the resources or inputs to be used for production will have no effect on the prices of these resources, that is, for the whole industry these resources or inputs are perfectly elastic in the short run. But whereas the expansion or contraction of output of the individual firm and therefore the changes in its demand for resources is not likely to affect their prices, the simultaneous expansion or contraction of all firms in the industry may mean a significant change in the demand for these resources and will therefore affect their prices. If expansion of industry output in the short run and therefore the increase in demand for resources raises the prices of these resources, then the cost curves of the individual firms will shift upward. On the other hand, if the expansion of the industry brings about a fall in the prices of resources, the cost curves of individual firms will shift downward. It may be that prices of some resources may rise and some others may fall with the expansion of the industry. In that case, the shift in the cost curves of the firms will depend upon whether the increase or decrease in resource prices is predominant.

When the cost curves of individual firms shift due to the change in resource prices, then the supply curve of industry cannot be obtained by summing up laterally the short-run supply curves of the firms, because then with every increase in the industry output, cost curves of firms change. In this case, therefore, when external effects are present, that is, when resource prices change with the expansion of industry, the short-run supply curve of the industry can be obtained by summing up the *equilibrium outputs* with different cost curves of all firms at each possible market price of the product.

THE EQUILIBRIUM OF THE COMPETITIVE INDUSTRY

The Concept of Equilibrium of the Industry

An industry is in equilibrium when there is no tendency for the industrial output to vary, that is, neither the existing firms have the tendency to expand output, nor to contract it and also no firm desires to enter it, nor any one wants to leave it. Now, the essential condition for the absence of any tendency for expansion or contraction of industry output is that the demand for the product of the industry and the supply of it by the industry are in balance. Unless the quantity demanded of the industry's product and the quantity supplied of it are equal, there will always be a tendency for the industry output to vary. If at a given price the quantity demanded of the product exceeds the quantity supplied of it by the industry, price of the product will tend to rise and the output of the industry will tend to be increased. On the other hand, if at a price the quantity demanded of the product falls short of the quantity supplied of it, the price and output of the industry will tend to fall. Thus, only when the quantity demanded and quantity supplied of the product of the industry are equal, there will be no tendency for the industry either to expand its output or to contract it. ***Thus an important condition for the industry to be in equilibrium is that it produces the level of output at which the quantity demanded and quantity supplied of its product are equal.***

Now, the output of the product of an industry can vary in two ways. First, the output of an industry can vary if the existing firms in it vary their output levels. And the firms will have no tendency to vary their output when they are individually in equilibrium by equating market price with marginal cost and thus maximizing their profits. Secondly, the output and therefore the supply of the product of an industry can vary by a change in the number of firms in it; the industry output will increase if new firms enter the industry and the industry output will decline if some of the existing firms leave it. Thus, given the demand for the product, an industry would be in equilibrium when neither the individual firms have incentive to change their output nor there is any tendency for the new firms to enter or for the existing firms to leave it. Therefore, besides the equality of demand and supply of the industry's product, two conditions which must be satisfied if there is to be equilibrium of the industry. First, each and every firm should be in equilibrium[1].

---

1. It should be noted here that, according to Marshall, for the equilibrium of the industry each firm in it may not be in equilibrium. To Marshall, equilibrium of the industry meant the equality of demand and supply of the industry's product, nothing more. According to Marshall, given the equilibrium of the industry some firms in it may be growing *i.e.,* expanding their output), some may be declining *(i.e.,* contracting their output), and some others may be holding their outputs constant. It is in this connection that Marshall evolved the concept of *representative firm,* the firm which was in equilibrium *(i.e.,* holding its output steady) when the industry was in equilibrium. There was a serious shortcoming in Marshall's concept of the equilibrium of the industry in that he did not demonstrate that for the industry to be in equilibrium, the outputs of growing firms are equal to the outputs of the declining firms. In the modern economic theory, Marshall's concept of representative firm has not been adopted and therefore in modern microeconomics, as stated in the text, for the industry to be in equilibrium, *all firms must also be in equilibrium.*

This will happen at the output of a firm where marginal cost is equal to marginal revenue and marginal cost curve cuts the marginal revenue curve from below. Second, the number of firms should be in equilibrium, *i.e.*, there should be no tendency for the firms either to move into or out of the industry. This will happen when all the entrepreneurs, *i.e.*, owners of the firms in the industry, are making zero economic profits which means they earn only ***'normal profits', that is, profits which are just sufficient to induce them to stay in the industry, and when no entrepreneur outside the industry thinks that he could earn at least normal profits if he were to enter it.***

Thus, the concept of normal profits is important in defining and describing equilibrium of the industry. If we assume that all entrepreneurs in a certain industry have the same opportunity costs, that is, the same transfer earnings if they leave the industry, then there would be a given fixed amount of normal profits for the whole industry. Every entrepreneur must earn at least this fixed amount of normal profits if he is to stay in the industry. If all the firms in the industry are earning profits above normal, there will be incentive for the firms outside the industry to enter it since there is every reason for the entrepreneurs outside the industry to expect that they would be able to earn at least normal profits if they enter. Thus, there will be a tendency for the firms in that industry to increase. If, on the other hand, the firms in the industry are earning profits below normal *(i. e.,* when they are incurring losses), it implies that the firms cannot cover their opportunity costs. Therefore, some of them will leave the industry and search for profits elsewhere. Thus the number of firms in that industry will tend to diminish. In conclusion, we can say that equilibrium of the industry *or full equilibrium,* as it is sometimes called, would be attained when the *number of firms in the industry* is in equilibrium, *(i.e.,* no movement into or out of the industry) and also *all individual firms in it are in equilibrium*, that is, they are equating marginal cost with marginal revenue, and *MC* curve cuts *MR* curve from below. It should be noted that normal profits of entrepreneur are included in the average cost of production. Therefore, if the price is equal to the average cost of production, it means that the entrepreneur is earning only normal profits.

Sometimes distinction is drawn between the *short-run and the long-run equilibrium of the industry*. In the short run only existing firms can make adjustment in their output while the number of firms remains the same, that is, no new firms can enter the industry and nor any existing firms can leave it. Since, in the short run, by definition, the entry or exit of the firms is not permitted, therefore for the short-run equilibrium of the industry, the condition of making only normal profits by the existing firms (or, in other words, the equality of average cost with average revenue) is not required. Thus, the industry is in short-run equilibrium when the short-run demand for and supply of the industry's product are equal and all the firms in it are in equilibrium. In the short-run equilibrium of the industry, though all firms must be in equilibrium, they all may be making supernormal profits or all may be having losses depending upon the demand conditions of the industry' s product. However, the concept of equilibrium of the industry is really relevant to the long run only because free entry into and free exit from the industry can occur only in the long run. Therefore, we shall discuss below the equilibrium of competitive industry in the long run.

From the foregoing analysis of the concept of industry equilibrium we arrive at the following three conditions for the equilibrium of the industry under perfect competition :

1. The long-run supply and the demand for the product of the industry should be in equilibrium;
2. All firms in the industry should be in long-run equilibrium by equating price with long-run marginal cost *($P = LMC$)*. In case this condition is fulfilled, firms would have adjusted the size of the plant; and

3. There should be no tendency for the new firms to enter the industry, nor for the existing firms to leave it. This would be so when firms are earning only normal profits (*i.e.*, zero economic profits with price -being equal to long-run minimum average cost (P = min. LAC).

In short, the conditions for the equilibrium of the competitive industry in the long run are :

$$Q_D = Q_S$$
$$P = LMC = \text{Min. } LAC$$

where Q_D stands for quantity demanded, Qs for quantity supplied, P denotes price, LMC and LAC denote long-run marginal and average cost respectively.

Let us now explain how the industry under perfect competition attains its equilibrium in the long run when all the above three conditions are fulfilled. It may be noted that our analysis of long-run equilibrium of the perfectly competitive firm made in the preceding section necessarily involves the equilibrium of the industry as well. Thus in Fig.28.8 when as a result of the entry of new firms the price of the product falls to OP_2 and the competitive firm reaches its long-run equilibrium position at the minimum long-run average cost producing level of output OQ_2 where price OP_2 = LMC = Min. LAC, the industry as a whole would also attain its equilibrium. This is so because all the firms in the industry (assuming identical cost functions) are in equilibrium and making only normal profits (*i.e.* zero economic profits). With earning of only normal profits, these will be no tendency for the firms to enter or exit the industry.

Only omission in our analysis of competitive equilibrium in the long run made in the context of Fig. 28.8 is that we have not drawn the demand and supply curves there though their role in determining the long-run competitive equilibrium through causing changes in price of the product with the entry of the new firms and as a consequence expansion in supply of output has been clearly brought out. In our present discussion we shall therefore explicitly draw the demand and supply curves of the industrial product along with the equilibrium adjustment of the competitive firm in the long-run to make abundantly clear our analysis of the equilibrium of the industry under perfect competition. Consider Fig. 28.11. Where in panel (a) demand and supply curves of the product of industry have been shown. Initially, DD and S_1S_1 are the demand and supply curves of the product respectively. It will be seen that these demand for and supply of the product are in equilibrium at price OP_1 when the industry produces OQ_1 output. A competitive firm shown in panel (*b*) takes this price OP_1 as given and maximises its profits by equating it with long-run marginal cost *(LMC)* after having adjusted its plant size. In this equilibrium position, the firm produces the level of output OM_2 and is making economic profits equal to the shaded are a $KDEP_1$ (Note that the scale on the horizontal axis in panel *(a)* is different from that in panel *(b)*). However, as explained earlier, this does not represent final situation of equilibrium of the firm. The large economic profits earned by the firms (assuming all other firms in the industry have same new cost functions) will attract other firms to enter the industry to make economic profits. The entry of new firms will lead to the expansion in output of the industry causing a rightward shift in the supply curve to the new position S_2S_2 in panel *(a)* resulting in lowering of price until it is equal to the minimum long-run average cost *(LAC)*. It will be seen that new supply curve S_2S_2 and the demand curve DD determine new price equal to OP_2 and the output by the industry increases to OQ_2. Now, it is this new market price of product OP_2, which the individual firms will take as given and equate it with their long-run marginal cost (LMC). It will be seen that price OP_2 is equal to long-run marginal cost curve at point F which is the minimum point of the long-run average cost LAC. It may be noted that with price OP_2, it will be no longer profitable for the firm to produce with plant represented by short-run average cost curve SAC_2. Therefore, the firm builds a new plant reflected by SAC_3 which has the lowest possible level of minimum average cost.

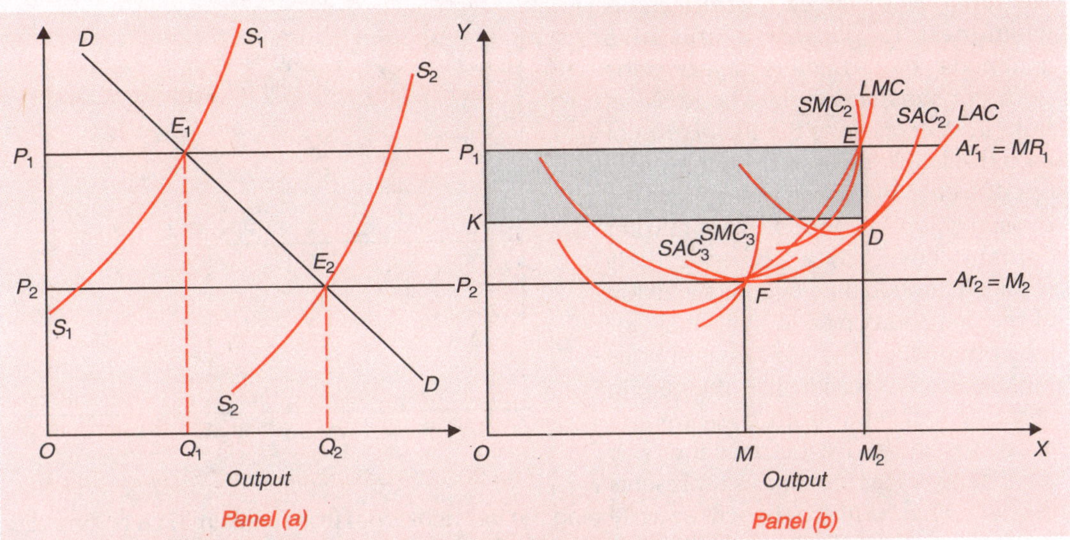

Fig. 28.11. *Long-Run Equilibrium Adjustment of Competitive Industry*

It will be seen from Fig. 28.11 that with price OP_2, the firm is in long-run equilibrium equating this price (P_2) with LMC as well as minimum LAC ($P_2 = LMC =$ Min. LAC) and is making zero economic profits or earning only normal profit. Theres is no longer any tendency for the new firms to enter the industry. Nor is there any tendency on the part of the existing firms to exit the industry as they are earning normal profits. Thus, since with price OP_2 (= LMC = Min. LAC) and industry output OQ_2, demand for and supply of the product of the industry are in balance and all firms in it are making only zero economic profits.

ECONOMIC EFFICIENCY OF PERFECTLY COMPETITIVE MARKET

We have explained above how in a perfectly competitive market price and output are determined through equilibrium between demand for and supply of goods. Now, an important question is how well do the competitive markets perform to allocate society's scarce resources? Do they use and allocate society's resources efficiently for satisfying the wants of the people ? To answer this question we must first explain what we mean by *economic efficiency or allocative efficiency*. ***The resources of a society are efficiently used if they are so used and allocated that the consumers get the maximum possible satisfaction. When such an efficiency has been achieved, it is then not possible through any reorganisation of resources and production of goods and services to make anyone better off without making someone worse off.*** Under such conditions of efficiency, the satisfaction of one individual can be increased only at the loss of utility by another. This concept of efficiency is generally referred to as *Pareto efficiency* as it was first developed by the Italian economist Vilfredo Pareto (1848-1923). We will use the concepts of consumer surplus and producer surplus to explain whether competitive markets achieve economic or allocative efficiency as defined above.

Consumer Surplus. Recall that consumer surplus obtained by the consumers from buying a product is the price that they are willing to pay over and above the market price which they actually pay for a commodity. It is important to note that ***demand curve of a commodity reflects what price the consumers are willing to pay for various units of a goods.*** This willingness to pay for a unit of a commodity by consumers measures the *utility or satisfaction* they hope to get from it. In economics the *well-being* of an individual is measured by the utility or satisfaction individuals obtain from the consumption of goods. The market demand curve of a commodity is obtained through the horizontal addition of the demand curves of individuals for the commodity. The consumer surplus obtained by all individuals is the gain in utility or well-being from consuming a good over and above the price they pay for it. Thus consumer surplus represents the *net gain of utility* or benefit or well-being the individuals get from consuming a commodity. It is measured by the area under the given demand curve as shown in Figure 28.12 where *DD′* is the demand curve of a commodity, *OP* is the market price as determined by demand for and supply of a commodity. The consumers will buy *OQ* quantity of the commodity and will pay total value equal to the *OPEQ* for the commodity while total value (equal to the money value of satisfaction they will get) which they are willing to pay for the commodity is equal to the total area under the demand curve upto the quantity *OQ* purchased, which is equal to the area *ODEQ*. Thus, total value they are willing to pay for *OQ* quantity of the commodity, that is, *ODEQ minus* the value *OPEQ* they actually pay for it gives us the amount of consumer surplus they obtain from buying the commodity. Remember consumer surplus measures the net gain or well-being by the consumer for buying the commodity from the market.

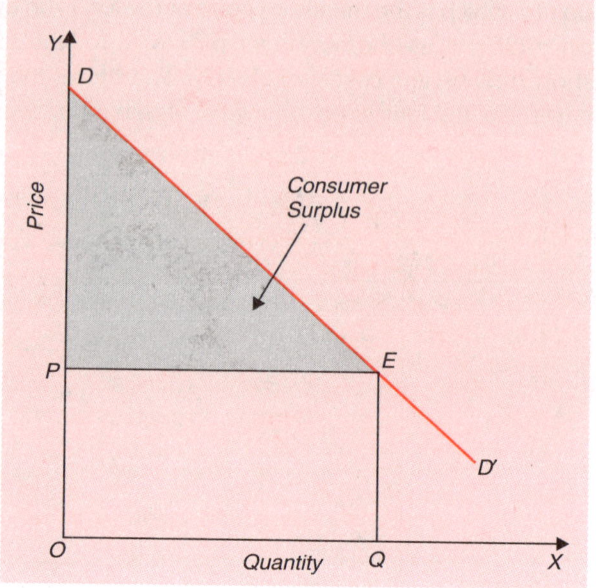

Fig. 28.12. *Measurement of Consumer Surplus*

Producer Surplus. *Similarly, producer surplus is the excess of market price at which producers sell the quantity of a commodity over and above the minimum price at which they would be willing to supply it.* The minimum price which the producers would accept to supply a unit of the commodity is its marginal cost which reflects the opportunity cost of resources used for its production. Consider Figure 28.13 where demand curve *DD* and supply curve *SS* of a commodity intersect at point *E* and determine *OP* as the market price and

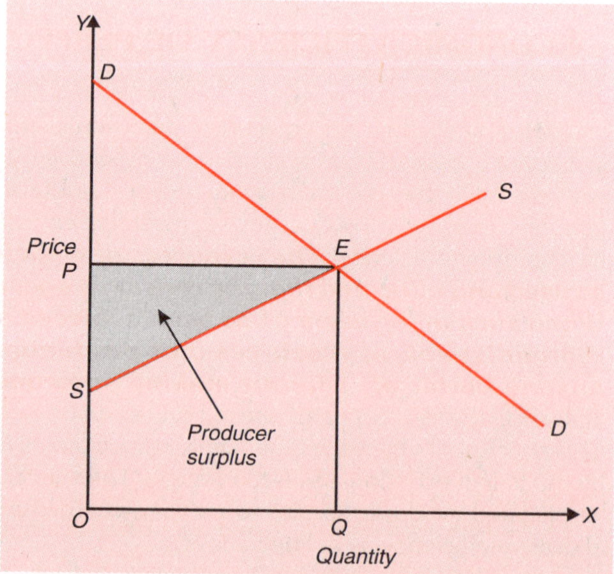

Fig. 28.13. *The Concept of Producer Surplus*

OQ as the quantity sold and bought. It will be seen from the supply curve *SS* of Figure 28.13 that producers produce the last Qth unit of the commodity at the marginal cost which is just equal to the market price *OP*. However, as is indicated by the supply curve *SS* the producers will be ready to supply the earlier successive units from zero to Qth unit at much less than the market price *OP*. Thus, from these earlier units the producers actually get more than their minimum acceptable supply price. The area *OSEQ* below the supply curve is indicator of the aggregate supply price of *OQ* units of the commodity produced and supplied by the producers. On the other hand, the total revenue earned by them is equal to the area *OPEQ* (market price *OP* x quantity *OQ* sold). Thus, the producers earn revenue equal to the shaded area *SEP* more than the aggregate supply price. This excess amount *SEP* over the aggregate supply price is the aggregate producer surplus earned by the producers. *The producer surplus earned by the producers is the measure of benefits obtained by them for producing and exchanging the commodity.*

Allocative Efficiency Under Perfectly Competitive Equilibrium

One of the most beneficial feature of perfectly competitive market is that it results in allocative efficiency which means that it enables the use of resources for production of goods that ensures maximum welfare benefits to the persons in a society. Allocative efficiency of perfectly competitive markets also implies the mutually beneficial exchange between consumers and producers of goods.That is, both are better off in participating in the exchange. Under conditions of perfectly competitive markets optimum production and exchange of goods takes place which ensures the achievement of maximum social welfare. This can be shown by the concept of producer surplus and consumer surplus.

Recall that consumer surplus measures the welfare gain to the consumers from buying a commodity equal to the amount which they are willing to pay (which reflects their utility derived from the commodity) over and above the market price they actually pay for the good which they buy from the producers. Consumer surpluse is measured by the area under the demand curve over the market price.

Thus, in Figure 28.14 where demand curve *DD* of consumers and supply curve *SS* of consumers through their intersection at point *E* determine market price *OP* and quantity *OQ* of the good produced and exchanged between them. Consumer surplus obtained by the consumers is equal to the area *DPE*. On the other hand, as explained above, *PES* is producer surplus obtained by the producers which measures the excess revenue obtained by them over and above the sum of marginal costs (*i.e.* supply price) incurred by them for producing *OQ* amount of the good.

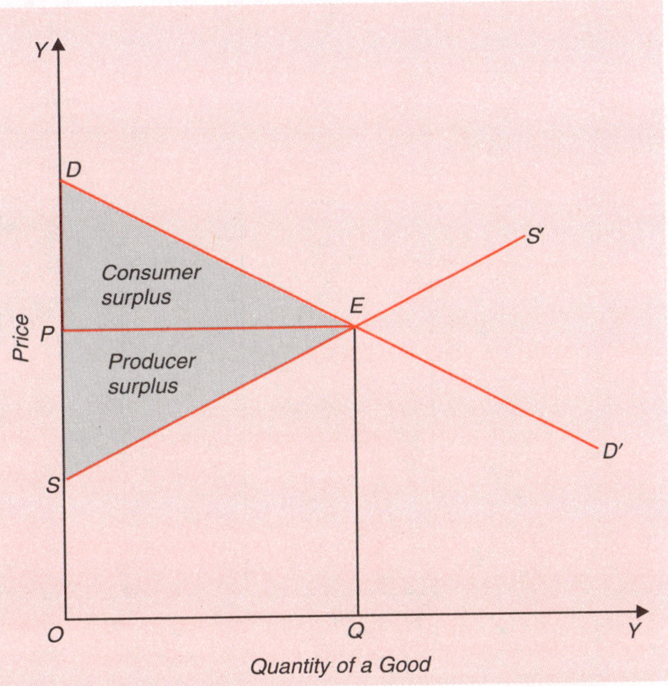

Fig. 28.14. *Maximisation of Total Economic Surplus*

It follows from above that both the consumers and producers gain from exchange and production of goods. ***From the society's point of view, the total gain is the sum of consumer surplus and producer surplus. This sum of consumer surplus and producer surplus, that is, the sum of areas DPE and PES is known as the total economic surplus.*** The allocative efficiency in consumption, production and exchange of goods and therefore maximum social benefit is attained when the total economic surplus (consumer surplus plus producer surplus) is maximised. And, as seen above, at price and output determined by demand for and supply of goods in a perfectly competitive market, this maximum total economic surplus is actually attained.

An alternative way of viewing the total of consumer surplus and producer surplus is to consider it as the *total benefits* obtained from the consumption of the two goods *over and above the total variable cost of producing a commodity*. Thus, the total benefit obtained by consuming *OQ* quantity of the good is the whole area *ODEQ* under the demand curve *DD′* which meaures the total utility or benefit obtained by the consumers and the area *OSEQ* is the sum of total costs of producing *OQ* quantity of the good. Thus, the area *DES* measures the total surplus (*i.e.*, the sum of consumer surplus and producer surplus). ***This sum of consumer surplus and producer surplus therefore measures the net social benefit from producing and consuming OQ quantity of the good.***

The key question is whether the total surplus is maximised at the competitive equilibrium as determined by demand for and supply of the good. If some other production and consumption of the good (or in other words, some other resource allocation to the good in question) leads to a higher total surplus, the output *OQ* of the good determined by competitive equilibrium would not be efficient. This is because it would then be possible to make consumers and producers better off collectively. On the other hand, if there is no alternative resource allocation to the good in question which generates a higher level of total surplus, the competitive equilibrium is economically efficient.

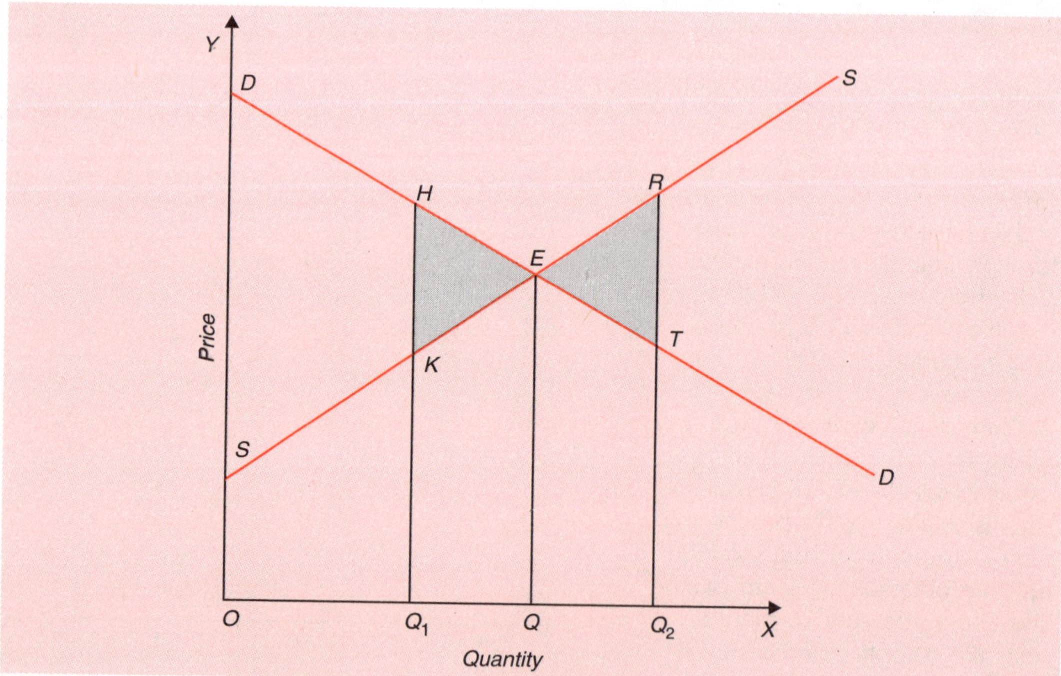

Fig. 28.15. *Efficiency of Perfectly Competitive Equilibrium*

To understand this consider Figure 28.15 where competitive equilibrium is attained by producing OQ quantity of the good. Now, suppose a smaller quantity OQ_1 of the good is produced, then as will be seen from Figure 28.15 the consumers and producers will suffer a loss of total economic surplus equal to the area HKE. Likewise, any other quantity smaller than OQ would mean a lower total economic surplus than that obtained from producing and consuming OQ quantity of the good by allocating required resources to its production.

If a greater quantity than OQ, say OQ_2 *is produced and consumed, the consumers would get less utility* (or welfare benefit) as indicated by the demand curve in the *range of quantity* QQ_2 which is lower than the cost of producing the good as indicated by the higher level of the supply curve in this quantity range (*i.e.*, QQ_2). Thus, the production of greater quantity OQ_2 of the good than the competitive output OQ leads to the loss of total economic surplus equal to the area ERT.

From above it follows that production of OQ quantity of the good competitive equilibrium ensures maximum total economic surplus and therefore leads to maximum social benefit. This is an important conclusion which tells us that ***competitive markets perform quite well in allocating scarce social resources.***

But perfect competition rarely exists in the real world. It is market forms of monopolies, oligopolies and monopolistic competition that exist in the real world and not perfect competition. We shall study in the next few chapters how market categories of monopolies, oligopolies and monopolistic competition create economic inefficiencies in resource allocation and hence loss of social welfare.

Further, the ***economic efficiency is achieved under conditions of perfect competition only when there do not exist any externalities, negative or positive.*** The existence of externalities causes divergence between private benefit and social benefit as well as between private cost and social cost. Thus, perfectly competitive equilibrium based on private cost and private benefit would not lead to the maximum social welfare when externalities are present.

Economic Efficiency and Equity

That under conditions of perfect competition the conclusion that welfare is maximum is based on the thinking that the total economic surplus is the true measure of social welfare. To consider so is to ignore the effect of distribution of output and income on social welfare. ***The equity, that is, fairness in distribution is as important as maximisation of total economic surplus.*** To consider the size of total economic surplus as the sole criterion of assessment of social welfare is to implicitly make the value judgement that a rupee gives each person the same satisfaction irrespective of whether the person is consumer or producer, rich or poor. To clarify this let us consider that price of a product is raised. As a result, the consumers would lose some consumer surplus and producers would gain some extra producer surplus. The criterion of total economic surplus is based on the net change in surplus in rupee terms. Suppose as a result of rise in price of a good consumers suffer a loss of consumer surplus of Rs. 1000 and producers gain extra producer surplus of Rs. 1000. Thus, the total economic surplus remains unchanged.

But, if consumers are poor households whereas producers are rich individuals, the redistribution of income from the poor consumers to the rich producers, the total economic surplus remaining the same, will lead to the *net* loss of social welfare. To conclude that in this case social welfare remains unchanged is based on the implicit assumption that the poor derive utility from Rs. 1000 equal to that of the rich. That is, marginal utility of one rupee is the same for the rich and the poor. This is a questionable assumption and involves value judgement which is not justified on any scientific grounds. In other words, ***maximising total economic***

surplus leads to economic efficiency but it will not be necessarily 'fair' or 'equitable'. The maximisation of total economic surplus does not capture the equity aspect of social welfare. In the light of this fact, the total economic surplus (*i.e.*, the sum of producer surplus and economic surplus) is not a very good measure of social well-being. Thus, maximisation of total surplus leads to the outcome which is economically efficient but it may not be necessarily fair or equitable.

It may be noted that some economists consider maximisation of total surplus as a valid criterion of social welfare as they think that once total surplus is maximised, it can be redistributed in accordance with society's notion of equity or fairness. It is argued that "*make the pie as big as possible and then distribute it according to society's notion of equity.*" However, in our view, it is difficult to redistribute output and income so as to ensure equity and thereby to increase social well-being. Besides, in the redistribution, demand and supply curves of a good which generated the maximum total surplus, are likely to change which may result in deviation of the outcome from the maximum total economic surplus (or economic efficiency).

ECONOMIC EFFICIENCY AND PERFECT COMPETITION: PARETO EFFICIENCY ANALYSIS

We have explained above the achievement of overall economic efficiency with the help of concepts of Consumer Surplus and Producer Surplus. However, in modern microeconomics, economic efficiency is explained with the help of Pareto criterion of efficiency or social welfare.

The Concept of Economic Efficiency

Vilfredo Pareto (1848-1923) was the first to part with this traditional approach to social welfare in two important respects. First, he rejected the notion of cardinal utility and its additive nature and, second, he detached welfare economics from the interpersonal comparison of utilities. Pareto's concept of maximum social welfare which is based upon ordinal utility and is also free from value judgements occupies a significant place in modern welfare economics. Therefore, his welfare or efficiency criterion avoids making interpersonal comparison of utility and still judges whether any change in economic organisation or public policy increases social welfare or economic efficiency. According to Pareto criterion of welfare or efficiency, a change is said to increase efficiency or social welfare if it makes some people better off without making any other member of the society worse off. Thus it is worth mentioning that some individuals becoming better off or worse off have to be judged not by anyone else but by the individuals themselves, that is, changes in individuals' welfare have to be based on their own estimation and not by any assessment by others. For example, if two individuals in a society exchange two goods, both will be better off because they do so voluntarily. Pareto optimum may not be a *sufficient* condition for attaining maximum social welfare but it is a *necessary* condition for it. ***Pareto optimum (often called Economic Efficiency) is a position from which it is impossible to make anyone better off without making someone worse off by any re-allocation of resources and outputs.*** In the words of Pareto, "We are led to define a position of maximum ophelimity (welfare) as one where it is impossible to make a small change of any sort such that the ophelimities of all the individuals, except those that remain constant, are either all increased or all diminished." Thus, in the Pareto optimum position it is not possible through any changes in allocation of resources among products and distribution of products among individuals to increase the welfare of some individuals of the society without reducing the welfare of any other.

The concept of economic efficiency or Pareto optimality has the following three aspects:

1. Productive Efficiency

2. Product-mix Efficiency

3. Distributive Efficiency

We explain below these three types of efficiency and how perfect competition fulfils these conditions.

Productive Efficiency

Production is Pareto-efficient when it is not possible to reallocate resources to produce more of some goods without producing less of any other good. That is, when through reallocation of resources, it is possible to produce some goods more without reduction in output of other goods, production is not efficient. It should be noted that productive efficiency has two aspects. First aspect of productive efficiency relates to the allocation of resources *within each firm*. Use of resources by a firm for production of a good or goods is efficient when it produces *any given output at the minimum possible cost or for a given cost-outlay (or the given amount of factors), it maximises output*. Under perfect competition, for any firm price of a product is given and constant, it will be maximising its profits if it uses its resources for production of goods in a way that minimises cost for a given level of output. Thus, profit-maximising firms working in perfectly competitive markets will be productively efficient.

The second aspect of productive efficiency relates to the ***allocation of resources among firms producing the same or different products.*** Allocation of resources among firms is efficient when all firms producing a product has the same marginal cost. If marginal costs of firms producing a product were not the same, then resources could be withdrawn from a firm whose marginal cost of producing a product is higher and be given to the firms whose marginal cost is lower and to minimise cost of producing a given output this reallocation of resources should continue until marginal cost in each firm using the resources and producing a product becomes the same.

It is worth noting that for the economy to work with production efficiency it must operate on the production possibility curve *PP* in Figure 28.16, such as at point *E* on it. An economy that is not productively efficient will operate at a point *inside* the production possibility curve such as a point *K* below *PP* curve in Figure 28.16. Operating at a point inside the production possibility curve, that is, when there is production inefficiency, implies that the economy can produce more of both the goods or can produce one good more without reducing the production of the other good, However, on a production possibility curve, the economy can move from one point to another, but in doing so it will increase the production of one good by reducing the production of the other goods. *At which point on the production possibility curve, the economy will operate depends on the preferences of the members of the society between two goods.*

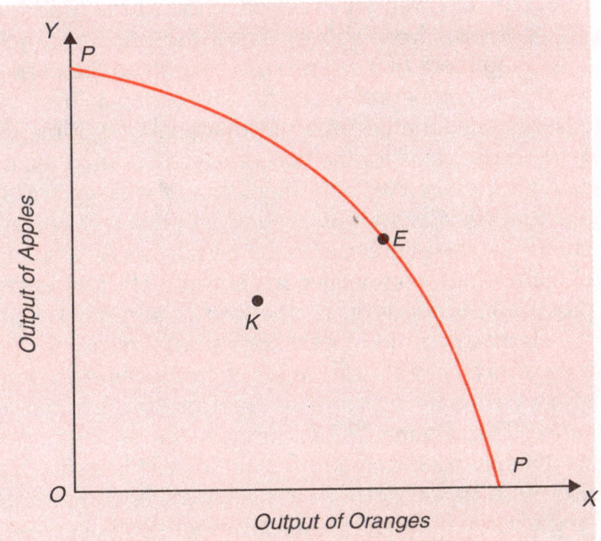

Fig. 28.16. *Production efficiency requires that the economy must operate on the production possibility curve.*

Allocative Efficiency: Optimum Product-Mix

For achieving overall economic efficiency it is not enough to distribute efficiently a given output of goods among consumers or to use resources efficiently for production of goods. The achievement of these exchange efficiency and production efficiency will not ensure maximum well-being, if the economy is producing *wrong* goods, that is, goods which people do not prefer. ***The product-mix efficiency means that allocation of resources among the production of various goods and services is in accordance with the preferences and demands of the people.*** If the economy is producing wrong mix of goods and services, that is, not producing goods and services in accordance with the preferences of the people, it will then be possible to produce more of one good and less of another to make all people better off or make some individuals better off without making anyone else worse off. Thus, allocative efficiency or product-mix efficiency relates to the choice among alternative points *on* the production possibility curve in accordance with the preferences of consumers.

Competitive markets are efficient as they produce goods which people want and prefer. To show that competitive markets are efficient, we have to show in equilibrium, it must not be possible to increase satisfaction of the people by producing more of one good and less of another. The condition for efficient allocation of resources among goods and services or efficient product-mix is that *marginal cost of producing each good or service must be equal to its market price*. The argument to show this runs as follows. Price of any good reflects an individual's willingness to pay for it or, in other words, it represents the value which a consumer places on the last unit of that good. When a consumer buys a good, he reveals that it is worth at least as much as the other things the same money could buy. Therefore, the current market price of a good that a consumer pays reflects the value he places on a good or in other words marginal benefit which he receives from it. On the other hand, marginal cost of a good reflects the opportunity cost of the resources that are used to produce the good. For example, if a firm employs a worker and pays him the market wage rate, this wage rate must be large enough to attract the worker either out of his giving up his leisure or away from producing other goods. The same argument applies to land, capital and other resources. Thus for using factors, labour, land, capital and other factors for production of a good, they must be paid at least their opportunity costs. Thus, marginal cost of producing a good reflects the opportunity costs of resources required for the production of the good.

It follows from above that if the price of a good exceeds marginal cost of producing it, producing more of it will provide benefits to the consumer in excess of its opportunity cost. As a result, the members of a society will get net gain from increasing its production. Similarly, if price of a good ends up at less than its marginal cost, it means resources are being used to produce the good whose value for the consumers is less than the opportunity cost of producing it. Therefore, producing less of it will be desirable from the viewpoint of social well-being. Now, since in competitive markets, equilibrium is reached when prices of various goods equal their marginal costs, it will not bring any net welfare gain to the consumers of a society from either producing more or less of any of them. Thus, competitive markets are efficient in respect of allocation of resources among the production of goods or, in other words, in respect of product-mix.

It may be noted that if *consumers' demands (i.e. preferences) between goods change, competitive markets will reallocate resources in accordance with the new demands or preferences of the consumers*. Suppose the economy is initially at point E_0 on the production possibility curve *PP'* in Figure 28.17. Suppose the preferences of consumers change in favour of apples. As a result, their demand for apples will increase and given their supply, price of apples will rise. With higher price of apples it will become more profitable to increase their production. At the same time, demand for oranges will decrease, and, given their supply, their prices will fall. At lower prices, the firms will reduce their production. Thus, as a result of change in consumers' preferences and consequently change in demand pattern for apples and oranges, the economy will shift from point E_0 to point E_1 on the production possibility curve *PP'* and at point E_1, it produces more apples and less oranges than at point E_0. Thus mix of products has changed in the economy reflecting the new preferences of consumers. Allocation of resources will also change; more resources will now be devoted to the production of apples than before.

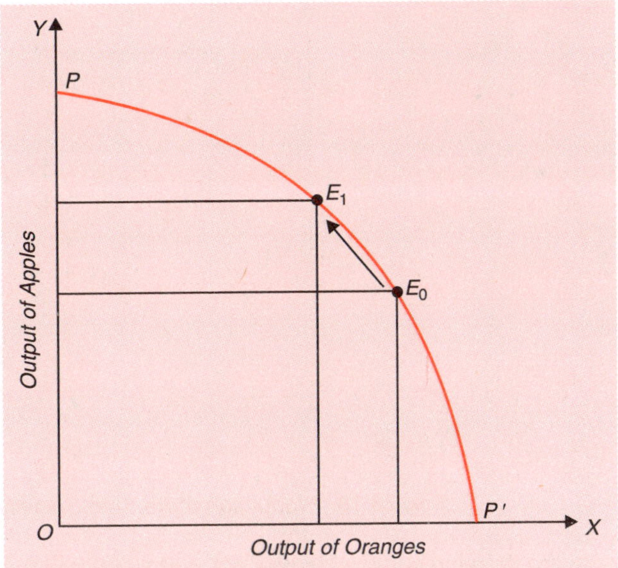

Fig. 28.17. *Change in Resource Allocation and Product-Mix following a Change in Demand for Goods*

Distributive Efficiency

Distributive efficiency means the distribution of a given output of goods between individuals in a society should be such that it should not be possible to make someone better off without making anyone else worse off. When such distributive efficiency is achieved there is no scope for exchange or trade between individuals which make all individuals better off or anyone better off without making someone else worse off. Perfectly competitive market ensures the achievement of distributive efficiency. In deciding about how much quantity of a good they should buy, the consumers equate marginal benefit which they receive from an additional unit of a good they buy with the marginal cost of that unit. Now, price which an individual is willing to pay for a unit of a good reflects marginal benefit which he obtains from that unit. Note that demand curve for a good represents price which individuals are prepared to pay for the good, that is, demand curve of an individual represents marginal benefit of various units of a commodity for the individuals. Market price of a good which an individual pays for the good, therefore, represents marginal benefit of the extra unit of the good he buys.

Now, in a perfectly competitive market, buyers are price takers and the same price they have to pay for a good. If all individuals face the same prices, they will equate their marginal benefit which they receive from the good with the same price. Hence, marginal benefits which they receive from a good will be the same. When marginal benefits of various individuals from consuming the goods are the same, any redistribution of the goods among them or any trading of the goods among them will not make all of them better off or make some better off without making other any one worse off. Hence, since *in a perfectly competitive market all individuals pay the same price for a good, distributive efficiency is achieved.*

MARKET FAILURES OF A PERFECTLY COMPETITIVE ECONOMY

However, even perfectly competitive economy fails to achieve economic efficiency or Pareto optimality. In other words, under some circumstances economic efficiency is not achieved even under perfect competition. These are generally referred to as market failures which we discuss below.

Externalities and Market Failure

A major source of market failure, which even occurs under perfect competition, is the existence of *externalities*, which may be negative or positive. Externalities are generated by the activities of firms which *harm or benefit others*. For example, *pollution of environment* by the productive activties of a firm *which harm others* but does not make any payment to them is an important negative externality which causes market failure to achieve economic efficiency, even under conditions of perfect competition.

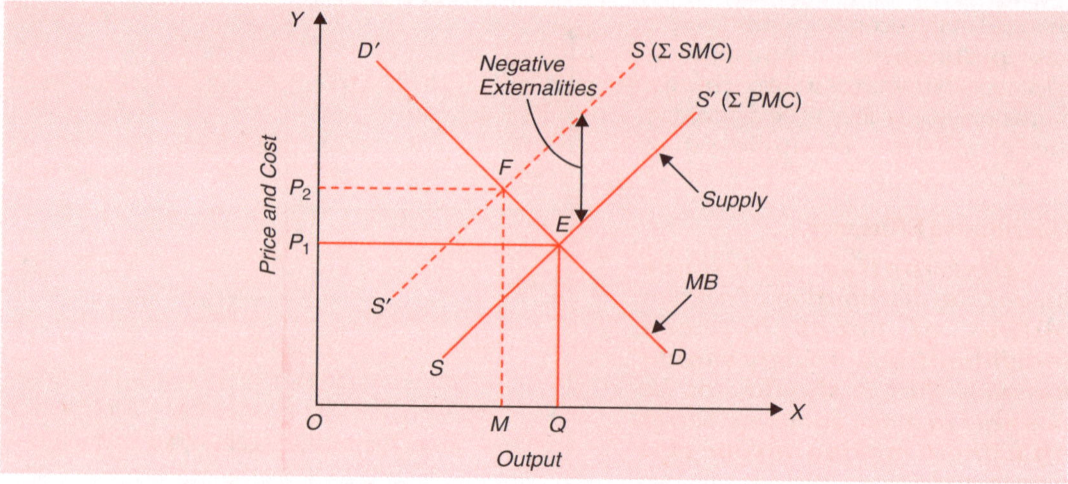

Fig. 28.18. *Production more than Socially Optimum Output Level*

The demand curve for any good represents marginal utility (or benefit) that the individuals obtain from consuming various amounts of the good. On the other hand, the supply curve of a product represents the sum of private marginal costs (ΣPMC) of production by various firms in the industry. Supply curve depicitng social marginal cost (SMC) will be above the supply curve based on private marginal cost (PMC) as $SMC = PMC$ + negative externalities. Since private firms do not take into account the negative externalities (e.g. external costs due to pollution created by them), to be in equilibrium or for maximisation of profits. They equate private marginal cost with price (Note that price of a commodity reflects marginal utility, that is, marginal benefit to the consumers). As will be seen from Fig. 28.18 when negative externalities are not taken into account by the perfectly competitive firm supply curve (which is the sum of private marginal cost curves) intersects the demand curve DD at point E and the equiilbrium is at output level OQ which is more than socially optimum output level OM at which supply curve $S'S'$ [which is obtained by adding negative externalities to PMC to obtain the supply curve $S'S'$ reflecting social marginal costs (SMC)] intersects the demand curve DD reflecting social marginal benefit (SMB). It is thus evident that the existence of negative externalities (such as the creation of pollution) causes more than socially optimal level of output being produced and therefore prevents the achievement of economic efficiency even when perfect competition prevails in the market.

Public Goods and Market Failure

Another source of economic inefficiency is found in case of public goods. Public goods are those goods which provide collective benefits to the members of a society, or, in other words, public goods are those which are collectively consumed by the members of society. The important examples of public goods are national defence, police protection, public health, flood control programme, to name a few. Their production provides benefits to all members of the society. In the production of these public goods, like private goods, the scarce productive resources such as labour, land and capital are used and therefore they should be efficiently used.

However, an important feature of public goods is that it is not possible to exclude or prevent those members of the society from consuming these goods who do not pay for them, that is, those

1. The beneficial and negative externalities in consumption and production will be explained in detail in a later chapter.

want to be '*free riders*'. Since public goods provide *collective benefit* to all members of the society, some members can enjoy their consumption without paying for them. In view of this non-payment of price by some members of the society, private producers driven as they are by profit maximisation would find unprofitable to produce them as they would not be able to cover fully their costs of production. As a result, in a competitive market economy public goods would be either not produced or produced in very little quantity. Therefore, public goods are generally produced or provided by the government through financing their production by taxing the people. Thus McConnel and Brue write, "The market system does not provide for social or public goods, despite its other virtues, the competitive price systems ignores the important class of goods and resources—national defence, flood control programmes and so forth—which can and do yield satisfaction to the consumers but which cannot be priced and sold through the market system".[2]

Imperfect Information

The third source of market failure to achieve efficiency under competitive conditions is imperfect information of the buyers and sellers of goods or factors. Efficiency of a competitive economy depends on the assumption that buyers of goods and services have perfect information about their quality and price, and the firms which buy inputs or factors for production have perfect information on their quality and price. The lack of perfect information can lead to wrong choices and inefficiency. For example buyers of goods do not have perfect information about the quality of goods they buy, especially the second-hand products such as used cars which may turn out to be lemons. Similarly, led by misleading advertisements the buyers may buy spurious drugs which may actually harm them rather than curing their diseases. The other important example of imperfect competition is provided by buying of life insurance which is difficult for the ordinary people to assess the terms and conditions of complex life insurance package which may lead to the wrong decisions being made by them.

On the other hand, the firms who are buyers of inputs do not have perfect information about their quality. For example, the firms lack information about the quality of workers hired by them. Besides the firms do not have perfect information about the likely return from different types of investment made by them. Thus imperfect information on the part of buyers of goods and inputs can lead to wrong choices and inefficiency even in a perfectly competitive economy.

Distribution of Goods and Economic Inefficiency

The contention that perfect competition will allocate resources efficiently and will thus maximise consumers' satisfaction is based on the assumption of *a given distribution of income*, however unequal it might be. Money income is distributed among members of society in some particular way and *results in a structure of demand* which determines who will get how much of the goods and services produced. The competitive market system works to produce goods and services according to the structure of demand (*i.e.* composition of outputs of goods and services demanded) determined by the given distribution of income. The market system then allocates resources to produce the goods and services (determined by distribution of income) to maximise the satisfaction of the individuals demanding the goods and services. Now, if distribution of money income is changed resulting in a different structure of demand for goods and services, the response of the working of the competitive market system would be to reallocate resources and maximise satisfaction of consumers by producing goods and services according to the *new* pattern of demand. Now, the pertinent question which allocation of resources is more efficient and provides the greatest satisfaction to the members of the society. There is no scientific answer to this question because it is not possible to make interpersonal

2. Campbell R. McConnel and Stanley L Brue, *Economics*, 11th edition, 1990, p. 514.

comparison of utility of various individuals of society. If it is assumed that people's capacity to get satisfaction is the same, the equal distribution of income among them and allocation of resources accordingly would be the most efficient one. However, in actual practice, people differ in regard to their capacity to obtain satisfaction from income because of their conditions of birth, environment, education, experiences in addition to their inherited mental and physical abilities. Such differences account for unequal distribution of income and wealth and capacities to obtain satisfaction from them. To quote McConnel and Brue again, "The basic point is that the distribution of income associated with the working of a purely competitive market system is quite unequal and therefore may lead to the production of triffles for the rich while denying the basic needs to the poor people ..... allocative efficiency is hardly a virtue if it comes in response to an income distribution which offends prevailing standards of equality".[3] It may be noted that many economists believe that the unequal distribution of income caused by the working of a market economy can be altered by the government by taxing the rich and spending the proceeds for the welfare of the poor.

NUMERICAL PROBLEMS ON PERFECT COMPETITION MODEL

Let us solve some numerical problems to make clear the conditions of profit maximisation under perfect competition.

Problem 1. *For a perfectly competitive firm, the following short-run function is given*

$$TC = 2 + 4Q + Q^2$$

If price of the product prevailing in the market is Rs. 8, at what level of output the firm will maximise profits ?

Solution. Since total revenue is equal to price multiplied by quantity of output, total revenue function is

$$TR = P \,.\, Q = 8Q$$
$$TC = 2 + 4Q + Q^2$$

We explain below the profit maximisation with both the *TR–TC* approach and *MC–MR* approach,

TR–TC Approach

Profits

$$\begin{aligned} \pi &= TR - TC \\ &= 8Q - (2 + 4Q + Q^2) \\ &= 8Q - 2 - 4Q - Q^2 \\ &= 4Q - 2 - Q^2 \qquad \ldots(i) \end{aligned}$$

Now, profits will be maximum at the output level at which first derivative of profit function with respect to the quantity of output equals 0. Thus, by taking the first derivative of profit function (*i*) and setting it equal to zero, we have :

$$\frac{d\pi}{dQ} = 4 - 2Q = 0$$

$$2Q = 4$$

$$Q^* = 2$$

MR–MC Approach

In this approach profits are maximum at the output level at which *MR* equals *MC*. We therefore first derive the marginal revenue and marginal cost from *TR* and *TC* functions.

3. McConnel and Brue, *op. cit.*, p. 513.

$$TR = 8Q \quad \text{...(ii)}$$

$$MR = \frac{dTR}{dQ} = 8$$

$$TC = 2 + 4Q + Q^2 \quad \text{...(iii)}$$

$$MC = \frac{d(TR)}{dQ} = 4 + 2Q$$

In order to determine profit-maximising output we set MR equal to MC. Thus,

$$MR = MC$$
$$8 = 4 + 2Q$$
$$2Q = 8 - 4 = 4$$
$$Q^* = 2.$$

Problem 2. *In a city there are a large number of firms selling a product and no single firm has any control over the price of the product. The following total revenue and cost functions are given for a single seller*

$$TR = 10Q$$
$$TC = 1000 + 2Q + 0.01Q^2$$

Determine how many units of the product a firm will produce per annum if it aims at profit maximisation. Also find out the total profits made by it in the equilibrium situation.

Solution. We determine MR and MC form the given revenue and cost functions. Thus,

$$TR = 10Q$$

$$MR = \frac{dTR}{dQ} = 10$$

(Note that since MR is constant, price will be equal to it.)

$$TC = 1000 + 2Q + 0.01Q^2$$

$$MC = \frac{d\,(TC)}{dQ} = 2 + 0.02Q$$

For profit maximisation

$$MC = MR$$
$$2 + 0.02Q = 10$$
$$0.02Q = 8$$
$$Q = \frac{8 \times 100}{2} = 400.$$

Profits

$$\pi = TR - TC$$
$$TR = P.Q = 10 \times 400 = 4000$$
$$TC = 1000 + 2 \times 400 + 0.01\,(400)^2$$
$$= 1800 + 1600 = 3{,}400$$
$$\pi = 4000 - 3400 = ₹\,600$$

Problem 3. *A firm producing bread is operating in a perfectly competitive market. The firm's variable cost function is given by*

$$TVC = 150Q - 20Q^2 + Q^3$$

where Q is level of output.

Determine below what price the firm should shut down production in the short run.

Solution. In the short run a firm will shut down operations if the price falls below the level of minimum average variable cost. So we first determine the minimum average variable cost.

$$AVC = \frac{TVC}{Q} = \frac{150\,Q}{Q} - \frac{20\,Q^2}{Q} + \frac{Q^3}{Q}$$

$$AVC = 150 - 20Q + Q^2$$

To determine the level of output at which average variable cost is minimum we take the first derivative of the *AVC* function and set it equal to zero.

$$\frac{d(AVC)}{dQ} = -20 + 2Q = 0$$

$$2Q = 20$$

$$Q = 10$$

Now, substituting the valve of Q in the *AVC* function we can know the minimum average variable cost.

$$AVC = 150 - 20 \times 10 + (10)^2$$

$$= 150 - 200 + 100 = 50$$

Thus, if price falls below ₹ 50 per unit the firm will shut down.

Problem 4. *A firm's total variable cost is given by the following :*

$$TVC = 75Q - 10Q^2 + Q^3$$

Will the firm produce the product if price of the product is ₹ 40 ?

Solution. A firm produces a product if price of the product exceeds its minimum average variable cost.

$$\text{AVC} = \frac{TVC}{Q} = \frac{75\,Q - 10\,Q^2 + Q^3}{Q}$$

$$= 75 - 10Q + Q^2 \qquad \ldots(i)$$

AVC is minimised at the output level at which

$$\frac{d\,(AVC)}{dQ} = 0$$

Taking the derivative of *AVC* we have :

$$\frac{d\,(AVC)}{dQ} = -10 + 2Q$$

Therefore, *AVC* will be minimum when

$$-10 + 2Q = 0$$

$$2Q = 10$$

$$Q = \;= 5$$

Now substituting the value of Q in equation for *AVC* we have

$$\text{Minimum } AVC = 75 - 10 \times 5 + 25$$

$$= 100 - 50 = 50$$

Thus, price of ₹ 40 of the product is less than the minimum average variable cost, the firm will not produce the product.

Problem 5. *Given the following short-run cost function of a firm*

$$TC = 1000 + 10Q^2$$

Derive the expression for firm's short-run supply curve.

Solution: A firm's short-run supply curve is firm's short-run marginal cost curve. To obtain marginal cost function we have to obtain the first derivative of total cost function. Thus,

$$MC = \frac{dTC}{dQ} = 2 \times 10Q = 20Q.$$

To get the short-run supply curve of a firm we set price equal to marginal cost. Thus,

$$P = 20Q$$

or $$Q = \frac{P}{20} \qquad ...(1)$$

Since the supply curve of a firm is that portion of marginal cost curve that lies above the minimum point of the average variable cost (*AVC*) curve. *AVC* is minimised at the output level where its first derivative equals zero. From the given cost function we find that *TFC* is 1000 and *TVC* is 10 Q^2.

$$AVC = \frac{TVC}{Q} = \frac{10Q^2}{Q} = 10Q$$

Setting its derivative equal to zero we have

$$\frac{d(10\,Q)}{dQ} = 0$$

or $$Q = 0$$

Thus, *AVC* is minimised when output (*Q*) is equal to zero. It therefore follows that the entire supply function found in (1) above, namely, $Q = P/20$ or $P = 20Q$ represents the short-run supply curve of the firm.

Problem 6. *A firm operating in a purely competitive environment is faced with a market price of ₹250 per unit of the product. The firm's total short-run cost function is*

$$TC = 6000 + 400Q - 20Q^2 + Q^3$$

(*i*) *Should the firm produce at this price in the short-run?*

(*ii*) *If the market price is ₹300 per unit, what will total profits (losses) be if the firm produces ten units of output? Should the firm produce at this price?*

(*iii*) *If the market price is greater than ₹300, should the firm produce at this price?*

Solution. (*i*) A firm will continue producing in the short run if price of the product of ₹ 250 exceeds the minimum average variable cost. So we have first to find out the minimum average variable cost.

Note that in the given cost function ₹ 6,000 is the total fixed cost because it does not contain any output element (*Q*). Thus,

$$TVC = 400Q - 20Q^2 + Q^3$$

$$AVC = \frac{TVC}{Q} = \frac{400\,Q - 20\,Q^2 + O^3}{Q}$$

$$AVC = 400 - 20Q + Q^2$$

To determine the level of output at which average variable cost is minimum, we take the first derivative of *AVC* function and set it equal to zero.

$$\frac{d(AVC)}{dQ} = -20 + 2Q$$

$$\text{Setting } \frac{d(AVC)}{dQ} = 0 \text{ we have}$$

$$-20 + 2Q = 0$$

$$2Q = 20$$

$$Q = 10$$

Substituting the value of Q in the AVC function we have

$$\text{Minimum } AVC = 400 - 20 \times 10 + (10)^2 = 300$$

Since the price of ₹ 250 is less than the minimum average variable cost of ₹ 300, the firm will not produce in the short run because it will not even recover variable costs.

(*ii*) If the market price of the product is ₹ 300, it may continue producing in the short run because it will be covering the variable costs fully, though it will not be recovering any part of the fixed costs and therefore suffering losses.

It should be noted that at price ₹ 300, the firm shall produce 10 units. This can be known by equating this price with marginal cost which is the profit-maximising condition under perfect competition. Thus,

$$MC = \frac{d(TVC)}{dQ} = 400 - 40Q + 3Q^2$$

$$MC = \text{Price} = 300$$

$$400 - 40Q + 3Q^2 = 300$$

$$Q = 10$$

Now
$$ATC = \frac{6000 + 400\,Q - 20Q^2 + O^3}{Q}$$

$$= \frac{6000}{Q} + 400 - 20Q + O^2$$

ATC at output 10= 600 + 400 – 200 + 100 = 900

Losses at Price ₹ 300 :

$$\pi = TR - TC$$

$$TR = P\,.\,Q - ATC \times Q$$

$$= (300 \times 10) - (900 \times 10)$$

$$= 3000 - 9000 = -6000$$

Thus, the firm will be suffering losses equal to ₹ 6,000 at price ₹ 300 per unit (that is, losses are equal to the total fixed cost).

Problem 7: *Suppose a firm is operating under perfectly competitive conditions in the market. It faces the following revenue and cost conditions:*

$$TR = 12Q$$

$$TC = 2 + 4Q + Q^2$$

Determine the equilibrium level of output using both the first order and second order conditions of equilibrium. Calculate total profits made.

Solution. Profits are maximised when the firm equates marginal cost with MR and marginal cost is rising. Thus, in order to obtain the equilibrium output we equate $MC = MR$.

$$TR = 12Q$$

$$MR = \frac{dTR}{dQ} = 12$$

$$MC = \frac{dTC}{dQ} = 4 + 2Q$$

In equilibrium,

$$MC = MR$$
$$4 + 2Q = 12$$
$$Q = 4$$

Total profits (π) $= TR - TC$

$$= 12Q - (2 + 4Q + Q^2)$$

Substituting $Q = 4$, we have

$$\pi = (12 \times 4) - 2 - (4 \times 4) - 16$$
$$= 48 - 34 = 14$$

Note that in order to ensure for the fulfillment of second order condition, we have to test whether *MC* is rising. For this, we take the derivative of *MC i.e.* we find second derivative of *TC*

Thus, $$MC = \frac{dTC}{dQ} = 4 + 2Q$$

$$\frac{d^2TC}{dQ^2} = + 2$$

The positive sign of the second derivative of *TC* implies that *MC* is rising.

Problem 8. *Suppose that revenue and total cost of a firm are given by the equations:*

$$R = 60Q$$

and $C = 10 + 5Q^2$, *(Q = output).*

Using TR-TC approach find what will be the profit-maximising output and total profit of the firm?

Solution :

$$\pi = TR - TC$$
$$= 60Q - 10 - 5Q^2 \qquad \ldots (i)$$

Profits will be maximum at the level of output at which the first derivative of total profit function = 0. Thus,

$$\frac{d\pi}{dQ} = 60 - 10Q$$

Setting $\frac{d\pi}{dQ}$ equal to zero we have

$$60 - 10Q = 0$$
$$10Q = 60$$
$$Q = 6$$

For the second order condition to be fulfilled, the second order derivative of profit function should be negative. Taking the second derivative of the profit function, we have

$$\frac{d^2\pi}{dQ^2} = -10$$

Thus, the second order condition is satisfied.

Substituting $Q = 6$ in the profit function, (*i*) we have

$$\pi = 60 \times 6 - 10 - 5(6)^2 = 360 - 10 - 5 \times 36$$
$$= 360 - 10 - 180 = ₹\,170$$

QUESTIONS FOR REVIEW

1. Explain the various features of a perfectly competitive market. How is price of a commodity determined under it?
2. What is meant by firm's equilibrium? Explain the conditions of short-run equilibrium of a firm under perfect competition. Is equality of marginal revenue with marginal cost sufficient condition for equilibrium of the firm?
3. Can a firm under perfect competition operate in the short run when it is making losses? If so, under what conditions?
4. When does a firm working under perfect competition decide to (*a*) shut down in the short run, (*b*) leave the industry in the long run ?
5. Explain the conditions of long-run equilibrium of a firm operating under conditions of perfect competition. A firm operating under perfect competition tends to be of optimum size. Explain. What is the significance of this for the consumer and the community as a whole?
6. "If there is free entry of new firms in the competitive industry, price must fall to the level of minimum long-run average cost." Explain.
7. "In the long-run equilibrium, every firm in a competitive industry earns zero profits. Why do not these firms leave the industry and go elsewhere to make some positive economic profits.?" Examine this statement.
8. A perfectly competitive firm has the following total cost function:

Total output (Units)	*Total cost (₹)*
0	20
1	30
2	42
3	55
4	69
5	84
6	100
7	117

How much will the firm produce if the price of the product in the market is ₹ 14 per unit? How will it change its output if price rises to ₹ 16 per unit?

[**Hint.** Under perfect competition *MR* = Price which is given to be equal to ₹ 14 or ₹16. For equating this *MR* or Price with *MC*, make the third column in the above table calculating *MC* at various levels of output and see at what output level *MC* = Price.]

9. (*a*) Explain the concept of supply curve. How is this relevant only under perfect competition ?

   (*b*) Derive a short-run supply curve of the firm operating under perfect competition. Explain that short-run supply curve of a firm always slopes upward.
10. What is meant by economic efficiency? Explain how economic efficiency is achieved under perfect competition.
11. Distinguish between *productive efficiency in resource use and allocative efficiency*. Explain how both are achieved under perfect competition.
12. Explain the concept of economic efficiency using the concepts of consumer surplus and producer surplus. Show how does a perfectly competitive market achieve economic efficie-ncy ? Does achievement of economic efficiency clash with the objective of equity ?
13. If a competitive firm's cost function is $C(q) = 100 + 10q - q^2 + \frac{1}{3} + q^3$, what is the firm's marginal cost function ? What is firm's profit maximising condition ?

APPENDIX TO CHAPTER 28

Competitive Equilibrium Under Differential Cost Conditions

Short-Run Equilibrium of the Firm: Differential Cost Conditions

We now pass on to explain the short-run equilibrium of firms when they are working under differential cost conditions. Differences in the quality of raw materials used by the various firms, differences in production techniques, differences in efficiency of managers employed by them, differences in the size of plants built by them and differences in the ability of the entrepreneurs themselves account for the differences in costs of the various firms. Some firms may enjoy the advantage of more convenient location, purer raw materials and more skilled managers that are not available to other firms. Under any of these differential cost conditions, cost curves of all firms will not be identical. We thus ***see that most of the cost-differences arise because various factors of production employed*** by different firms are heterogeneous and most important and relevant case is the case when different *entrepreneurs themselves are heterogenous*, that is, when entrepreneurs of various firms are of different efficiency and ability. More efficient firms employing better resources will have lower cost curves than others. For the sake of convenience we divide the firms having differential cost conditions into three categories *A, B* and *C* whose cost curves are shown in Fig. 28.19 represents short-run equilibrium of firms under differential cost conditions.

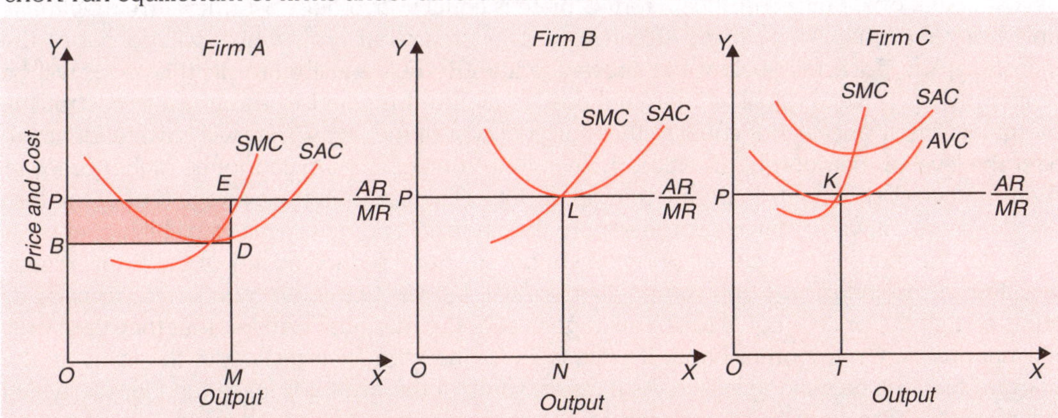

Fig. 28.19. *Short-Run Competitive Equilibrium under Differential Cost Conditions*

If price in the market is *OP*, then the firm of every category will adjust output where price *OP* equals its marginal cost. Firm *A* will be'in equilibrium at *E* and will be producing *OM* output, firm *B* will be in equilibrium at *L* and will be producing *ON*, firm *C* will be in equilibrium at *K* and will be producing *OT*. While for all the firms, price equals their marginal cost at equilibrium output, the firm A in equilibrium is making super-normal profits, the firm *B* is earning only normal profits and the firm *C* is making losses. This is so because cost conditions are different for the three firms. Thus, under conditions of different costs and in'short-run equilibrium, some firms in the industry may be earning super-normal profits, some may be making only normal profits and some others may be incurring losses.

Long-run Equilibrium of Firms : Differential Cost Conditions

What would be the long-run equilibrium position of the firms when they are operating under differential cost conditions. In this connection, the concept of marginal firm is relevant. A

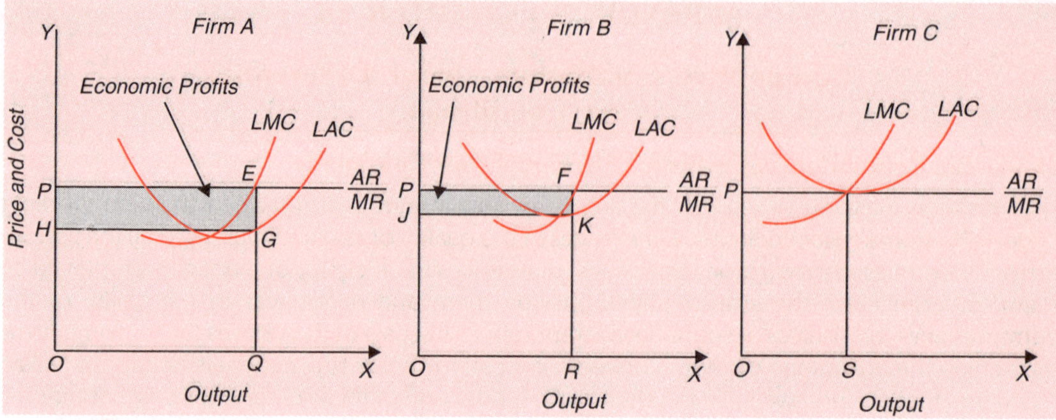

Fig. 28.20. *Long-Run Competitive Equilibrium under Differential Cost Conditions*

marginal firm is one which will be the first to leave the industry if price falls. The marginal firm is the highest-cost firm which earns only normal profits. Since the marginal firm is the highest-cost firm making only normal profits, it will be first to quit the industry if the price falls as with the fall in price its profits will sink below normal.

Fig. 28.20 represent long-run equilibrium of firms, which are of three categories in respect of cost conditions. For firms of category *C* price is equal to average cost, therefore they make only normal profits. Thus, firms of category *C* are marginal firms which will go out of the industry if the price falls below the present price *OP*. Full equilibrium, in this case, will be realised when price is equal to marginal cost of all the firms and to the average cost of the marginal firm. If price is not equal to the marginal cost of the firms, they will have tendency to alter the level of their output. Besides, price in long-run equilibrium cannot be higher or lower than average cost of the firm on the margin. If price is higher than the average cost of the firm on the margin, it will be earning profits more than normal and new firms with still higher costs will enter the industry, which will bring down the price and reduce profits of the firms already working in the industry. Long-run equilibrium will be reached when number of firms is so adjusted that the price is equal to the average cost of the marginal firms so that they earn only normal profits. On the other hand, if price is lower than the average cost of the firms on the margin, they will be making losses. As a result, some of the firms will leave the industry which will raise the price so that the firms left on the margin in the industry earn normal profits.

Fig. 28.20 represents long-run competitive equilibrium of firms under differential cost conditions. Three categories of firms in respect of cost are assumed and from each category one firm is shown. The price prevailing in the long run is *OP* which equals marginal cost of firm *A* at output *OQ*, marginal cost of firm *B* at output *OR*, and marginal cost of firm *C* at output *OS*. Besides, price *OP* is equal to average cost of the marginal firm *C* and therefore it makes only normal profits. But price *OP* is greater than average cost at equilibrium outputs of intra-marginal firms *A* and *B* and therefore they make super-normal profits. Price being equal to the marginal cost of all firms ensures equilibrium of all individual firms including the marginal one. The price being equal to average cost of the marginal firm guarantees that the marginal firm will be making only normal profits and therefore there will be no tendency for new firms to enter or for some of the existing firms to leave the industry.

The question now arises : Can't the new firms having lower cost than the marginal firm *C* enter the industry at price *OP* and earn profits more than normal? Our answer is in the negative because firms having lower costs than firm *C* would have already entered and would be working as intra-marginal firms. New firms having higher costs than category *C* will not enter since they will not be able to earn even normal profits. Besides, all firms in the industry incurring losses at price *OP* would have gone out of the industry in the long run so that for those who are left in the industry price *OP* is either greater than or at least equal to their average cost.

If price in the long run falls below *OP* in Fig. 28.20, the firms of category *C* will go out of the industry and some previous intra-marginal firms for which new price is equal to average cost will become marginal firms. We therefore conclude that in long-run competitive equilibrium under different cost conditions the output of individual firms and the number of firms in the industry is so adjusted that the following two conditions must be satisfied.

(1) *Price = MC of all firms ;*

(2) *Price = AC of the marginal firm.*

From above it follows that in long-run competitive equilibrium under differential cost conditions only the marginal firm will be of optimum size, because the equilibrium of only marginal firm is established at the minimum point of the average cost curve. The intra-marginal firms will be of more than optimum size, as are clear from Fig. 28.20.

Differential Cost Conditions and Economic Rent

We have explained above that in long-run competitive equilibrium under differential cost conditions, the marginal firm makes normal profits, while the intra-marginal firms which have lower costs than the marginal firm will earn profits more than normal. The lower costs of the intra-marginal firms and hence their abnormal profits are due to the fact that the intra-marginal firms employ better or more productive resources than those employed by the marginal firms.

Now, the question arises whether the prices of better or more efficient resources employed by the intra-marginal firms will not be bid up sufficiently high so as to wipe out the differences in costs between the marginal and intra-marginal firms. In fact, this would be so and the prices of the better or more efficient resources will be higher than those of the resources of the marginal firm to the extent of their extra efficiency. Competition among the firms in the long run ensures that differences in costs of the various firms due to differences in the efficiency of the various resources employed will disappear as a result of bidding up the prices of more efficient resources. For instance, if manager *A* employed by a firm runs the firm at ₹ 12,000 more cheaply per year than can the manager *B* employed by another firm, then manager A's salary will tend to be bid up until it is ₹ 12,000 higher per annum than the salary of manager *B*. If the firm employing manager *A* pays him only ₹10,000 more than *B*, it will then be in the interest of the other firm to try to get *A* by offering him to pay ₹ 11,000 more than *B* and it will pay firm employing *A* to try to keep him by offering him ₹ 11,500 more than *B* and so forth until the manager *A* is offered ₹ 12,000 more than *B*. We thus see that the lower costs or abnormal profits of intra-marginal firms made possible by the employment of more efficient resources tend to be paid out to the owners of those resources.

It follows from above that no differential profit advantage can be derived from employing better or more efficient resources, since extra payment equal to the reduction in costs made by them will have to be paid to the owners of these resources. In the other words, entire profit in excess of the normal will be obtained by the owners of more efficient resources. ***These extra payments made to the more efficient resources are over and above their transfer earnings, since their transfer earnings are already included in costs of production. These extra payments made to the more efficient resources over and above their transfer earnings are called rent in economics.*** This 'rent' is as

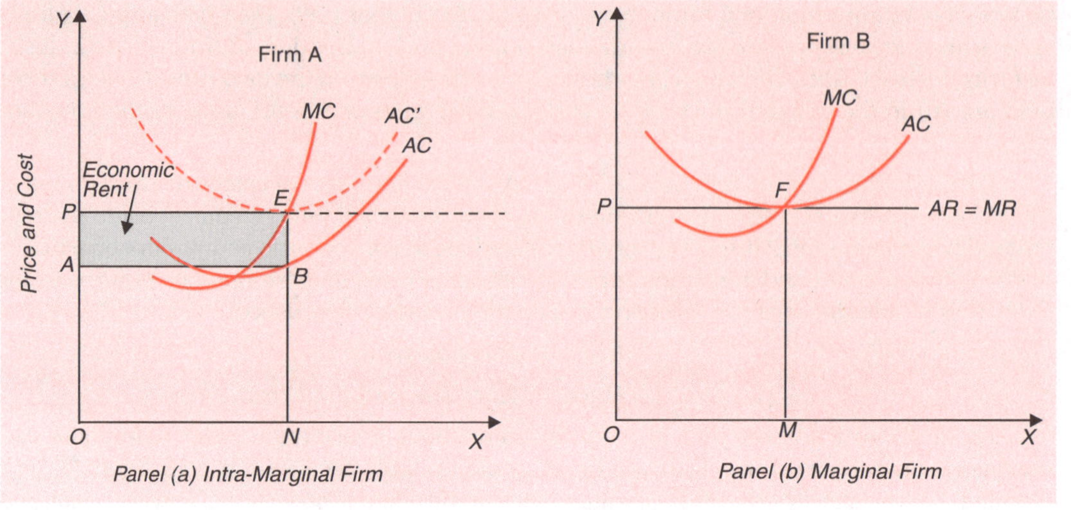

Fig. 28.21. *Economic Rent and Costs*

much a part of cost of production as any other payment. We therefore conclude that differential profit advantage enjoyed by the intra-marginal firms using more efficient resources is wiped out by the extra 'rent' they must pay. If an entrepreneur happens to own the more efficient resources himself, then no actual payment of rent by entrepreneur would take place. But the rent to more efficient resources will no doubt accrue, though it will be bagged by the entrepreneur himself, since he happens to own them. Rent is defined to be the part of the earnings of a factor which is over and above the minimum amount necessary to retain it in its given occupation. These excess earnings will accure to the more efficient units of a factor and will be received by him who happens to own them.

If the rent earned by the more efficient resources is therefore included in costs, then the long-run equilibrium of *all* firms under so called differential cost conditions will be established at the point of minimum average cost. This is illustrated in panels *(a)* and *(b)* of Fig. 28.21. Panel *(b)* of Fig. 28.21 represents the marginal firm and panel *(a)* represents an intra-marginal firm. *OP* is the price of the product. The price *OP* is equal to both marginal cost and average cost of the marginal firm. With price *OP*, the intra-marginal firm is in equilibrium at point *E* of the marginal cost. The average cost *AC* in panel (a) represents the cost of production exclusive of extra rent which has to be paid to the more efficient resources employed by it. The rent earned by the more efficient resources is equal to *ABEP*. Now, if this rent is included in the average cost, the average cost curve inclusive of the rent is represented by *AC′*. By including rent into total cost, we add a fixed amount which is independent of the firm's output (given the price of the product), the marginal cost curve *MC* will therefore cut *AC* as well as *AC′* at their minimum points. It is therefore clear that the long-run equilibrium of the intra-marginal firm will be fixed at the minimum point of the average cost curve inclusive of rent. Thus price is equal to both marginal cost and minimum average cost for all firms, marginal as well as intra-marginal. In fact, when average cost is understood to be inclusive of rent that has to paid to the more efficient units of the factors, there is no sense in calling some firms as marginal and some intra-marginal; the level of the average cost curve inclusive of rent will be the same for all firms and all will be making only normal profits.

Now suppose that the differences in the average cost are due to the differences in efficiency of entrepreneurs themselves while all other resources or factors used by the various firms are perfectly homogeneous. Then the rent of entrepreneurship will accrue to the more efficient entrepreneurs and they will therefore make more than normal profits, while the marginal entrepreneur will make only normal profits. Should then the rent of entrepreneurship be included in average cost just as the rent earned by the more efficient units of other factors of production is included in average cost. Similarity of the treatment demands that the rent of entrepreneurship be also included in average cost. If this is done, then price would be equal to marginal cost and average cost of all firms in long-run competitive equilibrium, even when some entrepreneurs would be more efficient than others. Further, our analysis shows that when ***economic rent earned by factors is included in*** cost of production, then ***every firm inequilibrium must be producing at the same minimum average cost in spite of the fact that some firms are more efficient than others.*** It will be seen in Fig. 28.21 that in equilibrium (with economic rent included in average cost) the firm A will be producing at cost *NE* which is equal to the average cost *MF* at which marginal firm *B* is producing.

It should, however, be pointed out that when either the efficiency of entrepreneurs or the quality of other factors varies the equilibrium output of all firms will not be the same, though all will be producing at the minimum point of their average cost curves inclusive of rent. The equilibrium and optimum output of the firms which have either more capable entrepreneurs or better type of other resources will be greater than the equilibrium and optimum output of the firms having either less capable entrepreneurs or less efficient other kinds of resources. For instance, the equilibrium (with economic rent included in average cost) the firm *A* will be producing at cost *NE* which is equal to the average cost *MF* at which marginal firm *B* is producing.

It should, however, be pointed out that when either the efficiency of entrepreneurs or the quality of other factors varies the equilibrium output of all firms will not be the same, though all will be producing at the minimum point of their average cost curves inclusive of rent. The equilibrium and optimum output of the firms which have either more capable entrepreneurs or better type of other resources will be greater than the equilibrium and optimum output of the firms having either less capable entrepreneurs or less efficient other kinds of resources. For instance, the equilibrium and optimum output of intra marginal of firm in panel (a) of Fig 28.21 is greater than the equilibrium and optimum output *OM* of the marginal firm is panel (*b*) of Fig. 28.21.

CHAPTER

29

Comparative Static Analysis of Equilibrium and Long-run Supply Curve of the Competitive Industry

Introduction

We have studied in the preceding two chapters that price of a product under perfect competition in determined by demand for and supply of the product. Thus, for the analysis of pricing in the long run under perfect competition we need to know the nature of the supply curve of the product of an industry. In the last chapter we saw that short-run supply curve of a product by an individual firm was the ***short-run marginal cost curve*** of the firm lying above the minimum point of the average variable cost curve. We further explained that the short-run supply curve of the competitive industry could be derived by the *horizontal summation* of the short-run supply curves of the firms in the industry. However, ***long-run supply curve of the industry cannot be obtained by summing up horizontally the supply curves of the firm.*** This is because when the industry expands, the long-run and short run cost curves shift due to external diseconomies and economies and with them the long-run equilibrium price also changes.

Comparative Static Analysis

In the derivation of long-run supply curve of a perfectly competitive industry we analyse the question ***how the supply by an industry responds in the long run to changes in demand.*** For instance, when the demand for the product increases, there will be adjustment of supply by the industry to meet the increase in demand. First, the existing firms expand their output. Secondly, new firms enter the industry resulting in larger supply of the product. With the increase in supply of the product both as a result of expansion of output by the industrial firms and the entry of new firms, the new equilibrium between demand and supply is established. In the derivation of long-run supply curve curve we see how the competitive industry makes adjustment from one equilibrium to another in response to changes in demand for a product. That is, in the explanation of ***long-run supply curve of the industry we make a comparative static analysis of industry equilibrium.*** Thus, a long-run supply curve of the industry shows the relationships between price and quantity supplied at various equilibrium points corresponding to different levels of demand. It is worth mentioning that all points on the long-run supply curve satisfy the following condition:

$$P = LMC = Min.LAC$$

However, it may be noted that the level of minimum average cost does not remain the same when the industry expands or contracts in response to the increase or decrease in demand for the product. The long-run average and marginal cost curves shift upward or downward or remain constant depends on the strength of external economies and diseconomies. How these externalities determine the long-run supply of the competitive industry will become clear from our comparative static analysis of the industry adjustment to the changes in demand. In our analysis of the derivation of long-run supply curve we assume that *technology and prices of other products* remain the same. The effect of changes in input prices and technology on competitive equilibrum will be explained at the end of this chapter. But, before analysing the derivation of long-run supply curve we will explain the concept of supply curve which it is important to remember is relevant in case of only perfectly competitive market structure.

The Concept of Supply Curve

Just as demand for a commodity refers to a schedule of the quantities of a commodity that will be purchased at different prices, similarly, the supply refers to a schedule of the quantities of a good that will be offered for sale at different prices. Supply curve is therefore a graphic representation of what quantities of a good will be offered for sale at all possible prices. Supply curve depicts the sellers' quantity reactions to various prices. Thus, the quantity supplied, like the quantity demanded, is a function of price. There is however an important difference between the reaction of the quantity supplied and demanded to changes in price of the good. Whereas the quantity demanded of a good generally increases with fall in price of the good and decreases with the rise in its price, the quantity supplied decreases with the fall in price of a good and increases with the rise in its price. In other words, while the quantity demanded has a negative or inverse relation with the price, the quantity supplied generally bears a positive or direct relation with the price. The positive relation between quantity supplied and price lies in the nature of the costs of production which generally rise as more quantity of a good is produced. This is because of positive relation between price and quantity supplied that the supply curve slopes upward from left to right. However, while the short-run supply curve always slopes upward to right, the long-run supply curve may slope either upward or downward, or it may be of a horizontal straight line depending upon whether the industry is working under increasing cost or decreasing cost or constant cost conditions. However, the upward-sloping supply curve showing increasing cost is more typical case even in the long run.

Supply-curve concept is relevant only in case of perfect competition. It is worth noting here that the concept of supply curve, as it is used in economic theory, is relevant only for the case of perfect or pure competition and it is quite inapplicable to the cases of imperfect competition —monopolistic competition, monopoly and oligopoly. This is because **the notion of supply curve refers to the question as to how much quantities of a commodity a firm will supply at various given prices.** In other words, notion of supply curve refers to the quantity reactions of a firm when the firm itself exercises no influence over the determination of price and takes price as a given datum for it and adjusts its quantity produced or supplied. Since only in perfect or pure competition a firm exercises no influence over the price which is determined by impersonal market mechanism of demand and supply, outside the control of individual firms, the concept of supply curve is relevant only for perfect or pure competition. So far as short-run supply curve of the industry under perfect competition is concerned, it is a mere lateral summation of the short-run supply curves of the firms.

However, under various forms of imperfect competition, an individual firm does not take the price as given and is not a mere quantity adjuster. In fact, under various forms of imperfect competition, a firm sets its own price. For a firm under imperfect competition, it is not a question of adjusting output or supply at a given price but of choosing *price-output combination* which maximizes its profits. Commenting on the relevance of supply curve, Prof. Baumol writes : The supply curve is, strictly speaking, a concept which is usually relevant only for the case of pure (or perfect) competition. The reason for this lies in its definition—the supply curve is designed to answer questions of the form, "How much will firm A supply if it encounters a price which is fixed at *P* dollars". But such a question is most relevant to the behaviour of firms that actually deal with prices over whose determination they exercise no influence."[1]

LONG-RUN SUPPLY CURVE UNDER PERFECT COMPETITION

In the long run the firms can change their capital equipment and the other fixed factors as well as the number of firms can vary in response to changes in the demand for a commodity. In the long run when the number of firms can enter and leave the industry the firm is in equilibrium at the minimum point of the long-run average cost curve where the long-run marginal cost curve intersects it. Thus, a firm under perfect competition in the long-run equilibrium is forced to produce only at one point of the long-run marginal cpst curve at which it cuts the average cost curve. Price in the long run is equal to both long-run marginal cost and minimum average cost. Therefore, the firm in the long run will produce and supply an output indicated by the minimum point of its long-run average cost curve, that is, its optimum size. Of course, this optimum size of the firm may change with the change in the number of firms in the industry. The long-run supply in the industry may be influenced by the changes in the optimum size of the firms (that is, long-run supply of output by individual firms) but it is mainly determined by the variation in the number of firms in the industry.

It should be noted that long-run supply curve is defined as the supply by the existing as well potential firms in the industry in the long run. A little reflection will show that the long-run supply curve of the industry cannot be the lateral summation of the long-run marginal cost curves of a given number of firms. This is because of three reasons. First, as explained above, *whole* of the long-run marginal cost curve does not constitute the long-run supply curve of an individual firm, ***only one point of the*** long-run marginal cost curve at which it cuts the average cost curve (that is, the minimum point of the average cost curve) constitutes the long-run supply of the individual firm. Secondly, the number of firms varies at different prices or at different demand conditions in the long run.

Thirdly, we cannot sum up any *existing* long-run marginal cost curves of the firms to obtain-the long-run supply curve of the industry because with the expansion of the industry in the long run cost curves of the firms shift due to the emergence of external economies and diseconomies. In order to know the output supplied by the firms of an industry in the long run, we need to know the position or level of the cost curves of the firms as well as the number of firms in the industry at a given demand and price of the product.

As we explained in a previous chapter, *external* economies and diseconomies are those which accrue to all firms in an industry as a result of the expansion of the industry as a whole. The creation of external economies by an expanding industry will shift the cost curves of the firms upward. On the other hand, the creation of external diseconomies will shift the cost curves of the firms downward. Whether a given industry will experience upward or downward shift in the cost curves depends upon the *net or combined effect* of the external economies and diseconomies. When with the expansion of an industry the external economies outweigh the external diseconomies so that there are *net external economies*, cost curves of the firms will shift downward. On the other hand, if with the expansion of an industry external diseconomies are stronger than the external economies so that there are *net external diseconomies,* cost curves of the firms will shift upward.

We thus see that external economies and diseconomies play a vital role in determining the shape of the long-run supply curve of the competitive industry. Whether a particular industry on expansion will experience the phenomenon of rising costs or falling costs or constant

1. W. Baumol, *Economic Theory and Operations Analysis,* Prentice Hall, 4th edition 1974, p. 342.

costs will depend upon the net result of external economies and diseconomies. The long-run supply curve of perfectly competitive industry will therefore have different shapes depending upon whether the industry in question is a *(i)* constant-cost industry ; *(ii)* increasing-cost industry or *(iii)* decreasing-cost industry.

It follows from above that at a given price the quantity supplied by an industry in the long run is determined by the optimum output of a firm in the long run (*i.e.*, output corresponding to minimum long-run average cost) multiplied by the number of firms in the industry at that price. With the change in price of the product following a change in demand conditions, the number of firms in the industry will change and also the cost curves of the firms will shift on account of the creation of external economies and diseconomies. As a result, the quantity supplied by the industry will change at a new price. The long-run supply curve of the industry may either be sloping upward or be a horizontal straight line or be sloping downward depending upon whether the industry in question is increasing-cost, constant cost, or decreasing cost. How the long-run supply curve under these types of cost conditions is obtained is explained below.

Long-run Supply Curve in Increasing-Cost Industry

When an industry expands in response to an increase in demand it experiences some external economies as well as some external diseconomies. Whereas external economies tend to reduce the cost and thereby shift the long-run cost curves downward, the external diseconomies tend to raise the costs and thereby shift the long-run cost curves upward. So we have an increasing-cost industry when external diseconomies outweigh the external economies, trial is, when there are *net external diseconomies.*

The external diseconomies which accrue to an expanding industry are generally the *rise in prices of materials or factors* used for production in the industry. As more firms enter the industry in response to the increase in demand for the product, the prices of scarce factors rise due to the increase in demand for them. In other words, more intensive bidding by the increased number of firms pushes up the prices of scarce materials. Wages of specialized labour, rent of land and the prices of scarce raw materials, capital equipment etc. are bound to rise as the demand for them increases as a result of the expansion of the industry. Generally, the same resources are used in different industries. As an industry expands, it has to take away the scarce resources from other industries by offering them higher prices. The rise in prices of the scarce factors raises the costs of production. Furthermore, the additional factors of production coming into the industry are generally less efficient or of inferior quality than the previous ones and this also brings about increase in cost of production as the industry expands. When these external diseconomies outweigh the external economies, the industry experiences rising costs and the average and marginal cost curves of the firms in the industry shift upward. Thus, Professor Heilbroner writes, "Industries may also experience long-run rising costs if their expansion pushes them up against factor scarcity of a stubbornly inelastic kind. Extractive industries, for example, may be forced to use progressively less accessible mineral deposits; or agricultural industries may be forced to use progressively less fertile or less-conveniently located land. Such industries would experience a gradual rise in unit costs as their output increased"[2].

Fig.29.1 illustrates the determination of long-run normal price in an increasing-cost industry. The left-hand side of the diagram in Fig. 29. 1 shows the long-run equilibrium of the firm at two different long-run normal prices, while the right-hand side of diagram shows the demand and supply curves of the industry with the horizontal scale compressed. To begin with, a given demand curve *DD* intersects the short-run supply curve SRS_1 at point *Q*. Therefore, the short-run price OP_0 is determined.

2. Robert L. Heilbroner, The *Economics Problem*, Prentics-Hall, 1970 p.512

From the left-hand side of the diagram it is seen that price OP_0 is equal to minimum long-run average cost of the firm. It means that the sizes of firms as well as the number of firms have already been fully adjusted to the given demand conditions as represented by the curve *DD*. Therefore, price OP_0 is also a long-run normal price corresponding to the demand conditions *DD*. Now, let us see what happens to the long-run normal price when a once for all

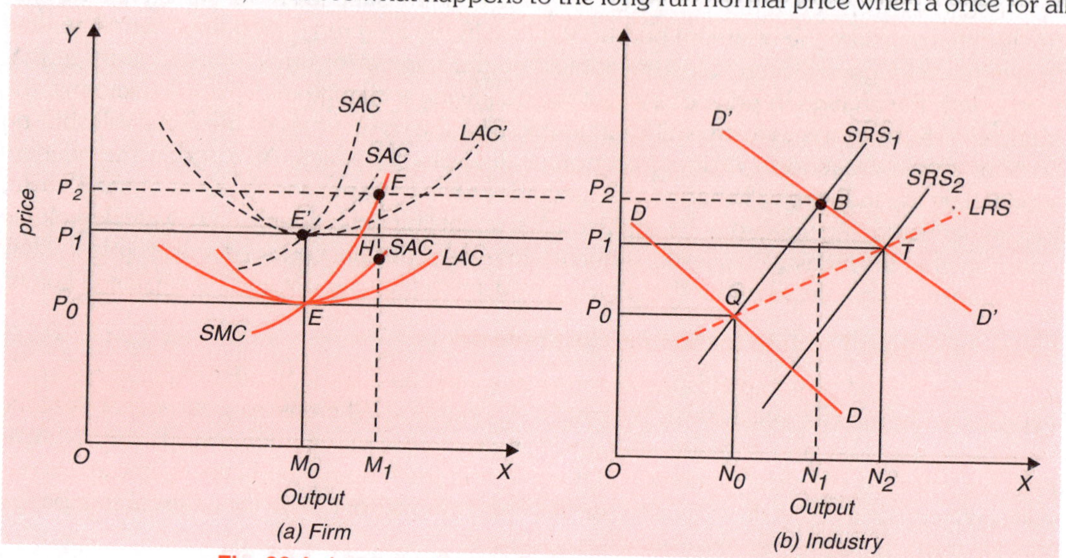

Fig. 29.1. *Long-run Supply Curve in Increasing-Cost Industry*

increase in demand from *DD* to *D′D′* occurs. In the short run price will rise to OP_2 *and* total quantity exchanged to ON_1 as a result of the given increase in demand. From the panel (a) of Fig. 29.1 it will be seen that the individual firm in the short run will expand its output along the short-run marginal cost curve and will be in equilibrium at point *F* on *SMC*. The firm will therefore expand output from OM_0 to OM_1. It will be further seen from the left-hand side of Fig. 29. 1 that the individual firm will be making supernormal profits equal to *FH per unit of output* in the short run at price OP_2. Lured by these supernormal profits new firms will enter the industry to produce the homogeneous product and will add to the supply of the product. As a result, the short-run supply curve will shift to the right. The new firms will continue entering the industry as long as supernormal profits are made and short-run supply curve will continue shifting rightward until its intersection with the new demand curve *D′D′* determines a price at which supernormal profits are reduced to zero.

It is evident form diagram 29.1 (*b*) above, that when short-run supply curve has shifted to the position SRS_2 due to the entry of a certain number of firms, it intersects the new demand curve *D ′D ′at* point *T* and determines the price OP_1 at which firms make only normal profits (*i.e.* economic profits, are reduced to zero). Price OP_1 is equal to the minimum average cost of the new long-run average -cost curve *LAC*. The long-run average cost curve has shifted upward from *LAC* to *LAC ′* due to increasing costs which come about with the expansion of the industry. Thus OP_1 is a long-run normal price and ON_2 is the new long-run quantity supplied corresponding to the demand conditions *D ′D ′*. Long-run price OP_1 is higher than the original long-run price OP_0 and also the quantity supplied ON_2 at price OP_1 is greater than the quantity supplied ON_0 at price OP_0. If points *Q* and *T* are joined together we get the long-run supply curve *LRS*. The long-run supply curve *LRS* slopes upward to the right in the present case because the industry is subject to increasing costs.

It follows from above that the long-run price of the product rises as demand increases in the case of increasing-cost industry. In other words, in the case of increasing-cost industry, more quantity of the product can be obtained or supplied only at a higher price. The extent to which the new long-run price differs from the original long-run price depends upon the extent to which the increase in cost occurs following the expansion of the industry. It must be borne in mind that *every point of the* long-run supply curve ***LRS represents a long-run equilibrium as the demand shifts to the right.*** It is clear from the analysis made above that the long-run supply curve of an increasing-cost industry slopes upward to the right and is more elastic than the short-run supply curve.

This case of increasing-cost industry or, in other words, ***rising supply price*** is believed to be the most typical of the competitive industries in the actual world. This is so because productive resources are scarce and are currently being used in various industries, therefore when an industry expands and requires more resources, it has to take away resources from others by paying higher prices for them. Thus, Samuelson writes : The case of increasing cost is "the normal one to be met in most sizable competitive industries. Why normal ? Because when a large industry (which has already achieved the economies of large-scale production) expands, it must coax men and other productive factors away from the other industries by bidding up their prices and thus its own cost. So the long-run supply curve will usually be sloping gently upward".[3]

Long-Run Supply-Curve in the Constant-Cost Industry

If an industry on its expansion gives rise to some external economies and external diseconomies which cancel each other so that the constituent firms do not experience any shift in their cost curves, then that industry is a constant-cost industry. In case of constant-cost industry, we have neither *net* external economies, nor *net* external diseconomies. An industry can also be a constant-cost industry if its expansion breeds neither external economies nor external diseconomies. As more firms enter an industry the demand for productive factors like raw materials, labour, chemicals, and machinery will increase and if prices of these productive resources go up as a result of the increase in demand, then the cost is bound to rise. It is therefore evident that an industry can be a constant-cost industry if it makes little impact on the market for these productive resources, that is, if its demand for productive resources is a negligible part of the total demand for them, so that the increase in demand for them by the industry does not push up their prices. To quote Prof. Samuelson, "only if the industry is small compared with the total of all other uses will Marshall's long-run supply curve be horizontal — which is called the case of constant cost"[4]. If the industry on its expansion does not create external diseconomies, it will be a constant-cost industry only when its expansion also does not give rise to any external economies.

Thus an industry can be constant cost in two ways. First, when the expansion of an industry creates both external economies and diseconomies but they cancel each other in their effect on costs, and second, when the expansion of an industry creates neither external economies, nor external diseconomies. Fig.29 .2 depicts the determination of long-run normal price in constant-cost industry. To begin with, a given demand curve *DD* intersects the short-run supply curve SRS_1 at point *Q* and short-run price *OP* is equal to the minimum long-run average cost of the firm. This means that the number of firms has already been fully adjusted to the given demand conditions. Therefore, price *OP* is also the long-run price corresponding to the demand conditions as represented by the curve *DD* and the quantity supplied by the

3. Paul A. Samuelson, *Economics,* 8thh edition, p. 366.
4. *Ibid,* p. 366.

industry is ON_0. Now suppose that the demand increases from *DD* to *D′D′*. As a result, price rises to *OP* ′ in the short run at which the short-run supply curve SRS_1 intersects the new demand curve *D* ′*D* ′. The quantity supplied by the industry increases to ON_1 in the short run. At price *OP* ′, a firm will be in equilibrium at *F* and will be producing OM_1, amount of the product. It will be seen from the figure that at price *OP* ′ the firm is making super-normal profits equal to *FH per* unit of output. This will attract other firms into the industry in question. As more firms enter the industry, the short-run supply curve will shift to the right. The new firms will go on entering the industry and short-run supply curve will go on shifting rightward until its intersection with the new demand curve *D′D′* determines a price at which super-normal profits of the firms disappear completely.

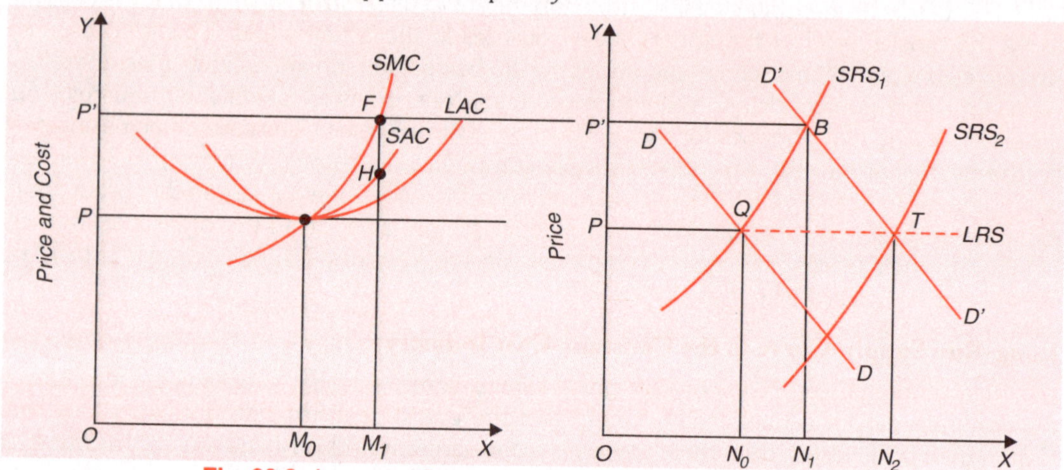

Fig. 29.2. *Long-run Supply Curve in a Constant-Cost Industry*

It will be seen from Fig.29.2 that when the short-run supply curve has shifted to SRS_2, it intersects the new demand curve *D* ′*D* ′ at *T* and once again determines price *OP* at which firms make only normal profits. Thus, price *OP* is also a long-run price corresponding to the demand curve *D′D′*. The cost curves of the firms have not shifted because external economies and diseconomies have offset each other's effect. As a result of the increase in demand the price went up in the short run but has returned to the original level of *OP* in the long run. In a constant-cost industry, long-run normal price remains the same whatever the level of demand. If points like *Q* and *T* are joined together we get a long-run supply curve *LRS* which is a horizontal straight line in the present case. It is thus clear that in the constant-cost industry new firms enter the industry without raising or lowering cost curves of firms and make available additional supplies of output at the same price which is equal to the minimum long-run average cost of the firms. Since long-run supply curve of the constant-cost industry is a horizontal straight line, any increase or decrease in demand will not produce any effect on the long-run price. In this case, increase or decrease in demand will in the long-run only change the supply of output by causing a change in the number of firms without producing any effect on the long-run normal price.

Here, a point is worth noting. While the long-run marginal cost curve of the firm will be sloping upward in its relevant part, the long-run supply curve of the industry in this case is a horizontal straight line. It is manifest from this that the long-run supply curve of an industry cannot be the lateral summation of the long-run marginal cost curves of the firms.

Long-run Supply Curve in the Decreasing-Cost Industry

When an industry grows in size by the increase in the number of firms, it may be that the external economies outweigh the external diseconomies so that there is a decline in the production cost of the firms. In other words, when an industry reaps **net external economies** as it expands, it is a decreasing-cost industry. There is every possibility of external economies to outstrip the external diseconomies when an industry grows in a new territory. In earlier stages of the growth of an industry in a new territory, not much diseconomies are created, while external economies are likely to accrue in greater amount. Costs may decline with the expansion of the industry due to the following external economies :

1. Some raw materials, tools and capital equipment may be made available to the industry at reduced prices because with the growth of industry some specialised subsidiary and correlated firms may spring up in the vicinity of the industry which produce them on a large scale and enjoy economies of scale and therefore can provide them to the expanding industry at the reduced prices.

2. Cheaper and better trained labour may become available with the expansion of the industry.

3. With the growth of industry, certain specialised firms may come into existence which work up its *waste products*. The industry can then sell its waste products at good prices, while previously it may be throwing them away.

4. As the industry expands it may become worthwhile to publish trade journals, to set up information centers and research institutions on collective basis which may help in discovering and diffusing technical knowledge concerning the industry.

Thus, while explaining the reasons for decreasing costs in an industry due to external economies, Robert L. Heilbroner writes : "The source of these changes in cost does not lie within the firm, in the relative efficiency of various factors mixed. Rather they are changes thrust upon the firm —for better or worse—by the interaction of the growing industry of which it is a part and the economy as a whole. A new industry, for example, by its very expansion may bring into being satellite firms that provide some of its necessary inputs ; and as the main new industry grows, the satellites also expand and thereby realise economies of scale that will benefit the main industry itself. The automobile industry, was surely an instance of such long-run falling costs (for a long period, at least) resulting from the economies of scale enjoyed by makers of tires, makers of batteries, and other equipments"[5].

In case the above-mentioned external economies are more powerful than the external diseconomies that may arise, the cost curves of all firms in the industry will shift to a lower position as the industry expands.

Long-run pricing in a decreasing cost industry is illustrated in Fig. 29.3. To start with, demand curve *DD* and short-run supply curves *SRS* intersect at *Q* and determine short-run price OP_0. Price OP_Q is also the initial long-run price since it is equal to the minimum long-run average cost of the firms which are therefore making only normal profits. With the increase in demand from *DD* to *D′D′*, short-run price rises to OP_2 and the quantity exchanged to ON_1. As a result of the rise in price from OP_2, each firm of the industry will expand output to OM_1 in the short run. Price OP_2 yields economic profits to the firms in the short run. These economic profits will attract other firms into the industry and as a result the industry will expand.

As the industry expands, short-run supply curve will shift to the right and owing to the decreasing-cost industry, cost curves of the firms will shift downward. The short-run supply curve will continue to shift to the right and cost curves of the firms continue to shift downward until the short-run supply curve reaches the position where it intersects the new demand curve *D′D′* at *T* and determines price OP_1 at which firms make only normal profits. Price OP_1 is

5. Robert L. Heilbroner, *The Economic Problem*, Prentice Hall, 1970, p. 512.

therefore long-run price corresponding to the demand curve $D'D'$. As is evident from panel *(b)* of Fig. 29.3, new long-run price OP_1 is lower than the original long-run price OP_0. Connecting points *Q* and *T*, we get the downward-sloping long-run supply curve *LRS*. We thus see that the long-run supply curve of a decreasing-cost industry slopes downward from left to right. In this case the greater supplies of the product will be forthcoming at reduced prices in the long run. Every increase in demand in this case will bring about a fall in the long-run price of the good. This is in sharp contrast to the increasing-cost industry in which case long-run price rises as the demand increases.

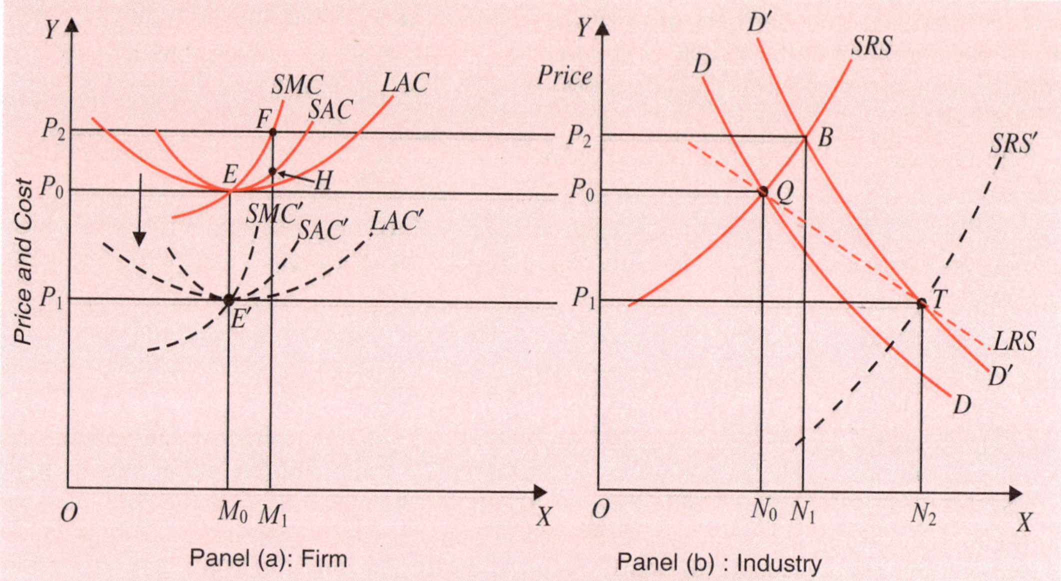

Fig.29.3. *Long-Run Supply Curve in a Decreasing-Cost Industry*

It follows from the analysis of long-run pricing made above that with the increases in demand, long-run price rises, remains constant, or falls depending upon whether the industry is subject to increasing cost, constant cost or decreasing cost.

CHANGE IN COMPETITIVE EQUILIBRIUM IN RESPONSE TO CHANGES IN INPUT PRICES AND TECHNOLOGY

Having discussed the determination of price and quantity of products in a competitive industry, we are now in a position to apply the theory of competitive pricing in the following two fields.

1. What is the response of price and output of a competitive industry to changes in prices of inputs and how it affects consumers and producers ?

2. How do changes in technology affect price and output of a competitive industry and to what extent the benefits of technological progress are passed on to consumers ?

In what follows we explain below the above two issues which are significant in understanding how economic policies regarding taxation, changes in input prices and technology affect consumers and producers.

Change in Price and Output of a Competitive Industry in Response to Rise in Input Prices

It is important to know how changes in input prices affect price and quantity produced and sold by a competitive industry. Input prices often change which bring about changes in prices and output of an industry. We first explain how equilibrium prices and quantity of an industry change when prices of inputs rise. Hike in prices of petrol, diesel and other petroleum products which are important inputs in industries and transport have an important effects on prices and outputs of industries. Similarly, rise in power rate, rise in excise duties on several raw materials used as inputs in industries raises the prices of inputs. Rise in prices of inputs raises the costs of production and causes upward shift in the cost curves, including the marginal

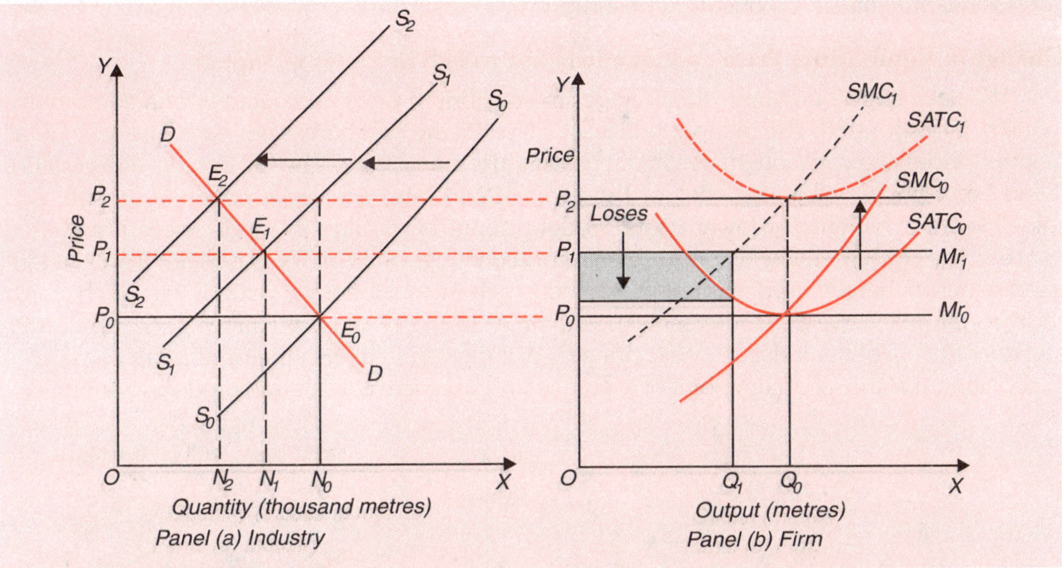

Fig. 29.4. *Response of Competitive Price and Output to Rise in Input Prices*

cost curves of the firms in the industry. The short-run supply curve of a competitive industry will shift as it is the summation of short-run marginal cost curves of the firms. Consider Figure29.4. In the left-hand panel initially demand curve *DD* and supply curve S_0S_0 of the industry intersect at point E_0 and determine equilibrium price equal to P_0 and quantity or output equal to N_0. Given price P_0, the firm is in equilibrium at the minimum point of initial short-run average total cost curve $SATC_0$ and is producing Q_0 amount of output by equating price = $MC = ATC$.

Now suppose prices of inputs rise which cause an upward shift in the cost curves (dotted) of the firms. With this, the short-run supply curve of the industry which will now be summation of the *new* short-run marginal cost curves of the firms shifts to the left to S_1S_1. The new short-run supply curve S_1S_1 of the industry intersects the given demand curve *DD* at point E_1 and determines a higher price P_1 and lower output N_1 It will be seen from the right-hand panel of Fig.29.4 that price has risen less than the rise in cost. If price of product had risen equal to rise in average cost of production, price would have risen to P_2. Instead, price has risen to P_1. The firm will now equate the higher price P_1 of the product with their new short-run marginal cost curves SMC_1. It will be seen from right-hand panel *(b)* that a firm will be in equilibrium by producing a lower output Q_1 and will be making losses equal to the shaded area. Since with rise in input prices and resultant rise in cost, price of product rises less than the rise in cost consumers do not bear the whole burden of rise in cost due to higher prices of inputs in the short run, a part of the burden is borne by the producers as they suffer losses.

However, the firms cannot continue making losses in the long run. As a result, some firms will leave the industry in the long run causing a shift in the supply curve of the industry further to the left so that it intersects the original demand curve *DD* and determine price P_2 which, as will be seen from the right-hand panel of Fig. 29.4 is equal to the new minimum average cost of $SATC_1$. It will be seen that in the long-run price has risen by P_0P_2, that is, by the full amount of rise in cost per unit due to rise in input prices. ***We therefore conclude that in the long run in a competitive industry, the whole burden of rise in costs caused by rise in prices of inputs has to be borne by the consumers in terms of higher price of the product that they have to pay.*** Besides, the consumers get less quantity of the product for consumption.

Change in Equilibrium Price and Quantity due to Fall in Prices of Inputs

We have explained above the changes in equilibrium price and quantity of a competitive industry in response to rise in input prices which shifts the cost curves upward. The case of fall in input prices and consequent decline in costs is just the reverse. The fall in costs as a result of fall in input prices will lower price of the product and raise equilibrium quantity bought and sold. How the benefits of lower costs brought about by decline in input prices are shared between the consumers and producers is illustrated in Figure 29.5. It will be seen from the left-hand panel *(a)* that initially the competitive industry is in equilibrium at point E_0 at which which short-run supply curve S_0S_0 intersects the demand curve *DD* and determines price equal to P_0 and quantity N_0 of the industry. With price P_0 being given, a firm in the right hand panel (b) is in equilibrium at the minimum point of average total cost curve $SATC_0$ and producing output Q_0.

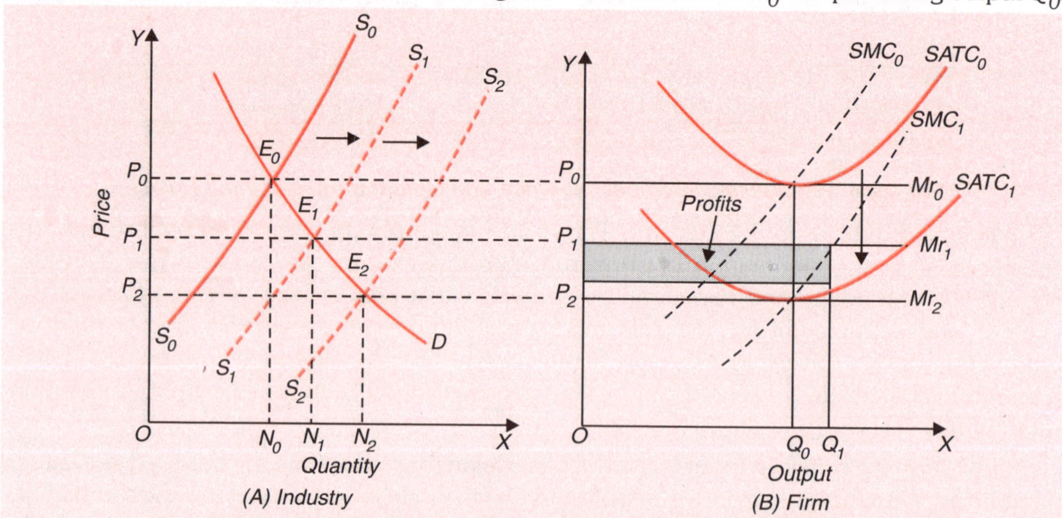

Fig. 29.5. *Response of Equilibrium Price and Quantity in a Competitive Industry to Fall In Prices of Inputs*

Now suppose that prices of inputs used in the industry fall that causes a downward shift in the cost curves to $SATC_1$ and SMC_1. With this the firms will supply a greater quantity of the product at the same price (or the same quantity of the product at a lower price). Since the short-run industry supply curve is summation of short-run marginal cost curves of firms, it will shift to the right to S_1S_1 (dotted) as will be seen from panel (a). The new supply curve S_1S_1 intersects the given demand curve *DD* at point E_1 and determines lower price P_1 and greater quantity N_1 Now, given the lower price P_1 the firms will equate it with their new short-run marginal cost curve SMC_1 (dotted) and produce output Q_1 It will be seen from panel (b) of Figure 29.5 producing output Q_1 at new price P_1 with lower costs, the firms will be making profits as shown by the shaded area in this short-run situation. Thus in the short run, the benefits of fall in costs due to decline in input prices are shared between the consumers and producers. The consumers gain because ***they have now to pay lower price for the***

product and the firms (i.e. producers) gain from making profits. It is worth noting that price of the product in the short run has not fallen by the full amount of the decline in costs. If price had fallen equal to the decline in cost, it would have declined from P_0 *to* P_2. Instead, in the short run price has fallen to P_1 only and therefore the firms are making profits in the short run due to greater decline in costs.

However, since in a competitive industry there is freedom of entry in the long run, lured by the economic profits earned by the existing firms in the short run new firms will enter the industry. As the new firms enter the industry, the short-run supply curve of the industry in panel (a) will shift further to the right. The new firms will continue to enter the industry until supply curve has shifted to S_2S_2. This new supply curve S_2S_2 intersects the given demand curve *DD* at point E_2 and determine price P_2 and quantity N_2 *of* the industry and, as will be observed from panel (b) of Figure 29.5, with price P_2 the firm is in equilibrium at the minimum point of the new short-run average cost curve $SATC_1$ and producing output Q_0. Note that where the output of firms remains the same at Q_0, supply by industry has increased because of entry of more firms to produce the product. The profits of the firms have been competed away in the long run due to entry of new firms as the price of the product has fallen by the full amount of the fall in cost. ***We conclude that under perfect competition in the long run benefits of lower costs due to fall in input prices have been fully passed on to the consumers in the form of lower price of the product and increase in output.***

RESPONSE OF PRICE AND OUTPUT OF THE COMPETITIVE INDUSTRY TO CHANGES IN TECHNOLOGY

Another important practical issue of pricing under perfect competition is how equilibrium price and output will change as a result of changes in technology. This issue can be examined at two levels. First, what is the response of price and output of a commodity when there occurs a single *once-for-all change in technology*. Second, what is the response of price and output when there is *continual changes in technology* that lowers cost per unit of output of a commodity. We analyse here the response of price and output to a *once-for-all change* in technology.

A Once-for-all Change in Technology

Industries often experience change in technology that results in lower cost of production. New techniques cannot put into use if investment in new plant and equipment embodying new technology is not made. Therefore, it takes time for a technological advance to spread through an industry. Suppose before the technological change occurs, the competitive industry is in long-run equilibrium with each firm making only normal profits *(i. e.* are in equilibrium with zero economic profits). Now suppose a technological change occurs which lowers cost curves of newly built plants. Since before the technological change competitive industry is in long-run equilibrium and therefore price is equal to average costs of the firms, the technological advance that lowers cost curves of newly built plants will enable the new firms which install new plants to make economic profits. The firms with old plants cannot make use of the new technology because it is not economically efficient to discard old plants if prevailing price exceeds average variable cost of production. Some firms whose plants are on the verge of being replaced will be quick to adopt the new improved technology. Thus, as a result of new firms building up new plants embodying new technology, their cost curves will shift downward. With lower costs, the firms will be willing to supply a larger quantity at the given price. Besides, initially since the price was equal to average cost, the lower cost will yield profits to the firms. Thus, the setting up of new plants embodying new technology will lead to the expansion in productive capacity.

As a result, the industry's short-run supply curve will shift to the right and lower price of the product. With the fall in price, profits of the firms with new plants will decline. This expansion in productive capacity and fall in price will continue until the new price as determined by demand and supply is once again equal to average total cost of production and profits are eliminated.

When firms having old plans are not able to cover even variable costs, they will scrap them and build a plant with new technology. Ultimately, the new long-run equilibrium will be established when all firms are using the new technology and price has become equal to the average total cost of production. This new long-run equilibrium is shown in Figure 29.6 where initially demand curve *DD* and supply curve S_1 of the industry determine price equal to P_1

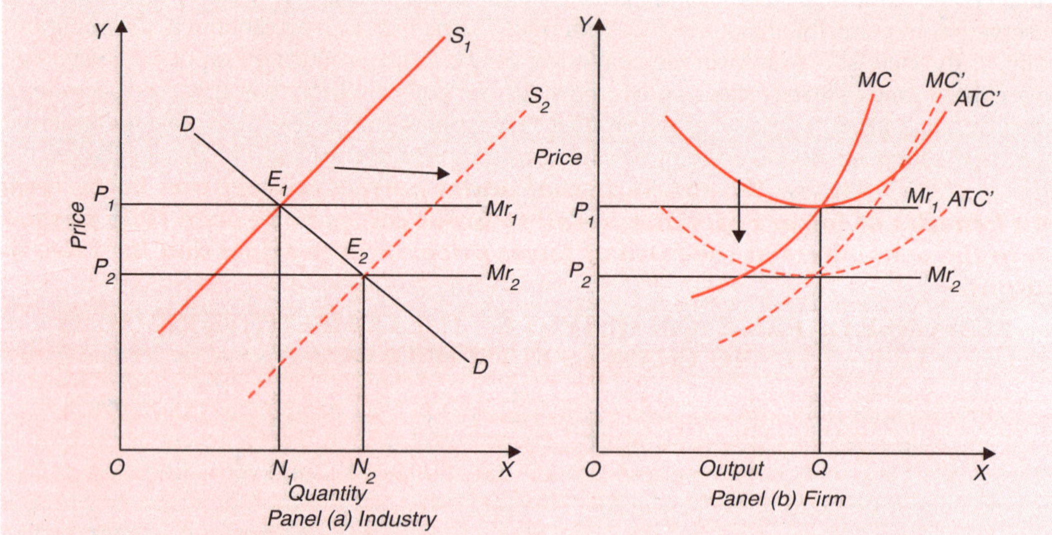

Fig. 29.6. *Long-run Adjustment to a Change in Technology*

which is equal to minimum average total cost of firms each of which is producing output *OQ*. Now suppose a once-for-all new technological change occurs causing average total cost curve and corresponding marginal cost curve to shift downward to the new dotted positions. With the expansion in capacity as a result of new technology supply curve of the industry shifts to S_2 which with the intersection of given demand curve determines price equal to P_2 which is equal to the minimum of new average total cost curve *ATC'* (dotted). Thus, a single once-for-all change in technology has resulted in lower price P_2 and a larger output N_2. [See panel (a) of Fig. 29.6.). Thus the benefits of new technology has been fully passed on to the consumers in the form of lower price and greater output for consumption.

QUESTIONS FOR REVIEW

1. What is meant by equilibrium of the industry ? How would you derive short-run supply curve of the competitive industry ?
2. What are external economies and external diseconomies? Give some examples. What role do they play in determining the long-run supply curve of a competitive industry ?
3. Derive long-run supply curve of (a) increasing-cost industry and *(b)* constant-cost industry working under conditions of perfect competition.
4. Suppose there is a permanent increase in demand for a product produced under conditions of

perfect competition. How will it affect (a) market price, *(b)* short-run price and *(c)* long-run price. Assume increasing-cost industry and illustrate diagrammatically.

5. Under what conditions long-run supply curve of a competitive industry can slope downward? If in such an industry demand for the product increases, how will its price change in (a) the short run and *(b)* the long-run? Illustrate diagrammatically.

6. Explain how it is possible for an industry to be a constant cost industry though each firm in the industry has increasing marginal costs.

7. "The supply curve is strictly speaking a concept which is usually relevant only for the case of pure (or perfect) competition" (Baumol). Explain.

8. It seems reasonable to conclude that the long-run supply curve of a typical competitive industry is upward sloping. Discuss.

9. Explain how will price and output of a competitive industry respond to (a) rise in prices of. inputs and *(b)* fall in prices of inputs. How will consumers and producers be affected in each case ?

10. How does an advance in technology affect price and output of a competitive industry ? To what extent the benefits of technological progress are passed on to the consumers ?

CHAPTER

30

Existence and Stability of Equilibrium Under Perfect Competition

Thus far, in our analysis of market equilibrium under perfect competition, we have implicitly assumed that a unique *stable* equilibrium exists. In the present chapter after briefly explaining the meaning of existence and uniqueness of equilibrium we shall make a detailed study of the conditions of stability of market equilibrium in both static and dynamic senses. Further, we shall explain these concepts with partial equilibrium analysis of demand and supply.

Existence of Equilibrium

Market equilibrium does not always exist at a positive price-quantity combination. Two possibilities of such non-existence of equilibrium are illustrated in Figure 30.1 where demand and supply curves do not intersect. In panel (a) of this figure the supply curve *SS* lies above the demand curve *DD* in the first quadrant of the two axes which shows the quantity demanded is

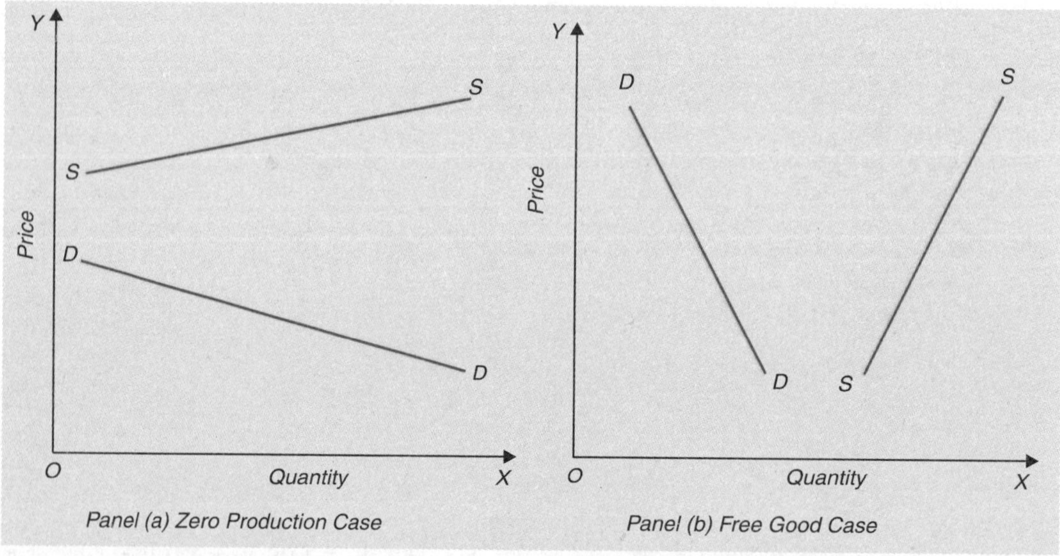

Fig. 30.1. Cases where market equilibrium does not exist

not equal to quantity supplied at any positive price-quantity combination. Since in this case supply price exceeds demand price at every positive quantity, no equilibrium exists in this case. Of course, theoretically it is conceivable that if demand and supply curves in panel *(a)* are extended to the left of the *Y*-axis, they might intersect in the second quadrant which would indicate the negative quantity of the good being supplied and bought which does not have any economic significance.

The demand for and supply of the good depicted in panel (a) of Figure 30.1 shows that the price which the consumers are willing to pay for the good is not enough to cover the cost incurred by the producers for their production. Thus, this case in which demand-supply equilibrium does not exist at a positive quantity shows that the good will not be produced. It is worth noting that the supply curve of a good lying above its demand curve implies that marginal cost of producing it is too high as compared to the demand price for it, that is, amount of money which people are willing to pay for it. This means that though it is technically possible to produce the commodity but it is not profitable to produce it and therefore it will not be produced. For example, though it is technically feasible to produce a pure gold car or pure gold lunch box, it will not be produced because its price will be too high that no one will demand it. Therefore, such commodities are not found in the market.

On the other hand, we find case of highly useful commodities which are available in such abundance in nature that marginal cost of production of a very large quantity of them is zero. Unless demand for them is too large, consumers can have them as much as they like free of charge. Therefore, such goods are called *free goods.* Air and water are chief examples of free goods. The case of free goods is depicted in panel *(b)* of Figure 30.2 where also demand and supply curves do not intersect. -***In this case of free goods, quantity supplied exceeds quantity demanded for every positive price of the good.*** Although air containing oxygen is very useful but it does not command a positive price because it is available in plenty in nature. Similarly, water in villages and towns is generally available in abundance and is a free good there, but in big cities like Delhi, because of the need for its purification and transportation and the expenses incurred on them, its marginal cost is positive and therefore water in big cities like Delhi has some small price (Note that it is because of the costs incurred on purifying and transporting Jamuna water that MCD in Delhi charges price for it).

We thus see from our above analysis that in the above two types of cases : (a) the goods which are not produced at all, and *(b)* the free goods where equilibrium between demand and supply does not exist, we can meaningfully interpret them.

Multiple Equilibria

Another problem concerning market equilibrium is that although it may *exist,* it may not

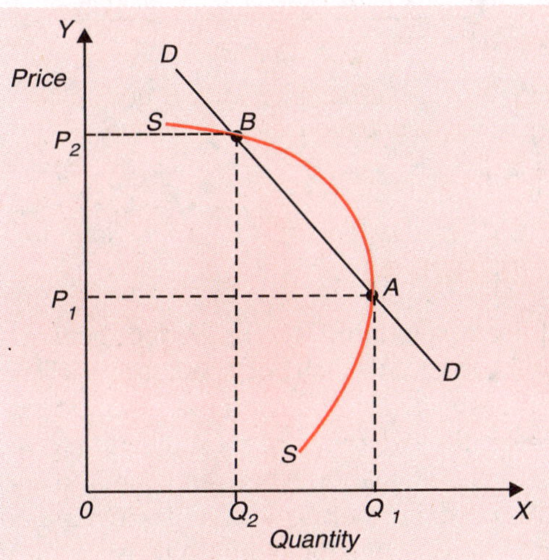

Fig. 30.2. *Supply curve bends backward: equilibrium is not unique.*

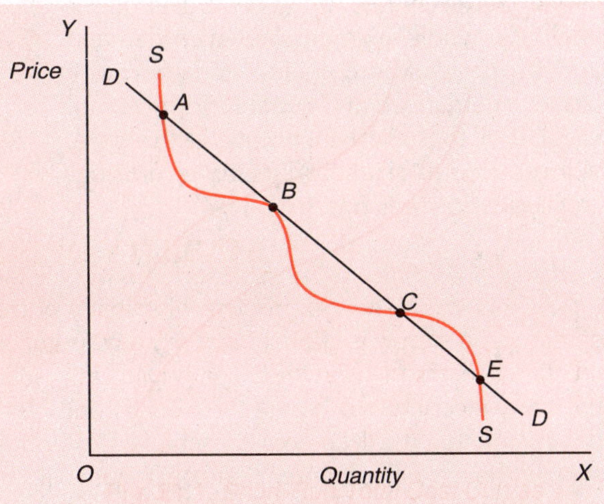

Fig. 30.3. *Multiple Equilibria*

be unique. That is, more than one equilibrium between demand and supply may exist at positive price-quantity combinations. Figure 30.2 illustrates one case in which equilibrium exists at two positive price-quantity combinations. In this, whereas demand curve *DD* is downward sloping throughout its length, the supply curve *SS* bends backward at higher prices. At two points *A* and *B* quantity demanded equals quantity supplied. Some evidences have been obtained which indicates supply curve of labour is backward-bending in some labour markets, especially in developing countries. It has been found that supply of labour increases in the beginning as wage rate rises but beyond a point with further increases in the wage rate it declines, that is, supply curve bends backward. As will be explained in a later chapter that at lower wage rates income of workers is low and therefore with the increase in the wage rate, they are induced to work for more hours and also more workers are attracted to work and offer their labour supply. But beyond a sufficiently high wage rate, if wage rate further rises, income of the workers increases to such an extent that they begin to prefer leisure to further earning more income. That is why labour supply curve bends backward at relatively higher wage rates. The problem in this case is that one cannot be certain out of these two equilibrium points where (*i.e.* at price P_1 or P_2) the market will settle.

Another case of multiple equilibria is illustrated in Figure 30.3 where both demand and supply have negative slopes but demand curve is sloping downward with a constant slope whereas supply curve has different slopes at different price ranges so that it intersects or meets the demand curve at three points. Thus in Figure 30.3, there are three points at which equilibrium between demand and supply exists. So in this case top it is theoretically inconclusive at which point the equilibrium will settle in the market. Another interesting case is presented in Figure 30.4 where there is whole range of vertical points (that is, a whole segment) at which demand and supply curves coincide and therefore quantity demanded and quantity supplied are equal at all these vertical points. In this case, whereas equilibrium quantity is unique, equilibrium price is not.

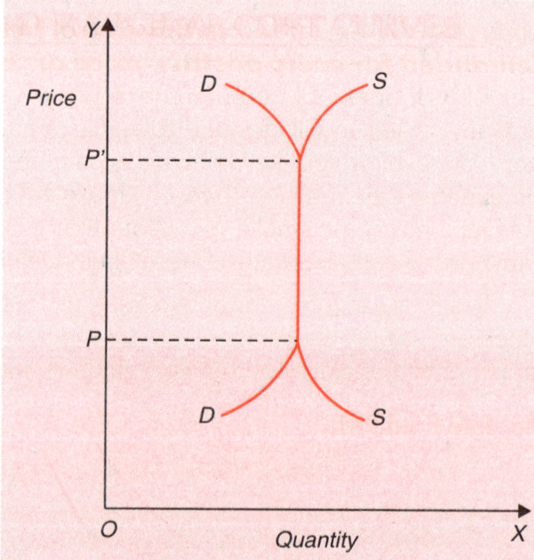

Fig. 30.4. *Equilibrium quantity is unique but equilibrium price is not unique*

STABILITY OF EQUILIBRIUM

We now turn to the problem of stability of market equilibrium. The equilibrium between demand and supply is attained at a price-quantity combination at which both buyers and sellers are satisfied about what they are buying and selling respectively and therefore they do not have any incentive to change their behaviour. However, the *existence* of an equilibrium does not ensure that it will be actually achieved. When there is disequilibrium between demand and supply, there is no guarantee that equilibrium will be restored. Furthermore, changes in demand due to changes in preferences of the consumers and changes in supply due to technological changes or variation in factor prices often occur which disturb the equilibrium. These changes either in demand or supply will define new equilibrium price but there is no guarantee that the new equilibrium price will be reached. Thus, when actual price differs from the equilibrium price due to certain disturbances, it is very relevant to ask whether some forces will come into operation which would cause the price to return to the equilibrium level. ***The equilibrium is stable, if following a disturbance in it, the equilibrium is established again, and unstable if the system tends to move away from the equilibrium situation.*** Whether or not equilibrium is restored when it is disturbed depends on the behaviour of the agents that is, buyers and sellers. For example, if market behaviour of buyers is such that they tend to bid up the price when quantity demanded exceeds the quantity supplied at a given price and the behaviour of sellers is such that they tend to lower it when the quantity supplied of a commodity is greater than quantity demanded of it, the equilibrium will be stable if it exists.

If demand curve is downward sloping *(i.e.* has a negative slope) and supply curve is upward sloping *(i. e.* has a positive slope) as is normally the case, the equilibrium between demand and supply, if it exists, will be stable. This is illustrated in Figure 30.5. At price P_1 the quantity supplied exceeds quantity demanded, (that is, at price P_1, excess demand is negative $ED < 0$). This means at price P_1 the sellers would not be able to sell the quantity they would like, that is, disequilibrium exists. According to the profit-maximising behaviour, in these circumstances the sellers would cut down production and bid down price until price P_0 is reached at which demand and supply are again in equilibrium. On the other land, if price is P_2 in Figure 30.5, the quantity demanded exceeds quantity supplied (that excess demand ED is positive), buyers would push up the price until P_0 is reached. Thus, with negatively sloping demand curve and positively sloping supply curve equilibrium when exists is stable as market price when disturbed moves toward equilibrium due to the assumed behaviour of buyers and sellers.

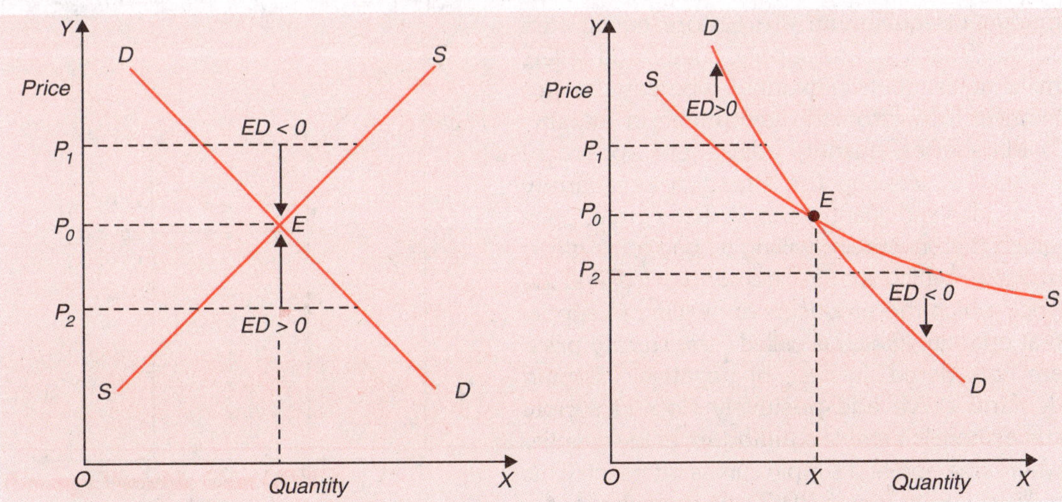

Fig. 30.5. *Stable Equilibrium* **Fig. 30.6.** *Unstable Equilibrium*

In Figure 30.6 both demand and supply curves are negatively sloping but the supply curve is less steep as compared to the demand curve. In this situation quantity demanded equals quantity supplied at price P_0. If the market price is initially at this equilibrium level P_0, it will stay there unless there is some external disturbance. However, if due to some disturbance, price happens to be P_1 which is above the equilibrium price P_0, quantity demanded exceeds quantity supplied (that is, $ED > 0$ where ED stands for excess demand), Now, given the behaviour pattern of buyers, they would tend to bid up the price and therefore the market price instead of returning to the equilibrium level P_0, will tend to move away from it. This shows the equilibrium at price P_0 in Fig. 30.6 is unstable. On the other hand, in Figure 30.6

if due to some disturbance, price happens to be P_2, which is below the equilibrium price, the quantity supplied exceeds the quantity demanded (that is, $ED < 0$), the sellers will tend to lower the price and price will not go up to the equilibrium level but will move away from it. This again shows the equilibrium at P_0 in Figure 30.6 represents unstable equilibrium.

Walrasian Price Adjustment and Marshallian Quantity Adjustment

Due to a certain external disturbance market may go out of equilibrium. This creates an adjustment in the market. But whether adjustment is made in price or quantity has been a controversial issue. Walras thought that it is price which is adjusted. When current price is below the equilibrium price, price is bid up and when current price is above the equilibrium, it is bid down. These changes in price are made on the basis of information from market about the nature of excess demand as to whether it is positive or negative (*i. e* $ED > 0$ or $ED < 0$).

It is useful to express mathematically Walrasian adjustment mechanism which considers adjustment in price over time when there is disequilibrium. Let $D(P)$ represent quantity demanded and $S(P)$ represent quantity supplied. Thus

$$\frac{dP}{dt} = D(P) - S(P) = ED(P) > 0$$

Thus, according to Walras, if $ED(P) > 0$, price goes up, that is, if quantity demanded exceeds quantity supplied, price will rise. On the contrary, if quantity demanded is less than quantity supplied, *i.e.* $ED(P) < 0$, price will fall.

On the other hand, according to Marshall it was quantity which was adjusted in case of market disequilibrium. To restore equilibrium between demand and supply, buyers and sellers make adjustments in quantity, whereas changes in prices follow from the adjustments in quantity. In Marshallian quantity adjustment approach, instead of viewing the situation as quantity demanded and quantity supplied *at a price,* price which the buyers are willing to pay for *a given quantity* (which is *called demand price)* and the price which the producers are willing to supply that quantity (which is called ' the *supply price* are considered. In case of negatively sloping demand curve and positively sloping supply curve, there is *a stable equilibrium* at the quantity where demand and supply curves intersect. This is illustrated in Figure 30.7. At the quantity Q_0 at which demand and supply curves intersect (that is, demand price equals supply price at the quantity Q_0), market equilibrium is reached and this equilibrium is stable even according to Marshallian approach, as was the case in Walrasian price adjustment approach. For example, suppose the quantity Q_1 is being produced and sold. It will be observed from figure 30.7 that for quantity Q_1, demand price which is equal to Q_1H exceeds the supply price which is equal to Q_1G (the price at which producers are willing to sell quantity Q_1 and which depends upon the marginal cost of production). Therefore, it is profitable for the producers to increase the quantity produced, and this adjustment in quantity continues until the quantity Q_0 is reached where demand price becomes equal to supply price. Further,

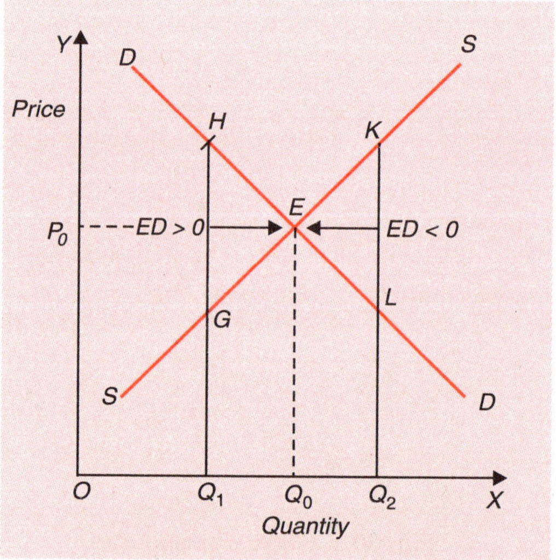

Fig. 30.7. *Stability of Equilibrium and Marshallian Quantity Adjustment*

it will be observed from Fig. 30.7 that if quantity happens to be Q_2, demand price at it is equal to Q_2L which is less than the supply price Q_2K at it. As a result, quantity will be reduced to the equilibrium quantity Q_0. This shows, according to Marshallian quantity adjustment approach, *equilibrium, at quantity* Q_0 in Figure 30.7 is *stable,* as was so under Walrasian price adjustment approach in this case of negatively-sloping demand curve and positively sloping supply curve.

However, in case of both demand and supply curves sloping downward with supply curve being less steep, as shown in Figure 30.8, the two approaches lead to different results. In this case whereas according to *Walrasian price adjustment, equilibrium is found to be unstable, under Marshallian quantity adjustment, the equilibrium at Q in Figure 30.8 is stable*. It will be seen from Figure 30.8 that if current quantity of commodity produced is Q_1 demand price exceeds supply price at it with the result that this would tend to increase the quantity until Q_0 is reached. On the contrary, if at any time output happens to be Q_2, demand price is less than supply price. Consequently, producers would be induced to reduce the quantity to Q_0 where demand price equals supply price and therefore quantity adjustment ceases.

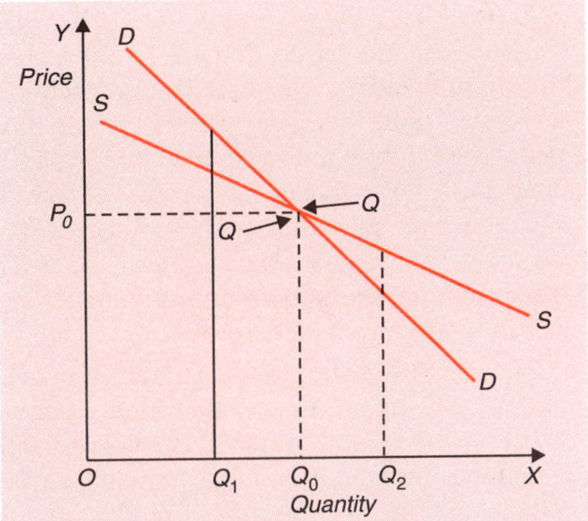

Fig. 30.8. *Under Marshallian Quantity Adjustment Approach, Equilibrium at Q_0 is Stable, under Walras Price Adjustment Approach equilibrium is Unstable.*

Let demand price at a quantity (Q) be denoted by $D^{-1}(Q)$ and supply price by $S^{-1}(Q)$, then $\frac{dQ}{dt}$ would show the change of quantity over time. In these mathematical terms, Marshallian adjustment mechanism can be mathematically expressed as follows,

$$\frac{dQ}{dt} = k\,[D^{-1}(Q) - S^{-1}(Q)] = k\,[(ED)^{-1}],\ k > 0$$

k being greater than zero means demand price exceeds supply price and as a result quantity increases. On the contrary, if k is less than zero ($k < 0$), demand price will be less than supply price, and the quantity will be reduced.

Static Stability Vs Dynamic Stability

Two types of stability of equilibrium may be distinguished. As mentioned above, when an equilibrium is disturbed, it creates an adjustment process in the market. For example, if price is below the equilibrium level, some buyers bid up the price leading to the restoration of equilibrium. Static analysis of stability does not consider how price and quantity change or adjust *through time* when there is disequilibrium between demand and supply; it merely considers the nature of change or tendencies that exist as to whether the market moves towards or away from equilibrium. It is important to note that stability conditions are derived from assuming a certain behaviour pattern on the part of buyers and sellers. We have made static analysis of stability of equilibrium and distinguished between Walrasian and Marshallian condition of static stability. We now turn to explain dynamic stability of equilibrium.

Dynamic stability considers how price and quantity change through time when the system is thrown into disequilibrium state. In other words, starting from a disequilibrium state, the dynamic analysis of stability investigates the *time path of the adjustment process* of the movement of price and quantity towards the equilibrium levels. It always takes time for the adjustment to be made in price and quantity and therefore instantaneous adjustment to the new equilibrium is not feasible. The process of dynamic adjustment is often explained through what is called recontracting model. According to this, buyers and sellers enter into series of provisional contracts about price and quantity until they reach a final equilibrium situation when recontracting ceases. Let us explain this recontracting in some greater detail.

Suppose that at an initial price, the quantity demanded by buyers is not equal to the quantity supplied, that is, there is, disequilibrium. Adjustment process starts and recontracting takes place. If at the new price there is still a discrepancy between demand and supply, the price will be further changed by what is called an auctioneer — a middle man through whom contracts are being made. This process of recontracting continues and price bids go on changing from period to period over the course of time until equilibrium price is reached at which quantity demanded equals quantity supplied. Thus, "equilibrium is stable in the dynamic sense *if the price converges to (or approximates the equilibrium over time* ; it is unstable if the price change is away from equilibrium".[1]

Dynamic stability not only depends on the *slopes* of demand and supply curves as does the static stability but also on the *margnitude* by which the market adjusts to the disequilibrium between demand and supply. It has been found that quite often there is overadjustment to the discrepancy between quantity demanded and supplied until right adjustment finally occurs over a period of time. For instance, if the equilibrium price of a commodity is Rs. 20/- but buyers actually bid for Rs. 15/-for it in the first instance and as a result positive excess demand emerges at this price. Now, realising the creation of excess demand *(i. e.* shortage of commodity at this lower price), the buyers overestimate the adjustment needed and bid a higher price, say Rs. 22/-, in the next period. Though each adjustment is made in the right direction but is larger in magnitude than needed for restoration of equilibrium. Thus dynamic analysis of stability also considers the *magnitude of reactions* to disturbances or imbalances.

Dynamic Stability with Lagged Adjustment : Cobweb Model

We shall now explain the notion of dynamic stability with a well known theorem often refered to as cobweb model. Cobweb theorem is the simplest model of economic dynamics when equilibrium reached over time between demand, supply and price is investigated. Producers' supply function (curve) shows how producers adjust their output to changes in price. At a higher price, they respond to produce more and at a lower price they cut down their production. But this adjustment in production in response to changes in price does not occur instantaneously but takes a good deal of time. Thus, there is a *time lag* between a change in price and appropriate adjustment in supply in response to it. The time gap between the decision to change the quantity supplied in response to a given price and its actually being supplied is known as *supply lag*. The supply lag is often found in case of agricultural commodities, animal rearing etc. For instance, it takes four-five months for wheat crop to be grown and raised.

It should be noted that the supply lag often result in *cyclical movements or oscillations* in price and quantity over time. The dynamic analysis of stability investigates whether these oscillations coverage to the equilibrium values or move away from them.

Cobweb Model. Let us explain the dynamics of cobweb model. We consider the market for wheat as an example of a market where the supply of wheat is a lagged function of price.

1. J. M. Henderson, R. E. Quandt, *Microeconomic Theory,* 2nd ed. 1971. p. 136 (Italics added) Note that dynamic stability has been defined in this quotation according to Walrasian condition of stability. In terms of Marshallian condition, dynamic stability can be defined in terms of the convergence of quantity through time to the equilibrium level.

In order to keep our analysis simple we assume that there is a one-year lag in the response of quantity supplied of wheat to a given market price of it. Thus

$$S_t = (P_{t-1})$$

which means that the quantity of wheat supplied in a year t depends on the price prevailing in the previous period (P_{t-1}). Further, in accordance with this the present year price (*i.e* P_1) will determine the quantity supplied in the next period (*i.e.* S_{t+1}).

On the side of demand function there is no lag, that is, the quantity demanded of this year depends on price of this year. The equilibrium price in any year is determined at the level at which the quantity ucmanded in any year t equals the quantity supplied in that year t. This means the price in a period adjusts to bring about equality in the quantity demanded in the year (D_t) and the quantity supplied in that year (S) which of course in this model is determined by the price prevailing in the previous year. It should be noted that there is perfectly inelastic supply in any year as in case of agricultural commodities like wheat no more quantity can be grown until next year to augment supply. Thus in any year t

$$D_t = S_t \text{ or, } D_t - S_t = 0 \qquad ...(1)$$

This is the equilibrium situation brought about by adjustment in price in a year. In any year there is clearing of the market, that is, no producer is left with unsold stocks and no consumer with unsatisfied demand. Possible time paths of change in price and consequently the nature of oscillations depends upon the particular demand and supply functions. The demand and supply functions according to cobweb model can be written as :

$$D_t = bP_t + a \qquad ....(i)$$

$$S_t = gP_{t-1} + C \qquad ....(ii)$$

where b and a in the demand function are constants ; whereas b is a slope coefficient showing relation between price of a commodity and demand for it, a is the constant intercept term. Similarly, g and C in the supply functions are constants ; whereas g denotes the slope coefficient showing the relation between price of a commodity and the quantity supplied which is forthcoming at it and C is the intercept term of this supply function.[2]

2. The possible time paths of price can be expressed mathematically as under :

Reproducing the demand and supply functions :

$$D_t = bP_t + a \qquad ....(i)$$

$$S_t = gP_{t-1} + C \qquad ....(ii)$$

In equilibrium

$$D_t - S_t = 0 \qquad ....(iii)$$

or,

$$bP_t + a - gP_{t-1} - C = 0$$

Solving for P_t we have

$$P_t = -\frac{a}{b} + \frac{gP_{t-1}}{b} + \frac{C}{b}$$

$$P_t = \frac{C-a}{b} + \frac{g}{b}P_{t-1} \qquad ....(iv)$$

Suppose to start with price $P = P_0$ when t = 0, the solution of the first order difference equation (iv) is

$$P_t = (P_0 - \frac{C-a}{b-g}\left(\frac{g}{b}\right)^t + \frac{C-a}{b-g} \qquad ....(v)$$

The above equation (v) describes the path of price over time. The equilibrium is dynamically stable if $P_t = P_{t-1} \rightarrow P_0$ as $t \rightarrow \infty$. If the absolute value of the slope of supply curve (*i.e.* $\frac{1}{|g|}$) is greater than that of demand curve (*i.e.* $\frac{1}{|b|}$), the price will tend towards the equilibrium price level and we will have a case of damped oscillations.

Now, the path of price as a function of time depends on the absolute values of the slope coefficient of the demand function [*i.e.* b in (i) above] and the slope coefficient of supply function (*i.e.* g in (*ii*) above)[2]. If the slope of the supply curve *i.e.* $\frac{1}{|g|}$ is greater (in absolute value) than the slope of the demand curve *i.e.* $\frac{1}{(a)}$ (that is, supply curve is *steeper* than the demand curve), we get the case of *damped oscillations,* which as will be seen from Figure 30.9 appears like a cobweb. Figure 30.9 describes the time path of price and quantity as we start from price-quantity combination (P_1, Q_1) Let us explain this path of price in greater detail. It will be seen from Figure 30.9 that demand and supply curves intersect at price P_0 and Q_0 which are therefore equilibrium quantity.

Suppose there is a disturbance such as drought which causes the output (quantity) of wheat to fall to Q_1. Now, with Q_1 as the quantity supplied and given the demand curve *DD,* the price P_1 is determined. From the supply curve *S* in Figure 30.9, it will be observed that at price P_1 the quantity supplied Q_2 will be forthcoming in the next year t_2. With Q_2 as the supply and the demand curve *DD* price P_2 is determined. Thus price falls from P_1 in year 1 to price P_2 in year 2. Now, as will be observed from Figure 30.9 price P_2 will induce the supply Q_3 in the next year 3. With Q_3 as the quantity supplied and demand curve *DD,* the price P_3 is the equilibrium price in period 3. This will further cause a change in supply in the next period and bringing about further change in price. But, as will be seen from Figure 30.9 price is oscillating but it damps, that is, tending towards the equilibrium price P_0. It is thus clear that in the present case when the absolute slope of the supply curve exceeds that of the demand curve we have damped oscillations in price, that is, price fluctuates but over a time it tends to move towards the equilibrium level. Therefore, the **cobweb model of damped oscillations represents the case of *stable dynamic equilibrium.*** It will be seen from panel (*b*) of Figure 30.9 which directly depicts the time path of price over the years and shows that over time the price tends to converge to the equilibrium level.

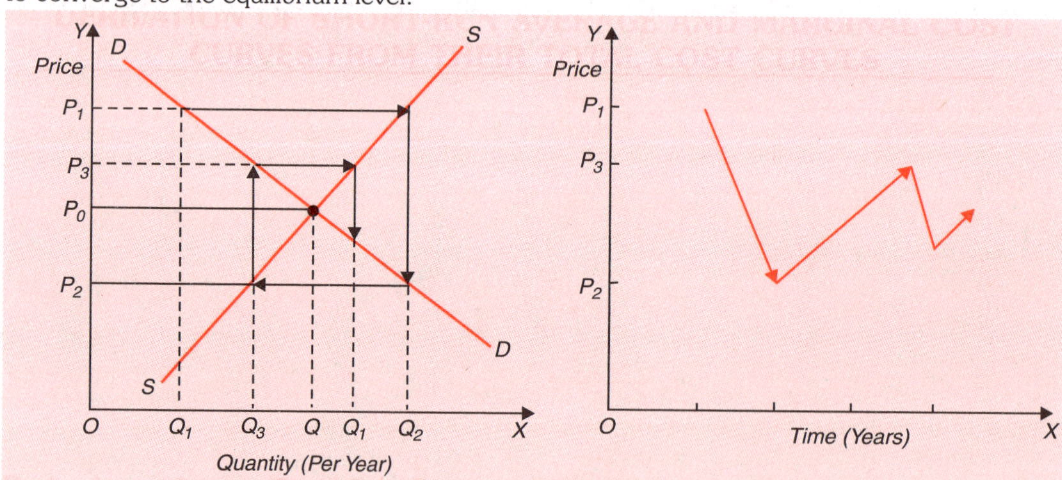

Fig. 30.9. *Damped Oscillations : Stable Dynamic Equilibrium*

Perpetual Oscillations. If the absolute slopes of the supply and demand curves are equal, we will get a cobweb model of perpetual oscillations as shown in Figure 30.10. The equal slopes ot supply and demand curves in economic sense imply that the response of quantity demanded and supplied to the changes in price is the same. Consider Figure 30.10. To start with, in year 1 the quantity of the good produced is Q_1 and, given the demand curve *DD,* the price P_1, is determined in year 1. Price P_1 in year 1 calls forth quantity produced and supplied

Q_2 in year 2. With Q_2 as the quantity supplied and the demand curve *DD*, a lower price P_2 is determined in year 2. It will be seen from supply curve *SS* that at the lower price P_2, the

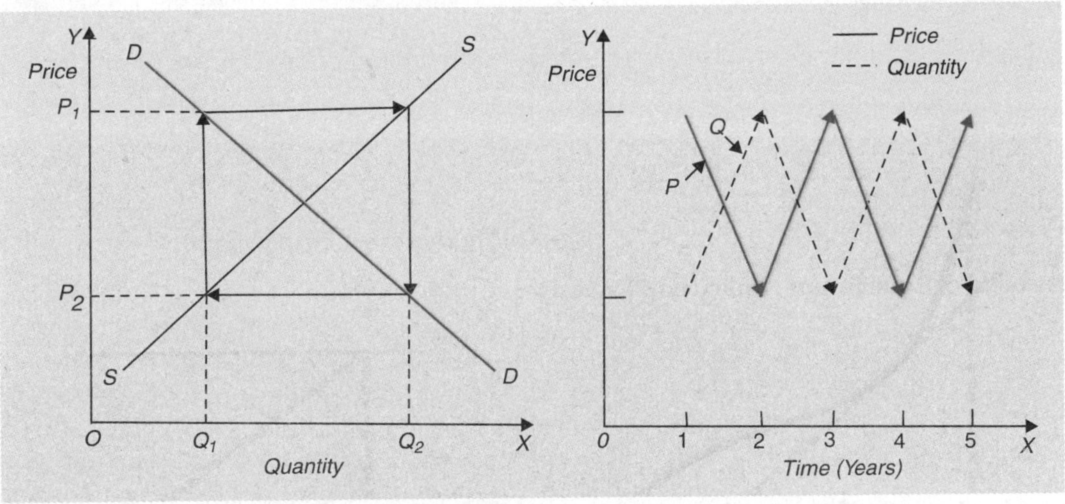

Fig. 30.10. *Cobweb Theorem : Perpetual Oscillations.*

producers reduce the quantity produced and supplied again to Q_1. With Q_1 as the quantity supplied and the demand curve *DD*, price again rises to P_1, in year 3 and so on. The price goes on fluctuating between P_1 and P_2 perpetually and quantity goes on oscillating ceaselessly between Q_1 and Q_2. It should be noted that these perpetual oscillations remain constant in amplitude. As will be seen from Figure 30.10(*b*) that in this case of perpetually oscillations, price and quantity do not move towards equilibrium price and quantity. Therefore, equilibrium once disturbed is never restored. In fact equilibrium is never attained in this case. It should be noted that when quantity is low, price is high, and when quantity is high, price is low.

Explosive Oscillations. Finally, we have cobweb model in which prices and quantities move further away from equilibrium instead of moving towards equilibrium as indicated by the intersection of demand and supply curves. This occurs when the *absolute value* of the slope of

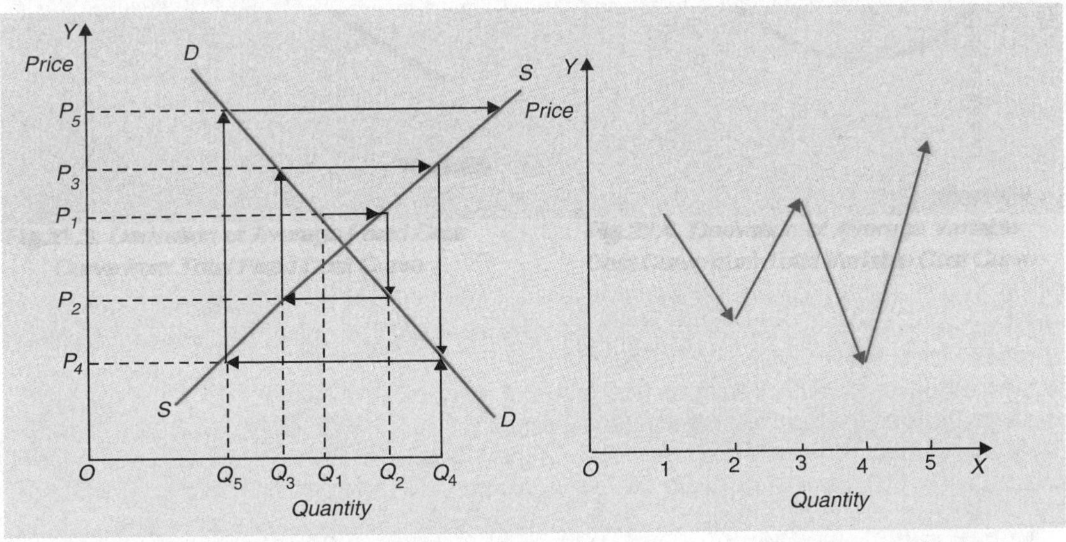

Fig. 30.11. *Cobweb Model: Explosive Oscillations and Unstable Dynamic Equilibrium*

the supply curve is less relative to that of the demand curve. In economic terms this implies that when the supply responds to changes in prices to a greater degree than the demand, the amplitude of oscillatons of price and quantity go on increasing over time and become too much excessive. Therefore, these ever-widening oscillations of price and quantity are called explosive oscillations and are depicted in Fig. 30.11. Starting from price P_1 in year1 it falls to P_2 in year 2 and then it goes up sharply to P_3 in year 3 and then have a drastic decline to P_4 in year 4. The price again rises sharply to P_5 in year 5 and so on. The price movements are also shown in panel *(b)* of Figure 30.11 where as will be seen price tends to move further away from the equilibrium indicated by the intersection of demand and supply curves. Thus, the explosive oscillations model represents an ***unstable dynamic equilibrium.***

Stability of Equilibrium : Policy Implications

The students are likely to gather impression that the discussion cf stability of equilibrium is a futile theoretical exercise without any economic significance. But this is far from truth. The stability of equilibrium of a market has important implications for economic policy. If a competitive market is in stable equilibrium, it implies that it can survive any external disturbances however large and drastic it may be. That is, if any disturbance causes disequilibrium the stable nature of market equilibrium ensures that certain forces will automatically come into play to bring it back into equilibrium. For instance, if due to certain factors, given the demand and supply curves, if price rises, that is, there is inflation in the economy, then if market equilibrium is stable, rise in price will be self-corrected without any interference from the Government. Similarly, if due to some reasons equilibrium is disturbed and consequently there prevail deflation and unemployment, the stability of equilibrium, if it is stable, ensures that the adjustment in wages, prices and labour employment would occur which will bring the market back into equilibrium without unemployment. This is a very important conclusion because if market equilibrium is stable and automatic correction of disequilibrium is possible, theoretically there is no need for Government interference in a free market economy in times of inflation, recession or unemployment.

On the contrary, if market equilibrium is unstable the Government has to play an important role by intervening in the economy to restore equilibrium. The economists who are in favour of market friendly approach tend to argue that less the interference by the Government in the working of a free market private enterprise system, the better it is. However, this argument in favour of free market and private sector is theoretically justified only if the market equilibrium is stable. In case of unstable market disequilibrium free competitive market could collapse under the pressure of either high inflation or recession. In fact, in the real world we witness unstable equilibrium in some commodity markets, labour markets, foreign exchange markets and therefore to rely on self-correction by the market would not be valid. Thus, the Government interference in the economy in case of unstable equilibrium is necessary to achieve equilibrium with stability in prices and to attain higher levels of income and employment.

CHAPTER

31

Kaldor and Sraffa on Incompatibility of Equilibrium with Perfect Competition

Controversy

We have explained earlier the conditions of equilibrium of both the firm and industry under perfect competition. But in case of both the firm as well as industry the question has often been raised as to whether under conditions or assumptions of perfect competition a determinate position of equilibrium really exists. It has been asserted by Piero Sraffa and Nicholas Kaldor that the ***equilibrium under perfect competition is incompatible with the conditions of perfect competition.*** In other words, no determinate position of equilibrium exists under perfect competition. Even if equilibrium position exists, there is no guarantee that it will be stable. In this chapter we will discuss the problem of determinateness of perfectly competitive equilibrium and will bring out under what conditions the equilibrium of the firm and industry is determinate.

Incompatibility of Fim's Equilibrium Under Perfect Competition and Decreasing Costs (Increasing Returns to Scale)

We have explained in the previous chapters that the equilibrium of the firm under perfect competition requires the fulfilment of two conditions. First, for the perfectly competitive firm to be in equilibrium at a level of output, marginal cost must be equal to price (or marginal revenue). Secondly, under perfect competition marginal cost must be *rising* at the equilibrium output. Now, when returns to factors are increasing, that is, when the marginal products of the factors are increasing, then the marginal cost would be declining. When marginal cost is declining throughout, the second order condition for the firm's equilibrium, that is, marginal cost must be rising at the equilibrium output would not be satisfied and therefore the equilibrium cannot exist under such conditions or, so to say, profit-maximising equilibrium output is indeterminate. When marginal cost is declining due to increasing returns, then at a given price which remains constant for a firm under perfect competition, it will be profitable for the firm to go on expanding its output. Therefore, unless the marginal cost curve rises (that is, unless the diminishing returns occur) and cut the marginal revenue curve (which under perfect competition is the same thing as the demand curve faced by an individual firm) from below, equilibrium of the firm is not possible. This is illustrated in Figure 31.1 where marginal cost curve *MC* is falling throughout, At point *F*, equilibrium is not possible though marginal cost is here equal to price (or *MR*). This is because at *F*, marginal cost is declining (or *MC* curve is cutting *MR* curve from above). As will be seen from Figure 31.1, if the firm expands output beyond point *F*, marginal cost becomes less than the price or *MR* and therefore it will be profitable to expand output. As long as *MC* curve is declining and price remains fixed at *OP* (which it does under perfect competition), the firm will continue expanding output until it swallows the whole market and establishes its monopoly. Thus increasing returns to scale for a firm (that is, declining marginal cost) would ultimately lead to the breakdown of perfect competition and establishment of monopoly or oligopoly.It is therefore said that **increasing returns to a firm and perfect competition are incompatible.** Thus, Professor Samuelson writes : "Under persisting decreasing costs for the firms, one or a few of them will "so expand their outputs as to become a significant part of the market for the industry's total output. We shall then end up with one of the following three cases :

(1) a single monopolist who dominates the industry.

(2) a few large sellers who together dominate the industry and who will later be called oligopolists.

(3) some kind of imperfection of competition that, in either a stable way or as a result of a series of intermittent price wars, represents an important departure from the economist's model of "perfect" competition wherein no firm has any control over industry price.[1]

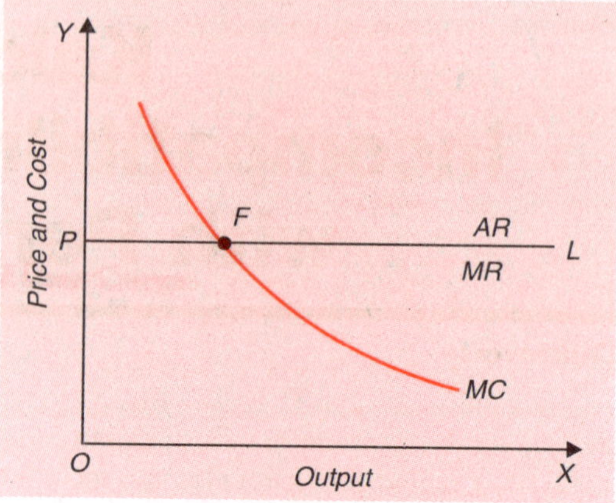

Fig. 31.1. *Incompatibility of Competitive Firm's Equilibrium under Decreasing Marginal Cost*

Incompatibility of Competitive Firm's Equilibrium with Constant Costs (Constant Returns)

Equilibrium of a competitive firm is not possible even under conditions of constant returns (or constant costs). When constant returns to factors prevail, marginal product of the factors remains the same and therefore marginal cost remains constant. If price (or *MR)* that prevails in the market is higher than marginal cost (which it should if the firm is to work in the iong run) then it will be profitable for the firm to go on expanding its output until perfect competition breaks down and monopoly is established. This is illustrated in Figure 31.2 where in the price prevailing in the market is *OH* and the marginal cost is *OK* which due to constant returns remains constant when output is expanded. Since price (or *MR)* remains higher than marginal cost *(MC)* throughout, it will be profitable for the firm to continuously expand its size or output. Therefore, under such circumstances, no equilibrium position exists, or in other words, equilibrium is indeterminate.

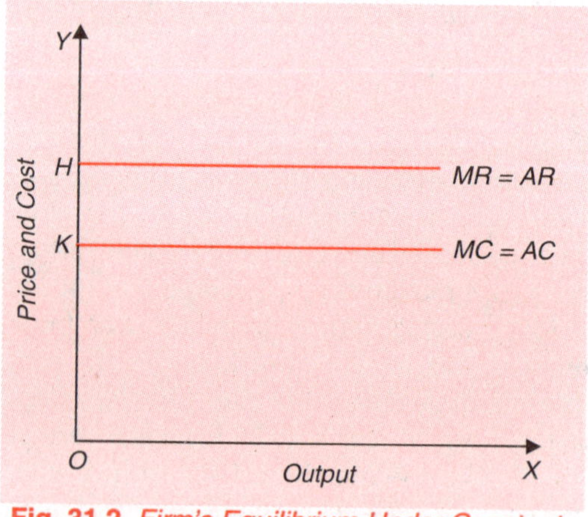

Fig. 31.2. *Firm's Equilibrium Under Constant Costs is Indeterminate.*

It should be noted that in Figure 31.2 nowhere both conditions of equilibrium [(*i*) *MC* = Price and (*ii*) *MC* must be rising at the equilibrium output] are satisfied. In this case, even the equilibrium condition of equality of *MC* with *MR* is not satisfied. We see that ***the equilibrium of the firm under conditions of perfect competition is incompatible even with constant returns or constant costs.***

1. P. A. Samuelson, *Economics,* 8th edition, p. 452.

We therefore conclude that under perfect competition equilibrium of the firm is possible only if marginal cost is rising so that it should cut the horizontal marginal revenue curve from below at the point of equality between *MR* and *MC* as is there at point *E* in Figure 31.3. In Figure 31.3, equilibrium of the firm is established at point *E* or output *OM* at which marginal

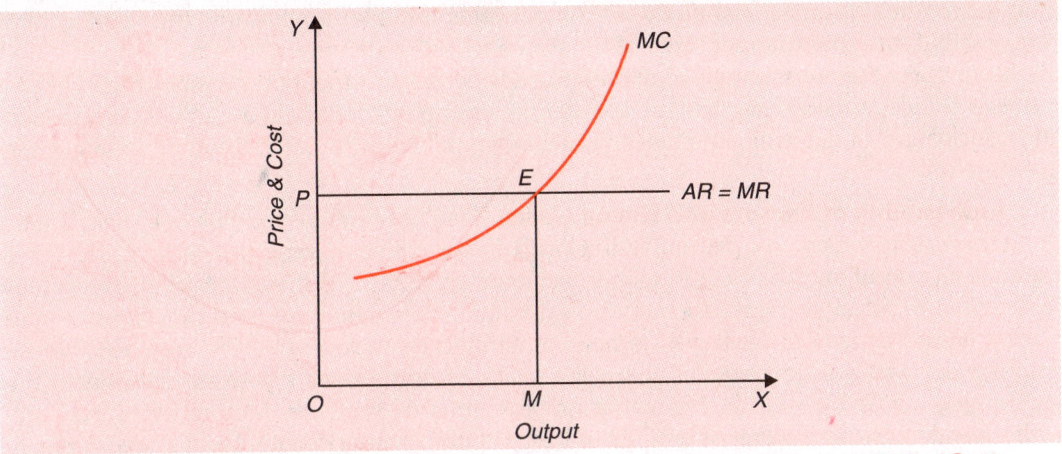

Fig. 31.3. *Determinate Firm's Equilibrium under Perfect Competition with Rising Cost*

cost is equal to marginal revenue and also marginal cost is rising at the point of equilibrium. It is not profitable to expand output beyond *OM* (or point *E*) because after it marginal cost is greater than price or marginal revenue.

Kaldor on Incompatibility of Firm's Long-Run Static Equilibrium with Perfect Competition

Nicholas Kaldor of Cambridge University in his now famous article *"The Equilibrium of the Firm"*[2] put forward the view that a long-run static equilibrium of the firm and perfect competition are incompatible. As we have seen above, the equilibrium of the firm under perfect competition is possible and determinate only when marginal cost is rising *(i.e.,* only under diminishing returns to factors). Now, Kaldor argues that in the long run under perfect competition, ***given static conditions,*** there is nothing which makes the cost curve of the individual firm to rise (relatively to the cost of the industry) and thus makes determinate equilibrium under perfect competition possible.

Kaldor argues that there is no doubt about the possibility of determinate equilibrium *in the short run* under perfect competition, since in the short run some factors are assumed to be fixed and the output is expanded by the increase in the amount of variable factors whose marginal product must decline (*i.e.*, the short-run marginal cost must rise) after a certain level of output due to the operation of the law of variable proportions. He thus writes : "In the short run (by definition) the supply of some factors is assumed to be fixed, and as the price of some other (freely variable) factors is given, costs per unit must necessarily rise after a certain point. (This follows simply from the assumption frequently styled "the law of non-proportional returns)"[3]. Therefore, according to Kaldor, problem of compatibility of equilibrium with the assumptions of perfect competition is ***essentially one of long-run equilibrium*** when all factors which the firm employs are freely variable in supply. It should be noted here that the assumptions of perfect competition are : *(i)* the price of the product is given for the firm ; *(ii)* prices of the factors are given for the firm and remain constant and unchanged when the firm expands its

2. This article by Kaldor was first published in *Economic Journal,* 1934 and is reprinted in Kaldor *"Essays on Value and Distribution"*, Gerald Ducworth and Co. 1960.
3. *Op. cit;* pp. 38-39.

level of output.

Now, it is the contention of Kaldor that ***given the assumptions of perfect competition and given that all factors are freely variable in the long run and all prices are constant, the costs (more particularly marginal cost) cannot rise,*** they must fall or remain constant when the firm expands its size. He enquires into the causes which *can possibly raise* the marginal cost of the firm and put limitation on the size of the firm and therefore make the determinate equilibrium under perfect competition possible. He rules out the possibilities of rise in marginal cost under the assumed conditions of perfect competition and concludes that determinate equilibrium is incompatible with perfect competition even in the long run.

Indivisibility of Factors and Rising Costs. First, he mentions the case of *indivisibilities of factors* due to which cost per unit in the long run falls for some ranges of output as the firm expands its output and then when all the technical economies due to indivisibilities are fully realised, unit cost of production reaches a minimum *after which it rises*. But, according to Kaldor, given that factors are freely variable, other efficient factors would be employed whose employment was not economical at smaller levels of output and therefore once again the economies would be reaped from the indivisibilities of the new factors employed and consequently the cost per unit of product will fall with the growth in output and size of the firm. This minimum unit cost with the new indivisible factors may be the same as with the previous ones. To quote him, with indivisibilities, "beyond a point costs may rise over a certain range, but (if in accordance with our assumptions), factors continue to be available at constant prices, afterwards they must again fall until they once more reach their minimum at the same level as before. The optimum point can then only be reached for certain outputs, but there is no reason why the successive optimum points should not be on the same level of average costs. Indivisibilities causing rising costs over certain ranges thus do not explain the limitation upon the size of the firm so long as ***all factors are freely variable*** and all prices are constant."[4] We thus see that, according to Kaldor, the factor of indivisibilities also cannot account for the rise in unit cost in the long run and therefore cannot make the long-run equilibrium of the firm determinate under perfect competition.

External Diseconomies and Rising Costs. Another factor which, according to Kaldor, can possibly raise unit cost as the size of the firm increases is of external diseconomies. Pecuniary external diseconomies, that is, the rise in factor prices are ruled out by definition, since it is assumed that factor prices remain constant for the firm because of the assumption of perfect competition in the factor market. The other external diseconomies which may arise are the scarcities *i.e.*, limited supplies of those factors which the firm does not directly employ but only indirectly uses them, for example, rising costs to the transporting company due to traffic congestion. But, according to Kaldor, such external diseconomies, even if they exist, are not relevant for the purpose of making long-run equilibrium of the individual firm determinate. This is because, "By definition they (external economies) affect all firms equally and therefore do not explain why the output of the individual firm remains relatively small (the number of firms in the industry relatively large), as they only gave a reason why the costs of the individual firm should be rising, but not why the costs of the individual firm should be ***rising relatively to the costs of the industry.*** The diseconomies therefore—in order that they should account for the limitation upon the size of the firm—must be internal"[5]

Fixity of Entrepreneurship and Rising Costs. Finally, marginal costs of a firm working

4. *Op. cit.*, p. 40.
5. *Op. cit.*, p. 40.

under perfect competition can rise in the long run ***if there is some factor whose supply is fixed even in the long run.*** And further, if conditions of perfect competition are to be preserved, such a fixed factor must be that "whose supply is fixed for the firm should at the same time have a flexible supply for the industry".[6] According to many economists there does exist such a fixed factor for the individual firm even in the long run. This is the factor of entrepreneurship which remains a single fixed factor in a firm and is also of variable supply to the industry as a whole. When with a fixed given unit of entrepreneur whose ability is limited, other factors are increased to expand output, diminishing returns to them occur due to the law of variable proportions and as a result the costs of the individual firm must rise after a certain level of output. "The fact that the firm is productive organisation under a single unit of control explains, therefore, by itself why it cannot expand beyond a certain limit without encountering increasing costs"[7]

But Kaldor does not accept the argument of fixity of entrepreneurship of an individual firm causing the rising costs and thereby make the perfect competition and long-run equilibrium of the firm compatible. He calls the entrepreneurship an ambiguous factor which possesses at least three different meanings. He argues, "what is generally called the "entrepreneurial function" can be either (1) risk or rather uncertainty bearing ; or (2) management which consists of two things : (a) supervision, (b) coordination...... ***which of these three functions can be considered as having a "fixed supply" in the long run"***[8] As regards uncertainty bearing he thinks it cannot have a fixed supply for the individual firm, especially in view of the fact that in corporate business or Joint Stock Company it is possible to spread the bearing of uncertainty over a great number of shareholders.

As far as the 'supervision' part of management is concerned, the firm can expand without loss of efficiency *(i.e.* without rising costs) by appointing more supervisors. As he says, "*is there any reason why it should not be possible to double output by doubling both, foremen and men ? An army of supervisors may be just as efficient (provided it consists of men of equal ability) as one supervisor alone*"[9] But Kaldor admits that the coordinating factor is a fixed factor in an individual firm and this can cause rising cost and thus makes the determinate solution to the firm's long-run equilibrium possible. He regards the coordinating factor as the essential part of the function of management which is concerned with the allocation of resources among the various lines of investment, with the adjustment of the productive concern to the continuous changes of economic data". He adds, "you cannot increase the supply of coordinating ability available to an enterprise alongside an increase in the supply of factors as it is the essence of coordination that every single decision should be made on a comparison with all other decisions already made or likely to be made, it must pass through a single brain. This does not imply, of course, that the task of coordination must necessarily, fall upon a single individual ; in modern business organisation, it may be jointly undertaken by a whole Board of Directors.. ......and it will not be possible at any rate beyond a certain point, to increase the supply of coordinating ability available to that enterprise by enlarging the Board of Directors"[10]. Thus Kaldor concedes that coordinating ability is a fixed and indivisible factor of production. "It is the one factor which in the long run is rigidly attached to the firm who, so to speak, lives and dies with it ; whose remuneration, therefore, is always price-determined".[11]

6. *Op. cit.* p. 41.
7. *Ibid, p. 42.*
8. *Op. cit,* p. 42 (italics mine).
9. *Ibid,* p. 43.
10. Ibid, p.43.
11. *Ibid,* p. 43.

However, according to Kaldor, cost curve is determined by the fixity of the supply of the coordinating ability but he asserts that this ***very fact renders the cost function of the individual firm indeterminate.*** This is because the coordinating ability, that is, the ability to adjust which imparts uniqueness and determinateness to the firm is an ***essentially dynamic function*** and which "is only required so long as adjustments are required; and the extent to which it is required ...... depends on the frequency and the magnitude of the adjustments to be undertaken". ***It is essentially a feature, not of equilibrium but of disequilibrium ;*** it is needed only so long as and in so far as the actual situation in which the firm finds itself deviates from the equilibrium situation"[12]

Kaldor further points -out that when a firm makes successive adjustment to a given data, the further coordinating tasks which are required to be done become less and less until finally in a long-run equilibrium situation coordinating ability is no more needed. In the state of equilibrium only supervision is required, which can be suitably increased and therefore no diseconomies can arise on account of this. Since coordinating ability is not required in the long-run equilibrium situation, any size of the business, however large, can be managed equally well. This, according to Kaldor, makes ***"the technically optimum size of the individual firm infinite (or indeterminate)".*** This means that long-run average cost curve is a horizontal straight line. With a given price under perfect competition and *constant long-run average cost,* the firm will tend to grow indefinitely. With this infinite growth, the firm will ultimately come to exercise a control over the price of the product and therefore will result in the breakdown of perfect competition. This makes the long-run equilibrium of the firm indeterminate. Hence Kaldor concludes that "under static assumption *(i.e.* a given constellation of economic data) there will be a continuous tendency for the size of the firm to grow and therefore ***long-period static equilibrium and perfect competition are incompatible assumptions".***

The above view of Kaldor is based upon the belief that firm's cost function can not be derived from the given economic data regarding factor prices and a given production function because "the relative position which the factor 'coordinating ability' occupies in that production function is not given independently of equilibrium but is a part of the problem of equilibrium itself."

Comments on Kaldor's View : From the above analysis it is clear that Kaldor makes the long-run cost function indeterminate by treating the factor of entrepreneurial and coordinating ability in a particular way. This particular treatment of entrepreneurial factor is not generally accepted by most of the modern economists. Most of the modern economists think that due to difficulties of management, coordination and control long-run cost curve of a firm slopes upward after a certain level of output. This rising cost curve puts a limit to the size of the firm working under conditions of perfect competition and makes the long-run equilibrium of the firm possible under it.

SRAFFA ON INCOMPATIBILITY OF COMPETITIVE EQUILIBRIUM WITH INCREASING RETURNS

Compatibility of increasing returns with the conditions of perfect competition has been difficult as well as a controversial issue in economic theory. Marshall believed that competitive equilibrium is possible under increasing returns, that is, when the firm and industry are experiencing decreasing-cost conditions. In the traditional value theory, while there was perfect agreement and harmony about almost every other thing, doubts were raised by many about

12. *Ibid.* p. 44.

the compatibility of competitive equilibrium in the context of increasing returns.[13] Thus Piero Sraffa who published a path breaking article entitled "The Laws of Returns under Competition" in *Economic Journal,*[14] in 1926 writes, "In the tranquil view which the modern theory of value presents us there is one dark spot which disturbs the harmony of the whole. This is represented by the supply curve, based on the laws of increasing and diminishing returns".[15]

It should be noted that Sraffa challenged the occurrence of both the increasing and-diminishing returns under conditions of perfect competition and tried to prove that it is constant cost (or constant returns) that can be validly assumed to be prevailing under conditions of perfect competition and in the framework of partial (or particular) equilibrium theory, with which Marshall was concerned. In fact Sraffa tried to prove that the ***equilibrium of the individual firm is incompatible with the assumptions of perfect competition.*** In other words, he showed that given the perfectly competitive assumptions, the firm would continue to grow or expand without reaching an equilibrium situation. According to him, it was the occurrence of diminishing returns due to which unit cost or marginal cost rises that the individual firm could be shown to be in determinate equilibrium under conditions of perfect competition. Under diminishing returns, a firm expands its size or output to the point where rising unit or marginal cost becomes equal to the given and constant price.

But Sraffa challenged the validity of the occurrence of diminishing returns or rising unit costs under perfect competition in the context of particular equilibrium theory in which the supply and demand conditions of a commodity are considered to *be independent* of the supply and demand of *other commodities.* He thus argues : "As regards diminishing returns, in fact ***if in the production of a particular commodity a considerable part of a factor is employed,*** the total amount of which is fixed or can be increased only at a more than proportionate cost, a small increase in the production of the commodity will necessitate a more utilization of that factor and this will affect in the same manner the cost of the commodity in question and the ***cost of other commodities*** into the production of which that factor enters; and since commodities into the production of which a common special factor enters are frequently, to a certain extent, substitutes for one another ..... the modification in their prices will not be without appreciable effects upon demand in the industry concerned"[16].

The rise in the price of substitutes and as a result its impact on the demand of the commodity in question whose output has been expanded in the first instance upsets the framework of particular equilibrium theory which, as stated above, assumes independence of demand and supply conditions of different commodities. Only if an industry uses a small part of a "constant factor", the small expansion of that industry and as a result the small increase in the demand for the factor will leave the price of the factor practically unaffected, and if the small expansion of the given industry takes place drawing marginal quantities of the constant

13. It should be noted that even before Sraffa laws of diminishing returns and increasing returns were the subject of controversy. In 1922, J. H. Clapham in his famous article entitled "Of Empty Economic Boxes" in *Economic Journal* criticized the laws of diminishing and increasing returns. But Clapham did not challenge the theoretical *validity* of these laws ; he only pointed out the immense difficulties of putting the real-world industries in the economic boxes labelled diminishing returns and increasing returns and so these economic boxes remain empty.' In other words, according to Clapham, we cannot say which real-world particular industries observe which law, or "What industries are in which boxes". See the whole debate in this connection in the following articles which are reprinted in *Readings in Price Theory,* AEA, pp. 119.-142 (1) J. H. Clapham, Of Empty Economic Boxes, (2) A. C. Pigou, Empty Economic Boxes: A Reply. (3) D. H. Robertson, These Empty Boxes. -
However, Piero Sraffa has challenged the theoretical validity of the laws of diminishing and increasing returns.

14. This article has been reprinted in *Readings in Price Theory.* AEA,.Reference to page numbers will be from this book.

15. *Op. cit.*

16. *Op. cit.*, pp. 184-85.

factor from other industries and therefore even if costs due to that factor rise, there will be rise in the cost of all industries using that factor. Therefore, according to Sraffa, "without upsetting the particular equilibrium analysis under perfect competition, it is difficult to account for unit or marginal cost curve to rise with the increase in the production of a commodity. Thus, he concludes, "the imposing structure of diminishing returns ***(that is, the rise in unit or marginal costs with the increase in output)*** is available only for the study of that minute class of commodities in the production of which whole of a factor of production is employed"[17]

Thus, in view of Sraffa, diminishing returns or rising unit and marginal costs do not prevail under conditions of perfect competition in case of most of the commodities. Now, as seen above, when the cost per unit or marginal cost does not rise, the firm under perfect competition cannot be in equilibrium. For the firm to be in equilibrium under perfect competition, unit or marginal cost must be rising.

Sraffa also criticized the increasing returns, that is, falling unit or marginal cost curve. No doubt, it was also recognised by Marshall and Pigou that increasing returns due to the *internal economies of scale* were not compatible with the perfect competition assumptions. As Sraffa points out, "reduction in cost connected with an increase in a firm's scale of production arising from *internal economies* or from the possibility of distributing the overhead charges over a large number of product units must be put aside as being incompatible with competitive conditions". Therefore, fall in unit costs of the firms which are compatible with perfect competition are those which are brought about by *external economies,* that is, economies, which arise from the forces external to the increase in the scale of the firm[18].

Now, it has been asserted by Sraffa that such external economies which do prevail are the result of *overall general industrial growth* and therefore are irrelevant for the purpose of particular equilibrium analysis of the determination of supply and price of a particular commodity. Further, according to him, those economies which are external to the firm but internal to the given particular industry are seldom found in actual practice. To quote him, "reductions in cost which are due to those *external* economies which result from the general progress of industrial environment, to which Marshall refers *(Principles* V, XI) must, of course, be ignored as they are clearly incompatible with the.conditions of the particular equilibrium of a commodity ....Those economies which are external from the point of view of the individual firm, but internal as regards the industry in its aggregate constitute *precisely the class which is seldom to be met with*"[19] Even if some such economies which are external to the firm but internal to the individual firm are present in the real world, they are not, according to Sraffa, likely to be brought about by *small* increases in production. He concludes, "supply curves showing decreasing costs (i. *e.,* increasing returns) are not to be found more frequently than their opposite."

From the above argument of Sraffa, two things follow : First, the diminishing and increasing returns and supply curve of the firm and the industry based on them showing variable costs at different levels of output or quantity supplied are not applicable to most of the industries under perfect competition. The variations in unit cost due to the changes in output under perfect competition can be found only in some exceptional industries. He therefore thinks that in case of most of the commodities produced under conditions of perfect competition cost per unit

17. *Ibid,* p. 185. (The sentence in the bracket is added by us). It should be noted that at the time Sraffa wrote his articles, concepts of marginal cost and marginal revenue were not developed. However, his argument remains unaffected whether we use unit cost or marginal cost.

18. *Ibid,* pp. 185-86.

19. Marshall himself wrote in his book *'Industry and Trade',* p. 198 "The economies of production on a large scale can seldom be allocated exactly to any one industry : they are in great measure attached to groups, often large groups of correlated industries".

must remain constant and therefore the unit cost curve and therefore the supply curve of the firm as well as of the industry under perfect competition should be horizontal straight line as shown by curve. *LRS* in Figure 31.4. Long-run supply curve of the industry has been drawn at the level of unit cost of production. In such a case when the supply curve is a horizontal straight line, there will be constant price in the long run, which, as will be seen in Fig. 31.4, will be equal to the unit cost of production whatever the level of output and demand. In this figure, price *OP*, which is equal to the unit cost of production, is determined by the intersection of demand and supply curves. Since in this case cost does not vary with output, any output demanded can be produced and supplied at the given constant cost. To quote him, "In normal cases, the cost of production of commodities produced competitively—as we are not entitled to take into consideration the causes which may make it rise or fall—must be regarded as constant in respect of small variations in the quantity produced. And so a *simple way of approaching the problem of competitive value, the old and now obsolete theory, which makes it dependent on the cost of production appears to hold its ground as the best available*"[20]

Secondly, it follows from Sraffa's argument that **under conditions of perfect competition, with product and factor prices remaining constant, the individual firm cannot be in equilibrium.** This is because in these conditions both the demand curve for the individual firm as well as unit cost curve will be horizontal straight lines and as shown in Figure 31.2 above, it will be profitable for the firm to go on expanding and growing indefinitely without reaching any determinate position of equilibrium. As we have discussed before, whether it is the constant costs or decreasing costs (*i.e.*, constant returns or increasing returns), the firm cannot be in equilibrium under conditions of perfect competition and will grow and expand enormously. As explained before, this expansion or growth of one firm will ultimately lead to the destruction of perfect competition and to the establishment of monopoly or oligopoly.

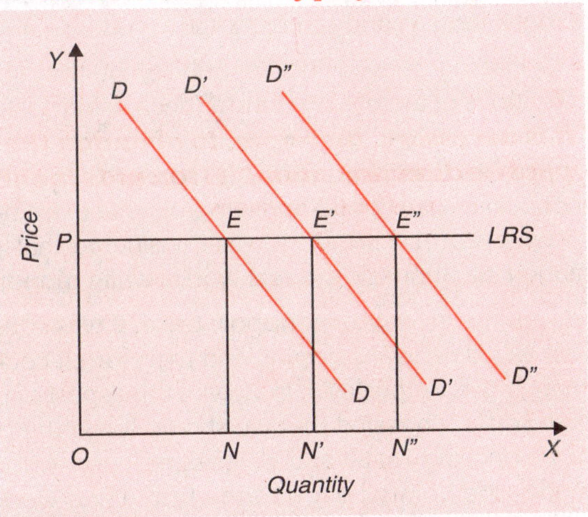

Fig. 31.4. *According to Sraffa, under perfect competition only constant costs can prevail.*

Until now we have been concerned with the destructive part of Sraffa's article. In this destructive part Sraffa demolished both the laws of diminishing and increasing returns and tried to prove that both these laws cannot operate under the assumed conditions of perfect competition model of particular equilibrium analysis. It should be noted that Sraffa did not dispute the occurrence of increasing returns (or even diminishing returns) *in the real world*. In fact he pointed out that many firms and industries in the real world experience increasing returns (decreasing costs). What he really disputed was the occurrence of these in the *theoretical model* of perfect competition in the context of partial equilibrium theory. We now turn to the second constructive part of Sraffa's article in which he examined the real-world situation and tried to make it compatible with the theory of imperfect competition.

20. *Ibid*, pp. 186-87. It should be noted that according to classical theory of value, price of a commodity is determined by the cost of production. In the case of constant cost case (horizontal long-run supply curve, as depicted by *LRS* curve in Figure 31.4), demand as a factor determining price becomes unimportant; for whatever the level of demand, long-run price remains unaffected.

Sraffa's Challenge to Perfect Competition Model and his Advocacy of the Adoption of Monopoly Model

It is in the second part of his article and in the context of discussing what limits the growth in the size of the firm under conditions of decreasing cost (increasing returns) that Sraffa made significant contributions to value theory. In this part he first posed Marshall's dilemma, which is also known as Sraffa's dilemma itself. Professor Shackle states Marshall's or Sraffa's dilemma as follows: "Perfect competition is the state of affairs where the individual firm can sell "as much as it likes" at a price which the market determines independently of this firm's output. If at each larger output, the firm's cost of production per unit of product is lower, what is there to prevent the firm's indefinite expansion ! But if the firm expands indefinitely, and thus swallows the whole market, where is perfect competition ?"[21]

In the second part of his article Sraffa provided a solution for the above-mentioned Marshall's dilemma. While providing a solution to Marshall's dilemma, Sraffa laid the foundation of imperfect competition theory which was later further developed and refined by Joan Robinson and E. H. Chamberlin[22]. Therefore, it is for this second constructive part that Sraffa's article is more famous and often quoted.

Having proved incompatibility of firm's equilibrium with perfect competition under conditions of increasing returns (decreasing costs), Sraffa begins his second part by suggesting, ***"It is necessary, therefore, to abandon the path of free competition and turn in the opposite direction, namely, towards monopoly".*** Before Sraffa, perfect competitions and monopoly were considered two opposite extreme cases with no intermediate market situations between them. Further, it was considered that perfect competition represented most of the market situations in the real world, while monopoly represented exceptional cases.

In the theory of monopoly price, it was considered that demand curve for the monopolist firm was downward sloping and therefore it could influence the market price of its product by changing its output level. In view of this aspect of pricing and output equilibrium under monopoly that Sraffa suggested that we should forgo the perfect competition model and find a solution of reconciling real-world decreasing costs with our price theory on the lines of monopoly model. He pointed out that the firm when working under decreasing costs conditions in the real world cannot grow indef-initely because the demand curve facing them was falling downward. That is, with the expansion in output, price of a product falls and therefore after a point it may become lower than the unit cost of production which may also be falling. ***Thus, it is the external factor, that is, demand or falling product price that puts a limit to the growth of the firms working under increasing returns (decreasing costs) conditions in the real world and not any internal factor which may bring about rising cost of production.*** We quote below a significant passage from his article in which he explains firm's equilibrium under decreasing costs with the falling demand curve.

"Everyday experience shows that a very large number of undertakings—and the majority of those which produce manufactured consumers' goods—work under conditions of individual diminishing costs. Almost any producer of such goods, if he could rely upon the market in which he sells his product being prepared to take any quantity of them from him at the current price, without any trouble on his part except that of producing them, would extend his business enormously.......Businessmen who regard themselves as being subject to competitive conditions

21. G.L.S. Shackle, *Years of High Theory.*

22. Chamberlin claims to have developed his monopolistic competition theory without having any opportunity to see Sraffa's article, whereas Mrs Joan Robinson pays tribute to Sraffa for his important contribution to the development of imperfect competition theory and says she got clues from Sraffa's article while developing her theory of imperfect competition.

would consider absurd the assertion that the limit to their production is to be found in the internal conditions of production in their firm, which do not permit of the production of a greater quantity without an increase in cost. ***The chief obstacle against which they have to contend when they want gradually to increase their production does not lie in the cost of production***—*which,* indeed, generally favours them in ***that direction—but in the difficulty of selling the larger quantity of goods without reducing the price or without having to face increased marketing expenses***. This necessity of reducing prices in order to sell a larger quantity of one's own product is only an aspect of the usually descending demand curve, with the difference that instead of concerning the whole of a commodity, whatever its origin, it relates only to the goods produced by a particular firm."[23]

Sraffa further goes on to explain that perfect competition in the real world does not prevail because various consumers show preference for the products of some firms over the others. This attachment of some consumers with a particular firm makes the competition imperfect and also creates downward sloping demand curve. Such a type of demand curve enables the firm to influence the price of the product. This makes the determinate equilibrium of the firm possible, even when it is working under conditions of decreasing costs. To quota Sraffa again, "the chief obstacle which hinders the free play of competition ...... and which renders a stable equilibrium possible, even when the supply curve for the product of each individual firm is descending—that is, the absence of indifference on the part of the buyers of goods as between the different producers. The causes of the preferences shown by any group of buyers for a particular firm are of the most diverse nature, and may range from 'long custom, personal acquaintance, confidence in the quality of the product, proximity, knowledge of particular requirements and the possibility of obtaining credit, to the reputation of a trade-mark, or sign or a name with high traditions, or to such special features of modelling or design in the product as—without constituting it a distinct commodity intended for the satisfaction of particular needs—have for their principal purpose that of distinguishing it from the products of other firms".[24]

It is clear from above that Sraffa challenged the two aspects of perrect competition theory. First, he explained that price for an individual firm is not a given and constant datum for it, but the firm even though it faces a lot of competition from other rival firms, exercises an influence over the price of its particular product. In order to sell more it has to reduce its price. This means that the demand curve confronting it is downward sloping. Secondly, the requirement of perfect competition is that a firm must necessarily be operating under individual rising costs (*i.e.* declining returns). Sraffa criticised this as unrealistic. Equilibrium of the firm under perfect competition in the context of decreasing costs, which in fact prevail in the real world, is indeterminate. As stated above, Sraffa made the determinate equilibrium of the firm possible by showing that demand curve facing a firm is sloping downward and this makes the establishment of determinate equilibrium possible.

As is evident from the quotation given above, Sraffa points out all those natural and artificial circumstances and causes such as differences in the quality of the product, differences in location, differences in the availability of obtaining goods on credit, trade-mark, trade name, differences in modelling or design of the products of different firms which explain a "willingness on the part of a group of buyers who constitute a firm's clientele to pay, if necessary, something extra in order to obtain the goods from a particular firm rather than from any other".[25] It is thus clear that Sraffa clearly visualized ***product differentiation as an important force causing***

23. *Op. cit,* pp. 190-91 (italics added)
24. *Ibid*
25. *Ibid.*

imperfection of competition, on which E. H. Chamberlin laid a great emphasis. Further, according to him, the preference of the product of one firm over the others due to product differentiation and consequently willingness of a buyer to pay somewhat higher price for a product manifests itself, over the relevant range, in the elasticity of the demand curve confronting a firm. Unlike the perfect competition, ***the elasticity of the demand curve facing a firm, due to the above mentioned product differentiation, is less than infinity.*** Moreover, Sraffa for the first time considered ***elasticity of demand for the firm's product as a measure of monopoly*** *power* involved in the given imperfect market situation. He thus writes : "We find that the majority of the circumstances which affect the strength of a monopolist...... exercise their influence essentially by affecting the elasticity of the demand curve for the monopolised goods. Whatever the causes may be, this is the only decisive factor in estimating the degree of independence which a monopolist has in fixing prices : ***the less elastic the demand for his product, the greater is his hold on his market***...... The significance of a moderate elasticity in the demand is that, although the monopolist has a certain freedom in fixing his prices, whenever he increases them he is forsaken by a portion of his purchasers, who prefer to spend their money in some other manner."[26]

From the above analysis, it is clear that short of explaining firm's equilibrium with marginal revenue and marginal cost, he explained all the important features of imperfect competition or monopolistic competition theory. This is most important, indeed revolutionary contribution to price theory. A further point regarding Sraffa is worth noting. Sraffa solved Marshall's dilemma not by showing the way in which real-world decreasing costs can be reconciled with perfect competition but by giving up the perfect competition model with its horizontal demand curve for the individual firm. He instead adopted the imperfect competition model with its downward-sloping demand curve for the individual firm. Thus, he reconciled decreasing costs (*i.e.* increasing returns) with imperfect competition which he thought prevailed in the real world.

Comments on Sraffa's Analysis

We have explained above the two parts of Sraffa's seminal article—the destructive and constructive parts. As far as the second constructive part of the Sraffa's article is concerned there is no doubt about his significant contributions to price theory for setting out the basis and necessity of imperfect competition theory. Further, he is also right in pointing out that it is demand or difficulty in selling more without reducing the price that ultimately puts the limit to the expansion of the firm and thus reconciling the real-world decreasing cost case with the economic theory.

But the destructive part of his article, namely, that under perfect competition both diminishing returns (increasing cost) and increasing returns (decreasing cost) cannot operate and therefore his contention that only the case of constant costs or returns is the valid proposition under perfect competition in the context of particular equilibrium theory, is not generally admitted. As explained above, with constant cost case, a perfectly competitive firm cannot be in determinate equilibrium position. This first destructive part of Sraffa's article is open to question from the viewpoint of modern economic theory. Diminishing returns or increasing cost in the case of both firm and industry is considered as a valid proposition under perfect competition in particular equilibrium analysis. Long-run cost curve of a firm under perfect competition first falls due to economies of scale and then rises after a certain level of output due to the *diseconomies of management* of a large-scale production. Stonier and Hague thus

26. *Op. cit.*,p. 191.
27. *Op. cit.*, pp. 191-92.

write, "The management of a firm is unlikely to be able to produce twice a given output as efficiently as it produces a given output, however long management is given to get used to having to do so. The total size of the management team can be increased or decreased but almost certainly not in proportion to output. Of course, if one really is dealing with a firm with a one-man entrepreneur, he will be completely indivisible. It is therefore reasonable to think that firms will still produce more cheaply at some scales of output than at others, even in the long run, if only because beyond a certain point management is difficult. Even in the long run, management is indivisible. Certain combinations of factors will thus produce at lower unit costs in the long run than others".[28]

We thus see that modern economists do believe that even under perfect competitive conditions, long-run cost first falls due to internal economies and then rises due to diseconomies of management.

Further, unlike that shown by Sraffa, *in case of particular industry as a whole* under perfect competition, case of increasing cost or diminishing returns is quite possible. Many industries on expansion find the prices of specific factors used by them rise. According to Sraffa, a particular industry producing a commodity will use these specific factors in larger quantities and further that these specific factors will also be used in the production of substitutes and/or complements and therefore to consider their total effect we should give up particular equilibrium analysis. But this need not be the case, for the specific factors used by an industry may not be used in other industries producing substitutes or complementary goods and therefore particular equilibrium analysis can be validly applied. Further, increasing cost or diminishing returns to the industries may be caused by the ***limited supplies of some factors.*** When these limited supplies are exhausted, other inputs will be used by the firms in the expanding industry, the fixed quantities of these limited factors will bring about diminishing returns. As regards the validity and compatibility of diminishing returns with perfect competitive conditions, Samuelson writes : "Long run expansion of an industry as more firms enter into the market and as each firm expands its output would produce *an increase in the market prices* of those factors of production that are in peculiarly heavy use in this industry ....What would be the effect upon the supply curve when an increase in industry output raises the prices of those factors of production peculiarly important in this industry ? It would certainly be to shift upward the marginal and other cost curves of the new and old firms."[29]

Even Decreasing Costs to the Industry is Compatible with Perfect Competition

Sraffa forcefully argued that decreasing costs to the industry was inconsistent with particular equilibrium theory of perfect competition and in this connection he refuted the *external economies* argument bringing about decreasing costs. He ruled out the external economies arising out of the correlated industries supplying the main industry with cheap material and equipment and some others using its by-products as irrelevant from the viewpoint of partial equilibrium analysis. In the opinion of the present author this is unduly restricting the scope of partial equilibrium analysis which can validly cover those cases of the growth of correlated industries which result from the expansion of a main particular industry. Moreover, this argument of Sraffa is against the ***method of analysis,*** that is, partial equilibrium analysis; he does not deny the existence of such external economies in the real world and their compatibility with perfect competition if general equilibrium analysis of the main industry, and its correlated industries is made. The very nature of external economies is such that it is hard to draw a line between a particular equilibrium analysis and general equilibrium analysis.

28. *A Textbook of Economic Theory,* 4th edition, 1972, p. 136.
29. Paul Samuelson, *Economics,* 8th edition 1970, p. 451.

Further, it may be debated as to whether those economies which are consistent with particular equilibrium analysis, that is, economies which are *external to the firm but internal to the industry,* existed in the real world in sufficiently large amounts so as to outweigh the external diseconomies. But the theoretical possibility and therefore compatibility of decreasing costs (increasing returns) with perfect competition cannot be denied. To quote Professor Samuelson again, "There is however the possibility that *external economies* could prevail in an industry. In such cases, expansion of industry output could shift downward the cost curves of a single firm and in the complicated adding of the resulting supplies of all firms, the industry supply curve could end up as downward sloping".[30]

It should be noted that Both Marshall and Pigou showed the compatibility of increasing returns (decreasing costs) in the industry with perfect competition on the basis of external economies. It is worth mentioning here that when there are *net external economies,* while the industry as a whole will be experiencing decreasing cost, the individual firms will be working at the rising portion of their long-run marginal cost curves, that is, the firms will be in equilibrium at the point where they are individually experiencing diminishing returns to scale. This is because with the expansion of the industry cost curves of the individual firms shift down due to net external economies, while the conditions of their individual long-run equilibrium remain the same, that is, long-run price must be equal to their both *LAC* and *LMC* and *LMC* must be rising at the point of equilibrium. It should be noted that the equality of long-run marginal cost *(LMC)* with long-run average cost *(LAC)* is achieved at the minimum point of the latter and the firm is in long-run equilibrium at the *optimum size.* At minimum point of *LAC*, *LMC′* is rising. This will be evident from Figure 31.5. In this figure, the demand curve for the product of the industry is *DD* which cuts the supply curve *LRS* at point *E* and determines price OP_1. Firm in the long run will be in equilibrium at output OM_1 (or point *H* on their *LMC*).

When in response to the increase in demand to *D′D′*, industry expands by the entry of new firms and in this process of expansion enough external economies are created, the cost curves of all firms, old as well as new, will shift below to the dotted position *LAC′* and *LMC′* in Figure 31.5.With demand curve *D′D′*, the industry will be in equilibrium at greater output ON_2 which is being supplied at lower price OP_2. This long-run supply curve of the industry is sloping downward. But with the downward shift in the cost curves to *LAC′* and *LMC′* of the firm as a result of expansion of the industry, *the individual firms will be in equilibrium at minimum point K of LAC which lies at the rising portion of their new long-run marginal cost curve LMC′*. Of course, the average and marginal costs of the firm have decreased, but that has been due to the *downward shift* in the cost curves, while they keep working in their new long-run equilibrium position at the rising part of their new marginal cost curve.[31]

30. *Op. tit.*, p. 456.

31. It should be pointed out here that in our reconciliation of decreasing costs (increasing returns) in the industry, we have followed A. C. Pigou who while defending Marshall pointed out that the firm under perfect competition is in long-run equilibrium at the optimum size (that is, output corresponding to the minimum long-run AC at which marginal cost is rising (that is, diminishing returns to the individual firm occurs). To explain increasing returns to the industry, he relied on external economies as we have done above. According to him, each firm was always in equilibrium at the point of rising marginal cost but the expansion of the industry (increase in the number of firms) would cause a downward shift in the cost curves of all firms and then again all would be working at *lower* minimum average cost at which marginal cost would be rising. As a result, the industry as a whole will be supplying more at a lower cost or price than before. However, it is worth mentioning that Mrs Joan Robinson is not convinced about Pigou's reconciliation of increasing returns (decreasing cost) to the industry with perfect competition conditions. In her later book she wrote: "Pigou tried to rescue Marshall by postulating an optimum firm ...... Pigou had to rely upon purely external economies, or "economies of large scale to the industry." Each firm was always working under conditions of rising marginal cost, but an increase in the number of firms would lower average cost at the minimum for all of them.... This fanciful construction, although it was demolished by Piero Sraffa more than forty years ago, is still used as the basis of the "theory of the firm" in modern textbooks *(Economic Heresies,* (pp. 58-59). We beg to differ with Joan Robinson and follow the view of most of the modern economists including that of Samuelson.

It is worth pointing out here that it is not necessary that when the long-run supply curve of the industry is downward sloping (having decreasing costs), firm's relevant cost curves should also be downward sloping. This is because as has been emphasized in earlier chapters, long-run supply curve of the industry is ***not obtained by the lateral summation of the cost curves of the firms.*** The long-run equilibrium of the firms under perfect competition is always at the minimum point of the long-run average cost at which long-run marginal cost is rising whether the industry's supply curve is upward sloping (increasing cost), is horizontal line (constant cost) or is downward sloping (decreasing cost).

Apart from the problem of compatibility of decreasing cost industry with perfect competition, another problem which is faced in connection with the decreasing-cost industry is that ***of stability of its equilibrium.*** Many economists have pointed out that decreasing-cost industry with its downward sloping supply curve cannot be in stable equilibrium and instability

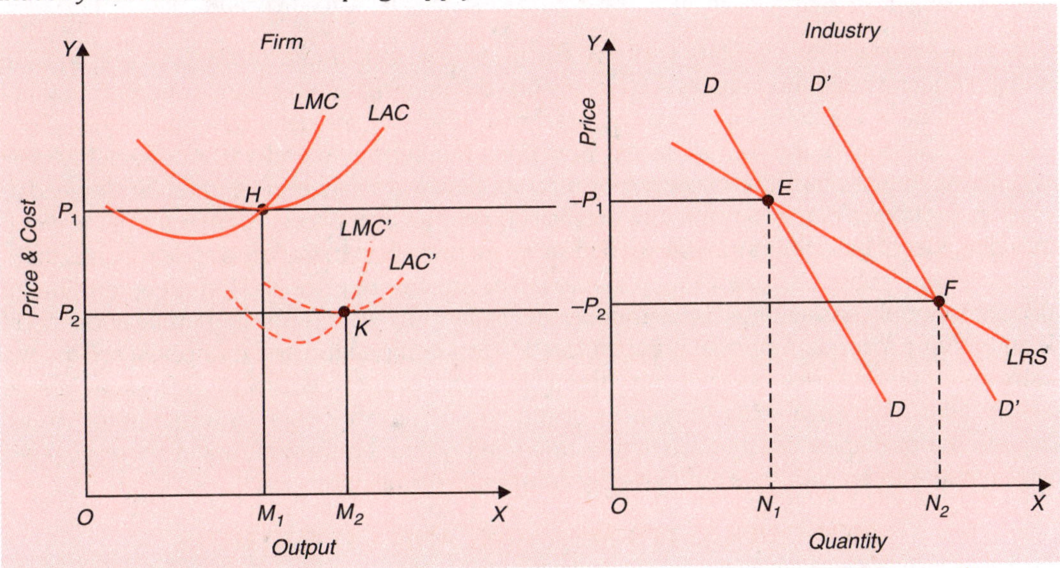

Fig. 31.5. Compatibility of Perfectly Competitive Equilibrium with Decreasing Costs (Increasing Returns)

in its price and output would be the feature of this industry. We have discussed this stability problem at length in the previous chapter.

Conclusion

From the foregoing analysis and discussion above, we derive the conclusion that whereas increasing returns to ***the individual firm are incompatible with the equilibrium under perfect competition, increasing returns (decreasing-cost conditions) to the industry due to external economies are quite compatible with perfect competition.*** But, as brought out above, Sraffa while discussing this problem of compatibility of increasing returns with perfect competition made significant contributions to the price theory by laying out the basis and necessity of imperfect competition theory. Thus Sraffa, though failed to demolish the perfect competition model and the validity of external economies from the point of view of particular equilibrium analysis, made a notable contribution in his constructive objective of developing the theory of imperfect competition wherein individual firms enjoy a good amount of monopoly power, though they also face a lot of competition from the rival firms.

CHAPTER

32

Price and Output Determination Under Monopoly

In a few previous chapters we have discussed the equilibrium of the firm and industry under perfect competition and as a consequence the determination of price and output under it. Monopoly is another important market form which merits detailed study in respect of output equilibrium of the firm as well as how price is determined under it. About eighty years ago it was thought that the existence of monopoly was an exceptional case. But nowadays monopolistic form of market structure extensively prevails in capitalist economies of the world, including that of India. Monopolistic market structure prevails in many large-scale manufacturing industries and public utility services. Therefore, the analysis of price and output determination under monopoly has assumed vital importance. Monopoly, as it is now generally understood, is an extreme form of imperfect competition. Perfect competition and monopoly are the two extreme opposite cases and between them the various intermediate market situations lie, which differ from each other in respect of the degree of monopoly. In this chapter we will explain the principles which underlie the price and output equilibrium under monopoly and will compare them with those of perfectly competitive equilibrium.

MONOPOLY: ITS MEANING AND CONDITIONS

What is monopoly ? ***Monopoly is said to exist when one firm is the sole producer or seller of a product which has no close substitutes***. Three points are worth noting in this definition. First, there must be a *single producer or seller of a product* if there is to be monopoly. This single producer may be in the form of an individual owner or a single partnership or a joint stock company. If there are many producers producing a product, either perfect competition or monopolistic competition will prevail depending upon whether the product is homogeneous or differentiated. On the other hand, when there are few producers or sellers of a product, oligopoly is said to exist. If then there is to be monopoly, there must be one firm in the field. Even literally monopoly means one seller. 'Mono' means one and 'poly' means seller. Thus monopoly means one seller or one producer.

But to say that monopoly means one seller or producer is not enough. A second condition which is essential for a firm to be called monopolist is that *no close substitutes for the product of that firm should be available.* If there are some other firms which are producing close substitutes for the product in question there will be competition between them. In the presence of this competition a firm cannot be said to have monopoly. Monopoly implies absence of all competition. For instance, there is one firm in India which produces 'Colgate' toothpaste but this firm cannot be called monopolist since there are many other firms which produce close substitutes of Colgate toothpaste such as Binaca, Forhans, etc. These various brands of toothpaste compete with each other in the market and the producer of any one of them cannot be said to have a monopoly. Thus the privilege of being the single seller of a product does not by itself make one a monopolist in the sense of possessing the market power to set the price. As a single seller, he may be a king without a crown.

We can express the second condition of monopoly in terms of cross elasticity of demand also. Cross elasticity of demand shows the degree of change in the demand for a good as a result of a change in the price of another good. Therefore, if there is to be monopoly ***the cross elasticity of demand between the product of the monopolist and the product of any other producer must be very small.***

The fact that there is one firm under monopoly means that other firms for one reason or another are prohibited to enter the monopolistic industry. In other words, *strong barriers to the entry of new firms exist* wherever there is one firm having a sole control over the production of a commodity. The barriers which prevent the firms to enter the industry may be economic in nature or else of institutional and artificial nature. In case of monopoly, barriers are so strong that they prevent entry of all firms except the one which is already in the field.

From above it follows that for the monopoly to exist, the following three conditions are necessary

1. There is a single producer or seller of a product.
2. There are no close substitutes for the product.
3. Strong barriers to the entry of new firms in the industry exist.

SOURCES OR CAUSES OF MONOPOLY

There are five major reasons or sources of monopoly. It is because of these reasons that monopolist enjoys a high degree of monopoly power. These sources relate to the factors which prevent the entry of new firms in an industry. Thus, these factors serve as barriers to the entry of new firms. We have explained earlier that strong barriers to the entry of new firms is an essential condition for the existence of monopoly. We explain below some of the important factors that serve as barriers to the entry of new firms and therefore constitute sources of monopoly.

1. Patents or Copyright. First important source of monopoly is that a firm may posses a patent or copyright which prevents others to produce the same product or use a particular production process. Generally, when the firms introduce *new products,* they get patent rights from the Government so that others cannot produce them. These patent rights are granted for a certain period of time. For example, when copying machine was invented, its inventor 'Xerox' company had monopoly in its production based on a patent granted to it by the Government. Likewise, when a new medicine is invented by a medical company, it gets, patent right from the Government so that it retains monopoly power over its production. Patents and copyrights constitute strong barrier to the entry of potential competitors.

2. Control over the Essential Raw Material. Another source of monopoly is a control by a particular firm over an essential raw material or input used in the production of a commodity. For example, before World War II, Aluminium Company of America exercised exclusive control over almost every source of bauxite, which is an essential input for the manufacture of aluminium, had the monopoly power over the production of aluminium in the USA. Likewise, OPEC (Organisation of Petroleum Exporting Countries) exercises monopoly power in the world over the supply of crude oil from the Middle East countries as it has control over the supply of crude oil of these countries.

3. Grant of Franchise by the Government. Another important reason for monopoly is the grant of franchise by the Government to a firm. A firm is granted the exclusive legal right to produce a given product or service in a particular area or region. For example, in a large part of Delhi Government has granted the exclusive right to TATA-owned Company NDPL to provide or distribute electricity in Delhi. Likewise, until a few years ago Mahanagar Telephone Nigam Ltd. (MTNL) enjoyed exclusive legal rights to provide land-line telephone service in Delhi. It may be noted that when a company is given a franchise to produce a particular product or provide a particular service by the Government, the Government keeps with itself the right to regulate its price and quality.

4. Economies of Scale: Natural Monopoly. Another important source of monopoly is significant economies of scale over a wide range of initial output. When significant economies of scale are present, ***long-run average cost of production goes on falling over a wide range of output and reaches a minimum at an output rate that is large enough for a single firm to meet the entire market demand at a price that is profitable.*** In such a situation if more than one firm operate to produce the product each firm must be producing the product at a higher than minimum level cost per unit. In such a situation each firm is inclined to cut price to increase its output and reduce average cost of the product. This leads to price warfare and one who survives in this economic warfare emerges as a monopolist.

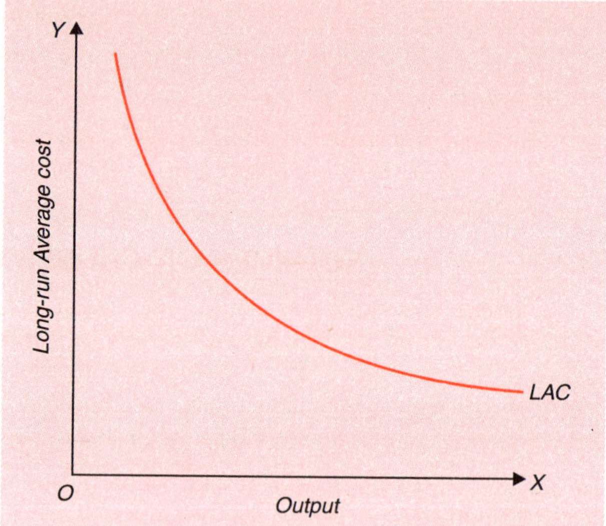

Fig. 32.1. *Significant Economies of Scale of a Natural Monopoly*

When there are significant economies of scale and as a result average cost decreases over a wide range of output (as shown in Fig. 32.1), *natural monopoly is said to exist.* Natural monopolies are regulated by the Government so that they should not charge high prices and exploit the consumers.

5. Advertising and Brand Loyalties of the Established Firms. Another important reason that prevents the entry of new competitors in the industry is the strong loyalties to the brands of the established firms and their heavy advertising campaigns to promote their brand. For example, strong loyalty of the consumers for 'Britannia Bread' makes it difficult for the potential competitors to enter. Further, for a long time in the USA the firm producing Coca Cola was well-established firm to produce a famous cold drink and no one dared to enter this field till Pepsi Cola, another giant, came and broke its monopoly. Huge advertising campaigns and customer service programmes are often undertaken to enhance the market power of the producer and prevent the entry of potential competitors. Besides, if well-established firms are expecting new potential competitors, they cut prices of their products so that potential competitors find it unprofitable to enter the industry.

THE NATURE OF DEMAND AND MARGINAL REVENUE CURVES UNDER MONOPOLY

It is important to understand the nature of the demand curve facing a monopolist. Whereas the demand curve facing *an individual firm* under perfect competition, as explained in a previous chapter, is a horizontal straight line, the demand curve facing the *whole industry* under perfect competition is sloping downward. This is so because the demand is of the consumers and the demand curve of consumers for a product usually slopes downward. The downward-sloping demand curve of the consumers faces the whole competitive industry. But an individual firm under perfect competition does not face a downward-sloping demand curve. This is because an individual firm under perfect competition is one among numerous firms constituting the industry so that it cannot affect the price by varying its individual level of output. A perfect competitive firm has to accept the ruling price as given and constant for it. It can sell as much as it likes at the ruling price of the product. Therefore, the demand curve facing an individual firm under perfect competition is a horizontal straight line at the level of prevailing price of the product. A perfectly competitive firm is a mere quantity adjuster; it has no influence over price.

But in the case of monopoly one firm constitutes the whole industry. Therefore, the entire demand of the consumers for a product faces the monopolist. Since the demand curve of the consumers for a product slopes downward, the monopolist faces a downward-sloping demand curve. If he wants to increase the sales of his good, he must lower the price. He can raise the price if he is prepared to sacrifice some sales. To put it in another way, monopolist can lower the price by increasing his level of sales and output, and he can raise the price by reducing his level of sales or output. A perfectly competitive firm merely adjusts the quantity of output it has to produce, price being a given and constant datum for it. But the monopolist encounters a more complicated problem. He cannot merely adjust quantity for a given price because each quantity change by it will bring about a change in the price at which product can be sold. Consider Fig. 32.2. *DD* is the demand curve facing a monopolist. At price *OP* the quantity demanded is *OM*, therefore he would be able to sell *OM* quantity at price *OP*. If he wants to sell greater quantity *ON*, then the price would fall to *OL*. If he restricts his quantity to *OG*, the price will rise to *OH*. Thus, every quantity change by him entails a change in price at which the product can be sold. Thus the problem faced by a monopolist is to choose the price-quantity combination which is optimum for him, that is, which yields him maximum possible profits.

Relation between Marginal Revenue and Price

It is important to know the relationship between marginal revenue and price under monopoly which faces a downward-sloping demand curve (*i.e.* average revenue curve). To explain this relationship let us write the expression for marginal revenue :

$$MR = \frac{\Delta TR}{\Delta Q} = \frac{\Delta(PQ)}{\Delta Q}$$

where ΔTR stands for change in total revenue, P for price and Q for quantity of output sold. Now consider Figure 32.3 where *DD* is the demand curve and when price falls from *OP* to *OP′*, the quantity demanded increases from *OQ* to *OQ′*. The change in total revenue [ΔTR or $\Delta(P.Q)$] is equal to the gain in revenue from extra unit sold (i.e. $P. \Delta Q$) following the decline in price and the loss in revenue incurred on all the previous intramarginal units due to the fall in price equals $Q. \Delta P$. Thus, for small values of ΔP and ΔQ, the change in total revenue can be obtained as under:

$$\Delta TR = P.\Delta Q + Q.\Delta P$$

Dividing both sides by ΔQ we have

$$\frac{\Delta TR}{\Delta Q} = P + Q \cdot \frac{\Delta P}{\Delta Q}$$

or $$MR = P + Q \cdot \frac{\Delta P}{\Delta Q} \qquad \ldots (i)$$

Since demand curve facing the monopolist is downward sloping, ΔP is *negative* whereas ΔQ is positive, the term $Q\frac{\Delta P}{\Delta Q}$ will be negative. It therefore follows from the above expression (*i*) that marginal revenue (*MR*) will be less than price (*P*)

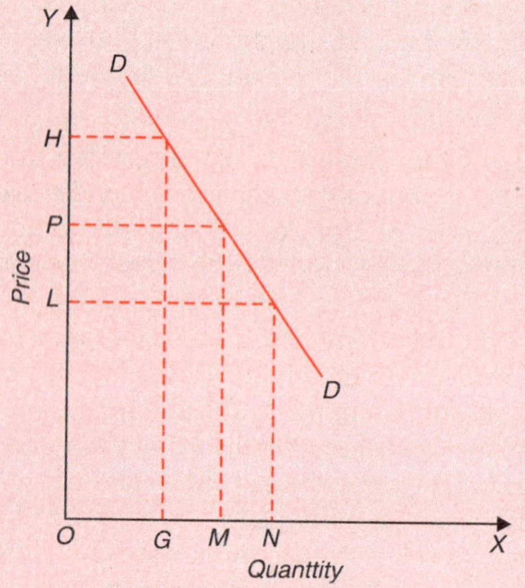

Fig. 32.2. *Demand curve of the monopolist slopes downward*

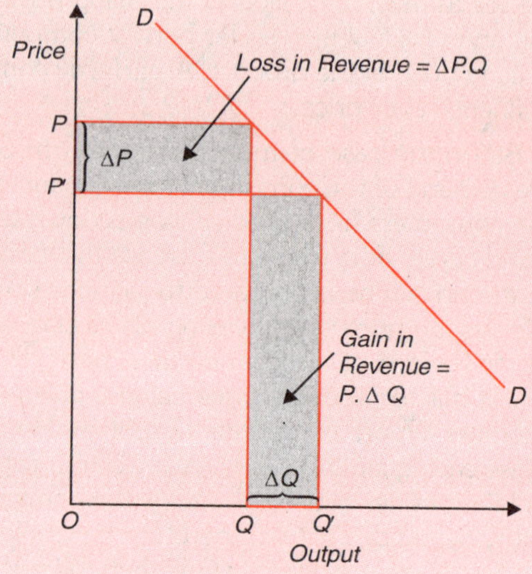

Fig. 32.3. *MR is less than price when demand curve Is downward sloping*

MR, Price and Elasticity of Demand Under Monopoly

By further manipulation of the expression (*i*) for marginal revenue we can explain relationship between marginal revenue, price and elasticity of demand. Let us *multiply and divide* by *P* the *second term* of the right-hand side of equation (*i*) above

$$MR = P + \frac{P}{P} Q. \frac{\Delta P}{\Delta Q}$$

$$= P + P. \frac{Q}{P} \cdot \frac{\Delta P}{\Delta Q} \qquad \ldots (ii)$$

Recall that price elasticity of demand, $e = \frac{\Delta Q}{\Delta P} \cdot \frac{P}{Q}$

Therefore, $$\frac{1}{e} = \frac{\Delta P}{\Delta Q} \cdot \frac{Q}{P}$$

Thus we see that the second term $\frac{\Delta P}{\Delta Q} \cdot \frac{Q}{P}$ in the expression (*ii*) for marginal revenue is the reciprocal of the price elasticity of demand. Therefore substituting $\frac{1}{e}$ for $\frac{\Delta P}{\Delta Q} \cdot \frac{Q}{P}$ in expression (*ii*) above we have

$$MR = P + P.\frac{1}{e} = P\left(1+\frac{1}{e}\right)$$

Since demand curve facing the monopolist has a negative slope, elasticity *e* will be negative. Therefore,

$$MR = P\left(1-\frac{1}{|e|}\right) \qquad ...(iii)$$

Since $1 - \frac{1}{|e|}$ is less than one, from the expression (*iii*) for the marginal revenue, it can be easily seen that marginal revenue will be less than price under monopoly. The expression (*iii*) also shows that *marginal revenue depends on the price of the product and price elasticity of demand.*

Thus, if for the monopolist elasticity of demand at a level of output equals one, its marginal revenue will be equal to zero. Thus, $MR = P(1-\frac{1}{1}) = 0$. If the *absolute value* of the price elasticity is greater than one, say, 2, his marginal revenue will be positive. Thus,

$$MR = P\left(1-\frac{1}{e}\right) = P\left(1-\frac{1}{2}\right) = \frac{1}{2}P$$

If the absolute value of the price elasticity is less than one, say, $\frac{1}{3}$, marginal revenue will be negative. Thus,

$$MR = P\left(1-\frac{1}{e}\right) = P\left(1-\frac{1}{1/3}\right) = P\,(1-3) = -\,2P$$

Demand curve facing the monopolist will be his average revenue curve. Thus the average revenue curve of the monopolist slopes downward throughout its length. We have seen above that marginal revenue is less than price when demand curve slopes downward. Therefore, marginal revenue curve will lie below the average revenue curve. When monopolist sells more, the price of his product falls, marginal revenue therefore must be less than price. In Fig. 32.4. *AR* is the average revenue curve of the monopolist and slopes downward, *MR* is the marginal revenue curve and lies below *AR* curve. At quantity *OQ* average revenue (or price) is *QR* or *OP* and marginal revenue is *QT* which is less than *QR*. We have explained that average and marginal revenue at a quantity are related to each other through elasticity of demand and in this connection we derived the

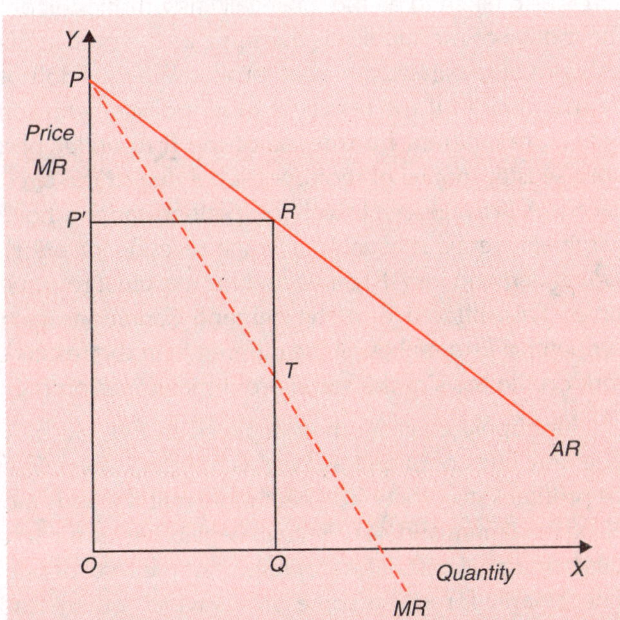

Fig. 32.4. *Average and Marginal Revenue Curves of the Monopolist*

following formula: $MR = \text{Price}\left(\frac{e-1}{e}\right) = P\left(1-\frac{1}{e}\right)$ where e stands for absolute value of elasticity.

Since AR is the same thing as price

Therefore, $$MR = AR\left(1-\frac{1}{e}\right)$$

Since the expression $1 - \frac{1}{e}$ will be less than unity, MR will be less than price, or price will be greater than MR. The extent to which MR curve lies below AR curve depends upon the value of the fraction $1 - \frac{1}{e}$.

The monopolist has a clearly distinguished demand curve for his product, which is identical with the consumers' demand curve for the product in question. It is also worth mentioning that, unlike oligopolist or a firm under monopolist competition, monopolist does not consider the repercussions of a price change by him upon those of other firms. Monopoly, as defined here, requires that the gap between the monopoly product and those of other firms is so large that changes in the price policies of the monopolist will not affect other firms and will therefore not evoke any readjustments of the price-output policies by these firms.

PRICE-OUTPUT EQUILIBRIUM UNDER MONOPOLY

Monopolist, like a perfectly competitive firm, tries to maximize his profits. Profit maximization assumption on which is based the equilibrium analysis of the perfectly competitive firm is also taken to be the most valid assumption about the behaviour of the monopolist too. The motive of monopolist is the same as the motive of the perfectly competitive firm, that is, both aim at maximizing money profits. We thus do not attribute any more sinister motive to the monopolist. If the results of monopolist's behaviour on the basis of profit maximization motive are different from those of the firm under perfect competition, it is not due to any more sinister motive of monopolist but due to the circumstances and situation in which he is placed. A firm under perfect competition faces a horizontal straight-line demand curve and marginal revenue is equal to average revenue (or price), but a monopolist faces a downward-sloping demand (or AR) curve and his marginal revenue curve lies below the average revenue curve. This difference in the demand conditions facing the monopolist and the perfectly competitive firm makes all the difference in the results of their equilibrium, even though both work on the basis of the same profit-maximization motive.

Monopoly equilibrium is depicted in Fig. 32.5. The monopolist will go on producing additional units of output as long as marginal revenue exceeds marginal cost. This is because it is profitable to produce an additional unit if it adds more to revenue than to cost. His profits will be maximum and he will attain equilibrium at the level of output at which marginal revenue equals marginal cost. If he stops short of the level of output at which MR equals MC, he will be unnecessarily foregoing some profits which otherwise he could make. In Fig.32.5 marginal revenue is equal to marginal cost at OM level of output. The firm will be earning maximum profits and will therefore be in equilibrium when it is producing and selling OM quantity of the product. If he increases his output beyond OM, marginal revenue will be less than marginal cost, that is, additional units beyond OM will add more to cost than to revenue. Therefore, the monopolist will be incurring a loss on the additional units beyond *OM* and will thus be reducing his total profits by producing more than *OM*. He is therefore in equilibrium at *OM* level of output at which marginal cost equals marginal revenue.

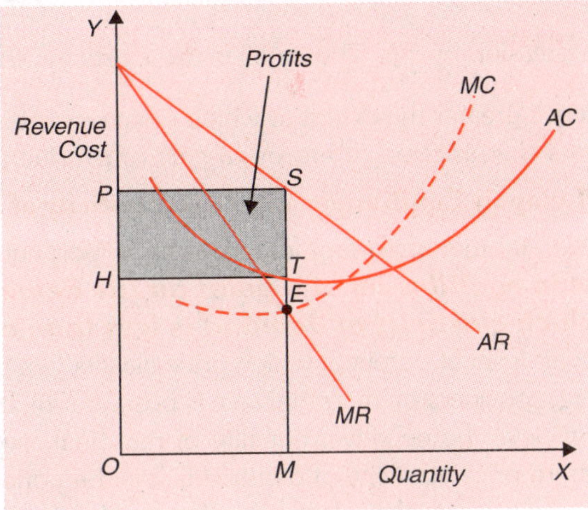

Fig. 32.5. *Firm's Equilibrium Under Monopoly : Mamimization of Profits*

It will be seen from the *AR* curve in Figure 32.5 that equilibrium output *OM* can be sold at price *MS* or *OP*. It therefore follows that the monopolist will produce output equal to *OM* and fix price of its product equal to *OP*. It will be further observed from Figure 32.5 that at the level of equilibrium output, average cost of production is equal to *MT*. With equilibrium price equal to *OP* or *MS*, the profit per unit is equal to *TS*. Profit per unit *TS* multiplied with output *OM* gives us the total economic profits made by the monopolist being equal to the shaded area *HTSP*.

Price and Marginal Cost Under Monopoly

There is a significant difference between monopoly equilibrium and perfectly competitive equilibrium. The price under perfectly competitive equilibrium is equal to marginal cost, but price exceeds marginal cost under monopoly. This is so because the monopolist, unlike perfectly competitive firm, faces a downward-sloping average revenue curve and his marginal revenue curve lies below average revenue curve. Therefore, in monopoly equilibrium when marginal cost is equal to marginal revenue, it is less than price (or average revenue). From Fig. 32.5 it will be noticed that at equilibrium output *OM*, marginal cost and marginal revenue are equal and both are here equal to *ME*, and are less than price or average revenue which is equal to *MS* = *OP*. It thus follows that price under monopoly is greater than marginal cost. But it is worth pointing out that although price under monopoly will not be equal to marginal cost it will stand in a certain relation to the marginal cost. We know that:

$$\text{Price} = MR\,\frac{e}{e-1}$$

where *MR* stands for marginal revenue and *e* for price elasticity of demand.

But, in equilibrium, $MR = MC$

Therefore, $$\text{Price} = MC\,\frac{e}{e-1}.$$

Since $\frac{e}{e-1}$ will be more than unity for a given value of elasticity, it follows that under monopoly :

$$\text{Price} > MC$$

Furthermore, from the fact that price $= MC\frac{e}{e-1}$ under monopoly it follows that the extent to which price would differ from marginal cost (*MC*) depends upon the value of elasticity on the average revenue curve at the point corresponding to the equilibrium output. The precise extent to which price will be greater than marginal cost (*MC*) will be given by the value of expression $\frac{e}{e-1}$. The smaller the elasticity, the greater the value of $\frac{e}{e-1}$ expression and hence greater the extent to which price would diverge from marginal cost. *Monopoly price is thus the function of marginal cost of production and elasticity of demand.*

Monopoly Equilibrium and Price Elasticity of Demand

Another important feature of monopoly equilibrium is that the ***monopolist will never be in equilibrium at a point on the demand curve or average revenue curve at which elasticity of demand is less than one.*** In other words, the monopolist will never fix his level of output at which price elasticity of demand or average revenue curve is less than one, provided the marginal cost is positive which is most usually the case. Since marginal cost can never be negative, equality of marginal revenue and marginal cost cannot be achieved where price elasticity of demand is less than one and marginal revenue is therefore negative. We know from the relationship between price elasticity and marginal revenue that whenever elasticity is less than one, marginal revenue is negative. Therefore, no sensible monopolist will produce on that portion of the demand or average revenue curve which gives him negative marginal revenue, that is, which reduces his total revenue, while the production of additional units adds to his total cost.

That the equilibrium of the monopolist will never be at the level of output at which price elasticity of demand on average revenue curve is less than one is illustrated in Figure 32.6. It will be seen from Figure 32.6 (upper panel) that up to *ON* level of output, *MR* is positive and total revenue is increasing as up to this output level, price elasticity of demand on the demand or average revenue curve is greater than one. Equilibrium will always lie where elasticity is greater than one. We know that at the middle point *R* of the straight-line demand or *AR* curve, elasticity is equal to one and corresponding to this unit elasticity point, marginal revenue is equal to zero. Below the middle point *R* on the average revenue curve, elasticity is less than one and marginal revenue is negative. The equilibrium of the monopolist will, therefore, never lie below the middle point of the average revenue curve *AR* as over this range, marginal revenue becomes negative and total revenue (*TR*) decreases as is evident from the falling *TR* curve beyond *ON* output. Thus, given that *MC* is positive, monopoly equilibrium cannot lie below the middle point of the average revenue curve where price elasticity is less than one. It will always lie above the middle point of the average revenue curve where elasticity is greater than one. The precise point on which monopoly equilibrium point lies depends, as already explained, upon the position of marginal cost curve and its intersection point with the marginal revenue curve.

Monopoly Equilibrium in Case of Zero Marginal Cost

There are however, some cases where marginal cost is zero, that is, it costs nothing to produce additional units of output. For instance, in case of mineral water spring, cost of production of mineral water is zero. Furthermore, in the very short period when a product is already on hand in excessive amount, it is not relevant to consider cost of production while determining the quantity of output to sell. In these cases where cost of production is either zero or is irrelevant to consider, the monopoly equilibrium will lie at a unit elasticity point on the demand curve. This is because in such cases monopolist has only to decide at which output the total revenue will be maximum. And total revenue is maximum at the output level at which marginal revenue is zero. When marginal cost is zero, the condition of profit maximisation, that is, the equality between marginal cost and marginal revenue can be achieved only at the output where the latter is also zero. It will be seen from upper panel of Fig. 32.6 that when marginal cost is zero, monopoly equilibrium will be achieved at *ON* level of output at which *MR* is zero. The price set by him in this situation will be *NR* or *OP*. *ON* quantity of output will yield maximum total revenue since beyond this marginal revenue becomes negative and total revenue will therefore start declining. Since cost of production is zero, the whole revenue will represent profits and because total revenue is maximum at *ON* output, the total profits will be maximum at this output. As at *ON* level of output *MR* is zero and, as already seen, corresponding to zero marginal revenue, elasticity of the demand on the average revenue curve is equal to one. We therefore conclude that when cost of production is zero, monopoly equilibrium will be established at a level where price elasticity of demand is one. If the marginal cost is positive, then, as explained above, monopolist will be in equilibrium at a point where price elasticity on average revenue curve is greater than one.

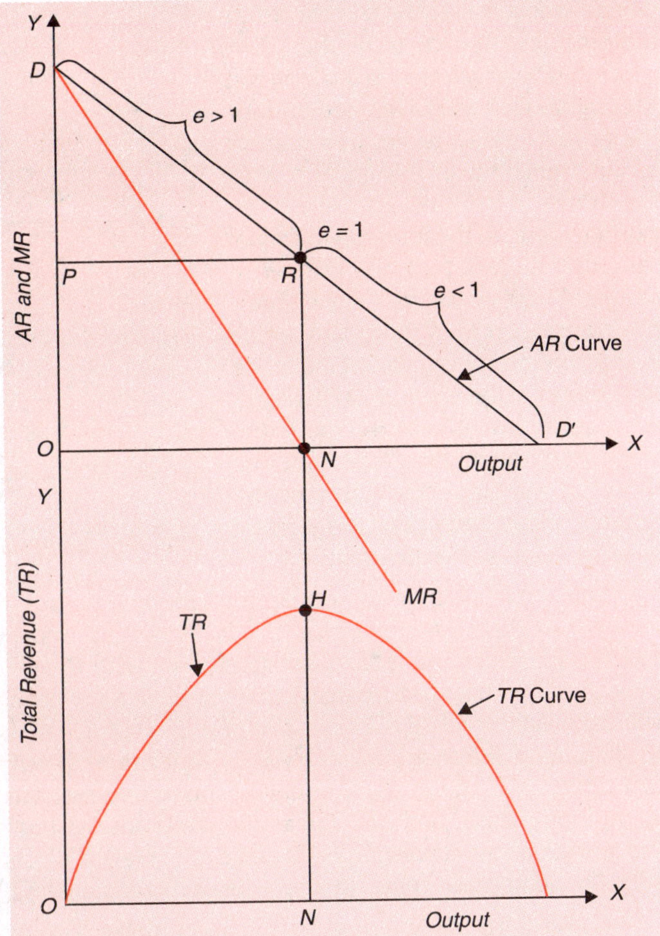

Fig. 32.6. *Monopolist cannot be in equilibrium at a level of output where elasticity of demand is less than one*

Long-Run Equilibrium under Monopoly

In the long run monopolist would make adjustment in the size of his plant. The long-run average cost curve and its corresponding long-run marginal cost curve portray the alternative plants, *i.e.*, various plant sizes from which the firm has to choose for operation in the long run. The monopolist would choose that plant size which is most appropriate for a particular level of demand. In the short run the monopolist adjusts the level of output while working with a given existing plant. His profit-maximizing output in the short run will be where to only the short-run marginal cost curve (*i.e.*, marginal cost curve with the existing plant) is equal to marginal revenue. But in the long run he can further increase his profits by adjusting the size of the plant. So in the long run he will be in equilibrium at the level of output where given marginal revenue curve cuts the long-run marginal cost curve. Fixing output level at which marginal revenue is equal to long-run marginal cost shows that the size of the plant has also been adjusted. That plant size is chosen which is most optimal for a given demand for the product. It should be carefully noted that, in the long run, marginal revenue is also equal to short-run marginal cost curve. But this short-run marginal cost curve is of the plant which has been selected in the long run keeping in view the given demand for the product. Thus while, in the short run, marginal revenue is equal only to the short-run marginal cost of a given existing plant, in the long run marginal revenue is equal to the long-run marginal cost as well as to the short-run marginal cost of that plant which is appropriate for a given demand for the product in the long run. In the long-run equilibrium, therefore, both the long-run marginal cost curve and the short-run marginal cost curve of the relevant plant intersect the marginal revenue curve at the same point.

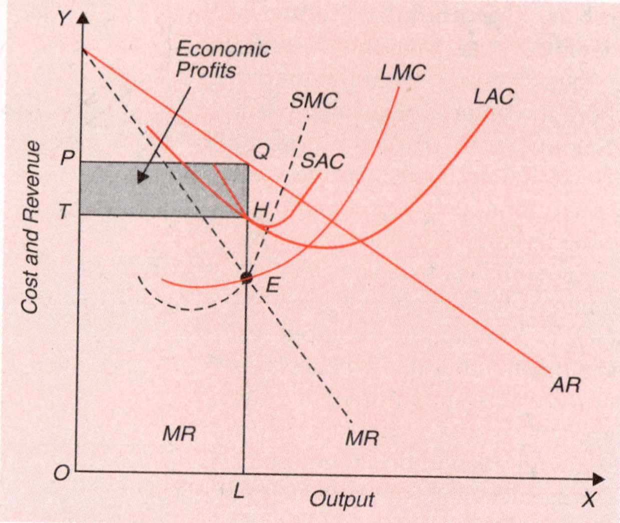

Fig. 32.7. *Long-run Equilibrium under Monopoly*

Further, it is important to note that, in the long run, the *firm will operate at a point on the long-run average cost curve* (*LAC*) at which the short-run average cost curve is tangent to it. This is because it is only corresponding to the tangency point of short-run average cost curve (*SAC*) with long-run average cost curve (*LAC*) that short-run marginal cost (*SMC*) of the optimal plant equals the long-run marginal cost (*LMC*). Figure 32.7 portrays the long-run equilibrium of the monopolist. He is in equilibrium at output *OL* at which long-run marginal cost curve *LMC* intersects marginal revenue curve *MR*. Given the level of demand as indicated by positions of *AR* and *MR* curves he would choose the plant size whose short-run average and marginal cost curves are *SAC* and *SMC*. He will be charging price equal to *LQ* or *OP* and will be making profits equal to the area of rectangle *THQP*.

It therefore follows that for the monopolist to maximize profits in the long run, the following conditions must be fulfilled

$$MR = LMC = SMC$$
$$SAC = LAC$$
$$P \geq LAC$$

The last condition implies in *long-run monopoly equilibrium* price of the product should be either greater than long-run average cost or at least equal to it. The price cannot fall below long-run average cost because in the long run the monopolist will quit the industry if it is not even able to make normal profits.

Long-Run Equilibrium Adjustment under Monopoly

In order to understand fully the difference between the short-run equilibrium and long-run adjustment under monopoly, it is necessary to show short-run equilibrium and long-run equilibrium in one figure. This is done in Fig. 32.8 which shows that for a given level of demand, the monopolist will be in short-run equilibrium at point *E* or at output OQ_1 if he has plant size SAC_1 at that time. But in the long run he would not be in equilibrium at *E* since in the long run he can also change the plant and will employ that plant which is most appropriate for a given level of demand. In the long run he will be in equilibrium at point *F* where marginal revenue curve cuts his long-run marginal cost curve. But every point of the long-run marginal cost curve corresponds to a point of some short-run marginal cost curve Long-run equilibrium point F at which marginal revenue curve cuts long-run marginal cost curve is also the point on short-run marginal cost curve SMC_2 which corresponds to the short-run average cost curve SAC_2. The plant having short-run cost curves SAC_2 and SMC_2 is optimal for him in the long run, given the level of demand as shown by AR and MR curves. It is now clear that the monopolist who was in equilibrium at E in the short run with the given plant having cost curves SAC_1 and SMC_1 has shifted to the plant having cost curves SAC_2 and SMC_2 in his long-run adjustment, level of demand being given. It will be noticed that, in the long run, the output has increased from OQ_1 to OQ_2 and price has fallen from OP to OJ. Profits have also increased in the long run; area $GHKJ$ is larger than the area $TRSP$.

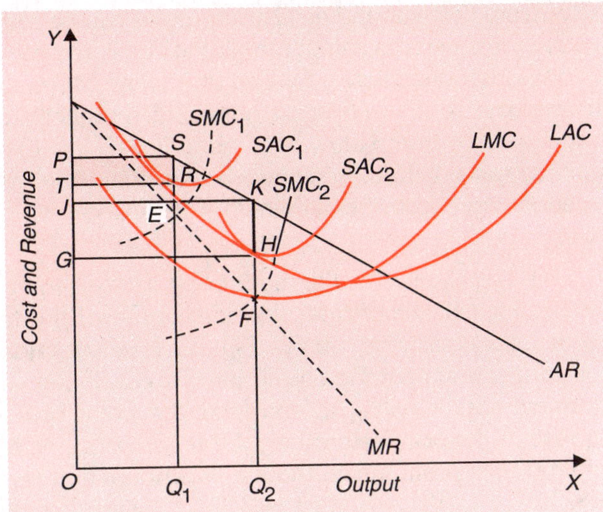

Fig. 32.8. *Shift from a Short-Run to Long-run Equilibrium Position under Monopoly*

MONOPOLY EQUILIBRIUM AND PERFECTLY COMPETITIVE EQUILIBRIUM COMPARED

We have explained, in the preceding chapters, equilibrium of a perfectly competitive firm and industry and also how price is determined under it. In the present chapter we have explained above the equilibrium under monopoly. It is now in the fitness of things to make a comparative study of the two. Only similarity between the two is that a firm both under perfect competition and monopoly is in equilibrium at the level of the output at which marginal revenue equals marginal cost. But there are many important points of difference which we spell out below.

Relationship Between Price and Marginal Cost. A significant difference between the two is that while *under perfect competition price equals marginal cost at the equilibrium output, in monopoly equilibrium it is greater than marginal cost.* Why? Under perfect competition average revenue curve is a horizontal straight line and therefore marginal revenue curve coincides with average revenue curve and as a result marginal revenue and average revenue are equal to each other at all levels of output. Therefore, under perfect competition at the equilibrium output marginal cost not only equals marginal revenue, but also equals average revenue, *i.e.*, price. On the other hand, average revenue curve confronting a monopolistic firm slopes downward and marginal revenue curve therefore lies below it. Consequently, under monopoly, average revenue (or price) is greater than marginal revenue at all levels of output. Hence, at equilibrium output of the monopolist where marginal cost equals marginal revenue, price stands higher than marginal cost. Thus, in perfectly competition equilibrium, Price = MR = MC. In monopoly equilibrium, Price > MC.

Monopoly Equilibrium Can Occur under All the three Cost-Conditions, namely, Increasing MC, Constant MC, and. Decreasing MC. A SeconcTimportant difference between the two is that while *under perfect competition, equilibrium is possible only when marginal cost is rising at the point of equilibrium, but monopoly equilibrium can be realised whether marginal cost is rising,remaining constant or falling at the equilibrium output.* This is so because the second order condition of equilibrium, namely, MC curve should cut MR

curve from below at the equilibrium point can be satisfied in monopoly in all the three cases, whether *MC* curve is rising, remaining constant or falling, whereas in perfect competition the second order condition is fulfilled only when MC curve is rising. Since in perfect competition the marginal revenue curve is a horizontal straight line, marginal cost curve can cut the marginal revenue curve from below only when it *(MC* curve) is rising. But under monopoly, marginal revenue curve is falling downward and, therefore, marginal cost curve can cut the marginal revenue curve from below whether it *(MC* curve) is rising, remaining at constant level, or falling.

The equilibrium of the monopolist in these three cases is shown in Fig. 32.9, 32.10 and 32.11. Fig. 32.9 illustrates the equilibrium of the monopolist when marginal cost curve is rising at the equilibrium output. Fig. 32.10 shows monopoly equilibrium when marginal cost is constant at and near the equilibrium output. In Fig. 32.11 monopolist is in equilibrium when marginal cost is falling at and near the point of equilibrium. In all these three cases, *OP* represents the price determined, *OM* represents the equilibrium output, and *RNQP* represents total positive profit made, though its amount differs in different cases.

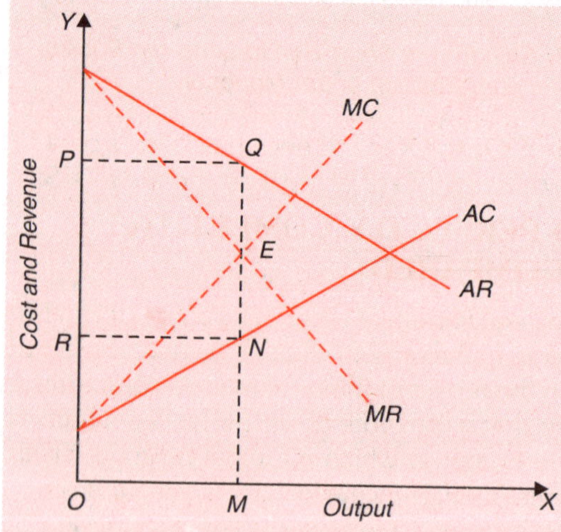

Fig. 32.9 *Monopoly Equilibrium in Case of Rising Marginal and Average Costs*

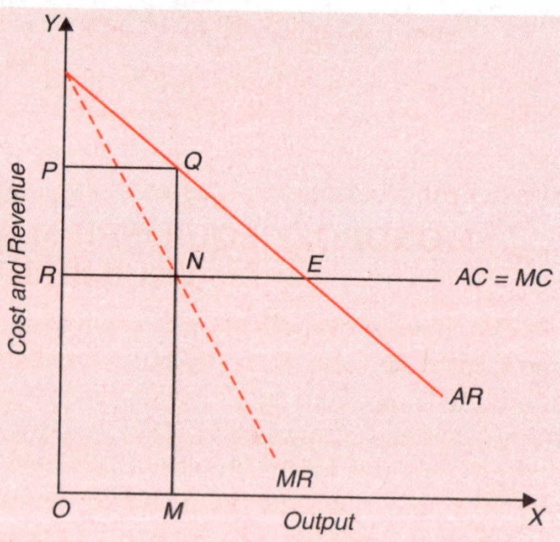

Fig. 32.10 *Monopoly Equilibrium in Case of Constant Marginal and Average Costs*

Long-Run Competitive Equilibrium, Monopoly Equilibrium and Optimum Size. Another significant difference between the two is that *whereas a perfectly competitive firm is in long-run equilibrium at the minimum point of the long-run average cost curve, monopolistic firm is generally in equilibrium at the level of output where average cost is still declining* and has not yet reached its minimum point. In other words, whereas a perfectly competitive firm tends to be of optimum size in the long run, a monopolist firm stops short of the optimum size. This is so because it pays a competitive firm to expand production so long as average cost is falling since average revenue and marginal revenue

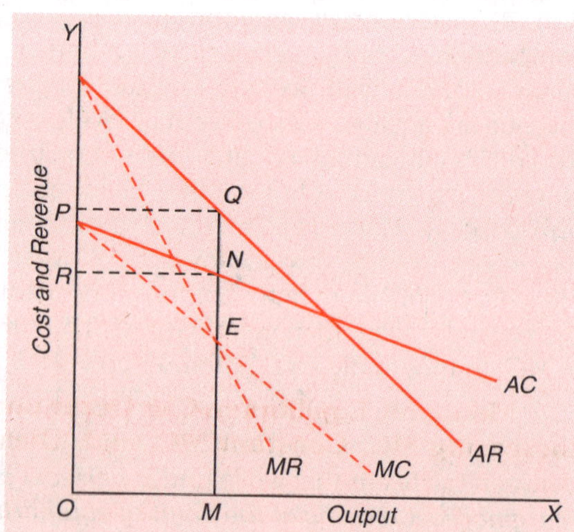

Fig. 32.11 *Monopoly Equilibrium in Case of Decreasing Marginal Cost*

remains constant, but it does not pay a monopolistic firm to expand production to the minimum point of the average cost curve because it is often not worthwhile for it to do so. More frequently, the marginal revenue curve of the monopolist intersects the marginal cost curve at the level of output at which average cost is still falling, as will be seen from Fig 32.7. On the other hand, in case of the competitive firm marginal revenue or price, in long-run equili-brium, is equal to both marginal cost and minimum average cost. In other words, profits of the competitive firm are, in the long run, maximum at the level of output at which long-run average cost is minimum.

Under Monopoly Supernormal Profits can Persist in the Long Run. Fourth important difference between the two is that *while the perfectly competitive firm is, in the long run, able to make only normal profits, a monopolist can make economic or supernormal profits even in the long run.* Under perfect competition, if firms in the short run are making profit above normal, the new firms will enter the industry to compete away these profits. But under monopoly the firm continues earning supernormal profits even in the long run since there are strong barriers to the entry of new firms in the monopolistic industry. It should not be understood from this that monopoly always guarantees supernormal profits. The monopoly can even make losses, though only in the short run. These short-run losses are not due to competition from any new firms but due to inadequate demand and relatively higher costs of production. The point is, if the monopolist, is the short run, in making profits above nominal they cannot be eliminated by the entry of new firms in the long run with the result that these supernormal profits will persist in the long run provided that the demand and cost situations are not changed unfavourably.

Monopolist can practise price discrimation to maximize profits, a competitive firm cannot do so. Last significant difference between monopoly and perfect competition is that while a *monopolist can discriminate prices for his good, a perfect competitor cannot.* The monopolist will by increasing his total profits by discriminating prices if he finds that elasticities of demand at the single monopoly price are different in different markets. But it is not possible for a firm under perfect competition to charge different prices from different buyers. This is because a seller under perfect competition confronts a perfectly elastic demand curve at the level of going market price. Therefore, if he tries to charge a bit higher price than the going market price from some buyers, they will turn to other sellers and purchase the same good at the going market pxrice. But the monopolist has the sole control over the supply of a product which has no close substitutes and therefore the demand curve of his product is very much less elastic. If the monopolist is able to break up his market into different parts on one basis or the other, it will be possible for him to discriminate prices in different parts of the market. But it will be profitable for him to charge different prices in the different parts only if the elasticity of demand at the single monopoly price is different in different parts.

Monopoly Equilibrium Price is Higher and Output Lower than under Perfect Competition. Another important difference between monopoly equilibrium and perfectly competitive equilibrium is that *under monopoly price is higher and output smaller than under perfect competition,* assuming demand and cost conditions in the two cases are the same. Suppose a number of firms are producing homogeneous products and pure or perfect competition in the sense that no one can individually affect the price exists among them. Price and output will be determined at the level where demand and supply curves intersect each other. Suppose that all the firms constituting the competitive industry combine together so as to form a monopoly. We assume that no economies, internal or external, accrue when the firms combine together so that the cost or supply conditions remain unchanged. Now, the price and output under monopoly are determined by the equality between marginal cost and marginal revenue.

Price-output equilibrium under perfect competition and monopoly are graphically shown in a single diagram (Fig. 32.12). Curves *DD* and *SS* are respectively demand and supply curves of the perfectly competitive industry. It should be noted that the supply curve *SS* of a product under perfect competition is obtained by horizontal summation of the marginal cost curves (ΣMC) of all the firms in the competitive industry. The two curves intersect each other at point *E* and as a result price *QE* or OP_1 and output *OQ* are determined under perfect competition. The marginal revenue curve *MR* is drawn corresponding to the demand curve *DD*. The supply curve *SS* of the perfectly competitive industry which is obtained by summing up laterally the marginal cost curves of the firms in it will now constitute the marginal cost curve under monopoly. It will be seen from Fig. 32.12 that the marginal revenue curve *MR* cuts the marginal cost curve *SS* (*i.e.* ΣMC) of the monopolist at point *B* and as a consequence monopoly price OP_2 and monopoly output *OM* are determined. It is thus clear that if cost conditions remain unchanged, the merger of firms to form monopoly has resulted in a higher price and a lower output of the product. As a result of monopoly coming into existence price has risen from OP_1 to OP_2 and output has fallen from *OQ* to *OM*. Monopolist thus restricts output to raise price.

Now, a pertinent question is whether cost conditions are likely to remain the same when a number of firms combine to become a monopoly ? In other words, whether some extra economies will not accrue when the monopoly comes into existence and works on a larger scale than that of a large number of separate firms under perfect competition. There are two opinions on this issue.

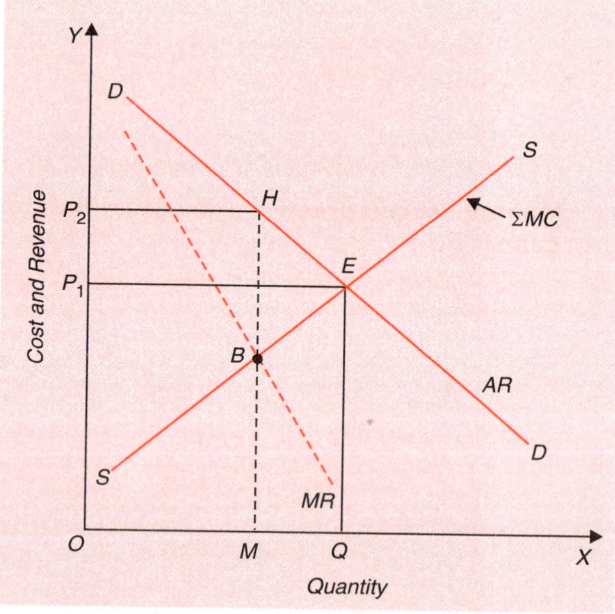

Fig. 32.12 *Under monopoly price is higher and output smaller than under perfect competition*

One view is that monopolist can introduce various economies such as greater specialization in the work by bringing about suitable lateral and vertical integration, organization of sales on a large scale, buying raw materials and machinery on a big order, getting cheap credit, discovering and introducing new methods of production, and undertaking various measures which are generally associated with rationalization. These economies, it is held, will lower the cost of production of the monopolist with the result that the marginal cost cure (*SS*) in case of monopoly in Fig. 32.12 will shift to a downward position when monopoly comes into existence. If these economies are good enough so that there is substantial downward fall in the cost curve, the monopoly price will be lower than the competitive price OP_1 or *QE* and monopoly output will be larger than the competitive output.

But in view of Joan Robinson, "perfect competition would bring about all the economies which monopoly could introduce".[1] She holds therefore that the cost curve will not shift downward as a result of the establishment of monopoly in place of the large number of firms working perfect competition. Thus, according to her, monopoly price is always higher and monopoly output always smaller than that under perfect competition.

1. See her *Economics of Imperfect Competition*, p.168

NUMERICAL PROBLEMS ON MONOPOLY EQUILBRIUM

Problem 1. *Let us illustrate the monopoly equilibrium with a numerical example. Suppose for a monopolist the following demand and total cost function are given. Find out how much he will produce and what price he will charge*

$$Q = 360 - 20\,P \text{ (demand function)}$$

$$TC = 6Q + 0.05Q^2 \text{ (cost function)}$$

Solution : In order to find the profit-maximizing solution we have to derive the marginal revenue and marginal cost from the demand and cost equations given above. In order to find out the marginal revenue we have to first obtain the total revenue function.

Thus we first derive the inverse demand function as under:

$$Q = 360 - 20P$$

$$20P = 360 - Q$$

$$P = 18 - 0.05\,Q \qquad \text{......}(i)$$

$$\text{Total revenue } (TR) = P.\,Q = 18Q - 0.05Q^2$$

Differentiating it with respect to output Q we can get MR. Thus

$$MR = \frac{\Delta TR}{\Delta Q} = \frac{\Delta(P.Q)}{\Delta Q} = 18 - 0.1Q \qquad \text{...}(ii)$$

Marginal cost can be obtained by differentiating the total function ($TC = 6Q + 0.05Q^2$). Thus, we have

$$MC = \frac{\Delta TC}{\Delta Q} = 6 + 0.1Q \qquad \text{...}(iii)$$

Since the profits of the monopolist will be maximized when he equates marginal revenue with marginal cost, setting $MR = MC$ we have

$$18 - 0.1Q = 6 + 0.1Q$$

$$0.2Q = 18 - 6 = 12$$

$$Q = 12.\frac{10}{2} = 60$$

To find out price we substitute the value of output Q in the demand function (*i*) above we have

$$P = 18 - 0.05Q$$

$$= 18 - 0.05 \times 60 = 18 - 3 = 15$$

To obtain total profits we calculate total revenue and total cost

$$TR = P.Q = 15 \times 60 = 900$$

$$TC = 6Q + 0.05Q^2 = 6 \times 60 + 0.05\,(60)^2$$

$$= 360 + \frac{5}{100} \times 3600 = 540$$

$$\text{Profit} = TR - TC = 900 - 540 = 360$$

Thus, output (Q) = 60; price (*P*) = ₹ 15 and profits = ₹ 360.

Problem 2. *A monopolist firm producing and supplying cooking gas to a city faces the following demand function*

$$Q = 400 - 20P$$

The firm has the following cost function

$$TC = 5Q + \frac{Q^2}{50}$$

Determine the quantity of the cooking gas he will produce and price he will charge to maximise profits. What will be amount of profits made by him ?

Solution. [Note that the given cost function does not contain the fixed cost component as all terms in it contain the element of output (Q). Therefore, this represents the long-run cost function as in the long run all factors are variable and there are no fixed costs.]

It should be carefully noted that for the problem of profit maximization for we are required to obtain total revenue function, from which marginal revenue can be derived. In order to obtain *TR* and *MR*, inverse demand function is required, that is, demand expressed in terms of "*Price as a function of quantity*". Thus,

$$Q = 400 - 20P$$

$$20P = 400 - Q$$

$$P = \frac{400}{20} - \frac{Q}{20}$$

Thus, inverse demand function is $P = 20 - \frac{Q}{20}$ ...(*i*)

Multiplying both sides by Q

$$PQ = TR = 20Q - \frac{Q^2}{20}$$

$$MR = \frac{d(TR)}{dQ} = 20 - \frac{Q}{10} \quad \text{...(ii)}$$

The given cost function is

$$TC = 5Q + \frac{Q^2}{50}$$

$$MC = \frac{d(TC)}{dQ} = 5 + \frac{Q}{25} \quad \text{...(iii)}$$

For profit maximisation

$$MR = MC$$

$$20 - \frac{Q}{10} = 5 + \frac{Q}{25}$$

$$\frac{Q}{25} + \frac{Q}{10} = 20 - 5 = 15$$

$$\frac{7Q}{50} = 15$$

$$7Q = 50 \times 15 = 750$$

Profit maximising output $Q^* = \frac{750}{7} = 107$ (rounded off)

To solve for P we substitute the value of Q^* in the demand function equation (*i*) above.

$$P = 20 - \frac{Q}{20}$$

$$P = 20 - \frac{107}{20} = 20 - 5.35 = 14.65$$

Thus, profit maximising price is ₹ 14.65.

Profits

$$\pi = TR - TC$$

$$TR = 14.65 \times 107 = 1568$$

$$TC = 5Q + \frac{Q^2}{50} = 5 \times 107 + \frac{(107)^2}{50} = 764$$

$$\pi = 1568 - 764 = 804.$$

Problem 3. *A monopolist has the following total cost function*

$$TC = 10 + 5Q$$

(1) If price elasticity of demand for his product is – 2, find out what price he will fix for his product.

(2) If the price elasticity of demand for his product changes to – 4, how will he change his price?

Solution :

(1)

$$TC = 10 + 5Q$$

$$MC = \frac{dTC}{dQ} = 5 \qquad ...(1)$$

The relationship between MR, price and price elasticity of demand (e) is

$$MR = P\left(1 + \frac{1}{e}\right)$$

Given that price elasticity of demand is – 2.

$$MR = P\left(1 + \frac{1}{-2}\right) = P\left(1 - \frac{1}{2}\right)$$

$$MR = \frac{1}{2}P \qquad ...(2)$$

In equilibrium,

$$MR = MC$$

$$\frac{1}{2}P = 5$$

$$P = 5 \times 2 = \text{Rs } 10$$

Given that

$$e = -4$$

$$MR = P\left(1 + \frac{1}{-4}\right) = P\left(1 - \frac{1}{4}\right) = \frac{3}{4}P$$

In equilibrium

$$MR = MC$$

$$\frac{3}{4}P = 5$$

$$P = 5 \times \frac{4}{3} = 6.67$$

Thus, with the increase in absolute value of price elasticity of demand, monopolist will reduce the price of his product.

Problem 4. *Suppose price elasticity of demand for the product of a monopolist is – 2.0. Show that price fixed by him will be twice the marginal cost of production.*

Solution. In price-output equilibrium of the monopolist

$$MR = MC$$

Since $$MR = P\left(1-\frac{1}{|e|}\right)$$

$$MC = P\left(1-\frac{1}{|e|}\right)$$

If $$e = -2.0$$

$$MC = P\left(1-\frac{1}{2}\right) = \frac{1}{2}P$$

or $$P = 2MC.$$

Problem 5. *Given the following linear demand and cost functions, show that monopolist will produce half the output under perfect competition*

$$Q = 300 - 2P \qquad \text{(Linear demand function)}$$

$$TC = 150 + 10Q$$

Solution : $$TC = 150 + 10Q$$

$$MC = \frac{dTC}{dQ} = 10 \qquad ...(i)$$

Now, the given linear demand function is

$$Q = 300 - 2P$$

$$2P = 300 - Q$$

$$P = 150 - 0.5Q \qquad ...(ii)$$

$$TR = PQ = 150Q - 0.5Q^2$$

$$MR = \frac{d(PQ)}{dQ} = 150 - Q \qquad ...(iii)$$

Output under perfect competition is determined where $MC = P$

Thus, under perfect competition

$$10 = 150 - 0.5Q$$

$$0.5Q = 150 - 10 = 140$$

Hence, $$Q_{pc} = 280 \qquad ...(iv)$$

In equilibrium under monopoly,

$$MR = MC$$

From (*iii*) we know $MR = 150 - Q$ and from (*i*) we know that $MC = 10$

Thus, in equilibrium under monopoly

$$150 - Q = 10$$

$$Q = 150 - 10 = 140$$

Thus, $$Q_m = 140 \qquad ...(v)$$

Comparing (*iv*) and (*v*) we find that output under monopoly is half of that produced under perfect competition.

ABSENCE OF SUPPLY CURVE UNDER MONOPOLY

An important feature of the monopoly equilibrium is that unlike a competitive firm, the *monopolist does not have the supply curve*. It is worthnoting that the supply curve shows how much output a firm will produce at various *given prices* of a product. The supply curve of a product by a firm traces out the ***unique price-output relationship,*** that is, against a given price there is a particular amount of output which the firm will produce and sell in the market. As explained in a previous chapter, the concept of supply curve is relevant only when the firm exercises no control over the price of the product and takes it given. Therefore, it is perfectly competitive firm which is a price taker and demand curve facing it is a horizontal straight line that unique price-output relationship is established. For a perfectly competitive firm, marginal revenue (*MR*) equals price and therefore to maximize profits, the firm equates the new higher price (*i.e.* new *MR*) with its marginal cost at higher level of output. In this way under perfect competition, marginal cost curve becomes the supply curve of the firm.

But for a monopoly firm demand curve slopes downward and marginal revenue (*MR*) curve lies below it. Therefore, a monopolist in order to maximize profits does not equate price with marginal cost; instead he equates marginal revenue with marginal cost. As a result, shifts in demand causing changes in price do not trace out a unique price-output series as happens in case of a perfectly competitive firm. In fact, under monopoly shifts in demand can lead to a change in price with no change in output or a change in output with no change in price or they can lead to changes in both price and output. This renders the concept of supply curve inapplicable and irrelevant under conditions of monopoly.

That, under monopoly, we do not get a series of unique price-output relationship or supply curve of a product is illustrated in Figure 32.13. Suppose the demand curve is initially D_1 corresponding to which MR_1 is the marginal revenue curve. Given the marginal cost curve *MC*, monopolist is in equilibrium at *OM* level of output and charging price OP_1. Now, suppose that demand curve shifts to the position D_2 corresponding to which MR_2 is the marginal revenue curve. It will be seen from Fig. 32.13 that the new marginal revenue curve MR_2 also intersects the given marginal cost curve *MC* at the same level of output *OM* as before the shift in the demand curve but the price has risen to OP_2. Thus we see that,

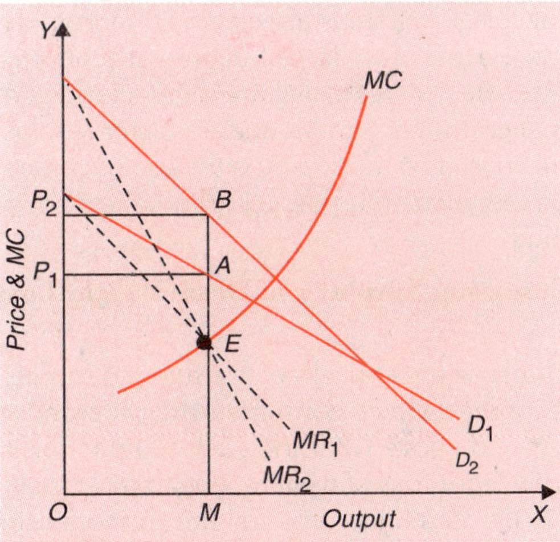

Fig. 32.13. *Under monopoly a shift in demand leading to the same output being supplied at two different prices*

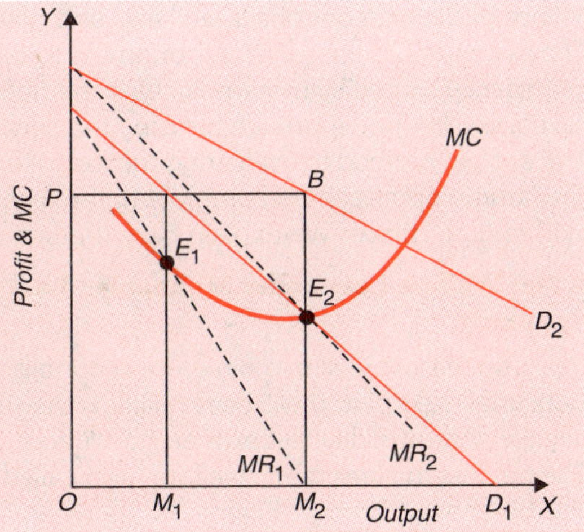

Fig. 32.14. *Under monopoly a shift in demand leading to a change in output supplied at the same price*

under monopoly, a shift in demand leads to the production and *supply of the same output at two different prices*. This clearly shows that there is no unique price-output relationship which is essential for the concept of supply curve to be applicable.

Figure 32.14 illustrates another special case where shift in demand leads to the *different levels of output being supplied at the same price*. Initially, with D_1 and MR_1 as the demand and marginal revenue curves respectively, the monopolist maximizes his profits by producing OM_1 and charging price OP. The shift in demand curve to D_2 and the marginal revenue curve to MR_2, the marginal cost curve MC cuts the new MR_2 curve at E_2 and it will be observed from Figure 32.14 that in the new equilibrium, the monopolist produces higher quantity OM_2 at the same price OP. This again shows that under monopoly there is no any *specific* quantity of the product supplied at a price.

To sum up, under monopoly, there is no supply curve associating unique output with a price. Shift in demand may lead to either change in price with the same output being produced and supplied or it may lead to the change in output with same price. However, usually the shift in demand would lead to the changes in both output and price. ***How price and output will change as a result of shift in demand depends not only on the marginal cost curve but also on the price elasticity of demand.*** The important thing to remember is that in sharp contrast to the case of a perfectly competitive firm, under monopoly marginal cost curve does not serve as the supply curve of the firm and further that there is no supply curve under monopoly depicting unique price-output relationship.

MONOPOLY, RESOURCE ALLOCATION AND SOCIAL WELFARE

Monopoly is often criticized that it causes misallocation of resources or economic inefficiency in resource allocation. *By economic efficiency we mean that resource allocation to the production of a good is such that it maximizes social welfare, that is, the satisfaction of the consumers*. Thus, whereas under perfect competition allocation of resources is pareto optimum and therefore social welfare is maximum, under monopoly resources are misallocated causing loss of social welfare.

As seen above, when a product is produced and sold under conditions of monopoly, the monopolist gains at the expense of consumers, who have to pay a price higher than the marginal cost of production. This results in loss of consumers' welfare. Which is greater ? Monopolist's gain or consumers' loss and how total social welfare is affected by a monopoly. The two methods are used by economists to measure the loss of welfare or degree of economic inefficiency caused by monopoly. One method to evaluate the loss in welfare is the adoption of partial equilibrium approach by using the concepts of consumer surplus and producer surplus. The second method to evaluating the loss of welfare caused by monopoly is the use of general equilibrium approach and employing the technique of production possibility curve and social indifference curves. We explain here the first method.

1. Net Welfare Loss under Monopoly: Loss of Consumer Surplus and Dead-Weight Loss Approach

To measure welfare gain or loss economists often use the concept of consumer's surplus. Consumer's surplus, it will be recalled, is the surplus of price which consumers are prepared to pay for a commodity rather than go without it over and above what they actually pay for it. The net loss in consumer's welfare, also called *dead weight loss* of welfare, due to monopoly, can be shown through Figure 32.15 where TD is the demand curve for the monopolist's product, MR is the corresponding marginal revenue curve. It is assumed that the industry is a constant cost industry so that average cost (AC) remains the same as output is increased and marginal cost is equal to it.

Under perfect competition, industry will be in equilibrium with ON output being produced and price OP_c or NA of the product is determined by the forces of demand for and supply of the product and is equal to marginal cost of production. It will be seen from Figure 32.15 that under perfect competition, price will be NA (or OP_c) which is equal to marginal cost at ON level of output. It will be seen from Figure 32.15 with OP_c or NA as the market price, buyers obtain consumers' surplus equal to area ATP_c. This is because total utility which they get by consuming ON output will be equal to the area $OTAN$ (*i.e.*, the area under the demand curve) and the total price they actually pay for it is measured by OP_cAN.

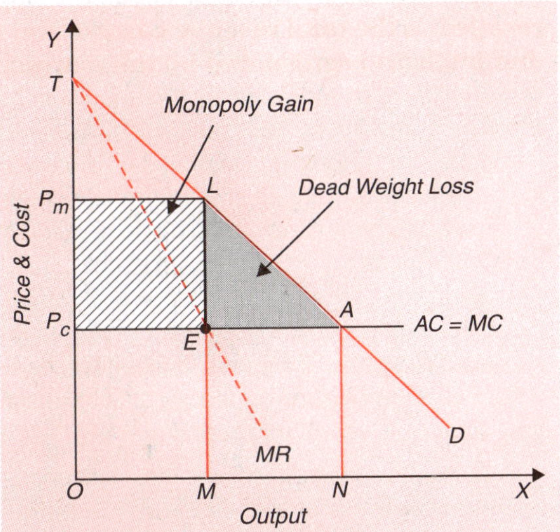

Fig. 32.15. *Welfare Loss due to Monopoly under Constant Cost Conditions*

Now, the monopolist would produce output OM of the product as this will maximize his profits (It will be seen from Fig. 32.15, that marginal revenue (MR) and marginal cost of the monopolist are equal at output level OM). The monopolist will set price OP_m or ML of the product. With output equal to OM and price OP_m, the monopolist gain is P_mLEP_c. On the other hand, with the rise in price to OP_m and fall in output to OM under monopoly, the consumer surplus has been reduced to LTP_m. That is, under monopoly consumers have suffered a loss of consumer surplus equal to the area ALP_mP_c. Out of the total loss of consumer surplus monopoly has gained profits equal to the area P_mLEP_c. Thus whereas consumers lose, the producers gain due to monopoly. In this way, there has been redistribution of income in favour of the monopolist. But the consumers' loss of consumer surplus is more than the gain of profits by the monopolist. It will be seen from Fig. 32.15 that there is net loss of consumer's welfare equal to the area of triangle LEA. Monopoly has caused this net welfare loss because it has reduced output from ON to OM. Between OM and ON outputs, consumers are prepared to pay higher price as indicated by portion of the demand or average curve in this region than the marginal cost which the society has to incur on producing units of output between OM and ON.

With lower production of the product by the monopolist, relatively less resources will be allocated to its production. For optimum allocation of resources or for being economically efficient (*i.e.* achieving pareto optimality) ON amount of the product, at which marginal cost equals price, should have been produced and resources allocated accordingly. To conclude, monopoly causes misallocation of resources and net loss of welfare (which is also known as *dead weight loss*) by not producing the level of output of the commodity at which price equals marginal cost of production. It should be noted that in addition to causing net welfare loss monopoly has also caused *transfer of income* away from the consumers. The monetary gain of the monopolist equal to the area P_mLEP_c represents this transfer of income to the monopolist producer; the monopolist has gained at the expense of consumers. Thus monopoly adversely affects income distribution in an economy. However, it is worth mentioning that in sharp contrast to this adverse distribution effect under which one's gain is other's loss, the net welfare loss measured by the area AEL represents a loss for which no one has gained. That is why it is often referred to as *dead-weight loss*. This is due to the economic inefficiency or misallocation of resources caused by monopoly.

Net Loss of Welfare under Monopoly in Case of Increasing Marginal Cost

In our above analysis of net welfare loss due to reduction in output and hike in the price by a monopolist as compared to the perfectly competitive equilibrium, it has been assumed that marginal cost curve is a horizontal straight line. When marginal cost curve is a horizontal straight line, the loss in welfare occurs only in consumer surplus. But when marginal cost curve is rising, the loss in welfare due to reduction in output by the monopolist will occur not only in reduction in consumer surplus but also in producer surplus. **Producer surplus, it will be recalled, is the total revenue earned over and over all the opportunity costs (explicit and implicit) represented by the marginal cost curve.** It may be noted that *maximum social welfare or economic efficiency is achieved when the sum of consumer surplus and producer surplus is the maximum*. In a perfectly competitive equilibrium where quantity demanded equals quantity supplied or price equals marginal cost, the sum of consumer surplus and producer surplus is maximum and therefore perfect competition ensures maximum social welfare or economic efficiency. But to be in equilibrium and maximize profits monopolist does not equate price with marginal cost. Instead, he equates marginal revenue with marginal cost and therefore reduces output and raises price and thereby causes loss of welfare. Loss in welfare as measured by the reduction in the sum of consumer surplus and producer surplus is illustrated in Figure 32.16. It will be seen that, under perfect competition, equilibrium will be at point *D* where price is equal to marginal cost (*MC*) and output *OQ* is being produced and price P_c is being charged.

Now, if monopoly comes into existence, the monopolist-producer will maximize profits by producing lower output *OM* and will charge higher price P_m. It will be observed that the loss in consumer surplus suffered by the buyers is equal to area P_cDAP_m. Due to the higher price charged by the monopolist, his gain in profits or producer surplus equals the rectangle P_cBAP_m. (It may be noted that this gain in producer surplus by the monopolist occurs at the expense of consumers who suffer a loss in consumer surplus and is equal to the price differential $P_m - P_c$ or *AB* times the monopoly output *OM*). Thus the gain in producer surplus represented by the area P_cBAP_m is just a transfer of income from the consumers to the monopolist. Net loss of consumer surplus or welfare is therefore the area of the triangle *ABD*.

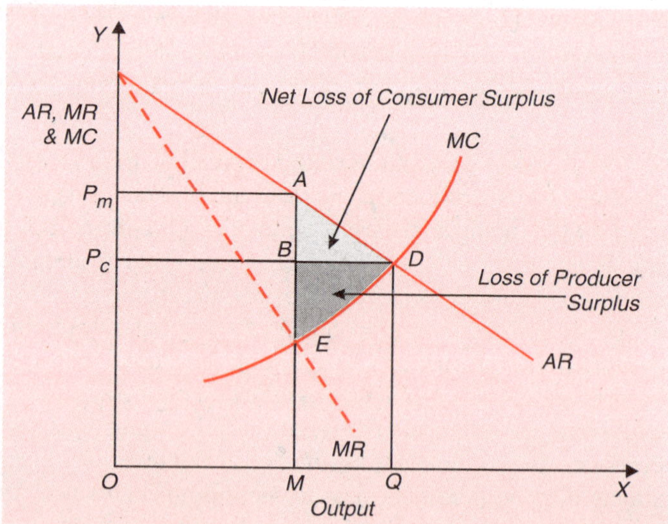

Fig. 32.16. *Dead-weight loss in welfare due to reduction in output and hike in price by the monopolist in case of increasing marginal cost*

However, in the situation depicted in Figure 32.16 where marginal cost is rising, apart from the net loss of consumer surplus, there is also a loss of producer surplus due to reduction in output by *QM* amount under monopoly. It will be seen from Figure 32.16 that under perfect competition with price equal to OP_c or *QD*, the extra revenue or producer surplus earned over and above the marginal costs in the region of *MQ* output equals the area *BDE* which is lost due to the reduction in output equal to *QM* by the monopolist. This loss in producer surplus *BDE* is also a *dead weight loss* caused by the inefficiency or lower production due to monopoly because this has not transferred to or benefited any other. Thus, the total dead weight loss of welfare caused by the monopoly is equal to the whole area *AED* which is the sum of net loss of consumer surplus (*ABD*) and the loss of producer surplus equal to *BDE* represents ***social cost of monopoly.***

It follows from the partial equilibrium approach to the measurement of loss of welfare that monopoly is economically inefficient and causes misallocation of resources as it does not extend production of a product to the level desired by the consumers. Some attempts have been made in recent years to measure statistically the loss in efficiency or welfare due to monopoly in the United States. A. C. Harberger estimated the aggregate loss in efficiency or welfare due to monopoly from 1924 to 1928 for the United States and found that this efficiency loss was one percent of national income (GNP) which was quite small[2]. However, Harberger's estimate has been criticised by G. J. Stigler[3] who pointed out some crucial flaws in the method adopted by Harberger to estimate the efficiency loss due to monopoly. Taking into account the objections by Stigler and making improvements in the method, Kamerschen[4] estimated that welfare loss due to monopoly for the period 1956-1961 in the United States was quite large, around 6 per cent of national income. However, the exact estimate of welfare or efficiency loss due to monopoly still remains a controversial issue.

NUMERICAL PROBLEM ON DEAD-WEIGHT LOSS

Problem 1. *A monopolist faces a demand curve, P = 700 — 2Q. If marginal cost is constant and is equal to 20. What is the amount of profits made by the monopolist? What is dead-weight welfare loss on account of monopoly ?*

Solution. For monopoly equilibrium, $MR = MC$.

The given demand curve is : $P = 100 - 2Q$

$$TR = P.Q = 100Q - 2Q^2$$

$$MR = \frac{d(TR)}{dQ} = \frac{d(PQ)}{dQ} = 100 - 4Q$$

Equating MR with MC (= 20) we have

$$100 - 4Q = 20$$

$$4Q = 100 - 20 = 80$$

$$Q = \frac{80}{4} = 20$$

To obtain equilibrium price we substitute $Q = 20$ in the given demand function. Thus,

$$P = 100 - 2 \times 20 = 100 - 40 = ₹\,60$$

Welfare is maximised when at the output produced price equals marginal cost as under conditions of perfect competition. Thus, equating price with marginal cost we have

$$P = MC$$

$$100 - 2Q = 20$$

$$2Q = 100 - 20 = 80$$

$$Q = 40.$$

2. A. C. Harberger, "Monopoly and Resource Allocation", *American Economic Review*, May, 1954.
3. G. J. Stigler, "The Statistics of Monopoly and Merger", *Journal of Political Economy*, February, 1956.
4. D. R Kamerschen, "An Estimation of the Welfare Losses from Monopoly in the American Economy", *Western Economic Journal*, Vol. 4,1966.

Dead-weight loss of welfare from monopoly is depicted in Figure 32.17. Consumer's surplus with output equal to 40 and price equal to 20 is equal to the area *DPE*. Monopoly restricts output to 20 and raises price to 60 or *OP*′. Therefore, under monopoly, consumer surplus is reduced to the area *DP*′*H*. Thus, consumers suffer a loss of welfare (*i.e.*, consumer's surplus) equal to the area *PP*′*HE*. The monopolist's profits as a result of restriction of output from 40 units to 20 units and raising of price of the product from 20 to ₹ 60, is equal to the area *PNHP*′ (*i.e.*, 40 × 20 = ₹ 800). But consumers suffer a greater loss of consumer surplus equal to the area *PP*′*HE*, that is, *NHE* more than the gain in profits of the monopolist. The welfare loss of consumers equal to the area *NHE* represents the *dead weight loss* of welfare and is

$$= \frac{1}{2}(40 \times 20) = \frac{1}{2}(800)$$

$$= 400$$

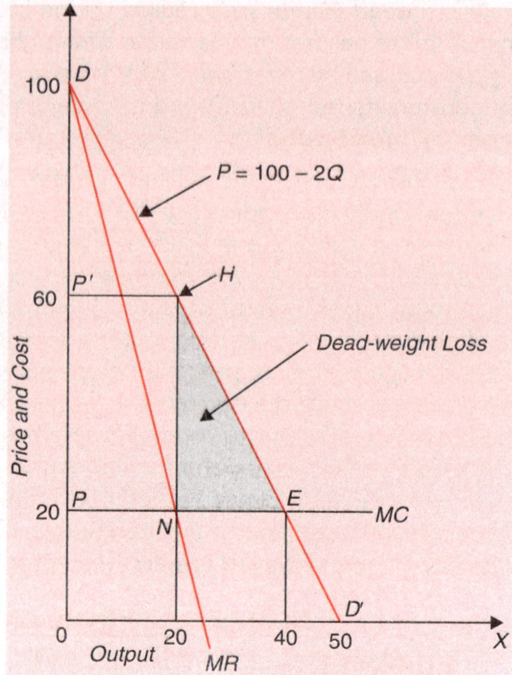

Fig. 32.17. *Dead-Weight Loss of Welfare*

This dead-weight loss represents social cost of monopoly.

QUESTIONS AND PROBLEMS FOR REVIEW

1. What is monopoly? Explain the three conditions necessary for the existence of monopoly.
2. Explain the relationship between average revenue, marginal revenue and price elasticity of demand under the conditions of monopoly.
3. Explain the equilibrium of a monopoly firm ? Show that price fixed by the monopolist is more than marginal cost of production.
4. How are price and output determined under monopoly ? Show that under monopoly price is higher and output smaller than under perfect competition.
5. Show that a monopolist will always operate on the elastic part of the demand curve.
6. A monopolist will never be in equilibrium on the *inelastic* ($e_p < 1$) portion of the demand curve. Explain.
7. A monopolistic firm has the following total cost function and demand function.

Price (Rupees)	*Quantity demanded (Units)*	*Total cost (Rs)*
8	5	20
7	6	21
6	7	22
5	8	23
4	9	24
3	10	25

Explain what price will be charged and what output will be produced.

[**Hint:** From the given data of price and quantity demanded, first find out total revenue (*TR* = *P*.*Q*). From *TR*, marginal revenue can be obtained at different levels of quantity demanded or sold. From total cost data, *MC* can be obtained. Then the output level at which *MC* = *MR*, will be the equilibrium output and price at that will be equilibrium price. In the above table, MC is constant at ₹ 1. When 6 units of sold, $MR = 2$ and when 7, units are sold, $MR = 0$, therefore the firm should produce 6 units of output to maximise its profits.]

8. How is monopoly power measured ? State Lerner's measure of degree of monopoly power. Show that degree of monopoly power is inverse of the price elasticity of demand.

9. A simple monopolist is in equilibrium. At the point of equilibrium the coefficient of price elasticity is – 2.0 and the marginal cost is Rs. 4.0. Calculate his equilibrium price. How will this price be affected by an increase in the fixed cost of the monopolist ? [**Hints** : In equilibrium, $MC = MR$

$$\text{Since } MR = P\left(1 - \frac{1}{|e|}\right)$$

Given $MC = 4$ and $e = -2$

$$\text{i.e., } 4 = P\left(1 - \frac{1}{2}\right)$$

$$P = 4 \times \frac{2}{1} = 8 \text{]}$$

10. When a monopolist is maximising profits, price is greater than marginal cost. Thus consumers will be paying more for additional units of output than it costs to produce. So why does not the monopolist produce more ?

11. A monopolist plans to produce 100 units of a commodity and observes that the price elasticity of demand at this output is 0.5. What advice would you give to the monopolist ?

[**Hints.** Since MR is negative at an output level where price elasticity is less than one, the monopolist will not be making maximum profits. In fact, he may be making losses if he pursues his plan. Therefore, the monopolist should restrict output of the commodity to the level where price elasticity of demand is greater than one and where his $MC = MR$]

12. A monopolist will never sell its product at a price less than its average total cost. Is it true or false ? Give reasons.

13. Explain why marginal revenue of a monopolist is less than the price charged.

14. Explain why a perfectly competitive firm will never operate when marginal cost is declining but a monopoly firm can do so.

15. If a price making monopolistic firm wants to maximise its sales revenue, it should :

(*a*) set the highest price it can get.

(*b*) set the lowest price it can get.

(*c*) choose a selling price at which the elasticity of demand for its product is unity.

(*d*) choose a selling price where the extra revenue received from the last unit sold exceeds the extra cost of making that unit.

Tick the right answer

16. Suppose that at the profit-maximising output, a monopolist price is twice as high as his marginal cost. What is the price elasticity of demand?

17. Does a monopolist always set his price above marginal cost ? Will he ever produce at the minimum point of long-run average curve.

[**Hints.** As explained in the text a monopolist always sets his price above marginal cost of production. Further, in the long run he usually produces less than the minimum point of LAC, that is, he produces with excess capacity in the long run. *However, this is not necessary* as it depends on the demand conditions facing him. If demand for his product is sufficiently large he may produce at or near the minimum point of long-run average curve, that is, produces with a optimal scale of plant and uses it at its full capacity (see Fig. 32.18). However, there is no certainty that monopolist will produce at this optimal level, as is the case under perfect competition. This is because unlike in competitive market conditions, no market forces operate under monopoly that compel the monopolist to work with optimum plant size and uses it at its full capacity.

18. A monopolist has attained equilibrium at a point on the demand curve where the coefficient of price elasticity is – 2.5 and the equilibrium price is Rs. 20.00. Calculate his marginal revenue.

19. What do you understand by 'dead-weight loss' of monopoly ? If the gains to producer be redistributed to consumers, would the "dead-weight loss" be eliminated ?

20. What is a social cost of monopoly ? If the gains to the monopolist could be redistributed to consumers, would the social cost of monopoly be eliminated. Explain briefly.

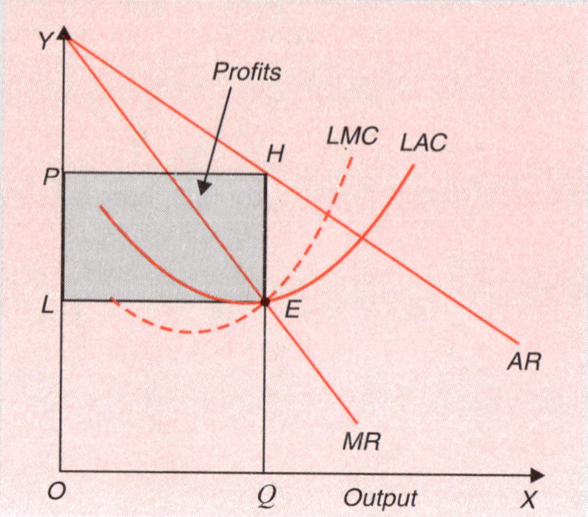

Fig. 32.18. *Monopolist working at the minimum point of LAC*

21. Let the demand function for an industry's output be $Q = 50 - 5P$, where P is price and Q is the output. Assume constant costs at Rs. 6 per unit of output.

(*i*) How much would a profit-maximising monopolist produce ? What would be the equilibrium price ?

(*ii*) Now assume the commodity is produced by a public sector undertaking which follows the *marginal cost pricing principle*. What would be the optimal quantity produced ?

[**Hints.** (*ii*) A public sector undertaking following marginal cost-pricing principle would set the price equal to marginal cost of production. Thus

$$Q = 50 - 5P \quad \text{...(1)}$$
$$5P = 50 - Q$$
$$P = 10 - 1/5Q \quad \text{...(2)}$$

Setting price (P) equal to marginal cost we have

$$6 = 10 - 1/5\,Q$$
$$1/5Q = 10 - 6 = 4, \text{ or } Q = 20]$$

22. Consider a shift in demand under monopoly. In two separate diagrams, show that this can result in:

(*i*) Different quantities being supplied at the same price.

(*ii*) Different prices supporting the same quantity. Hence show that a monopolist does not have a unique supply curve.

23. We write the percentage mark-up of price over marginal cost as $(P - MC)/P$. For a profit-maximising monopolist, how does this mark-up depend on the elasticity of demand ? Why can this mark-up be viewd as a measure of monopoly power ?

24. Show why supply curve does not exist under monopoly.

25. Explain how average revenue curve, marginal revenue curve and elasticity of demand are related to one another. Why should a monopoly firm not sell below the price where elasticity of demand is less than one?

26. Explain the long-run equilibrium under monopoly. Explain the adjustment process. How a monopoly firm will shift from the short-run equilibrium to the long-run equilibrium position. Why is monopoly profits not likely to be eliminated ?

27. Show how monopoly causes misallocation of resources and thereby causes loss of social welfare.

OR

Monopoly is said to be economically inefficient. Explain and show how it causes dead weight loss.

28. The demand curve facing a monopoly is $P = 100 - Q$. The firm's cost curve is $C(Q) = 10 + 5Q$. What is profit-maximising output

CHAPTER

33

Price Discrimination

MEANING OF PRICE DISCRIMINATION

Price discrimination refers to the practice of a seller to sell the same product at different prices to different buyers. A seller makes price discrimination between different buyers when it is both possible and profitable for him to do so. If the manufacturer of a refrigerator of a given variety sells it at ₹ 5000 to one buyer and at ₹ 5,500 to another buyer (all conditions of sale and delivery being the same in two cases), he is practising price discrimination.

Price discrimination, as defined above, is not a very common phenomenon. It is very difficult to charge different prices for the identical product from the different buyers. More often, the product is slightly differentiated to practise successfully price discrimination. Thus, the concept of price discrimination can be broadened to include the sale of the various varieties of the same good at prices which are not proportional to their marginal costs. Thus, G. Stigler defines price discrimination as ***"the sales of technically similar products at prices which are not proportional to marginal costs."***[1] On this definition, a seller is practicing price discrimination when he is charging different prices from different buyers for the different varieties of the same good if the differences in prices are not the same as or proportional to the differences in the costs of producing them. For example, if a book costs the publisher ₹ 50 per unit and its deluxe edition ₹ 65 per unit, then he will be practising price discrimination if he sells the ordinary edition at ₹ 70 per unit and the deluxe edition at ₹ 130 per unit. In this case, he is said to be practising price discrimination because the price difference between the two editions (₹ 130 – 70 = 60) is greater than the cost difference between them (₹ 65 – 50 = 10).

Though this second case of price discrimination is very relevant, but is more complicated. Therefore, for the purpose of analysis given below, we shall restrict ourselves to the simple case of price discrimination—the sale of the same product at different prices to different buyers. But the conclusions arrived at in this simple case will be generally valid in case of the more complicated case mentioned above.

Three types of price discrimination may be noted. Price discrimination may be (*a*) *personal*, (*b*) *local*, or (*c*) *according to use or trade*. Price discrimination is personal when a seller charges different prices from different persons. Price discrimination is local when the seller charges different prices from people of different localities or places. For instance, producer may sell a commodity at one price at home and at another price abroad. Discrimination according to use occurs when different prices of a commodity are charged according to the

1. G.J. Sitgler, *The Theory of Price*, revised edition, 1952, p. 215.

uses to which the commodity is put. For example, the electricity is usually sold at a cheaper rate for domestic uses than for commercial purposes.

Degrees of Price Discrimination

Prof. A.C. Pigou has distinguished between the following three types of price discrimination on another ground : (*i*) price discrimination of the first degree; (*ii*) price discrimination of the second degree; and (*iii*) price discrimination of the third degree.

Price Discrimination of the First Degree. Price discrimination of the first degree is also known as perfect price discrimination because this involves maximum possible exploitation of each buyer in the interest of the seller's profits. ***Price discrimination of the first degree is said to occur when the monopolist is able to sell each separate unit of the product at a different price.*** Thus under price discrimination of the 'first degree' every buyer is forced to pay the price which is equal to the maximum amount he is willing to pay rather than do without the good altogether. In other words, under perfect price discrimination, the seller leaves no consumer's surplus to any buyer. Perfect price discrimination requires that the seller makes a separate bargain with each of his buyers instead of setting just two or a few market prices each of which is available to a good number of buyers. This sort of price discrimination is also marked by the fact that the seller makes *an all or nothing* bargain with each buyer. In this all or nothing bargain, the total amount of money which a buyer is required to pay for a given unit of the good is the maximum amount which he is willing to pay for the unit of the good rather than go without it. Thus, the seller, under discrimination of the first degree, is able to deal individually with each buyer and is able to strike an all or nothing bargain. To sum up, the seller under first-degree price discrimination, charges each buyer the highest price he will be prepared to pay for each unit of the good he gets, and thus charges a separate price for each such unit. In other words, the seller forces the buyer to pay the maximum amount he is willing to pay for a given quantity of the good by threatening him with the alternative of denying him the good altogether. Perfect price discrimination is depicted in Fig. 33.1.

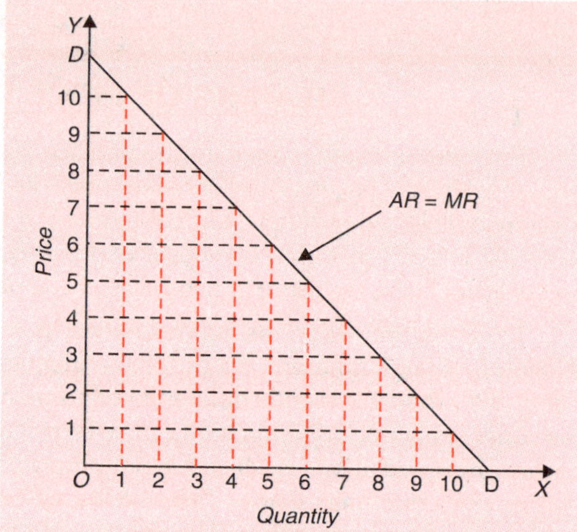

Fig. 33.1. *Price discriminating monopolist of the first degree extracts all the consumer surplus form the buyers*

Now, ***the monopolist practising perfect discrimination can extract from the buyer all the consumer surplus which he is getting by threatening him with the alternative of getting none of the good.*** Thus, the monopolist, under first-degree price discrimination, will charge from the buyers ₹ 10 for first unit, ₹ 9 for second unit, ₹ 8 for the third unit and so on for further units the monopolist will charge the highest price which a buyer is prepared to pay. As a result, the buyer will be left with no consumers surplus.

An important point about perfect price discrimination is worth noting. *While under simple monopoly,* marginal revenue curve of the seller lies below the demand curve of the buyer, under perfect price discrimination the demand curve of the buyer also becomes the marginal revenue curve of the seller. In the above illustration, the seller gets additional revenue of ₹ 10 from the first unit, that is, the price which he charges for the first unit, ₹ 9 from the second unit, *i.e.*, the price which he charges for the second unit ; ₹ 8 from the third unit, *i.e.*, the price which he charges for the third unit and so on. In other words, ₹ 10, ₹ 9, ₹ 8 and ₹ 7 are the successive marginal revenues of the seller. Under perfect price discrimination each unit of output is sold at a separate price. Each additional unit sold therefore adds to revenue an amount equal to the price for which it is sold. Under perfect price discrimination, the demand curve of the good is, therefore, also the marginal revenue curve of the seller.

Price Discrimination of the Second Degree. Price discrimination of the *second degree* would occur when a monopolist is able to charge ***separate prices for different blocks or quantities of a commodity from buyers*** and in this way he takes away a part, but not all of consumer surplus from them . Thus, under the second degree price discrimination a monopolist may charge a high price for first block of say 10 units, the medium price for the additional block of 10 units, and a lower price for additional 10 units of a commodity. For example, a monopolist may charge from a buyer a price of ₹ 50 per unit for the first 10 units, ₹ 40 per unit for the next 10 units and ₹ 30 per unit for the additional units of the commodity. As a result, some consumer's surplus is left with the buyers. This second degree price discrimination is depicted in Fig. 33.2.

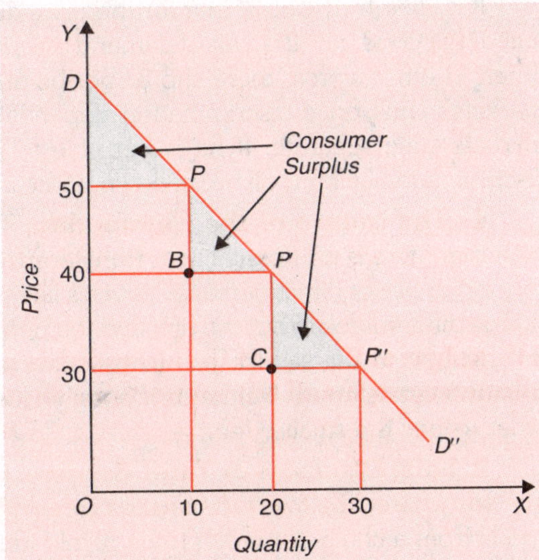

Fig. 33.2. *Different Groups Under Price Discrimination of the Second Degree*

Price Discrimination of the Third Degree. Price discrimination of the *third degree* is said to occur ***when the seller divides his buyers into two or more than two sub-markets or groups depending on the demand conditions in each sub-market and charges a different price in each sub-market.*** The price charged in each sub-market depends upon the output sold in that sub-market and the demand conditions of that sub-market. Price discrimination of the third degree is most common. A common example of such discrimination is found in the practice of a manufacturer who sells his product at a higher price at home and at a lower price abroad. Again, the third degree price discrimination is found when an electric company sells electric power at a lower price to the households and at a higher price to the manufacturers who use it for industrial purposes. In our analysis of price discrimination made below, we will assume only third degree price discrimination since this is usually more practicable as well as most commonly found in case of the real world.

WHEN IS PRICE DISCRIMINATION POSSIBLE ?

Two fundamental conditions are necessary for the price discrimination to become possible. First, price discrimination can occur only *if it is not possible to transfer any unit of the product from one market to another*. In other words, a seller can practise price discrimination only when he is selling in different markets which are divided in such a way that product sold by him in the cheaper market cannot be resold in the dearer market. Price discrimination by the original seller will break down if his buyers in the cheaper market purchase the product from him and resell it to the buyers of the dearer market. Buyers in the dearer market of the original seller will instead of buying from him will buy the product from the buyers of his cheaper market. Thus, a seller can charge different prices in the two markets when there is no possibility of the product being transferred from the cheaper market to the dearer market.

Second essential condition for price discrimination to occur is that ***it should not be possible for the buyers in the dearer market to transfer themselves into the cheaper market to buy the product or service at the lower price.*** For instance, if a doctor is charging a smaller fee from the poor than from the rich, then his price discrimination will break down if a rich man can pretend to be poor and pay a poor man's charges to the doctor.

It is clear from above that for the price discrimination to become practicable, neither the unit of the good, nor the unit of demand (*i.e.*, buyer) can be transferred from one market to the other. In other words, there should not be any seepage or communication between the two markets. Thus price discrimination depends upon the ability of the seller to keep his two markets quite separate. If he is not able to keep the different markets separate, the price discrimination by him will break down. Price discrimination is possible in the following cases.

1. The Nature of the Commodity. The nature of the commodity or service may be such that there is no possibility of transference from one market to the other. The most usual case is the sale of direct personal services like that of a surgeon or lawyer. The surgeons usually charge different fees from the rich and the poor for the same kind of operation. This is possible for them since the service has to be delivered personally by the surgeon and therefore, it cannot be transferred. Neither is it possible for the rich men to assume to be poor so easily in order to pay the smaller fee.

2. Long Distances or Tariff Barriers. Discrimination often occurs ***when the markets are separated by long distances or tariff barriers*** so that it is very expensive to transfer goods from a cheaper market to be resold in the dearer market. A monopolist manufacturer at Chennai may sell his product in one town, say Kolkata, at ₹ 20 and in another town, say Delhi, at ₹ 15. If the transport cost between Delhi and Kolkata is greater than ₹ 5 per unit it will not be worthwhile for the buyers in Delhi to transfer the goods to Kolkata on their own. Similarly, if a seller is selling his good in two different markets, say, in a home market which is protected by a tariff and in a foreign market without a tariff, he can take advantage of the tariff barrier and can raise the price of his product in the home market (which is protected by the tariff). As a result, he will be selling the product in the foreign market at a lower price than at home. ***This practice of selling the product at cheaper rates abroad than at home is often known as 'dumping'.***

3. Legal Sanction. In some cases there may be *legal sanction for price discrimination*. For example, an electricity company sells electricity at a lower price if it is used for domestic purposes and at a higher price if it is used for commercial purposes. In this case customers are liable to be fined if they use electricity for commercial purposes if the sanction has been granted for domestic purposes only. The same is the case with railways which charge different fares for travelling in First Class, and Second Class compartments. Though the service of carrying rendered in two classes of compartments slightly differs in each case but the differences in fares are out of proportion to the differences in comforts provided. So this is a clear case of price discrimination by legal sanction. It is unlawful and a criminal offence to travel in the first class with a ticket for the second class.

4. Preferences or Prejudices of the Buyers. Price discrimination may become possible due to *preferences or prejudices of the buyers*. The same good is generally converted into different varieties by providing different packings, different names or labels in order to convince the buyer that certain varieties are superior to others. Different prices are charged for different varieties, although they differ only in name or label. In this way the producers are usually able to break up their market and sell the so-called superior varieties to the rich people at higher prices and the so-called inferior varieties to the poor people. Sometimes there is some actual difference in the various varieties of the good, for instance, generally there is a difference in the paper used and quality of the binding between the deluxe edition and ordinary edition of a book, but the difference in prices of the two kinds of editions is more than proportional to the extra costs incurred on the deluxe edition. So, this is a clear case of price discrimination based on the preferences or prejudices of the various buyers of the product. It is worth quoting Joan Robinson in this connection. "Various brands of a certain article which in fact are almost exactly alike may be sold as different qualities under names and labels which induce rich and snobbish buyers to divide themselves from poor buyers, and in this way the market is split up and the monopolist can sell what is substantially the same thing at several prices.[2]"

Another case of price discrimination falling in this category is that when some people prefer to buy goods in a particular locality at a higher price. For example, if a seller has two shops, one in Connaught Place which is the most fashionable shopping centre in Delhi and another at Sadar Bazar which is very congested and ugly locality in Delhi, he may be selling the same product at a higher price in Connaught Place and at a lower price in Sadar Bazar. It is the fashionable and rich people who usually buy goods in Connaught Place and they will be prepared to pay a higher price rather than go for shopping in the congested and ugly locality of Sadar Bazar.

5. Ignorance and Laziness of Buyers. Price discrimination may become possible due to *ignorance and laziness of buyers*. If a seller is discriminating between two markets but the buyers of the dearer market are quite ignorant of that fact that the seller is selling the product at a lower price in another market, then price discrimination by the seller will persist. Price discrimination will also persist if the buyers of the dearer market are aware of the seller's act of selling the same product at a lower price in another market but due to laziness may not go for shopping in the cheaper market. In these cases if the ignorance is removed or laziness is given up, the price discrimination will break down.

6. Price discrimination may become possible ***when several groups of buyers require the same service for clearly differentiated commodities.*** For example, railways charge different rates of fare for the transport of cotton and coal. In this case price discrimination is possible since bales of cotton cannot be turned into loads of coal in order to take advantage of the cheaper rate of transport for coal.

Under which Market Structure Price Discrimination is Possible ?

We have seen above those conditions under which price discrimination is possible. Now, the question arises under what market form a seller can practise price discrimination. It is obvious that ***under perfect or pure competition no seller can charge different prices from different buyers for the same product.*** Under perfect or pure competition, there are many sellers selling the homogeneous product. If any seller tries to charge from some buyers a higher price than the prevailing market price, they will refuse to buy from him and will buy the same product at the prevailing price from other sellers. It is worth noting that under conditions of perfect or pure competition price discrimination cannot prevail even if the market can be easily divided into separate parts. This is so because if conditions of perfect or pure

2. Joan Robinson, *Economics of Imperfect Competition*, pp. 180-81.

competition prevail in each part of the whole market, then sellers will confront a perfectly elastic demand curve in each part and will like to sell the whole of his output in that part of the market in which the highest price prevails. But the attempt by all sellers to do so would force down the price to the competitive level so that a single price will prevail throughout the whole market. But if all sellers under perfect competition, combine or arrive at some understanding, then they can discriminate prices. ***"So long as market is perfect it is only if all sellers are combined or are acting in agreement that they can take advantage of the barriers between one part of a market and another to charge different prices for the same thing."***[3] However, it may be pointed out that if all sellers combine or enter into an agreement regarding price discrimination, perfect competition ceases to exist. We thus see that price discrimination is not possible under perfect competition.

Under monopolistic competition, price discrimination can occur. The degree of price discrimination practised depends upon the degree of imperfection in the market. The monopolistic competition prevails when the product is differentiated and every seller has some attached customers who will not move so readily from one seller to another. Therefore, if monopolistic competition exists and also the market can be divided into different parts by a seller, then price discrimination becomes possible. It should be noted that in this case an individual seller may not produce a single variety of the product but may produce various varieties of his product and thus may break up his market into different parts and charge different prices for different varieties of his good. Price discrimination will occur only if extra prices charged for the so-called superior varieties are not proportional to the extra costs incurred on them.

But ***price discrimination is more likely to occur when there is monopoly of the product by a single seller or when there is agreement among the various sellers selling the same product or service.*** Monopoly exists when there are no other sellers selling the same good or its close substitutes. Therefore, monopolist is in a position to charge different prices from different buyers for the same good. Price discrimination also usually occurs when there are various sellers selling the same product or same service but there is agreement among them for charging different prices from different groups of buyers. For instance, doctors have generally some understanding with each other to charge higher fees from the rich and lower fees from the poor.

WHEN IS PRICE DISCRIMINATION PROFITABLE ?

We have seen above under what conditions price discrimination is possible. Price discrimination may be possible yet it may not pay the monopolist to discriminate prices in the separate markets. In other words, the monopolist may be able to discriminate prices but it may not be profitable for him to do so. We have to see now under what conditions it is profitable for the monopolist to discriminate prices between the two markets. ***Price discrimination is profitable only if at a single monopoly price elasticity of demand in one market is different from price elasticity of demand in the other.*** Therefore, the monopolist will discriminate prices between two markets only when he finds that at the single monopoly price the price elasticity of demand of his product is different in the different sub-markets. We shall analyse below this condition for the profitability of price discrimination.

(*a*) **When Demand Curves in the Separate Markets are Iso-elastic.** If demand curves in the two markets are iso-elastic so that at every price the elasticity of demand in the two markets is the same, then it will not pay the monopolist to charge different prices in the

3. Joan Robinson, *Economics of Imperfect Competition*, p. 179.

two markets. Why? When elasticity of demand is the same in the two markets, it follows from the formula, $MR = AR\frac{e-1}{e}$ that marginal revenues in the two markets *at every price* (*i.e.*, every *AR*) of the good will also be the same. Now, if marginal revenue at every price of the product is the same in the two markets, it will not be profitable for the monopolist to transfer any amount of the good from one market to the other and thus to charge different prices of the good in the two markets.

(*b*) **When Elasticity of Demand is Different in Various Markets at the Single Monopoly Price.** It will be to the advantage of the monopolist to set different prices if price elasticities of demand in the two markets at the single monopoly price are not the same. In fact, if he wants to maximise profits he must discriminate prices if price elasticities of demand in the two markets *at the single monopoly price* are different. If the producer regards the two markets as one and charges a single monopoly price on the basis of aggregate marginal revenue and marginal cost of the output, he would not be maximising profits if elasticities of demand in the two markets at the single monopoly price are different. If price elasticity of demand is the same in the two markets at the single monopoly price, it will not pay the monopolist to discriminate between the two markets, even if the elasticities are different at other prices.

Suppose on the basis of aggregate marginal revenue and marginal cost, a monopolist fixes a single price (which is called the single monopoly price) and charges the same price in both the markets. If he now finds that price elasticity of demand at this single monopoly price is different he can increase his total profits by discriminating prices between the two markets. How is it profitable for the monopolist to charge different prices in the two markets when price elasticities of demand in them at the single monopoly price are different? This follows from the formula, $MR = AR\frac{e-1}{e}$. When average revenue in both the markets is the same, that is, when the monopolist charges a single monopoly price in both the markets, but price elasticities are different in the two markets, then marginal revenues in the two markets will be different. Suppose the single monopoly price is ₹ 15 and price elasticity of demand in markets *A* and *B* is 2 and 5 respectively. Then,

$$MR \text{ in market A} = AR_a \frac{e_a - 1}{e_a}$$

$$= 15\frac{2-1}{2} = 15 \times \frac{1}{2} = 7.5$$

$$MR \text{ in market } B = AR_b \frac{e_b - 1}{e_b}$$

$$= 15 \times \frac{5-1}{5}$$

$$= 15 \times \frac{4}{5} = 12$$

It is thus clear that marginal revenues in the two markets are different when price elasticities of demand at the single monopoly price are different. Further, from the above numerical example, it is evident that the marginal revenue in the market in which price elasticity is higher is greater than the marginal revenue in the market where price eelasticity is lower. Now, it is profitable for the monopolist to transfer some amount of the product from the market *A* where elasticity is less and, therefore, marginal revenue is low to the market *B* where elasticity is higher and, therefore, marginal revenue is larger. In this way, the loss of revenue by reducing sales in market *A* by some marginal units will be smaller than the gain in revenue from increasing sales in market *B* by those units. Thus, in the above example, if one unit of the product is withdrawn from market *A*, the loss in revenue will be ₹ 7.5, while with the addition to sales by one more unit of the product in market *B*, the gain in revenue will be about ₹ 12. It is thus clear that the transference of some units of the product will be profitable, when there is difference in price elasticities of demand and hence in marginal revenues.

It is worth mentioning that when some units of the product are transferred from market *A* to market *B*, price in market *A* will rise and price in the market *B* will fall. This means that the monopolist will now be discriminating prices between the two markets.

But here a relevant question arises: how long will it be profitable for the monopolist to continue shifting his product from the market with lower elasticity of demand to the market with higher elasticity of demand? It is worthwhile for the monopolist to go on transferring units from market *A* (with lower elasticity of demand) to market *B* (with higher elasticity of demand) until the marginal revenues in the two markets become equal. This is because as long as marginal revenue in market *B* is greater than that in market *A*, he will be making addition to revenue in market *B* by selling an additional unit of the product more than the loss he will be incurring in market *A* from reducing sales by one unit. When the marginal revenues in the two markets become equal as a result of transference of some units of output, it will no longer be profitable to shift more units of output from market *A* to market *B*. When the position of equality of the marginal revenues in the two markets is reached, he will be charging different prices in the two markets—a higher price in market *A* with lower elasticity of demand and a lower price in market *B* with a higher elasticity of demand.

PRICE AND OUTPUT EQUILIBRIUM UNDER PRICE DISCRIMINATION

We have explained above the conditions under which price discrimination is possible and profitable. We now turn to analyse the equilibrium of a discriminating monopolist. Under simple monopoly, a single price is charged for the whole output; but under price discrimination the monopolist will charge different prices in different sub-markets. First of all, therefore, the monopolist has to divide his total market into various sub-markets on the basis of differences in price elasticity of demand in them. The monopolist can divide his total market into *several sub-markets* according to the differences in demand elasticity, but for the sake of making our analysis simple we shall explain the case when the total market is divided into *two sub-markets*.

In order to reach the equilibrium position, the discriminating monopolist has to take two decisions: (1) how much total output should be produced; and (2) how the total output should be divided between the two sub-markets and what prices he should charge in the two sub-markets ?

The same marginal principle will guide the decision of the discriminating monopolist to produce a total output as that which guides a perfect competition or a simple monopolist. In other words, the discriminating monopolist will compare the marginal revenue with the marginal cost of output. But he has to find out first the aggregate marginal revenue (*AMR*) of the two sub-markets taken together and then compare this aggregate marginal revenue with the marginal cost of the total output. Aggregate marginal revenue curve is obtained by summing up laterally the marginal revenue curves of the sub-markets. Consider Fig. 33.3. MR_a is the marginal revenue curve in sub-market *A* corresponding to the demand curve D_a. Similarly, MR_b is the marginal revenue curve in sub-market B corresponding to the demand curve D_b. Now, the aggregate marginal revenue curve AMR, which has been shown in diagram (*iii*) of Fig. 33.3, has been derived by adding up laterally MR_a and MR_b. This aggregate marginal revenue curve depicts the total amount of output that can be sold in the two sub-markets taken together corresponding to each value of the marginal revenue. Marginal cost curve of the monopolist is shown by the curve MC in Fig. 33.3 (*iii*).

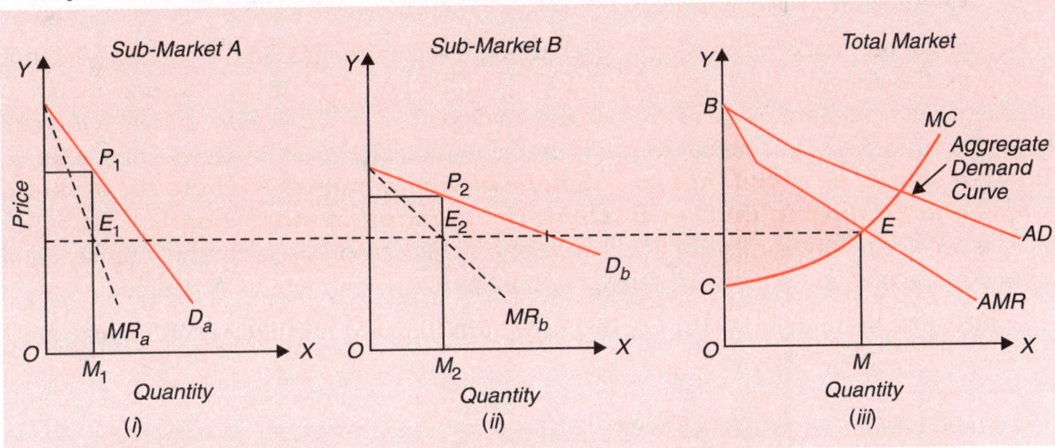

Fig. 33.3. *Determination of Total Output and Different Prices in the Two Markets*

The discriminating monopolist will maximise his profits by producing the level of output at which marginal cost curve MC intersects the aggregate marginal revenue curve AMR. It will be seen from Fig. 33.3 (*iii*) that profit-maximising output is OM, for only at OM aggregate marginal revenue (AMR) is equal to the marginal cost (MC) of the total output. Thus the discriminating monopolist will decide to produce OM level of output.

Once the total output to be produced has been determined the next task for the discriminating monopolist is to distribute the total output between the two sub-markets. He will distribute the total output OM in such a way that marginal revenues in the two sub-markets are equal. Marginal revenues in the two sub-markets must be equal if the profits are to be maximised. If he is so allocating the output in the two markets that the marginal revenues in the two are not equal, then it will pay him to transfer some amount of output from the sub-market in which the marginal revenue is less to the sub-market in which the marginal revenue is greater. Only when the marginal revenues in the two markets are equal, it will be unprofitable for him to shift any amount from one market to the other.

But for the discriminating monopolist to be in equilibrium it is essential not only that the marginal revenues in the two markets should be the same but that they should also be equal to the marginal cost of the whole output. Equality of marginal revenues in the two markets with marginal cost of the whole output ensures that the amount sold in the two markets will together be equal to the whole output OM which has been fixed by equalising aggregate marginal revenue with marginal cost. It will be seen from Fig. 33.3 [diagram (*iii*)] that at equilibrium output OM, marginal cost is ME. Now, the output OM has to be distributed in the two markets in such a way that marginal revenue in them should be equal to the marginal cost ME of the whole output. It is clear from the diagram (*i*) that OM_1 should be sold in sub-market A, because marginal revenue M_1E_1 at amount OM_1 is equal to marginal cost ME. Similarly, OM_2 should be sold in sub-market B, since marginal revenue $M_2 E_2$ at amount OM_2 is equal to the marginal cost ME of the whole output. To conclude, demand and cost conditions being given, the discriminating monopolist will produce total output OM and will sell amount OM_1 in sub-market A and amount OM_2 in sub-market B. It should be carefully noted that the total output OM will be equal to $OM_1 + OM_2$.

Thus, for the discriminating monopolist to be in equilibrium, the following conditions must be fulfilled:

1. $AMR = MC$
2. $MR_1 = MR_2 = MC$

Another important thing to know is what prices will be charged in the two markets. It is clear from the demand curve that amount OM_1 of the good can be sold at price M_1P_1 in sub-market A. Therefore, price M_1P_1 will be set in sub-market A. Likewise, amount OM_2 can be sold at price M_2P_2 in sub-market B. Therefore, price M_2P_2 will be set in sub-market B. Further, ***it should be noted that price will be higher in market A where the demand is less elastic than in market B where the demand is more elastic.*** Thus, price M_1P_1 is greater than the price M_2P_2. The relation between prices in the two markets and demand elasticities in them can be derived as follows.

We know that the following relationship between price, marginal revenue and price elasticity in a market holds good.

$$MR = \text{Price}\left(\frac{e-1}{e}\right)$$

Therefore, in sub-market A,

$$MR_a = P_a\left(\frac{e_a-1}{e_a}\right) \qquad \text{...}(i)$$

where P_a stands for price, MR_a for marginal revenue and e_a for price elasticity in market A. Likewise, in sub-market B,

$$MR_b = P_b\left(\frac{e_b-1}{e_b}\right) \qquad \text{...}(ii)$$

where P_b stands for price, MR_b for marginal revenue and e_b for price elasticity in market B. Since in equilibrium under price discrimination, $MR_a = MR_b$, from (*i*) and (*ii*) we get

$$P_a\left(\frac{e_a-1}{e_a}\right) = P_b\left(\frac{e_b-1}{e_b}\right)$$

$$\frac{P_a}{P_b} = \frac{\dfrac{e_b-1}{e_b}}{\dfrac{e_a-1}{e_a}} = \frac{\left(1-\dfrac{1}{e_b}\right)}{\left(1-\dfrac{1}{e_a}\right)}$$

Suppose absolute value of price elasticity in market A is equal to 2 and in market B it is equal to 3 then

$$\frac{P_a}{P_b} = \frac{\dfrac{3-1}{3}}{\dfrac{2-1}{2}} = \frac{\dfrac{2}{3}}{\dfrac{1}{2}}$$

$$= \frac{2}{3} \times \frac{2}{1} = \frac{4}{3}$$

Thus, when elasticities in markets A and B are 2 and 3 respectively, the prices in the two markets will be in the ratio of 4 : 3.

From the foregoing analysis it follows that the following two conditions are required to be satisfied for the equilibrium of a discriminating monopolist :

(1) Aggregate Marginal Revenue (AMR) = Marginal Cost (MC) of the total output.

(2) $MR_a = MR_b = MC$.

International Price Discrimination and Dumping

A special case of price discrimination occurs when a producer is selling in two markets, one in which he faces perfect competition, while in the other he has a monopoly. The demand curve for the product will be perfectly elastic for him in the market in which he faces perfect competition, while the demand curve will be sloping downward in the market in which he enjoys monopoly position. Such situation might occur when a producer sells his product in his home country in which he has a monopoly and in the world market which is perfectly competitive. Equilibrium in this situation is depicted in Fig. 33.4. In the home market in which the producer has a monopoly, demand curve or the average revenue curve AR^H is sloping downward. So does the marginal revenue curve MR^H. In the international or world market in which he faces perfect competition, the demand for his product is perfectly elastic. The average revenue curve AR^W of the producer in the world market is, therefore, a horizontal straight line and marginal revenue curve MR^W coincides with it. MC is the marginal cost curve of output. Aggregate marginal revenue (AMR) curve in this case is the composite curve $BFED$ which is the lateral summation of MR^H and MR^W. The marginal cost curve MC intersects the aggregate marginal revenue curve $BFED$ at point E and equilibrium output OM is determined. The total output OM is to be distributed between the home market and the world market in such a way that marginal revenue in each market is equal to each other and to the marginal cost ME. It is clear from Fig. 33.4 that when amount OR is sold in the home market, the marginal revenue is RF which is equal to marginal cost ME. Thus, out of total output OM, amount OR will be sold in the home market. From the curve AR^H, it is clear that price OP^H will be charged in the home market. Rest of the amount RM will be sold in the world market at price OP^W. Area $CEFB$ represents the total profits earned by the producer from both the markets. Price in the world market OP^W is lower than the price OP^H in the home market.

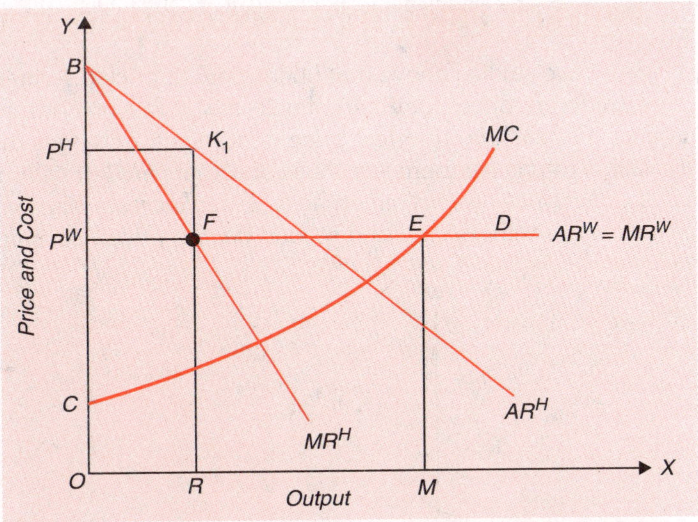

Fig. 33.4. *Equilibrium of the discriminating monopolist when he has a monopoly in the home market and faces perfect competition in the world market*

When a producer charges a lower price in the world market than in the home market, he is said to be dumping in the international market.

It is worth mentioning that difference in prices in the world market and home market is due to the differences in price elasticity of demand in them. In the domestic market, elasticity of demand is less and, therefore price charged is higher as compared to the international or world market where elasticity is high (in fact, it is equal to infinity), the price is lower.

Persistent Dumping Vs Predatory Dumping. It may be noted that the type of dumping which we have explained above is called *persistent dumping* by the economists. This persistent dumping is the most usual one and arises when a monopolist pursuing the objective of profit maximization perceives that there exist differences in price elasticity of demand in the domestic market and international market. He therefore finds that he can enlarge his profits by discriminating prices in the two markets. As mentioned above, the elasticity of demand is usually higher in the international market because there is severe competition among countries to sell their products in the world markets and also a relatively larger number of substitutes are available there. Thus, the monopolist maximises profits by charging higher price in the domestic market and lower price in the international market.

There is another type of dumping which is known as ***predatory dumping.*** Predatory dumping represents unfair method of competition because under it a producer deliberately sells his product in a foreign country at a lower price (even below his cost of production) in order to eliminate competitors and gain control of the foreign market for a short period of time. When the producer succeeds in his ulterior motive of gaining monopoly control of the foreign market, he then exploits the foreign buyers by substantially raising the price of his product and thus maximizing his long-run profits. It is this type of dumping that is severely criticised and opposed.

PERFECT PRICE DETERMINATION: OUTPUT DETERMINATION

We have studied above that under perfect price discrimination, the monopolist is able to charge different prices for different units and leaves no consumer surplus with the buyers of his product. For each unit perfect price discriminator charges maximum price which consumers are willing to pay for them and thus consumers are left with no consumer surplus. In this way with perfect price discrimination he is able to increase his revenue and profits more than what he gets under third degree and second degree price discrimination.

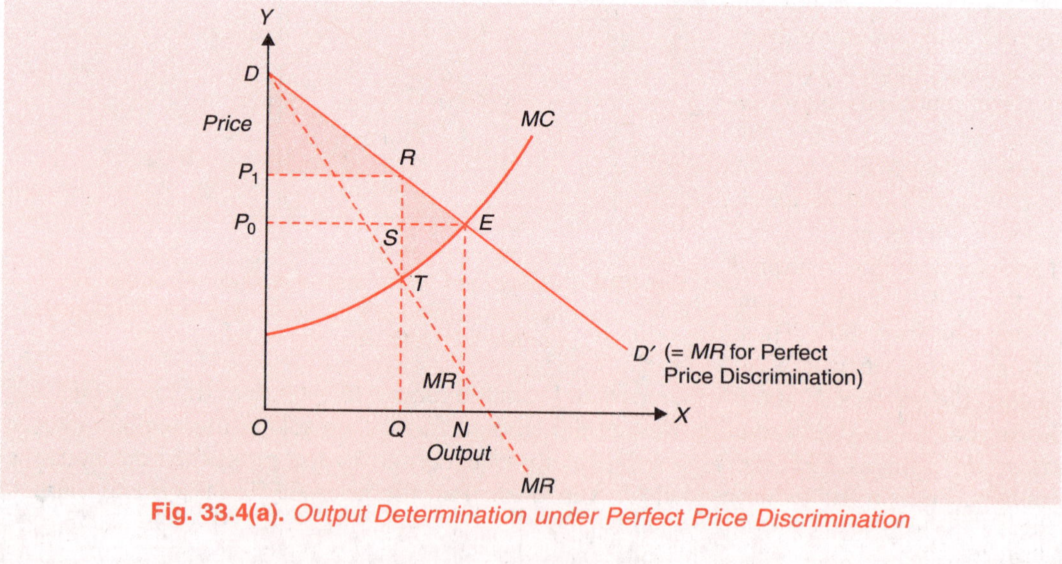

Fig. 33.4(a). *Output Determination under Perfect Price Discrimination*

Now, what output a monopolist practising perfect price discrimination will produce. For this it is important to understand what is marginal revenue (*MR*) curve of the perfect price discriminator. Since the perfect price discriminator charges the maximum price that the consumers are willing to pay for each unit, his marginal revenue from sale of different units of the product will be equal to the price of the units. As result, his marginal revenue curve will coincide with the market demand curve *DD′*. Consider Figure 33.4(a) where *DD′* is market demand curve forthe product which has been obtained by horizontal summation of all individual consumers' demand curves for the product. If the monopolist does not practice price discrimination and charges a single price (*i.e.* he is simple monopolist), his marginal revenue curve *MR* lies below the market demand curve *DD′*. The simple monopolist will equate his marginal revenue with marginal cost (*MR* = *MC*) to maximise profits. It will be seen from Figure 33.4(a) that the simple monopolist will produce *OQ* output corresponding to point *T* at which his *MR* = *MC* and charge price equal to OP_1 (= *QR*) and will leave consumer surplus equal to the area DP_1R with the buyers. However, since he produces less than the economically efficient output *ON* (at which Price = *MC*), there is dead-weight loss of welfare equal to area *TRE*.

Now, as explained above, a monopolist practising *perfect* price discrimination, marginal revenue (*MR*) curve will coincide with the market demand curve *DD′*. Therefore, perfect price discriminator will produce output *ON* at which his marginal cost (*MC*) curve intersects the market demand curve (*DD′*) which is also his marginal revenue curve. Thus in equilibrium at output *ON*, for monopolist practising perfect price discrimination marginal cost equals price as is the case of a firm working under perfect competition.

Since at equilibrium output ON of perfect price discriminator price equals marginal cost, there is no dead weight loss and he is achieving economic efficiency. In other words, dead-weight loss has been eliminated under perfect price discrimination. In fact, perfect price discriminator grabs the dead-weight loss for increasing his profits and consumers are left with no consumer surplus at all. Total profits of perfect price discriminating monopolist equal to the area *within* demand curve and *MC* curve upto the point *E*.

We reach paradoxical conclusion that when the monopolist who exploits his market power to the maximum extent under perfect discrimination, the degree of his monopoly power as measure by Lerner's Index $\left(\frac{P - MC}{P}\right)$ is found to be zero as price (*P*) is equal to marginal cost at equilibrium point *E* in Fig. 33.4 (a). Though he is exploiting the consumers to the maximum degree leaving no consumer surplus with them and yet he is producing economically efficient output and producers the same output as a perfectly competitive undustly would produce. This shows that Lerner's index is quite an inadequate measure of monopoly power and also economists' criterion of economic efficiency is a poor measure of social welfare as its does not consider how the gains in real income are distributed. In our example of perfect price discrimination, the benefits of increase in output under it are grabbed by the monopolist as his profits increase and consumer's real income declines as all their consumer surplus has been taken away by the perfect price discriminator.

CASE WHEN OUTPUT OF A COMMODITY IS POSSIBLE ONLY UNDER PRICE DISCRIMINATION

It is now proper to discuss whether the total output of the product under price discrimination will be greater than, equal to or smaller than output under simple monopoly in which a single price for the product is charged. There is no single rule in regard to the effect of price discrimination on output. Whether the price discrimination will increase output or reduce output or leave output unchanged depends upon the various conditions.

First of all, there are cases in which no output will be produced at all under simple monopoly. In such cases, output of the product is possible only under price discrimination. The fact that the average revenue under price discrimination is greater than the average revenue under simple monopoly has an important bearing over this question. If the average cost curve of a product lies above the demand curve for it throughout its length, then it will not be profitable for the simple monopolist to produce any output at all. He may find that if he breaks up the market and charges different prices in the various separate markets, it may be profitable for him to produce some output of the product. This is so because the average revenue obtained by discriminating prices in the two separate markets is greater than the average revenue under simple monopoly. The average revenue under price discrimination (*DAR*) may therefore be greater than the average cost, when average revenue under simple monopoly (*SAR*) is less than the average cost. This situation is depicted in Fig. 33.5 in which average cost of output is shown by the *AC* curve. D_1 is the demand curve facing the monopolist in one market and D_2 is the demand curve facing him in the other market. The composite curve *BRT* is the aggregate demand curve (*AD*) or the average revenue curve under simple monopoly (*SAR*).

It is evident from Fig. 33.5 that aggregate demand curve (*AD*) lies below the average cost curve *AC* throughout its length. In other words, average cost is greater than average revenue at all levels of output when a single price is charged for the product. For instance, suppose a simple monopolist decides to produce *OM* level of output, the single price which he will be able to charge from both markets is *MP* which is less than the average cost *MH*. So it will not pay the simple monopolist to produce *OM* output and charge the single price. But it will be profitable for him to produce *OM* output if he discriminates prices in the two markets. Under discrimination he may sell output OM_1 in one market at price M_1P_1 and output OM_2 in the other market at price M_2P_2 ($OM_1 + OM_2 = OM$). By discriminating prices in this way, suppose the average revenue obtained by him is equal to *MP′*. It will be seen from Fig. 33.5 that *MP′* is greater than the average cost *MH* of output *OM*. Thus, whereas it is not profitable for the simple monopolist to produce any output under single price system, it pays him to produce output by discriminating prices in the two markets.

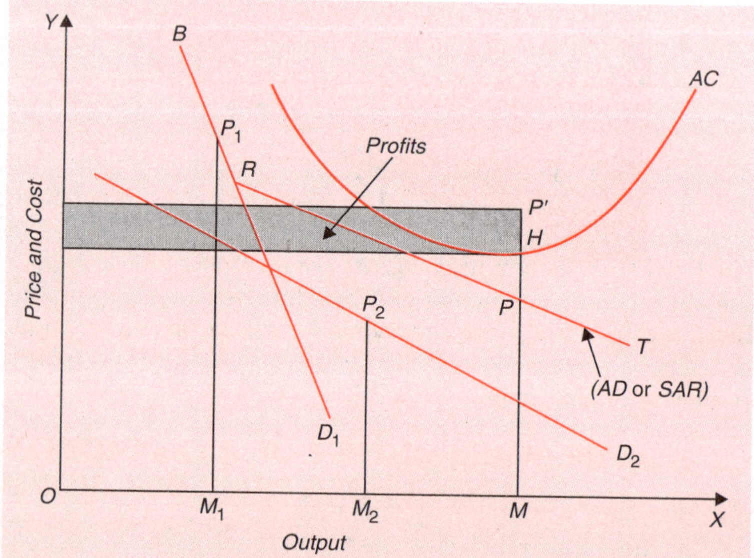

Fig. 33.5. *The Case Where Production is Possible only under Price Discrimination*

We have discussed above the extreme case when there will be no output without price discrimination. In less extreme cases, output under price discrimination can be larger than the output without price discrimination.

PRICE DISCRIMINATION AND SOCIAL WELFARE

Whether price discrimination promotes social welfare or not is difficult to say. Judgement as to whether price discrimination promotes social welfare partly depends upon whether with the adoption of price discrimination, total output of the product increases or not. If we put aside the output effect of price discrimination and consider the *distribution of a given output* in case when price discrimination is being practised, then economist's verdict would be that the price discrimination will adversely affect the social welfare since it will inefficiently allocate the output between the various consumers.

A necessary condition for the achievement of distributive (consumption) efficiency is that marginal rate of substitution (*MRS*) between any two goods must be the same for all consumers consuming the goods. This condition is violated under price discrimination. This is because, under price discrimination, different consumers face different prices and consequently the consumers will not have the same marginal rates of substitution between the goods in their equilibrium positions. In such a case satisfaction or welfare of some consumers can be increased without causing any reduction in the satisfaction or welfare of any other consumer. Thus, *for any given level of output*, the third-degree price discrimination will have an adverse effect on the consumption efficiency, that is, efficiency in the distribution of goods between the consumers and will therefore reduce welfare of the consumers. Thus we conclude that the condition for maximum social welfare that the marginal rate of substitution (MRS) of different consumers between any two goods should be the same, is violated by price discrimination. G.J. Stigler rightly writes : ***"given commodities and the buyers money incomes, all buyers can gain by the elimination of price discrimination, for price discrimination prevents them from reaching to the contract curve."***[4]

But the above argument against price discrimination is based on the assumption that the quantity of commodities produced of the goods is given. The question of their optimum distribution is analysed, by taking the given outputs of the goods. On the other hand, the total output that the monopolist sells in the two markets may increase or decrease as a result of price discrimination. Even monopolist who charges a single price produces less than the efficient or socially optimum output. And when as a result of price discrimination output falls, the inefficiency of monopoly is made even worse. However, when price discrimination leads to the increase in output, the effect of this increase in output on social welfare is positive. *Thus when the price discrimination leads to the increase in output, this extra output made possible by price discrimination has socially beneficial effect flowing from it and which should be put against the possible loss of social welfare due to misallocation of goods between the two individuals*. As we explained above, price discrimination in some cases leads to the increase in output. That is, output of a commodity in some cases is greater under price discrimination than under simple monopoly. Thus, from the point of view of output, especially when a society prefers a greater output to a smaller output, ***price discrimination in all those cases where it leads to the increase in output can be held to be promoting social welfare and is, therefore, justified.*** We agree with Mrs Joan Robinson when she writes:

"From the point of view of society as a whole, it is impossible to say whether price discrimination is desirable or not. From one point of view, therefore, ***price discrimination must be held to be superior to simple monopoly in all those cases in which it leads to an increase of output,*** and these cases are likely to be more common. But

4. G.J. Stigler, *The Theory of Price*, revised edition, pp. 93, 192.

against this advantage must be set the fact that *price discrimination leads to maldistribution of resources as between different uses*. Before it is possible to say whether discrimination is desirable or not it is necessary to weigh up the benefit from the increase in output against this disadvantage. In those cases in which discrimination will decrease output, it is undesirable on both counts."[5]

We may, however, add that one thing that we can say with certainty is that whether price discrimination leads to rise or fall in output as compared to ordinary monopoly, ***the total output under third-degree price-discrimination is less than the efficient or socially optimum output.*** This is because monopolist practicing price discrimination or not restricts output from the competitive level.

There is another important reason for which in some cases price discrimination is socially justified. This is the case when under a single uniform price, no output of a commodity is produced and only under price discrimination production of a commodity becomes profitable. Rail transportation is a case in point. It has been observed by many that if railway authorities are not permitted to charge higher fare from the rich people who travel in first or AC class, then it may not be profitable for the authorities to run the railways on a single uniform fare from all, rich and poor.

We have already graphically explained above with the aid of Fig. 33.5 that when aggregate demand curve (*AD*) for a commodity lies below the average cost curve throughout and, therefore, at no level of output average revenue (when single price is charged) is greater than the average cost, the commodity would not be produced at all with a single uniform price, because it is not profitable to do so. When in such cases, price discrimination is practised the average revenue under price discrimination (*DAR*) may become higher than the average cost of production, it becomes worthwhile or profitable to produce a commodity. In those cases, where under single uniform price no production is done and under price discrimination, production becomes possible (to be more exact, becomes profitable), then price discrimination is socially desirable and justified, if the production of that commodity is considered essential and important for the society. In such cases price discrimination leads to the production of goods and services that might otherwise be denied to the consumers.

Price Discrimination and Equity. Finally, price discrimination may be socially justified on grounds of equity. We have discussed above the desirability of price discrimination from the point of view of *efficiency criterion*. As regards *optimum distribution of goods* (that is, distributive efficiency), we have found that price discrimination leads to the maldistribution of the commodities between the individuals and thus violates the criterion of distributive efficiency. But this whole analysis of distributive efficiency is based on the given present distribution of income. If the present distribution of income is not considered equitable, then the mere distributive efficiency is not enough. ***Under price discrimination when price is raised for the rich and is lowered for the poor, it has a redistributive effect; the poor are benefited at the expense of the rich.*** Therefore, in order to reduce inequalities of personal real incomes, Government often itself practises price discrimination or when it controls prices in the private sector, it may permit or even encourage price discrimination. We thus see that equity criterion may outweigh the Pareto's efficiency criterion and may make the price discrimination socially justified.

We, therefore, conclude that from the point of view of distributive efficiency and optimum allocation of resources, ***given the present distribution of income,*** price discrimination is

5. John Robinson, *The Economics of Imperfect Competition*, p.206.(italics added)

not socially desirable. But from the point of view of expansion in output as well as ***for making the distribution of real incomes more equitable,*** price discrimination is socially justified. Thus, to pass judgement on the social desirability of a particular case of price discrimination, all these various considerations have to be weighed against each other.

NUMERICAL PROBLEM ON PRICE DISCRIMINATION

Problem. *Suppose a discriminating monopolist is selling a product in two separate markets in which demand functions are*

$$P_1 = 12 - Q_1$$
$$P_2 = 20 - Q_2$$

The monopolist's total cost function is

$$TC = 3 + 2Q$$

As an economic adviser you are asked to determine the prices to be charged in the two markets and amount of output to be sold in each market so that profits are maximised. You are also asked to calculate the total profits to be made from the strategy of price discrimination. What advise will you give?

Solution. As profits in case of price discrimination are maximised when $MR_1 = MR_2 = MC$, Therefore, we have to calculate the marginal revenue in the two markets from the given demand functions of the two markets.

Total revenue in market $1 = P_1Q_1 = 12Q_1 - Q_1^2$

$$MR_1 \text{ in market } 1 = \frac{\Delta(P_1Q_1)}{\Delta Q_1} = 12 - 2Q_1 \quad ...(1)$$

Total revenue in market $2 = P_2Q_2 = 20Q_2 - Q_2^2$

$$MR_2 \text{ in market } 2 = \frac{\Delta(P_2Q_2)}{\Delta Q_2} = 20 - 2Q_2 \quad ...(2)$$

We can derive the marginal cost from the total cost function

$$TC = 3 + 2Q$$

$$MC = \frac{\Delta TC}{\Delta Q} = 2$$

Profit-maximising amounts of output to be sold in the two markets are determined by applying the equilibrium condition $MR_1 = MR_2 = MC$ and solving the following equations:

$$MR_1 = MC$$
$$12 - 2Q_1 = 2$$
$$2Q_1 = 12 - 2 = 10$$
$$Q_1 = 5$$
$$MR_2 = MC$$
$$20 - 2Q_2 = 2$$
$$2Q_2 = 20 - 2$$
$$Q_2 = 18/2 = 9$$

Substituting these equilibrium outputs, Q_1 and Q_2 in the demand functions, we obtain the profit-maximising prices:

$$P_1 = 12 - Q_1 = 12 - 5 = 7$$
$$P_2 = 20 - Q_2 = 20 - 9 = 11$$

Total profits can be obtained in the usual way.

Total profits
$$\pi = (TR_1 + TR_2) - TC$$
$$= (P_1Q_1 + P_2Q_2) - (3 + 2Q)$$
$$= 7\,(5) + 11\,(9) - [3 + 2\,(5 + 9)]$$
$$= (35 + 99) - 31$$
$$= 134 - 31 = 103$$

QUESTIONS AND PROBLEMS FOR REVIEW

1. A monopolist is able to separate two markets. In one market, the demand can be expressed as $Q_1 = 14 - P_1$. In the second market the demand is $Q_2 = 20 - 2P_2$. The monopolist's *MC* (Marginal Cost) equals 4. Find the profit maximising output, its allocation between the two markets and the prices charged. What happens to profit ?
2. Define price discrimination. Under what conditions can a monopolist discriminate between different buyers in fixing the price of his product ? Under what conditions price discrimination is profitable ?
3. Explain the conditions under which monopolistic price discrimination is both possible and profitable.
4. Discuss the equilibrium of a monopolist, if one of the markets in which he operates is perfectly competitive.
   [**Hint.** This is the situation just like the dumping case discussed in the text.]
5. Distinguish between simple and discriminating monopoly. Show graphically how a discriminating monopolist attains equilibrium.
6. Suppose a monopolist sells his product in the home market and also exports a part of it. The foreign elasticity of demand for its product is below that of the domestic market. If consumer arbitrage between the two markets is impossible, how do the domestic and foreign prices compare ?
7. A firm supplies its product in two markets, demand being more elastic in one than in the other. Assuming that the firm aims to maximise its profits, show how the price and output in each market are determined.
8. A discriminating monopolist finds price elasticity of demand of his product –2.0 in one market and –1.5 in the other. What would be the ratio of prices charged by him in the two markets ?
9. What is Pareto efficiency in the distribution of goods between individuals? Show that price discrimination is not conducive to efficient distribution of goods.
10. When will a monopolist discriminate prices between buyers of his product ? *Is price discrimination socially justified* ?

CHAPTER

34

Measurement of the Degree of Monopoly Power

Monopoly is a matter of degree. Monopoly power is not only enjoyed by a pure monopolist but also by the producers and sellers of all those market categories in which monopoly element is present in a large or small measure. Thus producers or sellers in monopolistic competition and oligopoly enjoy monopoly power to a greater or lesser degree. By monopoly power we mean the amount of discretion which a producer or seller possesses in regard to the framing of his price and output policy. Monopoly power indicates the degree of control which a producer or seller wields over the price and output of his product. Now the question arises: what is the best method of measuring the degree of monopoly power. Various measures of monopoly power have been suggested by different economists but we shall discuss three of them below.

ELASTICITY OF DEMAND AS A MEASURE OF MONOPOLY POWER

The elasticity of demand for the product of a seller has long been regarded as indicator of the degree of monopoly power enjoyed by a seller. As we know that under pure or perfect competition, which is devoid of any monopoly element, demand curve confronting an individual seller or firm is perfectly elastic. Therefore, any departure from it would indicate the presence of some degree of monopoly. The extent to which a seller exercises control over the price and output of his product depends upon the elasticity of demand. Under pure or perfect competition with individual firm's demand curve for the product being perfectly elastic, the seller has no influence whatsoever over the price of his product. He takes the prevailing price in the market as given and constant and adjusts the level of his output accordingly. Thus under perfect or pure competition, a seller or firm enjoys absolutely no monopoly power.

When the demand curve is less than perfectly elastic, that is, when it slopes downward, as under various categories of imperfect competition (ordinary monopoly, monopolistic competition, oligopoly with and without product differentiation), some element of monopoly will be present indicating that the seller will enjoy some degree of monopoly power. With the demand curve for his product sloping downward, the seller can raise the price of his product, if he so likes, without losing all his customers. He can also fix a lower price than that of his rivals and thereby snatch some customers from them and thereby increases the quantity demanded of his product.

It is thus clear that when the demand curve falls downward (*i.e.*, when it is less than perfectly elastic), the seller possesses some discretion in shaping his policy with regard to the price he should charge for his product. The less the elasticity of demand for a seller's product, the greater the degree of monopoly control exercised by him and *vice versa*. When the elasticity of demand for his product is perfectly inelastic (demand curve being a vertical straight line), the seller can charge any price for his product howsoever high, the demand for his product remaining unchanged, he will enjoy absolute monopoly power[1]. Now, the greater the elasticity of downward sloping demand curve, the less the degree of monopoly power enjoyed by the firm.

A precise measure of monopoly power is given by the *inverse of* the elasticity of demand. Thus:

$$\text{Degree of monopoly power} = \frac{1}{e_p}$$

where e_p is the *absolute value* of price elasticity of demand. Thus when price elasticity of demand is $\frac{1}{4}$ or 0.25, the degree of monopoly power will be equal to $1/0.25 = 4$. If the elasticity of demand is 3, the degree of monopoly power will be equal to $1/e_p = 1/3$. It is thus clear that the less the elasticity of demand, the greater the monopoly power enjoyed by a seller, and the greater the elasticity of demand, the less the degree of monopoly power.

Critique

No doubt the price elasticity of demand is one indicator of the degree of monopoly power enjoyed by a seller in a certain market situation, but it is not a perfectly correct index of the strength of monopoly power. Given the level and shape of the downward-sloping demand curve of a seller, if the elasticity of demand is taken to be the measure of monopoly power, then the monopoly power possessed by the seller will vary at different levels of output, since at different points on the demand curve elasticity varies (with a straight-line demand curve, the elasticity at the middle point is equal to unity ; above the middle point, it is greater than one ; and below the middle point, it is less than unity). It follows that with one demand curve of a given shape and level, the degree of monopoly power judged by the elasticity of demand will be different at different points of the given demand curve. This looks very odd and unrealistic too.

Moreover, elasticity of demand as a measure of monopoly power fails in some oligopolistic industries where the competition between the few sellers is so acute and each of them is so much afraid of the price war that they do not compete on the basis of price, instead they take the prevailing price in the market as given and adjust their output on the basis of their non-price promotional effort such as product variation, advertising and other selling costs. Thus, in some cases of oligopoly, the demand curve facing an individual oligopolist, like that of a perfectly competitive seller, is known to be perfectly elastic, meaning thereby that monopoly power enjoyed by the oligopolist is zero. But no one can accept that few big firms which constitute the whole oligopolistic industry enjoy no monopoly power at all. We thus see that elasticity of demand as a measure of monopoly power may lead to quite misleading results in some cases.

LERNER'S MEASURE OF MONOPOLY POWER

Professor A. P. Lerner has put forward a measure of monopoly power which has gained great popularity and is most widely cited. Lerner takes perfect competition as the basis of departure for measuring monopoly power. He regards pure or perfect competition as the state of social optimum or maximum welfare and any departure from it would indicate the presence of some monopoly power leading to misallocation of resources or state of less than social optimum. As we know, in perfect competition price is equal to marginal cost of the

1. The case of a perfectly inelastic demand curve (demand curve being vertical straight line) is one concept of pure or absolute monopoly.

product in the equilibrium position. And it is this equality of price with marginal cost under perfect competition that ensures maximum social welfare or optimum allocation of resources.

Now when competition is less than pure or perfect, the demand curve facing a firm will be sloping downward and marginal revenue curve will lie below it. Consequently, when competition is less than perfect, that is, when it is imperfect, in a seller's equilibrium position, marginal cost will equal marginal revenue but price will stand higher than marginal cost or marginal revenue. This divergence between price and marginal cost, according to Lerner, is indicator of the existence of monopoly power. The greater this divergence between price and marginal cost, the greater the degree of monopoly power possessed by the seller. Based on this, Lerner has given the following precise index of monopoly power :

$$\text{Index of monopoly power} = \frac{P - MC}{P}$$

where P denotes price and MC denotes marginal cost at the equilibrium level of output.

When competition is pure or perfect, price (P) is equal to marginal cost and therefore Lerner's index of monopoly power is equal to zero indicating no monopoly power at all, for when price is equal to marginal cost, $P - MC$ will be equal to zero and the above formula will yield the value of index as zero.

Thus, under pure or perfect competition, Lerner's idex of monopoly power $\left(\frac{P-MC}{P}\right) = \frac{0}{P} = 0$. On the other hand, *when the monopolised product entails no cost of production, that is, when the product is a free good whose supply is controlled by one person, the marginal cost will be equal to zero* and Lerner's index of monopoly power $\left(\frac{P-MC}{P}\right)$ would be equal to one or unity. Thus when MC is equal to zero,

$$\frac{P - MC}{P} = \frac{P - 0}{P} = \frac{P}{P} = 1.$$

It is thus clear that Lerner's index of monopoly power can vary from zero to unity. Within this range, ***the greater the value of the index*** $\left(\frac{P-MC}{P}\right)$, ***the greater the degree of monopoly power possessed by the seller.*** For instance, if the price of a product is equal to ₹ 15 per unit and its marginal cost is ₹ 10, then the value of index will be $\frac{15-10}{15} = \frac{5}{15} = 1/3$ and when the price is equal to ₹ 20 and marginal cost is equal to 10, the index of monopoly power will be equal to $\frac{20-10}{20} = \frac{10}{20} = 1/2$.

Lerner's Index of Monopoly Power and Price Elasticity of Demand

Now, it has been shown that Lerner's index of monopoly power is nothing else but the inverse of the price elasticity of demand. We can prove this as follows :

Since at the equilibrium level, marginal cost is equal to marginal revenue, we can substitute in the above formula marginal revenue for marginal cost. Thus

$$\text{Lerner's index of monopoly power} = \frac{P - MC}{P}$$

$$= \frac{P - MR}{P} \qquad \ldots.(i)$$

We know that $MR = P\left(1 - \frac{1}{e}\right)$ where e is price elasticity of demand at the equilibrium output.

Thus, substituting $P\left(1 - \frac{1}{e}\right)$ for MR in (*i*) above we get,

$$\text{Lerner's index of monopoly power} = \frac{P - P\left(1 - \frac{1}{e}\right)}{P}$$

$$= \frac{P\left[1 - \left(1 - \frac{1}{e}\right)\right]}{P}$$

$$= 1 - 1 + \frac{1}{e}$$

$$= \frac{1}{e}.$$

It therefore follows that Lerner's index of monopoly power is equal to the inverse of price elasticity of demand. Thus degree of monopoly power can be judged by merely knowing the elasticity of demand at the equilibrium output. The degree of monopoly varies inversely with price elasticity of the demand for the good.

It is worth noting in this connection that while price elasticity of demand in Lerner' s index refers only to the price elasticity at the equilibrium output, in the first monopoly-power measure explained above the elasticity does not refer particularly to the equilibrium output.

Critique of Lerner's Measure of Monopoly Power

Lerner's measure has many shortcomings. Criticisms against it are almost the same which are levelled against the demand elasticity measure explained above. First, the chief shortcoming of Lerner's measure is its inability to measure the strength of monopoly and competitive elements in the *non-price competition* and in cases of product differentiation as in monopolistic competition and differentiated oligopoly. Lerner's index at the best measures the strengths of monopoly and competitive elements when the competition between the sellers is on the basis of price. When instead of competing on the basis of price the sellers in monopolistic competition and oligopoly compete on the basis of product variation, advertising and other forms of selling costs, Lerner's index fails to indicate truly the degree of monopoly and competition involved in such market structures. Suppose Lerner's monopoly index for a firm selling a differentiated product yields a high figure. But this does not necessarily mean that the seller will be possessing a high degree of monopoly power and facing less competition. It may be that the sellers of the various varieties of the product may not be competing on the basis of price and instead may be engaged in highly intensive competition in product variation and advertising and other forms of selling costs to promote the sales of their products.

On the basis of the above non-price factors some firms may enjoy greater monopoly control over their products than others. Thus E.H. Chamberlin righly says that elasticity and Lerner's index measures "pass over completely the important problems of competition and monopoly in the non-price area; quality and other aspects of the product including location and advertising and other forms of selling costs."[2]

Secondly, Lerner's measure is based upon only one aspect of monopoly, namely, its control over price which depends upon the availability and effectiveness of existing substitutes. It ignores the restraints on monopoly power put by the *potential substitutes* which would come to exist with the entry of new firms into the industry as a powerful factor limiting the monopoly power of the existing sellers. To quote Chamberlin again, "Neither elasticity nor the Lerner's Index measures anything the effectiveness of existing substitutes ; it gives no indication as to potential substitutes (the important problem of entry)."[3]

Thirdly, Lerner's index is criticized on the ground that monopoly power does not express itself only in the divergence of price from marginal cost, it also expresses itself in the restriction of output. Restriction of output may be the result of two measures, *underutilization* of plant capacity already built up or the *under-investment* by a firm when it is considering to build or expand the capacity. Lerner's formula does not take into account these important aspects of monopoly power.

Finally, Lerner' s measure has been criticized by Chamberlin on the ground that perfect competition with product homogeneity cannot be taken as a basis for measuring monopoly power of the sellers of real-world market structures with product differentiation. He asserts that perfect competition is quite imaginary, unreal and artificial since there is always product differentiation because of the difference in location, tastes and incomes of the people and the circumstances surrounding the sale of the products. He contends that it is of no use to measure the degree of monopoly by comparing an actual situation containing a blend of monopolistic and competitive elements with an artificially assumed state of perfect competition devoid of any monopoly elements. He thus says, "The upshot of these arguments is that in so far as products are actually heterogeneous by reasons of buyers' demands being dispersed over space and over a wide range of diverse tastes and incomes, it is completely artificial to conceive of purely competitive industries at all, and hence quite impossible to compare an actual situation, with its complex of monopoly and competitive elements, with an assumed state in which the monopoly elements were missing."[4]

Moreover, Chamberlin objects to treating perfect or pure competition as the *welfare ideal* or the state of *social optimum.* He argues that product differentiation is desired *per se* and therefore the welfare ideal must also be a state of maximum welfare when both monopoly and competitive elements (due to the presence of product differentiation) are involved. He thus says, "Not only the real world but also the welfare ideal, is a complex of monopoly and competition. It is only by considering both heterogeneity itself and the demand for it within an industry as non-existent or irrational (which I think to be the real meaning of Mrs. Robinson's imperfect competition) that it becomes possible to consider perfect competition as the welfare ideal. Mr. Lerner's index is explicitly designed to measure departures from such a social optimum, and follows in this respect imperfect, but not my monopolistic competition."[5]

---

2. E. H. Chamberlin, Measuring the Degree of Monopoly and Competition, printed in his *"Towards a General Theory of Value."* ,
3. E. H. Chamberlin, *op. cit.*
4. E. H. Chamberlin, *op. cit.* (Italics added).
5. Ibid

CROSS ELASTICITY OF DEMAND AS A MEASURE OF MONOPOLY POWER

Another method that has been suggested to measure monopoly power is the use of the concept of cross elasticity of demand. Probably, the concept of cross elasticity of demand to measure the degree of monopoly was first of all suggested by Kaldor[6], but it has been emphasized and popularised by Robert Triffin in his well known work ***'Value Theory and General Equilibrium Analysis'***. Cross elasticity of demand means the proportionate change in quantity demanded of a product as a result of a proportionate change in the price of another product. The cross elasticity of demand points to the degree of dependence of a firm's product upon the prices of other firms' products. If demand for a firm's product does not depend upon the prices of other firms' products, then that firm will be completely independent of price and output policies of others and the cross elasticity of demand for its product will be zero. The smaller the extent of cross elasticity of demand for the product of a firm, the greater the degree of monopoly power enjoyed by it and *vice versa*. The cross elasticity of demand between the products of two firms, *i* and *j*, can be written in the following algebraic form:

$$e_c = \frac{\Delta q_i}{q_i} \div \frac{\Delta p_j}{p_j} = \frac{\Delta q_i}{q_i} \times \frac{p_j}{\Delta p_j}$$

$$\frac{\Delta q_i p_j}{q_i \Delta p_j} = \frac{\Delta q_i p_j}{\Delta p_j q_i}$$

This means that cross elasticity of demand for the product of a firm *i* is the change in the relative quantity demanded of the product of firm *i* as a result of the relative change in the price of the product of another firm *j*. When the demand for the output of a firm or seller is not affected at all by the price of any other firm, the cross elasticity of demand for its product will be zero, that is, $\Delta q_i p_j / \Delta p_j q_i$ will be zero. Thus, when the cross elasticity of a firm's product with any product of another firm is zero, the firm will enjoy absolute monopoly power in pursuing his own price and output policy. Therefore, Robert Triffin ***defined pure monopoly as one the cross elasticity of demand for whose product is zero.*** The greater the cross elasticity of demand for a firm's product, the greater the degree of competition between the firms and less the degree of monopoly power. In perfect competition, the products sold by various firms are completely homogeneous and therefore perfect substitutes of each other. Therefore, if any firm under perfect competition lowers the price of its product, it will be able to attract all the customers of other firms with the result that demand for its rivals will be reduced to zero. Thus, according to Triffin and many others, the cross elasticity of demand between the products of various firms under perfect competition is infinite and therefore firms under perfect competition enjoy no monopoly power at all.

Thus pure monopoly having zero cross elasticity of demand enjoys absolute monopoly power and perfectly competitive firm having infinite cross elasticity of demand possesses zero monopoly power. But these are two limiting cases. Within these two limits, the less the coefficient of the cross elasticity of demand (that is, less the value of $\Delta q_i p_j / \Delta p_j q_i$), the greater the monopoly power and *vice versa*. Triffin has actually classified the various market structures on the basis of cross elasticity of demand.

6. N. Kaldor, Market Imperfections and Excess Capacity.

Criticism

Cross elasticity of demand as a measure of monopoly power has been severely criticized. First, it has been pointed out by several writers that ***cross elasticity of demand of any perfectly competitive firm with any other firm is also zero.*** They assert that if a purely competitive firm reduces its price to snatch away the customers of the rival firms it would be unable to satisfy all the demand at the lower price, because of its rising marginal costs when it expands its output. And the rising marginal costs are essential to pure or perfect competition, for decreasing or constant costs are incompatible with it. When a perfectly competitive firm reduces its price, it will not be able to meet much additional demand and therefore the sales of his rivals would not be perceptibly affected. In perfect competition by definition no firm is large enough to influence the demand or sales of other firms by its individual action.

Further, the cross elasticity of demand for the product of a firm under perfect or pure competition is also zero because it produces a product which has a very large number of perfect substitutes. Therefore, the effect of any change in price or output by a firm will spread over such a large number of firms that the impact on each of them will be so negligible that no one will take notice of it. Thus Professors Olson and Mcfarland of Princeton University (U.S.A.) rightly remark, "Because the number of firms producing very close or identical substitutes is so great no *one* of them will be noticeably affected when the pure competitor changes his price or output. If the pure competitor should attempt to raise his price unilaterally, the amount of substitution of the outputs of other firms for his firm's output will be considerable, since these other substitutes are virtually identical. ***But the crucial consideration is that no other one firm perceives any change because the number of firms involved is so large.***"[7]

Thus we see that according to the opinion of many modern economists cross elasticity of demand between a pure competitor's product and his rivals is zero. Now, when both in pure monopoly and pure competition, cross elasticity of demand is the same. it follows that the concept of cross elasticity of demand fails to distinguish the two extreme market structures—pure monopoly with absolute monopoly power and pure competition with no monopoly power. How can then it be used to measure the various degrees of monopoly power involved in various forms of imperfect competition ?

Moreover, cross elasticity of demand as a measure of monopoly power suffers from also the same shortcomings as the Lerner's measure. It thus does not take into account the restraint on monopoly power posed by the likelihood of the emergence of potential substitutes. Further, like Lerner's measure, it takes exclusively price as the basis of competition and ignores completely the elements of monopoly and competition involved in the *non-price area* such as quality of the product, differences in location, product variation, advertising and other forms of selling effort. Some firms may enjoy great monopoly power because of their large capacity to advertise and incur other selling costs, and others enjoy a good deal of monopoly power because their shops or factories are situated at a more favourable location than others. Cross elasticity fails to throw light on these aspects of monopoly power.

---

7. The Restoration of Monopoly and the Concept of Industry, *Quarterly Journal of Economics*, Vol. 76 (Nov. 1962). pp. 613-31 (italics added).

CHAPTER

35

Price and Output Under Bilateral Monopoly

In this chapter we propose to discuss how price and output are determined under bilateral monopoly which has been the subject of a good deal of controversy in economic theory. Bilateral monopoly is said to exist when a single seller of a product or input faces a single buyer of that. Thus, under bilateral monopoly, a seller or supplier is monopolist of his product or input, and the single buyer is monopsonist of that product or input. That is, under bilateral monopoly, ***monopolist faces the monopsonist.*** Since the seller has a monopoly of the commodity, no close substitutes of that commodity will be available. The seller has no other outlet to sell the commodity and the buyer has no other source from where he can buy that commodity. The case of bilateral monopoly is rarely found in the product market, but is often found in the input or factor markets. The important case of bilateral monopoly is found when a trade union which has a monopoly of selling labour services confronts a giant business corporation which has to buy labour from the trade union of labour and the issue is at what wage rate the exchange of labour should take place. Further, an exchange of two goods between two individuals is also in fact a case of bilateral monopoly which we havef already discussed in chapter on ***"Applications and Uses of Indifference Curves."*** In this chapter we shall confine ourselves to the question of price and quantity determination under bilateral monopoly in the product market and defer the question of wage determination under bilateral monopoly to a later chapter.

Price and Output under Bilateral Monopoly

Under bilateral monopoly in the market for a final product, the single buyer or monopsonist is a consumer. The firm which produces that product (which has no close substitutes) is the monopolist supplier or seller. Analysis of pricing and output under bilateral monopoly in the product market is almost the same as we made in case of the exchange of the two goods between two individuals. The concepts of indifference curves, Edgeworth Box and contract curve explained there are fully applicable to the present case. However, a slight difference is that in the present case the single buyer is the consumer who has *money* to offer for the product he demands and purchases. Therefore, we shall take one product which a monopolist produces and sells and the money which a single buyer of that product spends on it. But before discussing pricing and output under bilateral monopoly with the aid of indifference curves and contract curve, we shall explain them with the ordinary demand, marginal revenue and marginal cost curves. Consider Figure 35.1 where *DD* is the demand curve for the product of the buyer, which is based upon his marginal utility curve. Since there is a single buyer of the product, his demand curve *DD* would be the demand curve confronting the monopolist supplier and therefore *DD* would be average revenue *(AR)* curve for him. *MR* is the marginal revenue curve for the monopolist supplier corresponding to the demand curve *DD*. *MC* is the marginal cost curve of the monopolistic supplier.

Let us now explain the relevant curves for the monopsonist buyer. If the monopsonist buyer assumes that he has the full power to set price subject to the cost situation of the supplier, then he would consider marginal cost curve *MC* of the monopolist as his supply curve of the product. In other words, if he thinks he can force the supplier to accept price set by him, then he would be supplied by the supplier the quantity of the product at which his marginal cost equals the price set by the monopsonist buyer. Thus, if the monopsonist thinks he has the complete power to set the price, the marginal cost curve of the monopolist will indicate average supply prices at which various corresponding quantities of the product would be offered to him. Hence marginal cost curve *MC* of the monopolist is the supply curve or the curve of the average supply prices to him which in Figure 35.1 is labelled as *ASP*. Since the average supply

DD = *AR curve for the monpolist*

= *MU curve for the monopsonist*

MC = *Marginal cost curve of the monopolist seller*

= *Supply curve of the monopsonist buyer or it is the curve of average supply price (ASP)*

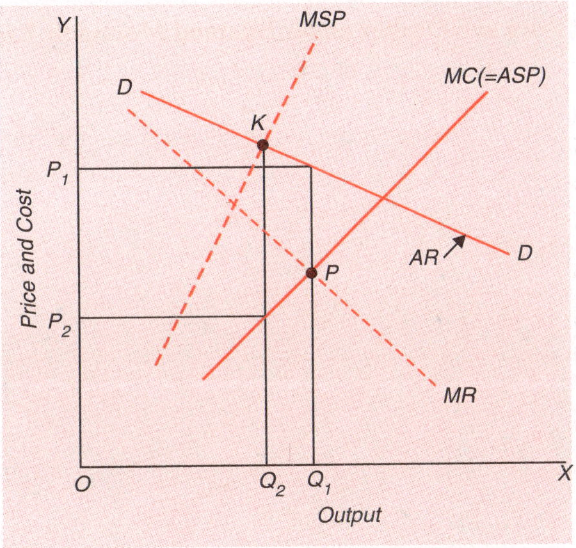

Fig. 35.1 . *Limits of Price and Output Under Bilateral Monopoly*

price *(ASP)* for the monopsonist rises as he obtains more quantity of the product, marginal supply price *(MSP)* and therefore the curve of marginal supply price (which may also be called marginal supply cost) will lie above the *ASP* curve, as is shown in the Figure 35.1 by the curve *MSP*. Thus, the curve of marginal supply price *(MSP)* is marginal to the curve of average supply price *(ASP)*.

Now, if the monopolist supplier thinks that, as a monopolist of the product, he has the usual power to determine any price and output on the demand curve of the buyer, then to maximize his own profits, he will equate his marginal cost with the marginal revenue. As will be seen from Figure 35. l, he will produce (or supply) OQ_1 and set price OP_1 at which marginal cost is equal to marginal revenue. In other words, most profitable price for the monopolist supplier is OP_1 and most profitable quantity produced and supplied is OQ_1.

On the other hand, the monopsonist buyer by assuming that he has the full power to set the price and in order to maximize his satisfaction he will equate his marginal supply price *(MSP)* with his marginal utility (or the price he is prepared to pay). Since demand curve *DD* indicates his marginal utility or the price he is prepared to pay, he will be maximizing satisfaction by purchasing OQ_2 at which average supply price is OP_2. It will be noticed from Figure 35.1 that price OP_2 is much lower than OP_1, that is, the price OP_1 which the monopolist wants to set is higher than the price OP_2 which the monopsonist wants to set.

It is clear from above that when both the buyer and supplier think themselves to be price markers and therefore act autonomously, they reach at different prices as well as at different quantities. But since by definition neither for buyer, nor for seller, any alternative course is open and both of them have to trade with each other, they have to agree on some price. Therefore, they will negotiate and bargain with each other. The actual price which may be agreed upon as a result of negotiation and bargaining may be anywhere between OP_1 and OP_2. Economic analysis does not help us to indicate exactly what price will emerge out of negotiation and bargaining, since it does not depend upon any economic factors. The exact price at which the settlement will be reached depends upon bargaining skill and power of the buyer and seller. Since price can end up anywhere between OP_1 and OP_2, *it is said to be indeterminate within these limits.*

Price and Output under Bilateral Monopoly Explained with the Help of Contract Curve

The concept of contract curve which we explained in an earlier chapter is very useful in explaining pricing and output under bilateral monopoly. We shall explain the case of bilateral monopoly when there is a single producer and supplier of a product. Consider Figure 35.2, in which on the *X*- axis is shown the quantity of product X and on the Y-axis the

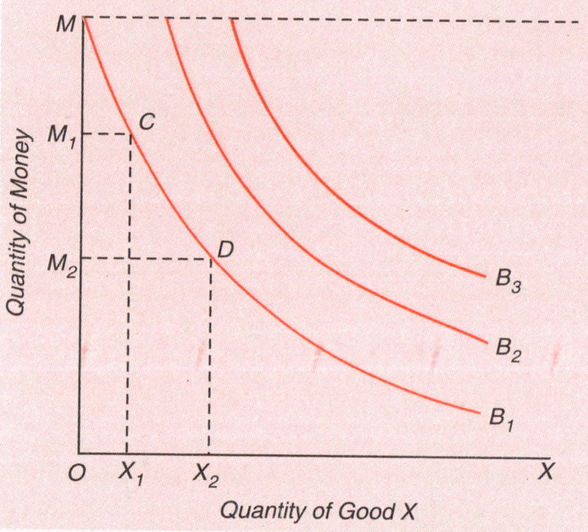

Fig. 35.2. *Indifference Curves of a Buyer*

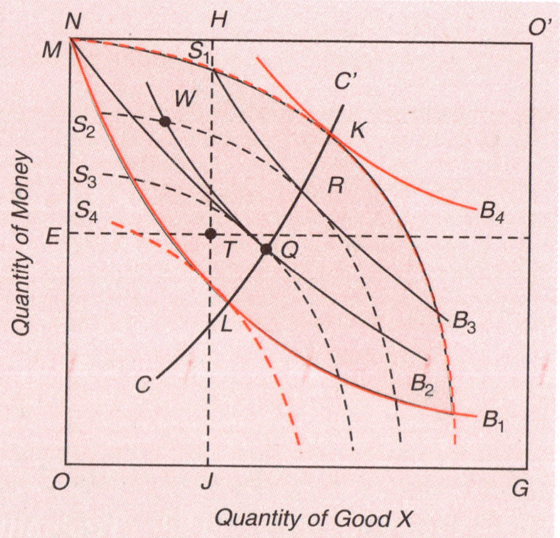

Fig. 35.3. *Price and Quantity Under Bilateral Monopoly is Indeterminate*

quantity of money is shown. We have drawn in Figure 35.2 the indifference curve B_1, B_2 and B_3 of the consumer (buyer) between money and the product *X*. Each indifference curve is the locus of all combinations of money and the product *X* which give the consumer equal satisfaction. However, the greater the level of indifference curve, the greater the level of buyer's satisfaction. Further, it has been assumed that buyer has *OM* amount of money which he can spend on the good. It should be noted that in the indifference curve diagram in Figure 35.2 we read downward from *OM*, the amount cf money which the buyer pays out for obtaining a certain quantity of the product *X*. Thus, if as a result of trading, the consumer ends up at point *C*, it means that he has paid MM_1 amount of money and has obtained OX_1 quantity of the product. Likewise if he ends up *at* point *D*, it means he has paid MM_2 amount of money and has obtained OX_2 quantity of the product.

Similarly, we can draw ***profit-indifference curves (or equal profit curves)*** between money and product X for the monopolist supplier of product X. *A profit indifference curve is the locus of all combinations of the quantity of product X supplied and the money which would yield equal amount of profit* (after deducting the cost of production) to the supplier. It should be noted that the maximum amount of product X that can be supplied by the monopolist supplier is determined by his productive capacity which we assume as a given fixed quantity (which in Figure 35.3 is taken to be *O 'N*). Out of this maximum production capacity level, the monopolist will supply the varying quantity of the product at various prices (we have not shown separately the indifference map of the monopolist supplier).

We can now combine the indifference maps of the monopsonist buyer and the monopolist supplier in an Edgeworth Box, as is shown in Figure 35.3. In this we have turned upside down the indifference map of the monopolist supplier and have joined the ends of the two axes. *O 'N* is the maximum supply capacity level of the product X of the monopolist supplier. Thus, the length of the vertical axis is equal to *OM*, the amount of money available with the monopsonist buyer and the length of horizontal axis is equal to *O 'N*, the maximum capacity level of the product of the monopolist. It should be noted that in Edgeworth Box presented in Figure 35.3, B_1, B_2, B_3 are indifference curves of the buyer which are convex to the origin and S_1, S_2, S_3 and S_4 are the equal-profit curves of the supplier which have been turned upside down and therefore are convex to the origin *O '*.

It should be noted any point in this Edgeworth Box represents *a trading point,* since this indicates where both the monopolist and monopolist (supplier and buyer) will end up after an act of trade or exchange. For instance, take point *T* which represents a particular trade between the buyer and the seller. At point *T*, the buyer has taken *OJ* quantity of product X and is having *OE* of money after trade, that is, he has paid *ME* amount of money for obtaining *OJ* (= *ET*) amount of the product X. The monopolist seller has sold *NH* (= *OJ*) of the product X and in return has obtained *ME* amount of money. The monopolist supplier is keeping the remaining capacity to supply equal to *O 'H* as unutilized.

Similarly, any other point in the Edgeworth Box diagram represents a trade or exchange between the buyer and the seller. Since there is a fixed supply of money *OM* available with the buyer, the amount of money he pays out to obtain X, goes to the seller and likewise there is a fixed capacity to supply of X with the seller. Whatever is supplied by the seller goes to the buyer and the remaining capacity remains unutilised with him. In Figure 35.3, B_1, B_2, B_3 and B_4 are the indifference curves of the buyer, S_1, S_2, S_3 and S_4 are the profit-indifference curves (equal profit curves) of the supplier:

By joining the points of tangency between the indifference curves of the buyer and supplier, we get a curve *CC '* which, as noted in Chapter 8, is called *contract curve.* This is because it is at any point on this curve that the trade or contract will take place. In order to analyse pricing and output under bilateral monopoly, ***we assume that the buyer and seller have decided to agree upon a certain price (i.e., rate of exchange) by negotiating with each other.*** We further suppose that they know each other's indifference map. When they open the negotiations, they will realise that for every point off the contract curvaj there will be some points on the contract curve *CC '* which will be advantageous to both of them.

Take, for instance, in the Edgeworth Box diagram point *W* which lies away from the contract curve CC *'* and at which therefore the two indifference curves of the buyer and seller (B_2 and S_2 respectively) intersect each other. It will be seen that *within* the area bounded by the indifference curves B_2 and S_2, higher indifference curves of both buyer and supplier will pass. Thus, the points lying between *Q* and *R* on the contract curve will be on the higher indifference curves (not actually drawn in the figure) of both the participants. Therefore, at any point on the contract curve between *Q* and *R* both the buyer and the seller will be better off than at point *W* because they will be on their higher indifference curves. Hence, even if they start negotiations by considering point *W*, they will ultimately come to any point between *Q* and *R* on the contract curve and exchange accordingly. We therefore see that from whatever point off the contract curve they open their negotiations, they will end up at a point on the contract curve. Thus, according to Prof. Baumol, "actual trading must end up somewhere along the contract curve, *CC* ′, for anywhere else it will be mutually advantageous to buyer and seller to renegotiate their deal, and only at a point on the contract curve will no such renegotiations be profitable to both."[1]

But it is worth mentioning that movement *along* the contract curve is not advantageous to both of them. As we move upward along the contract curve, the buyer will be reaching his higher indifference curves and the seller on his lower indifference curves. On the contrary, any downward movement on the contract curve will mean that buyer will become worse off and the seller better off. Economic analysis does not help to indicate *at what exact point* on the contract curve, the exchange between the buyer and seller will take place and accordingly what price as well as quantity of good will be determined. Since the trade between the buyer and seller can end up and therefore the price and output of the good can be determined ***at any point on the contract curve, economists say the price as well as quantity is indeterminate under bilateral monopoly.***

However, ***the range of indeterminacy (that is, the range of possible trading points and, therefore, the price and quantity) can be narrowed down.*** It is on any point on the arc *KL* of the contract curve CC ′ that trading between the two parties will take place. This can be easily explained. When the two parties do not trade with each other, they are at point *M* (or at *N* ; *M* and *N* coincide each other); the buyer has *OM* money and the supplier has *O* ′*N* quantity (capacity) to supply of good X. Thus *M* (or *N)* represents *no trade point.* It will be seen from the Figure 35.3 that indifference curve B_1 of the buyer and profit-indifference curve S_1, of the supplier pass through the point *M*. This implies that the buyer and the seller will refuse to trade, if the trade puts them at points which lie on the lower indifference curves than B_1, and S_1, respectively. In other words, the buyer will refuse to deal with the supplier, if the price fixed is such that he ends up at any point on an indifference curve which lies to the left of his indifference curve B_1, since it will mean trade will make him worse off than at *M*. Likewise, the supplier will refuse to deal, if it puts him to any point on a profit indifference curve which lies to the right of his profit indifference curve S_1, since this will make him worse off than at *M*. We have therefore shaded the area bounded by the indifference curves B_1 and S_1 of the buyer and the supplier irespectively. Moving from no deal point *M* to any point within the shaded area will be mutually advantageous to both of them and will therefore make both of them better off than at *M*. This is because any point within the shaded region will lie on their higher indifference curves than B_1 and S_1 respectively. Thus, the possible trading point (and therefore the determination of price and quantity) will be within the shaded region between the indifference curves through *M*. (that is, B_1 and S_1).

But, as explained above, corresponding to any point *off the* contract curve, there will be points *on* the contract curve which will be more advantageous to both of them, therefore the possible trading point will lie *on the arc LK* (which lies in the shaded region) of the contract curve *CC* ′. That is, beyond *L* and *Kon* the contract curve *CC* ′ the equilibrium or trading point between the two participants will not occur. We therefore conclude that ***the equilibrium price and quantity of the good will be determined anywhere on the arc LK of the contract curve CC ′.*** Beyond this, it is difficult to narrow down the range of possible points of final equilibrium or trading. Therefore, ***the determination of price and quantity under bilateral monopoly is indeterminate within the limits of the arc LK of the contract curve.*** The exact point on which the final equilibrium or trading point on the arc *LK* of the contract curve will lie depends upon the respective bargaining skill and strength of the two participants.

1. W. J. Baumol, *Economic Theory and Operations Analysis*, 3rd edition, p. 351.

Suppose the final equilibrium point lies at point Q. Both are better off at point Q than at M (no trade point); but the supplier is more better off than the buyer since Q lies on indifference curve S_3, of the supplier and on the indifference curve B_2 of the buyer. The price determined at the equilibrium point Q will be equal to the *slope* of the straight line MQ.

Depending upon the respective bargaining skill and strength the equilibrium or trading point can lie on R at which also both are better off than at M ; but here the buyer is more better off than the supplier. The price determined at the equilibrium point R will be equal to the slope of the straight line MR (not actually drawn in the figure). On the arc LK of the contract curve, as the trading or equilibrium point moves towards L, the supplier will be better off and the buyer worse off and as it moves towards K, the buyer would be better off and the supplier worse off. That is why contract curve is sometimes called *conflict curve*, because movement along it makes one better off and other worse off, though it is worth pointing out again that both would be better off at a point within the range LK of the contract curve than any point off it as well as than the no-trade point M. We, therefore, conclude that under bilateral monopoly and in the situation depicted in the figure, ***the price-quantity equilibrium is indeterminate within the range of the arc LK of the contract curve.***

It is worth mentioning here that the indeterminacy of price-quantity equilibrium does not mean that it is altogether impossible to give explanation of the economic phenomena (price and output under bilateral monopoly here). Indeed, our analysis of bilateral monopoly problem throws a good deal of light on the determination of price and output under it. Further, indeterminacy of equilibrium also does not mean that no final equilibrium position will be actually reached. In fact, the buyer and seller shall come to some price-quantity agreement. Thus, "*the indeterminacy means that the final solution is not fully predictable by economic analysis and this because the final outcome may not rest on economic considerations alone. Our simple analysis does, however, establish the boundaries of the final solution.*"[2]

It is worth mentioning here that by combining economics and psychology, Sidney Siegel and Lawrence E. Fouraker[3] have provided a theoretical solution to the bilateral monopoly. They have suggested that under bilateral monopoly there is a tendency on the part of the buyer and seller to *maximize joint profits*. The buyer and the seller then divide these profits according to some agreed formula. The tendency to maximize joint profits becomes very strong when the buyer and seller have quite good information about each other's wants and preferences. Thus, according to them, information about each other is a controlling force which determines the tendency to maximize joint profits.

Siegel and Fouraker also point out that the solution of the bilateral monopoly problem is also greatly influenced by the "*levels of aspiration*" of the buyer and the seller. Level of aspiration is a psychological concept and means the intensity of the desire to maximize. A person who has achieved a good success in the past from trading and hopes to perform better in the future will have a higher level of aspiration than the person who has met with failures in the past. But Prof. Baumol does not accept the joint-profit-maximization solution of the problem of bilateral monopoly. For the solution of indeterminacy problem of bilateral monopoly, according to Baumol, "Several suggestions have been offered, for example, the joint profit maximum point (the point which maximizes the sum of the profits of the buyer and seller together). However, it is difficult to see why one may expect that the bargainers should always be expected to end up at any one such point. For that reason, many economists have concluded that the bilateral monopoly problem is indeterminate."[4]

2. Charles L. Cole, *Microeconomics : A Contemporary Approach*, Harcourt Brace, Jovanovich, 1973, p. 257.
3. Sidney Siegel and Lawrence E. Fouraker, *Bargaining and Group Decision Making : Experiments in Bilateral Monopoly*, McGraw-Hill, New York, 1960.
4. *Op. cit.*, p. 351.

CHAPTER

36

Price and Output Determination Under Monopolistic Competition

Imperfect Competition : Monopolistic Competition and Oligopoly

Perfect competition and monopoly are rarely found in the real world and thus they do not represent, for the most part, the actual market situations. Therefore, the conclusions which follow from the theories of perfect competition were found to be inapplicable to the behaviour of business firms in the actual world. For instance, in the real world, firms were found to be enjoying 'internal economies of scale' which were incompatible with the theory of perfect competition. The urgent need was therefore felt to reformulate the theory of price so as to bring it nearer to the actual world. This was accomplished by E.H. Chamberlin and Joan Robinson who worked quite independently and brought out simultaneously "*The Theory of Monopolistic Competition*" and "*The Economics of Imperfect Competition*" respectively. Joan Robinson got the clues for her theory of imperfect competition from Sraffa who in his article "The Laws of Returns under Competitive Conditions" in *Economic Journal* asserted, ***"It is necessary, therefore, to abandon the path of free competition and turn in the opposite direction, namely, towards monopoly."***

Monopolistic competition theory of E.H. Chamberlin and imperfect competition theory of Joan Robinson, though similar in various ways differ in some important respects. The nutshell of these theories, especially of the theory of monopolistic competition, is that the perfect competition and pure monopoly are the two opposite limiting cases, lying between which is a series of intermediate cases, which differ from each other in relative strengths of monopoly and competitive elements, or in other words, in *degrees of imperfection*. It may be noted that the extreme limit of monopoly is reached when a seller does not face competition from any substitute product. Since every good has to compete with others for buyer's money income, every good is a substitute of others to some extent. It follows that the extreme limit of monopoly, which Sraffa denotes as *pure monopoly*, will be reached only when a single person or agency comes to have a "control over the supply of all economic goods." At the other extreme is pure or perfect competition in which case an individual seller has to compete with the products (of rival sellers) which are perfect substitutes of his own product, since products of all sellers are completely identical or homogeneous. Between these two extremes of pure monopoly and perfect competition, there are all gradations in which both the monopolistic and competitive elements are present. In the terminology of Robinson and Chamberlin, pure monopoly in the sense of a single seller of a product which has got no close substitutes is an extreme form of imperfect competition. ***The two important forms of imperfect competition are : (a) monopolistic competition, (b) oligopoly.***

The fundamental distinguishing feature of imperfect competition is that unlike that under perfect or pure competition, the demand curve confronting an individual firm under it slopes downward. As a result, the marginal revenue curve lies below it. Marginal revenue curve plays such a crucial role because of its definite relation with price and elasticity (MR = Price $\frac{e-1}{e}$). It is the nature of this relation which distinguishes a state of competition that is perfect from one that is impure or imperfect. The difference between marginal revenue and price at an output level depends upon the size of price elasticity of demand at it. Under perfect competition, price is equal to marginal revenue since price elasticity of demand is infinite, while under imperfect competition, price is greater than marginal revenue since price elasticity of demand is less than infinite. Therefore, the difference between the price and marginal revenue (or marginal cost) at equilibrium output is regarded as the *degree of monopoly*. Thus, the relative magnitudes of price and marginal revenue at equilibrium output help us to distinguish between different degrees of monopoly power in various market structures. The greater the difference between the price and the marginal revenue, the greater the degree of monopoly element and *vice versa*.

PRODUCT DIFFERENTIATION AND MONOPOLISTIC COMPETITION

The concept of monopolistic competition put forth by Chamberlin is a true revolutionary as well as more realistic than either perfect competition or pure monopoly. Before Chamberlin, monopoly and competition were regarded as two mutually exclusive alternatives; one would be absent when the other exists. On the other hand, according to Chamberlin, in most of the real world economic situations, both monopoly and competitive elements are present. Chamberlin's concept of monopolistic competition is thus a blending of competition and monopoly.

The distinguishing feature of monopolistic competition which makes it as a blending of competition and monopoly is the *differentiation of the product*. This means that the products of various firms are not homogeneous but differentiated though they are closely related to each other. Product differentiation does not mean that the products of various firms are altogether different. They are only slightly different so that they are quite similar and serve as close substitutes of each other. When there is any degree of differentiation of products, monopoly element enters the situation. And, the greater the differentiation, the greater the element of monopoly involved in the market situation. When there is a large number of firms producing differentiated products, each one has a monopoly of its own product but is subject to the competition of close substitutes. Since each is a monopolist and yet has competitors, we have a market situation which can be aptly described as "monopolistic competition." It is thus clear that monopolistic competition involves both the monopoly and competitive elements. Here, it is worth quoting Chamberlin himself "With differentiation appears monopoly and as it proceeds further, the element of monopoly becomes greater. Where there is any degree of differentiation whatever, each seller has an absolute monopoly of his own product, but is subject to the competition of more or less imperfect substitutes. Since each is a monopolist and yet has competitors we may speak of them as 'competing monopolists' and with peculiar appropriateness, of the forces at work as those of monopolistic competition."[1]

It is thus clear from above that in monopolistic competition, products are not identical as in perfect competition, but neither are they remote substitutes as in monopoly. The products of various sellers are fairly similar (but not the same) and serve as close substitutes of each other. Every seller has a monopoly of his own differentiated product but he has to face a stiff competition from his rival sellers which are selling close substitutes of his product.

1. E.H. Chamberlin, *The Theory of Monopolistic Competition, 7th ed., 1956, p. 64.*

Many examples of product differentiation can be given from the Indian scene. For instance, in India there are various manufacturers of toothpaste which produce different brands such as Colgate, Binaca, Forhans , Pepsodent , Signal, Neem etc. Thus, the manufacturer of 'Colgate' has a monopoly of producing it (nobody else can produce and sell the toothpaste with the name 'Colgate') but he faces competition from the manufacturers of Forhans, Binaca, Pepsodent etc. which are close substitutes of Colgate. The manufacturer of Colgate cannot therefore decide about his price-output policies without considering the possible reactions of rival firms producing close substitutes. Other examples of monopolistic competition are the producers of bathing soaps (Lux, Godrej, Breeze, Hamam, Palmolive, Jai etc.); the manufacturers of tooth brushes (Colgate, Dr. West's, Wisdom, Binaca, etc.); retailers' shops in the towns; barbers' shops in the towns, etc. We thus see that monopolistic competition corresponds more to the real world economic situation than perfect competition or monopoly.

A general class of product is differentiated if a basis exists for preferring goods of one seller to those of others. Such a basis for preference may be real or fancied, it will cause differentiation of the product. When such differentiation of the product exists, even if it is slight, buyers will be paired with sellers not in a random fashion (as in perfect competition) but according to their preferences. There are, broadly speaking, two bases of product differentiation. Firstly, differentiation may be based upon certain ***characteristics of the product itself*** such as exclusive patented features, trade marks and trade names, peculiarities of packages or wrappers if any, or difference in quality, design, colour or style. Real qualitative differences like those of materials used, design and workmanship are no doubt important means of differentiating products. But imaginary differences created through advertising, the use of attractive packets, the use of trade marks and brand names are more usual methods by which products are differentiated, even if physically they are identical or almost so. Secondly, differentiation may be based upon the ***conditions surrounding the sale of the product***. This means that product is differentiated if the services rendered in the process of selling the product by one seller or firm are not identical with those rendered by any other seller or firm. Thus, in retail trade to take only one instance, the conditions surrounding the sale of the product include "the convenience of the seller's location, the general tone or character of his establishment, his way of doing business, his reputation for fair dealing, courtesy, efficiency, and all others which attach his customers either to himself or to those employed by him".[2] If these and other intangible factors surrounding the sale of the product are different in case of different sellers, the product in each case will be different since the buyers take these intangible factors into consideration while making purchases. These factors like the patents, trade marks etc. serve as a basis for preference.

If the above two aspects of differentiation are borne in mind, then it will be quite manifest that virtually all products in the real world are more or less differentiated. It should be carefully noted that even when product differentiation is caused by the circumstances surrounding the sale of the products, both monopolistic and competitive elements are present. In retail trade, to take the above example, every product is rendered differentiated by the individuality of the establishment in which it is sold including the location factor, the general tone, reputation, goodwill of the establishment, way of dealing with customers etc. Each retail trader has complete and absolute control over the supply of his 'product' when this is taken to include location factor, general tone and reputation, way of dealing with the customers etc; this is the monopolistic aspect. Again, every retail trade is subject to the competition of other 'products' sold under different conditions and at different locations; this is the competitive aspect. Thus, as in the

2. E.H. Chamberlin, *op. cit.*, p. 68

case of patents and trade marks, both monopoly and competition are present in the case of 'products' differentiated by the conditions surrounding their sale.

Under monopoly, the demand curve for the product of the monopolist is given. But the demand curve for the product of an individual producer or seller under monopolistic competition cannot be taken as given since there exist, in monopolistic competition, close competitive interrelationships among various producers selling close substitutes. The demand curve for the product of an individual depends upon the nature and prices of its closely competing substitutes. Thus, according to Chamberlin, "Monopolistic competition concerns itself not only with the problem of an *individual equilibrium* (the ordinary theory of monopoly), but also with that of a *group equilibrium* (the adjustment of economic forces within a group of competing monopolists, ordinarily regarded as merely a group of competitors). In this, it differs both from the theory of competition and from the theory of monopoly".[3]

This leads us to Chamberlin's concepts of group and group equilibrium. Chamberlin has used the word group instead of industry in order to draw distinction between perfect competition and monopolistic competition. The word industry is generally used in economics in the context of pure or perfect competition and *refers to a collection of firms that produce homogeneous products*. But, as explained above, under monopolistic competition we have product hetrogeneity. Therefore, the word 'industry' loses its significance under monopolistic competition. Therefore, Chamberlin has used the word 'group'. ***By group he means "a number of producers whose goods are fairly close substitutes."*** We thus see that the Chamberlin's 'group' refers to a collection of firms that produce closely related but not identical products. It became necessary for Chamberlin to evolve the concept of 'group' as distinct from industry because in the case of group where products are differentiated there are special problems which are absent in the case of industry where products are homogeneous. The various firms in a given group produce products which are close substitutes of each other and therefore compete with each other in the market. The demand for the product of one producer depends upon the price and the nature of the products of his close rivals. These competitive inter-relationships among firms are absent in the case of an industry under pure or perfect competition since all of them produce homogeneous products and each of them can sell his entire supply of its product at the going market price.

An individual producer in the 'group' under monopolistic competition cannot therefore be treated in complete isolation from his rivals producing close substitutes, since the demand for his product depends upon the nature and price of the close substitutes. To quote Chamberlin: "From our point of view, each producer within the group is a monopolist, yet his market is interwoven with those of his competitors, and he is no longer to be isolated from them."[4]

Lastly, it may be noted that the sense in which the word 'competition' is generally used in the business world is in conformity more with the monopolistic competition than with the perfect competition. The phrases such as price cutting, under-selling, unfair competition, meeting competition, cut-throat competition, securing market etc. often used in the business world are irrelevant in the context of perfect competition. This is because each seller under so-called 'perfect competition' accepts the going market price and can dispose of his entire supply of the product without affecting price. For a perfect competitor there is no problem of choosing a price policy, problem of advertising in order to attract customers. Thus, the competition in the ordinary sense of the competitive phrases, just noted above, has meaning only in the

3. *Ibid.*, p. 69,
4. E.H. Chamberlin, *op. cit.* p.8.

context of monopolistic competition (and also of oligopoly) where products of various sellers are differentiated but closely related. Sellers really compete in the ordinary sense of the word only under the monopolistic competition and oligopoly.

IMPORTANT FEATURES OF MONOPOLISTIC COMPETITION

It is important to understand the important characteristics of monopolistic competition. The knowledge of these features will enable the students to know how this form of market structure is different from perfect competition and oligopoly. We explain below its important features.

1. A large number of firms. The first important feature of monopolistic competition is that under it there are a relatively large number of firms each satisfying a small share of the market demand for the product. Because there is a large number of firms under monopolistic competition, there exists stiff competition between them. Unlike perfect competition these large number of firms do not produce identical products. Instead, they produce and sell differentiated products which are close substitutes of each other. This makes the competition among firms real and tough.

Further, the fact that there is a large number of firms under monopolistic competition, size of each firm will be relatively small. This is unlike oligopoly where there are a few firms of big size.

2. Product differentiation. The second important feature of monopolistic competition is that the products produced by various firms are not identical but are slightly different from each other. Though different firms make their products slightly different from others, they remain close substitutes of each other. In other words, the products of various firms working under monopolistic competition are not the same but are similar. Therefore, their prices cannot be very much different from each other. It is because of the fact that their products are similar and close substitutes of each other that the various firms under monopolistic competition compete with each other.

3. Some influence over the price. Each firm under monopolistic competition produces a product variety which is close substitute of others. Therefore, if a firm lowers the price of its product variety, some customers of other product varieties will switch over to it. This means as it lowers the price of its product variety, quantity demanded of it will increase. On the other hand, if it raises the price of its product, some of its customers will leave it and buy the similar products from its competing firms. This implies that demand curve facing a firm working under monopolistic competition slopes downward and marginal revenue curve lies below it. This means that under monopolistic competition an individual firm is not a price taker but will have some influence over the price of its product. If it fixes a higher price, it will be able to sell a relatively smaller quantity of output. And if it fixes a lower price, it will be able to sell more. ***Thus under monopolistic competition, a firm has to choose a price-output combination which will maximise its profits.***

4. Non-price competition: Expenditure on advertisement and other selling costs. An important feature of monopolistic competition is that firms incur a considerable expenditure on advertisements and other selling costs to promote the sales of their products. Promoting sales of their products through advertisement is an important example of non-price competition. The expenditure incurred on advertisement is prominent among the various types of selling costs. The advertisement and other selling outlays by a firm change the demand for its product as well as its costs. Like the adjustments of price and product, a seller under monopolistic competition will also adjust the amount of his advertisement expenditure so as to maximise his profits. This problem of adjusting one's selling outlay is unique to monopolistic competition, because the firm under perfect competition has not to incur any expenditure on advertisement. The advertisement expenditure by a purely competitive firm will be without purpose since it can sell as much amount as it pleases at the going market price without any advertisement expenditure. The rival firms under monopolistic competition keenly compete with each other through advertisement by which they change the consumers' wants for their products and attract more customers. Thus, a full explanation of the equilibrium under monopolistic competition must also involve equilibrium in regard to the amount of expenditure on advertisement and other sales promotion activities.

5. Product variation. Another form of non-price competition which a firm under monopolistic competition has to face is the variation in products by various firms. A firm, under perfect competition, does not confront this problem, for the product is homogeneous under perfect competition. The problem of product variation under monopolistic competition exists because there is differentiation of products of various firms. The firm will try to adjust its product so as to conform more to the wishes of the buyers. The variation of the product may refer to a change in the quality of the product itself, technical changes, a new design, better materials, and it may mean only a new package or container. It may also mean more prompt or courteous service, and a different way of doing business. The amount of the product which a firm will be able to sell in the market depends in part upon the manner in which its product differs from others. Where the possibility of product differentiation exists, sales depend upon the skill with which a product is distinguished from others and made to appeal to a particular group of buyers. The profit maximisation principle applies to the choice of the nature of the product as to its price. In other words, a firm will choose that nature of the product, given its price, which gives it maximum profits. Therefore, in a full explanation of the firm's equilibrium under monopolistic competition we have also to explain product equilibrium in addition to price equilibrium and selling-costs equilibrium.

6. Freedom of entry and exit. This is another important feature of monopolistic competition. In a monopolistically competitive industry it is easy for the new firms to enter and the existing firms to leave it. Free entry means that when in the industry existing firms are making super-normal profits, the new firms enter the industry which leads to the expansion of output. As a result, price of product tends to fall in the long run. However, it may be noted that under monopolistic competition entry may not be as easy or free as under perfect competition. Whereas under perfect competition the new firms which enter the industry can produce identical products, but under monopolistic competition, the new firms can produce only new brands or product varieties which may initially find it difficult to compete with the already well-established brands and product varieties.

The Nature of Demand and Marginal Revenue Curves under Monopolistic Competition

It is important to understand the nature of the demand curve facing an individual firm under monopolistic competition. As has been explained in previous chapters, demand curve facing a firm working under perfect competition is perfectly elastic at the ruling market price since it has absolutely no control over the price of the product. On the contrary, a firm working under monopolistic competition enjoys some control over the price of its product since its product is somewhat differentiated from others. If a firm under monopolistic competition raises the price of its product, it will find some of its customers going away to buy other products. As a result, the quantity demanded of its product will fall. On the contrary, if it lowers the price, it will find that buyers of other varieties of the product will start purchasing its product and as a result the quantity demanded of its product will increase. It therefore follows that the demand curve facing an individual firm under monopolistic competition slopes downward.

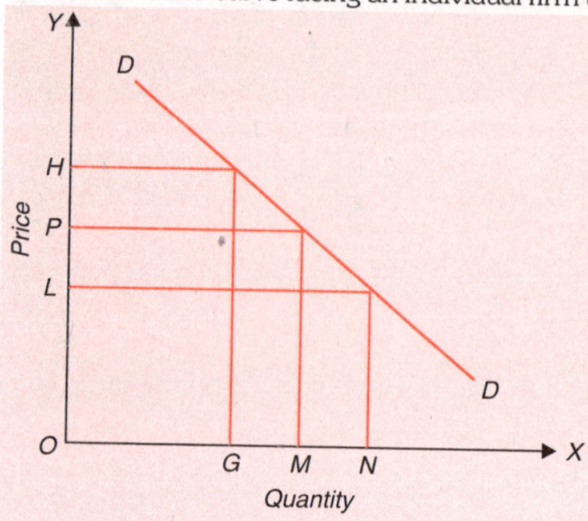

Fig. 36.1. *Demand Curve Facing a Monopolistically Competitive Firm*

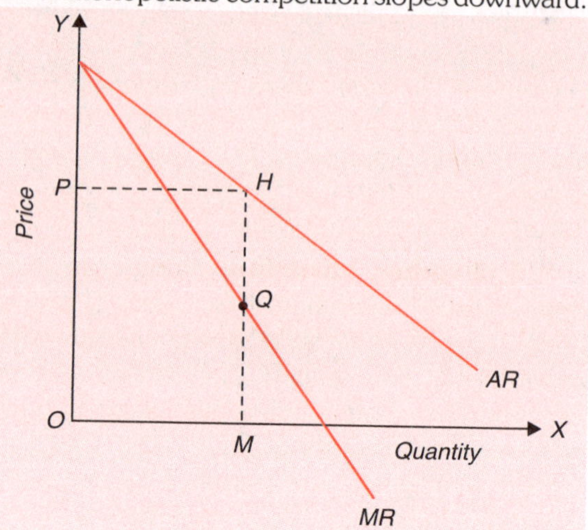

Fig. 36.2. *Average and Marginal Revenue Curves under Monopolistic Competition*

If a firm working under monopolistic competition wants to increase the sales of its product, it must lower the price. It can raise the price if it is prepared to sacrifice some sales. To put it in another way, a firm working under monopolistic competition can lower the price by increasing its level of sales and output. A perfectly competitive firm merely adjusts the quantity of output it has to produce, price being a given and constant datum for it. But a firm working under monopolistic competition faces a more complicated problem. It cannot merely adjust quantity at a given price because each quantity change by it will bring about a change in the price at which the product can be sold. Consider Fig. 36.1. *DD* is the demand curve facing an individual firm under monopolistic competition. At price *OP* the quantity demanded is *OM*. Therefore, the firm would be able to sell *OM* quantity at price *OP*. If it wants to sell greater quantity *ON*, then it will have to reduce price to *OL*. If it restricts its quantity to *OG*, price will rise to *OH*. Thus, every quantity change by it entails a change in price at which the product can be sold. Thus ***the problem faced by a firm working under monopolistic competition is to choose the price-quantity combination which is optimum for it, that is, which yields it maximum possible profits.***

Demand curve facing a firm will be his average revenue curve. Thus the average revenue curve of the monopolistically competitive firm slopes downward throughout its length. Since average revenue curve slopes downward, marginal revenue curve lies below it. This follows from usual average-marginal relationship. The implication of marginal revenue curve lying below average revenue curve is that the marginal revenue will be less than the price or average revenue. When a firm working under monopolistic competition sells more, the price of its product falls; marginal revenue therefore must be less than price. In Fig. 36.2 *AR* is the average revenue curve of the firm under monopolistic competition and slopes downward. *MR* is the marginal revenue curve and lies below *AR* curve. At quantity *OM*, average revenue (or price) is *OP* and marginal revenue is *MQ* which is less than *OP*. In an earlier chapter we have explained that average and marginal revenues at a level of output are related to each other through price elasticity of demand and in this connection we derived the following formula:

$$MR = AR\left(1-\frac{1}{e}\right)$$, where *e* stands for *absolute value* of price elasticity of demand.

PRICE-OUTPUT EQUILIBRIUM UNDER MONOPOLISTIC COMPETITION

A firm under monopolistic competition has to face various problems which are absent under perfect competition. Since the market of an individual firm under perfect competition is completely merged with the general one, it can sell any amount of the good at the ruling market price. But, under monopolistic competition, individual firm's market is isolated to a certain degree from those of its rivals with the result that its sales are limited and depend upon (1) its price, (2) the nature of its product, and (3) the advertising outlay it makes. Thus, the firm under monopolistic competition has to confront a more complicated problem than the perfectly competitive firm. Equilibrium of an individual firm under monopolistic competition involves equilibrium in three respects, that is, in regard to the price, the nature of the product, and the amount of advertising outlay it should make.

Equilibrium of the firm in respect of three variables simultaneously—price, nature of product, selling outlay—is difficult to discuss. Therefore, the method of explaining equilibrium in respect of each of them separately is adopted, keeping the other two variables given and constant. Moreover, as noted above, the equilibrium under monopolistic competition involves "individual equilibrium" of the firms as well as "group equilibrium." We shall discuss these two types of equilibrium first in respect of price and output and then in respects of product and advertising expenditure adjustments.

Individual Firm's Equilibrium under Monopolistic Competition

The demand curve for the product of an individual firm, as noted above, is downward sloping. Since the various firms under monopolistic competition produce products which are close substitutes of each other, the position and elasticity of the demand curve for the product of any of them depend upon the availability of the competiting substitutes and their prices. Therefore, the equilibrium adjustment of an individual firm cannot be defined in isolation from the general field of which it is a part. However, for the sake of simplicity in analysis, conditions regarding the availability of substitute products produced by the rival firms and prices charged for them are held constant while the equilibrium adjustment of an individual firm is considered in isolation. Since close substitutes for its product are available in the market, the demand curve for the product of an individual firm working under conditions of monopolistic competition is fairly elastic. Thus, although a firm under monopolistic competition has a monopolistic control over its variety of the product but its control is tempered by the fact that there are close substitutes available in the market and that if it sets too high a price for its product, many of its customers will shift to the rival products.

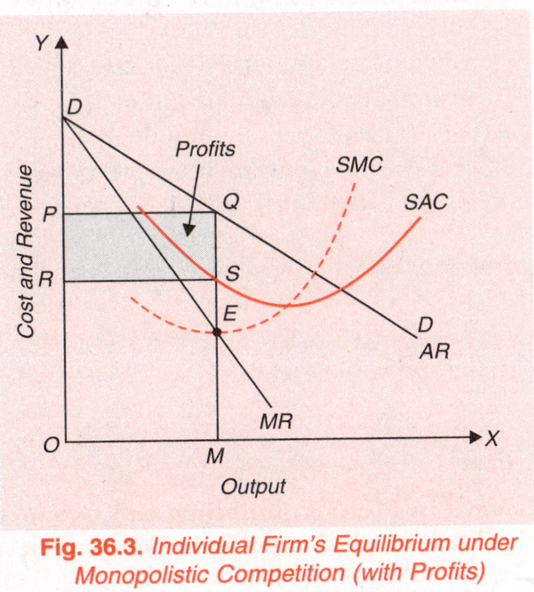

Fig. 36.3. *Individual Firm's Equilibrium under Monopolistic Competition (with Profits)*

Assuming the conditions with respect to all substitutes such as their nature and prices being constant, the demand curve for the product of a firm will be given. We further suppose that the product of the firm is held constant, only variables are price and output in respect of which equilibrium adjustment is to be made. The individual equilibrium under monopolistic competition is graphically shown in Fig. 36.3. *DD* is the demand curve for the product of an individual firm, the nature and prices of all substitutes being given. This demand curve *DD* is also the average revenue (*AR*) curve of the firm. *SAC* represents the short-run average cost curve of the firm, while *SMC* is the short-run marginal cost curve corresponding to it. It may be recalled that average cost curve first falls due to internal economies and then rises due to internal diseconomies.

Given these demand and cost conditions a firm will adjust its price and output at the level which gives it maximum total profits. Theory of value under monopolistic competition is also based upon the profit maximisation principle, as is the theory of value under perfect competition. Thus a firm in order to maximise profits will equate marginal cost with marginal revenue. In Fig. 36.3, the firm will fix its level of output at *OM*, for at *OM* output marginal cost is equal to marginal revenue. The demand curve *DD* facing the firm in question indicates that output *OM* can be sold at price *MQ* = *OP*. Therefore, the determined price will evidently be *MQ* or *OP*. In this equilibrium position, by fixing its price at *OP* and output at *OM*, the firm is making economic profits equal to the area *RSQP* which is maximum. It may be recalled that profits *RSQP* are in excess of normal profits because the normal profits which represent the minimum profits necessary to secure the entrepreneur's services are included in average cost curve *AC*. Thus, the area *RSQP* indicates the amount of supernormal or economic profits made by the firm.

In the short-run, the firm, in equilibrium, may make economic profits, as shown in Fig. 36.3 above, but it may make losses too if the demand conditions for its product are not so favourable relative to cost conditions. Fig. 36.4 depicts the case of a firm whose demand or average revenue curve *AR* for the product lies below the short average cost curve *SAC* throughout indicating thereby that no output of the product can be produced at positive profits. However, the firm is in equilibrium at output *ON* and setting price *NK* or *OT*, for by fixing price at *OT* and output at *ON*, it is rendering the losses to the minimum. In such an unfavourable situation there is no alternative for the firm except to make the best of the bad bargain.

We thus see that a firm in equilibrium under monopolistic competition, as under perfect competition, may be making economic profits or incurring losses depending upon the position of the short-run demand curve relative to the position of the average cost curve. Further, a firm may be making only normal profits even in the short run if the demand curve happens to be tangent to the short-run average cost curve.

It should be carefully noted that in individual equilibrium of the firm both in Fig. 36.3 and Fig. 36.4, the firm having once fixed price at *OP* and *OT* respectively will have no tendency to vary the price any more. If it varies its price upward, the loss due to fall in quantity demanded will be more than the gain made by the higher price. If it cuts down its price, the gain due to the increase in quantity demanded will be less than the loss due to the lower price. Hence, price will remain stable at *OP* and *OT* in the two cases respectively.

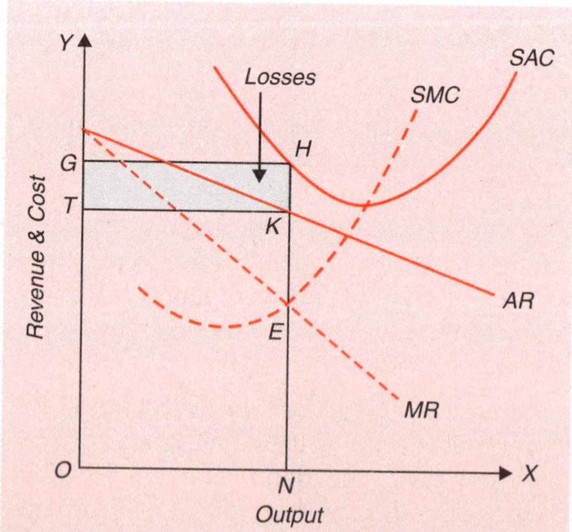

Fig. 36.4. *Individual Firm's Equilibrium under Monopolistic Competition (with Losses)*

Long-Run Firm's Equilibrium and Group Equilibrium under Monopolistic Competition

We may now turn to see how the 'group' comes to be in equilibrium. In other words, we have now to explain how the equilibrium adjustment of prices and outputs of a number of firms whose products are close substitues comes about. As explained above, each firm within a group has monopoly of its own particular product, yet its market is interwoven with those of his competitors who produce closely related products. The price and output decisions of a firm will affect his rival firms who may in turn revise their price and output policies. This dependence of the various producers upon one another is a prominent feature of monopolistic competition. The question now is: what characterises the system of relationship into which the group tends to fall as a result of producers's influence on each other ?

A difficulty faced in describing the group equilibrium is the vast diversity of conditions which exist in respect of many matters between the various firms constituting the group. The product of each firm has special characteristics and adapted to the tastes and preferences of its customers. The qualitative differences among the products lead to the large variations in cost and demand curves of the various firms. The demand curves of the products of various firms differ in respect of elasticity as well as position. Similarly, cost curves of the various firms differ in respect of shape and position. As a result of these heterogeneous conditions surrounding each firm, there will be differences in prices, outputs (scales of production) and profits of the various firms in the group. Putting this matter in another way, E.H. Chamberlin says: ***"The differentiation of the product is not, so to speak, 'uniformly spaced'; it is not distributed homogeneously among all the products which are grouped together. Each has its own individuality, and the size of its market depends on the strength of the preference for it over other varieties."***[5]

In order to simplify the analysis of equilibrium, Chamberlin ignores these diverse conditions surrounding each firm and takes an assumption what has been called "*uniformity assumption*". Thus Chamberlin says: ***"We, therefore, proceed under the heroic assumption that both demand and cost curves for all the 'products' are uniform throughout the group."***[6] Chamberlin points out that by taking this assumption we do not reduce the differentiation of products. Under the uniformity assumption, "It is required only that *consumer's preferences be evenly distributed among the different varieties*, and that differences between them be not such as to give rise to differences in cost."[7]

Further, to facilitate exposition of his theory, Chamberlin introduces a further assumption which has been called ***'symmetry assumption'*** by Prof. Stigler. It is that the number of firms being large under monopolistic competition, an individual's actions regarding price and output adjustment will have a negligible effect upon its numerous competitors so that they will not think of retaliation for readjusting their prices and outputs. He thus says, specifically, we assume for the present that any adjustment of price of a "product" by a single producer spreads its influence over so many of his competitors that the impact felt by any one is negligible and does not lead him to any readjustment of his own situation. A price cut, for instance, which increases the sales of him who made it draws inappreciable amounts from the markets of each of his many competitors, achieving a considerable result for the one who cut, but without making incursions upon the market of any single competitor sufficient to cause him to do anything he would not have done any way."[8]

5. *Op. cit.* p.82
6. *Ibid.*, p. 82
7. *Ibid*, p. 83 (*italics added*)
8. *Ibid., p.* 83

Given the above assumptions, we proceed to explain how under monopolistic competition an individual firm and a group of firms producing close substitutes come to be in equilibrium position. To begin with, suppose that the demand and cost curves of each of the firms in the group are *DD* and *AC* as depicted in Fig. 36.3. Each firm will set price *OP* at which short-run marginal cost is equal to marginal revenue and hence profits are maximum. Although all firms are making economic profits, there is no reason for any one to cut down price below *OP* because the sales gained thereby will be insufficient to make up the loss due to the lower price. These economic profits will, however, attract new firms into the field in the long run.

Here it may be pointed out that full freedom of entry cannot prevail under monopolistic competition. Entry can be fully free only if the new firms who propose to enter the field can produce exactly identical products as those of the existing firms. But under monopolistic competition, this is not possible. Therefore, entry in the full and strict sense cannot exist under monopolistic competition. However, new entrants are free to produce closely related products which are very similar to the products of the existing firms. Thus, ***under monopolistic competition there can be freedom of entry only in the sense of a freedom to produce close substitutes.***

Turning to the above argument, when the new firms lured by the economic profits enjoyed by the existing firms enter the field, the market would be shared between more firms and as a result the demand curve (or average revenue curve) for the product of each firm will shift downward *i.e.*, to the left. This process of entry of new firms and the resultant shift in the demand (average revenue) curve to the left will continue until the average revenue curve becomes tangent to the long-run average cost curve and the economic profits are completely wiped out. This is shown in Fig. 36.5 where average revenue curve is tangent the to the long-run average cost curve *LAC* at point *T*. Long-run marginal cost and marginal revenue curves intersect each other at point *E*, exactly vertically below *T*. ***Therefore, the firm is in long-run equilibrium by setting price QT or OP and producing OQ quantity of its product.*** Because average revenue is equal to average cost, the firm will be making only normal profits. Since all firms are alike in respect of demand and cost curves (by assumption), the average revenue of all will be tangent to their average cost curves and all firms will, therefore, be earning only normal profits. Because only normal profits are accruing to the firms there will be no more tendency for the new competitors to enter the field and the group as a whole will, therefore, be in equilibrium.

An important point is worth noting here. It is that ***a firm in long-run equilibrium under monopolistic competition makes only normal profits, as in perfect competition, but its price is higher and output smaller than under perfect competition.*** Under perfect competition, long-run equilibrium of the firm is established at the minimum point of the long-run average cost curve. In other words, a firm under perfect competition tends to be of the optimum size. But a firm in the long run under monopolistic competition, as is evident from Fig. 36.5, stops short of the optimum point and operates at the point at which long-run average cost is still falling. In Fig. 36.5 the firm produces output *OQ*, while a firm under perfect competition would have produced output *OR* at which long-run average cost is minimum. The firm under monopolistic competition can reduce its cost of production by expanding output to the point *R* but it will not do so because by expanding output beyond *OQ* it will be reducing price more than the average cost. It is, therefore, clear that by producing *OQ* instead of *OR*, the firm under monopolistic competition does not use its capacity fully. (The firm would be using its capacity fully, if it produces optimum or full capacity output *OR*). Thus capacity equal to *QR* is lying unused in the firm's long-run equilibrium under monopolistic competition. This ***unused capacity is called excess capacity which is a prominent feature of long-run equilibrium under monopolistic competition.***

Further, it may be noted that in the long-run equilibrium, firms under monopolistic competition make only normal profits as under perfect competition, but the price set under monopolistic competition is higher than the competitive price. In Fig. 36.5, price set in long-run equilibrium under monopolistic competition is QT while competitive price would have been equal to RL. This higher price under monopolistic competition is due to monopoly element contained in it. The monopoly element involved in monopolistic competition makes the demand or average revenue curve facing an individual firm downward sloping and a downward-sloping average revenue curve can be tangent to the long-run average cost curve only to the left of its minimum point.

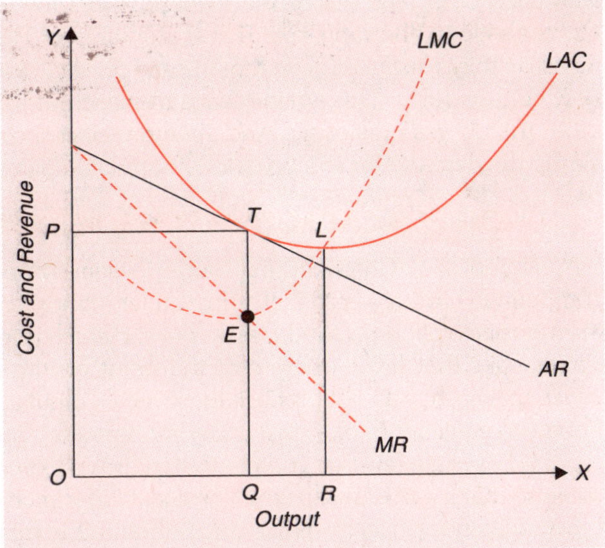

Fig. 36.5. *The Long-run Equilibrium : The group is in equilibrium when average revenue curves of the firms are tangent to their long-run average cost curves*

Thus price under monopolistic competition will be higher than the competitive price due to the monopoly element in monopolistic competition. But, in spite of the higher price, a firm under monopolistic competition will not be making profits above normal in the long run. We may, therefore, say that a ***firm under monopolistic competition, in the long-run equilibrium, charges higher price without enjoying monopoly profits.*** A significant result follows from this. It is that the non-existence of economic profits is no indicator of the absence of monopoly element. In long-run equilibrium under monopolistic competition, as seen above, the firm has monopoly power (it has a sole control over its own differentiated product with the result that demand curve for it slopes downward) but does not make any economic or supernormal profits. Further, the existence of economic profits does not necessarily mean the presence of monopoly power. Under perfect competition, a firm in the short run may enjoy economic or supernormal profits due to the increase in demand for the product. Thus it has been rightly said that ***"he skates on thin ice who identifies profits with monopoly and monopoly with profits."***

Another noteworthy point about long-run equilibrium under monopolistic competition is that with the increase in the number of firms in the long run ***demand curves facing individual firms will become more elastic in the sense that they will flatten out***. Although Chamberlin denies it, it is now commonly believed that as the number of firms gets larger in the long run, the cross elasticities of demand between the products of various firms will increase and as a result the demand curves of the firms will become more elastic (or graphically less steep). When, in the short run, economic profits are accruing to the firms due to the large demand for their brands or varieties of the product, lured by these economic profits the new firms will enter and try to produce brands or varieties as similar to the existing brands as possible. Thus, in the long run, products of various firms will become more similar or in other words, come closer together and as a result the demand curves facing individual firms will become more elastic. To put it in another way, the new firms which enter the group will come "in between" the old ones and thereby result in increasing the elasticities of demand curves (that is, make them flatten out).

Besides, the very fact that number of close substitutes in the long run increases due to the increase in the number of firms means that each brand will become more closely competitive with each other and hence the demand curve for the product of any one firm will become more elastic in the long run. Thus Stonier and Hague write: "If new producers enter the industry, this is likely to mean that instead of, say, twenty similar cars being produced there will now be, say, forty. This again means that each of the cars is likely to be more similar to each other than it was previously. And the more closely competitive substitutes there are, the more elastic the demand for the product of any one firm in the group will be."[9]

EXCESS CAPACITY UNDER MONOPOLISTIC COMPETITION

Theories of Chamberlin's monopolistic competition and Joan Robinson's imperfect competition have revealed that a firm under monopolistic competition or imperfect competition in long-run equilibrium produces an output which is less than socially optimum or ideal output. This means that firms operate at the point on the falling portion of long-run average cost curve, that is, they do not produce the level of output at which long-run average cost is minimum. Long-run equilibrium of a firm under monopolistic competition is achieved when the demand curve (or average revenue curve) facing a firm becomes tangential to the long-run average cost curve so that it earns only normal profits. Under such circumstances a firm can reduce average cost (and hence price) by expanding output to the minimum level of long-run average cost, but it will not do so because its profits are maximised (equality of marginal revenue with marginal cost is attained) at the level of output smaller than that at which its long-run average cost is minimum.

Society's productive resources are fully utilised when they are used to produce the level of output which renders long-run average cost minimum. Thus a monopolistically competitive firm produces less than the socially optimum or ideal output, that is, the output corresponding to the lowest point of long-run average cost curve. This is in sharp contrast to the position of the firm in long-run equilibrium under perfect competition, which operates at the minimum point of the long-run average cost curve. The amount by which the actual long-run output of the firm under monopolistic competition falls short of the socially ideal output is a measure of *excess capacity* which means unutilised capacity.

The existence of excess capacity under monopolistic competition can be understood from Figures 36.6 and 36.7. Figure 36.7 depicts the long-run position of a perfectly competitive firm which is in long-run equilibrium at the level of output *ON* corresponding to which long-run average cost is minimum. It is at output *ON* that the double condition of long-run equilibrium, namely Price = *MC* = *AC* is fulfilled. It is thus clear that firms under perfect competition produce socially ideal output. The production of output at the minimum point of long-run average cost is socially optimum as resources of the society are efficiently used and allocated. On the other hand, a firm under monopolistic competition depicted in Fig. 36.6 is in long-run equilibrium at output *OM* at which its marginal revenue is equal to long-run marginal cost and price is equal to average cost (Average revenue curve *AR* is tangential to average cost curve *LAC* at point *F* corresponding to output *OM*). It will be noticed that at output *OM* long-run average cost (*LAC*) is still falling and goes on falling up to output *ON*. This means that the firm can expand its production up to *ON* and reduce his long-run average cost to the minimum. Ideal output is the output at which long-run average cost is minimum. Therefore, the firm is ***producing MN less than the ideal output. Thus MN output represents the excess capacity which emerges under monopolistic competition.*** It is worth noting that the concept of

9. Stonier and Hague, *A Textbook of Economic Theory*, 4th edition, 1972, p.209

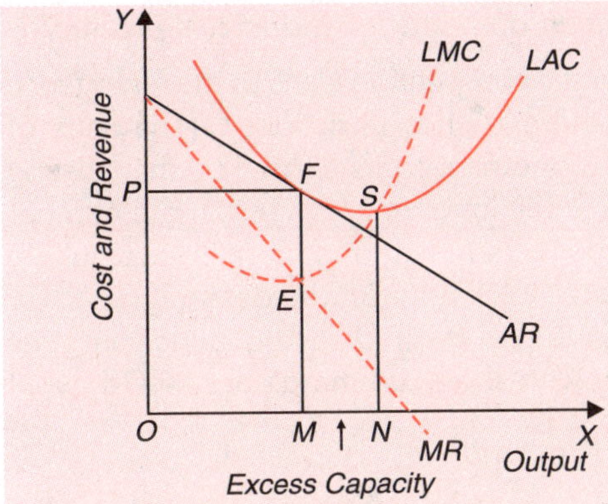

Fig. 36.6. *Excess Capacity under Monopolistic Competition*

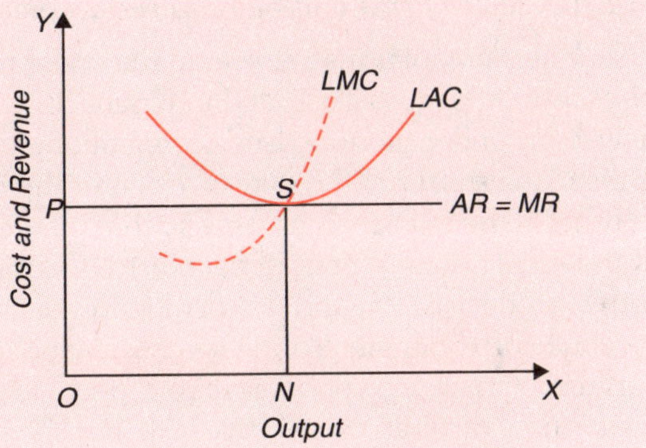

Fig. 36.7. *Ideal or Socially Optimum Output under Perfect Competition*

excess capacity refers only to the long run. This is because in the short run under any type of market structure (including perfect competition) there can be all sorts of departures from the ideal output reflecting incomplete adjustment to the existing market conditions.

Causes of Excess Capacity

What factors are responsible for the existence of excess capacity under monopolistic competition? It is due to the existence of excess capacity that average cost of production and price of product are higher and output smaller monopolistic competition than under perfect competition. There are three main causes of the emergence of excess capacity under monopolistic competition. First, the most important cause of the existence of excess capacity under monopolistic competition is ***downward-sloping demand curve (or average revenue curve) of the firm.*** A downward-sloping average revenue curve can be tangent to a U-shaped long-run average cost curve only at the latter's falling portion. It is only the horizontal demand curve or average revenue curve (as is actually found under perfect competition) which can be tangent to a U-shaped average cost curve at the latter's minimum point. From this, it also follows that the greater the elasticity of average revenue (or demand) curve confronting a monopolistically competitive firm, the less the excess capacity and *vice versa*. When the demand curve facing a firm is perfectly elastic, there is no excess capacity, as is the case under perfect competition.

Now, demand curve facing individual firms under monopolistic competition slopes downward due to *product differentiation* found in it. Various firms produce different varieties and brands of product and each has a certain degree of monopoly power over the variety or brand it produces for fixing price and output. If products were homogeneous, the demand curve would not have been downward sloping and long-run equilibrium would have been established at the minimum point of *LAC* without there being any excess capacity.

The second reason for the emergence of excess capacity under monopolistic competition, as has been emphasised by Chamberlin, ***is the entry of a very large a number of firms in the industry in the long run.*** Lured by excess profits in the short run new firms enter the industry in the long run. This results in sharing of market demand among many firms so that each firm produces a smaller output than its full or optimum capacity. There are too many grocery shops, too many cloth manufacturing firms, too many automobile parts producing firms, too many barber shops each operating with excess capacity. *In fact, under monopolistic competition, given the same demand and cost conditions, number of firms will be larger than even under perfect competition. This is because by expanding output to the minimum point* *of LAC, fewer firms will be required to meet the given demand for industry's product.*

How entry of firms in the long run under monopolistic competition leads to the emergence of excess capacity is illustrated in Figure 36.8. Since there are no restrictions on the entry of new firms under monopolistic competition, lured by economic profits earned by the existing firms in the short run the new firms enter the industry in the long run. As a result, the number of firms in the industry increases so that market demand is shared among more firms resulting in the reduction in output of each firm. Consider Figure 36.8. Initially, the demand curve for firm's product is D_2 and the firm is in equilibrium at output level Q_2 by equating marginal revenue corresponding to the given demand curve D_2 with short-run marginal cost (To avoid confusion, marginal revenue curve and short-run marginal cost curve are not drawn). The firm will be making economic profits in the short run. Output Q_2 represents the ideal output as at it the long-run average cost (*LAC*) is minimum and society's resources are used efficiently. Lured by economic profits earned by the existing firms, new firms enter the industry and as a result the demand curve facing each firm shifts to the left. The demand curve will go on shifting to the left until it becomes tangent to the long-run average curve *LAC* at point *T*. But with the shift in the demand curve to D_1, the profit-maximising quantity has fallen to Q_1. Thus with the entry of new firms the excess capacity equal to Q_1Q_2 has emerged in the firm. Besides, as a consequence, *the consumer pays a price higher than the minimum long-run average cost Q_2B.*

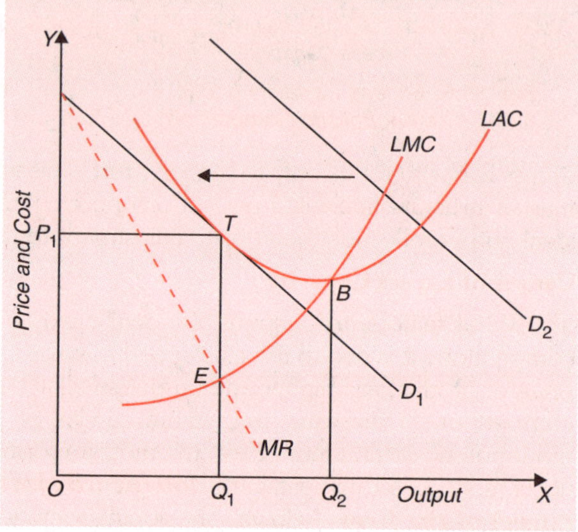

Fig. 36.8. *Emergence of Excess Capacity due to the Entry of Firms in the Long Run*

The conception and the measure of excess capacity as enunciated above is based upon a particular notion of ideal output. Marshall, Kahn[10], Harrod[11], Cassels[12] and Joan Robinson have regarded *ideal output or optimum size of the firm as that output at which its long-run average cost is minimum*. To quote Joan Robinson, "In a perfectly competitive industry each firm in full equilibrium will produce that output at which its average costs are minimum. Each firm will then be of the optimum size. If competition is imperfect, the demand curve for the output of the individual firm will be falling and the double condition of equilibrium can only be fulfilled for some output at which average cost is falling. The firms will, therefore, be of less than optimum size when profits are normal... It is only if conditions of perfect competition prevail that firms will be of the optimum size and there is no reason to expect that they will be of optimum size in the real world since in the real world competition is not perfect."[13]

How Excess Capacity is Beneficial ? However, many modern economists are of the view that excess capacity under monopolistic competition is *desirable in some respects.*

10. R.F. Kahn, "Some Notes on Ideal Output" , *Economic Journal,* XIV (1935), pp. 1-35.
11. R.F. Harrod, Doctrines of Imperfect Competition, *Quarterly Journal of Economics,* XLIX (1934-35), pp. 442-70.
12. J.M. Cassels, Excess Capacity and Monopolistic Competition, *Quartely Journal of Economics,* LI (1936-37), pp. 426-43.
13. Joan Robinson, *Economics of Imperfect Competition,* pp. 96-97.

According to them, excess capacity under monopolistic competition provides some benefits which increase consumer welfare. As mentioned above, the excess capacity comes into existence mainly due to product differentiation under monopolistic competition. Now, this *product differentiation leads to product variety* which is highly beneficial to the consumers. The ability to choose among a wide variety of clothes, furniture, restaurant meals and various types of product designs add greatly to the satisfaction or welfare of the consumers. Therefore, according to this view, social benefits of excess capacity should be weighed against the cost to the society of excess capacity.

PRICE-OUTPUT EQUILIBRIUM UNDER MONOPOLISTIC COMPETITION COMPARED WITH THAT UNDER PERFECT COMPETITION

It is useful to explain how price-output equilibrium under monopolistic competition differs from that under perfect competition.

1. Price is greater than MC under monopolistic competition. A significant difference between the two relates to the relation between price and marginal cost. Whereas in equilibrium under perfect competition, price is equal to marginal cost, in equilibrium under monopolistic competition price is greater than marginal cost. Since under perfect competition, an individual firm cannot influence the price of its product and takes price as given and constant, the demand or average revenue curve facing it is a horizontal straight line and marginal revenue (*MR*) is equal to average revenue (*AR*) or price. Therefore, under perfect competition when a firm equates marginal cost with marginal revenue so as to maximise its profits, the former also becomes equal to price.

On the other hand, under monopolistic competition, a firm exercises some control over the price of its product and the demand curve for it, representing prices at various quantities, slopes downward. As a result, marginal revenue (*MR*) curve lies below average revenue (*AR*) curve. Therefore, in order to maximise profits when a firm under monopolistic competition equates marginal cost with marginal revenue, price stands at a higher level than marginal cost. This is clear from Fig.36.9 where, in equilibrium, price determined is equal to *OP* or Q_1T, which is greater than marginal cost (Q_1E).

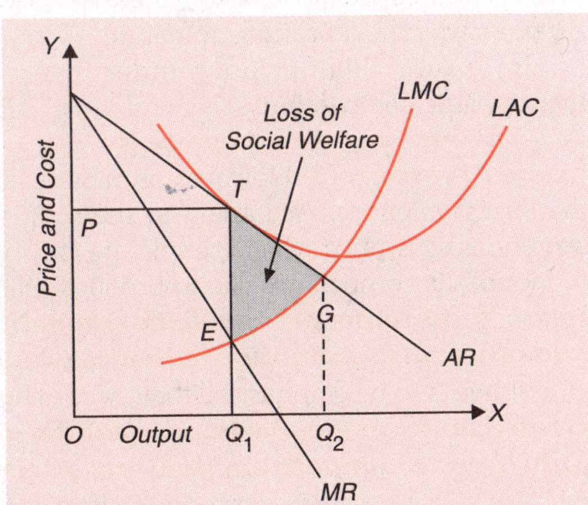

Fig. 36.9. *Inefficiency of Monopolistic Competition and Loss of Social Welfare*

It should be noted that ***producing level of output much less than at which marginal cost equals price implies a loss of social welfare.*** It should be noted that social welfare is maximum when output is extended to the point where price is equal to long-run marginal cost. It will be seen from Fig. 36.9 that such point is *G* where price or *AR* = *LMC*. But as will be seen from Fig. 36.9 the firm working under conditions of monopolistic competition produces OQ_1 in the long-run equilibrium. Thus, the area *TEG represents loss of social* welfare which is also called *dead weight loss*. This indicates inefficiency of monopolistic competition.

2. Long-run equilibrium under monopolistic competition is established at less than the technically efficient scale size

Another important difference between the equilibrium under monopolistic competition and perfect competition is that whereas a firm in long-run equilibrium under monopolistic competition produces less than its technically efficient scale (that is, the level of output at which long-run average cost is minimum), under perfect competition long-run equilibrium of the firm is established at the minimum point of the long-run average cost curve. In other words, a firm under perfect competition tends to be of economically most efficient size. But a firm under monopolistic competition, as is evident from Fig. 36.10 stops short of the technically efficient scale and operates in the long run at the point at which long-run average cost is still falling. In Fig. 36.10 the firm produces output *OQ*, while a firm under pure or perfect competition would have produced output *OR* at which long-run average cost is minimum. The firm under monopolistic competition can reduce its cost of production by expanding output to the point *R* but it will not do so because by expanding output beyond *OQ* it will be reducing price more than the average cost. It is, therefore, clear that by producing *OQ* instead of *OR* in the long run, the firm under monopolistic competition does not use its capacity fully. (The firm would be using its capacity fully if it produces output *OR* at which long-run average cost is minimum). Thus, capacity equal to *QR* lies unused in the firm under monopolistic competition. This unused capacity is called *excess capacity* which is a prominent feature of long-run equilibrium under monopolistic competition.

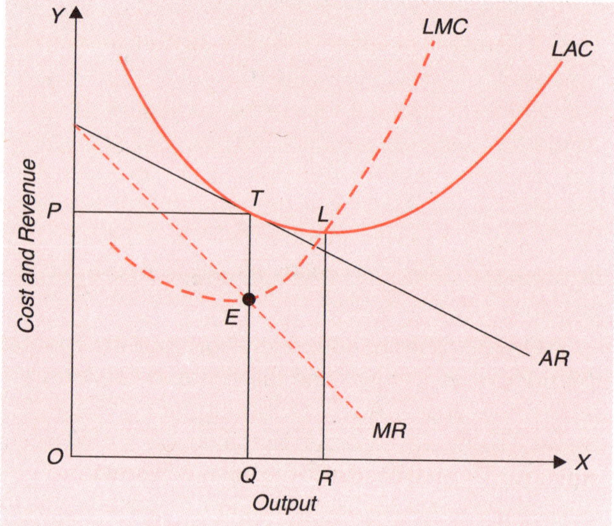

Fig. 36.10. *Production at less than Technically Efficient Scale*

This excess capacity represents waste of resources. However, as mentioned above, some economists do not consider *QR* as the excess capacity. According to them, this small loss of output and consequently higher average cost is price which people are paying for the product variety which they get under monopolistic competition due to product differentiation as compared to perfect competition. Further, ***firms under monopolistic competition spend a lot of money on advertisement and other sales promotion activities which also represents*** wastes of competition.

It needs to be emphasised that, according to Chamberlin, ***a lot of excess capacity is created under monopolistic competition as a result of entry of a large number of firms only if price competition does not prevail.*** If price competition prevails then there is not much excess capacity under monopolistic competition. However, in the long run many firms enter the industry so that market is shared among many and *in the absence of price competition* each produces much less than its full capacity.

3. Price under monopolistic competition is greater than competitive price.

Further, it may be noted that in the long-run equilibrium, firms under monopolistic competition make only normal profits as under perfect competition, but the price set under monopolistic competition is higher than competitive price, given the long-run average cost curve. In Fig. 36.10, price set in long-run equilibrium under monopolistic competition is *QT* while competitive price in the long run would have been equal to *RL*. This higher price under monopolistic competition is due to monopoly element contained in it. The monopoly element involved in monopolistic competition makes the demand or average revenue curve facing an individual firm downward sloping and a downward-sloping average revenue curve can be tangent to the long-run average cost curve only to the left of its minimum point.

Thus price under monopolistic competition will be higher than the perfectly competitive price due to the monopoly element in monopolistic competition. But, in spite of the higher price, a firm under monopolistic competition will not be making profits above normal in the long run. We may, therefore, say that a firm under monopolistic competition, in the long-run equilibrium, charges higher price without enjoying monopoly profits. A significant result follows from this. It is that the ***non-existence of super-normal profits is no indicator of the absence of monopoly element.*** In long-run equilibrium under monopolistic competition, as seen above, the firm has some monopoly power (it has a sole control over its own differentiated product) with the result that demand curve for it slopes downward) but it does not make any super-normal profits in the long run.

MONOPOLISTIC COMPETITION AND ECONOMIC EFFICIENCY

Perfect competition is said to be the ideal market form as it ensures maximum possible social welfare. In partial equilibrium analysis welfare is measuerd by the consumer surplus gained by the consumers and producer surplus earned by the producers. Under perfect competition, given the demand and cost conditions, the maximum possible sum of consumer surplus and producer surplus is achieved so that social welfare is maximised. Besides, under perfect competition in the long run firms operate at the minimum point of the long-run average cost curve which ensures maximum efficiency in the use of resources. According to this, not only *optimum scale of plant* (*i.e*, plant with minimum *LAC*) is set up but also that plant is operated at its *optimum* or *full capacity*, that is, at the minimum point of short-run average cost curve of the plant.

On the other hand, firms operating in monopolistic competitive environment earn zero economic profits in their long-run equilibrium but they operate with *two types of inefficiencies*. First, as discussed above in detail, firms operate in the long run with *excess capacity* which implies inefficiency or waste in the use of resources and this impedes the achievement of maximum social welfare. In long-run equilibrium under monopolistic competition, firms operate at less than the scale of output at which long-run average cost is minimum. In this long-run equilibrium situation, neither the optimum scale of plant is set up, nor the plant actually set up is operated at its optimum capacity (*i.e.*, at minimum point of short-run average cost). This implies higher cost and price as well as lower output than if production had been done at minimum point of *LAC*. Thus, the existence of excess capacity under monopolistic competition causes inefficiency in the use of resources and loss of consumer welfare.

The second type of inefficiency that prevails under monopolistic competition is called ***allocative inefficiency*** which refers to the misallocation of resources among products which also causes loss of welfare. ***Allocative efficiency is achieved if price of a product is fixed equal to the marginal cost of production.*** However, under monopolistic competition firms are in long-run equilibrium at the level of output at which price exceeds marginal cost of production. Consider Fig. 36.9, the firm is in long-run equilibrium at output OQ_1 at which *MR* equals *MC* but price fixed is Q_1T or *OP* which exceeds marginal cost Q_1E at the equilibrium output. The ideal output from the viewpoint of allocative efficiency is OQ_2 at which price equals *MC*. It will be observed from the *AR* curve in Fig. 36.9 that the price which consumers are willing to pay for additional units from Q_1 to Q_2 exceeds the marginal cost of production to be incurred by the society. If output were extended to Q_2 at which demand (*AR*) curve cuts the long-run marginal cost curve *LMC*, the total surplus (sum of consumer surplus and producer surplus) could be increased by an amount equal to the shaded area *ETG*. This shaded area *ETG* represents **dead weight loss of welfare.** This dead-weight loss accrues due to the monopoly element involved in monopolistic competition.

It may be recalled that monopoly element is present in monopolistic competition because products of different firms are differentiated and each of them has some control over the price of its product. Expansion of output to Q_2 requires allocation of more resources to the production of the product. By restricting output to Q_1 and thereby raising price of the product, firms operating under monopolistic competition do not allocate resources efficiently which cause dead-weight loss in social welfare. This is called dead-weight loss because there is no any compensating gain by any one else. Because of these inefficiences, monopolisitc competition was considered as socially undesirable form of market structure. However, many modern economists do not think so. This is for two reasons. First, the excess capacity that exists under monopolistic competition is very small because in the long run under monopolistic competition demand curve facing each firm becomes highly elastic as a result of the entry of new firms in the industry making available more close substitutes in the market.

Second, due to the demand (*AR*) curve becoming highly elastic in the long run monopolistic competition ensures that the difference between the price and marginal cost will also be very small which means whatever dead-weight loss in welfare occurs is not very significant. Above all there is gain or benefits to consumers because of ***product variety*** found in this market structure. Most consumers derive great satisfaction from the ability to choose among a wide variety of products and brands that exist under monopolistic competition. The gain in consumer welfare or benefits due to product diversity may be weighed against the cost of little inefficiency that prevails under monopolistic competition.

QUESTIONS AND PROBLEMS FOR REVIEW

1. What is monopolistic competition? Explain the important features of monopolistic competition.
2. What is product differentiation? What role does it play in the determination of price and output under monopolistic competition?
3. Analyse the short-run and long-run equilibrium of a firm working under monopolistic competition.
4. What is group equilibrium? Explain how group equilibrium is achieved under monopolistic competition.
5. (*a*) What is meant by excess capacity? Show that how a firm working under monopolistic competition works with excess capacity in the long run.

   (*b*) What causes excess capacity under monopolistic competition? Why is it undesirable?
6. Are there any benefits of excess capacity associated with monopolistc competition ?
7. What are wastes of competition? How are they found under monopolistic competition?
8. Compare price-output equilibrium under monopolistic competition with that under (*a*) perfect competition, (*b*) monopoly.
9. Explain Chamberlin's concept of excess capacity. What, according to him, is responsible for the emergence of excess capacity under monopolistic competition?
10. Explain the concept of economic efficiency. Evaluate economic inefficiency of firms operating under monopolistic competition.
11. "Monopolistically competitive industries are characterised by too many firms each of which produces too little."

CHAPTER 37

A Critique of Chamberlin's Theory of Monopolistic Competition

Superiority of Chamberlin's Approach

We have explained in the previous chapter Chamberlin's theory of monopolistic competition. Chamberlin's work has been both praised and criticized. Some have gone to the extent of saying that Chamberlin brought about a revolution in price theory, while some have bitterly criticized him. Stigler, Kaldor, Triffin and Harrod are among his critics. Various critics have criticised the different aspects of his theory. But even the critics have recognised the significance of Chamberlin's analysis and have hailed it as making a genuine break with the traditional price theory which viewed the different real-world markets as two mutually exclusive categories of perfect competition and monopoly. Chamberlin's approach of viewing many existing markets as blend of competitive and monopoly elements, his introduction of product differentiation, product variation and selling costs into the analytical framework of his monopolistic competition theory made a significant advance over the theories of perfect competition and monopoly existed before.

Thus, even G. Stigler, the most severe critic of Chamberlin's methodology, has paid rich tributes to him in the following words :

"Professor Chamberlin's work was a true revolutionary. Instead of assimilating observed market structures into exclusive classes such as competition and monopoly, he told us, we must throw off our theoretical heritage and look at the world with clear and candid eyes. Then we shall find that no simple dichotomy does justice to the rich variety of industrial organisation. True, there are (a very few) industries that closely resemble those studied by the economist of perfect competition. True, there are (perhaps more) firms that partake of the nature of monopoly as the concept was used in neoclassical economics. But vastly more often the firm displays a mixture of insulation from other rivals, by means of real or fancied product differences and of indirect rivalry by way of the (1) willingness of some consumers to shift among products and (2) the ability of firms to change their products. But these phenomena could not be explained with the help of neo-classical theory."[1] It is thus clear that Chamberlin introduced more realism into the price theory and by doing so he saved it from becoming mere institutional economics. To quote Stigler again, "The picture of economic life (picture of diversity and unsystematism) was not fundamentally new, but Professor Chamberlin's reaction was... (Chamberlin's vision was clearly a legitimate way of looking at economic life. One may even argue that it was more congruent with untutored observation, and in this sense more realistic."[2]

In spite of such praise showered on Chamberlin's theory of monopolistic competition, he has also come in for bitter criticism.

1. G. J. Stigler, *Five Lectures on Economic Problems* (London : Longman, Green and Co., 1949), p. !3.
2. *Ibid.*, p. 2.

1. Uniformity Assumption Challenged

In the first place Stigler and Kaldor have challenged the uniformity assumption made by Chamberlin in his theory. According to this assumption, demand and cost curves for all the products of the firms under monopolistic competition are taken to be identical or uniform. Thus, Chamberlin says, "We therefore proceed under the *heroic assumption* that both demand and cost curves for all 'products' are uniform throughout the group."[3] This uniformity assumption has been taken by Chamberlin in order to simplify his analysis of group equilibrium. According to Stigler, how can different products have uniform costs and demands. He is of the view that by making uniformity assumption Chamberlin "has implicity defined the group as a collection of physically homogeneous prqducts. The identity of costs and demand is otherwise meaningless."[4] It is because of the uniformity of costs and demands that Chamberlin has also assumed that prices of the products of various producers are identical. Stigler points out that "We simply cannot attach meaning to the statement that physically diverse things have the same price."[5]

Besides the assumption of identity of costs, demands and prices for all products, Chamberlin also assumes that buyers have perfect knowledge. Stigler asks, with uniform costs, demands and prices of the products of various firms on the one hand and perfect knowledge of the buyers on the other, will not the demand curves confronting each firm become perfectly elastic and thus making the situation as one of perfect competition and not monopolistic competition of downward-sloping demand curve ? Stigler therefore concludes "physical homogeneity possibly destroys at least temporarily Chamberlin's monopolistic competition." The sum and substance of Stigler's argument is that the picture of diversity in the real world which Chamberlin had presented in order to propound his theory of monopolistic competition has not in fact been incorporated in his theory because of his assumption of uniformity of demand and cost curves of all firms. This uniformity assumption in his view renders the products virtually homogeneous.

2. Symmetry Assumption Criticised

Stigler and Kaldor have also criticised the symmetry assumption made by Chamberlin in order to explain individual and group equilibria. This symmetry assumption relates to the presumption made by Chamberlin that the effect of a change in price and product made by one firm is spread uniformly over his competitors so that the effect in terms of reduction in demand on each of them is so much negligible that they do not think readjusting their prices or products in retaliation. Thus Chamberlin says, "specifically we assume for the present that any adjustment of price or of product by a single producer spreads its influence over so many of his competitors that the impact felt by any one is negligible and does not lead to any readjustment of his own action."[6] This assumption implies that cross elasticity of demand for a product is of the same order of magnitude with respect to any one of the rival products. By making this assumption Chamberlin was able to make the demand curve facing each firm *determinate.*

This assumption implies that even when there is product differentiation under monopolistic competition interdependence of firms on each other is non-existent. Critics point out that products are not uniformly and symmetrically differentiated from each other and that some are more near to each other than others. In view of this, the adjustment in price of the product or variation in the quality of the product by one producer will produce such a significant impact on his rivals whose products are more near to his product that they will definitely react and

3. E. H. Chamberlin, *The Theory of Monopolistic Competition.*
4. *Op. cit.*, p. 14.
5. *Op. cit.*, p. 15.
6. *Op. cit.*

readjust their prices or products. Stigler thus says, "Our vision tells us that we are unlikely to find symmetry, continuity or any sort of smoothness in the relationship among these products.[7]

Likewise, Kaldor is also of the opinion that there is no justification for assuming that cross elasticities of demand of a product will be of the *same order of magnitude with respect to the price* of all rival products as is suggested by symmetry assumption of Chamberlin. According to him, cross elasticities of demand between a product and others is larger with some and less with others. In view of this, Kaldor points out that, it is incorrect to assume that any adjustment of price or of product by a single producer will spread its influence *evenly* over all his competitors. Thus, according to Kaldor, "the different producers' products will never possess the same degree of substitutability in relation to any particular product. Any particular producer will always be faced with rivals who are nearer to him and others who are "farther off'. In fact, he should be able to class his rivals, *from his own point of view,* in a certain order according to the influence of their prices upon his own demand.... Each producer then is faced on each side with his nearest rivals, the demand for his own product will be most sensitive with respect to the prices of these; less and less sensitive as one moves further away from him."[8]

In view of the above Kaldor thinks that the effect of a single producer's change in his price or product will spread itself very much unevenly and the producers with whose products the degree of substitutability of his product is very large will be hurt more. Consequently, they will react by readjusting their prices or products. Therefore, Kaldor is of the view that under monopolistic competition other producers' prices and products cannot be assumed as "given" in drawing up the demand curve for a given producer, and the demand curve for a single producer's product is thus indeterminate under a monopolistic competition as is the case under conditions'of duopoly or oligopoly. He remarks, "The problems of duopoly are thus not merely concomitants of a situation where there are a small number of producers but arise in all cases where producers are selling substitute products, since the fact of imperfect substitutability necessarily involves the presence of the "scale" and thus of the small, number. "Duopoly" is thus seen not as a special class by itself but rather as "the leading species of a large genus."[9]

3. Challenge to Chamberlin's Concept of Group by Stigler and Triffin

Stigler and Robert Triffin have criticized Chxamberlin's group concept. As pointed out in the previous chapter, Chamberlin has used the word "group" in place of "industry" which he thinks applies to the collection of firms producing *homogeneous products,* as under perfect competition. In monopolistic competition, there is a difficulty in determining the precise boundaries of an industry because of the lack of homogeneity in the product. According to Chamberlin, a "group" is a collection of producers *of fairly close substitutes.* He defines a group thus :

"The group contemplated is one which has ordinarily been regarded as composing one imperfectly competitive market. A number of automobile manufacturers, of producers of pots and pans, of magazine publishers, or of retail shoe dealers. From our point of view, each producer within the group is a monopolist yet his market is interwoven with those of his competitors, and he is no longer to be isolated from them."[10]

Stigler concludes from the above description of group by Chambertin that his 'group' may be defined as ***"collection af firms whose cross elasticities of demand exceed some***

7. *Op. cit.*
8. Nicholas Kaldor Market Imperfections and Excess Capacity, printed in American Economic Association's *Readings in Price Theory,* pp. 389-90.
9. *Ibid.*, pp. 391-92.
10. E.H. Chamberlin, *Theory of Monopolistic Competition,* p. 81.

***pre-assigned value.*"** In Chamberlin's theory, the concept of group occupies an important place since he has distinguished his theory of monopolistic competition from the ordinary theory of monopoly by stating that whereas latter concerns only with individual equilibrium, the former analyses the individual equilibrium as well as the group equilibrium (that is, the adjustment of economic forces within a group of competing monopolies.) Moreover, group is important for Chamberlin's theory because it is through the group that he can explain the interdependence of differentiated products.

Stigler has called Chamberlin's group concept as very ambiguous. As stated above, to simplify his analysis of group equilibrium Chamberlin made two main assumptions : (1) uniformity assumption, that is, demand and cost curves for all the products in a group are uniform and (2) the symmetry assumption, that is, the impact of changes in price or product by one firm spreads uniformly over a large number of firms so that it does not evoke retaliation by any firm. According to Stigler, uniformity assumption renders the group as a collection of physically homogeneous products and therefore destroys his theory of monopolistic competition whose essence was diversity or product differentiation. He thus remarks, "by the uniformity assumption Chamberlin has implicitly defined the group as a collection of physically homogeneous products. The identity of costs and demand is otherwise meaningless and so also is the demand he proceeds to draw for a firm on the assumption that 'competitors' prices, are always identical. We simply cannot attach meaning to the statement that physically diverse things have the same price... This physical homogeneity possibly destroys Chamberlin's monopolistic competition."[11]

With this uniformity assumption, contrary to the picture of diversity found in the real world, Stigler argues that the tangency of average cost and demand curves which is deduced by Chamberlin for the group to be in equilibrium is of little importance. With the further introduction of symmetry assumption which implies that there is same degree of substitutability between the various products throughout the group Stigler remarks, "...now Chamberlin has utterly abandoned the picture with which his analytical technique was designed the deal: there is no variety and there is only one possible type of inter-relationship (substitution) between products. We probably have a Marshallian Industry."[12]

Furthermore, according to Stigler, if we recognise *asymmetry of substitution relationships* among firms, which exists in the real world economic life, then the group may include *all the firms in the economy.* This readily follows from the asymmetry of substitution relationship among firms ; taking a product of the given firm as our point of starting for finding out the substitution relationship we will find that each substitute has in turn its own substitutes so that *the adjacent cross elasticities* may not diminish, and even increase as we move farther away from the "base" firm in some technological or geographical sense.[13] Stigler further points out that the picture of diversity and unsystemmatism found in the real world shows that a large and a dominant role is often and perhaps usually played *by firm outside* a Chamberlin's group in determining prices and profits within that group. For all these reasons, Stigler argues that Chamberlin's group concept is ambiguous and serves no useful purpose and further that it destroys the very picture of diversity and unsystematism, with which Chamberlin's theory was meant to deal.

It should however be noted that the adoption of uniformity and symmetry assumptions by Chamberlin was only temporary and he later lifted these assumptions though separately in his analysis. By removing the symmetry assumption he points out that in that case problems of

11. Stigler, *op. cit.*, p. 15.
12. *Ibid.*, p. 17.
13. *Ibid.*, p. 15.

oligopoly or duopoly, namely, uncertainty regarding correct assumptions about the rivals' reactions would arise but from it he draws only this conclusion that prices under monopolistic competition will be higher than under pure competition. And by lifting the uniformity assumption he comes to the conclusion that the effect of diversity of demand and cost conditions will be that the demand curve would not be adjusted uniformly to the tangency position with the cost curves and some or all of the demand curves might be at various distances to the right of the point of tangency with the result that monopoly profits may be earned by all the firms in the group even in the long run.

But Stigler argues that from conclusions reached by Chamberlin with the lifting of twin assumptions of uniformity and symmetry, it is obvious that his theory of monopolistic competition contains no condition of equilibrium, it then only contains a definition of equilibrium. He further points out that the theory of monopolistic competition with the two assumptions lifted does not arrive at any determinate results about group equilibrium in monopolistic competition. To quote high again, "As a result, in the general case, we cannot make a single statement about economic events in the world we sought to analyse. It is true that many such statements are made by Chamberlin but nont follows rigorously from the ambiguous apparatus." In this connection, it should be further noted thai all of the definite comparisons between monopolistic competition and perfect competition are made by Chamberlin when both uniformity and symmetry are present. Moreover, these comparisons also depend upon a "further and technically inadmissible assumption that the cost curves of a firm will be the same under perfect competition and monopolistic competition, although there is no presumption that the size of the 'Group' will be the same in the two situations if they really differ."

It would be very appropriate to mention here the views of Robert Triffin in regard to the Chamberlin's group concept. Robert Triffin in his book *"Monopolistic Competition and General Equilibrium Theory"* has tried to develop an analytical apparatus which according to Stigler, "portrays faithfully the original picture of variety and unsystematism". In this he has not tried to divide the various firms in the economy into different industries or groups. He propounds the view that costs, demands and hence profits of each firm are functions *of all prices* in the econojny. In other words, profits of a firm $i = (p_1, p_2, p_3..p_n)$ where n is a very large number. Triffin generalises the theory of value and tries to analyse the interdependence among firms in the economy without bringing the concept of group or industry into his analysis. He remarks, ***"Product differentiation robs the concept of industry of both its definiteness and its service ability."***[14] **And further,** ***"In the general pure theory of value, "the group and the industry are useless concepts."***[15]

We have noted in an earlier chapter that, according to Chamberlin, monopolistic competition differs from the theory of monopoly only in containing group equilibrium. Now, if the group goes, then the theory of monopolistic competition is reduced to the theory of monopoly. In the end, it is worth noting that Chamberlin himself now admits that to classify industries or groups on the basis of market substitutability is quite arbitrary. But he still thinks that concept of group is not wholly without meaning and argues against discarding it completely as he thinks it useful to delimit a portion of the economic system and study it in some degree of isolation from the rest. His present view is obvious from the following statement which he later added as footnote to his book.

"It is not meant by this argument to discard completely the concept of an 'industry'. In many connections, it is obviously useful to delimit a portion of the economic system and study

14. Robert Triffin, *Monopolistic Composition and General Equilibrium Theory.*
15. Ibid.

it in some degree of isolation from the rest. And if this can be done, although entry is never "free", it is not wholly without meaning to speak of the relative ease with which this particular field may be entered in the sense of the relative ease with which substitutes for the particular products which compose the "industry" may be produced. One emerges from **any attempt to classify industries, however, with a feeling that it is all exceedingly arbitrary.** The *"common sense"* definition of industries in terms of which practical problems are likely to be studied seem to be based much more upon technological criteria than upon the possibility of market substitution."[16]

Now, it is purely a matter of opinion whether the concept of group or industry is useful and therefore be retained to convey the idea of a relatively greater extent to which a given number of firms are interdependent in the sense of the fairly close substitutability of their products. In the actual practice, not only do we speak of Oil Industry, Paper Industry, Cotton Textile Industry, Steel Industry and so on but also study their problems separately. But this actual classification of industries is based upon technologically similar products produced by each industry rather than on relatively greater substitutability of their products.

4. Monopolistic Competition and the Concept of Marginal Revenue

Professor Kaldor has criticized Chamberlin for belittling the importance of the concept of marginal revenue. The concept of marginal revenue has a special importance for imperfect competition or monopolistic competition since under it marginal revenue becomes distinct from price, while under perfect competition the two are the same. Therefore, marginal revenue has become closely associated with imperfect competition or monopolistic competition. It is with the equation to marginal revenue with the marginal cost that equilibrium output is known and profits maximized under imperfect competition. According to Chamberlin, marginal revenue is not unique to imperfect or monopolistic competition and the equation of marginal cost with marginal revenue is a necessary condition of profit maximization in all market categories including perfect competition. Therefore according to him, imperfect competition cannot be distinguished from pure or perfect competition on the basis of marginal revenue or on the basis of the equation of marginal cost with marginal revenue. He thus say that "it is perfectly obvious that the equation of marginal revenue and marginal cost is a general principle for the individual firm under any circumstances whatever, even under the purest of pure competition. It is, at bottom, only another way of saying that producers seek to maximize their profits, *and contributes nothing to distinguishing* ***"imperfect" competition from pure competition and monopoly.***"[17]

It is true that marginal revenue is not unique to imperfect competition and the equation of marginal cost with the marginal revenue is a necessary condition of equilibrium in all market forms. But Chamberlin does not realise that whereas under pure or perfect competition marginal revenue is not different from price, the two become different under conditions of imperfect competition. The, marginal revenue may not contain the "heart of the whole matter", but its discovery as a distinct and separate concept from price helped a great deal in developing the theory of imperfect competition. *We can distinguish* imperfect competition from the perfect one on the basis of the relationship between marginal revenue and price. Whereas under perfect competition, marginal revenue equals price, under imperfect competition marginal revenue is less than price. As described before in the explanation of the theory of imperfect competition, the magnitude of the difference between marginal revenue and price at a level of output depends upon the elasticity of demand at that output, $MR = \text{Price}\ [(e - 1)/e]$. The

16. E. H. Chamberlin, *Theory of Monopolistic Competition*, Footnote on page 202.
17. *Op. cit.*, p. 193 (italics supplied).

divergence of marginal revenue from price is so important a characteristic of imperfect competition that A. P. Lerner and Kaldor have measured the *degree of imperfection* or what is now popularly known as *degree of monopoly* by the magnitude of the difference between the marginal revenue and the price. The greater this difference, the greater the degree of imperfection or monopoly power.

Since at equilibrium output marginal revenue is equal to marginal cost, the relation between price and marginal revenue becomes the relation between price and marginal cost. With this relation in view and in conformity with our above argument, Kaldor remarks, "The heart of the whole matter which places the marginal revenue curve in such an important position is the relation of price to marginal cost. It is the nature of this relation which distinguishes a state of competition that is pure from one that is impure ; in one case price will be equal to marginal cost, in the other, it will be higher than marginal cost."[18]

It is thus clear that Chamberlin does not sufficiently recognise the significance of marginal revenue curve; he thinks too much in terms of average curves. He thinks marginal curves to be quite subordinate to average curves. He is on the wrong side when he criticizes Joan Robinson for her stating *double condition* for full or group equilibrium under imperfect competition, namely, marginal revenue must equal marginal cost and average revenue (or price) must equal average cost. He thinks that the equation of price with average cost is a sufficient condition for full equilibrium, since it inevitably includes the equality of marginal revenue with marginal cost. It is quite strange, as has been pointed out by Kaldor, that Chamberlin himself in the same article while refuting another criticism against his theory asserts that in his theory, the 'solution of tangency', *i.e.*, the equality of average cost with average revenue flows from certain heroic assumptions which are later dropped and is to be regarded as of only limited direct applicability, being mainly an expositional device, which represents an intermediate stage in the development of the theory."[19]

It is evident from this statement that when the two heroic assumptions (uniformity and symmetry) are lifted, Chamberlin drops the tangency of average revenue with the average cost curve as a condition of equilibrium in his monopolistic competition. Obviously, under such circumstances (that is, when the *AR* curve is not fallen to the tangency position), firms will be in equilibrium at the outputs where they are equating marginal cost with marginal revenue. Thus, the equation of marginal revenue with the marginal cost by all firms in Chamberlin's monopolistic competition is a necessary condition for their individual and collective equilibrium, while the equality of average revenue with average cost will be there only when there exists uniformity of demand and cost curves confronting the firms in monopolistic competition ('heoric assumption). Therefore, Professor Kaldor rightly criticizes Chamberlin on this point when he says that "what is essential for equilibrium under monopolistic competition, is equality of marginal cost and marginal revenue, whereas the equality of the average curves is merely an "expositional device."[20]

5. Number of Firms, Demand Elasticity and Market Imperfection

Another flaw pointed out by Kaldor in the monopolistic competition theory is the assertion of Chamberlin that lured by the excessive profits being earned by the existing firms as new firms enter the group and consequently the number of firms increases in the group, the elasticity of demand curves confronting the firms will not increase and therefore the degree of market imperfection will not be reduced. This view of Chamberlin is quite contrary to Joan Robison

18. Nicholas Kaldor, Monopolistic and Imperfect Competition, printed in his *Essays on Values and Dis-tribution.*
19. Chamberlin. *op.cit.*, p. 195.
20. Kaldor, *op. cit.*

who in her *"Economics of Imperfect Competition"* propounds that the new firms would come 'in between the old firms' as the number of firms increases with the result that the buyers' preferences between the various firms would be reduced which will raise the elasticities of demand of firms' products.[21] Increase in the elasticity of demand would mean the reduction in the degree of imperfection.

Kaldor also thinks that as new firms enter the industry in the long run, the new products would come in between the old products and the various products would come closer to one another. In other words, with a large number of firms the degree of substitutability between the products would increase. Therefore, as a result the cross elasticities of demand between them would Increase which will raise the elasticity of demand for each product in the group. As explained above, the degree of imperfection, as measured by the magnitude of difference between price and marginal revenue (or price and marginal cost) depends upon the elasticity of demand at the equilibrium output. The greater the elasticity, the less the difference between price and marginal revenue (or marginal cost) and therefore less the degree of market imperfection. To quote Kaldor, "The relevant fact, of course, is that such a shift to the left will increase the elasticity of demand at the equilibrium level of output and will therefore bring price necessarily nearer to marginal cost. Hence it will necessarily reduce the degree of market imperfection."[22]

As point out by Kaldor, the competitive field of the real world is *n-dimensional* rather *one-dimensional.* Therefore there are hundreds of ways in which products can be made more or lees similar, or more or less differentiated. It is because of this that when new firms enter the field, their new products will come in between the old ones which will raise the cross elasticities of demand for the products of monopolistically competitive group. This will make the demand curve for a product confronting a firm more elastic.

We therefore, agree with Kaldor that "despite Professor Chamberlin's protest, the idea that elasticities increase as the number of firms get large will continue to have astounding vitality".[23] And if the demand elasticity increases with the increase in the number of firms, the degree of imperfection cr monopoly power would decline.

6. Monopolistic Competition and Increasing Returns (Economies of Scale)

Professor Kaldor has argued that an important cause of the existence of imperfect or monopolistic competition is the existence of increasing returns or economies of scale. According to him, if the factors were perfectly divisible and consequently the economies of scale were absent, that is, if constant costs prevailed in the industry, such a large number of firms would enter into the industry that would establish the conditions of perfect competition. When the conditions of constant costs prevail in the industry and the firms are making excessive profits, according to Kaldor, these excessive profits under conditions of constant costs cannot be completely eliminated by the entry of more firms in the industry, so long as the elasticity of demand is less than infinity. As the new firms enter into the industry, the demand curve confronting each firm will shift to the left and will become more elastic. As a result, the demand for and the equilibrium output of a firm will decline but since costs are constant, the firm will still be making some profits by reducing output to the level where new marginal revenue equals marginal cost. Since profits cannot be completely wiped out in case of constant costs as long as the demand curve slopes downward even though slightly, *i.e.,* as long as demand elasticity is less than infinity, lured by these profits the new firms would continue to

21. Joan Robinson, *op. cit.,* p. 101.
22. Kaldor, *op., cit.*
23. Op. *cit.*

enter and consequently the output of each firm would continue to decline and the elasticity of demand would continue to increase until the firm's output is reduced to such an extent that it has completely lost its control over the price of the product or, in other words, until demand elasticity becomes infinite. When each firm is reduced to such a position, it will take price as given and will equate it with marginal cost (which would also be equal to average cost in this constant costs case). And this is perfect competition.

It is thus clear that in case of constant costs movement of the new firms into the industry will stop only when perfect competition is established. Thus Kaldor holds, "if we assume that economies of scale are completely absent *(i.e.,* long-run cost curves are horizontal), profits will never be eliminated altogether so long as the elasticity of demand is less than infinite...... the inflow of new producers will continue leading to a continuous reduction in the output of existing producers and a continuous increase in the elasticities of their demand until the latter *become 'infinite* and prices will equal average costs. There the movement will stop. But each "firm" will have reduced its output to such an extent that *it has completely lost its hold over the market."*[24] Demand becoming infinitely elastic and the firm having lost its control over the price implies the establishment of the conditions of perfect competition.

But Chamberlin has rejected the inherent association between monopolistic competition and economies of scale. He attacks Kaldor's view that if full divisibility of all factors is assumed and consequently economies of scale are completely absent, the free play of economic forces would necessarily establish perfect competition. He maintains that with the increase in the number of firms, the demand elasticity would not increase. Therefore, according to him, demand curve would not swing round to the horizontal position with the entry of a large number of firms and thus perfect competition would not be established. He says, "Now if high profits lead to an increase in the number of sellers, so that the curve moves to the left, it will remain of the same *slope*"[25] This is because he thinks, as explained in the previous section, that "large or small numbers indicate nothing necessarily as to the degree of substitutability between the products concerned."[26]

Further, Chamberlin thinks that economies of scale are not there because of indivisibility and even if all factors are perfectly divisible, economies of scale would not be absent. That is, perfect indivisibility of the factors does not make the cost curves horizontal. He even does not admit the possibility of constant costs. According to him, even if it is accepted that the demand curves become more elastic with the increase in the number of firms but cost curves were U-shaped then the profits would be eliminated as the demand curves are pushed to the left to the tangency position. When this happens,further movement of the firms would stop and group equilibrium would be reached without the demand curve becoming perfectly elastic or without the conversion of monopolistic competition into pure competition.

In the context of downward-sloping demand curve and constant costs, perfect divisibility of the factors would, according to him, lead to the absurd results by bringing into existence an infinite "number of infinitesimally small firms. He thus says, "If demand curves did *not* become horizontal, as has been argued in general above, we have an *absurd result.* The influx of firms would simply continue indefinitely (because there would always be profits under constant costs); and the final outcome would appear to be an *infinite number of infinitesimally small firms."*[27] Chamberlin concludes his answer to Kaldor's criticism regarding the conversion of monopolistic competition into perfect competition when there is perfect divisibility of the factors, and

24. Kaldor, Market Imperfection and Excess Capacity, printed in *Readings in Price Theory* (ABA), p. 394.
25. Chamberlin, *op. cit.*, p. 197.
26. *Ibid.*, p. 196.
27. *Op. cit.*

consequently the constant costs prevail, in the following words : "We may conclude that since infinite divisibility does nothing to the shape of the cost curves, and the number of firms does nothing for certain to the shape of the demand curves, there is no conversion of monopolistic into pure competition by any of these lines of reasoning."[28]

Whether perfect divisibility of factors implies the absence of economies of scale or not is a separate issue on which we have already commented upon in a previous chapter. But if the economies of scale are absent, that is, if the constant costs exist in an industry for one reason or another, we are inclined to agree with Kaldor's view that under the constant costs the number of firms in the industry would increase to such an extent and consequently output of each firm would be reduced to such a small magnitude that it will lose its control over price and accordingly will take price as given and equate it with marginal cost to determine its equilibrium output. This can happen even if the products remain slightly differentiated. In other words, we agree with Kaldor that in the case of constant costs, a free play of economic forces would establish pure or perfect competition. To quote Professor Kaldor :

"As the number of firms increases and demand curves move to the left, price necessarily moves nearer to marginal cost (which in constant cost case is also equal to average cost). There comes a point where producers no longer take into account their own influence upon price and proceed to equate price with marginal cost. At this point further movement will cease and pure competition is established. We can represent this situation by a horizontal demand curve if we like but this would be no more than a geometric expression of the assumption that producers take prices as given. The important point is that ***unless economies of large scale or rather the dis-economies of small-scale production set a limit to the inflow of competitors or "institutional monopolies" afford peculiar advantages to particular individuals, there can be no equilibrium until producers equate price with marginal costs, and equality of price with marginal cost is pure competition.***"[29]

We, therefore, unlike Chamberlin, come to the conclusion that the economies of scale (or increasing returns) are an important cause of the existence of monopolistic or imperfect competition. It also follows from this that the degree of market imperfections depends, among other things, on the extent to which economies of scale prevail. "If the economies of scale are rapidly exhausted (that is, at a relatively low level of output), the likelihood of there being a low degree of imperfection in competition is high and *vice versa.*" Further, as has been pointed out by Kaldor, the proposition that economies of scale are an important reason for the existence of monopolistic competition (monopoly elements in the competition) enables us to distinguish the *purely economic causes* of monopolies from the *institutional causes* of monopolies. Economies of scale are the economic causes of the imperfection or monopoly elements in competition, whereas the control over some important raw materials, patents etc., which confer advantages on some firms are the institutional causes of monopolistic elements.

Freedom of Entry and Monopolistic Competition

Another controversial issue in the theory of monopolistic competition is the concept of the 'freedom of entry'. Chamberlin in the original version of his theory of monopolistic competition assumed perfect freedom of entry into the monopolistically competitive group. He in his original version thus assumed that "entrance to the field in general and to every portion of it in particular was unimpeded." Kaldor in a paper ***"Market Imperfection and Excess Capacity"*** pointed out that this assumption of 'perfect freedom of entry' implies that

28. *Op. cit.,p.* 199.
29. Kaldor, *op. cit.*

"every producer could, if he wanted to, produce commodities completely identical to those of any other producer." It is obvious that freedom of enny in. this sense is incompatible with Chamberlin's monopolistic competition whose prominent feature is product differentiation.

Chamberlin agreed with Kaldor and realised his mistake of regarding 'freedom of entry' to be consistent with monopolistic competition with a differentiated product. Thus indicating his agreement with Kaldor, Chamberlin remarks, "Mr Kaldor has nightly pointed out that the statement that 'entrance to the field in general and to every portion of it in particular was unimpeded' implies that every producer could, if he wanted to, produce commodities completely identical to those of any producer... *Logically, this is what 'free entry' in its fullest sense must mean and it is quite incompatible with a differentiated product. With respect to the particular product produced by any individual firm under monopolistic competition, there can be no 'freedom of entry' whatever. No one else can produce a product identical with it, although he may be able to produce others which are fairly good substitutes for it.*[30] It is thus clear that, according to Chamberlin's later views, under monopolistic competition there can be freedom of entry only in a restricted sense of there being a liberty for others to produce only close substitutes. To quote him again, ***"Under monopolistic competition, then there can be freedom of entry only in the sense of a freedom to produce substitutes and in this sense freedom of entry is universal, since substitutes are entirely a matter of degree."***[31]

But this limited and restricted sense of "free entry" under monopolistic competition creates difficulties for Chamberlin's monopolistic competition theory. Chamberlin's theory of monopolistic competition involves the elimination of profits with the demand curves becoming tangent to the average cost curves by the entry of sufficient number of firms in the long run. New firms attract some of the customers from the existing firms to their own products and thereby reduce the demand for the products of the existing firms. But, if the new competitors can produce only those products which are close substitutes and not perfectly identical with those of the existing firms, it becomes highly doubtful whether the profits would be completely wiped out through the demand curves reduced to the tangency position.

Chamberlin himself is aware of this difficult problem in his theory created by the restricted sense of the freedom of entry. It is because of this difficulty that he remarks, "In order to give the concept meaning, ***it might be defined as freedom to produce substitutes within an arbitrarily delimited range of goodness, say a range sufficiently good to eliminate profits in excess of the necessary minimum."***[32] He adds, "We could not speak of freedom of entry in an industry, even in the limited sense here defined, unless profits for all producers in the industry were reduced to the minimum included in the cost curve."[33] But it is highly doubtful whether profits can be completely eliminated when there is freedom only to produce substitutes so long as the existing producers' products retain their differentiation and goodwill.[34] Thus in view of the restricted freedom of entry in the context of monopolistic competition, his tangency solution for the group equilibrium and the concept of excess capacity based on it becomes suspect.

Entangled into the complexities of his theory of group equilibrium and the inconsistency of the freedom of entry with a differentiated product, Chamberlin has argued for giving away the concept of freedom of entry altogether. He thus remarks, "The upshot of the matter

30. Chamberlin, *op. cit.*, pp. 200-201 (italics added).
31. *Ibid.*, p. 201.
32. *Ibid., p. 201.*
33. *Ibid.*, p. 201.
34. This point is more damaging to Chamberlin's theory in view of his stand that products do not come close to each other with the increase in the number of differentiated products due to the entry of new firms in the field. If the products remain as much differentiated as before, it is still more doubtful that profits would be competed away.

seems to be that the concept is not very useful and is even seriously misleading in connection with monopolistic com-petition. It is, in reality, a concept usually related to a market for a definite commodity and the fundamental difficulty, is that there is no such commodity under monopolistic competition beyond that produced by an individual firm."[35]

But he points out that his theory of monopolistic competition can be described without the concept of freedom of entry. According to him, only this much is essential that whenever profits exist under monopolistic competition, they would be reduced so far as possible by the new competitors producing substitutes for the existing ones. To quote him "In the matter of entry, all that we need to say is that wherever in the economic system there are profit possibilities they will be exploited so far as possible. The enjoyment of large profits by any particular firm is evidently an indication that others by producing close substitutes may be able to *compete some of them away.* The results may be very simply described without any concept of freedom or restriction of entry-without even the concept of an "industry": ***"Some firms in the system earn no profits in excess of the minimum counted as a cost, others earn more than this, and in various degrees."***[36]

But, as has been pointed out by Stigler whose views in this respect have been stated above, by making this later assertion Chamberlin virtually destroys his group equilibrium theory. With only some profits competed away, with some earning excessive profits (some more and some less), and with some earning only normal profits and the tendency of others to compete the excess profits away by producing close substitutes being always there, can it be said that group will ever be in equilibrium ? It is thus clear that in view of the limited freedom of entry the theory of group equilibrium cannot be sustained.[37]

Nor do we agree with Chamberlin that the concept of freedom of entry is quite useless and misleading in the context of imperfect or monopolistic competition. As has been maintained by Professor Kaldor that it is the concept of freedom of entry that enables us to distinguish between *institutional causes* of monopolies and restriction of entry from the *economic causes* of monopolies and oligopolies. Institutional causes of the restriction of entry refer to socially conferred privilege or unique advantages such as the ownership of patent rights, ownership of some scarce and more efficient raw materials and the like. On the other hand, the economic causes relate to the economics of scale which prohibit others to enter because the existing one is producing on a large scale. A new entrant can hope to compete only if he too sets up a plant of a sufficiently large scale but the market demand for the product might not be enough to enable both of them to operate with profit. Thus the economies of scale inhibit the potential competitors to enter in a field and compete with the established large-scale firms.

In this case, no institutional restrictions to the entry exist but the entry is prohibited because of the economies of scale. If there do not exist much economies of scale relative to demand in any industry, then the freedom of entry can be restricted only by the institutional causes. Entry can be said to be perfectly "free" if the socially conferred unique advantages enjoyed by the established producers are absent. As far as the economic causes of monopolies (or economies of scale) are concerned, we can say that in that case new firms are perfectly free to enter if they so like, but they wouid not enter because the prospects and possibilities of making profits by entering into the field are too bleak.

35. *Ibid., 203.*
36. *Ibid.*, 204.
37. It is not being suggested like Chamberlin that the concept of freedom of *entry* should be given up. What is contended here is that with the limited freedom of entry, the concept of group equilibrium in the context of monopolistic competition must go.

As a matter of fact, this economic cause of imperfect competition, monopolies or oligopolies became evident from Chamberlin's '*Theory of Monopolistic Competition*', and Kaldor regards this as a significant contribution made by Chamberlin to the economic theory. He therefore regrets over the Chamberlin's lately arguing for the abandonment of the concept of freedom of entry. He thus says :

"I particularly regret that Professor Chamberlin should have changed his views on this point. To have shown that the monopolised situations of the real world are quite compatible with "full freedom of entry," that is to say, with the complete absence of particular advantages vested in particular people, I have always regarded as one of the great achievements of the Theory of Monopolistic Competition. Up to the publication of this book, the idea of "monopoly was inevitably linked up in the'economist's mind as well as in the public mind, with the idea of a 'privilege,' the behaviour of monopolists might well have been described in terms of marginal curves but the causes of the existence of monopolists were generally sought in the possession of some unique advantage. ***Professor Chamberlin's theory of product differentiation has shown us that monopoly is purely a matter of degree*** and that monopolies of various degrees can exist without any "unique" advantage at all merely because the demand for a single variety of product is small relatively to the economies of scale in its production. To have shown that the limitations on competition can be due to purely economic causes, to the conditions of production and of consumption, and not only to the operations of that sinister group of individuals, the "institutional monopolies", the owner of patent rights and of mineral springs was a great step forward in economics and it should be placed to Chamberlin's credit despite his present disclaimer."[38]

It is thus clear that the concept of freedom of entry is helpful in knowing to which extent institutional causes (restrictions of entry) and economic causes (increasing returns) are responsible for the existence of particular monopolistic situations. "By doing away with the concept of freedom of entry, we shall no longer be able to distinguish between such monopolies as the Company store in a Company town, which owes its position to privilege and Henry Ford, who owes his position (largely if not entirely) to the economies of large scale production."[39]

Further, it is true, as has been asserted by Chamberlin, that there is no full freedom of entry in monopolistic competition with product differentiation. But, instead of making the concept of freedom of entry absolute, we can, as has been suggested by Kaldor, distinguish between *different degrees of freedom*. In any case, we have.to see how large is the range of substitutes over which extent the entry is free or closed. If the new firms can produce exactly identical products as the existing firms, the freedom of entry can be said to be full or perfect. If the new firms can produce close substitutes, degree of freedom of entry will be substantial. On the other hand, if the new competitors are able to produce only remote substitutes, the degree of freedom of entry will be very small. The closer the substitutes which the new producers can produce, the greater the degree of freedom of entry. Thus we can think of different degrees of freedom depending upon the elasticity of substitution of the products that could be produced by the new producers that enter into the group or industry to get a share in the excessive profits being earned by the existing producers.

Excess Capacity Criticism. The monopolistic competition theory has also been criticised on the basis of its conclusion that firms under it operate with excess capacity. We shall examine this criticism at length in the next chapter.

38. Kaldor, *op. cit.*
39. Ibid.

Conclusion

We have explained above the criticisms that have been levelled against Chamberlin's theory of monopolistic- competition. However, it will be wrong to get away with the impression that Chamberlins' contribution to price theory is insignificant. Despite some shortcomings, Chamberlin has made several important contributions to the price theory. Even his critics including Stigler and Kaldor have admitted the revolutionary character of his contributions. As stated in the beginning, incorporation of product differentiation, product variation and selling costs into the price theory by Chamberlin and importance given to monopolistic elements and oligopolies in his analysis of price formation in the real world are all his significant contributions to the economic theory. As a matter of fact, his analysis of monopolistic competition with a large number of firms producing various varieties of a product and with a falling demand curve for a particular variety has been incorporated as a part of what is called neoclassical price theory. Most of the modern textbooks of economics have adopted Chamberlin's monopolistic competition with a largs number of firms as a chief form of imperfect competition. To quote Stigler, a server critic of Chamberlin's theory, "The general contribution of the theory of monopolistic competition, on the other hand, seems to me indisputable; it has led to re-orientation and refinement of our thinking on monopoly. We are all now more careful to pay attention to the logical niceties of definitions of industries and commodities. We are now more careful to apply monopoly theory where it is appropriate. Thus importance of trade marks and of advertising and the need for study of product structure and evolution, have become more generally recognised."[40]

40. Stigler, *op. cit.*

CHAPTER

38

A Critical Evaluation of Excess Capacity of Doctrine Monopolistic Competition Theory

In chapter 36 we explained the doctrine of excess capacity in general. As stated there excess capacity is the amount by which actual output in the long run under monopolistic competition falls short of socially ideal output which was defined by Joan Robinson and others as the level of output corresponding to the minimum level of long-run average cost curve. Chamberlin explained the emergence of excess capacity as result of free entry of firms in the long run in the absence of price competition. Chamberlin explained the emergence of excess capacity with an alternative approach using the concepts of ***perceived demand curve and proportional demand curve.*** Before explaining these concepts of demand curve and critically examine chamberlin's concept of excess capacity, we will explain Cassel's two types of excess capacity.

Cassel's Two Concepts of Excess Capacity

Following Cassel,[1] excess capacity may be divided into two parts. This is illustrated in Figure 38.1. In the long run a firm under monopolistic competition is in equilibrium at output *OM* and is employing plant having short-run average cost curve SAC_1. Thus, from the viewpoint of the firm the plant of SAC_1 is an optimal one. But the firm is not utilizing the plant to its entire productive capacity, *i.e.*, the firm is not operating at the minimum point of SAC_1 but to the left of it. This means that firm is not efficiently or fully utilizing the plant (or resources embodied in the plant) *actually being employed* by it. The optimum use of the plant of SAC_1 is to produce with it output *OT*. But actually the firm produces with it only output *OM* since it is at *OM* that twin long-run equilibrium conditions of $MR = MC$ and $AR = AC$ are satisfied. Therefore, the difference between *OM* and *OT*, that is, output *MT* measures the excess capacity.

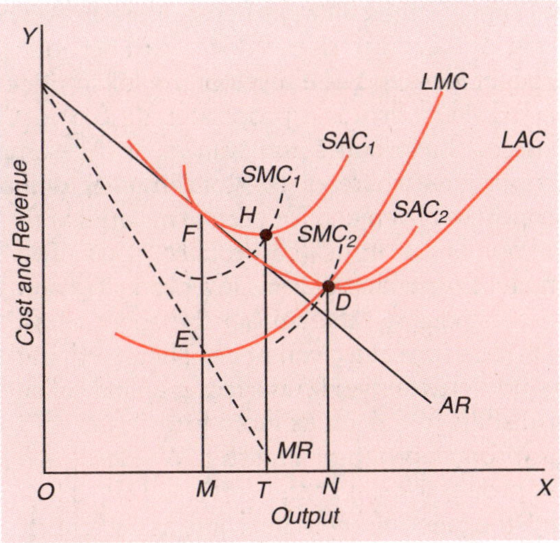

Fig. 38.1 *Two Concepts of Excess Capacity*

But, from the social point of view, the resources will be efficiently utilised if the firm employs a plant of SAC_2 and produces with

1. J. M. Cassels, Excess Capacity and Monopolistic Competition,- *Quarterly Journal of Economics*, LI (1936-37) pp. 426-43.

it output *ON*. The socially optimum output is therefore *ON*. Thus a portion of excess capacity represented by *TN* arises because socially ideal or optimum plant differs from an individual optimum plant. Social optimum requires that the firm should have employed resources represented by the plant size of SAC_2 and had worked it at the point *D*. But actually the firm employs resources represented by the plant size SAC_1. It follows that a firm in long-run equilibrium under monopolistic competition does not employ sufficient amount of society's potential resources to attain minimum average cost. Thus the total excess capacity from the. social point of view is *MN* of which *MT portion* arises because the firm does not operate the plant or resources it employs at its minimum average cost and the *TN* portion arises because individual and socially optimum plants differ.

Chamberlin's Concepts of Proportional and Perceived Demand Curves

The process of equilibrium adjustment under monopolistic competition has also been explained by two types of demand curves, namely, perceived demand curve and proportional demand curve. The demand curve facing an individual firm, as perceived by it, describes the demand for the product of one firm on the assumption that all other firms in the industry or group keep the *prices of their products constant*. The perceived demand curve shows the increase in quantity demanded of a product of a firm when a firm cuts down its price provided others keep their prices at the present level. On the contrary, it shows the fall in quantity demanded of the product of a firm which will occur if it raises its price on the assumption that others would not raise their prices. This type of demand curve in the present alternative approach, is known as *perceived demand curve* and is based upon the above important assumption.

On the other hand, *proportional curve* facing an individual shows the demand or sales of the product of a firm when the prices of all firms in a product-group or industry *change, all of them simultaneously in the same direction and by the same amount* so that they charge same or uniform price. Obviously, the proportional demand curve of a firm will be less elastic than its perceived demand curve, since equal change in price by all firms of the industry (or group) will prevent the shifting of customers from one seller to another. The proportional demand curve of each firm slopes downward because the market demand for the general class of the product increases as a result of the fall in price. In fact, the proportional demand curve facing an individual firm is a proportionate part of the total market demand curve for the general class of the product and will be of the same elasticity. Thus, since each firm gets some proportional share of the total market demand for the general class of the product, the proportional demand for each firm varies with the number of firms in a product-group. The greater the number of firms in a product-group (or the industry), the smaller the share of an individual firm at a given price. Therefore, the proportional demand curve facing an individual firm shifts to the left as more firms enter into the product-group or industry. We designate the proportional demand curve as *DD′* curve and, the perceived demand curve as *dd′* curve. The two types of demand curves are graphically shown in Fig. 38.2. The two demand curves have been shown to be interesecting at point *A* corresponding to price *OP* and quantity demanded *OQ*. This means that at price *OP*

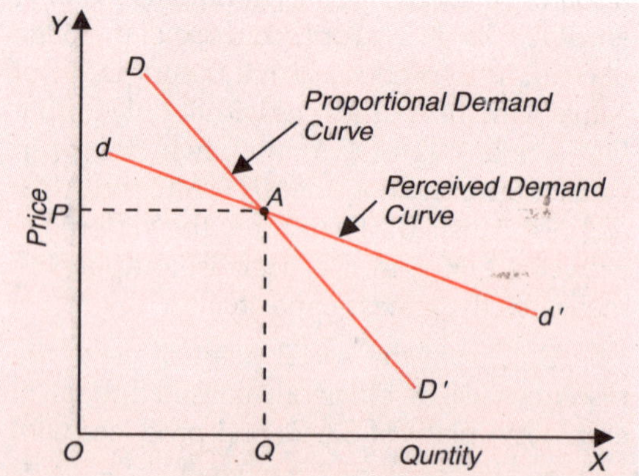

Fig. 38.2. *Chamberlin's Concepts of Perceived and Proportional Demand Curves*

of the product, the proportional share of each firm of the market demand for the industry product is equal to *OQ*. Since it is assumed that all firms charge the same price, all firms in the industry will be producing and selling *OQ* quantity and each charging *OP* price. Therefore, point A lies on the proportional demand curve. From the initial situation at A on the proportional demand curve *DD* ′ (with price equal to *OP* and quantity demanded of each equal to *OQ*), we can draw the perceived demand curve of a firm. An individual firm believes that if it makes small alternation in price, it will have negligible effect on each of its many competitors so that they will not think of readjusting their prices. Prices of others remaining unchanged at *OP*, an individual firm thinks that if it reduces its price, the sales or quantity demanded of its product will greatly increase as it will attract customers of other firms. Thus, an individual firm perceives that its demand is more elastic than the proportional demand curve and it can increase its profits by cutting down its price. Therefore, we construct the perceived demand curve *dd* ′ passing through point *A* as being more elastic than the proportional demand curve *DD* ′. However, it may be pointed out that since *each* firm in the product group will think independently that its price reduction will have a negligible effect upon each of his rivals and therefore assumes that others would keep their prices constant, the actual movement would not be along the perceived demand curve *dd* ′ but along the proportional demand curve *DD* ′ which shows actual sales by each firm when the prices of all change equally and are identical.

Short-Run Firm's Equilibrium Under Monopolistic Competition : Chamberlin's Alternative Approach

Price-output equilibrium of an individual firm in the short run in terms of two demand curves (proportional demand curves and perceived demand curve) is illustrated in Figure 38.3. Suppose the firm is initially at point *A* on the proportional demand curve *DD* ′. Firm's perceived demand curve $d_0d'_0$ which is more elastic than the proportional demand curve *DD* ′ has been drawn through point A. Each firm's share of demand for its product is equal to OQ_0 and all of them are charging uniform price OP_0.

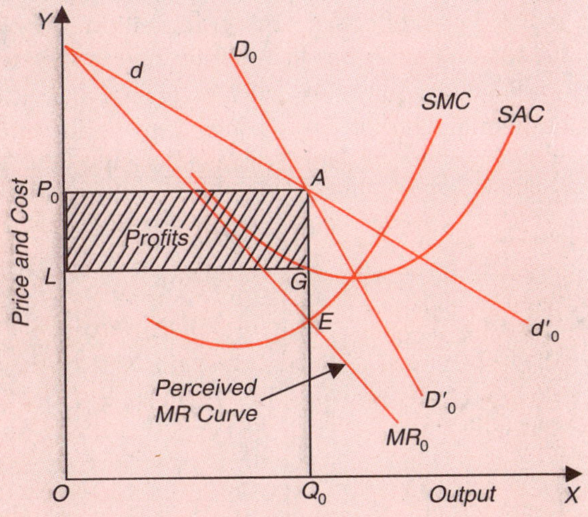

Fig. 38.3. *Short-run Equilibrium of the Firm under Monopolistic Competition: Proportional and Perceived Demand Curves Approach*

SAC and *SMC* are short-run average cost curve and short-run marginal cost curve respectively. Marginal revenue curve MR_0 corresponding the perceived demand curve dd'_0 has been drawn. *SMC* and MR_0 curves intersect at point *E* and accordingly output OQ_0 is equilibrium output of the firm and OP_0 is the equilibrium price charged with proportional and perceived demand curves cutting each other at point *A* in the present price-quantity equilibrium. It will be seen from Fig. 38.3 that price OP_0 exceeds average cost of production at OQ_0 output level and therefore the firm is making economic profits equal to the shaded area P_0AGL. Thus, according to Chamberlin's alternative approach, short-run equilibrium under monopolistic competition is reached at the price-output combination where *MR* = *MC* is such that corresponds to the point at which perceived demand curve *dd* ′ intersects the proportional demand curve *DD* ′.

Chamberlin's Concepts of Ideal Output and Emergence of Excess Capacity

The view of ideal output enunciated above rests upon the perfect or pure competition and its associated product homogeneity which gives rise to the horizontal demand curve confronting an individual firm under it and consequently the establishment of the long-run equilibrium of firm under perfect competition at the minimum point of the long-run average cost. The output at this minimum long-run average cost under perfect competition with product homogeneity is regarded as "ideal" from the viewpoint of social welfare. But Prof. Chamberlin argues that this ***"Competitive Ideal"*** cannot be considered as "ideal" under monopolistic competition.

According to Chamberlin, under monopolistic competition there is product differentiation which inevitably gives rise to the downward-sloping demand curve. Downward-sloping demand curve along with free entry into the product group and active price competition necessarily involves long-run equilibrium to the left of the minimum point of the long-run average cost curve. According to Chamberlin, product differentiation is desired *per se* and therefore the long-run equilibrium output of the monopolistically competitive firm under free entry and *active price competition* represents the "ideal output". This departure from the long-run equilibrium output under free entry and active price competition from the minimum average cost does not prevent the output to be ideal. Since this departure is only due to product differentiation which is desired by the consumers for its own sake.

Chamberlin regards product differentiation a quality of the product which entails a cost just as any other quality. The cost of product differentiation is represented by production to the left of the long-run minimum average cost curve. This means that "the difference between the actual long-run equilibrium output and output at minimum cost is then a measure, of the cost of producing differentiation rather than a measure of excess capacity".[5] But, according to Chamberlin, this is true only when effective price competition in the market is present, because it is only when effective price competition among the sellers is present that the buyers would have the degree of product differentiation they wish to purchase.

The ideal output as conceived by Chamberlin is illustrated in Figure 38.4. According to Chamberlin, the long-run equilibrium under monopolistic competition is established at the point where the subjective or perceived demand curve $d_p d'_p$ is tangent to the long-run average

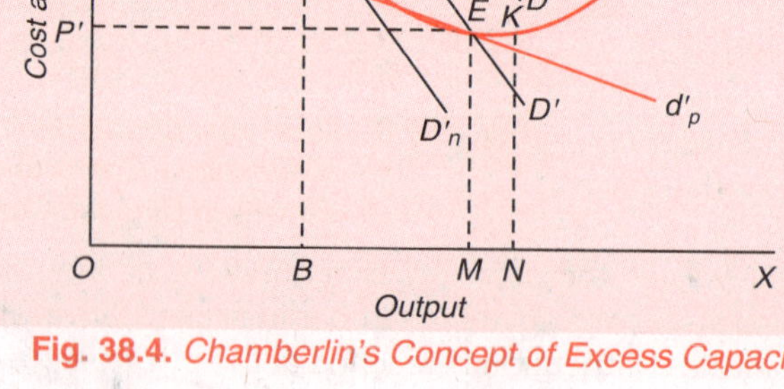

Fig. 38.4. *Chamberlin's Concept of Excess Capacity*

5. C. F. Ferguson, *Microeconomic Theory* (1966), p. 262.

cost curve and also market demand curve *DD'* curve cuts the *MC* curve at this point of tangency. This is achieved at point *E* where $d_p d'_p$ is tangent to *LAC* and *DD'* will be cutting *LAC* at this point. This long-run equilibrium point has been achieved after the adjustment in the number of firms in the 'group' has taken place and price competition has fully worked itself out. Corresponding to this long-run equilibrium point *E*, the firm is producing output *OM*. But point *E* lies on the falling portion of the long-run average cost curve. Chamberlin regards long-run equilibrium output *OM* corresponding to point *E* as the ideal output under monopolistic competition in which there is product differentiation. According to Chamberlin, output *ON* which corresponds to the minimum point of the long-run average cost curve *LAC* cannot represent ideal output under monopolistic competition involving product differentiation.

Thus, with active price competition when long-run equilibrium is at point *E* where perceived demand curve $d_p d_p$ is tangent to the long-run average cost curve and the firm is producing *OM* output which is ideal one under product differentiation, that is, there is no excess capacity. Therefore, ***according to Chamberlin, so long as there is active price competition in the market, monopolistic competition does not create excess capacity.*** In this view, excess capacity arises when there is free entry of firms but no price competition. Thus, it is the entry of firms in the long run in the monopolistically competitive group which, *in the absence of price competition*, gives rise to the excess capacity. In Figure 38.4, in the short run the firm is in equilibrium at point *S* at price *OP.* Since this price is higher than the average cost, firm will be making supernormal profits. This will attract other firms into the group. With the entry of firms into the industry, proportional demand curve *DD'* faced by the firm will be pushed to the left until it becomes tangential to the long-run average cost curve *LAC* and thereby pure profits are eliminated. In Figure 38.4, with the entry of the firms the proportional demand curve faced is shifted to the position $D_n D'_n$ where it is tangent to *LAC* at point *F.* Now the firm will be in stable equilibrium at point *F* and will be producing output *OB*, if there is no any price competition between the firms.

Now, in the absence of price competition between the firms the perceived demand curve *dd'* becomes irrelevant. Hence in the absence of price competition the perceived demand curve will not slide down the market demand curve $D_n D'_n$ and the firm will be in long-run stable equilibrium at point *F*, with price *OP* and producing *OB* output. Now, the ideal output according to Chamberlin is *OM*. Thus with free entry of firms and in the absence of price competition, the firm is producing *BM* less than the ideal output in long-run equilibrium under monopolistic competition. In Chamberlin's view *BM* represents excess capacity which is caused by the absence of price competition.

Chamberlin has given various reasons for the lack of price competition between the firms in monopolistic competition.[6] Firstly, the business firms may follow the policy of "to live and let live" and therefore they may not indulge in price cutting. They may set prices with reference to cost (including normal profits) rather than demand and accordingly seek only normal profits rather than maximum profits, more or less taking it granted that they will enjoy usual share of the total market demand. Secondly, the business firms in monopolistic competition may have entered into formal or tacit agreements. They might have formed 'price association' which builds up the spirit of 'maintaining price' among the competitors and prevents them from price cutting. Thirdly ***'business or professional ethics,*** also prevent them from disturbing the market by price cutting. It is generally considered unethical in the professions to compete on the basis of price. Fourth factor preventing price cutting is the fear of business firms that the lower price may lead the consumers to regard the particular product as of inferior quality. It is generally seen in the real world that many consumers blindly link quality with price.

6. *Op. cit.,pp.* 105-107.

In the fifth place, the business firms may make disguised or hidden price cuts while maintaining the price openly. Since open price cuts generally bring about retaliation from the rivals, it is considered desirable to give certain non-price concessions, offers and facilities free of charge, such as free coupons, premiums, etc., while displaying and charging the same price as competitors. All these extra non-price concessions or facilities are regarded as hidden price cuts. Finally, the prices may not be free to move at all being set by custom or tradition.

As pointed out above, if price competition is in fact absent, individual firms will have no perceived demand curve *dd'*. They will be concerned only with proportional demand curve *DD'* which represents the effects of price rise or price decline when all firms in the group simultaneously raise or reduce price. According to Chamberlin, the result of'the absence of price competition among the firms in monopolistic competition "is excess productive capacity for which there is no automatic corrective. Such excess capacity may develop, of course, under pure competition owing to miscalculation on the part of producers or to sudden fluctuations in demand or cost conditions. *But it is the peculiarity of monopolistic competition that it* may develop over long periods *with impunity,* prices always covering costs, and may, in fact, become permanent and normal through a failure of price competition to function. The surplus capacity is never cast off and the result is high prices and waste".[7] He further says that his theory of monopolistic competition "affords an explanation of such wastes in the economic system-wastes which are usually referred to as "wastes of competition". In fact they could never occur under pure competition. ***They are wastes of monopoly—of the monopoly dements in monopolistic competition.'***[8]

Harrod's Critique of the Excess Capacity Doctrine

The doctrine of excess capacity under monopolistic or imperfect competition has been criticised by some economists, especially by Harrod and Kaldor. According to Harrod, excess capacity theorem implies that the "rational" entrepreneur acts in an *inconsistent* manner. In monopolistically competitive equilibrium, as described by Chamberlin and Joan Robinson, Harrod points out that inconsistency arises because the entrepreneur is shown to be using *short-run marginal revenue curve* and a *long-run* marginal cost curve to determine optimal plant size and output. The behaviour of a rational entrepreneur in using short-run marginal revenue curve on the one hand and long-run marginal cost curve on the other is quite inconsistent. Harrod believes that the "consistent" entrepreneur will use the long-run marginal revenue curve with long-run marginal cost curve to determine his optimal output and size of the plant. Allowing for entry of other firms in the long run, the long-run marginal revenue curve (also the long.-run demand curve) is *more elastic* than the short-run marginal revenue curve. Consequently, the long-run marginal revenue curve will intersect the long-run marginal cost curve (long-run average revenue curve will be tangent to the long-run average cost curve) at a larger output than that shown to be determined by either Chamberlin or Joan Robinson and will be very close to the purely competitive output.

Furthermore, Harrod thinks that, in Chamberlin and Joan Robinson's analyses a firm is assumed to be very *short-sighted* in that it does not foresee the effect of its price policy on the entry of firms. He believes that firms behave in a far-sighted manner and take into account the likely effects of their price policy on entry of firms into industry. Chamberlin's model of monopolistic competition and Joan Robinson's theory of imperfect competition assume that the entrepreneur is highly rational, but extremely short-sighted. Harrod sarcastically remarks that Chamberlin and Joan Robinson's theories virtually say that "apparently, it is impossible to be an entrepreneur and not suffer from schizophrenia"[9] A far-sighted rational firm, according

7. *Ibid.*, p. 109.
8. *Ibid.* p. 109 (italics added).
9. R. F. Harrod. *op. cit.*

to him, would set a lower than short-run profit maximizing price to inhibit the entry of firms. Thus, a far-sighted firm would sacrifice the short-run profits to prevent the entry of firms. In fact, Harrod thinks that the rational and far-sighted firm will charge the price that will yield only normal profits even though short-run marginal revenue for that price and output is less than the short-run marginal cost. Harrod concludes the "imperfect competition does not usually tend to create excess capacity," Economists should therefore discard the "generally accepted doctrine to the contrary effect".[10]

Kaldor's Critique of the Theory of Excess Capacity

Professor Nicholas Kaldor, an eminent Cambrige economist, has also attacked the theory regarding the emergence of excess capacity under imperfect or monopolistic competition. Prof. Kaldor has selected Chamberlin's version of the creation of excess capacity in monopolistic competition. It may be noted at the outset that Kaldor does not absolutely deny the creation of excess capacity under monopolistic competition. But in his view the ***excess capacity which will arise in some circumstances will be very much less than that made out in Chamberlin's analysis.*** We have seen above that in Chamberlin's analysis, excess capacity arises when the new firms or entrepreneurs enter into industry or trade so that the demand curves facing firms are pushed to the position where 'they become tangential to the long-run average cost curve. In the absence of price competition, this results in the reduction of outputs of individual firms and rise in costs which represent excess capacity or waste of social resources.

According to Kaldor, it is because of the unrealistic assumptions made explicitly or implicitly by Chamberlin that high degree of excess capacity arises in monopolistic competition. If those particular assumptions are dropped, then Chamberlin's theory of the existence of a *large amount* of excess capacity breaks down. He thus says, "It would be most unfair therefore to criticise him on a point of logic since the logic of Prof. Chamberlin's analysis is indeed excellent. What he does not seem to be aware of is the degree of unreality involved in his initial assumption and the extent to which his main conclusions are dependent on those assumptions."[11]

1. First, it is assumed that there are a large number of producers or firms producing differentiated products which are close substitutes of each other. It follows from this that the demand curve for his product is downward sloping and that the cross elasticities of demand between the different producers' products is very large but not infinite.

2. Secondly, it is assumed in the theory that "consumers' ***preferences are fairly evenly distributed among the differentiated varieties."*** In view of this and further because of the fact that there are a large number of firms, the effect of variation in price or product by one firm is spread so thinly over a large number of its competitors that the impact felt by each of them is very negligible so that it does not lead to any readjustment or reaction from competitors. It is because of this assumption that prices of all the competitive firms are taken as given and the demand curve for a given firm is drawn up.

3. Thirdly, according to Kaldor, it is assumed in the monopolistic competition theory that no firm possesses an "institutional monopoly" over any of the product varieties and therefore the entry of new firms into the given group or industries is completely free.

4. Fourthly, the long-run cost curves of all firms are assumed to be falling up to a certain point, which implies ***that firms enjoy economies of scale up to a certain output.***

Given the above assumptions, Kaldor concludes that the excess capacity will arise in monopolistic competition in the long run as a result of the entry of new firms. If the firms are making supernormal profits in the short run, new firms will enter into the field and produce

10. *Ibid.*

close substitutes. As a result, the demand for the existing firms will be reduced, that is, the demand curves for their products will be pushed to the left. The process of entry of new firms will continue until the demand curve is driven to the position of being tangential to the average cost curve and thus profits are eliminated. This will mean equilibrium with excess capacity. "The effect of the entry of new competitors will not necessarily reduce the price of existing products, it may even raise them. The profits which the entrepreneur no longer earns will thus not be passed on to the consumer in the form of lower prices but are mainly absorbed in lower productive efficiency.[11] Therefore, Kaldor thinks that "There can be little doubt that, given these assumptions, the theory is unassailable. Any criticism therefore must be directed against the usefulness and the consistency of the assumptions selected."[12]

Kaldor admits that first assumption is justified but has challenged the other.three assumptions. He points out that cross elasticity of demand for a product of a firm is not of the same order of magnitude with respect to the prices of all products of competitors in the group (or industry). According to him, we cannot say that any variation in price or product by a single firm will spread its influence *evenly* over all his competitors. To quote him, "The different producers' products will never possess the same degree of substitutability in relation to any particular product. Any particular producer will always be faced with rivals who are near to him and others who are farther off. In fact, he should be able to class his rivals, *from his own point of view,* in a certain order according to the influence of their prices upon his own demand (which will not necessarily be of the same order as that applying to any particular rival of his)". Thus, according to Kaldor, the sellers or firms in monopolistic competition "cannot be grouped together in a lump but can at best be placed into a series. Each 'product' can be conceived as occupying a certain position on a 'scale' ; the scale being so constructed that those products are neighboring each other between which consumers' elasticity of substitution is the greatest.... Each producer then is faced on each side with his nearest rivals ; the demand for his own product will be most sensitive with respect to the prices of those ; less and less sensitive as one moves further away from him".[13]

The sum and substance of Kaldor's arguments is that even when the number of firms is very large as is the case under monopolistic competition, it *cannot* be assumed with good justification that the effect of variation *in price or product by a single producer* will spread itself *evenly* over a large number of his rivals and will be negligible for each of them individually so that they would not react in retaliation. In this way, Prof. Kaldor argues that rival producers' prices and products cannot be assumed as given and therefore the demand curve for a producer under monopolistic competition cannot be drawn up at all. Thus, demand curve for a single producer under monopolistic competition, like that under oligopoly or duopoly, is *indeterminate,* because it depends upon the large number of possible counter moves which his rivals may make in reaction to the former's price or product variation. Now, when the producer does not know the real demand curve facing him, the question that in the long run his demand curve will become tangential to average cost curve and consequently he will be in equilibrium with excess capacity does not arise.

Secondly, Kaldor points out that a producer while framing his price policy will not only take into consideration the existing competitors' reactions to his own actions but also the ***potential competition from new products,*** *i.e.,* the products of new or prospective entrants. A new product, he argues, must be placed in between certain two existing products. Thus, a new product will considerably affect the demand of his nearest 'neighbour's. In view of this

11. N. Kaldor, Imperfect Competition and Excess Capacity. *Readings in Price Theory (AEA).*
12. *Ibid, p. 388.*
13. *Ibid.,* p. 390.

potential competition, aproducer under monopolistic competition will act in *a farsighted manner* and charge a low price for his product and earn ordinary profits. This farsighted price policy will inhibit the entry of new competitors and as a result the producer will not be driven to the position of tangency with the average cost curve or, in other words, will not be driven to the state of excess capacity. "If a producer knows that if he charges a higher price today a competitor will appear tomorrow whose mere existence will put him in *a permanently worse position,* he will charge a price which will afford him only low profit, if only *he hopes to secure this profit permanently* ... And this 'foresight' will or at any rate may prevent him from being driven to a state of excess capacity".

Thirdly, Kaldor is of the view that if economies of scale are completely absent, the theory of excess capacity breaks down. We know that according to Kaldor economies of scale are absent if all productive factors are perfectly divisible. When there are no economies and dis-economies of scale, the long-run average cost will be a horizontal straight line and the long-run marginal cost curve will coincide with it. Now, when all factors are perfectly divisible, and hence the economies of scale completely absent, perfect competition must necessarily establish itself as a result of the free play of economic forces, product differentiation notwithstanding. With perfect competition, the demand curve is perfectly elastic or horizontal. Therefore, with horizontal cost as well as demand curves, there can be no question of the establishment of equilibrium with excess capacity. Now, the question arises as to how the perfect competition will establish itself when all economies of scale are completely absent. This is because when economies of scale are absent, that is, the long-run cost curves are horizontal, the profits will never be wiped out completely so long as elasticity of demand is less than infinite. When the new producers enter the field, the output of the individual firms will be reduced and the elasticities of their demand curves will increase, but in the case of horizontal average cost curve there will always be possibilities of making profits by the producers until the demand curve also becomes horizontal. But the demand curve becoming horizontal means the establishment of perfect competition. Thus, says Kaldor, "the inflow of new producers will continue, leading to a continuous reduction in the output of existing producers and a continuous increase in the elasticities of their demand until latter becomes infinite and will equal 'average costs'. There the movements will stop. ***But each 'firm' will have reduced its output to such an extent that it competely lost his hold over the market".***

If economies of scale exist due to the presence of indivisibilities, even then, according to Kaldor, excess capacity may not be created. This is because he thinks that when economies of scale exist, potential competition will never succeed in making the individual demand and cost curves tangential. In the presence of economies of scale, the entry of new firms into the field will stop much before the elasticity of demand becomes infinite. This is due to the increase in costs of the firms as the outputs of individual firms are reduced by the entry of new firms. But, Kaldor argues, "there is no reason to assume *that it will stop precisely at the point where the demand and cost curves are tangential.*"

Further, when the economies of scale are present, the new firms cannot enter the field with the expectation of making profits unless they set up sufficiently large-sized plant so as to avail of the economies of scale. But with their entry, the demand for every firm, especially his nearest neighbours and their own, will be reduced. With entry the demand may be reduced to such an extent that demand curves are pushed below the average cost curves and all are gone into losses. This fear of losses will prevent the entry of new firms. With this barrier to the entry, the demand curved of the existing firms will lie above the tangency with the average cost curve and will therefore be making profits, in which case they may not be working with much excess capacity. Thus, Prof. Kaldor concludes that ***"The same reason therefore which prevents***

competition from becoming 'perfect', i.e., indivisibilities will also prevent the complete elimination of profits". [14]

In the fourth place, Kaldor has criticised Chamberlin's excess capacity theory on the ground that *it assumes the absence of institutional monopoly.* Absence of institutional monopoly is implied in Chamberlin's analysis since he assumes that cost curves of all firms are identical. If the cost curves of different firms are different, it means low cost firms possess something which others do not possess. Thus differences in costs imply the presence of institutional monopolies. Such "institutional monopolies", according to Kaldor, "may consist of patents, copyrights, trade marks, or even a trade name. They may be conferred by law, by ownership, or merely by the will of the public".[14] He further elaborates, "Anything therefore which imposes higher costs on one producer than another whether it is the possession of unique resources by one entrepreneur or whether it is merely due to 'buyers' inertia' imposing a special 'cost of entry' on new producers implies to that extent the presence of 'institutional monopoly' ."[15] In fact, a large part of market imperfection in Chamberlin's monopolistic competition is due to the presence of institutional monopolies.

Now, the existence of these institutional monopolies can work both ways with regard to the generation of excess capacity. If the scales of differentiation of consumers between products of various producers remain constant, "institutional monopoly to the extent to which it is present will prevent the generation of excess capacity, since to that extent profits earned by one producer cannot be competed away by another producer."[16] But the presence of institutional monopoly, according to Kaldor, can work in the opposite direction also, namely, towards creating the excess capacity. This is because institutional monopoly by increasing the degree of imperfect competition reduces the elasticity of demand for the products of individual producers which tends to increase the excess capacity. Thus .Kaldor says, "Many types of institutional monopolies, however, by themselves increase the degree of market imperfect competition and to that extent are favourable to the generation of excess capacityi"[17] The net effect of these two opposing tendencies due to the existence of institutional monopolies may cancel out or may on balance either reduce or increase the excess capacity.

Lastly, Kaldor mentions another abstract assumption on which Chamberlin's theory of "excess capacity" is based, namely, that each producer produces only a *"single product".* It has been pointed out by the critics of Chamberlin that in reality many producers produce not one but a number of products together. It is said that if sufficiently large demand for one product does not exist (as happens when new firms enter the industry under monopolistic competition and consequently the demand for each producer is reduced) and therefore excess capacity arises, then the producers can take up the production of some other products also along with the first product and thereby can utilize the capacity fully. Thus we see that firms by diversifying their production, *i. e.,* by producing a number of products jointly can prevent the emergence of excess capacity. And, according to these critics, in the real world they do so.

But, in the opinion of Kaldor, the above argument concerning the avoidance of excess capacity by diversifying the production is not strictly accurate. In his view, whether or not increased competition due to the entry of new firms will bring about excess capacity, or rise in costs, depends upon "the nature of the cost-functions of the jointly produced products." He points out that in most cases, indivisible factors are not completely unspecialised 'spreading of production'[18] is always attended with some cost; *i.e.,* the physical productivity of a given

14. *Ibid.*, p. 394.
15. *Ibid.*, p. 396.
16. Ibid., p. 397.
17. *Ibid.* p. 397.

quantity of resources calculated in terms of any of the products will always be less, the greater the number of separate commodities they are required simultaneously to produce. That this is the case for a large proportion of jointly produced commodities is shown by the fact that the development of an 'industry' is always attended by 'specialisation' or 'disintegration', *i.e.*, the reduction of the number of commodities produced by single firms."[19]

Kaldor argues that if cost functions of jointly produced commodities are of the above nature, the increased competition not only by new firms but also by production of multiple products by the existing firms in reaction to the production of more than one product by some firms, the demand curve for each single product would become very much more elastic on account of the fact that each producer will be producing a very much smaller share of *each product* and the costs of production for each product will rise greatly due to the reason stated just above. As a result of such increased competition, the profits of producers would be eliminated, but costs of production will rise due to diversification of output by the producers. In such a situation, there will not exist much excess capacity in the sense in which Chamberlin and Joan Robinson use the term (namely, increase in output by firms would reduce cost per unit) since they will be utilising capacity by diversifying production, but there will be lot of *technical wastage and consequently higher costs* because "the physical productivity of resources will be less than it would be if each producer produced a smaller number of products and a large proportion of the total output of each."[21]

In conclusion, it may be noted that Kaldor criticizes the excess capacity theory in its rigid form, namely, the demand curves (or average revenue curves) would become tangential to the average cost curves as a result of the entry of new firms and the increased competition from them. He believes that there is likelihood of some excess capacity being created under imperfect competition, even if profits will not be completely wiped out. Of course, he is of the view that excess capacity so created would be of much smaller magnitude than that made out by Chamberlin and others of his way of thinking. To quote him, "there is a presumption that some degree of excess capacity will be generated even if profits will not be completely competed away : since 'indivisibilities by themselves will not offer a strong enough shield to prevent some rise in costs as a consequence of the intrusion of new competitors. ***Many of the objections therefor which can be brought against the theory if put forward in its rigid form (that demand curves will tend to become 'tangential' with the cost curves) do not affect the fundamental proposition that the*** effect of the competition of 'new entrants' and consequent reduction of the level of profits earned may take the form of a rise in costs rather than a reduction of prices."[22]

In case the economies of scale exist which prevent the competition from becoming perfect, then "the extent to which 'excess capacity' may be generated as a result of free competition .... will depend; *(i)* on the degree of shortsighted or farsightedness of producers (how far they take potential competition into account in deciding upon their price and product policy), *(ii)* the extent to which institutional monopolies are present .... *(iii)* the extent to which the various 'cross elasticities' of demand differ in order of magnitude."[23]

18. *Ibid.*, p. 397.
19. "Spreading of production" means producing a number of products jointly.
20. *Ibid.*, p. 402.
21. *Ibid.*, p. 402. ;
22. *Op. cit.*, p. 398 (italics added).
23. *Ibid.*, pp. 398-99.

Conclusion

The question of excess capacity under monopolistic competition has been widely discussed and besides Harrod and Kaldor, whose ideas have been explained above, other economists[24] have also participated in the debate over the excess capacity doctrine. These other economists have reached still different conclusions about excess capacity. As a matter of fact, the conclusions of various authors differ because each author introduces somewhat different assumptions to supplement those made by Chamberlin. It is only by further assumptions such as the producers are able to foresee the effects of his policies on the entry of potential competitors that Harrod and Kaldor arrived at different conclusions about excess capacity than Chamberlin. The other authors have arrived at still different conclusions by further modifying Chamberlin's assumptions. Therefore, the present author agrees with Professors K. J. Cohen and R. M. Cyert that "Harrod, Kaldor and other critics of the excess capacity theory really are developing their own models of imperfect competition rather than analysing the properties of Chamberlin's model."[25]

---

24. Special mention may be made of H. R. Edwards, "Price Formation in Manufacturing Industry and Excess Capacity", *Oxford Economic Papers, New* Series, 7. No. 1 (February, 1955), pp. 94-118 ; F. H. Hahn, Excess Capacity and Imperfect Competition. *Ibid.* 1 No. 3 (October 1955). pp. 229-40 : Paul Streeten, "Two Comments on the Articles by Mrs. Paul and Professor Hicks." *Ibid.* 259-64 and H.F. Lydall, "Conditions of New Entry and the Theory of Price", *Ibid.*, pp. 300-11.

25. K. J. Cohen and K. M. Cyert, *Theory of the Firm, Resource Allocation in a Market Economy* (1965), p. 226.

CHAPTER

39

Chamberlin's Monopolistic Competition Vs. Joan Robinson's Imperfect Competition Theories

Introduction

We saw in previous chapters that E. H. Chamberlin and Joan Robinson brought about a revolution in microeconomic theory by breaking with the perfect competition theory which dominated the economic scene till then. The two important works dealing with non-perfect competition, that is, *"Monopolistic Competition Theory"* by Mr. Chamberlin and *"The Economics of Imperfect Competition"* by Joan Robinson were independently written but were published in the same year (1933). For some time after the publication of these two theories, they were considered to be similar. In fact, many economists regarded 'monopolistic competition' and 'imperfect competition' as merely two different names for the same thing. But Chamberlin, from the very beginning, has been asserting and proving that his theory of monopolistic competition is quite different and dissimilar from Joan Robinson's theory of imperfect competition. The difference between the two theories, says Chamberlin, is not of mere terminology. He claims that there exists a fundamental difference in the conception of the problem and the treatment of various aspects of it.

Kaldor has dubbed Chamberlin to have fallen a victim to the general tendency among producers under monopolistic competition-a tendency which he so convincingly brings out-and accordingly ***"is trying to differentiate his product too far.."*** What Kaldor means is that there is not much difference between Chamberlin's theory of monopolistic competition and Joan Robinson's theory of imperfect competition and that Chamberlin is unnecessarily differentiating his theory. But now most economists have veered round to the view that the two theories are different in some important respects and further that Chamberlin's theory is more realistic description of economic phenomenon. Thus Samuelson remarks : **"With cogency and pertinacity, Chamberlin has always insisted on differentiating his product from that of Mrs. Robinson. *Posterity will agree.*"**[2] We discuss below in detail the differences between the two theories as claimed by Chamberlin.

Chamberlin Views Real-World Market Situations as Blend of Competition and Monopoly

The fundamental difference between the two theories is the difference in conception of the problem. Chamberlin regards most economic situations as composites of both competition and monopoly and explains price determination in the case where both competitive and monopolistic elements are present. The traditional .viewpoint, which held the stage before

1. Nicholas Kaldor, *Monopolistic and Imperfect Competition,* published in *'Essays on Values and Distribution'by him.*
2. Paul A. Samuelson : 'The Monopolistic Competition Revolution' printed in *Monopolistic Competition Theory: Studies in Impact* (Essays in Honour of Edward H. Chamberlin) edited by Robert E. Kuanne.

Chamberlin's theory was that monopoly and competition were mutually exclusive categories and thus the industries were classified as either perfectly competitive or monopolistic. Since in the traditional viewpoint monopoly and competition were regarded as mutually exclusive alternatives, elements of monopoly and competition were never visualised to be present together in any situation or industry. On the other hand, Chamberlin's monopolistic competition is the concept of a blending of competition and monopoly. Since most of the real-world market relations blend competitive with monopolistic traits, Chamberlin's theory is a more realistic description of the economic phenomenon.

Chemberlin rightly claims : "Monopolistic Competition is a challenge to the traditional viewpoint of economics that competition and monopoly are alternatives and that individual prices are to be explained in terms of either the one or the other. By contrast, it is held that most economic situations are composites of both competition and monopoly, and that, wherever this is the case, a false view is given by neglecting either'one of the two forces and regarding the situation as made up entirely (even though "imperfectly") of the other."[3] Thus, Chamberlin presents a new way of looking at the economic system. ***By considering real-world economic situations as blending of competition and monopoly and basing his theory of value on it, he made a revolutionary break with the past.*** Both competitive and monopolistic elements are present in the actual-world market situations because of the existence of product differentiation. Every seller is a *monopolist* of his own particular variety of the product, but at the same time he faces a *competition* from other varieties of the product which are close substitutes of his product variety. This product differentiation is the corner-stone of Chamberlin's theory of monopolistic competition.

This concept of blending of competition and monopoly is absent in Joan Robinson's *Imperfect Competition.* Chamberlin asserts and shows that Joan Robinson thinks of monopoly (in its ordinary sense) and competition as mutually exclusive alternatives. Chamberlin has produced evidences in support of his view that Robinson in her *'Economics of Imperfect Competition'* and later articles continues to regard competition and monopoly as mutually exclusive as it was held in the traditional economic thought. Chamberlin points out, for instance, that Robinson in her 'imperfect competition' considers the possibility of arranging "actual cases in a series of which pure monopoly would be the limit at one end and pure competition at the other" but rejects this as "involving insuperable diffi-culties". But it is in the intermediate cases between the two extreme limits of pure monopoly on the one hand and perfect competition on the other that both the elements of monopoly and competition are present in varying degrees. By not attempting to make gradations in between the two extreme limits, Robinson misses the opportunity of considering imperfectly competitive markets as involving elements of both monopoly and competition.

On the other hand, Chamberlin in his work *"Theory of Monopolistic Competition"* arranges the intermediate cases lying between the two extremes and views them as containing elements of both competition and monopoly in varying degrees. He thus writes : "Speaking more generally, if we regard monopoly as the antithesis of competition, its extreme limit is reached only in the case of control of the supply of all economic goods, which might be called a case of pure monopoly in the sense that all competition of substitutes is excluded by definition. At the other extreme is pure competition, where large classes of goods being perfectly standardized, every seller faces a competition of substitutes for his own product which is perfect. ***Between the two extremes there are all gradations, but both elements are always present, and must always 'be recognized. To discard either competition or monopoly is to falsify the result.'***"[4]

3. Edward H. Chamberlin, *Theory of Monopolistic Competition*, 6th edition, p. 204.
4. Edward H. Chamberlin, *op. cit.*, p. 63 (italics supplied).

Joan Robinson could not view most of the actual market relations as blend of competition and monopoly because of her inability to define commodity and monopoly in a correct and proper manner. She defines commodity with reference not to *a firm* but to an *industry* and her system is classification not of inter-firm relationship but of industries, each in every case producing a separate commodity and commodity of every industry is "homogeneous within itself." She could not therefore consider the differentiated commodities in an industry which serve as close substitutes and compete with one an other in the market. Because of this, monopoly arising out of differentiated commodity or product, as Chamberlin explains, was omitted by Joan Robinson. Her 'imperfectly competitive' industry produces a commodity which is 'homogeneous within itself.

Moreover, her concept of monopoly is quite strange. She uses two concepts of monopoly in her book which confuses the whole matter. Monopoly, according to her, merely refers to an individual seller or producer. She thus says : "Every individual producer has the monopoly of his own product that is sufficiently obvious and if a large number of them are selling in a perfect market the state of affairs exists which we are accustomed to describe as perfect competition."[5] On this definition, the individual seller, even under perfect competition, is a monopolist. What a strange definition of monopoly ? But she does not restrict herself to this definition alone. In Book IV, "The Comparison of Monopoly and Competitive Output", of her book, she describes monopoly in the conventional or traditional ***sense as the control over output of an industry by a single authority.***[6] Of course, she is aware that this latter definition is inconsistent with her logical conception of monopoly, as defined by her earlier. But the use of the two different concepts of monopoly makes her analysis confused.

It should be pointed out here that in the later usual concept of monopoly, Robinson considers monopoly to be *industry concept,* as it has always been till Chamberlin's analysis. Thus, according to her analysis, industries may be classified either monopolistic or competitive, and if the latter, either perfectly or imperfectly. It is therefore clear that in Robinson's analysis dichotomy between monopoly (in the usual sense) and competition appears to be as distinct as it is there in Pigou, Marshall, Taussing, or John Stuart Mill. Chamberlin says even the expression 'Imperfect Competition,' which is a purely negative one, shows that Robinson does not consider competition and monopoly as overlapping in real-world economic situations and therefore makes minimum interference with the traditional viewpoint of competition and monopoly being mutually exclusive alternatives. Chamberlin claims that his own expression "Monopolistic Competition" is better since it highlights the fact that most of the real-world economic situations contain both competitive and monopolistic elements. Thus he asserts " "The greater generality of monopolistic competition in picturing a continuum between the extremes of pure competition and pure monopoly although often credited to the two of us jointly simply does not exist in Mrs. Robinson's Imperfect Competition."[7]

Chamberlin Lays Stress on Product Differentiation

Another sharp contrast between the two theories is that while product differentiation is the corner-stone of Chamberlin's theory it does not find a significant place in Joan Robinson's theory of imperfect competition. It is due to product differentiation that monopoly element is present in monopolistic competition. That the various firms in most of the economic situations produce different products which are close substitutes of each other is a significant contribution

5. Joan Robinson, *The Economics of Imperfect Competition,* p. 5.
6. *Op. cit.,* p. 209.
7. Edward H. Chamberlin, *Towards a More General Theory of Value,* p. 29.

made by Chamberlin which has produced a great impact on microeconomic theory. On the other hand, Joan Robinson in her earlier reaction to Chamberlin's theory rejected the concept of product differentiation within an industry. Although Robinson in her *"Economics of Imperfect Competition"* speaks of preferences of buyers for the different sellers of an imperfectly competitive market, but her actual assumption of product homogeneity in her imperfect competition indicates that she considered the differences within any particular "commodity" of having little significance.

Joan Robinson in her *"Economics of Imperfect Competition"* does list the reasons which make different buyers prefer the good of one producer to those of another and therefore make the market imperfect. She thus points out that cost of transport, differences in quality of output of different producers, the differences in the facilities provided by different producers (such as quickness of service, good manners of salesmen, length of credit and attention paid to their individual wants), differences in prices, and influence exercised by advertisement are causes of imperfect competition. In spite of mentioning all these reasons as to why a buyer prefers one producer's product to another, she regards an imperfectly competitive industry producing a commodity which is for all practical purposes 'homogeneous within itself.'

Of course, she admits that the differences in the products of different firms due to which a customer buys from one producer rather than another makes it difficult to decide what precisely we mean by a *commodity*. But she leaves the matter here and does not give any more significance to the differences in the products of different firms constituting an imperfectly competitive industry and considers an imperfectly competitive industry producing a sufficiently homogeneous commodity. In fact, she entangled herself in defining and identifying "a commodity" of which she could not furnish a proper definition. Chamberlin's treatment in this regard is better ; he considers the output of every firm under monopolistic competition as constituting one product or commodity and the different firms under monopolistic competition produce different products or commodities which are close substitutes of each other. This difference in products or commodities or what he calls product differentiation, is the heart of Chamberlin's theory.

Chamberlin's Penetrating Analysis of Non-Price Competition, that is, Product Variation and Selling Costs

Another important difference between the two theories is that while in Chamberlin's theory of monopolistic competition, product variation and selling costs, which are two important forms of non-price competition, play an eminent role; in Robinson's imperfect competition, on the other hand, they do not play any part. It may be pointed out that Robinson recognizes in her imperfect competition theory that rival producers compete against each other in quality of the product, in advertisement, apart from changing the price, but she does not incorporate them in her theoretical analysis because she considers them to be difficult to do so. She thus says in the footnote on page 90 of her book, "The existence of competition which takes the form of providing facilities to the customer of improving the quality of goods, or advertisement, or any other form than a simple lowering of price is ***awkward from the point of view of theoretical analysis***'[8]

Robinson thus takes into account only price competition. A demand curve envisages only price competition, and it is the "downward sloping demand curve" with its separate and downward sloping marginal revenue curve that occupies a foremost position in her theory. In fact, as said earlier in this chapter, Mrs. Robinson defines imperfect competition in terms of the demand curve, namely, that imperfect competition is said to prevail when the demand

8. *Op. cit.*, p. 90 (italics supplied).

curve facing individual firms is downward sloping or less than perfectly elastic. By giving foremost place to the downward sloping demand curve in her imperfect competition she takes into account only price competition in her theoretical framework. Accordingly, Robinson does not explain the firm's equilibrium in regard to product adjustment and in regard to the amount of advertisement expenditure or selling costs it should incur.

On the other hand, an important contribution made by Chamberlin is that he assigns paramount place to the product variation and selling costs in his theoretical analysis. He accordingly discusses firm's equilibrium in regard to three variables–price, product and selling costs. Indeed, he points out that when competition is imperfect, the rival producers compete against each other more by varying the product and altering the magnitude of selling costs than by changing prices. The greater emphasis on the product variation and selling costs is a significant contribution made by Chamberlin to the price theory and in doing so he succeeded in reorienting the price theory and bringing it nearer to the real world.

By stressing on and incorporating only price competition in her theoretical framework, Robinson could not make a break with the past. She ignored the selling costs or advertisement expenditures in her discussion of firms' equilrbrium because they introduced complications into the 'all important' demand curve. Moreover, she points out that advertising expenditure can be treated like a price reduction from the viewpoint of the entrepreneur and thus she does not feel it necessary to introduce selling costs explicitly into her theoretical analysis and therefore fails to treat the selling costs as a separate variable. She thus says in her book : "Complications are introduced into the problem of the individual demand curve by the existence of advertising, but these have been ignored. It may be assumed that expenditure on advertisement necessary to increase the sales of firm can be treated as equivalent, from the point of view of the entrepreneur, to a reduction in price having the same effect upon sales."[9]

Furthermore, Robinson could not also pay much attention to the product adjustment by the firm because, as said above, she envisaged an imperfectly non-competitive industry with a sufficiently homogeneous commodity. It is thus clear that Chamberlin's emphasis on the product variation and selling costs and his treatment of them as separate variables in respect of which a firm has to make adjustment in order to be in equilibrium position makes an improvement over Robinson analysis. It should also be noted that Chamberlin's concept of monopolistic competition cannot be defined in terms of the demand curve or demand elasticity because to do so will narrow it down, like imperfect competition, to the price variable.

Analysis of Oligopoly Problem Neglected in Robinson's Imperfect Competition Theory

Another fundamental difference between the two authors is that whereas Robinson neglected the discussion of oligopoly problem which is crucial in the theory of imperfect competition, Chamberlin discussed oligopoly problem in detail and provided its own solution of it. The reason why she omitted oligopoly in her discussion of imperfect competition is again her preoccupation with the demand curve. The oligopoly problem presents a certain difficulty in the way of defining and analysing the demand curve and was therefore omitted by Robinson. As she herself says in a later article: "The reason oligopoly is neglected in *Economics of Imperfect Competition* is not that I thought it unimportant but that I could not solve it. I tried to fence it off by means of what unfortunately was a fudge in the definition of individual demand curve".[10]

9. *Op. dr.*, p. 21.
10. *Economics of Imperfect Competition Revisited.*

In fact, as pointed out by Chamberlin, imperfect competition defined as less than perfect demand elasticity, as is done by Robinspn, could not logically include more than a certain limited phases of oligopoly theory. In line with her definition of perfect and imperfect competitions, Joan Robinson tried to conceive the oligopoly problem in terms of demand elasticity. But the oligopoly cannot be defined in terms of demand elasticity. Under certain assumptions demand curve under oligopoly is perfectly elastic, as is the cause under perfect competition, while under other assumptions demand curve may be quite inelastic under oligopoly. Moreover, as Chamberlin rightly emphasizes, "different types of definitions of demand curves are required for different parts of the oligopoly problem ; and under certain assumptions demand curve simply cannot be drawn at all...... my own definitions were not in terms of elasticity, and in particular the oligopoly problem by its very nature defies definition in such terms."[11]

Thus omission of the treatment of oligopoly problem in Joan Robinson's *Economics of Imperfect Competition* is a serious lacuna, since the oligopoly is the predominant form of market in the real world. Chamberlin by devoting a good part of his book to the discussion of oligopoly problem showed awareness of the importance of oligopoly problem for understanding the behaviour of the business firms in the real world. Though oligopoly problem is still an unsettled question, Chamberlin's analysis made an improvement over the previous treatment of oligopoly problem and threw many valuable lights on the various aspects of it. Economists began to understand the oligopoly problem better after Chamberlin's analysis. Especially, his introduction of product differentiation into the oligopoly problem and his *"mutual dependence recognised"* of oligopoly made a genuine departure from the traditional analysis.

According to Chamberlin, Perfect Competition Cannot be regarded as Welfare Ideal

Another important difference between the two economists is while Joan Robinson considers perfect or pure competition to be 'ideal' from the viewpoint of economic welfare, Chamberlin does not think so. Chamberlin thus remarks: ***"The explicit recognition that product is differentiated brings into the open the problem of variety and makes it clear that pure competition may no longer be regarded as in any sense an 'ideal' for purposes of welfare economics."***[12] Pure or perfect competition can represent a 'welfare ideal' only under the assumptions *(a)* that products are homogeneous and *(b)* that people want homogeneous products in the sense that their demand for variety is unimportant or irrational and hence may be ignored. Both these assumptions are involved in Joan Robinson analysis (the first, is explicit and the second is implicit in her analysis). Chamberlin points out that products cannot be fully homogeneous in actual world, and further that people's liking and demand for variety is important and worth paying attention to and its fulfillment must be considered as promoting welfare. Even if perfect competition is regarded as a welfare ideal it will not be possible to achieve it because of the impossibility of having complete homogeneity of products. As Chamberlin says, "Retail shops, for example, could not all be located on the same spot, and personal differences between actors, singers, professional men, and businessmen could not be eliminated."[13]

Chamberlin further argues that even if it were possible to have complete homogeneity, or standardization of products'it will not be desirable from the point of view of welfare to standardize products beyond a certain point. "Differences in tastes, desires, incomes, and locations of buyers, and differences in the uses which they wish to make of commodities all indicate the need for variety."[14] This need for variety, according to Chamberlin, necessitates

11. E. H. Chamberlin, *Towards a More General Theory of Value.*
12. E. H. Chamberlin, *Theory of Monopolistic Competition*, p. 214.
13. *Ibid.*, p. 214. 3 *Ibid.* p. 214.

the substitution of the concept of a "competitive ideal' by an ideal involving both monopoly and competition. Therefore, in view of the product differentiation and the combination of monopoly and competitive elements in the actual markets, the relevant question is how much and what kinds of monopoly and what measure of social control will ensure 'welfare ideal'.

Furthermore, besides the ideal or optimum adjustment of price and output for the achievement of maximum welfare which is considered by conventional welfare theory, Chamberlin emphasizes that ***ideal adjustment of products and of selling outlays must also be explicity recognized as a pan of the welfare optimum.*** But since Joan Robinson does not pay much attention to product variation and selling outlays in her analysis of imperfect competition, the ideal adjustment of these two elements does not form a part of her welfare optimum.

It is clear from above that there is a sharp divergence between Chamberlin and Joan Robinson's concepts of welfare ideal.

Differences Regarding the Concept of Exploitation of Labour

The final important difference between the two theories is in respect of the exploitation of labour. Joan Robinson defines 'exploitation' as a wage less than the marginal physical product of labour valued at its selling price. In other words, according to Joan Robinson labour is exploited when it is paid a wage less than the *value of its marginal product (VMP).* She proves that under imperfect competition in the product market, labour inevitably gets less than the value of its marginal product, since it is paid according to marginal product multiplied by marginal revenue, that is, *marginal revenue product* or *MRP which* is less than the marginal product multiplied by the price. Since it is imperfect competition which generally prevails in the real world, labour is generally exploited by the entrepreneur. The entrepreneur, according to Joan Robinson, gets more than the value of his marginal product (that is, more than the marginal physical product multiplied by the price) and is thus the exploiter.

Now, according to Chamberlin, the payment of wage less than the value of the marginal product under imperfect or monopolistic competition does not indicate exploitation and therefore there is neither the exploiter nor exploited. According to Chamberlin, not only labour but all factors under monopolistic competition receive less than the value of their marginal physical products. This is because argument which is applicable to labour applies equally to all factors. Chamberlin argues that if under monopolistic competition all factors are paid rewards equal to the value of their marginal physical products *(VMP),* then the total incomes of all factors composing any firm will add up to more than the total revenue of the firm. How can then it be possible for the firm to pay the factor rewards equal to the value of their marginal products. Therefore, according to Chamberlin, the fact that some factors receive less than the value of marginal product does not mean that some other one will be receiving more than the value of the marginal product. As a matter of fact, ***under monopolistic competition all factors (including entrepreneur) get rewards according to a different principle, namely, according to the marginal revenue product (MRP)*** which is less than the value of marginal product. Thus no exploitation is indicated.

Joan Robinson, on the other hand, holds that all factors except entrepreneur receive rewards equal to marginal revenue product (that is, less than the value of marginal product). It is the entrepreneur in her theory that obtains income in excess of the value of his marginal product and is thus the exploiter of labour, Joan Robinson's conclusion about the exploitation of labour by the entrepreneur rests on the assumption that entrepreneur is an indivisible

14. *Ibid.* p. 214.

factor, one for each firm. Because entrepreneur is one and indivisible in a firm, according to Joan Robinson, "the marginal product of the entrepreneur to the firm has no meaning". Therefore, she takes into account the marginal product of the entrepreneur to an 'industry', in which case the marginal product of the entrepreneur can be found out by changing the number of firms. Under imperfect competition, the entrepreneur receives income in excess of the value of his ***marginal product to an 'industry'*** because if the entrepreneur employed in one firm is withdrawn and the other productive factors employed in this firm are distributed among other firms in the industry so that the number of firms in the industry is reduced by one, then the economies flowing from a larger output in each of the remaining firms in the industry would to an extent offset the loss of output due to reduction in the number of firms (or entrepreneurs) by one and thus diminish the loss of output.

Chamberlin challenges the above argument. The above reasoning, remarks Chamberlin, "applies not merely to entrepreneurship, but with equal force to any of the other factors. Any factor could be shown to have an excess of income over the value of its marginal product to the industry if, at the same time that a small quantity of it were removed, the resulting loss of product were offset, by reorganizing the remaining resources in the industry (including entrepreneurial ability) on a "more efficient" basis through increasing the degree of standardization of the product and reducing the number of firms". With respect to entrepreneurs, he says, "the argument no longer stands if we drop the assumption that varying entrepreneurs and varying firms are one and the same thing, and recognize, that in modern economic society, "entrepreneurship" seems to be as highly divisible and capable of being redistributed as any factor .... It would seem that, if entrepreneurship is taken to be divisible, there is no one left to assume the onus of 'exploitation'. Indeed, the search for an exploiter appears as a misdirected effort arising out of the extension of a competitive criterion of exploitation into a field where it is rendered inappropriate by the presence of monopoly."[15]

15. E. H. Chamberlin, *Theory of Monopolistic Competition*, pp. 217-18.

CHAPTER

40

Price and Output Determination Under Oligopoly

Introduction

We have studied price and output determination under three market forms, namely, perfect competition, monopoly, and monopolistic competition. However, in the real world economies we find that many of the markets or industries are oligopolistic. Oligopoly is an important form of imperfect competition. Oligopoly is said to prevail when there are few firms or sellers in the market producing or selling a product. In other words, when there are two or more than two, but not many, producers or sellers of a product, oligopoly is said to exist. Oligopoly is also often referred to as ***"Competition among the Few". The simplest case of oligopoly is duopoly which prevails when there are only two producers or sellers of a product.*** Analysis of duopoly raises all those basic problems which are confronted while explaining oligopoly with more than two firms.

Although there is no borderline between few and many but when the number of sellers of a product are two to ten, oligopoly situation is said to exist. When products of a few sellers are homogeneous, we talk of ***Oligopoly without Product Differentiation or Pure Oligopoly.*** On the other hand, when products of the few sellers or firms, instead of being homogeneous, are differentiated but close substitutes of each other, ***Oligopoly with Product Differentiation or Differentiated Oligopoly*** is said to prevail.

CHARACTERISTICS OF OLIGOPOLY

In oligopoly some special characteristics are found which are not present in other market structures. We discuss some of these characteristics below:

Interdependence. The most important feature of oligopoly is the interdependence in decision-making of the few firms which comprise the industry. This is because when the number of competitors is few, any change in price, output, product design etc. by a firm will have a direct effect on the fortune of its rivals, which will then retaliate in changing their own prices, output or products as the case may be. It is, therefore, clear that the oligopolistic firm must consider not only the market demand for the industry's product but also the reactions of the other firms in the industry to any action or decision it may take. Since more than one reaction-pattern is possible from the other firms, we have to make some assumptions about the reaction of the others before we can provide a definite and determinate solution of price-output fixation under oligopoly.

Importance of Advertising and Selling Costs. A direct effect of interdependence of oligopolists is that the various firms have to employ various aggressive and defensive marketing weapons to gain a greater share in the market or to prevent a fall in their market share. For this various firms have to incur a good deal of costs on advertising and on other measures of sales promotion. Therefore, there is a great importance of advertising and selling costs under conditions of market situation characterised by oligopoly. Prof. Baumol rightly says that "it is only under oligopoly that advertising comes fully into its own."[1] Under perfect competition, advertising by an individual firm is unnecessary in view of the fact that it can sell any amount of its product at the going price. A monopolist has also not to make any competitive advertisement since he is the only seller of a product. A monopolist may, perhaps, advertise when he has to inform the public about his introduction of a new model of his product or he may advertise in order to attract potential consumers who have not yet tried his product. Under monopolistic competition, advertising plays an important role because of the product differentiation that exists under it, but not as much important as under oligopoly. "Under oligopoly, advertising can become a life-and-death matter where a firm which fails to keep up with the advertising budget of its competitors may find its customers drifting off to rival products."[2]

In view of the fact that a firm in an oligopolistic industry competes by changing the advertisement costs, quality of the product, prices, output etc., the presence of competitive conditions in it can hardly be denied. To an oligopolist "Competition can consist not in the quiescent stalemate of perfect competition where there is no battle because there is never anyone strong enough to disturb the peace. Rather to him, true competition consists of the life of constant struggle, rival against rival, which one can only find under oligopoly (or, on a smaller scale, under conditions of monopolistic competition)."[3]

Group Behaviour. Further, another important feature of oligopoly is that for the proper solution to the problem of determination of price and output under it, analysis of group behaviour is important. Theories of perfect competition, monopoly and monopolistic competition present no difficult problem of making suitable assumption about human behaviour. In cases of perfect competition and monopolistic competition (with a large number of firms), the economists assume that the business firms behave in such a way as to maximise their profits. Assumption of profit maximisation gives overall good results in these situations where mass of people are involved and there is no interdependence of firms. On the other end, the theory of monopoly deals with a sole individual and it is also appropriate to assume profit maximising behaviour on his part.

But, the theory of oligopoly is a theory of *group behaviour* not of mass or individual behaviour, and to assume profit-maximising behaviour on the part of a producer of a group may not be very valid. In oligopoly, there are a few firms in a group which are very much interdependent. Given the present state of our economic and social science, there is no generally accepted theory of group behaviour. Do the members of a group will cooperate with each other in promotion of common interests or will they fight to promote their individual interests? Does the group possess any leader? If so, how does he get the others to follow him? These are some of the questions that need to be answered by the theory of group behaviour.

Indeterminateness of Demand Curve Facing an Oligopolist. Another important feature is the indeterminateness of the demand curve facing an oligopolist. The demand curve shows what amounts of its product a firm will be able to sell at various prices. Now, under perfect competition, an individual firm's demand curve is given and definite. Since a perfectly competitive firm is one among a large number of firms producing an identical product, it is incapable of influencing the price of its product by its own individual action. Therefore, a firm under perfect competition faces a perfectly elastic demand curve at the level of the going price in the market.

1. William J. Baumol, *Economic Theory and Operations Analysis,* 3rd ed., p. 352.
2. *Ibid,* p. 352.
3. *Ibid,* p. 352

On the other hand, a monopolist produces a product which has only remote substitutes. Therefore, a monopolist can safely ignore the effects of its own price changes on his distant rivals and, therefore, the monopolist faces a given and definite demand curve depending upon the consumer's demand for his product. Under monopolistic competition, where there is a large number of firms producing products which are close substitutes of each other, changes in price by an individual firm will have a negligible effect on each of its many rivals. Therefore, a firm under monopolistic competition can validly assume the prices of its rivals to remain unchanged when it makes changes in the price of its product. Thus, the demand curve for a firm under monopolistic competition can be taken as definite and is given by the buyers' preferences for its product.

But the situation under oligopoly is quite different because of interdependence of the firms in it. Under oligopoly, a firm cannot assume that its rivals will keep their prices unchanged when it makes changes in its own price. As a result of this, the demand curve facing an oligopolistic firm loses its definiteness and determinateness because it goes on constantly shifting as the rivals change their prices in reaction to price changes by a firm.

CAUSES FOR THE EXISTENCE OF OLIGOPOLIES

Oligopolies dominate in many industries in the free market economies. Some of the factors responsible for the existence of oligopolies are natural in the sense that they are based on underlying production technologies and demand conditions for the products and some are created by the firms themselves. We explain below both these causes of the existence of oligopolies.

1. Economies of Scale. One important reason that a market may have few firms is the existence of economies of scale. When the economies of scale are quite strong, then the market for a product may be too small to support a large number of firms. When economies of scale exist, average cost falls rapidly over a large range of increase in the level of output. As a result of large economies of scale, a few firms can fulfil the demand for the product by producing on a large scale and thus lowering their average cost of production. These economies of scale may be based on division of labour when production of a complex product is split up into several simple tasks each of which is accomplished by the specialised workers using machines in an assembly-line production. The use of division of labour and large-scale production is limited by the size of market, as was pointed out by Adam Smith in his well-known book "*Wealth of Nations*'. Therefore, big firms have advantage over small firms on account of economies of scale based on division of labour. The larger the scale of production, the lower the average variable cost of production.

A Large Amount of Fixed Cost. Apart from the falling average variable cost due to the use of greater degree of division of labour, economies of scale also exist due to a large fixed cost incurred on developing and designing a new product. If the sales by a firm of a new product that has been developed after incurring a large fixed cost increase, its average fixed cost declines. This helps the firm to recover its fixed cost if it is produced on a large scale resulting in a lower average fixed cost. With a lower average fixed cost at a large scale of product, the firm will be able to sell it at a lower price and compete away its rival firms producing on a small scale. Thus, Lipsey and Chrystal write, ***"With enormous development cost of some of today's high technology products, firms that can sell a large volume have a distinct pricing advantage over firms that sell a smaller volume.*** *Firms with large product development costs face downward-sloping average total cost curve even if their average variable costs are constant."*[4]

4. Lipsey and Chrystal, *Economics*, 10th edition., p. 200.

Economies of Scope. Similar to the economies of scale, there are economies of scope which arise in case of multiproduct firms when some of their resources can be used for the production of a number of products. ***Economies of scope arise when production of different products within one firm leads to the lower average cost of production than if they were produced in independent firms.*** Such economies of scope arise because some activities such as marketing and distribution can be shared by many products or there might be some skills available to the firm that can be used for the production of more than one product. The economies of scope also lower average cost of production and provide competitive advantage to large firms.

It follows from above that economies of scale arising out of division of labour and having a large fixed costs of product development and economies of scope enable a few large firms to lower unit cost of production. Market size of the product may be such that only a few large firms are able to exist and meet the demand for the product.

Barriers to Entry. A few firms in the industry may exist due to the barriers of entry. There are two types of barriers : technological and legal. A technological barrier to entry arises when the potential firms do not have the required knowledge or access to inputs as the existing firms. A legal barrier arises when government imposes restrictions on the entry of new firms to avoid harmful competition among the firms. For example, governments of many countries permit only a few firms to provide long-distance telephone calls or air-line services. Patents are another source of legal barriers to the entry of firms imposed by government as they provide incentives for future invention of new products.

Product Differentiation. When products produced by various firms are differentiated, it provides some market power to the producers of different varieties of the product. It may be noted that the names such as Maruti, Indica, Santro are the brand names of cars manufactures in India. When the existing firms enjoy good reputation for their brands of the product, it is difficult for the new firms to enter the market with the new products to compete the existing ones. Besides, the existing firms even make strategic threats to potential entrants against entering the market. Such threats may take the form of lowering the price of the product so as to make it unviable or unprofitable for the new entrants to operate in the industry. Product differentiation along with economies of scale are significant causes of the existence of oligopolies in the industry.

Firm-created Causes of Oligopolies. Product differentiation is not the only reason for the existence of a few big firms in the industries. Some existing firms may take strategic moves to take over other firms in the industry. Firms may grow and become big by *merging* with other firms. Firms may even drive out their rivals from the market by making them bankrupt through *predatory* practices. Thus, through takeovers, mergers and predatory practices, some firms in an industry become big and dominate it. By eliminating competitors, a few big firms are able to make large profits. However, the large profits made by the existing firms will attract the new firms in the industry. Therefore, unless the existing few firms can create and sustain strong barriers to the entry of new firms, oligopolies may not last long if they do not arise due to the technological factors such as economies of scale and scope.

Are Oligopolies due to Economies of Scale or Firms-Created Causes ?

As explained above, oligopolies exist both due to economies of scale and firms-created causes such as product differentiation, moves to prevent entry of new firms, takeover of other firms or merging with them. In some industries, the few firms dominate because due to the economies of scale efficient size of the firm is large enough relative to the size of the market so that only a few firms can meet the demand for the products. Harward economist Alfred D. Chandler in an important work has given evidence that the ***major reason for the existence***

of oligopolies in the United States, the United Kingdom and Germany is efficiency of the big firms gained through economies of scale and scope.

ARE PRICE AND OUTPUT UNDER OLIGOPOLY INDETERMINATE ?

We have explained above the various characteristics and problems of oligopoly. The readers will now like to know how the economists analyse the determination of price and output under oligopoly. Because of the interdependence of firms in oligopoly and the uncertainty about the reaction patterns of the rivals, the easy and determinate solution to the oligopoly problem is not possible. In other words, interdependence of firms in an oligopoly and consequently firm's reactions to each other's behaviour poses serious difficulties in establishing the theory of the determination of price and output in an oligopolistic market.

Interdependence of Firms in Oligopoly

A significant consequence of interdependence of firms in an oligopolistic market situation is that under it a *wide variety of behaviour patterns becomes possible*. "Rivals may decide to get together and co-operate in the pursuit of their objectives, at least so far as the law allows or, at the other extreme, they may try to fight each other to the death. Even if they enter into an agreement it may last or it may break down. And the agreements may follow a wide variety of patterns."[5] Therefore, a large variety of models analysing price-output determination under oligopoly have been evolved by the economists depending upon the different assumptions about the behaviour of the oligopolistic group and the reaction patterns of rivals to a change in price or output by a firm.

Another difficulty that arises from interdependence of oligopolistic firms is the ***indeterminateness of the demand curves facing individual firms.*** As has been stated earlier, because of the interdependence an oligopolistic firm cannot assume that its rival firms will keep their prices and quantities constant when it makes changes in its price. When an oligopolistic firm changes its price, its rival firms will retaliate or react and change their prices which in turn would affect the demand for the product of the former firm. Therefore, an oligopolistic firm cannot have sure and definite demand curve, since it keeps shifting as the rivals change their prices in reaction to the price changes made by it. Moreover, there is quite an uncertainty about the rival's reactions to a price change by one firm. That is, when an oligopoly firm cuts its price, whether its rivals will also cut their prices similarly, or whether they will keep their prices unchanged. If they cut their prices, whether they will cut their prices by the same amount, or by a smaller or greater amount. A definite and determinate demand curve for a firm can be drawn if its rival's prices remain unchanged or if it is known before hand that they will change their prices in a *certain particular way* in response to price changes by one firm. But under oligopoly there is no certainty about the reactions of the rivals to the price changes made by a firm. Hence the demand curve of an oligopolistic firm cannot be easily determined.

Now, when an oligopolist does not know the demand curve confronting him, what price and output he will fix cannot be ascertained by economic analysis. In other words, in view of the indeterminateness of demand curve for a firm under oligopoly, the solution for the determination of price and output under oligopoly cannot be provided by the economic theory. Under conditions of perfect competition, monopoly and monopolistic competition, an individual firm faces a determinate demand curve which has a corresponding definite marginal revenue curve. Then, on the basis of profit maximisation principle, the determinate solution to the price and output fixation under perfect competition, monopoly and monopolistic competition is found by the equality of marginal revenue with marginal cost. This solution cannot be applied

5. William J Baumol, *op. cit*, pp. 223–24.

to price and output determination under oligopoly without qualification or making some additional assumptions because the individual firm's demand curve and, therefore, the marginal revenue curve is indeterminate or unknown. Thus even if profit maximisation assumption is considered as valid under conditions of oligopoly, no determinate solution for price-output fixation can be provided because of the indeterminateness of demand curve.

Even when the firms of an oligopoly do not enter into collusion, tacit or formal, or choose a leader from among themselves and instead try to compete with each other no single and simple solution is possible as to how a firm will fix its price and output. This is because of the uncertainty about the reaction patterns of the rivals to a move by one firm. This uncertainty about the reaction patterns of competitors poses a serious analytical difficulty in the way of providing a determinate solution for the oligopoly problem. Quoting Prof. Baumol again, "When a businessman wonders about his competitors' likely response to some move which he is considering, he must recognize that his competitors, too, are likely to take this interdependence phenomenon into account. The firms attempts to outguess one another are then likely to lead to an ***interplay of anticipated strategies and counterstrategies which is tangled beyond hope of direct analysis.***"[6] Thus under oligopoly a firm is likely to imagine an infinite sequence of compounded hypotheses such as "If I make move A, he may consider making countermove B, but he may realise that I might then respond by making move C, in which case..., and so an *ad infinitum*."

Profit-Maximising Assumption Challenged in Case of Oligopoly

Again, a determinate solution to the price-output problem in other market forms (perfect competition, monopoly and monopolistic competition) is arrived at by assuming profit-maximising motive on the part of the firms. But some economists have challenged the validity of the profit-maximising hypothesis in oligopolistic situations. According to Prof. Rothschild, ***oligopolists aim at maximising their amount of stable profits over a long period of time rather than maximising profits at a time.***[7] On the other hand, Prof. Baumol thinks that in oligopolistic circumstances it is legitimate to assume ***sales maximising objective*** on the part of the firms.[8] Some other economists think that managers of oligopolistic firms maximise their own *utility function*. Still others like R.L. Morris think that firms try to maximise their *growth rate*. Finally, some economists assert that oligopolists do not maximise anything, they merely ***satisfice***. In other words, they aim to achieve satisfactory performance in terms of profits, sales, market share rather than maximum profits. All this controversy about the real objective of the firms relates especially to the oligopolistic firms. This controversy about the most probable objective of the oligopolists further introduces indeterminacy in the analysis of price and output under oligopoly.

In view of above, there is no single determinate solution of the oligopoly problem but a wide variety of possible solutions, each depending upon different assumptions. It is worth noting as to what exactly economists mean by *indeterminacy*. When no single solution of a problem is possible, economists generally say that the problem has no determinate solution. Thus economists usually speak of indeterminacy where mathematicians would speak of a multiplicity of solutions. Prof. Fritz Machlup explains the meaning of indeterminacy as follows:

"In a general way, economists speak of indeterminacy if not enough information is available to give a safe and unambiguous answer to a question before them. If they wish to solve a problem—for example, how the price of a certain commodity will change under certain

6. *Op. cit.*, p. 224 (italics added).
7. K.W. Rothschild, Price Theory and Oligopoly, *Economic Journal*, Vol. 57, 1947.
8. For Baumol's view about sales maximization objective, see chapter 45.

conditions—but find that the data which are assumed to be "given" *would permit of two or more perhaps of an infinite number of* answers, they will say that the problem has no determinate solution."[9]

VARIOUS APPROACHES TO DETERMINATION OF PRICE AND OUTPUT UNDER OLIGOPOLY

It may, however, be pointed out that in spite of what has been said above, economists have tried to provide a determinate solution to the oligopoly problem. But there is no any *single determinate solution, but a number of determinate solutions* depending upon different assumptions. The determinate solution to the oligopoly problem has been provided in the following ways.

Ignoring Interdependence. First, for providing a determinate solution to the price-output determination, some economists have assumed that oligopolistic firms *ignore interdependence.* Now, when interdependence disappears from decision-making of the oligopolistic firms, the demand curve facing them becomes determinate and can be ascertained. With this, the standard analysis of the theory of the firm can be applied to provide a determinate solution for price and output problem of oligopoly. Classical models of duopoly put forward by Cournot and Bertrand fall in this category. In both those models, oligopolistic interdependence has been ignored. Cournot[10] in his famous model assumed that each oligopolistic firm would set its output in the belief that its rival firm's output would remain constant. On the other hand, Bertrand[11] assumed that an oligopolistic firm would set its price in the belief that its rival firm would keep its price unchanged. But for providing a solution for price and output determination under oligopoly by ignoring the interdependence is a fundamentally mistaken approach. Rothschild rightly writes, "The determinate solution can be reached.... if it is assumed that the oligopolists do not take into account the effect of their action on the policy of their rivals as in the famous Cournot and Bertrand's solutions; ...But this type of approach is absolutely valueless, because it only solves the oligopoly problem by removing from the analysis its most essential differentiating aspect: the oligopolists' consciousness of their interdependence."[12]

Predicting Reaction Pattern and Counter-moves of Rivals. The second approach to provide a determinate solution to the price and output problem of oligopoly is to assume that oligopolistic firm is able to *predict the reaction patterns and counter-moves of his rivals*. In this approach various oligopoly models based on different assumptions regarding the particular reaction patterns have been propounded. Chamberlin[13] while recognizing that oligopolistic firms are conscious of their interdependence took some assumptions regarding the reaction pattern and provided a determinate solution according to which, under duopoly or oligopoly, monopoly output and price are determined so that *profits of duopolists (oligopolists) are jointly maximised*. P.M. Sweezy and Oxford economists, Hall and Hitch, assume that an oligopolist firm considers that while the price increase by it will not be followed by its rival firms, the price reduction will be matched by them. With such an assumption about the reaction pattern, demand curve facing an individual oligopolistic firm is of a kinked type with a kink at the current price. We shall discuss the kinked demand curve approach to oligopoly problem in

9. Fritz Machlup, The *Economics of Sellers' Competition,* p. 415 (italics added).
10. A. Cournot, "*Researches into the Mathematical Principles of the Theory of Wealth*", translated by Nathaniel T. Bacon, the Macmillan Co., New York, 1897.
11. J. Bertrand, "Theorie Mathematique de la Richesse Sociale", *Journal des Savants*, Paris, September 1893.
12. K.W. Rothschild, "Price Theory and Oligopoly", *'Economic Journal,'* Vol. 57, 1947, reprinted in *Reading in Price Theory* (AEA).
13. E.H. Chamberlin, *The Theory of Monopolistic Competition*, chapter 3 and Appendix A.

detail later in this chapter. Many other economists assuming other reaction patterns have propounded various other oligopoly models.

Cooperative Behaviour : Forming a Collusion to Maximise Joint Profits. The third approach to oligopoly problem assumes that oligopolistic firms, realising their interdependence, will pursue their common interests and will form a collusion, formal or tacit, that is, will enter into agreement and work in the pursuit of their common interests. They will maximise joint profits and share profits, market or output as agreed to between them. A variant of this approach is that firms in an oligopoly would accept one firm as a leader, which may be a dominant or low-cost firm, and they will follow their leader in the fixation of price of the product. Both the collusive and price leadership oligopoly models will be critically examined later in this chapter. In case of collusion and price leadership, the problem of indeterminateness of demand curve is not encountered.

Game Theory Approach to Oligopoly. Another significant approach to the oligopoly is that of the *theory of games*, put forward by Neumann and Morgenstern. In the theory of games, an oligopolistic firm does not guess at its rivals' reaction pattern, but *calculates the optimal moves by rival firms*, that is, their best possible strategies and in view of that adopts its own policies and counter-moves. The explanation of the application of the theory of games to the oligopoly problem will be discussed in a separate chapter in this book.

From our above analysis it follows that there is no single determinate solution to the price-output fixation under oligopoly. As said above, economists have developed a large number of models by taking different assumptions regarding the behaviour of the oligopolistic group (that is, whether they will cooperate together or fight with each other), regarding the objective they seek to achieve (that is, whether they are assumed to maximise individual or joint profits or they are assumed to maximise sales etc.), and regarding the *different reaction patterns* of rival firms to price and output changes by one firm.

COOPERATIVE VS. NON COOPERATIVE BEHAVIOUR : BASIC DILEMMA OF OLIGOPOLY

An important difference between oligopoly on the one hand and perfect competition and monopolistic competition on the other is that behaviour of oligopolistic firms can be strategic in deciding about their price and output policies. ***The strategic behaviour means that the oligopolistic firms must take into account the effect of their price-output decisions on their rival firms and on the reactions they expect from them.*** On the other hand, the firms working in perfect competition about their price and output and monopolistic competition while deciding about their price and output engage in non-strategic behaviour which means that while making decisions they do not take into account the likely reactions of their large number of competitors. Instead, in making decisions about their price and output, they are guided by their own demand and cost curves. The behaviour of monopolist is also non-strategic as he has no competitors with whom to compete and interact. A monopolist sets his price and output quite independently of others.

However, behaviour of an oligopolistic firm is a strategic one as it interacts with a few rivals who are affected by its decisions. There are mainly two types of strategies open to the oligopolists : ***compete with their rivals to promote their individual interests or cooperate with them to promote their mutual interests, namely, to maximise joint profits.*** This is the basic dilemma facing oligopolistic firms. The oligopolistic firms can make more profits as a group if they cooperate. However, any one oligopolistic firm can make more profits for itself by taking an appropriate price-output decision provided others continue to cooperate. In a perfectly competitive industry there are such a large number of firms that it is not possible to reach a cooperative solution unless some central authority enforce a cooperative decision on them. In contrast, in an oligopolistic industry the few firms can recognise their interdependence and realise the loss they may incur if they compete with each other instead of cooperating. Therefore, they can adopt cooperative behaviour to maximise their joint profits. In what follows we explain in brief the cooperative and non-cooperative behaviour in the context of oligopolistic market structure.

Cooperative Solution

If the few firms cooperate they can form a cartel *overtly* if permitted by law and *tacitly* if formal formation of cartel is prohibited by law. By deciding not to compete with each other they can decide to charge a monopoly price and reach an agreement on the outputs produced by each. In this way the cooperative behaviour results in maximisation of joint profits, that is, monopoly profits if they worked as one firm. We will explain later the *collusive oligopoly model which* provides an example of cooperative behaviour. However, we will see there how individual firms in a cartel has a tendency to cheat and try to undercut price to make more profits.

Another model of cooperative behaviour is *price-leadership model* where the few firms in an oligopolistic industry accept one firm as leader and accept the price set by it. Another cooperative model is put forward by Chamberlin who explains *how firms working independently* realise their interdependence and realise the prospects of making losses if they compete with each other. This leads them to charge a monopoly price which maximises their joint profits.

The Non-Cooperative Equilibrium : Nash Equilibrium

If few firms in the industry do not cooperate and compete with each other, even then they can reach an equilibrium, which is called *non-cooperative equilibrium*. This type of equilibrium is also called *Nash Equilibrium*, named after John Nash, the well-known US mathematician who was awarded the Nobel Prize in economics for his work in 1994[14], Nash equilibrium is reached when each firm thinks that *its present strategy is the optimum strategy given the present strategy of other firms*. That is, each firm in an oligopolistic industry has reached a strategy that it thinks is best under the circumstances provided others continue to follow their present strategies. The oldest model of duopoly was propounded by a French economist, A Cournot (1801-1876). In Cournot model the two firms do not cooperate but compete with each other. In Cournot's duopoly model each firm decides about the output it will produce, *assuming that its rival firm will keep its output constant at the present level*. Even competing through changes in output, the two duopolistic firms will reach the Nash equilibrium in which *each* thinks its present strategy (i.e. its present output of the product) is the best, given the output of the other firm. The other important model based on non-cooperative behaviour has been propounded by the French Mathematician Bertrand (1822-1900). In Bertrand model it is assumed that in making price decision, *a firm assumes that the other firm will keep its price constant*. After engaging in price war, in Bertrand model the duopolists will reach the equilibrium state when each firm thinks it is setting the best or optimum price, given the present price of the other firm.

From the foregoing analysis we see that economists have built models assuming both cooperative and non-cooperative behaviour of the firms.

---

14. On the whole life of John Nash a motion picture *'A Beautiful Mind'* has been made by the Hollywood. It is quite interesting to see this picture (now available in a CD form) to know the working of the mind of this great thinker.

COLLUSIVE OLIGOPOLY : CARTEL AS A COOPERATIVE MODEL

In order to avoid uncertainty arising out of interdependence and to avoid price wars and cut throat competition, firms working under oligopolistic conditions often enter into agreement regarding a uniform price-output policy to be pursued by them. The agreement may be either formal (open) or tacit (secret). But since formal or open agreements to form monopolies are illegal in most countries, agreements reached between oligopolists are generally tacit or secret. When the firms enter into such collusive agreements formally or secretly, collusive oligopoly prevails. But collusions are of two main types: (*a*) cartels and (*b*) price leadership. In a cartel type of collusive oligopoly, firms jointly fix a price and output policy through agreements. But under price leadership one firm sets the price and others follow it. The one which sets the price is a price leader and the others who follow it are its followers. The follower firms adopt the price of the leader even though they have to depart from their profit-maximising position, as they think that it is to their advantage not to compete with their leader and between themselves. In this present section we confine ourselves to explain the determination of price and output under the cartel type of collusive oligopoly and in the next section we will explain price and output determination under price-leadership form of collusive oligopoly.

Originally, the term 'cartel' was used for the agreement in which there existed a common sales agency which alone undertook the selling operations of all the firms that were party to the agreement. But now-a-days all types of formal or informal and tacit agreements reached among the oligopolistic firms of an industry are known as cartels. Since these cartels restrain competition among the member firms, their formations have been made illegal in some countries by the Governments passing laws against them. For instance, the formation of a cartel is illegal in U.S.A. under the Anti-Trust Laws passed there. However, in spite of the illegality of cartels they are still formed in U.S.A. through secret devices and by adopting some means or the other shrewd businessmen are able to evade the anti-monopoly laws.

Formal collusion or agreement among the oligopolists may itself take various forms. An extreme form of collusion is found when the member firms agree to surrender completely their rights of price and output determination to a 'Central Administrative Agency' so as to secure maximum joint profits for them. Formation of such a formal collusion is generally designated as *perfect cartel*. Thus under perfect cartel type of collusive oligopoly, the price and output determination of the whole industry as well as of each member firm is determined by the common administrative authority so as to *achieve maximum joint profits for the member firms.*

The total profits are distributed among the member firms in a way already agreed between them. The share from total profits of each member firm is not necessarily in proportion to the output quota it has to supply and the cost it incurs on it. The output quota to be produced by each firm is decided by the central administrative authority in such a way that the total costs of the total output produced is minimum. In fact, under perfect cartel, the central authority determines the separate outputs to be produced by the various members and the price they have to charge in the same way as a monopolist operating multiple plants would do. Now, the question arises as to what outputs different firms in a cartel will be asked to produce so that the total cost is made minimum. Total cost will be minimised when the various firms in the cartel produce such separate outputs so that their marginal costs are equal. This is because if the marginal costs of the member firms are not equal, then the marginal units of output could be produced at a smaller cost by the firms with a lower marginal cost than by those with a higher marginal cost.

Let us now see how the cartel works and determines its price and output. Let us assume that two firms have formed a cartel by entering into an agreement. We assume that the *cartel will aim at maximising joint profits for the member firms*. First of all, the cartel will estimate the demand curve of the industry's product. As the demand curve facing a cartel will be the aggregate demand curve of the consumers of the product, it will be sloping downward as is shown by the curve *DD* in Fig. 40.1(*c*). Marginal revenue curve *MR* showing the addition to cartel's revenue for successive additions to its output and sales will lie below the demand curve *DD*. Cartel's marginal cost curve (MC_c) will be given by the horizontal addition of the marginal cost curves of the two firms. This has been done in Fig. 40.1(*c*) where MC_c curve has been obtained by adding horizontally marginal cost curves MC_a and MC_b of firms *A* and *B* respectively. It should be noted that cartel's marginal cost curve MC_c, obtained as it is by horizontal addition of marginal cost curves of the two firms, will indicate the minimum possible total cost of producing each industry output on it; each industry's output being distributed among the two firms in such a way that their marginal costs are equal.

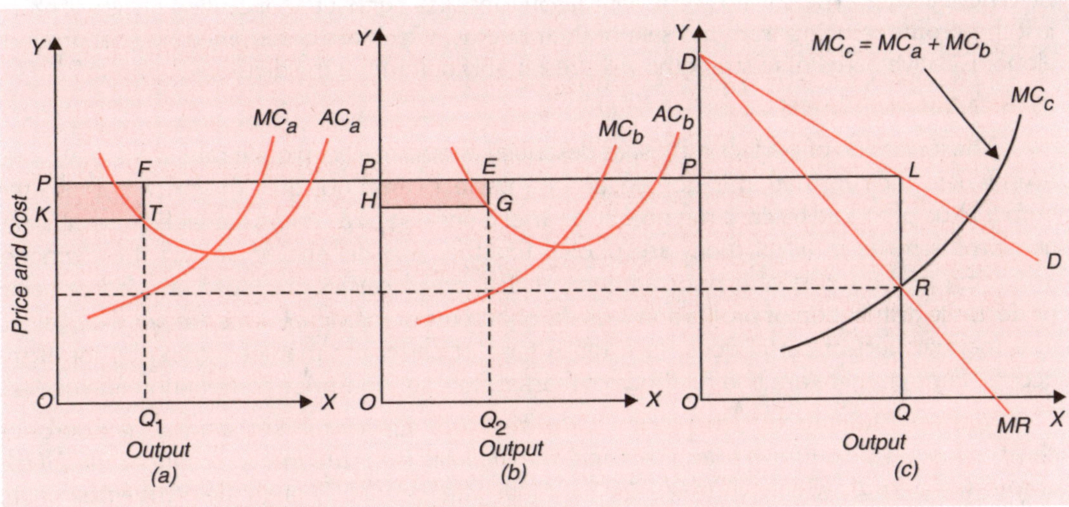

Fig. 40.1. *Price and Output Determination under Cartel: Joint Profit Maximisation*

Now, the cartel will maximise its profits by fixing the industry's output at the level at which *MR* and *MC* curves of the cartel intersect each other. It will be seen in Fig. 40.1(*c*) that *MR* and *MC* curves cut each other at point *R* or output *OQ*. It will also be seen from the demand curve *DD* that the output *OQ* will determine price equal to *QL* or *OP*. Having decided the total output *OQ* to be produced, the cartel will allot output quota to be produced by each firm so that the marginal cost of each firm is the same. This can be known by drawing a horizontal straight line from point *R* towards the *Y*-axis. It will be seen from the figure that when firm *A* produces OQ_1 and firm *B* produces OQ_2, the marginal costs of the two firms are equal. The output quota of firm *A* will be OQ_1, and of firm *B* will be OQ_2. It is worth noting that the total output *OQ* will be equal to the sum of OQ_1 and OQ_2.

Thus, the determination of output *OQ* and price *OP* and the outputs OQ_1 and OQ_2 by the two firms *A* and *B* will ensure the maximum joint profits for the member firms constituting the cartel. It will be seen from Fig. 40.1(*a*) that with output OQ_1 and cartel price *OP*, the profits made in firm *A* are equal to *PFTK* and with output OQ_2 and cartel price *OP* the profits made in firm *B* are equal to *PEGH*. The sum of profits, that is, the joint profits made by the cartel will be maximum under the given demand and cost conditions as they have been arrived at as a result of equating combined marginal cost (MC_c) with the combined marginal revenue

(*MR*). ***The allocation of output quota to each of them is made on the grounds of minimising cost and not as a basis for determining profit distribution.*** Prof. J.S. Bain rightly says, "There is no particular reason for believing that the operating firms will retain just the profits resulting from the sale of their quotas, which are determined on cost grounds alone. Relative bargaining strengths will presumably determine the division of profits."[15]

Market-Sharing Cartels

The formation of perfect cartels, as described above, has been quite rare in the real world even where their formation is not illegal. In a perfect cartel not only the price but also the output to be produced by each member of a cartel is decided by a central management authority and profits made in all of them are pooled together and distributed among the members according to the terms of a prior agreement. But when cartels are loose, instead of being perfect, the distribution of profits and fixation of outputs of individual firms are not determined in a manner perfect cartel does. In a loose type of cartel the market-sharing by the firms occurs. Further, there are two methods of market sharing: non-price competition and quotas.

Market-Sharing by Non-Price Competition. Under market sharing by non-price competition, *only a uniform price is set and, the member firms are free to produce and sell the amount of outputs* which will maximise their individual profits. Though the firms agree not to sell at a price below the fixed price they are free to vary the style of their product and the advertising expenditure and to promote sales in other ways. That is, the price being a fixed datum, the firms compete on non-price basis. If the different member firms have identical costs, then the agreed uniform price will be the monopoly price which will ensure maximisation of joint profits. But when there are cost differences between the firms as is generally the case, the cartel price will be fixed by bargaining between the firms. The level of this price will be such as will ensure some profits to high-cost firms.

But with cost differences such loose cartels are quite unstable. This is because the low cost firms will have an incentive to cut price to increase their profits and therefore they will tend to break away from the cartel. However, they may not openly charge lower price than the fixed one and instead cheat the other firms by giving secret price concessions to the buyers. However, as the rivals gradually lose their customers, the cheating by the low-cost firms will be ultimately discovered and consequently open price war may commence and cartel breaks down.

Market-Sharing by Output Quota. The second type of market-sharing cartel is the agreement reached between the oligopolistic firms regarding quota of output to be produced and sold by each of them at the agreed price. If all firms are producing homogeneous product and have same costs, the monopoly solution (that is, the maximisation of joint profits) will emerge with the market being equally shared by them. However, when costs of member-firms are different, the different quotas for various firms will be fixed and, therefore, their market shares will differ. The quotas and market shares in case of cost differences are decided through bargaining between the firms. During the bargaining process, two criteria are usually adopted to fix the quotas of the firms. One is the past level of sales of the various firms and the second is the productive capacity of the firms. However, the `past-period sales' and 'productive capacity' of various firms are not very firm criteria as they can be easily manipulated. Ultimately, the quotas fixed for various firms depend upon their bargaining power and skill.

The second common basis for the quota system and market sharing is the division of market regionwise, that is, the geographical division of the market between the cartel firms. In

15. J.S. Bain, *Pricing, Distribution and Employment*, 1953, p. 286.

this arrangement, price and also style of the product of cartel firms may vary.

Instability of a Cartel

It is worth noting that all types of cartels are unstable when there exists cost differences between firms. The low-cost firms always have a tendency to reduce price of the product to maximise their profits which ultimately results in the collapse of the collusive agreement. Further, if the entry of firms in the oligopolistic industry is free, the instability of the cartel is intensified. The new entrants may not join the cartel and may fix a lower price of the product to sell a large quantity. This may start a price war between the cartel firms and the new entrants. We thus see that the stability of the cartel arrangement is always in danger.

Graphical illustration. The strong incentive to cheat on the part of cartel members and consequently causing a break-down of a cartel is graphically illustrated in Fig. 40.2, where *DD* is market demand curve facing the cartel consisting of two firms *A* and *B*. MC_a in panel (*i*) is the marginal cost curve of the firm *A*. Similarly, there is marginal cost curve of firm *B*, (not shown in Fig. 40.2). Summing up horizontally marginal cost curves of the two firms forming a cartel we get the combined marginal cost curve MC_{a+b}. The cartel maximises its profits by equating *MR* with MC_{a+b} and accordingly output *OQ* and price *OP* in Panel (ii) of Fig. 40.2 are fixed. The output share of each firm will be fixed where marginal cost of each firm equals the combined marginal cost of the cartel members. Accordingly, the output share of firm *A* shown in panel (*i*) is Oq_a at which marginal cost of firm *A* equals the combined marginal cost *OT* or *QE* in the equilibrium situation. Oq_a will be the agreed share of output of firm *A*. To simplify our analysis we have not shown the cost situation of firm *B*, the other member of the cartel.

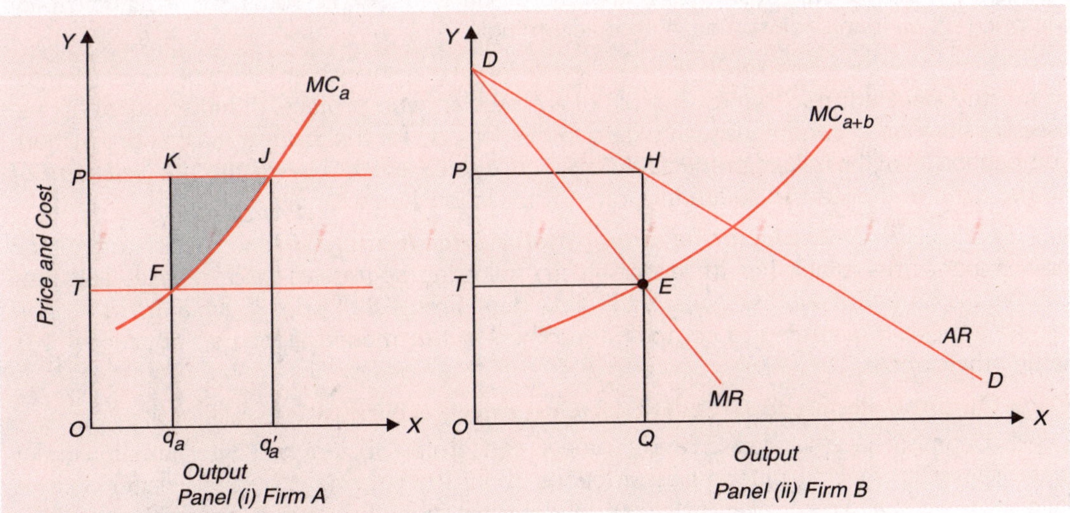

Fig. 40.2. *Instability of a Cartel Due to Cheating by a Member*

Thus, under the cartel agreement, firm *A* will be producing Oq_a, and charging price *OP*. Now, a glance at panel (*i*) in Fig. 40.2, reveals that given the price *OP*, fixed by the cartel, if the firm *A* increases its output from agreed share Oq_a to Oq'_a, it can increase its profits by the shaded area *FKJ*. This means that in order to increase its profits the firm *A* will have incentive to cheat by trying to produce and sell more at the agreed price *OP*. Similarly, the firm *B*, other member of the cartel (not shown in Fig. 40.2) will also find that it can increase its profits by violating the cartel agreement by producing and selling more than its agreed output share. To sum up, ***it is due to the promotion of self-interest by cartel members that accounts for the instability of cartel arrangements and frequent price wars.***

PRICE LEADERSHIP

As mentioned above, price leadership is an important form of collusive oligopoly. Under it, one firm sets the price, others follow it. Price leadership also comes into existence either through tacit or formal agreement. But as the formal or open agreement to establish price leadership are generally illegal, price leadership is generally established as a result of *informal and tacit understanding* between the oligopolists. The competing oligopolists in an informal meeting choose a leader and agree to follow him in setting price.

Types of Price Leadership

Price leadership is of various types. Firstly, there is a *price leadership by a low-cost firm.* In order to maximise profits the low-cost firm sets a lower price than the profit-maximising price of the high-cost firms. Since the high-cost firms will not be able to sell their product at the higher price, they are forced to agree to the low price set by the low-cost firm. Of course, the low-cost price leader has to ensure that the price which he sets must yield some profits to the high-cost firms—their followers.

Secondly, there is a ***price leadership of the dominant firm.*** Under this one of the few firms in the industry may be producing a vary large proportion of the total production of the industry and may, therefore, dominate the market for the product. This dominant firm wields a great influence over the market for the product, while other firms are small and are incapable of making any impact on the market. As a result, the dominant firm estimates its own demand curve and fixes a price which maximises its own profits. The other firms which are small having no individual effects on the price of the product, follow the dominant firm and accept the price set by it and adjust their output accordingly.

Thirdly, there is a ***barometric price leadership*** under which an old, experienced, largest or most respected firm assumes the role of a custodian who protects the interests of all. He assesses the market conditions with regard to the demand for the product, cost of production, competition from the related products etc. and *sets a price which is best from the viewpoint of all the firms* in the industry. Naturally, other firms follow him willingly.

Fourthly, there is ***exploitative or aggressive price leadership*** under which a very large or dominant firm establishes its leadership by following aggressive price policies and thus compel the other firms in the industry to follow him in respect of price. Such a firm will often initiate a move threatening to compete the others out of market if they do not follow it in setting their prices.

Price-Output Determination under Low-Cost Price Leadership

Economists have developed various models concerning price-output determination under price leadership making different assumptions about the behaviour of price leader and his followers. We shall first explain price-output determination under price leadership by a low-cost firm. In order to simplify our analysis we make the following assumptions:

(1) There are two firms, *A* and *B*. The firm *A* has a lower cost of production than firm *B*.

(2) The product produced by the two firms is homogeneous so that the consumers have no preference between them.

(3) Each of the two firms has equal share in the market. In other words, demand curve facing each firm will be the same and will be half of the total market demand curve of product.

Given the above assumptions, price and output determination under price leadership is illustrated in Fig. 40.3. Each firm is facing demand curve *Dd* which is half of the total market demand curve *DD* for the product. *MR* is the marginal revenue curve of each firm. AC_a and

MC_a are the average and marginal cost curves of firm A, and AC_b and MC_b are the average and marginal cost curves of firm B. Cost curves of firm A lie below the cost curves of firm B because we are assuming that firm A has a lower cost of production than firm B.

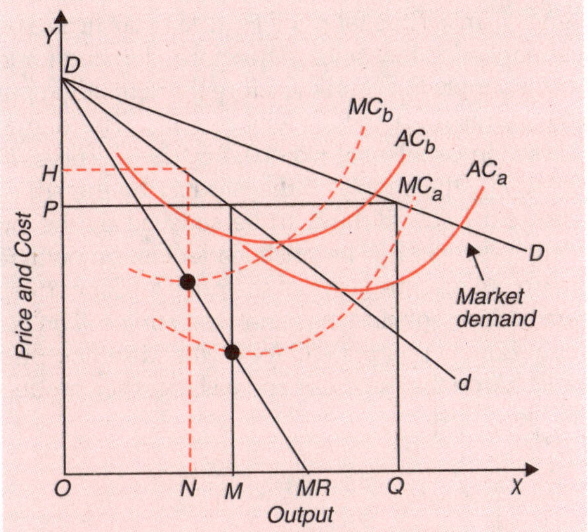

Fig. 40.3. *Price-Output Determination under Low-Cost Price Leadership*

The firm A will be maximising its profits by selling output OM and setting price OP, since at output OM, its marginal cost is equal to the marginal revenue. Firm B's profits will be maximum when it fixes price OH and sells output ON. It will be seen from the figure that profit-maximising price OP of firm A is lower than the profit-maximising price OH of firm B. Since the two firms are producing a homogeneous product, they cannot charge two different prices. Because the profit-maximising price OP of firm A is lower than the profit-maximising price OH of firm B, firm A will dictate price to the firm B or, in other words, firm A will win if there is price war between the two and will emerge as a price leader and firm B will be compelled to follow. Given these facts, the agreement reached between them, even though tacit it may be, will require that the firm A will act as the price leader and firm B as the price follower.

It should be noted that firm B after having accepted firm A as the price leader will actually charge price OP and produce and sell OM. This is because at price OP, it can sell OM output like firm A because the demand curve facing each firm is the same. Thus, both the firms will charge the same price OP and sell the same amount (OM). Note that the total output of the two firms will be $OM + OM = OQ$ which will be equal to the market demand for the good at price OP. But there is an important difference between the two. While firm A, the price leader, will be maximising its profits by selling output OM and charging price OP, the firm B will not be making maximum profits with this price-output combination because its profits are maximum at output ON and price OH. Therefore, profits earned by firm B by producing and selling output OM and charging price OP will be smaller than those of firm A because its costs are greater.

When the products of the price leader and his price followers are differentiated, then the price charged by them will be different but the prices charged by the followers will be only slightly different either way from that of the price leader and they will conform to a definite pattern of differentials.

Price-Output Determination Under Price Leadership by the Dominant Firm

We now proceed to explain the determination of price and output when there exists price leadership by a dominant firm which is having a large share of the market with a number of small firms as followers each of which has a small share of the market. To explain this we assume that the dominant firm knows the total market demand curve for the product. Further, the dominant firm also knows the marginal cost curves of the smaller firms whose lateral summation yields the total supply of the product by the small firms at various prices. This implies that from its past experience the dominant firm can estimate fairly well the likely supply of the product by the small firms at various prices. With this information, the leader can obtain his demand curve.

Consider panel (*a*) of Fig. 40.4 where *DD* is the market demand curve for the product, S_m is the supply curve the product of all the small firms taken together. At each price the leader will be able to sell the part of the market demand not fulfilled by the supply from the small firms. Thus, at price P_1, the small firms supply the whole of the quantity of the product demanded at that price. Therefore, demand for leader's product is zero. At price P_2, the small firms supply P_2C and therefore the remaining part of *CT* of the market demand will constitute the demand for the leader's product. The demand for leader's product has been separately shown in panel (*b*) of Fig. 40.4 by the d_L curve. P_2Z in panel *(b)* is equal to *C T* in panel *(a)*. At price P_3, the supply of the product by the small firms is zero. Therefore, the whole market demand P_3U will have to be satisfied by the price leader. Likewise, the other point of the demand curve for the price leader can be obtained. In panel (*b*) of Fig. 40.4. The MR_L is the marginal revenue curve of the price leader corresponding to his demand curve d_L. *AC* and *MC* are his average and marginal cost curves. The dominant price leader will maximise his profits by producing output *OQ* (or *PH*) and setting price *OP*. The followers, that is, the small firms will charge the price *OP* and will together produce *PB*. [*PH* in panel (*b*) equals *BS* of panel (*a*) in Fig. 40.4].

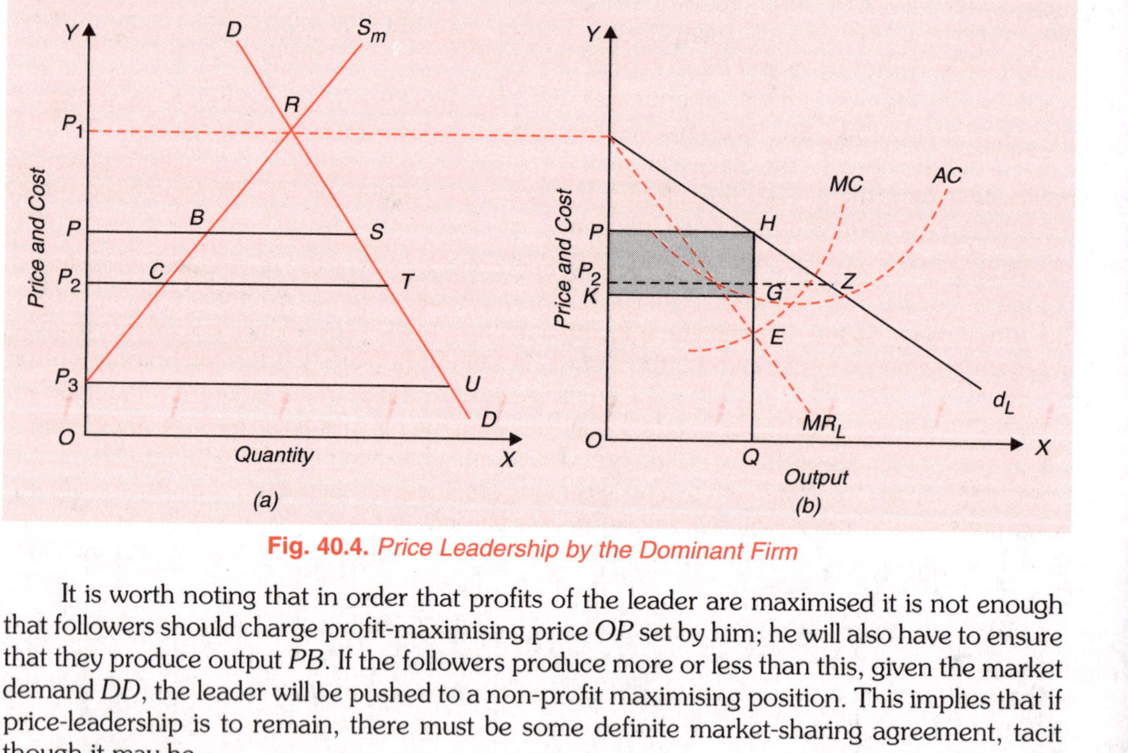

Fig. 40.4. *Price Leadership by the Dominant Firm*

It is worth noting that in order that profits of the leader are maximised it is not enough that followers should charge profit-maximising price *OP* set by him; he will also have to ensure that they produce output *PB*. If the followers produce more or less than this, given the market demand *DD*, the leader will be pushed to a non-profit maximising position. This implies that if price-leadership is to remain, there must be some definite market-sharing agreement, tacit though it may be.

Difficulties of Price Leadership

Price leadership involves many difficulties in the real world. First, the success of price leadership of a firm depends upon the correctness of his estimates about the reactions of his followers. If his estimates about the reactions of his rivals to price changes by it prove to be incorrect, then not only the success of his price policy but also his leadership in the market will be jeopardised. Secondly, when a price leader fixes a higher price than the followers would prefer, there is a strong tendency for the followers to make hidden price cuts in order to increase their shares of the market without openly challenging the price leader. A good number of devices which amount to secret price cutting are used by business firms. Some of these secret price-cutting devices are the offer of rebates, favourable credit terms, 'money back' guarantees, after-delivery free services, sale on the payment of price in easy installments with low rates of interest etc., and liberal entertainment of the buyers. Price leaders are generally fed up with the increasing number of concessions granted by their rivals and they make an open price cut to prevent further fall in their share of the market. In such circumstances price leadership becomes infructuous.

Another important difficulty of maintaining price leadership is the tendency on the part of the rivals to indulge in *non-price competition* to increase sales while charging the price set by the price leader. The devices used under 'non-price competition' include advertising and other methods of the sales promotion, like improvement of the quality of the product, in addition to the hidden price-product concessions mentioned above. While charging the same price, the rivals try to increase their share of the market by increasing the advertisement expenditure. As a result of this non-price competition, the price leader has also to adopt similar devices to prevent the fall in its sales or has to make outright cut in price in order to achieve his objective. In view of these facts, the price leader may not be able to maintain his leadership for a long time.

Further, there is a great limitation on the price leader to fix a high price of his product. This is because the high price will induce the rivals to make secret price cuts which will adversely affect the sales of the price leader. Moreover, a high price fixed by the price leader will attract new competitors into the industry which may not accept his leadership. Lastly, differences in costs also pose a problem. If the price leader has higher costs, then the high price fixed by him will, as mentioned above, induce the rivals to undercut price or will attract the entry of new firms into the industry. If the price leader has lower costs than his rivals, he will set a low price which will antagonise his rivals who will disturb him quite frequently.

KINKED DEMAND CURVE THEORY OF OLIGOPOLY

It has been observed that many oligopolistic industries exhibit an appreciable degree of price rigidity or stability. In other words, in many oligopolistic industries prices remain sticky or inflexible, that is, there is no tendency on the part of the oligopolists to change the price even if the economic conditions undergo a change. Many explanations have been given for this price rigidity under oligopoly and most popular explanation is the kinked demand curve hypothesis. The kinked demand curve hypothesis was put forward independently by Paul M. Sweezy[16], an American economist, and by Hall and Hitch[17], Oxford economists.

It is especially for explaining price and output *under oligopoly with product differentiation* that economists often use the kinked demand curve hypothesis. This is because when under oligopoly products are differentiated it is unlikely that when a firm raises its price, all customers would leave it because some customers are intimately attached to it due to product differentiation. As a result, demand curve facing a firm under differentiated oligopoly is not perfectly elastic. On the other hand, under oligopoly without product differentiation, when a firm raises its price, all its customers would leave it so that demand curve facing an oligopolist producing homogeneous product may be perfectly elastic. Further, under oligopoly without product differentiation, there is a greater tendency on the part of the firms to join together and form a collusion, formal or tacit, and, alternatively, to accept one of them as their leader in setting

16. Paul M. Sweezy, "Demand under Conditions of Oligopoly", *Journal of Political Economy*, Vol. XLVIII, August 1939, reprinted in American Economic Association, *Readings in Price Theory*.
17. R.L. Hall and C.J. Hitch, "Price Theory and Business Behaviour" *Oxford Economic Papers*, No. 2, May, 1939.

their price. No doubt, kinked demand curve has a special relevance for differentiated oligopoly, but it has also been applied for explaining price and output under oligopoly without product differentiation.

The demand curve facing an oligopolist, according to the kinked demand curve hypothesis, has a 'kink' at the level of the prevailing price. The kink is formed at the prevailing price level because the segment of the demand curve above the prevailing price level is highly elastic and the segment of the demand curve below the prevailing price level is inelastic. A kinked demand curve *dD* with a kink at point *K* has been shown in Fig. 40.5. The prevailing price level is *OP* and the firm is producing and selling the output *OM*. Now, the upper segment *dK* of the demand curve *dD* is relatively elastic and the lower segment *KD* is relatively inelastic. This difference in elasticities is due to the particular competitive reaction pattern assumed by the kinked demand curve hypothesis.

The competitive reaction pattern assumed by the kinked demand curve oligopoly theory is as follows:

Each oligopolist believes that if he lowers the price below the prevailing level, his competitors will follow him and will accordingly lower their prices, whereas if he raises the price above the prevailing level, his competitors will not follow his increase in price.

In other words, each oligopolistic firm believes that though its rival firms will not match his increase in price above the prevailing level, they will indeed match its price cut. These two different types of reaction of the competitors to the increase in price on the one hand and to the reduction in price on the other make the portion of the demand curve above the prevailing price level relatively elastic and the lower portion of the demand curve relatively inelastic. This is explained below:

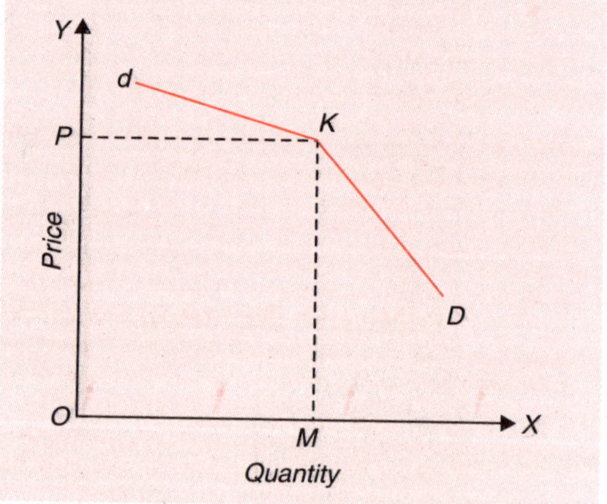

Fig. 40.5. *Kinked Demand Curve under Oligopoly*

(a) Price reduction. If an oligopolist reduces its price below the prevailing price level *OP* in order to increase his sales, his competitors will fear that their customers would go away from them to buy the product from the former oligopolist which has made a price cut. Therefore, in order to retain their customers they will be forced quickly to match the price cut. Because of the competitors quickly following the reduction in price by an oligopolist, he will gain in sales only very little. (His sales will increase not at the expense of his competitors but because of the rise in total quantity demanded due to the reduction in price of the good. In fact, each will gain in sales to the extent of a proportionate share in the increase in total demand). Very small increase in sales of an oligopolist following his reduction in price below the prevailing level means that the demand for him is inelastic below the prevailing price. Thus, the segment *KD* of the demand curve in Fig. 40.5 which lies below the prevailing price *OP* is inelastic showing that very little increase in sales can be obtained by a reduction in price by an oligopolist.

(b) Price increase. If an oligopolist raises his price above the pvailing level, there will be a substantial reduction in his sales. This is because as a result of rise in his price, his customers will withdraw from him and will go to his competitors who will welcome the new customers and will gain in sales. These happy competitors will have, therefore, no motivation to match the price rise. The oligopolist who raises his price will be able to retain only those customers who either have a strong preference for his product (if the products are differentiated) or who cannot obtain the desired quantity of the product from the competitors because of their limited productive capacity. Large reduction in sales following an increase in price above the prevailing level by an oligopolist means that demand with respect to increases in price above the existing one is highly elastic. Thus, in Fig. 40.5 the segment *dK* of the demand curve which lies above the current price level *OP* is elastic showing a large fall in sales if a producer raises his price.

It is now evident from above that each oligopolist finds himself placed in such a position that while, on the one hand, he expects his rivals to match his price cuts very quickly, he does not expect his rivals to match his price increases on the other. Given this expected competitive reaction pattern, each oligopolist will have a kinked demand curve *dKD* with the upper segment *dK* being relatively elastic and the lower segment *KD* being relatively inelastic.

Why Price Rigidity Under Oligopoly?

From what has been said above, it is easy to see why an oligopolist confronting a kinked demand curve will have no incentive to raise its price or to lower it. ***Since the oligopolist will***

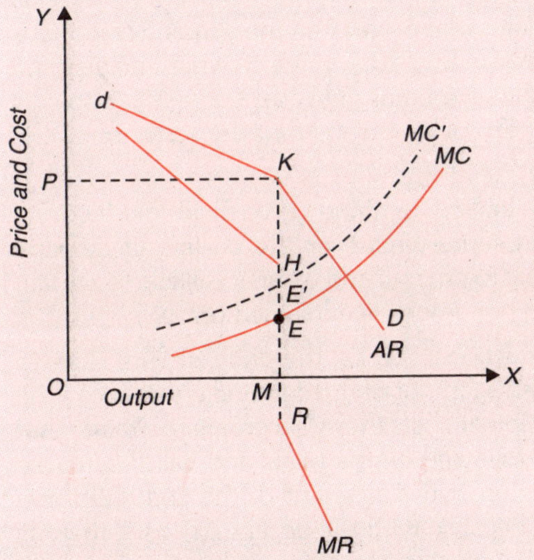

Fig. 40.6. *Changes in costs within limits do not affect the oligopoly price*

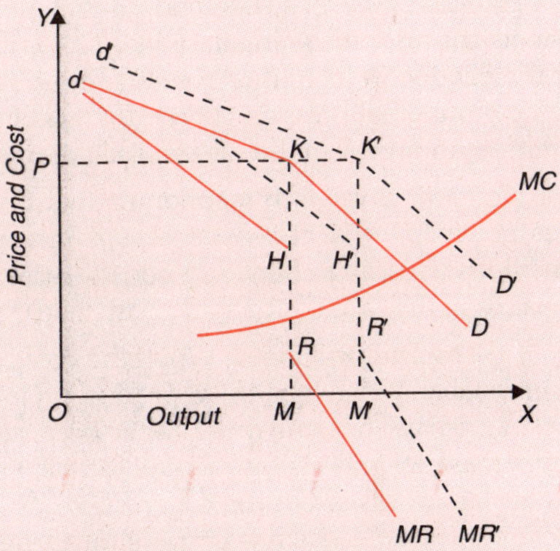

Fig. 40.7. *Changes in demand do not affect the oligopoly price*

not gain a large share of the market by reducing his price below the prevailing level, and will have substantial reduction in sales by increasing his price above the prevailing level, he will be extremely reluctant to change the prevailing price. In other words, each oligopolist will adhere to the prevailing price seeing no gain in changing it. Thus, rigid prices are explained in this way by the kinked demand curve theory. In Fig. 40.5, the prevailing price is *OP* at which kink is found in the demand curve *dKD*. The price *P* will tend to remain stable or rigid as every member of the oligopoly will not see any gain in lowering it or in increasing it. It should be noted that if the prevailing price *OP* is greater than average cost, more than normal profits will be made.

Further, it is worth mentioning that the oligopolist confronting a kinked demand curve will be maximising his profits at the current price level. For finding the profit-maximising price-output combination, marginal revenue curve *MR* corresponding to the kinked demand curve *dKD* has been drawn. It is worth mentioning that the marginal revenue curve associated with a kinked demand curve is discontinuous, or in other words, it has a broken vertical portion.

The length of the discontinuity depends upon the relative elasticities of two segments *dK* and *KD* of the demand curve at point *K*. The greater the difference in the two elasticities, the greater the length of the discontinuity. In Fig. 40.6 marginal revenue curve *MR* corresponding to the kinked demand curve *dKD* has been drawn which has a discontinuous portion or gap *HR*. Now, if the marginal cost curve of the oligopolist is such that it passes anywhere, say from point *E*, through the discontinuous portion *HR* of the marginal revenue curve *MR*, as shown in Fig. 40.6, the oligopolist will be maximising his profits at the prevailing price level *OP*, that is, he will be in equilibrium at point *E* or at the prevailing price *OP*. ***Since the oligopolist is in equilibrium, or in other words, maximising his profits at the prevailing price level, he will have no incentive to change the price.***

Furthermore, even if there are changes in costs, the price will remain stable so long as the marginal cost curve passes through the gap *HR* in the marginal revenue curve. In Fig. 40.6 when the marginal cost curve shifts upward from *MC* to *MC′* (dotted) due to the rise in cost, the equilibrium price and output remain unchanged since the new marginal cost *MC′* also passes from point *E′* through the gap *HR*.

Likewise, the kinked demand curve theory explains that even when the demand conditions change, the price may remain stable. This is illustrated in Fig. 40.7 in which when the demand for the oligopolist increases from *dKD* to *d′K′D′*, the given marginal cost curve *MC* also cuts the new marginal revenue curve *MR′* within the gap. This means that the same price *OP* continues to prevail in the oligopolistic market.

However, it is worth mentioning that from the kinked demand curve oligopoly theory it does not follow that the price always remains the same whenever the costs and demand conditions undergo a change. When the price is likely to change and when it is likely to remain inflexible in the face of changing costs and demand conditions is explained below:

(1) Decline in Costs. When the cost of production declines, the price is more likely to remain stable. When the cost of production falls, then segment of the demand curve above the current price will become more elastic because with lower costs there is a greater certainty that the increase in price by an oligopolist will not be followed by his rivals and will thus cause greater loss in sales. On the other hand, with lower cost the segment of the demand curve below the current price will become more inelastic because with the decline in costs, there is greater certainty that the reduction in price by an oligopolist will be followed by his rivals. With the upper segment becoming more elastic and the lower segment becoming more inelastic than before, the angle *dKD* will become less obtuse and hence the gap in the marginal revenue curve will increase. As a result of the increase in the gap (that is, the length of discontinuity) in the marginal revenue curve, the lower marginal cost curve is likely to pass through this gap showing that the price and output remain the same as before.

(2) Rise in Cost. *If there is a rise in the cost of the oligopolistic industry, the price is not likely to stay rigid.* When there is a rise in the cost of an industry, an oligopolist can reasonably expect that his increase in price will be followed by the others in the industry. Consequently, the segment of the demand curve above the prevailing price will become less elastic and thereby make the angle *dKD* more obtuse and this will narrow down the gap in the marginal revenue curve. With the smaller gap in the marginal revenue curve, the *higher marginal cost curve is likely to cut it above the upper point H* indicating that the equilibrium price will rise and the equilibrium output will fall. Thus, it follows from the kinked demand curve theory that price is not likely to remain stable in the event of rise in cost.

(3) Decrease in Demand. In case of decrease in demand, the price is very likely to remain inflexible and will not fall. When the demand decreases, it becomes more certain that if one oligopolist initiates the reduction in price, others will follow with the result that the lower segment of the demand curve will become more inelastic. On the other hand, in the face of a decline in demand it is very certain that the increase in price by one oligopolist will never be followed by others. As a result, the upper segment of the demand curve becomes more elastic, that is, it becomes more nearly horizontal. With the increase in the elasticity of the upper segment and the decrease in the elasticity of the lower segment, the gap in the marginal revenue curve becomes wider and therefore it is most likely that the given marginal cost curve will cross the marginal revenue curve inside the gap when the demand curve *dKD* shifts downward. This indicates that the price will remain unchanged in the case of decrease in demand.

(4) Increase in Demand. ***When the demand increases, the price is unlikely to remain stable; instead the price is likely to rise.*** In the event of increase in demand, an oligopolist can expect that if he initiates the increase in price, his competitors will most probably follow him. Therefore, the upper segment *dK* of the demand curve will become less elastic and the angle *dKD* will become more obtuse. As a result, the gap *HR* in the marginal revenue curve will decrease and if this gap decreases much, it is very likely that the marginal cost curve crosses the marginal revenue curve above the upper point *H*, that is, above the gap, indicating that the price will rise above *OP*.

From above, it is clear that the kinked demand curve analysis of oligopoly explains stability in price in the face of falling costs or declining demand, whereas, price is likely to rise when either the costs rise or demand increases. M.M. Bober, thus rightly writes:

"The kinky demand curve analysis points to the likelihood of price rigidity in oligopoly when a price reduction is in order and of price flexibility when conditions warrant a rise in price. There is hardly any disposition to lower the price when there is decline in demand or in costs, but the price may be raised in response to increased demand or to rising cost."[18]

Critical Apprisal of Kinked Demand Curve Theory

1. We saw above how the kinked demand curve theory of oligopoly provides an explanation of price rigidity under oligopoly. But there is a major drawback in the theory. It only explains why once an oligopoly price has been determined, it would remain rigid or stable, ***it does not explain how the price has been determined.*** There is nothing in the kinked demand theory which explains how the price which is prevailing is determined. In other words, whereas this theory shows why price tends to stay where it is, it tells us nothing about why the price is where it is. In Fig. 40.8 the kink occurs at the price *OP* because *OP* happens to be the prevailing or established price. The theory does not explain how the price got to be equal to *OP*. Sweezy's kinked demand curve theory does not explain at what level the kink in the demand curve is formed. In Fig. 40.8, we have shown two demand curves *dkD* and *d′k′D′*; the former has a kink at price *OP,* the latter has a kink at price *OP′*. Sweezy's theory does not explain at what price kink will, therefore, be formed and how the price will be determined. Once the price is determined somehow or other, Sweezy theory's explains how it will remain stable or rigid. Commenting upon kinked demand curve theory Prof. Silberston rightly writes, "The most interesting question is not 'why are prices sticky in the short run?' (if they are), but who decides what the price is to be and on what principles."[19]

However, it may be mentioned that the above criticism applies especially to P.M. Sweezy's version of the kinked demand curve analysis. Hall and Hitch's version of kinked demand curve analysis also explains the determination of oligopoly price. According to Hall and Hitch, equilibrium price is determined by average cost (including normal profits), that is, by the tangency between average cost curve and the demand curve, as shown in Fig. 40.9. However, Hall and Hitch version runs into difficulty when the average cost curve of the various firms in

18. M.M. Bober, *Intermediate Price and Income Theory.*

an oligopolistic industry are different.

2. Another shortcoming of the kinked-demand oligopoly theory is that it does not apply to the oligopoly cases of prices leadership and price cartels which account for quite a large part of the oligopolistic markets. When price leadership and price cartels exist in oligopolistic markets there is concerted behaviour in regard to the price changes and hence there is no kink in the demand curve in these cases.

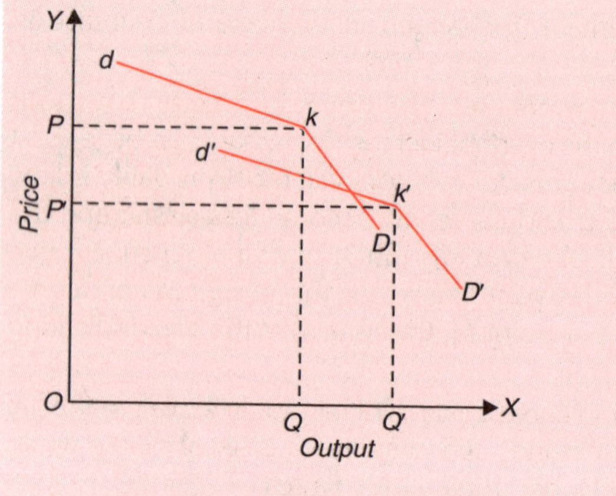

Fig. 40.8. *Two Kinked Demand Curves at Different Prices*

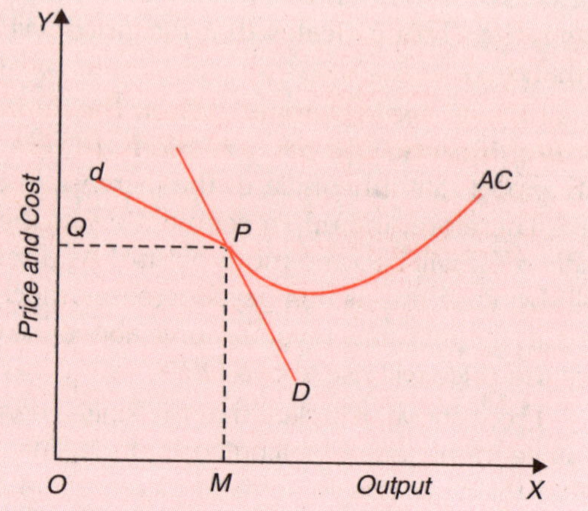

Fig. 40.9. *Full-Cost Pricing and Kinked Demand Curve*

3. Further, even in the case of pure oligopoly (*i.e.*, oligopoly with homogeneous products), the kinked demand curve theory does not furnish a complete explanation for price rigidity observed in oligopolistic markets. As explained earlier, from the kinked demand curve analysis it follows that prices are likely to remain stable when demand or cost conditions decrease, whereas under pure oligopoly prices are likely to rise in the case of increase in cost or demand.

4. Finally, it has been rightly asserted that explanation of price stability by Sweezy's kinked demand curve theory applies only to depression periods. In periods of depression, demand for the products decreases. As has been explained above, in the context of decreased demand, price in kinked demand curve theory is likely to remain sticky. But in periods of boom and inflation when the demand for the product is high and increasing, the price is likely to rise rather than remaining stable.

In conditions of boom and inflation, the kinked demand curve is of the type shown in Fig. 40.10 by the curve *dCD*. In this, the upper part *dC* of the demand curve is less elastic and the lower part *CD* is highly elastic. This is because under boom and inflationary conditions, it is expected that when one firm raises its price, its rival firms will follow, and if it cuts its price, they will not follow since the demand for their product is quite good due to boom conditions. Thus, during boom and inflationary conditions, the kinked demand curve is of quite different type from that postulated by Sweezy and Hall and Hitch. In Fig. 40.10 corresponding to the kinked demand curve *dCD*, the marginal revenue curve is *KLHG* with a broken part between *L* and *H*. Because of different types of kink, the marginal revenue curve in Fig. 40.10 is also of different types from the one shown earlier.

The important implication of this new type of kinked demand curve relevant to the conditions of boom and inflation is that under it price is unlikely to remain stable. Since under such a kinked demand curve, when costs of all firms increase and their marginal cost curves shift upward, there will be greater tendency to pass this increased costs on to the consumers by raising price, since if one firm does it, all are likely to follow it and therefore the quantity

19. Aubrey Silberston, Price Behaviour of Firms, *Economic Journal*, September 1970.

demanded of each firm will not decrease much.

Further, the price situation with this type of kinked demand curve is very unstable. As will be seen in Fig. 40.10 marginal cost curve *MC* while it does pass through the gap in the marginal revenue curve, *it cuts marginal revenue curve at two points, E and F.* Therefore, during periods of boom and inflation the price will not remain stable at *OP*, since the profits can be increased both by reducing the output to *ON*, and raising output to *OT*. Therefore, the firm (and its competitors too) may raise the price far above the current price *OP* to equate marginal revenue and marginal cost at the lower output *ON*. The firm even in boom conditions may decide to 'go it alone' and cut its price below *OP* so as to raise its output to *OT* and thus equate marginal revenue and marginal cost at higher level of output. We cannot say in advance whether in conditions of boom and inflation price will be raised or lowered but one thing is certain that it will not remain sticky at the current *OP* level.

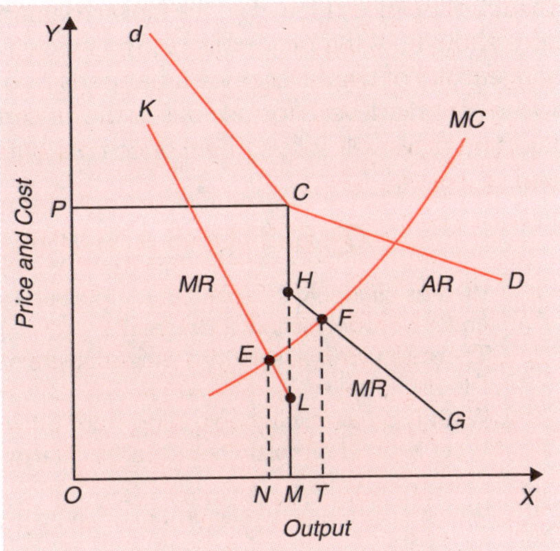

Fig. 40.10. *Kinked Demand Curve during Boom and Inflationary Conditions*

We therefore, conclude that from Sweezy as well as Hall and Hitch's versions of kinked demand curve theory, it follows that prices are likely to remain stable during depression periods but not during boom and inflationary periods. Our analysis shows that whether we use kinked demand curve of the type postulated by Sweezy as well as Hall and Hitch or an opposite type of the kinked demand curve, prices are unlikely to be stable during the boom periods.

Prof. Stigler's Critique of Kinked Demand Curve and his Empirical Study

Prof. George J. Stigler has made an empirical study of the behaviour of the oligopolies in order to test the theory of kinked demand curve.[20] His empirical study suggests that there does not exist any 'kink' in the demand curve confronting oligopolists. Prof. Stigler has, therefore, rejected the hypothesis of the kinked demand curve under oligopoly. It has been observed by him that in inflationary periods oligopolists do often follow one another's price rises, contrary to what is assumed in the kinked demand theory.

However, it may be pointed out that Prof. Stigler's statistical tests did not involve a sufficiently large number of producers and what might be indicated by a larger sample of producers is not at all clear from his study. Moreover, it should be noted that Prof. Stigler's empirical study refutes only the hypothesis of kinked demand curve, it does not question the price rigidity under oligopoly. There is considerable empirical evidence found by Prof. Stigler and many others of price rigidity under oligopoly. The point at issue is what is the proper explanation for this price rigidity. Despite Stigler's empirical study, many economists still believe in the explanation furnished by kinked demand curve theory regarding price stability, especially when price reductions are to be expected. However, as mentioned above, it seems clear that in cases of price leadership, formal agreements, price cartels, there cannot exist kink in the demand curve since there is concerted behaviour with respect to price in these cases. In other cases of oligopoly, 'kink' in the demand curve can exist. Whether it actually exists or not is still

20. Sec George J. Stigler, "The Kinky Oligopoly Demand Curve and Rigid Prices", *Journal of Political Economy*, Vol. LV, October, 1947, reprinted in American Economic Association's *Readings in Price Theory.*

a matter of opinion. However, the kinked demand curve analysis, as Professor Baumol remarks, "does show how the oligopolistic firm's view of competitive reaction patterns can affect the changeability of whatever price it happens to be charging."[21] It is worth noting that 'kink' at the current price level is formed due to the uncertainty by the oligopolists and their expectations that their rivals will follow their price-cuts but would not follow any increases in prices by them.

QUESTIONS AND PROBLEMS FOR REVIEW

1. What is oligopoly ? Explain the important features of oligopoly. Do you think price and output under oligopoly is indeterminate?
2. There is no unique solution to the problem of determination of price and output under oligopoly. Discuss.
3. What is collusive oligopoly ? How are price and output determined under it?
4. What is cartel ? Explain how a cartel determines price and output of a product to maximise joint profits.
5. Why are cartels generally unstable ? Why is there a tendency on the part of members of cartels to cheat ?
6. Explain Sweezy's kinked demand curve model of oligopoly. How does it explain price rigidity under oligopoly ?
7. What is non-price competition ? What role does it play in oligopolistic market situation ?
8. What alternative objectives to profit maximisation have been proposed which the firms working under oligopoly seek to achieve? Briefly explain them.
9. What are the different types of price leadership that may be established in oligopolistic market situation ? Assuming that there are two firms producing homogeneous products explain how price and output are determined where there is price leadership by
   (1) the lower cost firm, and (2) the dominant firm
10. What is kinked demand curve ? How does it help in explaining price rigidity under oligopoly?
11. Using the kinked demand curve model explain how the increase and reduction in marginal cost need not lead to any change in price or output.
12. What is meant by price rigidity ? Why are prices rigid under oligopoly ? Explain with the help of the kiked demand curve model.
13. What is Prisoner's Dilemma ? How does it help to explain the likelihood of firms opting for sub-optimal solution in oligopoly ?
14. What are the chief difficulties of maintaining price leadership in oligopolistic market situation? Examine the view that price leadership is likely to break down as there is generally a tendency on the part of the rival firms to indulge in *non-price competition* to promote their sales.
15. What is meant by interdependence of firms in oligopoly ? How does it affect price-output equilibrium of a firm ?
16. Explain briefly the various approaches that have been offered to explain the determination of price and output under oligopoly.
17. Explain Prisoner's Dilemma. How does it help to explain that cartels are quite unstable ?

21. William J. Baumol, *Economic Theory and Operations Analysis*, 1961.p.

CHAPTER

41

Classical Models of Oligopoly

Introduction

We shall now undertake the study of a number of models of oligopoly put forward by some classicial economists. The theory of non-collusive or uncoordinated oligopoly is one of the oldest theories of competition and monopoly or perhaps of all the theories of the behaviour of an individual firm. A model of oligopoly (duopoly case) was first of all put forth by Cournot, a French economist, in 1838.[1] Cournot's model of oligopoly was subjected to criticism in 1883 by Joseph Bertrand, a French mathematician, whose criticism of Cournot provided a substitute model of oligopoly. In 1897, Edgeworth, a famous Italian mathematician and economist, offered another model of oligopoly in an article published in an Italian journal.[2] Besides, Stackelberg, a German economist, and E.H. Chamberlin in also put forward their models of oligopoly. We will discuss below all these classical models of oligopoly.

It is useful to note here that the first three of these oligopoly models are based upon a behavioural assumption about an individual firm that it does not take into account rival's reactions to the output or price fixed by it. It is assumed in these three classical models of Cournot, Bertrand, and Edgeworth that an oligopolist believes that his rivals will keep their outputs or prices fixed, regardless of what output or price he fixes : In other words, each oligopolist believes that irrespective of his actions and their effect on the rival's business, his rivals would not react. That is to say, while deciding about his policy, the oligopolist does not take into account the possible reactions of his rivals in response to his actions. Such an assumption about rival's reactions is expressed by modern economists as ***zero conjectural variation*** of an oligopolist, that is, each oligopolist thinks or conjectures that the variations in rivals' output, price or any other variable reaction to his own variations is zero.[3] By taking conjectural variation of oligopolist as zero, these three classicial models ignore the mutual interdependence which is the heart of the oligopoly problem. It should be noted that in Cournot's model, it is rival's output which is assumed by an oligopolist to remain fixed at the present level, while he contemplates a certain change in his own ovvvvvutput. On the other hand, Bertand and Edgeworth in their models assume that the oligopolist believes that rival's *price* remains unchanged at the present level.

---

1. Augustin Cournot, *Researches into the Mathematical Principles of the Theory of Wealth* translated by N. T. Bacon. (New York, Macmillan, 1897).

2. F. Y. Edgeworth, *La Teoria Pura Del Monopoly,* Giormale degli Economist, Vol. XV, 1897. The English translation of this article appears in *Edgeworth's Papers Relating to Political Economy,* Vol. I, pp. 111.42 (London: Macmillan, 1925).

3. See W. Fellner, *Competition Among the Few* (New York, Alfred A. Knopf, 1949) pp. 71 ff. However, the use of this expression goes back to Ragnar Frisch in his article, Monopoly—Polypoly—The Concept of Force in the Economy (translated by W. Beckerman, *International Economic Papers,* Number 1).

In his famous work "*The Theory of Monopolistic Competition*" E.H. Chamberlin put forward another model of non-collusive oligopoly which is considered as an improvement over the three classical models of Cournot, Bertrand and Edgeworth as in ***Chamberlin's model it is assumed that oligopoly firms recognise their interdependence while fixing their output and price.*** Through his model Chamberlin arrives at a monopoly so1ution of pricing and output under oligopoly wherein firms jointly maximise their profits. Chamberlin's model will be discussed at the end of this chapter.

COURNOT'S DUOPOLY MODEL

As said above, Augustin Cournot, a French economist, published his theory of duopoly in 1838. But it remained almost unnoticed until 1880' s when Walras called the attention of the economists to Cournot's work. Cournot dealt with the case of duopoly. Let us first state the assumptions which are made by Cournot in his analysis of price and output under duopoly. First, Cournot takes the case of two identical mineral springs operated by two owners who are selling the mineral water in the same market. Their waters are identical. Therefore, ***his model relates to the duopoly with homogeneous products.*** Secondly, it is assumed by Cournot, for the sake of simplicity, that the owners operate mineral springs and sell water without any cost of production. Thus, in Cournot's model, cost of production is taken as zero; only the demand side of the market is analysed. It may be noted that the assumption of zero cost of production is made only to simplify the analysis. His model can be presented when cost of production is positive. Thirdly, the duopolists fully know the market demand for the mineral water—they can see every point on the demand curve. Moreover, the market demand for the product is assumed to be linear, that is, market demand curve facing the two producers is a straight line.

Lastly, Cournot assumes that each duoplist believes that regardless of his actions and their effect upon market price of the product, the rival firm will keep its output constant, that is, it will go on producing the same amount of output which it is presently producing. In other words, the duopolist will decide about the amount of output which is most profitable for him to produce in the light of his rival's present output and assumes that it remains constant. In other words, for determining the output to be produced, he will not take into account reactions of his rival in response to his variation in output and thus decides its level of output *independently*.

Cournot's Approach to Equilibrium

Suppose the demand curve confronting the two producers of the mineral water is the straight line *MD* as shown in Fig 41.1. Further suppose that *ON* = *ND* is the maximum daily output of each mineral spring. Thus, the total output of both the springs is *OD* = *ON* + *ND*. It will be seen from the figure that when the total output *OD* of both the springs is offered for sale in the market, the price will be zero. It may be noted here that if there was a perfect competition, the long-run equilibrium "price would have been zero and actual output produced equal to *OD*. This is because cost of production being assumed to be zero, price must also be zero so as to provide a no profit long-run equilibrium under perfect competition.

Assume for the moment that one producer A of the mineral water starts the business first. Thus, to begin with he will be monopolist. He will then produce daily *ON* output which is his maximum daily output, because his profits will be maximum at output *ON* [4] and will be

4. When cost of production is zero, the marginal cost will be zero. With demand curve *MD* as straight line, the marginal revenue curve will pass through the middle of *OD*, that is, through *N*. Thus, at *ON* output *MR* will be zero. Therefore, a monopolist with zero marginal cost will be in equilibrium at output *ON* where marginal revenue and marginal cost will be equal (both being zero at output *ON*). In such a situation, the monopolist will make maximum profits by producing output *ON*.

equal to *ONKP* (since the costs are zero, the whole revenue *ONKP* will be profits). The price which that producer will charge will be *OP.* Suppose now that the owner of the other spring enters into the business and starts operating his spring. This new producer *B* sees that the former producer *A* is producing *ON* amount of output. According to Cournot's behavioural assumption, the producer *B* believes that the former producer *A* will continue to produce *ON* $(= \frac{1}{2} OD)$ amount of output, regardless of what output he himself decides to produce. Given this belief, the best that the new producer can do is to regard segment *KD* as the demand curve confronting him. With his demand curve *KD,* the producer will produce *NH* $(= \frac{1}{2} ND)$ amount of output. The total output will now be *ON* + *NH* = *OH,* and the price will fall to *OP'*

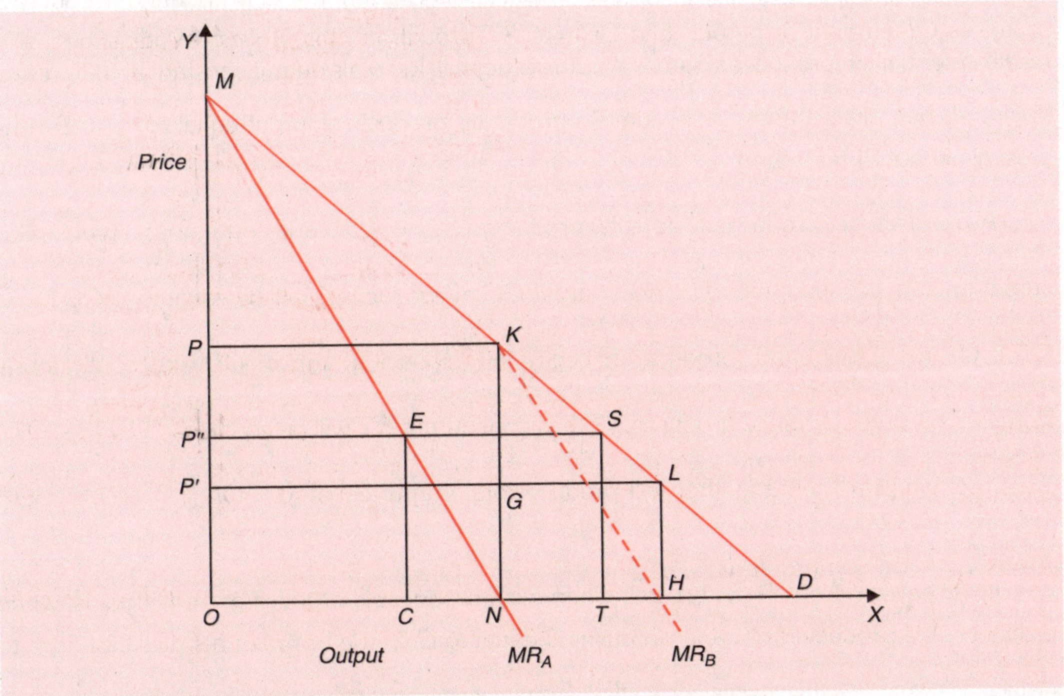

Fig. 41.1. *Cournot's Duopoly Solution*

or *HL* per unit. The total profits made by the two producers will be *OHLP'* which are less than *ONKP.* Out of total profits *OHLP '*, profits of producer *A* will be *ONGP '* and profits of producer *B* will be *NHLG.* Now that due to fall in price, profits of producer *A* are reduced from *ONKP* to *ONGP'* because of producer *B* producing output *NH,* the producer *A* will reconsider the situation. But he will assume that producer *B* will continue to produce output *NH.* With producer *B* producing output *NH,* the best that the producer A can do is to produce $\frac{1}{2}(OD - NH)$. He, will accordingly, reduce his output.

Now that producer *B* has been surprised by the reduction of output by producer *A* and he will also find that his share of total profits is less than that of producer *A*, he will reappraise his situation. Learning nothing from his earlier experience and believing that producer *A* will continue producing its new current level of output, the producer *B* will find his maximum profits by producing output equal to $\frac{1}{2}$ (*OD* – New Output of *A*). Producer *B*, accordingly, will increase his output. With this move of producer *B*, producer A will find his profits reduced. The producer *A* will therefore again reconsider his position and will find that he can increase his profits by producing output equal to $\frac{1}{2}$(*OD* – current output of producer *B*). This process of adjustment and readjustment by each producer will continue, producer *A* being forced gradually to reduce his output and producer *B* being able to increase his output gradually until the total output *OT* is produced ($OT = \frac{2}{3} OD$) and **each is producing the same amount of output equal to $\frac{1}{3}$ OD.** In this final position, producer *A* produces *OC* amount of output and producer *B* produces *CT* amount of output, and *OC* = *CT*. Throughout this process of adjustment and readjustment, each producer assumes that the other will keep his output constant at the present level and then always finds his maximum profits by producing output equal to $\frac{1}{2}$ (*OD*—the present output of the other).

As seen above, producer *A* starts by producing $ON = \frac{1}{2} OD$ and continuously reduces his output until he produces *OC*. The final output *OC* of producer *A* will be equal to $\frac{1}{3} OD$ (= $\frac{1}{2}$ *OT*). On the other hand, producer *B* begins by producing $\frac{1}{4}$th of *OD* and continuously increases his output until he produces *CT*. His final output *CT* will be equal to $\frac{1}{3} OD$ (= $\frac{1}{2} OT$). Thus the two producers together will produce total output equal to $\frac{1}{3} OD + \frac{1}{3} OD = \frac{2}{3} OD$ (= *OT*).

It will be seen from Fig. 41.1 that when each producer is producing $\frac{1}{3}$ *OD* (that is, when producer *A* is producing *OC* and producer *B* equal to *CT*), the best that his rival can do is to produce $\frac{1}{2}(OD - \frac{1}{3} OD)$ which is equal to $\frac{1}{3} OD = OC = CT$. Therefore, when each producer is producing $\frac{1}{3}$ *OD* so that the total output of the two together is $\frac{2}{3}$ *OD*, no one will expect to increase his profits by making any further adjustment in output. Thus, in Cournot's model of duopoly, *stable equilibrium* is reached when total output produced is $\frac{2}{3}$rd of *OD* and each producer is producing $\frac{1}{3}$rd of *OD*.

Comparison of Cournot Equilibrium with Perfectly Competitive Equilibrium and Monopoly Equilibrium.

It will be useful to compare the Cournot's duopoly solution with the monopolistic and the perfectly competitive solutions. If the two producers had combined and formed a coalition, then the output produced by them together will be the monopoly output *ON* and therefore, the price set will be the monopoly price *OP*. Monopoly output *ON* produced in case of coalition is much less than the output *OT* produced in Cournot's duopoly equilibrium. Further, the monopoly price *OP* charged in case of coalition is much greater than the price *OP″* determined in Cournot's duopoly equilibrium. In case of coalition, they will enjoy the monopoly profits *ONKP* which are maximum possible profits, given the demand curve *MD*. These monopoly profits can be shared equally by them. It will be seen from Fig. 41.1 that these monopoly profits *ONKP* made in case of coalition are much greater than the total profits *OTSP″* made by them in Cournot's duopoly equilibrium. It is thus clear that in case of the duopolists competing with each other as conceived by Cournot's duopoly solution, price and profits are lower and output is greater than if they had combined together and formed a monopoly.

On the other hand, if the market were perfectly competitive, the output would have been *OD* and price would have been zero. That is perfectly competitive solution would have resulted in greater output and lower price than under Cournot's duopoly equilibrium. Thus, under ***Cournot's duopoly solution, output is two thirds of the maximum possible output (i.e. purely competitive output) and price is two-thirds of he most profitable (i.e., monopoly) price.***

Extension of Cournot's Model to the Case of more than Two Firms

We saw above that under Cournot's duopoly solution, two producers produce $\frac{2}{3}$ *OD*, that is, two-thirds of the maximum possible output. His solution can be extended to those cases of oligopoly where there are more than two sellers. Thus, it can be shown in the same manner that if there were three producers, the total output would be $\frac{3}{4}$ th of *OD*, each of these three producing $\frac{1}{4}$ *OD*. In fact, the number of producers or sellers and the total output produced in Cournot's solution can be expressed in a general formula. Thus, if there are *n* producers, then under Cournot's solution, the total output produced will be $\frac{n}{n+1}$ of *OD* where *OD* is the maximum possible output. If there are 10 producers, the total 10 output under Cournot's solution will be $\frac{10}{10+1}$ of *OD*. Similarly, if there are 100 producers, the total output under Cournot's solution would be $\frac{100}{101}$ of *OD* and if there are a very large number of producers, the total output would be virtually *OD* (the purely competitive output) and the price would be purely competitive price (*i.e* , zero under the assumption of zero cost). The essential conclusion which follows is that "as the number of sellers increases from one to infinity the price is continually lowered from what it would be under monopoly conditions to what it would be under purely competitive conditions, and that for any number of sellers, it is perfectly determinate."[5]

Following Cournot, the costs of production in the above discussion of Cournot's oligopoly solution has been taken to be zero. However, it should be noted that above essential conclusion will not change if the cost curve with positive cost of production are introduced into the discussion.

Cournot's Duopoly Equilibrium as an Example of Nash Equilibrium

An American mathematician put forward a concept of equilibrium known after his name

5. E.H. Chamberlin, *The Theory of Monopolistie Competition*, p. 34.

as Nash Equilibrium. According to Nash, ***firms reach their equilibrium state when they are doing their best, given what its competitors are presently doing.*** In terms of price theory doing their best means maximising profits and what others are doing means what rate of output they are producing or what price they are charging or what advertising expenditure they are incurring to promote the sales of their products. When each firm is doing its best, given what others are doing, no one has any incentive to change its behaviour and hence equilibrium exists.

Now, in Cournot's model, equilibrium is achieved ***when each firm produces an output that maximises its profits, given the output produced by the rival firm and hence neither firm has any incentive to change its output. Hence, Cournot's Duopoly equilibrium is an example of Nash equilibrium.***

Cournot's Duopoly Model : Mathematical Illustration

Cournot's Duopoly model can be explained by presenting it in mathematical form. Let us assume the linear demand function

$$P = a - bQ \qquad \ldots(i)$$

where Q is the output of both the firms.

The above demand function can be written as

$$P = a - b(Q_a + Q_b) \qquad \ldots(ii)$$

where Q_a and Q_b are the outputs of firms A and B respectively.

In order to obtain total revenue of firm A, we multiply price (P) with output of firm A (i.e. Q_a). Thus,

$$TR_a = PQ_a = Q_a - bQ_a^2 - bQ_a - Q_b$$

Therefore, marginal revenue function for firm A is

$$\frac{d(TR_a)}{dQ_a} = MR_a = (a - bQ_b) - 2bQ_a \qquad \ldots(iii)$$

In order to maximise profits firm A would set what he perceives to be its marginal revenue equal to marginal cost. Let k be the marginal cost which remains constant. Thus, in equilibrium

$$(a - bQ_b) - 2bQ_a = k$$

$$Q_a = \frac{(a-k) - bQ_b}{2b} \qquad \ldots(iv)$$

The above equation (iv) states that the profit-maximising output Q_a of firm A depends on what other firm is producing, that is, Q_b. It describes how firm A will react to a rate of output produced by the rival firm. Therefore, the ***equation (iv) is called reaction function***. Similarly reaction function of firm B can be derived as

$$Q_b = \frac{(a-k) - bQ_a}{2a} \qquad \ldots(v)$$

It may be noted that equilibrium can be determined by solving the two reaction functions (iv) and (v) *simultaneously*. We shall illustrate it by taking a numerical example in a later section.

Cournot's Duopoly Equilibrium Explained with the Aid of Reaction Curves

Some economists have employed the reaction curves to explain Cournot's duopoly solution. The reaction curves may be output reaction curves or price reaction curves depending upon whether it is the output or the price which is the adjustment variable. Since, in Cournot's model, it is the output which is subject to the adjusting variation, output reaction carves are relevant. It should be carefully noted that these reaction curves refer not to the reactions which a seller expects will be forthcoming from his rivals but to the ***sellers own reactions*** to the moves of his rival.

In Fig. 41.1 output reaction curves of two producers (sellers *A* and *B* are shown, *MN* is the output reaction curve of *A* and *RS* is the output reaction curve of *B*. The output reaction curve *MN* of seller *A* shows how *A* will react to any change in output by *B*, that is, A's output reaction curve shows how much output he will decide to produce for each output of producer *B*. In other words, *A*'s output reaction curve indicates the most profitable output of *A* for each given output of *B*. Likewise, *B*'s output reaction curve *RS* shows how much output *B* will decide to produce (that is, what will be *B*'s most profitable output for each given output of *A*.). For example, if *B* produces output OB_1, *A*'s output reaction curve *MN* shows that A will produce output OA_2 in response to *B*'s output OB_1. Similarly, for all other outputs. On the

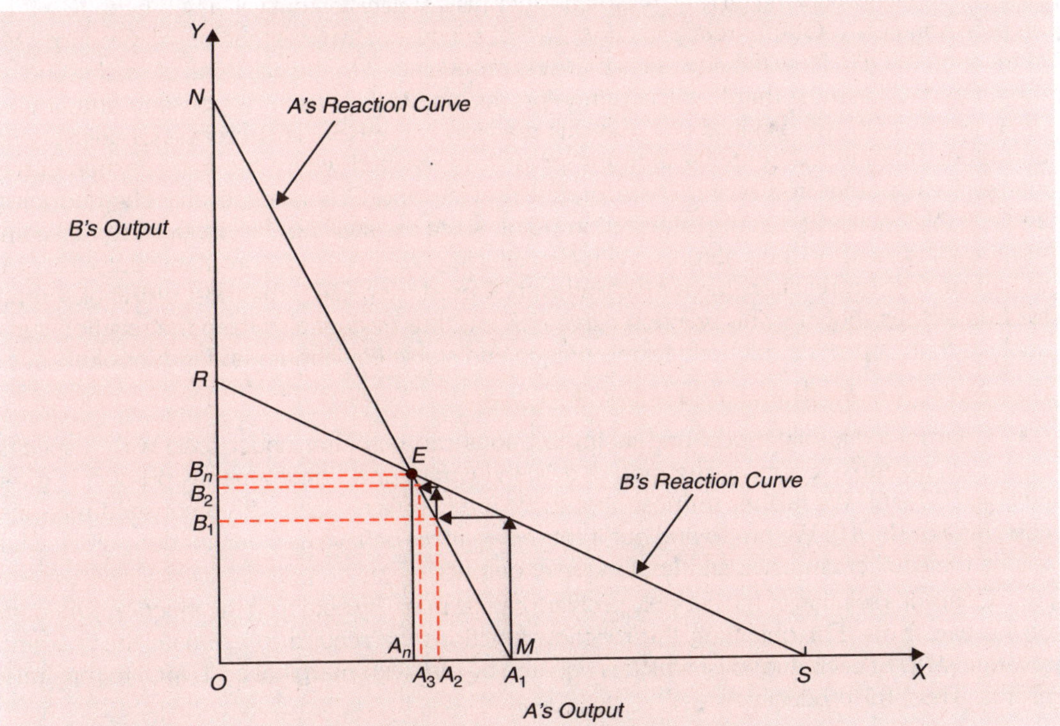

Fig. 41.2. Reaction Curves: Equilibrium in Cournot's Model

other hand, if *A* produces OA_2, *B*'s output reaction curve *RS* shows that *B* will produce OB_2, and so forth for all.other outputs.

It will be seen from Fig. 41.2 that output reaction curves have been drawn to be straight lines. This is because we are assuming that market demand curve for the product of duopolists is a straight line and that the marginal costs of production of both producers *A* and *B* are constant (at zero). It should be noted that output *OM* is the monopoly output since producer *A* will produce output *OM* (or OA_1) if producer *B*'s output is zero. In other words, producer A will produce and sell output *OM* if he were the monopolist. On the other hand, A will produce zero output if B's output is *ON*. Thus, *ON* represents the level of output which *B* must produce in order to force the producer *A* to produce zero output. Given the marginal costs as zero, the producer *A* will be forced to produce zero output when the price has fallen to zero and, therefore, production is no longer profitable. Output *ON* will be produced under conditions of pure competition since at output *ON* the price will be zero and therefore equal to marginal cost which is assumed to be zero in the present case. Thus, while *OM* is the monopoly output, *ON* is the purely competitive output. *RS* is the output reaction curve of *B* which indicates how much output producer *B* produces, given the level of output of producer *A*. We assume the two producers *A* and *B* to be completely identical, therefore, *OR* will be equal to *OM*, and *OS* will be equal to *ON*.

Output reaction curves, as interpreted above, can be used to explain Cournot's duopoly solution. Each producer, as before, assumes that his rival will continue producing the same amount of output regardless of what he might himself decide to produce. To begin with, suppose producer *A* goes into business first and is therefore initially a monopolist. Therefore, in the beginning *A* will produce output *OM* or OA_1. Suppose now *B* also enters into business. *B* will assume that *A* will keep his output constant at *OM* of *A*, he will produce OB_1. But when *A* sees that *B* is producing OB_1 he will reconsider his last decision but will assume that *B* will go on producing OB_1. Output reaction curve *NM* of producer *A* shows that he will produce OA_2 in reaction to OB_1. Now, when *B* sees that *A* is producing OA_2, he will think of readjusting his output and will assume that *A* will continue producing OA_2. Thus in response to output OA_2 of *A*, producer *B* will produce OB_2 (see his reaction curve RS). This process of adjustments and readjustments will continue until the point *E* is reached where the two reaction curves intersect each other and A and *B* are producing OA_n and OB_n respectively. The duopolists attain stable equilibrium at the intersection point, since they will not feel induced to make any further adjustments in their outputs. With *B* producing OB_n, A's most profitable output is OA_n as indicated by his reaction curve *MN*, and with A producing OA_n, the most profitable output for *B* is OB_n as shown by his reaction curve *RS*. It is thus evident also from the reaction curve analysis that Cournot's solution yields a unique and stable equilibrium under duopoly.

Cournot's Duopoly Model: A Numerical Example

Cournot's duopoly model and its implications can be better understood with a specific numerical example. Suppose the market demand curve for a homogeneous product is given by $P = 100 - Q$. We further suppose that there are two firms each with a constant marginal cost *(MC)* of Rs. 10. We are to find out if these two firms behave as Cournot duopolists, what will be the equilibrium price and total industry output.

Cournot's solution to the duopoly problem can be made by obtaining the *reaction functions* of the two firms. For obtaining the reaction functions we require to estimate the marginal revenue *(MR)* of each duopolist which is equated by him with marginal cost *(MC)* to maximise profits. Thus, for producer A

$$TR = P.Q_a$$

Where *TR* stands for total revenue which can be obtained from multiplying price with quantity produced and sold.

$$\text{As } P = 100 - Q,$$

$$TR_a = (100 - Q)Q_a$$

Since $$Q = Q_a + Q_b, \text{ we have}$$

$$TR_a = 100\,Q_a - (Q_a + Q_b)\,Q_a$$

$$= 100\,Q_a - Q_a^2 - Q_a\,Q_b$$

Now, $$MR_a = \frac{\Delta TR_a}{\Delta Q_a} = 100 - 2Q_a - Q_b$$

Now setting marginal revenue (*MR*) of producer A equal to marginal cost (*MC*) to maximise profits, we have

$$MR_a = MC$$
$$100 - 2Q_a - Q_b = 10$$
$$100 - 10 - Q_b = 2Q_a$$
$$90 - Q_b = 2Q_a$$
$$Qa = \frac{90 - Q_b}{2} = 45 - \frac{1}{2}Q_b$$

The equation $Q_a = 45 - \frac{1}{2}Q_b$ is the reaction function of firm *A*.

Similarly, reaction function of firm *B* can be derived which will be equal to $Q_b = \frac{90 - Q_a}{2}$ $= 45 - \frac{1}{2}Q_a$. Now, the two reaction function equations can be simultaneously solved to obtain the values of Q_a and Q_b. Thus

$$Q_a = 45 - \frac{1}{2}Q_b \quad ......(i)$$

$$Q_b = 45 - \frac{1}{2}Q_a \quad ......(ii)$$

Substituting the value Q_b in (*i*) we have

$$Q_a = 45 - \frac{1}{2}\left(45 - \frac{1}{2}Q_a\right)$$
$$= 45 - 22.5 + \frac{1}{4}Q_a$$
$$Q_a - \frac{1}{4}Q_a = 45 - 22.5 = 22.5$$
$$\frac{3}{4}Q_a = 22.5$$

or $$Q_a = 22.5 \times \frac{4}{3} = \frac{90}{3} = 30$$

Now substituting the value of Q_a (= 30) in (*ii*) above we have

$$Q_b = 45 - \frac{1}{2}30 = 30.$$

Thus, under Cournot's duopoly solution $Q_a = Q_b = 30$ and total industry output is 60 ($Q = Q_a + Q_b = 30 + 30 = 60$).

Now, substituting the value of Q in the market demand function we have,

$$P = 100 - Q$$
$$= 100 - 60 = 40$$

Thus price fixed in Cournot's duopoly model, price will be equal to Rs. 40.

Solution of Numerical Problem through Reaction Curves

From the above reaction functions of the two firms we can draw their reaction curves and obtain the Cournot' s solution where the two reaction curves intersect.

Thus, from the reaction function of $A\left(Q_a = 45 - \frac{1}{2}Q_b\right)$ we can obtain the amounts of output of A by assuming various levels of output which the firm B will produce

Thus, if $\quad Q_b = 0, Q_a = \left(45 - \frac{1}{2}Q_b\right) = \left(45 - \frac{1}{2} \times 0\right) = 45$

If $\quad Q_b = 90, Q_b = \left(45 - \frac{1}{2}90\right) = 0$

If $\quad Q_b = 60, Q_a = \left(45 - \frac{1}{2}60\right) = 15$

If $\quad Q_b = 30, Q_b = \left(45 - \frac{1}{2}30\right) = 30$

With the above information we can draw the reaction curve of firm A as shown in Figure

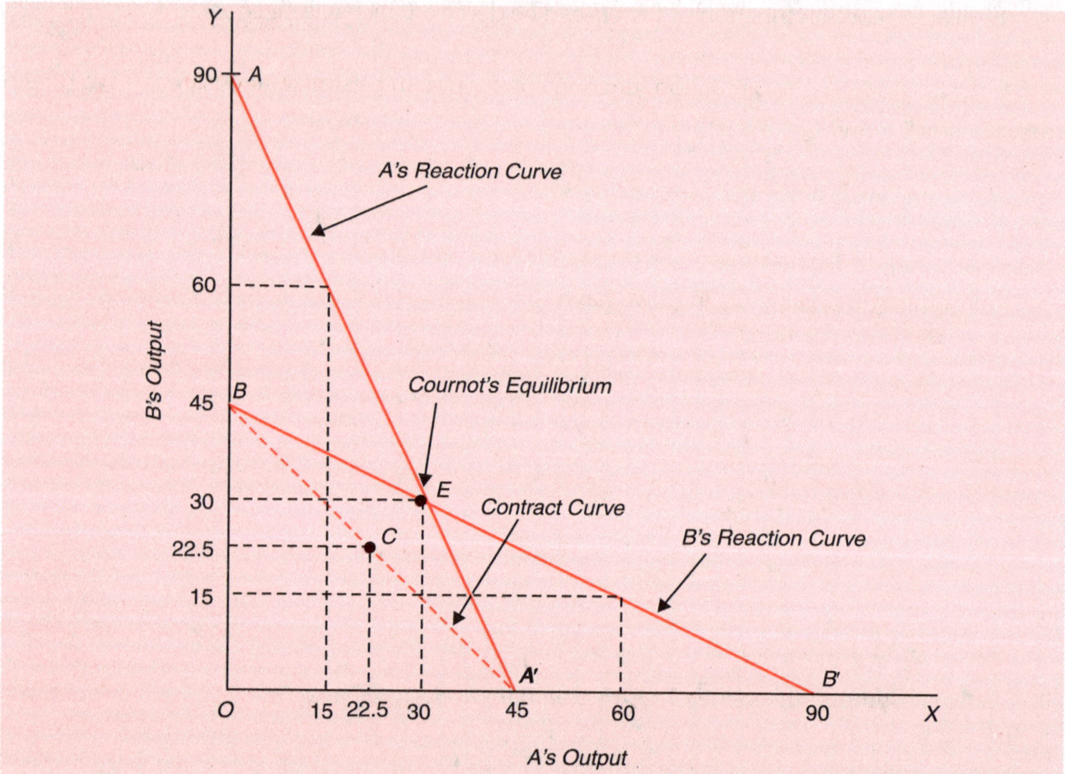

Fig 41.3. *Reaction Curves and Cournot Duopoly Solution*

41.3 by the reaction curve AA'. Similarly, from the reaction function of firm B we can calculate the amounts of output it will produce, given the amounts of output of firm A. Thus,

If $\quad Q_a = 0, Q_b = \left(45 - \frac{1}{2}Q_a\right) = \left(45 - \frac{1}{2}.0\right) = 45$

If $\quad Q_a = 90, Q_b = \left(45 - \frac{1}{2}90\right) = 0$

If $\quad Q_a = 60, Q_b = \left(45 - \frac{1}{2}60\right) = 15$

If $\quad Q_a = 30, Q_b = \left(45 - \frac{1}{2}.30\right) = 30$

On plotting the above data, we obtain reaction curves of *BB′* of firm *B*. It will be seen from Figure 41.3 that the reaction function curves of the two firms intersect at point *E* corresponding to 30 units of output of each firm. It may be noted that reaction function curves depict the profit-maxising outputs of each firm by assuming that the other firm's output remains constant. Thus, at point *E* where the reaction curves of firms *A* and *B* intersect, each firm maximises profits by producing 30 units of output by assuming that the other will also produce 30 units.

Comparison of Cournot Equilibrium with Collusion, Monopoly and Perfect Completion

Note that in Cournot equilibrium the total output of the two duopolists is equal to 30 + 30 = 60 which is greater than the monopoly output equal to 45 units of output (Note that if output of firm *B* is zero, the firm *A* produces 45 units. With firm *B's* output equal to zero, the firm *A* is monopolist and his profit-maximising output is 45). It follows that monopoly output is 45 units of output which is half of the perfectly competitive output of 90 units in the given circumstances. It is interesting to note that if instead of competing with each other, the two firms collude, they will maximise *total profits* and most probably will agree to share the profits equally. In case of collusion, they will in fact constitute a monopoly and their total profits are maximised at the level of output at which marginal revenue equals marginal cost. The monopoly output will be equal to 45 units and if they agree to share profits equally, each firm will produce 22.5 units. This can also be shown graphically in Figure 41.3. A straight line joining 45 units on each axis is drawn which is called *contract curve* which shows combination of outputs of firms A and *B*. Given the price and cost, if they agree to share profits *equally*, each will produce according to the mid point *C* of the contract curve, that is, each will produce 22.5 units. It is therefore evident that under collusion, the production is less and profits greater than in Cournot equilibrium.

That under collusion and forming a monopoly, the total output will be equal to 45 can be mathematically proved as under :-

As total profits are maximised by producing a level of output Q so that marginal revenue corresponding to market demand equals marginal cost of production (= ₹10). Thus

$$TR = PQ = (100 - Q)Q = 100Q - Q^2$$

$$MR = \frac{d(TR)}{dQ} = 100 - 2Q$$

Setting *MR* equal to *MC* (= 10), we determine the level of output which will be produced under collusion or monopoly

$$MR = MC$$

$$100 - 2Q = 10$$

$$2Q = 100 - 10 = 90$$

$$Q = 45$$

Any combination of outputs Q_a and Q_b of duopolists that adds up to 45 will maximise total profits. Thus, in case they agree to share profits evenly, their outputs, $Q_a = Q_b = 22.5$ with each producing half of total output.

It may be further noted that for determining perfectly competitive output in this case, we will have to set price equal to the marginal cost. Thus, for competitive output.

$$P = MC$$

$$100 - Q = 10$$

$$Q = 100 - 10 = 90$$

Thus we see that competitive output is greater than the output produced under Cournot equilibrium.

Evaluation of Cournot Duopoly Model

Cournot's model suffers from a basic flaw. According to Cournot model, in deciding its output each firm assumes that the other firm will keep its output constant, independent of what output it produces. Yet in the adjustment process to the equilibrium position the other firm does react to the output decision of its rival as it affects it profits except at the unique Cournot equilibrium point. Despite seeing this reaction of the rival firm, the duopolist do not learn from actual experience and continues to behave myopically and go on making the same naive assumption that the other firm will keep its output constant at the present level. A rational behaviour demands that duopolists should quickly recognise their mutual inter-dependence and act accordingly. Thus, Cournot model has been described as ***"no learning by doing model"***

Nevertheless, Cournot model occupies an important place in economic theory, for it formally describes equilibrium of the models of perfect competition and monopoly. Further, Cournot model is also useful as it presents a simple model of market structure from which the relationship between market power and market shares supplied by an individual firm can be derived and the tendency towards collusion and monopoly pricing and output fixation is clearly brought out.

BERTRAND'S DUOPOLY MODEL

Joseph Bertrand, a French mathematician, criticized Cournot's duopoly solution and put forth a substitute model of duopoly. According to Bertrand, there was no limit to the fall in price since each producer can always lower the price by underbidding the other and increasing his supply of output until the price becomes equal to his unit cost of production. There are some important differences in assumptions of Bertrand and Cournot's models of duopoly. In Bertrand's model, producers do not produce any output and then sell whatever price it can bring in. Instead, the producers first set the price of the product and then produce the output which is demanded at that price. Thus, in Bertrand's adjusting variable is price and not output.

In Cournot's model, each producer adjusts his output believing that rival will continue to produce the same output as he is doing at present, but in ***Bertrand's model each producer believes that his rival will keep his price constant at the present level whatever price he might himself set.*** Thus, in Bertrand's model, as in Cournot's, mutual interdependence of the duopolists is ignored. In other words, Bertrand's model also assumes zero conjectural variation. The difference is in the variable which is assumed to be constant. Whereas, in Cournot's model each producer (or seller) assumes his rival's output constant, in Bertrand's model, each producer (seller) assumes his rival's price constant. In Bertrand's model producers adjust their prices and not their outputs.

Furthermore, in Bertrand's model, it is not very important that the producer should know the correct market demand of their product, or should have identical view about the market demand. It is enough for each producer to know that he can capture the whole market by undercutting his rival. The other assumptions of Bertrand's model are the same as those of Cournot's model though their implications may be somewhat different. Thus, in Bertrand's model the products produced and sold by the two producers are completely identical and in no way differentiated. Its implication is that if a producer underbids the other, it can conquer the whole market (that is, snatch away all the customers from his rival). Further, the two producers have identical costs and also work under condition of constant marginal cost. Moreover, the productive capacity of the producers is unlimited, that is, there is no limit to their increase in the supply of output up to the maximum requirement of demand.

Let there be two producers *A* and *B*. Suppose that *A* goes into business first. Because *A* is the only producer at present he sets the price at the monopoly level, which is the most profitable for him. Now, suppose that *B* also enters into the business and starts producing the same product as produced by *A*. But *B* assumes that A will go on charging the same price which he is doing at present, irrespective of whatever price he himself might set. Further *B* finds that he can capture the whole market by slightly undercutting the price and thereby make substantial amount of profits. Accordingly, *B* sets a price slightly lower than A's price and as a result gets the entire demand of the product. A's sales, for the moment, falls to zero. Now, threatened with the loss of his entire business, producer A will reconsider his price policy. But while deciding about his new price policy he assumes that *B* will continue to charge the same price which he is doing at present. There are two alternatives open to him. First, he may match the price cut made by *B*, that is, he may charge the same price as *B* is now charging. In this case, he will secure half the market, the other half going to the producer *B*. Secondly, he may undercut *B* and set a slightly lower price than that of *B*. In this case, *A* will seize the entire market. Evidently, the latter course looks more profitable and thus *A* undercuts *B* and sets a price lower than *B*'s price.

But with the above move of *A*, producer *B* finding himself deprived of all his sales will react and think of changing his price. Since *B* also assumes A's price to remain fixed at the present level, whatever price he himself might set. Producer *B* has similarly two alternatives : he may match A's price or undercut him. Finding the undercutting more profitable, *B* will set a bit lower price than *A* and thus seize the whole market.

But again, *A* will be forced to undercut *B*. This price war (*i. e.* the process of undercutting) will go on until the price falls to the level of unit cost of production. Once the price has fallen to the level of unit cost of production, neither of them will like to cut the price further because in that case total costs would exceed total revenue and will therefore bring losses to the duopolists. Also, neither of them would like to raise the price, since in doing so either of them would be afraid of losing his entire business, given the belief that the other will go on charging the same lower price. Thus, when the price has fallen to the level of cost, neither of the duopolists have any incentive to lower the price further, or to raise it and, therefore, the equilibrium has been achieved. In ***Bertrand's model equilibrium is achieved when market price is equal to the average cost of production and the combined equilibrium output of the two duopolists is equal to the competitive output.***

It is evident from the above analysis of the Cournot and Bertrand' s models of duopoly that the fundamental assumption about the behaviour of the duopolists in the two models is similar. The duopolists in both models have erroneous and incorrigible belief that the rival will continue to do what he is presently doing regardless of what he himself might do. However, the basic assumption in the two models is not exactly the same. In Cournot's model, the basic assumption relates to the output policy, but in Bertrand's model, it relates to the price policy. Therefore, the two models yield different results. According to Cournot's model, equilibrium output is less than the purely competitive output and, therefore, the price is higher than the purely competitive price. But, according to Bertrand's model, output and price under duopoly are equal to those under pure or perfect competition.

EDGEWORTH DUOPOLY MODEL

F. Y. Edgeworth, a famous French economist, also attacked Cournot's duopoly solution. He criticised Cournot's assumption that each duopolist believes that his rival will continue to produce the same output irrespective of what he himself might produce. According to Edgeworht (as in Bertrand's model), each duopolist believes that his rival will continue to charge the same price as he is just doing irrespective of what price he himself sets. With this assumption, and taking the example of Cournot's "mineral wells", Edgeworth showed that no determinate equilibrium would be reached in duopoly.

The main difference between Edgeworth's model and Bertrand's model is that whereas in Bertrand, productive capacity of each duopolist is practically unlimited so that he could satisfy any amount of demand but in Edgeworth s model, the productive capacity of each duopolist is limited so that neither duopolist can meet entire demand at the lower price ranges. Each duopolist accepts as much demand of the product at a price as he can meet. It is not essential in Edgeworth's model that the products of dudpolists should be perfectly homogeneous, his argument will apply even if the products were close substitutes so that a slight price differential is sufficient for a good proportion of customers to switch from a higher priced product to a lower-priced product. However, in our analysis below we assume that the products of the two duopolists are perfectly homogeneous. Moreover, the cost conditions of the two duopolists need not be exactly same but must be similar.

Fig. 41.4 illustrates Edgeworth's model of duopoly. Since it is assumed that the products of two duopolists are completely identical, the market would be equally divided between the two duopolists at the same price of the product. Suppose *DC* and *DC′* represent the demand curves facing each duopolist. Suppose *OB* and *OB′* are the maximum possible outputs of the two duopolists respectively. If the duopolists form a collusion, they will set the monopoly price *OP* and will make maximum joint profits. Price *OQ* represents the price at which both duopolists sell their maximum possible outputs.

Suppose that the two duopolists happen to charge the price *OP*, then producers 1 and 2 will be producing and selling *OA* and *OA′* amounts of output respectively. Suppose now producer 1 thinks of revising his price policy. Producer 1 will believe that producer 2 will keep his price unchanged at *OP* regardless of whatever price he himself might charge. With producer 2's price remaining fixed at *OP*, producer 1 realises that if he sets the price slightly lower than *OP*, he will be able to attract a sufficient number of producer 2's customers so that he can sell his whole maximum output which he can produce. This would yield greater profits to producer 1 than he is making at present. Thus in Fig 41.4 if producer 1 lowers his price from *OP* to *OR*, he will be able to sell his entire maximum output *OB* and will make profits equal to *OBSR* which are greater than *OAEP*. Thus A would increase his profit by lowering his price.

But when producer 1 reduces his price, producer 2 will find most of his customers deserting him and his sales considerably reduced. Profits of producer 2 will accordingly fall considerably. As a result, producer 2 will think of making a counter move, but he too will assume that producer I will hold his price constant at *OR*. Producer 2 sees that if he cuts his price slightly below producer 1's price *OR*, say he fixes *OR′* he can take away enough customers of A to sell his entire maximum possible output *OB′*. Thus when producer 2 cuts his price to *OR′*, he sells his entire output *OB′* and makes profits equal to *OR′S′B′* which are greater than he was making before. As a result of this, sales and profits of producer 1 will greatly decline. Producer 1 will then react and will think that if he reduces his price a bit below *OR′*, he will be able to sell his whole maximum possible output *OB* by attracting customers of producer 2, still believing that producer 2 will keep his price fixed at *OR′*. Thus when producer 1 reduces his price, his profits will rise for a moment. But producer 2 will then react and reduce his price further in order to increase his profits. In this way, according to Edgeworth, the price cutting by two producers will continue until the price falls to the level *OQ* at which both producers sell their entire maximum possible outputs.

It will be seen Fig 41.4. that at price *OQ*, producers 1 and 2 are selling *OB* and *OB* ′ respectively (*OB* = *OB′*) and are making profits equal to *OBTQ* and *OB′T′Q′* respectively. When the price has been bid down to the level *OQ*, none of the producers will see any advantage to cut the price further. Since at price *OQ* each is selling the entire output he can produce, he will not be able to increase his profits because of his inability to increase his output further. But, according to Edgeworth, equilibrium is not attained at price *OQ*. Edgeworth argues that each producer will have no incentive to lower the price below *OQ*, but each will have incentive to raise it above *OQ*. Thus, Edgeworth says : "At this point it might seem that equilibrium would have been reached. Certainly it is not in the interest of either monopolist to lower the price still further. But it is in the interest of each to raise it." At price *OQ*, one of the two producers, say producer, 1, may realise that his rival producer 2 is selling his entire possible output *OB′* and serving half of the customers and cannot increase his output further to serve more customers. Thus producer 1 realises that he can serve the other half of the customers at the price which is most profitable for him and he will accordingly raise the price to *OP* at which he sells *OA* and earns profits *OAEP* which are larger than profits *OBTQ* at price *OQ*. Thus knowing that his rival has done his worst by putting his entire possible output on the market and that producer 2 cannot attract any of his *OA* units of demand because of his inability to produce more, producer 1 raises the price at *OP* and thereby increases his profits.

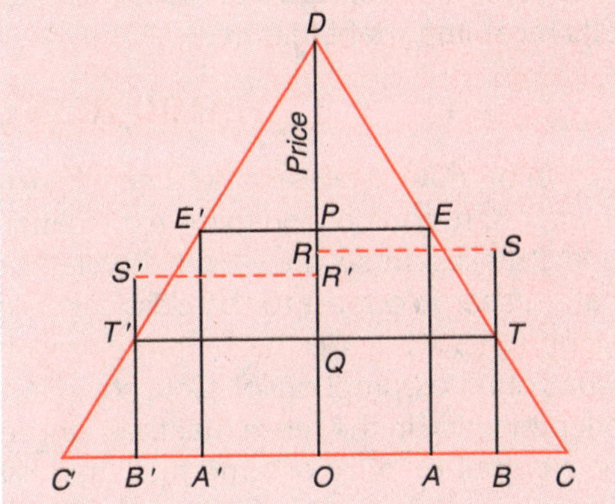

Fig. 41.4. *Edgeworth's Duopoly Solution*

But when producer 1 has raised the price to *OP*, producer 2 will realise that if he sets his price slightly below *OP*, he would still be able to sell *OB′* by attracting enough customers of producer 1 who is charging the price *OP* and, will therefore increase his profits. Accordingly, producer 2 raises his price to the level slightly below OP. But producer 1 then finding his customers deserting him and sales being reduced will believe that he can increases his profits by reducing his price slightly below producer 2's level. When he does so, then producer 2 will react, and so on. Thus, once again the process of competitive price cutting starts and the price again ultimately reaches the level OQ. But once the price has reached OQ, any of the producer will again raise it to *OP* and so on. In this way, price will oscillate between *OP* and *OQ*, gradually downward but upward in a jump. As said above, price *OP* is the monopoly price and price *OQ* is the competitive price. It follows from above that Edgeworth duopoly solution is one of perpetual disequilibrium, price constantly oscillating between the monopoly price and competitive price. Thus no determinate and unique equilibrium of duopoly is suggested by Edgeworth's duopoly model.

Comments over above Classical Models of Duopoly (Oligopoly)

In our analysis of three classical models of duopoly we saw that one common assumption in them is that the duopolists have zero conjectural variation, that is, while deciding about his output or price policy, each duopolist believes that his rival will hold output or price constant at the present level whatever he himself might do. Further, a producer remains unshaken in this erroneous belief even when he constantly finds himself to be proved incorrect since after his action the rival does react and changes his output or price. This is a chief logical error in classical models.

Furthermore, by assuming zero conjectural variation on the part of the duopolists (oligopolists), classical models ignore the mutual interdependence which is the chief characteristic of oligopoly. Thus, classical models provide solution for oligopoly problem by removing from it its most important feature.

CHAMBERLIN'S OLIGOPOLY MODEL

In his now famous work "*The Theory of Monopolistic Competition*" Chamberlin made an important contribution to the explanation of pricing and output under oligopoly. His oligopoly model makes an advance over the classical models of Cournot, Edgeworth and Bertrand in that, in sharp contrast to the classical models, his model is based on the assumption that the oligopolists recognise their interdependence and act accordingly. Chamberlin criticises the behavioural assumption of Cournot, Bertrand and Edgeworth that the oligopolists behave independently in the sense that they ignore their mutual dependence and while deciding about their output or price assume that their rivals will keep their output or price constant at the present level. According to him, oligopolists behave quite intelligently as they recognise their interdependence and learn from experience when they find that their actions, in fact cause the rivals to react and adjust their output level. This realisation of mutual dependence on the part of the oligopolists leads to the monopoly output being produced jointly and thus charging of the monopoly price. In this way, according to Chamberlin, ***maximisation of joint profits and stable equilibrium are achieved by the oligopolists even though they act in a non-collusive manner.*** Given identical costs they equally share these monopoly profits.

The process by which stable equilibrium under oligopoly is reached in Chamberlin's oligopoly model is illustrated in Figure 41.5. Chamberlin considers the case of a duopoly with zero cost of production of the two producers, *A* and *B*. Like Cournot he also assumes that the market demand curve for the product is linear. In Figure 41.5 *MD* represents this linear demand curve for the homogeneous product of the duopolists. As in Cournot's model, suppose producer *A* is the first to start production. He will view the whole market demand curve *MD* facing him and corresponding to which MR_1 is the marginal revenue curve. In order to maximise his profits he will equate marginal revenue with marginal cost (which is here taken to be equal to zero). It will be seen from Fig. 41.5 that he will be in equilibrium by making $MR = MC$ when he produces *OQ* output (*i.e.* half of *OD*), which is in fact the monopoly output, and will fix price equal to *OP*.

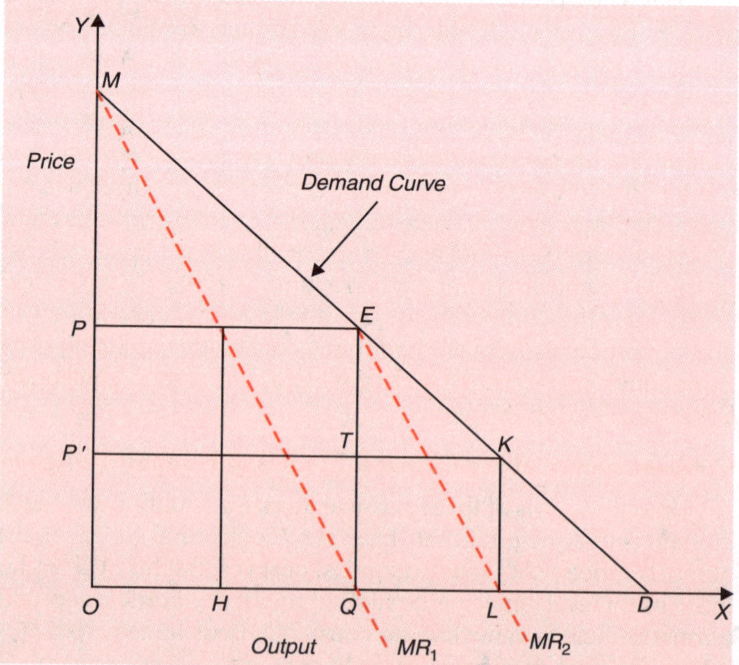

Fig. 41.5. *Chamberlin's Stable Model of Duopoly with Mutual Dependence Recognised*

Now, suppose producer *B* enters the market. He thinks, as in Cournot's model, that producer A would continue to produce *OQ* output and therefore views *ED* portion of the demand curve as the relevant demand curve facing him and corresponding to him MR_2 is the marginal revenue curve. With marginal cost being equal to zero, for maximing profits he will produce half of *QD*, that is, *QL* or at point *L* at which his marginal revenue curve MR_2 interesects the *X*-axis along which output is measured. With aggregate output *OL* (*OL* = *OQ of A* + *QL* of *B*), price will fall to the level *LKor OP '* with the result that profits earned by producer *B* will be equal to the area of rectangle *QLKT,* and due to the fall in price the profit of producer A will decrease from *OPEQ* to *OP 'TQ*.

However, from this point onward Chamberlin's analysis deviates from Cournot's model. Whereas in Cournot's model, the firm *A* will readjust his output and continue to assume that his rival will keep his output constant at *QL* level, but in Chamberlin's model producer *A* learns from his experience that they are interdependent. With the realisation of mutual-dependence, producer A decides to produce *OH* equal to output *(QL)* of producer *B* and half of monopoly output *OQ* so that the aggregate output of both of them is the monopoly output *OQ, (OQ* = *OH* of *A* + *QL* of *B*). With *OQ* as the aggregate output level, price will rise to *QE* or *OP.* Firm *B* also realises that in view of interdependence it is in the best interest for both of them to produce half of monopoly output and will therefore maintain output at the *QL* or *OH* level which is half of the monopoly output. Thus each producer producing half of monopoly output, will result in maximisation of joint profits though they do not enter into any formal collusion. In this way Chamberlin explains that duopolists behaving intelligently and realising their interdependence reach a stable equilibrium and they together produce monopoly output and charge monopoly price each sharing profits equally.

Comments. Chamberlin's model is an advance over the classical models in that the firms behave intelligently and recognise their interdependence. Their behaviour leads them to the ***monopoly solution of output and pricing which ensures maximisation of joint profits though they do not formally collude.*** This implies that firms have full information about the market demand curve and quickly learn from the experience and realise that the ultimate consequence of alternative chain of adjustments to rival's moves will be less profitable than sharing the monopoly profits equally with him.

Further, it is assumed in Chamberlin's model that the oligopolists know fully the costs of production of their rivals which enable them to arrive at a monopoly output and price which is in the best interest of all of them. Thus, unless all oligopolists have identical costs and demands, it seems impossible that the oligopolists will be able to reach monopoly solution, that is, maximisation of joint profits without collusion. It may be noted that ***even in a formal collusion there is always incentive on the part of rival firms to cheat by undercutting price to increase their individual profits.*** In Chamberlin's model of oligopoly without collusion, incentive for the firms to undercut price to increase their share of profit will be relatively more. Besides, Chamberlin's model has another great flaw as *it ignores the entry of new firms* and is thus a closed model. Due to the attraction of monopoly profits jointly earned by the existing firms, the new firms are likely to enter the industry. With the entry of new firms the attainment of stable equilibrium of oligopoly is unlikely to occur.

THE STACKELBERG MODEL

Introduction

In Stackelberg model, like in Cournot's model, firms adjust their outputs to maximise their profits. However, Stackelberg, a Germann economist, put forward an oligopoly model which is different from Cournot's model. In Cournot's model both firms in case of duopoly adjust their output independently and simultaneously assuming that the other's output will remain constant, that is, each duopolist in Cournot model does not think that his rival will react to his decision regarding output. ***In other words, in Cournot's model each firm does not recognise interdependence between them.***

Stackelberg model differs from Cournot's model in two respects. First, one firm recognises that his rival firm will take into account the quantity of output it decides to produce. Thus, firms recognise their interdependence and thus behave in a sophisticated manner. Secondly, in Stackelberg duopoly model the two firms do not take their decisions simultaneously; one firm fixes its output first, that is, it moves first to produce a quantity of a commodity. The other firm follows and produces its profit-maximising output by taking the output of the first mover as given and constant. That is, the follower behaves like a Cournot's duopolist. Stackelberg model shows that it is a advantageous for a firm to go first, that is, to become a leader so that others follow him.

The Follower's Problem

Let us start with the firm 2 which follows firm 1 which sets its output first. We assume that market demand foi the product is of the following form :

$$P = a - bQ$$

where a is constant intercept of the demand curve and b is the slope of the demand curve. Marginal cost of the production of both the firm is zero. P is price of the product and Q is output. Let output of firm 1 is denoted by Q_1 and output of firm 2 is denoted by Q_2 With this, the given demand function can be written as

$$P = a - b(Q_1 + Q_2) \quad \text{...(i)}$$

The follower firm 2 will decide about its profit-maximising output after firm 1 has taken its output decision, and further that firm 2 will fix its profit-maximising output taking the first mover firm 1 's output as given and constant. That is, the follower firm 2's output is given by Coumot's reaction curve which is obtained by a profit-maximisation by a firm taking the output of the other firm as given and constant. Recall that to derive Cournot's reaction curve, a firm equates marginal revenue with marginal cost, given the output of the rival firm. Thus, to determine the follower firm's profit-making output, given the output of the other firm, we obtain its marginal revenue function and then equate it with the given marginal cost.

To obtain total revenue of the follower firm 2, we multiply the inverse demand function equation (*i*) by its output which is denoted by Q_2 Thus

$$TR = PQ_2 = aQ_2 - bQ_1Q_2 - bQ_2^2$$

$$MR_2 = \frac{d(PQ_2)}{dQ_2} = a - bQ_1 - 2bQ_2$$

Setting MR_2 equal to marginal cost which is here given to be equal to zero we have

$$a - bQ_1 - 2bQ_2 = 0$$

$$2bQ_2 = a - bQ_1$$

$$Q_2 = \frac{a - bQ_1}{2b} \quad \text{.....(ii)}$$

The equation (*ii*) describes the reaction function curve of the follower firm 2.

Leader's Profit-Maximising Problem

Having explained how the follower firm will decide about its output, given the output of the leader, we now turn to explain how the leader firm will determine its profit - maximising output. According to Stackelberg model, the leader is a sophisticated firm which recognises that its output decision will influence the choice of output by the follower firm. The choice of profit-maximising output by the follower (firm 2), given an output of the other firm (in this case the output of the leader firm 1), is given by its reaction function curve as derived above. Hence making its output choice, the leader firm 1 will take into account the reaction function curve of the follower. Accordingly, in order to know the profit-maximising output of the leader, given the reaction function curve of the follower firm 1, we obtain the total revenue function of the leader firm 1. Thus, multiplying the given inverse demand function equation (*i*) by output Q_1 of the leader we have

$$TR_1 = PQ_1 = aQ_1 - bQ_1^2 - bQ_1Q_2 \quad \text{... (iii)}$$

Substituting the reaction function equation (*ii*) of the follower firm for Q_2 in the total revenue function of the leader firm 1 we have

$$PQ_1 = aQ_1 - bQ_1^2 - bQ_1\left(\frac{a - bQ_1}{2b}\right)$$

Simplifying it we get

$$PQ_1 = aQ_1 - bQ_1^2 - \frac{aQ_1}{2} + \frac{bQ_1^2}{2}$$

$$PQ_1 = \frac{1}{2}aQ_1 - \frac{1}{2}bQ_1^2$$

MR of the above total revenue function with respect to Q_1 is

$$MR_1 = \frac{d(PQ_1)}{dQ_1} = \frac{a}{2} - bQ_1 \quad \text{....(iv)}$$

To obtain profit-maximising output of the leader firm we equate marginal revenue obtained in equation (*iv*) above with marginal cost (*MC*) which is given to be equal to zero we get

$$\frac{a}{2} - bQ_1 = 0$$

$$bQ_1 = \frac{a}{2}$$

or leader's profit-maximising output, $Q_1^* = \dfrac{a}{2b}$ ....(*v*)

(Note that * mark over Q_1 indicates equalibrium or profit-maximising output)

Now in order to find out the follower firm 2's output we substitute the value of Q_1^* into the reaction function obtained in (*ii*) of the follower firm 2. Thus

$$Q_2 = \frac{a - bQ_1^*}{2b} = \frac{a - b\left(\frac{a}{2b}\right)}{2b}$$

$$Q_2 = \frac{a - \frac{a}{2}}{2b} = \frac{a\left(1 - \frac{1}{2}\right)}{2b} = \frac{\frac{a}{2}}{2b}$$

$$Q_2^* = \frac{a}{4b} \quad \text{....(vi)}$$

Thus, the output of leader firm 1 is $\frac{a}{2b}$ and the follower firm 2 is $\frac{a}{4b}$. We can obtain the price (P) of the product by substituting total output ($Q^* = Q_1^* + Q_2^*$) produced in the given demand function, $P = a - bQ^*$

Exercise 1. Given the demand function, P = 30 – Q, and the two firms 1 and 2 in an industry producing a product. Marginal cost of production of each firm is zero. Suppose firm 1 behaves as a Stackelberg's leader and firm 2 as its follower.

What output will be produced by them and what price will be determined ?

Solution. Follower firm 2 makes its decision after leader firm 1 assuming leader firm's output as given and constant. Here the constant term of the demand function, $a = 30$ and slope of the demand function $b = 1$.

Reaction function of the follower firm is : $Q_2 = \frac{a - bQ_1}{2b}$

or $$Q_2 = \frac{30 - Q_1}{2} = 15 - \frac{1}{2}Q_1 \quad \text{...(i)}$$

Total revenue of the leader firm 1 is

$$TR_1 = PQ_1 = 30Q_1 - Q_1(Q_1 + Q_2)$$

$$= 30Q_1 - Q_1^2 - Q_1Q_2 \quad \text{...(ii)}$$

Substituting $Q_2 = 15 - \frac{1}{2}Q_1$ in total revenue function equation (*ii*) of the leader firm we have

$$TR_1 = 30Q_1 - Q_1^2 - Q_1\left(15 - \frac{1}{2}Q_1\right)$$

$$= 30Q_1 - Q_1^2 - 15Q_1 + \frac{1}{2}Q_1^2$$

$$= 15Q_1 - \frac{1}{2}Q_1^2 \quad \text{...(iii)}$$

Marginal Reveue (MR_1) $\frac{d(TR_1)}{dQ_1}$ of the leader firm 1 is

$$= 15 - Q_1 \quad \text{...(iv)}$$

Setting MR_1 equal to marginal cost which is zero we have

$$15 - Q_1 = 0$$

$$Q_1^* = 15$$

Substituting the value of leader output Q_1, in the reaction function equation (*i*) of the follower firm 2 we have

$$Q_2^* = 15 - \frac{1}{2}Q_1$$

$$= 15 - \frac{1}{2} \times 15 = 7.5$$

Thus the leader firm's production is 15 and follower firm's output is 7.5. Hence total output (Q^*) is 15 + 7.5 = 22.5

To obtain price we substitute the total output of 22.5 in the given demand function. Thus

$$P = 30 - Q$$

$$= 30 - 22.5 = 7.5$$

Exercise 2. ***The Market demand curve for a Stackelberg leader and follower is given by P = 10 – Q. If each has a marginal cost of 2, what will be the equilibrium quantity and price for each producer.***

Solution. In this exercise we are given a positive marginal cost instead of zero marginal cost.

Follower's reaction function : Let us first derive follower's reaction function. The producer 2 is the follower

$$P = 10 - Q$$

or, $$P = 10 - (Q_1 + Q_2) \quad ...(i)$$

Multiplying the demand function equation (*i*) by the output Q_2 of producer 2 to obtain total revenue function we have

$$TR_2 = PQ_2 = 10Q_2 - Q_1Q_2 - Q_2^2$$

$$MR_2 = 10 - Q_1 - 2Q_2$$

Setting MR_2 equal to marginal cost we get the reaction function for the follower. Thus

$$10 - Q_1 - 2Q_2 = 2$$

$$2Q_2 = 10 - 2 - Q_1 = 8 - Q_1$$

$$Q_2 = 4 - \frac{1}{2}Q_1 \quad ...(ii)$$

Equation (*ii*) describes the reaction function equation for the follower.

Leader's Equilibrium: Demand function for the leader is

$$P = 10 - (Q_1 + Q_2)$$

Multiplying both sides by output Q_1 of leader we have

$$TR_1 = PQ_1 = 10Q_1 - Q_1^2 - Q_1Q_2 \quad ....(iii)$$

Substituting the value of $Q_2 = 4 - \frac{1}{2}Q_1$ *in* TR_1 equation (*iii*) we have

$$TR_1 = 10Q_1 - Q_1^2 - Q_1\left(4 - \frac{1}{2}Q_1\right)$$

$$= 10Q_1 - Q_1^2 - 4Q_1 + \frac{1}{2}Q_1^2$$

$$TR_1 = 6Q_1 - \frac{1}{2}Q_1^2$$

$$MR_1 = \frac{d(TR_1)}{dQ} = 6 - Q_1 \quad .....(iv)$$

Setting MR_1 equal to marginal cost (MC) we have

$$6 - Q_1 = 2$$

$$Q_1 = 6 - 2 = 4$$

Thus, the leader produces 4 units of the product.

Substuting $Q_1 = 4$ in the follower's reaction function equation (*ii*) we have

$$Q_2 = 4 - \frac{1}{2}Q_1 = 4 - \frac{1}{2} \times 4$$

$$= 2$$

Thus, the follower will produce 2 units of the product.

Total output = 4 + 2 = 6

Substituting the total output produced in the given demand function we get price at which the product will be sold. Thus

$$P = 10 - Q = 10 - 6$$

$$= 4$$

Thus price equals ₹ 4.

QUESTIONS FOR REVIEW

1. Explain how equilibirum output and price are determined in Cournot's duopoly model. State the underlying assumptions.
2. How is Cournot-Nash equilibrium determined ? Why is it stable ? Why don't the duopolists set the ourupt at joint-profit maximizing level by tacit collusion. *D. U. B.A. (Hons)* 2001

   [**Hint:** Cournot equilibrium is also called Cournot-Nash equilibrium.]
3. (a) Explain Cournot's duopoly model. What should the firms do to maximise their profits.

   (*b*) Bring out precisely the difference between Cournot equilibrium and profit maximising behaviour. *D.U. B.A. (Hons)* 1988
4. Explain Chamberlin's model of duopoly. How does it differ from Cournot's solution of duopoly problem.
5. Let the market for telecommunications equipment be represented by a duopoly where the two firms produce outputs q_1, and q_2 respectively. The inverse demand function is represented by $P = 100 - 2Q$ (where $Q = q_1 + q_2$). The marginal cost that each firm faces is 4:

   (*i*) What are the reaction functions of the Cournot's duopolists ?

   (*ii*) Calculate each firm's output and the market price at Cournot's equilibrium.

   D.U. B.A. (Hons) 2003

CHAPTER

42

Non-Price Competition: Selling Cost and Advertising

Introduction

Product variation and advertising are the two important instruments of non-price competition by firms. Product variation refers to the changes in some characteristics of the product (for example changing the quality of their product or improving the design of it and providing better service for their products) so as to make their products more appealing to the consumers.

Under monopolistic competition and oligopoly, the firms often compete through product variation and incurring selling costs or advertisement expenditure to increase the demand for their products and thereby increase revenue made. Advertising, salaries paid to staff employed for promotion of sales and other expenses on promotional activities constitute selling costs. Selling cost incurred by the firms in recent years have enormously increased. It has been estimated in recent years that in the USA more than $200 billion are spent on advertising annually. A single company McDonald, famous for its fast food spent as much as $ 2.50 billion on advertising in 1984. For firms working under conditions of monopolistic competition and oligopoly, besides adjustments of price, output and product, the important decision relates to how much selling cost or advertisement expenditure has to be taken so as to achieve the aim of profit maximisation. The first problem that is encountered in connection with selling costs is how they differ from production costs. The other important question which arises is why firms under monopolistic competition and oligopoly incur selling costs and not the firms working under conditions of perfect competition and monopoly. Further, how a firm will decide about the optimum level of selling costs or advertisement expenditure. And, lastly, what is the influence of selling costs on price and output of the product. We shall discuss all these questions concerning selling costs below.

Selling Costs Distinguished from Production Costs

The term "selling costs" is broader than advertisement expenditure. Whereas advertisement expenditure includes costs incurred only on getting the product advertised in newspapers and magazines, radio and television, selling costs include the salaries and wages of salesmen, allowances to retailers for the purpose of getting their product displayed by them, and so many other types of promotional activities, besides advertisement. Chamberlin who introduced the analysis of selling costs in price theory distinguished them from production costs. According to Chamberlin, cost of production includes all those expenses which are incurred to manufacture and provide a product to the consumer to meet his *given* demand or want, while the selling costs are those which are incurred to ***change, alter or create the demand for a product.*** Costs of production therefore include manufacturing costs, transportation costs, and cost of handling, storing and delivering a product to the consumers, since all of these activities add utilities to a good. And the addition or creation of utilities to satisfy the given wants is called *production* in economics. To quote Chamberlin, "Cost of production includes all expenses which must be met in order to provide the commodity or service, transport it to the buyer, and put it into his hands ready to satisfy his wants. On the other hand, ***selling costs include all outlays made in order to secure a demand or a market*** for the product. The former costs create utilities in order that given demands may be satisfied; the *latter create and shift the demand themselves.* A simple criterion is this : of all the costs incurred in the manufacture and sale of a given product, those which alter the demand curve for it are selling costs, and those which do not are costs of production."[1] The selling costs, according to Chamberlin, include "advertising in its many forms, salaries of salesmen and the expenses of sales departments and sales agencies (except where these agencies actually handle the goods), window displays, and displays and demonstrations of all kinds."[2]

It should be noted that transportation should not be construed as *increasing the demand,* as it apparently appears. This is because the transportation does not really increase the demand; it merely enables the producer to meet the demand of the consumer which is already there whether the transport cost is incurred by the producer or by the consumer himself. Likewise, a high site rent for a shop in a well-located area will increase the sales of the firm but cannot be considered as a part of selling costs, since in this the firm is meeting the given or existing demand for the product more accurately or exactly and not *altering* the demand for the product. By paying a high rent for a shop or a concern in the well-located area, the producer is merely adapting the product or himself more exactly to the given demand and not altering the demand or adapting his customers. Therefore, Chamberlin while drawing the distinction between production costs and selling costs writes that **those costs which are "*made to adapt the product to the demand are costs of production; those made to adapt the demand to the product are costs of selling.*"**[3]

It should however be noted that the distinction between production costs and selling costs cannot always be sharply made and there are cases where it cannot be said whether product is being adapted to meet the demand, or the demand is being adapted to sell the product. For instance, it is difficult to say whether the extra cost on attractive packaging is production cost or selling cost. However, as far as advertisement expenditure is concerned, there is little doubt about its being selling cost, since purpose of advertisement is to increase or create the demand for the product. Thus Chamberlin's distinction is quite applicable so far as advertisement is concerned. Because *advertising expenditure is the most important and dominant form of selling costs*, we in our analysis below shall use them interchangeably and discuss the various questions concerning selling costs by taking the case of advertisement expenditure.

Importance of Advertising and Other Selling Costs Under Monopolistic Competition and Oligopoly

As has been explained in previous chapters, there is no need for a firm working under perfect competition to undertake advertisement expenditure or to incur other selling costs, since, by assumption, the products produced by all firms in the perfectly competitive industry are homogeneous, and an individual firm can sell as much quantity of its product as it likes at the given price. If a perfectly competitive firm advertises for the product, the consumers who are influenced by it may purchase the product from other firms in the industry, since all are selling homogeneous products. Of course, the whole perfectly competitive industry, that is, all

1. Edward, H. Chamberlin, *The Theory of Monopolistic Competition*, 6th edition, p. 123 (italics added)
2. *Op. cit. p.* 124.
3. *Ibid*, p. 125.

firms together or their association may advertise to promote the sales of their product *at the expense* of the *products of other industries*. Such advertising is known as *promotional advertising*, as compared to competitive advertising with which we are here concerned. In India, there has been advertising by the *Terene* industry producing terylene fabrics for increasing the demand for its product at the cost of other kinds of fabrics. We, therefore conclude that under perfect competition, there can be promotional advertising by the whole industry but not the competitive advertising by individual firms to snatch away the customers from each other.

Under monopoly also, there is no competitive advertising, since, by definition, a monopolist produces a product which has no close substitutes. The monopolist only needs to inform or remind the buyers that a particular product is available and he need not emphasize the competitive nature of its product.Of course, the monopolist may advertise to promote his sales or demand of his product by providing information to the consumers about the existence and nature of his product but it will not be at the expense of its rivals, since no rivals producing close substitutes are there under monopoly. Hence the advertisement by the monopolist is informative and promotional and not competitive.

It is under monopolistic competition and oligopoly with product differentiation that advertisement and other selling costs become important as a competitive weapon at the disposal of a firm to increase its sales at the expense of others. This is because differentiated products produced by different firms under monopolistic competition and differentiated oligopoly are close substitutes of each other. Therefore, each firm under monopolistic competition tries to convince the buyers that its product is better than those of others in the industry. A firm under monopolistic competition and differentiated oligopoly may keep its price and product design constant and seek to increase the demand for its product by increasing the amount of advertisement expenditure and through it persuading the buyers that its brand of the product is of superior quality than others. Thus, this is competitive advertising which is aimed at attracting the customers to their product and weaning them away from the closely related products of the rivals. Thus, "***the fundamental aim of all 'competitive' advertising is to attract the customers' attention and to imprint the name of particular product on his mind' the aim is to persuade the consumer to put his hand in his pocket and buy the product in question...the main aim is to increase the sales of one firm at the expense of others and not to increase the sales of the 'group' as a whole.***"[4] For instance, we all know that all toothpastes are based upon the same chemical formula recommended by the medical science. But the firm producing Colgate through its radio and T.V. commercial programmes has been propagating that the toothpaste of Colgate variety is very much better than others and has special and superior qualities which are absent in other brands of toothpaste. The fundamental aim of Colgate advertisement is not to increase the aggregate demand for toothpaste in the country but to increase the demand for 'Colgate toothpaste' by competing away the buyers from other brands of toothpaste. Similarly, the manufacturers of other brands of toothpaste such as Binaca, Pepsodent, Close Up, etc. are also incurring expenditure on advertisement through various means and trying to convince the buyers that their particular brand of toothpaste is better than others. Such competitive advertisement by a firm often proves to be successful in its objective of increasing the demand for a particular brand of the product. Thus, as a result of advertisement demand curve facing an individual firm shifts to the right which indicates that at various prices, a greater quantity of the product can be sold than before.

It follows from above that in the presence of selling costs or advertisement, demand curve for a product cannot be taken as an objective fact given by the tastes or wants of the consumers.

4. Stonier and Hague, *op. cit.*, p. 222.

A firm can alter or shift the demand curve for its product through its own efforts by incurring advertisement expenditure and other forms of selling costs.

Effect of Selling Costs (Advertising Expenditure) on Demand

As explained above, *the purpose of advertising is to increase the demand, that is, to shift the demand curve for the product to the right.* However, these selling costs or advertising outlays are subject to the varying returns. That is, ***equal increments in advertising outlay first yield increasing returns and then eventually diminishing returns in terms of its effect on demand for the product.*** In the beginning, increases in advertising outlay will bring about increasing returns in raising demand for the product for two reasons. First, increase in advertising outlay (or selling costs) permits a firm to *repeat many times* the advertisement for the product. And this repetition of advertisement produces favourable effect on demand. "It is well established that repetition is essential if advertising is to make an impact on the consumer's mind. A single advertisement seen once will have at the most a negligible, and probably no effect on the consumer. The outlay for it is wasted. But continued advertising over a period of time and in different media is far more likely to impinge on the consumers' thoughts and consequent consumption choice".[5]

Second reason for occurrence of increasing returns as the advertisement outlay is increased in the beginning is the *economies of large scale* selling operations or advertising outlay. The main advantage is the *specialisation* which is made possible by the large-scale selling or advertising activity. To quote Prof. Hibdon again, "Large-scale activities permit the *use of specialised personnel with greater expertise and effectiveness*. There may also be *economies in the use of advertising media*. Greater total spending permits a shift in the technique and media that are used in the selling effort as well as the use of combinations of media."[6] As a result of the increasing returns from advertising outlay in the beginning, the demand increases more than proportionately to the equal increases in advertising outlay.

Eventually Diminishing Returns to Advertising Expenditure. But as the advertising outlay is stepped up, diminishing returns with respect to its demand raising effect are likely to set in eventually. First, this is because potential buyers differ in tastes, income and wealth. These differences among the potential buyers of the product mean that they will vary in their responses to selling operations or advertising by a firm. Initial advertisements will cause large increases in demand as the more susceptible buyers respond to advertisement. But further increase in advertisements is likely to bring about relatively less increases in demand as they fail to influence other buyers who do not prefer the good so much.

Second reason for the ultimate occurrence of diminishing returns from the increases in advertisement is that the existing buyers may not further increase the demand for the product as a result of more advertising by the firm. This is because ***as the consumer buys more of a product, its marginal utility to him falls.*** Further, in order to purchase one good more, he has to give up more of some other goods, his income being limited. As a result, the marginal utility of 'other goods' increases. Thus, on the one hand, the marginal utility of a good declines as it is purchased more under the influence of advertisement, and, on the other hand, the opportunity cost of buying this good increases on account of the rise in the marginal utility of 'other goods'. This makes the existing buyers of product reluctant to buy more units of it when advertising effort by a firm is greatly increased. Thus, this also causes diminishing returns to advertising outlay.

---

5. James E. Hibdon, *Price and Welfare Theory*, McGraw-Hill, 1969, p. 302.
6. *Op. cit.*, p. 302.

The effect of selling costs on the demand for the product and the varying returns in this connection are illustrated in Fig. 42.1. Demand curve before any advertisement expenditure is undertaken is D_0. Now, equal increments in advertisement expenditure successively bring about rightward shift in the demand curve to D_1, D_2, D_3 and D_4 respectively. We have assumed that the shift in the demand curve is parallel, while in the real world it may not be so. Because in the beginning there are increasing returns and then after a point diminishing returns occur, successive shifts in the demand curve differ in magnitude. At the given price OP, as a result of equal increments in advertising outlay, the quantity demanded increases from q_0 to q_1, q_1 to q_2, q_2 to q_3, and q_3 to q_4. It will be seen from Fig.42.1 that after D_3, diminishing returns to extra advertising outlay occur.

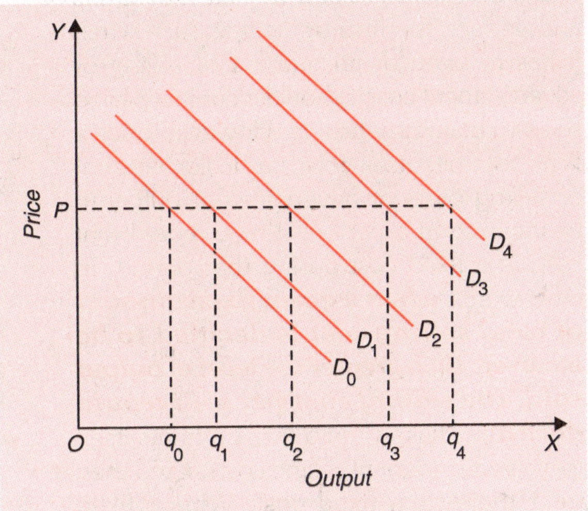

Fig. 42.1. *Increasing and Diminishing Returns to Advertising Expenditure or Selling Costs*

The Curve of Average Selling Cost

The concept of the curve of average selling cost should be carefully understood. When a firm has to plan what amount of advertising outlay (*i.e.*, selling costs), it should incur we treat the selling cost as a variable magnitude. Thus, with a certain amount of selling costs (advertising outlay) incurred in a period, the average selling cost or advertising cost per unit will depend upon the total output sold as a result of the rightward shift in the demand curve brought about by that amount of selling costs incurred and can be obtained from dividing the amount of advertisement costs incurred by the quantity of output sold. And as a firm plans to increase the amount of selling cost incurred in a period, the average selling cost will change depending, on the one hand, upon the increase in selling costs and, on the other, upon the resultant increase in output demanded (or sold) at a given price.As explained above, it is generally believed that *selling costs (advertisement outlay)* is subject to varying returns. In the beginning, increasing returns to selling costs are obtained, that is, equal increases in advertisement outlay cause more than proportionate increase in the amount demanded of the product at the given price. In other words, selling costs per unit of output will fall in the beginning. After a point diminishing returns to selling costs set in, increases in advertisement outlay would cause less than proportionate increases in the amount demanded of the product. In other words, after a point, average selling cost will rise. Hence, average selling cost in the beginning falls due to the increasing returns, reaches the minimum level and then rises due to the diminishing returns. Thus, the curve of average selling cost, like the ordinary average production cost curve, is U-shaped, which is shown in Fig.42.2 by the curve *ASC*.

However, the average selling cost curve *ASC* drawn in Fig. 42.2 should be carefully interpreted. It does not mean how the average selling cost per unit changes as output is increased. But it means the ***average selling cost per unit which is required to be undertaken to sell an extra unit of output.*** Ultimately, the average selling cost curve *ASC* will become vertical. This is because often the saturation point regarding the effect of extra selling costs on raising the demand for the product is reached, beyond which no further increases in selling costs causes any expansion in amount demanded of the product.

We have discussed above the nature of the average selling cost curve when the total selling cost is treated as a variable magnitude and, in fact, the firm treats it as such when it has to plan for an amount of selling or advertisement cost it should incur in a period so as to maximize profits. However, once a firm commits itself to a particular amount of selling costs or advertisement outlay to be incurred in a period, it may regard that cost as a fixed cost during that period. In other words, ***when a given fixed amount of total selling cost is decided to be incurred, then greater the level of output sold, the selling cost per unit would decline.*** Thus, when a firm commits itself to a given amount of selling costs, it will then treat them as a fixed cost. With a fixed amount of selling costs, average selling cost will fall as more units of output are sold.

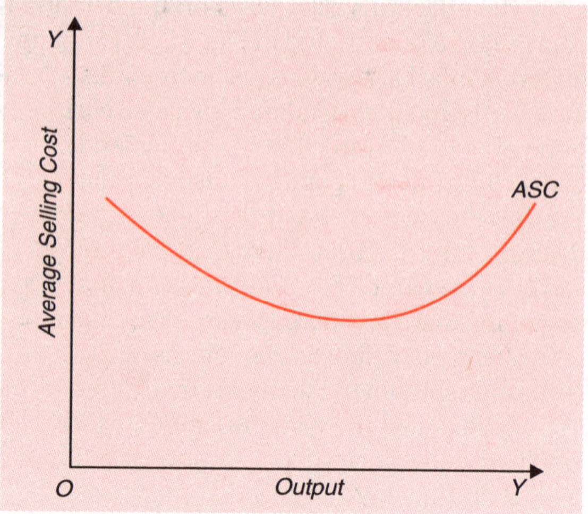

Fig. 42.2. *Average Selling Cost Curve When Total Selling Cost is Treated as a Variable*

OPTIMAL LEVEL OF ADVERTISING

As seen above, advertising not only increases demand for a firm's product, but it also raises the cost of the firm. A firm will undertake advertising only if it leads to the net increase in profits of the firm. A firm will go on increasing its advertisement expenditure if its ***marginal contribution to profit (MPC) from an additional unit of output is greater than the increase in advertising cost required to sell an additional unit of output***. The determination of optimal level of advertising is to apply the same marginal decision rule followed by a profit-maximising firm. The optimal level of advertising expenditure is determined at the level at which marginal contribution to profit (*MCP*) of advertising expenditure is equal to the marginal cost of advertising (*MCA*). Thus at the optimal level of advertising expenditure.

$$MCP = MCA$$

Let us elaborate this rule further. Marginal contribution to profit (*MCP*) is the difference between marginal revenue and marginal cost, as usually defined. Marginal revenue is the addition to total revenue earned from producing and selling an additional unit of output $\left(MR = \frac{\Delta TR}{\Delta Q}\right)$. Marginal cost is the addition to total cost of production by an extra unit of output produced. The marginal profit contribution (*MCP*) is therefore given by the difference between the marginal revenue (*MR*) and marginal cost of production (*MC*) of an additional unit of output. Thus,

$$MCP = MR - MC$$

On the other hand, marginal cost of advertising is the additional cost of advertisement (*MCA*) required for selling an additional unit of output. That is,

$$MCA = \frac{\Delta A}{\Delta Q}$$

where ΔA is change in cost of advertisement incurred on sale of an additional unit of output (*i.e.* ΔQ).

As stated above, the firm will go increasing its advertisement expenditure until marginal profit contribution (*MCP*) becomes equal to marginal advertisement cost (*MAC*). Thus at optimal or profit-maximising level of advertisement expenditure will be reached at the level where

$$MCP = MCA$$

Now,
$$MCP = MR - MC \text{ and}$$

$$MCA = \frac{\Delta A}{\Delta Q}$$

Thus, at the optimal level of advertising

$$MR - MC = \frac{\Delta A}{\Delta Q}$$

Since $MR = \frac{\Delta TR}{\Delta Q}$ and $MC = \frac{\Delta TC}{\Delta Q}$ we can state the condition for optimal level of advertisement expenditure as

$$\frac{\Delta TR}{\Delta Q} - \frac{\Delta TC}{\Delta Q} = \frac{\Delta A}{\Delta Q}$$

or
$$\frac{\Delta TR}{\Delta Q} = \frac{\Delta TC}{\Delta Q} + \frac{\Delta A}{\Delta Q}$$

Thus, if additional cost of advertisement is added to marginal cost of production and calling it as *marginal cost of production and sale* or MC^*, the condition for optimal level of advertising expenditure can be stated as under :

$$MR = MC^*$$

Thus, in the following analysis we will use this concept of marginal cost which is inclusive of marginal cost of advertisement expenditure. We explain and graphically illustrate the optimal level of advertising and determination of firm's equilibrium output and price in the following two cases:

1. Optimal level of advertising expenditure with price and product variety as given and constant.
2. Optimal level of advertising expenditure when both price and output are variable but product variety remains constant.

Optimum Level of Advertising Outlay (Selling Costs): With Price and Product Variety as Constants

An important question is how much selling costs (advertisement outlay), a firm will undertake so as to maximize its profits. In other words, what is the *optimum amount* of advertisement expenditure for a firm. The determination of optimal advertising outlay (selling cost) for the firm can be explained with the average and marginal cost curves. For explaining the optimal amount of advertising expenditure with average and marginal costs, we have to use the concept of average selling costs when advertisement outlay is taken to be variable. Consider Fig. 42.3 where *ASC* and *APC* are average selling costs and average production cost curves respectively. Average selling cost curve *ASC* has been superimposed over the average production cost curve *APC* to obtain average total cost curve *AC* (*AC* = *APC* + *ASC*). It should therefore be noted that the vertical distance between the *AC* and *APC* curves measures the average selling cost. *MC* is the marginal curve to the average total cost curve *AC*. We assume that price *OP* has already been fixed by the firm which is kept constant. Further, the nature of the product is also held unchanged and it is only the advertising expenditure which is varied and consequently demand curve shifts to the right and output sold increases.

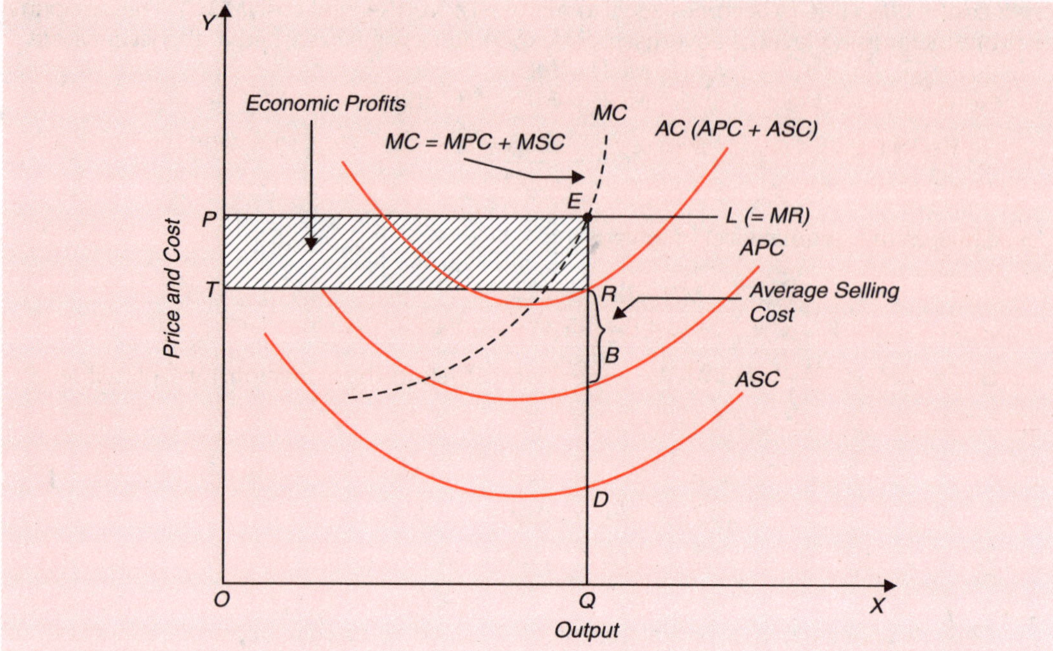

Fig. 42.3. *Optimal Level of Advertising Expenditure with Given Price and Product Variety*

Since price of the product remains fixed at *OP*, the horizontal line *PL* can be viewed as if it were a marginal revenue curve. This is because through increase in advertisement expenditure, a firm can sell more quantity of the product *without lowering price*. If the firm aims to maximize profits, then it will be in equilibrium regarding advertising outlay where the marginal cost (which is inclusive of both the increase in production cost and selling cost incurred on additional unit of output) is equal to the marginal revenue, *i.e.*, given price *OP*). It will be seen from Fig. 42.3 that marginal cost is equal to marginal revenue (or price) at *OQ* level of output at which profits will be maximized. With *OQ* as the output produced and sold, total profits made by the firm are equal to *PERT* and, as is evident from the figure, average selling cost incurred by the firm in its equilibrium position is equal to *QD* or *BR*. Therefore, the optimal amount of advertisement outlay, incurred by the firm will be equal to (*QD* or *BR*) multiplied by the output *OQ*.

Optimal Level of Advertising Expenditure or Selling Costs when Both Output and Price are Variables

Now, we shall explain the optimal level of advertising expenditure incurred by a monopolistically competitive firm to maximise its profits when it can influence both output and price through its advertising campaigns. In other words, we will now explain the profit-maximising or optimal combination of advertising expenditure, output and price. We shall, however, make our analysis with a two dimensional diagram. It may be emphasized again that advertisement expenditure or selling costs are an important form of *non-price competition*. Advertising represents a method by which a firm can increase the sales of its product and is an alternative to reduction in price of the product for promoting its sales. A firm can increase its sales by lowering the price of its product. But when it thinks price cutting is not prudent, the firm may attempt to promote sales through its advertising campaign. However, through advertisement or other forms of selling costs, a firm can increase both its output and price of its product. It may be noted that cost on advertisement or other forms of sales promotion activities of a firm depends in part also on how much advertising expenses or selling costs are being incurred by the rival firms.

Given the demand for the product of a firm and the amount of advertisement costs incurred by the rival firms, we get a U-shaped average selling cost curve which shows due to the greater effect of advertising on increase in demand and output in the beginning as advertising expenditure is stepped up, the average advertising cost (that is, selling cost per unit of output) falls. But beyond a certain level of advertising expenditure diminishing returns to additional advertising set in causing a rise in selling cost per unit of output. We obtain the average cost curve (*AC*) inclusive of average selling cost *by adding vertically* the average production cost (*APC*) and, average selling cost (*ASC*) curves. Note that the vertical distance between the average total cost curve (*AC*) and average production cost curve (*APC*) increases beyond a point due to the rise in average selling cost following the occurrence of diminishing returns to the increase in advertisement expenditure. The choice of combination of advertising, output and price that maximises the profits of the monopolistically competitive firm is illustrated in Fig. 42.4. We assume that in the absence of selling costs or advertising expenditure the demand for the product of the firm is given by the curve D_0.

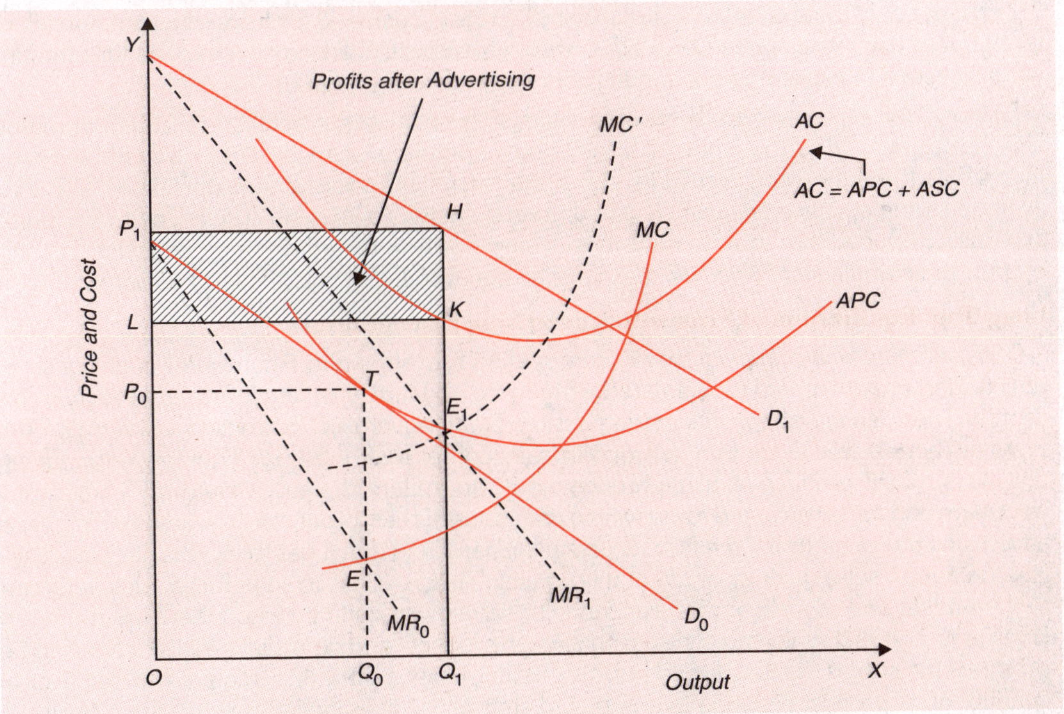

Fig. 42.4. *Optimal Levels of Advertising, Output and Price*

On the other hand, in the absence of advertising, *APC* is the average production cost curve which as usual is U-shaped and *MC* is the marginal cost curve associated with it. Prior to any advertising costs the firm is in equilibrium by producing OQ_o level of output and charging price OP_0 for its product. It will seen that in this equilibrium situation prior to any advertising costs, the firm is making zero economic profits since price is equal to average cost.

Now, in order to earn positive economic profits, the firm will attempt to raise demand for its product by launching an advertising campaign to attract customers. As it steps up its advertising expenditure the demand curve for its product will shift to the right. On the other hand, on account of increasing amount of expenditure incurred on advertisement, his average cost curve inclusive of advertising cost per unit will also shift above. It is worth noting that the average selling cost (*i.e.*, selling cost per unit of output) depends in part on the anticipated increase in output following the increase in demand for the product caused by the expansion in advertising expenditure. Since in the present model we are treating selling cost as a variable magnitude, marginal cost curve will also shift upward due to the additional advertising costs incurred as shown by the new higher marginal cost curve MC' which includes marginal advertising cost as well.

Let us assume that after a certain magnitude of advertising expenditure has been incurred the demand curve for firm's product has shifted up to the level D_1 and the marginal revenue curve corresponding to it has shifted up to the new position MR_1. Now, in order to determine the profit-maximising combination of output, price and advertising cost, the firm will equate marginal cost (inclusive of advertising cost) with marginal revenue corresponding to the demand curve reached after a certain successful advertising campaign. As will be observed from Fig. 42.4 that the new marginal cost curve MC' (inclusive of marginal selling cost) intersects the new MR_1 curve at point E_1 according to which profit maximising output is OQ_1 and price fixed will be equal to OP_1. In this equilibrium position, the firm will be making positive economic profits equal to the area of rectangle P_1HKL. Thus, it is evident that advertising has enabled the firm not only to raise its level of output by increasing demand for its product but also allows it to charge the higher price OP_1. Thus, through successful advertising expenditure the firm has succeeded in increasing economic profits from zero to P_1HKL.

Now, corresponding to the profit-maximising price-output equilibrium situation (output OQ_1 and price OP_1) the optimal advertising expenditure can be easily ascertained from Fig. 42.4. It will be seen from Fig. 42.4 that at profit-maximising output level OQ_1, the average selling cost is equal to E_1K (i.e. difference between AC and APC). The total optimal advertising expenditure in this profit-maximising position regarding three variables, namely, output, price and advertising, will therefore be equal to E_1K times the level of output OQ_1.

Long-Run Equilibrium of Firm with Advertising Expenditure

Equilibrium of a monopolistically competitive firm shown in Figure 42.4 is only a short-run equilibrium with regard to optimal advertising expenditure when the firm is making economic profits. These economic profits made possible by an advertising campaign will attract other firms as there is free entry in a monopolistically competitive industry. The new entrants into the industry will produce similar products and also imitate the successful firm's advertising campaign and advertise in the same way to gain sales of their products. As a result of increased advertising by competitors, the first successful firm will find that it has to increase its advertising expenditure to sell a given quantity of its product. That is, it has to send more sales personnel to the market and advertise more frequently to sell a given quantity when there are more rival firms in the market which are producing similar products and doing aggressive advertising to promote their sales. This will push up the selling costs of the firm required to sell a given quantity of its product resulting in an upward shift of the average selling cost curve (ASC).

Besides, as more firms producing similar products enter the industry, the demand and marginal revenue curves for the product will shift downward. Thus, the increased selling costs and reduction in demand for the product of the firm will tend to eliminate the economic profits in the long run. It may however, be noted that increased advertising by all the firms to promote sales of their products is likely to lead to an increase in demand for the product in general.

In Figure 42.5 we have shown that the long-equilibrium of the firm with advertising under monopolistic competition has been attained at output level OQ_2, where the demand curve D' and average cost curve AC inclusive of advertising (selling) costs has been brought to the new tangency position at point L. Thus, the firm in this long-run equilibrium position earns zero economic profits. It should be noted that the level of output OQ_2 by the firm in its long-run equilibrium position with advertising is greater than OQ_0 produced in long-run equilibrium without advertising. This implies that excess capacity will be reduced as a result of advertising in the long run. Thus, increased advertising by firms to promote their sales causes an increase in demand for the product in general leading to the reduction in excess capacity in each firm.

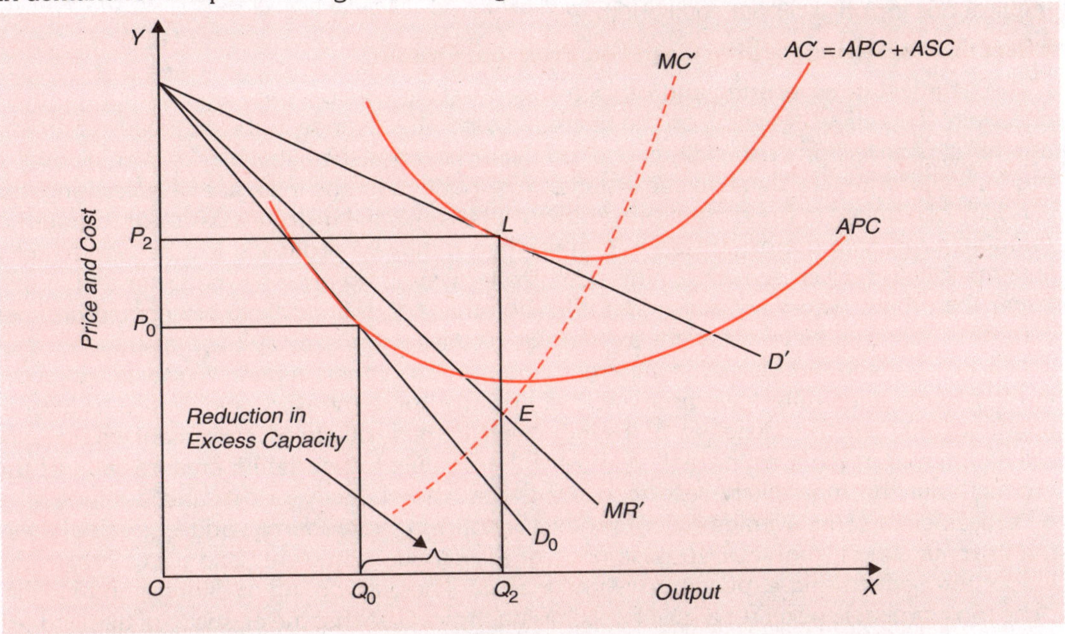

Fig. 42.5. *Long-Run Equilibrium with Advertising under Monopolistic Competition*

This helps in lowering average cost of production as the firms increase their size of plants and come closer to the optimum plant with which the product can be produced with minimum possible average cost. However, the consumers do not benefit from this lowering of average production cost because price does not fall due to the fact that whereas average production cost declines, the advertising cost per unit rises as a result of competitive advertising by the rival firms. Thus, whereas, on the one hand, advertising and other selling costs cause increase in demand for the product leading to the expansion in output by the firms, they, on the other hand, tend to raise the price of the product due to the increase in advertising cost per unit of output.

Effect of Advertising (Selling Costs) on Elasticity of Demand

We have seen above that as a result of advertising expenditure demand for the product increases, that is, demand curve shifts to the right. For the sake of convenience, we have assumed that the new demand curves after successive increase in advertising expenditure is undertaken are parallel to the old one, though in actual practice they need not be so. However, in this connection it is useful to consider whether when the demand increases and demand curve shifts to the right, elasticity of demand at each price remains the same, declines or rises. The purpose of competitive advertising or other forms of selling costs are to influence the consumers to buy a particular brand of the product rather than the other substitute brands of it. The intention of the producer who advertises for his brand of the product is to differentiate his brand more from the viewpoint of the consumers and try to prove his brand superior to others. Thus, if the purpose and intention of advertisements is achieved, then the consumers would begin to consider a particular brand of the product much superior to others. That is, they will now regard the other competitive brands as less closely substitutes than they were thinking before. This greater degree of differentiation and consequently fall in the elasticity of substitution will cause a decline in the elasticity of demand at each price as the demand curve shifts to the right under the influence of the advertisement. It is therefore, likely that the elasticity of demand should decline under the influence of advertising or other forms of selling costs. The extent to which elasticity will decline is of course very uncertain. As we shall see below, changes in elasticity of demand as a result of advertising expenditure have significant implications for price-output equilibrium.

Effect of Advertising (Selling Costs) on Price and Output

The effect of advertising and other forms of selling cost on price and output are quite uncertain. This effect depends, on the one hand, upon the change in the elasticity of demand as a result of advertising expenditure and, on the other, upon the behaviour of average cost of production. If when the demand curve shifts to the right under the influence of advertising, the elasticity of demand at the current price remains the same and *average cost of production is falling* sharply with the expansion in output, then it may be profitable for the firm to set a lower price after advertisement. In this case profit-maximising price will be lower and output larger than those before advertisement. On the other hand, if elasticity of demand declines very much as it shifts to the right as a result of advertisesment, and the average cost of production is rising sharply with the increase in production, then in order to maximize profits in the new situation after advertisement, the firm may raise the price and reduce its level of output. In this case, the advantage of the increase in demand due to advertisement expenditure will be enjoyed in the form of higher price of the product rather than increased sales of the product. But the most likely case to occur is that the elasticity of demand declines after advertisement and the average cost of product is not rising very sharply, and as result of these the firm may find it profitable to raise price of the product somewhat and also increase the output after advertising expenditure is undertaken. Thus, according to Stonier and Hague, "The most probable result for a profit maximising firm will be that the elasticity of demand will fall somewhat at each price, that the volume of demand will increase at each price and that price and output will both increase to some extent as a result of advertising campaign"[7]. And this is the case which we have considered in our analysis of advertising expenditure and depicted in Fig. 42.5. It will be seen from Fig. 42.5 that with successive increments in advertising expenditure price has risen from P_0 to P_2 and also output has increased from Q_0 to Q_2. Thus, in our analysis of Fig. 42.5 both price and output have increased as a result of advertisement outlay.

Evaluation of the Effect of Advertising

The net effect of advertising on consumer's welfare is a highly controversial issue. An eminent economist , J.K. Galbraith regards advertising expenditure as wasteful use of resources. Thus big firms through advertising manipulate the wants and tastes of the consumers and thereby create false needs of the consumers. Besides, they influence the consumers to buy certain varieties of a product at the expense of others while total output of the product does not increase. It is, however, true that advertising diverts resources from other goods to the particular product for which huge advertising expenditure by firms has been made.[8] It is worth noting that as a result of sales promotion through advertising consumers are lilkely to become *more loyal* to certain brand names or product varieties. This reduces the price elasticity of demand for the products of each firm in the long run which indicates that *advertising increases monopoly power* (note that monopoly power is measured by the reciprocal of price elasticity of demand). Increase in monopoly power also leads to the higher prices being charged by those firms who through successful advertising have established the superiority of their products in the minds of the consumers and thus reducing the price elasticity of demand for them.

However, the effect of advertising on price remains a controversial issue. A recent study

7. Stonier Hague, *op.cit.*, p. 226.
8. For a detailed discussion of the impact of advertising on price, output and consumer welfare, see William, Thomas A., "*Journal of Economic Literature*", June 1979, pp. 453-476.

of 150 major US industries by *E.W.* Eckard[9] has found that higher than average advertising expenditures relative to sales led to lower rates of increase in prices and higher rates of increase in output during 1963-1977. Thus, according to this study, advertising expenditure seems to increase rather than reduce competition. However, this beneficial effect of advertising has not been generally found by other authors. Contrary to the above view, others have argued that advertising provides information to the consumers and makes them aware of alternatives available to them about which they would otherwise be ignorant. According to this opposite view, advertising tends to *reduce consumer loyality to* particular brands leading to the increase in price elasticity of demand for the products of individual firms.[10] Advocates of advertising point out that it serves a useful social purpose by furnishing information and thereby reduce transaction costs of buying goods.

In their important studies Stigler[11] and Nelson"[12] have defended advertising expenditure by the firms on the ground that it *provides useful information to the consumers* about prices and availabilities of different alternative varieties of the product which *save their cost of search and shopping*. In the absence of advertising, according to them, the consumers are unlikely to find the best price for the product they want to purchase. Without advertising by the firms, it costs a good deal to the consumers on searching for products they want to buy. According to them, advertising leads to the reduction in prices of products and as a result consumers are better off. Besides, Nelson have found that the firms advertising their products have strong incentives to provide *useful and correct* information to consumers. Not only does the advertising reduce search costs of the consumers but also create brand awareness concerning better and inferior quality brands. Nelson distinguishes between what are called *search goods* and *experience goods*. Search goods include non-durable goods such as clothing, footwear, furniture, jewellery etc. The buyers can assess their quality by comparing among different brands and stores. Therefore, according to Nelson, in case of these search goods there is not much scope for befooling the people through misleading advertising.

On the other hand, experience goods are those durable and non-durable goods whose quality can be assessed only by trying them. Examples of experience goods are durable goods such as cars, electronic equipment, instruments and appliances and non-durable goods such as food products, tobacco products, drugs, beer, wine etc. According to Nelson, in case of these experience goods the consumers can be befooled at the first time of their purchasing them. They cannot be repeatedly befooled in their subsequent purchases of these experience goods as consumers come to know about their true quality when they try them first time. Therefore, Nelson concludes there is not much scope for misleading advertising of products. The firms, according to him, has a strong incentive to provide useful and truthful information to them.

In our view, however, contrary to the views of Prof. Nelson, the advertising expenditure by big firms in India is quite misleading. For example, both Coca Cola and Pepsi Cola through their heavy advertising campaigns have been claiming about the high quality and of safe nature of their drinks. But it has been found that their drinks actually contain more pesticides which are quite harmful for health of the people. Further, some studies in India have found that advertising by big Indian firms is competitive rather than informational. The firms undertake advertising expenditure to increase the demand for their brand of the product at the expense of others. Since all rival firms have indulged in this competitive advertising the result has been that the big firms only maintain their share of the market.

It follows from above that the effects of advertising are highly controversial and no firm conclusion can be drawn in general about their bad or beneficial effects.

9. E.W. Eckard, "Advertising, Concentration Changes and Consumer Welfare", *Review of Economics and Statistics*, May 1988.
10. Scherer, F.M., *Industrial Market Structure and Economic Performance*, 2nd Ed. Houghton Mifflin, 1980, p. 381.
11. George J. Stigler, " The Economics of Informations", *Journal of Political Economy*, June 1961.
12. Philip Nelson, "The Economic Consequences of Advertising", *Journal of Business*, April, 1975.

CHAPTER

43

Cost-Plus (or Mark-Up) Pricing Theory

Adding Mark-Up to Average Cost

So far we have explained those theories of price and output determination under oligopoly which are based on profit maximization assumption. After the marginalist revolution, profit maximisatipn by the firm is generally explained by the marginal analysis, that is, by the use of marginal revenue and marginal cost concepts. An important alternative approach to profit maximisation and marginal analysis is the ***cost-plus pricing theory*** which does not assume that rational firms seek to maximise profits. It may be pointed out in the beginning that cost-plus cost theory has been given several names. Cost-plus pricing theory is also known as ***full-cost pricing*** theory, or average cost pricing since in this theory price of a product is fixed on the basis of full average cost, that is, all costs per unit of output which also includes normal profit per unit of output. It is also called *mark-up pricing* theory, since this theory visualises that in order to fix price businessmen add a mark-up to their average cost of production.[1]

Cost-Plus Pricing Theory : Hall and Hitch's Version

Hall and Hitch of Oxford University made a root and branch attack on the marginal analysis and on the notion of profits maximization, and put forward the view that business firms in the real world fixed prices on the basis of direct cost (variable cost) per unit of output by adding to it overhead cost per unit and a margin of normal or conventional profits. To quote them, "the way in which businessmen decide what price to charge for their products and what output to produce, casts doubt on the general applicability of conventional analysis of price and output policy in terms of marginal cost and marginal revenue and suggest a mode of entrepreneurial behaviour which current economic doctrine tends to ignore."[2]

As has been mentioned in an earlier chapter, Hall and Hitch made an empirical study of the behaviour of business firms regarding fixation of prices of the products. In this study they interviewed 38 entrepreneurs of whom 33 were manufacturers of various products, 3 were retailers, and 2 were builders. From this empirical study they found, as is clear from the above quotation, that firms for fixing prices do not maximize profits by equating marginal cost with marginal revenue. It is worth mentioning here that they argued not only against marginal analysis of pricing by the firms but also challenged the notion that in fixing prices firms maximise their profits. Profit maximization, according to them, was a wrong way to approach the question of pricing by the business firms. Indeed they pointed out that business firms in the real world only tried to seek a satisfactory profits or, in other words, normal or conventional rate of profit. Thus, according to them, prices are fixed on the basis of full cost that is aveage direct

1. R. L. Hall and C. J. Hitch, Price Theory and Business Behaviour, *Oxford Economic Papers*, Vol. 2, 1939.
2. *Op. cit.*. p. 1

(variable) costs plus average overhead cost plus a satisfactory margin for profit. It should be noted that the average direct cost as well as average overhead cost is calculated on the basis of *expected output* in a period or on the basis of some conventional output.

Many reasons were provided by entrepreneurs as to why they fixed prices on the basis of cost-plus pricing. Firstly, they pointed out that if they fixed prices above average cost which would yield abnormal profits to them, ***there was the threat of actual or potential competitors*** competing away these profits. Further, they expressed ignorance of the concept of average and marginal revenue and also pointed out the absence of any data regarding marginal revenue and marginal cost. In view of the absence of data regarding *MC* and *MR*, how could they fix price on their basis. Furthermore, according to Hall and Hitch, in fixing prices of their products, entrepreneurs behave according to the moral principle that there is a price that *ought* to be charged and this price is the average cost price which includes normal profit and they think this is the right price that ought to be charged in periods of both good and bad business, that is, in period of both depression and boom. Thus, according to Hall and Hitch, there is not frequent changes in prices. Average-cost or cost-plus pricing, according to them, is the result of (*a*) tacit or open collusion, (*b*) considerations of long-run demand and costs, (*c*) moral conviction of firms and (*d*) uncertain effects of the increases and decreases in price.

They held that oligopolistic firms faced ***kinked demand curve*** and on account of this they emphasised stickiness of prices in the short run. As has been explained in a previous chapter, kinked demand curve with a kink at the current price, is formed on the assumption that the increase in price by an oligopolist will not be matched by its rivals, while the reduction in price will be immediately followed with the result that part of the demand curve above the current price will be highly elastic, whereas the part of the demand curve below the ruling price will be very much less-elastic.

Hall and Hitch combine cost-plus pricing, that is, average-cost pricing with kinked demand curve analysis. Current price is fixed on the basis of average-cost[3] (as defined above), and a kink in the demand curve is formed at this price. Average-cost pricing together with the kinked demand curve analysis is illustrated in Fig. 43.1. Suppose the firm decides to produce *OM* quantity of the product. This output, as pointed above, is fixed on the basis of expected sales in the period or on some conventional standard. With *OM* as the output, firm then calculates the (1) average direct cost incurred on labour, raw materials, etc. and (2) the average overhead cost incurred on capital equipment etc. He then adds to it his normal or conventional margin for profit. Addition of these three items yields full average cost, which let us suppose, is *MK* in Fig. 43.1. He will, therefore, set the price *OP* which is equal to *MK*. It will be noticed that the kink in the demand curve *dD* is formed at this price *OP* or *MK*.

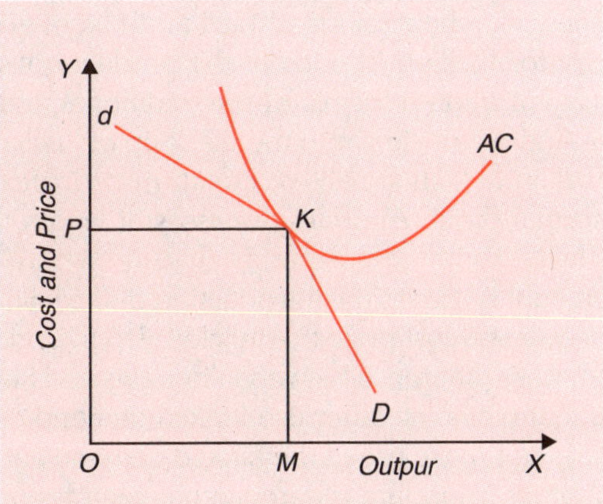

Fig. 43.1. *Average-Cost Pricing and Kinked Demand Curve*

Kinked demand curve analysis as used by Hall and Hitch along with his mark-up or average-

3. As we mentioned in an earlier chapter Sweezy version of kinked demand curve theory of oligopoly cannot explain how the current price came to be what it is. This flaw is not present in Hall and Hitch's version of kinked demand curve analysis.

cost pricing theory provides an explanation for the stability or rigidity of prices under oligopoly in the short run. Increases or decreases in demand will usually shift the kink to the right or left but will leave the price unchanged. But Hall and Hitch have mentioned the following two exceptions to this general rule in which case price of the product changes:

(1) If there is a large decrease in demand, and the demand remains at a low level for some time, there is every likelihood that price will be reduced so as to maintain output. According to Hall and Hitch, the explanation for this reduction in price in the context of depressed demand is that one entrepreneur may become panicky and his irrational behaviour forces the others to cut prices.

(2) If the average cost curves of all firms shift by similar amounts on account of changes in factor prices or technology, then this is "likely to lead to a revaluation of the "full cost" price. However, Hall and Hitch point out that "there will be no tendency for price to fall or rise more than the increase in wage and raw material costs."[4]

It should be noted that, given that the average cost curve falls for quite a large range of output, the cost-plus pricing suggests that price of the products will vary inversely with output; smaller levels of output will involve higher cost per unit and therefore, higher prices will be fixed. But, according to Hall and Hitch, the oligopolists will not produce small outputs and, therefore will not charge higher prices. This is because oligopolists (1) prefer price stability, (2) are prevented by the kink to raise price, and (3) they have propensity to produce larger levels of output or, in the words of Hall and Hitch, they desire to "keep plant running as full as possible, giving rise to a general feeling in favour of price concessions."[5]

Cost-Plus Pricing : Andrew's Version

Price Fixation according to Cost-Plus Principle. Prof. Andrews[6] also propounded a cost-plus principle of price fixation by businessmen. Andrews analysis is similar to that of Hall and Hitch, but there are some differences between the two. An important difference between the two lies in the use of the concept of "***costing margin***" by Andrews. The costing margin is conceived by Andrews as an addition to constant average direct cost and "will normally tend to cover the costs of the indirect factors of production and provide a normal level of net profit."[7] Thus, like the analysis of Hall and Hitch, addition of costing margin to the average variable cost for fixation of price of the product goes against the price fixation on the basis of profit-maximization principle of the traditional theory of value. Thus the concept of costing margin of Andrews is similar to the mark-up of Hall and Hitch, but there is a difference in that whereas Hall and Hitch visualise a *constant or inflexible* mark-up or a margin for overhead cost and normal profit, Andrews discusses at length the circumstances in which there might be some *flexibility* in the costing margin in response to competitive and market forces. As shall be brought out later, the introduction of flexibility in the costing margin brings Andrews' cost-plus or average-cost price theory closer to the price theory based on profit maximisation principle. Another difference between Andrews and Hall and Hitch's versions of cost-plus pricing theory is that while the latter use kinked demand curve along with average cost pricing, the former does not make use of the kinked demand curve hypothesis in his cost-plus pricing theory. Still another important difference between the two is that whereas Hall and Hitch consider that average cost varies with output and average cost curve is U-shaped, Andrews visualises that for a large relevant range of output, average direct (variable) cost remains constant.

4. *Op. cit.* p. 32.
5. *Ibid*, p. 28.
6. P.W.S Andrews, *Manufacturing Business*, Macmillan, London, 1949.
7. *Op. cit.* p. 184.

Andrews cost-plus pricing theory may be summarised as follows :

(*i*) The price which will be fixed by a business firm will equal *the estimated average direct cost* of production plus a costing margin. In other words, price will be equal to the 'full-cost' per unit of output.

(*ii*) Secondly, Andrews assumes on the basis of empirical investigations that average direct cost (*i.e.,* average variable cost) remains constant over a large range of output, provided the prices of direct factors (*i.e.*, variable factors) remain unchanged. Thus, according to Andrews, ***average direct cost curve is a horizontal straight line over a good part,*** if the prices of variable factors remain constant.

(*iii*) As said above, the costing margin will cover the cost per unit incurred on the indirect factors of production (*i.e.*, fixed factors) and the normal rate of profit. Once fixed, the costing margin will remain constant, whatever the level of output. However, costing margin will vary as a result of the permanent changes in the prices of indirect (*i.e.*, fixed) factors of production. As mentioned before, Andrews also visualises changes in the costing margin in response to the competitive and market forces.'

(*iv*) Fourthly, Andrews' analysis also suggests that, given the prices of direct factors of production, the price of the product will remain the same whatever the level of output.

(*v*) Lastly, at the price fixed on cost-plus basis, the given product will have a well-defined market and a ***firm will sell the amount of the product demanded at that price by the buyers.***

The theory of cost-plus pricing as put forward by Andrews is illustrated in Figure 43.2. Cost curve *AC* in this figure represents the average direct cost (*i.e.*, average variable cost). It will be seen that average direct cost curve *AC* is saucer-shaped, that is, it first falls, then remains constant for quite a large increase in output and then eventually rises. Corresponding to this, *MC* is the marginal cost curve; *MC* curve falls in the beginning and lies below *AC*, then it coincides with *AC* curve and eventually *MC* lies above *AC*. In order to proceed to fix the price, besides average direct cost a business firm has to calculate the total *indirect costs* (*i.e.*, fixed costs) and also the amount of profits it wishes to earn. The total indirect costs plus the amount of profits planned will yield a *fixed sum of money* which will remain constant for fixation of price in the short run. The 'costing margin', according to Andrews, is obtained from this fixed sum of money by dividing it by "some chosen output.

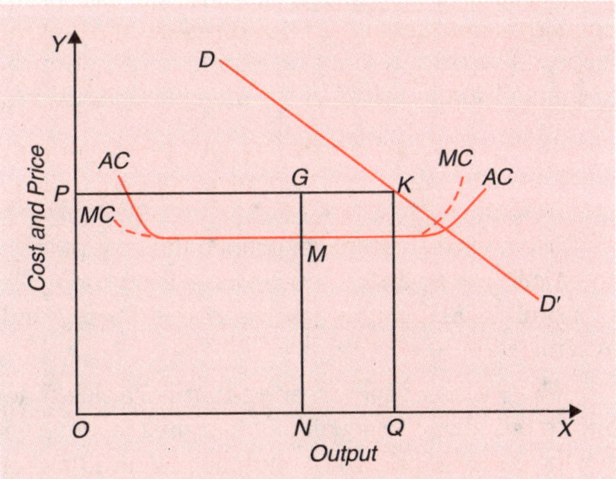

Fig. 43.2. *Price Fixation on the basis of Cost-Plus*

Determination of output for estimating costing margin. The chosen output used for the purpose of estimating costing margin can be determined in several ways. First, it may be fixed on the basis of ***capacity output of the given plant*** when by the capacity output Andrews means the maximum output that can be produced with the given plant. Output can be fixed by a business firm as some percentage of this capacity output. Secondly, the chosen output can be fixed on the basis of *sales of product made in the preceding production period*, or average of sales achieved over a number of previous production periods. Thirdly, the output may be determined on the basis of *expected sales in a future period* for which output is being produced.

If a new firm has to set the price of its product, or if the firm has introduced a new product for which it has to set the price, the above mentioned second way of choosing the output for estimating the costing margin is ruled out and in these circumstances only the first and third methods become relevant. In fact, when the firm is a new one or when an existing firm is introducing a new product, then the first and third methods of choosing output amount to the same thing. This is because the designed capacity of the plant will be determined by the expected sales of the product in the future periods.

In Fig. 43.2, let us assume that the firm has chosen output *ON* for estimating costing margin and for fixing price of the product. Further, suppose that if the given fixed sum of money, representing the total overhead (indirect) costs and the normal level of profits is divided by the chosen output *ON'* it yields *MG* amount which will be the costing margin to be added to the average direct cost for determining the price of the product. It will be seen from Figure 43.2 that at *ON* level of output, average direct cost is *NM*. If we add costing margin *MG* to *NM*, we get full-cost equal to *NG*. Thus, the price *OP* will be fixed equal to full cost *NG*. It should be noted that *price OP fixed on the basis of full cost NG will remain unchanged whatever the amount demanded and the actual output produced in the given period.* Now, if the demand for the product is given by the curve DD^1, then it will be seen from the Fig. 43.2 that at price *OP*, quantity *OQ* of the product will be demanded and therefore produced.[8] Now, even if the ***demand for the product increases or decreases, the price will remain unaltered at OP, provided the amount demanded lies within the range of constant average direct cost, that is, within its horizontal straight-line portion; and further provided that costing margin remains unaltered. Thus, we see that according to Andrews' version of cost-plus pricing theory also, price will change as a result of the changes in direct and indirect costs of production and not a result of alteration in demand.*** Thus, according to cost-plus theory "The price will not be altered in response to changes in demand, but only in response to changes in the prices of the direct and indirect factors.[9]

RECONCILIATION OF COST-PLUS PRICING WITH MARGINAL ANALYSIS

We have elaborately explained the cost-plus pricing theory. In spite of its being based on empirical investigations, cost-plus pricing theory has not found general acceptance among economists. Many have criticised this theory and have defended marginalism and profit maximization.

First, it has been asserted that cost-plus theory does not amount to the refutation of pricing based on the equality of marginal revenue with marginal cost (profit maximisation) and that the cost-plus pricing (or mark-up pricing as it is sometimes called) is ***quite consistent with the pricing based on marginal analysis and profit maximisztion.*** It has been asserted that costing margin or mark-up is chosen by considering and guessing what the price elasticity of demand for a particular product is. If the elasticity of demand for a product is greater, smaller mark-up is fixed; and if elasticity of demand for the product is less, greater mark-up is fixed. How the cost-plus pricing is consistent and compatible with marginal analysis of pricing is explained below.

---

8. It should be noted that output *OQ* must lie with in the maximum capacity output of the firm if the given demand is to be fully met. However, if *OQ* exceeds the maximum capacity and the firm has accumulated stock of the product from the previous periods, then it can draw upon the stocks to meet the demand.

9. W.J.L. Ryan, *Price Theory*, Macmillan, London, 1958, p. 377.

We know from our previous analysis of the relationship between price (*P*), elasticity (*e*) and marginal revenue (*MR*) that

$$P = MR\frac{e}{e-1}$$

Since, in equilibrium, $MR = MC$, it follows that

$$P = MC\frac{e}{e-1} \qquad ...(i)$$

Now, if constant costs prevail, as is generally the case in the real world, and is also assumed generally in cost-plus pricing theory, then marginal cost (*MC*) will be equal to the average variable cost (*AVC*). Therefore, writing *AVC* for *MC* in equation (*i*), we get

$$P = AVC\frac{e}{e-1}$$

or,

$$P = AVC\left(\frac{e-1}{e-1}+\frac{1}{e-1}\right)$$

$$= AVC\left(1+\frac{1}{e-1}\right)$$

$$P = AVC + AVC\,\frac{1}{e-1}$$

Therefore, Price $P = AVC$ + Mark-up

We, thus see that on the basis of profit maximization assumption, mark-up or costing margin is equal to $AVC\,\frac{1}{e-1}$, that is, a fraction of AVC.

Suppose price elasticity of demand of the product is 5, then mark-up $= AVC\,\frac{1}{e-1}$ $= AVC\,\frac{1}{5-1} = \frac{1}{4}$ *AVC*. That is, mark-up fixed will be 25% of *AVC*. Price will be equal to *AVC plus* 25% of *AVC* as mark-up.

It follows from above that pricing fixed on the basis of marginal revenue and marginal cost is consistent with the cost-plus pricing based on adding a mark-up to the average variable cost. Therefore, it is asserted that in cost-plus pricing, it does not necessarily mean that firms are not maximizing profits. Mark-up fixed on the basis of price elasticity of demand amounts to maximising profits. Thus, Prof. Bilas remarks, ***"The mark-up will vary from time to time with economic conditions as well as with seasonal changes. These variations bring about changes in the shape of the demand curve and in e. Therefore, when the businessman fixes prices at variable cost plus a mark-up and his mark-up charge is arrived at by a "feel of the market," we know that it is really a guess at the coefficient of price elasticity of demand and that economic theory is not necessarily being contradicted.***[10]

Similarly, Stonier and Hague write "*If full-cost pricing exists, it does not necessarily mean that firms behave very differently from the way economic theory suggests. Even if there is a widely-held convention in any industry charging 'full cost' prices, about what a 'satisfactory 'profit margin would be, this may well have been arrived at through an understanding, built up over time, of the sort of profit margins that competitive conditions in that industry usually*

10. R.A. Bilas, *Microeconomic Theory*, second edition, 1971, p. 233.

allows."[11]

But the whole synthesis established above between cost-plus pricing and marginal analysis of pricing is based upon the view (which has some empirical support too) that mark-up is fixed by taking into account price elasticity of demand for the product. Further, the above conclusion that average-cost pricing and marginal analysis of pricing based on profit maximization amount to the same thing is based upon the assumption that the average variable cost remains constant with changes in output. If average variable cost is not constant but changes with output, marginal cost in equilibrium will not be equal to *AVC* and, therefore, the synthesis established above will not hold good. Secondly, in bringing out the synthesis, it is assumed that mark-up is based on average variable cost (*AVC*) rather than the average total cost. If the mark-up is based on average total cost, then the error would be introduced and cost-plus pricing would not maximize profits.

It should be noted that there is little disagreement about the fact that firms in the real world follow average-cost or cost-plus pricing. There are enough empirical studies which support this cost-plus pricing. However, what is contended is that changing the mark-up with changes in the demand and other conditions means that firms are following profit maximising principle in fixing prices, although they may be pricing on the basis of average-cost or cost-plus. In fact, cost-plus pricing can be used whether the aim of the firm is to maximise short-run profits, long-run profits, total revenue from sales. Thus, Professor Hawkins remarks, "There is no reason why short-run profit maximisers, long-run profit maximisers and revenue maximiser should not all use cost-plus as a *means* of setting price. They could all, however, choose different mark-up in order to meet their objectives."[12]

A Critique of Cost-Plus Pricing

An important criticism of cost-plus pricing or full-cost pricing is that *why full-cost pricing is used*, in other words what is the motivation behind cost-plus pricing. To quote Hawkins again, "It is after all not enough just to say that in practice it (cost-plus pricing) is used, since no motivation is implied. And until the motivation is known, there is no way of predicting firms' responses to varying conditions or knowing why they choose any particular size of mark-up."[13]

It may, however, be noted that those who have propounded or supported the cost-plus pricing theory do point out the motivations for fixing full-cost price. One suggestion regarding the motivational aspect of full-cost pricing is that firms are '*satisficers*' and not '*maximizers*' that is, they aim to make a reasonable (or satisfactory) level of profit and not the maximum possible level. Therefore, according to them, margin or mark-up just includes this reasonable and satisfactory level of profit. Another, though a related one, is the suggestion that firms want only a ***fair or just rate of profit*** and it is immoral and unethical to charge more than a fair rate of profit.

The argument for cost-plus pricing that firms seek merely reasonable or fair rate of profit is thought by many economists to be unconvincing and unrealistic. The critics point out that a good deal of empirical evidence, including even that provided by Hall and Hitch, indicates that mark-up varies in response to changing economic conditions[14]. Now, if the firms want merely

11. Stonier and Hague, *A Textbook of Economic Theory*, 4th edition, 1972, p. 245.
12. Hawkins, *Theory of the Firm*, Macmillan, 1973, pp. 76-77.
13. *Op. cit.*, p. 74.
14. Besides the study of of Hall and Hitch, Business Behaviour and Price Policy, 1939, other empirical studies which find that mark-up or margin varies are (*i*) A.D. A. Kaplan, J. B. Dirlam and R. P. Lanzilotti, *Pricing in Big Business : A Case Approach*, Brookings Institution, Washington D.C. 1958.(2) B. Fog. *Industrial Pricing Policies*, translated by I.A. Bailey, North Holland Publishing Co., Amsterdam, 1960.

reasonable, fair or just profits, then why should they raise the mark-up or margin during the boom periods and lower it during the depression periods. Prof. Hawkins rightly asserts "the bulk of the evidence suggests that the size of the 'plus' margin varies; it grows in boom times and it varies with elasticity of demand and barriers to entry. It seems strange that people's concept of a 'fair' profit should generally vary so systematically with the ease of making profits.[15]

However, it should be noted that though the variation in the profit margin does not appear to be consistent with the notion of fair or just profits, but it is consistent with the '*satisficing*' behaviour as suggested by H. A. Simon.[16] According to Simon's satisficing behaviour people set an *aspiration level* regarding profits to be made. And when this aspired level of profit is achieved, they may raise the aspired level of profits which they hope and desire to achieve. This aspired level of profits need not be fixed at the maximum possible level. The point is that the motive of firm using full cost or cost-plus pricing need not be maximising short-run profits.

The second main reason for the use of average-cost or cost-plus pricing by businessmen which has been provided is that we live in a very uncertain world where due to lack of perfect information, demand for a product cannot be correctly predicted for the current month or the current year, let alone for the future years. And, it is asserted that the present price policy may affect the demand for product in the future years. It is further pointed out that in practice it is very difficult to determine what is the profit-maximizing or optimum price in view of the fact that so many variables affect this and firm has to estimate *all the permutations* of all the variables that influence the profit-maximizing (optimum) price.

In view of this Cyert and March[17] in their ***Behavioural Theory of the Firm*** suggest that for the firms it is better to use cost-plus pricing by applying a standard mark-up as a first approximation which, according to the experience of the firm, works reasonably well. They argue that the firm is then ready to supply whatever is demanded at that cost-plus price. Further, according to them, stocks can be used to cushion the effects of unexpected changes in demand. But, over a period of time, they argue that the firm may decide to change the plus-margin or mark-up in response to changing conditions (booms, slumps, degree of competition, and so on) and by doing experiments with different margins (mark-up), and learning from experience, they would be able to arrive at the proper mark-up. On this view, firms use cost-plus pricing because it is the best that they can do in a very uncertain world where conditions regarding demand, strength of competition, technology etc. are fast changing. Further, according to this view, whether pursuing this cost-plus pricing while varying the mark-up in response to the changing conditions, profits are actually maximized or not depends upon the skill and ability of the firms in making correct responses to the changing conditions.

Further, Machlup, a staunch supporter and defender of profit maximization, argues that the real point at issue is not whether in the real world firms try to maximize profits or not, but that whether the conclusions and predictions regarding firms behaviour derived from profit-maximization assumption are valid (or approximately so) description of the real world. He thinks that profit maximisation does lead us to the correct conclusions and predictions regarding the business behaviour in real world.[18]

---

15. *Op. cilt.*,p. 75.
16. H. A. Simon, Theories of Decision Making in Economics and Behavioural Sciences, *American Economic Review*, 1959.
17. Cyert and March, *Behaviral Theory of the Firm*, Prentice Hall, 1963, pp. 446.-47.
18. Machlup, Theories of the Firm : Marginalist, Behavioural, Managerial, *American Economic Review*, March 1967.

Further, it may be pointed out that empirical evidence against profit maximization which is based upon the interviews given by businessmen or the questionnaires which they have filled up are not beyond suspicion because what the people say they are doing may not be what they are doing. There are a good number of difficulties in knowing about the motivations of business firms, entrepreneurs and managers. Often they give contradictory answers to the various questions asked from them regarding profits and price. For instance, Lanzillotti[19], who interviewed a large number of American companies concluded that profit was not their dominant motive. But when the same companies were asked questions about pricing they replied that they did not change prices because it would not increase their long-run profits. This means that in changing prices, long-run profits was the main consideration, although to the question regarding profit motive they replied that profit was not their dominant motive. Likewise, E.A.G. Robinson and Kahn[20], among many others have pointed out that important elements of profit maximization or loss minimization principle actually entered into the pricing decisions of many of the businessmen investigated by Hall and Hitch.

Another, important criticism against average cost or full-cost pricing has been made by R.F. Kahn who has raised the interesting question on whose *average-cost*, price of a product will be fixed when a large or few firms compete to sell the same or similar product. According to him, if an industry is competitive in some sense, firms will not be able to fix their prices on their own full costs, regardless of the cost of others. Thus, there must be some firms on whose average cost the other firms will base their prices. That firm on the basis of whose cost the other firms in the industry will fix price will emerge as the price leader. Therefore, the theory of cost-plus pricing must consider the possibility of price leadership. Hall and Hitch did not analyse the price leadership satisfactorily while Andrews did not touch the subject. In fact, Andrews lays a much stress on the cosing margin, a firm *has to add* and therefore a firm in Andrews' analysis, according to Silberston pursues "defensive type of price policy, which .... is a policy more appropriate to a price follower than a price leader."[21]

Another reason or motive which has been pointed out for the adoption of average-cost (cost-plus) pricing is that the firms do not charge more than the normal or fair level of profits in order to forestall entry. That is, due to the fear of potential competition from the new firms that may enter the industry, the existing firms will use cost-plus pricing with only normal profits. Another reason which has been given for the use of the cost-plus pricing policy of the firm is that it can ameliorate the problem of uncertain competitors' reactions in oligopoly. The use of cost-plus pricing enables the firms of an industry to have tacit collusion regarding the price to be charged. The various firms in an oligopolistic industry recognizing their inter-dependence, come to use the same standard mark-up. With the use of same standard mark-up by all the firms in the industry, they can predict each other's reactions to changing conditions such as cost increases. The fact that firms apply a same standard mark-up to their costs, make their prices staying closely in line without any formal price collusion.

19. R. F. Lanzillotti, Pricing Objectives in Large Companies, *American Economic Review*, December 1958.
20. R. F. Kahn, Oxford Studies in the Price Mechanism, *Economic Journal*, March 1952.
21. Aubrey Silberston, Price Behaviour of Firms. *Economic Journal*, 1970

CHAPTER

44

Theory of Games and Strategic Behaviour

Introduction

In the previous chapter we have discussed those models of oligopoly which explain price and output under oligopoly by assuming objectives other than profit maximization. Another such model is to be found in the application of the theory of games to the oligopoly problem. Professor Neumann and Morgenstern in their book "*The Theory of Games and Economic Behaviour*" which was first published in 1944 provided *a new approach to many problems involving conflicting situations*. The game theory has been applied not only to the oligopoly but also to other economic questions like demand when uncertainty is present. Not only that, the game theory has been applied to the problems of subjects other than economics such as business administration, sociology, psychology, political science, military planning. The theory of games examines the outcome of a situation of interactions between the parties when they have *conflicting* interests. Basically, the game theory seeks to explain what is the rational course of action for an individual who is faced with an uncertain situation, the outcome of which depends not only upon his own actions but also upon the actions of others who too confront the same problem of choosing a rational strategic course of action. We shall describe below how the game theory explains his fundamental question. We shall confine ourselves only to the oligopoly problem. According to professors Neumann and Morgenstern,[1] in an oligopolistic market situation, individual oligopolist is faced with a problem of choosing a rational course of action, which is often called a strategy, keeping in view the possible reactions of his rivals whose reactions in turn would affect him. Thus, he confronts a problem similar to that of the player of any other game.

In a simple form of the game theory, the player has to choose among many possible courses of action which are called strategies. ***A strategy is thus a course of action or a policy which a player or a participant in a game will adopt during the play of the game.*** There are many possible strategies open to the individual among which he has to choose one at a time. In the case of oligopoly, the various alternative possible strategies which are relevant are: (a) changing the price, (b) changing the level of output, (c) increasing advertisement expenditure, and (d) varying the product. Changing the price may itself be divided into three strategies: (1) lowering the price, (2) raising the price, and (3) keeping the price unchanged. Similarly, the strategy of output may be (1) to increase the level of output, (2) to decrease output, and (3) to keep output constant. Likewise, increasing advertisement expenditure may further be divided into various strategies depending upon the various forms of advertisement,

1. John Von Neumann and Oskar Morgenstern, *Theory of Games and Economic Behaviour*, 3rd ed., New York-Wiley, 1964.

for instance, advertisement on radios, on television, in newspapers, in magazines, through handbills, through posters etc. Likewise, varying the product can be subdivided into various strategies depending upon the nature of the product to be chosen such as whether the colour of the package or the type of the package, or the quality of the product should be changed.

A basic feature of oligopoly is that each firm must take into account its rival's reactions to its own actions. For example, Maruti Udyog cannot ignore the effect of an increase in price of its product on the prices and profits of its rival firms and how they will respond to its move of rise in price of its product. Thus, it is clear that oligopolistic behaviour has some of the characteristics of a game where a player must know how his move will affect his rival, and how, assuming that he is rational, will react to his move.

Game theory highlights that, in an oligopolistic market, ***a firm behaves strategically, that is, it adopts strategic decision-making which means that while taking decisions regarding price, output, advertising etc. it takes into account how its rivals will react to its decisions and assuming them to be rational it thinks that they will do their best to promote their interests and take this into account while making decisions.*** Game theory sheds new light on some of the important issues faced in explaining decision-making by firms operating in oligopolistic markets. It explains why an individual firm decides to cheat on a cartel agreement. Further, it explains why and how firms operating in oligopolistic markets prevent the entry of new firms in the industry.

Cooperative and Non-Cooperative Games

Games which firms play can be either cooperative or non-cooperative. A game is cooperative if the firms (*i.e*, players in the game) can arrive at an enforceable or binding contract that permits them to adopt a strategy to maximise joint profits. Suppose making of a carpet costs Rs 500 but the buyers value it at Rs 1000. Fixation of price between Rs 500 and 1000 per carpet will yield profits. In this case, two firms producing carpet can cooperate with each other and adopt a joint price strategy to maximise their joint profits rather than competing with each other. ***If the two firms can sign a binding contract to share the profits between them from the production and sale of carpets, the game is called a cooperative game.***

On the other hand, a non-cooperative game is one where because of conflict of interests two firms cannot sign a binding contract. In most of the oligopolistic market situations binding contract, that is, contracts that are enforceable cannot be negotiated. Therefore, in oligopoly in most cases we find examples of non-cooperative games. ***In a situation of non-cooperative games while the competing firms take each other's actions into account but they take decisions independently and adopt strategies regarding pricing, advertising, product variation to promote their interests.***

It should be noted that a basic difference between a cooperative and non-cooperative game lies in the possibility of negotiating an enforceable contract. In cooperative games, negotiating binding or enforceable contracts are possible, in non-cooperative games they are not. In this chapter while explaining firms' decisions regarding pricing, advertising, we will be concerned mostly with non-cooperative games.

Note that there are games where the players move simultaneously. Each firm chooses a strategy before observing any action or strategy chosen by the rival firms. Not all games are of this type. In some games one player goes first and after which the other player reacts.

DOMINANT STRATEGY

How can firms decide about the optimal choice of a strategy ? Some strategies may be successful (that is, more profitable) if competitors make a *particular* choice, that is, take a particular decision but will not be successful if competitors make *other* choices. On the other hand, ***a dominant strategy is one which will be successful or optimal for a firm regardless of what others do, that is, no matter what strategy the rival firms adopt.***

Let us illustrate the dominant strategy in case of duopoly in the choice of whether to '*advertise*' or not. In this case, deciding in favour of advertising by a firm to promote its sales and hence profits or deciding not to advertise are the two strategies. Thus, '*Advertising*' or '*Not Advertising*' are the two strategies between which each firm has to make a choice. We assume there are two firms, *A* and *B* which have to make a choice between the two strategies. The outcome (or profits made) from the various combinations of two strategies chosen by the two firms are presented in the Table 44.1 in the form of payoff matrix. It should be noted that *outcome or profits* made by a firm by adopting a strategy is influenced by the choice of a particular strategy by the rival firm.

Table 44.1: *Matrix for Advertising Game*

		FIRM B	(*in ₹ Crores*)
		Advertising	*Not Advertising*
FIRM A	*Advertising*	A : 10 B : 5	A : 15 B : 0
	Not Advertising	A : 6 B : 8	A : 10 B : 2

It will be seen from the payoff matrix that if *both firms* adopt the strategy of '*Advertising*', the firm *A* will make profits of 10 crores and firm *B* will earn profits of 5 crores. If firm *A* decides to advertise and firm *B* decides not to advertise, profits of firm *A* are 15 crores and of firm *B* are zero. Similarly, if firm *A* decides not to advertise but firm *B* decides in favour of advertising, firm *A* makes profits of 6 crores and *B* of 8 crores. Further, if both firms go in for '*not advertising*' profits of *A* are 10 crores and of *B* are 2 crores.

Now, the question is what strategy each firm should choose. It is assumed that each firm is rational and will adopt a strategy which will ensure it more profits. Let us first consider choices and their outcome available for firm *A*. If the firm *B* adopts a strategy of '*Advertising*', profits of firm *A* are 10 crores if it also chooses strategy of advertising but only 6 crores if it chooses not to advertise. On the other hand, if firm *B* adopts strategy of '*Not Advertising*', profits of firm *A* are 15 crores if it opts for '*Advertising*' and profits of 10 crores if it also chooses strategy of '*Not Advertising*'.

It is thus clear from the payoff matrix, choice of strategy of '*Advertising*' by firm *A* is better or optimal since it ensures more profits whether firm *B* adopts strategy of '*Advertising*' or the strategy of '*Not Advertising*'. Thus, in the present payoff matrix, whatever strategy firm *B* adopts, for firm A strategy of **'*Advertising*' is optimal. *When payoff matrix of a game is such that a choice of one strategy is better regardless of whatever strategy the other firm chooses, the strategy is known as dominant strategy.*** In the present case choice of strategy of '*Advertising*' is a dominant strategy for firm A.

From the payoff matrix of the advertising game given in the Table 44.1, the sim[illegible] conclusion can be drawn for the optimal strategy to be adopted by firm *B*. Let us stat[illegible] choices that are open to firm *B*. If firm A adopts strategy of 'Advertising', the firm *B* makes profits of 5 crores if it also chooses strategy of 'Advertising' and zero if it chooses strategy of 'Not Advertising'. Thus, choice of strategy of 'Advertising' by firm B is better, if firm A opts for strategy of 'Advertising'. On the other hand, if firm A chooses strategy of 'Not Advertising', profits of firm *B* are 8 crores, if it chooses strategy of 'Advertising' and 2 crores if it adopts strategy of 'Not Advertising'. Thus, in this case too, choice of strategy of '*Advertising*' by firm *B* is optimal whatever strategy the firm *A* adopts. Thus, strategy of 'Advertising' is a dominant strategy for firm *B*.

Since it is assumed that both firms behave rationally each of them will choose strategy of 'Advertising' and the outcome will be profits of Rs 10 crores for firm A and Rs 5 crores for firm B.

It is important to note that all games do not have a dominant strategy for each player. To make it clear we make some changes in the payoff matrix and present them in Table 44.2. The payoff matrix in this table differs from the previous payoff matrix in that profits shown in the bottom right hand corner are different; they are ₹ 20 crores for firm A and ₹ 2 crores for firm *B* in case both adopt the strategy of 'Not Advertising'.

Table 44.2 : *Payoff Matrix for Advertising Game*

		FIRM B	
		Advertising	*Not Advertising*
FIRM A	Advertising	A : 10 B : 5	A : 15 B : 0
	Not Advertising	A : 6 B : 8	A : 20 B : 2

Note. *Numbers in the above table represent profits and are in crores.*

As will be seen from payoff matrix in Table 44.2, if firm *B* chooses strategy of 'Advertising' profits of firm A are ₹ 10 crores if it also opts for strategy of 'Advertising' and are ₹ 6 crores if it opts for strategy of 'Not Advertising'. Clearly, choice of strategy of 'Advertising' by firm A yields more profits and is therefore optimal if firm *B* adopts strategy of 'Advertising'. Now, if firm *B* chooses strategy of 'Not Advertising', profits of firm *A* are ₹ 15 crores, if it decides in favour of 'Advertising' strategy and its profits are ₹ 20 crores if it too adopts strategy of 'Not Advertising'. Thus, in this case given that firm *B* chooses strategy of 'Not Advertising' choice of strategy of 'Not Advertising' by firm *A* is optimal.

It follows from above that in the payoff matrix presented in Table 44.2, ***optimal strategy for firm A depends on which strategy the firm B adopts.*** Choice of strategy of 'Advertising' is optimal for firm *A*, given that the firm *B* adopts the strategy of 'Advertising'. On the other hand, choice of strategy of 'No Advertising' by firm *A* is better, given that the firm *B* adopts strategy of 'Not Advertising'. Thus, in this case there is no dominant strategy for firm *A*. The choice of an optimal strategy by firm *A* in the present case, that is, when dominant strategy does not exist, will be easier if firm *B* adopts a strategy before the firm *A* has to make its choice. But how a firm makes an optimal decision regarding choice of strategy if both firms must choose their strategies simultaneously, that is, at the same time. This is explained below.

hoice of an Optimal Strategy in the Absence of a Dominant Strategy

To decide about the optimal strategy by firm *A* when the choice of strategy by it depends at strategy the other firm *B* adopts, the *firm A must put itself in firm B's place*. For this the firm A has to know what strategy is the best from firm *B*'s point of view and further that it should assume that the firm *B* is rational and will therefore adopt the best strategy. From the payoff matrix given in Table 44.2, it will be seen that given that if the firm *A* chooses strategy of 'Advertising' the firm *B* will make profits equal to ₹ 5 crores if it adopts strategy of 'Advertising' and its profits will be equal to zero if it opts for 'Not Advertising' strategy. Further, if firm *A* chooses strategy of 'Not Advertising' profits of firm *B* will be ₹ 8 crores if it decides to advertise and only ₹ 2 crores if it decides not to advertise. Thus, for firm *B*, strategy of 'Advertising' is better no matter firm *A* adopts strategy of 'Advertising' or 'Not Advertising' and therefore the firm *A* can safely conclude that firm *B* will adopt this strategy of 'Advertising'.

Now, given that ***firm B will adopt strategy of 'Advertising'*** the firm A will choose its strategy; if it adopts strategy of 'Advertising' its profits will be ₹ 10 crores and if its adopts strategy of 'No Advertising', its profits will be ₹ 6 crores. Thus, given the firm *B*'s strategy of 'Advertising', the optimal strategy of firm A is that of 'Advertising' too. In this way both firms will reach the equilibrium ***state by choosing strategy of 'Advertising' and will have no incentive to deviate from it.*** It is quite logical outcome of the game because firm *A* is choosing the best strategy it can, given firm *B*'s strategy, and firm *B* is choosing the best strategy, given firm *A*'s strategy.

Nash Equilibrium

We may refer here to the concept of Nash equilibrium. Nash equilibrium is named after John F. Nash, an American mathematician and economist. We have explained above that in many games we do not have dominant strategies, but still the firms achieve equilibrium in the adoption of their strategies. The application of the concept of Nash equilibrium is quite relevant here. Nash equilibrium is a more general concept of equilibrium that is widely applicable and highly appealing. In the second advertising game whose payoff matrix is given in Table 44.2 and in which firm A has no dominant strategy we reached the conclusion that the equilibrium state is reached when firm A adopts strategy of 'Advertising', *given that the firm B will choose the strategy of 'Advertising'*. That is, firm A is making the best choice, given the choice by its rival firm *B* and firm *B* is choosing the best strategy, given the strategy of firm A. Therefore, they have no incentive to change their strategies. Hence, there exists an equilibrium, called Nash equilibrium.

Nash equilibrium describes a set of strategies where each player believes that it is doing the best it can, given the stragey of the other player or players.

In our above example of game 2 of advertising where firm A has no dominant strategy, each firm promotes its own interests and makes a best choice of strategy, given the other firm's strategy. In the above game, both firms *A* and *B* adopt strategy of 'Advertising' which is optimal for them. Since each is doing the best, given other's strategy and no one has a tendency to change it unilaterally, there exists Nash equilibrium. As no one has a tendency to deviate from the Nash equilibrium state, strategies chosen by them *are stable*.

Comparison Between Dominant Strategy and Nash Equilibrium

It is important to compare Nash equilibrium and equilibrium reached where each firm has a dominant strategy. Whereas *a dominant strategy equilibrium describes an optimal or best choice regardless of what strategy the other player adopts*, in Nash equilibrium each player adopts a strategy that is the best or optimal, *given the strategy other player adopts*. However, it may be noted that in some games we do not have Nash equilibrium and that some have more than one Nash equilibrium.

NEUMANN–MORGENSTERN GAME THEORY

There is a fundamental assumption in the Neumann-Morgenstern game theory which is worth mentioning. According to their game theory, ***an oligopolist while choosing his strategy will assume that his rivals will adopt a strategy which will be worst for him,*** that is, the rivals will adopt the policy which will be most unfavourable to him. That is to say, an oligopolist will adopt the policy of "*playing it safe*". Given this assumption, from among those strategies which provide him with various minimum gains, an oligopolist will select that one which is maximum in those minimum gains.

In order to discuss the solution of oligopoly problem suggested by Neumann-Morgenstern's theory of game, we suppose that an oligopolist knows the complete set of strategies open to him as well as those available to his rivals in the industry. Further, it is assumed that the struggle between the oligopolists is of the nature of "*strictly adversary game*". A strictly adversary game is one in which the outcome which is favourable from the viewpoint of one, is unfavourable to the other. Lastly, we take a **constant-sum game**, in which the outcomes to the two players, *i.e.*, oligopolists always add up to the same constant amount. Thus, in a constant sum game, one player's gain is always another player's loss. Thus, if the constant sum is profits of ₹ 10 which is to be shared between the two sellers, then if A receives ₹ 8, then *B* will be get ₹ 2, and if A gets ₹ 3, then *B* will obtain ₹ 7 and so on. In our explanation of the game theory below, we shall describe the behaviour of a pair of duopolists A and B, who compete for a given total profits of ₹ 10. When in a game aggregate of gain (+) and loss (–) is zero, the constant-sum game becomes a ***zero sum game***. In the oligopolistic market situation, if advertising compaign launched by a firm for promoting the sales of its product merely causes a *fixed number of consumers* to switch from other brands of the product to his brand without adding to the total demand of the product, it would be an example of a zero sum game.

Maximin and Minimax Strategies

Let us suppose that three strategies are open to *A* and three strategies are open to *B*. It is assumed that the duopolists are able to quantify the outcomes of the various combinations of different strategies. The various different strategies open to the duopolists and the effect on the profits of the various combinations of strategies are depicted in Table 44.3 which is called '*Payoff Matrix*'. The payoff matrix of a game represents the payoffs to each player for each combination of strategies that are chosen. In the Table 44.3 *A*'s strategies such A_1 A_2 and A_3 are represented in a column, and *B*'s strategies such as B_1, B_2 and B_3 are represented in a row. *A*'s payoff matrix in Table 44.3 *shows the amount of profits which accrue to A* as a result of the strategies adopted by him and his rival *B*.

Table 44.3 : *A's Payoff Matrix*

			B's Strategies		
		B_1	B_2	B_3	*Row Minima*
	A_1	2	8	1	1
A's Strategies	A_2	4	3	9	3
	A_3	5	6	7	5
Column maxima		5	8	9	

Thus, if *A* adopts strategy A_1 and *B* adopts strategy B_1, then the profits to *A* are ₹ 2. The profits to *B* will be the given constant sum (*i.e.* the profits of ₹ 10) minus the amount of profits which go to *A*. Therefore, in the above case (when *A* adopts strategy A_1 and *B* adopts strategy B_1) the profits of *B* will be Re. 10 – 2 = Re. 8. The profits of *B* are not shown in the table though they can be shown in a separate but the same type of table. In the table given above when *A* plays strategy A_1 and *B* plays strategy B_2 the profits to *A* will be

₹ 8. Likewise, if A selects strategy A_2 and B selects strategy B_3, the profits to A will be ₹ 9. Again, if A adopts strategy A_3 and B adopts strategy B_1, then the profits to A will be ₹ 5. Similarly, each of the other profit figures for A in the table corresponds to a particular combination of strategies chosen by A and B.

Now, given the payoff matrix of the above table, which strategies will be selected by A and B and what will be the outcome ? Suppose A has to choose his strategy before B chooses. As pointed out above, A will choose his strategy keeping in mind that B will adopt the most unfavourable strategy for him, that is, B will play that strategy which will provide minimum possible share of profits to A. Thus, if A decides to choose strategy A_1, then B can either choose strategy B_1 or B_2 or B_3. With A having adopted strategy A_1, if B adopts B_1, the profits to A will be ₹ 2; if he adopts B_2 the profits to A will be ₹ 8; if he adopts B_3, the profits to A will be Re. 1. It is clear that when A has adopted strategy A_1, B will cause A to get minimum profits (Re. 1) if he plays strategy B_3. Likewise, if A decides to select strategy A_2, then B would play strategy B_2 and will give in this way minimum possible profits (₹ 3) to A in this case. Again, if A adopts strategy A_3, then B will adopt strategy B_1, so as to cause minimum possible profits (₹ 5) to A in this case.

It is now obvious that A will choose strategy A_3 so that if B plays most unfavourable strategy even then he gets profits of Rs. 5 which is greater than the other minimum profits of Re. 1 and Rs. 3 in case of the selection of strategies A_1 and A_2 respectively. In other words, ***A will choose the strategy that gives him the maximum of the minimum profits he gets in three strategies.*** For the sake of convenience, minimum profits in each row are written in a new column entitled '*Row Minima*'. Thus while selecting his strategies A will look at the column of '*Row Minima*'. A will choose maximum of the row minima, that is, A will choose strategy A_3 which gives him maximum (₹ 5) of the minimum profits (v 1, 3 and 5). It is clear that ***A will follow a maximin strategy.***

When A has selected strategy A_3 and B comes to know of it, then B will adopt strategy B_1 because by doing so he will cause minimum possible gains (₹ 5) to A and will ensure maximum possible profits to himself. With A having adopted strategy A_3, if B adopts strategy B_2 or B_3, A's profit will be ₹ 6 or 7 respectively, that is, more than when he adopts strategy B_1. Thus when A has selected strategy A_3, B will select strategy B_1. With A having selected strategy A_3, B choosing strategy B_1, A will get profits of ₹ 5 as is seen from his Payoff Matrix in the above table and B will get profits of ₹ 10 – 5 = ₹ 5 (Here, by chance, the shares of the profits of the two are equal, they need not be necessarily equal in all cases.)

Now suppose that B has to choose his strategy first before A chooses his strategy. While making his choice of a strategy, B will also keep in mind that A will adopt the strategy which will be most undesirable for him (B). A's worst strategy for B will be one which will provide him (A) maximum possible profits and therefore reduces the share of profits to B to the minimum possible. The same table which shows profits or payoff to A can be made use of to explain the strategy to be adopted by B.

It will be seen from A's payoff Matrix that if B decides to choose strategy B_1, then if A chooses strategy A_1, the profits to him will be Re. 2 (and to B will be ₹ 8); if he chooses strategy A_2 the profits to him will be Rs. 4 (and to B will be ₹ 6); if he chooses strategy A_3, profits to him will be ₹ 5 (to B they will also be ₹ 5). It is thus clear that with B having decided to select strategy B_1, A will choose strategy A_3, because in this way, it will be getting maximum possible profits (₹ 5) and will be rendering the share of profits to B to the minimum possible. Now, if B selects strategy B_2, then A's worst strategy for B will be A_1, in which case share of profits to A will be ₹ 8 as seen from the table, the remaining ₹ 2 will go to B. Likewise, if B selects strategy B_3, A will select strategy A_2 so as to cause maximum possible profits (₹ 9) to him and minimum possible profits (Re. 1) to B.

Given the above reaction pattern of A, what strategy will be selected by B, that is, whether B will adopt strategy B_1 or B_2 or B_3. If he adopts strategy B_1, worst possible for him will be profits to A of ₹ 5 which are maximum in the given column. Similarly, if he adopts strategy B_2 worst possibility for him will be profits to A of ₹ 8 which is maximum in the new column. Further, if B adopts strategy B_3, worst possibility for him will be profits to A of ₹ 9 which is maximum in the column under B_3. In the above table various maxima of the columns have been written in a new row entitled '*Column Maxima*'. **The best course of action for *B* will be to choose *minimum of these maxima of columns*,** since by doing so he will ensure minimum possible profits to A and hence maximum possible profits to him. Thus, given the situation as depleted in the above Table 44.3, B will select strategy B_1 which provides to A profits of ₹ 5 which is minimum of the maxima of the column maxima. It follows therefore that ***B* will follow a *minimax strategy.*** When B has chosen strategy B_1 and announces it, A will examine his possible strategies and will naturally choose strategy A_3 since it gives him greater possible profits than A_1 or A_2.

We explained above the choice of strategies by A and B separately in two cases, first, when A chooses first before B makes a choice, and secondly when B has to choose first before A's chooses. It has been seen above that, given A's payoff matrix, as shown in the Table 44.3, in both cases A's choice is strategy A_3 and B's choice is strategy B_1. It should be noted that in *the actual game in the real world, neither A nor B has to choose first, they choose simultaneously.* But the foregoing argument nevertheless applies. Given the assumption that each expects worst from his rival, when both have to choose simultaneously, A will look at the row minima of his payoff matrix and will select maximum of the row minima, and B will look at the column maxima of A's payoff-matrix and will choose minimum of the column maxima. Given the A's payoff matrix, A will play *maximin strategy* and B will play *minimax strategy*. Thus even when both choose their strategies simultaneously, A will choose strategy A_3 because it is his maximin strategy and B will choose strategy B_1 because it is his minimax strategy. It is therefore clear that the *result is the same whether A chooses first, B chooses first or both choose simultaneously.*

Equilibrium (Saddle) Point

In payoff matrix in the above table the maximum of the row minima and the minimum of the column maxima are the same, that is, A's maximin strategy coincides with B's minimax strategy. When it happens so, the payoff matrix is said to possess an equilibrium point or, what is also technically called '*saddle point*'. In A's pay off matrix in the Table 44.3, pay-off 5 is an equilibrium or saddle point because the maximum of the row minima is 5 and minimum of the column maxima is also 5. Thus, A by choosing strategy A_3 and B by choosing strategy B_1 are in equilibrium, that is, they will have no incentive to change their strategies. When a payoff-matrix possesses an equilibrium point, then the maximin strategy is the most advantageous strategy open to one firm, *if the other employs a minimax strategy*. Actually, it is because of this that the pay-off entry of 5, in our table above that the maximin and minimax strategy combination is called an equilibrium point. In other words, when one firm employs a maximin strategy, the other is motivated to employ minimax strategy because that is how it can obtain the largest possible share of the profit. Conversely, if one firm plays minimax strategy, the other is motivated to employ the maximin strategy for the reason just mentioned above. In the words of Prof. Baumol, ***"Equilibrium points therefore possess an element of stability in that if one player adopts a strategy consistent with the attainment of such a point, the other player is also motivated to do so."***[2]

It is worth mentioning that when the maximum of row minima is not equal to the minimum

2. William J. Baumol, *Economic Theory and Operations Analysis,* Prentice Hall 2nd edition.

of column maxima, that is, when there is no equilibrium or saddle point in the pay-off matrix, then stable equilibrium would not be attained. In such cases, it matters a great deal who plays first and also it is helpful to know rival's strategy in advance. Various methods have been developed to provide solution in such a pay-off matrix which does not contain equilibrium or stable point. One of these methods is to permit the players to employ mixed strategies. A mixed strategy is a combination of two strategies with the probabilities assigned to these strategies. The technique of solving games involving mixed strategies is too complicated and its explanation is therefore not attempted here.

Critical Appraisal of Maximin Strategy

The maximin game theory as applied to the oligopoly problem has been questioned on some grounds. First, the fundamental assumption underlying the game theory, namely, that an oligopolist believes that his rival will do the worst and adopt his strategy keeping this in view has been questioned. It is pointed out that in essence this assumption about the behaviour of the entrepreneur (oligopolist) implies that he minimizes the chance of the maximum loss, that is, his policy is to "play safe". But such behaviour on the part of the oligopolist, it is said, is very pessimistic as well as conservative. In the real world, the entrepreneurs do not adopt such a cautious and pessimistic approach. They seek to increase their profits and share of the market and for that they often take risks. Commenting upon Neumann and Morgensterin's theory Ferguson and Kreps rightly remark : "This game theory may very well describe the type of the entrepreneur who is primarily intent upon maintaining solvency. It is a much less accurate description of the dynamic businessman who is constantly in quest of profit."[3]

Secondly, it is pointed out that the entrepreneurs in the real world do not possess the amount of knowledge assumed in the game theory. The entrepreneurs do not know even all the various strategies open to them, much less those open to their competitors. Moreover, the real world involves a good deal of uncertainty which has not been incorporated and also cannot be easily incorporated in the game theory.

In the third place, it is said that the oligopoly game is not a strictly adverse game, nor a constant sum game as granted in the theory of games. Contrary to these assumptions, the reduction in price by an oligopolist leads to the increase in the total quantity demanded and not a mere shift of customers from others. Besides, oligopolists do not fight over a lot of profits of a fixed size.

There is another flaw in the game theory. For the game theory to provide a definite solution, both the duopolists must be prudent, that is to say, both should play their maximin or minimax strategies. When one of the duopolists does not possess an adequate knowledge or is not very prudent or is prepared to take risks, then for any of these reasons he will not play minimax strategy. If this is so, then the adoption of maximin strategy by others will be unprofitable. In our example above, if B chooses strategy B_2 for any of the above reasons, then the selection of maximin strategy A_3 by A will not give him maximum possible share of the profits. With B having selected non-minimax strategy B_2, A will get maximum possible share of the profits if he plays strategy A_1. It is thus clear that when one of the duopolists is not prudent, the game theory cannot provide a solution. In the words of Professor Baumol ***"the prudent maximin strategy is only guaranteed to be good when playing against another prudent man."***[4]

It is evident from the above criticism that Neumann-Morgenstern game theory does not provide a complete and all agreed solution to the oligopoly problem. To quote Professors

3. C.E. Ferguson and J.M. Kreps, *Principles of Economics*, p. 531.
4. William J. Baumol, *Economic Theory and Operations Analysis*, p. 352.

Ferguson and Kreps again, "We can reasonably say that while their game theory points out some of the crucial aspects of competitive situations, it is not a model that offers a complete solution to the oligopoly problem".[5]

THE PRISONERS' DILEMMA AND OLIGOPOLY THEORY

The firms working in oligopolistic markets make decisions in the face of uncertainty about how their rivals will react to their moves. As explained above, game theory is a mathematical technique of analysing the behaviour of rival firms with regard to changes in prices, output and advertisement expenditure in the situations of conflicts of interest among individuals or firms. An important game model that has significant implications for the behaviour of the oligopolists is popularly known as prisoner's dilemma. Model of prisoner's dilemma explains how rivals behaving selfishly act contrary to their mutual or common interests. We first explain prisoner's dilemma with an example given originally while propounding this model.

Suppose two persons, Billa and Ranga have been caught for committing a bank robbery. Suppose the prosecution has no enough evidence for their committing the crime. In order to procure confession from them, they are interrogated in two separate rooms so that they cannot communicate with each other. While interrogating each accused, the police offers to Billa "If you confess to the crime (that is, cooperate with the police) while the other keeps silent (*i.e.* does not confess), you will be given imprisonment for only a short period, say, 1 year only but punish the other with 10 years imprisonment. If the other also confesses, then both of you would be sentenced to jail for 5 years". It is however known that if both prisoners do not confess, each can be jailed only for two years. The choices open to each accused are presented in payoff matrix which refers here to years of imprisonment in Table 44.4.

Table 44.4. *Prisoners' Dilemma*

		Ranga's Choice	
		Confesses	*Doesn't confess*
Billa's Choice	Confesses	Ranga : 5 years Billa : 5 years	Ranga : 10 years Billa : 1 year
	Doesn't confess	Ranga : 1 year Billa : 10 years	Ranga : 2 years Billa : 2 years

It will be seen that the outcome (*i.e.* length of sentence to each) is determined by the specific strategy, (that is, choice) adopted by each prisoner. The two strategies (choices) refer to (*i*) confess and (*ii*) and does not confess. If both Ranga and Billa confess, each gets 5 years imprisonment. If one confesses, but the other does not, the one who confesses (*i.e.* cooperate with the police) gets a very light punishment, namely, imprisonment for 1 year only and the one who doesn't confess is sentenced for 10 years imprisonment. It will be further seen from the table that if both do not confess (that is, they remain loyal and faithful to each other and do not cooperate with the police), both are sentenced to 2 years imprisonment.

Now, each prisoner faces an uncertainty regarding how the other person will behave, that is, whether or not he will confess. Though each person has to make an independent choice whether to confess or not but *the outcome, i.e. payoff depends on what the other does.*

Now, under these circumstances what choice will be made by the prisoners when they cannot communicate with each other and have to choose between the two alternatives independently. ***The model of prisoners' dilemma suggests that both behaving selfishly and working in self-interest confess to the crime and cheat each other.*** Since both confess,

5. *Op. cit.*, p. 531.

each will get imprisonment for 5 years. Why do they make this choice and confess can be shown as under. Take Ranga first, most probably, he would confess when he does not know how his co-accused will act. Ranga would reason like this : If I don't confess it is very likely that I will be imprisoned for 10 years as the other prisoner will most probably confess. If I confess, I will get 5 years imprisonment if the other one also confesses, and only one year imprisonment if he does not confess. So in the presence of uncertainty about the other person's choice, and behaving in self-interest, Ranga is likely to confess. Billa too reasoning similarly would confess. As a result, both prisoners would be sentenced for 5 years, though they would have received a lighter sentence of only two years if they had not confessed and remained loyal to each other. However, ***it is self-interest which leads each prisoner to confess and prevents them from attaining the best solution*** for themselves (2 years imprisonment) if both do not confess to the crime and remain loyal to each other. But the decision of each prisoner in favour of confession is quite rational because each person works in self-interest and tries to make the "*best*" of the "*worst outcomes*" in an uncertain situation.

Prisoners' Dilemma and Instability of a Cartel

The game of prisoners' dilemma is of important relevance to the oligopoly theory. The incentive to cheat by a member of a cartel (*i.e.* in the model of collusive oligopoly), and eventual collapse of cartel agreement is better explained with the model of prisoners' dilemma. Instead of two prisoners we take the two firms *A* and *B* which have entered into a cartel agreement and fixed the price and output each has to produce and sell (*i.e.* share of the market). The choice problem facing each member firm of the cartel is whether to cooperate and abide by the agreement and thus sharing the joint monopoly profits or to cheat the other and try to make higher individual profits. But if both cheat and violate the agreement, the cartel would breakdown and profits would fall to the competitive level. We will show that though both would lose by cheating others but, as seen in case of prisoners dilemma, their selfish behaviour leads them to cheat others. The payoff matrix for two member firms of a cartel from the various combinations of choices to be made by them is presented in Table 44.5.

Table 44.5 : *Payoff Matrix for Cartel Members*

		Firm A	
		Cheat	*Cooperate*
Firm *B*	Cheat (lower the price)	A : 5 lakhs B : 5 lakhs	A : 2 lakhs B : 25 lakhs
	Cooperate	A : 25 1akhs B : 2 lakhs	A : 15 lakhs B : 15 lakhs

It will be seen from this table if both firms cooperate and abide by the cartel agreement, they share monopoly profits; 15 lakhs to each of them (right-hand bottom). If both firms cheat, they violate the agreement and profits to each firm fall to the competitive level, ₹ 5 lakhs to each firm (left-hand top). If firm *A* cheats, while firm *B* abides by the agreement, firm *B*'s profits drop to low level of Rs. 2 lakhs and *A*'s profits rise to ₹ 25 lakhs (left hand bottom). On the other hand, if firm *B* cheats and firm *A* adheres to the agreement, profits of *A* decline to Rs. 2 lakhs and *B*'s profits shoot up to ₹ 25 lakhs (left-hand top).

It is evident from the payoff matrix that from the different choices made by the firms, each firm has a strong incentive to cheat. Under the prevailing circumstances, *A*'s best strategy is to cheat rather than cooperate. The same is true for firm *B* whose best strategy is also to cheat. Again, it is the pursuit of self-interest rather than common interest that prompts the firms to cheat other. Thus both firms will cheat and this will bring about the breakdown of the cartel.

Graphical Illustration: The strong incentive to cheat on the part of cartel members and consequently causing a breakdown of a cartel is graphically illustrated in Figure 44.1 where *DD′* is the market demand curve facing the cartel consisting of two firms *A* and *B*. MC_a and MC_b are the marginal cost curves of the firms *A* and *B* respectively. Summing up horizontally the cost curves we get the combined marginal cost curves MC_{a+b}. The cartel maximises its profits by equating *MR* with MC_{a+b} and accordingly output *OQ* and price *OP* is fixed. The two firms *A* and *B* produce and sell q_a and q_b respectively which is the agreed market share of the two firms (Note that output $OQ = Oq_a + Oq_b$.

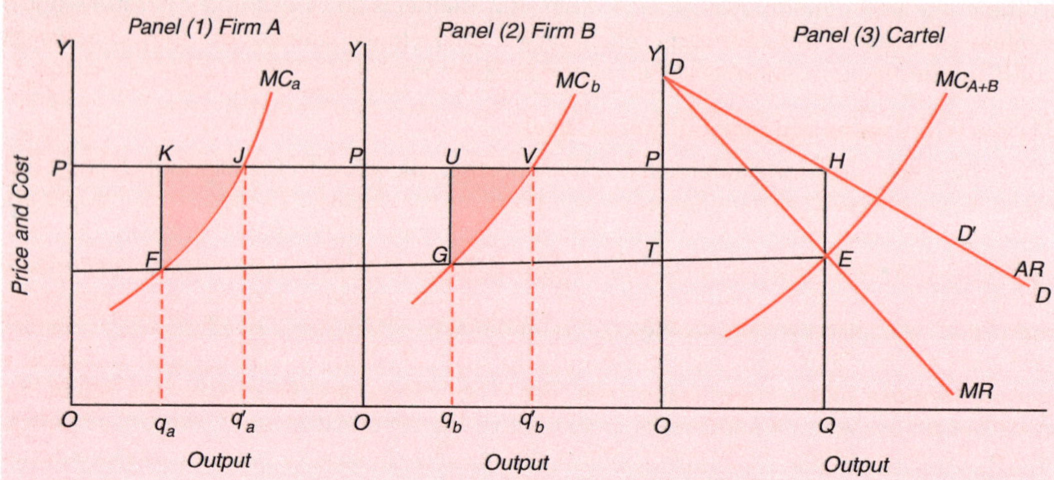

Fig. 44.1. *Instability of Cartel due to Cheating*

It will be seen from panel (1) that, at the price *OP*, if the firm *A* increases its output from q_a to q'_a, it can increase its profits by the shaded area *FKJ*. Similarly, firm *B* also thinks that given the price *OP* if it rises its output to q'_b, it can increase its profits by the shaded area by the *GUV*. Thus, to increase their own profits the firms have incentive to cheat by trying to produce and sell more at the agreed price. It is therefore the working of inner pressures and promotion of self-interest by cartel members that accounts for the instability of cartel arrangements.

REPEATED GAMES AND TIT-FOR-TAT STRATEGY

In our analysis of Prisoner's Dilemma it was assumed that game was played just once. While applying prisoner's dilemma type game to the case of a cartel we concluded that oligopolists like the prisoners lacking trust in each other and behaving selfishly cheated each other. This resulted in bad outcome (*i.e.* lower or no profits) for them. However, the firms facing prisoners' dilemma can increase their profits if they cooperate with each other. But such cooperation is unlikely to occur in a prisoners' dilemma type game played only once. In this game of prisoners' dilemma the players have only single apportunity to play a game (*i.e.* to confess or not). But in the real world oligopolists have to play games repeatedly as they have to set price and output over and over again.

In case of the working of a cartel at every point of time each firm has to decide whether to cheat or not. Behaving selfishly and having no trust in others, all member firms of a cartel cheat (that is, increase their output or undercut price) and as a result make only small profits. However, in case of repeated games the oligopolists may adopt a cooperative behaviour which enables them to earn large profits. Thus, when oligopolists play a repeated game, the analysis of a prisoners' dilemma type game played only once may not be correct.

In the case of a game played repeatedly players come to know how the others react to their moves and this in turn changes their strategic behaviour. Thus, in case of a repeated game, one firm has the opportunity to penalise the other for his previous bad behaviour. In this context it has been suggested that ***tit-for-tat strategy*** is the optimal strategy that will ensure cooperative behaviour of the players participating in a game[6]. Let us suppose an oligopolist firm *A* adopts a cooperative behaviour and charge a high price. Tit-for-tat strategy means that firm *A* will continue to charge high price so long as its rival firm *B* also continue to do so (*i.e.* adopts cooperative behaviour). But if firm *B* cheats and undercuts its price in a round, then in the next round firm *A* will retaliate and will also set a low price. Thus, the firm *B* knowing that the firm *A* is adopting a tit for tat strategy will have to take into account the possibility of the rival firm *A* retaliating in the next round. In case of repeated game, this tit-for-tat strategy results in cooperative behaviour among oligopolists.

However, whether tit-for-tat strategy will be viable depends on whether the repeated game is played indefinite or finite number of times. Let us first explain the outcome when repeated game is played indefinitely. We assume that there are two oligopolistic firms *A* and *B* and there are two possible strategies, namely, (1) charging a high price, and (2) charging a low price. The firms adopt tit-for-tat strategies. It may be mentioned again that according to tit-for-tat strategy ***what one firm does in the current period, the other firm will do in the next period.*** In the case of game of prisoners' dilemma which is played only once, if one firm cheats, the retaliation by the other firm in the next period does not arise as the game is over in the first round itself. However, in case of the repeated game, the other player (firm in our case) can penalise the other firm in the next period for any cheating by any player in the current period. It is assumed that a firm knows that its rival firm is adopting tit-for-tat strategy.

How tit-for-tat strategy is an optimal strategy and will result in cooperative behaviour on the part of the oligopolists is illustrated in payoff matrix given in Table 44.6.

Table 44.6 : *Payoff Matrix* (Figures in million rupees)

		Firm B's Strategies	
		Low Price	*High Price*
Firm A's Strategies	Low Price	A's Profits : 10 B's Profits : 10	A's Profits : 100 B's Profits : –50
	High Price	A's Profits : –50 B's Profits : 100	A's Profits : 50 B's Profits : 50

If game is played only once as in the above case of prisoners' dilemma, both firms will cheat and charge low price and, as will be seen from payoff matrix, they will earn profits only ₹ 10 million (see top left-hand box) while if they had cooperated and charged high price, they could have earned ₹ 50 million each (see bottom right-hand box). Under tit-for-tat-strategy in case of repeated game played for an indefinite period, suppose firm *A* starts with charging a high price and decides to continue charging the high price so long as the other firm also does likewise. But when the firm *B* cheats, that is, charges a low price, *B*'s profits rises to 100 millions in that round while the firm *A*'s profits have become negative (–50 million). Now, under the tit-for-tat strategy, the firm *A* will retaliate in the next round and set a low price.

6. See R. Axelord, "*The Evolution of Cooperation*" (New York : Basic Books, 1984).

When both charge low price, profits of each are 10 million (see upper left-hand box of Table 44.6). As the game is repeated indefinitely round after round, the cumulative loss of profits suffered by firm *B* will outweight his gain of profits in one round when it undercut the price. Thus, cheating (*i.e.* undercutting price in the present example) when the rivals are pursuing tit-for-tat strategy is not a profitable proposition. In this way the firms will learn that cooperative behaviour is the best course of action when each firm is pursuing the tit-for-tat strategy. When both cooperate and charge a high price, each firm will earn profits of ₹ 50 million in each round. (See bottom right-hand box in payoff matrix of Table 44.6). Thus, Hal Varian writes, ***"The tit-for-tat strategy does very well because it offers an immediate punishment for defection. It is also a forgiving strategy. It punishes the other player only once for each defection. If he falls into line and starts to cooperate, then tit for tat will reward the other player with cooperation. It appears to be a remarkably good mechanism for the efficient outcome in a prisoner's dilemma that will be played an indefinite number of times."***[7]

Let us now consider the case when the game is repeated a *finite* number of times, say in 10 rounds). Both players know that the game will be played 10 times and also that each is pursuing tit-for-tat strategy. Let us first consider 10th round which by assumption is the last round when the game will be played between the two firms. Whether they will cooperate each charging a high price or they will cheat each other by charging a low price. If firm *B* believes that its rival firm is rational will reason like this: Even knowing that the firm *A* is playing tit-for-tat strategy, the firm *B* will think since 10th round is the last round of playing the game and after that since the game is over, the firm *A* will have no chance to retaliate. Therefore, firm *B* will charge high price for the first 9 rounds but will choose to cheat, that is, will charge low price and make a large profits in the last 10th round (This is shown in the *bottom* left-hand side box of the payoff matrix of Table 44.6).

However, firm *A* will also reason likewise and will charge high price in the first 9 rounds but will plan to cheat (charge low price) in the last 10th round and will hope to make a large profits in the last 10th round thinking that firm *B* will have no chance to retaliate thereafter.

Thus, both thinking rationally will decide to choose the low price in the last 10th round and will not cooperate with each other. Hall Varian rightly writes, "Players cooperative because they hope that cooperation will induce further cooperation in the future. But this requires that there will always be the possibility of future play. Since there is no possibility of future play in the last round, no one will cooperate then".[8]

But what about next to the 10th round, that is, the 9th round. Firm *B* will reason that it should charge low price in this next to the last round because in any case there will be no cooperation between the two in the last round. But, of course, the Firm A being equally rational will also reason likewise and will plan to charge low price in the 9th round (*i.e.* next to the last round). The same reasoning can be repeated by both the firms for undercutting price, that is, for charging a low price in the 8th and earlier rounds as well, that is, for the rounds 8th, 7th, 6th etc. till the first round. Thus, when the game is played a *finite* number of times, even while pursuing tit-for-tat strategy the two firms will opt for *non-cooperative behaviour.* Thus, even with tit-for-tat strategy in case of repeated games to be played a *finite* number of times, we are stuck in 'Prisoners' Dilemma' without the outcome of the cooperative behaviour.

But cooperative outcome can come about even in this finite number of time for which the game is to be played if *a firm has a doubt about its competitor's rationality in pursuing tit-for-tat strategy* and its ability to reason out the logical implications of a finite time horizon as

7. Hal R. Varian, *Intermediate Microeconomics : A Modern Approach* (New York : WW Norton & Co., Fourth Edition, 1997,) p. 487.
8. Hall R. Varian, op. cit., p. 486.

explained above. Thus, if competing firms have doubts about whether the other firm is playing tit-for-tat or playing tit-for-tat blindly, this will make cooperative behaviour a good strategy. Besides, in this case of finite number of times the game is to be played cooperative behaviour can be regarded as a good strategy by the competing firms ***if the time is long enough and the firms are uncertain about how long will they be competing.*** Thus, "Most managers do not know how long they or their firms will be competing with their rivals and this also serves to make cooperative behaviour a good strategy. Although the number of months that the firms compete is probably finite, managers are unlikely to know just what the number is. As a result, the unraveling argument that begins with a clear expectation of undercutting in the last month no longer applies. As with an infinitely repeated game, it will be rational to play tit-for-tat".[9] Thus, in view of the fact that in most oligopolistic markets the game is in fact repeated over a long period and uncertain length of time and managers have doubts about how rationally their competitors behave, in case of repeated game for a finite number of times, the Prisoners' dilemma can have cooperative outcome.[10]

STRATEGIC MOVES

In the earlier sections it has been emphasised that oligopolists must realise that their own profits depend not only on their own decision and behaviour but also on the decision and behaviour of their rivals. This shows the importance of strategic moves by the oligopolists to enhance their profits. By making certain strategic moves an oligopolist can gain competitive advantage in the market. Thomas Schelling of Harvard University who has made an important contribution to the theory of strategic decision making defines the concept of strategic move in the following words : ***"A strategic move is one that influences the other person's choice in a manner favourable to one's self, by affecting the other person's expectations on how one's self will behave"***[11] For example, if Maruti Udyog threatens to retaliate by cutting the price of their cars to a level that would cause losses to its rival firms which produce Santro and Indica cars if they reduce their prices, this move of Maruti Udyog is a strategic move. This is because this threat is intended to ensure that the rival firms do not cut the prices of their cars.

Threat, Commitment and Credibility

For the strategic move of giving threat to be successful, there must be *commitment* that the firm making a threat will definitely carry it out. ***Only when there is commitment to carry out a threat that it becomes credible.*** If there is no commitment to carry out the threat, it will be an empty threat and will therefore not have the desired effect on the behaviour of the rivals. If a firm can convince its rival firms that it is committed to a particular move that it is making, then the rivals may cooperate without retaliating because they may think that they would lose more than they would gain from a long period of conflict with the firm making a move.

When a threat is credible is illustrated in the payoff matrix of firms *A* and *B* given in Table 44.7 where the profits of the two firms making different brands of cars are shown when they charge low price or high price for their cars. This payoff matrix shows that charging a high price is a dominant strategy for firm *A*, that is, whatever strategy (whether of charging a high price or low price) the rival firm *B* pursues, the strategy of charging a high price is optimal for

9. See Pindyek and Rubinfeld, op. cit., p. 466.
10. This result is based on the original research work done by David Kreps, Paul Milgrom, John Roberts, and Roberts Wilson, "Rational Cooperation in the Finitely Repeated Prisoners' Dilemma, *Journal of Economic Theory,* 1982, pp. 245-252."
11. Thomas C. Schelling, *The Strategy of Conflict,* (New York : Oxford University Press, 1960). Another important work that discusses strategic moves is by M. Porter, *Competitive Strategy* (New York : Free Press, 1980).

Table 44.7 : Payoff Matrix for a Pricing Game (in lacs)

		Firm B	
		Low Price	*High Price*
Firm A	Low Price	20, 20	20, 10
	High Price	30, 40	50, 30

(**Note:** *The first number in the pair shows profits of firm A, the second number shows profits of firm B*).

firm *A*. Thus, if firm *B* charges the low price, the firm *A* will earn profits of ₹ 20 lakhs if it charges a low price and ₹ 30 lakhs of it charges a high price. On the other hand, if the firm *B* charges a high price, the firm *A* will earn ₹ 20 lakhs if it charges a low price and ₹ 50 lakhs if it charges a high price. Thus, whether the firm *B* plays a low price strategy or a high price strategy, for firm *A*, high price strategy is the optimal strategy to adopt. It will be seen further from the payoff matrix of Table 44.7, that when the firm *A* will charge the high price, the firm *B* will opt for charging a low price and in this way will earn ₹ 40 lakhs instead of ₹ 30 lakhs if it charges the high price.

Under these circumstances (i.e. given the payoff matrix of Table 44.7) if firm *A* threatens firm *B* that it will charge a low price, this threat will be *incredible* or empty because the firm *B* knows that by charging a low price, the firm *A* will cause its profits to fall to ₹ 20 lakhs. Being an incredible threat the firm *B* will not take it seriously. As explained above, one way to make the threat credible is to make it binding and irreversible for one self. Thus, if a firm threatens to enter a particular market, it can make its threat credible if the potential firm buys a plant rather than lease it or enters into a long-term contract for buying raw materials. This shows that the firm which gives a threat to enter has made an irreversible commitment, and will therefore enter the market, come what may and this makes the threat credible. Take another example. If a firm commits to a price reduction if its rival firm lowers its price, then to make its commitment credible, it can make verbal or written agreement with the customers that it will match any price cut by its rival. On the other hand, if a particular firm has the image that it can easily ignore its particular commitment that it makes, then commitment is not credible and it will not pay much attention to the commitment made.

Another way for a firm to make the threat credible is to *build a reputation of irrationality* for carrying out its threat even if it has to lose some profits or even incur losses. This irrational reputation is developed when a firm has actually carried out its threat several times in the past (even at the expense of its profits). Thus, the threat of a firm with reputation of irrationality is a credible threat and its rivals will take serious note of it. Consider payoff matrix of Table 44.7 again. If the firm *A* is charging a high price and the *firm B is charging the low price,* they are earning profits of ₹ 30 and 40 lakhs respectively (see bottom left-hand corner of Table 44.7). Now, in order to increase its profits by forcing *B* to charge a high price, if the firm *A* having the reputation of irrational behaviour not only threatens but actually lowers its price to carry out its threat, then *B* will be induced to charge high price and as a result both firms will be charging high price and firm *A*'s profit will rise to ₹ 50 lakhs, but profits of the firm *B* will fall to ₹ 30 lakhs (see bottom right-hand corner). This is because in case of firm *A* lowering price and with firm *B* also charging a low price each will be making lower profits of ₹ 20 Lakhs. It is due to likely fall in profits as a result of firm *A* carrying out its threat that firm *B* is induced to charge the high price. It is important to note that though profits of the firm *B* has fallen to ₹ 30 lakhs because under threat from the firm *A* it has decided to cooperate, it is still greater than profits of ₹ 20 lakhs that it would earn if firm *A* had actually carried out its threat and both charged the low price.

In addition to what has been said about credible commitment, it may be noted that ***for a threat to be credible, the firm's commitment must be backed up with assets, skills and expertise, financial and technological powers to carry out the commitment.*** Besides, a firm's commitments are more credible if it has reputation and a long history of adhering to its commitments.

However, for tit-for-tat strategy to be successful certain conditions must be fulfilled. First, a reasonably *stable set of players* (that is, firms) is required for the successful working of tit-for-tat strategy. If the players (firms) change quite frequently co-operative behaviour between them is not likely to develop. Second, in tit-for-tat strategy for cooperative behaviour to be achieved, there must be *a small number of players* (firms). In case of a large number of competing firms, it is difficult to know what each firm is doing. As a result, cooperation cannot be enforced and generally breaks down when there are many firms confronting each other. Third, for the success of tit for tat strategy to induce cooperative behaviour it is assumed that each firm can quickly detect cheating by others and is able and willing to retaliate if the rivals do cheating. Fourth, *the demand and cost conditions must remain stable* for the success of tit-for-tat strategy. The failure to cooperate is quite often the result of changing demand or cost conditions. Uncertainties about demand or costs make it difficult for the firms to arrive at an implicit understanding of what cooperative behaviour requires. Lastly, as explained above, tit-for-tat strategy to induce cooperative behaviour, *the game is to be played either indefinitely* or for a long *uncertain* number of times.

ENTRY DETERRENCE

The existing firms, especially the monopolists try to prevent the entry of new firms as the entry of new firms reduce the profits of the existing firms. An important strategy for the existing firm to deter the entry of new firms in the market is the threat to lower price and thereby inflict losses on the potential entrant. However, such a threat by the existing firm will work only if it is credible. To illustrate whether threat is credible or not, consider the payoff matrix shown in Table 44.8. From this payoff matrix in Table 44.8, it follows that the threat by the existing firm *A* that if the potential firm *B* enters the market, as explained above, it will

Table 44.8 : *Payoff Matrix* *(Profits in lakhs)*

		Firm B (Potential Entrant)	
		Enter	*Stayout*
Firm A	Low Price	4, – 2	6, 0
(Existing Firm)	High Price	7, 2	10, 0

lower the price and impose loss on *B*, is not credible. It will be seen from the payoff matrix of Table 44.8 that before entry of firm *B* the firm A is charging high price and is making profits of ₹ 10 lakhs. (See bottom right-hand corner). Now, on entry by firm *B* in the market, if the existing firm charges a high price, the profits of the existing firm *A* are 7 lakhs and of the new firm *B* are 2 lakhs, and, on the other hand, if the existing firm *A* lowers the price to carry out its threat, the profits of firm A are 4 lakhs[12] and the new firm *B* incurs a loss of 2 lakhs. This shows that despite the entry of new firm *B*, it is profitable for the existing firm to charge a high price and earn profits of ₹ 7 lakhs which are greater than ₹ 4 lakhs in case it lowers the price in accordance with the threat held out. This, shows that threat is **not creditable. Unless the firm is irrational, it will not lower the price on the entry of new firm B.** And since the potential entrant knows this, the threat will not work and will not prevent the firm *B* from entering the market.

To make the threat credible the existing firm has to commit itself to resist the entry of the new firm *B* even at the expense of its profits. One way to make a credible commitment to resist the entry of the potential firm, is the *expansion of its capacity* by the existing firm before it is needed, that is, by *building excess capacity.*[13] Since for building of excess capacity, the existing firm will incur costs, there will be a change in the payoff matrix. The new payoff matrix given in Table 44.9 is the same as in the previous Table 44.8 except that after building

Table 44.9. *Payoff Matrix with Credible Commitment*

		Firm B (*Potential entrant*)	
		Enter	*Stayout*
Firm A	Low Price	4, −2	6, 0
(Existing firm)	High Price	3, 2	5, 0

excess capacity, firm *A*'s profits are ₹ 3 lakhs if he continues to charge the high price and Rs. 4 lakhs if it lowers the price. The profits of the existing firm *A* are now smaller even with the high price charged because of the costs incurred on building new capacity and sharing of the market with the new entrant. On the other hand, in case of low price being charged on the entry of new firm, the profits are the same, namely 4 lakhs as in the previous payoff in Table 32.8. This is because at the low price, the sales of the existing firm will increase resulting in greater revenue and as a result it will be able to utilise a part of the extra capacity built.

Thus, with low price the increase in revenue may cancel out the increase in costs due to the addition of extra capacity and therefore profits of the existing firm *A* remains the same by charging a low price. However, charging a low price by firm *A*, will cause losses of ₹ 2 lakhs to the new entrant (see upper left-hand corner). Thus, **realising that by entering the market, it will suffer a loss, the firm B will not enter the market and stay out.** Thus building of excess capacity before it is needed the existing firm commits itself to lowering price if the firm *B* dares to enter the market and thus makes its threat credible and deters the entry of the potential firm. Having built excess productive capacity, the existing firm *A* will charge a low price and make a profit of ₹ 4 lakhs instead of ₹3 lakhs if it charges a high price. Since the new firm *B* on entry will have to sell the product at the low price it will suffer a loss of ₹ 2 lakhs if it entered the market. Therefore, the firm *B* would not enter market and stay out. Thus, the existing firm *A* has succeeded in deterring entry by holding out a credible threat.

An alternative to building excess capacity is *creating a reputation for irrationality* in preventing entry of potential firms in the market even if it causes decline in profits for quite a long time. Thus, when a firm has good reputation for behaving irrationally, then even given the payoff matrix of Table 44.8, it will succeed in deterring entry. The reputation of irrationality of the existing firm creates a credible threat of price warfare if the potential firms enter the industry. As a matter of fact, in the real world it is reputation for irrationality that seems to work for deterring entry.

12. Note that fall in profits of the existing firm is due to (1) the market will now be shared between the two firms, and (2) lowering of price to deter entry.
13. For an elaborate analysis of the use of excess capacity to prevent entry, see J. Tirole *The Theory of Industrial Organisation* (Cambridge, MA : MIT Press, 1988).

QUESTIONS FOR REVIEW

1. Distinguish between cooperative game and non-cooperative game. Give examples.
2. Explain a dominant strategy. How is a stable equilibrium reached when a firm pursues its dominant strategy. How is equilibrium reached when there is no dominant strategy ?
3. What is Nash Equilibrium ? Does equilibrium in a prisoners' dilemma game represent Nash Equilibrium ?
4. What is prisoners' dilemma? How is it used to explain the instability of a cartel ?
5. Explain Neumann-Morgenstern theory of game ? On what grounds has it been criticised ?
6. What is a tit-for-tat strategy ? Why is it rational strategy when Prisoners' Dilemma type game is infinitely repeated ?
7. Explain the Prisoners' Dilemma game when it is repeated 15 times and both players are rational. Is tit-for-tat strategy optimal in this case ?
8. What is a "strategic move"? What are the conditions required for strategic move to be successful ?
9. What is a credible threat ? How can a threat be made credible ?
10. How does an incumbent firm succeed in deterring entry into the market by potential competitors ?
11. Can a threat of a price war deter entry by new firms ? What actions might a firm take to make this threat credible ?

CHAPTER

45

Sales Maximisation Model of Oligopoly Firm

Rationale for Sales Maximisation Hypothesis

Sales maximisation model of oligopoly of firm is another important alternative to profit maximisation model. This has been propounded by W. J. Baumol, an American Economist. In an earlier chapter we described the gist of Baumol's maximisation model and mentioned how Baumol challenges the profit maximisation assumption regarding business behaviour in these days of manager-dominated corporate form of business organisation and shows how sales maximisation is more valid and realistic assumption of business behaviour. Further, we pointed out there that sales maximisation was quite consistent with *rationality* assumption about business behaviour. We also noted there that sales maximisation model represented one of the managerial theories of the firms because in it the great importance had been given to the managerial role and to his pursuing self-interest in making price, output and advertising policies. Prof. Baumol thinks that *managers are more interested in maximizing sales than profits.*

It should be noted that by sales maximisation Baumol does not mean the maximisation of the *physical volume* of sales but the maximisation of *total revenue from sales*, that is, the dollar value of the sales made. Therefore, his theory is also known as ***revenue maximisation model.*** Further, Prof. Baumol does not ignore profit motive altogether. He argues that there is a *minimum acceptable level of profits* which must be earned by the management so as to finance future growth of the firm through retained profits and also to induce the potential shareholders for subscribing to the share capital of the company. Thus, according to him, management of oligopolistic firms *seeks to maximize sales or, in other words, total revenue subject to this minimum profit constraint*. He thus writes.

"*My hypothesis then is that oligopolists typically seek to maximise their sales subject to a minimum profit constraint. The determination of the minimum just acceptable profit level is a major analytical problem and I shall only suggest here that it is determined by long-run considerations. Profits must be high enough to provide the retained earnings needed to finance current expansion plans and dividends sufficient to make future issue of stocks attractive to potential purchasers. In other words, the firm will aim for that stream of profits which allows for the financing of maximum long-run sales. The business jargon for this is that management seeks to retain earnings in sufficient magnitude to take advantage of all reasonably safe opportunities for growth and to provide a fair return to shareholders*[1]."

With sales maximisation subject to minimum profit constraint as the objective of business firms, Baumol explains price-output determination by an oligopolistic firm, advertising

1. W.J. Baumol, On the Theory of Oilgopoly *Economica,* New Series,Vol. 25, 1958.

expenditure incurred by it, choice of output and input combinations by it, and the effect of changes in overhead costs on the price of products. He draws out the conclusions reached regarding these things in the sales maximisation model and how they differ from those of profit maximisation model. We explain below all these aspects of Baumol's sales maximisation model of oligopoly.

Sales Maximisation Model : Price-Output Determination of a Product without Advertising

We first explain Baumol's sales maximisation of an oligopoly firm in case when a firm produces a single product and does not undertake any expenditure on advertising or other promotional efforts. We further assume that firm's time horizon is a single period and in this period the firm seeks to maximise its sales revenue subject to a *minimum profit constraint*. The firm does not consider the effect of its price-output decision in the current period on price and output in the subsequent period. Besides, it is assumed that minimum profit constraint is *exogenously* determined by demands and expectations of shareholders and financing institutions of the firm. The firm must achieve this minimum level of profits so as to satisfy the shareholders and to prevent a fall in prices of firm's shares in stock exchange.

It is better to explain graphically price-output determination in Prof. Baumol's sales or total revenue maximisation model. Consider Figure 45.1 where the *Y*-axis measures total revenue, total cost and total profits in terms of rupees and the X-axis measures the total output. *TR* and *TC* are respectively total revenue and total cost curves. Since total cost curve *TC* starts from the origin, it means the diagram refers to the long-run cost-revenue situation. *TP* is the total profits curve which first rises and then after a point falls downward. Since total profits are the difference between total revenue and total costs at various levels of output, therefore total profits curve *TP* measures the vertical difference between the *TR* and *TC* curves at various levels of output.

If the firm aims at maximising profits, it will produce output *OA*. This is because corresponding to output *OA*, the highest point of the profit curve *TP* lies. But, as we have seen above, according to Prof. Baumol, the firm does not seek maximisation of profits. On the other hand, if the firm wants to maximise sales (or total revenue), it will fix output at level *OC* which is greater than *OA*. At output *OC* total sales revenue is CR_2 which is maximum in the diagram[2]. At this total sale revenue maximising output level *OC*, the firm is making total profits equal to *CG* which are less than the maximum attainable profits *AH*. It will be clear from the figure that total sales revenue maximisation output *OC* is larger than profit-maximising output *OA*. Prof. Baumol contends that the business firms aim at total sales revenue maximisation subject to a minimum profit constraint. Now, if *OM* is the minimum total profits which a firm wants to obtain, then *ML* is the minimum profit line.

Now, this minimum profit line *ML* cuts the total profits curve *TP* at point *E*. Therefore, if the firm wants total sales revenue maximisation subject to the minimum profits of *OM*, as has been contended by Prof. Baumol, then it will produce and sell output *OB*. At output *OB*, the firm will be having total revenue equal to BR_1 which is less than the maximum possible total revenue of CR_2. But the total revenue BR_1 is the maximum obtainable revenue to earn the

2. Note that total sales revenue is maximum at the level of output at which $MR = 0$ and price elasticity of demand is equal to unity. This is because at the maximum point of total revenue curve *TR*, its slope is equal to zero. Thus at point $R_2 = \frac{dTR}{dQ} = MR = 0$. It is known that corresponding to zero *MR*, price elasticity of demand is equal to unity.

minimum desirable profits *OM*. It should be noted that the firm can earn minimum profits *OM* even by producing output *ON* (minimum profit line *ML* also cuts the total profits curve *TP* at point *K*). But the total revenue at output *ON* is much less than that at output *OB*. Therefore, given the firm's objective of maximising total revenue subject to the minimum profit constraint, the firm will not produce output *ON* or at point *K*. It will be noticed from the figure that the output *OB* lies in between *OA* and *OC*, that is, it is larger than profit-maximising output *OA* but smaller than the total revenue-maximising output *OC*. Thus, in Prof. Baumol's model, oligopolistic firm will be in equilibrium at output *OB* and will be earning profits *BE* (or *OM*).

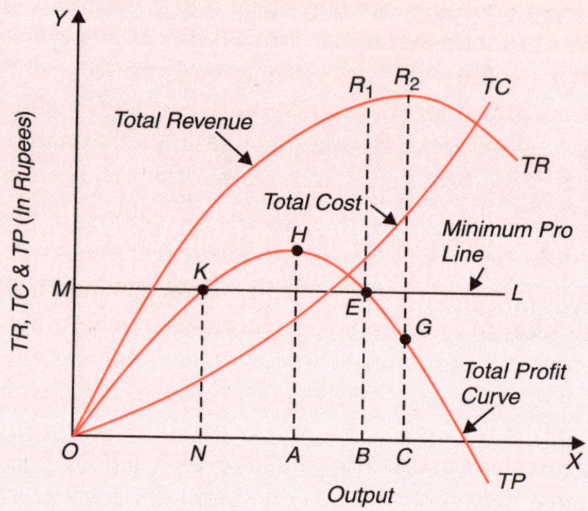

Fig. 45.1. *Prof. Baumol's Sales Maximization Model*

It should be carefully noted that the objective of total revenue (or sales) maximisation subject to the minimum profit constraint leads to a greater output and lower price than under profit maximisation. Price will be lower under revenue maximisation because the output under it, as seen above, is greater and given that demand or average revenue curve is sloping downward, the price will be less when output is larger. To quote Prof. Baumol "The profit maximizing output *OA* will usually be smaller than the one which yields either type of sales maximum, *OC* or *OB*. This can be proved with the aid of the standard rule that at the point of maximum profit marginal cost must equal marginal revenue. For marginal cost is normally a positive number (we can't usually produce more of a good for nothing). *Hence marginal revenue will also be positive when profits are at a maximum, i.e.*, further increase in output will increase total sales (revenue). Therefore, if at the point of maximum profit the firm earns more profit than the required minimum, it will pay the sales maximizer to lower his price and increase his physical output"[3].

The price charged at output *OB* will be equal to $\frac{\text{Total Revenue}}{\text{Output}}$, that is, $\frac{BR_1}{OB}$.

Now suppose the minimum acceptable profits are equal to *AH* (which are maximum possible profits under the given cost-revenue situation), then even under total revenue maximisation objective subject to the minimum profit constraint, the firm will produce the profit-maximising output *OA*. But it will produce output *OA* not to maximise profits but to maximise total revenue given the minimum profits constraint *AH*. Now, suppose the minimum acceptable profits for an entrepreneur are larger than *AH*, then it is obvious form the Figure

3. William J. Baumol, *Economic Theory and Operations Analysis*, 3rd. ed. pp. 326-27.

45.1 that, given the cost-revenue situations depicted in it, the firm cannot earn profits greater than *AH*. Therefore, the firm must either lower its minimum acceptable profit level or go out of the industry.

Sales Maximisation Model : Optimal Advertising Outlay

We know that firms in oligopolistic market conditions compete not only in terms of price but also in terms of advertising expenditure, product variation and special services offered to the buyers. Advertising expenditure is the chief form of non-price competition. We shall discuss here the question of optimal advertising expenditure to be incurred by an oligopolist and the conclusions reached in this connection will apply equally to the questions of optimal product adjustment and the optimal amount of special services to be provided by an oligopolist when he chooses to maximize sales (total revenue).

The important question in regard to the advertising is how much advertising expenditure a firm will make so as to achieve its objective. How much advertising outlay will be incurred by a firm is greatly influenced by the objective of the firm as to whether it seeks to maximize sales or profits. This optimal advertising expenditure from the viewpoints of both sales maximisation and profit maximisation is illustrated in Figure 45.2 in which advertising outlay is measured along the X-axis and total cost, total revenue and total profits on the *Y*-axis. Baumol takes an important assumption in connection with the effect of advertising outlay on total revenue or sales. He assumes, and he quotes empirical evidence for this, that the **increase in advertising outlay by a firm *will always raise the physical volume of sales*, though after a point these sales will increase at a diminishing rate.** Now, given the price of product, the total revenue (*i.e.* monetary value of the sales) will increase in proportion to the increase in the physical value of sales as a result of the increase in advertising outlay. Therefore, the increase in advertising outlay will always cause the total revenue to increase, though after a point diminishing returns are likely to set in.

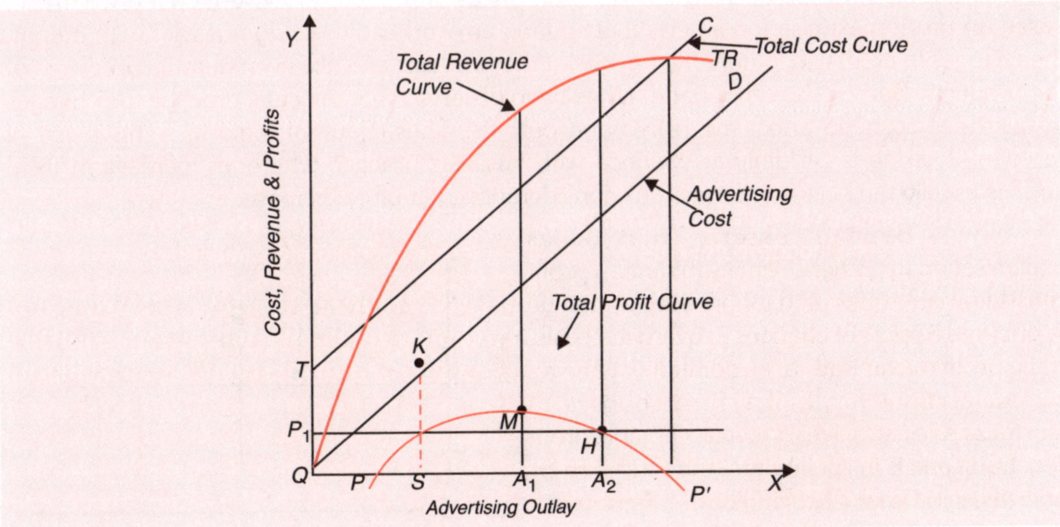

Fig. 45.2. *Optimal Advertising Outlay with Sales Maximisation and Profit Maximisation*

In Figure 45.2, *TR* is the total revenue curve which represents the change in total revenue as the advertising outlay is raised, *given the price of the product*. Curve *OD* represents the advertising cost and has been so drawn as to make 45° angle with *X*-axis. This is because we have simply transferred the advertising outlay shown on the *X*-axis to the vertical axis as advertising cost, (for instance $OS = SK$). The *other costs* of the firm incurred on fixed and variable factors are taken to be independent of the amount of advertising outlay. Therefore, by *adding a fixed amount of other costs* (equal to OT) to the advertising cost curve OD, we obtain the total cost curve TC. Finally, by taking out the difference between total revenue curve (TR) and total cost curve (TC) we draw the total profit curve PP'.

Now, it will be seen from Figure 45.2 that if the firm seeks to maximize its profits, it will incur advertising outlay equal to OA_1, at which the profit curve reaches its maximum point M. On the other hand, if P_1 is the minimum profit constraint and the firm chooses to maximize its total revenue with P_1 as the minimum profit constraint, it will spend OA_2 on advertisement which is greater than OA_1. We thus see that the objective of constrained revenue maximisation leads to a greater level of advertising outlay than the objective of profit maximisation. In this connection, it should be noted that here there is no possibility of *unconstrained sales or revenue maximum*, as is there corresponding to output OC in the previous Figure 45.1. This is because, unlike a reduction in price, *increase in advertising outlay always raises total revenue or sales* (by assumption). As a result, Baumol concludes that **"it will always pay the sales maximizer to increase his advertising outlay until he is stopped by the profit constraint, that is, until profit have been reduced to the minimum acceptable level. This means that sales maximizer will normally advertise no less than, and usually more than, do profit maximizers.** For, unless the maximum profit level A_1M is not greater than the required minimum P_1 it will be possible to increase advertising some what beyond the profit-maximizing level OA_1 without violating the profit constaint. Moreover, this increase will be desired since, by assumption, it will increase physical sales, and with them, dollar sales will rise proportionately."[4]

Sales Maximisation Model : Pricing and Changes in Fixed Costs

An important implication derived from sales maximisation hypothesis by Baumol is the effect of changes in fixed or overhead costs on prices of products. Conventional price theory based on profit maximisation asserts that so long as overhead costs do not vary with output, the changes in them would not affect prices of the products and nor even outputs produced of the products. But, on the other hand, it has been observed that in actual practice the changes in overhead costs do affect the prices and outputs. Thus, Baumol remarks "This piece of received doctrine is certainly at variance with business practice where an increase in fixed costs is usually the occasion for serious consideration of a price increase."[5]

Now, Baumol asserts that sales maximisation hypothesis with its minimum profit constraint can explain and rationalise the change in prices as a result of changes in overhead costs, while profit maximisation, as pointed out above, cannot account for it. If a firm chooses to maximize sales with a minimum acceptable profit constraint and is in equilibrium, then the **rise in overhead costs would bring about increase in total costs and as a result the profit of the firm will fall below the minimum acceptable profit level.** In order to prevent this fall in the profit level and to be in equilibrium again, the constrained sales-maximizing firm will reduce the

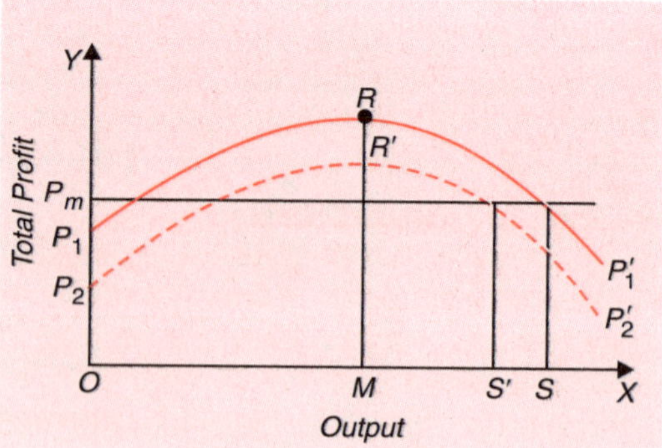

Fig.45.3. Increase in fixed costs lowers the level of output and raises price.

4. *Op. cit.*, p. 262
5. *Op. cit.*, pp. 257-59. (italics added).

production of the product so as to raise the selling price of the product.

The argument can be better understood with the help of Figure 45.3 where only total profit curves *bereft* of total cost and total revenue curves are shown. To begin with, suppose that, given a certain cost and revenue situation, total profit curve is $P_1P'_1$. If OP_m is the minimum profit constraint, then sales-maximizing firm, with OP_m as the minimum profit constraint, will be in equilibrium at output *OS*. On the other hand, profit-maximizing firm will be in equilibrium at output *OM*.

Now, suppose that there is an increase in overhead costs by the amount P_1P_2. With this increase in overhead costs, there will be a uniform downward shift in the total profit curve by the amount P_1P_2. Thus, after the shift, we get a total profit curve $P_2P'_2$ (dotted). It will be noticed from Figure. 45.3 that even with the new profit curve $P_2P'_2$, profit-maximising output remains at the same level *OM*. Thus, the increases in the overhead costs "reduce the height of the profit hill uniformly but they do not change the location of its peak. "But a sales-maximizing firm with OP_m as the profit constraint, will reduce output to OS'. This reduction in output will permit the firm to raise the selling price of the product. Thus, according to Baumol, with the hypothesis of sales maximisation with a minimum profit constraint we are better able to rationalise the businessman's behaviour regarding changes in prices and output in response to changes in overhead costs.

Like the effects of changes in overhead costs on prices and output, sales maximisation can also better explain the *impact of corporation income tax on prices and output*. It may be noted that corporation income tax is the tax on the profits of the public limited companies. The analysis of the effect of corporation income tax on the price and output is exactly the same as of change in overhead cost, and P_1P_2 in Figure. 45.3 can be treated as the amount of corporation income tax that has been imposed. According to conventional price theory based on profit maximisation, a firm cannot do anything to shift any part of the corporation income or profit tax to the consumer or its employees. Nor a profit-maximizing firm can gain anything by raising the price or changing its output as a result of the imposition of this corporation income tax on a company, provided the rates of the tax are so fixed that the greater the amount of profits earned before tax, the more it retains after the payment of tax. Hence, the output and price of a profit-maximizing firm remain unaltered as a result of the imposition of or changes in corporation income tax. Thus, according to Baumol, "The argument is almost exactly the same as the fixed cost analysis. The corporation tax reduces the height of the total profit curve, but it moves the peak of the curve neither to the right nor to the left."[6]

But if the firm's objective is maximisation of sales with a minimum profit constraint, the price will be raised and output reduced when corporation income tax is raised. To quote him, "when taxes are raised, the firm will be motivated to increase its price (and, therefore, to reduce its output) in order to make up its lost profits. The explanation of the shiftability of this apparently unshiftable tax is simple; the sales-maximizing firm will, in effect, have a reserve of profits which it has not claimed (it has not maximized profit) but which it can fall back on when driven to do so by a rise in tax costs, though it can get back to its old profits only by some sacrifice in its sales.[7]

Emphasis on Non-Price Competition in Sales Maximisation Model

Another important feature of sales-maximisation theory of the firm of Baumol is its emphasis on non-price competition in oligopoly as compared with the price competition. It

6. Op. cit., p. 264
7. *W.J. Baumol, On the Theory of Oligopoly, p. 266.*

has been observed by many economists that oligopolists are often very much reluctant to use price cutting to promote their sales. Baumol rightly argues that this reluctance on the part of the oligopolists to use price as a competitive weapon should not be explained merely by that they want to live in *quiet life*. This is because when competition under oligopoly does become more intense and vigorous, it may not be in terms of price cutting but in terms of non-price weapons, that is, in the form of more advertising expenditure, product modification, introduction of special services for the customers etc.

This greater propensity to indulge in non-price competition under oligopoly can be better explained with sales-maximisation objective rather with the profit maximisation objective. This is because as extra expenditure on advertising etc. increases the physical volume of sales, it must also increase the total revenue, whereas the effect of price cutting on the total revenue is doubtful. This is because, "a price reduction is a double-edged sword which, while it serves as an influence to increase total revenue in that it usually adds to the number of units which can be sold, simultaneously works in the opposite direction by reducing the revenue on each unit sold. In other words, as the economists know so well, depending on whether demand is or is not elastic, price cutting is an uncertain means for increasing dollar sales"[8]. The effect of price cutting on profits is more uncertain because if it fails to raise total revenue, it will most probably reduce profits because the increase in output as a result of reduction in price, will increase total costs. On the other hand, while the profitability of advertising, product modification, improved service is doubtful, their favourable effect on the sales is quite certain. Thus, according to Baumol, "the effect of advertising, improved services, etc. on sales is fairly sure while, very often, their profitability may be quite doubtful. Thus, ***sales maximisation makes for greater presumption that the businessman will consider non-price competition to be more advantageous alternative.***"[9]

Critical Appraisal of Sales Maximisation Model

Implication of sales maximisation thsory of Baumol is that price would be lower and output greater under sales maximisation than under profit maximisation. This is because, total revenue is maximized at the price-output level where marginal revenue is zero, while at the profit-maximizing level of output marginal revenue is positive, given that marginal costs are positive. We have explained above that even under sales maximisation with a minimum profit constraint, output will be greater and price lower than under profit maximisation objective. If this is true that oligopolists seek to maximize sales or total revenue, then the greater output and lower price will have a favourable effect on the welfare of the people.

As explained above, another implication of sales maximisation objective is that more advertising expenditure will be incurred under it. Further, under sales maximisation objective of oligopolists, price is likely to remain sticky and the firms are more likely to indulge in non-price competition. This is what actually happens in oligopolistic market situations in the real world. Another significant implication of Baumol's model is that "there may be a conflict between pricing in the long and short run. In a short-run situation where the scope of expansion in output is limited, revenue would often increase, if prices were raised ; but in the long run it might pay to keep price low in order to compete more effectively for a large share of the market. This price policy to be followed in the short rur would then depend on the expected repercussions of short-run decisions on long-run revenue.[10]

8. Baumol, *op. cit., p.* 266.
9. *Ibid, p* 266-67
10. A. Silberston, Price Behaviour of Firms, *Economic Journal*, 1970.

But sales maximisation model has not been without its critics. Shepherd[11] has asserted that an oligopolist confronts a kinked demand curve and that if the kink is quite large, total revenue (*i.e.*, sales) and total profits would be maximised at the same level of output. But Hawkins[12] has shown that Shepherd's conclusions are invalid if the oligopolistic firms indulge in any form of non-price competition such as advertising, product variation, improvement in service, etc. and normally in the real world they do so.

An important and convincing criticism against sales maximisation model has been made by Hawkins.[13] As has been noted above that, according to Baumol, sales maximizing firm will generally produce and advertise more than the profit-maximizing firm. But Hawkins has shown that this conclusion is generally invalid. According to him, in case of single-product firms, as compared with profit maximizing firm, sales maximizing firm will produce greater, smaller or same output and incur a greater, smaller or same advertising outlay. It all depends upon the responsiveness of demand or total revenue to advertising expenditure as compared with the responsiveness of demand and total revenue to price cuts. As regards multiproduct firms, which are generally found these days in the real world, in the static model, both sales maximisation and profit maximisation arrive at the same conclusion regarding choice of output and input combination.[14]

But, besides static model, Baumol has also developed a *growth model*[15] of a sales-maximizing firm from which, as has been shown by Williamson, different results follow as compared with profit maximizing firm.

In spite of the above criticism, the present author is of the view that Prof. Baumol's sales maximisation model is a significant alternative to profit maximisation and brings us closer to reality, for in many cases it explains, as we brought out above in the explanation of the model, the business behaviour in the real world better than profit maximisation. Even if in certain cases, sales and profit maximisation yield same or similar results, even then by providing interesting insight into managerial motivation in these days of manager-dominated big business corporations as well as by explicitly incorporating advertising and other forms of non-price competition in his model, Baumol has made a significant contribution to our price theory.

Exercise. *A firm faces a demand curve given by Q = 100-2P. Marginal and average costs for the firm are constant at Rs. 10 per unit. What output levels should the firm produce to (i) maximise profits and (ii) maximise sales revenue ? What are the respective profits at each output level ?*

---

11. W.G. Shepherd, On Sales Maximising and Oligopoly Behaviour, *Economica*, 1962.
12. C.J. Hawkins, 'On the Sales Revenue Maximization Hypothesis, *Journal of Industrial Economics*, April 1970.
13. C.J. Hawkins, "The Revenue Maximization Oligopoly Model", Comment, *American Economic Review*, March 1971.
14. See C.J. Hawkins, On the Sales Revenue Maximization Hypothesis', *Journal of Industrial Economics*, April 1970.
15. See W.J. Baumol's (1) *Business Behaviour, Value and Growth* 1957 (2) On the Theory of Expansion of the Firm, *American Economic Review*, Vol. 52 pp. 1078-87.

CHAPTER

46

Managerial Theories of the Firm: Marris and Williamson's Models

Managerial Models : Separation of Control from Ownership

In recent years, new theories of the firm have been developed which lay stress on the role of managers and their behavioural patterns in deciding about price and output under oligopoly. It has been pointed out that managers do not try to maximize profits but instead pursue other goals. Whether *the firms try to maximize profits also depends upon who controls the business conducted by them*. That is, whether the owner himself or their hired manager controls and directs the business is a very relevant question in this regard. In case of individual proprietorship and partnership, it is the owners themselves who take price and output decisions and perform other entrepreneurial functions. But these days the organizational set up of the firms, especially in case of big firms, is of the nature of joint stock companies or what are also called corporations. ***In the case of joint stock companies or corporations we find a separation between ownership and management.*** It is the shareholders who are the owners of the joint stock company and bear the risks of business. But price and output decisions are taken by hired managers. Under such a set up, profits of the business go to the shareholders and the managers are usually paid fixed salaries.

Now, it has been pointed out that it may be expected of the owner-entrepreneurs of individual proprietorship and partnership that they will try to maximize profits since it is in their interest to do so. But hired managers of joint stock companies cannot be expected to try to maximize profits since these profits are not to go to them; they are to go to shareholders. It may be true that when managers are able to earn more profits for shareholders, they may be rewarded by them in some form or the other, but there is great force and truth in the argument regarding managers not maximizing profits. The ***incentive to maximize profits is expected to be weaker on the part of persons who are not to get them.***

It is, of course, true that the assumption of profit maximisation has made our analysis of firm's behaviour in regard to price and output simple. But whether this assumption is true of the business behaviour in the real world is open to serious doubts. We shall critically examine in this chapter the important managerial theories of the firm which are especially relevant for fixation of price and output under oligopoly.

The important managerial theories of the firm which have been developed in recent years are managerial theories of Williamson and Marris. Like the sales maximisation theory of Baumol, managerial theories also do not admit the validity of profit maximisation hypothesis regarding the working of the business firms. All these managerial theories lay stress on the role of the manager and his seeking self-interest while making decisions regarding price, output, sales etc. of the corporate firms. Since the managers of corporate firms are motivated by considerations other than the maximisation of profits, their decisions regarding price, output etc. are likely to be different from those of the profit-maximizing firm.

It should be noted that Baumol's sales maximisation theory, discussed in the previous chapter, is also one type of the managerial theory of the firm. He has argued for the adoption of sales maximisation by a firm on the ground that, in his experience, managers always attempt to maximise sales rather than profits and that the prestige and goodwill of a manager depends upon the sales performance of the firm managed by him. Obviously, a manager cannot totally ignore profits because if the firm wants to survive, it must pay acceptable dividends to its existing shareholders and promise good dividends to those who purchase the new shares issued by the firm. Therefore, according to Baumol, managers of the firms aim to maximise sales revenue subject to a minimum profit level.

MARRIS'S MANAGERIAL THEORY OF FIRM

R. Marris[1] has put forward an important theory of the firm according to which managers do not maximise profits but instead, according to him, *they seek to maximise balanced rate of growth of the firm*. ***Maximisation of balanced rate of growth of the firm means maximisation of the rate of growth of demand for the products of the firm and rate of growth of capital supply.*** If G stands for balanced growth, G_d for the growth rate of demand for the product, G_c for the rate of growth of the capital supply, then the goal of the manager is :

$$\text{Maximise } G = G_d = G_c$$

In seeking to maximise the balanced growth rate, a manager faces the following two constraints :

(1) Managerial Constraint

(2) Financial Constraint

Managerial constraint refers to the strength of the managerial team and their skills. Financial constraint refers to the following three financial ratios :

(i) *ratio of debt* (*D*) *to total assets* (*A*) which is simply called *debt ratio* (*D/A*).

(2) *Liquidity ratio* which is the ratio of liquid assets of the firm to the total assets (L/A).

(3) *Retention ratio* (π_r/π) which refers to the ratio of retained profits to the total profits.

It is important to note that these financial variables determine the job security of the managers. If these financial ratios set by the manger crosses the prudent limits, they expose the firm to the risk of being taken over by others or the managers can be dismissed which can endanger their job security . Therefore, financial constraints are associated with the job security. Managers take into account job security while taking business decisions.

Rationale for Maximising Balanced Growth of the Firm

Now an important question is why managers seek to maximise the balanced growth rate of the firm, that is, why do they jointly maximise the rate of growth of demand for firm's products and the growth rate of capital supply. This is because by doing so they maximise their own utility function and the utility function of their owners. Before Marris, it was generally argued by the management theorists that the goals of manager and goals of the owner often cash because the utility functions which they try to maximise greatly differ. The utility function

1. R. Marris, A Model of Managerial Enterprise, *Quarterly Journal of Economics* (1963). Also R. Marris, *Theory of Managerial Capitalism*, Macmillan, 1964.

which managers seek to maximise include variables such as salaries, status, job security. On the other hand, utility function which owners seek to maximise include variables such as profits, capital supply, size of output, market share and image or reputation in the public.

According to Marris, despite the difference in the variables in the utility functions of managers and owners, the most of the variables included in both of them are positively correlated with a single variable, namely, the size of the firm. Further, according to him, the size of the firm may be measured by the level of output, capital supply, sales revenue or market share. However, Marris regards steady balanced growth rate over time as the objective of the managers because most of the variables such as sales, output, capital supply, included in their utility function also increase simultaneously so that maximising long-run growth of any variable amounts to maximising long-run growth of others.[2]

It is worth noting that, according to Marris, managers do not maximise the **absolute size** of the firm but **its rate of growth**, and the rate of growth of the firm is not the same thing as its absolute size from the viewpoint of managerial utility function. Marris argues that since growth of the firm is compatible with the interests of shareholders who are owners of the firm, there is no need to differentiate between the rate of growth of demand for firm's outputs (G_d) which managers want to maximise and rate of growth of capital supply (G_c) which owners want to maximise because in the state of equilibrium both the rates are equal.

It is clear from above that in Marris's model some variables in the manager's utility function such as salaries, status, power are strongly correlated with the rate of growth of demand for the products, and, therefore, managers' salaries will be higher and they will have more power and esteem, the faster the rate of growth of the firms. Besides, the higher growth of a firm also ensures better job security to the mangers.

Therefore, utility function of managers can be written as

$$U_M = f(G_D, S)$$

U_M = utility of managers

G_D = rate of growth of demand for output of the firm

S = measure of job security of managers

On the other hand, as seen above, utility of owners depend on the growth of capital supply which is positively correlated with the growth of profits.[3] Thus, owners' utility function can be written as

$$U_{owners} = f(G_c)$$

where G_c = rate of growth of capital supply

Following Penrose,[4] Marris thinks that the rate of growth of capital is subject to the constraint set by the decision making capacity of the managerial team. Besides, according to him, job security of the manager is determined by the weighted average of three financial ratios, namely, (1) debt-asset ratio (D/A), (2) the liquidity ratio (L/A), and (3) profit-retention ratio (π_r / π). These three financial ratios reflect the financial policy of the managers. Further, he is of the opinion that there is a saturation level for job security. Whereas after this saturation level marginal utility from the extra job security is zero, below this level, marginal utility from extra job security is infinite. With this constraint of job security, managerial utility function becomes :

2. See R. Marris, *A Model of Managerial Enterprise, op. cit.*

3. E. Penrose, *The Theory of Growth of the Firm*, Blackwell, 1959.

4. E. Penrose, Op. Cit.

$$U_m = (G_D)\ \overline{S}$$

where bar (–) on the job security variable S shows it acts as a constraint for utility maximisation of managers. That is, managers maximise their utility, that is, growth of demand for output subject to this job security constraint. Note that financial constraint is reflected in the job security constraint of a manager.

It thus follows from above that in Marris's model, a manager works under two constraints (*i*) managerial constraint set by the decision-making capacity of the managerial team and (*ii*) financial constraint determined by three financial ratios which are reflected in the job security of the managers.

Equilibrium of the Firm

In Marris's model, managers maximise their utility which depends on the rate of growth of demand for the products of the firm subject to the two constraints. It should be noted that in Marris's model, *firms grow by diversification*, that is, by undertaking the production of altogether new products or by producing new designs or models of the existing products. The utility function of the managers is therefore written as :

$$U_M = f(G_D)$$

On the other hand, as seen above, owners try to maximise their own utility which, according to Marris, depends not on profits but on the rate of growth of capital supply. Thus,

$$U_0 = f(G_c)$$

where U_0 = utility of owners

G_c = rate of growth of capital supply

Now, the firm will reach equilibrium position when it achieves *maximum rate of balanced growth rate* of demand for firms' product and growth rate of firm's supply of capital. Thus, for firm to be in equilibrium, the following condition must be fulfilled :

$$G_D = G_C = \text{maximum}$$

Therefore, in order to show the equilibrium of the firm we have to derive the function for the rate of growth of demand for the products (G_D) and function for the rate of growth of capital supply (G_C).

Rate of Growth of Demand for the Products (G_D). As mentioned above, the rate of growth of demand for products of a firm depends on the **rate of diversification**, that is, the introduction of the entirely new products per period which are not close substitutes of the competitors or the introduction by the managers per period of products which are close substitutes of existing firms' products. The second important factor on which rate of diversification depends is the proportion of successful new products, denoted by k. The proportion of successful new products depends on the ratio of diversification (*d*), the price of the product (*p*), expenditure on advertisement (*A*) and research and development (*R&D*). Thus, the function for the rate of growth of demand for the firms' products can be written as :

$$G_D = f(d, k)$$

Where

d = rate of diversification

k = proportion of successful new products

Rate of Growth of Capital Supply (G_c). Marris put forward the view that shareholders (*i.e.*, owners) of the firm pursue the objective of maximising rate of growth of capital supply which is taken as a measure of the growth of size of the firm. Capital supply of a corporate firm is given by summing up fixed assets, inventories, short-term assets and cash reserves. According to Marris, main source of capital supply of a firm is the growth in its profits which depends on profit-retention ratio which is decided by the managers. It may be noted that top managers of a firm cannot fix as high profit retention ratio as they would like. They have to distribute satisfactory dividends to keep shareholders happy and satisfied and also to avoid a fall in the prices of shares. If they do not do so, their job security will be endanagered. Besides profits, growth of capital supply depends on issue of new bonds or borrowing from banks.

Thus, three financial ratios, namely, debt-asset ratio, profit-retention ratio, liquidity ratio which are subjectively decided by managers through the financial coefficient a, which, as explained above, determines retained profits and hence determines the rate of growth of capital supply. Marris assumes that the rate of growth of capital supply is proportional to the magnitude of profits. Thus,

$$Q_C = a(\pi)$$

where π represents total profits per period

Secondly, tne rate of growth of capital supply depends on the average rate of profits earned by the firms which is denoted by m. It is worth noting that Marris takes price of products and its cost per unit as given and average profit margin (m) is obtained by deducting the cost per unit (C) average expenditure per unit on advertising A and research and development (R&D) activities (R & D) from price of the product. Thus,

$$m = P - C - (A) - (R\&D)$$

Since price and cost per unit is assumed to be given and constant by Marris, average profit margin is negatively associated with expenditure on advertising and research and development (R&D). Therefore, the higher the expenditure on advertisement and research and development activities, the lower will be the average rate of profit.

Thirdly, the growth of capital supply depends on the rate of diversification. This is because the magnitude of profits (π) per period which determines the capital supply is also a function of the rate of diversification. The higher the rate of diversification, the greater the rate of growth of capital supply.

Note that profits (π) per period depends on two things : (1) average profit margin (m) and the rate of diversification. Thus, profit function can be stated as under :

$$\pi = f(m,d)$$

where π = level of total profits per period

Substituting this profit function in the function governing supply of capital we have:

$$G_C = \bar{a}\ (\pi)$$

$$G_D = \bar{a}\ [f(m,d)]$$

where a is financial security coefficient.

The financial security coefficient is decided upon by the managers exogeneously and is taken to be constant by Marris in the formal model. However, in later stages of his formal model, he relaxes this assumption of constant financial security coefficient (a). However, it is important to note that so long as a is constant, growth of capital supply (G_C) and the magnitude of profits (π) are not **competing goals** and are positively related. The higher the level of profits means the higher the growth of capital supply.

Given the above functions regarding rate of growth of demand for products and rate of growth of capital supply the firm is in equilibrium when it is achieving the highest rate of balanced growth. ($G_D = G_C = G$ maximum)

Instrument Variables in Marris's Model

Instrument variables are policy variables which should be manipulated to achieve the objective of the firm. There are three instruments in Marris's model :

(1) the financial security coefficient

(2) rate of diversification

(3) the average profit margin.

An important policy instrument is to choose the value of financial security coefficient. The choice of a financial security coefficient depends on the financial policy of the manager. As seen above, financial security coefficient (*a*) is the weighted average of three financial ratios, namely, debt asset ratio, liquidity ratio and profit retention ratio. The manager can influence the growth rate by changing its three financial ratios. For instance, if he goes for a larger amount of borrowings and thus opt for high debt-asset ratio, growth of the firm can be accelerated. But a manager has to choose a prudent debt-asset ratio so that there is no risk for the firm to go bankrupt on account of the demands for greater interest payments and repayment of principal sum taken as loan.

Liquidity policy is also very important in its effect on the growth of the firm. Low liquidity ratio means much of the available funds with the firm have been invested to bring about a higher growth of output. But too low liquidity ratio also increases the risk for the firm to go bankrupt. Similarly, profit-retention ratio is also an important policy variable used by a manager. Profits are the most important source of supply of capital. Therefore, the greater the magnitude of retained profits, the greater the supply of capital which would ensure a higher growth of firm. But a higher profit-retention ratio means lower dividends for the shareholders which would make them unhappy and would therefore endanger manager's security. Therefore, a manager has to follow a prudent profit retention policy so as to keep the shareholders satisfied and also to avoid the fall in price of shares of the firm.

Further, **Marris takes price of the product as given** as determined by the oligopolist structure of industry. Hence adjustment in price is not an instrument variable in Marris's model. In Marris's model due to uncertainty of competitors response to changes in price and also imperfect knowledge of rival's strength, managers think it prudent to take the price as given and try to increase the demand for the product by increasing expenditure on advertisement. Marris also assumes that production cost per unit is given and not a policy variable.

The final important instrument variable is the ***choice of average profit margin (m).*** Since price and production cost are taken as given by Marris, average profit margin (*m*) can be affected by changing the level of advertisement (A) and expenditure on research and development (R&D). As mentioned above, the higher the level of expenditure on advertisement and research and development, the lower will be the profit margin, price and cost per unit being given.

It is evident from above that average profit margin in Marris's model is the residual and is negatively correlated with the expenditure on advertisement and research and development. Therefore, *m* is used as a proxy instrument for the policy variables of A and R&D.

EVALUATION OF MARRIS'S MODEL

An important contribution of Marris's model is the inclusion of financial policies in the decision making process by the managers of the firm. This has been done by incorporation of financial constraint as given by ***three financial ratios,*** namely, debt ratio, liquidity ratio and retention ratio which are set by managers of firms within prudent limits so as to ensure their job security. The fixation of these financial ratios are exogenous to the model and depends on the subjective sub-attitudes of the managers. Some other exogenous factors such as the demands of shareholders influence these financial ratios but the risk attitude of the managers is their prime determinant. However, manager's risk attitude is also governed by the past performance of the firm. If in the past the firm has shown better performance as a result of the present management and profit margin has been rising, the manager will feel encouraged to take more risk.

Marris's managerial model of has ingeneously ***found a solution which maximises utility of both the managers and owners.*** However, the balanced growth equilibrium of the firm depends on the variables in the various functions of the model which are crucially related to rate of growth of the firm. But the reconciliation of the goals of owners and managers may be true in case of steady growth but are unlikely to be true in condition of recession or sluggish demand.

Further, in this model of maximisation of rate of growth of the firm and maximisation of profits have been treated as conflicting goals. Commenting on this. Koutsoyiannis writes, " The model implies that both managers and owners perceive that the firm cannot simultaneously achieve maximum growth and maximum profits and that owners do in fact prefer the maximisation of the rate of growth, sacrificing some profits. Marris does not justify the preference of owners for capital growth over maximisation of profits."[5]

Besides, Marris in his model assumes the given costs and price structure which is not explained by his model. Further, he fails to explain inter-dependence among oligopolist firms which is an important characteristic of non-collusive oligopoly. This is a great lacuna in Marris's model.

Another shortcoming of Marris's model is his assumption that growth of the firm will continue to grow through diversification, that is, through development and introduction of *new products*. He does not realise that introduction new products will be imitated by the rival firms in the long run which will impede the growth of the firms. Besides, he thinks that anything can be sold to the consumers through well-organised market compaings. H. Townsend rightly points out that firms do not enjoy unlimited influence over consumer's demand. If one or two new products introduced by a firm flops in the market, the consumers are unlikely to try other new products of the firm, whatever the publicity."[6]

Further, Marris considers that the firm grows with introduction of products which have no close substitutes and therefore do not erode the markets of their competitors. This rules out the retaliatory reactions by the rival firms. This is a drawback in Marris's approach because successful new products are imitated by the competitors in the long run. Thus, the introduction of successful new products provide protection from competition only in the short run. In the long run markets for new products are eroded by imitation by the competitors. Koutsoyiannis rightly remarks, "Successful new products thus 'shelter' the firm from competition only in the

5. A. Koutsoyiannis, *Modern Microeconomics,* (London : MacMillan), 2nd edition 1979, p.368.
6. See H. Townsend, Competition and Big Business Firms; T. M. Rubczynslki (ed). A New Era in Competition (Blackwell, 1973).

short run, since in the long run this shelter is eroded by imitation. Secondly, this behaviour create interdependence of oligopolistic firms. Even if prices are assumed as given competition takes the form of new products. This sort of interdependence is not analysed by Marris."[7]

Lastly, another shortcoming of Marris's managerial model is its heavy reliance on the assumption that firms have their own "Research and Development (R&D)' division. In fact, most firms do not have such departments but rely on imitation of the inventions of other firms, or when this is not successful, they pay a royalty for using a patented invention.[8]

WILLIAMSON'S MANAGERIAL THEORY OF THE FIRM

But a full-fledged managerial theory of the firm has been put forward by O. E. Williamson[9] who emphasizes that ***managers are motivated by their self-interest and they maximse their own utility function.*** Again, the objective of utility maximisation by the managers is subject to the constraint that after-tax profits are large enough to pay acceptable dividends to the shareholders and also to pay for economically necessary investments (as opposed to discretionary investment expenditure by the managers).

It may however be pointed out that utility maximisation by the self-interest seeking managers, like sales maximisation model of Baumol, is possible only in a corporate form of business organisation where there exists separation between ownership and management. Thus, according to Cohen and Cyert, "This separation of ownership and management functions permit the managers of a firm to pursue their own self-interest, subject only to their being able to maintain effective control over the firm. In particular, if profits at any time are at an acceptable level, if the firm shows reasonable rate of growth over time and if sufficient dividends are paid to keep the stockholders happy, then the managers are fairly certain of retaining their power."[10]

Managerial Utility Function. According to Williamson, utility function of the self-seeking managers depends on the following factors:

(1) ***The salaries and other forms of monetary compensation*** which the managers obtain from the business firms. This is a major factor determining the utility of the managers since salary and other monetary rewards received by the manager from the firm determine his private expenditure and standard of living. However, according to Williamson, salary and other monetary compensations are not the total reward received by the managers from their firms and also these are not the only factor determining the utility of the managers.

(2) The second factor which influences the utility of the managers is ***the number of staff under the control of a manager.*** The greater the number of staff under the control of a manager, the greater the status and prestige of a manager and also the greater the power wielded by him. That is, the greater the number of staff under the control of a manager, the greater the salary and the amount of other monetary rewards . Because of these the number of staff personnel determines the utility which a manager obtains.

Since, according to Williamson, there is a close positive relationship between the number of staff and the manager's salary, he takes a single variable "*monetary expenditure on the staff*" in his formal model of utility maximisation by the manager rather than the two separate

7. A. Koutsoyiannis, *op. cit.*, p. 69.
8. *Ibid*, p. 369.
9. The important works by O. E. Williamson in which he has developed his managerial theory of the firm are (1) "A Model of Rational Managerial Behaviour" in R. M. Cyert and J. B. March, *A Behavioural Theory of the Firm*, Prentice Hall, 1963. (2) *The Economics of Discretionary Behaviour: Managerial Objectives in a Theory of the Firm*, Markham Publishing Co. Chicago, 1967.
10. Cohen and Cyert, *op. cit.* p. 354.

variables of salary and the number of staff.

(3) Thirdly, the manager's utility depends upon the amount of what Williamson calls "***Management slack***". This management slack consists of those **nonessential management perquisites** such as lavishly furnished offices, luxurious company cars, large expenses accounts etc. which are not necessary for the efficient and effective operation of the firm. The management slack also enters into the cost of production of the firm.

(4) Finally, utility derived by the manager from his job depends upon the ***magnitude of discretionary investment expenditure by the manager,*** that is, the amount of resources which the manager can spend according to his discretion. It should be noted that discretionary investment does not include those investment expenditures (such as periodic replacement of capital equipment) which are economically necessary for the survival of the firm. The magnitude of discretionary investment expenditure by a manager indicates the command over resources which he enjoys. By directing the flow of new investment by a firm, the manager determines in an important way the future growth of the firm.

Willianson's Managerial Discretional Model : Concepts of Actual, Discretionary and Reported Profits

Before explaining Williamson's formal model of managerial discretion, some concepts of profits used in it are worth nothing. Williamson has distinguished between three concepts of profits : (1) Actual profits (π), (2) Reported profits (π_r) and Minimum profits (π_0)

Actual profits are the difference between total revenue earned less the production costs (C) and expenditure on staff (S). Thus

$$\pi = R - C - S$$

where R = Total sales revenue

C = Production cost

S = Staff expenditure

Reported profits (π_r) are the difference between actual profits and nonessential managerial expenditure as represented by management slack. Thus

$$\pi_r = \pi - M \quad \text{... (1)}$$

where M represents management slack

Since $\pi = R - C - S$

$$\pi_r = R - C - S - M$$

Minimum profits (π_0) are the amount of profits (after tax) which are required to be paid as acceptable dividends to satisfy the shareholders who are the owners of the firm. If the shareholders do not get reasonable dividends they may sell their shares and thereby exposing the firm to the risk of being taken over by others, or alternatively they will vote for the dismissal of the top management. Both of these actions by the shareholders will reduce the job security of the top managerial team. Hence managers must give some minimum profits in the from of dividends to keep the shareholders satisfied so as to promote their job security. To meet this objective the reported profits must be large enough to be equal to minimum profit (π_0) plus the tax to be paid to the government. Thus :

$$\pi_r \geq \pi_0 + T$$

Discretionary profits (π_D) are the actual profits minus minimum profits and tax to be paid. Thus :

$$\pi_D = \pi - \pi_0 - T \qquad \text{... (2)}$$

where π_D = Discretionary profits

π = Actual profits

π_0 = Minimum profits

T = Tax to be paid to the government

Discretionary profits should be carefully distinguished from *discretionary investment*. Whereas, as seen above, discretionary profits are the amount left after minimum profits (π_0) and tax (T) are deducted from actual profits (π_D) = ($\pi - \pi_0 - T_5$), the discretionary investment equals reported profits minus minimum profits and tax. Thus

Discretionary Investment $\quad I_D = \pi_R - \pi_0 - T \qquad$ ... (3)

where π_R = reported profits

π_0 = minimum profits

T = Tax amount to be paid

Since difference between reported profits (π_R) and actual profits (π) arises due to management slack, discretionary profits (π_D) can be stated as under :

$$\pi_D = I_D + \text{expenditure due to management slack}$$

Thus, if management slack is zero

$$\pi_R = \pi \quad \text{and} \quad \pi_D = I_D$$

Managerial Utility Maximisation

As stated above, Williamson clubs the first two variables, namely (1) salary and other monetary compensations received by the manager and (2) number of staff under his control into a single variable. Utility of a manager in his model is a function of the following three variables :

$$U = U(S, M, I_D) \qquad \text{... (4)}$$

where, U denotes utility function

S stands for monetary expenditure on staff including salaries of managerial team

M stands for management slack

I_D stands for amount of discretionary investment

Maximisation of above utility function is subject to the minimum profit constraint. This means level of profits must be such so as to pay satisfactory profit to shareholders and pay for economically necessary investment (not included in discretionary investment).

In Williamson's managerial model, price is regarded as a function of output, the expenditure on staff and a demand shift parameter. Thus,

$$P = P(X, S, e)$$

where, P stands for the price function

X stands for the output level in a period

S stands for the expenditure on staff

e stands for a demand shift parameter

Graphic Representation of Williamson's Managerial Discretionary Model

In order to present a simplified Williamson's managerial model we assume that expenditure on account of managerial slack (M) is zero. Given this, managerial utility function becomes :

$$U_M = f(S, I_D)$$

When management slack (M) is zero, the reported profits equal actual profits, then from equation (3) above we have

$$I_D = \pi - \pi_0 - T \qquad \text{... (5)}$$

Substituting this formulation in managerial utility function we have :

$$U_M = f[S, (\pi - \pi_0 - T)] \qquad \text{... (6)}$$

Thus, we have the following simplified model of managerial function which has to be maximised subject to a constraint. Thus :

$$\text{maximise} : U_m = f[S, (\pi - \pi_0 - T)]$$

$$\text{Subject to: } \pi_r \geq \pi_0 + T$$

In order to find a graphic solution to the model we have to draw utility indifference curves of managers representing their utility function, This has been done in Fig. 46.1 where on the X-axis we measure expenditure on staff (S) and on the Y–axis the amount of discretionary profits. A managerial indifference curve shows various combinations of staff expenditure and discretionary profits which give equal satisfaction to the manager (note that discretionary profits in the present simplified model equal discretionary investment). These indifference curves are convex showing diminishing marginal rate of substitution of staff expenditure for discretionary profits. They do not intersect the axes[11] which means that managers will choose some positive values of both the staff expenditure and discretionary profits.

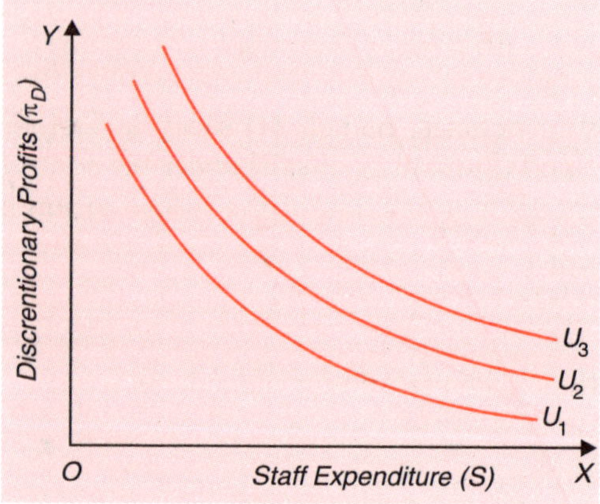

Fig. 46.1. *Utility Indifference Curves of Managers*

In Fig.46.2, we have shown the market relationship between profits and staff expenditure. As the expenditure on staff increases and as a result output expands, discretionary profits increase up to point S_1, and beyond this the discretionary profits start declining. When staff expenditure increases beyond C, discretionary profits become negative. Thus, staff expenditure being less than B and greater than C will not satisfy the minimum profit constraint π_0. In order to find equilibrium position of a manager we bring the indifference curves together with the discretionary profits curve in Fig. 46.3. It will be seen that the manager will maximise its utility at point E, where manager's indifference curve U_3 is tangent to the discretionary profit curve. It will be seen from the figure that in its equilibrium position, the manager will be incurring staff expenditure equal to S^* and making discretionary profits equal to S^*E. It will be further noticed that equilibrium profits will be less than the maximum profits while the staff expenditure will be more than the amount at which discretionary profits are maximum. This is due to managerial utility function according to which an optimum combination of discretionary profits and staff expenditure has to be achieved because both of them enter into managerial utility function. It should be noted that given that indifference curves have a negative slope, the equilibrium will be always be on the falling portion of the profit staff expenditure curve BC. This implies preference of managers for more staff expenditure in Williamson's model

11. Note that non-intersection of indifference curves with the axes implies that corner solutions are ruled out.

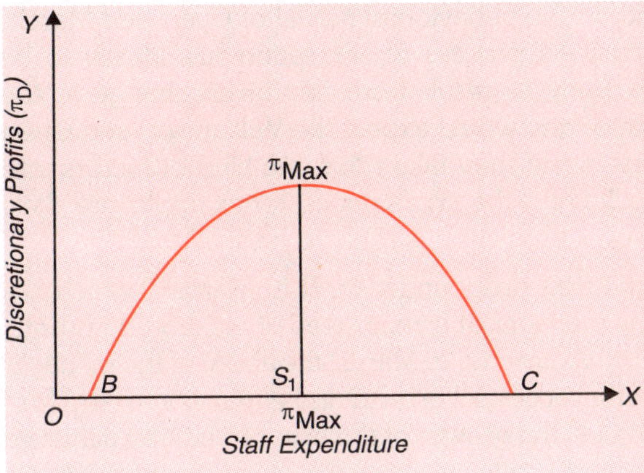

Fig. 46.2. *Dicretionary Profit Curve*

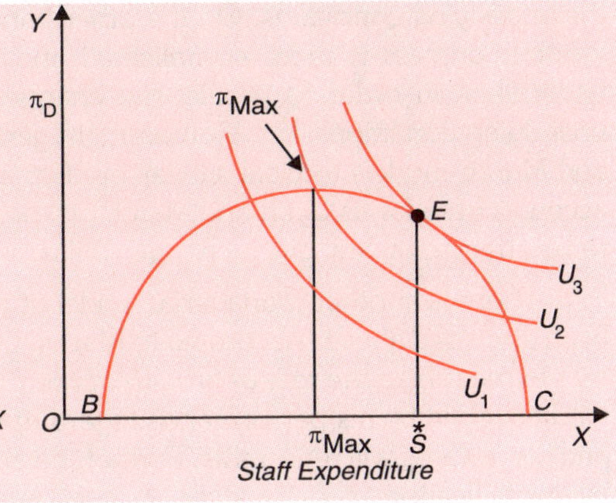

Fig. 46.3. *Equilibrium of Firm in Williamson's Model*

As compared to a profit-maximizing firm, utility-maximizing firm of Williamson's concept has a ***"higher staff expenditure and more management slack. No general statement can be made about the relative output levels for the two firms."***[12]

It may be pointed out that under conditions of perfect competition Williamson's utility maximisation model retains the result of profit maximisation model of the firm. But where competition is weak, that is, under conditions of oligopoly and monopoly, in Williamson's model expenditure on advertising, managerial luxuries (*i.e.*, management slack) will be greater (and therefore more management slack will be absorbed as a cost) and as a result costs of the firm will rise with a upward push to the price. When, under conditions of oligopoly and monopoly, demand weakens, in Williamson's utility maximisation model, the expenditure on staff, advertisement, managerial luxuries which are sources of high costs will be reduced and as a result the costs of the firm will decline with a downward push to the price.

It is interesting to compare the predictions of Williamson's model and profit-maximisation model of the firm when there is an increase in the profit tax rate or lump sum tax. According to Williamson's model, if the *profit-tax rate* on the firm is increased, there will be increase in the output and staff expenditure of the firm. This is because now that profits have been made less attractive by the imposition of higher tax rate, the manager will try to reduce the reported profits and for this they will increase the expenditure on staff and expand output. In other words, since utility of the manager from profits has been reduced by the higher tax rate on them, they will try to seek utility elsewhere by having more staff and more output.[13] However, if a *lump-sum tax* is imposed on the firm, Williamson's model implies that the firm will reduce its expenditure, particularly on staff. This is because with the imposition of a lump-sum tax, minimum profit constraint is raised and to earn the higher profits, the manager will try to reduce expenditure. On the other hand, a profit-maximising firm will not reduce or increase its expenditure and output whether a lump-sum tax is imposed or the rate of profit tax increased.

A merit of Williamson's model is that, like the profit-maximisation model of the firm, in it, given its assumption, *a solution can be found analytically* when there is any given change in

12. Cohen and Cyert, *op. cit.*, p. 361.
13. In contrast to Williamson's model, implications of sales maximization model of Baumol in the face of increase in the *profit-tax* rate are different. In Baumol's model, increase in the rate of profit tax will raise the minimum profit constraint, and therefore to obtain higher minimum-level of profits, the firm will try to reduce its expenditure.

the underlying conditions. On the other hand, in the behavioural model of Cyert and March, solution process is more complicated and in it "a process of simulation has ideally to be undertaken in order to predict the changes likely to result from any given change in the underlying conditions."[14] However, "in general one would expect the Williamson and Cyert and March models to yield similar predictions, since they take the same kind of factors into account. In so far as Cyert and March can predict how the firm's prices, for example, are likely to be affected by any given change, Williamson's prediction is likely to be similar."[15]

There is another managerial model of the firm propounded by R.L. Marris[16] which has been discussed above. According to Marris, the manager of firm, instead of maximizing profits, tries to *maximize the rate of growth of the firm*. According to Marris, the ability of the manager will be judged by his performance regarding the successful growth and expansion of the firm and his rewards will reflect this. Further, he argues, the growth of the firm can be best achieved by diversification.

Comments. Williamson has made various empirical studies from which he concludes that his managerial theory of the firm can better explain the pricing and output under oligopoly than the models based on profit maximisation. According to him, reactions of firms to changes in taxation, increase in expenditure on staff and managerial emoluments during periods of boom and drastic cut in these expenditure in recession and changes in compensation of the top executives, staff expenditure in general and managerial emoluments in response to changes in fixed costs can be better explained with his managerial model than the profit maximising model. In our view, however, the available evidence is not sufficient to prove the validity of his model. Besides, the conclusions of Williamson in favour of his managerial discretionary model are based on several implicit assumptions under the *ceteris paribus* clause. These assumptions are not likely to be fulfilled under dynamic conditions of shifts in demand and costs in boom and recession. Further, Williamson fails to explain pricing and output in those forms of oligopolistic market structure where there is strong rivalry among firms. Williamson model also does not take into account the *interdependence* of firms in oligopoly which is crucial for deciding about price and output under oligopoly.

Williamson in his model lays stress on the managerial discretion in determining not only output and price laid but also the level of staff expenditure and managerial emoluments. Williamson distinguished between desire of manager for discretionary action and the opportunity for managerial discretionary action. He measures the opportunity for managerial discretion by the concentration ratio in the industry (that is, the fewer firms in the industry) and the strength of barriers to the entry in the industry. He argued that the greater the concentration ratio in an industry, the stronger the barriers to the entry, the greater the opportunity for discretionary spending by the managers. Further, the proportionate representation of management on the board is, according to Williamson, a measure of desire of manager to act independently of sharehold+

ers of the firms. The critics have pointed out that this distinction between desire of management for discretionary behaviour and the opportunity for managerial discretion as drawn by Williamson, is not valid. This is because the greater number of managers on the board, the greater the desire for managerial discretionary behaviour. Thus, according to Koutsoyiannis, "It seems to us that the distinction between the *desire of managers* and the *opportunity of managers* for discretionary behaviour cannot be disentangled."[17]

14. Aubrey Silberston, Price Behaviour of Firms, *Economic Journal,* 1970.
15. Ibid.
16. R.L. Marris, *The Economic Theory of Managerial Capitalism*, Macmillan, London, 1964.
17. Koutsoyiannis, *Modern Microeconomics*, (*London : Macmillan*), Second Edition, 1979 p. 382.

CHAPTER

47

Behavioural Theory of the Firm: Satisficing Model

Introduction

In recent years behavioural approaches to the theory of the firm have been propounded which also do away with the assumption of profit maximisation. Indeed, these behavioural theories visualise that firms do not aim to maximise anything, neither profits, now sales and nor even utility. A distinctive feature of behavioural approach is that instead of hypothesizing about how business firms respond to various situations or how they should respond, it considers how the firms actually behave, that is, how they really take decisions in practice. These decisions relate to price of the product, level of output, sales strategy etc. From the evidence accumulated regarding the actual behaviour or decision-taking of the firms, logical argument has been used to build models regarding the behaviour of big business firms other than those whose actual decision-making processes were studied.

Like Marris's and Williamson's managerial models, the behavioural models also consider a large corporate business firm in which *ownership is separated from management.* It focuses on the organisational problems which arise from *within the internal structure of* these big business organisations and what is their impact on the decision-making process in them.

The advocates of the behavioural approach challenge not only the profit maximisation assumption but also the *omission of element of uncertainty from the conventional theory* of the firm. According to this behavioural approach, under conditions of uncertain demand or cost conditions while taking decisions regarding price, output, sales strategy, it is impossible to know whether profits are being maximised or not; the information required to estimate profits is not there. Most important of all, the advocates of behavioural approach lay stress on the *process of decision making within firms* for predicting decisions regarding price, output, sales, etc. of the firms. The behavioural model of the firm is based on the pioneering works of H.A. Simon[1] starting from his seminal article 'A behavioural Model of Rational Choice'. It was Simon who first of all put forward the view that the firms instead of maximising profits, normally ***satisfice***, that is, seek to have satisfactory performance with regard to profit, market shares, sales etc. Therefore, the behavioural theory is also called '*Satisficing Theory of the Firm*'. However, the behavioural model has been further developed by Cyert and March and Cohen and Cyert. Elaborating the behavioural approach Cohen and Cyert write ;

"*In particular, as one looks closely at the behaviour of actual firms, the justification for the*

1. Important works by H. A. Simon, in which he has developed his behavioural theory of the firm are: (1) A Behavioural Model of Rational Choice, *Quartely Journal of Economics,* Feb. 1955. (2) Theories of Decision Making in Economic and Behavioural Sciences, *American Economic Review,* June 1959. (3) *Models of Men,* Willey, New York, 1957.

assumption of profit maximisation seems to weaken. When one adds uncertainty to the firm's decision-making process, even defining the meaning of profit maximisation becomes difficult to do in an empirically meaningful way. The behavioural theory of the firm takes the position that arguments over motivation are somewhat fruitless. The critical issue is not whether one assumes profit-maximizing instead of satisficing behaviour. Instead, it is fruitful to develop an understanding of the process of decision-making within the firm."[2]

The Firm as a Coalition of Group with Conflicting Multiple Goals

A full-scale behavioural theory of the firm has been put forward by Cyert and March[3]. According to them, in these days of large-scale corporate type of business firms, we can no longer consider them as a *single major decision maker* (*i.e.*, the entrepreneur), but instead we should look at them as complex group or complex organisation *composed of various individuals and groups* whose interests may conflict with each other. Cyert and March call this complex organisation or group an *organisational coalition* which may include managers, stock holders, workers, suppliers, bankers, customers and so on. They assert that all of these different individuals participate in setting the *goals* of the organisation. To quote them, "the concept of a coalition assumes a different type of firm than we have been dealing with .....Hitherto the firm was implicitly regarded as controlled by an entrepreneur and the goals of the entrepreneur were the goals of the organisation. He purchased conformity to these goals by payments in the form of wages to workers, interest to capital sources and profits (when they existed) to himself."[4] According to the behavioural model of Cyert, March and Cohen, each group in this business organisation has its own set of *goals or demands* which are conflicting. For example, managers want high salaries and perks, workers want high wages and better pension, good condition of work, the shareholders want large profits and growing capital and so on. We explain these conflicting multiple goals below.

Conflicting Multiple Goals. Unlike the conventional theory of the firm with a single goal of profit maximisation, the behavioural theory of the firm does not accept that an organisation has a single goal to achieve. Instead, according to this theory, organisation has many goals. Cyert and March have mentioned five goals which the real-world firms generally possess. These are : (1) *production goal, (2) inventory goal, (3) sales goal, (4) market-share goal and (5) profit goal*. More important, they emphasize that different parts of the organisation have different goals. Goal regarding the level of production represents the demand of the coalition members connected with production, such as workers. Goal regarding the inventory level of finished goods reflects the demand of those members of organisational coalition who are connected with inventories such as salesmen and customers. Sales goal reflects the demands of those coalition members who are intimately connected with sales such as salesmen and also who regard amount of sales as necessary for survival and stability of organisation.

Likewise, market-share goal is affected by those coalition members who are greatly interested in comparative success of the organisation, for example, top-level managers, especially those who look after sales management. Finally, there is the profit goal which firstly meets the demands for accumulating resources so as to distribute them among shareholders as dividends, creditors as interest, and sub-units as increased budgets for them, and secondly it caters to the demands of management who are interested in showing their favourable performance by the amount of profits earned. Profit goal is generally set in terms of aspiration level with respect to the amount of money profits to be made. The profit goal may however be set in the form of

2. P.K.J. Cohen, and R.M. Cyert, *Theory of the Firm*, Prentice-Hall 1965, p. 33, (italics mine).
3. R.M. Cyert and J.C. March, *A Behavioural Theory of the Firm*, Prentice-Hall, 1963.
4. Cohen and Cyert, *op. cit.*, p. 331.

return on investment or profit share. It is the profit goal which is intimately connected with the pricing and output decision of a firm.

According to Cyert and March, the business firms are guided by the above five goals while taking decisions regarding price, output and sales strategy. It is worth noting that the above five goals are not mere theoretical hypothesis but have been found to be actually true by empirical investigations by Cyert and March. Further, according to them, all goals must be satisfied, but there is an ***implicit order of priority*** among them which is reflected in the way search activity takes place. It is also reflected in the speed and manner in which aspiration levels and goals regarding profit, production, sales, market share, and inventories are changed. Variations between firms as regard these latent priorities among the goals are explained, according to Cyert and March, by differences in the bargaining positions of the various members of organisational coalition in different firms.

The Aspiration Level and Satisficing Behaviour

The behavioral model as developed by Cyert, March and Cohen is based on the concept of *aspiration level* put forward by H.A. Simon. Simon points out that the most psychological theories assume that instead of maximising, rational men normally *satisfice*. Applying this to the business decisions, he suggests that instead of maximising profits, the firm aims at satisficing, that is, to achieve satisfactory overall performance of the firm as defined by the aspiration levels of goals set by it. Cyert and March adopt this satisficing behaviour on the basis of aspiration levels of various goals. They focus on explaining how business firms take decisions regarding price, output, sales strategy so as to achieve the satisfactory results in terms of the aspiration level of the goals set by it. Elaborating this viewpoint of the behavioural model, Koutosyiannis writes "The firm is satisficing organization rather than a maximising enterpreneur. The top management responsible for the coordination of the activities of the various members of the firms wishes to attain a satisfactory level of production to attain a satisfactory share of the market to earn a satisfactory level of profits, to divert a satisfactory percentage of the total receipts to research and development or to advertising, to acquire a satisfactory image and so on."[5]

Cyert and March regard the satisficing behaviour as *rational* and lays stress on Simon's concept of ***bounded rationality*** to justify satisficing behaviour of big corporate firms. The bounded rationality means the prudent behaviour under the given constraints. Satisficing is viewed as the attainment of the aspiration levels of goals which are finally set by the top management and ratified by the board of directors of the corporate firm. It is worth mentioning that goals are not set in terms of maximisation of some relevant magnitudes such as profits, sales, market share etc. but as the achievement of the aspiration levels of the goals set. Thus, the corporate business firms in this model are considered as satisficing organisations rather than the maximizes. Thus, the behavioural model, "redefines rationality. Traditional theory defined the rational firm as the firm that maximises profit (short-run and long-run). The behaviourist school is the only theory that postulates a satisficing behaviour of the firm which is rational given the limited information and limited computational abilities of the managers."

As aspiration level of a firm is based on its goal as well as its past experience, and in fixing it uncertainties are duly taken into account. If the actual performance of the firm reveals that a given aspiration level can be easily achieved, it will be revised upward. On the other hand, if it is found that a given aspiration level is difficult to be achieved, it will be lowered. Simon points out that when the actual performance of a firm falls short of an aspiration level, '*search*' *activity* is started to find out the ways of better *performance in the* future and therefore achieving the aspiration level.

5. A Koutosyiannis, op. cit. p. 390.

It may however be noted that according to Simon there is a limit to 'searching activities' which a firm will undertake, because for searching activity its gains must be balanced against its cost. That is why at the same time aspiration level is adjusted downward to a level which is more likely to be achieved. Since the firm limits its searching activity on account of its cost, it does not maximize profits. Therefore, while the firms behaving rationally aim at 'satisficing' rather than 'maximizing'.

Conflicts and their Resolution. According to Cyert and March, there does not prevail perfect harmony among various members of organisational coalition and conflicts among them often arise as regards goals, demands of the various members on the resources of the organisation and therefore organisation should be seen as a ***coalition of conflicting interests.*** These conflicts among the coalition members are resolved within the firm as a result of persuasion and accommodation of each other's viewpoint.

Further, these conflicts are reconciled by ***side payments*** which are in various monetary and non-monetary forms. An organisational coalition is viable if the payments made to the various coalition members are adequate to keep them in the organisation. If there are sufficient resources at the disposal of the organisation to meet all the demands of its members, the coalition is feasible one, otherwise not. Of course, since the demands of the members adjust to the actual payments and to their opportunity costs (*i.e.* transfer earnings), there is a *long-run tendency* for the payments and demands to be equal. But in the behavioural theory of Cyert and March, emphasis is laid on the *short-run relation between payments and demands* and on the imperfections in the factor markets.

Organisational Slack

In this connection, a great problem arises when the organisation is not able to accommodate the demands, which may be mutually conflicting and inconsistent, of its members because the available resources are not enough to do so. In this context, Cyert and March introduce the ***notion of organisational slack which is the excess of the actual payments to the various coalition members over and above what is required to keep them in the organisation. Thus slack consists in making payments to the various groups of coalition in excess of what is needed for the efficient working of the firm.*** To quote Cohen and Cyert, "Because of the frictions in the mutual adjustment of payments and demands, there is ordinarily a disparity between the resources available to the organisation and the payments required to maintain the organisation. The difference between total resources and total necessary payments is called *organisational slack*. ***Slack consists in payments to members of coalition in excess of what is required to maintain the organisation.*** Many interesting phenomena within the firm occur because slack is typically not zero".[6]

It is worth noting here that in conventional economic theory, organizational slack is zero, at least in equilibrium. Cyert and Cohen give various examples of organisational slack which exist in the business firms of the real world. "Many forms of slack typically exist: stock holders are paid higher dividends to keep stockholders (or banks) within the organisation; prices are set lower than necessary to maintain adequate income from customers; wages in excess of those required to maintain labour are paid; executives are provided with services and personal luxuries in excess of those required to keep them; sub-units are permitted to grow without real concern for the relation between additional payments and additional revenues; public services are provided in excess of those required"[7].

6. *Op, cit,* p. 353.
7. Cohen and Cyert, *op. cit.*, p. 353.

However, according to Cyert, March and Cohen, ***organisational slack plays a stabilising and adaptive role.*** When the external environments (*i.e.*, market conditions) are quite favourable, as under conditions of strong boom periods, the organisations secures excess resources which are paid as slack payments to meet the revised demands of those members of coalition whose demand adjusts more rapidly to the better achievement in good times. On the other hand, when the environment becomes less favourable, organisational slack serves as a cushion. In such times, scarcity of resources would tend to reduce the excess payments (*i.e.* organisational slack) to the various coalition members. If this organisational slack did not exist, the dwindling of resources in unfavorable times would have cut into the necessary payments of the members and thereby would have endangered the survival of the organisation. Thus organisational slack provides a pool of emergency resources.

The Process of Decision Making by the Firm

In this behavioural model, the goals of the firm as set by the top management are implemented through decision making at two levels, one at the level of top management itself and the second at the lower levels of management. Given the goals of the firm, the budgetary resources at the disposal of the firm are allocated among various departments/divisions according to their demands and goals set for them. However, managers of various departments bargain to obtain as large a share as possible from the budgetary resources. The top management retains some funds for use at its discretion at any point of time.

In approving proposals of various departments, two simple criteria are generally followed: the first is the *financial criterion* which examines whether the required funds are available, given the budgetary resources of the organisation. The second is the *improvement criterion* which assesses whether the implementation of the proposal will improve the condition of the organisation.

In the decision making process, the information is required to take appropriate decisions. However, gathering of information is not cost-less and requires budgetary resources. Cyert and March, following Simon, consider that search for information is not *undertaken* according to the marginalist rule, that is, up to the point at which marginal cost of information flow is equal to marginal benefit that would accrue to the firm.

Decision making at lower levels of Management. The decision making process at the lower levels of management is made with various degrees of freedom by departmental managers. With the given share of budget, the departmental managers enjoy considerable discretion in spending funds allotted to them. Besides, there is a lot of decentralisation in taking routine day-to-day decisions which is achieved through delegation of authority within each department or division.

Uncertainty Facing the Firm and its Impact on the Decision-Making Process. Unlike the traditional theory, the behaviourist model of Cyert and March considers the impact of two types of uncertainty. First type of uncertainty arises as a result of changes in consumer's tastes, invention of new methods of production and development of new products. In the behavioural theory this market uncertainty is overcome by business firms by underking only short-term planning and avoiding long-term planning. Thus the behavioral model implies that the firm does not consider long-term consequences of its decussions.

The second type of uncertainty arises out of competitor's reaction to the firm's decision. The behaviourist theory does not consider this type of uncertainty at all. This is because this model assumes that the existing firms have some form of *tacit collusion*. In this way the behaviourist model does not consider the interdepandence among oligopolistic firms which is a prominent feature of oligopolistic market structure. According to Cohen and March, through trade associations meetings, issue of information bulletins by the firms keep their competitors informed about the price, changes in the product and outlays they intend to make in future.

Price and Output Determination in the Behavioural Theory

What are the implications of this behavioural model for price formation. Cyert and March devised a simplified behavioural model of duopoly when the two duopolistic firms make decisions on price, output and sales strategy. In this model, each duopolistic firm is assumed to have three sets of goal (for profits, production and sales) and three basic decisions with regard to price, output and sales effort to make. In this model each duopolistic firm estimates demand and production cost and fixes its level of output. If this level of output does not yield the aspired level of profits, it then makes searches for ways to reduce costs and also re-estimates demand and, if necessary, lowers its profit goal. The other duopolistic firm also behaves in the same way. Price is fixed at the level of average direct cost (*i.e.*, average variable cost) plus a certain gross profit margin (for example, 20 per cent of the direct cost). Thus, in behavioural model, the cost-plus (*i.e.*, mark-up) pricing rule is followed. Though lower levels of management helps in calculating direct cost, final price decisions are taken by the top management.

The staff at lower level of management learn by experience though they are helped in their task by issuing a blue print containing rules to be followed by them. In the original Cyert and March model, multiple regression analysis was used to examine the extent to which firm's behaviour was sensitive to the variations in the internal parameters of the model. Afterwards Cohen and Cyert[8] produced a model in which simulation process was employed to explain the same general problem.

By taking data on demand, cost, market share, etc. and by using computer simulation, Cohen and Cyert compared the model's prediction with the actual behaviour of duopoly market faced by American Can Company and Continental Can Company. Most of the important moves by the two companies were predicted remarkably well by the model.

In the original behavioural model put forward by Cyert and March it was found that price was highly sensitive (i) to factors which bring about increases and decreases in the magnitude of organisational slack, (ii) to possible reduction of cost on advertisement and other sales promotion measures, and (iii) to adjustment in profit goals after actual profit achievement. For instance, if after the actual achievement, it was found that profits are low, then the organisation will explore the possibilities of reducing costs of production. For bringing about reduction in cost of production, the amount of organisational slack and also the expenditure on sales promotion measures may be cut down. The reduction in cost of production would enable the firm to reduce the price of the product. Further, if the coalition members were prepared to lower the profit goal, then the firm would more readily reduce the price of the product when difficult market situation arises. Thus, in the behavioural theory of the firm as presented by Cyert and March and also by Cohen and Cyert, close relationship between price, costs and profits has been stressed and price has been found to be highly sensitive to the factors influencing costs. The behavioral theory visualises the adjustment in cost of production and therefore price in response to the varying external market environments, whereas the conventional theory of the firm does not consider any such adjustments in cost of production because in this theory least-cost factor combination is achieved independently of market conditions regarding the product.

8. Cohen and Cyert have presented the behavioural theory of the firm in the book "*Theory of the Firm.*" Prentice Hall, 1965.

Thus, Silbertson[9] in his review article on **'*Price Behaviour of Firms' remarks,*** "The important difference between this type of model (*i.e.*, behavioural model), and more conventional models stems from the fact that this type of model lays emphasis on the process of decision taking, with its continuously changing goals, as the firm learns from its experience and adapts to it. An important corollary of this is that it lays much emphasis on cost reduction, whereas the assumption in conventional models is that for any given output, the least-cost combination of factors has been achieved".

Critical Evaluation of Behavioural Theory

The behaviourist model has made important contributions to the theory of the firm. It has provided a great insight in the process of goal formation and fixation of aspiration levels and also allocation of resources within firm. Its contribution also lies in analysing the stabilising role of organisation slack for a activity of the firm through changes in slack payments in periods of boom and depression, Further, unlike traditional theory of the firm, the behaviourist theory analyses resource allocation within firm and the decision-making process of a big corporate firm. It highlights the fact that the firm enjoys discretion in decision making and does not take the constraints of market environment as given and impossible to change. Prof. Koutsoyiannis is of the view that traditional theory of the firm and the behavioural theory are comlementary rather than substitutes. To quote him, the traditional theory stressed the role of the market (price) mechanism for the allocation of resources *between* the various sectors of the economy, while the behavioural theory examines the machanism of the resource allocation *within* the firm. Clearly, two theories are complementary rather than substitutes.

Behavioural approach has also been criticised on the ground that it uses a sledge hammer to crack a walnut. The question has been raised as to whether we should really try to construct mirror images of firms virtually assembling the decision-making process brick by brick for the purpose of predicting their behaviour as the behavioural approach does. Further, it has been asserted that instead of detailed, complicated and simulated model of firm's behaviour, simple model of profit-maximizing firm is sufficient for the prediction of price behaviour of the business firm and its response to increase in taxation in it. The staunch support for profit maximisation has come from Machlup[10]. According to him, "Even if formal accuracy demanded that we accept the maximisation of the decision-maker's total utility as the basic assumption, simplicity and fruitfulness speak for sticking with the postulate of maximisation of money profits for situations in which competition is effective. The question is not whether the firms of the real world will *really* maximise profits, or whether they even *strive* to maximise their money profits, but rather whether the *assumption* that this objective of the theoretical firms in the artificial world of our construction will lead to conclusions very different from those derived from admittedly more 'realistic assumptions'. He further adds, "some of the 'realistic assumption' proposed for inclusion in the theory can affect (by an unknown amount) the magnitude but not the direction of any change that is likely to result from a specified change in conditions".

It may however be pointed out that for drawing welfare conclusions from the changes in conditions, we need to know, as has been conceded by Machlup himself not merely the direction of change but also the magnitude. In welfare economics, to quote C.J. Hawkins, "We are interested in predicting more than just the direction of change. We need precise relationships such as '$MC = AR$ for all firms' or 'labour is paid its marginal physical product'. These relationships cannot be derived correctly except by having completely effective (*e.g.* in oligopoly),

9. Aubrey, Silberston, Price Behaviour of Firms, *Economic Journal*, 1970.
10. F. Machlup. Theories of the Firm : Marginalist, Behavioural, Managerial, *American Economic Review*, March 1967.

as Machlup himself concedes, managerial discretion may alter not just the extent of change but also its direction as the Williamson model has clearly demonstrated"[11]. Besides, the simulation approach of the behaviourist theory is only a predictive technique. It does not consider the conditions of entry of new firms in the industry and their effects on behavour of the existing firms.

In this model, it is considered that aspiration level will be adjusted downward whenever the goals, especially of achieving satisfactory rate of profits is not achieved. This rules out the theory of any objective criteria for assessment of satisfactory performance. Therefore, it is not clear in the behavioural theory what is satisfactory and what is unsatisfactory performance.

The behavioural theory has also been critcised on the ground of its belief that the firm behaves in a short-sighted manner as it considers that to overcome uncertainty of market environment the firms undertake only short-term planning. In our view, uncertainty of market environment cannot be successfully tackled by the firm by undertaking only short-term planning. As a matter of fact the business firms need to take a long-rum view of their business decisions and undertake a long-term planning if they want to grow.

A more serious drawback of the theory is that it rules out interdependence among oligopolistic firms by assuming tacit collusion among them. Thus the solution provided by them is quite unstable because collusion can be broken by any firm working contrary to the tacit collusive understanding. The instalitity of solution of behaviourist theory is more when entry of new firms is considered which are not a part of tacit collusion.

QUESTIONS FOR REVIEW

1. What is meant by satisficing behaviour ? Critically examine the view that corporate business firms are satisficers rather than maximizers.
2. The firm is a "Coalition of groups with conflicting goals". Explain the proposition of the behavioural model of the firm.
3. Explain the multiple goals of a corporate business firm. How are these goals formed and who set these goals.
4. What is meant by the aspiration level ? Explain this concept in the context of satisficing behaviour.
5. It is said that behavioural model of the firm redefinses rationality. How is it different from the concept of rationality of the traditional theory of the firm ?
6. Explain the decision making process of the oligopostic firm as conceived in the behavioural theory of the firm. Critically examine how it tables the problem of uncertainty faced by an oligopolistic firm.
7. What is meant by '*organisational slack*. Explain its role in the behavioural theory of the firm.
8. Compare the behavioural theory of the firm with the traditional theory of the firm. Are the two complementary or substitutes ?
9. How are price and output determined in the behavioural model ? Compare it with the marginalist rule of traditional theory of the firm.
10. Critically evaluate the behaviourist theory of the firm. On what grounds has it been criticised?
11. The behavioural theory resolves the core problem of oligopolistic interdependence by assuming tacit collusion of the firm in the industry. Explain and examine critically

11. C.J. Hawkins, *Theory of the Firm*, Macmillan, 1973, p. 73.

CHAPTER

48

Theory of Limit Pricing

Introduction

In our study of price determination we have finally reached the stage where we can explain some recent developments in price theory. In the traditional theories of monopoly and oligopoly, the existing firms do not worry about the potential entry of new firms and their behaviour and reactions. In the models of perfect competition, monopolistic competition, the effect of *actual entry* of new firms on price and output of the existing firms is studied. But the traditional oligopoly models of Cournot, Bertrand, Edgeworth and Chamberlin are closed models because they do not provide for the entry of new firms. The number of firms in these oligopoly models is assumed to be constant; only the reactions of the existing firms to the moves of rival firms are explained. Recently, it has been argued by several economists, prominent among whom are Bain, Sylos-Labini, Andrews, Modigliani, Jagdish Bhagwati that price-output decisions of the existing firms in oligopolistic markets are affected not only by the *actual* entry but also by the *potential* entry of firms.

An important issue that has been raised by these economists is that obigopolistic firms *do not maximise short-run profits*. Instead, they take a longer view of the situation and *seek to maximise profits over the long run* after allowing for potential entry of new firms that affect the profit possibilities. In his pioneering work 'A Note on Pricing in Monopoly and Oligopoly, (1949) followed by his book *'Barriers to New Competition'*, J. S. Bain put forward the theory of limit-pricing which in essence implies that firms do not maximise short-run profits because of the fear that the excessive or abnormal profits in the short run will induce the entry of new firms which will greatly reduce their profits in the long run. According to him, oligopolistic firms will not set a short-run profit-maximising price but instead charge a lower price that will prevent the entry of new firms in the industry. Thus, according to him, threat of potential entry is an important reason why collusive oligopoly does not charge the monopoly price. The theory of limit pricing or what is often called entry-preventing pricing has been further developed and generalised by Sylos-Labini, Modigliani and Jagdish Bhagwati. In the present chapter we will briefly explain the limit-pricing models put forward by these economists.

Basics of the Theory of Limit Pricing : Bain's Model

Bain's[1] theory of limit pricing relates to the case of collusive oligopoly. The central idea of his theory is the notion of limit price. Limit price is the highest price which the existing firms believe they can charge without attracting entry of new firms. In other words, *limit price is the entry preventing price.* In this analysis of limit pricing Bain assumes that products of the firms,

1. J. S. Bain has presented his theory of limit pricing in his two well known works (1) 'A Note on Pricing in Monoply and Oligopoly', *American Economic Review*, 1949. (2) *Barriers to New Competition* 'Harvard University Press, 1956.

both already established in the industry and the potential ones, are homogeneous. It is further assumed that the collusive oligopolists seek to maximise long-run profits. There is a given determinate demand curve for the industry product which remains unaltered and stable during price adjustments by the existing firms or change in price as a result of entry of new firms. Corresponding to this stable demand curve, there is marginal revenue curve.

The problem facing the collusive oligopolists is at what level limit price be set which prevents the entry of new firms. According to Bain, the limit price is determined by (a) the costs of the potential entrants, (b) price elasticity of demand for the industry product, (c) the size of the market, that is, the magnitude of demand for the product, (d) the number of established firms in the industry, and (e) on the level and shape of the long-rum average cost *(LAC)*. Figure 48.1 illustrates the essential features of limit-pricing theory. *DD′* is the market

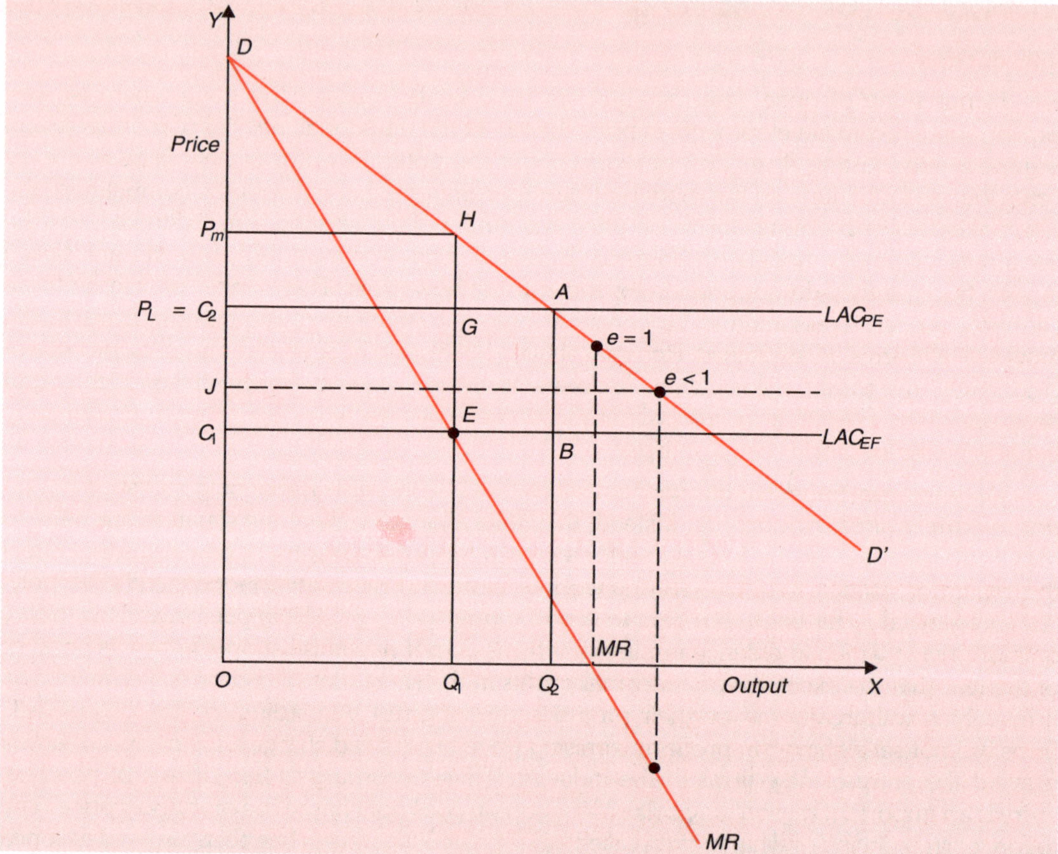

Fig. 48.1. *Limit Pricing Model*

demand facing the collusive oligopoly and *MR* is the corresponding revenue curve. Suppose the LAC_{EF} is the long-run average cost of the *existing* established collusive oligopolists. As LAC_{EF} is constant, *LMC* will be equal to it. If the collusive obgopoly wishes to maximise short-run profits it will set the price corresponding to the intersection (of LAC_{EF} (which is equal to LMC_{EF}) with the marginal revenue curve *MR*. It will be seen from Figure 48.1 that this short-run profit maximising price is equal to P_m (which is the monopoly price because we are considering the case of collusive oligopoly). But this short-run profit maximising price P_m is greater than the long-run average cost LAC_{PE} of the potential entrants. Consequently, the price P_m will attract entry of new firms in the industry. With entry of new firms, the established firms would lose a part of the market demand which would cause a shift in their demand curve to the left. Thus firms face uncertainty about the level of precise demand for their product as a result of the entry of new firms in the industry.

Now, if they set price P_L which is equal to the long-run average cost curve of the potential entrants *(LAC_{PE})*, they can quantity Q_2 of the product. The established collusive oligopolists will still earn profits as price P_L is greater than their long-run average cost LAC_{EF}. However, it will not be in the interest of potential rivals to enter the industry as the price P_L equals their average cost of production. If they enter the industry, the supply of the product will increase and, given the market demand curve, the price of the product will fall below their average cost of production. Thus, post-entry price will be less than the average cost of the potential entrants. If the potential firms enter the industry, they will suffer losses which therefore prevent them to enter at price P_L. Therefore, price P_L is known as the *limit price* as it is the price which the established firms can charge without inducing entry. It should be noted that at the limit price P_L, the established firms, unlike potential entrants, are making profits but profit margin per unit $C_1 P_L$ or $C_1 C_2$ is lower as compared to the case if they charge monopoly price.

It is worth mentioning that limit price is related to the existence of *barriers to entry*. In our analysis, it is the higher average cost of the potential entrants as compared to the established firms that acts as a barrier to their entry. And it is due to the absolute cost advantage enjoyed by the established firms that ensures their making profits even at the limit price and thus also succeeding in preventing entry of new firms. The established firms are making total profits equal to $C_1 C_2 AB$ which are less than short-run maximum profits C_1P_mHE. Firms are sacrificing some short-run profits as they expect they would be more than compensated for by higher profits earned in the long run with the entry-prevention strategy.

An important aspect of Bain's limit pricing theory is that with it Bain tried to explain the observed phenomenon of oligopolistic firms in some industries keeping their price at a level of demand where the price elasticity of demand was less than unity. A glance at Figure 48.1 will reveal that if the average cost of the potential entrants is *OJ*, the limit price will be set at this level. It will be further observed that at the price *OJ* on the given demand curve *DD′*, the price elasticity of demand is below unity as it corresponds to a point below the mid-point of the linear demand curve *DD′* and it will be further observed that marginal revenue is negative at this price. According to Bain, in order to prevent entry of potential firms, the oligopolists may set the limit price at the level *OJ* since it is still greater than their average cost of production (C_1) and therefore they make profits even at this price. If the oligopolists think it is in their best interest to adopt entry prevention strategy to promote maximisation of profits in the long run, they will set limit price at the level *OJ* under these circumstances.

Another interesting feature of Bain's limit pricing theory is that if the market demand and cost condition are such that monopoly price *(i.e* short-run profit-maximising price) is less than limit price ($P_m < P_L$), the oligopolists will charge the monopoly price to maximise their short-run profits because this will also serve to prevent entry and ensure maximum long-run profits.

It follows from above that Bain was able to explain why oligopolists charge price below the short-run profit maximising price. He explained that this was due to threat of potential entry of new firms. And they wished to prevent entry of potential firms as this ensures maximum long-run profits.

Barriers to Entry and Limit Price

In his later work *"Barriers to Entry"* (1956) Bain explained why oligopolists set price above the perfectly competitive price. According to him, limit price is set above the competitive price because of the existence of barriers to entry. In Bain's analysis of limit pricing the entry of a firm occurs when a *new firm* which enters the industry builds a *new productive capacity* that is not used for production prior to its entry. Further, Bain has put forward a concept which he calls ***'the condition of entry'*** which describes a margin by which the established oligopoly firms are able to raise their price above the perfectively-competitive price level *persistently* without inducing entry. In symbolic terms, the condition of entry has been written as :

$$E = \frac{P_L - P_c}{P_c} \qquad \ldots(i)$$

where E stands for the 'condition of entry' (that is, the *margin* by which the established firms can raise price above the competitive level), P_c stands for perfectly competitive price P_L stands for limit price. It should be noted that price under perfect competition equals long-run average cost ($P_c = LAC$).

Solving equation (*i*) above for P_L we have

$$P_L = P_c(1 + E)$$

The condition of entry or the extent of profit margin E by which the established firms can charge higher price as compared to the competitive price depends on the presence of various barriers to entry Bain has emphasised four such barriers to entry which are as under :—

1. ***Absolute Cost Advantage.*** The established firms enjoy some absolute cost advantage over the potential entrants. It is due to the cost advantage of the established firms that new firms on entry into the industry cannot compete with the already-existing firms.

2. ***Product Differentiation.*** The product differentiation gives individual firms a degree of control over the price of their product. The new firms cannot produce the same identical product, as produced by the established firms which may have earned a lot of goodwill for their products.

3. ***The Minimum Scale for the Efficient or Optimum production.*** Technology requires that a minimum size of plant at which average cost is minimum must be set up for production by a new firm on entry into industry.

4. ***Large Initial Capital Requirements.*** For setting up a new firm, a large amount of initial capital is required which may be difficult for the new firms to mobilise. This acts as a barrier to the entry of firms in an industry.

5. ***Economies of Scale.*** Economies of scale act as an important barrier to the entry of new firms. Economies of scale are of two types : ***real and pecuniary*** economies of scale. Real economies of scale may be technical, managerial or labour economies. Technical economies arise from the use of more efficient and specialised machinery. Managerial economies accrue to the firms due to the spreading of a fixed managerial input over a larger quantity of output. Labour economies result from the greater specialization and division of labour on a larger scale of production which enhance productivity of labour.

On the other hand, pecuniary economies of scale result from the bulk-buying of materials at preferential lower prices, lower transport costs which are realised when larger quantity of materials , and output are transported. Finally, pecuriary economies also occur due to lower advertising and other selling costs per unit of output when a large quantity of output is produced and sold.

SYLOS -LABINI MODEL OF LIMIT PRICING

Sylos-Labini[2] further modified and developed the limit pricing theory whose basis was laid by J.S. Bain. His analysis of limit pricing lays special emphasis on the economies-of-scale barrier to the entry of potential firms. His explanation of determinants of limit price is more precise and he also propounded a postulate about the behaviour pattern of established firms as well as potential entrants and is described as ***Sylos postulate.*** On the basis of Sylos's postulate and his analysis of determinants of limit price, Modigliani (1957) further refined it and presented a more general model of limit pricing which will be studied later.

Sylos-Labini considers a given market demand for a product with a unitary price elasticity of demand. The product is homogeneous and is being produced by few firms with a price leader. He assumes that there are three plant-sizes available with which various firms have to produce. Economies of scale accrue as the size of plant increases. However, because of rigid nature of technology assumed, the continuous *LAC* curve cannot be drawn. Instead, we have straight-line cost curves, the larger the plant size, the lower the average cost.

In Sylos-Labini model, price is set by the largest firm which is also the most efficient firm with the lowest average cost. The smaller firms cannot influence the price individually and are therefore price takers. However, the largest firm, the price leader, sets a price that is acceptable to all the firms in the industry but the price must be low enough to prevent entry of new firms. The price leader is fully aware of the costs of all plant sizes as well as the market demand for the product.

Further, Sylos-Labini assumes that the new firms which will enter the industry must set up the ***smallest size plant.***

Sylos's Postulate. Sylos makes an important behavioural assumption concerning the expectations of the established firms as well as of the potential entrants. First, according to Sylos' s postulate, the established firms expect that the new firm will not enter the industry if it estimates that with its entry price will fall below his average cost of production. Secondly, the new entrant expects that on his entry the established firms would keep their output constant at the preentry level so that the *increase in quantity demanded of* the product caused by the decline in its price due to its entry accrues entirely to it (*i.e.* the new firm).

Fixation of Limit Price

With the above assumptions made by Sylos, we can explain how the limit price is determined in this model. It should be noted that Sylos thinks that there is a normal rate of profit which must be earned by the firms if they are to stay in the industry. Thus, the minimum acceptable price must cover the average total cost *(ATC)* as well as the normal rate of profits. The minimum acceptable price is set according to full-cost pricing principle. Thus

$$P_i = ATC(1+r)$$

where P_i = the minimum acceptable price to the firm having *i*th plant size

ATC = Average total cost of *ith size plant*

r = normal rate of profit

Sylos limit pricing model is illustrated in Figure 48.2. *DD′* represents the market demand curve. AC_1, AC_2 and AC_3 are the average cost curves of the large-size, medium size, and small size plants respectively. The output OQ_S (which will be simply referred to as Q_s) is the

2. Sylos-Labini, *Oligopoly and Technical Progress,* Harvard University Press, Cambridge. 1957,

level of output with the minimum average cost of the small size plant. As noted above, it is assumed in the model that the new firm will enter the industry with this small size plant with average cost equal to AC_3. In view of various firms having different plant sizes with differential

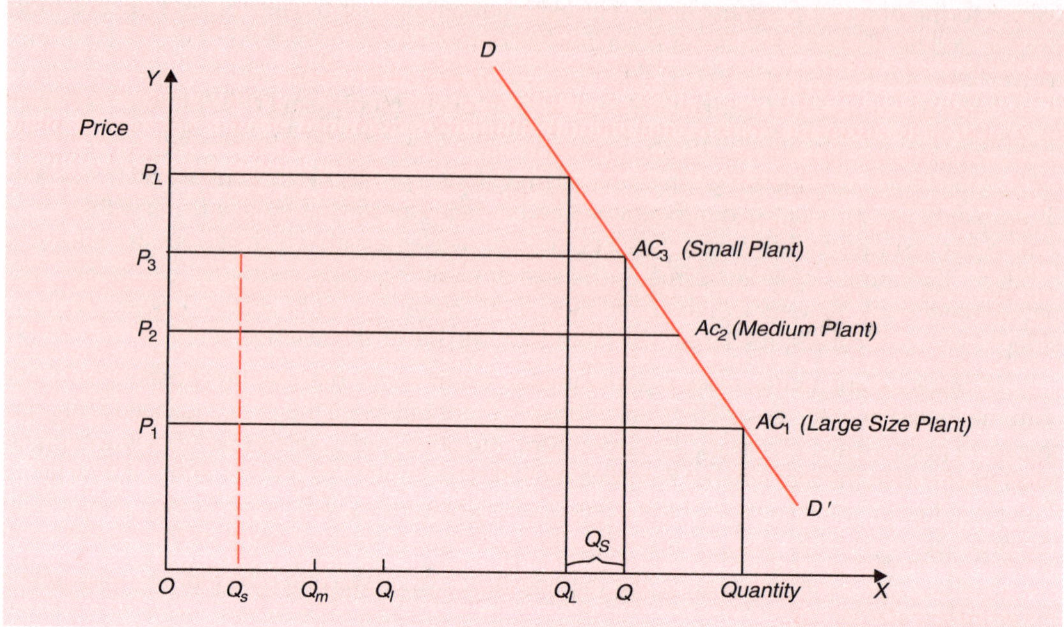

Fig. 48.2. *Determination of Limit Price : Sylos's Model*

costs, the price leader which is the most efficient firm with lowest average cost AC_1 will set a price which is acceptable to the least efficient firms having higher average cost AC_3. In Sylos's model, the most efficient firm, the price leader, does not think it profitable to compete away the smaller firms and instead in setting price he ensures that the least efficient firm with small-size plant continues to make at least normal profits and therefore the price fixed is acceptable to it. Accordingly, in our Figure 48.2, the most efficient firm will set a price above average cost AC_3 of the firms operating least efficient plant-size.

Now, exactly at what level above AC_3 the price leader will set the price ? As mentioned above, the price leader will set the price at a level which is above the average cost AC_3 of the least efficient firms and is therefore acceptable to them but which is also such that prevents entry of new firms in the industry. To determine this limit price the price leader has to ascertain the quantity demanded at price P_3 which is equal to AC_3 of the least efficient plant. It will be seen from Figure 48.2 that at price P_3, the quantity demanded of the product equals OQ. Given that the new firm can enter the industry with a plant size with productive capacity equal to OQ_s or simply Q_s, then $Q_L = Q - Q_s$ provides us the quantity of output corresponding to which price will be set. It will be seen from Figure 48.2 that quantity Q_L of output can be sold at price P_L. According to Sylos P_L is the limit price which will deter the entry of new firms. This is because if at the price P_L a new firm with an economically viable output Q_s enters the industry, the total supply of output $Q_L + Q_s$ will just exceed Q which will cause the price to fall just below the average cost AC_3 of the least efficient which is also the average cost of the new entrant (Note that in Sylos's model it is assumed that the new firm enters the industry ***with the least efficient plant size having average cost equal*** to AC_3 — this is the *scale barrier* emphasized by Sylos).

Now, according to Sylos, the potential entrant knows that with its entry and resultant increase in supply of output, price in the post-entry period will fall below its own average cost of production, he will not enter the industry. Thus P_L is the limit price that will be fixed to prevent entry into the industry. To quote Sylos, "The price tends to settle at a level immediately above the entry preventing price of the least efficient firms, which it is to the advantage of the largest and most efficient firms to let live"[3].

It should be noted that with limit price fixed at P_L all firms will make supernormal profits. The limit price P_L corresponding to output Q_L is the equilibrium price because it fulfills the two necessary conditions, namely, it is acceptable to all firms and also it prevents entry. However, it is worth mentioning that P_L *is* the upper limit of the limit price *(i.e.* entry preventing price). The price equal to P_3 is the lower limit. Thus equilibrium price cannot be higher than P_L, nor lower than P_3. In accordance with this, any output smaller than Q_L will not prevent the entry of new firms, while output larger than Q_L will deter entry into the industry. This is because as it will be noticed from Figure 48.2 that if the output produced by the established firms is less than Q_L, the new firm with output of Q_s will raise supply of output to less than Q and therefore price will not fall to the level of P_3 and consequently it will be worthwhile for the new firm to enter and thereby make profits. On the other hand, any output greater than Q_L will deter entry because new firm with minimum output Q_s will increase the supply of output to more than Q and consequently price will fall below AC_3 causing losses to the new firms :

From our above analysis of Sylos model it follows that the limit price is determined by the following factors :-

1. ***The absolute size of the market,*** that is, the market demand for the product. The greater the size of the market, the lower the limit price.
2. ***The price elasticity of demand.*** The greater the price elasticity of demand for the product, the lower the limit price that the established firms can set to prevent entry into the industry.
3. ***The technology of the industry.*** The technology determines the various sizes of plants and their average cost of product. As seen above, the technology also determines the minimum efficient plant size. The larger the minimum efficient plant size, the higher will be the limit price.

Modigliani's Model of Limit Pricing : Generalisation of Sylos's Model

Modigliani further developed the limit pricing model by relaxing some rigid assumptions concerning technology made by Sylos. With this he generalised Sylos's model retaining its assumption of *scale barrier* and *behavioural pattern* of the firms. In what follows we first describe assumptions made by Modigliani and then will explain his model of limit pricing.

Assumptions of Modigliani's Model

1. Modigliani assumes that the same technology is being used by all firms in the industry. The technology requires a minimum efficient plant size at which economies of scale are fully realised. Beyond this optimum scale, the long-run average cost (*LAC*) becomes a horizontal straight line. So the long-run average cost curve is L-shaped as shown in Figure 48.3 (panel *(a)*) and is the same for all firms.
2. As in Sylos's model, new firms enter the industry with the minimum efficient plant size, that is, with output $O\bar{q}$ (or simply $\bar{q}$) in panel (a) of Figure 48.3.

3. Sylos-Labini, *Oligopoly and Technical,* Harvard University Press, 1962,

3. The market demand for the product is known to both the established firms and the potential entrants. Moreover, homogeneous products are produced by the firms in the industry.
4. The behaviour pattern of the established firms and the potential entrants is the same as assumed in Sylos's postulate. As seen above, according to Sylos's postulate, the established firms expect that a new firm will not enter if it thinks that on his entry price of the product would fall below the long-run average cost (*i.e* level of its flat portion). On the other hand, potential entrants believes that even after its entry the established firms will keep their output constant at the pre-entry level.

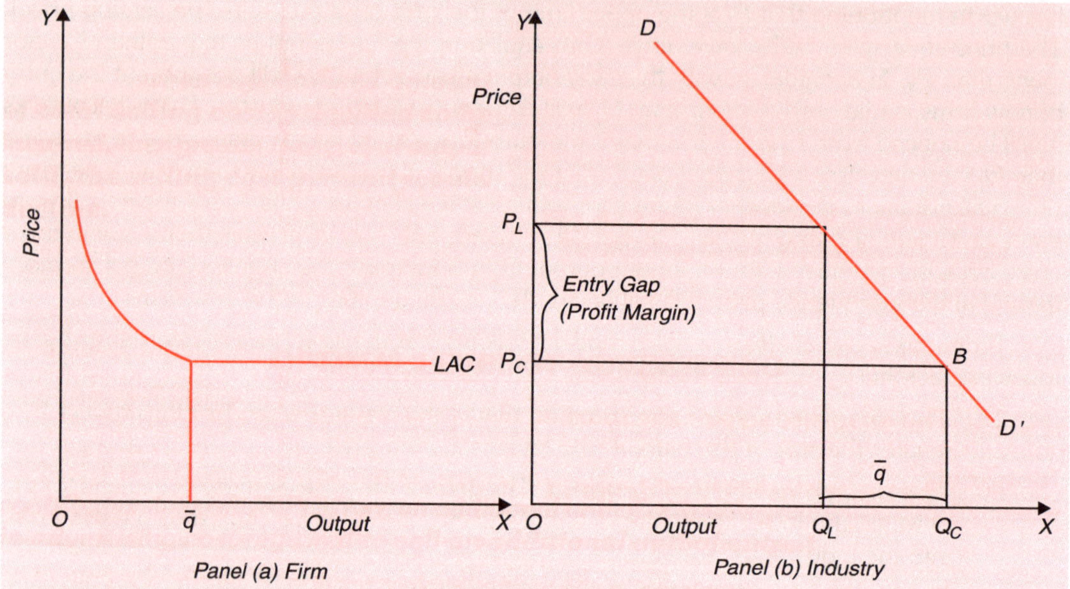

Fig. 48.3. *Modigliani's Model of Limit Pricing*

5. As in Sylos's model, Modigliani assumes that there exists a scale barrier, namely, the new firms cannot enter the industry with a plant size smaller than the minimum efficient size $\bar{q}$.
6. The largest firm in the industry acts as a price leader and he sets the price to prevent entry of new firms.

Determination of Limit Price in the Model

With the above assumptions Modigliani proceeds to show how the limit price is set above the level of competitive price. His model is illustrated in Figure 48.3 where *DD'* is the demand curve for the product. Since in the long run price is equal to long-run average cost (*LAC*), the competitive price is set at the level where the flat *LAC* curve (which is in fact the supply curve under perfect competition) intersects the given demand curve *DD'*. It will be observed from panel (*b*) of Figure that flat *LAC* curve intersects the demand curve *DD'* at point *B* and, accordingly, competitive price is P_c and the competitive output is Q_c.

Now, the established firms can charge a price higher than the competitive price P_c because of the existence of scale barrier. The problem before the price leader is at what level the price is set such that it prevents the entry of new firms. To obtain such a price, the total output which could be sold by all firms in the industry has to be determined. This depends on how much output a minimum efficient plant size, with which the new firm will enter, can produce. It will be seen from panel *(a)* that the minimum efficient plant size is given by the output equal to $\bar{q}$. If we subtract output $\bar{q}$ of the new entrant from competitive output Q_c we get $Q_L = Q_c - \bar{q}$ (see panel *b* in Figure 48.3). Corresponding to output Q_L, the price of the product equals P_L. Price P_L is the limit price which should be set to prevent entry of new firms in the industry. At price P_L the established firms would produce and sell quantity of output Q_L and will be making supernormal profits.

Now, fixation of limit price at the level P_L and output at level Q_L implies that if a new firm enters the industry and supplies an additional output $\bar{q}$ (the minimum quantity it can produce with least cost, the total output *would just* exceed competitive output Q_c and consequently the price would *just* fall below competitive price P_C = *LAC*. Thus, it will not be profitable for potential entrant which will therefore prevent the entry.

To conclude, once the quantity Q_L is determined the limit price P_L can be obtained from the given market demand curve for the product. It is worth mentioning that the limit price P_L is greater than the competitive price P_c because of the scale barrier. The difference $P_L - P_c$ is known as ***entry gap*** which represents the profit margin or premium by which the price can exceed the long-run average cost *(LAC)*. From the foregoing analysis it follows that the following factors determine the limit price and entry gap :-

(1) the demand for or market size of the product, that is, Q_c

(2) the price elasticity of demand for the product,

(3) the minimum efficient plant size

(4) the prices of factors and technology. Both of these determine the cost of production.

The above determinants of limit price are the same as in Sylos's model. Further, the limit price varies directly with minimum efficient plant *size*($\bar{q}$) and the competitive price (P_c = LAC). The greater the optimal plant size ($\bar{q}$), the smaller will be Q_L and therefore, given the demand curve, the higher will be limit price. Again, the higher the competitive price, the greater will be the limit price. On the other hand, the limit price varies inversely; with price elasticity of demand *(e)* and the absolute market size for the product (Q_c). A significant contribution of Modigliani lies in combining the above factors in an expression which shows how the various determinants are related to the limit price. The expression is as under :

$$P_L = P_c\left(1+\frac{\bar{q}}{Q_c.e}\right) \quad .....(i)$$

where P_L = the limit price

P_c = the competitive price

$\bar{q}$ = the minimum efficient plant size.

Q_c = the competitive output

The expression *(i)* showing the relationship between limit price and its determinants can be explained as under :-

In the neighbourhood of the competitive price P_c the price elasticity of demand can be written as under

$$e = \frac{\Delta Q}{Q} \div \frac{\Delta P}{P}$$

According to Sylos's postulate, the whole increase in demand accrues to the new entrant so that :

$$\Delta Q = Q_c - Q_L = \bar{q}$$

Further, at the competitive *price* P_c, the quantity sold is Q_c. Due to entry gap price rises from P_c *to* P_L so that

$$\Delta P = P_L - P_c$$

Substituting the values of ΔQ, ΔP, and Q in the elasticity measure we have

$$e = \frac{\bar{q}}{Q_c} \div \frac{P_L - P_c}{P_c} = \frac{\bar{q}}{Q_c} \times \frac{P_c}{P_L - P_c}$$

Solving for P_L we obtain

$$P_L = P_c\left\{1 + \frac{\bar{q}}{Q_c . e}\right\}$$

How the limit price changes with the minimum efficient plant size ($\bar{q}$) and price elasticity of demand (*e*) is graphically shown in Figures 48.4 and 48.5 respectively. It will be seen from Figure 48.4 that when minimum efficient plant size *increases* ($\bar{q}_2 > \bar{q}_1$,), the limit price increases from P_{L1} to P_{L2}.

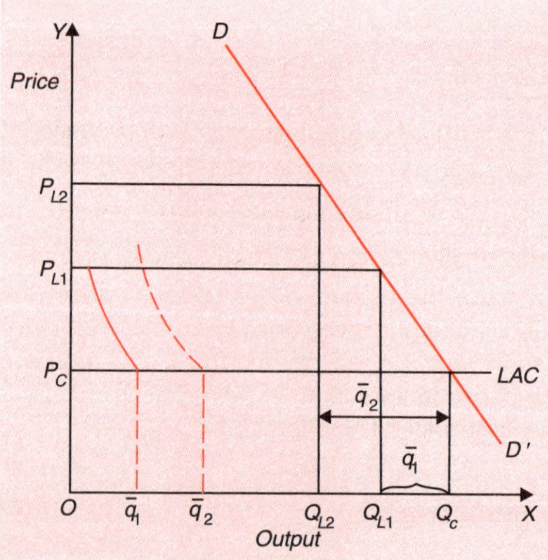

Fig. 48.4. *Limit price depends on the minimum efficient plant capacity. For* $\bar{q}_2 > \bar{q}_1$, $P_{L2} > P_{L1}$.

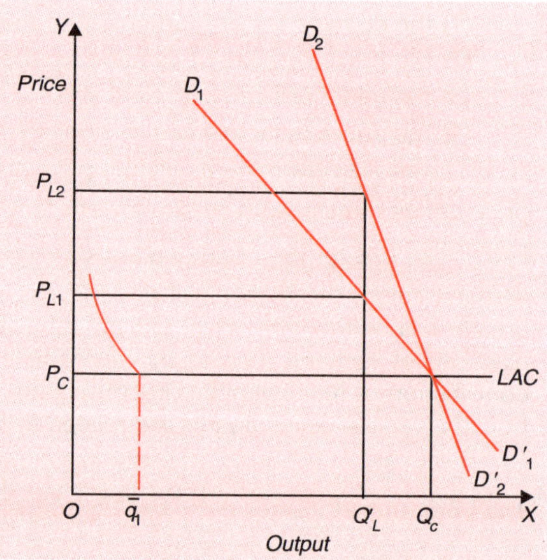

Fig. 48.5. *Limit Price is determined by price elasticity of demand. For* $e_2 > e_1$, $P_{L2} > P_{L1}$.

In Figure 48.5 two demand curves D_1D_1' and $D_2D'_2$ have been drawn. At the competitive price P_c, price elasticity of demand (e_2) on demand curve $D_2D'_2$ is greater than price elasticity of demand (e_1) on the demand curve $D_1D'_1$. It will be observed that limit price PL_2 fixed in case of less elastic demand, $D_2D'_2$, is higher than PL_1 fixed in case of more elastic demand $D_1D'_1$.

Bhagwati's Extension of Modigliani's Model

Prof. Bhagwati has further developed Modigliani's model and has also made it dynamic. First, Bhagwati's contribution lies in adding two more factors that determine the limit price.

These two additional determinants of limit price are (1) the number of firms in the industry and (2) the 'feel' of dissatisfaction of the consumers from the established firm. This feeling of dissatisfact measured by a special elasticity which is known as **Chagrin elasticity**, Secondly, he considered the changes in limit price in the framework of the *growing demand or market* for a commodity.

According to Bhagwati, as the new firms enter the industry and price of the product falls and the quantity demanded of the product increases; some of the new buyers will buy from the established firms who are known in the field and some new buyers will purchase from the new entrant. To make his analysis simple, Bhagwati assumes that increase in quantity demanded as a result of the fall is *shared equally* between the established firms and the new entrant. Let ΔQ stand for the increment in demand following the entry of new firm and resultant fall in price, N for the number of firms before the new one, $\bar{x}$ is the share of each in the increment in demand, then

$$\frac{\Delta Q}{N+1} = \bar{x}$$

or

$$\Delta Q = \bar{x}(N + 1) \qquad \text{... (1)}$$

The second factor emphasized by Bhagwati is that as a new firm enters the market and price falls, some of the consumers who were previously buying from the established firms switch to the new entrant as they had developed a feeling of dissatisfaction with the established firms thinking that they were exploiting them by charging higher prices before the entry of the new firm. As a result of the switching of customers, there is a certain decrease in the demand or sales of the established firm. Here a new concept *chagrin effect* has been introduced. Chagrin effect measures the proportionate decrease in quantity demanded *(i. e.* sales) of the established firms as the dissatisfied consumers switch to the new entrant and we denote it by β which has a positive sign.

Thus writing expression for the elasticity of demand of the established firms at competitive output Q_c and competitive price P_c we have

$$e = \frac{\Delta Q}{Q_c} \div \frac{\Delta P}{P}$$

Now from above we know that $\Delta Q = \bar{x}(N + 1)$. Substituting in the expression we have

$$e = \frac{\bar{x}(N+1)}{Q_c} \div \frac{\Delta P}{P} \qquad \text{...(2)}$$

$$\frac{\Delta P}{P} = \frac{P_L - P_c}{P_c}$$

Substituting $\frac{P_L - P_c}{P_L}$ for $\frac{\Delta P}{P}$ in (2) above and solving for P_L we have

$$P_L = P_c\{ 1 + \frac{\bar{x}(N+1)}{Q_c[(e+\beta(N+1)]} \qquad \text{....(3)}$$

It therefore follows that the two additional determinants of limit price P_L are the numbers of firms in the industry *(N +1)* and Chagrin effect which is denoted by β. To quote Prof. Bhagwati, "The premium obtainable in an industry will vary *directly* with (1) the minimum size of scale of most efficient production ($\bar{x}$) and the number of existing firms *(N)*; and *inversely* with (1) the size of the total market (Q_c) the price elasticity of industry demand and (3) the extent to which existing buyers will transfer custom to the entrant consequent upon entry."[4]

The expression (3) above represents determinants of limit price for a given market demand of a good. This has been extended further by Bhagwati to cover cases when dynamic changes in the market demand are occurring. If there is increment in demand by λ and proportion (*k*) of this increase goes to the new entrant, then the limit price is given by

$$P_L = \left\{1 + \frac{\bar{x} - k\lambda}{Q_c\left[\frac{e}{N+1} + \beta\right]}\right\} \quad \text{...(4)}$$

where Q_c represents the total quantity demanded at the competitive price after growth in demand has taken place. It will be seen that fraction k is inversely related to the limit price P_L. That is, if a higher proportion *(k)* of increase in demand accrues to the new entrant, the limit price (P_L) will be set at a lower level. This implies that entry is relatively easy in case of growth in demand for the product. The greater the growth in demand for the product, the less the premium by which the limit price will be higher than the competitive price.

From the above formulation (4) of the limit price an important result follows. This is that if $(k\lambda) > \bar{x}$, that is, if the *increase in demand* for the product accruing to the entrant exceeds the minimum efficient plant size, then entry in the industry cannot be prevented. This is because $(k\lambda) > \bar{x}$ means that on the entry of a firm and consequent increase in output would not cause the price to fall below the competitive price (= *LAC*) which is essential if entry of new firms is to be prevented. This implies profits to the new firm and this would induce its entry in the industry. Thus, in the case of faster growth in demand, the price strategy to forestall the entry of new firms becomes ineffective. Therefore, Prof. Bhagwati argues that in case of faster growth in demand, the entry prevention price policy becomes an ineffective instrument. Under these circumstances, according to him, entry-prevention strategy has to adopt other measures such as maintaining enough *spare productive capacity continuously* so that rate of production by the existing firms can be increased at the same pace as the growth in demand for the product. This however may be very expensive and unprofitable proposition. Moreover, this requires making of accurate forecast of the increasing demand. Such forecasting ability on the part of entrepreneurs is lacking. Prof. Bhagwati reaches a conclusion that if market demand for a product is increasing very rapidly (*i.e.* $(k\lambda > \bar{x})$, entry-prevention strategy cannot be based on adoption of price policy alone. The established firms have to adopt other ways and means to prevent entry of new firms. These ways and means adopted must ensure that the established firms themselves rather than potential entrants get the largest share of the growth in demand. According to Bhagwati, in growing markets, if the firms seek to forestall entry they should devise ways to increase their market share and adopt those policy instruments which are under their control.

Critical Evaluation of the Theory of Limit Pricing

In the foregoing analysis we have explained Bain, Sylos, Modigliani and Bhagwati's contributions to the theory of limit pricing. Bain, the pioneer in the theory of limit pricing, has made important contributions to the theory of oligopoly. He was the first to point out ***that potential entry or threat of entry*** has an important bearing on the pricing decisions of the existing firms. That the established firms take steps to prevent entry of new firms is an important idea made by Bain. He has rightly pointed out that in order to maximise long-run profits, the

4. J. Bhagwati, "Oligopoly Theory, Entry Prevention and Growth", *Oxford Economic Papers* 1970.

established firms who may be monopolist or oligopolist sacrifice some short run profits. Bain-Sylos-Modigliani have also validly laid stress on scale as one of the important factors preventing entry of new firms. However, the model of entry-preventing price policy suffers from serious limitations. First, these models assume that altogether a small *new* firm enters an industry. This however does not conform to the real world situation. It has been observed that it is not the *small new firms* but the well-established large firms in other industries who intend to diversify generally enter an industry. It may not be difficult for them to enter another industry and give tough competition to the existing firms in the industry. For example, in India large business houses of Birla, Tata, Reliance may enter any industry and succeed. The scale barriers, large capital requirements, absolute cost advantage of the existing firms over the potential entrants are not relevant in their case.

Besides, Bain-Sylos-Modigliani models of limit pricing concentrate on pursuing appropriate price policy alone. As a matter of fact, as has been pointed out by Bhagwati, often it is ***non-price competition*** such as advertising and other selling costs which is an effective instrument to deter the potential entrants. Further, in his limit price model Bain assumes that potential entrants believe that the existing firms will keep their price constant at pre-entry level by contracting their output is too optimistic assumption of the potential entrants. It implies that the established firms would have accommodating behaviour and would allow the entrant to gain any share of the market he likes while their own market share and profits are declining due to the fall in price as well as the decline in sales due to the entry of firms. Even Sylos's assumption that entrant expects that the established firms would keep their output constant at the pre-entry level in the post-entry period is a naive assumption which is neither realistic, nor the best alternative available to the established firms.

Further, Sylos's strategy in a way implies a defensive attitude in that the existing firms give up their initiative for price setting. Price will be virtually set by the new entrant, depending on the quantity he decides to sell in the market.[5] It has been argued that the established firms would like to retain their control on price and adopt other measures such as increasing their output, increasing advertising expenditure to prevent entry. This retaliatory strategy would lead to decline in price and the price may even fall below *LAC*. But, "depending, however, on their financial reserves and the length of time period over which established firms expect the price to remain below their *LAC,* they may find it profitable in the long run to start a price war and eliminate the entrant"[6]. It may be noted that in the real business world, we often find that established firms in the industry often adopt such measures to eliminate the new entrants. These elimination tactics also serve as a warning to the potential entrants in the future that they will meet the same fate.

Lastly, against Bain-Sylos-Modigliani's entry preventing price policy Andrews[7] and Bhagwati[8] have rightly argued that the best strategy for the established firms is the adoption *of mixed strategy,* according to which the established firms would first try to accommodate the new entrant and accordingly reduce their pre-entry output and partly allow the price to fall in the post-entry period. It has been argued that this is in conformity with the business behaviour in the real world. With this mixed strategy the established firms can continue to make super-normal profits. Further, they may launch an aggressive advertising campaign and they also step up other ways of non-price competition and thus making the survival of the entrant difficult and also thereby serve as a lesson to future potential entrants.

5. A. Koutsoyiannis, *Modern Microeconomics*, Macmillan, 2nd Edition, 1985, p. 312.
6. A. Koutsoyiannis, *op. cit.*, p. 312.
7. P.W.S. Andrews, *Manufacturing Business*, Macmillan, 1949.
8. J.N. Bhagwati, Oligopoly Theory, Entry Prevention and Growth, *Oxford Economic Papers*, 1970.

CHAPTER

49

Government Policies Towards Monopoly and Competition

Introduction

People look at monopolies with suspicion and they are considered as undesirable form of market structure. The existence of monopolies in an economy is an important cause of glaring income inequalities and monopolists wield a lot of economic power which they use to exploit both consumers and workers. Economists generally criticise monopolies as they restrict output and raise prices of their products. Thus monopolies and oligopolies not only increase income inequalities but also cause inefficiency in the allocation of resources of a society. In this chapter, we analyse the economic effects of monopolies and imperfect competition represented by oligopolies and what policies government can adopt to reduce their bad effects and to achieve economic efficiency.

THE DRAWBACKS OF MONOPOLIES AND LIMITED COMPETITION

The effect of monopolies and limited competition as in oligopolies is that they lead to economic inefficiency which reduce social welfare. There are four major sources of emergence of economic inefficiency under monopolies and oligopolies. First, *monopolies restrict output* and produce levels of output which are less than what are economically efficient. Second, there exists *managerial slack* under monopoly due to which cost per unit of output is higher. Thirdly, monopolies *spend less on research and development* and therefore, hampers technological progress. Fourth, monopolies and oligopolies often indulge in *rent-seeking activities* to raise or sustain their monopoly profits. We briefly explain below these drawbacks of monopolies and oligopolies.

1. Restriction of Output to Charge Higher Price

Monopolists, like firms working under perfect competitions, aim at maximising profits. But, as seen in the earlier chapters, to maximise profits a monopolist is able to charge higher price by restricting output of the product or service he produces. Given the same demand and cost conditions as prevailing in a competitive industry, the monopolist who maximises his profits at the output level at which his marginal cost equals marginal revenue, produces less than the competitive industry. Thus, by producing less and charging higher price, the monopolist works in an economically inefficient way and causes a loss of consumer welfare. Consider Fig. 49.1 where *DD* is the demand curve for a competitive industry consisting of a large number of firms. *SS* is the short-run supply curve of the competitive industry which is obtained by summing up the short-run marginal cost curves of the firms. The competitive industry is in equilibrium at point *E* at which demand curve and supply curve intersect and produces Q_c quantity of the product and price determined is equal to P_c. Note that under competitive equilibrium price P_c is equal to marginal cost of production at output level Q_c.

Now, with monopolist equating marginal revenue (*MR*) with marginal cost (*MC*) to maximise profits restricts output to Q_m and sets price equal to P_m. Note that when all competitive firms are merged to form a monopoly, supply curve *SS* of the competitive industry will become marginal cost (*MC*) curve of the monopolist . Thus, output under monopoly is lower and price higher than in a competitive industry and this leads to loss of consumer welfare.

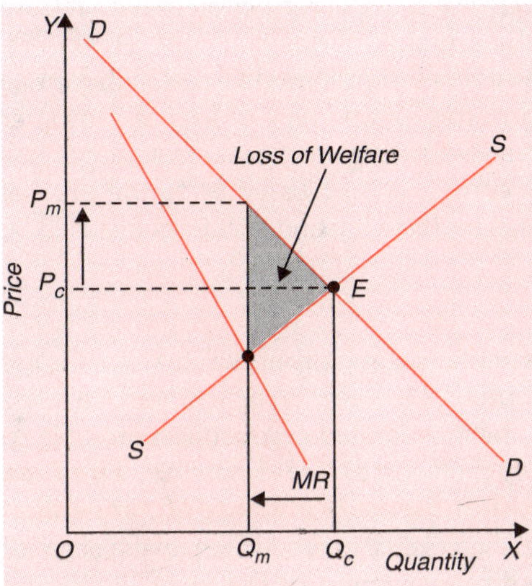

Fig. 49.1. *Monopolist restricts output to raise price*

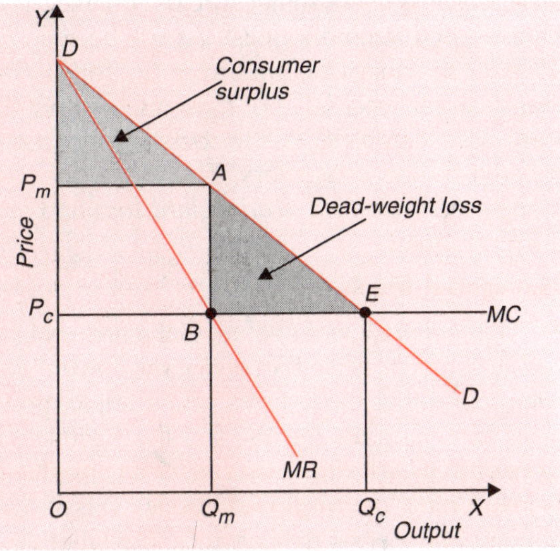

Fig. 49.2. *Dead-Weight Loss under Monopoly and Reduction in Consumer Surplus*

How monopoly causes loss of consumer welfare can be explained by reinterpreting the demand curve. On this interpretation, demand curve for a product shows ***how much money a consumer is willing to pay for an extra unit of the product*** as he consumes more quantity of the product. In other words, demand curve which depicts various prices at different quantities of goods purchased measures *marginal benefit* to a consumer of extra units of a product as he purchases more units of it. Since under perfect competition the output level is determined at which demand curve (which reflects marginal benefit) intersects the supply curve (which represents marginal cost curve), under it consumer welfare is maximised. Price paid by the consumers depicting marginal benefit is equal to marginal cost under perfect competition and this ensures maximum welfare. Alternatively, as explained in earlier chapters, allocative economic efficiency is achieved when total surplus (*i.e.*, the sum of consumer surplus and producer surplus) is maximised. Under perfect competition, the sum of consumer surplus and producer surplus) is maximised at output level Q_c in Fig. 49.1 at which demand curve *DD* intersects the supply curve *SS*.

On the other hand, by producing level of output at which price exceeds marginal cost, the monopolist reduces social welfare and causes allocative inefficiency. This is explicitly illustrated in Figure 49.2. To keep the analysis simple we assume that marginal cost curve (which is the supply curve under perfect competition) is a horizontal straight line which shows that marginal cost remains constant as output is increased. Under perfect competition as price is equated with marginal cost, output Q_c will be produced. With output Q_c and price P_c, consumer surplus enjoyed by consumers will be EP_cD. On the other hand, the monopolist will equate marginal cost with marginal revenue and will produce lower amount of output Q_m and charge higher price P_m. As a result, consumer surplus is reduced to AP_mD which represents the loss of consumer welfare equal to the area $AE\,P_cP_m$. But this loss of consumer welfare can be broken into two parts. First, the rectangle ABP_cP_m which represents the profits made by the monopolist by restricting output to Q_m and raising price to P_m. But this loss of consumer surplus is not a loss to the society as a whole. It is a transfer of income from the consumers to the monopolist as price of the product is raised and output reduced by the latter. But there is additional loss of consumer surplus equal to the area ABE because of restriction of output from Q_c to Q_m by the monopolist. As will be seen from the segment of demand curve AE in Fig. 49.2 for the units of output from Q_m to Q_c, the consumers are prepared to pay higher price than marginal cost (MC) of these units of output. Thus, this second type of loss of consumer surplus is a complete loss to society as no one in the society has gained as a result of this loss suffered by the consumers. Therefore, the loss of consumer surplus equal to the area of triangle ABE is called *dead-weight loss* and represents inefficiency and social cost caused by the monopolist.

Managerial Slack

It is generally pointed out that a firm which aims at maximising profits will try to minimise cost as far as possible for producing a given level of output. However, in actual practice it has been found that those firms which enjoy monopoly or face limited competition are able to make a lot of profits and also lack the incentives to keep their cost as low as possible. ***The lack of incentives to reduce costs as far as possible due to the absence of pressure of competition is known as 'managerial slack'.*** This also leads to inefficiency in production. In the absence of competition it is difficult to know whether or not management of the firms is efficient because it is always claimed by them that they are doing their best to keep their costs as low as possible. For example, before privatisation of telecom services BSNL (Bharat Sanchar Nigam Ltd.) had a monopoly of long distance telephone services and it charged very high prices but was always claiming that its costs were as low as possible. Now that there has been privatisation of Telecom services in India in the past few years with private companies such as Reliance, Tata, Hutch, Airtel have been permitted to provide long-distance telephone services, prices of them have fallen sharply. Now, under the pressure of competition with the private companies, even BSNL has substantially reduced the rates of long-distance calls. That shows there was a lot of managerial slack in BSNL and in fact it was not keeping its costs as low as possible. If it were not so, then how when it has to compete with the private companies it has been able to substantially cut the prices of long-distance calls.

Monopolies do not make Adequate Expenditure on Research and Development

It has often been found that because they do not have to face competition in selling their products, monopolies do not make enough expenditure to develop new products and new and better techniques of production. Since monopolists are able to make a large amount of profits without any effort to make progress in technology, there is lack of incentives on their part to make adequate effort and spend enough expenditure on research and development to develop new technologies which improve productivity and lower costs of production. Of course, there may be some exceptions to this general tendency on the part of monopolies. For example, it has been pointed out that the US telephone company AT & T made important innovations throughout the period when it held almost a monopoly position in providing telephone services in the United States. The invention of laser technology and transistor were two of its important contributions. However, Professor Stiglitz points out that ***"greater expenditure on research and development by AT & T was due to the regulation by government.*** He writes, AT & T was in a unique position. The prices it charged were set by government regulators and those prices were set that encouraged the expenditure of money on research. From this perspective

AT & T's research contribution was as much a consequence of government regulatory policy as of anything else."[1]

Rent-Seeking Activities of Monopolies

The last important source of economic inefficiency under monopoly is *their attempt to spend a lot of money in maintaining their monopoly position in the market rather than using their resources for productive purposes*. By maintaining their monopoly position, the monopolists continue making large monopoly profits. It may be noted that since these monopoly profits are over and above the opportunity costs of the capital invested by them and wages for the managerial services performed by the monopolists, they are often referred to as *monopoly rents*. Therefore, ***the attempts by the monopolists to maintain or acquire monopoly positions in some industries or in sale of some products or services so as to make monopoly profits is referred to as rent-seeking behaviour.***

Sometimes, monopoly position of a firm is the result of protection granted by government. Many developing countries grant a licence to a firm or few firms within their country to produce a product and thus providing a large market power or monopoly power to them which they use to make large profits. In addition, they ban the imports of some goods from abroad so as to prevent any competition from foreign manufacturers. To get these licences and protection from imports from abroad, these firms spend a lot of money for lobbying for them to maintain regulations that restrict competition and yield large profits to them. They liberally contribute to the election expenses of members of parliament and political parties. They even bribe bureaucrats to enforce regulations that favour them. Commenting on these rent-seeking activities, Prof. Stiglitz write ***"such activities are socially wasteful. Real resources (including labour times) are used to win favourable rules, not to produce goods and services. There is thus legitimate concern that the willingness of government to restrict competition will encourage firms to spend money on rent-seeking activities rather than on making a better product."***[2]

Further Disadvantages of Limited Competition

We have seen in the earlier chapters that oligopolies dominate the economy. In these oligopolies, there is limited competition among the few firms that operate to produce either the same or similar product. In oligopolies the output produced is lower than in perfect competition but is more than in monopoly. Though the expenditure on research and development to introduce new products and to discover superior techniques of production to reduce costs is quite intense under oligopoly, but other inefficiences are worse in oligopolies with limited competition. Oligopolistic firms spend more resources on practices to prevent entry of new firms in the industry so as to continue making large profits. An important way to deter entry of potential firms is to issue threat that if they dare to enter, they will reduce price to such a low level that the new entrants will suffer a great monetary loss. To make the threat credible, the existing oligopolistic firms *build excess capacity*. With excess capacity the existing firms can easily expand output to lower price of the product. This convince the potential entrants that if they enter the industry, the existing firms will lower price to compete them out. To deter entry the existing oligopolistic firms even resort to *predatory pricing*. ***Predatory pricing means the existing firms set price even below cost of production so as to inflict heavy losses on the new entrants.*** Unable to bear losses when the new entrants leave the industry, *the existing firms* raise prices so as not only to recover the earlier losses but to ensure

1. Joseph E, Stiglitz, *Economics, Second Edition,* p.290.
2. *Op. cit.*, p. 290

high sustained profits in future.

Besides, the oligopolists incur a lot of expenditure on competitive advertising to keep their market share in the product. Further, a large advertising expenditure is incurred to deter entry of potential entrants by influencing the consumers that their products are far better than others. However, the expenditure to deter entry may increase the profits of the existing oligopolistic firms facing limited competition but from the social point of view it involves wasteful expenditure and make consumers worse off. Thus, under oligopoly, firms facing limited competition operate with economic inefficiency.

PUBLIC POLICY TOWARDS MONOPOLY AND COMPETITION

Having discussed the drawbacks of monopolies and oligopolies, we will now explain how government intervenes to influence price charged and quantity produced by the firms working in monopolistic and oligopolistic markets. There are three ways in which government can influence these markets to achieve economic efficiency and to protect the interests of consumers.

1. *Nationalisation or Public Ownership* of the monopolistic and oligopolistic firms.
2. *Regulation of monopolies* so that they should charge such price and produce such quantities of goods which ensure economic efficiency and work in the best interests of public.
3. *To create competitive conditions and discourage monopolistc practices*.

It may be noted that the first two measures have been adopted to deal with monopolies, especially natural monopolies. In case of oligopolies, there is limited competition among the few firms and they often adopt certain business practices to prevent the entry of new firms or they join hand with each other to enter into agreements to promote collusion, formal or tacit. In this respect, the general public policy is to ***encourage competition.*** When encouraging competition does not work, government *passes legislation to enforce competition*.

We will discuss all the above three types of public policies to deal with monopolies and oligopolies.

Public Policy Towards Natural Monopoly : Nationalisation or Public Ownership

The first public policy approach towards natural monopoly is that government should take it under its ownership and run it as a nationalised enterprise. Before explaining the merits and demerits of public ownership of natural monopoly, it is necessary to clarify the meaning of natural monopoly. ***Natural monopoly in an industry is said to exist when there occur economies of scale over a large range of output due to which average cost of production steadly declines and the extent of market demand for a commodity is such that it can support only one big optimum-size firm.*** Under these circumstances a large-sized firm enjoying economies of scale and operating with a lower average cost of production can compete away the small-sized firms having higher average costs and can therefore succeed in establishing its monopoly. The examples of industries in which natural monopoly exists is distribution of electricity, water and gas in a city, rail transportation, air transportation, telephone services etc.

Let us first analyse how the working of a natural monopoly leads to economic inefficiency and causes loss of consumer's welfare. This is illustrated in Fig. 49.3 where *DD′* is the demand curve facing the natural monopolist. *ATC* is the average cost curve of the natural monopoly which, as will be seen from Fig. 49.3, is sloping downward throughout due to economies of scale. Marginal cost curve *MC* which shows changes in variable costs as extra units of output are produced is sloping downward. Note that average total cost curve *ATC* is falling throughout due to the economies of scale as more units of output are produced. Under perfect competition output Q_c will be produced at which marginal cost equals price of product P_c. But the natural monopoly maximises its profits by producing output Q_m at which its marginal revenue equals marginal cost and will set price equal to P_m and will make profits equal to $ABKP_m$. Natural monopoly is causing dead-weight loss equal to ANE and is, therefore, operating with economic inefficiency.

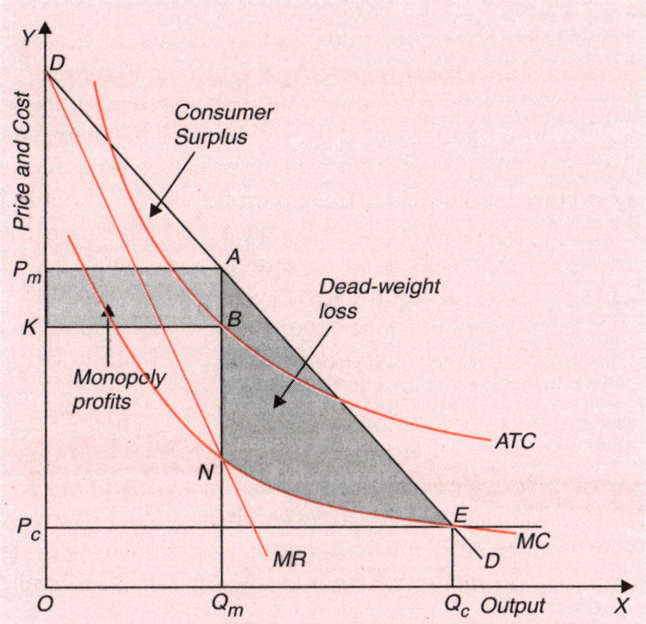

Fig. 49.3. *Profit Maximisation by a Natural Monopoly and its Economic Inefficiency*

But, as explained above, in the case of natural monopoly because of falling average cost throughout due to economies of scale, competition is ruled out. Under natural monopoly, average cost curve is declining throughout and marginal cost is less than it. Hence if a firm having a natural monopoly is asked to equate marginal cost with price, it will suffer losses as shown by the shaded area $EBSP_c$ in Fig. 49.4. If government wants the natural-monopoly firm to adopt this marginal-cost pricing policy it would have to grant subsidies to the firm equal to the shaded area. To finance subsidies, taxes would have to be imposed on the public. Thus grant of subsidies to the natural monopoly to make it work efficiently will impose costs on the society. Besides, it is very difficult to ascertain the amount of subsidies since the firm may inflate its costs.

As a result, instead of subsidising, government may decide to takeover the ownership of the firm having natural monopoly and operate it as a nationalised enterprise. In the UK this policy of nationalisation of natural monopolies in the field of railways, telephones, supply of electricity, gas and water was adopted during the period 1945 to 1951. In India too until recently the natural monopolies belonging to railways, post and telegraph, distribution of electricity and water, gas, telephone services have been in public ownership. In the last few years, distribution of electricity in cities like Delhi, Mumbai and Kolkata has been privatised. Also there has been privatisation of Telecom services and air transportation. But railways, post and telegraph are still in public ownership and are operated as nationalised enterprises.

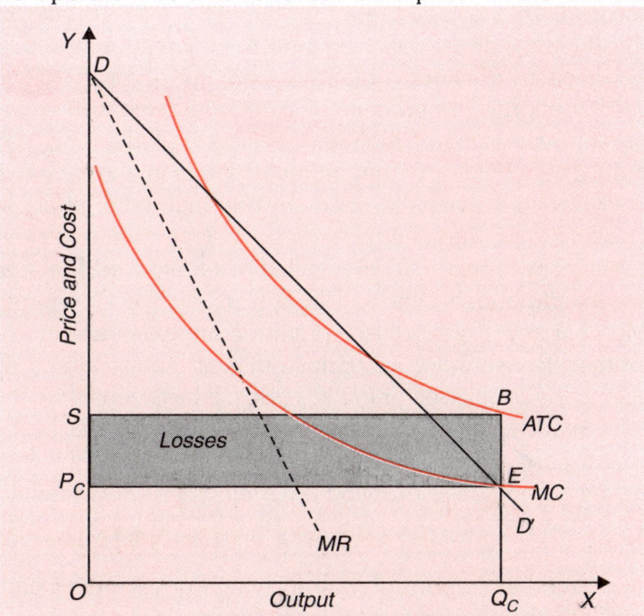

Fig. 49.4. *Natural Monopoly Making Losses on Equating MC with Price under Marginal Cost Pricing*

It was expected that, under government ownership, the natural monopolies would not abuse their monopoly power and would neither restrict output, nor charge high prices and thus work in public interest and achieve economic efficiency.

Problems of Nationalised Industries

But public ownership of natural monopolies has not been without problems. First, it has been pointed out that ***managers of public owned enterprises lack the incentives to minimise cost.*** Managers of a privately owned firms have incentives to minimise costs to make sufficient profits for the owners-shareholders in case of corporations to keep them satisfied. If the managers of a private firm are doing a bad job and not making sufficient profits, they will be fired by the owners of the firm. On the other hand, if bureaucrats who run a government-owned natural monopoly do a bad job, it is consumers and taxpayers who suffer because it is by taxing them that the losses of public-owned enterprises have to be met. The ability of managers of government-owned enterprises to obtain subsidies to cover the losses weaken their incentives to minimise cost. For the same reasons, bureaucrats who manage government-owned companies do not have any incentives to introduce any innovations to cut costs and improve the technology of production.

Besides, it has been found that in running public-sector enterprises governments often yield to temptation to interfere with the working of public sector undertakings to seek goals other than efficient operation. For example, in India, it has been observed that ***public sector undertakings have been overstaffed*** for sake of generating more employment. In Britain and some other European countries such as Sweden also the experience has been to provide public sector jobs to keep unemployment low, no matter whether extra employees are really required or not.

Further, as a result of incurring losses year after year public sector enterprises in the field of public utilities such as railways, electricity, telephone services etc. their investment plans have been severely constrained. For example in India losses of state electricity boards have been enormous which have adversely affected investment in the power sector. Government enterprises running the public utilities such as railways, electricity have been pressurised to provide some services at below their marginal cost, with the losses so incurred are made up by the profits made in other parts of business. This is often called *cross-subsidisation*. For example, the Indian Railways are required to maintain services on the loss-making routes which are financed by revenue obtained from more profitable routes. Another example of cross-subsidisation is the practice of Post and Telegraph Department of charging the same fee for delivering a piece of mail (e.g. registered letter or a parcel) between any two places within India as a whole or within any two points in a large city like Delhi.

Due to heavy losses made by nationalised or public sector enterprises and their inefficient working, there has been a tendency all over the world (including India) to sell these enterprises to the private sector. This is called *privatisation*. For example, in Delhi electricity distribution has been handed over to BSES (a Reliance Company) and NDPL (a Tata Company) . In Mumbai and Kolkata also, private companies are in charge of distribution of electricity. In Britain, British Telecom, British Gas and nationalised electricity and water companies were sold to the private sector in the 1980s. It has been found that after privatisation, these companies have made large profits and the prices of their shares have risen sharply. However, in order to cut costs, after privatisation these companies have made large cuts in employment and have contributed to growing unemployment in Britain and other European countries.

REGULATION OF NATURAL MONOPOLIES

Another important way in which government can deal with natural monopolies is to regulate their price and output. Privatisation can lead to more operational efficiency and enormous profits earned by the private owners but it cannot solve the basic problem and drawback of natural monopoly that it leads to a large market power enjoyed by private firms which exploits consumers by making enormous profits and causes loss of economic inefficiency. It is therefore necessary to regulate them and put restrictions on their behaviour so that they work in public interest and in economically efficient way. Therefore, even in Britain where previously nationalised industries in the field of public utilities have been privatised, regulatory commissions or committees have been appointed to regulate their behaviour.

Public Interest Theory and Marginal-Cost Pricing

One important theory of regulation is the *public interest theory*. According to public interest theory, the regulation of the firm having natural monopoly should be such as to ensure that it works with economic efficiency, that is, it should fix such price and output of the product or service that maximise the total surplus (sum of consumer surplus and producer surplus). Therefore, according to public interest theory, the regulation requires the firm to adopt *marginal-cost pricing*, as illustrated in Fig. 49.4. It will be seen from this figure that natural monopoly should be so regulated that it should charge price P_c and produce output Q_c at which marginal cost curve *MC* cuts the demand curve *DD′*. However, as explained above, with marginal-cost pricing the natural monopoly makes losses. This is because in a natural monopoly average total cost is falling throughout and marginal cost curve lies below it. Therefore, at output level at which marginal cost (*MC*) curve cuts demand curve and becomes equal to price, the average total cost will exceed price. As a result, with marginal cost equal to price the firm will make losses as shown by the shaded area in Fig. 49.4. Therefore, instead of charging such a low price that equals marginal cost and causes losses to the firm, the monopoly firm will just leave the industry. One response of public policy to this problem is to provide subsidy to the monopolist to compensate him for the losses. But, as pointed out above, to pay subsidy to the monopolist government will levy taxes on the people. However, taxation, as seen in an earlier chapter, involves dead-weight loss and reduce economic efficiency.

The second problem with marginal cost pricing as a regulatory policy is that it does not provide any incentive to reduce costs. Every firm working in a competitive market tries to minimise costs because lower costs mean more profits for it. But in case a of a regulated monopoly the firm knows whenever costs are reduced, the regulator will reduce prices and it will therefore not gain from making efforts to reduce costs. That is why to furnish incentives to reduce costs in actual practice regulators often allow the monopolists to retain some of the profits obtained through reduction in costs. However, this practice represents deviation from marginal-cost pricing.

Average-Cost Pricing

Due to the problems faced in marginal-cost pricing policy, especially when government does not want to give subsidies to the natural monopoly because of its financial costraint, average-cost pricing policy may be adopted. But if it is worthwhile to make investment in a public utility the monopolist must be assured of *fair return on capital*. The fair return on capital represents normal profits which are included in average cost of production. Thus, average-cost pricing policy regulates or fixes price equal to average cost of production which includes fair rate of return on capital invested by the firm. Consider Fig. 49.5. *DD′* is demand curve facing the firm owning a natural monopoly. *ATC* is the average total cost curve which includes fair return on capital invested. *MC* is the marginal cost curve. The regulator following average-cost pricing will set price P_a corresponding to which average total cost curve *ATC* intersects the given demand curve *DD′*. At this regulated price P_a, the firm will produce Q_a quantity of the product. It will be seen from Figure 49.5 that output Q_a is less than the output Q_c at which marginal cost (*MC*) equals price. Therefore, ***average-cost pricing leads to the level of output produced being less than the economically efficient output.*** As a result, average cost pricing causes *dead-weight loss of welfare* as shown by the shaded area.

The second problem facing average cost pricing policy is that under it monopoly firm has no incentive to reduce cost as it knows that if it cuts its costs, the regulatory authority will reduce the price and it will not therefore benefit from making efforts to reduce costs.

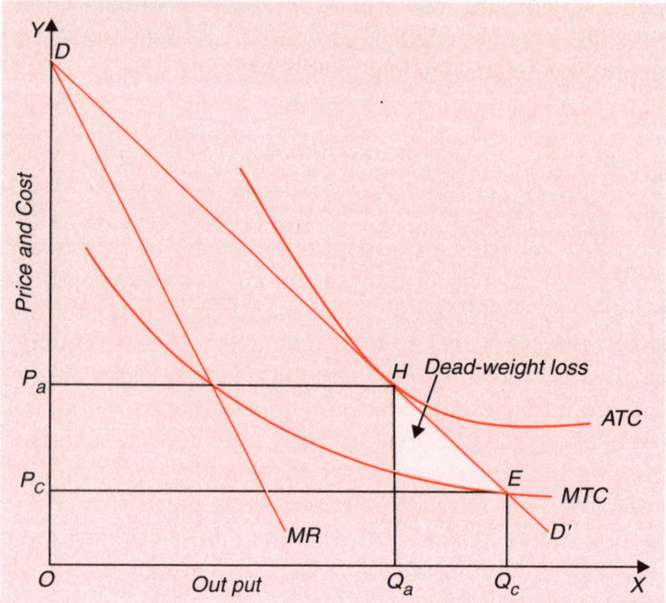

Fig. 49.5. *Average Cost Pricing to Regulate Natural Monopoly*

The third problem facing average-cost pricing is that since the firms are assured of a fair return on capital, they have a tendency to increase investment in capital as much as possible so as to obtain higher return on capital. This leads to too much investment. Besides, another problem of regulation through average-cost pricing is that firms have no incentives to innovate. This is because technological innovations reduce costs and as a result regualtors reduce price of the product, and therefore firms do not benefit from innovations introduced by them. In recent years, regulatory commissions in both the USA and the UK have realised that unless they reward the firms for introducing innovations, these will not be forthcoming. Therefore, in recent years business firms who by introducing technological innovations succeed in making profits, the regulators have allowed them to retain much of increased profits, at least for few years.

Capturing Regulators

But, the most serious problem of average-cost pricing is that ***regulators are often captured by the firms whom they are supposed to regulate.*** In contrast to public interest theory, according to capture theory, such regulations are framed that enable the monopolistic firms to maximise their producer surplus. So as a result of regulatory capture, regulatory authorities instead of trying to promote public interest, promote the interests of the monopoly firm. The monopoly firm often bribes the regulators to win them over. The fair return on capital is crucial for calculating average cost and fixing price on that basis. The monopoly firms often through bribe or otherwise succeed in misleading the regulators about true costs and fair return on capital. The managers of a monopoly firm often succeed in inflating their costs by spending a part of firm's revenues on inputs that are not really required. Keeping luxury cars, expensive office suits, lavish international travel, keeping company jets or helicopters, lavish entertainment expenditure are some of the ways in which monopoly firm inflates costs.

Explaining the reasons for capturing regulators based on experience of the UK and the US, Prof. Stiglitz writes, ***"regulators are pulled frequently into the cramps of those they regulate. This could happen through bribery and corruption but the much likelier way is just that over time employees of a regulated industry develop personal friendship with the regulators who in turn come to rely on their expertise and judgement. Worse, regulatory agencies (of necessity) tend to hire persons from the firms in the regulated industry. By the same token, regulators who demonstrate an "understanding " of the***

industry may be rewarded with good jobs in that industry after they leave government service"[3]. The above reasons apply equally well to India.

When the monopoly firm captures the regulator or succeeds in inflating the cost by misleading the regulator, the outcome is shown in Fig. 49.6. It will be seen from Fig. 49.6 that the firm of natural monopoly is maximising its profits by equating marginal cost (*MC*) with marginal revenue when it produces Q_m and charges P_m price. When the firm captures the regulator it makes the latter to fix price P_m which maximises its economic profits. The economic profits made by the monopoly firm in this situation when it captures regulator are shown by the shaded area P_aBHP_m in Fig. 49.6.

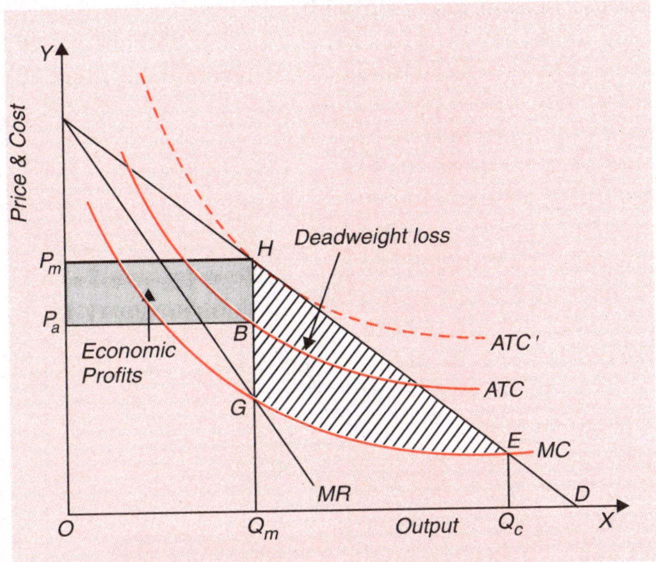

Fig. 49.6. *Outcome when Monopoly Firm Captures Regulator or Inflates Cost.*

The same outcome of profit maximising situation for the monopoly firm prevails if it succeeds in inflating its costs by misleading the regulator. With inflated costs, average total cost curve (*ATC*) shifts to the dotted position *ATC′* (inflated) which is tangent to the demand curve exactly vertically above the point *G* at which marginal cost equals marginal revenue and monopoly firm maximises its profits by producing output O_m. It will be further observed that with capturing the regulator or succeeding in inflating costs, dead-weight loss has increased to the stripped area *HGE*.

ENCOURAGING COMPETITION

The last way in which government can deal with natural monopoly is to encourage competition between firms, however imperfect competition it may be. This raises question as to how competition can be promoted in the field of natural monopoly when it is generally believed that competition in natural monopoly when average cost is falling over a large relevant range of output, is not viable. Suppose the two firms divide the market for a product of natural monopoly. Thus, we have duopolists competing in this natural monopoly industry. Why is competition not viable between the two ? This is illustrated in Fig. 49.7 where *ATC* is average total cost curve and *DD′* is the market demand curve for the product of natural monopoly which the two firms are sharing. If there were one monopolistic firm operating to meet the market demand, its profits would be maximised by producing output Q_m and charging price P_m. Now, when the two firms are sharing the market, suppose each is producing Q_d (half of Q_m) and its cost is AC_d. Now, any one firm can capture the entire market by cutting price below that of its rival firm. By expanding output beyond Q_d, it will be reducing its average cost. Having established its monopoly, it can set its price above AC_d and earn profits without worrying about the entry of any potential rivals trying to capture some of the profits. Potential rivals knows that on the entry by them the existing firm can afford to lower the price since it can

3. Joseph E. Stiglitz, *op. cit*, p. 291

enjoy economies of scale by expanding output. This deters the entry of new firms.

However, in the last three decades, in many countries efforts have been to introduce more competition in the industries of natural monopoly. In Britain bus services were deregulated and competition was promoted by allowing more firms to operate bus services. Competition has been introduced in telephone services in Britain by allowing more firms to use the cables already laid. In India too with the advances in telecom technology and advent of cellular telephones, more firms such as Airtel, Tata Indicom, Reliance have been allowed to provide telephone services. In Britain and India electricity generation has been separated from electricity distribution and more firms have been permitted to compete in generating electricity. Even electricity distribution has been privatised, different private firms have been given licenses to distribute electricity in specific areas.

In the USA and various countries of Europe and India too, airlines have been substantially deregulated and more than one air company has been allowed to compete. Thus, in India, Air Sahara, Jet Airways, Air Decean have been allowed to operate both within India and outside to compete with public sector companies. Increased competition has lowered fares and improved air services. Even there is now competition in the postal services with private courier companies providing the postal service.

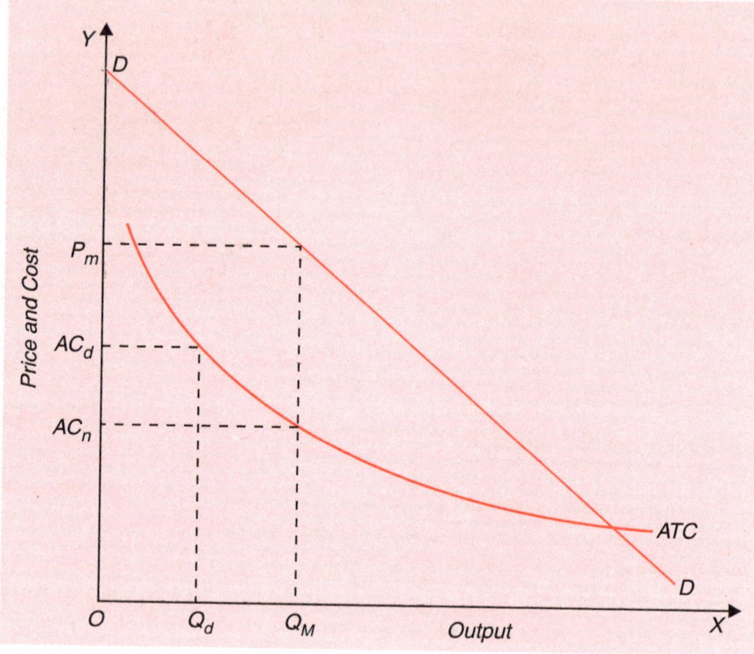

Fig. 49.7. *Natural Monopoly and Need for Competition*

But an important way monopoly firm can be subjected to competition is to allow imports of goods. When domestic monopolistic companies have to compete with the imported products, they will tend to charge lower prices to remain in business. However, competition from imports is more valid in case of other monopolistic and oligopolistic industries than in case of natural monopolies.

Increasing Competition through Anti-trust Law

In our above analysis, we have explained how public policy has tried to deal with natural monopolies. Government has also intervened to prevent *mergers* of the companies so as to prevent the creation of monopolies and to promote competition between them. When there is oligopoly, that is, there are a few firms in the industry, there is often a tendency among them to merge and form a cartel. A cartel is a collusive agreement among a number of firms aimed at restricting output and achieving larger profits for the member firms. In many countries *formation of cartel is illegal as it leads to monopoly and exploitation of the consumers*. However, international cartels such as famous OPEC (The Organisation of Petroleum Producing Countries) legally operate.

The oligopolies are regulated through enacting legislation such as *Anti-trust Law* which forbids the mergers of the firms which leads to the creation of monopolies. In the USA Sherman Anti-trust Law was passed in 1890 to reduce the market power of 'trusts' (oligopolies) that dominated the American economy at that time. The Sherman Act was amended in 1914 by the enactment of Clayton Act. Clayton Act of 1914 greatly strengthened the powers of government to proceed against any company or companies which try to create monopolies. According to this act, private law suits can also be filed in the courts if any company or companies which try to create monopoly or adopt monopolistic practices. It is this Anti-trust law that prevented Software giant Microsoft from buying Intuit in 1994. Similarly, the Department of Justice of the US started to enquire into the complaints of Microsoft competitors that the Microsoft monopolised the market for PC operating system (DOS and Windows) by making contracts with computer makers. These contracts made it difficult for firms producing other operating systems.

Recently, a US company Netscape, which produces a browser called Navigator complained against Microsoft that the latter was making available its web browser 'Internet Explorer' at a zero price which was unfair and monopolistic trade practice and not permissible under the US law. Microsoft's plea is that by making its Internet Explorer free of cost along with its Windows operating system it is giving consumers a greater value. The case is still pending in the court.

The Anti-trust laws provide government various ways in which it can intervene to promote competition. They give power to government to prevent mergers so as to prevent the creation of monopolies. The second, the anti-trust law empowers the government to break up companies to encourage competition. Thus, in the US a famous telecommunication company, AT&T was split up into eight small companies to encourage competition. Thirdly, antitrust laws prevent companies from coordinating their activities in ways that make markets less competitive.

It may be noted that all mergers of companies are not undesirable. Sometimes different firms merge not to reduce competition but to increase efficiency by joint operation and thus lower costs. The recent Indian Competition Act allows mergers of companies if they result in higher efficiency and lower costs but not in restricting competition. Some banks in India have merged in recent years to strengthen their financial position and to improve efficiency.

Thus crucial question is to examine whether formation of mergers of firms is to reduce competition or to improve efficiency and strengthen financial position. If merger is designed to reduce competition it is bad and undesirable, but if it is to improve efficiency and strengthen financial position of the firms without reducing competition it is desirable.

QUESTIONS FOR REVIEW

1. What is meant by managerial slack ? What does it mean when economists say that monopoly output is 'too little' or a monopoly price is "too high"? What benchmark do they use to claim this ?
2. Give reasons for the lack of incentives for the monopoly firm to lower costs as far as possible.
3. Why does a monopolistic firm lack incentives to make adequate expenditure on research and development (R & D) to make advances in technology ?
4. What is a natural monopoly ? Explain why average cost curve of a natural monopoly falls throughout ? What are the consequences of this ?
5. If regulatory authority of a natural monopoly sets price equal to marginal cost, what problem will arise ? How does nationalisation or regulation solve this problem?
6. What is public interest theory of regulation ? What price policy for a natural monopoly does it suggest ?
7. What is regulatory capture hypothesis? What are it consequences ?
8. How oligopolies are regulated so as to prevent them from merging and reducing competition?
9. Explain how competition is not viable in case of natural monopoly. How has government sought to promote competition in this case ?
10. What are the drawbacks of monopolies and limited competition ? Explain why there is need for regulation of monopolies and oligopolies with limited competition.

PART–V

THEORY OF DISTRIBUTION (PRICING OF FACTORS)

- Theory of Distribution: A General View
- Neo-classical Macro-Theory of Relative Distributive Shares
- Pricing of Factors in Competitive Markets
- Pricing of Factors in Imperfectly Competitive Markets
- Trade Unions, Collective Bargaining and Wages
- Theory of Rent
- Theories of Interest
- Theory of Profits
- Alternative Macro-Theories of Distribution

CHAPTER

50

Theory of Distribution: A General View

Functional vs. Personal Distribution

In the previous parts, we have discussed how the prices of products are determined in different market forms. The pricing of factors of production is the subject-matter of the present part. The theory of factor prices is popularly known as the *theory of distribution.* The distribution may be functional or personal. We are concerned with functional distribution in this book. The concept of functional distribution should be carefully distinguished from that of personal distribution. *Personal distribution* of national income or what is also known as *'size distribution of incomes'* means the distribution of national income among various individuals or persons in a society. As is well known, national income is not equally distributed among various individuals in the country. Some are rich, while others are poor. In fact, there are great inequalities of income between various individuals. Thus the theory of personal distribution studies how personal incomes of individuals are determined and how the inequalities of income emerge. On the other hand, in the theory *of functional distribution* we study how the various factors of production are rewarded for their services rendered in the pro-duction process. Factors of production have been classified by economists under four major heads *viz.*, land, labour, capital and enterprise. In the theory of functional distribution we study how the prices of these factors of production are determined. The prices of land, labour, capital and enterprise are called rent, wages, interest and profit respectively. Therefore, in the theory of functional dis-tribution we discuss how the rent of land, wages of labour, interest on capital and profits of entrepreneur are determined. To be brief, ***theory of functional distribution means the theory of factor pricing.*** To conclude, in the words of Professor Jan Pen, "in functional distribution, we are no longer concerned with individuals and their individual incomes, but with factors of production: labour, capital, land and something else that may perhaps best be called, 'entrepreneurial activity'. The theory examines how these factors of production are remunerated. It is primarily concerned with the price of a *unit* of labour, a *unit* of capital, a *unit* of land, and being an extension of price theory, it is sometimes called the theory of factor prices".[1]

The question that now arises is: Is it not the functional distribution that determines the personal distribution of national income. Personal distribution of income *only partly* depends upon functional distribution. How much income an individual will be able to get depends not only on the *price* of a particular factor he has but also on the *amount* of that factor he owns as well as the *prices* and the *amounts* of other productive factors which he may possesses. The ownership of resources is an institutional issue and is not determined by any economic factors but depends on legal property rights prevailing in a country. Thus the personal income of landlord depends not only on the rent but also on the amount of land he owns. Given the rent

1. Jan Pen, *Income Distribution,* Penguin Books, 1971, p. 16.

per acre, the greater quantity of land he owns, the greater will be his income. Further, the landlord may have lended some money to others for which he may be earning interest. The total income from interest on money will also add to his personal income. Thus, a person may be getting income from several sources *i.e.*, from the earnings of various factors of production. The earnings from all the sources will constitute his personal income. If our landlord does not do any other work and owns no other` factor of production, his personal income will depend on the rates of rent and interest and also on the amount of land he owns and has given on rent and the amount of money he has lent out.

Thus,"***Personal distribution* (or, *the size distribution of incomes*)** relates to individual persons and their income. The *way in which* that income was acquired often remains in the background. What matter is how much someone earns, not so much whether that income consists of wage, interest, profit, pension or whatever.[2] The total income from rent and interest will make up his personal income. Theory of personal distribution of income has therefore to explain not only how prices or rewards for factors such as rent of land, interest on capital are determined but also *how various people happen to own different quantities of these productive factors.* The theory of functional distribution, or the theory of factor prices, as it is often called, is thus only a part of theory of personal distribution.

Before we proceed further we would like to remove one confusion. It is that when we say how the prices of factors are determined, by that we do not really mean the prices of the factors *themselves.* By the prices of the factors, we mean the prices of their *services* or *use* for a period of time. Thus in factor pricing we do not study how the price or value of land as such is determined, instead we study how *the price for the use of land,* which is called rent, is determined. Similarly, in the theory of factor prices, we do not explain how the price of labourer as such is determined (the labourer never sells himself, he sells only his labour or *service* for a period), but we study how the price for the use or service of labour for a period, which is called the wage rate, is determined. It is only for the sake of convenience and brevity that we speak of pricing of factors while we actually mean the pricing of their *services* or *uses.*

Micro and Macro Theories of Distribution

Even the 'functional distribution' of income can be studied from two viewpoints *viz.*, micro and macro. The micro theory of distribution explains how the *rates of reward* for various factors of production are determined. In other words, the micro theory of distribution deals with the determination of *relative prices* of productive factors. It thus studies how the wage rate of labour, how the rate of rent on land, the rate of interest etc. are determined. On the other hand, the macro theory of distribution deals with the problem of the determination of *aggregate rewards* of various factors in the total national income. In other words, the macro distribution means the *relative shares* of various factors in national income. Therefore, the macro-theory of distribution is also known as the *theory of distributive shares.* Thus, the macro-theory of distribution or. distributive shares tells us as to how the share of labour in the national income.(*i.e.*, the total amount of all wages of all labourers in an economy) is determined. Similarly, the macro-theory of distribution explains how the share of rent in the national income (total amount of rent earned on all lands in the economy), the share of profit in the national income (the total amount of profits earned by all entrepreneurs in the country) are determined. To quote Professor Jan Pen again, "The theory of distributive shares attempts to explain the share of the total national income that each factor of production receives. It enquires into the percentage that labour receives of the whole, and also into the shares of interest, rent and profit. Now, individual income recipients disappear beyond the horizon.[3]

2. *Op. cit*, p. 15.
3. *Op. cit*, p. 18.

Theory of Distribution as a Special Case of Price Theory

It is worth mentioning here that in modern economic theory, theory of distribution is only a special case of the theory of price. As the prices of products are explained with the interaction of the demand for and supply of them, similarly distribution is conceived as the determination of prices of the factors which are also explained with interaction of demand for and supply of them. The income which a factor will obtain depends on the price determined by market, *i. e.,* demand and supply and the amount that will be used or employed of that factor. In other words, it is mainly the forces of free market, that is, demand and supply that go to determine the incomes of various factors and not any institutional framework such as ownership of property. Further, the association of various factors with particular social classes, such as land with land-owning class, capital with capitalists, and labour with the working class is also not emphasized. In fact, the factors are conceived merely as productive agents and distribution of income among them as merely functional rewards for their contribution to production. In other words, contemporary theory of distribution merely explains functional distribution of income and not a personal distribution of income.

The problem of income distribution in a free market economy reduces to the question of factor prices which are determined by demand for and supply of factors. Prof. A. K. Das Gupta describes the nature of contemporary distribution theory most candidly. He remarks, "distribution appears an extension of the theory of value..... *being just a problem of pricing of factors of production.* The two aspects of the economic problem are then integrated into a unified and logically self-consistent system. Value of a commodity is derived in the ultimate analysis from utility, and value of factors derived from productivity imputed by the commodities which they help in producing. The old tripartite division of factors into'land, labour and capital is retained but their old association with social classes is lost. Factors are conceived as just productive agents independently of the institutional framework within which they operate."[4]

MARGINAL PRODUCTIVITY THEORY OF DISTRIBUTION

We now turn to the question as to what determines the prices of factors of production. A theory which tries to answer this question and which has been fairly widely held by professional economists is known *as marginal productivity theory of distribution.* It may however be pointed out that in recent years its popularity has somewhat declined due to bitter criticisms levelled against it. The essence of this theory is that the price of a factor of production depends upon its marginal productivity. It also seems to be very fair that a factor of production should get its reward according to the contribution it makes to the total output, *i.e.* , its marginal productivity. Marginal productivity theory was first put forward to explain the determination of wage *i.e,* reward for labour but subsequently prices of other factors of production such as land, capital etc. also were explained with doctrine of marginal productivity.

The origin of the concept of marginal productivity can be traced to Ricardo and West. But both Ricardo and West applied the marginal productivity doctrine only td land. The concept of marginal productivity is implicit in the Ricardian Theory of Rent. But the idea of marginal productivity did not gain much popularity till the last quarter of 19th century, when it was re-discovered by economists like J.B. Clark, Jevons, Wicksteed, Walaras and later Marshall and J.R. Hicks popularised the doctrine of marginal productivity. It may however be pointed out that there are many versions of marginal productivity theory . Theories of marginal productivity propounded by various economists differ from each other in some respects. There are in fact so many versions of marginal productivity theory that Joseph Schumpeter has gone so far as

4. A. K. Das Gupta, *Tendencies in Economic Theory,* Presidential Address delivered at the 43rd Annual Conference of the Indian Economic Association, held at Chandigarh, December, 1960.

to remark that there are almost as many marginal productivity theories as there are ecomomists.[5] We shall explain here the views or versions of J. B. Clark, Marshall and Hicks, as these will provide all the points at issue concerning marginal productivity theory. Since marginal productivity theory has been mainly evolved for the determination of reward for labour, we shall discuss below its application to wage determination. But it should be understood to apply equally to the rewards of other factors of production.

Marginal Productivity Theory : Clark's Version

J. B. Clark, an American economist, developed marginal productivity theory of distribution in a number of articles and later on presented it in complete form as an explanation for the distribution of wealth in a country in his book *"The Distribution of Wealth"*. In order to bring out the fundamental factors at work in the mechanics of income distribution, Clark assumed a *completely static society,* free from the disturbances caused by economic growth or change. In other words, he assumed constant population, a constant amount of capital and unchanging techniques of production. ***"By isolating from the process of economic change and development***, Clark attempted to find the ***"natural values"*** of wages and other productive factors towards which all *actual values* in the real dynamic world around us tend at any moment of time."[6] Besides the assumption of static economy, he has also assumed perfect competition in the factor market and perfect mobility on the part of both labour and capital.

Besides assuming that total stock of capital remains constant, Clark also supposes that the ***form of capital*** can be varied at will. In other words, physical instruments of production can be adapted to varying quantities and abilities of available labour. Further, ***he treats labour as a homogeneous factor by taking identical labour units*** and discusses how the wage rate of labour is determined.

Optimal use or employment of a factor. Every rational employer or entrepreneur will try to utilize his existing amount of capital so as to maximize his profits. For this he will hire as many labourers (labour units) as can be profitably put to work with the given amount of capital. For an individual firm or industry, marginal productivity of labour will decline as more and more workers are added to the fixed quantity of capital. He will go on hiring more and more labour units as long as the addition made to the total product by a marginal labour unit is greater than the wage rate he has to pay for it. The employer will reach equilibrium position when the wage rate is just equal to the marginal product of labour.

Just consider the adjoining Fig. 50.1 where units of labour are represented on the X-axis and the marginal product of labour on the *Y*- axis. The *MP* curve shows the diminishing marginal product of labour as more units of it are employed. If the prevailing wage rate which an employer must pay is equal to *OW,* then it will be profitable for the employer to go on employing additional workers until the marginal product of labour becomes equal to the prevailing wage rate *OW.* It will be evident from Fig. 50.1 that if the prevailing wage rate is *OW,* then the employer will employ *OL* units of labour, since the marginal productivity of labour is equal to *OW* at *OL* employment of labour. He would not employ more than *OL* amount of labour as the marginal product of labour will fall below the wage rate *OW* and he would therefore be incurring losses on the employment of marginal workers beyond *OL*. Thus the employer would be maximizing his profits by equalizing the marginal product with the wage rate *OW.* Since perfect competition is assumed to be prevailing in the labour market, an individual firm or industry will have got no control over the wage rate. An individual firm or industry has therefore to determine only the number of factor units (labour in the present case) to which it

5. J. Schumpeter : *History of Economic Analysis*, p. 939.
6. A.M. Cartter : *Theory of Wages and Employment*, p. 14. (italics supplied)

has to give employment at the prevailing (existing) wage rate. Thus, at micro level *(i.e.,* for individual firm or industry) marginal productivity theory is the theory of employment.

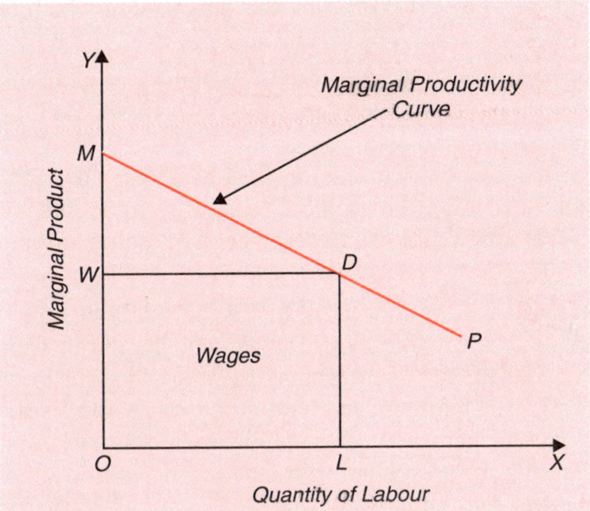

Fig. 50.1. *Wage rate is equalised with marginal productivity of labour*

Determination of a Factor Price

A marginal-product schedule or curve shows a particular wage-employment relationship. Since Clark has assumed a stationary state, ***he takes the total supply of labour available for employment in the whole economy as given and constant.*** In other words, in Clarkian analysis, aggregate supply curve of labour has been assumed to be *perfectly inelastic*, that is, it is of vertical shape.Given the total supply of labour in the economy, the wage rate will be determined by the marginal product of the availiable amount of labour assuming that all labour get employment. Given the aggregate amount of labour that is seeking employment, the wage rate that the labourers will secure will be equal to the *addition made to the total product* by the employment of the marginal unit of labour. In other words, if the total quantity of labour seeking employments is '*n*' units, then each unit of labour will get wage which will be equal to the difference between total production when *n* labour units were employed and that when *n* -1 labour units were employed. In other words, in the competitive labour market the wage rate will be ***determined by the marginal product of a given quantity of labour force.***

If the labourers compete with each other for obtaining jobs, they will bid the wage rate down if some of them find themselves unemployed. The employers will bid the wage rate up if the prevailing wage rate is smaller than the marginal product of available labour force. This is so because at the wage rate lower than marginal product the employers' demand for labour force will be more than the available number of labourers. Consider Fig. 50.2. In this figure, *MP* curve shows diminishing marginal product of labour as more units of labour are employed in the economy, assuming the quantities of other factors used as unchanged. Now, if the available quantity of labour force is *OL* in the whole economy, *LS* is the supply curve of labour which is perfectly inelastic. The marginal product of *OL* quantity of labour is *LD*. The wage rate will be determined by this marginal product *LD* and, therefore, equilibrium wage rate which will be determined by demand for and supply of labour in the

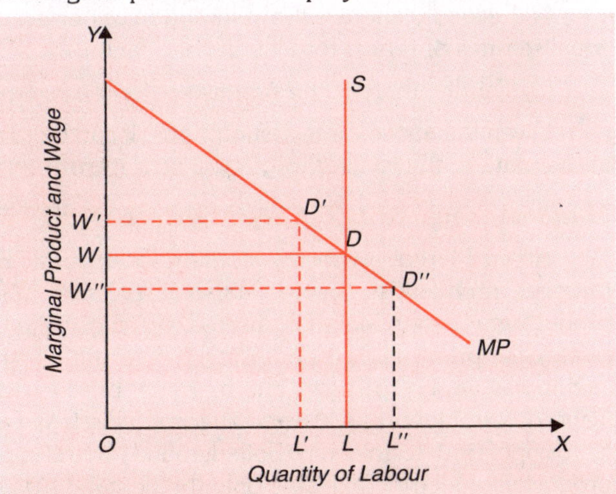

Fig. 50.2. *Wage rate is determined by marginal productivity*

market will be equal to *LD* or *OW.* At a higher wage rate *OW* ′, the employers will employ *OL*′ amount of labour leaving *LL*′ amount of labour unemployed. Unemployed workers in their attempt to get employment will bring the 'wage rate down to the level *OW* at which all are employed.

On the other hand, at a lower wage rate than *OW,* say *OW* ′′, the employers will demand *OL*″ amount of labour since their profits will be maximum if they are employing *OL*″ amount of labour at the wage rate OW″. But the available amount of labour is *OL*. Thus, at a lower wage rate than *OW*″ the demand for labour by the employers will be greater than the available supply of labour. In tlieir bid to get more labour, competition among employers will push the wage rate up to *OW* at which wage rate the employers demand just the same amount of labour which is actually available.

If the actually available labour force in the whole economy is *OL*″, that is, labour supply curve is vertical line *LD*″, then the marginal productivity of labour force in equiliburium will be *L*″*D*″ and therefore the wage rate will be equal to *OW*″. If the actual quantity of labour force is *OL*′, then the wage rate will be equal to *OW*′. Thus, given the quantity of labour in the country, wage rate is *determined* by marginal productivity of labour. One assumption which is implicit in the Clarkian marginal productivity theory as applied to the economy as a whole is that *of full employment*. In other words, it is assumed that the existing amount of labour in the economy is fully employed. To sum up 'in Clark's presentation, the marginal productivity of a given quantity of available labour determines.its wage level when we consider the market as a whole. In the disaggregated picture, however, where a single employer finds the wage level determined by the forces beyond his control, the marginal product of labour determines the level of employment.[7]

Clark's marginal productivity theory of distribution may be divided for analytical purposes into the following three component parts:-[8]

(1) There is the premise that a rational employer will be guided by the marginal productivity of the factor in determining the number of units of that factor he has to employ. This premise has been called by Prof. Cartter as *the* ***marginal productivity principle.*** (This is essentially based on the twin assumptions that die law of diminishing returns is working and that the employers are rational).

(2) Secondly, there is the assumption of perfect competition so that market forces tend to equalise rates of return for all units of a factor.

(3) Thirdly, there is the premise of long-run general equilibrium in all market.

Given the above three assumptions, it can be said that with a given fixed supply of labour in the market, the level of wages will be *determined* by the marginal product of labour.

Marginal Productivity Theory: Marshall-Hicks' Version

Alfred Marhall, who was contemporary of J. B. Clark, gave a different version of the marginal productivity theory. Marshall's version has been called by many as ***the*** marginal productivity theory. Marshall differed with those like Clark who held that wage rate (or for that matter, the price of any other factor) is determined by the marginal product of labour. Marshall said it was wrong to regard the marginal productivity principle or doctrine in the matter of wage determination as a *wage theory.* This is because he believed that wage rate (or any factor price) is determined by both demand for and supply of labour. According to him, Marginal productivity doctrine explains only the demand side of the problem. That is, given the wage

7. Allan M. Cartter, *Op. cit.*, p. 18
8.*Ibid.*, p. 18.

rate, a rational employer will employ as many units of labour as will equalize the wage rate with the marginal product of labour. At different wage rates, the employers will employ different amounts of labour units, depending upon the corresponding amount of the value of the marginal product. Thus, according to Marshall, the relationship between the wage rate and the marginal productivity of labour provides us with the demand curve of labour. For a complete theory as an explanation for wage determination, the supply curve of labour has also to be introduced into the analysis. The wage rate at which the upward-sloping supply curve of labour cuts the demand curve of labour (governed by the marginal productivity doctrine) will be *determined.* No doubt, the wage rate thus determined by demand and supply will be equal to the marginal product. It is worth quoting Marshall himself on this point: "This doctrine has sometimes been put forward as a theory of wages. But there is no valid ground for any such pretension..... Demand and supply exert equally important influence on wages, neither has a claim to predominance any more than has either blade of scissors or either pier of an arch....... (but) the doctrine throws into clear light the action of one of the causes that govern wages."[9]

It is clear from the above quotation from Marshall that he considered marginal productivity principle (which he calls the marginal productivity doctrine) as one of the two forces that *determine* wages, the other force being the supply of labour. Marshall believed that wages would tend to be equal to the marginal product, but he emphasised several times that the wages are not determined by marginal product, since like all other marginal quantities, marginal product is determined, *together with the price* (wage) by the interaction of demand and supply. In our view. However, the difference between Clark's version and Marshall's version lies in the nature of supply curve of a factor, e.g. of labour. While Clark considers labour supply curve of labour as perfectly inelastic at the given quantity of labour force. Marshall regards it as sloping upward.

Furthermore, Marshall ponted out that the marginal productivity doctrine plus the competitive conditions in the labour market would in the long run tend to make the wages of labour in different industries or *uses equal to eachother* and to the marginal product (assuming of course that labour is homogeneous). Another reason why Marshall rejected Clark' s version of marginal productivity theory and also therefore why he declined to call the marginal productivity doctrine as a theory of wages was his opposition to the use of the assumption of stationary state in his theory of distribution. As pointed out earlier, Clark' marginal productivity theory is dependent upon the rigid application of the stationary state abstraction Though Marshall made use of the technique of stationary state abstraction in his theory of product prices, but in his distribution theory he greatly qualified the technique of stationary state by introducing some dynamic elements in it. Marshall in his theory of distribution allowed for the gradual growth of population and for the changes in capital accumulation. Marshall pointed out that the changes in the real wages would, in the long run, affect the growth of population and, therefore, influence the size of labour force or supply of labour. Further, according to Marshall, the changes in the return on capital would greatly affect the present and future level of savings and would therefore bring about changes in capital accumulation. Clark in his theory of distribution had assumed away the changes in population (or labour force) and capital accumulation as a result of the changes in the factor rewards and thereby ignored the long-run repercussions of the changes in the factors rewards.

On another point also Marshall expressed his dissatisfaction with clark's version of marginal productivity theory and this difference was due to the fact that Marshall was more concerned with immediate short-run problems of individual employers. A relevant problem for the marginal productivity theory is to ascerain the marginal productivity of labour *separately* from the

9. Marshall, *Principles of Economics*, p. 518.

productive contribution of capital. This is because the employer (producer) has a joint demand for doses of combined labour and capitil. Clark, as *noted above,* **in order to find out the marginal productivity of labour separately assumed that the form of capital could be suitably adapted so that a given quantity of capital could be used with any number of labourers.** Since the adaptability or variation in the form of capital can be achieved only in the long run, Marshall did not adopt this technique of separating out the marginal productivity of labour. Instead, he evolved the concept of marginal **net** productivity of labour. Marginal *net* productivity of labour is obtained by measuring the marginal product of the joint addition of labour and capital and *subtracting from it the cost of capital*. The concept of marginal *net* product is essential and very useful for the employer who is to make short-run adjustments in the amount of labour used. It may however he pointed out that later writers such as Pigou,

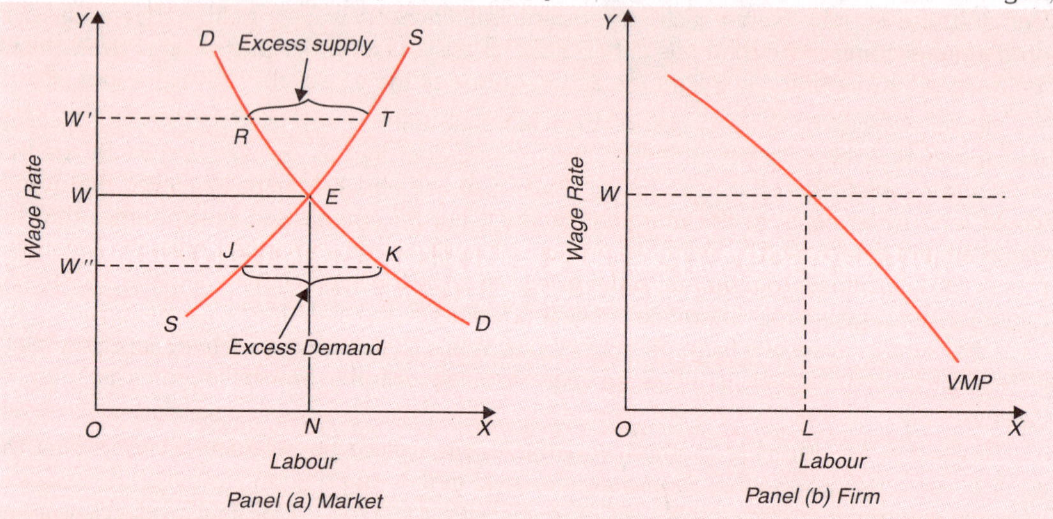

Fig. 50.3. *Wage Rate is Determined by Demand and Supply and is Equal to VMP of Labour.*

Robertson and Hicks did not adopt the concept of marginal *net* productivity of labour and instead like Clark, relied upon the adaptation of the form of capital in ascertaining labour's marginal productivity separately .

For the purpose of illustration, let us take the case of the factor labour and the price of its use, the wage rate, and explain how Marshall-Hicks' marginal productivity theory explains the determination of wages. It will be seen from Figure. 50.3 that the demand curve for labour as derived from the marginal productivity curve is given by *DD* which slopes downward to the right. On the other hand, supply curve of labour is sloping upward showing that as the wage rate rises, the amount of labour supplied to a given occupation or use will increase. Even for the economy as a whole, the supply curve of labour can slope upward indicating positive response of labour to the rise in the wage rate. It willL be seen from panel *(a)* of Fig. 50.3 that the demand and supply curves of labour intersect at point *E* and the labour market is in equilibrium with *OW as* the wage rate and *ON* quantity of labour employed. Thus, with the working of competitive forces, wage rate *OW* and level of employment *ON* are determined through the interaction of demand for and supply of labour. However, since demand curve for labour *DD* is a *horizontal summation of marginal products curves* of labour of all firms demanding labour from the market, wage rate so determined will be equal to marginal product of labour employed. If somehow wage rate *OW'* is prevailing, quantity demanded of labour *W'R* at this wage rate falls short of quantity supplied *W'T* at this wage rate. Under such a situation all workers who want work at this wage rate will not get jobs and will therefore become *involuntary* unemployd or, in other words, *exess supply* of labour will emerge. The competition among these unemployed workers will bring down the wage rate to the equilibrium level *OW*. On the other hand, if wage rate somehow is lower than *OW*, say *OW* ″, the excess demand for labour will emerge. This excess demand for labour will lead to the competition among employers which will result in rise in the wage rate to *OW*.

With *OW* as the given wage rate, it is evident from panel *(b)* of Figure 50.3 that each firm will employ *OL* amount of labour because with *OL* labour employment value of marginal produce *(VMP)* of labour is equal to the given wage rate. A firm operating under perfect competition equates the given wage rate with the value of marginal product of labour *(VMP)* so as to maximise profits.

Thus, according to Marshall and Hicks, under competitive conditions, wage rate and likewise other factor prices are determined by demand for and supply of a factor and are equal to value of the marginal product of the factor. It is however important to note that even in Marshall's model of marginal productivity theory which is also generally described as demand-supply theory of factor pricing, *full employment of labour prevails* is the equiliburium situation. Thus is Fig. 50.3, at the equilibrium wage rate *OW* that is determined by labour market equiliburium all those workers who want employment at this wage rate are in fact employed, that is, there is no involuntary unemployment. As noted above, in Clark's model and Marshall's model, the difference lies only in the nature of supply curve of labour. Whereas Clark considers supply curve of labour as perfectly inelastic at the given and constant labour force Marshall thinks it to be sloping upward. In both of them there is full employment of labour in the equilibrium situation.

Critical Evaluation of Marginal Productivity Theory

Marginal productivity theory has been a pillar in the neo-classical theory of income distribution and even in modern microeconomics it constitutes an important factor in the determination of factor prices. As mentioned above, there is no certainty as to what marginal productivity theory means or explains, since there exist many versions of the theory. Much of the criticism of the theory may be attributed to the conflicting interpretations of the theory given by its supporters. For instance, some of the protagonists of the theory believed that with the marginal productivity theory they not only succeeded in explaining the present system of distribution of income or the way how factor prices were determined but also succeeded in showing its *moral desirability*. In other words, they thought that the prices of factors are not only determined by marginal productivity but that the factors *ought to be paid* in accordance with their marginal productivity. In their view, factor prices are not only determined by and equal to marginal products but it is also socially just and ethically desirable that the various factors be paid according to their contribution to the total national product *i.e.,* equal to their marginal productivity.

In order to properly evaluate the marginal productivity theory, it is useful to remember that there are at least two views—Clarkian and Marshallian—of the marginal productivity theory differing mainly in their inclusiveness. Clarkian version of marginal productivity theory states that in the long run under conditions of competitive equilibrium and fixed factor supplies, factor prices are determined by marginal productivity and price of a factor in all its various uses will tend to be equal. On the other hand, Marshallian version says that only the demand for a factor is determined by marginal product of the factor. However, even in the Marshallian version the price of a factor, in equilibrium, will be equal to its marginal product and the price of a factor in all its various uses will tend to be equal in the long run.

Clarkian theory includes the Marshallian doctrine and claims more than the latter. As we shall see below, Marshallian doctrine which we preferred to call marginal productivity *principle* rather than *theory* in our above analysis, still constitutes the heart of modern theory of factor pricing, We shall diccuss below in detail the various objections raised against marginal productivity theory and shall indicate which objections are valid and which ones are based upon only misinterpretation of the theory and are thus misplaced. Most of the criticisms have been levelled against the Clarkian version, but some objections have been raised on the very concept of marginal product and therefore apply equally to the Marshallian principle of marginal productivity which is a fundamental doctrine of the modern theory of factor pricing.

1. Marginal Productivity theory is based on several unrealistic assumptions. It has often been argued that marginal productivity theory takes too many assumptions which are quite unrealistic. Therefore, it is concluded that theory has no validity. The theory of marginal productivity (Clarkian version) assumes a stationary state, perfect competition, perfect mobility of factors, equal bargaining power of buyers and sellers, and perfect knowledge, which are all far away from the actual conditions of the real world. World is not static. Instead, developments are continually taking place, making the actual world a dynamic one. Competition is not perfect, instead there are large imperfections in the factor markets which make any analysis of factor pricing based on the assumption of perfect competition quite useless. Bargaining powers of buyers and sellers of factor services, for instance, of employers and labourers, are not equal and thus make the exploitation of the weaker party possible.

"Prof. Paul Douglas[10], an advocate of marginal productivity theory, has given the following list of implicit assumptions made by marginal productivity theory.

(*i*) Employers are able to measure and predict in advance the marginal product of a factor.
(*ii*) There is free and complete competition among employers.
(*iii*) Labour knows its marginal productivity.
(*iv*) There is free and complete competition among workers for jobs.
(*v*) Capital is perfectly mobile.
(*vi*) Labour is perfectly mobile.
(*vii*) All labour is employed.
(*viii*) All capital is employed.
(*ix*) Bargaining power of labour and management are equal.
(*x*) Government does not interfere in the wage agreement.

At a first glance at these assumptions one gets the impression that a theory which makes such unrealistic assumptions can be hardly useful. But Prof. Douglas had made a strong plea in defence of this theory. He has *pointed out* that most of the assumptions are reasonably good description of actual long-run market conditions and are thus generally valid over time.

2. Under Imperfect Competition, factor rewards are not equal to value of marginal product. Another significant criticism levelled against marginal productivity theory (both Clarkian and Marshall-Hicks's versions) is that being based upon the assumption of perfect competition both in product and factor markets, it is unable to explain the determination of factor prices under conditions of imperfect competition in the factor and product markets. As we shall in the next chapter, following the developments of imperfect and monopolistic competition theories by Joan Robinson and Chamberlin, there emerged two concepts of marginal productivity, namely, marginal revenue product (*MRP*) and value of the marginal product (*VMP*). Thus, when there prevails imperfect competition in the product market (assuming perfect competition

10. Paul Douglas, *Theory of Wags*, p. 68.

in the factor market) a factor of production would not get remuneration equal to the value of the marginal product as it is generally presumed in the marginal productivity theory. Under imperfect competition in the product market, a factor of production is remunerated according to a different principle, namely, marginal revenue product *(MRP)* which is less than the value of the marginal product (*VMP*). According to Joan Robinson[11], a factor is *exploited* if it is paid less than the value of its marginal product, whereas in marginal productivity theory, as it was presented in neo-classical economic thought, there *was just and fair* distribution of total product; every factor getting equal to its contribution to the total production.

We are therefore of the view that in the context of imperfect competition in the product markets, marginal productivity theory needs to be modified.

3. Factors do not get reward equal to MRP in conditions of monopsony. If imperfect competition or monopsony prevails in the factor market, a factor will not get the reward even equal to its marginal revenue product *(MRP)*. Under imperfect competition or monopsony or oligopsony in the factor market, the firm to be in equilibrium, will equate marginal wage of labour with the marginal revenue product of labour and, as shall be seen later, this marginal wage is greater than the average wage or the wage rate which will be paid to the labour. We shall graphically explain this in the next chapter as to how the wage rate determined under conditions of monopsony is less than even the marginal revenue product (*MRP)* of labour. When a factor is paid less than its marginal revenue product, Joan Robinson calls it ***monopsonistic exploitation***[12]. We thus see that under monopsony or imperfect competition, factors do not get rewards equal to their marginal revenue product. Marginal productivity theory as it was presented by Marshall and Hicks, did not visualise the possibility of exploitation of labour or any other factor of production.

4. Marginal Productivity theory cannot explain rewards of the factors used in fixed proportions. Another serious shortcoming of marginal productivity theory is that it cannot explain the rewards of the factors which are used in fixed proportions. Marginal productivity takes it granted that a good degree of elasticity of substitution exists between the factors of production so that increase in one factor, keeping other factors constant, leads to the increase in the addition to the total product, that is, it has a *positive* marginal productivity and therefore gets *positive* reward for its contribution to production. But when the factors are used in fixed proportions, increase in one factor keeping the others constant, will not lead to any increase in total production at all. That is to **say, *in case af fixed proportions or fixed relations between the factors, marginal productivity of the factors will be zero.*** In view of their zero marginal productivity, according to the marginal productivity theory, their rewards or prices should also be zero.

But this is quite absurd; the factors of production, even when they have fixed relations with each other, obtain positive rewards. To quote Prof. J. Pen, "If the relation between labour and capital were fully fixed— as many people think it is— the traditional distribution theory would collapse. 'For if the relation between *L (i.e.,* labour) and *K(i.e.* capital) is fixed the marginal product of both is zero. An addition of a unit of labour, with equipment constant, yields nothing, any more than an extra amount of capital, without the addition of labour, would. In such a case the wage would also be zero, and also the interest. That is of course nonsense ; in fact a wage rate and an interest rate come about even with fixed relations between *L* and *K*, but the marginal productivity theory is no longer suitable for explaining them. Recourse must then be had to other principles.[13]

11. Joan Robinson, *Economics of Imperfect Competition*, p. 283.
12. *Ibid*, p. 295.
13. *Op. cit.*, p. 82.

5. Marginal productivity theory neglects the role of labour unions in influencing the wage rate. Still another serious drawback of marginal productivity theory is that, in its original and rigid version, trade unions or collective bargaining cannot raise the wages of labour without creating unemployment. Thus, according to this theory, trade unions are superfluous and collective bargaining by them is a futile activity. Given the downward-sloping nature of the marginal productivity curve, at the higher wage secured by the union, the employer will demand or employ less number of workers than before so that some labour will be rendered unemployed. But, as we shall see in a later chapter, increase in wage rate by the union does not always cause unemployment. Indeed, we shall study there that under conditions of monopsony, the increase in the wage rate by the union may be accompanied by the increase in employment rather than the creation of unemployment. As noted above, under conditions of imperfect competition, in the product and factor markets, labour (or any other factor) is exploited, that is, paid less than the value of its marginal product or less than its marginal revenue product. In this context trade unions can play a useful role of removing exploitation of labour by getting the wage rate raised to the level of value of marginal product or marginal revenue product.

6. Marginal productivity theory wrongly applied to the macro-analysis of wage-employment relashionship. Marginal productivity theory has also been criticised for its application to macroeconomic field and wrong conclusions drawn in this connection. At times of severe depression and huge unemployment during the thirties, A. C. Pigou, a famous neo-classical economist, argued on the basis of marginal productivity theory that cut in wages of labour in the whole economy would bring about increase in employment, since, given the falling marginal revenue productivity curve of labour, at a lower wage rate more labour will be employed and economy would be able to get out of depression. Thanks to J. M. Keynes who successfully challenged the above argument. According to him, what is valid in the case of a single industry or firm may not be valid for the economy as a whole. He argued for the macro-view of the problem, according to which wage is not only the cost of production to a firm or industry but also an income for the labourers who constitute a majority in the society. Therefore, according to Keynes, if all-round cut is made in the wages of the working class, their incomes will decline, which in turn would bring about a fall in the aggregate demand for goods. This fall in aggregate demand will adversely affect the employment opportunities and production in the economy. Thus, cut in wages, according to Keynes, instead of removing unemployment and depression will further deepen them. We thus see that application of marginal productivity theory to the macro level yields quite incorrect and invalid results.

7. Positive relationship between factor rewards and productivity ignored. Marginal productivity theory also ignores the positive interrelations between rewards of the factors and their productivity, especially between wages and the efficiency or productivity of labour. It has been pointed out that rise in wages has a favourable effect on the efficiency and productivity of labour. With higher wages workers can afford to have better standard of living and better health which will raise their productivity and efficiency. This positive relationship between wages and labour efficiency especially holds good in case of developing countries like India where the wage rates in many industries are even below the minimum subsistence level. With wages even below the subsistence level, workers remain underfed and undernourished and, as a result, unhealthy and inefficient. If following the rise in wages, efficiency and productivity of labour improve, then it may be worthwhile from the viewpoint of employers to raise wages. It has therefore sometimes been asserted that "higher wages are economical" or there is a '***economy of high wages***'. But, as mentioned above, marginal productivity theory completely ignores this favourable effect of higher wages on productivity of labour.

Now, if the favourable effect of higher wages on labour productivity is recognized, the unique level of wage-equilibrium arrived at in the marginal productivity theory is not valid. With every rise in the wage rate, there will be a different curve of marginal productivity of labour and a different wage-employment equilibrium. Thus there are various possible positions of wage-equilibrium depending upon the productivity and efficiency and there is a choice for the firm or the industry to select among them. That there is a *unique* wage equilibrium, as has been asserted by the strict and rigid version of marginal productivity theory, is therefore not acceptable.

8. Profit maximization assumption of marginal productivity theory criticised. Like the neo-classical theory ot pricing ot products, marginal productivity theory of distribution which has been developed by neo-classical economists is also a *marginal approach* to the problem and therefore assumes that the entrepreneurs or employers seek to *maximize profits.* It is only if the entrepreneurs are maximizers of profits that they will equate wage with marginal product of labour. If they do not seek to maximize profits, then they may employ the amount of labour at which marginal product of labour stands higher than the wage. Likewise, they may employ the number of workers at which the marginal product is lower than the wage. Just as Hall and Hitch have criticised the marginalist approach as it applies to product pricing on the ground that entrepreneurs do not maximize profits, R. A. Lester,[14] an American economist, has criticized the marginal productivity theory of distribution on the ground that entrepreneurs do not behave as maximizers of profits and therefore wages in the real world will differ from the marginal product of labour. Lester has provided empirical evidence in support of his views. But Machlup[15] and Pen[16] have defended the marginal productivity theory of distribution and the profit maximization assumption on which it is based. To quote Pen, "It is not necessary for every entrepreneur to be able to find the exact point of equilibrium, some will overshoot the equality of wage and marginal product, others will remain below it. However, the *trend is towards equality.* In this sense the theory gives only a rough approximation of equality, but as such it is probably not bad.[17]

9. Entrepreneurs are ignorant of marginal products of factors. Marginal productivity theory has also been challenged on the ground that it assumes that entrepreneurs are fully aware of their production function or, in other words, they know what are the marginal products of various factors and how they change with the expansion in their employment. In the empirical investigations when the entrepreneurs are asked whether for employing various factors of production they estimate their marginal productivities and take them into account, they flatly say 'no'. They generally reply to the economic investigator's question, "look, you are telling that I perform mental processes and calculations that I don't perform and in fact couldn't perform if I wanted to, because I do not know the production function. Your whole distribution theory is something you have made up. It's all very ingenious but there's no rhyme or reason to it.[18]

But many economists have tried to answer the above argument by pointing out that entrepreneurs may not be consciously calculating the marginal productivities of the various factors and taking the decisions according to these, but unconsciously or subconsciously they do behave according to the logic of marginal productivity, since they are out for maximum profits. Further, they point out that forces of competition compel them to behave in accordance

14. R. A. Lester, Shortcomings of Marginal Analysis for Wage Employment Problems, *American Economic Review*, 1946.
15. F. Machlup. Marginal Analysis and Empirical Research, *American Economic Review*, vol. 36, 1946.
16. J. Pen, *Income Distribution*, Penguin Books, 1971.
17. *Op. cit.*, p. 84.
18. J.Pen, *op.* cit., p. 85.

with the marginal productivity doctrine. Moreover, it is pointed out that there are many entrepreneurs working independently of one another to employ the various factors. Some may employ a factor at a reward which is higher than its marginal productivity and some others may employ it at a reward which is less than its marginal productivity. But the forces of competition will ensure that these discrepancies remain within bounds and on the average reward for a factor of production is approximately in line with its marginal product. Thus, according to J. Pen, "the hard struggle for survival keeps the discrepancies within bounds, the entrepreneur who gets right off course is destroyed by the market. Competition achieves a relation between K (capital) and L (labour) at which the marginal productivity theory more or less applies."[19]

It should be further noted that if factor rewards are approximately equal to their marginal products, marginal productivity theory would be correct and valid, economists do not insist on exact and precise equality of factor rewards with their marginal products. Professor Pen rightly remarks, "Through the use of differential quotients economists sometimes convey the impression of a misleading precision. We need that apparent exactitude to keep our mind on the rails, but we must not fall victim to it."[20]

10. Factors jointly' demanded do not have their separate marginal productivities. Another basic objection that has been raised against marginal productivity theory is that various factors are jointly demanded for the production of a commodity. That is, production of a commodity is the end result of cooperation of various factors and their *individual productivities cannot be separately estimated*. Further, all the factors are required to produce a commodity. Labur without the assistance of capital goods produce almost nothing and capital without the assistance of labour will not produce any thing at all. Now, when one cannot speak of the individual productivities of the factors at all or when we cannot calculate their individual productivities at all, then the question of rewarding the factors according to their marginal products cannot arise at all. This argument was forcefully advanced by English literary figures such as Bernard Shaw and Bertrand Russel. Bernard Shaw writes, "When a farmer and his labourers sow and reap a field, no body on earth can say how much of the wheat each of them has grown."[21] Likewise, Bertrand Russel writes, "In an industrial system a man never makes the whole of everything, but makes the thousandth part of a million things. Under these circumstances it is totally absurd to say that a man has the right to the produce of his own labour. Consider a porter on a railway whose business it is to shunt goods trains. What proportion of the goods carried can be said to represent the produce of his own labour ? The question is wholly insoluble,"[22]

It may be noted that many economists believe that there exists a good degree of elasticity of substitution between the factors and therefore one factor can be varied by a small amount keeping the other factors constant. In this way they argue that marginal products of various factors can be separately estimated.

11. Marginal Productivity Theory and Product Exhaustion Problem. A controversial problem concerning the marginal productivity theory is that if the various factors are remunerated in accordance with their marginal products, whether the total product would be just exhausted. Suppose there are two factors of production, labour and capital which are required for production of a commodity (ignore other factors). Now, the question is when wages to the labour are paid

19. *Op. cit.* p,. 86.
20. *Op. cit.* p,. 86.
21. Bernard Shaw, *Intelligent Woman's Guide to Socialism*, p. 21. Quoted by Dennis Robertson, *Principles of Economics*, The Fontana Library Edition, p. 186.
22. Bertrand Russel, *Prospects of Industrial Civilisation*, p. 146, quoted by Dennis Robertson, *Op. cit.'*, pp. 186-87.

equal to its marginal product, whether the remaining total product would be equal to capital's marginal product or less or more than it. This difficulty is called the ***adding up problem or product exhaustion problem*** of the marginal productivity theory of distribution. Whether total payment to factors equal to their marginal products does or does not exactly exhaust the total product depends on the form of the production function. If the production function is linearly homogeneous, or, in economic terms, constant returns to scale prevail, then with the aid of Euler theorem of mathematics it has been proved that total payments to factors equal to their marginal products would just exhaust the total product. But "The practical question is whether constant returns to scale do or do not occur in reality : once again, that differs entirely for the different branches of industry. At some places, there will not be enough income to remunerate everyone in accordance with marginal productivity, at other places something will be left. That too shows that the marginal productivity theory gives only a rough approximation of reality."[23]

12. Marginal productivity theory neglects the supply side of factor pricing. Another criticism, though based upon a wrong interpretation of the theory, is that the marginal productivity theory neglects the supply side of the factor pricing and merely describes the demand side of it. It is pointed out that the technique of equalization of marginal product of labour with wage and of marginal product of capital with interest and so on is that the entrepreneur who is out for maximum profits adjusts his employment of labour to a *given* wage rate and use of capital to a *given* interest rate. This theory does not explain how these given wage rate and given interest rate are *determined*. It is thus said the marginal productivity theory is more a theory of employment of labour or employment of capital rather a theory of wage determination or of interest determination. This has been asserted with reference to Clark's version of marginal productivity theory. As has been described above in the explanation of Clarkian version of marginal productivity theory that this version too becomes the theory of wage determination if it is applied to the economy as a whole and further that supply function (or curve) is taken to be *perfectly inelastic* at the full-employment level of labour. Thus Clark's version does not ignore the supply side but grants it perfectly inelastic at the level of full employment. As far as Marshall-Hicks's version of marginal productivity theory is concerned, it explicitly introduces an *elastic supply function of labour*, that is, quantity supplied of labour increases with the rise in the wage rate, and explains the wage determination through the interaction of demand and supply. We thus see that, if properly interpreted, marginal productivity theory takes into account both the demand for and supply of a factor.

13. Another important criticism of marginal productivity theory of distribution is that it does not explain the remuneration of entrepreneurs, that is, profits. Marginal productivity of a factor can be known if it can be varied by keeping the other factors fixed. But the entrepreneur in a firm is only one and fixed factor and variation in it is not possible. Therefore, marginal productivity of entrepreneur from the viewpoint of a firm is meaningless. If the single entrepreneur is withdrawn from the firm, keeping all other factors constant, the whole production process of the firm will collapse. And there is no meaning of adding one entrepreneur to a firm. The new entrepreneur will mean the establishment of altogether a new firm. It is because of this that in *neo-classical theory* of distribution, profit is shown as surplus or residual income and not as determined by marginal productivity.

14. Marginal productivity theory ignores the importance of power structure, and social institutions in determining factors rewards. Finally, the marginal productivity theory of distribution also does not give any importance to the power structure, social conventions,

23. J. Pen., *Op. cit.*, p. 85.

social status, and prestige of a group of workers in the determination of remuneration of various groups or classes of labour force. Professor Pen rightly writes that marginal productivity theory based on perfect competition "does not explain *discrimination* between men and women, between races and between social classes; it does not make it clear why top executives earn as much as do and why unions can push up wages."[24]

According to Pen, the high salaries drawn by the top executives of the firm cannot be explained by marginal productivity theory, since the concept of marginal productivity in their case is utterly vague and further that their remunerations can be explained only by the power structure. To quote him again, "remuneration of executives and staff work are fixed in another way : social conventions, the powers structure, considerations of prestige and status play a much larger part than marginal productivity. And that also holds good for the remuneration of the people not working in industry : of teachers, for instance (what is the marginal productivity of their contribution to the knowledge of economics ?) and of doctors (what is their marginal productivity to a human life ?). These are the sectors in which other laws apply than the derivatives of production. Economists often forget this."[25]

Conclusion

We have discussed above the various criticisms levelled against marginal productivity theory of distribution. Marginal productivity theory of distribution does not explain fully the determination of all factor prices. But marginal productivity of a factor is the most important *economic factor* governing the prices of factors. Other factors, such as power, social conventions, status and prestige do play a part in fixation of remunerations, but the economic factor of marginal productivity does exercise an important influence on the fixation of factor rewards.

EULER'S THEOREM AND PRODUCT EXHAUTION PROBLEM OR ADDING-UP PROBLEM

As soon as it was propounded that the factors of production are paid remunerations equal to their marginal products, a perplexing problem cropped up over which there has been a serious debate among the famous economists at that time. The perplexing problem which was posed was that if all factors were paid rewards equal to their marginal products, would the total product be just exactly exhausted ? In other words, if each factor is rewarded equal to its marginal product, the total product should be disposed of without any surplus or deficit. The problem of proving that the total product will be just exhausted if all factors are paid rewards equal to their marginal products has been called ***"Adding-up Problem" or Product Exhaustion Problem.***

Let us illustrate the product exhaustion problem by assuming that only two factors, labour and capital, are required for production. Let *a* stand for labour and *b* for capital. It should be remembered that marginal product of a factor can be known when it is varied, holding the other factors fixed. The reward to a variable factor can be shown as equivalent to marginal product when a certain quantity of the variable factor is used or employed. The reward for the fixed factor can then be shown as surplus (or residual income) of the total product over the marginally determined reward of the variable factor. Consider Figure 50.4 where labour has been treated as a variable factor and shown on the *X-axis* and capital has been taken as the fixed factor. If *OL* is the equilibrium amount of labour employed, the marginal product of labour is *LM* and wage rate determined according to this is *OW.* The total wage bill, that is, labour's share, is equal to *OLMW.* The total product produced is ΣMP, that is, the whole area

24. *Op. cit.*, p. 80.
25. *Op. cit.*, p. 86.

under the marginal productivity curve of labour *OSML*. Now the residual income, after marginally determined reward of labour *OLMW*, will go to capital as interest.

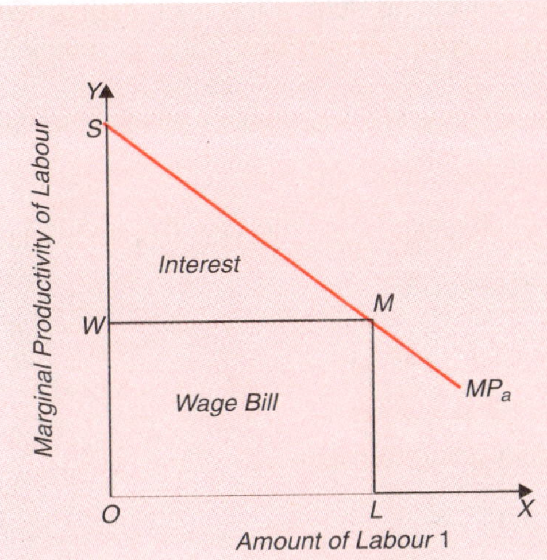

Fig. 50.4.

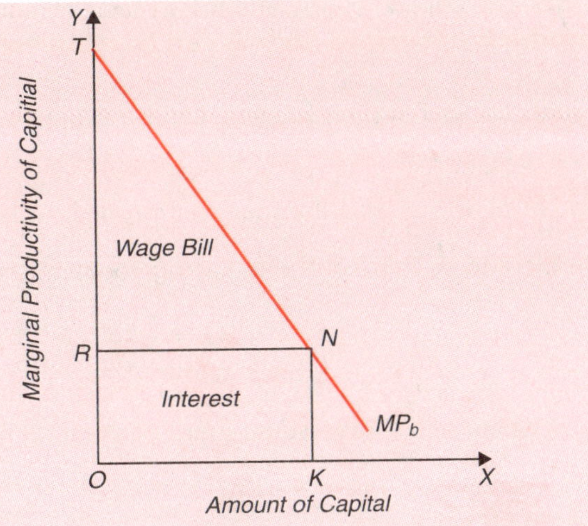

Fig. 50.5.

Thus, the total interest on capital will be equal to *OSML* – *OLMW*= *WMS*. With *OLMW as* marginally determined wages and *WMS as* residual income of interest, the total product is exhausted. But the problem of product exhaustion is to show that interest on capital determined as residual income is in fact equal to the marginal product of capital used multiplied by the amount of capital used. To show this, we have to treat capital as a variable factor and labour as a fixed factor. This has been done in Figure 50.5 by taking the same amount of labour used earlier as a fixed factor. Capital is now measured on the X-axis. If now the equilibrium amount of capital used is *OK, KN* is the marginal product of capital equal to which rate of interest *OR* is determined. Thus *OKNR* is the marginally determined interest income on capital. Now the residual income will go to the labour as wages. Thus in Figure 50.5 area *RNT is* the wage-bill which is determined as residual income.

Now, in order to show that payments in accordance with marginal productivity to both labour and capital would exactly exhaust the total product, it is required to be proved that the area *OKNR* in Figure 50.5 is equal to the area *WMS* in Figure 50.4, and area *RNTin* Figure 50.5 is equal to *OLMW* in Figure 50.4. In this way we will be able to show that the income of a factor determined as marginal is equal to the income of the factor determined as residual.

It should be noted that we have not proved the product exhaustion problem : we have only illustrated the problem itself.

Wicksteed's Solution of Product Exhaustion Problem

Philip Wicksteed was one of the first economists who posed this problem and provided a solution for it. Wicksteed applied a mathematical proposition called Euler's Theorem [26] to prove that the total product will be just exhausted if all the factors are paid equal to their marginal products. Let Q stand for the total output of the product, a stand for the factor labour and b stand for the factor capital and c stand for land. Assuming that there are only three factors employed for production. Then the adding-up problem implies that,

$$Q = MP_a \times a + MP_b \times b + MP_c \times c \quad .....(i)$$

26. This is after the name of its author *'Leonhard Euler'* (1907-1783), a Swiss mathematician.

That is, the marginal product of factor *a* multiplied by the amount of factor *a* plus the marginal product of factor *b* multiplied by the amount of factor *b* plus the marginal product of factor c multiplied by the amount of factor c equals the total product of the firm. ***Marginal products of various factors can be expressed as partial derivatives.*** Thus, the marginal product of labour (*i.e.*, factor a) can be expressed as $\frac{\delta q}{\delta a}$, and the marginal product of capital (factor *b*) as $\frac{\delta q}{\delta b}$ and the marginal product of land (factor c) as $\frac{\delta q}{\delta c}$, then for the adding-up problem to be fulfilled, the following equation must hold good:

$$Q = a\frac{\delta q}{\delta a} + b\frac{\delta q}{\delta b} + c\frac{\delta q}{\delta c} \qquad \text{......(ii)}$$

where $a\frac{\delta q}{\delta a}$ represents share of the total product going to capital.

$b\frac{\delta q}{\delta b}$ represents share of the total product going to land.

$c\frac{\delta q}{\delta c}$ represents share of the total product going to land.

Now, *Euler's theorem states that if Q is homogeneous function of the first decree, that is, if in Q =f (a, b, c) for any given increase in the variables a, b and c by an amount n, the output Q also increases by n, the equation (ii) above will hold good.* Thus homogeneous function of the first degree or linear homogeneous function is of the following form :

$$nQ = f(na, nb, nc)$$

According to Euler's theorem, for the linear homogeneous function :

$$Q = a\frac{\delta q}{\delta a} + b\frac{\delta q}{\delta b} + c\frac{\delta q}{\delta c}$$

Thus if *production function* is homogeneous of the first degree, then according to Euler's theorem the total product

$$Q = a\frac{\delta q}{\delta a} + b\frac{\delta q}{\delta b} + c\frac{\delta q}{\delta c}$$

where $\frac{\delta q}{\delta a}, \frac{\delta q}{\delta b}, \frac{\delta q}{\delta c}$ are partial derivatives of the production function and therefore represent the marginal products of lobour, capital, and land respectively. It follows, therefore, that if production function is homogeneous of the first degree (that is, where there are constant returns to scale), then, according to Euler's theorem, if the various factors, *a*, *b* and c are paid rewards equal to their marginal prod-ucts, the total product will be just exhausted, with no surplus or deficit.

Cobb-Douglas Production Function and Product Exhausion Problem. Let us demonstrate clearly the product exhausion problem with Euler's theorem by taking two factor Cobb-Douglas production, $Q = A L^a K^b$ which when $a + b = 1$, is homogeneous function of first degree (*i.e.* exhibits constant returns to scale) .

To study the distribution of the total product between the factors we have to determine marginal physical products of each factor by differenting the given production function with respect to labour and capital. Thus

$$MP_L = \frac{\partial Q}{\partial L} = AaL^{a-1}K^b$$

$$MP_K = \frac{\partial Q}{\partial K} = AbL^aK^{b-1}$$

Total payment to each factor is equal to the rate of reward per unit of the factor (which is taken to be equal to marginal proudct of a factor) multiplied by the amount of the factor employed. Thus

$$Y_L = \frac{\partial Q}{\partial L}.L = AaL^{a-1}K^b.L = aAL^aK^b \quad ...(1)$$

where Y_L stands for labour share *i.e.* real income of labour in the total product.

Since $AL^aK^b = Q$, from equation (1) we get

$$Y_L = aQ$$

Similarly, share of capital (Y_K) in the total product can be written as

$$Y_K = \frac{\partial Q}{\partial K}.K = bAL^aK^{b-1}.K = bAL^aK^b$$

Now, $AL^aK^b = Q$

Therefore $Y_k = bQ$

Total payment made to both the factors is the sum of the payments made to them. Thus,

$$Y = Y_L + Y_K = aQ + bQ = Q(a + b)$$

Now, if $a + b = 1$ in the given Cobb-Douglas production function, that is, if Cobb-Douglas production function is homogeneous of the first degree, then

$$Y = Q$$

We thus see that Euler's theorem is able to explain product exhaustion problem when production function is homogneous of the first degree. In the above way, Wicksteed, assuming constant returns to scale and applying Euler's theorem, proved the adding-up problem, that is, demonstrated that if all factors are paid equal to their marginal products, the total product will be just exactly exhausted.

Wicksteed's solution was criticised by Walras, Barone, Edgeworth and Pareto. It has been asserted by these writers that production function is not homogeneous of the first degree, that is, returns to scale are not constant in the actual world. Thus, Edgeworth satirically commented on Wicksteed's solution, ***"there is significance in this generalisation which recalls the Youth of philosophy. Justice is perfecy cube, said the ancient sage ; and rational conduct is a homogenous function, adds the modern savant."*** Critics have pointed out that production function is such that it yields U-shaped long-run average cost curve. The U-shape of the long-run average cost curve implies that up to a point, increasing returns to scale occur and after it diminishing returns to scale are found. In case a firm is still working under increasing returns to scale, then if all factors are paid equal to their marginal products, the total factor rewards would exceed the total product. On the other hand, if a firm is working under diminishing returns to scale, and all factors are paid equal to their marginal products, the total factor rewards would not fully exhaust the total product and will therefore leave a surplus. It follows that Euler's theorem does not apply and therefore the adding-up problem does not hold good when either there are increasing returns to scale or decreasing returns to scale.

Another drawback pointed out in Wicksteed's solution is that when there is constant returns to scale, the long-run average cost curve of the firm is a horizontal straight line, which is incompatible with perfect competition. (Under horizontal long-run average cost curve, the firm cannot have a determinate equilibrium position.) But competition was essential to the marginal productivity theory and therefore to Wicksteed's solution. Thus Wicksteed solution leads us to two contradictory things.

Wicksell, Walras, Barone, Samuelson and Hicks' Solution of Product Exhaustion Problem

After Wicksteed, Wicksell, Walras and Barone, each independently, advanced more satisfactory solution to the problem that marginally determined factor rewards would just exhaust the total product. These authors assumed that the typical production function was not homogeneous of the first degree, but was such that yielded U-shape long-run average cost curve. They pointed out that in the long run under perfect competition, the firm was in equilibrium at the minimum point of the long-run average cost curve. At the minimum point of the long-run average cost curve, the returns to scale are momentairly constant, that is, returns to scale are constant within the range of small variations of output. Thus the condition required for the marginally determined factor rewards to exhaust the total product, that is, the operation of constant returns to scale, was fulfilled at the minimum point of the long-run average cost curve, where a perfectly competitive firm is in long-run equilibrium. Thus, in the case of perfectly long-run equilibrium, if the factors are paid rewards equal to their marginal products, the total product would be just exactly exhausted.

As seen above, Wicksteed provided a solution to the product exhausion problem by assuring that production function was linearly homogenous, that is, constant returns to scale prevailed. Since all production functions are not linearly homogenous, the controversy remained unresolved whether or not, even under perfect competition and with the usual U-shape of long-run average cost curve with varying returns to scale, product-exhausion problem was valid. The credit for resolving this issue also goes to Hicks and Samuelson who showed that the ***solution to the product exhausion problem depended crucially on the market conditions of perfect competition and not on the property of production function. As a result of free*** entry and exit, the equilibrium of a firm under perfect competition in the long run ensures that the firms produce at the minimum point of the long-run average cost curve *LAC* (see Figure 50.6) where they make neither any economic profits, nor any losses. Now, if according to marginal productivity theory, factors are paid rewards equal to the value of their marginal products and the theory of perfect competition that in the long run the perfectly competitive firms earn zero economic profits, it follows that under perfect competition in both the product and factor markets the level of output and employment of factors (labour and capital) would be such as to satisfy the equilibrium conditions of factor employment and long-run competitive equilibrium with zero economic profits. We show below mathematically how under perfect competition in the product and factor markets, adding up problem is solved or product exhausion problem holds.

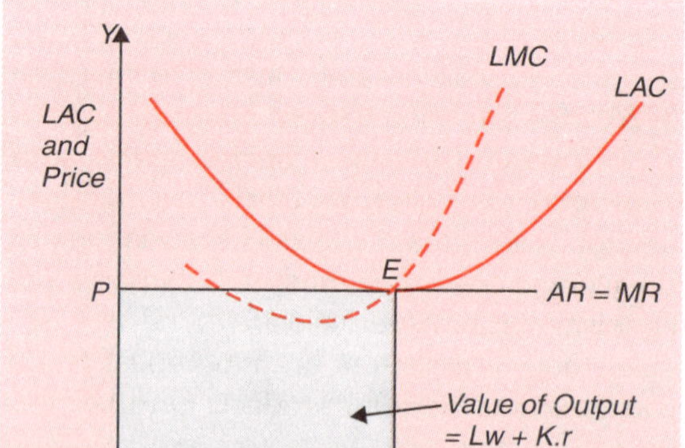

Fig. 50.6. *Total product is just exhausted with equilibrium at the minimum point of LAC under perfect competition.*

Mathematically, zero economic profit condition implies that the value of total output equals the total cost of production. Let *L* stand for labour, *K* for capital, *w* for wage rate, *r* for price of capital, *Q* for output of a product and *P* for the price of the product. According to the long-run perfectly competitive equilibrium at the minimum point E of LAC curve (See Figure 50.6) we have

$$\text{Value of output} = \text{Total cost}$$

$$P.Q = Lw + Kr \quad \text{....(1)}$$

Now, according to marginal productivity theory, factors are rewarded equal to value of their marginal products. Thus

$$w = VMP_L = P.MPP_L \quad \text{....(2)}$$

$$r = VMP_K = P.MPP_K \quad \text{.....(3)}$$

Substituting the values of w and r as obtained above in (2) and (3) respectively in (1) we have

$$PQ = L.P.MPP_L + K.P.MPP_K$$

Thus, for a given price P, if the factors (labour and capital) are paid equal to their marginal physical products (MPP_L and MPP_K), the total payments to labour and capital would be equal to the total product Q and thus total product would be just exhausted.

From above it is clear that it is the property of perfect competition, namely, that it ensures long-run equilibrium at the minimum point of the U-shaped long-run average cost curve with zero economic profits that solves the product exhaustion problem. It may, however, be noted that at the minimum point of the U-shaped LAC curve returns to scale are locally constant.

It follows from above that the two main solutions of the adding-up problem were offered. First, Wicksteed' s solution which assumed the operation of constant returns to scale. Secondly, the solution provided by Wicksell, Barone Walras, Samuelson and Hicks which assumed that the firms operated at the lowest point of the long-run average cost curve under perfect competition.

INTERRELATIONSHIPS BETWEEN VALUE, PRODUCTION AND DISTRIBUTION

Value, output, production and distribution are different parts of microeconomic theory but they are intimately related to each other. Because of this intimate interrelationship between value, production and distribution, microeconomic theory presents a unified and logically self-consistent picture of the working of the market economy.

Value and Distribution

Let us see first how distribution and value of output are interrelated to each other. As has been explained above, factors of production are remunerated according to the value of the marginal product (*VMP*) under conditions of perfect competition. But the value of the marginal product of a factor is the marginal physical product of the factor multiplied by the *price* of the product it helps to produce. The greater the price of the product, the greater will be the value of the marginal product of labour and hence the greater will be its wage or income. In fact, the demand curve for a factor is derived from the curve of value of marginal product (or marginal revenue product) of labour. If the value or price or the product which a factor produces goes up, the whole demand curve for labour will shift upward and, as a result, the price and income of the factor will rise. Indeed, the demand for a factor is said to be derived demand; it is derived from the demand for the products a factor helps to produce. Therefore, the value of the products and the income or price that a factor will obtain are closely related to each other.

Production and Distribution

Theories of production and distribution are also closely interrelated to each other. We have already explained in a previous chapter the relevance of the production theory for the theory of distribution. We have seen above in the explanation of the marginal productivity theory (both in Clarkian and Marshall-Hicks's versions) that payment to a factor is paid according to its marginal product, that is, its contribution to total production. The greater the marginal product of a factor, the greater the reward or income it will obtain. Now, the marginal product of a factor depends on the nature and form of production function.

As has been explained earlier, production function is written as $Q = f(L. K.)$ where Q stands for the total product, L stands for the amount of labour used, and K stands for the amount of capital used. If we increase L by a small amount keeping K constant, we can know how much increase in Q occurs and that increase is called a partial derivative of the production function. The derivative is written as $\frac{\delta Q}{\delta L}$. Likewise, we can keep L constant and increase K by a small amount, the increase in Q which will result from this is partial derivative of the production function with respect to K and is written $\frac{\delta Q}{\delta K}$. The economic terms for $\frac{\delta Q}{\delta L}$ and $\frac{\delta Q}{\delta K}$ are marginal products of labour and capital respectively. Marginal products of labour and capital play a vital role in the neo-classical theory of distribution (*i.e.* marginal productivity theory) which has been adopted by modern economists as well. Wages are equal to its marginal product of labour and interest on capital is equal to the marginal product of capital. As we have explained above in the critical evaluation of marginal productivity theory that this is not a fully adequate explanation of factor rewards or incomes, but this is no doubt a very important force determining the reward for a factor of production.

The principle that the equality of factor rewards with their marginal productivities is based upon the assumption that entrepreneurs seek to maximize profits. Professor Pen rightly writes, "the entrepreneur organizes production. It is not foolish to assume that he combines labour and capital in a proportion that is as advantageous as possible to him. Now if the wage that he has to pay to every worker is lower than the extra product that an extra worker supplies, it is to the entrepreneur's advantage to engage that worker. As long as the marginal productivity of capital is higher than the interest rate, he will want to get hold of more capital. Perhaps entrepreneur does not succeed in exactly achieving the optimum relations in his production process—complications occur ..... but ***nevertheless there is a constant force at work pursuing an equality of the remuneration of the factors of production and the marginal productivites.***"[27] He further remarks, "this simple truth, propagated by J. B. Clark, is important to start with, ***it supplies a synthesis between the production theory and the distribution theory.***"[28]

A particular feature of production function has a great relevance for the theory of distribution. And this is the diminishing marginal returns to a factor. We have seen above that entrepreneur goes on employing labour or capital until its marginal product declines to the level of the wage or the interest. If the marginal product of a factor, instead of diminishing, increases or remains constant, the above equality of factor rewards with marginal products cannot be achieved and the whole theory of distribution collapses.

27. J. Pen, *op. cit*, pp. 79-80.
28. *Ibid.*, p. 80.

Another important feature of production function which is crucially relevant for the theory of distribution is the *possibility of substitution* between the factors. If the productive factors have fixed or rigid relations, they would have to be used in a fixed proportion and in that case the marginal productivities would be zero and no theory of distribution can be based on zero marginal productivities of factors. The fact that a good deal of substituability between factors is present makes it possible to build a theory of distribution on the concept of marginal productivity. Prof. J. R. Hicks introduced the concept of *elasticity of substitution* between the factors and showed its importance for determining the distributive shares of its various factors. The concept of elasticity of substitution relates to the change in the proportion of the two factors used in response to the change in the ratio of the prices of the two factors. For instance, if the wages of labour rise relatively to the interest on capital, the entrepreneur will substitute capital for labour. The employment of capital will increase and that of labour will decline. This may reduce the distributive share of the product of labour and raise the distributive share of capital. We shall discuss the role of elasticity of substitution in determining the distributive shares of the various factors in detail in a later chapter.

Further, the possibility of substitution between the factors in the production function puts a limit on the power of the unions to raise wages and improve the levels of living of the working class. If the trade unions try to raise the wages and succeed in this, the entrepreneur will substitute capital for labour and as a result the employment of labour will fall, rendering some of the workers unemployed. This fear of unemployment being created prevents the trade unions to raise wages to a very high level.

From the foregoing analysis it follows that production is intimately related to production and the theory of distribution is based upon the theory of production.

QUESTIONS FOR REVIEW

1. Distinguish between personal and functional distribution of income. Is there any relation between the two ?
2. The mechanism of determination of factor prices does not differ fundamentally from that of prices of commodities. Discuss.
3. State and examine critically the marginal productivity theory of factor pricing.
4. How does Marshall-Hicks Verseon of Marginal Productivity Theory of Distribution differ from Clark's marginal productivity theory ?
5. Show that when factors are paid rewards equal to their marginal products, the total product would be just exhausted.
6. What is Euler's theorem ? Using Euler's theorem explain when factors are paid rewards equal to their marginal products, total product would be just exhausted.
7. Prove that the assumption of a homogeneous-of-degree one production function is not necessary for the marginal productivity theory of distribution.
8. What is '*Adding-up Problem*'? Using Cobb-Douglas production function, prove the adding-up problem in the theory of income distribution.
9. Explain how the theory of income distribution is related to the theory of production.
10. The theory of distribution is a mere extension of the theory of value. Discuss.
11. Show and explain that under conditions of imperfect competition in the product or factor markets, factors are not rewarded equal to the value of their marginal products.
12. Marginal productivity theory neglects the supply side of factors. Critically examine.
13. If wages are determined by marginal product of labour, trade unions are superfluous. Discuss.

CHAPTER

51

Neo-Classical Macro-Theory of Relative Distributive Shares

Neo-Classical Macro-Theroy of Distribution : Relative Shares of Labour and Capital

Marginal productivity theroy explained in the previous chapter is also called *neo-classical theory of distrubution* as it was propounded by neo-classical economists Neo-classical distrubution theory which was put forward to explain relative prices of factors has been extended to explain macro-distribution of national income, that is, to explain ***distributive shares of factors.*** Thus, it has been used to explain what determines the *relative* aggregate share of labour (*i.e.* total wages) and aggregate share of capital (*i.e.* total profits) in national income. As we have explained above, according to marginal productivity theory, marginal principle can be applied to *all factors* by taking them as variable factors and therefore their rewards equal to their marginal products are determined. Thus labour gets real wage rate equal to marginal product, capital gets rate of interest equal to its marginal product, land gets rent equal to its marginal product. The total *absolute* share of a factor is determined by its marginal product (*i.e.*, remuneration in real terms) multiplied by the amount of the factor used. Thus, the absolute share of labour in the national income is determined by the amount of labour used in production multiplied by its marginal product (or real wage rate), and so on. *The relative share of labour in the national income is its absolute share divided by the total national product.*

It should be noted that in neo-classicial marginal productivity theory, all factors are regarded as substitutes of each other, though to varying degrees. With the given and fixed supplies of factors, the marginal products of the various factors are known from the production function. With the knowledge of these marginal products of factors (equal to which real rewards for factors are determined), the absolute and relative shares of the factors can be found out. Take the case of labour whose amount we represent by *L*. Let *Q* stand for total output produced when *L* units of labour are given and employed. Then we can write the marginal product of labour as $\frac{\Delta Q}{\Delta L}$ which means change in output resulting from a marginal unit change in labour.

With $\frac{\Delta Q}{\Delta L}$ as the marginal product of labour and *L* as the total given quantity of labour used, the absolute share of labour will be:

$$= \frac{\Delta Q}{\Delta L} . L$$

Dividing the absolute share by the total national product (*Q*), we get the relative share of labour, which we represent by λ. Therefore,

$$\text{Relative Share of Labour in National Product, } \lambda = \frac{\Delta Q}{\Delta L} \cdot \frac{L}{Q}$$

$$\lambda = \frac{\Delta Q}{Q} \cdot \frac{L}{\Delta L}$$

$$= \frac{\Delta Q}{Q} \div \frac{\Delta L}{L}$$

But $\frac{\Delta Q}{Q} + \frac{\Delta L}{L}$ means the relative change in output as a result of relative change in the factor L.

In other words, $\frac{\Delta Q}{\Delta L} \cdot \frac{L}{Q}$ or $\frac{\Delta Q}{Q} \div \frac{\Delta L}{L}$ ***represents elasticity of output with respect to labour. It follows therefore that the relative share of labour in national income is equal to the elasticity of output with respect to labour.*** In numerical terms, if 1% change in the quantity of labour brings about a 25% change in the national product, then labour's share in national product will be 25%.

Likewise, relative share of capital, which we denote by k, can be ascertained. Let K stand for the amount of capital used. Therefore,

$$k = \frac{\Delta Q}{\Delta K} \cdot \frac{K}{Q}$$

$$= \frac{\Delta Q}{Q} \cdot \frac{K}{\Delta K}$$

$$= \frac{\Delta Q}{Q} \div \frac{\Delta K}{K}$$

which is the expression for the elasticity of total production with regard to capital. Thus ***relative share of capital in national income, k is equal to the elasticity of output with regard to capital.***

It therefore follows from above that according to neo-classical theory of distribution the relative shares of labour and capital in national income are equal to the output elasticities of these factors.

Changes in Absolute Shares of Labour and Capital

So far as absolute share of labour in national product (*i.e.*, national income) and changes in it as a result of changes in the quantity of labour is concerned, it can be better understood with the aid of the marginal productivity curve of the factor. Consider Figure 51.1. If OL is the given amount of labour, then its marginal product $\frac{\Delta Q}{\Delta L}$ or real wage rate will be OW. Absolute share of labour in the national product is $OW \times OL$, that is, the area of the rectangle $OLEW$. Now, suppose that the amount of labour increases to OL', the marginal product (or, the real wage rate) falls to OW'. Now, the absolute share of labour in national income will be equal to the area of new rectangle $OL'E'W'$. Now, whether this area of new rectangle $OL'E'W$ (and therefore new absolute share of labour in the national product) is greater than, or less than, or equal to the area of previous rectangle (*i.e.*, previous labour's share) depends upon whether the *elasticity of the marginal product curve* is greater than one, less than one, or equal to one. Thus, if the elasticity of marginal product curve is greater than one, labour's share in national income will increase with the increase in the quantity of labour relative to capital. And if this elasticity is less than one, labour's share will decline, and if it is equal to one, labour's share will remain the same with the increase in the quantity of labour, quantity of capital remaining constant.

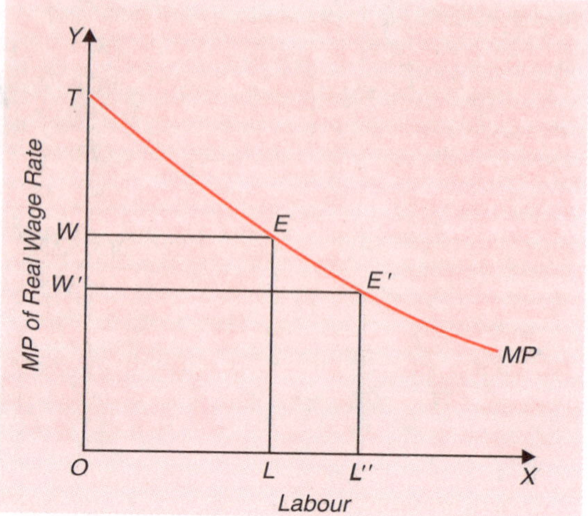

Fig. 51.1. Changes in Absolute Share of Labour and Elasticity of Marginal Product Curve

Since in neo-classical economic thought, the marginal productivity principle of rewarding a factor in accordance with its marginal product (*MP*), given its level of use or employment, is applied to all factors of production, remaining product *WET* must be only just sufficient for remunerating other factors of production. In this way, when all factors of production are paid rewards equal to their marginal products, the total product is just exhausted with no surplus or deficit. We have seen in the previous chapter that if we assume homogeneous production function of the first degree (*i.e.*, constant returns to scale) or consider the position of long-run equilibrium under perfect competition (minimum point of the long-run average cost curve, *LAC*) Euler theorem can be applied to prove that total product would in fact be just exhausted if all factors are paid remuneration equal to their marginal products.

In the neo-classical or marginal productivity theory of distributive shares, the two factors of production, labour and capital, have been generally considered. Whereas land has been considered to be included in capital, enterprises which receive profits are not considered at all. In fact, as mentioned earlier, in neo-classical economics, assuming perfect competition, entrepreneur's pure economic profits are zero in long-run equilibrium position. In neo-classical distribution theory, production function does not include entrepreneurs as an input. Thus, according to Pen "in neo-classical thought there are only two factors of production, so that $\lambda + k = 1$, but the thesis that the share of income is equal to the partial elasticity of production function can be applied without difficulty to any group within society. The share of carpenters is equal to the partial elastisity of the national production with respect to carpentry. The share of heavy clay is equal to the elasticity of national production with respect to heavy clay. ***Only in the case of the entrepreneurs does our formula fail to apply; this factor of production does not appear in the production function as an input. Pure profit does not fit into this story—something else will have to be found for that.***"[1]

Elasticity of Substitution and Changes in Relative Factor Shares in Neo-Classical Distribution Theory

As shown above, in neo-classical theory factor rewards are equal to their marginal products. Thus, real wage rate of labour (w) is equal to $\frac{\Delta Q}{\Delta L}$ or MP_L and real return on capital (r) is equal to $\frac{\Delta Q}{\Delta K}$ or MP_K.

1. *Op.cit.*, p. 171.

The relative share of labour in national income $= \frac{\Delta Q}{\Delta L}.\frac{L}{Q} = \frac{MP_L.L}{Q} = \frac{w.L}{Q}$ ....(1)

Likewise, relative share of capital in national income

$$= \frac{\Delta Q}{\Delta K}.\frac{K}{Q} = \frac{MP_K.K}{Q} = \frac{r.K}{Q} \quad ....(2)$$

Thus, the ratio of relative shares of labour and capital

$$= \frac{w.L}{Q} \div \frac{rK}{Q} = \frac{w.L}{rK} = \frac{w}{r}.\frac{L}{K} \quad ....(3)$$

Now, how this ratio of relative shares of labour and capital will change depend on the elasticity of substitution between the factors. The elasticity of substitution[1] shows the proportional change in capital-labour ratio by a given proportionate change in the ratio of factor prices $\left(\frac{w}{r}\right)$.

Now, consider the above equation (3) in which $\frac{w}{r}.\frac{L}{K}$ measures the ratio of relative shares of labour and capital. If relative price of labour rises, that is, if $\frac{w}{r}$ increases, this will induce the substitution of capital for labour and as a result capital-labour ratio (*K/L*) will increase (that is, $\frac{L}{K}$ ratio will decrease). If the elasticity of subsitution(σ) is less than one, say equal to 0.5, then 10 per cent increase in wage-rental ratio w/r will lead to the increase in capital-labour ratio *i.e.*,$\Delta\left(\frac{K}{L}\right)$ by only 5 per cent. Thus, given that the elasticity of substitution is less than one, then a given percentage increase in $\frac{w}{r}$ ratio will not cause the substitution of capital for labour in the same proportion as the wage rate rises relative to the price of capital with the result that relative share of labour $\frac{w.L}{r.K}$ (i.e. $\frac{w}{r}/\frac{K}{L}$) will increase.

On the other hand, if the elasticity of substitution between labour and capital is equal to unity, then 10 per cent increase in wage-rental ratio $\left(\frac{w}{r}\right)$ will lead to the substitution of capital for labour to the extent that capital-labour ratio (*K/L*) will also increase by 10 percent. This means that in case of unit elasticity of substitution between labour and capital, the ratio of relative factor shares $\left(\frac{w.L}{r.K} \text{or} \frac{w}{r}/\frac{K}{L}\right)$ will remain constant. That is, relative share of labour will

1. The elasticity substitution can be written as

$$\sigma = \frac{\Delta\left(\frac{k}{L}\right) \div \left(\frac{K}{L}\right)}{\Delta\left(\frac{w}{r}\right) \div \left(\frac{w}{r}\right)}$$ where σ stands for elasticity of substitution.

remain constant despite the factor that labour has become relatively more expensive.

In the case where production function is characterised by greater than unit elasticity of substitution between labour and capital, the rise in wage rate relative to the price of capital will cause more than proportionate change in the substitution of capital for labour and thus raising capital-labour ratio (K/L) substantially and thereby reducing the relative share of labour or $\frac{w.L}{r.K}$. To conclude, **given the two factor production function, if the price of labour rises relative to the price of capital, the relative share of labour will increase, remain unchanged or fall according as the elasticity of technical substitution between them is less than one, equal to one or greater than one.**

Now, take the opposite case. If the wage rate of labour falls relative to the rental[2] of capital so that $\frac{w}{r}$ decreases, and as a result $\frac{L}{K}$ ratio increases. *If elasticity of substitution is less than one (which means that the ratio L/K rises less than proportionate to the fall in w//r), the relative share of labour,* $\frac{w}{r} \cdot \frac{L}{K}$, *will decline relative to the share of capital.*

Now suppose w/r falls and as a result L/K rises, but the *elasticity of substitution is equal to one,* $\sigma = 1$; which means that the proportionate rise in L/K is equal to the proportionate fall in w/r. In this case, the ratio of relative shares $\frac{w.L}{r.K}$ will reamain the same as $\frac{w}{r}$ ratio falls. We thus see that changes in factor-ratio (L/K) as a result of changes in factor-price ratio (w/r) depend on the elasticity of substitution which determines the changes in the relative shares of factors, labour and capital, as the factor price ratio changes.

Now, if the wage rate falls relatively to the return on capital (r) and as a result the ratio w/r falls and consequently L/K ratio rises. If the elasticity of substitution between labour and capital is greater than one ($\sigma > 1$), the ratio of relative share of labour to capital $\frac{w}{r} \cdot \frac{L}{K}$ will increase as L/K ratio increases more than proportionately. Thus, according to Robertson, **"Labour's relative share will be more likely to increase the more substitutable it is for non-labour, the greater the ease with which increased supplies of it can, as if were, work their way into the productive process. The greater this ease, the less will the marginal productivity ot labour be reduced and the less will the marginal productivity of non-labour be raised as the supply of labour increases."**[3]

We thus see that in neo-classical theory whether elasticity of substitution is greater than one, less than one or equal to one is of great importance in determining changes reteiive distributive shares of various socio-economic groups. To examine the changes in relative snares of labour and capital, we are required to study the changes in factor-price ratio $\left(\frac{w}{r}\right)$ as well as factor ratio (L/K). Thus, given the fact that changes in $\frac{w}{r}$ ratio cause changes in K/L ratio and

2. Note that price of capital is also called rental.
3. D.H. Robertson, *Lectures on Economic Principles,* Fontana Library edition, p. 190.

vice versa, to judge the changes in relative income shares of the factors following the changes in *one of these ratios* will be incorrect, if the possibility of associated changes in *the other ratio* are not taken into account. Empirical studies have revealed that in the American economy over the post- War years, relative share of labour in national income has increased and the wage rate has also risen and also labour-capital ratio has declined (that is, capital-labour ratio has increased).

From our above analysis it follows that as a result ***of rise in w/r ratio and consequent decline in labour-capital ratio (or in other words increase is capital-labour ratio) the share of labour relative to capital will increase only if the elasticity of substitution is less than one.*** In fact, the empirical evidence is quite strong that the elasticity of substitution for the American economy and manufacturing sector as a whole is substantially less than one[4]. Thus empirical finding of elasticity of substitution being less than one is in accordance with the ***rise in relative wage rate as well as in the relative share of labour***in American economy in the post- War years. However, it will not be valid to conclude that in every industry in American economy and elsewhere, the elasticity of substitution between labour and capital is less than unity. In fact, C.E. Ferguson has found that many specific industries and product groups in America have a production function whose elasticity of substitution is greater than one[5]. In such industries, the relative share of labour in the total output of the industry has declined as a result of rise in wage rate relative to return on capital and consequent fall in labour-capital ratio (or rise in capital-labour ratio). In such industries the relative share of capital has increased even though its relative rate of return has fallen.

It follows from above that the relative shares of labour and capital change in response to the changes in their relative prices depending upon he elasticity of substitution, that is, on the responsiveness of factor proportions to the changes in the relative factor prices. But the observed changes in the relative shares over the years also depend upon the *nature of technological progress* that has taken place. Technological progress can be either neutral or biased. If it is biased it can be either capital-using or labour-using. Neutral technological *progress* shifts the production function in such a way that with constant *capital-labour ratio (i.e.,* factor proportions remaining unchanged), marginal rate of technical substitution and hence the factor price ratio $\left(\frac{w}{r}\right)$ remains the same. This leaves the relative shares of labour and capital unaffected under neutral technological progress.

If technological progress is of *capital-using i.e., capital-bias type,* it will reduce the marginal rate of technical substitution labour for capital ($MRTS_{LK}$) and hence factor price ratio $\left(\frac{w}{r}\right)$ with a capital-labour ratio remaining constant. This will reduce the relative income share of labour and increase the relative share of capital. On the other hand, if the technological change is of labour-using *(i.e.,* labour-biased), it will raise the marginal rate of technical substitution of labour for capital and hence the wage-rental ratio $\left(\frac{w}{r}\right)$ will rise, with a given constant labour-capital ratio, this will increase the income share of labour relative to capital. We explain below in detail the impact of the nature of technological progress on the relative income shares of the factors.

4. See J.W. Kendrick and Ryuzo Sato, Factor Prices, Productivity and Growth, *American Economic Review,* LIII, 1963, pp. 974-1090.
5. See C.E. Ferguson, "Cross-Section Production Functions and the Elasticity of Substitution in American Manufacturing Industry", *Review of Economics and Statistics,* XLV (1963), pp. 305-13 and Time-Series Production Functions and Technological Progress in American Manufacturing Industries, *Journal of Political Economy,* LXXIII, (1965), pp. 135-47.

TECHNOLOGICAL PROGRESS AND FACTOR SHARES IN INCOME

Being concerned with static analysis of factor shares we have so far assumed that production function remains constant over a period of time. However, in real life change in technology is continuously taking place which causes a shift in the production function and thereby brings about a change in marginal products of factors and therefore in marginal rate of technical substitution between labour and capital. Due to its effect on $MRTS_{LK}$ or ratio of MP_L/MP_K, the technological change affects income distribution or relative shares of factors.

Various Types of Technological Progress. Technological changes has been classified by J. R. Hicks into three categories (*i*) capital using, (*ii*) neutral and (*iii*) labour-using technological change. It may be noted that technological advancement implies that a given level of output can be produced with smaller quantities of factors and therefore isoquants shifts downward as a result of this. ***Technological change is said to be neutral, if at a given and constant capital-labour ratio, marginal rate of technical substitution*** $\left(= \frac{MP_L}{MP_K}\right)$ ***remains the same when due to the progress in technology isoquants representing production function shift downward.*** This is illustrated in panel (a) of Figure 51.2 . It will be seen from panel (a) that initially a firm is at isoquant Q producing level of output Q. OR is a linear ray from the origin

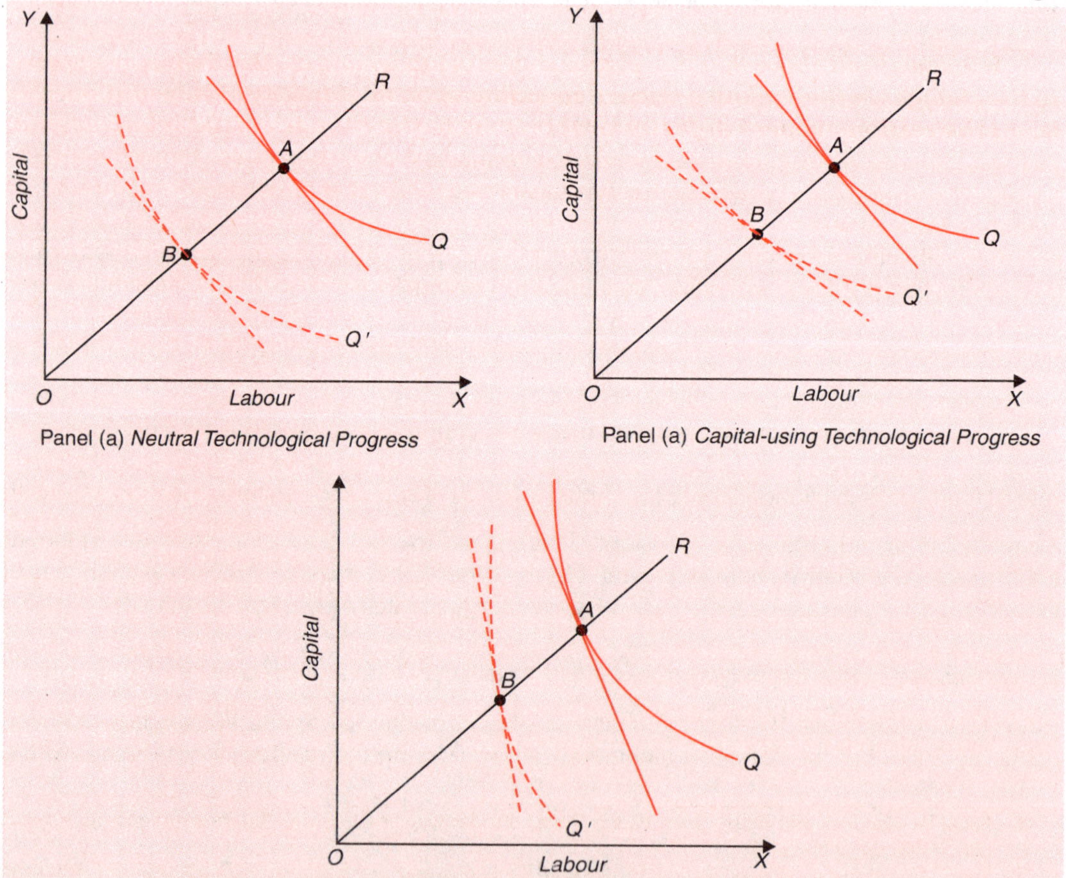

Panel (c) Labour-Using Technological Progress

Fig. 51.2. *Different Types of Technological Progress*

representing constant capital-labour ratio equal to its slope. Now, as a result of neutral technological progress isoquant representing level of output *Q* shifts downward to the new position *Q′* (dotted) and along the ray of constant capital-labour, *Q* ratio (*K/L*), the firm reaches at point *B*. It will be found that the slope of the tagent drawn at point *B* on the new isoquant, indicating $MRTS_{LK}$ *is* the same as at point *A* of the ray *OR* on the initial isoquant *Q′*. This occurs when the nature of technological change is such that it equally increases the marginal products of both labour and capital so that marginal rate of technical substitution ($MRTS_{LK}$) which is equal to the ratio of $MP_L MP_K$ remains the same.

Capital-Using Technological Progress. According to Hicks, technological progress is capital-using (or capital deepening) if it raises the marginal product of capital relative to labour. This means that with the shift in the isoquants representing production function, capital biased technological change will cause the marginal rate of technical substitution ($MRTS_{LK}$), which is ratio of marginal product of labour to marginal product of capital $\left(\frac{MP_L}{MP_K}\right)$, to decrease. Panel (*b*) of Figure 51.2 illustrates the capital-using technological change. It will be seen from panel (*b*) that the linear ray *OR* from the origin depicting-a given constant capital-labour *(K/L)* ratio intersects the initial isoquant *Q* at point *A* and the new isoquant *Q'* at point *B* after its downward shift due to the technological advancement. *A* glance at panel (*b*) will reveal that the slope of the tangent depicting $MRTS_{LK}$ drawn at point *B* on the isoquant *Q'is* less than at point *A* on the initial isoquant *Q*. This implies that marginal rate of technological substitution ($MRTS_{LK}$) has declined as a result of technological change showing that this is the case of capital using or capital-deepening technological progress.

Labour-Using Technological Change. Lastly, labour-using technological change occurs when it leads to the increase in marginal product of labour relative to marginal product of capital so that marginal rate of technical substitution of labour for capital ($MRTS_{LK}$) at the constant capital labour (*K/L*) ratio increases. Panel (c) of Figure 51.2 illustrates the case of labour-using technological change. With the improvement of technology.and consequent downward shift in isoquant representing a given level of output shifts from *Q* to *Q′*. It will be seen at point *B* on the ray *OR* the shope of the new isoquent *Q′* is greater than at point A on the initial isoquant *Q* which means that marginal rate of technical substitution of labour for capital ($MRTS_{LK}$) has increased with the change in technology, capital-labour ratio remaining constant. Thus, panel (c) represents the case of labour-using technological progress.

Technological Change and Relative Factor Shares

The nature of technological progress, whether it has capital-using or labour-using bias, has an important bearing on the income distribution between labour and owners of capital. This is explained below.

(*i*) When technological progress is *neutral*, relative shares of labour and capital will remain constant. This can be shown as under. As we know in equilibrium marginal rate of technical substitution of labour for capital is equal to the factor price ratio $\frac{w}{r}$ where *w* is the wage rate and *r* is the rental price of capital. (That is, $MRTS_{LK} = \frac{w}{r}$). Now, as explained above, when *neutral* technological change occurs and consequently isoquant shifts downward, $MRTS_{LK}$ remains the same at a constant capital-labour (*K/L*) ratio. This means that the ratio of factor prices $\left(\frac{w}{r}\right)$ which in equilibrium equals $MRTS_{LK}$ will remain the same. Thus, in Hicksian *neutral* technological change both factor price ratio $\left(\frac{w}{r}\right)$ and capital-labour ratio (K/L) remains constant, therefore the ratio of relative shares of labour and capital which is equal to $\frac{wL}{rK}$ will remain unchanged.

(*ii*) When *capital-using technological progress* occurs, at a constant capital-labour-ratio (*K/L*) marginal rate of technical substitution of labour for capital ($MRTS_{LK}$) declines. This means that in *equilibrium* the ratio of price of labour to the price of capital $\left(\frac{w}{r}\right)$ will decline, that is, r rises relative to (w), capital-labour-rario $\left(\frac{K}{L}\right)$ remaining constant. Note that in neoclassical theory prices of factors (w and r in the present case) are determined by their respective marginal products which means that factor price ratio $\left(\frac{w}{r}\right)$ will in equilibrium be equal to the ratio of marginal products $\left(\frac{MP_L}{MP_K}\right)$, that is, marginal rate of technical subsitution ($MRTS_{LK}$) between the two factors. Thus, in *case of capital-using technological progress where with constant capital-lobour rateo* $\left(\frac{K}{L}\right)$ *marginal rate of technical substitution declines and therefore* $\frac{w}{r}$ *falls, the ratio of relative factor shares* $\frac{wL}{rK}$ *will decline, that is, relative share of labour will fall, whereas relative* share of capital will increase.

(*iii*) **When there is labour - using technological progress,** at a constant capital-labour ratio $\left(\frac{K}{L}\right)$, marginal rate of technical subsitution ($MRTS_{LK}$) and hence $\frac{w}{r}$ ratio increases. Thus, in this case, the ratio of relative factor shares, $\frac{w.L}{r.K}$, increases as the ratio of wage-rental ratio $\frac{w}{r}$ increases with labour-capital ratio $\left(\frac{L}{K}\right)$ remaining constant. This means when *technological change is labour-using, relative share of labour will increase and the relative share of capital will decline.*

To sum up, relative share of labour (*i*) remains constant when technological progress is neutral; (*ii*) decreases when technological progress is capital-using, and (*iii*) increases when technological progress has a labour-using bias.

The analysis of relationship between technological progress and changes in relative shares made above which is based on the Hicksian definitions of the various types of technological change suffers from a drawback. It is that Hicksian classification of technological progress into capital-using, labour-using and neutral is based on a constant capital-labour (K/L) ratio. However, as is quite well known, *progress in technology not only causes change in marginal rate of substitution (or elasticity of substitution) but also the capital-labour* (K/L) *ratio*. Indeed, due to technological progress capital-labour (K/L) ratio has been continuously rising in the industrialised sectors of both the developed and developing countries. This has tended to increase the relative income share of capital. But where the trade union movement has been strong enough, the increase in capital-deepening (*i.e.*, rising K/L ratio) has also been accompanied by the increases of w/r ratio which has tended to prevent the fall in relative share of labour. We thus see that besides nature of technological change, the bargaining powers of the capitalists and the workers also influence the relative shares of labour and capital.

Cobb-Douglas Production Function and Distributive Shares of Labour and Capital

In neo-classical theory of distribution, it was fashionable for a long time to explain the distributive shares of labour and capital with linear Cobb-Douglas production function. This is because Cobb-Douglas production function has certain important properties which can show easily and elegantly the distributive shares of labour and capital. Furthermore, Cobb-Douglas production function proved to be ideal for explaining the *constancy of labour's share in national income*, which for a long time economists believed to be empirically true.

Linear Cobb-Douglas production function is of the following form :

$$Q = AL^{\alpha}K^{1-\alpha}$$

where L stands for labour, K for capital and Q for production. A and α are constants. A is an unimportant constant which depends on the choice of the units in which variables are expressed, whereas a is a very important constant which has to do with the distributive shares of labour and capital. This Cobb-Douglas production function possesses important properties some of which are worth mentioning here. First, it follows from this production function that production without capital is impossible, because L and K are multiplied by one another. Secondly, the sum of α and 1- α is equal to 1. This means that the above Cobb-Douglas production function represents constant returns to scale, that is, increase in the scale of production has no effect on productivity. If L and K are multiplied by a certain given number g, total production Q also increases by g times as large (For the proof that Cobb-Douglas production function implies constant returns to scale, an earlier chapter of this book).

The remarkable aspect of Cobb-Douglas production function is represented by exponent α which is proved to be equal to the elasticity of output with respect to labour. And the elasticity of output with regard to labour, as we have proved above, is equal to the relative share of labour in national income. Thus the exponent α in Cobb-Douglas production function measures the relative share of labour in national product. That the exponent α in Cobb-Douglas production function is equal to the elasticity of output with respect to labour and therefore to relative share of labour in national incomers proved below.

Since real wage rate (w) is equal to marginal product of labour $\left(\frac{\Delta Q}{\Delta L}\right)$, therefore, under linear Cobb-Douglas production function.

$$w = \frac{\Delta Q}{\Delta L} = \alpha AL^{\alpha-1}K^{1-\alpha}$$

Since absolute labour's share in national income can be obtained by multiplying the real wage rate with total quantity of labour, L, the absolute labour's share = $w.L = \frac{\Delta Q}{\Delta L}.L = \alpha AL^{\alpha-1+1}K^{1-\alpha}$

or $$w.L = \frac{\Delta Q}{\Delta L}.L = \alpha AL^{\alpha}K^{1-\alpha}$$

Now, relative labour' s share in national product can be obtained by dividing the absolute share by the total national product Q. Therefore, labour relative share = $\frac{w.L}{Q} = \frac{\Delta Q}{\Delta L}.\frac{L}{Q} = \frac{\alpha AL^{\alpha}K^{1-\alpha}}{Q}$

Since according to Cobb-Douglas production function,

$$Q = AL^{\alpha}K^{1-\alpha},$$

$$\text{Therefore, labour s relative share} = \frac{w.L}{Q} = \frac{\Delta Q}{\Delta L}.\frac{L}{Q} = \frac{\alpha AL^{\alpha}K^{1-\alpha}}{AL^{\alpha}K^{1-\alpha}}$$

$$= \frac{w.L}{Q} = \frac{\Delta Q}{\Delta L}.\frac{L}{Q} = \alpha$$

It should be noted that $\frac{\Delta Q}{\Delta L}.\frac{L}{Q}$ is the expression for the elasticity of output with respect to labour. We therefore conclude that in Cobb-Douglas production function labour' s relative share ir national product is equal to output elasticity with respect to labour or constant α which is the exponent of labour L in the function.

Likewise, exponent $1 - \alpha$ of K in the function measures capital's relative share in national income. We thus reach a remarkable conclusion regarding Cobb-Douglas production function with homogenous of first degree that the exponents are direct measure of the relative shares of labour and capital. According to the empirical investigations made by Cobb-Douglas, *i.e.* value of exponent α is 3/4 and therefore of exponent $1 - \alpha$ is 1/4. In other words, labour's relative share in national income is 75% and capital's relative share in it is 25%.

Another important conclusion regarding Cobb-Douglas production function is that the output etaslicities with respect to labour and capital, *i.e.*, a and $1 - \alpha$ respectively are "independent of the ratio K/L, *i.e.*, capital intensity or the amount of capital per worker. However much capital we pump into the production process, income distribution remains the same. In other words, according to this production function the shares of income are not influenced by capital accumulation. The price ratio of the factors of production *does* change with an increasing K/L. Real wages go up and the real rate of interest goes down. The degree of changes of these prices can be stated exacly. If the amount of capital per worker (i.e., $\frac{K}{L}$

ratio) increases by 1%, the interest-wage ratio under the Cobb-Dougls drops by 1%. The two variations (*i.e.*, r/w *and of* K/L) compensate one another, so that labour's relative share remains the same."[6]

Since responsiveness ot K/L to changes in r/w measures the elasticity of substitution, the above conclusion can also be reached in terms of elasticity of substitution. In linear Cobb-Douglas production function, elasticity of substitution between labour and capital is equal to one which means that as capital is accumulated and consequently real return on it (*i.e.*, marginal product of capital) falls, and consequently the factor price ratio r/w falls and the proportionate increase in capital-labour is equal to the proportionate increase in capital-labour is equal to the proportionate fall in r/w. As result, labour's relative share remains the same as more capital is accumulated. Thus, in neo-classical macro theory of distribution based on linear Cobb-Douglas production function, capital accumulation does not affect or determine relative shares ot labour and capital. Therefore, capital accumulation in neo-classical distribution theory has been discarded as a determinant of distributive shares.

Thus by applying Cobb-Douglas production function, neo-classical economist were able to show constancy of labour's relative share in national income. Commenting on it Professor Pen writes : "The Cobb-Douglas is, of course, ideal for explaining a constant share of labour. It was a god-send. Although its inventors were initially more interested in understanding the rate of growth than distribution, the function fitted perfectly into the then prevailing fashion of an *invariable* "λ (*i.e.*, labour's relative share). This, and the theoretical elegance of the Cobb-Douglas, explains its tremendous popularity. Numerous econometricians have taken it as starting point for empirical research. This has broadly confirmed what the investigators had in mind, *viz.*, an unchanging distribution."[7]

Solow's and SMAC Production Functions and Relative Shares of Labour and Capital

In the post-second world war period both in America and Britain it has been found that labour's relative share in national income has been rising and has not remained constant as it follows from linear Cobb-Douglas production function. Therefore, a new production function was needed to explain the rising share of labour. Prof. R. M. Solow[8] put forward a new production function which helped economists to explain the new situation. Solow's production function is as follows :

$$Q = (L^{\alpha} + K^{\alpha})^{1/\alpha}$$

where Q stands for total production, L for labour and K for capital, α is a constant. Though Solow's production function, like Cobb-Douglas' s production function, is linearly homogeneous (*i.e.* , exhibits constant returns to scale), there are some significant differences between the two. Firstly, in Solow's production function, elasticity of substitution is not equal to one but is equal to $\dfrac{1}{1-\alpha}$. As we shall see below that according to this value of elasticity there can be changes in distributive shares of labour and capital which could not occur if elasticity of substitution was equal to one. Secondly, unlike that of Cobb-Douglas production function, in Solow's production function the elasticity of output or production with respect to labour is not equal to its exponent, α but is equal to the following complicated expression :

6. Jan Pen, *op. cit.* p. 192.
7. *Op. cit.*,p. 193.
8. A Contribution to the Theory of Economic Growth, *Quarterly Journal of Economics*, 1956.

Elasticity of output or production with respect to labour = $\frac{L\alpha}{L^{\alpha}+K^{\alpha}}$, and

elasticity of output with respect to capital = $\frac{K\alpha}{L^{\alpha}+K^{\alpha}}$

The above expressions for elasticities of output are quite responsive or sensitive to changes in the factor ratio of *K* and *L*. This means that under Solow's production function, distribution of national income between labour and capital will depend on capital accumulation. "If more capital is introduced into production, the elasticity of production increases in respect of labour, and so does share of labour."[9]

We can express the effect of increase in capital intensity in Solow's production function in a better way by means of the elasticity of substitution. Solow's production function can hold with very different values of elasticity of substitution; elasticity of substitution can be less than one or also it can be greater than one. What is the actual value of the elasticity of substitution has to be found out by the econometricians through empirical studies. The value of elasticity of substitution is of crucial importance in determining the distributive shares of labour and capital. J.R. Hicks explained long time back that "a low elasticity of substitution means that the rapidly growing production factor must force itself into the production process at the expense of a relatively strong drop in prices. This drop in prices is by definition greater than the relative size of its amount. The net effect is that the income share of the fast grower drops. This might be called Hicks's Law. In fact capital is the more rapid grower of the two factors of production—therefore elasticity of substitution being less than one ($\alpha < 1$) implies a declining share of capital."[10] And declining share of capital with the capital accumulation and increase in capital intensity implies increase in the relative share of labour.

It is clear from the above analysis that elasticity of substitution is an important determinant of the distributive shares of labour and capital. In recent years much research workhas been done and new production functions known as **Constant Elasticity of Substitution Function** (shortly described as *CES* Functions) have been proposed. In these production functions elasticity of substitution, though not equal to one, remains constant as long as the function remains fixed, or in other words, elasticity of substitution remains constant or unchanged as capital-intensity increases. The most important type of the constant elasticity of substitution function is *SMAC* Function (Solow-Minhas-Arrow- Chenery Function)[11] known after the name of its inventors.

A good deal of empirical research has been done in the recent years on the basis of *SMAC* and other *CES* Functions in order to explain economic growth but as a by-product it has furnished the information regarding the actual value of elasticity of substitution between capital and labour and its consequent effect on income distribution. *This* empirical research has revealed that the *elasticity of substitution is almost always less than one and is approximately equal to* 0.6. This figure of elasticity of substitution ***"throws a new light on the mechanics of the society in which we live. It proves that the accumulation of capital is the worker's friend. Not only does labour productivity and thus prosperity increase as a result, but in***

9. Jan. Pen, *op. cit.*, p. 194.
10. J. Pen, 196.
11. K. Arrow, H. Chenery, B. Minhas and R. Solow, 'Capital Labour Substitution and Economic Efficiency', *Review of Economic Statistics*, 1961.
12. J. Pen, *op. cit.* 198.

addition increasing capital intensity leads to an increasing share of labour." [12] Elasticity of substitution being equal to 0.6 implies that for every 1% increase in capital intensity, the share of labour increases by about 0.2%. Professor Pen has found that it is *approximately* in accordance with reality in the United States and Britain. He thus writes : "in a country like the United States the amount of capital per worker has roughly doubled since the beginning of the century. That consequently leads to an increase in the share of labour 20%. And in fact the rise is of that order of size; labour's relative share was 55% in those days and is now about 70%, *i.e.*, an increase of 23%. We can also consider the pure share of capital, including land rent but excluding profit, which has fallen by about two-thirds since 1900 while the equation yields a drop of 60.%"[13]

Critical Evaluation of Neo-Classical Theory of Relative Shares

By laying stress on the nature of production function with its elasticity of substitution between labour and capital, neo-classical theory brings out certainly the most important factor which determines fne distributive shares in a society. As is clear from the quotation from Pen given above, the real changes in distributives shares *only roughly and approximately* accord with the predictions of neoclassical theory. A residue remains which remains unexplained. Therefore, besides production function and elasticity of substitution other factors also play a role in the determination of income distribution between labour and capital. One of these factors is the degree of monopoly in the economy as has been emphasized by Kalecki. The other factor is that wages and salaries have been pushed up *institutionally*, that is, *by the trade unions*. Further, conventions, prestige and social status also play a part in the determination of income distribution. Further, macro-level changes such as inflation and depression also affect the distribution of income.

Kaldor has criticized the neo-classical theory on the basis that it is difficult to measure capital which is required under neo-classical theory to find out marginal productivity of labour and capital. He thus writes : ***"The basic difficulty with the whole approach lies..... in the very meaning of 'capital' as a factor of production. Whilst land can be measured in acres per year and labour in man-hours. capital (as distinet from 'capital goods') cannot be measured in terms of physical units".*** [14]

Further, accorading to Kaldor, tne measurement of capital and hence the marginal rate of substitution between capital and labour can be obtained only if rate of profit is known before hand. And this involves, according to him, circular reasoning in the neo-classical theory of distribution. To quote him, "In fact the whole approach which regards the share of wages and profits in output as being determined by the marginal rate of substitution between capital and labour ..... is hardly acceptable to the present-day economists. Its inadequacy becomes evident as soon as it is realized that the 'marginal rate of substitution' between capital and labour—as distinct from the marginal rate of substitution between labour and land—can only be determined once the rate of profit and the rate of wages are already known. The same technical alternatives might yield very different 'marginal rates of substitution' according as the ratio of profits to wages is one thing or another."[15]

But, in the opinion of the present author even if the difficulty of measurement of capital is conceded, it remains true that the nature of production function and elasticity of substitution remain very important factors which determine income distribution in a society.

---

13. J.Pen, *op. cit*, p. 198.
14. N. Kaldor, *Alternative Theories of Distribution*.
15. **N. Kaldor, *op. cit.***

QUESTION FOR REVIEW

1. Explain and critically examine Neoclassical Macro Theory of Distribution.
2. Show how marginal productivity theory of distrubution explains relative share of labour and capital. Is it a valid explanation of changes in distrubutive shares of labour and capital ?
3. In the post Second war period labour's relative share in national income has risen in both the United States and Great Britain. How would you explain it will Neoclassical theroy of distribution.
4. Prior to the second world war, labour's share in national income remains constant in the major capitalist economies despite capital accumulation and economic growth. How would you explain it with Cobb-Douglas production function.
5. Write expressions for Solow production function and SMAC production function. How do they affect relative shares of labour and capital.
6. What is meant by elasticity of subsitution between factors? How does neoclassical theory of distribution explains relative shares of labour and capital in national income?
7. If elasticity of subsitution between labour and capital is less than one, how a rise in wage rate will affect their relative shares in national income.
8. Distinguish between neutral, capital-using and labour-using technological change. How do they affect relative shares labour and capital
9. Elasticity of substitution between labour and capital being less than one shows that accumulation of capital is the worker's friend. Not only does labour-productivity and thus prosperity increase as a result, but in addition increasing capital intensity leads to an increasing share of labour". Discuss.

CHAPTER

52

Pricing of Factors in Competitive Markets

Concepts of Factor Productivity

Before turning to the detailed study of how prices of factors of production are determined under conditions of perfect and imperfect competitions, it will be helpful for the proper understanding of the subject if we first explain the various concepts of productivity. The knowledge of these various concepts will greatly help in understanding the modern theory of factor prices. At the very outset it is desirable to make it clear why economists are interested at all in the productivity of a factor. We are concerned with productivity since the price which a factor will be able to get depends upon the value of its marginal product. Why? This is because the factors are demanded not because they directly satisfy the wants of the people. The factors are purchased to put them to work for producing goods which directly or indirectly satisfy the wants. Other things being equal, the greater the contribution made to the production of goods by a factor unit, the greater the price which it will be able to command in the market. Thus productivity of a factor is an important determinant of the price of a factor.

Average Product (AP). We have already explained the concepts of average physical productivity and marginal physical productivity in an earlier chapter. To repeat here, average physical product is the total production divided by the number of units of a factor employed.

$$\text{Average product } (AP) \text{ of a factor} = \frac{\text{total output}}{\text{total no. of units of a factor}}$$

Marginal Product (MP): Marginal physical product of a factor is the increase in total output caused by employing an additional unit of the factor, *quantity of other factors remaining fixed*. The fixed factors are, however, conceived to be adjusted or adapted in such a way that increased amount of the variable factor can be used with them.

Before the development of the theory of product pricing under imperfect competition (monopoly and monopolistic competition) by Joan Robinson and Chamberlin, the assumption of perfect competition in the product market was usually made while discussing the pricing of factors. Under perfect competition in the product market conversion of the marginal physical product into money terms merely involves multiplying the marginal physical product with the price of the product since the price of the product of an individual firm under perfect competition is a given and constant quantity. Money value of the marginal physical product under perfect competition thus means the marginal physical product multiplied by the price of the product. However, with the development of imperfect competition theory for the product markets two distinct concepts of marginal productivity have been evolved. They are :

(*i*) Marginal Revenue Product (*MRP*); and

(*ii*) Value of Marginal Product (*VMP*).

Marginal Revenue Product (MRP)

Marginal revenue product is the increment in the total value product caused by employing an additional unit of a factor, the expenditure on other factors remaining unchanged. In other words, marginal revenue product is the marginal physical product of the factor multiplied by the marginal revenue.

$$MRP = MPP \times MR$$

It is the marginal revenue product which is often termed as marginal product or marginal productivity.

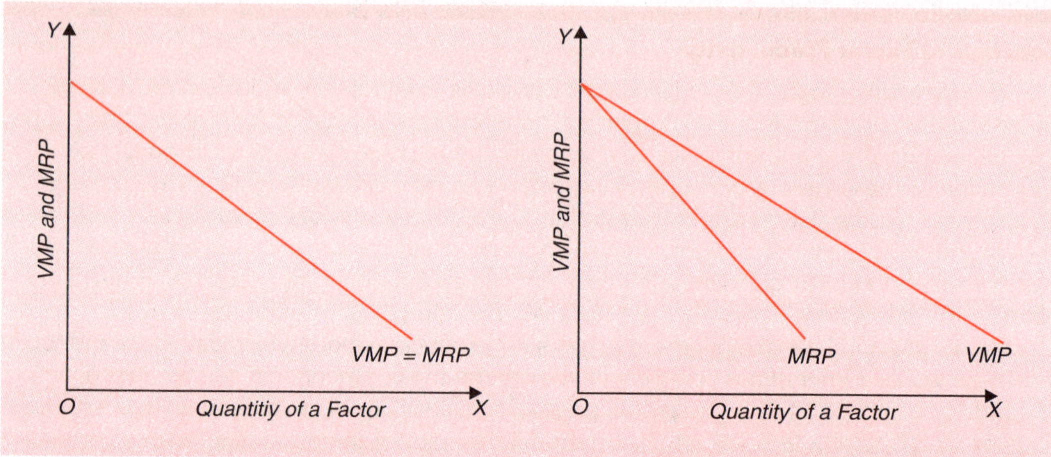

Fig. 52.1. *VMP and MRP under Perfect Competition in the Product Market*

Fig. 52.2. *VMP and MRP under Imperfect Competition in the Product Market*

Value of Marginal Product (VMP)

It means the marginal physical product of the factor multiplied by the price of the product (*i.e.* average revenue).

$$VMP = MPP \times \text{Price (or } AR)$$

Since under perfect competition the demand curve of the product facing an individual firm is perfectly elastic and therefore price and marginal revenue are equal, the value of marginal product and marginal revenue product are equal to each other as is shown in Fig. 52.1. But since in monopoly or imperfect competition, average revenue (or demand curve) is sloping downward and marginal revenue curve lies below the average revenue curve, price is not equal to marginal revenue. Therefore, in monopoly or in other forms of imperfect competition, marginal revenue product will not be equal to the value of marginal product. Since price is higher than marginal revenue under monopoly or monopolistic competition in the product market, the value of marginal product (*VMP*) will be greater than the marginal revenue product *(MRP)* and the marginal revenue product *(MRP)* curve will lie below the value of marginal product (*VMP*) curve as is shown in Fig. 52.2. Thus, in perfect competition *MRP* and *VMP* have identical meanings but in imperfect competition they diverge.

The distinction between Marginal Revenue Product (*MRP*) and the Value of Marginal Product (VMP) can be better understood from the following tables :

Table 52.1. Value of Marginal Product *(VMP)* and Marginal Revenue Product *(MRP)* in case of Perfectly Competitive Product Market

I	II	III	IV	V	VI	VII
Units of a Factor	*Total Output (Q)*	*Marginal Physical Product (MPP)*	*Price of Product* (P_x)	*Value of Marginal Product (VMP)* $MPP \times P_x$	*Total Revenue (TR)* $(Q \times P_x)$	*Marginal Revenue Product (MRP)*
1	25	25	2	50	50	50
2	70	45	2	90	140	90
3	110	40	2	80	220	80
4	145	35	2	70	290	70
5	172	27	2	54	344	54
6	191	19	2	38	382	38
7	199	8	2	16	398	16
8	199	0	2	0	398	0

In the *above* table perfect competition has been assumed to be prevailing in the product market. Therefore, price of the product (₹ 2) for an individual firm remains the same whatever the level of its output. As more units of labour are employed, total output (Q) is increasing but at a diminishing rate. That is to say, marginal physical productivity is declining (law of diminishing marginal returns has been assumed to be operating). Since *VMP* is equal to *MPP* × Price, *VMP* (Col. V) can be found by multiplying Col. III by Col IV. Thus when one labour unit is employed the marginal physical product is 25. Since the price of the product is ₹ 2, the value of marginal product (*VMP*) will be equal to 25 × 2 = 50 and so for the subsequent units of labour. It shall be noticed from Col. V that value of marginal product is declining as more units of labour are employed after the second unit. This is so because marginal physical product is declining due to the operation of law of diminishing returns.

Since in perfect competition in the product market *MR* is equal to price *(AR),* marginal revenue product *MRP* also can be found out by multiplying Col. III by Col. IV. Thus under perfect competition value of marginal product will be equal to marginal revenue product (compare Col. VII with Col. V). Since marginal revenue product productivity *(MRP)* can also be defined as the increment in the total revenue of a firm by employing an additional unit of a factor, it can be directly found out from Col. VI which shows the total revenue at the various levels of output.

MRP can be obtained by taking out the difference between the two successive total revenues. The difference in the two successive total revenues occurs due to the employment of an extra unit of a factor. Thus when two units of labour are employed, total revenue is ₹ 140 which is obtained by selling 70 units of output produced by 2 units of labour. When another labour unit is employed, the total output is 110 and total revenue obtained is ₹ 220. Thus, this additional unit of labour has added ₹ 80 (₹ 220 – ₹ 140) to the firm's total revenue. *MRP* of the subsequent units of labour can be found out in two ways : first, by multiplying marginal physical product *MPP* by *MR* (in the present case *MR* is equal to price); and secondly, by taking out the difference between the two successive total revenues caused by employing an additional unit of labour.

VMP and *MRP* under Imperfect Competition in the Product Market

Whereas value of marginal product and marginal revenue product are equal under perfect competition, they diverge if there is imperfect competition in the product market.

Table 52.2. *VMP* and *MRP* under Imperfect Competition

I	II	III	IV	V	VI	VII
Units of a Factor	*Total Output (Q)*	*Marginal Physical Product (MPP)*	*Price of Product (P)*	*Value of Marginal Product (VMP)*	*Total Revenue (TR) (P.Q)*	*Marginal Revenue Product (MRP)*
1	25	25	2.00	50.00	50	50
2	70	45	1.80	81.00	126	76
3	110	40	1.50	60.00	165	39
4	145	35	1.30	45.50	188.50	23.50
5	172	27	1.20	32.40	206.40	17.90
6	191	19	1.15	21.85	219.65	13.26
7	199	8	1.13	9.04	224.87	5.22
8	199	0	1.13	0.00	224.87	0.00

Under imperfect competition in the product market, average revenue curve or demand curve facing an individual firm slopes downward. In other words, as the firm increases its output (and sales), by employing more units of labour, the price of the product declines (see Col. IV in Table 52.2). Since the average revenue curve *(i.e.,* price curve) is falling downward under imperfect competition in the product market, *MR* curve will lie below it. In other words, *MR* will be less than *AR (i.e.,* price) of output. Since *VMP* is equal to *MPP* x Price and *MRP* is equal to *MPP* x *MR,* the two will not be equal to each other when imperfect competition prevails in the product market. *VMP* at various levels of labour employment which is shown in Col. V of Table 52.2 is obtained by multiplying *MPP* (Col. III) with price of the product which goes on falling (Col. IV). Thus when two units of labour are engaged, marginal physical product *(MPP)* is 45 and price of the product is ₹ 1.80. By multiplying 45 with ₹1.80 we get *VMP* equal to ₹ 81 which we write in Col. V corresponding to two units of labour. Likewise, *VMP* for other levels of labour employment can be found out.

In order to obtain *MRP* we have first to find out the total revenue at various levels of labour employment. The total revenue (Col. VI) is obtained by multiplying total output (Col. II) with price of the product (Col. IV). By finding out the difference between two successive total revenues, *MRP* can be obtained. Thus when two units of labour are employed, total revenue is ₹ 126 and when three units of labour are employed, the total revenue is ₹ 165. Increment in total revenue caused by the third unit of labour is thus equal to ₹ 165 – 126 = ₹ 39. Thus, *MRP* of labour when three units of it are employed is ₹ 39. Similarly, *MRP* of other levels of labour employment is found out and recorded in Col. VII. By comparing Col. V. and Col. VII, it will be clear that *VMP* and *MRP* are not the same and further that *MRP* is less than *VMP.* This is so because, as explained above, price and *MR* are not equal *(MR* is less than the price) for a firm facing imperfect competition in the product market. To sum up, under imperfect competition in the product market, *MRP* and *VMP* will diverge and *MRP* curve will lie below *VMP* curve.

Factor-Employment Equilibrium of a Firm: General Conditions

In Parts III and IV, we have discussed the conditions of firm's equilibrium in the product market in order to show what level of output it will produce so as to maximise its profits. In the present chapter we are concerned with the firm's equilibrium in the factor market. That is, we are here concerned with the equilibrium of the firm with respect to the amount of a factor (or productive service or resource) it has to employ. Of course, we explained in a previous chapter firm's equilibrium with regard to employment of a factor combination and found that in order to produce a given level of output at the minimum cost possible with given factor price, a firm will be in equilibrium when it is combining the various factors in such a way that marginal rate of technical substitution between any two factors is equal to their price ratio. ($MRTS_{LK} = \frac{w}{r}$). In terms of marginal product of factors we can say that a firm is in equilibrium in regard to the usage of factors so that

$$\frac{MP_L}{w} = \frac{MP_K}{r} = \frac{MP_d}{P_d}$$

where L, K and D stand for various factors of production, MP for marginal productivity of a factor, w, r and d are the prices of factors, labour, capital, and land respectively.

Using the above proportionality condition or equality of $MRTS_{LK}$ with factor price ratio $\left(\frac{w}{r}\right)$, we shall explain how a firm determines the absolute amount of a factor it has to use or employ and what factors govern its decision about this. There can be various possible situations in both the factor and product markets in which a firm may find itself. A firm may be facing perfect competition in both the factor and product markets. Or, there may prevail perfect competition for the firm in the factor market, but in the product market it may be a monopolist or working under imperfect competition. Further, while a firm may be a single buyer of a productive factor in the factor market (that is, the firm has a monopsony in the factor market) but has to face perfect competition in the product market. Still further, there may be firm's monopoly in both buying the factor and selling the product. In other words, there may be monopsony in the factor market as well as monopoly in the product market. Therefore we have to explain the firm's equilibrium in all the following possible situations :

(*a*) Perfect competition in both the factor and product markets;

(*b*) Perfect competition in the factor market, but monopoly or imperfect competition in the product market;

(c) Monopsony in the factor market but perfect competition in product market; and

(*d*) Monopsony in the factor market and monopoly in the product market.

As usual, in our analysis we assume that the entrepreneur who has to hire other factors of production is rational, *i.e.*, he tries to maximize his profits. In deciding about the number of units of a factor it has to employ, the rational entrepreneur will be guided by the change in cost as a result of employment of a factor unit and the change in revenue made by the sale of the additional output produced by that factor unit. The entrepreneur will compare the change in total value product with the change in cost of employing an extra unit of a factor. If the change in total revenue or value product resulting from the employment of an additional factor unit exceeds the additional cost of hiring it, it will be profitable for the firm to employ that unit.

Change in revenue resulting from the employment of an extra unit of the factor is called *Marginal Revenue Product (MRP)*, and the change in cost brought about by hiring an extra unit of the factor is called *Marginal Factor Cost (MFC)*. This is also called *marginal input cost* or *marginal expense (ME)* on a factor. The firm will go on employing more and more units of a factor as long as marginal revenue product of the factor exceeds the marginal factor cost of it. The firm will not employ an extra unit of a factor if its marginal factor cost is greater than its marginal revenue product, because it will not be profitable for the firm to do so. The profits of the entrepreneur will be maximum when it is employing a number of units of a factor at which its marginal revenue product equals its marginal factor cost. Therefore, the firm will achieve equilibrium in the employment of a factor when the following condition is satisfied:

Marginal Revenue Product = Marginal Factor Cost

$$MRP = MFC$$

As seen above, under perfect competition in the product market marginal revenue product *(MRP)* of a factor is equal to the value of its marginal product *(VMP)*, the condition of firm's equilibrium of a factor employment can be written

$$VMP = MFC$$

The equality *of MRP* with *MFC is* necessary but not a sufficient condition of firm's equilibrium in regard to the employment of the factor. For the firm to be in equilibrium position a second order condition must also be fulfilled. This second order condition is that the ***marginal revenue product curve must cut the marginal factor cost curve from above at the point of equilibrium.*** In other words, this second order condition states that for employment of a factor greater than the equilibrium level, marginal revenue product must be less than marginal factor cost; and for employment less than the equilibrium level, the marginal revenue product must be greater than the marginal factor cost. Thus, for the equilibrium level of employment, the following two conditions must be fulfilled :-

(1) $MRP = MFC$

(2) *MRP* curve must cut the *MFC curve from above*

OR

for employment greater than the equilibrium one, $MRP < MFC$, and

for employment less than the equilibrium one, $MRP > MFC$.

Under perfect competition in the product market, $MRP = VMP$ and perfect competition in the factor market, marginal factor cost curve is a horizontal straight line. Under these circumstances, *MRP* or *VMP* curve can cut *MFC* curve from above only if it is *declining* at the point of equilibrium. Thus, under perfect competition, the conditions for factor-employment equilibrium of the firm are :

(1) $VMP = MFC$

(2) *VMP* curve of the factor must be declining at the point of equilibrium.

Derived Demand for a Factor

According to the neo-classical theory of pricing of factors of production, under conditions of perfect competition it is the forces of demand for and supply of factors which determine their prices. It is therefore essential to understand first the nature of demand for factors of production. Demand for a factor differs in certain respects from the demand for consumer goods or products. Products or consumer goods are demanded because they satisfy the wants of the people directly. People demand food to satisfy the pangs of their hunger, they demand clothes to satisfy their want of providing a cover to their bodies and so forth. These products possess utility which directly satisfy the desires of the people and who are therefore willing to pay the price for these products.

But, unlike the products, the factors of production do not satisfy the wants of the people directly. The factors of production are demanded not because they directly satisfy the wants of the people who wish to buy them. Instead, they are demanded because they can be used to produce goods which then directly or indirectly satisfy human wants. Therefore, demand for factors of production is called *derived demand*. It is derived from the demand for the product they help to make. Thus, the demand for a factor ultimately depends upon the demands for goods it helps to produce. The greater the demand for goods a particular type of factor helps to make, the greater the demand for that type of factor. Just as demand for a good depends upon its utility, the demand for a factor depends upon the marginal productivity of a factor. In fact, as will be presently explained, the marginal productivity curve of the factor is the demand curve for that factor. The entrepreneur's demand for a factor of production is governed by the marginal productivity of the factor.

We shall first explain firm's equilibrium with regard to the employment of factors under conditions of perfect competition, the analysis of which will show how much quantity of a factor will be demanded by the firm.

Factor-Employment Equilibrium of a Firm in Competitive Markets

We explain the equilibrium of a factor employment by a firm working in competitive markets and therefore its demand for a factor by taking the example of labour. When there is perfect competition in the product market, an individual firm cannot influence the price of the product by changing its output level and therefore it has to take the ruling price in the market as given and only adjusts its output level so as to maximize its profits. Since for a perfectly competitive firm in the product market the price in the market is given and constant, the average revenue curve facing it is a horizontal straight line and marginal revenue curve coincides with it. For it, $AR = MR$. Therefore, a firm which is working under conditions of perfect competition in the product market the marginal revenue product of labour *(MRP)* will be equal to its value of marginal product (*VMP*). Thus under perfect competition in the product market, *MRP* and *VMP* curves of labour will be the same.

Perfect competition prevails in the labour market when :

(1) the labour is homogeneous and buyers[1] are identical from the sellers[2] point of view

(2) both buyers and sellers possess perfect information regarding the current factor prices (*i.e.* wage rate of labour) in the market;

(3) the number of buyers and sellers is very large ; and

(4) both buyers and sellers are free to enter or leave the market.

When a firm is confronting perfect competition in the labour market, it cannot affect the price of labour, that is, its wage rate, by varying its level of employment. A single firm's demand for labour is so small compared with the total demand for labour that any changes in its demand for labour will not affect its wage rate. It has to take the wage rate as given and constant for it. The firm can employ as many number of workers as it wishes at the prevailing wage rate. Therefore, ***the supply curve of the factor for a single firm under perfect competition in the labour market will be perfectly elastic (horizontal straight line) at the***

1. & 2. In the factor market, the *buyers* are the entrepreneurs or firms who have to buy the factors for producing goods, and the sellers are the owners of factors who have to supply these factors to the entrepreneurs. Workers supply labour, landlords supply land and so forth.

level of the prevailing wage rate. As a result, for a firm working under perfect competition in the labour market, the extra cost of hiring an extra unit of labour will be equal to the wage rate which remains unchanged. Thus, marginal factor cost on hiring labour under perfect competition in the labour market is equal to the wage rate of labour (*W* = *MFC*). 'This is shown in Fig. 52.3. In this figure, ruling wage rate of labour in the market is *OW*, which the firm has to accept as given and constant. Supply curve of the labour (or *AFC* curve) is a horizontal straight line and *MFC* curve coincides with it.

As explained above, the firm will continue employing more units of a factor as long as the marginal revenue product is greater than marginal factor cost and will achieve equilibrium position where marginal revenue product is equal to marginal factor cost, or where the marginal revenue product curve intersects the marginal factor cost curve. As in the present case when perfect competition prevails in both the labour and products markets, *MRP* is equal to *VMP* and *MFC* = *W*, we can state that a firm which is working under conditions of perfect competition will attain equilibrium at that level of labour employment where *VMP* (or *MRP*) of labour is equal to wage rate (= *MFC*). At point *E*, the second order condition is also satisfied since the *VMP* (or *MRP*) curve of labour is cutting *MFC* curve from above. It will be noticed from the Figure 52.3 that marginal revenue product of labour (*MRP*) is also equal to *MFC* at point *A*. But *A* cannot be the position of equilibrium since second order condition is not fulfilled. At point *A*, *VMP* or *MRP* curve is cutting *MFC* curve from below and it will be profitable for the firm to increase employment further. Thus, *E* is the point of equilibrium where *MRP* = *MFC* or *VMP* = Price of laour (*i.e.*, wage rate) as well as *VMP* curve is cutting *MFC* curve from above.

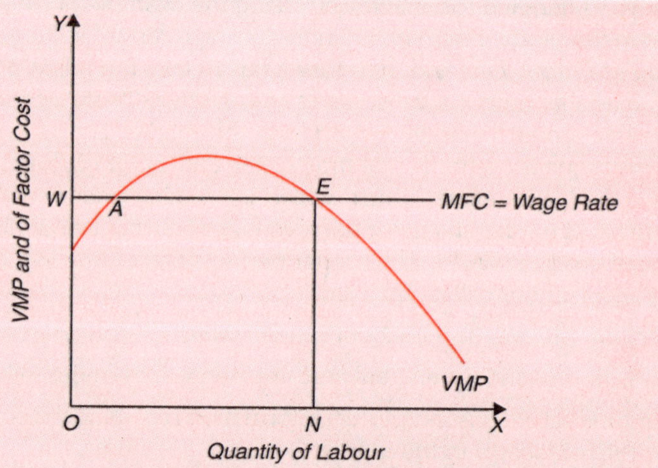

Fig. 52.3. *Employment of labour by a Firm*

To sum up, under perfect competition in both the labour and product markets

$$MRP = MFC = AFC \text{ (or Wage rate)}$$

Since *MRP* and *VMP* are equal when there is perfect competition in the product market, therefore

$$MRP = VMP = MFC = AFC \text{ (or Wage rate)}$$

Thus, we conclude that under perfect competition in both the markets, a factor of production, labour in our example, will get remuneraion equal to the value of its marginal product.

In order to know whether the firm is earning profits or losses we have so to draw average revenue product curve (*ARP)* as is shown Fig. 52.4. It will be seen from this figure that when the firm is in equilibrium at *ON* level of employment (*i.e.*, at point *E*) average revenue product (*ARP*) which is equal to *NR* is greater than average wage which is equal to *NE*. Therefore, *ER*

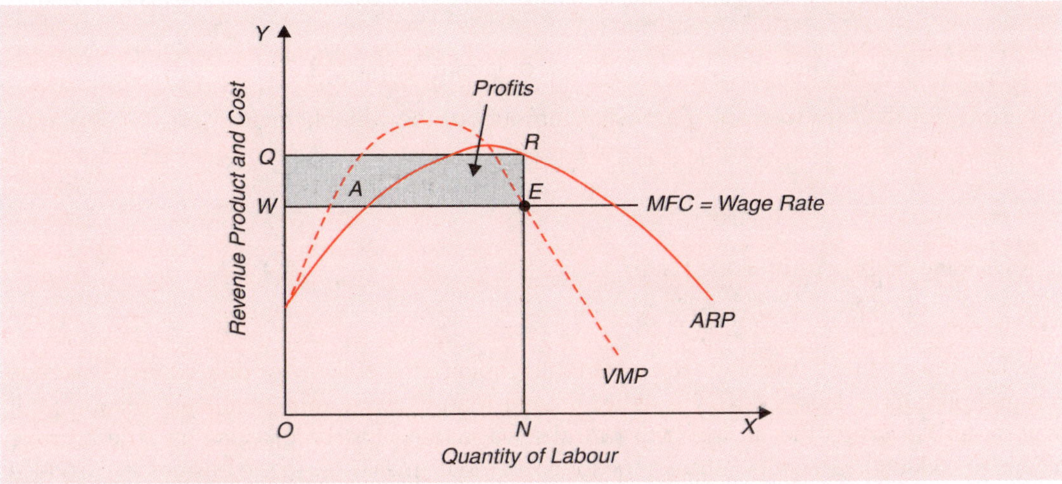

Fig. 52.4. *Demand for Labour : Labour-Employment Equilibrium and profit*

is the profit per unit of the factor. Rectangle *WERQ* is the total profit earned by the firm. Thus, with wage rate *OW* and equilibrium at *E,* the firm is making super-normal profits. Firm can earn such super-normal profits in the short run. But this cannot happen in the long run since by lure of these profits other firms will enter the labour market in the long run and hire labour and use it in the industry when it is yielding economic or super-normal-profits.

The Average Revenue Product and the Decision to Employ a Factor

It may be noted that the satisfaction of the marginal conditions for employing factors to maximise profits need not lead to the employment of a factor. The firm will employ a positive amount of a variable factor only if its contribution to total revenue product is at least equal to the variable costs incurred on it. This condition will be better understood if we express it in terms of the average revenue product of the variable factor.

As we know, the average revenue product of a factor is the total revenue earned per unit of the variable factor, say labour. Thus

$$ARP = \frac{TR}{L} \qquad .....(i)$$

where*TR* is the total revenue obtained by selling the total output produced by employing a given amount (*L*) of labour and *ARP* stands for the average revenue product of labour. But, total revenue (*TR*) is equal to the average revenue *(AR)* multiplied by the total output *(Q)* produced by employing a given quantity of the factor. It therefore follows

$$ARP = \frac{TR}{L} = \frac{AR.Q}{L} = AR.\frac{Q}{L} \qquad ......(ii)$$

Now, $\frac{Q}{L}$ represents the average physical product (*APP*) of labour. It follows from *(ii)* that

$$ARP \text{ of labour } = AR.APP$$

$$\text{and } TR = L.ARP$$

Suppose labour is the only variable factor used for production, then total variable cost *(TVC)* incurred for production will be equal to the total wages paid to the amount of labour employed. Thus in case of labour as the only variable factor,

$$TVC = w.L$$

where w is the wage rate and L is the amount of labour employed.

Now, for the firm to employ a positive amount of the variable factor,

$$TR \geq TVC$$

or,

$$L.ARP \geq wL$$

Dividing both sides by L we have

$$ARP \geq w$$

This means that in the short run a firm will employ a variable factor only when its average revenue product of labour *(ARP)* is either greater than its wage rate or at least equal to it. It may be further noted that in the long run, the wage rate must be greater than the average revenue product of labour, because in the long run the firm will stay in the business to produce a product when it covers not only the variable cost incurred on labour employed but also the costs incurred on other factors such as capital used along with labour. The decision to employ a positive amount of a variable factor is illustrated in Fig. 52.5. It will be seen from this figure that if the wage rate is W_2, the marginal factor cost on labour is given by the horizontal line MFC_2 which intersects the curve of marginal product of labour at point K. Thus, at point K, both the conditions of profit maximization are fulfilled, namely, MFC or $(W) = VMP$ and VMP curve of the labour is declining at point K. But the firm cannot be in equilibrium at point K, because wage rate W_2 exceeds the average revenue product *(ARP)* of labour and therefore

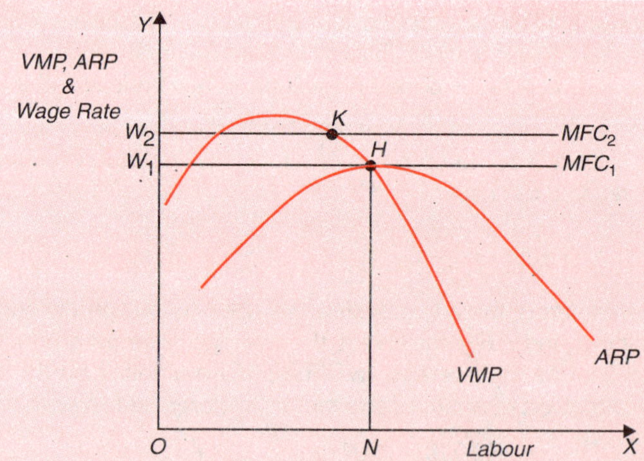

Fig. 52.5. *Labour will not be employed at a wage rate greater than ARP.*

employing labour at this wage rate means ihat the firm will not be covering even his labour costs (that is, variable costs) which it can avoid by deciding to shut down and not to employ labour. Similarly, *at any wage rate higher than the maximum ARP* (*i.e.* higher than w_1 in

Figure 52.5) the equality of wage rate with the value of marginal product of labour will be achieved where the wage rate is greater than average revenue product *(ARP)* of labour and therefore the employment of labour for production will bring losses to the firm because not only the fixed costs but also the variable costs on labour will not be covered. We thus see that ***the firm will decide to employ labour when wage rate is greater than or at least equal to the average revenue product ($w \geq ARP$).***

Derivation of Demand Curve for a Single Variable Factor

We have explained above how much amount of factor a firm under conditions of perfect competition in the factor market will employ and demand both in the short run and long run. We are now in a position to derive the *demand curve* for a factor of production under conditions of perfect competition, which with the intersection of supply curve of that factor will determine its price. The derivation nf demand curve for factor is illustrated in Fig. 52.6. It always pays an entrepreneur to go on hiring more and more units of a factor until its marginal revenue product equals its marginal factor cost. If there is a perfect competition in the factor market, then marginal factor cost will be equal to the market price of the factor which remains unaltered. As already explained, a perfectly competitive entrepreneur or buyer in the factor market will employ a factor of production to a point where its marginal revenue product equals its market price. In doing so, he will be maximizing his profits and will thus be in equilibrium position. Thus, in Fig. 52.6 if the market price of factor is OW_0, then the employer will hire or employ *ON* units of the factor since at *ON* units *MRP* of the factor is equal to its price OW_0. Thus at market price OW_o, *ON amount* of the factor will be demanded by the producer. If now the market price of factor falls to OW_1, the amount demanded of the factor will rise to *ON′* where marginal revenue product of the factor is equal to the new market price OW_1. If the factor price further falls to OW_2, then *ON″* quantity of the factor will be demanded by the firm (or entrepreneur).

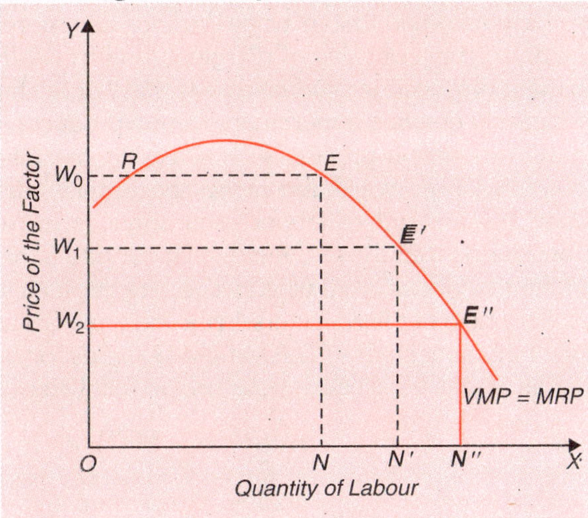

Fig. 52.6. *Derivation of Demand Curve for a Factor*

It is thus obvious that given the market price of the factor, we can read the quantity demanded of the factor by an entrepreneur from the marginal revenue product curve of the factor. The marginal revenue productivity curve usually first rises upward to a point and then slopes downward. But it, should be noted that only the downward sloping portion of the *VMP* curve forms the demand curve for that factor. This is so because the entrepreneur cannot be in equilibrium at the rising part of the *VMP* curve. For instance, in Fig. 52.6 with market price OW_0, the entrepreneur will not be in equilibrium at point *R*, since at *R*, value of marginal product curve is cutting marginal factor cost curve (which is here same as factor price curve) *from below*. With OW_0 as the price of the variable factor the entrepreneur will be in equilibrium at point *E* where *VMP* curve is cutting the factor price curve from above and will employ or demand *ON* amount of the factor. We thus conclude ***that under perfect competition in the factor market downward sloping part of the marginal value productivity (VMP) curve of the factor is the demand curve for the factor.***

Demand for a Factor (Labour) with More than One Variable Factors

In our analysis of demand curve for a single variable factor, labour in the foregoing analysis, we have assumed that as wage declines and more labour is demanded, the firm moves along the given curve of value of marginal product (*VMP*) which under perfect competition is equal to marginal revenue product curve *(MRP)* of the fator. This assumption is valid in the short run because in drawing a marginal revenue product curve of labour, the fixed cooperating factors in the production process such as capital are taken as given and constant. However, in the long run a firm would also make appropriate adjustment in the amount of capital employed when the amount of labour used changes in response to the changes in the wage rate. Considering that the two factors, labour and capital, are complementary, the increase in the amount of labour used, when wage rate declines, would lead the firm to adjust the quantity of capital (and other fixed factors) in the long run. Let us explain this by taking two-factor production function, namely, $Q = f(L.K)$ where Q stands for output of the product, L for labour and K for capital. In the equilibrium position the following condition holds :

$$\frac{MRP_L}{w} = \frac{MRP_K}{r}$$

where MRP_L and MRP_K are marginal revenue products of labour and capital respectively and w and r represent the prices of labour and capital respectively. Now, when the price of labour, that is, the wage rate falls, other things remaining the same, a firm moving along the *MRP* (or *VMP*) curve will demand more labour. However, the employment of more labour will raise the

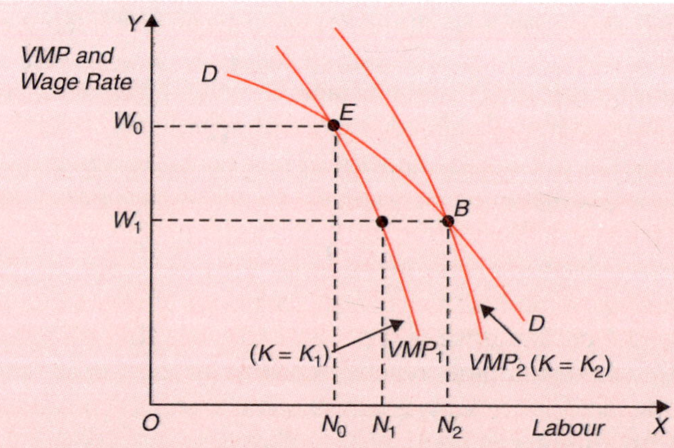

Fig. 52.7. *The Long-Run Demand for a Variable Factor (Labour) with Capital Adjustment*

marginal revenue productivity of capital if its amount remains unchanged causing disturbance in the above equilibrium condition. To minimise cost and thereby maximise profits, the firm will adjust the amount of capital employed. However, when the amount of capital is increased as more labour is employed following reduction in the wage rate, the whole marginal revenue product curve of labour would shift to the right. Thus, the demand for labour following the reduction in the wage rate will be determined in the long run by the equality of the lower wage rate with the new marginal revenue product of labour corresponding to the new amount of capital employed.

How the long-run demand curve of a variable factor is derived when capital is also adjusted is illustrated in Figure 52.7 where to begin with value of marginal product curve of labour VMP_1 has been drawn with a given amount of capital equal to K_1. It will be seen from the figure that at wage rate OW_0, the firm demands ON_0 amount of labour ($OW_0 = VMP_1$ at ON_0 amount of labour). Now, if the wage rate falls to OW_1 the firm would demand labour equal to

ON_1 provided the capital stock had remained constant at K_1. However, as explained above, the increase in the quantity demanded of labour at the lower wage rate OW_1 would raise the marginal revenue product of capital and therefore in the long run the firm would adjust the amount of capital. Suppose that by adjusting the capital stock the firm raises it to the new level K_2. The increase in capital to K_2 in the production process causes a rightward shift in the value of marginal product curve of labour to the new position VMP_2. With this new value of marginal product curve of labour VMP_2 obtained after adjusting the amount of capital to the level K_2 at the lower rate OW_1 the firm will demand ON_2 quantity of labour. Thus by joining points like *E* and *B*, we obtain the firm's long-run demand curve *EB* for labour when capital is also variable and adjusted appropriately . It will be seen from Figure 52.7 that firm's long-run demand curve for labour *EB* obtained after adjustment in the other factor, capital, is flatter than the *VMP* curves of labour .

We thus see that when more than one factor is variable, the value of marginal product *(VMP)* curve of a factor is not its demand curve. This is because various factors are jointly used in the production process of a good so that when the price of a factor changes leading to the change in its quantity demanded, it also causes changes in the use and employment of other factors. The changes in the amounts used of these 'other factors' in turn cause a shift in the marginal product of the factor whose price initially changes. As a matter of fact, a change in the price of a factor gives rise to two effects : a *substitution effect, output effect.* We explain below these two effects of a change in the price of a factor using two-factor production function $(Q) = f(L, K)$ where *Q* is output, and *L* and *K are* the factors of production, labour and capital.

Substitution Effect and Output Effect. Consider Figure 52.8. With the given factor prices, wage rate w_1 of labour and rental r_1 of capital, the iso-cost line is *AB* and the firm is producing level of output Q_1 by using OL_1 of labour and OK_1 of capital, price of capital remaining unchanged. Now suppose that the wage rate falls and as a result the iso-cost line shifts to *AC*. With this new iso-cost line *AC*, the firm is in equilibrium at point *R* producing a higher level of output Q_2 and using OL_2 of labour and OK_2 of capital. The movement from point *E* on isoquant Q_1 to point *R* on isoquant Q_2 as a result of fall in the wage rate of labour represents the price effect. This price effect can be divided into two separate effects : *a substitution effect* and *output effect*. To do so we have constructed a new iso-cost line *GH*, parallel to *AC* so that it represents the *new factor price ratio*, which is tangent to the initial isoquant Q_1 at point *S*. Equilibrium at point *S* on isoquant Q_1 instead of *E* is due to the substitution effect as the iso-cost line *GH* represents relatively cheaper labour as compared to the iso-cost line *AB*. As a result of this substitution effect the firm employs L_1L' more of labour and K_1K' less of capital than at the initial equilibrium point *E*.

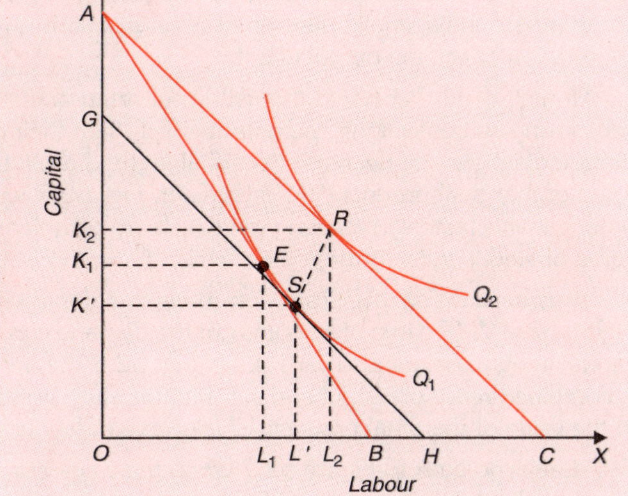

Fig. 52.8. *Substitution and Output Effects of a Change in Price of a Factor*

In Figure 52.8 the firm will not stay at *S*. This is because due to lower wage rate, *the firm will be spending less* on factor combination S with iso-cost line GH. At a lower wage rate of labour, with the *same total expenditure* the firm can buy more of labour or more of capital or more both of them. Thus, if the outlay on factors remains unchanged, the iso-cost line shifts to AC and as it will be seen from Figure 52.8 the firm attains equilibrium at point R on higher isoquant Q_2. The movement from factor combination S on isoquant Q_1 to point R on isoquant Q_2 is the result of output effect which causes the increase in employment of labour from OL' to OL_2 and increase in the use of capital from OK' to OK_2. This showns due to the combined effect of substitution effect and output effect of the fall in the wage rate the firm employs more of both labour and capital. The other factor capital increases as a result of fall in wage rate because output effect on it dominates over the substitution effect.

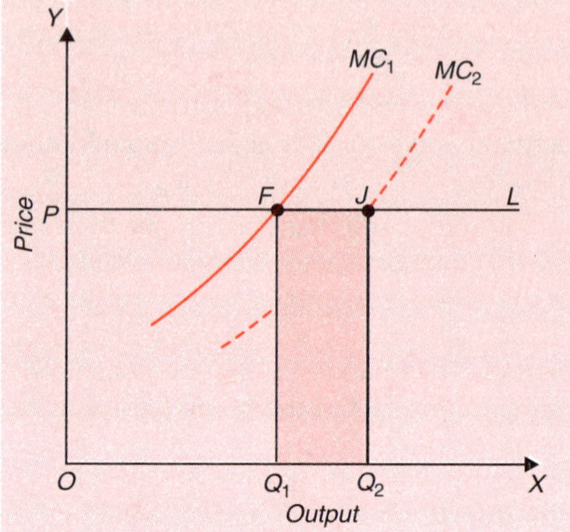

Fig. 52.9. *Rightward Shift in Marginal Cost Curve due to a Fall in the Wage Rate*

It may be noted that the profit-maxising firm will move from a lower isoquant Q_1 to the higher *isoquant* Q_2 depicting increase in output only when it is profitable to produce more. In fact it is so because the fall in wage rate of labour causes marginal cost of production to fall and as a result marginal cost curve shifts downward (i.e. to the right) as from MC_1 to MC_2 shown in Fig. 52.9. With this downward shift in MC curve, the price OP of output being given, a profit maximising firm will expand output from Q_1 to Q_2 (see Fig. 52.9). Increase in output will lead to the increase in the quantities used of both the factors (labour and capital). It is in fact due to the working of output effect that profit-maxising firm in Fig. 52.8 will not stay at point S on lower isoquant Q_1 and will move to higher isoquant Q_2 depicting higher level of output. In Fig. 52.8, the profit-maxising firm is finally in equilibrium at point R where the new iso-cost line AC representing lower wage rate is tangent to isoquant Q_2. At point R on isoquant Q_2 in this figure, more of both labour and capital are used as compared to initial equilibrium point E on isoquant Q_1 as a result of the combined effect of substitution effect and output effect.[3]

It may be further noted that when substitution effect of the fall in wage rate of labour is very strong and outweights the output effect, then their combined effect will be the increase in the use of labour and decrease in capital. In this case if capital is the only other variable factor value of marginal product (*VMP*) Curve in Fig. 52.7 will not shift to the right. There can be other variable factors in the long run which are complementary with labour due to which *VMP* curve of labour shifts to the right.

It is because of this expansion in capital along with labour due to output effect that in Figure 52.7 *VMP* curve of labour is not the demand curve of labour when other factors such as capital in our case are also variable. In Fig. 52.8 the net increase in capital from OK_1 to OK_2 is combined result of output and substitution effects of the fall in wage rate that causes a shift in the value of marginal product (*VMP*) curve of labour to the right.

Let us go back to Figure 52.7 when the wage rate falls from OW_0 to OW_1, the quantity demanded of labour increases. However, *the increase in demand for labour does not occur*

3. It should be noted that in case of perfect complementary factors with right-angled isoquants, the factor substitution effect is zero and the use of two factors increases due to output effect.

along the VMP_1 curve of labour when other factors can also vary, as they do at least in the long run. When wage rate falls and as a result use of labour expands and the level of output increases, the use of other cooperating factors such as capital will increase as well. Whereas the substitution effect of the reduction in wage rate tends to reduce the demand for a capital, the output effect which brings about an increase in demand for capital outweighs the substitution effect. Therefore in Fig. 52.7 more quantity of labour is demanded at a lower wage rate not only becaue more workers are employed at a lower wage rate but also because more complementary factor capital is used which shifts VMP curve of labour to the right. Thus, in Figure 52.7. It is due to the *net result* of these effects—substitution effect and output effect that the value of marginal product curve of labour shifts from VMP_1 to the new position VMP_2 and at the lower wage rate OW_1, more quantity of labour ON_2 is demanded as compared to ON_0 demanded at the higher wage rate OW_0. To conclude, when more than one factor is variable, with fall in the wage rate the firm does not move along the same *VMP* curve of labour but adjusting other factors switches over to the new *VMP* curve which lies to the right of the initial one. Thus by joining points *E* and *B* we obtain the demand curve of labour when other factors such as capital are also variable.

Competitive Industry's Demand for Labour

We now turn to explain competitive industry's demand curve for labour. We could obtain the demand curve for labour of the competitive industry by lateral summation of the labour demand curves of the individual firms constituting the industry if we assume that price of the product of the competitive industry remain constant or unchanged. This is however not realistic. When following the reduction in the wage rate all the firms in the industry employ more labour in the production of a commodity, the output of the commodity and therefore its supply in the market increases. This would result in lowering the price of the product.

It may be recalled that the marginal revenue product *(MRP)* of labour under perfect competition in the product market equals marginal physical product *(MPP)* of labour multiplied by the price of the product (under perfect competition $MRP_L = VMP_L = MPP_L \times$ Price of Product). Now, following the reduction in wage rate, as more labour is employed by all the firms in the competitive industry output expands bringing about a fall in the price of the product. This will cause a shift in the marginal revenue product curve of labour (MRP_L) to the left as shown in Figure 52.10 where when the price of the product falls from P_0 to P_1, the marginal product curve of labour shifts to the left to its new position MRP'_L *and* as will be seen from Figure 52.10 at the lower wage rate W_1 the firm demands and employs

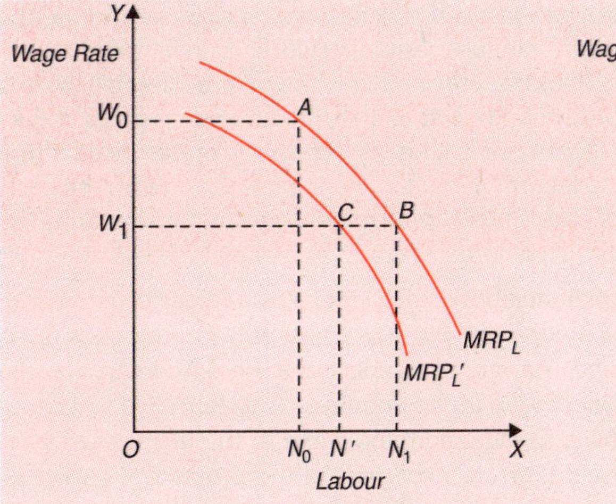

Fig. 52.10. *Shift in Firm's Demand Curve for Labour*

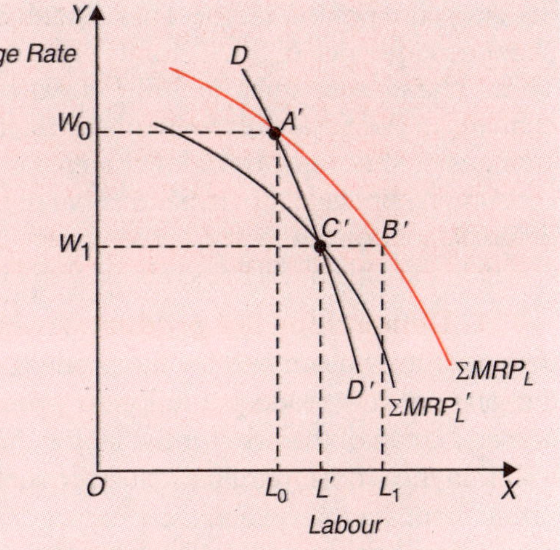

Fig. 52.11. *The Competitive Industry's Demand Curve for Labour*

labour ON' rather than ON_1 amount of labour which it would have demanded at the lower wage rate W_1 if the product price would have remained constant at P_0. This represents the ***product price effect*** on the demand for labour. It will be seen that when this price effect is taken into account, with the reduction in the wage rate from W_0 to W_1 the firm's demand for labour increases from ON to ON' and not to ON_1.

Having explained how a firm's demand for labour is affected by the change in price of the product, following the reduction in the wage rate, we can now derive the demand curve for labour of the competitive industry. This is illustrated in of Figure 52.11. At the wage rate OW_0, a competitive firm employs ON_0 amount of labour by equating wage rate OW_0 with the marginal revenue product of labour (MRP_L), price of the product equal to P_0 being given. [See Figure 52.10]. At the wage rate OW_0 the demand for labour of the industry as a whole can be obtained by the horizontal summation of the quantities demanded of labour by the given number of firms. Suppose there are 100 firms in the industry. By adding up horizontally the quantity demanded of labour by all the firms in the industry, that is, ΣMRP_L, with price of the product being equal to P_0 we get a point A' in panel *(b)* which shows that at wage rate OW_0 the industry demand for labour will equal OL_0 (*i.e.*, $OL_0 = ON_0 \times 100$ by adding up horizontally).

Now, when the wage rate falls to W_1 and with expansion in output or supply, price of the product falls to P_1 and consequently MRP curve of labour shifts to the left to the new position MRP'_L, in Fig. 52.10, a firm demands ON' quantity of labour. With this, the horizontal summation of the MRP_L curves to obtain the industry's demand curve for labour would also shift to the left to the new position $\Sigma MRP_L'$ with the price of the product equal to P_1. As will be seen from the Figure 52.11 that at the wage rate OW_0 the industry will demand OL_0 amount of labour and at the wage rate OW_1, the industry would demand OL' amount of labour rather than OL_1. Thus by joining points like A' and C', we obtain the industry's demand curve DD' of labour showing the quantity demanded of labour at different wage rates when product price effect of the change in the wage rate has been taken into account. It will be seen from Figure 52.11 that the industry's demand curve for labour DD' is *steeper or less elastic* than the marginal revenue product curves of labour of the firms.

DETERMINANTS OF DEMAND FOR FACTORS

We shall now explain those causes which bring about changes in the factor demand. In other words, we are to discuss those factors which cause shifts in the whole VMP curve or demand curve of the factor. These shifts or changes in factor demand are caused not by the change in the price of the factor itself but by other influences which work upon factor demand. These changes or shifts in VMP curve or demand curve of the factor are effected by the changes in the basic determinants of factor demand. Just as the demand curve of a product changes or shifts as a result of changes in income or changes in tastes or preferences of the consumers, similarly the demand curve of the factor will shift following the changes in the basic determinants of the factor demand curve. These basic determinants of factor demand, the variations in which will bring about shifts in factor demand curve, are explained below :

1. Demand for the product. As explained above, factor demand is a derived demand; derived from the demand for the product. The demand for a factor, therefore, depends upon demand for the product it helps to produce. As already explained, the *VMP* curve is the demand curve of the firm for the factor. Any change in the demand for the product will cause a shift in the whole marginal value productivity and the demand curve of the factor used in its production. An increase in the product demand, given the supply of the product, will raise its price. Hence the entire *VMP* curve which is obtained by multiplying marginal physical product by price will shift outward to the right when price rises following the increase in the demand for the product. On the other hand, decrease in the demand for the product, given the product supply, will lower its price. As a result, the *VMP* or demand curve of the factor will shift to the left (*i.e.*, downward).

2. Marginal physical productivity of the factor. Another determinant of the demand for a factor is its productivity. Like the changes in price of the product changes in marginal physical productivity will also cause a shift in the entire *MPP* or factor demand curve. For instance, increase in marginal physical productivity of labour will shift the demand curve of labour to the right (*i.e.*, outward). It may also be pointed out that historically we have experienced only increases in the physical productivity of the factors. *Decrease* in physical productivity, except under exceptional circumstances, has not been noticed. There are mainly three ways in which the marginal physical productivity of the factor can be increased. First, the *quality of the factor* may be improved. For instance, the labour productivity can be increased by making labour more educated and more skilful. Thus an improvement in the quality of the factor by enhancing its marginal productivity will cause outward shift in the factor demand curve.

Secondly, the marginal physical productivity of any factor depends upon the *quantity of the fixed cooperating factors* used with it. As seen above, the position of *MPP* curve of labour is dependent on the *quantity of capital* used with it. The greater the quantity of fixed cooperating capital used with labour, the higher the level of marginal physical productivity curve. As is shown in Fig. 52.12, as the quantity of fixed cooperating capital is increased, marginal physical product curve of labour shifts upward. When one unit of fixed factor 'capital' (*K*) is used, the marginal value product curve of labour is VMP_1. When the quantity of fixed factor 'capital' is increased to 2 units, value of marginal (*VMP*) curve of labour shifts outward to VMP_2 due to the increase in marginal physical product (*MPP*) of labour, price of the product remaining the same. With 3 units of capital, value of marginal product curve further shifts upward to VMP_3.

Thus, increase in the marginal physical product of labour as a result of increase in the quantity of capital (likewise, other cooperating fixed factors) will raise the *VMP* or factor demand curve outward to the right. It will be seen from Figure 52.12 that at the given wage rate *OW*, the quantity demanded of labour increases from ON_1 to ON_3 when as a result of increase in capital marginal physical product of labour increases, price of the product remaining the same.

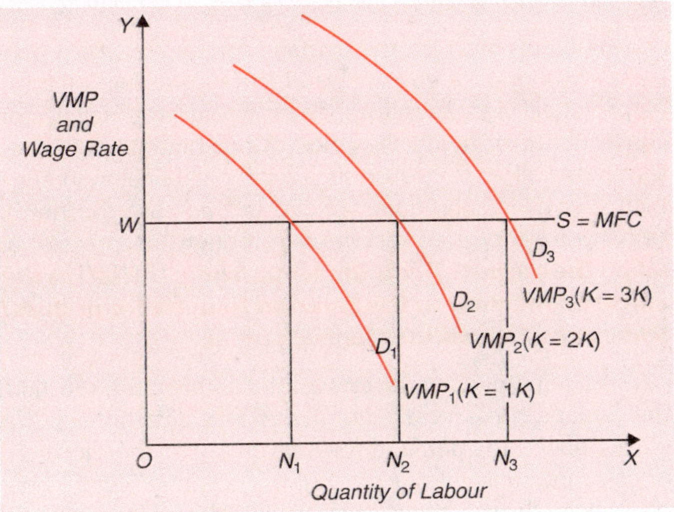

Fig. 52.12. *Increase in the demand for labour by a firm*

Thirdly, the marginal physical productivity is increased by the *advancement in technology*. The technological progress raises productivity by bringing about improvement in techniques of production. Hence, as a result of advance in technology, *VMP* curve or the demand curve of the factor will shift upward.

3. Price of other factors. Just as the demand for a commodity depends upon the prices of other related commodities, demand for a factor also depends upon the price of other related factors. But the effect of the changes in the price of related factors on the demand for a given factor would have different effects depending upon whether these related factors are substitutes or complements for the given factor. We first take the case of substitutes.

Suppose two factors, labour and machinery, are used for the production of a commodity. Now, labour and machinery are largely substitutes. We want to consider the effect on the demand for labour as a result of change in the price of machinery. If the price of machinery falls, so that machinery becomes relatively cheaper than labour, there would be large substitution of machinery for labour. Since machinery is now relatively cheaper than labour, it will pay the employer to use more machinery and less labour. Therefore, as a result of change in the price of machinery demand for labour will fall and machinery would be used in place of labour. Thus, the change in the price of machinery will have, as explained above, *substitution effect on* the demand for labour. As a result of the substitution effect of the fall in the price of machinery, the demand curve for labour will shift to the left. The extent to which the demand for labour will fall depends upon the extent to which it is possible to substitute machinery for labour.

But the change in the price of factor has not only a substitution effect but also *expansion or output effect.* The prices of factors govern the cost and price of the product. When, in our above example, the price of machinery falls, the cost of production of the product will decline and hence there would be fall in the price of the product. With the fall in the price of the product, more of it will be demanded. In response to greater demand, more output of the product would be made. The fall in the price of the machinery will thus lead to greater output of the product. To produce more output, more of labour as well as more of other factors including machinery will be required. This expansion in output due to the fall in the price of machinery, that is, output effect, would tend to increase the demand for labour. Thus, the fall in price of machinery has two opposite effects : first, substitution effect which tends to decrease the demand for labour ; and second, output effect (expansion effect) which tends to increase the demand for labour.

The net effect on the demand for labour would depend upon the relative strengths of these two opposite effects. But if the substitution effect is very large, it would outweigh the output effect and, therefore, there would be a net decrease in the demand for labour as a consequence of fall in the price of machinery. But, in some cases, a fall in the price of a substitute factor may cause such a large expansion in output that the output effect may more than offset the substitution effect. In that case the net effect would be the increase in the demand for the given factor, even though the price of a substitute factor has fallen. Thus, ***when the output effects are very strong, the fall in the price of a substitute factor may cause an increase in the demand for a factor in question, even though the two are to some extent substitutes for each other.***

To sum up, when factors are substitutes, the substitution and output effects tend to shift the demand curve for a factor in opposite directions. If the substitution effect is stronger than output effect, the demand for a given factor therefore changes in the same direction as the price of the substitute factor. But the output effect in some cases may be so strong that they overwhelm the substitution effect with the result that the demand for a given factor changes in the opposite direction to the price of the substitute factor. As a matter of fact, when as a result of fall in price of a factor, the demand for the other factor also increases due to the large output effect the two factors are said to be complementary, although some substitution effect is present.

But the change in the price of a complementary factor would have different effect on the demand for a given factor. Suppose two factors A and B are being used in the production of a commodity. Further suppose that A and B bear complementary relationship to each other. We are interested to know what happens to the demand for factor A, when the price of its complementary factor B changes. If the price of factor B falls, its quantity demanded will rise. Since B is complementary to A, when B will be used more due to fall in its price, it will necessitate more employment of factor A also. Thus the demand for factor A will increase as a consequence of the fall in the price of its complementary factor B. But this is not all. Output effect will also exercises their influence. When the price of B falls, cost of production will decline. As a result, the price of the product will fall which will bring about an increase in the quantity demanded of the product. Consequently, output of the product would be expanded. This increase in output will require more of both A and B. Thus the demand for factor A will rise due to not only complementary effect but also due to output effect. Thus complementary effect and output effect in the case of complementary factors work in the same direction, thereby reinforcing each other.

FACTORS DETERMINING ELASTICITY OF FACTOR DEMAND

We have explained above, the demand curve for a factor of production slopes downward. We have also brought out above what are the factors that determine the level and position of the demand curve of a factor. The implication of the downward-sloping demand curve for the factor is that when the price of the factor falls, greater quantity of it is demanded and *vice versa*. After knowing *the direction* of change in quantity demanded of the factor as a result of change in its price, we must now explain the *extent or degree* to which amount demanded of a factor changes following the change in its price. In other words, we must now explain the factors which govern the *elasticity* of demand for the factors. For instance, elasticity of demand for labour with respect to changes in wage rate is given by

$$e_L = \frac{\Delta L / L}{\Delta w / w} = \frac{\%\ \text{change in quantity of labour demanded}}{\%\ \text{change in wage rate}}$$

where L represents quantity demanded of labour and w for wage rate.

The elasticity of demand for labour depends upon the rate of decline in the *VMP* curve. The *VMP* curve has been obtained by multiplying the marginal physical products by the price of the product at various levels of factor employment. Therefore, the extent to which the labour demand increases in response to a fall in its wage rate, that is, the elasticity of labour demand, will primarily depend upon the rate of decline in marginal physical product of labour and rate of fall in price of the product as additional units of labour are employed. Now, the rate of decline in marginal physical productivity is controlled by *technical conditions of production* and the rate of fall in price is dependent on the *elasticity of demand for the product.* Thus the two important factors determining the elasticity of factor demand are technical conditions of production and the elasticity of demand for the product. The demand for a factor will be more elastic, if greater is the elasticity of demand for the product, and more slowly the marginal physical productivity of the factor falls when its employment rises and *vice versa*. We explain below in detail the various factors which govern the elasticity of demand for a factor.

1. Rate of Decline of Marginal Physical Product Curve. As explained above, elasticity of factor demand is dependent on the shape of marginal physical product curve. The more slowly the marginal physical product declines as additional units of a factor are added, the flatter and hence more elastic will be the *VMP* curve which, as explained above, is a demand curve for the factor. Thus more slow the decline in the marginal physical product, the greater will be the increase in employment or quantity demanded of the factor following the fall in its price. The rate of decline in marginal physical product is greater in the short run than in the long run because in the short run some of the factors are fixed in quantity and cannot be adjusted, while in the long run appropriate adjustment can be made in the quantities of all co-operating or fixed factors. In other words, in the long run, marginal physical product falls more gently or slowly, while in the short run it falls very rapidly. Therefore, elasticity of demand for the factor is greater in the long run than in the short run.

2. Possibility of Substitution. Another important factor governing the elasticity of demand for a factor is the possibility of substitution. The greater the number of available substitute factors for a given factor and the greater the elasticity of substitution between this factor and the others, the greater will be the elasticity of demand for the factor. If many close substitutes are available for a factor in question, then the rise in its relative price will cause substantial substitution of other factors for it and its quantity demanded will fall very much. For instance, handlooms and powerlooms are very close substitutes. If price of handlooms rises relatively, their quantity demanded will fall greatly since powerlooms will be substituted for them. Thus, the demand for handlooms tends to be elastic. On the contrary, if a factor of production has few and poor substitute factors, its demand will tend to be inelastic (*i.e.*, less elastic). To sum up, ***the elasticity of demand for a factor depends to a greater extent on the elasticity of substitution between this factor and others.***

The elasticity of supply of the substitute factors will also determine the elasticity of demand for a factor. The ability to substitute one factor for another can be prevented by the inelastic supplies of its substitute factors. The more elastic the supply of substitute factors, the more elastic will be the demand for the factors whose price changes. Besides, the demand for a factor is more elastic in the long run than in the short run because in the long run there are greater possibilities of substituting one factor for another.

3. Elasticity of Demand for the Product. Since demand for a factor of production is derived from demand for the products, elasticity of a factor demand depends on the elasticity of demand for the product it helps to produce. If the demand for the product is very elastic, then demand curve for the product will fall very slowly which means that price (and therefore *MR*) falls very slowly as output is increased. As a result, demand curve *VMP* for the factor which is obtained by multiplying *MPP* by price of the product will also fall very slowly and hence would be elastic. On the other hand, if the demand for the product is inelastic, then its demand curve will fall very rapidly which means that price of the product will also decline very sharply and hence the *VMP* curve (*i.e.*, the demand curve) of the factor will be inelastic. Thus, when the demand for the product is very elastic, relatively more output can be sold with only small reduction in the price of the product. Under such circumstances, a small change in the price of a factor used for production of that product will lead to a relatively large increase in the amount demanded of the factor.

To sum up, ***if demand for a product is highly elastic, then demand for the factor used in its production will be very elastic too. On the contrary, if demand for a product is relatively inelastic to changes in its price, the factor demand will also tend to be inelastic.***

4. Proportion of a Particular Factor Cost to the Total Production Cost. Finally, the elasticity of demand for a factor depends upon the relative importance of the factor in the production of the product. If a particular factor of production accounts for a greater proportion, say 75%, of the total production cost, then any change in the price of that factor will have a substantial effect on the total production cost and hence on the price and sales of the product.

As a result, the demand for the factor, which accounts for a greater proportion of the total production cost, tends to be elastic. Thus, if there is a small fall in the price of the factor accounting for 75% of the total cost, the cost of production and hence the price of the product will relatively fall greatly. With this large fall in price of the product, its quantity demanded will rise substantially so that more will be produced and sold. To produce substantially greater output, larger amount of the factor would be employed and demanded. In other words, in this case factor demand will be elastic. On the other hand, if a factor is insignificant in the production of a good and accounts for a relatively very little proportion of the total cost, its demand tends to be inelastic. It can be easily realised that a small change in the price of the factor which accounts for only .02 per cent of total cost would have insignificant effect upon the price of output and factor demand.

THE NATURE OF SUPPLY OF FACTORS

We now turn to the second determinant of factor prices. As said above, supply of factors also exercises an important influence on the prices of factors. Clark's version of marginal productivity theory takes full employment of productive factors as given and assumes that the supply of factors is perfectly inelastic. Therefore, in Clark's marginal productivity theory, demand for a factor plays an active and dominant role in the determination of factor prices. As pointed out earlier, Clark's marginal productivity theory was one-sided and viewed factor-price determination mainly from demand side alone. But following Marshall and Hicks, in the modern explanation of pricing of factors, role of both the demand and supply of factors is given equal importance. We have discussed above the nature of demand for factors and the factors determining it and its price elasticity of demand. In what follows we shall spell out the nature of supply of various factors. It is worth mentioning at the very outset that, unlike the demand for factors, the nature and behaviour of supply of various factors is not uniform. We shall explain in detail the nature of supply of various factors when we make analysis of the price determination of each factor separately. Here we shall indicate only the broad features of their supply.

It may be noted that supply curve of any factor represents the different quantities of that factor which are offered at various alternative prices. From the viewpoint of the nature of supply, factors may be divided into two classes : *original and produced factors.* Produced factors are the intermediate physical inputs such as capital equipment (*i.e* machinery, tools, components etc.), steel, cement, fertilizers, fuels which are themselves produced in some industries and are used as inputs or productive factors in other industries for production of other products. So far as supply curve of these produced factors is concerned, it is governed by the same laws of production which apply to the production and supply of goods produced by various industries. Therefore, supply curves of the produced inputs (factors) depend upon the changes in marginal cost of production. So long as marginal cost rises as output is expanded in industries such as machine-making, steel, fertilizers, marginal cost curve slopes upward and therefore the supply curve of these material inputs slopes upward. However, if the industries producing certain intermediate physical inputs experience decreasing costs as their output expands, their supply curve will be sloping downward.

Supply of Land

Land and labour are called original or primary factors of production as they are not produced in the industries. It is a free gift from nature and therefore its quantity is fixed by nature. More land cannot be produced in response to greater demand for it. Whatever the rent, high or low, for the use of land, its supply to the economy as a whole remains unchanged.

In other words, the supply of land to the entire economy does not depend on the price, *i.e.*, rent for its use. Hence, from the standpoint of the whole economy, the supply of land (which includes natural resources) is *perfectly inelastic*. Since supply of land is a free gift from nature

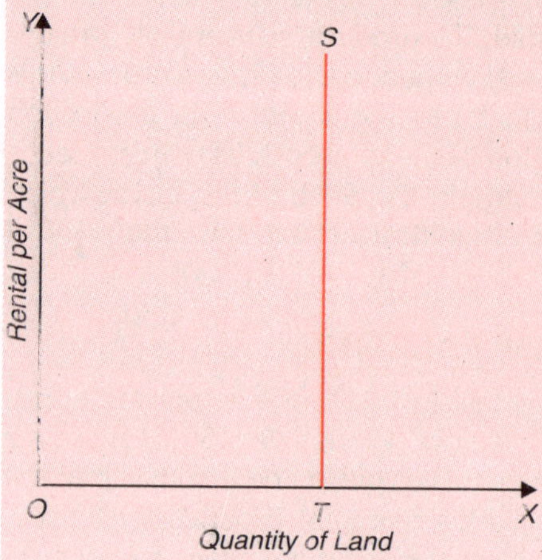

Fig. 52.13. *Perfectly Inelastic Supply Curve of Economy as a Whole*

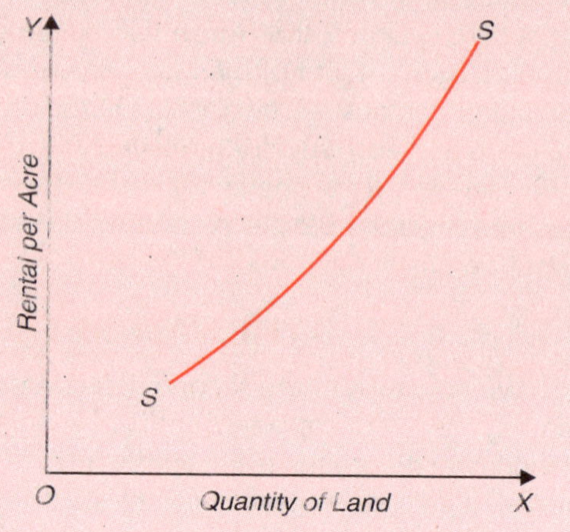

Fig. 52.14. *Somewhat Elastic Land for the Supply Curve of Land for a Particular Crop or Industry*

and not a produced factor, cost of production has no relevance for its supply. For the society as a whole, land has got no cost of production since society did not produce it; it got it free from nature.

But the supply of land to a *single use or to a particular* industry is not perfectly inelastic. The supply of land to a particular crop or industry can be increased by shifting of land from other crops or industries. By offering attractive rents, the supply of land for a particular use can be increased by taking it away from other competitive uses.

The supply of land for a particular crop or industry can be better explained with the help of the concept of ***transfer or alternative earnings. The transfer earnings of a factor may be defined as the earnings in the next best alternative use.*** Thus the transfer earnings of a piece of land under wheat is the amount of money earned by it if it is put to the cultivation of cotton, assuming that, after wheat, growing of cotton is the next best use of that piece of land. If that piece of land earns ₹ 5000 under wheat and ₹ 4000 under cotton, then ₹ 4000 is the transfer earnings of that piece of land. Now, a piece of land will be supplied to a particular use if at least its transfer earnings are paid to it. In our present example, if the earnings of this piece of land fall below ₹ 4000, then the piece of land will be withdrawn from the cultivation of wheat and put under cotton. As the earnings of land (*i.e.* rent) increases in one particular use, the land from other uses would be attracted towards it, so that the supply of land to the particular use in question would increase. Therefore, the ***supply curve of land to a particular use, crop or industry is elastic and slopes upward from left to right.*** This is shown in Figure 52.14.

SUPPLY OF CAPITAL

We now turn to the supply of capital which is a produced factor and occupies these days a paramount place in the production process. Here a distinction must be made between *real or physical capital, i.e.*, capital goods on the one hand *and financial capital* or *money capital* on the other, since the nature of their supply is quite different. Capital goods are produced factors as compared to the primary factors like land and labour which are not produced. Capital goods are produced by firms on the same basis as consumer goods. The nature of supply of consumer goods has been discussed in Part IV. The supply of capital goods is determined by the same factors as those which determine the supply of consumer goods. Since capital goods are reproducible, the cost of production exercises a significant influence over their supply. If the industry producing a capital good is subject to increasing costs, the supply curve of that capital good will be upward sloping indicating that more of it will be supplied at a higher price. And if the industry producing a certain capital good is working under constant cost conditions, the more of that capital good will be supplied at the same price and therefore its supply curve will be a horizontal straight line. However, once the durable capital goods have been produced, their supply is independent of their cost. But, over a period of time, cost is, no doubt, a determining factor of their supply.

As regards financial capital, the nature of its supply is very complex. The supply of financial capital depends upon the money supply in the economy, the savings of the people, their willingness to lend it or buy shares and bonds (*i.e.* their liquidity preference) and the ability as well as willingness of the banks to lend money to businessmen. An increase in the rate of interest has an important effect on the willingness of the people to save more and to accumulate more financial capital. Moreover, increase in the rate of interest exercises a strong effect in inducing the people to part with the money capital and lend it to businessmen or buy shares and bonds of companies. In other words, the rise in the rate of interest induces people to surrender liquidity and lend it to others.

Budget Constraint and Supply of Saving : Life Cycle Model

To understand the choice between present consumption and future consumption we use the concept of budget constraint. In the theory of consumer's behaviour with the help of budget constraint we analysed the choice between two goods by a consumer. In the present analysis of how much of his present income an individual will consume in the present and how much he will save, the budget constraint shows the choice between consumption in two periods. Let us first consider *life-time budget constraint* where the two time periods are working years and retirement years. In the working years an individual saves a part of his income so as to use the money so saved for consumption in the retirement period. Consider Figure 52.15. where on the horizontal axis we measure consumption and income in the working years and on the Y-axis we measure consumption in the retirement years. The income or wages of the individual in his working life is OY_0. In the extreme case an individual could consume his entire income or wages (OY_0) of his working life. If he does so he will save nothing for consumption in the period of his retirement from work. Generally, a rational individual thinks of the need for consumption in the years of his retirement.

On the other extreme case, he may save all his income or wages of the working years and consumes nothing. In this case he will earn interest on his savings which are either lent to others or kept in bank deposits. If we denote interest by r, then in case of saving his entire income (Y_0) of the working years the individual will have income equal to $Y_0(1 + r)$ for consumption in the period of retirement. It is important to note that our analysis of saving decision is based on ***life-cycle model. According to this model, individuals' consumption and saving decisions during a given year depends not only on his current consumption needs but also on his future consumption requirements during the rest of his life.*** To simplify our analysis, we assume that *an individual* lives in two periods (present period and the future period). Further, the present period is the period of his *working years* and the future period is of his *retirement years*.

It is evident that by saving, that is, postponing his consumption, he will be able to consume more goods in the future because he will have not only his saved money to spend but also interest earned on it. Thus, how much more consumption in future (*i.e.* retirement years) he will have for sacrifice of his consumption in the present (working years) depends on the rate of interest. For example, if interest rate is 10 per cent, then every one hundred rupees saved by him in the present year he will have ₹ 110 in the next year. If he saves ₹ 100 in the present period, he will have100 (1 + 0.1) to spend on goods for his consumption in the future. The cost of more consumption in future is sacrifice of his current consumption (*i.e.*, consumption in the working years) which he has to make for enjoying more consumption of goods in future. It is clear from above that relative price of consumption in the present period is 1 plus rate of interest (*i.e.* 1 + r).

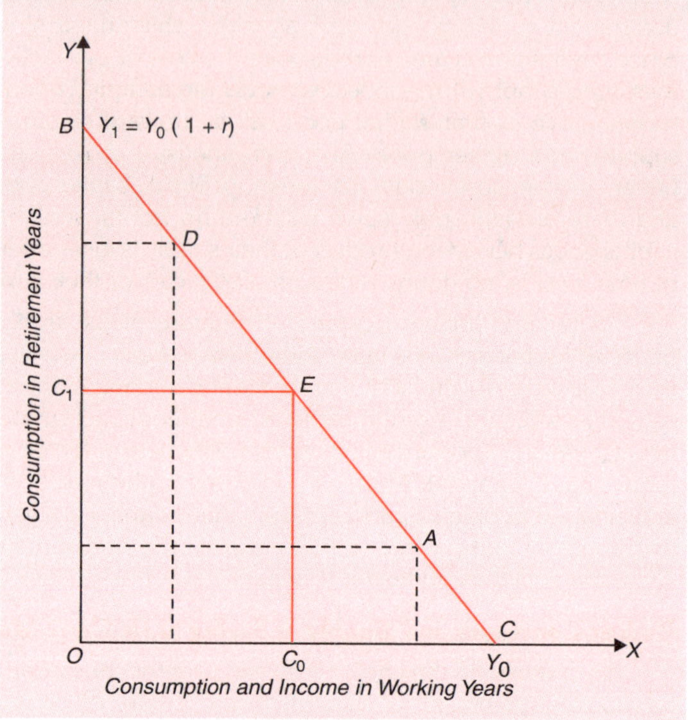

Fig. 52.15. *Life-Time Budget Constraint*

It is worth mentioning that in deciding about consumption and saving in the working years and consumption in the retirement years an individual is guided by *real rate* of interest and not merely *money* rate of interest. The difference between money rate of interest and real rate of interest arises due to the inflation that may be taking place over the years. Real rate of interest is money rate of interest minus rate of inflation. Thus, if money rate of interest is 10 per cent per annum and annual rate of inflation is 6 per cent, then real rate of interest will be 4 per cent per annum. In our example, we have divided the life span of an individual into two periods : the working years period and the retirement period. From the point of view of how much money he will have in real terms what matters is the length of time between when a person earns and saves and the time when he uses his savings for consumption in the retirement period and real rate of interest that he will earn on his savings.

In deciding about his choice about consumption and saving in the working years he will also take into account the *compound* rate of interest that he will earn on his savings and not merely the amount of savings he makes in the working years. For example, if rate of interest is simple 4 per cent and not compound rate of interest, then Re. 1 saved today and kept in bank deposits at 4% simple real *rate of interest* for 35 years, it will earn interest of

$35 \times \frac{4}{100} = ₹1.40$. Thus, Re. 1 saved will become equal to 1 + 1.40 = ₹ 2.40 after 35 years.

But if interest is 4 per cent compound interest rate, then Re. 1 saved today will earn interest in 35 years equal to $(1 + 0.04)^{35} = 2.94$ and thus $1 + 2.94 =$ ₹ 3.94 will be available for consumption after 35 years. This is just to illustrate the power of compound rate of interest. The slope of budget constraint is equal to $1 + r$ where r is rate of interest.

Now, consider the life-time budget constraint BC drawn in Figure 52.15. Which point an individual will choose on this budget line depends on his preference between present consumption and future consumption. A complete analysis of his choice requires the inclusion of his indifference curves between present consumption (*i.e.* consumption in working years) and consumption in the years of retirement. This indifference curve analysis of choice between present consumption and saving will be made in the next section. However we can consider some possible choices by the individual. Suppose the individual chooses point A on the budget constraint line BC. With his choice of point A, his consumption in the working life will be relatively large and saving for consumption in the years of retirement will be small. At the other extreme, he may choose point D in which case he will consume a very small amount of his income in the working period and save a relatively large amount of his income for future consumption. But empirical evidence shows that a typical individual chooses a middle position on the budget constraint such as point E in between the above two extreme cases. With his choice at point E, the individual consumes C_0 and saves $Y_0 - C_0$ in the working period and consumes C_1 in the retirement period. In his choice of point E on the budget constraint, the individual has *smoothened* his consumption, that is, his consumption in the working-life period is almost the same as in the period of retirement. This kind of saving behaviour which smoothens consumption over one's entire life span by providing sufficient saving for consumption in the years of retirement is called *life-cycle saving*.

Choice between Present Consumption and Future Consumption : Indifference Curve Analysis

We now examine with indifference curve analysis how an individual will choose between present and future consumption so as to maximise his total satisfaction over time. To make our analysis simple we consider only two time periods, working period and the retirement period. In real life there are more than two time periods over which consumption and saving decisions are made by an individual but the two-period model provides us useful insights into the basic issues involved. As mentioned above, the exchange of present consumption for future consumption is done through saving and lending these savings to others or keeping them in bank deposits which yield interest.

In our analysis we denote present period income by Y_0, future period income by Y_1, current consumption by C_0, future consumption by C_1 and rate of interest by r. Given his present income Y_0 and rate of interest (r), an individual has to decide how much he will consume in the present (*i.e.* C_0) and how much he will save for consumption in the future (*i.e.* C_1). The consumer's preferences between the present consumption and future consumption are represented by a set of indifference curves such as I_1, I_2 which are downward-sloping and convex to the origin as shown in Figure 52.16. The downward-sloping feature of indifference curves implies that the individual is willing to substitute some amount of present consumption for future consumption and the rate at which he is willing to substitute present consumption for future consumption depends on the particular pattern of consumption he likes to have.

The convexity of indifference curves implies that the individual would like to have some '*average' amount of consumption* in each period rather than extremely large consumption in the present and no or little consumption in the future or *vice versa*.

The Budget Constraint. To understand the choice, it is important to know the nature of budget constraint an individual faces in this regard. There are two possible kinds of consumption choices. First, he consumes his entire income in present period, that is, he consumes Y_0 in the present period and saves nothing for the future *(i.e.* next period). The second possibility is that he chooses to consume less than his present income and saves some for future consumption. That is, some present consumption is exchanged for more consumption in the future. How much more future consumption he will have for a given sacrifice of some consumption in the present depends on the rate of interest. Thus, if market real rate of interest is 10 per cent, then if he saves ₹ 100 in the present year, he will have ₹110 in the next year (110 = 100 + 10% of 100). In other words, he has exchanged ₹ 100 of the present consumption for consumption of ₹ 110 in the next year.

We now derive the budget constraint or what is called *intertemporal budget line* which has been shown by *BC* in Figure 52.16. We denote the individual's income in the present period by Y_0 and the next period's income by Y_1. In order to draw the intertemporal budget constraint we have to determine what would be the future income if the individual saves all his present income equal to Y_0. Given the interest rate equal to *r*, the next period's income will be $Y_1 = Y_0(1 + r)$. We represent it by point *B*.

Thus, if the individual decides to save his entire present income Y_0 for future consumption, then his next period's consumption which we denote by Y_1 will be

$$Y_1 = Y_0(1 + r)$$

We represent Y_1 by point *B* on the vertical axis in Fig. 52.16. If we join *B* with *C* we get the intertemporal budget line *BC* representing the budget constraint.

The slope of the budget constraint line *BC* = – (1+*r*). Thus the slope of the budget line equal to – (1 + *r*) depends on the market rate of interest *r*. It may be noted that ***rate of interest is in fact the return on saving.***

Intertemporal Choice ; Individual's Equilibrium

The pattern of individual's indifference curves depicts his preferences of present consumption over future consumption. In fact present consumption and future consumption can be regarded as two different goods. The slope of the indifference curve, that is, $\frac{\Delta C_1}{\Delta C_0}$ measures the marginal rate of substitution (*MRS*) between present consumption and future consumption and reflects his rate of time preference between the present and future consumption. On the other hand, as explained above, the slope of the budget line is given by – (1 + *r*) where *r* is rate of interest.

In his choice between present and future consumption, the consumer will try to maximise his satisfaction. But, as in consumer theory, the individual will be maximising his satisfaction where the given budget line *BC* is tangent to an indifference curve. It will be seen from Figure 52.16 that the individual is in equilibrium at point *E* on the indifference curve I_2. Thus the consumer's optimal equilibrium position is point *E* on indifference curve I_2 where his present

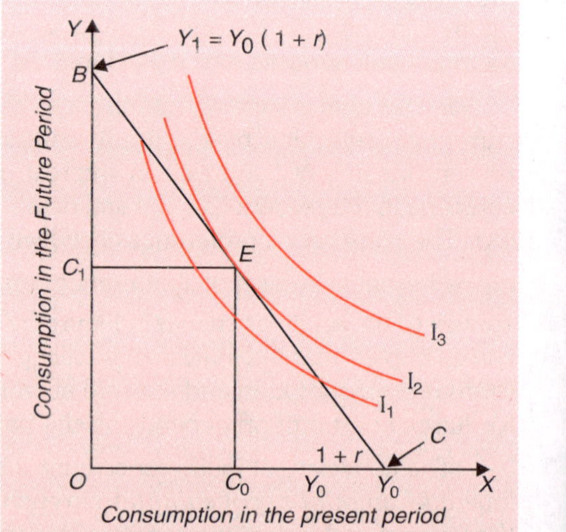

Fig. 52.16. *Choice between Present and Future Consumption: Life Saving Model*

consumption is C_0 and future consumption is C_1. With his equilibrium position at E his present consumption C_0 is less than his present income Y_0. That is, he is saving $Y_0 - C_0$ of his present income for consumption in the next period. He will lend this saving and earn interest on it so that his consumption in the next period is C_1. Thus, the individual saves a part of his income in the present period and lends it to others to earn interest.

It may be noted that at the equilibrium point E, the slope of indifference curve of the individual depicting his marginal rate of substitution between present consumption and future consumption ($MRS_{C_0C_1}$) is equal to the slope of the intertemporal budget line BC which in absolute terms is equal to $(1 + r)$. Thus, at equilibrium or optimal point E,

$$MRS_{C_0C_1} = (1 + r)$$

Saving and Interest Rate

It is useful to know what will be the impact of change in the rate of interest on individual's intertemporal choice or on his savings. This is depicted in Fig. 52.17. With the equilibrium position at E_0, suppose rate of interest rises. The rise in rate of interest will change the budget constraint. With a higher interest rate than the previous one, the new budget line $B'C$ will be steeper than the previous budget line BC. It will be seen from Fig. 52.17 that the new budget line $B'C$ representing higher rate of interest is steeper than the previous budget line BC. With this new budget line $B'C$ the individual is in equilibrium at point E_1 on his higher intertemporal indifference curve I_2 and is therefore better off than before. Besides, it will be noticed that with the new position E_1 of intertemporal choice on indifference curve I_2, the individual's present consumption has decreased from C_0 to C_0', that is, he has saved more at the higher rate of interest to increase his consumption in the future period by C_1C_1'.

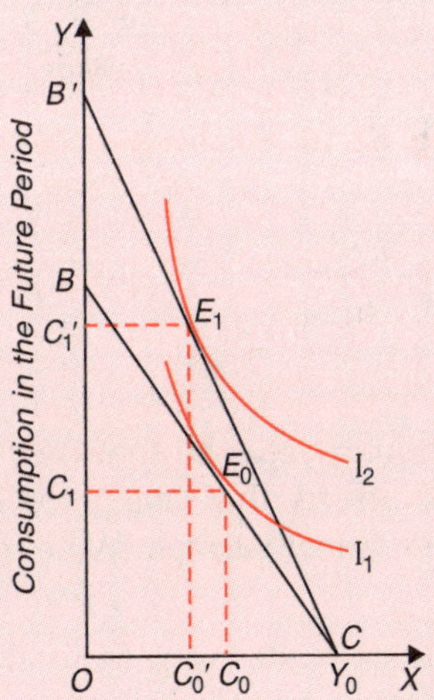

Fig. 52.17. *Impact of Rise in Interest Rate on Savings : Substitution Effect Dominates*

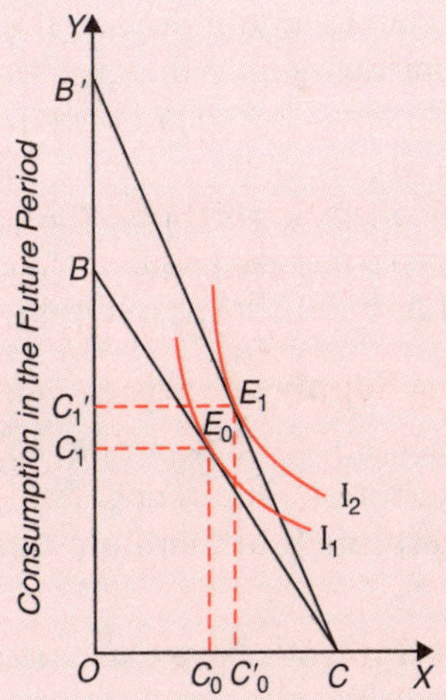

Fig. 52.18. *Impact of Rise in Interest Rate on Savings : Income Effect Dominates*

The effect of rise in interest rate has income effect as well as substitution effect. A rise in rate of interest increases income of the individual and therefore makes him better off. This induces him to consume more in the present. This is the income effect which tends to reduce savings. But the rise in interest rate also increases return on savings. This induces him to postpone consumption because every sacrifice of consumption (*i.e.* savings) will mean more consumption in the next period due to higher interest earned. This is substitution effect which tends to increase savings. Thus the substitution effect and income effect of rise in interest rate work in opposite direction. Therefore, net effect of rise in interest rate on saving is quite uncertain. Either of the two effects may dominate. As a result, higher interest rate may cause more or less savings. In Figure 52.18 we have shown the case when income effect dominates and therefore higher interest results in lower savings. However, empirical evidence about saving in the United States shows that substitution effect slightly outweighs the income effect. As a result, there is a small net positive effect of higher interest rate on savings.[4]

Supply Curve of Saving

As seen above, in Figure 52.17, a rise in the rate of interest induces the individual to save more. In this way, we can determine saving of an individual at different rates of interest. The higher the rate of interest, the greater is the supply of saving by him. By summing up the saving of various individuals at various rates of interest we can obtain market supply curve of saving which will slope upward showing positive relationship between rate of interest and saving. It may be noted that in case of some individuals who have a target of having a certain fixed level of income or consumption in future, a higher rate of interest will enable them to earn that fixed income by saving and lending less in this year. That is, for these individuals supply curve of saving will be backward sloping. However, those individuals who save and lend more at higher rates of interest predominate and therefore the overall supply curve of savings slopes upward, though at very high rates of interest backward-bending shape of the supply curve of saving cannot be ruled out. However, empirical evidence shows that a rise in interest rate has only a small positive effect on the rate of saving. The upward-sloping supply curve of saving has been shown in Figure 52.19 is quite small.

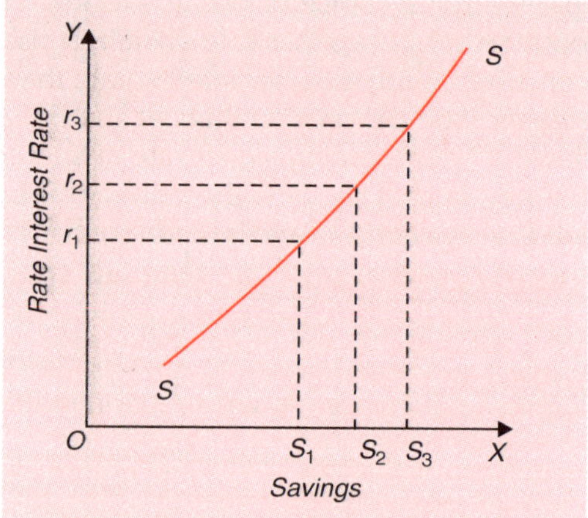

Fig. 52.19. *Positively-sloping Supply Curve of Saving*

Factors Affecting Supply of Saving

We have seen above that people save during working years so that they can consume enough in the years of retirement. And interest rate affects the saving for retirement. In addition to interest rate rate there are other factors that affect savings. We explain below all these factors.

1. Interest Rate. We have explained above that interest rate is one factor that determines supply of savings in the economy. The rise in interest rate generally brings about increase in supply of savings, though this effect is not significant. This is because rise in interest rate gives rise to two effects – income effect and substitution effect – which work in opposite direction. While income effect of rise in wage rate tends to reduce savings and its substitution effect tends to increase it. Since substitution effect generally dominates there is a net positive effect, though a small one, of rise in interest rate on supply of savings.

2. Income. Keynes emphasised that it is level of disposable income that determines,

4. See J. Stiglitz, *Economics*, Second Edition, 2002, p. 166.

savings. As income rises, both consumption and saving increase. However, according to Keynes, average propensity to consume declines as income increases and therefore saving rate rises at higher levels of income.

3. Social Security Provisions. Social security measures adopted by the government such as state pension, free health care lower savings. Generous pension scheme reduces the need for saving for the retirement years. Similarly, the provision of free health care through the National Health Service also reduces the need for savings to meet the medical expenses. It has been pointed by some economists that low saving rate of the UK and USA is mainly due to the comprehensive social security system in these countries.

4. Taxation System. Taxes also affect savings by individuals. In India and other countries income tax is the main direct tax levied on individuals' incomes including interest and dividend income. It has been pointed that income tax discourages saving. For people who keep their savings in bank deposits or use them for buying bonds and shares, tax on interest and dividends reduce after-tax return from them. ***"The tax on interest income substantially reduces the future pay-off from current saving and as a result reduces the incentives for people to save"***[5]. According to N.G. Mankiw, ***"Low rate of saving in the United States is at least partly attributable to tax laws that discourage savings."***[6]

Determinants of Aggregate Savings

Savings of all individuals in a society constitute aggregate savings of the economy. At any time, some individuals who are in working life save and others who are old and leading a retired life dissave. The retired people withdraw money from their bank accounts and/or sell shares and bonds to supplement income from their pension and other social security schemes. In determination of aggregate savings, *demographic factors* also play a role. A more slowly growing population has a proportionately larger population of old and retired people and this depresses aggregate saving rate of the economy.

Bequest Motive. An important factor that determines saving of a society is bequest motive. In order to leave behind a good amount of wealth for their children some rich people save during their life. If high inheritance taxes are levied, they would discourage saving on this account. Since bequest motive is an important reason for savings by individuals, especially the wealthy people, the lower inheritance taxes will have a large effect on increasing the saving rate of the economy.

Precautionary Motive. The people save for the unforeseen contingencies such as illness and periods of unemployment to protect themselves against these emergencies for which there is no insurance coverage.

Purchasing Power of Assets. The real value, that is, purchasing power of assets such as shares, bonds, houses possessed by the people, also influences savings of the people. If the prices of these assets rise, people feel better off than before. This induces them to consume more and therefore save less. It has been found that when prices of assets rise, people even get more loans from the banks and spend them for consumption purposes.

We have explained above some important factors that affect savings of a society.

SUPPLY OF LABOUR

The supply of labour can be viewed as supply of labour (working hours) of an indivdual, the supply of labour for an industry or occupation, and supply of labour for the economy as a whole. We begin with the annalysis of supply of labour (working hours) by an individual. As

5. See J. Stiglitz, op. cit p. 176.
6. N. Gregory Mankiw, *Principles of Economics,* Second Edition, 2001, p. 566

explained in Chapter 9 of application of indifference curve analysis, supply of labour by an individual depends on his choice of leisure by the individual for that time period. It should be noted that leisure is a desirable object which provides satisfaction to the individuals. On the other hand, work provides income to the individual with which he can buy goods and services to satisfy his wants. How much leisure an individual will be willing to sacrifice, that is, how many hours of work he will do, depends on the wage rate. We discuss below their choice between work (income) and leisure in detail with the help of indifference curves.

Work, Income and Leisure

Normally, the work-effort put in by the workers will vary in response to the changes in wage rates. We assume that the worker makes a contract with the employer to work for a certain wage rate per hour and that he is free to choose the number of hours he has to work in a week. This assumption, it may be pointed out, is not entirely realistic, because generally the workers are employed for a fixed number of hours in a week. The number of work-hours in a week may be fixed by law or by an agreement between the workers as a whole (or their trade unions) and the employer. Therefore, in actual practice, the worker may not be free to vary the number of hours he has to work. Even then, it may be pointed out that the workers can vary the number of hours to work in a week to some extent by choosing whether or not to work overtime, by taking leave on false pretexts, and by making similar other adjustments. This is the case with the workers who are employed on the basis of wage or salaries. Then, there are self-employed people such as farmers, business proprietors, independent professionals, etc. who can choose the number of hours they have to work in a week and their choice will depend upon the money rewards they are able to obtain for their work. In order to enunciate a general principle with regard to the supply of work-effort or labour by an individual worker we assume that the worker is completely free to vary the number of hours he has to work in a week.

Consider the worker's demand for income in exchange for the work-effort of labour he puts in. More income a worker has, more better off he will be. But, given the wage rate, more money income he can earn only by supplying more work-effort (or labour), that is, only by putting in more hours of work in a week. But more hours of work mean more sacrifice of leisure. It is therefore clear that given these circumstances a worker can have more income only by the loss of more leisure. And leisure, it should be noted, is a thing which provides satisfaction to the individual as do other goods of consumption. Therefore, the gain in satisfaction which a worker obtains as a result of earning more income by doing work has to be balanced against the loss of satisfaction he experiences as a result of the sacrifice of more leisure. It therefore follows that when the wage rate rises, whether or not a worker will offer to work more hours in a week depends upon his preference for leisure *vis-a-vis* income.

It needs to be emphasized that leisure does not mean 'doing nothing'. During the period of leisure, the worker may play with his children, do his gardening, listen to radio or watch television, visit the cinema, etc. Most of the consumption goods are enjoyed during the period of leisure. In fact, "Most of the good things of life must be enjoyed at leisure if they are to be enjoyed at all"[7] Having leisure strictly means *'not working for income'*. Income is demanded for spending on ordinary consumer goods. But, as explained above, leisure is also a thing that yields satisfaction to the worker. Therefore, a worker has to decide how many hours of work he should do and thereby earn income for spending on the consumption of consumer goods and how much leisure he should have.

7. Stonier and Hague, *op. cit.*, p. 305

When the wage rate rises, whether or not a worker will feel induced to work a larger number of hours depends upon his attitude towards income and leisure. In modern economic theory, relative preference between income and leisure are represented by indifference curves, with income represented on one axis and leisure on the other. Therefore, before explaining under what attitudes about income and leisure an individual will supply more hours of work in response to a rise in wage rate, we first explain the indifference curves between income and leisure.

Indifference Curves between Income and Leisure : Attitude Towards Work and Leisure

As said above, more income can be obtained, given the wage rate, by working for a larger number of hours, that is, by having smaller amount of leisure. In other words, more income can be obtained by sacrificing more of leisure. Thus, income and leisure are substitutes. Considering income and leisure as substitutes, indifference curves for an individual are drawn between income and leisure which depict his attitude towards income and leisure. Three such curves are shown in Fig. 52.20 where money income earned per week is measured on the Y-axis while X-axis represents, when read from left to right, hours of leisure enjoyed per week, and when read from right to left, hours of work supplied per week. As is known, there are 24 hours in all in a day or 168 hours in a week. In Fig 52.20, *OA* represents 24 hours which are the maximum up to which the individual can work for earning income in a day. An indifference curve between income and leisure shows the various combinations of income and leisure that yield equal satisfaction to the individual and among which he is therefore indifferent. It is assumed that more income is always preferable to less, other things remaining the same, .and also that more leisure is preferable to less leisure, other things remaining the same. Then, any combination on a higher indifference curve I_2 is preferable to any combination on a lower indifference curve I_1. Indifference curve I_3 is still higher and the combinations of income and leisure lying on it will be more desirable to the worker than the combinations lying on indifference curves I_2 and I_1.

The likely shape of the indifference curves for income and leisure is convex to the origin; they fall steeply first and then flatten out a little. This implies that when hours of leisure are small, utility of an hour of leisure is high and therefore relatively much income is required to be foregone for an hour of leisure to obtain the same level of satisfaction; and when the hours of leisure are many, utility of an hour of leisure is low and therefore relatively very less income is foregone to get an additional hour of leisure. This is the usual attitude towards income and leisure, and this makes the indifference curves between income and leisure as convex to the origin. There can be some exceptional patterns of attitudes towards income and leisure and accordingly the shapes of indifference curves in their case will be different. If an individual does not wish to have any leisure at all, his indifference curve for income and leisure will be perfectly flat, *i.e.* horizontal to the X-axis. If an individual likes to have as much leisure as possible, that is, he is too much fond of loafing about, passing time in recreation, sleeping etc. his indifference curve between income and leisure will be very highly steep. It is thus clear that different shapes of indifference curves reflect different patterns of attitude towards income and leisure. But, as said above, the usual shape of indifference curve between income and leisure is convex to the origin, first descending fast and then becoming flatter afterward.

Wage Line. How much money income an individual will earn depends not only upon the hours of work he puts in, but also on the wage rate per hour. Which particular combination of income and leisure in his indifference map of income and leisure the individual will choose, that is, how many hours he will decide to work and how many hours he will spend in leisure depends upon the wage rate per hour. Therefore, wage rate needs to be introduced into the diagram. As mentioned above, 24 hours are available to be spent on working for money income or for enjoying leisure time in a day. *OA* in Fig. 52.20 represents 24 hours. When the wage rate is ₹ 10 per hour, the worker will earn ₹ 240 if he works all the 24 hours during day. *OW* on the vertical axis represents money income of ₹ 240. Thus *AW* is the wage line whose slope represents the wage rate per hour. If the wage rate goes up to ₹ 12 per hour, the worker when working for all the 24 hours will earn money income of ₹ 288. Thus, as a result of hike in wage rate, the wage line will rotate upward to a new position.

Individual's Equilibrium between Income and Leisure : Optimum Choice of Work and Leisure

Fig. 52.20 depicts an indifference map representing an individual's desire for money income and leisure and his relative preference between different combinations of them. Suppose the wage rate is ₹ 10 per hour and the wage line is *AW*. The slope of the wage line *AW* represents the wage rate (that is, $\frac{OW}{OA}$ = the wage rate = $\frac{240}{24}$ = ₹ 10 per hour).

We assume the individual to be rational, that is, we assume that the individual will choose the combination of income and leisure so as to maximize his satisfaction. But in his attempt to maximize satisfaction, the individual is restricted by the time available with him and by the wage per hour which shows the rate at which time can buy money income. Given the constraints, the consumer will try to reach the highest possible indifference curve. Thus, in Fig. 52.20, given the wage line *AW* (which shows the wage rate per hour equal to $\frac{OW}{OA}$ = ₹ 10), the individual will be in equilibrium position (that is, will be maximizing his satisfaction) at a point on wage line *AW* which lies on the highest possible indifference curve. Such point is *E* at which the wage line *AW* is tangent to the indifference curve I_2. In this equilibrium position *E*, the individual is having *OL* leisure and *OM* money income. Further, he is working for *AL* hours of work. It is by working *AL* hours of work that he makes income equal to *OM*. It is therefore clear from the figure that at the given wage rate, he supplies *AL* amount of work-hours in a day.

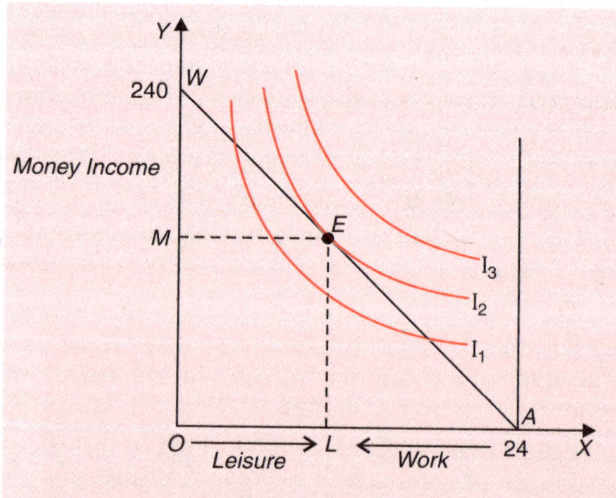

Fig. 52.20. *Equilibrium Regarding Income and Leisure*

Effect of Wage Increase on Work Effort: Income Effect and Substitution Effect

When the wage rate rises, the wage line will rotate upward and individual will be in equilibrium at a higher indifference curve. An important question which arises is : whether or not in the new equilibrium position reached as a result of the increase in the wage rate, the individual will offer to work for a larger number of hours than before. In other words, what will be the reaction of the individual to a rise in the wage rate? Before explaining the conditions under which the individual will supply more hours of work at the higher wage rate, we shall first show that the effect of the rise in wage rate can be divided into two component parts—the income effect and the substitution effect. In Fig. 52.21 when the wage rate rises and the wage

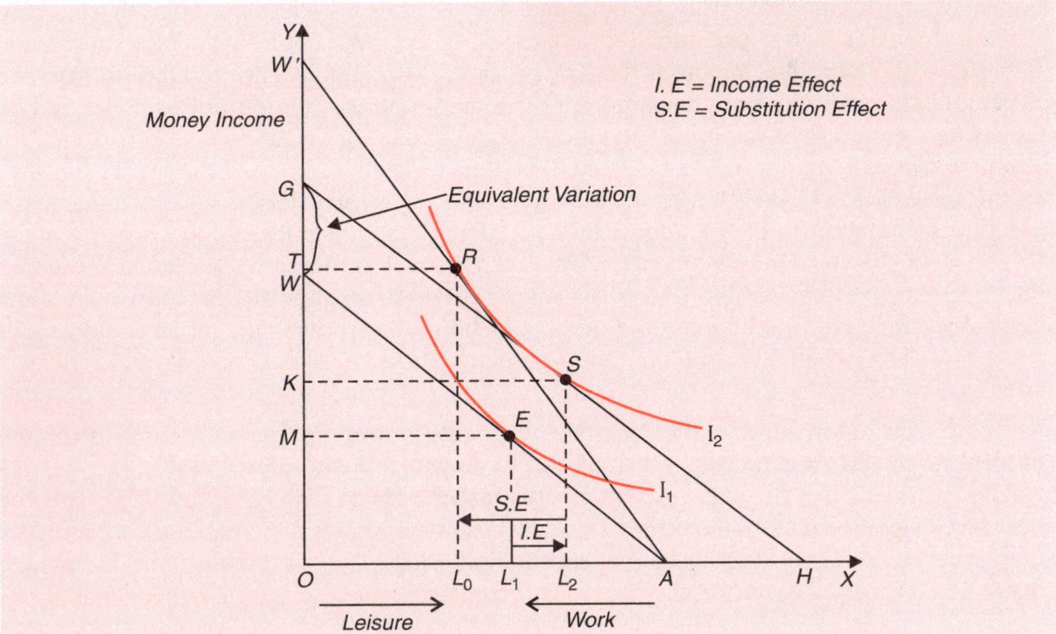

Fig. 52.21. *Work effort increases with the rise in the wage rate when the substitution effect is greater than the income effect.*

line shifts from *AW* to *AW'*, the individual moves from point *E* on indifference curve I_1 to the point *R* on indifference curve I_2. Thus when the wage rate rises, the individual reaches a higher indifference curve and is better off than before. It is as if the wage rate remained the same and a sum of money income equal to *WG* had been given to him. (Line *GH* has been drawn parallel to *AW* showing the wage rate as indicated by the wage line *AW.*) *WG is the equivalent variation in income.*

With the hypothetical wage line *GH,* the individual is in equilibrium at point *S* of indifference curve I_2. The movement from *E* to *S* is the result of working of the income effect caused by the increase in the wage rate. This increase in real income due to ***the increase in wage rate will induce the individual to consume more leisure as leisure is a normal good.*** This implies that as a result of this income effect, the individual increases his leisure by L_1L_2 and accordingly reduces his supply of labour (*i.e.* work hours) by L_1L_2. But the rise in the wage rate produces not only the income effect, but also what is known as substitution effect. Wage rate per work-hour is the opportunity cost of one hour spent in leisure. Thus, when the wage rate rises, each work-hour brings in more income than before, that is, ***the rise in the wage rate increases the opportunity cost of leisure and makes leisure relatively more expensive than before which induces the worker to consume less leisure and thus supply more labour.*** Therefore, as a result of substitution effect the individual moves from point *S* to point *R* along the indifference curve I_2 by substituting income for leisure.

It is clear from above that the movement from point *E* on indifference curve I_1 to point *R* on indifference curve I_2 due to the rise in the wage rate is the result of the operation of two forces. First, the income effect which operates along *ES* and brings the individual to indifference curve I_2 and thus makes him better off than before and, secondly, the substitution effect which operates along indifference curve I_2 and makes him move from *S* to *R* by substituting income for leisure. It should be noted that substitution effect of the rise in the wage rate always works in the direction of increasing the supply of labour (work hours) and reducing leisure. This is because when the wage rate rises the individual always tends to reduce leisure as this increase in the wage rate raises the opportunity cost of leisure. In Fig. 52.21 as a result of the substitution effect alone, the individual increases the work effort by L_2L_0 hours. As a result of the income effect alone, the individual can have more income and more leisure, or more income and no less leisure, or more leisure and no less income, depending upon his relative preference for income and leisure. In Fig. 52.21 as a result of the income effect alone of the rise in the wage rate the leisure is increased by L_1L_2 and income by *MK*. Increase in leisure by L_1L_2 means that work hours (or labour supply) is reduced by L_1L_2. Thus if income effect alone were operating, the labour supply would have been reduced by L_1L_2 hours. It is therefore clear that substitution effect and income effect of the rise in the wage rate work in opposite directions; while the substitution effect tends to increase the supply of labour (work hours), the income effect tends to reduce it. The net effect of the operation of the two effects will depend upon their relative strengths.

If the substitution effect of the rise in the wage rate is stronger than its income effect, the net result would be the increase in the supply of labour (*i.e.* work effort), that is, more hours would be worked when the wage rate rises. This case is depicted in Fig. 52.21 where income effect is reduction in work hours by L_1L_2, while substitution effect is increase in work effort by L_2L_0. As is obvious from the figure that substitution effect, L_2L_0 is greater than the income effect L_2L_0 by L_1L_0. Therefore, the net result is increase in work effort or supply of labour by L_1L_0 hours per day.

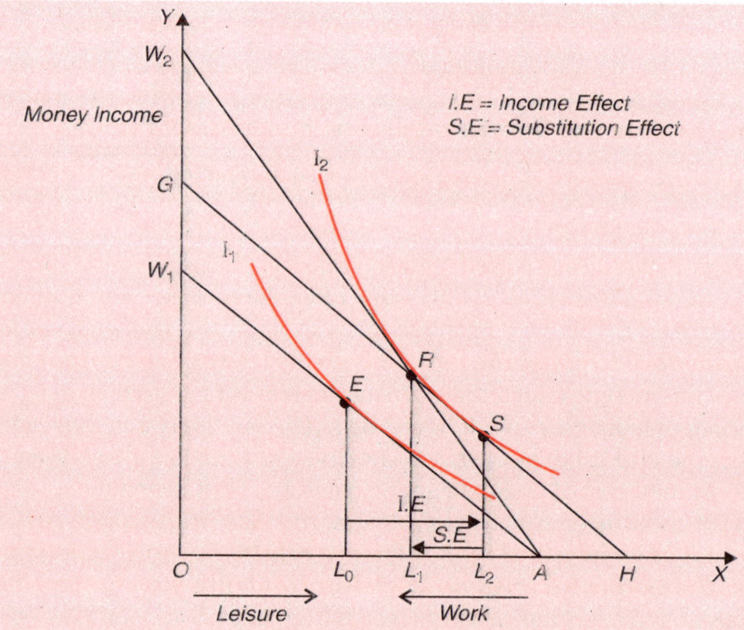

Fig. 52.22. *Work effort decreases with the rise in the wage rate when the substitution effect is smaller than the income effect*

On the other hand, if the income effect is stronger than the substitution effect, the work effort would be reduced as a result of the rise in the wage rate. This case is shown in Fig. 52.22 where income effect is the reduction in work effort by L_0L_2 and the substitution effect is L_2L_1 increase in hours of work effort. But income effect L_0L_2 is greater than substitution effect L_2L_1 by L_0L_1. Therefore, the net result is the reduction in work effort by L_0L_1, hours.

It is clear from above that whether an individual will supply more work effort or less as a result of the rise in the wage rate depends upon the relative strengths of the income and substituting effects, which in turn depends on the relative preference of individuals between income (work) and leisure. Thus, on theoretical grounds alone we cannot say whether labour supply (work hours) by an individual will increase following a particular increase in the wage rate.

Wage Offer Curve and Supply Curve of Labour

We now turn to explain the changes in the work effort or labour supplied by an individual worker due to the changes in the wage rate. Consider Fig. 52.23(*a*). To begin with, the wage line is A W_1; the slope of the wage line indicates the wage rate per hour. With wage line AW_1, the individual is in equilibrium at point *Q* on indifference curve I_1, and is working AL_1 hours in a week. Suppose the wage rate rises so that the new wage line is AW_2. With wage line AW_2, the individual is in equilibrium at point *R* on the indifference curve I_2 and is now working AL_2 hours which are more than before. If the wage rate further rises so that the new wage line is AW_3, the individual moves to the point *S* on indifference curve I_3 and works AL_3 hours which are more than AL_1 or AL_2. Suppose the wage rate further rises so that the wage line is AW_4. With wage line AW_4, the individual is in equilibrium at point *T* and works AL_4 hours. If points *Q, R, S* and *T* are connected, we get what is called *wage offer curve,* which shows the number

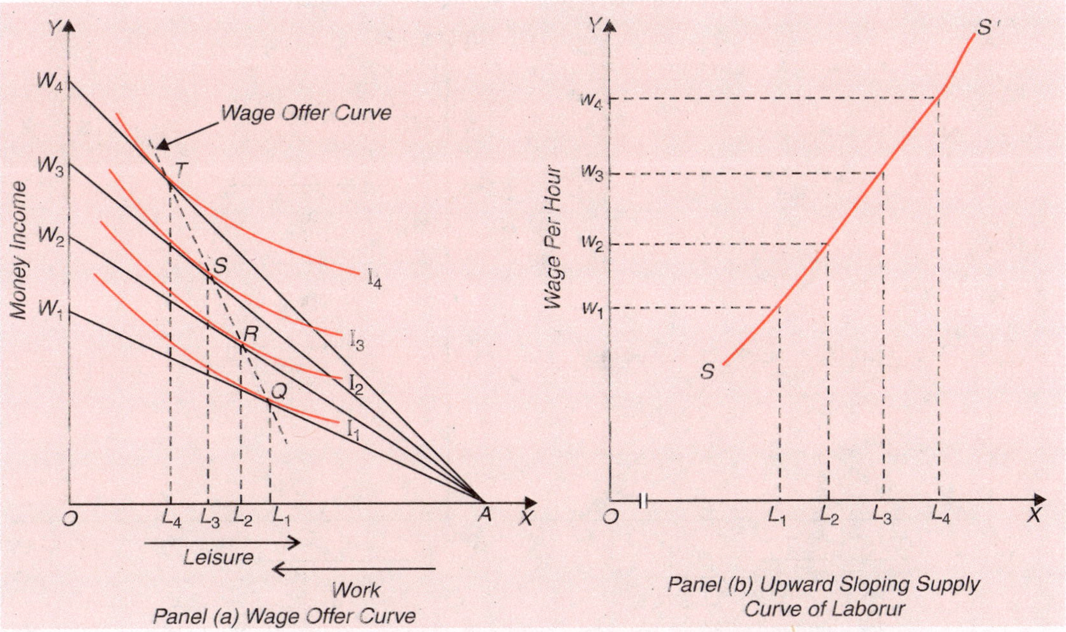

Fig. 52.23. *Derivation of Supply Curve of Labour*

of hours that an individual offers to work at various wage rates. It should be noted that the wage offer curve, strictly speaking, is not the supply curve of labour though it provides the same information as the supply curve of labour. The supply curve of labour is obtained when the wage rate is directly represented on the *Y*-axis and labour (*i.e.*, work effort) supplied at various wage rates on the X-axis reading from left to right. In Fig.52.23 (*b*) the supply curve of labour has been drawn from the information gained from Fig. 52.23 (*a*). Let the wage line AW_1 represents the wage rate equal to w_1, wage line AW_2 represents wage rate w_2, wage line AW_3 represents wage rate w_3 and wage line AW_4 represents wage rate w_4. It will be seen that as the wage rises from w_1 to w_4 and as a result the wage line shifts from AW_1 to AW_4 the number of hours worked, that is, the amount of labour supplied increases from L_1 to L_4. As a result, the supply curve of labour in Fig. 52.23(*b*) is upward sloping. The indifference map depicted in Fig. 52.23(*a*) is such that the substitution effect of the rise in the wage rate is stronger than the income effect of the rise in the wage rate so that the work effort supplied increases as the wage rate rises.

Backward-Bending Supply Curve of Labour. But the supply curve of labour is not always upward sloping. When an individual prefers leisure to income, then the supply of labour (number of hours worked) by an individual will decrease as the wage rate rises. This is because in such a case income effect which tends to reduce the work effort outweighs the substitution effect which tends to increase the work effort. In Fig. 52.24 such an indifference map is shown which yields a backward-sloping supply curve of labour which indicates that the number of hours worked per week decreases as the wage rate rises. AW_1, AW_2, AW_3 and AW_4 are the wage lines when the wage rates are w_1, w_2, w_3 and w_4 respectively. *Q*, *R*, *S* and *T* are the equilibrium points with the wage lines AW_1, AW_2, AW_3 and AW_4 respectively. It will be noticed from Figure 52.24 (*a*) that when the wage rate rises and as a consequence the wage line shifts from AW_1 to AW_4, the number of hours worked per week decreases from AL_1 to AL_4. In Fig. 52.24(*b*) supply curve of labour is drawn with *Y*-axis representing the hourly wage rate and *X*-axis representing number of hours worked per week at various wage rates.

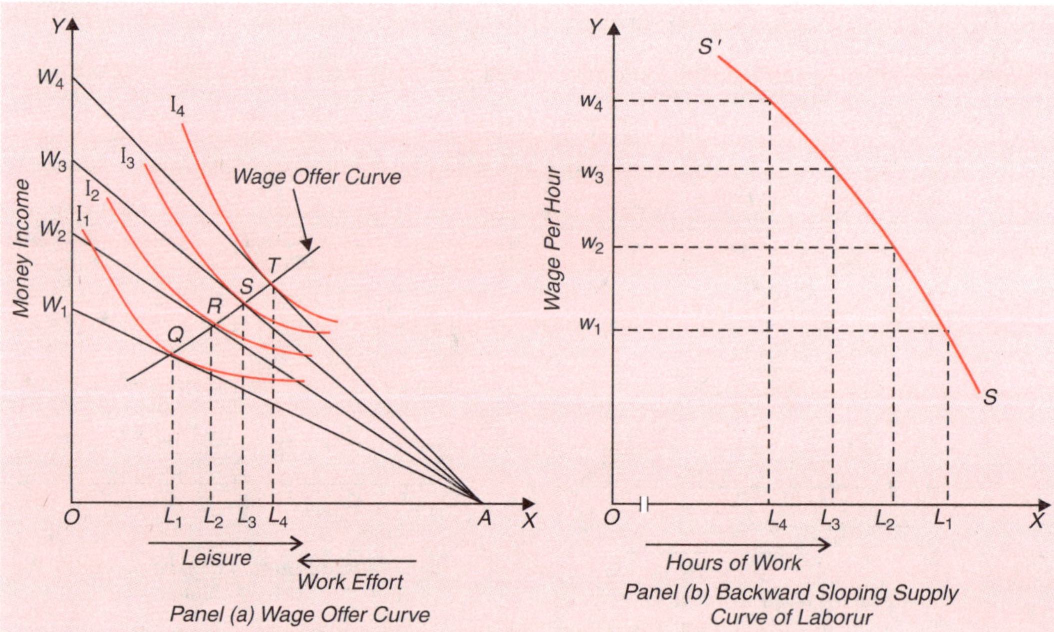

Fig. 52.24. *Backward-bending Supply Curve of Labour*

It will be seen from Fig. 52.24(*b*) that as the wage rate rises from w_1 to w_4, the supply of labour (*i.e.*, number of hours worked per week) decreases from OL_1 to OL_4. In other words, the ***supply curve of labour slopes backward***, that is, *it slopes upward from right to left.* It should be noted that it is the pattern of indifference curves between income and leisure, or in other words, it is the attitude towards income (work) and leisure that yields backward sloping supply curve. A glance at Fig. 52.24 (*a*) and Fig. 52.24(*b*) will reveal that the nature of indifference curves depends upon the relative preference between income and leisure. In Fig. 52.24 (*a*) indifference curves between income and leisure are such that the individual's preference for leisure is relatively greater than for income. In this case, when the wage rate rises, the individual enjoys more leisure due to larger income effect and accordingly reduces the number of hours worked per week.

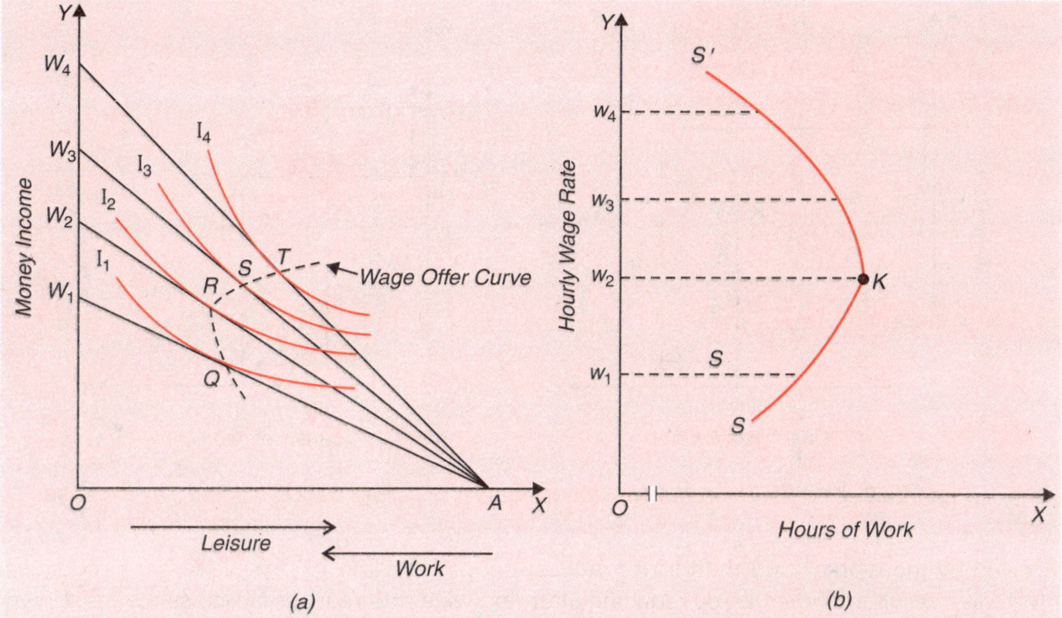

Fig. 52.25. *Backward Sloping Supply Curve of Labour Beyond a Certain Wage Rate*

But it generally happens that as the hourly wage rate rises from a very low level to a reasonably good level, the number of hours worked per day or week rises and as the hourly wage rate rises further, the number of hours worked per day or per week decreases. This is because an individual has some more or less *fixed minimum wants for goods and services* which he can satisfy with a certain money income. When the wage rate is so low that he is not earning sufficient money income to satisfy his more or less fixed minimum wants for goods and services, his preference for income will be relatively greater as compared to leisure, and, therefore, when the wage rate rises the individual will work more hours per week. When the wage rate has risen to a level which is sufficient to yield a sufficient money income for satisfying his fixed minimum wants, then for further increases in the wage rate the number of hours worked per week will decrease because now the individual can afford to have more leisure and also earn an income sufficient to meet his minimum wants for goods and services.

It follows from above that up to a certain wage rate the supply curve will slope upward from left to right and then for further increases in the wage rate the supply curve will bend backward. In the left hand panel of Fig. 52.25 an indifference map along with a set of wage lines AW_1, AW_2, AW_3, AW_4 (showing wage rates w_1, w_2, w_3, w_4 respectively) are shown. As the wage rate rises to w_2 and hecnce the wage line shifts to AW_2 the number of hours worked by the individual per week increases but when the wage rate further rises to w_3 and w_4 and hence the wage line shifts to AW_3 and AW_4, the number of hours worked by the individual decreases. From the right hand panel of Fig. 52.25 (*b*) it will be explicitly seen that the supply curve of labour slopes upward to the wage rate w_2 (that is, point *K*) and beyond that it slopes backward.

Tax Policy and Labour Supply

The effect of changes in tax rate on labour supply has an important influence on labour supply. This is because increase in tax rate, say income tax reduces the after-tax wage rate

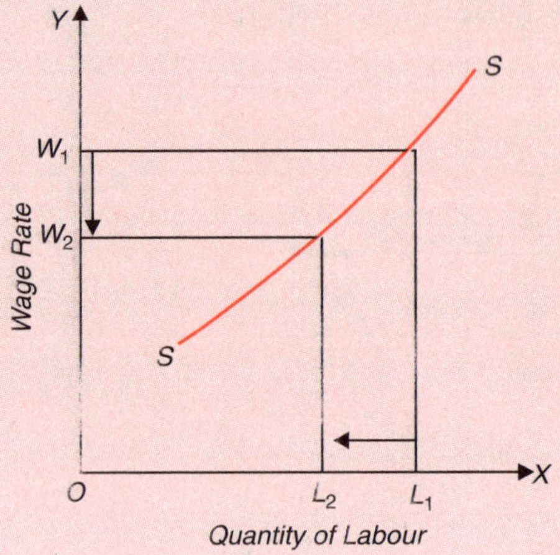

Fig. 52.26. *Income Tax reduces Labour Supply.*

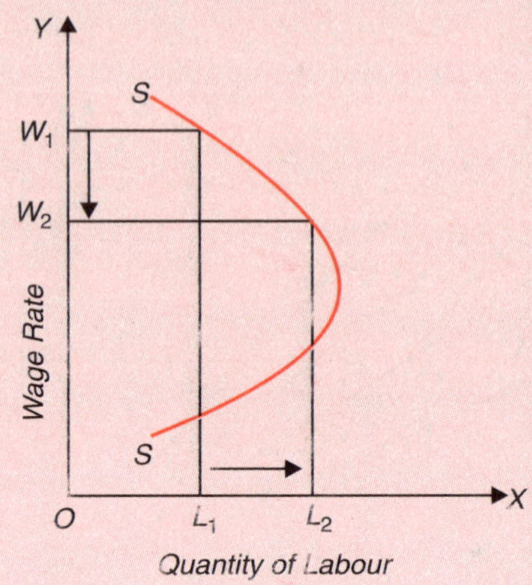

Fig. 52.27. *Income Tax increases Labour Supply.*

received by the worker and therefore it affects people's willing to provide larger productive effort. As a result, income tax, by reducing after-tax wage rate reduces labour supply as shown in Figure 52.26 where labour supply curve *SS* is upward sloping. Imposition of income tax reduces after-tax wage rate from W_1 to W_2 which induces *decrease* in the quantity of labour supplied from L_1 to L_2. However, if labour supply curve is backward-bending the imposition of a tax that reduces after-tax wage rate will *increase* labour supply as is shown in

Figure 52.27, where backward-bending supply curve of labour *SS* has been drawn. It will be seen from this Fig. 52.27 that when wage rate is reduced from W_1 to W_2 by increase in the tax rate, labour supply increases from OL_1 to OL_2 .

However, typical labour supply curve is upward sloping and in this case, as seen in Figure 52.26, increase in tax rate reduces work effort or labour supply.

With lesser productive effort or smaller labour supply as a result of imposition of tax economic performance of the economy is undermined and economic growth is adversely affected. In modern economics the analysis of effect of tax on labour supply is explained in the framework of substitution effect and income effect. There are two alternatives before an individual: either enjoy more leisure or do more work. When income tax is imposed, after-tax wage rate, that is, return from work diminishes and, therefore, opportunity cost of leisure falls. This induces the individual to substitute leisure for work effort. As a result of this substitution effect, supply of work effort is reduced. However, income effect of tax on income which reduces income will reduce leisure and increase labour supply. Generally, substitution effect dominates and therefore imposition of tax tends to reduce labour supply. To quote Eckstein, "If a worker has to pay taxes, say one half of his income from extra work, perhaps a lawyer working weekends, a doctor taking on additional patients or a sales-person making evening calls—his incentives will certainly be reduced."[8]

8. Otto, Eckstein, *Public Finance*, Prentice Hall.

Recently, the effect of tax policy on labour supply has been a subject of debate. In case of labour-supply by *men*, consensus among economists is that labour supply elasticity by men is positive but relatively low so that changes in tax rate have little effect on labour supplied by them and on their labour force participation rate. However, in case of *women*, reduction in after-tax wage rate has been found to have a large effect on their labour supply.

But some economists, especially those who believe in *supply-side economics,* are of the view that elasticity of men's labour supply is quite large. Therefore, according to them, very high tax rate on income that prevailed until the 1980s had a large disincentive effect on labour supply. Indeed, some advocates of supply-side economics laid so much emphasis on the adverse effect of tax on labour supply that they suggested that if tax rates were reduced, the high-income groups would supply so much more labour and their incomes would increase so much that government's revenue would increase even with lower rates of tax. Following this logic, income tax rates in the United States were reduced in the 1980s[9]. However, the prediction of supply-siders did not prove to be true. As mentioned above, the evidence in case of men indicates elasticity of labour supply is only small. As a result of tax cuts in the 1980s in the United States, *overall tax revenue* declined instead of increasing. However, *tax revenue from upper-income groups did increase.*[10] However, this increase in tax revenue from the rich does not seem to be the result of their putting in more work effort.

Two other explanations have been offered to explain the increase in tax revenue collected from the rich. First, the lower tax rates increased tax compliance by the rich and reduced tax evasion by them.[11] Lower tax rates not only reduced tax evasion but also "meant that the value of *avoiding taxes* through tax shelters fell and investors moved their money back into taxable activities"[12]. Second, as has been stressed by J. Stiglitz, a Nobel laureate in economics, after the tax cuts in the United States, "Wage inequality continued to increase over the period. The rich became richer not because they worked more hours but because they earned more per hour worked."[13] One important change in income tax system in the United States and India that has provided incentive to the married women to participate in the labour market is the separate treatment of wife and husband for taxation purposes. Previously, married couples (that is, husband and wife) were treated as a single entity and in the context of progressive income tax, this meant that they had to pay a higher marginal tax rate since their joint income was larger. As a result of tax reforms, husband and wife are treated as two *separate individuals* liable for tax payment. Thus, at present, each has to pay lower tax rate and as a result has a greater incentive to work on the basis of substitution effect. This change in tax policy has worked to increase substantially the labour supply by married women.

Labour Force Participation

Labour supply also increases as a result of rise in labour force participation rate. Labour force participation rate means the ratio of total population of working age which either works or is willing to work for pay. The children below the age of 15 and old people are excluded from labour force. A large number of women, especially married ones, do not want to work so they are also outside the labour force. The wealthy people who have inherited large wealth from their parents to support their families and do not want to work are also outside the labour force.

9. In India too income tax rates have been greatly reduced since 1991 when Dr. Manmohan Singh became Finance Minister and initiated economic reforms.

10. See J. Stiglitz, *Economics* 2000, p.169.

11. In the case of India, a noted Combridge economist, Nicholas Kaldor, argued that lower tax rates would check tax evasion and thereby increase tax compliance. Dr Manmohan Singh as FinanceMinister (1991-96) and P.C. Chidambaram later have provided this reason for reduction in income tax rates.

12. J. Stiglitz, *op. cit*, p. 169.

13. *Ibid.*

The decision about how much labour will be supplied can be divided into two parts: First, ***whether individuals work or are willing to work.*** Second, ***how much*** individuals work, that is, what amount of labour they supply. The decision of individual *whether* to work or express their willingness to work is called ***labour force participation decision***. In Figure 52.28 we have drawn the labour supply curve *S* of an individual. This shows how many hours of work the individual is willing to work at each wage rate. It will be seen that below wage rate W_R, the individual will not work, that is, will not participate in the labour force. Thus W_R is the minimum wage rate at which the individual will decide to work. Thus, minimum wage rate below which an individual is not willing to work is known as *reservation wage rate*. As the wage rate rises above W_R, the individual supplies more work-hours per week. Suppose for more than 100 hours per week the individual will not work whatever the wage rate. Therefore, at 100 hours per week labour supply curve of labour becomes perfectly inelastic.

Men except those who are either old or very rich who have inherited large wealth from their parents generally work or are willing to work. This is because they have to earn the livelihood for themselves and their families. Therefore, the minimum wage at which they offer their labour services or express their willingness to work is very low. The change in wage rate will affect men's decision as to how many hours they will work. ***The empirical evidence shows that elasticity of labour supply of men to changes in wage rate is quite small.***

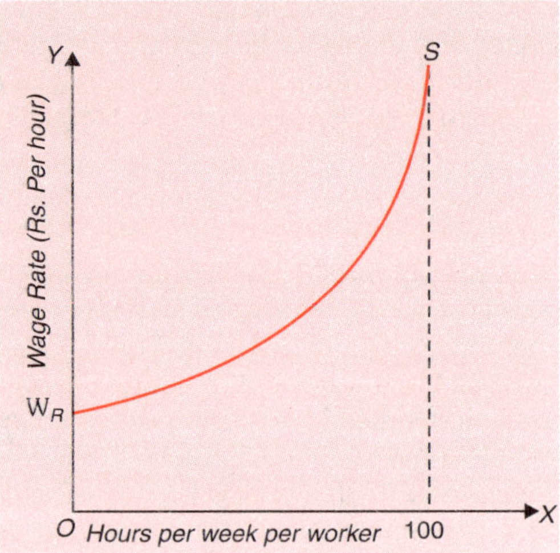

Fig. 52.28. *Individual's Labour Supply Curve*

In recent years in both the developed and developing countries women also participate in labour force. Previously, married women worked proportionately less. But in recent years even the proportion of married women in labour force has greatly increased. Even after child-birth married women are returning to work more quickly and in greater numbers than before. However, ***an important feature of labour supply by women is that it is more sensitive to changes in wage rates than that of men.*** Therefore, labour-supply curve of women is more elastic as compared with that of men. According to empirical evidence, elasticity of labour supply by women is equal to one. That is, one per cent change in wage rate brings about one per cent change in labour supplied by women.

Another important feature of women's labour supply is that in some developed countries such as the U.K. and the USA ***while labour force participation of men has declined, women's labour force participation has risen in the recent decades***[14]. The services sector has grown rapidly since 1980 in both the developed and developing countries (including India) and it has provided more employment opportunities to women. Thus increase in labour supply by women is due to two reasons. First, with rise in wage rate, women have offered more labour supply (*i.e.* work hours). Second, labour force participation rate of women has increased.

Supply Curve of Labour for the Economy as a whole

The supply curve of labour of a group of individuals or of the whole working force in the economy can be derived by summing up horizontally the supply curves of individuals. It may be

14. See J. Stiglitz, *op. cit*, pp. 166-67.

noted that the supply curve of labour for the economy as a whole will be upward sloping or downward sloping depending upon whether the relative number of individuals having upward-sloping supply curves is greater or less than those having backward-bending supply curves of labour. Further, different individuals will have backward bending portion in their supply curve at different wage ranges, which creates difficulties in finding the nature of supply curve of the whole working force. It is generally concluded that when the wage rate rises from the initially low level to a sufficiently good level, the total supply of labour to the economy as a whole increases (that is, supply curve for the economy as a whole slopes upward to a certain wage rate) and for further increases in the wage rate, the total supply of labour to the economy as a whole decreases (that is, beyond a certain wage rate, the total supply curve of labour slopes backward). Thus, the total supply curve of labour for the economy as a whole is generally believed to be of the shape depicted in Fig. 52.29.

In addition to the other factors, supply of labour to the whole economy depends on the following factors:

1. the size of population;
2. the age-composition of population ;
3. labour force participation rate, that is, the percentage of population who is willing or available for work;
4. the number of hours and days worked in a week, month or year; and
5. the intensity of work performed and the skills of workers.

The size of population is not influenced in any significant manner by the changes in the current wage rates. The advocates of the subsistence theory of wage believed that the size of population rises or falls with a rise or fall respectively in the wage rate, and from this they had deduced a law called "*Iron Law of Wages*". But the history has shown that rise in the wage rate may have just the opposite effect on the size of population from what the subsistence theory of wages conceives. Moreover, the historical experiences have revealed that the size of population is dependent upon the great variety of social, cultural, religious and economic factors among which wage rate plays only a minor determining role. Among the factors determining the supply of labour as enumerated above, the ability to work and the skills of the workers are also largely independent of the changes in the wage rate. However, the willingness to work may be influenced greatly by the changes in the wage rate. On the one hand, as wages rise, some persons will be induced to work more hours and others who do not work at lower wages may now be willing to supply their labour. But, on the other hand, as wages rise, some persons may be willing to work fewer hours and others like women may withdraw themselves from labour force, since the wages of their husbands have increased. Thus there are two conflicting responses to the rise in wages and therefore the exact nature of supply curve of labour is difficult to ascertain. ***It is, however, generally held that the total supply curve of labour rises up to a certain wage level and***

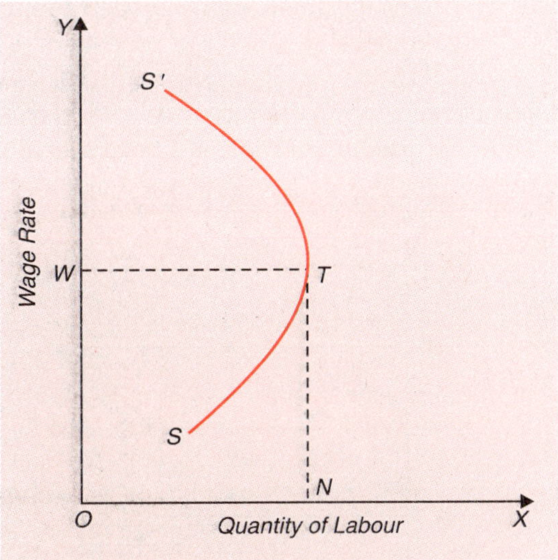

Fig. 52.29. *After a certain wage rate, supply curve of labour is backward bending.*

after that it slopes backward. This is shown in Fig. 52.29. As the wage rate rises up to *OW*, the total quantity supplied of labour increases, but beyond *OW*, the quantity supplied of labour diminishes as the wage rate is increased.

Supply Curve of Labour for an Industry or Occupaton

But so far as supply of labour to a particular industry is concerned, it is elastic and is upward sloping because as wages in an industry are increased, labourers from other industries will shift to this industry. The elasticity of the supply curve of labour to an industry will depend upon the transfer earnings of labourers, as is the case of supply of land from the viewpoint of a particular crop or industry.

Similar is the case of supply of workers to a particular occupation. If wages in one occupation go up, some persons from other similar occupations would be attracted to it and thus the supply of labour to that occupation will increase. Thus because of occupational shifts, the supply curve of labour to a particular occupation is elastic and rises upwards. The long-run supply curve of labour is more elastic than the short-run supply curve since, in the long run, besides the occupational shifts in the present labour force, new entrants to the labour market (who are now children) can also adopt that occupation by getting training for it in the very first instance.

WAGE DETERMINATION IN A PERFECTLY COMPETITIVE LABOUR MARKET

Like the prices of products, the prices of factors of production are also determined by demand and supply. Following Marshall-Hicks' version of marginal productivity theory of distribution, under conditions of perfect competition, prices of factors are explained to be determined by the equilibrium between demand for and supply of factors. Marshall and Hicks held that the price of a factor of production is determined by both the demand for and supply of the factor, but would be equal to the value of marginal product *(VMP)* of the factor. Thus, *in their view, price of the factor is not determined by the value of marginal product but is, in equilibrium, equal to it*. We have seen above how the demand for a factor of production depends upon its value of marginal product. We have also derived the demand curve of a factor of production of an industry. The supply curve of a productive factor is given by the curve showing the amounts of the factor offered by the owners of the factor at various factor prices. By taking labour as an example of a factor of production, we will explain how its price, that is, wage rate, is determined in a perfectly competitive labour market. The supply curve of labour or any other a factor to an industry or the economy as a whole *generally* slopes upward, at least in the relevant portion.

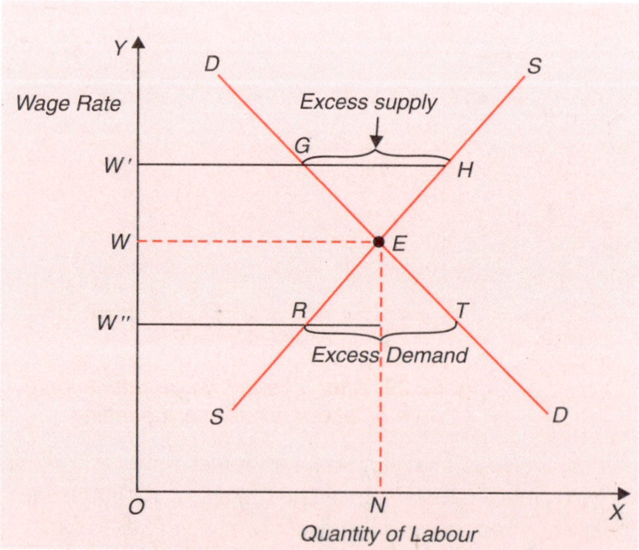

Fig. 52.30. *Equilibrium between demand for and supply of the labour to determine wage rate.*

Wage rate of labour ***is determined by the intersection of these demand and supply curves of labour.*** In other words, given the demand and supply curves of labour, its wage rate will adjust to the level at which the amount of the labour supplied is equal to the amount demanded. This is shown in Fig. 52.30 where *DD* is the demand curve and *SS* is the supply curve of labour. Only at wage rate *OW,* quantity of labour demanded is equal to its quantity supplied and accordingly the wage rate *OW* is thus determined. The price of labour cannot be determined at a level higher than or lower than *OW, i.e.,* other than the wage rate where amount demanded is equal to the amount supplied. For example, the wage rate cannot be established at the level *OW ′*, since at wage rate *OW′* the quantity offered for supply (*W ′H*) of labour is greater than the quantity demanded (*W ′G*) of it. As a result, the competition between these unemployed workers will force down the wage rate to the level *OW* where the quantity supplied is equal to the quantity demanded. Likewise, the wage rate cannot be determined at the level *OW ″* since at price *OW ″* the quantity demanded of the labour is greater than the quantity offered for supply at it. Thus at wage rate *W ″* excess demand for labour will emerge. Consequently, the competition among the producers demanding labour for production will push up the wage rate to the level *OW.*

Though wage rate of a labour is determined by demand for and supply of labour, yet it is equal to the value of marginal product of labour. This is illustrated by Fig. 52.31. It will be seen from Fig. 52.31 (*a*) that the equilibrium wage rate *OW* is determined in the labour market and *ON* is equilibrium quantity demanded and supplied of labour. An individual firm which demands labour will take the wage rate *OW* as given. It will now be seen from Fig. 52.31 (*b*) which depicts the position of a single firm that at wage rate *OW* the firm will employ or use *OM* quantity of the labour. This is so because in order to maximize its profits, the firm will equalize

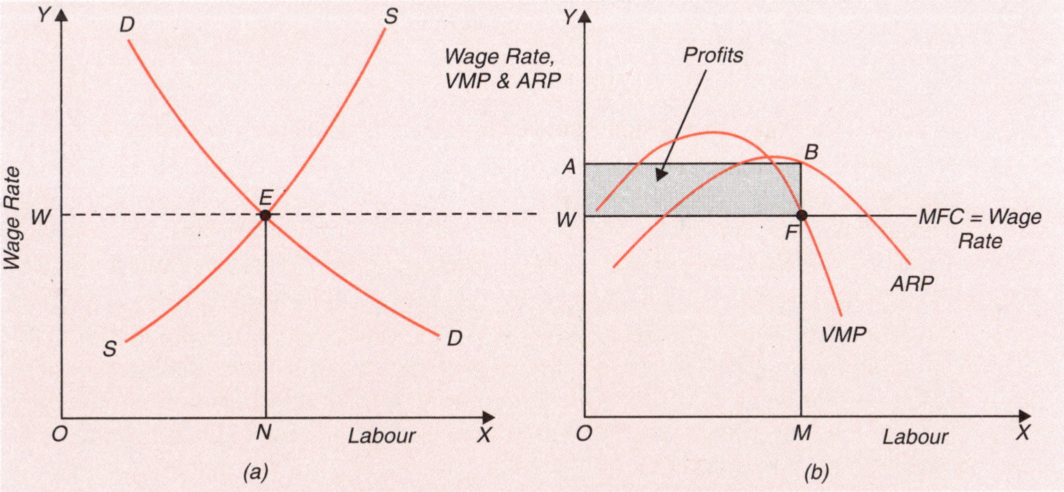

Fig. 52.31. *Factor price which is determined by demand for and supply of factor is equal to value of marginal product of the factor.*

the price of the factor with the *VMP* of the factor, and at *OM,* the wage rate of labour is equal to the marginal value product of labour. If the firm employs fewer than *OM* units of labour, then the *VMP* of labour will be greater than the given wage rate of labour or which will imply that there is still a scope for earning more profits by increasing the use of labour. If, on the other hand, the firm employs more than *OM* units of labour, *VMP* of labour will be less than the wage to be paid for it. As a result, the firm will incur losses on the marginal units and it will therefore be to the advantage of the firm to reduce the employment of labour. Thus firm maximizes its profits and is in equilibrium when it is employing *OM* amount of labour at which

VMP of labour is equal to its wage rate. ***To sum up, wage rate of labour in a perfectly competitive labour market is determined by demand for and supply of labour and is equal to the value of marginal product of labour.***

As is evident from Fig.52.31 (*b*), at price *OW*, the firm is earning super-normal profits, since in equilibrium *ARP* of labour is greater than the wage rate *OW* of labour. This can happen in the short run, but not in the long run. If firms are earning super-normal profits, more entrepreneurs will enter the market in the long run to purchase labour to produce the product made by that particular type of the labour. Entry of more entrepreneurs to the labour market will increase the demand for labour and as a result demand curve for labour in Fig. 52.31 (*a*) will shift outward to the right. This shift in demand curve due to rise in demand for labour is shown in panel (a) of Fig. 52.32. With this increase in demand, wage rate will rise to *OW*′. It is evident from Fig. 52.32(b) that with factor price *OW*′ the firm will be in equilibrium at *T* when it is employing *OM*′ amoumt of the factor. At *OM*′ amount of labour, the wage rate of labour is equal to *VMP* as well as *ARP* of labour. Since at *OM*′ wage rate is equal to the *ARP* of the factor, the firm is neither making super-normal profits, nor having losses.

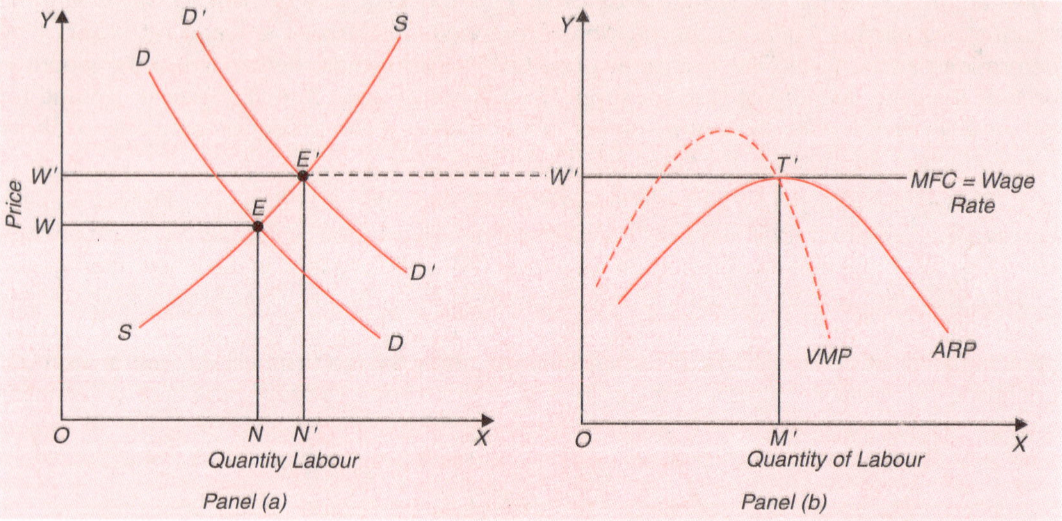

Fig. 52.32. *Determination of Wage Rate and Employment of Labour in the Long Run*

If, in the short run, firms are having losses, some firms will exit and stop purchasing that labour. As a result, the demand for labour will decrease. The demand curve will shift downward and to the left so that wage rate of labour will fall to a level at which the firms make zero profits. Thus, in the long run, under perfect competition in the factor market, price of the factor is equal to both *VMP* and *ARP* of the factor.

Long-run Wage rate = *MRP* = *ARP*.

To sum up, in the long run, as a result of the equilibrium between demand for and supply of labour wage rate is established at the level where the wage rate of labour is equal to both the VMP and ARP of labour.

We have seen above that when demand for a factor of production increases, given the supply curve of the factor, the factor price will rise. It is now left to be seen that what happens when the supply of a factor increases, given the demand curve of the factor. When the supply of a factor increases, the supply curve will shift to the right. This new supply curve will intersect the given demand curve at a lower price. Thus with the increase in the supply of a factor, its price will tend to fall. On the other hand, when the supply of a factor decreases, the supply curve will shift to the left and, given the demand curve, the price of the factor will rise.

As regards policy of factor owners, two results follow from our analysis. First, if the owner of a factor wants to raise the price of the service of their factor, they should try to increase the demand for their factor service. The demand for a factor increases, if the demand and price of the product rises, or the price of the substitute factor rises, or there is increase in the productivity of the factors due to the improvement in technology. Second, if factor owners want to maintain the price of their factor service(for example, wage rate of labour by workers) *i.e.*, to prevent their price from falling, they should not allow their supply to increase. This theory of factor pricing is based upon Marshall-Hicks' version of marginal productivity theory. In this theory, marginal productivity of a factor is an important economic force which determines the price of the factor. Therefore, this is subject to many criticisms which have been levelled against the marginal productivity theory and which we have already discussed in an earlier chapter.

DERIVATION OF DEMAND FUNCTION FOR A FACTOR

In this section we seek to derive a demand function for an input when both labour and capital inputs are variable. Let the following production function be given :

$$Q = \sqrt{LK} \qquad \text{...(1)}$$

Let w denote hourly wage rate of labour, r the price per unit of capital *(e.g.,* per machine hour). Thus the cost is

$$C = wL + rK \qquad \text{...(2)}$$

The task of the firm is to minimise cost for producing a level of output given the production function :

$$Q = \sqrt{LK} \text{ or } Q = L^{1/2} K^{1/2}$$

We have studied from both the graphical analysis and Lagrange method that cost for producing a level of output is minimised when marginal rate of technical substitution (or the ratio of marginal products of the two factors) equals the ratio of factor prices.

$$MRTS_{LK} = \frac{MP_L}{MP_K} = \frac{w}{r} \qquad \text{...(3)}$$

To find out the MP_L and MP_K we differentiate the production function ($Q = L^{1/2}K^{1/2}$) with respect to labour and capital. Thus

$$MP_L = \frac{\partial Q}{\partial L} = \frac{1}{2} L^{-1/2} K^{1/2}$$

$$MP_K = \frac{\partial Q}{\partial K} = \frac{1}{2} L^{1/2} K^{-1/2}$$

$$MRTS_{LK} = \frac{MP_L}{MP_K} = \frac{\frac{1}{2} L^{-1/2} K^{1/2}}{\frac{1}{2} L^{1/2} K^{-1/2}} = \frac{K}{L}$$

Substituting $\frac{K}{L}$ for $MRTS_{LK} \left(= \frac{MP_L}{MP_K} \right)$ in equation (3), we have

$$\frac{K}{L} = \frac{w}{r}$$

or $$K = \frac{w.L}{r} \qquad ...(4)$$

Now substituting $K = \frac{wL}{r}$ in the given production function ($Q = L^{1/2} K^{1/2}$) to obtain the relationship between labour and level of output, we have

$$Q = L^{1/2}\left(\frac{w.L}{r}\right)^{1/2}$$

Solving for L we get

$$L = w^{-1/2} r^{1/2} Q$$

or $$L = \left(\frac{r}{w}\right)^{\frac{1}{2}} .Q \qquad ...(5)$$

The equation (5) gives us the cost-minimisg quantity of labour for producing a given level of output. This also represents the long-run demand for labour input when both labour and capital are taken as variables.

Now, turning to the demand for capital (*i.e.* cost-minimising quantity of capital to be employed to produce the given output), we have seen above that

$$K = \frac{wL}{r}$$

or $$L = K \frac{r}{w} \qquad ...(6)$$

Substituting the value of $L = K \frac{r}{w}$ in the production function $Q = L^{1/2} K^{1/2}$) to obtain the relationship between capital and output we have

$$Q = \left(K \frac{r}{w}\right)^{1/2} . K^{1/2}$$

$$= K . r^{1/2} . w^{-1/2}$$

or $$K = w^{1/2} r^{-1/2} Q \qquad ...(7)$$

$w^{1/2} r^{-1/2} Q$ is the cost-minimising quantity of capital and represents the demand function for capital.

From equations (5) and (7) it is clear that demand for labour is a function of factor prices (w and r) and the level of output (Q). From equation (5) it follows that when wage rate rises quantity demanded of labour will decrease and *vice-versa*. Further, equation (5) shows that when price of capital rises, quantity demanded of labour will rise. Besides demand for labour is determined by the level of output (Q). Factor prices remaining constant, the greater the level of output, the greater the demand for labour. Similar conclusions hold good from equation (7) for the demand function for capital input.

NUMERICAL PROBLEMS

Problem 1. *Suppose a firm's production function is given by $Q = 12L - L^2$ where L is labour input per day and Q is output per day. Derive firm's demand for labour curve if output sells for ₹ 10 in a competitive market. How many workers will the firm hire per day when the wage rate is ₹ 30 per day ?*

Solution. For a firm working in a competitive market, demand for labour is determined by value of its marginal product (VMP). Since $VMP_L = P \times MP_L$, we first obtain marginal physical product of labour (MP_L) from the given production function. Thus,

$$Q = 12L - L^2$$

$$MP_L = \frac{dQ}{dL} = 12 - 2L$$

$$VMP = P \times MP_L = 10(12 - 2L)$$

$$VMP = 120 - 20L$$

Thus, demand for labour is given by

$$L_d = 120 - 20L$$

The firm will hire labour per day at which $VMP_L = w$. Using this and given that w = ₹ 30, we have

$$120 - 20L = 30$$

$$20L = 120 - 30 = 90$$

$$L = \frac{90}{20} = 4.5$$

The firm will hire 4.5 hours of labour per day.

Problem 2. *The demand for labour by a competitive industry is given by the following demand function :*

$$L_d = 1200 - 10w$$

where L_d is the labour demand per day and w is wage rate.

If labour supply curve is given by $L_s = 20w$, how much labour will be hired by the industry and what wage rate will it pay? Also find out how much economic rent will be earned by labour employed.

Solution. In a competitive labour market equilibrium wage rate and labour employment are determined by the intersection of labour demand and labour supply curves. Therefore equating demand for and supply of labour functions we have

$$1200 - 10w = 20w$$

$$30w = 1200$$

$$w = \frac{1200}{30} = 40$$

Substituting $w = 40$ in labour demand function we have

$$L_d = 1200 - 10w$$

$$= 1200 - 10 \times 40$$

$$= 800$$

Thus, 800 workers will be hired per day and wage rate of ₹ 40 per day will be paid to them.

Economic Rent. The economic rent earned by the quantity of a factor employed is its surplus earnings over and above its transfer earnings. Note that the transfer earnings of the units of a factor employed can be measured by the area under the supply curve of the factor. The total earnings of 800 workers employed at wage rate of ₹ 40 is

$L.w = 800 \times 40 =$ ₹ 3200

As is demonstrated in the accompanying diagram, the economic rent earned by 800 workers employed is given by half of the total earnings of workers (In Fig. 52.33 the total earnings of workers employed are given by the area of the rectangle *OLEW* and the economic rent of the workers is given by half of this area).

Economic Rent earned by 800 workers employed $= \frac{1}{2}(3200)$

= ₹ 1600 per day.

(Note: The diagram need not be drawn. We have drawn it to make it clear that in the present case of linear demand and supply curves, economic rent will be half of the total earnings of the workers employed.)

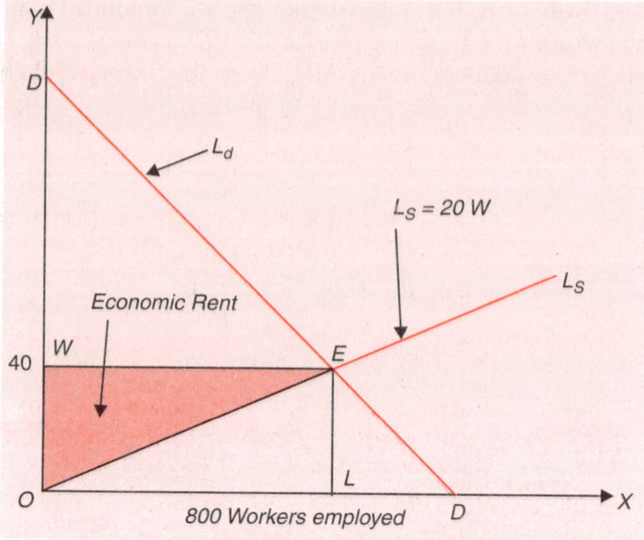

Fig. 52.33. *Economic Rent*

Problem 3. *Consider the following short-run production function (where X = variable input, Q = output).*

$$Q = 10X - 0.5X^2$$

Suppose the competitive firm sells its output for ₹ 10 per unit and it can obtain the variable input X at ₹ 20 per unit as much as it needs.

(a) *Determine the marginal revenue production function.*

(b) *Determine the marginal factor cost function.*

(c) *Determine the optimal value of X, given that the objective of the firm is to maximise profits.*

Solution. (a) Marginal revenue production function (*MRP*) is the first derivative of the total revenue function. Total revenue function can be obtained by multiplying the production function with price of output which is ₹ 10 per unit. Thus,

$$TR = PQ = 10(10X - 0.5X^2)$$
$$= 100X - 5X^2$$

$$MRP_X = \frac{dTR}{dX} = 100 - 10X \quad ...(1)$$

(b) Marginal factor cost function is the addition to total cost by using an extra unit of input. It is the first derivative of the total cost function $\left(MFC = \frac{dTC}{dX}\right)$. Since in the question, the price of the variable factor (*X*) is given and constant, *MFC* will be equal to the price of the variable input which is equal to ₹ 20 per unit). Thus,

$$MFC = 20 \quad ...(2)$$

(c) A firm which seeks to maximise profits will be making optimal use of the variable input when it is using its so much quantity at which its $MRP_x = MFC_x$. Thus, we can obtain the optimum value of the variable factor by equating the marginal revenue product function (equation 1) with marginal factor cost function (equation 2). Thus,

$$MRP_x = MFC_x$$
$$100 - 10X = 20$$
$$10X = 100 - 20 = 80$$
$$X = 8$$

Use of 8 units of the variable input X is optimal for the firm.

QUESTIONS FOR REVIEW

1. Explain how do people decide to make a choice about the number of hours they will work? Use indifference curve analysis to explain this choice.
2. How does a rise in wage rate affect labour supply ? Distinguish between income effect and substitution effect of rise in wage rate. How do they affect labour supply ?
3. Why is supply curve of labour of some individuals backward bending ?
4. Will increase in the wage rate always lead to an increase in the number of hours worked ? Why or why not ? *(D.U, B.A. (Hons. 2002)*
5. The saving decision is a decision of when to consume, today or tomorrow. Explain?
6. A principal motive of saving is to smooth consumption during working years and retirement years.
7. Explain the concept of budget constraint with regard to choice between consumption and saving. What is the factor that determines slope of the budget constraint in this regard ?
8. Explain with the help of indifference curve analysis how an individual will determine how much to consume and save in the present.
9. How will the rise in interest rate affect saving of individuals ? Distinguish between income effect and substitution effect of rise in interest rate. How do these effects influence the supply of savings ?
10. What are the factors that determine savings of individuals ?
11. How is a firm's demand curve for a variable factor input constructed when there is (*i*) only one variable input, (*ii*) several variable inputs in the production process.
12. What factors influence the elasticity of demand for a factor input ?
13. Derive graphically the competitive firm's demand curve for a variable factor when several variable factors are used.
14. How is demand for a factor of production a derived demand ? Explain the factors which influence the demand for factors.
15. Explain in terms of income effect and substitution effect how a backward bending supply curve of labour can come about.
16. How is the market demand for a variable factor of production derived from the demands of individual firms ? On what factors does the price elasticity of market demand for a factor depend ?
17. Assuming monopoly in the commodity market and perfect competition in the factor market, derive the demand curve for a variable factor when there are several variable factors.

(**Note:** When there is monopoly in the commodity market, marginal revenue is less than price. Therefore, in this question instead of using *VMP* curve of a variable factor we use *MRP* curve of the variable factor to derive the relevant demand curve.)

18. How are factor prices determined in a perfectly competitive factor market ? Show that the price of a factor in a perfectly competitive market is equal to the value of its marginal product (*VMP*).

CHAPTER

53

Pricing of Factors in Imperfectly Competitive Markets

Introduction

In the preceding chapter we have explained how the price of a factor of production is determined when there prevails perfect competition both in the product and factor markets. In the present chapter we will explain determination of the price of a factor when there is imperfect competition in the product and factor markets. As in the last chapter, we will explain the determination of factor prices in imperfectly competitive markets by taking the example of labour and the determination of its wage rate. The determination of wage rate of labour in imperfectly competitive markets will be explained in the following three cases :

1. When there prevails *perfect competition in the factor (labour) market and imperfect competition in the product market.*
2. When there is *monopsony in the factor (labour) market and perfect competition in the product market.*
3. When there is *monopsony in the factor market and monopoly in the product market.*

Before the theories of imperfect competition and monopolistic competition were introduced in economic theory no distinction was made between value of marginal product (*VMP*) and marginal revenue product (*MRP*). We have seen above that when there is imperfect competition, (*i.e.*, monopoly, oligopoly and monopolistic competition) in the product market, marginal revenue (*MR*) differs from the price of the product. As a result, under conditions of imperfect competition in the product market, marginal revenue product of the factor differs from value of the marginal product (VMP). This affects the demand for a factor and the price it will get under conditions of imperfect competition in the product market.

Wage Determination in Case of Perfect Competition in Labour Market and Imperfect Competition in Product Market

Since perfect competition is assumed to be prevailing in the labour market, wage rate will be determined by demand for and supply of labour, as explained in the previous chapter. But now the demand for the factor of production is determined not by the value of the marginal product (*VMP*) but by the marginal revenue product (*MRP*) of the factor. As we shall see below, in this case price of the factor, which is determined by demand for and supply of the factor, will be equal to the marginal revenue product, but will be ***less than the value of the marginal product (VMP) of the factor.***

The conditions of firm's equilibrium in factor market developed earlier will also apply in the present case. The firm working under perfect competition in factor market but monopoly or imperfect competition in the product market would also be in equilibrium position where *MRP* = *MFC* and *MRP* curve cuts *MFC* curve from above. But there are some differences between the present case and the case explained in the previous chapter.

Since in this case the firm is working under perfect competition in the labour market, it will not be able to affect the wage rate and therefore marginal labour cost (*MFC*), that is, supply curve of labour for an individual firm will be a horizontal straight line. Therefore, the firm will be in equilibrium, *i.e.*, maximising profits when *MRP* = *MFC* = wage rate. But because the firm in the present case is working under conditions of monopoly or imperfect competition in the product market, it will be able to exercise influence or control over the price of the product. *AR* curve for it will slope downward and *MR* curve will be below it. Consequently, *MRP of* labour which is equal to *MPP* × *MR* will not be equal to *VMP* which is equal to *MPP* × price of the product. Since *MR* is less than the price of the product under monopoly or imperfect competition, *MRP* would be less than *VMP* of labour. In symbolic terms :

$$MRP = MPP \times MR$$

$$VMP = \text{MPP} \times \text{Price of the product}$$

Since, under imperfect competition or monopoly in the product market, *MR* < Price of the product, therefore

$$MRP < VMP$$

In equilibrium in the labour market, the firm will make

$$\text{wage rate} = MRP$$

$$\text{Therefore, wage rate} = MRP < VMP$$

It is therefore concluded that *under conditions of monopoly or imperfect competition (i.e. monopolistic competition and oligopoly) in the product market, assuming perfect competition in the labour market, the labour will get wage rate less than value of its* marginal product.

The determination of wage rate and equilibrium of the firm when there is perfect competition in the labour market and imperfect competition or monopoly in the product market is shown in Fig.53.1. It will be seen from panel (*a*) of this figure that demand for and

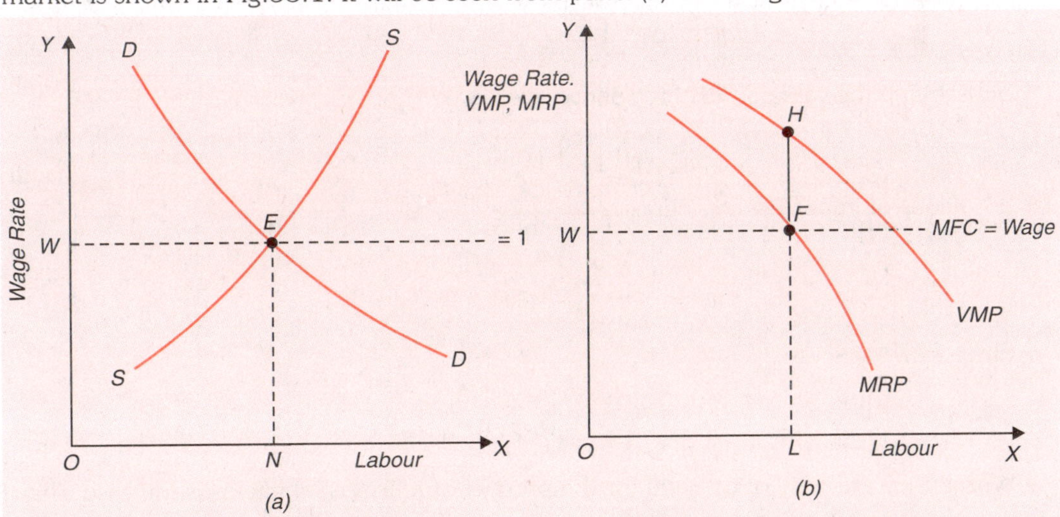

Fig. 53.1. *Wage Determination when there is Perfect Competition in the Labour Market and Imperfect Competition in the Product Market.*

supply of labour determine the wage rate equal to *OW.* Panel (*b*) of Figure 53.1 shows the equilibrium position of a firrn when there prevails imperfect competition in the product market.

Since *VMP* of labour is greater than *MRP* when there is imperfect competition in the product market, the *VMP* curve lies above *MRP* curve (for the sake of convenience, we have drawn only the downward-sloping portions *of MRP* and *VMP* curves). The firm will be in equilibrium at *F*, where it is equating wage rate with marginal revenue product *(MRP)* of labour. The equilibrium employment of the factor by a firm is *OL*. It will be noticed from the figure that the wage rate of labour *OW* is, in equilibrium, equal to marginal revenue product *LF* but is less than value of its marginal product which is equal to *LH*. Therefore, labour gets *HF* less than the value of its marginal product (VMP).

It may also be noted further that analysis of equilibrium made earlier when perfect competition prevails in the product market will also hold good in the present case. In the short run, the firms may make profits or suffer losses, but in the long run, in case there is monopolistic competition in the product market, adjustment will take place in the number of firms so that in the long run there are zero economic profits.

But no matter if it is short-run equilibrium or long-run equilibrium, the *wage rate will be less than the value of marginal product of labour (VMP_L) under conditions of monopoly or imperfect competition in the product market.*

It should be noted that exactly how much wage rate (*w*) will be less than the value of marginal product of labour $(VMP)_L$ depends on the *price elasticity of demand for the product* produced by the firm. The less the price elasticity of demand for the product, the greater the divergence between the wage rate (*w*) and the value of marginal product of labour (VMP_L). This can be shown as under :—

In labour-employment equilibrium when there is imperfect competition (monopoly) in the product market and perfect competition in the labour market:

$$w = MRP_L$$

$$= MR.MPP_L \qquad \text{....(i)}$$

Now, it will be recalled from the relationship between *AR*, *MR* and elasticity of demand that

$$MR = AR\left(1-\frac{1}{e}\right)$$

Substituting the value of *MR* in *(i)* above, we have

$$w = AR\left(1-\frac{1}{e}\right)MPP_L \qquad \text{(ii)}$$

Since *AR* = Price, rewriting *(ii)* above we have

$$w = \left(1-\frac{1}{e}\right)P.MPP_L$$

Since $P.MPP_L = VMP_L$

$$w = \left(1-\frac{1}{e}\right)VMP_L \qquad \text{...(iii)}$$

When price elasticity of demand for the product of a firm is infinite as is the case when perfect competition prevails in the product market, $\frac{1}{|e|} = 0$ and $\left(1-\frac{1}{|e|}\right) = 1$, it follows from the relation, $MR = P\left(1-\frac{1}{e}\right)$ that *MR* = Price or *P* in this case. Thus, in labour-employment equilibrium under perfect competition in the product market

$$w = \left(1 - \frac{1}{e}\right) P.MPP_L$$

$$= 1.P.MPP_L = VMP_L$$

But when there is imperfect competition (i.e. monopolistic competition and oligopoly) or monopoly in the product market, price elasticity of demand is less than infinite, the value of $(1 - \frac{1}{|e|})$ will be less than one. Therefore

$$w = \left(1 - \frac{1}{e}\right) VMP$$

Since $\left(1 - \frac{1}{e}\right)$ is less than one,

$$w < VMP$$

It will be seen that ***the lower the price elasticity of demand, the greater will be the difference between wage rate (w) and value of marginal product of labour (VMP_L).***

According to Joan Robinson,[1] a factor is *exploited* when it is paid less than the value of the marginal product *(VMP)*. Therefore, according to Joan Robinson, when imperfect competition prevails in the product market, labour and other factors, (*i.e.*, factors other than the entrepreneur) are exploited by the entrepreneur. But many economists, especially E. H. Chamberlin, do not agree with Robinson's definition of exploitation of labour. According to Chamberlin, a factor is exploited only when it is paid less than the marginal revenue product (*MRP*). As explained above, when there prevails imperfect or monopolistic competition (including monopoly and oligopoly) in the product market with perfect competition in the factor market, price of a factor is equal to the marginal revenue product, though it is less than the value of the marginal product. Therefore, according to Chamberlin, there is not any exploitation of labour or any other factor by the entrepreneur when imperfect competition exists in the product market, provided there is perfect competition in the factor market. We shall discuss this question of exploitation of labour at length in a later section.

FACTOR PRICING (WAGE DETERMINATION) UNDER MONOPSONY

What is Monopsony ? Monopsonist means a single buyer. There can be a single buyer in the product market as well as in the factor market. *Where there is a single buyer of a product, he is monopsonist in the product market.* However, we are concerned here with monopsonist in the factor market. Monopsony is said to exist in the factor market when there is a single buyer of a specific factor of production. For instance, when in a particular area, there is only one employer of a specific type of labour, he is monopsonist of that labour. Monopsony in the labour market also comes into existence when various employers of labour in an area form a collusion so far as recruitment of labour is concerned. Monopsony, while it is very rare in product markets, is more often found in factor markets.

Just as a monopolist in the product market faces a downward-sloping demand curve and can influence the price of the product by varying the level of his output, similarly a monopsonist in the factor market faces an upward-sloping supply curve of the factor. Accordingly,

1. Joan Robinson, *Economics of Imperfect Competition.*

monopsonist can affect the price of the factor by varying the level of its employment. As explained in the previous chapter, supply curve of labour to a particular industry or occupation is upward sloping indicating that at a higher wage rate more labour will be generally supplied. This is shown in Figure 53.2. Since as more labour is employed, a higher wage has to be paid to *all* workers, the addition made to total factor cost (or total labour cost in the present case) by employing an additional worker will be greater than the wage rate. Therefore, marginal factor cost *(MFC)* of labour will be above the supply curve of labour as shown in Figure 53.2.

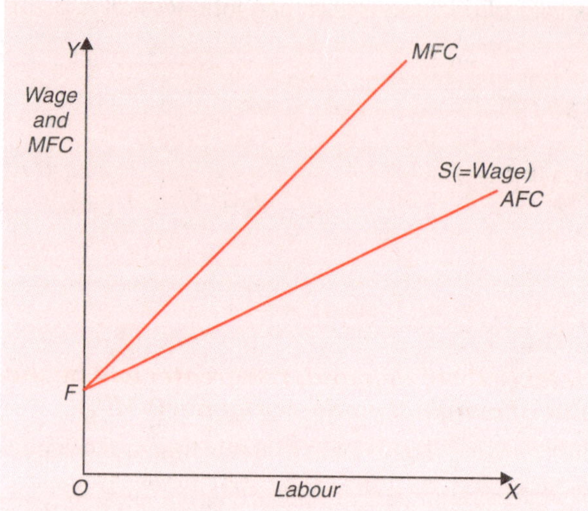

Fig. 53.2. *Supply Curve and Marginal Factor Cost Curve of Labour*

By restricting employment, it can lower the price of the factor. And if he wants to buy more amount of the factor, he will have to raise its price. Therefore, ***the supply curve of the factor or average cost (AFC) curve (i.e. wage curve) to the monopsonist will be rising upward to the right.***

Under monopsony in the labour market, a single buyer faces a large number of workers who are unorganised and whose geographical mobility of labour is very much limited. Monopsony may prevail when a big employer hires a proportionately very large number of a given type of labour so that he is in a position to influence the wage rate or it may prevail when various big employers have an understanding not to compete for labour and thus act as one in hiring labour. Thus, in the actual world, monopsony exists in the labour market when a large single employer or various employers acting as one confronts a large number of workers who are unorganised *(i.e.,* non-unionized) and who lack geographical mobility.

It should be noted that *non-organisation of labourers* into unions is an essential condition for the existence of monopsony, for when the labourers organise themselves into trade union, the supply of labour is channelled through the trade union and the trade union therefore becomes a sole seller of labour. When a single buyer—the employer—faces a single seller—the trade union—the market situation is one of bilateral monopoly and not of monopsony. Thus, monopsony will prevail when the workers are not organised into trade unions. Likewise, immobility of labour is also an essential condition for the existence of monopsony in the labour market. If the workers are sufficiently mobile so that they will move to places or industries where wages are higher, then the single employer in a local market will not possess a determining influence on wage rate paid to labour.

It is important to know the relationship between marginal factor cost (*MFC*) of labour, which is equal to *MRP* or *VMP* of labour in equilibrium and the wage rate paid to labour. This relationship is derived below. Assuming that labour is the only variable factor,

$$TFC = w.L$$

where *TFC* represents the total labour cost incurred, w is the wage rate paid to labour and L is the number of workers employed. The change in total labour cost caused by hiring additional worker is

$$\frac{\Delta TFC}{\Delta L} = w + \frac{L.\Delta w}{\Delta L}$$

or $$MFC = w + \frac{L.\Delta w}{\Delta L}$$

where *MFC* represents marginal factor cost of labour.

Multiplying and dividing by *w* of the right hand side of the above equation we have

$$MFC = w + \frac{L.\Delta w}{\Delta L}.\frac{w}{w}$$

$$= w\left(1 + \frac{L.\Delta w}{\Delta L.w}\right) = w\left(1 + \frac{L}{w}.\frac{\Delta w}{\Delta L}\right)$$

Now, $\frac{L}{w}.\frac{\Delta w}{\Delta L}$ is the *inverse* of the elasticity of supply curve of labour since the elasticity of supply of labour is equal to $\frac{\Delta L}{\Delta w}.\frac{w}{L}$

Thus, $$MFC = w\left(1 + \frac{1}{e_s}\right)$$

where e_s represents the elasticity of labour supply with respect to wage rate.

Since in labour-employment equilibrium $VMP_L = MFC_L$, it follows that

$$VMP = MFC = w\left(1 + \frac{1}{e_s}\right)$$

With an upward-sloping supply curve of labour, $\frac{1}{e_s}$ is positive, and the lower the elasticity of labour supply, the greater will be its inverse $\frac{1}{e_s}$. It follows therefore that under monopsony **in the labour market (along with perfect competition in the product market), the *amount by which* VMP (= MFC) is *greater than the wage rate (w) depends on the elasticity of labour supply* (e_s). *The less the elasticity of supply, the greater would be the divergence of the wage from VMP of labour.***

Wage Determination when there is Monopsony in the Labour Market and Perfect Competition in the Product Market

The non-organisation of workers into trade unions and immobility of the workers is essential for the existence of monopsony in the labour market. We shall now explain how wage rate is determined in a monopsonistic market situation. In a proper analysis of the same, we must know what type of market situation is confronted by the monopsonist in selling the product produced by the labour employed by him. We shall first explain the wage determination in the case where monopsony in the labour market is found with perfect competition in the product market. Then, we shall explain wage determination when monopsony in the labour market is found with monopoly in the product market, that is, where the monopsonist in the labour market is also the monopolist in the product market.

The demand curve of labour of the monopsonist, as of perfect competitor, is given by the curve of marginal revenue product. It should be noted that when perfect competition prevails in the product market, marginal revenue product will be equal to the value of the marginal product. Therefore, in this case, the curve of marginal revenue product will coincide with the curve of value of the marginal product.

The supply curve of labour to a monopsonist slopes upward as the S curve in Fig. 53.2 which indicates that to get more labour the monopsonist must pay higher wages. It should be noted that the supply curve of labour indicates the amounts of labour supplied at different wage rates. This supply curve of labour is also called average labour cost (*ALC*) or average factor cost (*AFC*) of labour. As labour supply curve is upward sloping, marginal factor cost of labour will be greater than the wage rate. That is why marginal factor cost (*MFC*) of labour lies above the supply curve of labour S.

The monopsonist will be in equilibrium where the marginal factor cost (*MFC*) of labour, *i.e.*, marginal labour cost (*MLC*) is equal to its marginal revenue product (*MRP*). It will be seen from Figure 53.3 that the marginal revenue product curve intersects the marginal factor cost (*MFC*) curve of labour at point E and thus the marginal factor cost (*MFC*) of labour is equal to its marginal revenue product at the level of labour employment OL_1. Further, it is evident from Fig. 53.3 that OL_1 amount of labour is forthcoming at OW_1 wage rate. Thus the monopsonist, in equilibrium, will employ OL_1 amount of labour and will pay OW_1 wage rate to the labourers. It will be clear from the figure that the wage rate (OW_1) determined under monopsony is smaller than value of marginal product (*VMP*) and marginal revenue product (*MRP*) of labour which is equal to the L_1E. Thus each worker gets EH less than his value of marginal product (*VMP*) and marginal revenue product. According to Joan Robinson, ***to pay a worker less than value of his marginal product is to exploit him.*** Therefore, in Fig. 53.3 exploitation of each worker done by the monopsonist is equal to EH. Because this exploitation is due to the existence of monopsony in the labour market, Joan Robinson calls it as the *monopsonistic exploitation*.

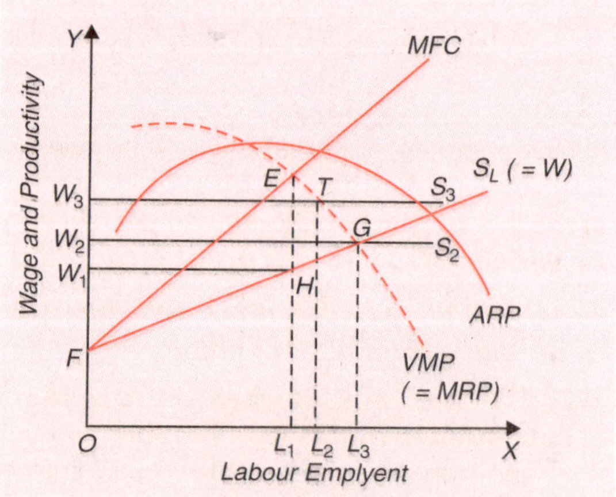

Fig. 53.3. *Wage Determination under Monopsony*

It should be noted that monopsony results in a lower wage rate and lower level of labour employment than under perfect competition in the labour market. Consider Fig. 53.3. If there were perfect competition in the labour market the equilibrium would have been at the point where the demand curve or *VMP* curve for labour intersects the supply curve S_L of labour. Therefore, under perfect competition in the labour market, the higher wage rate OW_2 and larger employment OL_3 would have been determined.

A very important conclusion can be derived from the above analysis of wage-employment equilibrium under monopsony in the labour market. It is that under conditions of monopsony in the labour market, trade unions can raise the wage rate without creating unemployment. In fact, it can be shown that a wage increase secured by trade unions under such circumstances will result in greater employment. Thus, in Fig. 53.3, if the wage rate is raised to OW_3 as a result of trade union's bargaining with the monopsonist, the employment offered by the monopsonist will increase from OL_1 to OL_2. This is because when the agreement is reached between the trade union and the monopsonist at wage OW_3, the average wage curve facing the monopsonist will become a horizontal straight line at the level of OW_3 and the marginal factor cost curve of labour will coincide with it. With this change, his equilibrium will be at point T corresponding to OL_2 level of employment.

However, there is a limit to such increases in both wage and employment, which we will explain in the next chapter.

Wage Determination When There is Monopsony in the Labour Market and Monopoly in the Product Market

Where there is monopoly in the product market, the curve of marginal revenue product will differ from the curve of the value of marginal product. The marginal revenue product curve (*MRP*) will be below the curve of the value of marginal product (*VMP*), for the marginal revenue is less than the average revenue when there is monopoly in the product market. The supply curve of labour S_L (wage curve *W*), as in the above case, slopes upward and the marginal factor cost curve (*MFC*) lies above it. The equilibrium of the monopsonist will be where the marginal revenue product equals marginal factor cost (*MFC*) of labour. In Fig. 53.4, the equilibrium of the monopsonist is at point *E* according to which wage *LH* or *OW* is determined and labour *OL* is employed.

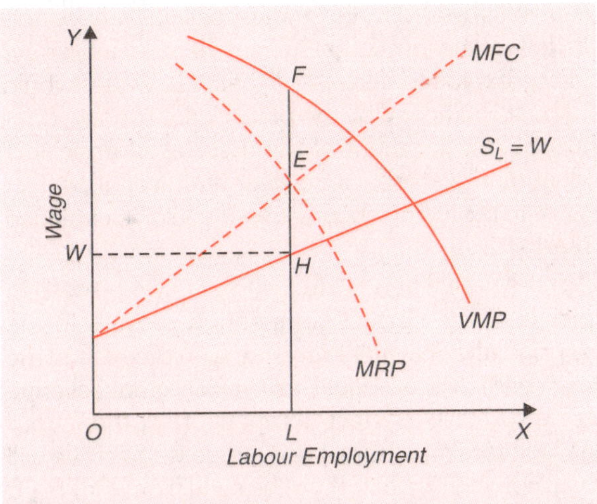

Fig. 53.4. *Wage Determination under Monopsony*

It will be seen from Fig. 53.4 that wage rate *LH* is not only less than marginal revenue product (*LE*) but is also less than the value of the marginal product (*LF*). The difference *EH* between marginal revenue product *LE* and the wage rate *LH* is due to the existence of monopsony in the labour market and has therefore been called by Joan Robinson as ***monopsonistic exploitation***. But the difference *FE* between the value of the marginal product *LF* and the marginal revenue product *LE* is due to the existence of monopoly in the product market. The worker gets *FE* amount less than his value of the marginal product because of the fact of monopoly in the product market and has therefore been designated as '*monopolistic exploitation*' by Joan Robinson. Thus, according to Joan Robinson, under monopsony-monopoly market situation, the worker is subjected to double exploitation; because of monopoly he gets less than the value of his marginal physical product and because of monopsony he gets less than his marginal revenue product.

EXPLOITATION OF LABOUR

We have explained above that labour is exploited when there prevails imperfect competition or monopoly in the product market as well as when there is imperfect competition or monopsony in the labour market. In the former case it is called monopolistic exploitation and in the latter it is called monopsonistic exploitation. In our above analysis we have followed Joan Robinson's approach to the exploitation of labour. As we saw in an earlier chapter, Robinson's definition of exploitation of labour is not accepted as valid by many economists, especially Chamberlin. It is therefore useful to discuss the concept of exploitation of labour and various meanings and interpretations of exploitation of labour that have been provided.

Pigou-Robinson's Concept of Exploitation

Joan Robinson, following A.C. Pigou, defined exploitation of labour as the payment to the labour which is less than its value of marginal product (*VMP*). And the value of marginal product is obtained by the marginal physical product multiplied by the selling price of the product. To quote Joan Robinson, "What is actually meant by exploitation, is, usually, that the wage is less than the marginal physical product of labour valued at its selling price".[2]

According to the above view, the exploitation of labour occurs when there is imperfect competition (or monopsony) in the buying of labour (*i.e.*, labour market) as well as when there is imperfect or monopolistic competition in the product market. Thus, on this definition, exploitation of labour cannot occur only when there is perfect competition in both the labour and product markets. Before the development of imperfect and monopolistic competition theories by Joan Robinson and Chamberlin it was believed that when there is imperfect competition in the labour market, labour would be exploited because in that case wages would be less than the marginal physical product of labour multiplied by the price of the product (that is, value of the marginal product, *VMP*). With the development of the theories of imperfect and monopolistic competition regarding product markets, it became clear that even if perfect competition prevailed in the labour market (that is, in buying of labour), labour could be exploited on account of imperfections in the product market.

Consider Figs 53.5 and 53.6. In Fig. 53.5 the case when perfect competition prevails in both the labour and product markets is depicted. Since perfect competition prevails in the market for the product produced by the firm, price and marginal revenue would be the same and therefore value of the marginal product (*VMP*) will be equal to the marginal revenue product (*MRP*) of labour. Further, since there also exists perfect competition in the labour market, the firm will have no control over the wage rate and therefore average wage curve will be perfectly elastic and marginal wage curve will coincide with it. It will be seen from Fig. 53.5 that firms would be in equilibrium at *ON* employment of labour where they are equating the

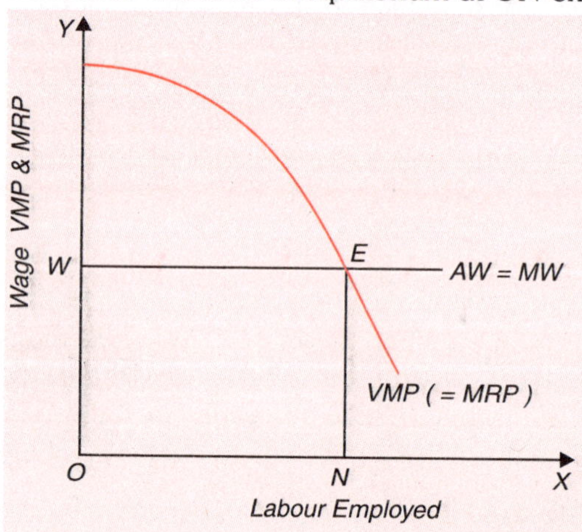

Fig. 53.5. *No labour exploitation exists under conditions of perfect competition in both the labour and product markets.*

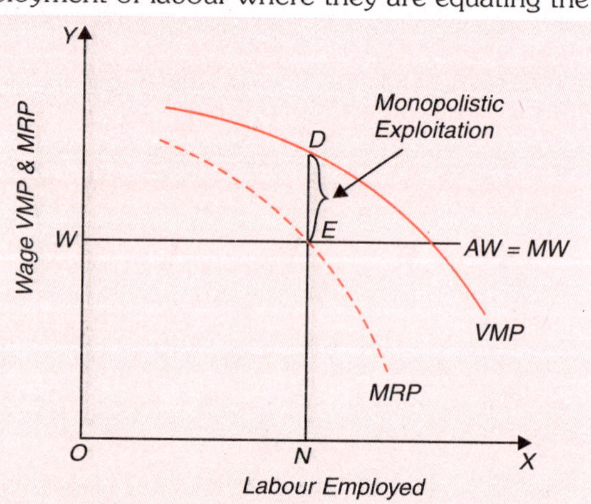

Fig. 53.6. *Labour is exploited when there is imperfect competition or monopoly in the product market even though perfect competition prevails in the labour market.*

wage rate with the value of the marginal product (*VMP*) which is equal to marginal revenue product (*MRP*). Thus, it is evident that under conditions of perfect competition in both the labour and product markets, labour is paid the wage rate equal to the value of its marginal product (*VMP*). On Pigou-Robinson's definition, no exploitation exists when perfect competition prevails in both the labour and product markets.

Now consider Figure 53.6 where the case when there prevails imperfect competition or monopoly in the product market, but there is perfect competition in the labour market. On

2. *Economics of Imperfect Competition*, p.282, and A.C. Pigou, *Economics of Welfare*, p.549.

Robinson-Pigou's definition labour will be exploited in this case. Since there is perfect competition in the labour market, average and marginal wage curves coincide and are perfectly elastic at the current wage rate. On account of imperfect competition or monopoly in the product market, marginal revenue is less than the price of the product and therefore the marginal revenue product (*MRP*) is less than the value of the marginal product (*VMP*) and therefore the curves of these two diverge from each other; *MRP* curve lies below the *VMP* curve. To be in equilibrium in this situation, a firm will equate wage with marginal revenue product. It will be seen from Fig. 53.6 that firm is employing *ON* amount of labour at which marginal revenue product is equal to the wage rate *OW*. It will be noticed from Fig. 53.6 that the value of the marginal product of *ON* amount of labour employed is *ND*, while it is being paid wage equal to marginal revenue product *NE* (*NE* = *OW*). And *OW* or *ND* is less than the value of marginal product *NE*. That is, labour is being paid less than the value of marginal product by the amount *ED* which, on Robinson-Pigou definition, represents exploitation of labour. Since this difference *ED* between the wage paid to labour and the value of marginal product of labour (in other words, divergence between *VMP* and *MRP*) has arisen on account of imperfect competition (including monopoly) in the product market, it has been termed as ***monopolistic axploitation*** by Joan Robinson.[3]

The divergence between the wage rate and the value of the marginal product (*VMP*) of labour can also arise on account of imperfect competition or monoprony in the labour market. When there is imperfect competition or monopsony in labour market, supply curve of labour (*i.e.*, average wage curve) is not perfectly elastic but is upward-sloping. As a result, marginal wage (*MW*) curve lies above the average wage *AW* curve. In this case divergence between wage (*i.e.*, average wage) and the value of the marginal product of labour arises on account if the difference between the marginal wage and average wage which is due to the monopsony or imperfect competition in the labour market. This divergence between the marginal wage and average wage and therefore between value of the marginal product and the wage rate exists even though there is perfect competition in the product market and therefore *MRP* and *VMP* are the same.

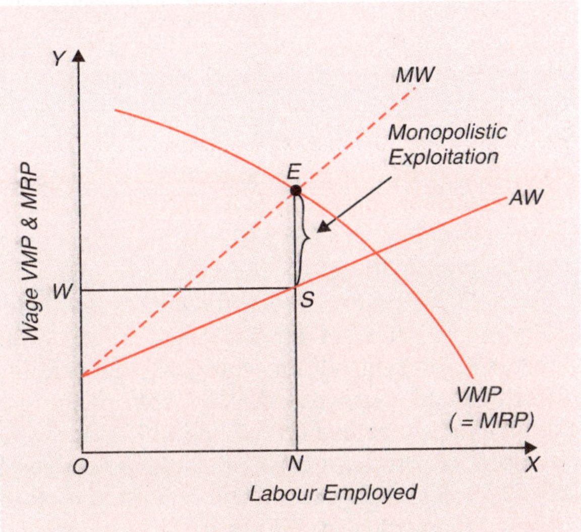

Fig. 53.7. *Monopsonistic Exploitation of labour*

Consider Figure 53.7 which depicts the exploitation of labour when there exists monopsony in the labour market and perfect competition in the market for the product. To be in equilibrium, firm will employ *ON* amount of labour corresponding to which marginal wage is equal to the marginal revenue product (which is here equal to *VMP*). The labour is being paid wage *OW* (= *NS*) which is less than the value of marginal product *NE* at *ON* amount of labour employed. The difference between the two is *ES* which represents exploitation of labour. Since exploitation *ES* in Fig. 53.7 has arisen on account of monopsony or imperfect competition in the labour market, it has been termed ***monopsonistic exploitation***

3. *Joan Robinson, Economics of Imperfect Competition*, Chapter 25.

of labour by Joan Robinson. Monopsonistic exploitation arises because the supply curve of labour is not perfectly elastic and therefore marginal wage curve lies above the average wage curve.

Now, as has been explained earlier, when there is imperfect competition (including monopoly and monopsony) in both the labour and product markets, labour would be subjected to *double exploitation, monopolistic as well as monopsonistic.* This case has been depicted in Fig. 53.4 (Given on an earlier page). On account of monopoly in the product market, the curve of marginal revenue product (*MRP*) lies below the curve of the value of the marginal product (*VMP*), and on account of imperfect competition (or monopsony in the labour market) marginal factor cost curve of labour (*MW*) lies above the average wage curve (*AW*). To be in equilibrium, the firm will equate marginal wage i.e. *MFC* with marginal revenue product and will therefore employ *OL* amount of labour. It will be seen from Fig. 53.4 that in this situation labour is being paid wage rate *OW* which is not only less than value of the marginal product *LF* but is also less than the marginal revenue product *LE* in equilibrium. As a result, according to Pigou-Robinson's concept of exploitation, the total exploitation of labour is *FH,* of which *EF* (the difference between *VMP* and *MRP*) is monopolistic exploitation and *EH* (the difference between wage and *MRP*) is monopsonistic exploitation.

It should be noted that Pigou-Robinson concept of exploitation of labour, namely, labour being paid less than the value of its marginal product (*VMP*), assumes perfect competition as the 'ideal' and the wage rate determined under it as the just, fair and proper. Any deviation from this perfectly competitive wage is regarded as exploitation. Thus according to Rothschild, "Professor Pigou, and following him Joan Robinson have made the *ideal of perfect competition* their starting point. Under the system the worker, would get, as we saw, a wage equal to the value of the marginal physical product. Every deviation from this is regarded as exploitation"[4]

The above concept of exploitation can be looked at from two viewpoints. First, it can be viewed as a *purely technical way* of describing the wage payments which are less than those which would have prevailed under conditions of perfect competition. In this purely technical viewpoint of exploitation, any evil design or sinister motive of the entrepreneur is not implied. Secondly, Pigou-Robinson's concept of exploitation can be viewed as the ***concept which regards perfect competition wages as the just, fair or right wages which ought to be paid by the entrepreneur to the labour.*** In this second sense emotional colouring is given to the concept of exploitation and sinister motive on the part of the entrepreneur is implied. Further, it is also implied in this second sense of exploitation that market price of a product reflects its social value. Pigou and to somewhat lesser extent Robinson regarded exploitation in this second sense, that is, from the viewpoint of emotional colouring and ethical standard. In the opinion of present author to regard "deviations from perfect competition" as unethical is unjustified and unwarranted. We therefore agree with Rothschild who writes : "This usage of exploitation... may be regarded as an implicit assumption that perfect competition wages are the 'right' or 'proper' wages of labour. There can be no doubt that such a moral undertone is part of Professor Pigou's definition, who stood under the influence of the newly developed marginal productivity theory; and to a lesser extent this is probably also true of Joan Robinson. It should be clear, however, that ***there is no any scientific reason to warrant such an assumption.*** By calling deviations from the perfect-competition equilibrium 'exploitation', it does not follow that ***this equilibrium has any superior ethical or political qualities."***[5]

4. K.W. Rothschild, *The Theory of Wages,* Augustus M. Kelley, New York, 1966.
5. *Ibid*, p. 103

Chamberlin's Critique of Pigou-Robinson's Concept of Exploitation

We have already mentioned in an earlier chapter that Chamberlin has criticised Pigou-Robinson's concept of exploitation and has provided his own concept of exploitation According to Chamberlin, under imperfect or monopolistic competition (in the product market), not only labour but all factors receive less than the value of their marginal products. This is because the argument which is applicable to labour applies equally to all factors. Chamberlin argues that under conditions of imperfect or monopolistic competition (in the product market) since marginal revenue is less than the price, if all factors are paid equal to the value of their marginal product, then the total payments to all factors will add up to more than the total revenue of the firm. How can then it be possible for the firm to pay the factors according to the value of their marginal product. According to Chamberlin, the fact that some factors receive less than the value of the marginal product does not mean that some other one will be receiving more than the value of the marginal product. According to him, ***when there is imperfect or monopolistic competition in the product market, all factors (including entrepreneurs) get rewards according to a different principle, namely, according to the marginal revenue product (MRP) which is less than the value of marginal product (VMP).***

In view of above, according to Chamberlin, *labour is exploited when it is paid less than the marginal revenue product* (*MRP*). Thus in the wage position depicted in Fig. 53.6 where imperfect (or monopolistic) competition or monopoly prevails in the product market and perfect competition in the labour market, labour is getting wage rate *OW* which is equal to marginal revenue product of labour *NE*, but is less than the value of the marginal product of labour, *ND*. Therefore, according to Chamberlin, in this condition, that is, when imperfect competition prevails in the product market and perfect competition in the labour market, no exploitation of labour exists, though on Pigou-Robinson's definition, labour is exploited in this situation because labour's wage is less than the value of marginal product.

In Figure 53.7 which depicts the wage situation when imperfect competition or monopsony prevails in the labour market, and perfect competition in the product market, labour is exploited both according to Chamberlin and according to Pigou-Robinson's concepts of exploitation, since in this case *MRP* is equal to *VMP* and wage paid to the labour is less than it. Further, in Figure 53.4 also where there is imperfect competition (or monopoly) in the product market and monopsony or imperfect competition in the labour market wage rate is less than both *VMP* and *MRP* and therefore labour exploitation would exist on Robinson-Pigou as well as on Chamberlin's definition of exploitation. But, on Chamberlin's definition, in Fig. 53.4 exploitation would be equal to *HE* only, whereas on Pigou-Robinson's definition, labour exploitation would be equal to *HF* which is equal to *HE* + *EF*.

It follows from above that on Chamberlin's definition, exploitation of labour results from monopsony or imperfect competition in the labour market, where the wage rate paid to the labour is less than the marginal revenue product (*MRP*). No doubt, Chamberlin's concept of exploitation is theoretically more sound and pinpoints a purely technical aspect of exploitation. However, emotional colouring is generally attached to the word exploitation, and this emotional colouring is not there in Chamberlin's concept of exploitation.

How can Labour Exploitation be Removed

We have discussed above the two concepts of exploitation and have also highlighted the conditions under which labour exploitation arises. Now, an important question is how this labour exploitation can be removed. That is, whether trade unions or Government can remove exploitation by raising the wages of workers or some other steps have to be taken to remove exploitation.

As far as *monopolistic exploitation* depicted in Fig. 53.6 by *ED* and a part *EF* in Fig. 53.4 which has arisen due to the imperfect competition in the product market is concerned it cannot be removed by raising wages by the trade unions. This is because, in this situation, if the trade unions succeed in raising wages, the employer will employ smaller amount of labour so as to equate the new high wage rate with the marginal revenue product of labour. But the important point to note is that with lower employment and higher wage rate, labour would still be exploited, for in this new wage position also, value of the marginal product (*VMP*) will be greater than the marginal revenue product (*MRP*) with which new higher wage will be equated by the employer. We thus see that *monopolistic exploitation of labour* as conceived by Joan Robinson cannot be removed by raising wages by trade unions or the government. Monopolistic exploitation can only be removed by *creating the conditions of perfect competition in the product market.* State can take measures for removing monopolistic conditions or imperfections from the product market.

But so far as monopsonistic exploitation of labour is concerned, it can be removed by raising wages through trade unions or state. We will explain this in an the next chapter.

NUMERICAL PROBLEMS

Problem 1. Suppose a firm has a monopsony in labour market. The firm can hire labour at the wage rate W = 10 + 4L. If its marginal revenue productivity function is given by MRP = 100 – L, what quantity of labour it will employ and what wage rate it will pay to them. Compare them with wage and employment levels that would exist if perfect competition prevailed in the labour market.

Solution. The firm will employ the quantity of labour at which its *MFC* of labour equals marginal revenue product (*MRP*) of labour.

To find marginal factor cost of labour, we first find total factor cost of labour by multiplying the given labour supply function $(W = 10 + 4L)$ by the amount of labour (*L*). Thus

$$TFC_L = L(10 + 4L) = 10L + 4L^2$$

We find MFC_L of labour by taking its first derivative. Thus $MFC_L = \dfrac{d(TFC)}{dL} = 10 + 8L$

Equating MFC_L with the given *MRP* function we have

$$10 + 8L = 100 - L$$

$$9L = 90$$

or $$L = \frac{90}{9} = 10$$

Thus the firm will employ 10 number of workers. To get wage rate we substitute $L = 10$ in the given labour supply function $(W = 10 + 4L)$. Thus

$$W = 10 + 4L$$

or $$W = 10 + 4 \times 10 = 50$$

Wage rate is ₹ 50.

Wage rate and employment level for a competitive labour market can be obtained by equating demand for labour function (*i.e. MRP* function) with supply of labour function (that is, wage function). Doing so we have

$$W = MRP$$
$$10 + 4L = 100 - L$$
$$5L = 90$$
$$L = 14$$

Under perfect competition 14 labour units will be employed as compared to 10 under monopsony. Wage rate in a competitive labour market can be obtained by substituting $L = 14$ in the supply function for labour (*i.e.* $W = 10 + 4L$). Thus substituting $L = 14$ in the supply function for labour,

$$W = 10 + 4L$$
$$= 10 + 4 \times 14$$
$$= ₹\ 66$$

Thus employment level (14) and wage rate (₹ 66) in a competitive labour market will be higher.

Problem 2. *A firm Balco has a monopsony in hiring labour while it sells its product in a perfectly competitive market. Its VMP = 14 – L and labour supply function is W = 2 + L.*

(a) *What are its profit-maximising quantity of labour used and wage rate paid to it ?*

(b) *Calculate the degree of monopsonistic exploitation of labour.*

(c) *How much labour will it employ if minimum wage of Rs. 8 is imposed on it by the government.*

Solution. To arrive at profit-maximising level of labour employment, the firm will equate marginal factor cost of labour (*MFC*) with value of marginal product (*VMP*) of labour. To find marginal factor cost of labour we have to find first the total factor cost (*TFC*) of labour. This can be obtained by multiplying the labour supply function ($W = 2 + L$) with the quantity of labour. Thus

$$TFC_L\ (i.e.,\ W.L) = L(2 + L) = 2L + L^2$$

$$MFC_L = \frac{d(TFC_L)}{dL} = 2 + 2L$$

Equating MFC_L with VMP of labour, we have

$$2 + 2L = 14 - L$$
$$3L = 14 - 2$$
$$L = 4$$

Thus 4 units of labour will be employed. To obtain wage rate we substitute $L = 4$ in the labour supply function. Thus

$$W = 2 + L = 2 + 4 = ₹\ 6$$

Thus wage rate paid is ₹ 6 per unit of labour.

(*b*) For measuring monopsonistic exploitation we calculate *MRP* (which is equal to *VMP* in the present case) at 4 units of labour. Therefore, substituting $L = 4$ in the demand for labour function (*i.e.* *VMP* function) we get

$$VMP = 14 - L$$

$$MRP = VMP = 14 - 4 = 10$$

Thus, while marginal revenue product (MRP) of labour is ₹ 10, labour is paid wage rate equal to ₹ 6. Thus ₹ 10 – 6 = ₹ 4 is *monopsonic exploitation per unit of labour*.

(c) With a minimum wage equal to ₹ 8 for the firm this will become marginal factor cost (*MFC*) of labour and it will equate it with the value of marginal product (*VMP*). Thus

$$8 = VMP = 14 - L \text{ or } L = 14 - 8 = 6$$

Thus with the imposition of minimum wage at a higher level, employment has also increased in this case of monopsony in the labour market.

Problem 3. The demand for computer engineers in the local market is given by $D_e = 760 - 0.1\,Q_e$ and their supply curve $S = 60 + 0.04\,Q_e$ where Q_e is the quantity of engineers.

(a) Calculate wage and employment levels that would prevail if market for engineers is perfectly competitive.

(b) If the engineers organise themselves into a power union, then

(i) What wage and employment the union will demand to maximise the total income of its members.

(ii) What wage and employment will the union demand to maximise the economic rent of its members?

Solution. (*a*) (Note that both the given demand and supply functions of engineers are inverse demand and supply functions. Therefore, the given inverse demand function can also be written as $W = 760 - 0.1Q_e$ and the given inverse supply function can be written as $W = 60 + 0.04Q_e$). To obtain wage and employment in a competitive market for engineers we have to equate the demand and supply functions. Thus

$$760 - 0.1Q_e = 60 + 0.04Q_e$$

$$760 - 60 = 0.04\,Q_e + 0.1\,Q_e$$

or

$$0.14\,Q_e = 700$$

$$Q_e = 700 \times \frac{100}{14} = 5000$$

To obtain the equilibrium wage rate at this level (*i.e.* 5000) of employment we substitute $Q_e = 5000$ in the supply function. Thus

$$S_e \text{ or } W = 60 + 0.04\,Q_e$$

$$W = 60 + 0.04 \times 5000$$

$$= 60 + 200 = 260$$

Thus the competitive level of employment of engineers is 5000 and wage rate is ₹ 260.

(*b*) (*i*) When the engineers organise themselves into a powerful union, there comes into existence monopoly in respect of sale of engineers' services. It will be remembered that a monopolist revenue is maximum when he sells the quantity of output corresponding to unit elasticity point of the demand curve facing him (that is, at the output level where *MR* is zero). Now, the labour union's marginal revenue function can be derived from the labour (demand function ($Q_e = 760 - 0.1\,Q_e$) by first obtaining from its total revenue function and, then taking its first derivative.

$$\text{Total revenue} \quad (TR) = Q_e(760 - 0.1\,Q_e)$$

$$\text{or} \quad TR = 760\,Q_e - 0.1\,Q_e^2$$

Differentiating it with respect to Q_e we have

$$MR = \frac{dTR}{dQ_e} = 760 - 0.2\,Q_e$$

Now, *total revenue (i.e. income) will be maximum at the level of employment* (Q_e) *at which MR = 0*. Therefore, setting *MR* function equal to zero we have

$$760 - 0.2\,Q_e = 0$$

$$760 = 0.2\,Q_e$$

$$Q_e = 760 \times \frac{10}{2} = 3800$$

To obtain the wage rate corresponding to employment of 3800 engineers we substitute $Q_e = 3800$ in the given inverse demand (*i.e.* wage) function for engineers, namely,

$$\begin{aligned} D_e\ (i.e.\ W) &= 760 - 0.1\,Q_e \\ &= 760 - 0.1 \times 3800 \\ &= 760 - 380 \\ &= ₹\ 380 \end{aligned}$$

Thus, to maximise income (*i.e.* wage bill) of its members the union will try to raise wage rate to Rs. 380 at an employment of 3800 engineers.

(*b*) (*ii*) The economic rent is the surplus over transfer earning or opportunity costs of the units of the factor employed. Further, it may be noted that supply function for labour ($W = 60 + 0.04\,Q_e$) is in fact the marginal cost function of labour for the union. Therefore, to maximise profits or economic rent (which is also called net revenue or surplus), the union will equate this marginal cost (*MR*) that has been found above to be equal to $760 - 0.2\,Q_e$. Thus equating marginal cost with this marginal revenue we have

$$60 + 0.04\,Q_e = 760 - 0.2\,Q_e$$

$$0.24\,Q_e = 760 - 60 = 700$$

$$Q_e = 700 \times \frac{100}{24} = 2917 \text{ (approx.)}$$

To get the wage rate corresponding to Q_e employment we substitute $Q_e = 2917$ in the demand function. Thus

$$D_e \text{ or } W = 760 - 0.1\,Q_e = 760 - 0.1 \times 2917$$

$$= 760 - 292 = 468 \text{ approx.}$$

Thus rent-maximising wage will be ₹ 468 and employment level will be 2917 engineers.

QUESTIONS FOR REVIEW

1. Discuss the circumstances under which a trade union can raise wages in an industry without affecting the level of employment adversely.
2. For a monopsonist what is the relationship between the supply of an input and themarginal expenditure (*i.e.* factor cost) on that input ?
3. Is it possible for a labour union to raise wages without reducing employment under conditions of :

   (*i*) Perfect competition in the labour market (*ii*) Monopsony in the labour market.
4. How far can labour unions succeed in raising both wages and employment under monopsonistic conditions ?
5. Show how under monopsony the imposition of a minimum wage law might lead to increased employment of labour.
6. When is labour said to be exploited ? What is monopolistic exploitation ? How does it differ from monopsonistic exploitation ? Which type of exploitation can be eliminated by trade unions ?
7. What is Joan Robinson's view of exploitation ? On what grounds has it been criticised? How does Chamberlin differ with it ?
8. A profit maximising firm's demand for labour is given by the equation $MRP_L = 200 - 4L$, where MRP_L is marginal revenue product of labour and L is the quantity of labour employed. The supply curve of labour facing the firm has the form

   $W = 10 + 3L$

   where W is the wage rate

(*a*) Determine what wage rate and employment will be fixed by the firm.

(*b*) Calculate the degree of exploitation of labour, if any.

(*c*) Suppose the equilibrium is disturbed by the creation of a labour union. What value of wage rate should the union bargain for in order to maximise employment ?

(**Hint.** From the labour supply function, first find out marginal factor cost (*MFC*) of labou and then equate it with MRP_L to obtain the value of labour employment (L). For similar solved problems see next chapter.)

CHAPTER

54

Trade Unions, Collective Bargaining and Wages

Superfluous Role of Trade Unions in Traditional Wage Theories

For a long time economists believed that trade unions and collective bargaining could not play an important role in raising the wages of workers or effecting improvements in their economic conditions. In other words, they thought that trade unions as an instrument to raise wages of workers or to improve their overall economic conditions are *ineffective and superfluous* and thus the collective bargaining by them is *a futile undertaking*. Therefore, in the leading nineteeth century wage theories, the role played by trade unions and collective bargaining in the determination of wages was entirely neglected. Thus, according to the *Subsistence Theory of Wage* or what is also known as the *Iron Law of Wages*, wage rate is determined by the subsistence level and that in the long run wage rate will remain equal to the subsistence level. Any increase in the wage rate, in the short run, above the minimum subsistence level will bring about increase in population and labour force by inducing the people to produce more children. As a result of this increase in population and labour force, the wage rate will again be depressed to the subsistence level. On the other hand, any fall in the wage rate below the subsistence level will lead to the starvation of the labour force which by increasing the death rate will cause reduction in population and shortage of labour which in turn will, in the long run, lead to the increase in the wage rate to the original subsistence level.

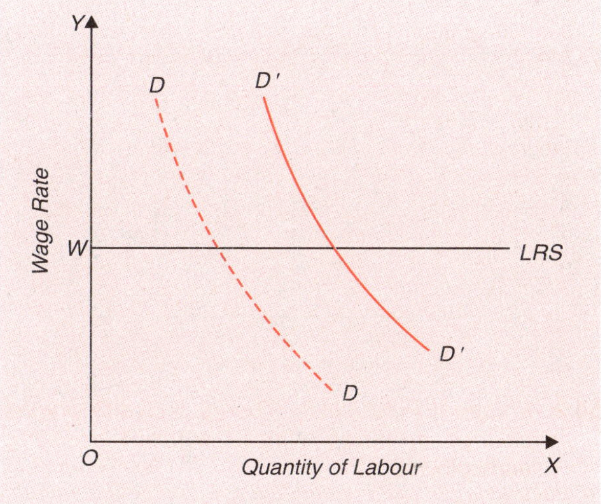

Fig. 54.1. *Subsistence Theory of Wages : Trade unions cannot raise wages above the subsistence level due to perfectly elastic nature of the long-run supply curve of labour.*

From above, it is clear that according to the Subsistence Theory or Iron Law of Wages, wage rate, in the long run, remains fixed or rigid at the subsistence level. In other words, according to this theory, long-run supply curve of labour *(LRS)* is perfectly elastic at the subsistence wage rate, as shown in Fig.54.1 where *OW* represents the subsistence wage rate. The perfectly elastic supply curve of labour implies that any attempt by the trade unions to raise wages of workers will be futile, for, as said above, increase in wage rate above the subsistence level will lead to the increase in population and working force and will therefore bring down the wage rate to the minimum level of subsistence. Furthermore, the perfectly elastic supply curve of labour in the long run implies that labourers cannot hope to receive higher wages or incomes above the minimum subsistence level, whatever the increases in long-run demand for labour and whatever the rise in their productivity in the long run. It will be seen from Fig.54.1 that when the demand for labour increases from *DD* to *D'D'*, the long-run equilibrium wage rate remains the same.

Similarly, *in Wage Fund Theory* also it is visualized that all-round increases in wages cannot be achieved by trade unions and collective bargaining. According to this theory, wages depend upon two things : (i) the wage fund or the circulating capital set aside for the purchase of labour, and *(ii)* the number of labourers seeking employment. Wages therefore cannot rise unless either the wage fund increases or the number of workers decreases. But because the theory takes the wage fund as fixed, wage could rise only by a reduction in the number of workers. It is therefore apparent that according to this theory the efforts of trade unions to bring about all-round increases in wages are futile. If they succeed in raising wages in one trade or industry, it can only be at the expense of workers in another trade or industry, since the wage fund is fixed and the trade unions have no control over population. It is therefore clear that trade unions and collective bargaining by them cannot raise wages for *labour class as a whole.*

Likewise, according to the marginal productivity theory of wages, with its assumptions of perfect competition and given supply of labour, trade unions cannot succeed in raising wages or cannot succeed in raising wages without creating unemployment. According to this theory, value of marginal product *(VMP)* curve is the employer's demand curve. Consider Fig. 54.2 where *VMP* is the value of marginal product curve of labour. With *OW* as the equilibrium wage rate in a competitive labour market, a single firm will employ *ON* quantity of labour. Now, if the wage rate is increased to *OW'* by the collective bargaining of trade union, *NN'* amount of workers would be rendered unemployed. If these unemployed workers are free to compete, they would press down the wage back to *OW.* If these *NN'* workers are, for one reason or the other, not free to compete, they will continue to remain unemployed. It is thus clear that, even according to marginal productivity theory, trade unions are unable to enhance wages or to enhance wages without creating unemployment.

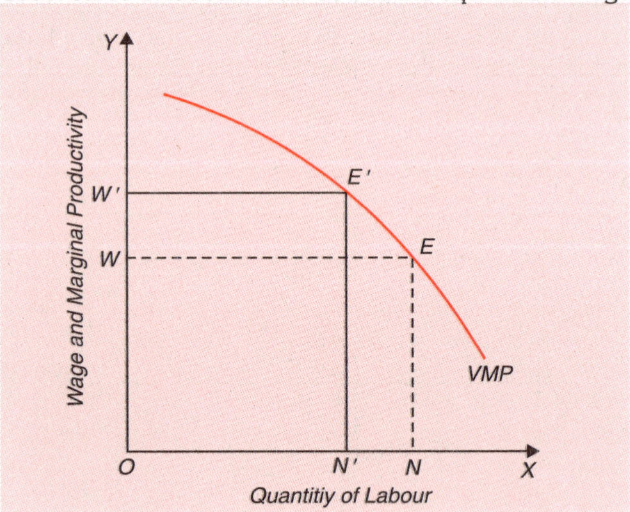

Fig. 54.2. *Marginal Productivity Theory ; Trade unions cannot enhance wages without creating unemployment.*

It is evident from above that in the famous wage theories of nineteenth century, there was no room for trade unions and collective bargaining in fixing and improving wages of the workers, though the conditions of the labour market were completely changed as a result of the emergence of the trade unions and their bargaining with the employers on behalf of the workers. The view about the futility of trade union also prevailed in the early twentieth century, even though many theorists expressed doubts about the correctness of this view. It was only in the 'thirties' of the twentieth century that role of trade unions and collective bargaining was introduced into the economic theory and significant place was accorded to them in fixing wages of the workers. The realisation of the fact that perfect competition only prevailed in some exceptional cases in the real world led to the reconsideration of whole price and wage theory. But the marginal productivity approach to the wage fixation was maintained; only the marginal productivity approach was extended to conditions of imperfect competition wherein scope for trade unions and collective bargaining in raising wages was shown.

Moreover, there has been emergence of two kinds of theories known as institutional and psychological theories of wage determination under trade unions. These theories do not try to reconcile the marginal productivity approach with the role of collective bargaining in the context of imperfect competition, but instead assign an eminent role to trade unions and collective bargaining in the wage determination, regardless of the marginal productivity doctrine. Thus, in these institutional and psychological theories, trade unions and collective bargaining do not enter through the back door but occupy a central place right from the beginning. In recent years there has been a due recognition of the role which the trade unions and collective bargaining play in the fixation of wages and various theories of bargaining have been advanced. Rather than being alternative explanations of wage determination under collective bargaining, these different bargaining theories of wages in fact bring out various factors which play a determining role in the bargaining process; different theories laying stress on different factors.

In what follows we first examine the effect of trade unions on wages and employment in (a) when there is perfect competition in the labour market and (*b*) when there is monopsony in the labour market. Then we will explain the circumstances and situations when labour unions can play a useful role in improving wages and living conditions of workers. Finally, we describe the determination of wage rate in the framework of bilateral monopoly model, that is, when a single buyer of labour, the monopsonist confronts a monopolistic seller of labour, the trade union, which collectively bargains with the employer on behalf of workers it represents.

Perfect Competition in the Labour Market: Trade Union and Wages

As explained in the previous chapter, when there is perfect competition in the labour market wage rate is determined by demand for and supply of labour. When there exists perfect competition in both the labour and product markets, demand for labour is derived from the value of marginal product *(VMP)* curve of labour. Wage rate determined through demand for and supply of labour is therefore equal to the value of marginal product of labour (wage rate = VMP_L). It may be noted that in a perfectly competitive labour market a large number of small firms who buy labour have to deal with a large number of unorganised workers. The diagram which explains the determination of wage rate in a perfectly competitive labour market is reproduced in Figure 54.3, where D_L is the demand curve tor laoour and S_L is the supply curve of labour. The intersection of these two curves determines the equilibrium wage rate equal to W_0 and number of workers L_0 are employed. Now suppose the workers organise themselves into a labour union which collectively bargains with the employers on their behalf. Holding a threat of strike the union presses for a higher wage rate, say W_1, and succeeds in getting this conceded. A glance at Figure 54.3 reveals that at the wage rate W_1, the employers demand and employ only OL_1 quantity of labour. Since labour is supplied through union and, given the agreed wage rate W_1, at which labour will be supplied to the employers, the labour supply curve assumes the shape of horizontal straight line W_1M at the wage rate W_1. It will be seen from Figure 54.3 that at wage rate W_1, employers demand and employ OL_1 (= W_1N) number of workers and thus creating unemployment. Though the reduction in employment is equal to L_0L_1 but unemployment created will be greater than this. This is because, as will be seen from the figure, at the wage rate W_1, the larger number of workers W_1M are willing to supply their labour services. As a result, the magnitude NM represents the excess supply of labour or the unemployment created by the establishment of a higher wage rate W_1 as a result of collective bargaining by the labour union as compared to the competitive wage rate W_o. Thus labour union has succeeded in raising wage rate but only at the expense of employment. The workers who are lucky enough to retain their employment are better off because their wage is now higher but those who lose jobs are worse off because it is very unlikely that they would get employment elsewhere even at the competitive wage rate.

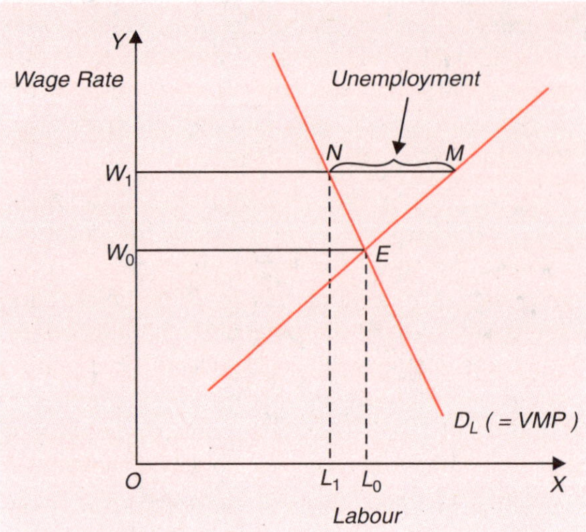

Fig. 54.3. *Effect of a labour union on wages and employment in a competitive labour market*

It may be noted that a trade union may benefit all workers, not just some of them. This can'be achieved if the demand for labour is *inelastic*. In case of inelastic demand, the increase in wage rate would result in higher total wage income, though level of employment falls. Consider Figure 54.3. With W_0 as the wage rate, and OL_0 as the level of employment, the total wage income equals $OW_0.OL_0$ or the area OL_0EW_0. At the higher wage rate W_1 achieved by the trade union the total wage income equals $OW_1.OL_1$ or area OL_1NW_1 which is greater than OL_0EW_0 because demand lor labour happens to be inelastic in this region of the demand curve for labour. Through some work-sharing arrangement or income-sharing arrangement, all workers can be benefited by the union as the total wage income has increased due to higher wage rate. However, demand for labour is not always inelastic. In case of elastic demand for labour, the higher wage rate achieved by union will not only greatly reduce employment but also result in lower total wage income. Therefore, in case of elastic demand for labour, the higher wage rate will benefit those who remain employed because they will be getting higher wage rate but those who are rendered unemployed would become worse off.

The Effect of a Trade Union in Case of Monopsony in the Labour Market

When there is monopsony in the labour market, trade union can succeed in increasing both wage and employment. To explain the effect of trade union in this case, let us first know the pre-union situation when the workers are unorganised and do not bargain collectively. Consider Figure 54.4.

In case of monopsony in the labour market, S_L is the labour supply curve depicting that the quantity of labour supplied increases as the wage rate increases. Since under monopsony in the labour market wage rate increases as more workers are hired, marginal labour cost, *MLC (i.e. MFC* of labour) lies above the supply curve of labour S_L. *VMP* (= *MRP*) curve represents the demand curve of labour as it has been assumed that perfect competition prevails in the product market. The monopsonist will maximise his profits by employing L_0 number of

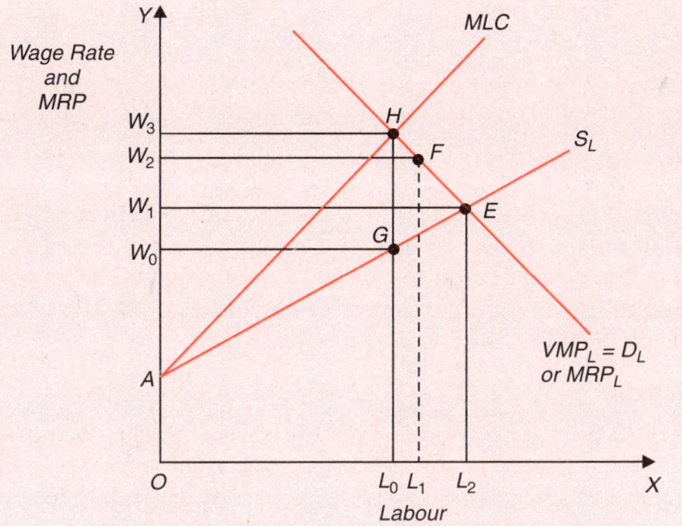

Fig. 54.4. *The Effect of a trade union on wages and employment in a monopsonistic labour market*

workers at which VMP_L or $MRP_L = MLC$ and will fix the wage rate equal to W_0.

Now suppose the workers organise themselves into union which collectively bargains with the monopsonist. Suppose the labour union set W_1 as the minimum wage at which labour will be supplied and in case this is not accepted, they would go on strike. Assuming that with the threat of strike they succeed in getting the wage rate W_1 accepted. With W_1 as the fixed wage rate, marginal labour cost now becomes a horizontal straight line W_1E which intersects the demand curve for labour (MRP_L) at point E indicating that at the wage rate W_1, the number of workers OL_2 will be employed. Thus, the trade union through collective bargaining has succeeded in raising wage rate from W_0 to W_1 and also increasing employment from L_0 to L_2. It is worth noting that wage-employment configuration, W_1, L_2 is the one that will be prevailing, had there been competitive labour market.

If the union sets a higher wage rate W_2 and gets it agreed, then the horizontal line W_2F becomes the marginal labour cost curve for the monopsonist and to be in equilibrium he equates it with marginal revenue product of labour (MRP_L) and, as will be seen from Fig. 54.4, will employ OL_1 number of workers which is smaller than L_2 but still greater than pre-unionised monopsony employment of L_0. Thus, even fixing a higher wage than the competitive one, the trade union has also caused employment level to rise to OL_1 as compared to employment OL_0 offered by the monopsonist. If union seeks to attain a higher wage rate it may set as high a wage rate as W_3. With W_3 as the wage rate W_3H is the marginal labour cost curve and consequently OL_0 workers will be employed by the monopsonist at this wage rate. That is, the level of employment is the same as was before the organisation of workers into union and undertaking collective bargaining but wage rate has gone up to quite a high level, Besides, it will be noticed that by raising wage rate to W_3, trade union has succeeded in eliminating monopsonistic exploitation.

It should be noted that if a union pursues a goal of maximising wage rate regardless of its effect on employment, it may set wage rate even higher than W_3. But a wage rate higher than W_3 implies the level of employment will fall below L_0 and some workers will be rendered unemployed which will threaten the solidarity of the union. Thus, the emergence of unemployment puts a limit to the power of trade union in seeking and setting a very high wage rate.

It follows from above that when there is monopsonistic labour market, the union can increase within a range both the wage rate and employment, It can maximise employment at L_2 and get the competitive wage rate W_1. It can attain a high wage rate W_3 and retain the pre-unionised level of employment L_0. In fact, within the range W_0 to W_3 of the wage rate it can set any wage rate without fear of unemployment being created. Further, it also follows that within a good range of wage fixation, even employment of labour increases as a result of collective bargaining by the union in monopsonistic labour market. This benefits not only the workers but also the consumers. With more employment of labour, total output increases. As a result, price falls which benefits the consumers.

Alternative Union Goals

Labour union enjoys monopoly power over the sale of labour to the employers. An important question is what it maximises or, in other words, what goals it pursues. It is evident from the foregoing analysis that outcome of collective bargaining by a union regarding wage and employment depends on the goal it pursues. The following possible goals of a labour union have often been mentioned :

1. The union seeks to ***maximise employment,*** especially it wishes to keep all its members employed.
2. The union may seek to **maximise *total wage income*** of its members.
3. The union may want to achieve maximum hourly wage rate and keep at least a core group of its members employed.
4. As a monopolist, a trade union may want to maximise profits or rent, that is, surplus income over and above the opportunity costs of the workers employed.

We will discuss these objectives with reference to Figure 54.5. Just as a monopolist seller of a product chooses a price-output combination on a demand curve facing him, similarly a union as a monopolist seller of labour can choose a point on the demand curve for labour D_L in Figure 54.5 which is in fact the marginal revenue product curve of labour *(MRP_L)*. This demand curve for labour D_L shows that as employment of labour increases, wage rate declines. We have also drawn in Figure 54.5 marginal revenue curve *MR* which is *marginal to the given demand curve D_L for labour.* Since as employment increases, wage rate falls, the addition to the revenue or income of the workers by employment of an additional worker will be less than the wage rate, marginal revenue curve lies below the demand curve of labour. S_L is the supply curve of labour which indicates as wage rate rises, more labour is supplied. Moreover, supply curve of labour represents the opportunity cost or transfer earnings of workers. Therefore, from the viewpoint of labour union, supply curve of labour S_L represents the *marginal cost (MC) of supplying labour.*

Now, if the objective of the union is to ***maximise employment of workers,*** it will set wage rate equal to W_1 at which L_4 quantity of labour is demanded and employed. If the union has L_4 members, all will be employed at wage rate W_1. As explained above, W_1 represents the wage rate of a competitive labour market and L_4 is the competitive level of labour employment and there is no monopsonistic exploitation of labour in this situation.

If a union aims at ***maximizing total wage income*** (that is, total revenue from labour employment), it will choose point on the demand curve for labour corresponding to which marginal revenue (*MR*) is zero. It will be seen from Figure 54.5 that it will fix wage rate equal to W_2 at which employment is L_3 and marginal revenue (*MR*) is zero. With this the total wage income is equal to the area OL_3BW_2 which is the maximum, given the demand curve for labour. It should be noted that this maximum income can be redistributed among its members by the union through employment or work-sharing arrangement or according to some other criterion.

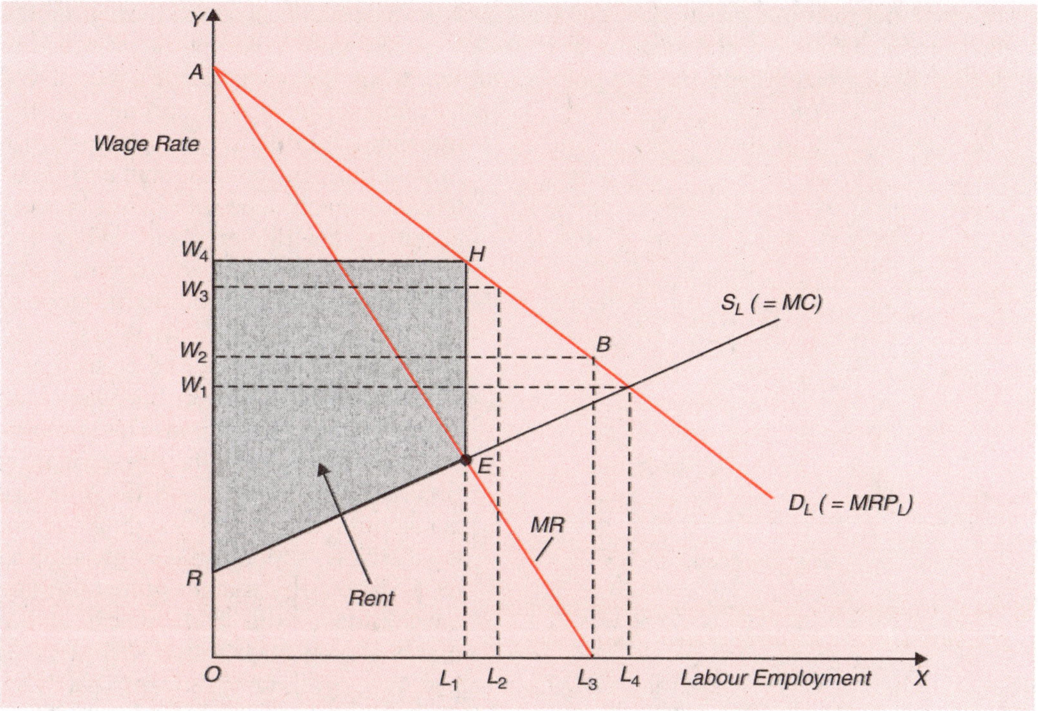

Fig. 54.5. *Alternative union Goals, Wages, and Employment*

Now, suppose that L_2 represents the core group of members of the union for whom it seeks maximum wage rate ensuring also that they remain employed. With this objective, the union will set higher wage rate equal to W_3, at which L_2 labour is employed.

Finally, if the union which is a single seller of labour is very powerful and behaves like a pure monopolist, it will seek to maximise its profits or net income over and above the opportunity costs. To maximise profits or net income, it will equate marginal labour cost (*MLC*) with marginal revenue (*MR*). It will be seen from Figure 54.5 that marginal labour cost curve (*MLC*) intersects marginal revenue curve *MR* at point *E*. Accordingly, the union behaving like a pure monopolist will fix wage rate equal to W_4 at which a lower level of employment L_1 is achieved. However, this lower level of employment and consequently creation of large-scale unemployment of its members will threaten the solidarity of the union and may ultimately lead to its break-up. It may be noted that these profits or net income over and above opportunity costs of labour are also called *rent* and in Figure 54.5 the shaded area $REHW_4$ represents these profits or rent earned.

POSITIVE ROLE OF TRADE UNIONS IN RAISING WAGES

As explained above, there was not much room for the bargaining in the marginal productivity theory in its earliest versions. First of all, a bargaining approach to wages was developed which indicates a scope for collective bargaining within the framework of marginal productivity theory. This was done by giving up some of the assumptions of marginal productivity theory which had been essential parts of its earlier versions. Then, with the emergence of the theories of imperfect competition, monopsony and oligopoly, bargaining approach within the framework of marginal productivity principle was considerably widened.

To begin with, static assumptions of marginal productivity theory have been challenged. It is accepted that marginal productivity curve is employer's demand curve and that, given the marginal productivity curve, the increase in the wage rate by trade union power, will lead to the creation of unemployment. But it is pointed out that when the wage increase is achieved through a successful bargaining, the marginal productivity curve may not remain the same but may shift above due to the rise in efficiency of workers brought about by the higher wage. When the efficiency and therefore the marginal productivity curve rises due to the increase in wages of the workers, the unemployment may not be created as a result of the increase in the wage rate secured by the trade union. This is shown in Fig. 54.6. Initially the marginal productivity curve is *MRP* and the equilibrium wage is *OW* and employment is *ON*. Now, suppose the wage is raised to *OW′* by the successful collective bargaining of the trade union. If the marginal productivity curve *MRP* remains unchanged, then at *OW′* wage rate, *ON′* men will be employed, which means that *NN′* number of men will be rendered unemployed. But if the rise in wage brings about a sufficient increase in efficiency and productivity so that the marginal productivity curve shifts upward to the dotted position, then unemployment will not be created. It will be seen from Fig. 54.6 that with the dotted marginal revenue productivity curve *MRP′*, *ON* men are employed at the higher wage rate *OW′*.

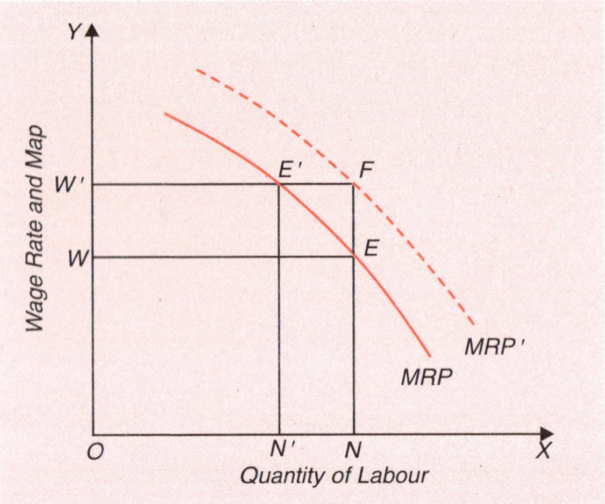

Fig. 54.6. *Increase in Marginal Revenue Productivity or Efficiency as a result of Rise in Wage Rate*

We thus see that if we consider the effect of the wage bargain on the increase in efficiency or marginal productivity, then the trade unions can succeed in raising wages without creating unemployment. Again, the increase in wages may force the employers to improve the efficiency of pro-duction process in which case also the marginal productivity curve shifts upward and as a result at the increased wage rate the same men may be employed. Again, the marginal revenue productivity curve may also shift above, if the increase in the wage rate brought about by collective bargaining is passed on to the consumers in the form of higher price of the product. In this case also the danger of unemployment being created will not be very much there and the higher wage rate will become the equilibrium wage rate equal to the new higher marginal revenue productivity. Therefore, the supporters of bargaining approach to wage fixation maintain that ***it is not so much the movements along the marginal productivity curve as it is the shifting of this curve that has to be considered when the impact of a wage bargaining is to be known.***

Similarly, when the wage rate is raised by collective bargaining, the supply of labour may fall so that the increased wage becomes the equilibrium wage without creating involuntary unemployment. Supply of labour can fall because when men are earning higher wages their women can stop working (that is, women withdraw themselves from labour force and stay at home) and children can be kept at school for a longer time. Further, at higher wages, individuals may work less hours in a week or smaller number of days in a month or year. Because of the reduction in the supply of labour at the higher wage rate, the higher wage rate may become the 'equilibrium' wage rate. Consider Fig 54.7 where *SS* ' is the supply curve of labour and *DD* ' is the demand curve for labour. Suppose the initial equilibrium is at point *P* where *ON* labour is employed at the wage rate OW_1. Suppose the trade union through collective bargaining succeeds in raising the wage rate to OW_2. As a result of this increase in the wage rate, *NM* amount of labour will be rendered unemployed but in the long run the higher wage rate leads to the reduction in the supply of labour (supply curve slopes backward) so that OW_2 is the new equilibrium wage that is determined and at which *OM* labour is employed.

It should be noted that at the new equilibrium point *Q*, labour *NM* is not unemployed, it has voluntarily withdrawn from employment at the higher wage OW_2. Further, it should be noted that at the new higher-level equilibrium where the supply of labour is less than before, the workers may get a larger proportion of the new higher national income and enjoy higher standards of leisure and education. (The national income will increase if the increase in output due to higher productivity at the increased wage rate is greater than the loss in output due to the reduction in the supply of labour.)

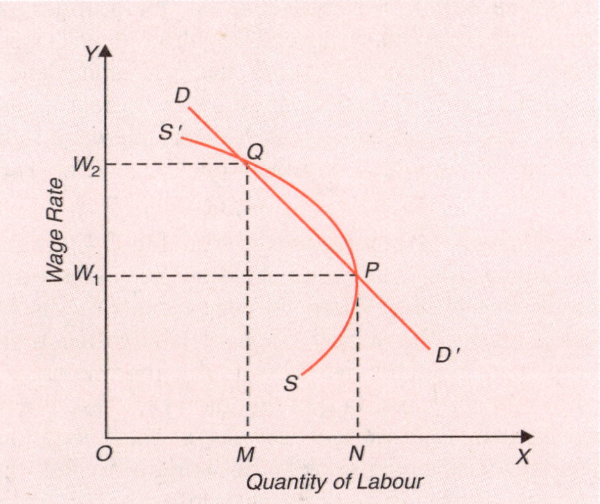

Fig. 54.7. *A higher wage secured by the union can become an equilibrium wage without involuntary unemployment if a part of the supply of labour withdraws itself from the labour force.*

It is clear from above that when the increase in wage rate is attained by trade unions through collective bargaining, there are such changes in the factors determining wage-employment situation that the increased wage becomes the equilibrium wage without creating unemployment. Prof. Rothschild rightly remarks : ***"The imposition of a higher wage may lead initially to some unemployment but may then produce such a change in the determinants of the wage-employment situation that the unemployment disappears and the higher wage becomes an equilibrium wage."*** [1]

Role of Trade Unions in raising Wages under Monopsony, Monopsonistic Discrimination and Imperfect Competition

It is evident from above that under perfect competition and in the framework of the marginal productivity theory conceived in dynamic terms, there is a good room for collective bargaining to raise wages. Further, the realisation that it is not the perfect competition, but the market forms of imperfect competition, oligopoly, monopoly, monopsony, oligopsony, etc. which mostly prevail in the real world, opened up new vistas for combining the marginal productivity analysis with the bargaining approach to the wage determination. The most striking case in these various forms of imperfect markets is of monopsony when there is a single buyer

1. K. W. Rothschild, Approaches to the Theory of Bargaining, published in *The Theory of Wage Determination*, edited by J.T. Dunlop, p. 284 (Italics supplied).

of labour. The monopsonist, as explained before, working on the marginal productivity principle equates marginal revenue product of labour with the marginal wage to be in equilibrium position. In such a situation, wage rate (*i.e.*, average wage) determined is less than the marginal revenue product of labour. It will be seen in Fig. 54.4 (given on an earlier page) that, under monopsony, wage rate OW_0 and employment OL_0 is determined. Under such circumstances, if workers organise themselves into trade unions, they can achieve increase in the wage rate without creating unemployment, indeed the employment will increase for some increases in the wage rate.

When the trade unions come into existence the supply of labour is channelled through it and the bargaining with the employer is on thė basis of 'all or nothing' at a particular wage rate demanded, that is, no supply of labour will be offered below the demanded and/or mutually agreed wage rate and the whole supply of labour will be offered at the mutually agreed wage. This means that the supply curve of labour under trade union becomes perfectly elastic at the demanded or mutually agreed wage rate. It will be seen from Fig. 54.4 that if the higher wage rate OW_1 is fixed under collective bargaining and the supply curve of labour assumes the perfectly elastic shape at OW_1, the new average wage curve W_1E will coincide with the marginal wage curve. It will be seen that, given the wage rate OW_1, the employer's equilibrium will be at point *E*, at which employment OL_2, which is greater than OL_0, will be offered by the employer.

It should be carefully noted from Fig. 54.4 that a powerful trade union can raise the wage rate up to OW_3, that is, equal to the marginal revenue productivity L_0H at the original level of employment OL_0. When the wage rate OW_3 is fixed under collective bargaining and as a consequence the supply curve of labour becomes perfectly elastic at the level OW_3, the employers' equilibrium will be at OL_0, the original level of employment. Thus under conditions of monopsony, a strong trade union can raise the wage rate to the level of value of marginal productivity L_0H without fear of creating unemployment. In the absence of trade union, the monopsonist would exploit the workers to the extent of *GH* It is therefore clear that the workers by organising themselves into the trade union and thereby collectively bargaining with the employer, can raise the wage rate up to the marginal revenue product of OL_0 number of workers and thus remove monopsonistic exploitation by the monopsonist.

Besides monopsony, even if there is imperfect competition in the labour market, the supply of labour to a firm, in the absence of organisation of labour into trade union, will be upward sloping and the marginal labour cost curve will lie above the average labour cost curve. In this case same result in regard to the effect of trade union on wage rate follows as is reached above in the case of monopsony.

The role of trade union to improve the lot of the workers can also be seen when there prevail the conditions ***of monopsonistic discrimination.*** Monopsonistic discrimination is said to prevail when the monopsonist pays different wages to the different workers. In our analysis of wage determination under conditions of monopsony we assumed that in order to secure additional supply of labour the employer must pay a higher wage. It was further assumed that the higher wage must be paid not only to the newcomers but also to all the existing employees. In such a case therefore marginal labour cost curve of labour (*i.e.*, marginal wage curve) lies above the supply curve of labour. However, under discriminating monopsony, the employer will pay the higher wage only to the newcomer and will continue to pay the previous employees the wage rate which is necessary to keep them in the firm. Thus it may be possible for the monopsonist to pay each worker only the minimum that is necessary to keep him in the firm. In other words, he will pay each worker according to his transfer earnings; workers with lower transfer earnings will be paid lower wages and workers with higher transfer earnings will be paid higher wages. Under monopsonistic discrimination, the employer will therefore strike a separate bargain with each worker he employs.[2] Under such discrimination the marginal labour cost curve will coincide with the supply curve of labour, since employing an additional worker just adds the wage paid to him to the labour cost. Therefore, under monopsonistic discrimination, the equilibrium will be reached where the supply curve of labour intersects the demand curve as under perfect competition. But it should be carefully noted that the profits made by the discriminating monopsonist would be considerably greater than under perfect competition as well as under simple monopsony.

Monopsonistic discrimination is quite common in the actual world where workers are unorganised and where due to fear of unemployment they have to accept the essential minimum wage. Under such circumstances, if the workers organise themselves into strong trade unions, they can force the monopsonist to stop discrimination and pay the same wage to all the workers of a given type and thereby can reduce his excess profits earned because of discrimination.

In developed countries as well as in established industries in the developing countries, the. organisation of labourers into powerful trade unions and thereby bargaining collectively with the employers, perfect monopsonistic discrimination (that is, discrimination between individual and individual) has vanished. But "group discrimination" is still very common in all countries, developed as well as developing. By group discrimination is meant the discrimination between different groups or sections of population. Thus, for the same work women are generally paid lower wages than men in many countries. In some countries, coloured people are likewise paid less wages than whjte men for the same work. Boys are also sometimes paid smaller wages than men. The group discrimination can be ended if the discriminated sections organise themselves into powerful trade unions and also by governmental action.

There is another special case which reveals that trade union can play a useful and successful role of improving the wages of the workers without causing adverse effects on employment. This case which is intensely associated with the idea of monopsony is of ***"collusion among employers".*** When there are a few large firms competing for the same kind of labour, they may realise that the increase in the demand for labour of one firm may raise wages so that *all of them* have to pay the higher wage rate. If one firm offers a higher wage to attract workers to itself from the other firms using the same type of labour, the others too will have to raise the wage in order to keep the workers with them. Under such circumstances the firms will develop a strong desire to avoid any competitive bidding for labour and spoiling the labour market. This may lead to open or tacit agreement among the firms not to raise wages.

But when there is collusion among firms not to raise wages, then the marginal productivity will not be even equalised with the marginal cost of labour. Under collusion among employers, the wage rate will be maintained at customary or agreed level even though the marginal revenue productivity will stand higher than the wage paid. Although the firm can increase his profits by expanding employment to the point where the marginal revenue productivity equals marginal cost of labour, but in doing so the firm will have to increase the wage rate which is prohibited under collusion. Under such conditions of collusion, the formation of a trade union by workers can force the employers to pay the wage equal to the marginal revenue productivity. Such a rise in the wage rate to the level of marginal productivity under pressure of trade union would not create any unemployment, because such a rise in the wage rate will only fill up the gap between the marginal revenue productivity and marginal cost of labour, and will not raise the latter above the former.

2. What we are in fact discussing *is perfect* monopsonistic discrimination.

Consider Fig. 54.8 where *OW* is the 'agreed' wage rate currently paid under collusion among employers and the firm is employing *ON* labour at this wage rate. Suppose now the demand for labour of the firm increases to *D'D'* and as a result the marginal revenue product of *ON* labour becomes *NP*. But because of collusion among employers prohibiting any increase in the wage rate, the firm will continue to pay the same wage rate *OW* even though the marginal revenue product of *ON* labour is greater than the wage rate by *RP*. It is evident from the figure that if the firm were free to increase the wage rate, it would have done so and expanded to the point *K* (where the marginal cost of labour equals the marginal revenue product) by snatching away some labour from the other firms. But under collusion he will go on paying the agreed wage rate *OW* and will employ *ON* labour even though his demand for labour has increased and the marginal revenue product of *ON* labour becomes *NP*. Therefore, under the pressure of trade union in the industry, the wage rate can be raised to the marginal productivity level *NP* without causing a decline in employment.

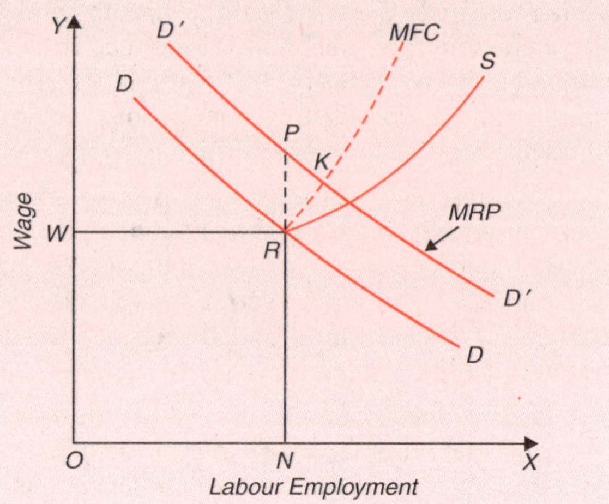

Fig. 54.8. *Wage rate can be raised by the labour union to the level of marginal revenue productivity when there is collusion among employers*

Furthermore, even in the case of oligopoly in the product market which so extensively prevails in the capitalist countries, the increase in the wage rate by the trade union may be achieved without creating unemployment. It is generally believed that the oligopolist confronts a 'kinked' demand curve (having a kink at the prevailing price of the product), corresponding to which the marginal revenue curve has a discontinuous or broken portion vertically below the kink. In such a case, when the increase in the wages rate occurs due to the collective bargaining by the trade union, the marginal cost curve shifts above, but for a moderate increase in the wage rate it will still cut the marginal revenue curve through its discontinuous portion, as has been seen in kinked demand curve model of oligopoly indicating thereby that the output remains unchanged despite the increase in the wage rate and consequently the rise in cost. No change in output as a result of the increase in the wage rate means that the employment will also remain the same, provided the employer does not substitute machinery for labour.

It follows therefore that in this case too the collective bargaining can succeed in raising the wage rate without adversely affecting the employment level. The oligopolistic market situation imposes a certain price and output policy on the employer due to which he is forced to swallow the whole increase in the wage bill following a moderate increase in the wage rate. Thus, in the oligopolistic market situation the trade union can succeed in raising wages by making inroads into the profits of the capitalist employer.

It is clear from the above analysis that trade unions are not superfluous and collective bargaining by them is therefore not a futile activity. In fact, the trade union can play a useful role in raising the wages of workers and can save them from the exploitation of the employers. Indeed, in many cases the trade unions can raise wages without creating unemployment.

WAGE DETERMINATION UNDER COLLECTIVE BARGAINING: BILATERAL MONOPOLY MODEL

Collective bargaining by trade union with an employer or, if it is industry-wide bargaining, with the employers' association represents a situation where a single seller faces a single buyer. Trade union of the firm or industry acts as a single voice representing the workers so that trade union becomes a single seller of labour to the employer. In other words, trade union has the monopoly oi selling labour. On the other hand, the employer, if he is monopsonist, or the employers' association is a single buyer of labour. Thus, under collective bargining a single buyer of labour faces a single seller of labour. Therefore, we are confronted here with a special case of bilateral monopoly and wage determination under trade unions or collective bargaining becomes a special case of price determination under bilateral monopoly. Analysis of wage determination under bilateral monopoly, as of product pricing under bilateral monopoly does not theoretically lead us to a certain particular wage at which agreement will be reached. Analysis of bilateral monopoly only brings out two limits —the upper limit sought by the union and the lower limit set by the employer—within which range the wage will be fixed. Actual wage rate fixed under collective bargaining will lie within that range and whether it will be nearer to the upper limit or to the lower limit depends upon the relative bargaining strengths of the union and employer. Apart from pointing to the range within which the wage will be determined, economic theory cannot lead us to conclude at which particular wage the agreement will be reached. Theoretically, the wage determination under collective bargaining within the range between upper and lower limits is indeterminate; wage may be set at any level within the range between the two limits.

However, it is useful to analyse the two limits or the range within which the wage rate will be fixed under collective bargaining. A difficulty crops up in the beginning if the analysis is in regard to the union behaviour. Just as economists have built up many models of oligopoly depending upon the assumptions in regard to the behaviour of the oligopolists, similarly many models of collective bargaining have been constructed depending upon the different assumptions in regard to the goals and behaviour of the union. A basic question in this regard is whether the trade unions are economic or political or politico-economic institutions. Again, even if aims of trade unions are purely economic, what economic policy will they pursue or what quantity will they seek to maximize. Thus, will the trade union seek the wage rate which would *maximize the income of its members* or will the trade union try to seek the wage which will *maximize the number of its members* ? Again, will the trade union strive to increase the wage rate to as high a level as possible without regard to the employment effect of its action, or will it seek some optimum combination of wage rate and employment. These are the different alternative objectives of trade unions which imply different patterns of their behaviour in their negotiation or bargaining with the employer.

Bilateral monopoly is a market form where a monopolist, the single seller of a product or service, sells to the monopsonist who is a single buyer of that product or service. In the present case the trade union is a single seller of labour, whereas the firm, if it is a monopsonist, is a single buyer of labour. The range of wage rates within which a particular wage rate will be settled can be easily explained with the diagram already presented earlier (see Figure 54.4 where the effect of a trade union on wages and employment in a monopsonistic labour market was discussed). Consider Figure 54.4 again. The employer would maximize his profits where marginal labour cost (*MLC*) equals marginal revenue product (MRP_L) of labour and as will be seen from Fig. 54.4 to achieve this he will wish to set wage rate equal to W_0 and employ L_0 number of workers. Thus W_0 is the minimum limit below which wage rate cannot fall. On the other hand, if the union seeks to maximise wage rate without creating unemployment it will demand wage rate W_3, at which, given the demand curve for labour D_L, OL_0 amount of labour is employed. Thus W_3 sets the upper limit to which wage rate can be raised. If the union sets higher wage rate than W_3 the employment will fall below L_0 and thus creating unemployment of some workers. Which particular wage rate will be ultimately settled between the two parties depends on their relative bargaining strengths.

A more sophisticated bilateral monopoly model of wage fixation is presented in Figure 54.9. In this Figure 54.9, marginal revenue curve *MR* which is marginal to the labour demand curve D_L (= MRP_L) has also been drawn which shows how much additional income or revenue

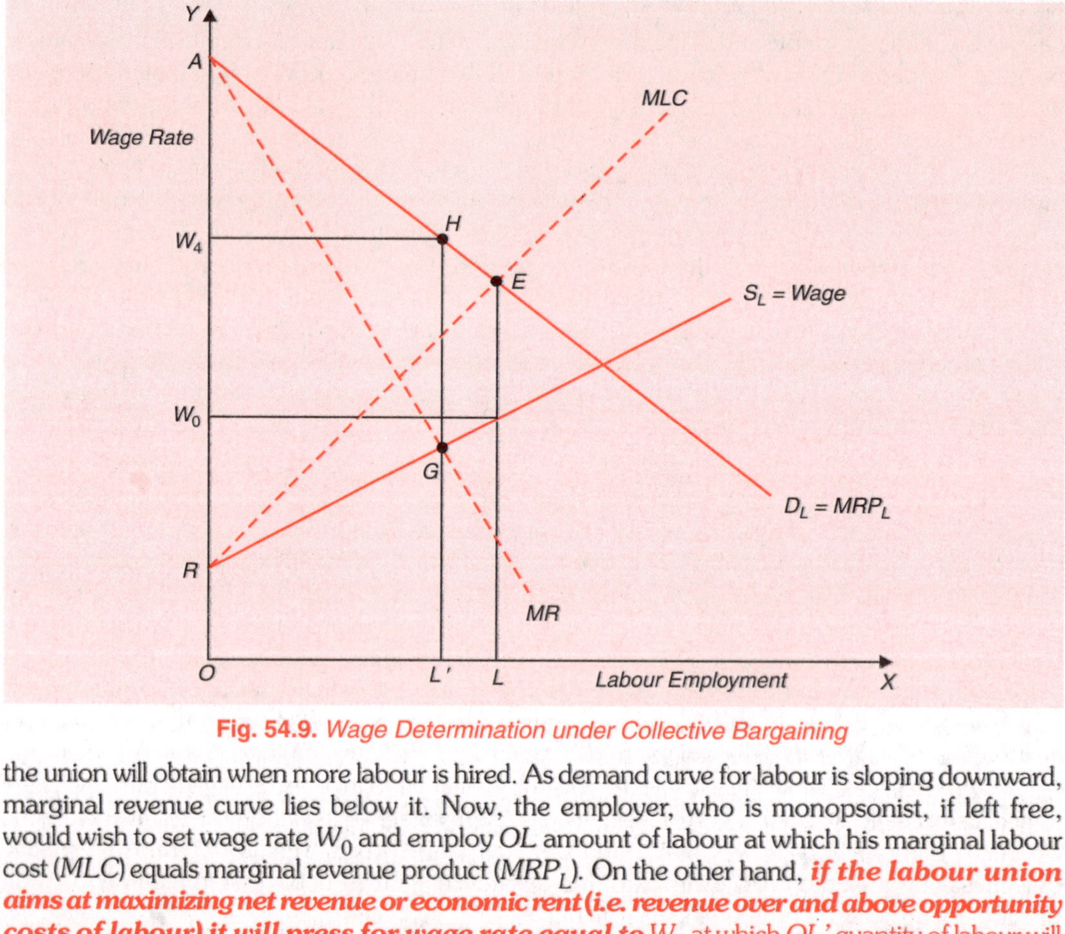

Fig. 54.9. *Wage Determination under Collective Bargaining*

the union will obtain when more labour is hired. As demand curve for labour is sloping downward, marginal revenue curve lies below it. Now, the employer, who is monopsonist, if left free, would wish to set wage rate W_0 and employ *OL* amount of labour at which his marginal labour cost (*MLC*) equals marginal revenue product (MRP_L). On the other hand, ***if the labour union aims at maximizing net revenue or economic rent (i.e. revenue over and above opportunity costs of labour) it will press for wage rate equal to*** W_4 at which *OL'* quantity of labour will be employed. It should be noted that this economic rent or surplus is maximised at the level of employment *L'* (in Figure 54.9) at which supply curve of labour representing marginal opportunity costs of workers intersects the marginal revenue curve of the union.

Thus W_4 is the upper limit of the wage rate sought by the union whereas W_0 is the lower limit. At which wage rate and employment settlement will be reached between the two parties depends on their bargaining powers and strategies. If the union can make a strong threat to strike, it might succeed in achieving a wage closer to W_4. On the other hand, if the employer makes a credible threat to declare lockout or hire non-union labour, it might secure a wage rate closer to W_0. The result is indeterminate.

WAGE DETERMINATION UNDER COLLECTIVE BARGAINING : FELLNER'S BILATERAL MONOPOLY MODEL[1]

In modern economic theory, it is granted that trade unions have *preference functions* or *indifference functions* between wages and employment. These preference or indifference functions of trade union which has the monopoly of selling labour take the place of supply curve (cost functions) of the monopolist in the product market. Now, the question arises as to what is the likely shape of the preference functions or indifference curves of the trade union. If the union seeks to achieve the maximum possible wage rate and cares nothing about the likely effect on the employment, the indifference curves will be horizontal straight lines, as shown in Fig. 54.10. Each successive indifference curve as we move upward on the *Y*-axis represents a higher level of satisfaction corresponding to the higher wage rate. Thus, indifference curve I_1 shows the levelof satisfaction of the union at wage rate OW_1. Similarly, the levels of

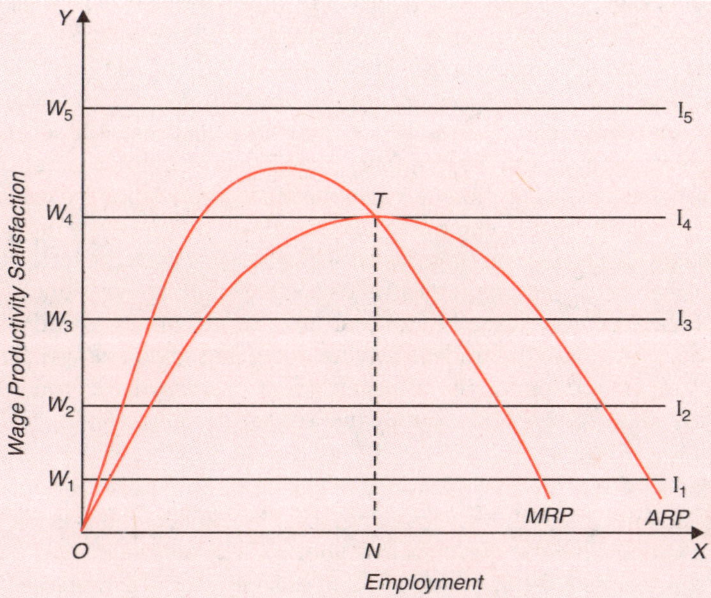

Fig. 54.10. *Upper and lower wage limits when the unions disregard the effect of wages on employment.*

satisfaction of the union at wage rate OW_2, OW_3, OW_4, OW_5 are respectively represented by indifference curves I_2, I_3, I_4, and I_5. The indifference curves have been so drawn as to indicate a *constant rise* in satisfaction between the successive indifference curves as we move upward. It will be noticed in Fig. 54.10 that as we move upward the distance between the successive indifference curves becomes larger indicating that as the wage rate is increased, successively larger increments in wage are required to yield a constant rise in satisfaction of the union. In Fig. 54.10, *ARP* represents average revenue productivity curve and *MRP* represents marginal revenue productivity curve.

If the union aims at achieving the maximum possible wage rate regardless of its effect on employment, the trade union, which is so powerful as to set the wage rate unilaterally, will choose the wage rate at which the corresponding indifference curve is tangent to the average

3. The analysis in this section is based upon an important work by William Fellner, *Competition Among the Few* (Newyork, Knofs, 1949): Chapter 10.

net revenue productivity curve (*ARP*). As Prof. Fellner says, "If the union possessed all the bargaining power.... that is, if it could set the conditions unilaterally, then with linear indifference map.... that wage line would be chosen which is tangential to *ARP*"[4]. In Fig. 54.10 the union will seek the wage rate OW_4 because indifference curve I_4 corresponding to the wage rate OW_4 is tangent to the average revenue productivity curve (*ARP*). It should be carefully noted that the trade union will not seek the wage rate above OW_4 though its satisfaction goes on increasing as the wage rate rises. This is because any wage rate higher than average revenue productivity will mean losses for the employer and he would rather stop production than to pay the wage rate higher than *ARP*. Therefore, the union even acting unilaterally will not try to set the wage rate higher than the maximum *ARP*. (We assume that the union knows the position of the average revenue productivity curve. Thus, in Fig. 54.10, I_4 is the highest possible indifference curve to which the union can reach and, therefore, wage rate OW_4 is the upper limit of the bargaining range which will be set by the union.

There will be a lower limit below which the wage rate cannot be set as a result of bargaining. If the employer possesses all the bargaining power, that is, if he can set the wage rate unilaterally, he will set the wage rate corresponding to this lower limit. It should be noted that the lower limit of the wage rate is that *which is still acceptable to the union.* There will be a certain wage rate lying on an indifference curve below which the trade union will not accept any wage rate at all; the trade union will call upon its members to go on strike than to accept the wage below a certain limit. For a single occupation or industry, the lower limit of the wage cannot be less than the transfer earnings, that is, the minimum wage rate that must be paid in order to keep the workers in the given occupation or industry. Moreover, it should be noted that the workers will remain the members of the union as long as they think that they benefit by it, that is, as long as the union can secure a wage higher than they would otherwise obtain in the state of being unorganised. Therefore, the trade union cannot afford to go below a certain lower limit, because its very existence depends upon ensuring to the workers a certain minimum wage. Employers will take this factor into account while setting the lower limit.

Further, the lower limit set by the employers will depend upon the business conditions, elasticity of demand for the product, elasticity of substitution between labour and capital, the wage rate being currently paid, the cost of living of the workers etc. It is evident that the lower limit is somewhat vague concept. Nevertheless, there will be a certain lower limit below which the wage will not be set as a result of the negotiations between the employer and the union.

As a result of the bargaining between the employer and the union, the wage rate will be fixed anywhere between the upper and lower limits, depending upon the relative bargaining strengths of the two parties. The actual wage rate fixed will be nearer to the upper limit, if the trade union is relatively more powerful. On the other hand, if the employer has a relatively greater bargaining power, the wage rate fixed will be nearer to the lower limit. Thus the distance between the upper and lower limits specifies the *bargaining range* within which the wage rate will be actually set. Economic theory cannot say exactly at what particular point the wage rate will be fixed within the bargaining range. Thus, the determination of actual wage rate under collective bargaining is *indeterminate.*

It may be carefully noted that the indifference curves between wages and employment are linear (*i.e.* horizontal straight lines) when the union does not bother about the effect on employment of the wage rate fixed, that is, when the union does not regard wage and employment as substitutes at all. With such behaviour of the union, then more employment cannot compensate for a wage loss. The trade union may adopt such an attitude to wages and employment when it is bargaining with the employer of a single firm. But when the bargaining

4. William Fellner, *Competition Among the Few*, p. 257.

is industry-wide so that the industrial trade union negotiates with the employers' association, the trade union will have to take into account the effect of wage on the employment in the industry. It may happen that the firms in the industry are working under differential cost conditions and for the wage rate fixed, some firms may not find worthwhile to operate and therefore close down. This will render the workers of these firms unemployed whose union may decide to break with the federal union of the industry and then strike separate bargains with their individual employers. Thus, the desire to maintain the unity of the trade unions will force the industrial trade union to take into account both wages and employment in its negotiations with the employer's representatives. Even the trade union of a single firm in its bargaining with the employer of the firm may take into account both wages and employment because of the fear that the workers which may be rendered unemployed as a result of the wage settled may turn against the union.

It is therefore unlikely that the trade union will maximize only the wage rate regardless of its effect on employment. It follows therefore that the ***trade union is likely to seek a certain optimum combination of wage and employment,*** considering the wage rate and the employment as substitutes to some extent. When, for the union, the wage rate and the level of employment are, in some degree, substitutes for each other, the preference functions or indifference curves of the union between the wage rate and the employment will be convex to the origin as depicted in Fig. 54.11. The fact that indifference curves between wage rate and employment are convex to the origin and *not downward-sloping straight lines* indicates that for the union, though wage and employment are substitutes, but they are not perfect substitutes of each other. Suppose that during the negotiation between the union and the employer, it is the wage rate which is to be settled, and the employer is free to offer the amount of employment he thinks to be most profitable at the wage rate settled. Now, given the wage rate, the profits of the employer will be maximum at the level of employment where the given wage rate equals the marginal revenue productivity. It follows therefore that the wage-employment combination which will be determined must lie on the marginal revenue productivity curve.

Now, the question is, with convex indifference curves, which wage rate the trade union

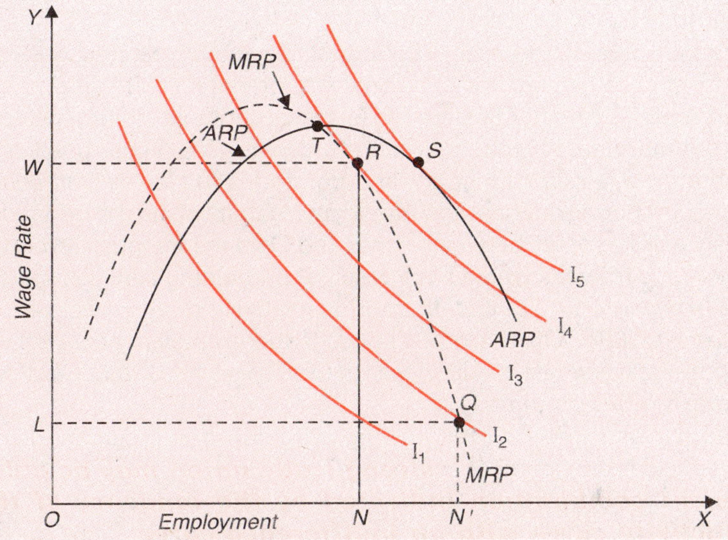

Fig. 54.11. *Upper and lower wage limits when bath wages and employment are taken into account by the union*

will choose. The trade union will obtain maximum possible satisfaction at the point on the given marginal revenue productivity curve to which an indifference curve of the union is tangent.

Therefore, the union will seek the wage rate corresponding to the point of the tangency in question. It will be noticed from Fig. 54.11 that the indifference curve I_4 is tangent to the *MRP* curve at point *R*. Corresponding to the tangency point *R*, the wage rate is *OW* at which employer will offer *ON* employment. Thus, the union will maximize its satisfaction by seeking the wage rate *OW*, at which the level of employment will be *ON*.

That the union will seek the wage corresponding to tangency point between its indifference curve with the given marginal revenue productivity curve, *provided the tangency in question lies below the ARP curve.* If the tangency between, the union's indifference curve and the marginal revenue productivity curve lies above the *ARP* curve (this can happen if the shape of union's indifference curves is different from that shown in Fig. 54. 11), then the union, instead of choosing the wage rate corresponding to the tangency point between the indifference curve and the *MRP* curve, will choose the wage corresponding to the highest point *T* of average revenue productivity curve *ARP*.

The wage rate corresponding to the tangency point between a union's indifference curve and the *MRP*, that is, point *R* in Fig. 54.11, or the wage rate equal to the highest average revenue productivity, that is, point *T* in Fig. 54.11, will be the upper limit set by the trade union as the case may be, above which the wage rate cannot be fixed.

As in case of horizontal straight-line union indifference curves, there will be a lower limit below which the wage rate will not be set in the present case of downward-sloping union's indifference curves. Let indifference curve I_2 be the minimum acceptable level of satisfaction for the union below which it will not accept any wage-employment combination. It should be carefully noted that the employer will like to move down along the *MRP* curve as far as possible, for his profits will be increasing as he moves down on the *MRP* curve. But, as the trade union moves downward on the *MRP* curve from the tangency point *R* it will be reaching on successively lower indifference curves indicating fall in the level of satisfaction of the union. But, as said above, there will be a minimum acceptable level of satisfaction of the trade union below which it will refuse to go. Thus, it is actually the minimum acceptable level of union's satisfaction which will set the lower limit to the settlement of the wage rate during bargaining between the trade union and the employer. If the employer possesses all the bargaining power, then the wage will be settled at this lower limit.

Let indifference curve I_2 represent the lowest acceptable level of satisfaction of the union. Since equilibrium settlement has to be on the marginal revenue productivity curve, the lower limit is represented by point *Q* where the lowest acceptable indifference curve I_2 of the union intersects the marginal revenue productivity curve *MRP*. Thus, point *R* is the upper limit above which the wage rate cannot go, and point *Q* is the lower limit below which the wage rate will not fall. Therefore, the wage-employment that will be determined as a result of collective bargaining will lie somewhere between *R* and *Q* on the marginal revenue productivity curve. That is, the wage rate determined as a result of bargaining between the employer and the union will lie between *OW* and *OL*. If union is relatively more powerful, the wage rate settled will be closer to *OW*. On the other hand, if the employer has a relatively greater bargaining strength, the wage rate will lie closer to *OL*. Thus, the distance *LW* is the range in which the wage rate is *indeterminate.*

It may be pointed out that in *an all or nothing bargaining* and demand for a wage rate together with a particular employment a ***strong trade union may be able to secure wage-employment combination indicated by the tangency of the average revenue productivity curve with an indifference curve.*** Thus, in Fig. 54.11, a powerful trade union, in an 'all or nothing' bargaining, will insist on and may be able to secure wage-employment combination represented by point *S* where indifference curve I_5 is tangent to average revenue productivity curve *ARP*.

HICKSIAN ANALYSIS OF WAGE DETERMINATION UNDER COLLECTIVE BARGAINING

In pure economic theory wage determination as a result of collective bargaining has been treated as price determination in the framework of a ***bilateral monopoly*** and was explained so by Edgeworth[5] as the result of bargaining between trade unions and employer or entrepreneur. Edgeworth explained that final settlement between labour union and employer may take place at a point on the contract curve which is the *locus* of the points of tangency of the indifference curves of the two parties. Since the final settlement between the trade union can occur at *any point* on the contract curve, there was a large range of indeterminacy about wage fixation. Whether the final settlement reached at a point on the contract curve between the two parties is favourable to the trade union or to the employer depends on their relative bargaining strength.

How the bargaining between the trade union and employer takes place and final settlement is reached has been explained by J.R. Hicks[6] through what he calls *employer's concession curve and union's resistance curve* which are drawn in Figure 54.12. Along the vertical axis we measure wage rate and along the horizontal axis we measure length of strike. Suppose *OW* is the wage rate in the market which the employer is willing to pay prior to trade union's pressure and bargaining with the employer. The trade union will demand higher wage rate. The instrument used by trade union of workes to get their demand conceded is the strike. Hicks uses two special curves to explain wage determination under collective bargaining. They are an *employer's concession curve and union's resistance curve.* Hicks asked the question to what extent can trade union pressure or force the employer to pay higher wages than they

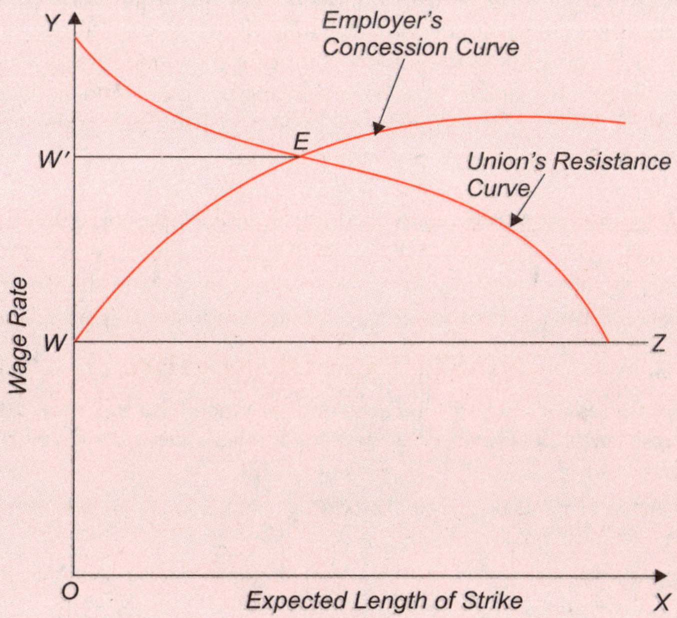

Fig. 54.12. *Hicks's Approach to Wage determination under Collective Bargaining*

would have obtained if there would have been no such pressure. The instrument of pressure, as mentioned above, is strike. To get its demand for higher wages conceded trade union threatens the employer that it will go on strike for a longer period.

5. See Edgeworth, *Mathematical Psychics*, London 1932.
6. J.R. Hicks, *The Theory of Wages*, London 1932

The employer would compare the cost of the higher wage and cost to him of the strike. The cost of the strike to the employer will depend on its expected duration, the size of his inventories and the state of the product market. If the employer thinks that the union is weak and the strike will fizzle out soon, the concession in terms of wage increase he will be inclined to offer will be small. The concession will rise as the expected staying power of the union and expected length of the strike rises. The employer's concession curve will rise, that is, it will slope upward and then flatten out at the maximum wage the employer is willing to pay rather than shut down his business.

On the other hand, the union's resistence curve slopes downward from the maximum wage demanded. As the strike proceeds further, union will get more information about the nature of employer's concession curve. The downward sloping union's resistance curve will ultimately cut the WZ line when members become desperate and are not willing to strike for any more period. According to J. R. Hicks, the equilibrium will be reached at point *E* where employer's concession curve and union's resistance curve intersect each other and corresponding wage rate is *OW′*. It will be seen from Fig. 54.12 that the new negotiated wage rate *OW′* as result of collective bargaining by the trade union is higher than the wage rate *OW* in the absence of trade union's pressure and collective bargaining by it. Since wage rate *OW′* is greater than *OW*, it means the collective bargaining by labour union has succeeded to achieve a higher wage rate for its member workers.

However, it is important to note that point *E* or new wage rate OW′ is only one possible point of equilibrium and not *the* equilibrium. In fact, OW′ represents just one point on the Edgeworthian contract curve. Even initial wage rate *OW* represents another point on the contract curve. Likewise, there are other possible points more or less away from the initial wage rate *OW*, depending on the shape and location of the employer's concession curve and union's resistance curve. Thus, though with the help of the given union's resistence curve and employer's concession curve Hicks was able to pinpoint the wage rate at which equilibrium will the reached, the wage rate under bilateral monopoly model and collective bargaining is indeterminate as it depends on the shape and location of the two curves which can differ as they depend on the relative strengths of the two parties.[7]

An interesting result follows from the Hicksian model of collective bargaining. "The degree of concession that labour union is likely to secure from the employer, given the expected length of the strike depends upon who the employer is. If it is the government, the concession curve is likely to be relatively low, it is easier for the Government to shift the prospective loss due to stoppage of work on to tax payers than it is for private industry to shift it on the consumers."[8]

QUESTIONS FOR REVIEW

1. What is (*a*) Subsistence theory of wages and (*b*) Wage-fund theory of wages. Show that in these classical theories of wages, trade unions can have no role in raising wages of labour.

2. "If wages are determined by marginal productivity of labour, then trade unions are superfluous". Do you agree ? Discuss.

3. In a competitive labour market, if trade union attempts to raise wage rate above the equilibrium wage rate, it will result in unemployment. Discuss using a diagram.

(**Hint.** Given the demand and supply curves of labour, attempt to raise wages causes unemployment. However, if with the rise in wages, marginal productivity curve of labour shifts upward adequately, or when the labour supply curve is backward sloping or when the

7. A.K. Dasgupta, *A Theory of Wage Policy* (New Delhi; 1976), Oxford University Press.
8. *Ibid.*

union restricts labour supply and as a result labour supply curve shifts to the left, then unemployment may not be created. For details see the text.)

4. Explain the role of trade unions in raising wages and employment and eliminating exploitation of labour in a free market economy.
5. What is monopsonistic exploitation of labour ? Show how far labour union can succeed in raising wages and eliminating exploitation of labour when the firm has a monopsony in labour market.
6. Why are wages and employment levels indeterminate when the union has monopoly power and the firm has monopsony power ?
7. If a trade union of labour faces a single buyer of labour, how would the wage rate and the level of employment be determined.
8. Wages and employment are indeterminate when a monopsonistic employer faces a monopolistic union. Explain.
9. Given the demand curve for labour (*i.e.* *MRP* curve of labour). Explain that

   (1) What wage rate the labour union will seek in order to *maximise employment?*

   (2) What will be wage rate and employment if union wants to increase the total wage income of its members ?

   (3) What will be the wage rate and employment if the union seeks to maximise rent earned by workers ?
10. What is bilateral monopoly ? Explain the determination of wages and employment when there is bilateral monopoly in labour market.
11. What is meant by collective bargaining ? Show that collective bargaining to raise wages need not always reduce employment.
12. Suppose both wages and employment enter into preference function of a labour union Using indifference curves between wages and employment, explain the upper and lower limits of wages and employment when a labour union bargains with a single buyer of labour.
13. Suppose that consultancy firm is monopsonist in the labour market for economic research assistants. The supply of such workers can be described by

$$P_L = 25 + 5Q_L$$

   where P_L is the price of labour (*i.e.* the wage rate) and Q_L is the number of workers. The consultancy firm's marginal revenue product function can be described as

$$MRP = 100 - 5Q_L$$

   (*i*) What wage rate (P_L) will the firm pay and how many workers will it hire ?

   (*ii*) What would happen to employment of labour if the Government sets a minimum wage of ₹ 60 (*i.e.* $P_L = 60$) ?
14. Explain Hicksian analysis of wage determination under collective bargaining through employer's concession curve and union's resistance curve. Is determination of wage rate in this analysis determinate ?

CHAPTER

55

Theory of Rent

Introduction

Having discussed the determination of reward for labour, we now turn to explain the determination of rent which is the price paid for the use of land. However, in modern economic theory, the term rent is used not only in the sense of reward for the use of land, but also in the sense of surplus earnings of the factors over their transfer earnings. In fact, in the second sense the concept of rent has been generalised so that it applies to surplus return over and above their transfer earnings of all factors of production, so that it is no longer peculiarly associated with land. We will first discuss the determination of land rent and will then explain the concept of rent as a generalised surplus return.

As mentioned before, distinguishing feature of land is that no human effort or sacrifice has been necessary to make it available to the society. Since land is not producible by man, its supply is absolutely inelastic, although its productivity can be increased by various improvements such as clearing, draining, introduction of irrigation facilities etc. These improvements are made by the efforts of man and therefore constitute capital goods. As the quantity of land available for use is scarce relative to demand, a price must be paid for its use. This price for the use of land, or what is commonly called *land rent,* is obtained by those people in the society in whom the ownership of land is vested. Since these private owners of land have not incurred any real costs to bring land into existence, the rent which they obtain is a surplus payment to them. The whole of the earnings of land, *i.e.,* land rent (excluding, of course, the return on capital investment in the form of improvements made on land by the owners) *are surplus,* since land is there in any case, and does not require any costs or human efforts to be made to bring it into existence. Thus, the term rent which was originally employed for the price paid for the use of land also came to be used for ***the surplus earnings of any factor of production in excess of the cost incurred to obtain its service.*** The land in its entirety to the whole society, being free gift of nature, does not require any cost to be paid in order to make it available to the society for use in production, the whole earnings of land are regarded as surplus. Thus, the whole earnings of land, from the viewpoint of society, become *economic rent.* We shall discuss this concept of rent in greater detail when we take up the explanation of the concept of rent as a generalised surplus return to all factors of production.

It should be noted that rent as a payment to the landlord for hiring or use of land by the tenant and the concept of rent as surplus over transfer earnings, which applies to all factors of production, are altogether different concepts and therefore should not be confused with each other. Modern economists generally call payment for hiring of land as ***land rent*** and surplus over transfer earnings as ***economic rent.*** Thus guarding us against confusing economic rent with land rent, Lipsey writes: "The term economic rent is a most unfortunate one. The adjective economic is often dropped and the economist often speaks of rent when he means economic rent, thus causing a confusion between the concept of a surplus over and above transfer earnings, and the payment made to landlords, for the hiring of land and buildings. When a tenant refers to his rent he is referring to what the pays his landlord, much of which is a transfer earning necessary to prevent the land and buildings in question from being transferred to some other use. It is important to guard against confusing the two concepts."[1]

The term rent is used in the following senses in modern economic theory :

1. First, the term rent refers to the rental made for the use of fixed factors of production whose existence is not dependant on any human effort or sacrifice. The chief example of the factor whose existence is not due to any effort or sacrifice made by man is land. Land to the society is a free gift from nature. Society has not incurred any cost to obtain the land. Moreover, land is not producible. So is the case with other natural resources. In fact, the term land, as used in economics, includes all natural resources. Since the supply of land and other natural resources are perfectly inelastic, therefore the term rent has also been defined as the price paid for the use of perfectly inelastic factors of production. As mentioned above, rent in this sense is often referred to as *land rent*.

2. Second, the term *economic rent* is employed for the surplus earned by a unit of a factor of production over and above the minimum earnings necessary to induce it to stay in the present use, industry or occupation. The minimum earnings which are required to keep a unit of a factor of production in its present occupation or industry are the earnings which that unit can obtain in its next best use or occupation. The earnings in the next best use or occupation are called transfer earnings. If a unit is not paid in its present employment at least the amount of money equal to its transfer earnings, it will then transfer itself to its next best use or occupation. Therefore, in this second sense, ***economic rent can also be defined as the payment to a unit of a factor of production in excess of its transfer earnings.***

3. Thirdly, Marshall extended the concept of rent to cover the earnings (net of depreciation and interest charges) of fixed capital equipment like machinery in the short run. The distinguishing characteristic of land is that its supply is perfectly inelastic and therefore its earnings depend mainly upon the demand for it. But, in the short-run period, fixed capital equipment like machinery is likewise perfectly inelastic in supply and cost of production is not relevant once it has been produced. Thus, in the short period, the earnings of fixed capital equipment depend mainly upon the demand conditions and are thus similar to land rent and have therefore been called rent by Marshall. Since these capital equipments are not permanently in fixed supply like land, and instead their supply is very much elastic in the long run, Marhsall preferred to call their earnings in the short period as ***Quasi Rent*** rather than rent.

Now we propose to discuss the above three concepts of rent as mentioned above. We start with the classical theory of rent which discusses the problem of payment for the use of land and other natural resources. '

RICARDIAN THEORY OF RENT

Classical theory of rent follows from the views of classical writers about the operation of law of diminishing returns in agriculture. Classical authors, West, Torrents, Malthus and Ricardo, each of them independently formulated the theory of differential rent. However, the classical theory of rent in the form presented and elaborated by David Ricardo has become more popular, though the idea of all of them concerning the land rent is fundamentally same. Ricardo gave credit to West and Malthus as his forerunner in the development of the theory of rent.

Ricardo defined rent as follows : "Rent is that portion of the produce of earth which is

1. Richard G. Lipsey, *An Introduction to Positive Economics*, 3rd edition, p. 350.

paid to the landlord for the use of the ***original and indestructible powers of the soil.*** It should be noticed that land rent, according to Ricardian definition, is a payment for the use of only land and is different from contractual rent which includes the return on capital investment made by the landlord in the form of hedges, drains, well and the like. When return on the capital investment made by the landowner is deducted from the contractual rent, what is left is pure land rent which is the price for the use of only land or "the original and indestructible powers of the soil."

It will generally facilitate the understanding of the Ricardian model of rent formation, if we clearly state the various assumptions made by him. First, Ricardo considers the supply of land from the viewpoint of the whole society and takes the quantity of land as completely fixed. No amount of higher price for the use of land can call forth an increased supply of it. Thus, the total supply of land is perfectly inelastic and unresponsive to any changes in rent. Secondly, he does not take into account the various alternative uses to which land can be put. He assumes the land to be used for growing a single composite crop 'corn'. The land has therefore been taken to be completely specific to one crop, *i.e.,* corn. In this way, in Ricardian model, either land is to be used for growing of corn or alternatively it has to be left idle. There are only two alternative uses of land : its use for growing of corn or no use at all. Thus ***he takes the transfer earnings of land as zero.*** No landowner would like to leave the land idle and therefore every landowner will be prepared to give it for any rent however little it may be provided the competition is perfect.

Thirdly, he assumes that land differs in quality. There are various grades of land, differing from each other in respect of fertility and location. Some pieces of land are more fertile than others and, as compared to others, some are more well located near the market centres.

Fourthly, he assumes that there is perfect competition in the market for land. In other words, there are many landowners who are to give their land on rent and there are many farmers who are to get land on rent for the purpose of growing corn. Further, each individual landowner and farmer has no influence over rent, *i.e.,* the price for the use of land.

Given the above assumptions, according to the classical theory, rent arises due to two reasons. First, if land is homogeneous, *i.e.,* of uniform quality, the scarcity of land relative to demand will give rise to rent. Ricardo calls it *scarcity rent.* Second, when land differs in quality *i.e.,* in fertility and location, the scarcity of superior grades of land will give rise to *differential rents.* We discuss below the emergence of scarcity and differential rents, as conceived in the classical theory.

Scarcity Rent

It is worth mentioning that in Ricardian differential approach too, demand and supply of land determine rent, though they are not directly shown to do so. The Ricardian theory can be expressed and explained directly in terms of demand for and supply of land. In the Ricardian treatment of rent, the supply of land for the economy as a whole is fixed, and the demand for land is derived from the demand for the "corn" produced by land. Thus, according to Lipsey, "The modern student of Economics will recognize in the Ricardian arguments the idea of derived demand. Landlords, Ricardo was saying, cannot just charge any price they want for land; the prices they get will depend on demand and supply. The supply of land is pretty well fixed and the demand depends on the price of corn. The higher the price of corn, the more profitable will it be to grow corn, the higher will be the demand for corn land, and the higher will be the price for its use."[2]

2.*Op. cit.* p. 349.

In the Ricardian model, it is assumed that land has only one use, that is, of growing com on it.' Therefore, no price is required to be paid to prevent land from transferring to other uses, that is, to uses other than growing corn. Further, the land has been considered for the economy as a whole. Therefore, the supply of land is a given and fixed quantity. Given these assumptions, supply curve of land is *perfectly inelastic.* Scarcity rent will arise only when the available quantity of land is scarce in relation to demand for it, which is derived from the demand for the corn. The Ricardian model of the determination of scarcity rent has been illustrated through demand and supply curves in Fig. 55.1 where *SS'* is the supply curve of land with *OS* as the available quantity of land. It is important to note that Ricardo did *not explicitly* explain the determination of land rent through demand and supply curves, but his model of land rent explains the emergence of rent as a result of supply of land becoming scarce in relation to demand for it. Therefore, we can explain the determination of land rent in Ricardian theory with the modern concepts of demand and supply curves.

It is assumed that all land is homogeneous and therefore no differences in fertility or location exist. It will be seen from Fig. 55.1 that various demand curves such as D_0D_0, D_1D_1, D_2D_2, and D_3D_3 and depend upon the various levels of demand for the product *i.e.,* corn. It should be noted that aggregate demand curve for land has been obtained by summing up the marginal revenue productivity curves of all farmers cultivating the land. Thus, as the demand for other factors, demand for land is also determined by its marginal revenue productivity. If, to begin with, demand curve for land is given by the curve D_0D_0, then *no rent on land will be charged* on hiring it. This is because with D_0D_0 as the demand curve, the available land *OS* is abundant in relation to the demand for it. With D_0D_0 as the demand curve, various farmers will use *OK* amount of land and as a result *KS* amount of land will remain idle or uncultivated. If the demand for land increases to D_1D_1, even then the rent of land will be nil, but now the whole

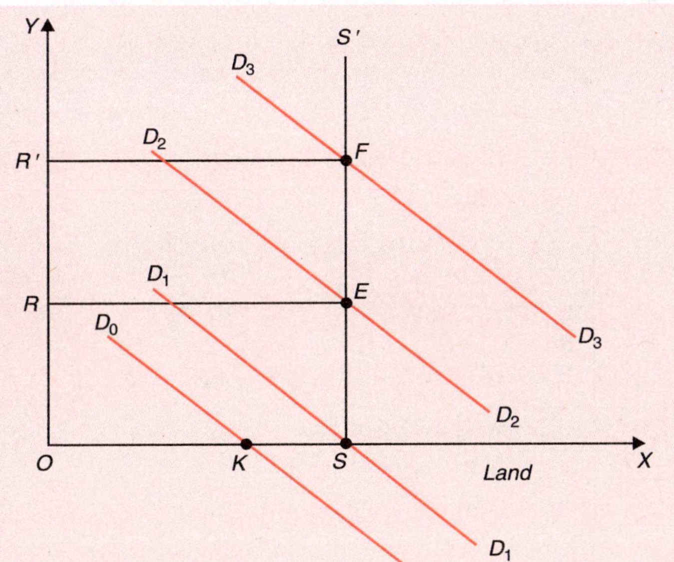

Fig. 55.1. *Ricardian Model: Determination of Land Rent through Demand and Supply Curves*

amount of available land *OS* will be cultivated. If the demand for land increases to D_2D_2, the demand for and supply of land will be in equilibrium at point *E* and the rent *OR* will be determined. With the further increase in demand for land to D_3D_3, rent rises to OR', whereas the supply of land remains fixed at OS. Demand for land can increase as a result of population growth which raises the consumption of corn or agricultural produce. This increased demand for corn or agricultural produce causes the demand curve for land to shift upward and thereby brings about a rise in the rent of land. We thus see that Ricardian model of determination of land rent can be better explained with demand and supply curves. There is an alternative way to explain the emergence and determination of rent in Ricardian theory which we explain below.

Rent as Surplus over Cost of Production. The emergence of land rent in the Ricardian theory can be easily explained by imagining that a new island is discovered and some people come to settle there. We suppose that all land in this island is completely homogeneous or is of uniform quality. In other words, all tracts of land in this island are equally fertile and equally well-situated. The quantity of land available for cultivation on this island is fixed and is therefore completely inelastic to changes in rent for its use. Land is to be used for the cultivation of a single crop "corn". Land is assumed to be having no other alternative uses. When the people come to settfe on this island, they will use the land for producing corn by applying labour and capital on it. When all the available land is not yet put into use, the price of corn will be equal to ***the average of labour and capital cost,*** with the farmers working at the minimum point of the average cost (exclusive of land rent) curve. The price of the corn must at least be equal to the average cost (exclusive of land rent) in the long run, if the use of labour and capital is to be worthwhile.

Since we are assuming perfect competition in the market for corn, the farmer's equilibrium will be established at the lowest point of long-run average cost curve (exclusive of rent). This is shown in Fig 55.2. The farmer is in equilibrium at OM level of output. The price of corn is OP which is equal to the minimum average cost ML (only labour and capital costs are included). Now with the growth of population on the island and with the development of the island's economy the demand for corn will increase so that the price of corn will temporarily rise above the average cost. Since all the available land is not yet brought under use, the rise of the

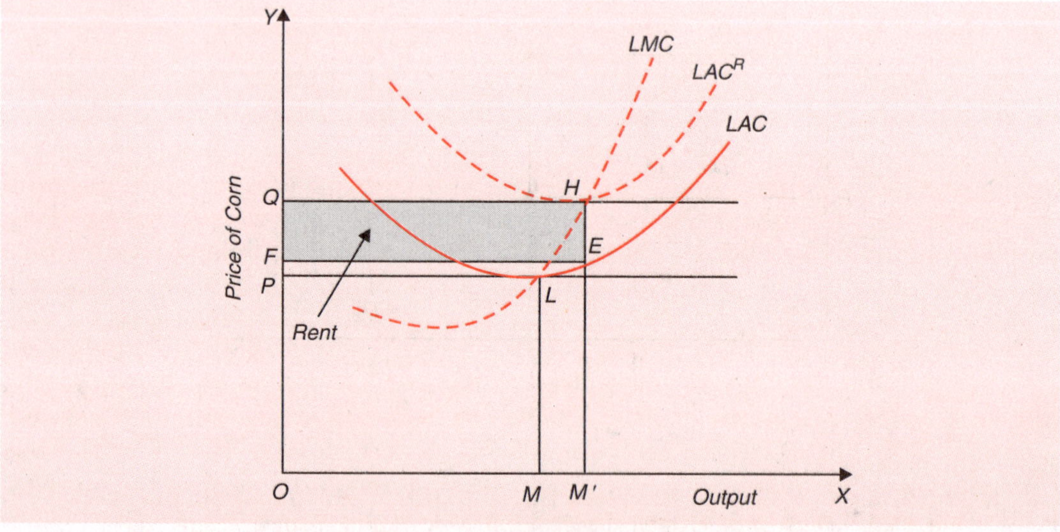

Fig. 55.2. *In Ricardian Theory rent arises as surplus over cost of production*

price of corn above the average cost will attract other new farmers who will bring the idle land under use for the production of corn. As the new farmers start production, the supply of corn will increase, with the result that the price of the corn will fall. Because the average cost of the new farmers will be the same as that of the old ones, the price of corn will fall back to the old level, that is, price *OP* in Fig. 55.2.

As long as some land is idle, the production of corn will be increased by bringing new land under cultivation. Thus, until land is not scarce, *i.e.,* some land is yet idle, the price of corn cannot rise *permanently* above the average of labour and capital costs. Since the price of corn is, in long-run equilibrium, equal to the average cost of only labour and capital, as long as all land is not fully used, ***there will be no surplus left to be earned as rent on land.*** In other words, it means that so long as there is some available land which is not yet brought into use, farmers will not have to pay any rent to the landlords for the use of their land.

Provided the competition among landlords is perfect (as is the case we are assuming here), the rent will not arise when there is still surplus land for use because the demand for land is relatively less than the supply of it. In other words, land is yet not scarce relative to demand. Price of anything arises only when it is scarce in relation to demand. If any landlord tries to charge any rent, when there is still some land lying idle with other landlords, farmers will go to take up that land for cultivation. The landlord need not be paid rent for the use of land since its only alternative use is keeping it idle. To sum up, so long as land is not scarce, rent cannot arise, since price of corn will be equal to the minimum average (labour and capital) cost. Suppose that the population continues increasing so that the demand for corn becomes so large that all available land is brought under cultivation. If the population of the island further increases beyond this, it will raise the demand for the product which will bring about rise in the price of corn above the minimum average (labour and capital) cost. Now, the price level cannot fall back to the original level *OP*; since no idle land is there to be taken up for production, all the land being already put in use. Suppose that the increase in demand for corn has resulted in the rise in its price from *OP* to *OQ*, each firm then expands its output so that marginal cost is equal to the new price *OQ*.

It will be seen from Fig. 55.2 that the farmer's equilibrium will be at point *H* at which marginal cost is equal to new price *OQ*. In this new equilibrium position, the firm will be producing *OM'* level of output. The expansion in output by the farmers will lower the price of corn to some extent, but it cannot bring the price back to its original level *OP*. This is so because if the demand is large enough that at the price *OP* which equals minimum average cost, the quantity demanded of the corn exceeds the quantity that can be produced and supplied at that price, the new price must stay above the price *OP*. We have assumed in our Fig. 55.2 that the new price finally settles at *OQ* level.

It is evident from the figure that a difference between the price of the corn and the average labour and capital cost has arisen. In other words, farmer earns more than the labour and capital cost incurred by him. While the average labour and capital cost incurred by him is *M'E*, the price of the corn is *M'H* (= *OQ*). Thus, the differential of *EH* between the price and the average labour and capital cost has arisen. This *EH* is the rent per unit of output which will be paid by the farmer to the landlord. Total rent to be paid by the farmer to the landlord will be *FEHQ*. This rent (difference between price and cost) cannot be competed away by the entry of more farmers in production since all land is already being employed for production. This rent has arisen because of the scarcity of land. In other words, rent arises due to the niggardliness of nature; nature has not provided land large enough to meet the level of demand by producing at the lowest level of average cost. The demand for corn has increased so much that the required output cannot be produced with total available supply of land at the minimum average cost (exclusive of rent). In order to meet the increased demand, output has to be expanded to the point *H* of marginal cost curve so that the new price *OQ* equals marginal cost. The marginal cost *M'H* which is equal to price *OQ* exceeds average cost *M'E* (incurred on labour and capital) by *EH*. Thus a differential *EH* between price and average cost emerges, which is rent of land required to be paid to the landlord.

It is clear from the foregoing discussion that, in the Ricardian theory, ***rent emerges as surplus over cost of production*** (labour and capital cost). Ricardo and other Classical writers did not consider rent as a part of the cost of production. However, if we take total rent *FEHQ* as fixed cost and add it to the average cost curve *LAC,* we shall get LAC^R (datted) which is shown above in Fig. 55.2.

Rent which we have discussed above is called *scarcity rent.* It is called scarcity rent because it arises due to the scarcity of homogeneous land. Since all land is homogeneous and there exists perfect competition among the landowners on the one hand and among the tenants on the other, all farmers will pay equal amount of rent. Because land has zero elasticity of supply *i.e.,* its quantity is fixed, the rise in rent will not bring more land into existence. Therefore, the essential feature of pure scarcity rent is that whereas a rise in the prices of other factors of production will bring about an increase in their supply, at any rate in the long run, a rise in rent cannot cause an increase in the supply of land. "Higher earnings can therefore persist for land even in the long run, whereas with other factors this is not very likely to happen because supply will increase to meet the increased demand. It is the fixity of its supply which distinguishes homogeneous land and its scarcity rent from other factors of production and their prices. Scarcity rent is essentially the result of the fact that land is in inflexible supply."[3]

Differential Rent

In the discussion of scarcity rent above, we have assumed that all land is homogeneous, *i.e.,* equally well fertile and equally well situated. This is however not a realistic assumption. In fact, Ricardo was most interested in showing the emergence of rent when the land differs in quality, *i.e.,* in fertility and situation. Some pieces of land are more fertile than others. Again, some pieces of land are more favourably situated than others. This is, they are located more near to the market centres, where the produce has to be sold, than others.

Fertility of tracts of land varies primarily because of the differences in the nature of the soil, temperature, rainfall and other climatic factors. With a given application of labour and capital, some pieces of land will yield more output per acre than others. Thus, the differences in fertility will bring about differences in the costs of production (exclusive of rent) of various farmers operating on the different grades of land. The farmers working on the superior or more fertile grades of land will have their average cost curve at a lower level than those working on the inferior or less fertile grades of land. Likewise, differences in location will cause differences in costs of various farmers because of the differences in transportation costs. In practice, land will be of numerous grades, shading off gradually from the best to the poorest. To simplify our analysis, we however assume that in our island there are three grades of land, *A* being the superior-most and C the poorest. *B* grade of land lies between *A* and C.

When people first come to island, they will take up the best grade land *A* for the production of corn. So long as some of grade *A* land is yet lying idle, there will be no rent. When with the increase in the population of the island or with the development of the island, the demand for corn increases, the whole of the grade *A* land will be put into use for the production of corn. At this stage each of the many farmers who will be using the grade *A* land will work at the lowest point of the average cost curve as shown in Fig. 55.3 (*a*). When once the whole of grade *A* land is brought into use and the demand for corn still further increases due to either the growth of population or the development of the island, two courses of action will be

3. Stonier and Hague, *A Textbook of Economic Theory,* 2nd edition, p. 283.

adopted. First, grade *B* land will also be taken up for production. Secondly, grade *A* land will be more intensively used, *i.e.*, more doses of labour and capital will be applied to the pieces of grade *A* land.

Now, the grade *B* land can be taken up for use only when the price sufficiently rises so that it covers the cost of production on grade *B* land. In other words, price must be high enough to cover the lowest average cost (exclusive of rent) of grade *B* land, otherwise it will not be worthwhile to cultivate it. In other words, if the price is lower than the lowest average labour and capital cost on grade *B* land, its cultivation will not pay back even the labour and capital cost incurred and therefore it will not be brought under cultivation. It is evident from Fig. 55.3 (*b*) that price must rise to *OP′* if grade *B* land is to be taken for cultivation. Now, suppose the demand for corn has risen so much that price of corn is *OP′* and therefore grade *B* land has been brought under cultivation. Thus, margin of cultivation has been extended to grade *B* land. In other words, grade *B* land is now on the *margin of extensive cultivation*. Every farmer cultivating the grade *B* land will operate at the lowest point of average cost curve *AC* in Fig. 55.3 (*b*). Since the price of corn *OP′* is equal to average labour and capital cost on grade *B* land there is no surplus over cost of production on grade *B* land and hence grade *B* land

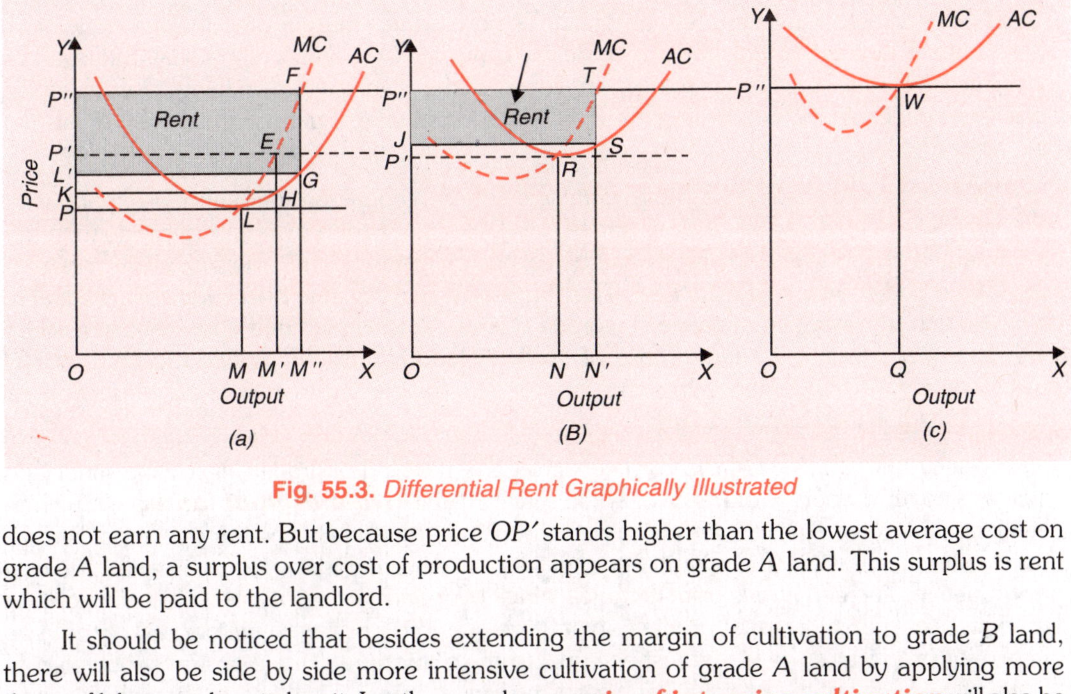

Fig. 55.3. *Differential Rent Graphically Illustrated*

does not earn any rent. But because price *OP′* stands higher than the lowest average cost on grade *A* land, a surplus over cost of production appears on grade *A* land. This surplus is rent which will be paid to the landlord.

It should be noticed that besides extending the margin of cultivation to grade *B* land, there will also be side by side more intensive cultivation of grade *A* land by applying more doses of labour and capital on it. In other words, ***margin of intensive cultivation*** will also be pushed forward. In terms of Fig. 55.3, it will mean that the farmers operating on grade *A* will not produce at the lowest point of average cost curve, they will also expand output to meet the increased demand. With the expansion in output, the marginal costs on farms of grade *A* land will rise. The price must rise to cover this increase in marginal cost, if the extra costs incurred on additions to capital and labour for expanding output are to be recovered. In Fig 55.3 (*a*) when the farmers of grade *A* land extend the margin of their intensive cultivation in response to increased demand, their new equilibrium position will be where the marginal cost is equal to new higher price *OP′*, that is, at point *E* on *MC* curve or at output *OM′*. It will be seen from Fig, 55.3 (*a*) that though new price *OP”* equals marginal cost *(M′E)*, but it stands higher than average of labour and capital cost which is equal to *M′H*, This surplus of price (or marginal cost) over average cost is land rent per unit of output which will have to be paid to the landlords. Total rent paid by the farmer will be equal to *KHEP′*.

It should be noticed that rent on grade *A* land would have arisen even if no more intensive cultivation was done and the output was restricted to *OM* level since the price *OP′* stands higher than the lowest average cost *ML* on grade *A* land. But, in practice, both the extensive and intensive margins are pushed further in order to meet the increase in demand and the surplus over cost of production, *i.e.*, land rent on intra-marginal lands arises because of both the more extensive and intensive cultivation. At this stage grade *B* land is *marginal land* which earns no rent and grade *A* land is ***intra-marginal land*** which earns rent equal to *KHEP′*. It should however be noted that rent on grade *A* land has arisen ***due to the scarcity of superior grade A land*** which makes it necessary to bring lower grade *B* land under cultivation.

Now suppose that population of the island further increases, which brings about further increases in demand for the produce of the land so that the price of the corn rises to *OP*". As a result of this, the grade *C* land will also be brought under cultivation and lands of grade *A* and *B* will be more intensively cultivated. Price *OP″* is equal to the minimum average cost of grade *C* land. There is no surplus earned over cost of production on grade *C* land and hence grade *C* land does not earn any rent. Grade *C* land is now on the margin of extensive cultivation. Thus, grade *C* land is the *marginal land*. Besides, at price *OP″*, lands of grade *A* and *B* will be more intensively cultivated by applying more doses of labour and capital on them. Consequently, output on grades *A* and *B* will be expanded to the point where the marginal cost equals the new price *OP″*.

It will be seen from Fig. 55.3 that with price of corn equal to *OP″* output is expanded to *OM″* on grade *A* land and to *ON′* on grade *B* land. Now, a surplus over cost of production has also emerged on grade *B* land. Total revenue earned on grade *B* land is now *ON′TP″*, whereas total labour and capital cost is *ON'SJ*. The surplus of total revenue over total cost is equal to *JSTP″* which represents rent earned by grade *B* land. As the result of the increase in price to *OP″*, the total revenue earned in case of grade *A* land is *OM"FP"*, while the total cost of production is *OM″ GL*. Hence the rent, that is, surplus earned over cost of production on grade *A* land has increased to *LGFP″*.

To sum up, with price of the corn equal to *OP*", the land of grade *C* is the marginal land and earns no rent, whereas the lands of grade *A* and *B* are ***intra-marginal lands,*** and higher-quality land of grade *A* is earning more rent than land of grade *B*. The important point to be noted about the classical (Ricardian) theory of rent is that rent does not form a part of the cost of production. As seen above, rent is the earnings over and above the cost of production. As rent does not enter into cost of production, it therefore does not determine price of corn. Price of corn (or produce of the land) must be equal to the minimum average cost of production of the marginal land, but the marginal land earns no rent. It is thus clear that, in Ricardian theory, rent is ***not price determining.*** In fact, in this theory rent is *price determined,* that is, it is price of corn which determines rent. To quote Ricardo, 'Corn is not high because a rent is paid, but a rent is paid because corn is high".

CRITICAL EVALUATION OF RICARDIAN THEORY OF RENT

So far as the determination of land rent is concerned and the forces which influence it, modern economists agree with the Ricardian theory of rent. Like Ricardo, modern economists are also of the view that rent of land arises because of its scarcity. Although Ricardo explained the determination of land rent through a ***'differential return'*** *approach* and not the basis of *direct* demand for and supply of land, and accordingly did not employ demand and supply curves to depict the determination of land rent, yet in Ricardian theory it is the forces of demand for and supply of land which determine the rent of land. Like modern economists, Ricardo too believed that demand for land is derived demand, it is derived from the demand for the produce of land, that is, what Ricardo called 'corn'. In the Ricardian theory with its differential approach, increase in the population of a country raises the demand for the corn and brings about rise in the land rent. In the modern approach based on direct interaction of demand and supply, the increase in population will shift the demand curve for land upward and thereby will push up the rent. Thus ***the demand-supply approach (or in other words, marginal productivity approach) of the modern economists and the differential return approach of Ricardo are alternative explanation of the same phenomenon and are in no sense contradictory;*** in both approaches forces of demand and supply play a crucial role in determination of rent. But the use of Ricardian differential approach does not provide any better understanding of the nature of rent than that of modern approach based on the use of direct demand and supply concepts. However, the adoption of Ricardian differential approach often leads to misunderstanding, for it suggests that rent of land requires a special theory for its explanation, that is, it may lead one to conclude that whereas rent of land can be explained with differential principle, the other factor rewards, wages of labour, interest on capital, etc. can be explained with demand and supply or marginal productivity principle. Obviously, such a conclusion would not be correct. We thus see that whereas there is no contradiction between differential theory of rent propounded by Ricardo and the modern theory based on direct use of demand and supply and the marginal productivity principle, there seems to be a little reason for the special theory of rent *(i.e.,* differential theory). Unity of economic thought and similarity of treatment requires land rent should also be explained directly with demand and supply curves as other factor prices.

Demand-Supply Analysis and Differential Rents

Modern economists also agree with Ricardo regarding differential rents arising on different kinds of land between which there are differences of fertility and location. In our above analysis of rent determination through demand and supply, we have assumed that all land is homogeneous. Therefore, a single uniform rent is determined. When there are differences in land, each kind of land would have its own separate demand and supply curves and consequently *differential rents* depending on their demand and supply will be determined. Thus, on demand and supply basis, even differential rents on different grades of land in respect of fertility and location can be explained.

Alternative Uses of Land, Land Rent, Cost of Production and Price

Ricardo explained the determination of land rent from the standpoint of the economy as a whole. He did not consider the question of rent payment from the point of view of a single industry or use. He did not consider the ***various different uses or industries*** for which land can be used. Since he confined himself to the whole land available in a society and a single use of it, he concluded that land rent from the point of view of the society as a whole is a surplus, superfluous and unnecessary payment. It is a surplus or unnecessary payment in the sense that it is not required to bring land into existence or use by the society. From the point of view of the economy as a whole, the total supply is inelastic, therefore the whole rent from land may be regarded as surplus or unnecessary payment. But this cannot be said of the land rent from the point of view of the individual industries or uses in which land is used. From the point of view of an industry producing a particular product, the necessary minimum payment for a factor is not the payment which will bring it into existence or use for the society but the payment which is required to induce that factor to remain in that particular industry or use rather than transfer itself to other industries or uses. "If land has various possible. uses, and it generally has, a relatively low land rent for the one use will lead to something different being done with the land. If houses yield too small a derived demand for land, and car parks a higher one, the property standing on it will be demolished and car parks will appear."[4] The minimum price or payment that must be paid to a unit of a factor in order to induce it to work in the particular industry or use is called transfer payment or transfer earning or transfer cost.

It should be noted that from the point of a particular industry transfer payments are as much a part of the supply price or cost of a product as any other element of cost. In order to obtain the land for any particular industry or use, it need to be paid a rent which is at least equal to the income it could earn in the next best alternative uses. Thus, this transfer price or payment will enter into cost of production and will determine the price of the product. Ricardo was therefore wrong when he asserted that rent does not enter cost of production of corn and therefore does not determine the price of the corn. Thus, according to modern economists, at least that part of land rent which is its transfer cost or earnings enters into the cost of production of the commodity produced by the land and therefore determines the price of the commodity as any other element of cost. Prof. Robertson expresses the modern viewpoint in regard to the land rent entering into the cost of production of a commodity in the following words: "The old phrase about rent not entering into cost.... conjures up to my mind a stately temple labelled costs of production with poor rent standing disconsolately on the mat outside ! ... from the point of view not only of the individual firm but of the individual industry the price paid for the use of land is exactly on all fours with the price paid for the use of the other factors of production."[5]

That the land rent enters into the cost of production and thus determines price of a commodity for the production of which land is used is quite evident if we consider the supply of land from the viewpoint of the individual farmer or any other individual use of land. For an individual farmer, the supply of land is perfectly elastic at the given rate of land rent. If an individual farmer does not pay this land rent, the land will get transferred to other farmers who will be ready to pay the current rate of land rent. It is therefore quite clear that for the individual farmer, the whole of land rent is a necessary payment and he therefore must include it in his cost of production on the basis of which price of the commodity will be determined. Jan Pen rightly writes : "Ricardo was right when he wrote: corn is not high because a rent is paid, but a rent is paid because corn is high. But that 'right' must be interpreted solely in the sense of inelastic supply curves that are confronted with a derived demand. If the latter is at a high level because end-product is expensive, a high land rent results from the market; that rent is not a cause but a consequence. However, ***one may not deduce from that the rent for the individual farmer is not a part of the costs.*** Not a single farmer would believe that, and rightly so. He simply has to pay for the land as for labour and for capital."[6]

We therefore see that Ricardo's view that rent of land does not enter into cost of production and therefore does not take part in the determination of the price of corn is quite wrong. He formed this view by considering land from the point of view of the whole society for which land is completely inelastic and has zero transfer cost. As a result, from the point of view of the society as a whole, the whole land rent is surplus and unnecessary payment. But, as Chamberlin writes, "Although rents may be surpluses from certain points of view, or for certain purposes, or subject to certain interpretations, they are to the individual producer no different from any

4. Jan Pen, *Income Distribution*, Penguin Books, 1971, p. 128.
5. D. H. Robertson, *Lectures on Economic Principles*, Fontana Library Edition, p. 204.
6. Jan Pen, op. *cit*, p. 128.

other money expense. They do not arise as a surplus from his own operations; they are a cost rigidly imposed upon him by the competition of his rivals for the use of rent-yielding property. They figure in the same way as do the wages of labour and the interest of capital in his computations as to the most advantageous proportion between the factors and as to the most advantageous scale of operations."[7]

To sum up, from the point of view of the individual industry and farmer or producer, land rent enters into cost of production, and therefore determines price. Ricardo was wrong in holding an opposite view that rent does not enter into cost of production and therefore does not determine price.

Land's Share in National Income and Stagnation of Economic Growth

Another aspect of Ricardian theory with which modern economists do not agree is the prediction by Ricardo, on the basis of his rent theory, that process of economic growth would come to an end and there will be economic stagnation. He argued that as the population increased, the demand for land would also increase. As a result, both the extensive and intensive margins would be pushed further and due to this rent of land will go up. According to him, in this process, share of land rent in the total national product will go up and share of profits will decline. Decline in profits means not much money will be available for financing the industry. Further, decline in the rate of profit will discourage inducement to invest. Consequently, further investment and growth process would come to a halt. But in actual practice things have not worked out in accordance with the prediction of Ricardo. To quote Jan Pen again, "The grandiose theory developed by D. Ricardo at the beginning of the nineteth century ... amounts to the fact that population growth and shortage of land will force up the share of land rent, as a result of which no money will be left for the financing of industry. Ricardo predicted stagnation of economic growth, but this prediction did not work out, nor has the increase in the share of rent of land occurred. ...There is in fact a clear shortage of land at many places, and especially in the cities this may lead to high prices and rents. This situation is not without its problems, but it is nothing like Ricardo's prediction."[8]

From the macro point of view, we shall discuss the Ricardian theory and share of the rent of land in national income in a later chapter.

THE CONCEPT OF ECONOMIC RENT AS A GENERALISED SURPLUS RETURN : MODERN CONCEPT OF RENT

In the modern economic theory the concept of economic rent has been generalised and extended to the surplus payments made to other factors of production besides land. In this connection two concepts of economic rent may be noted. First is the Ricardian concept of economic rent. As we saw above, Ricardo regarded land as a free gift of nature and considered the whole earnings of land as the economic rent. Later on, this Ricardian concept of rent has been extended to designate a part of the earnings of other factors of production—labour, capital and entrepreneurial ability—over and above the minimum necessary income required to induce the factors to do their work. Thus, in accord with Ricardo's concept, Joan Robinson says, "The essence of the conception of *rent is* the conception of a surplus earned by a particular part of a factor of production over and above the *minimum earnings necessary to induce it to do work.*"[9] Mrs. Joan Robinson defines the minimum payment required to be paid to labour and entrepreneur as follows: —"the minimum payment necessary to induce a labour

7. E.H. Chamberlin, *The Theory of Monopolistic Competition,* 1950.
8. *Op. cit.* p. 126.
9. *Economics of Imperfect Competition* (London, 1948), p. 102.

to continue to work with any given intensity is the real income which will maintain his physiological efficiency at an adequate level."... while "the necessary minimum for an entrepreneur is the level of earnings which is sufficient to prevent him from relapsing into the ranks of employed labour."[10]

A slightly different concept of economic rent dates back to Pareto. In the Paretian concept, economic rent is the excess payment to a factor over and above the minimum amount necessary to keep a factor in its *present occupation.* Thus according to Benham, economic rents are "the sum paid to the factors which need not be paid in order to retain the factors *in the industry.*"[11] Likewise, according to Boulding, economic rent is the payment to a factor "in excess of the minimum amount necessary to keep that factor in *its present occupation.*"[12] Mrs. Joan Robinson also discusses the question of surplus or economic rent from the viewpoint of individual industries or uses. She thus says, "from the point of view of an industry producing a particular commodity the necessary minimum payment for a factor is not the payment which will cause that factor to exist, but the payment which will cause it to take service in that particular industry rather than another."[5] And "the difference between the earnings actually received by a certain unit of a factor and its transfer price is its rent from the point of view of the industry."[13]

The Paretian concept of economic rent has also been defined in terms of transfer earnings, conceived as the earnings in the next best alternative occupation. Thus Paul Samuelson talking about economic rent of a labourer says, "we should term the excess of his income above the alternative wage he could earn elsewhere as a *pure rent.*"[14] Likewise, according to George Stigler, the rent of a factor'is "the excess of its return in the best use over its possible return in other uses."[15]

Now, the question arises: what is the difference between the Ricardian and Paretian concepts of economic rent, that is, what is the difference between the payment necessary ***to induce a factor to work*** **and the payment necessary** ***to keep a factor in the present occupation.*** The difference is that while the first concept (Ricardian economic rent) is concerned with whether or not a factor is supplied to the *economy as a whole,* the Paretian concept of rent is concerned with the question as to whether or not the factor is supplied to a particular present occupation or particular industry. Thus, a labourer must be paid wages equal to the subsistence amount, otherwise he will die of starvation and will therefore be not available to the economy for employment. In this sense the payment to a labourer in excess of the subsistence amount is the rent. Similarly, land being free gift of nature, no payment is required to be paid to land to make it available to the economy for production. Therefore, in the Ricardian sense, all the earnings of land are economic rent. But in the Paretian concept of economic rent, the supply of land or any other factor to the economy or society as a whole is not considered, but their supply to a particular industry or occupation is considered and the factors are considered as having *several alternative uses,* that is, factors are capable of being employed in various alternative industries or occupations. Moreover, in this Paretian concept, a factor is assumed to be currently employed in the best occupation or industry, that is, the occupation or industry in which the factor earns maximum income. The earnings in the next best occupation or industry is called *transfer earnings* of the factor. The i***ncome received by the factor in its present occupation or industry in excess of its transfer earnings is therefore called*** rent.

10. *Ibid*, p. 103.
11. Frederick Benham, *Economics,* 6th edition (London), p. 227.
12. K.E. Boulding, The Concept of Economic Surplus, *American Economic Review,* vol. 35, December 1945.
13. *Economics of Imperfect Competition,* p. 104.
14. *Op. cit,* p. 110.
15. Paul Samuelson, *Economics, 8th* edition.

Both the Ricardian and the Paretian concepts of economic rent are useful but recently Paretian concept has gained more popularity among the economists and is generally considered to be of great analytical value. Thus, commenting on the Ricardian and the Paretian concepts of economic rent, Professor Shepherd writes, "But of what analytical value is it to know that most factor income is in excess of the amount that will deter the factor from complete economic inactivity ....The reason for this sterility is that the price that will trigger a decision to do anything rather than *nothing* does not imply enough information about either the venue of society's wants or the economy's production possibilities. Paretian opportunity costs, on the other hand, give society's valuation of alternatives foregone and imply thereby an extensive matrix of product and factor supply and demand relationships, in short, propositions about economic welfare involve factor allocation among industries (occupations and commodities), not simply factor allocation between idleness on the one hand and *any* socially useful activity on the other."[17]

It is clear from above that other factors of production, labour, capital, entrepreneurship may also be found to be earning economic rent when they are getting payment greater than what is required to induce them to work in the present industry or use. Thus, in modern economic theory, ***economic rent is not merely confined to land, it also refers to the surplus payments made to units of other factors over and above what is necessary to keep them in the present industry or use.*** Thus, the units of other factors may also earn economic rent.

Economic rent arises when the supply of a factor is less than perfectly elastic.

Boulding[18] arid Joan Robinson[19] emphasized that whenever the supply of factor units to an industry or economy is not perfectly elastic, a part of the earnings of factor will consist of surplus or economic rent, since the full price they get are not necessary to make all the factor units available. If the supply is not perfectly elastic, some factor units will be available at a price lower than the price they wiil actually receive, the difference between the actual price and the one necessary to make them available is surplus or economic rent. We shall now explain below the concept of economic rent with special reference to land and will bring out the conditions under which it arises.

As explained above, in the classical (Ricardian) theory, the rent was conceived as a payment made to a factor of production whose total supply was completely inelastic or fixed. When the total supply of a factor is completely fixed or inelastic no price is needed to be paid in order to induce it to be available for production. Land is the main example of the factor of production whose total supply is fixed and completely inelastic to the economy as a whole. This is because land is a free gift of nature and is non-reproducible. Thus supply of land cannot be increased when the demand for it and hence the price for its use rises. On the contrary, even if the price of its use falls to zero, the total supply of land will remain unaffected. Land is there in any case and does not require to be paid any price in order to exist and become available for production. To put it in other words, the transfer earnings of land for economy as a whole are zero. Thus, to Ricardo and other classical economists, ***the whole earnings of land are functionless surplus,*** that is, whatever price the land happens to earn is not required to be paid for it in order to keep it in existence or to make it available to the society. Therefore, they regarded

16. George Stigler, *The Theory of Price,* 2nd edition, p. 99.
17. A. Ross Shepherd, "Economic Rent and the Industry Supply Curve". *Southern Economic Journal,* October, 1971.
18. K. E. Boulding, The Concept of Economic Surplus, *American Economic Review,* vol. 35, Dec. 1945.
19. *Economics of Imperfect Competition,* Ch. 8.

the whole price or earnings of land as economic rent defined as the surplus payment over and above what is required to be paid to make it available to the society. Thus, the term rent which in ordinary usage means the price or payment for hiring of land came to be used by economists as the ***title for the surplus earnings which the land receives.***

Since the whole price or payment made to land is surplus earnings in the sense defined above, the rent as a price for the use of land and rent as surplus earnings of land have often been wrongly used interchangeable, since they are conceptually different. Fig. 55.4 illustrates that whole of the earnings of land are economic rent from the viewpoint of the society. Suppose *OS* is the amount of land available to the society. The society then confronts a perfectly inelastic supply curve *SS'* of land. This perfectly inelastic supply curve *SS'* indicates that even if the price for the use of land falls to zero, its supply remains *OS*. Thus, the transfer earnings of land are zero. Curve *DD'* represents the demand for land of the society as a whole. As a result of the intersection of demand and supply curves of land, the rental *OR* per unit for the use of land is determined. Since transfer earnings are zero, the whole price *OR* will be the economic rent earned per unit of land. The total earnings of land will be *ORES* and whole of these earnings of land will represent economic rent, since the transfer earnings are zero.

The whole earnings of a factor can be surplus only if its supply is perfectly inelastic because of its being a free gift of nature and society having incurred no cost to make it available for production. Therefore, ***economic rent has also been defined as a payment for any factor whose supply is perfectly inelastic.*** Thus, economic rent refers to the payment for the use of land and other natural resources since it is the supply of land and other natural resources which are permanently in fixed supply.

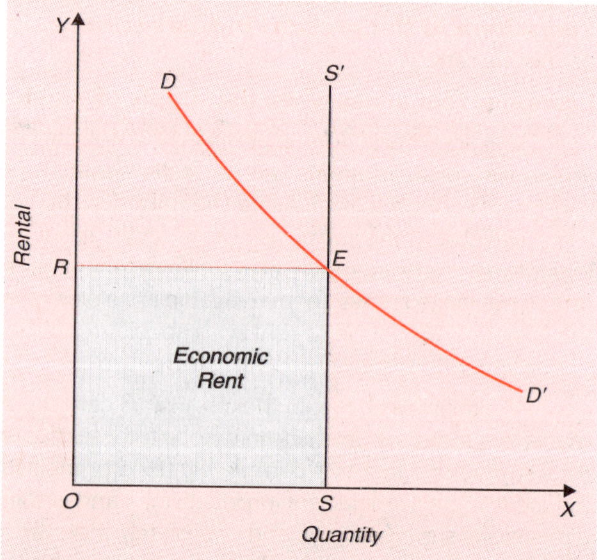

Fig. 55.4. *Whole Earnings are Economic Rent*

In the discussion of classical rent theory we have explained that economic rent arises due to the scarcity of land in relation to its demand. When the available supply of land is in plenty relative to its demand, there will be no price for its use and, therefore, no economic rent. Even the differential rents arise due to the scarcity. More fertile grades of land earn more rent because they are more scarce relative to their demand. So far, the modern economists are in complete agreement with Ricardo. The difference between Ricardo and modern economists arises due to the fact that whereas Ricardo considered the problem of land rent from the viewpoint of the economy or society as a whole, the modern economists also look at it from the standpoint of a particular industry (or use) and an individual producer. In Ricardian theory it is assumed that land is completely *specific* to the growing of one crop only, but in actual practice, land is used for the production of different competing crops.

According to the modern economists, it is only from die standpoint of the economy as a whole that land has perfectly inelastic supply. The supply of land for a particular use or industry is not perfectly inelastic. There are various uses or industries competing for the use of land. A unit of land being employed to produce a particular crop will be transferred to the production of other crops, if its earnings in the present use fall below the possible earnings in production of any other crop. It is therefore clear that from the viewpoint of a particular use or industry a payment has to be made for a unit of land so as to prevent it from being transferred to some other use or industry. *The payment or price which is necessary to keep a unit of factor (land in the present case) in a certain use or industry is called transfer earnings or transfer price,* because a payment or the price below this will cause it to be transferred elsewhere. Thus transfer earnings are the minimum earnings which must be paid to a unit of factor in order to induce it to remain in the present use or industry. The transfer earnings of a unit of a factor may also be defined as the amount of earnings which it can obtain in the next best alternative use, occupation or industry. This is because reduction in the earnings of a unit of factor in its present use, occupation or industry below its earnings in the next best alternative will cause it to transfer itself from the present use to its next best use. For instance, if a wheat growing industry has to keep land with it, then it must pay for the land at least its transfer earnings. Suppose, an acre of land currently employed in the production of wheat has its next best alternative of being used for the production of potato where it can earn ₹ 500. Thus, the transfer earnings of this acre of land is ₹ 500. Then, in order to keep this particular acre of land in the wheat industry, it must be paid at least ₹ 500, otherwise it will transfer itself to the potato growing industry. Now, if actually this acre of land is being paid ₹ 600 in the wheat industry, it will be earning economic rent of ₹ 100 which is the difference between actual earnings of ₹ 600 in the present use and its'transfer earnings of ₹ 500.

As the wheat industry uses more land, it will draw into it the land with successively higher supply prices. Thus, in Fig. 55.5, *A*th unit of land has a supply price equal to *AQ*. In other words, *AQ* must be paid to the *A*th unit of land in order to keep it in the wheat industry. Thus *AQ* represents the transfer earnings of *A*th unit of land. Similarly, *B*th unit of land must be paid *BR*, if it is to be attracted into or retained in the wheat industry. *BR* is therefore the transfer earnings of the *B*th unit of land. Likewise, transfer earnings of *C*th, *D*th, *E*th, *F*th and *G*th units of land are *CT, DU, EV, FW* and *GN* respectively. Demand curve *DD* of wheat industry for land and supply curve *SS* of land to it intersect at point *N* and thus determine *OP* as the price for the use of land.

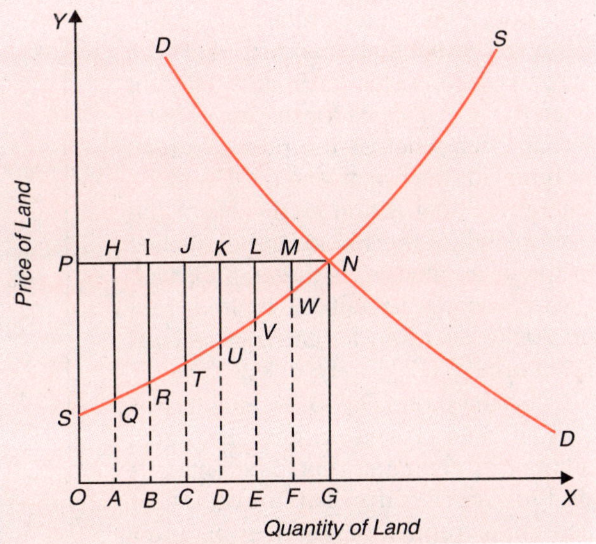

Fig. 55.5. *When the supply curve is less than perfectly elastic, a part of the earnings is economic rent and a part transfer earnings.*

Suppose all units of land are equally productive in respect of wheat production. Then all acres of land will get the same price as determined by demand of land for wheat production and supply of land to it. But if various units of land are *different in respect of other uses,* they will have different transfer earnings or different supply prices to the wheat industry, that is, they need to be paid different prices to attract them to the wheat industry. The units of land having larger earnings in other uses will need to be paid higher prices to attract them to the wheat industry and those with smaller earnings in the other uses will be required to be paid relatively smaller prices to draw them into the wheat industry. Under such conditions, therefore, the supply curve of land to the wheat industry will be upward sloping, as is shown by the curve *SS* in Fig. 55.5 indicating that price for the use of land determined is *OP* and *OG* is the equilibrium amount of land employed in the wheat industry.

It will be seen from Fig. 55.5 that Gth is the marginal unit of land employed in the wheat industry and further that the price *OP* per unit of wheat land is equal to transfer earnings *GN* of the marginal unit Gth of land. But, since we are assuming that all units of land are identical, *i.e.*, equally productive in respect of wheat, every unit of land employed in the wheat industry must get *OP* as the price for its use. Thus intra-marginal units, *A, B, C, D, E, F* will also be paid *OP* as the price for their use in wheat industry. But, it will be seen that whereas the price *OP* is equal to the transfer earnings of the marginal unit *G*, it is greater than the transfer earnings of the intra-marginal units, *A, B, C, D, E,* and *F.* That is to say, these intra-marginal units of land are paid by the wheat industry in excess of their transfer earnings. Thus, while the marginal unit of land employed in the wheat industry, that is, unit *G* does not earn any economic rent, the intra-marginal units of land will earn economic rent which will be equal to the price or earnings they get in the wheat industry minus their transfer earnings. Thus, *A*th unit of land obtains price *AH* (= *OP*) while its transfer earnings are only *AQ*. Therefore, *A*th unit of land earns *QH* as economic rent (*QH* = *AH* – *AQ*). Likewise, the economic rent earned by the *B*th, *C*th, *D*th, *E*th and *F*th units of land will equal to *RI, TJ, UK, VL* and *WM* respectively.

The total transfer earnings of the whole amount *OG* of land employed in the wheat industry is *OSNG*—the *area* under the supply curve up to point *G*. The total actual earnings made by the whole amount *OG* of land is *OPNG,* that is, the price *OP* multiplied by *OG*. The toal economic rent earned by the whole amount *OG* of land employed in the wheat industry is, therefore, the area *SNP* which is equal to the whole earnings *OPNG* minus the transfer earnings *OSNG*. It is now clear that whereas in the case of society as a whole, the whole earnings of land represents a surplus or economic rent, from the viewpoint of a single industry or use, a part of the earnings are transfer earnings (which must be paid in order to retain the land in the given use or industry) and only the remaining amount of earnings (*i.e.*, surplus over transfer earnings) represents economic rent.

Furthermore, a careful study of Fig. 55.5 will reveal that economic rent as a surplus over transfer earnings is different from the rent as price for the use of land. In Fig. 55.5 whereas the price per unit) or rental for the use of land is *OP* and the total price (that is, the total rent for the use of land) of the whole land employed in the given industry is the area *OPNG,* the total economic rent (*i.e*, the total rent as surplus over transfer earnings) earned is the area *SNP.*

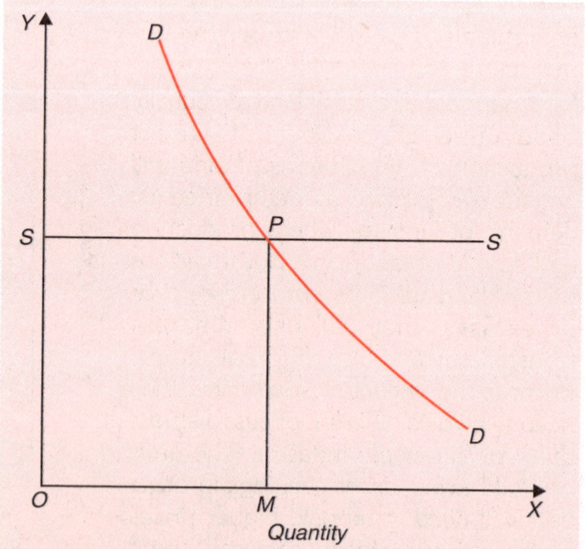

Fig. 55.6. *No economic rent is earned when the supply of a factor is perfectly elastic.*

Furthermore, Fig 55.5 makes it clear that all units of land do not earn equal amounts of economic rent; different units of land earn different amounts of economic rent depending upon their transfer earnings. Thus, economic rent earned by *A*th unit is *QH, B*th unit is *RI,*

Cth unit is *TJ* and so on. It should be noted that these differences in economic rent earned by different units of land are not due to the differences in their productivity in respect of wheat but due to the differences in their ability to earn in their next best uses.

When the supply of a factor is perfectly elastic, no economic rent is earned. Now, suppose that all units of land used in the wheat industry are not only identical in respect of wheat production but are also identical in respect of all other uses. In such circumstances, each unit of land employed in the wheat industry will have the same transfer earnings and therefore the supply curve of land for the wheat industry will be perfectly elastic as shown by *SS* curve in Figure 55.6. In this, therefore, the transfer earnings of every unit of land employed in the wheat industry is *OS*. In other words, every unit of land need to be paid equal to *OS* in order to retain it in the wheat industry. It will be seen in Figure 55.6 that price per unit for the use of land in the wheat industry as determined by demand for and supply of land in the wheat industry is also *OS*. Thus, every unit of land in the wheat industry gets *OS* and its transfer earnings is also *OS*. Therefore, in this case no unit of land in the wheat industry earns more than its transfer earnings, *i.e.*, no unit of land in the wheat'industry earns any economic rent. It is, therefore, ***clear that when the supply of any factor is perfectly elastic to an industry no unit of this factor will earn any economic rent.*** Further, it has been seen above, that whereas to the economy or society as a whole, the supply of land is perfectly inelastic and, therefore, the whole of its earnings are *economic rent,* the supply of land to an industry (the wheat industry in the above case) may be perfectly elastic and therefore earns no economic rent at all.

We have seen above that under certain circumstances some units of land from the viewpoint of industry may earn economic rent, *i.e.*, earnings in excess of their transfer earnings, and under some other conditions, land may not earn any economic rent at all. The same kind of analysis can be made for other factors as well. As pointed out above, the concept of ***economic rent is not merely confined to land, it applies to other factors of production as well. Thus labour, capital and entrepreneurs may also be earning economic rent when their supplies are less than perfectly elastic.*** Thus, consider the supply of a particular kind of workers in a given industry, all of which are being paid a certain uniform wage rate by the industry. But all these workers may be heterogeneous from the point of view of the other industries. As a result of this, they would have different transfer earnings and the supply curve of this kind of workers will be upward sloping (*i.e.*, less than perfectly elastic). Since all workers are getting the same wage rate in the industry which is determined by demand and supply, those workers whose transfer earnings are less than the wage rate will be getting economic rent or surplus. It will be seen from Fig. 55.7 that only the marginal (*i.e.*, *L*th worker) employed would not be obtaining any economic surplus or rent whereas all the intra-marginal units of labour before *L*th unit will be earning economic rent. In Fig. 55.7 the total economic rent earned by all the *intra-marginal* workers is equal to *WES*.

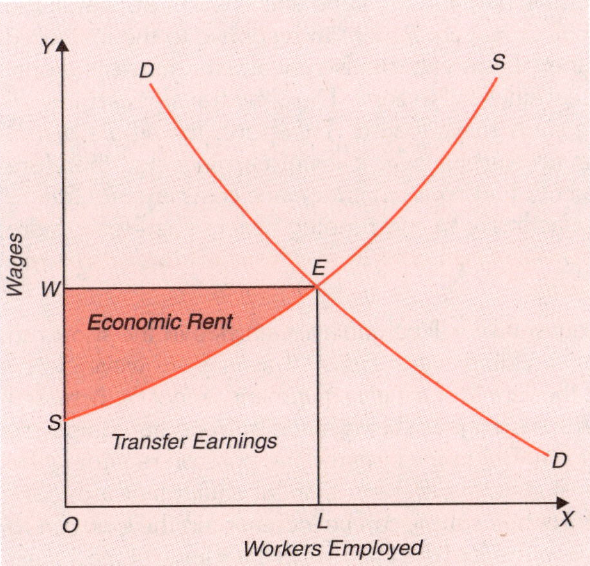

Fig. 55.7. *Economic Rent of Workers*

Likewise, entrepreneurs may be able to earn different amounts of profits in different industries. An entrepreneur will work in the industry in which he is able to get the greatest amount of profits and if his profits fall below a certain level, he will shift himself to the next best industry. But the additional amount of profits which he is able to earn in an industry over and above his transfer earnings (thats is, the profits in the next best profitable industry) are surplus or economic rent from the point of the given industry.

Similarly, a particular kind of capital equipment is not equally efficient from the viewpoint of all industries. It will therefore earn higher income for which it is best suited and will therefore earn over and above the necessary income that is required to keep that in the industry. This additional income, which owner of the capital equipment will get, will be economic rent from the standpoint of that industry. We thus see that all factors under certain circumstances may earn economic rent. But this economic rent will be different if we consider their supply from the standpoint of the economy as a whole than from the standpoint of the individual industry.

QUASI-RENT

The concept of quasi-rent was introduced in economic theory by Marshall. Marshall's concept of quasi-rent is the extension of the Ricardian concept of rent to the short-run earnings of the capital equipment (such as machinery, buildings etc.) which are in inelastic supply in the short run. The distinguishing characteristic of land is the fact that its supply is perfectly inelastic to changes in its price and therefore its earnings depend mainly upon the demand for it. But, in the short run, the fixed capital equipment such as machinery is likewise perfectly inelastic in supply and cost of its production is not relevant once it has been produced. During the short period, the earnings of specialized capital equipment depend mainly upon the demand conditions and are thus similar to land rent and have therefore been called rent by Marshall. Since the capital equipment is not permanently in fixed supply like land and instead their supply is very much elastic in the long run, Marshall preferred to call their earnings in the short period as quasi-rent rather than rent.

The quasi-rent is only a temporary surplus which is enjoyed by the owner of the capital equipment in the short run due to the increase in demand for it and which will disappear in the long run due to the increase in the supply of capital equipment in response to the increased demand. In the short run, specialized machinery has no alternative use and therefore its supply will remain fixed in the short run even if its earnings fall to zero. Thus, the transfer earnings of the capital equipment or machinery in the short run are zero. Therefore, the *whole of the earnings* of the machinery in the short run are surplus over transfer earnings and therefore represent rent. It may, however, be pointed out that some maintenance costs are required to be incurred in the short run to keep the machinery in the running order. Therefore, more precisely, the quasi-rent may be defined as ***'the short-run earnings of a machine minus the short-run cost of keeping it in running order."***

There is every reason to believe that quasi-rent will be generally earned in the short run by the capital equipment like machinery, buildings etc. This is because, however keen competition between entrepreneurs may be, the supply of capital equipment cannot be increased in the short run. Consequently, when very high earnings are being made from capital equipment they will not be competed away in the short run. But in the long run the position regarding the supply of capital equipment *(e.g.,* machines) is quite different. Capital equipment are man-made instruments of production and therefore their supply can be increased in the long run to meet the increased demand for them. Thus, as a result of the increase in the supply of machines, their excessive earnings will be competed away. In the long run, therefore, the competitive equilibrium is reached when the earnings from the capital equipment are just sufficient to maintain them in running order and provide only normal profits to entrepreneur. Thus, in the long run no surplus over cost of production is earned by the machines. Therefore, quasi-rent will disappear in the long-run competitive equilibrium. Professors Stonier and Hague rightly remark, "The supply of machines is fixed in the short run whether they are paid much money or little so they earn a kind of rent. In the long run this rent disappears for it is not a true rent, but only an ephemeral reward—a 'quasi-rent'."[20]

But the case of land is quite different. The supply of land being a free gift of nature and non-reproducible, its supply is perfectly inelastic in the short run as well as in the long run. Thus the surplus earnings or rent earned by land persist in the long run also. It is thus clear that the earnings of land and of capital equipment (machines etc.) are similar only in the short run. The analogy between the two does not hold in the long run because of the difference in the nature of their long-run supply. To quote Professors Stonier and Hague again, "In the long period, machines will stand on a very different footing from land or natural ability. For machines are produced by human effort whilst land or human ability are gift of nature. In the long run, therefore, the supply of land will not respond to an increase in demand for it, the supply of machines will. In the long run, therefore, land will earn rent but machines will, assuming competition, earn only just enough to make their existence worthwhile."[21]

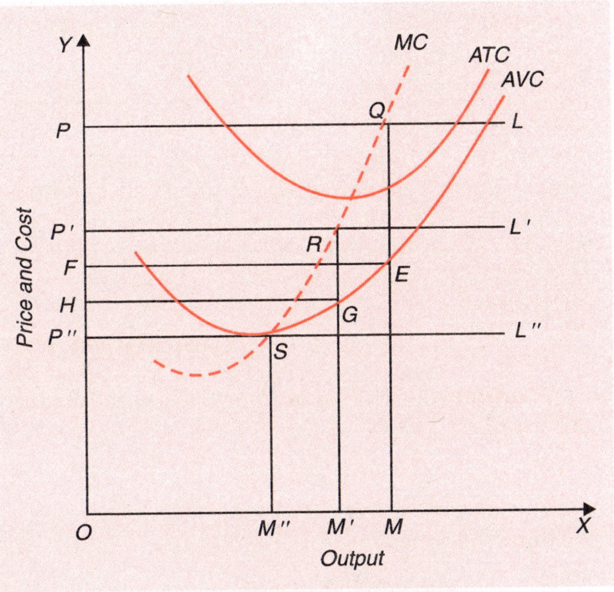

Fig. 55.8. Quasi-Rent

Production of a good is possible when a fixed factor is combined with some variable factors. The amount of variable factors used depends upon the level of output produced, while the quantity of the fixed factor remains unchanged during the short period. The variable costs must be recovered in the short run, otherwise the production would be stopped. Whatever excess earnings over and above the total variable costs are made are ascribed to the machines (*i.e.*, fixed factor). Therefore, quasi-rent has also been defined as the excess of total revenue earned in the short run over and above the total variable costs. Thus,

Quasi-Rent= Total Revenue Earned – Total Variable Costs

Since in the long run, all costs are variable and, in long-run competitive equilibrium, total receipts are equal to total costs (including normal profits to the entrepreneur), no excess earnings over and above the costs will accrue to the machines and therefore no quasi-rent will be earned by the machines. The earning of quasi-rent in the short run and its disappearance in the long run is illustrated in Fig. 55.8 whereas, as usual, output is measured on the X-axis and price and cost of output are measured on the Y-axis. *ATC* and *AVC* represent the average total cost and average variable cost curves respectively in the short run. It should be noted that

20. A. W. Stonier and B.C. Hague : *A Textbook of Economic Theory,* fourth edition, p. 329.
21. *Op. cif.*,p. 292.

the average variable costs, *AVC*, includes the cost incurred per unit of output on the variable factors such as labour, raw material etc. as well as the cost per unit of output for keeping the machinery in the working order during the short period. (As said above, the cost of maintaining the machinery in the working order during the short period is a part of the variable costs.)

Now suppose that the demand for the product is such that the price *OP* is determined. With price of the product *OP*, the price line faced by an individual entrepreneur is *PL* which represents the marginal revenue as well as the average revenue. With price line *PL*, the entrepreneur is in equilibrium at point *Q* and is producing *OM* level of output. It will be seen from the figure that the total revenue earned is *OMQP*, while total variable costs incurred is *OMEF*. The area *FEQP* represents the surplus of total revenue earned over total variable costs (*FEQP* = *OMQP* – *OMEF*). Thus *FEQP* is quasi-rent, that is, the short-run earnings of the machinery.

If now the demand for the product declines so that the price for the product falls to *OP* ′. With price *OP* ′, the price line is *P* ′*L*′ and equilibrium of the entrepreneur is at point *R* with output *OM* ′. Now the total revenue earned is *OM* ′*RP* ′ and the total variable cost is *OM* ′*GH*. Thus the quasi-rent earned by the machinery is now *HGRP* ′ (*HGRP* ′ = *OM* ′*RP* – *OM* ′*GH*). If the demand for the product further declines and the price falls to *OP* ″, the price line confronting the entrepreneur will be *P* ″*L*″ and he will be in equilibrium position at point *S*–the minimum point of the curve *AVC*. At point *S*, the total revenue earned is just equal to the total variable costs and the quasi-rent earned by the machinery has thus fallen to zero. The entrepreneur will close down production if the price falls below *OP* ″, for at a price below *OP* ″, it will not be realising fully even the variable costs. It is therefore clear that the quasi-rent cannot be negative.

NUMERICAL PROBLEM

Problem. *A big Indian Pharma Company Ranbaxy has a demand for specialised labour which is given by*

$$W = 80 - 0.1\, L_d$$

where w is wage rate and L_d is quantity demanded of labour. The supply L_s of the specialised labour to the company is completely inelastic at a level of 400

(*i*) *Draw the demand curve for labour and determine the equilibrium wage and the element of economic rent in that wage.*

(*ii*) *If the supply function for specialised labour for the company takes a normal upward-sloping form and is given by $W = 20 + 0.5\, L_s$, calculate the new equilibrium wage and the element of economic rent in it. Illustrate graphically.*

Solution. (*i*) To draw the demand curve of labour representing the given labour demand function ($W = 80 - 0.1\, L_d$) we need to know where the labour demand curve cuts the wage axis (*i.e.* *Y*-axis). It will cut the wage axis when labour used is zero. This can therefore be obtained by substituting $L_d = 0$ in the given demand function for labour. Thus $W = 80 - 0.1\,(0) = 80$. We therefore mark 80 on the *Y*-axis on which wage rate is measured.

Now, the given labour demand curve will cut the *X*-axis on which the quantity of labour demanded is measured when wage rate (*W*) is zero. Therefore, by substituting zero for *W* in the given demand function we have

$$0 = 80 - 0.1L$$

$$0.1L = 80$$

$$L = 80 \times \frac{10}{1} = 800$$

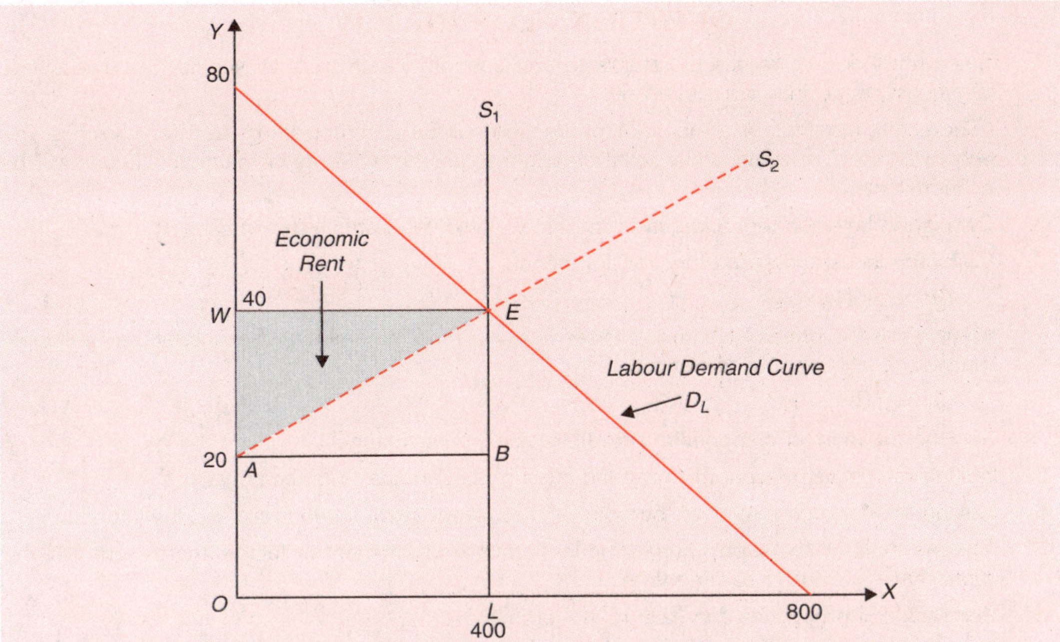

Fig. 55.9. *Equilibrium Wage and Employment, and Economic Rent*

We therefore mark 800 on the *X*-axis. By joining 800 on the *X*-axis with 80 on the *Y*-axis we get the demand for labour curve D_L. Since it is given that labour supply curve is perfectly inelastic at 400 and in equilibrium, $L_d = L_s$, we can get equilibrium wage rate by substituting labour-supply equal to 400 in labour-demand function. Thus

$$W = 80 - 0.1(400) = 80 - \frac{1}{10} \times 400 = 40$$

With 400 workers employed and ₹ 40 as wage rate, the total earnings of workers will be 40 × 400 = ₹ 16,000 or area *OLEW* in Figure 55.90. Since labour supply is perfectly inelastic at the level of 400, the transfer earnings in the present case is zero, the entire earnings of ₹ 16,000 or the entre area *OLEW* represents economic rent.

(*ii*) When the supply function takes the form $W = 20 + 0.1L$, we find the equilibrium level of employment by equating the given demand labour function with the new supply function. Thus

$$80 - 0.1L = 20 + 0.05L$$
$$0.15L = 80 - 20 = 60$$
$$L = 60 \times \frac{100}{15} = 400$$

Thus with new supply curve also, the equilibrium employment is 400 workers and given the same demand function, ₹ 40 will be the equilibrium wage. However, since the new supply curve S_2 starts from 20 on the *Y*-axis and crosses equilibrium point *E* corresponding to equilibrium wage rate of ₹ 40 the transfer earnings of labour with this will be the area *OAEL* whereas the total earnings are *OLEW*. Thus the area $AEW = \frac{1}{2}(20 \times 400) =$ ₹ 4000 which is half of the area *ABEW* represents economic rent in the present case.

QUESTIONS FOR REVIEW

1. Since rents do not represent returns to any economic activity, they should be taxed away. Would you treat quasi-rents similarly ?
2. "The actual earnings of a factor of production will be a composite of transfer earnings and economic rent". Explain under what conditions can the whole price paid to a factor will be economic rent.
3. Distinguish between rent and quasi-rent. How would you justify a tax on each of them?
4. Given the industry demand function for labour

   $$Q_L^D = 800 - 15P_L$$

   where P_L is the price of labour in rupees per day. Find the amount of economic rent if supply function of labour to the industry is

   $$Q_L^S = 50P_L + 50$$

   Assume that perfect competition prevails in the labour market.
5. Distinguish between economic rent and quasi-rent. Can quasi rent be negative ?
6. Distinguish between rent from the point of view of the firm, the industry and the economy.
7. The more elastic the supply curve, the less amount of payment to factors that is rent and the more that is a transfer earning. Explain.
8. Any factor of production can earn rent. Comment.
9. Distinguish between transfer earnings and economic rent of a factor. What proportion of total income of a factor would be economic rent if it has (1) a fully elastic supply curve, (2) a fully inelastic supply curve?

CHAPTER

56

Theories of Interest

Introduction

Having now discussed the determination of rent of land and wages of labour, we now pass on to the study of the theory of interest. Interest is a reward for capital. But there are two concepts of capital: physical capital and money or financial capital. Accordingly, there are two concepts of interest. One concept of interest is ***the real rate of interest*** which is the *rate of return* on physical capital such as machine, vehicle, tractor created for the purpose of producing more goods. A capital asset is used for production for several years and yields a stream of return over the years. A rate of return on it is obtained by calculating the present discounted value of the yields earned over the number of years for which capital asset is used for production.

The second concept of interest is the price paid for the use of borrowed funds from other and is often called ***money rate*** of interest. These funds are mainly used for investment in physical capital but they may also be used for consumption purposes. It is worth noting that money rate of interest is intimately related to the rate of return on physical capital. When the rate of return on a physical asset, that is, the real rate of interest, is higher than the market money rate of interest, then there will be greater investment in capital with the result that the rate of return on capital will fall. The equilibrium will be established when the rate of return becomes equal to the money rate of interest.

Classical economists have visualised interest as marginal productivity of physical capital but since physical capital has to be purchased with monetary funds, rate of interest becomes the rate of return over money invested in physical capital. As money to be invested in physical capital has to be saved by someone, interest also becomes the price for abstinence or waiting or time preference involved in the act of saving and lending it to others for investment in capital. There has been no complete agreement among the classical economists about the nature of interest. Some of them explained interest from the standpoint of the supply side, that is, savings, and therefore emphasized the role of abstinence, or waiting or time preference in the determination of interest. On the other hand, Knight and J.B. Clark explained the phenomenon of interest only from the viewpoint of the demand for capital and laid stress on the productivity of capital as a determining factor of interest. Irving Fisher, Bohm-Bawerk and some others explained the nature and determination of interest taking into account both the time preference (working on the supply side) and the productivity of capital (working on the demand side). It is evident that the classical economists emphasized the role of real factors such as thrift (*i.e.,* abstinence or waiting), time preference and productivity of capital in the determination of interest. Therefore, the classical theory is also known as *real theory* of interest.

On the other hand, neo-classical economists such as Wicksell, Ohlin, Haberler, Robertson, Viner etc. developed what is known as Loanable Funds or Neo-Classical Theory of interest.

These writers saw the interplay of monetary and non-monetary forces in the determination of the rate of interest. At their hands, interest theory ceased to be purely real or non-monetary theory. In their view, monetary factors along with the real factors determine the rate of interest. In a way loanable funds theory is a monetary theory of interest.

But monetary theory gained more recognition with the publication of Keynes' *General Theory*. According to Keynes, interest is purely a monetary phenomenon and as such it is determined by the demand for money (*i.e.*, liquidity preference) and the supply of money. According to him, *interest is a price not for the sacrifice of waiting or time preference but for parting with liquidity*. Since he emphasized the role of liquidity preference in the determination of the interest rate, his theory is known as ***liquidity preference*** theory of interest. Keynesian theory is purely a ***monetary theory.***

Some modern economists such as J.R. Hicks, A.P. Lerner and A.H. Hansen have brought about a synthesis between the classical and neo-classical theories on the one hand and Keynesian liquidity preference theory on the other. We shall discuss all these theories of interest in this chapter. It is worth noting that all these theories of interest seek to explain the determination of the rate of interest through the equilibrium between the forces of demand and supply. In other words, all these theories are ***demand and supply theories.*** The difference between the various theories of interest lies in the answer to the question : *demand for what and supply of what?* According to the classical theory, rate of interest is determined by *demand for savings to make investment and the supply of savings*. Loanable-funds theory seeks to explain the determination of the rate of interest through the equilibrium between *demand for and supply of loanable funds*. Besides savings, loanable funds consist of funds derived from other sources as well. Keynesian theory of interest explains the determination of interest through the equilibrium between the demand *for and supply of money*.

Another point worth mentioning is that a theory of interest has to explain two things. First, why does interest arise ? Secondly, how the rate of interest is determined ? All the three theories mentioned above explain both these aspects of interest.

CLASSICAL THEORY OF INTEREST

As has been mentioned above, this theory seeks to explain the determination of the rate of interest through the interaction of the demand for savings to make investment and the supply of savings. Since this theory explains the determination of the rate of interest by real forces such as thrift, time preference and productivity of capital, it is also called the *real theory* of interest. Various classical writers differ a good deal from each other in respect of their views about interest. Some of them laid emphasis on the forces governing the supply of savings. Thus they considered interest as a price for abstinence or waiting or time preference. Some others like J.B. Clark and Knight thought the marginal productivity of capital, which is a force that operates on the demand for savings, determines the rate of interest.

Fisher and Bohm-Bawerk explained the interest with both types of factors. There is a basic assumption that is common to all classical writers. It is that all of them assume full employment of resources. In other words, in their models if more resources are to be devoted to investment, that is, to the production of capital goods, some resources have to be withdrawn from the production of consumer goods.

According to this theory, money which is lent out to the entrepreneurs for investment in capital goods is to be made available by those who save out of their incomes. By abstaining from consumption they release resources for the production of capital goods. In order to induce people to save and refrain from consuming a part of their incomes, they must be offered some interest as a reward. To persuade them to save more, the higher rate of interest has to be offered. So far the various classical economists agreed but they differed in detail about the nature of interest. We shall discuss below the views of some of them.

Interest is a price for abstinence or waiting. It was Nasau Senior who first pointed out that saving involved a sacrifice of abstinence and interest is a price for this sacrifice. Any one who saves some money and is therefore able to lend it to others abstains from consuming a part of his income and in order to induce him to do so, he must be paid interest by the borrower. Thus, according to Senior, interest arises because of the abstinence involved in the act of saving. Without giving him the interest as compensation, the individuals will not like to undergo the sacrifice of abstaining from consumption. The idea of abstinence was criticised by some economists, in particular by Karl Marx, who pointed out that the rich people who are the main source of savings are able to save without making any real sacrifice of abstinence. They save because something is left over after they have indulged in consumption to their heart's desire. In order to avoid this criticism Marshall substituted the word *waiting* for "abstinence". According to him, when a person saves money and lends it to others, he does not abstain from consumption for all time ; he merely postpones consumption. But the individual who lends his savings has to wait until he gets back the money. Thus, the person who saves money and lends it to others undergoes the sacrifice of waiting. To induce people to save and wait some price has to be paid to them as compensation for making this sacrifice. According to this view, interest is a price for waiting.

Bohm-Bawerk's explanation of interest. The Austrian economist Bohm-Bawerk put forward another explanation of interest. According to him, interest arises because people prefer present goods to future goods of the same kind and quantity and, therefore, there is an agio, or premium on present goods as compared to future goods. People prefer present enjoyment to future enjoyment. In other words, future satisfaction when viewed from the present undergoes a discount. Interest is this discount which must be paid in order to induce people to lend money and therefore postpone present satisfaction to a future date. Bohm-Bawerk gave three reasons for the emergence of rate of interest. First, people have relatively greater needs or demands for goods in the present than in the future. In other words, present wants are felt more keenly than the future wants. As a result, demand for goods is greater in the present than in the future. The second reason advanced by Bohm-Bawerk is that people *underestimate future wants.* People underestimate future wants because (*i*) they lack imagination and therefore cannot judge the intensity of their future wants, (*ii*) they lack will and cannot resist the temptation of satisfying present wants and therefore undervalue their future wants, and (*iii*) the future is uncertain so that they think that they may or may not live to satisfy future wants. In view of all these, people prefer the satisfaction of present wants to future wants. Bohm-Bawerk describes this as an 'underestimate of future wants' which, according to him, is systematic irrationality.

Third reason for the emergence of interest given by Bohm-Bawerk is what he calls "technical superiority of present over future goods". This is so because the present goods can be used so as to make capital which involves roundabout and time-consuming methods of production and is more productive. Because of the greater productivity of capital, people prefer to have present goods which can be used as capital so that they have more goods in the future. They are therefore prepared to pay a premium or agio on the present goods as against future goods and this gives rise to interest.

Interest is paid because of time preference (Fisher's Theory). Irving Fisher, an eminent American economist, largely accepted Bohm-Bawerk's views about the nature of interest except that he criticised Bohm-Bawerk's third ground for interest, that is, the technical superiority of present over future goods. Fisher lays greater emphasis on time preference as a cause of interest. But along with time preference he also considered the role of marginal productivity of capital for which he used the term ***'rate of return over cost'*** as a factor that determines interest.

Rate of interest arises because people prefer present satisfaction to future satisfaction. They are therefore impatient to spend their incomes in the present. According to Fisher, interest is a compensation for the time preference of the individual. The greater the impatience to spend money in the present, that is, the greater the preference of individuals for the present enjoyment of goods to future enjoyment of them, the higher will have to be the rate of interest to induce them to lend money.

The degree of impatience to spend income in the present depends upon the size of the income, the distribution of income over time, the degree of certainty regarding enjoyment in the future and the temperament and character of the individual. The people whose incomes are large are likely to have their present wants more fully satisfied. Therefore, these rich people will discount the future at a relatively lower rate of interest (that is, their time preference will be less) and will be required to be paid a relatively lower rate of interest. As regards distribution of income over time, three kinds of situation are possible. The income may be uniform throughout one's life or may increase with age or decrease with age. If it is uniform, the degree of impatience to spend in the present will be determined by the size of the income and the temperament of the individual. If the income increases with age, it means the future is well provided for and the degree of impatience to spend money in the present (that is, time preference) will be greater. On the other hand, if the income decreases with age, the degree of impatience to spend money at present will be less.

As regards certainty of enjoyment in the future, if the individual is sure of enjoyment of income in the future, other things remaining the same, the impatience to spend money in the present will be less, that is, the degree of time preference will be smaller. Finally, the character and the temperament of the individual will also determine his time preference. A man of foresight will be less impatient to spend income in the present, that is, his rate of time preference will be less as compared to that of a spendthrift. The rate of time preference is also influenced by expectation of life. If a man expects to live long, his preference for spending income in the present will be comparatively low.

It is clear from the above analysis that Fisher, like Bohm-Bawerk, regarded the rate of interest as an agio on the present goods exchanged for future goods of the same kind. Fisher based his explanation of the rate of interest on his concept of income. According to him, interest is the link between expected future income values and the present capital values based on them. He says, "The value of the orchard depends upon the value of its crops and in this dependence lurks implicitly the rate of interest itself. The statement that 'capital produces income' is true only in the physical sense, it is not true in the value sense. On the contrary, income value produces capital value."[1]

As said above, Fisher also regarded productivity of capital which he first called *'rate of return over sacrifice'* and later ***'rate of return over cost,'*** as a determinant of interest. According to him, several different uses of capital which may yield different income streams are open to the owner of capital. He has to decide about the investment of his capital. The greater the expected income stream from use of capital, the greater will be the rate of interest. Another point worth mentioning is that Fisher introduced risk and uncertainly in his explanation of interest. According to him, individual has a choice of any *one* of a number of uncertain income streams so that instead of a single rate of interest representing the rate of exchange between

1. Irving Fisher, *Rate of Interest* (1907), p. 13.

this year and next year we now find a great variety of rates according to the risks involved.

Determination of the Rate of Interest in the Classical Theory

According to the classical theory of interest, rate of interest is determined by the supply of savings and demand for savings to invest. We have explained above the forces working on the side of supply of saving. Some classical economists laid stress on the abstinence or waiting involved in the act of savings and supply of them and some others emphasized the role of time preference as a determinant of the supply of savings. According to this theory, the money which is to be used for purchasing capital goods is made available by those who save from their current income. By postponing consumption a part of their income they release resources for the production of capital goods. It is assumed in this theory that savings are interest elastic. The higher the rate of interest, the more the savings which people will be induced to make. Besides, at higher rate of interest, savings would be forthcoming from those persons whose rates of time preference are more strongly weighed in favour of present satisfaction. The supply curve of savings will therefore slope upward to the right.

On the other hand, the demand for savings comes from the entrepreneurs or firms which desire to invest in capital goods. Capital goods are demanded because they can be used to produce further goods which can be sold to earn income. Thus capital goods have a revenue productivity like all other factors. For any given type of capital asset, *e.g.,* a machine, it is possible to draw a marginal revenue productivity curve showing the addition made to total revenue by an additional unit of a machine at various levels of the stock of that machine.

As said above, like other factors of production, capital has marginal revenue productivity. But the marginal revenue productivity of capital is a more complex concept than that of other factors because capital has a life of many years. A capital asset continues to yield returns for many years. But the future is quite uncertain. Therefore, the entrepreneurs have to judge the uncertainties of the future and estimate prospective yield or income from a capital asset after making allowance for maintenance and operating costs. In other words, they have to find out the *net expected return* of a capital asset. This net expected return is expressed as percentage of the cost of capital asset. The more capital assets of a given kind there are, the less income will be expected to accrue from a marginal unit of it. Therefore, the marginal revenue productivity curve of capital slopes downward to the right.

We have seen in the previous chapters that a firm under perfectly competitive factor market will hire a factor up to the point at which the price of that factor equals the marginal revenue productivity of the factor. The marginal revenue productivity from a capital asset can be regarded as marginal revenue productivity from the money invested in that capital asset. The *price* of money invested in capital assets is the rate of interest which a person has to pay on the borrowed funds. An entrepreneur will continue making investment in capital assets as long as the expected net rate of return, or in other words, marginal revenue productivity of capital or investment is grater than the rate of interest. Since the marginal revenue productivity curve of capital slopes downward, it will become profitable to purchase more capital goods as the rate of interest falls, *i.e.,* with the fall in the rate of interest more money will be demanded for investment. Thus, the investment demand curve relating the rate of interest with the investment demand will be downward sloping. In other words, investment demand is assumed to be interest-elastic.

The way in which the investment demand increases as the interest falls is illustrated in Fig. 56.1 where *II* is the investment demand curve showing the falling marginal revenue product of capital indicating the declining marginal net expected return as more investment is undertaken.

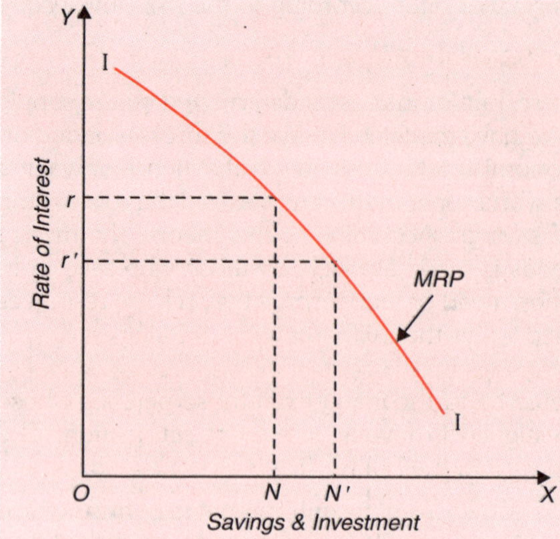

Fig. 56.1. *Investment Demand Curve*

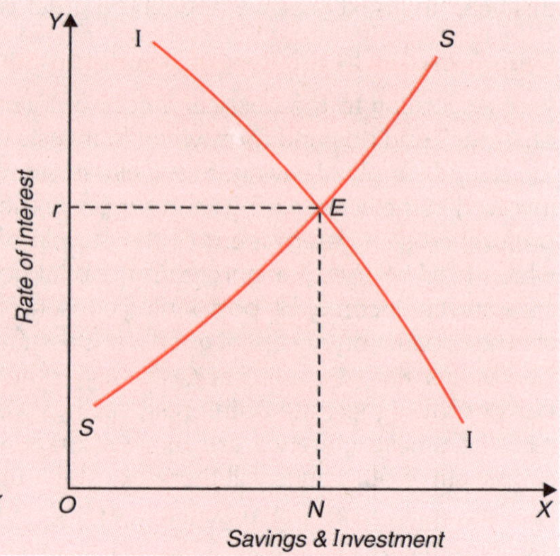

Fig. 56.2. *Classical Theory: Determination of Interest*

When rate of interest is *Or*, the entrepreneurs will make investment up to *ON*, for the marginal net expected return is equal to *Or* rate of interest when *ON* is the investment. If the rate of interest falls to *Or*′, then more capital projects will become profitable to be undertaken. Therefore, as a result of fall in rate of interest to *Or*′, investment increases to *ON*′.

It is clear from the above analysis that investment demand curve slopes downward to the right. With the change in rate of interest, investment will change.

Equilibrium between Demand and Supply. As seen above, according to the classical theory, the rate ot interest is determined by the intersection of the investment demand curve and the supply of savings curve—the curves showing the relation of investment and savings to the rate of interest. The way in which the rate of interest is determined by the intersection of investment demand and supply of savings is depicted in Fig. 56.2 where *II* is the investment demand curve and *SS* is the supply curve of savings. Investment demand curve *II* and the supply of savings curve *SS* intersect at point *E* and thereby determine *Or* as the equilibrium rate of interest. In this equilibrium position, *ON* is the amount of savings and investment. If any change in the demand for investment and supply of savings occur, the curves will shift accordingly and therefore the equilibrium rate of interest will also change.

Critical Appraisal of the Classical Theory of Interest

Classical theory of interest has been criticised on several grounds. J.M. Keynes made a strong attack on this theory and propounded a new theory of interest called liquidity preference theory. We shall consider below the various criticisms levelled against the classical theory of interest.

Full Employment Assumption. Classical theory of interest has been criticised for its assumption of fulf employment of resources which is said to be unrealistic. In the case of full employment of resources, more investment (*i.e.*, production of more capital goods) can take place only by curtailing consumption and thereby releasing resources from the production of consumption goods. Therefore, when full-employment of resources prevails, people have to be paid interest so as to induce them to abstain from consumption so that more resources should be devoted to the production of capital goods. But, when unemployed resources are found on a large scale there is no need for paying people to abstain from consumption or to postpone consumption and wait in order that more savings and investment should take place. More investment then can be undertaken by using unemployed or unutilized productive resources. Prof. Dillard rightly remarks : "Within the framework of a system of theory built on the assumption of full employment, the notion of interest as reward for waiting or abstinence is highly plausible. It is the premise that resources are typically fully employed that lacks plausibility in the contemporary world."[2]

Changes in Income Level Ignored. By assuming full employment the classical theory has ignored the changes in income level and their effect on savings and investment. Classical theory establishes a direct functional relationship between interest rate and the volume of savings. As the rate of interest goes up, more savings will take place. But at the higher rate of interest investment demand will be less with the result that interest will tend to fall to the level where savings and investment are in equilibrium. But this is not so realistic : first, because the direct functional relationship between savings and the rate of interest is doubtful, and secondly, because when more savings take place as a result of the rise in the rate of interest, these more savings should lead to more investment, as according to classical theory investment is governed by savings. Further, in the whole process of adjustment, change in income is not at all considered by the classical theory. As a matter of fact, when rate of interest rises and investment shrinks as a consequence, income will decline. With the decline in income, the saving will decline. Therefore, ***the equality between savings and investment are brought about not through changes in the rate of interest but through changes in income.***

Now, take the opposite case. If rate of interest falls, then, according to classical theory, the investment demand will increase. But at the lower rate of interest the greater supply of savings would not be forthcoming. Therefore, in classical theory more investment cannot take place even at lower rates of interest, because of the paucity of savings at lower rates of interest. But this is not what actually happens. At a lower rate of interest, more investment will be undertaken and increase in the investment will lead to the increase in income via multiplier. And out of increased income more would be saved. Again the tendency to equalise saving and investment is brought about by changes in income. Thus, the lower rate of interest through the increase in investment and income leads to the rise in saving. But this is quite contrary to the classical theory wherein at lower rate of interest small savings are made.

From the above analysis it follows that by neglecting the changes in income the classical theory is led into the error of viewing the rate of interest as the factor which brings about the equality of savings and investment. ***The classical theory ignores the changes in income level because it assumes full employment of resources.*** When the resources are fully employed, income level will remain constant, production techniques being given. Now, it was Keynes who abandoned the assumption of full employment and, therefore, considered the changes in income level and its relation with savings and investment. Quoting Prof. Dillard again, "The difference between the traditional theory of interest and Keynes money theory of interest is a fundamental aspect of the difference between the economics of full employment and the economics of less than full employment."[3]

Disincentive Effect of Lesser Consumption on Investment Ignored. According to the classical theory, more investment can occur only by cutting down consumption. More the reduction in consumption, the greater the increase in investment in capital goods. But as we know the demand for capital goods is a derived demand; it is derived from the demand for consumer goods. Therefore, the reduction in consumption, which means decrease in demand

2. D. Dillard, *Economics of J.M. Keynes*, p. 162.
3. *Op. cit.*, p. 160.

for consumer goods, will adversely affect the demand for capital goods and will thus lessen the inducement to invest. The disincentive effect of the fall in consumption on investment is glossed over by the classical theory.

As we shall see later, in Keynes's theory more investment does not occur at the expense of consumption. In Keynes's theory, in view of unemployment of resources, more investment is possible by utilizing the unemployed and underemployed resources. When investment increases, it leads to the increase in the income level. With the increase in incomes, people will consume more. Thus in Keynesian analysis more investment leads to more consumption, or in other words, investment and consumption go together. Keynesian analysis is more realistic in the context of unemployment of resources prevailing in the economy.

Independence of Savings Schedule from Investment Schedule Assumed. Another implication of assuming full employment and constant level of income is that investment demand schedule can change without causing a change in the savings schedule. For instance, according to classical theory, if investment demand curve *II* shifts downward to the dotted position *I'I'* (Fig. 56.3) because the profit prospects have lessened, according to classical theory, the new equilibrium rate of interest is *Or'* at which the new investment demand curve *I'I'* intersects the supply curve *SS* which remains unaltered. But this is quite untenable. As a result of fall in investment, income will decline. Since supply curve of savings is drawn with a given level of income, when income falls, there will be less savings than before and savings curve will shift to the left. But the classical theory does not take into account changes in the income level as a result of changes in investment and regards the savings schedule as independent of investment schedule which is not correct and realistic.

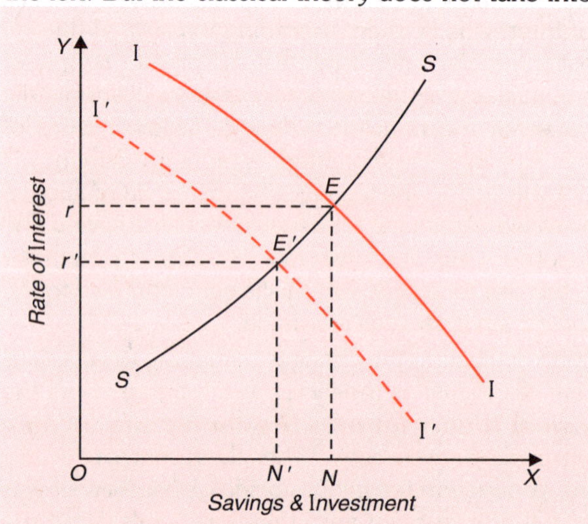

Fig. 56.3. According to classical theory, investment sehedule can change without affecting the saving schedule.

Indeterminateness. Finally, the classical theory, as pointed out by Keynes, is indeterminate. Position of the savings curve depends upon the income level, that is, the position of saving curve varies with the level of income. There will be different saving schedules for different levels of income. As income rises, the saving curve will shift to the right and as income falls the saving curve will shift to the left. Thus, we cannot know the position of the saving curve unless we already know the level of income, and if we do not know the position of the saving curve, we cannot know the rate of interest. It follows therefore that we cannot know what the rate of interest will be unless we already know what the income level is. But we cannot know the income level without already knowing the rate of interest because with the changes in the rate of interest investment will change which will in turn bring about changes in the income level. The classical theory therefore offers no determinate solution to the problem of interest rate determination and is therefore indeterminate.

Savings out of current income is not the only source of supply offunds. As we have seen, the classical theory considered only savings out of current income as constituting the supply of funds in the market. But savings out of current income is not the only source of capital supply. People have usually past hoarded savings, which they may dishoard in a period which will add to the supply of funds in the market. Further, now-a-days bank credit has become a very important source of investible funds which are also not taken into account by the classical theory.

We have critically explained the classical theory above. Some of the shortcomings of the classical theory were removed by the loanable funds theory which we now turn to explain.

LOANABLE FUNDS THEORY OF INTEREST

Another school of thought developed what is called loanable funds theory of interest. Among the principal economists who contributed to the development of loanable funds theory may be mentioned Wicksell, Bertil Ohlin, Robertson, Myrdal, Lindahl, Viner, etc. According to this theory, real forces such as thriftiness, waiting, time-preference and productivity of capital alone do not go to determine the rate of interest, monetary forces such as hoarding and dishoarding of money, money created by banks, monetary loans for consumption purposes also play a part in the determination of the rate of interest. Thus the exponents of the loanable funds theory saw the interplay of monetary and non-monetary forces in the determination of the rate of interest. We, therefore, see that loanable funds theory is a monetary theory of interest, although it is only partly monetary since it also recognises the importance of real forces such as thriftiness and productivity of capital in determination of rate of interest.

According to this theory, rate of interest is determined by the demand for and supply of loanable funds. The supply of loanable funds consists of savings out of disposable income, dishoarding, money created by the banks and disinvestment (*i.e.*, disentangling of fixed and working capital). The demand for loanable funds is composed of demand for investment, demand for consumption and demand for hoarding money. We explain below in detail these several sources of supply and demand of loanable funds.

Supply of Loanable Funds

Saving. Savings by individuals and households constitute the most important source of the supply of loanable funds. In the loanable funds theory savings are considered in either of the two ways. First, in the sense of *ex-ante* saving, that is, savings planned by individuals and households in the beginning of a period in the hope of expected incomes and anticipated expenditures on consumption, and secondly, in the sense of Robertsonian savings, that is, the difference between the income of the preceding period (which becomes disposable in the present period) and consumption of the present period. In both these senses of savings it is assumed that the amount of savings varies with rate of interest. More savings will be forthcoming at higher rates of interest and *vice versa.* It is granted that savings by individuals and households primarily depend upon the size of their income. But, given the level of income, savings vary with the rate of interest; the higher the rate of interest, the greater the volume of savings. Therefore, supply curve of savings slopes upward to the right.

Like individuals, business concerns also save. When the business is of the type of private enterprise or partnership, a part of the income from the business is used for consumption purposes and a part is kept for further expansion of the business. When the business is of the type of joint stock company, a part of the earnings is distributed as dividends to the shareholders and a part of the earnings of the company is retained undistributed which constitutes the *corporate savings*. Business savings depend partly upon the current rate of interest. A higher rate of the interest is likely to encourage internal business savings by the business firms as a substitute for borrowing from the loan market. These savings are mostly used for investment purposes by the business firms themselves and, therefore, most of them do not enter into the market for loanable funds. But these savings influence the rate of interest since they serve as substitute for borrowed funds and, therefore, reduce the market demand for loanable funds. In Fig. 56.4, the curve labelled as *S* indicates the supply curve of savings which slopes upward to the right.

Dishoarding. Dishoarding of the past accumulated savings constitutes another source of supply of loanable funds. Individuals may possess idle cash balances hoarded from the incomes of the previous periods wliich they may dishoard in a period. When people dishoard, the idle cash balances become active cash balances in the present period and thus add to the supply of loanable funds. People hoard money because of their preference for liquidity. When rate of interest rises or when the prices of bonds and shares decline, they may like to take advantage of these market movements and thus dishoard money for lending it to others or for purchasing bonds and shares. At a higher rate of interest, the individuals possessing idle cash balances will be induced to dishoard more money. At very low rates of interest, their parting with liquidity will not be rewarded sufficiently and, therefore they will hold on to money. It is evident that discarding is interest-elastic and, therefore, the curve of discarding slopes upward to the right as is shown in Fig. 56.4 by curve *DH*.

Bank Money. The banking system is another important source of the supply of loanable funds. The commercial banks by creating credit money advance loans to the businessmen and industries for investment. Banks can also reduce the supply of loanable funds by contracting their lending. Banks also purchase and sell securities and thereby affect the supply of loanable funds. The supply curve of funds provided by banks is to some degree interest-elastic. Generally speaking, the banks will lend more money at higher rates of interest than at lower ones. Therefore, supply curve of bank money also slopes upward to the right as is shown by the curve *BM* in Fig. 56.4.

Disinvestment. Disinvestment is another source of the supply of loanable funds. Disinvestment means disentangling of the present fixed and working capital. Usually a good amount of depreciation reserves is kept so as to replace the fixed capital when it is completely worn out. When there is a declining tendency in certain industries due to some structural changes in the economy, the entrepreneurs may not like to remain tied to those industries and therefore they may allow the existing stock of machines and other equipment belonging to those industries wear out without replacement. As a result, they may bring the depreciation reserves in the market for loanable funds. Similarly, working capital invested in business may be withdrawn gradually and made available as loanable funds. When disinvestment is decided to be undertaken, then not only the depreciation reserves but also a part of the revenue earned from the sale of output instead of going into capital replacement flows into the market for loanable funds. At higher rates of interest, the entrepreneurs will generally contemplate a greater amount of disinvestment. Prof. Bober rightly remarks, "Disinvestment is encouraged somewhat by a high rate of interest on loanable funds. When the rate is high, some of the current capital may not produce a marginal revenue product to match this rate of interest. The firm may decide to let this capital run down and to put the depreciation funds in the loan market."[5] It is therefore clear that disinvestment curve will also slope upward to the right, as is indicated by the curve *DI* in Fig.56.4.

By lateral summation of the curve of saving (*S*), dishoarding (*DH*), bank money (*BM*) and disinvestment (*DI*) we get in Fig. 56.4 the total supply curve of loanable funds *SL* which slopes

5. M.M. Bober, *Intermediate Price and Income Theory* (1955), p. 371.

upward to the right showing that a greater amount of loanable fund will be available at higher rates of interest and *vice versa*.

Demand for Lonable Funds

Having now explained the sources of supply of loanable funds, we now turn to explain the factors which determine the demand for loanable funds. Loanable funds theory also differs from the classical theory in its explanation of the demand for funds. Whereas the classical theory considers only the demand for funds for investment purposes, the loanable funds theory also considers the demand of loans for consumption and demand for hoarding money, apart from the demand of funds for investment. In considering the hoarding of money, loanable funds theory incorporates in itself the factor of liquidity preference on which Keynes later laid great stress as an important determinant of interest. We shall now explain these different sources of demand for loanable funds.

Investment Demand. Demand for investment constitutes an important factor working on the side of demand for loanable funds. Investment demand includes businessmen's borrowings for purchasing or making of new capital goods including the building up of inventories. The price of obtaining the loanable funds required to purchase or invest in capital goods is obviously the rate of interest. It will pay businessmen to demand and undertake investment of loanable funds up to the point where the expected net rate of return on investment equals the rate of interest. In the loanable funds theory, demand for investment depends upon the marginal revenue productivity of capital (or the marginal rate of return) in the same way as in the classical theory. When the rate of interest falls, businessmen will find it profitable to increase investment in capital goods with the result that their demand for loanable funds will increase. We thus see that demand for loanable funds for investment is interest-elastic; at a low rate of interest, there will be greater investment demand and *vice versa*. Therefore, the curve of investment demand for loanable funds slopes downward to the right as is shown by the curve *I* in Fig. 56.4.

Consumption Demand. Another important source of demand for loanable funds are the loans desired to be taken by the people for consumption purposes. Loans for consumption purposes are demanded by the people when they wish to make purchases in excess of their current incomes and idle cash resources. The loans for consumption purposes are demanded generally for buying durable-use goods such as houses, automobiles, refrigerators, television sets, air conditioners etc. Whereas a lower rate of interest will induce people to borrow more for consumption, the higher rate of interest will discourage borrowing for consumption. Therefore, consumption-demand curve for loanable funds slopes downward to the right and is shown by the curve labelled as *DS* in Fig. 56.4.

Demand for Hoarding. Lastly, demand for money to hoard is another important factor determining demand for loanable funds. Demand for hoarding money arises because of people's preference for liquidity, *i.e.*, for cash balances. Hoarded money represents idle cash balances. People save money when they do not spend all their disposable income on consumption. They can lend out their savings to others or purchase securities (i.e. bonds and shares) with their savings or invest their savings in real capital. Another alternative use of income saved (i.e., income not spent on consumption) is to hoard them, that is, to hold them as idle cash balances. People can also hoard money when they sell securities or assets owned by them and not spending the proceeds obtained therefrom. The important thing to understand is why people hoard money when they can earn some income by lending it to others or investing it in securities or capital assets. An important reason for the demand for hoarding money is that people like to take advantage of the changes in the rate of interest or changes in the prices of securities in the future. At higher current rates of interest, people will hoard less money because much of the money will be lent out to take advantage of the higher rates of interest, and people will hoard more money at lower rates of interest because loss suffered in hoarding money in this case will not be very much. It follows therefore that the curve of demand for hoarding money will also slope downward as is shown by the curve *H* in Fig. 56.4. An important point to be noted here is that the person who has a demand for funds to hoard himself supplies the funds for that purpose. A saver who hoards savings can be said to be supplying loanable funds and also demanding them to satisfy his liquidity preference.

By adding up horizontally the investment demand curve *I*, dissavings or consumption demand curve *DS,* and the hoarding demand curve *H,* we get *DL* curve in Fig. 56.4 as the total demand curve for loaable funds.

Equilibrium between Demand for and Supply of Loanable Funds. We have explained above the factors governing both the demand for and supply of loanable funds and have also derived the aggregate demand curve of loanable funds *DL* and the aggregate supply curve of loanable funds *SL.* Now, the rate of interest is determined by the intersection of the demand for loanable funds curve *DL* and the supply of loanable funds curve *SL,* as is illustrated in Fig. 56.4.

DL and *SL* curves intersect at point *E* and thereby determine the equilibrium rate of interest *Or.* At the equilibrium rate of interest *Or,* the loanable funds supplied and demanded are equal to *OM.* At any other interest rate either the demand for loanable funds will exceed the supply of loanable funds or the supply of loanable funds will exceed the demand for loanable funds and therefore there will be a change in the rate of interest until it reaches the level *Or* where demand for and supply of loanable funds are in equilibrium.

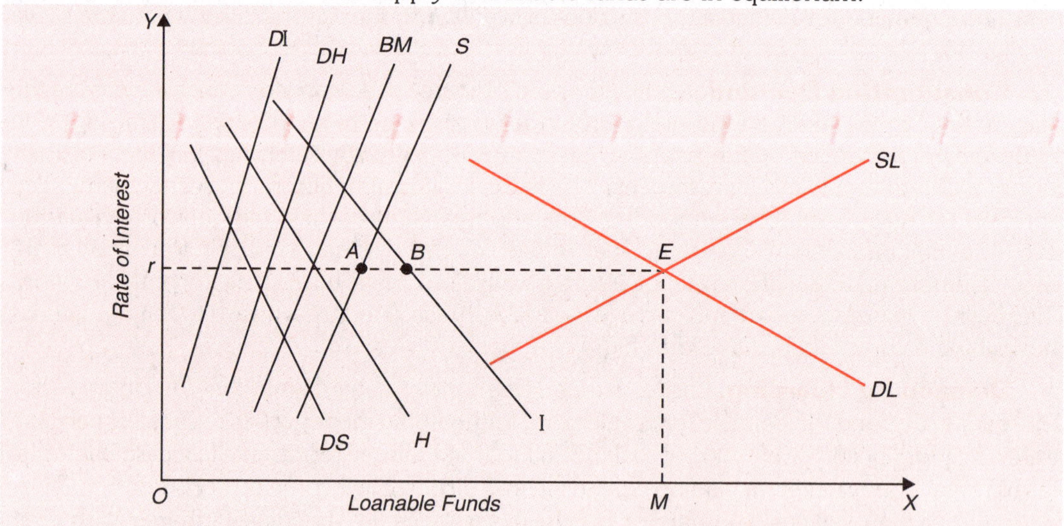

Fig. 56.4. *Determination of rate of interest through equilibrium between demand for and supply of loanable funds*

It should be noted that at the equilibrium rate of interest where aggregate demand for and supply of loanable funds are equal, planned savings and investment may not be equal, as is the case in Fig. 56.4. It will be seen from this figure that at equilibrium rate of interest *Or,* while saving is equal to *rA,* investment equals *rB.* As a result of investment being greater than savings, income will increase. With the increase in income, the savings curve *S* and the aggregate supply curve *SL* will shift to the right. And this shift in the savings and supply of loanable funds curve *SL* will cause a change in the rate of interest. We thus see that the rate of interest as determined by demand for and supply of loanable funds will not be stable one if there is inequality between saving and investment at that rate. This inequality will bring about a change in the income and thereby a change in the savings and supply of loanable funds. As a result, the rate of interest will tend to change. A stable equilibrium rate of interest will be achieved where intersection of the aggregate supply and demand curves of loanable funds determines the equilibrium rate of interest at which the saving and investment are also equal. But in a single period, the rate of interest at which quantities demanded and supplied of loanable funds are equal, will prevail in spite of the inequality of saving and investment, although the equilibrium rate of interest in such a situation will tend to change over some years through changes in income.

We have explained above the various components of demand for and supply of loanable funds and have shown how the equilibrium rate of interest is determined. We have taken the savings (*S*) on the supply side, dissavings (*DS*) on the demand side; dishoarding (*DH*) on the supply side and hoarding (*H*) on the demand side; investment (*S*) on the demand side and disinvestment on the supply side. We can further simplify our analysis of components of demand for and supply of loanable funds and bring out the conditions for the equilibrium rate of interest in a better way if we use *net* of saving (*i.e.*, savings *minus* dissavings), *net* of hoarding (*i.e.*, hoarding *minus* dishoarding) and *net* of investment (*i.e.*, investment *minus* disinvestment). This will become clear from the following :

We know that equilibrium rate of interest is determined where

Supply of loanable funds = Demand for loanable funds

or $$S + DH + BM + DI = I + DS + H$$

By taking *DS* to the left hand side and *DH* and *DI* to the right hand side we get

$$(S - DS) + BM = (I - DI) + (H - DH)$$

or $$\text{Net } S + BM = \text{Net } I + \text{Net } H$$

Or, Net saving + Bank money = Net Investment + Net hoarding

Thus we see that the rate of interest will be at the equilibrium level where the quantity supplied of net saving and bank money will be equal to the quantity demanded for net investment and net hoarding. This is the essence of the loanable funds theory of interest.

Critical Evaluation of Loanable Funds Theory

Loanable funds theory is superior to classical theory of interest. It has greatly improved our understanding of the forces working on the supply of and demand for loanable funds. It makes quite a comprehensive analysis of the determination of the rate of interest and takes into consideration all the relevant factors which have a bearing on the rate of interest, namely, saving or thriftiness, investment demand, hoarding and bank credit. However, loanable funds theory has been criticised by Keynes and Keynesians.

First, it was asserted by Keynes that the concept of hoarding as used in loanable funds theory was quite dubious. This is so because hoarding simply cannot increase or decrease as long as the amount of money remains the same. Money in circulation in an economy has to be in somebody's cash balances at any time. According to him, if the quantity of money remains the same, then the total amount of cash balances in the beginning and at the end of a period will be the same ; the greater hoarding of money by one person will be offset by the dishoarding by any other person. But this criticism of loanable funds theory is misplaced. As a matter of fact, the effective supply of money in a society does not merely depend upon the quantity of money, it also depends upon the velocity of circulation of money. And it is this velocity of circulation which changes as a result of hoarding or dishoarding and, therefore, involves the changes in the effective supply of money, although the amount of money in existence may have remained the same. Prof. G.N. Halm rightly writes, "The total quantity of money may well be the same in the beginning and at the end of the period, but the velocity of circulation of money may nevertheless have changed. And it is this change in the velocity of circulation of money which is partly caused by hoarding and dishoarding......An ***increase in idle balances at the expense of active balances is hoarding and results in a reduction in the velocity of circulation of money.*** The time duration of the idleness of money might change, changing at the same time the supply of loanable funds."[6]

Thus, we see that the hoarding can occur even if the quantity of money in circulation remains constant during a period and, therefore, Keynes's objection against the loanable funds theory on this ground is not valid. As a matter of fact, Keynes himself introduced distinction between ***'active'*** and ***'idle'*** balances. Now, as we noted in the quotation from Halm that an increase in ideal balances at the expense of active balances is hoarding and results in a reduction in the velocity of circulation of money. If the time duration of idleness of money *(i.e.,* period of rest between the two transfers) increases, it will mean hoarding which will reduce the supply of loanable funds and thus affect the determination of rate of interest.

Keynes also criticised the loanable funds theory on the ground that like classical theory it did not provide a determinate solution to the interest-rate determination and involved what was called circular reasoning. According to him, since saving is an important constituent of the supply of loanable funds, the supply of loanable funds curve will vary with the level of income which determines saving. We, therefore, cannot know the rate of interest unless we know what the level of income is. And we cannot know the level of income unless we know the rate of interest since rate of interest affects investment which in turn determines the level of income. Following Keynes, Hansen also disapproves loanable funds theory and maintains that "the schedule of loanable funds is compounded of savings plus net additions to loanable funds from new money and dishoarding of idle balances. But since the savings portion of the schedule varies with the level of disposable income, it follows that the total supply schedule of loanable funds also varies with income making the rate of interest indeterminate."[7]

Keynes was correct in criticizing the classical theory for its ignoring the effect of changes in the level of income upon the supply of saving but his criticism against loanable funds theory is not valid. This is because loanable funds theory seeks to explain the interest rate determination through *period analysis* with a lag of one period, which makes the theory quite determinate. In loanable funds theory, the supply of saving is regarded as being determined by the income of the preceding period and saving so determined along with other components of supply and the demand for loanable funds determine the rate of interest in the current period. The current rate of interest so determined affects the level of income in the succeeding period through investment. Prof. Halm rightly maintains that "It is not circular reasoning to say that income is influenced by investment, investment by rates of interest, rates of interest by the supply of loanable funds, the supply of loanable funds by savings, and ***savings in turn, by the income received in the last period.***"[8] We, therefore, conclude that charge against loanable funds theory that it is indeterminate is untenable. In fact, it is Keynes' s own liquidity preference theory of interest, as we shall see later, which is indeterminate.

Another charge against the loanable funds theory is that it is based upon the assumption of full employment of resources which does not hold in the real world. And the superiority of

6. G.N. Halm, *Monetary Theory,* 2nd ed. (1955) p. 344 (italics added),
7. A.H. Hansen, *Guide to Keynes,* p. 141.
8.G.N. Halm, *Op. cit.,* p. 147 (italics added).

Keynes's theory is sought to be proved on the basis of its being based upon realistic assumption of less than full employment. "The analysis of the loanable funds theory is built on the premise of full employment. Keynes, on the other hand, envisages that the economic system could be in a state of equilibrium.....at less than full employment. He builds his theory which may be applicable in such a society. This basic difference in the assumption accounts for the divergence in the analysis because people's response in both the societies will differ."[9] Professor Prasad seems to imply that loanable funds theory is inapplicable to the situation of less than full employment. But this is not correct interpretation of loanable funds theory. As we have seen above in the explanation of the loanable funds theory that it takes into account the increases in the level of income as a result of investment and their influence on savings. If the full employment were the assumption, how could the income increase ?

As a matter of fact, loanable funds theory is a synthesis between the classical theory and Keynes's liquidity preference theory since it takes into account the saving and investment demand of the classical theory as well as liquidity preference of Keynes's theory. By incorporating hoarding and dishoarding it considers the liquidity preference on which Keynes laid a great stress as an important factor determining the rate of interest. Besides, loanable funds theory has been described as dynamic. Thus Prof. H.G. Johnson has suggested that the Keynesian theory is 'static' seeking only to explain the state of affairs in a short-period equilibrium and how changes in circumstances will alter the equilibrium values, while the loanable funds theory is dynamic and seeks to explain precisely how interest and income move from one equilibrium level to another when circumstances have changed.[10]

KEYNES'S LIQUIDITY PREFERENCE THEORY OF INTEREST

In his epoch-making book, *"The General Theory of Employment, Interest and Money"* the late Lord Keynes gave a new view of interest. According to him, "Interest is the reward for parting wjth liquidity for a specified period."[11] A man with a given income has to decide first how much he is to consume and how much to save. The former will depend on, what Keynes calls, the *propensity to consume.* Given this propensity to consume, the individual will save a certain proportion of his given income. He now has to make another decision. Should he hold his savings ? How much of his resources will he hold in the form of ready money (cash or non-interest-paying bank deposits) and how much will he part with or lend depend upon what Keynes calls his *"liquidity preference"*. Liquidity preference means the *demand for money to hold* or the desire of the public to hold cash.

Demand for Money or Motives for Liquidity Preference

Liquidity preference of a particular individual depends upon several considerations. The question is : Why should the people hold their resources liquid or in the form of ready money, when they can get interest by lending such resources ? The desire for liquidity arises because of three motives: (*i*) the transactions motive, (*ii*) the precautionary motive, and (*iii*) the speculative motive.

The Transactions Motive. The transactions motive relates to the demand for money or need for cash for the current transactions of individual and business exchanges. Individuals hold cash in order "to bridge the interval between the receipt of income and its expenditure".

9. Brahmanand Prasad, Loanable Funds and Liquidity Preference in Interest Rate Determination (a paper read at *Indian Economic Conference,* Calcutta, 1966).
10. "Some Cambridge Controversies in Monetary Theory", *Review of Economic Studies,* Vol. XIX. No. 49(1951-52).
11. *Op. cit,* p. 167.

This is called the ***'Income Motive'.*** Most of the people receive their incomes by the week or the month, while the expenditure goes on day by day. A certain amount of ready money, therefore, is kept in hand to make current payments. This amount will depend upon the size of the individual's income, the interval at which the income is received and the methods of payments prevailing in the society.

The businessmen and the entrepreneurs also have to keep a proportion of their resources in ready cash in order to meet current needs of various kinds. They need money all the time in order to pay for raw materials and transport, to pay wages and salaries and to meet all other current expenses incurred by business firms. Keynes calls this as *'Business Motive'* for keeping money. It is clear that the amount of money held under this business motive will depend to a very large extent on the turnover (*i.e.*, the volume of trade of the firm in question). The larger the turnover, the larger in general will be the amount of money needed to cover current expenses.

Precautionary Motive. Precautionary motive for holding money refers to the desire of the people to hold cash balances for unforeseen contingencies. People hold a certain amount of money to provide for the danger of unemployment, sickness, accidents, and the other uncertain perils. The amount of money held under this motive will depend on the nature of the individual and on the conditions in which he lives.

Speculative Motive. The speculative motive relates to the desire to hold one's resources in liquid form in order to take advantage of market movements regarding the future changes in the rate of interest (or bond prices). The notion of holding money for speculative motive is a new typically Keynesian idea. Money held under the speculative motive serves as a store of value as money held under the precautionary motive does. But it is a store of money meant for a different purpose. The cash held under this motive is used to make speculative gains by dealing in bonds[12] whose prices fluctuate. If bond prices are expected to rise, which, in other words, means that the rate of interest is expected to fall, businessmen will buy bonds to sell when their prices actually rise. If, however, bond prices are expected to fall, *i.e.*, the rate of interest is expected to rise, businessmen will sell bonds to avoid capital losses. Nothing being certain in this dynamic world, where guesses about the future course of events are made on precarious basis, businessmen keep cash balances to speculate on the probable future changes in bond prices (or the rate of interest) with a view to making profits.

Given the expectation about the changes in the rate of interest in future, less money will be held under the speculative motive at a higher current or prevailing rate of interest arid more money will be held under this motive at a lower current rate of interest. The reason for this inverse correlation between money held for speculative motive and the prevailing rate of interest is that at a lower rate of interest less is lost by not lending money or investing it, that is, by holding on to money, while at a higher rate of interest holders of cash balances would lose more by not lending or investing.

Thus, the demand for money under speculative motive is a function of the current rate of interest, increasing as the interest rate falls and decreasing as the interest rate rises. Thus, demand for money under this motive is a decreasing function of the rate of interest. This is clear from Fig. 56.5. Along the *X*-axis is represented the speculative demand for money and along the *Y*-axis the rate of interest. The liquidity preference curve *LP* is a downward sloping towards the right signifying that the higher the rate of interest, the lower the demand for speculative motive, and *vice versa*. Thus, at the high current rate of interest *Or*, a very small

12. All securities and other such papers that yield a fixed and known rate of interest over a period of time are known as bonds.

amount *OM* is held for speculative motive. This is because at a high current rate of interest much money would have been lent out or used for buying bonds and therefore less money will be kept as inactive balances. If rate of interest falls to *Or'*, then a greater amount *OM'* is held under speculative motive. With the further fall in the rate of interest to *Or"*, money held under speculative motive increases to *OM"*. It will be seen from Fig. 56.5 that the liquidity preference curve *LP* becomes quite flat, *i.e.*, perfectly elastic at a very low rate of interest; it is horizontal line beyond point *E"* towards the right. This perfectly elastic portion of liquidity preference curve indicates the position of ***absolute liquidity preference*** of the people. That is, at a very low rate of interest people will hold with them as inactive balances any amount of money they come to have. This portion of liquidity preference curve with absolute liquidity preference has been called ***liquidity trap*** by J.M. Keynes.

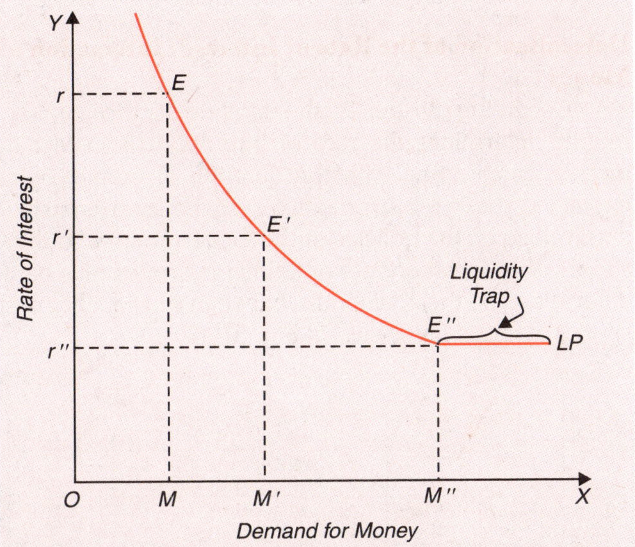

Fig. 56.5. *Liquidity Preference for Speculative Motive*

But demand for money to satisfy the speculative motive does not depend so much upon what the current rate of interest is, as on expectations of changes in the rate of interest. If there is a change in the expectations regarding tfie future rate of interest, the whole curve or schedule of liquidity preference for speculative motive will change accordingly. Thus, if the public on balance expect the rate of interest to be higher (*i.e.*, bond prices to be lower) in the future than had been previously supposed, the speculative demand for money will increase and the whole liquidity preference curve for speculative motive will shift upward.

If the total supply of money is represented by *M*, we may refer to that part of *M* held for transactions and precautionary motive as M_1 and to that part held for the speculative motive as M_2. Thus $M = M_1 + M_2$. The money held under the transactions and precautionary motives, *i.e.* M_1, is completely interest-inelastic unless the interest rate is very high. The amount of money held as M_1, that is, for transactions and precautionary motive, is mainly a function of the size of income and business transactions together with the contingencies growing out of the conduct of personal and business affairs. We can write this in a functional form as follows:

$$M_1 = L_1(Y) \qquad \ldots.(i)$$

where *Y* stands for income, L_1 for liquidity preference function, and M_1, for money held under the transactions and precautionary motive.

The above function implies that money held under the transactions and precautionary motive is a function of income.

On the other hand, money demanded for speculative motive, *i.e.*, M_2, as explained above, is primarily a function of the rate of interest. This can be written as :

$$M_2 = L_2(r) \qquad \ldots.(ii)$$

where r stands for the rate of interest, L_2 for liquidity preference function for speculative motive.

Since total supply of money $M = M_1 + M_2$, we get from (*i*) and (*ii*) above

$$M = L_1(Y) + L_2(r) \qquad \text{....}(iii)$$

It follows from (*iii*) above that given the supply of money M (and also income) the rate of interest will be determined by the liquidity preference.

Determination of the Rate of Interest : Interaction of Liquidity Preference and Supply of Money

According to Keynes, the demand for money, *i.e.*, the liquidity preference and supply of money determines the rate of interest. It is in fact the liquidity preference for speculative motive which along with the quantity of money determines the rate of interest. We have explained above the speculative demand for money in detail. As for the supply of money, it is determined by the policies of the Government and the Central Bank of the country. The total supply of money consists of coins plus notes plus bank deposits. How the rate of interest is determined by the equilibrium between the liquidity preference for speculative motive and the supply of money is shown in Fig. 56.6.

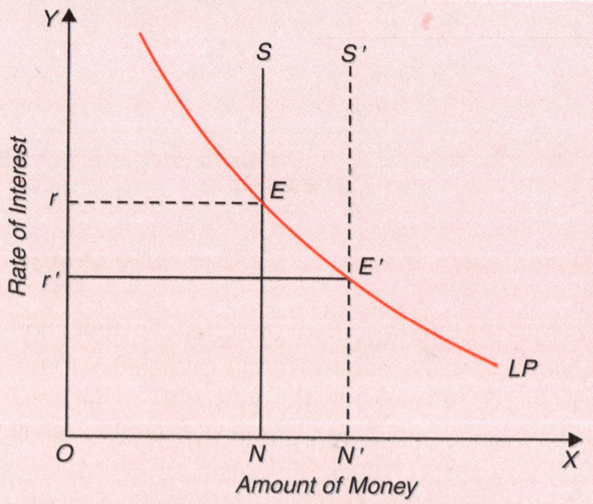

Fig. 56.6. *Equilibrium between Demand for and Supply of Money*

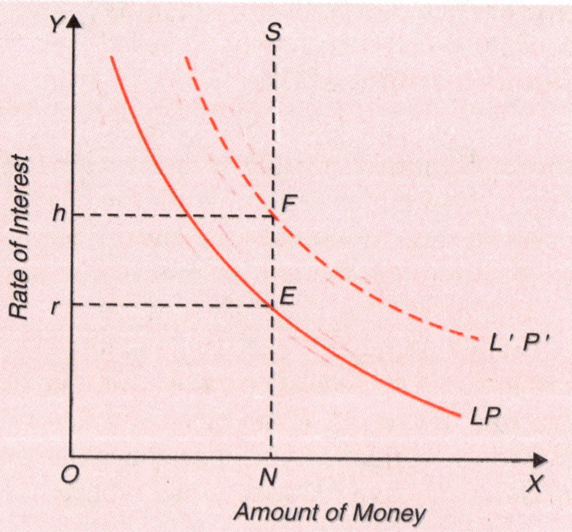

Fig. 56.7. *Effect of Increase in Liquidity Preference on the Rate of Interest*

In Fig. 56.6, *LP* is the curve of liquidity preference for speculative motive. In other words, *LP* curve shows the demand for money for speculative motive. To begin with, *ON* is the quantity of money available for satisfying liquidity preference for speculative motive. Rate of interest will be determined where the speculative demand for money is in balance or equal to the fixed supply of money *ON*. It is clear from the figure that speculative demand for money is equal to *ON* quantity of money at *Or* rate of interest. Hence *Or* is the equilibrium rate of interest. Assuming no change in expectations, an increase in the quantity of money (via open market operations) for the speculative motive will lower the rate of interest. In Fig. 56.6, when the quantity of money increases from *ON* to *ON'*, the rate of interest falls from *Or* to *Or'* because the new quantity of money *ON'* is in balance with the speculative demand for money at *Or"* rate of interest. In this case we move down along the curve. Thus, given the schedule or curve of liquidity preference for speculative motive, an increase in the quantity of money brings down the rate of interest.

But the act of increase in the quantity of money may cause a change in the expectations of the public and thereby cause an upward shift in liquidity preference curve for speculative motive bringing the rate of interest up. But this is not certain. "New developments may only cause wide differences of opinion leading to increased activity in the bond market without necessarily causing any shift in the aggregate speculative demand for money schedule. If the balance of market expectation is changed, there will be *shift* in the schedule. Central Bank policy designed to increase the money supply may therefore be met by an upward shift of speculative demand function leaving the rate of interest virtually unaffected."[13] Thus, a large increase in the quantity of money may exert only a small influence on the rate of interest in certain circumstances.

It is worth mentioning that shift in liquidity preference schedule or curve can be caused by many other factors which affect expectations and might take place independently of changes in the quantity of money by the Central Bank. Shifts in the liquidity function may be either downward or upward depending on the way in which the public interprets a change in events. If some change in events leads the people on balance to expect a higher rate of interest in the future than they had previously supposed, the liquidity preference for speculative motive will increase which will bring about an upward shift in the curve of liquidity preference for speculative motive and will raise the rate of interest.

In Fig. 56.7, assuming that the quantity of money remams unchanged at *ON,* the increase in the liquidity preference curve from *LP* to *L'P '*, the rate of interest rises from *Or* to *Oh* because at *Oh,* the new speculative demand for money is in equilibrium with the supply of money *ON*. It is worth noting that when the liquidity preference for speculative motive increases from *LP* to *L'P'*, the amount of money held does not increase ; it remains *ON* as before. Only the rate of interest rises from *Or* to *Oh* to equate the new liquidity preference for speculative motive with the available quantity of money *ON*.

Thus we see that Keynes explained interest in terms of purely monetary forces and not in terms of real forces like productivity of capital and thrift which formed the foundation-stones of both classical and loanable fund theories. According to him, demand for money for speculative motive together with the supply of money determines the rate of interest. He agreed that the marginal revenue product of capital tends to become equal to the rate of interest but the rate cf interest is not determined by marginal revenue productivity of capital. Moreover, according to him, interest is not a reward for saving or thriftiness or waiting but for parting with liquidity. Keynes asserted that it is not the rate of interest which equalises saving and investment. But this equality is brought about through changes in the level of income.

Critical Appraisal of Keynes's Liquidity Preference Theory of Interest

1. Keynes ignored real factors in the determination of interest. First, it has been pointed out that rate of interest is not a purely monetary phenomenon. Real forces like productivity of capital and thriftiness or saving also play an important role in the determination of the rate of interest. Keynes makes the rate of interest independent of the demand for investment funds. In fact, it is not so independent. The cash-balances of the businessmen are largely influenced by their demand for capital investment. This demand for capital-investment depends upon the marginal revenue productivity of capital. Therefore, the rate of interest is not determined independently of the marginal revenue productivity of capital (marginal efficiency of capital) and investment demand. When investment demand increases due to greater profit prospects or, in other words, when marginal revenue productivity of capital rises, there will be greater demand for investment funds and the rate of interest will go up. But Keynesian theory

13. A.H. Hansen, *A Guide to Keynes*, p. 133.

does not account for this. Similarly, Keynes ignored the effect of the availability of savings on the rate of interest. For instance, if the propensity to consume of the people increases, savings would decline. As a result, supply of funds in the market will decline which will raise the rate of only LM curve which shows various rates of interest at different levels of income interest.

2. Keynesian theory is also indeterminate. Exactly the same criticism applies to Keynesian theory itself on the basis of which Keynes rejected the classical and loanable funds theories. Keynes's theory of interest, like the classical and loanable funds theories, is indeterminate. According to Keynes, rate of interest is determined by the speculative demand for money and the supply of money available for satisfying speculative demand. Given the total money supply, we cannot know how much money will be available to satisfy the speculative demand for money unless we know how much the transactions demand for money is. And we cannot know the transactions demand for money unless we first know the level of income because money held under transactions motive depends on the level of income. Thus the Keynesian theory, like the classical, is indeterminate. "In the Keynesian case the supply and demand for money schedules cannot give the rate of interest unless we already know the income level; in the classical case the demand and supply schedules for saving offer no solution until the income is known. Precisely the same is true of loanable fund theory. Keynes criticism of the classical and loanable-fund theories applies equally to his own theory,[14] In fact, as we shall see below from Keynes's liquidity preference theory, we can derive only *L.M.* curve which shows various rates of interest at different levels of income when money market is in equilibrium.

3. No liquidity without savings. According to Keynes, interest is a reward for parting with liquidity and is in no way a compensation and inducement for saving or waiting. But without saving how can the funds be available to be kept as liquid and how can there be question of surrendering liquidity if one has not already saved money. Jacob Viner rightly maintains, "Without saving there can be no liquidity to surrender." Therefore, the rate of interest is vitally connected with saving which is neglected by Keynes in the determination of interest.

It follows from above that Keynesian theory of interest is also not without flaws. But importance Keynes gave to liquidity preference as a determinant of interest is correct. In fact, the exponents of loanable funds theory incorporated the liquidity preference in their theory by laying greater stress on hoarding and dishoarding. We are inclined to agree with Prof. D. Hamberg when he says, "Keynes did not forge nearly as *new* a theory as he and others at first thought. Rather, his great emphasis on the influence of hoarding on the rate of interest constituted an invaluable addition to the theory of interest as it had been developed by the loanable funds theorists who incorporated much of Keynes's ideas into their theory to make it more complete."[15]

SYNTHESIS BETWEEN CLASSICAL AND KEYNES'S THEORIES OF INTEREST: IS-LM CURVE MODEL

We have noted above that both the classical theory and Keynes' liquidity preference theory of interest are indeterminate and quite inadequate. Renowned economists, Hicks and Hansen, have brought about a synthesis between the classical and Keynes' theories of interest and have thereby succeeded in propounding an adequate and determinate theory of interest through the intersection of what are called *IS* and *LM* curves. They are of the opinion that the classical and loanable funds theories amount to the same thing. According to them, the difference between these two theories, *i.e.*, classical and loanable funds, lies only in the meaning of

14. A.H. Hansen, *A Guide to Keynes*, p. 141.
15. D. Hamberg, *Business Cycles*, p. 183.

savings. The Pigovian supply schedule of savings amounts to the same thing as the Robertsonian or Swedish supply of loanable funds. Through derivation the *IS* curve from the classical theory and *LM* curve from Keynes' liquidity preference theory they have brought about a synthesis

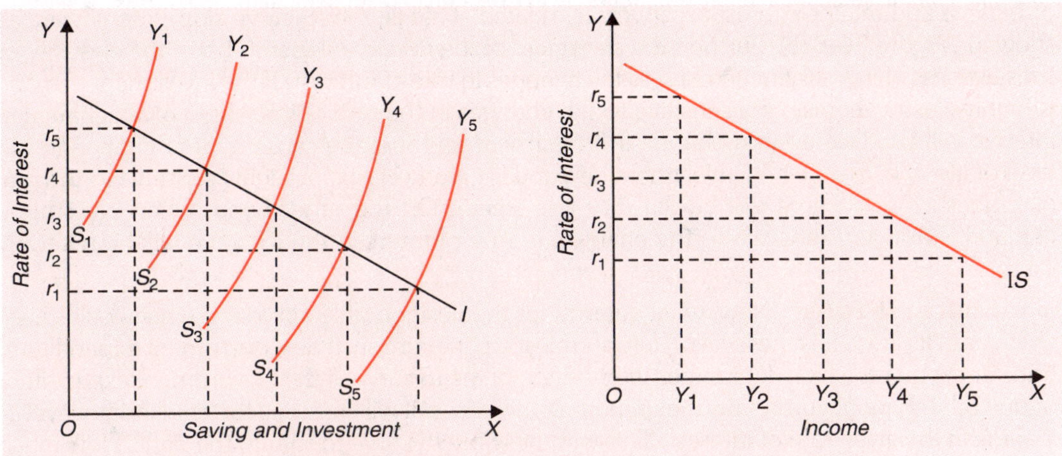

Fig.56.8. *Derivation of IS Curve from the Classical Theory*

between the classical and Keynes' theories of interest to provide an adequate and determinate theory of the rate of interest. From the classical theory they get a family of saving curves at various income levels. From these various saving curves at various income levels together with the given investment demand curve, the *IS* curve is derived. This *IS* curve tells us what will be the various rates of interest at different levels of income, given the investment demand curve and a family of saving curves at different levels of income. On the other hand, from Keynes' formulation, the *LM* curve is obtained from a family of liquidity preference curves corresponding to various income levels together with the given stock of money supply. This is because as the level of income increases, people would like to hold more money under the transactions motive. That is, the higher the level of income, the higher would be the liquidity preference curve. With the given supply of money, the different levels of liquidity preference curves corresponding to various levels of income would determine different rates of interest. This yields *LM* curve which depicts the various combinations of interest and income level at which money market is in equilibrium. Now, Hicks and Hansen show that with the intersection of *IS* and *LM* curves, both the interest and income are simultaneously determined. Thus the classical and Keynes' theories taken together help us in obtaining an adequate and determinate theory of interest. In what follows we explain how the *IS* curve is derived from the classical theory, and the *LM* curve from Keynes' theory. Further, we will explain what factors determine the shape and the levels of *IS* and *LM* curves.

Derivation of the *IS* Curve

In Fig. 56.8 *IS* curve is derived. As the income rises, the savings curve shift to the right and the rate of interest which equalises savings and investment falls. In Fig. 56.8 (*b*) we measure income (*Y*) on the *X*-axis and plot the corresponding rates of interest determined by the equality of savings and investment on the *Y*-axis. Thus, when income is Y_2 the relevant savings curve is S_2Y_2 and the corresponding rate of interest that equalizes savings and investment is r_4. Similarly, for other levels of income rates of interest that equalise savings and investment can be obtained and plotted. Since, as income increases, rate of interest falls, the *IS* curve slopes downward.

Thus, *IS* curve relates the rates of interest with the levels of income at which intended savings and investment are equal. In other words, the *IS* curve depicts the various combinations of levels of interest and income at which intended savings being equal to investment, **goods market is in equilibrium.** Since with the increase in income the savings curve shifts to the right, its intersection with the investment demand curve will lower the rate of interest, the level of income and rate of interest are inversely related. That is, the *IS* curve slopes downward as shown in Figure 56.8 (*b*). Further, the steepness of the *IS* curve depends upon the elasticity or sensitiveness of investment demand to the changes in rate of interest. If the investment demand is highly elastic, that is, very sensitive to the changes in the rate of interest, a given change in interest will produce a large change in investment and thereby cause a large change in the level of income. Thus when investment demand is greatly elastic or highly sensitive to the rate of interest, the *IS* curve will be flat (*i.e.* less steep). On the other hand, when investment demand is not very sensitive to the changes in rate of interest, the *IS* curve will be relatively steep.

Shift in *IS* curve : Now, what determines the position of *IS* curve and what would cause changes in its level. It is the level of autonomous expenditure such as Government expenditure, transfer payments which determines the position of the *IS* curve. If the Government expenditure or any other type of autonomous expenditure increases, it will increase the equilibrium level of income at the given rate of interest. This will cause the *IS* curve to shift to the right. How much does the *IS* curve shift following an increase in autonomous expenditure depends on the size of multiplier. A reduction in Government expenditure or transfer payments will shift the *IS* curve to the left.

Derivation of the *LM* Curve

The *LM* curve can be derived from the Keynesian liquidity preference theory of interest. Liquidity preference or demand for money to hold depends upon transactions motive and speculative motive. It is the money held for transactions motive which is a function of income. The greater the level of income, the greater the amount of money held for transactions motive and therefore the higher the level of liquidity preference curve. Thus, we can draw a family of liquidity preference curves at various levels of income. Now, the intersection of these various

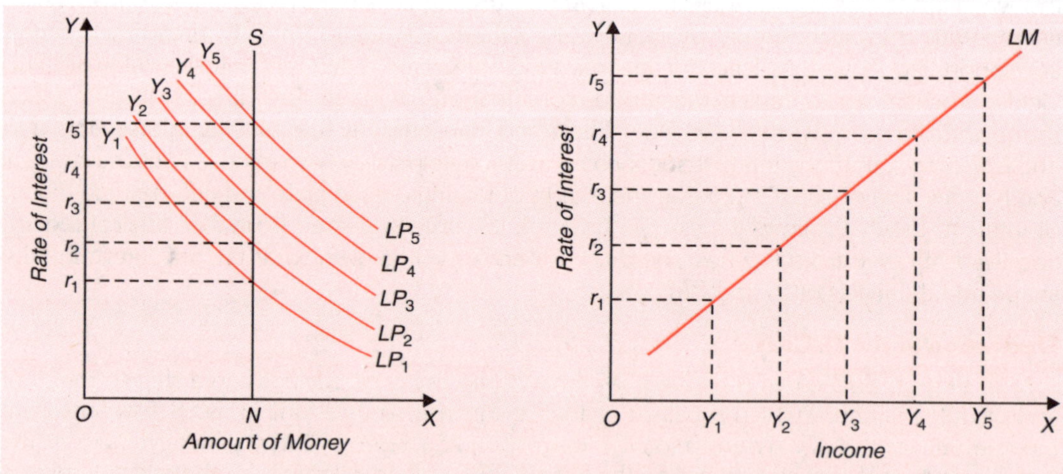

Fig. 56.9. *Derivation of LM Curve from a Family of Liquidity Preference Curves*

liquidity preference curves corresponding to different income levels with the supply curve of money fixed by the monetary authority would give us the *LM* curve which relates the rate of interest with the level of income as determined by *money-market equilibrium* corresponding to different levels of liquidity preferefice curve (Fig. 56.9). The *LM* curve tells us what the various rates of interest will be (given the quantity of money and the family of liquidity preference curves) at different levels of income. But the liquidity preference curves alone cannot tell us what exactly the rate of interest will be. In Fig. 56.9. (*a*) and (*b*) we have derived the *LM* curve from a family of liquidity preference curves. As income increases liquidly preference curve shifts outward and therefore the rate of interest which equates supply of money with demand for money rises. In Fig. 56.9 (*b*) we measure income on the *X*-axis and plot the income levels corresponding to the various interest rates determined at those income levels through money-market equilibrium by the equality of demand for and supply of money in Fig. 56.9 (*a*).

The Slope and Position of the *LM* Curve

It will be noticed from Figure 56.9 (*b*) that the *LM* curve slopes upward to the right. This is because with higher levels of income, demand for money (that is, the liquidity preference curve) is higher and consequently the money-market equilibrium, that is, the equality of the given money supply with liquidity preference curve, occurs at a higher rate of interest. This implies that rate of interest varies directly with income. It is important to know which factors determine the slope of the *LM* curve. There are two factors on which the slope of the *LM* curve depends. First, the responsiveness of demand for money (*i.e.*, liquidity preference) to the changes in income. As the income increases, say from Y_1 to Y_2, the liquidity preference curve shifts from LP_1 to LP_2, that is, with an increase in income, demand for money would increase for being held for transactions motive, $L_1 = f(Y)$. This extra demand for money would disturb the money-market equilibrium and for the equilibrium to be restored the rate of interest will rise to the level where the given money supply curve intersects the new liquidity preference curve corresponding to the higher income level. It is worth noting that in the new equilibrium position, with the given stock of money supply, money held under the transactions motive will increase whereas the money held for speculative motive will decline. The greater the extent to which demand for money for transactions motive increases with the increase in income, the greater the decline in the supply of money available for speculative motive and, given the liquidity preference schedule for speculative motive, the higher the rise in the rate of interest and consequently the steeper the *LM* curve, $r = f(M_2, L_2)$ where M_2 is the stock of money available for speculative motive and L_2 is the money demand or liquidity preference function for speculative motive.

The second factor which determines the slope of the *LM* curve is the elasticity or responsiveness of demand for money (*i.e.*, liquidity preference for speculative motive) to the changes in rate of interest. The lower the elasticity of liquidity preference with respect to the changes in interest rate, the steeper will be the *LM* curve. On the other hand, if the elasticity of liquidity preference (money-demand function) to the changes in the rate of interest is high, the *LM* curve will be relatively flat or less steep.

Shifts in the *LM* Curve : Another important thing to know about the *IS-LM* curve model is to know what brings about shifts in the *LM* curve or, in other words, what determines the position of the *LM* curve. As seen above, a *LM* curve is drawn with a given stock of money supply. Therefore, when the money supply increases, given the liquidity preference function, it will lower the rate of interest at the given level of income. This will cause *LM* curve to shift to the right. On the other hand, if money supply is reduced, given the liquidity preference (money demand) function, it will raise the rate of interest at the given level of income and will therefore cause the *LM* curve to shift above and to the left.

The other factor which causes a shift in the *LM* curve is the change in liquidity preference (money demand function) for a given level of income. If the liquidity preference function for a given level of income shifts upward, this, given the stock of money, will lead to the rise in the rate of interest. This will bring about a shift in the *LM* curve to the left. On the contrary, if the liquidity preference function for a given level of income declines, it will lower the rate of interest and will shift the *LM* curve down and to the right.

Intersection of the *IS* and *LM* Curves: Simultaneous Determination of Interest and Income

The *IS* curve and the *LM* curve relate the two variables : (*a*) income and (*b*) the rate of interest. Income and the rate of interest are therefore determined together at the point of intersection of these two curves, *i.e., E* in Fig. 56.10. The equilibrium rate of interest thus determined is Or_3 and the level of income determined is OY_3. At this point, income and the rate interest stand in relation to each other such that (1) investment and saving are in equilibrium and (2) the demand for money is in equilibrium with the supply of money (*i.e.,* the desired amount of money is equal to the actual supply of money). It should be noted that *LM* curve has been drawn by taking the supply of money as fixed.

Thus, a determinate theory of interest is based on : (1) the investment-demand function, (2) the saving function (or, conversely, the consumption function), (3) the liquidity preference function, and (4) the quantity of money. We see, therefore, that according to Hicks and Hansen, both monetary and real factors, namely, productivity, thrift, and the monetary factors, that is, the demand for money (liquidity preference) and supply of money play a part in the determination of the rate of interest. Any change in these factors will cause a shift in *IS* or *LM* curve and will therefore change the equilibrium level of the rate of interest and income.

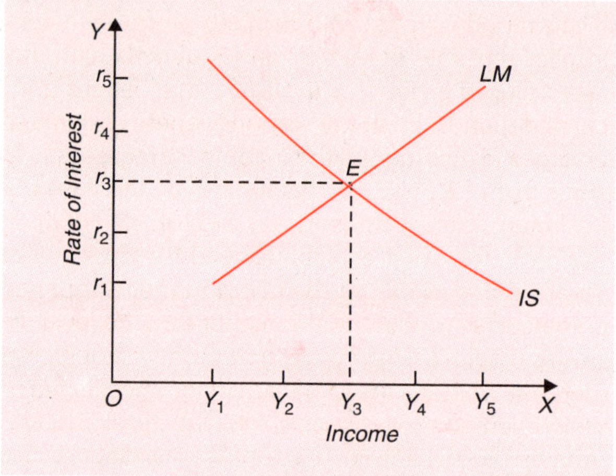

Fig. 56.10. *Simultaneous Determination of Interest and Income*

Hicks-Hansen theory explained above has succeeded in integrating the theory of money with the theory of income .determination. And by doing so, as we shall see below, it has succeeded in synthesising the monetary and fiscal policies. Further, with Hicks-Hansen analysis, we are better able to explain the effect of changes in certain important economic variables such as desire to save, the supply of money, investment, liquidity preference on the rate of interest.

Changes in the Supply of Money. Let us first consider what will happen if the supply of money is increased by the action of the Central Bank. Given the liquidity preference schedule, with the increase in the supply of money, more money will be available for speculative motive at a given level of income which will cause the interest rate to fall. As a result, the *LM* curve will shift to the right. With this rightward shift in the *LM* curve in the new equilibrium position, rate of interest will be lower and the level of income greater than before. This is shown in Figure 56.11. where with a given supply of money, *LM* and *IS* curves intersect at point *E*. With the increase in the supply of money, *LM* shifts to the dotted position *LM'* and with *IS* schedule remaining unchanged, new equilibrium is at point *G* corresponding to which rate of interest is lower and level of income greater than at *E*. Now, suppose that instead of increasing the supply of money, Central Bank of the country takes steps to reduce the supply of money. With the reduction in the supply of money, less money will be available for speculative motive at each level of income and as a result, the *LM* curve will shift to the left of *E,* and the *IS* curve remaining unchanged, in the new equilibrium position (as shown in Figure 56.11) the rate of interest will be higher and the level of income smaller than before.

Changes in the Desire to Save or Propensity to Consume : Let us consider what happens to the rate of interest when desire to save or, in other words, propensity to consumer changes. When people's desire to saive falls, that is, when propensity to consume rises, the aggregated demand will increase and therefore, level of national income will rise at each rate of interest. As a result, the *IS* curve will shift outward to the right. In Figure 56.12 suppose with a certain given fall in the desire to save (or increase in the propensity to consume), the *IS* curve shifts rightward to the position *IS′*. With *LM* curve remaining unchanged, the new equilibrium position will be established at *H* corresponding to which rate of interest as well as

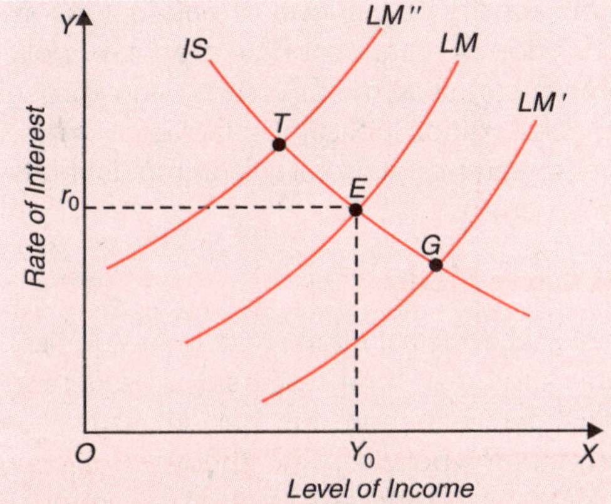

Fig. 56.11. *Impact of Change in Supply of Money*

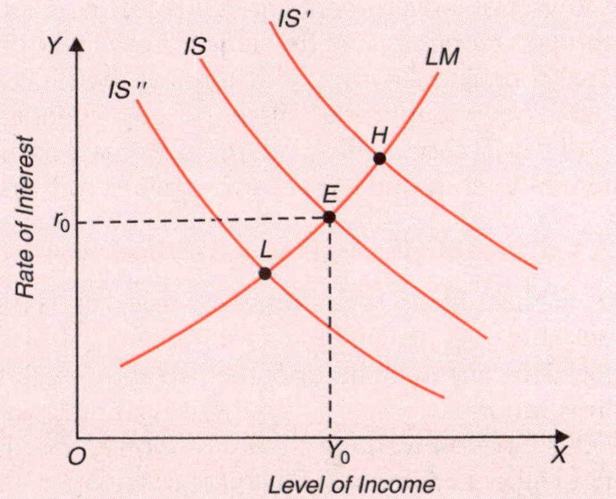

Fig. 56.12. Impact of Change in Propensity to Save on Rate of Interest and Income

level of income will be greater than at *E*. Thus, a fall in the desire to save has led to the increase in both rate of interest and level of income. On the other hand, if the desire to save rises, that is, if the propensity to consume falls, aggregate demand will decline which will cause the level of national income to fall for each rate of interest and as a result the *IS* curve will shift to the left. With this, and *LM* curve remaining unchanged, the new equilibrium position will be reached to the *left* of *E* (as shown in Figure 56.12) corresponding to which both rate of interest and level of national income will be smaller than at *E*.

Changes in Investment and Government Expenditure : Changes in investment and Government expenditure will also shift the *IS* curve. If either the private investment increases or Government steps up its expenditure, aggregate demand will increase and this will bring about the increase in national income through the multiplier process. This will shift *IS* schedule to the right, and, given the *LM* curve, the rate of interest as well as the level of income will rise. On the contrary, if somehow private investment expenditure falls or the Government reduces its expenditure, the level of national income will fall. With this, *IS* curve will shift to the left and, given the *LM* curve, both the rate of interest and level of national income will fall.

Changes in Liquidity Preference : Changes in liquidity preference will bring about changes in the *LM* curve. If the liquidity preference of the people rises, the *LM* curve will shift to the left. This is because higher liquidity preference, given the supply of money, will raise the rate of interest corresponding to each level of national income. With the leftward shift in the *LM* curve, given the *IS* curve, the equilibrium rate of interest will rise and the level of national income will fall.

On the contrary, if the liquidity preference of the people falls, the *LM* curve will shift to the right. This is because, given the supply of money, the downward shift in the liquidity preference curve means that corresponding to each level of income there will be lower rate of interest. With rightward shift in the *LM* curve, given the *IS* curve, the equilibrium rate of interest will fall and the equilibrium level of national income will increase.

We thus see that changes in propensity to consume (or desire to save), investment or Government expenditure, the supply of money and the liquidity preference will cause shifts in either *IS* or *LM* curves and will thereby bring about changes in the rate of interest as well as in national income. Hicks-Hansen integration of classical and Keynesian theories of interest clearly shows that Government can influence the economic activity or the level of national income through monetary and fiscal measures. Through adoption of an appropriate monetary policy (*i.e.* changing the supply of money) the Government can shift the *LM* curve and through pursuing an appropriate fiscal policy (expenditure and taxation policy) the Government can shift the *IS* curve. Thus both monetary and fiscal policy can play a useful role in regulating the rate of interest and level of economic activity in the country.

A Critique of Hicks-Hansen Synthesis or IS-LM Curve Model

Hicks-Hansen synthesis of classical and Keynesian theories of interest makes a significant advance in explaining the determination of the rate of interest. It represents a more general, inclusive and realistic approach to the interest rate determination. Further, Hicks-Hansen integration succeeds in synthesising fiscal with monetary policies, and theory of income determination with the theory of money. But Hicks-Hansen synthesis of interest theories is not without limitations. First, it is based upon the assumption that the rate of interest is quite flexible, that is, free to vary and not rigidly fixed by a Central Bank. If the rate of interest is quite inflexible, then the appropriate adjustments explained above will not take place. Secondly, the synthesis is also based upon the assumption that investment is interest-elastic, that is, investment varies with the rate of interest. If investment is interest-inelastic, then also the Hicks-Hansen synthesis breaks since the required adjustments do not occur .

Thirdly, Don Patinkin[16] and Milton Freidman have criticised Hicks-Hansen synthesis as being too artificial and over-simplified. In their view, division of the economy into two sectors—monetary and real—is artificial and unrealistic. According to them, monetary and real sectors are quite interwoven and act and react on each other. Further, Patinkin has pointed out that *Hicks-Hansen synthesis has ignored the possibility of changes in the price level of commodities*. According to him, the various economic variables such as supply of money, propensity to consume or save, investment, and liquidity preference not only influence the rate of interest and the level of income but also the prices of commodities and services. He has suggested a more integrated and general equilibrium approach which involves the simultaneous determination of not only the rate of interest and the level of income but also of prices of commodities and services. We shall not discuss here the views of Professor Patinkin because that will land us into the details of macroeconomics.

However, in modern economics, IS-LM curve model of determination of rate of interest and level of national income is widely believed to be correct explanation of determination of interest and level of national income is widely believed to be correct explanation of determination of interest. Besides IS-LM model incorporates the influence of both the monetary and real factors in the determination of rate of interest.

16. Don Patinkin, *Money; Interest and Prices*, Harper and Row, 1965.

WHY MONEY INTEREST RATE IS POSITIVE

Keynes's View. It is useful to explain why money interest rate is positive. We first explain it with the Keynesian theory of interest. According to Keynesian viewpoint, liquidity preference is absolute or infinite at very low positive interest rate, say 2 to 3 per cent rate of interest. According to him, when money interest rate falls to very low level the people are likely to expect that rate of interest will not fall further, in fact they expect it to rise in future. This discourages them to part with liquidity to lend it to others or to buy bonds. Therefore, they tend to hold any an amount of money at such low, though positive, interest rate. It is said that there is liquidity trap at low positive money interest rate. In this situation all the additional money which the Central Bank of a Counitry will crate will be absorbed or kept by them without causing any fall in the interest rate. Consider Figure 56.13 where *LP*. In represents liquidity preference curve

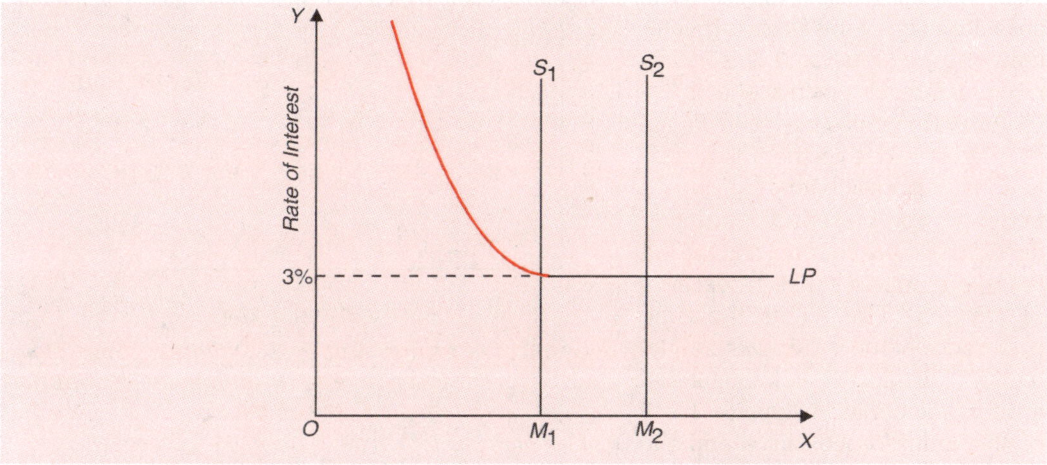

Fig. 56.13. Money Rate of Interest Money Supply remains positive

of the people which becomes horizontal or absolute at very low (3%) interest rate. With M_1 as the supply of money equilibrium interest rate is 3% which is considered to be very low by the people. Now, if the Central Bank creates new money and as a result money supply increases to M_2 . Due to the existence of liquidity trap interest rate remains unchanged at positive 3% money interest rate.

Fisher's Analysis. There is more important explanation of positive interest rate. According to Irving Fisher, a classical economist, whose explanation of interest is quite well known, not only *money interest rate* but also *real interest rate* is *normally* positive. In Fisher's analysis real interest rate is determined on the one hand by people's *impatience* to consume now rather than in the future (that is, people prefer present consumption) to future consumption and there is a certain rate of time preference of the people and on the other by the *productivity of capital* (which involves roundabout method of production) in which savings are inverted. If people prefer present consumption to future consumption and capital is productive (i.e. it has net productivity), then the real interest rate will be positive and not zero.

Fisher's analysis of determination of interest has been explained with Figure 56.14 in which indifference curves between present consumption and future consumption and also production posibility curve have been drawn. An indifference curve represents individual's preference for present consumption over future consumption. This positive preference for present consumption gives *vertical bias* to the indifference curves. On the other hand, the production possibilities curve *TT′* represents the productivity of capital (or rates of return) at various levels of investment. The net positive productivity of capital makes the production possibility curve also *vertically biased.* These indifference curves and production possibility curve are shown in Fig. 56.14. 45 line *OZ* represents equal consumption in the present and the next year. According to Fisher's theory, rate of interest is determined both by individuals' time preference and net marginal productivity of capital. At the equilibrium position *E*, the slopes of the indifference curve U_2 and production possibility curve *TT'* are equal. The slope of the tangent *kk'* drawn to these curves at the equilibrium point *E* is equal to $1 + i$ where *i* is the rate of interest. If the absolute value of this slope is greater than one (*i.e.* $1 + i > 1$), this means rate of interest is positive (that is, $i > 0$). According to Fisher, positive rate of interest is due to the impatience to consume now (that is, individual's preference of present consumption over future consumption) and the net return on capital (*i.e.* net productivity of capital). Thus, it is the time preference of the individuals and net marginal productivity of capital that ensures the conmon slope (= $1 + i$) of the indifference curve and the production possibility curve at the equilibrium point to be greater than one. ***This explains rate of interest will be generally positive and cannot be zero.***

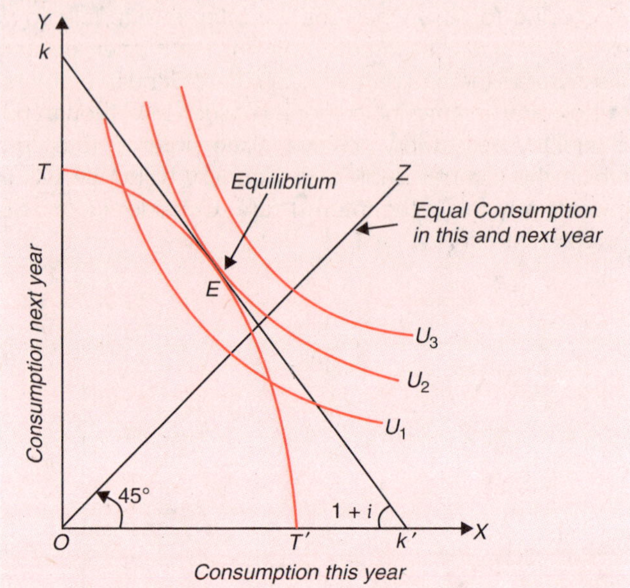

Fig. 56.14. *Fisher's Analysis of Interest: Both Time Preference and Productivity of Capital Determine Rate of Interest*

However, in case the absolute slope at the tangency point of indifference curve with the production possibilities curve is equal to one (*i.e.*, $1 + i = 1$), the real rate of interest will be zero ($i = 0$). This can happen if the individual is *neutral* between present consumption and future consumption and at the equilibrium point production possibility curve shows no net return on capital. However, the neutrality between present consumption and future consumption on the part of individual is not a normal behaviour. Further, capital has a net productivity which makes the production possibility curve having a slope greater than one.

To conclude, zero rate of interest can occur if people's behaviour regarding present and future consumption is not normal and capital does not show any net return. ***Thus, given the normal behaviour of the people regarding present and future consumption, and positive net productivity of capital, rate of interest cannot be zero if it is to be determined freely by market forces and not administered by government or Central Bank of the country.***

It may be noted here that in India in some recent years it has been observed that real rate of interest on bank deposits and other saving instruments have been negative. How do we explain this strange or unusual phenomenon. Remember that real rate of interest is equal to money interest rate minus rate of inflation. As in recent years (2008 – 2011) annual money rates of interest on bank deposits for the maturely period upto 3 years has been in the range of 6 per cent to 8 per cent while rate of inflation based on Consumer Price Index (CPI) has been above 10 per cent per annum which implies negative real rate of interest. Thus, it is high rate of inflation that has caused negative real interest rate. However, the negative real interest rates on bank deposits have not been without bad consequences. They have discouraged people to save in the form of bank deposits. The people have tended to be invest their savings in gold, jewellery and real estate whose prices have gone up yielding people high positive rates of return. However, people are still keeping a good amount of their savings in the form of bank deposits because they conseder them safe. Besides, people save and keep their savings as bank deposits not merely to earn interest rate. They need money for transaction purposes, for education and marriage of their children and for meeting contingencies such as illness.

CHAPTER

57

Theory of Profits

Introduction

After having discussed the determination of rent of land, wages of labour and interest on capital, we now pass on to the study of profits which are said to be the reward for enterprise, the fourth factor of production. No doubt profits are associated with entrepreneur and his functions but the economists from time to time have expressed diverse and conflicting views about the nature, origin and role of profits. Till today, there is no complete agreement among economists about the true nature and origin of profits. As a matter of fact, there has been perhaps no topic in the whole economic theory which has been in such a confused and tangled state as the theory of profits.

A part of the confusion in the theory of profits is due to the lack of agreement among economists about the true or proper function of the entrepreneur. Some have held the view that the function of the entrepreneur is to organise and co-ordinate the other factors of production. According to them, entrepreneur earns profits for his performing this function. On this view, enterprise is a special type of labour and profits a special form of wages. Some others have described the entrepreneur as performing joint and inseparable functions of *responsibility (i.e.,* ultimate risk bearing) and *control (i.e.,* ultimate decision making). The entrepreneur earns profits because he takes a risk of incurring losses when his price and output policies prove to be incorrect in view of the future business movements. Schumpeter has assigned to the entrepreneur the role of an innovator and profits as a reward for his introducing innovations. Lastly, F. H. Knight has emphasized uncertainty in the economy as a factor which gives rise to profits and bearing of uncertainty is the task of the entrepreneur.

Besides, some economists have described profits as ***non-functional income.*** Thus J.M. Keynes expressed the view that profits resulted from the favourable movements of the general price level. Joan Robinson, E.H. Chamberlin and M. Kalecki have associated profits with the imperfect competition and monopoly. According to them, the greater the degree of imperfection or, in other words, the greater the degree of monopoly power, the greater the profits made by the entrepreneur. Thus, profit has been associated by F. H. Knight with uncertainty, by Schumpeter with innovations, by Hawley with risk-bearing, and by Joan Robinson, E.H. Chamberlin and M. Kalecki with the degree of monopoly power. As a matter of fact, profits arise from all these sources. Therefore, no single explanation or theory of profits is adequate; each omits some crucial factors and fails to bring out some important economic phenomena having a relation with profits. Prof. B. S. Keirstead, therefore, expresses the view that profits originate from monopoly, successful innovation and a correct estimate of uncertain future. He thus says, "Profits may come to exist as a result of monopoly or monopsony, as a reward for innovation, as a reward for the correct estimate of uncertain factors, either particular to the industry or general to the whole economy."[1]

1. B.S. Keirstead, *Capital, Interest and Profits* (1959), p. 6.

It is worth mentioning that profits are ***residual income*** left after the payment of the contractual rewards to other factors of production. The entrepreneur while engaging other factors of production enters into contract with them. He thus pays wages to the workers, rent on the land employed, interest on the loans taken at the rate already fixed by contracts. In fact, the entrepreneur makes payments to these factors much in advance of the realisation of the values of the output produced after sale of the product. What is left after paying the contractual rewards of other factors employed is the profit of entrepreneur. Thus profits are ***non-contractual income*** and therefore they may be positive or negative, whereas the contractual income of other factors such as wages, rent and interest are always positive and never negative. It should be further noted that ***pure profits*** of the entrepreneur are found by subtracting from the gross residual income the ***imputed values of rent and interest*** on the self-owned land and capital employed by the entrepreneur and also the ***imputed wages*** for his work of routine management.

PROFIT AS A DYNAMIC SURPLUS

A popular conception of profits is that they arise in a dynamic economy, that is, in an economy where changes are taking place. In a static economy where nothing changes there can be no profits. It was J.B. Clark who first propounded that profits are a dynamic surplus. He argued that in a stationary state where no changes in conditions of demand and supply are occurring, the prices paid to the factors on the basis of their marginal productivity would exhaust the total value production and no profits would accrue to the entrepreneur. Profits result when selling prices of the goods exceed their cost of production. Now, in a competitive long-run equilibrium, price equals average cost of production (including normal profits which are in fact wages for routine supervision and management) and therefore no pure profits are made. Now, if no changes either in the conditions of demand or in the conditions of supply occur, competitive equilibrium will persist and therefore no profits will be earned by the entrepreneur. On the contrary, if due to the changes in either demand or supply, price exceeds cost of production, profits will emerge. If due to these changes, price falls below the cost of production, negative profits, that is, losses, will accrue to the entrepreneur. It is evident that changes disturb the equilibrium and thereby give rise to profits. In other words, profits arise due to ***disequilibrium*** caused by the changes in demand and supply conditions. Prof. Stigler rightly says, "Firms in a competitive industry may receive profits.....because of a state of disequilibrium....these profits can arise even if all entrepreneurs are identical, for disequilibrium can characterise a whole industry. If prices are higher, or costs lower than were anticipated, entrepreneurs will receive a return in excess of the alternative product of their resources. If prices were lower or costs higher than were anticipated, entrepreneurs will receive less than the alternative product of their resources, *i.e.*, negative profits. Positive profits may persist for a long time if firms outside the industry are slow to enter the industry and negative profits can persist as long as specialised equipment yields more when used in the industry than when used elsewhere, say as scrap."[2]

It should be noted that these disequilibrium profits arise from ***unanticipated* changes in demand or cost conditions.** If the changes could have been foreseen in advance, then suitable adjustments could have been made according to the anticipated changes so that forces of competition would have driven profits to zero.

Now the question is, what changes occur in the economy and give rise to profits ? J. B. Clark mentioned five changes that occur in a dynamic economy and which give rise to profits.

2. G.J. Stigler, *The Theory of Price* (revised edition, 1952), p. 181.

These five changes are : changes in the quantity and quality of human wants, changes in methods or techniques of production, changes in the amount of capital, and changes in the forms of business organisation. These changes are constantly taking place and bring about the divergence between price and cost and thereby give rise to profits, positive or negative. If the demand for a commodity increases due to the increase in population or increase in the incomes of the people or due to the increase in consumers' preference for the commodity, the price of the commodity will rise, and if cost remains the same, profits would accrue to the entrepreneurs producing the commodity. On the other hand, cost of production may go down as a result of the adoption of a new technique of production, or as a result of cheapening of the raw material, and if price remains constant or does not fall to the same extent, the profits would emerge.

Apart from the five changes mentioned by Clark, there are other changes also which occur in the economy. All the changes which take place and as a result of which profits arise in a dynamic economy may be classified into two types : (1) ***innovations*** and (2) ***exogenous changes.*** Innovations represent changes which are introduced by individual entrepreneurs themselves. The entrepreneur earns large profits from introducing innovations such as a new product, a new and cheaper method of production, a new method of marketing the product, a new way of advertisement. The innovational changes may either reduce cost or increase the demand for the product and thereby bring profits into existence. Those entrepreneurs who introduce successful innovations earn large profits. But as the innovation gets known to other entrepreneurs or they adopt similar other innovations, profits which arose because of a particular innovation tend to disappear. But new innovations are being continuously introduced by the entrepreneurs and profits continue to arise out of them.

Exogenous changes refer to those changes which are external to the firms or industries in an economy. These changes affect all firms in an industry or sometimes all the industries in the economy. Examples of exogenous changes are breaking out of wars, occurrence of sometimes periods of inflation and rising prices and sometimes business depression and falling prices, changes in the monetary and fiscal policies of government affecting favourably or unfavourably, changes in the technology of production, changes in tastes and preferences of the consumers, changes in income and spending habits of the people, changes in the availability of substitute products, alteration in the legislative and legal environment affecting the industries, and changes in preferences between income and leisure. All these changes affect either the cost or demand of the products and give rise to profits, positive or negative as the case may be. For instance, during war when prices of goods mount up, and costs lag behind, the entrepreneurs make a lot of profits. Similarly, when inflation occurs due to the increased demand for goods caused by rising incomes, increasing population and expansion in the money supply, the huge profits accrue to the firms. On the contrary, when period of depression comes due to the fall in effective aggregate demand, firms suffer huge losses and some may go into liquidation. During periods of depression, all prices, rents, wages, and interest tend to fall but because of the non-contractual nature, profits fall sharply and even become negative.

Here the views of Prof. F. H. Knight about dynamic changes giving rise to profits are worth mentioning. According to him, "Dynamic changes give rise to a peculiar form of income only in so far as the changes and their consequences are unpredictable in character..... It cannot, then, be the change which is the cause of profits, since if the law of change is known, as in fact is largely the case, no profits can arise. The connection between change and profits is uncertain and always indirect. Change may cause a situation out of which profit will be made, if it brings about ignorance of the future ......It is not dynamic change, nor any change as such which causes profits, but divergence of actual conditions from those which have been expected and on the basis of which business arrangements have been made. For satisfactory explanation of profit we seem to be thrown back from the dynamic theory to the *uncertainty of the future*."[3]

As far as unpredictable, unforeseen changes and uncertainty about the future giving rise to profits are concerned, there can be no disagreement with Prof. Knight. But with his assertion that dynamic changes as such are not the cause of profits, one can differ. Against Knight's view it may be pointed out that if there is no change there will be no uncertainty about the future and therefore no profits. Thus the factor of change is fundamental in bringing profits into existence. Professors Stonier and Hague rightly maintain, "In an economy where nothing changes, there can be no profits. There is no uncertainty about the future, so there are no risk and no profits."[4]

INNOVATIONS AND PROFITS : SCHUMPETER'S THEORY OF PROFITS

Successful innovations as important dynamic changes and as source of profit has been, in brief, explained above. But since innovation has been signed out as a very important factor responsible for the occurrence of profits to the entrepreneurs, it requires to be dealt with separately. It has been held by Joseph Schumpter that the main function of the entrepreneur is to introduce innovations in the economy and profits are reward for his performing this function. Now, what is innovation ? Innovation, as used by Schumpeter, has a very wide connotation. Any *new* measure or policy adopted by an entrepreneur to reduce his cost of production or to increase the demand for his product is an innovation. Thus, innovations can be divided into two categories.

First type of innovations are those which reduce cost of production, or in other words, which change the production functions. In this first type of innovations are included the introduction of a new machinery, new and cheaper technique or process of production, exploitation of a new source of raw material, a new and better method of organising the firm, etc. Second type of innovations are those which increase the demand for the product, or in other words, which change the demand or utility function. In this category are included the introduction of a new product, a new variety or design of the product, a new and superior method of advertisement, discovery of new markets etc. If an innovation proves successful, that is, if it achieves its aim of either reducing the cost of production or enhancing the demand for the product, it will give rise to profit. Profits emerge because due to successful innovation either cost falls below the prevailing price of the product or the entrepreneur is able to sell more and at a better price than before. It should be noted that profits accrue not to him who conceives innovation nor to him who finances it but to him who introduces it. Further, whenever any new innovation is contemplated to be introduced, it always calls for a new combination of factors or realloction of resources.

It is here worth mentioning that profits caused by a particular innovation are only temporary and tend to be competed away as others imitate and also adopt that. An innovation ceases to be new or novel, when others also coime to know of it and adopt it. When an entrepreneur introduces a new innovation, he is first in a monopoly position, for the new innovation is confined to him only. He therefore makes large profits. When after some time others also adopt it in order to get a share, profits will disappear. If the law allows and the entrepreneur is able to get his new innovation, *e.g.*, new product patented, then he will continue to earn profits.

3. F. H. Knight, *Risk, Uncertainty and Profits*, pp. 37-38.
4. Stonier and Hague, *A Textbook of Economic Theory*, 2nd edition, p. 327.

But in a competitive economy and without patent laws, the existing competitors or the new firms will soon adopt any successful innovation and profits would be eliminated. But in a competitive and progressive economy the entrepreneurs always continue to introduce new innovations and thus profits continue emerging out of them. Thus.Prof. Stigler says, "Unless one can construct a permanent monopoly, such profits as are realized by successful innovation are essentially transitional and will be eliminated by the attempts of other firms to share them. But these profits may exist for a considerable time because of the ignorance of other firms of their existence or because of the time required for the entry of new firms. More important, the successful innovator can continuously seek new disequilibrium profits since the horizon of conceivable innovations is unlimited."[5]

We have seen above that innovations are important source of profits. Obtaining profits is a necessary incentive for the entrepreneurs to conceive and introduce innovations which help the economic development of the country. Since innovations, if successful, yield profits and profit is also the motive to introduce innovations, profits are both the cause and effect of innovations.

RISK, UNCERTAINTY AND PROFITS : KNIGHT'S THEORY OF PROFITS

An important theory associates profit with risk and uncertainty. According to F. H. Knight, profit is a reward for uncertainty bearing. Even before Knight, F. B. Hawley and A. C. Pigou had pointed out that entrepreneurs earned profits because they had to bear the risks of undertaking production. But Knight has greatly developed the theory of profits based on uncertainty. He has distinguished between risk and uncertainty on the one hand and predictable and unpredictable changes on the other. According to him, dynamic changes give rise to profits in so far as changes and their consequences are unpredictable in character. Only those changes whose occurrence cannot be known before hand give rise to profit.

As we have noted above, if there were no changes or if the changes were foreseen and predictable, there would have been no uncertainty about the future and no profits. Profits arise because of the uncertainty of future. If the future conditions could be completely foreknown in the present, then competition would certainly adjust things to the ideal state where all prices would equal costs and profits would not emerge. Thus, it is our ignorance about the future and uncertainty of it that give rise to profits. In other words, it is the divergence of actual conditions from those which have been expected and on the basis of which business arrangements have been made that give rise to uncertainty and profits. Prof. A. K. Dass Gupta rightly maintains, "Uncertainty is thus a permanent feature of economic system. It is one of the limitations of human ingenuity that it cannot unearth the contents of the future. Trained instincts of businessmen coupled with statistical information may go a long way, but in so far as the course of nature (both physical and human) is anything but rhythmical, the future would always remain more or less of mystery."[6] He further writes : "So long as entrepreneurs start operations with imperfect knowledge about the state of the market and so long as the anticipated marginal product of the hired factors deviates from their actual product, so long a surplus would persist."[7]

We thus see that entrepreneurs have to undertake the work of production under conditions of uncertainty. In advance they have to make estimates of the future conditions regarding demand for the product and other factors which affect price and costs. In view of their estimates and anticipations, they make contract with the suppliers of factors of production in advance at

5. G. J. Stigler, *op. cit.*, p. 182.
6. A.K. Dass Gupta, *The Conception of Surplus in Theoretical Economics*, p. 188.
7. *Ibid*, p. 188.

fixed rates of remuneration. They realise the value of the output produced by the hired factors after it has been produced and sold in the market. But a good deal of time is spent in the process of producing and selling the product. It follows, therefore, that a good time gap elapses between the contracts made by the entrepreneur with the factors of production at fixed rates and the realisation of sale proceeds from the output made by them. As mentioned before, these contracts are based upon anticipations about the future conditions. But between the time of contracts and the sale of the output many changes may take place which may upset anticipations for good or for worse and thereby give rise to the profits, positive and negative. Now, if the conditions prevailing at the time of the sale of output could be known or predicted when the entrepreneurs enter into contractual relationships with the factors of production about their rates of remuneration, there would have been no uncertainty and, therefore, no profits. Thus ***uncertainty, that is, ignorance about the future conditions of demand and supply, is the core of profits.*** It should be noted that positive profits accrue to those entrepreneurs who make correct estimate of the future or whose anticipations prove to be correct. Those whose anticipations prove to be incorrect will have to suffer losses.

We thus see that profit is a residual and non-contractual income which accrues to the entrepreneurs because of the fact of uncertainty. The entrepreneur is unhired factor; he hires others for work of production. It is, therefore, entrepreneur who bears uncertainty and earns profits as a reward for that. J.F. Weston who has been a prominent exponent and supporter of uncertainty theory of profits explains the emergence of profits in the following way : "Under uncertainty total product may not be equal to total costs (explicit and implicit) *because plans are not fulfilled.* How this occurs is briefly indicated. Two classes of owners of productive services are distinguished. First, those with rates of compensation fixed in advance of the determination of the results of operations, are called *hired factors* and receive contractual returns. Second, those with rates of compensation dependent upon the results of operation are referred to as *unhired factors* who receive non-contractual or residual returns. Whatever the basis upon which contractual relationships have been entered, actual results will not have been accurately foreseen because of uncertainty. Hence whatever ***the basis upon which contractual commitments have been made events actually do not turn out that way.*** This is the significance of economic profit. ***It is not possible to plan in advance exactly what total product or total costs will be.***"[8]

Now, the question is what changes cause uncertainty ? As has been explained earlier, there are *two types of changes* which take place and are responsible for conditions of uncertainty. First type of changes refer to the innovations (for example, introduction of a new product or a new and cheaper method of production etc.) which are introduced by the entrepreneurs themselves. These innovations not only create uncertainty for the rivals or competitors who are affected by them but they also involve uncertainty for the entrepreneur who introduces them, for one cannot be certain whether a particular innovation will be definitely successful. The second type of changes which cause uncertainty are those which are external to the firms and industries. These changes are: changes in tastes and fashions of the people, changes in Government policies and laws especially taxation, wage and labour policies and laws, movements of prices as a result of inflation and depression, changes in the incomes of the people, changes in production technology etc. All these changes cause uncertainty and bring profits, positive or negative, into existence.

We have seen above that entrepreneurs work under conditions of uncertainty and that

8. J. Fred Weston, A Generalized Uncertainty Theory of Profit, *American Economic Review,* XL (March 1950), (Italics added).

they bear uncertainty and earn profits as a reward for that. Here a distinction drawn by F. H. Knight between ***insurable risk* and *non-insurable risk*** is worth mentioning. Because of the changes that are continuously occurring in the economy, entrepreneur has to face many risks. But all risks do not cause uncertainty and give rise to profits. It is only ***non-insurable risks*** that involve uncertainty and the entrepreneur earns profits for bearing these non-insurable risks. This raises the question as to what kind of risks are insurable and what non-insurable. The entrepreneur faces risks like fire, theft, accident etc. which may cause him huge losses. But these risks of fire, theft, accident etc. can be insured against on the payment of a fixed premium. Insurance premium is included in the cost of production. Thus, no uncertainty arises due to insurable risks as far as individual entrepreneurs are concerned and therefore they cannot give rise to profits.

Only those risks can be insured the probability of whose occurrence can be calculated. Thus, an insurance company knows by its calculation on the basis of past statistics that how much percentage of the factories will catch fire in a year. On the basis of this information, it will fix the rate of premium and is able to insure the factories against this risk. But there are risks which cannot be insured and therefore they have to be borne by the entrepreneurs. These non-insurable risks relate to the outcomes of the price-output decisions to be taken by the entrepreneurs. Whether it will pay him to increase output, reduce output and what will be the outcome in terms of profits or losses as a result of his particular output decision. Again, whether it will pay him to lower price or to raise it and when he takes a particular price decision whether he would make profits or losses. Similarly, he has to face risks as a result of his decisions regarding mode of advertisement and outlay to be made on it, product variation etc. For taking all these decisions he has to guess about demand and cost conditions and there is always risk of suffering losses as a result of these decisions. No insurance company can insure the entrepreneurs against commercial losses which may emerge out of decisions regarding price, output, product variation and also against the losses which may fall upon the entrepreneurs due to the structural, cyclical and other exogenous changes which take place in the economy. It is, therefore, clear that ***it is non-insurable risks that involve uncertainty and give rise to profits.*** To quote Knight, "It is 'uncertainty' distinguished from insurable risk that effectively gives rise to the entrepreneurial form of organisation and to the much condemned 'profit' as an income form."[9]

Knight's theory rightly emphasised that uncertainty in a dynamic business environment gives rise to profits. The bearing of uncertainty is an important function to be performed by the entrepreneurial class in a society. This makes the profits as functional income that is earned for performing the function of uncertainty bearing. But all profits are not functional nor do they arise due to uncertainty. As we have studied in the theories of monopoly, monopolisitc competition, oligopoly in product markets and monopsony in factor markets, that a significant amount of profits arises due to the monopoly power enjoyed by the producers. Knight's theory ignores the fact of monopoly power giving rise to profits. M. Kalecki whose theory of profits we will discuss below propounded that monopoly power was an important source of profits in modern free-market economies. It is also worth mentioning that monopoly profits can arise even in a stationary economy where no changes are taking place.

Further, in our view that while the profits may emerge as a result of dynamic changes, innovations and uncertainty but the ***appropriation*** of profits by the recipients is *institutionally* determined. The *separate* theories must be developed to explain the *origin* of profits and *sharing out* of profits. For instance, Weintraub points out that "The entrepreneur's function is

9. 'Social Economic Policy', *Canadian Journal of Economics and Political Science* (26 Feb. 1960), p. 31.

directed and executed with an eye towards profit making, *the sharing of profits is an entirely separate issue."*[10] Likewise, R.A. Gordan states : "It is important to bear in mind that accounting for the *origin* and *existence* of an income does not in itself explain its allocation to particular persons or classes. The way in which a given income accrues to various individuals will depend largely on how those individuals fit into the ***institutional setting*** which prevails. Thus, though 'pure profits' may be explainable in terms of change, uncertainty and friction (essentially a nonfunctional explanation), the fact that these gains go to particular persons is related not to exercise of entrepreneurial function, but rather to the ***nature and distribution of ownership rights.***"

MONOPOLY THEORY OF PROFITS

We have explained above that profits can originate from dynamic changes, innovations, and from making a correct estimate of future under conditions of uncertainty. But monopoly is another source of profits. Monopolistic position gives rise to profits both in static and dynamic conditions. Monopolist commands a control over the price of a product and therefore manages to make profits by virtue of his monopoly power. He raises price by restricting his level of output and thereby makes profits. Monopoly is a matter of degree only. Monopoly power is exercised not only by a pure monopolist which produces a product which has no close substitutes but also to somewhat lesser extent by the producers working under monopolistic competition and oligopoly. We have seen in our chapters on product pricing under imperfect competition that monopoly element is present in various categories of imperfect competition, namely, pure monopoly, monopolistic competition and oligopoly. It is due to this monopoly element in these categories of imperfect competition that demand curve slopes downward in them. Thus, monopoly power is associated with downward-sloping demand curve.

We have seen in our chapters on pricing and output under pure monopoly, monopolistic competition and oligopoly that due to monopoly power and resultant downward-sloping demand curve, firm's equilibrium, that is, equality between marginal revenue and marginal cost, is reached at a price which is higher than marginal cost of production. Further, the price so determined is often higher than average cost of production which yields positive profits to the firm enjoying monopoly power to a greater or smaller degree. Owing to the strong barriers for the entry of new firms, the firms working under pure monopoly and oligopoly continue to make supernormal profits even in the long run. Even under monopolistic competition with a large number of firms, due to product differentiation entry into the industry is not fully free, as was later realised by Chamberlin himself. Product differentiation gives a firm a certain degree of monopoly power in setting his own price and no new firms can produce exactly the same product as that of any existing firm under monopolistic competition. With only restricted entry of firms under monopolistic competition, demand curve does not fall, even in the long run, to the tangency position with the average cost curve so that the entrepreneurs working under monopolistic competition also continue to enjoy positive profits by virtue of their monopoly power. Commenting on monopoly as a source of profits, Professor Pen writes, "The real monopolist—the one and only supplier in a branch of industry—is rare, but in many cases a breath of monopoly pervades competition. One brand is not the same as another—the one and only supplier in a branch of industry—is rare, but in many cases a breath of monopoly pervades competition. One brand is not the same as another—economists call that product differentiation, and as a result an element of monopoly power creeps into the market that yields an extra profit for the supplier. He can fix his own price, which is impossible under

10. Weintraub, *An Approach to the Theory of Income Distribution*, p. 203.

perfect competition, and perhaps he extends his volume of production a little less than he would otherwise have done. In some cases this limitation of production is an obvious danger; contrived scarcity leads to profit for a small group and to harm for the public."[11]

As we have discussed in a previous chapter, A. P. Lerner has provided a quantitative measure of the degree of monopoly present in any market situation. Lerner's quantitative measure of the degree of monopoly is based on the fact that whenever monopoly power is present and as a result demand curve is downward-sloping, price set by the producer will deviate from marginal cost. Further, this measure of degree of monopoly power is based upon ideal market situation of perfect competition, in which monopoly element is completely absent and in equilibrium price is equal to marginal cost. According to Lerner, if p stands for price and m for marginal cost, the difference $p - m$ measures the deviation from perfect competition ideal, or in other words, the extent of monopoly power present in any real market situation.

The difference, $p - m$, expressed as a fraction of price, p, that is, $\frac{p-m}{p}$ is Lerner's measure of degree of monopoly. Now, it has been asserted by many exponents of monopoly theory of profits, especially M. Kalecki, that the greater the degree of monopoly $\left(\frac{p-m}{p}\right)$, the greater the size of profits earned by the entrepreneur or firm. According to M. Kalecki, the degree of monopoly as given by Lerner's measure, $\frac{p-m}{p}$, is the most important factor determining the volume of profits; indeed, according to him, it is the only determinant of the level of profits.

It should be noted that the degree of monopoly power of a firm, or in other words, its power to set price above marginal cost of production depends upon the *elasticity of the demand curve* facing him. We have already proved in on earlier chapter that the Lerner's measure of degree of monopoly $\left(\frac{p-m}{p}\right)$ is equal to price reciprocal of price elasticity of demand (*i.e.*, l/ e). That is, the smaller the elasticity of demand for a product, the greater the degree of monopoly power. But the elasticity of demand for a firm's product depends on the extent to which product is different from others; the greater the extent to which its product is differentiated, the less the elasticity aad consequently the greater the degree of monopoly.

The second factor on which the monopoly power of a firm depends is its share in the market or in the total output of the industry. The greater its share in the industrial output or market for the product, the greater the extent of monopoly power wielded by a producer. This is because the greater its share in the market or total output of the market, the greater will be his freedom and independence in setting the price. Now, with the monopoly power gained by the extent of distinctiveness of his product and his share in the total output or market, the producer succeeds in setting price above cost of production and thereby earns supernormal profits for himself.

It is often pointed out that monopoly power possessed by a producer is no guarantee of positive profits, if demand for the product is inadequate and cost of production is high. In case of unfavourable demand-cost situations, producers working under pure monopoly, monopolistic competition and oligopoly enjoying varying degrees of monopoly power can make losses. In

11. Jan Pen, *Income Distribution*, Penguin Books, p. 134.

fact, in earlier chapters we too have shown that producers under pure monopoly and monopolistic competition respectively make losses in the short run in spite of the monopoly power possessed by them when the demand conditions for the product produced by them are not favourable. Thus, according to Professor Bober, "he skates on thin ice who identifies profits with monopoly and monopoly with profits."[12]

No doubt there is a good deal of possibility of losses being earned in the short run by firms under monopolistic competition (when there is a large number of firms), but the possibility of losses in case of pure monopoly and oligopoly should not be exaggerated. Pure monopoly and oligopoly generally go together with big business which is organised on corporate basis. Big corporate firms working under pure monopoly and oligopoly and enjoying a lot of monopoly power do not take the consumer's demand as given but seek to ***manipulate and create*** demand and have enough resources to do so. Through product variation, advertisements and other sales promotion devices, big corporate firms having a good deal of monopoly power ***succeed in shifting the demand curve for their product.*** Thus through the devices of persuasive advertisement, product variation and other sales promotion activities the big firms with greater monopoly power see to it that the demand curve for their product remains above cost of production yielding them a good deal of profits.

Further, firms with varying degrees of monopoly power not only exploit the consumers by setting a higher price and thereby earn profits but often they are also often ***monopsonist or oligopsonist in various factor markets.*** With their monopsonistic power they also exploit the factors, especially labour, and pay them less than their marginal revenue products. By exploiting the hired factor, they increase their share of profits.

Monopoly power of a firm manifests itself in its ability to raise price of the product. But if a firm sets a higher price and thereby earns excessive profits, it will attract other firms into the industry and will reduce the monopoly power of the existing firms and eliminate excessive profits. Therefore, authors such as F. Machlup[13], F. H. Hahn[14] and Jean Marchal[15] have emphasized that in order that the monopoly power be enduring and lasting and therefore firms continue to enjoy monopoly profits, there must be ***strong barriers to the entry of firms.*** Thus monopoly power and the profits accruing because of that ultimately depends on the restrictions on the entry of firms. Control over the supply of an essential raw material, legal restrictions in certain cases such as patent rights, the existence of goodwill enjoyed by the existing firms, reputation of brands and trade names of the products of existing firms, economies of large-scale production and difficulty of organising production on a large scale are some of the important factors that put restrictions on the entry of firms and make possible the earning of the monopoly profits by the existing firms enjoying a high degree of monopoly power.

Critical Evaluation of Monopoly Theory of Profits

It is certainly true that monopoly is a good source of profits. Theories of imperfect competition and monopolistic competition by Joan Robinson and Chamberlin involving downward-sloping demand curve with its implication of price-setting power made a significant contribution not only to price theory as such but also to the profit theory. But Kalecki's assertion that monopoly is the ***only source or determinant*** of profits is not right. Dynamic changes, innovations by the entrepreneurs themselves, uncertainty are also important causes of profits and in any adequate explanation of profits these things can hardly be neglected. Further, there

12. M.M. Bober, *Intermediate Price and Income Theory.*
13. Fritz Machlup, Competition, Pilopoly and Profit, *Economica,* Vol. XI, 1942.
14. F. H. Hahn, A Note on Profit and Uncertainty, *Economica,* Vol. XIV, 1947.
15. Jean Marchal, The Construction of a New Theory of Profits, *American Economic Review,* Vol. XLI, 1954.

is no any contradiction between uncertainty and monopoly theories of profits. As has been asserted by F. H. Hahn[16], market imperfections in monopolistic competition and oligopoly increase uncertainty and further that this uncertainty makes the entry of firms more difficult. Thus the theory which attributes profits to monopoly power only supplements the uncertainty theory of profits rather than replace it.

Kalecki's concept of the degree of monopoly $\left(\frac{p-m}{p}\right)$ and profits resting on it has been criticized. For instance, measure of the degree of monopoly $\left(\frac{p-m}{p}\right)$ is zero under perfect competition, since price (p) is equal to marginal cost (m) under it. It implies that under perfect competition with zero degree of monopoly the share of profits (*i.e.*, capital) will be zero and the share of labour will be 100% which is obviously unrealistic and ridiculous. To quote Pen, "Unfortunately upon closer examination the Kaleckian theory proves disappointing. We have a presentiment of this when we examine what happens under perfect competition, *i.e.*, a neo-classical world. Then the formula produces odd results : the degree of the monopoly is zero, and the share of labour is 100%. But nevertheless capital remains scarce and productive — it is improbable that it would receive no remuneration. Now, of course, it may be argued that Kalecki's theory was not designed for such a world but all the same it ought to be able to embrace this borderline case as well."[17]

It should be noted that much of the criticisms against monopoly theory of profits is against Kalecki's measure of degree of monopoly and its association with profits. That monopoly is an important cause and source of profits cannot be denied. Kalecki particularly used *macro* degree of monopoly and explained with it the distributive shares of profits and wages in national income. We will discuss this Kalecki's macro-theory of distribution based on Lerner's concept of degree of monopoly in the next chapter.

QUESTIONS FOR REVIEW

1. There can be no profits in a stationary state. Discuss.
2. "Profit is the reward for making innovations". Do you consider this statement as an adequate explanation for profits?
3. What is the role of profit in a free market economy ? Is there a conflict between profit earning and social welfare ?
4. Explain why profits are zero in a competitive equilibrium of an industry.
5. Profit is a reward for bearing uncertainty. Discuss.
6. Critically examine Kalecki's theory that profits arise due to monopoly power enjoyed by the producers in a capitalist economy.
7. 'Profits are a dynamic surplus' Critically examine.
8. Profits arise due to disequilibrium caused by unanticipated changes in price or costs. Discuss.

16. *Op. cit.* p. 291.
17. *Op. cit.* p. 177.

CHAPTER

58

Alternative Macro-Theories of Distribution

PROBLEM OF DISTRIBUTIVE SHARES

We have explained in the last few chapters how the prices of the various factors of production, such as land, labour, capital and enterprise, are determined. The theory of the determination of factor prices, that is, rent, wages, interest and profits, is known as the theory of distribution since on these prices it depends to a good extent how the national income and output will be distributed among the owners of these factors of production. We may again remind the student that we in economic theory are concerned *with functional or factoral* distribution of income *(i.e.,* distribution of income between the factors as rewards for their contribution to output) and not with *personal* distribution of income (*i.e,* the distribution of income among various individuals in the society). The two types of distribution, though quite distinct, are greatly interrelated. Given the distribution of the ownership of non-human resources such as land, factories, capital equipment as determined by the society's structure of property rights, the personal distribution of income will depend upon the prices of the various factors.

But our approach so far to the problem of distribution has been mainly neo-classical. At the hands of the neo-classical writers, the theory of distribution became mainly the theory of the determination of relative factor prices rather than the distribution of national income among the aggregative shares of rents, wage and profits in the society. Thus the neo-classical theory which has been incorporated in most of the modern textbooks of economics has been concerned with the process of the determination of *factor prices* : rent, wage, interest, and with the demand for a factor by an individual firm or industry. In other words, in the neo-classical theory the distribution of income has been treated as a micro-economic problem. It does not provide us with an answer to an important question of how the *aggregate shares* of the various factors such as labour and capital are determined. In other words, it does not explain how the *shares* of total wage income *(i.e.,* the total share of the labour class) or total profits *(i.e.,* the total share of the property owning class) are determined. How the total *shares* of the various categories of income are determined is the subject-matter of the *Macro-Theory of Distribution.* This is also called the ***Aggregative Theory of Income Distribution.*** Thus, whereas micro-theory of distribution deals with the analysis of the determination of the *relative prices of the factors,* macro-theory of distribution is concerned with the analysis of the determination ***of relative shares of the factors*** in the total national income. Therefore, macro-theory of distribution is also known as ***theory of distributive shares.***

The interest in this problem of distribution of income into factoral shares goes back to Ricardo who emphasised that how the national output is distributed among the various social classes—landlords, workers and capitalists—is the principal problem in economic analysis. It may be noted that Ricardo's interest in the problem of determination of distributive shares was not so much due to the importance of this question *per se* but because he thought that the theory of distribution was crucial to understand the working of the whole economic system and the forces which determine its growth. Thus, Prof. Kaldor remarks, "Ricardo's concern in the problem of distribution was not due, or not only due, to the interest in the question of distributive shares *per se,* but to the belief that the theory of distribution holds the key to an understanding of the whole mechanism of the economic system—of the forces governing the rate of progress, of the ultimate incidence of taxation, of the effects of protection and so on. It was through the laws which regulate distributive shares that he was hoping to build what in present-day parlance we would call 'a simple macro-economic model'."[1]

The present-day concern with the macro-theory of distribution has been aroused by the empirical finding that ***share of wages in national income*** remained constant in the present-day advanced capitalist economies till the end of the second World War in spite of the fact that in these countries there was a good deal of changes in techniques of production and a rapid progress in terms of per capita income and capital accumulation relative to labour during this period. It was only by explaining what determines the shares of wages, profits, etc., in the national income that some economists were able to account for the historical constancy of the labour share in the national income. It is worth mentioning that the historical constancy of labour share in national income is contrary to what Ricardo had thought. Ricardo was of the view that as the economy develops, relative shares of wages, profits and rent would vary. Ricardo wrote in the preface to his book, "in different stages of society the *proportions* of the whole produce of earth which will be allotted to each of these (three) classes under the names of rent, profit and wages will be essentially ***different.***"[2]

In chapter 51 we discussed the neo-classical theory of macro-distribution based on marginal productivity theory. We shall discuss below various alternative theories which explain the determination of aggregative share of wages, profits, etc., in the national income. These alternative theories which explain the distributive shares can be classified under the following four heads :

(1) The Ricardian or Classical Theory.

(2) The Marxian Theory.

(3) Kalecki's Degree of Monopoly Theory.

(4) Keynesian or Kaldor's Theory.

We shall explain below each of these theories separately.

RICARDIAN OR CLASSICAL THEORY OF INCOME DISTRIBUTION

In Ricardo's theory the economy is divided into two broad sectors—agriculture and industry.. But the agricultural sector occupies a crucial place in the Ricardian model, since it is the forces working in the agricultural sector that determine the distributive shares in the industry. Besides, Ricardo's theory is based upon three assumptions. First, it is assumed that law of diminishing returns operates in agriculture. That is, when more labour is applied to the agricultural land, average and marginal products of labour diminish. Secondly, Ricardo assumes the Malthusian law of population according to which the population will increase if the wage rate rises above the minimum subsistence level, and the population will decrease if the wage rate falls below it. With the changes in population as a result of variation in the wage rate above and below the subsistence level, the wage rate tends to be equal to the subsistence level in the long run.

1. N. Kaldor, Alternative Theories of Distribution, *Review of Economic Studies*. Vol. 23, pp. 83-100, reprinted in his '*Essays on Value and Distribution.*"
2. Quoted by Kaldor in his "*Alternative Theories of Distribution*".

Thirdly, Ricardo regards profits as a necessary incentive for capital accumulation which is the key to economic growth.

Ricardo discusses the distribution of national output among the three shares of rents, wages and profits. According to Prof. Kaldor, the Ricardian theory of income distribution is based upon two separate principles, the ***'marginal principle'*** and the ***'surplus principle'***. With the help of the marginal principle the Ricardian theory explains the determination of the share of rent in the national output and with the surplus principle, the theory explains how the remaining national output (that is, national output *less* rent) is divided between wages and profits. As is well known, the rent in the Ricardian theory is the difference between the product of labour on "marginal land" (*i.e.,* the land that yields output just sufficient to cover cost of production) and the product on the'superior lands. If both extensive as well as intensive margins of cultivation are taken into account, then the rent of a land is equal to the difference between its total product and the production costs (of labour) incurred on it.

Since in the Ricardian theory production cost per unit of labour, in equilibrium position, must be equal to the marginal productivity of labour, the total costs of production will be given by the marginal product of labour multiplied by the number of units of labour employed. On the other hand, total product can be obtained by multiplying the average productivity with the amount of labour employed. The difference between the total product and the total production costs will represent the rent of land. On a little reflection it will be clear that the difference between the marginal productivity and the average productivity of labour on a given land will be equal to the rent earned from land per unit of labour employed and the total rent will be equal to the difference between the average product and marginal product multiplied by the number of units of labour employed. To quote Prof. Kaldor, "Rent is the difference between the product of labour on marginal land and the product on average land, or (allowing for the intensive as well as extensive margins) the ***difference between the average and marginal labour productivity.***"[3]

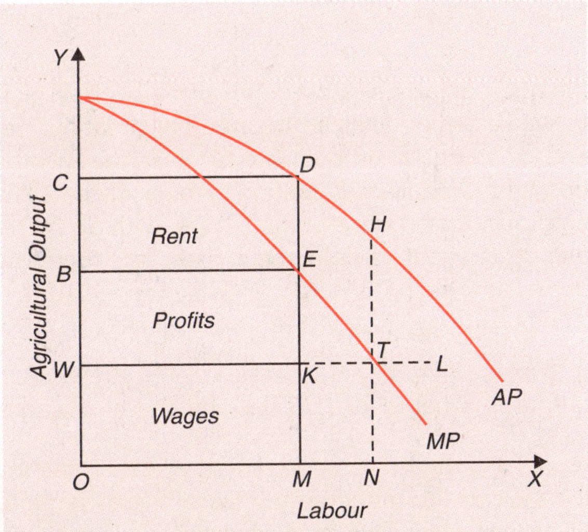

Fig. 58.1. *Determination of Relative Shares in the Ricardian Macroeconomic Model*

How the Ricardian theory explains the determination of relative shares of rents, wages, and profits with the use of the marginal principle and the surplus principle is illustrated in Figure 58.1,[4] which depicts the situation in the agricultural sector of the economy. In this figure, *X*-axis measures the amount of labour employed on the agricultural land, and the *Y*-axis measures the agricultural product produced. *AP* and *MP* curves respectively represent the average and marginal productivity of labour. Both *AP* and *MP* curves are downward sloping because of the operation of the law of diminishing returns. If we suppose *OM* labour is employed in the agriculture, then the marginal product of labour is *ME* and the average product of labour is *MD*. The difference between the marginal product and the average product is equal to *ED*. As explained above, the difference

3. N. Kaldor, *op. cit.*

4. This diagram is adapted from Kaldor's article referred above.

between the average and marginal product of labour represents the rent earned on land per unit of labour employed. Thus *ED* is the rent of land per unit of labour employed. The total rent earned by land is equal to the area *BEDC* (that is, *ED* multiplied by *BE*). Thus out of the total product *OMDC*, the share of rent is *BEDC*.

Now, the remaining product *OMEB* is to be divided between labour and capital. It is worth mentioning here that in the Ricardian theory wage rate of labour is *not* determined by the marginal productivity of labour as is generally assumed in neo-classical economics. In the Ricardian theory the marginal product is assumed to be equal to the sum of wages and profits. The wage rate in Ricardo's analysis is determined by the minimum subsistence level, a level which is just sufficient to keep the labour force living at a minimum subsistence (which in Ricardo's analysis is determined both by biological and cultural factors). Suppose the minimum subsistence level is given by *OW* amount of the agricultural output (*i.e.*, corn). Then the wage rate that will be determined in the long run is *OW*. Since the marginal product of labour is the sum of wages and profit in the Ricardian system, the distance *KE* (= *WB*) measures the rate of profit per unit of labour employed. Now, with *OM* as the labour employed *and OW as* the wage rate, the share of wages will be *OMKW*. Thus, from the remaining output *OMEB* (*i.e.*, output less rent), the share of wages (labour's share) is equal to *OMKW*. The rest of the output, *WKEB*, will be the share of profits in the total output. It is thus clear that profits in the Ricardian theory are regarded as a residual income which are left after the payments of wages and rents have been made. In other words, profits are the *surplus* of total product over wages and rents.

We in Figure 58.1 have assumed that *OM* is the amount of labour employment. But now the question arises, what determines this level of labour employment ? It should be noted that in the Ricardian analysis the number of labour employed is not determined by the wage rate and the marginal productivity curve. In the Ricardian theory the level of employment depends upon the capital accumulation in the economy. As more capital is accumulated, more labour is employed to produce goods. Thus, with an increase in the capital stock, demand for labour and therefore its employment rises. It is therefore clear that the level of employment in the agricultural sector is determined by the available capital stock.

As we saw above, with *OM* as labour employment the share of profits in the agricultural output is equal to *WKEB* and the share of wages is *OMKW*. The *resulting* ratio, $\frac{\text{Profits}}{\text{Wages}}$, represents the percentage rate of profit on the investment made. In the equilibrium position, the percentage money rate of profits on capital investment must be the same in agriculture and in industry. This is so because, given their mobility, capital funds would move from one sector to the other until the rate of profit becomes equal in both the sectors. But it is a special feature of the agricultural sector that money rate of profit in it cannot be different from that measured in terms of its own product, *i.e.*, corn rate of profit. This is because in the agricultural sector both the input (wage fund used for payment to labour) and output are the same commodity, namely, corn.

But in the manufacturing industry the input and output are different commodities. Whereas the input in the manufacturing industry are wages in terms of corn paid to the labour, the output is in terms of manufactured goods. Now the input (corn-wage) is a fixed quantity determined by the minimum subsistence level and also, ***given the state of technical knowledge,*** the output per worker in terms of manufactured goods is also fixed. It follows that the money rate of profit in the industry cannot change as a result of the variation either in the corn-wage or in output per worker because both of these are fixed. The only way in which the money rate of profit in the industry can change and can become equal, in equilibrium, to the money rate of profit in agriculture is through changes in the relative prices of industrial goods in terms of agricultural product. Thus, ***the money rate of profit in industry must become equal to the corn-rate of profit in the agriculture and not the other way around.*** Therefore, in the Ricardian scheme, the money rate of profit in the industry depends upon the corn-rate of profit in agriculture (which is equal to the money rate of profit in agriculture). It follows therefore that ***money rate of profit in manufacturing industry*** depends upon the corn-rate of profit in agriculture. The fall in the corn-rate of profit in the agriculture will bring about a fall in the money rate of profit in the manufacturing industry too.

Now, it is important to know what happens to the relative distributive shares as the economic growth takes place. Since it is the behaviour of the agricultural sector which is crucial to the determination of relative shares of profits, wages and rents in the economy, we start with the development in the agriculture. With capital accumulation, labour employment and output expands in agriculture. As a result of increase in labour employment and output, the demand for labour will increase. Increase in the demand for labour will cause the rate of wages to rise above the minimum subsistence or the 'natural' level. This will bring about the increase in population. This increase in population will bring down the wage rate to the minimum subsistence level through the increase in the supply of labour, but it will also lead to the increase in demand for agricultural output.

As output is expanded in agriculture to meet the increase in demand for agricultural oufput by employing more labour, the average and marginal products of labour will decline due to the operation of the principle of diminishing returns. In Figure 58.1 average and marginal products of labour fall as more labour is employed, since the *AP* and *MP* curves are sloping downward due to the diminishing returns. This means that when labour employment in agriculture is increased and agricultural output expands, the ***rent will increase because, as we have seen above, rent is the difference between the average and marginal products of labour.*** A glance at Figure 58.1 will reveal that the vertical distance between the *AP* and *MP* curves increases with the increase in the number of labour employed. With *OM* labour employed, the difference between average product (*AP*) and marginal product (*MP*), that is, rent on land per unit of labour is *ED* and it will be seen that to the right of *M*, the difference between the two goes on rising. Thus, given the state of technical knowledge, the development in agriculture will bring about rise in land rents.

Besides, the fall in average and marginal products of labour means the rise in the cost of production. This is because agricultural output increases less than in proportion to the increase in labour. As a result of the rise in unit cost of production, the prices of agricultural output will increase. With the higher price of corn or of agricultural output, the *greater money wage* will have to be paid to the labourers so that they should maintain the subsistence standard of living. But it should be noted that while wages in terms of money would rise, ***the wages in terms of corn will not change and will remain fixed at the minimum subsistence level (OW) in the long run.*** An important thing to note is that in the Ricardian model, though the real wage rate will remain fixed at *OW* in the long run, the share of wages in the total product will increase with the expansion of output and employment in agriculture. This is apparent from Figure 58.1 where when labour employment in agriculture increases up to *ON*, the total wages share rises to the area *OWTN* which is greater than the wages share *OWKM* at *OM* level of employment. Both the absolute and the relative share of wages in the total product has increased.

It should be noted that the increase in wages share occurs at the expense of profits which shrink continuously with the increase in output and employment. That the profits will decline is quite evident from Figure 58.1. As seen above, profit earned per unit of labour is the difference between the marginal product of labour and the subsistence wage paid to the labourers. It will be seen from Fig. 58.1 that the distance between the marginal product (*MP*) and the minimum subsistence wage line *WL* to the right of point *K* (*or* at labour employment greater than *OM)* goes on declining till it completely disappears at point *T* or at labour employment *ON* where the marginal product of labour has become equal to the subsistence wage *OW.* That is, profit goes on declining as employment increases beyond *M* till it falls to zero at the *ON* level of employment. It is thus clear that while the relative share of wages increases, the share of profits declines and becomes zero as output and employment are expanded in agriculture. It should be noted that it is because of the diminishing returns in agriculture (*i.e.,* falling marginal product of labour) which is responsible for the decline in profits.

Now, the question is, what happens to the distributive shares in the industrial sector as output and employment expand in agriculture? In the Ricardian model, the profit would decline even in the manufacturing industry. This is because as a result of rise in prices of agricultural output the money cost of the subsistence level will increase and therefore the industries would have to pay higher wages to their workers.[5] The rise in wages of the workers means that profits of the manufacturers would decline. Thus profits in the manufacturing industry would decline because of the operation of diminishing returns in agriculture and the consequent rise in cost and prices of agricultural output, even though industries themselves may not be subject to diminishing returns. Besides this, as we have explained above, if it is assumed that capital is quite mobile, the profit rate in the industry must fall too when the profit rate in the agriculture declines, or else capital would move from one sector to the other. The reason behind this is the same as has been just noted above, namely, that the profit in the industry will decline when the profit in agriculture falls because the prices of agricultural output will rise forcing the industrialists to pay high wages.

We have seen above that in the Ricardian macro-economic model, there fs continuous tendency towards a declining rate of profit both in the agricultural and industrial sectors of the economy. In the Ricardian theory, profit has been regarded as a necessary incentive for capital accumulation in the economy. When profit rate declines, the rate of capital accumulation falls and ultimately when the rate of profit is reduced to zero, investment and capital accumulation would cease to exist and the economy would reach the state of stagnation where further growth will completely stop. This is the conclusion of Ricardo's theory.

We can sum up the Ricardian theory of aggregate income distribution and the development in the economy in the following words of Prof. Patterson, "Given the assumption of a constant technology and a constant 'natural' wage in real terms, the relative share of wages in the total output will increase with a rising level of output and employment. The relative share of profit will decline and ultimately fall to zero. This is the point at which the economy reaches the infamous 'Stationary' state of classical theory, a gloomy situation in which all accumulation, population growth and technical progress cease. The basic causal force in this scheme is the fact of diminishing returns in agriculture, a grim tendency which can only by postponed temporarily by technical progress. Technical progress cannot, in other words, prevent the ultimately disappearance of profit and the onset of a stationary state."[6]

5. Whereas agricultural sector itself produces goods, *i.e.,* corn in terms of which real wage rate is fixed. The rise in the money wages as a result of rise in agricultural prices due to the diminishing returns does not affect the agriculture, since the real wage—wage in terms of corn—remains the same. But, as explained above, for the industrial sector this is not so. Because the industries do not produce corn on which wages will be spent, even in the case of constant real-wage in terms of corn they would have to pay higher money wages and this would affect their profits.
6. Wallace C. Patterson, *Income, Employment and Economic Growth* (New York, 1962), p. 430.

Paul Davidson has opined that whereas Ricardian theory is quite clear about the increase in the relative share of wages in the total product in course of economic growth and this takes place at the expense of profits, but Ricardo was not so much certain and definite about the change in relative share of rent in the total product during the course of development. But, if with the growth in output and employment the economic system behaves as has been depicted in Figure 58.1, the relative share of rent will increase along with the rise in the total share of wages. This is because the gap between the average product and marginal product (which is equal to rent) goes on widening with the successive increases in the employment of labour.

Criticism of Ricardian Macro-Theory of Distribution

Ricardo's theory was the first bold and imaginative attempt to explain the crucial problem of income distribution into relative functional shares of rent, wages and profits. But this theory suffers from various weaknesses.

First, actual events in the course of development have been quite contrary to what Ricardo had predicted on the basis of his theory. Thus, contrary to Ricardo's contention, the relative share of wages in the total product has not increased. Empirical research has revealed that the relative labour share (wages) in national income remained constant till the end of the Second World War in the Western capitalist countries. Further, even the tendency towards the declining rate of profit, as had been predicted by Ricardo on the basis of diminishing returns, has also not been actually found. The share of profits in the total product also remained more or less constant till the end of the Second World War. Furthermore, there has been rapid economic progress in the capitalist countries. Contrary to Ricardo's gloomy prognosis that the economies would inevitably move towards the stationary state, there has been a rapid economic growth in these economies. We thus see that actual events have not vindicated the Ricardian theoretical system and Ricardo has proved to be a poor prophet.

Secondly, Ricardo's analysis is unsatisfactory because it is tied too closely to the principle of diminishing returns. It is on the basis of the operation of diminishing returns that Ricardo had concluded that the share and the rate of profit will fall whereas the shares of wage and rent will increase. According to Ricardo, technical progress cannot be so rapid as to suspend the operation of diminishing returns. However, technical progress has been actually so rapid that it has kept the operation of diminishing returns in abeyance. It is the rapid rate of technical progress that has caused a high rate of economic growth and development.

Thirdly, Ricardo had assumed Malthusian law of population, namely, that population would increase if the real wage rate rose above the subsistence level. This is quite incorrect and has also been falsified by the actual experience in the Western countries. Population does not increase with every increase in real wages. Actually, the increase in the wage rate and per capita income in advanced Western countries have tended to reduce the birth rate and therefore the growth of population.

THE MARXIAN THEORY OF INCOME DISTRIBUTION

The Marxian theory of aggregate income distribution is derived from the Ricardian theory, even though his analysis reaches diametrically opposite conclusions about the behaviour of the distributive shares in the total product. Thus Prof. Kaldor remarks, "The Marxian theory is essentially an adaptation of Ricardo's 'surplus theory'."[7] Marx's theory of distribution is an important aspect of his general theory of development of capital since he thought that changes in the distributive shares affect crucially the course of development in a capitalist economy.

The Marxian analysis of income distribution rests on the *labour theory of value,* which Marx took over from Adam Smith and Ricardo. According to Marx's labour theory of value, the value of a commodity is determined by the labour time necessary for its production. ***It is the labour alone that is the ultimate source of all value.*** According to Marx, equipment and raw materials do not create value ; they merely transfer their own value to the commodity. On the other hand, labour creates more value than the value of labour power expended on the production of goods and services. In other words, it is the unique characteristic of labour power that it creates more value than its own value. The value of labour power is determined by the cost of reproduction of labour, that is, by the value of goods and services that are required to maintain the labourers at the minimum subsistence level. In other words, the value of labour power means the minimum subsistence wages which are just sufficient to keep the labourers living and intact. The value of labour power implies the supply price of labour—the price at which the workers offer their labour for use by the capitalists in the productive process. But, as said above, the labour produces more than the value of its labour power, that is, more than the output required for its minimum subsistence standard.

Labour theory of value and the concept of value of labour power as being equal to the minimum subsistence level are crucial to Marxian theory because they form the basis of Marx's ***theory of surplus value*** which in turn explains the distribution of aggregate income into wages and profits in a capitalist economy.[8] Since labour creates more value product than its own cost or value of labour power, that is, more than the minimum subsistence output, the surplus emerges which is expropriated by the capitalists who happen to own the material means of production such as capital equipment, land and raw materials with which labour is employed to produce goods and services. This surplus value represents profits of the capitalists. According to Marx, the surplus value or profits which are created by labour over and above their value of labour power or subsistence requirements are unjustifiably expropriated by the capitalist class. In other words, the surplus value or profit extracted from labour by the capitalists represents the ***exploitation of labour.***

It is through the ownership of non-human means of production that the capitalists are able to exploit the labour class and extract surplus value from it. Thus, the share of profits in the total value of output depends upon the magnitude of surplus value extracted from it. Prof. Patterson rightly remarks, "The notion of surplus value is crucial to the Marxian theory of income distribution; surplus value is the source of all profits and thus the amount of surplus that can be expropriated by the capitalist class will determine the relative share of profits in the income total."[9]

In the Marxian analysis, the total value of output is composed of three elements. First, it consists of the value of the capital and raw materials consumed in the production of goods and services. Marx calls this as ***constant capital*** which is written as C. Secondly, the total value output contains the value of labour power used in the production of goods and services, that is, the total wages in terms of minimum subsistence wages paid to the workers. Marx calls this as ***variable capital*** which is written as V. Thirdly, the total value output contains the ***surplus value*** which is created by the labourers over and above the value of their labour power and which, as seen above, is bagged by the capitalist class as profits. Thus,

$$\text{Total value output} = \text{constant capital} + \text{variable capital} + \text{surplus value}$$
$$= C + V + S$$

C, as said above, stands for capital consumption. It should be noted that in case of the whole

7. N. Kaldor, *Alternative Theories of Distribution.*
8. It should be noted that Marx considers two classes—workers and capitalists—between which total income is to be distributed. He regards profits as the income of the property owning class. Therefore, rent from land is included in his profits.
9. Wallace, C. Patterson, *op. cit.*, p. 432.

economy C will contain only the consumption of fixed capital, since raw materials are intermediate products and their value will be included in the value of final goods produced. If we subtract the value of C from the total output, we get the ***net output*** which will consist of value of the labour power or variable capital (V) and the surplus value (S). V and S are wages share and profits share respectively in the net output. Thus

$$\text{Net output} = V + S$$

$$= \text{wages share} + \text{profits share}$$

$$\frac{\text{profits share}}{\text{wages share}} = \frac{S}{V}$$

The ratio $\frac{S}{V}$ has been called by Marx as the ***rate of exploitation.*** It is this rate of exploitation $\frac{S}{V}$ which represents the ratio of profits share to the wages share in the national income. A rise in this ratio means the increase in the rate of exploitation and hence increase in the profits share relative to wages share in the national income; a fall in this ratio means the relative decrease in the profits shares and the relative increase in the wages share in the national income. To quote Professor Patterson again, "The ratio of profit share to the wage share is of key importance in Marx's analysis because this ratio S/V is more than a measure of the rate of exploitation; a change in S/V means that a change has taken place in the relative share of wages and non-wage (*i.e.,* profits) income in the total output. Consequently, if we understand how Marx thought that this ratio would change in response to the' basic forces at work in the capitalistic system, we grasp the essence of the Marxian theory of income distribution."[10]

According to Marx, the forces at work in a capitalist economic system bring about the increase in the rate of exploitation of labour. The basic force at work is the competition among the capitalists to increase the rate of exploitation, that is, the ratio S/V and thereby enlarge their profits share relative to wages share. But, how the capitalists are able to do this? First thing to understand in this connection is Marx, like Ricardo, believed that the market wage rate tended to be equal to the minimum subsistence level in the long run. In other words, wage rate, according to Marx, cannot rise above the subsistence level except in the very short run.

However, reason given by Marx for the existence of the minimum subsistence wages is different from what Ricardo thought it to be. According to Ricardo, it was the increases in population in case of rise in wages above the subsistence level that kept the wages tied to the subsistence level. In Marx's analysis, it is the prevailing excess of labour supply over the demand for labour that prevents the wages from rising above the minimum subsistence level. Because of the continuous excess of labour supply over demand, there comes to exist a large amount of unemployed workers which Marx called ***"the reserve army of labour".*** It is therefore the existence of reserve army of labour (*i.e.,* the unemployed) that prevents the wages from going above the minimum subsistence level. Now, why does supply of labour remain excess relative to demand for it ? "Marx assumed that as capitalist enterprise progresses at the expense of pre-capitalistic enterprise more labourers are released through the disappearance of the non-capitalist or handicraft units than are absorbed in the capitalist sector owing to the difference in productivity per head between the two sectors. As long as the growth of capitalist enterprise is at the cost of a shrinkage of pre-capitalist enterprise the increase in the supply of wage-

10. *Op. cit.*, p. 432.

labour thus tends to run ahead of the increase in the demand for wage labour."[11]

The wages being fixed at the minimum subsistence level, the measures which bring about the increase in the output of labour will raise the rate of exploitation and therefore the profits of the capitalists. According to Marx, the capitalists who own the material means of production ***compete with each other*** to increase the rate of exploitation (S/V) which is the same thing as the increase in profit share relative to wage share. Thus Professor Patterson remarks, "In the Marxian theory competition takes the form of a struggle among the owners of the material instruments of production to increase the rate of exploitation and this comes to the same thing, the non-wage share in the income total."[12]

There are three ways of increasing the surplus value or rate of exploitation. In the first place, this can be done by ***lengthening the working day***. When the workers are forced to work for a higher number of hours in a day than before, the total output increases and, given the wages paid to them, the surplus value expropriated by the capitalists and therefore the rate of exploitation increases. Secondly, the surplus value or rate of exploitation may be raised by ***increasing the intensity of labour,*** that is, forcing the workers to do greater amount of work while keeping the working day constant. However, the extent to which the surplus value can be increased in these two ways is very limited. The third and, according to Marx, a major way in which the capitalist can increase the surplus value is ***raising the physical productivity of workers through technical progress.*** Technical progress involves the improvements in techniques of production. Workers working with better and improved techniques produce more than before while working the same number of hours in a day and with same intensity and as a result the total output produced by them increases. With wages remaining constant at the minimum subsistence level, the difference between the total output and the subsistence output as a result of technical progress increases and hence the surplus value or rate of exploitation increases.

But technical progress can be achieved only if there is capital accumulation. As a result, the competition among the capitalists seeking to increase the surplus value forces them to accumulate capital, that is, to make investment. But in the Marxian scheme, as has been pointed out by Kaldor, capital accumulation or investment activity is not motivated by the lure of profit, but it is the necessity forced on them by the competitive straggle among the capitalists. Thus speaking about the motives behind capital accumulation, Prof. Kaldor says,

"For Ricado this was simply to be explained by the lure of a high rate of profit. Capitalists accumulate voluntarily so long as the rate of profit exceeds the minimum 'necessary compensation' for the risks and trouble encountered in the productive employment of capital. For Marx, however, accumulation by capitalist enterprise is not a matter of choice but a necessity, due to the competition among the capitalists themselves. This in turn was explained by the existence of economies of large-scale production (together with the implicit assumption that the amount of capital employed by any particular capitalist is governed by his own accumulation). Given the fact that the larger the scale of operations, the more efficient the business, each capitalist is forced to increase the size of his business through the re-investment of his profits if he is not to fall behind in the competitive struggle."[13]

We thus see that as technical progress and capital accumulation proceed apace and capitalist economic system develops, the surplus value extracted from the workers or rate of their exploitation will increase as a result of the competitive struggle among the capitalists.

---

11. Kaldor, *op. cit.*
12. *Op. cit.*, p. 433.
13. Kaldor, *op. cit.*

Consequently, with the development of capitalist economic system, the relative share of wages (labour's share) in the national income will fall and the relative share of profits (capitalists' share) will rise. Therefore, the development of the capitalist economy involves the steady worsening of the living conditions of the working classes. This has been called by Marx as ***"the immiseration of the proletariat"*** or ***"the law of increasing misery of the working classes".*** According to this law, technical progress and capital accumulation in a capitalist society and consequently the growth in national income must lead to the fall in the relative share of wages in national income and the rise in the relative share of profits.

It is thus clear that about the changes in the relative share with development of the capitalist system Marx reaches a conclusion which is diametrically opposed to the conclusion of Ricardo who thought that with the development of the capitalist economy, relative share of wages will increase and the relative share of profits will decline. Professor Patterson rightly points out that in the Marxian macroeconomic model of income distribution, "the fundamental cause of decline in the relative share of wages is technical progress, the fruits of which entirely go to the owners of the physical instruments of production. The alleged increasing misery of the working class does not come from any decline in the level of real wages, since their 'misery' does not increase in any absolute sense ; it is the result instead of the failure of real wages to advance along with gains in productivity. This is the heart of Marx's theory of distribution."[14]

Although Marx concluded that the *relative share* of profits will increase with the development of capitalist economic system as a result of technical progress and capital accumulation, he, however, following Ricardo, took the view that with capital accumulation the *rate of profit* will be falling.[15] It should therefore be carefully noted that in view of Marx, whereas *relative share* of profits increases, ***the rate of profit declines*** as the capitalist economy develops. This looks like a contradiction but Marx proved their co-existence.[16] But unlike Ricardo, Marx did not explain the falling rate of profit on the basis of operation of diminishing returns. He explained this tendency of declining rate of profit on the basis of the increase in what he called the ***"organic composition of capital".*** Organic composition of capital is the ratio of constant capital (*C*) to the total capital (*C* + *V*). Thus, organic *C* composition of capital is $\frac{C}{C+V}$. Now, the rate of profit is equal to the ratio of total surplus value (*S*) to the total capital (*C* + *V*) employed, that is, rate of profit is equal to $\frac{S}{C+V}$.

Let *P* stand for the rate of profit and then we have the following relationship :

$$P = \frac{S}{C+V}$$

$$P = \frac{S}{V} \cdot \frac{V}{C+V}$$

14. *Op. cit.,p.* 434.
15. Kaldor, *op. cit.*
16. It has been pointed by several authors that falling rate of profit does not necessarily follow from Marxian theory but Marx definitely held the view and he tried to prove it that there is a tendency of the falling rate of profit. Moreover, Marx employed this tendency of falling rate of profit to explain the ultimate collapse of the capitalist system.

$\frac{V}{C+V}$ is the ratio of variable capital to the total capital. If we subtract $\frac{C}{C+V}$ from one, we will get the ratio of variable capital to the total capital $\frac{V}{C+V}$, because the total capital is equal to $C + V$. Therefore,

$$P = \frac{S}{V}\left(1-\frac{C}{C+V}\right)$$

From the above equation it follows that if *S/V* (the rate of exploitation) remains constant, the rate of profit will decline if $\frac{C}{C+V}$, *i.e.*, organic composition of capital increases. Thus while holding that relative share of profits will increase, Marx also took the stand that the rate of profit will decline in the capitalist economy as a result of capital accumulation and consequent increase in the organic composition of capital. In the modern terminology we can say that Marx was of the view that as more capital is accumulated and capital-output ratio rises in productive processes or, in other words, as more capital-intensive production techniques are employed, the rate of profit will fall.

Critique of the Marxian Theory of Distribution

Marxian theory has been criticised on several grounds. Marx has proved to be a bad prophet. Prediction which he made on the basis of his theory has not come true and the actual events have not taken the Marxian line. Marx had predicted that relative share of wages in the national income would fall and the economic conditions of the workers would deteriorate. All this has not come true. Empirical research has found that share of wages in the national income remained constant in the Western capitalist countries till the end of forties[17], instead of falling as predicted by Marx, the workers have obtained a due share from the increases in physical productivities brought about by the technical progress and capital accumulation in the capitalist countries. As a result, the living conditions of the workers have greatly improved so that they have now become less revolutionary.

Besides, there has not been found any tendency of the falling rate of profit. On the basis of the falling rate of profit and the concentration of purchasing power in the hands of the few, Marx predicted that the capitalist economies would have periodic crises and ultimately the system would collapse. Actual events have falsified this gloomy forecast of Marx. Of course, there have been trade cycles in the capitalist economies in these economies but in spite of these short-run fluctuations these economies have made phenomenal progress in the last 150 years or so, so that they have now become affluent countries. Prof. Patterson rightly remarks, "Marx thought the capitalistic system would be increasingly wrecked by crises of greater and greater severity until finally it would collapse amid an uprising of the working class that would usher in the era of communism. Marx proved to be a bad prophet concerning not only the behaviour of the wage share in the national income, but also the long-term development of capitalism.[18]

Further, there is a great theoretical flaw in Marx's contention of falling rate of profit with the increase in organic composition of capital. Several authors[19] have pointed out that law of

17. Quite Contrary to Marx's view recent evidence shows that in the Post-Second World War period, wages share in national income in the USA has increased.
18. Patterson, *op. cit.*, p. 435.
19. Joan Robinson, *An Essay in Marxian Economics*, pp. 75-82 and N. Kaldor, *Altemative Theories of Distribution*.

the falling rate of profit cannot really be derived from the law of the increasing organic composition of capital. Since Marx believes that the real wages of the workers remain fixed at the subsistence level, then as a result of increase in organic composition of capital due to capital accumulation and technical progress, the output per head will greatly increase and, given the real wages constant at the subsistence level, the surplus value (*i.e.*, the profits) earned by the capitalists will greatly increase and will secure a rising rate of profit. In this context Prof. Kaldor's views are worth quoting. He says, "Since Marx assumes that the supply price of labour remains unchanged in terms of commodities, when the organic composition of capital and hence output per head rises, there is no more reason to assume that an increase in 'organic composition' will yield a lower rate of profit to an higher rate. For even if output per man were assumed to increase more slowly than ('constant' plus 'variable') capital per man, the 'surplus value' per man (the excess of output per man over the given minimum subsistence wages) will necessarily increase faster than output per man, and may thus secure a rising rate of profit even if there is diminishing productivity to successive additions to the fixed capital per unit of labour."[20]

Lastly, Marx's theory of income distribution is based upon the labour theory of vafue which is not acceptable to the modern economists. Marx's analysis of surplus value or exploitation of labour is directly based upon his contention that all value is created by labour while capital merely transfers his own value to the value of the commodity. Capital adds greatly to the productivity of the proces and does create a good deal of value. To deny this is to show one's prejudice. Moreover, labour theory of value is only a variant of the cost of production theory. But as was pointed out long ago by Marshall that only costs of prodiuction (costs of labour as well as capital) do not determine price or value. The value also depends upon marginal utility or the demand for the commodity. The price or value of commodity is determined by the interaction of the forces of both demand and supply. Therefore, Marx's thesis that value of a commodity is determined by the necessary labour time required to produce it is quite obsolete and not acceptable to the modern economists. Thus when labour theory of value is wrong, the theory of surplus value and exploitation based upon it falls to the ground.

KALECKI'S 'DEGREE OF MONOPOLY' THEORY OF DISTRIBUTIVE SHARES

An important theory of distributive shares was advanced by M. Kalecki[21] who explained that distribution of national income into profits and wages depends upon the degree of monopoly in the economy. It is worth mentioning in the beginning that Kalecki applied Lerner's micro-economic degree of monopoly ($\frac{p-m}{p}$; where p stands for price, and m for marginal cost) to the macro-level. Thus, he used average or macro-economic degree of monopoly by estimating the average of the degree of monopoly of all individual enterprises in the economy.

It should be noted that in Kalecki's formulation of the degree of monopoly marginal cost includes cost of labour and raw materials per unit of output. Further, in Kalecki's theory cost of labour only includes wages of manual labour, since he has lumped salaries— the wages of white collar workers with the incomes of the capitalist class. Thus, p–m indicates income per unit of output of the capitalist class which includes entrepreneurial profits (inclusive of dividends)

20. Kaldor, *op. cit.*

21. M. Kalecki, The Distribution of National Income, in his *Essays on the Theory of Economic Fluctuations*, reprinted in *The Theory of the Firm*, edited by G.C. Archibald, Penguin Modern Economic Readings, 1971. The reference to page numbers will be from the later book.

and aggregate overhead costs (interest, depreciation and salaries).

In order to explain the determination of distributive shares of capitalist class and labour in national income, Kalecki has made two assumptions. First, he assumes that the short-period marginal cost curve is equal to the short-period average cost on manual labour and raw materials to a certain point corresponding to 'practical capacity' . Secondly, he assumes that output in the firms in the actual world is below this maximum practical capacity. Thus he assumes the existence of excess capacity in the economy. "In the real world an enterprise is seldom employed beyond the 'practical capacity* a fact which is therefore a demonstration of general market imperfections and widespread monopolies or oligopolies."[22]

Taking the above assumptions, Kalecki explains his theory as follows :

Lerner' s measure of degree of monopoly of a *single firm* is the ratio of the difference between price *(p)* and marginal cost (*m*) to price, or

$$\mu = \frac{p-m}{p},$$

where μ indicates the degree of monopoly.

Since Kalecki assumes constant costs, marginal cost will be equal to average cost, and therefore in the above formula we can substitute average cost *'a'* for marginal cost '*m*' , and therefore can write the formula of degree of monopoly of a single firm as follows :

$$\mu = \frac{p-a}{p} \qquad \text{...}(i)$$

or,

$$p\mu = (p-a) \qquad \text{....}(ii)$$

(*p* – *a*) is the difference between the price of the product and average cost on manual labour and raw materials per unit of output. Thus this difference (*p* – *a*) is made up of entrepreneurial profits, interest, depreciation and salaries and therefore represents *gross capitalist income* (inclusive of salaries) *per unit of output* of the employer. For obtaining total gross capitalist income of the single employer, we have to multiply the two sides of the equation (*ii*) derived above by the total production of the single firm.

Let *x* stand for the total production of the firm. Multiplying both sides of the equation (*ii*) by *x* we obtain

$$xp\mu = x(p-a) \qquad \text{....}(iii)$$

Therefore, *x* (*p* – *a*) represents the total gross capitalist income (inclusive of salaries) of the employer. In order to obtain the gross capitalist income of the economy as a whole where there are a large number of firms, we have to sum up the gross capitalist incomes of *all the firms* in the economy. With such summation, the equation (*iii*) can be written as :

$$\Sigma xp\mu = \Sigma x(p-a) \qquad \text{....}(iv)$$

Thus $\Sigma x(p-a)$ equals the gross capitalist income of ***all the firms*** of the economy taken together. And Σxp will be equal to the total value of the output of all goods produced and sold in the economy. Thus Σxp represents ***aggregate turnover*** of the whole economy which we may write as *T*. Thus $T = \Sigma xp$. It should be noted that the aggregate turnover *T* is made up of the value of gross national product plus the value of the raw materials produced and sold. If we divide both sides of the equation *(iv)* derived above by the aggregate turnover *T*,

22. Kalecki, *op. cit.*,

$$\frac{\Sigma xp\mu}{T} = \frac{\Sigma x(p-a)}{T}$$

Since $T = \Sigma xp$

$$\frac{\Sigma xp\mu}{\Sigma xp} = \frac{\Sigma x(p-a)}{T}$$

$\frac{\Sigma xp\mu}{\Sigma xp}$ is the expression for the weighted average of the micro-degrees of monopoly u, or in other words, it is the expression for the macro degree of monopoly which we write as $\bar{\mu}$.

$$\bar{\mu} = \frac{\Sigma x(p-a)}{T} \quad \text{...}(v)$$

or macro-degree of monoply= $\frac{\text{gross capitalist income}}{\text{aggregate turnover}}$

It follows from the above equation (v) that "The relative share of gross capitalist incorne and salaries in the aggregate turnover is with great approximation equal to the average degree of monopoly."[23] It is evident from the formula of the equation (v) that given the costs of the raw materials, which are included in a, the increase in the average degree of monopoly power $\bar{\mu}$ will cause the share of gross capitalist income or profits rise at the expense of labour share. Thus, according to Kalecki, "The distribution of the product of industry is at every moment determined by the degree of monopoly. Our formula therefore holds both for the short period and the long run, even though it was deduced on the basis of, so to speak, pure short period considerations. And contrary to the usual view ***neither inventions nor the elasticity of substitution between capital and labour have any influence on the distribution of income.***"[24]

Labour's Share in National Income and Degree of Monopoly

Kalecki was more interested in showing the dependence of labour's share in national income on the average or macro degree of monopoly in the economy. If A stands for the national income and W for the total wage bill in the economy, then $A - W$ will represent the gross capitalist's income of the economy[25]. But, as explained above, gross capitalist's income is also equal to $\Sigma x(p - a)$. Substituting $A - W$ for $\Sigma x(p - a)$ in equation (v) derived above, we get

$$\bar{\mu} = \frac{\Sigma x(p-a)}{T}$$

$$\bar{\mu} = \frac{A-W}{T} \quad (vi)$$

Multiplying both sides by T/W, we get

$$\bar{\mu} \cdot \frac{T}{W} = \frac{(A-W)}{T} \cdot \frac{T}{W}$$

23. *Op. cit.*,p.222.
24. *Ibid*, p., 223.
25. It should be noted that value of national product or national income A is not the same thing as aggregate turnover. Whereas national income consists of the value of only final goods, aggregate turnover T is made of value of final goods plus the value of intermediate goods such as raw materials.

$$\bar{\mu} \cdot \frac{T}{W} = \frac{A-W}{W}$$

$$\bar{\mu} \cdot \frac{T}{W} = \frac{A}{W} - 1$$

or
$$\frac{A}{W} = 1 + \bar{\mu} \cdot \frac{T}{W}$$

Writing the reciprocal of the above, we obtain

$$\frac{W}{A} = \frac{1}{1+\bar{\mu} \cdot \frac{T}{W}} \quad \text{(vii)}$$

$\frac{W}{A}$, that is $\frac{\text{wages}}{\text{national income}}$, represents the relative share of wages in national income. From the question (*vii*) it is evident that the relative share of wages in national income (*W/A*) is inversely related to degree of monopoly power $\bar{\mu}$, and *T/W*. The formula shows clearly that the increase in the degree of monopoly power will reduce the relative share of wages (*i.e.*, manual labour's share). The labour's share will be reduced not only because of the rise in the degree of monopoly power $\bar{\mu}$ "but also because *T/W* is increased by a rise in the degree of monopoly since this raises prices in relation to wages."[26]

It should be further noted that, according to Kalecki, apart from a change in the degree of monopoly, *T/W can* also change as a result of the *change in the price of basic raw materials* in relation to wage costs in the industries. As is mentioned above, the aggregate turnover *T* consists of the value of all outputs (including raw materials) and this value is found out by multiplying the physical outputs with their prices. Therefore, when the prices of the basic raw materials change, the aggregate turnover *T* will change and consequently *T/W* will also change which, given the degree of monopoly, will affect the share of wages in national income (*W/A*). The increase in price of basic raw materials and hence in *T/W* will reduce the labour's share (*W/A*) and vice versa. To quote Kalecki, "It is obvious from the formula that with a given degree of monopoly, the relative share of manual labour falls when *T/W* increases, consequently a rise in the prices of 'basic raw materials' as compared with wage cost by raising *T/W* must lower the relative share of manual labour."[27] Kalecki derives two conclusions from his analysis of labour's share in national income : "(1) A rise of the degree of monopoly causes a decrease in the relative share of manual labour W/A. (2) A rise of prices of 'basic raw materials' in relation to wage-cost causes a fall in *W/A* but in a much lesser proportion."[28]

How Kalecki Explains Constancy of Labour's Share in National Income

A lot of empirical evidence revealed that labour's share in national income remained more or less constant in many capitalist countries till at least the end of the Second World War. It was a big problem to explain the constancy of wages share in national income. With his degree of monopoly theory of distribution, Kalecki explained this constancy in the labour's share. He did so by bringing into his analytical model colonial countries which supplied raw materials to the capitalist countries which ruled them. Without the exploitation of the colonial countries by the capitalist countries, labour's share in national income in the capitalist countries

26. *Op. cit.*. pp. 227-28 .

would have declined. Thus, according to Kalecki's theory, the workers in the capitalist countries are parties to the exploitation of colonial countries and they have benefited from it.

According to Kalecki there has been increasing concentration in the industries in the capitalist countries and the firms are becoming bigger and bigger which have raised the degree of monopoly in the economy. Many branches of industry have become oligopolistic and many oligopolies have been converted into cartels. If only the factor of increasing degree of monopoly were operating, this would have caused a decline in the relative share of labour. But, as has been brought out above, the prices of basic raw materials also influence the labour's share in national income. And the prices of these basic raw materials supplied by the colonial countries to the capitalist countries fell due to the change in the terms of trade against the former. This fall in the prices of basic raw materials tended to increase the labour's share in national income. Thus, according to Kalecki, increasing degree of monopoly was counter-balanced by the fall in the prices of basic raw materials with the result that labour's share in national income remained more or less constant.

Kalecki has been able to explain the constancy of labour's share in national income even during the course of business cycle. According to Kalecki, the prices of raw materials and degree of monopoly change in slump and boom periods of the business cycles in such a way that labour's share in national income remains constant. Kalecki argues that in the slump cartels are created to save profits and also there is reluctance on the part of entrepreneurs to make price cuts for fear of inducing the competitors to do likewise. With this, the gap between the price and marginal cost increases and as a result, the degree of monopoly increases during the slump. The increase in the degree of monopoly during the slump *tends to reduce* the share of labour in the national income. But the fall in the prices of raw materials during the slump *tends to raise it*. Thus, the two forces which determine the share of labour in national income work in the opposite direction and therefore counter-balance each other, as a result of which labour's share in national income remains constant in the slump.

On the other hand, according to Kalecki, in the boom period of the business cycle, when the trade revives, cartels are dissolved because of improving prospects of independent activity and the entry of others in the industry. As a result, competition increases during the boom which reduces the degree of monopoly. The reduction in the degree of monopoly tends to raise the labour's share in national income during the boom period, but the rise in the prices of raw material during the boom tends to reduce it. Thus, again the two forces offset each other in the boom period and as a consequence labour's share in national income remains constant even during the boom. Thus, Kalecki concludes : "If we look at our data on the relative share of manual labour in the national income we see that in general it does not change much during the business cycle. But the prices of basic raw materials fall in the slump and rise in the boom as compared with wages, and this tends to raise it in the boom. If the relative share of manual labour remains more or less constant, it can be concluded that the degree of monopoly tends to increase in the depression and decline in the boom."[29]

Critique of the 'Degree of Monopoly Theory' of Distribution

Kalecki was able to explain the stability of labour's share in national income in the capitalist countries which puzzled economists for a long time. Further, the degree of monopoly or competition is an important factor that determines profits and hence distributive shares in national income. But his theory is not without flaws and has been widely criticized.

---

27. *Op. cit., p. 228.*
28. *Op. cit.,p. 228.*

In the first place, Jan Pen has pointed out that Kalecki by attributing profits to the degree of monopoly *alone* has glossed over other factors in causing profits and affecting distributive shares. Further, according to him, the use of Lerner's concept of degree of monopoly at the macro-level leads us to wrong conclusions regarding profits. To quote Pen, "In some theories, especially that of M. Kalecki on distributive shares, the degree of monopoly occupies a central position; ***it is the only determinant of the level of profits.*** Now this seems exaggerated to me. For one of the difficulties with this concept is that it is so hard to use macro-economically. The marginal costs lie at a different level per firm; efficient firms have a lower cost curve than inefficient ones. .Now if the efficient firms make extra profits, this is caused by a bonus on having a lead. If we use the macro-economic degree of monopoly, the danger threatens that we shall ascribe part of the profit that has been made as a result of differences in the efficiency to the existence of monopoloid situations. This of course distorts the causes of income distribution."[30]

Attacking Kalecki's theory further, Pen writes: "It is certainly true that the degree of competition is important. However, there are other forces in operation that likewise influence profits and interest, and which may not be described by words such as 'monopoly' and 'competition'. One such force is the shortage of capital. Another factor, which is probably highly important, is 'the existence of cost differentials between firms'. If efficient and inefficient firms work side by side, large differential profits may occur. These do not disappear through competition nor are they determined by the existence of monopolies. Differential profits is a category of income which simply cannot be fitted into Kalecki's system. And, worse still, these bonuses for higher productivity appear in his mind as the consequences of monopoly—a typical example of how to turn wine to water."[31]

Secondly, Kalecki has ignored the power of labour altogether, he has stressed only on the power of the capitalists. And this makes his analysis a biased description of the present-day capitalism. As has been emphasized by J.K. Gailbraith[32], labour unions exercise a countervailing power to the power of the capitalists owning the manufacturing industries and tend to reduce the degree of monopoly in the economy and consequently raise the labour's share in national income. But "Kalecki passes over the position of power of the unions—he sees only the power of the capitalists, so that a reduction in the degree of monopoly through countervailing power remains outside the picture."[33]

Further, in view of the present author, the labour unions through their collective bargaining power have succeeded in wresting monetary advantages which are passed on in the form of higher prices to the general consuming public. This has resulted in what has been called cost-inflation and which has reduced the real incomes of other classes in the society. In developing countries like India organised labour force both in the private and public sectors has succeeded in raising its wages which are in part responsible for inflation in the country. Further, these enhanced wages have reduced the surpluses in the industrial sector, especially in the public sector which could have been utilized for generating employment and income for those who are unorganised and live below the poverty line. The point is that the trade unions are a force to reckon with and through their monopoly power they have tended to increase the share of organised labour at the expense of the unorganised labour force. Like the monopoly power of the capitalist class, the monopoly power of the labour unions too affects the distributive shares

29. *Op. cit.*, pp. 231.32
30. *Op. cit.*,p. 135.
31. *Op. cit.*,p. 177.
32. J.K. Galbraith, *American Capitalism.*
33. Jan Pen, *op.cit.*, p. 177.

of the various classes in the society. But Kalecki has ignored the monopoly power of the labour unions and its effect on the distribution of income in the society; perhaps it did not suit his purpose.

Further, Kalecki wrongly established positive relation between industrial concentration and the degree of monopoly. According to Kalecki, the greater the concentration in the industry, the greater the profit margin (*i.e.*, the gap between the price and cost of production) and therefore the greater the degree of monopoly power of an individual enterprise. Further, according to Kalecki, the large oligopolistic concerns in an industry have a propensity to enter into collusion or form a cartel and thereby increase the degree of monopoly further. All this has been challenged. Thus Pen asserts, "It is a cheap illusion to believe that large concerns help one another furtively. It is easy to describe oligopoly as a few firms hand in glove with one another. But the reader who is familiar with the business world knows that the competition between giant concerns can be particularly fierce, also as regards prices. Concerns struggle for markets; and in the process they are not always afraid to lower prices. Sometimes oligopolistic competition leads to unstable market conditions, and prices drop. It is of course true that the increase in the market share of the giant concerns also causes their share in the total profit to increase. However, that is not the point; what is at issue with the degree of monopoly is the profit *margin*. In general it has not been proved that this is higher for large firms than for small ones. Small firms sometimes need a higher profit margin to stay in business, and they often succeed in charging relatively high prices."[34]

Kaldor has criticized Kalecki's theory for its association with the price elasticity of demand. As has been explained earlier, 'degree of monopoly power' is equal to the reverse of the price elasticity of demand. Actually, Kalecki visualised that monopolistic or oligopolistic firms fixed their profit margins or mark-ups on the basis of the price elasticity of demand. Commenting upon Kalecki's theory, Kaldor writes : "On closer inspection, however, the elasticity of the demand curve facing the individual firm turned out to be no less of a broken reed than its counterpart, the elasticity of substitution between factors. There is no evidence that firms in imperfect markets set their prices by reference to the elasticity of their sales function, or that short-period pricing is the outcome of any deliberate attempt to maximize profits by reference to an independent revenue and a cost function. Indeed the very notion of a demand curve for the product of a single firm is illegitimate if the prices charged by different firms cannot be assumed to be independent of each other."[35]

We conclude that Kalecki has emphasized only one factor which has a bearing on income distribution. It is certainly true that firms with a price-setting power will affect the distribution of income. But the importance of other factors should not be ignored.

KALDOR'S OR KEYNESIAN THEORY OF INCOME DISTRIBUTION

Professor Kaldor[36] has put forward a theory of income distribution which occupies an important place in the theories of aggregate income distribution as well as in theories of economic growth, since growth in his theory depends upon distribution of income between profits and wages. Kaldor has called hia theory as the *Keynesian theory of distribution,*[37] since he employs Keynes' theoretical framework or Keynesian apparatus of thought to explain the factors on which distribution of income between profits and wages depends. Moreover, it is called the Keynesian theory because Kaldor thinks that evidence can be produced to show that

34. *Op. cit.*, p. 178.
35. N. Kaldor, Alternative Theories of Distribution, *Review of Economic Studies*, vol. 23, pp. 83-100.
36. Nicholas Kaldor, *op. cit.*
37. Kaldor's Theory is also known as *Neo-Keynesian Theory of Distribution*.

"at some stage in the development of his idea, Keynes came near to formulating such a theory."[38]

Kaldor also divides the national income into two parts— wages and profits– which are respectively the share of labour class and the property owning class. Thus profits are defined as the incomes of the property owning class and therefore include ordinary profits, rents and interest. Wages comprise not only the reward for manual labour but salaries as well. Before we explain Kaldor's theory of income distribution, it is essential to state the assumptions which Kaldor makes to show on what factors the distribution of national income into wages and profits depends. First, he assumes that a state of full employment prevails in the economy so that total output or income is given. Secondly, he assumes that marginal propensities to save (or consume) are constant for the wage earners and the property owners and further that marginal propensity to save of the workers is smaller than that of capitalists, the profit receivers. The important aspects of Kaldorian theory can be stated algebraically in a series of equations:

Suppose W stands for total or aggregate wages and P stands for total profits and further that S_w stands for aggregate savings out of wages and S_p for aggregate savings out of profits, then :

$$Y = W + P \qquad ...(i)$$

The above equation is simply an identity which says that total national income (Y) is composed of the sum of aggregate wages and aggregate profits.

Now, in an equilibrium position, intended (or *ex ante*) savings must be equal to intended (or *ex ante*) investment. Since we are dealing with an equilibrium state at full employment, therefore

$$I = S \qquad ...(ii)$$

Now the total savings in the society is the sum of aggregae savings out of wages and aggregate savings out of profits. Therefore

$$S = S_w + S_p \qquad ...(iii)$$

Taking the investment as given and if we represent average propensity to save of the wage earners by s_w and average propensity to save of the profit earners by s_p, then

$$S_w = s_w \times W$$

and,

$$S_p = s_p \times P$$

From (*ii*) and (*iii*) it follows that

$$I = s_p.P + s_w.W \qquad ...(iv)$$

From (*i*) above we know that

$$W = Y - P$$

Therefore, substituting $Y - P$ in (*iv*) for W, we get

$$I = s_p P + s_w (Y - P)$$

$$I = s_p P + s_w Y - S_w P$$

$$I = (s_p - s_w) P + s_w Y$$

Dividing both sides by national income (Y) we get

$$\frac{I}{Y} = (s_p - s_w)\frac{P}{Y} + s_w$$

38. Kaldor, *op. cit.*

Dividing both sides by (s_p - s_w) and rearranging the above equation we obtain

$$\frac{P}{Y} = \frac{1}{s_p - s_w}\frac{I}{Y} - \frac{s_w}{s_p - s_w}$$

Since *P* stands for profits and *Y* for national income, therefore

$$\frac{\text{Profit}}{\text{National income}} = \frac{1}{s_p - s_w}\frac{I}{Y} - \frac{s_w}{s_p - s_w}$$

The above equation shows that, given the saving propensities of the capitalists and the wage earners (i. e., s_p and s_w), *ratio of profits to national income* $\left(\frac{P}{Y}\right)$ *depends on the ratio of investment to national income* $\left(\frac{I}{Y}\right)$. *Increase in the investment-income ratio,* $\frac{I}{Y}$, *that is, rise in the rate of investment, will bring about an increase in share of profits in income* $\left(\frac{P}{Y}\right)$ *and the corresponding decrease in the share of wages in the income,* $\frac{W}{P}$.

In the above Kaldor's model, investmnt or rather the ratio of investment to total income, as in Keynesian theory, has been treated as an independent variable, that is, it is regarded as unresponsive to change in the propensities to save (s_p and s_w). Further, Kaldor's model of income distribution holds good only if the saving propensity of the capitalists (*i.e.*, profit receivers) and the wage earners differs and further that if marginal propensity to save out of profits is greater than the marginal propensity to save out of wages. That is, the model operates if

$$s_p \neq s_w$$

and $$s_p > s_w$$

The system will be unstable if propensity to save out of profits, s_p, is less than the propensity to save out of wages. This is because if $s_p < s_w$, then when the investment decreases and consequently there is a fall in prices, this would bring about a fall in demand which would in turn cause a further fall in prices and so on. Thus in case of $s_p < s_w$, a fall in prices would be cumulative and the system will be unstable. Likewise, if $s_p < s_w$, the rise in the prices would bring about an increase in demand and will generate a further rise in prices. Thus $s_p > s_w$ is an essential condition for stability in the system. According to Kaldor, "The degree of stability of the system depends on the difference of marginal propensities, *i.e.*, on $\frac{1}{s_p - s_w}$, which may be defined as ***'coefficient of sensitivity of income distribution'***, since it indicates the change in the share of profits in income which follows from a change in the share of investment in output. Not only this assumption $s_p > s_w$ is essential for stability, it is also a necessary condition for the increase in the share of profits in the national income when the ratio of investment to income, *I*/*Y*, increases,"[39] The underlying idea is that ***given the level of income (because Kaldor assumes full employment), the only way in which the saving-income ratio can rise***

39. Kaldor, *op. cit.* (italics added)

and become equal to the higher investment-income ratio so that new equilibrium is achieved can be either through the change in the propensities to save which Kaldor rules out by assuming the values of s_w and s_p constant, or through a shift in the distribution of real income from the wage earners with lower propensity to save to the capitalist class with higher propensity to save.

The important aspect of Kaldor's model is that *share of profit in the national income is a function of investment-income ratio, the greater the investment-income ratio, the greater the share of profits in the national income and vice versa.* When there is a state of full employment, the increase in the investment outlay can bring about a new equilibrium with higher level of real investment if it causes in real terms both the increase in investment-income ratio, *I/Y*, and the saving-income ratio, *S/Y*. Now, if as a result of increase in investment expenditure the saving-income ratio in real terms does not rise, the price would rise continuously. Thus, in the Kaldorian theory, shift in the distribution of income in favour of the capitalist class is essential if there is to be continued full-employment equilibrium with the higher level of real investment in the economy.

The question arises, how the changes in distribution of income in favour of the capitalists (profit receivers) occur as a result of the increase in the investment expenditure. This occurs through the mechanism of the changes in the price level. Given the level of full employment, when the investment expenditure increases, there is a general rise in prices. Now because, according to Kaldor, wages lag behind prices, the profit margins of the capitalists rise. Thus the rise in prices and the failure of the money wages to rise at the same time, will bring about an increase in the share of profits in the national income and corresponding decrease in the wages share. Because the propensity to save out of profits is greater than the propensity to save out of wages, the change in the distribution of income in favour of profit receivers caused by the rise in the general level of prices will bring about the increase in the overall level of savings in the economy. The new equilibrium is achieved when through the above process the saving-income ratio has risen so as to be equal to the higher investment-income ratio. Therefore, Prof. Patterson rightly remarks, "The key importance to the Kaldorian system is the assumption that the propensity to save of profit recipients is greater than that of wage earners. Without this assumption, the real saving-output ratio would not rise, irrespective of any alteration in the distribution of income, and thus the system would be unstable."[40]

Finally, mention may be made of the two constraints imposed by Kaldor to make his model of income distribution yield economically meaningful results.

They are:

$$w > w_{min} \qquad \ldots(1)$$

and

$$P/Y > m \qquad \ldots(2)$$

The implication embodied in the constraint (1) is that the wage rate (w) should be above a certain minimum level which is determined by the cost of conventional subsistence. It should be so, for only then the real wages could permit of a decline due to the rise in the price level so as to bring about a redistribution of incomes in favour of profits. And thus only then could it be possible for the savings to increase and equilibrium growth to be established when investment exceeded the *ex-ante* savings.

In the same way, the constraint (2) implies that the profit margins must also be above a certain minimum below which entrepreneurs, regardless of the demand conditions, would not reduce prices any more. Fulfilment of this constraint implies that entrepreneurs would willingly

40. Patterson, *op. cit.*, p. 444.

accept lower profit margins that are associated with price reductions during conditions of deficient demand (*i.e.* excess of *ex ante* saving). In the absence of this constraint, an excess of savings over investment in the conditions of full employment, instead of being rectified through a fall in prices and profit margins, would be eliminated by a fall in income and employment.

In effect, the aforesaid two constraints are required to ensure the effective operations of the Kaldorian adjustment mechanism (changes in price level relative to money wages in response to the disequilibrium between *ex-ante* saving and investment which regulates profit margins *(P/Y)* in accordance with the level of savings required to be generated to feed investment.

Hence, the operation of the redistributive mechanism which is the crux of Kaldorian theory of income distribution would take place only if the constraints (1) and (2) hold good. Failing this, profits would get determined in some different way and it would be necessary to assume "a purely non-Keynesian system where there is necessarily just enough investment to finance full employment where, in other words, savings govern investment, not the other way round".

Critical Appraisal of Kaldor's Theory of Distribution

Kaldor's model of income distribution highlights the fact that saving and investment combine to determine, *inter alia,* the distribution of income. And it is the manner of distribution of income which *inter alia* determines chiefly the ultimate size of national income.

Another distinctive feature of the model is that here ***it is the changes in the distribution rather than changes in the level of income that provide the adjustment mechanism between saving and investment.*** This aspect stems from the view that saving adjusts passively to investment, the latter having no dependence on the saving propensities in the society. The entrepreneurial investment decisions play a much larger role than that allowed by the marginal productivity theory of distribution. Indeed, the saving decisions are subsequential and not consequential in investment decisions of entrepreneurs. Having built a macro-model of income distribution around this central feature, Kaldor's analysis makes a definite advance towards providing a more realistic explanation of the observed phenomenon.

However, there are certain shortcomings which make Kaldor's exposition rather rigid and less acceptable. For instance, the constraints embodied in (1) and (2) render the model somewhat useless in the context of reality. The constraint (1) purports to say that the money wages ought to be more than socially acceptable minimum level of subsistence. It is only then that the workers' resistance to the necessary reduction in real wages as a result of the rise in price level in response to the excess of investment over *ex ante* saving would not be too formidable. Implicit in this assumption is the implication that the decline in the workers' living standards up to a biological subsistence level would be frictionless. That is to say, they would offer no resistance to the fall in their levels of living till the biological subsistence level is reached. Therefore, the assumption is that the workers would start demanding rise in money wages only once this biological subsistence is reached.

But such an assumption lacks realism. It is quite doubtful that such a behaviour on the part of the workers would actually be there. There exist strong trade union movements and also escalation clauses in the wage contracts especially in the developed countries, so that it is very unlikely for the wages to be flexible downwards. Actually, the fall in real wages would be resisted by demands for higher money wages.

Indeed, there are serious doubts as to whether workers would be willing to accept any fall in real wages before, what has been termed by Joan Robinson "inflation barrier", sets in. To put it in more exact words, before the workers resist any reduction in real wages by demands for higher wages, the inflationary pressures set in. And with the inflationary spiral on, higher prices of consumer goods relative to the money wages entail a lower real consumption by the workers. So for a while the real wages may decline without setting up pressures on the part of the workers to increase the money wages rates. But soon a limit to the fall in real wages is reached and money wage rates start rising.

When money wage rates increase, money expenditure would also increase. And a vicious circle of money wages chasing prices would set in. What shall happen in such a situation in regard to the investment decisions ? There would be a keen desire of the entrepreneurs to invest. But increased investment could take place in the Kaldorian system only when there is a commensurate decline in real wages. Thus, there occurs a head-on conflict between the entrepreneurs' desire to invest and the refusal of the wage-earners to accept a level of real wages which that investment would entail. Something must give way in a situation like this. Either the investment will be curtailed through the operation of certain checks that come into being or the system explodes in a hyper-inflation.[41]

In view of the aforesaid, it is quite unlikely that there could be adequate reduction in real wages through a decline in money wages to eliminate the disequilibrium between investment and *ex ante* saving . And unless the real wages decline adequately, the adjustment mechanism will fail to operate. It is only when the reduction in real wages is enough to bring about a degree of income redistribution that is in consonance with the needs of eliminating the excess investment that the adjustment mechanism could work fully. And any partial workability of the adjustment mechanism is insufficient for Kaldor's theory to provide an explanation to the income shares.

Kaldor's theory is also defective in another way. It ignores the realationship between the share of profits and marginal products, elasticities of substitution and the life of capital. Whether there is reasonable substitutability of factors or absence of it will have a considerable influence on the distributive shares of capitalists and the wage-earners. Thus, the omission to take cognizance of the relationship between the share of profits and the substitutability between factors damages the Kaldorian analysis to a great extent. The model works in a situation where there is a strong complementarity of factors of production.

However, the most serious omission in Kaldor's model is with regard to the impact of technical progress on the income distribution as between the capitalists and the workers. Technical progress is complementary or otherwise to investment, *i.e.,* embodied or disembodied one. In the former it causes the benefits from *new* investment to rise throughout time. And in the latter it causes the benefits from *existing* investments to rise over time. Thus, it is not that high investment shorn of technical progress function through some 'widow's curse' would by itself produce and alone be responsible for a higher rate of profit to accrue and continue. Kaldor having constructed his model of income distribution in complete disregard of this very potent factor, thus, lacks realism.

In fact, in the face of technical progress and rising productivity of labour, Kaldor's exposition would need to be reversed a great deal. For in that event real wages could rise even when price level is rising. But so long as the rise in the level of prices takes place at a slower rate than the rise in the productivity of labour, the relative share of labour in income *(W/Y)* could fall and that of capitalist *(P/Y)* rise. And this is all that is essential for Kaldor's theory of income distribution to work. However, this argument is based on the assumption that the trade union of workers is more concerned about their absolute level of real wages than their relative income shares. Actually, this may not be so in the real world, for there is quite a bit of evidence that suggests that labour is quite aware of the profit margins in making their wage demands.

41. Joan Robinson, *The Accumulation of Capital*, p. 48.

Indeed most of the 'cost-push' inflation in the recent years has its basic root cause in the attempts on the part of the labour and the capitalists to swell up their respective shares of the national income.

Turning to the constraint (2), it tells us that the entrepreneurs would accept reductions in their profit margins up to a certain minimum so as to wipe out excess of full-employment savings over investment *(i.e.,* in conditions of deficient aggregate demand). But it is really not clear as to whether entrepreneurs would accept any reductions in prices and profit margins. The commonly observed phenomenon of prices being rigid in the downward direction is well known especially in the developed countries. Rather than adjusting prices, the producers generally prefer to make adjustments in terms of output during the periods of deficient demand.

Moreover, it is not merely sufficient that the firms should be prepared to accept *some* reductions in profit margins. The reductions have to be adequate enough so that the particular minimum P/Y is in conformity with the macro-economic equilibrium. The very fact that there may be too much monopoly power concentrated in the hands of the entrepreneurs may jam the process of adjustment needed for the equilibrium to be restored.

Above all, it is not always necessary that all reductions in the level of prices be accompanied by reductions in the profit margins (P/Y), since technical progress may, on the other hand, cause the unit costs to decline more than the fall in the prices. Kaldor's theory completely ignores such a possibility. Thus, to the extent that fall in prices fails to bring about commensurate fall in P/Y, the redistributive mechanism for wiping out the deficiency in aggregate demand would fail to work. And so to that extent a downward departure from full employment would ensue.

Hence, it follows from the above mentioned arguments that there may be a serious degree of inflexibility of relative income shares in the Kaldor model. Consequently, his model leaves us completely in the dark in respect of the mechanism that governs the limits on W/Y and P/Y. And the very factor of the rigidity of shares in this model implies that it fails to offer any satisfactory alternative to the marginal productivity theory of distribution.

Kaldor has brought out a very important factor, namely, investment-income ratio, which determines the shares of profits and wages in national income. However, Kaldor's theory is much restricted by the assumptions he makes. First, Kaldor regards investment as an independent of savings ratio and propensities to save. He himself admits that his theory ceases to hold good if the investment is not an independent variable.[42]

Secondly, Kaldor proves that how the relative share of profits in the national income, given the conditions of full employment, will increase when investment is undertaken to increase the capacity, but he does not provide us with an explanation as to how the distributive shares will be affected by the increases in investment and the resultant expansion in output and real income ***below the level of full employment.*** Thus, with full employment as an assumption, Kaldor's analysis has a distinct classical flavour, even though he makes use of Keynesian framework of income theory.

Lastly, Kaldor has failed to incorporate human capital in his theory, attention being concentrated on physical capital (material instruments of production). As a result of the rise in investment-income ratio and consequently the determination of the conditions of wage earners in which are included the highly skilled workers, engineers, managers, scientists (which constitute the human capital) will adversely affect the human capital of the country and will therefore bring about the reduction in real income and output. Thus "the failing of the theory to incorporate human capital leaves the theory too simple to explain the complexities of the real world."

42. Kaldor, *op. cit.*

PART–VI

GENERAL EQUILIBRIUM ANALYSIS AND WELFARE ECONOMICS

- General Equilibrium Analysis
- Welfare Economics: An Introduction
- Concept and Conditions of Pareto Optimality
- New Welfare Economics: Compensation Principle
- Grand Utility Possibility Frontier and Welfare Maximisation
- Market Failures, Externalities and Public Goods
- Social Welfare Function and Theory of Social Choice

CHAPTER

59

General Equilibrium Analysis

Partial Equilibrium and General Equilibrium Analysis

In the previous chapters we have focussed on explaining the determination of price and quantity of a commodity or a factor and the working of its market viewed in isolation of what happens to other commodities and factors. We have analysed how equilibrium price and quantity of a commodity or a factor is determined through demand and supply, assuming prices of other commodities and factors would remain the same when changes occur in the price of the commodity under consideration. That means the effect, if any, of the changes in price of a commodity on the demand for other commodities is ignored. This type of analysis where we do not take into account the inter-relationship or inter-dependence between prices of commodities or between prices of commodities and factors of production is called *partial equilibrium analysis.* In this partial equilibrium analysis each product or factor market is considered as independent and self-contained for the proper explanation of the determination of price and quantity of a commodity or a factor.

However, partial equilibrium analysis is not useful and relevant to apply when there is strong inter-relationship between commodities or between factors. Thus when markets for various commodities and factors are interdependent, that is, when changes in the price of a commodity or a factor have important repercussions on the demand for other commodities or factors, partial equilibrium analysis would not yield correct results. In such cases when there is significant inter-relationship between various markets or that the changes in one market would significantly affect others, we should employ general equilibrium analysis which considers ***simultaneous equilibrium*** of all markets taking into account all effects of changes in price in one market over others. It may be mentioned that both types of equilibrium analysis are useful, each being valuable in its own way.

Partial equilibrium analysis is useful when the changes in conditions in one market have little repercussions on other markets. However, when the changes in conditions in one market have significant effects on other markets, general equilibrium analysis should be used. For example, in partial equilibrium analysis when we consider the determination of market price of a commodity we assume that prices of other goods do not change. Thus, a rise in price of petrol following imposition of a tax on it would cause little effect on the prices of goods such as wrist watches, drapers, bowling balls, and in turn there would be negligible feedback effect of changes in prices of these goods on the demand and price of petrol. If prices of petrol and of only these commodities are to be considered and since there are little repercussions of changes in prices of petrol on these other commodities, the use of partial equilibrium analysis of price determination of petrol would be quite reasonable.

However, when market for automobiles is considered, the rise in price of petrol would have an important effect on their demand and price. Therefore, the assumption of partial equilibrium analysis that prices of automobiles would remain constant, when the price of petrol changes, would be seriously wrong. This is because petrol and automobiles being *complements* to each other, their markets are inter-related and mutually inter-dependent and therefore changes in their prices would significantly affect each other. In such cases when there exist inter-relationship and inter-dependence of the markets for goods (whether they are complements or substitutes), the general equilibrium analysis should be used. In general equilibrium analysis, all prices are considered variable and the analysis of simultaneous determination of equilibrium in all markets is made.

In fact when we look at the economic system as a whole, there is a great deal of inter-relationship and inter-dependence among various markets for commodities and factors and there are a large number of decision-making agents—consumers, producers, workers (who supply labour) and other resource owners. All these agents are self-interested and would behave to maximize their goals; consumers would maximize their utility, and producers would maximize their profits. A comprehensive analysis of the economic system when prices and quantities of all commodities and factors are considered as variable and which would take into account all inter-relationships and inter-dependence could be made only through general equilibrium analysis. The general equilibrium would occur when markets for all commodities and factors and all decision-making agents—consumers, producers, resource owners–are simultaneously in equilibrium.

To sum up, ***partial equilibrium analysis focuses on explaining the determination of price and quantity in a given product or factor market when one market is viewed as independent of other markets. On the other hand, general equilibrium analysis deals with explaining simultaneous equilibrium in all markets when prices and quantities of all products and factors are considered as variables.*** Thus, in general equilibrium analysis inter-relationship among markets of all products and factors are explicitly taken into account.

This chapter dwells upon the conditions of general equilibrium of a competitive economy *i.e.*, the economy in which all product and factor markets are perfectly competitive. We shall concentrate on the conditions of general equilibrium with regard to the following three aspects:

1. the distribution of goods and services for consumption among individuals in the society;
2. the allocation of productive factors to the production of various goods and services; and
3. the composition of production (or output mix) together with the distribution of consumption.

In this chapter,'we shall discuss whether a general equilibrium *exists* at all. Although the question of existence of general equilibrium is an abstract one, it is very important because many propositions of economics rest on the existence of general equilibrium. We shall also spell out in case general equilibrium exists, whether it is *unique.*

General Equilibrium of Exchange and Consumption : A Pure Exchange Economy Model

First, we shall explain general equilibrium in a pure exchange economy. In this pure exchange system, we assume that there is no production. That is, we consider the case when two goods are provided to the individuals in the economy from outside the system. To keep our analysis simple we assume that there are (1) *two goods,* a specific bundle of which has been made available to the individuals for consumption; and (2) there are *two individuals* between which exchange of goods has to take place and equilibrium reached with regard to the distribution of the specific amounts of these two goods.

Edgeworth Box and General Equilibrium of Exchange. In this, two goods, two individuals (2 × 2) model of pure exchange, the famous Edgeworth Box diagram has been employed to explain the general equilibrium of distribution of two goods between two individuals. In what follows we first explain the concept of Edgeworth Box and then analyse the general equilibrium in this pure exchange system. Consider Figure 59.1 where a box with certain fixed dimensions has been drawn. Along the *X*-axis we measure the commodity *X* and along the Y-axis, the commodity *Y*. The total available amount of commodity *X* is OX_0 and of commodity *Y* is OY_0. The available amounts of the two commodities, OX_0 and OY_0, determine the dimension of the box. The quantity of *X* available with the individual *A* is measured from left to right along the *X*-axis with bottom left-hand corner O_A as the origin. And, quantity of commodity *Y* available with the individual *A* is measured along the Y-axis from bottom to top with the origin O_A. For individual *B*, the top right hand corner O_B has been taken as the origin and with the given quantities of *X* and *Y*, the quantity of *X* available for consumption for individual *B* is measured, right to left, from origin O_B, and the quantity of *Y* available for *B* is measured, top to bottom, from the origin O_B.

It follows from above that Edgeworth Box has fixed dimensions representing the maximum available quantities of *X* and *Y* to be distributed between the two individuals. We further assume that the two individuals between them will entirely consume all the available quantities of the two goods. It may be noted that a point in the Edgeworth Box represents a particular distribution pattern of two goods between the two consumers. This implies that if the two individuals trade goods with each other and accordingly move from one point in the Edgeworth Box to another, the quantities purchased and sold of each good would be equal. Thus, with

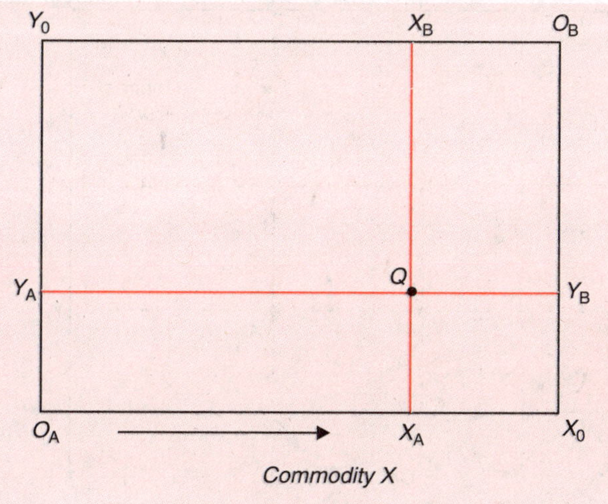

Fig. 59.1. *Edgeworth Box*

trade or exchange of goods, it is the distribution or consumption of two goods of the two individuals that will change, the total quantities of the two goods remaining constant.

In the Edgeworth Consumption Box we also draw the indifference curves of the two individuals *A* and *B* depicting their scale of preferences between the two goods. As we move upward from bottom left to top right, the satisfaction of individual *A* increases and that of *B* decreases, that is, *A* moves to successively higher indifference curves and individual *B* to successively lower indifference curves.

With the above assumptions, the general exchange equilibrium would lie somewhere on the contract curve, that is, the line which passes through the tangency points of indifference curves of the two individuals. At these tangency points of indifference curves, *MRSxy* of individual *A* equals that of individual *B*. Thus, the general equilibrium of exchange will occur when the following condition holds good :

$$MRS^A_{xy} = MRS^B_{xy}$$

Since a point on the contract curve lies within the Edgeworth box with the fixed quantities of the two goods, the equilibrium reached at a point on the contract curve after exchange or trading between the two individuals implies that the distribution for consumption of the two goods between the two individuals would just exhaust the available quantities of the two goods.

From above it cannot be known at which specific point or location of the contract curve, the general equilibrium of exchange will be reached. This is because the equality of *MRSxy* of the two individuals exists at all points of the contract curve. However, ***if we know the initial distribution of two goods between the two individuals we can pinpoint the boundaries within which the general equilibrium of exchange would lie.*** Consider Figure 59.2. If the initial distribution of two goods between the two individuals is represented by point *C* where individual *A* has X_{AI} amount of good *X* and Y_{AI} amount of good *Y*. The remaining quantity of good *X*, that is, $X_0 - X_{AI} = X_{BI}$ *would be allocated to individual B and the remaining* $Y_0 - Y_{AI} = Y_{BI}$ amount of good *Y* would go to individual *B*. At this initial distribution of goods *X* and *Y* with two individuals *A* and *B* (This is also generally referred to as initial endowments of goods to two individuals) the indifference curves of two individuals are intersecting. Now, this initial

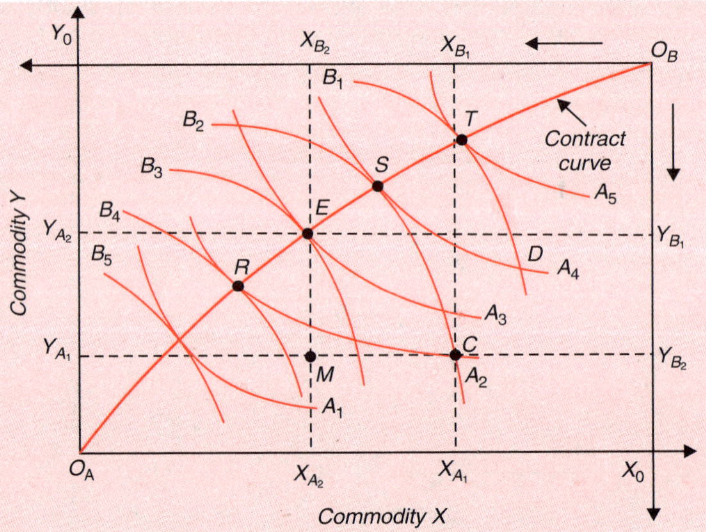

Fig. 59.2. *General Equilibrium of Exchange*

distribution or endowments of goods at point *C* cannot be the position of equilibrium for the two individuals, because the two individuals can gain in welfare or, in other words, can become better off if they exchange some amounts of the goods possessed by them and move to the contract curve. That is, if the individuals think that they can benefit from trading or exchange, they will trade with each other. As long as they think there are possibilities of becoming better off, they will trade with each other by exchanging goods and end up at the contract curve. With the initial distribution of two goods as implied by point *C*, if the two individuals through exchange of goods between them move to the point *R* on the contract curve, individual *B* reaches on his higher indifference curve and therefore becomes better off and *A* is no worse off as he remains on the same indifference curve as in his initial distribution point *C*. On the other hand, if through exchange they move to point *S* on the contract curve, individual *A* becomes better off and individual *B* no worse off as compared to the initial position *C*. And if through trading and exchange of goods they move to any point between *R* and *S* on the contract curve both the individuals will gain from trading as they will be reaching their respective higher indifference curves.

With initial distribution at point C and through exchange of goods nearer they move to point *R* on the contract curve, individual *B* will benefit more and nearer they move to point *S* on the contract curve, the individual *A* will gain more as compared to the initial distribution position *C*. Where exactly on the contract curve, their equilibrium position of exchange will lie depends upon the bargaining power of each individual. With their almost equal bargaining power, their equilibrium position of exchange on the contract curve may lie at point *E* where the two individuals gain almost equally as a result of exchange. Thus, if the initial distribution of two individuals is not on the contract curve, there will be tendency on the part of individuals to trade or exchange goods between themselves and to move to a point on the contract curve because in doing so, they will be increasing their satisfaction.

It is evident from the foregoing analysis that given the initial endowment or distribution point *C* the general equilibrium of exchange can occur somewhere between *R* and *S* on the contract curve. ***On all points between R and S, the exchange equilibrium can exist. Although equilibrium will exist at a point on the contract curve, there is no unique position of exchange equilibrium; all points between R and S on the contract curve are possible equilibrium positions.*** If instead of point *C*, the initial distribution or endowments of goods to the two individuals is given by point *D* where the indifference curves A_4 and B_1, of the two individuals are intersecting, the exchange equilibrium will occur anywhere on the segment *ST of* the contract curve. It should be noted that in the pure exchange economy model which we are considering here, income of an individual is given by the initial endowment of goods to him. Thus, it is the *initial income distribution* and the relative bargaining strengths of the individuals that determine a position of general equilibrium on the contract curve.

It should be further noted that given the initial distribution indicated by point *C* and the bargaining strengths of the two individuals if point *E* on the contract curve is the position of exchange equilibrium actually reached, then individual *A* has exchanged the amount of commodity *X* equal to $X_{A1} - X_{A2}$ for the amount of commodity *Y* equal to $Y_{A2} - Y_{A1}$. Since point *E* lies on the contract curve which is the locus of the tangency points of indifference curves of the two individuals, marginal rate of substitution between the two goods (MRS_{xy}) of individual *A* equals marginal rate of substitution between the two commodities (MRS_{xy}) of individual *B*. Now, if instead of personal bargaining, *perfect competition prevails in an exchange economy,* each individual takes the prices of two goods as given, even then the general equilibrium will be reached at a point on the contract curve where their MRS_{xy} are equal to the same price ratio (P_x/P_y). The general equilibrium of exchange attained has the following important features :

1. The general equilibrium of exchange occurs at a point on the contract curve where the marginal rate of substitution between the two goods (MRS_{xy}) of the two individuals is the same. ***The exchange equilibrium cannot be at a point in the Edgeworth Box which is not on the contract curve.*** This is because at a point which is not on the contract curve, indifference curves of two individuals intersect each other and therefore their MRS_{xy} are not equal to each other.
2. Since any equilibrium point on the contract curve such as point *E* would lie within the

Edgeworth Box, drawn with the given amounts of two goods, the exchange of goods between the two individuals when they move to the equilibrium point on the contract curve would imply that quantity sold of each good equals the quantity purchased of that good. That is, markets for the two goods would clear. For example, in Figure 59.2 on moving to the equilibrium position *E* on the contract curve individual *A* relative to his initial endowment of goods is selling good *X* and buying good *Y*. The opposite is true of individual *B* who buys good *X* and sells good *Y*. The quantity sold and purchased of each good must equal each other. If this does not happen, the two markets will not clear and shortages or surpluses would emerge.

3. The general exchange equilibrium determines not only the final distribution of two goods between the individuals but also a rate of exchange of goods between the two individuals. In Fig. 59.2 in the equilibrium position at *E* on the contract curve quantity *MC* of *X* has been exchanged for *ME* of commodity *Y*. This indicates the relative prices at which the exchange of goods takes place between the two individuals.
4. The general equilibrium of exchange does not lead to the determination of *absolute prices* of goods but only ***relative prices of goods.*** This will be explained in detail later in this chapter.
5. The general equilibrium of exchange is *not unique*; it may occur at any point on the contract curve depending on the *initial endowments of goods* of the individuals. Even with a given initial endowments of goods of the individuals (such as point *C* in Fig. 59.2), the exchange equilibrium *may occur at any point on the segment* of the contract curve within the boundaries defined by the indifference curves of the two individuals that intersect at the initial point.

General Equilibrium of Production

We now extend our analysis of general equilibrium to the sphere of production. Production of goods requires the use of inputs or factors of production. The level of production of goods depends upon the allocation of resources to them. As emphasized in the beginning, the general equilibrium analysis takes into account the mutual inter-dependence of markets. Now, we are not only concerned with the mutual inter-dependence of markets for goods between themselves but also between product markets and factor markets. To keep our analysis simple we shall assume that two factors or inputs, labour and capital, are required for the production of two goods *X* and *Y*. This analysis of general equilibrium by taking two goods and two factors will enable us to capture the essential characteristics of the general equilibrium of production. Besides taking 2×2 model, we make the following assumptions:

1. All units of labour are homogeneous so that they receive equal remunerations for their contribution to the production of goods. So is the case with all units of capital.
2. The available quantities of the two factors, labour and capital are *fixed* in the economy and both of them are fully employed and utilised.
3. There is smooth production function for each good so that production factors, labour and capital, can be freely transferred from one good to the other.
4. Technology is given which together with the factor endowments limits the production possibilities.

It may be mentioned here that there are four markets in the model considered here : two factor markets of labour and capital, and two product markets of goods *X* and *Y*.

With the above assumptions we shall analyse the general equilibrium of production in all the four markets. It may be emphasized again that the various markets are inter-related. For example, if more labour is employed in the production of good X, then, given its fixed supply, some labour will have to be withdrawn from the production of good Y. Changes in labour allocation to the production of goods would also have repercussions on the use of capital in the production of two goods. It is indeed the task of general equilibrium analysis to determine the pattern of relative prices and quantities of goods and factors at which all markets clear together, that is, prices and quantities at which demand and supply in each of the four markets are brought into equilibrium simultaneously.

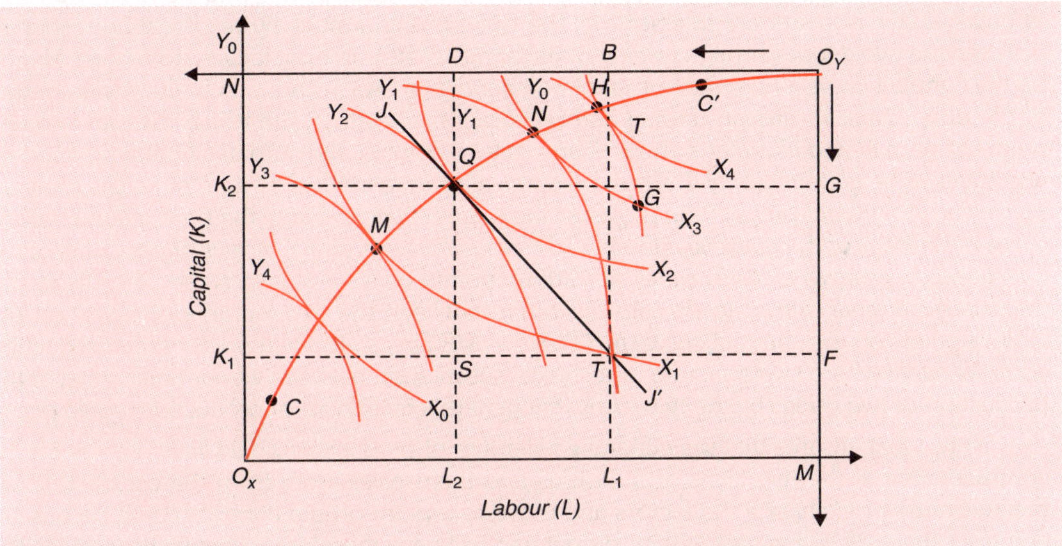

Fig. 59.3. *General Equilibrium of Production*

Edgeworth Production Box and General Equilibrium of Production

As in case of general equilibrium of exchange or consumption, the general equilibrium of production can also be analysed with the help of Edgeworth Box diagram. In case of Edgeworth Production Box, dimensions of the box represent the available fixed quantities of the two factors, labour and capital. Thus, in the Edgeworth Production Box as shown in Figure 59.3, along the horizontal axis we measure the quantity of labour and along the vertical axis we measure the quantity of capital. In this box various isoquants are also drawn for the products X and Y. For good X, various isoquants representing successively higher levels of output such as X_0, X_1, X_2 etc. are drawn with the bottom left hand corner O_x as their origin. For good Y, various isoquants such as Y_0, Y_1, Y_2 representing successively higher levels of output of Y are drawn with top right hand corner O_y as the origin. The isoquant map of each good exhibits their production function. As constructed, isoquants of good X imply that the good X is relatively capital-intensive and isoquants for good Y imply that good Y is relatively labour-intensive. This means that for any given factor price ratio, that is, ratio of price of labour to the price of capital (w/r), minimization of cost for *a* ***given level of output*** of good X requires higher capital-labour ratio (K/L) than that of good Y.

It is important to note that any point in the Edgeworth Box represents *a* ***particular allocation of labour and capital*** between the two industries, one producing good X and the other producing good Y. Various points in the box represent different alternative allocation of factors between the two commodities. For example, point T in the box shows that O_xL_1 (or

K_1T) amount of labour and O_XK_1 (or L_1T) amount of capital are allocated to the production of X and the remaining amount of labour *TF* and the remaining amount of capital *TC* are allocated to the production of good *Y*. It will be seen from Figure 59.3 that the points *M, Q, N* etc. represent different allocation of factors from the point *T*.

Now, a smooth curve *CC'* joining the tangency points of isoquants of X and Y has been drawn. This is called the *production contract curve.* It can be shown that the general equilibrium of production would occur somewhere on this production contract curve. The allocation of factors implied by a point *away from the contract curve* such as point *T* cannot be the possible position of general equilibrium of production. This is because from the point *T* where X-isoquant and Y-isoquant are intersecting, the two firms can move by re-allocating resources between the two goods (through trading or exchange of resources of factors) to a point *M* or *N* on the contract curve where the output of one good increases without the reduction in output of the other. And, if through trading and reallocation of factors, the two firms move to any point between *M* and *N on* the contract curve, say to point *Q*, the outputs of both the goods *X* and *Y* would be greate than at *T*. Thus, resource allocation implied by a point on the contract curve leads to greater output than those off the contract curve. Since the production contract curve is the locus of the tangency points of the isoquants of X and Y, slopes of isoquants of the two goods are equal to each other at various points on it. Because slope of an isoquant measures marginal rate of technical substitution between the two factors ($MRTS_{Lk}$) on the various points on the contract curve, $MRTS^x_{LK} = MRTS^y_{LK}$. It is at a point of the production contract curve where marginal rate of technical substitution between labour and capital in the production of two goods by the two firms that general equilibrium of production would occur.

Now, what ensures that the general equilibrium of production would lie at a point on the contract curve. If the two firms or industries find themselves away from the contract curve, they wil trade or exchange the factors and move to a point on the contract curve because in doing so they will be increasing their output and will have therefore incentive to move to the contract curve. It should be noted that if the production is done by the firms at a point on the contract curve, one firm can increase production only at the cost of reduction in output of the other firm. Thus, if the firms move from point *M* to *N*, the production of *X* increases while the production of *Y* decreases. It is worth mentioning that *point of general equilibrium of production is not unique* since it may occur at any point on the production contract curve, depending on a starting point, that is, initial allocation of a fixed amount of factors (labour and capital) to the production of two goods. For example, if the initial allocation of factors is denoted by point *T* in Figure 59.3, then with reallocation through trading of factors, the two firms can move to and attain general equilibrium at any point on the segment *MN* of the production contract curve. Further with a different initial allocation of the fixed amount of factors, say point G in the Edgeworth Box, there will be a different point of production equilibrium lying anywhere on the segment *HN* of the contract curve.

It is worth noting that with initial factor allocation point *T*, if the general equilibrium of production occurs at point *Q* on the contract curve, it will determine not only the quantities of factors allocated to the two goods but also the equilibrium ratio of factor prices, that is, the ratio of wage rate of labour to the rental price of capital $\left(\frac{w}{r}\right)$ so that *QS* of capital is exchanged for *ST* of labour.

Besides, the point of general equilibrium or production will also determine the product-mix (that is, outputs of two goods X and *Y*) produced. Thus, if general equilibrium of production occurs at point *Q* on the contract curve, it means that output X_2 of good X and output Y_2 of good *Y* are being produced in the production equilibrium situation.

From the foregoing analysis it follows that the general equilibrium of production requires not only the ***simultaneous equilibrium of the two factor markets determining*** allocation of resources between the production of the two goods but also the ***simultaneous equilibrium of the product markets*** of two goods X and *Y* indicating quantity demanded of each good equals the quantity supplied.

Transformation Curve and General Equilibrium of Production

In our above analysis we have shown the output of two goods *X* and *Y* through isoquants in the *factor space* of the Edgeworth Production Box. To bring outputs of two goods directly into the picture and to clearly show the equilibrium in markets for goods, we require to display outputs of the two goods in the *output space.* This is done through a familiar concept of *transformation curve* which is also known as *production possibility curve.* A transformation curve shows the alternative combinations of two goods that can be produced with the given fixed amounts of the factors. The transformation curve is derived from the contract curve of production in the space by mapping or plotting the various output combinations of two goods directly in *output space* corresponding to the various points of the contract curve. In Figure 59.4 transformation curve is drawn from the production contract curve in Figure 59.3. For example, corresponding to point *Q* on the contract curve *CC'* in Figure 59.3 indicating X_2 level *of* output of good *X* and Y_2 level of output of good Y, we plot the point *Q'* in the output space of Figure 59.4. Likewise, point *N'* corresponding to point *N* on the contract curve, point *M'* corresponding to the point *M* of the contract curve are plotted and on joining such points as *N'*, *Q'*, *M'* we get the transformation curve *TT'*. **A transformation curve shows how one good is transformed into another by transferring resources from the production of one good into the production of the other.**

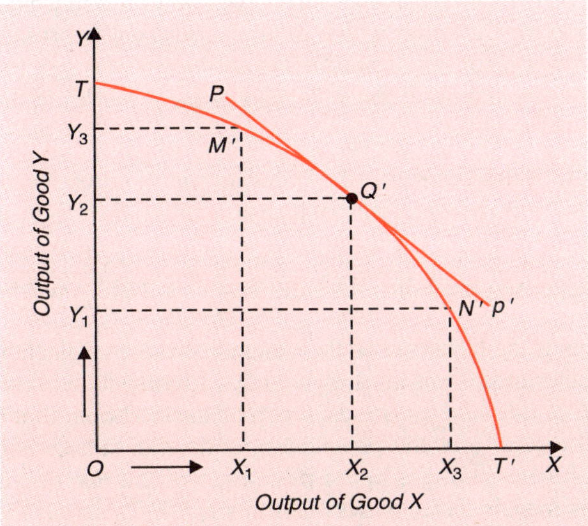

Fig. 59.4. *Transformation Curve and General Equilibrium of Production*

Two aspects of the transformation curve are worth noting. First, it is concave to the origin which implies that the amount of commodity *Y* which has to be given up or sacrificed in order to produce an additional unit of *X* goes on increasing as we produce more of good X. This implies the operation of diminishing return to scale in the production of X. In case returns to scale increase, the transformation curve obtained would be convex to the origin. We will get a straight line transformation curve when returns to scale are constant. Thus the shape of the transformation curve depends upon the nature of the production function of a commodity.

Secondly, the slope of the transformation curve at a point measures the marginal rate of transformation between the two goods. Marginal rate of transformation of good *X* for good

$Y(MRT_{xy})$ indicates the amount by which the production of good Y has to be reduced to produce one more unit of good X with the help of resources released from the reduction in output of good Y, that is, MRT_{xy} is the rate at which one good is transformed into another and is equal to the ratio of marginal costs of production of the two goods. Thus

$$MRT_{xy} = \frac{MC_x}{MC_y} 0.$$

GENERAL EQUILIBRIUM OF PRODUCTION AND EXCHANGE

Having now explained the conditions of exchange equilibrium and production equilibrium separately we are now in a position to explain the ***simultaneous general equilibrium of production and exchange***. The problem of the overall general equilibrium is as follows. Can a set of prices exist at which quantities demanded of goods by the consumers are fulfilled by the quantities supplied of the goods by the producers who use factors for the production of goods and the set of factor prices which equate demand for them with their available supplies.

To explain the general equilibrium of production and exchange together, we need to draw a transformation curve. There are several points on the transformation curve; each represents a different production equilibrium indicating a different output-mix of the two goods. Each point of the transformation curve corresponds to a point on the production contract curve which shows all combinations of two goods which satisfy the condition of general equilibrium of production. A slope at a point on the transformation curve shows the marginal rate of transformation (MRT_{xy}) of one good for the other which in equilibrium will represent the ratio of prices of two goods. The general equilibrium of production can occur at any of the points on the given transformation curve depending upon the initial allocation of factors in the production of two goods.

Now, an important question is, which of the points on the transformation curve, or, in other words, which price ratio of commodities or marginal rate of transformation (MRT_{xy}) will be the equilibrium ratio ? The general equilibrium level of price ratio $\left(\frac{P_X}{P_Y}\right)$ or MRT_{xy} will be one which on the one hand maximizes profits of the firms and on the other maximizes satisfaction of consumers. To analyse the general equilibrium of output-mix, we have to introduce in our analysis the consumers preference pattern or demand for goods. It can be easily shown that if MRS_{xy} *of* the consumers is not equal to the MRT_{xy} *in* the production, consumer satisfaction will not be maximised with the result that further changes in the price ratio of the two goods and output-mix will tend to occur. Since the marginal rate of transformation MRT_{xy} shows the rate at which one good is 'transformed' into another in the production process and marginal rate of substitution measures the rate at which consumers are willing to exchange one good for the other, equilibrium cannot be reached unless the two rates are equal. Thus, only when MRT_{xy} equals MRT_{xy}, planned product-mix, that is, the quantities of two goods, will be consistent with the preferences of consumers and ensure general equilibrium of production and exchange. This can be made clear with a simple numerical example. For instance, if at a given output-mix of two goods X and Y, MRT_{xy} *of* the producers of the economy is $3Y/X$ and MRS_{xy} *of* consumers equals $2Y/1X$. Thus, in this case MRS_{xy} of consumers is less than MRT_{xy} *of* producers. That is, the economy can produce 3 units of Y by foregoing one unit of good X while the consumers are willing to exchange or buy 2 units of Y for one unit of X.

MRS_{xy} of consumers being less than MRT_{xy} of producers implies that greater quantity of commodity X and smaller quantity of commodity Y is being produced than desired by the consumers. Obviously, if the economy reduces the production of X by one unit and produces 3 units more of Y and give them to the consumers, their satisfaction or welfare will increase as they are willing to get even 2 units of Y for the sacrifice of one unit of X. Thus consumers' satisfaction can be raised by expanding the production of Y and reducing the production of X until the two rates, namely, MRS_{xy} of consumers and MRT_{xy} of producers become equal. General equilibrium will thus be reached if with adjustment in output-mix of the two commodities, MRT_{xy} equals MRS_{xy}. In a free-market economy, the interaction between producers and consumers would ensure such adjustment which will bring about product-mix that will equate MRS_{xy} *of* consumers with MRT_{xy} of producers and thus ensuring maximum consumers' satisfaction.

The general equilibrium of production together with the general equilibrium of exchange (or consumption) requires that the marginal rate of transformation not only be equal to marginal rate of substitution (MRS_{xy}) of the consumers but also MRS_{xy} of the two consumers be equal to each other. As seen earlier, if the MRS_{xy} *of* the two individuals are not equal, they will increase their satisfaction by trading goods with each other until their MRS_{xy} become equal to each other.

Thus, for the achievement of general equilibrium of production and exchange we arrive at the following condition :

$$MRT_{xy} = MRS^A_{xy} = MRS^B_{xy}$$

The overall general equilibrium of production and exchange is illustrated in Figures 59.5 and 59.6. Consider Figure 59.5 where a transformation curve TT' is drawn. Let us consider the point L on the transformation curve TT'. At point L, the output OM of good X and output

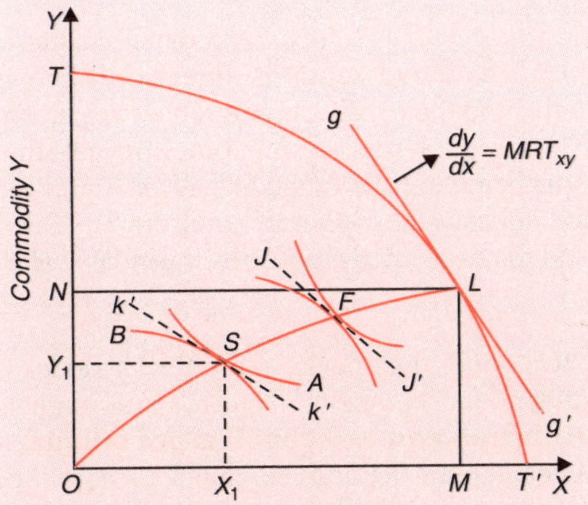

Fig. 59.5. *General Disequilibrium: $MRT_{xy} > MRS_{xy}$*

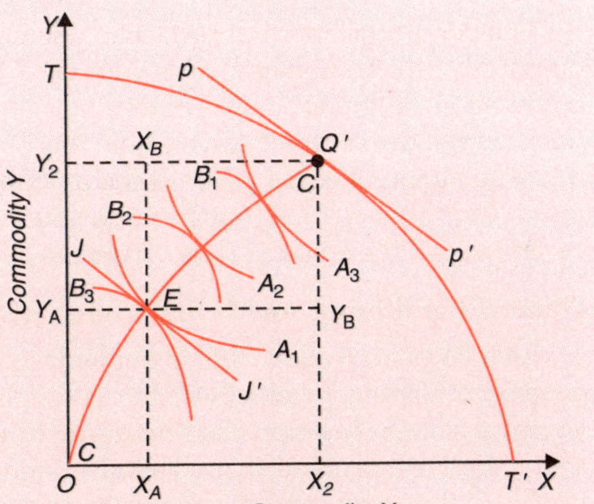

Fig. 59.6. *General Equilibrium of Production and Exchange: $MRS_{xy} = MRT_{xy}$*

ON of good Y is being produced. With OM quantity of good X and ON quantity of good Y, Edgeworth Box has been made. With the given preference pattern of the two consumers, their indifference curves have been drawn within the box which are tangent to each other at point S and their MRS_{xy} is indicated by the slope of the tangent line kk'. A glance at Figure 59.5 shows that MRS_{xy} of consumers at point S is less *than* MRT_{xy} of producers at point L indicating that production-mix is inconsistent with consumer's preferences. This shows the system is in disequilibrium indicating that greater quantity of X and smaller quantity of Y is being produced than demanded by the consumers. In response to this disequilibrium situation and to maximize their profits producers would tend to produce more of Y and less of X and this process of adjustment in output-mix will continue until the MRT_{xy} in production is brought into equality with MRS_{xy} of consumers. With this equality, general equilibrium of production and exchange (consumption) would be attained. This general equilibrium is shown in Figure 59.6 where at position Q' on the transformation curve TT' OX_2 level of output of X and OY_2 level of output of Y are being produced and MRT_{xy} *at* point Q' equals MRS_{xy} *at* E (slopes of JJ' and PP' are equal). Producers are in equilibrium as at Q' marginal rate of transformation (MRT_{xy}) equals the price ratio $\left(\frac{P_x}{P_y}\right)$ as measured by the slope of pp'. There is general equilibrium of exchange or consumption as MRS_{xy} of the two individuals are the same (their indifference curves being tangent to each other at point E). There is joint equilibrium of production and exchange as the $MRTxy$ which determines price ratio $\left(\frac{P_x}{P_y}\right)$ at point Q also equals MRS_{xy} of the two individuals according to the consumption equilibrium point E. Thus, with point Q' on the transformation curve TT' and point E on the contract curve drawn in the Edgeworth Box made from point Q', the following condition of general equilibrium of production and consumption is fulfilled.

$$MRT_{xy} = \left(\frac{P_x}{P_y}\right) = MRS^A_{xy} = MRS^B_{xy}$$

General equilibrium of production determines total output X_2 of commodity X and total output Y_2 of commodity Y. It is with OX_2 and OY_2 as the dimensions, Edgeworth Box is drawn and indifference curves of two individuals depicting their scale of preferences are drawn with CC' as the contract curve within this box. Consumption equilibrium point E reveals that out of total output X_2 of good X, the amount X_A is being consumed by individual A and the remaining amount of X goes to individual B for consumption. Out of total output Y_2 of commodity Y, the amount Y_A is consumed by A and the remaining amount by the individual B.

General Equilibrium and Initial Endowment

It follows from above that in our two factors, two goods, two persons (2 × 2 × 2) model of general equilibrium, together with the assumption that perfect competition prevails in all markets we arrive at the conclusion that ***the general equilibrium can exist* but it is not unique.** It should be further noted that solution of general equilibrium depends on initial allocation of factors to the two goods. It is the initial allocation of factors to the two goods that determines a point on the contract curve at which production equilibrium is attained. This production equilibrium also determines the relative factor prices and the amount of factors (labour and capital) used in production. The amount of factors used and relative factor prices together determine the incomes of the consumers. Consumers who are not only demanders of goods but also lend the services of their factors and derive income from them. Assuming that constant returns to scale prevail, the incomes earned from factors will just exhaust total product. It is these factoral incomes that constitute the initial endowment or distribution of income in the Edgeworth consumption box. In our analysis we have found that the general equilibrium of production which occurs at point Q' on the transformation curve TT' in Figure 59.6 corresponds to the point Q on production contract curve of the Edgeworth Production Box in Figure.59.3

and consumption equilibrium point E is obtained on the consumption contract curve in the Edgeworth Box drawn through point Q' in Fig. 59.6 .This position of general equilibrium of production and consumption indicates ***that factor markets of labour and capital and product markets of goods X and Y are simultaneously in equilibrium*** and determine the following things :

(1) relative prices of factors (w & r) as indicated by the slope of the line joining initial point T to the equilibrium point Q on the contract curve in Figure 59.3.

(2) allocation of factors between products X and Y as indicated by point Q in Figure 59.3.

(3) relative prices of product X and Y as measured by the slope of the price line PP' in Figure 59.6.

(4) the product-mix, that is, the levels of output of goods X and Y as given by point Q' in Figure 59.6.

(5) the distribution of goods X and Y between the two individuals as indicated by point E in Figure 59.6.

General Equilibrium Determines only Relative Prices

It is important to note that micro-economic theory is concerned with analysing the factors that determine relative prices and not absolute prices. Relative price means price of a good or a factor as compared to the price of another good or a factor. In other words, by relative prices we mean the ratio of prices of goods and ratio of prices of factors. That micro-economic theory concerns with relative prices is made quite clear in the analysis of general equilibrium analysis. In our analysis of general equilibrium when we talked about the determination of factor prices, it was the ratio of factor prices (*i.e.*, the ratio of price of labour to the price of capital, $\frac{w}{r}$) as measured by the common slope of the isoquants at the tangency points of the relevant isoquants that was determined. In fact, we did not explain how absolute prices, namely, wage rate of labour, w and price of capital, r were determined. Likewise, in general equilibrium analysis we do not concern ourselves with the determination of absolute prices of goods ; we only show how general equilibrium determines the *ratio of prices* of two goods *i.e.* $\left(\frac{P_x}{P_y}\right)$.

Thus we found that in Figure 59.6 general equilibrium is established at point Q' on the transformation curve TT' where $MRT_{xy} = MRS^B_{xy} = MRS^A_{xy}$ and saw that this yields relative prices of goods X and Y, that is, the ratio $\left(\frac{P_x}{P_y}\right)$ which is measured by the slope of the transformation curve at that equilibrium point Q' and not the absolute prices.

An important thing to note is that because it is the relative and not absolute prices that result from the general equilibrium analysis that doubling or halving of *all prices* so that relative prices remain the same would not bring any change in the equilibrium position. For example, suppose the relative prices of two goods X and Y, $\frac{P_x}{P_y}$, as measured by the marginal rate of transformation at point Q' in Figure 59.6 is 2/1 and the relative price of labour and capital (w/r) as measured by the slope of the isoquants at point Q in Figure 59.3 is 3/1. Further suppose price of good X is ₹ 20 and the price of good Y is 10, so that relative product price is 20/10 = 2/1 and the price of labour (w) is ₹ 30 and the price of capital (r) is ₹ 10, so the relative factor price w/r equals 3/1. *Now, if all prices are doubled,* P_x = ₹ 40, P_Y = ₹ 20, w = ₹ 60 and r = ₹ 20, then the relative prices of products $\frac{P_x}{P_y} = \frac{40}{20} = \frac{2}{1}$ and relative factor prices $\frac{w}{r} = \frac{60}{20} = \frac{3}{1}$. Since all relative prices have remained the same despite the change in their absolute levels, the position of general equilibrium would remain unaltered. In real terms nothing would change. Consumers would have twice the payments or income but would buy exactly the same quantities of goods X and Y. Each firm would receive double the total revenue than before but would buy and employ the same amounts of factors at double the prices. Thus, *it is the relative prices that are significant* in determining the real outcome — production, employment of factors, income distribution and the distribution of goods between the individuals. That is why micro-economic theory lays stress on the determination of relative prices. To conclude, general equilibrium analysis yields relative and not absolute prices. If absolute prices of all products and all factors change by a same percentage, the real situation would remain unchanged.

GENERAL EQUILIBRIUM AND PERFECT COMPETITION

We have explained above the general equilibrium of exchange and production separately and then simultaneously. We have shown that general equilibrium in all the three aspects can exist. However, the general equilibrium of exchange and production, separately as well as simultaneously, can occur at any point on the contract curve depending on the *initial endowment of goods* (that is income) and *bargaining strengths* of the individuals. However, if perfect competition is assumed to be prevailing in both the product and factor markets, the general equilibrium *can be unique* but it will still depend on the given initial endowment of goods (that is, initial income distribution). That under perfect competition general equilibrium can exist and depends on the initial endowments is shown as under :

Perfect Competition and General Equilibrium of Exchange

We will explain first general equilibrium of exchange under competitive conditions. With perfect competition in the buying and selling of goods no individual can influence the prices of goods; he takes the prices as given and constant. Thus, with given prices of goods X and Y, consumer A maximises his satisfaction by equating his marginal rate of substitution (MRS_{xy}) with the given price ratio. Thus

$$MRS^A_{xy} = \frac{P_x}{P_y} \qquad ...(i)$$

Similarly, the individual B would be maximizing his satisfaction when

$$MRS^B_{xy} = \frac{P_x}{P_y} \qquad ...(ii)$$

Since under perfect competition both the individuals will be facing the same set of prices, from (*i*) and (*ii*) we get

$$MRS^A_{xy} = MRS^B_{xy} = \frac{P_x}{P_y}$$

Now consider Figure 59.7. Suppose the initial endowments of individuals A and B is given by point C. Further suppose that the prevailing perfectly competitive price ratio $\left(\frac{P_x}{P_y}\right)$ is denoted by the slope of the price line *PP′* which is drawn through the initial endowment point C. In fact, the price line *PP′* passing through initial endowment point C becomes the budget line for the two consumers. With the initial endowment of the two individuals represented by point C and the perfectly competitive price-ratio line *PP′* the two individuals in their attempt to maximise satisfaction will trade goods with each other and move to a unique point *E* on the contract curve where their indifference curves are tangent to the given price line *PP′*. In this way, by adding the assumption of perfect competition in the sale and purchase of goods and starting from initial endowment point *C* we have reached the unique point *E* where the general equilibrium of exchange occurs on the *segment RS* of the contract curve. With position *C* as the starting point and point *E* where they reach equilibrium position individual *A* has sold good X and purchased good Y, whereas individual *B* has purchased good X and sold good Y. Price ratio of the two goods is given by the slope of the budget line *PP*'. At equilibrium at *E* with the budget line *PP*' (*i.e.* price ratio) the quantity of good X demanded by *B* equals the quantity of good X supplied by *A* and, similarly, quantity demanded of good *Y* equals the quantity supplied of good Y. As a result, markets for the two goods are in equilibrium and therefore general equilibrium of exchange exists. Note that a general equilibrium refers to a set of prices at which quantity demanded of goods equals their quantity supplied. We thus see that general equilibrium is consistent with perfect competition.

However, it may be noted that not all prices are consistent with general equilibrium under perfect competition. For instance, price ratio of the two goods represented by the price line *KK*' which also passes through the initial endowment point C. With this price ratio or price line *KK*', individual *A* is in equilibrium at point G and individual *B* is in equilibrium at point *H*, the ' markets of goods X and *Y* are not in equilibrium as the MRS_{xy} of the two individuals are not equal to $\frac{P_x}{P_y}$ at the same point. While individual *B* demands less of good X, the individual *A* is willing to supply more of it, that is, surplus of good X emerges in the market. As regards good Y, with price ratio line *KK*', individual *A* demands more of good Y than individual *B* is willing to supply it. Thus with price ratio line *KK*', the competitive markets of two goods are not in equilibrium.

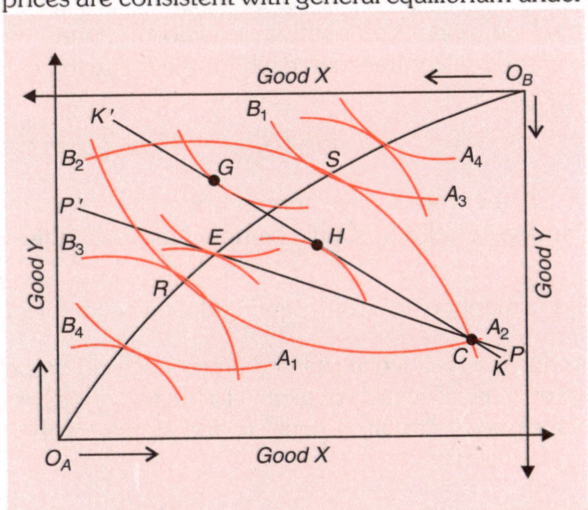

Fig. 59.7. *General Equilibrium of Exchange under Perfectly Competitive Conditions*

It should be emphasised again that the equilibrium of exchange on the segment *RS* of the contract curve in Fig. 59.7 is reached by assuming that C is the initial endowment of goods (*i.e.* initial income) of the two individuals. With a different initial endowment point in the Edgeworth box, we will obtain a different point of exchange equilibrium on the contract curve.

Perfect Competition and General Equilibrium of Production

General equilibrium of production requires the determination of allocation of resources among the firms which use the factors for production of goods. We have seen above that general equilibrium of production occurs at a point on the production contract curve where the $MRTS_{LK}$ in the production of commodity X equals the $MRTS_{LK}$ in the production of commodity Y. With perfect competition prevailing in the factor markets, factor-price ratio $\left(\frac{w}{r}\right)$ will be given for each firm. In order to minimise cost for producing a given output, a firm will be in equilibrium when $MRTS_{LK} = \frac{w}{r}$.

Now, what ensures that the general equilibrium of production would occur at a point on the contract curve. As we are assuming factor markets are competitive, it is the competitive forces that would bring the economy in equilibrium at a point on the contract curve. If the two firms find themselves away from the contract curve, they will trade or exchange the factors and move to a point on the contract curve because in doing so they will be increasing their output and will have therefore incentive to move to the contract curve. To produce a given level of output of a commodity, each firm will minimise its cost of production by equating marginal rate of technical substitution between factors ($MRTS_{LK}$) with the *same* factor price ratio $\frac{w}{r}$ where w stands for the wage rate of labour and r for the rental price of capital. To conclude, under competitive conditions general equilibrium of production would occur at a point on the contract curve where the following condition holds:

$$MRTS^{x}_{LK} = MRTS^{y}_{LK} = \frac{w}{r}$$

If the competitive forces bring the economy to be in general equilibruim at point Q in Figure 59.3, it should be noted that JJ' is the price line which passes through the initial endowment point T representing the given factor-price ratio $\left(\frac{w}{r}\right)$. The general equilibrium of production reached at point Q under perfect competition in the factor markets will determine not only the allocation of factors to the two goods as implied by point Q but also the equilibrium factor-price ratio (w/r) equal to the slopes of the isoquants of X and Y at point Q of the contract curve.

Alternative Proof of General Equilibrium of Production under Competitive Economy

There is an alternative way of showing that the general equilibrium of production under competitive conditions would lie on the contract curve. In the competitive labour market, a profit maximizing firm or industry would employ so much labour that brings wage rate (W) equal to the value of marginal product (VMP_L) of labour. Likewise, in the competitive market for capital, the profit maximizing firms in the industries would equate the rental price of capital (r) with the value of the marginal product of capital (VMP_K). Now, under conditions of perfect competition, factors are paid remunerations equal to the value of their marginal products. All units of a factor whether employed in industry X or industry Y will get the same remuneration equal to the value of its marginal product. Thus, in industry X producing good X,

$$VMP_L = w$$

where VMP_L = Value of marginal product labour and w = Wage rate

Since value of marginal product of a factor equals the marginal physical product of the factor multiplied by the price of the product, we get

$$P_x MP_L = w \qquad (i)$$

where P_x is the price of the product X and MP_L is the marginal physical product of labour.

Likewise, the rental price of capital (r) would equal the value of marginal productivity of capital (VMP_K).

$$VMP_K = r$$

$$P_x MP_K = r \qquad (ii)$$

Dividing (*i*) by (*ii*),

$$\frac{P_x MP_L}{P_x MP_K} = \frac{w}{r}$$

$$\frac{MP_L}{MP_K} = \frac{w}{r}$$

Since under competitive conditions factor price-ratio (w/r) would be the same for the firms producing X and those producing Y. Thus

$$\left(\frac{MP_L}{MP_K}\right)^x = \frac{w}{r}$$

and
$$\left(\frac{MP_L}{MP_K}\right)^y = \frac{w}{r}$$

The factor price-ratio (w/r) *being the same for both the industries* X and Y.

$$\left(\frac{MP_L}{MP_K}\right)^x = \left(\frac{MP_L}{MP_K}\right)^y = \frac{w}{r} \qquad (iii)$$

Since the marginal rate of technical substitution between the two factors equals the ratio of marginal physical product of labour to the marginal physical product of capital, from *(iii)* it follows that if competitive conditions prevail,

$$MRTS_{LK}^{x} = MRTS_{LK}^{y} = \frac{w}{r}$$

Perfect Competition and General Equilibrium of Production and Exchange

In a two factors, two goods and two consumers (2 × 2 × 2) model we have explained above that the general equilibrium of production and exchange occurs at a point where the following condition is fulfilled :

$$MRT_{xy} = MRS_{xy}^{A} = MRS_{xy}^{B}$$

As explained earlier, marginal rate of transformation between two goods, MRT_{xy} is equal to the ratio of marginal cost of production of two commodities. Thus,

$$MRT_{xy} = \frac{MC_x}{MC_y}$$

Now, if perfect competition is prevailing in the goods markets, then the individual firms producing the goods would equate the given price of a good with its marginal cost of production. Thus

$$MC_x = P_x \text{ and } MC_y = P_y$$

The slope of the production transformation curve measures the marginal rate of transformation (MRT_{xy}). Thus, given the market prices of goods for the firms as is the case under perfect competition, the general equilibrium of production will occur at a point on the production transformation curve where marginal rate of transformation equals the ratio of prices of goods. Thus, in equilibrium under perfect competition,

$$MRT_{xy} = \frac{MC_x}{MC_y} = \frac{P_x}{P_y} \quad \text{...}(i)$$

Such a general equilibrium of production is represented by point Q on the transformation curve TT in Figure 59.8 where the price line PP' is tangent to it. Note that the slope of the price line PP' measures the given ratio of competitive prices of the two goods $\left(\frac{P_x}{P_y}\right)$. Thus general equilibrium of production at point Q on the production transformation curve TT' determines the product-mix; X_0 of good X and Y_0 of good Y.

It follows from above that given the factor endowments of the economy and the nature of production function (*i.e.*, technology) under perfect competition the general equilibrium of production reaches a unique position on the transformation curve of the economy and a unique position on the corresponding contract curve in the Edgeworth Production Box.

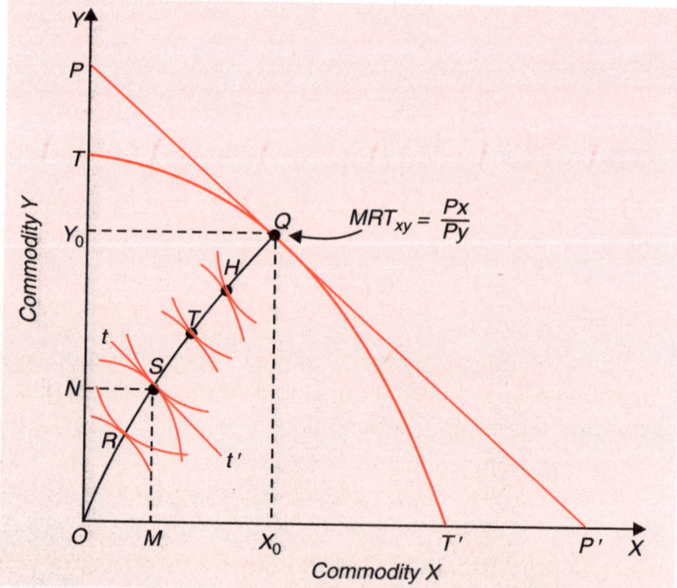

Fig. 59.8. *General Equilibrium of Production and Exchange*

Now, we have to see how in general equilibrium under perfect competition, this equilibrium product mix is to be distributed for consumption between the two individuals. We know that in order to maximise satisfaction, consumers equate their marginal rate of substitution between the two goods (MRS_{xy}) with the ratio of the given competitive prices of the two goods. Thus, in equilibrium under perfect competition,

$$MRS^A_{xy} = \frac{P_x}{P_y} \text{ and } MRS^B_{xy} = \frac{P_y}{P_y} x \quad \ldots(ii)$$

Since the consumers and producers (firms) face the same price ratio of the two goods, from conditions (*i*) and (*ii*) above we have

$$MRT_{xy} = MRS^A_{xy} = MRS^B_{xy} = \frac{P_x}{P_y}$$

This general equilibrium of production and exchange is shown in Figure 59.8 where from point Q at the transformation curve we have made Edgeworth box with dimension X_0 of good X and Y_0 of good Y. It will be observed from Figure 59.8 that at its point S on the contract curve, the slope of the indifference curve of the two individuals measuring the marginal rate of substitution between two goods is equal to the slope of the price line PP'. Thus, with perfect competition we are able to determine a unique position of general equilibrium of production and exchange at a point on the contract curve.

It may however be re-emphasized that even this position of general equilibrium depends on the *initial allocation af fixed amounts* of two factors to the two goods which in turn is determined by the *initial* endowments or distribution of goods (*i.e.* distribution of real income) between the two individuals. With a different initial allocation of factors to the two goods or different initial endowments of goods of the two individuals even with perfect competition we would have reached a different position of general equilibrium of production and exchange.

QUESTIONS FOR REVIEW

1. Distinguish between partial and general equilibrium. What does the contract curve indicate in Eegeworth Box diagram?
2. What is meant by general equilibrium ? Using Edgeworth-box diagram, explain general equilibrium of a pure exchange economy. When is general equilibrium analysis more useful?
3. In an economy characterised by two consumers, two commodities show how general equilibrium of exchange is attained. State your assumption clearly.
4. What is the marginal rate of transformation? Explain with its help how general equilibrium of production is attained in case of two commodities. Also show that marginal rate of transformation of one good for another is equal to the ratio of marginal costs producing the two goods.
5. Point out the inadequacies of partial equilibrium analysis. Under what conditions can the existence of meaningful general equilibrium solution be guaranteed?
6. Define a contract curve. What determines the final location of the two parties on the contract curve ? In what sense is the contract curve a locus of optimal locations ?
7. Define and illustrate diagrammatically general equilibrium in an economy with perfectly competitive factor and product markets. State and explain clearly the conditions in which a general equilibrium will exist for such an economy.
8. "General equilibrium of exchange occurs at a point on the exchange contract curve." Explain. Can there the two such points?
9. Absolute prices are indeterminate in a model of general equilibrium analysis. True or false. Explain.
10. "General equilibrium analysis is solely concerned with relative prices" Explain.
11. 'The general competitive equilibrium is Pareto optimum'. Discuss.

CHAPTER

60

Welfare Economics: An Introduction

WHAT WELFARE ECONOMICS IS ABOUT

So far we have been concerned with the analysis of what has been called positive economics which explains merely "how it is". That is, we have been concerned with explaining how prices of products and factors are determined and further on the basis of these prices how the allocation of resources is made in a private enterprise economy. Now, in this part of the book we shall discuss whether any allocation of resources is efficient or not. By efficiency in economics we mean whether any state or situation regarding resource allocation maximizes social welfare or not. In welfare economics attempt is made to establish criteria or norms with which to judge or evaluate alternative economic states and policies from the viewpoint of efficiency or social welfare. These criteria or norms serve as a basis for recommending economic policies which will increase social welfare. Thus, according to Prof. Lange, "Welfare economics establishes norms of behaviour which satisfy the requirements of social rationality of economic activity."[1] The term "social rationality" of economic activity is to be interpreted as that activity which ensures optimum allocation of resources and therefore guarantees maximum social welfare. To quote him again, "The norms of behaviour established by welfare economics are supposed to guarantee the optimal allocation of economic resources of the society."[2] Putting it more specifically, Prof. Baumol writes, "Welfare Economics has concerned itself mostly with policy issues which arise out of the allocation of resources, with the distribution of inputs among the various commodities and the distribution of commodities among various consumers."[3] And it may be emphasized again that allocation of resources is efficient or optimum when social welfare is maximum.

The inter-relationship among various parts of the economy means that certain particular change in one part of the economy affects resource allocation in all other parts of it. Thus, a central problem in welfare economics relates to whether a particular change in resource allocation will increase or decrease social welfare. However, an almost insurmountable difficulty which is faced in welfare economics is that it is not possible to measure social welfare *objectiviely,* for it involves making interpersonal comparison of utilities or welfares of different individuals comprising the society. In order to avoid making interpersonal comparison of utility, whose scientific nature has been challenged, among others, by Lord Robbins, economists have mostly used what is known as ***Pareto optimality*** criterion for evaluating whether social welfare increases or decreases as a result of a specific change in economic state, situation or policy. According to Pareto criterion of optimality or efficiency, ***any change that makes at least one individual better off without making any other worse off is an improvement in social welfare.*** Of

1. O.P. Lange, *Political Economy,* Vol. I p. 317.
2. *Ibid.*
3. J. Baumol, *Economic Theory and Operations Analysis,* 4th edition, 1978, p. 406.

course, when a certain change makes every one in the society better off, social welfare will undoubtedly increase. On the other hand, social welfare will decrease if a certain change makes no individual better off while it makes at least one individual worse off. With the aid of this criterion we can define the state of maximum social welfare or what is known as ***Pareto optimality or economic efficiency.*** Economic state or situation is said to be Pareto-optimal or efficient in which allocation of resources is such that by any rearrangement of them it is not possible to make any individual better off without making any other worse off. This concept of Pareto optimality or economic efficiency is the basis of welfare economics and has a large number of applications in applied economics. We shall explain the conditions which ensure Pareto optimality and also critically evaluate Pareto's welfare criterion in the next chapter at length.

Pareto criterion and the concept of Pareto optimality does not embrace those changes in economic state which make some persons better off and others worse off. This is because such changes involve interpersonal comparisons of utility which were ruled out by Pareto and his followers. Kaldor and Hicks propounded a welfare criterion, which is known as compensation principle, to judge those changes in situation which make some persons better off and others worse off. They have claimed that their welfare criterion does not involve interpersonal comparison of utility and value judgements. It is asserted that Kaldor and Hicks rehabilitated welfare economics from the damaging criticism of Lord Robbins and founded a "*New Welfare Economics*" free from value judgements or interpersonal comparison of utility. In the development of new welfare economics, Scitovsky and Little have also made significant contributions. The critical evaluation of "New Welfare Economics" forms the subject-matter of a separate chapter.

After discussing new welfare economics we shall study the concept of the *social welfare function* propounded by Bergson and Samueson. According to this social welfare concept, any attempt to establish propositions in welfare economics without the introduction of explicit value judgements is sterile. Bergson-Samuelson social welfare function as well as Arrow's analysis of how to obtain social welfare function from preferences of individuals shall be discussed at the end of this part. Welfare economics has been a controversial subject in recent years because it involves value judgements about which there is a sharp difference of opinion among economists.

Now-a-days the establishment of a welfare state is the fundamental objective of modern democratic Governments. In order to achieve this objective the State attempts to satisfy the wants of each and every individual of the society. Non-satisfaction of wants gives pain to a man and its satisfaction, a pleasure. The word 'pleasure' is associated with welfare. Some wants always remain unsatisfied and give pain to an individual whereas some are always satisfied or are in the process of being satisfied that increases welfare. The fact remains that the welfare is the result of the satisfaction or removal of wants. It can be concluded from this fact that to increase the welfare of a man his wants must be satisfied. According to Prof. J.K. Mehta, if we compare the two periods of time, then "a given man has greater welfare in that period in which a larger number of his wants have been satisfied. Conversely, we can say that the smaller the number of wants (of given intensities) that remain unsatisfied, the greater is the welfare."[4]

INDIVIDUAL WELFARE AND SOCIAL WELFARE

In welfare economics we do not confine ourselves to the economics of individual welfare but go beyond that. Actually, we study the 'economics of social welfare' under the title 'welfare economics.' An individual's welfare at any given time or during a period of time is measured by the amount of satisfaction that he enjoys at the time or during that period of time. He

4. J.K. Mehta and Mahesh Chand, *A Guide to Modern Economics*, Somaiya Publications, Bombay, 1970, p.180.

always tries his best to maximise his satisfaction. Various attempts have been made, especially by natural scientists, to give some objective meaning to an individual's welfare. The daily intake of calories, the level of the personality (which some psychologists seem to think is an objective entity), longevity[5]—all these have been suggested at one time or another to increase individual welfare. But all these are arbitrary and for quite a long time the economists' conception has been a subjective one. That welfare is a state of mind or in other words, "the elements of welfare are the states of consciousness"[6] is generally accepted by the economists. Some objectivity can be introduced by linking individual welfare very closely to individual choice. In other words, a person's welfare map can be defined to be identical with his preference map. It means that a person's welfare is maximum in his most preferred position. If a person chooses the position *A* rather than *B*, his welfare is higher in *A* than in *B*. Thus individual choices reflect the individual welfare because whatever is chosen by an individual is thought to give him maximum satisfaction.

Individual welfare is a function of so many economic and non-economic variables. Classical economists distinguished between 'general welfare' and 'economic welfare'. To Pigou economic welfare was a part of general welfare which could 'be brought directly or indirectly into relation with the measuring rod of money.'[7] But money is a very unsatisfactory measuring rod. Therefore, economists regard general welfare as being determined by a large number of economic and non-economic variables. Welfare economics proceeds on the assumption that all non-economic variables remain unchanged or they are exogenous. It means that they can influence the economic variables without being influenced by them. Weather is a good example of it which influences individual welfare but remains unaffected by it.

However, the concept of social or group welfare is a bit intricate one. Social welfare is composed of two words—social and welfare. Social is derived from the noun society. We must know what a society is. In simple words, when people help one another to satisfy their wants they are said to form a society in respect of the satisfaction of those wants. The wants they co-operate to satisfy can be called socialized wants. People can never be taken to form a society irrespective of their wants because all the wants are never satisfied. The term welfare refers to the satisfaction of wants. Therefore, social welfare refers to the satisfaction of socialized wants. In this sense if some people are better off than before due to satisfaction of non-socialised wants, that is, which they satisfy by their individual efforts, social welfare cannot be said to have increased. But for analytical convenience it is generally assumed in economics that all wants of the people are socialized. Thus, every addition to the welfare of an individual would constitute a component of social welfare.

Welfare being a subjective thing, it resides in human mind. Welfare of an individual consists of psychic utilities or satisfactions obtained by him. Since society cannot be regarded as an organic whole having its own mind like individuals, therefore social welfare is not something which resides in the mind of the society. It is also not possible to use the method of a *social choice* for judging social welfare objectively because society does riot choose any position unanimously. It is true, majorities often agree but we are interested in the welfare of each and every member of the society. Thus, the only alternative left to us is to define ***social welfare as a sum total of the satisfactions of all the individuals in a society.*** Now the problem is who will undertake the job of aggregation of the satisfactions of different individuals. We are to find out such a sensitive man whose mind records the pains and pleasures of the different members of the society correctly. Since such a sensitive man cannot be found in the society, correct measurement of social welfare is not possible.

5. Radhakamal Mukerjee. *The Political Economy of Population.*
6. A.C. Pigou, *Economics of Welfare,* 4th edition, Macmillan & Co. Ltd., London, 1932.
7. *Ibid.*

Three Concepts of Social Welfare

Prof. Graff has distinguished three concepts of social welfare.[8] The first concept of social or group welfare is the paternalist one which describes the views of a paternalist authority or State and not of the individuals in the society. According to this concept, the preferences of. the individual members of the society may be ignored and the State or a paternalist authority or a dictator uses its own ideas about social welfare; social welfare increases when that paternal authority or the dictator thinks it so.

The second concept of social welfare is one which has been used by V. Pareto and his followers. According to this Paretian concept, social welfare is simply the function of the welfares of various individuals in a society. If some persons in a society are made better off and none worse off, social welfare increases and if some are made worse off and none better off, it decreases. But if some are made better off and some worse off, then, according to Paretian concept, we cannot know what has happened to the welfare of the society. The Paretian concept of social welfare rules out interpersonal comparison of utility or welfare and rests only on a generally accepted ethical view that "it is good that if somebody is made better off while nobody is worse off." But since in most cases of changes in economic organisation and policy, at least some people are made worse off, the Paretian concept of social welfare is of limited value for most of the real world economic problems.

The third concept of social welfare involves interpersonal comparison of utility which is to be made by introducing explicit value judgements. This concept of social welfare has been propounded by Bergson and Samuelson in their now well-known theory of social welfare function. Thus they have described the ordinal utility functions of the various persons in the society with the help of a social welfare function. These economists are of the opinion that changes in social welfare cannot be assessed without making interpersonal comparisons of utility and therefore without making value judgements. It is because of this that this concept of social welfare is able to judge the welfare implications of even those changes in economic organisation and policies that make some people better off and others worse off.

Various concepts of social welfare have been referred to above. Economists generally do not accept the paternalist or dictatorial concept of social welfare. Some economists such as Robbins and his followers tried to separate economics from ethics but now-a-days there is consensus among economists that welfare economics cannot be separated from ethics. Bergson, Samuelson, Little, Arrow and others are of the opinion that value judgements are most important in welfare economics. But the fact remains that social welfare and changes in it cannot be measured accurately due to heterogeneity of the interests of the society.

ROLE OF VALUE JUDGEMENTS IN WELFARE ECONOMICS

It is important to explain the role of value judgements in welfare economics. Since welfare economics is concerned with the social desirability or otherwise of economic policies, value judgements play a crucial role. As mentioned above, by value judgements or values is meant the conceptions or ethical beliefs of the people about what is good or bad. These conceptions regarding values of the people are based on ethical, political, philosophical and religious beliefs of the people and are not based on any scientific logic or law. There is a great controversy regarding whether value judgements should have any role to play in welfare economics. Robbins and followers have been asserting that the inclusion of value judgements would make our

8. J. De V. Graff. *Theoretical Welfare Economics*, Cambridge University Press, 1957, pp. 7-11.

subject unscientific and therefore, according to them, economists should refrain from making value judgements. On the other hand, majority of modern economists are of the view that economists should not fight shy of making value judgements if there is a wide consensus about them among the community. Using his knowledge of economics together with these value judgements he should comment upon the social desirability or otherwise of certain policies and issues. Professor Paul Streeten rightly says, "Economists cannot and should not refrain from making value judgements if their studies are to be more than a purely formal technique of reasoning, an algebra of choice. The technique, the algebra, is important and ought to be as scientific as possible, but it is significant only as a means to study of wealth and welfare and of the way to improve them"[9]

It should be noted that as far as the welfare of individual is concerned, though difficult to measure in cardinal terms, economists can measure it in ordinal terms and by observing the act of choice of the individual. For instance, if an individual chooses *A* rather than *B*, it shows that his welfare is greater in *A* than in *B*. Thus, choice by an individual is an objective test for knowing and comparing his welfare in different economic states. Therefore, what promotes individual welfare or not can be tested and verified. However, when welfare economics has to judge the social welfare or group welfare, it encounters difficulties, because the measurement of social welfare is not an easy task and contains value judgements and interpersonal comparisons of utility. This is because the society or group whose welfare we have to judge cannot be regarded as an organic whole, having its own mind. Therefore, social welfare, unlike individual welfare, is not something which resides in the mind of the society. We cannot derive propositions of social welfare from choice of individuals comprising the society, because various individuals choose differently and, therefore, there is no unanimous social choice. Individual choices differ because various individuals have different tastes, preferences and ethical beliefs and therefore different value judgements. The vital issues in welfare economics are concerned with social welfare and devising certain criteria to judge the social welfare. Therefore, welfare economics cannot be purely objective or free from value judgements.

It is worth noting that ***Pareto evolved the concept of social welfare which is said to be free from any value judgements,*** because it is not based upon any interpersonal comparison of utility. According to Pareto, the social welfare depends upon the welfare of the individuals comprising the society and, according to him, if at least one individual is made better off by certain economic reorganisation and no one being made worse off, the social welfare increases, that is, if any economic reorganisation increases the welfare of one without reducing the welfare of any other, then the social welfare increases. When a certain economic state is reached, when through any reorganisation it is not possible to make at least one individual better off with no other being worse off, this is called the state of maximum social welfare or ***Pareto optimum.*** However, Paretian concept of social welfare is confined to only limited issue of welfare economics. Generally, when any economic reorganisation increases the welfare of some, it would generally reduce the welfare of some others and therefore, in this case, Pareto criteria will not apply and following Robbins economists object to making interpersonal comparison of utility to derive welfare propositions, since interpersonal comparison of utility is based upon value judgements.

However, Kaldor and Hicks by propounding a compensation principle laid the foundations of ***New Welfare Economics*** which is supposed to be free from value judgements. According

9. Paul Streeten, Economics and Value Judgements, *Quarterly Journal of Economics*, 1950, p. 595.

to this compensation principle, if a change in economic organisation increases the welfare of some and reduces the welfare of others, and those who gain in welfare are able to compensate the losers and still be better off than before, then the change in economic organisation will increase social welfare. However, Kaldor-Hicks welfare criterion has been subjected to criticisms. The claim of Kaldor and Hicks that their criterion is free from value judgements or ethical assumptions has been contested. To quote Professor Baumol, "Both the Kaldor and the Scitovsky tests operate on the basis of an implicit and unacceptable value judgement. By using a criterion involving potential money compensation, they set up a concealed inter-personal comparison on a money basis."[10] He further writes, "It is no answer to this criticism to say that these criteria are just designed to measure whether production, and hence, potential welfare, are increased by a policy change that these criteria dis-entangle the evaluation of a production change from that of the distribution change by which it is accompanied. Consider a change in *production* which increases gin output but reduces the output of whiskey. If *X* likes highballs but *Y* prefers martins, the question whether this is an increase in production is inextricably tied in with the question of the distribution of these beverages between *X* and *Y*."[11]

In the end we may note that Professor Bergson has pursued a different line of approach to welfare economics. He has propounded the concept of social welfare function in which a set of value judgements is *explicitly* introduced and with this social welfare function, the economists can judge the social desirability of certain economic reorganisations or policy changes. These value judgements, according to Bergson, "must be determined by its compatibility with the values prevailing in the community the welfare of which is being studied."[12] Followers of Bergson like Samuelson and I.M.D. Little are of the view that welfare economics cannot be separated from value judgements, because any statement about increase or decrease of social welfare necessarily involves value judgements. On the rightness of Bergson's social welfare function, and his introduction of explicit value judgements in it, Prof. Baumol writes, "Essentially the Bergson criterion must be judged right, if not very helpful. To decide whether *B* is better than *A*, we must certainly employ some value judgements, and unless these judgements are explicit they must be treated with suspicion."[13] Likewise, Professor K. E. Boulding writes: "One must admit that the task of making value judgements explicit is very important. It is obviously preposterous to suppose that one can set up criteria for judgement which are somehow independent of ethical norms."[14]

Thus, according to several modern economists such as Samuelson, Little, Boulding, welfare economics cannot be purged of value judgements. In fact, the study of welfare economics has been developed to make policy recommendations to promote social welfare. And for doing so economists cannot escape from introducing ethical norms or value judgements since we all take interest in the question concerning happiness and welfare of the society. "Welfare economics and ethics cannot, then, be separated. They are inseparable because the welfare terminology is a value terminology.....Getting rid of value judgements would be throwing the baby away with the bathwater. The subject is one about which nothing interesting can be said

10. Nicholas Kaldor, Welfare Propositions in Welfare Economics, *Economic Journal,* 1939, and J.R. Hicks, Foundations of Welfare Economics, *Economic Journal,* 1939.

11. *Op. cit.,p.* 530.

12. A. Bergson, On the Concept of Social Welfare, *Quarterly Journal of Economics,* 1954.

13. *Op. cit.,* p. 404.

14. K.E. Boulding, "Welfare Economics" in B.E. Haley (ed) *A.E.A., A Survey of Contemporary Economics,* Richard D. Irwin, 1952.

without value judgements for the reason that we take a moral interest in welfare and happiness".[15]

It should not be gathered from above that the explicit introduction of value judgements makes the study of welfare economics unscientific. In spite of the explicit introduction of value judgements in welfare studies, the economist's approach can still be scientific in the sense that he scientifically deduces the welfare propositions from the given value judgements.

15. I.M.D. Little, *A Critique of Welfare Economics,* Oxford University Press, 2nd Edition, 1957.

CHAPTER

61

Concept and Conditions of Pareto Optimality

PARETO CRITERION OF SOCIAL WELFARE: EQUILIBRIUM APPROACH

The concept of Pareto optimum or economic efficiency stated above is based on a welfare criterion put forward by Pareto. Pareto criterion states that if any reorganisation of economic resources does not harm anybody and makes someone better off, it indicates an increase in social welfare. If any reorganisation or change makes everybody in a society better off, it will, according to Pareto, undoubtedly mean increase in social welfare. Thus, in the words of Prof. Baumol "any change which harms no one and which makes some people better off (in their own estimation) must be considered to be an improvement."[1] Pareto criterion can be explained with the help of Edgeworth Box diagram which is based on the assumptions of ordinal utility and non-interpersonal comparison of utilities. Suppose two persons *A* and *B* form the society and consume two goods *X* and *Y*. The various levels of their satisfaction by consuming various combinations of the two goods have been represented by their respective indifference curves.

In Figure 61.1, O_A *and* O_B are the origins for the utilities of two persons A and *B* respectively. $I_{a1}, I_{a2}, I_{a3}, I_{a4}$ and $I_{b1}, I_{b2}, I_{b3}, I_{b4}$ are their successively higher indifference curves. Suppose the initial distribution of goods X and Y between the members of the society, *A* and *B*, is represented by point *K* in the Edgeworth Box. Accordingly, individual *A* consumes O_AG of *X* + *GK* of *Y* and is at the level of satisfaction represented by indifference curve I_{a3}. Similarly, individual *B* consumes *KF of X* + *KE* of *Y* and gets the satisfaction represented by indifference curve Ib_1. Thus the total given volume of goods *X* and *Y* is distributed between *A* and *B*. In this distribution, individual *A* consumes relatively larger quantity of good *Y* and individual *B* of good *X*. Now, it can be shown with the aid of Pareto's welfare criterion that a movement from

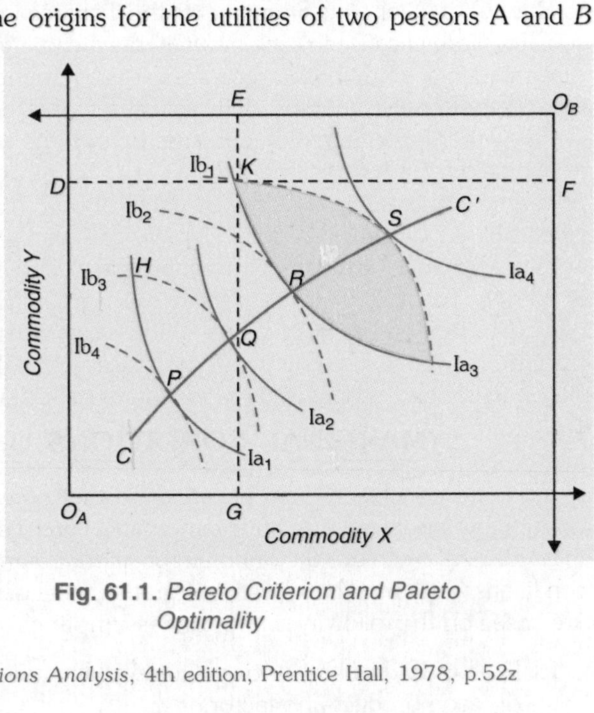

Fig. 61.1. *Pareto Criterion and Pareto Optimality*

1. W.J. Baumol, *Economic Theory and Operations Analysis*, 4th edition, Prentice Hall, 1978, p.52z

the point *K* to a point such as *S* or *R* or any other point in the shaded region will increase social welfare.

Any movement from *K* to *S* through redistribution of two goods between two individuals increases the level of satisfaction of *A* without any change in the satisfaction of B because as a result of this *A* moves to his higher indifference curve I_{a4}, and *B* remains on his same indifference curve Ib_1 (*K* and *S* lie on *B*'s same indifference curve Ib_1). In other words, as a result of the movement from *K* to *S*, individual *A* has become better off whereas individual *B* is no worse off. Thus, according to Pareto criterion, social welfare has increased following the movement from *K* to *S* and therefore *K* is not the position of economic optimum. Similarly, the movement from *K* to *R* is also desirable from the point of view of social welfare because in this individual *B* becomes better off without any change in the satisfaction of individual *A*. Therefore, both the positions *S* and *R* are better than *K*. The tangency points of the .various indifference curves of the two individuals of the society are the Pareto optimum points and the locus of these points is called '*contract curve*' or '*conflict curve*'.

Pareto Criterion and Utility Possibility Curve

Pareto criterion can also be explained with the help of Samuelson's utility possibility curve. ***Utility possibility curve is the locus of the various combinations of utilities obtained by two persons from the consumption of a particular bundle of goods.*** In Figure 61.2, *CV* is a utility possibility curve which shows the various levels of utilities obtained by two individuals *A* and *B* of the society resulting from the redistribution of a fixed bundle of goods and its consumption by them. According to Pareto criterion, a movement from *Q* to *R*, or *Q* to *D*, or *Q* to *S* represents the increase in social welfare because in such movements the utility of either *A* or *B* or both increases. *A* movement from *Q* to *R* implies that the utility or welfare of *B* increases, while that of *A* remains the same. On the other hand, a movement from *Q* to *S* implies that while *A* has become better off, *B* is no worse off. And a movement from *Q* to *D* or any other point on the segment between *R* and *S* will mean increase in welfare or utility of both the individuals. Thus points *R*, *D* and *S* are preferable to *Q* from the point of view of social welfare. But unfortunately Pareto criterion does not help us in evaluating the changes in welfare if the movement as a result of redistribution is from the point *Q* to a point outside the segment *RS*; such as point *E* on the utility possibility curve *CV* because this involves interpersonal comparison of utility. As a result of the movement from point *Q* to *E*, the utility of *A* decreases while that of *B* increases. In such circumstances, Pareto criterion cannot tell us as to whether social welfare increases or decreases.

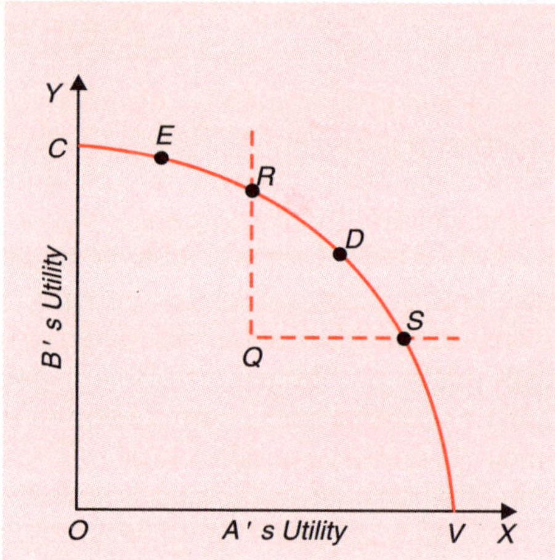

Fig. 61.2. *Pareto Criterion*

MARGINAL CONDITIONS OF PARETO OPTIMUM

Pareto concluded from his criterion that competition leads the society to an optimum position but he did not give any mathematical proof of it, nor he derived the marginal conditions to be fulfilled to achieve the optimum position. Later on, Lerner and Hicks derived the marginal conditions which must be fulfilled for the attainment of Pareto optimum. These marginal conditions are based on the following important assumptions :

1. Each individual has his own ordinal utility function and possesses a definite amount of each product and factor.

2. Production function of every firm and the state of technology is given and remains constant.
3. Goods are perfectly divisible.
4. A producer tries to produce a given output with the least-cost combination of factors.
5. Every individual wants to maximise his satisfaction.
6. Every individual purchases some quantity of all goods.
7. All factors of production are perfectly mobile.

Given the above assumptions, various marginal conditions (first-order conditions) required for the achievement of Pareto optimum or maximum social welfare are explained below :

1. The Optimum Distribution of Products among the Consumers: Efficiency in Exchange. The first condition relates to the optimum distribution of the goods among the different consumers composing a society at a particular point of time. The condition is : "The marginal rate of substitution between any two goods must be the same for every individual who consumes them both."[2] Marginal rate of substitution of one good for another is the amount of one good necessary to compensate for the loss of a marginal unit of another to maintain a constant level of satisfaction. So long as the marginal rate of substitution *(MRS)* between two goods is not equal for any two consumers, they will enter into an exchange which would increase the satisfaction of both or of one without decreasing the satisfaction of the other.

This condition can be better explained with the help of the Edgeworth Box diagram. In Figure 61.3, goods *X* and *Y*, which are consumed by two individuals *A* and *B* composing a society are represented on the *X* and *Y* axes respectively. O_A and O_B are origins for *A* and *B* respectively. I_{a1}, I_{a2}, I_{a3} and I_{b1}, I_{b2}, I_{b3} are the indifference curves showing successively higher level of satisfaction of consumers *A* and *B* respectively. *CC* ′ is the contract curve passing through various tangency points *Q*, *R*, *S* of the indifference curves of *A* and *B*. The marginal rates of substitution *(MRS)* between the two goods for individuals *A* and *B* are equal on the various points of the contract curve *CC* ′. Any point outside the contract curve does not represent the equality of *MRS* between the two goods for two individuals *A* and *B* of the society.

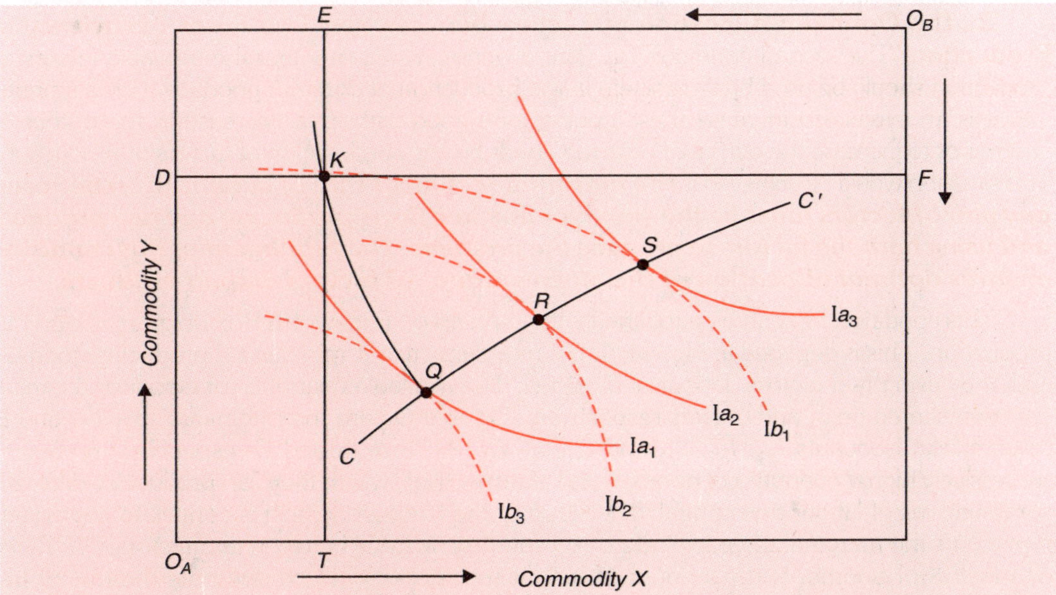

Fig. 61.3. *The Optimum Distribution of Goods*

2. M.W. Reder, *Studies in the Theory of Welfare Economics*, Columbia University Press, New York, 1947, p. 24.

Let us consider point K where indifference curves I_{a1} and I_{b1} of individuals A and B respectively intersect each other instead of being tangential. Therefore, at point K marginal rate of substitution between two goods X and Y (MRS_{xy}) of individual A is not equal to that of B. With the initial distribution of goods as represented by point K, it is possible to increase the satisfaction of one individual without any decrease in that of the other or to increase the satisfaction of both by redistribution of the two goods X and Y between them. A movement from K to S increases the satisfaction of A without any decrease in B's satisfaction. Similarly, a movement from K to Q increases B's satisfaction without any decrease in A' s satisfaction. The movement from K to R increases the satisfaction of both because both move to their higher indifference curves. Thus, a movement from K to Q or to S or any other point on the segment SQ of the contract curve will, according to Pareto criterion, increase the level of social welfare.

From above it follows that movement from any other point away from the contract curve to a point on the *relevant segment* of the contract curve will mean increase in social welfare. At any point off the contract curve in the Edgeworth Box, the indifference curves of the two individuals will intersect which will mean that MRS_{xy} of two individuals is not the same. And, as explained above, this indicates that through exchange of some units of goods between them, they can move to some point on the contract curve where the social welfare (that is, welfare of two individuals taken together) will be higher.

Since the slope of an indifference curve represents the marginal rate of substitution (MRS_{xy}), at every point of the contract curve, which represents tangency points of the indifference curves, MRS_{xy} of two individuals are equal. Therefore, points on the contact curve represent the maximum social welfare. However, a movement along the contract curve in either direction will make one individual better off and the other worse off since it will put one individual on his successively higher indifference curves and the other on his successively lower indifference curves. Thus, every point on the contract curve denotes maximum social welfare in the Paretian sense but we cannot say anything about the best of them with the help of Pareto criterion.

2. The Optimum Allocation of Factors between any Two Firms : Efficiency in Production. The second condition for Pareto optimum requires that the available factors of production should be used by the society in the production of different goods in such a manner that it is impossible to increase the output of one good without a decrease in the output of another or to increase the output of both the goods by any re-allocation of factors of production. This situation would be achieved if ***the marginal technical rate of substitution between any pair of factors must be the same for any two firms producing any two products and using both the factors to produce the products. The fulfillment of this condition ensures optimal allocation of the given amount of factors among products.***

This condition too can be explained with the help of Edgeworth Box diagram relating to production. This is depicted in Fig. 61.4. Let us assume two firms A and B producing goods X and Y by using two factors, labour and capital. The available quantities of labour and capital are represented on X and Y axes respectively. O_A and O_B are the origins for firms A and B respectively. Isoquants I_{a1}, I_{a2}, I_{a3} and I_{b1}, I_{b2}, I_{b3} of firms A and B respectively represent successively higher quantities of goods X and Y respectively which they can produce by different combinations of labour and capital. The slope of the isoquant, which is convex to the origin, represents the marginal technical rate of substitution (*MRTS*) between two factors. *MRTS* of one factor for another is the amount of one factor necessary to compensate the loss of the marginal unit of another so that the level of output remains the same. So long as the *MRTS* between two factors for two firms producing goods X and Y is not equal, total output can be increased by transfer of factors from one firm to another. In terms of the given diagram any movement from *K* to *S* or to *Q* raises the output of one firm without any decrease in the output of the other. The total output of the two firms increases when through redistribution of factors between the two firms, a movement is made from the point *K* to the point *Q* or *S* on the contract curve. A glance at Figure 61.4 will reveal that movement from point *K* off the contract curve to the point *R* on the contract curve will raise the output of both the firms individually as well as collectively. Therefore, it follows that corresponding to a point off the contract curve there will be some points on the contract curve production at which will ensure greater total output of the two firms. As the contract curve is the locus of the tangency points of the isoquants of two firms, the marginal rate of substitution of the two firms is the same at every point of the contract curve *CC′*. It, therefore, follows that on the contract curve at every point of which *MRTS* between the two factors of two firms is the same, the allocation of factors between the two firms producing *X* and *Y* respectively is optimum. When the allocation of factors between the two firms is such that they are producing at a point on the contract curve, then no re-allocation of factors will increase the total output of the two firms taken together.

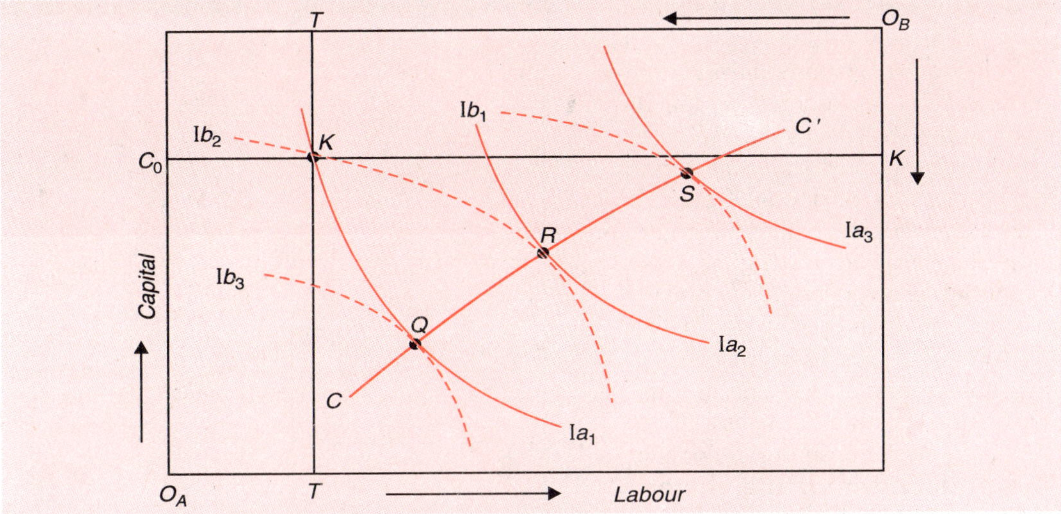

Fig. 61.4. *The Optimum Allocation of Factors between two Firms*

But it is worth mentioning that there are several points on the contract curve and each of them represents the optimum allocation of labour and capital as between the two firms producing goods *X* and *Y*. But which one of them is best cannot be said on the basis of Pareto criterion because movement along the contract curve in either direction represents such factor re-allocation which increases the output of one and reduces the output of another firm.

3. The Optimum Direction of Production: Efficiency in Product-Mix. The third condition relates to the production of goods in accordance with consumer's preferences. This is also called overall condition of Pareto optimality or allocative efficiency. The fulfillment of this condition determines the optimum quantities of different commodities to be produced with given factor endowments. That is, the fulfillment of this condition ensures Pareto optimality with regard to product-mix. This condition states that ***"the marginal rate of substitution between any pair of products for any person consuming both must be the same as the marginal rate of transformation (for the community) between them."***[3] When this condition is fulfilled resources of a society will be allocated to the production of various goods in accordance with consumers' preferences. One way of proving this condition

3. Reder, *op. cit.*, p. 30.

of Pareto optimality is to take a representative consumer who reflects society's preferences between the two goods. The preferences of this representative consumer reflect the preferences of the society as a whole. The second method to explain this condition of Pareto optimality is the technique of drawing an Edgeworth Box where the indifference curves of the two consumers composing a society are drawn. We explain this condition through both these methods. First consider Fig. 61.5 in which we draw indifference curves reflecting preferences of the society between the two commodities.

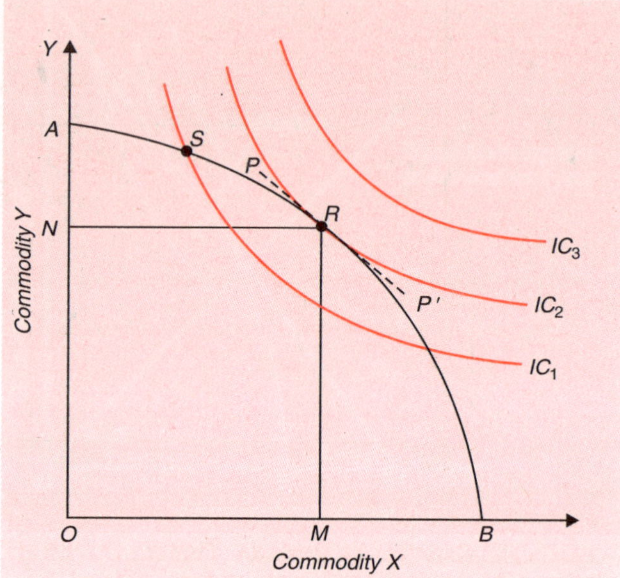

Fig. 61.5. *Optimum Direction of Production : Optimum Product-Mix*

In Fig. 61.5 commodities *X* and *Y* have been represented on the *X* and Y_1 axes respectively. *AB* is a community's transformation curve between a pair of goods *X* and *Y*. This curve represents the maximum amount of good *X* that can be produced for any quantity of good *Y*, given the amounts of other goods that are produced and fixed supplies of available resources. IC_1 and IC_2 are the indifference curves of a representative consumer reflecting the preferences of the society between the two goods, the slope of which represents the marginal rate of substitution between the two goods of the society. The MRT_{xy} of the community and MRS_{xy} of the consumers of the society are equal to each other at point *R* at which the community's transformation curve is tangent to the indifference curve IC_2 of the consumers. Point *R* represents optimum composition of production in which commodities *X* and *Y* are being produced and consumed in *OM and ON* quantities. This is because of all the points on the community's transformation curve, point *R* lies at the highest possible indifference curve IC_2 of the consumer. For instance, if a combination of goods *X* and *Y* represented by *S* is being produced and consumed ; the consumer would be at a lower level of welfare because *S* lies on his lower indifference curve IC_1 which intersects the community's transformation curve instead of being tangential to it. Tangents drawn to the indifference curve and the transformation curve at the point *S* will intersect each other showing their slopes are not equal, that is, MRS_{xy} of the consumer is not equal to the MRT_{xy} of the society. With the situation at *S* there is a possibility of moving the consumer to a higher indifference curve by changing the direction or composition of production *i.e.* by increasing the production of *X* and reducing the production of *Y*. Thus, the optimum direction of production (or product-mix) is established at point *R* where community's transformation curve is tangent to the indifferent curve of a representative consumer in the society.

Let us now explain this condition of Pareto optimality with Edgeworth-box technique taking two consumers comprising a society. Consider the two Figures 61.6 and 61.7. Take Figure 61.6 first where *TT'* is the society product-transformation curve and suppose that output of two commodities OX_1 of *X* and OY_1 of *Y* is being produced by working at point *L*. Given this point *L* an Edgeworth Box has been drawn with OX_1 of commodity *X* and OY_1 of commodity *Y* being the dimensions of the box. The indifference curves of the two consumers *A* and B are also drawn, taking O as the origin for A and L for the origin of B. Starting from some initial endowment in the box, consumers through trading with each other have moved to

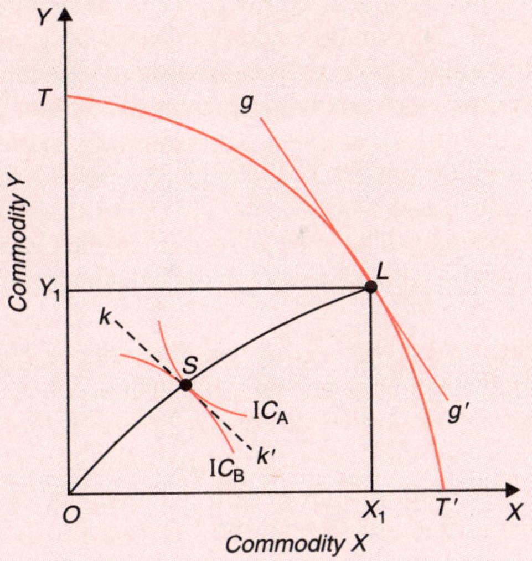

Fig. 61.6. *Product-Mix is Pareto Sub-Optimal*

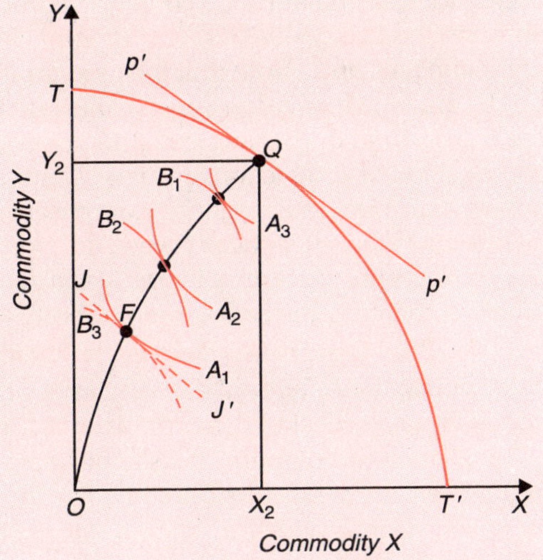

Fig. 61.7. *Product-Mix is Pareto Optimal*

the consumption-efficient point S on the contract curve where their indifference curves are tangent to each other. Slope of the common tangent indicates their marginal rate of substitution of the two consumers between the two goods. We have also drawn a tangent gg' to the transformation curve TT' at point L which indicates the marginal rate of transformation between the two goods (MRT_{xy}). It will be seen from Figure 61.6 that the marginal rate of transformation MRT_{xy} of the society at point L exceeds that of marginal rate of substitution (MRS_{xy}) of the two consumers; the slope of tangent gg' is greater than the slope of tangent kk' to the indifference curves of the individuals. Suppose MRT_{xy} is 3, while marginal rate of substitution of the consumers is 1. This means that by reducing the production of commodity X by one unit, it can produce 3 units of commodity Y, while for the loss of one unit of X the consumers are willing to take one unit of Y, their satisfaction remaining constant. Thus, if the producers in the society reduce the production of X by one unit and produce 3 units more of Y, after compensating the consumers' one unit loss of X by each of them, the extra one unit of Y produced can be given to either of the consumers increasing his satisfaction, without making the other individual worse off or equally divide the extra one unit between the two consumers and thus making both of them better off.

We thus see that the composition of production of two goods at L is not in accordance with the preferences of the consumers since with this either consumer can be made better off without the other being made worse off or both can be made better off by re-allocating resources between the production of commodities X and Y. Thus, the production at L on the transformation curve and consumption of goods at S is not Pareto optimum. The consumers' welfare can be increased by diverting resources from the production of X to the production of Y. This is shown in Figure 61.7 where by re-allocating resources we have reached at point Q on the production transformation curve TT' where greater quantity Y_2 of commodity Y and smaller quantity X_2 of commodity X is being produced. The tangent pp' drawn to the transformation curve at point Q measures the marginal rate of transformation (MRT_{xy}) between the two goods. Taking quantities of goods OX_2 and OY_2 as dimensions we have drawn Edgeworth Box in the output space. The contract curve showing the tangency points of the indifference curves of two individuals have been drawn within this box.

Now, it will be seen that if the two consumers attain equilibrium at point *F* on the contract curve, their common marginal rate of substitution as measured by the slope of the tangent *JJ'* drawn to their indifference curves at point *F* is equal to the marginal rate of transformation between the two goods (MRT_{xy}) at point *Q* on the transformation curve indicated by the slope of the tangent *pp'*. (Note that the tangent *jj'* to the indifference curves is parallel to the tangent *pp'* to the transformation curve.) This implies that product-mix being produced at point *Q* on the transformation curve is consistent with the preferences of the two consumers. Therefore, composition of production at point *Q* and consumption pattern of individuals at point *F* would ensure maximum satisfaction and represent Pareto optimal product-mix. This is because having attained equilibrium at these points, through any further re-allocation of resources and changing the product-mix we cannot increase satisfaction of one without reducing the satisfaction of the other, or increase the satisfaction of both.

4. The Optimum Degree of Specialisation. This is the condition necessary for determining the optimum level of output of each product by every firm. If a firm produces two goods, it has to decide the proportion of the resources to be used for the production of two goods. If the Pareto optimality is to be attained *"the marginal rate of transformation between any two products must be the same for any two firms that produce both."*[4] This condition tells to which degree any firm should specialize in order to maximise the total output of that product by all firms.

Let us first explain this condition for achievement of Pareto optimality with a numerical example. Suppose the marginal rate of transformation between two goods *X* and *Y* of firm *A* is 3 :1 and of firm *B*, is 2 : 1. That is

$$MRT_{xy} \text{ of Firm } A = \frac{\Delta Y}{\Delta X} = \frac{3}{1}$$

$$MRT_{xy} \text{ of Firm } B = \frac{\Delta Y}{\Delta X} = \frac{2}{1}$$

It will be recalled that marginal rate of transformation *A* being equal to 3 implies that it can produce 3 units of *Y* by sacrificing one unit of *X* (that is, devoting resources released from reduction in output of *X* by one unit). MRT_{xy} of firm *B* implies that it can produce 2 units of *Y* by reducing output of *X* by one unit and thus releasing resources. It follows that if resources by the two firms are reallocated so that firm A shifts some resources from X to *Y* and firm *B* from *Y* to *X*, the total output of two goods will increase. Thus if firm A produces one unit less of *X* and the resources so released are devoted to *Y*, it will produce 3 units of *Y* whereas the loss in production of *X* is one unit. On the other hand, if firm *B* produces 2 units less of *Y* and resources so released are allocated to the production of good *X*, there will be gain in one unit of *X* for the loss of 2 units of *Y*. Thus, with this rearrangement of resources in the two firms the combined output of the two firms of good *Y* will increase by one unit, while the combined output of X will remain the same. If the MRT_{xy} between the two goods in the two firms is the same, the re-allocation of resources between the two goods would not lead to the increase in combined output or increase in output of one good without loss of output of another-. Let us explain this condition with the help of transformation or production possibility curves of the two firms.

In Figure 61.8 (a) and 61.8 (b), *FT* and *GH* are the transformation curves of firms *A* and *B* respectively. They have been drawn on the assumption of increasing costs (that is, diminishing returns) conditions. A transformation curve is a locus of various combinations of

4. M.W. Reder, *op. cit*, p. 27.

two goods which a firm can produce by fully utilizing its given resources. The slope of the transformation curve represents the marginal rate of transformation (*MRT*) between two goods.

Suppose in Fig. 61.8 firm A is producing *OL* of *X* and *OQ* or *LC* of *Y* and firm *B* is producing *OE* of *X* and *ED* of *Y*. Thus the total output of both the firms is *(OL + OE)* of *X* and *(LC + ED)* of *Y*. Now we have to prove that total output of goods *X* and *Y* will increase if the two firms specialise in accordance with their relative efficiency in the production of two goods. In Figures 61.8 (*a*) and (*b*) we have drawn tangents to the transformation curves of firms *A* and *B* at their current production at points *C* and *D* respectively. The slopes of these tangents to the

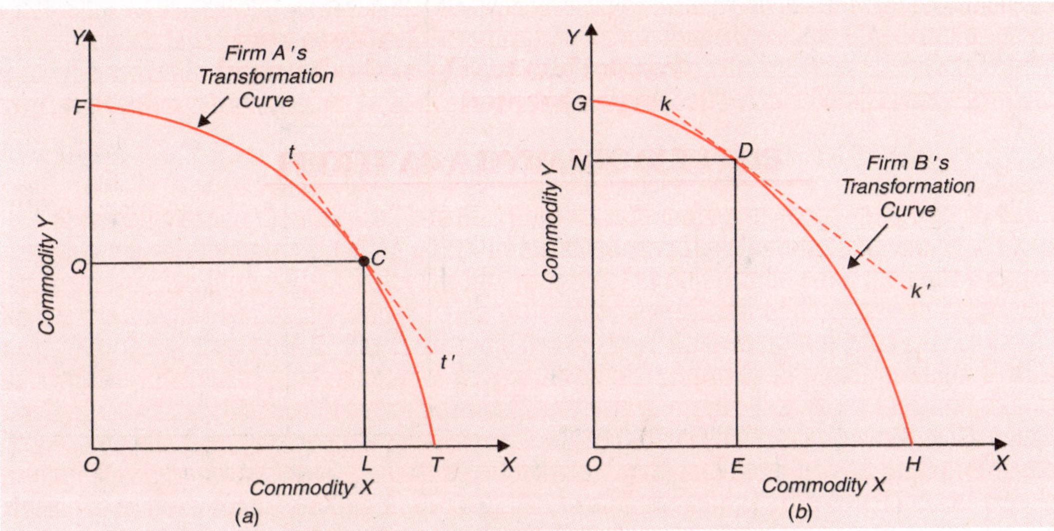

Fig. 61.8. *The Optimum Degree of Specialisation*

transformation curves indicate the opportunity costs of commodity X in the two firms (opportunity cost $= \dfrac{\Delta Y}{\Delta X}$ = slope). It will be seen from the figures that the slope of tangent *tt'* on firm *A*'s transformation curve is greater than the slope of tangent *kk'* on firm B's transformation curve. There will be gain in total output of goods X and *Y* if firm A reduces output of commodity *X* and increases the output of commodity *Y* and, on the contrary, firm *B* should reduce output of Y and devote the resources so released to the production of X until the slopes of the transformation curves in the two become equal. To sum up, Pareto-optimum is achieved from the viewpoint of the degree of specialisation when the two firms produce such combinations of goods that the slope of the transformation curve of the two firms is the same.

5. The Optimum Factor-Product Relationship. The fifth marginal condition of Pareto optimum relates to optimum factor-product relationship. It states, ***"The marginal rate of transformation between any factor and any product must be the same for any pair of firms using the factor and producing the product."***[5] It may be noted that the marginal rate of transformation of factor into a product means how many units of a product are produced by an additional unit of a factor. Therefore, this condition simply states that the marginal product of any factor in producing a particular product must be the same in all firms producing that product. If this marginal condition is not met,[6] a switching around of inputs can give us something for nothing, it can increase one or both outputs without any increase in input use.

5. W. J. Baumol, *Economic Theory and Operations Analysis*, 4th edition, 1977, p. 507.
6. M.W. Reder, *op. cit.*, pp. 32-33.

This condition can be explained with the help of Figures 61.9 (a) and 61.9 (b) in which units of factor labour have been measured on the horizontal axis from *right to left* and output of a product on the vertical axis. It will be seen from these figures that as the amount of labour used increases, the total output of the product increases but at a diminishing rate. The curve *QP* in Figure 61.9 (a) shows as more units of labour are used in Firm *A*, output of the product increases but at a diminishing rate. Similarly, the curve *NM* in Figure 61.9 (b) shows as more labour is employed total product increases but at a diminishing rate. It should be noted

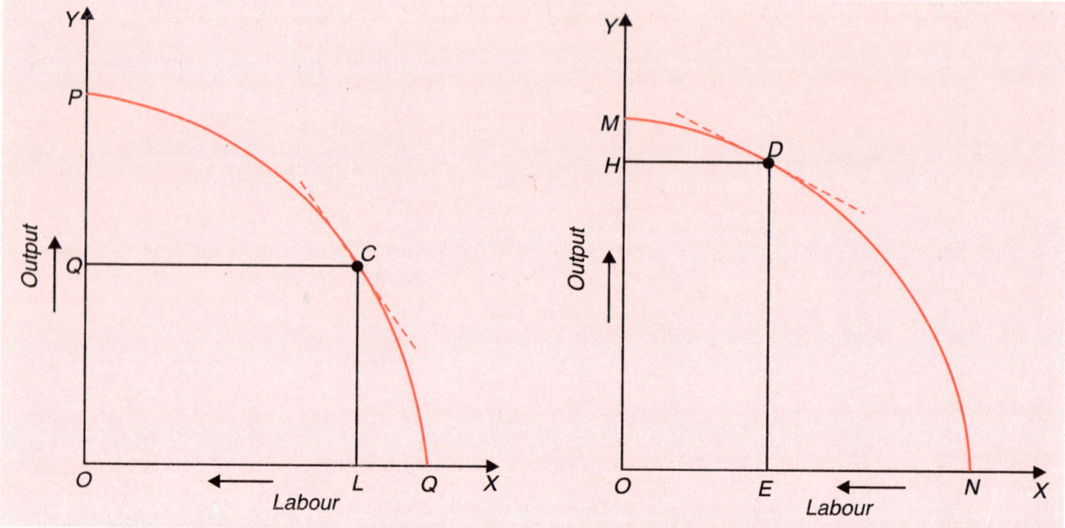

Fig. 61.9. *The Optimum Factor-Product Relationship*

here that it is an input (labour in our figures) that is being transformed into output. The slope of the transformation curve in the present case $\left(\frac{\Delta Q}{\Delta L}\right)$ will therefore measure the marginal product of labour. It will be seen from the figures that the marginal product of labour is greater in firm *A* than in *B* (as will be known from the slopes of tangents drawn at points *C* and *D* to the transformation curves of the two firms), then total output of the product will increase if labour is shifted from firm *B* to firm *A*. The total output will be maximised and Pareto optimality attained in the use of labour in the two firms when through re-allocation of labour between the two firms the marginal rate of transformation of labour into product (*i.e. MP* of labour) becomes the same.

6. The Optimum Allocation of a Factor's Time. The sixth marginal condition relates to the optimum allocation of a factor's time, particularly human labour time as between 'work for money income' and 'leisure'. To achieve the optimum position ***"the marginal rate of substitution between the amount of (product) X received for aiding in its production (by a given firm) and the time spent in rendering this aid must be the same for each unit owner as the marginal rate of transformation between the time of his factor unit spent in aiding production (in this way) and the (product) X."***

Thus, according to this condition, in case of factor 'labour' the marginal rate of substitution between leisure and 'work for money income' must be equal to the marginal rate of transformation between labour time and the product. There is an inverse relationship between leisure and money income *i.e.* if a person enjoys more leisure he receives less money income for he would be working for smaller time. Thus, an indifference curve of the factor (labourer) can be constructed by joining the various combinations of money income and leisure which give equal satisfaction to the factor owner (individual labourer). The slope of this indifference curve represents the marginal rate of substitution between leisure and income. Similarly, each factor unit owner has a transformation curve between a factor unit's time and the product. If a factor works for more hours, he produces more output of any commodity. Every point on the transformation curve represents the marginal rate of transformation between factor unit's time and the product. *The optimum allocation of factor's time requires that the marginal rate of substitution between leisure and income of the factor must be equal to the marginal rate of transformation between factor's time and product.* If the *MRS* between leisure and income is greater than the *MRT* between factor's time and product, the satisfaction of the individual can be increased by transferring a factor unit's time from work to leisure. Optimum position is reached when the two become equal to each other. This is illustrated in Figure 61.10.

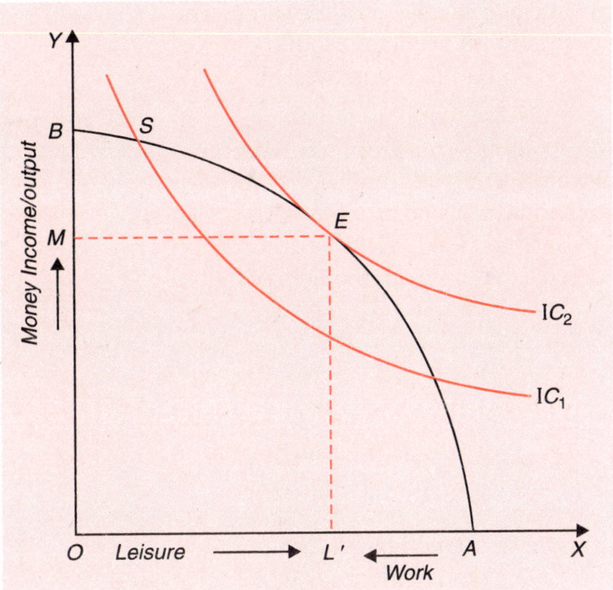

Fig. 61.10. *The Optimum Allocation of a Factor's Unit Time*

In Fig. 61.10 the work has been measured on the *X*-axis from right to left and output of product (which yields income) on the *Y*-axis, taking *A* as the zero point of the work and origin *O* as zero output level of the product. *AB* is a transformation curve representing the diminishing marginal rate of transformation between work and the product because of the concavity of the curve, the work (working hours) done being represented from right to the left. IC_1 and IC_2 are the indifference curves of the factor owners, each representing a given level of satisfaction derived from the various combinations of income and leisure. Optimum position is attained at point *E* where the transformation curve *AB* is tangent to the indifference curve IC_2. Both the curves have equal slope at point *E* representing the equality of *MRT* and *MRS*. Obviously point *S* in the diagram is not an optimum position because at point *S* indifference curve IC_1 and transformation curve *AB* intersect each other instead of being tangential to each other. From point *S* there is the possibility of moving to a point *E* on higher indifference curve IC_2, which is tangential to the transformation curve by substituting leisure for income.

7. Inter-Temporal Optimum Allocation of Money Assets. The seventh condition relates to the inter-temporal allocation over time of money capital. Thus this condition relates to the lenders and borrowers of capital or money assets. It states that the rate of interest at which an individual is willing to lend capital must be equal to its marginal productivity to the borrower. In other words, this condition states that the marginal rate of substitution between money funds at any pair of times (say t_1, and t_2) must be the same for every pair of individuals or firms including pairs, one member of which is a firm and the other an individual. For instance, if an individual *A* is prepared to give ₹ 100 at any time t_1 for ₹ 110 to be received at time t_2, while an individual *B* is prepared to give ₹100 at time t_1 for more than ₹110 (say ₹ 115) at time t_2, then the marginal rate of substitution between money capital at these pairs of times for the two individuals is not the same. The social welfare will increase if individual A lends ₹ 100 to the individual B.

It is also worth noting that to reach the optimum position, the optimum amount of lending and borrowing for each individual and firm must take place in a given period of time. This condition can be explained with the help of Figure 61.11. In Figure 61.11 money income in the present and in the future have been shown on the X and Y - axes respectively.

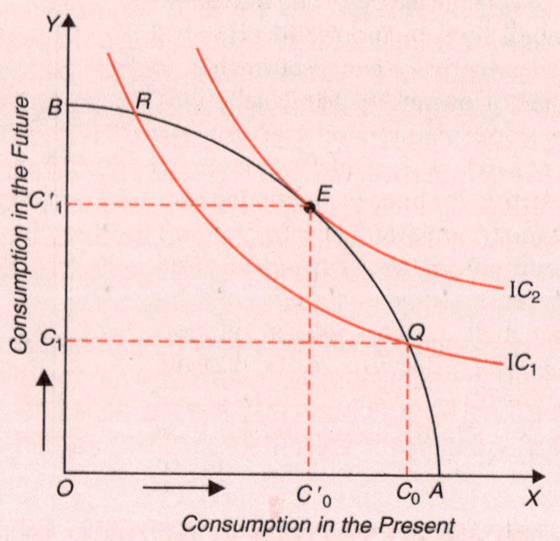

Fig. 61.11. *The Optimum Amount of Lending and Borrowing*

IC_1 and IC_2 are inter-temporal indifference curves of the lender. An inter-temporal indifference curve is the locus of various combinations of present and future money incomes which give equal satisfaction to the lender. The curve is convex to the origin which represents the diminishing marginal rate of substitution of future income for present income. A lender wants to forego successively lower present income for a certain amount of future income. Similarly, AB is the inter-temporal production possibility curve of the borrower which is concave to the origin due to decreasing marginal productivity of capital. Point Q on the production possibility curve is the initial endowment of the individual.

The inter-temporal production possibility curve AB and the intertemporal indifference curve IC_2 are tangential to each other at E. Therefore, E is the optimum position of the individual. where marginal rate of substitution of the individual lender between present income and future income is equal to the marginal rate of substitution (more accurately marginal rate of transformation) between present income and future income of the borrower. Since IC_1 intersects the time production possibility curve AB at point Q, it cannot be optimum positions because there is a possibility of lender moving to his higher time indifference curve such as IC_2. With optimal position at E the individual would consume C_0' in the present and C'_1 in the future. This means that he has reduced his current consumption by C_0C_0' so that he should have greater consumption in the future. This further implies that he is lender of money and his lending will be equal to C_0C_0'. It should be noted that if this initial endowment point was R, his optimal consumption would have been less than his present consumption. In that case he would have been a borrower.

Thus, for a Pareto optimum all the above seven marginal conditions must be satisfied.

The Second-Order and Total Conditions

The marginal or the first-order conditions explained above are *'necessary'* but not *sufficient* for the attainment of maximum social welfare because the marginal conditions by themselves do not guarantee maximum welfare, for the marginal conditions can be fulfilled even at the level of minimum welfare. To attain the maximum welfare position second-order conditions together with the marginal conditions must be satisfied. The second-order conditions require that all indifference curves are convex to the origin and all transformation curves concave to it in the neighbourhood of any position where marginal conditions are satisfied.

But even the satisfaction of both (first- and second-order conditions) does not ensure the largest maximum welfare because even when marginal conditions (first and second order) are fulfilled, it may still be possible to move to a position where social welfare is greater. To attain the maximum social welfare, another set of conditions which are called by Hicks as the *'total conditions'* must also be satisfied. The total conditions state, "that if welfare is to be a maximum, it must be impossible to increase welfare by producing product not otherwise produced or by using a factor not otherwise used."[7] If it is possible to increase welfare by such activities the optimum position is not determined by marginal conditions alone.

Therefore, welfare will be really maximum if the marginal as well as total conditions are satisfied. But such a Pareto optimum too is not a unique one. It is one of a large number of optima. The whole analysis of conditions of Pareto optimality assumes a given distribution of income. With a change in the distribution of income Pareto optimality will be achieved with different output-mix of various products and different allocation of various factors among products. Thus, a new optimum will emerge due to redistribution of income and there are no criteria to judge whether the new optimum is better or worse than the previous social optimum because this can be known only with the help of some value judgements regarding income distribution which has been ruled out by the Pareto criterion.

A Critical Evaluation of Pareto Criterion and Pareto Optimality

Pareto criterion and the concept of Pareto optimality or maximum social welfare based on it occupies a significant place in welfare economics. To judge the efficiency of an economic system, the notion of Pareto optimality has been used to bring out the gains of trading or exchange of goods between individuals. But even Pareto criterion which rules out comparing those changes in policies which make some people worse off has been a subject of controversy and has been criticised on several grounds.

First, it has been alleged that Pareto criterion is not completely free from value judgements. The supporters of Pareto criterion claim that it provides us with an 'objective' criterion of efficiency. However, this has been contested. Against Pareto criterion it has been said that to say that a policy change which makes some better off without others being worse off increases social welfare is itself a value judgement. This is because we recommend such changes which pass Pareto criterion. The implication of this assertion will become obvious when the persons who gain as a result of policy change are the rich and those who remain where they were before are poor. Therefore, to say on the basis of Pareto criterion that whenever any policy change which, without harming anyone, benefits some people regardless of whoever they may be, increases social welfare is a value judgement which may not be accepted by all.

Second, an important limitation of Pareto criterion is that it cannot be applied to judge the social desirability of those policy proposals which benefit some and harm others. But those policy changes are quite rare which do not harm at least some individuals in the society. Thus, Pareto criterion is of limited applicability as it cannot be used to pronounce judgements on a majority of policy proposals which involve conflict of preferences of two individuals. Thus, according to P. K. Patnaik, "Pareto criterion fails seriously when it comes to comparing alternatives. Whenever there is conflict of preferences of two individuals with respect to two alternatives, the criterion fails to rank those two alternatives no matter what the preferences of the rest of individuals in the society might be".[8] To evaluate social desirability of those policy changes which benefit some and harm others, we need to make interpersonal comparison of

7. Reder, *op. cit.*, p. 37.
8. Prasanta K. Patnaik, Some Aspects of Welfare Economics. *The Indian Economic Journal*, Conference Number, 1974, p. 68C.

utility which Pareto criterion refuses to do. Thus, "Pareto criterion works by sidestepping the crucial issue of interpersonal comparison and income distribution, that is, by dealing only with cases where no one is harmed so that the problem does not arise".[9]

Another shortcoming of Pareto criterion and notion of maximum social welfare based on it is that *it* ***leaves a considerable amount of indeterminacy in the welfare analysis*** since every point on the contract curve is Pareto-optimal. For instance, in Fig. 61.1, every point such as *P, Q, R, S* on the contract curve is Pareto-superior to any point such as *K* and *H* which lies off the contract curve. Movement from one point on the contract curve to another as a result of change in economic policy, that is, through re-distribution of commodities makes one individual better off and the other worse off, that is, one gains at the expense of the other. This means that on the basis of Pareto criterion, social alternatives lying on the contract curve cannot be compared since with any movement on the contract curve one individual gains and the other loses, that is, it involves redistribution of income or welfare. Therefore, to compare various alternatives lying on the contract curve and to choose between them, inter-personal comparison and value judgements regarding proper distribution of income need to be made. However, Pareto refused to make value judgements and sought to put forward a value-free or objective criterion of welfare.

It, therefore, follows that on the basis of Pareto criterion where the change from an alternative lying off the contract curve to an alternative on the contract curve is judged to increase social welfare but this cannot be said of the change from one position on the contract curve to another on it. But as there are infinite number of points on the contract curve all of which are Pareto optimal, no choice can be made out of them on the basis of Pareto criterion. To remove this indeterminacy and to choose among the alternatives lying on the contract curve one needs to make some additional value judgements beyond what is implied in the Pareto criterion. Henderson and Quandt hold a similar view when they assert, ***"The analysis of welfare in terms of Pareto optimality leavs a considerable amount of indeterminacy in the solution : there are infinite number of points which are Pareto optimal."*** They further remark that, 'The indeterminacy is the consequence of considering an increase in welfare to be unambiguously defined only if an improvement in one individual's position is not accompanied by a deterioration of the position of another. The indeterminacy can only be removed by further value judgements."[10]

Above all, a chief drawback of Pareto optimality analysis is that it accepts the prevailing income distribution and no attempt is made to find an optimal distribution of income, since it is thought that there does not exist any objective, value-free and scientific way of finding optimal distribution of income. Thus, Pareto optimality analysis remains either silent or biased in favour of *status quo* on the issue of income distribution. Further, Pareto optimality analysis may lead to recommend the prevailing situation where a majority of the population lives on the subsistence level or below the poverty line while a few live a life of affluence. Thus, "Ultimately, the Paretian approach can be considered the welfare economists' instrument *par excellence* for the circumvention of the issue of income distribution."[11]

It may also be mentioned that for any initial distribution of income (that is, for any given distribution of goods) between the individuals, there will be several Pareto optimal positions. Consider Figure 61.3 corresponding to point *K*, the points on the segment *RS* on the contract curve *CC′* will represent Pareto optimal positions. Likewise, corresponding to a given distribution of income (*i.e.* distribution of goods) as represented by point *H*, the points on the segment *PQ*

9. W.J. Baumol, *Economic Theory and Operations Analysis*, 4th ed. 1977. Prentice Hall, p. 527.
10. J. M. Henderson, and R. E. Quandt, *Microeconomic Theory*, 2nd edition, 1971, p. 265.
11. Baumol, *op. cit.* p. 503.

of the contract curve CC' will be Pareto-optimal. Thus corresponding to a different distribution of income, there will be different Pareto optima. In the Paretian analysis there is no way of evaluating whether one pattern of income distribution is better than the other.

Prof. Amartya Sen's Critique of Pareto Optimality

Further, criticising Pareto criterion Prof. Amartya Sen has pointed out that the success that the criterion of Pareto optimality has achieved in judging the desirability of a social state or a policy change is very limited. To quote him, "A Social state is described as Pareto optimal if and only if no one's utility can be raised without reducing the utility of someone else. This is a very limited kind of success and in itself may or may not guarantee much. ***A state can be Pareto optimal with some people in extreme misery and others rolling in luxury, so long as the miserable cannot be made better off without cutting into the luxury of the rich.***"[12] So, according to him, this is not a good and adequate criterion for juding social welfare.

Further, Prof. Sen has criticised Pareto optimality on the basis that it identifies well-being with utility and captures the efficiency aspects only of utility-based accounting. It may be noted that utility is interpreted in two ways. Firstly, it is said to mean ***'happiness'.*** Secondly, it is interpreted in the ***sense of 'desire-fulfillment'. He is of the view that utility does not always reflect well-being. To quote him, "To judge the well-being of a person exclusively in metric of happiness or desire-fulfillment has some obvious limitations.*** These limitations are particularly damaging in the context of interpersonal comparison of well-being. Since the extent of happiness reflects what one would expect and how the social 'deal' seems in comparison with that."[13] He is of the view that people living a life of great misfortune with little hope and opportunities may get more utility or happiness even from small gains. But that should not be interpreted that there is a significant improvement in their well-being. The measure of utility in the sense of happiness may not reveal the true picture about the state of his deprivation. He thus writes: "The hopeless beggar, precarious landless labourers, the dominated housewife, the hardened unemployed or the over-exhausted coolie may all take pleasure in small mercies, and manage to suppress intense suffering for the necessity of continued survival, but it would be ethically deeply mistaken to attach correspondingly small value to the loss of their well-being because of their survival strategy."[14]

According to Prof. Sen, even in case of desire-fulfilment, the same problem arises, because "the hopelessly deprived lack the courage to desire much, and their deprivations are muted and deadened in scale of desire-fulfillment."

The sum and subsistence of Sen's criticism is that the concept of utility used in judging Pareto optimality whether it is interpreted in terms of happiness or desire-fulfillment is seriously inadequate and insufficient for judging a person's well-being. To quote him, "Well-being is ultimately a matter of valuation, and while happiness and fulfilment of desire may well be valuable for the person's well-being, they cannot — on their own or even together — adequately reflect the value of well-being."[15]

It is thus clear that welfare or well-being of individuals depends on a wide range of variables than those associated with utility which is derived from the consumption of goods and services and amount of leisure enjoyed. Welfare or well-being also depends on such variables as political and environmental factors, personal and political freedom individuals enjoy, disposition of their

12. Amartya Sen, *On Ethics and Economics,* Oxford University Press, 1990, pp. 31-32.
13. *Ibid.*
14. Amartya Sen, *Op.cit.*, pp. 45-46.
15. *Ibid.*, p. 46.

neighbours. For an adequate measure of well-being these variables cannot be ignored. "In comparing different economic systems or comparing different ways of organising a given economy, the possibility that some of these variables might be affected cannot be ignored. Thus, a reorganisation that gives everyone more income and leisure might not improve the welfare of the community if at the same time it limits individual freedoms or requires the abandonement of cherished cultural traditions."[16]

In the end, it may be pointed out that Pareto criterion is not altogether usless. It is useful in the sense that, "by throwing out the Pareto inoptimal alternatives, it reduces the range within which socially best alternatives are to be looked for, and therefore does serve as a useful first step. The trouble arises if one gets so fascinated with this first step that one does not try to go any further, but that can hardly be called a defect of Pareto criterion."[17] Moreover, as has been pointed out above, Pareto analysis has been used to bring out the gains from trading or exchange of goods between the two individuals.

PERFECT COMPETITION AND PARETO OPTIMALITY: FIRST THEOREM OF WELFARE ECONOMICS

In our above analysis we have explained the various marginal conditions of attaining Pareto optimality or, in other words, optimum allocation of resources. It has been claimed by several economists that perfect competition is an ideal market form which ensures the attainment of Pareto optimality or maximum social welfare as it fulfils all the marginal conditions required for the purpose. Essentially Pareto optimality involves efficiency in the use and allocation of resources at the disposal of a community. As seen above, if Pareto efficiency is not achieved it implies one can be made better off without anyone being made worse off. In this case there is scope of increasing social welfare by reorganisation of resources, say through a public policy. An important feature of general equilibrium reached in perfectly competitive markets leads to maximum social welfare or economic efficiency in the sense of Pareto optimality. This is known as the ***first or fundamental theorem of welfare economics.*** According to this theorem, general equilibrium attained in perfectly competitive markets for goods and factors exhausts all possbilities of increasing welfare of the individuals from exchange between them or the use and allocation of resources in the production of different goods. In other words, the first or fundamental theorem of welfare economics postulates that general competitive equilibrium is Pareto opimal. We shall show below how perfectly competitive equilibrium leads to the first theorem of welfare economics. In what follows we shall show how equilibrium under perfect competition satisfies all the marginal conditions required for the achievement of Pareto optimum. We shall further explain what are the major obstacles in the way of maximizing social welfare or achieving Pareto optimality.

Perfect Competition and Optimal Distribution of Goods or Efficiency in Exchange

The condition for Pareto optimality with regard to the distribution of goods among consumers requires that the marginal rate of substitution (*MRS*) between any two goods, say X and Y, must be the same for any pair of consumers. Let A and B be the two consumers between whom two goods X and Y are to be distributed. Under perfect competition prices of all goods are given and same for every consumer. It is also assumed that consumers try to maximize their satisfaction subject to their budget constraint. Now, given the prices of two goods, consumer A will maximize his satisfaction when he is buying the two goods X and Y in such amounts that:

16. P. Else, P. Curwen, *Principles of Microeconomics,* Unwin, Hyman, London, 1990, p. 324.
17. Prasanta K. Patnaik, *op. cit,* p. 688.

$$MRS_{xy}^{A} = \frac{P_x}{P_y} \quad ...(i)$$

Likewise, the consumer *B* will also be in equilibrium (maximise his satisfaction) when he is purchasing and consuming the two goods *X* and *Y* in such amounts that:

$$MRS_{xy}^{B} = \frac{P_x}{P_y} \quad ...(ii)$$

Since this is essential condition of perfect competition that prices of goods are the same or uniform for all consumers, the price ratio of the two goods $\left(\frac{P_x}{P_y}\right)$ in equations (*i*) and (*ii*) above will be the same for consumers *A* and *B*. It, therefore, follows from equations (*i*) and (*ii*) above that under conditions of perfect competition marginal rate of substitution between two goods *X* and *Y* will be equal for the two consumers. That is,

$$MRS_{xy}^{A} = MRS_{xy}^{B}$$

This result will hold good between any pair of goods for any pair of consumers.

Perfect Competition and Optimal Allocation of Factors between Firms

The second marginal condition for Pareto optimality relates to the optimal allocation of factors among the production of various goods. This condition requires that for the optimal allocation of factors marginal rate of technical substitution *(MRTS)* between any two factors, say labour and capital of any pair of firms must be the same in the production of any product. This condition is also satisfied by perfect competition. For a firm working under perfect competition prices of factors it employs are given and constant and it is in equilibrium (that is, minimizes cost for a given level of output) at the combination of factors where the given isoquant is tangent to an iso-cost line. As is well known, the slope of the isoquant represents marginal rate of technical substitution between the two factors and the slope of the iso-cost line measures the ratio of the prices of two factors. Thus, under perfect competition, a cost-minimizing firm *A* producing good *X* will equate *MRTS* between labour and capital with the price ratio of these two factors. Thus under perfect competition :

$$MRTS_{LK}^{A} = \frac{w}{r} \quad ...(i)$$

where w and r are the prices of labour and capital respectively and $MRTS_{LK}^{A}$ is the marginal rate of technical substitution between labour and capital in the production of good *X* by firm *A*. Similarly, firm *B* producing good *X* and working under perfect competition will also equate his marginal rate of technical substitution between the two factors with their price ratios. Thus

$$MRS_{LK}^{B} = \frac{w}{r} \quad ....(ii)$$

Since under perfect competition, prices of factors are the same for all the firms, each firm will adjust the use of factors in such a way its his marginal rate of technical substitution (*MRTS*) between labour and capital in the production of a good is equal to the *same factor price ratio*. In other words, $\frac{w}{r}$ will be the same for all of them and to this $MRTS_{LK}$ of the firms producing different commodities will be made equal. It, therefore, follows from (*i*) and (*ii*) above that under perfect competition :

$$MRTS_{LK}^{A} = MRTS_{LK}^{B}$$

We thus see that perfect competition ensures optimal allocation of resources as between different firms using these resources for production of commodities.

Perfect Competition and Allocative Efficiency (Optimum Direction of Production)

The most important condition for the attainment of Pareto optimum is one which refers to the optimum direction or composition of production. In other words, this condition requires how much amounts of different goods should be produced and resources allocated accordingly. This refers to the general condition for optimum allocation of resources which has also been called the condition for ***Allocative Economic Efficiency.*** This condition states that marginal rate of substitution between any two commodities for any consumer should be the same as the marginal rate of transformation for the community between these two commodities.

Under conditions of perfect competition, each firm to be in equilibrium produces so much output of a commodity that its marginal cost is equal to the price of the commodity. Thus, for firms in perfect competition, $MC_x = P_x$, $MC_y = P_y$, where MC_x and MC_y are marginal costs of production of commodities X and Y respectively and P_x and P_y are prices of commodities X and Y. Therefore, it follows that firms in perfect competition will be in equilibrium when they are producing commodities in such quantities that

$$\frac{MC_x}{MC_y} = \frac{P_x}{P_y}$$

The ratio of marginal costs of two commodities represents the marginal rate of transformation between them. Therefore, for each firm working under perfect competition :

$$MRT_{xy} = \frac{MC_x}{MC_y} = \frac{P_x}{P_y} \qquad \text{...}(i)$$

When there prevails perfect competition on the buying side, each consumer maximises his satisfaction and is in equilibrium at the point where the given budget line is tangent to his indifference curve. In other words, each consumer is in equilibrium when :

$$MRS_{xy} = \frac{P_x}{P_y} \qquad \text{...}(ii)$$

Since, under perfect competition, *the ratio of prices of two commodities* $\left(\frac{P_x}{P_y}\right)$ *is the same for a consumer and a producer,* it follows from (*i*) and (*ii*) above that

$MRS_{xy} = MRT_{xy}$

Likewise, this will hold good for any other pair of commodities. Thus, perfect competition satisfies the marginal condition required for the Pareto allocative efficiency or optimal product-mix. This is shown in Figure 61.12 where at the tangency point Q between indifference curve IC_2 reflecting the preferences of the consumer and the transformation curve TT' representing the production possibilities of the community, the general equilibrium occurs under perfect competition. At this equilibrium point Q, OM quantity of product X and ON quantity of product

Y are being produced and the consumer is at its highest possible indifference curve IC_2 and $MRS_{xy} = MRT_{xy}$. Any deviation from this product-mix (OM of X and ON of Y) will lower the welfare of consumers. Thus, the competitive equilibrium at point Q represents Pareto optimal direction of production, or allocative efficiency.

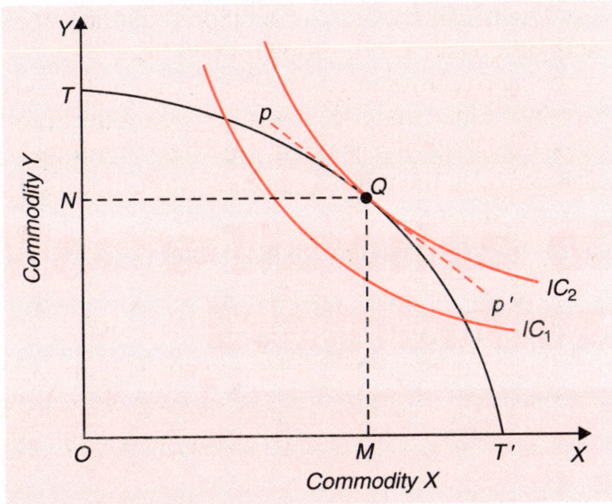

Fig. 61.12. *Pareto-Optimal Mix of Output under Perfect Competition*

Perfect Competition and Optimum Degree of Specialisation

Pareto optimality with regard to the degree of specialisation in production by various firms requires that the marginal rate of transformation *(MRT)* between any two products must be the same for any two firms that produce the two products. Let us assume two firms *A* and *B* each producing the two products *X* and *Y*. The Pareto optimum with regard to the degree of specialisation of products requires that :

$$MRT_{xy}^{A} = MRT_{xy}^{B}$$

where MRT_{xy} represents marginal rate of transformation between products *X* and *Y*.

Now, a firm working under perfect competition and producing two products will equalise marginal rate of transformation between *X* and *Y* (MRT_{xy}) with the price ratio of the two products so as to maximise its profits. A multi-product firm will be in equilibrium where a given transformation curve is tangent to an iso-revenue line. The tangency of the iso-revenue curve with the transformation curve implies the equality of marginal rate of transformation between the two products with the price ratio of the two products. Since under perfect competition prices of all products are the same or uniform for all firms, the firms are merely price takers having no individual influence over the prices of the products. As a result, all firms under perfect competition will equate their marginal rate of transformation between the two products with the same ratio of prices of the products. This will render the marginal rate of transformation between the two products equal for all firms. In terms of notations used above, under perfect competition the firm *A* will be in equilibrium when :

$$MRT_{xy}^{A} = \frac{P_x}{P_y}$$

Similarly, under perfect competition the firm *B* will be in equilibrium when :

$$MRT_{xy}^{B} = \frac{P_x}{P_y}$$

Since product price ratio $\left(\frac{P_x}{P_y}\right)$ is the same for both the firms, it follows that under perfect competition :

$$MRT_{xy}^{A} = MRT_{xy}^{B}$$

The fulfillment of this condition regarding optimal degree of specialisation under perfect competition can also be shown in another way. As is quite well known, a firm under perfect competition equates price with marginal cost of production of a commodity in order to maximise its profits. Since marginal cost of every product produced by a firm under perfect competition will be equalised with its price, the ratio of marginal costs of two products produced by the firm will be equal to the ratio of prices of two products. Thus, the firm A will be in equilibrium under perfect competition with :

$$\frac{MC_x^A}{MC_y^A} = \frac{P_x}{P_y}$$

Likewise, the firm B will be in equilibrium when

$$\frac{MC_x^B}{MC_y^B} = \frac{P_x}{P_y}$$

Since prices of two products, P_x and P_y, are the same for all the firms working under perfect competition, the price ratio of the products, $\frac{P_x}{P_y}$, will also be the same. It therefore follows from above that:

$$\frac{MC_x^A}{MC_y^B} = \frac{MC_x^A}{MC_y^B}$$

Now, the ratio of marginal costs of two products $\frac{MC_x}{MC_y}$ represents the marginal rate of transformation between the two products (MRT_{xy}). Hence the marginal rate of transformation between the two products ($MRTS_{xy}$) will be the same for the two firms. Thus

$$MRT_{xy}^A = MRT_{xy}^B$$

Perfect Competition and Optimum Factor-Product Relationship

The fourth condition required for the achievement of Pareto optimality states that marginal rate of transformation between any factor and any commodity must be the same for any pair of firms using the factor and producing a product. Marginal rate of transformation between a factor and a commodity implies marginal physical product *(MP)* of the factor in the production of that commodity.

Therefore, this condition requires that marginal physical product of a factor must be the same for all firms using the factor and producing a commodity. This condition is also satisfied under conditions of perfect competition. To be in equilibrium a firm under perfect competition in the factor market will employ such an amount of the factor that equates price of the factor with the value of the marginal product (*VMP*) of the factor. Now, value of the marginal product of the factor is marginal physical product of the factor *(MPP)* multiplied by the price of the commodity (P_x). Let us take labour as an example of a factor of production and w as the price of labour, that is, its wage rate. Thus,

$$VMP \text{ of a factor} = MP_L P_X$$

It follows from above that under perfect competition for any firm A to be in equilibrium,

$$w = VMP_L^A = MP_L^A . P_x$$

$$\frac{w}{P_x} = MP_L^A \qquad ...(i)$$

Likewise, for another firm B to be in equilibrium :

$$w = VMP_L^B = MP_L^B . P_X$$

or,

$$\frac{w}{P_x} = MP_L^B \qquad ....(ii)$$

Since under perfect competition price of factor w as well as the price of product (P_x) is the same for all firms, it follows from (*i*) and (*ii*) above that :

$$MP_L^A = MP_L^B \qquad ...(iii)$$

That is, marginal physical product of a factor is the same in both firms A and B producing a commodity. This will hold good for any pair of firms working under perfect competition.

FUNDAMENTAL THEOREM OF WELFARE ECONOMICS : A CRITIQUE

It has been shown above that ***perfectly competitive equilibrium is Pareto optimal.*** This is called fundamental theorem of welfare economics. This is also called the **invisible hand theorem**. The belief that competitive market economy provides an efficient means of allocating scarce resources goes back to Adam Smith who argued in his famous book "*Wealth of Nations*" that individuals who pursue their self-interest they operating through market promote the welfare of others and welfare of the society as a whole. Thus individual consumers seek to maximise their own satisfaction and producers pursue to maximise their own profits. Thus, even though promoting the interests of the society as a whole is not a part of their intention but they are led by the forces of market system to promote the interest of the society as a whole.

We have proved above that perfect competition in the market satisfies (1) Pareto's optimum condition of exchange, that is, MRS_{xy} of any pair of individuals under it is the same, (2) Pareto's optimum condition of production, that is, $MRTS_{LK}$ of any pair of firms using the two factors for producing products under it is the same, and (3) Pareto's condition for optimal direction of production (*i.e.* optimum product-mix), namely MRT_{XY} in production equals MRS_{XY} of consumers. (For details regarding proofs of these and other conditions see above pages.)

However, the conditions under which a perfect competitive market system achieves Pareto optimality or what is also called ***economic efficiency*** are quite restrictive. One important condition for the achievement of Pareto optimality is that the general competitive equilibrium exists. This requires that all markets concerned are in equilibrium simultaneously. If one market is not in equilibrium for some reason, the condition for Pareto optimality would be violated which would leave unutilised the opportunities for Pareto improvement.

The second important requirement for the validity of the fundamental theorem of welfare economics is that ***second order conditions for equilibrium must be fulfilled.*** This implies that consumer preferences (or indifference curves) are convex and also producers production sets (*i.e.* isoquants) are convex. This implies that consumers marginal rate of substitution and producers marginal rate of technical substitution ($MRTS_{LK}$) must be diminishing at or near the equilibrium point. Further, production transformation curves must be concave if Pareto optimality is to be achieved. The existence of perfect competition does not guarantee that these second order conditions will be fulfilled. In this context it may be noted that in many areas of production there prevail ***increasing returns to scale.*** In case of increasing returns to scale equality *of*

MRT_{xy} with MRS_{xy} does not ensure Pareto optimality. The third condition required for the fulfillment of fundamental theorem of welfare economics is that **externalities** in production and **externalities** in consumption do not exist. The assumption of the absence of production externalities implies that production choices by any firm do not affect the production possibilities of other firms. Similarly, the assumption of the absence of consumption externalities implies that production decisions of the firms do not affect the consumption possibilities of the consumers. In case these externalities in production and consumption exist, the competitive equilibrium will not achieve Pareto optimality from the social point of view. How externalities prevent the achievement of Pareto optimality and lead to loss of social welfare will be explained in detail in a later chapter.

Lastly, it is important to note that the competitive equilibrium under the conditions mentioned above ensures Pareto optimality or efficiency in use and allocation of resources. It has nothing to do with desirable distribution of welfare. In other words, ***it ensures Pareto efficiency not social justice.*** Pareto optimality analysis assumes the initial factor endowment as given. Initial inequalities in the ownership of assets or factor endowments causes inequalities which leads to non-optimal distribution of goods and services and therefore loss of social welfare. We will explain in detail in a later section how always ensure pare to optimality.

PERFECT COMPETITION AND THE SECOND THEOREM OF WELFARE ECONOMICS

We have explained above how perfectly competitive general equilibrium leads to the first or fundamental theorem of welfare economics, that is, competitive equilibrium is Pareto optimum. There is also a second theorem of welfare economics according to which for every Pareto optimal situation there is a competitive equilibrium, given the initial income distribution or factor endowment. Take for instance the case of Pareto optimality of exchange. When the indifference curves, are convex to the origin, every efficient allocation (*i.e.* Pareto optimal distribution) on the contract curve for exchange is a competitive equilibrium for some given *initial distribution of goods or allocation of factors* (*i.e.*income) among individuals. This implies that *whatever the initial disribution of income in a* society the corresponding Pareto optimality or economic efficiency with regard to exchange and distribution of goods among the individuals can be reached through perfectly competitive equilibrium. Consider Figure 61.13 where allocation of goods, between two individuals is shown. If initial distribution of goods between the two goods is given by point K, then perfect competition can lead to the determination of price ratio of goods as shown by price line P_1P_1 so that through exchange the two individuals can reach at point S which depicts higher level of welfare for both and as it lies at the contract curve, it is Pareto optimal.

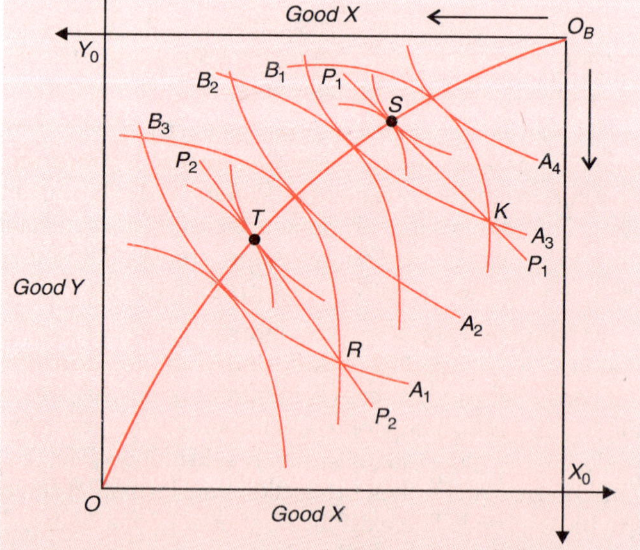

Fig. 61.13. *Proving the Second Theorem of Welfare Economics*

Similarly, if initial distribution of goods (*i.e.* real income) is given by point *R*, then perfect competition can determine price ratio of the two goods as given by price line P_2P_2 so that through exchange the two individuals can reach point *T* on the contract curve which is Pareto optimal.

DOES PERFECT COMPETITION ALWAYS ENSURE PARETO OPTIMALITY AND MAXIMUM SOCIAL WELFARE ?

Many economists have fallen into trap of believing that perfect competition always attains Pareto optimality and maximises social welfare. However, this is not true. Firstly, perfect competition does not guarantee that second-order conditions required for the achievement of Pareto optimality will also be fulfilled. According to second-order conditions needed for the attainment of Pareto optimality consumer indifference curves and production isoquants must be convex. That is, for the equilibrium under perfect competition marginal rates of substitution between goods and marginal rates of technical substitution between any two factors must be declining at or near the equilibrium points. There is nothing in the perfect competition that guarantees the fulfilment of this condition and as a result Pareto optimality or economic efficiency in the use and allocation of resources may not be achieved. Further, another second-order condition for attainment of Pareto optimality requires that the production transformation curve between two goods must be concave in the relevant region. If the production transformation curve in relevant region is convex, then the equality of *MRS* between two goods with the *MRT* between them would not ensure Pareto optimality or maximum social welfare though perfect competition might be prevailing in the markets for two goods. Consider Fig. 66.14 where production transformation curve *PP'* in the relevant region is convex to the origin due to good *X* being produced under conditions of increasing returns to scale. IC_1, IC_2 are social indifference curves (in output space) of the society. It will be observed from this figure that at point *A*, marginal rate of transformation (MRT_{xy}) in production equals marginal rate of substitution of consumers and this apparently satisfies the condition of Pareto optimality. But this does not represent efficient allocation of resources because second-order condition of concavity of production transformation at point *A* is not satisfied. In fact, it is at point *B* on the transformation curve which is Pareto-efficient because marginal rate of transformation is diminishing at point *B* and therefore transformation curve is concave to the origin at this point.

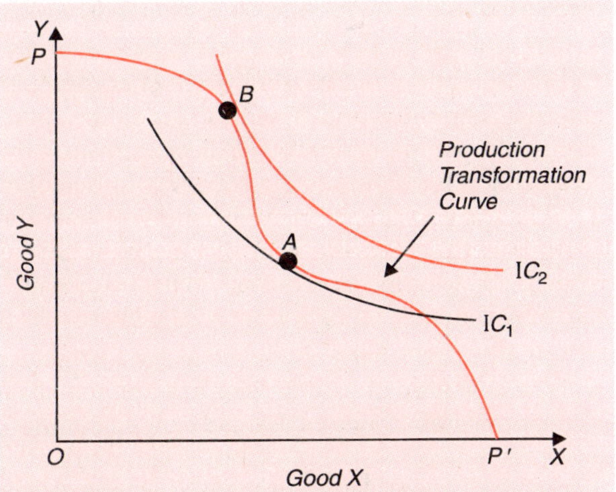

Fig. 61.14. *Increasing Returns and Competitive Equilibrium*

In the real world in several areas of production we find that increasing returns to scale occur and due to them production transformation curves are convex rather than being concave to the origin. Thus in the context of increasing returns to scale Pareto efficiency cannot be achieved even though conditions of perfect competition may prevail in the goods markets.

Another important qualification to the assertion that perfect competition ensures Pareto optimality is that perfect competition yields Pareto optimality in the sense that it puts the economy on some point on the utility possibility curve. As seen earlier, all points on the utility possibility curve are Pareto optimum. Which is best out of all of them is left undecided and indeterminate in Paretian analysis. There is no guarantee that perfectly competitive equilibrium will coincide with a best or bliss point. Such a best or *bliss point* can be obtained if value judgements are made, but Pareto ruled out making inter-personal comparison of utility and value judgements.

Further, there is no reason to believe that perfect competition necessarily maximises social welfare. The equilibrium point achieved under perfect competition depends on factor ownership and to say that perfect competition maximises social welfare is to assert that existing factor ownership is socially desirable (More will be said on this point later). In this context of inequality in factor ownership, to attain the *bliss point* the society will have to redistribute wealth (*i.e.* factor ownership through lump-sum transfers or through other types of taxes) so as to move the economy along a utility possibility curve from actual competitive equilibrium point to the bliss point.[19]

Lastly, the belief that competitive equilibrium maximises social welfare is based on the concept of utility as a measure of well-being. It has been explained above in the critical evaluation of Pareto criterion that Prof. Amartya Sen has rightly challenged that 'utility is not a good measure of welfare' (for all points of criticism of Prof. Amartya Sen, see above pages).

Besides, when externalities, that is, external economies and diseconomies in production and consumption, are present, perfect competition will not lead to Pareto optimality. When external economies and diseconomies either in production or consumption are present, social marginal cost (or benefit) will diverge from private marginal cost (benefit). Now, perfect competition only ensures the equality of price of a product with the private marginal cost and not with the equality of price with the social marginal cost. Thus, the existence of externalities will prevent the achievement of Pareto optimality or efficient allocation of resources even when perfect competition prevails in the economy. How the occurrence of externalities obstructs the achievement of maximum social welfare will be explained at length in a later chapter.

Further, even if the above two factors, namely, non-fulfilment of the second-order conditions and the existence of externalities are not actually found, the perfect competition will not lead to economic efficiency or Pareto optimality (that is, optimum allocation of resources) if the given distribution of income is not optimal from the viewpoint of social welfare. As mentioned before, analysis of Pareto optimality accepts the prevailing income distribution which may be far from the optimum distribution. There is nothing in perfect competition which ensures optimum distribution of income. That the distribution of income is an important factor determining social welfare is now widely recognised by the economists.

Finally, there is another factor which prevents the achievement of Pareto optimality or maximum social welfare even when perfect competition prevails in the economy. This factor relates to the employment or utilisation of available resources. Pareto optimality will not be attained if the available resources are not fully employed or utilised. This is because if some of the available resources are unemployed or unutilized, then the society could produce more of a commodity by employing the unemployed resources and therefore without cutting down the production of any other commodity. Now, when it is possible to produce more of a commodity without reduction in the output of another, then the society could make either all individuals better off or at least some better off without making others worse off. If the economy is operating at a point inside its transformation curve (*i.e.* production possibility curve), it would not then be employing or utilizing its resources fully and it would then be possible to increase

19. See Graff on this point, *op. cit.*, pp. 77-79.

the output of both commodities (represented on the two axes) or to increase the output of one commodity without reducing the output of the other. Thus, any position of working inside the transformation or production possibility curve cannot be a position of Pareto optimality. Therefore, for the economy to achieve Pareto optimality it must work at some point on the given production possibility curve implying full employment of resources. Full employment of available resources is therefore a necessary condition for the attainment of Pareto optimality. But it is important to note that perfect competition does not guarantee full employment of resources and therefore does not necessarily lead to the achievement of Pareto optimality.

It follows from above that perfect competition though a necessary condition is not a sufficient condition for Pareto optimality. Therefore, a free enterprise economy characterised by perfect competition ensures efficient allocation of resources or maximum social welfare cannot be accepted without some qualifications. And these qualifications are : (1) the second- order conditions are satisfied, (2) the externalities in production and consumption are absent, (3) prevailing distribution of income is optimal from the social point of view, and (4) available resources are fully employed. It may also be noted that in present-day free enterprise capitalist economies perfect competition is an exception rather than the rule. In present-day capitalist economies, it is monopolies, oligopolies and monopolistic competition which largely prevail. And, as shall be seen in a later chaper these market forms serve as a great obstacle for the achievement of Pareto optimality or optimum allocation of resources.

FAILURES OF MARKET AND ROLE OF GOVERNMENT

We have explained above the various concepts of economic efficiency and have seen how a perfectly competitive market succeeds in achieving exchange efficiency, production efficiency and allocative efficiency. As a result, competitive market achieves maximum possible well-being of the people of a society. In an economy characterised by perfectly competitive markets, government performs only its basic functions, namely, to maintain law and order in the economy, to enforce property rights and contracts made by the people while making market transactions.

There is a good deal of difference of opinions among economists regarding whether markets in the actual world can be relied upon to achieve economic efficiency, prosperity of the people and acceptable distribution of resources and incomes. On the one extreme, there are economists like Fredrich von Hayek of Austria and Milton Friedman of the United States who believe that markets in the real world are highly competitive and free market economies are quite successful in achieving economic efficiency, prosperity and desirable distribution of income. They think that wherever there are departures from ideal of perfectly competitive markets, intervention of government will not improve the working of the economy.

However, the dominant view among mainstream economists is that though perfectly competitive markets are ideal and serve as useful benchmark with which the outcome of actual markets can be compared, there are significant failures of market system. According to them, government intervention can bring about improvements in the allocation of resources and distribution of incomes. Many markets in the economy are not sufficiently competitive and there are firms which wield great market power and restrict output of goods and raise their prices. Government can intervene and regulate them, especially natural monopolies where competition is non-viable. Besides, government can take measures to check monopolistic and restrictive trade practices to encourage competition in the economy. Through passing laws government can declare illegal the mergers such as a cartel which lead to monopolies.

Some economists lay emphasis on failures of market which arise due to **imperfect information** that prevails in the real world. In perfectly competitive markets, it is assumed that both the firms and buyers have perfect information about the quality of workers, and return which they will receive from investment. However, in the real world firms do not have perfect information about the quality of workers hired by them. Firms do not have perfect information on the likely returns from different types of investment made by them.

Some economists lay stress on the existence of **negative externalities** which prevent the competitive markets to achieve economic efficiency. In this connection *pollution of environment* by the productive activities of firms which harm others and is an important example of the failures of markets to achieve economic efficiency. Another significant failure of market is the *existence of unemployment* which exists on a large scale in the free market economies. The existence of unemployment implies that some resources, especially labour, are lying idle and putting them to use will enable us to produce more of some goods without reducing the production of any other.

Besides, there are **public goods** which are collectively consumed by the members of a society and it is not possible to exclude anyone who does not pay for them from consuming them or enjoying their services. The important examples of public goods are national defence, law and order, lighthouses. Since people who do not pay for them cannot be excluded from consuming them or enjoying their service, it is not profitable for private firms to produce them. Therefore, government has to provide these public goods.

We have explained above the cases when markets do not perform well and therefore government intervention is needed to improve market efficiency. However, it does not *necessarily* mean that government intervention will definitely improve efficiency. ***Just as there are market failures, there are government failures too.*** However, in our view, role of government is essential in the economy to achieve social objectives of efficiency, improvement in distribution of income, reducing unemployment and to provide public goods. Various market failures are explained in detail in a later chapter.

QUESTIONS FOR REVIEW

1. In welfare economics attempt is made to establish criteria or norms to judge the social desirability of economic policies. Explain.
2. What is meant by social welfare ? Is it possible to measure social welfare without interpersonal comparison of utility ?
3. What is meant by economic efficiency ? Is it right to ignore equity in distribution when it clashes with the objective of economic efficiency ?
4. What is new welfare economics ? Explain its approach to social welfare.
5. Explain three concepts of social welfare mentioning in each case the approach to the inter-personal comparison of utility.
6. What is meant by value judgements ? Explain their role in welfare economics.
7. Define economic efficiency ? Explain Pareto's three conditions for achievement of economic efficiency.
8. State Pareto's criterion of social welfare and explain it using Edgeworth Box diagram.
9. Explain the concept of utility possibility curve. How would you explain Pareto's criterion of social welfare with utility possibility curve ?
10. What is Pareto optimality ? State and explain the conditions of Pareto optimality regarding (1) distribution of goods between individuals, (2) allocation of resources between firms and (3) direction of production.
11. Pareto criterion does not give us a sufficient basis for ordering states from the viewpoint of social welfare. Examine critically.
12. State and explain Pareto optimality criterion. How far is it useful in suggesting policies that will make the community better off ?

13. Perfect competition will tend to yield an optimal allocation of resoruces. Discuss.
14. State and explain diagrammatically the marginal conditions for a Pareto-optimal distribution of goods and resources in a two factors, two commodities, two consumers model.
15. "Pareto criterion works by sidestepping the crucial issue of interpersonal comparison and income distribution." (Baumol) Discuss.
16. Pareto's analysis leaves a considerable amount of indeterminacy in maximisation of social welfare. Discuss.
17. Pareto optimality is necessary but not a sufficient condition for social welfare maximisation. Discuss.
18. The collapse of the communist regime in Eastern Europe and Soviet Union can be attributed to economic inefficiencies. Discuss.
19. Show that a general competitive equilibrium is also Pareto optimal.
20. There is no unique Pareto-optimal allocation in an economy. True or false ? Explain
21. When perfectly competitive markets are in equilibrium, the three conditions for economic efficiency regarding exchange, allocation of factors among products and direction of production are satisfied.

CHAPTER

62

New Welfare Economics: Compensation Principle

Introduction

Pareto laid the foundation of the modern welfare economics by formulating the concept of social optimum which is based on the concept of ordinal utility and is free from interpersonal comparisons of utilities and value judgements. He aimed at formulating a value-free objective criterion designed to test whether a proposed policy change increases social welfare or not. Pareto criterion states simply that an economic change which harms no one and makes someone better off indicates an increase in social welfare. Thus, this criterion does not apply to those economic changes which harm some and benefit others. In terms of Edgeworth Box diagram Pareto criterion fails to say as to whether or not social welfare increases as movement is made in either direction along the contract curve because it rejects the notion of interpersonal comparison of utility. As we have seen in the last chapter, every tangency point of the two indifference curves on the contract curve represents a Pareto optimum. There is thus no any unique Pareto optimum position. This criterion does not tell us about changes in the level of social welfare if one moves on the contract curve from one tangency point to another because such movement harms one and benefits the other. Thus the analysis of welfare in terms of Pareto optimality leaves a considerable amount of indeterminacy, for there are numerous Pareto optimum points on the contract curve. Economists like Kaldor, Hicks and Scitovsky have made efforts to evaluate the changes in social welfare resulting from any economic reorganisation which harms somebody and benefits the others. These economists have sought to remove indeterminacy in the analysis of Pareto optimality. They have put forward a criterion known as the ***'compensation principle'*** on the basis of which they claim to evaluate those changes in economic policy or an organisation which make some individual better off and others worse off. The 'compensation principle' is based on the following assumptions:

1. The satisfaction of an individual is independent of the others and he is the best judge of his welfare.
2. There exist no externalities of consumption and production.
3. The tastes of the individuals remain constant.
4. The problems of production and exchange can be separated from the problems of distribution. Compensation principle accepts the level of social welfare to be a function of the level of production. Thus, it ignores the effects of a change in distribution on social welfare.
5. Utility can be measured ordinally and interpersonal comparisons of utilities are not possible.

Given the above assumptions, a criterion of compensation principle can be discussed. Kaldor, Hicks and Scitovsky have claimed to formulate a value-free objective criterion of measuring the changes in social welfare with the help of the concept of 'compensating payments'.

Kaldor-Hicks Welfare Criterion : Compensation Principle

Nicholas Kaldor was the first economist to give a welfare criterion based on compensating payments. Kaldor's criterion helps us to measure the welfare implications of a movement in either direction on the contract curve in terms of Edgeworth box diagram. According to Kaldor's welfare criterion, if a certain change in economic organisation or policy makes some people better off and others worse off, then that change will increase social welfare if those who gain from the change could compensate the losers and still be better off than before. In the words of Prof. Baumol, "Kaldor's criterion states that a change is an improvement if those who gain evaluate their gains at a higher figure than the value which the losers set upon their losses."[1] Thus, if any policy change benefits any one section of the society (gainers) to such an extent that it is better off even after the payment of compensation to the other section of the society (losers) out of the benefits received, then that change leads to increase in social welfare. In Kaldor's own words, "In all cases... where a certain policy leads to an increase in physical productivity and thus in aggregate real income... it is possible to make everybody better off without making anybody worse off. It is quite sufficient... to show that even if all those who suffer as a result are fully compensated for their loss, the rest of the community will still be better off than before."[2] Prof. J.R. Hicks supported Kaldor for employing compensation principle to evaluate the change in social welfare resulting from any economic reorganisation that benefits some people and harms the others. This criterion states that, "If *A* is made so much better by the change that he could compensate *B* for his loss and still have something left over, then the reorganisation is unequivocal improvement."[3] In other words, a change is an improvement if the losers in the changed situation cannot profitably bribe the gainers not to change from the original situation. Hicks has given his criterion from the losers' point of view, while Kaldor had formulated his criterion from gainers' point of view. Thus the two criteria are really the same though they are clothed in different words. That is why they are generally called by a single name 'Kaldor-Hicks criterion'.

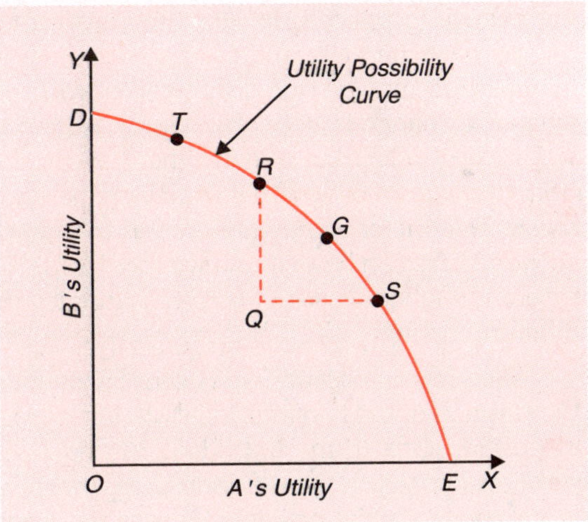

Fig. 62.1. *Kaldor-Hicks Criterion Explained with Utility Possibility Curve*

Kaldor-Hicks criterion can be explained with the help of the utility possibility curve. In Fig 62.1 ordinal utility of two individuals *A* and *B* is shown on *X* and *Y* axes respectively. *DE* is the utility possibility curve which represents the various combinations of utilities obtained by individuals *A* and *B*. As we move downward on the curve *DE,* utility of *A* increases while that of *B* falls. On the other hand, if we move up on the utility curve *ED,* utility of B increases while that of *A* falls.

Suppose the utilities obtained by *A* and *B* from the distribution of income or output

1. W. J. Baumol, *Economic Theory and Operations Analysis,* 4th Ed., 1977, p. 530.
2. N. Kaldor, "Welfare Propositions of Economics and Interpersonal Comparison of Utility", *Economic Journal,* Sept. 1939.
3. J.R. Hicks, The Foundations of Welfare Economics, *Economic Journal,* Vol. XIX, December 1939

between them are represented by point *Q* inside the utility possibility curve *DE*. Let us assume that as a result of some change in economic policy, the two individuals move from point *Q* to point *T* on the utility possibility curve *DE*. As a result of this movement, utility of individual *B* has increased while the utility of *A* has declined, that is, B has become better off and *A* has become worse off than before. Therefore, this movement from point *Q* to point *T* cannot be evaluated by means of Pareto criterion. Of course, points such as *R, G, S* or any other point on the segment *RS* of the utility possibility curve *DE* are socially preferable to point *Q* on the basis of Pareto criterion. But since the movement from *Q* to *T* involves interpersonal comparison of utility it cannot be said whether or not social welfare increases on the basis of Pareto criterion. However, the compensation principle propounded by Kaldor-Hicks enables us to say whether or not social welfare has increased as a result of movement from *Q* to *T*. According to Kaldor-Hicks criterion, we have to see whether the individual *A* who gains with the movement from position *Q* to position *T* could compensate the individual *A* who is loser and still be better off than before. Now, it will be seen from Figure 62.1 that utility possibility curve *DE* passes through points *R, G* and *S*. This means that by mere redistribution of income between the two individuals, that is, if individual *B* gives some compensation to individual *A* for the loss suffered, they can move from position *T to* the position *R*. It is evident from the figure that at position *R* individual *A* is as well off as at the position *Q* but individual *B* is still better off as compared to the position *Q*. It means due to a policy change and consequent movement from position *Q* to position *T*, the gainer (individual *B)* could compensate the loser (individual *A)* and is still better off than at *Q*. Therefore, according to Kaldor-Hicks criterion, social welfare increases with the movement from position *Q* to position *T* because from *T* they could move to the position *R* through mere redistribution of income.

It is noteworthy that, according to Kaldor-Hicks criterion, compensation may not be actually paid to judge whetner or not social welfare has increased. It is enough to know whether the gainer *could* compensate the loser for the loss in his welfare and still be better off. Whether redistribution of income (that is, payment of compensation) should be actually made following the change in policy is left for the Government to decide. If it is *possible* for the gainer to compensate the loser and still be better off, the economists can say that social welfare has increased. It may be noted that gainer can compensate the losers and still be better off only when the change in economic policy leads to the increase in output or real income. That is why Kaldor and Hicks claim that they have been able to distinguish between ***change in output*** from ***change in distribution.*** When their criterion is satisfied by any change in the situation, it means that the economy has moved to a productively more efficient position and as a result social welfare can be said to have increased. Now, whether redistribution of income is actually made through payment of compensation by the gainers to the losers, according to them, is a different matter.

Now, the implications of Kaldor-Hicks criterion become more clear if through redistribution the position of the two individuals changes from *T* to *G* (see Fig. 62.1). It is quite manifest that at position *G* both the individuals *A* and *B* are better off than at the position *Q*. Thus the position *T* to which the two individuals moved as result of a certain change in economic policy is superior to initial position *Q* from the viewpoint of social welfare, since from position *T* movement can be made, merely through redistribution of income to position G where both are better off as compared to the position *Q*.

It may be noted that in the situation depicted in Figure 62.1, the change in economic policy brings about a movement from a position inside the utility possibility curve to a point on it. Now let us see what happens to social welfare if as a result of the adoption of a certain economic policy the utility possibility curve moves outward and the two individuals move from a point on the utility possibility curve to a point on a higher utility possibility curve. It can be shown that, according to Kaldor-Hicks criterion, such a movement causes an improvement in social welfare. Consider Figure.62.2. *UV* is the original utility possibility curve and *Q* represents the position at which the two individuals are initially placed. Now suppose utility possibility curve shifts outward to the new position *U′ V′* and the two individuals are placed at point *R* on it. In movement from *Q* on *UV* to *R* on *U′ V′* the utility of *A* has increased and that of *B* has declined. But position *R* denotes greater social welfare on the basis of Kaldor's criterion when compared to the position *Q* on the original utility possibility curve *UV* because with *U′ V′* as the utility possibility curve it is possible to move, through mere redistribution of income, from position *R* to position *S* where the individual *B* has been fully compensated for his loss of utility, the individual *A* is still better off as compared to position *Q*. To conclude, any change in the economy that moves the individuals from a position on a lower utility possibility curve to a position on a higher utility possibility curve increases social welfare.

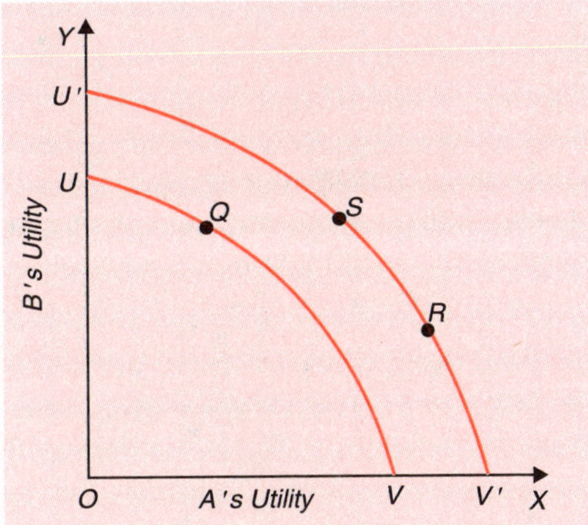

Fig. 62.2. *Kaldor-Hicks Welfare Criterion*

Scitovsky Paradox

Scitovsky pointed out an important limitation of Kaldor-Hicks criterion that might lead to contradictory results. He showed that if some situation position *B* is shown to be an improvement over position *A* on Kaldor-Hicks criterion, it may be possible that position *A* is also shown to be an improvement over *B* on the basis of the same criterion. For getting consistent results when position *B* has been revealed to be preferred to position *A* on the basis of a welfare criterion, then position *A* must not be preferred to position *B* on the same criterion. According to Scitovsky, Kaldor-Hicks criterion involves such contradictory and inconsistent results. Since Scitovsky was the first to point out this paradoxical result in Kaldor-Hicks criterion, it is known as 'Scitovsky Paradox'.

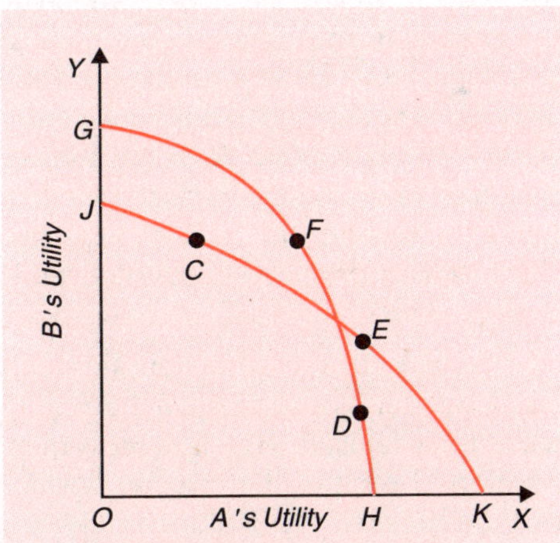

Fig. 62.3. *Scitvosky Paradox*

How Kaldor-Hicks criterion may lead to contradictory results in some situation is depicted in Figure 62.3. In this figure *JK* and *GH* are the two utility possibility curves which intersect each other. Now suppose that the initial position is at point *C* on *JK*. Further suppose that due to a certain policy change, utility possibility curve changes and takes the position *GH* and the two individuals find themselves at position *D*. Position *D* is superior to position *C* on the basis of Kaldor-Hicks criterion because from position *D* movement can be made through mere income redistribution to position *F* at which individual *B* has been fully compensated but individual *A* is still better off as compared to the original position *C*. Thus movement from position *C* to position *D* satisfies Kaldor-Hicks criterion. But, as has been pointed out by Scitovsky, reverse movement from position *D* on the new utility possibility curve *GH* to the position *C* on the old utility possibility curve *JK* also represents an improvement on Kaldor-Hicks criterion, that is, *C is* socially better than *D* on Kaldor-Hicks criterion. This is because from position *C* movement can be made by mere redistribution of income to position *E* on the utility possibility curve *JK* on which position *C* lies and which also passes through the position *E*. And, as will be observed from Fig. 62.3, at position *E* that while *A* is "as well off as at position *D*, the individual *B is* still better off than at *D*. We thus see that the movement from position *C* to position *D* due to a policy change is passed by the Kaldor-Hicks criterion and also the movement back from position *D* to position *C* is also passed by the Kaldor-Hicks criterion. This implies that *D* is socially better than *C* on this criterion and *C* is also socially better than *D* on the same criterion. So Kaldor-Hicks criterion leads us to contradictory and inconsistent results. It is mentionworthy that these contradictory results are obtained by Kaldor-Hicks criterion when following a policy change new utility possibility curve intersects the former utility possibility curve. After bringing out the possibility of contradictory results in Kaldor-Hicks criterion Scitovsky formulated his own criterion which is generally known as Scitovsky's Double Criterion.

Scitovsky's Double Criterion of Welfare

To rule out the possibility of contradictory results in Kaldor-Hicks test, Scitovsky formulated a double criterion which requires the fulfilment of Kaldor-Hicks test and also the fulfilment of the reversal test. It means that a change is an improvement if the gainers in the changed situation are able to persuade the losers to accept the change and simultaneously losers are not able to persuade the gainers to remain in the original situation. Scitovsky's double criterion can also be explained with the help of utility possibility curve. In Figure 62.4, *CD* and *EF* are the two utility possibility curves which do not intersect each other at any point. Suppose there is a change from position *Q* on the utility possibility curve *CD* to the position *G* on the utility possibility curve *EF* as a result of the adoption of a new economic policy. Such a movement is an improvement on Kaldor-Hicks criterion because *G* lies on the utility possibility curve *EF* passing through point *R*. From the position *G*, movement can be made to the position *R* simply by redistributing the income between the two individuals. And *R* is better than *Q* because the utility of both the individuals is greater at *R* as compared to the position *Q*. Thus the Kaldor-Hicks criterion is satisfied and therefore change from *Q* to *G* will increase social welfare.

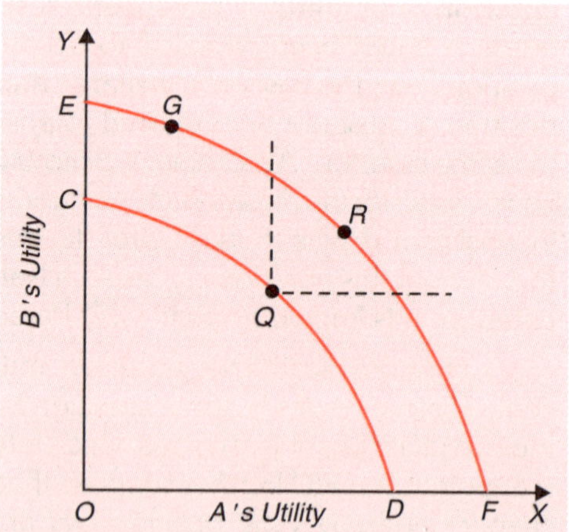

Fig. 62.4. *Scitovsky's Double Criterion*

Now, let us see, what happens to the reversal test. It must also be satisfied, if the Scitovsky double test is to be fulfilled. That is, a movement from the position *G* back to the original position *Q must not be passed* by Kaldor-Hicks criterion if Scitovsky's reversal test is to be satisfied. It is evident from Figure 62.4 that from position *Q* we cannot move to any other position on the utility possibility curve *CD* merely through redistribution of income which is socially better than *G* (that is, which raises utility of either *A* or *B*, the utility of the other remaining constant or which raises the utility of both). We thus see that while movement from position *Q* to *G* is passed by Kaldor-Hicks criterion, reverse movement from position *G* to position *Q* is not passed by Kaldor-Hicks criterion. Hence, in Figure Fig.62.4 the movement from the position *Q* to *G* satisfies Scitovsky's criterion. Thus when the two utility possibility curves are non-intersecting and change involves movement from a position on a lower utility possibility curve to a position on a higher utility possibility curve, the change raises social welfare on the basis of Kaldor-Hicks-Scitovsky criterion. This happens only when a change brings about increase in aggregate output or real income.

A Critique of the Compensation Principle

The compensation principle as developed by Kaldor, Hicks and Scitovsky has been a topic of much discussion in welfare economics since 1939. Prof. Kaldor was the first to give a criterion to judge the changes in social welfare when an economic change benefits some people and harms the others. Later Hicks also supported this criterion in 1940, though he put it in different words; Scitovsky tried to improve the Kaldor-Hicks criterion by formulating his own double criterion. These welfare economists have claimed that they have succeeded in developing a welfare criterion based on ordinal concept of utility and also which is free from any value judgements. But compensation principle has been bitterly criticised by the various welfare economists.

First, Little has pointed out that Kaldor did not formulate a new welfare criterion at all because he assumed welfare to be a function of increase in production or efficiency irrespective of the changes in distribution. Thus, according to Little, Kaldor has given only a definition of 'increase in wealth' or 'increase in efficiency'. Kaldor himself has interpreted the compensation principle in this sense as he says that, "when the production of wealth goes up, some income distribution could be found which makes some people better off, and no one worse off than before". However, as desired income distribution via compensation is only hypothetical, therefore, according to Little, it is not a welfare test but a definition of 'economic efficiency' in terms of over-compensation.

Second, compensation principle is ***not free value judgements*** as is claimed by its propounders. It involves implicit value judgements. Prof. Baumol and Little are of the opinion that the contention of Prof. Kaldor that the changes which enable the gainers to compensate the losers and still be better off are good changes, is itself a value judgement. According to Little, to say that a policy which meets the Kaldor-Hicks criterion increases output or "efficiency" of society is, in effect, to recommend it. According to him, Kaldor and Hicks have coined a *definition* of "efficiency" whose implicit ethical implications or value judgements will hardly find favour with many people. Compensation is after all only hypothetical; it is consistent with making the poor yet poorer. Thus, according to Little, if the value judgements implicit in Kaldor-Hicks criterion are made explicit, then the claim of Kaldor and Hicks that they have discovered a criterion of detecting increases in wealth, production or efficiency free from value judgements is hardly acceptable.

Third, likewise, Baumol is also of the view that Kaldor-Hicks criterion is based upon unacceptable implicit value judgements. "By using a criterion involving potential money compensations, they set up a concealed interpersonal comparison on a money basis."[4] If an individual *A* evaluates his gain from a change worth ₹ 500 whereas another individual *B* evaluates his loss due to that economic change at ₹ 75, we cannot conclude that social welfare has increased; for if the loser is poor and the gainer a rich one, it may be possible that loss of satisfaction of the poor from ₹ 75 is far greater than the addition to the satisfaction of the rich by ₹ 500 because the marginal significance of one rupee to a poor is far greater than that of the rich. Thus without actual compensation, the change would mean a major loss of welfare to the poor individual *B* and a trivial gain of welfare to the rich individual *A* even if it passes the Kaldor criterion with flying colours. To. quote Baumol again, "The Kaldor and Scitovsky criteria

4. Baumol, *op. cit*, p. 530.

have thus ducked the basic problem of the interpersonal comparison required to evaluate a policy change which harms X but aids Y. They duck it by saying implicitly that the recommendation should be based on X's and Y's relative willingness and ability to pay for what they want."[5]

Fourth, Kaldor-Hicks have claimed that through compensation principle they have been able to separate a production change from the distribution change by which it is accompanied. For instance, as a result of a policy change output of Coca-Cola increases and that of whisky decreases. Now, if individual X prefers Coca-Cola but Y prefers whisky, the question whether there has occurred any increase in production is inseparably connected with the distribution of these beverages between X and Y. In many cases it is, therefore, difficult to say whether or not production has increased without considering how the output or real income is being distributed.

Moreover, Kaldor and Hicks think that the level of production is the main determinant of social welfare and the distribution a secondary one. But this is quite untenable. This is because welfare has dual aspect: absolute and relative. People are dissatisfied not only because they are poor but more because other people are very rich. If all the people would have been poor they would not have been dissatisfied very much. Thus, a lower total output equitably distributed ensures greater social welfare than larger output inequitably distributed.

Fifth, Gorman is of the opinion that Scitovsky's double criterion can avoid contradictory results only when the choice is to be made from only two positions. This criterion does not help us if the choice of a position is to be made from more than two possible positions. Moreover, Prof. Samuelson refers to a more basic drawback in Scitovsky's double criterion. Scitovsky's criterion is satisfied if utility possibility curve in one situation lies above the utility possibility curve of the other situation in the ***neighborhood of both actual observed points.*** But Samuelson asserts that "the complete test for an increase in welfare requires the utility possibility curve after the change to be nowhere inside the corresponding utility possibility curve before the change and at least somewhere outside it. In other words, every welfare position attainable before the change must be attainable after together with at least one position that was not attainable before."[6]

Sixth, Prof. Baumol, Little and Arrow point out another major flaw in compensation principle that it does not envisage social welfare. This principle proves the social desirability of change in the social state on the basis of the criterion that gainers *could* compensate the losers and still be better off than before. These critics are of the opinion that policy changes which would increase social welfare when accompanied by actual compensation need not lead to improvement in social welfare if compensation is not actually made. Dr. Rothenberg has given a very good example to illustrate this. He supposes an initial social state in which a firm adopts a new invention and as a result the cost of production of the firm is reduced but it throws the competitors out of industry and the workers become unemployed. Let us suppose that the gainer firm from the invention can compensate the losers out of its increased income and still be better off. If the compensation is not actually made in the changed situation, social welfare will decrease as the welfare loss suffered by the workers rendered unemployed will be very large indeed. As a matter of fact, there is no guarantee that compensation will be actually made in such cases. Thus, so long as compensation is hypothetical, a change might make the rich richer and the poor yet poorer and therefore reduce social welfare.

It follows from above that a basic flaw in Kaldor-Hicks compensation principle is that it refers to ***potential welfare rather than actual welfare*** since it does not envisage that compensation should be actually made. In the absence of actual compensation one cannot say whether or not actual social welfare has increased as a result of a certain policy change unless

5. *Op. cit.* p. 530.

6. P. A. Samuelson, *Oxford Economic Papers,* January 1950.

one is prepared to make some value judgements. Therefore, making value judgements, especially that concerns distribution of income or welfare, is quite indispensable in welfare economics. And economists should not fight shy of making those value judgements which are widely accepted by the people.

It may also be noted that if compensation is actually made, then Kaldor-Hicks criterion is quite unnecessary, for in that case only Pareto criterion will be sufficient to judge the effect of a policy change on social welfare.

Seventh, ***compensation principle does not take into account the external effects*** on consumption and production. The exponents of compensation principle are of the opinion that an individual's welfare depends solely upon his own level of production and consumption and is not affected by the production and consumption activities of the others. But this is not a realistic assumption because a person's level of satisfaction (or dissatisfaction) depends to a large extent upon the consumption of goods and services by other persons. A person is more satisfied as his ***relative economic position*** in the society is improved. Thus, if an economic change leaves a person where he was before but makes some other individuals better off, he will not feel as well-off as in the original situation, that is, his level of welfare will fall. The gains by some individuals from a policy change have usually unfavourable external effects on the welfare position of those whose position is said to have remained unchanged.

Thus compensation principle has been criticised on several grounds, especially for its unacceptable implicit value judgements. Because of the above limitations of compensation criteria of Kaldor, Hicks and Scitovsky, some economists, especially Bergson, Samuelson and Arrow, have propounded a concept of social welfare function, which incorporates explicit value judgements to evaluate the welfare implications of policy changes and also to find out a unique social optimum.

QUESTIONS FOR REVIEW

1. What is compensation principle of judging change in social welfare brought about by the adoption of an economic policy ? Is compensation considered in this principle real or hypothetical ?
2. State Kaldor-Hicks criterion of judging social welfare, Explain with the help of utility possibility curve how it judges the social welfare impact of an economic policy which makes some persons better off and others worse off.
3. Show how Kaldor-Hicks criterion helps in solving the problem of indeterminacy involved in Pareto's analysis of maximisation of social welfare.
4. "Pareto criterion does not give us sufficient basis of ordering states. The Kaldor-Hicks-Scitovsky criteria do not carry us much further." Examine critically. *[B.A.(Hons)D.U. 1984]*
5. Does Kaldor-Hicks-Scitovsky criteria give us sufficient basis for ordering states from the viewpoint of social welfare? Give reasons for your answer. *[B.A. (Hons) D.U 1993]*
6. In proposing compensation criterion Kaldor and Hicks claimed that they succeeded in giving a welfare criterion which was free from value judgements. Do you agree ? Discuss.
7. In what way is Scitovsky criterion an improvement over Kaldor-Hicks criterion ? Do you agree with the view that Scitovsky criterion does not remove all the weaknesses of Kaldor-Hicks criterion? Discuss. *[B.A.(Hons) D. U. 1996]*
8. How far can Kaldor-Hicks-Scitovsky criteria be considered an improvement over Pareto's criterion of social welfare ? Discuss.
9. Show that alternative *A* being better than *B* on Kaldor-Hicks criterion does not rule out the possibility that alternative *B* is better than *A* on Kaldor-Hicks criterion.
10. "The Kaldor and Scitovsky criteria have ducked the basic problem of the interpersonal comparison of utility required to evaluate a policy change which *harms* X but *aids* Y" (Baumol). Do you agree ? Discuss.

CHAPTER

63

Grand Utility Possibility Frontier and Welfare Maximisation

Introduction

An alternative approach, which is more thorough and comprehensive, to maximization of social welfare has been recently developed.[1] It may, however, be noted at the very outset that this approach is based on Pareto-optimality analysis and the concept of social welfare function. It is more thorough and comprehensive in the sense that it approaches the problem of maximization of social welfare from the viewpoint of general equilibrium analysis and explains simultaneous determination of (*a*) the unique allocation of factors into different products, (*b*) unique output of different products and (*c*) unique distribution of products between individuals which ensure maximum social welfare. From these we draw a curve, known as *"Grand Utility Possibility Frontier"* which shows the distribution of utility or welfare between individuals, given the Pareto-efficient outputs of two products, Pareto-efficient allocation of factors into two products. But there are infinite number of points on a grand utility possibility frontier, all of which are Pareto-efficient. In order to remove the indeterminacy this approach makes use of the concept of social welfare function. Together with grand utility possibility frontier, social welfare function enables us to find a determinate and unique solution regarding maximum social welfare as well as the desired distribution of welfare between the two individuals. In this general equilibrium analysis of production, exchange and distribution of welfare, the following assumptions are generally made :

1. First, there exists a given amount of two factor endowments. These factors, say,capital (*K*) and labour (*L*), are homogeneous and perfectly divisible.
2. Two homogeneous goods are produced and the production function for each is given and remains constant. Besides, each production function is smooth (*i.e.* of continuous curve type), exhibits constant returns to scale and further that isoquants are convex to the origin, that is, marginal rate of technical substitution (*MRTS*) diminishes along any isoquant.
3. A society which comprises two individuals, *A* and *B*, each of whom has a given and constant ordinal preference function exhibited by a set of smooth indifference curves which are convex to the origin. For the sake of convenience, the levels of satisfaction or utility are measured through arbitrary numerical indices. In accordance with this, the indifference curves of each individual are labelled as *I, II, III, IV* etc.
4. A social welfare function depicting the aggregate welfare of two individuals as well as distribution of welfare (in their own preference scales) between them. The social welfare function permits a unique preference ordering among all possible states *i.e.* situations. It is worth noting that the formulation of a social welfare function requires value judgements to be made regarding the distribution of welfare between the individuals, *X* and *Y*.

1. The analysis of this approach is based upon Francis M. Bator, "The Simple Analytics of Welfare Maximization," *American Economic Review*, Vol. XLVII, 1957.

We shall now explain, step by step, how the above approach derives a Grand Utility Possibility Frontier and then with the aid of social welfare function how it arrives at a point of *"Constrained Bliss'* or maximum possible social welfare.

From Factor Endowments and Production Functions to the Production Possibility Curve

According to assumption (1) above, there are given amounts of two factors or inputs—labour and capital. Assume that the fixed amounts of these inputs are $\bar{L}$ and $\bar{K}$ respectively. These given amounts of factor endowments, $\bar{L}$ and $\bar{K}$ will determine the dimensions of the Edgeworth Box diagram redrawn in Figure 63.1 (*a*). $O_F\bar{L}$ and $O_F\bar{K}$ represent the amounts of labour and capital available in the economy and these are measured along the X and Y axes respectively in the Edgeworth box drawn in Fig 63.1 (*a*), Thus the space covered in between these dimensions in Fig. 63.1 (*a*) represents the *input space*. I_F, II_F, III_F, IV_F, V_F are the successively higher isoquants representing successively greater output of food for which O_F is the origin. I_C, II_C, III_C, IV_C, V_C are the successively higher isoquants representing successively greater output of cloth for which O_C is the origin. It will be seen from Figure 63.1 (*a*) that Q_1, Q_2, Q_3, Q_4, and Q_5 are the tangency points of the isoquants of food and cloth.The curve O_FO_C is the locus of these tangency points of the isoquants and therefore represents production contract curve. As explained in a previous chapter, each point on this contract curve represents Pareto-optimal allocation of factors in the production of food and cloth, since marginal rate of technical substitution between two factors is the same at the tangencies represented by the contract curve O_FO_c.

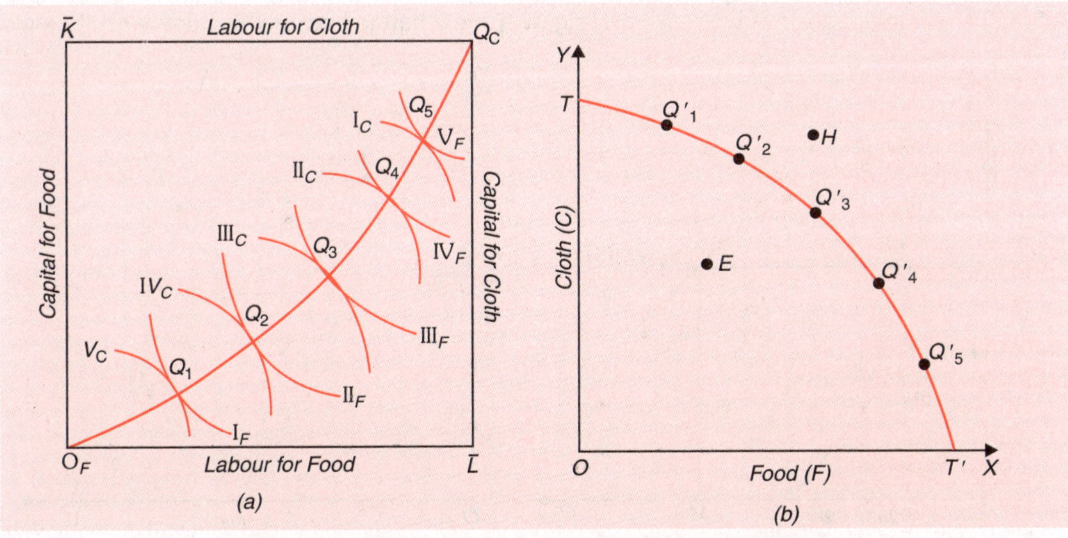

Fig. 63.1. *Derivation of Production Possibility Frontier*

Now, by mapping the production contract curve O_FO_C from input space into output space, we can obtain the production possibility curve. This is done in Figure 63.1 (*b*) where the two axes represent the outputs of two commodities—food and cloth. As we move up on the contract curve O_FO_C, in Fig. 63.1(*a*), the output of food increases whereas the output of cloth decreases. Corresponding to point Q_1 representing the output levels of food and cloth as given by their isoquants I_F and V_C respectively in the input space, we plot the point Q'_1 in the output space in Figure 63.1 (*b*). Likewise, corresponding to the points, Q_2, Q_3, Q_4 and Q_5 of the contract curve O_FO_C in the input space ot Figure 63.1 (*a*) we plot the points Q'_2, Q'_3, Q'_4 and Q'_5, respectively in the output space in Figure 63.1 (*b*). By joining these points Q'_1,

Q'_2, Q'_3, Q'_4 etc. in the output space we get the curve TT' in Figure 63.1 (*b*) which is called the production possibility frontier or the transformation curve. Production possibility frontier depicts the various combinations of two commodities (food and cloth) which are capable of being produced with a given resource endowment.

Any combination of outputs of two commodities lying outside the production possibility frontier such as point *H* in Fig. 63.1 (*b*) is unattainable since to produce such a level of output a larger resource endowment will be needed. On the other hand, any combination of outputs of the two commodities lying inside the production possibility frontier such as point *E* in Fig. 63.1 (*b*) is Pareto-inoptimal, since it would imply a needless sacrifice of commodities due to the underutilization or unemployment of available resource endowment. Therefore, a society which seeks to maximize social welfare will try to achieve an equilibrium position on its production possibility frontier.

It is noteworthy that the slope of the production possibility frontier represents the marginal rate of transformation (*MRT*) between two commodities. In other words, the slope of the production possibility curve indicates how much additional cloth can be produced when some factors are transferred from food production to cloth production, given that factors are optimally reallocated so as to satisfy Pareto condition for factor substitution.

From the Production Possibility Curve to the Grand Utility Possibility Frontier

Next step in the present approach is to derive a "grand" utility posibility frontier from the production possibility frontier. On the production possibility curve let us select a point Q_3 which represents O_AM output of food and O_AN output of cloth in Fig. 63.2 (*a*). Taking O_AM and O_AN as the dimensions we make an Edgeworth exchange box. In this Edgeworth box we

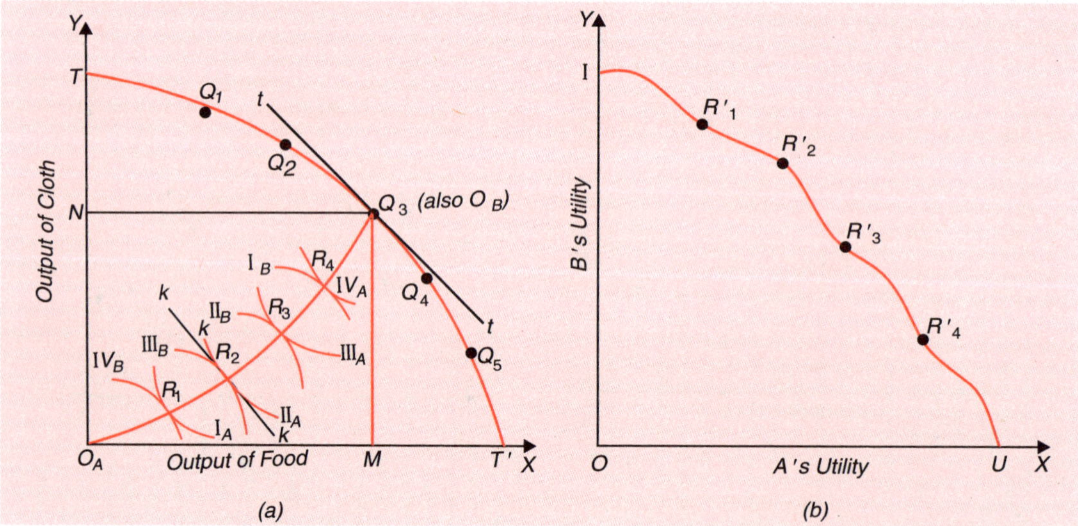

Fig. 63.2. *Derivation of Utility Possibility Curve from Production Possibility Frontier*

draw the indifference curves I_A, II_A, III_A, etc. of individual *A* for whom 0_A has been taken as the origin. Point Q_3 has been taken as the origin for the individual *B* and indifference curves I_B, II_B, III_B, IV_B of individual *B* have been drawn with Q_3 as the origin. On joining the tangencies of the indifference curves of the two individuals we get the exchange contract curve O_AQ_3, which represents Pareto-optimal positions regarding the distribution of the two goods between the two individuals, since subjective marginal rates of substitution *(MRS)* of the two individuals are equal at these tangency points. As we move up from point O_A towards Q_3 on the contract curve, the individual A goes to his successively higher indifference curve and individual B to his successively lower indifference curve.

Now, the exchange contract curve which represents the Pareto-optimal distribution of the goods between two individuals in the output space can be transformed into the utility space so as to obtain the utility possibility frontier. As there will be different exchange contract curves corresponding to different points of the production possibility curve, one utility possibility curve will correspond to a particular point on the production possibility curve. How the utility possibility curve is derived from an exchange contract curve is illustrated in Fig. 63.2 (*b*) where the two axes represent the utility level of the two individuals. As mentioned above, corresponding to point Q_3 on the production possibility curve TT' the exchange contract curve is given by O_AQ_3. Now at point R_1 individual A is at the utility level I_A (measured in ordinal index) and individual B is at his utility level IV_B. Thus, corresponding to point R_1 on the contract curve in the output space of Fig. 63.2 (*a*) we have plotted point R'_1 in utility space in Figure 63.2 (*b*). Likewise, corresponding to point R_2 in the commodity output space in Figure 63.2 (*a*), we plot the point R'_2 in the utility space in Figure 63.2 (*b*). Similarly, R'_3 and R'_4 are plotted in the utility space corresponding to the points R_3 and R_4 in the commodity space. By joining points R'_1, R'_2, R'_3 etc. we get the utility possibility curve in Fig. 63.2(*b*) corresponding to the exchange contract curve O_AQ_3 in Fig. 63.2(*a*) which in turn corresponds to output combination represented by point Q_3 on the given production possibility frontier $T'T'$.

We can take other points such as Q_1, Q_2, Q_4, Q_5 of the production possibility curve $T'T'$ in Fig. 63.2 (*a*) and determine the different contract curves corresponding to the different points (output combinations) of the production possibility curve. In this way we will get a number of utility possibility curves corresponding to different points of the production possibility curve.

It may be noted that a single utility possibility curve corresponding to an exchange contract curve such as the curve IU in Fig 63.2 (*b*), alone does not help us much in obtaining the solution for maximum social weltare, as it shows an infinite number of utility pairs of two individuals corresponding to infinite number of tangency points on a given exchange contract curve. But the principle that for general equilibrium to be reached, marginal rate of transformation between goods (*MRT*) should be equal to the marginal rate of substitution (*MRS*) between them of individuals, helps us to remove one "infinity" dimension and get a single point on a utility possibility curve which is relevant to a given exchange contract curve. Now, a glance at Figure 63.2 (*a*) will reveal that the marginal rate of transformation in production at point Q_3 is given by the slope of length *tt*. It will be further seen that the tangent *kk* drawn at the tangency point R_2 on the contract curve O_AQ_3 is parallel to the tangent *tt*. As the slope of tangent drawn to the indifference curves indicates the subjective marginal rate of substitution (*MRS*) *of* the individuals, it follows that at point R_2 on the contract curve the marginal rate of substitution between food (*F*) and cloth *C* of the two individuals which are equal to each other are also equal to the marginal rate of transformation in production. Thus, at point R_2 in Figure 63.2 (*a*) and R'_2 in 63.2 (*b*).

$$MRT_{FC} = MRS^A{}_{FC} = MRS^B{}_{FC}$$

Thus it is only one point R'_2 on the utility possibility curve which is relevant, for it is only this which satisfies the Pareto condition that marginal rate of transformation in production must be equal to the subjective marginal rate of substitution of the individuals. Likewise, other utility possibility curves corresponding to different contract curves formed relative to different points on the production possibility curve can be drawn and different optimal points (a single optimum point on each utility possibility curve) on them which satisfy the condition of equality of marginal rate of transformation with subjective marginal rates of substitution can be determined. By joining such relevant points of the various utility possibility curves, we get what is called "Grand Utility Possibility Frontier" each point of which indicates utility possibility point corresponding to a given point on the production possibility frontier, given that the equality of marginal rate of transformation in production with the marginal rate of substitution is satisfied. In Fig. 63.3 we have shown only two utility possibility curves *IU* and *I′U′* at which P'_2 and R'_2 are the relevant utility possibility points respectively which satisfy the condition of equality of marginal rate of transformation with the subjective marginal rate of substitution between them. Grand utility possibility curve *VV′* (thick curve) which connects these optimal, relevant utility possibility points which satisfy Pareto optimal conditions of factor substitution, exchange and production.

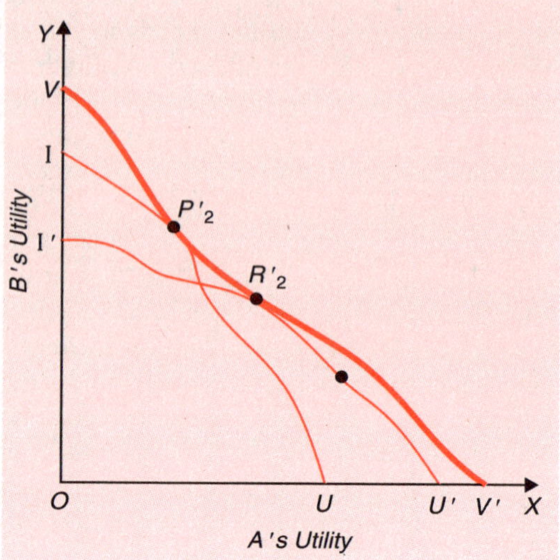

Fig. 63.3. *Grand Utility Possibility Frontier*

Thus, as the output-mix is different at different points on a production possibility curve, at each point of the production possibility curve separate Edgeworth exchange box will be constructed and separate contract curve will be generated. Each contract curve will yield a separate utility possibility curve on which there will be a single optimal point which satisfies the equality of unique marginal rate of transformation with the subjective marginal rate of substitution. In this way we derive a grand utility possibility frontier each point of which represents *(a)* unique combination of utility levels of two individuals associated with *(b)* unique distribution of output of commodities between the two individuals corresponding to (c) equality between the marginal rate of transformation and marginal rate of substitution of food for cloth, *(d)* a particular combination of outputs of food and cloth on a given production possibility curve and further that *(e)* each combination of outputs of food and cloth represents a unique allocation of factor endowments between the production of food and cloth.

We thus see that a lot of Pareto optimality analysis is involved in deriving a grand utility possibility frontier. But even a grand utility possibility frontier does not provide us with a single determinate solution for maximization of social welfare, since there are infinite number of points on this frontier which are all Pareto optimal. Therefore, in order to provide a determinate solution, this approach makes use of the concept of social welfare function.

From the Grand Utility Possibility Frontier to the Point of Constrained Bliss

Social welfare function together with grand utility possibility frontier enables us to find a unique solution for the problem of maximization of social welfare. How a social welfare function is formulated will be discussed at length in the next chapter. It will be suffice to mention here that a social welfare function depends on the welfare positions of two individuals in their own preference scales. As mentioned before, the construction of social welfare function requires value judgements regarding distribution of welfare is a very difficult job unless the society is governed by a dictator. In the case of the existence of a dictator in the society, individual preference function of the dictator will be the social welfare function. We shall explain in detail in the next chapter how a social welfare function is constructed through democratic procedures and what are the difficulties involved in this. Social welfare function is generally represented by the ***social indifference curves***, each of which indicates utility combinations of two individuals which yield equal level of aggregate welfare of two individuals (*i.e.* equal social welfare). The higher the level of social indifference curve, the greater the level of social welfare.

Now let us superimpose grand utility possibility frontier on the social indifference curves representing social welfare function to find a unique optimum of maximum social welfare position. In Fig. 63.4 social indifference curves W_1, W_2, W_3 and W_4 representing the social welfare function have been combined with the grand utility possibility curve VV′. Social indifference curve W_3 and grand utility possibility frontier *VV′* are tangential to each other at point *Q*, which represents the maximum possible social welfare, given the factor endowments, state of technology and preference orders of the individuals. Point *Q* at W_3 is known as the point of *constrained bliss.* Social welfare represented by the social indifference curve W_4 is higher than W_3 but it is not possible to attain it, given the technology and factor endowments. Thus we have a unique optimum point from among a large number of Pareto optimum points on the grand utility possibility curve, at which the social welfare is the maximum. The point of constrained bliss represents the unique pattern of production of goods, unique distribution of goods between the individuals and unique combination of factors employed to produce the goods.

It is worth noting that Pareto optimal position may be inferior to non-Pareto optimal position from the point of view of social welfare. In Fig. 63.4 point *S* lies in the given grand utility possibility curve and therefore represents a Pareto optimal position. But *S* is inferior to poinr *R* which as compared to point *S* which is a non-Pareto optimal position lies on a higher social indifference curve W_2. Point *S* lies on the relatively lower social indifference curve W_t and thus represents a lower level of social welfare. *R* is a non-Pareto optimum because it lies below the grand utility possibility frontier *VV′*.

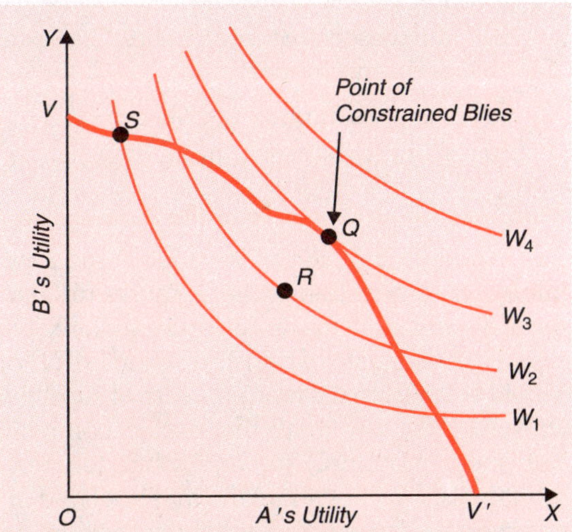

Fig. 63.4. *Maximization of Social Welfare: Point of Constrained Bliss*

Thus *R* is superior to *S* from the point of view of social welfare because anybody, who determines the social welfare function, considers *R* to be superior to *S*. Point *R* represents the distribution of utility between two individuals *A* and *B* different from the point *S*. Value judgements about the distribution of welfare between the two individuals consider position *R* superior to point *S* from the viewpoint of social welfare although *R* is not a Pareto optimum position. However, it is important to note that point *Q* of constrained bliss or maximum possible social welfare is a Pareto optimal or economically efficient and also represents the optimum distribution of welfare between the two persons given by the particular social welfare function. Thus, this ***unique solution of constrained bliss combines the value judgements about equity or distributive justice with the economic efficiency or Pareto optimality.***

CHAPTER

64

Market Failures, Externalities and Public Goods

In an earlier chapter we have seen that how perfectly competitive market ensures Pareto optimality or what is also called economic efficiency. This implies that competitive market system helps to achieve the state of maximum social welfare such that any reallocation of resources cannot make some people better off without reducing the welfare of someone else. However, under some circumstances the market system cannot lead to this optimum situation of Pareto efficiency (*i.e.* the state of maximum social welfare). These circumstances due to which market fails to achieve economic efficiency or maximum social welfare have been called *market failures*. There are three main causes of market failure. They are :

1. the existence of monopoly or imperfect competition;
2. the presence of externalities, *i.e.*, external economies and diseconomies in production and consumption; and
3. the consumption of public goods.

We shall explain below these obstacles at some length.

Monopoly as an Obstacle to the Attainment of Pareto Optimality

An important complaint against monopoly (and as a matter of fact against all forms of imperfect competition) is that it causes misallocation of productive resources and thus hinders the achievement of maximum social welfare. The crucial condition required for Pareto optimality is that marginal rate of transformation (*MRT*) of the community between any two commodities should be equal to the marginal rate of substitution (*MRS*) between these commodities of every consumer. We saw above that perfect competition satisfies this condition of Pareto optimality. But under monopoly (or any other form of imperfect competition such as oligopoly or monopolistic competition) the marginal rate of transformation of the community between two commodities is not equal to the marginal rate of substitution between them of the consumers. Consequently, monopoly does not ensure optimum allocation of resources and services as an obstacle to the attainment of maximum social welfare. The reason for this is that a monopolist does not equate price of his product with marginal cost of production; he restricts output and charges higher price than marginal cost. Assume that there are two commodities, X and Y, and further that the commodity X is being produced under conditions of monopoly whereas the commodity Y is being produced under conditions of perfect competition. Since the commodity X is being produced under conditions of monopoly, the price (P_x) of commodity X will be greater than marginal cost (MC_X) of its production. Thus, $P_x > MC_X$. But since the commodity Y is being produced under conditions of perfect competition, price (P_y) of commodity Y will be equal to its marginal cost (MC_y) of production. That is, $P_y = MC_y$.

It therefore follows that:

$$\frac{MC_x}{MC_y} < \frac{P_x}{P_y}$$

Since the ratio of marginal costs of two commodities $\left(\frac{MC_x}{MC_y}\right)$ represents the marginal rate of transformation (MRT_{xy}) between them, therefore,

$$MRT_{xy} < \frac{P_x}{P_y} \quad \text{...(i)}$$

But the consumers in order to be in equilibrium will equate their marginal rate of substitution between two commodities (MRS_{xy}) with the price ratio of the two commodities $\left(\frac{P_x}{P_y}\right)$. This is because each individual consumer will take the prices of commodities as given and constant for him. Thus, for consumers,

$$MRS_{xy} = \frac{P_x}{P_y} \quad \text{...(ii)}$$

From (*i*) and (*ii*) above it follows that under conditions of monopoly in the production of X

$$MRT_{xy} < MRS_{xy}$$

or

$$MRS_{xy} > MRT_{xy}$$

That is, when monopoly exists in the production of a commodity marginal rate of substitution between commodities will be greater than the marginal rate of transformation. In other words, consumers would like the commodity under monopoly production to be produced more but monopolists would not be producing the desired quantity of the commodity and will, therefore, be causing loss of satisfaction and misallocation of resources.

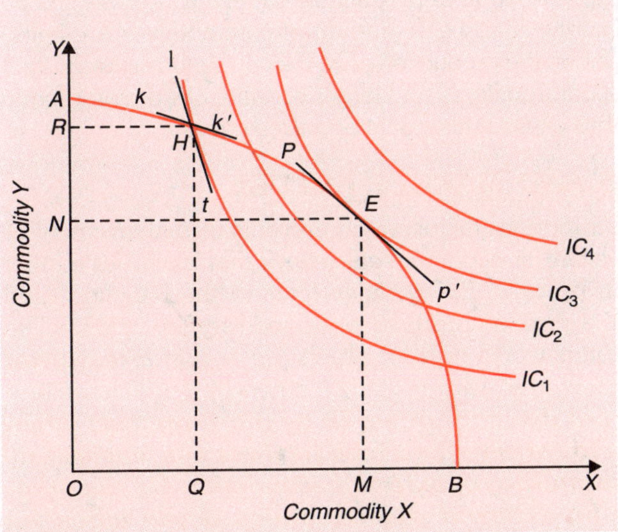

Fig. 64.1. *Monopoly as an Obstacle to Maximization of Social Welfare*

That monopoly causes loss of social welfare and misallocation of resources will become very clear by considering Figure 64.1. It will be seen from this figure that the transformation curve of the community AB is tangent to the community indifference curve IC_3 at point E. Therefore, at point E marginal rate of transformation (MRT_{xy}) of the community between two commodities is equal to the marginal rate of substitution (MRS_{xy}) of the community. Thus E represents maximum possible level of social welfare and the combination of two commodities being produced *(i.e. OM* of *X* and *ON* of *Y)* represents optimum allocation of resources. But when the commodity *X* is being produced under conditions of monopoly, the equilibrium will not be at point *E* but instead it will be at point *H*. This is because, under monopoly, producers would be equating marginal rate of transformation (*MRT*) or ratio of marginal costs $\left(\frac{MC_x}{MC_y}\right)$ with the ratio of marginal revenues $\left(\frac{MR_x}{MR_y}\right)$ and not with the ratio of prices of two goods $\left(\frac{P_x}{P_y}\right)$. Since consumers would be equating marginal rate of substitution (MRS_{xy}) with the price ratio of two goods, the marginal rate of transformation in the equilibrium position at point *H* will not be equal to the marginal rate of substitution. This is quite obvious from Figure 64.1 wnere at point *H* transformation curve *AB* and consumers' indifference curve$1C_1$ are intersecting each other. This implies that slopes of transformation curve *AB* at point *H*, which indicates marginal rate of transformation, and the slope of consumers' indifference curve IC_1 which indicates marginal rate of substitution, will not be the same. It will be observed from Figure 64.1 that at point *H* marginal rate of substitution between two goods (MRS_{xy}) *is* greater than the marginal rate of transformation *(*MRT_{xy}) between them as tangent *ll'* drawn to point *H* on indifference curve IC_1, is steeper than the tangent *kk'* drawn to point *H* on transformation curve *AB*. This means that consumers' preference is that good *X* should be produced more but because of the existence of monopoly in the production of commodity *X* it is not being produced to their desired quantity. As a result, the level of satisfaction or welfare of the consuming community is at a lower level than possible under the given production conditions. Consuming community's satisfaction will be greater at point *E* which lies on indifference IC_3 but under conditions of monopoly in the production of *X*, equilibrium is at point *H* which lies on the lower indifference curve IC_1. Thus monopoly causes loss of satisfaction or welfare. This loss of satisfaction or welfare is due to the fact that monopoly is not optimally allocating its resources to the production of commodity *X* according to the consumers' preferences. Given the transformation curve and consuming community's indifference map, the optimal production pattern is represented by the point *E* where *OM* amount of commodity *X* and *ON* amount of commodity *Y* are being produced. But under conditions of monopoly in the production of *X*, the equilibrium is established at point *H* where smaller quantity *OQ* of commodity *X* and larger quantity *OR* of commodity *Y* are being produced. Thus monopoly has caused misallocation of resources.

EXTERNALITIES AND MARKET FAILURE

The existence of externalities is an important factor which prevents the achievement of Pareto optimality (or maximum social welfare or economic efficiency), that is, causes market failure, even when perfect competition prevails. Externalities refer to the beneficial and detrimental effects of an economic unit (a firm, a consumer or an industry) on others. The beneficial externalities created by a consumer or a firm for others are known as ***external economies*** and detrimental or negative externalities imposed on others by a productive firm or a consumer are also known as ***external diseconomies. To be more precise, when an economic unit creates benefits for others for which he does not receive any payment, there exist beneficial externalities or external economies. On the other hand, detrimental externalities or external diseconomies occur when an economic unit inflicts costs on others for which he does not make any payment.***

It is noteworthy that the term externalities covers both the external economies and external diseconomies. When for a productive firm there exist external economies, that is, beneficial external effects, then the private marginal cost of the firm will be higher than the social marginal cost, since the firm will not take into account benefits external to it *(i.e.* benefits created for others). And the market price fixed on the basis of private marginal cost will not reflect the social marginal cost which will be lower when external economies occur. Similarly, when with the expansion of a firm detrimental externalities or external diseconomies occur, then the private marginal cost will be lower than the social marginal cost, since the firm will not take into account the harms it causes to other's by its activity. Thus when a firm expands its production, it increases the smoke it emits and thereby harms others health who live in the surrounding areas. The others may suffer from respiratory diseases and have to incur extra medical expenditure. Besides, living of people become quite unpleasant in the surrounding areas due to cloud of noxious fumes emitted and huge noise created. Therefore ***when a firm's activities create detrimental externalities, its private marginal cost would be lower then the social marginal cost*** as the extra external costs it imposes on others are not counted in calculating private marginal costs. Thus, when external diseconomies occur, price fixed on the basis of private marginal cost will be lower than that determined on the basis of social marginal cost.

It follows from above that ***in the absence of externalities,*** all costs incurred and all benefits received by producers and consumers will be reflected in market prices and that there will not be any divergence between private and social costs (or benefits). But, when externalities (external economies and diseconomies) occur, market prices determined on the basis of private costs and benefits will not truly reflect social costs and therefore divergence is caused between private and social costs (or benefits).

It follows from above that externalities arise primarily due to the fact that the effects regarding costs, output, employment, labour skills, technological capabilities of the activities of a producer or consumer on others or society as a whole are not reflected in market prices and therefore ***market prices do not truly reflect social costs.*** We shall give below a few examples of externalities, that is, external economies and diseconomies in production and consumption. The basic idea behind the belief that a competitive price system is optimal is based on the fact that a producer benefits himself only by benefiting the society because he makes available certain goods and services to the society. In other words, by promoting his own interests he promotes the interests of society as well. But there are so many cases in production and consumption "when members of the economy do things which benefit others in such a way that they can receive no payment in return or where their actions are detrimental to others and involve no commensurate cost to themselves."[1] Thus, due to externalities there arises the divergence between social and private costs and between social and private benefits.

Positive or Beneficial Externalities in Production

As the firm expands its scale of production, it becomes possible for the firm to produce a unit of product at a relatively lower cost due to ***internal economies*** of large-scale production. On the other hand, ***external economies*** occur when the expansion of a firm's output creates benefits, part of which goes to others. A firm may create external benefits for others in two ways : *(a)* By expanding its production, the firm may render a direct service to others such as training the labourers by its manpower training programme and thus benefit the other firms by making available skilled and trained labourers when they have to pay no cost or only nominal cost, *(b)* By expanding its production a firm may make the supply of some inputs cheaper for

1. Baumol, *op. cit.*, p. 517.

all the firms in the industry. For example, an expansion in the production of an engineering firm may increase the demand for steel. And if the steel production is subject to internal economies of large-scale production, then the expansion of steel industry following the increase in its demand will lower its cost and price. Another example of external economies is provided by the construction of a bridge or a highway which reduces transport cost and increases the land values in the neighbouring areas. Still another example of external economies of production is provided by the pumping of water from a mine. If a firm pumps out water from its mine 'A', it will lower the cost of pumping water from mine '*B*' owned by another firm. Similarly, bees of producers of honey create benefits for the owners of nearby orange groves, for the bees help pollinate oranges in the groves. On the other hand, orange groves create external economies for the honey producers since the orange groves provide nectar for the bees producing honey. In all these cases, a firm incurs costs for its own production but the benefits arising out of it are also reaped by others who pay no price for them.

Negative or Detrimental Externalities

Let us explain some external diseconomies of production. There are a good number of external diseconomies which may be created by the productive activity of a firm. The pollution of air by the factories through emitting smoke and the wastes of factories poured into streams or ocean create health hazard for men, especially those who live in the surrounding areas. For these external harms caused to the other members of the society, the firms are not required to pay any price. A factory owner pays nothing to the residents of the neighbouring colony who happen to be the victims of pollution by the factory. Another example of external diseconomies is provided by a firm or industry which has to keep more trucks on the road to do its business. This will overcrowd the road which will increase the transportation costs of other firms or industry which had to carry its own goods by trucks. The expanding firm or industry does not pay any price for the higher transport cost incurred by others.

Externalities in Consumption

Beneficial externalities or external economies in consumption arise when the consumption of a person creates beneficial effects on others. Many examples of external economies can be given. For example, the satisfaction of a telephone owner increases with the increase in the number of telephone owners because he can now contact a larger number of persons on telephone. Likewise, if a person maintains a beautiful garden or lawn, he not only raises his own satisfaction but also that of others, especially his neighbours who also enjoy the look of his garden or lawn. Similarly, when a person maintains his car in such a way that it is quite safe to drive it and also does not emit any smoke, it will also improve others' safety and health and therefore welfare. In this category, we may also include the expenditure incurred by the parents on educating their sons. This will not only benefit them and their sons but also other members of the society. This is because the education makes a person civilised and better citizen and therefore whoever comes in contact with him, derives satisfaction from him. Thus, in the presence of external economies in consumption the social utility exceeds the private utility and therefore divergence between social and private benefits is caused when external economies in consumption prevail.

On the contrary, detrimental externalities or external diseconomies of consumption occur when a person's consumption creates unfavourable impact on other consumers. A good example of it is provided by the conspicuous consumption of a person who through demonstration effect causes a lot of dissatisfaction to his friends and neighbourers who now feel themselves inferior to him. Likewise, when a person purchases candy bars for his children it will make his neighbouring children unhappy because their parents cannot afford to buy these for them. Likewise, loud music played by your neighbour may disturb you and cause a lot of dissatisfaction. Also falls in this category the purchasing of a new Maruti SX4 car by your friend because now your Maruti 800 in your own eyes becomes old. More examples of such external diseconomies of consumption can be given.

HOW EXTERNALITIES CAUSE MARKET FAILURE

The existence of beneficial and detrimental exernalities, that is, external economies and diseconomies explained above play a significant role in determining the activities of production and consumption in the economy. A pertinent question is how these externalities can lead to the misallocation of resources and thereby act as an obstacle to the attainment of Pareto optimality and thus causes market failure to achieve maximum social welfare. When externalities in production and consumption prevail and as a result divergence is caused between private and social costs and between private and social benefits, the economy guided by the market prices alone, even when perfect competition prevails, will fail to achieve optimum allocation of resources (or, in other words, result in failure of market to attain maximum social welfare). When external economies, that is, beneficial externalities occur in production, private marginal cost will be greater than the social marginal cost and when external diseconomies in production are present, private marginal cost will be lower than social marginal cost.

Under these circumstances therefore a firm which creates external benefits for others will not produce its product to the extent social interest requires. This is because equating price with the private marginal cost, which is higher than the social marginal cost will result in under-production of the product. Thus in this case of the existence of external economies in production, output of the product determined on the basis of private marginal cost, will be less than the socially optimal level of output. This is illustrated in Figure 64.2 where *SS* represents the supply curve for the product of the industry which has been obtained by summing up the private marginal cost curves of firms. Due to the existence of external economies (beneficial

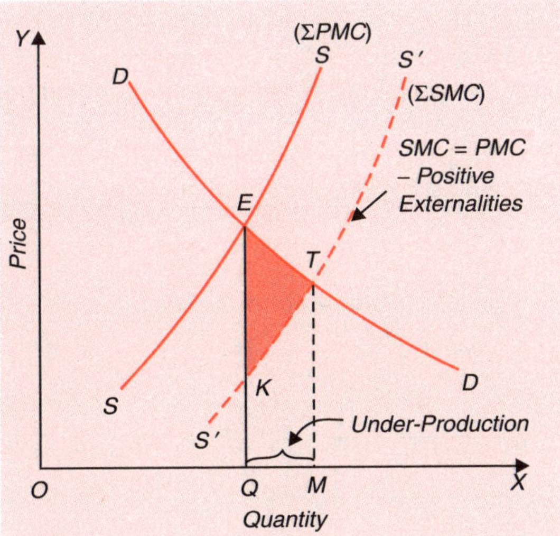

Fig. 64.2. *Positive or Beneficial Externalities Cause less than Socially Optimum Output.*

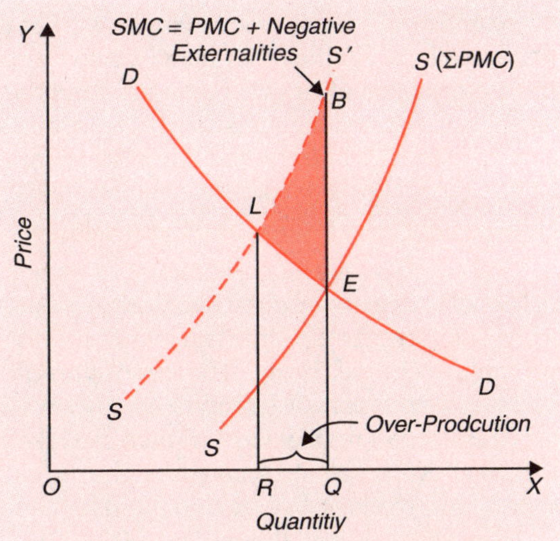

Fig. 64.3. *Negative Externalities Cause more than Pareto Optimal Output.*

externalities) marginal social cost will be smaller than the private marginal costs. Therefore, the supply curve *S′S′* (dotted) of the product reflecting social marginal cost will be lower than the supply curve *SS* based on private marginal costs. The supply curve reflecting social cost is lower because it takes into account external economies generated by the production in the industry, while private cost does not take into account these beneficial externalities. It will be seen from Figure 64.2 that the given demand curve *DD* and the supply curve *SS*, based upon the private marginal cost of production, intersect at point E and thus determine OQ as the actual amount of the product produced. But the socially optimum output is OM at which the supply curve $S'S'$ reflecting social marginal cost intersects the given demand curve. It is thus evident that the product is being produced in smaller quantity than the socially optimum output OM. Thus the ***existence of external economies (beneficial externalities) results in under-production and loss of social welfare equal to the area ETK.***

On the other hand, when there exist negative externalities (that is, detrimental externalities) in production, private marginal cost will be lower than the social marginal cost since the former will not take into account costs or harms imposed on others. Therefore, when external diseconomies are present, equating price with private marginal cost will result in over-production of the product, that is, more than socially optimum output will be produced. This also represents market failure and is illustrated in Figure 64.3. It will be seen that the supply curve SS based on private marginal costs intersects the demand curve at point E and thus determines OQ amount of output. Supply $S'S'$ (dotted) which takes into account external diseconomies and therefore reflects social cost lies at a higher level and intersects the demand curve at point L and therefore socially optimum output will be OR. Thus, it follows ***when detrimental externalities (negative externalities) in production are present, equating price with private marginal cost will result in over-production of the product, that is, more than socially optimum output will be produced and will cause loss of social welfare equal to the area ELB.***

Externalities in Consumption and Market Failure

When there are external economies in consumption, then the demand curve tor the product determined on the basis of private marginal utility will be lower than that based on social marginal utility, for the former will fail to reflect the external economies in consumption being generated. Therefore, in this case too output determined on the basis of private marginal utility and demand will result in lower output than the socially optimum level that is, will cause market failure. On the other hand, when there exist external diseconomies in consumption the private marginal utility will be higher than the social marginal utility, since the former will not take into account the external diseconomies. As a result, when external diseconomies in consumption are present, the output determined on the basis of private marginal utility (benefit) will be more than the socially optimum level and therefore represents market failure.

Government Intervention and Externalities

Where there are a good amount of external benefits or external costs, the Government intervenes to take appropriate measures to promote social well-being. The imposition of taxes and provision of subsidies are the two important measures that Government can take to tackle the problems created by the presence of externalities. We explain them below.

Taxation. When there is excess production by firms due to the *creation of negative externalities*, for example, pollution of environment by 'firm' or industry by their productive activity the Government can impose per unit tax so that private marginal cost (*PMC*) curve inclusive of per unit tax shifts above to the level of social marginal cost (*SMC*) so that equilibrium of the firm is at optimum level of output. Consider Fig. 64.4 with detrimental

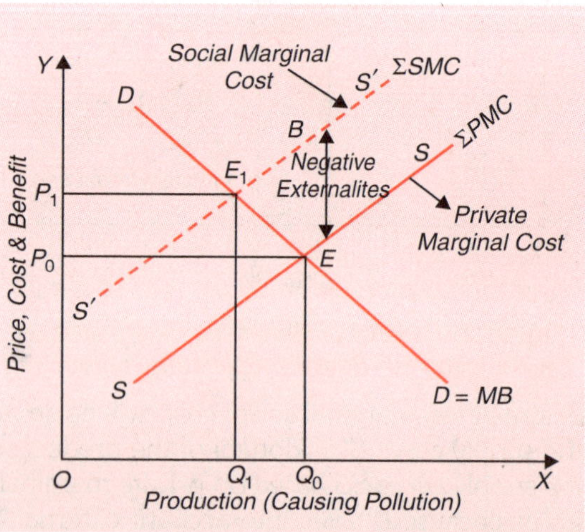

Fig. 64.4. *Imposition of Tax on the Production of Polluting Industry to Achieve Optimal Level of Output*

external effects of creating pollution the industry produces *OQ* output at which supply curve *SS* based on private marginal costs of the firms cuts demand curve *DD* reflecting marginal benefits (MB) at point *E* and is producing output Q_1Q_0 more than the optimal level. If the Government imposes per unit tax equal to *EB*, private marginal cost (*PMC*) of the firms shown by the supply curve *SS* will shift up and conincide with social marginal cost curves *SMC* shown by the supply curve *S′S′* (dotted). With this tax per unit, the industry will be in equilibrium at point E_1 where supply cruve *S′S′* cuts the demand curve *DD* and produces optimum output level *OQ*. In this way taxation solves the problem of over-production in case of negative externalities and ensures efficient level of output.

Provision of Subsidies. On the other hand, to promote social well-being and achieve Pareto optimum level of output the Government provides subsidies to those activities which are believed to generate external benefits. That is, positive externalities. Thus education is subsidised by the Government not only because it creates equal opportunities for all people of a country but also because it generates positive or beneficial externalities. For example, it has been found that educated people commit less crimes, an external benefit so that the Government has to spend less on prevention of crime. Besides, the academic research which is a byproduct of the education system, benefits all people when it discovers useful things for them and also makes significant contribution to economic growth. If education is provided by profit-making enterprises, its private marginal cost will be greater than social marginal cost and it will be produced les than the optimal level as shown in Fig. 64.5 where without any subsidy *OQ* level of output is produced which is less than the optimal level *OM*. If Government provides subsidy per unit equal to *EK*, the supply curve will shift below to the level of *S′S′* (dotted) so that the industry now produces socially optimal output *OM* at which supply curve *S′S′* based on social marginal cost (*SMC*) cuts the demand curve *DD*.

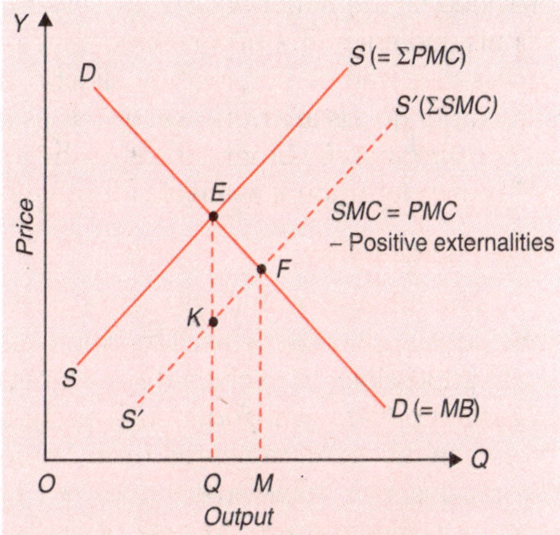

Fig. 64.5. *Provision of subsidies in case of Positive externalities to achieve Efficient level of output*

PUBLIC GOODS AND MARKET FAILURE

The existence of public goods provides us another important source of market failure.Public goods though socially valuable but, for reasons explained below, they cannot be supplied by private sector companies. It is due to the possession of certain properties by public goods that makes it difficult if not impossible for the markets to achieve pareto optimality or economic efficiency. Two essential characteristics of public goods are that they are ***non-rival* and *non-exclusive in consumption***. Let us explain these characteristics of public goods in some details.

Non-Rivalry in Consumption

In order to explain what are non-rival goods, it is better to know first what are *rival goods*. A rival good is one of which when one unit is consumed by an individual, that very unit cannot be consumed by another. For example, if Rekha consumes an apple, any other person, say Karishma, cannot eat the same very apple. Of course, Karishma can get another apple for her consumption from the market by paying a price for it. Similarly, if Amit drinks Pepsi Cola, Bela cannot drink the same very pack of Pepsi Cola, that is, two individuals cannot consume the same very Pepsi Cola; its consumption by one individual excludes others to consume it. Thus goods like apples, Pepsi Cola, shirts, machines and several such other goods, the consumption of which reduce their availability for other persons, are called rival goods. Rival goods cannot be public goods, they are private goods.

On the other hand, public goods are non-rival in consumption. National defence, parks, television signals, flood control project, pollution control project, lighthouse in the sea are some examples of public goods. Thus all persons of a nation can enjoy (consume) equally the security provided by the national defence system. All persons of a city can benefit from the television signals and enjoy the programme telecast. The enjoyment provided by a park, if there is free access to it, can be obtained by all who visit it. National defence, parks, television signals and such other goods are non-rival goods as their consumption by one individual does not exclude its consumption by others. That is, the consumption of a non-rival good by an individual does not reduce its amount available for others to consume. To conclude, public goods are non-rival.

Non-Excludability

The other essential characteristic of a public good is non-excludability in distribution of their consumption benefits. This non-exclusive nature of a public good implies that it is difficult, if not impossible, to exclude those from consuming them who are not willing to pay for them. In case of private rival goods such as shirts, cars, Pepsi Cola, apples, those who do not pay for them can be easily prevented from consuming them or receiving benefits from them because the producer or seller simply does not provide them these goods, if they have not paid their price. On the contrary, in case of public goods, either it is not possible or it is very costly to prevent those people who do not pay for these goods. We will explain later that it is due to the feature of non-excludiability of public goods that accounts for the failure of market in case of these goods to ensure Pareto efficiency.

For example, national defence is a public good and is provided to all members of a society and its benefits are available to all equally irrespective of whether some people pay taxes for it or not. It is difficult if not impossible to exclude those people from receiving benefits of security provided by national defence system who do not pay for it. Likewise, if a lighthouse is constructed in a sea, it provides light for all the ships whether any one of them pays for it or not and it is not possible to prevent those who do not pay from receiving light from the light-house. This inability to exclude those who do not pay for receiving benefits also applies in case of other public goods such as television signals, pollution control project to provide clear air, flood control projects, parks etc.

Free - Rider's Problem and Public Goods

It is easy to show how non-excludiability of a public good can lead to market failure, that is, failure of market to achieve Pareto efficiency. As explained above, non-excludiability of public goods arises because producers are not able to prevent those from consuming or enjoying benefits from these goods who do not pay their share of cost. There is a problem called a ***free-rider's problem*** which states that because people cannot be excluded from consuming public goods or enjoying benefits from them, there is incentive for persons in these situations to free ride and try to enjoy benefits from reduced pollution, parks, television signals, light house without paying for them. These persons want to get something for nothing and rely on others to make purchases of public goods whose benefits they will also automatically get.

Due to this free-rider problem or inability of producers of public goods to prevent those who do not pay for receiving benefits from them that a profit-maximising firm will either not produce a public good or produce too little of it. This creates economic inefficiency or Pareto non-optimality. Let us take an example of this free-rider's problem in case of public goods leading to economic inefficiency. Suppose the construction of a dam to check floods which cause a lot of damage in a city is required. This dam when built will protect equally all people of the city from the damages due to floods. However, some people of the city would not like to pay for the dam with the hope that others would pay for it and they because of non-excludability would also enjoy its benefits. But in view of this incentive to free ride, adequate revenue to cover costs of building the dam cannot be provided and, therefore, no private entrepreneur would consider it worthwhile to construct the dam to control floods. Similarly, the production of other public goods such as lighthouse, television signals, pollution abatement projects would not be extended to the socially desirable level in view of the non-excludability and incentive to free ride.

Public Goods and Pareto Efficiency

Before explaining further how the free-rider's problem results in less than socially optimal production of public goods, it is important to understand how Pareto optimal level of production of public good is determined. Because public goods are non-rival in consumption, some modifications are required in formulation of Pareto optimality conditions. To illustrate the conditions of Pareto optimality in case of public goods we take the case of a society composed of two persons *A* and *B* and the public good is the pollution control project aimed to clean air which if produced would benefit both of them. But the two persons may not perceive to receive the same amount of marginal benefits from this pollution control measure. In other words, they may have different evaluation of the marginal benefits of pollution control measure. Each person will place some value on the pollution control. The marginal benefits they obtain or values they place on the different quantities of pollution abatement are depicted in Figure 64.6. Due to differences in tastes or perceptions of two individuals, the curve showing their marginal benefits from the pollution-free air are different, the curves MB_A and MB_B depict the marginal benefits obtained by individuals *A* and *B* respectively from the varying quantities of pollution-free air.

The marginal benefit curve can also be interpreted as the price which the individuals are willing to pay for the different quantities of pollution-free air. Thus, it will be seen from the marginal benefit curves that individual *A* will be willing to pay price Q_1A_1 for OQ_1 quantity of pollution-free air, whereas individual *B* is willing to pay Q_1B_1 for the same OQ_1 quantity of the pollution-free air. Similarly, for OQ_2 quantity of the pollution-free air, the individual *A* is wiling to pay price equal to Q_2A_2 and individual *B* is willing to pay price equal to Q_2B_2. Therefore, the marginal benefit curves can be interpreted as the demand curves of the individuals for pollution-free air. It should also be noted that the marginal benefits or the price which the individuals are willing to pay depend on the values they place on the different quantities of the pollution-free air.

In order to determine the Pareto-optimal quantity of pollution-free air we need the total market demand curve or the aggregate marginal benefit curve of the individuals comprising the society. Market demand curve for a public good cannot be obtained in the way market demand curve is obtained in case of private goods. Since a private good is rival in consumption, the market demand curve of it is obtained by adding up sideways *(i.e.* horizontal addition) of the demand curves (i.e. marginal benefit curves) of the two individuals. But, as explained above, public goods are non-rival in consumption, that is, in case of public goods same units of output can be consumed by various people at the same time. Therefore, different individuals can pay for the same units of a public good at the same time. Thus, a pollution control project renders the air of a town free of pollution to some degree from which everybody in the town is benefited and should pay for it. Consider Figure 64.6, where it will be seen that individual A is prepared to pay price Q_1A_1 for OQ_1 quantity of pollution-free air and the individual B is prepared to pay price Q_1B_1 for the *same* OQ_1 quantity of pollution-free air which he enjoys or consumes at the same time as individual A. Thus, for OQ_1 quantity of clean air, the total price which the two individuals are willing to pay equals $Q_1A_1 + Q_1B_1 = Q_1M$. Similarly, for the same OQ_2 quantity of pollution-free air, individual A is prepared to pay price equal to Q_2A_2, and individual B is prepared to pay price equal to Q_2B_2. Thus, the total price which the individuals together are willing to pay for the same OQ_2 quantity of the good is equal to the sum of these two prices, *i.e.* $Q_2A_2 + Q_2B_2 = Q_2N$. It therefore follows that in case of a public good market demand curve is derived by summing up *vertically* the demand curves of the individuals because each individual consumes the same units of the good at the same time.

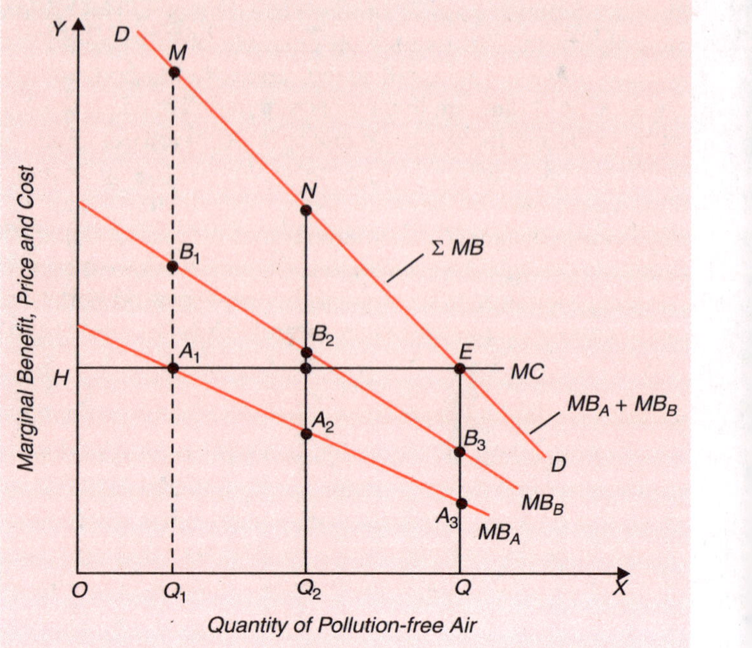

Fig. 64.6. *Public Good, Pareto Optimum and Market Failure*

Having now obtained the market demand curve of a public good we can now show what will be the Pareto-efficient output of a public good. In this connection it should be noted that a society has to bear the costs it incurs on labour and materials to produce pollution-free air. Pareto-efficient output is determined at a level at which price the individuals together are willing to pay for the good (that is, aggregate benefit), equals the marginal cost of production. Suppose the marginal cost of production is equal to OH per unit and remains constant. In Figure 64.6, with OH as the constant marginal cost, MC is the marginal cost curve. It will be observed from the figure that price which the two individuals together are willing to pay equals marginal cost (MC) at OQ quantity of pollution-free air. As said above, price which the persons are willing to pay indicates the aggregate marginal benefit. Thus, aggregate marginal benefit and marginal cost of production are equal at OQ level of output of pollution-free air. If resources are allocated to the pollution control project to the extent that OQ quantity of pollution-free air is produced at which price (marginal benefit) equals marginal cost incurred, the social welfare (*i.e.*, the aggregate benefits of the two individuals) will be maximum. Thus OQ is Pareto-efficient level of output of the public good.

How Public Goods Cause Market Failure

But a private firm will produce Pareto optimum output ***OQ only if each individual pays a price equal to the marginal benefit.*** At OQ output marginal benefit of pollution-free air is QA_3 for individual A and QB_3 for individual B. If both are willing to pay prices equal to these marginal benefits, the aggregate price per unit which they together will pay for

Pareto-efficient quantity OQ amounts to OH or $QE = QA_3 + QB_3$. In this way total revenue collected by the private firm will cover the cost of pollution control project which cleans the air and therefore will be worthwhile for the private firm to undertake the pollution control project.

But, as explained above, due to inability of the producer of a public good to exclude those who do not pay and want to be free-riders, the costs of optimal level of output cannot be covered by a private producer. Therefore, in this situation too little or even none of the public good will be produced though the marginal benefits of additional units *(i.e.,* the value the individuals place on these additional units) exceeds the social marginal costs of producing these units. Thus, private production and functioning of market in case of public good do not lead to Pareto efficiency in the provision of public goods.

It may be further noted that in case of two individuals composing a society, there may not be much problem for an individual trying to be a free-rider because of his being constantly watched and pressured, but in the real world a society consists of *many* persons. There is incentive to the persons for misrepresenting the values they place *(i.e.* the benefits they receive) on public goods such as national defence, pollution control project, flood control programme, television signals, and apparently claiming that they have little interest in the provision of these public goods. Since a large number of individuals are involved, each one is likely to think that his not paying for the public good will not make much difference to the overall revenue and the public good will be produced and he will be able to enjoy its benefits without making any contribution. This, of course, would be true if one individual tries to be a free-rider. But, as is likely the case, if many individuals and may even all of them thinking in a similar way try to be free riders, then as explained above in Figure 64.4 enough revenue cannot be collected to cover the cost of production of a public good. In this situation there will be no production of a public good at all, at least its Pareto optimal quantity would not be produced. Thus the production of highly important and useful public goods such as national defence, pollution control project, flood control project, television signals may not be undertaken at all if we rely on private sector and market. This is a glaring example of the market failure.

An interesting way of explaining market failure to achieve Pareto efficiency in case of public goods is to emphasise that marginal cost of allowing a person to consume the public good is zero *once it is produced,* even if it is possible to prevent him from consuming the commodity. Thus, parks, television signals, flood control projects etc. having been produced, the cost of letting additional consumers to consume these goods or their services is zero. For example, within good limits a visitor to a public park who has not paid is not to affect the enjoyment of the park by those who have paid for it, and it costs the society or a private producer nothing for this additional person visiting the park and enjoying (consuming) it. In fact he would be made better off and no one would be worse off because no more resources of the society are used when the additional person is allowed to enjoy the park (*i.e.* marginal cost is zero). Now, if the marginal cost of permitting additional persons to consume the good is zero, then Pareto efficiency requires that price of the public good should be zero. But the total cost of production of public goods is not zero; to produce public good is indeed very expensive. To meet these total costs of production private producer sets a positive price to cover cost. Consequently, price set will be higher than marginal cost and less than Pareto-optimal quantity will be consumed. Thus production of a public good by the private sector does not lead to Pareto-optimality in allocation of the good. In other words, market fails to achieve Pareto efficiency.

In view of the private sector not undertaking the production of public goods due to non-profitability, the government produces their optimum output and finance them through imposing taxes on the people.

THEORY OF THE SECOND BEST

We have explained in an earlier chapter that satisfaction of Pareto criterion and the marginal conditions of Pareto optimality lead to economic efficiency or maximum social welfare. Applying the Pareto criterion and marginal conditions we found that movement from a point inside the production possibility frontier to a point on it will increase social welfare. In this chapter we have explained above that due to the existence of monopoly or imperfections in some markets or in case of externalities and public goods all marginal conditions of Pareto optimality are not fulfilled.

Now, a pertinent question has been raised by Profs. Lipsey and Lancaster in their theory of second best[2]. According to them, if it is not possible to satisfy *all* conditions of Pareto efficiency (or if it is not possible to satisfy these conditions in all markets) and consequently best solution, that is, maximum social welfare situation is unattainable, whether or not efforts should be made to achieve the *second best* position by satisfying the remaining marginal conditions of Pareto optimum or satisfying these conditions in the remaining markets if in some markets they are not fulfilled. In their theory of second best they assert that this second best solution will not lead to the increase in social welfare. Let us give a concrete example. Suppose a monopoly exists in one market and Government takes steps to make this market competitive, *it would appear* that social welfare will increase (as price and marginal cost will be equated in this market) irrespective of whether in *some other markets* competition cannot be enforced and therefore in them Pareto optimal conditions cannot be satisfied. According to the second best theory, this will not lead to the increase in social welfare. That is, the second best solution is not desirable.

The formal proof of the second best theorem is a bit complicated and difficult. Therefore, we will present their argument with its graphic representation. Consider Figure 64.5 where production possibility frontier PP' has been drawn on which all points are Pareto-efficient. According to Lipsey and Lancaster, it is sometimes better to move *inside* to the production possibility curve to achieve a higher level of social welfare in case all marginal conditions are not satisfied. To demonstrate this, social welfare curves (also called community indifference curves) have also been drawn in Figure 64.7 like the indifference curves of the individual. These social welfare curves represent combinations of two products X and Y which yield the same level of welfare to the society. Further, the higher the level of a social welfare curve, the higher the level of social welfare. It will be seen from Figure 64.5 that point H at which social welfare curve is tangent to the production possibility curve PP' shows the maximum social welfare point satisfying all the

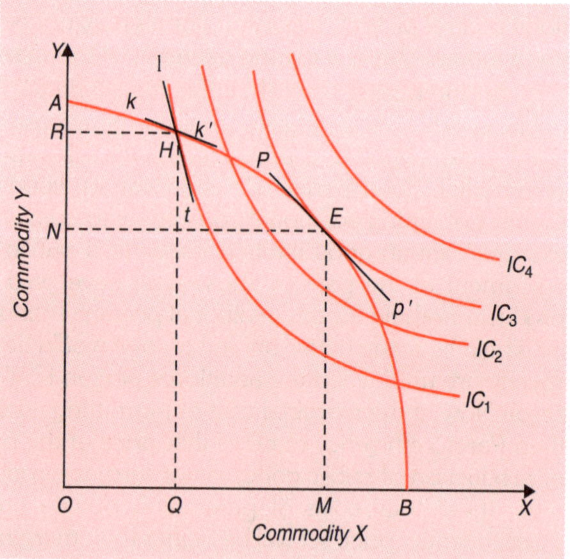

Fig. 64.7. *Graphic Demonstration of the Theory of Second Best*

2. R.G. Lipsey, and Kelvin Lancaster, The General Theory of Second Best, *Review of Economic Studies*, Vol. 24, 1956-57, pp. 11-32.

marginal conditions of Pareto-optimality. Now, suppose due to the existence of monopoly in the markets for two goods, the socially best point H is unattainable. Further suppose that due to the existence of monopolies only combinations lying on the line CC' are attainable. Suppose the economy is at present at point L on the attainable line CC'. Now, if Pareto optimality is to be achieved we can move from a point L which is inside the production possibility curve to point A or B on production possibility curve pp' which are also on the attainable line CC'. However, as will be seen from the figure, moving to point A or B on the production possible curve would put us on a lower social welfare curve W_1. If instead we move from point L to the point E which is *interior* to the production possibility curve PP' which is therefore Pareto-inefficient but yields a higher level of welfare (as indicated by social welfare curve W_2.) as compared to the point L. Thus, the theory of second best asserts that when one of the marginal conditions for Pareto optimality is not satisfied (in the present example, the existence of monopoly does not satisfy the condition of optimum direction of production, namely, MRS_{xy} is not equal to MRT_{xy}), it may be better to violate other marginal conditions of Pareto optimality to achieve maximum possible social welfare.

The theory of the second best has been used to question the desirability of advocating competitive pricing in ***some particular markets*** when it is known that Pareto conditions do not hold in other markets. However, the supporters of such piecemeal policies in making some markets more competitive for achieving Pareto optimality argue that as the markets in questions are unrelated, it does not matter for attaining maximum social welfare that in other markets conditions for Pareto efficiency are not fulfilled. Advocates of the latter policy argue that *when markets are relatively independent or unrelated, marginal cost pricing increases* social welfare. Thus, "the theory of second best applies most strongly when markets are closely related : that is, they either produce complementary goods like bread and butter, or one market is an intermediate supplier of another as in the case of tyre makers supplying automobile producers"[3].

QUESTIONS FOR REVIEW

1. What is meant by optimum allocation of resources ? Show that monopoly leads to misallocation of resources.
2. What are the major sources of competitive market failure ? Explain briefly in each case why the competitive market does not always operate efficiently.
3. What are public goods ? What limits the possibility of the private production of public goods ?
4. (*a*) What are the characteristics of a pure public good ?

   (*b*) What do you understand by the *free-rider problem* ? How does it lead to non-pareto optimal production in case of public goods ?
5. What is public good ? What are the economic implications of public goods ?
6. Write a note on the role of externalities and public goods in causing market failure.
7. Competitive markets fail due to market power, incomplete information, externalities and presence of public goods. Explain these concepts in support of your answer.
8. When external costs are associated with the production of some goods, should the outputs of the goods on efficiency grounds be limited to a level at which the external costs are zero ? Why or why not ?

3. S. Charles Maurice and Own R. Phillips, *Economic Analysis : Theory and Application*, Irwin, 1989.

9. Explain and graphically show that when there are external economies and diseconomies in production, market would not provide a Pareto optimum.
10. Explain the theory of second best. In which cases does it apply ?
11. What are external diseconomies ? Give some examples. Show taxes on industries or services which create external diseconomies improve economic efficiency.
12. How do externalities cause market failure ? In what ways the Government should intervenue to correct market failure.

CHAPTER

65

Social Welfare Function and Theory of Social Choice

Introduction

The concept of 'Social Welfare Function' was propounded by A. Bergson in his article *'A Reformulation of Certain Aspects of Welfare Economics'* in 1938. Prior to it various concepts of social welfare function had been given by different welfare theorists but they failed to provide a satisfactory solution to the problem of maximisation of social welfare. Bentham talked of welfare in terms of ***'the greatest happiness of the greatest number.'*** Neo-Classical welfare theorists discussed the problem of social welfare on the basis of cardinal measurability of utility and interpersonal comparison of utility. Analysis of Pareto optimality maximises social welfare by satisfying various marginal conditions of production, distribution and allocation of resources among products. But unfortunately they are not fulfilled due to the existence of various externalities and imperfections in the market. Moreover, Pareto optimality analysis fails to measure the changes in welfare resulting from any change which benefits one section of society and harms the other. Compensation principle as given by Kaldor-Hicks-Scitovsky attempts to measure the changes in social welfare resulting from such economic changes which harm some and benefit others through hypothetical compensating payments. Compensation theorists claimed to give a *value-free objective criterion* based on ordinal concept of utility but, as seen in a previous chapter, these criteria are not operationally feasible.

By providing the concept of social welfare function Bergson and Samuelson have attempted to provide a new approach to welfare economics. They have put forward the concept of social welfare function that considers only the ordinal preferences of individuals. They agree to Robbins' view that interpersonal comparison of utility involves value judgements but they assert that without making some value judgements, economists cannot evaluate the impact of changes in economic policy on social welfare. Thus, according to them, welfare economics cannot be separated from value judgements. According to them, welfare economics is essentially a normative study. But the approach to study it must be scientific despite the fact that the use of value judgements in it is unavoidable.

The Classical Social Welfare Function

Before making a detailed study of the Bergson-Samuelson's social welfare function, a brief explanation of some alternative welfare functions will be useful as it will bring out the different ethical judgements made in them. An important social welfare function was put forward by Bentham, Pigou and Marshall. According to them, social welfare is the ***sum of cardinal utilities*** obtained by all members of a society. In algebraic form, the classical social welfare function can be written as :

$$W = U_1 + U_2 + \text{.............} + U_n$$

where W denotes social welfare, U_1, U_2 etc. represent the cardinal utilities of the individual members of the society.

The goal of a society is to maximise social welfare, that is, the aggregate of the utilities of the individuals comprising the society. In the classical welfare function it is further assumed that the law of diminishing marginal utility applies to money income. Given this, maximum social welfare (utility) will be achieved if income is so distributed that marginal utility of income is equal for all individuals in the society. The neo-classical economists make further assumption that various individuals have the same tastes and therefore same capacity for satisfaction with the result that their utility functions are alike. With these assumptions, ***according to classical welfare function, maximisation of social welfare is achieved only with equal distribution of income.***

A Critique. There are many limitations of classical welfare function and is therefore not accepted by modern economists. This is for two reasons. First, classical welfare function is based on cardinal measurement of utility which has been rejected by the modern economists. In the opinion of modern economists, utility is an ordinal concept and cannot be measured cardinally. Second, classical welfare function assumes that utilities derived by individuals from consumption of goods can be compared interpersonally and can also be added up. This is also not accepted by modern economists who think that interpersonal comparison of utility is not scientific and therefore cannot be validly made. Let us elaborate on this point. Suppose Government adopts a fiscal policy which transfers income from an individual A to B so that A becomes better off and B worse off. According to neo-classical economists we can not only measure cardinally the gain in utility by A and loss in utility by B but also can compare the gain and loss of utility by the two persons. However, for making such interpersonal comparison of utility value judgement is needed because there is no scientific and objective way of making such comparison. Various scholars can make different ethical judgements to evaluate whether gain in utility of A is greater or less than the loss of utility of B.

Finally, classical welfare function makes an important ethical assumption that social welfare is the *sum* of cardinal utilities of individuals comprising the society. This implies that *same weight* is given to a drunkard as to a learned professor of economics. This ethical assumption has been considered as invalid by modern economists. Therefore, policy recommendations based on classical social function, such as equal income distribution and progressive income taxation, are unacceptable unless they are justified and supported by other methods.

Pareto's Social Welfare Function

We have already critically examined Pareto's criterion for social welfare and the concept of Pareto optimality based on it. Here, a passing reference to Pareto's social welfare function is called for as it will help in comparing it with other social welfare functions. According to Pareto'social welfare function, when one individual is made better off with no else becoming worse off, social welfare increases, and, on the contrary, when one individual is made worse off without any one becoming better off, social welfare decreases. Further, maximum social welfare is attained when through any reorganisation of production and distribution of goods and reserources no one can be made better off without any one being made worse off, that is, when no one's utility can be raised without reducing the utility of others. This *maximum social welfare situation* is also called **Pareto optimality or economic efficiency.**

It should be noted that in Pareto's welfare function no interpersonal comparison of utility is made. Only a broad value judgement is made that it is a good thing to make one or some persons better off without making anybody worse off. Pareto's welfare function has been criticized on the ground that ***it is of limited operational significance*** because as a result of reorganisation and adoption of new economic policies, some people become better off and others worse off and therefore in this case *on the basis of Pareto criterion* it cannot be said whether social welfare increases, decreases or remains the same. Pareto's social welfare function and the concept of Pareto optimality based on it has recently come in for severe criticism by Prof. Amartya Sen. Sarcastically he writes, **"A state can be Pareto optimal with some people in extreme misery and others rolling in luxury, so long as the miserable cannot be made better off without cutting into the luxury of the rich."**[1] Prof. Sen laments that Pareto's welfare function pays no attention to distributiorial considerations of utility or welfare. He deplores that Pareto's welfare optimum is rooted in self-seeking behaviour of individuals which he thinks is not something interesting in welfare economics. To quote him again, "In the small box to which welfare economics got confined with Pareto optimality as the only criterion of judgement and self-seeking behaviour as the only basis of economic choice, the scope of saying something interesting in welfare economies became exceedingly small."[2]

Maximin or Rawlsian Social Welfare Function

Another important social welfare function has been proposed by the noted philosopher John Rawls.[3] Rawls begins his welfare analysis by considering a society as being in an *'initial position'* in which no individual knows what his final utility position will be. The problem he poses is that what type of welfare criterion would be adopted by the society when it is in such an *initial* position where everybody has to behave under uncertainty about how the welfare criterion chosen will ultimately affect his utility or welfare. Assuming that individuals are *risk averse,* he asserts that such a welfare criterion will be chosen that departure from perfect equality would be made only when with unequal distribution of utilities, the *worst off* individual is actually better off than under equality. Rawlsian social welfare function can be written as

$$W(U_1, U_2, \ldots\ldots\ldots U_n) = \min (U_1, U_2, \ldots\ldots U_n)$$

Thus, this social welfare function implies that social welfare of resource allocation depends only on the worst off individual, that is, person with minimum utility

BERGSON-SAMUELSON SOCIAL WELFARE FUNCTION

Bergson-Samuelson social welfare function is an ordinal index of society's welfare and *is a function of the utility level of all individuals* constituting the society. Bergson-Samuelson Social Welfare Function can be written in the following manner :

$$W = W(U_1, U_2, U_3 \ldots\ldots U_n)$$

where W represents the social welfare, $U_1, U_2, U_3 \ldots\ldots U_n$ represent the ordinal utility indices of different individuals of the society. The ordinal utility index of an individual depends upon the goods and services he consumes and the magnitude and kind of the work he does and the leisure he enjoys.

Bergson-Samuelson social welfare function is essentially based on three propositions. First, as stated above, like the Paretian concept of social welfare, Bergson-Samuelson social welfare function depends solely on the utility or welfare of the individual members of the community and no one else. Though this proposition does not explicitly considers welfare of the people in other communities it does not rule out the concern for people in other communities. This is because welfare of each member of the community can be reduced or increased by the well-being of the people of other communities. However this does imply that a community has *no collective interest* over and above the interests of its individual members.

1. Amartya Sen, *On Ethics and Economies,* Oxford University Press, Delhi, 1990, p. 34.
2. *Ibid.*
3. J. Rawls, *A Theory of Social Justice,* Harvard University Press, 1971.

The second important proposition on which this social welfare function rests is that individual utilities or welfare denoted by U_1, U_2, U_3 etc depends on individual's *own* evaluation of their welfare rathar than of any one else. Therefore, this approach to social welfare has been described as *'individualistic'*. It may however be noted that governments of various countries have passed laws which are not consistent with this proposition. Some laws restrict people from getting pleasure or utility from smoking, drinking alcohol, taking drugs etc. On the other hand, some laws compel people to consume certain things such as education to primary level. However, "the notion that unless there are specific reasons to the contrary, individuals should be free to act in the light of their own personal assessments of their own welfare is a fundamental one in market-oriented economies and therefore needs to be taken into account in appraising the potential efficiency of such economies."[4]

Social Welfare Function and Value Judgements. The important thing to note about Bergson-Samuelson social welfare function is that in its construction *explicit* value judgements are introduced. Value judgements determine the form of the social welfare function ; with a different set of value judgement, the form of social welfare function would be different. Social welfare function is thus not *unique* ; its form varies with different value judgements. Value judgements are essentially ethical notions which are introduced from outside economics. The value judgements required to construct social welfare function may be obtained through democratic process through voting by individuals or it may have to be imposed on the society in a dictatorial manner. Whether the form of social welfare function is decided through democratic method of voting and majority rule or it is arrived at through consensus, the form of social welfare function depends upon the value judgements of those who promulgate them since it expresses their views regarding the effect which the utility level of each individual has on the social welfare. In the words of Prof. Scitovsky, "The social welfare function can be thought of as a function of each individual's welfare which in turn depends both on his personal well-being and on his appraisal of the distribution of welfare among all members of the community".[5]

Since the value judgements required for the formulation of social welfare function are not of the economist himself and instead they are introduced from outside economics they are not obtained through any scientific method. It has been claimed that social welfare function has solved the basic problem of welfare economics, since it thinks unnecessary for the economists themselves to make value judgements concerning what is a desirable distribution of welfare as between individuals constituting the society. In other words, economist need not himself decide about what is the most desirable distribution of welfare. He can take value judgements regarding distribution as given from outside economics.

Social Welfare Function is Individualistic. Bergson's social welfare function is called individualistic social welfare function because it reflects individual's own evaluation of their welfare rather than of any one else. Further individuals' welfare or utility depends on economic variables such as goods and services consumed and leisure enjoyed which have a direct effect on individuals' own welfare. The ordinal utility level of an individual is function of his own consumption of goods and services and not of others. Moreover, the utility level of an individual depends on his own evaluation of desirability or usefulness of different goods and services consumed which depends upon his tastes. An individual may derive more utility from the consumption of liquor whereas another individual may derive very nominal utility or no utility at all from it.

---

4. Peter Else & Peter Curwen, *Principles of Microeconomics*, (London, Unwin Hyman, 1990, p. 324.
5. T. Scitovsky, *The State of Welfare Economics*, printed in *Papers on Welfare and Growth*, George Allen and Unwin Ltd., 1964, p. 184.

The social welfare function and its form depends upon the value judgements of the person or institution whom the society has authorised to decide. The authorised person or institution may be any body but for true value judgements regarding the social welfare he must be unbiased because changes in social welfare will depend upon his value judgements. "These judgements as to what constitutes justice and virtue in distribution may be those of the economist himself or those set up by the legislature, by some other governmental authority or by some other unspecified person or group."[6] A social welfare function can be attained by common consensus or it may be forced upon the society by a dictator.

In modern age of democratic governments people elect their representatives who constitute the Government. The political party which has a majority forms the Government and rules the country. The representatives' Government formed by the majority rule formulates various policies on the basis of value judgements and it is expected of it that all the policy decisions by the Government will aim at maximising social welfare rather than maximising the welfare of an individual or a particular section of the society.

Bergson and Samuelson expressed the view that all value judgements used to construct the social welfare function must be consistent which implies that if in a given situation A is preferred to B and B is preferred to C, then A must be preferred to C. This is nothing new to students of economics as this is the well-known assumption of transitivity in social choice among various alternatives.

Representation of Bergson-Samuelson Social Welfare Function through Social Indifference Curves

We can explain the social welfare function with the help of social indifference curves or welfare frontiers. Let us assume a society of two persons. In such a case social welfare function can be represented with the help of social indifference curves. In Fig. 65.1 the utilities of individuals A and B have been represented on the horizontal and vertical axes respectively. W_1, W_2 and W_3 are the social indifference curves representing successively higher levels of social welfare. A social indifference curve is a locus of the various combinations of utilities of A and B which results in an equal level of social welfare. The properties of social indifference curve are just like those of individual consumer's indifference curves. Given a family of social indifference curves, the effects of a proposed change in policy on social welfare can be evaluated. In terms of Fig. 65.1 any policy change that moves the economy from Q to T is an improvement. Similarly, a movement from Q to S or from R to S also represents an improvement in social welfare and a movement from T to Q or T to S represents a decrease in social welfare. A movement along the same social indifference curve represents no change in level of social welfare. It is worth noting that the considerations of fairness and equity are incorporated into

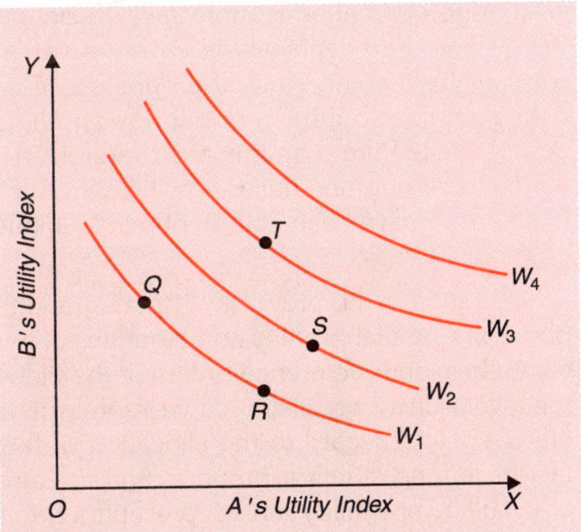

Fig. 65.1. *Social Indifference Curves Depicting Social Welfare Function*

6. W. J. Baumol, *Economic Theory and Operations Analysis*, 4th edition, p. 531.

the social welfare function and are reflected in the shapes of social indifference curves. Thus, it is only on the basis of social welfare function incorporating value judgements regarding distribution of welfare among individuals that we are able to say whether or not society as a whole has become better off when *A*'s utility increases and *B*'s utility decreases. Thus in Figure 65.1 if a change causes the two individuals *A* and *B* to move from point *R* to *Q* it implies that individual *B* has become better off and *A* has become worse off, that is, *B*'s utility increases while that of *A* decreases. But since points *R* and *Q* lie on the same social indifference curve, social welfare remains the same. This means that in movement from point *R* to *Q*, loss of utility by *A* has been evaluated to be equal to the gain in utility by *B*. Thus in the construction of social welfare function curve interpersonal comparison of utility and, therefore, value judgements have been made.

Similarly, if a change is effected which shifts the individual from point *Q* to point *S* in social welfare function depicted in Fig. 65.1 social welfare increases but with this change *B*'s utility has declined and *A*'s utility has increased. Thus, in the evaluation of social welfare, gain in utility of *A* has been adjudged to be of greater value as compared to the loss of utility of *B*, when the two move from point *Q* to point *S*. Thus, it is now clear that in the construction of social welfare functions curves as shown in Fig. 65.1 interpersonal comparison of utility and value judgements have been made.

Analysis of Pareto optimality failed to provide a 'unique optimum solution' which represents maximum social welfare. There are a large number of solutions which are optimum on the basis of Pareto criterion. In terms of Edgeworth box diagram every point on the contract curve represents the optimum position. In terms of Grand Utility Possibility Frontier, all points on it are Pareto optimal or economically efficient. But Pareto criterion does not tell us the best of them. Thus, Paretian analysis leaves us with a lot of indeterminacy in the choice of maximum social welfare point. Now, the significance of social welfare function is that it enables us to obtain a unique optimum position regarding social welfare. This unique optimum position is best of all the Pareto optima and therefore ensures the maximum social welfare. By including the concept of grand utility possibility frontier along with Bergson-Samuelson social welfare function we have been able to obtain a unique optimum position or maximum social welfare position.

As seen in the previous chapter, grand utility possibility frontier is a locus of the various physically attainable utility combinations of two persons when the factor endowment, state of technology and preference orders of the individuals are given. In other words, every point on the grand utility possibility curve represents the position of Pareto optimality or economic efficiency with regard to the allocation of the products among the consumers, allocation of factors among different products and the direction of production. Thus, every point on the grand utility possibility curve represents a Pareto optimum or economic efficiency as judged by Pareto criterion and as we move from one point to another on it the utility of one individual increases while that of the other falls. As explained above, social indifference curves depicting social welfare function obtained on the bases of value judgement *regarding fairness or equity in distribution of welfare*. Thus, welfare analysis by combining grand utility possibility frontier showing Pareto optimality or economic efficiency with the concept of social welfare function representing equitable distribution as obtained by value judgements made enables us to arrive at a **solution for maximum social welfare *which combines efficiency with equity.***

Maximum Social Welfare : Point of Constrained Bliss

Now, let us superimpose grand utility possibility curve on the social indifference curves representing social welfare function to find a unique optimum position of social welfare. In Fig.

65.2 social indifference curves W_1, W_2, W_3 and W_4 representing the social welfare function have been drawn along with the grand utility possibility curve VV'. Social indifference curve W_3 is tangent to the grand utility possibility curve VV' at point Q. Thus, point Q represents the maximum possible social welfare given the factor endowments, state of technology and preference scales of the individuals. Point Q is known as the point of *constrained bliss* since, given the constraints regarding factor endowments and the state of technology, Q is the highest possible state of social welfare which the society can attain. Social welfare represented by the social indifference curve W_4 is higher than social indifference curve W_3 passing through Q but it is not possible to attain it, given the technology and factor endowment.

Thus, from among a large number of Pareto optimum points on the grand utility possibility curve, we have a unique optimum point Q at which the social welfare is the maximum. Optimum point Q not only represents economic efficiency as it lies on the grand utility possibility curve but also equitable distribution as judged by the ethical judgement made by the society. The point of constrained bliss represents the unique pattern of production of goods, unique distribution of goods between the individuals and unique combination of factors employed to produce the goods. In order to know these, we can go back from optimum point Q on the grand utility possibility curve to Edgeworth exchange box to locate the distribution of

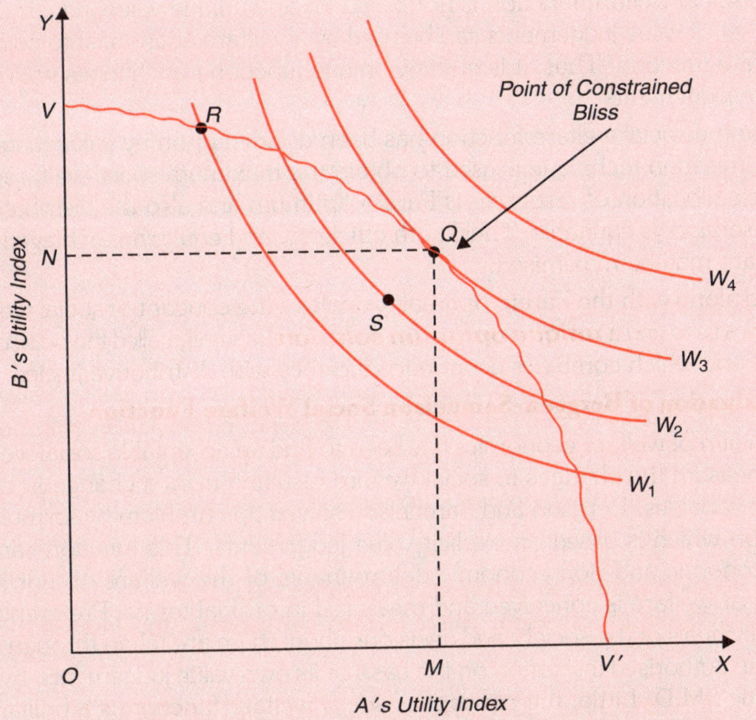

Fig. 65.2. *Social Welfare Function and Position of Constrained Bliss*

goods and utility between the two individuals. To locate the position of optimum allocation of resources we have to go to the corresponding Edgeworth production contract curve and trace the optimum point with the fixed amount of resources and technology and given the *initial endowment* of individuals.

It may be further noted that there is often a ***conflict between efficiency and equity.*** For example, in Figure 65.2 point R lying on the grand utility possibility frontier is the position of economic efficiency and, on the other hand, position S is *interior* to the grand utility possibility curve VV' and is therefore economically inefficient. But point S lies on a higher social indifference curve W_2 than point R lying on a lower social indifference curve W_1. This means economically less efficient position S yields higher level of social welfare than the position R of economic efficiency. This is ***because as judged by the society position S represents more equitable distribution than position R. Thus, it is sometimes in social interest to choose inefficient allocation of resources, if the truly optimum situation Q is unattainabie. In order to achieve equitable distribution of welfare, that is, to satisfy society's concept of equity, some inefficiency in resources allocation is accepted.***

The following features ot the Bergson-Samuelson social welfare function are worth noting:

1. The Bergson-Samuelson social welfare function is based on explicit value judgements and involves interpersonal comparisons of utility in ordinal terms.
2. In Bergson's social welfare function, the maximum social welfare position is completely determined as a result of the introduction of value judgements regarding distribution of welfare among individuals.
3. This social welfare function is not based on any unique value judgements. Instead, any set of value judgements can be used by a welfare economist to construct a social welfare function. Thus, it is not any unique function but changes with the change in value judgements.
4. Once the social welfare function has been decided upon by value judgements, the maximisation technique is used to obtain the maximum social welfare position at which allocation of resources is Pareto optimum and also the distribution of goods and services is equitable. Thus, both efficiency and equity are achieved so that social welfare may be maximised.
5. Used along with the Pareto optimality analysis the concept of social welfare function enables us to find a ***unique optimum solution*** generally called the point *of constrained bliss* and which combines economic efficiency with distributive justice.

A Critical Evaluation of Bergson-Samuelson Social Welfare Function

The main aim of welfare economics has been to find an acceptable social welfare function which could measure the changes in social welfare resulting from a change in economic and non-economic variables. Bergson and Samuelson solved this problem by formulating a social welfare function which is based on explicit value judgements. This function can incorporate the various economic and non-economic determinants of the welfare of individuals. In this function utility or welfare is conceived and measured in ordinal terms. Preferences or utilities of different individuals of the society and decisions about them are taken through a democratic method or by an authorised institution on the basis of its own value judgements. Even according to its bitter critic I.M.D. Little, the concept of social welfare function is a brilliant theoretical construct which completes the formal mathematical system of welfare economics. Pareto optimality analysis does not help us in providing a unique solution to the problem of maximizing social welfare. As seen above, with the help of social welfare function we can measure the changes in social welfare even when one individual becomes better off and another worse off by making some distributional value judgements in the form of social welfare function. Bergson-Samuelson's social welfare function incorporating explicit value judgements is an improvement over earlier attempts such as compensation principle advanced by Kaldor, Hicks and Scitovsky. However economists have pointed out some important drawbacks in the concept of social welfare function.

Limited Practical Significance. Little, Streeten and Baumol have pointed out that social welfare function is of limited practical significance. According to Little, the social welfare function can neither be used in a democratic state nor even in a totalitarian one because in them there would be as many vague social welfare functions as there are individuals. Social welfare function, to quote Little, is only "a formal device necessary to a perfectly general abstract system of 'welfare', which is devoid of any practical significance."[7] Likewise, Paul Streeten also thinks that social welfare function is a highly formal concept which has hardly any relation with the important facts of social life and choice. To quote him, "No political programme or individual value standard would fit the model of a social welfare function of the required type."[8] Prof. Baumol is also of the opinion that the concept of social welfare is of limited practical value as it does not tell us how to get the value judgements which it requires for its construction. Though Bergson criterion of social welfare function, writes Baumol, "provides us with a highly useful frame of reference, unfortunately it does not come equipped with a kit and a set of instructions for collecting the welfare judgements which it requires. Thus it still leaves us with the difficult part of the job unsolved."[9]

Impossibility of Constructing a Social Welfare Function from Individual Preferences. A highly damaging drawback of social welfare function has been pointed out by K.J. Arrow who has shown that social welfare function cannot be constructed on the basis of value judgements arrived at through democratic process of majority rule in group decision-making. Arrow has proved that the majority rule leads to contradictory results or intransitivity of social choices when individuals are asked to make a choice from among *more than two* alternatives available to them. Therefore, Prof. Arrow concludes that a social welfare function which is based on mere ordinal preferences cannot in principle be constructed from the preferences of all the individuals comprising a society. Of course, social welfare function can be set up on the basis of value judgements of an individual who can impose his will on the society but that will reflect the aims and aspirations of an absolute dictator. The contradiction pointed out by Prof. Arrow has been explained below in detail.

Bergson-Samuelson's social welfare function approach is individualistic. The concept of social welfare function is based on the proposition that it is individuals that count and social welfare function is derived from individuals' preferences. Individual welfare is assumed to be based on individuals' own evaluation of their utility rather than of anyone else. The approach is thus individualistic. This is not always desirable. In some cases individuals do not know what is good or best for them. Thus the use of drugs and alcohol to derive pleasure may be in their evaluation promoting their welfare, but by consuming these harmful things they may be harming themselves. Further, the individuals may not be spending adequately on education, health which truly increase their welfare. It is with a view to promote social welfare that the Government puts restrictions on individual's consumption of certain goods such as drugs, alcohol, blue films on the one hand, and compel the consumption of some goods such as education services on the other.

Welfare depends on a wider range of variables than those associated with utility. Social welfare function approach is based on the utility which an individual derives from economic variables such as consumption of goods and services. Apart from these economic variables, welfare or well-being of individuals depends on a whole range of political and environmental variables such as enjoyment of human rights, political freedom, pollution-free environment.

7. I.M.D. Little, *A Critique of Welfare Economics*, p. 123.
8. Paul Streeten, Appendix to Gunnar Myrdal's *The Political Elements in the Development of Economic Theory*, p. 216.
9. Baumol, *op. cit.*, p. 531.

Thus, "in comparing different economic systems or in comparing different ways of organising a given economy, the possibility that some of these variables might be affected cannot be ignored. Thus a reorganisation that gives everyone more income and leisure ***might not improve the welfare of the community if at the same time it limits individual freedom or requires the abandonment of cherished cultural traditions.***"[10]

Prof. Amartya Sen's Critque : Judging welfare or well-being in terms of utility is of limited significance.

Prof. Amartya Sen has criticised modern welfare economics covenng both Pareto efficiency and social welfare function on the ground that utility is not a true indicator of well-being. To quote him, "A difficulty with welfarism arises from the particular interpretation of well-being that utility provides. To judge the well-being of a person exclusively in the metric of happiness or desire-fulfilment has some obvious limitations. These limitations are particularly damaging in the context of interpersonal comparisons .of well-being."[11] He further adds, "A person who has had a life of misfortune, with very little opportunities, and rather little hope, may be more easily reconciled to deprivations than others reared in more fortunate and affluent circumstances. ***The metric of happiness may, therefore, distort the extent of deprivation, in a specific and biased way.*** The hopeless beggar, the precarious landless labourer, the dominated housewife, the hardened unemployed or the over-exhausted coolie may all take pleasures in small mercies and manage to suppress intense suffering for the necessity of continuing survival, but ***it would be ethically deeply mistaken to attach a correspondingly small value to the loss of their well-being because of the survival strategy***"[12].

It follows from above that Amartya Sen has criticised the concept of social welfare based on utility which means psychological reactions of individuals to goods and services which they consume. Prof. Sen shifts the focus on promoting ***positive freedoms*** of individuals for assessing the change in their welfare following a change in organisation or public policy. He defines freedom as ***'capabilites to function'*** as to what persons can do or cannot do. It is capabilities to function that reflect freedom in the positive sense and determine well-being or welfare of the people.[13]

ARROW'S THEORY OF SOCIAL CHOICE

Bergson and Samuelson made significant contribution to welfare economics by introducing explicit value judgements in the form of social welfare function. However, Bergson and Samuelson did not deal with the question as to how to get these value judgements or what these value judgemens could be for constructing a social welfare function. It was this problem left untouched by Samuelson and Bergson, which was explored by Arrow in his path-breaking work *"Social Choice and Individual Values"*. Prof. Arrow pointed out that the construction of social welfare function which reflects the preferences of all individuals constituting a society is an impossible task. The main contention of Arrow is that it is very difficult to set up reasonable democratic procedures for the aggregation of individual preferences into a social preference for making a social choice. Arrow has proved a general theorem according to which it is impossible to construct a social ordering which will in some way reflect the individual ordering of all the members of the society.

10. P. Else and P. Curwin, *Principles of Microeconomics,* Unwin Hyman, London, 1990. p. 324 (Italics added).
11. Amartya Sen, *On Ethics and Economics,* Oxford University Press, Delhi, 1990. pp. 45-46. (italics added).
12. *Ibid.*
13. See his well-known article, "The Concept of Well-Being" a Silver Jubilee Lecture at Institute of Economic Growth, Delhi University.

In the original version of Bergson-Samuelson social welfare function, welfare of an individual was thought to depend solely upon the goods and services consumed by him alone and not by others. Hence, an individual ordering of alternative 'social states' reflected his tastes and not of others. On the other hand, Arrow has pointed out that ***individual's ordering of social states does not depend exclusively upon the commodities consumed but also on the amounts of various types of collectives such as municipal services, parks, sanitation, erection of statues of famous men,*** etc. He has argued that welfare results of collective activity cannot be evaluated by an individual solely on the basis of his consumption. Instead, individual ordering of social states will depend on his own consumption as well as on the consumption of others in a society. Individual ordering of alternative social states reflects his value judgements which are also called simply *'values'* by Arrow. According to Arrow, it is ordering of social states according to the *values* of individuals as distinct from the individual *tastes* which should be determined for construction of a valid social welfare function.

Arrow's Conditions of Social Choice

We have seen earlier that the value judgements of a superman or a dictator about social welfare may not be valid due to various types of biases in human mind. As a result, a superman's or dictator's value judgements or values do not truly reflect the social choice. Arrow was the first welfare economist who attempted to lay down reasonable necessary conditions for achieving the social ordering which reflects the desire or the ordering of all individuals of the society. There are many ways in which social choice can be derived. Choice may be made by a dictator or through custom and tradition, or by some spiritual or religious head as was done in a traditional society or by individuals comprising a society through voting. The problem of social choice is easiest in a dictatorial rule in which all the social choices are made by the dictator and all the individuals comprising the society are compelled to accept it. Similarly, in a traditional society various religious and spiritual rules or customs make the problem of the social choice very easy. No individual can disregard the social choice made by a religious and spiritual head.

But the problem of making a soical choice based on individual ordering becomes difficult in a democratic society in which every individual is free to have his own individual ordering of various social states. Now, a pertinent question is as to whether the social choice can consistently be derived from individual orderings. Prof. Arrow has laid down certain necessary conditions which social choices must satisfy in order to reflect the individual orderings. He has laid down the following five conditions which must be met for an acceptable social welfare function. In fact, these conditions reflect the value judgements of Arrow himself.

Condition 1 : Transitivity or Consistency, The first condition mentioned by Arrow is that social choices must be consistent or transitive. Transitivity of the social choices implies that if an alternative *A* is socially preferred to alternative *B* and alternative *B* is socially preferred to alternative *C,* then alternative C will not be socially preferred to alternative *A.* If alternative *C* is found to be socially preferred to *A,* then the condition of transitivity would be violated and the choice would be inconsistent. It may be mentioned that the question of transitivity arises only when the social ordering has the properties of convexity. By *convexity* we mean that the various alternatives must be related to each other by preference or by indifference. Thus two alternatives are said to be related or connected if for any pair of alternatives *A* and *B,* either *A* is preferred to *B* or *B* to *A* or there is indifference between the two. Thus, the condition of transitivity must be found in the social choice because it has been considered by Arrow as a condition for consistent social choice.

Condition 2: Responsiveness to Individual Preferences. The second condition is that social ordering must depict 'responsiveness to individual preferences'. It states that social ranking must respond positively to the individual ranking. This means that the social choices must change in the same direction as the choices of the individuals constituting the society. To quote Arrow, "The social welfare function is such that the social ordering responds positively to alteration in individual value or at least not negatively."[14] This implies that social choice reflects the values of different individuals of the society and it changes as the individual values change. Suppose an alternative *A* is socially preferred to *B* on the basis of a set of individual orderings. If change occurs in the ordering of individuals so that some individuals prefer alternative *A* more strongly than before and no one's preference for it declines, then *A* must remain socially preferred to *B*. It is worth mentioning that this condition would be violated "if there were some individuals against whom society discriminates in the sense that when their desire for some alternative increases relative to other alternatives, the social desirability of that alternative is reduced."[15]

Condition 3 : The Condition of Non-Imposition. The third condition is of 'non-imposition'. This states that social choices must not be imposed independently of individual preferences. For instance, it implies that if no individual in the society prefers alternative *B* to alternative *A* and any one or few other individuals in the society prefer alternative *A* to alternative *B*, then society must prefer *A* to *B*. This condition implies that the choice of an alternative by the society must satisfy Pareto criterion. This also implies that the social choice must not be determined by any one outside the community.

Condition 4 : The Condition of Non-Dictatorship. The fourth condition relates to the existence of non-dictatorship. It states that social choices must not be dictated by any one individual in the community. For instance, *A* must not be socially preferred to *B* only because any one individual in the society prefers *A* to *B* irrespective of the preferences of other individuals. If this condition is violated, then the individual whose preferences are regarded as social preferences will in fact be a dictator. This condition implies that the social choices must be determined by the democratic method of voting by all individuals rather than dictatorial one of imposition of his will by an individual.

Condition 5 : Independence of Irrelevant Alternatives. The fifth condition is of independence of irrelevant alternatives. According to this, social ranking of any two alternatives is determined *exclusively* by individual ranking of these two alternatives alone and should not be affected at all by individual preferences with respect to other alternatives. In other words, a most preferred alternative out of a given set of available alternatives must be independent of (that is, not affected by) other alternatives, which are not available. Suppose three alternatives, *A*, *B* and *C*, are available and society prefers *A* to *B* and *B* to *C*. If C were no longer available, then this condition implies that it must not be the case that society then prefers *B* to *A*. Thus, the social preference of *A* over *B* depends only on individual preferences of just these two alternatives, *A* and *B*, and not on any other alternative which is not immediately relevant.

The above five conditions of Arrow reflect his value judgements and they seem to be quite reasonable set of conditions for making social choices in a free democratic society. However, Arrow has shown that it is impossible to make social choices without violating at least one of the above five conditions. In other words, it is not possible to construct a social welfare function on the basis of individual values that satisfy all the above conditions. Arrow

14. K.J. Arrow, *Social Choice and Individual Values.*
15. Quandt and Henderson, *Microeconomic Theory,* 2nd edition, 1971, p. 285.

has specially demonstrated through his general impossibility theorem that when the choice is between *more than two* alternatives, then the individual's voting or expression of preferences for them would lead to inconsistent or contradictory results so that no valid social choice can be made by the majority rule. We will explain below Arrow's impossibility theorem.

Arrow's Impossibility Theorem

After discussing the social choice and individual values, Arrow proved his famous impossibility theorem in terms of abstract mathematics and symbolic logic. From this he concludes that it is not possible to pass.from the individual preferences to the social preferences so as to construct a social welfare function. According to Arrow's theorem, "If we exclude the possibility of interpersonal comparisons of utility, then the only method of passing from individual tastes to social preferences which will be satisfactory and which will be defined for a wide range of sets of individual ordering are either imposed or dictatorial."

The democratic procedure for reaching a social choice or group decision is the expression of their preferences by individuals through free voting. Social choice will be determined by the majority rule. But Arrow has demonstrated through his impossibility theorem mentioned above that consistent social choices cannot be made without violating the consistency or transitivity condition. The social choice on the basis of majority rule may be inconsistent even if individual preferences are consistent. Arrow first considers a simple case of *two* alternative social states and proves that in this case group decision or social choice through a majority rule yields a social choice which can satisfy all the five conditions. But when there are more than two alternatives, majority rule fails to yield a social choice without violating at least one of the five conditions. Thus, in case of more than two alternatives, social welfare function based on individual preferences cannot be constructed.

Let us illustrate the proof of the impossibility theorem with the help of Table 65.1 given below. In this table three individuals *A*, *B* and *C* who constitute the society have been shown to have voted for three alternative social states *X*, *Y* and *Z*, by writing 3 against the most preferred alternative, writing 2 for the next preferred alternative and 1 for the least preferred alternative. A glance at the table will reveal that individual *A* prefers *X* to *Y*, *Y* to *Z*, and therefore *X* to *Z*. Individual *B* prefers *Y* to *Z*, *Z* to *X* and therefore *Y* to *X*. And individual *C* prefers *Z* to *X*, *X* to *Y* and therefore *Z* to *Y*. It is clear that two individuals (i.e. majority) *A* and *C* prefer *X* to *Y* and the majority (individuals *A* and *B*) prefer *Y* to *Z* and also the majority (individuals *B* and *C*)

Table 65.1. Ranking of Alternatives by Individuals and Social Choice

	Alternative Social States		
	X	Y	Z
A	3	2	1
B	1	3	2
C	2	1	3

prefer *Z* to *X*. Thus, we see that majority rule leads to inconsistent social choices because on the one hand *X* has been preferred to *Z* by the majority and on the other hand *Z* has also been preferred to *X* by the majority which is quite contradictory or inconsistent. Prof. Arrow, therefore, concludes that it is impossible to derive a social ordering of different conceivable alternative social states on the basis of the individual ordering of those social states without violating at least one of the value judgements as expressed in the five conditions. This is in essence his impossibility theorem.

We have shown above how Arrow has proved that it is impossible to construct a social welfare function based on all individual preferences without involving inconsistency or non-contradictory social ranking. It is worth mentioning that in reaching this conclusion Arrow has assumed that only *ranking i.e.* ordinal preferences of individuals be considered which means that no weight should be given to the intensity of preferences. For, it is very difficult to measure the intensity of feelings of different individuals with regard to various social states such as the erection of a social overhead capital such as bridges, tunnels, sanitation work or parks etc. It should be further noted that if weights are assigned to individual preferences *i.e.* if the intensity of individual preferences are considered, then consistent and non-contradictory social choice is possible. Thus, according to Baumol, "In deciding whether to allocate labour to the production of some drug needed to treat a rare but dangerous disease or to the manufacture of Scrabble sets we may *recognize* that, compassion aside, *more people* will want the Scrabble sets than the medicine. Yet on the crudest sort of interpersonal comparison of benefits, we may decide that the public as a whole will gain more from the production of the medicine because its ***potential users feel much more strongly*** about their preference then do the others"[16]

Arrow's Consequences

From his five conditions mentioned above, Arrow has derived three consequences. It is from these consequences that he derives general impossibility theorem explained above. Let us take these consequences in case of three alternatives *X, Y* and *Z* available to two individuals *A* and *B*. According to consequence 1, whenever the two individuals prefer *X* to *Y* then irrespective of the rank of the third alternative *Z*, the society will prefer *X* to *Y*. According to consequence 2, if in a given social choice, the will of individual *A* prevails against the opposition of individual *B*, then the will of *A* will certainly prevail in case individual *B* is indifferent or agrees with *A*. According to consequence 3, if individuals *A* and *B* have exactly conflicting interests in the choice between two alternatives *X* and *Y*, then the society will be indifferent between *X* and *Y*. It is interesting to note that the simple proof of impossibility theorem follows from the consequence 3. For instance, if individual *A* prefers *X* to *Y*, and individual *B* prefers *Y* to *Z*, then according to consequence 3, the society will be indifferent as between the two alternatives, *A* and *B*. If this does not hold good, then Arrow's condition of non-existence of a dictator will be violated. For instance, if individual *A* prefers *X* to *Y* and individual *B* prefers *Y* to *Z* and if society opts for *X*, then *A* will be a dictator inasmuch as his choice will always be a social choice. It follows from above that Arrow has demonstrated that social welfare function based on all individual preferences cannot be constructed without violating at least one of his seemingly simple and reasonable conditions.

Amartya Sen on Arrow's Impossibility Theorem

An important contribution of Amartya Sen in welfare economics is to clearly bring out the implications of Arrow's impossibility theorem and resolving it. As stated above, according to Arrow's impossibility theorem making a social choice through the democratic process of 'majority voting' can lead to inconsistent results and a choice can be made in such a situation through the decision by a dictator. About Arrow's impossibility theorem Sen writes, "This is an extraordinary impressive and elegant theorem – one of the most beautiful analytical results in

16. W. J. Baumol, *Economic Theory and Operations Analysis*, 3rd edition, p. 407. (italics supplied)

the field of social science." In fact Sen resolved this problem of inconsistency involved in Arrow's theorem by pointing out that in such a situation for making a decision regarding social choice through democratic mechanism more information is needed to make a rational social choice for maximising social welfare. With this additional or more information it is quite possible to arrive at a rational social choice in a democracy which involves taking a decision after free discussion and consensus. To quote Amartya Sen, "Arrow's theorem does not in fact show what the popular interpretation frequently takes it to show. It establishes, in effect, not the impossibility of rational choice but the impossibility that arises when we try to ***base social choice on a limited class of information.***"[17]

He thus resolves the impossibility of making a rational choice that maximises social welfare by laying emphasis on additional or different information from the majority rule for making a rational social choice. Arrow's impossibility theorem, Sen writes, "does not at all rule out decision mechanisms that use more or different information bases than voting rules do. In taking a social decision on economic matters it would be natural for us to consider other information."[18]

For showing how majority rule is inadequate mechanism for resolving economic disputes he gives a very convincing example of dividing a cake among three persons, 1, 2, and 3, with the assumption that each person votes to maximise only her own share of the cake. He points out any division of the cake among three persons, the majority (*i.e.* two persons in the present example) can be made better off by taking a part of any one's share (say person 1's share) and then dividing it between the two. Those, who constitute the majority, if asked would vote for taking the share of the third and distribute the same between them. Amartya Sen rightly points out that, "This way of 'improving' the social outcome would work – given that social judgement is by majority rule – even if the person thus victimised (viz.) happens to be the poorest of the three. Indeed, we can continue taking away more and more from the poorest person and dividing the loot between the richer two – all the time making a majority improvement. This process of "improvement" can go on until ***the poorest has no cake left to be taken away***"

Thus decision rules on information base consisting only of preference ranking of the persons without any notice being taken of who is poorer than whom or who gains and who loses how much from redistribution of income or any other information is quite inadequate for making a rational choice. To conclude in the words of Amartya Sen, "The information base for this class of rules, of which the majority decision procedure is a prominent example, is thus extremely limited, and it is certainly quite inadequate for making informed judgements about welfare economic problems. This is not primarily because it leads to inconsistency (as generalised in the Arrow theorem) but because we cannot really make social judgement with so little information."[19]

ALTERNATIVE SOCIAL CHOICE THEORIES

We have discussed above the theory of social choice based upon Pareto criterion and Bergson-Samuelson social welfare function. Depending on the social welfare function adopted, there are alternative theories of social choice. We have seen that it is difficult to obtain Bergson-Samuelson social welfare function which is based on universally accepted or democratically

17. Amartya Sen, *Development as Freedom*, Oxford University Press, 2000, p.p. 250-51.
18. *Op. cit.*, p. 251.
19. *Op. cit.*, p. 252.

chosen value judgements. Arrow's impassibility theorem shows that *majority voting* in favour of a particular choice is not possible.

It will be useful to explain how other social welfare criteria or welfare functions explained above lead to a social choice about resource allocation and distribution of utility.

Classical Utilitarian Welfare Criterion

As explained above, classical social welfare function regards social welfare as the *sum* of utilities of all individuals of the society. *In this utilitarian welfare function utilities of all individuals in the society are given equal weights.* If there are '*n*' individuals in the society, utilitarian welfare function can be written as

$$W = U_1 + U_2 + U_3 \ldots\ldots + U_n$$

If the capacity to get pleasure from consuming goods is the same of all members of the society, then the above utilitarian welfare function will lead to equal distribution of goods. However, under this social welfare function, distribution of goods produced is considered superior, if individuals who enjoy most from consuming certain goods are given more of these goods, other things remaining the same. Thus, in this case, there is non-egalitarian distribution of goods and this is judged as superior according to the utilitarian social welfare function.

Utilitarian social welfare function has been generalised in which different weights are assigned to utilities of various individuals. If the weight assigned to utility of individual 1 is α, to the utility of individual 2 is α_2 and so on, then the generalised utilitarian social welfare function can be written as

$$W = \alpha_1 U_1 + \alpha_2 U_2 \ldots\ldots\ldots + \alpha_n U_n$$

These different weights depends on some criteria, such as higher weights are given to the utilities of hard working people, the colour of the skin of the people (under the former apartheid system of South Africa), boys and men as against girls and women (due to gender bias in India).

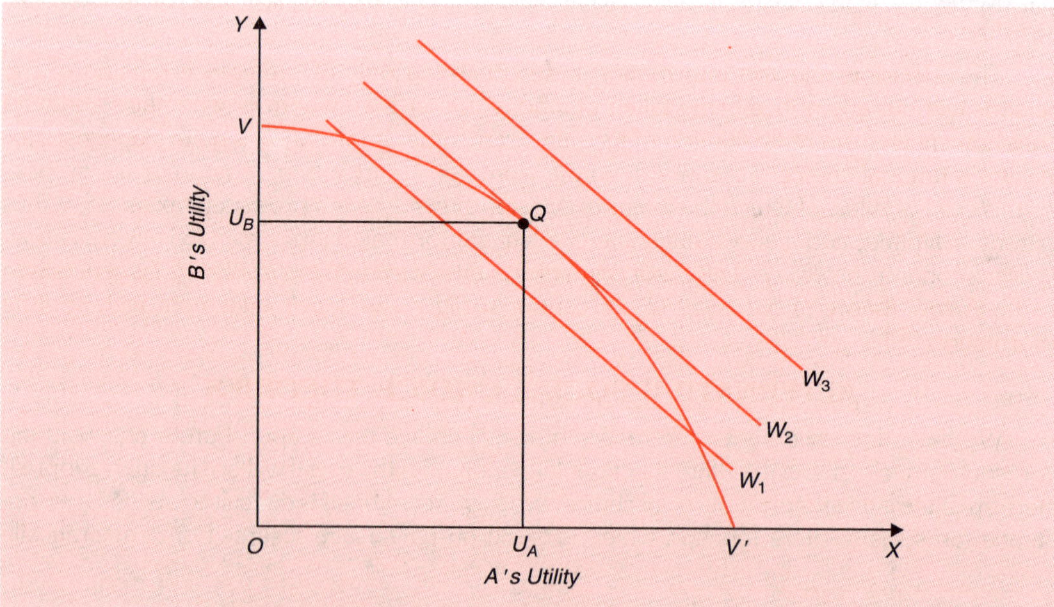

Fig. 65.3. *Utilitarian Welfare Criterion for Social Choice*

According to this social welfare function, social welfare indifference curves W_1, W_2, W_3 are straight lines with −1 slope and are parallel to each other as shown in Figure 65.3. As will be seen from this figure, the sum of utilities of the two individuals ($U_A + U_B$) is maximum at point Q at which social indifference curve W_2 is tangent to the grand utility possibility frontier VV'. Thus, subject to the constraints of grand utility possibility frontier, choice of Q is socially optimum choice according to the classical welfare function. It may be noted that optimum point Q implies a certain allocation of two goods, X and Y, between individuals A and B and this allocation can be derived from Edgeworth exchange box diagram. Remember the allocation of two goods between the individuals will lie on the contract curve in the Edgeworth box where the indifference curves of the individuals are tangent to each other.

Rawls' Concept of Social Justice and Welfare Criterion

John Rawls[20], a philosopher of Harvard, has put forward a strongly egalitarian criterion of social justice in making a social choice. His social welfare criterion is primarily concerned with the distribution of real income rather than subjective utilities. *Rawls believes that society should maximise the welfare of the poorest, that is, the worst-off member of society who is the person with minimum level of utility.* According to him, the largest weight should be given to utility of the person with lowest level of utility. Rawls' social welfare function is written as

$$W = \min (U_1, U_2, \ldots\ldots\ldots U_n)$$

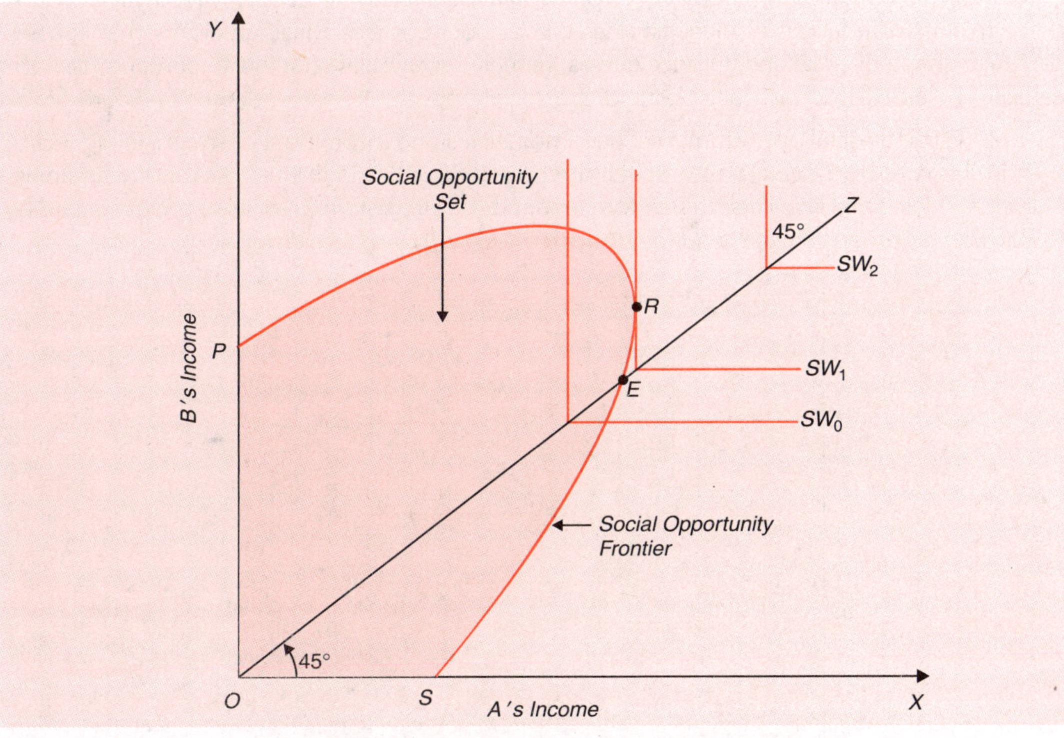

Fig. 65.4. *Rawls' Social Welfare Criterion*

20. John Rawls, *A Theory of Justice*, (Cambridge: Harvard University Press), 1971.

According to social welfare criterion based on this social welfare function relatively equal distribution of goods maximises social welfare. Rawls' welfare criterion is depicted in Figure 65.4 where along with *X*-axis *A*'s income and along with *Y*-axis *B*'s income are measured. It is assumed that there are two individuals in a society. The curve *PRES* is the social opportunity frontier which shows the various possibilities of obtaining incomes by the two individuals. According to Rawlsian social welfare criterion inequality of incomes in a society is justified only to the extent it increases income or welfare of the least well-off person. In this figure a 45° line *OZ* has been drawn which shows equal distribution of income between the two individuals. Social welfare contours (*i.e.* social indifference curves) in Rawls' social welfare function are rectangular with corners at the 45° equality line. In the social opportunity set *PRES* (shaded area), the optimum point is *E* which lies on the social opportunity frontier from which the 45° equality line *OZ* passes. Therefore, at point *E* on the social opportunity frontier incomes of two individuals *A* and *B* are equal.

Now, suppose a certain economic reorganisation or change in public policy shifts the position of the two individuals from point *E* on the 45° equality line to point *R* on the social opportunity frontier above and to the right of point *E*. This change in position from point *E* to point *R* implies that individual *B* has gained more than the individual *A*. However, less advantaged individual *A* has also benefited from change from equality position *E* to inequality position *R*. However, according to Rawlsian criterion, inequality of incomes is better than equality only if it benefits the least advantaged person. That the inequality point *R* is better than the equality point *E* is revealed by the fact that point *R* lies on higher social indifference SW_1. It may lowever be noted this result in favour of inequality has come about because Rawlsian criterion assumes a particular shape of social indifference curves, namely rectangular shape with corner at the 45° equality line and also a particular shape of the social opportunity set as shown in Figure 65.5.

However, if social opportunity set has a negative slope throughout as shown in Fig. 65.5, then in this case by moving on the social opportunity frontier individual *B* cannot gain unless individual *A* loses and vice versa. Therefore, under these circumtances social optimum according to Rawlsian approach always requires **absolute equality of income.**

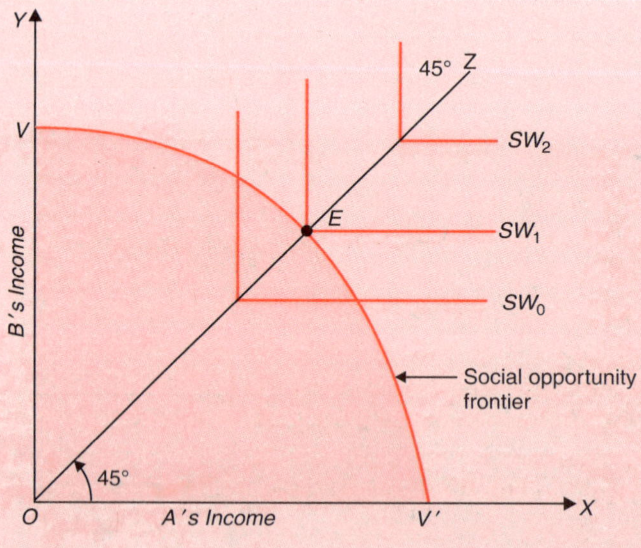

Fig. 65.5. *Rawlsian Optimum Lies on the 45° Equality Line*

PART–VII

INTERTEMPORAL CHOICE AND MARKETS WITH ASYMMETRIC INFORMATION

- Interest, Saving and Investment: Intertemporal Choice
- Information Problem and Markets with Asymmetric Information

CHAPTER

66

Interest, Saving and Investment: Intertemporal Choice

Introduction

An important branch of microeconomics is concerned with explaining intertemporal choices or, in other words, optimal allocation of resources over time. In this chapter we will examine various types of intertemporal choices of an individual. First, we examine the choice of an individual between present and future consumption, that is, how much of his current income he will consume in the present year and how much he will save and lend so as to increase his income and consumption in the future. The individual aims to maximise his total or joint satisfaction from the present and future consumption, given his endowment position. On the other hand, we will explain the case of an individual who borrows against his future income to maximise his satisfaction from the present and future consumption. Thus we will explain the intertemporal choice of both the lender and the borrower.

The examples of individuals who refrain from consuming all their current income so that they are able to increase future income and consumption are quite common. However, the examples of individuals who borrow against their future income so as to spend in the present can also be provided. For example, students of professional courses often borrow against their higher anticipated future incomes when they get jobs. Likewise, in India farmers often borrow for current consumption against their standing crops which are to be reaped in future. Thus, through lending and borrowing, present income can be exchanged for future income and *vice-versa.*

The second way in which present income can be exchanged for future income is releasing some resources from the production of consumer goods and using them for the production of capital goods such as machines, factories so that future income and consumption be raised. In other words, some current income can be saved so that these savings are invested for the production of capital goods. In this way physical capital goods or assets as well as human capital (such as education, skills, health etc.) can be accumulated to raise future incomes and standards of living. It is thus clear that lending and borrowing, saving and investment involve intertemporal choice, that is, choice between the present and future consumption. This intertemporal choice is of crucial importance as on it depends the growth of the economy.

In what follows we will first explain intertemporal choice between present and future consumption by an individual which maximises his total satisfaction over time, that is, joint satisfaction from the present and future consumption. This will enable us to explain the determination of rate of interest through borrowing and lending equilibrium.

Intertemporal Choice : Lending

We now examine how an individual will choose between present and future consumption so as to maximise his total satisfaction over time (we consider only two time, periods, this year and the next year). As mentioned above, the exchange of present consumption for future consumption and *vice-versa* is done through lending and borrowing.

This intertemporal choice is depicted in Fig. 66.1 where U_1, U_2, U_3, etc. are indifference curves representing preferences between consumption this year and consumption next year. BW_0 is the budget line whose slope measures the rate of exchange between consumption this year and consumption in the next year. In other words, the slope of the budget line depends on the rate of interest which is in fact the price of lending and borrowing income. We assume that the individual has income of Y_0 (= ₹ 60) in the present year and expects to have income Y_1 (= ₹ 30) in the next year, that is, he is initially at point A on the budget line. This initial position at A is generally referred to as individual's ***endowment position***. It should be noted

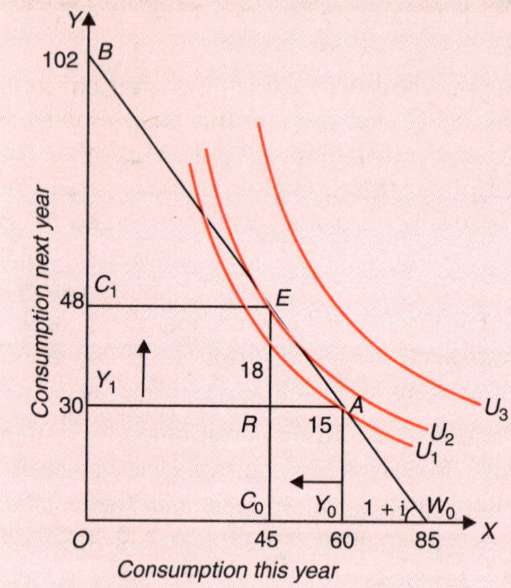

Fig.66.1 *(a) Intertemporal Consumption Choice: Lending*

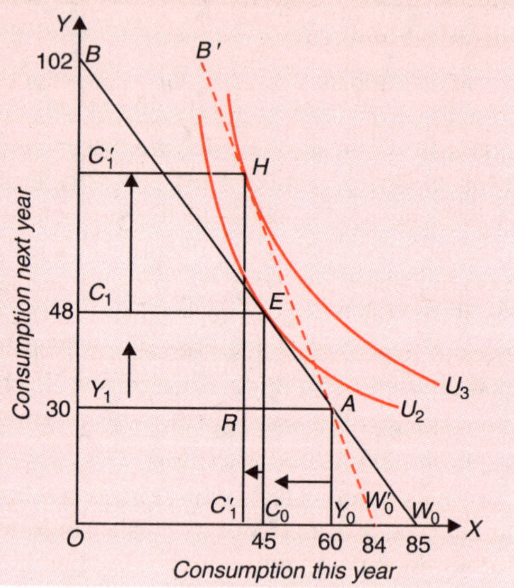

Fig. 66.1. *(b) Effect of Rise in Rate of Interest on Consumption and Saving*

that ***individual's consumption need not be equal to his present income*** Y_0 and his consumption next year need not be equal to his future income Y_1. This is because he can refrain from consuming all his present income in this year and lend a part of it to others or he can borrow against next year's income to increase his present consumption. In this choice between consumption this year and the next year, the individual will try to maximise his total satisfaction in the two periods. A glance at Figure 66.1*(a)* reveals that the consumer will be in equilibrium at point E where the budget line BW_0 is tangent to the indifference curve U_2. In this optimal choice his consumption this year is C_0 (= 45 units) and consumption next year is C_1 (= 48 units). With his endowment position at A, equilibrium at point E implies that he has lended $Y_0 - C_0$ (= 15 units) this year and his consumption next year has risen by $C_1 - Y_1$ (48 –30 =18) units. In other words, he has exchanged 15 units of the present year consumption for 18 units of consumption in the next year. The slope of the budget line is given by :

$$\frac{ER}{AR} = -\frac{18}{15} = -1.2, \text{ or } -(1 + 0.2)$$

Besides, this means that the sacrifice of 15 units of consumption this year has given him 3 units of extra consumption next year. That is, real rate of interest is 18 – 15/15 = 3/15 = 0.2 or 20 per cent.

Thus, the slope of the budget line is

$$\frac{ER}{AR} = \frac{C_1 - Y_1}{Y_0 - C_0} = -(1 + 0.2) = -(1 + i)$$

where i stands for the rate of interest.

The negative sign implies the downward-sloping nature of the budget line. That is, in order to earn interest and thereby increase his consumption and income in the next year he has to reduce his consumption in the present year. It will be seen from Fig. 66.1 (*a*) that individual has sacrificed his present consumption by ($Y_0 - C_0$) or 15 units to increase his consumption in the next year from Y_1 to C_1 (*i.e.* by 18 units). Thus, through lending he has redistributed his endowment into present and future consumption.

It is worth noting that if the individual saves and lends all his present income Y_0 (= 60) of this year, given the interest rate of 0.2, which determines the slope of budget line BW_0, he will receive additional income of 60 (1 + 0.2) = 72 next year (In that case his total income next year will be 30 + 72 = 102). Though an individual can do this but by doing so he will not be maximising his total satisfaction.

It is clear from above that ***interest is a premium received by the individual next year by lending Re. I this year.*** Putting it alternatively, interest is the excess of the price P_1 received next year over the price P_0 of this year. Thus

$$P_1 = P_0 (1 + i) \qquad \ldots(i)$$

or

$$\frac{P_1}{P_0} = 1 + i \qquad \ldots(ii)$$

where interest i is the excess of P_1 over P_0.

If interest is 0.2 *i.e.* 20 per cent, then by lending Re.1 today (*i.e.* P_0) we get Re.1 (1 + i) or 1(1 + 0.2) next year which is denoted by P_1. In our above example, the individual lends ₹ 15 at the rate of interest 0.2 and receives next year amount equal to 15 (1 + 0.2) = 18 from the borrower. It, therefore, follows that Re. 1 + 0.2 next year is worth Re. 1 today, if rate of interest is 0.2 or 20 per cent per annum.

From (*ii*) above it follows that slope of the budget line BW_0 is equal to – (1 + i) or in absolute terms (1 + i)

Effect of Rise in Interest Rate on Lending. Consider Fig. 66.1 (*b*). If the interest rate rises, the budget line will become steeper. At a higher rate of interest individual will usually save more, that is, will cut down his consumption more. For example, in Fig. 66.1(*b*) with endowment position at A the rise in interest rate to 25 per cent, the slope of the new budget line $B' W'_0$ will be equal to I + i = 1. + 0.25 = 1.25

Note that the new budget line $B'W_0'$ will pass through the endowment position A and will be steeper than the previous budget line. It will be seen from Fig. 66.1 (*b*) that the new budget line $B' W'_0$ is tangent to the higher indifference curve U_3 at point H and in this new optimal or equilibrium choice, he reduces his consumption further to C'_0 and in exchange his consumption next year increases by $C_1 C'_1$. In other words, at a higher rate of interest he has saved and lended more than at the lower rate of interest. Since as a result of ***rise in rate of***

interest, the lender has moved from a lower difference curve U_2 to the higher indifference curve U_3, he has become better off.

Supply Curve of Lending

As seen above, in Fig. 66.1*(b)* a rise in the rate of interest induces the individual to save and lend more. In this way we can determine the lendings of an individual at different rates of interest. The higher the rate of interest, the greater is the supply of lendings by him. By summing up the lendings of various individuals at various rates of interest we can obtain market supply curve of lending which will slope upward showing positive relationship between rate of interest and lending. It may be noted that in case of some individuals who have a target of having a certain fixed level of income or consumption in the future, a higher rate of interest will enable them to earn that fixed income by saving and lending less in this year. That is, for these individuals supply curve of lending will be backward sloping. However, those individuals who lend more at higher rates of interest predominate and therefore overall supply curve of lending slopes upward, though at very high rates of interest backward-bending shape of supply curve of lending cannot be ruled out.

Intertemporal Choice : Borrowing

We now turn to analyse borrowing by individuals. Individuals whose endowment position lies to the left of the optimal-choice point *E* in Fig. 66.2*(a)* will borrow money instead of lending, that is, they will dissave in the present and borrow. Let point *S* in Fig. 66.2*(a)* represent the endowment position of an individual with Y_0 income in the present year and Y_1 next year. But given the same preferences between the present and future consumption as depicted by his indifference curves and U_2 the intertemporal optimum choice of this individual

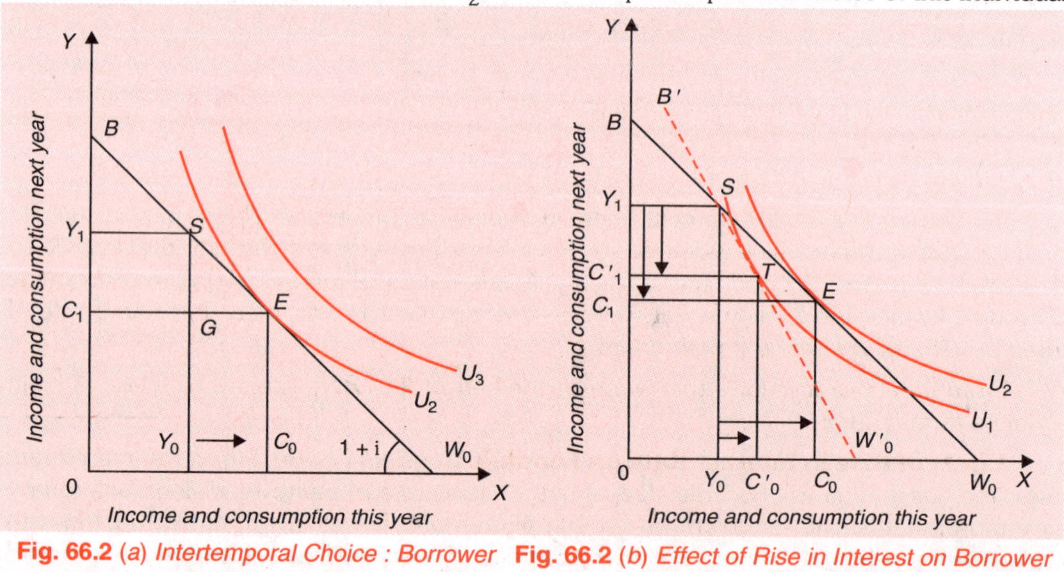

Fig. 66.2 *(a) Intertemporal Choice : Borrower* Fig. 66.2 *(b) Effect of Rise in Interest on Borrower*

is given by point *E* on indifference curve U_2. This means he consumes C_0 in this year and C_1 next year. As compared to his preferred consumption pattern, he has less income in the present and more in the next year. He, therefore, ***borrows in the present against his future income to maximise his satisfaction over the two years.*** From Fig. 66.2*(a)* it will be seen that he borrows $C_0 - Y_0$ to raise his consumption this year. For each unit he borrows, he will pay $1 + 0.2 = 1.2$ next year, given 0.2 or 20 per cent as the rate of interest.

Now, if the rate of interest rises, say to 0.3, that is, 30 per cent, the intertemporal budget line becomes $B'W'_0$ which is steeper than BW_0. It will be seen from Fig. 66.2*(b)* that the new budget line $B'W'_0$ is tangent to the indifference curve U_1 at point *T* which shows that his borrowings has declined to $C'_0 - Y_0$ at a higher rate of interest. It therefore follows that there is negative relationship between rate of interest and the amount of borrowing, showing individual borrows less at higher rates of interest and *vice-versa*. Accordingly, the curve of borrowing of an individual slopes downward. By adding horizontally the borrowings of various individuals we get the demand curve for borrowing (D_B) which slopes downward as shown in Fig. 66.3.

Borrowing-Lending Equilibrium : Determination of Rate of Interest

By bringing demand for borrowing and supply of lending curves together we can show what rate of interest is determined through borrowing-lending equilibrium. This has been shown in Fig. 66.3 where S_L is the supply curve of lending which slopes upward and D_B is the demand curve of borrowing which slopes downward as explained above. It will be seen from Fig. 66.3 that borrowing and lending are in equilibrium at rate of interest *i* (= 0.2). Thus 0.2 or 20 per cent is the equilibrium rate of interest determined by the interaction of borrowings and lendings by individuals. If the rate of interest is greater than 0.2, say it is 0.25, there will be excess supply of lending over demand for borrowing As a result, rate of interest will fall down to 0.2. On the other hand, if rate of interest is lower than the equilibrium rate of interest *i* or 0.2, the supply of lending falls short of demand for borrowing pushing the rate of interest up to the equilibrium level 0.2.

Endowed or Present Wealth and Consumption. From the foregoing analysis it follows that when allowance is made for lending and borrowing *it is not the current income that limits consumption choices or saving* of an individual but the value of what is called his *present or endowed wealth*. It is therefore important to understand the concept of *present or endowed wealth of an individual.* ***Present or endowed wealth is the present market value of the current and future incomes of an individual.*** Confining ourselves to the two-period analysis, present wealth of an individual is equal to the income of this year plus the present value of next year's income.

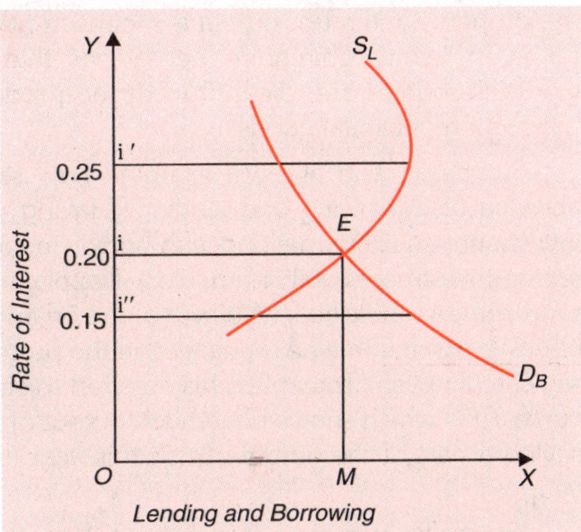

Fig. 66.3. *Borrowing-Leding Equilibrium Determination of Market Rate of Interest*

Thus, individual's present or endowed wealth is given by

$$W_0 = Y_0 + \frac{Y_1}{1+i}$$

where W_0 stands for the present wealth, Y_0 for the present year's income, Y_1 for next year's income and *i* for market rate of interest. Note that present value of next year's income is obtained by discounting it at the market rate of interest.

In our above analysis, (Figure 66.1) where individual has income equal to 60 units in the current year and 30 units in the next year and market rate of interest is 0.2 or 20 per cent, the present wealth of the individual is

$$W_0 = Y_0 + \frac{Y_1}{1+i} = 60 + \frac{30}{1+0.2} = 85$$

It will be seen from Fig. 66.1(*a*) that the budget line meets the *X*-axis at $W_0 = 85$. When rate of interest rises to 0.25, the value of the present wealth becomes

$$W_0 = 60 + \frac{30}{1+0.25} = 60 + \frac{30}{1.25} = 84$$

Change in endowed or present wealth through changes in the market rate of interest plays an important role in individual's intertemporal choices between present and future consumption.

It has been seen above in Fig. 66.1(*b*) that rise in the rate of interest causing a change in the present wealth has induced the individual to save and lend more. Further, like an increase in income, increase in wealth of an individual will cause an outward shift in the budget line which will permit the individual to consume more this year as well as next year.

SAVING–INVESTMENT EQUILIBRIUM : INTERTEMPORAL PRODUCTION ARD CONSUMPTION DECISIONS

In our above analysis of lending-borrowing equilibrium made above, we have assumed that there are no *net savings*; while lenders save and lend some income, borrowers dissave and borrow the income. In borrowing-lending equilibrium, what lenders wish to lend (*i.e.* save) is exactly equal to what the borrowers (*i.e.* dissave) at the equilibrium rate of interest. Thus, in our ***borrowing-lending model described above, net savings being zero, there is no investment.*** In other words, our above model of lending and borrowing is a *pure exchange model* involving no production or investment decision. It may be noted that real investment means the creation or production of new capital goods which add to the productive capacity of the economy and raises output and consumption in future years. In our analysis we now allow for investment which requires net savings, that is, a part of current income is saved, or in other words, resources are released from the production of consumer goods and devoted to the production of capital goods.

To begin with, we will examine how saving-investment equilibrium is reached in the absence of borrowing and lending. Having explained that we will turn to explain saving-investment equilibrium along with borrowing and lending. To make clear the fundamentals of saving-investment equilibrium, we will explain it by taking the case of Robinson Crusoe which represents an individual who lives alone on an island isolated from any exchange with anyone else. We assume that he is engaged in the production and consumption of a single commodity, say catching fish. To explain his decision to save and invest, we draw a production possibility curve *TT′* which shows how much output of fish he can produce and consume next year by saving a part of the output of fish this year (that is, by refraining from its consumption this year).

It may be stressed again that investment refers to the creation of new capital goods. In the case of isolated Robinson Crusoe who instead of devoting all his available time in catching (*i.e.* producing) fish and consuming this year, may decide to devote some of his time for building a net (which is a capital asset) to catch more fish next year. In other words, he saves a part of his current output of fish which he could produce if he devoted all his current time in catching fish. Note that ***in this non-exchange economy (that is, without borrowing and lending) Robinson Crusoe's saving and investment are done by the same person and are one and the same thing.***

In Fig. 66.4 let us assume that initial endowment position is given by point A on the production possibility curve TT' which shows he can transform some output of fish this year (Y_0) to the output of fish next year (Y_1) through building a fishing net in the current year and therefore sacrificing some current output and consumption. Now suppose that starting from his endowment position A he decides to save and invest a part of current output of fish. As explained above, he can do this by spending some of the available time of this year for building a fishing net which he uses next year to catch more fish. Consider Fig. 66.4 with his endowment at A, he cuts down his production and consumption of fish this year to C_0 (that is, he saves and invests equal to $Y_0 - C_0$ amount of current output of fish) and devotes the time so released from catching fish this year for building the net, a capital asset. With this fishing net he is able to increase his output and consumption of fish to C_1 next year. Thus, the fishing net has enabled him to catch $C_1 - Y_1$ (= 65 – 30 = 35) more fish next year. In terms of numbers, saving and investment of $Y_0 - C_0$ = 15 units has enabled him to increase output of fish by $C_1 - Y_1$ = 35 units in the next year and accordingly on the production transformation curve TT' he moves from endowment position A to optimal choice point E. The rate of return is therefore equal to (35 – 15)/15 = 20/15 = 1.33 or 133 per cent.

Now, if individual decides to increase his saving and investment further to $C'_0 - Y_0$ (= 25), that is, if he cuts down consumption of this year to 50, he will move to point R on the production transformation curve TT', the average yield of return falls, (15–10)/10 = 5/10, that is, 50 per cent. ***This falling rate of return with the increase in investment is due to the operation of the law of diminishing returns.***

In Figure 66.4 we have also drawn indifference curves of Robinson Crusoe reflecting his preferences between his present and future consumption. Note that the slope of an indifference curve at a point measures the marginal rate of substitution of present for future consumption (MRS_{01}) which means how much he is willing to obtain next year for a unit sacrifice of fish this year. Starting from his initial endowment position A Robinson Crusoe moves to his optimal point E at which indifference curve U_2 is tangent to the production possibility curve TT'. It may be noted that at the initial endowment point A the indifference curve U_1 is intersecting the production possibility curve TT'. A look at point A shows that slope of the production possibility curve at this endowment point A which measures the marginal rate of transformation (MRT_{01}) is greater than his marginal rate of substitution of present consumption for future consum-ption (MRS_{01}). To put it in other words, at endowment point A the rate of return on investment is greater than the rate of time preference between his present consumption and future

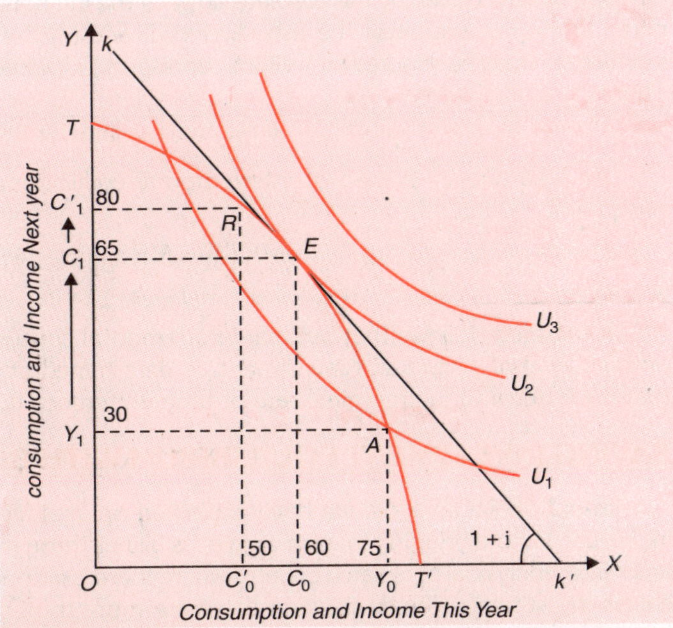

Fig. 66.4. *Saving-Investment Equilibrium : Intertempoal Production and Consumption Optimum : Robinson Crusoe Case*

consumption given by the slope of indifference curve U_1 at it. That is, the rate of return which he receives is greater than the amount of extra output or consumption which he is willing to receive for a unit sacrifice of his present consumption. Therefore, Robinson Crusoe moves up on the production possibility curve from his endonment point A to the tangency point E at which the slopes of the production possibility curve TT' and the higher indifference curve U_2 are equal. Thus, under the given circumstances, U_2 is the highest possible indifference curve to which Robinson Crusoe can go. Therefore, the particular choice of present and future consumption represented by point E is the optimum for him and saving and investment he is making at this point is of optimal level. If he saves and invests more and moves up further on the production possibility curve to the position R on it, he will go below the indifference U_2 indicating that he is going away from the optimum saving and investment level.

To sum up, choice of optimal saving and investment is determined by the equality of the marginal rate of transformation (MRT_{01}) of present consumption for future output and the marginal rate of substitution of present for future consumption. While marginal rate of transformation of present consumption for future output (MRT_{01}) is measured by the absolute slope of the production possibilities curve, marginal rate of substitution of present for future consumption is known by the absolute slope of an indifference curve. Since at the optimal choice point E the production possibility curve TT' is tangent to the indifference curve U_2, $MRT_{01} = MRS_{01}$.

Now gross marginal rate of transformation MRT_{01} can be broken into two parts, first the opportunity cost (that is, one fish sacrificed this year) and, secondly, the extra units of fish produced, which is called the net return. Thus

$$MRT_{01} = 1 + r$$

where r is the extra units of output and is called net return on investment.

Likewise, marginal rate of substitution of present consumption for future consumption (MRS_{01}) which is given by the absolute slope of the indifference curve can also be split into two parts: (I) the repayment of the fish sacrificed; and (2) the extra net reward received for the sacrifice and may be denoted by k which represents individual's marginal rate of time preference. Thus

$$MRS_{01} = 1 + k$$

As seen above, in case of intertemporal equilibrium or optimal choice of saving and investment

$$MRT_{01} = MRS_{01}$$

or $$1 + r = 1 + k \quad \text{or} \quad r = k$$

It therefore follows that optimal intertemporal consumption stream, or in other words, optimal level of saving and investment, is determined at the point where marginal rate of return r is equal to the marginal rate of time preference (k).

SAVING-INVESTMENT EQUILIBRIUM WITH BORROWING AND LENDING

In our above analysis, we have explained optimal level of saving and investment of an individual without bringing in exchange possibilities through borrowing and lending. In case of an isolated individual or isolated country where there is no one to lend or trade saving necessarily equals investment. However, when there are more than one individual or country and as a result there are possibilities of borrowing and lending, saving and investment may not be equal. In such a **case the problem before an individual or a country is to choose not only**

an optimal level of saving and investment but also optimal borrowing and lending. This optimal choice is depicted in Fig. 66.6 where TT' represents production possibilities of transforming present consumption into future output or income. The slope of the production possibility curve indicates the marginal rate of transformation of the present output for future output and is written as MRT_{01}. As shown above,

$$MRT_{01} = 1 + r$$

where r represents the rate of return on investment

We can draw an intertemporal budget line passing through every point of the production possibility curve. This intertemporal budget line represents exchange possibilities in the market for an individual who through borrowing or lending can select optimum consumption stream, that is, consumption this year and consumption next year. It may be recalled that the slope of the intertemporal budget line equals $1 + i$ where i stands for market rate of interest at which an individual can borrow or lend. Thus, whereas an isolated Robinson Crusoe can choose only optimal level of saving and investment to maximise his satisfaction, individual in the present case can also benefit from exchange possibilities, that is, from borrowing and lending in the market in order to maximise his satisfaction over time. Individual has to make a two-fold choice. First, he has to determine the optimum level of investment so as to maximise his present or endowed wealth. Secondly, given the level of present wealth, he has to decide the optimum consumption stream in this year and the next year through borrowing or lending. Given the production possibility curve TT' and individual's endowment position A at it, the individual is having income Y_0 this year and Y_1 next year.Passing through A on the production possibility curve we have drawn in Fig. 66.5 an intertemporal budget line B_0W_0 whose slope has been determined by the market rate of interest (i) and its level or location by the magnitude of present wealth. As explained above, corresponding to the point A on the budget line B_0W_0, the value of the present wealth is OW_0 (which we simply write as W_0) and is equal to the distance from the origin at which the budget line B_0W_0 meets the X-axis. We have seen above that the value of present wealth is the market value of income of this year and income of the next year. Note that the market value of next year's income is obtained by disounting next year's income at the market rate of interest. Thus

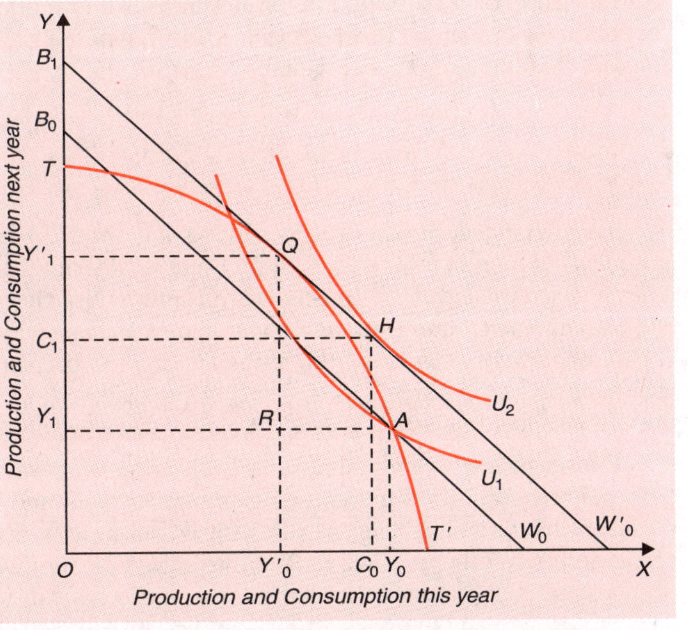

Fig. 66.5. *Saving -Investment Equilibrium with Borrowing and Lending*

Present wealth, $$W_0 = Y_0 + \frac{Y_1}{1+i}$$

where Y_0 is present year's income, Y_1 is income of the next year and i is the market rate of interest.

Likewise, various parallel budget lines whose slope equals $1 + i$ and pass through various points of the given production possibility frontier TT' can be drawn, each of which represents a certain magnitude of present wealth. In order to determine the optimum level of investment and accordingly optimum income stream in this year and next, he will aim at maximizing the magnitude of present wealth. For this end in view, he will try to reach the highest possible budget line on the given production possibility frontier. It will be seen from Fig. 66.5 that B_1W_0' is the highest possible budget line which is tangent to production possibility curve TT' at point Q. Corresponding to this budget line $B_1W'_0$, the magnitude of present wealth is given by

$$W'_0 = Y'_0 + \frac{Y'_1}{1+i}$$

W'_0 is the maximum attainable present wealth under the given circumstances. At the tangency point Q representing the maximum possible present wealth, marginal rate of transformation of present output (or income) for future output or income (MRT_{01}) is equal to the absolute slope of the budget line (*i.e.* $1 + i$), where i is the market rate of interest. Thus, at point Q of maximum present wealth.

$$MRT_{01} = (1 + i)$$

Since $$MRT_{01} = 1 + r$$

Therefore, $$1 + r = 1 + i \quad \text{or} \quad r = i$$

Thus at tangency point Q, representing optimal income stream rate of return on investment (r) equals the market rate of interest (i). Point Q determines the optimal level of investment as it has enabled the individual to achieve maximum possible value of present wealth by reaching highest attainable intertemporal budget line. It will be seen from Fig. 66.5 that starting from endowment point A to reach the tangency point Q on the production possibility frontier, he has made investment equal to $Y_0 - Y'_0$ or the distance AR to achieve the maximum possible present wealth.

However, it is worth noting that in the present case of exchange possibilities, point Q does not represent the optimum consumption stream and $Y_0 - Y'_0$ or distance AR does not represent his optimal saving as the individual can now finance a part of his investment by borrowing from others. Thus, having maximised present wealth by undertaking optimal level of investment, the individual will now maximise his satisfaction by making optimal choice between present and future consumption. He will achieve this through exchange in the market (that is, through borrowing or lending). As seen before, his optimal consumption choice will be at the point where the highest attainable budget line $B_1W'_0$ representing maximum possible present wealth W'_0 is tangent to the indifference curve showing individual's preference between present and future consumption. It will be seen from Fig. 66.5 that the budget line $B_1W'_0$ is tangent to the indifference curve U_2 at point H corresponding to which the individual consumes C_0 in the present year and C_1 next year.

It must be repeated that the slope of the indifference curve indicates marginal rate of substitution of present consumption for future consumption (MRS_{01}) which equals I + k. At the tangency point H the slope of intertemporal budget line B_1W_0', that is, $1 + i$ is equal to the slope of indifference curve U_2. Thus at the optimal consumption point H

$$MRS_{01} = 1 + i$$

Since $$MRS_{01} = 1 + k$$

where, k is the rate of the time preference, therefore at the optimum consumption point H.

$$MRS_{01} = 1 + k = 1 + i \quad or \quad k = i$$

This means at the optimal consumption stream point H rate of time preference (k) is equal to the market rate of interest (i). It will be noticed from Figure 66.5 that at the optimal consumption point H the individual saves $Y_0 - C_0$ but, as seen above, he makes investment equal to $Y_0 - Y'_0$. Thus, the total optimal investment made by him is financed partly by his own savings equal to $Y_0 - C_0$ and partly by borrowing equal to $C_0 - Y'_0$. In this way he maximises his satisfaction over time (*i.e.* in the two-periods case here) by first making optimal level of investment and then choosing optimum level of consumption in the present and future by exchanging, that is, through borrowing. Thus, in his attempt to maximise his satisfaction in the two periods he makes best possible use of the production possibilities thrown up by the production possibility frontier as well as the optimum use of the exchange or consumption possibilities represented by the intertemporal budget line whose slope is determined by the market rate of interest.

Determination of Market Interest Rate with Saving and Investment, Borrowing and Lending

We can now explain the determination of market rate of interest through equilibrium between saving and investments in the economy when exchange possibilities of lending and borrowing are present. As seen before, we can add the intended investments and intended savings of all individuals at various rates of interest to obtain the aggregate investment demand curve and aggregate supply curve of savings of the economy. The rate of interest is determined at the level at which aggregate investment demand curve I_D and aggregate supply curve S_S of savings intersect each other as shown in Fig. 66.6. In it at rate of interest i the investment demand equals supply of savings. At any other rate of interest which is higher or lower than i, the two are not equal which will cause readjustment in rate of interest bringing intended savings and intended investment equal to each other. Thus the condition for equilibrium rate of interest is :

$$I(i) = S(i).$$

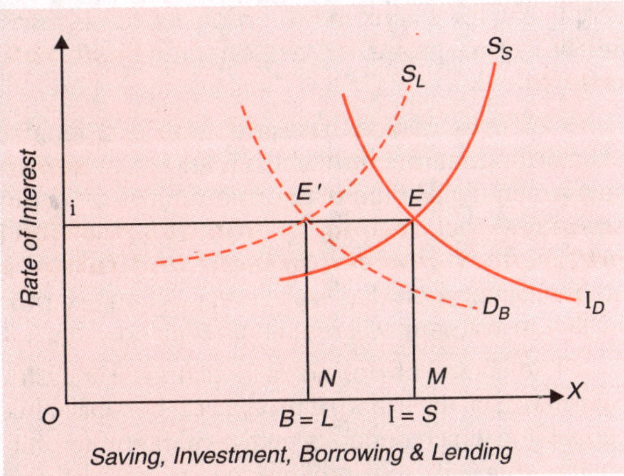

Fig. 66.6. *Determination of Interest Rate with Saving and Investment and Borrowing and Lending*

Alternatively, determination of equilibrium rate of interest is shown by the intersection of demand curve D_B for borrowing and supply curve S_L of lending. As seen before, at the equilibrium rate of interest $S_L = D_B$ which in our Fig. 66.6 occur at point E' or rate of interest i. Note that saving-investment equilibrium and lending-borrowing equilibrium occur at the same rate of interest. This can be proved as under :

As regards the borrowers, they can either invest by saving themselves or by borrowing from others. Thus

$$I = S + D_B \quad \text{...(i)}$$

As regards the lenders, they can use their saving either for investment by themselves or for lending others. Thus

$$S = I + S_L \quad \text{....(ii)}$$

Bringing the equations (*i*) and (*ii*) together and keeping in view that in equilibrium intended savings (*S*) = intended investment (*I*), we have

$$I + S_L = S + D_B$$

or

$$S_L = D_B$$

Thus we see that lending-borrowing equilibrium and saving-investment equilibrium occur at the same rate of interest. However, it is important to note that at the equilibrium rate of interest aggregate amount borrowed (and lent) can be either more or less than the aggregate amount invested (and saved). Thus in Fig. 66.6 at the equilibrium rate of interest *i* amount invested equals *OM* whereas amount borrowed equals *ON*. This happens because the difference ***NM* amount of investment is financed by self-resources by the investors.**

INVESTMENT DECISIONS AND NET PRESENT VALUE RULE

Our intertemporal analysis of investment and interest made above has an important practical application for decision making of a business firm. Managers of private business firms and public enterprises have often to decide which investment projects are to be undertaken. For example, a business manager has often to decide whether he should build a new plant, purchase a new high-tech computer, should he scrap the old machine, how much to invest in research and development (R & D) or advertising and so forth. As investment projects yield return over a number of years, they involve streams of cash flows (*i.e.* a sequence of incomes and costs). Our intertemporal analysis of lending and borrowing, saving and investment made above is very useful for examining the problem of his investment decisions. Whether or not to make investment in a project is based on some ***basic rules or what are also called investment criteria.***

Before explaining these important decision rules it is necessary to make clear the meaning of an important theorem which is known as ***separation theorem.***[1] Our analysis of saving-investment equilibrium with opportunities of lending and borrowing which is depicted in Fig. 66.6 shows that ***optimal production position is quite independent of individual's preferences between present and future consumption.*** Even if indifference curve map reflecting individual's preference changes, production optimum point *Q*, that is, optimum level of investment will remain unaffected. This is known as ***Separation Theorem.***

The choice of optimal production or investment position (point *Q* in our Fig. 66.5) is determined by the shape of production possibility frontier *TT′* and the slope of the intertemporal budget line which depends on the market rate of interest. The budget line in no way depends on the shape of the indifference curves of the lenders and borrowers which depict their preferences between the present and future consumption. However, it may be noted that separation theorem applies only if the markets for lending and borrowing are perfect and transaction costs are nil. If the transactions involve a good deal of cost, the investment decision, that is, choice of optimum production point on the production possibility curve, will in part depend on the preference of the individual for the present consumption over future consumption, that is, in this case, the amount of investment will depend on the willingness to save.

Note that in case of any isolated individual such as Robinson Crusoe in our above analysis separation theorem does not apply because he has no exchange possibilities of lending or borrowing and therefore his investment and consumption choice are the same. In his case investment is necessarily self-financed and therefore his preferences between the present and future consumption which determines his saving must also determine his investment decision. In fact, as explained above, saving and investment in case of isolated Robinson Crusoe are one and the same thing.

1. See T. Harshleifer and A. Glazer, *Price Theory and Application*, 5th ed. Prenctice Hall, India, 1993, p. 404

Net Present Value Rule for Investment Decision : Choice of a Project

An investment project yields a return in the form of a stream of dated incomes and it also involves cost to be incurred in the present. For instance, for a project such as investment for purchasing a machine, building a factory, acquiring an educational or technical skill, an individual has to incur costs in the current year. Returns from an investment project are obtained as cash flows of income or output in future years. An important decision rule for investment is the net present value criterion. The basis of this criterion or rule is that a ***unit of a commodity or a rupee next year is worth less than a unit of the commodity or rupee this year.*** Therefore, income or output flow from a project accruing at different times cannot be simply added to determine whether or not to make investment in the project. The reason for this is returns in future years have to be discounted at the market rate of interest. First, we will make our analysis of choice of investment projects when two periods are involved, that is, the present year and the next year. In an investment project, since in the present year cost is incurred, cash flow is negative. The returns start from the next year in the form of increase in income or in output, the cash flows are positive in the future years. In the choice of project a firm is guided by the ***principle of maximisation of wealth***. Investment in a project which increases wealth is desirable. Further, as mentioned earlier, while making investment decision, the firm will calculate the net present value of a project. The ***net present value of a project is the value today of the net cash flows in the future year obtained by discounting them at the market rate of interest minus the cost incurred on the project in the current year.*** Note that costs incurred on maintenance of a machine or any other type of project have to be subtracted from receipts or income flows to obtain the net cash flows for the future years. A project which will yield income only from a year now and has no scrap value, present value is given by

$$NPV = -C_0 + \frac{R_1}{1+i}$$

where NPV denotes the net present value of a project, C_0 is the cost of the project in the current year and will therefore be negative, R_1 is the net cash flow in the next year and i is the market rate of interest.

If the net present value of an investment project is positive, this means it increases wealth of the business firm. As the objective of the firm is to maximise its wealth, it will be desirable to undertake the project if its net present value is positive. Thus, we get a decision rule for deciding about investment in a project.

Net Present Value Decision Rule I : ***Approve or undertake any project whose net present value is positive and reject any project whose net present value is zero or negative.***

Let us illustrate this rule.

Example I. *If an investment project costs ₹ 10,000, market rate of interest is 15 per cent per annum, and it yields return of ₹ 16,100 in the next year.*

Sol. The net present value of the project is given by

$$NPV = -C_0 + \frac{R_1}{1+i}$$

$$NPV = -10{,}000 + \frac{16{,}100}{1+0.15}$$

$$= -10{,}000 + \frac{16{,}100}{1.15}$$

$$= -10{,}000 + 16{,}100 \times \frac{100}{115}$$

$$= -10{,}000 + 14{,}000 = ₹\,4{,}000$$

Thus, net present value of the project is positive and therefore undertaking of this project will increase wealth of the firm by ₹ 4,000. Therefore, investment in this project should be made.

Take another example.

Example 2. *Suppose a firm is planning to purchase a machine which costs ₹ 20,000 and interest is 10 per cent per annum and anticipated yield from it next year is ₹ 22,000 and at the end of the next year the machine has no salvage or scrap value. Is it worthwhile to approve the project?*

Sol. Net present value of the machine (*NPV*) $= -C_0 + \frac{R_1}{1+i} = -20{,}000 + \frac{22{,}000}{1+0.1}$

$$= -20{,}000 + \frac{22{,}000}{1.1}$$

$$= -20{,}000 + 22{,}000 \times \frac{10}{11} = 0$$

Thus the net present value of the machine is zero. It is not worthwhile to make investment in the machine. However, it may be noted that if the yield from the machine next year exceeds ₹ 22,000, its net present value will become positive and it will then be desirable to purchase it for the production of a commodity. Note that if the yield next year remains ₹ 22,000 but rate of interest falls below 10 per cent, the net present value will again become positive and it will be worthwhile to make investment in the machine.

Example 3. *Suppose a firm is considering to invest in a project. Its cost this year is ₹ 1 lakh and its yield in year one from now is ₹ 1.25 lakh and its scrap value is zero. What is the highest rate of interest at which the project should be undertaken?*

Sol. To determine the required value of the rate of interest (i), we should make the net present value equal to zero . Thus

$$NPV = -C_0 + \frac{R_1}{1+i} = 0$$

$$-1{,}00{,}000 + \frac{1{,}25{,}000}{1+i} = 0$$

$$\frac{1{,}25{,}000}{1+i} = 1{,}00{,}000$$

or $$1{,}00{,}000\,(1+i) = 1{,}25{,}000$$

$$1 + i = \frac{1{,}25{,}000}{1{,}00{,}000} = \frac{5}{4}$$

$$i = \frac{5}{4} - 1 = 0.25$$

This means if the rate of interest is 0.25, that is, 25 per cent, the net present value of project is zero. Thus, if the rate of interest falls below 25 per cent, the net present value will become positive. Thus the project should be undertaken for any value of the rate of interest below 25 per cent.

Net Present Value Rule 2 : Choice Among Multiple Projects

In our above analysis we have been concerned with explaining a rule regarding whether or not a project should be approved for investment. Now, we will discuss the choice by a firm when several projects are available for investment. In this case we need to compare the net present values of the various projects. The project which has the highest net present value should be undertaken. The project with the highest net present value will make the greatest contribution to the objective of maximising wealth by a firm. Thus, in case of choice among multiple projects we arrive at the following rule : ***"If the two or more mutually exclusive projects are available for investment, undertake the project which has the highest net present value."***

It may be pointed out that we face difficulties in the use of this rule when projects, instead of being mutually exclusive, are *interdependent*, that is, undertaking of a project may change the benefits or returns from the other projects. For instance, a project of flood control may increase the benefits or revenue from the project of growing wheat on an agricultural farm. In case of these interdependent projects we have to modify the rule. In this case we should compare not the net present values of individual projects but various 'sets' of interdependent projects. Thus, for the choice of a single project from various projects, they must be mutually exclusive, that is, independent of each other.

Let us illustrate this decision rule concerning mutually exclusive multiple projects by giving an example.

Example : Two projects A and B are available to a firm. Cost in the current year and net cash flow in the next year of each is given below. Which project a firm should choose if market rate of interest is 10 per cent per annum ?

Project	*Cost this year*	*Net cash flow in the next year*
Project A	100 lakh	120 lakh
Project B	150 lakh	180 lakh

$$\text{Net present value } NPV \text{ of Project A} = -C_0 = \frac{R_1}{1+i}$$

$$= -100 + \frac{120}{1+0.10} = -100 + 120 \times \frac{10}{11}$$

$$= -100 + 109.09 = 9.09$$

$$\text{Net present value } NPV \text{ of Project B} = -150 + \frac{180}{1.1}$$

$$= -150 + 180 \times \frac{10}{11} = -150 + 163.63 = 13.63$$

Thus, net present value of project *B* is greater than the net present value of project *A*. Therefore, the firm which aims at maximising wealth should undertake project *B*.

Net Present Value Rule for Investment Decisions : Multiperiod Case

Many investment projects yield a stream of returns (*i.e.* cash flows) beyond two periods.

The present value rule applies in this case too. However, we have to extend the net present value rule to deal with several years. Return or net cash flow of ₹ 1000 occurring in the third year is worth less than ₹ 1000 occurring in the second year. Likewise, ₹ 1000 accruing in the fourth year is less than ₹ 1000 accruing in the third year. Therefore, in a multiperiod case the net present value of a project can be obtained as under :

$$NPV = -C_0 + \frac{R_1}{1+i} + \frac{R_2}{(1+i)^2} + \frac{R_3}{(1+i)^3} + \ldots + \frac{R_n}{(1+i)^n}$$

where NPV is the present value of the project, C_0 is the cash flow during the current year (It is negative in case of an investment project as cost has to be incurred on a project in the current year) R_1, R_2, R_3..........R_n are the positive net cash flows in the form of income after first, second, third year and so on. Let us explain the net present value rule for the investment decision in a multiperiod case.

Example : *Suppose a firm is considering to buy a machine today for ₹ 25,000. The use of this machine in the production process of a commodity causes firm's net income to rise by ₹ 15,000 in each of the next two years. Assume the rate of interest is 10 per cent and machines has no scrap value. Is it desirable for the firm to purchase the machine?*

Sol. $$NPV = -C_0 + \frac{R_1}{1+i} + \frac{R_2}{(1+i)^2}$$

$$= -25{,}000 + \frac{15{,}000}{1+0.1} + \frac{15{,}000}{(1+0.1)^2}$$

$$= -25{,}000 + 15{,}000 \times \frac{10}{11} + 15{,}000 \times \frac{10}{11} \times \frac{10}{11}$$

$$= -25{,}000 + 13{,}636.4 + 12{,}396.7 = 1033.1$$

Thus we find net present value of the machine is positive and therefore it will increase the wealth of the firm by ₹ 1,033. It is therefore desirable to make investment in it.

If the machine creates net revenue of ₹ 15,000 in one more year, the net present value will further increase, making the machine more wealth generating. In case a machine yields net return in the third year also, we extend our equation to the third year as well and calculate the net present value. Thus

$$NPV = -C_0 + \frac{R_1}{1+0.1} + \frac{R_2}{(1+0.1)^2} + \frac{R_3}{(1+0.1)^3}$$

Further, if at the end of two years the machine has some scrap value, say equal to Z, then value Z will also be discounted at the given market rate of interest. Thus, in this case

$$NPV = -C_0 + \frac{R_1}{1+0.1} + \frac{R_2}{(1+0.1)^2} + \frac{Z}{(1+0.1)^3}$$

Present Value of an Annuity with Perpetual Constant Annual Yield

An interesting case is of annuity with a constant stream of net cash flows for ever (*i.e.*, in perpetuity), starting from a year now. The net present value of such an annuity is given by

$$PV = \frac{R}{i}$$

where R is stream of payments which an investor receives starting from a year now, i is the rate of interest This can be proved as follows :

$$PV = \frac{R}{1+i} + \frac{R}{(1+i)^2} + \frac{R}{(1+i)^3} \text{.....indefinitely}$$

In the above R can be factored out. Therefore,

$$PV = R\left[\frac{1}{1+i} + \frac{1}{(i+i)^2} + \frac{1}{(1+i)^3} + ...\infty\right] = \frac{R}{i}$$

Let us provide an example.

Suppose a bond yields a sum of ₹ 6,000 per annum indefinitely, starting from a year now. Assuming rate of interest is 12 per cent, its present value is given by

$$PV = \frac{R}{i} = \frac{6000}{0.12} = \frac{6000}{12/100} = 50,000$$

This is because if ₹ 50,000 are invested at 12 per cent rate of interest, it will yield Rs. 6,000 every year for ever $\left(50,000 \times \frac{12}{100} = 6000\right)$

Effect of Change in Rate of Interest on the Present Value

It is important to note that the rate of interest has an important bearing on the present value of an investment project. ***The lower the rate of interest, the higher the present value of a project and vice versa.*** Thus, in our above example present value of an annuity, with a constant annual yield of ₹ 6,000 for ever, if the rate of interest falls to 10 per cent, its present value will be

$$PV = \frac{R}{i} = \frac{6000}{0.10} = 6000 \times \frac{100}{10} = 60,000$$

Thus, at a lower rate of interest the present value of the annuity has increased. This not only applies to the case of an annuity with a constant yield indefinitely but also to our earlier examples of present values of investment projects which yield cash flows for a limited number of years and also if annual yields are not constant.

It is also important to note here that cost of an investment project (for example, purchasing a machine) may not be incurred entirely in the current period, some cost also occurs every year for its maintenance. Therefore, when finding out net present value of a project, we need to consider *net cash flows* of the projects. In order to obtain these net cash flows, from the extra revenue generated by a project, the cost incurred on it for its maintenance and operation has to be subtracted from it. Further, as mentioned above, the projects have some scrap value, therefore when finding out present value of a project, the present value of its scrap value has also to be included in the stream of net cash flows of a machine or any other project.

Application of Present Value Rule to Education or Human Capital

Our analysis of present value of investment project has an important application in the field of education. Note that in line with the physical capital, persons with education of some standard are regarded as human capital because higher education increases their productivity and lifetime earnings. Therefore, expenditure on education is regarded as investment by the economists. Various studies have been made in the USA and other developed countries for estimating present values of lifetime earning of persons with Bachelor's and Post-graduate degree of education. These studies reveal that people with college and university education earn higher salaries as compared to the salaries of the persons with only high school degree which indicates the importance of investment in education. These studies also compare the lifetime earnings of the persons with higher education in various fields such as engineering, economics, computer science, physics. Note that for comparing the lifetime earnings of the various educated people, it is the present values of their lifetime earnings that are considered. One such study made in the USA assumes that earnings from the college education begin in the 5th year after admission to college and end in the 40th year for calculating the present value of lifetime earnings for the Bachelor Degrees in various fields. Considered in this way, the present value equation takes the following special form :

$$PV = \frac{R_5}{(1+i)^5} + \frac{R_6}{(1+i)^6} + \frac{R_7}{(1+i)^7} + \ldots\ldots + \frac{R_{40}}{(1+i)^{40}}$$

In different studies, calculations of the present values have been made assuming different per cent rates of interest. Findings of one such study are given in Table 66.1 for the sake of illustration.

Table 66.1 : Present Values of Lifetime Earnings with Bachelor's Degree in Various Fields

Mathematics	\$ 432,068
Economics	\$ 339,482
Computer Science	\$ 306,753
Political Science	\$ 300,000
Physics	\$ 282,758
Psychology	\$ 262,127
Agriculture Science	\$ 225,116
Biological Sciences	\$ 215,691
Sociology	\$ 213,590

Source : A Study by A Razin and J.D. Campbell, quoted in *'Price Theory and Applications'* by Hirshleifer and Glazer, 5th ed. Prentice Hall India, p. 411.

In the above calculations of present value, interest rate has been taken to be equal to 3 per cent. It may however be noted that the above estimates do not exactly indicate the importance of investment in education. This is because earning of higher income is only one objective of acquiring education.

QUESTIONS FOR REVIEW

1. Explain clearly the meaning of time preference. Explain the minimum value that rate of interest can take.
2. Show how an individual who lives in only two periods chooses his intertemporal investment and consumption levels when borrowing-lending as well as productive opportunities are open to him.
3. An individual allocates a fixed income Y between consumption today (C_1) and tomorrow (C_2) in order to maximise his utility $U(C_1, C_2)$. The constant one period rate of interest is r.
   (*a*) What is the budget constraint?
   (*b*) Show that in equilibrium MRS (of C_1 for C_2) equals $(1 + r)$

(c) Show that if r increases, then C_2 cannot go down but C_1 can move in any direction.

4. In a world of pure exchange (without intertemporal productive opportunities) show graphically how each individual with a fixed wealth constraint chooses a preferred intertemporal pattern of consumption.

5. In terms of intertemporal budget line and intertemporal preferences, examine the impact of a change in the interest rate on savers' and borrowers' well-being. Can you determine the impact of the increase in the interest rate on each group's current and future consumption assuming that both current and future consumption are normal goods ?

6. Explain the rule for calculating present discounted value of a perpetual income stream. What is the worth of a perpetuity paying ₹ 10,000 per year when the rate of interest is 8 per cent per annum ?

7. Given the following three projects, which project has the maximum net discounted present value assuming the market rate of interest as 8% ? *[D.U. BA(Hons), 1987]*

(i) Project *A* which yields an income of ₹ 200 per year indefinitely into the future.

(ii) Project *B* which yields ₹ 400 per year for two years

(iii) Project *C* which yields ₹ 100 today and ₹ 200 after 2 years

8. For a certain project the anticipated cash flows are ₹ 100 at present and ₹ 125 next year. What is the present value when the interest rate is 10% ? What is the highest rate of interest at which the project should be undertaken ?

9. Calculate the market equilibrium value for the following assets. Assume the market rate of interest is 10%.

(i) A bond that pays ₹ 100 interest per year for two years and is paid off at ₹ 1000 at the end of two years

(ii) A building that will earn ₹ 100 per year for two years and then will earn ₹ 50 per year indefinitely into the future.

10. What is the internal rate of return on an investment ? Calculate the internal rate of return on an investment yielding ₹ 25,000 after one year and costing ₹ 20,000. Suppose instead that this investment yielded nothing in the first year and ₹ 30,000 after two years, what would be its internal rate of return ?

11. An investment pays ₹ 100 per year for ever starting a year from now. What is its present value if the rate of interest is 10 per cent ? What is its present value if the rate of interest is 20 per cent?

12. Suppose the interest rate is 10 per cent. What is the value of a coupon bond that pays ₹ 80 per year for each of the next five years and then makes principal repayment of ₹ 1000 in the sixth year? What is the value of the bond if interest rate is 15 per cent?

13. What is the net present value (NPV) criterion for investment decision? How is net present value of investment projects calculated? If all the cash flows for the project are certain, what discount rate should be used to calculate the NPV ?

14. How is the present value of a bond calculated ? If the interest rate is 5 per cent, what is the present value of a perpetuity that pays ₹ 1000 per year for ever ?

APPENDIX TO CHAPTER 66

Cost-Benefit Analysis

Meaning

In the foregoing chapters we have been mainly concerned with the business decision making by private enterprises which are driven mainly by profit motive. In the selection of investment projects the private firms take into account only the internal direct effects (that is, cash flows accruing to them and the costs they have to incur) and do not take the longer and wider view of their activities from the social point of view. As seen in the previous chapter the private sector firms follow the net present value criterion for acceptance or rejection of investment projects. But public enterprises and non-profit institutions have to take a broader social repercussions of their resource allocation and investment decisions. That is, they take into account both internal (direct) and external (indirect) effects of their business decisions. An analytical model called cost-benefit analysis is used to analyse the wider impact of resource allocation and investment decisions, especially by public enterprises. Properly understood, it is *Social Cost-Benefit* Analysis of investment projects though the word 'social' is often omitted. Thus in social cost-benefit analysis, we estimate both direct (i.e., internal) and indirect (i.e., external) costs of a project to the society as well as its direct and indirect benefits to the society.Therefore, *cost-benefit analysis is especially used for analysing the desirability of public sector investment programme and is a counter part of capital budgeting which is used to evaluate any investment project by a private enterprise.* Explaining the essence of cost-benefit analysis Prest and Turvey who are the pioneers of the technique of cost-benefit analysis write, "Cost-benefit analysis is a practical way of assessing the desirability of projects where it is important to take a long view (in the sense of looking at repercussions in the distant future as will as the nearer future) and a wider view (in the sense of allowing for side-effects of many kinds and many persons, industries, regions, etc.), i.e., it implies the enumeration and evaluation of all relevant costs and benefits"[1]. It is important to note that in estimating social costs of a project market prices of resources are not used as they are generally distorted; they are distorted due to the imposition of taxes by the Government or due to the market imperfection or monopoly power of the resource owners. Instead, specially devised prices called ***shadow prices*** which reflect the opportunity costs or true scarcity values of the resources used.

It is worth noting that public sector enterprises and non-profit institutions face the same problems of resource allocation and investment as the private sector. But in deciding about them while the public sector enterprises take a wider view and consider both internal and external effects of their decisions, the private sector, guided by profit considerations alone, adopts a narrow view and takes into account only internal effects of their business decisions, disregarding the external effects which may be harmful or beneficial. Thus in cost-benefit analysis we are not concerned with internal benefits and internal costs of an investment project to be undertaken by a private firm. The cost-benefit analysis enumerates and evaluates *all social benefits* and *all social costs* of a project or expenditure

1. Prest and Turvey, *Economic Journal,* December, 1975.

programme in contrast to the capital budgeting technique used by private firms which take into account only their private costs and private benefits to judge the desirability of an investment project. Besides, since benefits from an investment project are reaped mostly in in future years and costs are also incurred for a long period in future, it is ***discounted social benefits and discounted social costs that are*** compared to decide about the desirability of a project. However, for discounting social benefits and costs of an investment project, it is ***social discount rate*** that is often used.

The Use of Cost-Benefit Analysis

As mentioned above, the technique of cost-benefit analysis is particularly used when *a long and wider view* of the effects of a particular project or expenditure programme is needed. As in case of capital budgeting by private firms cost-benefit analysis is generally used in case when the economic effects of a project or an investment expenditure programme or policy change *accrue in future years*. However, unlike the capital budgeting by private firms, the cost-benefit analysis attempts to estimate all direct economic effects as well as indirect spill-over effects.

Cost benefit analysis is used to assess whether a particular project or specific public expenditure programme should be accepted or rejected. In order to do so benefits, both direct and indirect, of a project or specific public expenditure programme and similarly the costs to be incurred on the project over the years are estimated. Then the *present value* of both the benefits and costs over the future years are estimated using an appropriate discount rate from social point of view. It follows from above that cost-benefit analysis is a method of evaluating public projects and expenditure programmes for making decisions regarding the desirability of the projects to be undertaken. Accordingly, it is used to assess big public expenditure schemes such as building dams and airports, controlling diseases (for example, malaria control programme), planning for defence and safety, and spending for health, education and research.

Cost-Benefit Criterion

Having calculated the present values of both benefits and costs at a given social discount rate then the two are compared. If using the given social discount rate *present value of benefits from a project or other investment programme exceeds the present value of costs, the said project or investment programme is accepted for being undertaken*. On the other hand, if present value of benefits is less than the present value of costs, the proposed project or expenditure programme is economically inefficient and should therefore be rejected.

Besides being used to evaluate the economic justification of the entire project or programme, the cost-benefit analysis is used to determine whether the size of project or programme under implementation be increased and if so by what extent. Such decision is usually made by using traditional marginal analysis by estimating additional benefits from the proposed increase in size and additional costs to be made. Thus the objective of public sector decision-making regarding whether it is building of an airport or regulating a public utility (such as electricity generation and distribution) is wider than maximising private profits which guides private sector decision. *In making a decision the Government or public enterprise has not only to consider benefits that accrue as revenue to the enterprise but also the external benefits (beneficial externalities) that accrue to other members of the socially*. Likewise, the cost-benefit analysis considers not only the costs that are paid by the enterprise but also the external costs (i.e., external diseconomies) (including environment pollution) it inflicts on others by its activity.

General Steps (or Stages) of Cost-Benefit Analysis

There are no simple rules which Government or any public authority should follow to undertake cost-benefit analysis. The following four general stages or steps are involved in conducting cost-benefit analysis.

Let us explain the above stages in some detail of undertaking cost-benefit analysis.

Step 1. In stage 1 we are concerned with assessing whether the proposed investment project or expenditure programm is appropriate from the wider social point of view taking into account all the *externalities* (that is, both beneficial and harmful external effects) of the investment project. Obviously, the project will be considered as appropriate for being undertaken if there are *significant beneficial externalities* so that they exceed the cost of the project. However, the appropriateness of the project depends on the objective function to be maximised. This objective function is set by the Government or in a democracy by the parliament which represents the people.

Step 2. The step or stage - 2 requires identifying and enumerating all external benefits and costs many of which may be intangible such as noise, pollution, beauty and healthly environment. There are both direct and indirect (external) benefits and costs of

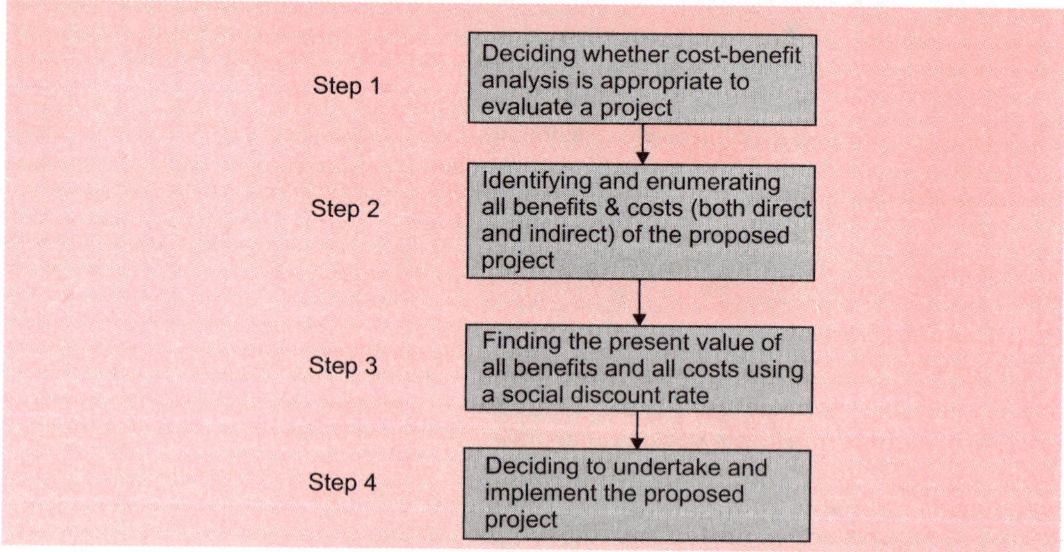

Fig. 66A.1. *Steps (or Stages) of Cost-Benefit Analysis*

an investment project. The direct or internal benefits of a project can be measured by the extra quantity of goods and services produced if the project is undertaken compared to the conditions without it. Thus, the direct benefits of an irrigation project is the quantity of extra crop produced net of extra costs in the form of more labour, seeds and equipment used as compared to the non-irrigated land. On the other hand, direct costs include capital costs incurred on capital equipment, machines installed, land acquired to undertake and implement the project and the operating and maintenance costs incurred over the life span of the project.

In addition to the direct effects of an investment project, there are invariably ***indirect or external effects.*** These indirect or external beneficial effects are classified into two types, (1) **real or technological and (2) the pecuniary effects.** The real external benefits may include reduction in costs to be incurred on other Government programmes. For example, the construction of irrigation dam may lead to reduction in flooding and soil erosion which would reduce the Government outlay on flood control and anti-soil erosion programmes. Such real indirect or external benefits are counted in cost-benefit studies.

On the other hand, *indirect (external) pecuniary benefits* are not generally included in the enumeration of benefits and costs in a cost-benefit study. These external pecuniary benefits accrue in the form of increased volume of business or increase in land values as a consequence of undertaking a project. Thus the areas in Delhi which fall near Metro railway routes has caused increase in land values in these areas. Besides, the shops and restaurants which exist in the areas surrounding the metro-lines have found increase in the volume of their business. These indirect or external pecuniary benefits are purely distributional and not counted in cost-benefit studies of Metro-railways.

Similarly, indirect multiplier effects and induced investment effects which result from Government investment projects are also generally not counted (except in some special circumstances) since they would occur whether investment made is by the public sector or private sector. For example, if the objective of Government investment programme is regional development, undertaking a local investment project may induce local investment, create multiplier effect on generation of income and employment resulting in reduction of regional unemployment. Since regional development forms a part of objective function to be maximised, some include them in their cost-benefit studies of regional investment programme.

Steps 3. In the stage 3 the evaluation of the identified externalities are made. However, such evaluation is quite a difficult task as it involves also evaluating intangible externalities such as noise, pollution, green environment.

The evaluation of tangible benefits of an investment project is relatively simple as the extra output of goods and services resulting from an investment project can be valued on the basis of their prevailing market prices. However, the intangible benefits accruing such as increase in beauty, healthy environment and direct benefits of human lives saved as a result of health-care programmes, and accident-prevention expenditure programmes is conceptually very difficult if not impossible. For example, what is the value of human life saved ?

As regards costs, it is worth noting that in cost-benefit analysis, costs are measured as ***opportunity costs*** as the social value forgone since the resources have to be withdrawn from other activities to the implementation of the proposed project.[2] For example, if for undertaking an irrigation project, 50 per cent of required labour is withdrawn from the ranks of unemployed labour force the social opportunity cost of such labour is zero and ought to be calculated as such in cost-benefit analysis though the workers employed will be paid market wages. The same holds in case of *idle land* used for a project. With no alternative use, the opportunity cost of idle land is zero. This is so despite the fact that Government has actually to pay compensation to the landowners for acquiring this idle land. This compensation will affect only the distribution of benefits from the project for use of land and not the social cost of the project.

All the benefits and costs (both internal and external) over the life span of the project have to discounted to obtain their present values. In this connection a difficult decision has also to be made about appropriate social discount rate. Besides, constraints placed on cost-benefit analysis have also to be taken into account.

Steps 4. Lastly, in stage 4 on the basis of valuation made in stage-3, decision has to be taken in stage 4 regarding whether to undertake the proposed investment project or it should be rejected. This will be mainly done on the basis of cost-benefit criterion. If the present value of all benefits (both internal and external) exceeds the present value of all

2. See E.J. Mishan, *Cost-Benefit Analysis, An Introduction*, Praeger Publishers, 1971, ph. 7-8.

costs (both internal and external) of the project, it should be accepted. However, the decision in this regard, especially if the project is in the public sector, political considerations also play a part in making the decision regarding undertaking of the proposed project.

Conclusion

It follows from above that the cost-benefit analysis is a method of evaluating investment project or other public expenditure programme by identifying and evaluating all relevant costs and benefits (both internal and external). A proposed project has to be undertaken, if the present value of all benefits exceeds the present value of all costs. Initially cost-benefit analysis was developed to evaluate public sector investment project but is now being used by decision making by the private sector as *environment awareness* has greatly increased in recent years because Government imposes taxes on the firms for their harmful externalities and provide subsidies to them if they generate beneficial externalities.

Importance of Cost-Benefit Analysis

Social Cost-benefit analysis is highly significant for development planning in developing countries. The significant benefit of cost-benefit analysis is that it can guide investment decisions, especially for the public sector. Given the constraint of resources, on the basis of cost-benefit analysis, the Government can choose the most beneficial among them. The Government can use the social-cost benefit analysis even for evaluating the effects of private investment projects. This helps the Government for formulating its policies to either support or discourage certain private investment projects. The Government can support private investment projects by providing subsidies or provide financial support through financial institutions. The Government can discourage them by imposing taxes if the social costs exceed social benefits of the private investment project.

The significance of cost benefit analysis can be better recognised when we consider that alternative method of resource allocation is market mechanism which uses *market prices* of goods and services which do not reflect true social benefits and costs of investment projects. As mentioned above, social cost-benefit analysis takes into account wider and broader social benefits and costs incorporating both the *direct and indirect effects* of an investment. To quote Thirwall, **"The technique of cost-benefit analysis is recommended for the appraisal of publicly financed projects in order to allocate resources in a way that is most profitable to the society, recognising that the market prices of goods and factors of production do not necessary reflect their social values and costs respectively and given that the society is concerned with the future level of consumption as well as the present, the level of current saving may be suboptimal."**[3]

Ensuring Optimal Use of Scarce Resources. Planning in developing countries requires a lot of investment in infrastructure and heavy industries projects such as building of highways, airports, irrigation dams and canals, power plants, steel plants and communication network. These projects have indirect beneficial effects which are crucial for acceleration of economic growth and generation of employment opportunities. However, these investment projects require not only financial resources which are scarce in developing countries but also foreign exchange, skilled or technically trained manpower, a lot of energy resources (such as coal, petroleum oil). The desirability of the investment of these investment projects relating to infrastructure and basic heavy industries cannot be analysed on the basis of market prices of goods and factors. Hence cost-benefit analysis which uses shadow prices reflecting opportunity costs or true scarcity values of resources used in investment projects is essential for optimum use of scarce resources in development planning.

3. A.P. Thirwall, *Growth and Development with Special Reference to Developing Economics,* Macmellan, 2004, 7th edition, pp. 373-374.

Importance for Planning. Thus cost benefit analysis is of vital importance in economic planning for growth and employment generation in developing countries. It is on the basis of cost benefit analysis that those investment projects are chosen in a five year plan which help in achieving the objectives of the plan. Since through cost-benefit analysis different investment projects are ranked in accordance with their contributions to the plan objectives relating to GDP growth and employment generation, priorities can be assigned which projects be undertaken in a plan period. Little and Mirrlees consider the appraisal of various investment projects on the basis of cost-benefit analysis as a *sine quo non* of economic planning for development.[4]

Besides, cost-benefit analysis help in promoting social interest rather than any sectional or group interest. If the projects are selected on the basis of social cost benefit analysis, it becomes, difficult for any vested interests or groups of the people to oppose them if they do not suit their narrow interests.[5]

QUESTIONS FOR REVIEW

1. What is cost-benefit analysis ? How does it differ from capital budgeting ?
2. Explain the use of cost-benefit analysis. What types of benefits and costs are included in cost-benefit analysis ?
3. Explain the various steps involved in making cost-benefit analysis of Government's investment project.
4. Explain the cost-benefit criterion which is used to evaluate the desirability of undertaking an investment project by the Government.
5. How are benefits of an investment project yielding benefits over a number of future years are compared with costs incurred over the years ? Explain
6. Explain the importance of cost-benefit analysis for developing countries, especially for planning of projects for growth and employment.

4. I.M.D. Little and Mirrlees, "*Manual of Industrial Projects in Developing Countries*", OECD, 1969.
5. See Stephen A Marglin, *Public Investment Critera*, George Allen & Unwin, London, 1973.

CHAPTER 67

Information Problem and Markets with Asymmetric Information

In the earlier chapters we explained the model of perfect competition in the product market. In this perfect competition model it is assumed that market participants, namely, the consumers of a product and its producers (i.e., firms), had perfect information about the price, availability and quality of the products. Thus under it, the consumers know about what products are available in the market and at what prices and where they are available. Besides, they know fully well the quality of the products available, that is, their various attributes and characteristics. In other words, they have full knowledge of the *opportunity set* available to them. The consumers also know their preferences of various goods and can tell at what rate they are willing to exchange one good for another, for example, wheat for cloth or oranges for apples, Further, students who consume education service and paying for it know fully well how much they will benefit from it.

In the perfect competition, the firms, the producers of goods, are fully informed about the most efficient technique available for producing goods, the productivity of workers hired by them. They know the efficiency with which workers are actually doing their jobs. Besides, firms are perfectly informed about the quality of other inputs and the prices at which they are available from various sources. Finally, the firms know about the prices at which they can sell not only today but in the future too. Indeed in perfect competition model they fully know the demand and supply curves of their products produced by them.

The Information Problem

However, in the real world the households and the firms do not have full information about the price, quality and availability of the products. In fact, they have only *imperfect information* about opportunity set available to them. Perfect competition model often misleads us in the situations characterised by imperfect information. A leading example of imperfect information is **asymmetric information** about the quality of **used goods,** for example, used cars in the market. By asymmetric information we mean one party in the market for used cars does not know (i.e. has no perfect information) about the quality of the product being sold. In case of used cars while the sellers know about the true quality of their products, the buyers do not know the quality of the used cars which may turn out to be *'lemons'* (that is, defective pieces). Similarly, asymmetric information also occurs while the workers who sell their labour services know their ability and efficiency, the firms who hire them are not well informed about it.

* This chapter draws heavily on Joseph E Stiglitz work. Joseph E Stiglitz won a Nobel Prize in Economics for his significant contribution to the imperfect information problem and its related lemon problem. A brief review of Stiglitz appears in his book, *'Economics''* published by Norton & Co. in whose third edition (2002) is written with co-authrship with Walsh.

Economists such as Joseph E. Stiglitz of the University of California and Akerlof have incorporated imperfect information of the households and firms in their models of market equilibrium. They emphasize certain economic phenomena such as *lemon problem,* hiring of suitable persons for the jobs can be explained well only by incorporating imperfect information in economic models of functioning of markets. Stiglitz and Walsh write, ***"Prices and markets provide the basis of the economy's incentive system. But there are some information problems that markets do not handle or do not handle well. And the imperfect information sometimes inhibits the ability of the market to perform the tasks they perform so well when information is complete."***[1]

According to Stiglitz, for bringing economics closer to the real world one should appreciate the problem of information faced by the firms (*i.e.* producers and employees) and the buyers of the products. In this context the example of insistence by employers about the possession of college graduate degree for certain jobs is worth mentioning. The possession of college graduate degree conveys information to the employers about their quality or productivity of the person applying for particular jobs. Thus Stiglitz and Walsh write, "College graduates may receive a higher income than high school graduates, not only because they have learned things in college that make them productive but also because their college degree conveys valuable information to employers. Employers cannot easily learn in an interview which applicants for a job will be productive. College graduates are, on average, more productive workers .... It may simply have enabled firms to sort more easily students who are productive from the less productive."[2]

Price system in a competitive economy provides an efficient solution to the information problem. Prices play a significant role in bringing about coordination in productive activities of the firms. It is the prices of products that convey information to the firms about the economic scarcity of the products. The *high prices* of certain products convey information to the firms what people prefer and adjust their productive activity accordingly. The *relative prices* of goods tell the firms at what rate the consumers are willing to exchange various goods, that is, their trade-offs. They are guided by the prices in deciding about what goods are to be produced and in what quantities. Thus ***prices serve as a signal to the firms of marginal benefits of producing extra units of various goods.*** And this is all that the firms need to know about for deciding about their productive activity.

Likewise, prices of inputs convey information to the firms about the extent of their scarcity. On the basis of market prices of inputs they decide what inputs and in what quantities to be used for producing various commodities. They try to economise on the relatively more scarce inputs and use relatively more cheap inputs. But, as pointed out by Stiglitz, there are some information problems that markets do not handle well. And imperfect information sometimes inhibits the ability of markets to perform the tasks they perform well when information is complete.

Therefore, when there is imperfect information, for getting correct information buyers and firms are willing to pay for it. Information can be considered as a good like any other good and like other goods it has a price. Investors spend a lot of money on newspapers, business magazines that provide them information about shares and bonds of companies, other investment opportunities such as mutual funds. By subscribing to them people pay a price for the information they provide. The growth of internet has reduced the costs of getting various types of valuable information which was earlier difficult to obtain.

---

1. Joseph E Stiglitz and Carl E Walsh, *Economics,* 3rd edition, 2002, Norton and Co.
2. Stiglitz and Walsh, *op. cit.* p. 234.

However, despite the growth of information technology, market for information is far from perfect. Two factors are responsible for it. First, information is not exactly like any other good. While in case of other goods buyers can have a look at them and know its components and attributes. But, correct information is not easy to get when you buy it. Advertisements in the newspapers generally give misleading information to the people. Some writers in business magazines give biased information about the stocks and mutual funds of various companies, the quality of various cars, etc. Of course, the sellers of information either through advertisements in newspapers, or television and electronic media appear to say 'Trust us we are giving you correct information'. However, the people and the firms are generally sceptical about the correctness of this information conveyed to them.

Even if a consumer or a firm buys certain information which it thinks will provide benefit and is worth paying for it, information it gets is far from perfect. Getting information is quite costly. Consumers as well as firms can be victims of inaccurate or imperfect information. A profit-maximizing firm hires workers as long as marginal revenue (MRP) of workers exceeds the wage rate. How can a firm judge the productivity of workers who apply for a job. Likewise, the consumers are often misled by advertisements informing them by the firms that their oil can blacken their hair naturally or can grow new hair and remove their baldness. Their claims turn out to be untrue.

It follows from above that imperfect information is a fact of life. We will discuss below how it affects economic behaviour of the consumers and firms and what are the solutions to this.

THE MARKET FOR LEMONS AND ADVERSE SELECTION

Asymmetric Information

In the perfect competition model it is assumed that sellers and buyers are perfectly and equally informed about the quality of goods being sold in the market. This assumption is valid if it is either quite easy to verify the quality of goods or it is not costly to ascertain which goods are of high quality and which goods are of low quality. In view of the known differences in qualities of various goods, the different prices of the goods will then reflect the quality differences between them.

When it is not easy to know about the quality of goods or it is costly to get information about them and the buyers and sellers of goods are not equally informed about the quality of goods, then there is asymmetric information. Thus, ***asymmetric information means the market situation when the buyers and sellers have a different information while making a transaction.***

The various examples of markets with asymmetric information can be given. An important example of asymmetric information is of the market for used cars. In this case the sellers are better informed than the buyers about quality of the used cars that are being sold. The theory of lemons was first developed in connection with the sale of used cars. Some used cars are of bad or low quality (*i.e.* they are lemons) and others are of good quality. While the sellers know whether the cars they are selling are 'lemons' or of good quality but the buyers do not know about whether they are lemons or of good quality. The other examples of markets with asymmetric information are ***provision of insurance service and labour market.*** The customer is better informed than the insurance company about the probability of his getting ill. In case of labour market, different workers have different productivities and it is difficult for the employer to know the productivity of the workers and other employees.

The problem about the asymmetric information is that it leads to market failure, that is, failure to achieve Pareto efficiency. We shall discuss below the markets with asymmetric information and the problems it gives rise to.

The Market for Lemons

The important example of market with asymmetric information is the market for lemons. In the market for lemons, the buyers and sellers have different information about the quality of the goods being bought and sold. **The word lemon is used to describe a defective or low quality product**[3]. Let us consider the market for used cars. We assume that the used cars are of different qualities; some of them are of good quality while others are just lemons. The bad quality cars *(i.e.* lemons) quite often break down and require a lot of repairs. However, while the sellers of used cars fully know the quality of their used cars, the buyers are uncertain about their quality due to lack of information. Therefore, the market for used cars is an important example of asymmetric information. It is important to note that though some of the used cars available for sale are of bad quality, but all sellers of used cars, whether of good quality or bad quality, claim that their car is of good quality. The buyers of course cannot know which of the used cars are of good quality and which are just lemons. Therefore, ***the price of the used car in the market depends on the average quality of the used car offered for sale.*** This is because the buyers being uninformed about the quality of the used cars will not be willing to pay more than what an average quality used car is worth. This means that the owners of bad quality cars will get price for their used cars more than what they are worth. This has an important consequence. The owners of good quality used cars will not be able to get the price for their better quality cars since the price determined in the market for used cars will be equal only to what average quality used cars are worth. As a result, the owners of good quality used cars will withdraw their cars from the market. This will reduce the number of used cars available for sale in the market. With this the average quality of used cars offered for sale will also go down and so also the price of the used cars. This will cause some more car owners whose used cars are relatively of good quality to go out of the market for used cars. This process of withdrawing from the market for used cars will go on until only bad quality used cars, that is, lemons, are left for sale in the market. This phenomenon is called ***adverse selection as due to asymmetric information on the part of sellers and buyers the bad quality products drive out the good quality products from the market leaving only lemons left in the market.***

Thus adverse selection occurs when an informed party to a bargain or contract conceals information about the true quality of the product from the other uninformed party leading to the latter getting unexpected poor quality of the product.

Adverse Selection. It is evident from above that adverse selection occurs when the average quality of the used cars for sale drastically declines. The mix of the good quality used cars and lemons changes adversely as price falls. This is the consequence of imperfect information on the part of buyers of used cars. This is illustrated in Fig. 67.1. In panel (a) of Fig. 67.1 along the *X*-axis the price of used cars is measured and on the *Y*-axis the average quality of used cars being sold in the market is measured. As explained above, as price of used cars rises, their average quality rises and, on the other hand, as price of used cars falls, their average quality declines rapidly because good quality used cars are withdrawn from the market. Therefore, the ***average quality curve QL of used cars slopes upward to the right.***

Panel (*b*) of Figure 67.1 depicts tfte market equilibrium of the used cars. In this Panel (b) *SS′* is the supply curve of the used car which is sloping upward. As price rises, the number of used cars supplied in the market increases because, as explained above, at a higher price even the relatively good quality used cars are also supplied in the used cars market. *DD′* is the

3. Nobel Laureate George Akerlof was the first economist who discussed the problem posed by asymmetric information in market for lemons. See his paper, "The Market for Lemons: Qualitative Uncertainty and the Market Mechanism," *The Quarterly Journal of Economics*, August 70, pp. 488-500.

demand curve for used cars. It has a peculiar shape as it slopes upward in the beginning but bends backward after a point. This is because, as explained above, with the fall in price average quality of used

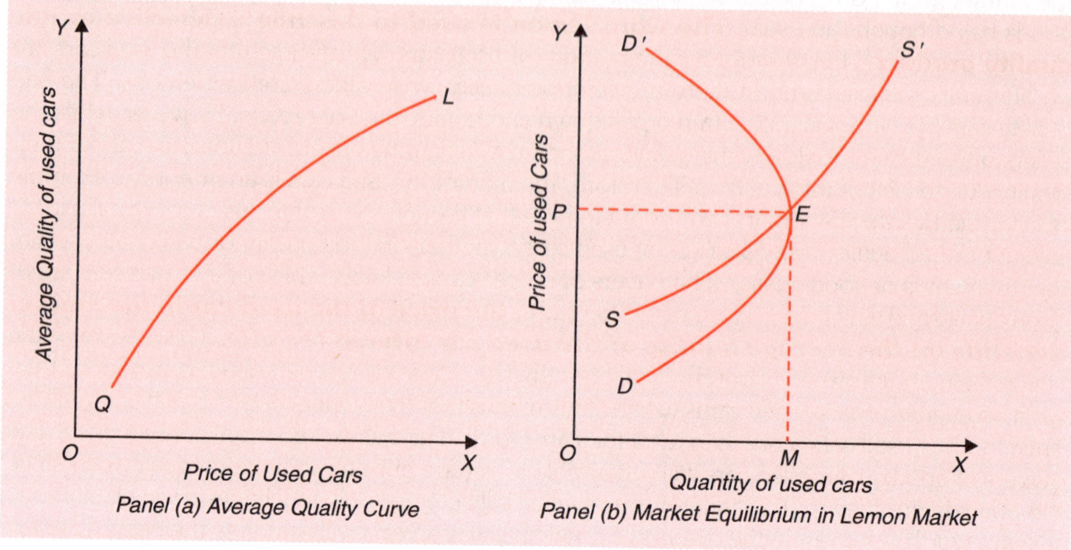

Fig. 67.1. *Market for Lemons*

cars declines. The demand for used cars depends not only on price but also on the quality of used cars offered for sale in the market. Thus as price of used cars falls, their average quality decreases rapidly, their quantity demanded falls. This causes the demand curve to bend backward at lower prices of the used cars. It will be seen from panel (*b*) that market equilibrium is reached at point *E* and price *OP* and quantity *OM* of the used cars are determined.

It follows from above that one consequence of imperfect information on the part of the buyers (that is, asymmetric information between buyers and sellers) is that *there are relatively few buyers and sellers,* that is, market for used cars becomes *thin*. In some circumstances, the market for used cars may cease to exist when there is imperfect or asymmetric information. Stiglitz and Walsh rightly write, "The used car market is a thin one, those who for one reason or another want to buy a used car always want to drive a better car. But mixed in with these are people who are trying to dump their lemons. The buyers cannot tell the lemons apart from good cars. Rather than risk it, they simply do not buy (of course the fact that demand is low drives down the price, increasing the proportion of lemons. It is a vicious circle)."[4]

Asymmetric Information and the Market Failure

The example of sale of used cars brings out how asymmetric information leads to market failure, that is, failure to achieve Pareto efficiency. This is due to the *externality* between the seller of high-quality and low-quality used cars. When some individual try to sell their low-quality cars, they affect the buyers' perceptions of the quality of the average car available for sale in the market. This causes reduction in the price that they are willing to pay for the used cars available in the market which hurts the individuals who want to sell their good or high-quality cars. Because of asymmetric information, that is, the buyers cannot easily determine the quality of used cars, they can do so only after they have purchased them and used them for a while. As seen above, the asymmetric information creates the lemons problem and drives

4. Stiglitz, *op. cit, p.* 291.

good cars out of the market and thereby harms the welfare of the owners of good quality cars who want to sell their cars. Thus, externality created by asymmetric information prevents the achievement of Pareto efficiency and creates market failure.

Measures Adopted to Solve the Problem of Adverse Selection

The lemouns problems arises because the sellers of good used cars are not able to inform accurately to the buyers about the quality of their cars. To solve this problem, some institutions have been developed to deal with the problem. The first institution that has come about into existence is of used car dealers who provide *guarantees* for the cars they sell. The well-reputed dealers who want to keep their goodwill in the market give assurance for the quality of cars bought through them. Besides, there are automobile service centres that check the quality of used cars for a certain fee. The buyers of used cars can thus get information about the quality of the used cars from these testing centres.

Some other devices that have been developed to solve the problem of quality uncertainty are the use of brand names, the practice of providing franchisees (such as Apollo Hospitals, franchisees of NIIT etc.), Chain stores etc. These brand names and franchisees of some reputed companies also provide assurance about the good quality of goods or services being provided. As we shall see below with regard to insurance market, the devices of *coinsurance* and the *deductibles* have been adopted to tackle the problem of moral hazard that arises due to asymmetric information.

The Insurance Market and Adverse Selection

After Akerlof who first analysed the lemons problem created by asymmetric information in the market for used cars, his analysis has been extended to the markets for insurance, financial credit and labour employment. These other markets are also characterised by asymmetric information. In this section we will study how Akerlof's analysis has been applied to the insurance market.

In the case of insurance, the insurance company has less information about the state of health of the individuals who want to get their life insured or want insurance for sickness or in case of general insurance about the accident proneness of their cars, etc. Let us take the case of insurance against illness. Suppose there are two groups of individuals who want to insure for the risk of illness. One group of individuals belongs to high risk group. There are H number of individuals who constitute the high risk group. The second group is of low risk individuals and there are L number of them. The possibility of their becoming ill and therefore becomes entitled to claim insurance money is P_H and P_L respectively. The individuals belonging to both these groups get themselves insured and the insurance company is not able to distinguish between them. While insurance company does not know the true state of their health, the individuals, that is, the buyers of insurance, are fully informed about the likelihood of their becoming ill. Thus, this is a case of asymmetric information. The weighted average probability of their becoming ill is

$$\overline{P} = P_H \cdot \frac{H}{H+L} + P_L \cdot \frac{L}{H+L}$$

where $\overline{P}$ stands for the weighted average probability of illness. Obviously, $P_H > \overline{P} > P_L$. Suppose the cost of insurance is C. If the insurance company is to recover at least the cost of insuring them against illness, then the insurance premium to cover both the high-risk and low-risk individuals which we denote by I is given by

$$I \geq C\overline{P}$$

As the individuals know their risk of becoming ill, as is being assumed here, while the individuals with low risk (P_L) may not be willing to buy the insurance, given the above insurance premium, the individuals with high risk will be very much eager to buy it. Because $\bar{P} > P_L$, the insurance premium will be much greater than CP_L in case of low-risk individuals. Therefore, the low-risk individuals are likely to drop out and in that case to recover the insurance cost of high-risk individuals, the insurance company will have to raise the rate of insurance premium. As a result, only the high risk individuals will buy the insurance and the ***individuals with low risk of illness will go without insurance.*** Thus, as in case of used cars, the problem of adverse selection also arises in case of insurance market. In fact, the term adverse selection was first used in case of health insurance because the insurance companies ***do not get unbiased selection of individuals who buy insurance policy and it is only the high-risk individuals who purchase it.*** In such a situation the insurance claims will *mostly* be made by the individuals with high risk and as a result the insurance company *who charges premium rate on the basis of average risk* of both kinds of individuals with high-risk and low risk of illness will go bankrupt.

However, various measures have been proposed to overcome the problem of adverse selection. First, the insurance company can offer the low-risk individuals to get coinsurance (under the coinsurance scheme the individuals share a portion of the loss with the insurance company) or get some ***deductibility scheme*** (that is, get some amount deducted from the claim for the loss suffered). The insurance company can offer various individuals to make a choice among different schemes with different rates of coinsurance, the amounts of deductibles, length of contract etc. From the choices made the insurance company can know the risk characteristics of various individuals willing to buy insurance and adjust the insurance premium accordingly.

From above it follows that some schemes have been devised to tackle the problem of adverse selection in connection with health insurance. But one thing is certain from above that there ***cannot be a single insurance premium policy.*** There can be at least two insurance policies, one for high-risk individuals who get complete insurance and the other for low-risk individuals who get insurance with a large deductible. In this case the low-risk individuals get only partial insurance. However, given the fact that there is not only two groups of individuals with either high risk or low risk but a continuum of individuals with several probabilities, there can be no equilibrium in the insurance market that ensures market efficiency.[5]

It may be emphasized that the problem of adverse selection in health insurance arises because insurance company cannot fix their rates of premium on the *average incidence* of illness in the population. Therefore, to solve the problem of adverse selection, *compulsory purchase plan of insurance* by a group of people containing both high-risk and low-risk individuals and an insurance company fixing its premium rate on the basis of *average incidence* of health problem has been adopted in some cases. In such a situation it is claimed that each of the individuals comprising compulsory purchase group can be made better off. The high-risk individuals are better off because they buy insurance at a rate that is relatively lower than the risk they face and the low-risk individuals can purchase insurance at a rate less than the rate that would be prevailing ***when only high-risk people purchased it.*** Such compulsory insurance plans with some variation have been extensively adopted. For example, all teachers of a college or university can be brought under the compulsory health insurance plan with the insurance company fixing its premium rate on the basis of average risk of health problem faced by the teachers. Similarly, all employees of a factory can be asked to participate in the

5. See M Rothschild and J. Stiglitz, "Equilibrium in Competitive Insurance Market: An Essay on the Economics of Imperfect Information", *Quarterly Journal of Economics,* November 1976.

compulsory insurance plan. But the scheme of compulsory purchase plan is repugnant to most of the economists who lay stress on 'free choice' as a means of achieving Pareto efficiency. But a compulsory purchase plan of insurance restricting choice of individuals ensures Pareto efficiency by tackling the adverse consequences of the existence of externality between the low- risk and high-risk individuals. In this connection, it may be noted that some employers offer health insurance plans to their employees as ***a part of the package of fringe benefits.*** As a set of all employees with low-risk and high-risk of illness participate in the health plan, the insurance company can fix its premium rate on the basis of average risk and also the problem of adverse selection is eliminated. But in this case cost of insurance plan is borne by the employer and the employees get it as an incentive to work for the employer.

The Problem of Moral Hazard

Another problem that often arises in the insurance market is that of moral hazard. **The moral hazard refers to a person or firm's behaviour which may change after buying insurance so that *it increases the probability of theft, fire, illness or other accident*.** In other words, moral hazard is opportunistic act of an insured person who takes advantage of the ill-informed company or person (i.e. insuring company or agent) through his unobserved fraudulent behaviour. This is because when a person buys insurance, the loss from an accident, fire or getting ill is shifted from the person to the insurance company. Therefore, when insured against risk, a person takes less care or takes fewer precautions to avoid accident, fire, illness or any other disaster, the probability of the accident, illness or any other disaster which is insured increases. And when the accident, illness or any other insured disaster occurs, the person or firm often inflates the loss suffered. This opportunistic behaviour of the insured person due to asymmetric information raises the cost of insurance of the insurance company. For example, if a person gets his car insured for theft and accident. Knowing that the loss occurred as a result of an accident will be borne by the insurance company, he will drive the car more carelessly after buying insurance and thus increasing the probability of accident taking place.

Take another example, say of medical insurance involving moral hazard. After buying medical insurance, individuals usually spend less on health care which increases the probability of their getting ill. Besides, they are likely to spend more on treatment when fall ill than if they had no insurance. This behaviour on the part of individuals increases the amount payable by the insurance companies on account of mediclaim.

Similarly, in case of fire insurance, the firms are likely to take fewer precautions such as installation of fire detector system and thereby increasing the probability of a fire and in addition, the firms inflate the loss of property damaged if fire actually occurs. In fact, the probability of fire rises very much, if the property is insured for an amount greater than its true value.

It is worth noting that if the care taken by an individual who buys insurance is observable, then there is no problem. In case care is observable, the insurance company can fix its premium on the basis of the amount of care taken by the person or firm. Thus, in real life the insurance companies usually charge different rates from firms which have a fire sprinkler system in their building; or to charge smokers higher premium rates than non-smokers for health insurance. In these cases the firms try to discriminate among those who buy insurance depending on the care or choices they make that affect the probability of damage.

But the problem of moral hazard arises because the insurance companies cannot observe all the relevant actions regarding care the individuals take after buying insurance. If the problem of moral hazard is not reduced, it could lead to the very high insurance costs and premium rates which would defeat the very purpose of insurance. The purpose of insurance is to distribute the given risks of a large monetary loss among many individuals or firms participating in an insurance programme. But if the facility of available insurance increases the total risks and claimed losses, then insurance does not prove to be efficient and it may not be even possible to provide insurance.

Insurance companies have tried to reduce or overcome the problem of moral hazard. One method generally adopted by the insurance companies is ***specifying the precautions that individuals or firms buying insurance must take to be eligible for making a claim.*** For example, the insurance company might require that individual must get medical check-up annually to continue enjoying health insurance. Similarly, the insurance companies may charge higher premium from drivers involved in accidents, may require the installation of fire detector system by the firms as a condition for providing insurance to them. By specifying these conditions, the insurance company attempts to reduce the probability of illness, accident or fire and thereby reduce the possible claims on it.

Another method often adopted by the insurance companies to reduce the problem of moral hazard is that of *coinsurance.* In coinsurance the individual or firm shares a good portion of a potential loss with the insurance company. That is, in case of coinsurance, the insurance company insures only a part of the possible loss or value of property insured. The idea behind such a proposal is that when the individual or firm shares a good part of potential loss with the insurance company, the individual or firm will take more care and precautions to avoid losses.

A similar proposal to overcome the problem of moral hazard is the provision made in the insurance policy that includes a large ***"deductible"*** under which the insured individual or firm has to pay a part of the claim. This also ensures that the insured individual will have incentive to take some amount of care.

Moral Hazard and Allocative Inefficiency

Moral hazard is not only a problem for insurance companies. It also affects the ability of the market to achieve efficient resource allocation. This is illustrated in Figure 67.2 where we have shown the demand curve for driving in kilometres per week. The demand curve D is sloping downward to the right. This is because at the higher cost of driving, the individuals switch over to other means of transportation. To begin with, let us suppose the *cost of driving per kilometre* includes the cost of insurance and the insurance company can *measure correctly* the number of kilometres driven. Thus in this case the problem of moral hazard does not arise. The owner-driver knows the more driving by him will increase his insurance premium and therefore his total cost of driving will increase. For example, as will be seen from Figure 67.2 when the cost of car driving is ₹ 15 per kilometre, (including ₹ 5 per kilometre of insurance cost), the driver will do car driving 200 kilometres per week. Since there is no problem of moral hazard, marginal utility of car driving for 200 kilometres is equal to marginal cost of driving (₹ 15) per kilometre. 200 kilometres car driving is socially efficient level.

However, the problem of moral hazard arises because it is very difficult for an insurance company to monitor driving habits of individuals and further that insurance premium does not depend on the number of kilometres driven. Once a car owner buys a car insurance policy he has to pay a given insurance premium for a week, month or a year. Therefore, the owner-driver thinks that any additional accident cost will be borne by the insurance company and further that since the ***insurance premium does not vary with the number of kilometres driven,*** he will have therefore incentive to drive car more kilometres than without insurance. Without the insurance premium of ₹ 5 per kilometre, the cost of driving per kilometre will now be ₹ 10 (that is, ₹ 15 – 5 = 10). It will be seen that from Figure 67.2 that at the cost of driving ₹ 10 per kilometre, the owner-driver will drive 300 kilometres per week which is more than the socially efficient number of 200 kilometres. Thus it is clear that the problem of moral hazard leads to socially inefficient kilometres of driving activity.

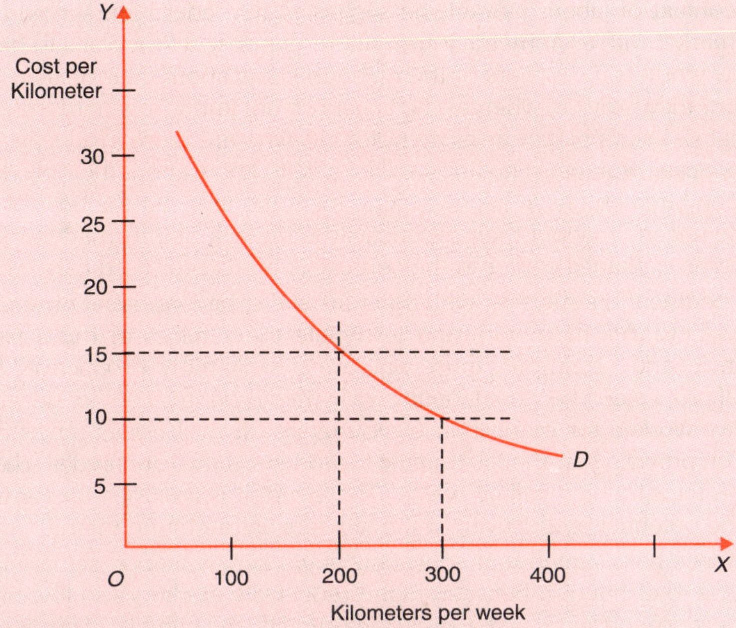

Fig. 67.2. *Moral Hazard and Allocative Inefficiency*

MARKET SIGNALLING: PROVIDING INFORMATION

In the earlier section of this chapter we have explained how asymmetric information leads to the lemons problem. Since sellers know more about the quality of their products than the buyers, the buyers assume that products offered for sale are of low quality. **This results in fall in price of the product and ultimately only low-quality products, that is, lemons are sold in the market, the good quality products having been driven out of the market.** This is called the adverse selection which is the consequence of asymmetric information. Similarly, in case of insurance market we have seen that since the insurance companies cannot know who are high-risk individuals and who are low-risk individuals in order to provide insurance at an appropriate rate of insurance premium, the result is again of adverse selection, that is, only high-risk individuals buy insurance at high premiums. In the extreme case such high rates of insurance premiums may come about that no one is willing to buy insurance and the insurance market even ceases to exist. Similarly, as shall be explained at length below, the problem of adverse selection occurs in case of employment of workers by the employers who cannot distinguish between high-productivity and low-productivity workers while deciding to employ them.

The problem of adverse selection caused by asymmetric information has been sought to be resolved through *market signalling*. It has been proposed that if sellers of high-quality products, low-risk individuals or more productive workers can somehow inform or send signals to the potential customers about their superior quality, the problem of adverse selection can be mostly overcome. A firm *can send signals* that indicates the high quality of its products to its potential buyers by adopting *brand names*, and by offering *guarantees and warranties*. The firm whose products are of low quality cannot offer guarantees and warranties since it will be very costly to do so.

In case of employment of workers education serves as a good signalling device regarding the productivity of workers. Michael Spence showed that in some markets the sellers could send signals to the potential buyers conveying them about the better quality of their products.

In the context of labour market, he suggested that education served as a good signal[6] in a labour market with asymmetric information. Suppose a firm plans to hire some new workers. The new workers (*i.e.* sellers of their labour) know about their quality, that is, productivity of the labour they provide, whereas the buyers do not know how hard they work, how skilful they are. That is, the employer firms do not know who are more productive workers and who are less productive workers. The firms will be able to know about their productivity only after they have been hired and have been working for some time. At the time of hiring them the firms are quite uncertain about their productivity. This lack of information may lead to the adverse selection as explained earlier in the context of market for used cars and insurance market.

A pertinent question is, why don't firms first hire workers, observe them for some time to know how well they work and terminate the services of those workers who have low productivity and retain only those who are actually more productive? However, this is not a practical proposition because labour laws in many countries do not permit the firing of workers who have worked for more than 6 months in a firm. Besides, firms have to invest a lot of money on providing on-the-job training to workers. If they are fired at a later time, the resources spent on their training will go waste. Therefore, it is much better for the firms if they know about the potential productivity of the workers before hiring them.

Spence has claimed that education of workers is a good signal that can be used by the employers to distinguish between high-productivity workers and low-productivity workers. A person's education level can be easily measured by the number of years of schools, the degrees obtained, the college or university where he studied, the grade or marks obtained etc. The education undoubtedly can raise one's productivity. But as has been stressed by Spence in his model of signalling that ***even if education does not improve one's productivity, it will still be a useful signal of productivity*** because it is easier and less costly for more productive persons to obtain a higher level of education as compared to the low-productivity persons. More productive persons are more intelligent, highly motivated, more hard-working and are therefore likely to obtain a higher level of education which can be used as a signal of their higher productivity to enable them to get highly lucrative jobs. For all these reasons firms are also right in thinking that education is a signal of productivity.

Spence in his important contribution regarding education as a signal emphasized that education is a good signal if cost of acquiring it is less by a more productive worker as compared to the low productive worker. We explain below his model of signalling in some detail.

Spence Model of Signalling

Suppose P_H represents the productivity of high-quality workers and they are H in number and P_L represents the productivity of low-quality of workers whose number is L. The total number of workers seeking jobs are therefore $H + L$. If H workers are paid wages equal to their marginal productivity P_L and L workers are paid wages equal to their marginal productivity P_L, then there will be efficient use of labour. But, since the employers are unable to distinguish between high-productivity P_L workers and low-productivity workers, it is not possible to achieve Pareto efficiency in labour use. The *weighted average* productivity of workers which we represent by $\overline{P}$ is given by

$$\overline{P} = P_H \cdot \frac{H}{H+L} + P_L \cdot \frac{L}{H+L}$$

$$P_H > \overline{P} > P_L$$

In view of the fact that it is not possible for the employers to distinguish between high and

6. See Michael Spence, *Market Signalling*, Cambridge, MA Harvard University Press, 1974.

low productivity workers, they may pay each worker equal to their *average* marginal productivity $\bar{P}$ as obtained above. Paying workers equal to their average marginal productivity rather than their own marginal productivity would violate the conditions of achieving Pareto efficiency.

Let us suppose as Spence does that though education does not cause increase in productivity of workers, it *costs less* for more productive workers (*H*) to acquire education as compared to the less productive workers. Using education as a signal of their higher marginal productivity, the educated workers are able to get jobs and are paid high wages. On the other hand, low-quality workers are unable to get education because it is either not easy for them to get education or is very costly for them to acquire education which can serve as signal to get employment.

Spence showed that a number of conditions must be fulfilled if education is to serve as a good signalling device in the job market and equilibrium is achieved that ensures market efficiency in the sense that more productive workers in fact get employment and are paid equal to the value of their marginal products.

The conditions stipulated by Spence in his signalling model can be stated as under. Let C_H the cost of education for high-productivity workers and C_L the cost of education of the low-productivity workers.

1. The first essential condition of Spence's model of education as a successful signalling device for higher productivity is $C_H < C_L$, that is, it costs less for high-productivity workers to acquire education.
2. The second condition is : $C_L > P_H - P_L$, that is, it costs more for low-productivity workers to acquire education for using as a necessary signal than the differential in productivity and therefore the differences in wages paid to the two types of workers.
3. $C_H < P_H - P_L$, that is, it *costs less* to high productivity workers to invest in education so as to use it as a signal than the differential in productivity that is *perceived* to result from possessing that signal.

Those having acquired education to use it as a signal are paid a wage $W_H = P_H$ and those who have not acquired educational signal are paid a wage $W_L = P_L$. The following equilibrium condition follows from the above conditions :

$$C_H < (P_H - P_L) < C_L \qquad \text{...(i)}$$

According to the above equilibrium condition, since $C_H < (P_H - P_L)$, *high productivity workers find it worthwhile to invest in acquiring education as a signal and get job at the wage rate equal to their high productivity,* P_H, *and, on the other hand, since* $(P_H - P_L) < C_L$ or $C_L > (P_H - P_L)$, *the low productivity workers do not find it worthwhile to invest in acquiring education as a signal for perceived high productivity and are satisfied with accepting the low wage rate equal to* P_L.

The above equilibrium condition (*i*) is called *separating equilibrium.* It shows how the two groups of workers separate themselves for acquiring education as a signal, to get jobs. However, the equilibrium condition (*i*) is a ***necessary but not the sufficient condition*** for the success of education as a signalling device. For example, suppose that the equilibrium condition (*i*) is satisfied but *all* workers before they invest in acquiring education are paid a wage equal to their average productivity $\bar{P}$. Because, as stated above, $C_L > P_H - P_L$, it does not pay the low-productivity workers to invest in acquiring education to serve as signal to get high-paid jobs. However, even though $C_H < P_H - P_L$ but at the same time $C_H > P_H - \bar{P}$, then even high-productivity workers would not find it sufficient to induce them to invest in acquiring education. Hence in view of being presently paid wage equal to the average productivity $\overline{P}$, the wage differential $(P_H - \overline{P})$ is considered by the high-productivity workers being not worthwhile to invest in acquiring education as a signal to earn wage rate equal to P_H. Under these circumstances, both the low-productivity workers and high-productivity workers would have no incentive to acquire education as signal. Hence the equilibrium condition (*i*) derived above is a necessary but a sufficient condition for the success of education as a signal.

Spence's model of treating education as a mere signalling device has been criticised on the ground that it represents a social waste of resources. Based on the assumption that acquiring education does not lead to the increase in true productivity and merely serves as a signal of *perceived* productivity, high productivity workers are induced to spend a lot of time (even years) simply to invest in acquiring education to act as successful signal of **high perceived productivity.** Thus, commenting on Spence's model, Griffiths and Wall write, "The *efficiency gain is* that of more appropriate allocation of high-productivity employees after the educative signal is acquired; the *efficiency loss* is the resources used up by society in providing some individuals with educational opportunities merely to serve as a non-productive signalling device; and, of course, the *opportunity cost* of work foregone by high-productivity workers during the educational process."[7]

THE PRINCIPAL-AGENT PROBLEM

In the modern corporate companies there is a separation of ownership from control between shareholders who are the owners and the managers who actually organise and control the working of the companies. The owners (shareholders in case of corporate companies) are often referred to as *principals* and the managers who organise, manage and control the business firm are called *agents*. In this case of separation of ownership from control of the business firms, the *principal-agent problem* arises. The principal-agent problem refers to the situation when the managers pursue their goals such as high salaries, power, prestige, perquisites even at the cost of the owners (*i.e.* their principals)[8]. Whereas the shareholders want to maximise their profits or present value of the net worth of their companies, managers who pursue their own goals often take decisions which are contrary to the goal of the owners.

Asymmetric information plays a role in this principal-agent relationship. The managers, that is, agents possess information which is not available to the owners. The owners could acquire information through research activity and extensive and costly monitoring of the managers. Since it is very costly and also not possible to gather all the required information to fully overcome the asymmetry in information, it is quite unlikely that the owners (*i.e.*, principals) will undertake such costly activity. As a result, due to the lack of adequate information by the owners, the managers (*i.e.* agents) have ample freedom to behave discretionally and take decisions to promote their own interests rather than the interests of the owners. It is important to note that the principal-agent problem exists not only in private corporate enterprises but also in public enterprises. We briefly explain below this agency relationship problem in both the sectors.

The Principal-Agent Problem in Private Sector

In large private corporate enterprises, an individual or an institution holds a relatively very small part of the share capital in the enterprise. This fact makes it difficult to obtain adequate information about how efficiently the managers are working. Theoretically, an important function of the owners or their representatives is to monitor the managers' functioning.

7. Allan Griffiths and Stuart Wall, *Intermediate Microeconomics, Theory and Application,* London Addison Wesley Longman Ltd .,1996. P.476.
8. See E.F.Fauna, "Agency Problems of the Theory of the Firm" in *Journal of Political Economy,* April 1980.

But, as noted above, it is very costly for an individual shareholder to gather sufficient information to monitor the decision-making by the managers.

But managers can pursue which objectives which conflict with the interests of their principals (*i.e.* owners). First, it has been pointed out that managers try to maximise the growth or sales of the firm rather than profits or net worth of the firms. The more rapid growth in output or sales or increase in market share provide larger cash flows which help the managers to get more perks or perquisites. The other objective that is often said to be pursued by the managers is maximisation of their utility by them. As Williamson has suggested that the utility which a manager gets from his job depends not only on salaries, but also on respect from the peers, power to control the corporation, the large subordinate staff they have, the fringe benefits and other perks they enjoy and a long tenure of the job.

However, in a private corporate enterprise there are limitations to managers' ability to pursue objectives which conflict with the maximisation of owners' profits or net worth of the firms. First, shareholders can raise objections when they find that managers are not working efficiently and as a result they are not getting adequate dividend or when the value of the stock of the firm is not increasing. They can in extreme cases can get the managers dismissed, of course with the help of the board of directors who monitor managerial activities.

But what are the ways to overcome this principal-agent problem so as to improve the efficiency of the business organisation.

Takeover by other owners. If a business firm is poorly managed and its owners are unable to properly control and monitor the managerial actions, it may be taken over by other firms who are quite tough and adept in controlling management. When a firm is poorly managed, the old owners are happy to sell out to the new firms. There is every possibility that the new firms dispense with the services of the existing managers. Therefore, the threat of takeover often induces the management to improve its performance to avoid being taken over. Thus one way in which the performance of poorly managed companies may be improved is through the threat posed by potential takeover.

Long-Term Contracts. An important way of dealing with the principal-agent problem is to enter into long-term contracts such as ***profit-sharing contracts*** with managers so that they have the incentive to pursue the objective of profit maximisation in their own interest. It may however be noted that the objective of owners' profit-sharing contract is to promote managers' effort and work, but the payment scheme under the contract must be based on measured output of his efforts, that is, profits. The other examples of long-term contracts are *many years' service contracts with CEO and other senior managers*. These long period service contracts enable managers to take a long-term view and devise such strategies that ensure large profits over a long period of time.

Providing Part-Ownership. A more popular way of coping with the principal-agent problem is to *give the managers a financial stake in the better performance of the firm*. Many corporate companies in India and abroad have stock purchase plans whereby managers can buy equity shares of the company at less than market price. These partial ownership plans provide incentive to managers to maximise firm's profits and to act in accordance with the interests of the firm's owners. An important research study has found that if managers own between 5 and 10 per cent of the stock of a firm, the firm is likely to perform better in terms of profitability than if they own less than 5 per cent.[9]

Incentive Pay. Incentive Pay Schemes are quite common method of coping with principal-agent problem. In these incentive pay schemes, management salaries and bonuses are related to company's profitability or high salaries or bonuses are given to the managers who succeed

9. See R. Morck, A Shliefer and R Vishny, "Manaagement Ownership and Corporate Performance" *Journal of Financial Economics*, March 1988.

in meeting profit targets set for them. It has been found that markets for managers come into existence. Those managers who secure high profits for the firms because of their better performance earn high salaries. Thus profit-linked salaries give incentive to managers to maximise profits or net worth of the firms which is consistent with the interests of the owners. Thus, to quote Pindyck and Rubinfeld, ***"When it is impossible to measure effort directly, an incentive structure that rewards outcome of high levels of effort can induce agents to aim for the goals that the owners set."***[10]

Despite the above measures that may be taken to cope with the principal-agent problem, the means by which the shareholders can control and monitor management functioning are limited and imperfect. The principal-agent problem exists not only between owners and managers of firms but also between *owners and workers.* The workers, like managers, may pursue their own interests rather than maximising profits or net worth of the firm. Some incentive schemes, similar to those for managers, such as bonus payment to the workers and profit-sharing arrangement with them as a reward for putting in a high level of work-effort, have often been adopted to induce workers to show better performance. In this connection efficiency wage theory has been offered which explains that better paid workers would put in large effort to create more output and profits for the owners. We will explain this wage efficiency theory in a later section.

The Principal-Agent Problem in Public Enterprises

The principal-agent relationship also exists in public enterprises. Managers of public enterprises are more interested in increasing their power, perks, staff. All these can be achieved when the business is expanded beyond their efficient level. Since it is very expensive to monitor and control the behaviour of managers of public enterprises, they tend to be inefficient. Thus in India it has been found that public enterprises suffer from inefficiency and low profitability due to lack of effective monitoring of the behaviour of managers. Checks by ministries and legislatures on management of public enterprises are not likely to be effective because managers are better informed about problems and functioning of their enterprises. Lack of market forces controlling them also makes managers of public enterprises inefficient because a good number of public enterprises in India are 'state monopolies'.

In order to improve the efficiency and profitability of public sector managers, they should be recruited through professional job market instead of being appointed from IAS cadre. When public sector managers know that if they pursue improper objectives, their services can be terminated, they would try to perform efficiently. Though they should be given autonomy in their day-to-day functioning and decision-making, overall checks or controls must be exercised by legislatures, parliamentary committees and Government's Audit and Accounting Authorities. Above all, if public enterprises produce same or similar products or services as the private enterprises, they can be opened up to competition. For example, in India the managerial efficiency of MTNL and BSNL has greatly improved when telecommunication sector has been opened up and private enterprises have been allowed to operate in this sector. Similarly, the managerial efficiency of public sector banks has started improving not only because of intense competition among them but also because of the competition they now face from good private and foreign banks which under the new economic policy have been allowed to expand significantly. Thus competition for public sector managements can be as effective as competition among private enterprises for ensuring their efficient working and proper managerial behaviour.

EFFICIENCY WAGE THEORY

Efficiency wage theory is a recent development in the analysis of determination of wages and employment. As shall be explained below, an interesting feature of this theory is that it helps to explain that whereas wage rate remained at above the competitive equilibrium rate,

10. R.S. Pindyck and D.L. Rubinfeld, *Microeconomics,* Prentice Hall of India, 1995, p. 613.

substantial unemployment of labour prevails in a competitive economy. Given the competitive labour market, the existence of such unemployment could not be expected if unemployed workers were willing to work for a lower wage than that received by the employed workers. The question that arises is that under such circumstances why firms do not lower wages and increase employment and thereby raise their profits and eliminate involuntary unemployment.

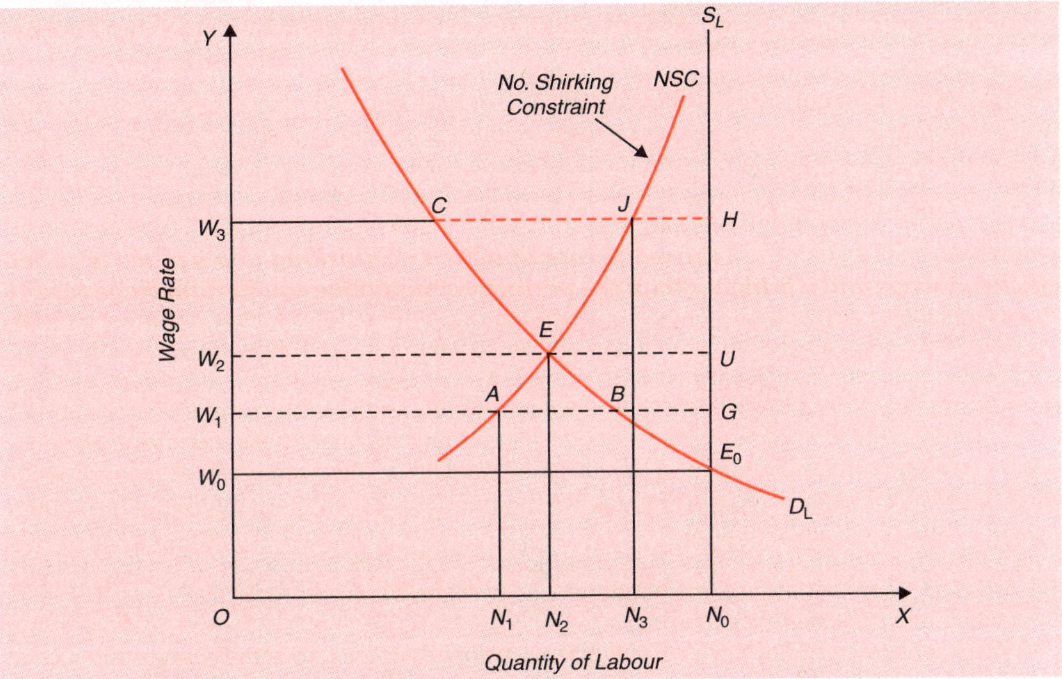

Fig. 67.3. *Efficiency Wage and Unemployment in a Non-Shirking Model.*

Efficiency wage theory makes a different assumption than the simple competitive model of wage determination which is based on the assumption that productivity of labour is independent of wage rate paid to labour. On the contrary the ***efficiency wage theory assumes that productivity or efficiency of labour, that is, output per hour or per day, depends on the level of wage rate paid to it.***

According to the efficiency wage theory, ***it is difficult for the firms to accurately know about workers' productivity*** and therefore the workers can shirk work and do not put in their best efforts in raising their productivity. As a result, since the firms cannot monitor workers' productivity, they also encounter principal-agent problem arising from asymmetric information between the owners of the firms and the workers. Therefore, the efficiency wage theory suggests that the firms willingly pay higher than the equilibrium competitive wage rate in order to provide incentive to workers not to shirk work (*i.e.* not to slack off). But since firms have limited or imperfect information about worker's productivity, the workers who shirk cannot be fired for shirking.

Let us illustrate the efficiency wage theory with a diagram. The shirking model assumes that perfectly competitive labour market prevails and all workers are equally productive and get the same wage. But once they are employed they can either work productively or shirk. But, as mentioned above, the firms employing them have imperfect information about their true productivity, they are not likely to be fired for shirking. The model works as follows.

D_L curve in Figure 67.3 represents the demand for labour and S_L is the supply curve of labour which for sake of simplicity is assumed to be perfectly inelastic at ON_0 number of workers. Given the competitive market, wage rate is determined at the level of W_0 corresponding to which demand curve D_L of labour intersects the supply curve S_L. If the firm pays its workers the competitive wage rate W_0, the workers will have incentive to shirk. This is because firm's managers having limited information about workers' productivity are unable to detect workers who are shirking and even if they are able to detect those who are shirking and fire them, these workers can readily get employment elsewhere at the current wage rate as there does not exist any unemployment at this wage rate. As a result, the workers have little incentive to put in their best work-effort to become more productive and are likely to shirk.

In order to ensure that the workers do not shirk, a firm must pay workers a higher wage than the perfectly competitive wage rate W_0 in Figure 67.3. With the wage rate higher than W_0, the workers will not shirk because if they are fired by the firm for shirking they will be able to get employment in some other firms only at the lower competitive wage rate W_0. Since they would not like to give up present higher pay job, they are induced to work more productively and not shirk. Therefore, if the difference in wage rates is large enough, the shirking by workers can be prevented Thus ***the wage rate at which no shirking takes place is called efficiency wage and it is higher than the perfectly competitive equilibrium wage rate.***

But since all firms in the labour market face the problem of shirking, in order to avoid shirking by workers all of them would pay efficiency wage rate, that is, wage rate higher than the competitive equilibrium wage rate W_0. This however does not mean that workers will now be motivated to shirk. This is because at a wage rate higher than the competitive equilibrium wage rate W_0, quantity demanded of labour is less than the quantity supplied of it and as a result involuntary unemployment of labour emerges. Under these circumstances, even when *all firms pay efficiency wage rate* (*i.e.* higher than the equilibrium wage rate W_0), the workers will not shirk because if when fired by a firm for shirking, they will remain unemployed (perhaps for a long time) before they get jobs at the efficiency wage rate with some other firms. Thus, the prospect of remaining unemployed induces workers to work productively and not shirk even when all firms pay efficiency wage.

Now, what determines the level of efficiency wage. According to some economists such as J. Yellen[11], J. Stiglitz[12], the minimum wage that the workers are required for not shirking is inversely related to the level of unemployment. For example, in Figure 67.3 if wage rate is W_1, the level of unemployment equal to AG (which is equal to N_1N_0) must be there to induce workers not to shirk. If wage rate is W_2, then the unemployment level of $EU (= N_2N_0)$ is required to prevent shirking by the workers. Further, if wage rate is W_3, then JH ($= N_3N_0$) must be the level of unemployment needed to prevent shirking by workers. Thus, the no-shirking constraint curve is upward sloping that indicates the efficiency wage rate (that is, the wage rate that must be paid to prevent shirking) is higher, the smaller the level of unemployment. It may be noted that as efficiency wage is higher, the non-shirking constraint (*NSC*) curve gets nearer and nearer the given vertical supply curve S_L of labour but never crosses it.

The equilibrium efficiency wage rate is determined at the level where non-shirking constraint (*NSC*) curve intersects the demand curve D_L of labour. It will be seen from Figure 67.3 that W_2 is the equilibrium efficiency wage rate because corresponding to this wage rate non-shirking constraint curve (*NSC*) intersects the demand for labour curve D_L at point E. Why W_2 is the equilibrium efficiency wage rate? At the wage rate W_2, the actual demand or employment of labour is W_2E or ON_2 and therefore actual unemployment will be EU which is the level of unemployment required to induce workers not to shirk. On the other hand, if wage rate is W_1, actual unemployment will be equal to BG whereas level of unemployment equal to AG is required to prevent shirking by workers. Therefore, efficiency wage rate will tend to rise.

If wage rate is W_3, the actual unemployment CH is higher than the level of unemployment JH required to prevent shirking. As a result, efficiency wage rate falls. Thus equilibrium is reached at the efficiency wage rate W_2 at which actual unemployment equals the level of

11. J. Yellen, "Efficiency Wage Models of Unemployment, *American Economic Review*, May 1984.

12. J. Stiglitz, "The Causes and Consequences of the Dependence of Quality of Price, *Journal of Economic Literaure*, March 1987.

unemployment required to avoid shirking by workers. Therefore, W_2 is the equilibrium efficiency wage rate at which unemployment equal to *EU* (that is, N_2N_0) prevails. Note that equilibrium efficiency wage rate W_2 is higher than competitive equilibrium wage rate W_0 at which all who want employment are in fact employed and therefore there is no unemployment. Thus, no shirking model or efficiency wage model explains why higher than competitive wage rate is paid to the workers while there exists substantial unemployment in a competitive economy.

Application. Although efficiency wage model is highly simplified, it helps to explain a number of real world phenomenon. The chief example of application of efficiency wage theory was by Henry Ford, who has been a major producer of automobiles in the United States. In 1914 Henry Ford took a famous decision to raise the minimum daily wage from \$2.34 to \$5 a day for labour. Besides, he reduced the length of the working day from 9 to 8 hours. This was an unprecedented decision as it was quite unusual for a firm to announce that it would double the wage rate it pays to his workers.

Although Henry Ford was criticised by other producers for his policy of paying higher wages to his labour, it paid him good dividends. Henry Ford not only succeeded in maintaining a stable labour force but also could hire workers who were on an average more productive. According to the evidence available, productivity in Ford's factory increased by 51 per cent and absenteeism had been halved. The higher wages resulted in fewer layoffs and discharges, and workers worked hard and more productively. As a result his average cost declined and profitability greatly increased. Ford's profits increased from \$ 30 million in 1914 to \$ 60 million in 1916. Ford himself later said that his decision to raise wage rate "was one of the finest cost-cutting moves we ever made."[13] According to modern economists, what Ford did was to pay an efficiency wage.[14]

To what extent the efficiency wage theory is applicable to developing countries like India, I leave it for the readers to think about it. However the present author is of the view that Indian industrialists do not have such progressive and innovative outlook as Henry Ford had. It may be noted that apart from the efficiency wage theory explained above, in India and other developing countries the productivity of workers depends on the wage rate for nutritional reasons as well. If poor Indian workers are paid better wages, they would afford to purchase more and better food which would make them healthier and more productive than at present.

QUESTIONS FOR REVIEW

1. What is asymmetric information ? Explain why asymmetric information between buyers and sellers leads to market failure when a market is otherwise perfectly competitive.
2. Explain why Lemons in the used cars market drive out good quality used cars.
3. Explain the lemons problem in the market for used goods. How can this problem be overcome ?
4. Adverse selection is the direct result of asymmetric information. Explain. How can the problem of adverse selection be overcome?
5. Distinguish between adverse selection and moral hazard problem in insurance markets. Can one exist without the other ?
6. How are signalling devices used by sellers to convince buyers that their products are of high quality ? Explain.
7. What is a moral hazard problem ? How is moral hazard problem related to externalities faced by insurance companies ? How can it be overcome?
8. Why might managers of firms be able to achieve objectives other than profit maximisation, the goal of the firm's shareholders ?
9. Explain the principal-agent problem. How can the managers be induced to promote the interests of their owners ?
10. How are incentive pay and profit-sharing payment schemes likely to resolve principal-agent problem ?
11. What is an efficient wage ? Why is it profitable for the firm to pay an efficiency wage ?
12. Explain the efficiency wage theory. Is it relevant in case of India ?

13. Henry Ford, *My Life and Work,* 1922, p. 147.
14. See D. Raff and L Summers, "Did Henry Ford Pay Efficiency Wages". *Journal of Labour Economics,* 1987.